SOCIAL SECURITY LEGISLATION 2017/18

VOLUME III: ADMINISTRATION, ADJUDICATION AND THE EUROPEAN DIMENSION

SOCIAL SECURITY LEGISLATION 2017/18

General Editor
Nick Wikeley, M.A. (Cantab)

VOLUME III: ADMINISTRATION, ADJUDICATION AND THE EUROPEAN DIMENSION

Commentary by

Mark Rowland, LL.B.
Judge of the Upper Tribunal

Robin White, M.A., LL.M.
Emeritus Professor of Law, University of Leicester
Formerly Judge of the Upper Tribunal

Consultant Editor
Child Poverty Action Group

SWEET & MAXWELL

THOMSON REUTERS

Published in 2017 by
Thomson Reuters
trading as Sweet & Maxwell,
Registered in England & Wales. Company number 1679046.
Registered office and address for service:
5 Canada Square, Canary Wharf, London E14 5AQ.

Typeset by Servis Filmsetting Ltd, Stockport, Cheshire
Printed and bound by CPI Group (UK) Ltd, Croydon, CR0 4YY

For further information on our products and services,
visit www.sweetandmaxwell.co.uk

No natural forests were destroyed to make this product.
Only farmed timber was used and re-planted.

A CIP catalogue record for this book is
available from the British Library

ISBN 978-0-414-06409-6

CHILD POVERTY ACTION GROUP

The Child Poverty Action Group (CPAG) is a charity, founded in 1965, which campaigns for the relief of poverty in the United Kingdom. It has a particular reputation in the field of welfare benefits law derived from its legal work, publications, training and parliamentary and policy work, and is widely recognised as the leading organisation for taking test cases on social security law.

CPAG is therefore ideally placed to act as Consultant Editor to this 4-volume work—**Social Security Legislation 2017/18**. CPAG is not responsible for the detail of what is contained in each volume, and the authors' views are not necessarily those of CPAG. The Consultant Editor's role is to act in an advisory capacity on the overall structure, focus and direction of the work.

For more information about CPAG, its rights and policy publications or training courses, its address is 30 Micawber Street, London, N1 7TB (telephone: 020 7837 7979—website: *http://www.cpag.org.uk*).

FOREWORD

It is immensely reassuring to have available to those who prepare and attend hearings a steadfast source of reliable information and guidance, in a familiar format, that will effectively assist us in our common endeavour to deliver access to justice for those seeking redress. In the face of ongoing complex reform as well as the continuing development of the jurisprudence applicable to the existing legislation it remains an essential reference and I am happy to once again endorse the publication of these volumes. We owe a tremendous debt of gratitude to all those who contribute to making the Social Security Legislation series such a success.

Judge John Aitken
Chamber President, Social Entitlement Chamber
Social Security and Child Support,
Criminal Injuries Compensation,
Asylum Support.

PREFACE

Administration, Adjudication and the European Dimension is Volume III of *Social Security Legislation 2017/18*. The companion volumes are Volume I: *Non-Means Tested Benefits and Employment and Support Allowance*; Volume II: *Income Support, Jobseeker's Allowance, State Pension Credit and the Social Fund*; Volume IV: *Tax credits and HMRC-administered Social Security Benefits;* and Volume V: *Universal Credit*. The "year" in the title of the works relates to the tax/contribution year, and conveys the period the books (and the Supplement) are designed to cover.

Each of the volumes in the series provides the text of UK legislation (and in this volume also European treaties and legislation) clearly showing the form and date of amendments, and is up to date to April 10, 2017. The commentary in this volume includes references to some later case law. Provisions specific to social security administration or adjudication have been retained as far as possible in this volume, but where a separate scheme exists for particular types of payments, it has sometimes been more practical to reproduce the procedural provisions alongside the substantive provisions in Volume I.

Copy for this year includes all the small, but significant, amendments resulting from the introduction of the new bereavement benefit, and incorporation of all the changes included in the most recent Supplement. There has also been a steady stream of significant case-law on material in this volume to accommodate in the commentary. It is probably fair to say that the introduction of the new bereavement benefit and the continuing introduction of universal credit, and of personal independence payments, have been the Government's key priorities in social security implementation and there has been comparatively little other legislation.

Neither the outcome of the EU referendum of June 23, 2016 nor the Prime Minister's letter of March 29, 2017 triggering art.50 of the Treaty on European Union immediately alters the United Kingdom's membership of the Union. The United Kingdom will remain a Member State and European Union law will continue to apply until the exit arrangements provided for in art.50 are completed.

As always, revising and updating the legislative text and commentary has required considerable flexibility on the part of the publisher and a great deal of help from a number of sources, including CPAG as advisory editor to the series. We remain grateful for this assistance in our task of providing an authoritative reflection on the current state of the law. To maximise space for explanatory commentary in books which seem to grow in size year on year, we have provided lists of definitions only where the commentary to the provision is substantial, or where reference to definitions is essential for a proper understanding. Users of the book should always check whether particular words or phrases they are called on to apply have a particular meaning ascribed to them in legislation. Generally the first or second regulation in each set of regulations contains definitions of key terms (check the

"Arrangements of Regulations" at the beginning of each set for an indication of the subject matter covered by each regulation). There are also definition or "interpretation" sections in primary legislation.

Users of the series and its predecessor works have over the years contributed to their effectiveness by providing valuable comments on our commentary, as well as pointing out where the text of some provision has been omitted in error, become garbled, or not been brought fully up to date. In some cases, this has drawn attention to an error which might otherwise have gone unnoticed. In providing such feedback, users of the work have helped to shape the content and ensure the accuracy of our material, and for that we continue to be grateful. We hope that users of the work will continue to provide such helpful input and feedback. Please write to, or email, the General Editor of the series: Professor Nick Wikeley, c/o School of Law, University of Southampton, Highfield, Southampton SO17 1BJ, (njw@soton.ac.uk); and he will pass on any comments received to the appropriate commentator.

Our gratitude continues to go to the President of the Social Entitlement Chamber of the First-tier Tribunal and his colleagues there for continuing the now long tradition of help and encouragement in our endeavours.

August 2017

Mark Rowland
Robin White

CONTENTS

USING THIS BOOK: AN INTRODUCTION TO LEGISLATION AND CASE LAW

Introduction

This book is not a general introduction to, or general textbook on, the law relating to social security but it is nonetheless concerned with both of the principal sources of social security law—*legislation* (both primary and secondary) and *case law*. It sets out the text of the most important legislation, as currently in force, and then there is added commentary that refers to the relevant case law. Lawyers will be familiar with this style of publication, which inevitably follows the structure of the legislation.

This note is designed primarily to assist readers who are not lawyers to find their way around the legislation and to understand the references to case law, but information it contains about how to find social security case law is intended to be of assistance to lawyers too.

Primary legislation

Primary legislation of the United Kingdom Parliament consists of *Acts of Parliament* (also known as *Statutes*). They will have been introduced to Parliament as *Bills*. There are opportunities for Members of Parliament and peers to debate individual clauses and to vote on amendments before a Bill is passed and becomes an Act (at which point the clauses become sections). No tribunal or court has the power to disapply, or hold to be invalid, an Act of Parliament unless it is inconsistent with European Union law.

An Act is known by its "short title", which incorporates the year in which it was passed (e.g. the Social Security Contributions and Benefits Act 1992), and is given a chapter number (abbreviated as, for instance, "c.4" indicating that the Act was the fourth passed in that year). It is seldom necessary to refer to the chapter number but it appears in the running heads in this book.

Each *section* (abbreviated as "s." or, in the plural, "ss.") of an Act is numbered and may be divided into *subsections* (abbreviated as "subs." and represented by a number in brackets), which in turn may be divided into *paragraphs* (abbreviated as "para." and represented by a lower case letter in brackets) and *subparagraphs* (abbreviated as "subpara." and represented by a small roman numeral in brackets). Subparagraph (ii) of para.(a) of subs.(1) of s.72 will usually be referred to simply as "s.72(1)(a)(ii)". Upper case letters may be used where additional sections or subsections are inserted by amendment and additional lower case letters may be used where new paragraphs and subparagraphs are inserted. This accounts for the rather ungainly s.171ZS of the Social Security Contributions and Benefits Act 1992 (in Vol.IV).

Sections of a large Act may be grouped into a numbered *Part*, which may even be divided into *Chapters*. It is not usual to refer to a Part or a Chapter unless referring to the whole Part or Chapter.

Where a section would otherwise become unwieldy because it is necessary to include a list or complicated technical provisions, the section may simply refer to a *Schedule* at the end of the Act. A Schedule (abbreviated as "Sch.") may be divided into paragraphs and subparagraphs and further divided into heads and subheads. Again, it is usual to refer simply to, say, "para.23(3)(b)(ii) of Schedule 3". Whereas it is conventional to speak of a section *of* an Act, it is usual to speak of a Schedule *to* an Act.

When Parliament wishes to change the law, it may do so by passing a new Act that amends a previous Act or it may do so by passing a freestanding Act, although even then consequential amendments to other legislation are usually required. Thus, for instance, when incapacity benefit was introduced by the Social Security (Incapacity for Work) Act 1994, the changes were largely made by inserting sections 30A to 30E and Part XIIA into the Social Security Contributions and Benefits Act 1992 and repealing the provisions in that Act dealing with sickness and invalidity benefit. In contrast, when jobseeker's allowance was introduced by the Jobseekers Act 1995, it was decided that the main provisions relating to the new benefit would be found in the 1995 Act itself and the 1992 Act was amended only so as to repeal, or amend, the provisions dealing with, or referring to, unemployment benefit.

When there has been a proliferation of Acts or Acts have been very substantially amended, the legislation may be consolidated in a new Act, for which there is a fast track procedure in Parliament. Only limited amendments may be made by a consolidation Act but such an Act reorganises and tidies up the legislation. Because social security law is so frequently amended, it tends to be consolidated every decade or two. The last consolidation Acts relevant to this book were the Social Security Contributions and Benefits Act 1992 (in Vols I, II and IV) and the Social Security Administration Act 1992 (in this volume).

Secondary legislation

Secondary legislation (also known as *subordinate legislation* or *delegated legislation*) is made by *statutory instrument* in the form of a set of *Regulations* or a set of *Rules* or an *Order*. The power to make such legislation is conferred on ministers and other persons or bodies by Acts of Parliament. To the extent that a statutory instrument is made beyond the powers (in Latin, ultra vires) conferred by primary legislation, it may be held by a tribunal or court to be invalid and ineffective. Secondary legislation must be laid before Parliament. However, most secondary legislation is not debated in Parliament and, even when it is, it cannot be amended although an entire statutory instrument may be rejected.

A set of Regulations or Rules or an Order has a name indicating its scope and the year it was made and also a number, as in the Social Security (Disability Living Allowance) Regulations 1991 (SI 1991/2890) (the 2890th statutory instrument issued in 1991). Because there are over 3,000 statutory instruments each year, the number of a particular statutory instrument is important as a means of identification and it should usually be cited the first time reference is made to that statutory instrument.

Sets of Regulations or Rules are made up of individual *regulations* (abbreviated as "reg.") or *rules* (abbreviated as "r." or, in the plural, "rr."). An Order is made up of *articles* (abbreviated as "art."). Regulations, rules and articles may be divided into paragraphs, subparagraphs and heads. As in Acts, a set of Regulations or Rules or an Order may have one or more Schedules attached to it. The style of numbering used in statutory instruments is the same as in sections of, and Schedules to, Acts of Parliament. As in Acts, a large statutory instrument may have regulations or rules grouped into Parts and, occasionally, Chapters. Statutory instruments may be amended in the same sort of way as Acts.

Northern Ireland legislation

Most of the legislation set out in this series applies only in Great Britain, social security not generally being an excepted or reserved matter in relation to Northern Ireland. However, Northern Irish legislation—both primary legislation, most relevantly in the form of *Orders in Council* (which, although statutory instruments, had the effect of primary legislation in Northern Ireland while there was direct rule from Westminster) and *Acts of the Northern Ireland Assembly*, and subordinate legislation, in the form of *statutory rules*—has, until recently, largely replicated legislation in Great Britain so that much of the commentary in this book will be applicable to equivalent provisions in Northern Ireland legislation. Latterly, there has been a greater reluctance to maintain parity with Great Britain and, initially at least, the provisions in the Welfare Reform Act 2012 were not replicated in Northern Ireland.

However, following a lengthy impasse, on November 18, 2015, the Northern Ireland Assembly consented to the stalled Northern Ireland (Welfare Reform) Bill 2015 being taken forward by the Westminster Parliament and approved the welfare clauses of the Welfare Reform and Work Bill as initially introduced at Westminster and the draft Welfare Reform (Northern Ireland) Order 2015. Subsequently, the Northern Ireland (Welfare Reform) Act 2015 received the Royal Assent on November 25, 2015. The purpose of the Act was to provide a power by Order in Council to legislate for welfare reform in Northern Ireland and confer power on the Secretary of State or on a Northern Ireland department to make further provision by regulations or order.

The Welfare Reform (Northern Ireland) Order 2015 (SI 2015/2006) was duly made and came into force on December 10, 2015. The Order makes provision equivalent to the Welfare Reform Act 2012 and will implement the reforms contained in that Act in Northern Ireland with some limited specific changes. The Order confers powers on the Northern Ireland Department for Social Development (now renamed the Department for Communities) to make regulations with respect to the reforms in Northern Ireland. The reforms are gradually being rolled out across the jurisdiction in 2016 and 2017 (see e.g. the Welfare Reform (Northern Ireland) Order 2015 (Commencement No. 1) Order 2016 (SR No 46/2016).

In addition, the Northern Ireland Act 1998 (Modification) Order 2016 (SI 2016/160) adds the Welfare Reform Act 2012 and the Welfare Reform (Northern Ireland) Order 2015, together with certain pensions legislation to the legislation listed in s.87(6) of the Northern Ireland Act 1998 (which requires the Secretary of State for Work and Pensions and the Minister with responsibility for social security in Northern Ireland to consult each other to ensure, to the extent they agree, that the relevant legislation achieves single systems of social security, child support and pensions for the UK).

To that extent parity in welfare provision has been restored. Alongside these statutory changes the Northern Ireland Executive has announced allocations from Executive funds to 'top-up' the UK welfare arrangements in Northern Ireland, so as to mitigate the effects of these changes, with a review planned for 2018/2019.

European Union legislation

The United Kingdom is a Member State of the European Union, and European Union legislation has effect within the United Kingdom. The outcome of the EU referendum of June 23, 2016 does not immediately alter the United Kingdom's membership of the Union; the United Kingdom will remain a Member State and European Union law will continue to apply until such time as the exit arrangements provided for in art.50 of the Treaty on European Union are completed. The primary legislation is in the form of the *Treaties* agreed by the Member States. Relevant subordinate legislation is in the form of *Regulations,* adopted to give effect to the provisions of the Treaties, and *Directives,* addressed to Member States and requiring them to incorporate certain provisions into their domestic laws. Directives are relevant because, where a person brings proceedings against an organ of the State, as is invariably the case where social security is concerned, that person may rely on the Directive as having direct effect if the Member State has failed to comply with it. European Union Treaties, Regulations and Directives are divided into *Articles* (abbreviated as "Art.") United Kingdom legislation that is inconsistent with European Union legislation may be disapplied. The most relevant provisions of European Union legislation are set out in Part III of this volume.

Finding legislation in this book

If you know the name of the piece of legislation for which you are looking, use the list of contents at the beginning of each volume of this series which lists the pieces of legislation contained in the volume. That will give you the paragraph reference to enable you to find the beginning of the piece of legislation. Then, it is easy to find the relevant section, regulation, rule, article or Schedule by using the running heads on the right hand pages. If you do not know the name of the piece of legislation, you will probably need to use the index at the end of the volume in order to find the relevant paragraph number but will then be taken straight to a particular provision.

The legislation is set out as amended, the amendments being indicated by numbered sets of square brackets. The numbers refer to the numbered entries under the heading "AMENDMENTS" at the end of the relevant section, regulation, rule, article or Schedule, which identify the amending statute or statutory instrument. Where an Act has been consolidated, there is a list of "DERIVATIONS" identifying the provisions of earlier legislation from which the section or Schedule has been derived.

Finding other legislation

Legislation in both its amended and its unamended form may now be found on *http://www.legislation.gov.uk* and so the "Blue Volumes" at *http://lawvolumes.dwp.gov.uk/the-law-relating-to-social-security/* are no longer being updated (as from October 2015). Northern Ireland social security legislation may be found at *http://www.communities-ni.gov.uk/law_relating_to_social_security*. European Union legislation may be found at *http://eur-lex.europa.eu/collection/eu-law.html*.

Interpreting legislation

Legislation is written in English and generally means what it says. However, more than one interpretation is often possible. Most legislation itself contains definitions. Sometimes these are in the particular provision in which a word occurs but, where a word is used in more than one place, any definition will appear with others. In an Act, an interpretation section is usually to be found towards the end of the Act or of the relevant Part of the Act. In a statutory instrument, an interpretation provision usually appears near the beginning of the statutory instrument or the relevant Part of it. In the more important pieces of legislation in this series, there is included after every section, regulation, rule, article or Schedule a list of "DEFINITIONS", showing where definitions of words used in the provision are to be found.

However, not all words are statutorily defined and there is in any event more to interpreting legislation than merely defining its terms. Decision-makers and tribunals need to know how to apply the law in different types of situations. That is where case law comes in.

Case law and the commentary in this book

In deciding individual cases, courts and tribunals interpret the relevant law and incidentally establish legal principles. Decisions on questions of legal principle of the superior courts and appellate tribunals are said to be binding on decision-makers and the First-tier Tribunal, which means that decision-makers and the First-tier Tribunal must apply those principles. Thus the judicial decisions of the superior courts and appellate tribunals form part of the law. The commentary to the legislation in this series, under the heading "GENERAL NOTE" after a section, regulation, rule, article or Schedule, refers to this *case law*.

Much case law regarding social security benefits is still in the form of decisions of Social Security Commissioners and Child Support Commissioners. However, while there are still Commissioners in Northern Ireland, which has a largely separate judiciary and tribunal system, the functions of Commissioners in Great Britain were transferred to the Upper Tribunal and allocated to the Administrative Appeals Chamber of that tribunal on November 3, 2008. Consequently, social security case law is increasingly to be found in decisions of the Upper Tribunal.

The commentary in this series is not itself binding on any decision-maker or tribunal because it is merely the opinion of the author. It is what is actually said in the legislation or in the judicial decision that is important. The legislation is set out in this series, but it will generally be necessary to look elsewhere for the precise words used in judicial decisions. The way that decisions are cited in the commentary enables that to be done.

The reporting of decisions of the Upper Tribunal and Commissioners

About 50 of the most important decisions of the Administrative Appeals Chamber of the Upper Tribunal are selected to be "reported" each year in the Administrative Appeals Chamber Reports (AACR), using the same criteria as were formerly used for reporting Commissioners' decisions in Great Britain. The selection is made by an editorial board of judges and decisions are selected for reporting only if they are of general importance and command the assent of at least a majority of the relevant judges. The term "reported" simply means that they are published in printed form as well as on the Internet (see *Finding case law*, below) with headnotes (i.e. summaries) and indexes, but there are two other important consequences of a decision being reported. Reported decisions are available in all tribunal venues and can be consulted in local social security offices and some main libraries. They also have a greater precedential status than ordinary decisions (see *Judicial precedent* below).

A handful of Northern Ireland Commissioners' decisions are also selected for reporting in the Administrative Appeals Chamber Reports each year, the selection being made by the Chief Social Security Commissioner in Northern Ireland.

Citing case law

As has been mentioned, much social security case law is still to be found in decisions of Social Security Commissioners and Child Support Commissioners, even though the Commissioners have now effectively been abolished in Great Britain.

Reported decisions of Commissioners were known merely by a number or, more accurately, a series of letters and numbers beginning with an "R". The type of benefit in issue was indicated by letters in brackets (e.g. "IS" was income support, "P" was retirement pension, and so on) and the year in which the decision was selected for reporting or, from 2000, the year in which it was published as a reported decision, was indicated by the last two digits, as in *R(IS) 2/08*. In Northern Ireland there was a similar system until 2009, save that the type of benefit was identified by letters in brackets after the number, as in *R 1/07 (DLA)*.

Unreported decisions of the Commissioners in Great Britain were known simply by their file numbers, which began with a "C", as in *CIS/2287/2008*. The letters following the "C" indicated the type of benefit in issue in the case. Scottish and, at one time, Welsh cases were indicated by a "S" or "W" immediately after the "C", as in *CSIS/467/2007*. The last four digits indicated the calendar year in which the case was registered, rather than the year it was decided. A similar system operated in Northern Ireland until 2009, save that the letters indicating the type of benefit appeared in brackets after the numbers and, from April 1999, the financial year rather than the calendar year was identified, as in *C 10/06-07 (IS)*.

Decisions of the Upper Tribunal, of courts and, since 2010, of the Northern Ireland Commissioners are generally known by the names of the parties (or just two of them in multi-party cases). Individuals are anonymised through the use of initials in the names of decisions of the Upper Tribunal and the Northern Ireland Commissioners and occasionally in the names of decisions of courts. In this series, the names of official bodies may also be abbreviated (e.g. "SSWP" for the Secretary of State for Work and Pensions, "HMRC" for Her Majesty's Revenue and Customs, "CMEC" for the Child Maintenance and Enforcement Commission and "DSD" for the Department for Social Development in Northern Ireland). Since 2010, decisions of the Upper

Tribunal and of Northern Ireland Commissioners have also been given a "flag" in brackets to indicate the subject matter of the decision, which in social security cases indicates the principal benefit in issue in the case. Thus, the name of one jobseeker's allowance case is *SSWP v JB (JSA)*.

Any decision of the Upper Tribunal, of a court since 2001 or of a Northern Ireland Commissioner since 2010 that has been intended for publication has also given a *neutral citation number* which enables the decision to be more precisely identified. This indicates, in square brackets, the year the decision was made (although in relation to decisions of the courts it sometimes merely indicates the year the number was issued) and also indicates the court or tribunal that made the decision (e.g. "UKUT" for the Upper Tribunal, "NICom" for a Northern Ireland Commissioner, "EWCA Civ" for the Civil Division of the Court of Appeal in England and Wales, "NICA" for the Court of Appeal in Northern Ireland, "CSIH" for the Inner House of the Court of Session (in Scotland), "UKSC" for the Supreme Court and so on). A number is added so that the reference is unique and finally, in the case of the Upper Tribunal or the High Court in England and Wales, the relevant chamber of the Upper Tribunal or the relevant division or other part of the High Court is identified (e.g."(AAC)" for the Administrative Appeals Chamber, "(Admin)" for the Administrative Court and so on). Examples of decisions of the Upper Tribunal and a Northern Ireland Commissioner with their neutral citation numbers are *SSWP v JB (JSA)* [2010] UKUT 4 (AAC) and *AR v DSD (IB)* [2010] NICom 6.

If the case is reported in the Administrative Appeals Chamber Reports or another series of law reports, a reference to the report usually follows the neutral citation number. Conventionally, this includes either the year the case was decided (in round brackets) or the year in which it was reported (in square brackets), followed by the volume number (if any), the name of the series of reports (in abbreviated form, so see the Table of Abbreviations at the beginning of each volume of this series) and either the page number or the case number. However, before 2010, cases reported in the Administrative Appeals Chamber Reports or with Commissioners' decisions were numbered in the same way as reported Commissioners' decisions. *Abdirahman v Secretary of State for Work and Pensions* [2007] EWCA Civ 657; [2008] 1 W.L.R. 254 (also reported as *R(IS) 8/07*) is a Court of Appeal decision, decided in 2007 but reported in 2008 in volume 1 of the Weekly Law Reports at page 254 and also in the 2007 volume of reported Commissioners' decisions. *NT v SSWP* [2009] UKUT 37 (AAC), *R(DLA) 1/09* is an Upper Tribunal case decided in 2009 and reported in the Administrative Appeals Chamber Reports in the same year. *Martin v SSWP* [2009] EWCA Civ 1289; [2010] AACR 9 is a decision of the Court of Appeal that was decided in 2009 and was the ninth decision reported in the Administrative Appeals Chamber Reports in 2010.

It is usually necessary to include the neutral citation number or a reference to a series of reports only the first time a decision is cited in any document. After that, the name of the case is usually sufficient.

All decisions of the Upper Tribunal that are on their website have neutral citation numbers. If you wish to refer a tribunal or decision-maker to a decision of the Upper Tribunal that does not have a neutral citation number, contact the office of the Administrative Appeals Chamber (*adminappeals@hmcts.gsi.gov.uk*) who will provide a number and add the decision to the website.

Decision-makers and claimants are entitled to assume that judges of both the First-tier Tribunal and the Upper Tribunal have immediate access to reported decisions of Commissioners or the Upper Tribunal and they need not provide copies, although it may sometimes be helpful to do so. However, where either a decision-maker or a claimant intends to rely on an unreported decision, it will be necessary to provide a copy of the decision to the judge and other members of the tribunal. A copy of the decision should also be provided to the other party before the hearing because otherwise it may be necessary for there to be an adjournment to enable that party to take advice on the significance of the decision.

Finding case law

The extensive references described above are used so as to enable people easily to find the full text of a decision. Most decisions of any significance since the late 1990s can be found on the Internet.

Decisions of the Upper Tribunal and of the Commissioners in Great Britain may be found at *https://www.gov.uk/administrative-appeals-tribunal-decisions*. This includes reported decisions since 1991 and other decisions considered likely to be of interest to tribunals and tribunal users since about 2000, together with a few older decisions. Decisions of Commissioners in Northern Ireland may be found on *https://www.communities-ni.gov.uk/services/northern-ireland-digest-case-law*.

The Administrative Appeals Chamber Reports, which include not only reported decisions of the Administrative Appeals Chamber of the Upper Tribunal but also reported decisions of the Northern Ireland Commissioners and decisions of the courts in related areas of law, are available on the HMCTS website at *http://www.osscsc.gov.uk/Decisions/adminAppealsChamberReports.htm*. They are also published by the Stationery Office in bound volumes which follow on from the bound volumes of Commissioners' decisions published from 1948.

Copies of decisions of the Administrative Appeals Chamber of the Upper Tribunal or of Commissioners that are otherwise unavailable may be obtained from the offices of the Upper Tribunal (Administrative Appeals Chamber) or, in Northern Ireland, from the Office of the Social Security and Child Support Commissioners.

Decisions of a wide variety of courts and tribunals in the United Kingdom may be found on the free website of the British and Irish Legal Information Institute, *http://www.bailii.org*. It includes all decisions of the Supreme Court and provides fairly comprehensive coverage of decisions given since about 1996 by the House of Lords and Privy Council and most of the higher courts in England and Wales, decisions given since 1998 by the Court of Session and decisions given since 2000 by the Court of Appeal and High Court in Northern Ireland. Some earlier decisions have been included, so it is always worth looking and, indeed, those decisions dating from 1873 or earlier and reported in the English Reports may be found through a link to *http://www.commonlii.org/uk/cases/EngR/*.

Decisions of the European Court of Justice (concerned with the law of the European Union) are all to be found on *http://curia.europa.eu*.

Decisions of the European Court of Human Rights are available at *http://www.echr.coe.int*.

Most decisions of the courts in social security cases, including decisions of the European Court of Justice on cases referred by United Kingdom courts and tribunals, are reported in the Administrative Appeals Chamber Reports or with the reported decisions of Commissioners and may therefore be found on the same websites and in the same printed series of reported decisions. So, for example, *R(I)1/00* contains Commissioner's decision *CSI/12/1998*, the decision of the Court of Session upholding the Commissioner's decision and the decision of the House of Lords in *Chief Adjudication Officer v Faulds*, reversing the decision of the Court of Session. The most important decisions of the courts can also be found in the various series of law reports familiar to lawyers (in particular, in the *Law Reports*, the *Weekly Law Reports*, the *All England Law Reports*, the *Public and Third Sector Law Reports*, the *Industrial Cases Reports* and the *Family Law Reports*) but these are not widely available outside academic or other law libraries, although the *All England Law Reports* are occasionally to be found in the larger public libraries. See the Table of Cases at the beginning of each volume of this series for all the places where a decision mentioned in that volume is reported.

If you know the name or number of a decision and wish to know where in a volume of this series there is a reference to it, use the Table of Cases or the Table of Commissioners' Decisions 1948–2009 in the relevant volume to find the paragraph(s) where the decision is mentioned.

Judicial precedent

As already mentioned, decisions of the Upper Tribunal, the Commissioners and the higher courts in Great Britain become *case law* because they set binding precedents which must be followed by decision-makers and the First-tier Tribunal in Great Britain. This means that, where the Upper Tribunal, Commissioner or court has decided a point of legal principle, decision-makers and appeal tribunals must make their decisions in conformity with the decision of the Upper Tribunal, Commissioner or court, applying the same principle and accepting the interpretation of the law contained in the decision. So a decision of the Upper Tribunal, a Commissioner or a superior court explaining what a term in a particular regulation means, lays down the definition of that term in much the same way as if the term had been defined in the regulations themselves. The decision may also help in deciding what the same term means when it is used in a different set of regulations, provided that the term appears to have been used in a similar context.

Only decisions on points of law set precedents that are binding and, strictly speaking, only decisions on points of law that were necessary to the overall conclusion reached by the Upper Tribunal, Commissioner or court are binding. Other parts of a decision (which used to be known as obiter dicta) may be regarded as helpful guidance but need not be followed if a decision-maker or the First-tier Tribunal is persuaded that there is a better approach. It is particularly important to bear this in mind in relation to older decisions of Social Security Commissioners because, until 1987, the right of appeal to a Commissioner was not confined to points of law.

Where there is a conflict between precedents, a decision-maker or the First-tier Tribunal is generally free to choose between decisions of equal status. For these purposes, most decisions of the Upper Tribunal and decisions of Commissioners are of equal status. However, a decision-maker or First-tier Tribunal should generally prefer a reported decision to an unreported one unless the unreported decision was the later decision and the Commissioner or Upper Tribunal expressly decided not to follow the earlier reported decision. This is simply because the fact that a decision has been reported shows that at least half of the relevant judges of the Upper Tribunal or the Commissioners agreed with it at the time. A decision of a Tribunal of Commissioners (i.e. three Commissioners sitting together) or a decision of a three-judge panel of the Upper Tribunal must be preferred to a decision of a single Commissioner or a single judge of the Upper Tribunal.

A single judge of the Upper Tribunal will normally follow a decision of a single Commissioner or another judge of the Upper Tribunal, but is not bound to do so. A three-judge panel of the Upper Tribunal will generally follow a decision of another such panel or of a Tribunal of Commissioners, but similarly is not bound to do so, whereas a single judge of the Upper Tribunal will always follow such a decision.

Strictly speaking, the Northern Ireland Commissioners do not set binding precedent that must be followed in Great Britain but their decisions are relevant, due to the similarity of the legislation in Northern Ireland, and are usually regarded as highly persuasive with the result that, in practice, they are generally given as much weight as decisions of the Great Britain Commissioners. The same approach is taken in Northern Ireland to decisions of the Upper Tribunal on social security matters and to decisions of the Great Britain Commissioners.

Decisions of the superior courts in Great Britain and Northern Ireland on questions of legal principle are almost invariably followed by decision-makers, tribunals and the Upper Tribunal, even when they are not strictly binding because the relevant court was in a different part of the United Kingdom or exercised a parallel – but not superior – jurisdiction.

Decisions of the European Court of Justice come in two parts: the Opinion of the Advocate General and the decision of the Court. It is the decision of the Court which is binding. The Court is assisted by hearing the Opinion of the Advocate General before itself coming to a conclusion on the issue before it. The Court does not always follow its Advocate General. Where it does, the Opinion of the Advocate General often elaborates the arguments in greater detail than the single collegiate judgment of the Court. Decision-makers, tribunals and Commissioners must apply decisions of the European Court of Justice, where relevant to cases before them, in preference to other authorities binding on them.

The European Court of Human Rights in Strasbourg is quite separate from the European Court of Justice in Luxembourg and serves a different purpose: interpreting and applying the European Convention on Human Rights, which is incorporated into United Kingdom law by the Human Rights Act 1998. Since October 2, 2000, public authorities in the United Kingdom, including courts, Commissioners, tribunals and decision-makers have been required to act in accordance with the incorporated provisions of the Convention, unless statute prevents this. They must take into account the Strasbourg case law and are required to interpret domestic legislation, so far as it is possible to do so, to give effect to the incorporated Convention rights. Any court or tribunal may declare secondary legislation incompatible with those rights and, in certain circumstances, invalidate it. Only the higher courts can declare a provision of primary legislation to be incompatible with those rights, but no court, tribunal or Upper Tribunal can invalidate primary legislation. The work of the Strasbourg Court and the impact of the Human Rights Act 1998 on social security are discussed in the commentary in Part IV of this volume.

See the note to s.3(2) of the Tribunals, Courts and Enforcement Act 2007 in Part V of this volume for a more detailed and technical consideration of the rules of precedent.

Other sources of information and commentary on social security law

For a comprehensive overview of the social security system in Great Britain, CPAG's *Welfare Benefits and Tax Credits Handbook*, published annually each spring, is unrivalled as a practical introduction from the claimant's viewpoint.

From a different perspective, the Department for Work and Pensions publishes the 14-volume *Decision Makers' Guide* at *https://www.gov.uk/government/collections/decision-makers-guide-staff-guide* and the new *Advice for Decision Making*, which covers personal independence payment, universal credit and the "new" versions of Jobseeker's Allowance and Employment and Support Allowance, at *https://www.gov.uk/government/publications/advice-for-decision-making-staff-guide*. Similarly, Her Majesty's Revenue and Customs publish manuals relating to tax credits, child benefit and guardian's allowance, which they administer, see *http://www.hmrc.gov.uk/thelibrary/manuals-a-z.htm*. (Note that the *Child Benefit Technical Manual* also covers guardian's allowance.) These guides and manuals are extremely useful but their interpretation of the law is not binding on tribunals and the courts, being merely internal guidance for the use of decision-makers.

There are a number of other sources of valuable information or commentary on social security case law: see in particular publications such as the *Journal of Social Security Law*, CPAG's *Welfare Rights Bulletin*, *Legal Action* and the *Adviser*. As far as online resources go there is little to beat *Rightsnet* (*http://www.rightsnet.org.uk*). This site contains a wealth of resources for people working in the welfare benefits field but of special relevance in this context are Commissioners'/Upper Tribunal Decisions section of the "Toolkit" area and also the "Briefcase" area which contains summaries of the decisions (with links to the full decisions). Sweet and Maxwell's online subscription service *Westlaw* is another valuable source (*http://www.westlaw.co.uk*), as is the Merrill Corporation's *Casetrack* (*http://www.casetrack.com/ct/casetrack.nsf/index?openframeset*) and LexisNexis *Lexis* (*http://www.lexis.com*).

Conclusion

The internet provides a vast resource but a search needs to be focused. Social security schemes are essentially statutory and so in Great Britain the legislation which is set out in this series forms the basic structure of social security law. However, the case law shows how the legislation should be interpreted and applied. The commentary in this series should point the way to the case law relevant to each provision and the Internet can then be used to find it where that is necessary.

CHANGE OF NAME FROM DEPARTMENT OF SOCIAL SECURITY TO DEPARTMENT FOR WORK AND PENSIONS

The Secretaries of State for Education and Skills and for Work and Pensions Order 2002 (SI 2002/1397) makes provision for the change of name from the Department of Social Security to Department for Work and Pensions. Article 9(5) provides:

"(5) Subject to article 12 [which makes specific amendments], any enactment or instrument passed or made before the coming into force of this Order shall have effect, so far as may be necessary for the purposes of or in consequence of the entrusting to the Secretary of State for Work and Pensions of the social security functions, as if any reference to the Secretary of State for Social Security, to the Department of Social Security or to an officer of the Secretary of State for Social Security (including any reference which is to be construed as such as reference) were a reference to the Secretary of State for Work and Pensions, to the Department for Work and Pensions or, as the case may be, to an officer of the Secretary of State for Work and Pensions."

CHANGES IN TERMINOLOGY CONSEQUENT UPON THE ENTRY INTO FORCE OF THE TREATY OF LISBON

The Treaty of Lisbon (Changes in Terminology) Order 2011 (SI 2011/1043) (which came into force on April 22, 2011) makes a number of changes to terminology used in primary and secondary legislation as a consequence of the entry into force of the Treaty of Lisbon on December 1, 2009. The Order accomplishes this by requiring certain terms in primary and secondary legislation to be read in accordance with the requirements of the Order. No substantive changes to the law are involved.

The changes are somewhat complex because of the different ways in which the term "Community" is used, and the abbreviations "EC" or "EEC" are used. References to the "European Community", "European Communities", "European Coal and Steel Communities", "the Community", "the EC", and "the EEC" are generally to be read as references to the "European Union".

The following table shows the more common usages involving the word "Community" in the first column which are now to be read in the form set out in the second column:

Original term	**To be read as**
Community treaties	EU treaties
Community institution	EU institution
Community instrument	EU instrument
Community obligation	EU obligation
Enforceable Community right	Enforceable EU right
Community law, or European Community law	EU law
Community legislation, or European Community legislation	EU legislation
Community provision, or European Community provision	EU provision

Provision is also made for changes to certain legislation relating to Wales in the Welsh language.

Relevant extracts from the Order can be found in Part III of this volume.

THE MARRIAGE (SAME SEX COUPLES) ACT 2013

The Marriage (Same Sex Couples) Act 2013 (c.30) provides in s.3 and Schs 3 and 4 that the terms "marriage", "married couple" and being "married" in existing and future legislation in England and Wales are to be read as references to a marriage between persons of the same sex. The same approach is taken to any legislation about couples living together as if married. This is subject to certain specified exclusions contained in Sch.4 and in any Order providing for a contrary approach to be taken.

Schedule 2 to The Marriage (Same Sex Couples) Act 2013 (Consequential and Contrary provisions and Scotland) Order 2014 (SI 2014/560) contains a substantial list of contrary provisions to s.11(1) and (2) and paras 1 to 3 of Sch.3 to the 2013 Act. Most of these relate to specific enactments, but note that Pt 2 of the Schedule provides that s.11(1) and (2) do not apply to "EU instruments". This term is defined in Sch.1 to the European Communities Act 1972 (as amended) as "any instrument issued by an EU institution". It refers mainly to Regulations, Directives, Decisions, recommendations and opinions issued by the institutions.

TABLE OF CASES

TABLE OF COMMISSIONERS' DECISIONS 1948–2009

Northern Ireland Commissioners' Decisions from 2010 and all Upper Tribunal decisions will be found in the Table of Cases above.

TABLE OF ABBREVIATIONS USED IN THIS SERIES

1975 Act	Social Security Act 1975
1977 Act	Marriage (Scotland) Act 1977
1979 Act	Pneumoconiosis (Workers' Compensation) Act 1979
1986 Act	Social Security Act 1986
1996 Act	Employment Rights Act 1996
1998 Act	Social Security Act 1998
2002 Act	Tax Credits Act 2002
2004 Act	Gender Recognition Act 2004
2006 Act	Armed Forces Act 2006
2008 Act	Child Maintenance and Other Payments Act 2008
2013 Act	Marriage (Same Sex Couples) Act 2013
2014 Act	Marriage and Civil Partnership (Scotland) Act 2014
A1P1	Art.1 of Protocol 1 to the European Convention on Human Rights
AA	Attendance Allowance
AA 1992	Attendance Allowance Act 1992
AAC	Administrative Appeals Chamber
AACR	Administrative Appeals Chamber Reports
A.C.	Law Reports, Appeal Cases
A.C.D.	Administrative Court Digest
Admin	Administrative Court
Admin L.R.	Administrative Law Reports
Administration Act	Social Security Administration Act 1992
Administration Regulations	Statutory Paternity Pay and Statutory Adoption Pay (Administration) Regulations 2002
AIP	assessed income period
All E.R.	All England Reports
All E.R. (E.C.)	All England Reports (European Cases)
AMA	Adjudicating Medical Authorities
AO	Adjudication Officer
AOG	*Adjudication Officers Guide*
art.	article
Art.	Article
ASD	Autistic Spectrum Disorder
ASPP	Additional Statutory Paternity Pay

A.T.C.	Annotated Tax Cases
Attendance Allowance Regulations	Social Security (Attendance Allowance) Regulations 1991
AWT	All Work Test
BA	Benefits Agency
Benefits Act	Social Security Contributions and Benefits Act 1992
B.H.R.C.	Butterworths Human Rights Cases
B.L.G.R.	Butterworths Local Government Reports
Blue Books	*The Law Relating to Social Security*, Vols 1–11
B.P.I.R.	Bankruptcy and Personal Insolvency Reports
B.T.C.	British Tax Cases
BTEC	Business and Technology Education Council
B.V.C.	British Value Added Tax Reporter
B.W.C.C.	Butterworths Workmen's Compensation Cases
c.	chapter
C	Commissioner's decision
C&BA 1992	Social Security Contributions and Benefits Act 1992
CAA 2001	Capital Allowances Act 2001
CAB	Citizens Advice Bureau
CAO	Chief Adjudication Officer
CB	Child Benefit
CBA 1975	Child Benefit Act 1975
CBJSA	Contribution-Based Jobseeker's Allowance
C.C.L. Rep.	Community Care Law Reports
CCM	HMRC *New Tax Credits Claimant Compliance Manual*
C.E.C.	European Community Cases
CERA	cortical evoked response audiogram
CESA	Contribution-based Employment and Support Allowance
CFS	chronic fatigue syndrome
Ch.	Chancery Division Law Reports; Chapter
Citizenship Directive	Directive 2004/38/EC of the European Parliament and of the Council of April 29, 2004
CJEC	Court of Justice of the European Communities
CJEU	Court of Justice of the European Union
Claims and Payments Regulations	Social Security (Claims and Payments) Regulations 1987
Claims and Payments Regulations 1979	Social Security (Claims and Payments) Regulations 1979
Claims and Payments Regulations 2013	Universal Credit, Personal Independence Payment, Jobseeker's Allowance and Employment and Support Allowance (Claims and Payments) Regulations 2013
CM	Case Manager

CMA	Chief Medical Adviser
CMEC	Child Maintenance and Enforcement Commission
C.M.L.R.	Common Market Law Reports
C.O.D.	Crown Office Digest
COLL	*Collective Investment Schemes Sourcebook*
Community, The	European Community
Computation of Earnings Regulations	Social Security Benefit (Computation of Earnings) Regulations 1978
Computation of Earnings Regulations 1996	Social Security Benefit (Computation of Earnings) Regulations 1996
Consequential Provisions Act	Social Security (Consequential Provisions) Act 1992
Contributions and Benefits Act	Social Security Contributions and Benefits Act 1992
Contributions Regulations	Social Security (Contributions) Regulations 2001
COPD	chronic obstructive pulmonary disease
CP	Carer Premium; Chamber President
CPAG	Child Poverty Action Group
CPR	Civil Procedure Rules
Cr. App. R.	Criminal Appeal Reports
CRCA 2005	Commissioners for Revenue and Customs Act 2005
Credits Regulations 1974	Social Security (Credits) Regulations 1974
Credits Regulations 1975	Social Security (Credits) Regulations 1975
Crim. L.R.	Criminal Law Review
CRU	Compensation Recovery Unit
CSA 1995	Children (Scotland) Act 1995
CSIH	Inner House of the Court of Session (Scotland)
CSM	Child Support Maintenance
CS(NI)O 1995	Child Support (Northern Ireland) Order 1995
CSOH	Outer House of the Court of Session (Scotland)
CSPSSA 2000	Child Support, Pensions and Social Security Act 2000
CTA	Common Travel Area
CTA 2009	Corporation Tax Act 2009
CTA 2010	Corporation Tax Act 2010
CTB	Council Tax Benefit
CTC	Child Tax Credit
CTC Regulations	Child Tax Credit Regulations 2002
CTF	child trust fund
CTS	Carpal Tunnel Syndrome
DAC	Directive 2011/16/ EU (Directive on administrative co-operation in the field of taxation)

DAT	Disability Appeal Tribunal
dB	decibels
DCA	Department for Constitutional Affairs
DCP	Disabled Child Premium
Decisions and Appeals Regulations 1999	Social Security Contributions (Decisions and Appeals) Regulations 1999
Dependency Regulations	Social Security Benefit (Dependency) Regulations 1977
DfEE	Department for Education and Employment
DHSS	Department of Health and Social Security
Disability Living Allowance Regulations	Social Security (Disability Living Allowance) Regulations
DIY	do it yourself
DLA	Disability Living Allowance
DLA Regs 1991	Social Security (Disability Living Allowance) Regulations 1991
DLAAB	Disability Living Allowance Advisory Board
DLADWAA 1991	Disability Living Allowance and Disability Working Allowance Act 1991
DM	Decision Maker
DMA	Decision-making and Appeals
DMG	*Decision Makers' Guide*
DMP	Delegated Medical Practitioner
DP	Disability Premium
DPT	diffuse pleural thickening
DPTC	Disabled Person's Tax Credit
DRO	Debt Relief Order
DSD	Department for Social Development (Northern Ireland)
DSM IV; DSM-5	Diagnostic and Statistical Manual of Mental Disorders of the American Psychiatric Association
DSS	Department of Social Security
DTI	Department of Trade and Industry
DWA	Disability Working Allowance
DWP	Department for Work and Pensions
DWPMS	Department for Work and Pensions Medical Service
EAA	Extrinsic Allergic Alveolitis
EAT	Employment Appeal Tribunal
EC	European Community
ECHR	European Convention on Human Rights
ECJ	European Court of Justice
E.C.R.	European Court Reports
ECSC	European Coal and Steel Community

ECSMA	European Convention on Social and Medical Assistance
EEA	European Economic Area
EEC	European Economic Community
EESSI	Electronic Exchange of Social Security Information
E.G.	Estates Gazette
E.G.L.R.	Estates Gazette Law Reports
EHC plan	education, health and care plan
EHIC	European Health Insurance Card
EHRC	European Human Rights Commission
E.H.R.R.	European Human Rights Reports
EL	employers' liability
E.L.R	Education Law Reports
EMA	Education Maintenance Allowance
EMP	Examining Medical Practitioner
Employment and Support Allowance Regulations	Employment and Support Allowance Regulations 2008
EPS	extended period of sickness
Eq. L.R.	Equality Law Reports
ERA	evoked response audiometry
ERA scheme	Employment, Retention and Advancement scheme
ES	Employment Service
ESA	Employment and Support Allowance
ESA Regs 2013	Employment and Support Allowance Regulations 2013
ESA Regulations	Employment and Support Allowance Regulations 2008
ESA WCAt	Employment and Support Allowance Work Capability Assessment
ESC	employer supported childcare
ESE Scheme	Employment, Skills and Enterprise Scheme
ESE Regulations	Jobseeker's Allowance (Employment, Skills and Enterprise Scheme) Regulations 2011
ESES Regulations	Jobseeker's Allowance (Employment, Skills and Enterprise Scheme) Regulations 2011
ETA 1973	Employment and Training Act 1973
ETA(NI) 1950	Employment and Training Act (Northern Ireland) 1950
ETS	European Treaty Series
EU	European Union
Eu.L.R.	European Law Reports
EWCA Civ	Civil Division of the Court of Appeal (England and Wales)
EWHC Admin	Administrative Court Division of the High Court (England and Wales)

IS Regs	Income Support Regulations
IS Regulations	Income Support (General) Regulations 1987
ISA	Individual Savings Account
ISBN	International Standard Book Number
ITA 2007	Income Tax Act 2007
ITEPA 2003	Income Tax, Earnings and Pensions Act 2003
I.T.L. Rep.	International Tax Law Reports
I.T.R.	Industrial Tribunals Reports
ITS	Independent Tribunal Service
ITTOIA 2005	Income Tax (Trading and Other Income) Act 2005
IVB	Invalidity Benefit
IW (General) Regs	Social Security (Incapacity for Work) (General) Regulations 1995
IW (Transitional) Regs	Incapacity for Work (Transitional) Regulations
Jobseeker's Allowance Regulations	Jobseeker's Allowance Regulations 1996
Jobseeker's Regulations 1996	Jobseeker's Allowance Regulations 1996
JSA	Jobseeker's Allowance
JSA 1995	Jobseekers Act 1995
JSA (NI) Regulations	Jobseeker's Allowance (Northern Ireland) Regulations 1996
JSA (Transitional) Regulations	Jobseeker's Allowance (Transitional) Regulations 1996
JSA Regs 1996	Jobseeker's Allowance Regulations 1996
JSA Regs 2013	Jobseeker's Allowance Regulations 2013
JS(NI)O 1995	Jobseekers (Northern Ireland) Order 1995
J.S.S.L.	Journal of Social Security Law
J.S.W.L.	Journal of Social Welfare Law
K.B.	Law Reports, King's Bench
L.& T.R.	Landlord and Tenant Reports
LCW	limited capability for work
LCWA	Limited Capability for Work Assessment
LCWRA	limited capability for work-related activity
LDEDC Act 2009	Local Democracy, Economic Development and Construction Act 2009
LEA	local education authority
LEL	Lower Earnings Limit
LET	low earnings threshold
L.G. Rev.	Local Government Review
L.G.L.R.	Local Government Reports
L.J.R.	Law Journal Reports
LRP	liable relative payment
L.S.G.	Law Society Gazette
Luxembourg Court	Court of Justice of the European Union (also referred to as CJEC and ECJ)

MA	Maternity Allowance
MAF	Medical Assessment Framework
Maternity Allowance Regulations	Social Security (Maternity Allowance) Regulations 1987
MDC	Mayoral development corporation
ME	myalgic encephalomyelitis
Medical Evidence Regulations	Social Security (Medical Evidence) Regulations 1976
MEN	Mandatory Employment Notification
Mesher and Wood	*Income Support, the Social Fund and Family Credit: the Legislation* (1996)
M.H.L.R.	Mental Health Law Reports
MHP	mental health problems
MIF	minimum income floor
MIG	minimum income guarantee
Migration Regulations	Employment and Support Allowance (Transitional Provisions, Housing Benefit and Council Tax Benefit (Existing Awards) (No.2) Regulations 2010
MP	Member of Parliament
MRSA	methicillin-resistant Staphylococcus aureus
MS	Medical Services
MWA Regulations	Jobseeker's Allowance (Mandatory Work Activity Scheme) Regulations 2011
MWAS Regulations	Jobseeker's Allowance (Mandatory Work Activity Scheme) Regulations 2011
NCB	National Coal Board
NDPD	Notes on the Diagnosis of Prescribed Diseases
NHS	National Health Service
NI	National Insurance
N.I..	Northern Ireland Law Reports
NICA	Northern Ireland Court of Appeal
NICom	Northern Ireland Commissioner
NICs	National Insurance Contributions
NINO	National Insurance Number
NIRS 2	National Insurance Recording System
N.L.J.	New Law Journal
NMC	Nursing and Midwifery Council
Northern Ireland Contributions and Benefits Act	Social Security Contributions and Benefits (Northern Ireland) Act 1992
N.P.C.	New Property Cases
NRCGT	non-resident capital gains tax
NTC Manual	Clerical procedures manual on tax credits
NUM	National Union of Mineworkers
NUS	National Union of Students
OCD	obsessive compulsive disorder

Ogus, Barendt and Wikeley	A. Ogus, E. Barendt and N. Wikeley, *The Law of Social Security* (1995)
Old Cases Act	Industrial Injuries and Diseases (Old Cases) Act 1975
OPB	One Parent Benefit
O.P.L.R.	Occupational Pensions Law Reports
OPSSAT	Office of the President of Social Security Appeal Tribunals
Overlapping Benefits Regulations	Social Security (Overlapping Benefits) Regulations 1975
P	retirement pension case
P. & C.R.	Property and Compensation Reports
para.	paragraph
Pay Regulations	Statutory Paternity Pay and Statutory Adoption Pay (General) Regulations 2002; Statutory Shared Parental Pay (General) Regulations 2014
PAYE	Pay As You Earn
PC	Privy Council
PCA	Personal Capability Assessment
PCC	Police and Crime Commissioner
PD	Practice Direction; prescribed disease
Pens. L.R.	Pensions Law Reports
Pensions Act	Pension Schemes Act 1993
PEP	Personal Equity Plan
Persons Abroad Regulations	Social Security Benefit (Persons Abroad) Regulations 1975
Persons Residing Together Regulations	Social Security Benefit (Persons Residing Together) Regulations 1977
PIE	Period of Interruption of Employment
PILON	pay in lieu of notice
Pilot Scheme Regulations	Universal Credit (Work-Related Requirements) In Work Pilot Scheme and Amendment Regulations 2015
PIP	Personal Independence Payment
P.I.Q.R.	Personal Injuries and Quantum Reports
Polygamous Marriages Regulations	Social Security and Family Allowances (Polygamous Marriages) Regulations 1975
PPF	Pension Protection Fund
Prescribed Diseases Regulations	Social Security (Industrial Injuries) (Prescribed Diseases) Regulations 1985
PSCS	Pension Service Computer System
Pt	Part
PTA	pure tone audiometry
P.T.S.R.	Public and Third Sector Law Reports
PTWR 2000	Part-time Workers (Prevention of Less Favourable Treatment) Regulations 2000

PVS	private and voluntary sectors
Q.B.	Queen's Bench Law Reports
QBD	Queen's Bench Division
QCS Board	Quality Contract Scheme Board
QEF	qualifying earnings factor
QYP	qualifying young person
r.	rule
R	Reported Decision
R.C.	Rules of the Court of Session
REA	Reduced Earnings Allowance
reg.	regulation
RIPA	Regulation of Investigatory Powers Act 2000
RMO	Responsible Medical Officer
rr.	rules
RR	reference rate
RSI	repetitive strain injury
RTI	Real Time Information
R.V.R.	Rating & Valuation Reporter
s.	section
S	Scottish Decision
SAP	Statutory Adoption Pay
SAPOE Regulations	Jobseeker's Allowance (Schemes for Assisting Persons to Obtain Employment) Regulations 2013
SAWS	Seasonal Agricultural Work Scheme
SAYE	Save As You Earn
SB	Supplementary Benefit
SBAT	Supplementary Benefit Appeal Tribunal
SBC	Supplementary Benefits Commission
S.C.	Session Cases
S.C. (H.L.)	Session Cases (House of Lords)
S.C. (P.C.)	Session Cases (Privy Council)
S.C.C.R.	Scottish Criminal Case Reports
S.C.L.R.	Scottish Civil Law Reports
Sch.	Schedule
SDA	Severe Disablement Allowance
SDP	Severe Disability Premium
SEC	Social Entitlement Chamber
SEN	special educational needs
SERPS	State Earnings Related Pension Scheme
ShPP	statutory shared parental pay
ShPP Regulations	Statutory Shared Parental Pay (General) Regulations 2014
SI	Statutory Instrument

SIP	Share Incentive Plan
S.J.	Solicitors Journal
S.J.L.B.	Solicitors Journal Law Brief
SLAN	statement like an award notice
S.L.T.	Scots Law Times
SMP	Statutory Maternity Pay
SMP (General) Regulations 1986	Statutory Maternity Pay (General) Regulations 1986
SPC	State Pension Credit
SPC Regulations	State Pension Credit Regulations 2002
SPCA 2002	State Pension Credit Act 2002
SPL Regulations	Shared Parental Leave Regulations 2014
SPP	Statutory Paternity Pay
ss.	sections
SS (No.2) A 1980	Social Security (No.2) Act 1980
SSA 1975	Social Security Act 1975
SSA 1977	Social Security Act 1977
SSA 1978	Social Security Act 1978
SSA 1979	Social Security Act 1979
SSA 1981	Social Security Act 1981
SSA 1986	Social Security Act 1986
SSA 1988	Social Security Act 1988
SSA 1989	Social Security Act 1989
SSA 1990	Social Security Act 1990
SSA 1998	Social Security Act 1998
SSAA 1992	Social Security Administration Act 1992
SSAC	Social Security Advisory Committee
SSAT	Social Security Appeal Tribunal
SSCBA 1992	Social Security Contributions and Benefits Act 1992
SSCB(NI)A 1992	Social Security Contributions and Benefits (Northern Ireland) Act 1992
SSCPA 1992	Social Security (Consequential Provisions) Act 1992
SSD	Secretary of State for Defence
SSHBA 1982	Social Security and Housing Benefits Act 1982
SSHD	Secretary of State for the Home Department
SSI	Scottish Statutory Instrument
SS(MP)A 1977	Social Security (Miscellaneous Provisions) Act 1977
SSP	Statutory Sick Pay
SSP (General) Regulations	Statutory Sick Pay (General) Regulations 1982
SSPA 1975	Social Security Pensions Act 1975
SSPP	statutory shared parental pay
SSWP	Secretary of State for Work and Pensions

State Pension Credit Regulations	State Pension Credit Regulations 2002
S.T.C.	Simon's Tax Cases
S.T.C. (S.C.D.)	Simon's Tax Cases: Special Commissioners' Decisions
S.T.I.	Simon's Tax Intelligence
STIB	Short-Term Incapacity Benefit
subpara.	subparagraph
subs.	subsection
T	Tribunal of Commissioners' Decision
T.C.	Tax Cases
TCA 1999	Tax Credits Act 1999
TCA 2002	Tax Credits Act 2002
TCC	Technology and Construction Court
TCEA 2007	Tribunals, Courts and Enforcement Act 2007
TCGA 1992	Taxation of Chargeable Gains Act 2002
TCTM	*Tax Credits Technical Manual*
TEC	Treaty Establishing the European Community
TENS	transcutaneous electrical nerve stimulation
TEU	Treaty on European Union
TFC	tax-free childcare
TFEU	Treaty on the Functioning of the European Union
TIOPA 2010	Taxation (International and Other Provisions) Act 2010
TMA 1970	Taxes Management Act 1970
T.R.	Taxation Reports
Transfer of Functions Act	Social Security Contributions (Transfer of Functions etc.) Act 1999
Tribunal Procedure Rules	Tribunal Procedure (First-tier Tribunal)(Social Entitlement Chamber) Rules 2008
UB	Unemployment Benefit
UC	Universal Credit
UC Regs 2013	Universal Credit Regulations 2013
UCITS	Undertakings for Collective Investments in Transferable Securities
UKAIT	UK Asylum and Immigration Tribunal
UKBA	UK Border Agency of the Home Office
UKCC	United Kingdom Central Council for Nursing, Midwifery and Health Visiting
UKFTT	United Kingdom First-tier Tribunal Tax Chamber
UKHL	United Kingdom House of Lords
U.K.H.R.R.	United Kingdom Human Rights Reports
UKSC	United Kingdom Supreme Court
UKUT	United Kingdom Upper Tribunal

Forfeiture Act 1982

(1982 c.34)

Arrangement of Sections

An Act to provide for relief for persons guilty of unlawful killing from forfeiture of inheritance and other rights; to enable such persons to apply for financial provision out of the deceased's estate; to provide for the question whether pension and social security benefits have been forfeited to be determined by the Social Security Commissioners; and for connected purposes.
[13th July 1982]

1.—(1) In this Act, the "forfeiture rule" means the rule of public policy which in certain circumstances precludes a person who has unlawfully killed another from acquiring a benefit in consequence of the killing. 1.2

(2) References in this Act to a person who has unlawfully killed another include a reference to a person who has unlawfully aided, abetted, counselled or procured the death of that other and references in this Act to unlawful killing shall be interpreted accordingly.

General Note

There is a general rule of English law that a person should not benefit from his or her wrongdoing. More specifically, the forfeiture rule has the effect that, generally, a person who has unlawfully killed another forfeits his or her right to any benefit that might otherwise have been acquired as a result of the death, e.g. an inheritance under a will or an indemnity under an insurance policy. In *R. v National Insurance Commissioner, Ex p. Connor* [1981] Q.B. 758 (also reported as an appendix to *R(G) 2/79*), the forfeiture rule was applied to prevent a woman convicted of the manslaughter of her husband from obtaining entitlement to widow's benefit. A Tribunal of Commissioners subsequently held that it also applied to entitlement to a Category B retirement pension based on a victim's contribution record (*R(P) 1/88*). The same rule applies in Scotland (*Burns v Secretary of State for Social Services* 1985 S.L.T. 351 (also reported as an appendix to *R(G) 1/83*)). 1.3

This Act was passed following *Connor*, the purpose being to mitigate the effect of the forfeiture rule where its operation could be harsh. Thus s.2 permits courts to modify the effect of the rule where it would otherwise prevent a person from obtaining certain interests in property and s.3 provides that the rule shall not preclude a person from applying to a court for certain types of financial provision. Section 4 deals with the rule's application to social security benefits. Section 5 provides that there may be no modification in a case of murder.

The leading modern case on the forfeiture rule is *Dunbar v Plant* [1998] Ch. 412, in which it was held that, since the coming into force of this Act, a strict approach should be taken to the question of whether death has been caused by criminal conduct and any mitigation should be achieved through a modification of the effect of the rule, so that some of the earlier cases, in which regard was had to the degree of culpability in deciding whether the rule applied at all, should no longer be followed. The rule applies where a court or the Upper Tribunal finds that a crime causing death has been committed, even if the relevant person has not been convicted of any crime or the criminal conduct was not the most immediate cause of death. Thus, in *Dunbar v Plant*, the rule was held to apply in the case of a woman who had survived a suicide pact, where she had not been prosecuted but her actions amounted to aiding and abetting suicide (which is a crime under the Suicide Act 1961 even though suicide itself is not). It follows from this strict approach that the forfeiture rule applies in any case where a person has been convicted of manslaughter, including manslaughter on the ground of diminished responsibility (*R(FP) 1/05*), and it seems likely that it would now also be found to apply in a case of causing death by dangerous driving. The rule can apply even where the person concerned has been prosecuted and acquitted of manslaughter, provided that the court or Upper Tribunal is nonetheless satisfied that the offence has been committed (*Gray v Barr* [1970] 2 Q.B. 626, upheld on appeal [1971] 2 Q.B. 554), although the Upper Tribunal is unlikely to go behind an acquittal unless satisfied that there is material evidence that was not available to the criminal court (*R(G) 2/90*). The rule also applies if the action bringing about the death occurred abroad, provided it would have amounted to a crime in Great Britain (*R(G) 1/88*). Subsection (2) recognises that acting as an accessory to a crime may be enough to cause the forfeiture rule to apply and, in *R(FG) 1/04*, it was held that a person convicted under s.4 of the Offences against the Person Act 1861 of soliciting to murder was likely to have "counselled . . . the death of [the victim]" for the purposes of the subsection.

The forfeiture rule does not apply where a person is of unsound mind to the extent of being incapable of committing a crime (*Re Houghton, Houghton v Houghton* [1915] 2 Ch. 173).

1.4 **2.** *Omitted.*

1.5 **3.** *Omitted.*

[6Upper Tribunal] to decide whether rule applies to social security benefits

1.6 **4.**—(1) Where a question arises as to whether, if a person were otherwise entitled to or eligible for any benefit or advantage under a relevant enactment, he would be precluded by virtue of the forfeiture rule from receiving the whole or part of the benefit or advantage, that question shall (notwithstanding anything in any relevant enactment) be determined by [6the Upper Tribunal].

[1(1A) Where [6the Upper Tribunal] determines that the forfeiture rule has precluded a person (in this section referred to as "the offender") who has unlawfully killed another from receiving the whole or part of any such benefit or advantage, [6the Upper Tribunal] may make a decision under this subsection modifying the effect of that rule and may do so whether the unlawful killing occurred before or after the coming into force of this subsection.

(1B) [6The Upper Tribunal] shall not make a decision under subsection (1A) above modifying the effect of the forfeiture rule in any case unless [6it] is satisfied that having regard to the conduct of the offender and of the deceased and to such other circumstances as appear to [6the Upper Tribunal] to be material, the justice of the case requires the effect of the rule to be so modified in that case.

(1C) Subject to subsection (1D) below, a decision under subsection (1A) above may modify the effect of the forfeiture rule in either or both of the following ways—

(a) so that it applies only in respect of a specified proportion of the benefit or advantage;

(b) so that it applies in respect of the benefit or advantage only for a specified period of time.

(1D) Such a decision may not modify the effect of the forfeiture rule so as to allow any person to receive the whole or any part of a benefit or advantage in respect of any period before the commencement of this subsection.

(1E) If [[6]the Upper Tribunal] thinks it expedient to do so, [[6]the Upper Tribunal may direct that its] decision shall apply to any future claim for a benefit or advantage under a relevant enactment, on which a question such as is mentioned in subsection (1) above arises by reason of the same unlawful killing.

(1F) It is immaterial for the purposes of subsection (1E) above whether the claim is in respect of the same or a different benefit or advantage.

(1G) For the purposes of obtaining a decision whether the forfeiture rule should be modified the Secretary of State may refer to [[6]the Upper Tribunal] for review any determination of a question such as is mentioned in subsection (1) above that was made before the commencement of subsections (1A) to (1F) above (whether by [[6]the Upper Tribunal] or not) and shall do so if the offender requests him to refer such a determination.

(1H) Subsections (1A) to (1F) above shall have effect on a reference under subsection (1G) above as if in subsection (1A) the words "it has been determined" were substituted for the words "[[6]the Upper Tribunal] determines".]

(2) [[6]Tribunal Procedure Rules may make provision] for carrying this section into effect; and (without prejudice to the generality of that) the rules may, in relation to the question mentioned in subsection (1) above or any determination under that subsection [[2] or any decision under subsection (1A) above]—

(a) apply any provision of any relevant enactment, with or without modifications, or exclude or contain provisions corresponding to any such provisions; [[6]. . .]

(b) [[6]. . .]

(3) [[6]. . .]

(4) [[6]. . .]

(5) In this section—

[[6]. . .]; and

"relevant enactment" means any provision of the following and any instrument made by virtue of such a provision:

the Personal Injuries (Emergency Provisions) Act 1939,
the Pensions (Navy, Army, Air Force and Mercantile Marine) Act 1939,
the Polish Resettlement Act 1947,
[[3] . . .],
[[2] the Social Security Acts 1975 to 1991],
[[3] the Social Security Contributions and Benefits Act 1992],
[[5] section 1 of the Armed Forces (Pensions and Compensation) Act 2004],

[4 the Pension Schemes Act 1993],
[7 Part 1 of the Pensions Act 2014],
[8 section 30 of that Act],

and any other enactment relating to pensions or social security prescribed by regulations under this section.

AMENDMENTS

1. Social Security Act 1986 s.76 (July 25, 1986).
2. Statutory Sick Pay Act 1991 s.3(1)(c) (February 12, 1991).
3. Social Security (Consequential Provisions) Act 1992 ss.3 and 4 and Sch.2 para.63.
4. Pension Schemes Act 1993 Sch.8 para.15 (February 7, 1994).
5. Armed Forces (Pensions and Compensation) Act 2004 s.7(1) (April 6, 2005).
6. Transfer of Tribunal Functions Order 2008 (SI 2008/2833) Sch.3 para.38 (November 3, 2008).
7. Pensions Act 2014 Sch.12 para.1 (April 6, 2016).
8. Pensions Act 2014 Sch.16 para.1 (April 6, 2017).

DEFINITIONS

"forfeiture rule"—see s.1(1).
"offender"—see subs.(1A).
"relevant enactment—see subs.(5).

GENERAL NOTE

Subsection (1)–(1H)

1.7 Until November 3, 2008, the powers provided for in this section were exercised by Social Security Commissioners.

Subsections (1A) to (1H) were added after a Tribunal of Commissioners held that subs.(1) gave Commissioners power only to decide whether the forfeiture rule applied and did not give them any power to modify it (*R/G) 1/84*, *R(G) 2/84*, *R(P) 1/84*). Whenever a claimant's entitlement to a social security benefit under a "relevant enactment" (see subs.(5)) arises at least partly in consequence of the death of someone the claimant has killed, there is likely to arise the question whether the killing was unlawful and the forfeiture rule applies. The Secretary of State or other authority responsible for determining entitlement to benefit is then bound to refer the case to the Upper Tribunal so that it can decide under subs.(1) whether the forfeiture rule does apply (see the note to s.1) and, if so, whether it should be modified under subs.(1A).

The forfeiture rule cannot be modified in a case of murder (see s.5). However, the Act recognises that in other cases the forfeiture rule is capable of being unduly harsh and so the Upper Tribunal may modify the effect of the rule. The paramount consideration when considering modification is the culpability of the claimant (*Dunbar v Plant* [1998] Ch. 412). The Upper Tribunal has a broad discretion and may even decide that the forfeiture rule should have no effect at all, although that will be rare (*R(G) 1/98*, holding *R(G) 3/90* to have been implicitly overruled). Equally, though, the Upper Tribunal may decline to modify the effect of the forfeiture rule. In *R(G) 1/91*, a Commissioner refused to modify the rule where the Court of Appeal had quashed a conviction for murder and substituted a verdict of manslaughter on the ground of diminished responsibility because the trial judge had failed adequately to address the jury in relation to two written medical reports put to a defence witness in cross-examination when the prosecution had failed to call the authors of the reports to give evidence. The Commissioner, who was not bound by the same rules of evidence, held that the weight of evidence was against a finding of diminished responsibility and pointed to a finding of murder, although he acknowledged that s.5 did not apply because the claimant did not actually stand convicted of murder. In *R(FP) 1/05*, where the claimant's plea of guilty to manslaughter on the ground of diminished responsibility had been accepted, a Commissioner considered the claimant's culpability to be low but he still refused to modify the forfeiture rule because only 47p pw was at stake and he considered that the effect of the forfeiture rule was not harsh but was just. In *Henderson v Wilcox* [2015] EWHC 3469 (Ch), the High Court decided not to modify the forfeiture rule in a case where there had been a conviction for manslaughter on the basis of an absence of intention to kill or cause serious injury, rather than on the ground of diminished responsibility, although a hospital order had been made under s.37 of the Mental Health Act 2013. The assault had been a serious one and the culmination of a series of attacks for at least several months and, although the assailant had had a low IQ and had been frustrated by having to assume the role of carer of his mother in circumstances where he did not have the necessary life skills, he had had a good understanding of what he was doing and that it was wrong. The judge said: "Sympathy for the applicant is not . . . the guiding factor for the court, as Patten J made clear in *Dalton v Latham* [2003] EWHC 796 (Ch). I must be satisfied that justice requires modification of the forfeiture rule." On the other hand, in *In re Land, decd.* [2006] EWHC 2069 (Ch); [2007] 1 W.L.R. 1009, where the claimant was too late to apply for modification of the forfeiture rule under s.2 of this Act so as to be able to inherit under his mother's will, s.3 was applied instead and it was held that the court was not precluded from making reasonable financial provision for the claimant under the Inheritance (Provision for Family and Dependants Act) 1975. The claimant, who had again been his mother's carer, had been sentenced to four years' imprisonment for manslaughter on the basis, it appeared, of gross negligence. The judge said: "the picture that presents itself to me is one of the inadequacy to meet the challenges presented by the deceased's condition, an inability to recognise that inadequacy, and a hesitancy in turning to outside help. The claimant must be and has been punished for the wrong that he did; he has also been punished by being deprived of the provision which the Deceased intended for him. But he should not be further punished by being deprived of the reasonable provision that he might otherwise expect under the 1975 Act."

Modification under this section is usually in the form of an order directing that the forfeiture rule will have effect only for a certain period or that it will have effect only to reduce benefit by a certain proportion or both (subs.(1C)).

Subsection (2)

See the Tribunal Procedure (Upper Tribunal) Rules and, in particular, rr. 26 and 47. **1.8**

Subsection (5)

Although the term "relevant enactment" includes war pensions schemes made **1.9** under the first three statutes mentioned in the definition, it does not include the main war pensions scheme covering former members of the Armed Forces injured or killed due to service before April 6, 2005, which is not made under those enactments. This is presumably because that scheme contains its own, rather broader, forfeiture provision in respect of which decisions are made by the Secretary of State for Defence with a right of appeal to the First-tier Tribunal (War Pensions and Armed Forces Compensation Chamber) in England and Wales or a Pensions Appeal Tribunal in Scotland or Northern Ireland. The war pensions schemes to which this Act applies are the scheme covering civilians injured by enemy action in the Second World War, various schemes covering merchant seaman and other civilians who served afloat in that conflict and the scheme covering members of the Polish Armed Forces who served under British command, none of which schemes has a forfeiture provision. On the other hand, the Armed Forces Compensation Scheme that applies in respect of members of the Armed Forces injured or killed due to service since April 6, 2005 is a "relevant enactment" for the purposes of this

PART XIII

ADVISORY BODIES AND CONSULTATION

The Social Security Advisory Committee and the Industrial Injuries Advisory Council

PART XIV

SOCIAL SECURITY SYSTEMS OUTSIDE GREAT BRITAIN

Co-ordination

Reciprocity

PART XV

MISCELLANEOUS

Travelling expenses

Offences

National Insurance Numbers

Industrial injuries and diseases

182C. Requirement is apply for National Insurance Number
183. *Omitted.*
184. Control of pneumoconiosis.

Workmen's compensation etc.

185. *Omitted.*

Supplementary benefit etc.

186. *Omitted.*

Miscellaneous

187. Certain benefit to be inalienable.
188. *Omitted.*

PART XVI

GENERAL

Subordinate legislation

189. Regulations and orders—general.
190. Parliamentary control of orders and regulations.

Supplementary

191. Interpretation—general.
192. Short title, commencement and extent.

SCHEDULES:

1. Claims for benefit made or treated as made before 1st October 1990.
2.–9. *Omitted.*
10. Supplementary benefit etc.

PART I

CLAIMS FOR AND PAYMENTS AND GENERAL ADMINISTRATION OF BENEFIT

Necessity of claim

Entitlement to benefit dependent on claim

1.—(1) Except in such cases as may be prescribed, and subject to the following provisions of this section and to section 3 below, no person shall be 1.18

entitled to any benefit unless, in addition to any other conditions relating to that benefit being satisfied—

(a) he makes a claim for it in the manner, and within the time, prescribed in relation to that benefit by regulations under this Part of this Act; or

(b) he is treated by virtue of such regulations as making a claim for it.

[2(1A) No person whose entitlement to any benefit depends on his making a claim shall be entitled to the benefit unless subsection (1B) below is satisfied in relation both to the person making the claim and to any other person in respect of whom he is claiming benefit.

(1B) This subsection is satisfied in relation to a person if—

(a) the claim is accompanied by—

(i) a statement of the person's national insurance number and information or evidence establishing that that number has been allocated to the person; or

(ii) information or evidence enabling the national insurance number that has been allocated to the person to be ascertained; or

(b) the person makes an application for a national insurance number to be allocated to him which is accompanied by information or evidence enabling such a number to be so allocated.

(1C) Regulations may make provision disapplying subsection (1A) above in the case of—

(a) prescribed benefits;

(b) prescribed descriptions of persons making claims; or

(c) prescribed descriptions of persons in respect of whom benefit is claimed,

or in other prescribed circumstances.]

[10 (2) Where under subsection (1) a person is required to make a claim or to be treated as making a claim for a benefit in order to be entitled to it, the person is not entitled to it in respect of any period more than 12 months before the date on which the claim is made or treated as made.

(2A) But subsection (2) does not apply—

(a) to a disablement benefit or reduced earnings allowance, or

(b) in a case where a claim for the benefit is made or treated as made by virtue of section 3(2).]

(3) Where a person purports to make a claim for benefit on behalf of another—

[7 (za) for personal independence payment by virtue of section 82 of the Welfare Reform Act 2012; or]

(a) for an attendance allowance by virtue of section 66(1) of the Contributions and Benefits Act; [7 . . .]

that other shall be regarded for the purposes of this section as making the claim, notwithstanding that it is made without his knowledge or authority.

(4) In this section and section 2 below "benefit" means—

[8 (za) universal credit;]

[9 (zb) state pension or a lump sum under Part 1 of the Pensions Act 2014;]

[10 (zc) bereavement support payment under section 30 of the Pensions Act 2014;]

(a) benefit as defined in section 122 of the Contributions and Benefits Act;

[1 (aa) a jobseeker's allowance;]

[4 (ab) state pension credit;]

[5 (ac) an employment and support allowance,]

[7 (ad) personal independence payment.]
(b) any income-related benefit.
(5) This section (which corresponds to section 165A of the 1975 Act, as it had effect immediately before this Act came into force) applies to claims made on or after 1st October 1990 or treated by virtue of regulations under that section or this section as having been made on or after that date.
(6) Schedule 1 to this Act shall have effect in relation to other claims.

AMENDMENTS

1. Jobseekers Act 1995 Sch.2 para.38 (October 7, 1996).
2. Social Security Administration (Fraud) Act 1997 s.19 (December 1, 1997).
3. Welfare Reform and Pensions Act 1999 Sch.8 para.16 (April 24, 2000).
4. State Pension Credit Act 2002 s.11 and Sch.1 paras 1–2 (April 7, 2003).
5. Welfare Reform Act 2007 s.28 and Sch.3, para.10 (October 27, 2008).
6. Welfare Reform Act 2012 s.31 and Sch.2 para.3 (February 25, 2013).
7. Welfare Reform Act 2012 Sch.9 para.8 (April 8, 2013).
8. Welfare Reform Act 2012 Sch.2 para.4 (February 25, 2013 for regulation making purposes only).
9. Pensions Act 2014 s.56(4), s.23 and Sch.12, para.9 (April 6, 2016).
10. Pensions Act 2014 s.31 and Sch.16 para.21 (April 6, 2017).

DERIVATION

Social Security Act 1975 s.165A. **1.19**

DEFINITIONS

"the 1975 Act"—see s.191.
"claim"—*ibid.*
"disablement benefit"—*ibid.*
"the Contributions and Benefits Act"—*ibid.*
"income-related benefit"—*ibid.*
"prescribe"—*ibid.*

GENERAL NOTE

Subsection (1)

The general rule is that there cannot be entitlement to benefit unless a claim is made for it. But note that this is a general rule, not a universal one. The general rule is subject to special cases for which special provision is made, and to the provisions of this section. "Benefit" for the purposes of this section is defined in para.(4). Section 1 applies to claims made on or after October 1, 1990. Schedule 1 deals with earlier claims. **1.20**

The introduction of the predecessor of s.1 was precipitated by the decision of the House of Lords in *Insurance Officer v McCaffrey* [1984] 1 W.L.R. 1353 that (subject to an express provision to the contrary) a person was entitled to benefit if he met the conditions of entitlement even though he had not made a claim for that benefit. Claiming went to payability, not entitlement. This was contrary to the long-standing assumption of the Department and was corrected with effect from September 2, 1985.

Section 3, which is excluded from the operation of s.1, deals with late claims for bereavement benefit where the death of the spouse is difficult to establish.

Secretary of State for Work and Pensions v Nelligan, R(P)2/03 [2003] EWCA Civ 555, Judgment of April 15, 2003, is the Court of Appeal's decision on the appeal against the Commissioner's decision in *CP/3643/2001*. The Commissioner had concluded that s.43(5) of the Contributions and Benefits Act 1992 contained an exception to the general rule that there must always be a claim for benefit. He decided that a married woman does not need to claim *both* a Category A *and* a Category B pension in order to obtain payment of the latter. The Court of Appeal allowed the appeal. It concluded that s.43(5) only applied where there had been a claim for *both* a Category A *and* a Category B retirement pension. There was no derogation from the general principle in s.1 of the Administration Act 1992. The Court of Appeal considered that s.43 was about making a choice between two competing entitlements rather than about establishing entitlement to benefit.

Subsections (1A)–(1C)

1.21 These provisions were inserted by s.19 of the Social Security Administration (Fraud) Act 1997 and came into force on December 1, 1997. The effect of subss. (1A) and (1B) is to impose an additional condition of entitlement to benefit where subs.(1)(a) applies (i.e. in the normal case). Claimants will not be entitled to benefit unless when making a claim they provide a national insurance (NI) number, together with information or evidence to show that it is theirs, or provide evidence or information to enable their NI number to be traced, or apply for a NI number and provided sufficient information or evidence for one to be allocated to them. This requirement for an NI number applies to both claimants and any person for whom they are claiming, except in prescribed circumstances (subs.(1C)). See reg.2A of the Income Support Regulations, and the Jobseeker's Allowance Regulations, for who is exempt and note the different dates from which this requirement bites for these benefits.

In *CH/4085/2007,* the Commissioner described subs.(1B) as "a most unsatisfactory provision in a number of respects" (para.17). The Commissioner notes that there are no regulations governing the issue of national insurance numbers, and regards *CIS/345/2003* as wrong in taking the view that reg.9 of the Crediting and Treatment of Contributions, and National Insurance Numbers Regulations 2001 governed this. But the primary legislation was not, in the view of the Commissioner so incomplete as to be unworkable in the case before him. He counsels that regulations should be made in case the primary legislation does prove unworkable in a different factual situation. The case before him concerned an application which had been made by post by a local authority on behalf of a claimant for housing benefit. The Commissioner explains:

> "25. More important is the issue at the heart of this appeal: what is meant by 'information or evidence enabling [a national insurance] number to be so allocated'. The problem, which appears not to have been anticipated by the draftsman, is that it is not possible for a claimant to satisfy the Secretary of State that a national insurance number should be allocated by way of a postal application. What the Secretary of State actually requires in order to allocate a national insurance number is sufficient evidence to show that the applicant does not already have a national insurance number (i.e., the evidence that would be required under section 1(1B)(a)(ii) so as to enable a national insurance number to be found if one had been allocated), information that a claim for a benefit requiring an application for a national insurance number has been, or is to be, made and information as to identity so that the Secretary of State can be satisfied that the claimant is genuine. It is the information as to identity that is the difficulty. A local authority should satisfy itself as to the identity of those in respect of whom benefit is claimed but the Secretary of State does not rely on the local authority doing so. Instead, the person concerned is called to "an evidence of identity interview" at a jobcentre and is told what evidence to bring, it being made plain that photocopies are not accepted. The interview enables the person's face to be compared with a photograph in a passport, makes it unnecessary for valuable original documents as to identity to be sent by post and enables a person to be questioned to test his or her statements. However, it has not been the understanding of the parties that the application is only 'made' at the interview.
>
> 30. Against this background, the phrase 'information or evidence enabling [a national insurance] number to be so allocated' cannot, in my judgment, extend to information and evidence provided at an interview. This is clear from the fact that the application must be 'accompanied' by the information and evidence and, in

any event, if Parliament had intended to include the information that is provided at interview, it would in my view simply have made entitlement conditional on a national insurance number being allocated, which it has deliberately not done so as not to delay the award of benefit. Moreover, the legislation does not specify what information or evidence must be sent with the application because regulation 9(1A) of the 2001 Regulations does not apply. A person can be expected to send only what he or she has been told to send and the source of that information is likely to be those administering the benefit being claimed. The jobcentre will presumably ask for information that could have been sent in advance and has been omitted such as, for instance, information as to the applicant's place of birth, which was not included with the information originally sent by the local authority on behalf of the claimant's husband in this case. It cannot be right that a claimant should be penalised because a local authority acting on her husband's behalf neglects to include information that can perfectly well be provided subsequently. In my judgment, the information and evidence mentioned in the legislation is only that information and evidence that the person concerned could reasonably have been expected to send when the application was made. . . . .

31. However, that is not to say that a failure to attend an interview or to supply all the information required will not be relevant to entitlement to benefit. If a person does not take all the steps necessary to obtain a national insurance number after supplying the initial information and evidence, an adjudicating authority may be entitled to infer that the application for a national insurance number was not genuine, or has ceased to be genuine, and therefore not sufficient to satisfy the statutory condition of entitlement. That could justify revision or supersession of an award. Thus, while I agree . . . that the tribunal should have found that the claimant had supplied sufficient information and evidence to satisfy section 1(1B)(b), I accept that [counsel for the local authority] is entitled to draw attention to the failure to attend the interview.

32. On the other hand, evidence of a failure to attend an interview is insufficient to show that an application was not, or has ceased to be, genuine. Regard must at least be had to the cause of the failure but even a lack of good cause may not indicate a lack of intention to pursue an application. Social security legislation makes specific provision for cases where a person has failed to attend a jobcentre to 'sign on' or has failed to attend a medical examination. Here, no specific provision is made but adjudicating authorities must act fairly. Some enquiry must be made as to why the person failed to attend the interview and as to whether the person will attend another one. If no reply is received, it may be appropriate to infer that there was never any intention of obtaining a national insurance number, but that was not the position here."

Subsection (2)

This provision imposes an overall limit of 12 months to the entitlement to benefit before the date of claim. Not all benefits are caught by subs.(1) and there is a further exclusion in para.(b). Regulation 19 of and Sch.4 to the Claims and Payments Regulations impose the ordinary time-limits for claiming and since April 1997 allow the limits in the cases of income support, JSA, family credit and disability working allowance (and their successor benefits) to be extended for a maximum of three months only in tightly defined circumstances. The test of good cause has been abandoned. Where there is such an extension, the claim is then treated as made on the first day of the period for which the claim is allowed to relate (reg.6(3)). Although the drafting is not at all clear, the reference in subs.(2) to the 12-month limit from the date on which the claim is made or is treated as made seems to make the limit start from the date fixed by reg.6(3). However, reg.19(4) prevents an extension of the time-limit for the benefits covered by reg.6(3) leading to entitlement earlier than three months before the actual date of claim. But the restriction seems to stem from that regulation and not from s.1(2), or the earlier forms set out in Sch.1. 1.22

Note that from April 1997 the time limit for claiming social fund maternity and funeral payments is three months (Claims and Payments Regulations, reg.19(1) and Sch.4, paras 8 and 9) and there is no longer any provision allowing claims for these payments to be made outside this time limit.

Subsection (3)

1.23 Subsection (3) deals with a particular situation which may arise in connection with claims to attendance allowance and disability living allowance. In general, there is no objection to claims being made by someone on behalf of another person, though the Department will require a clear indication that the agent is acting with the express authority of the person claiming.

Subsection (4)

1.24 This subsection contains the definition of "benefit" for the purposes of the section.

The starting point is the definition of benefit in s.122 of the Contributions and Benefits Act, which (so far as current benefits are concerned) refers to benefits under Pts II–V of the Contributions and Benefits Act. Specific provisions of para.(4) add jobseeker's allowance, an employment and support allowance, State pension credit, and any income-related benefit.

Though fairly comprehensive, this list does not include child benefit and winter fuel payments. On the latter see *CIS/2337/2004*, para.9. This does not mean that claims are not required for those benefits (indeed provision is made for claims elsewhere in the social security legislation), but it does mean that s.1 does not apply in relation to entitlement to benefit being dependent upon a claim.

It can be argued that the form of decision will differ depending upon whether a claim is a condition of entitlement. It is at least arguable that, if a claim is not a condition of entitlement and no claim has been made but a person claims to be entitled to the benefit, any decision should be in the form that there is a nil award. By contrast, if an adverse decision is made because no claim has been made where a claim is a condition of entitlement, then the form of the decision should be that there is no entitlement. This fine distinction is unlikely to impress those seeking a benefit, but may assist in drawing a distinction between the majority of cases where s.1 makes a claim a condition of entitlement, and the much smaller class of cases where s.1 does not apply.

Subsection (5)

1.25 There were a number of different versions of the section from which this section is derived and subs.(5) indicates that this section is limited to claims made on or after October 1, 1990. Schedule 1 sets out the earlier variations of the section. In many cases concerning claims to benefit care will need to be taken to apply the law as at the date of the claim. There is a particular risk of error where appeals are being reheard after the considerable delays inherent in successful appeals. Obviously, as time goes by this risk will diminish and eventually disappear.

Retrospective effect of provisions making entitlement to benefit dependent on claim

1.26 **2.**—(1) This section applies where a claim for benefit is made or treated as made at any time on or after 2nd September 1985 (the date on which section 165A of the 1975 Act (general provision as to necessity of claim for entitlement to benefit), as originally enacted, came into force) in respect of a period the whole or any part of which falls on or after that date.

(2) Where this section applies, any question arising as to—

(a) whether the claimant is or was at any time (whether before, on or after 2nd September 1985) entitled to the benefit in question, or to any other benefit on which his entitlement to that benefit depends; or

(b) in a case where the claimant's entitlement to the benefit depends on the entitlement of another person to a benefit, whether that other person is or was so entitled,

shall be determined as if the relevant claim enactment and any regulations made under or referred to in that enactment had also been in force, with any necessary modifications, at all times relevant for the purpose of determining the entitlement of the claimant, and, where applicable, of the other person, to the benefit or benefits in question (including the entitlement of any person to any benefit on which that entitlement depends, and so on).

(3) In this section "the relevant claim enactment" means section 1 above as it has effect in relation to the claim referred to in subsection (1) above.

(4) In any case where—

(a) a claim for benefit was made or treated as made (whether before, on or after 2nd September 1985, and whether by the same claimant as the claim referred to in subsection (1) above or not), and benefit was awarded on that claim, in respect of a period falling wholly or partly before that date; but

(b) that award would not have been made had the current requirements applied in relation to claims for benefit, whenever made, in respect of periods before that date; and

(c) entitlement to the benefit claimed as mentioned in subsection (1) above depends on whether the claimant or some other person was previously entitled or treated as entitled to that or some other benefit,

then, in determining whether the conditions of entitlement to the benefit so claimed are satisfied, the person to whom benefit was awarded as mentioned in paragraphs (a) and (b) above shall be taken to have been entitled to the benefit so awarded, notwithstanding anything in subsection (2) above.

(5) In subsection (4) above "the current requirements" means—

(a) the relevant claim enactment, and any regulations made or treated as made under that enactment, or referred to in it, as in force at the time of the claim referred to in subsection (1) above, with any necessary modifications; and

(b) subsection (1) (with the omission of the words following "at any time") and subsections (2) and (3) above.

DERIVATION

Social Security Act 1975 s.165B. 1.27

DEFINITIONS

"the 1975 Act"—s.191.
"benefit"—see s.1(1).
"claim"—see s.191.
"claimant"—*ibid.*

GENERAL NOTE

There are a number of benefits where entitlement can depend on whether a person was entitled to a benefit at some earlier date (e.g. on reaching pensionable age). While the predecessor of s.1 clearly governed such questions from September 2, 1985, onwards, it was arguable that in relation to earlier dates the *McCaffrey* principle (see note to s.1(1) above) had to be applied. *R(S) 2/91* decided that that 1.28

argument was correct. The predecessor of s.2 was inserted by the Social Security Act 1990 to reverse the effect of that decision and to do so retrospectively back to September 2, 1985.

The form of s.2 is complex and the retrospective effects are difficult to work out. It only applies to claims made or treated as made on or after September 2, 1985 (subs.(1)). Thus very late appeals or very long good causes for late claim might not be affected. Then on any such claim if a question of entitlement at any other date arises (including dates before September 2, 1985) that question is to be decided according to the principle of s.1 as it was in force at the relevant time (subs.(2)). The only exception to this is that if for any period benefit has been awarded following a claim, that beneficiary is to be treated as entitled to that benefit even though under the current requirements he would not be (subs.(4)).

Work-focused interviews and work-related activity

[1 Claim or full entitlement to certain benefits conditional on work-focused interview.

1.29 **2A.**—(1) Regulations made make provision for or in connection with—

(a) imposing, as a condition falling to be satisfied by a person who—

(i) makes a claim for a benefit to which this section applies, and

[4 (ii) has not attained pensionable age at the time of making the claim (but see subsection (1A)),]

a requirement to take part in [4 one or more work-focused interviews];

(b) imposing at a time when—

(i) a person [4 has not attained pensionable age and is] entitled to such a benefit, and

(ii) any prescribed circumstances exist,

a requirement to take part in [4 one or more work-focused interviews] as a condition of that person continuing to be entitled to the full amount which is payable to him in respect of the benefit apart from the regulations.

[4 (1A) For the purposes of subsection (1) a man born before [8 6 December 1953] is treated as attaining pensionable age when a woman born on the same day as the man would attain pensionable age.]

(2) The benefits to which this section applies are—

(a) income support;

(b) housing benefit;

(c) council tax benefit;

(d) widow's and bereavement benefits falling within section 20(1)(e) and (ea) of the Contributions and Benefits Act [9 . . .];

(e) incapacity benefit;

(f) severe disablement allowance; and

(g) [2 carer's allowance].

[6 (2A) No requirement may be imposed by virtue of this section on a person who—

(a) is not a member of a couple, and

(b) is responsible for, and a member of the same household as, a child under the age of one.

(2B) For the purposes of subsection (2A)(b) regulations may make provision—

(a) as to circumstances in which one person is to be treated as responsible or not responsible for another;
(b) as to circumstances in which persons are to be treated as being or not being members of the same household.]

(3) Regulations under this section may, in particular, make provision—
(a) for securing, where a person would otherwise be required to take part in interviews relating to two or more benefits—
(i) that he is only required to take part in one interview, and
(ii) that any such interview is capable of counting for the purposes of all those benefits;
(b) for determining the person by whom interviews are to be conducted;
(c) conferring power on such persons or the designated authority to determine when and where interviews are to take place (including power in prescribed circumstances to determine that they are to take place in the homes of those being interviewed);
(d) prescribing the circumstances in which persons attending interviews are to be regarded as having or not having taken part in them;
(e) for securing that the appropriate consequences mentioned in subsection (4)(a) or (b) below ensue if a person who has been notified that he is required to take part in an interview—
(i) fails to take part in the interview, and
(ii) does not show, within the prescribed period, that he had good cause for that failure;
(f) prescribing—
(i) matters which are or are not to be taken into account in determining whether a person does or does not have good cause for any failure to comply with the regulations, or
(ii) circumstances in which a person is or is not to be regarded as having or not having good cause for any such failure.

(4) For the purposes of subsection (3)(e) above the appropriate consequence of a failure falling within that provision are—
(a) where the requirement to take part in an interview applied by virtue of subsection (1)(a) above, that as regards any relevant benefit either—
(i) the person in question is to be regarded as not having made a claim for the benefit, or
(ii) if (in the cases of an interview postponed in accordance with subsection (7)) that person has already been awarded the benefit, his entitlement to the benefit is to terminate immediately;
(b) where the requirement to take part in an interview applied by virtue of subsection (1)(b) above, that the amount payable to the person in question in respect of any relevant benefit is to be reduced by the specified amount until the specified time.

(5) Regulations under this section may, in relation to any such reduction, provide—
(a) for the amount of the reduction to be calculated in the first instance by reference to such amount as may be prescribed;
(b) for the amount as so calculated to be restricted, in prescribed circumstances, to the prescribed extent;
(c) where the person in question is entitled to two or more relevant benefits, for determining the extent, and the order, in which those

benefits are to be reduced in order to give effect to the reduction required in his case.

(6) Regulations under this section may provide that any requirement to take part in an interview that would otherwise apply to a person by virtue of such regulations—

(a) is, in any prescribed circumstances, either not to apply or not to apply until such time as is specified;

(b) is not to apply if the designated authority determines that an interview—

(i) would not be of assistance to that person, or

(ii) would not be appropriate in the circumstances,

(c) is not to apply until such time as the designated authority determines, if that authority determines that an interview—

(i) would not be of assistance to that person, or

(ii) would not be appropriate in the circumstances,

until that time;

and the regulations may make provision for treating a person in relation to whom any such requirement does not apply, or does not apply until a particular time, as having complied with that requirement to such extent and for such purposes as are specified.

(7) Where—

(a) a person is required to take part in an interview by virtue of subsection (1)(a), and

(b) the interview is postponed by or under regulations made in pursuance of subsection (6)(a) or (c),

the time to which it is postponed may be a time falling after an award of the relevant benefit to that person.

[[7] (7A) Information supplied in pursuance of regulations under this section shall be taken for all purposes to be information relating to social security.]

(8) In this section—

[[6] "couple" has the meaning given by section 137(1) of the Contributions and Benefits Act;]

"the designated authority" means such of the following as may be specified, namely—

(a) the Secretary of State,

(b) a person providing services to the Secretary of State,

(c) a local authority,

[[3] (ca) subject to subsection (9), a county council in England,]

(d) [[3] subject to subsection (9),] a person providing services to, or authorised to exercise any function of, [[3] any authority mentioned in paragraph (c) or (ca)];

"interview" (in subsections (3) to (7)) means a work-focused interview;

"relevant benefit", in relation to any person required to take part in a work-focused interview, means any benefit in relation to which that requirement applied by virtue of subsection (1)(a) or (b) above;

"specified" means prescribed by or determined in accordance with regulations;

"work-focused interview", in relation to a person, means an interview conducted for such purposes connected with employment or training in the case of that person as may be specified;

and the purposes which may be specified include purposes connected with a person's existing or future employment or training prospects or needs, and (in particular) assisting or encouraging a person to enhance his employment prospects.]

[3 (9) A county council in England or a person providing services to, or authorised to exercise any function of, such a council may be specified as the designated authority only in relation to interviews with persons to whom the council is required to make support services available under section 68(1) of the Education and Skills Act 2008 (support services: provisions by [5 local authorities]).]

AMENDMENTS

1. This section was added by the Welfare Reform and Pensions Act 1999 ss.57–58 with effect from November 11, 1999.

2. The Regulatory Reform (Carer's Allowance) Order 2002 (SI 2002/1457) art.1 (September 1, 2002 for the purpose of making regulations; April 1, 2003 for all other purposes).

3. Education and Skills Act 2008 Sch.1 para.45 (January 26, 2009).

4. Welfare Reform Act 2009 s.35(2) (February 10, 2010).

5. Education and Skills Act 2008 Sch.1 para.45 (May 5, 2010; commenced by an amendment).

6. Welfare Reform Act 2009 s.3(2) (October 6, 2011 for the purpose of making regulations) (October 31, 2011 for all other purposes).

7. Welfare Reform Act 2009 s.34(1) (January 12, 2010).

8. Pensions Act 2011 Sch.1 para.3 (January 3, 2012).

9. Pensions Act 2014 s.31 and Sch.16 para.22 (April 6, 2017).

[1 Full entitlement to certain benefits conditional on work-focused interview for partner

2AA.—(1) Regulations may make provision for or in connection with imposing, at a time when— 1.30

(a) a person ("the claimant") who—

[6 (i) has not attained pensionable age (but see subsection (1A)), and

(ii) has a partner who has also not attained pensionable age,]

is entitled to a benefit to which this section applies at a higher rate referable to his partner, and

(b) prescribed circumstances exist.

A requirement for the partner to take part in [6 one or more work-focused interviews] as a condition of the benefit continuing to be payable to the claimant at that rate.

[6 (1A) For the purposes of subsection (1) a man born before 6 December 1953 is treated as attaining pensionable age when a woman born on the same day as the man would attain pensionable age.]

(2) The benefits to which this section applies are—

(a) income support;

(b) an income-based jobseeker's allowance other than a joint-claim jobseeker's allowance;

(c) incapacity benefit;

(d) severe disablement allowance; [6 . . .]

(e) [3 carer's allowance] [6; and]

[4 (f) an employment and support allowance.]

(3) For the purposes of this section a benefit is payable to a person at a higher rate referable to his partner if the amount that is payable in his case—

(a) is more than it would be if the person concerned was not a member of a couple; or
(b) includes an increase of benefit for his partner as an adult dependant of his.

(4) Regulations under this section may, in particular, make provision—

(a) for securing, where the partner of the claimant would otherwise be required to take part in work-focused interviews relating to two or more benefits—
 (i) that the partner is required instead to take part in only one such interview; and
 (ii) that the interview is capable of counting for the purposes of all those benefits;
(b) in a case where the claimant has more than one partner, for determining which of those partners is required to take part in the work-focused interview or requiring each of them to take part in such an interview;
(c) for determining the persons by whom work-focused interviews are to be conducted;
(d) conferring power on such persons or the designated authority to determine when and where work-focused interviews are to take place (including power in prescribed circumstances to determine that they are to take place in the homes of those being interviewed);
(e) prescribing the circumstances in which partners attending work-focused interviews are to be regarded as having or not having taken part in them;
(f) for securing that if—
 (i) a partner who has been notified of a requirement to take part in a work-focused interview fails to take part in it, and
 (ii) it is not shown (by him or by the claimant), within the prescribed period, that he had good cause for that failure,

the amount payable to the claimant in respect of the benefit in relation to which the requirement applied is to be reduced by the specified amount until the specified time;

(g) prescribing—
 (i) matters which are or are not to be taken into account in determining whether a partner does or does not have good cause for any failure to comply with the regulations; or
 (ii) circumstances in which a partner is or is not to be regarded as having or not having good cause for any such failure.

(5) Regulations under this section may, in relation to a reduction under subsection (4)(f), provide—

(a) for the amount of the reduction to be calculated in the first instance by reference to such amount as may be prescribed;
(b) for the amount as so calculated to be restricted, in prescribed circumstances, to the prescribed extent;
(c) where the claimant is entitled to two or more benefits in relation to each of which a requirement to take part in a work-focused interview applied, for determining the extent to, and the order in, which those benefits are to be reduced in order to give effect to the reduction required in his case.

(6) Regulations under this section may provide that any requirement

to take part in a work-focused interview that would otherwise apply to a partner by virtue of the regulations—

(a) is, in any prescribed circumstances, either not to apply or not to apply until the specified time;

(b) is not to apply if the designated authority determines that such an interview would not be of assistance to him or appropriate in the circumstances;

(c) is not to apply until such time as the designated authority determines (if that authority determines that such an interview would not be of assistance to him or appropriate in the circumstances until that time);

and the regulations may make provision for treating a partner to whom any such requirement does not apply, or does not apply until a particular time, as having complied with that requirement to such extent and for such purposes as are specified.

[7 (6A) Information supplied in pursuance of regulations under this section shall be taken for all purposes to be information relating to social security.]

(7) In this section—

[2 "couple" has the meaning given by s.137(1) of the Contributions and Benefits Act;]

"designated authority" means such of the following as may be specified, namely—

(a) the Secretary of State,

(b) a person providing services to the Secretary of State,

(c) a local authority, and

[5 (ca) subject to subsection (8), a county council in England, and]

(d) [5 subject to subsection (8),] a person providing services to, or authorised to exercise any function of, [5 any authority mentioned in paragraph (c) or (ca)];

"partner" means a person who is a member of the same couple as the claimant;

"specified" means prescribed by or determined in accordance with regulations;

and

"work-focused interview" has the same meaning as in section 2A above.]

[5 (8) A county council in England or a person providing services to, or authorised to exercise any function of, such a council may be specified as the designated authority only in relation to interviews with persons to whom the council is required to make support services available under section 68(1) of the Education and Skills Act 2008 (support services: provisions by [8 local authorities]).]

Amendments

1. Inserted by the Employment Act 2002 s.49 (July 5, 2003).
2. Civil Partnership Act 2004 s.254 and Sch.24 para.55 (December 5, 2005).
3. Welfare Reform Act 2007 Sch.7(3) (July 3, 2007).
4. Welfare Reform Act 2007 s.28 and Sch.3 para.10 (October 27, 2008).
5. Education and Skills Act 2008 Sch.1 para.46 (January 26, 2009).
6. Welfare Reform Act 2009 s.35 (February 10, 2010).
7. Welfare Reform Act 2009 s.34 (January 12, 2010).
8. Education and Skills Act 2008 Sch.1 para.45 (May 5, 2010; commenced by an amendment).

[1 Supplementary provisions relating to work-focused interviews

1.31 **2B.**—(1) Chapter II of Part I of the Social Security Act 1998 (social security decisions and appeals) shall have effect in relation to relevant decisions subject to and in accordance with subsections (3) to (8) below (and in those subsections "the 1998 Act" means that Act).

(2) For the purposes of this section a "relevant decision" is a decision made under regulations under section 2A above that a person—

(a) has failed to comply with a requirement to take part in an interview which applied to him by virtue of the regulations, or

(b) has not shown, within the prescribed period mentioned in section 2A(3)(e)(ii) above, that he had good cause for such a failure.

[3 (2A) For the purposes of this section a "relevant decision", in relation to regulations under section 2AA above, is a decision that—

(a) the partner of a person entitled to a benefit has failed to comply with a requirement to take part in an interview which applied to the partner by virtue of the regulations, or

(b) it has not been shown within the prescribed period mentioned in section 2AA(4)(f)(ii) above that the partner had good cause for such a failure.]

(3) Section 8(1)(c) of the 1998 Act (decisions falling to be made under or by virtue of certain enactments are to be made by the Secretary of State) shall have effect subject to any provisions of regulations under section 2A [4 or 2AA] above by virtue of which relevant decisions fall to be made otherwise than by the Secretary of State.

(4) For the purposes of each of sections 9 and 10 of the 1998 Act (revision and supersession of decisions of Secretary of State) any relevant decision made otherwise than by the Secretary of State shall be treated as if it were such a decision made by the Secretary of State (and accordingly may be revised by him under section 9 or superseded by a decision made by him under section 10).

(5) Subject to any provisions of regulations under either section 9 or 10 of the 1998 Act, any relevant decision made, or (by virtue of subsection (4) above) treated as made, by the Secretary of State may be—

(a) revised under section 9 by a person or authority exercising functions under regulations under section 2A [4 or 2AA] above other than the Secretary of State, or

(b) superseded under section 10 by a decision made by such a person or authority,

as if that person or authority were the Secretary of State.

(6) Regulations shall make provision for conferring (except in any prescribed circumstances) a right of appeal under section 12 of the 1998 Act (appeal to [5First-tier Tribunal]) against—

(a) any relevant decision, and

(b) any decision under section 10 of that Act superseding any such decision, whether made by the Secretary of State or otherwise.

(7) Subsections (4) to (6) above apply whether—

(a) the relevant decision, or

(b) (in the case of subsection (6)(b)) the decision under section 10 of the 1998 Act,

is as originally made or has been revised (by the Secretary of State or otherwise) under section 9 of that Act; and regulations under subsection (6) above may make provision for treating, for the purposes of section 12 of that Act, any decision made or revised otherwise than by the Secretary of State as if it were a decision made or revised by him.

(8) Section 12 of the 1998 Act shall not apply to any decision falling within subsection (6) above except in accordance with regulations under that subsection.

(9) In [2. . .]

(b) section 72(6) of the Welfare Reform and Pensions Act 1999 (supply of information),

any reference to information relating to social security includes any information supplied by a person for the purposes of an interview which he is required to take part in by virtue of section 2A [4 or 2AA] above.

(10) In this section "interview" means a work-focused interview within the meaning of section 2A above.]

AMENDMENTS

1. Welfare Reform and Pensions Act 1999 s.57 (November 11, 1999).
2. Employment Act 2002 (2002 c.22) s.54 and Sch.8 (November 24, 2002).
3. Employment Act 2002 (2002 c.22) s.54 and Sch.7 (July 5, 2003).
4. Employment Act 2002 (2002 c.22) s.53 and Sch.7 (July 5, 2003).
5. The Transfer of Tribunal Functions Order 2008 (SI 2008/2833) art.102 (November 3, 2008).

[1 Optional work-focused interviews

2C.—(1) Regulations may make provision for conferring on local authorities functions in connection with conducting work-focused interviews in cases where such interviews are requested or consented to by persons to whom this section applies. 1.32

(2) This section applies to[3 . . .] [3 —

(a) persons making claims for or entitled to any of the benefits listed in section 2A(2) above or any prescribed benefit; and

(b) partners of persons entitled to any of the benefits listed in section 2AA(2) above or any prescribed benefit;]

and it so applies regardless of whether such persons have, in accordance with regulations under section 2A [3 or 2AA] above, already taken part in interviews conducted under such regulations.

(3) The function which may be conferred on a local authority [4 or on a county council in England] by regulations under this section include functions relating to—

(a) the obtaining and receiving of information for the purposes of work-focused interviews conducted under the regulations;

(b) the recording and forwarding of information supplied at, or for the purposes of, such interviews;

(c) the taking of steps to identify potential employment or training opportunities for persons taking part in such interviews.

[4(3A) Regulations under this section may confer functions on a county council in England only in relation to interviews with persons to whom the council is required to make support services available under section 68(1) of the Education and Skills Act 2008 (support services: provision by [5 local authorities]).]

(4) Regulations under this section may make different provision for different areas or different authorities.

for the circumstances and manner in which payment may be made to one person on behalf of another for any purpose, which may be to discharge, in whole or in part, an obligation of the person entitled to the benefit or any other person;

(r) for making a payment on account of a benefit, or conferring a right to make a reduction [4 . . .] on account, where no claim has been made and it is impracticable for one to be made immediately;

(s) for making a payment on account of a benefit, or conferring a right to make a reduction [4 . . .] on account, where a claim has been made but it is impracticable for the claim or an appeal, reference, review or application relating to it to be determined immediately;

(t) for making a payment on account of a benefit, or conferring a right to make a reduction [4 . . .] on account, where an award has been made but it is impracticable to institute the benefit immediately;

(u) generally as to administration.

(2) Regulations under this section may include [6provision in relation to council tax benefit that prescribed provisions shall apply instead of prescribed provisions of Part I or II of the Local Government Finance Act 1992, or that prescribed provisions of either of those Parts shall not apply] or shall apply subject to prescribed amendments or adaptations.

[7(3) References in subsection (2) above to either of the Parts there mentioned include references to regulations made under the Part concerned.]

AMENDMENTS

1. Local Government Finance Act 1992 Sch.9 para.12(1)(a) (July 1, 1992: substituted from March 6, 1992 but affected provision was not in force until July 1, 1992).
2. Local Government Finance Act 1992 Sch.9 para.12(1)(b) (July 1, 1992: substituted from March 6, 1992 but affected provision was not in force until July 1, 1992).
3. Child Support, Pensions and Social Security Act 2000 Sch.7 para.21(2) (November 1, 2000).
4. Local Government Finance Act 1992 Sch.9 para.12(1)(c) (July 1, 1992: substituted from March 6, 1992 but affected provision was not in force until July 1, 1992).
5. Social Security Act 1998 Sch.8 para.1 (July 2, 2001 as SI 2001/2316).
6. Local Government Finance Act 1992 Sch.9 para.12(2) (July 1, 1992: substituted from March 6, 1992 but affected provision was not in force until July 1, 1992).
7. Local Government Finance Act 1992 Sch.9 para.12(3) (July 1, 1992: substituted from March 6, 1992 but affected provision was not in force until July 1, 1992).

GENERAL NOTE

1.48 In relation to the abolition of council tax benefit, s.6 is repealed by the Welfare Reform Act 2012 Sch.14(1) para.1 with effect from April 1, 2013, subject to savings and transitional provisions as set out in SI 2013/358.

Relationship between community charge benefits

1.49 **7.**—(1) Regulations may provide for a claim for one relevant benefit to be treated, either in the alternative or in addition, as a claim for any other relevant benefit that may be prescribed.

(2) Regulations may provide for treating a payment made or right conferred by virtue of regulations—

(a) [1 . . .]
(b) under section 6(1)(r) to (t) above,

as made or conferred on account of any relevant benefit that is subsequently awarded or paid.

(3) For the purposes of subsections (1) and (2) above relevant benefits are—

(a) any benefit to which section 5 above applies; and
(b) [2 council tax benefit].

AMENDMENTS

1. Welfare Reform Act 2012 Sch.14(11) para.1 (April 1, 2013).

2. Local Government Finance Act 1992 Sch.9 para.13 (July 1, 1992: substituted from March 6, 1992 but affected provision was not in force until July 1, 1992).

DERIVATION

Social Security Act 1986 s.51B. 1.50

DEFINITIONS

"claim"—see s.191.
"prescribed"—*ibid.*

[1 Sharing of functions as regards certain claims and information

7A.—(1)Regulations may, for the purpose of supplementing the persons or bodies to whom claims for relevant benefits may be made, make provision— 1.51

(a) as regards housing benefit or council tax benefit, for claims for that benefit to be made to—
  (i) a Minister of the Crown, or
  (ii) a person providing services to a Minister of the Crown;
(b) as regards any other relevant benefit for claims for that benefit to be made to—
  (i) a local authority,
  (ii) a person providing services to a local authority, or
  (iii) a person authorised to exercise any function of a local authority relating to housing benefit or council tax benefit.

[4 (c) as regards any relevant benefit, for claims for that benefit to be made to—
  (i) a county council in England,
  (ii) a person providing services to a county council in England, or
  (iii) a person authorised to exercise any function a county council in England has under this section.]

(2) Regulations may make provision for or in connection with—

(a) the forwarding by a relevant authority of—
  (i) claims received by virtue of any provision authorised by subsection (1) above, and
  (ii) information or evidence supplied in connection with making such claims (whether supplied by persons making the claims or by other persons);
(b) the receiving and forwarding by a relevant authority of information or evidence relating to social security [3 or work] matters supplied by, or the obtaining by a relevant authority of such information or evidence from—

it in the manner, and within the time, prescribed in relation to health in pregnancy grant by regulations under section 5.

(2) No person is entitled to health in pregnancy grant unless subsection (3) or (4) is satisfied in relation to her.

(3) This subsection is satisfied in relation to a person if her claim for health in pregnancy grant is accompanied by—

(a) a statement of her national insurance number and information or evidence establishing that that number has been allocated to her; or

(b) information or evidence enabling the national insurance number that has been allocated to her to be ascertained.

(4) This subsection is satisfied in relation to a person if she makes an application for a national insurance number to be allocated to her which is accompanied by information or evidence enabling a national insurance number to be allocated to her.

(5) The Commissioners for Her Majesty's Revenue and Customs may by regulations make provision disapplying subsection (2) in the case of prescribed descriptions of persons making a claim.]

AMENDMENT

1. Added by Health and Social Care Act 2008 s.132(3) (July 21, 2008 in relation to enabling the exercise on or after July 21, 2008 of any power to make orders or regulations and defining expressions relevant to the exercise of any such power; January 1, 2009 in relation to England and Wales; not yet in force otherwise).

GENERAL NOTE

1.65 Health in pregnancy grant was a short-lived benefit. It was only made available to those who had reached the 25th week of their pregnancy by January 1, 2011: see s.3 of the Savings Accounts and Health in Pregnancy Grants Act 2010.

Child benefit

Necessity of application for child benefit

1.66 **13.**—(1) Subject to the provisions of this Act, no person shall be entitled to child benefit unless he claims it in the manner, and within the time, prescribed in relation to child benefit by regulations under section 5 above.

[1 (1A) No person shall be entitled to child benefit unless subsection (1B) below is satisfied in relation to him.

(1B) This subsection is satisfied in relation to a person if—

(a) his claim for child benefit is accompanied by—

(i) a statement of his national insurance number and information or evidence establishing that that number has been allocated to him; or

(ii) information or evidence enabling the national insurance number that has been allocated to him to be ascertained; or

(b) he make an application for a national insurance number to be allocated to him which is accompanied by information or evidence enabling such a number to be so allocated.

(1C) Regulations may make provision disapplying subsection (1A) above in the case of—

(a) prescribed descriptions of persons making claims, or

(b) prescribed descriptions of children [2 or qualifying young persons] in respect of whom child benefit is claimed,

or in other prescribed circumstances.]

(2) Except where regulations otherwise provide, no person shall be entitled to child benefit for any week on a claim made by him after that week if child benefit in respect of the same child [2 or qualifying young person] has already been paid for that week to another person, whether or not that other person was entitled to it.

AMENDMENTS

1. Welfare Reform and Pensions Act 1999 s.69 (May 15, 2000).
2. Child Benefit Act 2005 Sch.1 Pt 1 para.20 (April 10, 2006).

DERIVATION

CBA 1975 s.6. 1.67

GENERAL NOTE

There is a general bar on receiving child benefit if it has already been paid to someone else in respect of the same child even though that other person was not entitled to it. 1.68

The rules relating to claims for and payments of child benefit are now to be found in the Claims and Payments Regulations 1987.

See reg.38 of the Child Benefit (General) Regulations 2006 in Volume 1 for an escape route from the application of the rule in subs.(2).

Section 13A Omitted. 1.69

Statutory sick pay

Section 14 Omitted. 1.70

Statutory maternity pay

Section 15 Omitted. 1.71

[1Payments in respect of mortgage interest etc.

Payment out of benefit of sums in respect of mortgage interest etc.

15A.—(1) This section applies in relation to cases where— 1.72
(a) mortgage interest is payable to a qualifying lender by a person ("the borrower") who is entitled, or whose partner, former partner or qualifying associate is entitled, to [9 universal credit;] income support [2 . . .] [8 an income-based jobseeker's allowance or an income-related employment and support allowance]; and
(b) a sum in respect of that mortgage interest is or was brought into account in determining [9maximum amount for the purposes of universal credit or] the applicable amount for the purposes of income support [2 . . .] [8 an income-based jobseeker's allowance or an income-related employment and support allowance] in the case of the borrower or the partner, former partner or qualifying associate;

and any reference in this section to "the relevant beneficiary" is a reference to the person whose [9 maximum amount for the purposes of universal credit or] applicable amount for the purposes of income support or [2 . . .] [8 an income-based jobseeker's allowance or an income-related employment and support allowance] is or was determined as mentioned in paragraph (b) above.

[3 (1A) This section also applies in relation to cases where—

(c) mortgage interest is payable to a qualifying lender by a person (also referred to as "the borrower") who is, or whose partner, or former partner or qualifying associate is, entitled to state pension credit; and

(d) a sum in respect of that mortgage interest is or was brought into account in determining the appropriate minimum guarantee for the purposes of state pension credit in the case of the borrower or the partner, former partner or qualifying associate;

and any reference in this section to "the relevant beneficiary" includes a reference to the person whose appropriate minimum guarantee for the purposes of state pension credit is or was determined as mentioned in paragraph (b) above.]

(2) Without prejudice to paragraphs (i) and (p) of section 5(1) above, regulations may, in relation to cases where this section applies, make provision—

(a) requiring that, in prescribed circumstances, a prescribed part of any relevant benefits [3 (other than state pension credit)] to which the relevant beneficiary is entitled shall be paid by the Secretary of State directly to the qualifying lender and applied by that lender towards the discharge of the liability in respect of the mortgage interest;

[3 (aa) authorising or requiring that, in prescribed circumstances, a prescribed part of any state pension credit to which the relevant beneficiary is entitled may (or, as the case may be, shall) be paid by the Secretary of State directly to the qualifying lender and shall be applied by that lender towards the discharge of the liability in respect of the mortgage interest;]

(b) for the expenses of the Secretary of State in administering the making of payments under the regulations to be defrayed, in whole or in part, at the expense of qualifying lenders, whether by requiring them to pay prescribed fees or by deducting and retaining a prescribed part of the payments that would otherwise be made to them under the regulations or by such other method as may be prescribed;

(c) for requiring a qualifying lender, in a case where by virtue of paragraph (b) above the amount of the payment made to him under the regulations is less than it would otherwise have been, to credit against the liability in respect of the mortgage interest (in addition to the payment actually made) an amount equal to the difference between—

(i) the payment that would have been so made, apart from paragraph (b) above; and

(ii) the payment actually made;

and, in any such case, for treating the amount so credited as properly paid on account of benefit due to the relevant beneficiary;

(d) for enabling a body which, or person who, would otherwise be a qualifying lender to elect not to be regarded as such for the purposes of this section, other than this paragraph;

(e) for the recovery from any body or person—

(i) of any sums paid to that body or person by way of payment under the regulations that ought not to have been so paid; or

(ii) of any fees or other sums due from that body or person by virtue of paragraph (b) above;

(f) for cases where the same person is the borrower in relation to mortgage interest payable in respect of two or more different loans; and

(g) for any person of a prescribed class or description who would otherwise be regarded for the purposes of this section as the borrower in relation to any mortgage interest not to be so regarded, except for the purposes of this paragraph;

but the Secretary of State shall not make any regulations under paragraph (b) above unless he has consulted with such organisations representing qualifying lenders likely to be affected by the regulations as he considers appropriate.

(3) The bodies and persons who are "qualifying lenders" for the purposes of this section are—

[4 (a) a deposit taker;]

(b) [4 . . .]

[4 (c) an insurer;]

(d) any county council, [5 county borough council,] district council . . . or London Borough Council,

(e) the Common Council of the City of London,

[6 (ee) any council constituted under section 2 of the Local Government etc (Scotland) Act 1994]

(f) the Council of the Isles of Scilly,

(g) any new town corporation,

and such bodies or persons not falling within the above paragraphs as may be prescribed.

(4) In this section—

[3 "appropriate minimum guarantee" has the meaning given by section 2(3) of the State Pension Credit Act 2002;]

[4 "deposit taker" means—

(a) a person who has permission under [10 Part 4A] of the Financial Services and Markets Act 2000 to accept deposits, or

(b) an EEA firm of the kind mentioned in paragraph 5(b) of Schedule 3 to that Act which has permission under paragraph 15 of that Schedule (as a result of qualifying for authorisation under paragraph 12 of that Schedule) to accept deposits;

"insurer" means—

(a) a person who has permission under [10 Part 4A] of the Financial Services and Markets Act 2000 to effect and carry out contracts of insurance, or

(b) an EEA firm of the kind mentioned in [paragraph 5(d)] of Schedule 3 to that Act which has permission under paragraph 15 of that Schedule (as a result of qualifying for authorisation under paragraph 12 of that Schedule) to effect and carry out contracts of insurance;]

"mortgage interest" means interest on a loan which is secured by a mortgage of or charge over land, or (in Scotland) by a heritable security, and which has been taken out to defray money applied for any of the following purposes, that is to say—

(a) acquiring any residential land which was intended, at the time of the acquisition, for occupation by the borrower as his home;
(b) carrying out repairs or improvements to any residential land which was intended, at the time of taking out the loan, for occupation by the borrower as his home;
(c) paying off another loan; or
(d) any prescribed purpose not falling within paragraphs (a) to (c) above;

but interest shall be regarded as mortgage interest by virtue of paragraph (c) above only to the extent that interest on that other loan would have been regarded as mortgage interest for the purposes of this section had the loan not been paid off;

"partner" means—

(a) any person [[7] who is married to, or a civil partner of, the borrower] and who is a member of the same household as the borrower; or
(b) any person [[7] who is neither married to, nor a civil partner of, the borrower but who lives together with the borrower as [[11] if they were a married couple], otherwise than in prescribed circumstances;

and "former partner" means a person who has at some time been, but no longer is, the borrower's partner;

"qualifying associate", in relation to the borrower, means a person who, for the purposes of income support, [[3] or an income-based jobseeker's allowance], [[8]state pension credit or an income-related employment and support allowance], [[9] or universal credit] falls to be treated by regulations under Part VII of the Contributions and Benefits Act [[8], the State Pension Credit Act 2002 or Part 1 of the Welfare Reform Act 2007], [[6] or Part 1 of the Welfare Reform Act 2012] as responsible for so much of that expenditure which relates to housing costs (within the meaning of those regulations) as consists of any of the mortgage interest payable by the borrower, and who falls to be so treated because—

(a) the borrower is not meeting those costs, so that the person has to meet them if he is to continue to live in the dwelling occupied as his home; and
(b) the person is one whom it is reasonable, in the circumstances, to treat as liable to meet those costs;

"relevant benefits" means such of the following benefits as may be prescribed, namely—

[[9](za) universal credit]
(a) benefits, as defined in section 122 of the Contributions and Benefits Act;
[[2] (aa) a jobseeker's allowance;]
(b) income support;
[[3] (c) state pension credit;]
[[8] (d) an employment and support allowance;]

"residential land" means any land which consists of or includes a dwelling.

[[4] (4A) The definitions of "deposit taker" and "insurer" in subsection (4) must be read with—

(a) section 22 of the Financial Services and Markets Act 2000;
(b) any relevant order under that section; and

(c) Schedule 2 to that Act.]

[11 (4B) . . .]

(5) For the purposes of this section, regulations may make provision—

(a) as to circumstances in which residential land is or is not to be treated as intended for occupation by the borrower as his home; or

(b) as to circumstances in which persons are to be treated as being or not being members of the same household.]

AMENDMENTS

1. Social Security (Mortgage Interest Payments) Act 1992 s.1 and Sch. para.1 (July 1, 1992; the equivalent amendment to the Social Security Act 1986 came into force on March 16, 1992).

2. Jobseekers Act 1995 Sch.2 para.40 (October 7, 1996).

3. State Pension Credit Act 2002 s.14 and Sch.2 (July 2, 2002 for the purpose only of making regulation; fully in force October 6, 2003).

4. The Financial Services and Markets Act 2000 (Consequential Amendments and Repeals) Order 2001 (SI 2001/3649) (October 6, 2003).

5. Local Government (Wales) Act 1994 Sch.8 para.11 (April 1, 1996).

6. Local Government etc. (Scotland) Act 1994 Sch.13 para.175 (April 1, 1996).

7. Civil Partnership Act 2004 s.254 and Sch.24 para.57 (December 5, 2005).

8. Welfare Reform Act 2007 s.28 and Sch.3 para.10 (October 27, 2008).

9. Welfare Reform Act 2012 s.31 and Sch.2 para.6 (February 25, 2013).

10. Financial Services Act 2012 s.114 and Sch.18 para.74(2) (April 1, 2013).

11. The Marriage (Same Sex Couples) Act 2013 (Consequential and Contrary Provisions and Scotland) Order 2014 (SI 2014/560) art.23 (March 13, 2014).

DEFINITION

"Contributions and Benefits Act"—see s.191.

GENERAL NOTE

Section 15A authorises the regulations which set out the meat of the scheme for direct payment to lenders of the element of housing costs in relation to income-based benefits to cover mortgage interest and supplies some basic definitions. The main provisions are in Sch.9A to the Claims and Payments Regulations. **1.73**

With effect from December 16, 2014, art.29 and Sch.5 para.9 of the Marriage and Civil Partnership (Scotland) Act 2014 and Civil Partnership Act 2004 (Consequential Provisions and Modifications Order 2001 (SI 2014/3229) amended the definition of "partner" by substituting a definition in the same terms as the existing definition. However, the existing definition applied only to England and Wales; the new definition applies to England, Wales, Scotland and Northern Ireland.

Emergency payments

Emergency payments by local authorities and other bodies

16.—(1) The Secretary of State may make arrangements— **1.74**

(a) with a local authority to which this section applies; or

(b) with any other body,

for the making on his behalf by members of the staff of any such authority or body of payments on account of benefits to which section 5 above applies in circumstances corresponding to those in which the Secretary of State himself has the power to make such payments under subsection (1)(r) of that section; and a local authority to which this section applies shall have power to enter into any such arrangements.

(2) A payment under any such arrangements shall be treated for the purposes of any Act of Parliament or instrument made under an Act of Parliament as if it had been made by the Secretary of State.

(3) The Secretary of State shall repay a local authority or other body such amount as he determines to be the reasonable administrative expenses incurred by the authority or body in making payments in accordance with arrangements under this subsection.

(4) The local authorities to which this section applies are—

(a) a local authority as defined in section 270(1) of the Local Government Act 1972, other than a parish or community council;

(b) the Common Council of the City of London; and

(c) a local authority as defined in section 235(1) of the Local Government (Scotland) Act 1973.

DERIVATION

1.75 Social Security Act 1988 s.8.

PART II

ADJUDICATION

1.76 *Repealed.*

PART III

OVERPAYMENTS AND ADJUSTMENTS OF BENEFIT

GENERAL NOTE

Overview of overpayments

1.77 The overpayments landscape has changed. There are now two distinct systems for recovering benefit which has been overpaid, though there remain some similarities between the two systems.

Overpayments that are automatically recoverable

1.78 Provision has been made by the Welfare Reform Act 2012 for the recovery of overpaid benefit whatever the circumstances in which the overpayment has arisen. Overpayments under this new system, which might conveniently be thought of as recovery under the 2013 rules, are automatically recoverable. The relevant provisions are to be found in ss.71ZB–71ZF, and the Social Security (Overpayments and Recovery) Regulations 2013 (paras 2.869–2.914 below). The benefits subject to this new regime are:

- Universal credit;
- New-style Contributory Jobseeker's Allowance where the claim was made on or after April 29, 2013;
- New-style Contributory Employment and Support Allowance where the claim was made on or after April 29, 2013; and
- the housing credit element of state pension credit.

In addition there are three further situations in which an overpayment is always recoverable:

- where the late payment of income has resulted in a person being paid more income support, income-based jobseeker's allowance, income-based employment and support allowance, or pension credit: s.74 of the SSAA 1992;
- where too much mortgage interest has been paid to the beneficiary's lender where the beneficiary is in receipt of income support, income-based jobseeker's allowance, income-based employment and support allowance, or pension credit: Sch.9A para.11 of the Claims and Payments Regulations; and
- where too much benefit has been credited to a beneficiary's bank account: s.71(4) of the SSAA 1992.

Appeals are available against decisions that an overpayment is automatically recoverable but the grounds for a successful appeal will relate to the formalities rather than what might be called the merits of recovery, though it may be possible to appeal against any decision changing entitlement if something has gone wrong in that respect.

Overpayments which are sometimes recoverable

This is the traditional territory of overpayment recovery and applies to all benefits other than those mentioned above and overpayments of housing benefit. 1.79
The relevant rules are to be found in s.71 of the SSAA 1992 and the Social Security (Payments on Account, Overpayments and Recovery) Regulations 1988 (paras 2.915–2.955 below). Under this system, the overpayment can only be recovered if:

- the decision awarding benefit has been changed; and
- there has been a failure to disclose a material fact or misrepresentation of a material fact; and
- the overpayment was caused by the failure to disclose or the misrepresentation.

Misrepresentation etc.

Overpayments—general

71.—(1) Where it is determined that, whether fraudulently or otherwise, 1.80
any person has misrepresented, or failed to disclose, any material fact and in consequence of the misrepresentation or failure—

(a) a payment has been made in respect of a benefit to which this section applies; or

(b) any sum recoverable by or on behalf of the Secretary of State in connection with any such payment has not been recovered,

the Secretary of State shall be entitled to recover the amount of any payment which he would not have made or any sum which he would have received but for the misrepresentation or failure to disclose.

[[1](2) Where any such determination as is referred to in subsection (1) above is made, the person making the determination shall [[2] in the case of the Secretary of State or a [[14] First-tier Tribunal], and may in the case of [[14] the Upper Tribunal] or court]—

(a) determine whether any, and if so what, amount is recoverable under that subsection by the Secretary of State, and

(b) specify the period during which that amount was paid to the person concerned.]

(3) An amount recoverable under subsection (1) above is in all cases recoverable from the person who misrepresented the fact or failed to disclose it.

(4) In relation to cases where payments of benefit to which this section applies have been credited to a bank account or other account under arrangements made with the agreement of the beneficiary or a person acting for him, circumstances may be prescribed in which the Secretary of State is to be entitled to recover any amount paid in excess of entitlement; but any such regulations shall not apply in relation to any payment unless before he agreed to the arrangements such notice of the effect of the regulations as may be prescribed was given in such manner as may be prescribed to the beneficiary or to a person acting for him.

(5) [[12] . . .]

[[4] (5A) Except where regulations otherwise provide, an amount shall not be recoverable [[12] under subsection (1) or under regulations under subsection (4)] unless the determination in pursuance of which it was paid has been reversed or varied on an appeal or [[2] has been revised under section 9 or superseded under section 10 of the Social Security Act 1998]].

(6) Regulations may provide—

(a) that amounts recoverable under subsection (1) above or regulations under subsection (4) above shall be calculated or estimated in such manner and on such basis as may be prescribed;

(b) for treating any amount paid to any person under an award which is subsequently determined was not payable—

(i) as properly paid; or

(ii) as paid on account of a payment which it is determined should be or should have been made,

and for reducing or withholding any arrears payable by virtue of the subsequent determination;

(c) for treating any amount paid to one person in respect of another as properly paid for any period for which it is not payable in cases where in consequence of the subsequent determination—

(i) the other person is himself entitled to a payment for that period; or

(ii) a third person is entitled in priority to the payee to a payment for that period in respect of the other person,

and for reducing or withholding any arrears payable for that period by virtue of the subsequent determination.

(7) [[18] . . .]

(8) Where any amount paid [[16] . . .] is recoverable under—

(a) subsection (1) above;

(b) regulations under subsection (4) [[18] . . .] above; or

(c) section 74 below,

it may, without prejudice to any other method of recovery, be recovered by deduction from prescribed benefits.

(9) Where any amount paid in respect of a [[11] couple] is recoverable as mentioned in subsection (8) above, it may, without prejudice to any other method of recovery, be recovered, in such circumstances as may be prescribed, by deduction from prescribed benefits payable to either of them.

[[17] (9A) Regulations may provide for amounts recoverable under the provisions mentioned in subsection (8) above to be recovered by deductions from earnings.

(9B) In subsection (9A) above "earnings" has such meaning as may be prescribed.

(9C) Regulations under subsection (9A) above may include provision—

(a) requiring the person from whom an amount is recoverable ("the beneficiary") to disclose details of their employer, and any change of employer, to the Secretary of State;

(b) requiring the employer, on being served with a notice by the Secretary of State, to make deductions from the earnings of the beneficiary and to pay corresponding amounts to the Secretary of State;

(c) as to the matters to be contained in such a notice and the period for which a notice is to have effect;

(d) as to how payment is to be made to the Secretary of State;

(e) as to a level of earnings below which earnings must not be reduced;

(f) allowing the employer, where the employer makes deductions, to deduct a prescribed sum from the beneficiary's earnings in respect of the employer's administrative costs;

(g) requiring the employer to keep records of deductions;

(h) requiring the employer to notify the Secretary of State if the beneficiary is not, or ceases to be, employed by the employer;

(i) creating a criminal offence for non-compliance with the regulations, punishable on summary conviction by a fine not exceeding level 3 on the standard scale;

(j) with respect to the priority as between a requirement to deduct from earnings under this section and—

(i) any other such requirement;

(ii) an order under any other enactment relating to England and Wales which requires deduction from the beneficiary's earnings;

(iii) any diligence against earnings.]

(10) Any amount recoverable under the provisions mentioned in subsection (8) above—

(a) if the person from whom it is recoverable resides in England and Wales and the county court so orders, shall be recoverable [[21] under section 85 of the County Courts Act 1984] or otherwise as if it were payable under an order of that court; and

(b) if he resides in Scotland, shall be enforced in like manner as an extract registered decree arbitral bearing a warrant for execution issued by the sheriff court of any sheriffdom in Scotland.

[[5](10A)[[19] . . .]

(10B)[[19] . . .]

(11) This section applies to the following benefits—

[[20] (za) state pension or a lump sum under Part 1 of the Pensions Act 2014;]

(a) benefits as defined in section 122 of the Contributions and Benefits Act;

[[6](aa) [[19] . . .]

[[9](ab) state pension credit;]

[[13](ac) [[19] . . .]

[[22](ad) personal independence payment;]

[23 (ae) bereavement support payment under section 30 of the Pensions Act 2014;]
(b) [7 . . .] income support;
(c) [10 . . .]
(d) [10 . . .]
(e) any social fund payments such as are mentioned in section 138(1)(a) or (2) of the Contributions and Benefits Act; and
[15 (ea) health in pregnancy grant; and]
(f) child benefit."

[11 (12) In this section, "couple" has the meaning given by section 137(1) of the Contributions and Benefits Act.]

AMENDMENTS

1. Social Security (Overpayments) Act 1996 s.1(2) (for determination made after July 24, 1996).
2. Social Security Act 1998 Sch.7 (July 5, 1999).
3. Social Security (Overpayments) Act 1996 s.1(3) (for determinations made after July 24, 1996).
4. Social Security (Overpayments) Act 1996 s.1(4) (for determinations made after July 24, 1996).
5. Jobseekers Act 1995 s.32(1) (October 7, 1996).
6. Jobseekers Act 1995 Sch.2 (October 7, 1996).
7. Jobseekers Act 1995 Sch.3 (October 7, 1996).
8. Tax Credits Act 2002 s.51 and Sch.4 (February 26, 2003 for the purpose of making regulations only; April 1, 2003 for the purpose of transfer of functions only; for remaining purposes date to be appointed).
9. State Pension Credit Act 2002 s.14 and Sch.2 (July 2, 2002 for the purposes of making regulations only; fully in force October 6, 2003).
10. Tax Credits Act 2002 s.60 and Sch.6 (April 8, 2003).
11. Civil Partnership Act 2004 s.254 and Sch.24 para.58 (December 5, 2005).
12. Welfare Reform Act 2007 s.44 (July 3, 2007).
13. Welfare Reform Act 2007 s.28 and Sch.3 para.10 (October 27, 2008).
14. The Transfer of Tribunal Functions Order 2008 (SI 2008/2833) art.103 (November 3, 2008).
15. Health and Social Care Act 2008 s.132(4) (January 1, 2009 in relation to England and Wales; not yet in force otherwise).
16. Welfare Reform Act 2012 s.150(2) (May 9, 2012).
17. Welfare Reform Act 2012 s.106 (July 1, 2012).
18. Welfare Reform Act 2012 s.147 and Sch.14 Pt 11 (April 1, 2013).
19. The Welfare Reform Act 2012 (Commencement No.8 and Savings and Transitional Provisions) Order 2013 (SI 2013/358) art.5(4) brings into force provisions of the Welfare Reform Act 2012 repealing subs.(10A) and (10B), as well as subs.(11)(aa) (jobseeker's allowance), and 11(ac) (employment and support allowance). However, art.5(6) provides that jobseeker's allowance and employment and support allowance "remain benefits to which section 71 of the 1992 Act applies to the extent that those benefits have been claimed before 29th April 2013." (April 29, 2013).
20. Pensions Act 2014, s.56(4), s.23 and Sch.12, para. 11 (April 6, 2016).
21. Tribunals, Courts and Enforcement Act 2007, Sch.13, para.102 (April 6, 2014).
22. Welfare Reform Act 2012, Sch.9, para.10 (June 10, 2013).
23. Pensions Act 2014 s.31 and Sch.16 para.25 (April 6, 2017).

GENERAL NOTE

1.81 The structure of the following commentary is as follows:

Introduction

A complex body of case-law has built up on the proper application of s.71, which has included some significant changes of approach over time. What follows is a commentary on the current state of the case-law as it applies to typical benefit arrangements today without the detail of its historical development. For that, readers are referred to the more lengthy annotations in earlier editions of this work. **1.82**

The regulations to which this section makes reference are the Social Security (Payments on Account, Overpayments and Recovery) Regulations 1988 (paras 2.915–2.955 below).

For an overview of the new landscape for overpayments, see the general note appended to the heading to Pt III of this Act (paras 1.77–1.79 above).

The basic requirements

A decision maker dealing with an overpayment question must: **1.83**

- make an "entitlement decision" by revising or superseding all relevant decisions awarding benefit during the period for which the overpayment is sought;
- where necessary offset the benefit paid against any residual amount of benefit under the entitlement decision;
- determine the period during which the overpayment occurred;
- calculate the amount of the recoverable overpayment;
- make an "overpayment decision" specifying the amount that is recoverable, the period of the overpayment, and the person from whom it is recoverable, and set out the basis for recovery; and
- give a decision on whether and on whom to apply a civil penalty ("a penalty decision").

On civil penalties, see the annotations to ss.115C and 115D of the SSAA 1992.

Before addressing these requirements in more detail, one or two general points about the application of s.71 need to be made.

Limitation periods

Arguments that overpayments are not recoverable because of the application of limitation periods applicable to the recovery of debts in actions before the courts have long been held to be destined to fail: *R(SB) 5/91*. The matter has been put completely beyond doubt by the amendment made by the amendment to s.38 of the **1.84**

Limitation Act 1980 and by s.108 of the Welfare Reform Act 2012. The amendment is to have effect as if it came into force at the same time as s.38 of the Limitation Act 1980, except for the purposes of proceedings brought before the coming into force of the section, that is, on March 8, 2012 (which was the date s.108 entered into force).

Recovery at common law not possible

1.85 The Supreme Court has confirmed that s.71 is the only route to recovery of overpayments of social security benefits to the exclusion of any common law entitlement to recover the money: *CPAG v SSWP* [2010] UKSC 54.

Recovery of overpayments and bankruptcy

1.86 A number of cases have considered the interrelationship between s.71 and the bankruptcy provisions of the Insolvency Act 1986. It seems that the timing of determinations under s.71 will be relevant in deciding whether a discharged bankrupt is freed from liability for deductions from benefit in repayment of an overpayment of benefit.

R (Steele) v Birmingham CC [2005] EWCA Civ 1824 concerned an overpayment of jobseeker's allowance. The claimant was awarded the benefit in December 1999. In September 2001, he was adjudged bankrupt on his own petition. In March 2002 an overpayment decision was made by the Secretary of State. Recovery of the overpayment was by means of deductions from benefit. The deductions were suspended during the period of bankruptcy, but were started again when the claimant was discharged from his bankruptcy. The claimant argued that the payments were a contingent liability within the meaning of the Insolvency Act 1986 and therefore he was released from this debt following his discharge from bankruptcy. In judicial review proceedings at first instance, the claimant was successful. However, the decision was successfully appealed by the Secretary of State. The Court of Appeal ruled that the claimant was under no obligation or liability to repay the overpaid benefit until a determination was made under s.71. No such determination had been made before the date of his bankruptcy. It followed that the overpaid amount was not a bankruptcy debt for the purposes of a release on discharge from bankruptcy under s.281(1) of the Insolvency Act 1986.

Different timings applied in *R (Balding) v Secretary of State for Work and Pensions* [2007] EWCA Civ 1327. The claimant was in receipt of income support. An overpayment determination was made in July 1994. In June 1995 the claimant, on his own petition, was adjudged to be bankrupt. The claimant was discharged from bankruptcy in June 1998. The Secretary of State sought to recover the overpayment by deductions from the claimant's benefit, arguing that such deductions were outside the scope of the bankruptcy legislation. The Court of Appeal upheld the decision of the Administrative Court: [2007] EWCA 759 (Admin) and praised the judgment of Davis J. in the court below for its depth of analysis of the issues involved. Regardless of the method of recovery chosen by the Secretary of State (deductions from benefit or recovery in debt proceedings in the courts), there was a liability to repay money under an enactment. Discharge from bankruptcy wiped out the liability to repay the sum under the insolvency legislation.

In *SSWP v Payne* [2011] UKSC 60 the Supreme Court brought the law in relation to bankruptcy and debt relief orders into line, ruling that *Balding* was correctly decided, and raising a question mark over the correctness of aspects of a House of Lords decision in the Scottish case of *Mulvey v Secretary of State for Social Security* [1997] UKHL 10. The decision of the administrative court in *R v Secretary of State for Social Security, ex p. Taylor and Chapman* was wrongly decided. The effect of the decision in *Payne* is that the Secretary of State loses the power to recoup overpayments on the making of a bankruptcy order just as he does on the making of a debt relief order (at [23]).

From whom can recovery be sought

Section 71 refers to the possibility of recovery from "any person" and the provision has been interpreted as widely as these sweeping words suggest. Therefore, recovery can be sought from claimants, their appointees, their spouses or partners, their children, their solicitors, and their personal representatives. However, where recovery is sought other than from the claimant, special considerations will apply where recovery can only be triggered by a misrepresentation or a failure to disclose a material fact. In particular, careful consideration will need to be given to the question of whether the party against whom recovery is sought was under an obligation to disclose facts to the Secretary of State. 1.87

Appointees: the term "appointee" means a person who has been appointed by the Secretary of State under reg.33 of the Claims and Payments Regulations to administer a particular benefit on behalf of a person unable to act. It does not include a person holding a Power of Attorney for a claimant who has not been made an appointee under reg.33: see *CA/1014/1999*, discussed in *CSDLA/1282/2001* and *CIS/242/2003*. 1.88

The leading authority is the decision of a Tribunal of Commissioners in *R(IS) 5/03*, which was set up to resolve a difference between the decisions in *CIS/332/1993* and *R(IS) 5/00*. *CIS/332/1993* had ruled that the acts of the appointee, when acting as such, are treated as acts of the claimant and so recovery is only available from the claimant (or the claimant's estate) and not the appointee. *R(IS) 5/00* had ruled that recovery was available from the appointee, the claimant's mother, who had not disclosed an increase in the claimant's savings. *R(IS) 5/03* concerned an overpayment which had arisen when income support continued in payment at the previous rate when the costs of the claimant's accommodation in a nursing home were met wholly by the health authority. The claimant's mother was her appointee under an appointment made by the Secretary of State for all benefit purposes. The appointee had failed to inform the Department that the costs of her daughter's accommodation in a nursing home were fully met by the health authority.

The Tribunal of Commissioners draws on the common law relating to agency but recognises that the social security context requires certain modifications to the common law rules applicable in a contractual situation. This is justified, in particular, because normal agency principles come into play where the principal has delegated authority to an agent. In the social security context, no such delegation exists, since it is the payer (the Secretary of State) who authorises another to act on behalf of persons unable to act for themselves. The benefit recipient, where reg.33 of the Claims and Payments Regulations applies, is not a party to the delegation of powers. It had been argued by the appellant and CPAG that to render the appointee personally liable would produce a situation in which, for example, social workers might be unwilling to undertake responsibilities as appointees to the disadvantage of benefit recipients. The Tribunal of Commissioners in preferring the principles set out in *R(IS) 5/00*, and concluding that *CIS/332/1993* is wrongly decided, mollified the impact of their decision by finding that there are exceptions to the liability of an appointee. Generally, both the claimant and the appointee will be liable for overpayments resulting from misrepresentations or failure to disclose. There are two exceptions to this rule. The first is that only the appointee will be liable for the overpayment if the appointee has retained the benefit instead of paying it to or applying it for the benefit of the claimant. The second exception is that the appointee will not be liable if the appointee has acted with "due care and diligence". This will avoid an appointee becoming personally liable where they make a wholly innocent representation, because some change in the claimant's affairs has not been made known to the appointee, and the appointee has not failed to exercise the powers of appointee in such a manner that they could be held to be at fault.

Despite the inevitable intricacies which always seem to arise in the manifold scenarios in which overpayments of benefits arise, this decision now makes it clear that the starting point is that both the claimant and any appointee are liable for overpayments of benefit subject to the two qualifications set out in *R(IS) 5/03*.

1.89 **Personal representatives:** it had been made clear in *Secretary of State for Social Services v Solly* [1974] 3 All E.R. 922 that recovery from the estate of a deceased person was possible. *R(SB) 28/83* is an example of recovery from the claimant's personal representative. However, tribunals are not the place in which objections to liability by the executor on the grounds, for example, that the estate has already been distributed are to be resolved. Those are matters concerning a decision to pursue recovery (which were reserved under the old adjudication system for the Secretary of State) rather than liability for the overpayment and may need adjudication in court: *R(SB) 1/96*.

In *R(1S) 6/01* the Commissioner held that the Secretary of State has no power under s.71 to seek recovery from the estate of a deceased claimant where there are no duly constituted personal representatives. The Secretary of State is not, however, without any powers in such circumstances, since "he could have made application to the High Court for a limited grant of administration under s.116 of the Supreme Court Act 1981. The court can apparently make a limited grant of that kind for a variety of purposes." (At para.38.)

1.90 **Spouses and partners:** special considerations arise where recovery is sought from spouses or partners. In *CIS/619/1997* the Commissioner follows *CIS/13742/1996* in holding that s.71 requires a review of the claims of both husband and wife before reg.13 of the Payments on Account Regulations can be used to offset benefit payable to one spouse against an overpayment that is recoverable from the other spouse. Tribunals faced with such cases should have regard to these two decisions in dealing with an appeal before them. The Commissioner also questions the propriety of inclusion in papers relating to the wife's appeal of details concerning the husband where she had maintained throughout that she was living separately from him. He suggests that there might be breach of confidentiality in relation to the husband's affairs, and appears to urge that such cases may be ones in which consideration would need to be given to disclosure of the husband's affairs to the tribunal as distinct from disclosure to the claimant. He recognises that this in turn gives rise to issues touching on the requirement to provide a fair hearing for the claimant and of natural justice.

1.91 **Agents:** in *Tkachuk v SSWP*, reported as *R(IS) 3/07*, the Court of Appeal agreed with the Commissioner that a number of provisions in social security legislation supplement or modify the common law of agency. It would accordingly not always be the case that knowledge of an agent is attributed to the principal. In *VB v SSWP* [2008] UKUT 15 (AAC) which concerned the attribution of knowledge by a financial advisor who was not the claimant's appointee, the judge said:

> "79. In my view it would be a quite unwarranted extension of the scope of section 71 to hold that where a claimant's advisor is aware of a material fact, the claimant herself is necessarily fixed with knowledge of that same fact by means of importing the common law rules of agency."

Evidence required to sustain a decision that an overpayment is recoverable

1.92 It is for the Secretary of State to show on the balance of probabilities all the facts which are needed to justify the recovery of any overpayment: *R(SB) 6/85*, at para.5 and *DG v SSWP (DLA)* [2011] UKUT 14 (AAC), at [75]. This means that the Secretary of State should adduce evidence to support all elements required for a proper overpayment decision. This will include documentary evidence which is reasonably available: see *C1/06-07 (IS)* and *CIS/1462/2006*. Tribunals need to be alert to whether a paper submission adduces adequate evidence to show that all of the requirements are met where, as is commonplace, there is no representative of the Secretary of State before the tribunal. Where the Secretary of State has been given every opportunity to prove the statutory conditions but has manifestly failed to do so, and does not appear before a First-tier Tribunal (in this case after an adjournment with directions), then it is entirely appropriate to find against the Secretary of State: *FW v SSWP (IS)* [2010] UKUT 374 (AAC).

Where the Secretary of State seeks to adduce surveillance evidence, questions can arise as to the legitimacy of the surveillance. In such cases the existence of authorisation under the Regulation of Investigatory Powers Act 2000 will be relevant. How the system operates and its compatibility with art.8 ECHR is discussed in *DG v SSWP (DLA)* [2011] UKUT 14 (AAC), [43]–[47] and see annotations to art.8 ECHR.

In *JF v SSWP (DLA)* [2015] UKUT 267 (AAC) and *AF v SSWP (DLA)* [2015] UKUT 266, Judge Wikeley sets out the due process requirements that apply in overpayment cases where the claimant's credibility is in issue. Care must be taken to consider all the evidence, to show why a discretion to consider an issue not raised in this appeal was exercised, to make clear findings of fact which reflect all the evidence before it, and to be very careful about considering even part of the evidence in the absence of the claimant (part of a DVD was viewed by the tribunal while the claimant was not in the room).

Missing documents: There is no presumption that missing documents contain material favourable to a claimant: *R(IS) 11/92*. Where a key document (for example, a claim form as in *CG/3049/2002*) has gone missing, a tribunal should seek to reconstruct the form from the best evidence available. However, a tribunal should not engage in guesswork, nor make any assumptions about who is most likely to have made a mistake: *CG/3049/2002*, at para.14. **1.93**

Evidence of a criminal conviction: In *R(S) 2/80*, the Commissioner ruled that the fact of a conviction should not be ignored and should have a bearing on any appeal relating to benefit. The initial burden must lie on the insurance officer, now Secretary of State, to show that a conviction is related to the benefit in issue in the appeal and covered the same period, although the onus of proof then shifts to the claimant to show that, notwithstanding the conviction, the claimant is entitled to the benefit in issue. **1.94**

This and other authorities have been considered in *AM v SSWP (DLA)* [2013] UKUT 94 (AAC). The case concerned the recovery of an overpayment against both the claimant and her appointee, who was her husband. The appointee was prosecuted and convicted of an offence under s.112(1D) SSAA 1992. The judge held that the criminal conviction against the appointee was not conclusive in any way against the claimant herself and was only of very limited effect as against the appointee.

After reviewing the earlier authorities, the judge considered that *R(S) 2/80* was wrongly decided in so far as it finds that a conviction leads to the legal burden of proof being shifted. The judge held that:

(a) the fact that the strict rules of evidence do not apply in social security cases does not mean that a tribunal can take into account matters that are not probative;

(b) on the basis of the decision of the Court of Appeal in *Hollington v Hewthorn* [1943] K.B. 587, a conviction has no probative value as it represents only the opinion of the relevant judge or jury;

(c) applying *Hunter v Chief Constable of the West Midlands Police* [1982] A.C. 529 there is a general rule of public policy that the use of a civil action to initiate a collateral attack on the decision of a criminal court is an abuse of process in the absence of fresh evidence which entirely changes an aspect of the case;

(d) this applies in social security cases to a limited extent only, as entitlement to benefits is required by statute to be determined by a specialist tribunal with a superior knowledge of social security law and, where appropriate, with members with medical expertise and a disability qualification; and

(e) in any event it is necessary for tribunals to examine very carefully the factual and legal basis of any conviction, looking at the charges, the evidence, and the findings of fact of the court, and also, where there is a guilty plea, at the facts admitted by the guilty plea, which may not be everything included in the charges.

Finally, the judge found that although the conviction was subsequent to the decision under appeal it could still be taken into account notwithstanding s.12(8)(b) of the Social Security Act 1998.

In *Newcastle CC v LW* [2013] UKUT 123, the same judge applied these principles in a case concerning an overpayment of housing benefit in which the claimant had pleaded guilty to a criminal charge relating to her failure to disclose that she was living together with a man as husband and wife. She argued that she had pleaded guilty to the offence to avoid facing more serious charges relating to mortgage fraud. The judge ruled that, on public policy grounds, the claimant could not resile from her guilty plea on appealing to the tribunal against the overpayment decision. However, the tribunal must look carefully at the conviction and the plea in order to be clear what it was that she had admitted, as well as the extent to which she should, as a consequence, be precluded from challenging the basis of the overpayment decision.

See also *JCW v SSWP (IS)* [2015] UKUT 283 (AAC).

The requirement for revision or supersession of all decisions in the overpayment period

1.95 Section 71(5A) requires, with only limited exceptions, that the decision awarding benefit must be revised under s.9 SSA 1998 or superseded under s.10 SSA 1998 (or reversed or varied on an appeal). Such a decision is commonly referred to as "the entitlement decision". This requirement is fundamental to recovery under s.71(1) and the absence of an entitlement decision renders any overpayment decision of no effect. A tribunal will err in law if it fails to consider whether there are grounds for a revision or supersession: *RH v SSWP (DLA)* [2015] UKUT 453 (AAC). However, there is nothing to preclude the Secretary of State from starting the whole process afresh if it transpires that there is no proper entitlement decision: *R(IS) 13/05* and *AG v SSWP* [2010] UKUT 291 (AAC).

An entitlement decision determines just that: entitlement to benefit. So, a decision that a couple are living together as husband and wife is *not* an entitlement decision since it is merely a precursor to an entitlement decision: *SSWP v AM* [2010] UKUT 428 (AAC).

The exceptions to the requirement for a prior entitlement decision are:

(a) Where the facts and circumstances of the misrepresentation or failure to disclose do not provide the basis for revising or superseding the decision: Payments on Account Regulations 1988 reg.12. The DMG gives as examples of such cases the correction of accidental errors and irregular encashments: para.09032.

(b) Certain JSA overpayments to 16 and 17 year olds: SSAA 1992 s.71A.

The Secretary of State should ensure that evidence is provided that an entitlement decision has been made prior to the overpayment decision, which has been sent to the claimant. The best evidence is a copy of the decision accompanied by a copy of the letter sent to the claimant communicating that decision. Computer printouts are commonly presented as evidence, although these are only acceptable if they are comprehensible and are explained.

1.96 Often entitlement decisions and overpayment decisions are made at the same time or within a short period of each other. However, sometimes the time lag is much longer. Plainly an entitlement decision attracts its own appeal if the claimant takes issue with its correctness. An appeal against an overpayment decision after the expiry of the time for an appeal against the entitlement decision does not constitute an appeal against the entitlement decision and this can cause difficulties for the person from whom recovery is sought since the Secretary of State argues that the underlying factual basis has been established by either the initial decision or a failed appeal against the entitlement decision. That is, however, not correct. The judge in *SSWP v IM (IS)* [2010] UKUT 428 (AAC) ruled that, when making findings of fact, the effect of s.17(2) SSA 1998 on the finality of decisions is that neither the Secretary of State nor a tribunal is bound by findings of fact made in the course of dealing with an entitlement decision when dealing with an overpayment decision. The same conclusion was reached in *KJ v SSWP (DLA)* [2010] UKUT 452 (AAC), where the judge said:

> "16. This demonstrates, yet again, the unsatisfactory consequences which can ensue if entitlement and overpayment appeals are not heard together. In effect, the decision of the First Tribunal in this case was a complete waste of time. The Claimant was entitled to reargue in the overpayment appeal the issues of fact decided by the First Tribunal."

The decision of a Tribunal of Commissioners in *R(IB) 2/04* is the lead authority on the extent to which a tribunal can cure a defect in an entitlement decision so that the overpayment decision will not fail. This ruled that tribunals have power to remedy defects in decisions where they were not so serious as to render the decision in issue wholly incoherent. In general a Secretary of State's decision which altered the original decision with effect from the date of the original decision should be treated as a revision under s.9 and a Secretary of State's decision which altered the decision from a later date should be treated as a supersession under s.10. However, there must be something which can properly be regarded as a decision; a document which has so little coherence or connection to the legal powers of the decision maker cannot properly be regarded as a decision.

SS v SSWP (JSA) [2013] UKUT 233 (AAC) contains some useful observations of dealing with cases where the Secretary of State's decision-making is arguably incoherent in that there is inconsistency of decision-making resulting in considerable lack of clarity as to whether there has been a proper revision or supersession of the entitlement decision.

To be effective, a decision must not only be made but must also be communicated to its recipient. As long ago as 2003, in *R v SSHD, ex p. Anufrijeva* [2003] UKHL 36, the House of Lords had ruled, in the context of an asylum decision, that where a statutory scheme contemplated notification of some decision affecting a person, the affected person is entitled to notification of the decision if it is to have legal effect. Lord Steyn said: **1.97**

> "Notice of a decision is required before it can have the character of a determination with legal effect because the individual concerned must be in a position to challenge the decision in the courts if he or she wishes to do so. This is not a technical rule. It is simply an application of the right of access to justice. That is a fundamental and constitutional principle of our legal system . . . ." (At [26].)

In the social security context, an issue can arise in relation to the timing of the making of the decision, its effective date, and the notification of the decision to the claimant. What is clear is that there must be an entitlement decision prior to or at the latest contemporaneous with the overpayment decision. A decision of the Northern Ireland Court of Appeal in *Hamilton v Department for Social Development* [2010] NICA 46 ruled that failure to notify one of the two entitlement decisions in issue was corrected when it was incorporated by reference in the notification of the overpayment decision. Her appeal rights had not been compromised.

In *SSWP v Deane* [2010] EWCA Civ 699, the Court of Appeal ruled that there was no obligation on the English Court of Appeal to follow decisions of the Northern Ireland Court of Appeal but that where the decision of the Northern Ireland court relates to a statutory provision which is the same as that applicable in England and Wales, then it should be followed in order to avoid "the wholly undesirable situation arising of identically worded legislation . . . being applied in inconsistent ways." (Per Ward L.J. at [26].)

The decision in the *Hamilton* case is considered in *DK v SSWP (IS)* [2011] UKUT 230 (AAC): see [10]–[17]. Difficulties do seem to arise, as explained in *DK v SSWP,* because the DWP's computerised system is only able to handle supersession decisions taking effect no more than 14 months before the date of the decision. Rather than making the whole decision by hand, the DWP appears to engage in a double act: using the computer for the maximum period the programme will permit, and making a manual decision in relation to any earlier period. This has resulted in some cases in the computer-generated decision being sent to the claimant but not the one based on a manual record. A question then arises as to whether the decision based on the manual record has been properly notified to the claimant.

1.98 *SSWP v AD (IS)* [2011] UKUT 184 is just such a case. It contains a useful analysis of the effect of the *Hamilton* case, and raises some doubts about the circumstances in which communication of an overpayment decision can properly encompass a notification of an entitlement decision. These doubts arise from the decision in *CPC/3743/2006*, followed in *CIS/527/2010*, requiring that there are proper decisions altering entitlement for all parts of the period of the claimed overpayment as at the date on which the recoverability decision is made.

Both the *Hamilton* decision and *SSWP v AD* are the subject of analysis in *LL v SSWP (IS)* [2013] UKUT 208. The judge describes the making of an entitlement decision as the internal aspect of the rule in s.71(5A) and its notification as the external aspect of the rule. He confirms that both steps must have been taken before a recoverability decision is made. In general supersession decisions take effect on the day on which they are made, although certain non-advantageous decisions based on a change of circumstances may take effect from an earlier date. Some cases will accordingly require clear recognition of both the internal aspects of the requirements of s.71(5A), as well as the date from which the entitlement decision takes effect. These three temporal aspects of an entitlement decision should not be confused. The judge also indicates that his view of the *Hamilton* decision is that it decides only that simultaneous notification of an entitlement decision and a recoverability decision is legally permissible where the notification was sufficiently clear to enable its recipient to appreciate that it served the dual function of notifying both an entitlement decision and an overpayment decision in terms which ensured a right of appeal in respect of both decisions. Like the judge in *SSWP v AD*, the judge in *LL v SSWP* has some reservations about whether simultaneous notification of the entitlement decision and the overpayment decision is compatible with s.71(5A). This is because an entitlement decision had not been perfected by notification at the time the recoverability decision was made. In such cases, the requirements of s.71(5A) have not been met at the time when the recoverability decision is made. Furthermore, s.12(8)(b) of the SSA 1998 means that facts obtained after the date of the decision (that is, the communication of a relevant entitlement decision) under appeal cannot be taken into account.

Intention

1.99 The use of the words "whether fraudulently or otherwise" show that there is no need to prove any fraudulent intent. Wholly innocent mistakes by claimants can result in recoverable overpayments: *R(SB) 28/83*; *R(SB) 9/85*; and *R(SB) 18/85*. Innocent misrepresentations are easy to imagine. However, it may be better to think of non-fraudulent failures to disclose rather than innocent failures, since non-disclosures involve some breach of a duty to disclose. In *R(SB) 28/83* it was suggested that the duty to disclose extends to matters relevant to the claim to benefit which a person with reasonable diligence would have been aware.

This interpretation of the section is confirmed by the Court of Appeal in *Page and Davis v Chief Adjudication Officer*, published as a supplement to *R(SB) 2/92*, where Dillon L.J. said:

> "The whole burden of the phrase 'whether fraudulently or otherwise' must be . . . that it is to apply even if the misrepresentation is not fraudulent, in other words, if it is innocent. No other construction makes any sense, in my view, of this particular subsection."

Misrepresentation

A misrepresentation can arise by a positive or deliberate act or as a result of omission: *R(SB) 9/85*; and may be a written statement, an oral statement, or even in some cases the result of silence (as when part of a claim form is left blank): *R(SB) 18/85*. Innocent misrepresentations are caught as well as deliberate misrepresentations; what is relevant is that there is some statement which is untrue for whatever reason: *Page v CAO (CA)* reported as appendix to *R(SB) 2/92* and *CSIS/0345/2004*. 1.100

However, it is essential in every case to identify with some accuracy exactly what the misrepresentation is on which the Secretary of State: see, for example, *NS v SSWP (CA)* [2014] UKUT 7 (AAC) in making the recoverability decision. It will not be enough simply to indicate that the claimant must have got something wrong. This can involve careful analysis of all the evidence in cases involving overpayments of benefit over significant periods of time. It is not enough for a decision maker or tribunal simply to assert that a claimant must have misrepresented something in a claim form or claim forms. It will not suffice to argue that there must have been misrepresentations because the claimant received benefit to which subsequent findings suggest that they were not entitled. There must be some evidence of the misrepresentation or misrepresentations on which the award of benefit was found: *MK v SSWP (DLA)* [2011] UKUT 12 (AAC).

In providing information, claimants are not expected to be aware of the technicalities of social security legislation: *CTC/4025/2003*. In *KW v SSWP* [2009] UKUT 143 (AAC), the judge said:

> " . . . people are not to be accused or made liable for misrepresentation when they truthfully answer the questions they are actually asked, understanding the language used in its ordinary simple sense, instead of the different and more elaborate questions they *might* have been asked if the focus had been on some more artificial and restricted meaning." (At [41].)

The need to take a reasonable approach to responses to questions put to claimants is illustrated in *EL v SSWP* [2008] UKUT 4 (AAC). The Secretary of State sought to argue that a claimant had misrepresented his circumstances by not providing a response to the question, "Please use this space to tell anything else you think we might need to know" on the claim form. The claimant was a Mexican national who had been given limited leave to remain in the United Kingdom on the condition that he have no recourse to public funds. His employment had come to an end and he had claimed and been awarded income-based jobseeker's allowance. The judge concluded that failure to respond to so open-ended a question cannot constitute a misrepresentation. Failure to reply to a specific question would generally constitute a misrepresentation, although failure to respond to a question couched in such general terms would not. The claimant had been asked no question about his immigration status. The overpayment was accordingly not recoverable. 1.101

It has long been accepted that a written statement may be qualified by an oral statement; it is often asserted by claimants that a form does not accurately reflect everything that was said. While generally claimants bear responsibility for the contents of forms, if it is accepted that an oral qualification has not been properly noted, this may preclude the written representation from being a misrepresentation: *R(SB) 18/85*.

A written misrepresentation may also be qualified or modified when that written communication is read in conjunction with other written communications which should be before the decision-maker in making the decision which resulted in the overpayment of benefit: *R(SB) 2/91*, at paras 10–13. In such cases, it goes without saying that careful findings of fact are vital. Tribunals should call for originals (or clear copies) of statements signed by persons which are claimed to be the misrepresentation on which an overpayment decision is founded.

In *R(SB) 3/90* the Commissioner holds that there can still be a misrepresentation of a material fact even where there has been an earlier disclosure of that fact (at para.11). Although disclosure prevents any recovery of an overpayment based on 1.102

the failure to disclose head, a misrepresentation by declaration on a claim form that a claimant had no money coming in when superannuation payments from a former employer were in payment, receipt of which had previously been disclosed, overrides that disclosure. The Commissioner specifically states that the Department is entitled to rely on statements in the current claim form and is under no duty to check back to see whether those statements are consistent with earlier disclosures. So it remains incumbent on claimants to be meticulous in their completion of claim forms even after a course of dealing with the Department. The reasoning of the Commissioner in *R(SB) 3/90* is implicitly approved by the Court of Appeal in *Morrell v SSWP* [2003] EWCA Civ 526; *R(IS) 6/03*, [38]–[48].

CSU/03/1991 adds a gloss to *R(SB) 3/90. CSU/03/1991* was a case in which two forms had been submitted by the claimant containing conflicting information about the claimant's pension position. When he initially claimed unemployment benefit, he disclosed on Form UB461 the correct amount of his pension expressed as a weekly amount. However, a few days later he erred in recording on Form UB81(PEN) the pension as £293.75 per *year* rather than per *month*. The claimant's argument was that in considering his claim the adjudication officer should have had regard to both documents and that this would have indicated the error and no overpayment would have resulted. The adjudication officer sought to argue that there was no obligation to check back to see whether any inconsistent information was given in earlier documents. The Commissioner held that something had clearly gone wrong in the Department; both documents should have been before the adjudication officer in determining this claim and the adjudication officer could not rely on *R(SB) 3/90* as the basis for recovering the overpayment of benefit which resulted from the adjudication officer's reliance on the incorrect figure on the Form UB81(PEN).

ED v SSWP [2009] UKUT 161 (AAC), adds a further gloss on *R(SB) 3/90*. The Upper Tribunal judge observed:

> "... *R(SB) 3/90* and *Morrell* are not to be interpreted as meaning that whenever a misrepresentation of material fact has been made nothing that has gone before can ever be relevant to the question of whether a subsequent overpayment of benefit was in consequence of the misrepresentation. In *R(SB) 3/90* the question was of linking back into previous claims whose administration had been completed. In *Morrell,* the provision of income by the claimant's mother was something that in its nature was capable of stopping or being interrupted at any time, so that there was no necessary inconsistency between the information given earlier by the local authority and a 'no' answer on the review form. Those decisions do not exclude the consideration of all the circumstances of particular cases and the fundamental test must in accordance with *Duggan* be that of causation, whether the misrepresentation or failure to disclose was *a* cause, possibly amongst other causes, of the subsequent overpayment." (At [27].)

1.103 In *CIS/5117/1998*, the Commissioner addresses the question of the extent to which silence can constitute a misrepresentation. The claim form for income support had been completed by an officer of the Department and read back to him. The form indicated that the claimant was married and living with his wife. None of the questions about his wife, particularly about her earnings or other income, had been answered. The tribunal found as a fact that the claimant had not been asked questions about his wife's earnings or other income by the Department's officer. An overpayment decision went on appeal to the tribunal which found that there had been no misrepresentation or failure to disclose in the circumstances of this case. The adjudication officer appealed. The Commissioner upheld the tribunal; the only substantial issue was whether or not the claimant made a misrepresentation by his silence when he made the claim on which the award of income support was based.

The Commissioner concludes that *R(SB) 18/85* applied to this case. The claimant had answered all of the questions put to him by the officer of the Department and the form was not read over to the claimant in its entirety. In these circumstances, says the Commissioner, the claimant's "misrepresentation" that the information on the form was complete "was qualified by the fact that he had supplied all the information for which he had been asked" in circumstances where the officer had given him no opportunity to answer the relevant questions about his wife's earnings, gave no indication that such matters might be material to benefit entitlement and did not read back the entries on the claim form to confirm their correctness. The facts of this case are unusual and appear to represent a failure by the Department to follow its own recommended procedures. However, where such unusual circumstances are established, the claimant's silence does not amount to a misrepresentation. In so far as *CIS/645/1993* suggests that silence as to material facts known to the claimant amounts to a misrepresentation, that decision must be read as referring to a deliberate decision to say nothing on a matter known to be material.

Now that most benefit payments are paid direct into a bank account, there are fewer cases involving the signing of declarations, yet there are still declarations at the end of claim forms, and on Jobcentre Plus coupons (Form ES25JP). The key to good decision making is to consider carefully the terms of the declaration. Many older postal claims forms were in terms that the information on the form is true and complete *as far as the claimant was aware*. These qualifying words protected a claimant against an innocent misrepresentation arising as a result of something they did not know at the time. More modern declarations are not qualified in this way but are a simple declaration that the information on the form is true and complete. A declaration in these terms does not protect a claimant from an innocent misrepresentation arising because of things they do not know when completing the form: *Jones & Sharples v CAO)* [1994] 1 All E.R. 225 (CA), reported as *R(IS) 7/94*, and *CIS/674/1994*; see also *Franklin v CAO* (CA), reported as *R(IS) 16/96*.

Mental capacity and misrepresentation

CSB/1093/1989 explores in some detail issues concerning mental capacity in overpayment cases. The particular question addressed was the extent to which claimants are entitled to escape the normal consequences of material misrepresentations by contending that they were mentally incapacitated at the time when they signed the relevant document. The case concerned an overpayment of supplementary benefit which had arisen when, over a period of six months, the claimant misrepresented that her son was still a member of the family for benefit purposes when he had left school and had undertaken a Youth Training Scheme. It was argued on behalf of the claimant that her mental condition, combined with effects of antidepressant drugs, was such that she could not be held responsible for putting her signature to the declarations in connection with the benefit claim. There is a discussion of the possibility of pleading *non est factum* (that the mind did not go with the pen with the result that the signature is to be treated as not having been made). The Commissioner stresses the narrow nature of the defence of *non est factum* and the difficulty of applying the doctrine to the realities of a modern social security system. As established in *Saunders v Anglia Building Society* [1971] A.C. 1004, three conditions must be met for a plea of *non est factum* to succeed: 1.104

(a) The claimant was under a disability, which might include being illiterate.

(b) The document signed was fundamentally, radically or totally different from that which the person thought they were signing.

(c) The person signing the document was not careless in doing so, and took such precautions as ought to have been taken in all the circumstances to ascertain the content and significance of the document.

In the *Saunders* case, Purchas L.J. had stressed the need for satisfying each of the three conditions set out above, particularly the third one. The overall effect is that the plea is unlikely to be available where the claimant has made a claim. A claimant who has the capacity to make a claim also has the capacity to make a representation affecting it: *CG/4494/1999 (T)*, [18].

The Commissioner in *CSB/1093/1989* indicates at paras 17 and 18 that he believes that the case of *Re Beaney, deceased* [1978] 1 W.L.R. 770, which was not concerned with social security at all, might be of assistance to tribunals. Mrs Beaney was an old lady whose health had been deteriorating for some time. She executed a transfer of a house to her eldest daughter in circumstances where all parties present at the signing of the document, including a solicitor who was an old friend of Mrs Beaney's late husband, thought that she understood what she was doing. Medical evidence, however, was that she had advanced senile dementia and her mental state was such that she could not have understood what she was doing. The two younger children sought a declaration that the transfer was void for want of capacity. The judge stated in his judgment that the degree or extent of understanding required in respect of any instrument is relative to the particular transaction which it is to effect. The more trivial the transaction, the lower the requisite degree of understanding. The Commissioner indicates that regard must be had to this test and that the key question is whether a claimant at the time of signing realised that they were signing a document in connection with a claim to benefit which could result in the payment of benefit. If the answer is negative, then s.71 cannot be applied to that claimant.

1.105 In difficult cases all the evidence will need to be considered over the period under review. So lucid letters written by the claimant about benefit in the relevant period will be relevant evidence of capacity. The most important evidence will be that of expert medical witnesses, whose views are to be preferred, as in *Re Beaney*, to the views of witnesses who are without medical qualifications.

In *CAO v Sheriff* (CA) reported as *R(IS) 14/96*, the Court of Appeal concluded that, even where a receiver has been appointed by the Court of Protection, a claimant who signs a claim form for benefit is capable of making a misrepresentation as to the facts upon which payment of benefit is based. Nor can such a person defeat a claim to repayment of overpaid benefit by arguing that they lacked capacity to make a representation. Nourse L.J. said:

> "If the representor need not know of the material fact misrepresented, I cannot see why it should make any difference if she does not know that she is making a representation. That no doubt would make the misrepresentation more innocent. But it would not take it outside s.53(1) [now s.71(1)]. So that can be no ground for saying that the misrepresentation was not made by the claimant."

Millett L.J. put it even more bluntly:

> ". . . it does not avail a recipient of benefit from whom the Secretary of State seeks repayment of benefit on the ground that he misrepresented a material fact to deny that he had mental capacity to make the representation."

R(IS) 4/06 places formidable hurdles in the path of a claimant seeking to rely on an argument that a claimant did not know what they were doing when completing a claim form. The decision is authority for three key propositions. First, even if the doctrine of *non est factum* applied to social security, which was doubtful, there was no evidence that the form was fundamentally different from the form the claimant thought he was signing and he could reasonably have taken precautions to ascertain its contents and significance (*Lloyds Bank Plc v Waterhouse* [1993] 2 F.L.R. 97 followed, at [9]–[23]). Secondly, there is a difference between acting deliberately and acting dishonestly or fraudulently and it is possible for a claimant to make an innocent misrepresentation by omission (see [30] and [31]). Thirdly, the language of the declaration signed by the claimant could not be read other than as a guarantee that the form had been completed in a way that accurately set out all details that might affect entitlement to the benefit claimed and hence was a misrepresentation and not a failure to disclose (*CAO v Sherriff*, reported as *R(IS) 14/96*, followed, at para.39).

Failure to disclose

Note that where something is not disclosed on a *claim* for benefit which results in an overpayment, the basis of recovery under s.71(1) can only be misrepresentation. This is because the duties which give rise to a failure to disclose relate to beneficiaries. At the point of claim, a person is a claimant and not yet a beneficiary: *CPC/196/2012*. 1.106

However, in *R(SB) 40/84*, at para.12, the Commissioner ruled that a tribunal may switch from failure to disclose to misrepresentation as the basis for the recovery provided that the following conditions are met:

(a) the tribunal has told the appellant that they have such a course of action under consideration;

(b) the misrepresentation relied upon has been clearly identified; and

(c) the appellant has been afforded an adequate opportunity to address the changed basis of recovery without being disadvantaged by surprise.

An adjournment may be necessary to enable an appellant to give full consideration to the implications of the changed basis upon which recovery is to be considered.

Failure to disclose is now much more closely linked to specific instructions given to beneficiaries by the Secretary of State than it once was. Except in the case of jobseeker's allowance, the Secretary of State may require beneficiaries to provide information or evidence in relation to their continuing entitlement to benefit: reg.32(1) of the Claims and Payments Regulations.

Beneficiaries have a duty to provide such information or evidence as the Secretary of State may require in connection with payment of a benefit awarded: reg.32(1A) of the Claims and Payments Regulations.

Except in the case of jobseeker's allowance, beneficiaries have a duty to notify the Secretary of State of any change of circumstances which they might reasonably be expected to know might affect continuing entitlement to benefit.

There are specific duties in relation to jobseeker's allowance to be found in reg.24 of the JSA Regulations. This is why jobseeker's allowance is omitted from the application of reg.32(1) and (1B) but not reg.32(1A).

The decision of the Tribunal of Commissioners in *CIS/4348/2003*, affirmed on appeal to the Court of Appeal as *B v SSWP* [2005] EWCA Civ 929 reported as *R(IS) 9/06* (leave to appeal to the House of Lords was refused—the claimant made an application to the Court of Human Rights which ruled on February 14, 2012, that there had been no violation of art.14 when read with art.1 of Protocol 1), overturns some leading authorities of long standing in ruling, in essence, that there is no overriding requirement applying in every case that disclosure must be reasonably expected of the claimant before an overpayment of benefit can be recovered on the grounds of the failure to disclose. The duty to disclose flows from the statutory provisions quoted above. Then following propositions were common ground: 1.107

(a) There can be a wholly innocent failure to disclose, exemplified by those who do not disclose some material fact because they do not appreciate that it is a material fact.

(b) Persons cannot fail to disclose for the purposes of s.71 a matter unless it is known to them. Whether a matter is known to someone is determined by applying a subjective test.

(c) A material fact for the purposes of s.71 is a fact which is objectively material to the decision to award benefit.

(d) Failure to disclose is not the same as mere non-disclosure. "It imports a breach of some obligation to disclose" (see [13]).

The duty of disclosure flowing from reg.32(1A) is almost always unqualified, but see *LH v SSWP (RP)* [2017] UKUT 249 (AAC) below. It relates to specific matters which a claimant or other beneficiary has been instructed to disclose. In meeting this obligation no question arises concerning the mental capacity of the person required to furnish the information. It is not open to claimants to argue that they were unable to respond to an unambiguous request because, as a result of mental incapacity, they did not understand the request. The Tribunal of Commissioners considers what protection there is for claimants whose capacity may affect their ability to handle their affairs. Two protections are identified. First, there is the possibility that an appointee is appointed to act on their behalf. The Tribunal of Commissioners notes that, where no appointment has been made, "the higher courts have in the past taken a fairly robust approach to submissions based on a lack of capacity" (at para.64). Secondly, there is the possibility that the Secretary of State will exercise the discretion not to recover the overpayment in the particular circumstances of any given case, though the Tribunal comments that it is not "aware of any published guidelines on the exercise of this discretion." (See para.65.)

Decision makers and other adjudicating authorities will need to determine whether a failure to disclose arises in the context of the duty in reg.32(1A) or 32(1B) of the Claims and Payments Regulations. Where reg.32(1A) is in issue, the focus should be on the specific instructions given to the claimant or other person: were there clear and unambiguous instructions of the need to disclose specific facts which have not been disclosed? The relevant instructions may be found in claim forms, notes accompanying claim forms, award notifications and leaflets accompanying these, as well as specific instructions addressed to a person. Such forms and leaflets change from time to time and a copy of the instructions at the relevant time should be provided for tribunals where a person appeals.

1.108 In *R(IB) 4/05* the Commissioner follows the decision in *CIB/3925/2003* to the effect that the advice given to recipients of incapacity benefit about exempt work are couched in terms which do not *require* notification to the DWP before undertaking such work, though it was accepted that undertaking the work without giving the required notice had the result that entitlement to incapacity benefit ceased. The advice to benefit recipients could not be said to be "unambiguous" such that non-disclosure of undertaking such work could ground recovery of any overpayment of incapacity benefit.

This approach is confirmed in the decision of the Court of Appeal in *Hooper v SSWP* [2007] EWCA Civ 495, reported as *R(IB) 4/07*, which concerned an overpayment that had arisen when a recipient of incapacity benefit had started work without notifying the Secretary of State. The Commissioner had taken the view that a direction in a factsheet given to the claimant that "you should tell the office . . . before you start work" constituted a requirement because it was a "polite way of wording an instruction". The Court of Appeal disagreed. There was no reason why the language used could not be clearer in indicating a formal requirement to notify by using the word "must" rather than "should". Dyson L.J. said, "The context is not one which demanded politeness at the expense of clarity." (At [57].) In the course of his judgment, Dyson L.J. expressly approves the reasoning of Commissioners Mesher and Howell in *CIB/3925/2003* and *R(IB) 4/05*.

A rather broader enquiry is required where reg.32(1B) is in issue. Here there remains a need to consider whether, in all the circumstances of the case, disclosure can reasonably be expected.

There will be rare cases where the duty to disclose under reg.32(1A) or reg.32(1B) is not unqualified: *LH v SSWP (RP)* [2017] UKUT 249 (AAC). The claimant was in receipt of a state retirement pension, and claimed a dependency increase for his wife. The wife subsequently became entitled to a state retirement pension on her own right. An overpayment arose because the dependency increase was not adjusted to take account of the wife's own retirement pension. The Secretary of State initially argued that the claimant had failed to disclose the receipt by his wife of her own state retirement pension. However, on closer enquiry it was accepted that the claimant had been in contact with the Department about the effect of an award of a state retirement pension for his wife. The Secretary of State then changed his argument: the claimant could reasonably be expected to disclose the annual uprating of his benefit and had failed to do so. Judge Wright takes a new view on the concept of disclosure, and resurrects aspects of *R(SB) 15/87* in that disclosure is not limited to a breach of reg.32. There are still occasions in which disclosure is not reasonably to be expected: see, in particular, paras 58–69 of the decision. Disclosure of annual uprating, which was in issue in this case, is such an example.

In *SS v SSWP* [2009] UKUT 260 (AAC), the judge ruled that the standard letter advising incapacity benefit claimants that their entitlement to incapacity credits had ended because, as a result of a personal capability assessment, they were to be treated as available for work, "implied very strongly that, if the effect of the decision about incapacity credits was that the Claimant ceased to be entitled to income support, Jobcentre Plus would take steps to terminate the income support award." (See [11].) It followed that there was no breach of the obligation to disclose under reg.32(1B) of the Claims and Payments Regulations and that any overpayment of income support which arose in those circumstances would not be recoverable. **1.109**

A common ground of appeal against an overpayment decision based on failure to disclose a change in entitlement to one benefit which affects another benefit is that the Secretary of State must be aware of the change and this means there has been no failure to disclose. However, *Hinchy v SSWP* [2005] UKHL 16, reported as *R(IS) 7/05*, established that claimants are not entitled to make assumptions about the administrative arrangements for communications between parts of the DWP, and are certainly not entitled to assume the existence of effective channels of communication between one office and another. Lord Hoffmann, giving the lead opinion in the House of Lords, considered that the line of authority established in the relevant Commissioners' decisions reflected the realities of benefit administration and went on to say:

> "32. . . . The claimant is not concerned or entitled to make any assumptions about the internal administrative arrangements of the department. In particular, she is not entitled to assume the existence of infallible channels of communication between one office and another. Her duty is to comply with what the Tribunal called the 'simple instruction' in the order book. . . . For my part, I would approve the principles stated by the Commissioners in *R(SB) 15/87* and *CG/4494/99*. The duty of the claimant is the duty imposed by regulation 32 or implied by section 71 to make disclosure to the person or office identified to the claimant as the decision maker. The latter is not deemed to know anything which he did not actually know."

Lady Hale agreed, noting that there was nothing intrinsically wrong in requiring disclosure from the claimant of information known to one part of the DWP which may or may not be known to another part of the DWP. Lady Hale has some reservations about whether the requirement to disclose the termination of the disability living allowance was made sufficiently clear in this case but concedes that this goes to findings of fact rather than a question of law.

The case law in this area is not entirely clear. In *CIS/1887/2002*, the Commissioner ruled that there can be no failure to disclose where both benefits in question were being handled by the same local office, even where the benefits were being handled by different sections of that local office. The claimant submitted a claim for both income support and incapacity benefit to the same office. Income support was awarded and an award of incapacity benefit was subsequently made. The claimant did not tell the local office of this award and his income support continued to be paid resulting in a substantial overpayment of that benefit. The Commissioner, following *CSB/0677/1986*, concluded:

> "21. It is also in my judgment a principle established beyond question that for the purposes of section 71 there is no 'failure to disclose' where the material fact in question is already known to the person or office to whom, under the principle laid down by the House of Lords in *Hinchy*, notification would otherwise have to be made. This too I take to be axiomatic and not called in question by anything said in the recent decision of their Lordships. It may be the kind of point Lord

> Hoffmann had in mind when he said 'a disclosure which would be thought necessary only by a literal-minded pedant . . . need not be made', though perhaps a true pedant would be the least likely to think disclosure necessary in such circumstances, taking the (accurate) view that there can be no question of 'disclosure' to a person or entity of something that he or it knows already.
>
> 22. In my judgment the question of liability under section 71 is concluded in favour of the claimant, and against the Department's view as accepted by the tribunal, by the fact that all questions affecting both of the interconnected benefits involved in this case were being dealt with by the single local benefits office at the same address; and there was nothing in any of the correspondence, literature or other evidence put before the tribunal to show that the staff from time to time dealing with the relevant incapacity benefit and income support questions were separately identified to the claimant or any else as different 'offices'; or that the need to track down and notify any separate individual or section of individuals within that same office at the same address was either reasonably to be expected mf the claimant or in any way brought to his attention. On the contrary, all the material before the tribunal pointed to the opposite conclusion, and that has been reinforced by the further submissions and explanations of the system in such an office provided for me for the purposes of this appeal."

ME v SSWP (SPC) [2016] UKUT 12 (AAC) illustrates the need for careful enquiry. The appellant was the subject of an overpayment decision in relation to an award of pension credit on the basis that he had failed to disclose receipt of an occupational pension. The appellant had made disclosures to Jobcentre Plus by telephone. On close enquiry and from a telephone number on a letter (other than the relevant award letter which was no longer available) from the Pension Service sent to the appellant, it appeared that the telephone numbers on letters he had received from both Jobcentre Plus and the Pension Service may well have been identical, which could have resulted in his having made the disclosure required of him by the Pension Service. Since the Secretary of State could not produce the original award letter, the Secretary of State accepted that he could not show, on the balance of probabilities, that there had been a failure to disclose.

1.110 In cases where different benefits are being handled by different parts of the DWP, and notification from one of them to the other does take place, the arguments now focus on the question of causation: whether the failure to disclose resulted in the overpayment. These issues are discussed in the section of this commentary headed "Causation" at paras 1.115–1.116 below.

In *CIS/1996/2006* and *CIS/2125/2006* the Commissioner alludes to the negative consequences of the decision in *B v SSWP* in noting that there can be no obligation on a claimant's partner to disclose, and so, if the partner was the only person who knew the material fact, there can be no failure to disclose. The pertinent paragraph of the decision reads:

> "As the submissions . . . on behalf of the Secretary of State in each of these appeals are right to concede, the tribunal's findings of facts and reasons were insufficient to show how the duty of disclosure it placed on the appellant arose. Moreover in my judgment the tribunal misdirected itself in holding that the facts could bring him within regulation 32(1B) of the Claims and Payments Regulations at all. That provision, as the decision rightly said, imposes a duty; but a person in this appellant's position is not one of the people on whom that duty is expressed to be imposed. An income support claimant's partner, whose details have to be included in the claim, does not thereby become another claimant; is not a 'beneficiary' (an expression which is undefined, but in this context must mean a person with some entitlement to the relevant benefit); or a person 'by whom' the benefit awarded, not to the partner but to the claimant in his or her own right, is receivable. Nor is the income support under such an award receivable by the claimant in any sense as agent for or 'on behalf of ' a partner

merely because that partner's existence and resources are disclosed in the claim and taken into account in calculating the applicable amount, and thus the net overall level of benefit, appropriate to the *claimant* on the claim and any resulting award." (See [14].)

JM v SSWP [2010] UKUT 135 (AAC) illustrates the need to analyse carefully what is in issue in an overpayment recoverability decision. The claimant had been in receipt of the lowest rate of the care component on the grounds that she could not cook a main meal for herself. She subsequently asked for the mobility component to be added but raised no issue relating to the care component. The mobility component was added. It was then established that she was working as a cleaning supervisor and that her mobility was, in fact, far in excess of the description of her walking ability on which the award had been based. Those circumstances also called into question her entitlement to the care component. An entitlement decision was made removing entitlement to both components from their initial award and an overpayment decision was made seeking recovery. A First-tier tribunal confirmed the entitlement decision and the Upper Tribunal judge on appeal found no fault with it. However, the First-tier tribunal had not sufficiently examined the basis for recovery of the overpaid benefit. It was accepted that there had been a serious misrepresentation of her walking ability by the claimant, which was "simply and obviously far beyond any genuine margin of error or imprecise description" (see [22]). Regardless, the appellant had not made any representations beyond statements made at the time of the original award of just the care component and that had been based on her claim supported only by her GP. The First-tier tribunal had, in the opinion of the Upper Tribunal judge, been right to conclude that an overpayment of the care component could only arise if the Secretary of State could establish that there had been a failure to disclose a material fact. The Upper Tribunal judge observes:

> "What the evidence showed was that in making her application in early November 2004 to have the mobility component added to her existing disability living allowance award, the claimant simply said nothing about her care needs because she was not asked to. On her own admission and the tribunal's findings, she knew she could in fact cook a main meal for herself all along, and knew the basis for her existing award of care component was a mistaken assumption that she could not reasonably do so. What she did then was simply to keep mum, and not volunteer any information to the department from which they could see they had made a mistake." (See [27].)

The Upper Tribunal judge notes that prior to *R(IS) 9/06 B v SSWP* disclosure 1.111
by the appellant would have been regarded as being reasonably to be expected, but following that decision, the proper enquiry was to ask whether she had been required to disclose her knowledge that she had been awarded the care component on a mistaken basis. The judge concludes that none of the requirements imposed on the appellant required her to disclose information concerning her care needs or specifically on her ability to cook a main meal for herself. In all the circumstances the Secretary of State had not shown a required basis for recovery of the overpaid care component of the disability living allowance.

One of the issues which arose in *AS v SSWP (CA)* [2015] UKUT 592 (AAC); [2016] AACR 22, concerned the burden of proof which falls on the Secretary of State where claimants state that they have made disclosure by way of telephone communication with the Department. The issue arose in an overpayment case involving a claimed failure to disclose earnings on making a claim for carer's allowance where the existence of those earnings only came to light some years later. On the first question, the claimant's representative argued, relying on *CSB/347/1983* and *R(SB) 10/85*, that, in the face of the claimant's evidence that he had disclosed his earnings in a telephone call to the Department, the Secretary of State was required as a matter of law to adduce evidence as to the procedures in place at the relevant office of the Department at the relevant time, and could not merely adduce evidence that no record of the telephone conversation could be found. Judge Wright does not consider that *R(SB) 10/85* supports the proposition to be found in *CSB/347/1983*. Furthermore, even if *CSB/347/1983* constituted a principle of law in December 1983 when it was decided, it did not survive the approach advocated in *Kerr v Department for Social Development* [2004] UKHL 23; *R 1/04(SF)* which explained that the inquisitorial approach adopted in tribunals meant that "it will rarely be necessary to resort to concepts taken from adversarial litigation such as the burden of proof" (para.63). Under s.12(8)(a) of the Social Security Act 1998 what evidence is or is not needed in any case will depend on the facts of the case. The circumstances of the case before Judge Wright did not put in issue the procedures for recording telephone conversations. Judge Wright concludes:

> "43. Accordingly, in so far as the comments in *CSB/347/1983* about telephone recording systems was laying down a rule of law, in my judgment it should no longer be followed."

In *R(A) 2/06*, the Commissioner considered the extent to which oral representations by an officer of the DWP can have an impact on the statutory duty to disclose. The case concerned a claimant with an appointee who was in a care home. When the local authority took over the payment of the care home fees, no disclosure was made and attendance allowance continued to be paid resulting in an overpayment of that benefit. In the run-up to the change of legislation which resulted in the local authority payment of the care home fees, the daughter (who was the appointee) was visited by a Customer Liaison Manager. In evidence, the appointee said that the Customer Liaison Manager "told me that the visit . . . would initiate any action required with regard to my mother's benefit changes when council funding started and there was no need for me to take any further action." (See [6] of the Decision.) The Commissioner accepts that a particular duty to provide information is capable of being modified by an oral representation made by an officer of the DWP, though it will be vital that careful findings of fact are made about such representations and their context. Finally, the Secretary of State must present evidence to show any duty to disclose; such a duty will not be implied and any assumption made by the Secretary of State that there is a duty to disclose is likely to be challenged in overpayment cases.

It follows from *Hinchy* that disclosure must be made to the local office handling the benefit claim in question. The disclosure may be in writing, though it need not be. In practice any disclosure not in writing will be reduced to writing by someone in the DWP. All disclosures must be made as soon as is practicable after the event which triggers the need for them.

A decision by Commissioner Stockman in Northern Ireland could well have implications for analogous cases elsewhere in the United Kingdom: *RM v Department for Communities C8/16-17 (JSA)*. The appeal concerned an overpayment of jobseeker's allowance. The obligations corresponding to those found in reg.32 of the Claims and Payments Regulations are in reg.24 of the JSA Regulations. In Northern Ireland, the instruction given to claimants is to notify either the Department for Social Development or his or her employment adviser (who was at the time an employee of the Department for Employment and Learning—the two departments have since been unified as the Department for Communities). The claimant told his employment adviser that his partner was working. The employment adviser told the claimant to notify someone in the Department for Social Development, but the claimant (a Lithuanian national) did not do so and said he had not understood the instruction to do so.

Commissioner Stockman rules that disclosure was complete when notice was given to the employment adviser, and it was not open to the employment adviser to vary the statutory requirement by oral instruction.

A further question was whether there was a continuing duty to disclose. Commissioner Stockman distinguished *R(SB) 15/87* and *R(SB) 54/83* because communication in those cases was not to an officer in the section handling the benefit in respect of which the overpayment arose. Here the claimant had complied with the directions he had received by giving notice to his employment adviser.

1.112 A continuing duty to disclose will arise where disclosure is made by someone other than the claimant. However, it should be noted that *R(SB) 15/87* establishes that where disclosure is made by a third party (other than an appointee, personal representatives, guardians and both members of joint claim couples), such notification is sufficient only if all the following conditions are met:

(a) the information is given in connection with the claimant's benefit entitlement and in compliance with any instructions from the Secretary of State;

(b) the claimant is aware that the information has been provided; and

(c) in the circumstances it is reasonable for the claimant to believe that it is unnecessary that further action is taken.

CIS/14025/1996 establishes that such third party disclosures must be adequate to alert an officer of the DWP that it is a disclosure on behalf of another in respect of their benefit entitlement. Mere casual or incidental disclosure will not suffice.

If, following a disclosure by a third party, nothing changes, the claimant may well be under a continuing duty to disclose. This is illustrated by *WW v HMRC (CHB)* [2011] UKUT 11 (AAC). The claimant was in receipt of child benefit but her entitlement ceased when the child was taken into care. The claimant did not disclose the change in the child's circumstances to HMRC but it was found that she had certain dealings with officers of the DWP. The judge found that, in the course of one of those dealings, the officer of the DWP had indicated that the change of circumstances would be reported to HMRC with the result that payment of child benefit would cease. That did not happen. The judge ruled that an officer of the DWP has ostensible authority to make oral representations to pass on information to HMRC. This was based in part on the absence of any complete separation of the administration of child benefits between the DWP and HMRC. However, when the promised onward transmission of information did not take place, the claimant should have noticed that child benefit was still in payment and done something about this. She could only escape liability to repay three months worth of child benefit.

TM v SSWP (ESA) [2015] UKUT 109 (AAC) concerned an overpayment which arose on a conversion decision from entitlement to income support to entitlement to income-related ESA. The conversion decision was made in ignorance of the fact that the claimant had capital exceeding £16,000. It was eventually conceded that this could only be recovered on the grounds of a failure to disclose. The claimant's representative raised a number of arguments in support of his client's appeal. He argued that, as the alleged failures to disclose occurred while the claimant was entitled to income support, it could not be the basis for recovery in relation to ESA. Judge Rowland rejected that argument:

> "As long as there was a duty to make disclosure and the failure to disclose the material facts has caused the overpayment, it does not matter that the duty to disclose arose in respect of a different benefit from the one in respect of which it is submitted that the overpayment is recoverable." (para.7).

A further argument was that, as at the date of the award, the Secretary of State was fully aware of the claimant's capital but made a mistake for which the Secretary of State was wholly responsible. Judge Rowland said:

> "... it is difficult to see how any overpayment arising under the award ... can be said to have been in consequence of the claimant's failure to disclose his capital if the Secretary of State already knew about the capital then and the decision was based on a mistake for which only he was responsible, unless, perhaps, the claimant was aware that the award was wrongly made."

Since this issue had not been fully explored by the First-tier Tribunal, the appeal was remitted for a rehearing.

where there may have been a case control or a reminder at the relevant time in 2005, and as to what happened in relation to those procedures."

SSWP v SS (SPC) [2013] UKUT 272 (AAC) considers when the chain of causation is broken and how a tribunal should proceed when an argument on this issue arises in the course of the hearing. The judge rules that it will be a breach of natural justice to fail to adjourn a hearing to enable the Secretary of State to respond to arguments that the chain of causation has been broken (at [6]). Whether and when the chain of causation is broken is a question of fact but a failure to respond immediately to information arising from a Generalised Matching Service Scan will not necessarily result in a break in the chain of causation (see especially [15]). The case includes a review of some earlier case-law.

BD v SSWP (PC) [2016] UKUT 162 (AAC) contains a detailed account (at paras 8-9) of arrangements for computerised communications between various parts of the Department and the expectations as to action that would be taken on those communications. The case also considers the application of the principles set out in *GJ v SSWP (IS)* and *SSWP v SS (SPC)*.

The calculation of the overpayment

1.117 *KP v RB of Kensington and Chelsea (HB)* [2014] UKUT 393 (AAC) determines that a compensation order made by the Crown Court does not act as a cap on the amount of overpaid housing benefit and excess council tax benefit which is recoverable.

There are two linked aspects of the calculation of the overpayment: the period of the overpayment and the amount of the overpayment. Both must be specified in the overpayment decision. It is not at all uncommon to see variations both in dates and amounts where there is an appeal against an overpayment decision. It is for the Secretary of State to determine both the period and the amount of the overpayment. Tribunals may be called upon to check the accuracy of the determination.

In *CS/366/1993* the Commissioner gives advice on the level of proof of payment of a benefit recovery of which is being sought. This is an issue which can come up in overpayment appeals, when a claimant either directly or indirectly puts in issue whether they have ever received the money which the adjudication officer, or now decision-maker, says is recoverable. The Commissioner reminds tribunals that the burden of proof is on the balance of probabilities. Where there is evidence of entitlement to and payment of benefit that may be sufficient to show that the benefit was paid. It certainly is in the absence of any challenge by the claimant. Equally, no higher burden will lie with the adjudication officer if the claimant does not adduce evidence that they did not receive the benefit but simply asked the adjudication officer to prove that the benefit was paid.

In *R(SB) 11/86* it was held that underpayments of benefit during the relevant period could be taken into account. The sums to be deducted in calculating recoverable amounts are governed by reg.13 of the Payments on Account Regulations.

1.118 A schedule showing how the overpayment is calculated is normally included in the appeal papers, although great care must be taken in simply adopting these, especially if there is any variation of the decision under appeal. The tribunal may, for example, find that an overpayment is recoverable for a different period. This will affect the amount recoverable. The need for tribunals to state expressly the sum which is recoverable and how it is calculated was stressed in *R(SB) 9/85*. This advice was repeated in *R(SB) 11/86* where the Commissioner helpfully approves the practice of leaving a difficult recalculation to the adjudication officer *provided that* it is made clear that the claimant or the adjudication officer may refer the matter back to the tribunal in the event of any particular difficulty or disagreement arising. The approach tribunals should adopt is to recalculate benefit in the light of the facts as found by them to determine the amount of the overpayment: *R(SB) 20/84* and *R(SB) 10/85(T)*.

In *CIS/442/1992* the Commissioner reminds tribunals of the proper procedure to follow when the calculation of the amount of the overpayment is initially left for determination by the parties. Where reference back to the tribunal is necessary, then that reference should be to the same tribunal which dealt with the issue of liability (at para.5). Should it prove necessary to refer the case back to a differently constituted tribunal, then both the issue of liability and the issue of calculation will need to be considered at the adjourned hearing (at para.7). A different tribunal should only hear the case if satisfied that it is not practicable to reconvene the original tribunal (at para.7).

Where capital is in issue, then the rules on diminishing capital are likely to come into play. This is governed by reg.14 of the Payments on Account Regulations. This provides for the reduction of the figure of capital resources at quarterly intervals from the beginning of the period of the overpayment period by the amount overpaid in respect of the listed benefits in the previous quarter. No other reduction of the actual amount of capital resources is allowed: reg.14(2).

For the proper approach to whether arrears in respect of a period of suspension may be set off against an overpayment in respect of an earlier period, see *MR v SSWP (IS)* [2013] UKUT 588 (AAC).

The method of recovery

Whether a recoverable overpayment is actually recovered, and if so, how, are matters for the Secretary of State, and do not concern tribunals. Nevertheless, it is worth noting the judgment of the Supreme Court in *SSWP v Payne* [2011] UKSC 60, in which the court ruled that the DWP cannot recover overpayments of benefit or Social Fund loans by deductions from benefit where that overpayment or loan has been included in a Debt Relief Order (DRO) in insolvency proceedings. The Supreme Court went on to consider the position following the making of a bankruptcy order and decided that it should be the same for bankruptcy as for DROs. In other words, there is no power to make deductions from benefits following the making of a bankruptcy order, just as after a DRO. **1.119**

Direct payments to bank accounts

Section 71(4) provides for the automatic recovery of overpaid benefit arising from incorrect payments into bank accounts. Subsection (4) provides an independent ground for recovering overpayments resulting from the use of payments to a bank account or other similar account. Recovery will only be available if the claimant received, before agreeing to such method of payment, notice in the form specified in reg.11 of the Payments on Account Regulations. If the conditions in reg.11 are not satisfied, an overpayment may still be recoverable under s.71(1). **1.120**

Tax credits: substitution of subs(8)–(9)

Section 71(8)–(9) is, with effect from October 5, 1999, by virtue of s.2 and Pt. IV para.10 of Sch.2 to the Tax Credits Act 1999, to be read as follows in any case where the overpayment was made in respect of tax credits: **1.121**

"(8) An amount recoverable under subsection (1) above in any year of assessment—

(a) shall be treated for the purposes of Part VI of the Taxes Management Act 1970 (collection and recovery) as if it were tax charged in an assessment and due and payable;
(b) shall be treated for the purposes of section 203(2)(a) of the Income and Corporation Taxes Act 1988 (PAYE) as if it were an underpayment of tax for a previous year of assessment.

(8A) Where—

(a) an amount paid in respect of a claim is recoverable under subsection (1) above; and
(b) a penalty has been imposed under section 9(1) of the Tax Credits Act 1999 (penalties for fraud etc.) on the ground that a person fraudulently or negligently made an incorrect statement or declaration in connection with that claim,

the amount shall carry interest at the rate applicable from the date on which it becomes recoverable until payment.

(9) The rate applicable for the purposes of subsection (8A) above shall be the rate from time to time prescribed under section 178 of the Finance Act 1989 for those purposes."

See *Larusai v SSWP* [2003] EWHC 371 (Admin), discussed in the annotations to reg.13 of the Payments on Account Regulations, for the relationship between working families tax credit and benefits administered by the DWP in relation to recovery of overpayments of benefits administered by the DWP.

The amnesty in the Welfare Reform and Pensions Act 1999 s.68

1.122 Note that s.68 of the Welfare Reform and Pensions Act 1999 (paras 1.592–1.597 above) provides that certain overpayments of benefit are not to be recoverable. One of the key conditions is that the overpayment decision was given before June 1, 1999. In dealing with overpayments the provisions of that section should be checked to determine whether they exclude recovery in the now unlikely event that a decision prior to 1999 is in issue.

[1 Overpayments out of social fund

1.123 **71ZA.**—(1) Subject to subsection (2) below, section 71 above shall apply in relation to social fund payments to which this section applies as it applies in relation to payments made in respect of benefits to which that section applies.

[2(2) Section 71 above as it so applies shall have effect as if the following provisions were omitted, namely—

(a) in [3 . . .] subsection (5A), the words

"reversed or varied on an appeal or";

(b) [3 . . .]

(c) subsections (7), (10A) and (10B).]

[4 (2A) Subsection (9A) of section 71 above as it so applies shall have effect as if the reference to amounts recoverable under the provisions mentioned in subsection (8) of that section were to amounts recoverable under subsections (1) and (4) of that section by virtue of subsection (1) above.]

(3) This section applies to social fund payments such as are mentioned in section 138(1)(b) of the Contributions and Benefits Act.]

AMENDMENTS

1. Social Security Act 1998 s.75(1) (October 5, 1998).
2. Note that until ss.9, 10 and 38 of the 1998 Act come into force, subs.(2) is substituted by para.8 of Sch.6 to the Act.
3. Welfare Reform Act 2007 Sch.8 (July 3, 2007).
4. Welfare Reform Act 2012 s.106 (July 1, 2012).

GENERAL NOTE

1.124 Section 75(2) of the Social Security Act 1998 provides that s.71ZA applies to social fund overpayment decisions made on or after October 5, 1998.

[[1] *Recovery of benefit payments*

Recovery of overpayments of certain benefits

71ZB.—(1) The Secretary of State may recover any amount of the following paid in excess of entitlement— 1.125

(a) universal credit,
(b) jobseeker's allowance,
(c) employment and support allowance,
(d) *except in prescribed circumstances, housing credit (within the meaning of the State Pension Credit Act 2002).*

(2) An amount recoverable under this section is recoverable from—
(a) the person to whom it was paid, or
(b) such other person (in addition to or instead of the person to whom it was paid) as may be prescribed.

(3) An amount paid in pursuance of a determination is not recoverable under this section unless the determination has been—
(a) reversed or varied on an appeal, or
(b) revised or superseded under section 9 or section 10 of the Social Security Act 1998,

except where regulations otherwise provide.

(4) Regulations may provide that amounts recoverable under this section are to be calculated or estimated in a prescribed manner.

(5) Where an amount of universal credit is paid for the sole reason that a payment by way of prescribed income is made after the date which is the prescribed date for payment of that income, that amount is for the purposes of this section paid in excess of entitlement.

(6) In the case of a benefit referred to in subsection (1) which is awarded to persons jointly, an amount paid to one of those persons may for the purposes of this section be regarded as paid to the other.

(7) An amount recoverable under this section may (without prejudice to any other means of recovery) be recovered—
(a) by deduction from benefit (section 71ZC);
(b) by deduction from earnings (section 71ZD);
(c) through the courts etc (section 71ZE);
(d) by adjustment of benefit (section 71ZF).]

AMENDMENT

1. The Welfare Reform Act 2012 (Commencement No. 8 and Savings and Transitional Provisions) Order 2013 (SI 2013/358) art.5(2) (April 29, 2013).

GENERAL NOTE

Note that this section is not fully in force. Article 5(3)(a) of the Welfare Reform Act 2012 (Commencement No.8 and Savings and Transitional Provisions) Order 2013 (SI 2013/358) provided for the amending s.105(1) of the WRA 2012 to have effect in so far as it was not already in force "except in so far as it inserts section 71ZB(1)(d) of the 1992 Act and the word 'and' immediately preceding it" (the italicised text above). The Commencement No.8 Order was then modified by art.23(3) of the Welfare Reform Act 2012 (Commencement No.9 and Transitional and Transitory Provisions and Commencement No. 8 and Savings and Transitional Provisions (Amendment)) Order 2013 (SI 2013/983), which provides that new s.71ZB(1)(b) and (c) "come into force on 29th April 2013 only in so far as they relate respectively to a new style JSA award and a new style ESA award". 1.126

Sections 71ZB to 71ZF concern the new style provisions on the recovery of overpayments. See the commentary in *Volume V Universal Credit* of this series.

[1 71ZC Deduction from benefit

1.127 (1) An amount recoverable from a person under section 71ZB may be recovered by deducting the amount from payments of prescribed benefit.

(2) Where an amount recoverable from a person under section 71ZB was paid to the person on behalf of another, subsection (1) authorises its recovery from the person by deduction—

(a) from prescribed benefits to which the person is entitled,

(b) from prescribed benefits paid to the person to discharge (in whole or in part) an obligation owed to that person by the person on whose behalf the recoverable amount was paid, or

(c) from prescribed benefits paid to the person to discharge (in whole or in part) an obligation owed to that person by any other person.

(3) Where an amount is recovered as mentioned in paragraph (b) of subsection (2), the obligation specified in that paragraph shall in prescribed circumstances be taken to be discharged by the amount of the deduction.

(4) Where an amount is recovered as mentioned in paragraph (c) of subsection (2), the obligation specified in that paragraph shall in all cases be taken to be so discharged.]

AMENDMENT

1. Welfare Reform Act 2007 s.105 (see note on commencement below).

COMMENCEMENT

1.128 New ss.71ZB to 71ZH are inserted after s.71ZA by s.105 of the Welfare Reform Act 2012. The Welfare Reform Act 2012 (Commencement No.2) Order 2012 (SI 2012/1246) brings ss.71ZC, 71ZD and 71ZE into force for certain purposes. Article 2 of the Order provides that the basis on which these amendments are made is as follows:

"(4) 1st July 2012 is the day appointed for the coming into force of the following provisions of the Act—

(a) section 105(1) (recovery of benefit payments), to the extent that it inserts section 71ZC(1) (deduction from benefit) of the Administration Act, for the purpose only of prescribing under section 71ZC(1) the benefits from which deductions may be made in order to recover the penalties;

(b) section 105(1) to the extent that it inserts section 71ZD (deduction from earnings) of the Administration Act; . . . .

(5) 1st October 2012 is the day appointed for the coming into force of the following provisions of the Act—

(a) section 105(1) (recovery of benefit payments) to the extent that it inserts sections 71ZC(1) (deduction from benefit) and 71ZE (recovery by court action) of the Administration Act, for the purpose only of enabling recovery of the penalties to take place by those methods; . . . .".

[1 71ZD Deduction from earnings

1.129 (1) Regulations may provide for amounts recoverable under section 71ZB to be recovered by deductions from earnings.

(2) In this section "earnings" has such meaning as may be prescribed.

(3) Regulations under subsection (1) may include provision—

(a) requiring the person from whom an amount is recoverable ("the beneficiary") to disclose details of their employer, and any change of employer, to the Secretary of State;
(b) requiring the employer, on being served with a notice by the Secretary of State, to make deductions from the earnings of the beneficiary and to pay corresponding amounts to the Secretary of State;
(c) as to the matters to be contained in such a notice and the period or which a notice is to have effect;
(d) as to how payment is to be made to the Secretary of State;
(e) as to a level of earnings below which earnings must not be reduced;
(f) allowing the employer, where the employer makes deductions, to deduct a prescribed sum from the beneficiary's earnings in respect of the employer's administrative costs;
(g) requiring the employer to keep records of deductions;
(h) requiring the employer to notify the Secretary of State if the beneficiary is not, or ceases to be, employed by the employer;
(i) creating a criminal offence for non-compliance with the regulations, punishable on summary conviction by a fine not exceeding level 3 on the standard scale;
(j) with respect to the priority as between a requirement to deduct from earnings under this section and—
  (i) any other such requirement;
  (ii) an order under any other enactment relating to England and Wales which requires deduction from the beneficiary's earnings;
  (iii) any diligence against earnings.]

AMENDMENT

1. Welfare Reform Act 2007 s.105 (see note on commencement below).

COMMENCEMENT

New ss.71ZB to 71ZH are inserted after s.71ZA by s.105 of the Welfare Reform Act 2012. The Welfare Reform Act 2012 (Commencement No.2) Order 2012 (SI 2012/1246) brings ss.71ZC, 71ZD and 71ZE into force for certain purposes. Article 2 of the Order provides that the basis on which these amendments are made is as follows: 1.130

"(4) 1st July 2012 is the day appointed for the coming into force of the following provisions of the Act—
(a) section 105(1) (recovery of benefit payments), to the extent that it inserts section 71ZC(1) (deduction from benefit) of the Administration Act, for the purpose only of prescribing under section 71ZC(1) the benefits from which deductions may be made in order to recover the penalties;
(b) section 105(1) to the extent that it inserts section 71ZD (deduction from earnings) of the Administration Act; . . . .

(5) 1st October 2012 is the day appointed for the coming into force of the following provisions of the Act—
(a) section 105(1) (recovery of benefit payments) to the extent that it inserts sections 71ZC(1) (deduction from benefit) and 71ZE (recovery by court action) of the Administration Act, for the purpose only of enabling recovery of the penalties to take place by those methods; . . . .".

(d), 7(2A)(d) or (4)(d), 8(3)(aa), (4)(d) or 9(2A)(d) of the Social Security Fraud Act 2001.

(2) An amount recoverable under this section is recoverable from—

(a) the person to whom it was paid, or

(b) such other person (in addition to or instead of the person to whom it was paid) as may be prescribed.

(3) Regulations may provide that amount recoverable under this section are to be calculated or estimated in a prescribed manner.

(4) Where universal credit or a jobseeker's allowance is claimed by persons jointly, an amount paid to one claimant may for the purposes of this section be regarded as paid to the other.

(5) Sections 71ZC to 71ZF apply in relation to amounts recoverable under this section as to amounts recoverable under section 71ZB.]

AMENDMENT

1. The Welfare Reform Act 2012 (Commencement No. 8 and Savings and Transitional Provisions) Order 2013 (SI 2013/358) art.5(2) (April 29, 2013).

GENERAL NOTE

1.136 The significance of the words in italics in s.71ZH(1)(b) is that this paragraph is repealed with effect from April 29, 2013 but is maintained in force for certain purposes: see The Welfare Reform Act 2012 (Commencement No. 9 and Transitional and Transitory Provisions and Commencement No. 8 115A and Savings and Transitional Provisions (Amendment)) Order 2013 (SI 2013/983) art.7(1)(e).

Recovery of jobseeker's allowance: severe hardship cases

1.137 **71A.**—(1) Where—

(a) a severe hardship direction is revoked; and

(b) it is determined by [2 the Secretary of State] that—

(i) whether fraudulently or otherwise, any person has misrepresented, or failed to disclose, any material fact; and

(ii) in consequence of the failure or misrepresentation, payment of a jobseeker's allowance has been made during the relevant period to the person to whom the direction related,

[2 the Secretary of State] may determine that [2 he] is entitled to recover the amount of the payment.

(2) In this section—

"severe hardship direction" means a direction given under section 16 of the Jobseekers Act 1995; and

"the relevant period" means—

(a) if the revocation is under section 16(3)(a) of that Act, the period begining with the date of the change of circumstances and ending with the date of the revocation; and

(b) if the revocation is under section 16(3)(b) or (c) of that Act, the period during which the direction was in force.

(3) Where a severe hardship direction is revoked, the Secretary of State may certify whether there has been misrepresentation of a material fact or failure to disclose a material fact.

(4) If the Secretary of State certifies that there has been such misrepresentation or failure to disclose, he may certify—

(a) who made the misrepresentation or failed to make the disclosure; and

(b) whether or not a payment of jobseeker's allowance has been made in consequence of the misrepresentation or failure.

(5) If the Secretary of State certifies that a payment has been made, he may certify the period during which a jobseeker's allowance would not have been paid but for the misrepresentation or failure to disclose.

(6) A certificate under this section shall be conclusive as to any matter certified.

(7) Subsections (3) and (6) to (10) of section 71 above apply to a jobseeker's allowance recoverable under subsection (1) above as they apply to a jobseeker's allowance recoverable under section 71(1) above.

(8) The other provisions of section 71 above do not apply to a jobseeker's allowance recoverable under subsection (1) above.]

AMENDMENTS

1. Jobseekers Act 1995 s.18 (October 7, 1996).
2. Social Security Act 1998 Sch.7 para.82 (October 18, 1999).

GENERAL NOTE

Section 16 of the Jobseekers Act 1995 enables the Secretary of State to direct that a person under the age of 18 is to qualify for JSA in order to avoid severe hardship. The direction may be revoked on the ground of change of circumstances (s.16(3)(a)) or on the ground that the young person has failed to pursue an opportunity, or rejected an offer, of training without good cause (s.16(3)(b)) or on the ground that mistake as to or ignorance of a material fact led to the determination that severe hardship would result if JSA was not paid (s.16(3)(c)). A special provision is needed for recovery in cases of misrepresentation or failure to disclose because the revocation of the direction is not a review which can found action under s.71 and it appears that it does not enable the decision on entitlement to JSA to be reviewed for any period before the date of the revocation. Note that the Secretary of State's certificate is conclusive on almost every issue (subs.(3)–(6)). The provisions of s.71 about the mechanics of recovery apply. 1.138

Special provision as to recovery of income support

72. [1. . .] 1.139

AMENDMENT

1. Repealed by Jobseekers Act 1995 Sch.3 (October 7, 1996).

Adjustments of benefits

Overlapping benefits—general

73.—(1) Regulations may provide for adjusting [8 state pension under Part 1 of the Pensions Act 2014 or] benefit as defined in section 122 of the Contributions and Benefits Act [1, or a contribution-based jobseeker's allowance] [6 or a contributory employment and support allowance] which is payable to or in respect of any person, or the conditions for [2 receipt of that benefit] where— 1.140

(a) there is payable in his case any such pension or allowance as is described in subsection (2) below; or
(b) the person is, or is treated under the regulations as, undergoing

medical or other treatment as an in-patient in a hospital or similar institution.

(2) Subsection (1)(a) above applies to any pension, allowance or benefit payable out of public funds (including any other benefit as so defined, whether it is of the same or a different description) which is payable to or in respect of—

(a) the person referred to in subsection (1);
(b) that person's [4 wife, husband or civil partner];
(c) any [5 . . .] dependent of that person; or
(d) the [4 wife, husband or civil partner] of any adult dependant of that person.

(3) Where but for regulations made by virtue of subsection (1)(a) above two persons would both be entitled to an increase of benefit in respect of a third person, regulations may make provision as to their priority.

[3(4) Regulations may provide for adjusting—

[8 (za) state pension under Part 1 of the Pensions Act 2014;]
(a) benefit as defined in section 122 of the Contributions and Benefits Act;
(b) a contribution-based jobseeker's allowance, or
[6(c) a contributory employment and support allowance,]

payable to or in respect of any person where there is payable in his case any such benefit as is described in subsection (5) below.]

(5) Subsection (4) above applies to any benefit payable under the legislation of any member State other than the United Kingdom which is payable to or in respect of—

(a) the person referred to in that subsection;
(b) that person's [4 wife, husband or civil partner];
(c) any [4 . . .] dependent of that person; or
(d) the [4 wife, husband or civil partners] of any adult dependant of that person.

[7 (6) Personal independence payment is to be treated for the purposes of this section as if it were benefit as defined in section 122 of the Contributions and Benefits Act.]

AMENDMENTS

1. Jobseekers Act 1995 Sch.2 para.49(2)(a) (June 11, 1996).
2. Jobseekers Act 1995 Sch.2 para.49(2)(b) (June 11, 1996).
3. Jobseekers Act 1995 Sch.2 para.49(3) (June 11, 1996).
4. Civil Partnership Act 2004 s.254 and Sch.24 para.59 (December 5, 2005).
5. Child Benefit Act 2005 Sch.1 Pt 1 para.21 (April 10, 2006).
6. Welfare Reform Act 2007 s.28 and Sch.3 para.10 (October 27, 2008).
7. Welfare Reform Act 2012, Sch.9, para.11 (April 8, 2013).
8. Pensions Act 2014, s.56(4), s.23 and Sch.12, para.12 (April 6, 2016).

DERIVATION

1.141 SSA 1975 s.85 as amended.

GENERAL NOTE

1.142 See the Hospital In-Patients Regulations and Overlapping Benefits Regulations.

Income support and other payments

1.143 **74.**—(1) Where—

(a) a payment by way of prescribed income is made after the date which is the prescribed date in relation to the payment; and
(b) it is determined that an amount which has been paid by way of income support [2 . . .] [2, an income-based jobseeker's allowance [3 state pension credit or an income-related employment and support allowance]] would not have been paid if the payment had been made on the prescribed date,

the Secretary of State shall be entitled to recover that amount from the person to whom it was paid.

(2) Where—
(a) a prescribed payment which apart from this subsection falls to be made from public funds in the United Kingdom or under the law of any other member State is not made on or before the date which is the prescribed date in relation to the payment; and
(b) it is determined that an amount ("the relevant amount") has been paid by way of [5 universal credit or] income support [2 . . .] [2, an income-based jobseeker's allowance [3, state pension credit or an income-related employment and support allowance]] that would not have been paid if the payment mentioned in paragraph (a) above had been made on the prescribed date,

then—
(i) in the case of a payment from public funds in the United Kingdom, the authority responsible for making it may abate it by the relevant amount; and
(ii) in the case of any other payment, the Secretary of State shall be entitled to receive the relevant amount out of the payment.

(3) Where—
(a) a person (in this subsection referred to as A) is entitled to any prescribed benefit for any period in respect of another person (in this subsection referred to as B); and
(b) either—
(i) B has received income support [1 or an income-based jobseeker's allowance] for that period; or
(ii) B was, during that period, a member of the same family as some person other than A who received income support [1 or an income-based jobseeker's allowance] for that period; and
(c) the amount of the income support [4 an income-based jobseeker's allowance or an income-based employment and support allowance] has been determined on the basis that A has not made payments for the maintenance of B at a rate equal to or exceeding the amount of the prescribed benefit,

the amount of the prescribed benefit may, at the discretion of the authority administering it, be abated by the amount by which the amounts paid by way of income support . . . [4, an income-based jobseeker's allowance or an income-related employment and support allowance] exceed what it is determined that they would have been had A, at the time the amount of the income support [1or an income-based jobseeker's allowance] was determined, been making payments for the maintenance of B at a rate equal to the amount of the prescribed benefit.

(4) Where an amount could have been recovered by abatement by virtue of subsection (2) or (3) above but has not been so recovered, the Secretary of State may recover it otherwise than by way of abatement—

(a) in the case of an amount which could have been recovered by virtue of subsection (2) above, from the person to whom it was paid; and
(b) in the case of an amount which could have been recovered by virtue of subsection (3) above, from the person to whom the prescribed benefit in question was paid.

(5) Where a payment is made in a currency other than sterling, its value in sterling shall be determined for the purposes of this section in accordance with regulations.

AMENDMENTS

1. Jobseekers Act 1995 Sch.2 para.50 (October 7, 1996).
2. State Pension Credit Act 2002 s.14 and Sch.2 (July 2, 2002 for the purposes of making regulations only; fully in force October 6, 2003).
3. Welfare Reform Act 2007 s.28 and Sch.3 para.10 (October 27, 2008).
4. The Employment and Support Allowance (Miscellaneous Amendments) Regulations 2008, (SI 2008/2428) reg.23 (October 27, 2008).
5. Welfare Reform Act 2012 s.31 and Sch.2 para.7 (February 25, 2013).

DERIVATION

1.144 Social Security Act 1986 s.27.

DEFINITION

"prescribed"—see s.191.

GENERAL NOTE

1.145 This is an important provision, which is often overlooked. In *R(IS) 14/04* the Commissioner confirms that there is an appeal against a determination that there is a recoverable overpayment under this section to an appeal tribunal under the Social Security Act 1998 in the following terms:

> ". . . a determination made by the Secretary of State under section 74(1) that a particular amount of income support has been paid to the claim but would not have been so paid had he received his prescribed income payments at the prescribed date, and in consequence is legally recoverable from him under the terms of section 74(1), is an appealable decision within the jurisdiction of the tribunal under section 12 Social Security Act 1998. The appeal does not however extend to any subsequent question of whether or how to enforce any liability so established, which is an administrative or discretionary matter for the Secretary of State." (para.21)

The question which arises under this section is whether there has been a payment of a prescribed benefit which would not have been made had prescribed income been paid to the claimant on the prescribed date.

CIS/5048/2002 illustrates the limitations of this section. The claimant had been receiving income support for herself and her husband. The claimant's husband had applied for, and was awarded, incapacity benefit for himself which he had not disclosed to his wife. The result was an overpayment of income support, which the Secretary of State sought to recover under s.74. The Commissioner ruled on the appeal:

> "10. Two subsections of section 74 were invoked in the submission to the tribunal, subsections (2) and (4). Subsection (2) allows, on the facts of this case, an abatement of the incapacity benefit paid to the husband. It does not authorise any deduction from the claimant. There is nothing in the subsection that allows recovery from 'the other' member of a married or unmarried couple (other than joint claimants). For the record, I indicated in a direction that I do not see how section 74(3) could be applied here either, and the secretary of state's represen-

taive has not disputed this. As I noted in those directions, there is in any event no mention of subsection (3) anywhere in the papers. Subsection (4) applies where an abatement could have been made under subsection (2) or subsection (3) but has not been made. As applied with subsection (2) it allows recovery from the person from whom the abatement could have been retained the husband, not the claimant. So neither of the preconditions for subsection (4) to be applicable to the claimant are present. The decision of the tribunal therefore cannot stand. Equally, neither can the decision of the Secretary of State.

11. I have not considered whether section 74(1) could apply to the claimant because it has not been put in issue. The secretary of state's representative makes the suggestion, which I agree is the best way forward in this case, that the appropriate action is for me to set aside the decision of the Secretary of State and refer the matter back to the Secretary of State. That I do. The Secretary of State can make further decisions about overpayment if he so decides, and those decisions will have their own rights of appeal. He will note the comments of the solicitors about the inapplicability of section 71 to the claimant."

Subsection (1)

Prescribed income is defined in reg.7(1) of the Social Security (Payments on account, Overpayments and Recovery) Regulations 1988 ("the Overpayments Regulations"). The prescribed date under reg.7(2) is, in general, the first day of the period to which that income relates. If as a result of that income being paid after the prescribed date, more benefit is paid than would have been paid if the income had been paid on the prescribed date, the excess may be recovered. Note that the right to recover is absolute and does not depend on lack of care on the claimant's part, or on the effect of this section having been pointed out. That approach is confirmed in *CIS/625/1991*, where the Commissioner rejected the argument that there had to be an investigation of what an adjudication officer would in practice have done if the income had been paid on time. An example would be where a claimant has not been paid part-time earnings when they were due and as a result has been paid income support on the basis of having no earnings. Once the arrears of wages are received, the excess benefit would be recoverable. Late payment of most social security benefits is covered in subss.(2) and (4), but can also come within subs.(1). For instance, if a claim is made for child benefit and while a decision is awaited income support is paid without any deduction for the amount of the expected child benefit, then if arrears of child benefit are eventually paid in full (i.e. the abatement procedure of subs.(2) does not work) the "excess" income support for the period covered by the arrears is recoverable under subs.(1) or (4). 1.146

It is essential that the dates on which prescribed income was due to be paid and on what dates due payments would have affected income support entitlement should be determined: *R(SB) 28/85* and *CIS/625/1991*.

Subsection (2)

Prescribed payments are listed in reg.8(1) of the Overpayments Regulations and include most social security benefits, training allowances and social security benefits from other EC countries. As under the excess income support or JSA, if the abatement mechanism breaks down, the Secretary of State may recover the excess under subs.(4). 1.147

In *CIS/12082/1996* and *CIS/4316/1999* the same Commissioner ruled that art.111 of EC Reg.574/72 does not preclude the application of s.74(2). *CIS/4316/1999* illustrates the application of s.74(2) in the context of the complex rules for determining entitlement to retirement pension where contributions have been made in more than one Member State of the European Union.

In *CIS/764/2002* the Commissioner says,

"I conclude in the present case (although the issue may need eventually to be argued out in some other case) that when there has been an abatement under section 74(2) of the Social Security Administration Act 1992, the relevant amount of income support is to be treated as if had not been paid as income support. Therefore it cannot be touched by a subsequent decision about the recoverability of an overpayment of income support under section 71. I rest that on the overall context of sections 71 and 74, if the conclusion is not required by regulations 5 and 13(a) of the Payments Regulations." (para.22)

The Commissioner had concluded that the requirements of regs 5 and 13(a) of the Payments on Account Regulations required the same result: see para.20 of the decision.

In *PT v SSWP (JSA)* [2013] UKUT 372 (AAC), the judge explained that s.74(2) "is concerned with cases where a claimant in receipt of an income-related benefit is entitled to arrears of another benefit (or other payment from public funds) that would have fallen to be taken into account as income and so would have reduced entitlement to the income-related benefit had it been paid at the correct time." (At [10].) It does not cover the situation of a person where an error in the Department has resulted in a failure to recoup overpaid jobseeker's allowance from arrears of an employment and support allowance. The only way such a sum could be recouped was through the operation of reg.5 of the Social Security (Payments on account etc) Regulations 1988. As s.74(2) did not apply, s.74(4) could not apply to justify recovery under s.74.

Subsection (5)

1.148 *R(SB) 28/85* had revealed problems in valuing a payment of arrears in a foreign currency which might cover quite a long period during which exchange rates varied. This provision authorises regulations to be made to deal with the conversion. See reg.10 of the Payments Regulations, which appears to require the actual net amount received to be taken into account, reversing the effect of *R(SB) 28/85*.

[1 Payment of benefit where maintenance payments collected by Secretary of State

1.149 **74A.**—(1) This section applies where—

(a) a person ("the claimant") is entitled to a benefit to which this section applies;

(b) the Secretary of State is collecting periodical payments of child or spousal maintenance made in respect of the claimant or a member of the claimant's family; and

(c) the inclusion of any such periodical payment in the claimant's relevant income would, apart from this section, have the effect of reducing the amount of the benefit to which the claimant is entitled.

(2) The Secretary of State may, to such extent as he considers appropriate, treat any such periodical payment as not being relevant income for the purposes of calculating the amount of benefit to which the claimant is entitled.

(3) The Secretary of State may, to the extent that any periodical payment collected by him is treated as not being relevant income for those purposes, retain the whole or any part of that payment.

(4) Any sum retained by the Secretary of State under subsection (3) shall be paid by him into the Consolidated Fund.

(5) In this section—

"child" means a person under the age of 16;

"child maintenance", "spousal maintenance" and "relevant income" have such meaning as may be prescribed;

[2 "couple" has the meaning given by section 137(1) of the Contributions and Benefits Act;]

"family" means—

(a) [2 couple];

(b) a [2 couple] and a member of the same household for whom one of them is, or both are, responsible and who is a child or a person of a prescribed description;

(c) except in prescribed circumstances, a person who is not a member of a [2 couple] and a member of the same household for whom that person is responsible and who is a child or a person of a prescribed description;

[2 . . .]

(6) For the purposes of this section, the Secretary of State may by regulations make provision as to the circumstances in which—

(a) persons are to be treated as being or not being members of the same household;

(b) one person is to be treated as responsible or not responsible for another.

(7) The benefits to which this section applies are [4 universal credit,] income support, an income-based jobseeker's allowance [3, an income-related employment and support allowance] and such other benefits (if any) as may be prescribed.]

AMENDMENTS

1. Child Support Act 1995 s.25 (October 1, 1995).
2. Civil Partnership Act 2004 s.254 and Sch.24 para.60 (December 5, 2005).
3. Welfare Reform Act 2007 s.28 and Sch.3 para.10 (October 27, 2008).
4. The Welfare Reform Act 2012 (Commencement No. 9 and Transitional and Transitory Provisions and Commencement No. 8 and Savings and Transitional Provisions (Amendment)) Order 2013 (SI 2013/983) art. 3(1)(b) (April 29, 2013).

GENERAL NOTE

See reg.2 of the Social Security Benefits (Maintenance Payments and Consequential Amendments) Regulations 1996 for definitions of "child maintenance", "spousal maintenance" and "relevant income" and regs 3–5 for other points of interpretation. 1.150

75.–77. *Omitted.* 1.151

Social fund awards

Recovery of social fund awards

78.—(1) A social fund award which is repayable shall be recoverable by the Secretary of State. 1.152

(2) Without prejudice to any other method of recovery, the Secretary of State may recover an award by deduction from prescribed benefits.

(3) The Secretary of State may recover an award—

(a) from the person to or for the benefit of whom it was made;

(b) where that person is a member of a [3 couple], from the other member of the couple;

(c) from a person who is liable to maintain the person by or on behalf of whom the application for the award was made or any person in relation to whose needs the award was made.

[1 (3A) Where—

(a) a jobseeker's allowance is payable to a person from whom an award is recoverable under subsection (3) above; and

(b) that person is subject to a bankruptcy order,

a sum deducted from that benefit under subsection (2) above shall not be treated as income of his for the purposes of the Insolvency Act 1986.

(3B) Where—

(a) a jobseeker's allowance is payable to a person from whom an award is recoverable under subsection (3) above; and

(b) the estate of that person is sequestrated,

a sum deducted from that benefit under subsection (2) above shall not be treated as income of his for the purposes of the Bankruptcy (Scotland) Act [6 2016].]

(4) Payments [4 out of the social fund] to meet funeral expenses may in all cases be recovered, as if they were funeral expenses, out of the estate of the deceased, and (subject to section 71 above) by no other means.

[3 (5) In this section "couple" has the meaning given by section 137(1) of the Contributions and Benefits Act.]

(6) For the purposes of this section—

(a) a man shall be liable to maintain his wife [3 or civil partner] and any children of whom he is the father; and

(b) a woman shall be liable to maintain her husband [3 or civil partner] and any children of whom she is the mother;

(c) a person shall be liable to maintain another person throughout any period in respect of which the first-mentioned person has, on or after 23rd May 1980 (the date of the passing of the Social Security Act 1980) and either alone or jointly with a further person, given an undertaking in writing in pursuance of immigration rules within the meaning of the Immigration Act 1971 to be responsible for the maintenance and accommodation of the other person; and

(d) "child" includes a person who has attained the age of 16 but not the age of 19 and in respect of whom either parent, or some person acting in place of either parent, is receiving [5 universal credit,] income support [2 or an income-based jobseeker's allowance].

(7) Any reference in subsection (6) above to children of whom the man or the woman is the father or mother shall be construed in accordance with section 1 of the Family Law Reform Act 1987.

(8) Subsection (7) above does not apply in Scotland, and in the application of subsection (6) above to Scotland any reference to children of whom the man or the woman is the father or the mother shall be construed as a reference to any such children whether or not their parents have ever been married to one another.

(9) A document bearing a certificate which—

(a) is signed by a person authorised in that behalf by the Secretary of State; and

(b) states that the document apart from the certificate is, or is a copy of, such an undertaking as is mentioned in subsection (6)(c) above, shall be conclusive of the undertaking in question for the purposes of this section; and a certificate purporting to be so signed shall be deemed to be so signed until the contrary is proved.

AMENDMENTS

1. Jobseekers Act 1995 s.32(2) (October 7, 1996).
2. Jobseekers Act 1995 Sch.2 para.51 (October 7, 1996).
3. Civil Partnership Act 2004 s.254 and Sch.24, para.61 (December 5, 2005).
4. Welfare Reform Act 2012 s.70 and Sch.8, para.2 (April 1, 2013).
5. The Welfare Reform Act 2012 (Commencement No. 8 and Savings and Transitional Provisions) Order 2013 (SI 2013/358) art.5(5) (April 29, 2013).
6. Bankruptcy (Scotland) Act 2016 (Consequential Provisions and Modifications) Order 2016 (SI 2016/1034) art.7 and Sch.1 para.9 (November 30, 2016).

DERIVATIONS

Subss.(1)–(3): Social Security Act 1986 s.33(5)–(7). 1.153
Subs.(4): 1986 Act s.32(4).
Subs.(5): 1986 Act s.33(12).
Subss.(6)–(9): 1986 Act ss.26(3)–(6) and 33(8).

DEFINITION

"prescribed"—see s.191.

GENERAL NOTE

Subsections (1)–(3)

These provisions give the framework for recovery of social fund loans. See the Social Fund (Recovery by Deductions from Benefits) Regulations 1988. 1.154

Income support and JSA are prescribed benefits for the purposes of subs.(2) (reg.3(a) and (c) of the Social Fund (Recovery by Deductions from Benefits) Regulations). In *Mulvey v Secretary of State for Social Security*, *The Times*, March 20, 1997, the House of Lords on March 13, 1997 held that where deductions were being made from benefit under subs.(2) when the claimant was sequestrated (the Scottish equivalent of a declaration of bankruptcy), the Secretary of State was entitled to continue to make the deductions. If that were not so, the gross benefit would become payable to the claimant, who would thus gain an immediate financial advantage from sequestration, a result which Parliament could not have intended.

> "Prior to sequestration the [claimant] had no right to receive by way of income support more than her gross entitlement under deduction of such sum as had been notified to her by the [Secretary of State] prior to payment of the award by the [Secretary of State]. This was the result of the statutory scheme and she could not have demanded more. The [Secretary of State's] continued exercise of a statutory power of deduction after sequestration was unrelated thereto and was not calculated to obtain a benefit for him at the expense of other creditors. The only person who had any realistic interest in the deductions was the [claimant] from which it follows that the [Secretary of State] was not seeking to exercise any right against the permanent trustee." (Lord Jauncey)

The view of the Inner House of the Court of Session was thus approved. See the notes in the 1996 edition for the earlier decisions in *Mulvey*.

English bankruptcy law is not the same as Scottish sequestration law. However, in *R. v Secretary of State for Social Security, Ex p. Taylor and Chapman, The Times*, February 5, 1996, Keene J. reached the same conclusion as the Inner House in *Mulvey* in relation to the effect of s.285(3) of the Insolvency Act 1986 in these circumstances. The deductions in *Chapman* were not being made under subs.(2) 1.155

but from the claimant's retirement pension under s.71(8) in order to recover an overpayment of income support, but it was accepted that the position was the same in both cases. Keene J. rejected a submission by the Secretary of State that the operation of s.285(3) was precluded in this situation, but held that it did not prevent the deductions under subs.(2) and s.71(8) being made. The Secretary of State was not seeking to go against "the property of the bankrupt" within the terms of s.285(3) as the claimants' entitlement under the 1992 Act was to the net amount of benefit. In *Mulvey* (above) Lord Jauncey said this about the contrary argument:

> "Even more bizarre would be the situation where overpayments obtained by fraud were being recovered by deduction from benefits. On sequestration the fraudster would immediately receive the gross benefit. It is difficult to believe that Parliament can have intended such a result."

Note that s.32 of the Jobseekers Act 1995 amends both ss.78 and 71 to provide that amounts deducted under subs.(2) or s.71(8) from JSA payable to a bankrupt person are not to be treated as income for the purposes of the Insolvency Act 1986 and the Bankruptcy (Scotland) Act 1985 (in effect giving preference to the DSS over other creditors, although the House of Lords in *Mulvey* rejected such a comparison).

These decisions now need to be read in the light of the judgment of the Supreme Court in *SSWP v Payne* [2011] UKSC 60, which took the view that *Taylor and Chapman* was wrongly decided. The Supreme Court decided that the Secretary of State lost the power to seek recovery of social fund loans on the making of either a bankruptcy order, or a debt relief order in insolvency proceedings.

Subsection (4)

1.156 Subsection (4) contains an important provision for the recovery of any payment for funeral expenses out of the estate of the deceased. Regulation 8 of the Social Fund Maternity and Funeral Expenses (General) Regulations lists sums to be deducted in calculating the amount of a funeral payment. These include assets of the deceased which are available before probate or letters of administration have been granted. The old reg.8(3)(a) of the Single Payments Regulations required the deduction of the value of the deceased's estate, but since it might take some time for the estate to become available, the provision in subs.(4) is preferable.

The funeral payment is to be recovered as if it was funeral expenses. Funeral expenses are a first charge on the estate, in priority to anything else (see *R(SB) 18/84*, paras 8 and 10, for the law in England and Scotland). *CIS/616/1990* decides that the right to recover is given to the Secretary of State. The adjudication officer (and the tribunal) has no role in subs.(4).

The only other method of recovery is under s.71, which applies generally where there has been misrepresentation or a failure to disclose and does depend on a review of entitlement by an adjudication officer followed by a determination of an overpayment.

Subsections (6)–(9)

1.157 See the notes to s.105.

Northern Ireland payments

Recovery of Northern Ireland payments

1.158 **79.** Without prejudice to any other method of recovery—

(a) amounts recoverable under any enactment or instrument having effect in Northern Ireland and corresponding to an enactment or instrument mentioned in section 71(8) above shall be recoverable by deduction from benefits prescribed under that subsection;

(b) amounts recoverable under any enactment having effect in Northern Ireland and corresponding to section 75 above shall be recoverable by deduction from benefits prescribed under subsection (4) of that section; and

(c) awards recoverable under Part III of the Northern Ireland Administration Act shall be recoverable by deduction from benefits prescribed [1 under section 71(8).]

DERIVATIONS

Paragraph (a): Social Security Act 1986 s.53(7A). **1.159**
Paragraph (b): 1986 Act s.29(8).
Paragraph (c): 1986 Act s.33(8A).

AMENDMENT

1. Welfare Reform Act 2012 s.70 and Sch.8 para.3 (April 1, 2013).

DEFINITIONS

"the Northern Ireland Administration Act"—see s.191.
"prescribed"—*ibid.*

Adjustment of child benefit

Child benefit—overlap with benefits under legislation of other member States

80. Regulations may provide for adjusting child benefit payable in respect of any child [1 or qualifying young person] in respect of whom any benefit is payable under the legislation of any member State other than the United Kingdom. **1.160**

DERIVATION

CBA 1975 s.4A. **1.161**

AMENDMENT

1. Child Benefit Act 2005 Sch.1 Pt 1 para.22 (April 10, 2006).

PART IV

RECOVERY FROM COMPENSATION PAYMENTS

Repealed. **1.162**

PART V

INCOME SUPPORT AND THE DUTY TO MAINTAIN

Failure to maintain—general

1.163 **105.**—(1) If—

(a) any person persistently refuses or neglects to maintain himself or any person whom he is liable to maintain; and

(b) in consequence of his refusal or neglect [5 universal credit,] income support [1 . . .] [3 , an income-based jobseeker's allowance or an income-related employment and support allowance] is paid to or in respect of him or such a person,

he shall be guilty of an offence and liable on summary conviction to imprisonment for a term not exceeding 3 months or to a fine of an amount not exceeding level 4 on the standard scale or to both.

(2) For the purposes of subsection (1) above a person shall not be taken to refuse or neglect to maintain himself or any other person by reason only of anything done or omitted in furtherance of a trade dispute.

[4 (3) Subject to subsection (4), for the purposes of this Part, a person shall be liable to maintain another person if that other person is—

(a) his or her spouse or civil partner, or

(b) a person whom he or she would be liable to maintain if sections 78(6)(c) and (9) had effect for the purposes of this Part.]

[1 (4) For the purposes of this section, in its application to an income-based jobseeker's allowance [3 or an income-related employment and support allowance], a person is liable to maintain another if that other person is his or her spouse [2 or civil partner].]

AMENDMENTS

1. Jobseekers Act 1995 Sch.2 para.53 (October 7, 1996).
2. Civil Partnership Act 2004 s.254 and Sch.24, para.62 (December 5, 2005).
3. Welfare Reform Act 2007 s.28 and Sch.3 para.10 (October 27, 2008).
4. Child Maintenance and Other Payments Act 2008 s.45(1) (July 14, 2008).
5. The Welfare Reform Act 2012 (Commencement No. 9 and Transitional and Transitory Provisions and Commencement No. 8 and Savings and Transitional Provisions (Amendment)) Order 2013 (SI 2013/983) art.3(1)(b) (April 29, 2013).

Recovery of expenditure on benefit from person liable for maintenance

1.164 **106.**—(1) Subject to the following provisions of this section, if income support [2 or universal credit] is claimed by or in respect of a person whom another person is liable to maintain or paid to or in respect of such a person, the Secretary of State may make [3 an application] against the liable person to [3 the family court] for an order under this section.

(2) On the hearing of [3 an application] under this section the court shall have regard to all the circumstances and, in particular, to the income of the liable person, and may order him to pay such sum, weekly or otherwise, as it may consider appropriate, except that in a case falling within

section 78(6)(c) above that sum shall not include any amount which is not attributable to income support [2 or universal credit] (whether paid before or after the making of the order).

(3) In determining whether to order any payments to be made in respect of income support [2 or universal credit] for any period before the [3 application]was made, or the amount of any such payments, the court shall disregard any amount by which the liable person's income exceeds the income which was his during that period.

(4) Any payments ordered to be made under this section shall be made—

(a) to the Secretary of State in so far as they are attributable to any income support [2 or universal credit] (whether paid before or after the making of the order);

(b) to the person claiming income support [2 or universal credit] or (if different) the dependant; or

(c) to such other person as appears to the court expedient in the interests of the dependant.

(5) [3 . . .]

(6) [3 For the references to the family court there shall be substituted references to the sheriff.]

(7) [1 . . .]

DERIVATION

Social Security Act 1986 s.24. **1.165**

AMENDMENTS

1. Child Maintenance and Other Payments Act 2008 Sch.8 para.1 (July 14, 2008).

2. The Welfare Reform Act 2012 (Commencement No. 9 and Transitional and Transitory Provisions and Commencement No. 8 and Savings and Transitional Provisions (Amendment)) Order 2013 (SI 2013/983) art.3(1)(b) (April 29, 2013).

3. Crime and Courts Act 2013 Sch.11(1) para.128(1) (April 22, 2014).

DEFINITION

"child"—see ss.105(3) and 78(b).

Recovery of expenditure on income support: additional amounts and transfer of orders

107.[1 . . .] **1.166**

AMENDMENT

1. Repealed by Child Maintenance and Other Payments Act 2008 Sch.8 para.1 (October 27, 2008).

Reduction of expenditure on income support: certain maintenance orders to be enforceable by the Secretary of State

108.—(1) This section applies where— **1.167**

(a) a person ("the claimant") who is the parent of one or more children is in receipt of income support [4 or universal credit] either in respect of those children or in respect of both himself and those children; and

(b) there is in force a maintenance order made against the other parent ("the liable person")—
   (i) in favour of the claimant or one or more of the children, or
   (ii) in favour of some other person for the benefit of the claimant or one or more of the children,

and in this section "the primary recipient" means the person in whose favour that maintenance order was made.

(2) If, in a case where this section applies, the liable person fails to comply with any of the terms of the maintenance order—

(a) the Secretary of State may bring any proceedings or take any other steps to enforce the order that could have been brought or taken by or on behalf of the primary recipient; and

(b) any court before which proceedings are brought by the Secretary of State by virtue of paragraph (a) above shall have the same powers in connection with those proceedings as it would have had if they had been brought by the primary recipient.

(3) The Secretary of State's powers under this section are exercisable at his discretion and whether or not the primary recipient or any other person consents to their exercise; but any sums recovered by virtue of this section shall be payable to or for the primary recipient, as if the proceedings or steps in question had been brought or taken by him or on his behalf.

(4) The powers conferred on the Secretary of State by subsection (2)(a) above include power—

(a) to apply for the registration of the maintenance order under—
   (i) section 17 of the Maintenance Orders Act 1950;
   (ii) section 2 of the Maintenance Orders Act 1958; or
   (iii) the Civil Jurisdiction and Judgments Act 1982; [2 or
   (iv) Council Regulation (EC) No 44/2001 of 22nd December 2000 on jurisdiction and the recognition and enforcement of judgments in civil and commercial matters; and]

[4 (aa) to apply for recognition and enforcement of the maintenance order under the Maintenance Regulation, to the extent permitted by Article 64 of the Regulation; and]

(b) to make an application under section 2 of the Maintenance Orders (Reciprocal Enforcement) Act 1972 (application for enforcement in reciprocating country).

(5) Where this section applies, the prescribed person shall in prescribed circumstances give the Secretary of State notice of any application—

(a) to alter, vary, suspend, discharge, revoke, revive, or enforce the maintenance order in question; or

(b) to remit arrears under that maintenance order;

and the Secretary of State shall be entitled to appear and be heard on the application.

(6) Where, by virtue of this section, the Secretary of State commences any proceedings to enforce a maintenance order, he shall, in relation to those proceedings, be treated for the purposes of any enactment or instrument relating to maintenance orders as if he were a person entitled to payment under the maintenance order in question (but shall not thereby become entitled to any such payment).

(7) Where, in any proceedings under this section in England and Wales, the court makes an order for the whole or any part of the arrears due under

the maintenance order in question to be paid as a lump sum, the Secretary of State shall inform [4 the Lord Chancellor] of the amount of that lump sum if he knows—

(a) that the primary recipient either—

(i) received legal aid under the Legal Aid Act 1974 in connection with the proceedings in which the maintenance order was made, or

(ii) was an assisted party, within the meaning of the Legal Aid Act 1988, in those proceedings, or

[1(iii) received services funded by the Legal Services Commission as part of the Community Legal Service; and]

[5 (iv) was provided with civil legal services (within the meaning of Part 1 of the Legal Aid, Sentencing and Punishment of Offenders Act 2012) under arrangements made for the purposes of that Part of that Act; and]

(b) that a sum remains unpaid on account of the contribution required of the primary recipient—

(i) under section 9 of the Legal Aid Act 1974 in respect of those proceedings, or

(ii) under section 16 of the Legal Aid Act 1988 in respect of the costs of his being represented under Part IV of that Act in those proceedings, [1 or

(iii) by virtue of section 10 of the Access to Justice Act 1999 in respect of services funded by the Legal Services Commission as part of the Community Legal Service.]

[5 (iv) under regulations under sections 23 or 24 of the Legal Aid, Sentencing and Punishment of Offenders Act 2012 in respect of civil legal services (within the meaning of Part 1 of that Act) provided under arrangements made for the purposes of that Part of that Act,]

as the case may be.

[3 (8) In this section "maintenance order"—

(a) in England and Wales, means—

(i) any order for the making of periodical payments which is, or has at any time been, a maintenance order within the meaning of the Attachment of Earnings Act 1971;

(ii) any order under Part 3 of the Matrimonial and Family Proceedings Act 1984 (overseas divorce) for the making of periodical payments;

(iii) any order under Schedule 7 to the Civil Partnership Act 2004 for the making of periodical payments;

(b) in Scotland, means any order, except an order for the payment of a lump sum, falling within the definition of "maintenance order" in section 106 of the Debtors (Scotland) Act 1987, but disregarding paragraph (h) (alimentary bond or agreement).]

[6 (9) In this section "the Maintenance Regulation" means Council Regulation (EC) No 4/2009 including as applied in relation to Denmark by virtue of the Agreement made on 19th October 2005 between the European Community and the Kingdom of Denmark.]

AMENDMENTS

1. Access to Justice Act 1999 Sch.4 para.48 (April 1, 2000).

2. The Civil Jurisdiction and Judgments Order 2001 (SI 2001/3929) art.5 and Sch.3 (March 1, 2002).

3. Child Maintenance and Other Payments Act 2008 Sch.7 para.2(2) (October 27, 2008).

4. The Welfare Reform Act 2012 (Commencement No. 9 and Transitional and Transitory Provisions and Commencement No. 8 and Savings and Transitional Provisions (Amendment)) Order 2013 (SI 2013/983) art.3(1)(b) (April 29, 2013).

5. Legal Aid, Sentencing and Punishment of Offenders Act 2012 Sch.5(1) para.41 (April 1, 2013).

6. Civil Jurisdiction and Judgments Order 2011 (SI 2011/1484) Sch.7 para.14 (June 18, 2011).

DERIVATION

1.168 Social Security Act 1986 s.24B.

Diversion of arrested earnings to Secretary of State—Scotland

1.169 **109.**—(1) Where in Scotland a creditor who is enforcing a maintenance order or alimentary bond or agreement by a current maintenance arrestment or a conjoined arrestment order is in receipt of [2 universal credit,] income support [1 or an income-related employment and support allowance] the creditor may in writing authorise the Secretary of State to receive any sums payable under the arrestment or order until the creditor ceases to be in receipt of [2 universal credit,] income support [1 or an income-related employment and support allowance] or in writing withdraws the authorisation, whichever occurs first.

(2) On the intimation by the Secretary of State—

(a) to the employer operating the current maintenance arrestment; or

(b) to the sheriff clerk operating the conjoined arrestment order;

of an authorisation under subsection (1) above, the employer or sheriff clerk shall, until notified by the Secretary of State that the authorisation has ceased to have effect, pay to the Secretary of State any sums which would otherwise be payable under the arrestment or order to the creditor.

AMENDMENTS

1. Welfare Reform Act 2007 s.28 and Sch.3 para.10 (October 27, 2008).

2. The Welfare Reform Act 2012 (Commencement No. 9 and Transitional and Transitory Provisions and Commencement No. 8 and Savings and Transitional Provisions (Amendment)) Order 2013 (SI 2013/983) art.3(1)(b) (April 29, 2013).

DERIVATION

1.170 Social Security Act 1986 s.25A.

PART VI

ENFORCEMENT

Inspection and offences

[1 Authorisations for investigators.

109A.—(1) An individual who for the time being has the Secretary of State's authorisation for the purposes of this Part shall be entitled, for any one or more of the purposes mentioned in subsection (2) below, to exercise any of the powers which are conferred on an authorised officer by sections 109B and 109C below. **1.171**

(2) Those purposes are—

(a) ascertaining in relation to any case whether a benefit is or was payable in that case in accordance with any provision of the relevant social security legislation;

(b) investigating the circumstances in which any accident, injury or disease which has given rise, or may give rise, to a claim for—

(i) industrial injuries benefit, or

(ii) any benefit under any provision of the relevant social security legislation,

occurred or may have occurred, or was or may have been received or contracted;

(c) ascertaining whether provisions of the relevant social security legislation are being, have been or are likely to be contravened (whether by particular persons or more generally);

(d) preventing, detecting and securing evidence of the commission (whether by particular persons or more generally) of benefit offences.

(3) An individual has the Secretary of State's authorisation for the purposes of this Part if, and only if, the Secretary of State has granted him an authorisation for those purposes and he is—

(a) an official of a Government department;

(b) an individual employed by an authority administering housing benefit or council tax benefit;

(c) an individual employed by an authority or joint committee that carries out functions relating to housing benefit or council tax benefit on behalf of the authority administering that benefit; or

(d) an individual employed by a person authorised by or on behalf of any such authority or joint committee as is mentioned in paragraph (b) or (c) above to carry out functions relating to housing benefit or council tax benefit for that authority or committee.

(4) An authorisation granted for the purposes of this Part to an individual of any of the descriptions mentioned in subsection (3) above–

(a) must be contained in a certificate provided to that individual as evidence of his entitlement to exercise powers conferred by this Part;

(b) may contain provision as to the period for which the authorisation is to have effect; and
(c) may restrict the powers exercisable by virtue of the authorisation so as to prohibit their exercise except for particular purposes, in particular circumstances or in relation to particular benefits or particular provisions of the relevant social security legislation.

(5) An authorisation granted under this section may be withdrawn at any time by the Secretary of State.

(6) Where the Secretary of State grants an authorisation for the purposes of this Part to an individual employed by a local authority, or to an individual employed by a person who carries out functions relating to housing benefit or council tax benefit on behalf of a local authority—
(a) the Secretary of State and the local authority shall enter into such arrangements (if any) as they consider appropriate with respect to the carrying out of functions conferred on that individual by or in connection with the authorisation granted to him; and
(b) the Secretary of State may make to the local authority such payments (if any) as he thinks fit in respect of the carrying out by that individual of any such functions.

(7) The matters on which a person may be authorised to consider and report to the Secretary of State under section 139A below shall be taken to include the carrying out by any such individual as is mentioned in subsection (3)(b) to (d) above of any functions conferred on that individual by virtue of any grant by the Secretary of State of an authorisation for the purposes of this Part.

(8) The powers conferred by sections 109B and 109C below shall be exercisable in relation to persons holding office under the Crown and persons in the service of the Crown, and in relation to premises owned or occupied by the Crown, as they are exercisable in relation to other persons and premises.

[2 (9) This section and sections 109B to 109C below apply as if—
(a) the Tax Credits Act 2002 were relevant social security legislation, and
(b) accordingly, child tax credit and working tax credit were relevant social security benefits for the purposes of the definition of "benefit offence".]]

AMENDMENTS

1. Inserted by the Child Support, Pensions and Social Security Act 2000 c.19, Sch.6 para.2 (April 2, 2001).
2. Welfare Reform Act 2012 s.122 (June 6, 2012).

[1 Power to require information.

1.172 **109B.**—(1) An authorised officer who has reasonable grounds for suspecting that a person—
(a) is a person falling within subsection (2) [2 or (2A)] below, and
(b) has or may have possession of or access to any information about any matter that is relevant for any one or more of the purposes mentioned in section 109A(2) above,

may, by written notice, require that person to provide all such information described in the notice as is information of which he has possession, or to which he has access, and which it is reasonable for the authorised officer to require for a purpose so mentioned.

(2) The persons who fall within this subsection are—

(a) any person who is or has been an employer or employee within the meaning of any provision made by or under the Contributions and Benefits Act;

(b) any person who is or has been a self-employed earner within the meaning of any such provision;

(c) any person who by virtue of any provision made by or under that Act falls, or has fallen, to be treated for the purposes of any such provision as a person within paragraph (a) or (b) above;

(d) any person who is carrying on, or has carried on, any business involving the supply of goods for sale to the ultimate consumers by individuals not carrying on retail business from retail premises;

(e) any person who is carrying on, or has carried on, any business involving the supply of goods or services by the use of work done or services performed by persons other than employees of his;

(f) any person who is carrying on, or has carried on, an agency or other business for the introduction or supply, to persons requiring them, of persons available to do work or to perform services;

(g) any local authority acting in their capacity as an authority responsible for the granting of any licence;

(h) any person who is or has been a trustee or manager of a personal or occupational pension scheme;

(i) any person who is or has been liable to make a compensation payment or a payment to the Secretary of State under section 6 of the Social Security (Recovery of Benefits) Act 1997 (payments in respect of recoverable benefits); and

[16 (ia) a person of a prescribed description;]

(j) the servants and agents of any such person as is specified in any of paragraphs (a) to [16 (ia)] above.

[3 (2A) The persons who fall within this subsection are—

(a) any bank;

[4 (aa) the Director of National Savings;]

(b) any person carrying on a business the whole or a significant part of which consists in the provision of credit (whether secured or unsecured) to members of the public;

[5 (c) any insurer;]

(d) any credit reference agency (within the meaning given by section 145(8) of the Consumer Credit Act 1974 (c. 39));

(e) any body the principal activity of which is to facilitate the exchange of information for the purpose of preventing or detecting fraud;

(f) any person carrying on a business the whole or a significant part of which consists in the provision to members of the public of a service for transferring money from place to place;

(g) any water undertaker or sewerage undertaker, [6 Scottish Water or any local authority which is to collect charges by virtue of an order under section 37 of the Water Industry (Scotland) Act 2002 (asp 3);]

[7 (h) any person who—

(i) is the holder of a licence under section 7 of the Gas Act 1986 (c. 44) to convey gas through pipes, or

(ii) is the holder of a licence under section 7A(1) of that Act to supply gas through pipes;]

[8 (i) any person who (within the meaning of the Electricity Act 1989 (c. 29)) distributes or supplies electricity;]

(j) any person who provides a telecommunications service;

(k) any person conducting any educational establishment or institution;

(l) any body the principal activity of which is to provide services in connection with admissions to educational establishments or institutions;

(m) the Student Loans Company;

(n) any servant or agent of any person mentioned in any of the preceding paragraphs.

(2B) Subject to the following provisions of this section, the powers conferred by this section on an authorised officer to require information from any person by virtue of his falling within subsection (2A) above shall be exercisable for the purpose only of obtaining information relating to a particular person identified (by name or description) by the officer.

(2C) An authorised officer shall not, in exercise of those powers, require any information from any person by virtue of his falling within subsection (2A) above unless it appears to that officer that there are reasonable grounds for believing that the identified person to whom it relates is–

(a) a person who has committed, is committing or intends to commit a benefit offence; or

(b) a person who (within the meaning of Part 7 of the Contributions and Benefits Act) is a member of the family of a person falling within paragraph (a) above.

(2D) Nothing in subsection (2B) or (2C) above shall prevent an authorised officer who is an official of a Government department and whose authorisation states that his authorisation applies for the purposes of this subsection from exercising the powers conferred by this section for obtaining from–

(a) a water undertaker or [9 Scottish Water,]

(b) any person who (within the meaning the Gas Act 1986) supplies gas conveyed through pipes,

(c) any person who (within the meaning of the Electricity Act 1989) supplies electricity conveyed by distribution systems, or

(d) any servant or agent of a person mentioned in any of the preceding paragraphs,

any information which relates exclusively to whether and in what quantities water, gas or electricity are being or have been supplied to residential premises specified or described in the notice by which the information is required.

(2E) The powers conferred by this section shall not be exercisable for obtaining from any person providing a telecommunications service any information other than information which (within the meaning of section 21 of the Regulation of Investigatory Powers Act 2000) is communications data but not traffic data.

(2F) Nothing in subsection (2B) or (2C) above shall prevent an authorised officer from exercising the powers conferred by this section for requiring information, from a person who provides a telecommunications service, about the identity and postal address of a person identified by the authorised officer solely by reference to a telephone number or electronic address used in connection with the provision of such a service.]

(3) The obligation of a person to provide information in accordance with a notice under this section shall be discharged only by the provision of that information, at such reasonable time and in such form as may be specified in the notice, to the authorised officer who—

(a) is identified by or in accordance with the terms of the notice; or
(b) has been identified, since the giving of the notice, by a further written notice given by the authorised officer who imposed the original requirement or another authorised officer.

(4) The power of an authorised officer under this section to require the provision of information shall include a power to require the production and delivery up and (if necessary) creation of, or of copies of or extracts from, any such documents containing the information as may be specified or described in the notice imposing the requirement.

[[10] (5) No one shall be required under this section to provide—

(a) any information that tends to incriminate either himself or, in the case of a person who is [[11] married or is a civil partner, his spouse or civil partner]; or
(b) any information in respect of which a claim to legal professional privilege or, in Scotland, confidentiality as between client and professional legal adviser, would be successful in any proceedings;

and for the purposes of this subsection it is immaterial whether the information is in documentary form or not.]

[[13] (6) Provision may be made by order—

(a) adding any person to the list of persons falling within subsection (2A) above;
(b) removing any person from the list of persons falling within that subsection;
(c) modifying that subsection for the purpose of taking account of any change to the name of any person for the time being falling within that subsection.

(7) In this section—

[[13] "bank" means—

(a) a person who has permission under Part IV of the Financial Services and Markets Act 2000 (c. 8) to accept deposits;
(b) an EEA firm of the kind mentioned in paragraph 5(b) of Schedule 3 to that Act which has permission under paragraph 15 of that Schedule (as a result of qualifying for authorisation under paragraph 12 of that Schedule) to accept deposits or other repayable funds from the public; or
(c) a person who does not require permission under that Act to accept deposits, in the course of his business in the United Kingdom;]

"credit" includes a cash loan or any form of financial accommodation, including the cashing of a cheque;

[[14] "insurer" means—

(a) a person who has permission under Part IV of the Financial Services and Markets Act 2000 to effect or carry out contracts of insurance; or
(b) an EEA firm of the kind mentioned in paragraph 5(d) of Schedule 3 to that Act, which has permission under paragraph 15 of that Schedule (as a result of qualifying for authorisation under paragraph 12 of that Schedule) to effect or carry out contracts of insurance;]

"residential premises", in relation to a supply of water, gas or electricity, means any premises which–
(a) at the time of the supply were premises occupied wholly or partly for residential purposes, or
(b) are premises to which that supply was provided as if they were so occupied; and
"telecommunications service" has the same meaning as in the Regulation of Investigatory Powers Act 2000 (c. 23).]
[[15] (7A) The definitions of "bank" and "insurer" in subsection (7) must be read with—
(a) section 22 of the Financial Services and Markets Act 2000;
(b) any relevant order under that section; and
(c) Schedule 2 to that Act.]]

AMENDMENTS

1. Inserted by the Child Support, Pensions and Social Security Act 2000 Sch.6 para.2 (April 2, 2001).
2. Social Security Fraud Act 2001 s.1(2) (April 30, 2002).
3. Social Security Fraud Act 2001 s.1(2) (April 30, 2002).
4. Social Security Administration Act 1992 (Amendment) Order 2002 (SI 2002/817) art.2(a) (April 30, 2002).
5. Social Security Administration Act 1992 (Amendment) Order 2002 (SI 2002/817) art.2(b) (April 30, 2002).
6. Water Industry (Scotland) Act 2002 (Consequential Modifications) Order 2004 (SI 2004/1822) Sch.1(1) para.16(a) (July 14, 2004).
7. Social Security Administration Act 1992 (Amendment) Order 2002 (SI 2002/817) art.2(c) (April 30, 2002).
8. Social Security Administration Act 1992 (Amendment) Order 2002 (SI 2002/817) art.2(d) (April 30, 2002).
9. Water Industry (Scotland) Act 2002 (Consequential Modifications) Order 2004 (SI 2004/1822) Sch.1(1) para.16(b) (July 14, 2004).
10. Social Security Fraud Act 2001 s.1(3) (April 30, 2002).
11. Civil Partnership Act 2004 Sch.24(4), para.64 (December 5, 2005).
12. Social Security Fraud Act 2001 s.1(4) (February 26, 2002).
13. Social Security Administration Act 1992 (Amendment) Order 2002 (SI 2002/817) art.3(a)(i) (April 1, 2002).
14. Social Security Administration Act 1992 (Amendment) Order 2002 (SI 2002/817) art.3(a)(ii) (April 1, 2002).
15. Social Security Administration Act 1992 (Amendment) Order 2002 (SI 2002/817) art.3(b) (April 1, 2002).
16. The Welfare Reform Act 2012 (Commencement No. 10) Order 2013 (SI 2013/1250) art.3 (June 17, 2013).

[[1] Power of Secretary of State to require electronic access to information

1.173 **109BA.**—(1) Subject to subsection (2) below, where it appears to the Secretary of State—
(a) that a person falling within section 109B(2A) keeps any electronic records,
(b) that the records contain or are likely, from time to time, to contain information about any matter that is relevant for any one or more of the purposes mentioned in section 109A(2) above, and
(c) that facilities exist under which electronic access to those records is

being provided, or is capable of being provided, by that person to other persons,

the Secretary of State may require that person to enter into arrangements under which authorised officers are allowed such access to those records.

(2) An authorised officer—

(a) shall be entitled to obtain information in accordance with arrangements entered into under subsection (1) above only if his authorisation states that his authorisation applies for the purposes of that subsection; and

(b) shall not seek to obtain any information in accordance with any such arrangements other than information which relates to a particular person and could be the subject of a requirement under section 109B above.

(3) The matters that may be included in the arrangements that a person is required to enter into under subsection (1) above may include—

(a) requirements as to the electronic access to records that is to be made available to authorised officers;

(b) requirements as to the keeping of records of the use that is made of the arrangements;

(c) requirements restricting the disclosure of information about the use that is made of the arrangements; and

(d) such other incidental requirements as the Secretary of State considers appropriate in connection with allowing access to records to authorised officers.

(4) An authorised officer who is allowed access in accordance with any arrangements entered into under subsection (1) above shall be entitled to make copies of, and to take extracts from, any records containing information which he is entitled to require under section 109B.]

AMENDMENT

1. Inserted by the Social Security Fraud Act 2001, s.2(1) (April 30, 2002).

[1 Powers of entry.

109C.—(1) An authorised officer shall be entitled, at any reasonable time and either alone or accompanied by such other persons as he thinks fit, to enter any premises which— 1.174

(a) are liable to inspection under this section; and

(b) are premises to which it is reasonable for him to require entry in order to exercise the powers conferred by this section.

(2) An authorised officer who has entered any premises liable to inspection under this section may—

(a) make such an examination of those premises, and

(b) conduct any such inquiry there,

as appears to him appropriate for any one or more of the purposes mentioned in section 109A(2) above.

(3) An authorised officer who has entered any premises liable to inspection under this section may—

(a) question any person whom he finds there;

(b) require any person whom he finds there to do any one or more of the following—

(i) to provide him with such information,
(ii) to produce and deliver up and (if necessary) create such documents or such copies of, or extracts from, documents,

as he may reasonably require for any one or more of the purposes mentioned in section 109A(2) above; and

(c) take possession of and either remove or make his own copies of any such documents as appear to him to contain information that is relevant for any of those purposes.

(4) The premises liable to inspection under this section are any premises (including premises consisting in the whole or a part of a dwelling house) which an authorised officer has reasonable grounds for suspecting are—

(a) premises which are a person's place of employment;
(b) premises from which a trade or business is being carried on or where documents relating to a trade or business are kept by the person carrying it on or by another person on his behalf;
(c) premises from which a personal or occupational pension scheme is being administered or where documents relating to the administration of such a scheme are kept by the person administering the scheme or by another person on his behalf;
(d) premises where a person who is the compensator in relation to any such accident, injury or disease as is referred to in section 109A(2)(b) above is to be found;
(e) premises where a person on whose behalf any such compensator has made, may have made or may make a compensation payment is to be found.

(5) An authorised officer applying for admission to any premises in accordance with this section shall, if required to do so, produce the certificate containing his authorisation for the purposes of this Part.

(6) Subsection (5) of section 109B applies for the purposes of this section as it applies for the purposes of that section.]

AMENDMENT

1. Inserted by the Child Support, Pensions and Social Security Act 2000 Sch.6 para.2 (April 2, 2001).

1.175 **[1 Class 1, 1A, 1B or 2 contributions: powers to call for documents etc.**

[2 **110ZA**—(1) Schedule 36 to the Finance Act 2008 (information and inspection powers) applies for the purpose of checking a person's position as regards relevant contributions as it applies for the purpose of checking a person's tax position, subject to the modifications in subsection (2).

(2) That Schedule applies as if—

(a) references to any provision of the Taxes Acts were to any provision of this Act or the Contributions and Benefits Act [3 or the National Insurance Contributions Act 2014] relating to relevant contributions,
(b) references to prejudice to the assessment or collection of tax were to prejudice to the assessment of liability for, and payment of, relevant contributions,
(c) the reference to information relating to the conduct of a pending appeal relating to tax were a reference to information relating to the conduct of a pending appeal relating to relevant contributions, and

(d) [4 paragraphs 21, 21A, 35(4A)(c), 36, 37(2) and (2A), 37A and 37B] of that Schedule (restrictions on giving taxpayer notice where taxpayer has made tax return) were omitted.]

[5 (2A) Part 3 of Schedule 38 to the Finance Act 2012 (power to obtain tax agent's files etc.) applies in relation to relevant contributions as in relation to tax and, accordingly—

(a) the cases described in paragraph 7 of that Schedule (case A and case B) include cases involving conduct or an offence relating to relevant contributions,

(b) (whether the case involves conduct or an offence relating to tax or relevant contributions) the papers and other documents that may be sought under that Part include ones relating to relevant contributions, and

(c) the other Parts of that Schedule apply so far as necessary to give effect to the application of Part 3 by virtue of this subsection.]

(3) In this section "relevant contributions" means Class 1, Class 1A, Class 1B or Class 2 contributions.]

AMENDMENTS

1. National Insurance Contributions and Statutory Payments Act 2004 s.7 (April 6, 2005).
2. Finance Act 2008 Sch.36(10) para.84 (April 1, 2009: substitution has effect subject to savings provision specified in SI 2009/404 art.9).
3. National Insurance Contributions Act 2014 s.7(5) (April 6, 2014).
4. Finance Act 2009, s.96 and Sch.48 (Appointed Day, Savings and Consequential Amendments) Order 2009 (SI 2009/3054) Sch.1 para.3(b) (April 1, 2010).
5. Finance Act 2012 Sch.38(7) para.56 (April 1, 2013).

Section 110A–112 omitted. **1.176**

[1 Breach of regulations

113.—(1) Regulations and schemes under any of the [2 legislation to which this section applies] may provide that any person who contravenes, or fails to comply with, any provision contained in regulations made under [2 that legislation]— **1.177**

(a) in the case of a provision relating to contributions, shall be liable to a penalty;

(b) in any other case, shall be guilty of an offence under [2 any enactment contained in the legislation in question].

[3 (1A) The legislation to which this section applies is—

(a) the relevant social security legislation; and

(b) the enactments specified in section 121DA(1) so far as relating to contributions, [4 . . .].]

(2) Any regulations or scheme making such provision as is mentioned in subsection (1)(a) above shall—

(a) prescribe the amount or rate of penalty, or provide for how it is to be ascertained;

(b) provide for the penalty to be imposed by the [5 Inland Revenue]—

(i) within six years after the date on which the penalty is incurred; or

(ii) where the amount of the penalty is to be ascertained by reference to the amount of any contributions payable, at any

4. Welfare Reform Act 2012 ss.113–115 (May 8, 2012).

5. The Social Security (Penalty as Alternative to Prosecution) (Maximum Amount) Order 2015 (SI 2015/202) reg.2 (April 1, 2015).

1.180 *Section 115B Omitted.*

[1 Civil penalties

Incorrect statements

1.181 **115C.**—(1) This section applies where—

(a) a person negligently makes an incorrect statement or representation, or negligently gives incorrect information or evidence—
  (i) in or in connection with acclaim for a relevant social security benefit, or
  (ii) in connection with an award of a relevant social security benefit,
(b) the person fails to take reasonable steps to correct the error,
(c) the error results in the making of an overpayment, and
(d) the person has not been charged with an offence or cautioned, or been given a notice under section 115A, in respect of the overpayment.

(2) A penalty of a prescribed amount may be imposed by the appropriate authority—

(a) in any case, on the person,
(b) in a case where the person ("A") is making, or has made, a claim for the benefit for a period jointly with another ("B"), on B instead of A.
(c) The error results in the making of an overpayment, and
(d) the person has not been charged with an offence or cautioned, or been given a notice under section 115A, in respect of the overpayment.

(3) Subsection (2)(b) does not apply if B was not, and could not reasonably be expected to have been, aware that A had negligently made the incorrect statement or representation or given the incorrect information or evidence.

(4) A penalty imposed under subsection (2) is recoverable by the appropriate authority from the person on whom it is imposed.

(5) Sections 71ZC, 71ZD and 71ZE apply in relation to amounts recoverable by the appropriate authority under subsection (4) as to amounts recoverable by the Secretary of State under section 71ZB (and, where the appropriate authority is not the Secretary of State, those sections so apply as if references to the Secretary of State were to that authority).

(6) In this section and section 115D—"appropriate authority" means—

(a) the Secretary of State, or
(b) an authority which administers housing benefit or council tax benefit;

"overpayment" has the meaning given in section 115A(8), and the reference to the making of an overpayment is to be construed in accordance with that provision;

"relevant social security benefit" has the meaning given in section 121DA(7).]

AMENDMENT

1. This provision inserted by Welfare Reform Act 2012 s.116 (May 10, 2012 for the purpose of making regulations; October 1, 2012 for all other purposes).

GENERAL NOTE

Civil penalties were introduced with effect from October 1, 2012 as part of the strategy to reduce both fraud and error in the benefit system. However, civil penalties can only be imposed where no benefit fraud is involved. They cannot be applied where an overpayment arises solely from official error within the DWP or HMRC. DMG 09420 indicates that there must be a recoverable overpayment of £65.01 or more before a civil penalty can be imposed. This would appear to be DWP policy since no minimum amount is specified in primary or secondary legislation. 1.182

Penalty decisions will be added to overpayment decisions; overpayments are defined broadly in s.115A(8). This means that where a civil penalty is imposed, there will be three relevant decisions in cases under s.71(1): the entitlement decision revising or superseding decisions on entitlement; the overpayment decision determining that there is a recoverable overpayment; and the penalty decision imposing a civil penalty. For overpayment decisions under the 2013 rules (see annotations immediately under the heading to Pt.III SSAA 1992 above at paras 1.77–1.79).

The prescribed amount of the penalty under this section is £50: Social Security (Civil Penalties) Regulations 2012 reg.2. Civil penalties are only available where the overpayment period began on, or falls wholly after October 1, 2012.

There are four conditions required for the imposition of a penalty: 1.183

(a) the overpayment does not involve fraud: subs.(1)(d);
(b) there has been an incorrect statement, representation, information or evidence made or given negligently by the person upon whom the penalty is imposed in connection with a claim or an award of benefit (which is defined broadly in s.121DA(7)): subs.(1)(a);
(c) the person has failed to take reasonable steps to correct the error: (subs.(1)(b); and
(d) the error has resulted in the overpayment: subs.(1)(c).

Some of the issues these conditions raise—such as causation under subs.(1)(c)—may well be resolved in determining whether there is a recoverable overpayment under s.71(1), although others will involve additional findings of fact. Since negligence is required before a penalty can be imposed, the wholly innocent misrepresentation will not attract a civil penalty, even though it may ground an overpayment decision. Negligence is a question of fact but will include consideration of whether the person acted carelessly without paying sufficient intention to the importance of making correct statements in relation to benefit matters. Findings of fact will also be needed on whether reasonable steps have been taken to correct the error.

Subsections (2) and (3) make provision for a civil penalty to be imposed on the other half of a joint claim couple. However, this is only the case if that other party could reasonably be expected to have been aware that the first party had negligently made an incorrect statement or representation or given incorrect information or evidence.

[1 Failure to disclose information

115D.—(1) A penalty of a prescribed amount may be imposed on a person by the appropriate authority where— 1.184

(a) the person, without reasonable excuse, fails to provide information or evidence in accordance with requirements imposed on the person

by the appropriate authority in connection with a claim for, or an award of, a relevant social security benefit,
(b) the failure results in the making of an overpayment, and
(c) the person has not been charged with an offence or cautioned, or been given a notice under section 115A, in respect of the overpayment.

(2) A penalty of a prescribed amount may be imposed on a person by the appropriate authority where—
(a) the person, without reasonable excuse, fails to notify the appropriate authority of a relevant change of circumstances in accordance with requirements imposed on the person under relevant social security legislation,
(b) the failure results in the making of an overpayment, and
(c) the person has not been charged with an offence or cautioned, or been given a notice under section 115A, in respect of the overpayment.

(3) Where a person is making, or has made, a claim for a benefit for a period jointly with another, and both of them fail as mentioned in subsection (1) or (2), only one penalty may be imposed in respect of the same overpayment.

(4) A penalty imposed under subsection (1) or (2) is recoverable by the appropriate authority from the person on whom it is imposed.

(5) Sections 71ZC, 71ZD and 71ZE apply in relation to amounts recoverable by the appropriate authority under subsection (4) as to amounts recoverable by the Secretary of State under section 71ZB (and, where the appropriate authority is not the Secretary of State, those sections so apply as if references to the Secretary of State were to that authority).

(6) In this section "relevant change of circumstances, in relation to a person, means a change of circumstances which affects any entitlement of the person to any benefit or other payment or advantage under any provision of the relevant social security legislation.]

AMENDMENT

1. This provision inserted by Welfare Reform Act 2012 s.116 (May 10, 2012 for the purpose of making regulations; October 1, 2012 for all other purposes).

GENERAL NOTE

1.185 While s.115C deals with civil penalties imposed where there have been incorrect statements, s.115D deals with civil penalties imposed where there has been a failure to disclose or provide information or evidence. There are separate provisions dealing with a failure to provide required information or evidence (subs.(1)); and with a failure to notify a relevant change of circumstances (subs. (2)).

There are three conditions required for the imposition of a penalty under subs.(1):
(a) the overpayment does not involve fraud: subs.(1)(c);
(b) there has been a failure by the person upon whom the penalty is imposed, without reasonable excuse, to provide information of evidence required by the Secretary of State in connection with a claim or an award of benefit (which is defined broadly in s.121DA(7)): subs.(1)(a); and
(c) the failure has resulted in the overpayment: subs.(1)(b).

There are three conditions required for the imposition of a penalty under subs.(2):
(a) the overpayment does not involve fraud: subs.(2)(c);
(b) there has been a failure by the person upon whom the penalty is imposed, without reasonable excuse, to notify a relevant change of circumstances in

connection with a claim or an award of benefit (which is defined broadly in s.121DA(7)): subs.(2)(a); and

(c) the failure has resulted in the overpayment: subs.(2)(b).

Relevant change of circumstances is defined in subs.(6).

Findings of fact will be needed on whether any circumstances put forward by the person upon whom the penalty has been imposed constitute a reasonable excuse for the failure issue. This is likely to include consideration of the timing of any action where late notification has been given.

In joint claims, where there has been a failure by both parties to provide information or evidence, or to notify a relevant change of circumstances, a penalty can only be imposed on one of them: subs.(3).

In *VT v SSWP (IS)* [2016] UKUT 178 (AAC), [2016] AACR 42, Judge Rowland makes two important rulings.

First, even if all the conditions for the imposition of a civil penalty are met, including claimants' lacking a reasonable excuse for a failure to disclose material facts, the imposition of a civil penalty is still a matter of discretion.

Secondly, Judge Rowland confirms, accepting the Secretary of State's submission, that there is a right of appeal in respect of the imposition of a penalty. The Secretary of State shifted his ground during the course of the appeal, and Judge Rowland notes that the present state of the legislation is "unsatisfactory".

Section 116–121D omitted. **1.186**

[Interpretation of Part VI

[1] **121DA.**— (1) In this Part "the relevant social security legislation" means the provisions of any of the following, except so far as relating to contributions, [2 . . .] statutory sick pay or statutory maternity pay, that is to say— **1.187**

(a) the Contributions and Benefits Act;
(b) this Act;
(c) the Pensions Act, except Part III;
(d) section 4 of the Social Security (Incapacity for Work) Act 1994;
(e) the Jobseekers Act 1995;
(f) the Social Security (Recovery of Benefits) Act 1997;
(g) Parts I and IV of the Social Security Act 1998;
(h) Part V of the Welfare Reform and Pensions Act 1999;
[3 (hh) the State Pension Credit Act 2002;]
[4 (hi) Part 1 of the Welfare Reform Act 2007;]
[5 (hj) Part 1 of the Welfare Reform Act 2012;]
[6 (hk) Part 4 of that Act;]
[10 (hl) Part 1 of the Pensions Act 2014;]
(i) the Social Security Pensions Act 1975;
(j) the Social Security Act 1973;
(k) any subordinate legislation made, or having effect as if made, under any enactment specified in paragraphs (a) to (j) above.

(2) In this Part "authorised officer" means a person acting in accordance with any authorisation for the purposes of this Part which is for the time being in force in relation to him.

(3) For the purposes of this Part—

(a) references to a document include references to anything in which information is recorded in electronic or any other form;
(b) the requirement that a notice given by an authorised officer be in writing shall be taken to be satisfied in any case where the contents of the notice—

(i) are transmitted to the recipient of the notice by electronic means; and
(ii) are received by him in a form that is legible and capable of being recorded for future reference.

(4) In this Part "premises" includes—
(a) moveable structures and vehicles, vessels, aircraft and hovercraft;
(b) installations that are offshore installations for the purposes of the Mineral Workings (Offshore Installations) Act 1971;
(c) places of all other descriptions whether or not occupied as land or otherwise;

and references in this Part to the occupier of any premises shall be construed, in relation to premises that are not occupied as land, as references to any person for the time being present at the place in question.

(5) In this Part—
"benefit" includes any payment, credit or loan;
[7 "benefit offence" means—
(a) any criminal offence in connection with a claim for a relevant social security benefit;
(b) any criminal offence in connection with the receipt or payment of any amount by way of such a benefit;
(c) any criminal offence committed for the purpose of facilitating the commission (whether or not by the same person) of a benefit offence;
(d) any attempt or conspiracy to commit a benefit offence; and

"compensation payment" has the same meaning as in the Social Security (Recovery of Benefits) Act 1997.

(6) [8 . . .]

(7) In this section [9 "relevant social security benefit" means a benefit under any provision of the relevant social security legislation; and] "subordinate legislation" has the same meaning as in the Interpretation Act 1978.]

AMENDMENTS

1. Child support, Pensions and Social Security Act 2000 s.67 (April 2, 2001).
2. Tax credits Act 2002 Sch.6 (April 8, 2003).
3. State Pension credit Act 2002 Sch.2 para.12 (July 2, 2002).
4. Welfare Reform Act 2007 Sch.3 para.10(12) (October 27, 2008).
5. Welfare Reform Act 2012 Sch.9 (April 29, 2013).
6. Welfare Reform Act 2012 Sch.9 para.12 (April 8, 2013).
7. Social Security Fraud Act 2001 s.1(7) (April 30, 2002).
8. Welfare Reform Act 2012 Sch.14 (April 1, 2013).
9. Social Security Fraud Act 2001 s.1(8) (April 30, 2002).
10. Pensions Act 2014 s.56(4), s.23 and Sch.12, para.13 (April 6, 2016).

PART VII

INFORMATION

1.188 **121E.–123.** *Omitted.*

The Registration Service

Provisions relating to age, death and marriage

1.189 **124.**—(1) Regulations made by the Registrar General under section 20 of the Registration Service Act 1953 or section 54 of the Registration of Births,

Deaths and Marriages (Scotland) Act 1965 may provide for the furnishing by superintendent registrars and registrars, subject to the payment of such fee as may be prescribed by the regulations, of such information for the purposes—

(a) of the provisions of the Contributions and Benefits Act to which this section applies;

[1 (aa) of the provisions of Parts I and II of the Jobseekers Act 1995;]

[3 (ab) of the provisions of the State Pension Credit Act 2002;]

[6 (ac) of the provisions of Part 1 of the Welfare Reform Act 2007;]

[8 (ad) of the provisions of Part 1 of the Welfare Reform Act 2012;]

[9 (ae) of the provisions of Part 4 of that Act;]

[11 (af) of the provisions of Part 1 of the Pensions Act 2014; and]

[12 (ag) of section 30 of the Pensions Act 2014; and]

(b) of the provisions of this Act so far as they have effect in relation to matters arising under those provisions,

including copies or extracts from the registers in their custody, [10 (or in the case of marriages converted from civil partnerships, copies or extracts from the register of conversions)] as may be so prescribed.

(2) This section applies to the following provisions of the Contributions and Benefits Act—

(a) Parts I to VI except section 108;

(b) Part VII, so far as it relates to income support and [5 . . .];

(c) Part VIII, so far as it relates to any social fund payment such as is mentioned in section 138(1)(a) or (2);

(d) Part IX;

(e) Part XI; and

(f) Part XII.

(3) Where the age, marriage or death of a person is required to be ascertained or proved for the purposes mentioned in subsection (1) above, any person—

(a) on presenting to the custodian of the register under the enactments relating to the registration of births, marriages and deaths, in which particulars of the birth, marriage or death (as the case may be) of the first-mentioned person are entered, a duly completed requisition in writing in that behalf; and

(b) on payment of a fee of [2 £3.50] in England and Wales and [7 £10.00] in Scotland,

shall be entitled to obtain a copy, certified under the hand of the custodian, of the entry of those particulars.

[10 (3A) Where it is required to be ascertained or proved for the purposes mentioned in subsection (1) above, that a civil partnership has been converted into a marriage, any person—

(a) on presenting to the superintendent registrar in whose district the conversion took place, a duly completed requisition in writing in that behalf; and

(b) on payment of a fee of £10.00;

is entitled to obtain a copy, certified under the hand of the superintendent registrar, of the entry relating to that marriage in the register of conversions.]

(4) Requisitions for the purposes of [10 subsections (3) and (3A)] above shall be in such form and contain such particulars as may from time to time be specified by the Registrar General, and suitable forms of requisition shall, on request, be supplied without charge by superintendent registrars and registrars.

(c) each registrar of births and deaths,

to furnish the Secretary of State, [3or the Inland Revenue, for the purposes of their respective functions] under the Contributions and Benefits Act [1, the Jobseekers Act 1995] [2the Social Security (Recovery of Benefits) Act 1997] [4, the Social Security Act 1998] [5, the State Pension Credit Act 2002] [6, Part 1 of the Welfare Reform Act 2007] [7, Part 1 of the Welfare Reform Act 2012] [8, Part 4 of that Act] [9, Part 1 of the Pensions Act 2014] [10, section 30 of that Act] and this Act and the functions of the Northern Ireland Department under any Northern Ireland legislation corresponding to [1any of those Acts], with the prescribed particulars of such deaths as may be prescribed.

(2) The regulations may make provision as to the manner in which and the times at which the particulars are to be furnished.

AMENDMENTS

1. Jobseekers Act 1995 Sch.2 para.60 (October 7, 1996).
2. Social Security (Recovery of Benefits) Act 1997 s.33 and Sch.3 para.5 (October 6, 1997).
3. Social Security Contributions (Transfer of Functions, etc.) Act 1999 s.1(1) and Sch.1 para.25 (April 1, 1999).
4. Social Security Act 1998 s.86 and Sch.7 (dates as for implementation of SSA 1998 for various benefits as set out on para.1.88 of this volume).
5. State Pension Credit Act 2002 s.14 and Sch.2 (July 2, 2002 for the purpose of making regulations only; fully in force October 6, 2003).
6. Welfare Reform Act 2007 s.28 and Sch.3 para.10 (October 27, 2008).
7. The Welfare Reform Act 2012 (Commencement No. 9 and Transitional and Transitory Provisions and Commencement No. 8 and Savings and Transitional Provisions (Amendment)) Order 2013 (SI 2013/983) art.3(1)(b) (April 29, 2013).
8. Welfare Reform Act 2012 Sch.9 para.16 (June 10, 2013).
9. Pensions Act 2014 s.56(4), s.23 and Sch.12, para.16 (April 6, 2016).
10. Pensions Act 2014 s.31 and Sch.16 para.29 (April 6, 2017).

DERIVATION

1.194 Social Security Act 1986 s.60.

DEFINITIONS

"the Contributions and Benefits Act"—see s.191.
"the Northern Ireland Department"—*ibid.*
"prescribed"—*ibid.*

Personal representatives—income support and supplementary benefit

Personal representatives to give information about the estate of a deceased person who was in receipt of income support or supplementary benefit

1.195 **126.**—(1) The personal representatives of a person who was in receipt of [4 universal credit,] income support [1, an income-based jobseeker's allowance] [2, state pension credit] [3, an income-related employment and support allowance] or supplementary benefit at any time before his death shall provide the Secretary of State with such information as he may require relating to the assets and liabilities of that person's estate.

(2) If the personal representatives fail to supply any information within 28 days of being required to do so under subsection (1) above, then—

(a) the appropriate court may, on the application of the Secretary of State, make an order directing them to supply that information within such time as may be specified in the order; and

(b) any such order may provide that all costs (or, in Scotland, expenses) of and incidental to the application shall be borne personally by any of the personal representatives.

(3) In this section "the appropriate court" means—

(a) in England and Wales, a county court;

(b) in Scotland, the sheriff;

and any application to the sheriff under this section shall be made by summary application.

AMENDMENTS

1. Jobseekers Act 1995 Sch.2 para.61 (October 7, 1996).

2. State Pension Credit Act 2002 s.14 and Sch.2 (July 2, 2002 for the purpose of making regulations only; fully in force October 6, 2003).

3. Welfare Reform Act 2007 s.28 and Sch.3 para.10 (October 27, 2008).

4. The Welfare Reform Act 2012 (Commencement No. 9 and Transitional and Transitory Provisions and Commencement No. 8 and Savings and Transitional Provisions (Amendment)) Order 2013 (SI 2013/983) art.3(1)(b) (April 29, 2013).

DERIVATION

Social Security Act 1986 s.27A. 1.196

GENERAL NOTE

Under s.71(3) an overpayment which would have been recoverable from a person may be recoverable from that person's estate (*Secretary of State for Social Services v Solly* [1974] 3 All E.R. 922, *CSSB 6/1995*). Section 126 provides a specific obligation for the estate to provide information about the assets in it. However, s.126 only applies to the estates of income support, income-based JSA or supplementary benefit claimants. It does not apply to all benefits. Nor does it apply to anyone other than a recipient of income support, JSA or supplementary benefit. Sometimes a person other than a recipient may become liable to recovery by making a misrepresentation or failing to disclose a material fact: *R(SB) 21/82* and *R(SB) 28/83*. See the note to s.71(3). 1.197

126A. *Omitted.* 1.198

127.–128A. *Repealed by Sch.2 to the Social Security Administration (Fraud) Act 1997 (July 1, 1997).* 1.199

Statutory sick pay and other benefits

Section 129 Omitted. 1.200

Section 130 Omitted. 1.201

Section 131 Omitted. 1.202

Section 132 Omitted. 1.203

Section 132A Omitted. 1.204

Furnishing of addresses for maintenance proceedings, etc.

1.205 **133.** The Secretary of State may incur expenses for the purpose of furnishing the address at which a [1person] is recorded by him as residing, where the address is required for the purpose of taking or carrying on legal proceedings to obtain or enforce an order for the making by the [1person] of payments—

(a) for the maintenance of the [1 person's spouse, former spouse, civil partner or former civil partner]; or

[1 (b) for the maintenance or education of any child of the person, or of any child of the person's spouse, former spouse, civil partner or former civil partner.]

DERIVATION

1.206 SSA 1975 s.161.

AMENDMENT

1. Civil Partnership (Pensions and Benefit Payments) (Consequential, etc. Provisions) Order 2005 (SI 2005/2053) Sch.1(2) para.6(2) (December 5, 2005).

[1 *Universal Credit Information*

Supply of universal credit information

1.207 **133A.**—(1) This section applies to information that is held by—

(a) the Secretary of State; or

(b) a person providing services to the Secretary of State, in connection with the provision of those services,

that relates to an award of universal credit.

(2) Information to which this section applies may be supplied to—

(a) a local housing authority;

(b) a licensing authority; or

(c) a person authorised to exercise any function of a local housing authority or a licensing authority,

for use in connection with obtaining a rent repayment order in respect of an award of universal credit or recovering an amount payable under such an order.

(3) For the purposes of this section—

"licensing authority" means a person designated by order under section 3 of the Housing (Wales) Act 2014(1);

"local housing authority" has the meaning given by section 261 of the Housing Act 2004(2); and

"rent repayment order" means a rent repayment order as referred to in section 73 or 96 of the Housing Act 2004 or section 32 of the Housing (Wales) Act 2014.]

AMENDMENT

1. Inserted by The Universal Credit and Miscellaneous Amendments (No.2) Regulations 2014 (SI 2014/2888), reg.9(1) (November 26, 2014).

134.–149. *Omitted.* 1.208

PART X

REVIEW AND ALTERATION OF BENEFITS

GENERAL NOTE

Sections 150-154 concern the review and alteration of benefits, and are principally concerned with the annual up-rating of benefits. They are not reproduced here to save space. However, provisions relating to up-rating in the Welfare Benefits Uprating Act 2013 and the four-year freeze on benefits in s.11 of the Welfare Reform and Work Act 2016 are set out later in this volume. 1.209

PART XI

COMPUTATION OF BENEFITS

Effect of alteration of rates of benefit under Parts II to V of Contributions and Benefits Act

155.—(1) This section has effect where the rate of any benefit to which this section applies is altered— 1.210

(a) by an Act subsequent to this Act;
(b) by an order under [4 section 150, 150A or 152] above; or
(c) in consequence of any such Act or order altering any maximum rate of benefit;

and in this section "the commencing date" means the date fixed for payment of benefit at an altered rate to commence.

(2) This section applies to benefit under Part II, III, IV or V of the Contributions and Benefits Act.

(3) Subject to such exceptions or conditions as may be prescribed, where—

(a) the weekly rate of a benefit to which this section applies is altered to a fixed amount higher or lower than the previous amount; and
(b) before the commencing date an award of that benefit has been made (whether before or after the passing of the relevant Act or the making of the relevant order),

except as respects any period falling before the commencing date, the benefit shall become payable at the altered rate without any claim being made for it in the case of an increase in the rate of benefit or any review of the award in the case of a decrease, and the award shall have effect accordingly.

(4) Where—

(a) the weekly rate of a benefit to which this section applies is altered; and
(b) before the commencing date (but after that date is fixed) an award is made of the benefit,

the award either may provide for the benefit to be paid as from the commencing date at the altered rate or may be expressed in terms of the rate appropriate at the date of the award.

(5) Where in consequence of the passing of an Act, or the making of an order, altering the rate of disablement pension, regulations are made varying the scale of disablement gratuities, the regulations may provide that the scale as varied shall apply only in cases where the period taken into account by the

assessment of the extent of the disablement in respect of which the gratuity is awarded begins or began after such day as may be prescribed.

(6) Subject to such exceptions or conditions as may be prescribed, where—

(a) for any purpose of any Act or regulations the weekly rate at which a person contributes to the cost of providing for a child [2 or qualifying young person], or to the maintenance of an adult dependant, is to be calculated for a period beginning on or after the commencing date for an increase in the weekly rate of benefit; but

(b) account is to be taken of amounts referable to the period before the commencing date,

those amounts shall be treated as increased in proportion to the increase in the weekly rate of benefit.

(7) So long as sections 36 and 37 of the National Insurance Act 1965 (graduated retirement benefit) continue in force by virtue of regulations made under Schedule 3 of the Social Security (Consequential Provisions) Act 1975 or under Schedule 3 to the Consequential Provisions Act, regulation may make provision for applying the provisions of this section—

[1(a) to the amount of graduate retirement benefit payable for each unit of graduated contributions,

(b) To increased of such benefit under any provisions made by virtue of section 24(1)(b) of the Social Security Pensions Act 1975 or section 62(1)(a) of the Contributions and Benefits Act, and

(c) to any addition under section 37(1) of the National Insurance Act 1965 (addition to weekly rate of retirement pension for [3 widows, widowers and surviving civil partners]) to the amount of such benefit].

AMENDMENTS

1. Pensions Act 1995 s.131(3) (July 19, 1995).
2. Child Benefit Act 2005 Sch.1 Pt 1 para.23 (April 10, 2006).
3. Civil Partnership (Pensions and Benefit Payments) (Consequential, etc. Provisions) Order 2005 (SI 2005/2053) Sch.1(2) para.9 (December 5, 2005).
4. Pensions Act 2007 Sch.1(5) para.23 (July 26, 2007: insertion has effect as specified in 2007 c.22 s.5(3) and (7)).

DERIVATION

1.211 SSA 1986 s.64.

[1Power to anticipate pensions up-rating order

1.212 **155A.**—(1) This section applies where a statement is made in the House of Commons by or on behalf of the Secretary of State which specifies—

(a) the amounts by which he proposes, by an order under [4 [5 150, 150A or 151A] above (as the case may be)] above, to increase—

(i) the weekly sums that are payable by way of [5 a state pension under Part 1 of the Pensions Act 2014,] retirement pension [2 or shared additional pension]; or

(ii) the amount of graduated retirement benefit payable for each unit of graduated contributions; and

(b) the date of which he proposes to bring the increases into force ("the commencing date").

(2) Where before the commencing date and after the date on which the statement is made, an award is made of [5 a state pension,] a retirement pension [3, a shared additional pension] or a graduated retirement benefit, the award may provide for the pension or benefit to be paid as from the commencing date at the increased rate or may be expressed in terms of the rate appropriate at the date of the award.]

AMENDMENTS

1. Social Security Act 1998 s.76 (November 16, 1998).
2. Welfare Reform and Pensions Act 1999 Sch.12 para.25(3) (December 1, 2000).
3. Welfare Reform and Pensions Act 1999 Sch.12 para.25(3) (December 1, 2000).
4. Pensions Act 2007 Sch.1(5) para.24 (July 26, 2007: substitution has effect as specified in 2007 c.22 s.5(3) and (7)).
5. Pensions Act 2014, s.56(4), s.23 and Sch.12, para.22 (April 6, 2016).

Up-rating under sections 150 above of pensions increased under section 52(3) of the Contributions and Benefits Act.

[1**156.**—(1) This section applies in any case where a person is entitled to a Category A retirement pension with an increase, under section 52(3) of the Contributions and Benefits Act, in the additional pension on account of the contributions of a spouse [2 or civil partner] who had died. 1.213

(2) Where in the case of any up-rating order under section 150 above—

(a) The spouse's [2 or civil partner's] final relevant year is the tax year preceding the tax year in which the up-rating order comes into force, but

(b) The person's final relevant year was an earlier tax year,

then the up-rating order shall not have effect in relation to that part of the additional pension which is attributable to the spouse's [2 or civil partner] contributions.

(3) Where in the case of any up-rating order under section 150 above—

(a) The person's final relevant year is the tax year preceding the tax year in which the up-rating order comes into force, but

(b) The spouse's [2 or civil partner's] final relevant year was an earlier tax year,

Then the up-rating order shall not have effect in relation to that part of the additional pension which is attributable to the person's contributions.]

AMENDMENTS

1. Pensions Act 1995 s.130(1) (July 19, 1995).
2. Civil Partnership Act 2004 s.254 and Sch.24 para.66 (December 5, 2005).

DERIVATION

SSPA 1975 s.23(2A). 1.214

Effect of alteration of rates of child benefit

157.—(1) Subsections (3) and (4) of section 155 above shall have effect where there is an increase in the rate or any of the rates of child benefit as they have effect in relation to the rate of benefit to which that section applies. 1.215

(2) Where in connection with child benefit—

(a) any question arises in respect of a period after the date fixed for the commencement of payment of child benefit at an increased rate—

(i) as to the weekly rate at which a person is contributing to the cost of providing for a child [1 or qualifying young person]; or
(ii) as to the expenditure that a person is incurring in respect of a child [1 or qualifying young person]; and
(b) in determining that question account falls to be taken of contributions made or expenditure incurred for a period before that date,

the contributions made or expenditure incurred before that date shall be treated as increased in proportion to the increase in the rate of benefit.

DERIVATION

1.216 CBA 1975 s.5(6).

AMENDMENT

1. Child Benefit Act 2005 Sch.1 Pt 1 para.24 (April 10, 2006).

Treatment of excess benefit as paid on account of child benefit

1.217 **158.**—(1) In any case where—
(a) any benefit as defined in section 122 of the Contributions and Benefits Act or any increase of such benefit ("the relevant benefit or increase") has been paid to a person for a period in respect of a child [1 or qualifying young person]; and
(b) subsequently child benefit for that period in respect of the child [1 or qualifying young person] becomes payable at a rate which is such that, had the relevant benefit or increase been awarded after the child benefit became payable, the rate of the relevant benefit or increase would have been reduced,

then, except in so far as regulations otherwise provide, the excess shall be treated as paid on account of child benefit for that period in respect of the child [1 or qualifying young person].

(2) In subsection (1) above "the excess" means so much of the relevant benefit or increase as is equal to the difference between—
(a) the amount of it which was paid for the period referred to in that subsection; and
(b) the amount of it which would have been paid for that period if it had been paid at the reduced rate referred to in paragraph (b) of that subsection.

DERIVATION

1.218 SS(MP)A 1977 s.17(4).

AMENDMENT

1. Child Benefit Act 2005 Sch.1 Pt 1 para.25 (April 10, 2006).

GENERAL NOTE

1.219 This provision avoids increases of benefits overlapping with, in particular, increase of child benefit. See also paras (4) and (5) of reg.2 of the Fixing and Adjustment of Rates Regulations.

Effect of alteration in the component rates of income support

1.220 **159.**—(1) Subject to such exceptions and conditions as may be prescribed, where—

(a) an award of income support is in force in favour of any person ("the recipient"); and
(b) there is an alteration in any of the relevant amounts, that is to say—
(i) any of the component rates of income support;
(ii) any of the other sums specified in regulations under Part VII of the Contributions and Benefits Act; or
(iii) the recipient's benefit income; and
(c) the alteration affects the computation of the amount of income support to which the recipient is entitled,

then subsection (2) or (3) below (as the case may be) shall have effect.

(2) Where, in consequence of the alteration in question, the recipient becomes entitled to an increased or reduced amount of income support ("the new amount"), then, as from the commencing date, the amount of income support payable to or for the recipient under the award shall be the new amount, without any further decision of [1the Secretary of State], and the award shall have effect accordingly.

(3) Where, notwithstanding the alteration in question, the recipient continues on and after the commencing date to be entitled to the same amount of income support as before, the award shall continue in force accordingly.

(4) In any case where—
(a) there is an alteration in any of the relevant amounts; and
(b) before the commencing date (but after that date is fixed) an award of income support is made in favour of a person,

the award either may provide for income support to be paid as from the commencing date, in which case the amount shall be determined by reference to the relevant amounts which will be in force on that date, or may provide for an amount determined by reference to the amounts in force at the date of the award.

(5) In this section—

"alteration" means—
(a) in relation to—
(i) the component rates of income support; or
(ii) any other sums specified in regulations under Part VII of the Contributions and Benefits Act,

their alteration by or under any enactment whether or not contained in that Part; and
(b) in relation to a person's benefit income, the alteration of any of the sums referred to in [4 section 150, 150A or 151A] above—
(i) by any enactment; or
(ii) by an order under [2 section 150, 150A [4, 151A] or 152] above,

to the extent that any such alteration affects the amount of his benefit income;

"benefit income", in relation to any person, means so much of his income as consists of—
(a) benefit under the Contributions and Benefits Act, other than income support; [3 . . .]
[4 (za) state pension under Part 1 of the Pensions Act 2014;]
[3 (aa) personal independence payment; or]
(b) a war disablement pension or war widow's pension;

"the commencing date" in relation to an alteration, means the date on which the alteration comes into force in the case of the person in question;

"component rate", in relation to income support, means the amount of—

(a) the sum referred to in section 126(5)(b)(i) and (ii) of the Contributions and Benefits Act; or

(b) any of the sums specified in regulations under section 135(1) of that Act; and

"relevant amounts" has the meaning given by subsection (1)(b) above.

AMENDMENTS

1. Social Security Act 1998 Sch.7 para.95 (November 29, 1999 for purposes specified in SI 1999/3178 art.2(1) and Sch.1; not yet in force otherwise).
2. Pensions Act 2007 Sch.1(5) para.25 (July 26, 2007: insertion has effect as specified in 2007 c.22 s.5(3) and (7)).
3. Welfare Reform Act 2012 Sch.9 para.18 (April 8, 2013).
4. Pensions Act 2014 (Consequential Amendments) Order 2016 (SI 2016/931) art.2(2) (September 16, 2016).

DERIVATION

1.221 Social Security Act 1986 s.64A.

DEFINITIONS

"the Contributions and Benefits Act"—see s.191.
"war disablement pension"—*ibid.*
"war widow's pension"—*ibid.*

GENERAL NOTE

1.222 The general rule under s.159 is that if there is an alteration in the prescribed figures for personal allowances, premiums, the relevant sum (i.e. assumed "strike pay" in trade dispute cases), or any social security benefits which count as income for income support purposes (subss.(1) and (5)), then any consequent change in the amount of income support which is payable takes effect automatically without the need for a decision (subs.(2)).

[1 Effect of alteration of rates of a jobseeker's allowance

1.223 **159A.**—(1) This section applies where—

(a) an award of a jobseeker's allowance is in force in favour of any person ("the recipient"); and

(b) an alteration—

 (i) in any component of the allowance, or

 (ii) in the recipient's benefit income,

affects the amount of the jobseeker's allowance to which he is entitled.

(2) Subsection (3) applies where, as a result of the alteration, the amount of the jobseeker's allowance to which the recipient is entitled is increased or reduced.

(3) As from the commencing date, the amount of the jobseeker's allowance payable to or for the recipient under the award shall be the increased or reduced amount, without any further decision of [2 the Secretary of State]; and the award shall have effect accordingly.

(4) In any case where—

(a) there is an alteration of a kind mentioned in subsection (1)(b); and
(b) before the commencing date (but after that date is fixed) an award of a jobseeker's allowance is made in favour of a person,

the award may provide for the jobseeker's allowance to be paid as from the commencing date, in which case the amount of the jobseeker's allowance shall be determined by reference to the components applicable on that date, or may provide for an amount determined by reference to the components applicable at the date of the award.

(5) In this section—

"alteration" means—

(a) in relation to any component of a jobseeker's allowance, its alteration by or under any enactment; and
(b) in relation to a person's benefit income, the alteration of any of the sums referred to in [3 section [5 150, 150A or 151A]] above by any enactment or by an order under section [5 150, 150A or 151A] above, to the extent that any such alteration affects the amount of the recipient's benefit income;

"benefit income", in relation to a recipient, means so much of his income as consists of—

(a) benefit under the Contributions and Benefits Act; or
[4 (aa) personal independence payment; or]
[5 (za) state pension under Part 1 of the Pensions Act 2014;]
(b) a war disablement pension or war widow's pension;

"the commencing date" in relation to an alteration, means the date on which the alteration comes into force in relation to the recipient;

"component", in relation to a jobseeker's allowance, means any of the sums specified in regulations under the Jobseekers Act 1995 which are relevant in calculating the amount payable by way of a jobseeker's allowance.]

AMENDMENTS

1. Jobseekers Act 1995 s.24 (October 7, 1996).
2. Social Security Act 1998 Sch.7 para.96 (October 18, 1999).
3. Pensions Act 2007 Sch.1(5) para.26 (July 26, 2007: insertion has effect as specified in 2007 c.22 s.5(3) and (7)).
4. Welfare Reform Act 2012 Sch.9 para.19 (April 8, 2013).
5. Pensions Act 2014 (Consequential Amendments) Order 2016 (SI 2016/931) art.2(3) (September 16, 2016).

DEFINITIONS

"the Contributions and Benefit Act"—see s.191.
"war disablement pension"—*ibid.*
"war widow's pension—*ibid.*

GENERAL NOTE

This section has the same effect for income-based JSA as s.159 does for income support. 1.224

[1 Effect of alterations affecting state pension credit]

159B.—(1) Subject to such exceptions and conditions as may be prescribed, subsection (2) or (3) below shall have effect where— 1.225

(a) an award of state pension credit is in force in favour of any person ("the recipient"); and

[1 159C Effect of alteration of rates of an employment and support allowance

1.226 (1) Subject to such exceptions and conditions as may be prescribed, subsection (2) or (3) shall have effect where—

(a) an award of an employment and support allowance is in force in favour of any person ("the recipient"), and
(b) an alteration—
  (i) in any component of the allowance,
  (ii) in the recipient's benefit income, or
  (iii) in the recipient's war disablement or war widow's or widower's pension,

affects the computation of the amount of the employment and support allowance to which he is entitled.

(2) Where, as a result of the alteration, the amount of the employment and support allowance to which the recipient is entitled is increased or reduced, then, as from the commencing date, the amount of the employment and support allowance payable in the case of the recipient under the award shall be the increased or reduced amount, without any further decision of the Secretary of State; and the award shall have effect accordingly.

(3) Where, notwithstanding the alteration, the recipient continues on and after the commencing date to be entitled to the same amount by way of an employment and support allowance as before, the award shall continue in force accordingly.

(4) Subsection (5) applies where a statement is made in the House of Commons by or on behalf of the Secretary of State which specifies—

(a) in relation to any of the items referred to in subsection (1)(b)(i) to (iii), the amount of the alteration which he proposes to make by an order under [2 section 150, 150A [4, 151A] or 152] or by or under any other enactment, and
(b) the date on which he proposes to bring the alteration into force ("the proposed commencing date").

(5) If, in a case where this subsection applies, an award of an employment and support allowance is made in favour of a person before the proposed commencing date and after the date on which the statement is made, the award—

(a) may provide for the employment and support allowance to be paid as from the proposed commencing date at a rate determined by reference to the amounts of the items referred to in subsection (1)(b)(i) to (iii) which will be in force on that date, or
(b) may be expressed in terms of the amounts of those items in force at the date of the award.

(6) In this section—

"alteration" means—

(a) in relation to any component of an employment and support allowance, its alteration by or under any enactment;
(b) in relation to a person's benefit income, the alteration of any of the sums referred to in [4 section 150, 150A or 151A] by any enactment or by an order under [2 [4 section 150, 150A, 151A] or 152] to the extent that any such alteration affects the amount of his benefit income;
(c) in relation to a person's war disablement pension or war widow's or widower's pension, its alteration by or under any enactment;

"benefit income", in relation to a person, means so much of his income as consists of benefit under the Contributions and Benefits Act [4, state pension under Part 1 of the Pensions Act 2014] [2 or personal independence-payment];

"the commencing date", in relation to an alteration, means the date on which the alteration comes into force in relation to the recipient;

"component", in relation to an employment and support allowance, means any of the sums specified in regulations under Part 1 of the Welfare Reform Act 2007 which are relevant in calculating the amount payable by way of an employment and support allowance;

"war disablement pension" and "war widow's or widower's pension" have the same meaning as in section 159B.]

AMENDMENTS

1. Welfare Reform Act 2007 s.28 and Sch.3 para.10 (October 27, 2008).

2. Pensions Act 2007 Sch.1(5) para.28 (October 27, 2008: insertions came into force on July 26, 2007 but could not take effect until the commencement of the Welfare Reform Act 2007 Sch.3 para.10(23) on October 27, 2008 and has effect as specified in 2007 c.22 s.5(3) and (7)).

3. Welfare Reform Act 2012 Sch.9 para.21 (April 8, 2013).

4. Pensions Act 2014 (Consequential Amendments) Order 2016 (SI 2016/931) art.2(5) (September 16, 2016.)

[1 Effect of alterations affecting universal credit

159D.—(1) Subject to such exceptions and conditions as may be prescribed, subsection (2) or (3) shall have effect where— 1.227

(a) an award of universal credit is in force in favour of any person ("the recipient"), and

(b) an alteration—

(i) in any element of universal credit,

(ii) in the recipient's benefit income,

(iii) in any amount to be deducted in respect of earned income under section 8(3)(a) of the Welfare Reform Act 2012,

(iv) in any component of a contribution-based jobseeker's allowance,

(v) in any component of a contributory employment and support allowance, or

(vi) in such other matters as may be prescribed, affects the computation of the amount of universal credit to which he is entitled.

(2) Where, as a result of the alteration, the amount of universal credit to which the recipient is entitled is increased or reduced, then, as from the commencing date, the amount of universal credit payable in the case of the recipient under the award shall be the increased or reduced amount, without any further decision of the Secretary of State; and the award shall have effect accordingly.

(3) Where, notwithstanding the alteration, the recipient continues on and after the commencing date to be entitled to the same amount by way of universal credit as before, the award shall continue in force accordingly.

(4) Subsection (5) applies where a statement is made in the House of Commons by or on behalf of the Secretary of State which specifies—

(a) in relation to any of the items referred to in subsection (1)(b)(i) to (vi), the amount of the alteration which he proposes to make by an

Implementation of increases in income support due to attainment of particular ages

1.229 **160.**—(1) This section applies where—

(a) an award of income support is in force in favour of a person ("the recipient"); and

(b) there is a component which becomes applicable, or applicable at a particular rate, in his case if he or some other person attains a particular age.

(2) If, in a case where this section applies, the recipient or other person attains the particular age referred to in paragraph (b) of subsection (1) above and, in consequence—

(a) the component in question becomes applicable, or applicable at a particular rate, in the recipient's case (whether or not some other component ceases, for the same reason, to be applicable, or applicable at a particular rate, in his case; and

(b) after taking account of any such cessation, the recipient becomes entitled to an increased amount of income support,

then, except as provided by subsection (3) below, as from the day on which he becomes so entitled, the amount of income support payable to or for him under the award shall be that increased amount, without any further decision of [1 the Secretary of State], and the award shall have effect accordingly.

(3) Subsection (2) above does not apply in any case where, in consequence of the recipient or other person attaining the age in question, some question arises in relation to the recipient's entitlement to [1 personal independence payment, or] any benefit under the Contributions and Benefits Act, other than—

(a) the question whether the component concerned, or any other component, becomes or ceases to be applicable, or applicable at a particular rate, in his case; and

(b) the question whether, in consequence, the amount of his income support falls to be varied.

(4) In this section "component", in relation to a person and his income support, means any of the sums specified in regulations under section 135(1) of the Contributions and Benefits Act.

Amendments

1. Social Security Act 1998 Sch.7 para.97 (November 29, 1999).
2. Welfare Reform Act 2012 Sch.9 para.22 (April 8, 2013).

Derivation

1.230 Social Security Act 1986 s.64B.

Definition

"the Contributions and Benefits Act"—see s.191.

General Note

1.231 Section 160 extends the process begun by s.159 of taking routine adjustments in the amount of income support out of the ordinary mechanism of review.

[1Implementation of increases in income-based jobseeker's allowance due to attainment of particular ages

160A.—(1) This section applies where— 1.232

(a) an award of an income-based jobseeker's allowance is in force in favour of a person ("the recipient"); and

(b) a component has become applicable, or applicable at a particular rate, because he or some other person has reached a particular age ("the qualifying age")

(2) If, as a result of the recipient or other person reaching the qualifying age, the recipient becomes entitled to an income-based jobseeker's allowance of an increased amount, the amount payable to or for him under the award shall, as from the day on which he becomes so entitled, be that increased amount, without any further decision of [2 the Secretary of State]; and the award shall have effect accordingly.

(3) Subsection (2) above does not apply where, in consequence of the recipient or other person reaching the qualifying age, a question arises in relation to the recipient's entitlement to—

(a) a benefit under the Contributions and Benefits Act; [3. . .]

[3 (aa) personal independence payment; or]

(b) a jobseeker's allowance.

(4) Subsection (3)(b) above does not apply to the question—

(a) whether the component concerned, or any other component, becomes or ceases to be applicable, or applicable at a particular rate, in the recipient's case; and

(b) whether, in consequence, the amount of his income-based jobseeker's allowance falls to be varied.

(5) In this section "component", in relation to a recipient and his jobseeker's allowance, means any of the amounts determined in accordance with regulations made under section 4(5) of the Jobseekers Act 1995.]

AMENDMENTS

1. Jobseekers Act 1995 s.25 (October 7, 1996).
2. Social Security Act 1998 Sch.7 para.98 (October 18, 1999).
3. Welfare Reform Act 2012 Sch.9 para.23 (April 8, 2013).

DEFINITION

"the Contributions and Benefits Act"—see s.191.

GENERAL NOTE

See s.160. 1.233

[1 160B Implementation of increases in employment and support allowance due to attainment of particular ages

(1) This section applies where— 1.234

(a) an award of an employment and support allowance is in force in favour of a person ("the recipient"), and

(b) a component has become applicable, or applicable at a particular rate, because he or some other person has reached a particular age ("the qualifying age").

(2) If, as a result of the recipient or other person reaching the qualifying age, the recipient becomes entitled to an employment and support allowance of an increased amount, the amount payable to or for him under the award shall, as from the day on which he becomes so entitled, be that increased amount, without any further decision of the Secretary of State; and the award shall have effect accordingly.

(3) Subsection (2) does not apply where, in consequence of the recipient or other person reaching the qualifying age, a question arises in relation to the recipient's entitlement to

[2 (a) a benefit under the Contributions and Benefits Act; or

(b) personal independence payment.]

(4) Subsection (2) does not apply where, in consequence of the recipient or other person reaching the qualifying age, a question arises in relation to the recipient's entitlement to an employment and support allowance, other than—

(a) the question whether the component concerned, or any other component, becomes or ceases to be applicable, or applicable at a particular rate, in the recipient's case, and

(b) the question whether, in consequence, the amount of his employment and support allowance falls to be varied.

(5) In this section, "component", in relation to a recipient and his employment and support allowance, means any of the amounts determined in accordance with regulations made under section 2(1)(a) or 4(2)(a) of the Welfare Reform Act 2007.]

AMENDMENTS

1. Welfare Reform Act 2007 s.28 and Sch.3 para.10 (October 27, 2008).
2. Welfare Reform Act 2012 Sch.9 para.24 (April 8, 2013).

PART XII

FINANCE

1.235 **161.–166.** *Omitted.*

The social fund

1.236 **167.**—(1) The fund known as the social fund shall continue in being by that name.

(2) The social fund shall continue to be maintained under the control and management of the Secretary of State and payments out of it shall be made by him.

(3) The Secretary of State shall make payments into the social fund of such amounts, at such times and in such manner as he may with the approval of the Treasury determine.

(4) Accounts of the social fund shall be prepared in such form, and in such manner and at such times, as the Treasury may direct, and the Comptroller and Auditor General shall examine and certify every such account and shall lay copies of it, together with his report, before Parliament.

(5) The Secretary of State shall prepare an annual report on the social fund.

(6) A copy of every such report shall be laid before each House of Parliament.

DERIVATIONS

Subs.(1): Social Security Act 1986 s.32(1). **1.237**
Subss.(2)–(6): 1986 Act s.32(5)–(7B).

Allocations from social fund

s.168. Repealed. **1.238**

Adjustments between social fund and other sources of finance

169.—(1) There shall be made— **1.239**

(a) out of the social fund into the Consolidated Fund or the National Insurance Fund;

(b) into the social fund out of money provided by Parliament or the National Insurance Fund,

such payments by way of adjustment as the Secretary of State determines (in accordance with any directions of the Treasury) to be appropriate in consequence of any enactment or regulations relating to the repayment or offsetting of a benefit or other payment under the Contributions and Benefits Act [1 or the State Pension Credit Act 2002].

(2) Where in any other circumstances payments fall to be made by way of adjustment—

(a) out of the social fund into the Consolidated Fund or the National Insurance Fund; or

(b) into the social fund out of money provided by Parliament or the National Insurance Fund,

then, in such cases or classes of cases as may be specified by the Secretary of State by order, the amount of the payments to be made shall be taken to be such, and payments on account of it shall be be made at such times and in such manner, as may be determined by the Secretary of State in accordance with any direction given by the Treasury.

AMENDMENT

1. State Pension Credit Act 2002 s.14 and Sch.2 (July 2, 2002 for the purpose of making regulations only; fully in force October 6, 2003).

DERIVATION

Social Security Act 1986 s.85(11) and (12). **1.240**

DEFINITION

"the Contributions and Benefits Act"—see s.191.

PART XIII

ADVISORY BODIES AND CONSULTATION

The Social Security Advisory Committee and the Industrial Injuries Advisory Council

The Social Security Advisory Committee

1.241 **170.**—(1) The Social Security Advisory Committee (in this Act referred to as "the Committee") constituted under section 9 of the Social Security Act 1980 shall continue in being by that name—

(a) to give (whether in pursuance of a reference under this Act or otherwise) advice and assistance to the Secretary of State in connection with the discharge of his functions under the relevant enactments;

(b) to give (whether in pursuance of a reference under this Act or otherwise) advice and assistance to the Northern Ireland Department in connection with the discharge of its functions under the relevant Northern Ireland enactments; and

(c) to perform such other duties as may be assigned to the Committee under any enactment.

(2) Schedule 5 to this Act shall have effect with respect to the constitution of the Committee and the other matters there mentioned.

(3) The Secretary of State may from time to time refer to the Committee for consideration and advice such questions relating to the operation of any of the relevant enactments as he thinks fit (including questions as to the advisability of amending any of them).

(4) The Secretary of State shall furnish the Committee with such information as the Committee may reasonably require for the proper discharge of its functions.

(5) In this Act—

"the relevant enactments" means—

(a) the provisions of the Contributions and Benefits Act [1, this Act and the Social Security (Incapacity for Work) Act 1994], except as they apply to industrial injuries benefit and Old Cases payments;

[2 (aa) the provisions of the Jobseekers Act 1995;] and

[3 (ab) section 10 of the Child Support Act 1995;]

[4 (ac) the provisions of the Social Security (Recovery of Benefits) Act 1997; and]

[5 (ad) the provisions of Chapter II of Part I of the Social Security Act 1998 and section 72 of that Act;]

[6 (ae) sections 60, 72 and 79 of the Welfare Reform and Pensions Act 1999;]

[7 (af) section 42, sections 62 to 65 and [14 sections 69 and 70 of the Child Support Pensions and Social Security Act 2000;]

[8 (ag) sections 7 to 11 of the Social Security Fraud Act 2001;]

[9 (ah) the provisions of the State Pension Credit Act 2002;]

[11 (ai) section 7 of the Age-Related Payments Act 2004;]

[12 (aia) the provisions of Part 1 of the Welfare Reform Act 2007;]

[13 (aj) sections 32 and 33 of the Welfare Reform Act 2007;]
[14 (ak) the provisions of Part I of the Welfare Reform Act 2012;]
[15 (al) Part 4 of that Act;]
[16 (am) the provisions of Part 1 of the Pensions Act 2014;]
[17 (an) section 30 of the Pensions Act 2014;]
(b) the provisions of Part II of Schedule 3 to the Consequential Provisions Act, except as they apply to industrial injuries benefit; and

"the relevant Northern Ireland enactments" means—
(a) the provisions of the Northern Ireland Contributions and Benefits Act and the Northern Ireland Administration Act, except as they apply to Northern Ireland industrial injuries benefit and payments under Part I of Schedule 8 to the Northern Ireland Contributions and Benefits Act; and
[2 (aa) any provisions in Northern Ireland which correspond to provisions of the Jobseekers Act 1995; and]
[3 (ab) any enactment corresponding to section 10 of the Child Support Act 1995 having effect with respect to Northern Ireland; and]
[4 (ac) any provisions in Northern Ireland which correspond to provisions of the Social Security (Recovery of Benefits) Act 1997; and]
[5 (ad) any provisions in Northern Ireland which correspond to provisions of Chapter II of Part I of the Social Security Act 1998 and section 72 of that Act;]
[6 (ae) any provisions in Northern Ireland which correspond to sections 60, 72 and 79 of the Welfare Reform and Pensions Act 1999;]
[7 (af) any provisions in Northern Ireland which correspond to section 42, any of sections 62 to 65, and [14 sections 69 and 70 of the Child Support Pensions and Social Security Act 2000;]; and]
[8 (ag) any provisions in Northern Ireland which correspond to sections 7 to 11 of the Social Security Fraud Act 2001, and]
[9 (ah) any provisions in Northern Ireland which correspond to provisions of the State Pension Credit Act 2002; and]
[12 (aia) any provisions in Northern Ireland which correspond to Part 1 of the Welfare Reform Act 2007;]
[13 (aj) any provisions in Northern Ireland which correspond to sections 32 and 33 of the Welfare Reform Act 2007;]
[14 (ak) the provisions of Part I of the Welfare Reform Act 2012;]
[15 (al) any provisions in Northern Ireland which correspond to Part 4 of that Act;]
[16 (am) any provisions in Northern Ireland which correspond to the provisions of Part 1 of the Pensions Act 2014;]
[17 (an) any provisions in Northern Ireland which correspond to section 30 of the Pensions Act 2014;]
(b) the provisions of Part II of Schedule 3 to the Social Security (Consequential Provisions) (Northern Ireland) Act 1992, except as they apply to Northern Ireland industrial injuries benefit; and
[10 (c) section 32(6) of the Pension Schemes (Northern Ireland) Act 1993;]

and in this definition—
(i) "Northern Ireland Contributions and Benefits Act" means the Social Security Contributions and Benefits (Northern Ireland) Act 1992;

reference to the Committee or the Council of any regulations contained in either—

(a) a statutory instrument made before the end of the period of 6 months beginning with the coming into force of the enactment under which those regulations are made; or

(b) a statutory instrument—

(i) which states that it contains only regulations made by virtue of, or consequential upon, a specified enactment; and

(ii) which is made before the end of the period of 6 months beginning with the coming into force of that specified enactment.

(6) In relation to regulations required or authorised to be made by the Secretary of State in conjunction with the Treasury, any reference in this section to the Secretary of State shall be construed as a reference to the Secretary of State and the Treasury.

(7) In this section "regulations" means regulations under any enactment, whenever passed.

1.246 **174.–176.** *Omitted.*

PART XIV

SOCIAL SECURITY SYSTEMS OUTSIDE GREAT BRITAIN

Co-ordination

1.247 **Section 177:** *repealed by the Northern Ireland Act 1998, Sch.15 (December 2, 1999).*

1.248 **Section 178:** *repealed by the Northern Ireland Act 1998, Sch.15 (December 2, 1999).*

Reciprocal agreements with countries outside the United Kingdom

1.249 **179.**—(1) For the purpose of giving effect—

(a) to any agreement with the government of a country outside the United Kingdom providing for reciprocity in matters relating to payments for purposes similar or comparable to the purposes of legislation to which this section applies, or

(b) to any such agreement as it would be if it were altered in accordance with proposals to alter it which, in consequence of any change in the law of Great Britain, the government of the United Kingdom has made to the other government in question,

Her Majesty may by Order in Council make provision for modifying or adapting such legislation in its application to cases affected by the agreement or proposed alterations.

(2) An Order made by virtue of subsection (1) above may, instead of or in addition to making specific modifications or adaptions, provide generally that legislation to which this section applies shall be modified to such extent

as may be required to give effect to the provisions contained in the agreement or, as the case may be, alterations in question.

(3) The modifications which may be made by virtue of subsection (1) above include provisions—

(a) for securing that acts, omissions and events having any effect for the purposes of the law of the country in respect of which the agreement is made have a corresponding effect for the purposes of this Act, [1 the Jobseeker's Act 1995], [2 Chapter II of Part I of the Social Security Act 1998] [3 Part II of the Social Security Contributions (Transfer of Functions, etc.) Act 1999] [5, Part III of the Social Security Contributions (Transfer of Functions etc.) (Northern Ireland) Order 1999] [6, the State Pension Credit Act 2002] [7, Part 1 of the Welfare Reform Act 2007] [9 , Part 1 of the Welfare Reform Act 2012] [, Part 4 of that Act] [11 , Part 1 of the Pensions Act 2014] [12, Part 5 of that Act] and the Contributions and Benefits Act (but not so as to confer a right to double benefit);

(b) for determining, in cases where rights accrue under such legislation and under the law of that country, which of those rights is to be available to the person concerned;

(c) for making any necessary financial adjustments.

(4) This section applies—

(a) to the Contributions and Benefits Act;

(aa) [1 to the Jobseeker's Act 1995];

(ab) [2 to Chapter II of Part I of the Social Security Act 1998];

(ac) [3 to Part II of the Social Security Contributions (Transfers of Functions, etc.) Act 1999]; and

[4(ad) to Part III of the Social Security Contributions (Transfer of Functions etc.) (Northern Ireland) Order 1999;]

[5(ae) to the State Pension Credit Act 2002; and]

[7(af) to part 1 of the Welfare Reform Act 2007;]

[9 (ag) to Part 1 of the Welfare Reform Act 2012; and]

[10 (ah) to Part 4 of that Act;]

[11 (ai) to Part 1 of the Pensions Act 2014;]

[12 (aj) to Part 5 of the Pensions Act 2014;]

(b) to this Act,

except in relation to the following benefits—

(i) community charge benefits;

(ii) payments out of the social fund;

(iii) Christmas bonus;

(iv) statutory sick pay; and

(v) statutory maternity pay.

(5) The power conferred by subsection (1) above shall also be exercisable in relation to regulations made under the Contributions and Benefits Act [8, this Act or Part I of the Welfare Reform Act 2007] [11 or Part 1 of the Pensions Act 2014] [12 or section 30 of that Act] and concerning—

[9 (za) universal credit;]

(a) income support;

[1(aa) jobseeker's allowance];

[5(ab) state pension credit];

[7(ac) employment and support allowance;]

[11 (ad) state pension under Part 1 of the Pensions Act 2014;]

[12 (ae) bereavement support payment;]

(b) [6 . . .];

(c) [6 . . .];
(d) housing benefit; or
(e) child benefit.

Amendments

1. Jobseekers Act 1995 Sch.2 (April 22, 1996).
2. Social Security Act 1998 Sch.7 (July 5, 1999).
3. Transfer of Functions Act 1999 Sch.7 (April 1, 1999).
4. Social Security Contributions (Transfer of Functions etc.) (Northern Ireland) Order 1999 (April 1, 1999).
5. State Pension Credit Act 2002 s.14 and Sch.2 (July 2, 2002 for the purpose of making regulations only; fully in force October 6, 2003).
6. Tax Credits Act 2002 s.60 and Sch.6 (April 8, 2003).
7. Welfare Reform Act 2007 s.28 and Sch.3 para.10 (October 27, 2008).
8. The Social Security (Miscellaneous Amendments) (No.3) Regulations 2011 (SI 2011/2425) reg.3 (October 31, 2011).
9. The Welfare Reform Act 2012 (Commencement No. 9 and Transitional and Transitory Provisions and Commencement No. 8 and Savings and Transitional Provisions (Amendment)) Order 2013 (SI 2013/983) art.3(1)(b) (April 29, 2013).
10. Welfare Reform Act 2012 Sch.9 para.27(3) (April 8, 2013).
11. Pensions Act 2014 s.23 and Sch.12 para.25 (July 7, 2015).
12. Pensions Act 2014 s.31 and Sch.16 para.33 (February 8, 2017).

Derivation

1.250 SSA 1975 s.143 as amended and CBA 1975 s.15 as amended.

General Note

1.251 For further information reciprocal arrangements, see annotations to s.113, of the Contributions and Benefits Act 1992.

For a discussion on how s.179 acts to modify other social security provisions, see *Campbell v Secretary of State for Work and Pensions* [2005] EWCA Civ 989.

[1 Exchange of information with overseas authorities]

1.252 **179A.**—(1) This section applies where it appears to the Secretary of State—
(a) that there are arrangements in force for the exchange of relevant information between him and any authorities in a country outside the United Kingdom ("the overseas country"); and
(b) that the arrangements and the law in force in the overseas country are such as to ensure that there are adequate safeguards in place against any improper use of information disclosed by the Secretary of State under this section.

(2) For the purpose of facilitating the carrying out by authorities in the overseas country of any function relating to anything corresponding to, or in the nature of, a social security benefit, the Secretary of State may make any such disclosure of relevant information to authorities in the overseas country as he considers necessary to give effect to the arrangements.

(3) It shall be the duty of the Secretary of State to take all such steps as may be reasonable for securing that relevant information disclosed to him in accordance with the arrangements is not used for any purpose for which its use is not expressly or impliedly authorised by or under the arrangements.

(4) This section does not apply where provision is in force under section 179 above for giving effect to the arrangements in question.

(5) The purposes for which information may be required to be disclosed to the Secretary of State under section 122D above or section 116D of the Northern Ireland Administration Act (information required from authorities administering housing benefit or council tax benefit) shall be deemed to include the further disclosure of that information in accordance withthis section.

(6) In this section "relevant information" means any information held by the Secretary of State or any authorities in a country outside the United Kingdom for the purposes of any functions relating to, or to anything corresponding to or in the nature of, a social security benefit.]

AMENDMENT

1. Inserted by the Social Security Fraud Act 2001 ss.1 and 5 (February 14, 2003).

PART XV

MISCELLANEOUS

180.–182B. *Omitted.* 1.253

National insurance numbers

[1 Requirement to apply for national insurance number

182C.—(1) Regulations may make provision requiring a person to apply for a national insurance number to be allocated to him. 1.254

[2(1A) Regulations under subsection (1) above may require the application to be made to the Secretary of State or to the Inland Revenue.]

(2) An application required by regulations under subsection (1) above shall be accompanied by information or evidence enabling such a number to be allocated.]

AMENDMENTS

1. Social Security Administration (Fraud) Act 1997 Sch.1 para.9 (July 1, 1997).

2. Social Security Contributions (Transfer of Functions, etc.) Act 1999 s.1(1) and Sch.1 para.31 (April 1, 1999).

GENERAL NOTE

See subss.(1A)–(1C) of s.1, inserted by s.19 of the Social Security Administration (Fraud) Act, which make having, or applying for, a national insurance number a condition of entitlement to benefit in most cases. 1.255

183. *Omitted.* 1.256

Control of pneumoconiosis

184. As respects pneumoconiosis, regulations may provide— 1.257

(a) for requiring persons to be medically examined before, or within a prescribed period after, becoming employed in any occupation in relation to which pneumoconiosis is prescribed, and to be medically examined periodically while so employed, and to furnish information required for the purposes of any such examination;

(b) for suspending from employment in any such occupation, and in such other occupations as may be prescribed, persons found on such an examination—
 (i) to be suffering from pneumoconiosis or tuberculosis, or
 (ii) o be unsuitable for such employment, having regard to the risk of pneumoconiosis and such other matters affecting their susceptibility to pneumoconiosis as may be prescribed;

(c) for the disqualification for the receipt [1 personal independence payment, or benefit as defined in section 122 of the Contributions and Benefits Act,] in respect of pneumoconiosis of any person who fails without good cause to submit himself to any such examination or to furnish information required by the regulations or who engages in any employment from which he has been suspended as mentioned in paragraph (b) above;

(d) for requiring employers—
 (i) to provide facilities for such examinations,
 (ii) not to employ in any occupation a person who has been suspended as mentioned in paragraph (b) above from employment in that occupation or who has failed without good cause to submit himself to such an examination,
 (iii) to give to such officer as may be prescribed the prescribed notice of the commencement of any prescribed industry or process;

(e) for the recovery on summary conviction of monetary penalties in respect of any contravention of or failure to comply with any such requirement as is mentioned in paragraph (d) above, so, however, that such penalties shall not exceed £5.00 for every day on which the contravention or failure occurs or continues;

(f) for such matters as appear to the Secretary of State to be incidental to or consequential on provisions included in the regulations by virtue of paragraphs (a) to (d) above or section 110(1) of the Contributions and Benefits Act.

AMENDMENT

1. Welfare Reform Act 2012 Sch.9 para.30 (April 8, 2013).

1.258 **185.** *Omitted.*

Supplementary benefit etc.

1.259 **186.** *Omitted.*

Miscellaneous

Certain benefit to be inalienable

1.260 **187.**—(1) Subject to the provisions of this Act, every assignment of or charge on—
[5 (za) universal credit;]
[6 (zb) state pension under Part 1 of the Pensions Act 2014;]

(a) benefit as defined in section 122 of the Contributions and Benefits Act;
[1(aa) a jobseeker's allowance;]
[2(ab) state pension credit;]
[3(ac) an employment and support allowance;]
[4(ad) personal independence payment]
[7 (ae) bereavement support payment under section 30 of the Pensions Act 2014;]
(b) any income-related benefit; or
(c) child benefit,

and every agreement to assign or charge such benefit shall be void; and, on the bankruptcy of a beneficiary, such benefit shall not pass to any trustee or other person acting on behalf of his creditors.

(2) In the application of subsection (1) above to Scotland—

(a) the reference to assignment of benefit shall be read as a reference to assignation, "assign" being construed accordingly;
(b) the reference to a beneficiary's bankruptcy shall be read as a reference to the sequestration of his estate or the appointment on his estate of a judicial factor under section 41 of the Solicitors (Scotland) Act 1980.

(3) In calculating for the purposes of section 5 of the Debtors Act 1869 or section 4 of the Civil Imprisonment (Scotland) Act 1882 the means of any beneficiary, no account shall be taken of any increase of disablement benefit in respect of a child or of industrial death benefit.

AMENDMENTS

1. Jobseekers Act 1995 Sch.2 para.72 (October 7, 1996).
2. State Pension Credit Act 2002 s.14 and Sch.2 (July 2, 2002 for the purposes of making regulations only; fully in force October 6, 2003).
3. Welfare Reform Act 2007 s.28 and Sch.3 para.10 (October 27, 2008).
4. Welfare Reform Act 2012 Sch.9 para.31 (April 8, 2013).
5. The Welfare Reform Act 2012 (Commencement No. 9 and Transitional and Transitory Provisions and Commencement No. 8 and Savings and Transitional Provisions (Amendment)) Order 2013 (SI 2013/983) art.3(1)(b) (April 29, 2013).
6. Pensions Act 2014, s.56(4), s.23 and Sch.12, para.26 (April 6, 2016).
7. Pensions Act 2014 s.31 and Sch.16 para.34 (April 6, 2017).

DERIVATIONS

Social Security Act 1975 s.87. **1.261**
"the Contributions and Benefits Act"—see s.191.
"income-related benefit"—*ibid.*

GENERAL NOTE

The House of Lords in *Mulvey v Secretary of State for Social Security*, *The Times*, March 20, 1997 dealt with the part of s.187(1) providing that, on bankruptcy or sequestration of a beneficiary, benefit does not pass to the trustee in bankruptcy. It held that the purpose was "to make clear beyond peradventure that the permanent trustee [the Scottish equivalent of the trustee in bankruptcy] could have no interest in any entitlement of a debtor to receive any of the social security benefits to which it applied" (Lord Jauncey). The Secretary of State's obligation to make payment of benefit is owed to the beneficiary and cannot be owed to the trustee in bankruptcy or permanent trustee. See the notes to s.78(2) for the situation where deductions are being made from benefit for the repayment of social fund loans or the recovery of overpayments. **1.262**

10. Welfare Reform Act 2009 s.2(4) (November 12, 2009).
11. Welfare Reform Act 2012 s.104(1) (February 25, 2013).
12. Welfare Reform Act 2012 s.147 and Sch.14 Pt 1; and SI 2013/358 art.8(c) (April 1, 2013).

GENERAL NOTE

1.265 In accordance with s.2(1) of the Tax Credits Act 1999, this section is to be read, in relation to tax credit, as if references to the Secretary of State were references to the Treasury or, as the case may be, the Board.

DERIVATIONS

1.266 SSA 1975 ss.113, 133, 166 and 168 as amended.

Parliamentary control of orders and regulations.

1.267 **190.**—(1) Subject to the provisions of this section, a statutory instrument containing (whether alone or with other provisions)—

[11 (zza) an order under section 115A(3B);]

[12 (zzb) regulations under section 115C(2) or 115D(1) or (2);]

[13 (za) regulations under section 132A(4);]

(a) an order under [10 section 141, 143, 145, 150, 150A, [14 151A,] or 162(7)] above; or

[7(aza) any order containing provision adding any person to the list of persons falling within section 109B(2A) above; or]

[8(aa) the first regulations to be made under section 2A;]

[9 (ab) the first regulations to be made under section 2AA;]

(b) regulations under [3section 154] above,

shall not be made unless a draft of the instrument has been laid before Parliament and been approved by a resolution of each House of Parliament.

(2) Subsection (1) above does not apply to a statutory instrument by reason only that it contains regulations under section 154 above which are to be made for the purpose of consolidating regulations to be revoked in the instrument.

(3) A statutory instrument—

(a) which contains (whether alone or with other provisions) orders or regulations made under this Act by the Secretary of State [5, the Treasury or the Inland Revenue]; and

(b) which is not subject to any requirement that a draft of the instrument be laid before and approved by a resolution of each House of Parliament,

shall be subject to annulment in pursuance of a resolution of either House of Parliament.

(4) [1 . . .]

AMENDMENTS

1. Social Security Act 1998 Sch.7 (November 29, 1998).
2. Social Security Act 1998 Sch.7 (April 6, 1999).
3. Social Security (Recovery of Benefits) Act 1997 Sch.3 (October 6, 1997).
4. Social Security Administration (Fraud) Act 1997 Sch.1 (July 1, 1997).
5. Transfer of Functions Act 1999 Sch.3 (April 1, 1999).
6. Welfare Reform and Pensions Act 1999 Sch.13 (April 6, 2000).
7. Social Security Fraud Act 2001 s.20 (February 26, 2002).
8. Welfare Reform and Pensions Act 1999 Sch.12 paras 79 and 83 (November 11, 1999).

9. Employment Act 2002 s.53 and Sch.7 (July 5, 2003).
10. Pensions Act 2007 Sch.1(5) para.30 (July 26, 2007: insertion has effect as specified in 2007 c.22 s.5(3) and (7)).
11. Welfare Reform Act 2012 s.114(2) (May 8, 2012).
12. Welfare Reform Act 2012 s.116(2) (May 10, 2012).
13. National Insurance Contributions Act 2006 s.7(3) (March 30, 2006).
14. Pensions Act 2014 s.56(4), s.23 and Sch.12, para.27 (April 6, 2016).

General Note

In accordance with s.2(1) of the Tax Credits Act 1999, this section is to be read, in relation to tax credit, as if references to the Secretary of State were references to the Treasury or, as the case may be, the Board. **1.268**

Derivation

SSA 1975 s.167 as amended and CBA 1975 s.22. **1.269**

Supplementary

Interpretation—general

191. In this Act, unless the context otherwise requires— **1.270**

"the 1975 Act" means the Social Security Act 1975;

"the 1986 Act" means the Social Security Act 1986;

"benefit" means benefit under the Contributions and Benefits Act [1 and includes [26 universal credit,] [29 state pension under Part 1 of the Pensions Act 2014,] a jobseeker's allowance] [19 . . .] , [27 state pension credit, an employment and support allowance [32, personal independence payment and bereavement support payment under section 30 of the Pensions Act 2014]];

[9 "billing authority" has the same meaning as in Part 1 of the Local Government Finance Act 1992;]

"Christmas bonus" means a payment under Part X of the Contributions and Benefits Act;

"claim" is to be construed in accordance with"claimant";

"claimant" (in relation to contributions under Part I and to benefit under Parts II to IV of the Contributions and Benefits Act) means—

(a) a person whose right to be excepted from liability to pay, or to have his liability deferred for, or to be credited with, a contribution, is in question;

(b) a person who has claimed benefit;

and includes, in relation to an award or decision a beneficiary under the award or affected by the decision;

"claimant" (in relation to industrial injuries benefit) means a person who has claimed such a benefit and includes—

(a) an applicant for a declaration under [3 section 29 of the Social Security Act 1998] that an accident was or was not an industrial accident; and

(b) in relation to an award or decision, a beneficiary under the award or affected by the decision;

[. . .]

[. . .4]

"the Consequential Provisions Act" means the Social Security (Consequential Provisions) Act 1992;

[5"contribution" means a contribution under Part I of the Contributions and Benefit Act;]

[6"contribution-based jobseeker's allowance" has the same meaning as in the Jobseekers Act 1995;]

"contributions card" has the meaning assigned to it by section 114(6) above;

"the Contributions and Benefits Act" means the Social Security Contributions and Benefits Act 1992;

[21 "contributory employment and support allowance" means a contributory allowance under Part 1 of the Welfare Reform Act 2007 (employment and support allowance);]

[28 . . .]

"disablement benefit" is to be construed in accordance with section 94(2)(a) of the Contributions and Benefits Act;

"the disablement questions" is to be construed in accordance with section 45 above;

"dwelling" means any residential accommodation, whether or not consisting of the whole or part of a building and whether or not comprising separate and self-contained premises;

[9"financial year" has the same meaning as in the Local Government Finance Act 1992;]

"5 year general qualification" is to be construed in accordance with section 71 of the Courts and Legal Services Act 1990;

"housing authority" means a local authority, a new town corporation

"house benefit scheme" is to be construed in accordance with section 134(1) above;

[1"income-based jobseeker's allowance" has the same meaning as in the Jobseekers Act 1995;]

"income-related benefit" means—

(a) income support;

(b) [8 working families tax credit]

(c) [8 disabled person's tax credit]

(d) housing benefit; and

[2(e) council tax benefit];

[21 "income-related employment and support allowance" means an income-related allowance under Part 1 of the Welfare Reform Act 2007 (employment and support allowance);]

"industrial injuries benefit" means benefit under Part V of the Contributions and Benefits Act, other than under Schedule 8;

[10"Inland Revenue" means the Commissioners of Inland Revenue]

. . .10;

. . .11;

"local authority" means—

(a) in relation to England . . .12, the council of a district or London borough, the Common Council of the City of London or the Council of the Isles of Scilly;

[11(aa) in relation to Wales, the council of a county or county borough;] and

(b) in relation to Scotland [12a council constituted under section 2 of the Local Government etc. (Scotland) Act 1994];

"medical examination" includes bacteriological and radiographical tests and similar investigations, and "medically examined" has a corresponding meaning;

"medical practitioner" means—

(a) a registered medical practitioner; or

(b) a person outside the United Kingdom who is not a registered medical practitioner, but has qualifications corresponding (in the Secretary of State's opinion) to those of a registered medical practitioner;

"medical treatment" means medical, surgical or rehabilitative treatment (including any course of diet or other regimen), and references to a person receiving or submitting himself to medical treatment are to be construed accordingly;

[[24] "money purchase contracted-out scheme" is to be construed in accordance with [[30] section 7B] of the Pensions Act"]

"new town corporation" means—

[[22] (a) in relation to England—

(i) a development corporation established under the New Towns Act 1981; or

(ii) the Homes and Communities Agency so far as exercising functions in relation to anything transferred (or to be transferred) to it as mentioned in section 52(1)(A) to (d) of the Housing and Regeneration Act 2008;

[[25] (iii) the Greater London Authority so far as exercising its new towns and urban development functions;]

(ab) in relation to Wales—

(i) a development corporation established under the New Towns Act 1981; and

(ii) the Welsh Ministers so far as exercising functions in relation to anything transferred (or to be transferred) to them as mentioned in section 36(1)(A)(i) to (iii) of that Act; and]

(b) in relation to Scotland, a development corporation established under the New Towns (Scotland) Act 1968;]

[[20] "the Northern Ireland Department" means the Department for Social Development but—

(a) in section 122 and sections 122B to 122E also includes the Department of Finance and Personnel; and

(b) in sections 121E, 121F, 122, 122ZA, 122C and 122D also includes the Department for Employment and Learning;]

"the Northern Ireland Administration Act" means the Social Security (Northern Ireland) Administration Act 1992;

"occupational pension scheme" has the same meaning as in [[15]section 1] of the Pensions Act;

"the Old Cases Act" means the Industrial Injuries and Diseases (Old Cases) Act 1975;

"Old Cases payments" means payments under Part I of Schedule 8 to the Contributions and Benefits Act;

[[17]"pensionable age" has the meaning given by the rules in paragraph 1 of Schedule 4 to the Pensions Act 1995];

"the Pensions Act" means the [[15]Pension Schemes Act 1993];

"personal pension scheme" has the meaning assigned to it by [[15]section 1 of the Pensions Act] [[15]and "appropriate", in relation to such a scheme, shall be construed in accordance with [[30] section 7B(6)], of that Act] "prescribe" means prescribe by regulations; [23 and "prescribed" must be construed accordingly;]

"President" means the President of social security appeal tribunals; disability appeal tribunals and medical appeal tribunals;

"rent rebate", [. . .18] and "rent allowance" shall be construed in accordance with section 134 above;

[. . .18]

[19 "state pension credit" means state pension credit under the State Pension Credit Act 2002;]

"tax year" means the 12 months beginning with 6th April in any year;

"10 year general qualification" is to be construed in accordance with section 71 of the Courts and Legal Services Act 1990; and

[31 "universal credit assessment period" means an assessment period for the purposes of Part 1 of the Welfare Reform Act 2012;]

"widows benefit" has the meaning assigned to it by section 20(1)(e) of the Contributions and Benefits Act.

AMENDMENTS

1. Jobseekers Act 1995 Sch.2 (April 22, 1996).
2. Local Government Finance Act 1992 Sch.9 (March 6, 1992).
3. Social Security Act 1998 Sch.7 (July 7, 1999).
4. Social Security (Recovery of Benefits) Act 1997 Sch.3 (October 6, 1997).
5. Social Security Administration (Fraud) Act 1997 Sch.1 (July 1, 1997).
6. Jobseekers Act 1995 Sch.2 (April 22, 1996).
7. Housing Benefit Act 1996 Sch.13 (April 1, 1997).
8. Tax Credits Act 1999 Sch.1 (October 5, 1999).
9. Local Government Finance Act 1992 Sch.9 (March 6, 1992).
10. Transfer of Functions Act 1999 Sch.1 (April 1, 1999).
11. Social Security (Incapacity for Work) Act 1994 Sch.1 (April 13, 1995).
12. Local Government etc. (Scotland) Act 1994 Sch.14 (April 1, 1996).
13. Local Government (Wales) Act 1994 Sch.16 (April 1, 1996).
14. Local Government etc. (Scotland) Act 1994 Sch.13 (April 1, 1996).
15. Pension Schemes Act 1993 Sch.8 (February 7, 1994).
16. Social Security Administration (Fraud) Act Sch.1 (July 1, 1997).
17. Pensions Act 1995 Sch.4 (July 19, 1995).
18. Housing Act 1996 Sch.13 (April 1, 1997).
19. State Pension Credit Act 2002 s.14 and Sch.2 (July 2, 2002 for the purpose of making regulations only; fully in force October 6, 2003).
20. Employment Act 2002 s.53 and Sch.7 (September 9, 2002).
21. Welfare Reform Act 2007 s.28 and Sch.3, para.10 (October 27, 2008).
22. Housing and Regeneration Act 2008 Sch.8 para.61 (December 1, 2008).
23. Welfare Reform Act 2007 Sch.5 para.10 (July 3, 2007).
24. The Pensions Act 2007, (Abolition of Contracting-out for Defined Contribution Pensions Schemes) (Consequential Amendments) (No. 2) Regulations 2011 (SI 2011/1724) reg.2 (April 6, 2012).
25. Localism Act 2011 Sch.19 para.31 (April 1, 2012).
26. Welfare Reform Act 2012 s.31 and Sch.2 para.31 (February 25, 2013).
27. Welfare Reform Act 2012 s.91 and Sch.9 para.32 (February 25, 2013).
28. Welfare Reform Act 2012 s.147 and Sch.14 Pt 1; and SI 2013/358 art.8(c) (April 1, 2013).
29. Pensions Act 2014, s.56(4), s.23 and Sch.12, para.28 (April 6, 2016).
30. Pensions Act 2014, s.56(4), s.23 and Sch.13, para.57 (April 6, 2016).
31. The Universal Credit and Miscellaneous Amendments (No.2) Regulations 2014 (SI 2014/2888) reg.7(1)(c) (November 26, 2014).
32. Pensions Act 2014 s.31 and Sch.16 para.35 (April 6, 2017).

DERIVATIONS

SSA 1975 s.168 and Sch.20. 1.271
Short title, commencement and extent.

192.—(1) This Act may be cited as the Social Security Administration Act 1992. 1.272

(2) This Act is to be read, where appropriate, with the Contributions and Benefits Act and the Consequential Provisions Act.

(3) The enactments consolidated by this Act are repealed, in consequence of the consolidation, by the Consequential Provisions Act.

(4) Except as provided in Schedule 4 to the Consequential Provisions Act, this Act shall come into force on 1st July 1992.

(5) The following provisions extend to Northern Ireland—

[. . .[1]];

[[2]]

section 170 (with Schedule 5);

[[3] section 171(with schedule 6);]

[section 177 (with Schedule 8);

and this section.

(6) Except as provided by this section, this Act does not extend to Northern Ireland.

AMENDMENTS

1. Social Security Act 1998 Sch.7 (October 5, 1999).
2. Social Security (Recovery of Benefits) Act 1997 Sch.3 (October 6, 1997).
3. Northern Ireland Act 1998 Pt VIII s.89(9) (December 2, 1999).

SCHEDULES

SCHEDULE 1

CLAIMS FOR BENEFIT MADE OR TREATED AS MADE BEFORE 1ST OCTOBER 1990 1.273

Claims made or treated as made on or after 2nd September 1985 and before 1st October 1986

1. Section 1 above shall have effect in relation to a claim made or treated as made on or after 2nd September 1985 and before 1st October 1986 as if the following subsections were substituted for subsections (1) to (3)—

"(1) Except in such cases as may be prescribed, no person shall be entitled to any benefit unless, in addition to any other conditions relating to that benefit being satisfied—

(a) he makes a claim for it—
 (i) in the prescribed manner; and
 (ii) subject to subsection (2) below, within the prescribed time; or
(b) by virtue of a provision of Chapter VI of Part II of the 1975 Act or of regulations made under such a provision he would have been treated as making a claim for it."

"(2) Regulations shall provide for extending, subject to any prescribed conditions, the time within which a claim may be made in cases where it is not made within the prescribed time but good cause is shown for the delay.

(3) Notwithstanding any regulations made under this section, no person shall be entitled to any benefit (except disablement benefit or industrial death benefit) in respect of any period more than 12 months before the date on which the claim is made."

Claims made or treated as made on or after 1st October 1986 and before 6th April 1987

2. Section 1 above shall have effect in relation to a claim made or treated as made on or after 1986 and before 6th April 1987 as if the subsections set out in paragraph 1 above were substituted for subsections (1) to (3) but with the insertion in subsection (3) of the words "reduced earnings allowance" after the words "disablement benefit".

Pension Scheme or, from 2002, the new "second state pension" scheme. However, until April 15, 2016, employees were able to "contract out" of the liability to make contributions for an additional pension provided they were making contributions to an approved occupational or personal pension scheme. The Pensions Schemes Act 1993, provides for guaranteed minimum pensions from contracted-out occupational pension schemes. See Vol.1 of this work for both Acts.

Over a working life, a person may have contributed both to an additional pension under one or both of the state schemes and to one or more occupational or personal pension schemes. Where a guaranteed minimum pension is payable under an occupational scheme to a person entitled to an additional pension under the State Earnings-Related Pension Scheme, overlap is avoided by s.46 of the 1993 Act which provides for an adjustment to the Category A retirement pension. This involves the determination of a number of questions, some of which are to be determined by the Secretary of State and some of which are allocated to the Her Majesty's Revenue and Customs (to whom the functions of the Commissioners for Inland Revenue have been transferred by the Commissioners for Revenue and Customs Act 2005 s.5(2)) by this section. In *R(P) 1/04*, the Commissioner held that it was for the Secretary of State to determine entitlement to a Category A retirement pension and to identify the occupational pension schemes relevant to that entitlement, for the Inland Revenue to determine entitlement to a guaranteed minimum pension in respect of each occupational pension scheme and for the Secretary of State to aggregate the guaranteed minimum pensions and decide on the amount of any reduction of the Category A retirement pension under s.46 of the 1993 Act.

Section 170(6) and (7) provides for appeals against decisions of Her Majesty's Revenue and Customs relating to guaranteed minimum pensions to be heard by the First-tier Tribunal as though it were a social security case rather than a tax case. However, it was pointed out in *R(P) 1/04* that there can be no appeal until a formal decision is issued and that the Inland Revenue did not always issue a formal decision unless a calculation was disputed. In those circumstances, as any dispute was likely to be raised first in a challenge to the final decision issued by the Secretary of State, it was suggested that it might be necessary for the Secretary of State or an appeal tribunal to refer a question to the Inland Revenue for formal determination even though regs 11A and 38A of the Social Security and Child Support (Decisions and Appeals) Regulations 1999 did not strictly apply.

Perhaps surprisingly, an appeal against a refusal to issue a contracting-out certificate is one type of case that falls, by virtue of this section, to be treated as a social security case. However, where a question arises as to whether a particular claimant was in contracted-in or contracted-out employment for the purpose of ascertaining his entitlement to a pension, it arises as part of a question as to his liability to pay contributions or as to what contributions have been paid and so is a question falling within the jurisdiction of the tax authorities by virtue of s.8(1)(c) or (e) of the Social Security Contributions (Transfer of Functions, etc.) Act 1999 (*CP/3833/2003*).

Employment Tribunals Act 1996

(1996 c.17)

ARRANGEMENT OF SECTIONS

An Act to consolidate enactments relating to industrial tribunals and the Employment Appeal Tribunal.

[22nd May 1996]

General Note

This Act started life as the Industrial Tribunals Act 1996 but was given its new short title by s.1(2) of the Employment Rights (Dispute Resolution) Act 1998, which also renamed the tribunals themselves, with effect from August 1, 1998. 1.279

Power to provide for recoupment of benefits

16.—(1) This section applies to payments which are the subject of proceedings before [1 employment tribunals] and which are— 1.280

(a) payments of wages or compensation for loss of wages,
(b) payments by employers to employees under sections 146 to 151, sections 168 to 173 or section 192 of the Trade Union and Labour Relations (Consolidation) Act 1992,
(c) payments by employers to employees under —
(i) Part III, V, VI or VII,
(ii) section 93, or
(iii) Part X,
of the Employment Rights Act 1996, or
(d) payments by employers to employees of a nature similar to, or for a purpose corresponding to the purpose of, payments within paragraph (b) or (c),

and to payments of remuneration under a protective award under section 189 of the Trade Union and Labour Relations (Consolidation) Act 1992.

(2) The Secretary of State may by regulations make with respect to payments to which this section applies provision for any or all of the purposes specified in subsection (3).

(3) The purposes referred to in subsection (2) are—

(a) enabling the Secretary of State to recover from an employer, by way of total or partial recoupment of jobseeker's allowance [3 , income support or income-related employment and support allowance]—
(i) a sum not exceeding the amount of the prescribed element of the monetary award, or
(ii) in the case of a protective award, the amount of the remuneration,
(b) requiring or authorising an [1employment tribunal] to order the payment of such a sum, by way of total or partial recoupment of [3 jobseeker's allowance, income support or income-related employment and support allowance], to the Secretary of State instead of to an employee, and
(c) requiring an [1employment tribunal] to order the payment to an employee of only the excess of the prescribed element of the monetary award over the amount of any [5 universal credit,] jobseeker's allowance [3 , income support or income-related employment and support allowance] shown to the tribunal to have been paid to the employee and enabling the Secretary of State to recover from the employer, by way of total or partial recoupment of the benefit, a sum not exceeding that amount.

(4) Regulations under this section may be framed—

(a) so as to apply to all payments to which this section applies or to one or more classes of those payments, and

[3 (b) so as to apply to all or any of the benefits mentioned in subsection (3).]

(5) Regulations under this section may—

(a) confer powers and impose duties on [1 employment tribunals] or [2 . . .] other persons,

(b) impose on an employer to whom a monetary award or protective award relates a duty—

(i) to furnish particulars connected with the award, and

(ii) to suspend payments in pursuance of the award during any period prescribed by the regulations,

(c) provide for an employer who pays a sum to the Secretary of State in pursuance of this section to be relieved from any liability to pay the sum to another person,

[2(cc) provide for the determination by the Secretary of State of any issue arising as to the total or partial recoupment in pursuance of the regulations of a jobseeker's allowance, unemployment benefit [5 universal credit,] a jobseeker's allowance, unemployment benefit [3 , income support or income-related employment and support allowance],

(d) confer on an employee a right of appeal to [4the First-tier Tribunal] against any decision of the Secretary of State on any such issue, and]

(e) provide for the proof in proceedings before [1 employment tribunals] (whether by certificate or in any other manner) of any amount of [5 universal credit,] jobseeker's allowance [3 , income support or income-related employment and support allowance] paid to an employee.

(6) Regulations under this section may make different provision for different cases.

AMENDMENTS

1. Employment Rights (Dispute Resolution) Act 1998 s.1(2) (August 1, 1998).
2. Social Security Act 1998 Sch.7 para.147 (October 18, 1999).
3. Welfare Reform Act 2007 s.28(1) and Sch.3 para.15(1) and (2) (October 27, 2008).
4. Transfer of Tribunal Functions Order 2008 (SI 2008/2833) Sch.3 para.137 (November 3, 2008).
5. Universal Credit (Consequential, Supplementary, Incidental and Miscellaneous Provisions) Regulations 2013 (SI 2013/630) reg.11(1) to (3) (April 29, 2013).

DEFINITIONS

"income-based jobseeker's allowance"—see s.17(4).
"income-related employment and support allowance"—see s.17(5).
"monetary award"—see s.17(3).
"the prescribed element"—*ibid.*

GENERAL NOTE

1.281 See the Employment Protection (Recoupment of Benifits) Regulations 1996.

Recoupment: further provisions

17.—(1) Where in pursuance of any regulations under section 16 a sum has been recovered by or paid to the Secretary of State by way of total or partial recoupment of [2 universal credit,] jobseeker's allowance [1 , income support or income-related employment and support allowance]— 1.282

(a) no sum shall be recoverable under Part III or V of the Social Security Administration Act 1992, and

(b) no abatement, payment or reduction shall be made by reference to the [2 universal credit,] jobseeker's allowance [1 , income support or income-related employment and support allowance] recouped.

(2) Any amount found to have been duly recovered by or paid to the Secretary of State in pursuance of regulations under section 16 by way of total or partial recoupment of jobseeker's allowance shall be paid into the National Insurance Fund.

(3) In section 16—

"monetary award" means the amount which is awarded, or ordered to be paid, to the employee by the tribunal or would be so awarded or ordered apart from any provision of regulations under that section, and

"the prescribed element", in relation to any monetary award, means so much of that award as is attributable to such matters as may be prescribed by regulations under that section.

(4) In section 16 "income-based jobseeker's allowance" has the same meaning as in the Jobseekers Act 1995.

[1 (5) In this section and section 16 "income-related employment and support allowance" means an income-related allowance under Part 1 of the Welfare Reform Act 2007 (employment and support allowance).]

AMENDMENTS

1. Welfare Reform Act 2007 s.28(1) and Sch.3 para.15(1), (3) and (4) (October 27, 2008).

2. Universal Credit (Consequential, Supplementary, Incidental and Miscellaneous Provisions) Regulations 2013 (SI 2013/630) reg.11(1) and (4) (April 29, 2013).

Social Security (Recovery of Benefits) Act 1997

(1997 c.27)

ARRANGEMENT OF SECTIONS

Introductory

Certificates of recoverable benefits

SCHEDULES:

Schedule 1—Compensation payments.
  Part I—Exempted payments.
  Part II—Power to disregard small payments.
Schedule 2—Calculation of compensation payment.
Schedule 3—*Omitted.*
Schedule 4—*Omitted.*

An Act to re-state, with amendments, Part IV of the Social Security Administration Act 1992.

[19th March 1997]

GENERAL NOTE

This Act provides for the recovery by the Secretary of State from those liable to pay compensation for an injury or disease (or from schemes making equivalent payments where the person who would otherwise be liable to pay compensation was uninsured) of an amount equal to the amount of social security benefits he has paid to the victims. As the long title says, the Act is to "re-state, with amendments," Pt IV of the Social Security Act 1992, which was a true consolidation measure and re-enacted s.22 of, and Sch.4 to, the Social Security Act 1989 which first introduced a scheme like this for recovering benefits. This Act is not a consolidation measure because, while a number of the provisions are the same as under the old schemes, the amendments make some fundamental changes. **1.284**

The Compensation Recovery Unit of the Department for Work and Pensions is at Durham House, Washington, Tyne and Wear NE38 7SF. It administers this legislation and similar legislation, outside the scope of this book, relating to the recovery of certain costs to the health service. A fairly detailed guide to its procedures is obtainable from its webpage: *https://www.gov.uk/government/collections/cru.*

A person making a compensation payment in consequence of an accident injury or disease (whether voluntarily or pursuant to a court order or agreement or otherwise—see s.1(3)—unless the payment is exempt—see s.1(2) and Sch.1) *must* apply under s.4 to the Compensation Recovery Unit for a "certificate of recoverable benefits" *before* making the payment. Under s.5, that certificate should specify the amount of relevant benefits (listed in col.2 of Sch.2) paid, or expected to be paid within the "relevant period" (which will end when the compensation payment is made if the maximum period of five years has not already elapsed—see s.3), *in respect of* the accident, injury or disease (see the definition of "recoverable benefit" in s.1(4)(c) which refers back to s.1(1)(b)). The compensator must then pay to the Secretary of State a sum equal to the total amount of those recoverable benefits (s.6) and pay to the victim the compensation payment. Certain parts of the compensation payment may be reduced to reflect the benefits received by the victim during the "relevant period" (s.8), but benefits paid after that period must be ignored in the assessment of damages (s.17).

Sections 10–14 provide for reviews of, and appeals against, certificates of recoverable benefits.

Introductory

Cases in which this Act applies

1.—(1) This Act applies in cases where— **1.285**

(a) a person makes a payment (whether on his own behalf or not) to or in respect of any other person in consequence of any accident, injury or disease suffered by the other, and

(b) any listed benefits have been, or are likely to be, paid to or for the other during the relevant period in respect of the accident, injury or disease.

(2) The reference above to a payment in consequence of any accident, injury or disease is to a payment made—

(a) by or on behalf of a person who is, or is alleged to be, liable to any extent in respect of the accident, injury or disease, [1. . .]

(b) in pursuance of a compensation scheme for motor accidents[1 , or

(c) under the Diffuse Mesothelioma Payment Scheme (established under the Mesothelioma Act 2014);]

but does not include a payment mentioned in Part I of Schedule 1.

(3) Subsection (1)(a) applies to a payment made—

(a) voluntarily, or in pursuance of a court order or an agreement, or otherwise, and

(b) in the United Kingdom or elsewhere.

(4) In a case where this Act applies—

(a) the "injured person" is the person who suffered the accident, injury or disease,

(b) the "compensation payment" is the payment within subsection (1)(a), and

(c) "recoverable benefit" is listed benefit which has been or is likely to be paid as mentioned in the subsection (1)(b).

AMENDMENT

1. Mesothelioma Act 2014 s.11 and Sch.1 paras. 1 and 2 (March 31, 2014).

DEFINITIONS

"compensation scheme for motor accidents"—see s.29.
"listed benefit"—*ibid.*
"payment"—*ibid.*
"the relevant period"—see s.3.

GENERAL NOTE

1.286 The principle behind this legislation is that, where a person is liable under the law to compensate a victim of any accident, injury or disease, that person should also compensate the Secretary of State for the social security benefits paid to the victim in respect of that accident, injury or disease during the "relevant period" as defined in s.3. In practice, the scheme is operated with the co-operation of insurance companies and subs.(2) provides that relevant payments include those made through certain schemes set up to ensure payments are made to victims where the person liable was not insured. The key questions are therefore those posed by subs.(1): whether the payment is made "in consequence of any accident, injury or disease" and whether benefits have been paid "in respect of" that particular accident, injury or disease.

In *Rand v East Dorset Health Authority* [2001] P.I.Q.R. Q1, this Act was held not to apply where parents of a child were awarded damages in respect of the defendants' negligence in failing to inform them before the child's birth that the child would be suffering from Down's Syndrome. It had been claimed that the child would have been aborted had the parents received the information and the damages had been awarded purely for economic loss resulting from negligent mis-statement and so were not awarded "in consequence of any accident, injury or disease suffered by the [parents]". That decision was distinguished in *R(CR) 4/03*, which was also a case of medical negligence. There, a doctor was alleged to have failed to recognise symptoms of diabetes in a woman in an advanced stage of pregnancy. It was claimed that, had the symptoms been detected, the condition would have been confirmed and an emergency Caesarean section could have been performed with a high chance of the child being born alive. As it was, the child died in utero and labour had to be induced and the mother suffered a major depressive episode. Compensation was claimed not only under the Fatal Accidents Act 1976 (which compensation is exempt under reg.2 of the Social Security (Recovery of Benefits) Regulations 1997) but also for the mother's psychiatric injury. The case was settled. The Commissioner held that compensation was paid in consequence of an accident, injury or disease suffered by the mother. The Commissioner also commented that the phrase "accident, injury or disease" was an "odd one" because it was not clear how benefits might be paid in respect of an accident if there was neither injury nor disease. He suggested that there might be little difference between an "accident" and an "injury" in this context.

The crucial question in most cases arising under this Act is whether listed benefits have been paid "in respect of" the accident, injury or disease within the meaning that phrase has in subs.(1)(b), so as to fall within the scope of the term "recoverable benefit" as defined in subs.(4)(c).

For a benefit to be paid "in respect of " an accident, injury or disease, the accident, injury or disease must be an effective cause of the payment of benefit and an accident may cease to be an effective cause of disablement if its effects have worn off and been replaced by the effects of a worsening pre-accident condition (*R(CR) 1/01*). In *R(CR) 3/03*, it was held that only benefits the payment of which was caused by the relevant disease were paid "in respect of" the disease and that ordinary principles of causation applied, having regard to the conditions of entitlement to each benefit. A relevant accident, injury or disease could therefore cease to be an effective cause of the payment of benefit even if its effects had not worn off. It was enough merely for it to be shown that the benefit would have been paid due to a pre-existing condition even if the relevant disease had not been developed. In that case, the claimant was paid compensation in respect of asbestos–induced disease but the evidence was that the claimant was suffering from other, longer-standing, conditions that contributed to his disablement and were getting worse. The Commissioner found the claimant would have become incapable of work from a certain date even if he had not suffered from the asbestos-induced disease and therefore that the asbestos-induced disease ceased to be a cause of the payment of benefits paid in respect of incapacity from that date, although it had accelerated the onset of incapacity. In relation to disability living allowance, he found that the asbestos-related disease had been a contributory factor in the claimant's entitlement to the mobility component throughout that part of the "relevant period" for which it had been paid but that it had never been a contributory factor in the claimant's entitlement to the care component. Thus, part of the incapacity benefits listed in the original certificate of recoverable benefits and all of the care component of disability living allowance were not recoverable but the rest of the incapacity benefits and all of the mobility component were recoverable.

Conversely, where the other cause of disablement arises *after* the relevant accident, benefit that would have been paid as a result of the relevant accident if the other cause had not arisen is attributable to the relevant accident, whereas benefit that would not have been paid but for the other cause of disablement is attributable to that other cause. In *R(CR) 2/04*, the claimant had returned to work for another employer after the relevant accident, even though he was still suffering from some minor disablement, and then suffered a second industrial accident, following which he was incapable of work again. The Commissioner found that the incapacity was initially attributable to the second accident because the claimant would have been able to continue working but for that accident. However, the effects of that accident then wore off and the effects of the relevant accident worsened and the Commissioner found that there came a time when the claimant would have been incapable of work 1.287

due to the relevant accident even if the second accident had not occurred so that the payment of benefits became attributable to the relevant accident again.

Where a claimant undergoes a medical operation as a result of an accident, injury or disease and the operation causes further disablement, benefits paid in consequence of that further disablement will have been paid "in respect of" the accident (*CCR/2046/2002*). The same applied where the claimant suffered a psychological reaction due to stress caused by a misdiagnosis due to the misreading of an X-ray that was required by the relevant accident, although it was suggested that the result might have been different if it had been proved that the misdiagnosis had been due to negligence (*CCR/4307/2000*).

Where there has been medical negligence, compensation may be paid in respect of any injury or disease caused by the negligence. In *CCR/1022/2006*, it was pointed out that it is important to distinguish between the effects of the accident, injury or disease that led to the claimant being admitted to hospital and the effects of the medical negligence that occurred while he was a patient there. "The question for the tribunal was whether, had there not been the delay in arranging the MRI scan and therefore a delay in surgery, the appellant would have qualified for disability living allowance at the rate at which it was awarded or at a lower rate. If the answer was 'yes', the benefit was to that extent not recoverable."

1.288 A similar approach was taken in *AW v SSWP (CR)* [2011] UKUT 223 (AAC), despite the parties not having drawn the judge's attention to any of the Commissioners' decision in this area and the Secretary of State having inappropriately relied upon *Hassall v Secretary of State for Social Security* [1995] 1 W.L.R. 812 (also reported as *R(CR) 1/95*) (see below). The claimant, who was already suffering from some disablement as a result of earlier injures sustained while he was in the army, suffered serious injuries in a motor cycle accident and during the course of treatment was infected with MRSA as a result of negligence by the hospital. That infection, rather than his injuries, required the amputation of his left leg. The Secretary of State sought to recover disability living allowance from compensation received by the claimant from the hospital and the claimant's appeal was dismissed by the First-tier Tribunal. The Upper Tribunal approved the First-tier Tribunal's approach to the case, in which it had considered that the issue was whether the claimant would have been entitled to disability living allowance if the amputation had not occurred, although it allowed the claimant's appeal on the ground that the First-tier Tribunal had not adequately considered the effects of the injuries sustained by the claimant while in the army.

However, where a claimant had accepted £50,000 in respect of a claim that injuries from a particular date were due solely to medical negligence, it was necessary to adopt a consistent approach and the claimant was not entitled to argue that the injuries he had suffered after that date were entirely due to the accident that had led him to be hospitalised rather than to the medical negligence (*CCR/2232/2006*).

The need for consistency between the approach taken by a party to court proceedings and the approach taken by the same party in proceedings under this Act is not confined to medical negligence cases and such consistency is expected from compensators as well as from claimants. In *R(CR) 1/07*, where a compensator settled a claim made on the basis that psychiatric injury was due to a particular cause, the compensator was not entitled to argue that the injury was due to a cause not covered by the claim and that the compensator was therefore not in fact liable in respect of the injury in consequence of which the compensation was paid. Attention was drawn to the word "alleged" in s.1(2)(a). Compensators must therefore pay careful attention to the certificate of recoverable benefits when deciding whether to compromise a case that could be defended. It is important to note that the principal issue in both *CCR/2232/2006* and *R(CR) 1/07* was whether the compensation had been paid in respect of a particular injury (in circumstances where it could not plausibly be claimed to have been paid in respect of some other injury or damage), rather than whether the benefits listed in the certificate of recoverable benefits were paid in respect of the injury. The issue therefore did not fall within the scope of the right of appeal conferred by s.11.

Benefits that ought not to have been paid at all—because they were paid under a mistake of fact or medical opinion or law, whether deliberately induced by the claimant or not—cannot be said to have been paid "in respect of " an accident, injury or disease (*R(CR) 1/02*, a decision of a Tribunal of Commissioners, and *Eagle Star Insurance v Department for Social Development*, a decision of the Court of Appeal in Northern Ireland reported as *R1/01(CRS)*). It follows that, if it is shown that benefit was paid at too high a rate, only that part of the benefit properly paid was paid "in respect of " the accident, injury or disease (*R(CR) 1/03*). See further the note to s.11. **1.289**

However, in *R1/05(CRS)*, it was held that benefits paid as a result of bureaucratic delay between the date of a medical examination and a consequent supersession decision do not necessarily cease to be recoverable.

There is no provision for reducing the amount of recoverable benefit because some other benefit would have been paid to the claimant if the relevant accident or injury had not occurred or the relevant disease had not been developed. Furthermore, income support is paid "in respect of " an accident if it is paid on the basis of the claimant being incapable of work due to the accident, even if the claimant would have been paid income support on some other basis if the accident had not happened (*Hassall v Secretary of State for Social Security* [1995] 1 W.L.R. 812 (also reported as *R(CR) 1/95*)). Where a claimant might be at risk of having compensation reduced under s.8 in respect of post-accident benefits paid in place of pre-accident benefits, he or she may need to include a claim for the loss of the pre-accident benefits in the claim for compensation (*ibid.*, and *Neal v Bingle* [1998] Q.B. 466), although this is less of a problem under this Act than it was under the legislation it replaced. In *R1/06 (CRS)*, the Commissioner followed *Hassall* when deciding that the whole of income support awarded during the relevant period on the grounds of incapacity caused by the accident was recoverable notwithstanding that part of it was attributable to dependants acquired by the claimant after the relevant accident. It would not have been necessary for benefit to be paid in respect of the dependants if the accident had not occurred. In *R(CR) 1/96*, the claimant was a hairdresser injured in a road accident. She was awarded income support on the basis of incapacity for work and later, after she became capable of light work, on the basis that she was available for work, although she was still unfit for work as a hairdresser. The Commissioner held that the income support paid on the basis of the claimant's availability for work was paid "otherwise than in consequence of the accident". It is suggested that this part of the decision is based on a misreading of *Hassall* and would probably not be followed by the Upper Tribunal if the issue were to arise again. *Hassall* was concerned with income support paid on the basis of availability for work *before* the accident but there seems no reason why such a benefit should not be recoverable when a claimant has lost employment as the result of an accident, particularly as jobseeker's allowance, which has replaced income support when a claimant is capable of, and available for, work is clearly listed in Sch.2. However, the issue may not arise for determination because, in practice, the Secretary of State seldom seeks recovery of jobseeker's allowance (see *R(CR) 2/04*, at para.19).

There may be a question as to whether benefit paid in consequence of a disease for a period before the beginning of the "relevant period" is recoverable (see the note to s.3).

[[1]Lump sum payments: regulation-making power

1A.—(1) The Secretary of State may by regulations make provision about the recovery of the amount of a payment to which subsection (2) applies (a "lump sum payment") where— **1.290**

(a) a compensation payment in consequence of a disease is made to or in respect of a person ("P") to whom, or in respect of whom, a lump sum payment has been, or is likely to be, made, and

(b) the compensation payment is made in consequence of the same disease as the lump sum payment.

(2) This subsection applies to—

(a) a payment made in accordance with the Pneumoconiosis etc. (Workers' Compensation) Act 1979 ("the 1979 Act"),

(b) a payment made in accordance with Part 4 of the Child Maintenance and Other Payments Act 2008, [2. . .]

(c) an extra-statutory payment (within the meaning given by subsection (5)(d) below)[2 , and

(d) a payment under the Diffuse Mesothelioma Payment Scheme (established under the Mesothelioma Act 2014),

(but this subsection does not apply to a payment within paragraph (d) in a case where the compensation payment is itself such a payment).]

(3) Regulations under this section may, in particular—

(a) make provision about the recovery of the amount of a lump sum payment made to or in respect of a dependant of P;

(b) make provision enabling the recovery of the amount of a lump sum payment from a compensation payment (including provision enabling the recovery of an amount which reduces the compensation payment to nil);

(c) enable the amount of a lump sum payment made before commencement to be recovered from a compensation payment made after commencement;

(d) make provision about certificates in respect of lump sum payments;

(e) apply any provision of this Act, with or without modifications.

(4) References in subsection (1) to a payment made in consequence of a disease—

(a) are references to a payment made [2 as specified in section 1(2)(a) or (c)] in respect of the disease, but

(b) do not include references to a payment mentioned in Part 1 of Schedule 1.

(5) In this section—

(a) "commencement" means the date on which this section comes into force,

(b) "compensation payment" means a payment within section 1(1)(a) above,

(c) "dependant" has the meaning given by section 3 of the 1979 Act, and

(d) "extra-statutory payment" means a payment made by the Secretary of State to or in respect of a person following the rejection by the Secretary of State of a claim under the 1979 Act.]

AMENDMENTS

1. Child Maintenance and Other Payments Act 2008 s.54 (June 10, 2008 for the purpose only of making regulations and October 1, 2008 for other purposes).

2. Mesothelioma Act 2014 s.11 and Sch.1 paras 1 and 17 (March 31, 2014).

DEFINITIONS

"commencement"—see subs.(5).

"compensation payment"—*ibid.*

"dependant"—*ibid.*
"extra-statutory payment"—*ibid.*
"lump sum payment"—see subs.(1).
"payment"—see s.29.
"regulations"—*ibid.*

GENERAL NOTE

The Social Security (Recovery of Benefits) (Lump Sum Payments) Regulations 2008 are made under this section (and other provisions of this Act). They provide a scheme for the recovery of payments within the scope of subs.(2) that have been made by the Secretary of State in respect of death or disablement due to pneumoconiosis or mesothelioma from a person making a compensation payment on or after October 1, 2008 in respect of the relevant disease. The main differences between the scheme created by the Regulations and the scheme under the Act are that there is no five-year "relevant period" as there is under s.3 of the Act and that the Regulations also apply where the lump sum payment and compensation payment have been made to a dependant of the person who was suffering from the disease. Regulations 4 and 5 define the scope of the scheme, and s.1(3) of the Act applies with "Section 1A(1)(a)" substituted for "Subsection (1)(a)". Regulations 8–13 are broadly equivalent to ss.4–9 of the Act and reg.2 applies ss.10–34 (except ss.16, 24, 25, 32 and 34(2)) of, and Sch.1 to the Act, with modifications. Most of the modifications are minor, but s.15 is completely substituted. Regulations 7 and 14–19 make provision equivalent to regs 2, 9, 3, 4, 6, 10 and 11, respectively, of the Social Security (Recovery of Benefits) Regulations 1997. 1.291

Compensation payments to which this Act applies

2. This Act applies in relation to compensation payments made on or after the day on which this section comes into force, unless they are made in pursuance of a court order or agreement made before that day. 1.292

DEFINITION

"compensation payment"—see s.1(4)(b).

GENERAL NOTE

By virtue of the Social Security (Recovery of Benefits) Act 1997 (Commencement Order) 1997 (SI 1997/2085), this section came into force on October 6, 1997. Where a court order or agreement was made before that date, the recovery provisions of Pt IV of the Social Security Administration Act 1992 continue to apply, unless the accident or injury occurred before January 1, 1989 (or, in the case of a disease, benefit was claimed before January 1, 1989), in which case benefits will not be recoverable by the Secretary of State at all (see s.81(7) of the 1992 Act). Regulation 12 of the Social Security (Recovery of Benefits) Regulations 1997 makes transitional provision for cases arising under the 1992 Act. 1.293

Lump sum payments within the scope of s.1A(2) may be recovered only where the compensation payment was made on or after October 1, 2008 (see reg.6 of the Social Security (Recovery of Benefits) (Lump Sum Payments) Regulations 2008).

"The relevant period"

3.—(1) In relation to a person ("the claimant") who has suffered any accident, injury or disease, "the relevant period" has the meaning given by the following subsections. 1.294

(2) Subject to subsection (4), if it is a case of accident or injury, the

relevant period is the period of five years immediately following the day on which the accident or injury in question occurred.

(3) Subject to subsection (4), if it is a case of disease, the relevant period is the period of five years beginning with the date on which the claimant first claims a listed benefit in consequence of the disease.

(4) If at any time before the end of the period referred to in subsection (2) or (3)—

(a) a person makes a compensation payment in final discharge of any claim made by or in respect of the claimant and arising out of the accident, injury or disease, or

(b) an agreement is made under which an earlier compensation payment is treated as having been made in final discharge of any such claim,

the relevant period ends at that time.

DEFINITIONS

"claimant"—see subs.(1).
"compensation payment"—see s.1(4)(b).
"listed benefit"—see s.29.

GENERAL NOTE

1.295 Subsection (2) identifies the beginning of the "relevant period" if the compensation is paid in consequence of an accident or injury and subs.(3) identifies the beginning of the "relevant period" if compensation is paid in consequence of a disease.

It was observed in *R(CR) 4/03* that this section implies that "accident" and "injury" are indistinguishable in this Act in cases where the injury is due to an accident, because subs.(2) clearly envisages them occurring on the same specific date, rather than contemplating the injury being the, possibly long-standing and possibly delayed, result of an accident. It was also observed that this section requires a distinction to be drawn between an "injury" and a "disease" and that that might not always be straightforward. It may be noted that the Social Security (Industrial Injuries) (Prescribed Diseases) Regulations 1985 in fact include prescribed injuries as well as diseases (see also s.108(1)(b) of the Social Security Contributions and Benefits Act 1992). It is unclear when the "relevant period" begins if a disease is caused by an accident and benefit in respect of the disease is not claimed until some time after the date of the accident.

If s.1(1)(b) and (4)(c) and subs.(3) of this section are all read literally, it appears that there is a possibility of more than five years' worth of benefit being recovered where compensation is paid in consequence of a disease. That is because the "relevant period" appears to run from the date of claim, rather than the date from which benefit is awarded. Typically, arrears of disablement benefit in respect of a prescribed disease are paid in respect of a period of three months before the date of claim, although the payment of those arrears is obviously made after that date and within the "relevant period". It may be arguable that one or more of the provisions should not be read literally on the basis that it is unlikely that it was intended that more than five years' worth of benefit should be recoverable, although the counter-argument is that the possibility of arrears being caught should have been obvious to the draftsman and could easily have been avoided if it was unintended.

Subsections (2) and (3) provide for a "relevant period" of five years but subs.(4) shortens it if compensation is paid sooner. As benefits payable after the "relevant period" are not recoverable (s.1(1)(b) and (4)(c)) and are ignored in the calculation of damages (s.17), it is likely to be in the interests of a compensator and, usually, a claimant to settle a claim for compensation as soon as possible.

Certificates of recoverable benefits

Applications for certificates of recoverable benefits

4.—(1) Before a person ("the compensator") makes a compensation payment he must apply to the Secretary of State for a certificate of recoverable benefits. 1.296

(2) Where the compensator applies for a certificate of recoverable benefits, the Secretary of State must—

(a) send to him a written acknowledgement of receipt of his application, and

(b) subject to subsection (7), issue the certificate before the end of the following period

(3) The period is—

(a) the prescribed period, or

(b) if there is no prescribed period, the period of four weeks,

which begins with the day following the day on which the application is received.

(4) The certificate is to remain in force until the date specified in it for that purpose.

(5) The compensator may apply for fresh certificates from time to time.

(6) Where a certificate of recoverable benefits ceases to be in force, the Secretary of State may issue a fresh certificate without an application for one being made.

(7) Where the compensator applies for a fresh certificate while a certificate ("the existing certificate") remains in force, the Secretary of State must issue the fresh certificate before the end of the following period.

(8) The period is—

(a) the prescribed period, or

(b) if there is no prescribed period, the period of four weeks,

which begins with the day following the day on which the existing certificate ceases to be in force.

(9) For the purposes of this Act, regulations may provide for the day on which an application for a certificate of recoverable benefits is to be treated as received.

DEFINITIONS

"compensator—see subs.(1).
"compensation payment"—see s.1(4)(b).
"existing certificate"—see subs.(7).
"prescribed—see s.29.
"recoverable benefit"—see s.1(4)(c).
"regulations"—see s.29.

GENERAL NOTE

No period has yet been prescribed for the purposes of subss.(3)(a) or (8)(a). By virtue of s.21, the consequence of the Secretary of State failing to issue a certificate of recoverable benefits within the specified period is that no benefits are recoverable and the victim is entitled to the full compensation without deduction. However, for s.21 to apply, the application for the certificate of recoverable benefits must have been accurate and it must have been acknowledged. The Compensation Recovery Unit asks compensators to tell them if an acknowledgement has not been received within 14 days. 1.297

Potential compensators must notify the Compensation Recovery Unit of any claim within 14 days of the claim being received (see s.23 and regulations made under it). This is usually done by completing form CRU1 (obtainable from the Unit's webpage: *https://www.gov.uk/government/collections/cru*) and it enables the Unit to start collecting the relevant information from the offices responsible for the payment of benefits. The Unit sends to the potential compensator a form CRU4 which is the form the compensator must use to obtain the certificate of recoverable benefits. Form CRU4 can also be used by a compensator to obtain, for the purposes of negotiation with the victim, an informal indication of the benefits that have been paid, although the Unit stresses that the accuracy of such an indication depends on how much information they have to hand at that time and a formal certificate of recoverable benefits issued later may be based on more up-to-date information. The victim is, of course, entitled to that information as well and can obtain it directly from the office or offices responsible for payment. A copy of any formal certificate is sent to the injured person (or other person expected to receive the compensation), thus ensuring compliance with s.5(5).

A fresh certificate, issued under subs.(5) after a previous certificate has expired, may include benefits not included in the previous certificate (*SSWP v Lanarkshire Health Board (CR)* [2014] UKUT 177 (AAC).

This section does not apply in respect of the recovery of lump sum payments within the scope of s.1A(2). See, instead, reg.8 of the Social Security (Recovery of Benefits) (Lump Sum Payments) Regulations 2008.

Subsection (9)

1.298 See reg.7(2) of the Social Security (Recovery of Benefits) Regulations 1997.

Information contained in certificates

1.299 **5.**—(1) A certificate of recoverable benefits must specify, for each recoverable benefit—

(a) the amount which has been or is likely to have been paid on or before a specified date, and

(b) if the benefit is paid or likely to be paid after the specified date, the rate and period for which, and the intervals at which, it is or is likely to be paid.

(2) In a case where the relevant period has ended before the day on which the Secretary of State receives the application for the certificate, the date specified in the certificate for the purposes of subsection (1) must be the day on which the relevant period ended.

(3) In any other case, the date specified for those purposes must not be earlier than the day on which the Secretary of State received the application.

(4) The Secretary of State may estimate, in such manner as he thinks fit, any of the amounts, rates or periods specified in the certificate.

(5) Where the Secretary of State issues a certificate of recoverable benefits, he must provide the information contained in the certificate to—

(a) the person who appears to him to be the injured person, or

(b) any person who he thinks will receive a compensation payment in respect of the injured person.

(6) A person to whom a certificate of recoverable benefits is issued or who is provided with information under subsection (5) is entitled to particulars of the manner in which any amount, rate or period specified in the certificate has been determined, if he applies to the Secretary of State for those particulars.

DEFINITIONS

"benefit"—see s.29.
"compensation payment"—see s.1(4)(b).
"injured person"—see s.1(4)(a).
"recoverable benefit"—see s.1(4)(c).
"the relevant period"—see s.3.

GENERAL NOTE

Note that only "recoverable" benefits should be specified on the certificate and, by virtue of s.1(1)(b) and (4)(c), that means benefits listed in col.2 of Sch.2 that have been, or are likely to be, paid to or for the victim during the relevant period *in respect of* the accident, injury or disease. Thus, not all benefits paid, or to be paid, during the relevant period should be specified in the certificate; only those that are attributable to the accident, injury or disease are recoverable. See the note to s.1. 1.300

For reviews of, and appeals against, certificates of recoverable benefits, see ss.10–14.

This section does not apply in respect of the recovery of lump sum payments within the scope of s.1A(2). See, instead, reg.9 of the Social Security (Recovery of Benefits) (Lump Sum Payments) Regulations 2008.

Liability of person paying compensation

Liability to pay Secretary of State amount of benefits

6.—(1) A person who makes a compensation payment in any case is liable to pay to the Secretary of State an amount equal to the total amount of the recoverable benefits. 1.301

(2) The liability referred to in subsection (1) arises immediately before the compensation payment or, if there is more than one, the first of them is made.

(3) No amount becomes payable under this section before the end of the period of 14 days following the day on which the liability arises.

(4) Subject to subsection (3), an amount becomes payable under this section at the end of the period of 14 days beginning with the day on which a certificate of recoverable benefits is first issued showing that the amount of recoverable benefit to which it relates has been or is likely to have been paid before a specified date.

DEFINITIONS

"amount of the recoverable benefits"—see s.9(4)(b).
"compensation payment"—see s.1(4)(b).
"recoverable benefit"—see s.1(4)(c).

GENERAL NOTE

The compensator may recoup some of the payment by reducing under s.8 the amount of compensation paid to the victim. However, the additional cost of benefits paid to the victim during the relevant period falls on the compensator. The compensator may not appeal against the certificate of recoverable benefits until the compensation has been paid (s.11(3)). 1.302

This section does not apply in respect of the recovery of lump sum payments within the scope of s.1A(2). See, instead, reg.10 of the Social Security (Recovery of Benefits) Lump Sum Payments) Regulations 2008.

Recovery of payments due under section 6

1.303 **7.**—(1) This section applies where a person has made a compensation payment but—

(a) has not applied for a certificate of recoverable benefits, or

(b) has not made a payment to the Secretary of State under section 6 before the end of the period allowed under that section.

(2) The Secretary of State may—

(a) issue the person who made the compensation payment with a certificate of recoverable benefits, if none has been issued, or

(b) issue him with a copy of the certificate of recoverable benefits or (if more than one has been issued) the most recent one,

and (in either case) issue him with a demand that payment of any amount due under section 6 be made immediately.

(3) The Secretary of State may, in accordance with subsections (4) and (5), recover the amount for which a demand for payment is made under subsection (2) from the person who made the compensation payment.

(4) If the person who made the compensation payment resides or carries on business in England and Wales and a county court so orders, any amount recoverable under subsection (3) is recoverable by execution issued from the county court or otherwise as if it were payable under an order of that court.

(5) If the person who made the payment resides or carries on business in Scotland, any amount recoverable under subsection (3) may be enforced in like manner as an extract registered decree arbitral bearing a warrant for execution issued by the sheriff court of any sheriffdom in Scotland.

(6) A document bearing a certificate which—

(a) is signed by a person authorised to do so by the Secretary of State, and

(b) states that the document, apart from the certificate, is a record of the amount recoverable under subsection (3),

is conclusive evidence that that amount is so recoverable.

(7) A certificate under subsection (6) purporting to be signed by a person authorised to do so by the Secretary of State is to be treated as so signed unless the contrary is proved.

DEFINITIONS

"compensation payment"—see s.1(4)(b).
"payment"—see s.29.
"recoverable benefit"—see s.1(4)(c).

GENERAL NOTE

1.304 This section provides a simple way of recovering not only sums due under s.6 from compensators who have followed the proper procedures but also sums due from those who have failed to apply for a certificate of recoverable benefits at all. For reviews of, and appeals against, certificates issued under s.7(2)(a), see ss.10–14.

This section does not apply in respect of the recovery of lump sum payments within the scope of s.1A(2). See, instead, reg.11 of the Social Security (Recovery of Benefits) (Lump Sum Payments) Regulations 2008.

Reduction of compensation payment

8.—(1) This section applies in a case where, in relation to any head of compensation listed in column 1 of Schedule 2— 1.305

(a) any of the compensation payment is attributable to that head, and
(b) any recoverable benefit is shown against that head in column 2 of the Schedule.

(2) In such a case, any claim of a person to receive the compensation payment is to be treated for all purposes as discharged if—

(a) he is paid the amount (if any) of the compensation payment calculated in accordance with this section, and
(b) if the amount of the compensation payment so calculated is nil, he is given a statement saying so by the person who (apart from this section) would have paid the gross amount of the compensation payment.

(3) For each head of compensation listed in column 1 of the Schedule for which paragraphs (a) and (b) of subsection (1) are met, so much of the gross amount of the compensation payment as is attributable to that head is to be reduced (to nil, if necessary) by deducting the amount of the recoverable benefit or, as the case may be, the aggregate amount of the recoverable benefits shown against it.

(4) Subsection (3) is to have effect as if a requirement to reduce a payment by deducting an amount which exceeds that payment were a requirement to reduce that payment to nil.

(5) The amount of the compensation payment calculated in accordance with this section is—

(a) the gross amount of the compensation payment, and
(b) the sum of the reductions made under subsection (3),

(and, accordingly, the amount may be nil).

DEFINITIONS

"amount of the recoverable benefit"—see s.9(4)(b).
"compensation payment"—see s.1(4)(b).
"gross amount of the compensation payment"—see s.9(4)(a).
"payment"—see s.29.
"recoverable benefit"—see s.1(4)(c).

GENERAL NOTE

Under the scheme replaced by this Act, the compensation payment was reduced by the whole amount of benefits paid within the relevant period in respect of the accident, injury or disease, even if the compensation had been awarded solely in respect of pain and suffering (*CSS/36/1992*). The effect was that the compensator almost always passed the entire cost of the recovery of benefits on to the injured person. This could produce unfair results, because the claimant's compensation for pain and suffering was eroded, particularly in two types of cases. The first was where the benefits were paid in respect of, say, a need for personal care (i.e. where the care component of disability living allowance was paid) for which the claimant had not claimed compensation because, say, the care was provided by a spouse free of charge. To some extent this could be avoided by claimants inventing new and cumbersome claims for loss based on the effects of the legislation for recovery of benefits. The second was a less tractable problem, which arose because most claims for compensation are settled and there is likely to be an element of compromise. If 1.306

a claim for loss of earnings was settled on the basis that was inconsistent with the basis of a claim for benefits, the recovery of benefits from the claimant could appear disproportionate (*CCR/8023/1995*). Whether that was unfair or not depended on whether or not the basis of settlement more accurately reflected the truth than the basis of the claim for benefit, but there could obviously be unfairness where there was a genuine compromise of the claim for compensation but the real burden of repaying the Secretary of State fell wholly on the claimant, rather than being shared by the compensator.

Under the new scheme, the compensator bears the cost of the alleged wrong-doing, being able to pass the cost on to the claimant only to the extent that he has paid relevant compensation to the claimant. Schedule 2 sets out three relevant heads of compensation (lost earnings, cost of care and loss of mobility) and sets out beside each of them the benefits in respect of which a deduction may be made under this section. Where a court makes an award of damages, it must quantify the amount allowed in respect of each of the heads of compensation set out in Sch.2 (s.15(2)). It is then for the compensator to make the appropriate deduction under s.8. Disputes as to the proper amount to be deducted under s.8 are not unusual. The legislation does not make explicit provision for the resolution of such disputes. Presumably, if the parties have become aware in the course of pre-trial negotiations that there is an issue as to the operation of s.8, the court can be asked to deal with that issue at the same time as assessing damages. What is quite clear is that the issue is to be determined by a court and not on an appeal to a tribunal under s.11. See *R(CR) 2/03* and *R(CR) 2/04*. In those decisions it was suggested that the issue could be determined in enforcement proceedings if it had not been dealt with by the judge at trial. Most cases, of course, are settled. Amendments to the Civil Procedure Rules have since made it clearer that the question whether a deduction is being properly made needs to be considered *before* a defendant's offer of settlement is accepted (see the note to s.16).

Where a payment into court is made, the compensator must state whether any deduction has been made under this section (see the note to s.16). Where a case is settled without there being a payment into court, the parties will no doubt have had regard to the operation of this section in reaching the settlement but it will usually be presumed that there was no reduction under this section unless the agreement expressly records such a reduction. It is important for the parties to record such a reduction if it is intended that the claimant should bring an appeal before a tribunal challenging the recoverability of benefits, because a claimant has a right of appeal only if there has been a reduction (see s.11(2)(b)). Otherwise only the compensator has a right of appeal. The question of who should bear the cost or risk of such an appeal can be a matter to be taken into account in negotiating a settlement but the settlement must be worded appropriately if it is to have the intended effect. Section 11(3) provides that an appeal may be brought only after the claim giving rise to the compensation payment has been disposed of, so that the Secretary of State does not get caught up in arguments between the claimant and the compensator as to the amount of compensation and the proper application of s.8. Where an application for review or an appeal by either party is successful in a case where there was a reduction of the compensation payment under this section, the refund is made to the compensator who must make a new calculation under this section (reg.11(4) and (5) of the Social Security (Recovery of Benefits) Regulations 1997). This has the effect that a compensator has no practical interest in appealing where the compensation payment has been reduced by the whole amount of recoverable benefits (*R(CR) 2/03*). The compensator has an interest only to the extent to which the amount of recoverable benefits *has not* been reflected in a reduction under this section, just as a claimant has an interest only to the extent to which the amount of recoverable benefits *has* been reflected in a reduction. Where, following a review or appeal, a compensator is obliged to make a further payment to the Secretary of State in a case where there was a reduction under this section, there are limited circumstances in which the reduction may be recalculated and the claimant may be required to make a refund to the compensator (*ibid.*, reg.11(6) and (7)).

Although neither s.8 nor Sch.2 refers to the period in respect of which recoverable benefits may be taken into account, it was suggested in *R(CR) 2/04* that benefits should be deducted under s.8 only in so far as they are payable in respect of the period for which compensation in respect of the relevant head of damages has been paid. The Commissioner also suggested that the calculation under s.8 should be made *before* the amount of compensation is reduced to take account of contributory negligence. However, as he also held that the proper operation of s.8 was a matter for the courts and not for tribunals or Commissioners, those suggestions are obiter dicta. 1.307

This section does not apply in respect of the recovery of lump sum payments within the scope of s.1A(2). See, instead, reg.12 of the Social Security (Recovery of Benefits) Lump Sum Payments) Regulations 2008. Nor does it apply in respect of the recovery of payments under the Diffuse Mesothelioma Payment Scheme established under the Mesothelioma Act 2014. See instead s.8A, below.

[1 Reduction of payment under Diffuse Mesothelioma Payment Scheme

8A.—(1) This section applies instead of section 8 in a case where the compensation payment is a payment under the Diffuse Mesothelioma Payment Scheme. 1.308

(2) The gross amount of the compensation payment—

(a) is to be reduced by the amount of the recoverable benefit, and

(b) accordingly, is to be reduced to nil in any case where the amount of the recoverable benefit is equal to or greater than the gross amount of the compensation payment.

(3) Any claim of a person to receive the compensation payment is to be treated for all purposes as discharged if—

(a) the person is paid the gross amount of the compensation payment less the amount of the recoverable benefit, or

(b) the amount of the recoverable benefit is equal to or greater than the gross amount of the compensation payment and the person is given a statement by the scheme administrator saying that the compensation payment has been reduced to nil.]

AMENDMENT

1. Mesothelioma Act 2014 s.11 and Sch.1 paras. 1 and 3 (March 31, 2014).

DEFINITIONS

"compensation payment"—see s.1(4)(b).
"gross amount of the compensation payment"—see s.8(4)(a).
"payment"—see s.29.
"recoverable benefit"—see s.1(4)(c).
"scheme administrator"—see s.29.

GENERAL NOTE

The Diffuse Mesothelioma Payment Scheme is established under the Mesothelioma Act 2014 (see Vol.I). 1.309

Section 8: supplementary

9.—(1) A person who makes a compensation payment calculated in accordance with section 8 [1 or 8A] must inform the person to whom the payment is made— 1.310

(a) that the payment has been so calculated, and
(b) of the date for payment by reference to which the calculation has been made.

(2) If the amount of a compensation payment calculated in accordance with section 8 [[1] or 8A] is nil, a person giving a statement saying so is to be treated for the purposes of this Act as making a payment within section 1(1)(a) on the day on which he gives the statement.

(3) Where a person—
(a) makes a compensation payment calculated in accordance with section 8 [[1] or 8A], and
(b) if the amount of the compensation payment so calculated is nil, gives a statement saying so,

he is to be treated, for the purpose of determining any rights and liabilities in respect of contribution or indemnity, as having paid the gross amount of the compensation payment.

(4) For the purposes of this Act—
(a) the gross amount of the compensation payment is the amount of the compensation payment apart from section 8 [[1] or 8A], and
(b) the amount of any recoverable benefit is the amount determined in accordance with the certificate of recoverable benefits.

AMENDMENT

1. Mesothelioma Act 2014 s.11 and Sch.1 paras. 1 and 8 (March 31, 2014).

DEFINITIONS

"compensation payment"—see s.1(4)(b).
"gross amount of the compensation payment"—see subs.(4)(a).
"payment"—see s.29.
"recoverable benefit"—see s.1(4)(c).

GENERAL NOTE

1.311 This section does not apply in respect of the recovery of lump sum payments within the scope of s.1A(2). See, instead, reg.13 of the Social Security (Recovery of Benefits) (Lump Sum Payments) Regulations 2008. Presumably it is intended that the heading of the section should be read since the 2014 amendments as referring to s.8A as well as s.8.

Reviews and appeals

Review of certificates of recoverable benefits

1.312 **10.**—[[1](1) Any certificate of recoverable benefits may be reviewed by the Secretary of State—
(a) either within the prescribed period or in prescribed circumstances; and
(b) either on an application made for the purpose or on his own initiative.]

(2) On a review under this section the Secretary of State may either—
(a) confirm the certificate, or
(b) (subject to subsection (3)) issue a fresh certificate containing such variations as he considers appropriate[[1] or
(c) revoke the certificate.]

(3) The Secretary of State may not vary the certificate so as to increase the total amount of the recoverable benefits unless it appears to him that the variation is required as a result of the person who applied for the certificate supplying him with incorrect or insufficient information.

[2 (4) The scheme administrator of the Diffuse Mesothelioma Payment Scheme may not apply for a review under this section.]

AMENDMENTS

1. Social Security Act 1998 Sch.7 para.149 (March 4, 1999 for the making of regulations, November 29, 1999 for other purposes).

2. Mesothelioma Act 2014 s.11 and Sch.1 paras 1 and 4 (March 31, 2014).

DEFINITIONS

"amount of the recoverable benefits"—see s.9(4)(b).
"prescribed"—see s.29.
"recoverable benefit"—see s.1(4)(c).
"regulations"—see s.29.
"scheme administrator"–*ibid.*

GENERAL NOTE

This section is applied with modifications to cases concerned with the recovery of payments within the scope of s.1A(2) (see the Social Security (Recovery of Benefits) (Lump Sum Payments) Regulations 2008 reg.2 and Sch.1 para.3). 1.313

Subsection (1)

Note that the Social Security Act 1998 does not abolish the concept of review in this context. No period has been prescribed, so an application for review may be made at any time. The circumstances in which a decision may be reviewed are prescribed by regs 9 and 9ZA of the Social Security and Child Support (Decisions and Appeals) Regulations 1999 and are very broad. 1.314

Generally, a certificate of recoverable benefits is accompanied by a notice to the effect that there is a right of appeal in relation to the certificate only if the Secretary of State has considered an application for review of the certificate, in which case an application for review is a necessary precursor to an appeal (see reg.9ZB of the Social Security and Child Support (Decisions and Appeals) Regulations 1999). Note that subs.(3) provides protection on a review that is lacking on an appeal. There does not seem to be any reason why there should not be a further review after an appeal has been brought. In *CCR/3391/2005*, it was said that the Secretary of State should always consider reviewing a decision against which an appeal has been brought, so as to prevent unnecessary appeals reaching tribunals. "In effect, a submission to a tribunal should be an explanation for the Secretary of State not reviewing the decision in the light of the grounds of appeal." That approach is still necessary where the appellant has provided on the appeal evidence that was not before the Secretary of State either when the certificate of recoverable benefits was issued or when the benefits concerned were awarded so that there is a factual issue upon which the Secretary of State has not previously made a decision.

Subsection (3)

This is an important provision. Once a certificate has been issued, it cannot be varied on review so as to increase the amount of recoverable benefits unless the person who applied for the certificate (the compensator) caused the error. Where the compensator has provided incorrect or insufficient information as a result of being given incorrect or insufficient information by a claimant who knew it to be incorrect or insufficient and who provided it with intent to limit the amount of a reduction under s.8, the compensator may be able to recover from the claimant 1.315

of Appeal in Northern Ireland). It follows that, on an appeal brought under this section as modified and applied to the recovery under the Social Security (Recovery of Benefits) (Lump Sum Payments) Regulations 2008 of lump sum payments made under the Pneumoconiosis etc. (Workers' Compensation) Act 1979, the compensator is in principle entitled to argue that the payment made to the claimant under the 1979 Act ought not to have been made (*Aviva Insurance Ltd v SSWP* [2015] UKUT 613 (AAC); [2016] AACR 29). Similarly, a tribunal is entitled to find that benefit was paid at too high a rate (*R(CR) 1/03*). In *C2/01–02(CRS)*, a Commissioner in Northern Ireland held that it was not the tribunal's function to substitute their judgment for the authority who awarded benefit and that the question was whether benefit had reasonably been awarded. Thus, if the awarding authority could properly have awarded benefit in respect of the relevant accident, injury or disease on the evidence before them and there is no new evidence, it will be impossible to show that benefit was awarded otherwise than in respect of the accident, injury or disease. However, in many cases a tribunal considering an appeal under s.11 will have before them evidence that was not before the authority awarding benefit and in those circumstances the tribunal's judgment will be the only one that can be applied. Where benefit may be awarded on a number of different bases and it is being alleged that benefit ought not to have been awarded or that the disablement justifying the award was not caused by the relevant accident, injury or disease, it is important for the tribunal to be able to infer from the evidence on which basis the benefit in question was actually awarded because only then is it possible to determine whether the claimant's circumstances justified that award. For instance, it is a gross over-simplification to believe that incapacity benefit or employment and support allowance is paid because a person is actually incapable of work (see, in relation to employment and support allowance, the Employment and Support Allowance Regulations 2008 in Vol.I of this work). Establishing that the claimant was in fact capable of work may therefore not demonstrate a lack of entitlement. A statutory assessment is applicable to most claimants of incapacity benefit and an argument that a claimant ought not to have been treated as satisfying that assessment on account of the relevant accident, injury or disease requires evidence focused on the activities considered in such an assessment. Moreover, some claimants are not required to be assessed in the usual way and are treated as being incapable of work or having limited capability for work under various deeming provisions. Again, a submission that benefit was not properly paid would have to focus on the terms of those regulations. In particular, before such an initial assessment is actually carried out, a claimant is usually treated as incapable of work on the basis of medical certificates provided by a doctor. In *R(CR) 2/02*, it was suggested by the Tribunal of Commissioners that as long as a claimant was providing such certificates referring to the relevant disease, benefit was properly awarded in respect of that disease whether or not the claimant was actually incapable of work or would actually have satisfied a personal capability assessment. Doubtless, there would be exceptions where, for instance, a claimant was working and so was required to be treated as capable of work or as not having limited capability for work. It may also be arguable that, where a claimant had obtained the medical certificate by misleading his doctor as to the severity of his or her condition or, perhaps, where the doctor plainly ought not to have given a certificate, benefit can be said not to have been properly paid in respect of the relevant accident, injury or disease but, given that a medical certificate merely certifies that the claimant was advised not to work and is not actually a certificate that the person is incapable of work (see Sch.1 to the Social Security (Medical Evidence) Regulations 1976), it will not be easy to demonstrate that a certificate was inappropriate. In any event, *R(CR) 2/02* was distinguished in *R(CR) 1/04*. In the latter case, incapacity benefit had been awarded pending the carrying out of a personal capability assessment on the basis of medical certificates supplied by the claimant's doctor, which referred to an eye injury sustained when a fire extinguisher had gone off accidentally. The Commissioner found that the eye injury caused by the fire extinguisher had in fact had no disabling effect on the claimant after a week and that the disablement was the result of a pre-existing condition in the claimant's eye and, later, from both that cause and a depressive illness. In those circumstances, he held that the incapacity benefit had not been paid "in respect of" the relevant accident, notwithstanding that the claimant had been deemed to be incapable of work on the strength of the medical certificates.

Paragraph (d) permits an appeal where there is a dispute as to whether the Act applies at all because, for instance, it is claimed that compensation was not paid "in consequence of any accident, injury or disease" (see the note to s.1). If this paragraph is read with para.(b), it is plain that a claimant or compensator is also entitled to argue that a payment of compensation was not paid in respect of a particular injury and that benefits paid in respect of that injury should not have been brought into account. However, such an argument can be advanced only where it can be shown that the compensation was in fact paid in respect of some other injury or damage. Thus, in *CCR/2232/2006*, where the claimant had received £50,000 damages on the basis that injuries after a particular date were due solely to medical negligence, he was not entitled to argue on an appeal under this section that the injury was due to the accident that led to him being hospitalised rather then to the medical negligence and, in *R(CR) 1/07*, where a compensator settled a claim made on the basis that psychiatric injury was due to a particular cause, the compensator was not entitled to argue that the injury was due wholly to a cause not covered by the claim for compensation. 1.319

Note that no appeal lies under this section against a compensator's decision to make a reduction under s.8. Any dispute about such a reduction must be determined by the court seised of the claim for compensation, either when compensation is assessed or in enforcement proceedings. A claimant should not accept a payment into court or an offer of settlement if he or she is not prepared to accept that s.8 has been applied reasonably or at least that the net award of compensation is adequate (see *R(CR) 2/03* and *R(CR) 2/04*).

Subsection (2)

A compensator always has a right of appeal but in fact has no interest in appealing insofar as the amount of compensation was reduced under s.8, due to the effect of reg.11(5) of the Social Security (Recovery of Benefits) Regulations 1997 which requires the recalculation of the s.8 reduction if the appeal is successful (*R(CR) 2/03*). An injured person has a right of appeal only if there has been a s.8 reduction. In any appeal under this section, any other person who could have appealed is made a party to the proceedings (see the definition of "respondent" in the Tribunal Procedure (First-tier Tribunal) (Social Entitlement Chamber) Rules 2008). In *CCR/3425/2003*, the Commissioner said that, as a claimant was entitled to be a party to a compensator's appeal only where there had been a deduction under s.8, it was to be inferred that the right to respond arose because the claimant might be entitled to a refund from the compensator under reg.11(5) of the 1997 Regulations, rather than because the Secretary of State might decide to revise or supersede an award of benefit, if the compensator was successful. Accordingly, as the claimant did not support the compensator's appeal and did not seek a refund, he had suffered no material loss when he had been misled by a letter from the Department suggesting that he need not attend the hearing. If both the claimant and the compensator appeal, the Compensation Recovery Unit should inform the tribunal and ask for the appeals to be heard together (*CCR/2231/2003*). 1.320

Subssections (2A) and (2B)

See regs 9ZB and 29(6) of the Social Security and Child Support (Decisions and Appeals) Regulations 1999, which generally require a person to seek a review of a decision before lodging an appeal but enable the Secretary of State to treat a purported appeal as an application for a review. 1.321

Subsection (3)

An appeal cannot be brought until after the compensation claim has been fully disposed of and the s.6 payment has been paid to the Secretary of State. A claim is not 1.322

finally disposed of until any appeal against a court's order or judgment is determined (*Williams v Devon CC* [2003] EWCA Civ. 365 (*The Times*, March 26, 2003)) and so presumably the reference to the s.6 payment having been made must include any further payments required under reg.9 of the Social Security (Recovery of Benefits) Regulations 1997 in the event of a claimant's appeal being successful and requiring a further payment of compensation to be made. Generally, payment of compensation is made following the settlement of a claim, which implies agreement by the claimant as to the net amount of compensation to be paid after any reduction under s.8. However, where a court assesses compensation, it is not obliged at that stage to assess the appropriate amount of any reduction under s.8. That is left to the compensator. It was suggested in *R(CR) 2/04* that if the claimant wishes to challenge the amount of a s.8 reduction, he or she can do so in enforcement proceedings brought on the basis that the compensator has not fully satisfied the court's judgment.

See r.22(2)(d) of the Tribunal Procedure (First-tier Tribunal) (Social Entitlement Chamber) Rules 2008 for the time within which an appeal to a tribunal must be brought.

Subsection (5)

1.323 Regulations made under this subsection have all been revoked except for reg.29(6) of the Social Security and Child Support (Decisions and Appeals) Regulations 1999, made under subs.(5)(c). Note that a tribunal considering an appeal under this section has no express power either to refer the victim for examination or to examine him themselves because the primary legislation contains no power equivalent to s.20 of the Social Security Act 1998 under which r.25 of the Tribunal Procedure (First-tier Tribunal) (Social Entitlement Chamber) Rules 2008 is made.

Reference of questions to [2 the First-tier Tribunal]

1.324 **12.**—[1(1) The Secretary of State must refer an appeal under section 11 to an [2 the First-tier Tribunal].]

(2) [1. . .]

(3) In determining [1 any appeal under section 11], the tribunal must take into account any decision of a court relating to the same, or any similar, issue arising in connection with the accident, injury or disease in question.

(4) On [1 an appeal under section 11 [2 the First-tier Tribunal]] may either—

(a) confirm the amounts, rates and periods specified in the certificate of recoverable benefits, or

(b) specify any variations which are to be made on the issue of a fresh certificate under subsection (5) [1 or

(c) declare that the certificate of recoverable benefits is to be revoked.]

(5) When the Secretary of State has received [1the decision of the tribunal on the appeal under section 11, he must in accordance with that decision] either—

(a) confirm the certificate against which the appeal was brought, or

(b) issue a fresh certificate [1 or

(c) revoke the certificate.]

(6) [1 . . .]

(7) Regulations [1 . . .] may (among other things) provide for the nondisclosure of medical advice or medical evidence given or submitted following a reference under subsection (1).

(8) [1 . . .]

AMENDMENTS

1. Social Security Act 1998 Sch.7 para.151 and Sch.8 (November 29, 1999).

2. Transfer of Tribunal Functions Order 2008 (SI 2008/2833) Sch.3 paras 138 and 140 (November 3, 2008).

DEFINITIONS

"recoverable benefit"—see s.1(4)(c).
"regulations"—see s.29.

GENERAL NOTE

This section is applied with modifications to cases concerned with the recovery of payments within the scope of s.1A(2) (see the Social Security (Recovery of Benefits) (Lump Sum Payments) Regulations 2008 reg.2 and Sch.1 para.5). **1.325**

Subsection (1)

The primary legislation includes no provision equivalent to s.20 of the Social Security Act 1998. Therefore, even when the tribunal includes a medically qualified panel member, the tribunal has no express power to examine the victim, although there is also no express prohibition on such an examination. Presumably the victim could consent to an examination. There is not even any express power to refer a victim for examination but it is difficult to see any objection to there being such a reference, provided the victim were to consent and some arrangement could be made for the payment of an examining doctor. **1.326**

Subsection (3)

Note that the tribunal need only "take into account" any decision of a court; it is not bound by such a decision. This is partly because it would be unfair on the Secretary of State to be bound by a decision in proceedings to which he was not a party (*R(CR) 1/02*). Most proceedings before courts are settled and do not result in reasoned decisions but claimants and compensators are expected to act before a tribunal in a manner that is consistent with the way they have settled a case or, in the case of a claimant, have claimed benefits. Thus a tribunal should be slow to accept an argument advanced by a compensator that is inconsistent with a section 8 deduction that it has made, unless the claimant agrees that the deduction should not have been made, and, equally, a tribunal should be slow to accept an argument advanced by a claimant that is inconsistent with the basis on which compensation was obtained or benefits were claimed (*R(CR) 2/03*). Where a claimant had accepted £50,000 in respect of a claim that injury in respect of which benefits had been paid was due solely to medical negligence, he was not entitled to argue that the benefits were paid otherwise than in respect of that injury (*CCR/2232/2006*). **1.327**

Similarly, where a compensator had settled a claim made on the basis that psychiatric injury was due to a particular cause, the compensator was not entitled to argue that the injury was due wholly to a cause not covered by the claim for compensation (*R(CR) 1/07*).

Subsection (4)

In *CCR/4/1993* and *CSCR/1/1995*, Commissioners held that, on appeals, the Secretary of State was entitled to refer to the tribunal questions which related to benefits that were not on the original "certificates of total benefit" (the forerunners of certificates of recoverable benefits). In the first case the Commissioner held that, on an appeal, all matters were at large. In the second case, the Commissioner took a narrower approach and held that a tribunal was strictly confined to the issues referred to it by the Secretary of State but that, in that case, the new benefits were within the scope of the reference. The Commissioner noted the contrast between the position on appeal and the limitation, now contained in s.10(3), with respect to reviews and warned of the perils of appealing. **1.328**

Under the new legislation as amended, what are before the tribunal by virtue of subs.(1) are the "appeal" under s.11 and all matters that can fairly be said to arise within that appeal—and within the jurisdiction of the tribunal bearing in mind its constitution (see the note to subs.(1) above). There is no provision in this Act equivalent to s.12(8)(a) of the Social Security Act 1998, but it is suggested that the approach should be the same: the tribunal may deal with issues not expressly raised by the notice of appeal but is not bound to do so, provided it exercises that discretion judicially.

Subsection (7)

1.329 Since Tribunal Procedure Rules have replaced regulations made by the Secretary of State, this provision has fallen into disuse. See now r.14(2)–(6) of the Tribunal Procedure (First-tier Tribunal) (Social Entitlement Chamber) Rules 2008.

Appeal to [2Upper Tribunal]

1.330 **13.**—(1) [2. . .]

(2) An appeal [2 to the Upper Tribunal under section 11 of the Tribunals, Courts and Enforcement Act 2007 which arises from any decision of the First-tier Tribunal under section 12 of this Act] may be made by—

(a) the Secretary of State,

(b) the person who applied for the certificate of recoverable benefits,

[1(bb) (in a case where that certificate was issued under section 7(2)(a)) the person to whom it was issued, or]

(c) (in a case where the amount of the compensation payment has been calculated in accordance with section 8 [3 or 8A]) the injured person or other person to whom the payment is made

[3 but the scheme administrator of the Diffuse Mesothelioma Payment Scheme may not appeal under this section.]

(3) [2. . .]

(4) [1. . .]

AMENDMENTS

1. Social Security Act 1998 Sch.7 para.152 and Sch.8 (November 29, 1999).

2. Transfer of Tribunal Functions Order 2008 (SI 2008/2833) Sch.3 paras 138 and 141 (November 3, 2008).

3. Mesothelioma Act 2014 s.11 and Sch.1 paras 1, 6 and 8 (March 31, 2014).

DEFINITIONS

"compensation payment"—see s.1(4)(b).

"injured person"—see s.1(4)(a).

"scheme administrator"—see s.29.

GENERAL NOTE

1.331 This section is applied with modifications to cases concerned with the recovery of payments within the scope of s.1A(2) (see the Social Security (Recovery of Benefits) (Lump Sum Payments) Regulations 2008 reg.2 and Sch.1 para.6). It does not add anything to s.11(2) of the 2007 Act.

Reviews and appeals: supplementary

1.332 **14.**—(1) This section applies in cases where a fresh certificate of recoverable benefits is issued as a result of a review under section 10 or an appeal under section 11.

(2) If—

(a) a person has made one or more payments to the Secretary of State under section 6, and

(b) in consequence of the review or appeal, it appears that the total amount paid is more than the amount that ought to have been paid,

regulations may provide for the Secretary of State to pay the difference to that person, or to the person to whom the compensation payment is made, or partly to one and partly to the other.

(3) If—

(a) a person has made one or more payments to the Secretary of State under section 6, and

(b) in consequence of the review or appeal, it appears that the total amount paid is less than the amount that ought to have been paid,

regulations may provide for that person to pay the difference to the Secretary of State.

(4) Regulations under this section may provide—

(a) for the re-calculation in accordance with section 8 [[1] or 8A] of the amount of any compensation payment,

(b) for giving credit for amounts already paid, and

(c) for the payment by any person of any balance or the recovery from any person of any excess,

and may provide for any matter by modifying this Act.

AMENDMENT

1. Mesothelioma Act 2014 s.11 and Sch.1 paras 1 and 8 (March 31, 2014).

DEFINITIONS

"compensation payment"—see s.1(4)(b).
"payment"—see s.29.
"recoverable benefit"—see s.1(4)(c).
"regulations"—see s.29.

GENERAL NOTE

See reg.11 of the Social Security (Recovery of Benefits) Regulations 1997. 1.333

This section is applied with modifications to cases concerned with the recovery of payments within the scope of s.1A(2) (see the Social Security (Recovery of Benefits) (Lump Sum Payments) Regulations 2008 reg.2 and Sch.1 para.7). Regulation 19 of the 2008 Regulations makes provision equivalent to reg.11 of the 1997 Regulations.

Courts

Court orders

15.—(1) This section applies where a court makes an order for a compensation payment to be made in any case, unless the order is made with the consent of the injured person and the person by whom the payment is to be made. 1.334

(2) The court must, in the case of each head of compensation listed in column 1 of Schedule 2 to which any of the compensation payment is attributable, specify in the order the amount of the compensation payment which is attributable to that head.

DEFINITIONS

"compensation payment"—see s.1(4)(b).
"injured person"—see s.1(4)(a).

GENERAL NOTE

1.335 A substituted version of this section is applied to cases concerned with the recovery of payments within the scope of s.1A(2) (see the Social Security (Recovery of Benefits) (Lump Sum Payments) Regulations 2008 reg.2 and Sch.1 para.8).

Subsection (2)

1.336 A court hearing a case within five years of a relevant accident must specify the amount of the compensation awarded that was attributable to any particular head in col.1 of Sch.2 in respect of the whole five-year period, because the court cannot know when payment of the sum awarded will actually be made (*Mitchell v Laing*, 1998 S.C. 342). Nonetheless, the compensator was to deduct only those benefits that had been paid or were due to be paid up until the date of the payment of the sum awarded by the court.

The court's view must be taken into account by any tribunal considering an appeal against a certificate of recoverable benefits (see s.12(3)) and, presumably, also by the Secretary of State considering a review (see reg.9(d) of the Social Security and Child Support (Decisions and Appeals) Regulations 1999). However, the principal purpose of s.15(2) is to enable s.8 to be operated properly. There is no express requirement to state the period in respect of which each head of the compensation is paid (which, it has been suggested in *R(CR) 2/04*, is a material fact limiting the amount of any deduction under s.8) but that information will usually be clear from the court's reasoning.

Payments into court

1.337 **16.**—(1) Regulations may make provision (including provision modifying this Act) for any case in which a payment into court is made.

(2) The regulations may (among other things) provide—

(a) for the making of a payment into court to be treated in prescribed circumstances as the making of a compensation payment,

(b) for application for, and issue of, certificates of recoverable benefits, and

(c) for the relevant period to be treated as ending on a date determined in accordance with the regulations.

(3) Rules of court may make provision governing practice and procedure in such cases.

(4) This section does not extend to Scotland.

DEFINITIONS

"compensation payment"—see s.1(4)(b).
"recoverable benefit"—see s.1(4)(c).
"payment"—see s.29.
"prescribed"—*ibid.*
"regulations"—*ibid.*
"relevant period"—see s.3.

GENERAL NOTE

Subssections (1) and (2)

1.338 Regulation 8 of the Social Security (Recovery of Benefits) Regulations 1997 provides that a payment into court is treated as a compensation payment under the

Social Security (Recovery of Benefits) Act 1997 and a current certificate of recoverable benefits must be lodged with it (reg.8(1)). However, the liability of the compensator under s.6 of the Act to pay the Secretary of State the recoverable benefits does not arise until notice has been given that all or part of the payment into court has been paid to the victim (reg.8(2)). If the payment into court is accepted by the victim within 21 days, the "relevant period" under s.3 is taken to have ended on the date the money, or the last part of it, was paid into court (reg.8(3)). If, however, the case is settled after that 21 days have expired and the money is paid to the victim by consent in satisfaction of the claim, the "relevant period" is taken to have ended on the date on which the application to the court for the payment is made (reg.8(4)). If all or part of the money in court is paid to the victim following an order of the court, the "relevant period" is taken to have ended on the date of the order (reg.8(5)). If the whole of the payment into court is returned to the defendant, the making of the payment into court ceases to be treated as the making of a compensation payment and there is no liability to pay anything to the Secretary of State (reg.8(7)).

Subsection (3)

Part 36 of the Civil Procedure Rules deals with offers to settle cases in England and Wales. Rule 36.22 provides— **1.339**

"(1) In this rule and rule 36.11—

(a) "the 1997 Act" means the Social Security (Recovery of Benefits) Act 1997;
(b) "the 2008 Regulations" means the Social Security (Recovery of Benefits) (Lump Sum Payments) Regulations 2008;
(c) "recoverable amount" means—
  (i) "recoverable benefits" as defined in section 1(4)(c) of the 1997 Act; and
  (ii) "recoverable lump sum payments" as defined in regulation 4 of the 2008 Regulations;
(d) "deductible amount" means—
  (i) any benefits by the amount of which damages are to be reduced in accordance with section 8 of, and Schedule 2 to, the 1997 Act ("deductible benefits"); and
  (ii) any lump sum payment by the amount of which damages are to be reduced in accordance with regulation 12 of the 2008 Regulations ("deductible lump sum payments"); and
(e) "certificate"—
  (i) in relation to recoverable benefits is construed in accordance with the provisions of the 1997 Act; and
  (ii) in relation to recoverable lump sum payments has the meaning given in section 29 of the 1997 Act as applied by regulation 2 of, and modified by Schedule 1 to, the 2008 Regulations.

(2) This rule applies where a payment to a claimant following acceptance of a Part 36 offer would be a compensation payment as defined in section 1(4)(b) or 1A(5)(b) of the 1997 Act.

(3) A defendant who makes a Part 36 offer should state either—
(a) that the offer is made without regard to any liability for recoverable amounts; or
(b) that it is intended to include any deductible amounts.

(4) Where paragraph (3)(b) applies, paragraphs (5) to (9) of this rule will apply to the Part 36 offer.

(5) Before making the Part 36 offer, the offeror must apply for a certificate.

(6) Subject to paragraph (7), the Part 36 offer must state—
(a) the gross amount of compensation;
(b) the name and amount of any deductible amount by which the gross amount is reduced; and

(c) the net amount of compensation.

(7) If at the time the offeror makes the Part 36 offer, the offeror has applied for, but has not received, a certificate, the offeror must clarify the offer by stating the matters referred to in paragraphs (6)(b) and (6)(c) not more than 7 days after receipt of the certificate.

(8) For the purposes of rule 36.17(1)(a), a claimant fails to recover more than any sum offered (including a lump sum offered under rule 36.6) if the claimant fails upon judgment being entered to recover a sum, once deductible amounts identified in the judgment have been deducted, greater than the net amount stated under paragraph (6)(c).

(Section 15(2) of the 1997 Act provides that the court must specify the compensation payment attributable to each head of damage. Schedule 1 to the 2008 Regulations modifies section 15 of the 1997 Act in relation to lump sum payments and provides that the court must specify the compensation payment attributable to each or any dependant who has received a lump sum payment.)

(9) Where—

(a) further deductible amounts have accrued since the Part 36 offer was made; and

(b) the court gives permission to accept the Part 36 offer,

the court may direct that the amount of the offer payable to the offeree shall be reduced by a sum equivalent to the deductible amounts paid to the claimant since the date of the offer.

(Rule 36.11(3)(b) states that permission is required to accept an offer where the relevant period has expired and further deductible amounts have been paid to the claimant)"

The effect of CPR r.36.17 is that a failure to recover a sum greater than the amount offered under Pt.36 is usually that the claimant has to pay any costs incurred by the defendant after the latest date the offer could have been accepted without the permission of the court. Rule 36.22(8), which makes it clear that the relevant sum for the purposes of the comparison is the net amount after deductions have been made under s.8. CPR r.36.17 is modified by r.36.21 in cases started under the pre-action protocols for "Low Value Personal Injuries Claims" arising out of road traffic accidents or employers' liability or public liability claims but no longer proceeding under those protocols, but r.36.21(3)(c) has the same effect in such cases as r.36.22(8) does in other cases.

Benefits irrelevant to assessment of damages

1.340 **17.** In assessing damages in respect of any accident, injury or disease, the amount of any listed benefits paid or likely to be paid is to be disregarded.

DEFINITION

"listed benefit"—see s.29.

GENERAL NOTE

1.341 This section is applied with modifications to cases concerned with the recovery of payments within the scope of s.1A(2) (see the Social Security (Recovery of Benefits) (Lump Sum Payments) Regulations 2008 reg.2 and Sch.1 para.9).

Benefits are disregarded not only when assessing damages but also when calculating interest on the damages, so that recoverable benefits are not to be deducted from damages for loss of earnings before calculating the interest due (*Wisely v John Fulton (Plumbers) Ltd, Wadey v Surrey CC* [2000] 1 W.L.R. 820 (HL)).

This section is not an overriding mandatory provision within the scope of Art.16 of Regulation (EC) No.864/2007 so that, in *Syred v Powszechny Zaklad Ubezpreczen (PZU) SA* [2016] EWHC 254 (QB); [2016] 1 W.L.R. 3211 where the claimant was severely injured in a road accident in Poland and the Regulation had the effect that quantum fell to be determined by Polish law subject to any overriding mandatory provision of English law, Polish law was applied and required credit to be given for benefits when assessing damages. A "nil" certificate had been issued in that case but, even if recoverable benefits had been paid during the "relevant period", the ruling would probably have made a difference only in respect of benefits that had been received, or were likely to be received, after the "relevant period" had ended. That is because applying the compensatory principle of Polish law would presumably have had the same effect as is achieved by s.8 in respect of the "relevant period" and the compensator could not have expected to be entitled to reduce the amount of damages twice in respect of the same benefits.

Reduction of compensation: complex cases

Lump sum and periodical payments

18.—(1) Regulations may make provision (including provision modifying this Act) for any case in which two or more compensation payments in the form of lump sums are made by the same person to or in respect of the injured person in consequence of the same accident, injury or disease. 1.342

(2) The regulations may (among other things) provide—

(a) for the re-calculation in accordance with section 8 of the amount of any compensation payment,

(b) for giving credit for amounts already paid, and

(c) for the payment by any person of any balance or the recovery from any person of any excess.

(3) For the purposes of subsection (2), the regulations may provide for the gross amounts of the compensation payments to be aggregated and for—

(a) the aggregate amount to be taken to be the gross amount of the compensation payment for the purposes of section 8,

(b) so much of the aggregate amount as is attributable to a head of compensation listed in column 1 of Schedule 2 to be taken to be the part of the gross amount which is attributable to that head;

and for the amount of any recoverable benefit shown against any head in column 2 of that Schedule to be taken to be the amount determined in accordance with the most recent certificate of recoverable benefits.

(4) Regulations may make provision (including provision modifying this Act) for any case in which, in final settlement of the injured person's claim, an agreement is entered into for the making of—

(a) periodical compensation payments (whether of an income or capital nature), or

(b) periodical compensation payments and lump sum compensation payments.

(5) Regulations made by virtue of subsection (4) may (among other things) provide—

(a) for the relevant period to be treated as ending at a prescribed time,

(b) for the person who is to make the payments under the agreement to be treated for the purposes of this Act as if he had made a single compensation payment on a prescribed date.

(6) A periodical payment may be a compensation payment for the purposes of this section even though it is a small payment (as defined in Part II of Schedule 1).

GENERAL NOTE

1.347 No regulations have been made under this section.

The section is nonetheless applied with modifications to cases concerned with the recovery of payments within the scope of s.1A(2) (see the Social Security (Recovery of Benefits) (Lump Sum Payments) Regulations 2008 reg.2 and Sch.1 para.12).

Compensation payments to be disregarded

1.348 **21.**—(1) If, when a compensation payment is made, the first and second conditions are met, the payment is to be disregarded for the purposes of sections 6 and 8 [1 or 8A].

(2) The first condition is that the person making the payment—

(a) has made an application for a certificate of recoverable benefits which complies with subsection (3), and

(b) has in his possession a written acknowledgement of the receipt of his application.

(3) An application complies with this subsection if it—

(a) accurately states the prescribed particulars relating to the injured person and the accident, injury or disease in question, and

(b) specifies the name and address of the person to whom the certificate is to be sent.

(4) The second condition is that the Secretary of State has not sent the certificate to the person, at the address, specified in the application, before the end of the period allowed under section 4.

(5) In any case where—

(a) by virtue of subsection (1), a compensation payment is disregarded for the purposes of sections 6 and 8 [1 or 8A], but

(b) the person who made the compensation payment nevertheless makes a payment to the Secretary of State for which (but for subsection (1)) he would be liable under section 6,

subsection (1) is to cease to apply in relation to the compensation payment.

(6) If, in the opinion of the Secretary of State, circumstances have arisen which adversely affect normal methods of communication—

(a) he may by order provide that subsection (1) is not to apply during a specified period not exceeding three months, and

(b) he may continue any such order in force for further periods not exceeding three months at a time.

AMENDMENT

1. Mesothelioma Act 2014 s.11 and Sch.1 paras 1 and 8 (March 31, 2014).

DEFINITIONS

"compensation payment"—see s.1(4)(b).
"injured person"—see s.29.
"payment"—see s.29.
"prescribed—*ibid.*
"recoverable benefit"—see s.1(4)(c).

GENERAL NOTE

1.349 If a certificate of recoverable benefits is not issued within four weeks (subject to subs.(6)) following receipt and acknowledgement of a full and accurate application, the Secretary of State loses his right of recovery. It is clear from subs.(4) that the late issue of a certificate will not do. However, if the compensator makes a payment to the Secretary of State in error—perhaps in reliance on an expired certificate—the Secretary of State is not obliged to pay it back because the dispensation under this section ceases to apply (subs.(5)). For the date on which an application is treated as received, see reg.7(2) of the Social Security (Recovery of Benefits) Regulations 1997 which is made under s.4(9).

This section is applied with modifications to cases concerned with the recovery of payments within the scope of s.1A(2) (see the Social Security (Recovery of Benefits) (Lump Sum Payments) Regulations 2008 reg.2 and Sch.1 para.13).

Subsection (3)

For the prescribed particulars, see reg.7(1) of the Social Security (Recovery of **1.350**
Benefits) Regulations 1997.

Subsection (4)

The period allowed under s.4(3) and (8) is four weeks, but see s.21(6). **1.351**

Subsection (5)

It is not clear whether the Secretary of State can, by issuing an out of time cer- **1.352**
tificate, insist on obtaining more than the payment made by the compensator or whether he is confined to accepting what has been sent, which is likely to have been based on an earlier certificate.

22. *Omitted.* **1.353**

Provision of information

23.—(1) Where compensation is sought in respect of any accident, injury **1.354**
or disease suffered by any person ("the injured person"), the following persons must give the Secretary of State the prescribed information about the injured person—

(a) anyone who is, or is alleged to be, liable in respect of the accident, injury or disease, and
(b) anyone acting on behalf of such a person.

(2) A person who receives or claims a listed benefit which is or is likely to be paid in respect of an accident, injury or disease suffered by him, must give the Secretary of State the prescribed information about the accident, injury or disease.

(3) Where a person who has received a listed benefit dies, the duty in subsection (2) is imposed on his personal representative.

(4) Any person who makes a payment (whether on his own behalf or not)—

(a) in consequence of, or
(b) which is referable to any costs (in Scotland, expenses) incurred by reason of,

any accident, injury or disease, or any damage to property, must, if the Secretary of State requests him in writing to do so, give the Secretary of State such particulars relating to the size and composition of the payment as are specified in the request.

(5) The employer of a person who suffers or has suffered an accident, injury or disease, and anyone who has been the employer of such a person at any time during the relevant period, must give the Secretary of State the prescribed information about the payment of statutory sick pay in respect of that person.

(6) In subsection (5) "employer" has the same meaning as it has in Part XI of the Social Security Contributions and Benefits Act 1992.

[1 (6A) The following persons must give the Secretary of State the prescribed information for the purposes of this Act—

(a) the scheme administrator of the Diffuse Mesothelioma Payment Scheme, and

(b) any person providing services to the scheme administrator.]

(7) A person who is required to give information under this section must do so in the prescribed manner, at the prescribed place and within the prescribed time.

(8) Section 1 does not apply in relation to this section.

AMENDMENT

1. Mesothelioma Act 2014 s.11 and Sch.1 para.19 (March 31, 2014).

DEFINITIONS

"employer"—see subs.(6).
"injured person"—see subs.(1) (and subs.(8), disapplying s.1).
"listed benefit"—see s.29.
"payment"—*ibid.*
"prescribed"—*ibid.*
"the relevant period"—see s.3.
"scheme administrator"—see s.29.

GENERAL NOTE

1.355 Regulations 3, 4, 5 and 6 of the Social Security (Recovery of Benefits) Regulations 1997 are made under subss (1), (2), (5) and (7) respectively.

This section is applied with modifications (which, among other things, disapply subss.(5), (6) and (8)) to cases concerned with the recovery of payments within the scope of s.1A(2). See the Social Security (Recovery of Benefits) (Lump Sum Payments) Regulations 2008 reg.2 and Sch.1 para.15. Regulations 15, 16 and 17 of the 2008 Regulations respectively make provision equivalent to regs 3, 4 and 6 of the 1997 Regulations.

Power to amend Schedule 2

1.356 **24.**—(1) The Secretary of State may by regulations amend Schedule 2.

(2) A statutory instrument which contains such regulations shall not be made unless a draft of the instrument has been laid before and approved by resolution of each House of Parliament.

DEFINITION

"regulations"—see s.29.

Provisions relating to Northern Ireland

1.357 **25.–27.** *Omitted.*

General

The Crown

28. This Act applies to the Crown. **1.358**

GENERAL NOTE

This is effectively a new provision because s.104 of the Social Security Administration Act 1992 was never brought into force (see Social Security (Consequential Provisions) Act 1992 Sch.4 para.3). It is applied to cases concerned with the recovery of payments within the scope of s.1A(2) (see the Social Security (Recovery of Benefits) (Lump Sum Payments) Regulations 2008 reg.2). **1.359**

General interpretation

29. In this Act— **1.360**

[2. . .]

"benefit" means [4 universal credit] any benefit under the Social Security Contributions and Benefits Act 1992, a jobseeker's allowance [1, an employment and support allowance] [3, personal independence payment] or mobility allowance,

[2. . .]

"compensation scheme for motor accidents" means any scheme or arrangement under which funds are available for the payment of compensation in respect of motor accidents caused, or alleged to have been caused, by uninsured or unidentified persons,

"listed benefit" means a benefit listed in column 2 of Schedule 2,

"payment" means payment in money or money's worth, and related expressions are to be interpreted accordingly,

"prescribed" means prescribed by regulations, and

"regulations" means regulations made by the Secretary of State.

[5 "scheme administrator", in relation to the Diffuse Mesothelioma Payment Scheme, has the meaning given by section 18 of the Mesothelioma Act 2014.]

AMENDMENTS

1. Employment and Support Allowance (Consequential Provisions) (No.2) Regulations 2008 (SI 2008/1554) reg.50(1) and (2) (October 27, 2008).
2. Transfer of Tribunal Functions Order (SI 2008/2833) Sch.3 paras 138 and 142 (November 3, 2008).
3. Welfare Reform Act 2012 s.91 and Sch.9 paras 34 and 35 (April 8, 2013).
4. Welfare Reform Act 2012 s.31 and Sch.2 paras 40 and 41 (April 29, 2013).
5. Mesothelioma Act 2014 s.11 and Sch.1 para.7 (March 31, 2014).

GENERAL NOTE

This section is applied with modifications to cases concerned with the recovery of payments within the scope of s.1A(2) (see the Social Security (Recovery of Benefits) (Lump Sum Payments) Regulations 2008 reg.2 and Sch.1 para.18). In particular, "certificate" is defined as meaning "a certificate which includes amounts in respect of recoverable benefits and of recoverable lump sum payments, including where any of those amounts are nil". **1.361**

Regulations and orders

1.362 **30.**—(1) Any power under this Act to make regulations or an order is exercisable by statutory instrument.

(2) A statutory instrument containing regulations or an order under this Act (other than regulations under section [1 11(2A) or] 24 or an order under section 34) shall be subject to annulment in pursuance of a resolution of either House of Parliament.

[1 (2A) A statutory instrument containing regulations under section 11(2A) may not be made unless a draft of the instrument has been laid before and approved by a resolution of each House of Parliament.]

(3) Regulations under section 20, under section 24 amending the list of benefits in column 2 of Schedule 2 or under paragraph 9 of Schedule 1 may not be made without the consent of the Treasury.

(4) Subsections (4), (5), (6) and (9) of section 189 of the Social Security Administration Act 1992 (regulations and orders—general) apply for the purposes of this Act as they apply for the purposes of that.

DEFINITIONS

"benefit"—see s.29.
"regulations"—*ibid.*

AMENDMENT

1. Welfare Reform Act 2012 s.102(6) and Sch.11 paras 9 and 11 (February 25, 2013 for regulation-making purposes and April 29, 2013 for all other purposes).

GENERAL NOTE

1.363 This section is applied to cases concerned with the recovery of payments within the scope of s.1A(2) (see the Social Security (Recovery of Benefits) (Lump Sum Payments) Regulations 2008 reg.2).

1.364 **31.** *Omitted.*

Power to make transitional, consequential etc. provisions

1.365 **32.**—(1) Regulations may make such transitional and consequential provisions, and such savings, as the Secretary of State considers necessary or expedient in preparation for, in connection with, or in consequence of—

(a) the coming into force of any provision of this Act, or
(b) the operation of any enactment repealed or amended by a provision of this Act during any period when the repeal or amendment is not wholly in force.

(2) Regulations under this section may (among other things) provide—

(a) for compensation payments in relation to which, by virtue of section 2, this Act does not apply to be treated as payments in relation to which this Act applies,
(b) for compensation payments in relation to which, by virtue of section 2, this Act applies to be treated as payments in relation to which this Act does not apply, and
(c) for the modification of any enactment contained in this Act or referred to in subsection (1)(b) in its application to any compensation payment.

DEFINITIONS

"compensation payment"—see s.1(4)(b).
"payment"—see s.29.
"regulations"—*ibid.*

GENERAL NOTE

See reg.12 of the Social Security (Recovery of Benefits) Regulations 1997. **1.366**

33. *Omitted.* **1.367**

Short title, commencement and extent

34.—(1) This Act may be cited as the Social Security (Recovery of Benefits) Act 1997. **1.368**

(2) Sections 1 to 24, 26 to 28 and 33 are to come into force on such day as the Secretary of State may by order appoint, and different days may be appointed for different purposes.

(3) Apart from sections 25 to 27, section 33 so far as it relates to any enactment which extends to Northern Ireland, and this section this Act does not extend to Northern Ireland.

GENERAL NOTE

Some regulation-making powers were brought into force on September 3, 1997 but the main provisions of the Act came into force on October 6, 1997 (see the Social Security (Recovery of Benefits) Act 1997 (Commencement Order) 1997 (SI 1997/2085)). **1.369**

Subss.(1) and (3) are applied to cases concerned with the recovery of payments within the scope of s.1A(2) (see the Social Security (Recovery of Benefits) (Lump Sum Payments) Regulations 2008 reg.2).

SCHEDULES

SCHEDULE 1

COMPENSATION PAYMENTS

PART I

Exempted payments

1. Any small payment (defined in Part II of this Schedule). **1.370**

2. Any payment made to or for the injured person under section 35 of the Powers of Criminal Courts Act 1973 or section 249 of the Criminal Procedure (Scotland) Act 1995 (compensation orders against convicted persons).

3. Any payment made in the exercise of a discretion out of property held subject to a trust in a case where no more than 50 per cent. by value of the capital contributed to the trust was directly or indirectly provided by persons who are, or are alleged to be, liable in respect of—

(a) the accident, injury or disease suffered by the injured person, or
(b) the same or any connected accident, injury or disease suffered by another.

4. Any payment made out of property held for the purposes of any prescribed trust (whether the payment also falls within paragraph 3 or not).

5. Any payment made to the injured person by an insurance company within the meaning of the Insurance Companies Act 1982 under the terms of any contract of insurance entered into between the injured person and the company before—

claimed damages in respect of her continuing liability to her landlord. The judge awarded her 5/7ths of the rent settlement and he held that that compensation was not for loss of earnings but for the destruction of the business. The Court of Appeal held that it was "compensation for earnings lost" and that the compensator was therefore entitled to deduct from that compensation the amount of relevant benefits paid to the claimant.

By reg.16 of the Employment and Support Allowance (Transitional Provisions, Housing Benefit and Council Tax Benefit) (Existing Awards) (No.2) Regulations 2010 (SI 2010/1907), this Act is applied with effect from October 1, 2010 for the purposes of enabling the Secretary of State to recover employment and support allowance paid in consequence of a "conversion decision" if a compensation payment is made. This is achieved by treating a conversion decision as though it were a decision as to a person's entitlement to an employment and support allowance which had been made on a claim. Whether it was really necessary to include this Act within the scope of reg.16 seems doubtful.

1.376 "Compensation for earnings lost" includes interest on damages for loss of earnings (*Griffiths v British Coal Corp* [2001] EWCA Civ 336; [2001] 1 W.L.R. 1493).

Given the way that ss.6 and 8 operate together, compensation for lost earnings presumably includes compensation for loss of *potential* earnings in the case of a person who was not employed at the time of a relevant accident or who was in temporary employment only. A benefit is recoverable only if it was paid "in respect of" the relevant accident, injury or disease (see the note to s.1).

"Compensation for cost of care" includes damages for services in the nature of care and domestic assistance given gratuitously, because the object of the legislation is to avoid double recovery as well as avoiding loss to the Secretary of State who had become liable to pay the benefits (*Griffiths v British Coal Corp* [2001] EWCA Civ 336; [2001] 1 W.L.R. 1493).

"Compensation for loss of mobility" in para.3, col.1 refers only to compensation for patrimonial (i.e. financial) loss, such as the cost of fares for journeys by bus or taxi, and does not refer to any element of solatium (i.e. compensation for pain and suffering or loss of amenity) (*Mitchell v Laing*, 1998 S.C. 342).

1.377 Schedules 3 and 4: *Omitted.*

Social Security Act 1998

(1998 c.14)

ARRANGEMENT OF SECTIONS

PART I

DECISIONS AND APPEALS

CHAPTER I

GENERAL

Decisions

Appeals

4. to 7. *Repealed.*

CHAPTER II

SOCIAL SECURITY DECISIONS AND APPEALS

Decisions

8. Decisions by Secretary of State.
9. Revision of decisions.
10. Decisons superseding earlier decisions.
10A. Reference of issues by Secretary of State to Inland Revenue.
11. Regulations with respect to decisions.

Appeals

12. Appeal to First-tier Tribunal.
13. Redetermination etc. of appeals by tribunal.
14. Appeal from First-tier Tribunal to Upper Tribunal.
15. Application for permission to appeal against a decision of the Upper Tribunal.

Procedure etc.

16. Procedure.
17. Finality of decisions.
18. Matters arising as respects decisions.

Medical examinations

19. Medical examination required by Secretary of State.
20. Medical examination required by appeal tribunal.

Suspension and termination of benefit

21. Suspension in prescribed circumstances.
22. Suspension for failure to furnish information etc.
23. Termination in cases of failure to furnish information.
24. Suspension and termination for failure to submit to medical examination.

Appeals dependent on issues falling to be decided by Inland Revenue

24A. Appeals dependent on issues falling to be decided by Inland Revenue.

Part III

Benefits

Part IV

Miscellaneous and Supplemental

An Act to make provision as to the making of decisions and the determination of appeals under enactments relating to social security, child support, vaccine damage payments and war pensions; to make further provision with respect to social security; and for connected purposes.

[21st May 1998]

PART I

DECISIONS AND APPEALS

CHAPTER I

GENERAL

Decisions

Transfer of functions to Secretary of State

1.379 **1.** *Omitted.*

Use of computers

1.380 **2.**—(1) Any decision, determination or assessment falling to be made or certificate falling to be issued by the Secretary of State under or by virtue of a relevant enactment, or in relation to a war pension, may be made or issued not only by an officer of his acting under his authority but also—

(a) by a computer for whose operation such an officer is responsible; and

(b) in the case of a decision, determination or assessment that may be made or a certificate that may be issued by a person providing services to the Secretary of State, by a computer for whose operation such a person is responsible.

(2) In this section "relevant enactment" means any enactment contained in—

(a) Chapter II of this Part;

(b) the Social Security Contributions and Benefits Act 1992 ("the Contributions and Benefits Act");

(c) the Administration Act;

(d) the Child Support Act;

(e) the Social Security (Incapacity for Work) Act 1994;

(f) the Jobseekers Act 1995 ("the Jobseekers Act");

(g) the Child Support Act 1995; [1 . . .]

(h) the Social Security (Recovery of Benefits) Act 1997 [2 . . .]

[1 (i) the State Pension Credit Act 2002;]

[2(j) Part 1 of the Welfare Reform Act 2007;] [4 . . .]

[4 (k) Part 1 of the Welfare Reform Act 2012;] [5 . . .]

[3 (l) Part 4 of that Act;]

[5 (m) Part 1 of the Pensions Act 2014] [6 or

(n) section 30 of the Pensions Act 2014].

(3) In this section and section 3 below "war pension" has the same meaning as in section 25 of the Social Security Act 1989 (establishment and functions of war pensions committees).

AMENDMENTS

1. State Pension Credit Act 2002 Sch.1 para.5 and Sch.3 (July 2, 2002 for the purpose of exercising any power to make regulations or orders and April 7, 2003 for other purposes).

2. Welfare Reform Act 2007 Sch.3 para.17(1) and (2) (July 27, 2008).
3. Welfare Reform Act 2012 s.91 and Sch.9 paras 37 and 38 (April 8, 2013).
4. Welfare Reform Act 2012 s.31 and Sch.2 paras 43 and 44 (April 29, 2013).
5. Pensions Act 2014 s.23 and Sch.12 paras 31 and 32 (April 6, 2016).
6. Pensions Act 2014 s.31(5) and Sch.16 paras 37 and 38 (April 6, 2017).

DEFINITIONS

"the Administration Act"—see s.84.
"the Child Support Act"—*ibid.*
"relevant enactment"—see subs.(2).
"war pension"—see subs.(3).

GENERAL NOTE

This section applies as though the Pension Schemes Act 1993 were a relevant enactment (Pension Schemes Act 1993 s.170(1)). **1.381**

In *C3/07-08(IS)*, a Deputy Commissioner in Northern Ireland was highly critical of the failure of computer-generated letters issued in Northern Ireland to reflect the statutory provisions for decision-making in the Northern Ireland equivalent to this Act. He held a decision that failed adequately to inform the recipient of her rights to seek reasons or to appeal to be so defective as to be invalid.

Use of information

3.—(1) Subsection (2) below applies to information relating to [2 any of the matters specified in subsection (1A) below] which is held— **1.382**

(a) by the Secretary of State or the Northern Ireland Department; or
(b) by a person providing services to the Secretary of State or the Northern Ireland Department in connection with the provision of those services.

[2 (1A) The matters are—

(a) social security [3 . . .] or war pensions;
[3 (aa) child support [5 . . .];]
(b) employment or training;
(c) private pensions policy;
(d) retirement planning:]
[4 (e) the investigation or prosecution of offences relating to tax credits.]
[6 (f) the Diffuse Mesothelioma Payment Scheme.]]

(2) Information to which this subsection applies—

(a) may be used for the purposes of, or for any purposes connected with, the exercise of functions in relation to [2 any of the matters specified in subsection (1A) above]; and
(b) may be supplied to, or to a person providing services to, the Secretary of State or the Northern Ireland Department for use for those purposes.

(3) [1 . . .]

(4) In this section "the Northern Ireland Department" means the Department of Health and Social Services for Northern Ireland [1 or the Department for Employment and Learning in Northern Ireland].

[2 (5) In this section—

"private pensions policy" means policy relating to occupational pension schemes for personal pension schemes (within the meaning given by section 1 of the Pension Schemes Act 1993);

"retirement planning" means promoting financial planning for retirement.]

AMENDMENTS

1. Employment Act 2002 Sch.6 paras 1 and 4 (September 9, 2002).
2. Pensions Act 2004 Sch.10 para.1 (November 18, 2004).
3. Child Maintenance and Other Payments Act 2008 s.57(1) and Sch.7 para.3(1) and (2) (April 6, 2010).
4. Welfare Reform Act 2012 s.127(10) (May 8, 2012).
5. Public Bodies (Child Maintenance and Enforcement Commission: Abolition and Transfer of Functions) Order 2012 (SI 2012/2007) art.3(2) and Sch. para.64(a) (August 1, 2012).
6. Mesothelioma Act 2014 s.11 and Sch.1 paras 1 and 21 (March 31, 2014).

DEFINITIONS

"the Administration Act"—see s.84.
"the Northern Ireland Department"—see subs.(4).
"private pensions policy"—see subs.(5).
"retirement planning"—*ibid.*
"war pension"—see s.2(3).

GENERAL NOTE

1.383 This section provides for the sharing of what would otherwise be confidential information between the Department for Work and Pensions in Great Britain and departments in Northern Ireland. See also the Social Security Investigation Powers (Arrangements with Northern Ireland) Regulations 2007 (SI 2007/271). Most, if not all, of those functions of the Department of Health and Social Services (which is now the Department of Health) that are relevant to this section were transferred to a new Department for Social Development in 1999 (which has now been merged into the Department for Communities).

Provision is made for functions under this section to be exercised on behalf of the Secretary of State by the Scottish Ministers (see s.93(1) of the Scotland Act 1998 and art.2(1)(b) of the Scotland Act 1998 (Agency Arrangements) (Specification) Order 2014 (SI 2014/1892)), because the Scottish Ministers exercise relevant functions relating to employment and training.

Appeals

1.384 **4.** [1 . . .]

AMENDMENT

1. Transfer of Tribunal Functions Order 2008 (SI 2008/2833) Sch.3 paras 143 and 144 (November 3, 2008).

1.385 **5.–7.** [1 . . .]

AMENDMENT

1. Transfer of Tribunal Functions Order 2008 (SI 2008/2833) Sch.3 paras 143 and 145–147 (November 3, 2008), subject to a saving under art.1(5).

GENERAL NOTE

1.386 These sections made provision for appeal tribunals, to whom appeals lay under s.12 and from whom appeals lay to Social Security Commissioners under s.14. Both the appeal tribunals and Commissioners also had functions under other legislation. Subject to one exception, the functions of appeal tribunals constituted under this Act and Commissioners have been transferred respectively to the First-tier Tribunal and the Upper Tribunal. The exception is the determination by appeal tribunals of appeals referred by Scottish Ministers under s.158 of the Health and Social Care (Community Health and Standards) Act 2003 and the determination by Commissioners of appeals against such determinations under s.159. Those functions relate to the recovery of National Health Service charges in Scotland and could not be transferred because health is a devolved function in Scotland. Therefore, although ss.5–7 are repealed for all other purposes, art.1(5) of the Transfer of Tribunal Functions Order 2008 has the effect that those provisions, and a number of other provisions relating to the appointment of appeal tribunals and Commissioners and their procedural rules, remain in force in Scotland for the purposes of the 2003 Act. The Personal Injuries (NHS Charges) (Reviews and Appeals) (Scotland) Regulations 2006 (SSI 2006/593) make procedural provision for these appeals and reg.8(2) applies a number of otherwise revoked regulations in Pts IV and V of the Social Security and Child Support (Decisions and Appeals) Regulations 1999 Regulations for those purposes.

If there were in fact any such appeals, the Scottish Parliament might perhaps legislate to redirect the appeals to another tribunal or court. In England and Wales, s.158 of the 2003 Act has been amended by the 2008 Order and now provides for the Secretary of State to refer appeals to the First-tier Tribunal. See the Personal Injuries (NHS Charges) (Reviews and Appeals) and Road Traffic (NHS Charges) (Reviews and Appeals) (Amendment) Regulations 2006 (SI 2006/3398), as amended, for procedural provisions.

CHAPTER II

SOCIAL SECURITY DECISIONS AND APPEALS

Decisions

Decisions by Secretary of State

8.—(1) Subject to the provisions of this Chapter, it shall be for the Secretary of State— **1.387**

(a) to decide any claim for a relevant benefit;
(b) [6 . . .] [1and]
(c) subject to subsection (5) below, to make any decision that falls to be made under or by virtue of a relevant enactment; [1 . . .]
(d) [1 . . .]

(2) Where at any time a claim for a relevant benefit is decided by the Secretary of State—

(a) the claim shall not be regarded as subsisting after that time; and
(b) accordingly, the claimant shall not (without making a further claim) be entitled to the benefit on the basis of circumstances not obtaining at that time.

(3) In this Chapter "relevant benefit" [2 . . .] means any of the following, namely—

(a) benefit under Parts II to V of the Contributions and Benefits Act;
[8 (aa) universal credit;]
[9 (ab) state pension or a lump sum under Part 1 of the Pensions Act 2014;]

[10 (ac) bereavement support payment under section 30 of the Pensions Act 2014;].

(b) a jobseeker's allowance;

[5(ba) an employment and support allowance]

[7(baa) personal independence payment;]

[3(bb) state pension credit;]

(c) income support;

(d) [4 . . .];

(e) [4 . . .];

(f) a social fund payment mentioned in section 138(1)(a) or (2) of the Contributions and Benefits Act;

(g) child benefit;

(h) such other benefit as may be prescribed.

(4) In this section "relevant enactment" means any enactment contained in this Chapter, the Contributions and Benefits Act, the Administration Act, the Social Security (Consequential Provisions) Act 1992 [3, the Jobseekers Act [5, the State Pension Credit Act 2002 [8, Part 1 of the Welfare Reform Act 2007, Part 1 of the Welfare Reform Act 2012] [7 [9, Part 4 of that Act or Part 1 of the Pensions Act 2014]]] [10 or section 30 of that Act], other than one contained in—

(a) Part VII of the Contributions and Benefits Act so far as relating to housing benefit and council tax benefit;

(b) Part VIII of the Administration Act (arrangements for housing benefit and council tax benefit and related subsidies).

(5) [1 Subsection (1)(c) above does not include any decision which under section 8 of the Social Security Contributions (Transfer of Functions, etc.) Act 1999 falls to be made by an officer of the Inland Revenue.]

AMENDMENTS

1. Social Security Contributions (Transfer of Functions, etc.) Act 1999 Sch.7, para.22 (April 1, 1999).

2. Welfare Reform and Pensions Act 1999 s.88 and Sch.13 (April 6, 2000).

3. State Pension Credit Act 2002 Sch.1 para.6 (July 2, 2002 for regulation-making and order-making purposes and April 7, 2003 for other purposes).

4. Tax Credits Act 2002 Sch.6 (April 8, 2003, subject to a saving in respect of outstanding questions concerning work families' tax credit and disabled person's tax credit—see Tax Credits Act 2002 (Commencement No.4, Transitional Provisions and Savings) Order 2003 (SI 2003/962) art.3(1)–(3)).

5. Welfare Reform Act 2007 Sch.3 para.17(1) and (3) of and July 27, 2008 for other purposes (March 18, 2008 for regulation-making purposes).

6. Welfare Reform Act 2012 s.147 and Sch.14 Pt.8 (April 1, 2013).

7. Welfare Reform Act 2012 s.91 and Sch.9 paras 37 and 39 (February 25, 2013 for regulation-making purposes and April 8, 2013 for other purposes).

8. Welfare Reform Act 2012 s.31 and Sch.2 paras 43 and 45 (February 25, 2013 for regulation-making purposes and April 29, 2013 for other purposes).

9. Pensions Act 2014 s.23 and Sch.12 paras 31 and 33 (April 6, 2016).

10. Pensions Act 2014 s.31(5) and Sch.16 paras 37 and 39 (April 6, 2017).

DEFINITIONS

"the Administration Act"—see s.84.

"claim"—by virtue of s.39(2), see s.191 of the Social Security Administration Act 1992.

"claimant"—see s.39(1) and, by virtue of s.39(2), see s.191 of the Social Security Administration Act 1992.

"the Contributions and Benefits Act"—see s.84.
"Inland Revenue"—by virtue of s.39(2), see s.191 of the Social Security Administration Act 1992 but note that the Inland Revenue has been merged into Her Majesty's Revenue and Customs by the Commissioners for Revenue and Customs Act 2005.
"the Jobseekers Act"—see s.84.
"prescribed"—*ibid.*
"relevant benefit"—see subs.(3).
"relevant enactment"—see subs.(4).

General Note

This section makes general provision for initial decisions by the Secretary of State. However, by Tax Credits Act 1999 s.2(1)(b) and Sch.2 para.5(b)(i), the functions of making initial decisions in respect of working families' tax credit and disabled person's tax credit (both now abolished) were transferred to officers of the Inland Revenue. By s.50(2)(e) of the Tax Credits Act 2002, the Secretary of State's functions under this Act relating to child benefit and guardian's allowance were transferred to the Board of Inland Revenue with effect from April 7, 2003. The Inland Revenue has now been merged into Her Majesty's Revenue and Customs, by the Commissioners for Revenue and Customs Act 2005. **1.388**

By regs 6 and 16 of the Employment and Support Allowance (Transitional Provisions, Housing Benefit and Council Tax Benefit) (Existing Awards) (No. 2) Regulations 2010 (SI 2010/1907), the whole of Ch.II of Pt I of the 1998 Act is applied with effect from October 1, 2010 for the purposes of enabling the Secretary of State to make, revise and supersede a "conversion decision" moving a claimant from incapacity benefit to employment and support allowance and to enable "any other matter to be determined in connection with any person's entitlement or continuing entitlement to an award of an employment and support allowance by virtue of these Regulations". This is achieved by treating a conversion decision as though it were a decision as to a person's entitlement to an employment and support allowance which had been made on a claim.

Subsection (1)

The Secretary of State must investigate any claim and ensure that the claimant is asked the appropriate questions so that he or she has a reasonable opportunity to produce material evidence. See under the heading *The inquisitorial role of the tribunal and the burden of proof* in the note to s.3(1) of the Tribunals, Courts and Enforcement Act 2007 in Part V below. Much of what is said in that note under the heading *Evidence* is also relevant to the Secretary of State's consideration of a claim, as is what is said under the heading *Relying on decisions of other bodies*. Thus, where another body has made a decision on a question relevant to a claim for benefit, it is not necessary for the Secretary of State to consider that question from scratch as though the other decision did not exist, provided the other body made a considered decision on the point. He is entitled, in the absence of anything to compel a contrary conclusion, to regard the existence of that decision as satisfactory evidence (*R(H) 9/04*) of the facts found by that body. However, he is not bound to reach the same conclusion as the other body and must take account of any new evidence or any contrary submission made by the claimant. **1.389**

In *C v Secretary of State for Work and Pensions (Zacchaeus 2000 intervening)* [2015] EWHC 1607 (Admin), it was held that delays of thirteen and ten months in making decisions on claims for personal independence payment were unlawful—the Secretary of State must act reasonably in allocating resources in the light of the volume of applications, the resources available and the need to ensure fairness and consistency (see *R v Secretary of State for Social Services, ex parte CPAG* [1990] 2 QB 540 and *R.(S) v Secretary of State for the Home Department* [2007] EWCA Civ 546; [2007] Imm AR 781 at [51]) —but did not breach the European Convention on

entitled to employment and support allowance under reg.30 was a decision made under s.8(1)(c) so that the claimant would have a right of appeal under s.12. That could be important if it were again decided that the claimant did not have limited capability for work because it could be argued that benefit should at least have been awarded until that later decision was made. However, the Upper Tribunal reached no firm conclusion because the question had turned out to be academic as it had subsequently been decided that the claimant did have limited capability for work.

Subsection (3)

1.392 It having been pointed out that the lack of any reference in subs.(3) to mobility allowance meant that there was no power to revise or supersede a decision relating to mobility allowance so as to be able to recover an overpayment (*CDLA/2999/2004*), the Social Security Act 1998 (Prescribed Benefits) Regulations 2006 prescribe a number of benefits payable under the Social Security Act 1995 and the Supplementary Benefits Act 1976. The benefits prescribed were all abolished before the 1998 Act came into force and are unemployment benefit, sickness benefit, invalidity benefit, attendance allowance (as paid to those under 65), mobility allowance and supplementary benefit.

The provisions of Ch.II of Pt I of the 1998 Act are applied to decisions under ss.2 and 3 of the Age-Related Payments Act 2004, not by virtue of regulations made under this subsection but by s.5(5) of the 2004 Act.

Subsection (5)

1.393 Under s.8(1)(e) of the Social Security Contributions (Transfer of Functions, etc.) Act 1999 and the Commissioners for Revenue and Customs Act 2005, it is for Her Majesty's Revenue and Customs to determine whether contributions of a particular class have been paid in respect of any period. Thus, it is for Her Majesty's Revenue and Customs to determine the amount of contributions paid but it is for the Secretary of State to decide any question about the interpretation or application of the Social Security (Earnings Factor) Regulations 1979 (*R(IB) 1/09*).

However, any question as to the amount of contributions paid for graduated retirement benefit remains a matter for Secretary of State (*R(P) 1/08*) as are the questions whether a person is entitled to "credits" (Sch.3 para.17 to the Social Security Act 1998, *CIB/2338/2000*) or is entitled to home responsibilities protection (Sch.3 para.16). It also appears that any dispute as to which is the relevant contribution year in respect of any claim is a matter for the Secretary of State, so that the effect of *Secretary of State for Social Security v Scully* [1992] 1 W.L.R. 927 (reported also as *R(S) 5/93*) is reversed and the effect of *R(G) 1/82* is restored. The Secretary of State's decisions are appealable under s.12.

Revision of decisions

1.394 **9.**—(1) [1 . . .] Any decision of the Secretary of State under section 8 above or section 10 below may be revised by the Secretary of State—

(a) either within the prescribed period or in prescribed cases or circumstances; and

(b) either on an application made for the purpose or on his own initiative;

and regulations may prescribe the procedure by which a decision of the Secretary of State may be so revised.

(2) In making a decision under subsection (1) above, the Secretary of State need not consider any issue that is not raised by the application or, as the case may be, did not cause him to act on his own initiative.

(3) Subject to subsections (4) and (5) and section 27 below, a revision under this section shall take effect as from the date on which the original decision took (or was to take) effect.

(4) Regulations may provide that, in prescribed cases or circumstances, a revision under this section shall take effect as from such other date as may be prescribed.

(5) Where a decision is revised under this section, for the purpose of any rule as to the time allowed for bringing an appeal, the decision shall be regarded as made on the date on which it is so revised.

(6) Except in prescribed circumstances, an appeal against a decision of the Secretary of State shall lapse if the decision is revised under this section before the appeal is determined.

AMENDMENT

1. Welfare Reform Act 2012 s.147 and Sch.14 Pt.8 (April 1, 2013).

DEFINITION

"prescribed"—see s.84.

GENERAL NOTE

This section applies to decisions under ss.2 and 3 of the Age-Related Payments Act 2004 (see s.5(5) of the 2004 Act). In relation to child benefit and guardian's allowance, the functions of the Secretary of State under this section were transferred with effect from April 7, 2003 to the Board of Inland Revenue (Tax Credits Act 2002 s.50(2)(e)). The functions of the Secretary of State in relation to the former working families' tax credit and disabled person's tax credit were similarly transferred to officers of the Inland Revenue from October 5, 1999 (Tax Credit Act 1999 s.2(1)(b) and Sch.2). The Inland Revenue has now been merged into Her Majesty's Revenue and Customs, by the Commissioners for Revenue and Customs Act 2005. **1.395**

This section also applies to most decisions of Her Majesty's Revenue and Customs made under s.170(2) of the Pensions Schemes Act 1993, by virtue of s.170(4).

By regs 6 and 16 of the Employment and Support Allowance (Transitional Provisions, Housing Benefit and Council Tax Benefit) (Existing Awards) (No. 2) Regulations 2010 (SI 2010/1907), the whole of Ch.II of Pt I of the 1998 Act is applied with effect from October 1, 2010 for the purposes of enabling the Secretary of State to make, revise and supersede a "conversion decision" moving a claimant from incapacity benefit to employment and support allowance and to enable "any other matter to be determined in connection with any person's entitlement or continuing entitlement to an award of an employment and support allowance by virtue of these Regulations". This is achieved by treating a conversion decision as though it were a decision as to a person's entitlement to an employment and support allowance which had been made on a claim.

Subsection (1)

Under the Social Security Administration Act 1992, provision was made for the "review" of decisions. Such reviews are replaced by "revisions" under s.9 and "supersessions" under s.10. Note that only a decision of the Secretary of State may be revised whereas a decision of the Secretary of State *or* of a tribunal or a Commissioner may be superseded. Apart from that, there is little that can be gleaned from the primary legislation as to the difference between revision and supersession. The most obvious distinction between the two concepts probably lies in the date from which the new decision takes effect. Where a decision is revised, the revised decision has effect from the effective date (or what should have been the effective date) of the original decision (see s.9(3)). On a supersession, the new decision takes effect from the date on which it is made and does not affect any past period, subject to limited provision for backdating in some cases (s.10(5)). A related distinction is that there is no appeal under s.12 against a refusal to revise under **1.396** s.9. Formally, there is only a right of appeal against the original decision but s.9(5) extends the time for appealing against the original decision if it is revised, although not always if there is a refusal to revise (see the annotation to subs.(5)). By contrast, an appeal may be brought under s.12 against any decision under s.10. Beyond all that, no indication is given by the primary legislation as to the circumstances in which a revision of a decision is more appropriate than a supersession or vice versa. For that information, one must look at regs 3 and 4 of the Social Security and Child Support (Decisions and Appeals) Regulations 1999, regs 5–11 of the Child Benefit and Guardian's Allowance (Decisions and Appeals) Regulations 2003 and regs 5, 6 and 8–19 of the Universal Credit, Personal Independence Payment, Jobseeker's Allowance and Employment and Support Allowance (Decisions and Appeals) Regulations 2013 relating to revisions and at reg.6 of the 1999 Regulations, reg.13 of the 2003 Regulations and regs 22–31 of the 2013 Regulations relating to supersession. There would still be some overlap between the two procedures if it were not for reg.6(3) of the 1999 Regulations, reg.15 of the 2003 Regulations, and reg.32 of the 2013 Regulations which provide that a decision that may be revised cannot be superseded (save in limited circumstances where the revision could not take into account a further ground of supersession).

Happily, an application for supersession may be treated as an application for revision and vice versa (regs 3(10) and 6(5) of the 1999 Regulations regs 7(1)(a) and 14(1)(a) of the 2003 Regulations and regs 20(1) and 33(1) of the 2013 Regulations), so that it is not fatal if claimants or their advisors do not fully understand the difference when making the application.

Despite, or perhaps because of, this flexibility, experience shows that decisions are not always issued in the correct form. Indeed, it is often Departmental practice to issue decisions that state the outcome without stating whether the decision is a revision or supersession. It has been suggested that that is not necessarily improper when the decision is first issued to the claimant but that the decision ought nonetheless to have been made in the appropriate form so that, if there is a request for reasons or an appeal, the true basis of the decision can be explained (*CIB/313/2002*). However, strong criticisms have been made of the Secretary of State's failure in many circumstances to record any decision at all in the proper form (see *CPC/3891/2004* and *R(IS) 13/05*). Even where a decision is made in terms of a revision or supersession, there are occasions when the wrong type of decision is issued. This is unfortunate because the distinction between revision and supersession is very important when an appeal is lodged. While an appeal following a revision or refusal to revise lies against the original decision, an appeal following a supersession or refusal to supersede lies against the later decision. It is particularly important for a decision terminating an award to be issued in the correct form if the Secretary of State or Her Majesty's Revenue and Customs intends subsequently to make a decision to the effect that there has been a recoverable overpayment, because s.71(5A) of the Social Security Administration Act 1992 generally requires there to have been a revision or supersession before an overpayment can be recovered (*CIS/3228/2003*, *R(IS) 13/05*). Section 71(5A) recognises that, unless an award is either revised or else superseded on a ground that makes the supersession retrospective by virtue of reg.7 of the 1999 Regulations, reg.16 of the 2003 Regulations, or regs 34–37 of the 2013 Regulations, the original award still governs entitlement in respect of the period before the decision terminating it was made and it cannot be shown that any benefit was overpaid.

1.397 For the circumstances in which a tribunal may give a decision in terms of supersession on an appeal following a revision or refusal to revise and vice versa, see the note to s.12(2), where it is suggested that many of the difficulties identified would be removed if some ground for revision were instead grounds for supersession. In deciding whether revision or supersession was the more appropriate remedy, the draftsmen of the Regulations appear to have placed too much emphasis on the date from which a decision is effective and too little on the lack of an appropriate right of appeal against a decision given in terms of revision and the lack of any express provision for correcting on appeal a decision-maker's mistaken choice as to the appropriate procedure for making a change to an earlier decision.

Section 9(1) provides that "any decision . . . under section 8 above or section 10 below" may be revised. However, in s.12(1) there is reference to "any decision . . . under section 8 or 10 above (whether as originally made or as revised under section 9 above)" and similar words referring to section 9 are to be found in s.10(1)(a). Do those references to s.9 in ss.10 and 12 suggest that references to decisions under ss 8 and 10 normally include decisions that have been revised? Or does the fact that there are references to s.9 in ss.10 and 12 but none in s.9 itself suggest that a decision that has already been revised cannot be revised again? In *CIS/3535/2003*, the Deputy Commissioner preferred the former approach and said, obiter, that a decision that has already been revised may be revised again and that the time for bringing an application under reg.3(1) of the Social Security and Child Support (Decisions and Appeals) Regulations 1999 starts again from the date the revision is notified.

Subsection (2)

Note that the Secretary of State "need not", but nonetheless may, consider additional issues. On an appeal following a revision or refusal to revise, the decision under appeal is the original decision (see subs.(5) read with s.12(1)). The tribunal's duty to consider issues is determined by the issues raised by the appeal (see s.12(8)(a)) rather than by the issues raised by the earlier application for revision because it is not obliged to consider independently the merits of the revisions or refusal to revise. **1.398**

Subsection (4)

See reg.5 of the Social Security and Child Support (Decisions and Appeals) Regulations 1999, reg.12 of the Child Benefit and Guardian's Allowance (Decisions and Appeals) Regulations 2003 and reg.21 of the Universal Credit, Personal Independence Payment, Jobseeker's Allowance and Employment and Support Allowance (Decisions and Appeals) Regulations 2013 which provide that the principal exception to the general rule is where a ground for the revision is that the original decision was made effective from the wrong date in the first place. **1.399**

Subsection (5)

This allows a claimant to appeal against a revised decision. However, it does not apply where a decision is not revised. On the other hand, the time for appealing against a decision that has not been revised is extended where the application for revision was made in circumstances where "mandatory reconsideration" applied (see r.22(2)(d)(i) of the Tribunal Procedure (First-tier Tribunal) (Social Entitlement Chamber) Rules 2008) or was otherwise made under reg.3(1) or (3) of the Social Security and Child Support (Decisions and Appeals) Regulations 1999 reg.5 of the Universal Credit, Personal Independence Payment, Jobseeker's Allowance and Employment and Support Allowance (Decisions and Appeals) Regulations 2013 (see r.22(2)(d)(ii) of, and para.5(c) of Sch.1 to, the 2008 Rules). In other cases, it will generally be wise for any person asking for a revision to lodge an appeal at the same time so that, if the decision is not revised, the claimant will not have to bring a late appeal. The fact that a claimant was waiting for a decision on an application for revision may be regarded as a compelling reason for admitting an appeal late, but a claimant would be unwise to take that for granted. If, the claimant having lodged both an application for revision and an appeal, the decision is not revised, the appeal will proceed. If the decision is revised, the appeal will lapse under subs.(6) only if the revised decision is more advantageous to the claimant than the original decision. This subsection then applies to such a case, enabling the claimant to appeal against the decision as revised. If the original decision is revised otherwise than to the advantage of the claimant, the appeal will not lapse but the claimant will be given another month to make representations in the light of the revision. **1.400**

In a case where an application for revision is made otherwise than under reg.3(1) and (3) of the Social Security and Child Support (Decisions and Appeals) Regulations 1999 and more than 13 months has elapsed since the original decision, so that no appeal may be brought against it, there is no way of challenging by way of an appeal a refusal to revise the decision (see *R(IS) 15/04* and *Beltekian v Westminster CC* [2004] EWCA Civ 1784 (reported as *R(H) 8/05*), in which no attempt appears to have been made to argue that subs.(5) should be read as including a refusal to revise in the same way that s.12(9) must be read as referring to a refusal to supersede). Recourse must be had to judicial review. It follows that, although a refusal to revise a decision may include a refusal to supersede the decision and an appeal might be brought against the refusal to supersede, it is not permissible for the First-tier Tribunal when deciding such an appeal to substitute a decision in terms of revision, at least where the refusal to revise is explicit (*R(IS) 15/04*, applied in *AW v SSWP (IB)* [2013] UKUT 20 (AAC)). Attention was drawn in *JA v SSWP (DLA)* [2014] UKUT 44 (AAC) to anomalies that can flow from this approach, given some of the circumstances in which decisions must be revised rather than superseded.

Subsection (6)

1.401 See reg.30 of the Social Security and Child Support (Decisions and Appeals) Regulations 1999, reg.27 of the Child Benefit and Guardian's Allowance (Decisions and Appeals) Regulations 2003 and reg.52 of the Universal Credit, Personal Independence Payment, Jobseeker's Allowance and Employment and Support Allowance (Decisions and Appeals) Regulations 2013.

Decisions superseding earlier decisions

1.402 **10.**—(1) Subject to [1 subsection (3)] [4 . . .] below, the following, namely—

(a) any decision of the Secretary of State under section 8 above or this section, whether as originally made or as revised under section 9 above; [3 ...]

[3(aa) any decision under this Chapter of an appeal tribunal or a Commissioner; and]

(b) any decision under this Chapter [2 of the First-tier Tribunal or any decision of the Upper Tribunal which relates to any such decision]

may be superseded by a decision made by the Secretary of State, either on an application made for the purpose or on his own initiative.

(2) In making a decision under subsection (1) above, the Secretary of State need not consider any issue that is not raised by the application or, as the case may be, did not cause him to act on his own initiative.

(3) Regulations may prescribe the cases and circumstances in which, and the procedure by which, a decision may be made under this section.

(4) [1 . . .]

(5) Subject to subsection (6) and section 27 below, a decision under this section shall take effect as from the date on which it is made or, where applicable, the date on which the application was made.

(6) Regulations may provide that, in prescribed cases or circumstances, a decision under this section shall take effect as from such other date as may be prescribed.

[3 (7) In this section—

"appeal tribunal" means an appeal tribunal constituted under Chapter 1 of this Part (the functions of which have been transferred to the First-tier Tribunal);

"Commissioner" means a person appointed as a Social Security Commissioner under Schedule 4 (the functions of whom have been transferred to the Upper Tribunal), and includes a tribunal of such persons.]

AMENDMENTS

1. Social Security Contributions (Transfer of Functions, etc.) Act 1999 Sch.7 para.23 (April 1, 1999).
2. Transfer of Tribunal Functions Order 2008 (SI 2008/2833) Sch.3 paras 143 and 148 (November 3, 2008).
3. Welfare Reform Act 2012 s.103 and Sch.12 para.4 (November 3, 2008).
4. Welfare Reform Act 2012 s.147 and Sch.14 Pt.8 (April 1, 2013).

DEFINITIONS

"appeal tribunal" –see subs.(7).
"Commissioner"—*ibid.*
"prescribed"—see s.84.

GENERAL NOTE

Transitional provisions in the various commencement orders bringing this Act into force (see the note to s.87), provide for the supersession under this section of decisions made by the various adjudicating authorities that existed under earlier legislation and, in *CI/1800/01*, the Commissioner construed a reference to adjudicating medical authorities as including medical appeal tribunals so as to enable a claimant to apply for supersession of a decision of a medical appeal tribunal that had continuing effect. However, in *CDLA/2999/2004*, the Commissioner declined to find any power to supersede an award of mobility allowance (which was a benefit that was replaced by the mobility component of disability living allowance in April 1992) made by an adjudication officer in 1986. 1.403

The practical effect of *CDLA/2999/2004* has now substantially been reversed by the Social Security Act 1998 (Prescribed Benefits) Regulations 2006, which prescribes mobility allowance (and certain other benefits) for the purposes of s.8(3)(h) of this Act, and by the Social Security Act 1998 (Commencement Nos.9 and 11) (Amendment) Order 2006 (SI 2006/2540), which amends transitional provisions relating to the replacement of sickness and invalidity benefit by incapacity benefit and to the replacement of attendance allowance for people under 65 and mobility allowance by disability living allowance.

The insertion of subs.(1)(aa) retrospectively makes transitional provision (previously assumed to be unnecessary) expressly enabling decisions of appeal tribunals and Commissioners made before November 3, 2008 to be superseded.

This section applies to decisions under ss.2 and 3 of the Age-Related Payments Act 2004 (see s.5(5) of the 2004 Act). 1.404

In relation to child benefit and guardian's allowance, the functions of the Secretary of State under this section were transferred with effect from April 7, 2003 to the Board of Inland Revenue (Tax Credits Act 2002 s.50(2)(e)). The functions of the Secretary of State in relation to the former working families' tax credit and disabled person's tax credit were similarly transferred to officers of the Inland Revenue from October 5, 1999 (Tax Credit Act 1999 s.2(1)(b) and Sch.2). The Inland Revenue has now been merged into Her Majesty's Revenue and Customs, by the Commissioners for Revenue and Customs Act 2005.

This section also applies to most decisions of Her Majesty's Revenue and Customs made under s.170(2) of the Pensions Schemes Act 1993, by virtue of s.170(4).

By regs 6 and 16 of the Employment and Support Allowance (Transitional Provisions, Housing Benefit and Council Tax Benefit) (Existing Awards) (No. 2) Regulations 2010 (SI 2010/1907), the whole of Ch.II of Pt 1 of the 1998 Act is applied with effect from October 1, 2010 for the purposes of enabling the Secretary of State to make, revise and supersede a "conversion decision" moving a claimant from incapacity benefit to employment and support allowance and to enable "any other matter to be determined in connection with any person's entitlement or continuing entitlement to an award of an employment and support allowance by virtue of these Regulations". This is achieved by treating a conversion decision as though it were a decision as to a person's entitlement to an employment and support allowance which had been made on a claim.

Subsection (1)

1.405 For the distinction between revision and supersession, see the note to s.9(1). Note that an application for supersession may be treated as an application for revision and vice versa (regs 3(10) and 6(5) of the Social Security and Child Support (Decisions and Appeals) Regulations 1999 regs 7(1)(a) and 14(1)(a) of the Child Benefit and Guardian's Allowance (Decisions and Appeals) Regulations 2003 and regs 20(1) and 33(1) of the Universal Credit, Personal Independence Payment, Jobseeker's Allowance and Employment and Support Allowance (Decisions and Appeals) Regulations 2013).

Also, under reg.6(5) of the 1999 Regulations or reg.33(1) of the 2013 Regulations, the provision of information to the Secretary of State may be treated as an application for supersession. There are no other provisions specifying what constitutes an application for supersession. In *CI/954/2006*, the Commissioner doubted that giving information to a medical adviser during an examination was to be treated as an application for supersession, although the Secretary of State could have superseded on his own motion in the light of the information.

Often departmental procedures require a claimant to complete a claim form for what is really a supersession rather than a claim. This can lead to confusion. One example is the practice of requiring claimants of income support who move to a new address to complete a new claim. If this is not done promptly, a claimant may find that there is a gap in benefit payments that is not subsequently made up. The grounds upon which benefit is withheld in those circumstances may be somewhat dubious. In *CI/954/2006*, it was pointed out that where a claimant is in receipt of disablement benefit and suffers another industrial accident, a claim in respect of the subsequent accident may have to be treated in the alternative as an application for supersession of the original award, because, following *R(I) 4/03*, aggregation of assessments of disablement is an alternative to the making of two separate awards. One practical difference is that claims may be backdated but supersessions in those circumstances cannot, which the Commissioner suggested is anomalous. The Commissioner also pointed out that an application for supersession of an assessment of disablement needed to be treated also as an application for supersession of the underlying award if proper effect was to be given to any supersession of the assessment of disablement (see the annotations to regs 6 and 26 of the 1999 Regulations, below). Similarly, in *ED v SSWP* [2009] UKUT 206 (AAC) it was held that a claimant was applying for supersession of an earlier tribunal's decision, rather than making a new claim, when he had an existing award of disablement benefit in respect of one injury and was seeking to reopen the question whether he was suffering from a loss of faculty in respect of another condition following the earlier tribunal's decision that he was not.

It was held in *PH v SSWP (DLA)* [2013] UKUT 268 (AAC) that the Secretary of State is entitled to extend the period of an award of disability living allowance by way of supersession. It is unlikely that he would often wish to do so, rather than requiring the claimant to make a renewal claim, but the point was important in that case because the question that arose was whether the First-tier Tribunal, standing in the shoes of the Secretary of State, had the power to extend the period of an award when allowing an appeal against a supersession decision that had prematurely ended an award with the result that the claimant had not made a renewal claim.

Subsection (2)

1.406 A person may appeal against aspects of a decision superseding an earlier decision notwithstanding that the decision maker did not address his or her mind to those aspects of the decision on the supersession, having done so only when making the earlier decision (*MF v Redcar and Cleveland BC (HB)* [2015] UKUT 634 (AAC)). Thus, although, when superseding and terminating an award of contributory employment and support allowance on the ground that 365 days have elapsed without the claimant having been in the support group, the Secretary of State is entitled to rely on their previous decision that the claimant did not have a limited capability for work-related activity, the claimant is entitled to raise on an appeal against the supersession decision the question whether they did have a limited capability for work-related activity at the date of the supersession decision (*MC v SSWP (ESA)* [2014] UKUT 125 (AAC); [2014] AACR 35). However, where an issue is not raised by an appeal, the fact that it was not raised before the Secretary of State either may be a factor the tribunal should take into account when deciding whether to consider the issue on the appeal (see s.12(8)(a)).

Subsection (3)

See regs 6 and 8 of the Social Security and Child Support (Decisions and Appeals) Regulations 1999, regs 13 and 14 of the Child Benefit and Guardian's Allowance (Decisions and Appeals) Regulations 2003 and regs 22–31 and 33 of the Universal Credit, Personal Independence Payment, Jobseeker's Allowance and Employment and Support Allowance (Decisions and Appeals) Regulations 2013. **1.407**

Where a person applies for supersession and the Secretary of State decides that the case and circumstances are not among those prescribed by reg.6 of the 1999 Regulations (or, equally, reg.13 of the 2003 Regulations), it has now been established that the Secretary of State may issue a decision refusing to supersede the original decision, rather than superseding it but without making any change (see *Wood v Secretary of State for Work and Pensions* [2003] EWCA Civ 53 (reported as *R(DLA) 1/03*)). It is not entirely clear whether he may still, as an alternative approach, supersede the original decision without making any change, but the distinction is of little practical importance. See the note to reg.6 of the 1999 Regulations.

Subsection (5)

In *R(IB)2/04*, the Tribunal of Commissioners decided that where a claimant has applied for supersession in order to obtain an increase of benefit but the Secretary of State supersedes the award so as to reduce entitlement, the supersession is made on the Secretary of State's own initiative and not on the claimant's application. Therefore, subject to the effect of any regulations made under subs. (6), it is effective from the date of the decision and not the date of the claimant's application. Similarly, where the Secretary of State's supersession decision is not less favourable than the original decision but the claimant appeals and the tribunal not only does not allow the appeal but also makes a decision even less favourable than the original decision, the tribunal's decision is usually effective from the date of the Secretary of State's supersession decision. See paras 95–97 of the Tribunal's decision. **1.408**

Where a decision has been made that invalid care allowance is not payable because incapacity benefit is in payment and reg.4 of the Social Security (Overlapping Benefits) Regulations 1977 precluded the payment of both benefits, a decision to resume payment of invalid care allowance after payment of incapacity benefit ceases is a decision under s.8 and not a supersession under s.10 (*Secretary of State for Work and Pensions v Adams* [2003] EWCA Civ 796 (reported as *R(G) 1/03*)). This means that, where there has been a delay in reinstating payment of invalid care allowance, the decision is nonetheless automatically effective from the date when payment of incapacity benefit ceased, rather than from a later date determined by s.10(5).

Subsection (6)

See reg.7 of, and Schs 3A to 3C to, the Social Security and Child Support (Decisions and Appeals) Regulations 1999 reg.16 of the Child Benefit and Guardian's Allowance (Decisions and Appeals) Regulations 2003 and regs 34–37 of **1.409** the Universal Credit, Personal Independence Payment, Jobseeker's Allowance and Employment and Support Allowance (Decisions and Appeals) Regulations 2013.

[1 *Reference of issues by Secretary of State to Inland Revenue*

References of issues by Secretary of State to Inland Revenue

1.410 **10A.**—(1) Regulations may make provision requiring the Secretary of State, where on consideration of any claim or other matter he is of the opinion that there arises any issue which under section 8 of the Social Security Contributions (Transfer of Functions, etc.) Act 1999 falls to be decided by an officer of the Inland Revenue, to refer the issue to the Inland Revenue.

Regulations under this section may—

(a) provide for the Inland Revenue to give the Secretary of State a preliminary opinion on any issue referred to them,

(b) specify the circumstances in which an officer of the Inland Revenue is to make a decision under section 8 of the Social Security Contributions (Transfer of Functions, etc.) Act 1999 on a reference by the Secretary of State,

(c) enable or require the Secretary of State, in specified circumstances to deal withany other issue arising on consideration of the claim or other matter pending the decision of the referred issue, and

(d) require the Secretary of State to decide the claim or other matter in accordance with the decision of an officer of the Inland Revenue on the issue referred to them, or in accordance with any determination of the [2 First-tier Tribunal or Upper Tribunal] made on appeal from [2 the tribunal's decision].]

Amendments

1. Social Security Contributions (Transfer of Functions, etc.) Act 1999 Sch.7 para.24 (July 5, 1999).

2. Transfer of Tribunal Functions and Revenue and Customs Appeals Order 2009 (SI 2009/56) Sch.1 paras 247 and 248 (April 1, 2009).

Definitions

"claim"—by virtue of s.39(2), see s.191 of the Social Security Administration Act 1992.

"Inland Revenue"—*ibid*, but note that the Inland Revenue has been merged into Her Majesty's Revenue and Customs by the Commissioners for Revenue and Customs Act 2005.

"prescribed"—see s.84.

"tax appeal Commissioners"—see s.39(1).

General Note

1.411 See reg.11A of the Social Security and Child Support (Decisions and Appeals) Regulations 1999 and reg.42 of the Universal Credit, Personal Independence Payment, Jobseeker's Allowance and Employment and Support Allowance (Decisions and Appeals) Regulations 2013.

Some decisions fall to be made by Her Majesty's Revenue and Customs by virtue of s.170 of the Pensions Schemes Act 1993 (rather than by virtue of s.8 of the Social Security Contributions (Transfer of Functions, etc.) Act 1999) but the Secretary of State may nevertheless refer to Her Majesty's Revenue and Customs issues for determination under the 1993 Act notwithstanding that regulations under this section do not apply (*R(P) 1/04*).

Regulations with respect to decisions

11.—(1) Subject to the provisions of this Chapter and the Administration Act, provision may be made by regulations for the making of any decision by the Secretary of State under or in connection with the current legislation, or the former legislation, including a decision on a claim for benefit. **1.412**

(2) Where it appears to the Secretary of State that a matter before him involves a question of fact requiring special expertise, he may direct that in dealing with that matter he shall have the assistance of one or more experts.

(3) In this section—

"the current legislation" means the Contributions and Benefits Act, the Jobseekers Act [[1], the Social Security (Recovery of Benefits) Act 1997 [[2] , the State Pension Credit Act 2002 [[3], Part 1 of the Welfare Reform Act 2007, Part 1 of the Welfare Reform Act 2012 [[4] , Part 4 of that Act and Part 1 of the Pensions Act 2014]]]] [[5] and section 30 of that Act];

"expert" means a person appearing to the Secretary of State to have knowledge or experience which would be relevant in determining the question of fact requiring special expertise;

"the former legislation" means the National Insurance Acts 1965 to 1974, the National Insurance (Industrial Injuries) Acts 1965 to 1974, the Social Security Act 1975 and Part II of the Social Security Act 1986.

AMENDMENTS

1. State Pension Credit Act 2002 ss.11 and 21 and Sch.1 para.7 and Sch.3 (July 2, 2002 for the purpose of exercising any power to make regulations or orders and April 7, 2003 for other purposes).
2. Welfare Reform Act 2007 Sch.3 para.17(1) and (4) (October 27, 2008).
3. Welfare Reform Act 2012 ss.31 and 91 Sch.2 para.46 and Sch.9 para.40 (February 25, 2013).
4. Pensions Act 2014 s.23 and Sch.12 paras 31 and 34 (April 6, 2016).
5. Pensions Act 2014 s.31(5) and Sch.16 paras 37 and 40 (April 6, 2017).

DEFINITIONS

"the Administration Act"—see s.84.
"benefit"—by virtue of s.39(2), see s.191 of the Social Security Administration Act 1992.
"claim"—*ibid.*
"Contributions and Benefits Act"—see s.84.
"the current legislation"—see subs.(3).
"expert"—*ibid.*
"the former legislation"—*ibid.*
"the Jobseeker's Act"—see s.84.

GENERAL NOTE

In relation to the former working families' tax credit and disabled person's tax credit, the power to make regulations was transferred to the Commissioners of Inland Revenue and the other functions of the Secretary of State were transferred to officers of the Inland Revenue, with effect from October 5, 1999 (Tax Credits Act **1.413**

1999, s.2(1)(b) and Sch.2, paras 5(b)(iii) and 8(a)). In relation to child benefit and guardian's allowance, powers and functions were similarly transferred to the Inland Revenue by the Tax Credits Act 2002 (see s.50(2)(e)). The Inland Revenue has now been merged into Her Majesty's Revenue and Customs, by the Commissioners for Revenue and Customs Act 2005.

Subsection (1)

1.414 See in particular reg.28 of the Social Security and Child Support (Decisions and Appeals) Regulations 1999 and reg.51 of the Universal Credit, Personal Independence Payment, Jobseeker's Allowance and Employment and Support Allowance (Decisions and Appeals) Regulations 2013.

Appeals

Appeal to [2 First-tier Tribunal]

1.415 **12.**—(1) This section applies to any decision of the Secretary of State under section 8 or 10 above (whether as originally made or as revised under section 9 above) which—

(a) is made on a claim for, or on an award of, a relevant benefit, and does not fall within Schedule 2 to this Act; [1 or]

(b) is made otherwise than on such a claim or award, and falls within Schedule 3 to this Act; [1 . . .]

(c) [1 . . .]

[1 (2) In the case of a decision to which this section applies, the claimant and such other person as may be prescribed shall have a right to appeal to [2 the First-tier Tribunal], but nothing in this subsection shall confer a right of appeal –

[3(a) in relation to a prescribed decision, or a prescribed determination embodied in or necessary to a decision;

(b) where regulations under subsection (3A) so provide.]]

(3) Regulations under subsection (2) above shall not prescribe any decision or determination that relates to the conditions of entitlement to a relevant benefit for which a claim has been validly made or for which no claim is required.

[3(3A) Regulations may provide that, in such cases or circumstances as may be prescribed, there is a right of appeal under subsection (2) in relation to a decision only if the Secretary of State has considered whether to revise the decision under section 9.

(3B) The regulations may in particular provide that that condition is met only where—

(a) the consideration by the Secretary of State was on an application,

(b) the Secretary of State considered issues of a specified description, or

(c) the consideration by the Secretary of State satisfied any other condition specified in the regulations.

(3C) The references in subsections (3A) and (3B) to regulations and to the Secretary of State are subject to any enactment under or by virtue of which the functions under this Chapter are transferred to or otherwise made exercisable by a person other than the Secretary of State.]

[5 (3D) In the case of a decision relating to child benefit or guardian's allowance, the making of any appeal under this section against the decision as originally made must follow the Commissioners for Her Majesty's Revenue and Customs first deciding, on an application made for revision of that decision under section 9, not to revise the decision.]

(4) Where the Secretary of State has determined that any amount is recoverable under or by virtue of section 71 [4 , 71ZB, 71ZG, 71ZH,] or 74 of the Administration Act, any person from whom he has determined that it is recoverable shall have the same right of appeal to [2 the First-tier Tribunal] as a claimant.

(5) In any case where—

(a) the Secretary of State has made a decision in relation to a claim under Part V of the Contributions and Benefits Act; and

(b) the entitlement to benefit under that Part of that Act of any person other than the claimant is or may be, under Part VI of Schedule 7 to that Act, affected by that decision,

that other person shall have the same right of appeal to [2 the First-tier Tribunal]as the claimant.

(6) A person with a right of appeal under this section shall be given such notice of a decision to which this section applies and of that right as may be prescribed.

(7) Regulations may –

[3(a) make provision as to the manner in which, and the time within which, appeals are to be brought;

(b) provide that, where in accordance with regulations under subsection (3A) there is no right of appeal against a decision, any purported appeal may be treated as an application for revision under section 9.]

(8) In deciding an appeal under this section, [2 the First-tier Tribunal]—

(a) need not consider any issue that is not raised by the appeal; and

(b) shall not take into account any circumstances not obtaining at the time when the decision appealed against was made.

(9) The reference in subsection (1) above to a decision under section 10 above is a reference to a decision superseding any such decision as is mentioned in paragraph (a) or (b) of subsection (1) of that section.

AMENDMENTS

1. Social Security Contributions (Transfer of Functions, etc.) Act 1999 Sch.7 para.25 (April 1, 1999).

2. Transfer of Tribunal Functions Order 2008 (SI 2008/2833) Sch.3 paras 143 and 149 (November 3, 2008).

3. Welfare Reform Act 2012 s.102(1)–(4) (February 25, 2013).

4. Welfare Reform Act 2012 s.105(6) (April 29, 2013).

5. Tax Credits, Child Benefit and Guardian's Allowance Reviews and Appeals Order 2014 SI 2014/886 art.4(1) (April 6, 2014).

DEFINITIONS

"the Administration Act"—see s.84.

"claim"—by virtue of s.39(2), see s.191 of the Social Security Administration Act 1992.

"claimant"—see s.39(1) and, by virtue of s.39(2), see s.191 of the Social Security Administration Act 1992.

"the Contributions and Benefits Act"—see s.84.
"prescribed"—*ibid.*
"relevant benefit"—see s.8(3).

GENERAL NOTE

1.416 This section provides only for appeals against decisions made by the Secretary of State under ss.8 and 10 of this Act. However, it applies to decisions under ss.2 and 3 of the Age-Related Payments Act 2004 by virtue of s.5(5) of the 2004 Act) and is also applied to other decisions of the Secretary of State by reg.9 of the Social Security (Work-focused Interviews for Lone Parents) and Miscellaneous Amendments Regulations 2000 reg.15 of the Social Security (Jobcentre Plus Interviews) Regulations 2002 and reg.14 of the Social Security (Jobcentre Plus Interviews for Partners) Regulations 2003, all of which are concerned with decisions that claimants have failed without good cause to attend interviews.

It also applies—with only the modification that references to the Secretary of State are to be construed as references to the Board of Inland Revenue or to an officer of the Inland Revenue—so as to provide for appeals against decisions relating to child benefit and guardian's allowance (by virtue of the Tax Credits Act 2002 Sch. para.50), against decisions relating to the former working families' tax credit and disabled person's tax credit (by virtue of the Tax Credits Act 1999 Sch.2 para.21), against penalties imposed under s.9(1), (3)(a) or (5)(a) of the 1999 Act (by virtue of Sch.4 para.3(2) of the 1999 Act) and against decisions given under s.170 of the Pension Schemes Act 1993 in respect of retirement pensions (by virtue of s.170(6) of the 1993 Act). The Inland Revenue has now been merged into Her Majesty's Revenue and Customs, by the Commissioners for Revenue and Customs Act 2005.

Quite separate rights of appeal to the First-tier Tribunal are given under s.4 of the Vaccine Damage Payments Act 1979 (in respect of vaccine damage payments—see Volume I of this work), under ss.11 and 12 of the Social Security (Recovery of Benefits) Act 1997 (in respect of the recovery of benefits from those making compensation payments in respect of personal injury), under reg.10(2B) of the Employment Protection (Recoupment of Jobseeker's Allowance and Income Support) Regulations 1996 (in respect of the recovery of benefits from those making compensation payments in employment tribunal proceedings), under s.50 of the Child Maintenance and Other Payments Act 2008 (in respect of mesothelioma lump sum payments), under reg.25 of the Diffuse Mesothelioma Payment Scheme Regulations 2014 and under s.56 of the Childcare Payments Act 2014.

1.417 Separate rights of appeal to the First-tier Tribunal are also conferred by ss.21(9) and 22 of the Child Trust Funds Act 2004, but subss.(7) and (8)(b) of this section are applied in modified form to such appeals by reg.6 of the Child Trust Funds (Non-tax Appeals) Regulations 2005 (SI 2005/191) (which were originally made under s.24(5) of the 2004 Act and remain valid under the new s.23(6)). See Vol. IV for the 2004 Act and the Child Trust Funds (Appeals) Regulations 2005, made under subs.(7) as so applied.

Until April 1, 2009, a version of subs.(1) of this section, substituted for subs (1) and (2), and modified versions of subss.(7) and (8)(b) were applied to appeals under the Tax Credits Act 2002 by reg.4 of the Tax Credits (Appeals) Regulations 2002 (SI 2002/2926). However, those Regulations then lapsed insofar as they applied in Great Britain for reasons explained in *JI v HMRC (TC)* [2013] UKUT 199 (AAC) and alternative provision has now been made (see Vol.IV).

Numerous statutes and regulations outside the scope of this work also provide rights of appeal to the First-tier Tribunal in classes of case allocated to the Social Entitlement Chamber.

Subsection (1)

1.418 This section provides only for appeals against decisions under ss.8 and 10 of this Act (but see the note above). Challenges to decisions under s.9 are brought by appealing against the original decision rather than the s.9 decision. The phrase "decision . . . under section . . . 10" includes a decision to refuse to supersede (*Wood v Secretary of State for Work and Pensions* [2003] EWCA Civ 53 (reported as *R(DLA) 1/03*)), notwithstanding the terms of subs.(9).

There cannot be an appeal unless there has been a decision under s.8 or s.10 and so a tribunal had no jurisdiction to consider a challenge to the Secretary of State's failure to exercise his power to make a winter fuel payment without a claim (*R(IS) 12/05*). In *CIS/4088/2004*, the Commissioner considered that there must have been a decision refusing to make a payment in circumstances where the claimant had previously received a winter fuel payment and it was erroneously believed within the Department for Work and Pensions that no further payment could be made in the absence of a claim after the claimant had ceased to be entitled to incapacity benefit, but that decision was doubted in *CIS/840/2005*.

A lacuna in subs.(1) was explored in *R(IS) 14/04*, where the claimant had purported to appeal to an appeal tribunal against a decision to the effect that benefit was recoverable from him under s.74 of the Social Security Administration Act 1992. The Commissioner agreed with the tribunal that a right of appeal could not arise under subs.(1)(b) because there was no reference in Sch.3 to decisions under s.74 of the 1992 Act, although paras 5 and 6 of the Schedule refer to recoverability decisions made under s.71 of the 1992 Act and subs.(4) shows that it is intended that claimants should be entitled to appeal against decisions under either s.71 or s.74. He concluded that the right of appeal arose under subs.(1)(a) because the decision under s.74 "is sufficiently related to the award of income support on which the excess payment has been made". The same reasoning was applied in *VT v SSWP (IS)* [2016] UKUT 178 (AAC); [2016] AACR 42, where it was held that there was a right of appeal against the imposition of a civil penalty under s.115D of the Social Security Administration Act 1992.

The scope of an appeal

The scope of the First-tier Tribunal's jurisdiction must depend on the scope of the decision which is the subject of the appeal. Paragraph (a) provides for an appeal against any decision made *on* a claim or award. Section 20(1)(a) and (b) of the Social Security Administration Act 1992 drew a distinction between a "claim" and a "question" and s.36 expressly enabled a tribunal to deal with any question first arising before them and not previously considered by an adjudication officer. The new legislation does not use the terms "claim" and "question" and there is no provision similar to the old s.36. However, this may not make much difference. In *CIB/2338/2000*, the Commissioner held that the only type of "decision" that could be appealed was an "outcome" decision which is "a useful expression to refer to decisions that have, in crude terms, an impact on a claimant's pocket". He pointed out that an appeal lay only against decisions under ss.8 and 10. Section 8(1)(a) provides only that the Secretary of State shall "decide any claim". Section 8(1)(c) provides for the making of "any decision that falls to be made under or by virtue of any enactment" but the Commissioner did not construe that as referring to the individual determinations that are the building blocks of a decision on a claim for benefit. He understood it to refer to the making of decisions in relation to, say, crediting of earnings for contributions purposes. Section 10 refers to the supersession of decisions under s.8 or decisions of tribunals or Commissioners on appeal against from s.8 decisions. Therefore, there is no appeal against a decision on what used to be called a "question". In *CIB/2338/2000*, that meant that there was no appeal solely against the determination that the claimant was incapable of work; the appeal was against the consequential decision that he was not entitled to a "credit". This approach, which was endorsed by a Tribunal of Commissioners in *R(IB) 2/04*, makes it unnecessary for there to be a provision equivalent to the old s.36 expressly providing for a tribunal to deal with an issue that has not been considered by a decision-maker, because it is implicit that, if a tribunal has rejected a ground upon which the decision-maker has made an "outcome decision", it is necessary (subject to **1.419** s.12(8)(a)) for the tribunal to consider such other issues as are necessary in order to substitute its own "outcome decision" for the decision-maker's. However, this is all subject to two qualifications. First, Sch.3 to the Act and reg.26 of the Social Security and Child Support (Decisions and Appeals) Regulations 1999 make provision for appeals to be brought against certain freestanding decisions that are not "outcome decisions". Secondly, there are circumstances in which a tribunal is not obliged to substitute an "outcome decision" for one under appeal but may, in effect, remit the case to the Secretary of State or Her Majesty's Revenue and Customs (*R(IS) 2/08*, discussed in more detail in the annotation to subs.(2) below).

Accurately identifying the scope of the appeal may be very important in some cases.

By virtue of s.12(1)(b) there is a right of appeal against an assessment of disablement for industrial disablement benefit, as a freestanding decision (see para.9 of Sch.3 to the Act and reg.26 of the Social Security and Child Support (Decisions and Appeals) Regulations 1999). In *R(I) 5/02*, the Tribunal of Commissioners held that a tribunal considering such an appeal had no jurisdiction to consider a refusal of benefit consequent upon the assessment of disablement. It is not clear how the two decisions were notified to the claimant in that case but it has been suggested that an appeal against an assessment of disablement should be treated as being also an appeal against the refusal of benefit, unless the Secretary of State is prepared to treat it as an application for revision of the refusal of benefit (*CI/1547/2001*). This is because, if there is no appeal against the refusal of benefit, it would have to be revised or superseded to give effect to a successful appeal in respect of the assessment of disablement. It does not appear that any such revision or supersession could be effective from the beginning of the period of assessment if action for revision or supersession is taken only after the tribunal's decision.

There are other circumstances where a decision against one decision should be taken to be also an appeal against another decision, even where the other decision is implicit and has not actually been recorded. Thus, in *R(JSA) 2/04*, it was held that, where a claimant seeks benefit for the period between the end of one award and a new claim, an appeal against a refusal to backdate the new claim must sometimes be treated as being also an appeal against the termination of that previous award, because the latter may be the decision that is really being challenged. Similarly, in *CS v SSWP (DLA)* [2011] UKUT 509 (AAC), an appeal against a decision in respect of entitlement was held also to have been an appeal against a separate decision that an overpayment was recoverable. In *Abbas v Secretary of State for Work and Pensions* [2005] EWCA Civ 652, where the claimant had made a continuation claim for disability living allowance and the Secretary of State's response was to supersede the existing award and terminate it before it had originally been due to end, it was necessary for the appeal against the supersession decision to be treated also as an appeal against a disallowance of the continuation claim because otherwise, even if the claimant showed that she satisfied the conditions for entitlement to disability living allowance, benefit could not be awarded in respect of any period after the original renewal date.

Subsection (2)

1.420 For regulations made under this subsection, see regs 25 and 27 of the Social Security and Child Support (Decisions and Appeals) Regulations 1999, regs 24 and 25 of the Child Benefit and Guardian's Allowance (Decisions and Appeal) Regulations 2003 and regs 49 and 50(2) of the Universal Credit, Personal Independence Payment, Jobseeker's Allowance and Employment and Support Allowance (Decisions and Appeals) Regulations 2013.

Even where an appeal to the First-tier Tribunal must be lodged with a decision-maker, the decision-maker is not entitled to refuse to refer the case to a tribunal if he considers that the tribunal has no jurisdiction to hear it. It is for the tribunal to determine whether it has jurisdiction to hear a case (*R(I) 7/94*) and, if the decision-maker were to refuse to refer an appeal to the tribunal, it would be open to the tribunal to consider whether it had jurisdiction and, if it had, to determine the appeal without the appeal having been passed to it (*R(H) 1/07*).

The nature of an appeal to the First-tier Tribunal

For the investigatory approach of the First-tier Tribunal and its approach to evidence, see the note to s.3(1) of the Tribunals, Courts and Enforcement Act 2007. 1.421

An appeal to the First-tier Tribunal is a rehearing (*R(F) 1/72*); it is not just a review of the decision under appeal. The tribunal stands in the shoes of the decision-maker and has the power to consider any issue and make any decision the decision-maker could have made (*R(IB) 2/04*). Thus, when considering an appeal against a decision that a claimant of employment and support allowance does not have limited capability for work-related activity, the First-tier Tribunal may consider whether the claimant had a limited capability for work (*AE v SSWP (ESA)* [2014] UKUT 5 (AAC); [2014] AACR 23). A person may appeal against aspects of a decision superseding an earlier decision notwithstanding that the decision-maker did not address his or her mind to those aspects of the decision on the supersession, having done so only when making the earlier decision (*MF v Redcar and Cleveland BC (HB)* [2015] UKUT 634 (AAC)). Thus, on an appeal against a decision superseding and terminating an award of contributory employment and support allowance on the ground that 365 days have elapsed without the claimant having been in the support group, the claimant is entitled to raise the question whether they did have a limited capability for work-related activity at the date of the supersession decision (*MC v SSWP (ESA)* [2014] UKUT 125 (AAC); [2014] AACR 35). Moreover, where the Secretary of State has a broad discretion, e.g. as to the period of disqualification for jobseeker's allowance to be imposed when a person leaves his employment voluntarily without just cause, the tribunal has to substitute its own judgment for that of the Secretary of State, rather than merely considering whether the Secretary of State has acted reasonably (*CJSA/1703/2006*). The same approach applies in contexts other than social security law (see *R(AF) 3/07*, *MC v SSD* [2009] UKUT 173 (AAC) and *Ofsted v GM* [2009] UKUT 89 (AAC); [2010] AACR 21). However, not only does the First-tier Tribunal have no less power than the Secretary of State, it also has no greater power and so is equally unable to supersede an earlier decision of a tribunal on the ground of mistake of law (*NH v CMEC* [2009] UKUT 183 (AAC); [2010] AACR 21).

In *R(H) 6/06*, it was said that "a right of appeal against an exercise of discretion that is non-justiciable because the relevant considerations cannot be discerned must be limited to points of law". In other words, it would be a review rather than a true appeal. A discretion is non-justiciable only if the relevant considerations are policy matters requiring "essentially non-legal judgments" (*R(H) 3/04*) and legislation does not normally confer a right of appeal to a tribunal against such a decision unless it expressly limits the right to points of law. If legislation appears to confer such a right in respect of a non-justiciable decsion, there may arise questions as to the construction or validity of the legislation, as in *R(H) 6/06*. In *R(H) 1/08*, the Commissioner pointed out that the mere fact that different people might legitimately exercise their judgment differently on the same facts does not make the judgment a discretion and, if there is a discretion, does not make it non-justiciable. It has not been suggested that any appeal under s.12 is capable of raising a non-justiciable issue.

The powers of the First-tier Tribunal

There is nothing in s.12 to indicate what powers a tribunal has when it allows an appeal, and, although it stands in the shoes of the decision-maker and can make any decision the decision-maker could have made, it is therefore also open to a tribunal to set aside a decision and, in effect, to remit the case to the original decision-maker where that appears to be more appropriate than substituting its own decision. Examples of cases where that might be done are where a recoverability decision 1.422

should have been made against a person who is not a party to the appeal *(R(H) 6/06)* or where issues first arise in the course of an appeal (*R(IS) 2/08*, where it was made clear that the tribunal must nonetheless deal with the issues originally raised in the appeal). Thus, although an appeal to a tribunal normally lies only against an "outcome decision" (*R(IB) 2/04*), a tribunal hearing an appeal against an "outcome decision" is not always obliged to substitute another such decision. The Tribunal of Commissioners said, at para.48 of *R(IS) 2/08*—

> "When an appeal against an outcome decision raises one issue on which the appeal is allowed but it is necessary to deal with a further issue before another outcome decision is substituted, a tribunal may set aside the original outcome decision without substituting another outcome decision, provided it deals with the original issue raised by the appeal and substitutes a decision on that issue. The Secretary of State must then consider the new issue and decide what outcome decision to give. In that outcome decision, he must give effect to the tribunal's decision on the original issue unless, at the time he makes the outcome decision, he is satisfied that there are grounds on which to supersede the tribunal's decision so as, for instance, to take account of any changes of circumstances that have occurred since he made the decision that was the subject of the appeal to the tribunal. Because his decision is an outcome decision, the claimant will have a right of appeal against it."

The Tribunal of Commissioners gave the following additional guidance at [55(2)]—

> "Where a tribunal, having dealt with the issues originally raised in an appeal, is not able immediately to give an outcome decision, it must decide whether to adjourn or whether to remit the question of entitlement to the Secretary of State. The technical difficulty of the outstanding issues and the likelihood of a further appeal if the entitlement question is remitted will be relevant considerations. The tribunal should consider whether the Secretary of State would be in a better position to decide the issue and to seek further information from the claimant. It may have to balance the desirability of a decision being made as quickly as possible against the desirability of it being made as accurately as possible, given that an appeal on a point of fact will not lie against a decision of the tribunal on any fresh issue. The wishes of the parties should be taken into account."

However, what the First-tier Tribunal cannot do is provide a remedy that the decision-maker could not provide in a decision under s.8 or 10. Thus, if delay in deciding a case is such as to breach an appellant's rights under art.6 of the European Convention on Human Rights, the First-tier Tribunal cannot, on an appeal under this section, provide any remedy for that breach (*AS v SSWP (CA)* [2015] UKUT 592 (AAC); [2016] AACR 22).

Correcting procedural errors by the Secretary of State

1.423 In *R(IB) 2/04*, a Tribunal of Commissioners considered in depth the jurisdiction of tribunals and the extent to which tribunals are limited, or not limited, by the terms of the decision against which an appeal has been brought. They noted that s.12 makes no positive provision at all as to a tribunal's powers so that those powers must be found by a process of implication. They therefore considered the case law on adjudication before the 1998 Act came into force (in particular, *R(F) 1/72*, *R(P) 1/55*, *R(SB) 1/82* and *R(SB) 42/83*). That led to the conclusion that an appeal to an appeal tribunal under s.12 is by way of rehearing. At para.24, the Tribunal said:

> "As a matter of principle, on such an appeal the tribunal may make any decision which the officer below could have made on the legal questions before that officer. That principle encompasses dealing with new questions so as to reach the right

result on an appeal, within the limit that the appeal tribunal has no jurisdiction (in the absence of express legislation to that effect) to determine questions which fall outside the scope of that which the officer below could have done on the proper legal view of the issues before him, by way of a claim or an application or otherwise."

They pointed out, at para.31, that s.12(8)(a) reinforces that approach because it is implicit in that provision that an appeal tribunal is not limited to considering issues actually raised by the parties.

Against that background, the Tribunal considered three issues concerning the powers of tribunals: whether supersession decisions can be substituted for revision decisions and vice versa, whether defects in supersession decisions can be remedied, and whether a tribunal can make a decision less favourable to a claimant than the decision under appeal. (Other issues considered by the Tribunal are noted in the annotations to regs 3 and 6 of the Social Security and Child Support (Decisions and Appeals) Regulations 1999).

Can supersession decisions be substituted for revision decisions and vice versa?

The Tribunal's decision on this issue is based on their view of the nature of appeals following supersession decisions under s.10 and revision decisions under s.9. In the former case, the appeal is, both in form and in substance, an appeal against the decision to supersede or not to supersede. Where there has been a revision or a refusal to revise, any appeal is, in form, against the original decision because s.12(1) does not provide for an appeal against the decision under s.9 but reg.31(2) of the Social Security and Child Support (Decisions and Appeals) Regulations 1999 extends the time for appealing against the earlier decision as revised or, where the revision or non-revision was under regs 3(1) or (3), not revised. If there is a refusal to revise under, say, reg.3(5)(a) on the ground of "official error", the time for appealing is not extended which may have the consequence that the refusal to revise cannot be challenged save by way of judicial review (*R(IS)15/04* , approved by the Court of Appeal in *Beltekian v Westminster CC* [2004] EWCA Civ 1784 (reported as *R(H) 8/05*)). However, where a claimant is entitled to appeal following a refusal to revise a decision on the ground of "official error", he or she must show that the original decision did arise from an official error if the appeal is to be allowed. Therefore, the Tribunal held at para.40 of *R(IB)2/04*, an appeal following a revision or refusal to revise is, in substance, an appeal against the decision under s.9, even if in form it is an appeal against the original decision. 1.424

The parties nonetheless argued that the legislation did not allow a tribunal to give a supersession decision on appeal from a revision decision and vice versa, although counsel for the claimants submitted that it should readily be implied that a revision decision included a refusal to supersede and that a supersession decision included a refusal to revise. However, the Tribunal considered that the result of taking the approach advocated by the parties had too often been absurd. At para.50, they said:

"The meaning of a statutory provision which is so clear that it admits only one possible construction cannot be altered or departed from by reference to the consequences, however inconvenient or anomalous. However, in our judgement the statutory provisions relevant to this issue fail by some margin to reach the degree of clarity which would bring that principle into play. In these circumstances, in ascertaining the legislature's intention, it is quite proper to have regard to the potential consequences of possible alternative constructions, in the context of the statutory scheme as a whole. In the field of benefit decisions and appeals procedure, we consider it proper, in construing the relevant provisions, to assume that the legislature did not intend to create a scheme which would be likely to lead to impracticable or indeed absurd results in a significant number of cases. On the contrary, we proceed on the basis that the legislature intended the provisions relating to decisions and appeals (and in particular those relating to provisions changing the effect of a previous decision) to form at least a reasonably workable scheme."

Having given examples of some of the more absurd consequences of the parties' submissions, the Tribunal held, at para.55:

> "In our judgment, if an appeal tribunal decides that the Secretary of State's decision under Section 9 or Section 10 changing or refusing to change a previous decision was wrong then (subject to the restriction in Section 12(8)(b), if relevant) it has jurisdiction to make the revision or supersession decision which it considers the Secretary of State ought to have made, even if that means making a decision under Section 9 when the Secretary of State acted only under Section 10, and vice versa."

1.425 They rejected the need to resort to the theory of implied decisions on the ground that "the 1998 legislation could not have been intended to involve consideration of such arid technicalities and complications" (at para.59). However, in *R(IS)15/04*, the same Tribunal, sitting a few weeks later resiled somewhat from what they had said in both [55] and [59] of *R(IB)2/04*. In *R(IS)15/04* (subsequently approved by the Court of Appeal in *Beltekian v Westminster CC* [2004] EWCA Civ 1784 (reported as *R(H) 8/05*)), the Secretary of State had expressly both superseded and refused to revise a decision. The claimant appealed but was out of time for appealing against the original decision and so was unable to challenge the refusal to revise although he could challenge the supersession. The Tribunal of Commissioners held that the appeal tribunal had had no jurisdiction to substitute a revision for the supersession, saying, at para.78:

> "It seems to us, in those circumstances, if an appeal tribunal were permitted to substitute a revision decision for the supersession decision, that would in effect be to permit by the back door what is not permitted by the front door, namely an appeal against the refusal to revise."

Obscurely, they added that "[i]t would have been a different matter if the Secretary of State had not made a decision (whether express or implied) on the issue of revision for official error". It is not clear why they took that view, which, strictly speaking, is obiter, particularly as it is not clear what they meant by an implied decision, given their rejection of the theory in *R(IB)2/04*. It is suggested that the theory of implied decisions would always treat a decision in terms of supersession as an implied refusal to revise, even if the issue of official error had not expressly been considered, because it is a precondition of any supersession decision that there are no grounds for revision (see reg.6(3) of the Social Security and Child Support (Decisions and Appeals) Regulations 1999, which allows only a technical exception to that general rule). However, in *CDLA/1707/2005*, the Deputy Commissioner applied the approach of the Tribunal of Commissioners and substituted for a refusal to supersede an award of benefit a decision revising the award on the ground of "official error". In *JS v SSWP (DLA)* [2014] UKUT 44 (AAC), the judge suggested that, had the issue been central to the case, he would have given the Chamber President an opportunity to direct that a three-judge panel should consider the question whether a revision on a ground other than "official error" could properly be substituted for a supersession. He drew attention to further anomalies that can arise if there is no such power (see the note to reg.3(5) of the 1999 Regulations).

Can defects in supersession decisions be remedied?

1.426 The Tribunal of Commissioners in *R(IB)2/04* held that an appeal tribunal can remedy defects in a decision such as failing to acknowledge that an existing decision needed superseding, failing to state the grounds of supersession or relying on the wrong grounds of supersession.

> "72. . . . there may be some decisions made by the Secretary of State which have so little coherence or connection to legal powers that they do not amount to decisions under Section 10 at all. . . .
>
> 73. If, however, the Secretary of State's decision was made under Section 10 (as

to which, see paragraph 76 below), . . . the appeal tribunal has jurisdiction, on appeal, to decide whether the outcome arrived at by that decision (i.e. either to change or not to change the original decision) was correct. . . .
76. In our judgment a decision should generally be regarded as having been made under Section 10, regardless of the form in which it may be expressed, if it has the effect of terminating an existing entitlement from the date of the decision (or from some later date than the effective date of the original decision). . . . Similarly, a decision should generally be regarded as having been made under Section 9 if it changes the original decision with effect from the effective date of that decision."

The implication of the Tribunal's decision appears to be that an appeal tribunal should limit its decision to holding that the Secretary of State's decision was invalid only in cases where the Secretary of State's decision is completely incoherent and the nature of the decision cannot be implied or where the Secretary of State had no power to make any decision at all. Another implication of a tribunal being entitled to correct defects in decisions of the Secretary of State is that it will often be unnecessary for a tribunal to consider the exact nature of the decision of the Secretary of State that is under appeal; it will usually be enough to consider what he *should* have decided (*R(IS) 2/08*). Indeed, in *SSWP v AM (IS)* [2010] UKUT 428, it was noted that there is no statutory requirement to record a decision in writing and, in *SSWP v JM (SPC)* [2013] UKUT 72 (AAC), it was said that the implication was that notice of a decision need not necessarily record the precise wording of the decision although it was also said that there were good reasons why it should. In the latter case, the judge was satisfied that a decision was a supersession because it had obviously "involved the mental processes required for a supersession" (since it was the correct decision on the Secretary of State's understanding of the substantive law and the facts) and the First-tier Tribunal was held to have erred in law in finding the decision to be inchoate. See also *DB v SSWP (SPC)* [2013] UKUT 74 (AAC).

The Tribunal of Commissioners in *R (IB) 2/04* went on to say, at para.82, that it is necessary for an appeal tribunal chairman to "perfect" or "recast" a defective decision in the tribunal's decision notice only "if either (i) the decision as expressed is wrong in some material respect (e.g. states an incorrect ground of appeal) or (ii) there is likely to be some particular practical benefit to the claimant or to the adjudication process in future in reformulating the decision". However, if a statement of reasons is requested, giving reasons for the tribunal's decision is likely to involve explaining how any defects in the Secretary of State's decision were approached.

The ability of a tribunal to correct defects in a decision of the Secretary of State **1.427** means that, where the Secretary of State wrongly applied the personal capability assessment as amended by regulations that had been held to be ultra vires, the tribunal was entitled to substitute a decision by applying the unamended test (*R(IB)5/05*).

The approach taken in *R(IB)* 2/04 has been followed by a Tribunal of Commissioners in Northern Ireland (*BMcD v DSD (DLA)* [2011] NICom 175; [2013] AACR 29) but they suggested a degree of caution: "principally in order to ensure that the perception of the independence of the appeal tribunal is not damaged" and also "to ensure that the appellant is aware of the effect that the exercise of the power to remedy defects may have on the issues of the case".

Can a tribunal make a decision less favourable to a claimant than a supersession decision under appeal?

The Tribunal held that an appeal tribunal could make a decision less favourable **1.428** to a claimant than a supersession decision under appeal. This followed both from the Tribunal's view as to the nature of an appeal to an appeal tribunal and from the terms of s.12(8)(a), implicitly providing that a tribunal may consider issues not raised by the parties. However, the Tribunal made two important comments at paras 94 and 97 of their decision.

First, a tribunal must consciously exercise the discretion in s.12(8)(a) to consider a point not raised by the parties and, if a statement of reasons is requested, must explain in that statement why the discretion was exercised in the manner it was. For the points to be taken into account when exercising the discretion, see the annotation to s.12(8)(a) below.

Secondly, where the tribunal's decision is even less favourable to the claimant than the original decision that was the subject of the supersession decision under appeal, the tribunal's decision is "effectively the exercise by the tribunal of the Secretary of State's power to supersede 'on his own initiative" and so, by virtue of s.10(5), the decision is usually effective from the date of the Secretary of State's decision under appeal rather than from the date of the claimant's application for supersession.

1.429 Although the First-tier Tribunal is therefore entitled to make a decision less favourable to a claimant than the one under appeal, a Commissioner discouraged tribunals from doing so in borderline cases. In *CDLA/2738/2007*, it was said—

> "The tribunal was entitled to take the view that the claimant was not virtually unable to walk but the Secretary of State was equally entitled to take the opposite view. Where a tribunal's findings are not materially different from the Secretary of State's and the Secretary of State's conclusion in favour of the claimant is not perverse, a tribunal should be slow to interfere and must, in accordance with *R(IB) 2/04*, give reasons for considering it necessary to do so."

In *CDLA/884/2008*, he said —

> "8. An increasing number of appeals before Commissioners seem to be cases where a tribunal has made a decision less favourable to the claimant than the one the claimant was challenging before the tribunal. It is not surprising that appeals should be brought before Commissioners in such cases, particularly as the consequence of any such decision is that there will have been an overpayment, the recoverability of which will have been left undetermined by the tribunal. Tribunals need to be aware of the dangers of being both prosecutor and judge, one of which is the risk of making errors unprompted by the parties. Such errors are too common and are contributing significantly to the caseload of Commissioners. It is particularly unfortunate that two of the several errors made by the tribunal in the present case were on points in respect of which a Tribunal of Commissioners had relatively recently given clear guidance.
> 9. There are other risks in being both prosecutor and judge. The most obvious is that there can be a perception that the tribunal has prejudged the case. Of course a tribunal has an inquisitorial or investigative role but here it is noteworthy that the tribunal, having apparently formed the (not unreasonable) view on the papers that the claimant's entitlement to any disability living allowance was doubtful, started the proceedings by warning the claimant that his existing award was at risk and advising him that he could withdraw his appeal. The claimant having declined to withdraw his appeal, the tribunal then launched straight into the question of the claimant's entitlement to the mobility component, by questioning him about how he had got to the hearing, without first listening to what the claimant had to say about his needs for care which was the issue upon which he had brought his appeal. It is little wonder that the claimant says, in effect, that he formed an early view that the tribunal was more interested in its own agenda than in what he had to say."

He pointed out that it was not necessarily enough to give a claimant an opportunity to withdraw his appeal; it had been said in *R(IB) 2/04* that the claimant had to be given sufficient notice to enable him to prepare his case on the new issue, which meant being given notice of the case against him where that would not be obvious to him.

> "10. . . . A tribunal is in a difficult position. If it gives the claimant too robust a warning at the beginning of a hearing, it runs the risk of giving the impression of having prejudged the case. If it does not give such a robust warning, the warning may not adequately convey to the claimant the case he or she needs to consider

resisting with the consequence that a decision not to withdraw the appeal, or not to ask for an adjournment, is not fully informed. This is a powerful reason for tribunals refraining from making decisions less favourable to claimants than the decisions being challenged, except in the most obvious cases (e.g., where the evidence is overwhelming or the facts are not in dispute and no element of judgment is involved or where the law has been misapplied by the Secretary of State) or after an appropriate adjournment. In such obvious cases, a failure expressly to state why a tribunal has considered a point not in issue between the parties will not necessarily render the tribunal's decision erroneous in point of law; in less obvious cases, the absence of a reason for considering the point may suggest that the discretion to do so has not been exercised properly.

11. If a tribunal does not consider the correctness of an award that is not directly in issue before it, it does not follow that it should do nothing if it has doubts about the award. The chairman is at liberty to draw the doubts to the Secretary of State's attention in the decision notice and can arrange for the parties to be sent a copy of the record of proceedings (including his or her note of evidence) without them having to request it. That would enable the Secretary of State to consider a supersession or revision and, in disability living allowance cases, would often avoid the possibility of there having been an overpayment, which is often a consequence of a tribunal considering the issue and which often worries claimants more than the mere cessation of entitlement."

In both cases, the Commissioner restored the Secretary of State's decision. In practice, cases often turn on the claimant's own oral evidence which, if unfavourable to the claimant, is unlikely to be in dispute and, provided the findings of fact are such as to make it clear why the claimant could not be entitled to benefit in the light of that evidence, a tribunal is unlikely then to be found to have erred in not expressly stating why it took the point on its own initiative. An adjournment is also unlikely to be necessary where a case can be determined on the basis of the claimant's own oral evidence and where it could not reasonably be argued that the claimant was entitled to benefit in the light of that evidence. The cases where most care is needed are those truly on a borderline and those where a claimant might be able to provide further evidence if given an opportunity to do so.

In *BK v SSWP* [2009] UKUT 258 (AAC), the Upper Tribunal judge rejected **1.430** an argument that the First-tier Tribunal had failed to act impartially when, after a represented claimant had declined an opportunity to ask for an adjournment, it made a decision less favourable to the claimant than the one being challenged. She said that the First-tier Tribunal's inquisitorial role meant that it ought to investigate an unappealed element of an award if it had a "real doubt" about it. This is not necessarily inconsistent with the approach taken in *CDLA/884/2008* because "real doubt" is a ground for investigating a case rather than a ground for reaching a different conclusion from that reached by the Secretary of State, particularly where grounds for supersession would be required. The comments in *CDLA/884/2008* were concerned mainly with the position after such investigation as is possible at a hearing—which in practice usually consists simply of asking the claimant a few questions—has been concluded.

In *C15/08-09(DLA)*, a Northern Ireland Commissioner has expressed a more fundamental disagreement with the approach taken in *CDLA/884/2008*, stating that, "[w]here the appeal tribunal has any doubt concerning the validity of the decision under appeal, where that decision incorporates an existing award, it is under a duty to undertake a full investigation of the legitimacy of the existing award and determine whether that award is correct".

However, in *AP-H v SSWP (DLA)* [2010] UKUT 183 (AAC), the judge disagreed with both *BK v SSWP* and *C15/08-09(DLA)* insofar as they suggested that there was a duty to consider issues not raised by the appeal. He emphasised that *R(IS) 2/04* made it plain there was a discretion, albeit one that had to be exercised judicially. Nonetheless, he rejected an argument, based on *CDLA/884/2008*, to the effect that the First-tier Tribunal had erred in considering an undisputed award that was not "clearly wrong". He said that the First-tier Tribunal was entitled to consider any issue and that *CDLA/884/2008* was concerned with the question whether it was clear why it had done so in a case where no reason had been given. Looking at the evidence in the case before him, he was satisfied that it *was* clear why the First-tier Tribunal had considered an award that was not in dispute.

The point made in *CDLA/884/2008* about the need to give a claimant an adequate opportunity to put his or her case was repeated in *BTC v SSWP (PIP)* [2015] UKUT 155 (AAC), where it was pointed out that, in any case where the First-tier Tribunal takes a new point, "the claimant will not have had advance notice of the issue, as would be the case if the Secretary of State had been required to give grounds for opposing the appeal under Rule 24(2)(e) of the Tribunal Procedure (First-tier Tribunal) (SEC) Rules 2008" and it was held that "the tribunal's decision to consider on its own initiative whether to remove mobility component led to precisely the kind of unprompted error envisaged in *CDLA/884/2008*. The tribunal's failure to invite the claimant to put her case with regard to the distance from her home to her G.P.'s surgery and with regard to what she did while on holiday, when she could not possibly know that those matters would be crucial to the tribunal's decision, deprived the claimant of the opportunity to correct any errors by the tribunal and amounted to serious breaches of the requirement of fairness."

Vexatious litigants

1.431 The courts have power to make orders barring litigants who persistently bring inappropriate proceedings from bringing further proceedings without permission. This raises the question of the extent to which such orders apply so as to bar a person from exercising a right of appeal to a tribunal.

An extended civil restraint order made against a vexatious litigant in a county court does not prevent the litigant from appealing to the First-tier Tribunal and participating fully in the proceedings (*JW v SSWP* [2009] UKUT 198 (AAC)). Indeed, even when made by the Court of Appeal, an "extended civil restraint order" or "general civil restraint order" can extend only to civil proceedings in a county court, the High Court or the Court of Appeal, because such orders are made under Practice Direction 3C to supplement r.3.11 of the Civil Procedure Rules which apply only in those courts.

On the other hand, differing views have been expressed by the Upper Tribunal as to whether a "civil proceedings order" or an "all proceedings order" made under s.42 of the Senior Courts Act 1981 prevents a person from appealing to the First-tier Tribunal without the permission of the High Court. It is well established that the word "courts" in s.42 has a wide meaning that includes tribunals. In *IB v Information Commissioner* [2011] UKUT 370 (AAC), the Upper Tribunal decided that both the First-tier Tribunal and the Upper Tribunal were courts for the purposes of s.42. However, in *AO v Shepway DC (HB)* [2013] UKUT 9 (AAC), the judge disagreed and held that a civil proceedings order did not preclude a claimant from bringing an appeal before the First-tier Tribunal without the permission of the High Court, at last in a social security case. Considerations which led him to his conclusion included the fact that such cases can be concerned with entitlement to income-related benefits of last resort, that a vexatious litigant cannot bring a case before the First-tier Tribunal without there being a decision against which to appeal, that the First-tier Tribunal has ample powers to deal with hopeless appeals, and that in practice it is impossible to administer a bar because every case would have to be checked against the list of vexatious litigants.

Subsection (3)

1.432 See the note to Sch.2 to the Social Security and Child Support (Decisions and Appeals) Regulations 1999 in which it is suggested that either much of that schedule is ultra vires or else this subsection is of no practical effect.

Subsections (3A)–(3C)

Regulations under subs.(3A) may effectively require would-be appellants to apply for a revision of the decision being challenged before appealing. See reg.3ZA of the Social Security and Child Support (Decisions and Appeals) Regulations 1999 and reg.7 of the Universal Credit, Personal Independence Payment, Jobseeker's Allowance and Employment and Support Allowance (Decisions and Appeals) Regulations 2013. This is known as "mandatory reconsideration". Previously, there was a practice of considering revising a decision (under reg.3(4A) of the 1999 Regulations on the papers after an appeal has been lodged. The intention is to reduce the number of appeals by introducing a more intensive revision process *before* an appeal is lodged in which claimants are telephoned so that they can discuss their cases. **1.433**

The Social Security Advisory Committee considered the impact of "mandatory reconsideration" in a study published in July 2016 (Occasional Paper No.18), which may be found at *https://www.gov.uk/government/publications/government-response-ssac-report-on-decision-making-and-mandatory-reconsideration* (accessed April 2017), together with the Government's responses.

Subsection (3D)

This subsection is plainly intended to have the same sort of effect as regulations made under subs.(3A). However, if read literally, it not only requires a person to apply for a revision before appealing but if the revision is only partially successful, requires them to apply for further revisions until HMRC makes a decision refusing to revise the decision at all. It may, perhaps, be arguable that a revision includes a decision "not to revise" to the extent that it gives the claimant less than had been sought in the application for revision. **1.434**

Subsection (4)

Although this subsection assumes that a claimant has a right of appeal against a decision under s.74 of the 1992 Act, such decisions are not mentioned in Sch.3. However, in *R(IS)14/04*, the Commissioner held that a claimant was entitled to appeal against a decision under s.74 by virtue of subs.(1)(a) of this section, rather than subs.(1)(b). **1.435**

Subsection (7)

Provision for the time and manner in which appeals are to be brought is now made in Tribunal Procedure Rules and so regulations made under subs.(7)(a) have all been revoked except for regs 29A and 30 of the Child Benefit and Guardian's Allowance (Decisions and Appeals) Regulations 2003. Regulation 3ZA(5) of the Social Security and Child Support (Decisions and Appeals) Regulations 1999 and reg.7(5) of the Universal Credit, Personal Independence Payment, Jobseeker's Allowance and Employment and Support Allowance (Decisions and Appeals) Regulations 2013 have been made under subs.(7)(b). **1.436**

Subsection (8)(a)

In *CDLA/1000/2001*, it was held that the question whether an issue is "raised by the appeal" is to be determined by reference to the substance of the appeal and not just the wording of the letter of appeal. The claimant was in receipt of the mobility component of disability living allowance and was seeking the care component. The Commissioner decided that, as the claimant had attributed some of his care needs to the arthritis that caused his mobility difficulties, it was impossible for the tribunal to consider the care component without also considering the basis of the award of the mobility component. Therefore, the claimant's entitlement to the mobility component was raised by his appeal in respect of the care component. The Commissioner also held that the claimant had no preserved right to the protection formerly accorded to life awards of one component when a claimant had sought the other. That protection had been swept away when Pt II of the Social Security Administration Act 1992 was repealed by the Social Security Act 1998. **1.437**

Paragraph (a) confers a discretion. In *CI/531/2000*, the Commissioner considered a standard submission by the Secretary of State in appeals relating to the diagnosis of industrial diseases in which it was said that the only issue before the tribunal was the diagnosis question and that, if the tribunal decided that question in the claimant's favour, it was not possible for them to go on and consider whether to award benefit. The Commissioner held the submission to be wrong in law but that the discretion to consider other issues must be exercised judicially. He pointed out that it was often desirable to deal with disablement at the same time as diagnosis but he said that natural justice required that the claimant (and, it can be added, the Secretary of State) be warned that disablement would also be considered and that when a tribunal dealt with a factual issue that had not previously been considered, the result was that the claimant was deprived of any appeal on the facts (and, it may be added, any application for revision under reg.3(1)(b) of the Social Security and Child Support (Decisions and Appeals) Regulations 1999). However, as already noted in relation to subs.(1), it was held in *CIB/2338/2000* that appeals lie only against "outcome decisions" and not against determinations of mere "questions". It follows that, in any case where a claimant has claimed disablement benefit, a determination that he or she is not suffering from a prescribed disease will be a determination made for the purpose of deciding that disablement benefit is not payable and any challenge to the determination will be made in an appeal against the refusal of benefit. If, on such an appeal, a tribunal decides that the claimant *was* suffering from the prescribed disease at the date the Secretary of State's decision was given, can the tribunal refuse to go on and determine all the other issues that must be determined if a decision is to be made as to whether or not to award benefit? In the light of *R(IS) 2/08*, the answer is now clearly "yes" and, in situations like that arising in *CI/531/2000*, it is often very much easier for everyone if the tribunal leaves the Secretary of State to make a new "outcome decision" than it would be if it does so itself. Thus, it may be that the only error in the Secretary of State's submission in *CI/531/2000* was that it was written in terms of what the tribunal could legally do rather than in terms of what it could do as a matter of practicality without obtaining further submissions.

The approach taken in *R(IS) 2/08* gives greater effect to subs.(8)(a) than the alternative approach would, but the provision would in any event apply where a tribunal could give an "outcome decision" without considering any new issue. In some instances considering a new issue may be to the considerable disadvantage of the claimant who has appealed to the tribunal.

1.438 In *R(IB) 2/04* at paras 93 and 94, the Tribunal of Commissioners held that, where an appeal tribunal is minded to make a decision less favourable to the claimant than the one under appeal and the respondent has not invited them to make such a decision, the appeal tribunal must address their minds to the power conferred by subs.(8)(a) not to consider the issue. The discretion is one to be exercised judicially, taking into account all the circumstances of the particular case. Furthermore, the tribunal's decision is likely to be held to be erroneous in point of law if the statement of reasons does not show that there has been a conscious exercise of the discretion.

> "In exercising the discretion, the appeal tribunal must of course have in mind, in particular, two factors. First, it must bear in mind the need to comply with Article 6 of the Convention and the rules of natural justice. This will involve, at the very least, ensuring that the claimant has had sufficient notice of the tribunal's intention to consider superseding adversely to him to enable him properly to prepare his case. The fact that the claimant is entitled to withdraw his appeal any time before the appeal tribunal's decision may also be material to what Article 6 and the rules of natural justice demand. Second, the appeal tribunal may consider it more appropriate to leave the question whether the original decision should be superseded adversely to the claimant to be decided subsequently by the Secretary of State. This might be so if, for example, deciding that question would involve factual issues which do not overlap those raised by the appeal, or if it would necessitate an adjournment of the hearing."

See also *BMcD v DSD (DLA)* [2011] NICom 175; [2013] AACR 29, a decision of a Tribunal of Commissioners in Northern Ireland.

The same approach is required where a tribunal takes a new point against the Secretary of State. In *CH/3009/2002*, a decision had been made on a claim that could have been treated also as an application for the revision of a decision terminating an earlier award. The Commissioner held that, although it followed from *R(IB) 2/04* that the tribunal had the power to give a decision in terms of revision, the question of revision could be left to the Secretary of State. Thus, subs.(8)(a) can be seen as providing an alternative course of action to the adjournment that will sometimes be required where a new point is taken, although the Commissioner deciding *CH/3009/2002* did comment that, depending on the terms of the Secretary of State's decision, it might not be possible for a claimant to get the case back before a tribunal given the decision of the Tribunal of Commissioners in *R(IS) 15/04* (subsequently approved by the Court of Appeal in *Beltekian v Westminster CC* [2004] EWCA Civ 1784 (reported as *R(H) 8/05*)). It is suggested that the position might be no different if there were an adjournment because the Secretary of State could presumably make a decision before the tribunal was reconvened.

In considering how the discretion conferred by para.(a) should be exercised, a **1.439**
tribunal ought to have regard (among other things) to the adequacy of any alternative action that the claimant or Secretary of State might take to have the new issue taken into account and, if it is not obvious, ought to draw attention to that alternative action (*CDLA/15961/1996*). If an entirely new point is being taken at a hearing, it is necessary for the parties to have the opportunity of dealing with it but that does not necessarily mean there must be an adjournment because it ought to be possible for most points to be adequately considered immediately. If a party has deliberately chosen not to attend, the question whether there should be an adjournment so that he or she may consider the new point may be more complicated. There are three options: to refuse to consider the new point, to consider it immediately or to adjourn. A lot will depend on the nature of the issue and whether any advance notice was given of it, as well as the possibility of applying for a revision or supersession on the new ground. A wise appellant who wishes to raise a new point will give both the tribunal and the Secretary of State notice as soon as possible. However, if the Secretary of State chooses not to be represented at a hearing, it may be thought that he can hardly complain about not being allowed to comment on any evidence the claimant may give.

Subsection (8)(a) implies a power to consider new issues but makes it clear that there are limits to the extent to which the inquisitorial role of a tribunal imposes a duty to consider such issues. As was said by a Tribunal of Commissioners in *R(SB) 2/83*,

> "Everything will depend on the circumstances in any given instance. We would be slow to convict a tribunal of failure to identify an uncanvassed factual point in favour of the claimant in the absence of the most obvious and clear cut circumstances."

In particular, where a claimant has an apparently competent representative, it is not always necessary for a tribunal to explore matters not raised by the representative (see *CSDLA/336/2000*, in which the Commissioner reviews the authorities and emphasises the summary nature of proceedings before tribunals). Thus, in *CSIB/160/2000*, the representative identified the descriptors in issue on the all work test and the tribunal were entitled to assume that the representative knew the claimant's case and so therefore the tribunal did not err in not considering other descriptors. In *CH/2484/2006*, the Deputy Commissioner said that "it would be unrealistic—especially in a case like this where both parties were represented—to expect tribunals to read every clause of a tenancy agreement in case a representative fails to rely on a clause which might be helpful to his case". He also said—

> "To the extent that the local authority is dissatisfied with the outcome of this case, that perhaps highlights the need for thorough preparation of a local

> authority's factual case in advance of tribunal hearings, so that all the points can be raised there. Even the most thoroughly prepared appeal to a Commissioner is not an adequate substitute for doing so, for the reason that, however strongly a Commissioner might doubt the factual correctness of a tribunal decision . . ., the Commissioner's doubts are irrelevant in the absence of an error of law. And it will seldom be an error of law for a tribunal to fail to deal with a point that a local authority representative has not raised before it."

Even less is a tribunal required to investigate issues when a representative has declined to make submissions on them having been given a specific opportunity to do so (*CSIB/588/1998*).

1.440 However, sometimes issues raised by the evidence but overlooked by otherwise competent professional representatives are so fundamental that a tribunal will err in not dealing with them. That was the case in *R4/01(IS)*, a decision of a Tribunal of Commissioners in Northern Ireland. The claimant's executor had appealed to a tribunal against a decision that £63,735.31 had been overpaid to the claimant and was recoverable from her estate because the claimant had failed to disclose capital assets in the form of land. The executor was represented by counsel. The case was argued on the basis that there had been disclosure but it was stated that, although the legal interest in the land was vested in the claimant, the land had been regarded as belonging to her brother. The Tribunal of Commissioners held that that clearly raised the question whether the claimant had any beneficial interest in the land and that the appeal tribunal had erred in failing to consider that issue notwithstanding that it had not been raised by counsel representing the executor. The issue had been fundamental to the appeal. However, the Tribunal of Commissioners also said that an appeal tribunal must have a reasonable expectation that important and fundamental issues will be brought to its attention by professional representatives. Given the professional representation, if the issue of the property being regarded as belonging to the brother had not been mentioned by a witness at the hearing itself, the appeal tribunal would have been entitled to conclude it had been dropped.

The Court of Appeal in Northern Ireland has, in *Mongan v Department for Social Development* [2005] NICA 16 (reported as *R3/05 (DLA)*), taken a similar approach to that taken by Commissioners and the approach taken in *Mongan* has been expressly endorsed by the Court of Appeal in England and Wales (*Secretary of State for Work and Pensions v Hooper* [2007] EWCA Civ 495 (reported as *R(IB) 4/07*). In *Mongan*, the Court held that the identical wording of the Northern Ireland equivalent of s.12(8)(a) suggests "that the tribunal would not be absolved of the duty to consider relevant issues simply because they have been neglected by the appellant or her legal representatives and that it has a role to identify what issues are at stake on the appeal even if they have not been clearly or expressly articulated by the appellant." There is no duty "to exhaustively trawl the evidence to see if there is any remote possibility of an issue being raised by it" but issues "clearly apparent from the evidence" must be considered.

> "[17] Whether an issue is sufficiently apparent from the evidence will depend on the particular circumstances of each case. Likewise, the question of how far the tribunal must go in exploring such an issue will depend on the specific facts of the case. The more obviously relevant an issue, the greater will be the need to investigate it. An extensive enquiry into an issue will not invariably be required. Indeed, a perfunctory examination of the issue may often suffice. It appears to us, however, that where a higher rate of benefit is claimed and the facts presented to the tribunal suggest that an appellant might well be entitled to a lower rate, it will normally be necessary to examine the issue, whether or not it has been raised by the appellant or her legal representatives.
>
> [18] In carrying out their inquisitorial function, the tribunal should have regard to whether the party has the benefit of legal representation. It need hardly be said that close attention should be paid to the possibility that relevant issues might be overlooked where the appellant does not have legal representation. Where an appellant

is legally represented the tribunal is entitled to look to the legal representative for elucidation of the issues that arise. But this does not relieve them of the obligation to enquire into potentially relevant matters. A poorly represented party should not be placed at any greater disadvantage than an unrepresented party."

In that case, the claimant had sought the higher rate of the mobility component of disability living allowance but the Court held that the arguments and evidence presented to the tribunal were such that it should have been alert to the need to investigate entitlement to the lower rate of the mobility component, whether or not that question was raised by the claimant's solicitor.

In *C37/09-10 (DLA)*, a Northern Ireland Commissioner has interpreted that as **1.441** meaning that a concession made by a representative should not be accepted without the tribunal first looking behind it to see whether it was properly made, but that goes much further than the approach to concessions taken in most cases (see above) and, it is suggested, a tribunal is entitled to have regard to an explicit concession when considering whether an issues arises that is "clearly apparent from the evidence". Indeed, it is striking that the appellant claimant in that case did not resile from the concession even on the appeal to the Commissioner.

Moreover, in *CDLA/4099/2004*, the Commissioner held that a tribunal had not erred in law in failing to deal with an issue when the claimant had an adequate alternative remedy. The claimant had applied for supersession of an award of disability living allowance. The application was treated as effective from the date it was received and, on appeal, the case was argued before the tribunal on that basis because the claimant's representative wrongly considered that an award of benefit for a period before the application could be considered on a subsequent application for revision. In fact, the tribunal could, by virtue of s.12(8)(a), have considered entitlement to benefit during that earlier period (because reg.7(6) of the Social Security and Child Support (Decisions and Appeals) Regulations 1999 would have applied if the claimant's proposed argument in respect of that earlier period had been accepted). However, the Commissioner held that the tribunal had not been *bound* to consider entitlement during that earlier period because the claimant still had an adequate alternative remedy in a further application for supersession.

It follows from the power under s.12(8)(a) to deal with issues not raised in an appeal that it is open to the First-tier Tribunal to deal with issues raised by a respondent to a multi-party case without it being necessary for the respondent to cross-appeal or submit a respondent's notice. However, in *John v Information Commissioner* [2014] UKUT 444 (AAC) where the Upper Tribunal reached a similar conclusion in relation to appeals under the Freedom of Information Act 2000, it referred to *Birkett v Department for the Environment, Food and Rural Affairs* [2011] EWCA Civ 1606 and held that the First-tier Tribunal could exercise its case-management powers to prevent unfairness to an appellant as a result of a new point being raised at a late stage. This can apply both ways, by way of enforcement of the time limits in the Tribunal Procedure (First-tier Tribunal) (Social Entitlement Chamber) Rules 2008 for appeals, responses and replies, in which parties are expected to include their grounds for challenging or defending the decision under appeal (see rr.22–24).

Subsection (8)(b)

By contrast with para.(a), para.(b) confers no discretion. In the light of reg.3(9) **1.442** of the Social Security and Child Support (Decisions and Appeals) Regulations 1999 and s.9(5) of the Act, when a decision has been revised under s.9, "the time when the decision appealed against was made" must refer to the date on which the original decision was made. Paragraph (b) is therefore consistent with the approach that any change of circumstances requires a new claim or a supersession under s.10 and it reverses the effect of *R(S)2/98*. Paragraph (b) did not apply where the appeal was brought before May 21, 1998 when this Act received the Royal Assent and Sch.6, para.3 (which made transitory provision preventing social security appeal tribunals and disability appeal tribunals from taking account of circumstances not obtaining at the date of the decision under appeal) came into force. In such a case, a tribunal had still to consider the claimant's entitlement to benefit throughout the period to the date of its decision or down to the date from which another decision was effective (*CIB/213/1999*).

In *NC v SSWP (ESA)* [2015] UKUT 147 (AAC), it was pointed out that the draftsman of s.12(8)(b) may not have foreseen that, in the absence of an equivalent provision in s.10, regulations under s.10(3) might enable a supersession to take account of circumstances not obtaining at the time of the Secretary of State's decision. It is not easy to see how a decision of the Secretary of State to supersede a decision on the ground of an anticipated change of circumstances (see reg.6(2)(a)(ii) of the Social Security and Child Support (Decisions and Appeals) Regulations 1999) can be upheld by the First-tier Tribunal.

However, it is important to note that para.(b) does not prevent a tribunal having regard to evidence that was not before the Secretary of State and came into existence after the decision was made or to evidence of events after the decision under appeal was made for the purpose of drawing inferences as to the circumstances obtaining when, or before, the decision was made (*R(DLA) 2/01*, *R(DLA) 3/01* and *BMcD v DSD (DLA)* [2011] NICom 175; [2013] AACR 29, a decision of a Tribunal of Commissioners in Northern Ireland).

This creates particular difficulties where entitlement to benefit depends on a prognosis. Thus, in *R(DLA) 3/01*, the claimant would be entitled to disability living allowance only if she was likely to satisfy the relevant conditions for six months. She was recovering from an operation. The Commissioner held that, in such a case, a tribunal was entitled to take account of the actual rate of recovery, even though the evidence of that arose after the date of the decision under appeal, provided that the fact that the claimant had not recovered as quickly as originally expected merely reflected the natural vagaries of an uncertain recovery process. Untoward circumstances arising after the date of the decision had to be disregarded, whether that operated to the claimant's advantage or to her disadvantage. Thus the fact that a claimant recovering from a heart attack developed pneumonia after the Secretary of State's decision was made would have to be ignored. So too would a dramatic improvement in a claimant's condition due to the use of a new drug. A similar case came before a Commissioner in *CDLA/2878/2000*. The claimant was a nurse who became incapacitated due to a slipped disc. She claimed disability living allowance on August 31, 1999, had a successful operation on December 17, 1999 and was able to return to work on February 14, 2000. The tribunal said simply that disability living allowance could not be awarded because there was no evidence that the claimant could have satisfied the conditions of entitlement from February 14, 2000, which was less than six months from the date of claim. The Commissioner set aside the tribunal's decision on the ground that the tribunal had not considered whether, at the date of claim, it had been likely that she would cease to satisfy the conditions of entitlement within six months. He directed the new tribunal to determine that likelihood on the basis of what was known at the date of claim.

1.443 A contention that subs.(8)(b) did not apply to changes of circumstances occurring between the date of a decision made in advance and the date from which the decision was effective was rejected by a Tribunal of Commissioners in *R(DLA) 4/05* who pointed out that s.8(2)(b) precluded the Secretary of State from taking account of any such change of circumstances that he might anticipate. However, they stressed that they were not disagreeing with the approach taken in *R(DLA) 3/01* and also that the Secretary of State (when making an advance award) could take account of the effects of the mere passage of time, such as the claimant attaining a certain age or the qualifying period for a benefit being completed. Consequently, a tribunal may take account of the effect of the mere passage of time after the date of the Secretary of State's decision in any case where the Secretary of State could have made an advance award of disability allowance under reg.13A of the Social Security (Claims and Payments) Regulations 1987. In *Secretary of State for Work and Pensions v Bhakta* [2006] EWCA

Civ 65 (reported as *R(IS) 7/06*), the Court of Appeal approved *R(DLA) 4/05* and applied it to an income support case where an advance award could have been made under reg.13. The case was one where the only reason that the claimant had not been found by the Commissioner to be habitually resident at the date of the Secretary of State's decision was that a sufficient period of residence had not elapsed by that date. Regulation 13 has been amended with effect from May 23, 2007 so as to exclude that class of case (and all claims by "persons from abroad") from the scope of the regulation, but the principle confirmed in *Bhakta* remains good in other contexts. *R(DLA) 4/05* has also been followed by a Tribunal of Commissioners in Northern Ireland (*R3/05 (DLA)*).

In *CDLA/3293/2000*, a case where the claimant had appealed against a decision of the Secretary of State to make no award of disability living allowance, the Commissioner held that s.12(8)(b) did not preclude a tribunal from using hindsight to fix the length of an award that they considered should be made. Similarly, in *PH v SSWP (DLA)* [2013] UKUT 268 (AAC), it was held that the First-tier Tribunal is entitled to extend the original period of an award of disability living allowance when allowing an appeal against a supersession decision that had prematurely ended the award (which had had the result that the claimant had not made a renewal claim before the original award would have ended). The judge suggested that, in that case, the First-tier Tribunal should have extended the award for long enough to enable the claimant to make an effective renewal claim. Since by the time he decided the appeal to the Upper Tribunal the claimant had made a new claim, the judge substituted for the First-tier Tribunal's decision an award terminating on the day before the day from which the new claim was effective. He said:

> "Section 12(8)(b) is clearly intended to prevent the First-tier Tribunal from having regard to such changes of circumstances as a change in a claimant's condition but I do not think that the legislature contemplated that the First-tier Tribunal should ignore administrative events such as the making of a new claim if that would force it to make a potentially overlapping award that might require unscrambling through a further supersession decision."

However, in *CDLA/3722/2000*, an appeal tribunal was held not to be entitled to use hindsight to reduce the period of a claimant's award to less than the minimum period of six months. At the time of the Secretary of State's decision she was likely to satisfy the conditions for disability living allowance for six months. In fact, she had a course of treatment and got better much earlier than had been expected. The Commissioner held that the tribunal were obliged to turn a blind eye to the improvement and the Secretary of State would not be able to supersede the decision so as to prevent benefit being paid for longer than the claimant's condition merited.

The Commissioner deciding *R(DLA) 3/01* observed that s.12(8)(b) required tri- 1.444
bunals to indulge in the sort of artificial exercise that is frowned upon in modern courts where judges are not expected to close their eyes to reality and he referred to *Charles v Hugh James Jones and Jenkins (a firm)* [2000] 1 All E.R. 289, 299–301. Section 12(8)(b) is of particular importance in disablement benefit cases where tribunals can usually themselves examine the claimant (see reg.52 of the Social Security and Child Support (Decisions and Appeals) Regulations 1999) and must be careful to distinguish between those of their findings that are relevant to circumstances obtaining at the time of the decision under appeal and those that are not.

Section 12(8)(b) applies to changes of legal circumstances as well as changes of factual circumstances so that, as one might expect, the First-tier Tribunal usually has to apply the law as it was in force when the Secretary of State made his decision. However, the First-tier Tribunal may be obliged to give effect to retrospective legislation passed after the date of the Secretary of State's decision. Although the passing of a retrospective Act of Parliament is itself a change of circumstances (*Chief Adjudication Officer v McKiernon* (reported as *R(I) 2/94*)), a retrospective Act passed after the Secretary of State has made a decision can alter the legal circumstances obtaining at the time of his decision. Thus it was held in *Secretary of State for Work and Pensions v Reilly* [2016] EWCA Civ 413; [2017] Q.B. 257; [2017] AACR 14 at [137] that, where the Secretary of State has made a decision on the basis of regulations that have been subsequently held to be ultra vires and the regulations are then retrospectively validated by Act of Parliament, the Secretary of State is entitled to rely on the effect of that Act in responding to an appeal against his decision.

In *CIS/2428/1999*, it was pointed out that a literal interpretation of s.12(8)(b) would prevent a tribunal from taking account of a cause for a late claim which existed before the claim was made and had ceased to exist before the Secretary of State's decision on the claim. The Commissioner considered that that would be absurd and would prevent adjudication on a case falling within reg.19(5) of the Social Security (Claims and Payments) Regulations 1987. He extended the principle behind *R(DLA) 3/01* and held that a circumstance "obtains" at the date of decision if it is a circumstance, whenever it occurred, that is relied on by a claimant in justifying a late claim. The principle has been further extended in *CJSA/2375/00*. In that case, the claimant had failed to attend two courses and had been disqualified from jobseeker's allowance for two weeks in respect of the first failure and four weeks in respect of the second failure. The disqualification for four weeks was permitted only because there had been a previous disqualification. The claimant appealed against both disqualifications and the appeals came before two different tribunals. The appeal against the first disqualification was allowed. The second appeal was dismissed and the claimant appealed to the Commissioner. The Commissioner said that, following the decision of the first tribunal, the Secretary of State should have revised the second disqualification under reg.3(6) of the Social Security and Child Support (Decisions and Appeals) Regulations 1999, so as to reduce the period to two weeks. However, as the Secretary of State had not done so, the second tribunal should have reduced the period, notwithstanding that the decision of the first tribunal had been given after the Secretary of State's decision on the second disqualification. The Commissioner said:

> "In a case like this, an appeal tribunal is entitled to take account of any factor known to it that relates to a past period or past event that was relevant to the decision under appeal, even if the position at the date of the hearing is different from that at the date of the decision. This gives section 12(8)(b) a sensible operation. It allows an appeal tribunal to substitute a decision on factors relevant to the period the Secretary of State had considered. But it prevents the tribunal from trespassing into the period after that date by taking account of factors that are only relevant to that later period.
>
> I repeat that I have not defined the words used in section 12(8)(b). I have simply tried to give them a sensible operation in circumstances like those involved in this case. I emphasise that I have been concerned in this decision with past periods or events. I have not been concerned with cases where the Secretary of State has had to speculate on the likely future course of events, such as the qualifying period for a disability living allowance, which I considered in [*R(DLA) 3/01*]".

Similar contortions were required in *CJSA/2472/2005*. In this case, entitlement to jobseeker's allowance had been terminated on the ground that the claimant had to be treated as not being available for work because the restrictions he had put on his availability were more restrictive than those recorded in his jobseeker's agreement. He had already, before the termination of his entitlement to benefit, applied for a variation of his jobseeker's agreement. That application had been only partially successful and the claimant had appealed against both the variation of his jobseeker's agreement and the termination of his entitlement to jobseeker's allowance. The Commissioner held that the Secretary of State, a tribunal or a Commissioner may direct that a varied jobseeker's agreement be given retrospective effect so that it has effect from the date of the application for variation. The consequence of the Commissioner allowing the claimant's appeal in respect of the jobseeker's agreement and making such a direction in that case was that, if the claimant signed the varied agreement, the circumstances obtaining at the date of the decision in respect of entitlement to jobseeker's allowance would be changed, affecting the operation of s.12(8)(b). He therefore adjourned the appeal in respect of entitlement to jobseeker's allowance in order to give the claimant the opportunity to sign the varied jobseeker's agreement, pointing out that the Secretary of State would be able to revise the termination of entitlement if the agreement were signed.

Section 12(8)(b) would be unobjectionable if, like s.12(8)(a), it said "need not" instead of "shall not". As it is, it introduces an unwelcome element of technicality into appeals to tribunals that are generally supposed to be user-friendly. As the cases demonstrate, this is particularly so where "outcome decisions" in respect of entitlement are dependent on other decisions. In less complex cases, the remedy for a claimant is to make a new claim, or application for supersession, whenever there is an event that might be regarded as a new circumstance. There may be some cases where the wise claimant will make such claims or applications at regular intervals while an appeal is pending. The Secretary of State would then be obliged to make separate decisions on each claim or application (because the power to refer claims or applications to a tribunal so that they can be considered with a pending appeal has been abolished) and there would be a separate right of appeal against each decision. However, experience suggests that claimants do not consider new claims or applications to be necessary while an appeal is pending, even though some of the literature provided to them makes the suggestion, and so the reality may be that claimants lose benefit that they would undoubtedly have been entitled to but for s.12(8)(b). **1.445**

Note that where a claimant does make a new claim or application for supersession pending an appeal, the Secretary of State is now empowered to revise the decision made on that claim or application in the light of the decision given on appeal (reg.3(5A) of the Social Security and Child Support (Decisions and Appeals) Regulations 1999). This makes it unnecessary for claimants to lodge repeated appeals based on the same grounds, but it remains necessary to lodge a further appeal if the point in issue arises out of a change of circumstances since the decision that was the subject of the original appeal.

Of course, s.12(8)(b) can work in a claimant's favour if there has been a new circumstance since the decision under appeal that would have reduced his or her entitlement to benefit. It may well be that the Secretary of State could not supersede the tribunal's decision (see the note to reg.6(2)(a) of the Social Security and Child Support (Decisions and Appeals) Regulations 1999). See *CDLA/3722/2000*, mentioned above. Giving effect to the tribunal's decision in the claimant's favour might, in some cases, give rise to an overpayment that was recoverable under s.71 of the Social Security Administration Act 1992 on the basis that the change of circumstances should have been disclosed to the Secretary of State so that the decision under appeal could have been superseded before the appeal was heard. However, in a case where the Secretary of State had refused benefit altogether in the decision under appeal and benefit had then been awarded by the tribunal on the basis of their findings as to the circumstances obtaining at the date of the Secretary of State's decision, it seems unlikely that there would have been any duty on the claimant to disclose any changes of circumstances while the appeal was pending. Even if the Secretary of State does have power to supersede a tribunal's decision in the light of a change of circumstances arising before the decision was given, another problem facing the Secretary of State may be continued ignorance of the new circumstance. He does not always send a representative to tribunal hearings and he does not usually ask for a copy of the record of proceedings or a full statement of the tribunal's findings and reasoning. Unless a tribunal refers in the short decision notice, recorded under r.33(2)(a) of the Tribunal Procedure (First-tier Tribunal) (Social Entitlement Chamber) Rules 2008, to a change of circumstances mentioned at the hearing, the Secretary of State may remain ignorant of it for ever and, of course, the tribunal will have been obliged by s.12(8)(b) to ignore the change when awarding benefit.

Although an element of discretion in s.12(8)(b) might make it much easier to do justice, a provision similar to s.12(8)(b) has been held not to be incompatible with the European Convention on Human Rights even in the context of asylum claims (*AS (Somalia) v Secretary of State for the Home Department* [2009] UKHL 32; [2009] 1 W.L.R. 1385).

Subsection (9)

1.446 In *Wood v Secretary of State for Work and Pensions* [2003] EWCA Civ 53 (reported as *R(DLA) 1/03*), the Court of Appeal overruled *R(DLA) 6/02* and held that the phrase "a decision superseding" should be read as "a decision taken pursuant to the power to supersede", so as to permit an appeal against a refusal to supersede. Rix L.J. conceded that that left this subsection as "a fairly redundant provision".

Redetermination etc. of appeals by tribunal

1.447 **13.**—(1) This section applies where an application is made [2 to the First-tier Tribunal for permission to appeal to the Upper Tribunal from any decision of the First-tier Tribunal under section 12 or this section].

(2) [2 . . .]

(3) If each of the principal parties to the case expresses the view that the decision was erroneous in point of law, [2the First-tier Tribunal] shall set aside the decision and refer the case for determination by a differently constituted [2the First-tier Tribunal].

[1(4) In this section and section 14 below "the principal parties" means—

(a) the persons mentioned in subsection (3)(a) and (b) of that section, and

(b) where applicable, the person mentioned in subsection (3)(d) and such a person as is first mentioned in subsection (4) of that section.]

AMENDMENTS

1. Social Security Contributions (Transfer of Functions, etc.) Act 1999 Sch.7 para.26 (April 1, 1999).

2. Transfer of Tribunal Functions Order 2008 (SI 2008/2833) Sch.3 paras 143 and 150 (November 3, 2008), subject to a saving under art.1(5).

DEFINITION

"the principal parties"—see subs.(4).

GENERAL NOTE

1.448 By reg.7 of the Child Trust Funds (Non-tax Appeals) Regulations 2005 (SI 2005/191), this section is applied in a modified form to appeals under ss.21(9) and 22 of the Child Trust Funds Act 2004 (see Vol.IV) but, as the modifications involve the omission of subs.(3), which is now the only operative part of the section, and as the only reference to "principal parties" in s.14 has been repealed, the continued application of this section to those cases seems entirely pointless. Until April 1, 2009, this section was also applied in a similarly modified form to appeals under the Tax Credits Act 2002 but, as explained in the note to s.12, the regulation applying it has lapsed in relation to cases in Great Britain.

Indeed, it is not easy to see why this section has not been completely repealed for ordinary social security cases as well. Subsection (2) provided a power to set aside a decision where a tribunal chairman considering an application for leave to appeal against a decision of the tribunal considered that the decision was erroneous in point of law. That was obviously a useful power, enabling unnecessary appeals to be avoided, and it has been extended to all decisions of the First-tier Tribunal against which there is a right of appeal by s.9 of the Tribunals, Courts and Enforcement Act 2007. Subsection (2) has been repealed (subject to a saving for reasons explained in the note to ss.5–7) because it would add nothing to s.9 of the 2007 Act.

Now, subs.(3) is the only operative part of the section. It is a strange provision, *requiring* a judge to set aside a decision of the First-tier Tribunal if the principal parties express the view that it was erroneous in point of law, whether or not he or she agrees. It would be unobjectionable if it conferred a *power* to set aside a decision with which all the parties were dissatisfied but it is the duty to do so that creates the difficulty. The First-tier Tribunal will always have included a judge, whereas it is very rare for any party to be represented by a lawyer. Yet, if the parties express the view, no matter how unreasonably, that the decision is erroneous in point of law, their view prevails and the judge must set the decision aside. It is not even necessary for the parties to agree on the error of law. It might, perhaps, be arguable that, in some cases, different parts of a decision of a tribunal are different decisions for the purposes of this section but that will not always be possible. The First-tier Tribunal may have steered carefully between two extreme views advanced by the parties, all to no avail. If re-determining tribunals took the same approach and the parties remained stubborn, the litigation could go on for ever unless action were taken to avoid subs.(3) coming into play. There is no scope for a judge to take the view that the case would be better determined by the Upper Tribunal than by the First-tier Tribunal differently constituted.

Happily, the necessity of applying subs.(3) seldom arises because it is comparatively rare for all parties to assert that there is an error of law in a tribunal's decision. **1.449** This is largely because it is unnecessary to ascertain the views of a respondent to an application for permission to appeal, since granting permission is not a final determination of the parties' rights and refusing permission is a decision in favour of the respondent. Most applications for permission are made by claimants. However, for some reason that may owe more to history rather than principle, where the Secretary of State applies for permission to appeal, it is the practice of the Social Entitlement Chamber of the First-tier Tribunal always to seek the view of the claimant before determining the application. That might be necessary if the judge were contemplating reviewing the decision instead of granting permission but is unnecessary otherwise. If, in those circumstances, the claimant asserts that the tribunal's decision is erroneous in point of law the judge will be bound to set the decision aside.

The other circumstance where this section may be brought into play is where both parties seek permission to appeal against a decision. However, a decision may not be set aside under this section once one such application for permission to appeal has been determined and permission has been either granted or refused (*CF/6923/1999*, but see *CIB/2949/2005*, where the Commissioner suggested that this might have been too broadly expressed).

It seems unlikely that this section will be found to apply where the First-tier Tribunal has refused to admit an application for permission because it was late (see r.38(5)(b) of the Tribunal Procedure (First-tier Tribunal) (Social Entitlement Chamber) Rules 2008).

Note that, where a decision is set aside, the case must be referred to a differently **1.450** constituted tribunal. It is usual for the decision that has been set aside to be included in the papers before the new tribunal.

That is not inappropriate. Even if their findings of fact cannot be relied upon, issues identified by the first tribunal may well be of assistance to the new tribunal, although it must be careful not to be influenced by the discredited findings (*Swash v Secretary of State for the Home Department* [2006] EWCA Civ 1093; [2007] 1 W.L.R. 1264). There may, however, be special circumstances in which the legally qualified panel member setting the first decision aside considers that the interests of justice require the case to be heard by a tribunal that has not seen that decision and he or she will be able to issue appropriate directions to ensure that that happens (*ibid.*).

In *CIB/4193/2003*, a decision made on a consideration of the papers was set aside and a new paper consideration was arranged without that being made clear to the claimant who had decided that she wanted to attend a hearing. The Commissioner set aside the second decision and suggested that claimants should be given an opportunity to ask for a hearing when a decision is set aside under this section.

In *CIS/4533/2001*, it was held that there was no appeal against a setting aside under this section but that was because a decision under this section was then made by a legally qualified panel member whereas the right of appeal was expressed as being against a decision of an appeal tribunal. Since the coming into force of the Tribunals, Courts and Enforcement Act 2007, different considerations would apply.

Appeal from [2First-tier Tribunal to Upper Tribunal]

1.451 **14.**—(1) [2. . .]

(2) [1 . . .]

(3) [1 . . .] An appeal [2 to the Upper Tribunal under section 11 of the Tribunals, Courts and Enforcement Act 2007 from any decision of the First-tier Tribunal under section 12 or 13 above lies] at the instance of any of the following—

(a) the Secretary of State;
(b) the claimant and such other person as may be prescribed;
(c) in any of the cases mentioned in subsection (5) below, a trade union; and
(d) a person from whom it is determined that any amount is recoverable under or by virtue of section 71 or 74 of the Administration Act.

(4) In a case relating to industrial injuries benefit an appeal [2 to the Upper Tribunal under section 11 of the Tribunals, Courts and Enforcement Act 2007 from any decision of the First-tier Tribunal under section 12 or 13 above lies] at the instance of a person whose entitlement to benefit is, or may be, under Part VI of Schedule 7 to the Contributions and Benefits Act, affected by the decision appealed against, as well as at the instance of any person or body such as is mentioned in subsection (3) above.

(5) The following are the cases in which an appeal lies at the instance of a trade union—

(a) where the claimant is a member of the union at the time of the appeal and was so immediately before the matter in question arose;
(b) where that matter in any way relates to a deceased person who was a member of the union at the time of his death;
(c) where the case relates to industrial injuries benefit and the claimant or, in relation to industrial death benefit, the deceased, was a member of the union at the time of the relevant accident.

(6) Subsections [1. . .] (3) and (5) above, as they apply to a trade union, apply also to any other association which exists to promote the interests and welfare of its members.

(7) [2 . . .]
(8) [2 . . .]
(9) [2 . . .]
(10) [2 . . .]
(11) [2 . . .]
(12) [2 . . .]

AMENDMENTS

1. Social Security Contributions (Transfer of Functions, etc.) Act 1999 Sch.7 para.27 (April 1, 1999).
2. Transfer of Tribunal Functions Order 2008 (SI 2008/2833) Sch.3 paras 143 and 151 (November 3, 2008), subject to a saving under art.1(5).

DEFINITIONS

"the Administration Act"—see s.84.
"claimant"—see s.39(1) and, by virtue of s.39(2), see s.191 of the Social Security Administration Act 1992.
"the Contributions and Benefits Act"—*ibid.*
"industrial injuries benefit"—by virtue of s.39(2), see s.191 of the Social Security Administration Act 1992.
"prescribed"—see s.84.

GENERAL NOTE

Originally, this section provided for a right of appeal to a Social Security Commissioner from a decision of an appeal tribunal and it also introduced Sch.4, providing for the appointment of Commissioners. The right of appeal has now been replaced by the right of appeal to the Upper Tribunal under s.11 of the Tribunals, Courts and Enforcement Act 2007. However, the repeals of subsections (7)–(12) are subject to a saving for the reason given in the note to ss.5–7. **1.452**

Now this section merely makes provision as to who may appeal in social security cases. Subsections (3) and (4) probably add little to s.11(2) of the 2007 Act, which provides that "any party" has a right of appeal. Section 11(2) certainly means that the failure to exercise the power to make regulations under subs.(3)(b) to the same extent as the equivalent power in s.12(2) of this Act no longer creates any substantial difficulty. Subsections (5) and (6) reproduce provisions in earlier legislation which fell into disuse in the 1970s or 1980s. The modern approach of trade unions and other organisations is to act as a representative of a member rather than appealing in their own right.

In relation to cases where the original decision was made by Her Majesty's Revenue and Customs (i.e. cases under s.170 of the Pension Schemes Act 1993 or cases concerning the former working families' tax credit or disabled person's tax credit or, now child benefit or guardian's allowance), this section applies with the modification that the reference to the Secretary of State are to be read as a reference to Her Majesty's Revenue and Customs (Pensions Schemes Act 1993 s.170(7), Tax Credits Act 1999 Sch.2 para.21 and Sch.4 para.3(2), Tax Credits Act 2002 Sch.4, para.15 and Commissioners for Revenue and Customs Act 2005 s.4(1)).

By reg.8 of the Child Trust Funds (Non-tax Appeals) Regulations 2005 (SI 2005/191), this section is applied in a rather more modified form to appeals under ss.21(9) and 22 of the Child Trust Funds Act 2004 (see Vol.IV). Until April 1, 2009, this section was also applied, with similar modifications, to appeals under the Tax Credits Act 2002 but, as explained in the note to s.12, the regulation applying it has lapsed in relation to cases in Great Britain.

Application for permission to appeal against a decision of the Upper Tribunal

15.—(1) [1 . . .] **1.453**

(2) [1 . . .]

(3) [1 An application for permission to appeal from a decision of the Upper Tribunal in respect of a decision of the First-tier Tribunal under section 12 or 13] may only be made by—

(a) a person who, before the proceedings before the [1 Upper Tribunal] were begun, was entitled to appeal to the [1 Upper Tribunal] from the decision to which the [1 Upper Tribunal's] decision relates;

(b) any other person who was a party to the proceedings in which the first decision mentioned in paragraph (a) above was given;

(c) any other person who is authorised by regulations to apply for [1 permission];

[1 . . .]

(4) [1 . . .]

(5) [1 . . .]

AMENDMENT

1. Transfer of Tribunal Functions Order 2008 (SI 2008/2833) Sch.3 paras 143 and 152 (November 3, 2008), subject to a saving under art.1(5).

GENERAL NOTE

1.454 Originally, this section provided for a right of appeal to an appellate court from a decision of a Social Security Commissioner. The equivalent right of appeal from a decision of the Upper Tribunal is now provided by s.13 of the Tribunals, Courts and Enforcement Act 2007. Now this section merely makes provision as to who may appeal in social security cases. It will seldom be necessary for a person to rely on this section rather than s.13(2) of the 2007 Act, which provides that "any party" has a right of appeal and therefore the continued application of this section to appeals under ss.21(9) and 22 of the Child Trust Funds Act 2004, by reg.10 of the Child Trust Funds (Non-tax Appeals) Regulations 2005 (SI 2005/191), seems unnecessary. Until April 1, 2009, this section was also applied to appeals under the Tax Credits Act 2002 but, as explained in the note to s.12, the regulation applying it has lapsed in relation to cases in Great Britain. The repeal of most of this section and the amendments to subs.(3) are subject to a saving so as to enable a person to appeal to the Court of Session against a decision of a Social Security Commissioner under s.159 of the Health and Social Care (Community Health and Standards) Act 2003 (see the note to ss.5–7).

[1 Functions of Senior President of Tribunals

1.455 **15A.**—(1) The Senior President of Tribunals shall ensure that appropriate steps are taken by the First-tier Tribunal to secure the confidentiality, in such circumstances as may be prescribed, of any prescribed material, or any prescribed classes or categories of material.

(2) [2 . . .]

(3) [2 . . .]]

AMENDMENTS

1. Transfer of Tribunal Functions Order 2008 (SI 2008/2833) Sch.3 paras 143 and 153 (November 3, 2008).

2. Deregulation Act 2015, s.79 (May 26, 2015).

GENERAL NOTE

1.456 This section replaced paras 7 and 10 of Sch.1 when that Schedule was repealed in 2008, but the duty under subs.(2) to make an annual report to the Secretary of State on the standards achieved by him or her in the making of decisions against which an appeal lay to the First-tier Tribunal was abolished in 2015. The Senior President may delegate his functions under this section to another judge, e.g. the President of the Social Entitlement Chamber of the First-tier Tribunal (see s.8 of the Tribunals, Courts and Enforcement Act 2008).

Procedure

16.—(1) Regulations ("procedure regulations") may make any such provision as is specified in Schedule 5 to this Act. **1.457**

(2) [[1] . . .]

(3) It is hereby declared—

(a) [[1] . . .]

(b) that the power to provide for the procedure to be followed in connection with the making of decisions by the Secretary of State includes power to make provision with respect to the formulation of the matters to be decided, whether on a reference under section 117 of the Administration Act or otherwise.

(4) *Omitted.*

(5) *Omitted.*

(6) [[1] . . .]

(7) [[1] . . .]

(8) [. . .]

(9) [. . .]

Amendment

1. Transfer of Tribunal Functions Order 2008 (SI 2008/2833) Sch.3 paras 143 and 154 (November 3, 2008), subject to a saving under art.1(5).

Definitions

"the Administration Act"—see s.84.
"procedure regulations"—see subs.(1).

General Note

The repeal of most of this section is subject to a saving for reasons explained in the note to ss.5–7. **1.458**

Subsection (1)

See the Social Security and Child Support (Decisions and Appeals) Regulations 1999, the Child Benefit and Guardian's Allowance (Decisions and Appeals) Regulations 2003 and the Universal Credit, Personal Independence Payment, Jobseeker's Allowance and Employment and Support Allowance (Decisions and Appeals) Regulations 2013. By reg.11 of the Child Trust Funds (Non-tax Appeals) Regulations 2005 (SI 2005/191), this subsection is applied to appeals under ss. 21(9) and 22 of the Child Trust Funds Act 2004. See Vol.IV for that Act and the Child Trust Funds (Appeals) Regulations 2005 which are made under this subsection as so applied. Until April 1, 2009, it was also applied to appeals under the Tax Credits Act 2002 but, as explained in the note to s.12, the regulation applying it has lapsed in relation to cases in Great Britain. **1.459**

Subssections (4) and (5)

These subsections are to be repealed by the Social Security Contributions (Transfer of Functions, etc.) Act 1999 Sch.7 para.28, presumably at the same time as the only provisions that would have given them practical effect and which have never been brought into force. **1.460**

Finality of decisions

1.461 **17.**—(1) Subject to the provisions of this Chapter [[1] and to any provision made by or under Chapter 2 of Part 1 of the Tribunals, Courts and Enforcement Act 2007], any decision made in accordance with the foregoing provisions of this Chapter shall be final; and subject to the provisions of any regulations under section 11 above, any decision made in accordance with those regulations shall be final.

(2) If and to the extent that regulations so provide, any finding of fact or other determination embodied in or necessary to such a decision, or on which such a decision is based, shall be conclusive for the purposes of—

(a) further such decisions;
(b) decisions made under the Child Support Act; and
(c) decisions made under the Vaccine Damage Payments Act.

AMENDMENT

1. Transfer of Tribunal Functions Order 2008 (SI 2008/2833) Sch.3 paras 143 and 155 (November 3, 2008).

DEFINITIONS

"the Child Support Act"—see s.84.
"the Vaccine Damage Payments Act"—see s.84.

GENERAL NOTE

1.462 By reg.12 of the Child Trust Funds (Non-tax Appeals) Regulations 2005 (SI 2005/191), this section is applied with substantial modifications to appeals under ss.21(9) and 22 of the Child Trust Funds Act 2004 (see Vol.IV). Similarly, reg.3 of the Childcare Payments (Appeals) Regulations 2016 (SI 2016/1078) applies this section to appeals under the Childcare Payments Act 2014, with substantial modifications the precise effects of which are not entirely clear (see Vol.IV).Until April 1, 2009, it was also applied in modified form to appeals under the Tax Credits Act 2002 but, as explained in the note to s.12, the regulation applying it has lapsed in relation to cases in Great Britain.

Subsection (1)

1.463 This re-enacts s.60(1) of the Social Security Administration Act 1992. Decisions are "final" subject to appeals and revisions or supersesssions. Therefore, it is not possible to sue the Secretary of State in negligence in respect of a decision (*Jones v Department of Employment* [1989] Q.B. 1) although an action could lie in misfeasance. That does not prevent the Department for Work and Pensions being sued in respect of bad advice. The finality of decisions does not prevent decisions being challenged by way of judicial review (*R. v Medical Appeal Tribunal, Ex p. Gilmore* [1957] 1 Q.B. 574, a decision made before there was a right of appeal from a medical appeal tribunal to a Commissioner) although the reluctance of the High Court to allow such challenges when there is a statutory right of appeal means that they are confined to exceptional cases.

Subsection (2)

1.464 See reg.10 of the Social Security and Child Support (Decisions and Appeals) Regulations 1999 (in relation to decisions as to whether or not a person is incapable of work) and regs 5(2) and 6(1) of the Social Security (Industrial Diseases) (Prescribed Diseases) Regulations 1985 (in relation to whether or not a person has been suffering from a prescribed disease). Note that there is no express provision re-enacting s.60(2) of the 1992 Act which provided that, as a general rule, a finding in one decision was *not* conclusive for the purpose of any other decision. However, it is suggested that such an express provision is not necessary and that, in the absence of any rule of evidence to the contrary, a person or body making a decision is entitled to rely on an earlier finding but is not bound to do so. If that were not the approach to be taken in the absence of any express provision, subs. (2) would be unnecessary. Thus, as was pointed out in *CIB/3327/2004*, although a decision as to whether or not a person was incapable of work that was made on a claim for incapacity benefit was conclusive for the purposes of credits in respect of incapacity for work (by virtue of reg.10 of the 1999 Regulations), a decision as to whether or not a person was engaged in remunerative work made on a claim for jobseeker's allowance was not conclusive for the purposes of credits in respect of involuntary unemployment.

There is no power to make decisions under this Act conclusive for the purpose of decisions under the Social Security (Recovery of Benefits) Act 1997. Therefore, a tribunal considering an appeal under s.11 of that Act is entitled to find that benefit was not paid in respect of an accident, even if that conclusion is inconsistent with the benefit having been awarded at all *(R(CR) 1/02)*. Similarly, *CIS/1330/2002* holds that a finding of fact within a decision as to a claimant's entitlement to benefit is not conclusive for the purposes of a decision as to whether an overpayment has been made and is recoverable. In *SSWP v AM (IS)* [2010] UKUT 428 (AAC), the judge took a subtly different approach from that taken in *CIS/1330/2002* and held that "an entitlement decision necessarily establishes that there has been an overpayment, because it proves that the amount paid during a particular period was more than the claimant was entitled to" although he also held, consistently with *CIS/1330/2002*, that "when making findings of fact, the effect of section 17(2) of the 1992 Act is that the decision maker or tribunal dealing with the overpayment recoverability decision cannot be bound by the findings in relation to those facts made in the course of dealing with the entitlement decision". The difference in approach is therefore of little, if any, practical importance. Again, it was held in *CIS/3605/2005* that an erroneous decision on entitlement was a valid revision or supersession decision for the purposes of s.71(5A) of the Social Security Administration Act 1992, so as to enable the Secretary of State to recover an overpayment, but was not conclusive as to the amount of the overpayment, with the result that only the amount actually overpaid was recoverable. This approach was applied in *CA/2650/2006*, where a tribunal had found a claimant not to be ordinarily resident in Great Britain from October 27, 2003, when she had moved abroad, and had upheld a decision superseding her award of attendance allowance from that date. On an appeal against a second tribunal decision to the effect that an overpayment from October 27, 2003 to January 4, 2004 was recoverable from the claimant, the Commissioner found that she had ceased to be ordinarily resident in Great Britain only from January 4, 2004 (even though she was also resident abroad) and so she had not been overpaid benefit as a result of any failure to disclose a material fact. Accordingly, he allowed her appeal. However, under the law as it then stood, the first tribunal ought to have superseded her award only from the date of supersession in February 2004. The Commissioner pointed out that, even if the claimant had in fact ceased to be ordinarily resident in Great Britain on October 27, 2003, the first tribunal would have wrongly decided that she had not been entitled to attendance allowance from then until January 4, 2004, but that decision was final by virtue of s.17(1) of the Social Security Act 1998. Moreover, if she had ceased to be ordinarily resident, she would have actually been overpaid during that period because, had she reported the fact that she had moved overseas straightaway, her award would have been terminated immediately. He considered that, in those circumstances, he would have been bound to find that there had been an overpayment and that it was recoverable, despite the first tribunal's error. That suggestion is, strictly speaking, obiter dicta. However, the same Commissioner returned to the point in *CIB/2762/2007* in circumstances where a supersession had been made effective from a date before it was made, when, under the defective legislation then in force, that was not permissible even though the claimant had been overpaid and it was arguable that she had failed to disclose a material fact. The claimant had appealed against a later decision that the overpayment was recoverable and the Commissioner held that the tribunal considering the appeal against the recoverability was bound to find that there had been an overpayment but he said that the appropriate course of action would have been to adjourn and allow the Secretary of State to revise the supersession decision on the ground of official error and then revise the overpayment decision in the claimant's favour, causing the appeal to lapse.

Note that s.29(4) makes an industrial accident declaration conclusive for the purposes of any claim for industrial injuries benefit in respect of that accident. That provision is not applied in respect of the onset of industrial diseases. However, in *Secretary of State for Work and Pensions v Whalley* [2002] EWCA Civ 166 (reported as *R(I) 2/03*), the Court of Appeal held that a finding as to the date of onset of an industrial disease made in the context of a claim for disablement benefit was binding in respect of a later claim for reduced earnings allowance. The Court appears to have accepted an argument advanced by the Secretary of State that s.60(1) of the 1992 Act made the finding binding and that s.60(2) was concerned only with "preliminary matters such as the precise symptoms displayed at any particular time". This is, in effect, an argument that was rejected by the Tribunal of Commissioners in *R(CR) 1/02*. *Whalley* was considered in *R(I) 2/04*, in which it was held that the reason that a finding as to a date of onset of an industrial disease is conclusive lies in reg.6(1) of the Social Security (Industrial Injuries) (Prescribed Diseases) Regulations 1985 rather than in s.17. It was pointed out that in *Whalley* the issue had been whether a finding that the claimant was *not* suffering from a prescribed disease so that there was *no* date of onset was conclusive and that that had turned on the finality of a decision on a diagnosis question under the pre-1998 Act system of adjudication, which in turn had precluded a finding in a later claim for disablement pension that there had been an earlier date of onset. In *R(I) 5/04*, it was held that, while a finding that a claimant had suffered from a prescribed disease from a particular date was conclusive as to the date of onset by virtue of reg.6(1) of the 1985 Regulations, a finding that the claimant had *not* been suffering from a prescribed disease was not conclusive under the new system of adjudication in the context of the legislation then in force, but was merely final in respect of the period up to the date of the decision of the Secretary of State in which the finding was made. However, reg.5(2) of the 1985 Regulations was introduced with effect from March 18, 2005 to reverse *R(I) 5/04* by providing that a negative finding is now also conclusive.

1.465 In *LS v LB Lambeth (HB)* [2010] UKUT 461 (AAC); [2011] AACR 27, the three-judge panel was invited to consider whether the First-tier Tribunal had been bound by a decision of a legally qualified panel member of an appeal tribunal to admit an appeal that it considered ought not to have been admitted because the legally qualified panel member had had no power to admit it. The majority held that it was unnecessary to decide whether the First-tier Tribunal had had a discretion to reconsider the legally qualified panel member's decision because it found the First-tier Tribunal's decision to be erroneous in point of law on another ground and substituted a decision that the legally qualified panel member's decision would not be reconsidered. The implication is that the First-tier Tribunal was at least not bound to reconsider the legally qualified panel member's decision. The issue arose because, in *Watt v Ahsan* [2007] UKHL 51; [2008] A.C. 696, the House of Lords held that an employment tribunal had been bound by a decision of the Employment Appeal Tribunal, dismissing an appeal from the employment tribunal's ruling made in the same proceedings to the effect that it had jurisdiction to consider the case before it, notwithstanding that a subsequent decision of the Court of Appeal in different proceedings had overruled the Employment Appeal Tribunal's decision. It might just have been arguable that the legally qualified panel member's determination would have been a "determination embodied in or necessary to such a decision" so as to have brought s.17(2) of the Social Security Act 1998 into play had the issue arisen in the context of an ordinary social security decision, but there is no equivalent to s.17(2) in para.11 of Sch.7 to the Child Support, Pensions and Social Security Act 2000, which provides for the finality of decisions in housing benefit cases, and so the point did not arise in *LS v LB Lambeth (HB)*. On the other hand, the First-tier Tribunal's power under r.5(3)(e) of the Tribunal Procedure (First-tier Tribunal) (Social Entitlement Chamber) Rules 2008 to deal with an issue as a preliminary issue would be undermined if a decision on a preliminary issue were not binding in the same proceedings. Section 17 appears more concerned with whether a decision made in one set of proceedings is binding on a decision-maker or tribunal concerned with another set of proceedings than with whether a decision of a tribunal binds it for the purposes of further steps in the same proceedings.

In *CM v HMRC (TC)* [2014] UKUT 272 (AAC), the Upper Tribunal suggested that, where there were competing claims for child tax credit, the second claimant could be added as a party to an appeal brought by the first claimant, on the basis that the decision would then be binding on both claimants. If a person is added as a party to proceedings and has all the rights of a party to make representations and is made properly aware of the issues, there is no reason in principle (absent s.17(2)) why findings of fact made in any proceedings to which he or she is a party should not be binding on him or her. However, in an ordinary social security case, there are procedural difficulties, since presumably a separate decision would have subsequently to be made in respect of the second claimant's award and the implication of s.17(2) cannot be ignored. On the other hand, even if the decision to which both claimants were parties was not formally binding, it would obviously carry practical weight and arguably sufficient weight to justify any appeal that required the issue to be reargued being struck out under r.8(3)(c) of the Tribunal Procedure (First-tier Tribunal) (Social Entitlement Chamber) Rules 2008 on the ground of a lack of any reasonable prospect of success in the absence of compelling new evidence or some other compelling reason.

Matters arising as respects decisions

18.—(1) Regulations may make provision as respects matters arising— **1.466**

(a) pending any decision under this Chapter of the Secretary of State, [1 or the First-tier Tribunal or any decision of the Upper Tribunal which relates to any decision of this Chapter of the First-tier Tribunal] which relates to—

(i) any claim for a relevant benefit; [1 or]

(ii) any person's entitlement to such a benefit or its receipt; [1 or]

(iii) [1 . . .]

(iv) [1 . . .]

(b) out of the revision under section 9 above or on appeal of any such decision.

(2) Regulations under subsection (1) above as it applies to child benefit may include provision as to the date from which child benefit is to be payable to a person in respect of a child [2 or qualifying young person] in a case where, before the benefit was awarded to that person, child benefit in respect of the child [2 or qualifying young person] was awarded to another person.

Amendments

1. Social Security Contributions (Transfer of Functions, etc.) Act 1999 Sch.7 para.29 (April 1, 1999).
2. Child Benefit Act 2005, Sch.1, para.26 (April 10, 2006).
3. Transfer of Tribunal Functions Order 2008 (SI 2008/2833) Sch.3 paras 143 and 156 (November 3, 2008).

do, contain similar powers to require claimants to attend medical examinations and associated penalties for failure to comply. Regulation 9 of the Social Security (Personal Independence Payment) Regulations 2013 (see Vol.I) makes rather different provision for a person to be required to "participate in a consultation" "with a person approved by the Secretary of State". Note also that this section applies only to references by the Secretary of State: separate provision is made under s.20 for references required to assist tribunals.

Subsection (1) is in permissive terms and does not require that a person be referred to a health care professional for examination and report. Therefore, the Secretary of State is entitled to, and should, consider whether an examination is really necessary in a case where a claimant has contended that (e.g. for mental health reasons) he or she has good cause for not attending any examination. If the Secretary of State is satisfied that the claimant cannot reasonably be expected to attend for an examination but also considers that there is insufficient evidence upon which to make a decision awarding benefit, it may be appropriate for him to make a decision not to award the benefit. However, there may be adequate written evidence to justify an award. See *CG v SSWP (II)* [2015] UKUT 400 (AAC).

1.469 A health care professional is entitled to decline to examine a person in the absence of a chaperon and a claimant's unreasonable refusal to allow a chaperon to be present may constitute failing without good cause to submit to an examination (*CIB/2011/2001*). However, it may still be possible for a report to be completed on the basis of informal observations and a lengthy conversation with the claimant, without there having been an examination within the terms of this section, and the health care professional's opinion may be taken into account as evidence, provided the decision-maker or tribunal can identify the factual basis on which the opinion was given (*CDLA/2466/2007*), although, in *CDLA/4208/2004*, the Commissioner criticised a tribunal for referring to opinions formed by a doctor in those circumstances as "clinical findings".

For the recovery of expenses incurred in attending an examination, see s.20A.

Subsection (3)

1.470 What the decision is, depends on what the question was. It may be a decision to reject a whole claim but it may be a decision to award benefit but on a basis less favourable to the claimant than would otherwise have been the case. The claimant will usually be able to appeal against the decision (and apply for revision under s.9) and will be entitled to argue that he did have good cause for failing to comply with the request. He or she would also be entitled to argue that the decision was less favourable than was required by subs.(3), having regard to what was really in issue. The other remedy open to a claimant is to make a new claim (if benefit was not awarded) or make a new application for a supersession (if there is some continuing entitlement). The consequence will be to raise the question again and the Secretary of State will be obliged to make a new decision, which he will not be able to make under subs.(3) unless the claimant has failed without good cause to comply with a new request to attend for, or submit to, a medical examination.

Where the First-tier Tribunal allows an appeal against a decision made under subs.(3), it has the power to give a substantive decision on the claimant's entitlement to benefit but it will rarely be able to do so without adjourning either for an examination or to give the Secretary of State an opportunity to make further submissions (*CG v SSWP (II)* [2015] UKUT 400 (AAC)). It cannot direct the health care professional to carry out a domiciliary visit for the purpose of a medical examination under this section, but it can make a suggestion to that effect. (It can only direct a domiciliary visit when exercising its own power to refer a case to a health care professional under s.20(2).)

It is suggested that what amounts to "good cause" under this provision is the same as under all similar provisions where benefit claimants are required to attend medical examinations. A number of decisions on the meaning of "good cause" were considered in *AF v SSWP* [2009] UKUT 56 (AAC) in the context of reg.8(2) of the Social Security (Incapacity for Work) (General) Regulations 1995. It was emphasised that the integrity of the social security scheme depends on there being appropriate tests in place, so that, in the absence of "good cause" a person who decides as a matter of principle not to attend an examination must be taken to accept the consequence that benefit is likely to be refused. On the other hand, reference was made to *R(S) 9/51* where the claimant was a Christian Scientist and the Commissioner accepted that an objection based on a firm religious conviction, rather than mere prejudice or distaste for the process, would amount to "good cause". See, further, the annotation to subss.(1) and (2), above.

Medical examination required by appeal tribunal

20.—(1) This section applies where an appeal has been brought under section 12 above against a decision on a claim for a relevant benefit, or as to a person's entitlement to such a benefit [1 . . .]. 1.471

(2) [3 The First-tier Tribunal may, if conditions prescribed by Tribunal Procedure Rules] are satisfied, refer the person—

(a) in respect of whom the claim is made; or

(b) whose entitlement is at issue,

to a [2 health care professional approved by the Secretary of State] for such examination and report as appears to [3 the First-tier Tribunal] to be necessary for the purpose of providing [3 it] with information for use in determining the appeal.

[3 . . .]

[2 (2A) The power under subsection (2) to refer a person to a healthcare professional approved by the Secretary of State includes power to specify the description of health care professional to whom the person is to be referred.]

(3) At a hearing before [3 the First-tier Tribunal, except in cases or circumstances prescribed by Tribunal Procedure Rules,] the tribunal—

(a) may not carry out a physical examination of the person mentioned in subsection (2) above; and

(b) may not require that person to undergo any physical test for the purpose of determining whether he satisfies the condition mentioned in section 73(1)(a) of the Contributions and Benefits Act.

AMENDMENTS

1. Social Security Contributions (Transfer of Functions, etc.) Act 1999 Sch.7 para.31 (April 1, 1999).

2. Welfare Reform Act 2007 s.62(1), (3) and (4) (July 3, 2007).

3. Transfer of Tribunal Functions Order 2008 (SI 2008/2833) Sch.3 paras 143 and 157 (November 3, 2008).

DEFINITIONS

"claim"—by virtue of s.39(2), see s.191 of the Social Security Administration Act 1992.

"the Contributions and Benefits Act"—see s.84.

"health care professional"—see s.39(1).

"medical examination"—by virtue of s.39(2), see s.191 of the Social Security Administration Act 1992.

"relevant benefit"—see s.8(3).

General Note

Subssections (2) and (2A)

1.472 A reference may be made only if there arises one or more of the issues listed in Sch.2 to the Tribunal Procedure (First-tier Tribunal (Social Entitlement Chamber) Rules 2008 (see r.25(3)). For the recovery of expenses incurred in attending an examination, see s.20A. Note that this section and the rules made under it apply only to cases under s.12 of this Act and not to other cases before the First-tier Tribunal. Note also, that the examination may not require a person to undergo a physical test for the purpose of determining whether that person is unable to walk or virtually unable to do so (see r.25(4)).There is no statutory penalty for failing to attend for, or submit to, a medical examination required by an "eligible person" or requested by a health care professional making a report under this section. Such a penalty is unnecessary as it is open to the tribunal to draw such inferences from the failure as appear proper when deciding the medical issues arising before them.

It is not the practice for the First-Tier Tribunal to obtain reports from the claimant's own doctors as a matter of course. However, claimants sometimes expect that that will be done. In *R(M) 2/80*, the claimant's consultant wrote suggesting that the Mobility Allowance Unit obtain medical evidence from his department. They did not do so. The Commissioner held that the claimant should have been told that her consultant's suggestion would not be followed up and that it would be up to her to obtain any further evidence if she so wished. Similar approaches were taken in *CI/13/1986* and *CA/133/1988*. These decisions were applied in *CIB/16604/1996* where the claimant wrote in his letter of appeal that "you are quite free to check my hospital and [doctor's] records". Neither the claimant nor the adjudication officer attended the hearing before the tribunal. The Commissioner held that there had been a breach of the rules of natural justice because the claimant reasonably believed that the tribunal would have before them his medical records and he was therefore prevented from providing relevant evidence in the sense that he could not reasonably be expected to produce evidence he thought the tribunal already had. That case was distinguished in *CIB/5030/1998* because there was evidence before the Commissioner that the Independent Tribunal Service issued a leaflet making it clear that claimants' doctors would not automatically be approached by the Benefits Agency, the Department of Social Security or the tribunal. The Commissioner held that it was not reasonable for the claimant to believe that the tribunal would have before them evidence from his doctors. That was so even though the claimant said that he had misunderstood the leaflet and thought he had only to give his consent. The Commissioner considered that there was no basis for that misunderstanding.

Subsection (3)

1.473 See r.25(2) and (4) of the Tribunal Procedure (First-tier Tribunal (Social Entitlement Chamber) Rules 2008. In *CDLA/433/1999*, it was held that carrying out a physical examination in breach of the forerunner of this subsection was not an error of law rendering a decision liable to be set aside but relying on evidence from the examination would have been. Observing a claimant during a hearing is not a physical examination or test (*R(DLA) 1/95*). In *R4/99(IB)*, the Commissioner in Northern Ireland said that a tribunal were entitled to use all their senses, including sight, in assessing evidence before them. In *R1/01(IB)*, a Tribunal of Commissioners in Northern Ireland adopted both those views. They held that the phrase "may not carry out a physical examination" suggests some formal process beyond mere observing and that a tribunal is not prohibited from looking at an injury if it is either readily visible or if the claimant wishes them to see it. They said that the tribunal had erred in simply rejecting the claimant's request to look at his knee. The tribunal should either have acceded to the request or else they should have given the claimant the opportunity of obtaining alternative evidence. A tribunal should not simply refuse such a request, unless they consider the evidence unnecessary or irrelevant. The Tribunal of

Commissioners said that the legislation prohibits a tribunal from asking to see a part of the claimant's body but it does not prevent the claimant from asking the tribunal to look. Nor does it prevent the tribunal from looking at what they can see without making any request. However, they are not entitled to do more than observe and, except in a case within the scope of r.25(2), a tribunal member ought not to accede to a request to feel a lump or manipulate a limb. If such evidence is necessary, the tribunal should adjourn in order to obtain a report. That decision was followed in *MA v SSWP (ESA)* [2015] UKUT 290 (AAC), where the First-tier Tribunal had invited the claimant to lift his trouser legs so that the medically qualified member could determine whether or not there was muscle wasting. Nonetheless, in the circumstances of that case, the Upper Tribunal held that the error was not material and it upheld the First-tier Tribunal's decision that the claimant was not entitled to employment and support allowance. However, in *R(DLA) 5/03*, the Commissioner noted the distinction between a "physical examination" and a "physical test" and held that the prohibition on tests for the purpose of determining whether a claimant is unable, or virtually unable, to walk did not prevent a tribunal from asking a claimant to demonstrate activities for other purposes. He further said that a tribunal might be entitled to draw inferences from a refusal to comply with such a request, depending on the reasonableness of the request and any reasons given by the claimant for not complying. In *GL v SSWP* [2008] UKUT 36 (AAC), it was suggested that testing a claimant's ability to estimate time by asking him for how long he had been sitting in the tribunal hearing was "approaching, if not crossing," the line between observing a claimant and conducting a physical examination, but that seems inconsistent with *R(DLA) 5/03* and to overlook the word "physical" used in both subparagraphs. In *R(IB) 2/06*, it was held that examining x-rays is not a "physical examination" but that a tribunal was entitled to decline to look at x-rays on the ground that it did not have the expertise to analyse them. However, in such a case, the tribunal was obliged to consider whether to adjourn to obtain a report, which would involve considering whether it was likely that such a report would assist the tribunal in determining the point in issue before it.

[1 Travelling and other allowances

20A.—(1) The Lord Chancellor may pay to any person required under this Part (whether for the purposes of this Part or otherwise) to attend for or to submit to medical or other examination or treatment such travelling and other allowances as the Lord Chancellor may determine. 1.474

(2) In subsection (1) the reference to travelling and other allowances includes compensation for loss of remunerative time but such compensation shall not be paid to any person in respect of any time during which the person is in receipt of remuneration under section 28 of, or paragraph 5 of Schedule 2 to, the Tribunals, Courts and Enforcement Act 2007 (assessors and judges of First-Tier Tribunal).]

AMENDMENT

1. Transfer of Tribunal Functions Order 2008 (SI 2008/2833) Sch.3 paras 143 and 158 (November 3, 2008).

GENERAL NOTE

This section replaces para.4(1)(b) (and para.4(2) so far as relevant) of Sch.1 of this Act, which has been repealed. 1.475

Suspension and termination of benefit

Suspension in prescribed circumstances

1.476 **21.**—(1) Regulations may provide for—

(a) Suspending payments of a relevant benefit, in whole or in part, in prescribed circumstances;

(b) the subsequent making in prescribed circumstances of any or all of the payments so suspended.

(2) Regulations made under subsection (1) above may, in particular, make provision for any case where—

(a) it appears to the Secretary of State that an issue arises whether the conditions for entitlement to a relevant benefit are or were fulfilled;

(b) it appears to the Secretary of State that an issue arises whether a decision as to an award of a relevant benefit should be revised (under section 9 above) or superseded (under section 10 above);

(c) an appeal is pending against a decision of [[2] the First-tier Tribunal, the Upper Tribunal] or a court; or

(d) an appeal is pending against the decision given in a different case by a [[2] the Upper Tribunal] or a court, and it appears to the Secretary of State that if the appeal were to be determined in a particular way an issue would arise whether the award of a relevant benefit (whether the same benefit or not) in the case itself ought to be revised or superseded.

(3) For the purposes of subsection (2) above, an appeal against a decision is pending if—

(a) an appeal against the decision has been brought but not determined;

(b) an application for [[2] permission] to appeal against the decision has been made but not determined; or

(c) in such circumstances as may be prescribed, an appeal against the decision has not been brought (or, as the case may be, an application for [[2] permission] to appeal against the decision has not been made) but the time for doing so has not yet expired.

(4) [[1] . . .]

AMENDMENTS

1. Social Security Contributions (Transfer of Functions, etc.) Act 1999 Sch.7 para.32 (April 1, 1999).

2. Transfer of Tribunal Functions Order 2008 (SI 2008/2833) Sch.3 paras 143 and 159 (November 3, 2008).

DEFINITIONS

"prescribed"—s.84.
"relevant benefit"—see s.8(3).

GENERAL NOTE

1.477 See regs 16 and 20 of the Social Security and Child Support (Decisions and Appeals) Regulations 1999 regs 18 and 21 of the Child Benefit and Guardian's Allowance (Decisions and Appeals) Regulations 2003 and regs 44 and 46 of the Universal Credit, Personal Independence Payment, Jobseeker's Allowance and Employment and Support Allowance (Decisions and Appeals) Regulations 2013.

Suspension for failure to furnish information etc.

22.—(1) The powers conferred by this section are exercisable in relation to persons who fail to comply with information requirements. 1.478

(2) Regulations may provide for—

(a) suspending payments of a relevant benefit, in whole or in part;

(b) the subsequent making in prescribed circumstances of any or all of the payments so suspended.

(3) In this section and section 23 below "information requirement" means a requirement, made in pursuance of regulations under [2 section 5(1A)] of the Administration Act, to furnish information or evidence needed for a determination whether a decision on an award of benefit to which that section applies should be revised under section 9 or superseded under section 10 above.

[1 (4) Subsection (3A) of section 5 of the Administration Act (which glosses paragraph (hh) in the case of state pension credit) shall apply in relation to subsection (3) above as it applies in relation to paragraph (hh) of subsection (1) of that section.]

AMENDMENTS

1. State Pension Credit Act 2002 Sch.1 para.8 (July 2, 2002 for the purpose of exercising any power to make regulations or orders and October 6, 2003 for other purposes).

2. Welfare Reform Act 2012 s.99(5) (February 25, 2013).

DEFINITIONS

"the Administration Act"—see s.84.
"information requirement"—see subs.(3).
"prescribed"—see s.84.
"relevant benefit"—see s.8(3).

GENERAL NOTE

See reg.17 of the Social Security and Child Support (Decisions and Appeals) Regulations 1999, reg.19 of the Child Benefit and Guardian's Allowance (Decisions and Appeals) Regulations 2003 and reg.45 of the Universal Credit, Personal Independence Payment, Jobseeker's Allowance and Employment and Support Allowance (Decisions and Appeals) Regulations 2013. 1.479

Termination in cases of failure to furnish information

23. Regulations may provide that, except in prescribed cases or circumstances, a person— 1.480

(a) whose benefit has been suspended in accordance with regulations under section 21 above and who subsequently fails to comply withan information requirement; or

(b) whose benefit has been suspended in accordance with regulations under section 22 above for failing to comply with such a requirement,

shall cease to be entitled to the benefit from a date not earlier than the date on which payments were suspended.

DEFINITIONS

"information requirement"—see s.22(3).
"prescribed"—see s.84.

GENERAL NOTE

1.481 See reg.18 of the Social Security and Child Support (Decisions and Appeals) Regulations 1999, reg.20 of the Child Benefit and Guardian's Allowance (Decisions and Appeals) Regulations 2003 and reg.47 of the Universal Credit, Personal Independence Payment, Jobseeker's Allowance and Employment and Support Allowance (Decisions and Appeals) Regulations 2013.

Suspension and termination for failure to submit to medical examination

1.482 **24.** Regulations may make provision—

(a) enabling the Secretary of State to require a person to whom a relevant benefit has been awarded to submit to medical examination;

(b) for suspending payments of benefit, in whole or in part, in a case of a person who fails to submit himself to a medical examination to which he is required to submit in accordance with regulations under paragraph(a) above;

(c) for the subsequent making in prescribed circumstances of any or all of the payments so suspended;

(d) for entitlement to the benefit to cease, except in prescribed cases or circumstances, from a date not earlier than the date on which payments were suspended.

DEFINITIONS

"medical examination"—by virtue of s.39(2), see s.191 of the Social Security Administration Act 1992.

"prescribed"—see s.84.

"relevant benefit"—see s.8(3).

GENERAL NOTE

1.483 See reg.19 of the Social Security and Child Support (Decisions and Appeals) Regulations 1999.

[1*Appeals dependent on issues falling to be decided by Inland Revenue*

Appeals dependent on issues falling to be decided by Inland Revenue

1.484 **24A.**—(1) Regulations may make provision for [2 the First-tier Tribunal or Upper Tribunal], where on any appeal there arises any issue which under section 8 of the Social Security Contributions (Transfer of Functions, etc.) Act 1999 falls to be decided by an officer of the Inland Revenue, to require the Secretary of State to refer the issue to the Inland Revenue.

(2) Regulations under this section may—

(a) provide for the appeal to be referred to the Secretary of State pending the decision of the Inland Revenue,

(b) enable or require the Secretary of State, in specified circumstances, to deal with any other issue arising on the appeal pending the decision on the referred issue, and

(c) enable the Secretary of State, on receiving the decision of an officer of the Inland Revenue, or any determination of the [3 First-tier Tribunal or Upper Tribunal] made on appeal from his decision—

(i) to revise his decision,
(ii) to make a decision superseding his decision, or
(iii) to refer the appeal to the [2 First-tier Tribunal or Upper Tribunal] for determination.]

AMENDMENTS

1. Social Security Contributions (Transfer of Functions, etc.) Act 1999 Sch.7 para.33 (July 5, 1999).
2. Transfer of Tribunal Functions Order 2008 (SI 2008/2833) Sch.3 paras 143 and 160 (November 3, 2008).
3. Transfer of Tribunal Functions and Revenue and Customs Appeals Order 2009 (SI 2009/56) Sch.1 paras 247 and 249 (April 1, 2009).

DEFINITION

"Inland Revenue"—by virtue of s.39(2), see s.191 of the Social Security Administration Act 1992 but note that the Inland Revenue has been merged into Her Majesty's Revenue and Customs by the Commissioners for Revenue and Customs Act 2005.

GENERAL NOTE

See reg.38A of the Social Security and Child Support (Decisions and Appeals) Regulations 1999 and reg.43 of the Universal Credit, Personal Independence Payment, Jobseeker's Allowance and Employment and Support Allowance (Decisions and Appeals) Regulations 2013. **1.485**

Decisions and appeals dependent on other cases

Decisions involving issues that arise on appeal in other cases

25.—(1) This section applies where— **1.486**
(a) a decision by the Secretary of State falls to be made under section 8, 9 or 10 above in relation to a particular case; and
(b) an appeal is pending against the decision given in another case by [1the Upper Tribunal] or a court (whether or not the two cases concern the same benefit).

(2) In a case relating to a relevant benefit, the Secretary of State need not make the decision while the appeal is pending if he considers it possible that the result of the appeal will be such that, if it were already determined, there would be no entitlement to benefit.

(3) If the Secretary of State considers it possible that the result of the appeal will be such that, if it were already determined, it would affect the decision in some other way—
(a) he need not, except in such cases or circumstances as may be prescribed, make the decision while the appeal is pending;
(b) he may, in such cases or circumstances as may be prescribed, make the decision on such basis as may be prescribed.

(4) Where the Secretary of State acts in accordance with subsection (3)(b) above, following the determination of the appeal he shall if appropriate revise his decision (under section 9 above) in accordance with that determination.

(5) For the purposes of this section, an appeal against a decision is pending if—

(a) an appeal against the decision has been brought but not determined;
(b) an application for leave to appeal against the decision has been made but not determined; or
(c) in such circumstances as may be prescribed, an appeal against the decision has not been brought (or, as the case may be, an application for leave to appeal against the decision has not been made) but the time for doing so has not yet expired.

(6) In paragraphs (a), (b) and (c) of subsection (5) above, any reference to an appeal, or an application for leave to appeal, against a decision includes a reference to—

(a) an application for, or for leave to apply for judicial review of the decision under section 31 of the Supreme Court Act 1981; or
(b) an application to the supervisory jurisdiction of the Court of Session in respect of the decision.

AMENDMENT

1. Transfer of Tribunal Functions Order 2008 (SI 2008/2833) Sch.3 paras 143 and 161 (November 3, 2008).

DEFINITIONS

"prescribed"—see s.84.
"relevant benefit"—see s.8(3).

GENERAL NOTE

Subsection (1)

1.487 This section applies only where a decision falls to be made by the Secretary of State (or, in relation to decisions under s.170 of the Pension Schemes Act 1993 or in respect of child benefit or guardian's allowance, Her Majesty's Revenue and Customs—see s.170(7) of the 1993 Act (if it is not construed too literally) and ss.50(2)(e) and 51 of, and Sch.4 para.15 to, the Tax Credits Act 2002). See s.26 where a decision falls to be made by a tribunal. No appeal lies against a decision under this section (see Social Security and Child Support (Decisions and Appeals) Regulations 1999 Sch.2 para.7, Child Benefit and Guardian's Allowance (Decisions and Appeals) Regulations 2003 Sch.2 para.4 and Universal Credit, Personal Independence Payment, Jobseeker's Allowance and Employment and Support Allowance (Decisions and Appeals) Regulations 2013 Sch.3 para.8).

"Court" is not defined for the purposes of this section (compare s.27(7)) but the context in which the word appears limits its scope. There must be an appeal pending against a decision "in another case" of the Upper Tribunal or a court. This includes an application for judicial review of a tribunal decision (see subs.(6)) but not an application for judicial review of a decision of the Secretary of State or Her Majesty's Revenue and Customs or, in a housing benefit case, a local authority. However, an appeal to the Court of Appeal against a decision of the High Court, or to the Inner House of the Court of Session from a decision of the Outer House, on judicial review of the Secretary of State, Her Majesty's Revenue and Customs or a local authority would appear to be caught. A reference to the European Court of Justice by a Commissioner is certainly not caught. The words in parenthesis tend to suggest that the court must be concerned with some sort of social security benefit as does the general context of the provision and the need to have some sort of practical boundary. Otherwise, it might be suggested that, say, an appeal to the House of Lords from a decision of the Court of Appeal dealing with the meaning of the word "misrepresentation" in a marine insurance policy was a relevant appeal (because it might possibly assist with the understanding of that word in s.71 of the Social Security Administration Act 1992).

Subssections (2) and (3)

The Secretary of State (or Her Majesty's Revenue and Customs) must consider two separate issues. The first is whether a possible result of the appeal would affect the decision before him. The Secretary of State would be a party to most such appeals and it is to be hoped that he does not indulge in too much wishful thinking. The word "possible" is broad. And what is the meaning of "result of the appeal"? Is it confined to the ratio decidendi or is it sufficient that the Secretary of State considers that there might be some useful obiter dicta? The second issue the Secretary of State (or Her Majesty's Revenue and Customs) must consider is whether he should not make the decision or should decide it in accordance with subs.(3)(b) or whether he should ignore the fact that there is an appeal pending. He has a broad discretion and much will depend on such circumstances as the number of cases, the amount of money at stake, hardship to the claimants and the degree of probability that the court's decision will provide significant assistance with the determination of the cases before him. **1.488**

For regulations under subs.(3)(b), see reg.21(1)–(3) of the Social Security and Child Support (Decisions and Appeals) Regulations 1999, reg.22(1)–(3) of the Child Benefit and Guardian's Allowance (Decisions and Appeals) Regulations 2003 and reg.53(1) of the Universal Credit, Personal Independence Payment, Jobseeker's Allowance and Employment and Support Allowance (Decisions and Appeals) Regulations 2013.

Subsection (4)

The revision usually has effect from the same date as the original decision (see s.9(3)). **1.489**

Subsection (5)

See reg.21(4) of the Social Security and Child Support (Decisions and Appeals) Regulations 1999, reg.22(4) of the Child Benefit and Guardian's Allowance (Decisions and Appeals) Regulations 2003 and reg.53(2) of the Universal Credit, Personal Independence Payment, Jobseeker's Allowance and Employment and Support Allowance (Decisions and Appeals) Regulations 2013. **1.490**

Appeals involving issues that arise on appeal in other cases

26.—(1) This section applies where— **1.491**

(a) an appeal ("appeal A") in relation to a decision under section 8, 9 or 10 above is made to [1 the First-tier Tribunal, or from the First-tier Tribunal to the Upper Tribunal] and

(b) an appeal ("appeal B") is pending against a decision given in a different case by [1 the Upper Tribunal] or a court (whether or not the two appeals concern the same benefit).

(2) If the Secretary of State considers it possible that the result of appeal B will be such that, if it were already determined, it would affect the determination of appeal A, he may serve notice requiring [1 First-tier Tribunal or Upper Tribunal]—

(a) not to determine appeal A but to refer it to him; or

(b) to deal withthe appeal in accordance with subsection (4) below.

(3) Where appeal A is referred to the Secretary of State under subsection (2)(a) above, following the determination of appeal B and in accordance with that determination, he shall if appropriate—

(a) in a case where appeal A has not been determined by the [1 First-tier Tribunal], revise (under section 9 above) his decision which gave rise to that appeal; or

(b) in a case where appeal A has been determined by the [1 First-tier Tribunal], make a decision (under section 10 above) superseding the tribunal's decision.

(4) Where appeal A is to be dealt with in accordance with this subsection, the [1 First-tier Tribunal or Upper Tribunal] shall either—

(a) stay appeal A until appeal B is determined; or

(b) if the [1 First-tier Tribunal or Upper Tribunal] considers it to be in the interests of the appellant to do so, determine appeal A as if—

(i) appeal B had already been determined; and

(ii) the issues arising on appeal B had been decided in the way that was most unfavourable to the appellant.

In this subsection "the appellant" means the person who appealed or, as the case may be, first appealed against the decision mentioned in subsection (1)(a) above.

(5) Where the [1 First-tier Tribunal or Upper Tribunal] acts in accordance with subsection (4)(b) above, following the determination of appeal B the Secretary of State shall, if appropriate, make a decision (under section 10 above) superseding the decision of the [1 First-tier Tribunal or Upper Tribunal] in accordance withthat determination.

(6) For the purposes of this section, an appeal against a decision is pending if—

(a) an appeal against the decision has been brought but not determined;

(b) an application for leave to appeal against the decision has been made but not determined; or

(c) in such circumstances as may be prescribed, an appeal against the decision has not been brought (or, as the case may be, an application for leave to appeal against the decision has not been made) but the time for doing so has not yet expired.

(7) In this section—

(a) the reference in subsection (1)(a) above to an appeal to [1 the Upper Tribunal] includes a reference to an application for leave to appeal to [1 the Upper Tribunal]; and

(b) any reference in paragraph (a), (b) or (c) of subsection (6) above to an appeal, or to an application for leave to appeal, against a decision includes a reference to—

(i) an application for, or for leave to apply for, judicial review of the decision under section 31 of the Supreme Court Act

(ii) an application to the supervisory jurisdiction of the Court of Session in respect of the decision.

(8) Regulations may make provision supplementing that made by this section.

AMENDMENT

1. Transfer of Tribunal Functions Order 2008 (SI 2008/2833) Sch.3 paras 143 and 162 (November 3, 2008).

DEFINITION

"prescribed"—see s.84.

GENERAL NOTE

Subsection (1)

1.492 See the note to s.25(1) for the meaning of "court". See also subss.(6) and (7).

Subsection (2)

It is for the Secretary of State (or, in relation to decisions under s.170 of the Pension Schemes Act 1993 or in respect of child benefit or guardian's allowance, Her Majesty's Revenue and Customs—see s.170(7) of the 1993 Act (if it is not construed too literally) and ss.50(2)(e) and 51 of, and Sch.4, para.15 to, the Tax Credits Act 2002) to identify both appeal B and appeal A although there is no reason why one notice may not be issued in respect of several appeals A. As in s.25(2) and (3), the Secretary of State (or Her Majesty's Revenue and Customs) must first make a judgment as to the possible effects of the decision in appeal B and must then consider whether to serve notice under this subsection. It will not always be appropriate to do so. If the Secretary of State does decide to issue the notice, he must go on to decide whether the tribunal should be required to refer appeal A to him under para.(a) or to deal with the appeal in accordance with subs. (4) under para.(b). Which option is appropriate will depend on the circumstances of the case. **1.493**

It may be thought to be unobjectionable that there be specific provision as to the way appeals should be handled while the decision in a "test case" is awaited, but to be highly objectionable that the decision as to the appropriate procedure should lie wholly in the hands of the Secretary of State who is a party in appeal A and is usually a party in appeal B. The perception that this provision was desirable appears to have arisen out of an occasion when the then President of social security appeal tribunals directed tribunals to determine a vast number of appeals notwithstanding the fact that an appeal against a Social Security Commissioner's decision was pending in the courts. This resulted in some thousands of extra appeals being brought before the Commissioners. It may be thought that this is unlikely to be repeated. In practice the Secretary of State is very often content to allow tribunals to manage blocks of "lookalike" cases without resorting to serving a notice under this section and where a notice is served it is usually after consultation with the relevant Chamber President. There can be an advantage to a claimant in having a notice served under this section where a tribunal might award some benefit on appeal A even if that appeal is determined on the basis that appeal B is determined adversely to the claimant. The claimant is then not deprived of that benefit while appeal B is awaiting final determination. It might be better if the legislation merely allowed the Secretary of State to seek a general direction in respect of a block of similar cases from the relevant Chamber President. As it is, any challenge to the Secretary of State's judgment must be by way of an application for judicial review.

Subsection (3)

Presumably para.(b) exists in case appeal A was decided in ignorance of the notice requiring it not to be determined. The decision is not rendered ineffective and so operates until it is superseded. It is not clear what happens if either party appeals against it. **1.494**

Subsection (4)

It is for the tribunal to decide whether para.(a) or para.(b) should apply in any particular case. Paragraph (b) is unlikely to be used a great deal unless either the claimant asks for it to be used or else the tribunal is fairly sure that the decision on appeal B is unlikely to assist the claimant. A judgment as to what is the most unfavourable way in which the issues arising on appeal B might be decided requires that the tribunal be given considerable information about the appeal, including pleadings, so that it can be established what the issues really are. **1.495**

Subsection (5)

The supersession is effective from the date from which the tribunals decision would have been effective had it been decided in accordance with the decision in "Appeal B", the test case (reg.7(33) of the Social Security and Child Support **1.496**

(Decisions and Appeals) Regulations 1999 reg.16(8) of the Child Benefit and Guardian's Allowance (Decisions and Appeals) Regulations 2003 and reg.27(4) of the Universal Credit, Personal Independence Payment, Jobseeker's Allowance and Employment and Support Allowance (Decisions and Appeals) Regulations 2013).

Subsection (6)

1.497 See reg.22 of the Social Security and Child Support (Decisions and Appeals) Regulations 1999 reg.23 of the Child Benefit and Guardian's Allowance (Decisions and Appeals) Regulations 2003 and reg.54 of the Universal Credit, Personal Independence Payment, Jobseeker's Allowance and Employment and Support Allowance (Decisions and Appeals) Regulations 2013.

Cases of error

Restrictions on entitlement to benefit in certain cases of error

1.498 **27.**—(1) Subject to subsection (2) below, this section applies where—

(a) the effect of the determination, whenever made, of an appeal to [3the Upper Tribunal] or the court ("the relevant determination") is that the adjudicating authority's decision out of which the appeal arose was erroneous in point of law; and

(b) after the date of the relevant determination a decision falls to be made by the Secretary of State in accordance with that determination (or would, apart from this section, fall to be so made)—

(i) in relation to a claim for benefit;

(ii) as to whether to revise, under section 9 above, a decision as to a person's entitlement to benefit; or

(iii) on an application made under section 10 above for a decision as to a person's entitlement to benefit to be superseded.

(2) This section does not apply where the decision of the Secretary of State mentioned in subsection (1)(b) above—

(a) is one which, but for section 25(2) or (3)(a) above, would have been made before the date of the relevant determination; or

(b) is one made in pursuance of section 26(3) or (5) above.

(3) In so far as the decision relates to a person's entitlement to a benefit in respect of—

(a) a period before the date of the relevant determination; or

(b) in the case of a widow's payment, a death occurring before that date,

it shall be made as if the adjudicating authority's decision had been found by [3the Upper Tribunal] or court not to have been erroneous in point of law.

(4) In deciding whether a person is entitled to benefit in a case where his entitlement depends on his having been entitled to the same or some other benefit before attaining a particular age, subsection (3) above shall be disregarded for the purpose only of deciding whether he was so entitled before attaining that age.

(5) Subsection (1)(a) above shall be read as including a case where—

(a) the effect of the relevant determination is that part or all of a purported regulation or order is invalid; and

(b) the error of law made by the adjudicating authority was to act on the basis that the purported regulation or order (or the part held to be invalid) was valid.

(6) It is immaterial for the purposes of subsection (1) above—

(a) where such a decision as is mentioned in paragraph (b)(i) falls to be made, whether the claim was made before or after the date of the relevant determination;

(b) where such a decision as is mentioned in paragraph (b)(ii) or (iii) falls to be made on an application under section 9 or (as the case may be) 10 above, whether the application was made before or after that date.

(7) In this section—

"adjudicating authority" means—

(a) the Secretary of State;

(b) any former officer, tribunal or body; or

(c) any officer, tribunal or body in Northern Ireland corresponding to a former officer, tribunal or body;

"benefit" means—

(a) benefit under Parts II to V of the Contributions and Benefits Act, other than Old Cases payments;

(b) benefit under Part II of the Social Security Act 1975 (in respect of a period before July 1, 1992 but not before April 6, 1975);

(c) benefit under the National Insurance Act 1946 or 1965, or the National Insurance (Industrial Injuries) Act 1946 or 1965 (in respect of a period before April 6, 1975);

(d) a jobseeker's allowance;

[1 (dd) state pension credit;]

[2 (de) an employment and support allowance;]

[4 (df) personal independence payment;]

[7 (dg) bereavement support payment under section 30 of the Pensions Act 2014;]

(e) any benefit corresponding to a benefit mentioned in [1 paragraphs (a) [7 to (dg)] above]; and

(f) any income-related benefit [5 *universal credit*];

[6 (g) state pension or a lump sum under Part 1 of the Pensions Act 2014;]

"the court" means the High Court, the Court of Appeal, the Court of Session, the High Court or Court of Appeal in Northern Ireland, the House of Lords or the Court of Justice in the European Community;

"former officer, tribunal or body" means any of the following, that is to say—

(a) an adjudication officer or, in the case of a decision given on a reference under section 21(2) or 25(1) of the Administration Act, a social security appeal tribunal, a disability appeal tribunal or a medical appeal tribunal;

(b) an adjudicating medical practitioner appointed under section 49 of that Act or a specially qualified adjudicating medical practitioner appointed in accordance with regulations under section 62(2) of that Act; or

(c) the National Assistance Board, the Supplementary Benefits Commission, the Attendance Allowance Board, a benefit officer, an insurance officer or a supplement officer.

(8) For the purposes of this section, any reference to entitlement to benefit includes a reference to entitlement—

those powers once he knows the limits of the powers. This is despite the fact that Parliament could not have known the extent to which the powers would be exceeded. Henry VIII could hardly have asked for more.

Subsection (7)

1.503 Note that the First-tier Tribunal is not an "adjudicating authority". Quite why a social security appeal tribunal giving a decision on a reference should have been included as a "former tribunal" is unclear because there was no reason to suppose that their view of the law would necessarily be consistent with that held by the Department of Social Security. Perhaps the draftsman had a particular case in mind. The inclusion of disability appeal tribunals and medical appeal tribunals is even more obscure as there was no power to refer cases to them under the provisions cited. The inclusion of the Court of Appeal in Northern Ireland in the definition of "court" is interesting as a decision of that court is not, strictly speaking, binding in Great Britain. Such a decision is, however, highly persuasive and should usually be followed. The implication is that, if the Secretary of State does decide to follow a decision of the Court of Appeal in Northern Ireland, the decision before him "falls to be made . . . in accordance with" the decision of the court for the purpose of subs. (1).

Subssections (9) and (10)

1.504 No regulations have yet been made under these powers.

Correction of errors and setting aside of decisions

1.505 **28.**—(1) Regulations may make provision with respect to—

(a) the correction of accidental errors in any decision [4 of the Secretary of State] or record of a decision [4 of the Secretary of State] made under any relevant enactment;

(b) [4. . .]

[4. . .]

[1 (1A) In subsection (1) "decision" does not include [4 any decision of the First-tier Tribunal or] any decision made by an officer of the Inland Revenue, other than a decision under or by virtue of Part III of the Pensions Schemes Act 1993.]

(2) Nothing in subsection (1) above shall be construed as derogating from any power to correct errors [4. . .] which is exercisable apart from regulations made by virtue of that subsection.

(3) In this section "relevant enactment" means any enactment contained in—

(a) this Chapter;

(b) the Contributions and Benefits Act;

(c) the Pension Schemes Act 1993;

(d) the Jobseekers Act; [2 . . .]

(e) the Social Security (Recovery of Benefits) Act 1997; [2 [3 . . .]]

[2 (f) the State Pension Credit Act 2002;] [3[5 . . .]]

[3 (g) Part 1 of the Welfare Reform Act 2007;]

[5 (h) Part 1 of the Welfare Reform Act 2012; [6 . . .]

(i) Part 4 of that Act;] [6 or

(j) Part 1 of the Pensions Act 2014 [7 or section 30 of that Act].]

AMENDMENTS

1. Social Security Contributions (Transfer of Functions, etc.) Act 1999 Sch.7 para.34 (July 5, 1999).

2. State Pension Credit Act 2002 Sch.1 para.10 and Sch.3 (July 2, 2002 for regulation-making purposes and April 7, 2003 for other purposes).

3. Welfare Reform Act 2007 Sch.3 para.17(1) and (6) (March 18, 2008 for regulation-making purposes and July 27, 2008 for other purposes).

4. Transfer of Tribunal Functions Order 2008 (SI 2008/2833) Sch.3 paras 143 and 164 (November 3, 2008).

5. Welfare Reform Act 2012 ss.31 and 91 Sch.2 paras 43 and 48 and Sch.9 paras 37 and 42 (February 25, 2013).

6. Pensions Act 2014 s.23 and Sch.12 paras 31 and 36 (April 6, 2016).

7. Pensions Act 2014 s.31(5) and Sch.16 paras 37 and 42 (April 6, 2017).

DEFINITIONS

"Contributions and Benefits Act"—see s.84.

"Inland Revenue"—by virtue of s.39(2), see s.191 of the Social Security Administration Act 1992 but note that the Inland Revenue has been merged into Her Majesty's Revenue and Customs by the Commissioners for Revenue and Customs Act 2005.

"the Jobseekers Act"—see s.84.

"prescribed"—see s.84.

"relevant enactment"—see subs.(3).

GENERAL NOTE

See reg.9A of the Social Security and Child Support (Decisions and Appeals) Regulations 1999 and reg.38 of the Universal Credit, Personal Independence Payment, Jobseeker's Allowance and Employment and Support Allowance (Decisions and Appeals) Regulations 2013. This section is no longer concerned with the correction and setting aside of tribunal decisions, for which see now para.15 of Sch.5 to the Tribunals, Courts and Enforcement Act 2007. **1.506**

Industrial accidents

Decision that accident is an industrial accident

29.—(1) Where, in connection with any claim for industrial injuries benefit, it is decided that the relevant accident was or was not an industrial accident— **1.507**

(a) an express declaration of that fact shall be made and recorded; and
(b) subject to subsection (3) below, a claimant shall be entitled to have the issue whether the relevant accident was an industrial accident decided, notwithstanding that his claim is disallowed on other grounds.

(2) [2 . . .]

(3) The Secretary of State, [1the First-tier Tribunal or the Upper Tribunal] (as the case may be) may refuse to decide the issue whether an accident was an industrial accident, if satisfied that it is unlikely to be necessary to decide the issue for the purposes of any claim for benefit and this Chapter shall apply as if any such refusal were a decision on the issue.

(4) Subject to sections 9 to 15 above, any declaration under this section that an accident was or was not an industrial accident shall be conclusive for the purposes of any claim for industrial injuries benefit in respect of that accident.

(5) Where subsection (4) above applies—
(a) in relation to a death occurring before April 11, 1988; or
(b) for the purposes of section 60(2) of the Contributions and Benefits Act,

it shall have effect as if at the end there were added the words "whether or not the claimant is the person at whose instance the declaration was made".

(6) For the purposes of this section (but subject to section 30 below), an accident whereby a person suffers personal injury shall be deemed, in relation to him, to be an industrial accident if—
(a) it arises out of and in the course of his employment;
(b) that employment is employed earner's employment for the purposes of Part V of the Contributions and Benefits Act; and
(c) payment of benefit is not under section 94(5) of that Act precluded because the accident happened while he was outside Great Britain.

(7) A decision under this section shall be final except that sections 9 and 10 above apply to a decision under this section that an accident was or was not an industrial accident as they apply to a decision under section 8 above if, but only if, the Secretary of State is satisfied that the decision under this section was given in consequence of any wilful non-disclosure or misrepresentation of a material fact.

AMENDMENTS

1. Transfer of Tribunal Functions Order 2008 (SI 2008/2833) Sch.3 paras 143 and 165 (November 3, 2008).
2. Welfare Reform Act 2012, s.68(1) (December 5, 2012).

DEFINITIONS

"benefit—by virtue of s.39(2), see s.191 of the Social Security Administration Act 1992.
"claim"—*ibid.*
"claimant"—see s.39(1) and, by virtue of s.39(2), see s.191 of the Social Security Administration Act 1992.
"Contributions and Benefits Act"—see s.84.
"industrial injuries benefit"—by virtue of s.39(2), see s.191 of the Social Security Administration Act 1992.

GENERAL NOTE

1.508 This section re-enacts s.44 of the Social Security Administration Act 1992 with only minor changes. It provides for the Secretary of State to make a declaration that a person has suffered an industrial accident, whether or not the claim has any prospects of success on other grounds, although, under subs.(3), the Secretary of State (or a tribunal) may refuse to determine that question if it is unlikely there will ever be a claim for benefit.

Subsection (2) used to provide that a declaration could be made even if there was no claim for benefit. Since a declaration must be made if there is a claim for benefit and a future claim might succeed even if the present one does not, the repeal does not prevent a person from seeking a declaration if minded to do so but it does make it unnecessary to advertise the existence of a right to seek a declaration without a claim, and it has the effect that a claimant cannot be criticised for not seeking a declaration when suffering no relevant symptoms.

A determination that there was or was not an industrial accident is conclusive for the purposes of later claims for benefit (unless it is set aside on appeal or is revised or superseded). However, it is important to note that this section is expressed to be subject to s.30, so that a decision under this section which implies that a person has suffered personal injury as a result of an accident does not require anyone to find that the claimant has suffered disablement as a result of the injury even though the two decisions may appear, in the circumstances of the case, to contradict one another.

The usual rights of appeal apply to declarations under this section, but the power to revise or supersede such decisions is strictly limited, by subs.(7), to cases of *wilful* non-disclosure or misrepresentation of a material fact. **1.509**

Where the Secretary of State has decided that a claimant has not suffered an industrial accident and the claimant appeals against that decision, a tribunal may exercise the power conferred by subs.(3) to refuse to decide the issue on the ground that it is unlikely to be relevant to any claim to benefit (*CI/1297/2002*). That refusal to decide the issue must replace the Secretary of State's decision, and will make an important difference if the tribunal is wrong and there ever is a claim for benefit, because the Secretary of State's decision would have been conclusive by virtue of subs.(4) and the scope for revision or supersession would have been limited by virtue of subs.(7). In *CI/732/2007*, the Commissioner accepted a submission by the Secretary of State to the effect that it was also open to a tribunal to refuse to make a declaration where a claimant had suffered a vaccination reaction as the result of a vaccination in the course of her employment. A vaccination reaction is normal and so the claimant had not suffered an industrial accident, because there had been no unexpected or untoward event. The Secretary of State's submission was in the claimant's favour because its acceptance meant the claimant was not precluded from advancing new medical evidence in the future to show that other ill health was attributable to the vaccination, which would lead to a finding that she had suffered an industrial accident.

Effect of decision

30.—(1) A decision [1 . . .] that an accident was an industrial accident is to be taken as determining only that paragraphs (a), (b) and (c) of subsection (6) of that section are satisfied in relation to the accident. **1.510**

(2) Subject to subsections (3) and (4) below, no such decision is to be taken as importing a decision as to the origin of any injury or disability suffered by the claimant, whether or not there is an event identifiable as an accident apart from any injury that may have been received.

(3) A decision that, on a particular occasion when there was no event so identifiable, a person had an industrial accident by reason of an injury shall be treated as a decision that, if the injury was suffered by accident on that occasion, the accident was an industrial accident.

(4) A decision that an accident was an industrial accident may be given, and a declaration to that effect be made and recorded in accordance with section 29 above, without its having been found that personal injury resulted from the accident.

(5) Subsection (4) above has effect, subject to the discretion under section 29(3) above, to refuse to decide the issue if it is unlikely to be necessary for the purposes of a claim for benefit.

AMENDMENT

1. Welfare Reform Act 2012 s.68(2) (December 5, 2012).

DEFINITIONS

"benefit"—by virtue of s.39(2), see s.191 of the Social Security Administration Act 1992.

"claim"—*ibid.*
"claimant"—see s.39(1) and, by virtue of s.39(2), see s.191 of the Social Security Administration Act 1992.

GENERAL NOTE

1.511 This section replaces s.60(3) of the Social Security Administration Act 1992. The drafting of the new provision is a great improvement (or was until subs.(1) was amended – the repealed words showed that the reference to "that section" is to s.29). The overall effect is the same. A finding that there has been an industrial accident does not prevent it from being found that there has been no loss of faculty resulting from the accident even if the two decisions appear to be inconsistent. This is so even in a case where a person suffers a heart attack and the only "accident" found was the heart attack itself. Another decision-maker is still entitled to hold that the heart attack was not the result of an accident. This provision was first introduced by the National Insurance Act 1972 to reverse the effect of *Jones v Secretary of State for Social Services* [1972] A.C. 944 (also reported as an appendix to *R(I) 3/69*). It is less important than it used to be now that all material decisions are made by the Secretary of State and there is no longer the old division of jurisdiction between adjudication officers and adjudicating medical authorities. However, it still has significance where different decision-makers deal with the question whether there was an industrial accident and the question whether the claimant suffers a loss of faculty as a result of the accident (e.g. where a tribunal reverses a decision to the effect that there was no industrial accident but does not go on and deal with the other questions arising on the claim). In *CI/105/1998*, it was pointed out that, quite apart from cases where the accident is indistinguishable from the injury suffered, there are cases where an indication that an accident was one giving rise to personal injury is a necessary part of a decision-maker's reasoning because it may help to explain why a declaration is made in respect of that alleged cause of the injury rather than another. However, it was also made clear that the effect of the forerunner of this section was that any view as to causation expressed when making the decision that an accident was an industrial accident could be only provisional.

Other special cases

Incapacity for work

1.512 **31.**—(1) Regulations may provide that a determination that a person is disqualified for any period in accordance with regulations under section 171E of the Contributions and Benefits Act shall have effect for such purposes as may be prescribed as a determination that he is to be treated as capable of work for that period, and vice versa.

[1 (1A) Regulations may provide that a determination that a person is disqualified for any period in accordance with regulations under section 18(1) to (3) of the Welfare Reform Act 2007 shall have effect for such purposes as may be prescribed as a determination that he is to be treated as not having limited capability for work for that period, and vice versa.]

(2) Provision may be made by regulations for matters of such descriptions as may be prescribed to be determined by the Secretary of State, notwithstanding that other matters fall to be determined by another authority.

(3) Nothing in this section shall be taken to prejudice the generality of the power conferred by section 17(2) above.

AMENDMENT

1. Welfare Reform Act 2007 Sch.3 para.17(1) and (7) (March 18, 2008 for regulation-making purposes and October 27, 2008 for other purposes).

DEFINITIONS

"Contributions and Benefits Act"—see s.84.
"prescribed"—*ibid.*

GENERAL NOTE

Subssections (1) and (1a)

See reg.10 of the Social Security and Child Support (Decisions and Appeals) Regulations 1999. **1.513**

Subsection (2)

See reg.11 of the Social Security and Child Support (Decisions and Appeals) Regulations 1999. **1.514**

Industrial diseases

32. Regulations shall provide for applying the provisions of this Chapter, subject to any prescribed additions or modifications, in relation to decisions made or falling to be made under sections 108 to 110 of the Contributions and Benefits Act. **1.515**

DEFINITIONS

"Contributions and Benefits Act"—see s.84.
"prescribed"—*ibid.*

GENERAL NOTE

See the Social Security (Industrial Injuries) (Prescribed Diseases) Regulations 1985, as amended by art.4(8) of and Sch.8 to the Social Security Act 1998 (Commencement No.8 and Savings and Consequential and Transitional Provisions) Order 1999, (in Vol.I) and reg.12A of the Social Security and Child Support (Decisions and Appeals) Regulations 1999. **1.516**

Christmas bonus

33.—(1) A decision by the Secretary of State that a person is entitled or not entitled to payment of a qualifying benefit in respect of a period which includes a day in the relevant week shall be conclusive for the purposes of section 148 of the Contributions and Benefits Act. **1.517**

(2) In this section, expressions to which a meaning is assigned by section 150 of that Act have that meaning.

DEFINITIONS

"Contributions and Benefits Act"—see s.84.
"qualifying benefit"—by virtue of subs.(2), see s.150 of the Social Security Contributions and Benefits Act 1992.
"relevant week"—*ibid.*

General Note

1.518 This replaces s.67 of the Social Security Administration Act 1992.

Housing benefit and council tax benefit

1.519 **34.–35.** *Omitted.*

Social fund payments

1.520 **36.–38**. *Repealed.*

Supplemental

[1 Certificates

1.521 **39ZA.** A document bearing a certificate which—

(a) is signed by a person authorised in that behalf by the Secretary of State, and
(b) states that the document, apart from the certificate, is a record of a decision of an officer of the Secretary of State,

shall be conclusive evidence of the decision; and a certificate purporting to be so signed shall be deemed to be so signed unless the contrary is proved.]

Amendment

1. Transfer of Tribunal Functions Order 2008 (SI 2008/2833) Sch.3 paras 143 and 166 (November 3, 2008).

General note

1.522 This section partially replaces para.13 of Sch.1 to this Act, which has been repealed. However, there is no longer any provision for certifying decisions of tribunals.

Computer records often need some interpretation in order to make them intelligible. However, a certificate is conclusive only to the extent that it authenticates the record of the decision. This section does not make the certificate conclusive to the extent that the certificate purports also to interpret the record of the decision.

It does not follow from the fact that a certified copy of a decision is conclusive evidence of the decision that other evidence cannot be relied upon, although such other evidence would not be conclusive (*JM v SSWP (ESA)* [2013] UKUT 234 (AAC); [2014] AACR 5 at [74]).

Interpretation etc. of Chapter II

1.523 **39.**—(1) In this Chapter—

[4. . .]

[2 "claimant", in relation to a joint-claim couple claiming a joint-claim jobseeker's allowance (within the meaning of the Jobseekers Act 1995), means the couple or either member of the couple;]

[6 "claimant", in relation to a couple jointly claiming universal credit, means the couple or either member of the couple;]

[4. . .]

[3 "health care professional" means—

(a) a registered medical practitioner,

(b) a registered nurse,
(c) an occupational therapist or physiotherapist registered with a regulatory body established by an Order in Council under section 60 of the Health Act 1999, or
(d) a member of such other profession regulated by a body mentioned in section 25(3) of the National Health Service Reform and Health Care Professions Act 2002 as the Secretary of State may prescribe;]

"relevant benefit" has the meaning given by section 8(3) above;

[5. . .]

(2) Expressions used in this Chapter to which a meaning is assigned by section 191 of the Administration Act have that meaning in this Chapter.

(3) Part II of the Administration Act, which is superseded by the foregoing provisions of this Chapter, shall cease to have effect.

AMENDMENTS

1. Social Security Contributions (Transfer of Functions, etc.) Act 1999 Sch.7 para.35 (April 1, 1999).
2. Welfare Reform and Pensions Act 1999 Sch.7 para.17 (March 19, 2001).
3. Welfare Reform Act 2007 s.62(1) and (5) (July 3, 2007).
4. Transfer of Tribunal Functions Order 2008 (SI 2008/2833) Sch.3 paras 143 and 167 (November 3, 2008), subject to a saving under art.1(5).
5. Transfer of Tribunal Functions and Revenue and Customs Appeals Order 2009 (SI 2009/56), Sch.1, paras 247 and 250 (April 1, 2009).
6. Welfare Reform Act 2012, s.31 and 91, Sch.2, paras 43 and 49 (February 25, 2013 for regulation-making purposes and April 29, 2013 for other purposes).

DEFINITION

"the Administration Act"—see s.84.

GENERAL NOTE

By reg.14 of the Child Trust Funds (Non-tax Appeals) Regulations 2005 (SI 2005/191), this subsection is applied with some modifications to appeals under ss.21(9) and 22 of the Child Trust Funds Act 2004 (see Vol.IV). Until April 1, 2009, it was also applied in modified form to appeals under the Tax Credits Act 2002 but, as explained in the note to s.12, the regulation applying it appears to have lapsed in relation to cases in Great Britain. 1.524

Definitions omitted by virtue of the Transfer of Tribunal Functions Order 2008 remain in force for the purpose explained in the note to ss.5–7.

"health care professional"

Until 2007, all medical examinations were carried out by registered medical practitioners. However, as the focus on examinations for social security purposes is usually the functional effects of a medical condition, the expertise of nurses, occupational therapists and physiotherapists may be as relevant and so provision is now made for many medical examinations to be carried out by a health care professional falling within this definition. This may result in a physiotherapist making an assessment in respect of a person suffering from a mental disorder. In *ST v SSWP (ESA)* [2014] UKUT 547 (AAC); [2015] AACR 23, the three-judge panel recorded evidence given to it about the recruitment, training and assessment of health care professionals and it held that the weight to be given to a physiotherapist's opinion in relation to mental health issues is a matter for the decision-maker or tribunal. The professional qualification of a health care professional is usually recorded in the relevant report but not having that information or not knowing the precise areas of expertise of the health care professional does not necessarily require the First-tier 1.525

Tribunal to reject opinions expressed in the report (*JM v SSWP (ESA)* [2013] UKUT 234 (AAC); [2014] AACR 5, at [76]).

From June 29, 2010, reg.3 of the Social Security (Disability Living Allowance) (Amendment) Regulations 2010 (SI 2010/1651), made under this section, provides—

> "**Health care professionals**
>
> **3.** For the purposes of section 39(1) of the Social Security Act 1998 (meaning of health care professional), in relation to a claim for disability living allowance under section 73(1AB) of the Social Security Contributions and Benefits Act 1992, the following persons are health care professionals –
>
> (a) an optometrist registered with the General Optical Council;
> (b) an orthoptist registered with the Health Professions Council."

Note, therefore, that optometrists and orthoptists are health care professionals only for the purposes of claims to the mobility component of disability living allowance made on the ground of severe visual impairment.

The effect of s.39 and the 2010 Regulations made under it is that all health care professionals must be "registered" members of their professions. In relation to doctors and nurses, this is because s.39 must be read with s.5 of, and Sch.1 to, to the Interpretation Act 1978 which provide that, unless the contrary intention appears—

"Registered" in relation to nurses and midwives, means registered in the register maintained under article 5 of the Nursing and Midwifery Order 2001 by virtue of qualifications in nursing or midwifery, as the case may be.

"Registered medical practitioner" means a fully registered person within the meaning of the Medical Act 1983 who holds a licence to practise under that Act.

It was held in *RO v SSWP (ESA)* [2016] UKUT 402 (AAC) that a claimant required to attend for, or submit to, a medical examination by a health care professional is entitled to make a reasonable request for proof that a purported healthcare professional is in fact a health care professional. However, the First-tier Tribunal did not err in finding that an offer extended to the claimant at the assessment centre to check the assessor's credentials on the Nursing and Midwifery Council website was sufficient. It did not matter that the website did not contain photographs so that the identity of the health care professional could not also be checked.

Chapter III

Other Decisions and Appeals

1.526 **40.–47.** *Omitted.*

Part II

Contributions

1.527 **48.–66.** *Omitted.*

Part III

Benefits

67.–76. *Omitted.* 1.528

Part IV

Miscellaneous and Supplemental

Pilot schemes

77.—(1) Any regulations to which this subsection applies may be made so as to have effect for a specified period not exceeding 12 months. 1.529

(2) Any regulations which, by virtue of subsection (1) above, are to have effect for a limited period are referred to in this section as "a pilot scheme".

(3) A pilot scheme may provide that its provisions are to apply only in relation to—

(a) one or more specified areas of localities;
(b) one or more specified classes of person;
(c) persons selected—
   (i) by reference to prescribed criteria; or
   (ii) on a sampling basis,

(4) A pilot scheme may make consequential or transitional provision with respect to the cessation of the scheme on the expiry of the specified period.

(5) A pilot scheme ("the previous scheme") may be replaced by a further pilot scheme making the same, or similar, provision (apart from the specified period) to that made by the previous scheme.

(6) In so far as a pilot scheme would, apart from this subsection, have the effect of—

(a) treating as capable of work any person who would not otherwise be so treated; or
(b) reducing the total amount of benefit that would otherwise be payable to any person,

it shall not apply in relation to that person.

(7) Subsection (1) above applies to—

(a) regulations made under section 171D of the Contributions and Benefits Act (incapacity for work: persons treated as incapable of work); and
(b) in so far as they are consequential on or supplementary to any such regulations, regulations made under any of the provisions mentioned in subsection (8) below.

(8) The provisions are—

(a) subsection (5)(a) of section 22 of the Contributions and Benefits Act (earnings factors);
(b) section 30C of that Act (incapacity benefit);
(c) [1 . . .];
(d) subsection (1)(e) of section 124 of that Act (income support) and,

3. Transfer of Tribunal Functions Order 2008 (SI 2008/2833) Sch.3 paras 143 and 169 (November 3, 2008), subject to a saving under art.1(5).
4. Welfare Reform Act 2012 s.102(1) and (5) (February 25, 2013).

GENERAL NOTE

1.535 The omitted provisions remain in force for the purpose explained in the note to ss.5–7.

Reports by Secretary of State

1.536 **81.** [[1] . . .]

AMENDMENT

1. Welfare Reform Act 2012 s.143 (May 8, 2012).

1.537 **82.** *Omitted.*

1.538 **83.** *Omitted.*

Interpretation: general

1.539 **84.** In this Act—

"the Administration Act" means the Social Security Administration Act 1992;

"the Child Support Act" means the Child Support Act 1991;

"the Contributions and Benefits Act" means the Social Security Contributions and Benefits Act 1992;

"the Jobseekers Act" means the Jobseekers Act 1995;

"the Vaccine Damage Payments Act" means the Vaccine Damage Payments Act 1979;

"prescribe" means prescribe by regulations.

1.540 **85.** *Omitted.*

1.541 **86.** *Omitted.*

Short title, commencement and extent

1.542 **87.**—(1) This Act may be cited as the Social Security Act 1998.

(2) This Act, except—

(a) sections 66, 69, 72 and 77 to 85, this section and Schedule 6 to this Act; and
(b) subsection (1) of section 50 so far as relating to a sum which is chargeable to tax by virtue of section 313 of the Income and Corporation Taxes Act 1988, and subsections (2) to (4) of that section,

shall come into force on such day as may be appointed by order made by the Secretary of State; and different days may be appointed for different provisions and for different purposes.

(3) An order under subsection (2) above may make such savings, or such transitional or consequential provision, as the Secretary of State considers necessary or expedient—

(a) in preparation for or in connection with the coming into force of any provision of this Act; or

(b) in connection with the operation of any enactment repealed or amended by a provision of this Act during any period when the repeal or amendment is not wholly in force.

(4) This Act, except—

(a) section 2 so far as relating to war pensions;

(b) sections 3, 15, 45 to 47, 59, 78 and 85 and this section; and

(c) section 86 and Schedules 7 and 8 so far as relating to enactments which extend to Northern Ireland,

does not extend to Northern Ireland.

(5) The following provisions of this Act extend to the Isle of Man, namely—

(a) in section 4, subsections (1)(c) and (2)(c);

(b) sections 6 and 7 and Schedule 1 so far as relating to appeals under the Vaccine Damage Payments Act;

(c) sections 45 to 47 and this section;

(d) paragraphs 5 to 10 of Schedule 7 and section 86(1) so far as relating to those paragraphs; and

(e) section 86(2) and Schedule 8 so far as relating to the Vaccine Damage Payments Act.

DEFINITION

"Vaccine Damage Payments Act"—see s.84.

GENERAL NOTE

Subssections (2) and (3)

The following commencement orders have been made: SI 1998/2209, SI 1998/2708, SI 1999/418, SI 1999/526, SI 1999/528, SI 1999/1055, SI 1999/1510, SI 1999/1958, SI 1999/2422, SI 1999/2739, SI 1999/2860, and SI 1999/3178. The main provisions relating to social security adjudication were brought into effect at different times, depending on the benefit in issue, according to the following timetable: **1.543**

Industrial injuries benefit; Guardian's allowance; Child benefit; Pension Schemes Act 1993—July 5, 1999 (see, primarily, SI 1999/1958).

Retirement pension; Widow's benefit; Incapacity benefit; Severe disablement allowance; Maternity allowance—September 6, 1999 (see, primarily, SI 1999/2422).

Working families' tax credit; Disabled person's tax credit—October 5, 1999 (see, primarily, SI 1999/2739).

Attendance allowance; Disability living allowance; Invalid care allowance; Jobseeker's allowance; Credits of contributions or earnings; Home responsibilities protection; Vaccine damage payments—October 18, 1999 (see, primarily, SI 1999/2860).

All other purposes (including income support)—November 29, 1999 (see, primarily, SI 1999/3178).

SCHEDULES

SCHEDULE 1

[1. . .] **1.544**

AMENDMENT

1. Transfer of Tribunal Functions Order 2008 (SI 2008/2833) Sch.3 paras 143 and 171 (November 3, 2008), subject to a saving under art.1(5).

GENERAL NOTE

1.545 This Schedule remains in force for the limited purpose explained in the note to ss.5–7.

SCHEDULE 2

DECISIONS AGAINST WHICH NO APPEAL LIES

Jobseeker's allowance for persons under 18

1.546 **1.** In relation to a person who has reached the age of 16 but not the age of 18, a decision—
(a) whether section 16 of the Jobseekers Act is to apply to him; or
(b) whether to issue a certificate under section 17(4) of that Act.

Christmas bonus

1.547 **2.** A decision whether a person is entitled to payment under section 148 of the Contributions and Benefits Act.

Priority between persons entitled to [3 carer's allowance]

1.548 **3.** A decision as to the exercise of the discretion under section 70(7) of the Contributions and Benefits Act.

Priority between persons entitled to child benefit

1.549 **4.** A decision as to the exercise of the discretion under paragraph 5 of Schedule 10 to the Contributions and Benefits Act.

Persons treated as if present in Great Britain

1.550 **5.** A decision whether to certify, in accordance with regulations made under section 64(1), 71(6), 113(1) or 119 of the Contributions and Benefits Act, that it is consistent with the proper administration of that Act to treat a person as though he were present in Great Britain.

[1 *Work-focused interviews*

1.551 **5A.** A decision terminating or reducing the amount of a person's benefit made in consequence of any decision made under regulations under section 2A [4 or 2AA] of the Administration Act (work-focused interviews).]

Alteration of rates of benefit

1.552 **6.** A decision as to the amount of benefit to which a person is entitled, where it appears to the Secretary of State that the amount is determined by—
(a) the rate of benefit provided for by law; or
(b) an alteration of a kind referred to in—
(i) section 159(1)(b) of the Administration Act (income support); [2 . . .]
(ii) section 159A(1)(b) of that Act (jobseeker's allowance) [2 or
(iii) section 129B(1)(b) of that Act (state pension credit)]][5 , or
(iv) section 159C(1)(b) of that Act (employment and support allowance).] [7 or
(v) section 159D(1)(b) of that Act (universal credit).]

Increases in income support due to attainment of particular ages

1.553 **7.** A decision as to the amount of benefit to which a person is entitled, where it appears to the Secretary of State that the amount is determined by the recipient's entitlement to an increased amount of income support or income-based jobseeker's allowance in the circumstances referred to in section 160(2) or 160A(2) of the Administration Act.

Reduction in accordance with reduced benefit direction

1.554 **8.** A decision to reduce the amount of a person's benefit in accordance with a reduced benefit direction (within the meaning of section 46 of the Child Support Act).

[6 *Reduction on application of benefit cap*

8A. A decision to apply the benefit cap in accordance with regulations under section 96 of the Welfare Reform Act 2012.] 1.555

Power to prescribe other decisions

9. Such other decisions as may be prescribed. 1.556

AMENDMENTS

1. Welfare Reform and Pensions Act 1999 s.81 and Sch.11 para.87 (November 11, 1999).
2. State Pension Credit Act 2002 s.11 and Sch.1 para.11 (July 2, 2002 for the purpose of exercising any power to make regulations or orders and October 6, 2003 for all other purposes).
3. Regulatory Reform (Carer's Allowance) Order 2002 (SI 2002/1457) art.2(1) and Sch. para.3(b) September 2002 for the purposes of exercising powers to make subordinate legislation and October 28, 2002 for all other purposes).
4. Employment Act 2002. s.53 and Sch.7 para.51 (July 5, 2003).
5. Welfare Reform Act 2007 Sch.3 para.17(1) and (8) (October 27, 2008).
6. Welfare Reform Act 2012 s.97(6) (April 15, 2013).
7. Welfare Reform Act 2012 s.31 and Sch.2 paras 50(1) and (2) (April 29, 2013).

DEFINITIONS

"the Administration Act"—see s.84.
"benefit"—by virtue of reg.39(2), see s.191 of the Social Security Administration Act 1992.
"the Child Support Act"—see s.84.
"the Contributions and benefits Act"—*ibid.*
"the Jobseekers Act"—*ibid.*
"prescribed"—*ibid.*

GENERAL NOTE

Paragraphs 3 and 4

In *TD v SSWP (CSM)* [2013] UKUT 282 (AAC); [2014] AACR 7, the Upper Tribunal held that para.4 did not involve a breach of art.6 of the European Convention on Human Rights because, there being no guidance in the legislation or regulations as to how the discretion to award child benefit to one parent rather than the other in a case where they shared care equally, the issue was non-justiciable in the sense in which that term was used in *R(H) 3/04* and *R(H) 6/06* so that an appeal to the First-tier Tribunal would effectively be confined to points of law and judicial review provided an adequate alternative remedy. That decision was followed in *SSWP v AK (CA)* [2014] UKUT 415 (AAC) insofar as it was held that para.3 was also not inconsistent with the European Convention on Human Rights. However, it was held that, while para.3 precluded an appeal against a decision as to which of two people caring for the relevant disabled person and otherwise entitled to carer's allowance should receive the allowance, it did not preclude an appeal brought on the ground that the other potential claimant was not in fact caring for the disabled person. 1.557

Paragraph 6(a)

A decision under reg.22A of the Income Support (General) Regulations 1987, reducing the amount of income support payable to a person while an appeal against a decision that the claimant is capable of work is pending, is not a decision on the "rate of benefit" within para.6(a). (*Re Smyth's Application* [2001] N.I. 393, QBD (NI), in which Kerr J. considered the equivalent provision in the Social Security (Northern 1.558

Ireland) Order 1998). Similarly, it was held in *MM v SSWP (ESA)* [2012] UKUT 443 (AAC) that para.6(a) did not prohibit an appeal against a decision that a prisoner was entitled to employment and support allowance at the rate of nil, it being arguable that he was entitled to it at a higher rate. In both cases, the appeal was not about the rate of benefit prescribed in relation to a class of person but about whether the claimant fell within that class. The judge deciding *MM* commented that para.6(a) seemed unnecessary and "owes more to history than anything else".

Paragraph 9

1.559 See Sch.2 to the Social Security and Child Support (Decisions and Appeals) Regulations 1999 Sch.2 to the Child Benefit and Guardian's Allowance (Decisions and Appeals) Regulations 2003. and Sch.3 to the Universal Credit, Personal Independence Payment, Jobseeker's Allowance and Employment and Support Allowance (Decisions and Appeals) Regulations 2013.

SCHEDULE 3

DECISIONS AGAINST WHICH AN APPEAL LIES

PART I

BENEFIT DECISIONS

Entitlement to benefit without a claim

1.560 **1.** In such cases or circumstances as may be prescribed, a decision whether a person is entitled to a relevant benefit for which no claim is required.

2. If so, a decision as to the amount to which he is entitled.

Payability of benefit

1.561 **3.** A decision whether a relevant benefit (or a component of a relevant benefit) to which a person is entitled is not payable by reason of—

(a) any provision of the Contributions and Benefits Act by which the person is disqualified for receiving benefit;
(b) regulations made under section 72(8) of that Act (disability living allowance);
(c) regulations made under section 113(2) of that Act (suspension of payment); [1 . . .]
(d) [8 . . .]
[5 (da) [8 . . .]]
[1 (e) [6 . . .]] [2 or
(f) section [7 6B,] 7, 8 or 9 of the Social Security Fraud Act 2001][4 ; [10 . . ..]
(g) section 18 of the Welfare Reform Act 2007];
[10 (h) regulations made under section 85(1) or 86(1) of the Welfare Reform Act 2012;
(i) section 87 of that Act.]

[9 **3A.** A decision as to the amount of a relevant benefit that is payable to a person by virtue of regulations under section 6B, 7, 8 or 9 of the Social Security Fraud Act 2001.]

Payments to third parties

1.562 **4.** Except in such cases or circumstances as may be prescribed, a decision whether the whole or part of a benefit to which a person is entitled is, by virtue of regulations, to be paid to a person other than him.

Recovery of benefits

1.563 **5.** A decision whether payment is recoverable under section 71 or 71A of the Administration Act.

6. If so, a decision as to the amount of payment recoverable.

6A. *Not yet in force.*

[11 **6B.** A decision as to the amount of payment recoverable under section 71ZB, 71ZG or 71ZH of the Administration Act.]

[12 *State pension: prisoners and overseas residents*

6C. A decision that a state pension under Part 1 of the Pensions Act 2014 is not payable by reason of regulations under section 19 of that Act (prisoners). **1.564**

6D. A decision that a person is not entitled to increases in the rate of a state pension under Part 1 of the Pensions Act 2014 by reason of regulations under section 20 of that Act (overseas residents).]

Industrial injuries benefit

7. A decision whether an accident was an industrial accident for the purposes of industrial injuries benefit. **1.565**

Jobseekers' agreements

8. A decision in relation to a jobseeker's agreement as proposed to be made under section 9 of the Jobseekers Act, or as proposed to be varied under section 10 of that Act. **1.566**

[3 *State pension credit*

8A. A decision whether to specify a period as an assessed income period under section 6 of the State Pension Credit Act 2002. **1.567**

8B. If so, a decision as to the period to be so specified.

8C. A decision whether an assessed income period comes to an end by virtue of section 9(4) or (5) of that Act.

8D. If so, a decision as to when the assessed income period so ends.]

Power to prescribe other decisions

9. Such other decisions relating to a relevant benefit as may be prescribed. **1.568**

PART II

CONTRIBUTIONS DECISIONS

10.–15. *Omitted.* **1.569**

16. A decision whether a person was (within the meaning of regulations) precluded from regular employment by responsibilities at home.

17. A decision whether a person is entitled to be credited with earnings or contributions in accordance with regulations made under section 22(5) [13 or (5ZA)] of the Contributions and Benefits Act.

18.–29. *Omitted.* **1.570**

AMENDMENTS

1. Child Support, Pensions and Social Security Act 2000 s.66 and Sch.9 Pt V (October 15, 2001).
2. Social Security Fraud Act 2001 s.12(2) (April 1 2002).
3. State Pension Credit Act 2002 Sch.1 para.12 (July 2, 2002 for the purpose of exercising any power to make regulations or orders and October 6, 2003 for other purposes).
4. Welfare Reform Act 2007 Sch.3 para.17(1) and (9) (October 27, 2008).
5. Welfare Reform Act 2009 s.1(4) and Sch.3 para.4 (November 12, 2009).
6. Welfare Reform Act 2009 Sch.7 (March 22, 2010).
7. Welfare Reform Act 2009 Sch.4 para.10 (April 1, 2010).
8. Welfare Reform Act 2012 s.46(4) (October 22, 2012).
9. Welfare Reform Act 2012 s.31 and Sch.2 paras 43 and 51 (April 1, 2013).
10. Welfare Reform Act 2012 s.91 and Sch.9 paras 37 and 43 (April 8, 2013).
11. Welfare Reform Act 2012 s.105(7) (April 29, 2013).
12. Pensions Act 2014 s.23 and Sch.12 paras 31 and 37 (April 6, 2016).
13. Pensions Act 2014 (Consequential Amendments) Order 2016 (SI 2016/931) art.3 (September 15, 2016).

DEFINITIONS

"the Administration Act"—see s.84.
"benefit"—by virtue of reg.39(2), see s.191 of the Social Security Administration Act 1992.
"claim"—*ibid.*
"the Child Support Act"—see s.84.
"the Contributions and Benefits Act"—*ibid.*
"industrial injuries benefit"—by virtue of s.39(2), see s.191 of the Social Security Administration Act 1992.
"the Jobseekers Act"—s.84.
"prescribed"—*ibid.*
"relevant benefit"—see s.8(3).

GENERAL NOTE

1.571 By reg.16 of, and para.5 of Sch.2 to the Employment and Support Allowance (Transitional Provisions, Housing Benefit and Council Tax Benefit) (Existing Awards) (No. 2) Regulations 2010 (SI 2010/1907), (as amended by reg.15 of the Employment and Support Allowance (Transitional Provisions, Housing Benefit and Council Tax Benefit) (Existing Awards) (No. 2) (Amendment) Regulations 2010 (SI 2010/2430)), this Schedule is modified with effect from October 1, 2010 for the purpose of migrating claimants from incapacity benefit to employment and support allowance. It is to be read as though there were inserted—

> *"Conversion of certain existing awards into awards of an employment and support allowance*
>
> **8E.** A conversion decision within the meaning of the Employment and Support Allowance (Transitional Provisions, Housing Benefit and Council Tax Benefit) (Existing Awards) (No. 2) Regulations 2010."

Paragraph 3

1.572 A decision under art.13(2) of the Convention on Social Security between Great Britain and Jamaica that a person is not permanently incapacitated for work is not a decision under s.113 of the Social Security Contributions and Benefits Act 1992 disqualifying a person from benefit, even though it may lead to such a decision, and therefore it does not fall within para.3(a) (*Campbell v Secretary of State for Work and Pensions* [2005] EWCA Civ 989).

Paragraphs 5 to 6B

1.573 It was suggested in *VT v SSWP (IS)* [2016] UKUT 178 (AAC); [2016] AACR 42 that these paragraphs may be otiose because, in *R(IS) 14/04* and that decision respectively, it has been held that decisions as to the recoverability of benefits under s.74 of the Social Security Administration Act 1992 and the imposition of civil penalties under s.115D of that Act fall within the scope of s.12(1)(a) of this Act (and so are appealable), with the implication that the decisions covered by these paragraphs as to the recoverability of other payments also do so, rather than falling within s.12(1)(b).

Paragraph 6A is to be inserted by s.105(7) of the Welfare Reform Act 2012 when housing credit is introduced for claimants of state pension credit.

Paragraph 9

1.574 Regulation 26 of the Social Security and Child Support (Decisions and Appeals) Regulations 1999 is made under para.9 and so too are reg.50(1) of, and Sch.3 to, the Universal Credit, Personal Independence Payment, Jobseeker's Allowance and Employment and Support Allowance (Decisions and Appeals) Regulations 2013.

Parasgraphs 10 – 29

Paragraphs 10–15 and 18–29 have never been brought into force and are all to be repealed by the Social Security Contributions (Transfer of Functions, etc.,) Act 1999 Sch.7 para.36 but so far the repealing provision has been brought into effect only in respect of para.23 (twice! See SI 1999/527 and SI 1999/1662). The jurisdictions which would have been conferred on appeal tribunals were instead transferred to the tax commissioners. Paragraphs 16 and 17, on the other hand, introduce new rights of appeal to tribunals where none existed before 1999. In *CIB/3327/2004*, the Commissioner commented on the lack of arrangements within the Department for Work and Pensions for proper decisions to be made in respect of the crediting of earnings or contributions. In particular, it appeared that such decisions as were made did not include information about the new right of appeal conferred by para.17. Arrangements have been made under s.17 of the Social Security Contributions (Transfer of Functions, etc.) Act 1999 for Her Majesty's Revenue and Customs to make decisions on behalf of the Secretary of State in respect of matters falling within the scope of para.16 (mentioned in *SF v SSWP (HRP)* [2013] UKUT 175 AAC), in which it was pointed out that, notwithstanding that HMRC makes the decisions, appeals lie within the jurisdiction of the Social Entitlement Chamber of the First-tier Tribunal rather than the Tax Chamber) and in respect of some matters falling within the scope of para.17. These arrangements appear not to cover decisions relating to the crediting of earnings or contributions in respect of unemployment or incapacity for work, although *CIB/3327/2004* revealed some confusion among staff as to the division of responsibility between the Department for Work and Pensions and HMRC. Further criticism of the handling of credits cases was voiced in *CIB/1602/2006*. In particular, the Commissioner criticised instructions to staff causing them to make undisclosed assumptions about contributions and credits issues instead of issuing decisions in respect of such issues informing claimants of their rights of appeal. **1.575**

The function of making decisions in respect of Class 3 credits to those entitled to them by virtue of being entitled to child benefit has been transferred to HMRC who administer child benefit itself (National Insurance Contribution Credits (Transfer of Functions) Order 2009 (SI 2009/1377) with effect from April 6, 2010. However, nearly all the provisions of this Act continue to apply to such decisions, as though references to the Secretary of State were references to HMRC.

Schedule 4

[1. . .] **1.576**

Amendment

1. Transfer of Tribunal Functions Order 2008 (SI 2008/2833) Sch.3 paras 143 and 172 (November 3, 2008), subject to a saving under art.1(5).

General note

This Schedule remains in force for the limited purpose explained in the note to ss.5–7. **1.577**

Schedule 5

Regulations as to Procedure: Provision Which may be Made

1. Provision prescribing the procedure to be followed in connection with— **1.578**

(a) the making of decisions or determinations by the Secretary of State, [1. . .] and

(b) the withdrawal of claims, applications, appeals or references falling to be decided or determined by the Secretary of State, [1. . .].

2. [1. . .]

3. Provision as to the form which is to be used for any document, the evidence which is to be required and the circumstances in which any official record or certificate is to be sufficient or conclusive evidence.

4. Provision as to the time within which, or the manner in which—

(a) any evidence is to be produced; or

(b) any application, reference or appeal is to be made.

5. [1. . .]

6. [1. . .]

7. [1. . .]

8. [1. . .]

9. Provision for the non-disclosure to a person of the particulars of any medical advice or medical evidence given or submitted for the purposes of a determination.

AMENDMENT

1. Transfer of Tribunal Functions Order 2008 (SI 2008/2833) Sch.3 paras 143 and 173 (November 3, 2008), subject to a saving under art.1(5).

GENERAL NOTE

1.579 This Schedule no longer enables regulations to be made in respect of the procedure before tribunals, having been replaced by Sch.5 to the Tribunals, Courts and Enforcement Act 2007, but the omitted provisions remain in force for the purpose explained in the note to ss.5–7. By reg.11(5) of the Child Trust Funds (Non-tax Appeals) Regulations 2005 (SI 2005/191), this Schedule is applied to appeals under ss.21(9) and 22 of the Child Trust Funds Act 2004 with the modification that "the Secretary of State" is omitted from both places where it occurs in para.1, which makes that paragraph redundant. Until April 1, 2009, it was also applied in similarly modified form to appeals under the Tax Credits Act 2002 but, for reasons explained in the note to s.12, the regulation applying it has lapsed in relation to cases in Great Britain. It is still applied, with references to the Board substituted for references to the Secretary of State, to child benefit and guardian's allowance decisions and appeals (Tax Credits Act 2002 Sch.4 para.15).

See the Social Security and Child Support (Decisions and Appeals) Regulations 1999, the Child Benefit and Guardian's Allowance (Decisions and Appeals) Regulations 2003 and, in Vol.IV, the Child Trust Funds (Appeals) Regulations 2005.

SCHEDULES 6 TO 8

1.580 *Omitted.*

Social Security Contributions (Transfer of Functions, etc.) Act 1999

(1999 C.2)

ARRANGEMENT OF SECTIONS

PART I

GENERAL

PART II

DECISIONS AND APPEALS

PART III

MISCELLANEOUS AND SUPPLEMENTAL

SCHEDULES

Omitted.

An Act to transfer from the Secretary of State to the Commissioners of Inland Revenue or the Treasury certain functions relating to national insurance contributions, the National Insurance Fund, statutory sick pay, statutory maternity pay or person schemes and certain associated functions relating to benefits; to enable functions relating to any of those matters in respect of Northern Ireland to be transferred to the Secretary of State, the Commissioners of Inland Revenue or the Treasury; to make further provision, in connection with the functions transferred, as to the powers of the Commissioners of Inland Revenue, the making of decisions and appeals; to provide that rebates payable in respect of members of money purchase contracted-out pension schemes are to be payable out of the National Insurance Fund; and for connected purposes.

[25th February 1999]

PART I

GENERAL

1.–7. *Omitted.* **1.582**

PART II

DECISIONS AND APPEALS

Decisions by officers of Board

8.—(1) Subject to the provisions of the Part, it shall be for an officer of the Board— **1.583**

(a) to decide whether for the purposes of Parts I to V of the Social Security Contributions and Benefits Act 1992 a person is or was an earner and, if so, the category of earners in which he is or was to be included,

So too do matters relating to the payment of contributions for graduated retirement benefit, which were not contributions of a "class" and so do not fall within the scope of s.8(1)(c) of this Act with the result that they remain within the scope of s.8(1)(c) of the 1998 Act (*R(P)1/08*). Note, however, that s.17 permits the Secretary of State to make arrangements for Her Majesty's Revenue and Customs to discharge his decision-making functions in relation to those matters.

Moreover, s.23 of this Act permits the functions listed in s.8 to be transferred back to the Secretary of State and also permits other functions of the Secretary of State relating to contributions to be transferred to HMRC. Under these powers, the function of making decisions in respect of Class 3 "credits" to those entitled to them by virtue of being entitled to child benefit has been transferred to HMRC (who administer child benefit itself) with effect from April 6, 2010. However, nearly all the provisions of the Social Security Act 1998 continue to apply to such decisions, as though references to the Secretary of State were references to HMRC (National Insurance Contribution Credits (Transfer of Functions) Order 2009 (SI 2009/1377)).

1.585 **9.–16.** *Omitted.*

Arrangements for discharge of decision-making functions

1.586 **17.**—(1) The Secretary of State may make arrangements with the Board for any his functions under Chapter II of Part I of the Social Security Act 1998 in relation to—

(a) a decision whether a person was (within the meaning of regulations) precluded from regular employment by responsibilities at home, or

(b) a decision whether a person is entitled to be credited with earnings or contributions in accordance with regulations made under section 22(5) [1 or (5ZA)] of the Social Security Contributions and Benefits Act 1992,

to be discharged by the Board or by officers of the Board.

(2) No such arrangements shall effect the responsibility of the Secretary of State or the application of Chapter II of Part I of the Social Security Act 1998 in relation to any decision.

(3) *Omitted.*

AMENDMENT

1. Pensions Act 2014 (Consequential and Supplementary Amendments) Order 2016 (SI 2016/224) art.5 (April 6, 2016).

DEFINITIONS

"the Board"—see s.27, but note that the functions of the Board have been transferred to Her Majesty's Revenue and Customs by the Commissioners for Revenue and Customs Act 2005.

"contributions"—see s.27.

GENERAL NOTE

1.587 Questions about home responsibilities protection and the crediting of earnings or contributions are questions that are relevant to a person's contributions record, but they are nonetheless decisions within the jurisdiction of the Secretary of State and there are rights of appeal to the Social Entitlement Chamber of the First-tier Tribunal (see the Social Security Act 1998 Sch.3 paras 16 and 17). Despite this, decisions about home responsibilities protection are made by Her Majesty's Revenue and Customs under an arrangement under this section. So too are most decisions about "credits" other than those related to incapacity for work or availability for work, which are made by the Secretary of State because a person claiming benefit on the ground of incapacity for work or availability for work is usually treated also as claiming "credits". It appears that there is also an arrangement under this section in respect of questions concerning records of payment of contributions for graduated retirement benefit (*R(P)1/08*). However, notwithstanding that HMRC makes decisions where there are such arrangements, appeals still lie within the jurisdiction of the Social Entitlement Chamber of the First-tier Tribunal rather than the Tax Chamber. As explained in *SF v SSWP (HRP)* [2013] UKUT 175 AAC), this is because the decisions are not made under s.8 and so the right of appeal is still conferred by para.16 of Sch.3 to the Social Security Act 1998 and not by s.11 of this Act with the consequence that appeals do not fall within exception (i) of art.6(c) of the First-tier Tribunal and Upper Tribunal (Chambers) Order 2010 (SI 2010/2655), set out in the note to s.7 of the Tribunals, Courts and Enforcement Act 2007, below).

18.–19. *Omitted.* 1.588

Part III

Miscellaneous and Supplemental

20.–26. *Omitted.* 1.589

Interpretation

27. In this Act, unless a contrary intention appears— 1.590
"the Board" means the Commissioners of Inland Revenue;
"contributions" means contributions under Part I of the Social Security Contributions and Benefits Act 1992.

General Note

"the Board" 1.591
The functions of the Commissioners of Inland Revenue have now been transferred to the Commissioners for Her Majesty's Revenue and Customs by s.5(2) of the Commissioners for Revenue and Customs Act 2005.

Short title, commencement and extent

28.—(1) This Act may be cited as the Social Security Contributions (Transfer of Functions, etc.) Act 1999. 1.592
(2) *Omitted.*
(3) *Omitted.*

Welfare Reform and Pensions Act 1999

(1999 c.30)

Arrangement of Sections

Parts I to IV (*omitted*)

Part V

to be recoverable; quite what this means in the context of the section is not clear. Subsection (6) refers to circumstances which take the overpayment out of the scope of subs.(2). There are both issues of timing and of culpability in the section which it is difficult to understand. Clearly subs.(6) is intended to exempt culpable overpayments from the amnesty, but the drafting is obscure.

Supply of information for certain purposes

1.597 **72.** —(1) The Secretary of State may by regulations make such provision for or in connection with any of the following matters, namely—

(a) the use by a person within subsection (2) of social security information [[1] , or information relating to employment or training,] held by that person,

(b) the supply (whether to a person within subsection (2) or otherwise) of social security information [[1] , or information relating to employment or training,] held by a person within that subsection,

(c) the relevant purposes for which a person to whom such information is supplied under the regulations may use it, and

(d) the circumstances and extent (if any) in and to which a person to whom such information is supplied under the regulations may supply it to any other person (whether within subsection (2) or not),

as the Secretary of State considers appropriate in connection with any provision to which subsection (3) applies or in connection with any scheme or arrangements to which subsection (4) applies.

(2) The persons within this subsection are—

(a) a Minister of the Crown;

(b) a person providing services to, or designated [[2] (specifically or by description)] for the purposes of this section by an order of, a Minister of the Crown;

(c) a local authority (within the meaning of the Administration Act); [[3] . . .]

[[4] (ca) a county council in England; and]

(d) a person providing services to, or authorised to exercise any function of, [[5] any authority mentioned in paragraph (c) or (ca)] [[6] , or]

[[6] (e) Part 1 of the Welfare Reform Act 2012.]

(3) This subsection applies to any provision made by or under—

[[7] (a) any of sections 2A to 2F and 7A of the Administration Act,]

(b) section 60 of this Act, [[8] . . .]

(c) the Jobseekers Act 1995 [[9] , [[10] . . .]]

[[9] (d) Part 1 of the Welfare Reform Act 2007.]

(4) This subsection applies to—

(a) any scheme designated by regulations under subsection (1), being a scheme operated by the Secretary of State (whether under arrangements with any other person or not) for any purposes connected with employment or training in the case of persons of a particular category or description;

(b) any arrangements of a description specified in such regulations, being arrangement made by the Secretary of State for any such purposes.

(5) Regulations under subsection (1) may, in particular, authorise information supplied to a person under the regulations—

(a) to be used for the purpose of amending or supplementing other information held by that person; and
(b) if it is so used, to be supplied to any other person, and used for any purpose, to whom or for which that other information could be supplied or used.

(6) In this section—

"relevant purposes" means purposes connected with—
(a) social security, child support or war pensions, or
(b) employment or training;

"social security information" [11 . . .] means information relating to social security, child support or war pensions and in this subsection "war pensions" means war pensions within the meaning of section 25 of the Social Security Act 1989 (establishment and functions of war pensions committees).

(6A) [12 . . .]

(7) Any reference in this section to [13 information relating to, or purposes connected with, employment or training includes information relating to, or purposes connected with,] the existing or future employment or training prospects or needs of persons, and (in particular) assisting or encouraging persons to enhance their employment prospects.

AMENDMENTS

1. Welfare Reform Act 2009 s.34(4)(a) (January 12, 2010).
2. Welfare Reform Act 2012 s.134(2) (May 8, 2012).
3. Education and Skills Act 2008 Sch.2 para.1 (January 26, 2009).
4. Education and Skills Act 2008 Sch.1(2) para.74(2)(a) (March 30, 2010).
5. Education and Skills Act 2008 Sch.1(2) para.74(2)(b) (March 30, 2010).
6. Universal Credit (Consequential, Supplementary, Incidental and Miscellaneous Provisions) Regulations 2013 (SI 2013/630) reg.15(b) (April 29, 2013).
7. Welfare Reform Act 2009 s.2(5) (November 12, 2009).
8. Welfare Reform Act 2007 Sch.8 para.1 (October 27, 2008).
9. Welfare Reform Act 2007 Sch.3 para.18 (October 27, 2008).
10. Universal Credit (Consequential, Supplementary, Incidental and Miscellaneous Provisions) Regulations 2013 (SI 2013/630) reg.15(a) (April 29, 2013).
11. Welfare Reform Act 2012 s.134(3)(a) (May 8, 2012).
12. Welfare Reform Act 2012 s.134(3)(b) (May 8, 2012).
13. Welfare Reform Act 2009 s.34(4)(b) (January 12, 2010).

Social Security Fraud Act 2001

(2001 c.11)

ARRANGEMENT OF SECTIONS

Loss of benefit provisions

(2) In subsection (1)(b)—

(a) "the appropriate penalty provision" means section 115A of the Administration Act (penalty as alternative to prosecution) or section 109A of the Social Security Administration (Northern Ireland) 1992 (the corresponding provision for Northern Ireland);

(b) "appropriate authority" means—

(i) in relation to section 115A of the Administration Act, the Secretary of State or an authority which administers housing benefit or council tax benefit, and

(ii) in relation to section 109A of the Social Security Administration (Northern Ireland) Act 1992, the Department (within the meaning of that Act) or the Northern Ireland Housing Executive.

(3) Subsection (4) does not apply by virtue of subsection (1)(a) if, because the proceedings in which the offender was convicted constitute the [4 current] set of proceedings for the purposes of section 7, the restriction in subsection (2) of that section applies in the offender's case.

(4) If this subsection applies and the offender is a person with respect to whom the conditions for an entitlement to a sanctionable benefit are or become satisfied at any time within the disqualification period, then, even though those conditions are satisfied, the following restrictions shall apply in relation to the payment of that benefit in the offender's case.

(5) Subject to subsections [4 (5A)] to (10), the sanctionable benefit shall not be payable in the offender's case for any period comprised in the disqualification period.

[3 (5A) The Secretary of State may by regulations provide that, where the sanctionable benefit is universal credit, the benefit shall be payable, during the whole or a part of any period comprised in the disqualification period, as if one or more of the following applied—

(a) the amount payable were reduced in such manner as may be prescribed;

(b) the benefit were payable only if there is compliance by the offender with such obligations with respect to the provision of information as may be imposed by the regulations;

(c) the benefit were payable only if the circumstances are otherwise such as may be prescribed;

(d) any amount of the benefit payable in prescribed circumstances were recoverable by the Secretary of State.]

(6) Where the sanctionable benefit is income support, the benefit shall be payable in the offender's case for any period comprised in the disqualification period as if the applicable amount used for the determination under section 124(4) of the Social Security Contributions and Benefits Act 1992 of the amount of the offender's entitlement for that period were reduced in such manner as may be prescribed.

(7) The Secretary of State may by regulations provide that, where the sanctionable benefit is jobseeker's allowance, any income-based jobseeker's allowance shall be payable, during the whole or a part of any period comprised in the disqualification period, as if one or more of the following applied—

(a) the rate of the allowance were such reduced rate as may be prescribed;

(b) the allowance were payable only if there is compliance by the offender with such obligations with respect to the provision of information as may be imposed by the regulations;

(4) In relation to cases in which the benefit is jobseeker's allowance, the provision that may be made by virtue of subsection (2) is provision that, in the case of the offender's family member, any income-based jobseeker's allowance shall be payable, during the whole or a part of any period comprised in the relevant period, as if one or more of the following applied—

(a) the rate of the allowance were such reduced rate as may be prescribed;

(b) the allowance were payable only if there is compliance by the offender or the offender's family member, or both of them, with such obligations with respect to the provision of information as may be imposed by the regulations;

(c) the allowance were payable only if the circumstances are otherwise such as may be prescribed.

[[1] (4A) In relation to cases in which the benefit is state pension credit, the provision that may be made by virtue of subsection (2) is provision that, in the case of the offender's family member, the benefit shall be payable for the whole or any part of any period comprised in the relevant period as if the rate of the benefit were reduced in such manner as may be prescribed.]

[[2] (4B) In relation to cases in which the benefit is employment and support allowance, the provision that may be made by virtue of subsection (2) is provision that, in the case of the offender's family member, any income-related allowance shall be payable, during the whole or a part of any period comprised in the relevant period, as if one or more of the following applied—

(a) the rate of the allowance were such reduced rate as may be prescribed;

(b) the allowance were payable only if there is compliance by the offender or the offender's family member, or both of them, with such obligations with respect to the provision of information as may be imposed by the regulations;

(c) the allowance were payable only if circumstances are otherwise such as may be prescribed.]

(5) In relation to cases in which the benefit is housing benefit or council tax benefit, the provision that may be made by virtue of subsection (2) is provision that, in the case of the offender's family member, the benefit shall be payable, during the whole or a part of any period comprised in the relevant period, as if one or both of the following applied—

(a) the rate of the benefit were reduced in such manner as may be prescribed;

(b) the benefit were payable only if the circumstances are such as may be prescribed.

(6) Where—

(a) the conviction of any member of a person's family for any offence is taken into account for the purposes of any restriction imposed by virtue of any regulations under this section, and

(b) that conviction is subsequently quashed,

all such payments and other adjustments shall be made in that person's case as would be necessary if no restriction had been imposed that could not have been imposed had the conviction not taken place.

[[3] (7) Where, after the agreement of any member of a person's family ("M") to pay a penalty under the appropriate penalty provision is taken into account for the purposes of any restriction imposed by virtue of any regulations under this section—

(a) M's agreement to pay the penalty is withdrawn under subsection (5) of the appropriate penalty provision, or

(b) it is decided on an appeal or in accordance with regulations under the Social Security Act 1998 or the Social Security (Northern Ireland) Order 1998 that [4 any overpayment made] to which the agreement relates is not recoverable or due,

all such payments and other adjustments shall be made as would be necessary if no restriction had been imposed that could not have been imposed had M not agreed to pay the penalty.

(8) Where, after the agreement ("the old agreement") of any member of a person's family ("M") to pay a penalty under the appropriate penalty provision is taken into account for the purposes of any restriction imposed by virtue of any regulations under this section, the amount of [4 any overpayment made] to which the penalty relates is revised on an appeal or in accordance with regulations under the Social Security Act 1998 or the Social Security (Northern Ireland) Order 1998—

(a) if there is a new disqualifying event for the purposes of section 6B consisting of M's agreement to pay a penalty under the appropriate penalty provision in relation to the revised overpayment or M being cautioned in relation to the offence to which the old agreement relates, the new disqualification period for the purposes of section 6B falls to be determined in accordance with section 6C(4)(a), and

(b) in any other case, all such payments and other adjustments shall be made as would be necessary if no restriction had been imposed by or under this section that could not have been imposed had M not agreed to pay the penalty.

(9) In this section "the appropriate penalty provision" has the meaning given by section 6B(2)(a).]

AMENDMENTS

1. State Pension Credit Act 2002 Sch.2 para.46 (July 2, 2002 for the purpose of exercising any power to make regulations or orders and October 6, 2003 for other purposes).

2. Welfare Reform Act 2007 Sch.3 para.23(1), (4) and (5) (March 18, 2008 for regulation-making purposes and October 27, 2008 for other purposes).

3. Welfare Reform Act 2009 Sch.4 para.4 (January 12, 2010 for regulation-making purposes and April 1, 2010 for all other purposes).

4. Welfare Reform Act 2012 s.113(8)(b) (May 8, 2012).

5. Welfare Reform Act 2012 s.31 Sch.2 paras 56 and 61(1)–(4) (February 25, 2013).

DEFINITIONS

"benefit"—see s.13.

"disqualifying benefit"—see s.6A(1).

"family"—by virtue of s.13, see s.137(1) of the Social Security Contributions and Benefits Act 1992.

"income-based jobseeker's allowance"—by virtue of s.13, see s.1(4) of the Jobseekers Act 1995.

"the offender"—see subs.(2)(c).

"the offender's family member"—see subs.(2)(a).

"prescribed"—see s.11(1).

"the appropriate penalty provision"–see subs.(9).

"the relevant period"—see subs.(2)(b).
"state pension credit"—see s.13.

GENERAL NOTE

This section allows the loss of benefit to be incurred by another member of the offender's family where that other person is claiming an income-related benefit that takes account of the offender's membership of the family. **1.609**

Subsections (1)(a), (b), (bc), (c) and (d), (3), (4), (4B) and (5) have formally been repealed with effect from April 1, 2013 in so far as they apply to council tax benefit, subject to a saving (Welfare Reform Act 2012 s.147 and Pt 1 of Sch.14; Welfare Reform Act 2012 (Commencement No.8 and Savings and Transitional Provisions) Order 2013 (SI 2013/358) arts 8(c) and 9 and Sch.4).

Power to supplement and mitigate loss of benefit provisions

10.—(1) The Secretary of State may by regulations provide for any social security benefit to be treated for the purposes of [3 sections 6A to 9] — **1.610**

(a) as a disqualifying benefit but not a sanctionable benefit; or
(b) as neither a sanctionable benefit nor a disqualifying benefit.

(2) The Secretary of State may by regulations provide for any restriction in section [36B,] 7, 8 or 9 not to apply in relation to payments of benefit to the extent of any deduction that (if any payment were made) would fall, in pursuance of provision made by or under any enactment, to be made from the payments and paid to a person other than the offender or, as the case may be, a member of his family.

(3) In this section "social security benefit" means—

(a) any benefit under the Social Security Contributions and Benefits Act 1992 or the Social Security Contributions and Benefits (Northern Ireland) Act 1992; [1 . . .]
(b) any benefit under the Jobseekers Act 1995 or the Jobseekers (Northern Ireland) Order 1995 (S.I. 1995/2705 (N.I. 15));
[1 (bb) any benefit under the State Pension Credit Act 2002 or under any provision having effect in Northern Ireland corresponding to that Act; or]
[2 (bc) any benefit under Part 1 of the Welfare Reform Act 2007 (employment and support allowance) or under any provision having effect in Northern Ireland corresponding to that Part;]
[4 (bd) any benefit under Part 1 of the Welfare Reform Act 2012 (universal credit) or under any provision having effect in Northern Ireland corresponding to that Part;]
[5 (be) any benefit under Part 4 of the Welfare Reform Act 2012 (personal independence payment) or under any provision in Northern Ireland which corresponds to that Part;]
[6 (bf) state pension or a lump sum under Part 1 of the Pensions Act 2014 or under any provision in Northern Ireland which corresponds to that Part;]
[7 (bg) bereavement support payment under section 30 of the Pensions Act 2014 or under any provision in Northern Ireland which corresponds to that section;]
(c) any war pension.

AMENDMENTS

1. State Pension Credit Act 2002 Sch.2 para.47 and Sch.3 (July 2, 2002 for the purpose of exercising any power to make regulations or orders and October 6, 2003 for other purposes).
2. Welfare Reform Act 2007 Sch. para.23(1) and (6) (March 18, 2008 for regulation-making purposes and October 27, 2008 for other purposes).
3. Welfare Reform Act 2009 Sch.4 para.5 (January 12, 2010 for regulation-making purposes and April 1, 2010 for all other purposes).
4. Welfare Reform Act 2012 ss.31 and Sch.2 paras 56 and 62 (April 1, 2013).
5. Welfare Reform Act 2012 s.91 and Sch.9 paras 45 and 47 (April 8, 2013).
6. Pensions Act 2014 s.23 and Sch.12 paras 39 and 41 (April 6, 2016).
7. Pensions Act 2014 s.31(5) and Sch.16 paras 43 and 45 (April 6, 2017).

DEFINITIONS

"benefit"—see s.13.
"disqualifying benefit"—see s.6A.
"family"—by virtue of s.13, see s.137(1) of the Social Security Contributions and Benefits Act 1992.
"sanctionable benefit"—see s.6A.
"social security benefit"—see subs.(3).
"war pension"—by virtue of s.13, see s.25 of the Social Security Act 1989.

Loss of benefit [6 orders and] regulations

1.611 **11.**—(1) In [3 sections 6B to 10] "prescribed" means prescribed by or determined in accordance with regulations made by the Secretary of State.

(2) Regulations under any of the provisions of [3 sections 6B to 10] small be made by statutory instrument which (except in the case of regulations to which subsection (3) applies) shall be subject to annulment in pursuance of a resolution of either House of Parliament.

(3) A statutory instrument containing (whether alone or with other provisions)—

(a) a provision by virtue of which anything is to be treated for the purposes of section [3 6B or] 7 as a disqualifying benefit but not a sanctionable benefit,
(b) a provision prescribing the manner in which the applicable amount is to be reduced for the purposes of section [3 6B (6),] 7(3) or 9(3),
(c) a provision the making of which is authorised by section [3 [4 6B(5A), (7)], (8), (9) or (10)] [4 7(2A), (4)] [1, (4A)] [2,(4B)] or (5), 8(4) or [4 9(2A), (4)] [1, (4A)] [2,(4B)] or (5), or
(d) a provision prescribing the manner in which the amount of joint-claim jobseeker's allowance is to be reduced for the purposes of section 8(3)(a),
[5 (e) regulations under section 6B(14) or an order under section 6B(15), or]
[6 (f) an order under section 7(10A),". . .]

shall not be made unless a draft of the instrument has been laid before, and approved by a resolution of, each House of Parliament.

(5) The provision that may be made in exercise of the powers to make regulations that are conferred by [3 sections 6B to 10] shall include different provision for different areas.

AMENDMENTS

1. State Pension Credit Act 2002 Sch.2 para.48 (July 2, 2002 for the purpose of exercising any power to make regulations or orders and October 6, 2003 for other purposes).
2. Welfare Reform Act 2007 Sch. para.23(1) and (7) (March 18, 2008 for regulation-making purposes and October 27, 2008 for other purposes).
3. Welfare Reform Act 2009 Sch.4 para.6 (January 12, 2010 for regulation-making purposes and April 1, 2010 for all other purposes).
4. Welfare Reform Act 2012 s.31 Sch.2 paras 56 and 63(1) and (2) (February 25, 2013).
5. Welfare Reform Act 2012 s.118(1) and (8)(b) (February 25, 2013 for regulation-making purposes and April 1, 2013 for other purposes).
6. Welfare Reform Act 2012 ss.118(1) and (8)(a) and (c), and 119(1)–(12) (April 1, 2013).

DEFINITION

"the Administration Act", by virtue of s.18, means the Social Security Administration Act 1992.

Consequential amendments

12. *Omitted.* **1.612**

Interpretation of [3 sections 6A to 12]

13.—In this section and [3 sections 6A to 12]— **1.613**

"benefit" includes any allowance, payment, credit or loan;

[3 "cautioned", in relation to any person and any offence, means cautioned after the person concerned has admitted the offence; and caution is to be interpreted accordingly;]

[3 . . .]

"family" has the same meaning as in Part 7 of the Social Security Contributions and Benefits Act 1992;

"income-based jobseeker's allowance", "joint-claim jobseeker's allowance" and "joint-claim couple" have the same meanings as in the Jobseekers Act 1995;

[2 "income-related allowance" has the same meaning as in Part 1 of the Welfare Reform Act 2007 (employment and support allowance);]

[3 . . .]

"sanctionable benefit" has the meaning given by [3 section 6A(1)];

[1 "state pension credit" means state pension credit under the State Pension Credit Act 2002;]

"war pension" has the same meaning as in section 25 of the Social Security Act 1989 (establishment and functions of war pensions committees).

AMENDMENTS

1. State Pension Credit Act 2002 Sch.2 para.49 (July 2, 2002 for the purpose of exercising any power to make regulations or orders and October 6, 2003 for other purposes).
2. Welfare Reform Act 2007 Sch. para.23(1) and (8) (March 18, 2008 for regulation-making purposes and October 27, 2008 for other purposes).
3. Welfare Reform Act 2009 Sch.4 para.7 (January 12, 2010 for regulation-making purposes and April 1, 2010 for all other purposes).

Tax Credits Act 2002

(2002 c. 21)

ARRANGEMENT OF SECTIONS

PART 1

TAX CREDITS

1.614 1.–48. *Omitted.*

PART 2

CHILD BENEFIT AND GUARDIAN'S ALLOWANCE

Transfer of functions etc.

49. Functions transferred to Treasury.
50. Functions transferred to Board.
51.–52. *Omitted.*
53. General functions of Commissioners for Revenue and Customs.
54. Transitional provisions.
55.–57. *Omitted.*

PART 3

SUPPLEMENTARY

Information etc.

58. Administrative arrangements.
59. *Omitted.*

Other supplementary provisions

60.–64. *Omitted.*
65. Regulations, orders and schemes.
66. Parliamentary etc. control of instruments.
67. Interpretation.
68.–70. *Omitted.*

Schedules 1.–6. *Omitted.*

An Act to make provision for tax credits; to amend the law about child benefit and guardian's allowance; and for connected purposes.

[8th July 2002]

General Note

Part 1 of the Act provides for child tax credit and working tax credit which are dealt within Vol.IV of this work. 1.615

Part 2 of the Act transfers functions relating to child benefit and guardian's allowance from the Department for Work and Pensions to the Treasury and the Board of Inland Revenue which has now been merged into Her Majesty's Revenue and Customs. Those benefits remain social security benefits despite the change in responsibility for them and administration and adjudication remain under the Social Security Administration Act 1992 and the Social Security Act 1998, although new secondary legislation has been made.

1.–48. *Omitted.* 1.616

Part 2

Child Benefit and Guardian's Allowance

Transfer of functions etc.

Functions transferred to Treasury

49.—(1) The functions of the Secretary of State under— 1.617

(a) section 77 of the Social Security Contributions and Benefits Act 1992 (c.4) (guardian's allowance: Great Britain),
(b) Part 9 of that Act (child benefit: Great Britain), except [1 . . .] paragraphs 5 and 6(1) of Schedule 10,
(c) section 80 of the Social Security Administration Act 1992 (c.5) (overlap with benefits under legislation of other member States: Great Britain), and
(d) section 72 of the Social Security Act 1998 (c.14) (power to reduce child benefit for lone parents: Great Britain),

are transferred to the Treasury.

(2) The functions of the Northern Ireland Department under—

(a) section 77 of the Social Security Contributions and Benefits (Northern Ireland) Act 1992 (c.7) (guardian's allowance: Northern Ireland),
(b) Part 9 of that Act (child benefit: Northern Ireland), except [1 . . .] paragraphs 5 and 6(1) of Schedule 10,
(c) section 76 of the Social Security Administration (Northern Ireland) Act 1992 (c.8) (overlap with benefits under legislation of other member States: Northern Ireland), and
(d) Article 68 of the Social Security (Northern Ireland) Order 1998 (1998/1506 (N.I. 10)) (power to reduce child benefit for lone parents: Northern Ireland),

are transferred to the Treasury.

(3) The functions of the Secretary of State under Part 10 of the Social Security Administration Act 1992 (c.5) (review and alteration of benefits: Great Britain) so far as relating to child benefit and guardian's allowance are transferred to the Treasury.

(4) The functions of the Northern Ireland Department under sections 132

to 134 of the Social Security Administration (Northern Ireland) Act 1992 (c. 8) (review and alteration of benefits: Northern Ireland) so far as relating to child benefit and guardian's allowance are transferred to the Treasury.

AMENDMENT

1. Child Benefit Act 2005 s.3 and Sch.2 (April 10, 2006).

DEFINITION

"the Northern Ireland Department": see s.67.

GENERAL NOTE

1.618 This section transfers policy responsibility for child benefit and guardian's allowance (i.e. making the regulations as to entitlement and fixing the rates) from the Secretary of State for Work and Pensions to the Treasury.

Functions transferred to Board

1.619 **50.**—(1) The functions of the Secretary of State and the Northern Ireland Department under the provisions specified in subsection (2), so far as relating to child benefit and guardian's allowance, are transferred to the Board.

(2) The provisions referred to in subsection (1) are—

(a) the Social Security Contributions and Benefits Act 1992 (c.4),
(b) the Social Security Administration Act 1992, except Part 13 (advisory bodies and consultation: Great Britain),
(c) the Social Security Contributions and Benefits (Northern Ireland) Act 1992 (c. 7),
(d) the Social Security Administration (Northern Ireland) Act 1992, except Part 12 (advisory bodies and consultation: Northern Ireland),
(e) Chapter 2 of Part 1 of the Social Security Act 1998 (c.14) (social security decisions and appeals: Great Britain),
(f) Chapter 2 of Part 2 of the Social Security (Northern Ireland) Order 1998 (1998/1506 (N.I. 10)) (social security decisions and appeals: Northern Ireland), and
(g) any subordinate legislation made under any of the provisions specified in section 49 or any of the preceding provisions of this subsection.

(3) This section has effect subject to section 49.

DEFINITIONS

"the Board"—see s.67, but note that the functions of the Board have been transferred to Her Majesty's Revenue and Customs by the Commissioners for Revenue and Customs Act 2005.

"the Northern Ireland Department"—*ibid.*

GENERAL NOTE

1.620 While s.49 transfers policy responsibility for child benefit and guardian's allowance to the Treasury, this section transfers operational responsibility (i.e. administration and adjudication) from the Secretary of State for Work and Pensions to the Board of Inland Revenue, whose functions have now been transferred to Her Majesty's Revenue and Customs by the Commissioners for Revenue and Customs Act 2005. The primary legislation governing administration and adjudication remains the same (subject to consequential amendments made by s.51 and Sch.4

and repeals under s.60 and Sch.6) but the Board made new subordinate legislation (see the Child Benefit and Guardian's Allowance (Administrative Arrangements) Regulations 2003, the Child Benefit and Guardian's Allowance (Administration) Regulations 2003 and the Child Benefit and Guardian's Allowance (Decisions and Appeals) Regulations 2003).

Consequential amendments

51. *Omitted.* 1.621

52. *Omitted.* 1.622

[1 General functions of Commissioners for Revenue and Customs

53.—The Commissioners for Her Majesty's Revenue and Customs shall be responsible for the payment and management of child benefit and guardian's allowance.] 1.623

AMENDMENT

1. Commissioners for Revenue and Customs Act 2005 s.50 and para.90 of Sch.4 (April 18, 2005).

Transitional provisions

54.—(1) Any function covered by section 49 which is a function of making subordinate legislation may be exercised by the Treasury at any time after the passing of this Act if the subordinate legislation made in the exercise of the function comes into force after the commencement of that section. 1.624

(2) Any function covered by section 50 which is a function of making subordinate legislation may be exercised by the Board at any time after the passing of this Act if the subordinate legislation made in the exercise of the function comes into force after the commencement of that section.

(3) Nothing in section 49 or 50 affects the validity of anything done by or in relation to the Secretary of State or the Northern Ireland Department before its commencement.

(4) Anything (including legal proceedings) relating to any functions transferred by section 49, or any property, rights or liabilities transferred by section 52(1), which is in the course of being done or carried on by or in relation to the Secretary of State or the Northern Ireland Department immediately before the transfer may be continued by or in relation to the Treasury.

(5) Anything (including legal proceedings) relating to any functions transferred by section 50, or any property, rights or liabilities transferred by section 52(2), which is in the course of being done or carried on by or in relation to the Secretary of State or the Northern Ireland Department immediately before the transfer may be continued by or in relation to the Board.

(6) Anything done by the Secretary of State or the Northern Ireland Department for the purposes of or in connection with any functions transferred by section 49, or any property, rights or liabilities transferred by section 52(1), which is in effect immediately before the transfer has effect afterwards as if done by the Treasury.

(7) Anything done by the Secretary of State or the Northern Ireland Department for the purposes of or in connection with any functions transferred by section 50, or any property, rights or liabilities transferred by section 52(2), which is in effect immediately before the transfer has effect afterwards as if done by the Board.

(8) The Treasury is substituted for the Secretary of State or the Northern Ireland Department in any subordinate legislation, any contracts or other documents and any legal proceedings relating to any functions transferred by section 49, or any property, rights or liabilities transferred by section 52(1), made or commenced before the transfer.

(9) The Board are substituted for the Secretary of State or the Northern Ireland Department in any subordinate legislation, any contracts or other documents and any legal proceedings relating to any functions transferred by section 50, or any property, rights or liabilities transferred by section 52(2), made or commenced before the transfer.

(10) Any order made under section 8 of the Electronic Communications Act 2000 (c.7) which—

(a) modifies provisions relating to child benefit or guardian's allowance, and

(b) is in force immediately before the commencement of this subsection,

is to continue to have effect for the purposes of child benefit and guardian's allowance, despite subsection (7) of that section, until regulations made by the Board under section 132 of the Finance Act 1999 (c.16) which are expressed to supersede that order come into force.

DEFINITIONS

"the Board"—see s.67, but note that the functions of the Board have been transferred to Her Majesty's Revenue and Customs by the Commissioners for Revenue and Customs Act 2005.

"the Northern Ireland Department"—*ibid.*

GENERAL NOTE

1.625 Subsections (1) and (2) came into force on the passing of the Act (s.61), but the remaining provisions of this Part came into force for the purpose of making subordinate legislation on February 26, 2003, for the purpose of the transfer of functions on April 1, 2003 and for the purpose of entitlement to payment of child benefit and guardian's allowance on April 7, 2003 (Tax Credits Act 2002 (Commencement No.2) Order 2003).

Subsection 10

1.626 The Social Security (Electronic Communications) (Child Benefit) Order 2002 remains in force.

1.627 **55.–57.** *Omitted.*

PART 3

SUPPLEMENTARY

Information etc.

Administrative arrangements

58.—(1) This section applies where regulations under— **1.628**

(a) section 4 or 6 of this Act,

(b) section 5 of the Social Security Administration Act 1992 (c.5), or

(c) section 5 of the Social Security Administration (Northern Ireland) Act 1992 (c.8),

permit or require a claim or notification relating to a tax credit, child benefit or guardian's allowance to be made or given to a relevant authority.

(2) Where this section applies, regulations may make provision—

(a) for information or evidence relating to tax credits, child benefit or guardian's allowance to be provided to the relevant authority (whether by persons by whom such claims and notifications are or have been made or given, by the Board or by other persons),

(b) for the giving of information or advice by a relevant authority to persons by whom such claims or notifications are or have been made or given, and

(c) for the recording, verification and holding, and the forwarding to the Board or a person providing services to the Board, of claims and notifications received by virtue of the regulations referred to in subsection (1) and information or evidence received by virtue of paragraph (a),

(3) "Relevant authority" means—

(a) the Secretary of State,

(b) the Northern Ireland Department, or

(c) a person providing services to the Secretary of State or the Northern Ireland Department.

DEFINITIONS

"the Board"—see s.67, but note that the functions of the Board have been transferred to Her Majesty's Revenue and Customs by the Commissioners for Revenue and Customs Act 2005.

"relevant authority"—see subs.(3).

"tax credit"—by virtue of s.67, see s.1(2).

GENERAL NOTE

See the Child Benefit and Guardian's Allowance (Administrative Arrangements) Regulations 2003. **1.629**

59. *Omitted.* **1.630**

Other supplementary provisions

60.–64. *Omitted.* **1.631**

Regulations, orders and schemes

1.632 **65.**—(1) Any power to make regulations under sections 3, 7 to 13, 42 and 43, and any power to make regulations under this Act prescribing a rate of interest, is exercisable by the Treasury.

(2) Any other power to make regulations under this Act is exercisable by the Board.

(3) Subject to subsection (4), any power to make regulations, orders or schemes under this Act is exercisable by statutory instrument.

(4) The power—

(a) of the Department of Health, Social Services and Public Safety to make schemes under section 12(5), and

(b) of the Northern Ireland Department to make orders under section 62(1),

is exercisable by statutory rule for the purposes of the Statutory Rules (Northern Ireland) Order 1979 (S.I. 1979/1573 (N.I. 12)).

(5) Regulations may not be made under section 25 or 26 in relation to appeals in Scotland without the consent of the Scottish Ministers.

(6) Regulations may not be made under section 39(6) or 63(8) without the consent of the Lord Chancellor [[1], the Department of Justice in Northern Ireland] and the Scottish Ministers.

(7) Any power to make regulations under this Act may be exercised—

(a) in relation to all cases to which it extends, to all those cases with prescribed exceptions or to prescribed cases or classes of case,

(b) so as to make as respects the cases in relation to which it is exercised the full provision to which it extends or any less provision (whether by way of exception or otherwise),

(c) so as to make the same provision for all cases in relation to which it is exercised or different provision for different cases or classes of case or different provision as respects the same case or class of case for different purposes,

(d) so as to make provision unconditionally or subject to any prescribed condition,

(e) so as to provide for a person to exercise a discretion in dealing with any matter.

(8) Any regulations made under a power under this Act to prescribe a rate of interest may—

(a) either themselves specify a rate of interest or make provision for any such rate to be determined by reference to such rate or the average of such rates as may be referred to in the regulations,

(b) provide for rates to be reduced below, or increased above, what they otherwise would be by specified amounts or by reference to specified formulae,

(c) provide for rates arrived at by reference to averages to be rounded up or down,

(d) provide for circumstances in which alteration of a rate of interest is or is not to take place, and

(e) provide that alterations of rates are to have effect for periods beginning on or after a day determined in accordance with the regulations in relation to interest running from before that day as well as from or from after that day.

(9) Any power to make regulations or a scheme under this Act includes

power to make any incidental, supplementary, consequential or transitional provision which appears appropriate for the purposes of, or in connection with, the regulations or scheme.

AMENDMENT

1. Northern Ireland Act 1998 (Devolution of Policing and Justice Functions) Order 2010 (S.I. 2010/976), Sch.18 paras 59 and 60 (April 12, 2010).

DEFINITIONS

"the Board"—see s.67, but note that the functions of the Board have been transferred to Her Majesty's Revenue and Customs by the Commissioners for Revenue and Customs Act 2005.

"prescribe"—see s.67.

Parliamentary etc. control of instruments

66.—(1) No [1 order or] regulations to which this subsection applies may be made unless a draft of the instrument containing [1 the order or regulations] (whether or not together with other provisions) has been laid before, and approved by a resolution of, each House of Parliament. 1.633

(2) Subsection (1) applies to—

[1 (za) an order made by the Treasury under section 36A(8) or 36C(9),

(zb) regulations made under section 36A(5) or 36C(4),]

(a) regulations prescribing monetary amounts that are required to be reviewed under section 41,

(b) regulations made by virtue of subsection (2) of section 12 prescribing the amount in excess of which charges are not taken into account for the purposes of that subsection, and

(c) the first regulations made under sections 7(8) and (9), 9, 11, 12 and 13(2).

(3) A statutory instrument containing—

(a) [1 an order or] regulations under this Act,

(b) a scheme made by the Secretary of State under section 12(5),or

(c) an Order in Council under section 52(7),

is (unless a draft of the instrument has been laid before, and approved by a resolution of, each House of Parliament) subject to annulment in pursuance of a resolution of either House of Parliament.

(4) A statutory instrument containing a scheme made by the Scottish Ministers under section 12(5) is subject to annulment in pursuance of a resolution of the Scottish Parliament.

(5) A statutory rule containing a scheme made by the Department of Health, Social Services and Public Safety under section 12(5) is subject to negative resolution within the meaning of section 41(6) of the Interpretation Act (Northern Ireland) 1954 (c. 33 (N.I.)).

AMENDMENT

1. Welfare Reform Act 2012 s.120(4) (February 1, 2013).

Interpretation

67.—In this Act— 1.634

"the Board" means the Commissioners of Inland Revenue,

(a) the Department for Social Development;
(b) the Department of Finance and Personnel;
(c) the Department for Employment and Learning.

(8) For the purposes of this section any reference to functions relating to social security includes a reference to functions relating to—

(a) statutory payments as defined in section 4C(11) of the Social Security Contributions and Benefits Act 1992;
(b) maternity allowance under section 35 of that Act;
(c) statutory payments as defined in section 4C(11) of the Social Security Contributions and Benefits (Northern Ireland) Act 1992;
(d) maternity allowance under section 35 [1 or 35B] of that Act.

(9) This section does not limit the circumstances in which information may be supplied apart from this section.

(10) *(amends s.3 of the Social Security Act 1998)*

COMMENCEMENT

1.640 Section 127 of the Welfare Reform Act 2012 entered into force on May 9, 2012 by virtue of s.150(2) of the Act and provides for information sharing between the Secretary of State and HMRC. Although the Act applies generally only to England and Wales and Scotland under s.149(1), the provisions in s.127(1)–(9) apply to England and Wales, Scotland and Northern Ireland under s.149(2) of the Welfare Reform Act 2012.

AMENDMENTS

1. The Social Security (Maternity Allowance) (Participating Wife or Civil Partner or Self-employed Earner) Regulations 2014 (SI 2014/606) reg.4 (April 1, 2014).
2. Public Bodies (Child Maintenance and Enforcement Commission: Abolition and Transfer of Functions) Order 2012 (SI 2012/2007) Sch.1(1) para.102(b) (August 1, 2012).
3. Childcare Payments Act 2014 (Commencement No.1) Regulations 2016 (SI 2016/763) (July 20, 2016).

Information-sharing involving local authorities etc.

Information-sharing in relation to provision of overnight care etc.

1.641 **130.** —(1) This section applies where a local authority holds information falling within subsection (2) in relation to a person who is receiving or is likely to receive a relevant service.

(2) The information referred to in subsection (1) is—

(a) information as to the fact of the provision or likely provision of the service;
(b) information about when the provision of the service begins or ends or is likely to do so;
(c) other prescribed information relating to the service provided and how it is funded (including the extent to which it is funded by the recipient).

(3) In this section "relevant service" means—

(a) a service consisting of overnight care in the individual's own home provided by or on behalf of a local authority;
(b) a residential care service provided by or on behalf of a local authority;
(c) a service consisting of overnight hospital accommodation.

(4) In subsection (3)(c) "hospital accommodation" means—
(a) in relation to England, hospital accommodation within the meaning of the National Health Service Act 2006 which is provided by [1 . . .], an NHS trust or an NHS foundation trust;
(b) in relation to Wales, hospital accommodation within the meaning of the National Health Service (Wales) Act 2006 which is provided by a Local Health Board or an NHS trust;
(c) in relation to Scotland, hospital accommodation within the meaning of the National Health Service (Scotland) Act 1978 which is provided by a Health Board or Special Health Board but excluding accommodation in an institution for providing dental treatment maintained in connection with a dental school.
(5) The local authority may—
(a) itself use the information for purposes relating to the payment of a relevant benefit to the individual, or
(b) supply the information to a person specified in subsection (6) for those purposes.
(6) The persons referred to in subsection (5) are—
(a) the Secretary of State;
(b) a person providing services to the Secretary of State;
(c) a local authority;
(d) a person authorised to exercise any function of a local authority relating to a relevant benefit;
(e) a person providing services relating to a relevant benefit to a local authority.
(7) In this section "relevant benefit" means—
(a) universal credit;
(b) [2 . . .]
(c) [2 . . .]
(d) any prescribed benefit.
(8) Regulations under subsection (7)(d) may not prescribe a benefit provision for which is within the legislative competence of the Scottish Parliament.

COMMENCEMENT

By virtue of the Welfare Reform Act 2012 (Commencement No.1) Order 2012 (SI 2012/863) March 20, 2012 was the appointed day for the entry into force of s.130 for the purpose only of exercising the power to make regulations, and May 8, 2012 was the appointed day for its full entry into force. **1.642**

AMENDMENTS

1. The Health and Social Care Act 2012 (Consequential Amendments) Order 2013 (SI 2013/594) art.7 (April 1, 2013).
2. Welfare Reform Act 2012 Sch.14(1) para.1 (April 1, 2013, subject to savings and transitional provisions specified in SI 2013/358).

GENERAL NOTE

See The Social Security (Information-sharing in relation to Welfare Services etc.) Regulations 2012 (SI 2012/1483) as amended for the prescription of the information which may be shared. **1.643**

Information-sharing in relation to welfare services etc.

1.644 **131.** — (1) The Secretary of State, or a person providing services to the Secretary of State, may supply relevant information to a qualifying person for prescribed purposes relating to welfare services or council tax.

(2) A qualifying person who holds relevant information for a prescribed purpose relating to welfare services may supply that information to—

(a) the Secretary of State, or

(b) a person providing services to the Secretary of State, for a prescribed purpose relating to a relevant social security benefit.

(3) A qualifying person who holds relevant information for a prescribed purpose relating to welfare services, council tax or housing benefit may—

(a) use the information for another prescribed purpose relating to welfare services, council tax or housing benefit;

(b) supply it to another qualifying person for use in relation to the same or another prescribed purpose relating to welfare services, council tax or housing benefit.

(4) Relevant information supplied under subsection (1) or (3) to a qualifying person may be supplied by that person to a person who provides qualifying welfare services for purposes connected with the provision of those services.

(5) In subsection (4) services are qualifying welfare services if—

(a) a local authority, or

(b) a person who is a qualifying person by virtue of subsection (11)(g), contributes or will contribute to the expenditure incurred in their provision.

(6) The Secretary of State may not exercise the power in subsection (3) to prescribe purposes for which information may be supplied by a qualifying person so as to prescribe an excepted purpose in relation to excepted information held by a Welsh body.

(7) In subsection (6)—

(a) excepted information is information held by the Welsh body that—

(i) is not supplied by, or derived from information supplied to another person by, the Secretary of State or a person providing services to the Secretary of State or a person engaged in the administration of housing benefit, and

(ii) is held only for an excepted purpose;

(b) an excepted purpose is a purpose relating to a matter provision for which—

(i) is within the legislative competence of the National Assembly for Wales, or

(ii) is made by the Welsh Ministers, the First Minister for Wales or the Counsel General to the [1 Welsh Government].

(8) The Secretary of State may not exercise the power in subsection (3) to prescribe purposes for which information may be supplied by a qualifying person so as to prescribe an excepted purpose in relation to excepted information held by a Scottish body.

(9) In subsection (8)—

(a) excepted information is information held by the Scottish body that—

(i) is not supplied by, or derived from information supplied to another person by, the Secretary of State or a person providing services to the Secretary of State or a person engaged in the administration of housing benefit, and

(ii) is held only for an excepted purpose;

(b) an excepted purpose is a purpose relating to a matter provision for which is within the legislative competence of the Scottish Parliament.

(10) Subsections (1) to (4) do not apply in a case where the supply or use of information is authorised by section 130.

(11) In this section "qualifying person" means—

(a) a local authority;

(b) a person authorised to exercise any function of such an authority relating to welfare services or council tax;

(c) a person providing services to a local authority relating to welfare services or council tax;

(d) an authority which administers housing benefit;

(e) a person authorised to exercise any function of such an authority relating to housing benefit;

(f) a person providing to such an authority services relating to housing benefit; or

(g) a person prescribed or of a description prescribed by the Secretary of State.

(12) In this section—

"council tax" includes any local tax to fund local authority expenditure;

"person engaged in the administration of housing benefit" means—

(a) an authority which administers housing benefit,

(b) a person authorised to exercise any function of such an authority relating to housing benefit, or

(c) a person providing to such an authority services relating to housing benefit;

"relevant information" means information relating to—

(a) any relevant social security benefit, or

(b) welfare services;

"relevant social security benefit" has the meaning given in section 121DA(7) of the Social Security Administration Act 1992;

"Scottish body" means—

(a) a local authority in Scotland,

(b) a person authorised to exercise any function of such an authority relating to welfare services,

(c) a person providing to a local authority in Scotland services relating to welfare services, or

(d) a person prescribed or of a description prescribed by the Secretary of State;

"welfare services" includes services which provide accommodation, support, assistance, advice or counselling to individuals with particular needs, and for these purposes "assistance" includes assistance by means of a grant or loan or the provision of goods or services;

"Welsh body" means—

(a) a local authority in Wales,

(b) a person authorised to exercise any function of such an authority relating to welfare services,

(c) a person providing to a local authority in Wales services relating to welfare services, or

(d) a person prescribed or of a description prescribed by the Secretary of State.

COMMENCEMENT

1.645 By virtue of the Welfare Reform Act 2012 (Commencement No.1) Order 2012 (SI 2012/863) March 20, 2012 was the appointed day for the entry into force of s.131 for the purpose only of exercising the power to make regulations; and May 8, 2012 was the appointed day for its full entry into force.

AMENDMENT

1. Wales Act 2014 s.4(4)(a) (February 17, 2015).

GENERAL NOTE

1.646 See The Social Security (Information-sharing in relation to Welfare Services etc.) Regulations 2012 (SI 2012/1483) as amended for the prescription of the information which may be shared.

Unlawful disclosure of information supplied under section 131

1.647 **132.** — (1) A person to whom subsection (2) applies is guilty of an offence if the person discloses without lawful authority any information—

(a) which comes to the person by virtue of section 131(1), (3) or (4), and
(b) which relates to a particular person.

(2) This subsection applies to—

(a) a person mentioned in section 131(11)(a) to (c);
(b) a person who provides qualifying welfare services (within the meaning of section 131);
(c) a person who is or has been a director, member of the committee of management, manager, secretary or other similar officer of a person mentioned in paragraph (a) or (b);
(d) a person who is or has been an employee of a person mentioned in paragraph (a) or (b).

(3) A person guilty of an offence under this section is liable—

(a) on conviction on indictment, to imprisonment for a term not exceeding two years or a fine or both, or
(b) on summary conviction, to imprisonment for a term not exceeding twelve months or a fine not exceeding the statutory maximum or both.

(4) It is not an offence under this section—

(a) to disclose information in the form of a summary or collection of information so framed as not to enable information relating to any particular person to be ascertained from it;
(b) to disclose information which has previously been disclosed to the public with lawful authority.

(5) It is a defence for a person ("D") charged with an offence under this section to prove that at the time of the alleged offence—

(a) D believed that D was making the disclosure in question with lawful authority and had no reasonable cause to believe otherwise, or
(b) D believed that the information in question had previously been disclosed to the public with lawful authority and had no reasonable cause to believe otherwise.

(6) A disclosure is made with lawful authority if it is so made for the purposes of section 123 of the Social Security Administration Act 1992.

(7) This section does not affect that section.

(8) Regulations under section 131(11)(g) may include provision for applying the provisions of this section to—

(a) a person who is a qualifying person within the meaning of section 131 by virtue of the regulations, or

(b) a person associated with such a qualifying person by reason of the person's office or employment or otherwise.

(9) In relation to an offence under this section committed in England and Wales before the commencement of section 154(1) of the Criminal Justice Act 2003 (increase in maximum term that may be imposed on summary conviction of offence triable either way) the reference in subsection (3)(b) to twelve months must be taken to be a reference to six months.

COMMENCEMENT

Welfare Reform Act 2012 (Commencement No.1) Order 2012 (SI 2012/863) (May 8, 2012). 1.648

GENERAL NOTE

See The Social Security (Information-sharing in relation to Welfare Services etc.) Regulations 2012 (SI 2012/1483) as amended for the prescription of the information which may be shared. 1.649

Sections 130 to 132: supplementary

133. — (1) In sections 130 and 131— 1.650

"benefit" includes any allowance, payment, credit or loan;

"local authority" means—

(a) a county or district council in England;

(b) an eligible parish council (within the meaning of Chapter 1 of Part 1 of the Localism Act 2011);

(c) a London borough council;

(d) the Common Council of the City of London in its capacity as a local authority;

(e) the Council of the Isles of Scilly;

(f) a county or county borough council in Wales;

(g) a council constituted under section 2 of the Local Government etc. (Scotland) Act 1994;

"prescribed" means prescribed in regulations made by the Secretary of State.

(2) Any power to make regulations under sections 130 and 131 includes power—

(a) to make different provision for different purposes, cases and areas;

(b) to make such incidental, supplemental, consequential, transitional or saving provision as the Secretary of State thinks necessary or expedient.

(3) Regulations under sections 130 and 131 must be made by statutory instrument.

(4) A statutory instrument containing regulations under section 130 or 131 is subject to annulment in pursuance of a resolution of either House of Parliament.

COMMENCEMENT

1.651 By virtue of the Welfare Reform Act 2012 (Commencement No.1) Order 2012 (SI 2012/863) March 20, 2012 was the appointed day for the entry into force of s.133(1)–(4); and May 8, 2012 was the appointed day for its full entry into force.

GENERAL NOTE

1.652 See The Social Security (Information-sharing in relation to Welfare Services etc.) Regulations 2012 (SI 2012/1483) as amended for the prescription of the information which may be shared.

Welfare Benefits Up-rating Act 2013

(2013 C.16)

ARRANGEMENT OF SECTIONS

An Act to make provision relating to the up-rating of certain social security benefits and tax credits.

[26th March 2013]

GENERAL NOTE

1.654 This Act, which entered into force on October 1, 2013 (The Welfare Benefits Up-rating Act 2013 (Commencement) Order 2013 (SI 2013/2317) is part implementation of the Government's plan to reduce welfare expenditure. Under the Social Security Administration Act 1992 the Secretary of State is required to review the value of benefits in the light of changes in prices and to make annual uprating orders, subject to Parliamentary approval, in the light of those changes. The Treasure is under a similar obligation under the Tax Credits Act 2002.

The Act provides that working age benefits will be up-rated by 1 per cent in 2014–15 and 2015–16. Working age benefits are the main rates of income support, jobseeker's allowance, employment and support allowance, and housing benefit, the work-related activity group component of employment and support allowance, maternity allowance, and statutory adoption, maternity, paternity and sick pay. Corresponding payment under universal credit are also covered. In addition increases in the couple element and lone parent element of working tax credit and the child element of tax credit are also limited to 1 per cent. Rounding of the resulting sums will be done to the nearest five pence.

Be it enacted by the Queen's most Excellent Majesty, by and with the advice and consent of the Lords Spiritual and Temporal, and Commons, in this present Parliament assembled, and by the authority of the same, as follows:

Up-rating of certain social security benefits for tax years 2014–15 and 2015–16

1.—(1) The Secretary of State must, in each of the tax years ending with 5 April 2014 and 5 April 2015, make an order by statutory instrument increasing each of the relevant sums by 1%. **1.655**

For the meaning of the "relevant sums" see paragraph 1 of the Schedule.

(2) [1 Subject to subsection (2A), an] order under this section must be framed so as to bring the variations to which it relates into force—

(a) in the week beginning with the first Monday in the tax year following that in which the order is made, or

(b) on an earlier date in April specified in the order;

and the provision that may be made under this subsection includes provision bringing the variation in a particular sum into force on different dates for different purposes.

[1 (2A) An order under this section shall be framed so that—

(a) any variation of the relevant sums referred to in paragraphs 1(j) to (l) of the Schedule (sums specified under Part 1 of the Welfare Reform Act 2012) comes into force in relation to a person on the relevant day; and

(b) any other variation to which the order relates comes into force, for the purposes of determining the amount of universal credit to which a person is entitled, on the relevant day.

(2B) In subsection (2A) "relevant day", in relation to a person, means the first day of the first universal credit assessment period in respect of the person which begins on or after—

(a) the Monday of the week specified in subsection (2)(a), or

(b) any earlier date specified under subsection (2)(b).

(2C) In subsection (2B) "universal credit assessment period" means an assessment period for the purposes of Part 1 of the Welfare Reform Act 2012.]

(3) The Secretary of State may, in providing for an increase under subsection (1), adjust the amount of the increase so as to round any sum up or down to the extent the Secretary of State thinks appropriate.

(4) After making an order under this section, the Secretary of State must lay before Parliament a copy of a report by the Government Actuary or the Deputy Government Actuary giving that Actuary's opinion on the likely effect on the National Insurance Fund of the parts of the order that relate to sums payable out of the Fund.

(5) Subsection (1) does not apply in relation to a tax year if, on the review in that tax year under section 150(1) of the Social Security Administration Act 1992, the Secretary of State determines that the general level of prices in Great Britain has not increased, or has increased by less than 1%, over the period under review.

(6) Where subsection (1) applies in relation to a tax year, the draft of any up-rating order laid before Parliament by virtue of the review in that tax year under section 150(1) of the Social Security Administration Act 1992 must not include provision increasing any of the relevant sums.

(7) In this section a reference to the Secretary of State, in relation to the sums mentioned in section 150(1)(i) of the Social Security Administration Act 1992, is a reference to the Treasury.

(8) A reference in any enactment, other than this Act and sections 189

and 190 of the Social Security Administration Act 1992, to an order under section 150 of that Act includes a reference to an order under this section.

(9) Nothing in section 166 of the Social Security Administration (Northern Ireland) Act 1992 applies in relation to an order made by the Treasury under section 132 of that Act which corresponds to an order made under this section.

AMENDMENT

1. The Universal Credit and Miscellaneous Amendments (No.2) Regulations 2014 (SI 2014/2888), reg.7(2) (November 26, 2014).

Up-rating of tax credits for tax years 2014–15 and 2015–16

1.656 **2.**—(1) The Treasury must, in each of the tax years ending with 5 April 2014 and 5 April 2015, make an order by statutory instrument increasing each of the relevant amounts by 1%.

For the meaning of the "relevant amounts" see paragraph 2 of the Schedule.

(2) An order under this section must be framed so that it has effect in relation to awards of tax credits for the tax year following that in which the order is made.

(3) The Treasury may, in providing for an increase under subsection (1), adjust the amount of the increase so as to round any amount up or down to the extent the Treasury think appropriate.

(4) Subsection (1) does not apply in relation to a tax year if, on the review in that tax year under section 41 of the Tax Credits Act 2002, the Treasury determine that the general level of prices in the United Kingdom has not increased, or has increased by less than 1%, over the period under review.

(5) Where subsection (1) applies in relation to a tax year, the Treasury must not exercise any other power to vary any of the relevant amounts if that variation would take effect in relation to awards of tax credits for the tax year following that in which the order is made.

Short title, interpretation, commencement and extent

1.657 **3.**—(1) This Act may be cited as the Welfare Benefits Up-rating Act 2013.

(2) In this Act "tax year" means a period beginning with 6 April in one year and ending with 5 April in the next.

(3) This section comes into force on the day on which this Act is passed.

(4) The other provisions of this Act come into force on such day as the Secretary of State or the Treasury may by order made by statutory instrument appoint; and different days may be appointed for different purposes.

(5) Section 1(1) to (7) and paragraph 1 of the Schedule extend to England and Wales and Scotland only.

(6) Section 1(9) extends to Northern Ireland only.

(7) The other provisions of this Act extend to England and Wales, Scotland and Northern Ireland.

SCHEDULE Sections 1 and 2

MEANING OF THE "RELEVANT SUMS" AND THE "RELEVANT AMOUNTS"

The "relevant sums" for the purposes of section 1 **1.658**

1. The "relevant sums" for the purposes of section 1 are the sums—
(a) specified in paragraph 1 of Schedule 2 to the Income Support (General) Regulations 1987 (S.I. 1987/1967);
(b) specified in paragraph 1 of Schedule 3 to the Housing Benefit Regulations 2006 (S.I. 2006/213);
(c) mentioned in section 150(1)(i) and (j) of the Social Security Administration Act 1992;
(d) specified in regulations under section 4(2) of the Jobseekers Act 1995;
(e) specified in paragraph 1 of Schedule 1 to the Jobseeker's Allowance Regulations 1996 ;
(f) specified in regulations under section 2(1)(a) of the Welfare Reform Act 2007;
(g) specified in regulations under section 2(4)(c) of the Welfare Reform Act 2007, so far as relating to the component under section 2(3) of that Act;
(h) specified in paragraph 1 of Schedule 4 to the Employment and Support Allowance Regulations 2008 ;
(i) specified in regulations under section 4(6)(c) of the Welfare Reform Act 2007, so far as relating to the component under section 4(5) of that Act;
(j) specified in regulations under section 9(2) of the Welfare Reform Act 2012;
(k) specified in regulations under section 10(3) of the Welfare Reform Act 2012 in respect of an amount to be included under section 10(2) of that Act (but where more than one sum is so specified, only the smaller or smallest of those sums is a "relevant sum");
(l) specified in regulations under section 12(3) of the Welfare Reform Act 2012 in respect of needs or circumstances of a claimant prescribed by virtue of section 12(2)(a) of that Act (but not in respect of needs or circumstances prescribed by virtue of section 12(2)(b)).

The "relevant amounts" for the purposes of section 2

2. The "relevant amounts" for the purposes of section 2 are the monetary amounts— **1.659**
(a) specified in Schedule 2 to the Working Tax Credit (Entitlement and Maximum Rate) Regulations 2002 for the basic element, the 30 hour element, the second adult element and the lone parent element;
(b) specified in regulation 7(4)(c) and (f) of the Child Tax Credit Regulations 2002.

Welfare Reform and Work Act 2016

(2016 c.7)

ARRANGEMENT OF SECTIONS

SCHEDULE 1

An Act to make provision about reports on progress towards full employment and the apprenticeships target; to make provision about reports on the effect of certain support for troubled families; to make provision about life changes; to make provision about the benefit cap; to make provision about social security and tax credits; to make provision for loans for mortgage interest and other liabilities; and to make provision about social housing rents.

[16 March 2016]

Freeze of certain social security benefits for four tax years

1.661 **11.**—(1) For each of the tax years ending with 5 April 2017, 5 April 2018, 5 April 2019 and 5 April 2020, the amount of each of the relevant sums is to remain the same as it was in the tax year ending with 5 April 2016.

(2) For each of the tax year ending with 5 April 2017, 5 April 2018, 5 April 2019 and 5 April 2020, the rates of child benefit are to remain the same as they were in the tax year ending with 5 April 2016.

(3) A review under section 150(1) of the Social Security Administration Act 1992 (review of whether certain benefits have retained their value) in the tax years ending with 5 April 2016, 5 April 2017, 5 April 2018 and 5 April 2019 need not cover any of the relevant sums or the rates of child benefit.

(4) A draft up-rating order which is laid before Parliament under section 150(2) of that Act in the tax years ending with 5 April 2016, 5 April 2017, 5 April 2018 and 5 April 2019 need not cover any of the relevant sums or the rates of child benefit.

(5) In each of the tax years ending with 5 April 2016, 5 April 2017, 5 April 2018 and 5 April 2019, the Secretary of State must lay before Parliament a copy of a report by the Government Actuary or the Deputy Government Actuary giving that Actuary's opinion on the likely effect of the provision in subsection(1) on the National Insurance Fund in the following tax year, so far as that provision relates to any sums payable out of the Fund.

(6) In this section –

"child benefit" –

(a) in relation to England and Wales and Scotland, has the same meaning as in Part 9 of the Social Security Contributions and Benefits Act 1992;
(b) in relation to Northern Ireland, has the same meaning as in Part 9 of the Social Security Contributions and Benefits (Northern Ireland) Act 1992;

"the relevant sums" means the sums described in paragraph 1 of Schedule 1;

"tax year" means a period beginning with 6 April in one year and ending with 5 April in the next.

SCHEDULE 1 Sections 11 and 12

MEANING OF "THE RELEVANT SUMS" AND "THE RELEVANT AMOUNTS"

1. "The relevant sums" for the purposes of section 11 are the sums— 1.662

(a) specified in paragraph 1 of Schedule 2 to the Income Support (General) Regulations 1987 (S.I. 1987/1967);
(b) specified in paragraph 1 of Schedule 3 to the Housing Benefit Regulations 2006 (S.I. 2006/213);
(c) specified in paragraph 25 of Schedule 3 to the Housing Benefit Regulations 2006 (S.I. 2006/213);
(d) specified in regulations under section 4(2) of the Jobseekers Act 1995;
(e) specified in paragraph 1 of Schedule 1 to the Jobseeker's Allowance Regulations 1996 (S.I. 1996/207);
(f) specified in regulations under section 2(1)(a) of the Welfare Reform Act 2007;
(g) specified in regulations under section 2(4)(c) of the Welfare Reform Act 2007, so far as relating to the component under section 2(3) of that Act;
(h) specified in paragraph 1 of Schedule 4 to the Employment and Support Allowance Regulations 2008 (S.I. 2008/794);
(i) specified in regulations under section 4(6)(c) of the Welfare Reform Act 2007, so far as relating to the component under section 4(5) of that Act;
(j) specified in regulations under section 9(2) of the Welfare Reform Act 2012;
(k) specified in regulations under section 10(3) of the Welfare Reform Act 2012 in respect of an amount to be included under section 10(2) of that Act (but where more than one sum is so specified, only the smaller or smallest of those sums is a "relevant sum");
(l) specified in regulations under section 12(3) of the Welfare Reform Act 2012 in respect of needs or circumstances of a claimant prescribed by virtue of section 12(2)(a) of that Act (but not in respect of needs or circumstances prescribed by virtue of section 12(2)(b)).

2. *Not reproduced; concerns tax credits*

PART II

REGULATIONS

SECTION A

DWP-ADMINISTERED BENEFITS

NOTE

References to 1992 Acts in pre-1992 Regulations

Some regulations made before the consolidation of social security legislation in 1992 still refer to provisions in the earlier legislation even though they have been replaced by provisions of the Social Security Contributions and Benefits Act 1992 or Social Security Administration Act 1992. This is technically acceptable because those references are deemed to be references to that have replaced them but is apt to be confusing.

In order to be as helpful as possible to users of this volume, the authors have, wherever practicable, inserted in square brackets reference to the relevant provisions of the 1992 legislation.

However, some of the older regulations contain many references to legislation which has either been repealed or is only of significance to those able to retain an entitlement to a defunct benefit. In these cases, reference has generally been left to the earlier legislation. Equally, in some regulations, it was considered that it might mislead if the interpretation regulation was amended.

Readers should therefore note that the material appearing in square brackets is the authors' amendment to include reference to the 1992 legislation. Such amendments have no official standing. All other references to legislation are as they appear in the current version of the regulations printed in this volume.

The Social Security (Civil Penalties) Regulations 2012

(SI 2012/1990)

IN FORCE OCTOBER 1, 2012

ARRANGEMENT OF REGULATIONS

The Secretary of State for Work and Pensions makes the following Regulations in exercise of the powers conferred by sections 115C(2), 115D(1) and (2), 189(1) and 191 of the Social Security Administration Act 1992.

In accordance with section 190(1) of that Act, a draft of this instrument was laid before Parliament and approved by a resolution of each House of Parliament

This instrument contains only regulations made by virtue of section 116(1) of the Welfare Reform Act 2012 and is made before the end of the period of 6 months beginning with the coming into force of that section.

In so far as these Regulations relate to housing benefit and council tax benefit, in accordance with section 176(1) of the Social Security Administration Act 1992(5), consultation has taken place with organisations appearing to the Secretary of State to be representative of the authorities concerned.

Citation, commencement and interpretation 2.2

1. (1) These Regulations may be cited as the Social Security (Civil Penalties) Regulations 2012 and come into force on 1st October 2012.

(2) In these Regulations, "the Act" means the Social Security Administration Act 1992.

Prescribed amount of penalty: section 115C of the Act 2.3

2. The prescribed amount of the penalty for the purpose of section 115C(2) of the Act (incorrect statements etc.) is £50.

Prescribed amount of penalty: section 115D(1) of the Act 2.4

3. The prescribed amount of the penalty for the purpose of section 115D(1) of the Act (failure to provide information) is £50.

Prescribed amount of penalty: section 115D(2) of the Act 2.5

4. The prescribed amount of the penalty for the purpose of section 115D(2) of the Act (failure to notify appropriate authority of a relevant change of circumstances) is £50.

The Social Security (Claims and Information) Regulations 1999

(SI 1999/3108)

ARRANGEMENT OF REGULATIONS

The Secretary of State for Social Security, in exercise of the powers conferred upon him by sections 2C, 7A, 189(1), (4) and (5) and 1919 of the Social Security Administration Act 1992 and sections 72 and 83(1) and (4) to (8) of the Welfare Reform and Pensions Act 1999 and of all other powers enabling him in that behalf, after consultation in respect of provisions in these Regulations relating to housing benefit and council tax benefit with organisations appearing to him to be representative of the authorities concerned, by this instrument, which contains only regulations made by virtue of or consequential upon sections 58, 71 and 72 of the Welfare Reform and Pensions Act 1999 and which is made before the end of a period of 6 months beginning with the coming into force of those provisions, hereby makes the following Regulations:

Citation and commencement

2.7 **1.** These Regulations may be cited as the Social Security (Claims and Information) Regulations 1999 and shall come into force on 29th November 1999.

Interpretation

2.8 **2.** In these Regulations,—

"the Act" means the Welfare Reform and Pensions Act 1999;

"the Child Support Acts" means the Child Support Act 1991 and the Child Support Act 1995;

"the Council Tax Benefit Regulations" means the Council Tax Benefit (General) Regulations 1992;

"the Housing Benefit Regulations" means the Housing Benefit (General) Regulations 1987;

"relevant authority" means a person within section 72(2) of the Act.

Work-focused interview

3. A work-focused interview is an interview conducted for any or all of the following purposes— 2.9

(a) assessing a person's prospects for existing or future employment (whether paid or voluntary);
(b) assisting or encouraging a person to enhance his prospects of such employment;
(c) identifying activities which the person may undertake to strengthen his existing or future prospects of such employment;
(d) identifying current or future employment or training opportunities suitable to the person's needs; and
(e) identifying educational opportunities connected with the existing or future employment prospects or needs of the person.

Additional functions of local authorities

4.—(1) A local authority to whom Part I of Schedule I to these Regulations applies may conduct a work-focused interview with, or provide assistance to, a person to whom paragraphs (2) and (3) apply, where the interview or assistance is requested or consented to by that person. 2.10

(2) This paragraph applies to a person who resides in a postcode district identified in Part I of Schedule 2 to these Regulations.

(3) This paragraph applies to any person making a claim for, or entitled to, any benefit specified in paragraph (4) and applies whether or not a person has had an interview in accordance with regulations made under section 2A of the Administration Act(d).

(4) The benefits specified in this paragraph are—

(a) income support;
(b) housing benefit;
(c) council tax benefit;
(d) widow's benefit;
(e) bereavement benefits;
[3 (ea) bereavement support payment under section 30 of the Pensions Act 2014;]
(f) incapacity benefit;
(g) severe disablement allowance;
(h) [2 carer's allowance];
(i) a jobseeker's allowance;
(j) disability living allowance.

(5) For the purposes of paragraph (1), the request or consent may be made or given to—

(a) the local authority conducting the interview or giving the assistance;
(b) any person who, or authority which, may be specified as a designated authority for the purposes of section 2A(8) of the Administration Act; or
(c) a person designated an employment officer for the purposes of section 9 of the Jobseekers Act 1995.

(6) For the purposes of carrying out functions under paragraph (1), a local authority may in particular—

(a) obtain and receive information or evidence for the purpose of any work-focused interview to be conducted with that person;

(b) arrange for the work-focused interview to be conducted by one of the following—

(i) the Secretary of State;

(ii) a person providing services to the Secretary of State; or

(iii) a person providing services to, or authorised to exercise any function of, the local authority;

(c) forward information supplied for the purpose of a work-focused interview to any person or authority conducting that interview;

(d) take steps to identify potential employment or training opportunities for persons taking part in work-focused interviews;

(e) [1 . . .];

(f) take steps to identify—

(i) obstacles which may hinder a person in taking up employment or training opportunities;

(ii) educational opportunities which may assist in reducing or removing such obstacles; and

(g) record information supplied at a work-focused interview.

AMENDMENTS

1. The Social Security (Work-focused Interviews for Lone Parents) and Miscellaneous Amendments Regulations 2000 (SI 2000/1926) Sch.2 (August 14, 2000).

2. The Social Security Amendment (Carer's Allowance) Regulations 2002 (SI 2002/2497) Sch.2 (October 28, 2002).

3. The Pensions Act 2014 (Consequential, Supplementary and Incidental Amendments) Order 2017 (SI 2017/422) art.16 (April 6, 2017).

Further provisions as to claims

2.11 *Regulation 5 amends the Claims and Payments Regulations 1987; the changes are incorporated in those regulations.*

War Pensions and Child Support

2.12 **6.**—(1) Where a person resides in the area of an authority to which Part I or II of Schedule 1 to these Regulations refers, he may make a claim for a war pension, or submit an application under the Child Support Acts to any office [1 of a relevant authority] displaying the **one** logo (whether or not that office is situated within the area of the local authority in which the person resides).

(2) Any change of circumstances arising since a claim or application was made in accordance with paragraph (1) may be reported to the office to which that claim or application was made.

(3) The areas to which this paragraph refers are those areas which are within both—

(a) the area of a local authority identified in Part I or II of Schedule1 to these Regulations, and

(b) a postcode area identified in Part I or II of Schedule 2 to these Regulations.

(4) A person making a claim or application to a participating authority in accordance with paragraph (1) shall comply with any requirements for the time being in force in relation to—

(a) claims for war pensions or applications under the Child Support Acts;

(b) the provision of information and evidence in support of such claims or applications,

as if those requirements also applied to the participating authority.

(5) A participating authority shall forward to the Secretary of State—

(a) any claim for a war pension or application under the Child Support Acts made in accordance with this regulation;

(b) details of changes of circumstances reported to the authority in accordance with this regulation; and

(c) any information or evidence—

(i) given to the authority by the person making a claim or application or reporting the change of circumstances; or

(ii) which is relevant to the claim or application or the change reported and which is held by the authority.

(6) For the purpose of this regulation, a "participating authority" means any authority or person to whom a claim or application may be made or change of circumstances reported in accordance with paragraphs (1) and (2).

AMENDMENT

1. The Social Security (Work-focused Interviews for Lone Parents) and Miscellaneous Amendments Regulations 2000 (SI 2000/1926) Sch.2 (August 14, 2000).

Holding information

7. A relevant authority to whom information or evidence relating to social security matters [[1], or information relating to employment or training] is supplied or by whom such information or evidence is obtained, including information obtained under regulation 8(2), may— 2.13

(a) make a record of that information or evidence; and

(b) hold the information or evidence, whether as supplied or as recorded.

AMENDMENT

1. The Social Security (Claims and Information) (Amendment) Regulations 2010 (SI 2010/508) reg.2(2) (April 6, 2010).

Provision of information

8.—(1) A relevant authority may give information or advice to any person, or to a person acting on his behalf, concerning— 2.14

(a) a claim he made, or a decision given on a claim he made, for a social security benefit or a war pension;

(b) an application he made, or a decision given on an application he made, under the Child Support Acts.

(2) For the purpose of giving information or advice in accordance with paragraph (1), a relevant authority may obtain information held by any other relevant authority.

9. Claims for Housing Benefit

2.15 *Amends the Housing Benefit Regulations*

10. Consequential Amendments to the Housing Benefit Regulations

2.16 *Further amends the Housing Benefit Regulations*

11. Claims for Council Tax Benefit

2.17 *Amends the Council Tax Benefit Regulations*

12. Consequential Amendments to the Council Tax Benefit Regulations

2.18 *Further amends to the Council Tax Benefit Regulations*

Information

2.19 **13.**—(1) A relevant authority which holds social security information may—

(a) use that information—

(i) in connection with arrangements [1 . . .] made under section 2 of the Employment and Training Act 1973;

(ii) for any purpose to which regulations 3, 4 and 6 of these Regulations, or any regulations inserted by these Regulations, apply; or

(iii) for purposes connected with the employment or training of the persons to whom it relates;

(b) supply the information—

(i) to any other relevant authority to enable that authority to carry out a work-focused interview or any function conferred upon it by these Regulations or by regulations inserted by these Regulations;

(ii) in so far as relevant for the purpose for which it is being provided, to any person in respect of whom the person undertaking the work-focused interview is notified has a vacancy or is about to have a vacancy in his employment or at his place of employment;

(iii) to any person (an "employment zone provider") to whom payments are made by the Secretary of State in accordance with section 60(5)(c)(i) of the Act (special schemes for claimants for jobseeker's allowance);

(iv) to any other relevant authority in connection with any scheme operated by, or any arrangements made by, the authority for purposes connected with employment or training;

[1 (v) to any other relevant authority in connection with arrangements made under section 2 of the Employment and Training Act 1973, in particular for use by that authority in connection with the provision of advice, support and assistance which persons may need in order to acquire or enhance their skills and qualifications with a view to improving their prospects of finding and retaining employment.]

[1 (1A) A relevant authority which holds employment or training information about a person ("P") may supply that information to another relevant authority for use by that second authority in connection with the provision to P (pursuant to arrangements made by the Secretary of State) of advice, support and assistance which P may need in order to acquire or enhance P's skills and qualifications with a view to improving P's prospects of finding and retaining employment.]

(2) An employment zone provider may supply to any other relevant authority information relating to any person participating in a scheme for which he receives a payment under section 60(5)(c)(i) of the Act where the information may be relevant to the person's benefit entitlement.

(3) Where the work-focused interview is undertaken by a relevant authority other than the authority which obtained the information, then the authority supplying the information shall, for the purposes of that interview, supply any other social security information held by them.

(4) A relevant authority which holds social security information [1 or information relating to employment or training] may supply that information to any other relevant authority for the purposes of research, monitoring or evaluation in so far as it relates to [1 any of the purposes] specified in paragraph (5).

(5) The purposes [1 . . .] are—

(a) work-focused interviews;

(b) any purpose for which regulations 3, 4 and 6 of these Regulations, or any regulations inserted by these Regulations, applies;

(c) any scheme or arrangements made by the Secretary of State connected with employment or training; [1 . . .]

(d) section 60 of the Act.

[1 (e) any arrangements made by the Secretary of State of the nature referred to in paragraph (1)(b)(v) or (1A); and

(f) monitoring the retention of employment.]

AMENDMENT

1. The Social Security (Claims and Information) (Amendment) Regulations 2010 (SI 2010/508) reg.2(3) (April 6, 2010).

Purposes for which information may be used

14.—(1) The purposes for which information supplied in connection with matters referred to in paragraph (2) may be used are for— 2.20

(a) the processing of any claim for a social security benefit or a war pension or for an application for a maintenance assessment under the Child Support Act 1991;

(b) the consideration of any application for employment by a person to whom information is supplied in connection with any employment opportunity;

(c) the consideration of the training needs of the person who supplied the information;

(d) any purpose for which a work-focused interview may be conducted;

(e) the prevention, detection, investigation or prosecution of offences relating to social security matters.

[1 (f) assessing the employment or training needs of the person to whom the information relates;

(g) evaluating the effectiveness of training, advice, support and assistance provided;

(h) monitoring the retention of employment.]

(2) The matters referred to in this paragraph are—

(a) work-focused interviews; or

(b) any other provision in or introduced by these Regulations.

AMENDMENT

1. The Social Security (Claims and Information) (Amendment) Regulations 2010 (SI 2010/508) reg.2(4) (April 6, 2010).

Information supplied

2.21 **15.** Information supplied to a person or authority under these Regulations—

(a) may be used for the purposes of amending or supplementing information held by the person or authority to whom it is supplied; and

(b) if it is so used, may be supplied to another person or authority, and used by him or it for any purpose, to whom or for which that other information could be supplied or used.

Partners of claimants on jobseeker's allowance

2.22 **16.**—(1) The social security information specified in paragraph (2) may be supplied by a relevant authority to the partner of a claimant for a jobseeker's allowance where—

(a) the allowance has been in payment to the claimant, or would have been in payment to him but for section 19 of the Jobseekers Act 1995 (circumstances in which jobseeker's allowance is not payable) for a period of six months or more;

(b) the allowance remains in payment or would be in payment but for that section; and

(c) the partner is being invited to attend the office of the relevant authority for purposes connected with employment or training.

(2) The information which may be supplied is—

(a) that jobseeker's allowance is in payment to the claimant or would be in payment to him but for section 19 of the Jobseekers Act; and

(b) that payment has been made to the claimant or would have been so made but for section 19, for a period of at least six months.

(3) In this regulation, "partner" has the same meaning as in the Jobseeker's Allowance Regulations 1996 by virtue of section 1(3) of those Regulations.

Partners of claimants

2.23 **17.**—(1) The social security information specified in paragraph (4) may be supplied by a relevant authority to the partner of a claimant for a qualifying benefit where [1 . . .] [1 one or more of the qualifying benefits has been payable to the claimant for at least six months.]

(2) The qualifying benefits are—

(a) a jobseeker's allowance;
(b) income support;
(c) incapacity benefit;
(d) severe disablement allowance;
(e) [2 carer's allowance]
(3) [1 . . .]
(4) The information which may be supplied is—
(a) that a qualifying benefit is or has been payable to the claimant;
(b) the period for which the qualifying benefit has been payable.
(5) In this regulation, [3 "partner"] means one member of [3 a couple] of which the claimant is also a member [3, and "couple" has the same meaning as in regulation 1(3) of the Jobseeker's Allowance Regulations 1996"].

AMENDMENTS

1. The Social Security (Claims and Information and Work-focused Interviews for Lone Parents) Amendment Regulations 2001 (SI 2001/1189) reg.2 (April 23, 2001).
2. The Social Security Amendment (Carer's Allowance) Regulations 2002 (SI 2002/2497) Sch.2 (October 28, 2002).
3. The Civil Partnership (Pensions, Social Security and Child Support) (Consequential etc. Provisions) Order 2005 (SI 2005/2877) (December 5, 2005).

Consequentials

18. *Omitted.* 2.24

The Social Security (Claims and Information) Regulations 2007

(SI 2007/2911)

IN FORCE OCTOBER 31, 2007

ARRANGEMENT OF REGULATIONS

The Secretary of State for Work and Pensions makes the following Regulations in exercise of the powers conferred by sections 5(1)(a), 7A(1), (2) and (6)(d), 7B(2) and (5), 189(1) and (4) to (6) and 191 of the Social Security Administration Act 1992.

In accordance with section 176(1)(a) of that Act, as regards provisions in the Regulations relating to housing benefit and council tax benefit, he has consulted organisations appearing to him to be representative of the authorities concerned.

The Social Security Advisory Committee has agreed that proposals in respect of these Regulations should not be referred to it.

Citation, commencement and interpretation

2.26 **1.**—(1) These Regulations may be cited as the Social Security (Claims and Information) Regulations 2007 and shall come into force on 31st October 2007.

(2) In regulations 4 and 5 "the Administration Act" means the Social Security Administration Act 1992.

(3) In regulations 2 to 4—

"specified benefit" means one or more of the following benefits—

(a) attendance allowance;

[2 (b) bereavement support payment under section 30 of the Pensions Act 2014;]

(c) [2 . . .];

(d) carer's allowance;

(e) disability living allowance;

1(ee) employment and support allowance;]

(f) incapacity benefit;

(g) income support;

(h) jobseeker's allowance;

(i) retirement pension;

(j) state pension credit;

(k) widowed parent's allowance;

(l) winter fuel payment;

"the Secretary of State" includes persons providing services to the Secretary of State;

"local authority" includes persons providing services to a local authority and persons authorised to exercise any function of a local authority relating to housing benefit or council tax benefit.

AMENDMENTS

1. Social Security (Miscellaneous Amendments) (No. 3) Regulations 2010 (SI 2010/840) reg.8 (June 28, 2010).

2. The Pensions Act 2014 (Consequential, Supplementary and Incidental Amendments) Order 2017 (SI 2017/422) art.30 (April 6, 2017).

Use of social security information: local authorities

2.27 **2.**—(1) This regulation applies where social security information held by a local authority was supplied by the Secretary of State to the local authority and this information—

(a) was used by the Secretary of State in connection with a person's claim for, or award of, a specified benefit; and

(b) is relevant to that person's claim for, or award of, council tax benefit or housing benefit.

(2) The local authority must, for the purposes of the person's claim for, or award of, council tax benefit or housing benefit, use that information without verifying its accuracy.

(3) Paragraph (2) does not apply where—

(a) the information is supplied more than twelve months after it was used by the Secretary of State in connection with a claim for, or an award of, a specified benefit; or

(b) the information is supplied within twelve months of its use by the Secretary of State but the local authority has reasonable grounds for believing the information has changed in the period between its use by the Secretary of State and its supply to the local authority; or

(c) the date on which the information was used by the Secretary of State cannot be determined.

Use of social security information: Secretary of State

3.—(1) This regulation applies where social security information held by the Secretary of State was supplied by a local authority to the Secretary of State and this information— 2.28

(a) was used by the local authority in connection with a person's claim for, or award of, council tax benefit or housing benefit; and

(b) is relevant to that person's claim for, or award of, a specified benefit.

(2) The Secretary of State must, for the purposes of the person's claim for, or award of, a specified benefit, use that information without verifying its accuracy.

(3) Paragraph (2) does not apply where—

(a) the information is supplied more than twelve months after it was used by a local authority in connection with a claim for, or an award of, council tax benefit or housing benefit; or

(b) the information is supplied within twelve months of its use by the local authority but the Secretary of State has reasonable grounds for believing the information has changed in the period between its use by the local authority and its supply to the Secretary of State; or

(c) the date on which the information was used by the local authority cannot be determined.

Social security information verified by local authorities

4.—(1) This regulation applies where social security information is verified by a local authority by virtue of regulations made under section 7A(2)(e) of the Administration Act and forwarded by that local authority to the Secretary of State. 2.29

(2) The Secretary of State must, for the purposes of a person's claim for, or award of, a specified benefit, use this information without verifying its accuracy.

(3) Paragraph (2) does not apply where—

(a) the Secretary of State has reasonable grounds for believing the social security information received from the local authority is inaccurate; or

(b) the Secretary of State receives the information more than four weeks after it was verified by the local authority.

Specified benefits for the purpose of section 7B(3) of the Administration Act

5. The benefits specified for the purpose of section 7B(3) of the Administration Act are— 2.30

(a) a "specified benefit" within the meaning given in regulation 1(3);

(b) housing benefit; and

(c) council tax benefit.

Regs 6–10 amend other legislation and the amendments are incorporated in the relevant regulations.

The Social Security (Claims and Payments) Regulations 1987

(SI 1987/1968) (AS AMENDED)

ARRANGEMENTS OF REGULATIONS

PART I

General

PART II

Claims

PART III

Payments

PART IV

Third Parties

PART V

Extinguishment

PART VI

Mobility Component of Disability Living Allowance and Disability Living Allowance for Children

PART VII

Miscellaneous

SCHEDULES

Whereas a draft of this instrument was laid before Parliament and approved by resolution of each House of Parliament:

Now therefore, the Secretary of State for Social Services, in exercise of the powers conferred by sections 165A and 166(2) of the Social Security Act 1975, section 6(1) of the Child Benefit Act 1975, sections 21(7), 51(1)(a) to (s), 54(1) and 84(1) of the Social Security Act 1986 and, as regards the revocations set out in Schedule 10 to this instrument, the powers specified in that Schedule, and all other powers enabling him in that behalf by this instrument which contains only regulations made under the sections of the Social Security Act 1986 specified above and provisions consequential on those sections and which is made before the end of a period of 12 months from the commencement of those sections, makes the following Regulations:

PART I

GENERAL

Citation [1 , commencement and application]

1. —[1 (1)] These Regulations may be cited as the Social Security (Claims and Payments) Regulations 1987 and shall come into operation on 11th April 1988. 2.32

(2) *Omitted.* 2.33

[1 (3) These Regulations do not apply to universal credit (within the meaning of Part 1 of the Welfare Reform Act 2012) or personal independence payment (within the meaning of Part 4 of that Act).]

AMENDMENT

1. The Universal Credit, Personal Independence Payment, Jobseeker's Allowance and Employment and Support Allowance (Claims and Payments) Regulations 2013 (SI 2013/380), reg.4 and Sch.3, para.(2) (April 8, 2013).

GENERAL NOTE

The Universal Credit, Personal Independence Payment, Jobseeker's Allowance and Employment and Support Allowance (Claims and Payments) Regulations 2013 (SI 2013/380) govern claims and payments for a personal independence payment. These regulations are extended to cover claims for universal credit and to the contribution-based forms of jobseeker's allowance and employment and support allowance with effect from April 29, 2013. 2.34

Interpretation

2.35 **2.**—(1) In these Regulations, unless the context otherwise requires—

[20 . . .];

[27 "the 1992 Act" means the Social Security Administration Act 1992;]

[23 "the 2000 Act" means the Electronic Communications Act 2000;]

[22 "the 2002 Act" means the State Pension Credit Act 2002;]

[33 "the 2013 Regulations" means the Universal Credit, Personal Independence Payment, Jobseeker's Allowance and Employment and Support Allowance (Claims and Payments) Regulations 2013;]

[22 "advance period" means the period specified in regulation 4E(2);]

[30 "appropriate office" means an office of the Department for Work and Pensions and where any provision in these Regulations relates to a claim, notice or other information, evidence or document being received by or sent, delivered or otherwise furnished in writing to an appropriate office, include a postal address specified by the Secretary of State for that purpose.]

[36 "bereavement benefit means—

(a) a bereavement payment referred to in section 36 of the Contributions and Benefits Act as in force immediately before it was repealed by paragraph 8 of Schedule 16 to the Pensions Act 2014;

(b) a bereavement allowance referred to in section 39B of the Contributions and Benefits Act as in force immediately before it was repealed by paragraph 13 of Schedule 16 to the Pensions Act 2014;

(c) widowed parent's allowance;

"bereavement support payment" means bereavement support payment under section 30 of the Pensions Act 2014;]

[21 "the Board means the Commissioners of Inland Revenue; and references to "the Board" in these regulations have effect only with respect to working families tax credit;]

[11 "claim for asylum" has the same meaning as in the Asylum and Immigration Appeals Act 1993;]

"claim for benefit" includes—

(a) an application for a declaration that an accident was an industrial accident;

(b) [3. . .]

(c) an application for [14a revision under section 9 of the Social Security Act 1998 or a supersession under section 10 of that Act of] a decision for the purpose of obtaining any increase of benefit [6in respect of a child or adult dependant under the Social Security Act 1975 or an increase in disablement benefit under section 60 (special hardship), 61 (constant attendance), 62 (hospital treatment allowance) or 63 (exceptionally severe disablement) of the Social Security Act 1975], but does not include any other application for [14 a revision under section 9 of the Social Security Act 1998 or a supersession under section 10 of that Act] of a decision;

[15 "Contributions and Benefits Act" means the Social Security Contributions and Benefits Act 1992;]

[34 "couple" means

(a) two people who are married to, or civil partners of, each other and are members of the same household; or
(b) two people who are not married to, or civil partners of, each other but are living together as a married couple;]

[17 "Crown servant posted overseas" means a person performing the duties of any office or employment under the Crown in right of the United Kingdom who is, or was prior to his posting, ordinarily resident in the United Kingdom;]

[13 "'disabled person's tax credit' and 'working families' tax credit" shall be construed in accordance with section 1(1) of the Tax Credits Act 1999]

[23 "electronic communication" has the same meaning as in section 15(1) of the 2000 Act;]

[29 "'the Employment and Support Allowance Regulations'" means the Employment and Support Allowance Regulations 2008;]

[22 "guarantee credit" is to be construed in accordance with sections 1 and 2 of the 2002 Act;]

[26 . . .]

[10 "the Jobseekers Act" means the Jobseekers Act 1995;

"jobseeker's allowance" means an allowance payable under Part I of the Jobseekers Act;

"the Jobseeker's Allowance Regulations" means the Jobseeker's Allowance Regulations 1996;]

[16 "joint-claim couple" and "joint-claim jobseeker's allowance" have the same meaning in these Regulations as they have in the Jobseekers Act by virtue of section 1(4) of that Act;]

[29 "'limited capability for work'" has the same meaning as in section 1(4) of the Welfare Reform Act";]

"long-term benefits" means any retirement pension, [24 a shared additional pension] a widowed mother's allowance, a widow's pension, [15widowed parent's allowance, [36 . . .]] attendance allowance, [5disability living allowance], [19 carer's allowance], [12. . .], any pension or allowance for industrial injury or disease and any increase in any such benefit;

[25 . . .];

"partner" means one of a [25 couple]; [4. . .]

[9 "pension fund holder" means with respect to a personal pension scheme or retirement annuity contract, the trustees, managers or scheme administrators, as the case may be, of the scheme or contract concerned;]

[9 "personal pension scheme" has the same meaning as in section 1 of the Pension Schemes Act 1993 in respect of employed earners and in the case of self-employed earners, includes a scheme approved by the Board of Inland Revenue under Chapter IV of Part XIV of the Income and Corporation Taxes Act 1988;]

[22 "qualifying age" has the same meaning as in the 2002 Act by virtue of section 1(6) of that Act;]

[11 "refugee" means a person recorded by the Secretary of State as a refugee within the definition in Article 1 of the Convention relating to the Status of Refugees done at Geneva on 28th July 1951 as extended by Article 1(2) of the Protocol relating to the Status of Refugees done at New York on 31st January 1967;]

[20 "relevant authority" means a person within section 72(2) of the Welfare Reform and Pensions Act 1999;]

[9 "retirement annuity contract" means a contract or trust scheme approved under Chapter III of Part XIV of the Income and Corporation Taxes Act 1988;]

[24 "shared additional pension" means a shared additional pension under section 55A [35 or 55AA] of the Contributions and Benefits Act;]

[22 "state pension credit" means state pension credit under the 2002 Act;]

[32 "universal credit" means universal credit under Part 1 of the Welfare Reform Act 2012;]

[25 . . .]

"week" means a period of 7 days beginning with midnight between Saturday and Sunday.

[29 " 'the Welfare Reform Act' " means the Welfare Reform Act 2007;]

[15 "widowed parent's allowance" means an allowance referred to in section 39A of the Contributions and Benefits Act;]

[31 "working age benefit" means any of the following—

(a) [36 . . .];
(b) an employment and support allowance;
(c) incapacity benefit;
(d) income support;
(e) a jobseeker's allowance;
(f) widowed mother's allowance;
(g) widowed parent's allowance;
(h) widow's pension.]

(2) Unless the context otherwise requires, any reference in these Regulations to—

(a) a numbered regulation, Part or Schedule is a reference to the regulation, Part or Schedule bearing that number in these Regulations and any reference in a regulation to a numbered paragraph is a reference to the paragraph of that regulation having that number;
(b) a benefit includes any benefit under the Social Security Act 1975 [SSCBA], child benefit under Part I of the Child Benefit Act 1975, income support [22 state pension credit] [7, family credit and disability working allowance under the Social Security Act 1986 [SSCBA] and any social fund payments such as are mentioned in section 32(2) (a) [1and section 32(2A)] of that Act [SSCBA, s.138(1)(a) and (2)] [35 , state pension under Part 1 of the Pensions Act 2014] [10and a jobseeker's allowance under Part I of the Jobseekers Act] [29, a shared additional pension] [36, bereavement support payment] or an employment and support allowance under Part 1 of the Welfare Reform Act.

[10(2A) References in regulations 20, 21 (except paragraphs (3) and (3A)), 29, 30, 32 to 34, 37 (except paragraph (1A)), 37A, 37AA (except paragraph (3)), 37AB, 37B, 38 and 47 to "benefit", "income support" or "a jobseeker's allowance", include a reference to a back to work bonus which, by virtue of regulation 25 of the Social Security (Back to Work Bonus) Regulations 1996, is to be treated as payable as income support or, as the case may be, as a jobseeker's allowance [24 . . .] [29 , a shared additional pension or an employment and support allowance under Part 1 of the Welfare Reform Act].]

(3) For the purposes of the provisions of these Regulations relating to the making of claims every increase of benefit under the Social Security Act 1975 [SSCBA] shall be treated as a separate benefit [12. . .].

[22 (4) In these Regulations references to "beneficiaries" include any person entitled to state pension credit.]

AMENDMENTS

1. The Social Security (Common Provisions) Miscellaneous Amendments Regulations 1988 (SI 1988/1725) reg.3 (November 7, 1988).
2. Transfer of Functions (Health and Social Security) Order 1988 (SI 1988/1843) art.3(4) (November 28, 1988).
3. The Social Security (Medical Evidence, Claims and Payments) Amendment Regulations 1989 (SI 1989/1686) reg.3 (October 9, 1989).
4. The Social Security (Miscellaneous Provisions) Amendment Regulations 1991 (SI 1991/2284) reg.5 (November 1, 1991).
5. The Social Security (Claims and Payments) Amendment Regulations 1991 (SI 1991/2741) reg.2(a) (February 3, 1992).
6. The Social Security (Miscellaneous Provisions) Amendment Regulations 1992 (SI 1992/247) reg.9 (March 9, 1992).
7. The Social Security (Claims and Payments) Amendment Regulations 1991 (SI 1991/2741) reg.2(b) (March 10, 1992).
8. The Social Security (Claims and Payments) Amendment (No.4) Regulations 1994 (SI 1994/3196) reg.2 (January 10, 1995).
9. Income-related benefit Schemes and Social Security (Claims and Payments) (Miscellaneous Amendments) Regulations 1995 (SI 1995/2303) reg.10(2) (October 2, 1995).
10. The Social Security (Claims and Payments) (Jobseeker's Allowance Consequential Amendments) Regulations 1996 (SI 1996/1460) reg.2(2) (October 7, 1996).
11. The Income Support and Social Security (Claims and Payments) (Miscellaneous Amendments) Regulations 1996 (SI 1996/2431) reg.7(a) (October 15, 1996).
12. The Social Security (Claims and Payments) Amendment Regulations 1999 (SI 1999/2358) reg.2 (September 20, 1999) and The Child Benefit, Child Support and Social Security (Miscellaneous Amendments) Regulations 1996 (SI 1996/1803) reg.18 (April 7, 1997).
13. The Tax Credits (Claims and Payments) (Amendment) Regulations 1999 (SI 1999/2572) reg.3 (October 5, 1999).
14. The Social Security Act 1998 (Commencement No.9 and Savings and Consequential and Transitional Provisions) Order 1999 (SI 1999/2422) Sch.7 (September 6, 1999).
15. The Social Security (Benefits for Widows and Widowers) (Consequential Amendments) Regulations 2000 reg.9 (SI 2000/1483) (April 9, 2001).
16. The Social Security (Joint Claims: Consequential Amendments) Regulations 2000 (SI 2000/1982) reg.2(2) (March 19, 2001).
17. Tax Credits (Miscellaneous Amendments No.4) Regulations 2002 (SI 2002/696) reg.2 (July 23, 2002).
18. Social Security (Electronic Communications) (Child Benefit) Order 2002 (SI 2002/1789) art.2 (October 28, 2002); revoked with effect from December 1, 2003.
19. The Social Security Amendment (Carer's Allowance) Regulations 2002 (SI 2002/2497) Sch.2 (October 28, 2002).
20. Social Security Act 1998 Sch.6 (November 29, 1999).
21. Tax Credits (Claims and Payments) (Amendment) Regulations 1999 (SI 1999/2572) reg.3 (October 5, 1999).
22. State Pension Credit (Consequential, Transitional and Miscellaneous Provisions) Regulations 2002 SI 2002/3019 reg.3 (April 7, 2003).
23. The Social Security (Electronic Communications) (Carer's Allowance) Order 2003 (SI 2003/2800) reg.2 (December 1, 2003).
24. The Social Security (Shared Additional Pension) (Miscellaneous Amendments) Regulations 2005 (SI 2005/1551) (July 6, 2005).
25. The Civil Partnership (Pensions, Social Security and Child Support) (Consequential etc. Provisions) Order 2005 (SI 2005/2887) (December 5, 2005).

26. The Social Security (Miscellaneous Amendments) (No.2) Regulations 2006 (SI 2006/832) reg.2 (April 10, 2006).
27. The Social Security (Claims and Payments) Amendment (No.2) Regulations 2006 (SI 2006/3188) (December 27, 2006).
28. The Social Security (Miscellaneous Amendments) (No.2) Regulations 2007 (SI 2007/1626) (July 3, 2007).
29. The Employment and Support Allowance (Consequential Provisions) (No. 2) Regulations 2008 (SI 2008/1554) reg.10 (October 27, 2008).
30. The Social Security (Miscellaneous Amendments) (No.2) Regulations 2009 (SI 2009/1490) reg.2 (July 13, 2009).
31. The Social Security (Miscellaneous Amendments) (No. 6) Regulations 2009 (SI 2009/3229) reg.2 (April 6, 2010).
32. The Universal Credit (Consequential Supplementary, Incidental and Miscellaneous Provisions) Regulations 2013 (SI 2013/630) reg.29(2) (April 29, 2013).
33. The Social Security (Miscellaneous Amendments) (No. 2) Regulations 2013 (SI 2013/1508) reg.2(2) amends reg.2(1) (July 29, 2013).
34. The Marriage (Same Sex Couples) Act 2013 (Consequential Provisions) Order 2014 (SI 2014/107) reg.10 (March 13, 2014).
35. The Pensions Act 2014 (Consequential, Supplementary and Incidental Amendments) Order 2015 (SI 2015/1985) art.9(2) (April 6, 2016).
36. The Pensions Act 2014 (Consequential, Supplementary and Incidental Amendments) Order 2017 (SI 2017/422) art.10 (April 6, 2017).

GENERAL NOTE

2.36 Section 15(1) of the Electronic Communications Act 2000 defines "electronic communication" as follows:

> "'electronic communication' means a communication transmitted (whether from one person to another, from one device to another or from a person to a device or vice versa)—
> (a) by means of a telecommunication system (within the meaning of the Telecommunications Act 1984); or
> (b) by other means but while in an electronic form;"

With effect from December 16, 2014, art.29 and Sch.6 para.6 of the Marriage and Civil Partnership (Scotland) Act 2014 and Civil Partnership Act 2004 (Consequential Provisions and Modifications Order 2001 (SI 2014/3229) amended the definition of "couple" by substituting a definition in the same terms as the existing definition. However, the existing definition applied only to England and Wales; the new definition applies to England, Wales, Scotland and Northern Ireland.

PART II

CLAIMS

Claims not required for entitlement to benefit in certain cases

2.37 **3.**—[17—(1)] It shall not be a condition of entitlement to benefit that a claim be made for it in the following cases—

[15 (za) in the case of a Category A or B retirement pension, where the beneficiary is a person to whom regulation 3A applies;]

(a) In the case of a Category C retirement pension where the beneficiary is in receipt of—
 (i) another retirement pension under the Social Security Act 1975; or

(ii) widow's benefit under Chapter 1 of Part II of that Act; or

(iii) benefit by virtue of section 39(4) of that Act corresponding to a widow's pension or a widowed mother's allowance;

[19 (iv) widowed parent's allowance;]]

(b) in the case of a Category D retirement pension where the beneficiary—

(i) was ordinarily resident in great Britain on the day on which he attained 80 years of age; and

(ii) is in receipt of another retirement pension under the Social Security Act 1975;

(c) age addition in any case;

[10 (ca) in the case of a Category A retirement pension where the beneficiary—

(i) is entitled to any category of retirement pension other than a Category A retirement pension; and

(ii) becomes divorced or the beneficiary's civil partnership is dissolved;]

[11 (cb) in the case of a Category B retirement pension where the beneficiary is entitled to either a Category A retirement pensions or to a graduated retirement benefit or to both and

(i) the spouse or civil partner of the beneficiary becomes entitled to a Category A retirement pension [18 or a state pension under section 4 of the Pensions Act 2014]; or

(ii) the beneficiary marries or enters into a civil partnership with a person who is entitled to a Category A retirement pension [18 or a state pension under section 4 of the Pensions Act 2014];]

[14 or

(iii) the spouse or civil partner of the beneficiary dies having been entitled to a Category A retirement pension [18 or a state pension under section 4 of the Pensions Act 2014] at the date of death;]

(d) in the case of a Category A or B retirement pension [18 or a state pension under Part 1 of the Pensions Act 2014]—

(i) where the beneficiary is a woman over the age of 65 and entitled to a widowed mother's allowance [6 or widowed parent's allowance], on her ceasing to be so entitled; or

(ii) where the beneficiary is a woman under the age of 65 and in receipt of widow's pension [19 . . .], on her attaining that age

[10 . . .]

[19 . . .]

(e) [1in the case of retirement allowance]

(f) [2. . .]

(g) [3 in the case of a jobseeker's allowance where—

(i) payment of benefit has been suspended in the circumstances described in regulation 16(2) of the Social Security and Child Support (Decisions and Appeals) Regulations 1999; and

(ii) the claimant whose benefit has been suspended satisfies the conditions of entitlement (apart from the requirement to claim) to that benefit immediately before the suspension ends.]

(h) [5 in the case of income support where the beneficiary—

(i) is a person to whom regulation [8 . . .] [7 or 6(5)] of the Income

only in a case where, on the day which falls 8 weeks before the day on which the beneficiary reaches pensionable age, the beneficiary—

(a) is in receipt of an exempt benefit, or would be in receipt of it but for that benefit not being payable as a result of the application of any of the legislation listed in paragraph (7); and

(b) is neither entitled to, nor awaiting the determination of a claim for, a non-exempt benefit.

(4) Receipt of a written notification under paragraph (1) does not affect the requirement that a beneficiary who—

(a) before reaching pensionable age, informs the Secretary of State that they want their entitlement to a Category A or B retirement pension to be deferred in accordance with section 55(3)(a) of the Contributions and Benefits Act(a); or

(b) after reaching pensionable age, elects to be treated as not having become entitled to either a Category A or B retirement pension in accordance with regulation 2 of the Social Security (Widow's Benefit and Retirement Pensions) Regulations 1979(b),

must make a claim in order subsequently to be entitled to a Category A or B retirement pension.

(5) For the purposes of paragraph (3)(a), a beneficiary who is in receipt of an exempt benefit includes a beneficiary who—

(a) has been awarded such a benefit on or before the day which falls 8 weeks before the day on which the beneficiary reaches pensionable age; and

(b) has not yet received the first payment of that benefit.

(6) For the purposes of this regulation—

"exempt benefit" means any of the following—

(a) an employment and support allowance;

(b) income support;

(c) a jobseeker's allowance;

(d) long-term incapacity benefit;

(e) state pension credit; and

"non-exempt benefit" means any of the following—

(a) carer's allowance;

(b) short-term incapacity benefit;

(c) severe disablement allowance;

(d) widowed mother's allowance;

(e) widow's pension.

(7) The legislation referred to in paragraph (3)(a) is—

(a) section 19 of the Jobseekers Act(a)(circumstances in which a jobseeker's allowance is not payable);

(b) section 20A of that Act(b)(denial or reduction of joint-claim jobseeker's allowance);

(c) regulations made by virtue of any of the following provisions of the Jobseekers Act—

(i) section 8(2)(a)(c)(attendance, information and evidence);

(ii) section 17A(5)(d)(d)(schemes for assisting persons to obtain employment: "work for your benefit" schemes etc.);

(iii) paragraph 7(1)(a) of Schedule A1(e)(persons dependent on drugs etc.);

[2 (ca) any provision of the Social Security Fraud Act 2001 and regulations made by virtue of any such provision.]

(d) regulation 18 of the Social Security (Incapacity for Work) (General) Regulations 1995(f) (disqualification for misconduct etc.); and
(e) regulation 157 of the Employment and Support Allowance Regulations (disqualification for misconduct etc.).]

AMENDMENTS

1. Social Security (Exemption from Claiming Retirement Pension) Regulations 2010 (SI 2010/1794) reg.2 (November 2, 2010).
2. The Social Security (Exemption from Claiming Retirement Pension) Regulations 2011 (SI 2011/1554) reg.3A (October 11, 2011).

Making a claim for benefit

4.—(1) [[13] Subject to [[21] paragraphs (10) to (11B)], every] claim for benefit [[7]other than a claim for income support or jobsseeker's allowance] shall be made in writing on a form approved by the Secretary of State [[3]for the purpose of the benefit for which the claim is made], or in such other manner, being in writing, as the Secretary of State [[8] or the Board] may accept as sufficient in the circumstances of any particular case. 2.40

[[7] (1A) [[21] Subject to paragraph (11A), in the case of] a claim for income support or jobseeker's allowance, the claim shall—
(a) be made in writing on a form approved by the Secretary of State for the purpose of the benefit for which the claim is made;
(b) unless any of the reasons specified in paragraph (1B) applies, be made in accordance with the instructions on the form; and
(c) unless any of the reasons specified in paragraph (1B) applies, include such information and evidence as the form may require in connection with the claim.

(1B) The reasons referred to in paragraph (1A) are—
(a) [[10] subject paragraph (IBA)—
 (i) the person making the claim is unable to complete the form in accordance with the instructions or to obtain the information or evidence it requires because he has a physical, learning, mental or communication difficulty; and
 (ii) it is not reasonably practicable for the claimant to obtain assistance from another person to complete the form or obtain the information or evidence; or
(b) the information or evidence required by the form does not exist; or
(c) the information or evidence required by the form can only be obtained at serious risk of physical or mental harm to the claimant, and it is not reasonably practicable for the claimant to obtain the information or evidence by other means; or
(d) the information or evidence required by the form can only be obtained from a third party, and it is not reasonably practicable for the claimant to obtain such information or evidence from such third party; or
(e) the Secretary of State is of the opinion that the person making the claim [[10]or, in the case of claim for a jobseeker's allowance by a joint-claim couple, either member of that couple,] has provided sufficient information or evidence to show that he is not entitled to the benefit for which the claim is made, and that it would be inappropriate to

require the form to be completed or further information or evidence to be supplied.

[10 (1BA) In the case of a joint-claim couple claiming a jobseeker's allowance jointly, paragraph (1B)(a) shall not apply to the extent that it is reasonably practicable for a member of a joint-claim couple to whom that sub-paragraph applies to obtain assistance from the other member of that couple.]

(1C) If a person making a claim is unable to complete the claim form or supply the evidence or information it requires because one of the reasons specified in sub-paragraphs (a) to (d) of paragraph (1B) applies, he may so notify an appropriate office by whatever means.]

[18 (1D) In calculating any period of one month for the purposes of paragraph (7) and regulation 6(1A)(b), there shall be disregarded any period commencing on a day on which a person is first notified of a decision that he failed to take part in a work-focused interview and ending on a day on which he was notified that that decision has been revised so that the decision as revised is that he did take part.]

(2) [8In the case of a claim for working families' tax credit, where a married or unmarried couple is included in the family, the claim shall be made by whichever partner they agree should so claim.

(2A) Where, in a case to which paragraph (2) applies, the partners are unable to agree which of them should make the claim, the Board may in their discretion determine that the claim shall be made by the partner who, on the information available to the Board at the time of their determination, is in their opinion mainly caring for the children.]

(3) [5Subject to paragraph (3C),] in the case of a [16 couple], a claim for income support shall be made by whichever partner they agree should so claim or, in default of agreement, by such one of them as the Secretary of State shall in his discretion determine.

[2(3A) In the case of a married or unmarried couple where both partners satisfy the conditions set out in [8 section 129(1) of the Social Security Contributions and Benefits Act 1992], a claim for [8 disabled persons tax credit] shall be made by whichever partner they agree should so claim, or in default of agreement, by such one of them as [8 the Board] shall determine.]

[4(3B) For the purposes of income-based jobseeker's allowance—

(a) in the case of a [16 couple], a claim shall be made by whichever partner they agree should so claim or, in default of agreement, by such one of them as the Secretary of State shall in his discretion determine;

(b) [10 (b) where there is no entitlement to a contribution-based jobseeker's allowance on a claim made—

(i) by a member of a joint-claim couple, he subsequently claims a joint-claim jobseeker's allowance with the other member of that couple, the claim made by the couple shall be treated as having been made on the date on which the member of that couple made the claim for a jobseeker's allowance in respect of which there was no entitlement to contribution-based jobseeker's allowance;

(ii) by one partner and the other partner wishes to claim incomebased jobseeker's allowance, the claim made by that other partner shall be treated as having been made on the date on which the first partner made his claim;]

(c) where entitlement to income-based jobseeker's allowance arises on the expiry of entitlement to contribution-based jobseeker's allowance consequent on a claim made by one partner and the other partner then makes a claim—

(i) the claim of the first partner shall be terminated; and

(ii) the claim of the second partner shall be treated as having been made on the day after the entitlement to contribution-based jobseeker's allowance expired.]

[5(3C) In the case of a claim for income support for a period to which [9 regulation 21ZB(2)] of the Income Support (General) Regulations 1987 (treatment of refugees) refers, the claim shall be made by the refugee or in the case of a [16 couple] both of whom are refugees, by either of them.]

(4) Where one of a [16 couple] is entitled to income support under an award and, with his agreement, his partner claims income support that entitlement shall terminate on the day before that claim is made or treated as made.

[6(5) Where a person who wishes to make a claim for benefit and who has not been supplied with an approved form of claim notifies an appropriate office (by whatever means) of his intention to make a claim, he [10or if he is a member of a joint-claim couple, either member of that couple] shall be supplied, without charge, with such form of claim by such person as the Secretary of State [8 or the Board] may appoint or authorise for that purpose.]

[4(6) [12 Subject to paragraphs (6A) to (6D),] A person wishing to make a claim for benefit shall—

(a) if it is a claim for a jobseeker's allowance, unless the Secretary of State otherwise directs, attend in person at an appropriate office or such other place, and at such time, as the Secretary of State may specify in his case in a [10notification under regulation 23 or 23A] of the Jobseeker's Allowance Regulations;

(b) if it is a claim for any other benefit, deliver or send the claim to an appropriate office.]

[12 (6A) [19 This paragraph applies to a person]—

(a) who has attained the qualifying age and makes a claim for—

(i) an attendance allowance, [29 widowed parent's allowance] a carer's allowance, a disability living allowance or incapacity benefit; or

(ii) a retirement pension of any category [27 , a state pension under Part 1 of the Pensions Act 2014] [15 or a shared additional pension] for which a claim is required or a winter fuel payment for which a claim is required under regulation 3(1)(b) of the Social Fund Winter Fuel Payment Regulations 2000;

(b) who has not yet attained the qualifying age and makes a claim for a retirement pension [27 , a state pension under Part 1 of the Pensions Act 2014] [15 or a shared additional pension] in advance in accordance with regulation 15(1); [17 . . .]

[19 (c) who makes a claim for income support; or

(d) who has not attained the qualifying age and who makes a claim for a carer's allowance, disability living allowance [22, incapacity benefit or an employment and support allowance.]]

(6B) A person to whom paragraph (6A) applies may make a claim by sending or delivering it to, or by making it in person at—

(a) an office designated by the Secretary of State for accepting such claims; [17 . . .]

[19 (b) the offices of—

(i) a local authority administering housing benefit [25 . . .]

(ii) a county council in England,
(iii) a person providing services to a person mentioned in head (i) or (ii),
(iv) a person authorised to exercise any function of a local authority relating to housing benefit [25 . . .], or
(v) a person authorised to exercise any function a county council in England has under section 7A of the Social Security Administration Act 1992,

if the Secretary of State has arranged with the local authority, county council or other person for them to receive claims in accordance with this sub-paragraph.]

(6C) Where a person to whom paragraph (6A) applies makes a claim in accordance with paragraph (6B)(b), on receipt of the claim the local authority or other person specified in that sub-paragraph—

(a) shall forward the claim to the Secretary of State as soon as reasonably practicable;
(b) may receive information or evidence relating to the claim supplied by—
   (i) the person making, or who has made, the claim; or
   (ii) other persons in connection with the claim,

   and shall forward it to the Secretary of State as soon as reasonably practicable;
(c) may obtain information or evidence relating to the claim from the person who has made the claim, but not any medical information or evidence except for that which the claimant must provide in accordance with instructions on the form, and shall forward the information or evidence to the Secretary of State as soon as reasonably practicable;

[19(cc) may verify any non-medical information or evidence supplied or obtained in accordance with sub-paragraph (b) or (c) and shall forward it to the Secretary of State as soon as reasonably practicable;]

(d) may record information or evidence relating to the claim supplied or obtained in accordance with sub-paragraphs (b) or (c) and may hold the information or evidence (whether as supplied or obtained or as recorded) for the purpose of forwarding it to the Secretary of State; and
(e) may give information and advice with respect to the claim to the person who makes, or who has made, the claim.

[14 (6CC) Paragraphs (6C)(b) to (e) apply in respect of information, evidence and advice relating to any claim by a person to whom paragraph (6A) applies, whether the claim is made in accordance with paragraph (6B)(b) or otherwise.]

(6D) The benefits specified in paragraph (6A) are relevant benefits for the purposes of section 7A of the Social Security Administration Act 1992.]

[22 (7) If a claim, other than a claim for income support or jobseeker's allowance, is defective at the date it is received in an appropriate office or office specified in paragraph (6B) where that paragraph applies—

(a) the Secretary of State shall advise the claimant of the defect; and
(b) if a properly completed claim is received within one month, or such longer period as the Secretary of State may consider reasonable, from the date on which the claimant is [23 first] advised of the defect, the Secretary of State shall treat the claim as properly made in the first instance.

(7ZA) If a claim, other than a claim for income support or jobseeker's allowance, has been made in writing but not on the form approved for the time being—

(a) the Secretary of State may supply the claimant with the approved form; and

(b) if the form is received properly completed within one month, or such longer period as the Secretary of State may consider reasonable, from the date on which the claimant is supplied with the approved form, the Secretary of State shall treat the claim as properly made in the first instance.]

[10 (7A) In the case of a claim for income support, if a defective claim is received, the Secretary of State shall advise the person making the claim of the defect and of the relevant provisions of regulation 6(1A) relating to the date of claim.

(7B) In the case of a claim for a jobseeker's allowance, if a defective claim is received, the Secretary of State shall advise—

(a) in the case of a claim made by a joint-claim couple, each member of the couple of the defect and of the relevant provisions of regulation 6(4ZA) relating to the date of that claim;

(b) in any other case, the person making the claim of the defect and of the relevant provisions of regulation 6(4A) relating to the date of claim.]

(8) A claim, other than a claim for income support or jobseeker's allowance, which is made on the form approved for the time being is, for the purposes of these Regulations, properly completed if completed in accordance with the instructions on the form and defective if not so completed.

[8(8A) Where—

(a) the Board determine under paragraph (2A) that a claim for working families' tax credit shall be made by the partner who in their opinion is mainly caring for the children,

(b) a claim for working families' tax credit is made by that partner on the form approved for the time being, and

(c) the claim is not completed in accordance with the instructions on the form by reason only that, in consequence of the other partner not agreeing which of them should make the claim, it has not been signed by the other partner

the Board may in their discretion treat that claim as completed in accordance with the instructions on the form for the purposes of paragraph (8), notwithstanding that it has not been signed by the other partner in accordance with those instructions.]

(9) In the case of a claim for income support or jobseeker's allowance, a properly completed claim is a claim which meets the requirements of paragraph (1A) and a defective claim is a claim which does not meet those requirements.]

[11 (10) This regulation shall not apply to a claim for state pension credit [22, subject to regulation 6(1G)], [20 or an employment and support allowance.]

[28 (11) A claim for the following benefits may be made by telephone call to a telephone number specified by the Secretary of State for the purpose of the benefit for which the claim is made, unless the Secretary of State directs, in any particular case, that the claim must be made in writing—

(a) graduated retirement benefit;

(b) a shared additional pension;

(c) a retirement pension;
(d) a state pension under Part 1 of the Pensions Act 2014;
[29 (e) widowed parent's allowance;
(ea) bereavement support payment;]
(f) a social fund payment for funeral expenses or winter fuel payment;
(g) industrial injuries benefit.]

[21 (11A) A claim for income support or jobseeker's allowance may be made by telephone call to the telephone number specified by the Secretary of State where such a claim falls within a category of case [22 for which the Secretary of State accepts telephone claims, or in any other case where the Secretary of State is willing to do so]

(11B) Paragraph (11A) shall apply unless in any particular case the Secretary of State directs that the claim must be made in writing.]

[22 (12) A claim made by telephone in accordance with paragraph (11) or (11A) is properly completed if the Secretary of State is provided with all the information required to determine the claim and the claim is defective if not so completed.

(13) Where a claim made by telephone is defective—
(a) in the case of a claim other than a claim for income support or jobseeker's allowance, paragraph (7) applies;
(b) in the case of a claim for income support, paragraph (7A) applies; and
(c) in the case of a claim for jobseeker's allowance, paragraph (7B) applies,

except that references to a defective claim being received or received in an appropriate office or office specified in paragraph (6B) where that paragraph applies are to be read as references to a defective claim being made by telephone and the reference in paragraph (7)(b) to a properly completed claim being received is to be read as a reference to a claim made by telephone being properly completed.]

[22 . . .]

AMENDMENTS

1. The Social Security (Miscellaneous Provisions) Amendment Regulations 1990 (SI 1990/2208) reg.8 (December 5, 1990).

2. The Social Security (Claims and Payments) Amendment Regulations 1991 (SI 1991/2741) reg.3 (February 3, 1992).

3. The Social Security (Miscellaneous Provisions) Amendment Regulations 1992 (SI 1992/247) reg.10 (March 9, 1992).

4. The Social Security (Claims and Payments) (Jobseeker's Allowance Consequential Amendments) Regulations 1996 (SI 1996/1460) reg.2(4) (October 7, 1996).

5. The Income Support and Social Security (Claims and Payments) (Miscellaneous Amendments) Regulations 1996 (SI 1996/2431) reg.7(b) (October 15, 1996).

6. The Social Security (Miscellaneous Amendments) (No.2) Regulations 1997 (SI 1997/793) reg.2(4) (April 7, 1997).

7. The Social Security (Miscellaneous Amendments) (No.2) Regulations 1997 (SI 1997/793) reg.2 (October 6, 1997).

8. The Tax Credits (Claims and Payments) (Amendment) Regulations 1999 (SI 1999/2572) reg.4 (October 5, 1999).

9. The Social Security (Immigration and Asylum) Consequential Amendments Regulations 2000 (SI 2000/636) (April 3, 2000).

10. The Social Security (Joint Claims: Consequential Amendments) Regulations 2000 (SI 2000/1982) reg.2(3) (March 19, 2001).

11. State Pension Credit (Consequential, Transitional and Miscellaneous Provisions) Regulations 2002 (SI 2002/3019) reg.4 (April 7, 2003).

12. The Social Security (Claims and Payments and Miscellaneous Amendments) Regulations 2003 (SI 2003/1632) reg.2(2) (July 21, 2003).
13. The Social Security (Claims and Payments and Payments on account, Overpayments and Recovery) Amendment Regulations 2005 (SI 2005/34) reg.2 (May 2, 2005).
14. The Social Security, Child Support and Tax Credits (Miscellaneous Amendments) Regulations 2005 (SI 2005/337) reg.7 (March 18, 2005).
15. The Social Security (Shared Additional Pension) (Miscellaneous Amendments) Regulations 2005 (SI 2005/1551) (July 6, 2005).
16. The Civil Partnership (Pensions, Social Security and Child Support) (Consequential etc. Provisions) Order 2005 (SI 2005/2887) (December 5, 2005).
17. The Social Security (Miscellaneous Amendments) (No.2) Regulations 2006 (SI 2006/832) (April 10, 2006).
18. The Social Security (Work-focused Interviews) Regulations 2000 (SI 2000/897) (April 3, 2000).
19. The Social Security (Claims and Information) Regulations 2007 (SI 2007/2911) (October 31, 2007).
20. The Employment and Support Allowance (Consequential Provisions) (No.2) Regulations 2008 (SI 2008/1554) reg.12 (October 27, 2008).
21. The Social Security (Miscellaneous Amendments) (No. 5) Regulations 2008 (SI 2008/2667) reg.2 (October 30, 2008).
22. The Social Security (Miscellaneous Amendments) (No.2) Regulations 2009 (SI 2009/1490) reg.2 (July 13, 2009).
23. The Social Security (Miscellaneous Amendments) (No.4) Regulations 2009 (SI 2009/2655) reg.3 (October 26, 2009).
24. Social Security (Claims and Payments) Amendment (No.3) Regulations 2010 (SI 2010/1676) reg.2 (July 29, 2010).
25. The Council Tax Benefit Abolition (Consequential Provision) Regulations 2013 (SI 2013/458) reg.3 (April 1, 2013).
26. The Social Security (Miscellaneous Amendments) Regulations 2014 (SI 2014/591) reg.3 (April 28, 2014).
27. The Pensions Act 2014 (Consequential, Supplementary and Incidental Amendments) Order 2015 (SI 2015/1985) art.9(4) (April 6, 2016).
28. Social Security (Claims and Payments) Amendment Regulations 2016 (SI 2016/544) reg.2 (June 15, 2016).
29. The Pensions Act 2014 (Consequential, Supplementary and Incidental Amendments) Order 2017 (SI 2017/422) art.10 (April 6, 2017).

Definitions

"appropriate office"—see reg.2(1).
"benefit"—see reg.2(2).
"claim for benefit"—see reg.2(1).
"jobseeker's allowance"—*ibid.*
"married couple"—*ibid.*
"partner"—*ibid.*
"refugee"—*ibid.*
"unmarried couple"—*ibid.*

General Note

Introduction

Note that this regulation does not apply to claims for state pension credit, or for an employment and support allowance: para.(10). 2.41

Section 1 of the Administration Act requires a claim to be submitted for any benefit to which the section applies except where regulations otherwise prescribe (see reg.3), as a condition of entitlement to benefit. This largely removes the effect of the decision of the House of Lords in *Insurance Officer v McCaffrey* [1984] 1 W.L.R. 1353, though some doubt remained in relation to entitlement prior to September 2, 1985, when the first version of s.1 was implemented. This is now resolved by s.2 of the Administrative Act.

The claims system is largely predicated on a system of written claims, but recent amendments now make provision for telephone claims.

2.42 A fine line used to be drawn between the responsibilities of the Secretary of State and the adjudicating authorities under this regulation. It has been consistently held that it is for the Secretary of State to say whether a document (not in the prescribed form) is acceptable as "sufficient in the circumstances of the particular case," but the duty lies on the adjudicating authorities to decide whether such a document is a claim for benefit: *R(U) 9/60* and *R(S) 1/63*. It may be significant that in both these cases the Commissioner concluded that a document accepted by the Secretary of State did not constitute a claim for benefit. It is sometimes argued that the Secretary of State's authority under para.(1) extends to determining the date of the claim. This is not so. The sole issue reserved for the Secretary of State under para.(1) is whether the *form* of the claim (if not on a prescribed form) is acceptable as a claim. It is left for decision makers and tribunals to determine the date of the claim and what has been claimed once the Secretary of State has determined that it is in acceptable form: *R(SB) 5/89* confirmed in *CU/94/1994*. This distinction now largely disappears with the abolition of adjudication officers.

Novitskaya v London Borough of Brent (SSWP intervening) [2009] EWCA Civ 1260; [2010] AACR 6, is a judgment on a housing benefit claim, but the propositions stated by the Court of Appeal must relate to the general concept of a claim for benefit. The Court of Appeal ruled that a claim did not need to be in any particular form, nor did it need to name a benefit, but it must raise the possibility of its being a claim for benefit. Referring to *R(S) 1/63*, Arden L.J. said:

> "19. While this is a very helpful decision, excessive reliance should not be placed on the Commissioner's statement that the intention to claim benefit should appear on the face of the document alleged to constitute a claim. Claims are no different from any other document requiring interpretation and it is now well-established that the meaning of documents should be ascertained in the light of the relevant surrounding facts (*Investors Compensation Scheme Ltd v West Bromwich Building Society* [1998] 1 WLR 896). Thus, it may be possible to infer that a claim is being made from some other document. The Commissioner refers to the possibility that an accompanying letter might be enough to make it clear that another document was making a claim. In my view this is certainly legally possible."

A claim not in the prescribed form would be a defective claim, but that defect would be capable of being corrected, and would not necessarily defeat the claim altogether. In response to the judgment the Department has three principles for determining guidance in Memo DMG 3/10, which suggests the application of three principles of determining whether a claim not on an official claim form is a claim for benefit (albeit defective):

(1) The contested document should be able to be read as a claim for benefit and not simply as a request for information.

(2) A particular benefit does not necessarily have to be named; but there is a clear inference that the vaguer the document the less likely it will be that decision maker will conclude that it is a defective claim for benefit rather than some other communication.

(3) The contested document should not be considered in isolation, but should be read in the context of any accompanying documents or statements made to the Department by the author of the document.

The issue of whether tribunals have jurisdiction to consider the decision of the Secretary of State as to when a claim was validly made where it is initially defective has been considered in cases *R(IS) 6/04* and *CIS/758/2002*. The Commissioner, in *R(IS) 6/04,* ruled that the absence of a right of appeal was incompatible with art.6 of the European Convention, and so disapplied the provision in Sch.2 to the Decisions and Appeals Regulations in so far as it was necessary to do so in order to ensure that the claimant was entitled to appeal against a decision as to whether or when a claim had been validly made in accordance with this regulation. This has restored the position to that which previously applied before the SSA 1998 entered into force: see *R(U)9/60.* 2.43

On the substance of what is required for a valid claim, the Commissioner has this to say:

> "I do not think an over-literal approach should be taken in this context: if, for example, all the figures required to determine entitlement are supplied and identified sufficiently clearly when the claimant submits his claim, either in answers recorded on the claim form itself or in annexed documents to which those answers expressly or impliedly refer, then it would in my judgment be open to a tribunal to hold on the facts that there has been no *material* failure such as to render the claim and the information supplied with it incomplete, even if admittedly the claimant has not complied with the instructions to the letter by repeating the actual figures in the boxes on the form itself. In addition, it seems to have been regarded as a defect fatal to the *claim* that he only gave details of his bank, and not of a Post Office, in the part of the form that asked him about the method of *payment* he preferred if benefit was in due course awarded." (para.54)

and:

> "I direct the tribunal that for this purpose they should concern themselves only with the matters and information necessary to determine entitlement to the benefit claimed. It seems to me that both sides are right in saying, as Mr Wright submits and Mr Spencer very fairly agrees in the most recent written submissions, that the requirements in regulation 4(1A)(b)–(c) strictly concern the information and evidence required in connection with the *claim* so as to enable it to be determined; not such things as the administrative arrangements for payment of any benefit that may subsequently be awarded on that claim. Thus even though it is of course convenient and sensible for the claimant to be asked about these at the same time and to put them on the same form, the omission of such additional details as the Post Office, needed (if at all) only for payment purposes (and as Mr Spencer points out, not in any event crucial or binding so far as the Secretary of State is concerned, under regulation 20 of the Claims and Payments regulations) does not render an otherwise complete claim defective." (para.56)

CIS/758/2002 added a gloss on this case in relation to defective claims for income support or a jobseeker's allowance, namely that the mandatory four week time limit for correcting defects on the claim form is not contrary to Convention rights protected by the Human Rights Act 1998 when compared with the longer discretionary time limit allowed for correcting defects in claims for other benefits. This is said to be because income support and income-based jobseeker's allowance are not possessions for the purposes of the protection of property rights under art.1 of Protocol 1 of the European Convention, although that proposition is almost certainly no longer good law following the decision of the Grand Chamber in the *Stec* case: see annotations to art.1 of Protocol 1 at para 4.90.

Once a claim has been made, it may only be withdrawn before it has been adjudicated upon by an adjudication officer (now decision maker): *R(U)2/79* and *R(U)7/83* and see reg.5(2).

Paragraph (1)

2.44 Unless provision is made for telephone claims, para.(1) provides that claims must be made in writing, normally on an official form, although the Secretary of State may accept some other kind of written claim. In such a case, under para.(7), the Secretary of State may require the claimant to fill in the proper form. If this is done in the proper time the claim is treated as duly made in the first instance. It no longer seems possible for an oral claim to be accepted, but see below on telephone claims. However, see reg.6(1)(aa) for the position when a claimant contacts an office with a view to making a claim.

Note also *R(SB) 9/84* where a Tribunal of Commissioners holds that where a claim has been determined, the Secretary of State must be deemed, in the absence of any challenge at the time, to have accepted that the claim was made in sufficient manner. See the notes to reg.33. See also *CDLA/1596/1996* in which the Commissioner set aside the tribunal's decision because they had failed to consider whether they should refer to the Secretary of State the question whether the claimant's application for review should be treated as a claim under para.(1).

MS v SSWP (JSA) [2016] UKUT 206 (AAC) establishes that the defective claim rule in reg.4(1) is limited to information or evidence required by the claim form and not that required at a later interview. Judge Wright said:

> "10. It is thus apparent from the wording of regulation 4(9) that the statutory 'defective claim' is limited to a claim which does not meet the requirements of regulation 4(1A) alone. Moreover, and most importantly for the purposes of this appeal, the information or evidence (the lack of which, or failure to provide which may render a claim defective) has to be information or evidence that has been required by the claim form as the . . . words ['as the form may require'] in regulation 4(1A)(c) and the 'required by the form' language in regulation 4(1B) in my judgment make evident. Information or evidence required other than by the claim form, at a follow-up interview for example, cannot therefore make the claim 'defective' if not provided."

In *SSWP v BM (RP)* [2016] UKUT 419 (AAC), the claimant had deferred his entitlement to a retirement pension for some years. He sent in a letter on March 6, 2015 claiming his retirement pension and stating that he would "like to receive any back-dated payments from my 65th birthday onwards to which I am entitled." The claimant died on 11 March. The administrator of the claimant's estate subsequently completed a formal claim form, but the Secretary of State only awarded retirement pension including three months' arrears prior to the date of claim. The letter setting out the decision said that the administrator did not have the option of choosing a lump sum payment on behalf of the claimant's estate because the claimant had not made the claim before he died. The First-tier Tribunal found as a fact that the letter had been received by the Department on March 9, that it was a valid claim, and that the claimant had made clear that he wanted a lump sum payment. But, in the alternative, if he had not, he was deemed to have chosen a lump sum because of para.A1(2) of Sch.5 to the Contributions and Benefits Act.

Two issues were before the Upper Tribunal: (1) whether the First-tier Tribunal had erred in law in concluding that the Department received the letter on March 9; and (2) whether the claim was procedurally effective. Judge Markus QC analyses the case law on posting and its receipt, and rejects the argument that the First-tier Tribunal had erred in applying s.7 of the Interpretation Act 1978; the tribunal had rather made a finding of fact that was open to it in the light of the all the circumstances. There was, just to mention one factor, no date stamp on the claimant's letter. Judge Markus QC says, in a context in which the Department admitted receipt of the letter but asserted that it was not received until March 12:

> "The tribunal was entitled to take judicial notice of Royal Mail practice and to find, in the absence of any evidence to the contrary, that it was likely that collection and delivery occurred accordingly." (para.21)

Judge Markus QC also upholds the First-tier Tribunal's finding that the letter constituted a claim. The Secretary of State argued that the administrator was not able to perfect the claim by providing the information missing from the initial letter. Judge Markus disagreed; *R(IS) 3/04* did not apply; the Claims and Payments Regulations make different provision for claims to income support and claims to retirement pension. In this case, the administrator must have been acting under an appointment covered by reg.30(1)—and not reg.30(6)—and this enabled the administrator to perfect the claim. Finally, Judge Markus sees no error of law in the First-tier Tribunal's concluding that the import of the claimant's letter of 6 March was that he wanted a lump sum payment.

Paragraphs (1A)–(1C)

These provisions, together with reg.6(1A) and (4A)–(4AB), introduce the so-called 2.45
"onus of proof" changes for claims for income support and JSA from October 6, 1997. The aim is to place more responsibility on claimants for these benefits to provide information and evidence to support their claim (see the DSS's Memorandum to the Social Security Advisory Committee (SSAC) annexed to the Committee's report (Cmnd. 3586) on the proposals). SSAC supported this principle but considered that it was "premature to introduce penalties for failure to provide information when it is more likely that the current problems lie more with the forms and procedures than with dilatory or obstructive claimants". As the Committee pointed out, the current claim forms are lengthy, complex and difficult for many people to understand, and moreover in the past told claimants not to delay sending in the claim form even if they had not got all the required information. Furthermore, since income support and income-based JSA are basic subsistence benefits, claimants have every incentive to cooperate in providing all the information needed to get an early payment. Thus SSAC's main recommendation was that the claim forms and guidance to claimants should first be revised and tested "before introducing new penalties, which together with the proposed changes to backdating rules [see reg.19], will only serve to complicate the social security system and penalise the most disadvantaged claimants". But this recommendation was rejected by the Government, although the final form of the regulations did take limited account of some of SSAC's other recommendations.

Under the rules, in order for a claim for income support or JSA to be validly made, it must be in writing (unless telephone claims are permitted) on a properly completed approved form (there is no longer any provision for the Secretary of State to accept any other kind of written claim) and all the information and evidence required by the form must have been provided (para.(1A)). However, the requirement to complete the form fully or to provide the required evidence does not apply in the circumstances set out in para.(1B). The list in para.(1B) is exhaustive and there is no category of analogous circumstances. If any of sub-paras (a)–(d) of para.(1B) do apply, the person can inform an appropriate office (defined in reg.2(1)) "by whatever means" (e.g. verbally or through a third party) (para.(1C)). Note that the obligation to provide information and evidence only relates to that required by the claim form; if a claim is accepted as validly made it will still be open to the Department to seek further information if this is required in order to decide the claim, but this will not alter the date of claim.

See reg.6(1A) for the date of claim for an income support claim and reg.6(4A)–(4AB) for the date of claim for JSA claims (and note the differences).

Thus the major effect of these rules is that there is a requirement to produce the 2.46
specified information and evidence *before* a claim is treated as having been made (although see reg.6(1A) and (4A)–(4AB) for the date of claim). Whether the necessary evidence has been produced or whether a claimant is exempt under para.(1B) will, however, now be subject to appeal to a tribunal, on the application, by analogy, of the principle established in *R(IS) 6/04*. The contrary position which has been set out in earlier editions and was approved by the Commissioner in *CJSA/69/2001* would seem to be inconsistent with the approach adopted in *R(IS) 6/04*.

For a decision addressing the proper approach to a case in which a person seeks to resurrect a claim for income support some considerable time after sending in a letter indicating an intention to claim income support, see *IJ v SSWP (IS)* [2013] UKUT 302 (AAC).

For a decision exploring issues which can arise when an electronic claim for a jobseeker's allowance goes wrong, see *CW v SSWP (JSA)* [2016] UKUT 114 (AAC).

Note also s.1(1A) of the Administration Act, under which claimants will not be entitled to benefit unless they satisfy requirements relating to the provision of national insurance numbers.

Paragraphs (2) and (2A)

2.47 In working families' tax credit cases, if a couple is involved, the claim may be made by either partner.

Paragraph (3)

2.48 In income support cases, where a couple is involved, either partner can be the claimant, except in the case of a refugee under para.(3C). There is a free choice. If the couple cannot jointly agree who should claim, the Secretary of State is to break the tie. There are still some differences in entitlement according to which partner is the claimant, particularly since only the claimant is required to be available for work. In addition, head (b) of para.12(1) of Sch.2 to the Income Support Regulations (disability and higher pensioner premium) can only be satisfied by the claimant. But there is now no long-term rate and the full-time employment of either partner excludes entitlement to income support. See reg.7(2). Under the Income Support (Transitional) Regulations transitional protection is lost if the claimant for the couple changes. *CIS 8/1990* and *CIS 375/1990* challenged this rule on the grounds that it was indirectly discriminatory against women (since in 98 per cent of couples (at that time) the man was the claimant). Following the European Court of Justice's decision in the *Cresswell* case that income support is not covered by EC Directive 79/7 on equal treatment for men and women in social security (see the notes to reg.36 of the Income Support Regulations), the claimants could not rely on European law. The Commissioner also rejects a submission that the Sex Discrimination Act 1975 prevented the discriminatory effect of regs 2 and 10 of the Transitional Regulations. Paragraph (4) below deals with changes of partner.

Paragraph (3A)

2.49 Under para.(3A), if both partners in a couple satisfy the conditions of entitlement for a disabled person's tax credit, they may choose which one of them is to claim. If they cannot choose, the Secretary of State makes the decision.

Paragraph (3B)

2.50 Sub-paragraph (a) applies the normal income support rule for couples to income-based JSA. Sub-paragraphs (b) and (c) make provision about the deemed date of the claim for income-based JSA by one partner when a claim for contribution-based JSA by the other partner fails or entitlement comes to an end.

Paragraph (3C)

2.51 Where one of a couple is a refugee, the claim for income support must be made by that partner. If both are refugees, there is a free choice.

CIS/3438/2004 concerned a claim for income support by a Turkish woman admitted to the United Kingdom as a refugee. She claimed income support on August 6, 2003 enclosing a letter from the Home Office dated July 16, 2003 acknowledging her refugee status. She had also been instructed to provide the Department with details of any support provided to her as an asylum seeker by the Home Office. She did not include such a letter with her claim form because she did not have such a letter. It did not exist because it had not at that time been provided by the Home Office. The required information was subsequently obtained and provided to the

Department. The claim for income support made on August 6, 2003 was rejected on the ground that the claimant had failed to comply with the requirement in reg.4(1A) to "include such information and evidence as the form may require in connection with the claim." The tribunal upheld the decision refusing the claim. The Commissioner concludes that there was no proper basis for finding a claimant, in these circumstances, to be in breach of reg.4(1A) by not submitting a document which she did not have at the time with the claim form. While it would be proper to require submission of the information, it was an error of law to treat the claim which had been made as a nullity.

Paragraph (4)

If there is a change of claimant within a couple in the middle of a continuing income support claim, the claims are not to overlap. The change is a matter of a new claim for benefit, not review as it was for supplementary benefit (*R(SB) 1/93*). In *CSIS 66/1992* the Commissioner rejects the argument that para.(4) combined with s.20(9) of the Social Security Act 1986 (SSCBA s.134(2)) meant that a change of claimant could not be backdated. If the claimant could show good cause for her delay in claiming, regs 19(2) and 6(3) enabled her claim to be backdated to the date from which she had good cause (subject to the then what was then a 12-month limit in reg.19(4)). Duplication of payment could be avoided by the AO reviewing the claimant's husband's entitlement for any past period in respect of which the claimant was held to be entitled to benefit and applying reg.5(1) and (2), Case 1, of the Payments Regulations. By becoming the claimant the wife qualified for a disability premium. There is a specific provision in para.19 of Sch.7 to the Income Support Regulations for arrears of a disability premium in these circumstances. 2.52

Paragraph (5)

Regulation 4(5) imposes a duty on the Department to provide a claim form in the circumstances set out there. The effect of a failure by the Department to comply with that duty is considered in *R (IS) 4/07*, which also reviews the earlier authorities on the point. The specific issue raised was whether a breach of reg.4(5) results in suspension of the operation of the time limits for claiming. The Commissioner concludes that it does not. However, the provisions of reg.19 on backdating would be available to a claimant who sought to have a claim backdated in such circumstances. 2.53

Paragraph (6)

The claim must be delivered or sent to the appropriate office, though increasing provision is now being made for telephone or electronic claims. 2.54

For a discussion of some evidential and practical issues in relation to the making of a claim and the timing of it, see *SSWP v LM (IS)* [2015] UKUT 202 (AAC).

For JSA, a claimant wishing to make an initial claim must normally go in person to the nearest Job Centre to obtain a claim pack from the new jobseeker receptionist. An appointment will then be made for the claimant to return, usually within five days, for a new jobseeker interview. This is all part of the concept of "active signing". The claim will be treated as made on the date of the first attendance, if it is received properly completed within a month (reg.6(1)(aa) and (4A)).

For a decision exploring issues which can arise when an electronic claim for a jobseeker's allowance goes wrong, see *CW v SSWP (JSA)* [2016] UKUT 114 (AAC).

Paragraphs (6A)–(6D)

Note the rules in these paragraphs which relate to claims for the named benefits by those who have attained "the qualifying age". This is defined in reg.2 by reference to s.1(6) of the State Pension Credit Act 2002, which provides: 2.55

In this Act " 'the qualifying age' " means—

(a) in the case of a woman, pensionable age; or

(b) in the case of a man, the age which is pensionable age in the case of a woman born on the same day as the man.

Pensionable age for women is currently 60, but between 2010 and 2020 will rise gradually until it reaches 65 in line with men: see s.126 and Sch.4 to the Pensions Act 1995 for the detail.

Paragraphs (7) and (8)

2.56 Paragraph (7), which does not apply to claims for income support or JSA (for which see para.(7A)), deals with written claims not made on the proper form (for which, see para.(1)), and situations where the proper form is not completed according to the instructions (see para.8)). The Secretary of State may simply treat this as an ineffective attempt to claim, but also has power to refer the form back to the claimant. Then there is one month (extendable by the Secretary of State) to complete the form properly, in which case the claim is treated as made on the date of the original attempt to claim (see reg.6(1)(b)). Note also *R(SB) 9/84*; see the note to para.(1).

CP/3447/2003 concerned a claim for an adult dependency increase to a retirement pension for the claimant's wife. The claimant had made his claim for retirement pension at the proper time in advance of his 65th birthday indicating on the claim form that he wished to claim the increase for his wife. Adult dependency increase is, by virtue of reg.2(3) of the Claims and Payments Regulations, treated as a separate benefit requiring a separate claim. The Department failed to pick up the statement in the retirement pension claim form and did not send the claimant a further form to complete. In the following year, the claimant wrote to ask whether he was getting the increase after a query on his tax return. The required form was then issued to him. He completed it and it was clear that he should have been receiving the increase all along. The Secretary of State refused to pay it back to the start of the retirement pension on the grounds that the claim was received following the enquiry and could only be backdated three months from that date. By the time the appeal came before the tribunal, the Secretary of State accepted that the decision was wrong. The issue turned on the proper interpretation of reg.4(7). In particular, what was the date on which the claim was made 'in the first instance' in this case. Was it the date on which the claimant wrote his letter asking about his entitlement to the increase of his wife, or was it the indication in his original claim form for retirement pension indicating that he wanted the increase for his wife?

The Commissioner concluded,

> "In those circumstances, given that (a) a claim in writing for the increase is now accepted as having been made in the first instance by the claimant in early 1999 as part of the original claim for his pension, and (b) the Secretary of State did in fact exercise his powers in regulation 4(7) to supply the claimant with the approved form which was returned duly completed well within the month stipulated, the conditions under which the Secretary of State is bound to treat the claim as if it had been duly made "in the first instance" are in my judgment satisfied in reference to the *original* date of claim in 1999, not just the enquiry letter the following year. Since the requirement to treat the claim as duly made "in the first instance" is mandatory once the conditions are met, there is no further exercise of discretionary or administrative judgment for the Secretary of State to make under regulation 4(7) before the effect in terms of entitlement to benefit can be properly determined. Although it was only in response to the further enquiry that the form was eventually supplied the Secretary of State could not in my judgment possibly rely on that as an argument for saying that the existence of the first claim should be ignored, when the failure to supply the form in the first instance was admittedly an administrative error by his own local officials and should never have happened at all." (para.15)

The Commissioner does, however, note that in so finding in the particular circumstances of this case, he is not to be taken as pronouncing as a matter of general principle that ticking boxes on a form in the expectation of receiving a further form ought in every case to constitute making a claim in writing for the benefit in question. (para.14)

Paragraph (7A)

There are special rules in reg.4 where the benefit claimed is income support. In 2.57
CIS/3173/2003, the claimant had contacted an office of the Department with a view to making a claim for income support on October 14, 2002, and she had subsequently completed an income support claim form on October 24, 2002, but did not include payslips with that form. These were required since she declared that she was doing "therapeutic work" (actually work accepted as permitted for the purposes of incapacity benefit). The Department contacted the claimant on December 18, 2002 regarding the missing payslips. These were provided on December 19, 2002. The decision maker awarded income support only from December 19, 2002. The tribunal upheld that decision. The Commissioner also concludes that there was no entitlement until December 19, 2002. He concludes that the claim form sent in without the accompanying payslips was a defective claim under sub-para.(7A) with the consequences stated there, but that reg.6(1A) makes provision only for one month's leeway in providing the information or evidence required to cure the defect. More than one month had passed here, and accordingly no claim which complied with the requirement of reg.4(1A) was made until December 19, 2002. It did not matter that the Department had not requested the payslips earlier. The Commissioner has granted leave to appeal in this case.

Paragraphs (7A), (7B) and (9)

If a claim for income support or JSA is defective (on which see para.(9)), the 2.58
Secretary of State will simply advise the claimant of the defect and of the rules in reg.6(1A) (for income support claims) or reg.6(4A) (for JSA claims) as appropriate. It will then be up to the claimant to comply with those provisions if he is in a position to do so.

Paragraphs (11)–(14)

These paragraphs make provision, in a system which has previously been based 2.59
upon a requirement for written claims, for telephone claims for retirement pension and graduated retirement pension. Telephone claims will take the form of an interview between an officer of the Department and the claimant whose answers will be input directly into the Department's computer system. A decision on the claim may be made on the spot, since entitlement to pensions can very often be determined easily by reference to information already held in Departmental records. These paragraphs make provision for telephone claims, but reserve the Secretary of State's power to insist upon a written claim. Provision is also made for treating a telephone claim as a defective claim and allowing a period for the defect to be remedied.

[1 Further provisions as to claims

4A.—(1) Where a claimant resides in both— 2.60

(a) the area of a local authority specified in Part I or II of Schedule 1 to the Social Security (Claims and Information) Regulations 1999; and
(b) a postcode district identified in Part I or II of Schedule 2 to the Social Security (Claims and Information) Regulations 1999,

any claim for a benefit to which paragraph (2) applies may be made to any office displaying the one logo (whether or not that office is situated within the area of the local authority in which the claimant resides).

(2) The benefits to which this paragraph applies are—

(a) a jobseeker's allowance;

(b) income support;
(c) incapacity benefit;
(d) [2 carer's allowance];
(e) severe disablement allowance;
(f) widow's benefit;
(g) bereavement benefits;
(h) disability living allowance.

(3) A claim made in accordance with paragraph (1), other than a claim for income support or a jobseeker's allowance, shall be made in writing on a form approved by the Secretary of State for the purpose of the benefit to which the claim is made, or in such other manner, being in writing, as the person to whom the claim is made may accept as sufficient in the circumstances of the particular case.

(4) In the case of a claim for income support or a jobseeker's allowance, the provisions of regulation 4(1A) to (1C) shall apply.

(5) In its application to the area of any authority specified in Part I or II of Schedule 1 to the Social Security (Claims and Information) Regulations 1999, the "appropriate office" in these Regulations includes also an office of an authority or person to whom claims may be made in accordance with paragraph (1).

(6) In these Regulations, a "participating authority" means any local authority or person to whom claims may be made in accordance with paragraph (1).

AMENDMENTS

1. This regulation inserted by The Social Security (Claims and Information) Regulations 1999 (SI 1999/3108) reg.5 (November 29, 1999).

2. The Social Security Amendment (Carer's Allowance) Regulations 2002 (SI 2002/2497) Sch.2 (October 23, 2002).

Forwarding claims and information

2.61 **4B.**—(1) A participating authority may—

(a) record information or evidence relating to any social security matter supplied by or obtained from a person at an office displaying the **one** logo, whether or not the information or evidence is supplied or obtained in connection with the making of a claim for benefit;
(b) give information or advice with respect to any social security matter to persons who are making, or have made, claims for any benefit to which regulation 4A(2) applies [2 or for state pension credit.]

(2) A participating authority shall forward to the Secretary of State—

(a) any claim for benefit, other than a claim for housing benefit [3 . . .], together with any information or evidence supplied to the authority in connection with that claim; and
(b) any information or evidence relating to any other social security matter, except where the information or evidence relates solely to housing benefit [3 . . .] given to the authority by a person making a claim for, or who has claimed, a benefit to which regulation 4A(2) applies.]

AMENDMENTS

1. This regulation inserted by The Social Security (Claims and Information) Regulations 1999 (SI 1999/3108) reg.5 (November 29, 1999).
2. State Pension Credit (Consequential, Transitional and Miscellaneous) Regulations 2002 (SI 2002/3019) reg.4 (April 7, 2003).
3. The Council Tax Benefit Abolition (Consequential Provision) Regulations 2013 (SI 2013/458) reg.3 (April 1, 2013).

[1 Electronic claims for benefit

4ZC.—(1) Any claim for benefit in relation to which this regulation applies, and any certificate, notice, information or evidence given in connection with that claim, may be made or given by means of an electronic communication, in accordance with the provisions set out in Schedule 9ZC. 2.62

[5 "(2) This regulation applies to the following benefits—
(a) carer's allowance;
(b) attendance allowance;
[6 (ba) bereavement support payment;]
(c) disability living allowance;
(d) graduated retirement benefit;
(e) a jobseeker's allowance;
(f) a retirement pension;
(g) state pension under Part 1 of the Pensions Act 2014;
(h) shared additional pension;
(i) industrial injuries benefit;
(j) an employment and support allowance.]

AMENDMENTS

1. The Social Security (Electronic Communications) (Carer's Allowance) Order 2003 (SI 2003/2800) reg.2 (December 1, 2003).
2. The Social Security (Electronic Communications) (Miscellaneous Benefits) Order 2005 (SI 2005/3321) (January 30, 2006).
3. The Social Security (Electronic Communications) Order 2011 (SI 2011/1498) (February 1, 2012).
4. The Pensions Act 2014 (Consequential, Supplementary and Incidental Amendments) Order 2015 (SI 2015/1985) art.9(5) (April 6, 2016).
5. Social Security (Claims and Payments) Amendment Regulations 2016 (SI 2016/544) reg.2 (June 15, 2016).
6. The Pensions Act 2014 (Consequential, Supplementary and Incidental Amendments) Order 2017 (SI 2017/422) art.10 (April 6, 2017).

GENERAL NOTE

CW v SSWP (JSA) [2016] UKUT 114 concerned an attempt to claim jobseeker's allowance online which went wrong. The claimant attempted to make a claim online, but receive no acknowledgement of it. She subsequently wrote to her local Jobcentre about the failed attempt to claim online. The response was that there was no record of an online claim and that the claimant should make a claim. The claimant then (well over a month after her initial attempt) made an online claim which was recorded, and she subsequently attended an interview at her local Jobcentre. She sought an award back-dated to her initial attempt to make an online claim, but this was refused. Judge Mitchell notes that the electronic date of claims rules are to be found in Schedule 9ZC, which requires that "information 2.63

shall not be taken to have been delivered to an official computer system by means of an electronic communication unless it is accepted by the system to which it is delivered" para.4(3) of Sch.9ZC). Furthermore, paragraph 6 contains a presumption that an electronic claim has not been received if it has not been recorded on an official computer system. He then concludes that the backdating provisions in regulation 19 of the Claims and Payments Regulations could not assist the claimant, since it would be distorting language to apply the provisions about the use of the post and the telephone to online communications. However, the tribunal had not fully enquired as to when the claimant had first enquired about benefit after the failure of the online claim—the evidence suggested that she had written a letter about this earlier than the first letter in the tribunal documents. He accordingly remitted to appeal for a fresh hearing at which this issue could be explored.

[1 Electronic claims for benefit

2.64 **4C.**—(1) Any claim for benefit in relation to which this regulation applies, and any certificate, notice, information or evidence given in connection with that claim, may be made or given by means of an electronic communication, in accordance with the provisions set out in Schedule 9C.

(2) This regulation applies in relation to child benefit.]

AMENDMENT

1. Inserted by the Social Security (Electronic Communications) (Child Benefit) Order 2002 (SI 2002/1789) art.3 (October 28, 2002).

[1 Making a claim for state pension credit

2.65 **4D.**—(1) A claim for state pension credit need only be made in writing if the Secretary of State so directs in any particular case.

(2) A claim is made in writing either—

(a) by completing and returning in accordance with the instructions printed on it a form approved or provided by the Secretary of State for the purpose; or

(b) in such other written form as the Secretary of State accepts as sufficient in the circumstances of the case.

(3) A claim for state pension credit may be made in writing whether or not a direction is issued under paragraph (1) and may also be made [5 . . .] in person at an appropriate office [3 . . .].

[3 (3A) A claim made in writing may also be made at an office designated by the Secretary of State for accepting claims for state pension credit.]

[7 (4) A claim made in writing may also be made at the offices of—

(a) a local authority administering housing benefit [3 . . .];

(b) a county council in England;

(c) a person providing services to a person mentioned in sub-paragraph (a) or (b);

(d) a person authorised to exercise any functions of a local authority relating to housing benefit [3 . . .]; or

(e) a person authorised to exercise any function a county council in England has under section 7A of the Social Security Administration Act 1992,

if the Secretary of State has arranged with the local authority, county council or other person for them to receive claims in accordance with this paragraph.]

[3 (5) Where a claim is made in accordance with paragraph (4), the local authority or other specified person—
(a) shall forward the claim to the Secretary of State as soon as reasonably practicable;
(b) may receive information or evidence relating to the claim supplied by the person making, or who has made, the claim to another person, and shall forward it to the Secretary of State as soon as reasonably practicable;
(c) may obtain information or evidence relating to the claim from the person who has made the claim and shall forward it to the Secretary of State as soon as reasonably practicable;
[7(cc) may verify any non-medical information or evidence supplied or obtained in accordance with sub-paragraph (b) or (c) and shall forward it to the Secretary of State as soon as reasonably practicable;]
(d) may record information or evidence relating to the claim supplied or obtained in accordance with sub-paragraph (b) or (c) and may hold the information or evidence (whether as supplied or obtained or as recorded) for the purpose of forwarding it to the Secretary of State; and
(e) may give information and advice with respect to the claim to the person who makes, or has made, the claim.]

[3 (5A) Paragraph (5)(b) to (e) applies in respect of information, evidence and advice relating to any claim for state pension credit, whether it is made in accordance with paragraph (4) or otherwise.]

(6) A claim for state pension credit made in person [5 . . .] is not a valid claim unless a written statement of the claimant's circumstances, provided for the purpose by the Secretary of State, is approved by the person making the claim.

[5 (6A) A claim for state pension credit may be made by telephone call to the telephone number specified by the Secretary of State.

(6B) Where the Secretary of State, in any particular case, directs that the person making the claim approves a written statement of his circumstances, provided for the purpose by the Secretary of State, a claim made by telephone is not a valid claim unless the person complies with the direction.

(6C) A claim made by telephone in accordance with paragraph (6A) is defective unless the Secretary of State is provided, during that telephone call, with all the information he requires to determine the claim.

(6D) Where a claim made by telephone in accordance with paragraph (6A) is defective, the Secretary of State is to provide the person making it with an opportunity to correct the defect.

(6E) If the person corrects the defect within one month, or such longer period as the Secretary of State considers reasonable, of the date the Secretary of State [8 first] drew attention to the defect, the Secretary of State shall treat the claim as if it had been duly made in the first instance.]

(7) A [4 couple] may agree between them as to which partner is to make a claim for state pension credit, but in the absence of an agreement, the Secretary of State shall decide which of them is to make the claim.

(8) Where one member of a [4 couple] ("the former claimant") is entitled to state pension credit under an award but a claim for state pension credit is made by the other member of the couple, then, if both members of the couple confirm in writing that they wish the claimant to be the other

member, the former claimant's entitlement shall terminate on the last day of the benefit week specified in paragraph (9).

(9) That benefit week is the benefit week of the former claimant which includes the day immediately preceding the day the partner's claim is actually made or, if earlier, is treated as made.

(10) If a claim for state pension credit is defective when first received, the Secretary of State is to provide the person making it with an opportunity to correct the defect.

(11) If that person corrects the defect so that the claim then satisfies the requirements of paragraph (2) and does so within 1 month [6 or such longer period as the Secretary of State considers reasonable] of the date the Secretary of State [8 first] drew attention to the defect, the claim shall be treated as having been properly made on the date—

(a) the defective claim was first received by the Secretary of State or the person acting on his behalf; or

(b) if regulation 4F(3) applies, the person informed an appropriate office [1 or other office specified in regulation 4F(3)] of his intention to claim state pension credit.

(12) [5 Paragraph (6E) and (11) do] not apply in a case to which regulation 4E(3) applies.

(13) State pension credit is a relevant benefit for the purposes of section 7A of the Social Security Administration Act 1992.]

AMENDMENTS

1. Inserted by The State Pension Credit (Consequential, Transitional and Miscellaneous) Regulations 2002 (SI 2002/3019) reg.4 (April 7, 2003).

2. The Social Security (Claims and Payments and Miscellaneous Amendments) Regulations 2003 (SI 2003/1632) reg.2 (July 21, 2003).

3. The Social Security, Child Support and Tax Credits (Miscellaneous Amendments) Regulations 2005 (SI 2005/337) reg.7 (March 18, 2005).

4. The Civil Partnership (Pensions, Social Security and Child Support) (Consequential etc. Provisions) Order 2005 (SI 2005/2887) (December 5, 2005).

5. The Social Security (Miscellaneous Amendments) (No.2) Regulations 2006 (SI 2006/832) (July 24, 2006).

6. The Social Security (Miscellaneous Amendments) (No.3) Regulations 2006 (SI 2006/2377) (October 2, 2006).

7. The Social Security (Claims and Information) Regulations 2007 (SI 2007/2911) (October 31, 2007).

8. The Social Security (Miscellaneous Amendments) (No.4) Regulations 2009 (SI 2009/2655) reg.3 (October 26, 2009).

9. The Council Tax Benefit Abolition (Consequential Provision) Regulations 2013 (SI 2013/458) reg.3 (April 1, 2013).

[1 Making a claim before attaining the qualifying age

2.66 **4E.**—(1) A claim for state pension credit may be made, and any claim made may be determined, at any time within the advance period.

(2) The advance period begins on the date which falls 4 months before the day on which the claimant attains the qualifying age and ends on the day before he attains that age.

(3) A person who makes a claim within the advance period which is defective may correct the defect at any time before the end of the advance period.]

AMENDMENT

1. Inserted by the State Pension Credit (Consequential, Transitional and Miscellaneous) Regulations 2002 (SI 2002/3019) reg.4 (April 7, 2003).

[1 Making a claim after attaining the qualifying age: date of claim

4F.—(1) This regulation applies in the case of a person who claims state pension credit on or after attaining the qualifying age. 2.67

(2) The date on which a claim is made shall, subject to paragraph (3), be—

(a) where the claim is made in writing and is not defective, the date on which the claim is first received—

(i) by the Secretary of State or the person acting on his behalf; or

(ii) in a case to which regulation 4D(4) relates, in the office of a person specified therein;

(b) where the claim is not made in writing but is otherwise made in accordance with regulation 4D(3) [4 or (6A)] and is not defective, the date the claimant provides details of his circumstances by telephone to, or in person at, the appropriate office or other office designated by the Secretary of State to accept claims for state pension credit; or

(c) where a claim is initially defective but the defect is corrected under regulation [4 4D(6E) or (11)], the date the claim is treated as having been made under that regulation.

(3) If a [3 person wishing to make a claim]—

(a) informs [3 (by whatever means) an appropriate office [2, or other office designated by the Secretary of State for accepting claims for state pension credit or the office of the person specified in regulation 4(D)] of his intention to claim state pension credit; and

(b) subsequently makes the claim in accordance with regulation 4D within 1 month of complying with sub-paragraph (a), or within such longer period as the Secretary of State may allow,

the claim may, where in the circumstances of the particular case it is appropriate to do so, be treated as made on the day the claimant first informed [2 an office specified in subparagraph (a)] of his intention to claim the credit.]

AMENDMENTS

1. Inserted by the State Pension Credit (Consequential, Transitional and Miscellaneous) Regulations 2002 (SI 2002/3019) reg.4 (April 7, 2003).

2. The Social Security (Claims and Payments and Miscellaneous Amendments) Regulations 2003 (SI 2003/1632) reg.2 (July 21, 2003).

3. Social Security (Housing Benefit, Council Tax Benefit, State Pension Credit and Miscellaneous Amendments) Regulations 2004 (SI 2004/2327) reg.8 (October 6, 2004).

4. The Social Security (Miscellaneous Amendments) (No. 2) Regulations 2006 (SI 2006/832) (July 24, 2006).

GENERAL NOTE

The amendments to reg.4 of the Claims and Payments Regulations are significant in that they may provision for much greater co-operation between the Department and local authorities in relation to the receipt of claims for benefits administered by these agencies. 2.68

Claims under these provisions may be directed to an office designated by the

Secretary of State for accepting such claims. In relation to benefits administered by the Department, the party receiving the claim is under a duty to forward the claim to the Department as soon as reasonably practicable.

[1 Making a claim for employment and support allowance by telephone

2.69 **4G.**—(1) A claim ("'a telephone claim'") for an employment and support allowance may be made by telephone call to the telephone number specified by the Secretary of State.

(2) Where the Secretary of State, in any particular case, directs that the person making the claim approves a written statement of his circumstances, provided for the purpose by the Secretary of State, a telephone claim is not a valid claim unless the person complies with the direction.

(3) A telephone claim is defective unless the Secretary of State is provided, during that telephone call, with all the information he requires to determine the claim.

(4) Where a telephone claim is defective, the Secretary of State is to advise the person making it of the defect and of the relevant provisions of regulation 6(1F) relating to the date of claim.

(5) If the person corrects the defect within one month, or such longer period as the Secretary of State considers reasonable, of the date the Secretary of State [2 first] drew attention to the defect, the Secretary of State must treat the claim as if it had been properly made in the first instance.]

AMENDMENTS

1. The Employment and Support Allowance (Consequential Provisions) (No. 2) Regulations 2008, (SI 2008/1554) reg.13 (October 27, 2008).

2. The Social Security (Miscellaneous Amendments) (No.4) Regulations 2009 (SI 2009/2655) reg.3 (October 26, 2009).

GENERAL NOTE

2.70 In *TR v SSWP (ESA)* [2013] UKUT 555 (AAC) the judge draws attention to the distinction between the provision of information (as required by this and similar regulations) and the provision of information *and evidence*, which is required elsewhere in the regulations. The judge says that information "comprises facts" whereas evidence requires some documentary evidence to support those facts (see [7]).

[1 Making a claim for employment and support allowance in writing

2.71 **4H.**—(1) A claim ("a written claim") for employment and support allowance need only be made in writing if the Secretary of State so directs in any particular case but a written claim may be made whether or not a direction is issued.

(2) A written claim must be made on a form approved for the purpose by the Secretary of State and be made in accordance with the instructions on the form.

(3) A claim in writing may also be made at the offices of—

(a) a local authority administering housing benefit [3 . . .];

(b) a person providing to such an authority services relating to housing benefit [3 . . .]; or

(c) a person authorised to exercise the function of a local authority relating to housing benefit [3 . . .],

if the Secretary of State has arranged with the local authority or person

five per cent or less was for private purposes. The Secretary of State argued that this was irrelevant since a claim could not be altered after it had been determined. The tribunal accepted the argument. The Commissioner notes that there is nothing in reg.5 which prevents a claimant from seeking to explain an answer in a way which is different from how the decision-maker interpreted it. He goes on to raise the question whether there might be a difference for the purpose of reg.5(1) between a claim and evidence on a claim, but does not seek to answer the question.

Regulation 5(1) would appear to be drafted sufficiently widely that it would encompass an amendment not only to the claim, but also to the evidence on which the claim is based. The underlying purpose of the regulation appears to be to ensure that the decision is based on full circumstances obtaining when the claim is determined. So, for example, a claimant might wish to include new members of his family to the claim, or correct an error on the claim form which has just been noticed. Both would appear to be within reg.5(1).

Paragraph (2)

In *CJSA/3979/1999* the Commissioner explores the possibility of a claimant's being able to withdraw a claim where there has been an award of benefit for an indefinite period. The Commissioner concludes, 2.75

> "If the original claim is for an indefinite period, so that the award is for an indefinite period, I do not think that the claim can later be converted into one for a definite period. The original claim cannot be unmade or amended. . . . However, it does not necessarily follow from that that a claim cannot be withdraw for a prospective period even though there is a current indefinite award. In a sense there has already been an adjudication on that period through the making of an indefinite award, but only in a fairly technical sense. If a claimant unequivocally says that he wishes his claim to stop at the current date or that he wishes to withdraw his claim for the future, why should that not be given effect? Some regard should be had for the autonomy of claimants. . . . I conclude that even where there is a current award of benefit, a claimant may with-draw a claim on a prospective basis." (para.24)

But the Commissioner goes on to indicate that the termination of the indefinite award should be the subject of adjudication in order to ensure that the withdrawal is properly made and not, for example, the result of coercion or improper inducement. In the case before the Commissioner, one issue raised was whether the claimant had been coerced into withdrawing a claim to JSA by threats to investigate whether he had been working for certain periods prior to those in respect of which he was interviewed.

R(H) 2/06 concerned the interpretation of a provision of the Housing Benefit (General) Regulations 1987 (SI 1987/1971) in identical terms to reg.5(2). The Commissioner ruled that, although in some cases it may be possible to make a fresh claim which can be backdated to cover the period of a claim which has been withdrawn, the consequence of a genuine and effective withdrawal is, in the absence of any provision permitting reinstatement, to prevent any award from being made on the claim after the withdrawal took effect. Although different considerations might apply to claimants who are not fully able to manage their affairs or to understand the consequences of their actions, claimants who are not subject to any such disability would normally have to establish that the withdrawal of the claim was induced by some factor such as threatening or overbearing behaviour, deception or similar improper conduct in order to show that the notice of withdrawal of a claim was not a genuine expression of the claimant's intention at the time when the notice was given.

Date of claim

6.—(1) [3Subject to the following provisions of this regulation] [29 or regulation 6A (claims by persons subject to work-focused interviews)] the date on which a claim is made shall be— 2.76

(a) in the case of a claim which meets the requirements of regulation 4(1), the date on which it is received in an appropriate office;

[12(aa) in the case of a claim for—

[30 . . .]

[30 . . .]

jobseeker's allowance if first notification is received before 6th October 1997; or

income support if first notification is received before 6th October 1997;

which meets the requirements of regulation 4(1) and which is received in an appropriate office within one month of first notification in accordance with regulation 4(5), whichever is the later of—

(i) the date on which that notification is received; and

(ii) the first date on which that claim could have been made in accordance with these Regulations;]

(b) in the case of a claim which does not meet the requirements of regulation 4(1) but which is treated, under regulation 4(7) as having been [36 properly] made, the date on which the claim was received in an appropriate office in the first instance.

[23 (c) in the case of a claim made by telephone in accordance with [34 regulation 4(11) or (11A), the date [36 the claim is properly completed;]

(d) in the case of a claim made by telephone which is defective but which is treated, under regulation [36 4(13)(a) as having been properly] made, the date of that telephone call.]

[21 (1ZA) In the case of a claim made in accordance with regulation 4(6B)—

(a) paragraph (1) shall apply in relation to a claim received at an office specified in that regulation as it applies in relation to a claim received at an appropriate office; and

(b) paragraph (1A) shall apply in relation to an office specified in that regulation as it applies in relation to an appropriate office.]

[13 (1A) In the case of claim for income support—

(a) subject to the following sub-paragraphs, the date on which a claim is made shall be the date on which a properly completed claim is received in an appropriate office [36 or a claim made by telephone is properly completed] or the first day in respect of which the claim is made if later;

(b) where a properly completed claim is received in an appropriate office [36 or a claim made by telephone is properly completed] within one month of first notification of intention to make that claim, the date of claim shall be the date on which that notification is [36 made or is] deemed to be made or the first day in respect of which the claim is made if later;

(c) a notification of intention to make a claim will be deemed to be made on the date when an appropriate office receives—

(i) a notification in accordance with regulation 4(5); or

(ii) a defective claim.]

[18a (1B) Subject to paragraph (1C), in the case of a claim for working families' tax credit or disabled person's tax credit which meets the requirements of regulation 4(1) and which is received in an appropriate office within one month of first notification in accordance with regulation 4(5)—

(a) where the claimant is entitled to that credit on the date on which that notification is received ("the notification date") and the first day of the period in respect of which that claim is made is on or before the notification date, the date on which a claim is made shall be the notification date; or

(b) where the claimant is not entitled to that credit on the notification date but becomes so entitled before the date on which the claim is received, the date on which the claim is received, the date on which a claim is made shall be—

(i) the date on which the claimant becomes so entitled, or

(ii) if later, the first day of the period in respect of which the claim is made provided that it is not later than the date on which the claim is received.

(1C) Paragraph (1B) shall not apply in the case of a claim which is received in an appropriate office—

(a) in the case of working families' tax credit, within the period specified opposite that credit at paragraphs (a) or (aa) in column (2) of Schedule 4(a); or

(b) in the case of disabled person's tax credit, within the period specified opposite that credit in paragraphs (a) or (b) in column (2) of Schedule 4.]

[[18b] unless the previous award of working families' tax credit or disabled person's tax credit was terminated by virtue of regulation 49ZA of the Family Credit (General) Regulations 1987 or regulation 54A of the Disability Working Allowance (General) Regulations 1991.]

[[27] (1D) Subject to paragraph (1E) and without prejudice to the generality of paragraph (1), where a properly completed claim for incapacity benefit is received in an appropriate office within one month of the claimant first notifying such an office, by whatever means, of his intention to make that claim, the date of claim shall be the date on which that notification is made or the first day in respect of which the claim is made if later.

(1E) For the purposes of paragraph (1D), a person [[32] . . .] may notify his intention and may send or deliver his claim to an office specified in regulation 4(6B)]

[[36] (1F) In the case of a claim for an employment and support allowance, the date on which the claim is made or treated as made shall be the first date on which—

(a) a claim made by telephone is properly completed, or a properly completed claim is received in an appropriate office, or office mentioned in regulation 4H(3);

(b) a defective claim is received or made but is treated as properly made in the first instance in accordance with regulation 4G(5) in the case of a telephone claim, or 4H(7) in the case of a written claim; or

(c) the Secretary of State is notified of an intention to claim and within one month or such longer period as the Secretary of State considers reasonable of first notification, a claim made by telephone is properly completed, or a properly completed claim is received in an appropriate office, or office mentioned in regulation 4H(3),

or the first day in respect of which the claim is made, if later.

(1G) In paragraph (1F) "properly completed" has the meaning assigned by regulation 4(8) in the case of a written claim and 4(12) in the case of a telephone claim.]

(2) [[1]. . .]

[[1](3) In the case of a claim for income support, [[14] working families' tax credit, disabled person's tax credit] [[12]or jobseeker's allowance] [[5]. . .], where the time for claiming is extended under regulation 19 the claim shall be treated as made on the first day of the period in respect of which the claim is, by reason of the operation of that regulation, timeously made.

(4) Paragraph (3) shall not apply when the time for claiming income support [14 working families' tax credit, disabled person's tax credit] or jobseeker's allowance]] has been extended under regulation 19 and the failure to claim within the prescribed time for the purposes of that regulation is for the reason only that the claim has been sent by post.]

[18 (4ZA)Where a member of a joint-claim couple notifies the employment officer (by whatever means) that he wishes to claim a jobseeker's allowance jointly with the other member of that couple, the claim shall be treated as made on the relevant date specified in accordance with paragraphs (4ZB) to (4ZD).

(4ZB) Where each member of a joint-claim couple is required to attend under regulation 4(6)(a)—

(a) if each member subsequently attends for the purpose of jointly claiming a jobseeker's allowance at the time and place specified by the employment officer and complies with the requirements of paragraph (4AA)(a), the claim shall be treated as made on whichever is the later of the first notification of intention to make that claim and the first day in respect of which the claim is made;

(b) if, without good cause, either member fails to attend for the purpose of jointly claiming a jobseeker's allowance at either the time or the place so specified or does not comply with the requirements of paragraph (4AA)(a), the claim shall be treated as made on the first day on which a member of the couple attends at the specified place and complies with the requirements of paragraph (4AA)(a).

(4ZC) Where only one member of the couple is required to attend under regulation 4(6)(a)—

(a) subject to the following paragraphs, the date on which the claim is made shall be the sate on which a properly completed claim is received in an appropriate office [36 or a claim made by telephone is properly completed] or the first day in respect of which the claim is made, if later, provided that the member of the couple who is required to attend under regulation 4(6)a) does so attend;

(b) where a properly completed form is received in an appropriate office [36 or a claim made by telephone is properly completed] within one month of first notification of intention to make that claim, the date of claim shall be the date of that notification;

(c) if, without good cause, the member of the couple who is required to attend under regulation 4(6)(a) fails to attend for the purpose of making a claim at either the time or place so specified or does not comply with the requirements of paragraph (4AA), the claim shall be treated as made on the first day on which that member does attend at that place and does provide a properly completed claim.

(4ZD) Where, as at the day on which a member of a joint-claim couple ("the first member") notifies the employment officer in accordance with paragraph (4ZA), the other member of that couple is temporarily absent from Great Britain in the circumstances specified in regulation 50(6B) of the Jobseeker's Allowance Regulations, the date on which the claim is made shall be the relevant date specified in paragraph (4ZB) or (4ZC) but nothing in this paragraph shall treat the claim as having been made on a day which is more than three months after the day on which the first member notified the employment officer in accordance with paragraph (4ZA).

[[13](4A) Where a person [[18]who is not a member of a joint-claim couple] notifies the Secretary of State (by whatever means) that he wishes to claim a jobseeker's allowance—

(a) if he is required to attend under regulation 4(6)(a)—

(i) if he subsequently attends for the purpose of making a claim for that benefit at the time and place specified by the Secretary of State and complies with the requirements of paragraph (4AA) [[18](b)], the claim shall be treated as made on whichever is the later of first notification of intention to make that claim and the first day in respect of which the claim is made;

(ii) if, without good cause, he fails to attend for the purpose of making a claim for that benefit at either the time or place so specified, or does not comply with the requirements of paragraph (4AA) [[18](b)], the claim shall be treated as made on the first day on which he does attend at that place and does provide a properly completed claim;

(b) if under regulation 4(6)(a) the Secretary of State directs that he is not required to attend—

(i) subject to the following sub-paragraph, the date on which the claim is made shall be the date on which a properly completed claim is received in an appropriate office [[36] or a claim made by telephone is properly completed] or the first day in respect of which the claim is made if later;

(ii) where a properly completed claim is received in an appropriate office [[36] or a claim made by telephone is properly completed] within one month of first notification of intention to make that claim, the date of claim shall be the date of that notification.

[[18] (4AA) Unless the Secretary of State otherwise directs, a properly completed claim for shall be provided [[36] or made]—

(a) in a case to which paragraph (4ZA) applies, at or before the time when a member of the joint-claim couple is first required to attend for the purpose of making a claim for a jobseeker's allowance;

(b) in any other case, at or before the time when the person making the claim for a jobseeker's allowance is required to attend for the purpose of making a claim.]

(4AB) The Secretary of State may direct that the time for providing [[36] or making] a properly completed claim may be extended to a date no later than the date one month after the date of first notification of intention to make that claim.]

(4B) Where a person's entitlement to a jobseeker's allowance has ceased in any of the circumstances specified in regulation 25(1)(a), (b) or (c) of the Jobseeker's Allowance Regulations (entitlement ceasing on a failure to comply) and—

(a) where he had normally been required to attend in person, he shows that the failure to comply which caused the cessation of his previous entitlement was due to any of the circumstances mentioned in regulation 30(c) or (d) of those Regulations, and no later than the day immediately following the date when those circumstances cease to apply he makes a further claim for jobseeker's allowance; or

(b) where he had not normally been required to attend in person, he shows that he did not receive the notice to attend and he immediately makes a further claim for jobseeker's allowance,

that further claim shall be treated as having been made on the day following that cessation of entitlement.

(4C) Where a person's entitlement to a jobseeker's allowance ceases in the circumstances specified in regulation 25(1)(b) of the Jobseeker's Allowance Regulations (failure to attend at time specified) and that person makes a further claim for that allowance on the day on which he failed to attend at the time specified, that claim shall be treated as having been made on the following day.]

[[11](4D) In the case of a claim for income support to which regulation 4(3C) (claim by refugee) refers, the claim shall be treated as made [[15] on the date on which his claim for asylum was recorded by the Secretary of State as having been made.]

[[2](5) Where a person submits a claim for attendance allowance [[6]or disability living allowance or a request under paragraph (8)] by post and the arrival of that [[6]claim or request] at an appropriate office is delayed by postal disruption caused by industrial action, whether within the postal service or elsewhere, the [[6]claim or request] shall be treated as received on the day on which it would have been received if it had been delivered in the ordinary course of post.]

[[3](6) Where—

(a) on or after 9th April 1990 a person satisfies the capital condition in section 22(6) of the Social Security Act 1986 [SSCBA, s.134(1)] for income support and he would not have satisfied that condition had the amount prescribed under regulation 45 of the Income Support (General) Regulation 1987 been £6,000; and

(b) a claim for that benefit is received from him in an appropriate office not later than 27th May 1990;

the claim shall be treated as made on the date [[4]not later than 5th December 1990] determined in accordance with paragraph (7).

(7) For the purpose of paragraph (6), where—

(a) the claimant satisfies the other conditions of entitlement to income support on the date on which he satisfies the capital condition, the date shall be the date on which he satisfies that condition;

(b) the claimant does not satisfy the other conditions of entitlement to income support on the date on which he satisfies the capital condition, the date shall be the date on which he satisfies the conditions of entitlement to that benefit.]

[[6](8) [[8]Subject to paragraph (8A [[21] and (8B)]),] where—

(a) a request is received in an appropriate office for a claim form for disability living allowance or attendance allowance; and

(b) in response to the request a claim form for disability living allowance or attendance is issued from an appropriate office; and

(c) within the time specified the claim form properly completed is received in an appropriate office,

the date on which the claim is made shall be the date on which the request was received in the appropriate office.

[[8](8A) Where, in a case which would otherwise fall within paragraph (8), it is not possible to determine the date when the request for a claim form was received in an appropriate office because of a failure to record that date, the claim shall be treated as having been made on the date 6 weeks before the date on which the properly completed claim form is received in an appropriate office.]

[21 (8B) In the case of a claim for disability living allowance or attendance allowance made in accordance with regulation 4(6B), paragraphs (8) and (8A) shall apply in relation to an office specified in that regulation as they apply in relation to an appropriate office.]

(9) [9In paragraph (8) and (8A)]—

"a claim form" means a form approved by the Secretary of State under regulation 4(1); "properly completed" has the meaning assigned by regulation 4(8);

"the time specified" means 6 weeks from the date on which the request was received or such longer period as the Secretary of State may consider reasonable.]

[7(10) Where a person starts a job on a Monday or Tuesday in any week and he makes a claim for [14 disabled person's tax credit] in that week the claim shall be treated as made on the Tuesday of that week.

(11) [14 . . .]

[12 (12) [14 . . .] Where a person has claimed [14 disabled person's tax credit] and that claim ("the original claim") has been refused, and a further claim is made in the circumstances specified in paragraph (13), that further claim shall be treated as made—

(a) on the date of the original claim; or
(b) on the first date in respect of which the qualifying benefit was payable, whichever is the later.

(13) The circumstances referred to in paragraph (12) are that—

(a) the original claim was refused on the ground that the claimant did not qualify under section 129(2) of the Contributions and Benefits Act;
(b) at the date of the original claim the claimant had made a claim for a qualifying benefit and that claim had not been determined;
(c) after the original claim had been determined, the claim for the qualifying benefit was determined in the claimant's favour; and
(d) the further claim for [14 disabled person's tax credit] was made within three months of the date that the claim for the qualifying benefit was determined.

(14) [14 . . .]

(15) In paragraphs (12) and (13) "qualifying benefit" means any of the benefits referred to in section 129(2) of the Contributions and Benefits Act.

[31 (15A) Paragraphs (16) to (34) shall not apply in any case where it would be advantageous to the claimant to apply the provisions of regulation 19 (time for claiming benefit.)]

[16 (16) Where a person has claimed a relevant benefit and that claim ("the original claim") has been refused in the circumstances specified in paragraph (17), and a further claim is made in the additional circumstances specified in paragraph (18), that further claim shall be treated as made—

(a) on the date of the original claim; or
(b) on the first date in respect of which the qualifying benefit was [19 awarded],

whichever is the later.

(17) The circumstances referred to in paragraph (16) are that the ground for refusal was—

(a) in the case of severe disablement allowance, that the claimant's disablement was less than 80 per cent;

(b) [27 . . .];

(c) in any case, that the claimant [19, a member of his family or the disabled person] had not been awarded a qualifying benefit.

(18) The additional circumstances referred to in paragraph (16) are that—

[19(a) a claim for the qualifying benefit was made not later than 10 working days after the date of the original claim and the claim for the qualifying benefit had not been decided;

(b) after the original claim had been decided the claim for the qualifying benefit had been decided in favour of the claimant, a member or his family or the disabled person; and]

(c) the further claim was made within three months of the date on which the claim for the qualifying benefit was decided.

(19) Where a person has been awarded a relevant benefit and that award ("the [31 "original award") has been terminated or reduced or payment under that award ceases in the circumstances] specified in paragraph (20), and a further claim is made in the additional circumstances specified in paragraph (21), that further claim shall be treated as made—

(a) on the date of termination of the original award; or

(b) on the first date in respect of which the qualifying benefit [19 is [28 awarded or] [31 re-awarded or becomes payable again]],

whichever is the later.

[28 (20) The circumstances referred to in paragraph (19) are—

(a) that the award of the qualifying benefit has itself been terminated or reduced by means of a revision, supersession, appeal or termination of an award for a fixed period in such a way as to affect the original award; [31 . . .]

(b) at the date the original award was terminated the claimant's claim for a qualifying benefit had not been decided] [31 or]

[31 (c) that the qualifying benefit has ceased to be payable in accordance with—

(i) regulation 6(1) of the Social Security (Attendance Allowance) Regulations 1991 or regulation 8(1) of the Social Security (Disability Living Allowance) Regulations 1991 because the claimant is undergoing treatment as an in-patient in a hospital or similar institution, or

(ii) regulation 7 of the Social Security (Attendance Allowance) Regulations 1991 or regulation 9 of the Social Security (Disability Living Allowance) Regulations 1991 because the claimant is resident in certain accommodation other than a hospital.]

(21) [31 Subject to paragraph (21A), the additional] referred to in paragraph (19) are that—

(a) after the original award has been terminated the claim for the qualifying benefit is decided in [19 favour of the claimant, a member of his family or the disabled person]; [31 or]

[31 (b) the qualifying benefit is re-awarded following revision, supersession or appeal; or

(c) the qualifying benefit is re-awarded on a renewal claim when an award for a fixed period expires; or

(d) the cessation of payment ends when the claimant leaves the hospital or similar institution or accommodation referred to in paragraph(20)(c); and

the further claim [34 for a relevant benefit] referred to in paragraph (19), is made within three months of the date [34 of the decision to award, re-award, or recommence payment of the qualifying benefit on the grounds that sub-paragraph (a), (b), (c) or (d) was satisfied.]]

[31 (21A) Paragraph (21) applies whether the benefit is re-awarded when the further claim is decided or following a revision of, or an appeal against, such a decision.]

(22) In paragraphs (16) to (21) [19 . . .] [27, (30) and (33)]—

"relevant benefit" means any of the following, namely—

(a) benefits under Parts II to V of the Contributions and Benefits Act except incapacity benefit;

(b) income support;

(c) a jobseeker's allowance;

(d) a social fund payment mentioned in section 138(1)(a) or (2) of the Contributions and Benefits Act;

(e) child benefit;

[24 (f) state pension credit]

"qualifying benefit" means—

(a) in relation to severe disablement allowance, the highest rate of the care component of disability living allowance;

(b) in relation to invalid care allowance, any benefit referred to in section 70(2) of the Contributions and Benefits Act;

(c) in relation to a social fund payment in respect of maternity or funeral expenses, any benefit referred to in [37 regulation 5(1)(a) or 7(4)(a) of the Social Fund Maternity and Funeral Expenses (General) Regulations 2005];

(d) any other relevant benefit which [19, when it is awarded or re-awarded,] has the effect of making another relevant benefit payable or payable at an increased rate;

"the disabled person" means the person for whom the invalid care allowanced claimant is caring in accordance with section 70(1)(a) of the Contributions and Benefits Act.

[19 "family" has the same meaning as in section 137(1) of the Contributions and Benefits Act or, as the case may be, section 35(1) of the Jobseekers Act [24, and in the case of state pension credit "member of his family" means the other member of a couple where the claimant is a member of a [25 . . .] couple].]

(23) Where a person has ceased to be entitled to incapacity benefit, and a further claim for that benefit is made in the circumstances specified in paragraph (24), that further claim shall be treated as made—

(a) on the date on which entitlement to incapacity benefit ceased; or

(b) on the first date in respect of which the qualifying benefit was payable,

whichever is the later.

(24) The circumstances referred to in paragraph (23) are that—

(a) entitlement to incapacity benefit ceased on the ground that the claimant was not incapable of work;

(b) at the date that entitlement ceased the claimant had made a claim for a qualifying benefit and that claim had not been decided;

(c) after entitlement had ceased, the claim for the qualifying benefit was decided in the claimant's favour; and

(d) the further claim for incapacity benefit was made within three months of the date on which the claim for the qualifying benefit was decided.

(25) In paragraphs (23) and (24) "qualifying benefit" means any of

the payments referred to in regulation 10(2)(a) of the Social Security (Incapacity for Work) (General) Regulations 1995.

(26) In paragraph [27 (18)(a) and (c), 21(a), (24) and (30) and in paragraph (18)(b)] where the word appears for the second time, "decided" includes the making of a decision following a revision, supersession or an appeal, whether by the Secretary of State, [35 the First-tier Tribunal, the Upper Tribunal] or the court.]

(27) Where a claim is made for [14 working families' tax credit or disabled person's tax credit], and—

(a) the claimant had previously made a claim for income support or jobseeker's allowance ("the original claim");
(b) the original claim was refused on the ground that the claimant or his partner was in remunerative work; and
(c) the claim for [14 working families' tax credit or disabled person's tax credit] was made within 14 days of the date that the original claim was determined,

that claim shall be treated as made on the date of the original claim, or, if the claimant so requests, on a later date specified by the claimant.

(28) Where a claim is made for income support or jobseeker's allowance, and—

(a) the claimant had previously made a claim for [20 working tax credit] ("the original claim");
(b) the original claim was refused on the ground that the claimant or his partner was not in remunerative work [20 for the purposes of that tax credit]; and
(c) the claim for income support or jobseeker's allowance was made within 14 days of the date that the original claim was determined,

that claim shall be treated as made on the date of the original claim, or, if the claimant so requests, on a later date specified by the claimant.]

(29) In the case of a claim for an increase of severe disablement allowance or of invalid care allowance in respect of a child or adult dependant, [17 paragraph (16) and (19)] shall apply to the claim as if it were a claim for severe disablement allowance or, as the case may be, invalid care allowance.

[19 (30) Where—

(a) a claimant was awarded income support or income-based jobseeker's allowance ("the original award");
(b) the original award was termination and [31 . . .], the claimant, a member of his family or the disabled person claimed a qualifying benefit; and
(c) the claimant makes a further claim for income support or income-based jobseeker's allowance within 3 months of the date on which the claim for the qualifying benefit was decided,

the further claim shall be treated as made on the date of termination of the original award or the first date in respect of which the qualifying benefit is awarded, whichever is the later.]

[22 (31) Subject to paragraph (32), where—

(a) a person—
  (i) has attained pensionable age, but for the time being makes no claim for a Category A retirement pension; or
  (ii) has attained pensionable age and has a spouse [26 or civil partner]

who has attained pensionable age, but for the time being makes no claim for a Category B retirement pension;

(b) in accordance with regulation 50A of the Social Security (Contributions) Regulations 2001, (Class 3 contributions: tax years 1996–97 to 2001–02) the Commissioners of Inland Revenue subsequently accept Class 3 contributions paid after the due date by the person or, in the case of a Category B retirement pension, the spouse [26 or civil partner];

(c) in accordance with regulation 6A of the Social Security (Crediting and Treatment of Contributions, and National Insurance Numbers) Regulations 2001 the contributions are treated as paid on a date earlier than the date on which they were paid; and

(d) the person claims a Category A or, as the case may be, a Category B retirement pension,

the claim shall be treated as made on—

(i) 1st October 1998; or

(ii) the date on which the person attained pensionable age in the case of a Category A retirement pension, or, in the case of a Category B retirement pension, the date on which the person's spouse [26 or civil partner] attained pensionable age,

whichever is later.

(32) Paragraph (31) shall not apply where—

(a) the person's entitlement to a Category A or B retirement pension has been deferred by virtue of section 55(2)(a) of the Contributions and Benefits Act (increase of retirement pension where entitlement is deferred); or

(b) the person's nominal entitlement to a Category A or B retirement pension is deferred in pursuance of section 36(4) and (7) of the National Insurance Act 1965 (increase of graduated retirement benefit where entitlement is deferred),

nor where sub-paragraph (a) and (b) both apply.]

[27 (33) [31 Subject to paragraph 34, where] a person makes a claim for a carer's allowance [34 or for an increase in carer's allowance in respect of an adult or child dependent] within 3 months of a decision made—

(a) on a claim;

(b) on revision or supersession; or

(c) on appeal whether by [35 the First-tier Tribunal, the Upper Tribunal] or the court,

awarding a qualifying benefit to the disabled person, the date of claim [34 shall be treated as the first day of the benefit week in which the award of the qualifying benefit became payable.]

[31. . . .]

[34 (34) Where the decision awarding a qualifying benefit is made in respect of a renewal claim where a fixed period award of that benefit has expired, or is due to expire, the date of claim for carer's allowance shall be treated as the first day of the benefit week in which the renewal award of qualifying benefit became payable.]

[38 (35) A claim for attendance allowance or the care component of disability living allowance which is in respect of a period beginning on or before 18th October 2007 but which is made after that date, is to be treated as made on 18th October 2007 where—

(a) on or after 8th March 2001, the claimant had an award of that benefit;

(b) the Secretary of State made a superseding decision to end that award on the ground that there had been, or it was anticipated that there would be, a relevant change of circumstances as a result of the claimant's moving, or planning to move, from Great Britain to an EEA state or Switzerland;
(c) that superseding decision was confirmed on appeal; and
(d) the claimant has not received an extra-statutory payment in respect of the benefit being claimed.

(36) A claim for carer's allowance which is in respect of a period beginning on or before 18th October 2007 but which is made after that date, is to be treated as made on 18th October 2007 where—
(a) on or after 8th March 2001, the claimant had an award of that benefit;
(b) the Secretary of State made a superseding decision to end that award on the ground that there had been, or it was anticipated that there would be, a relevant change of circumstances as a result of—
   (i) the claimant's moving from Great Britain to an EEA state or Switzerland; or
   (ii) the claimant no longer caring for a severely disabled person, as defined in section 70(2) of the Contributions and Benefits Act, because that person's award of attendance allowance or the care component of disability living allowance had ended, or would end, by virtue of a superseding decision made on the ground of that person's moving from Great Britain to an EEA state or Switzerland; and
(c) the claimant has not received an extra-statutory payment in respect of that allowance.

(37) In paragraphs (35)(d) and (36)(c), "extra-statutory payment" means a payment made by the Secretary of State, in respect of attendance allowance, the care component of disability living allowance or carer's allowance which, but for the superseding decision referred to in paragraph (35)(b) or, as the case may be, (36)(b), would have been payable from 18th October 2007.]

AMENDMENTS

1. The Social Security (Claims and Payments) Amendment Regulations 1988 (SI 1988/522) reg.2 (April 11, 1988).

2. The Social Security (Medical Evidence, Claims and Payments) Amendment Regulations 1989 (SI 1989/1686), reg.4 (October 9, 1989).

3. The Social Security (Claims and Payments) Amendment Regulations 1990 (SI 1990/725) reg.2 (April 9, 1990).

4. The Social Security (Miscellaneous Provisions) Amendment Regulations 1990 (SI 1990/2208) reg.9 (December 5, 1990).

5. The Social Security (Miscellaneous Provisions) Amendment Regulations 1991 (SI 1991/2284) reg.6 (November 1, 1991).

6. The Social Security (Claims and Payments) Amendment Regulations 1991 (SI 1991/2741) reg.4 (February 3, 1992).

7. The Social Security (Claims and Payments) Amendment Regulations 1991 (SI 1991/2741) reg.4 (March 10, 1992).

8. The Social Security (Claims and Payments) Amendment (No.3) Regulations 1993 (SI 1993/2113) reg.3 (September 27, 1993).

9. The Social Security (Claims and Payments) Amendment Regulations 1994 (SI 1994/2319) reg.2 (October 3, 1994).

10. The Social Security (Claims and Payments) (Jobseeker's Allowance Consequential Amendments) Regulations 1996 (SI 1996/1460) reg.2(5) (October 7, 1996).

11. The Income Support and Social Security (Claims and Payments) (Miscellaneous Amendments) Regulations 1996 (SI 1996/2431) reg.7(c) (October 15, 1996).
12. The Social Security (Miscellaneous Amendments) (No.2) Regulations 1997 (SI 1997/793) reg.3 (April 7, 1997).
13. The Social Security (Miscellaneous Amendments) (No.2) Regulations 1997 (SI 1997/793) reg.3(3) and (5) (October 6, 1997).
14. The Tax Credits (Claims and Payments) (Amendment) Regulations 1999 (SI 1999/2572) reg.5 (October 5, 1999).
15. The Social Security (Immigration and Asylum) Consequential Amendments Regulations 2000 (SI 2000/636) reg.5 (April 3, 2000).
16. The Social Security and Child Support (Miscellaneous Amendments) Regulations 2000 (SI 2000/1596) reg.3(a) (June 19, 2000).
17. The Social Security and Child Support (Miscellaneous Amendments) Regulations 2000 (SI 2000/1596) reg.3(b) (June 19, 2000).
18. The Social Security (Joint Claims: Consequential Amendments) Regulations 2000 (SI 2000/1982) reg.2(4) (March 19, 2001).
18a. The Tax Credits (Claims and Payments) (Amendment) Regulations 2001 (SI 2001/567) (April 10, 2001).
18b. The Tax Credits (Claims and Payments) Amendment (No.3) Regulations 2001 (SI 2001/892) (April 10, 2001).
19. The Social Security (Claims and Payments and Miscellaneous Amendments) Regulations 2002 (SI 2002/428) reg.2 (April 2, 2002).
20. The Social Security (Working Tax Credit and Child Tax Credit) (Consequential Amendments) Regulations 2003 (SI 2003/455) Sch.4 (April 1, 2003).
21. The Social Security (Claims and Payments and Miscellaneous Amendments) Regulations 2003 (SI 2003/1632) reg.2 (July 21, 2003).
22. Social Security (Retirement Pensions) Amendment Regulations 2004 (SI 2004/2283) reg.2 (September 27, 2004).
23. The Social Security (Claims and Payments and Payments on account, Overpayments and Recovery) Amendment Regulations 2005 (SI 2005/34) reg.2 (May 2, 2005).
24. The Social Security, Child Support and Tax Credits (Miscellaneous Amendments) Regulations 2005 (SI 2005/337) reg.7 (March 19, 2005).
25. The Social Security (Civil Partnerships) (Consequential Amendments) Regulations 2005 (SI 2005/2878) (December 5, 2005).
26. The Civil Partnership (Pensions, Social Security and Child Support) (Consequential etc. Provisions) Order 2005 (SI 2005/2877) (December 5, 2005).
27. The Social Security (Miscellaneous Amendments) (No.2) Regulations 2006 (SI 2006/832) (April 10, 2006).
28. The Social Security (Miscellaneous Amendments) (No.3) Regulations 2006 (SI 2006/2377) (October 2, 2006).
29. The Social Security (Work-focused Interviews) Regulations 2000 (SI 2000/897) (April 3, 2000).
30. The Tax Credits (Claims and Payments) (Amendment) Regulations 2001 (SI 2001/567) (April 10, 2001).
31. The Social Security (Miscellaneous Amendments) (No.4) Regulations 2007 (SI 2007/2470) (September 24, 2007).
32. The Social Security (Claims and Information) Regulations 2007 (SI 2007/2911) (October 31, 2007).
33. The Employment and Support Allowance (Consequential Provisions) (No.2) Regulations 2008 (SI 2008/1554) reg.13 (October 27, 2008).
34 The Social Security (Miscellaneous Amendments) (No.5) Regulations 2008 (SI 2008/2667) reg.2 (October 30, 2008).
35. The Tribunals, Courts and Enforcement Act 2007 (Transitional and Consequential Provisions) Order 2008 (SI 2008/2683) reg.43 (November 3, 2008).
36. The Social Security (Miscellaneous Amendments) (No.2) Regulations 2009 (SI 2009/1490) reg.2 (July 13, 2009).

37. The Social Security (Miscellaneous Amendments) Regulations 2010 (SI 2010/510) reg.3(2) (April 6, 2010).
38. The Social Security (Disability Living Allowance, Attendance Allowance and Carer's Allowance) (Miscellaneous Amendments) Regulations 2011 (SI 2011/2426) reg.3 (October 31, 2011).

DEFINITIONS

"appropriate office"—see reg.2(1).
"claim for asylum"—*ibid.*
"claim for benefit"—*ibid.*
"jobseeker's allowance"—*ibid.*

GENERAL NOTE

Introduction

2.77 Claims are generally not made until received in any appropriate office.

R(SB)8/89 concerns the date of a claim for a single payment of supplementary benefit, but, since the date of claims for most benefits is also the date of receipt in the office of the Department, the decision is directly in point in relation to these benefits. The Commissioner's comments are worth quoting at length since the determination of the date of claim is often an issue arising on appeals:

> "In order for the claim to be made it is not alone necessary for the claimant to despatch the form but it is also necessary for the office of the Department to receive it. In my judgment if the office of the Department puts it out of its power to receive the claim by closing its offices and also arranging with the Post Office not to deliver mail on the days upon which the office is closed, then it put it out of its power to receive the claim. It may be that the claim can be received by the office of the Department whether such office is open or closed, but it cannot be received in circumstances where the Department arranges that mail should not be delivered. In her submission to me the adjudication officer now concerned refers to no deliveries being made by the Post Office on days upon which the office of the Department are [*sic*] closed. It will be a question of fact for the new tribunal to find whether such is by arrangement between the Department and Post Office and then to consider whether the Department has put it out of its power to receive claims on a Saturday. If they come to the conclusion that it did and find that in the normal course of delivery on that day then such is the date of claim." (At para.7.)

Where claim packs are sent out for disability living allowance and attendance allowance, it is not the practice of the Department (in contrast to the position where enquiries are made about other benefits) to follow the matter up if no completed claim is returned. The Claims and Payments Regulations clearly do not require such action, but it is understood that a number of welfare rights units are concerned that the variation in practice may operate to the disadvantage of claimants. It is, of course, the receipt of a completed claim (or at least some document which can be regarded as a claim under reg.4) which constitutes a claim under the regulations.

Establishing whether a person has claimed, and, if so, the date of a claim can arise with some frequency before tribunals. In *CP/4104/2004* the Commissioner reminds tribunals of the need to check on both departmental policies of destruction of documents and available computer records in assessing whether a claimant has made a claim. It may be necessary to receive evidence as to what a computer printout actually means. The core advice is not to accept unquestioningly assertions by the Department that it has no record of a claim or enquiry. In the case before the Commissioner that assertion was made to the tribunal, but on further enquiry turned out not to be the correct position.

Regulation 6 is one of the longest social security regulations, and is full of twists and turns. Great care should be taken in reading the regulation in any case raising questions concerning the date of claim.

Paragraph (1)

A properly completed claim on the proper form is made on the date that it is received in a benefit office. For a decision on the proper approach where the Department contends that a claim form has not been received, see *SSWP v ZVR (CA)* [2013] UKUT 515 (AAC). 2.78

There are many complications around this basic rule following the introduction of JSA and the severe restriction on the backdating of claims under reg.19 from April 1997.

R(SB) 8/89 holds that if the Department puts it out of its power to receive a claim, as by closing its office and arranging with the Post Office not to deliver mail, e.g. on a Saturday, then if that day is the day on which the claim would have been delivered, it is the date of claim. It can be said that by making the arrangement with the Post Office the Department constitute the Post Office bailees of the mail (see *Hodgson v Armstrong* [1967] Q.B. 299 and *Lang v Devon General Ltd* [1987] I.C.R. 4). The Commissioner does not deal expressly with the situation where the office is closed, but there is no arrangement about the mail, e.g. if an office is closed on a Saturday and the Saturday and Monday mail is all stamped with the Monday date in the office. Here, principle would suggest that if it can be shown that in the normal course of the post delivery would have been on the Saturday, then the Saturday is the date of receipt and the date of claim. If a claimant proves a delivery by hand when the office is closed, the date of delivery is the date of receipt.

Note also *CIS/4901/2002* relating to arrangements between the Department and the Post Office for the handling of mail, which is reported in more detail in the annotations to reg.19. 2.79

Levy v Secretary of State for Work and Pensions [2006] EWCA Civ 890, reported as *R(G) 2/06* considered the applicability to social security claims of the rebuttable presumption in s.7 of the Interpretation Act 1978 that a letter put in the post is delivered to its addressee. The Court of Appeal ruled that reg.6(1) was not ultra vires. The next question was whether s.7 of the Interpretation Act 1978 applied. Dyson L.J. (with whom Hallett and Pill L.JJ. agreed) concluded that the provision has no application in this context. Even if s.7 did apply, its application would appear to be excluded by the words "unless the contrary intention appears" in s.7 of the Interpretation Act. The Court of Appeal concludes that "It is plain that regulation 6(1) requires that the claim be received in fact and not merely that it be sent." (para. 32 of the judgment). It follows that *CIS/306/2003* and *CG/2973/2004* correctly analyse the legal position and that *CSIS/48/1992* and *CIS/759/1992* are wrong in so far as they suggest otherwise.

Paragraph (1A)

This provides that the date of claim for an income support claim will be the date a properly completed claim (i.e. one that complies with reg.4(1A)) is received (or the first day claimed for, if later). But if such a claim is received within one month of the date that the person first contacted the Department with a view to making a claim, or a previous defective claim (i.e. one that does not comply with reg.4(1A)), the date of claim will be the date of that initial contact or defective claim (or the first day claimed for, if later). Thus if more than a month elapses before the claimant complies with the requirements of reg.4(1A), the date of claim will be the date of that compliance (unless the rules on backdating apply: see reg.19(4)–(7)). See further the note to reg.4(1A)–(1C). 2.80

In *R(IS) 10/06* the Commissioner considers whether there is any priority in the claims covered by reg.6(1A)(c). He concludes:

> "16. On further consideration, I now realise that I was wrong to be concerned about the absence of any specified priority between the two heads of reg.6(1A)(c).

17. This only appears puzzling if the heads in that provisions are read in isolation from subparagraph (b). Subparagraph (c) is expressed as a deeming provision. Its function, though, is more akin to a definition. It sets out the circumstances in which a person is tread as notifying an intention to make a claim. If heads (i) and (ii) are read into paragraph (b), it reads:

> 'where a properly completed claim is received in an appropriate office within one month of first notification of intention to make that clauim, *which may be shown by (i) a notification in accordance with regulation 4(5) or (ii) a defective claim*, the date of claim shall be the date on which that notification is deemed to be made or the first day in respect of which the claim is made if later.'

Set out like that, no issue of priority arises. The claimant is given a choice to rely on one month from the date of notification or from the date of defective claim."

It is worth noting that the view of the Department is that this decision conflicts with *R(IS)14/04* (which, the Department contends, holds that the one-month period runs from the *first* point of contact; that is, the request for the claim form or the submission of the defective claim form), and argues that the *R(IS)14/04* should be followed in preference to *R(IS) 10/06.*

In *R(IS) 3/04* the Commissioner rules that it is not possible for a valid claim to income support to be made where a claimant dies having given notification of intention to make a claim but not having perfected the claim before his death by completing and submitting a claim form. The case concerned a situation in which the claim was completed and submitted by the executor of the claimant's will.

Paragraph (3)

2.81 For these benefits, if the time for claiming is extended under reg.19, the claim is treated as made at the beginning of the period for which the claim is deemed to be in time. Initial claims for working families tax credit and disabled person's tax credit and claims for income support and JSA have to be made on the first day of the period claimed for (Sch.4, paras 6, 7 and 11).

Paragraph (4)

2.82 The interaction of this provision with others is far from clear. It does not look as though it can apply directly in a case where the decision maker has extended the time for claiming by up to a month under reg.19(6). If the claim is not actually made (i.e. received: para.(1)) within the extended period, the claim is not timeously made and para.(3) above does not apply anyway. Postal delay is not a circumstance listed in reg.19(5) (replacing the old good cause rule), but may be relevant to the reasonableness of the delay in claiming. See also reg.19(7).

Paragraphs (4A)–(4AB)

2.83 In the case of JSA, if the person attends the Job Centre for the purpose of making a claim when required to do so and provides a properly completed claim (i.e. with all the necessary information: see reg.4(1A) and (9)), the date of claim will be the date the person first contacted the Job Centre (or the first day claimed for, if later) (para.(4)(a)(i) and (4AA)). Note the *discretion* to extend the time for delivery of a properly completed claim form under para.(4AB); unlike income support (and JSA postal signers) the month's allowance to return the fully completed claim form is not automatic. Note also para.(4A)(a)(ii) which provides that if the person fails to comply with these requirements without good cause the date of claim will be the date that he does comply. Thus if the person does have good cause for not so complying, presumably para.(4A)(a)(i) will apply when he does attend and does provide a fully completed claim form (and note the discretion in relation to the claim form under para.(4AB)). For claimants who are not required to attend the Job Centre in person (i.e. who are allowed to apply by post), their claim will be treated as made on the day they first contacted the Job Centre with a view to making a claim (or on the first day claimed for, if later) if a properly completed claim is received within one month, or the date the properly completed claim is received if more than one month has elapsed (para.(4A)(b)). See further the note to reg.4(1A)–(1C)).

In *CG/4060/2005* the Commissioner decided that reg.6(4AB) applied only to claims for a jobseeker's allowance, and so was of no assistance to persons claiming carer's allowance.

Paragraphs (4B) and (4C)

These paragraphs deal with certain cases where entitlement to JSA has ceased because of a failure to attend the Job Centre or to provide a signed declaration of availability and active search for employment, so that a new claim is necessary. **2.84**

Paragraph (4D)

These are special rules for claims by refugees. **2.85**

Paragraphs (6) and (7)

These provisions create a special rule on the increase of the capital limit for income support to £8,000. Where, from April 9, 1990, a claimant has capital of more than £6,000 but not more than £8,000, a claim made before May 28, 1990, can be back-dated to the date on which all the conditions of entitlement are satisfied. **2.86**

Paragraph (10)

Where a claimant starts work on a Monday or Tuesday and makes a claim for disability working allowance at any time in that week (i.e. Sunday to Saturday), the claim is treated as made on the Tuesday. **2.87**

Paragraphs (12)–(15)

Where a claim for disabled persons tax credit is disallowed on the ground that a qualifying benefit is not payable, although a claim for that benefit has been made, and later the qualifying benefit is awarded, a fresh claim for the tax credit made within three months of the award of the qualifying benefit is to be treated as made on the date of the original claim (or the date from which the qualifying benefit is awarded, if later). This rule is made necessary by the restrictions from April 1997 on the backdating of claims under reg.19 and on the effect of reviews. **2.88**

Paragraph (22)

The definition of "relevant benefit" does not include personal independence payment, and so does not count as a "qualifying benefit" for the purpose of the backdating provisions in reg.6(16)–(21). The Department has advised CPAG the omission is an oversight and will be remedied by regulations in 2015, and that, in the meantime, the Department will treat personal independence payment as if it were a "relevant benefit." The Department has, however, subsequently advised that it now has no current plans to amend the regulations to this effect. **2.89**

Paragraphs (31) and (32)

These provisions "get around" the 12-month limitation on back-dating set out in s.1(2) of the Administration Act in relation to claims for retirement pension. They enable claimants to go back as far as October 1, 1998 in certain circumstances. The Explanatory Memorandum to the regulations indicates that the intended beneficiaries of the provisions are those who did not receive notice that their contribution records were deficient for the tax years 1996/97 to 2002/02 because the annual Deficiency Notice procedure which identifies such cases and advises customers of the need to consider making voluntary contributions to make good the shortfall did not take place in those years. **2.90**

Paragraphs (35) and (36)

These paragraphs accommodate the consequences of the judgment of the Court of Justice in *Commission v European Parliament and Council* (C-299/05) [2007] E.C.R. I-8730, which determined that attendance allowance, carer's allowance, **2.91** and the care component of a disability living allowance constitute sickness benefits within Regulation 1408/71 (which are exportable by the beneficiary), and not special non-contributory benefits (which are not exportable).

Claims by persons subject to work-focused interviews

2.92 [[1]**6A.**—[[2] (1) This regulation applies to any person who is required to take part in a work-focused interview in accordance with regulations made under section 2A(1)(a) of the Social Security Administration Act 1992.]

(2) Subject to the following provisions of this regulation, where a person takes part in a work-focused interview, the date on which the claim is made shall be—

(a) in a case where—

(i) the claim made by the claimant meets the requirements of regulation 4(1), or

(ii) the claim made by the claimant is for income support and meets the requirements of regulation 4(1A),

the date on which the claim is received in the appropriate office.

(b) in a case where a claim does not meet the requirements of regulation 4(a) but is treated, under regulation 4(7), as having been duly made, the date on which the claim was treated as received in the appropriate office in the first instance;

(c) in a case where—

(i) first notification of intention to claim income support is made to an appropriate office, or

(ii) a claim for income support is received in an appropriate office which does not meet the requirements of regulation 4(1A),

[[5] (d) without prejudice to sub-paragraphs (a) and (b), where a properly completed claim for incapacity benefit is received in an appropriate office within one month of the claimant first notifying such an office, by whatever means, of his intention to make that claim, the date of claim shall be the date on which that notification is made or the first day in respect of which the claim is made if later.]

the date of notification of, as the case may be, the date the claim is first received where the properly complete claim form is received within 1 month of notification or the date the claim is first received, or the day on which a properly completed claim form is received where these requirements are not met.

(3) In a case where a decision is made that a person is regarded as not having made a claim for any benefit because he failed to take part in a work-focused interview but subsequently claims such a benefit, in applying paragraph (2) to that claim no regard shall be had to any claim regarded as not having been made in consequence of that decision.

(4) Paragraph (2) shall not apply in any case where a decision has been made that the claimant has failed to take part in a work-focused interview.

[[4] (5) In regulation 4 and this regulation, "work-focused interview" means an interview which [. . .] [is conducted for such purposes connected with employment or training as are specified under section 2A of the Social Security Administration Act 1992.]

AMENDMENTS

1. Regulation inserted by The Social Security (Work-focused Interviews) Regulations 2000 (SI 2000/897) (April 3, 2000).

2. The Social Security (Jobcentre Plus Interviews) Regulations 2001 (SI 2001/3210) (October 22, 2001).
3. Social Security (Jobcentre Plus Interviews) Regulations 2002 (SI 2002/1703) Sch.2 (September 30, 2002).
4. Social Security (Working Neighbourhoods) Regulations 2004 (SI 2004/959) reg.22 (April 26, 2004).
5. The Social Security (Miscellaneous Amendments) (No.2) Regulations 2006 (SI 2006/832) (April 10, 2006).

Evidence and information

7.—(1) [3Subject to paragraph (7),] every person who makes a claim for benefit shall furnish such certificates, documents, information and evidence in connection with the claim, or any question arising out of it, as may be required by the Secretary of State [4 or the Board] and shall do so within one month of being required to do so or such longer period as the Secretary of State [5Board] may consider reasonable. **2.93**

[6 (1A) A claimant shall furnish such information and evidence as the Secretary of State may require as to the likelihood of future changes in his circumstances which is needed to determine—

(a) whether a period should be specified as an assessed income period under section 6 of the 2002 Act in relation to any decision; and
(b) if so, the length of the period to be so specified.

(1B) The information and evidence required under paragraph (1A) shall be furnished within 1 month of the Secretary of State notifying the claimant of the requirement, or within such longer period as the Secretary of State considers reasonable in the claimant's case.

(1C) In the case of a claimant making a claim for state pension credit in the advance period, time begins to run for the purposes of paragraphs (1) and (1B) on the day following the end of that period.]

(2) [3Subject to paragraph (7),] where a benefit may be claimed by either of two partners or where entitlement to or the amount of any benefit is or may be affected by the circumstances of a partner, the Secretary of State may require the partner other than the [5claimant to do either or both of the following, within one month of being required to do so or such longer period as the Board may consider reasonable—

(a) to certify in writing whether he agrees to the claimant making or, as the case may be, that he confirms the information given about his circumstances;
(b) to furnish such certificates, documents, information and evidence in connection with the claim, or any question arising out of it, as the Board may require.]

claimant to certify in writing whether he agrees to the claimant making the claim or, as the case may be, that he confirms the information given about his circumstances [4working families tax credit or disabled persons tax credit].

(3) In the case of a claim for [4working families' tax credit] or [4disabled person's tax credit], the employer of the claimant or, as the case may be, of the partner shall [4within one month of being required to do so or such longer period as the Board may consider reasonable] furnish such certificates, documents, information and evidence in connection with the claim or any question arising out of it as may be required by the Secretary of State [4Board].

[2 (4) In the case of a person who is claiming [4 disabled person's tax credit, working families' tax credit], [3 income support] [6 jobseeker's allowance [7 state pension credit or employment and support allowance.] where that person or any partner is aged not less than 60 and is a member of, or a person deriving entitlement to a pension under, a personal pension scheme, or is a party to, or a person deriving entitlement to a pension under, a retirement annuity contract, he shall where the [5 Board so require, within one month of being required to do so or such longer period as the Board may consider reasonable] Secretary of State so requires furnish the following information—

(a) the name and address of the pension fund holder;

(b) such other information including any reference or policy number as is needed to enable the personal pension scheme or retirement annuity contract to be identified.

(5) Where the pension fund holder receives from the Secretary of State [5Board] a request for details concerning the personal pension scheme or retirement annuity contract relating to a person or any partner to whom paragraph (4) refers, the pension fund holder shall [5, within one month of the request or such longer period as the Board may consider reasonable] provide the Secretary of State [5Board] with any information to which paragraph (6) refers.

(6) The information to which this paragraph refers is—

(a) where the purchase of an annuity under a personal pension scheme has been deferred, the amount of any income which is being withdrawn from the personal pension scheme;

(b) in the case of—

(i) a personal pension scheme where income withdrawal is available, the maximum amount of income which may be withdrawn from the scheme; or

(ii) a personal pension scheme where income withdrawal is not available, or a retirement annuity contract, the maximum amount of income which might be withdrawn from the fund if the fund were held under a personal pension scheme where income withdrawal was available,

calculated by or on behalf of the pension fund holder by means of tables prepared from time to time by the Government Actuary which are appropriate for this purpose.]

[3(7) Paragraphs (1) and (2) do not apply in the case of jobseeker's allowance.]

[4(8) Every person providing childcare in respect of which a claimant to whom regulation 46A of the Family Credit (General) Regulations 1987 applies is incurring relevant childcare charges, including a person providing childcare on behalf of a school, local authority, childcare scheme or establishment within paragraph (2)(b), (c) or (d) of that regulation, shall furnish such certificates, documents, information and evidence in connection with the claim made by the claimant, or any question arising out of it, as may required by the Board, and shall do so within one month of being required to do so or such longer period as the Board may consider reasonable.

(9) In paragraph (8) "relevant childcare charges" has the meaning given by regulation 46A(2) of the Family Credit (General) Regulations 1987.]

AMENDMENTS

1. The Social Security (Claims and Payments) Amendment Regulations 1991 (SI 1991/2741) reg.5 (March 10, 1992).

2. Income-related Benefit Schemes and Social Security (Claims and Payments) (Miscellaneous Amendments) Regulations 1995 (SI 1995/2303) reg.10(3) (October 2, 1995).

3. The Social Security (Claims and Payments) (Jobseeker's Allowance Consequential Amendments) Regulations 1996 (SI 1996/1460) reg.2(6) (October 7, 1996).

4. The Tax Credits (Claims and Payments) (Amendment) Regulations 1999 (SI 1999/2572) reg.6 (October 5, 1999).

5. For tax credits purposes only: The Tax Credits (Claims and Payments) (Amendment) Regulations 1999 (SI 1999/2572) reg.6 (October 5, 1999).

6. State Pension Credit (Consequential, Transitional and Miscellaneous) Regulations 2002 (SI 2002/3019) reg.4 (April 7, 2003).

7. The Employment and Support Allowance (Consequential Provisions) (No.2) Regulations 2008 (SI 2008/1554) reg.15 (October 27, 2008).

Definitions

"benefit"—see reg.2(2).
"claim for benefit"—see reg.2(1).
"jobseeker's allowance"—*ibid.*
"partner"—*ibid.*
"pension fund holder"—*ibid.*
"personal pension scheme"—*ibid.*
"retirement annuity contract"—*ibid.*

General Note

From time to time, decision makers have suggested that a person is not entitled to benefit because they have failed to furnish the Secretary of State with information within the one month referred to in reg.7(1). *R(IS)4/93* was just such a case. The adjudication officer decided that the claimant was not entitled to income support because the claimant had failed—inter alia to provide sufficient evidence as to the amount of capital held. The tribunal confirmed the adjudication officer's decision and the claimant appealed to the Commissioner. **2.94**

Deputy Commissioner Mesher (as he then was) concluded that both the adjudication officer and the tribunal had misunderstood the operation of reg.7(1). Drawing on the reasoning of the Court of Appeal in *R. v Secretary of State for Social Services Ex p. Child Poverty Action Group* [1990] 2 Q.B. 540, the Deputy Commissioner explains that reg.7(1) is concerned with the responsibilities of the Secretary of State to collect information so that the Secretary of State can submit a claim to an adjudication officer for determination:

> "Once such a submission is made, it is simply irrelevant whether or not the claimant has satisfied the Secretary of State under reg.7(1) of the Claims and Payments Regulations or whether or not the claimant has furnished sufficient information for the Secretary of State to refer the claim to the adjudication officer. Those matters are entirely for the Secretary of State [see para.11 of *R(SB)29/83*]. Once the claim is submitted to him under section 98(1) [now s.20(1) of the Administration Act], the adjudication officer's duty is to take it into consideration and, so far as practicable, dispose of it within 14 days of its submission (Social Security Act 1975, s.99(1)) [now s.21(1) of the Administration Act]. As decided by the Court of Appeal in the passage quoted above, the adjudication officer has the power to make further investigations or call for further evidence before determining the claim. Or he may determine the claim on the evidence currently available, especially if he considers that the claimant has already had a reasonable opportunity of producing the required information or evidence." (At [13].)

The Deputy Commissioner goes on to advise that adjudication officers and tribunals when presented with a claim for determination (whether initially or on appeal) must focus on the "essential elements of entitlement directly" in the light of the evidence available. Since claimants generally have the burden of showing on the balance of probabilities that they meet the conditions of entitlement, the absence of information from the claimant will often result in a finding against them.

2.95 The Deputy Commissioner does not spell out how tribunals should proceed if the absence of information means that the tribunal cannot make any findings of fact. There will be cases where there is insufficient information to find positively some fact which results in there being no entitlement. In these rare cases where a claimant's reluctance to participate defeats the inquisitorial jurisdiction of tribunals, it is open to the tribunal to decide the matter purely on the burden of proof. In such cases the proper approach is for the tribunal:

— to record no findings of fact, or perhaps only those that are proved, *avoiding* the inclusion of reference to those issues on which facts cannot be found;
— to record in the decision that the claimant is not entitled to the benefit on the claim made on such and such a day because they have not proved on the balance of probabilities that they meet the conditions of entitlement for the benefit; and
— to explain fully in the reasons for the decision what the relevant conditions of entitlement are and why the tribunal is unable to make findings of fact on all the material issues.

R(IS)4/93 has been referred to and disapproved by the Court of Appeal in Northern Ireland in *Kerr v Department for Social Development* [2002] NICA 32, Judgment of July 4, 2002. That decision went an appeal to the House of Lords. The decision of the House of Lords in *Kerr v Department for Social Development*, [2004] UKHL 23; [2004] 1 W.L.R. 1372 (appendix to *R1/04(SF)*) was handed down on May 6, 2004. The discussion in the House of Lords broadened from the considerations which had taken place in the courts below. The comments, in particular of Baroness Hale, on the decision-making process are discussed in detail in the annotations to s.3(1) of the Tribunals, Courts and Enforcement Act 2007. The House of Lords dismissed the appeal. In their opinions, no mention is made of *R(IS) 4/93* which had been disapproved in the reasons of the Court of Appeal. Notwithstanding the absence of any comment, its authority must be considerably weakened by the dismissal of the appeal. However, it is suggested that it will still provide some useful guidance in those cases where, despite the best endeavours of the adjudicating authorities to collect all the evidence needed to determine a claim for benefit, they remain short of evidence on key matters. For a discussion of the similar provisions in relation to the adjudication of housing benefit and council tax benefit claims see the decision of the Tribunal of Commissioners in *R(H) 3/05*.

In *CIS/51/2007* and *CIB/52/2007* the Commissioner comments on the relationship between regs 4–6A, and reg.7. The context was a claim which left some uncertainty about the claimant's identity (the national insurance number provided did not correspond to the identity of the claimant) and the correctness of his address (enquiries to the address given had resulted in denials that the claimant had ever lived there). The Commissioner notes that there are requirements for making a claim under the regulations, which are a matter of form and procedure, and that these should be distinguished from "the obvious and universal necessity for any person making such a claim to substantiate it by showing he meets the qualifying conditions for entitlement". This is a matter of fact and evidence (para. 8). The provisions of reg.7(1) apply only to those who have made something that can be identified as a procedurally effective claim. That is determined by applying the rules in reg.4 to 6A. A claim which raises questions about the identity of the claimant may be a claim. Establishing identity is a matter of fact and evidence. If claimants cannot establish these matters, then they have failed to comply with the reasonable evidence requirements, and it will be appropriate to determine that they have not met the conditions of entitlement.

Attendance in person

8.—(1) [[1]. . .] 2.96

(2) Every person who makes a claim for benefit [[1] (other than a jobseeker's allowance)] shall attend at such office or place and on such days and at such times as the Secretary of State [[2] or the Board] may direct, for the purpose of furnishing certificates, documents, information and evidence under regulation 7, if reasonably so required by the Secretary of State [[2] or the Board].

AMENDMENTS

1. The Social Security (Claims and Payments) (Jobseeker's Allowance Consequential Amendments) Regulations 1996 (SI 1996/1460) reg.2(7) (October 7, 1996).

2. The Tax Credits (Claims and Payments) (Amendment) Regulations 1999 (SI 1999/2572) reg.20 (October 5, 1999).

DEFINITIONS

"benefit"—see reg.2(2).
"claim for benefit"—see reg.2(1).

GENERAL NOTE

There seems now to be no direct sanction for a failure to comply with reg.8(2) in relation to benefits other than JSA. For JSA obligations, see reg.23 of the Jobseeker's Allowance Regulations. 2.97

Interchange with claims for other benefits

9.—(1) Where it appears that a person who has made a claim for benefit specified in column (1) of Part I of Schedule 1 may be entitled to the benefit specified opposite to it in column (2) of that Part, any such claim may be treated by the Secretary of State [[1] or the Board] as a claim alternatively, or in addition, to the benefit specified opposite to it in that column. 2.98

(2) Where it appears that a person who has claimed any benefit specified in Part II of Schedule 1 in respect of a child may be entitled to child benefit in respect of the same child, the Secretary of State may treat the claim alternatively, or in addition, for the benefit in question as a claim by that person for child benefit.

(3) Where it appears that a person who has claimed child benefit in respect of a child may be entitled to any benefit specified in Part II of Schedule 1 [[2]. . .] in respect of the same child, the Secretary of State may treat the claim for child benefit as a claim alternatively, or in addition, by that person for the benefit in question specified in that Part.

(4) Where it appears that a person who has made a claim for benefit other than child benefit is not entitled to it, but that some other person may be entitled to an increase of benefit in respect of him, the Secretary of State may treat the claim as if it were a claim by such other person for an increase of benefit in respect of the claimant.

(5) Where it appears that a person who has made a claim for an increase of benefit other than child benefit in respect of a child or adult dependant is not entitled to it but that some other person may be entitled to such an increase of benefit in respect of that child or adult dependant, the Secretary

of State may treat the claim as if it were a claim by that other person for such an increase.

(6) Where it appears that a person who has made a claim for a guardian's allowance in respect of any child is not entitled to it, but that the claimant or the wife or husband of the claimant, may be entitled to an increase of benefit for that child, the Secretary of State may treat the claim as if it were a claim by the claimant or the wife or husband of the claimant for an increase of benefit for that child.

[3 (7) In determining whether he [1 or they] should treat a claim alternatively or in addition to another claim (the original claim) under this regulation the Secretary of State shall treat the alternative or additional claim, whenever made, as having been made at the same time as the original claim.]

Amendments

1. The Tax Credits (Claims and Payments) (Amendment) Regulations 1999 (SI 1999/2572) regs 20 and 22 (October 5, 1999).

2. The Child Benefit, Child Support and Social Security (Miscellaneous Amendments) Regulations 1996 (SI 1996/1803) reg.19 (April 7, 1997).

3. The Social Security (Miscellaneous Provisions) Amendment Regulations 1992 (SI 1992/247) reg.12 (March 9, 1992).

General Note

2.99 This invaluable provision removes some of the rigour of ensuring that a claimant chooses the right benefit to claim and is not prejudiced by making a mistaken choice. The regulation now also covers interchange of claims for child benefit with claims for other benefits. There was originally some doubt over whether a decision to treat a claim as one in the alternative was for the adjudicating authorities or the Secretary of State.

In *R. v Secretary of State for Social Security Ex p. Cullen and Nelson* (*The Times*, May 16, 1997 reported as *R(A) 1/97*), the Court of Appeal confirmed the decision of Harrison J. in *Cullen* (November 16, 1996) and reversed the decision of the Commissioner in *Nelson* (*CA 171/1993*). In both cases, unsuccessful claims for supplementary benefit had been made prior to April 11, 1988. At that time, the 1979 Claims and Payments Regulations allowed the Secretary of State to treat a claim for supplementary benefit as in the alternative a claim for attendance allowance. The Claims and Payments Regulations 1987, which came into effect on April 11, 1988, contained no such power. In 1991 (*Cullen*) and 1993 (*Nelson*) claims for attendance allowance were made and it was sought to have the supplementary benefit claims treated as claims for attendance allowance. The Court of Appeal held that the Secretary of State had no power to do so, so that the Commissioner in *CA/171/1993* was wrong to refer the question to the Secretary of State for determination. Once the 1979 Regulations were revoked, the Secretary of State could no longer exercise a power which no longer existed. As the Secretary of State had only had a discretion under the 1979 Regulations whether or not to treat a supplementary benefit claim as in the alternative a claim for attendance allowance, the claimants had no accrued rights which were preserved on the revocation of the 1979 Regulations under s.16 of the Interpretation Act 1978.

[1 Claim for incapacity benefit [3 , severe disablement allowance or employment and support allowance] where no entitlement to statutory sick pay or statutory maternity pay]

2.100 **10.**—(1) Paragraph (2) applies to a claim for incapacity benefit or severe] disablement allowance for a period of incapacity for work of which the claimant gave his employer a notice of incapacity under regulation 7 of the Statutory Sick Pay (General) Regulations 1982, and for which he has been informed in writing by his employer that there is no entitlement to statutory sick pay.

[3 (1A) Paragraph (2) also applies to a claim for an employment and support allowance for a period of limited capability for work in relation to which the claimant gave his employer a notice of incapacity under regulation 7 of the Statutory Sick Pay (General) Regulations 1982, and for which he has been informed in writing by his employer that there is no entitlement to statutory sick pay.]

(2) A claim to which this paragraph applies shall be treated as made on the date accepted by the claimant's employer as the first day of incapacity, provided that he makes the claim—

(a) within the appropriate time specified in paragraph 2 of Schedule 4 beginning with the day on which he is informed in writing that he was not entitled to statutory sick pay; or

(b) [2 . . .]

(3) Paragraph (4) applies to a claim for maternity allowance for a pregnancy or confinement by reason of which the claimant gave her employer notice of absence from work under [section 164(4) of the Social Security Contributions and Benefits Act 1992] and regulation 23 of the Statutory Maternity Pay (General) Regulations 1986 and in respect of which she has been informed in writing by her employer that there is no entitlement to statutory maternity pay.

(4) A claim to which this paragraph applies shall be treated as made on the date when the claimant gave her employer notice of absence from work or at the beginning of the 14th week before the expected week of confinement, whichever is later, provided that she makes the claim—

(a) within three months of being informed in writing that she was not entitled to statutory maternity pay; or

(b) [2 . . .]

AMENDMENTS

1. The Social Security (Claims and Payments) Amendment (No.2) Regulations 1994 (SI 1994/2943) reg.3 (April 13, 1995).

2. The Social Security (Miscellaneous Amendments) (No.2) Regulations 1997 (SI 1997/793) reg.4 (April 7, 1997).

3. The Employment and Support Allowance (Consequential Provisions) (No.2) Regulations 2008 (SI 2008/1554) reg.16 (October 27, 2008).

Special provisions where it is certified that a woman is expected to be confined or where she has been confined

11.—(1) Where in a certificate issued or having effect as issued under the Social Security (Medical Evidence) Regulations 1976 it has been certified that it is to be expected that a woman will be confined, and she makes a claim for maternity allowance in expectation of that confinement any such claim may, unless the Secretary of State otherwise directs, be treated as a claim for [1 incapacity city benefit] [3 , severe disablement allowance or employment and support allowance] made in respect of any days in the period beginning with either— 2.101

(a) the beginning of the 6th week before the expected week of confinement; or

(b) the actual date of confinement, whichever is the earlier, and ending in either case on the 14th day after the actual date of confinement.

(2) Where, in a certificate issued under the Social Security (Medical Evidence) Regulations 1976 it has been certified that a woman has been confined and she claims maternity allowance within [2 three months] of that date, her claim may be treated in the alternative or in addition as a claim for incapacity benefit [3 , severe disablement allowance or employment and support allowance] for the period beginning with the date of her confinement and ending 14 days after that date.

AMENDMENTS

1. The Social Security (Claims and Payments) Amendment (No.2) Regulations 1994 (SI 1994/2943) reg.4 (April 13, 1995).

2. The Social Security (Miscellaneous Amendments) (No.2) Regulations 1997 (SI 1997/793) reg.5 (April 7, 1997).

3. The Employment and Support Allowance (Consequential Provisions) (No.2) Regulations 2008, (SI 2008/1554) reg.17 (October 27, 2008).

GENERAL NOTE

2.102 In *R(S)1/74* the Commissioner held that a similarly worded predecessor to this regulation which made similar, though not identical, provision neither confers title to sickness benefit nor restricts the right to it. The regulation does no more than define the period for which, having made an unsuccessful claim to maternity allowance, a woman may be treated as having made a claim to incapacity benefit. There is nothing to prevent her seeking to prove incapacity for some period or periods additional to that to which her claim is taken to relate.

2.103 *Regulation 12 revoked by The Social Security (Claims and Payments on account, Overpayments and Recovery) Amendment Regulations 1989 (SI 1989/136) (February 27, 1989).*

Advance claims and awards

2.104 **13.**—(1) Where, although a person does not satisfy the requirements of entitlement to benefit on the date on which a claim is made, the [3 Secretary of State] is of the opinion that unless there is a change of circumstances he will satisfy those requirements for a period beginning on a day (the relevant day") not more than 3 months after the date on which the claim is made, then [3 the Secretary of State] may—

(a) treat the claim as if made for a period beginning with the relevant day; and

(b) award benefit accordingly, subject to the condition that the person satisfies the requirements for entitlement when benefit becomes payable under the award.

(2) [3 A decision pursuant to paragraph (1)(b) to award benefit may be revised under section 9 of the Social Security Act 1998] if the requirements for entitlement are found not to have been satisfied on the relevant day.

(3) [2 [6. . .] Paragraphs (1) and (2) do not apply] to any claim for maternity allowance, [6 . . .], [4 state pension credit] retirement pension or increase, [8 state pension under Part 1 of the Pensions Act 2014,] [5 a shared additional pension] [6 . . .] [1 disability living allowance], or any claim within regulations 11(1)(a) or (b).

(4)–(8) [6 . . .]

[6 (9) Paragraphs (1) and (2) do not apply to—

(a) a claim for income support made by a person from abroad as defined in regulation 21AA of the Income Support (General) Regulations 1987 (special cases: supplemental—persons from abroad); [7 . . .]

(b) a claim for a jobseeker's allowance made by a person from abroad as defined in regulation 85A of the Jobseeker's Allowance Regulations (special cases: supplemental—persons from abroad).] [7 and

(c) a claim for an employment and support allowance made by a person from abroad as defined in regulation 70 of the Employment and Support Allowance Regulations (special cases: supplemental—persons from abroad).]

AMENDMENTS

1. The Social Security (Claims and Payments) Amendments Regulations 1991 (SI 1991/2741) reg.13 (March 9, 1992).

2. The Social Security (Claims and Payments) Amendment Regulations 1994 (SI 1994/2319) reg.3 (October 3, 1994).

3. The Social Security Act 1998 (Commencement No 9, and Savings and Consequential and Transitional Provisions) Order 1999 (SI 1999/2422) Sch.7 (September 6, 1999).

4. State Pension Credit (Consequential, Transitional and Miscellaneous) Regulations 2002 (SI 2002/3019) reg.6 (April 7, 2003).

5. The Social Security (Shared Additional Pension) (Miscellaneous Amendments) Regulations 2005 (SI2005/1551) reg.2 (July 2, 2005).

6. The Social Security, Housing Benefit and Council Tax Benefit (Miscellaneous Amendments) Regulations 2007 (SI 2007/1331) (May 23, 2007).

7. The Employment and Support Allowance (Consequential Provisions) (No. 2) Regulations 2008 (SI 2008/1554) reg.18 (October 27, 2008).

8. The Pensions Act 2014 (Consequential, Supplementary and Incidental Amendments) Order 2015 (SI 2015/1985) art.9(6) (April 6, 2016).

GENERAL NOTE

This regulation contains a useful power in the case of the specified benefits to make awards in advance, subject to revision if the conditions of entitlement are found not to be satisfied as at the date the award takes effect. But amendments following the Court of Appeal's decision in *Secretary of State for Work and Pensions* v. *Bhakta,* [2006] EWCA Civ. 65 exclude advance awards for persons from abroad in relation to the habitual residence test. **2.105**

The weight of authority on the proper interpretation of reg.13(1) is that a claim is to be treated as continuously made until it is determined: see *AW v SSWP (IB)* [2013] UKUT 20 (AAC), [15]–[19], and the authorities cited there.

Advance award of disability living allowance

[1 **13A.**—(1) Where, although a person does not satisfy the requirements for entitlement to disability living allowance on the date on which the claim is made, the [2 Secretary of State] is of the opinion that unless there is a change of circumstances he will satisfy those requirements for a period beginning on a day ("the relevant day" not more than 3 months after the date on which the claim is made, then [2 the Secretary of State] may award disability living allowance from the relevant day subject to the condition that the person satisfies the requirements for entitlement on the relevant day. **2.106**

(2) Where a person makes a claim for disability living allowance on or

after 3rd February 1992 and before 6th April 1992 the adjudicating authority may award benefit for a period beginning on or after 5th April 1992 being a day not more than three months after the date on which the claim was made, subject to the condition that the person satisfies the requirements for entitlement when disability living allowance becomes payable under the award.

(3) [[2] A decision pursuant to paragraph (1) or (2) to award benefit may be revised under section 9 of the Social Security Act 1998] if the requirements for entitlement are found not to have been satisfied when disability living allowance becomes payable under the award.]

AMENDMENTS

1. The Social Security (Claims and Payments) Amendment Regulations 1991 (SI 1991/2741) reg.7 (February 3, 1992).

2. The Social Security Act 1998 (Commencement No.11 and Transitional Provisions) Order 1999 (SI 1999/2860) Sch.3 (October 18, 1999).

GENERAL NOTE

2.107 In *CSDLA/852/2002*, and repeated in *CSDLA/553/2005* the Commissioner explains:

> "4. Regulation 13A thus permits an award of DLA where a claim is made no more than three months before the date from which the award takes effect, if the DM considers that by that date the claimant will satisfy the three months qualifying period for DLA and is then likely so to satisfy the qualifying conditions for a further six-month period. The claim subsists until the matter is determined by the DM (s.8(2)(a) of the Social Security Act 1998).
> 5. A claim is to be treated as being continuously made until it is determined. Therefore, although Regulation 13A only benefits the claimant if the claim is made within the relevant three-month period, it applies provided that the DLA conditions in question are satisfied by the date of the Secretary of State's decision under appeal and seemed likely to continue for both the three-month qualifying period and the six-month prospective period, so that the Secretary of State could then have made an advance award.
> 6. The issue for the tribunal was, therefore, whether . . . when the claim was decided by the Secretary of State (and beyond which circumstances could not be taken because of section 12(8)(b) of the Social Security Act 1998), circumstances existed, (even if proved by later evidence not available to the DM at the time) which justified an award under regulation 13A."

A different Commissioner had come to the same conclusion in *CDLA/3071/2005*. In *KH v SSWP* [2009] UKUT 54 (AAC), the judge also came to the same conclusion by slightly different reasoning. Regulation 6(8) of the Claims and Payments Regulations did not require the date of claim to be regarded as the date a claim form was requested (provided that it was returned within six weeks or such longer period as the Secretary of State chooses to accept), since this would deprive Regulation 13A of much of its significance. The judge says:

> "12. As I have said, there is no reason to give effect to regulation 6(8) beyond its context and purpose. Regulation 13A, in contrast to regulation 6(8), is concerned with the future, not the past. There is no need or reason to allow that provision to control the power to make an advance award. The natural meaning of 'the date on which the claim is made' in the context of regulation 13A is the date on which it is received. If the Secretary of State's argument is correct, the effectiveness of regulation 13A is significantly reduced. Potentially six weeks (or longer at the Secretary of State's discretion) may have past before the claim is even

received and further weeks may pass while the Secretary of State obtains medical evidence and decides the claim. In that context, there may be little or no scope for an advance award if the 3 months begins on the date the claimant asked for a claim pack."

[1 Advance claim for and award of disability working allowance

13B.—(1) Where a person makes a claim for disability working allowance on or after 10th March 1992 and before 7th April 1992 the adjudicating authority may— **2.108**

(a) treat the claim as if it were made for a period beginning on 7th April 1992; and

(b) An award benefit accordingly, subject to the condition that the person satisfies the requirements for entitlement on 7th April 1992.

(2) An award under paragraph (1)(b) shall be reviewed by the adjudicating authority if the requirements for entitlement are found not to have been satisfied on 7th April 1992.]

AMENDMENT

1. The Social Security (Claims and Payments) Amendment Regulations 1991 (SI 1991/2741) reg.7(2) (March 10, 1992).

DEFINITION

"adjudicating authority"—see reg.2(1).

GENERAL NOTE

This allowed an advance claim in the few weeks immediately before the start of the scheme on April 7, 1992. **2.109**

[1 [2 Further claim for and award of disability living allowance or attendance allowance

13C.—(1) A person entitled to an award of disability living allowance or attendance allowance may make a further claim for disability living allowance or attendance allowance, as the case may be, during the period of 6 months immediately before the existing award expires.] **2.110**

(2) Where a person makes a claim in accordance with paragraph (1) the [3 Secretary of State] may—

(a) treat the claim as if made on the first day after the expiry of the existing award ("the renewal date"); and

(b) award benefit accordingly, subject to the condition that the person satisfies the requirements for entitlement on the renewal date.

(3) [4 A decision pursuant to paragraph (2)(b) to award benefit may be revised under section 9 of the Social Security Act 1998] if the requirements for entitlement are found not to have been satisfied on the renewal date.]

AMENDMENTS

1. The Social Security (Claims and Payments) Amendment Regulations 1991 (SI 1991/2741) reg.8 (February 3, 1992).

2. The Social Security, Child Support and Tax Credits (Miscellaneous Amendments) Regulations 2005 (SI 2005/337) reg.7 (March 18, 2005).

3. The Social Security Act 1998 (Commencement No.11, and Savings and Consequential and Transitional Provisions) Order 1999 (SI 1999/2860) Sch.3 para.2 (October 18, 1999).

General Note

2.111 This permits a continuation claim for disability living allowance to be made during the last six months of an existing award.

In *CDLA/14895/1996*, it was held that reg.13C(2) should not be applied until it has been considered whether, if the claim were treated as an application for review under s.30(13) of the Social Security Administration Act 1992, there would be grounds for review. If there are grounds for review, the existing award should be reviewed. Otherwise, the claim should be treated as a renewal claim, effective only from the end of the existing award.

The relationship of this regulation and the prohibition on tribunals of considering circumstances obtaining after the date of claim under s.12(8)(b) of the Social Security Act 1998 was considered in *CDLA/3848/2001*, where the Commissioner said,

> "In my judgment it is implicit in Reg.13C of the 1987 Regulations that circumstances occurring between the date of a decision on a renewal claim and the renewal date can (and therefore must) be taken into account by an appeal tribunal.
> . . .
> Regulation 13C(2), having stated that the Secretary of State may treat the claim as if made on the renewal date, goes on to provide that he may 'award benefit accordingly.' That means that the task of a decision maker (and appeal tribunal on appeal) is to determine whether the conditions for disability living allowance will be (or were) satisfied *on the renewal date*. It is in my view implicit that circumstances which occur between the date of the decision maker's decision and the renewal date can be taken into account by an appeal tribunal. It cannot have been the intention of s.12(8)(b) and Reg.13C, read together, that an appeal tribunal is prevented from taking into account changes in circumstances relevant to the very issue which it has to decide. If it were to ignore such changes, the effect of its decision would not be to 'award benefit accordingly' (i.e. on the basis of a claim treated as made on the renewal date)."

A Scottish Commissioner agreed with this reasoning in deciding an appeal relating to a claim for an attendance allowance, where there is no corresponding provision. Though disability living allowance and attendance allowance are separate benefits, there is no logical reason why there should not be similar provision in relation to renewal claims. However, there is not. The Commissioner in *CSA/248/2002* had to decide the effect of a tribunal's only deciding matters down to the date of the decision, and whether this had constituted an error of law. The Commissioner concluded that the renewal claim could be competently made in advance of the expiry of the existing award (at paras 12 and 13). But the Commissioner found himself compelled to conclude that s.12(8)(b) did apply to the renewal of an attendance allowance claim (at para.19).

2.112 In *CDLA/4331/2002*, it was held that, when hearing an appeal from a decision on a renewal claim effective from the claimant's 16th birthday, a tribunal is required to determine the appeal on the basis that that the claimant was 16, even if she was only 15 at the date of the Secretary of State's decision. The approach taken was different from that in *CDLA/3848/2001*, but the result was the same on the facts of the case. In *C12/2003–04 (DLA)*, a Commissioner in Northern Ireland expressly disagreed with *CDLA/3848/2001* and concluded that the Secretary of State was not entitled to refuse benefit at all until the date from which the renewal claim would have been effective. A tribunal, faced with an appeal against a disallowance of a renewal claim made before the date from which a new award would have been effective, therefore had no power to do more than set aside the Secretary of State's decision as having been made without jurisdiction, leaving the Secretary of State to make a new decision.

This conflict of authority has now been resolved in a decision of a Tribunal of Commissioners in *R(DLA)4/05*. The Tribunal of Commissioners departs from the reasoning in both *CDLA/3848/2001* and *C12/2003–04 (DLA)*. *CDLA/3848/2001* had failed to take into account that effect had to be given to the provisions of ss.8(2)(b) and 12(8)(b) of the Social Security Act 1998 in the context of renewal claims. This precluded the Secretary of State from taking into account any circumstances not obtaining at the date of the decision. This meant that the Secretary of State had to determine the renewal claim on the basis of circumstances existing at the time the decision was made. In so doing they dissent from paras 106–107 of another decision of a Tribunal of Commissioners in *R(IB)2/04* (see below) which had indicated that renewal claims required prediction. The later Tribunal of Commissioners concludes that this part of the earlier decision was made without full argument and consideration of the implications of s.8(2)(b). They consider that, if a change of circumstances before the renewal date is anticipated, best practice would be to defer the making of the decision until closer to the renewal date in order to know whether the anticipated change had indeed materialised. The Tribunal's disagreement with the Northern Ireland decision in that reg.13C(2)(b) only permits the imposition of a condition in the case of an advance award that all the conditions of entitlement exist as at the renewal date. So the Secretary of State did have power to disallow a renewal claim before the renewal date.

The earlier decision of the Tribunal of Commissioners in *R(IB)2/04* had, in its third issue, addressed the question of whether the power to revise in reg.13C(3) is a free-standing one, or whether reg.3 of the Decisions and Appeals Regulations needs to be established before a decision on a renewal claim can be altered under reg.13C(3). The Tribunal of Commissioners concludes that there is no need for a ground for revision under reg.3 of the Decisions and Appeals Regulations to exist to trigger a reg.13C(3) revision. However, in the usual case where the issue concerns the condition of the claimant at the renewal date, "it can be exercised only on the ground that the claimant's condition has either improved between the date of decision and the renewal date to a greater extent than anticipated by the decision maker or has not deteriorated during that period to the extent anticipated by the decision maker." (para.13 of the summary of conclusions on issues of law.' This conclusion must, however, now be read in the light of the decision of the Tribunal of Commissioners in the later decision referred to above.

[1 Advance claims for an award of state pension credit

13D.—(1) Paragraph (2) applies if— 2.113

(a) a person does not satisfy the requirements for entitlement to state pension credit on the date on which the claim is made; and

(b) the Secretary of State is of the opinion that unless there is a change of circumstances he will satisfy those requirements—

 (i) where the claim is made in the advance period, when he attains the qualifying age; or

 (ii) in any other case, within 4 months of the date on which the claim is made.

(2) Where this paragraph applies, the Secretary of State may—

(a) treat the claim as made for a period beginning on the day ("the relevant day") the claimant—

 (i) attains the qualifying age, where the claim is made in the advance period; or

 (ii) is likely to satisfy the requirements for entitlement in any other case; and

(b) if appropriate, award state pension credit accordingly, subject to the condition that the person satisfies the requirements for entitlement on the relevant day.

(3) An award under paragraph (2) may be revised under section 9 of the Social Security Act 1998 if the claimant fails to satisfy the conditions for entitlement to state pension credit on the relevant day.]

[2 (4) This regulation does not apply to a claim made by a person not in Great Britain as defined in regulation 2 of the State Pension Credit Regulations (persons not in Great Britain).]

AMENDMENTS

1. Inserted by the State Pension Credit (Consequential, Transitional and Miscellaneous Provisions) Regulations 2002 (SI 2002/3019) reg.6 (April 7, 2003).

2. The Social Security, Housing Benefit and Council Tax benefit (Miscellaneous Amendments) Regulations 2007 (SI 2007/1331) (May 23, 2007).

Advance claim for and award of maternity allowance

2.114 **14.**—(1) Subject to the following provisions of this regulation, a claim for maternity allowance in expectation of confinement, or for an increase in such an allowance in respect of an adult dependent, and an award on such a claim, may be made not earlier than 14 weeks before the beginning of the expected week of confinement.

(2) A claim for an increase of maternity allowance in respect of an adult dependant may not be made in advance unless, on the date when made, the circumstances relating to the adult dependant concerned are such as would qualify the claimant for such an increase if they occurred in a period for which she was entitled to a maternity allowance.

Advance notice of retirement and claim for and award of pension

2.115 **15.**—(1) A claim for a retirement pension of any category, and for any increase in any such pension, [8 or a state pension under Part 1 of the Pensions Act 2014] [6 or a shared additional pension] and an award on such a claim, may be made at any time not more than 4 months before the date on which the claimant will, subject to the fulfilment of the necessary conditions, become entitled to such a pension.

(2) [1. . .]

(3) [1. . .]

(4) [1. . .]

[2 (5) Where a person claims a Category A or Category B retirement pension and is, or but for that claim would be, in receipt of [3 incapacity benefit] [4. . .] for a period which includes the first day to which the claim relates, then if that day is not the appropriate day for the payment of retirement pension in his case, the claim shall be treated as if the first day of the claim was instead the next following such pay day.

(6) Where the spouse of such a person as is mentioned in paragraph (5) above claims a Category A or Category B retirement pension and the first day of that claim is the same as the first day of the claim made by that person, the provisions of that paragraph shall apply also to the claim made by the spouse [7 or civil partner].]

(7) For the purposes of facilitating the determination of a subsequent claim for a Category A, B or C retirement pension [8 or a state pension

under Part 1 of the Pensions Act 2014], a person may at any time not more than 4 months before the date on which he will attain pensionable age, and notwithstanding that he [5 intends to defer his entitlement to a Category A or Category B retirement pension] [8 or a state pension under Part 1 of the Pensions Act 2014] at that date, submit particulars in writing to the Secretary of State in a form approved by him for that purpose with a view to the determination (in advance of the claim) of any question under the Act [8 or the Pensions Act 2014] relating to that person's title to such a [8 pension] [5. . .] and subject to the necessary modifications, the provisions of these regulations shall apply to any such particulars.

AMENDMENTS

1. Social Security Act 1986 (October 1, 1989).
2. The Social Security (Abolition of Earnings Rule) (Consequential) Regulations 1989 (SI 1989/1642) reg.2(2) (October 1, 1989).
3. The Social Security (Claims and Payments) Amendment (No.2) Regulations 1994 (SI 1994/2943) reg.5 (April 13, 1995).
4. The Social Security (Claims and Payments) (Jobseeker's Allowance Consequential Amendments) Regulations 1996 (SI 1996/1460) reg.2 (October 7, 1996).
5. The Social Security (Abolition of Earnings Rule) (Consequential) Regulations 1989 (SI 1989/1642) reg.2(3) (October 1, 1989).
6. The Social Security (Shared Additional Pension) (Miscellaneous Amendments) Regulations 2005 (SI 2005/1551) (July 6, 2005).
7. The Civil Partnership (Pensions, Social Security and Child Support) (Consequential etc. Provisions) Order 2005 (SI 2005/2877) (December 5, 2005).
8. The Pensions Act 2014 (Consequential, Supplementary and Incidental Amendments) Order 2015 (SI 2015/1985) art.9(7) (April 6, 2016).

GENERAL NOTE

In *CP/1074/1997* a Commissioner had to consider the proper approach to be taken to the determination of a date of birth in relation to a claim for retirement pension. The claimant had been born in the Punjab, and his year of birth had been consistently stated on a number of documents as 1931, but there was no clear evidence of the day he was born in that year. On September 13, 1995 he made a claim for retirement pension, but the adjudication officer treated his date of birth as December 31, 1931 and concluded that the claim made on September 13, 1995 could not be accepted. This would have required the claimant to have been born no later than January 13, 1931 in order to be within the four months provided for in reg.15(1). The claimant adduced evidence that he had been born on December 18, 1930, but his was not accepted by the tribunal. In dealing with the appeal the Commissioner addresses a number of arguments put forward on behalf of the claimant. The Commissioner accepted that the claimant did not need to prove a particular date of birth, merely that he had reached retirement age by a particular date. He did not, however, accept a second argument which was based on the application of a mathematical approach to the evidential test of the balance of probabilities. The claimant argued that as each day passed in the year in which it was accepted that a person was born, it became more probable that the person had been born by that day in the year. By the beginning of July it could therefore be said that it was more probable than not that the claimant had been born by that date. In such circumstances, the practice of the adjudication officer in using the last day of the year as the date of birth was an error of law. The Commissioner rejects this argument, citing *Re JS (a minor)* [1980] 1 All E.R. 1061, for the proposition that the concept of evidential probability is not the same as the mathematical concept. The Commissioner approves the proposition in that case that the civil burden of 2.116

expiration of an existing award of [6 disabled person's tax credit or working families' tax credit], entitlement shall begin on the day after the expiration of that award.]

[10 (1D) Except in a case where regulation 22D(1) or (2) applies, for the purpose only of determining the day from which retirement pension payable in arrears under regulation 22C is to become payable, where entitlement would otherwise begin on a day which is not the first day of the benefit week, entitlement shall begin on the first day of the benefit week next following.]

[11 (1E) Except in a case where regulation 22DA applies, for the purpose only of determining the day from which state pension under Part 1 of the Pensions Act 2014 payable in arrears under regulation 22CA is to become payable, where entitlement would otherwise begin on a day which is not the first day of the benefit week, entitlement shall begin on the first day of the benefit week next following.]

(2) Where there is a change in the rate of any benefit to which paragraph (1) applies [8 (other than widowed mother's allowance and widow's pension)] the change, if it would otherwise take effect on a day which is not the [8 first day of the benefit week] for that benefit, shall take effect from the [8 first day of the benefit week] next following.

[8 (2A) Subject to paragraph (2B), where there is a change in the rate of [12 . . .], widowed mother's allowance, widowed parent's allowance or widow's pension, the change, if it would otherwise take effect on a day which is not the first day of the benefit week, shall take effect from the first day of the benefit week next following.

(2B) Paragraph (2A) shall not apply in a case where an award of benefit is terminated and benefit is paid in arrears.

(2C) Where a benefit specified in paragraph (2A) is paid in advance and the award is terminated, the termination, if it would otherwise take effect on a day which is not the first day of a benefit week, shall take effect on the first day of the benefit week next following.]

[9 (2D) [10 Where an award of retirement pension] is terminated due to the death of the beneficiary, the termination shall take effect on the first day of the benefit week next following the date of death.

(2E) Except in a case where [10 paragraph (2F) or] regulation 22D(2) applies, where a retirement pension is paid in arrears under regulation 22C and there is a change in the rate of that benefit, the change, if it would otherwise take effect on a day which is not the first day of the benefit week, shall take effect from the start of the benefit week in which the change occurs.]

[10 (2F) Except in a case where regulation 22D(2) applies, where a retirement pension is paid in arrears under regulation 22C and a change in the rate of that benefit takes effect under an order made under section 150 or 150A of the 1992 Act (annual up-rating of benefits, basic pension etc.) the change, if it would otherwise take effect on a day which is not the first day of the benefit week, shall take effect on the first day of the benefit week next following.]

[11 (2G) Except in a case where paragraph (2H) applies, where—

(a) a state pension under Part 1 of the Pensions Act 2014 is paid in arrears under regulation 22CA; and

(b) there is a change in the rate of that benefit,

the change, if it would otherwise take effect on a day which is not the first day of the benefit week, shall take effect from the start of the benefit week in which the change occurs.

(2H) Where—

(a) a state pension under Part 1 of the Pensions Act 2014 is paid in arrears under regulation 22CA; and

(b) a change in the rate of that benefit takes effect under an Order made under section 150, 150A or 151A of the 1992 Act,

the change, if it would otherwise take effect on a day which is not the first day of the benefit week, shall take effect on the first day of the benefit week next following.]

[1 (3) For the purposes of this regulation the first day of the benefit week—

(a) in the case of child benefit [5 and guardian's allowance] is Monday,

(b) in the case of [6 disabled person's tax credit or working families' tax credit] is Tuesday, and

[8 (c) in any other case is—

(i) when paid in advance, the day of the week on which the benefit is payable in accordance with regulation 22 (long-term benefits) or 22A ([12 bereavement support payment], widowed mother's allowance, widowed parent's allowance and widow's pension;

(ii) when paid in arrears, the first day of the period of 7 days which ends on the day on which the benefit is payable in accordance with [9 regulation 22, 22A or [11 , 22C or 22CA]]]

(4) The benefits specified for exclusion from the scope of paragraph (1) are [4 jobseeker's allowance], [3 incapacity benefit], [7,employment and support allowance] maternity allowance, [1. . .], severe disablement allowance, income support [6, state pension credit] [8 , [12 bereavement support payment], widowed parent's allowance] [9 , retirement pension payable in arrears under regulation 22C] [11 , state pension under Part 1 of the Pensions Act 2014 payable in arrears under regulation 22CA] [1. . .] and any increase of those benefits.

Amendments

1. The Social Security (Claims and Payments) Amendment Regulations 1988 (SI 1988/522) reg.3 (April 11, 1988).

2. The Social Security (Claims and Payments) Amendment Regulations 1991 (SI 1991/2741) reg.9 (March 10, 1992).

3. The Social Security (Claims and Payments) Amendment (No.2) Regulations 1994 (SI 1994/2943) reg.6 (April 13, 1995).

4. The Social Security (Claims and Payments) (Jobseeker's Allowance Consequential Amendments) Regulations 1996 (SI 1996/1460) reg.2(9) (October 7, 1996).

5. The Social Security (Claims and Payments) Amendment Regulations 1999 (SI 1999, No.2358) reg.2 (September 20, 1999).

6. State Pension Credit (Consequential, Transitional and Miscellaneous Provisions) Regulations 2002, (SI 2002/3019) reg.7 (April 7, 2003).

7. The Employment and Support Allowance (Consequential Provisions) (No.2) Regulations 2008 (SI 2008/1554) reg.19 (October 27, 2008).

8. The Social Security (Claims and Payments) Amendment Regulations 2009 (SI 2009/604) reg.2 (April 6, 2009).

9. The Social Security (Miscellaneous Amendments) (No.6) Regulations 2009 (SI 2009/3229) reg.2(3) (April 6, 2010).

10. The Social Security (Miscellaneous Amendments) Regulations 2010 (SI 2010/510) reg.3(3) (April 6, 2010).

11. The Pensions Act 2014 (Consequential, Supplementary and Incidental Amendments) Order 2015 (SI 2015/1985) art.9(9) (April 6, 2016).
12. The Pensions Act 2014 (Consequential, Supplementary and Incidental Amendments) Order 2017 (SI 2017/422) art.10 (April 6, 2017).

DEFINITIONS

"benefit"—see reg.2(2).
"jobseeker's allowance"—see reg.2(1).
"week"—*ibid.*

GENERAL NOTE

2.122 This regulation restates in part the rules formerly contained in reg.16(10) of the Claims and Payments Regulations 1979. In *R(P)2/73* it was held that the effect of a similarly worded predecessor to reg.16(10) was not just to make benefit payable from the next pay day but to make it begin on that day. The Commissioner made clear, though, that the regulation was concerned with "payability not title". The new wording does not appear wholly to resolve the difficulty, since para.(1) is prefaced by the intention only to concern itself with payability, though later the word "entitlement" is used. Presumably that means "entitlement to payment of benefit" and not title to the benefit itself. There are occasions where title to the benefit arising on an earlier date than the first date of payment has significant consequences.

[1 Date of entitlement under an award of state pension credit for the purpose of payability and effective date of change of rate

2.123 **16A.**—(1) For the purpose only of determining the day from which state pension credit is to become payable, where the credit is awarded from a day which is not the first day of the claimant's benefit week, entitlement shall begin on the first day of the benefit week next following.

(2) In the case of a claimant who—

(a) immediately before attaining the qualifying age was entitled to income support [4 or universal credit] [2, income-based jobseekers allowance or income-related employment and support allowance] and is awarded state pension credit from the day on which he attains the qualifying age; or

(b) was entitled to an income-based jobseeker's allowance [4 or universal credit] after attaining the qualifying age and is awarded state pension credit from the day which falls after the date that entitlement ends,

entitlement to the guarantee credit shall, notwithstanding paragraph (1), begin on the first day of the award.

(3) Where a change in the rate of state pension credit would otherwise take effect on a day which is not the first day of the claimant's benefit week, the change shall take effect from the first day of the benefit week next following.

[3 (4) For the purpose of this regulation, "benefit week" means—

(a) where state pension credit is paid in advance, the period of 7 days beginning on the day on which, in the claimant's case, that benefit is payable;

(b) where state pension credit is paid in arrears, the period of 7 days ending on the day on which, in the claimant's case, that benefit is payable.]

AMENDMENTS

1. State Pension Credit (Consequential, Transitional and Miscellaneous Provisions) Regulations 2002 (SI 2002/3019) reg.7 (April 7, 2003).

2. The Employment and Support Allowance (Consequential Provisions) (No.2) Regulations 2008 (SI 2008/1554) reg.20 (October 27, 2008).

3. The Social Security (Miscellaneous Amendments) Regulations 2010 (SI 2010/510) reg.3(4) (April 6, 2010).

4. The Universal Credit (Consequential Supplementary, Incidental and Miscellaneous Provisions) Regulations 2013 (SI 2013/630) reg.29(3) (April 29, 2013).

Duration of awards

17.—(1) Subject to the provisions of this regulation and of section [1 37ZA(3) of the Social Security Act 1975 (disability living allowance) and section] 20(6) [2 and (6F)] of the Social Security Act 1986 [4 working families' tax credit and disabled person's tax credit] [SSCBA, ss.71(3), 128(3) and 129(6)] a claim for benefit shall be treated as made for an indefinite period and any award of benefit on that claim shall be made for an indefinite period. 2.124

[3 (1A) Where an award of income support or an income-based jobseeker's allowance is made in respect of [7 a couple] and one member of the couple is, at the date of claim, a person to whom section 126 of the Contributions and Benefits Act or, as the case may be, section 14 of the Jobseekers Act applies, the award of benefit shall cease when the person to whom section 126 or, as the case may be, section 14 applies returns to work with the same employer.]

(2) [3. . .]

(3) [6 Except in the case of claims for and awards of state pension credit,] if [3. . .] it would be inappropriate to treat a claim as made and to make an award for an indefinite period (for example where a relevant change of circumstances is reasonably to be expected in the near future) the claim shall be treated as made and the award shall be for a definite period which is appropriate in the circumstances.

(4) In any case where benefit is awarded in respect of days subsequent to the date of claim the award shall be subject to the condition that the claimant satisfies the requirements for entitlement [5. . .]

(5) The provisions of Schedule 2 shall have effect in relation to claims for [3a jobseeker's allowance] made during periods connected with public holidays.

AMENDMENTS

1. The Social Security (Claims and Payments) Amendment Regulations 1991 (SI 1991/2741) reg.10 (February 3, 1992).

2. The Social Security (Claims and Payments) Amendment Regulations 1991 (SI 1991/2741) reg.10 (March 10, 1992).

3. The Social Security (Claims and Payments) (Jobseeker's Allowance Consequential Amendments) Regulations 1996 (SI 1996/1460) reg.2(10) (October 7, 1996).

4. The Tax Credits (Claims and Payments) (Amendment) Regulations 1999 (SI 1999/2572) regs 24 and 25 (October 5, 1999).

5. The Social Security Act 1998 (Commencement No.12 and Consequential and Transitional Provisions) Order 1999 (SI 1999/3178) Sch.6 (November 29, 1999).

6. State Pension Credit (Consequential, Transitional and Miscellaneous Provisions) Regulations 2002 (SI 2002/3019) reg.8 (April 7, 2003).

7. The Civil Partnership (Pensions, Social Security and Child Support) (Consequential etc. Provisions) Order 2005 (SI 2005/2877) (December 5, 2005).

DEFINITIONS

"benefit"—see reg.2(2).
"claim for benefit"—see reg.2(1).
"jobseeker's allowance"—*ibid.*
"the Jobseekers Act"—*ibid.*

GENERAL NOTE

2.125 In general awards are to be made for an indefinite period (para.1), subject to revision or supersession where the claimant's circumstances change such that the entitlement is reduced or removed. An award of benefit can only be terminated by supersession. In *CIS/4167/2003* the Commissioner queries whether terminations of indefinite awards have always been accompanied by the required supersession decision. In the case before him an award had been closed without the making of a supersession decision in circumstances where this suggested possible standard practice.

Paragraph (3) deals with short-term situations and allows awards for a fixed period, except in the case of state pension credit.

The effect of para.(1) is that awards of most benefits are now made for an indefinite period. Entitlement only ceases where there has been a revision or supersession which establishes that the conditions of entitlement are no longer met. In earlier times, there was a distinct tendency on reviews for adjudication officers to argue that it was for the claimant to establish continuing entitlement to the benefit, whereas the true position was that, where an indefinite award had been made, it was for the decision maker to show that there were good grounds to revise or supersede the award: see generally *R(S) 3/90.*

2.126 In *CIS/620/1990*, the Commissioner stressed that the requirements of reg.17 were not a mere technicality. An indefinite award of benefit can only be terminated on review if it its shown on review (under the earlier legislation) that the conditions of entitlement cease to be met. In any other circumstances the original award continues. Any purported subsequent award of benefit cannot overlap with the earlier award. Indeed there would be no jurisdiction to make a subsequent award since the matter is res judicata: see paras 8 and 11 of *CIS/620/1990.*

The power to review or supersede an award of benefit will arise under s.9 (revision, which takes effect from the operative date of the decision being revised) or s.10 (supersession, which takes effect from the date of the supersession decision) of the Social Security Act 1998. There must be grounds on which the decision maker can determine that the conditions of entitlement have ceased to exist. Some are specific to certain benefits while others are more general in application. Reference should be made to the annotations to ss.9 and 10 of the 1998 Act, as well as to Pt II of the Decisions and Appeals Regulations and the commentary on these regulations, if any issue under reg.17 arises.

2.127 *Regulation 18 revoked by The Social Security (Claims and Payments) (Jobseeker's Allowance Consequential Amendments) Regulations 1996 (SI 1996/1460) (October 7, 1996).*

[1 Time for claiming benefit

2.128 **19.**—(1) Subject to the following provisions of this regulation, the prescribed time for claiming any benefit specified in column (1) of Schedule 4 is the appropriate time specified opposite that benefit in column (2) of that Schedule.

(2) The prescribed time for claiming the benefits specified in paragraph (3) is three months beginning with any day on which, apart from satisfy-

ing the condition of making a claim, the claimant is entitled to the benefit concerned.

(3) The benefits to which paragraph (2) applies are—

(a) child benefit;

(b) guardian's allowance;

(c) [13 . . .];

(d) invalid care allowance or carer's allowance;

(e) maternity allowance;

(f) [13 . . .];

[10 (ff) . . .]

(g) widow's benefit;

[17 (ga) subject to paragraph (3B), widowed parent's allowance;

(gb) subject to paragraph (3BA), bereavement support payment;]

(h) [11 . . .] any increase in any benefit (other than income support or jobseeker's allowance) in respect of a child or adult dependant.

[16 (i) state pension credit]

[17 . . .]

[11 (3B) The time prescribed for claiming [17 widowed parent's allowance] in respect of the day on which the claimant's spouse [12 or civil partner] has died or may be presumed to have died where—

(a) less than 12 months have elapsed since the day of the death; and

(b) the circumstances are as specified in section 3(1)(b) of the Social Security Administration Act 1992 (death is difficult to establish),

is that day and the period of 12 months immediately following that day if the other conditions of entitlement are satisfied.]

[17 (3BA) The prescribed time for claiming bereavement support allowance in respect of—

(a) the rate set out in regulation 3(2) or (5) of the Bereavement Support Payment Regulations 2017 (rate of bereavement support payment); and

(b) the date on which the claimant's spouse or civil partner died,

is 12 months beginning with the date of that death.]

[15 (3C) In any case where the application of paragraphs (16) to (34) of regulation 6 would be advantageous to the claimant, this regulation shall apply subject to those provisions.]

(4) Subject to paragraph (8), in the case of a claim for income support, jobseeker's allowance, [3 working families' tax credit or disabled persons' tax credit], where the claim is not made within the time specified for that benefit in Schedule 4, the prescribed time for claiming the benefit shall be extended, subject to a maximum extension of three months, to the date on which the claim is made, where—

(a) any [7 one or more] of the circumstances specified in paragraph (5) applies or has applied to the claimant; and

(b) as a result of that circumstance or those circumstances the claimant could not reasonably have been expected to make the claim earlier.

(5) The circumstances referred to in paragraph (4) are—

(a) the claimant has difficulty communicating because—

(i) he has learning, language or literacy difficulties; or

(ii) he is deaf or blind,

and it was not reasonably practicable for the claimant to obtain assistance from another person to make his claim;

(b) except in the case of a claim for jobseeker's allowance, the claimant was ill or disabled, and it was not reasonably practicable for the claimant to obtain assistance from another person to make his claim;

(c) the claimant was caring for a person who is ill or disabled, and it was not reasonably practicable for the claimant to obtain assistance from another person to make his claim;

(d) the claimant was given information by an officer of the [3 Department for Work and Pensions] [or in a case to which regulation 4A applies, a representative of a relevant authority] or the Board which led the claimant to believe that a claim for benefit would not succeed;

(e) the claimant was given written advice by a solicitor or other professional adviser, a medical practitioner, a local authority, or a person working in a Citizens Advice Bureau or a similar advice agency, which led the claimant to believe that a claim for benefit would not succeed;

(f) the claimant or his partner was given written information about his income or capital by his employer or former employer, or by a bank or building society, which led the claimant to believe that a claim for benefit would not succeed;

(g) the claimant was required to deal with a domestic emergency affecting him and it was not reasonably practicable for him to obtain assistance from another person to make his claim; or

(h) the claimant was prevented by adverse weather conditions from attending the appropriate office.

(6) In the case of a claim for income support jobseeker's allowance, [3working families' tax credit or disabled person's tax credit] [7 where the claim is not made within the time specified for that benefit in Schedule 4, the prescribed time for claiming the benefit shall be extended, subject to a maximum extension of one month, to the date on which the claim is made, where—

(a) any one or more of the circumstances specified in paragraph (7) applies or has applied to the claimant; and

(b) as a result of that circumstance or those circumstances the claimant could not reasonably have been expected to make the claim earlier.]

(7) The circumstances referred to in paragraph (6) are—

(a) the appropriate office where the claimant would be expected to make a claim was closed and alternative arrangements were not available;

(b) the claimant was unable to attend the appropriate office due to difficulties with his normal mode of transport and there was no reasonable alternative available;

(c) there were adverse postal conditions;

(d) the claimant [7 or, in the case of income support jobseeker's allowance, the claimant or his partner] was previously in receipt of another benefit, and notification of expiry of entitlement to that benefit was not sent to the claimant [7 or his partner, as the case may be,] before the date that his entitlement expired;

[9 (e) in the case of a claim for working families' tax credit, the claimant had previously been entitled, or the partner of the claimant had previously been entitled in relation to the claimant, to income support or jobseeker's allowance and the claim for working families' tax credit was made within one month of—

(i) the expiry of entitlement to income support ignoring any period in which entitlement resulted from the person entitled not being treated as engaged in remunerative work by virtue of regulation 6(2) and (3), or paragraphs (5) and (6) of regulation 6 of the Income Support (General) Regulations 1987; or

(ii) the expiry of entitlement to jobseeker's allowance;]

(f) except in the case of a claim for working families' tax credit or disabled persons' tax credit, the claimant had ceased to be a member of a married or unmarried couple within the period of one month before the claim was made; [2 . . .]

(g) during the period of one month before the claim was made a close relative of the claimant had died, and for this purpose "close relative" means partner, parent, son, daughter, brother or [2 sister; or]

[9 (h) in the case of a claim for disabled person's tax credit, the claimant had previously been entitled to income support, jobseeker's allowance, incapacity benefit or severe disablement allowance and the claim for disabled person's tax credit was made within one month of—

(i) the expiry of entitlement to income support ignoring any period in which entitlement resulted from the claimant being treated as engaged in remunerative work by virtue of paragraphs (2) and (3) or paragraph (5) and (6) of the Income Support (General) Regulations 1987; or

(ii) the expiry of entitlement to jobseeker's allowance, incapacity benefit or severe disablement allowance;

(ha) in the case of a claim for disabled person's tax credit, the partner of the claimant had previously been entitled in relation to the claimant to income support or jobseeker's allowance, and the claim for disabled person's tax credit was made within one month of—

(i) the expiry of entitlement to income support ignoring any period in which entitlement resulted from the partner of the claimant not being treated as engaged in remunerative work by virtue of paragraphs (2) and (3) or paragraph (5) and (6) of the Income Support (General) Regulations 1987; or

(ii) the expiry of entitlement to jobseeker's allowance;]

[6 (i) in the case of a claim for a jobseeker's allowance by a member of a joint-claim couple where the other member of that couple failed to attend at the time and place specified by the Secretary of State for the purposes of regulation 6.]

[14 (j) the claimant was unable to make telephone contact with the appropriate office where he would be expected to notify his intention of making a claim because the telephone lines to that office were busy or inoperative.]

(8) This regulation shall not have effect with respect to a claim to which [4 regulation 21ZB] of the Income Support (General) Regulations 1987 (treatment of refugees) applies.]

AMENDMENTS

1. The Social Security (Miscellaneous Amendments) (No.2) Regulations 1997 (SI 1997/793) reg.6 (April 7, 1997).

2. The Social Security (Claims and Payments and Adjudication) Amendment (No.2) Regulations 1997 (SI 1997/2290) reg.6 (October 13, 1997).

3. The Secretaries of State for Education and Skills and for Work and Pensions Order 2002 (SI 2002/1397) art.18, (September 30, 2002).
4. The Social Security (Immigration and Asylum) Consequential Amendments Regulations 2000 (SI 2000/636) reg 5 (April 3, 2000).
5. The Social Security (Benefits for Widows and Widowers) (Consequential Amendments) Regulations 2000 (SI 2000/1483) reg.9 (April 9, 2001).
6. The Social Security (Joint Claims: Consequential Amendments) Regulations 2000 (SI 2000/1982) reg.2(5) (March 19, 2001).
7. The Social Security (Claims and Payments and Miscellaneous Amendments) Regulations 2002 (SI 2002/428) reg.3 (April 2, 2002).
8. The Social Security (Claims and Payments and Miscellaneous Amendments) (No.3) Regulations 2002 (SI 2002/2660) reg.2 (April 1, 2003).
9. The Tax Credits Schemes (Miscellaneous Amendments No.4) Regulations 2000 (SI 2000/2978) reg.10 (November 28, 2000).
10. Social Security (Claims and Payments) Amendment (No.2) Regulations 2004 (SI 2004/1821) reg.2(a) (October 6, 2004).
11. Social Security (Claims and Payments) Amendment (No.2) Regulations 2005 (SI 2005/777) reg.2 (April 11, 2005).
12. The Social Security (Civil Partnerships) (Consequential Amendments) Regulations 2005 (SI 2005/2878) (December 5, 2005).
13. The Social Security (Claims and Payment) Regulations 2005 (SI 2005/455) reg.3 (April 6, 2006).
14. The Social Security (Miscellaneous Amendments) (No.3) Regulations 2006 (SI 2006/2377) (October 2, 2006).
15. The Social Security (Miscellaneous Amendments) (No.4) Regulations 2007 (SI 2007/2470) (September 24, 2007).
16. The Social Security (Miscellaneous Amendments) (No. 4) Regulations 2008 (SI 2008/2424) reg.2 (October 6, 2008).
17. The Pensions Act 2014 (Consequential, Supplementary and Incidental Amendments) Order 2017 (SI 2017/422) art.10 (April 6, 2017).

DEFINITIONS

"appropriate office"—see reg.2(1).
"jobseeker's allowance"—*ibid.*
"married couple"—*ibid.*
"partner"—*ibid.*
"unmarried couple"—*ibid.*

GENERAL NOTE

Introduction

2.129 Regulation 19 was completely re-drafted in April 1997 to remove references to good cause and with it decades of case law. Administrative complexity in dealing with back-dated claims was said to justify the new approach introduced in 1997. New case law is now emerging which suggests that the more limited grounds for back-dating may not be quite as restrictive as appears at first sight. It remains true that appeals concerning back-dating require a meticulous attention to fact-finding and careful attention to the words of reg.19 as interpreted in Commissioners' decisions.

There are now broadly two groups of benefits: those which must be claimed on the day in respect of which the situation giving rise to the claim first occurs, and those where a three months time limit is allowed for claiming. There are also two groups of benefits where issues of backdating arise.

The first group of benefits is income support, jobseeker's allowance whether income-based or contribution-based, working families' tax credit, and disabled person's tax credit. For this first group, there are two possible extensions available. They may be backdated for up to three months if the conditions set out in paras (4) and (5) are met. If the conditions are met, the backdating is mandatory. There is also the possibility of an extension of the time limit for claiming for up to one month if a different set of conditions set out in paras (6) and (7) are met.

The second group of benefits is child benefit, guardian's allowance, carer's allowance, maternity allowance, certain widowhood benefits (see para.(3)(h)), and increases of benefit (other than income support and jobseeker's allowance) in respect of a child or adult dependent. Those benefits listed in Sch. 4 for which the time limit is three months can also be included in this second group: incapacity benefit; disablement benefit and increases; reduced earnings allowance; and social fund payment for funeral expenses. For these benefits there is a three month time limit for claiming, which means that whatever the reasons for any delay in claiming, they can be backdated for up to three months. **2.130**

The regulation does not apply to claims within reg.21ZB of the Income Support General Regulations. These set out special rules for claims for income support for a person who has submitted a claim for asylum on or after April 3, 2000 and is treated as a refugee. See commentary on the regulation in Vol.II.

Regulation 19 can only apply where there is a claim which is properly constituted for the purposes of reg.4: *CIS/157/2001*.

Note that reg.19 does not apply to claims for winter fuel payments: *CIS/2337/2004*, para.19.

RR v SSWP (JSA) [2017] UKUT 50 (AAC) concerned an online claim for jobseeker's allowance which the claimant asked to be back-dated for two years. There was some dispute as to whether there was an undetermined claim from the earlier date, though the First-tier Tribunal found that there was not. Judge Poynter makes the important point that the effect of a decision covering a two-year period was that such a decision would determine all and any claims that may have been extant in relation to that period. There can only be one outcome decision for any given period. (paras 30-31).

Paragraph (1): the time limits

Paragraph (1) sets out the time limits for those benefits listed in Sch.4 to the regulations. These include income support. **2.131**

If a claimant signs an ordinary income support claim form which contains no question asking from what date benefit is claimed, the claim will be interpreted as a claim for an indefinite period from the date on which the claim is made. If claimants wish to claim for a past period, that must be expressly stated: *R(SB) 9/84*, at para.11. But note that in *CIS/2057/1998* the Commissioner accepted that a claimant who had put on her claim form "disabled—aged 16" had indicated an intention to claim income support from her 16th birthday. If, before a decision is made on an ordinary claim, a claimant indicates a wish to claim for a past period, that can operate as an amendment of the original claim taking effect on the original date. But if, after there has been a decision on the claim, the claimant indicates such a wish (as often happens when the original claim has been successful), it is generally assumed that such a claim can only be treated as a fresh claim on the date on which it is made, and that any question of back-dating under reg.19(4) has to be assessed according to that date of claim.

Paragraphs (2) and (3): benefits for which the time limit for claiming is three months

The prescribed time for claiming the benefits listed in para.(3) is three months beginning the any day of potential entitlement. The contrast between this formulation of backdating and the technique adopted for income-related benefits may be important. If the claimant was entitled to the benefit (apart from the requirement to make a claim for the benefit) where the three-month time limit applies, the payment of benefit can be backdated for three months without any reason being shown for the delay in claiming. **2.132**

Paragraphs (4) and (5): claims for income support and jobseeker's allowance

2.133 *(1) Introduction:* Although it is common to speak of the backdating of claims, it should be appreciated that the technique adopted in para.(4) is to extend the time for claiming for a past period forward from the first day of that period. There is an immediate problem in the working of the three month time limit. If, on May 31 in any year, a claim is made for income support for the period from February 1 to May 30 in that year, it appears that the time for claiming for the whole period cannot be extended under para.(4) because to do so would go beyond the maximum period of three months permitted under the regulation. It does not matter that one of the listed circumstances has made it reasonable for the claim not to have been made earlier. The claim could be amended before a decision is made on it so as to make it a claim from March 1 to May 30, that is, the maximum permitted period of backdating.

It follows that it would be good practice for decision-makers in dealing with a claim which inevitably breaks the maximum period of backdating not to decide the claim, but to invite the claimant to amend the period claimed for.

An alternative approach would be for a decision-maker to treat a claim for an extension of the time limit for claiming beyond three months as being a claim for the maximum permitted period. It seems likely that most claimants, if asked, would say that they would prefer this approach if the alternative was the total rejection of the claim for an extension of the time limit for claiming.

2.134 Although reg.5(1) only provides for a claim to be amended before a determination of it, it does not explicitly state that a claim may not be amended after a determination has been made. Thus if an amendment is made before, or even at, an appeal hearing, it is suggested that a tribunal would be able to deal with the claim for an extension, as amended. Since the tribunal is conducting a complete rehearing of all the issues under appeal, it may also wish to consider whether to treat the claim as simply being a claim for the maximum period allowed for an extension whatever period was initially requested by the claimant. It certainly seems doubtful that the intention was that only claims for extensions of up to three months could be considered under para.(4). This view is supported by *CJSA/3994/1998* where the Deputy Commissioner held that a claimant who had asked for his claim to be backdated for nearly a year should be treated as asking for the time for his making his claim to be extended to the maximum permitted by the regulations.

In *R(IS) 16/04*, the Commissioner follows the approach adopted in *CIS/849/1998* and *CJSA/3994/1998* (the correctness of which was conceded by the Secretary of State) to the effect that a claim can be taken as including a claim for a period starting with the earliest date which would make the claim in time.

Note too that *R(IS) 3/01* holds that the maximum period of extension should be calculated backwards from the date of actual claim, not forwards from the first day of the period expressly claimed for.

2.135 In *R(IS) 16/04*, the Commissioner rules that the question of reasonableness under regs 19(4)(b) and 19(6)(b) can only be asked in relation to each particular period of claim, and not the totality of any delay. The Commissioner gives as an example the position of a claimant who delays making a claim for income support for several months, but who then makes a claim. Just after he posts the claim form, there is a strike by postal workers which holds up delivery of the claim for some weeks. The fact that the claimant could have claimed earlier than he did should not defeat his reliance on adverse postal conditions in relation to the claim he actually made.

For an interesting case concerning the position of jurors and benefits, see *CIS/1010/2003*.

2.136 *(2) The test to be satisfied under paras (4) and (5):* There are two questions which must be answered before there can be an extension of the time for claiming. The first is that one of the circumstances listed in para.(5) has applied to the claimant. There is no condition that the circumstances must have applied *throughout* the period claimed for or continues to apply at the date of claim. Such considerations may come in under the second question, which is whether as a result of the circumstances or a combination of them, the claimant could not reasonably have been expected to make the claim earlier. This approach is explicitly set out in the reported Northern Ireland decision *R2/01(IS)*. Thus, if a claimant who has been affected, for example, by illness delays unreasonably after recovery from the illness in making the claim, the request for an extension of the time limit for claiming will fail on the second ground. Such a claim could also fail if there has been unreasonable delay at some earlier stage before one of the listed circumstances applies.

Just as careful findings of fact were the secret of good decision-making under the old good cause rules, so too similar attention to detail will be required under the rules introduced in 1997. This will include findings of fact on key dates, and precision in making findings about what a claimant has been told and by whom.

Note that the list of circumstances set out in para.(5) is exhaustive, and there is no category of analogous circumstances to deal with meritorious cases which were not foreseen by the draftsman: *CJSA/3121/1998*, para.9. Ignorance of one's rights or of the procedure for claiming, whether reasonable or otherwise, does not feature in the circumstances listed in para.(5).

Finally, since the maximum period of backdating is now three months (previously it was 12 months), will this change the qualitative nature of the decision-making? Perhaps not, when the restrictive grounds on which the Secretary of State can extend the period to one month as set out in paras (6) and (7) are considered.

(3) Paragraphs (5)(a), (b), (c) and (g): reasonable practicability of obtaining assistance: Several of the paragraphs provide, in addition to a primary set of circumstances, a further requirement, namely that "it was not reasonably practicable for the claimant to obtain assistance from another person to make his claim". In *CIS/2057/1998*, the Commissioner points out that the question is whether it is reasonable practicable for the claimant to seek assistance from another person to make the claim, not whether it is reasonable practicable for another person to take the initiative in offering assistance. **2.137**

The corresponding words of the Northern Ireland regulations have been considered by the Chief Commissioner in Northern Ireland. In *C12/98 (IS)* the Chief Commissioner notes, having regard to the two-stage test set out in para. (4), that:

> "'reasonably practicable for him to obtain assistance' . . . must mean something other than 'can reasonably have been expected to make the claim earlier', otherwise there would be no need for the two sub-paragraphs to consist of different terminology in qualifying reasonableness." (See para.11.)

The Chief Commissioner adds:

> " . . . I accept that [the adjudication officer] is correct in submitting that regulation 19(5)(b) places an obligation on a sick or disabled person to seek assistance with his or her claim unless it is not practicable for him to obtain it; but while it might be more likely that someone who suffers a mental health problem could satisfy the provisions of regulation 19(4) and (5), it is necessary for the Adjudicating Authorities to look at the circumstances of each case and they are not entitled to make an assumption that a person suffering from a mental health problem would automatically be unable to seek assistance from another person to make a claim."

The circumstances in which it will and will not be reasonably practicable to obtain assistance from another person are so varied that, once again, full and careful findings or fact are the key to good decision making in all claims involving consideration of this issue.

(4) Paragraph (5)(a): difficulty communicating: This sub-para. concerns difficulties of communication arising because a person has learning, language or literacy **2.138**

difficulties, or because a person is deaf or blind. The words "deaf" or "blind" are not defined and so should be given their ordinary meaning, namely and respectively a person without hearing and a person without sight. Those who are hearing impaired or visually impaired may not be properly described as deaf or blind, but might well fall within the scope of someone who has difficulty communicating because of learning, language or literacy difficulties. Note that those who are deaf and blind must have difficulty communicating as a result of that disability and, additionally, must show that it was not reasonably practicable to obtain assistance from another person to make the claim. This is certainly an area where the qualification of *reasonable* practicability will be important.

In *CIS/2057/1998* the claimant had learning difficulties. She made a claim for income support which was awarded. Later her mother requested on her behalf that benefit be backdated to her sixteenth birthday (no-one had been appointed to act on behalf of the claimant). The tribunal erred in taking the view that the claimant had a supportive family who should have taken the initiative in finding out about her benefit entitlement. The proper approach was to determine (and the Commissioner so found) whether the claimant came within sub-para.(a)(i) and then to ask whether it was reasonably practicable for her to obtain assistance, not whether it was reasonably practicable for her family to provide it.

2.139 *(5) Paragraph (5)(b): illness and disability:* This sub-paragraph does not apply to claims for jobseeker's allowance. It deals with those many situations in which a person's delay is caused by illness or disability. In *CIS/610/1998* (discussed below in relation to sub-para.(d)) the Commissioner noted that the tribunal should have investigated the nature of the claimant's illness and whether this prevented him from queuing.

The first determination is the nature and dates of the person's illness or disability. The illness or disability must be compounded by its not being reasonably practicable for the claimant to obtain assistance from another person to make the claim.

2.140 *(6) Paragraph (5)(c): caring responsibilities:* This sub-para. offers an escape route for those with caring responsibilities. The situation in which the sub-para. applies are likely to be (but not expressed exclusively to be) situations where a period of intensive caring arises, or perhaps where another carer becomes unavailable and the claimant has stepped in to help. It is easy to think of circumstances where the circumstances will be satisfied, but also easy to think of rather more marginal cases. The sub-para. also requires the claimant to show that it was not reasonably practicable to obtain assistance from another person to make the claim.

2.141 *(7) Paragraph (5)(d): information from an officer of the Department leading a claimant to believe that a claim for benefit would not succeed:* This has proved to be a troublesome provision which the Department sought to argue was much narrower in its scope than its interpretation by the Commissioners. Note that there is no requirement that the claimant's belief that a claim would not succeed was reasonable in all the circumstances. But an unreasonably held belief might result in the claimant's failing the test in para.(4)(b).

Note that in [13] and [14] of *R(IS) 4/07* the Commissioner ruled that a breach of reg. 4(5) of the Claims and Payments Regulations (duty to provide a claim form) does not suspend time limits for making a claim.

A very common problem is the gap in benefit which often occurs when claimants transfer from jobseeker's allowance to income support because they have become incapable of work. It was thus perhaps predictable that the first Commissioners' decisions on the 1997 backdating rules would stem from this issue.

2.142 In *CIS/610/1998* the claimant, who had been claiming a jobseeker's allowance, took a Form Med. 3 issued by his GP to the Benefits Agency. There was a queue so he approached a security guard. The guard advised him that he did not need to fill in any forms, took his medical certificate, and wrote his national insurance number in a logging-in book. A week later the claimant received an incapacity benefit claim form through the post. He completed it and took it to the Benefits Agency. While in the queue, he was advised by another claimant that he needed to complete an income support claim form with his incapacity benefit claim form. He checked this advice when he reached the counter and then submitted claims for both benefits. The adjudication officer refused to backdate the claim for income support. The matter came before the Commissioner for consideration.

The Commissioner concluded on the facts of this case that the security guard was an "officer of the Department". The information supplied by the guard to the claimant could have left the claimant with the impression that he did not need to make another claim in connection with his transfer from a jobseeker's allowance to income support, and that in that sense any new claim would not succeed.

However, in *S K-G v SSWP (JSA)* [2014] UKUT 430 (AAC) Judge Wikeley decided that reg.19(5)(d) does not apply either to information in a standard DWP letter or to information on the direct.gov website to claims being made online or by telephone. Regulation 19(5)(d) is directed to "the situation where a claimant is given information by a DWP officer as part of some specific interchange or transaction relevant to their personal circumstances" (para.17). Furthermore, reg.19(5)(d) is not directed to official information about the process or method of claiming (para.21).

In *SSWP v PG (JSA)* [2015] UKUT 616 (AAC), Judge Wright disagrees with Judge Wikeley's conclusions in *SK-G v SSWP (JSA)* [2014] UKUT 430 that information on the Department's website does not constitute information given by an officer of the Department within reg.19(5)(d). Judge Wright had the benefit of argument in an oral hearing and provides detailed consideration of the process by which information finds its way onto the Department's website (paras 18-20)—in this case the *DirectGov* website. Judge Wright concludes that information on the website is capable of falling within the scope of reg.19(5)(d).

In *CIS/1721/1998* the claimant was given an incapacity benefit claim form when she went to the Job Centre with a medical certificate after fracturing her wrist. Two weeks later her claim for incapacity benefit was refused and she was advised to claim income support. The adjudication officer refused to backdate the claim.

The Commissioner accepts that the implication of the advice to claim incapacity **2.143**
benefit was that the claimant would be entitled to that benefit and not to income support. He considered that this was a reasonable belief on her part (incapacity benefit, if payable, would have exceeded her income support applicable amount). The Commissioner also took account of reg.4(5). The official to whom she produced the medical certificate should have supplied her with an income support claim form. A failure to supply this form would also have led her to believe that there was no entitlement to income support.

CIS/3749/1998 expands on this point. The Commissioner states that claimants were entitled by reason of reg.4(5) to assume that they had been given the right forms for the benefits they requested, and, if they were not, sub-para.(d) should clearly be considered. The claimant in this case had been receiving an income-based jobseeker's allowance, so there was at least a reasonable possibility that a claim for incapacity benefit would fail for lack of contributions. The Commissioner also drew attention to the fact that a failure to provide the right form brought reg.4(7A) into effect which would give the Secretary of State a discretion at accept a late claim.

In *CIS/3994/1998* (followed in *CSIS/815/2004*) the claimant had received advice that he was not entitled to income support on making two enquiries of the Department. That advice seemed to be correct in the light of the evidence of what the claimant had told the Department when he telephoned. The tribunal had ruled that this was not enough to bring the claimant within sub-para.(5)(d) in that the information he had received was reasonable. The Deputy Commissioner could find no such qualification in the sub-para.; the claimant had made an enquiry and

his employer's appeal procedures. This advice was confirmed in writing in a letter produced by the tribunal hearing in January 1998. The Commissioner states that the reason the sub-para. required the advice to be in writing was to avoid any doubt or argument as to the contents of that advice. If before the decision made by the decision-maker or tribunal, the advice was confirmed in writing, these difficulties were avoided and the advice amounted to written advice for the purposes of the sub-para. The reasoning is questionable since the wording of the provision appears to require the written advice to be what leads the claimant to believe that a claim will not succeed. The Commissioners' approach could also raise difficulties now that tribunals cannot take account of any circumstances not obtaining at the time when the decision appealed against was made: s.12(8)(b) of SSA 1998.

The group of advisers within the sub-paragraph is drawn widely, and covers a wide range of agencies.

2.147 In *CIS/1107/2008* the Commissioner ruled that reg.19(5)(e) was broad enough to include advice given by officials in the visa section of the British Embassy in Addis Ababa. The appellant had, incorrectly, been issued with a two year visa with a restriction on recourse to public funds. This resulted in his not claiming income support until he had received the correct visa which was for indefinite leave to remain with no restriction in relation to recourse to public funds.

As with sub-para.(5)(d), there is no requirement that the claimant's belief that a claim would not succeed was reasonable in all the circumstances. But an unreasonably held belief might result in the claimant's failing the test in para.(4)(b).

2.148 *(9) Paragraph (5)(g): domestic emergencies:* These circumstances are rather surprisingly included in para.(5) when they might more appropriately be included within the Secretary of State's discretion, since it is difficult to think of circumstances which would meet the requirements of the sub-para. which would last more than a month. Perhaps the distinction originally lay in the mandatory nature of the extension where para.(5) is satisfied compared with the discretionary nature of the extension in para.(7), but if that is the distinction, there are circumstances listed in para.(7) which should also be in para.(5). The extension in para.(6) is mandatory following the April 2002 amendment.

2.149 *(10) Paragraph (5)(h): adverse weather conditions:* Again these circumstances will usually be of very limited duration save in the more remote parts of the country, and the circumstances seem more appropriate for determination under the Secretary of State's decision-making under para.(6).

2.150 *(11) Paragraphs (6) and (7): the decision-maker's one-month decision:* As originally drafted, this was the Secretary of State's discretion to extend the time limit for claiming up to one month and applies to claims for income support, jobseeker's allowance, working families' tax credit and disabled person's tax credit. The Secretary of State could extend the time limit for claiming for any period up to a maximum of one month,

- if the Secretary of State considered that to do so would be consistent with the proper administration of benefit, and
- any of the circumstances in para.(7) applied.

The April 2002 amendment makes this a mandatory list of special circumstances which justify a one month extension to the time limit for claiming. The reference to consistency with the proper administration of benefit happily disappears. Once again the list is exhaustive and has no category of analogous circumstances.

In *CJSA/3659/2001* the Commissioner notes that decisions under reg.19(6) and (7), which contain the requirement that the Secretary of State in the circumstances set out in these paragraphs extend the time limit for claiming to one month, are within the jurisdiction of tribunals. This flows from the provision in para.5(a) of

Sch.2 to the Decisions and Appeals Regulations which excludes from the list of Secretary of State's decisions against which no appeal lies a decision under reg.19 as to the time for claiming benefit. This is drafted widely enough to bring within the tribunal's jurisdiction not only the matters in reg.19(4) and (5), but also those in reg.19(6) and (7). It follows that tribunals must consider both sets of rules relating to extension of the time limit for claiming.

Note in relation to these provisions, reg.6(1)(aa) and (1A) for the automatic allowance of one month to return the claim forms in the cases mentioned there, and note the discretionary rule in reg.6(4B) in relation to claims for a jobseeker's allowance.

It would seem that the principle of *CSIS/61/1992* still applies that in every case 2.151
where a claim is made outside the time limit specified in Sch.4, the Secretary of State should consider the use of the operation of the extension under para.(6) before the claim is referred to a decision-maker for decision. If this has not been done, a tribunal may decide to adjourn for the matter to be considered. There may also be cases where information comes to light in the hearing which makes it appropriate to adjourn to enable the decision maker to re-consider the matter.

It is sometimes argued that the circumstances envisaged in sub-para.(7)(a) are exceptional, as when an office closes unexpectedly due to flooding or industrial action. It is submitted that this is to apply too narrow an interpretation to the words. The sub-para. surely covers situations where a claim would need to be made on a Saturday, but the office is closed and the claim is submitted on the following Monday.

There has been a decision on reg.19(7)(b), which may be limited to some rather special facts: *CSJSA/0811/2006*. It concerned a claimant's lack of funds to pay the ferry fare from Islay to the mainland. He argued that this meant that he was unable to attend the appropriate office due to difficulties with his normal mode of transport and there was no reasonable alternative available. The Deputy Commissioner, in remitting the appeal for determination a new tribunal, considered that "difficulties" in this context could include an inability to pay. He then addressed the issue of whether there was any reasonable alternative, and interpreted the regulation here as referring to reasonable alternative transport. Finally, it was necessary to consider whether the claimant could reasonably have been expected to make the claim earlier than he did. Here the issue was whether earlier claim by telephone was a reasonable course of action for the claimant to have taken. This would require consideration of any enquiry made by the claimant about telephone claims, and whether the claimant did as much as could reasonably be expected of him. If, having done that, he remained ignorant of the possibility of a telephone claim, then he would not fall foul of the provision in reg.19(6)(b).

In *CIS/4901/2002* the Commissioner considered what is meant by the term 2.152
"adverse postal conditions" as used in reg.19(7)(c), but ultimately decided the case on different grounds. The circumstances of the case were that the claimant had received some claim forms in the post but no reply paid envelope had been provided. The forms were completed and mailed to the Department in an envelope provided by the claimant to which he affixed a single first class stamp. However, the correct postage was more than this. It was not received by the Department. A second claim was made and benefit paid from a later date; the claimant sought to have this claim backdated to the date of an enquiry made of the Jobcentre about his benefit entitlement which had resulted in his being advised to claim income support or incapacity benefit, and in his being sent the first set of forms. Eventually, the first set of forms was returned to the claimant by the Post Office endorsed by the Revenue Protection Section indicating that insufficient postage had been attached to the letter. Some £0.77 needed to be paid for the forms to be delivered. A second endorsement was to the effect that the package had "not [been] called for." It was established that there was, in relation to the Benefit Office to which the claimant had sent the first set of forms, an arrangement under which the Post Office adopted a different policy from that which normally applies in relation to under-stamped mail. The normal practice is to advise the addressee that mail

awaits them and is available on payment of the amount of the underpayment plus handling fee. The practice which it was accepted should have been adopted in this case was for the forms to have been delivered and for the amount of the underpayment to be included in a bulk surcharge arrangement with the Department. It would seem to flow from the detailed reasoning of the Commissioner in the case that he would accept that there might be an argument to bring the failure of such arrangements within the ambit of the phrase "adverse postal conditions." However, he decided the case on the basis that the Post Office in holding the first set of claim forms was the bailee for the Department and so the original forms are to be treated as being in the hands of the Department between the date of its receipt until they were returned to the claimant. This was sufficient to ground entitlement to the benefit from the earlier date.

In *R(IS) 16/04*, the Commissioner accepts that delays in post arriving over the Christmas period constitute adverse postal conditions within para.(7)(c).

In *CJSA/3960/2006*, the Deputy Commissioner ruled that a delay of two working days beyond the maximum period within which a letter should have been delivered constituted "adverse postal conditions". The mere fact of the delay established that there were adverse postal conditions. A second issue arose in the case on the interpretation of the words "before the date that his entitlement expired" in reg.19(7)(d). The Deputy Commissioner ruled that a decision that a person was not entitled to income support from February 4, 2006 meant that the claimant's entitlement ended on February 3, 2006, since "her entitlement expired on the very last moment of the Friday but before the very first moment of the Saturday." (See para.20.)

In *CJSA/0743/2006* the Commissioner ruled that the words "another benefit" in reg.19(7)(d) referred to a different benefit. He said, "I consider that the natural meaning of the work in that context is 'different'" (See para.9.)

2.153 *(12) Paragraph (8) CJSA/4383/2003* concerns the relationship of the 28 day time limit for claiming income support by asylum seekers who have received notification that they have been accepted as having refugee status under reg.21ZB(2) of the Income Support General Regulations. Provided income support is claimed within this time limit, the award can be backdated to the date of the asylum application. Because of delays inherent in the determination of such claims, this can be a very substantial period. In the appeal before the Commissioner, the issue arose as to whether a person within the ambit of reg.21ZB(2) lost all ability to use the provisions of reg.19(4) and (5) to seek backdating of a claim for income support. The Secretary of State had argued that the reg.19(8) had this effect. The Commissioner disagreed for the following reasons:

> "17. . . . In my view this is to misunderstand the legislative framework. The starting point is section 1 of the Social Security Administration Act 1992, which (in virtually all cases) requires a claim to be made as a precondition of entitlement to benefit. Section 5 of the 1992 Act then grants the Secretary of State various regulation-making powers in relation to claims. In the exercise of these powers, the Social Security (Claims and Payments) Regulations 1987 have been made. Regulation 19(1) of, and Schedule 4 to, those Regulations sets out the basic rules for claiming various benefits and the time limits that apply. Thus the general rule is that claims for income support or jobseeker's allowance must be made on 'the first day of the period in respect of which the claim is made'. Regulation 19(4) and (5) then provide, by way of exception to this general principle, that the prescribed period for claiming these benefits can be extended for up to three months if 'good cause', as defined by the Regulations, can be established.
> 18. However, regulation 19(4) is expressly stated to be subject to regulation 19(8). The purpose of regulation 19(8) is to provide that those claimants who can avail themselves of regulation 21ZB are not to be caught by the standard limit of three months on backdating entitlement to income support. A success-

ful applicant for asylum, who claims arrears of income support within 28 days of receiving the Home Office's notification, is a person who makes 'a claim to which regulation 21ZB [. . .] of the Income Support (General) Regulations 1987 (treatment of refugees) applies'. In that situation regulation 19(8) then provides that 'this regulation' (i.e. the normal three month rule) 'shall not have effect'. In other words, the claim for arrears of benefit, if made within the 28 day time limit, may be backdated by many more than three months and indeed right back to the date of the asylum application. This is supported by regulation 6(4D) of the 1987 Regulations, which deems the claim so made to have been made actually at the much earlier date when asylum was applied for—see the obiter opinion of Mrs Deputy Commissioner Rowley in *CIS/579/2004* (at paragraph 43.4).
19. In my view, therefore, there are not two entirely separate and mutually exclusive regimes, which appears to be the Secretary of State's contention. The correct position in law is that a person in the claimant's situation may be able to make a claim for backdated benefit in accordance with regulation 19(4) and (5). Just because he is a successful applicant for asylum does not take him out of that regime. However, if he had made his claim within 28 days of the Home Office letter, he might have his entitlement to benefit backdated to the date of his original application for asylum, by virtue of regulation 21ZB, regardless of the normal three month rule in regulation 19(4)."

PART III

PAYMENTS

[1 Time of payment: general provision

20. Subject to regulations 21 to 26B, benefit shall be paid in accordance with an award as soon as is reasonably practicable after the award has been made.] 2.154

AMENDMENT

1. Inserted by The Social Security (Miscellaneous Amendments) (No.2) Regulations 2006 (SI 2006/832) reg.2 (April 10, 2006).

DEFINITION

"benefit"—see reg.2(2).

20A.—[1 . . .] 2.155

AMENDMENT

1. The Social Security (Miscellaneous Amendments) (No.2) Regulations 2006 (SI 2006/832) reg.2 (April 10, 2006).

Direct credit transfer

21.—[12 (1) The Secretary of State may arrange for benefit to be paid by way of direct credit transfer into a bank or other account nominated by the person entitled to benefit or a person acting on their behalf.] 2.156
(2) [9 . . .]
(3) [2Subject to paragraph (3A)] benefit shall be paid in accordance with

paragraph (1) within seven days of the last day of each successive period of entitlement [9 . . .] [7or, so far as concerns working familiar tax credit, within such time as the Board may direct]

[2(3A) Income Support shall be paid in accordance with paragraph (1) within 7 days of the time determined for the payment of income support in accordance with Schedule 7.]

[6(3B) Where child benefit is payable in accordance with paragraph (1), [9 an arrangement under that paragraph] shall also have effect for any guardian's allowance to which the claimant is entitled and that allowance shall be paid in the same manner as the child benefit due in his case.

(3C) Where guardian's allowance is payable in accordance with paragraph (1), [9 an arrangement under that paragraph] shall also have effect for the child benefit to which the claimant is entitled and that child benefit shall be paid in the same manner as the guardian's allowance which is due in his case.]

(4) In respect of benefit which is the subject of an arrangement for payment under this regulation, the Secretary of State [7or the Board] may make a particular payment by credit transfer otherwise than is provided by paragraph (3) [2or (3A)] if it appears to him [7or them] appropriate to do so for the purpose of—

(a) paying any arrears of benefit, or

(b) making a payment in respect of a terminal period of an award or for any similar purpose.

(5) [11 . . .]

[8 (5A) In relation to payment of a joint-claim jobseeker's allowance, references in this regulation to the person entitled to benefit shall be construed as references to the member of the joint-claim couple who is the nominated member for the purposes of section 3B of the Jobseekers Act.]

(6) [5. . .]

AMENDMENTS

1. The Social Security (Miscellaneous Provisions) Amendment Regulations 1992 (SI 1992/247) reg.15 (March 9, 1992).

2. The Social Security (Claims and Payments) Amendment (No.2) Regulations 1993 (SI 1993/1113) reg.2 (May 12, 1993).

3. The Social Security (Claims and Payments) Amendment Regulations 1994 (SI 1994/2319) reg.4 (October 3, 1994).

4. The Social Security (Claims and Payments) Amendment Regulations 1994 (SI 1994/2319) reg.8 (April 13, 1995).

5. The Social Security (Claims and Payments) Amendment Regulations 1996 (SI 1996/672) reg.2(3) (April 4, 1996).

6. The Social Security (Claims and Payments) Amendment Regulations 1999 (SI 1999/2358) reg.2 (September 20, 1999).

7. The Tax Credits (Claims and Payments) (Amendment) Regulations 1999 (SI 1999/2572) regs 20, 23 and 24 (October 5, 1999).

8. The Social Security (Joint Claims: Consequential Amendments) Regulations 2000 (SI 2000/1982) reg.2(6) (March 19, 2001).

9. The Social Security (Claims and Payments and Miscellaneous Amendments) (No.2) Regulations 2002 (SI 2002/2441) reg.2 (April 6, 2003).

10. The Social Security (Miscellaneous Amendments) (No.2) Regulations 2006 (SI 2006/832) reg.2 (April 10, 2006).

11. The Social Security (Miscellaneous Amendments) Regulations 2012 (SI 2012/757) reg.15(2) (April 1, 2012).

12. The Universal Credit and Miscellaneous Amendments (No.2) Regulations 2014 (SI 2014/2888), reg.5(2) (November 26, 2014).

DEFINITIONS

"appropriate office"—see reg.2(1).
"partner"—*ibid.*

GENERAL NOTE

Until May 12, 1993, it was not possible for income support to be paid by direct credit transfer. 2.157

[1 Delayed payment of lump sum

21A.—(1) The regulation applies where— 2.158
(a) a person ("P") is entitled to a lump sum under, as the case may be—
(i) Schedule 5 to the Contributions and Benefits Act (pensions increase or lump sum where entitlement to retirement pension is deferred);
(ii) Schedule 5A to that Act (pension increase or lump sum where entitlement to share additional pension is deferred); or
(iii) Schedule 1 to the Social Security (Graduated Retirement Benefit) Regulations 2005 (further provisions replacing section 36(4) of the National Insurane Act 1965: increases of graduated retirement benefit and lump sums);
[2 (iv) section 8 of the Pensions Act 2014 (choice of lump sum or survivor's pension in certain cases); or
(v) Regulations under section 10 of the Pensions Act 2014 (inheritance of graduated retirement benefit) which makes provision corresponding or similar to section 8 of that Act;]

or
(b) the Secretary of State decides to make a payment on account of such a lump sum.

(2) Subject to paragraph (3), for the purposes of section 7 of the Finance (No. 2) Act 2005 (charge to income tax of lump sum), P may elect to be paid the lump sum in the tax year ("the later year of assessment") next following the tax year which would otherwise be the applicable year of assessment by virtue of section 8 of that Act (meaning of "applicable year of assessment" in section 7).

(3) P may not elect in accordance with paragraph (2) ("a tax election") unless he elects on the same day as he chooses a lump sum in accordance with, as the case may be—
(a) paragraph A1 or 3C of Schedule 5 to the Contributions and Benefits Act;
(b) paragraph 1 of Schedule 5A to that Act;
(c) paragraph 12 or 17 of Schedule 1 to the Social Security (Graduated Retirement Benefit) Regulations 2005;
[2 (d) section 8 of the Pensions Act 2014;
(e) Regulations under section 10 of the Pensions Act 2014 which make provision corresponding or similar to section 8 of that Act,]

or within a month of that day.

(4) A tax election may be made in writing to an office specified by the Secretary of state for accepting such elections or, except where in any particular case the Secretary of State directs that the election must be made in

writing, it may be made by telephone call to the number specified by the Secretary of State.

(5) If P makes a tax election, payment of the lump sum, or any payment on account of the lump sum, shall be made in the first month of the later year of assessment or as soon as reasonably practicable after that month, unless P revokes the tax election before the payment is made.

(6) If P makes no tax elections in accordance with paragraph (2) and (3), or revokes a tax election, payment of the lump sum or any payment on account of the lump sum shall be made as soon as reasonably practicable after P—

(a) elected for a lump sum, or was treated as having so elected; or

(b) revoked a tax election.

(7) If P dies before the beginning of the later year of assessment—

(a) any tax election in respect of P's lump sum shall cease to have effect; and

(b) no person appointed under regulation 30 to act on P's behalf may make a tax election.

(8) In this regulation "the later year of assessment" has the meaning given by section 8(5) of the Finance (No. 2) Act 2005.]

AMENDMENTS

1. The Social Security (Deferral of Retirement Pensions, Shared Additional Pension and Graduated Retirement Benefit) (Miscellaneous Provisions) Regulations 2005 (SI 2005/2677) (April 6, 2006).

2. The Pensions Act 2014 (Consequential, Supplementary and Incidental Amendments) Order 2015 (SI 2015/1985) art.9(10) (April 6, 2016).

Long term benefits

2.159 **22.**—[5 (1) Subject to the provisions of this regulation and [8 regulations 22A, 22C and 25(1)], long term benefits may be paid at intervals of [6 four weekly in arrears, weekly in advance or, where the beneficiary agrees, at intervals not exceeding 13 weeks in arrears.]

(1A) [9 Subject to paragraph (1B), disability] living allowance shall be paid at intervals of four weeks.]

[9 (1B) The Secretary of State may, in any particular case or class of case, arrange that attendance allowance or disability living allowance shall be paid at such other intervals not exceeding four weeks as may be specified.]

(2) Where the amount of long-term benefit payable is less than[4 £5.00] a week the Secretary of State may direct that it shall be paid (whether in advance or in arrears) at such intervals as may be specified not exceeding 12 months.

(3) Schedule 6 specifies the days of the week on which the various long term benefits are payable.

AMENDMENTS

1. The Social Security (Claims and Payments) Amendment Regulations 1991 (SI 1991/2741) reg.12(a) (February 3, 1992).

2. The Social Security (Claims and Payments) Amendment Regulations 1991 (SI 1991/2741) reg.12(b) (February 3, 1992).

3. The Social Security (Claims and Payments) Amendment (No.4) Regulations 1994 (SI 1994/3196) reg.5 (January 10, 1995).

4. The Social Security (Claims and Payments and Adjudication) Amendment Regulations 1996 (SI 1996/2306) reg.22(2) (October 7, 1996).
5. The Social Security (Claims and Payments and Miscellaneous Amendments) (No.2) Regulations 2002 (SI 2002/2441) reg.2 (April 6, 2003).
6. The Social Security (Miscellaneous Amendments) (No.5) Regulations 2008 (SI 2008/2667) reg.2 (October 30, 2008).
7. The Social Security (Claims and Payments) Amendment Regulations 2009 (SI 2009/604) reg.2 (April 6, 2009).
8. The Social Security (Miscellaneous Amendments) (No. 6) Regulations 2009 (SI 2009/3229) reg.2(4) (April 6, 2010).
9. The Social Security (Miscellaneous Amendments) Regulations 2010 (SI 2010/510) reg.3(5) (April 6, 2010).

[1 [2 . . .] widowed mother's allowance, widowed parent's allowance and widow's pension

22A.—(1) Subject to paragraphs (2) and (4), [2 . . .] widowed mother's allowance, widowed parent's allowance and widow's pension shall be paid fortnightly in arrears on the day of the week specified in paragraph (3). 2.160

(2) The Secretary of State may, in any particular case or class of case, arrange that a benefit specified in paragraph (1) be paid on any other day of the week.

(3) The day specified for the purposes of paragraph (1) is the day in column (2) which corresponds to the series of numbers in column (1) which includes the last 2 digits of the person's national insurance number—

(1)	*(2)*
00 to 19	Monday
20 to 39	Tuesday
40 to 59	Wednesday
60 to 79	Thursday
80 to 99	Friday.

(4) The Secretary of State may, in any particular case or class of case, arrange that the beneficiary be paid weekly in advance or in arrears or, where the beneficiary agrees to be paid in such manner, at intervals of four or 13 weeks in arrears.]

Amendments

1. Inserted by The Social Security (Claims and Payments) Amendment Regulations 2009 (SI 2009/604) reg.2 (April 6, 2009).
2. The Pensions Act 2014 (Consequential, Supplementary and Incidental Amendments) Order 2017 (SI 2017/422) art.10 (April 6, 2017).

[1 Payment of [2 . . .] widowed mother's allowance, widowed parent's allowance and widow's pension at a daily rate

22B.—(1) Where entitlement to a [2 . . .] widowed parent's allowance begins on a day which is not the first day of the benefit week, it shall be paid at a daily rate in respect of the period beginning with the day on which entitlement begins and ending on the day before the first day of the following benefit week. 2.161

(2) Where the Secretary of State changes the day on which a benefit mentioned in paragraph (5) is payable, the benefit shall be paid at a daily

rate in respect of any day for which payment would have been made but for that change.

(3) An award of benefit mentioned in paragraph (5) shall be paid at a daily rate where—

(a) the award is terminated;

(b) entitlement ends on a day other than the last day of the benefit week; and

(c) the benefit is paid in arrears.

(4) Where benefit is paid at a daily rate in the circumstances mentioned in paragraph (3), it shall be so paid in respect of the period beginning with the first day of the final benefit week and ending on the last day for which there is an entitlement to the benefit.

[2 . . .]

(6) Where benefit is payable at a daily rate in the circumstances mentioned in this regulation, the daily rate shall be 1/7th of the weekly rate.]

AMENDMENTS

1. Inserted by The Social Security (Claims and Payments) Amendment Regulations 2009 (SI 2009/604) reg.2 (April 6, 2009).

2. The Pensions Act 2014 (Consequential, Supplementary and Incidental Amendments) Order 2017 (SI 2017/422) art.10 (April 6, 2017).

GENERAL NOTE

2.162 Note that the Social Security (Transitional Payments) Regulations 2009 (SI 2009/609) make provision for the payment of a one-off transitional payment and an adjusting payment of benefit. Regulation 2 provides for a one-off transitional payment to be made where payments to persons in receipt of income support, widowed mother's allowance, widowed parent's allowance and widow's pension are changed from weekly in advance to weekly in arrears. Regulation 3 makes provision for an adjusting payment of benefit to be made where payments to persons in receipt of incapacity benefit, income support, severe disablement allowance, widowed mother's allowance, widowed parent's allowance and widow's pension are changed from weekly in arrears to fortnightly in arrears. Regulation 4 makes provision for the recovery of an adjusting payment of benefit.

[1 Retirement pension

2.163 **22C.**—(1) This regulation applies in relation to payment of a retirement pension to persons who reach pensionable age on or after April 6, 2010, other than to a person to whom paragraph (7) applies.

(2) Subject to paragraphs (4) to (6), a retirement pension shall be paid weekly, fortnightly or four weekly (as the Secretary of State may in any case determine) in arrears on the day of the week specified in paragraph (3).

(3) The day specified for the purposes of paragraph (2) is the day in column (2) which corresponds to the series of numbers in column (1) which includes the last 2 digits of the person's national insurance number—

(1)	(2)
00 to 19	Monday
20 to 39	Tuesday
40 to 59	Wednesday
60 to 79	Thursday
80 to 99	Friday

(4) The Secretary of State may, in any particular case or class of case, arrange that retirement pension be paid on any other day of the week.

(5) The Secretary of State may, in any particular case or class of case, arrange that the beneficiary be paid in arrears at intervals of 13 weeks where the beneficiary agrees.

(6) Where the amount of a retirement pension payable is less than £5.00 per week the Secretary of State may direct that it shall be paid in arrears at such intervals, not exceeding 12 months, as may be specified in the direction.

(7) This paragraph applies to a man who—

(a) was in receipt of state pension credit in respect of any day in the period beginning with the day 4 months and 4 days before the day on which he reaches pensionable age and ending on April 5, 2010; or

(b) was in continuous receipt of state pension credit from April 5, 2010 until a day no earlier than the day 4 months and 4 days before the day on which he reaches pensionable age.]

AMENDMENT

1. Inserted by The Social Security (Miscellaneous Amendments) (No.6) Regulations 2009 (SI 2009/3229) reg.2(5) (April 6, 2010).

[1 State pension under Part 1 of the Pensions Act 2014

22CA.—(1) This regulation applies in relation to payment of a state pension under Part 1 of the Pensions Act 2014. 2.164

(2) State pension is to be paid in arrears.

(3) The Secretary of State may arrange to pay state pension at intervals of—

(a) one week;

(b) two weeks, if the beneficiary was in receipt of a working age benefit immediately before becoming entitled to the state pension which was paid fortnightly;

(c) four weeks;

(d) 13 weeks, if the beneficiary agrees; or

(e) such length not exceeding 12 months as the Secretary of State may choose, if—

(i) the Secretary of State makes a direction specifying that length; and

(ii) the amount of the state pension payable is less than £5.00 per week.

(4) State pension is to be paid—

(a) on the day in column (2) which corresponds to the series of numbers in column (1) which includes the last 2 digits of the person's national insurance number; or

(b) In any particular case or class of case, on any other day of the week that the Secretary of State may choose.

(1) Last 2 digits national insurance number	*(2) Day to be paid state pension*
00 to 19	Monday
20 to 39	Tuesday

40 to 59	Wednesday
60 to 79	Thursday
80 to 99	Friday]

AMENDMENT

1. Added by The Pensions Act 2014 (Consequential, Supplementary and Incidental Amendments) Order 2015 (SI 2015/1985) art.9(11) (April 6, 2016).

[1 Payment of retirement pension at a daily rate

2.165 **22D.**—(1) Where the entitlement of a person (B) to a retirement pension begins on a day which is not the first day of the benefit week in the circumstances specified in paragraph (3), it shall be paid at a daily rate in respect of the period beginning with the day on which entitlement begins and ending on the day before the first day of the following benefit week.

(2) Where in respect of a retirement pension—

(a) the circumstances specified in paragraph (3) apply,

(b) B's entitlement to that benefit begins on a day which is not the first day of the benefit week, and

(c) a change in the rate of that benefit takes effect under an order made under [2 section 150 or 150A] of the 1992 Act (annual up-rating of basic pension etc.) on a day, in the same benefit week, subsequent to the day on which B's entitlement arose,

it shall be paid at a daily rate in respect of the period beginning with the day on which entitlement begins and ending on the day before the first day of the following benefit week.

(3) The circumstances referred to in paragraphs (1) and (2) are where—

(a) the retirement pension is paid in arrears,

(b) B has not opted to defer entitlement to a retirement pension under section 55 of the Contributions and Benefits Act(13), and

(c) B—

(i) was in receipt of a working age benefit in respect of any day in the period beginning with the day 8 weeks and a day before B reaches pensionable age and ending immediately before the day B reaches such age, or

(ii) has reached pensionable age and is a dependent spouse of a person who is in receipt of an increase for an adult dependant under section 83 or 84 of the Contributions and Benefits Act.

(4) Where benefit is payable at a daily rate in the circumstances mentioned in this regulation, the daily rate which shall apply in respect of a particular day in the relevant period shall be 1/7th of the weekly rate which, if entitlement had begun on the first day of the benefit week, would have had effect on that particular day.

(5) In this regulation, "benefit week" means the period of 7 days which ends on the day on which, in B's case, the benefit is payable in accordance with regulation 22C.]

AMENDMENTS

1. Inserted by The Social Security (Miscellaneous Amendments) (No.6) Regulations 2009 (SI 2009/3229) reg.2(5) (April 6, 2010).

2. The Social Security (Miscellaneous Amendments) Regulations 2010 (SI 2010/510) reg.3(6) (April 6, 2010).

[1 Payment of state pension under Part 1 of the Pensions Act 2014 at a daily rate

22DA.—(1) State pension under Part 1 of the Pensions Act 2014 is to be paid at a daily rate where— 2.166

(a) the day on which a person's first benefit week begins is after—

(i) the day on which the person reaches pensionable age; or

(ii) where the person has deferred their state pension under sections 16 and 17 of the Pensions Act 2014, the first day in respect of which the person makes a claim for their state pension; or

(b) the day on which a person's last benefit week begins is before the day on which the person dies.

(2) The period for which a daily rate is to be paid is—

(a) where paragraph (1)(a) applies, the period—

(i) beginning on the day on which the person reaches pensionable age or the first day in respect of which the person makes a claim for their state pension; and

(ii) ending on the day before the day on which the person's first benefit week begins; or

(b) where paragraph (1)(b) applies, the period beginning on the day on which the person's last benefit week begins and ending on the day on which the person dies.

(3) The daily rate at which state pension is payable under this regulation is 1/7th of the weekly rate which would have had effect on the day if a weekly rate had been payable.

(4) In this regulation, "benefit week" means the period of 7 days ending on the day on which the person's state pension is payable in accordance with regulation 22CA(4).]

AMENDMENT

1. Added by The Pensions Act 2014 (Consequential, Supplementary and Incidental Amendments) Order 2015 (SI 2015/1985) art.9(12) (April 6, 2016).

[1 Child benefit and guardian's allowance.]

23.—(1) Subject to the provisions of this regulation [3 . . .], child benefit shall be payable as follows:— 2.167

(a) in a case where a person entitled to child benefit elects to receive payment weekly in accordance with the provisions of Schedule 8, child benefit shall be payable weekly from the first convenient date after the election has been made;

(b) in any other case child benefit shall be payable in the last week of each successive period of four weeks of the period of entitlement.

(2) Subject to paragraph (3) and regulation 21, child benefit payable weekly or four-weekly shall be payable on Mondays or Tuesdays (as the Secretary of State may in any case determine) [2 by means of serial orders or on presentation of an instrument for benefit payment]

(3) In such cases as the Secretary of State may determine, child benefit shall be payable otherwise than—

(a) by means of serial order [2or on presentation of an instrument for benefit payment,]

(b) on Mondays or Tuesdays, or

(c) at weekly or four-weekly intervals,

and where child benefit is paid at four-weekly intervals in accordance with paragraph (1)(b) the Secretary of State shall arrange for it to be paid weekly if satisfied that payment at intervals of four weeks is causing hardship.

[1 (3A) Where a claimant for child benefit is also entitled to guardian's allowance, that allowance shall be payable in the same manner and at the same intervals as the claimant's child benefit under this regulation.]

(4) The Secretary of State shall take steps to notify persons to whom child benefit is payable of the arrangements he has made for payment so far as those arrangements affect such persons.

AMENDMENTS

1. The Social Security (Claims and Payments) Amendment Regulations 1999 (SI 1999/2358) reg.2(5) (September 20, 1999).

2. The Social Security (Claims and Payments) Amendment (No.4) Regulations 1994 (SI 1994/3196) reg.6 (January 10, 1995).

3. The Social Security (Claims and Payments and Miscellaneous Amendments) (No.2) Regulations 2002 (SI 2002/2441) reg.2 (April 1, 2003).

[1 Incapacity benefit, maternity allowance and severe disablement allowance

2.168 **24.**—(1) Subject to [3 . . .] [4 paragraphs (3) and (3A)], incapacity benefit [4 , maternity allowance] and severe disablement allowance shall be paid fortnightly in arrears unless [4 in any particular case or class of case], the Secretary of State arranges otherwise.

[4 "(1A) Subject to paragraph (1B), the benefits specified in paragraph (1) shall be paid on the day of the week specified in paragraph (1C).

(1B) The Secretary of State may, in any particular case or class of case, arrange that a benefit specified in paragraph (1) be paid on any other day of the week.

(1C) The day specified for the purposes of paragraph (1A) is the day in column (2) which corresponds to the series of numbers in column (1) which includes the last 2 digits of the person's national insurance number—

(1)	(2)
00 to 19	Monday
20 to 39	Tuesday
40 to 59	Wednesday
60 to 79	Thursday
80 to 99	Friday.

]

(2) [4 . . .]

(3) If the weekly amount of incapacity benefit or severe disablement allowance is less than £1.00 it may be paid in arrears at intervals of 4 weeks.

[2 (3A) Where the amount of incapacity benefit payable after reduction for pension payments under section 30DD of the Social Security Contributions and Benefits Act 1992 (including any reduction for other purposes) is less than £5.00 per week, the Secretary of State may direct that it shall be paid [4 in arrears] at such intervals as may be specified not exceeding 12 months.]

(4) [4 . . .]]

AMENDMENTS

1. Regulation.24 substituted by The Social Security (Claims and Payments) Amendment (No.2) Regulations 1994 (SI 1994/2943) reg.9 (April 13, 1995); words in heading to and certain words in regulation deleted by The Social Security (Claims and Payments) (Jobseeker's Allowance Consequential Amendments) Regulations 1996 (SI 1996/1460) reg.2(13) (October 7, 1996).

2. The Social Security (Incapacity Benefit) Miscellaneous Amendments Regulations 2000 (SI 2000/3210) reg.3 (April 6, 2001).

3. The Social Security (Claims and Payments and Miscellaneous Amendments) (No.2) Regulations 2002 (SI 2002/2441) reg.2 (April 8, 2003).

4. The Social Security (Claims and Payments) Amendments Regulations 2009 (SI 2009/604) reg.2 (April 6, 2009).

Payment of attendance allowance and constant attendance allowance at a daily rate

25.—(1) Attendance allowance [1or disability living allowance] [2. . .] shall be paid in respect of any person, for any day falling within a period to which paragraph (2) applies, at the daily rate (which shall be equal to 1/7th of the weekly rate) and attendance allowance [1 or disability living allowance] [2. . .] payable in pursuance of this regulation shall be paid weekly or as the Secretary of State may direct in any case. 2.169

(2) This paragraph applies to any period which—

(a) begins on the day immediately following the last day of the period during which a person was living in [3 a hospital specified in or other accommodation provided as specified in regulations made under [section 72(8) of the Social Security Contributions and Benefits Act 1992] ("specified hospital or other accommodation")]; and

(b) ends—

(i) if the first day of the period was a day of payment, at midnight on the day preceding the [3 4th] following day of payment, or

(ii) if that day was not a day of payment, at midnight on the day preceding the [3 5th] following day of payment, or

(iii) if earlier, on the day immediately preceding the day on which [3 he next lives in specified hospital or other accommodation],

if on the first day of the period it is expected that, before the expiry of the period of [3 28 days] beginning with that day, he will return to [3 specified hospital or other accommodation].

(3) An increase of disablement pension under [section 104 of the Social Security Contributions and Benefits Act 1992] where constant attendance is needed ("constant attendance allowance") shall be paid at a daily rate of 1/7th of the weekly rate in any case where it becomes payable for a period of less than a week which is immediately preceded and immediately succeeded by periods during which the constant attendance allowance was not payable because regulation 21(1) of the Social Security (General Benefit) Regulations 1982 applied.

AMENDMENTS

1. The Social Security (Claims and Payments) Amendment Regulations 1991 (SI 1991/2741) reg.13(a) (April 6, 1992).

2. The Social Security (Disability Living Allowance and Claims and Payments) Amendment Regulations 1996 (SI 1996/1436) reg.3 (July 31, 1996).

3. The Social Security (Claims and Payments) Amendment Regulations 1991 (SI 1991/2741) reg.13(b)–(f) (April 6, 1992).

Income support

2.170 **26.**—(1) [3 Subject to regulation 21 (direct credit transfer), Schedule 7] shall have effect for determining the [6 . . .] time at which income support is to be paid, [. . .5] and the day when entitlement to income support is to begin.

(2) [6 . . .]

[2 (3) [6 . . .].]

(4) Where the entitlement to income support is less than 10 pence or, in the case of a beneficiary to whom [1 section 23(a)] of the Social Security Act 1986 [SSCBA, s.126] applies, £5, that amount shall not be payable unless the claimant is also entitled to payment of any other benefit with which income support [2may be paid] under arrangements made by the Secretary of State.

AMENDMENTS

1. The Social Security (Claims and Payments) Amendment Regulations 1988 (SI 1988/522) reg.6 (April 11, 1988).

2. The Social Security (Claims and Payments and Payments on account, Overpayments and Recovery) Amendment Regulations 1989 (SI 1989/136) reg.2 (February 27, 1989).

3. The Social Security (Claims and Payments) Amendment (No.2) Regulations 1993 (SI 1993/1113) reg.3 (May 12, 1993).

4. The Social Security Act 1998 (Commencment No.12 and Consequential and Transitional Provisions) Order 1999 (SI 1999/3178) Sch.6 (November 29, 1999).

5. The Social Security and Child Support (Miscellaneous Amendments) Regulations 2000 (SI 2000/1596) reg.4(1) (June 19, 2000).

6. The Social Security (Miscellaneous Amendments) (No.2) Regulations 2006 (SI 2006/832) reg.2 (April 10, 2006).

[1 Jobseeker's allowance

2.171 **26A.**—(1) Subject to the following provisions of this regulation, jobseeker's allowance shall be paid fortnightly in arrears unless in any particular case or class of case the Secretary of State arranges otherwise.

(2) The provisions of paragraph 2A of Schedule 7 (payment of income support at times of office closure) shall apply for the purposes of payment of a jobseeker's allowance as they apply for the purposes of payment of income support [5 . . .]

(3) Where the amount of a jobseeker's allowance is less than £1.00 a week the Secretary of State may direct that it shall be paid at such intervals, not exceeding 13 weeks, as may be specified in the direction.

(4)–(8) [. . .4].

AMENDMENTS

1. The Social Security (Claims and Payments) (Jobseeker's Allowance Consequential Amendments) Regulations 1996 (SI 1996/1460) reg.2(14) (October 7, 1996).

2. The Social Security (Miscellaneous Amendments) (No.4) Regulations 1998 (SI 1998/1174) reg.8(3)(a) (June 1, 1998).

3. The Social Security Act 1998 (Commencement No.12 and Consequential and Transitional Provisions) Order 1999 (SI 1999/3178) Sch.6 (November 29, 1999).

4. The Social Security and Child Support (Miscellaneous Amendments) Regulations 2000 (SI 2000/1596) reg.4(2) (June 19, 2000).

5. The Secretaries of State for Education and Skills and for Work and Pensions Order 2002 (SI 2002/1397) art.18 (June 27, 2002).

DEFINITIONS

"jobseeker's allowance"—see reg.2(1).
"the Jobseeker's Allowance Regulations"—*ibid.*
"partner"—*ibid.*
"week"—*ibid.*

[1 State pension credit

26B.—(1) Except where [3 paragraph (2) or regulation 26BA] applies, state pension credit shall be payable on Mondays, but subject, [2 to regulation 21 where payment is by direct credit transfer]. 2.172

(2) [3 Subject to regulation 26BA, state pension credit] shall be payable—

[4 (a) on the same day as any—

(i) state pension under Part 1 of the Pensions Act 2014; or

(ii) retirement pension,

is payable to the claimant; or]

(b) on such other day of the week as the Secretary of State may, in the particular circumstances of the case, determine.

(3) [2 . . .]

(4) State pension credit paid [2 otherwise than in accordance with regulation 21] shall be paid weekly in advance.

(5) Where the amount of state pension credit payable is less than £1.00 per week, the Secretary of State may direct that it shall be paid at such intervals, not exceeding 13 weeks, as may be specified in the direction.

(6) [2 . . .]

(7) [2 . . .].]

AMENDMENTS

1. Inserted by State Pension Credit (Consequential, Transitional and Miscellaneous Provisions) Regulations 2002 (SI 2002/3019) reg.9 (April 7, 2003).

2. The Social Security (Miscellaneous Amendments) (No.2) Regulations 2006 (SI 2006/832) reg.2 (April 10, 2006).

3. The Social Security (Miscellaneous Amendments) (No.6) Regulations 2009 (SI 2009/3229) reg.2(6) (April 6, 2010.

4. The Pensions Act 2014 (Consequential, Supplementary and Incidental Amendments) Order 2015 (SI 2015/1985) art.9(13) (April 6, 2016).

[1 Intervals for payment of state pension credit

26BA.—(1) Where state pension credit is payable to a person who reaches pensionable age on or after 6th April 2010, other than a person to whom regulation 22C(7) applies, it shall be paid weekly, fortnightly or four weekly (as the Secretary of State may in any case determine) in arrears on the day of the week specified in paragraph (2). 2.173

(2) The day specified for the purposes of paragraph (1) is the day in column (2) which corresponds to the series of numbers in column (1) which includes the last 2 digits of the person's national insurance number—

(1)	(2)
00 to 19	Monday
20 to 39	Tuesday

40 to 59	Wednesday
60 to 79	Thursday
80 to 99	Friday

(3) The Secretary of State may, in any particular case or class of case, arrange that state pension credit be paid on any other day of the week.

(4) Where the amount of state pension credit payable is less than £1.00 per week the Secretary of State may direct that it shall be paid in arrears at such intervals, not exceeding 13 weeks, as may be specified in the direction.]

AMENDMENT

1. Inserted by The Social Security (Miscellaneous Amendments) (No.6) Regulations 2009 (SI 2009/3229) reg.2(7) (April 6, 2010).

[1 Employment and support allowance

2.174 **26C.**—(1) Subject to paragraphs (3) to (7), employment and support allowance is to be paid fortnightly in arrears on the day of the week determined in accordance with paragraph (2).

(2) The day specified for the purposes of paragraph (1) is the day in column (2) which corresponds to the series of numbers in column (1) which includes the last 2 digits of the claimant's national insurance number—

(1)	(2)
00 to 19	Monday
20 to 39	Tuesday
40 to 59	Wednesday
60 to 79	Thursday
80 to 99	Friday

(3) The Secretary of State may, in any particular case or class of case, arrange that the claimant be paid otherwise than fortnightly.

(4) The Secretary of State may, in any particular case or class of case, arrange that employment and support allowance be paid on any day of the week and where it is in payment to any person and the day on which it is payable is changed, it must be paid at a daily rate of 1/7th of the weekly rate in respect of any of the days for which payment would have been made but for that change.

(5) Where the weekly amount of employment and support allowance is less than £1.00 it may be paid in arrears at intervals of not more than 13 weeks.

(6) Where the weekly amount of an employment and support allowance is less than 10 pence that allowance is not payable.

(7) The provisions of paragraph 2A of Schedule 7 (payment of income support at time of office closure) apply for the purposes of payment of employment and support allowance as they apply for the purposes of payment of income support.]

AMENDMENT

1. The Employment and Support Allowance (Consequential provisions) (No.2) Regulations 2008 (SI 2008/1554) reg.21 (October 27, 2008).

General Note

Note that Pt 4 of Sch.2 to the Employment and Support Allowance (Transitional Provisions, Housing Benefit and Council Tax Benefit) (Existing Awards) (No.2) Regulations 2010 (SI 2010/1907) (as amended) contains modifications of reg.26C for the purposes of the transition to employment and support allowance. 2.175

[1 [2 Working families' tax credit and disabled persons' tax credit]]

27.—(1) Subject to regulation 21 [3and paragraph (1A)] [2working families' tax credit] and [2disabled persons' tax credit] shall be payable in respect of any benefit week on the Tuesday next following the end of that week by means of a book of serial orders [3or on presentation of an instrument for benefit payment] unless in any case the Secretary of State arranges [4 Board arrange] otherwise. 2.176

[5 (1A) Subject to paragraph (2), where an amount of [2 working families' tax credit] and [2 disabled persons' tax credit] becomes payable which is at a weekly rate of note more than £4.00, that amount shall, if the Secretary of State so directs [4 Board so direct], be payable as soon as practicable by means of a single payment; except that if that amount represents an increase in the amount of either of those benefits which has previously been paid in respect of the same period, this paragraph shall apply only if that previous payment was made by means of a single payment.]

(2) Where the entitlement to [2working families' tax credit] and [2 disabled persons' tax credit] is less than 50 pence a week that amount shall not be payable.]

Amendments

1. Reg.27 substituted by The Social Security (Claims and Payments) Amendment Regulations 1991 (SI 1991/2741) reg.14 (April 6, 1992).

2. The Tax Credits (Claims and Payments) (Amendment) Regulations 1999 (SI 1999/2752) regs 24 and 25 (October 5, 1999).

3. The Social Security (Claims and Payments) Amendment (No.3) Regulations 1993 (SI 1993/2113) reg.3(4) (October 25, 1993).

4. For tax credits purposes only, these words are substitue for the words "Secretary of State arranges": The Tax Credits (Claims and Payments) (Amendment) Regulations 1999 (SI 1999/2572) reg.12(a) (October 5, 1999).

5. The Social Security (Claims and Payments) Amendment (No.3) Regulations 1993 (SI 1993/2113) reg.3(4) (October 25, 1993).

Fractional amounts of benefit

[1 **28.**—(1) Subject to paragraph (2),] where the amount of any benefit payable would, but for this regulation, include a fraction of a penny, that fraction shall be disregarded if it is less than half a penny and shall otherwise be treated as a penny. 2.177

[1 (2) Where the amount of any maternity allowance payable would, but for this regulation, include a fraction of a penny, that fraction shall be treated as a penny.]

Amendment

1. Social Security (Claims and Payments) Amendment (No.2) Regulations 2002 (SI 2002/1950) reg.2 (September 2, 2002).

DEFINITION

"benefit"—see reg.2(2).

[1 Payments to persons under age 18

2.178 **29.**—Where benefit is paid to a person under the age of 18 (whether on his own behalf or on behalf of another) [2 . . .] [2 a direct credit transfer under regulation 21 into any such person's account, or the receipt by him of a payment made by some other means] shall be sufficient discharge to the Secretary of State [3 or the Board].]

AMENDMENTS

1. The Social Security (Claims and Payments etc.) Amendment Regulations 1996 (SI 1996/672) reg.2(4) (April 4, 1996).
2. Social Security (Claims and Payments and Miscellaneous Amendments) (No.2) Regulations 2002 (SI 2002/2441) reg.6 (October 23, 2002).
3. The Tax Credits (Claims and Payments) (Amendment) Regulations 1999 (SI 1999/2572) reg.30 (October 5, 1999).

DEFINITION

"benefit"—see reg.2(2).

Payments on death

2.179 **30.**—(1) On the death of a person who has made a claim for benefit, the Secretary of State [1or the Board] may appoint such person as he [1or they] may think fit to proceed with the claim [15 and any related issue of revision, supersession or appeal].

(2) Subject to [12 paragraphs (4) and (4A)], any sum payable by way of benefit which is payable under an award on a claim proceeded with under paragraph (1) may be paid or distributed by the Secretary of State to or amongst persons over the age of 16 claiming as personal representatives, legatees, next of kin, or creditors of the deceased (or, where the deceased was illegitimate, to or amongst other persons over the age of 16), and the provisions of regulation 38 (extinguishment of right) shall apply to any such payment or distribution; and—

(a) [13 a direct credit transfer under regulation 21 into any such person's account, or the receipt by him of a payment made by some other means,] shall be a good discharge to the Secretary of State [1or the Board] for any sum so paid; and
(b) where the Secretary of State is satisfied [1or the Board is satisfied] that any such sum or part thereof is needed for the benefit of any person under the age of 16, he [1or they] may obtain a good discharge therefor by paying the sum or part thereof to a person over that age who satisfies the Secretary of State [1or the Board] that he will apply the sum so paid for the benefit of the person under the age of 16.

(3) Subject to paragraph (2), any sum payable by way of benefit to the deceased, payment of which he had not obtained at the date of his death, may, unless the right thereto was already extinguished at that date, be paid or distributed to or amongst such persons as are mentioned in paragraph (2), and regulation 38 shall apply to any such payment or distribution, except that, for the purpose of that regulation, the period of 12 months shall

be calculated from the date on which the right to payment of any sum is treated as having arisen in relation to any such person and not from the date on which that right is treated as having arisen in relation to the deceased.

(4) [[19] Subject to paragraph (4B), paragraphs] (2) and (3) shall not apply in any case unless written application for the payment of any such sum is made to the Secretary of State [[1]or the Board] within 12 months from the date of the deceased's death or within such longer period as the Secretary of State [[1]or the Board] may allow in any particular case.

[[12] (4A) In a case where a joint-claim jobseeker's allowance has been awarded to a joint-claim couple and one member of the couple dies, the amount payable under that award shall be payable to the other member of that couple.]

[[19] (4B) A written application is not required where—

(a) an executor or administrator has not been appointed;

(b) the deceased was in receipt of a retirement pension [[20] , a state pension under Part 1 of the Pensions Act 2014] of any category or state pension credit including where any other benefit was combined for payment purposes with either of those benefits at the time of death;

(c) the sum payable by way of benefit to the deceased is payable to a person who was the spouse or civil partner of the deceased at the time of death; and

(d) either—

(i) the spouse or civil partner and the deceased were living together at the time of death; or

(ii) they would have been living together at the time of death but for the fact that either or both of them were in a residential care or a nursing home or in a hospital.]

(5) [[16] Subject to paragraphs (5A) to [[20] (5H),] where the conditions specified in paragraph (6) are satisfied, a claim may be made on behalf of the deceased to any benefit other than [[2]jobseeker's allowance,] income support, [[14], state pension credit] [[3]working families' tax credit or disabled person's tax credit] or a social fund payment such as is mentioned in section 32(2)(a) [[4]and section 32(2A)] of the Social Security Act 1986 [[5], or reduced earnings allowance or disablement benefit], to which he would have been entitled if he had claimed it in the prescribed manner and within the prescribed time.

[[18] (5A) Subject to paragraphs (5B) to (5G), a claim may be made in accordance with paragraph (5) on behalf of the deceased for a Category A or Category B retirement pension or graduated retirement benefit provided that the deceased was not married or in a civil partnership on the date of his death.

(5B) But, subject to paragraphs (5C) to (5G), a claim may be made in accordance with paragraph (5) on behalf of the deceased for a Category A or Category B retirement pension or graduated retirement benefit where the deceased was a married woman or a civil partner on the date of death if the deceased's widower or surviving civil partner was under pensionable age on that date and due to attain pensionable age before 6th April 2010.

(5C) Where a claim is made for a shared additional pension [[20] or a state pension under Part 1 of the Pensions Act 2014] under paragraph (5) or for a retirement pension or graduated retirement benefit under paragraphs (5) and (5A) or (5B), in determining the benefit to which the deceased would have been entitled if he had claimed within the prescribed time, the prescribed time shall be the period of three months ending on the date of his death and beginning with any day on which, apart from satisfying the condition of making a claim, he would have been entitled to the pension or benefit.

(5D) Paragraph (5E) applies where, throughout the period of 12 months ending with the day before the death of the deceased person, his entitlement to a Category A or a Category B retirement pension, shared additional pension or graduated retirement benefit was deferred in accordance with, as the case may be—

(a) section 55 of the Contributions and Benefits Act (pension increase or lump sum where entitlement to retirement pension is deferred);
(b) section 55C of that Act (pension increase or lump sum where entitlement to shared additional pension is deferred); or
(c) section 36(4A) of the National Insurance Act 1965(**c**) (deferment of graduated retirement benefit).

(5E) Where a person claims under paragraph (5) or under paragraphs (5) and (5A) or (5B) the deceased shall be treated as having made an election in accordance with, as the case may be—

(a) paragraph A1(1)(a) of Schedule 5 to the Contributions and Benefits Act (electing to have an increase of pension), where paragraph (5D)(a) applies;
(b) paragraph 1(1)(a) of Schedule 5A to that Act (electing to have an increase of a shared additional pension) where paragraph (5D)(b) applies; or
(c) paragraph 12(1)(a) of Schedule 1 to the Social Security (Graduated Retirement Benefit) Regulations 2005 (electing to have an increase of benefit), where paragraph (5D)(c) applies.

(5F) [20 Paragraphs (5G) and (5H) apply]

(a) the deceased person was a widow, widower or surviving civil partner ("W") who was married to, or in a civil partnership with, the other party of the marriage or civil partnership ("S") when S died;
(b) throughout the period of 12 months ending with the day before S's death, S's entitlement to a Category A or a Category B retirement pension or graduated retirement benefit was deferred in accordance with, as the case may be, paragraph (5D)(a) or (c); and
(c) W made no statutory election [20 , or choice under section 8(2) of the Pensions Act 2014 or Regulations under section 10 of that Act which make provision corresponding or similar to section 8(2),] in consequence of the deferral.

(5G) Where a person claims under paragraphs (5) and (5A) the deceased [20 (referred to as W in paragraph (5F))] shall be treated as having made an election in accordance with, as the case may be—

(a) paragraph 3C(2)(a) of Schedule 5 to the Contributions and Benefits Act (electing to have an increase of pension), where paragraph (5D)(a) applies; or
(b) paragraph 17(2)(a) of Schedule 1 to the Social Security (Graduated Retirement Benefit) Regulations 2005 (electing to have an increase in benefit), where paragraph (5D)(c) applies.]

[20 (5H) Where a person makes a claim under paragraph (5) for a state pension under Part 1 of the Pensions Act 2014, the deceased (referred to as

W in paragraph (5F)) shall be treated as having made a choice to be paid a state pension under—

(a) section 9 of the Pensions Act 2014 (survivor's pension based on inheritance of deferred old state pension) in accordance with section 8(2)(b) of that Act; or

(b) Regulations under section 10 of the Pensions Act 2014 which make provision corresponding or similar to section 9 of that Act in accordance with Regulations under section 10 which make provision corresponding or similar to section 8(2)(b).]

(6) [6Subject to the following provisions of this regulation,] the following conditions are specified for the purposes of paragraph (5)—

(a) Within six months of the death an application must have been made in writing to the Secretary of State for a person, whom the Secretary of State thinks fit to be appointed to make the claim, to be so appointed;

(b) a person must have been appointed by the Secretary of State to make the claim;

(c) there must have been no longer period than six months between the appointment and the making of the claim.

[7(6A) Where the conditions specified in paragraph (6B) are satisfied, a person may make a claim for reduced earnings or disablement benefit, including any increase under [section 104 or 105 of the Social Security Contributions and Benefits Act 1992], in the name of a person who had died.

(6B) [8Subject to the following provisions of this regulation,] the conditions specified for the purposes of paragraph (6A) are—

(a) that the person who had died would have been entitled to the benefit claimed if he had made a claim for it in the prescribed manner and within the prescribed time;

(b) that within 6 months of a death certificate being issued in respect of the person who has died, the person making the claim has applied to the Secretary of State to be made an appointee of the person who has died

[9(ba) that person has been appointed by the Secretary of State to make the claim]

(c) the claim is made within six months of the appointment.]

[10(6C) Subject to paragraph (6D), where the Secretary of State certifies that to do so would be consistent with the proper administration of the Social Security Contributions and Benefits Act 1992 the period specified in paragraphs (6)(a) and (c) and (6B)(b) and (c) shall be extended to such period, not exceeding 6 months, as may be specified in the certificate.

(6D)(a) Where a certificate is given under paragraph (6C) extending the period specified in paragraph (6)(a) or (6B)(b), the period specified in paragraph (6)(c) or (6B)(c) shall be shortened by a period corresponding to the period specified in the certificate;

(b) no certificate shall be given under paragraph (6C) which would enable a claim to be made more than 12 months after the date of death (in a case falling within paragraph (6)) or the date of a death certificate being issued in respect of the person who has died (in a case falling within paragraph (6B)); and

(c) in the application of sub-paragraph (b) any period between the date when an application for a person to be appointed to make a claim is made and the date when that appointment is made shall be disregarded.]

(7) A claim made in accordance with paragraph (5) [[11]or paragraph (6A)] shall be treated, for the purposes of these regulations, as if made by the deceased on the date of his death.

(8) The Secretary of State [[1]or the Board] may dispense with strict proof of the title of any person claiming in accordance with the provisions of this regulation.

(9) In paragraph (2) "next of kin" means—

(a) in England and Wales, the persons who would take beneficially on an intestacy; and

(b) in Scotland, the persons entitled to the moveable estate of the deceased on intestacy.

AMENDMENTS

1. The Tax Credits (Claims and Payments) (Amendment) Regulations 1999 (SI 1999/2572) regs 13, 20 and 22 (October 5, 1999).

2. The Social Security (Claims and Payments) (Jobseeker's Allowance Consequential Amendments) Regulations 1996 (SI 1996/1460) reg.2(15) (October 7, 1996).

3. The Tax Credits (Claims and Payments) (Amendments) Regulations 1999 (SI 1999/2572) regs 24 and 25 (October 5, 1999).

4. The Social Security (Claims and Payments) Amendment Regulations 1991 (SI 1991/2741) reg.15 (March 10, 1992).

5. The Social Security (Common Provisions) Miscellaneous Amendments Regulations 1988 (SI 1988/1725) reg.3(6) (November 7, 1988).

6. The Social Security (Claims and Payments) Amendment (No.3) Regulations 1993 (SI 1993/2113) reg.3(5)(a) (September 27, 1993).

7. Paragraphs (6A) and (6B) inserted by The Social Security (Miscellaneous Provisions) Amendment Regulations 1990 (SI 1990/2208) reg.11(3) (December 5, 1990).

8. The Social Security (Claims and Payments) Amendment (No.3) Regulations 1993 (SI 1993/2113) reg.3(5)(a) (September 29, 1993).

9. The Social Security (Claims and Payments) Amendment Regulations 1994 (SI 1994/2319) reg.5 (October 3, 1994).

10. Paragraphs (6C) and (6D) inserted by The Social Security (Claims and Payments) Amendment (No.3) Regulations 1993 (SI 1993/2113) reg.3(5)(b) (September 27, 1993).

11. The Social Security (Miscellaneous Provisions) Amendment Regulations 1990 (SI 1990/2208) reg.11(4) (December 5, 1990).

12. The Social Security (Joint Claims: Consequential Amendments) Regulations 2000 (SI 2000/1982) reg.2(7) (March 19, 2001).

13. Social Security (Claims and Payments and Miscellaneous Amendments) (No.2) Regulations 2002 (SI 2002/2441) reg.7 (October 23, 2002).

14. State Pension Credit (Consequential, Transitional and Miscellaneous Provisions) Regulations 2002 (SI 2002/3019) reg.10 (April 7, 2003).

15. The Social Security, Child Support and Tax Credits (Miscellaneous Amendments) Regulations 2005 (SI 2005/337) reg.7 (March 18, 2005).

16. The Social Security (Claims and Payments) Amendment Regulations 2005 (SI 2005/455) reg.4 (April 6, 2006).

17. The Social Security (Shared Additional Pension) (Miscellaneous Amendments) Regulations 2005 (SI 2005/1551) reg.3 (April 6, 2006).

18. The Social Security (Retirement Pensions and Graduated Retirement Benefit) (Widowers and Civil Partnership) Regulations 2005 (SI 2005/3078) reg.4 (April 6, 2006).

19. The Social Security (Miscellaneous Amendments) (No.4) Regulations 2007 (SI 2007/2470) (September 24, 2007).

20. The Pensions Act 2014 (Consequential, Supplementary and Incidental Amendments) Order 2015 (SI 2015/1985) art.9(14) (April 6, 2016).

General Note

Note the decisions referred to in the annotations to reg.33. **2.180**

It would seem that the power of appointment in reg.30(1) on the death of the claimant is a separate appointment from that under reg.33. It would follow that where a claimant has an appointee under reg.33 and dies, there should at least be confirmation of continuation of the appointment under reg.33 to enable the appointee to act under reg.30. The better course, since there are specific requirements in the regulation, would be for a separate appointment to be made.

In *CIS/1423/1997* the Commissioner holds, at para.21 of his decision, that the plain words of reg.30 do not allow the Secretary of State to appoint a person to represent the claimant or their estate in the context of a decision for the recoverability of an overpayment from the claimant's estate.

Note that paras (4)–(7) contain a special power of appointment to enable *a claim* to be made after a person's death.

R(IS)3/04 discusses aspects of reg.30 at paras 14–17 of the decision. The Commissioner notes that reg.30(5) is the only provision permitting claims to be made in respect of deceased persons, and reg.30(5) expressly does not apply to income support.

Death of claimant pending appeal to the Commissioner

It sometimes happens that the claimant dies while the appeal is pending before the Commissioner. In such cases the surviving partner may not wish to take on an appointment enabling the matter to continue, and there may be no personal representatives because there is no estate. The result is that, where there is a claimant's appeal, there is no one who can withdraw the appeal. In such circumstances, the practice of the Commissioners is to treat the appeal as abated: see *R(S)7/56*, *R(I)2/83* and *R(SB)25/84*. For all practical purposes the matter is then closed, though the possibility remains that the matter could be revived on application. This could happen if, for example, the Secretary of State chose to appoint someone to act for the deceased claimant. The most likely appointee would be the Official Solicitor, but is difficult to imagine circumstances in which it would be appropriate to take such action. In overpayment cases, care should be taken to ensure that the Benefits Agency has given an assurance that it will not seek recovery from the estate before treating an appeal as abated, since abatement of a claimant's appeal without such an assurance would not preclude recovery against the estate. **2.181**

The use of the abatement procedure is not appropriate where the appellant is the adjudication officer. In such cases, the proper course of action is for the adjudication officer to withdraw the appeal: *R(I)2/83*, at para.6.

In *CIS/1340/1999* the Commissioner was considering an appeal involving a substantial overpayment of benefit in which the claimant had died since filing the appeal. No executors or administrators were appointed, and the claimant's husband did not respond to an invitation by the Department to consider applying to be the claimant's appointee. The Commissioner comments on the reference in these annotations that care should be taken to obtain an assurance that the Benefits Agency will not seek to recover the overpayment from the estate before treating the appeal as abated. He states that he does not consider that proposition to flow from the cases, and that *R(I)2/83* is merely authority for the proposition that, where such an assurance is available in an overpayment case, it may be appropriate to dismiss the appeal rather than merely declare it abated. At para.20, he says,

> "But I see no reason why, before declaring the appeal abated or indeed striking it out, I should require an assurance to be sought from the Secretary of State that recovery of the overpayment will not be pursued. So long as the original decision of the adjudication officer stands the Secretary of State should be entitled to recover the overpayment. If he does so and there is anyone who has an interest in

ensuring that it is not recovered, that person will be able to take steps to have the appeal reinstated."

The appeal was declared abated.

[1 Payment of arrears of joint-claim jobseeker's allowance where the nominated person can no longer be traced

2.182 **30A.** Where—

(a) an award of joint-claim jobseeker's allowance has been awarded to a joint-claim couple;

(b) that couple ceases to be a joint-claim couple; and

(c) the member of the joint-claim couple nominated for the purposes of section 3B of the Jobseekers Act cannot be traced,

arrears on the award of joint-claim jobseeker's allowance shall be paid to the other member of the former joint-claim couple.]

AMENDMENT

1. The Social Security Amendment (Joint Claims) Regulations 2001 (SI 2001/518) reg.5 (March 19, 2001).

Time and manner of payments of industrial injuries gratuities

2.183 **31.**—(1) This regulation applies to any gratuity payable under [Part V of the Social Security Contributions and Benefits Act 1992].

[2 (1A) In the case of a person who made a claim for benefit in accordance with regulation 4A(1), a change of circumstances may be notified to a relevant authority at any office to which the claim for benefit could be made in accordance with that provision.]

(2) Subject to the following provisions of this regulation, every gratuity shall be payable in one sum.

(3) A gratuity may be payable by instalments of such amounts and at such times as appear reasonable in the circumstances of the case to the adjudicating authority awarding the gratuity if—

(a) the beneficiary to whom the gratuity has been awarded is, at the date of the award, under the age of 18 years, or

(b) in any other case, the amount of the gratuity so awarded (not being a gratuity payable to the widow of a deceased person on her remarriage) exceeds £52 and the beneficiary requests that payments should be made by instalments.

(4) An appeal shall not be brought against any decision that a gratuity should be payable by instalments or as to the amounts of any such instalments or the time of payment.

(5) Subject to the provisions of regulation 37 (suspension), a gratuity shall—

(a) if it is payable by equal weekly instalments, be paid in accordance with the provisions of regulation 22 insofar as they are applicable; or

(b) in any case, be paid by such means as may appear to the Secretary of State to be appropriate in the circumstances.

AMENDMENTS

1. The Social Security Act 1998 (Commencement No.12 and Consequential and Transitional Provisions) Order 1999 (SI 1999/3178) Sch.6 (November 29, 1999).
2. The Social Security (Claims and Information) Regulations 1999 (SI 1999/3108) (November 29, 1999).

[5 Information to be given and changes to be notified

32.—(1) Except in the case of a jobseeker's allowance, every beneficiary and every person by whom or on whose behalf, sums by way of benefit are receivable shall furnish in such manner [12 . . .] as the Secretary of State may determine [12 and within the period applicable under regulation 17(4) of the Decisions and Appeals Regulations] such information or evidence as the Secretary of State may require for determining whether a decision on the award of benefit should be revised under section 9 of the Social Security Act 1998 or superseded under section 10 of that Act. 2.184

(1A) Every beneficiary and every person by whom, or on whose behalf, sums by way of benefit are receivable shall furnish in such manner and at such times as the Secretary of State may determine such information or evidence as the Secretary of State may require in connection with payment of the benefit claimed or awarded.

(1B) Except in the case of a jobseeker's allowance, every beneficiary and every person by whom or on whose behalf sums by way of benefit are receivable shall notify the Secretary of State of any change of circumstances which he might reasonably be expected to know might affect—

(a) the continuance of entitlement to benefit; or
(b) the payment of benefit

as soon as reasonably practicable after the change occurs by giving notice [8 of the change to the appropriate office—

(i) in writing or by telephone (unless the Secretary of State determines in any particular case that notice must be in writing or may be given otherwise than in writing or by telephone; or
(ii) in writing if in any class of class he requires written notice (unless he determines in any particular case to accept notice given otherwise than in writing)]]

[7 (1C) In the case of a person who made a claim for benefit in accordance with regulation 4A(1), a change of circumstances may be notified to a relevant authority at any office to which the claim for benefit could be made in accordance with that provision.]

(2) Where any sum is receivable on account of an increase of benefit in respect of an adult dependant, the Secretary of State may require the beneficiary to furnish a declaration signed by such dependant confirming the particulars respecting him, which have been given by the claimant.

[2(3) In the case of a person who is claiming income support, state pension credit . . . [11, a jobseekers allowance or an employment and support allowance], where that person or any partner is aged not less than 60 and is a member of, or a person deriving entitlement to a pension under, a personal pension scheme, or is a party to, or a person deriving entitlement to a pension under, a retirement annuity contract, he shall where the Secretary of State so requires furnish the following information—

(a) the name and address of the pension fund holder;
(b) such other information including any reference or policy number

as is needed to enable the personal pension scheme or retirement annuity contract to be identified.

(4) Where the pension fund holder receives from the Secretary of State a request for details concerning a personal pension scheme or retirement annuity contract relating to a person or any partner to whom paragraph (3) refers, the pension fund holder shall provide the Secretary of State with any information to which paragraph (5) refers.

(5) The information to which this paragraph refers is—

(a) where the purchase of an annuity under a personal pension scheme has been deferred, the amount of any income which is being withdrawn from the personal pension scheme;

(b) in the case of—

(i) a personal pension scheme where income withdrawal is available, the maximum amount of income which may be withdrawn from the scheme; or

(ii) a personal pension scheme where income withdrawal is not available, or a retirement annuity contract, the maximum amount of income which might be withdrawn from the fund if the fund were held under a personal pension scheme where income withdrawal was available,

calculated by or on behalf of the pension fund holder by means of tables prepared from time to time by the Government Actuary which are appropriate for this purpose.]

[[6] (6) This regulation shall apply in the case of state pension credit subject to the following modifications—

(a) [[10] in connection with the setting of a new assessed income period], the information and evidence [[10] which the Secretary of State may require] to be notified in accordance with this regulation includes information and evidence as to the likelihood of future changes in the claimant's circumstances needed to determine—

(i) whether a period should be specified as an assessed income period under section 6 of the 2002 Act in relation to any decision; and

(ii) if so, the length of the period to be so specified; and

[[9] (b) except to the extent that sub-paragraph (a) applies, changes to an element of the claimant's retirement provision need not be notified if—

(i) an assessed income period is current in his case; [[12] or]

[[12] (ii) the period applicable under regulation 17(4) of the Decisions and Appeals Regulations has not expired;

. . .

(7)) In this regulation, "the Decisions and Appeals Regulations" means the Social Security and Child Support (Decisions and Appeals) Regulations 1999.]

Amendments

1. The Social Security (Miscellaneous Provisions) Amendment (No.2) Regulations 1992 (SI 1992/2595) reg.4 (November 16, 1992).

2. Income-related benefit Schemes and Social Security (Claims and Payments) (Miscellaneous Amendments) Regulations 1995 (SI 1995/2303) reg.10(4) (October 2, 1995).

3. The Social Security (Claims and Payments) (Jobseeker's Allowance Consequential Amendments) Regulations 1996 (SI 1996/1460) reg.2(16) (October 7, 1996).
4. The Tax Credits (Claims and Payments) (Amendment) Regulations 1999 (SI 1999/2572) reg.14 (October 5, 1999).
5. The Social Security and Child Support (Miscellaneous Amendments) Regulations 2003 (SI 2003/1050) reg.2 (May 5, 2003).
6. State Pension Credit (Consequential, Transitional and Miscellaneous Provisions) Regulations 2002 (SI 2002/3019) reg.11 (April 7, 2003).
7. The Social Security (Claims and Payments and Miscellaneous Amendments) Regulations 2003 (SI 2003/1632) reg.2 (July 21, 2003).
8. The Social Security (Notification of Change of Circumstances) Regulations 2003, SI 2003/3209 reg.2 (January 6, 2004).
9. The State Pension Credit (Transitional and Miscellaneous Provisions) Amendment Regulations 2003 (SI 2003/2274) (October 6, 2003).
10. The Social Security (Students and Miscellaneous Amendments) Regulations 2008 (SI 2008/1599) reg.3 (August 25, 2008).
11. The Employment and Support Allowance (Consequential provisions) (No.2) Regulations 2008 (SI 2008/1554) reg.22 (October 27, 2008).
12. The Social Security (Suspension of Payment of Benefits and Miscellaneous Amendments) Regulations 2012 (SI 2012/824) (April 17, 2012).

DEFINITIONS

"appropriate office"—see reg.2(1).
"beneficiary"—see Social Security Act 1975, Sch.20.
"benefit"—see reg.2(2).
"jobseeker's allowance"—see reg.2(1).
"pension fund holder"—*ibid.*
"personal pension scheme"—*ibid.*
"retirement annuity contract"—*ibid.*

GENERAL NOTE

A Tribunal of Commissioners in *CIS/4348/2003* ruled that the duty to disclose **2.185** under s.71 of the Administration Act flowed from the provisions of reg.32. Note that the duty applies to beneficiaries and "every person by whom or on whose behalf, sums by way of benefit are receivable". The latter group includes appointees under reg.33.

The Tribunal of Commissioners draws a clear distinction between the two duties set out in reg.32. There is a duty in regs 32(1) and (1A) to notify the Secretary of State or Board of Inland Revenue of any matter where the Secretary of State or the Board has given unambiguous directions for the disclosure of the matter. There is no question of deciding in such cases whether disclosure was reasonably to be expected to the claimant. Any failure to disclose such information will render any overpayment of benefit resulting from the failure to disclose recoverable.

By contrast the duty in reg.32(1B) is to notify changes of circumstances which a benefit recipient might reasonably be expected to know might affect the continuance of entitlement to benefit or the payment of benefit. The Tribunal of Commissioners concludes that it is only in these cases that it is necessary to consider whether disclosure by the claimant was in all the circumstances reasonably to be expected.

The distinction may be easier to make in theory than in practice, but, given **2.186** the different consequences of failure to disclose under the two separate duties, it will be necessary to consider very carefully the source of any obligation to provide the Secretary of State or Her Majesty's Revenue and Customs with information and the specificity of that information. So, a requirement to disclose that children are no longer living with the claimant but had been taken into care (as was the case in *CIS/4348/2003*) which is clearly set out in documentation given to the claimant, will give rise to the duty to disclose under the first duty. Arguments about the claimant's capacity are not relevant. By contrast, failure to disclose some unspecified set of circumstances which might affect benefit entitlement will fall under the second duty, and will require consideration of whether disclosure in all the circumstances of the case could reasonably be expected of the claimant.

In *CDLA/2328/2006* the Commissioner said:

> " . . . There is nothing wrong in a tribunal relying on one paragraph rather than the other. The duties under paragraphs (1A) and (1B) are cumulative. The tribunal was entitled to rely on either duty. A finding that a claimant was in breach of paragraph (1B) is not rendered wrong in law just because the claimant was also in breach of paragraph (1A). What the tribunal must do is to rely on one or the other and make clear which." (See para.20.)

In interpreting the duty under paragraph (1A), the Commissioner stresses the distinction between information gathering and decision making. The claimant is required to report facts which might show that entitlement is affected. It is then for the decision maker to decide whether to investigate further, if necessary, and to make a decision on whether entitlement is in fact affected by the change in circumstances. The Commissioner says:

> "23. The interpretation of the duties must reflect their nature and purpose. So the duty to report 'if things get easier for you' is not a duty to report 'if you believe that you are no longer virtually unable to walk'. Nor does this duty necessarily require a comparison between the claimant's abilities and disabilities at the time of the original award and those current at the time when the Secretary of State says a change should have been reported. That comparison does not arise until the later decision-making stage. The notes deal only with the earlier information-gathering stage. It is important not to confuse the issue whether the claimant failed to report a change of circumstances (an information-gathering question) and the issue whether that change was material to his entitlement (a decision-making question).
>
> 24. The duty does not set the focus of comparison on the time of the original award. If it did, it would become increasingly burdensome as time passes. In this case it would require the claimant to remember precisely how disabled he had been 18 years previously. The duty, like all the duties, is continuously speaking. It is to report if at any time things are easier for the claimant. That means easier by reference to the preceding period. Obviously that has to be applied in a reasonable time frame. It would not be necessary to report if a claimant were feeling a bit better today than yesterday. The test has to be applied over a period that is sufficient to show overall a sustained improvement or deterioration, taking account of any usual variation. This is not precise, but that is because it is a matter of judgment for each case."

2.187 On the interpretation of para.(1B) the Commissioner says:

> "28. . . . If the Secretary of State has issued an instruction to the claimant or to claimants generally, that will found a duty under paragraph (1A) and there should be no need to rely on paragraph (1B). There may be circumstances in which the Secretary of State could not rely on paragraph (1A) and could only rely on the instructions under paragraph (1B), but I have not been able to imagine one. But, assuming that this is possible, I accept that the notes issued by the Secretary of State are relevant under paragraph (1B). The instructions they contain may inform what is reasonable to expect a claimant to know. It would

usually be reasonable for a claimant to know the contents of those instructions. (I do not exclude the possibility that it may not be reasonable for the claimant to know everything that is in the Secretary of State's notes. For example, this may, perhaps, not be reasonable on account of the claimant's mental state.) And the notes may be so comprehensive that, in a particular case, there is no need to consider anything else. But the duty under paragraph (1B) is defined by the terms of that paragraph. The instructions given to claimants do not define that duty. They are merely evidence of what it was reasonable to expect the claimant to know. And the duty to report may be wider than any instructions given by the Secretary of State. For example, it may be reasonable for the claimant to realise from questions in a claim pack that a particular matter is relevant to entitlement, even if the notes issued by the Secretary of State do not specifically refer to them.

29. For completeness, I will mention that the focus under paragraph (1B) is different from that under paragraph (1A). There the duty refers to entitlement, but only whether the claimant might reasonably be expected to know a change of circumstances *might* affect entitlement. It is not necessary for the claimant to understand the actual impact that a change will have, but the focus is different from that appropriate to the duty imposed under paragraph (1A). A comparison with his disablement at the time of the award may be justified. But it is also possible to envisage cases in which a claimant ought reasonably to realise that a change of circumstances might affect entitlement without undertaking a comparison with the time of the award. For example, a claimant's mobility may improve to such an extent that no reasonable person would consider that the claimant was virtually unable to walk."

In *GJ v SSWP* [2010] UKUT 107 (AAC), the Judge rules (at [18]–[21]) that reg.32 does not require a claimant to notify the local office with information which the local office handling the claim has provided. This would be pointless and such a requirement would not be lawful in regulations made under s.5 of the Administration Act.

Note that there is no general requirement that the form of disclosure must be in writing, though any disclosure will often be reduced to writing and signed by the claimant.

In *CSDLA/1282/2001* the Deputy Commissioner held that, where there was no appointment by the Secretary of State under reg.33, but there was a Power of Attorney, then benefit was not receivable by the person holding the Power of Attorney, and accordingly that person was under no duty to provide information under reg.32. **2.188**

Note that Pt 3 of Sch.1 and Pt 4 of Sch.2 to the Employment and Support Allowance (Transitional Provisions, Housing Benefit and Council Tax Benefit) (Existing Awards) (No.2) Regulations 2010 (SI 2010/1907) (as amended) contains modifications of reg.32 for the purposes of the transition to employment and support allowance.

[1 Alternative means of notifying changes of circumstances

32ZZA.—(1) In such cases and subject to such conditions as the Secretary of State may specify, the duty in regulation 32(1B) to notify a change of circumstances may be discharged by notifying the Secretary of State as soon as reasonably practicable— **2.189**

(a) where the change of circumstances is a birth or death, through a relevant authority, or a county council in England, by personal attendance at an office specified by that authority or county council, provided the Secretary of State has agreed with that authority or county council for it to facilitate such notification; or

(b) where the change of circumstances is a death, by telephone to a telephone number specified for that purpose by the Secretary of State.

(2) In this regulation "relevant authority" has the same meaning as in the Housing Benefit Regulations 2006. [3 . . .]]

AMENDMENTS

1. Inserted by The Social Security (Notification of Changes of Circumstances) Regulations 2010 (SI 2010/444) reg.2 (April 5, 2010).

2. The Council Tax Benefit Abolition (Consequential Provision) Regulations 2013 (SI 2013/458) reg.3 (April 1, 2013).

[1 Information given electronically

2.190 **32ZA.**—(1) Where this regulation applies a person may given any certificate, notice, information or evidence required to be given and in particular may give notice or any change of circumstances required to be notified under regulation 32 by means of an electronic communication, in accordance with the provisions set out in Schedule 9ZC.

[2 (2) This regulation applies in relation to an award of—

(a) attendance allowance;

[6 (aa) bereavement support payment;]

(b) carer's allowance;

(c) disability living allowance;

(d) an employment and support allowance;

[3 (da) incapacity benefit;]

(e) income support;

(f) a jobseeker's allowance];

[3 (g) retirement pension;

(h) state pension credit;]

[4 (i) state pension under Part 1 of the Pensions Act 2014;]

[5 (j) industrial injuries benefit.]

AMENDMENTS

1. The Social Security (Electronic Communications) (Carer's Allowance) Order 2003 SI 2003/2800 reg.2 (December 1, 2003).

2. The Social Security (Electronic Communications) Order 2011 (SI 2011/1498) reg.4(3) (June 20, 2011).

3. The Social Security (Electronic Communications) (No.2) Order 2011 (SI 2011/2943) (January 23, 2012).

4. The Pensions Act 2014 (Consequential, Supplementary and Incidental Amendments) Order 2015 (SI 2015/1985) art.9(15) (April 6, 2016).

5. Social Security (Claims and Payments) Amendment Regulations 2016 (SI 2016/544) reg.2 (June 15, 2016).

6. The Pensions Act 2014 (Consequential, Supplementary and Incidental Amendments) Order 2017 (SI 2017/422) art.10 (April 6, 2017).

[1 Information given electronically

2.191 **32A.**—(1) Where this regulation applies a person may give any certificate, notice, information or evidence required to be given and in particular may give notice of any change of circumstances required to be notified under regulation 32 by means of an electronic communication, in accordance with the provisions set out in Schedule 9C.

(2) This regulation applies in relation to child benefit.]

AMENDMENT

1. Social Security (Electronic Communications) (Child Benefit) Order 2002 (SI 2002/1789) art.4 (October 28, 2002).

[1 Information relating to awards of benefit

32B. —(1) Where an authority or person to whom paragraph (2) applies has arranged with the Secretary of State for the authority or person to receive claims for a specified benefit or obtain information or evidence relating to claims for a specified benefit in accordance with regulation 4 or 4D, the authority or person may— 2.192

(a) receive information or evidence which relates to an award of that benefit and which is supplied by—
 (i) the person to whom the award has been made; or
 (ii) other persons in connection with the award,
 and shall forward it to the Secretary of State as soon as reasonably practicable;
(b) verify any information or evidence supplied; and
(c) record the information or evidence supplied and hold it (whether as supplied or recorded) for the purpose of forwarding it to the Secretary of State.

(2) This paragraph applies to—
(a) a local authority administering housing benefit [3 . . .];
(b) a county council in England;
(c) a person providing services to a person mentioned in sub-paragraph (a) or (b);
(d) a person authorised to exercise any function of a local authority relating to housing benefit [3 . . .];
(e) a person authorised to exercise any function a county council in England has under section 7A of the Social Security Administration Act 1992.

(3) In paragraph (1), "specified benefit" means one or more of the following benefits—
(a) attendance allowance;
(b) [5 . . .]
(c) [5 . . .]
(d) carer's allowance;
(e) disability living allowance;
[1 (ee) employment and support allowance;]
(f) incapacity benefit;
(g) income support;
(h) jobseeker's allowance;
(i) retirement pension;
(j) state pension credit;
(k) widowed parent's allowance;
(l) winter fuel payment.]
[4 (m) state pension under Part 1 of the Pensions Act 2014.]

AMENDMENTS

1. The Social Security (Claims and Information) Regulations 2007 (SI 2007/2911) (October 31, 2007).

2. The Social Security (Miscellaneous Amendments) (No.2) Regulations 2009 (SI 2009/1490) reg.2 (July 13, 2009).

3. The Council Tax Benefit Abolition (Consequential Provision) Regulations 2013 (SI 2013/458) reg.3 (April 1, 2013).
4. The Pensions Act 2014 (Consequential, Supplementary and Incidental Amendments) Order 2015 (SI 2015/1985) art.9(16) (April 6, 2016).
5. The Pensions Act 2014 (Consequential, Supplementary and Incidental Amendments) Order 2017 (SI 2017/422) art.10 (April 6, 2017).

PART IV

THIRD PARTIES

Persons unable to act

2.193 **33.**—(1) Where—

(a) a person is, or is alleged to be, entitled to benefit, whether or not a claim for benefit has been made by him or on his behalf; and
(b) that person is unable for the time being to act; and either
(c) no [6 deputy] has been appointed by the Court of Protection [6 under Part 1 of the Mental Capacity Act 2005 or receiver appointed under Part 7 of the Mental Health Act 1983 but treated as a deputy by virtue of the Mental Capacity Act 2005] with power to claim, or as the case may be, receive benefit on his behalf; or
(d) in Scotland, his estate is not being administered by [4 a judicial factor or any guardian acting or appointed under the Adults with Incapacity (Scotland) Act 2004 who has power to claim or, as the case may be, receive benefit on his behalf],

the Secretary of State [2 or the Board] may, upon written application made to him by a person who, if a natural person, is over the age of 18, appoint that person to exercise, on behalf of the person who is unable to act, any right to which that person may be entitled and to receive and deal on his behalf with any sums payable to him.

[7 "(1A) Where a person has been appointed under regulation 82(3) of the Housing Benefit Regulations 2006 or regulation 63(3) of the Housing Benefit (Persons who have attained the qualifying age for state pension credit) Regulations 2006 by a relevant authority within the meaning of those Regulations to act on behalf of another in relation to a benefit claim or award, the Secretary of State may, if the person agrees, treat him as if he had appointed him under paragraph (1).]

(2) Where the Secretary of State has made [2 or the Board have made] an appointment [4, or treated an appointment as made,] under paragraph (1)—

(a) he [2 or they] may at any time revoke it;
(b) the person appointed may resign his office after having given one month's notice in writing to the Secretary of State [2 or the Board] of his intention to do so;
(c) any such appointment shall terminate when the Secretary of State is notified [2 or the Board are notified] that a receiver or other person to whom paragraph (1)(c) or (d) applies has been appointed.

(3) Anything required by these regulations to be done by or to any person

who is for the time being unable to act may be done by or to the receiver, [4 judicial factor or] guardian, if any, or by or to the person appointed under this regulation or regulation 43 [1(disability living allowance for a child)] and [3 . . .] [3 a direct credit transfer under regulation 21 into the account of any person so appointed, or the receipt by him of a payment made by some other means] shall be a good discharge to the Secretary of State [2 or the Board] for any sum paid.

AMENDMENTS

1. The Social Security (Claims and Payments) Amendment Regulations 1991 (SI 1991/2741) reg.16 (February 3, 1992).
2. The Tax Credits (Claims and Payments) (Amendment) Regulations 1999 (SI 1999/2572) regs 15, 20, 22 and 23 (October 5, 1999).
3. Social Security (Claims and Payments and Miscellaneous Amendments) (No.2) Regulations 2002 (SI 2002/2441) reg.8 (October 23, 2002).
4. The Social Security, Child Support and Tax Credits (Miscellaneous Amendments) Regulations 2005 (SI 2005/337) reg.7 (March 18, 2005).
5. The Housing Benefit and Council Tax Benefit (Consequential Provisions) Regulations 2006 (SI 2006/217) Sch.2 para.2 (March 6, 2006).
6. The Social Security (Miscellaneous Amendments) (No.4) Regulations 2007 (SI 2007/2470) (September 24, 2007).
7. The Council Tax Benefit Abolition (Consequential Provision) Regulations 2013 (SI 2013/458) reg.4 (April 1, 2013).

DEFINITIONS

"benefit"—see reg.2(2).
"claim for benefit"—see reg.2(1).

GENERAL NOTE

Appointment under the powers contained in reg.33 should be carefully distinguished from situations in which a person is appointed under a private arrangement as an adviser to a claimant: see *Tkachuk v Secretary of State for Work and Pensions*, reported as *R(IS) 3/07*, and *VB v SSWP* [2008] UKUT 15 (AAC). 2.194

Even if no appointment has been made, a claim made by a person unable to act, or by an "unauthorised person" on their behalf, is still valid (*CIS/812/1992*, applying para.8 of *R(SB) 9/84* where a Tribunal of Commissioners holds that in the absence of any challenge at the time the Secretary of State must be deemed to have accepted that the claim was made in sufficient manner). In *Walsh v CAO* (Consent Order, January 19, 1995) the Court of Appeal also applied *R(SB)9/84* when setting aside *CIS/638/1991* in which the Commissioner had held that a claim made on behalf of a person unable to act by a person who had not been formally appointed was a nullity.

Note that any subsequent appointment has retrospective effect (*R(SB)5/90*).

In *CIS/642/1994* the claimant's husband was her appointee under reg.33. She died before the tribunal hearing. The Commissioner holds that the tribunal decision was a nullity because there had been no appointment under reg.30 (deceased persons). Appointments under reg.30 were a distinct and different form of appointment from reg.33 appointments. He dissents from para.8 of *R(SB)9/84* and repeats his view (see *CIS/638/1991*) that it is open to adjudication officers and tribunals (and Commissioners) to determine that a claim is a nullity in cases where a person is unable to act and there has been no valid appointment. This is out of step with the current weight of authority. 2.195

CIS/812/1992 also confirms that, in relation to the pre-April 1997 form of the rules for backdating claims, if there has been no appointment it is only necessary to decide whether the claimant has good cause for a late claim; it is not necessary to consider the reasonableness of the failure to claim of a person who has been acting informally on his behalf. The Commissioner declines to follow paras 12 and 13 of *R(IS)5/91* since this could not be reconciled with paras 9 and 10 of *R(SB)9/84* (which was a Tribunal of Commissioners' decision). See also *CSB/168/1993* which takes a similar view and contains a useful summary of the authorities on this issue.

Under the current form of reg.19(5) the test is also of the claimant's personal circumstances, if there is no appointee, but those circumstances sometimes expressly include whether there is anyone who could help the claimant.

2.196 The Secretary of State's normal practice in making appointments is not to make an appointment generally but to limit it to a specific benefit: see *R(IS)5/91*. *R(IS)5/91* concerned the effect of an appointment for supplementary benefit purposes on a subsequent income support claim following the 1988 changes. There is some doubt whether such a limited appointment has survived the changes brought about then. There is now a single regulation governing appointments, and some argue that, at a consequence appointments are for all benefits. Tribunals do, however, continue to see appointments limited to certain benefits. The message is that the scope of the appointment needs to be considered in every case where it is relevant, though in the absence of any limiting conditions, there is a strong case for considering that it applies to all benefits.

Where a claimant has died, the Secretary of State may appoint a person to act: *R(SB)8/88*. Unless the Secretary of State does so, the tribunal has no jurisdiction to proceed in the absence of action by a personal representative under a grant of probate or letters of administration.

In *CSDLA/1282/2001*, the Deputy Commissioner concludes, following *CA/1014/1999*, that a person holding a Power of Attorney is not a person made an appointee under reg.33: see para.18.

2.197 In *R(SB)5/90*, Commissioner Goodman clarifies the decision in *R(SB)8/88* in holding that the appointment of a person to act by the Secretary of State operates retrospectively. Thus, so far as tribunals are concerned, an appointment after the date of the appeal but before the date of the hearing will be sufficient to ground jurisdiction. The power of appointment is to be found in reg.30(1).

Note that the power of appointment under this regulation is a separate power of appointment from that under reg.30 which arises on the death of the claimant, or where a claim is made after death, a potential claimant.

On the liability of appointees in respect of overpayments of benefit, see the discussion in the notes to s.71 of the Administration Act.

The practice of the Secretary of State in making appointments under reg.33 appears to vary. Since April 1988 there has been a single regulation governing appointments and the regulation is drafted in sufficiently wide terms to encompass a single appointment to cover all social security benefits; it covers "any sums payable to him". Previously there were separate sets of regulations covering means-tested and non-means-tested benefits, and it was the interaction of the sets of regulations which was primarily in issue in *R(IS)5/91*. The experience of tribunals appears to be that in some cases the appointment is for all benefits, and in other cases it is limited to particular benefits. Indeed, in some cases it is not clear what the scope of the appointment is, as when a claimant asks for an appointment in relation to a particular benefit and the appointment is made in general terms. The nature of the appointment seldom seems to be an issue upon which the appeal turns.

See also annotation to reg.30.

Payment to another person on the beneficiary's behalf

2.198 **34.**—[3 (1) Except in a case to which paragraph (2) applies,] the Secretary of State [2 or the Board] may direct that benefit may be paid, wholly or in part, to [1 another natural person] on the beneficiary's behalf if such a direction as to payment appears to the Secretary of State [2 or the

Board] to be necessary for protecting the interests of the beneficiary, or any child or dependant in respect of whom benefit is payable.

[3 (2) The Secretary of State may direct that a joint-claim jobseeker's allowance shall be paid wholly or in part to a natural person who is not a member of the joint-claim couple who is the nominated member for the purposes of section 3B of the Jobseekers Act if such a direction as to payment appears to the Secretary of State to be necessary for protecting the interests of the other member of that couple or, as the case may be, both members of that couple.]

AMENDMENTS

1. The Social Security (Miscellaneous Provisions) Amendment (No.2) Regulations 1992 (SI 1992/2595) reg.5 (January 4, 1993).

2. The Tax Credits (Claims and Payments) (Amendment) Regulations 1999 (SI 1999/2572) reg.20 (October 5, 1999).

3. The Social Security (Joint Claims: Consequential Amendments) Regulations 2000 (SI 2000/1982) reg.2(8) (March 19, 2001).

DEFINITIONS

"beneficiary"—see Social Security Act 1975 Sch.20.
"benefit"—see reg.2(2).
"child"—see 1986 Act s.20(11).

[1 Deductions of mortgage interest which shall be made from benefit and paid to qualifying lenders

34A.—(1) [2 In relation to cases to which section 15A(1) or (1A) of the Social Security Administration Act 1992] (payment out of benefit of sums in respect of mortgage interest etc.) applies and in the circumstances specified in Schedule 9A, such part of any relevant benefits to which a relevant beneficiary is entitled as may be specified in that Schedule shall be paid by the Secretary of State directly to the qualifying lender and shall be applied by that lender towards the discharge of the liability in respect of that mortgage interest [4 or, insofar as the payment exceeds that liability, in accordance with paragraph 4A of that Schedule.]. 2.199

[3 (1A) Paragraph (1) shall only apply in relation to a relevant beneficiary who is entitled to state pension credit where he is entitled to a guarantee credit.]

[4 (2) The provisions of Schedule 9A shall have effect in relation to payments made under this regulation.]

AMENDMENTS

1. The Social Security (Claims and Payments) Amendment Regulations 1992 (SI 1992/1026) reg.3 (May 25, 1992).

2. State Pension Credit (Consequential, Transitional and Miscellaneous Provisions) Regulations 2002 (SI 2002/3019) reg.12 (April 7, 2003).

3. The State Pension Credit (Consequential, Transitional and Miscellaneous Provisions) (No. 2) Regulations 2002 (SI 2002/3197) (April 7, 2003).

4. The Social Security (Claims and Payments) Amendment Regulations 2010 (SI 2010/796) reg.2 (April 8, 2010).

DEFINITIONS

"qualifying lender"—see Administration Act s.15A(3).
"relevant beneficiary"—see Administration Act s.15A(1).
"relevant benefits"—see Administration Act s.15A(4).

[1 Deductions of mortgage interest which may be made from benefits and paid to qualifying lenders in other cases

2.200 **34B**.—(1) In relation to cases to which section 151A(1A) of the Social Security Administration Act 1992 applied (others than those referred to in regulation 34A(1A))—

(a) in the circumstances specified in paragraph 2A(1) of Schedule 9A; and
(b) in either of the further circumstances specified in paragrpag 2A(2) of that Schedule,

such part of any relevant benefits to which a relevant beneficiary is entitled as may be paid by the Secretary of State directly to the qualifying lender and shall be applied by that lender towards the discharge of the liability in respect of that interest [2 or, insofar as the payment exceeds that liability, in accordance with paragraph 4A of that Schedule.].

[2 2) The provisions of Schedule 9A shall have effect in relation to payments made under this regulation.]

AMENDMENTS

1. The State Pension Credit (Consequential, Transitional and Miscellaneous Provisions) (No. 2) Regulations 2002 (SI 2002/3197) (April 7, 2003).
2. The Social Security (Claims and Payments) Amendment Regulations 2010 (SI 2010/796) reg.2 (April 8, 2010).

[1 [3Deductions which may be made from benefit and paid to third parties

2.201 **35.**—(1) Except as provided for in regulation 34A and Schedule 9A, deductions] may be made from benefit and direct payments may be made to third parties on behalf of a beneficiary in accordance with the provisions of Schedule 9 [4 and Schedule 9B].

(2) Where a social fund payment for maternity or funeral expenses [2or expenses for heating which appear to the Secretary of State to have been or to be likely to be incurred in cold weather] is made, wholly or in part, in respect of a debt which is, or will be, due to a third person, [5 . . .] [5 payment may be, and in the case of funeral expenses shall be, made to that person and where an instrument of payment is made to that person it may be sent to the beneficiary].

AMENDMENTS

1. The Social Security (Claims and Payments) Amendment Regulations 1988 (SI 1988/522) reg.7 (April 11, 1988).
2. The Social Security (Common Provisions) Miscellaneous Amendments Regulations 1988 (SI 1988/1725) reg.3 (November 7, 1988).
3. The Social Security (Claims and Payments) Amendment Regulations 1992 (SI 1992/1026) reg.4 (May 25, 1992).
4. The Social Security (Claims and Payments) Amendment Regulations 2001 (SI 2001/18) reg.2 (January 31, 2001).

5. Social Security (Claims and Payments and Miscellaneous Amendments) (No.2) Regulations 2002 (SI 2002/2441) reg.9 (April 8, 2003).

Definitions

"beneficiary"—see Social Security Act 1975 Sch.20.
"benefit"—see reg.2(2).

General Note

Child support payments

Regulation 35 and Sch.9 make provision for various deductions from benefit to be paid to third parties. These include payments in lieu of child support payments, which are at the bottom of the list of priorities. A new Sch.9B was introduced dealing specifically with child support maintenance and payments to persons with care. But the relationship between Sch.9B deductions and those arising under Sch.9 is not spelled out, so that it is unclear whether flat rate child support liabilities take precedence over other deductions from benefit under Sch.9. **2.202**

The policy response appears to be that child support deductions from a range of benefits will set apart from the rest of the direct payments scheme rather than take precedence over them. So child support deductions will, as a matter of policy rather than law, be taken without regard to other Sch.9 deductions. Administrative arrangements will ensure that where only one of a child support deduction and another deduction can be taken, priority will be given to the child support deduction. The provisions of Sch.9B kick in in April 2002, although Sch.9B was inserted in January 2001. It is said to be the intention that existing child support cases will continue to be dealt with under the provisions of Sch.9 with conversion to the new scheme at some later common date.

This is all a most unsatisfactory way of sorting out deficiencies in the clarity of the legislative scheme.

Regulation 35A revoked by The Social Security (Care Homes and Independent Hospitals) Regulations 2005 (SI 2005/2687) (October 24, 2005). **2.203**

Payment to a partner as alternative payee

36.—[3(1)] [1 Except where a wife has elected in accordance with regulation 6A of the Social Security (Guardian's Allowances) Regulation 1975 (prescribed manner of making an election under section 77(9) of the Social Security Contributions and Benefits Act 1992) that guardian's allowance is not to be paid to her husband,] where one of a married or unmarried couple residing together is entitled to child benefit [2 working families' tax credit, disabled person's tax credit] [1 or guardian's allowance] the Secretary of State [2 or the Board] may make arrangements whereby that benefit as well as being payable to the person entitled to it, may, in the alternative, be paid to that person's partner on behalf of the person entitled. **2.204**

[3 (2) Where a person is entitled to a winter fuel payment within the meaning of the Social Fund Winter Fuel Payment Regulations 2000 and—

(a) that person is one [4 member of a] couple of a member of a polygamous marriage;
(b) the other member of that couple or another member of that marriage

("the other person") is in receipt of income support [5 , an income-based jobseeker's allowance or an income-related employment and support allowance] and

(c) both members of the couple or marriage are living together within the meaning of regulation 1(3)(b) of those Regulations,

the Secretary of State may pay the winter fuel payment to the other person on behalf of the person entitled notwithstanding that [6 in the qualifying week the other person has not yet attained the qualifying age].]

AMENDMENTS

1. The Social Security (Claims and Payments) Amendment Regulations1999 (SI 1999/2358) reg.2(6) (September 20, 1999).

2. The Tax Credits (Claims and Payments) (Amendment) Regulations 1999(SI 1999/2752) regs 20, 24 and 25 (October 5, 1999).

3. The Social Security (Claims and Payments and Miscellaneous Amendments) (No.3) Regulations 2002 (SI 2002/2660) reg.2 (November 2, 2002).

4. The Civil Partnership (Pensions, Social Security and Child Support) (Consequential etc. Provisions) Order 2005 (SI 2005/2877) (December 5, 2005).

5. The Employment and Support Allowance (Consequential provisions) (No.2) Regulations 2008 (SI 2008/1554) reg.23 (October 27, 2008).

6. The Social Security (Equalisation of State Pension Age) Regulation 2009 (SI 2009/1488) reg.6 (April 6, 2010).

2.205 *Regulation 36A revoked by The Social Security (Claims and Payments) Amendment Regulations 1991 (SI1991/2741) reg.18 (April 6, 1992).*

PART V

[1 . . .] EXTINGUISHMENT

AMENDMENT

1. Words in heading omitted by The Social Security Act 1998 (Commencement No.8, and Savings and Consequential and Transitional Provisions) Order 1999 (SI 1999/1958) Sch.9 (July 5, 1999).

2.206 *Regulations 37–37B revoked by The Social Security Act 1998 (Commencement No.8, and Savings and Consequential and Transitional Provisions) Order 1999 (SI1999/1958), Sch.9 (July 5, 1999).*

Extinguishment of right to payment of sums by way of benefit where payment is not obtained within the prescribed period

2.207 **38.**—(1) [1Subject to paragraph (2A), the right to payment of any sum by way of benefit shall be extinguished] where payment of that sum is not obtained within the period of 12 months from the date on which the right is to be treated as having arisen; and for the purposes of this regulation the right shall be treated as having arisen—

(a) in relation to any such sum contained in an instrument of payment which has been given or sent to the person to whom it is payable, or to a place approved by the Secretary of State [4 or the Board] for collection by him (whether or not received or collected as the case may be)—

(i) on the date of the said instrument of payment, or

(ii) if a further instrument of payment has been so given or sent as a replacement, on the date of the last such instrument of payment;

[3(aa) [8 . . .];]

(b) in relation to any such sum to which sub-paragraph (a) does not apply, where notice is given (whether orally or in writing) or is sent that the sum contained in the notice is ready for collection on the date of the notice or, if more than one such notice is given or sent, the date of the first such notice;

[7 (bb) in relation to any such sum which [9 the Secretary of State has] arranged to be paid by means of direct credit transfer into a bank or other account, on the due date for payment of the sum;]

(c) in relation to any such sum to which [3 none of (a), [8 . . .] or [7 (b) or (bb) apply], on such date as the Secretary of State determines [4 or the Board determine].

(2) The giving or sending of an instrument of payment under paragraph (1)(a), or of a notice under paragraph (1)(b), shall be effective for the purposes of that paragraph, even where the sum contained in that instrument, or notice, is more or less than the sum which the person concerned has the right to receive.

[1(2A) Where a question arises whether the right to payment of any sum by way of benefit has been extinguished by the operation of this regulation and the [5 Secretary of State] is satisfied that—

(a) [5 he] first received [4 or the Board first received] written notice requesting payment of that sum after the expiration of 12 months; and

(b) from a day within that period of 12 months and continuing until the day the written notice was given, there was good cause for not giving the notice; and

[2(c) [5. . .] either—

(i) [5. . .] no instrument of payment has been given or sent to the person to whom it is payable and [5. . .] no payment has been made under the provisions of regulation 21 ([6 direct] credit transfer); or

(ii) that such instrument has been produced to [5 the Secretary of State] and [5. . .] no further instrument has been issued as a replacement,]

the period of 12 months shall be extended to the date on which the [5 Secretary of State] decides that question, and this regulation shall accordingly apply as though the right to payment had arisen on that date.]

(3) For the purposes of paragraph (1) the date of an instrument of payment is the date of issue of that instrument or, if the instrument specifies a date which is the earliest date on which payment can be obtained on the instrument and which is later than the date of issue, that date.(4) This regulation shall apply to a person authorised or appointed to act on behalf of a beneficiary as it applies to a beneficiary.(5) This regulation shall not apply to the right to a single payment of any industrial injuries gratuity or in satisfaction of a person's right to graduated retirement benefit.

AMENDMENTS

1. The Social Security (Medical Evidence, Claims and Payments) Amendment Regulations 1989 (SI 1989/1686) reg.7 (October 9, 1989).
2. Social Security (Claims and Payments) Amendment (No.3) Regulations 1993 (SI 1993/2113) reg.3(8) (September 27, 1993).
3. Social Security (Claims and Payments Etc.) Amendment Regulations 1996 (SI 1996/672) reg.2(5) (April 4, 1996).
4. The Tax Credits (Claims and Payments) (Amendment) Regulations 1999(SI 1999/2572) reg.20 (October 5, 1999).
5. The Social Security Act 1998 (Commencement No.9, and Savings and Consequential and Transitional Provisions) Order 1999 (SI 1999/2422) Sch.7 (September 6, 1999).
6. Social Security (Claims and Payments and Miscellaneous Amendments) (No.2) Regulations 2002 (SI 2002/2441) reg.10 (April 8, 2003).
7. The Social Security, Child Support and Tax Credits (Miscellaneous Amendments) Regulations 2005 (SI 2005/337) reg.7 (March 18, 2005).
8. The Social Security (Miscellaneous Amendments) (No.2) Regulations 2006 (SI 2006/832) reg.2 (April 10, 2006).
9. The Social Security (Miscellaneous Amendments) Regulations 2012 (SI 2012/757) reg.15(3) (April 1, 2012).

DEFINITIONS

"beneficiary"—see Social Security Act 1975 Sch.20.
"benefit"—see reg.2(2).
"instrument for benefit payment"—see reg.2(1).

GENERAL NOTE

2.208 In *CDLA/2807/2003* the Commissioner said,

"It seems to me quite impossible to say in circumstances where the operative decision is that no benefit is payable that any right to payment, let alone a right to payment of any amount that has been quantified, is in existence. There could be no right to payment until that decision has been altered in some way. Regulation 38 simply cannot have any operation in such circumstances."

In *CU/2604/1999*, the Commissioner said,

"The subject of regulation 38 is the 'right to payment of any sum'. The regulation sets out various rules for ascertaining the date on which that right is to be treated as having arisen. This includes the rule in regulation 38(1)(c). However, there must *first* be a right to payment of a *sum*. The word 'sum' means something otherwise it could have been omitted and left the provision meaning something slightly different. . . . In my view, if the amount has not been quantified, there is no 'sum', even if there has been identified a basis for quantifying it. Contrary to what has been argued on behalf of the Secretary of State, the fact that the tribunal later quantified the amount does not affect the fact it had not bee quantified at the time when the adjudication officer sought to extinguish the right to payment. If there is no sum, then the right to payment of it cannot arise, and cannot be extinguished under regulation 38." (See para.17.)

In *CDLA/2609/2002*, the Commissioner offers a helpful overview of reg.38:

"15. I start with the overall scheme of regulation 38 of the Claims and Payments Regulations. It is concerned not with payment of benefit in a general sense, but with the extinguishment of a 'right to payment of any sum by way of benefit' (regulation 38(1)). The basic condition for such extinguishment is that 'payment of that sum is not obtained within the period of 12 months from the date on which the right is to be treated as having arisen'. Mr Commissioner Levenson has in decision *CU/2604/1999* (in the papers under that reference, but now reported as *R(U)1/02*) stressed that some meaning must be given to the word 'sum'. So he held there that where a Commissioner had decided that unemployment benefit was payable to a claimant for a specified period, without quantifying the amount of benefit, there was no sum identified to which a right of payment attached which could be extinguished. Likewise, it seems to me that some weight must be attached to the use of the term 'any sum by way of benefit' and to the test being in terms of 'obtaining' payment of such a sum. The use of language does not point towards a situation where benefit of a sufficiently ascertainable amount has been merely been awarded by a decision on entitlement and payability, so that the Secretary of State is under an obligation to pay the benefit as soon as reasonably practicable (Claims and Payments Regulations, regulation 20). It points towards a situation where a particular sum has been allocated to the claimant and some steps along the administrative process of making payment have been taken, leaving the claimant with some relatively mechanical steps to take to 'obtain' payment.

16. That view is also consistent with the provisions of subparagraphs (a) to (b) of regulation 38(1), which define the dates on which the right to payment of a sum by way of benefit is to be treated as having arisen in certain circumstances. The rules are that: where the claimant has been given or sent an instrument of payment or an instrument has been made available for collection, the right arises on the date of the instrument or any replacement instrument (subparagraph (a)); where a sum is payable by means of an instrument for benefit payment (see regulation 20A), the right arises on the first date on which payment could be obtained by that means (subparagraph (aa)); and, where subparagraph (a) does not apply and notice is given or sent that the sum is available for collection, the right arises on the date that the notice is sent (subparagraph (b)). It makes perfect sense to say in all those situations that a right to payment of the particular sum by way of benefit had arisen and that, if the claimant does not take the other necessary steps to get paid (even in a situation, for instance, where a letter gets lost in the post), payment has not been obtained. The final provision in regulation 38(1), the crucial provision in this case, is subparagraph (c), under which the right to payment is to be treated as having arisen:

> '(c) in relation to any such sum to which none of (a), (aa) or (b) apply, on such date as the Secretary of State determines or the [Board of Inland Revenue] determine.'

17. It is plainly arguable that subparagraph (c) does not give the Secretary of State an unfettered discretion to choose any date whatsoever, but must be interpreted in accordance with the overall scheme and scope of regulation 38(1) and by reference to the circumstances of subparagraphs (a) to (b). It is true that regulation 38(2A) on good cause is drafted on the assumption that regulation 38(1) can apply in a case where no instrument of payment was given or sent to the claimant, but I do not think that that undermines what I have said above. Miss Topping submitted that, although subparagraph (c) might exclude irrational or completely unreasonable choices, it certainly allowed the Secretary of State to determine that a right to payment of a sum by way of benefit arose on the date on which a weekly payment of benefit would have been made in the ordinary course of things, even though no administrative steps at all had actually been taken towards making payment."

It is a common feature of social security benefit that the right to payment of **2.209** benefit does not survive a delay of more than 12 months in obtaining payment of it. The determination of the date on which the right to payment is treated as arising may be crucial and is a matter for the Secretary of State (or Board of the Inland Revenue as appropriate).

Only where reg.38(2A) applies does any issue for the adjudicating authorities arise. Then it is only whether the right to payment has been extinguished, but it will still be for the Secretary of State to determine "whether there should be a replacement instrument." (See [7]).

Cases in which the claimant says that no giro was received are governed by *R(IS) 7/91* under which questions of payment were held not to be questions relating to the award of benefit.

Unravelling those matters which are for the adjudicating authorities and those matters which do not attract a right of appeal will become more complicated under the new system under which there adjudication officers have been abolished and all decisions are taken by the Secretary of State with some attracting a right of appeal and others not.

Note that *R(P)3/93* was concerned with the version of this regulation in force until September 27, 1993, and has no application to the present version of the regulation.

Good cause

2.210 The test of good cause is the test which formerly existed under the replaced reg.19 of the Claims and Payments Regulations. Reference to the 1996 edition of *Non Means Tested Benefits: The Legislation* contains a detailed account of the case law, but the classic definition of good cause is that found in *R(S)2/63:*

> "In Decision *CS371/49* the Commissioner said 'Good cause' means, in my opinion, some fact which, having regard to all the circumstances (including the claimant's state of health and the information which he had received and that which he might have obtained) would probably have caused a reasonable person of his age and experience to act (or fail to act) as the claimant did.' This description of good cause has been quoted in countless cases. It has stood the test of time. In our judgment it is correct. The word 'fact' of course includes a combination of events happening either simultaneously or in succession."

PART VI

[[1]MOBILITY COMPONENT OF DISABILITY LIVING ALLOWANCE AND DISABILITY LIVING ALLOWANCE FOR CHILDREN]

AMENDMENT

1. The Social Security (Claims and Payments) Amendment Regulations 1991 (SI 1991/2741) reg.19(a) (February 3, 1992).

2.211 *Regulations 39–41 revoked by The Social Security (Claims and Payments) Amendment Regulations 1991 (SI 1991/2741), reg.19(b) (February 3, 1992).*

Cases where allowance not to be payable

2.212 **42.**—(1) Subject to the provisions of this regulation, [[1]disability living allowance by virtue of entitlement to the mobility component] shall not be payable to any person who would otherwise be entitled to it in respect of any period—

(a) during which that person has the use of an invalid carriage or other vehicle provided by the Secretary of State under section 5(2) of and Schedule 2 to the National Health Service Act 1977 or section 46 of the National Health Service (Scotland) Act 1978 which is a vehicle propelled by petrol engine or by electric power supplied for use on the road and to be controlled by the occupant; or

(b) in respect of which that person has received, or is receiving, any payment—

(i) by way of grant under the said section 5(2) and Schedule 2 or section 46 towards the costs of running a private car, or

(ii) of mobility supplement under the Naval, Military and Air Forces etc., (Disablement and Death) Service Pensions Order 1983 or the Personal Injuries (Civilians) Scheme 1983 or under the said Order by virtue of the War Pensions (Naval Auxiliary Personnel) Scheme 1964, the Pensions (Polish Forces) Scheme 1964, the War Pensions (Mercantile Marine) Scheme 1964 or an Order of Her Majesty in relation to the Home Guard dated 21st December, 1964 or 22nd December, 1964 or in relation to the Ulster Defence Regiment dated 4th January, 1971,

or any payment out of public funds which the Secretary of State is satisfied is analogous thereto.

(2) A person who has notified the Secretary of State that he no longer wishes to use such an invalid carriage or other vehicle as if referred to in paragraph (1)(a) and has signed an undertaking that he will not use it while it remains in his possession awaiting collection, shall be treated, for the purposes of this regulation, as not having the use of that invalid carriage or other vehicle.

(3) Where a person in respect of whom [[1]disability living allowance] is claimed for any period has received any such payment as referred to in paragraph (1)(b) for a period which, in whole or in part, covers the period for which the allowance is claimed, such payment shall be treated as an aggregate of equal weekly amounts in respect of each week in the period for which it is made and, where in respect of any such week a person is treated as having a weekly amount so calculated which is less than the weekly rate of [[1] mobility component of disability living allowance to which, apart from paragraph (1), he would be entitled], any allowance to which that person may be entitled for that week shall be payable at a weekly rate reduced by the weekly amount so calculated.

(4) In a case where the Secretary of State has issued a certificate to the effect that he is satisfied—

(a) that the person in question either—

(i) has purchased or taken on hire or hire-purchase; or

(ii) intends to purchase or take on hire or hire-purchase a private car or similar vehicle ("the car") for a consideration which is more than nominal, on or about a date (not being earlier than 13th January, 1982) specified in the certificate ("the said date");

(b) that that person intends to retain possession of the car at least during, and to learn to drive it within, the period of 6 months or greater or lesser length of time as may be specified in the certificate ("the said period") beginning on the said date; and

(c) that the person will use [[1] disability living allowance by virtue of entitlement to the mobility component] in whole or in part during the said period towards meeting the expense of acquiring the car, paragraph (1)(a) shall not apply, and shall be treated as having never applied, during a period beginning on the said date and ending at the end of the said period or (if earlier) the date on which the Secretary of State cancels the certificate because that person has parted with possession of the car or for any other reason.

AMENDMENT

1. The Social Security (Claims and Payments) Amendment Regulations 1991 (SI 1991/2741) reg.20 (February 3, 1992).

Children

2.213 **43.**—(1) In any case where a claim for [[1]disability living allowance] for a child is received by the Secretary of State, he shall, in accordance with the following provisions of this regulation, appoint a person to exercise, on behalf of the child, any right to which he may be entitled under the Social Security Act 1975 in connection with [[1]disability living allowance] and to receive and deal on his behalf with any sums payable by way of [[1]that allowance].

(2) Subject to the following provisions of this regulation, a person appointed by the Secretary of State under this regulation to act on behalf of the child shall—

(a) be a person with whom the child is living; and
(b) be over the age of 18 [[2] or, if the person is a parent of the child and living with him, be over the age of 16]; and
(c) be either the father or mother of the child, or, if the child is not living with either parent, be such other person as the Secretary of State may determine; and
(d) have given such undertaking as may be required by the Secretary of State as to the use, for the child's benefit, of any allowance paid.

(3) For the purpose of paragraph (2)(a), a person with whom a child has been living shall, subject to paragraph (4) and to the power of the Secretary of State to determine in any case that the provisions of this paragraph should not apply, be treated as continuing to live with that child during any period—

(a) during which that person and the child are separated but such separation has not lasted for a continuous period exceeding [[1]12 weeks]; or
(b) during which the child is absent by reason only of the fact that he is receiving full-time education at a school; or
(c) during which the child is absent and undergoing medical or other treatment as an in-patient in a hospital or similar institution; or
(d) during such other period as the Secretary of State may in any particular case determine:

Provided that where the absence of the child under (b) has lasted for a continuous period of 26 weeks or the child is absent under (c), that person shall only be treated as continuing to live with that child if he satisfies the Secretary of State that he has incurred, or has undertaken to incur, expenditure for the benefit of the child of an amount not less than the allowance payable in respect of such period of absence.

(4) Where a child in respect of whom an allowance is payable, is, by virtue of any provision of an Act of Parliament—

(a) committed to, or received into the care of, a local authority; or
(b) subject to a supervision requirement and residing in a residential establishment under arrangements made by a local authority in Scotland;

any appointment made under the foregoing provisions of this regulation shall terminate forthwith:

Provided that, when a child is committed to, or received into, care or is made subject to a supervision requirement for a period which is, and when it began was, not intended to last for more than [1 12 weeks] the appointment shall not terminate by virtue of this paragraph until such period has lasted for 8 weeks.

(5) In any case where an appointment on behalf of any child in the care of, or subject to a supervision requirement under arrangements made by, a local authority is terminated in accordance with paragraph (4), the Secretary of State may, upon application made to him by that local authority or by an officer of such authority nominated for the purpose by that authority, appoint the local authority or nominated officer thereof or appoint such other person as he may, after consultation with the local authority, determine, to exercise on behalf of the child any right to which that child may be entitled under the Act in connection with the allowance and to receive and deal on his behalf with any sums payable to him by way of [1 disability living allowance] for any period during which he is in the care of, or, as the case may be, subject to a supervision requirement under arrangements made by, that authority.

(6) Where a child is undergoing medical or other treatment as an inpatient in a hospital or similar institution and there is no other person to whom [1 disability living allowance] may be payable by virtue of an appointment under this regulation, the Secretary of State may, upon application made to him by the [4 health authority] [1 National Health Service Trust] [3 NHS Foundation Trust] or, as the case may be, social services authority, controlling the hospital or similar institution in which the child is an in-patient, or by an officer of that authority [1 or Trust] nominated for the purpose by the authority, appoint that authority [1 or Trust] or the nominated officer thereof or such other person as the Secretary of State may, after consultation with that authority [1 or Trust], determine, to exercise on behalf of the child any right to which that child may be entitled in connection with the allowance and to receive and deal on his behalf with any sums payable to him by way of [1 disability living allowance] for any period during which he is an in-patient in a hospital or similar institution under the control of that authority [1 or Trust].

(7) For the purposes of this regulation—

[4 . . .]

[2 "child" means a person under the age of 16;]

"child's father" and "child's mother" include a person who is the child's father or mother by adoption or would be such a relative if an illegitimate child had been born legitimate;

[4 "health authority" means—

(a) [5 . . .]

(b) in relation to Wales, a Health Authority established under section 8 of that Act; and

(c) in relation to Scotland, a Health Board within the meaning of the National Health Service (Scotland) Act 1978;]

"hospital or similar institution" means any premises for the reception of and treatment of persons suffering from any illness, including any mental disorder, or of persons suffering from physical disability, and any premises used for providing treatment during convalescence or for medical rehabilitation;

"local authority" means, in relation to England and Wales, a local authority as defined in the Local Government Act 1972 and, in relation to Scotland, a local authority as defined in the Local Government (Scotland) Act 1973;

"social services authority" means—

(a) in relation to England and Wales, the social services committee established by a local authority under section 2 of the Local Authority Social Services Act 1970; and

(b) in relation to Scotland, the social work committee established by a local authority under section 2 of the Social work (Scotland) Act 1968.

AMENDMENTS

1. The Social Security (Claims and Payments) Amendment Regulations 1991 (SI 1991/2741) reg.21 (February 3, 1992).

2. The Social Security, Child Support and Tax Credits (Miscellaneous Amendments) Regulations 2005 (SI 2005/337) reg.7 (March 18, 2005).

3. The Health and Social Care (Community Health and Standards) Act 2003 (Supplementary and Consequential Provisions) (NHS Foundation Trusts) Order 2004 (SI 2004/696) art.3 and Sch.3 (March 11, 2004).

4. The National Health Service Reform and Health Care Professions Act 2002 (Supplementary, Consequential etc. Provisions) Regulations 2002 (SI 2001/2469) Sch.1 Pt.2 (October 1, 2002).

5. National Treatment Agency (Abolition) and the Health and Social Care Act 2012 (Consequential, Transitional and Saving Provisions) Order (SI 2013/235) art.11 and Sch.2 Pt.1 para.11 (April 1, 2013).

Payment of [1 disability living allowance] on behalf of a beneficiary

2.214 **44.**—(1) Where, under arrangements made or negotiated by Motability, an agreement has been entered into by or on behalf of a beneficiary in respect of whom [1 disability living allowance is payable by virtue of entitlement to the mobility component at the higher rate] for the hire or hire-purchase of a vehicle, the Secretary of State may arrange that any [1 disability living allowance by virtue of entitlement to the mobility component at the higher rate payable] to the beneficiary shall be paid in whole or in part on behalf of the beneficiary in settlement of liability for payments due under that agreement.

(2) Subject to regulations 45 and 46 an arrangement made by the Secretary of State under paragraph (1) shall terminate at the end of whichever is the relevant period specified in paragraph (3), in the case of hire, or paragraph (4), in the case of a hire-purchase agreement.

(3) In the case of hire the relevant period shall be—

(a) where the vehicle is returned to the owner at or before the expiration of the [3 . . .] term of hire, the period of the [3 . . .] term; or

(b) where the vehicle is retained by or on behalf of the beneficiary with the owner's consent after the expiration of the original term of hire [3, other than where sub-paragraph (d) applies,], the period of the original term; or

(c) where the vehicle is retained by or on behalf of the beneficiary otherwise than with the owner's consent after the expiration of the original term of hire or its earlier termination, whichever is the longer of the following periods—

(i) the period ending with the return of the vehicle to the owner; or

(ii) the period of the original term of hire.

[3; or

(d) where the original term of hire is extended by an agreed variation of the agreement, the period of the extended term.]

(4) In the case of a hire-purchase agreement, the relevant period shall be—

(a) the period ending with the purchase of the vehicle; or

(b) where the vehicle is returned to the owner or is repossessed by the owner under the terms of the agreement before the completion of the purchase, the original period of the agreement.

[2(5) In this regulation "Motability" means the company, set up under that name as a charity and originally incorporated under the Companies Act 1985 and subsequently incorporated by Royal Charter].

AMENDMENTS

1. The Social Security (Claims and Payments) Amendment Regulations 1991 (SI 1991/2741) reg.22 (February 3, 1992).

2. The Social Security (Miscellaneous Provisions) Amendment Regulations 1990 (SI 1990/2208) reg.13 (December 5, 1990).

3. The Social Security, Child Support and Tax Credits (Miscellaneous Amendments) Regulations 2005 (SI 2005/337) reg.7 (March 18, 2005).

[1 Recovery of expenses

44A.—(1) Paragraph (2) applies where— 2.215

(a) an agreement referred to in regulation 44(1) has been entered into; and

(b) a relevant provider is receiving payments of disability living allowance in settlement of liability for payments due under that agreement.

(2) The Secretary of State may require the relevant provider to make payments to meet the reasonable expenses of the Secretary of State in administering the making of the payments of disability living allowance to the relevant provider.

(3) The method by which the expenses under paragraph (2) are to be met is for the Secretary of State to issue an invoice to the relevant provider setting out the expenses that have been incurred and for the relevant provider to pay the sum stated to the Secretary of State.

(4) The first invoice issued by the Secretary of State may recover expenses incurred between 21st July 2016 and the date of the invoice.

(5) Subsequently the Secretary of State may issue invoices no more frequently than annually and only in respect of expenses incurred since the period covered by the previous invoice.

(6) The expenses that the Secretary of State may take into account for the purposes of paragraph (2) include—

(a) the salaries and other costs relating to the employment of staff wholly engaged in the administering of the payments of disability living allowance and where staff have other responsibilities, an apportioned amount of those costs; and

(b) overheads, including rent and other shared costs, relating to those staff.

(7) In determining what expenses were reasonably incurred in administering the making of payments of disability living allowance to a relevant provider, the Secretary of State must have regard to any agreement between the Secretary of State and the relevant provider concerning the level of service to be provided by the Secretary of State in the making of such payments to that relevant provider.]

AMENDMENT

1. Inserted by the Social Security (Expenses of Paying Sums in Relation to Vehicle Hire) Regulations 2016 (SI 2016/674) reg.3 (July 21, 2016).

Power for the Secretary of State to terminate an arrangement

2.216 **45.** The Secretary of State may terminate an arrangement for the payment of [1disability living allowance by virtue of entitlement to the mobility component at the higher rate] on behalf of a beneficiary under regulation 44 on such date as he shall decide—

(a) if requested to do so by the owner of the vehicle to which the arrangement relates, or

(b) where it appears to him that the arrangement is causing undue hardship to the beneficiary and that it should be terminated before the end of any of the periods specified in regulation 44(3) or 44(4).

AMENDMENT

1. The Social Security (Claims and Payments) Amendment Regulations 1991 (SI 1991/2741) reg.23 (February 3, 1992).

Restriction on duration of arrangements by the Secretary of State

2.217 **46.** The Secretary of State shall end an arrangement for the payment of [1 disability living allowance by virtue of entitlement to the mobility component at the higher rate] on behalf of a beneficiary made under regulation 44, where he is satisfied that the vehicle to which the arrangement relates has been returned to the owner, and that the expenses of the owner arising out of the hire or hire-purchase agreement have been recovered following the return of the vehicle.

PART VII

MISCELLANEOUS

[1 Instruments of payment

2.218 **47.**—(1) Instruments of payment issued by the Secretary of State shall remain his property.

(2) Any person having an instrument of payment shall, on ceasing to be entitled to the benefit to which the instrument relates, or when so required by the Secretary of State, deliver it to the Secretary of State or such other person as he may direct.]

AMENDMENT

1. Inserted by The Social Security (Miscellaneous Amendments) (No.2) Regulations 2006 (SI 2006/832) reg.2 (April 10, 2006).

Revocations

2.219 **48.** The regulations specified in column (1) of Schedule 10 to these regulations are hereby revoked to the extent mentioned in column (2) of that Schedule, in exercise of the powers specified in column (3).

Savings

49. [1. . .] 2.220

AMENDMENT

1. The Social Security (Miscellaneous Provisions) Amendment (No.2) Regulations 1992 (SI 1992/2595) reg.6 (November 16, 1992).

GENERAL NOTE

Regulation 49 maintained in force regulations about claims and reviews relating to supplementary benefit and family income support. See *CIS/465/1991*. Because its terms led to the mistaken impression that the substantive terms of the schemes survived the repeal of the Supplementary Benefits Act 1976 and the Family Income Supplements Act 1970 by the Social Security Act 1986, reg.49 has been revoked from November 16, 1992. See *R(SB) 1/94*. It is not immediately apparent that reg.49 was necessary in order to allow claims to be made for supplementary benefit for periods prior to April 11, 1988, and reviews of entitlement for such periods to be carried out. Therefore its revocation may have no effect on such matters. See Sch.10 to the Administration Act. However, *CSB 168/1993* is to the contrary. 2.221

In *CIS/12016/1996* a Commissioner, after a detailed review of the legal issues, concluded that from November 16, 1992, it has been impossible for an effective claim to be made for supplementary benefit. This was in spite of the powerful argument that an underlying entitlement to supplementary benefit for a period before April 11, 1988, and the right to pursue a remedy in respect of that entitlement could be preserved by s.16(1) of the Interpretation Act 1978 on the revocation of the supplementary benefit legislation. The reason was that any remedy protected would be under reg.3(1) of the Supplementary Benefit (Claims and Payments) Regulations 1981, which required a claim for weekly supplementary benefit to be made in writing on a form approved by the Secretary of State or in such other manner as the Secretary of State accepted as sufficient. In *CIS/12016/1996* the claim was made in a letter in July 1993. By that date, the Secretary of State had no power to accept the manner of claim as sufficient, because the 1981 Regulations no longer existed. Since the Secretary of State's power was discretionary, the claimant had no accrued right which could be preserved by s.16(1). It had been held in *R. v Secretary of State for Social Security Ex p. Cullen* (November 21, 1996), now confirmed by the Court of Appeal (*The Times*, May 16, 1997, and see the notes to reg.9) that the hope of having a discretion to treat a claim for supplementary benefit as in the alternative a claim for attendance allowance was not preserved by s.16(1) as an accrued right. The same had to apply to the power to accept claims as made in sufficient manner.

Note also *CIS/7009/1995* which confirms that it was not possible to make a late claim for National Assistance after the start of the supplementary benefit scheme on November 24, 1966. There were no savings provisions to enable claims for National Assistance to succeed after that date (see *CSB 61/1995*).

SCHEDULE 1

PART I

BENEFIT CLAIMED AND OTHER BENEFIT WHICH MAY BE TREATED AS IF CLAIMED IN ADDITION OR IN THE ALTERNATIVE

Benefit claimed (1)	Alternative benefit (2)	
[1 Incapacity benefit]	[1 Severe disablement allowance]	2.222
[2 . . .]	[2 . . .]	
Severe disablement allowance	[1 Incapacity benefit]	

[2 . . .]	[2 . . .]
[1 Incapacity benefit for a woman]	[1 Maternity allowance]
Severe disablement allowance for a woman	Maternity allowance
[11 Employment and support allowance for a women]	[11 Maternity allowance]
Maternity allowance	[1 Incapacity benefit [11, severe disablement allowance or employment and support allowance]
A retirement pension of any category	Widow's benefit [9 or bereavement benefit]
A retirement pension of any category	A retirement pension of any other category a shared additional pension [3 or graduated retirement benefit]
[1 An increase of incapacity benefit]	An increase of severe disablement allowance
Attendance allowance	An increase of disablement pension where constant attendance is needed
An increase of disablement pension where constant attendance is needed	Attendance allowance [4 or disability living allowance]
An increase of severe disablement allowance	[1 An increase of incapacity benefit]
Income support	[5 . . .] [4 . . .] or [10 carer's allowance]
[6 Widow's benefit [9 or bereavement benefit]]	[6 A retirement pension of any category or graduated retirement benefit]
[4 Disability living allowance]	[4 Attendance allowance or an increase of disablement pension where constant attendance is needed]
[4 Attendance allowance or an increase of disablement pension where constant attendance is needed]	[4 Disability living allowance]
[7 Disabled person's tax credit]	[7 Working families' tax credit]
[7 Working families' tax credit]	[7 Disabled person's tax credit]
[13 Bereavement benefit	Bereavement support payment
Bereavement support payment	Bereavement benefit]
[12 A state pension under any section of Part 1 of the Pensions Act 2014]	[12 A state pension under any other section of Part 1 of the Pensions Act 2014 or bereavement benefit]
[12 Bereavement benefit]	[12 A state pension under Part 1 of the Pensions Act 2014]

In this part of this Schedule—

(a) Reference to an increase of any benefit (other than an increase of disablement pension where constant attendance is needed) are to an increase of that benefit in respect of a child or adult dependant;

(b) "widow's benefit" means widow's benefit under [Part II of the Social Security Contributions and Benefits Act 1992] and benefit by virtue of section [78(9)] of that Act corresponding to a widow's pension or a widowed mother's allowance.

Part II

Interchange of Claims for Child Benefit with Claims for Other Benefits

2.223 [8 . . .]
Guardian's allowance
Maternity allowance claimed after confinement

Increase of child dependant by virtue of [sections 80 and 90 of the Social Security Contributions and Benefits Act 1992], or regulations made under [section 78(9)] of that Act.

AMENDMENTS

1. The Social Security (Claims and Payments) Amendment (No.2) Regulations 1994 (SI 1994/2943) reg.10 (April 13, 1995).
2. The Social Security (Claims and Payments) (Jobseeker's Allowance Consequential Amendments) Regulations 1996 (SI 1996/1460) reg.2 (October 7, 1996).
3. The Social Security (Claims and Payments) Amendment Regulations 1988 (SI 1988/522) reg.8 (April 11, 1988).
4. The Social Security (Claims and Payments) Amendment Regulations 1991 (SI 1991/2741) reg.25 (February 3, 1992).
5. The Social Security (Miscellaneous Provisions) Amendment (No.2) Regulations 1992 (SI 1992/2595) reg.7 (November 16, 1992).
6. The Social Security (Miscellaneous Provisions) Amendment Regulations 1990 (SI 1990/2208) reg.14 (December 5, 1990).
7. The Tax Credits (Claims and Payments) (Amendment) Regulations 1999 (SI 1999/2572) regs 24 and 25 (October 5, 1999).
8. The Child Benefit, Child Support and Social Security (Miscellaneous Amendments) Regulations 1996 (SI 1996/1803) reg.20 (April 7, 1997).
9. The Social Security (Benefits for Widows and Widowers) (Consequential Amendments) Regulations 2000 (SI 2000/1483) reg.9 (April 9, 2001).
10. The Social Security Amendment (Carer's Allowance) Regulations 2002 (SI 2002/2497) Sch.2 (October 28, 2002).
11. The Employment and Support Allowance (Consequential provisions) (No.2) Regulations 2008 (SI 2008/1554) reg.24 (October 27, 2008).
12. The Pensions Act 2014 (Consequential, Supplementary and Incidental Amendments) Order 2015 (SI 2015/1985) art.9(17) (April 6, 2016).
13. The Pensions Act 2014 (Consequential, Supplementary and Incidental Amendments) Order 2017 (SI 2017/422) art.10 (April 6, 2017).

SCHEDULE 2 — **Regulation 17(5)**

SPECIAL PROVISIONS RELATING TO CLAIMS FOR [1JOBSEEKER'S ALLOWANCE] DURING PERIODS CONNECTED WITH PUBLIC HOLIDAYS

1.—(1) In this Schedule— 2.224

(a) "public holiday" means, as the case may be, Christmas Day, Good Friday or a Bank Holiday under the Banking and Financial Dealings Act 1971 or in Scotland local holidays; and "Christmas and New Year holidays" and "Good Friday and Easter Monday" shall be construed accordingly and shall in each case be treated as one period;
(b) "office closure" means a period during which an [1 office of the Department for Education an Employment] or associated office is closed in connection with a public holiday;
(c) in computing any period of time Sundays shall not be disregarded.

(2) Where any claim for [1a jobseeker's allowance] is made during one of the periods set out in paragraph (3), the following provisions shall apply—

(a) a claim for [1a jobseeker's allowance] may be treated by [2 the Secretary of State as a claim for that benefit for period, to be specified in his decision, not exceeding 35 days after the date of the claim where that claim is made during the period specified in sub-paragraph (a) of paragraph (3), or 21 days after the date of claim where the claim is made during the period specified in either sub-paragraph (b) or (c) of paragraph (3);
(b) on any claim so treated, benefit may be awarded as if the provisions of paragraph (4) of regulation 17 applied.

(3) For the purposes of paragraph (2) the periods are—

(a) in the case of Christmas and New Year holidays, a period beginning with the start of the 35th day before the first day of office closure and ending at midnight between the last day of office closure and the following day;

(b) in the case of Good Friday and Easter Monday, a period beginning with the start of the 16th day before the first day of the office closure and ending at midnight between the last day of office closure and the following day;

(c) in the case of any public holiday, a period beginning with the start of the 14th day before the first day of office closure and ending at midnight between the last day of office closure and the following day.

AMENDMENTS

1. The Social Security (Claims and Payments) (Jobseeker's Allowance Consequential Amendments) Regulations 1996 (SI 1996/1460) reg.2 (October 7, 1996).
2. The Social Security Act 1998 (Commencement No.11 and Transitional Provisions) Order 1999 (SI 1999/2860) Sch.3 (October 18, 1999).

2.225 *Schedule 3 revoked by The Social Security (Claims and Payments) (Jobseeker's Allowance Consequential Amendments) Regulations 1996 (SI 1996/1460) reg.2 (October 7, 1996).*

SCHEDULE 4

PRESCRIBED TIME FOR CLAIMING BENEFIT

2.226

Description of benefit (1)	Prescribed time for claiming benefit (2)
1. [1 Jobseeker's allowance]	[1 The first day of the period in respect of which the claim is made]
[2 **2.** Incapacity benefit or severe disablement allowance]	[2 The day in respect of which the claim is made and period of [3 3 months] immediately following it.]
3. Disablement benefit (not being an increase of benefit)	As regards any day on which, apart from satisfying the condition of making a claim, the claimant is entitled to benefit, that day and the period of 3 months immediately following it.
4. Increase of disablement benefit under section 61 (constant attendance), or 63 (exceptionally severe disablement) of the Social Security Act 1975.	As regards any day which apart form satisfying the conditions that there is a current award of disablement benefit and the making of a claim, the claimant is entitled to benefit, that day and the period of 3 months immediately following it.
5. Reduced earnings allowance	As regards any day on which apart from satisfying the conditions that there is an assessment of disablement of not less than one percent. and the making of a claim, the claim is entitled to the allowance, that day and the period of 3 months immediately following it.
6. Income support	The first day of the period in respect of which the claim is made.
7. [4 Working families' tax credit]	(a) Where [4 working families' tax credit] has previously been claimed and awarded the period beginning 28 days before and ending 14 days after the last day of that award; [5 (aa) where [4 disabled person's tax credit] has previously been claimed and awarded the period beginning 42 days before and ending 14 days after the last day of that award of [4 disabled person's tax credit]] (b) Subject to [5 (a) and (aa)], the first day of

	the period in respect of which the claim is made; (c) where a claim for [4 working families' tax credit] is treated as if made for a period beginning with the relevant day by virtue of regulation 13 of these Regulations, the period beginning on 10th March 1992 and ending on 6th April 1992]
8. Social fund payment in respect of maternity expenses	[17 (a) In a case where regulation 5(3)(a) of maternity expenses the Social Fund Maternity and Funeral Expenses (General) Regulations 2005 applies ("the 2005 Regulations"), the period beginning 11 weeks before the first day of the expected week of confinement and ending 3 months after the actual date of confinement. [18 (b) In a case where regulation 5(3)(b) of the 2005 Regulations applies, the period beginning with the date on which the claimant becomes responsible for the child and ending 3 months after that date.] (c) In a case where regulation 5(3)(c) of the 2005 Regulations applies, the period beginning with the date on which an order referred to in that sub-paragraph is made and ending 3 months after that date. (d) In a case where regulation 5(3)(d) of the 2005 Regulations applies, the period beginning with the date on which the guardianship takes effect and ending 3 months after that date. (e) In a case where regulation 5(3)(e) of the 2005 Regulations applies, the period beginning with the date on which the child is placed with the claimant or the claimant's partner for adoption and ending 3 months after that date. (f) In a case where regulation 5(3)(f) of the 2005 Regulations applies, the period beginning with the date on which the adoption— (i) takes effect in respect of an adoption mentioned in section 66(1)(c) or (d), or (ii) is recognised under section 66(1)(e), of the Adoption and Children Act 2002, and ending 3 months after that date.]
9. Social fund payment in respect of funeral expenses	[8 The period beginning with the date of death and ending 3 months after the date of the funeral.]
9A. [9 . . .]	
10. Increase of disablement benefit under [10 section 60 of the Social Security Act 1975 on grounds of special hardship or] section 62 of the Social Security Act 1975 on the grounds of receipt of hospital treatment.	A regards any day on which, apart form satisfying the conditions that there is a current award of disablement benefit and the making of a claim, the claimant is entitled to benefit, that day and the period 3 months immediately following it.
[11 **11.** [12 Disabled person's tax credit]	(a) Where [12 disabled person's tax credit] has previously been claimed and awarded the period beginning 42 days

	before and ending 14 days after the last day of that award; (b) where [12 working families' tax credit] has previously been claimed and awarded the period beginning 28 days before and ending 14 days after the last day of that award of [12 working families' tax credit]; (c) subject to (a) and (b), the first day of the period in respect of which the claim is made; (d) where a claim for [12 disabled person's tax credit] is made by virtue of regulation 13B(1), the period beginning on 10th March 1992 and ending on 6th April 1992.]
[13 **12.** . . .]	
[14 **13.** Retirement pension of any category [19 or state pension under Part 1 of the Pensions Act 2014]	As regards any day on which apart from satisfying the condition of making a claim, the claimant is entitled to the pension, that day and the period of 12 months immediately following it.]
[14 **14.** Graduated retirement benefit	As regards any day on which, apart from satisfying the condition of making a claim, the claimant is entitled to benefit, that day and the period of 12 months immediately following it.]
[15 **15.** Shared additional pension	As regards any day on which, apart from satisfying the condition of making a claim, the claimant is entitled to the pension, that day and the period of 12 months immediately following it.]
[16 **16.** Employment and support allowance	The day in respect of which the claim is made and the period of three months immediately following it.]

For the purposes of this Schedule—

"actual date of confinement" means the date of the [17 birth] of the child or, if the woman is confined of twins or a greater number of children, the date of the [17 birth] of the last of them; and

"confinement" means labour resulting in the [17 birth] of a living child, or labour after [17 24] weeks of pregnancy resulting in the [17 birth] of a child whether alive or dead.

Amendments

1. The Social Security (Claims and Payments) (Jobseeker's Allowance Consequential Amendments) Regulations 1996 (SI 1996/460) reg.2 (October 7, 1996).
2. The Social Security (Claims and Payments) Amendment (No.2) Regulations 1994 (SI 1994/2943) reg.12 (April 13, 1995).
3. The Social Security (Miscellaneous Provisions) (No.2) Regulations 1997 (SI 1997/793) reg.7 (April 7, 1997).
4. The Tax Credits (Claims and Payments) (Amendment) Regulations 1999 (SI 1999/2572) regs 24 and 25 (October 5, 1999).
5. The Social Security (Claims and Payments) Amendment Regulations 1991 (SI 1991/2741) reg.26 (March 10, 1992).
6. The Social Security (Miscellaneous Provisions) Amendment Regulations 1991 (SI 1991/2284) reg.10 (November 1, 1991).
7. The Social Security (Social Fund and Claims and Payments) (Miscellaneous Amendments) Regulations 1997 (SI 1997/792) reg.8 (April 7, 1997).

8. The Social Security (Claims and Payments and Adjudication) Amendment Regulations 1996 (SI 1996/2306) reg.6 (October 7, 1996).
9. The Social Security (Miscellaneous Provisions) Amendment Regulations 1991 (SI 1991/2284) reg.11 (November 1, 1991).
10. The Social Security (Claims and Payments) Amendment Regulations 1988 (SI 1988/522) reg.9 (April 11, 1988).
11. The Social Security (Claims and Payments) Amendment Regulations 1991 (SI 1991/2741) reg.26(b) (March 10, 1992).
12. The Tax Credits (Claims and Payments) (Amendment) Regulations 1999 (SI 1999/2572) regs 24 and 25 (October 5, 1999).
13. The Social Security (Miscellaneous Amendments) (No.4) Regulations 2008 (SI 2008/2424) reg.2C3 (October 6, 2008).
14. The Social Security (Claims and Payments) Amendment Regulations 2005 (SI 2005/455) reg.5 (April 6, 2006).
15. The Social Security (Shared Additional Pension (Miscellaneous Amendments) Regulations 2005 (SI 2005/1551) reg.3 (April 6, 2006).
16. The Employment and Support Allowance (Consequential provisions) (No.2) Regulations 2008 (SI 2008/1554) reg.24 (October 27, 2008).
17. The Social Fund Maternity Grant Amendment Regulations 2010 (SI 2010/2760) reg.3 (December 13, 2010).
18. The Social Fund Maternity Grant Amendment Regulations 2011 (SI 2011/100) reg.4 (January 24, 2011).
19. The Pensions Act 2014 (Consequential, Supplementary and Incidental Amendments) Order 2015 (SI 2015/1985) art.9(18) (April 6, 2016).

General Note

Sometimes there is a need to be very precise about dates. *CIB/2805/2003* was just such a case. The Deputy Commissioner notes that the formulation used in relation to incapacity benefit (and, it should be noted, in relation to several other benefits) is to specify the time limit by reference to the day of claim and a period of three months immediately following it. The Deputy Commissioner rules that this means that the claimant gets the day of claim and a full three months immediately following the date in respect of which the claim is made. This gave the claimant two more days than the Secretary of State had calculated. 2.227

Schedule 5 revoked by The Social Security (Claims and Payments and Adjudication) Amendment Regulations 1996 (SI 1996/2306) reg.7 (October 7, 1996). 2.228

SCHEDULE 6 **Regulation 22(3)**

Days for Payment of Long Term Benefits

[1 Attendance allowance and disability living allowance

1. Subject to the provisions of regulation 25 (payment of attendance allowance, constant attendance allowance and the care component of a disability living allowance at a daily rate) attendance allowance shall be payable on Mondays and disability living allowance shall be payable on Wednesdays, except that the Secretary of State may in a particular case arrange for either allowance to be payable on any other day of the week and where it is in payment to any person and the day on which it is payable is changed, it shall be paid at a daily rate of 1/7th of the weekly rate in respect of any of the days for which payment would have been made but for that change.] 2.229

2. [2. . .]

Industrial injuries benefit

3. Any pension or allowance under [Part V of the Social Security Contributions and Benefits Act 1992], including any increase, shall be payable on Wednesdays. 2.230

[5Carer's allowance]

2.231 **4.** [5carer's allowance] shall be payable on Mondays, except that where a person is entitled to that allowance in respect of a severely disabled person by virtue of regulation 3 of the Social Security (Invalid Care Allowance) Regulations 1976 the [5carer's allowance] shall be payable on Wednesdays.

Retirement pension

2.232 **5.** [8 Subject to regulation 22C, retirement pension] shall be payable on Mondays, except that—

(a) where a person became entitled to a retirement pension before September 28, 1984, that pension shall be payable on Thursdays;

[3(b) where—

(i) a woman was entitled to a widow's benefit, or

(ii) a man or a woman was entitled to a bereavement benefit,

immediately before becoming entitled to a retirement pension, that pension shall be payable on [4 . . .] [4 the day of the week which has become the appropriate day for payment of such a benefit to him in accordance with paragraph 6];]

(c) where a woman becomes entitled to a retirement pension immediately following the payment to her husband of an increase of retirement pension in respect of her, the retirement pension to which she becomes entitled shall be payable on the same days as those upon which the retirement pension of the husband is payable;

(d) the Secretary of State may, notwithstanding anything contained in the foregoing provisions of this paragraph, arrange for retirement pension to be payable on such other day of the week as he may [4 . . .] [4 where payment is by credit transfer, or in the circumstances of any particular case, determine];

(e) where, in relation to any person, any particular day of the week has become the appropriate day of the week for the payment of retirement pension, that day shall thereafter remain the appropriate day in his case for such payment.

Shared additional pension

2.233 [6 **5A.** Shared additional pension shall be payable on Mondays, except that—

(a) where a retirement pension is payable to the claimant, it shall be payable on the same day as the retirement pension; or

(b) the Secretary of State may, notwithstanding the provisions of sub-paragraph (a), arrange for a shared additional pension to be payable on such other day of the week as he may, in the circumstances of any particular case, determine.]

Widowed mother's allowance and widow's pension

2.234 **6.** Widowed mother's allowance [7 . . .]

7. [1. . .]

AMENDMENTS

1. The Social Security (Claims and Payments) Amendment Regulations 1991 (SI 1991/2741) reg.27 (April 6, 1992).

2. The Social Security (Claims and Payments) Amendment Regulations 1999 (SI 1999/2358) reg.2 (September 20, 1999).

3. The Social Security (Benefits for Widows and Widowers) (Consequential Amendments) Regulations 2000 (SI 2000/1483) reg.9 (April 9, 2001).

4. Social Security (Claims and Payments and Miscellaneous Amendments) (No.2) Regulations 2002 (SI 2002/2441) reg.11 (October 23, 2002).

5. The Social Security Amendment (Carer's Allowance) Regulations 2002 (SI 2002/2497) Sch.2 (October 28, 2002).

6. The Social Security (Shared Additional Pension) (Miscellaneous Amendments) Regulations 2005 (SI 2005/1551) (July 6, 2005).

7. The Social Security (Claims and Payments) Amendments Regulations 2009 (SI 2009/604) reg.2 (April 6, 2009).

8. The Social Security (Miscellaneous Amendments) (No.6) Regulations 2009 (SI 2009/3229) reg.2(8) (April 6, 2010).

SCHEDULE 7 **Regulation 26**

[15 TIME OF PAYMENT AND COMMENCEMENT OF ENTITLEMENT IN INCOME SUPPORT CASES]

Manner of payment

1. Except as otherwise provided in these Regulations income support shall be paid in arrears in accordance with the award.] **2.235**

Time of payment

2. Income support shall be paid in advance where the claimant is— **2.236**

(a) in receipt of retirement pension; or

(b) over pensionable age and not in receipt of [9. . .] [7incapacity benefit or severe disablement allowance and is not a person to whom section 126 of the Social Security Contributions and Benefits Act 1992 (trade disputes) applies] unless he was in receipt of income support immediately before the trade dispute began; or

(c) [16 subject to paragraph 2ZA] in receipt of widow's benefit [13or [17 widowed parent's allowance]] and is not [14 . . .] providing or required to provide medical evidence of incapacity for work; or

(d) a person to whom [1section 23(a)] of the Social Security Act 1986 [SSCBA, s.127] applies, but only for the period of 15 days mentioned in that subsection.

[16 2ZA. Paragraph 2(c) shall only apply where a widow's benefit or a [17 widowed parent's allowance] is paid in advance.]

[2**2A.**—(1) For the purposes of this paragraph—

(a) "public holiday" means, as the case may be, Christmas Day, Good Friday or a Bank Holiday under the Banking and Financial Dealings Act 1971 or in Scotland local holidays, and

(b) "office closure" means a period during which an office of the Department of Social Security or associated office is closed in connection with a public holiday.

(2) Where income support is normally paid in arrears and the day on which the benefit is payable by reason of paragraph 3 is affected by office closure it may for that benefit week be paid wholly in advance or partly in advance and partly in arrears and on such a day as the Secretary of State may direct.

(3) Where under this paragraph income support is paid either in advance or partly in advance and partly in arrears it shall for any other purposes be treated as if it was paid in arrears.]

[3**3.** (1) Subject to [7sub-paragraph (1A) and to] any direction given by the Secretary of State in accordance with sub-paragraph (2), income support in respect of any benefit week shall, if the beneficiary is entitled to a relevant social security benefit or would be so entitled but for failure to satisfy the contribution conditions or had not exhausted his entitlement, be paid on the day and at the intervals appropriate to payment of that benefit.

[7(1A) Subject to sub-paragraph (2), where income support is paid to a person on the grounds of incapacity for work, that entitlement commenced on or after 13th April 1995, and no relevant social security benefit is paid to that person, the income support shall be paid fortnightly in arrears.]

(2) The Secretary of State may direct that income support in respect of any benefit week shall be paid at such intervals and on such days as he may in any particular case or class of case determine.

3A.—(1) Income support for any part-week shall be paid in accordance with an award on such day as the Secretary of State may in any particular case direct.

(2) In this paragraph, "part-week" has the same meaning as it has in Part VII of the Income Support (General) Regulations 1987.]

4. [1In this Schedule]—

"benefit week" means, if the beneficiary is entitled to a relevant social security benefit or would be so entitled but for failure to satisfy the contribution conditions or had not exhausted his entitlement, the week corresponding to the week in respect of which that benefit is paid, and in any other case a period of 7 days beginning or ending with such day as the Secretary of State may direct;

[1"Income Support Regulations" means the Income Support (General) Regulations 1987;] and

"relevant social security benefit" means [9. . .] [7incapacity benefit], severe disablement allowance, retirement pension [12 [17 widowed parent's allowance]] or widow's benefit.

Payment of small amounts of income support

2.237 **5.** Where the amount of income support is less than £1.00 a week the Secretary of State may direct that it shall be paid at such intervals as may be specified not exceeding 13 weeks.

Commencement of entitlement to income support

2.238 **6.**—(1) Subject to sub-paragraphs (3) and (4), in a case where income support is payable in arrears entitlement shall commence on the date of claim.

(2) [[1]Subject to sub-paragraphs (2A) and (3)], in a case where, under paragraph 2, income support is payable in advance entitlement shall commence on the date of claim if that day is a day for payment of income support as determined under paragraph 3 but otherwise on the first such day after the date of claim.

[[1](2A) Where income support is awarded under regulation 17(3) for a definite period which is not a benefit week or a multiple of such a week entitlement shall commence on the date of claim.

(3) In a case where regulation 13 applies, entitlement shall commence on the day which is the relevant day for the purposes of that regulation [[5] except where income support is paid in advance, when entitlement shall commence on the relevant day, if that day is a day for payment as determined under paragraph 3 but otherwise on the first day for payment after the relevant day].]

(4) [[1]. . .]

[[9](5) If a claim is made by a claimant within 3 days of the date on which he became resident in a resettlement place provided pursuant to section 30 of the Jobseekers Act or at a centre providing facilities for the rehabilitation of alcoholics or drug addicts, and the claimant is so resident for the purposes of that rehabilitation, then the claim shall be treated as having been made on the day the claimant became so resident.]

(6) Where, in consequence of a further claim for income support such as is mentioned in sub-paragraph 4(7) of Schedule 3 to the Income Support (General) Regulations 1987, a claimant is treated as occupying a dwelling as his home for a period before moving in, that further claim shall be treated as having been made on the date from which he is treated as so occupying the dwelling or the date of the claim made before he moved in to the dwelling and referred to in that sub-paragraph, whichever is the later.

7. [. . .[12]].

AMENDMENTS

1. The Social Security (Claims and Payments) Amendment Regulations 1988 (SI 1988/522) reg.10 (April 11, 1988).

2. Transfer of Functions (Health and Social Security) Order 1988 (SI 1988/1843); The Social Security (Claims and Payments and Payments on account, Overpayments and Recovery) Amendment Regulations 1989 (SI 1989/136) reg.2(b) (February 27, 1989).

3. The Social Security (Medical Evidence, Claims and Payments) Amendment Regulations 1989 (SI 1989/1686) reg.8 (October 9, 1989).

4. The Social Security (Miscellaneous Provisions) Amendment Regulations 1990 (SI 1990/2208) reg.15 (December 5, 1990).

5. The Enterprise (Scotland) Consequential Amendments Order 1991 (SI 1991/387) art.2 and Sch.(April 1, 1991).

6. The Social Security (Miscellaneous Provisions) Amendment Regulations 1992 (SI 1992/247) reg.17 (March 9, 1992).

7. The Social Security (Claims and Payments) Amendment (No.2) Regulations 1994 (SI 1994/2943) reg.14 (April 13, 1995).

8. The Social Security (Claims and Payments etc.) Amendment Regulations 1996 (SI 1996/672) reg.2(6) (April 4, 1996).

9. The Social Security (Claims and Payments) (Jobseeker's Allowance Consequential Amendments) Regulations 1996 (SI 1996/1460) reg.2(24) (October 7, 1996).

10. The Social Security (Miscellaneous) Amendment (No.4) Regulations 1998 (SI 1998/1174) reg.8(3)(b) (June 1, 1998).

11. The Social Security Act 1998 (Commencement No.12 and Consequential and Transitional Provisions) Order 1999 (SI 1999/3178) Sch.6 (November 29, 1999).

12. The Social Security and Child Support (Miscellaneous Amendments) Regulations 2000 (SI 2000/1596) reg.5 (June 19, 2000).

13. The Social Security (Benefits for Widows and Widowers) (Consequential Amendments) Regulations 2000 (SI 2000/1483) reg.9 (April 9, 2001).
14. The Social Security, Child Support and Tax Credits (Miscellaneous Amendments) Regulations 2005 (SI 2005/337) reg.7 (March 18, 2005).
15. The Social Security (Miscellaneous Amendments) (No.2) Regulations 2006 (SI 2006/832) reg.2 (April 10, 2006).
16. The Social Security (Claims and Payments) Amendments Regulations 2009 (SI 2009/604) reg.2 (April 6, 2009).
17. The Pensions Act 2014 (Consequential, Supplementary and Incidental Amendments) Order 2017 (SI 2017/422) art.10 (April 6, 2017).

General Note

Paragraph 2

These categories of claimant are paid income support in advance. Apart from pensioners and most widows, those returning to work after a trade dispute are covered. **2.239**

Paragraphs 3 and 4

Where a claimant meets the conditions of entitlement for one of the benefits listed as a "relevant social security benefit," the income support benefit week, pay-day and interval of payment is the same as for that benefit. Thus, those incapable of work are paid fortnightly in arrears (reg.24(1)), although under reg.24 the Secretary of State can arrange payment of incapacity benefit at other intervals (e.g. weekly), in which case income support follows suit. Otherwise the benefit week is to be defined by the Secretary of State. Income support paid for a definite period under reg.17(3) need not be in terms of benefit weeks. Paragraph 3A provides that payments for part-weeks may be made as the Secretary of State directs. **2.240**

Paragraph 6

The general rule for income support paid in arrears is that entitlement begins on the date of claim. The first payment on the pay day at the end of the first benefit week (or the second benefit week in the case of the unemployed) can thus be precisely calculated to include the right number of days. Payments can then continue on a weekly basis. **2.241**

If income support is paid in advance, then, as for supplementary benefit, entitlement begins on the next pay day following the claim or coinciding with the date of claim.

Where the award is for a definite period under reg.17(3) entitlement begins with the date of claim (sub-para.(2A)). Sub-paragraph (3) deals with the special case of advance awards. Sub-paragraphs (5) and (6) cover other special cases.

SCHEDULE 8 — **Regulation 23(1)(a)**

Election to Have Child Benefit Paid Weekly

1. A person to whom benefit is payable for an uninterrupted period beginning before and ending after March 15, 1982 may make an election, in accordance with paragraph 3, that benefit be payable weekly after that date, if either— **2.242**

(a) he makes the election before the end of the 26th week from the day on which benefit was payable for the first four weeks in respect of which the Secretary of State made arrangements for four-weekly payment to the person entitled in accordance with regulation 21 or regulation 23(1)(b); or

(b) he was absent from Great Britain on the March 15, 1982 for one of the reasons specified in paragraph 4 and he makes the election before the end of the 26th week of the period beginning with the first week in respect of which benefit became payable to him in Great Britain on his return.

2. Subject to paragraph 5, a person entitled to benefit may make an election, in accordance with paragraph 3, that benefit be paid weekly if he satisfies either of the following conditions—

(a) he is a lone parent within the meaning set out in regulation 2(2) of the Child Benefit and Social Security (Fixing and Adjustment of Rates) Regulations 1976, or]

(b) he, or his spouse residing with him or the person with whom he is living as husband and wife, is receiving income support, [[2]an incomed-based jobseeker's allowance], [[3] or payment in accordance with an award of family credit or disability working allowance which was awarded with effect for a date falling before 5th October 1999.]

3. An election for benefit to be payable weekly under paragraphs 1 or 2 shall be effected by giving notice in writing to the Secretary of State delivered or sent to the appropriate office and shall be made when it is received.

4. An election may not be made under paragraph 1(b) unless the person's absence abroad on the March 15, 1982 was by reason of his being—

(a) a serving member of the forces, as defined by regulation 1(2) of the Social Security (Contributions) Regulations 1979, or

(b) the spouse of such a member, or

(c) a person living with such a member as husband and wife.

5. Every person making an election for benefit to be paid weekly under paragraph 2 shall furnish such certificates, documents and such other information of facts as the Secretary of State may, in his discretion, require, affecting his right to receive payment of benefit weekly and in particular shall notify the Secretary of State in writing of any change of circumstances which he might reasonably be expected to know might affect the right to receive payment of benefit weekly, as soon as reasonably practicable after the occurrence thereof.

6. Where a person makes an election, in accordance with this regulation, for benefit to be paid weekly, it shall continue to be so payable—

(a) in the case of an election under paragraph 1, so long as that person remains continually entitled to benefit, or

(b) in the case of an election under paragraph 2, so long as that person remains continually entitled to benefit and the conditions specified in that paragraph continue to be satisfied.

7. A person who has made an election that benefit be payable weekly may cancel it at any time by a notice in writing delivered or sent to the appropriate office; and effect shall be given to such a notice as soon as is convenient.

AMENDMENTS

1. The Child Benefit, Child Support and Social Security (Miscellaneous Amendments) Regulations 1996 (SI 1996/1803) reg.21 (April 7, 1997).

2. The Social Security (Claims and Payments) (Jobseeker's Allowance Consequential Amendments) Regulations 1996 (SI 1996/1460) reg.2 (October 7, 1996).

3. The Social Security and Child Support (Tax Credits) Consequential Amendments Regulations 1999 (SI 1999/2566) Sch.8 (September 5, 1999).

SCHEDULE 9 **Regulation 35**

DEDUCTIONS FROM BENEFIT AND DIRECT PAYMENT TO THIRD PARTIES

Interpretation

2.243 **1.** [[20]—(1)] In this Schedule—

[[11]"the Community Charges Regulations" means the Community Charges (Deductions from Income Support (No.2) Regulations 1990;

"the Community Charges (Scotland) Regulations" means the Community Charges (Deductions from Income Support) (Scotland) Regulations 1989;]

[[21]"contribution-based jobseeker's allowance" [[52] (except where used in sub-paragraph

(2)(b)] means any contribution-based jobseeker's allowance which does not fall within the definition of "specified benefit";]

[43 "contributory employment and support allowance" [52 (except where used in sub-paragraph (3)(b)] means any contributory employment and support allowance which does not fall within the definition of "specified benefit"]

["the Council Tax Regulations" mean the Council Tax (Deductions from Income Support) Regulations 1993;]

"family" in the case of a claimant who is not a member of a family means that claimant [31 and for the purposes of state pension credit "a family" comprises the claimant, his partner, any additional partner to whom section 12(1)(c) of the 2002 Act applies and any person who has not attained the age of 19, is treated as a child for the purposes of section 142 of the Contributions and Benefits Act and lives with the claimant or the claimant's partner;];

[11"the Fines Regulations" means the Fines (Deductions from Income Support) Regulations 1992;]

[6"5 per cent of the personal allowance for the single claimant aged not less than 25" means where the percentage is not a multiple of 5 pence the sum obtained by rounding that 5 per cent to the next higher such multiple;

[35 "hostel" means a building—

(a) in which there is provided for persons generally, or for a class of persons, accommodation, otherwise than in separate and self-contained premises, and either board or facilities of a kind set out in paragraph 4A(1)(d) below adequate to the needs of those persons and—

(b) which is—

(i) managed by or owned by a housing association registered with [48 the Regulator of Social Housing of the Welsh Ministers]

[44 (ii) managed or owned by a registered social landlord which is registered in accordance with [53 Part 2 of the Housing (Scotland) Act 2010]]

(iii) operated other than on a commercial basis and in respect of which funds are provided wholly or in part by a government department or a local authority; or

(iv) managed by a voluntary organisation or charity and provides care, support or supervision with a view to assisting those persons to be rehabilitated or resettled within the community, and

(c) which is not—

(i) a care home;

(ii) an independent hospital; or

(iii) an establishment run by the Abbeyfield Society including all bodies corporate or incorporated which are affiliated to that Society, and

(d) in sub-paragraph (b)(iv) above, "voluntary organisation" shall mean a body the activities of which are carried out otherwise than for profit, but shall not include any public or local authority;]

"housing authority" means a local authority, a new town corporation, [44. . .] or the Rural Development Board for Rural Wales;]

[36 "the Housing Benefit Regulations" mean the Housing Benefit Regulations 2006;

"the Housing Benefit (State Pension Credit) Regulations" mean the Housing benefit (Persons who have attained the qualifying age for state pension credit) Regulations 2006;]

[20"housing costs" means any housing costs met under—

(a) Schedule 3 to the Income Support Regulations but—

(i) excludes costs under paragraph 17(1)(f) of that Schedule (tents and tent sites); and

(ii) includes costs under paragraphs 17(1)(a) (ground rent [34 . . .]) and 17(1)(c) (rentcharges) of that Schedule but only when they are paid with costs under paragraph 17(1)(b) of that Schedule (service charges); or

(b) Schedule 2 to the Jobseeker's Allowance Regulations but—

(i) excludes costs under paragraph 16(1)(f) of that Schedule (tents and tent sites); and

(ii) includes costs under paragraphs 16(1)(a) (ground rent and feu duty) and 16(1)(c) (rentcharges) of that Schedule but only when they are paid with costs under paragraph 16(1)(b) of that Schedule (service charges);]

[31 (c) Schedule II to the State Pension Credit Regulations but—

(i) excludes costs under paragraph 13(1)(f) of that Schedule (tents and sites); and

Housing costs

2.245 **3.**—(1) Subject to [7sub-paragraphs (4) to (6)] and paragraph 8, where a beneficiary who has been awarded the specified benefit or his partner is in debt for any item of housing costs which continues to be applicable to the beneficiary in the determination of his applicable amount [31 or appropriate minimum guarantee], the [25Secretary of State] may, if in [27 his] opinion it would be in the interests of the family to do so, determine that the amount of the award of the specified benefit ("the amount deductible") calculated in accordance with the following sub-paragraphs shall be paid in accordance with sub-paragraph 2(3).

(2) [7Subject to sub-paragraphs (2A) and (3)], the amount deductible shall be such weekly aggregate of the following as is appropriate:—

(a) in respect of any debt to which sub-paragraph (1) applies, or where the debt owed is in respect of an amount which includes more than one item of housing costs, a weekly amount equal to 5 per cent. of the personal allowance for a single claimant aged not less than 25 [1. . .] for such period as it is necessary to discharge the debt, so however that in aggregate the weekly amount calculated under this sub-paragraph shall not exceed 3 times that 5 per cent;

(b) for each such debt—

(i) in respect of mortgage payments, the weekly amount of the mortgage payment in that case; and

(ii) for any other housing item, the actual weekly cost necessary in respect of continuing needs for the relevant items,

and the [25Secretary State] may direct that, when the debt is discharged, the amount determined under sub-paragraph (b) shall be the amount deductible.

[7(2A) Where a payment falls to be made to a third party in accordance with this Schedule, and—

(a) more than one item of housing costs falls to be taken into account in determining the beneficiary's applicable amount; and

(b) in accordance with [16paragraph 4(8) or (11) or] [15paragraph 18] of Schedule 3 to the Income Support Regulations [20or, as the case may be, paragraph 4(8) or (11) or paragraph 17 of Schedule 2 to the Jobseeker's Allowance Regulations] [43 or paragraph 6(10) or (13) or paragraph 19 of Schedule 6 to the Employment and Support Allowance Regulations] [31 or paragraph 5(9) or (12) or paragraph 14 of Schedule II to the State Pension Credit Regulations] an amount is not allowed or a deduction falls to be made from the amount to be met by way of housing costs,

then in calculating the amount deductible, the weekly aggregate amount ascertained in accordance with sub-paragraph (2) shall be reduced by an amount determined by applying the formula—

$$C \times \frac{B}{A}$$

where—

A = housing costs;

B = the item of housing costs which falls to be paid to a third party under this Schedule;

C = the sum which is not allowed or falls to be deducted in accordance with [15paragraph 4(8) or (11) or paragraph 18] of Schedule 3 to the Income Support Regulations. [20or, as the case may be, paragraph 4(8) or (11) or paragraph 17 of Schedule 2 to the Jobseeker's Allowance Regulations][31 or paragraph 5(9) or (12) or paragraph 14 of Schedule II to the State Pension Credit Regulations]] [43 or paragraph 6(10) or (13) or paragraph 19 of Schedule 6 to the Employment and Support Allowance Regulations]

(3) Where the aggregate amount calculated under sub-paragraph (2) is such that paragraph 2(2) would operate to prevent any payment under this paragraph being made that aggregate amount shall be adjusted so that 10 pence of the award is payable to the beneficiary.

(4) Sub-paragraph (1) shall not apply to any debt which is either—

(a) in respect of mortgage payments and the beneficiary or his partner has in the preceding 12 weeks paid sums equal to [8or greater than] 8 week's mortgage payments due in that period; or

(b) for any other item of housing costs and is less than half the annual amount due to be paid by the beneficiary or his partner in respect of that item,

unless, in either case, in the opinion of the adjudicating authority it is in the overriding interests of the family that paragraph (1) should apply.

[7(5) No amount shall be paid pursuant to this paragraph in respect of mortgage interest in any case where a specified part of relevant benefits—

(a) is required to be paid directly to a qualifying lender under regulation 34A and Schedule 9A; or

(b) would have been required to be paid to a body which, or a person who, would otherwise have been a qualifying lender but for an election given under paragraph 9 of Schedule 9A not to be regarded as such.

(6) In sub-paragraph (5), "specified part" and "relevant benefits" have the meanings given to them in paragraph 1 of Schedule 9A.]

Miscellaneous accommodation costs

[9**4.**—(1) Where an award of income support [32, jobseeker's allowance or [43, state pension credit or employment and support allowance]]— 2.246

(a) [32 in the case of income support] is made to a person [35 residing in a care home, an Abbeyfield Home or an independent hospital] as defined in regulation [28 2(1)] of the Income Support Regulations [20 or [32 in the case of jobseeker's allowance], regulation 1(3) of the Jobseeker's Allowance Regulations], [43 or in the case of employment and support allowance, regulation 2(1) of the Employment and Support Allowance Regulations] or]

[57 (b) in the case of income support, jobseeker's allowance or employment and support allowance, is made to person who is in accommodation provided under section 3(1) of, and Part 2 of the Schedule to, the Polish Resettlement Act 1947(2) (provision by the Secretary of State of accommodation in camps); or

(c) in the case of state pension credit, is made to a person residing in—

(i) a care home as defined in regulation 1(2) of the State Pension Credit Regulations;

(ii) an independent hospital as defined in regulation 1(2) of those Regulations;

(iii) an establishment run by the Abbeyfield Society (including all bodies corporate or incorporate which are affiliated to the Society); or

(iv) accommodation provided under section 3(1) of, and Part 2 of the Schedule to, the Polish Resettlement Act 1947 where the person requires personal care,]

[32 or to a person who is only temporarily absent from such accommodation] the [25 Secretary of State] may determine that an amount of the specified benefit shall be paid direct to the person or body to whom the charges in respect of that accommodation are payable, [32 or to a person who is only temporarily absent from such accommodation] but, [32 except in a case where accommodation is provided under section 3(1) of, and Part II of the Schedule to, the Polish Resettlement Act 1947] or where the accommodation is [2run by a voluntary organisation either for purposes similar to the purposes for which resettlement units are provided] or which provides facilities for alcoholics or drug addicts, only if the adjudicating authority is satisfied that the beneficiary has failed to budget for the charges and that it is in the interests of the family.

[32 (2) Subject to sub-paragraphs (3) and (3A), the amount of any payment of income support, jobseeker's allowance [43, state pension credit or employment and support allowance] to a third party determined under sub-paragraph (1) shall be—

(a) in a case where the beneficiary is not in accommodation [35 . . .] as specified in [57 sub-paragraph (1)(c)(ii)], an amount equal to the award of income support, jobseeker's allowance, [43, guarantee credit or employment and support allowance] payable to the claimant but excluding an amount, if any, which when added to any other income of the beneficiary as determined in accordance with regulation 28 of the Income Support Regulations, regulation 93 of the Jobseeker's Allowance Regulations [43, regulation 90 of the Employment and Support Allowance Regulations] or regulation 17 of the State Pension Credit Regulations will equal the amount prescribed in respect of personal expenses in sub-paragraph (2A); and

(b) in any other case, the amount of the award of income support, jobseeker's allowance [43, guarantee credit or employment and support allowance], excluding the amount allowed by sub-paragraph (2A) in respect of personal expenses.

(2A) The amount in respect of personal expenses where a beneficiary is in accommodation referred to in paragraphs 4(1)(a) [57 (b) or (c)]shall be—

(a) for a single person the sum of [58 £24.25];

(b) for a couple where both members of the couple are in such accommodation, [58 £24.25]; for each member;

(c) for a member of a polygamous marriage where more than one member is in such accommodation, [58 £24.25]; for each member in such accommodation.

(3) This sub-paragraph shall apply where an award is made of—

(a) income support calculated in accordance with Part VII of the Income Support Regulations (calculation of income support for part-weeks); or
(b) jobseeker's allowance calculated in accordance with Part XI of the Jobseeker's Allowance Regulations (part-weeks);
(c) state pension credit for a period of less than a week calculated under regulation 13A of the State Pension Credit Regulations (part-weeks), or a part week payment of state pension credit calculated otherwise. [43 or
(d) employment and support allowance for a period of less than a week calculated in accordance with Part 14 of the Employment and Support Allowance Regulations (periods of less than a week).]

(3A) Where sub-paragraph (3) applies then the amount of any payment to a third party determined under sub-paragraph (1) shall be an amount calculated in accordance with sub-paragraph (2)(a) or (b) as appropriate except that in respect of—
(a) the income of the beneficiary, if any; and
(b) the amount allowed for personal expenses by sub-paragraph (2A) above,
the amount shall be the amount used in the calculation under the provisions listed in sub-paragraph (3)(a), (b) or (c), divided by 7 and multiplied by the number of days in the part-week and no payment shall be made to a third party where the Secretary of State certifies it would be impracticable to do so in that particular case.]

(4) Where the amount calculated under sub-paragraph [32 (2) or (3A) is such that paragraph 2(2) would operate to prevent any payment under this paragraph being made the amount shall be adjusted so that 10 pence of the award is payable to the beneficiary.]

[6Hostel payments

2.247 **4A.**—(1) This paragraph applies to a beneficiary if—
(a) [45 the beneficiary] has been awarded specified benefit; and
[45 (b) either the beneficiary or the beneficiary's partner—
(i) is resident in a hostel and has claimed housing benefit in the form of a rent rebate or rent allowance; or
(ii) is resident in approved premises under section 13 of the Offender Management Act 2007; and]
(c) [45 . . .]
(d) the charge for [45 the hostel or approved premises, as the case may be,] includes a payment, whether direct or indirect, for one or more of the following services—
(i) water;
(ii) a service charge for fuel;
(iii) meals;
(iv) laundry;
(v) cleaning (other than communal areas).

(2) Subject to sub-paragraph (3) below, where a beneficiary [8 . . .] has been awarded specified benefit the [25 Secretary of State] may determine that an amount of specified benefit shall be paid to the person or body to whom the charges referred to in subparagraph (1)(d) above are or would be payable.

(3) The amount of any payment to a third party under this paragraph shall be either—
(a) the aggregate of the amounts determined by a housing authority in accordance with the provisions specified in sub-paragraph (4); or
(b) if no amount has been determined under paragraph (a) of this sub-paragraph, an amount which the adjudicating authority estimates to be the amount which is likely to be so determined.

[36 (4) The provisions referred to in sub-paragraph (3)(a) above are regulation 12(6) of, and paragraphs 1(a)(ii) and (iv), 2, 3, 4 and either 6(1)(b) or 6(2) or 6(3) or 6(4) of Schedule 1 to, the Housing Benefit Regulations or, as the case may be, the Housing Benefit (State Pension Credit) Regulations;]

(5) [36 . . .]

[20(6) Where—
(a) an award of income support is calculated in accordance with regulation 73(1) of the Income Support Regulations (calculation of income support for part-weeks);
(b) an award of jobseeker's allowance is calculated in accordance with regulation 150(1) of the Jobseeker's Allowance Regulations (amount of a jobseeker's allowance payable), [43 or
(c) an award of employment and support allowance is calculated in accordance with regulation 165 of the Employment and Support Allowance Regulations (entitlement of less than a week etc.),]

the amount of any payment of income support or, as the case may be, jobseeker's allowance [43 or employment and support allowance] payable to a third party determined under sub-paragraph (2) above shall be an amount calculated in accordance with sub-paragraph (3)(a) or (b) above divided by 7 and multiplied by the number of days in the part-week, and no payment shall be made to a third party under this sub-paragraph where the Secretary of State certifies that it would be impracticable to do so in that particular case.]]

Service charges for fuel, and rent not falling within paragraph 2(1)(a)

5.—(1) Subject to paragraph 8, this paragraph applies to a beneficiary if— 2.248

(a) he has been awarded the specified benefit; and

(b) he or his partner is entitled to housing benefit in the form of a rent rebate or rent allowance [46 or is resident in approved premises under section 13 of the Offender Management Act 2007]; and

(c) [unless sup-paragraph (1A) applies] he or his partner has arrears of rent which equal or exceed four times the full weekly rent payable and—

(i) there are arrears of rent in respect of at least 8 weeks and the landlord has requested the Secretary of State to make payments in accordance with this paragraph; or

(ii) there are arrears of rent in respect of less than 8 weeks and in the opinion of the [25 Secretary of State] it is in the overriding interests of the family that payments shall be made in accordance with this paragraph.

[42 (1A) This sub-paragraph applies where the rent includes charges for services included under paragraph 4A(1)(d) and the arrears for these services exceeds £100.00.]

[46 (1B) For the purposes of sub-paragraphs (1) and (1A), references to "rent" include charges incurred in respect of accommodation in approved premises under section 13 of the Offender Management Act 2007.]

[51 (2) For the purposes of sub-paragraph (1) arrears of rent do not include any amount which falls to be deducted under regulation 74 of the Housing Benefit Regulations (non-dependant deductions) or, as the case may be, regulation 55 of the Housing Benefit (State Pension Credit) Regulations (non-dependant deductions) when assessing a person's housing benefit.

(3) [46 The adjudicating authority shall determine that a weekly amount of the specified benefit awarded to the beneficiary shall be paid to his or his partner's landlord if—

(a) he or his partner is entitled to housing benefit and in calculating that benefit a deduction is made under [36 regulation 12(3) of the Housing Benefit Regulations or, as the case may be, the Housing Benefit (State Pension Credit) Regulations] in respect of either or both of water charges or service charges for fuel; and

(b) the amount of the beneficiary's award is not less than the amount of the deduction,

and the amount to be paid shall be equal to the amount of the deduction.

(4) [36. . .].

[20(5) A determination under this paragraph shall not be made without the consent of the beneficiary if the aggregate amount calculated in accordance with sub-paragraphs (3) and (6) exceeds [38 a sum calculated in accordance with paragraph 8(4);]

[31 (5A) [38 . . .]]

(6) In a case to which sub-paragraph (1) [42 or (1A)] applies the adjudicating authority may determine that a weekly amount of the specified benefit awarded to that beneficiary equal to 5 per cent. of the personal allowance for a single claimant aged not less than 25 [6 . . .] shall be paid to his landlord [46 , or the person or body to whom charges are payable in respect of the residence of the beneficiary or the beneficiary's partner in approved premises under section 13 of the Offender Management Act 2007,] until the debt is discharged.

[8(7) Immediately after the discharge of any arrears of rent to which sub-paragraph (1) [42 or (1A)] applies and in respect of which a determination has been made under sub-paragraph (6) the adjudicating authority may, if satisfied that it would be in the interests of the family to do so, direct that an amount, equal to the amount by which the eligible rent is to be reduced by virtue of [36 regulation 12(3) of the Housing Benefit Regulations or, as the case may be, the Housing Benefit (State Pension Credit) Regulations] in respect of charges for water or service charges for fuel or both, shall be deductible.]

Fuel costs

6.—(1) [31 Subject to sub-paragraphs (6) and (6A)] and paragraph 8, where a beneficiary who has been awarded the specified benefit or his partner is in debt for any [55 fuel item] to an 2.249

amount not less than the rate of personal allowance for a single claimant aged not less than 25 and continues to require [55 the fuel in respect of which the debt arose ("the relevant fuel")] the [5 Secretary of State], if in its opinion it would be in the interests of the family to do so, may determine that the amount of the award of the specified benefit ("the amount deductible") calculated in accordance with the following paragraphs shall be paid to the person or body to whom payment is due in accordance with paragraph 2(3).

(2) The amount deductible shall, in respect of any fuel item, be such weekly aggregate of the following as is appropriate:—

[6(a) in respect of each debt to which sub-paragraph (1) applies ("the original debt"), a weekly amount equal to 5 per cent of the personal allowance for a person aged not less than 25 for such period as is necessary to discharge the original debt, but the aggregate of the amounts, calculated under this paragraph shall not exceed twice 5 per cent of the personal allowance for a single claimant aged not less than 25;]

(b) except where current consumption is paid for by other means (for example prepayment meter), an amount equal to the estimated average weekly cost necessary to meet the continuing needs for [55 the relevant fuel], varied, where appropriate, in accordance with sub-paragraph (4)(a)[55 ", plus such weekly amount as is required to meet any payments required to be made under a green deal plan within the meaning of section 1 of the Energy Act 2011 ("the 2011 Act").]

(3) [6 . . .]

(4) Where an amount is being paid direct to a person or body on behalf of the beneficiary or his partner in accordance with a determination under sub-paragraph (1) and [27 a decision which enbodies that determination falls to be reviewed]—

(a) where since the date of that determination the average weekly cost estimated for the purpose of sub-paragraph (2)(b) has either exceeded or proved insufficient to meet the actual cost of continuing consumption so that in respect of the continuing needs for [55 the relevant fuel] the beneficiary or his partner is in credit or, as the case may be, a further debt has accrued, the adjudicating authority may determine that the weekly amount calculated under that paragraph shall, for a period of 26 weeks [8or such longer period as may be reasonable in the circumstances of the case], be adjusted so as to take account of that credit or further debt;

(b) where an original debt in respect of any fuel item has been discharged the adjudicating authority may determine that the amount deductible in respect of that fuel item shall be the amount determined under sub-paragraph (2)(b).

(5) [6 . . .]

[20(6) Subject to paragraph 8, a determination under this paragraph shall not be made without the consent of the beneficiary if the aggregate amount calculated in accordance with sub-paragraph (2) exceeds [38 a sum calculated in accordance with paragraph 8(4).]

[31 [38 . . .]]

(7) [6 . . .]

[55 (8) In this paragraph, "fuel item" means—

(a) any charge for mains gas, including for the reconnection of mains gas; and

(b) any charge for mains electricity, including any charge for the disconnection or reconnection of mains electricity and including any payments required to be made under a green deal plan within the meaning of section 1 of the 2011 Act.]

[6 Water charges

2.250 **7.**—(1) This paragraph does not apply where water charges are paid with rent; and in this paragraph "original debt" means the debt to which sub-paragraph (2) applies, [13 including any disconnection or reconnection charges and any other costs (including legal costs) arising out of that debt].

(2) Where a beneficiary or his partner is liable, whether directly or indirectly, for water charges and is in debt for those charges, the [25 Secretary of State] may determine, subject to paragraph 8, that a weekly amount of the specified benefit shall be paid either to a water undertaker to whom that debt is owed, or to the person or body authorised to collect water charges for that undertaker, [8 but only if [27 the Secretary of State] is satisfied that the beneficiary or his partner has failed to budget for those charges, and that it would be in the interests of the family to make the determination.]

(3) Where water charges are determined by means of a water meter, the weekly amount to be paid under sub-paragraph (2) shall be the aggregate of—

(a) in respect of the original debt, an amount equal to 5 per cent of the personal allowance for a single claimant aged not less than 25 years; and

(b) the amount which the [25 Secretary of State] estimates to be the average weekly cost necessary to meet the continuing need for water consumption.

(4) Where the sum estimated in accordance with sub-paragraph (3)(b) proves to be greater or less than the average weekly cost necessary to meet continuing need for water consumption so that a beneficiary or his partner accrues a credit, or as the case may be a further debt, the adjudicating authority may determine that the sum so estimated shall be adjusted for a period of 26 weeks [8 or such longer period as may be reasonable in the circumstances of the case] to take account of that credit or further debt.

(5) Where water charges are determined other than by means of a water meter the weekly amount to be paid under sub-paragraph (2) shall be the aggregate of—

(a) the amount referred to in sub-paragraph (3)(a); and

(b) an amount equal to the weekly cost necessary to meet the continuing need for water consumption.

(6) Where the original debt in respect of water charges is discharged, the [25 Secretary of State] may direct that the amount deductible shall be—

(a) where water charges are determined by means of a water meter, the amount determined under sub-paragraph (3)(b) taking into account any adjustment that may have been made in accordance with sub-paragraph (4); an

(b) in any other case, the amount determined under sub-paragraph (5)(b).

(7) Where the beneficiary or his partner is in debt to two water undertakers—

(a) only one weekly amount under sub-paragraph (3)(a) or (5)(a) shall be deducted; and

(b) a deduction in respect of an original debt for sewerage shall only be made after the whole debt in respect of an original debt for water has been paid; and

(c) deductions in respect of continuing charges for both water and for sewerage may be made at the same time.

[20 (8) Subject to paragraph 8 (maximum amount of payments to third parties), a determination under this paragraph shall not be made without the consent of the beneficiary if the aggregate amount calculated in accordance with sub-paragraphs (3), (4), (5) and (6) exceeds [38 a sum calculated in accordance with paragraph 8(4).]

[31 [38 . . .]]

[10 Payments in place of payments of child support maintenance

7A.—[12(1) Subject to paragraph (2), where [26 the Secretary of State] (within the meaning of section 13 of the Child Support Act 1991) has determined that section 43 of that Act and regulation 28 of the Child Support (Maintenance Assessments and Special Cases) Regulations 1992 (contribution to maintenance by deduction from benefit) apply in relation to a beneficiary or his partner, the [25 Secretary of State] shall (subject to paragraph 8), if it is satisfied that there is sufficient specified benefit in payment, determine that a weekly amount of that benefit shall be deducted by the Secretary of State for transmission to the person or persons entitled to it.] 2.251

(2) Not more than one deduction shall be made under [12sub-paragraph (1)] in any one benefit week as defined in paragraph 4 of Schedule 7.

(3) [18Subject to sub-paragraph (4),] the amount of specified benefit to be paid under this paragraph shall be the amount prescribed by regulation 28(2) of the Child Support (Maintenance Assessments and Special Cases) Regulations 1992 for the purposes of section 43(2)(a) of the Child Support Act 1991 [18 . . .].]

[18(4) Where, apart from the provisions of this sub-paragraph, the provisions of paragraphs 8(1) and 9 would result in the maximum aggregate amount payable equalling 2 times 5 per cent of the personal allowance for a single claimant aged not less than 25 years, the amount of specified benefit to be paid under this paragraph shall be one half of the amount specified in sub-paragraph (3).]

[21Arrears of child support maintenance

7B.—(1) Where a beneficiary is entitled to contribution-based jobseeker's allowance [43 or contributory employment and support allowance] and an arrears notice has been served on the beneficiary, the Secretary of State may request in writing that an amount in respect of arrears of child support maintenance be deducted from the beneficiary's jobseeker's allowance [43 or contributory employment and support allowance]. 2.252

(2) Where a request is made in accordance with sub-paragraph (1), the [25 Secretary of State] shall determine that an amount in respect of the arrears of child support maintenance shall be deducted from the beneficiary's jobseeker's allowance [43 or contributory employment and support allowance] for transmission to the person entitled to it.

(3) Subject to sub-paragraphs (4) and (5), the amount to be deducted under subparagraph

(2) shall be the weekly amount requested by the Secretary of State, subject to a maximum of one-third of the age-related amount applicable to the beneficiary under section 4(1)(a) of the Jobseekers Act.

[43 (3A) Subject to sub-paragraphs (4) and (5), the amount to be deducted from the beneficiary's employment and support allowance under sub-paragraph (2) is the weekly amount requested from the beneficiary's employment and support allowance by the Secretary of State, subject to a maximum of one-third of the amount applicable to the beneficiary under regulation 67(2) of the Employment and Support Allowance Regulations (prescribed amounts).]

(4) No deduction shall be made under this paragraph where a deduction is being made from the beneficiary's contribution-based jobseeker's allowance [43 or contributory employment and support allowance] under the Community Charges Regulations, the Community Charges (Scotland) Regulations, the Fines Regulations or the Council Tax Regulations.

(5) Where the sum that would otherwise fall to be deducted under this paragraph includes a fraction of a penny, the sum to be deducted shall be rounded down to the next whole penny.

(6) In this paragraph—

"arrears notice" means a notice served in accordance with regulation 2(2) of the Child Support (Arrears, Interest and Adjustment of Maintenance Assessments) Regulations 1992; and

"child support maintenance" means such periodical payments as are referred to in section 3(6) of the Child Support Act 1991.]

[39 **Eligible loans**

2.253 **7C.** —(1) In this paragraph—

"borrower" means a person who has, either solely or jointly, entered into a loan agreement with an eligible lender in respect of an eligible loan and who is, for the time being, entitled to an eligible benefit;

"eligible lender" means—

(a) a body registered under section 1 of the Industrial and Provident Societies Act 1965 (societies which may be registered);

(b) a credit union within the meaning of section 1 of the Credit Unions Act 1979 (registration under the Industrial and Provident Societies Act 1965);

(c) a charitable institution within the meaning of section 58(1) of the Charities Act 1992 (interpretation of Part II);

(d) a body entered on the Scottish Charity Register under section 3 of the Charities and Trustee Investment (Scotland) Act 2005 (Scottish Charities Register),which, except for a credit union, is licensed under the Consumer Credit Act 1974 and which may be determined by the Secretary of State as an appropriate body to which payments on behalf of the borrower may be made in respect of loans made by that body;

[42 (e)a community interest company within the meaning of Part 2 of the Companies (Audit, Investigations and Community Enterprise) Act 2004,]

"eligible loan" means a loan made by a lender, who is at that time an eligible lender, to a borrower except a loan—

(a) which is secured by a charge or pledge;

(b) which is for the purpose of business or self-employment; or

(c) which was made by means of a credit card;

"loan agreement" means an agreement between the eligible lender and the borrower in respect of an eligible loan.

(2) In this paragraph "eligible benefit" means—

(a) carer's allowance;

(b) the following contributory benefits—

(i) incapacity benefit;

(ii) retirement pension; [37. . .]

[37 (iii) state pension under Part 1 of the Pensions Act 2014; or]

(c) the following benefits—

(i) income support;

(ii) jobseeker's allowance;

(iii) state pension credit.

[43 (iv) employment and support allowance.]

(3) Where the conditions set out in sub-paragraph (4) are met the Secretary of State may deduct a sum from an eligible benefit to which the borrower is entitled equal to 5 per cent. of the personal allowance for a single [42 claimant] aged not less than 25 and pay that sum to the eligible lender towards discharge of the sum owing under the loan agreement at the date of the application.

(4) The conditions referred to in sub-paragraph (3) are—

(a) the borrower has failed to make payments as agreed with the eligible lender for a period of 13 weeks before the date of the application and has not resumed making payments;

(b) the borrower has given his written permission to the eligible lender to provide to the Secretary of State personal data within the meaning of section 1 of the Data Protection Act 1998 (basic interpretive provisions);

(c) the eligible lender has agreed that no interest or other charge will be added to the amount owed at the date of the application;

(d) no sum is being deducted under this paragraph;

(e) no sum is being deducted from the borrower's eligible benefit under section 71(8) of the 1992 Act (overpayments-general) at the date of the application; and

(f) no sum is being deducted from the borrower's eligible benefit under section 78 of the 1992 Act (recovery of social fund awards) at the date of the application.

(5) The Secretary of State shall notify the borrower and the eligible lender in writing of a decision to make a deduction under this paragraph.

(6) The Secretary of State may make deductions under this paragraph only if the borrower is entitled to an eligible benefit throughout any benefit week.

[[56] (6A) The Secretary of State shall not make deductions from a benefit mentioned in sub-paragraph (2) where the borrower is in receipt of any benefit within the meaning of "eligible benefit" in paragraph 11(8) (eligible loans) of Schedule 6 (deductions from benefit and direct payment to third parties) to the 2013 Regulations unless the amount of benefit mentioned in that definition is insufficient to meet the deduction.]

(7) The Secretary of State shall not make deductions from a benefit mentioned in sub-paragraph (2)(a) where the borrower is in receipt of another eligible benefit unless that benefit is one mentioned in sub-paragraph (2)(b) and is insufficient to enable the deduction to be made or is a benefit mentioned in sub-paragraph (2)(c) and the amount is insufficient to meet the deduction plus 10 pence.

(8) The Secretary of State shall not make deductions from a benefit mentioned in sub-paragraph (2)(b) where the borrower is in receipt of a benefit mentioned in sub-paragraph (2)(c) unless the amount of that benefit is insufficient to meet the deduction plus 10 pence.

(9) The Secretary of State shall cease making deductions from an eligible benefit [[49] under this paragraph] if—

(a) there is no longer sufficient entitlement to an eligible benefit to enable him to make the deduction;

(b) entitlement to all eligible benefits has ceased;

(c) a sum is deducted from the borrower's eligible benefit under section 71(8) of the 1992 Act;

(d) an eligible lender notifies the Secretary of State that he no longer wishes to accept payments by deductions;

(e) the borrower's liability to make payment in respect of the eligible loan has ceased;

(f) the lender has ceased to be an eligible lender; or

(g) the borrower no longer resides in Great Britain.

(10) The sums deducted from an eligible benefit by the Secretary of State under this paragraph shall be paid to the eligible lender.

(11) The Secretary of State shall notify the borrower in writing of the total of sums deducted by him under any application—

(a) on receipt of a written request for such information from the borrower; or

(b) on the termination of deductions.

(12) Where a deduction is made under this paragraph from a specified benefit, paragraph 8 (maximum amount of payment to third parties) is to have effect as if—

(a) in sub-paragraph (1) for "and 7A" there were substituted", 7A and 7C"; and

(b) in sub-paragraph (2) for "and 7"there were substituted", 7 and 7C.]

[[41] **Integration loans**

7D. Subject to paragraphs 2(2), 8 and 9, where a person has an integration loan which is recoverable by deductions, any weekly amount payable shall be equal to 5 per cent of the personal allowance of a single claimant aged not less than 25 years, including where the loan is a joint loan.] **2.254**

[[49] **Tax credits overpayment debts and self-assessment debts**

7E.—(1) In this paragraph— **2.255**

"self-assessment debt" means any debt which—

(a) has arisen from submission of a self-assessment to Her Majesty's Revenue and Customs under section 9 of the Taxes Management Act 1970 (returns to include self-assessment); and
(b) is recoverable under Part 6 of that Act;

"tax credits overpayment debt" means any debt which is recoverable under section 29 of the Tax Credits Act 2002 (recovery of overpayments).

(2) Where the conditions set out in sub-paragraph (3) are met, the Secretary of State may deduct from a specified benefit to which the beneficiary is entitled a sum which is up to a maximum of 3 times 5 per cent of the personal allowance for a single claimant aged not less than 25 and pay that sum to Her Majesty's Revenue and Customs towards discharge of any outstanding tax credits overpayment debt or self-assessment debt owed by the beneficiary to Her Majesty's Revenue and Customs.

(3) The conditions mentioned in sub-paragraph (2) are—

(a) that the beneficiary has given written consent to Her Majesty's Revenue and Customs for deductions to be made from a specified benefit towards discharge of any outstanding tax credits overpayment debt or self-assessment debt owed by the beneficiary to Her Majesty's Revenue and Customs; and
(b) no sum is being deducted under this paragraph.

(4) The Secretary of State shall cease making deductions from a specified benefit under this paragraph if—

(a) there is no longer sufficient entitlement to a specified benefit to enable deductions to be made;
(b) entitlement to all specified benefits has ceased;
(c) the beneficiary withdraws consent for the Secretary of State to make deductions from a specified benefit; or
(d) the beneficiary is no longer liable to repay any tax credits overpayment debt or self-assessment debt.

(5) The Secretary of State shall notify the beneficiary in writing of the total sums deducted under this paragraph—

(a) on receipt of a written request for such information from the beneficiary; or
(b) on the termination of deductions.

(6) Where a deduction is made under this paragraph from a specified benefit, paragraph 8 (maximum amount of payment to third parties) is to have effect as if—

(a) in sub-paragraph (1) for "and 7A" there were substituted ", 7A and 7E"; and
(b) in sub-paragraph (2) for "and 7D" there were substituted ", 7D and 7E".

Maximum amount of payments to third parties

2.256 **8.**—(1) The maximum aggregate amount payable under [19paragraphs] 3(2)(a), 5(6), 6(2)(a)[6, 7(3)(a)[11, 7(5)(a) and 7A]] [22. . .] [11, and [34 regulation 5 of the Council Tax Regulations and regulation 4 of the Fines Regulations] [41, and in respect of an integration loan which is recoverable by deductions] shall not exceed an amount equal to 3 times 5 per cent of the personal allowance for a single claimant aged not less than 25 years.

(2) The maximum [5aggregate] amount payable under [6 paragraphs 3(2)(a), 5, 6 [41, 7 and 7D]] shall not without the consent of the beneficiary, exceed [38 a sum calculated in accordance with sub-paragraph (4).]

[31 (2A) In the case of state pension credit, the maximum aggregate amount payable under paragraphs 3(2)(a), 5, 6, and 7 shall not, without the consent of the beneficiary, exceed a sum equal to 25 per cent. of the appropriate minimum guarantee less any housing costs under Schedule II to the State Pension Credit Regulations which may be applicable in the particular case.]

(3) [22. . .]

[38 (4) The sum referred to in sub-paragraph (2) is—

(a) where the claimant or partner does not receive child tax credit, 25 per cent of—
  (i) in the case of income support, the applicable amount for the family as is awarded under sub-paragraphs (a) to (d) of regulation 17(1) (applicable amounts) or sub-paragraphs (a) to (e) of regulation 18(1) (polygamous marriages) of the Income Support Regulations;
  (ii) in the case of jobseeker's allowance, the applicable amount for the family as is awarded under paragraphs (a) to (e) of regulation 83 (applicable amounts) or sub-paragraphs (a) to (f) of regulation 84(1) (polygamous marriages) of the Jobseeker's Allowance Regulations; or
  (iii) in the case of state pension credit, the appropriate minimum guarantee less any housing costs under Schedule 2 to the State Pension Credit Regulations 2002 which may be applicable in the particular case;

[50 (iv) in the case of an employment and support allowance, the applicable amount for the family as is awarded under paragraph (1)(a) and (b) of regulation 67 (prescribed amounts) or paragraph (1)(a) to (c) of regulation 68 (polygamous marriages) of the Employment and Support Allowance Regulations; or]

(b) where the claimant or his partner receives child tax credit, 25 per cent of the sum of—

(i) the amount mentioned in [54 sub-paragraphs (a)(i) to (iv)], which applies to the claimant;

(ii) the amount of child benefit awarded to him or his partner by the Board under Part 2 of the Tax Credits Act 2002; and

(iii) the amount of child tax credit awarded to him or his partner by the Board under section 8 of that Act.]

Priority as between certain debts

[11**9.**—(1A) Where in any one week— 2.257

(a) more than one of the paragraphs 3 to [49 7A, 7C or 7E] are applicable to the beneficiary; or

(b) one or more of those paragraphs are applicable to the beneficiary and one or more of the following provisions, namely, [22. . .] [34 regulation 3 of the Community Charges Regulations, regulation 3 of the Community Charges (Scotland) Regulations, regulation 4 of the Fines Regulations [41, regulation 5 of the Council Tax Regulations and regulation 9 of the Integration Loans for Refugees and Others Regulations 2007] also applies; and

(c) the amount of the specified benefit which may be made to third parties is insufficient to meet the whole of the liabilities for which provision is made;

the order of priorities specified in sub-paragraph (1)(B) shall apply.

(1B) The order of priorities which shall apply in sub-paragraph (1)(A) is—

(za) [22. . .]

(a) any liability mentioned in paragraph 3 (housing costs) [44 paragraph 4 (miscellaneous accomodation costs) or paragraph 4A (hostel payments)];

(b) any liability mentioned in paragraph 5 (service charges for fuel and rent not falling within paragraph 2(1)(a));

(c) any liability mentioned in paragraph 6 (fuel costs);

(d) any liability mentioned in paragraph 7 (water charges);

(e) any liability mentioned in [34 regulation 3 of the Community Charges Regulations (deductions from income support etc.), regulation 3 of the Community Charges (Scotland) Regulations (deductions from income support etc.) or any liability mentioned in regulation 5 of the Council Tax Regulations (deduction from debtor's income support etc.)];

(f) any liability mentioned in [34 regulation 4 of the Fines Regulations (deductions from offender's income support etc.)];

(g) any liability mentioned in paragraph 7A (payments in place of payments of child support maintenance).]

[41 (ga) any liability to repay an integration loan which is recoverable by deductions.]

[39 (h) any liability mentioned in paragraph 7C (liability in respect of loans).]

[49 (i) any liability mention in paragraph 7E (tax credits overpayment debts and self-assessment debts.).]

(2) As between liability for items of housing costs liabilities in respect of mortgage payments shall have priority over all other items.

(3) As between liabilities for items of gas or electricity the [25 Secretary of State] shall give priority to whichever liability it considers it would, having regard to the circumstances and to any requests of the beneficiary, be appropriate to discharge.

(4) [6. . .]

AMENDMENTS

1. The Social Security (Claims and Payments) Amendment Regulations 1988 (SI 1988/522) reg.11 (April 11, 1988).

2. The Social Security (Claims and Payments and Payments on account, Overpayments and Recovery) Amendment Regulations 1989 (SI 1989/136) reg.2(7) (February 27, 1989).

3. The Social Security (Claims and Payments and Payments on account, Overpayments and Recovery) Amendment Regulations 1989 (SI 1989/136) reg.2(7) (April 10, 1989).

4. The Social Security (Medical Evidence, Claims and Payments) Amendment Regulations 1989 (SI 1989/1686) reg.9 (October 9, 1989).
5. The Social Security (Miscellaneous Provisions) Amendment Regulations 1990 (SI 1990/2208) reg.16 (December 5, 1990).
6. The Social Security (Miscellaneous Provisions) Amendment Regulations 1991 (SI 1991/2284) regs 12–20 (November 1, 1991).
7. The Social Security (Claims and Payments) Amendment Regulations 1992 (SI 1992/1026) reg.5 (May 25, 1992).
8. The Social Security (Miscellaneous Provisions) Amendment (No.2) Regulations 1992 (SI 1992/2595) reg.8 (November 16, 1992).
9. The Social Security (Miscellaneous Provisions) Amendment (No.2) Regulations 1992 (SI 1992/2595) Sch.1 para.8 (April 1, 1993).
10. The Social Security (Claims and Payments) Amendment Regulations 1993 (SI 1993/478) reg.2 (April 1, 1993).
11. The Deductions from Income Support (Miscellaneous Amendments) Regulations 1993 (SI 1993/495) reg.2 (April 1, 1993).
12. The Social Security (Claims and Payments) Amendment (No.3) Regulations 1993 (SI 1993/2113) reg.3 (September 27, 1993).
13. The Social Security (Claims and Payments) Amendment Regulations 1994 (SI 1994/2319) reg.7 (October 3, 1994).
14. The Social Security (Claims and Payments) Amendment (No.2) Regulations 1994 (SI 1994/2943) reg.15 (April 13, 1995).
15. The Social Security (Income Support and Claims and Payments) Amendment Regulations 1995 (SI 1995/1613) reg.3 and Sch.2 (October 2, 1995).
16. The Social Security (Income Support, Claims and Payments and Adjudication) Amendment Regulations 1995 (SI 1995/2927) reg.3 (December 12, 1995).
17. The Social Security (Claims and Payments etc.) Amendment Regulations 1996 (SI 1996/672) reg.2(7) (April 4, 1996).
18. The Child Support (Maintenance Assessments and Special Cases) and Social Security (Claims and Payments) Amendment Regulations 1996 (SI 1996/481) reg.5 (April 8, 1996).
19. The Child Support (Maintenance Assessments and Special Cases) and Social Security (Claims and Payments) Amendment Regulations 1996 (SI 1996/481) reg.6 (April 8, 1996).
20. The Social Security (Claims and Payments) (Jobseeker's Allowance Consequential Amendments) Regulations 1996 (SI 1996/1460) reg.2(26) (October 7, 1996).
21. The Social Security (Jobseeker's Allowance Consequential Amendments) (Deductions) Regulations 1996 (SI 1996/2344) reg.25 (October 7, 1996).
22. The Social Security and Child Support (Miscellaneous Amendments) Regulations 1997 (SI 1997/827) reg.7(2) (April 7, 1997).
23. The Social Security (Child Maintenance Bonus) Regulations 1996 (SI 1996/3195) reg.16(2) (April 7, 1997).
24. The Social Security (Miscellaneous Amendments) Regulations 1997 (SI 1997/454) reg.8(10) (April 6, 1997).
25. The Social Security Act 1998 (Commencement No.11 and Transitional Provisions) Order 1999 (SI 1999/2860) Sch.3 (October 18, 1999).
26. The Social Security Act 1998 (Commencement No.7 and Consequential and Transitional Provisions) Order 1999 (SI 1999/1510) Sch.4 (June 1, 1999).
27. The Social Security Act 1998 (Commencement No.12 and Consequential and Transitional Provisions) Order 1999 (SI 1999/3178) Sch.6 (November 29, 1999).
28. The Social Security Amendment (Residential Care and Nursing Homes) Regulations 2002 (SI 2002/398) reg.2(2) (April 8, 2002).
29. The Social Security Amendment (Residential Care and Nursing Homes) Regulations 2002 (SI 2002/398) reg.2(3) (April 8, 2002).

30. Social Security (Claims and Payments and Miscellaneous Amendments) (No.2) Regulations 2002 (SI 2002/2441) reg.12 (October 23, 2002).
31. State Pension Credit (Consequential, Transitional and Miscellaneous Provisions) Regulations 2002 (SI 2002/3019) reg.14 (April 7, 2003).
32. The Social Security (Third Party Deductions and Miscellaneous Amendments) Regulations 2003 (SI 2003/2325) reg.2 (October 6, 2003).
33. The Social Security (Claims and Payments) Amendment Regulations 2004 (SI 2004/576) (April 12, 2004 of first benefit pay day thereafter).
34. Social Security (Claims and Payments) Amendment (No.2) Regulations 2005 (SI 2005/777) reg.3 (April 11, 2005).
35. The Social Security (Care Homes and Independent Hospitals) Regulations 2005 (SI 2005/2687) (October 24, 2005).
36. The Housing Benefit and Council Tax Benefit (Consequential Provisions) Regulations 2006 (SI 2006/217) Sch.2 para.2 (March 6, 2006).
37. The Social Security (Miscellaneous Amendments) (No.2) Regulations 2006 (SI 2006/832) reg.2 (April 10, 2006).
38. The Social Security (Miscellaneous Amendments) (No.3) Regulations 2006 (SI 2006/2377) (October 2, 2006).
39. The Social Security (Claims and Payments) Amendment (No. 2) Regulations 2006 (SI 2006/3188) (December 27, 2006).
40. The Social Security Benefits Up-rating Regulations 2009 (SI 2009/607) (April 6, 2009).
41. The Social Security (Claims and Payments) Amendment (No.2) Regulations 2007 (SI 2007/1866) (July 31, 2007).
42. The Social Security (Miscellaneous Amendments) Regulations 2008 (SI 2008/698) reg.3 (April 14, 2008).
43. The Employment and Support Allowance (Consequential provisions) (No.2) Regulations 2008 (SI 2008/1554) reg.26 (October 27, 2008).
44. The Social Security (Miscellaneous Amendments) (No.6) Regulations 2008 (SI 2008/2767) reg.3 (November 17, 2008).
45. The Social Security (Miscellaneous Amendments) (No.2) Regulations 2009 (SI 2009/1490) reg.2 (July 13, 2009).
46. The Social Security (Miscellaneous Amendments) Regulations 2010 (SI 2010/510) reg.3(7) (April 6, 2010).
47. The Social Security Benefits Up-rating Regulations 2013 (SI 2013/599) reg.4 (April 8, 2013).
48. Housing and Regeneration Act 2008 (Consequential Provisions) (No. 2) Order (SI 2010/671) art.4 and Sch.1 (April 1, 2010).
49. Social Security (Claims and Payments) Amendments (No. 2) Regulations 2010 (SI 2010/870) reg.2 (April 30, 2010).
50. Employment and Support Allowance (Transitional Provisions, Housing Benefit and Council Tax Benefit (Existing Awards) (No. 2) Regulations 2010 (SI 2010/1907) reg.26 (October 1, 2010).
51. The Social Security (Miscellaneous Amendments) Regulations 2011 (SI 2011/674) reg.4 (April 1 *or* April 4, 2011).
52. The Social Security (Miscellaneous Amendments) (No. 3) Regulations 2011 (SI 2011/2425) reg.8 (October 31, 2011).
53. The Housing (Scotland) Act 2010 (Consequential Provisions and Modifications) Order 2012 (SI 2012/700) art.4 and Sch. para.10 (April 1, 2012).
54. The Social Security (Miscellaneous Amendments) Regulations 2012 (SI 2012/757) reg.12(4) (April 1, 2012).
55. The Social Security (Miscellaneous Amendments) Regulations 2013 (SI 2013/443) reg.3 (April 2, 2013).
56. The Social Security (Miscellaneous Amendments) (No. 2) Regulations 2013 (SI 2013/1508) reg.2(3) (July 29, 2013).
57. The Social Security (Miscellaneous Amendments) (No. 3) Regulations 2013 (SI 2013/2536) reg.5(3) (October 29, 2013).

58. The Social Security Benefits Up-rating Regulations 2017 (SI 2017/349) reg.4 (April 1, 2017).

DEFINITIONS

"adjudicating authority"—see reg.2(1).
"beneficiary"—see Social Security Act 1975 Sch.20.
"family"—see 1986 Act, s.20(11) (SSCBA s.137(1)).
"instrument for benefit payment"—see reg.2(1).
"jobseeker's allowance"—*ibid.*
"partner"—*ibid.*
"qualifying lender"—see Administration Act s.15A(3).

Note that these references are only to phrases defined outside Sch.9 itself. See para.1 for definitions special to Sch.9.

GENERAL NOTE

2.258 The provisions for part of weekly benefit to be diverted direct to a third party are of great importance in determining the actual weekly incomes of claimants. There have been changes in the provisions on fuel and water charges and Sch.9A now deals specifically with payments of mortgage interest.

On deductions in respect of rent arrears under para.5(6), *R(IS) 14/95* holds that the arrears must be proved, at least where these are disputed. In addition, the existence of an arguable counterclaim in possession proceedings is a matter that an adjudicating authority might properly take into account in deciding whether to exercise the discretionary power to make deductions under para.5(6).

See annotations to reg.35 for comment on the precedence to be accorded to child support payments and the relationship between Sch.9 and Sch.9B.

[1 SCHEDULE 9A

DEDUCTIONS OF MORTGAGE INTEREST FROM BENEFIT AND PAYMENT TO QUALIFYING LENDERS

Interpretation

2.259 **1.** In this Schedule—

[9. . .]

"Income Support Regulations" means the Income Support (General) Regulations 1987;

[7"relevant benefits" means—

[19 (a) income support, or income support and any incapacity benefit or severe disablement allowance where—
(i) either benefit is paid with income support in a combined payment in respect of any period; and
(ii) the income support alone is insufficient for the purpose of this Schedule;]

(b) [16 . . ..]

(c) income-based jobseeker's allowance;] [17

[30 (ca) contribution-based jobseeker's allowance where—
(i) both income-based jobseeker's allowance and contribution-based jobseeker's allowance are in payment, and
(ii) the income-based jobseeker's allowance alone is insufficient for the purposes of this Schedule;]

[19 (d) state pension credit, or state pension credit and any retirement pension, incapacity benefit or severe disablement allowance where—
(i) one of those benefits is paid with state pension credit in a combined payment in respect of any period; and
(ii) the state pension credit alone is insufficient for the purpose of this Schedule;]

[26 (e) income-related employment and support allowance;]

[30 (f) contributory employment and support allowance where—

(i) both income-related employment and support allowance and contributory employment and support allowance are in payment, and

(ii) the income-related employment and support allowance alone is insufficient for the purposes of this Schedule;]

[32. . ..]

"specified part" shall be construed in accordance with paragraph 3.

Specified circumstances for the purposes of Regulation 34A

[5**2.** The circumstances referred to in regulation 34A are that— 2.260

[8(a) [17 the amount to be met under—

(i) Schedule 3 to the Income Support Regulations; or

(ii) Schedule 2 to the Jobseeker's Allowance Regulations; or

(iii) Schedule II to the State Pension Credit Regulations,] or

[26 (iv) Schedule 6 to the Employment and Support Allowance Regulations,]

by reference to the standard rate [21 . . .] and, in the case of income support, to any amount payable in accordance with paragraph 7 of Schedule 3 to the Income Support Regulations;] and

(b) the relevant benefits to which a relevant beneficiary is entitled are payable in respect of a period of 7 days or a multiple of such a period.]

[23 Specified circumstances for the purposes of Regulation 34B

2A.—(1) The circumstances referred to in regulation 34B are that— 2.261

(a) the relevant beneficiary is entitled to a savings credit as construed in accordance with sections 1 and 3 of the 2002 Act and not to a guarantee credit; and

(b) sub-paragraphs (a) and (b) of paragraph 2 apply.

(2) The further circumstances referred to in that regulation are that —

(a) the relevant beneficiary has requested the Secretary of State in writing to make such payments to the qualifying lender; or

(b) the Secretary of State has determined that it would be in the relevant beneficiary's interests, or in the interests of his family to make such payment to the qualifying lender.

(3) In making the determination referred to in sub-paragraph (2)(b), the Secretary of State shall have regard to whether or not the relevant beneficiary is in arrears with his payments to the qualifying lender.

(4) For the purposes of sub-paragraph (2)(b), "a family" comprises the relevant beneficiary, his partner, any additional partner to whom section 12(1)(c) of the 2002 Act applies and any person who has not attained the age of [25 20], is treated as a child for the purposes of section 142 of the Contributions and Benefits Act and lives with the relevant beneficiary or the relevant beneficiary's partner.]

SPECIFIED PART OF RELEVANT BENEFIT

3. [5(1) Subject to the following provisions of this paragraph, the part of any relevant benefits which, as determined by the [14 Secretary of State in accordance with regulation 34A, shall be paid] directly to the qualifying lender ("the specified part") is[8, in the case of income support,] a sum equal to the amount of mortgage interest to be met in accordance with paragraphs 6 and 8 to 10 of Schedule 3 to the Income Support Regulations (housing costs) together with an amount (if any) determined under paragraph 7 of that Schedule (transitional protection) [8or, in the case of jobseeker's allowance, a sum equal to the amount of mortgage interest to be met in accordance with paragraphs 6 to 9 of Schedule 2 to the Jobseeker's Allowance Regulations] [26 or, in the case of employment and support allowance, a sum equal to the amount of mortgage interest to be met in accordance with paragraphs 8 to 11 of Schedule 6 to the Employment and Support Allowance Regulations].] 2.262

[17 (1A) Subject to the following provisions of this paragraph, the part of state pension credit which, as determined by the Secretary of State in accordance with regulation 34A, shall be paid directly to the qualifying lender, is a sum equal to the amount of mortgage interest to be met under paragraph 7 of Schedule II to the State Pension Credit Regulations.]

(2) [5. . .]

(3) Where, in determining a relevant beneficiary's applicable amount for the purposes of income support [[26 income-based jobseeker's allowance or income-related employment and support allowance] [17 or a relevant beneficiary's appropriate minimum guarantee in state pension credit]]—

(a) a sum in respect of housing costs is brought into account in addition to a sum in respect of mortgage interest; and

(b) in accordance with [5paragraph 4(8) or (11) or paragraph 18] of Schedule 3 to the

Income Support Regulations [8or, as the case may be, [17 paragraph 5(9) or (12) or paragraph 14 of Schedule II to the State Pension Credit Regulations or] paragraph 4(8) or (11) or paragraph 17 of Schedule 2 to the Jobseeker's Allowance Regulations] [26 or paragraph 6(10) or (13) or 19 of Schedule 6 to the Employment and Support Allowance Regulations] an amount is not allowed or a deduction falls to be made from the amount to be met under [8either of those Schedules],

then the specified part referred to in [17 sub-paragraph (1) or (1A)] of this paragraph is the mortgage interest minus a sum calculated by applying the formula—

$$C \times \frac{B}{A}$$

[5where—

A = housing costs within the meaning of paragraph 1 of Schedule 3 to the Income Support Regulations [8or, as the case may be, [17 paragraph 1 of Schedule II to the State Pension Credit Regulations or] paragraph 1 of Schedule 2 to the Jobseeker's Allowance Regulations] [26 or paragraph 1 of Schedule 6 to the Employment and Support Allowance Regulations];

B = the housing costs to be met in accordance with paragraphs 6 and 8 to 10 of Schedule 3 to the Income Support Regulations (housing costs) together with an amount (if any) determined under paragraph 7 of that Schedule (transitional protection) [8or, as the case may be, [17 paragraph 7 of Schedule II to the State Pension Credit Regulations or] paragraphs 6 to 9 of Schedule 2 to the Jobseeker's Allowance Regulations] [26 or paragraphs 8 to 11 of Schedule 6 to the Employment and Support Allowance Regulations]; and

C = the sum which is not allowed or falls to be deducted in accordance with paragraph 18 of Schedule 3 to the Income Support Regulations [8or, as the case may be, [17 paragraph 5(9) or (12) or paragraph 14 of Schedule II to the State Pension Credit Regulations or] paragraph 4(8) or (11) or paragraph 17 of Schedule 2 to the Jobseeker's Allowance Regulations] [26 or paragraph 19 of Schedule 6 to the Employment and Support Allowance Regulations].]

(4) [17 Except where the relevant benefit is state pension credit,] Where a payment is being made under a policy of insurance taken out by a beneficiary to insure against the risk of his being unable to maintain repayments of mortgage interest to a qualifying lender, then the amount of any relevant benefits payable to that lender shall be reduced by a sum equivalent to so much of the amount payable under the policy of insurance as represents payments in respect of mortgage interest.

(5) [9. . .]

(6) [9. . .]

(7) [5. . .]

(8) Where the amount of any relevant benefits to which a relevant beneficiary is entitled is less than the sum which would, but for this sub-paragraph, have been the specified part, then the specified part shall be the amount of any relevant benefits to which the relevant beneficiary is entitled less 10p.

[15 (9) In the case of a person to whom regulation 6(5) of the Income Support Regulations applies, no part of any relevant benefit shall be paid directly by the Secretary of State to a qualifying lender.]

[17 (10) In sub-paragraph (1), the relevant benefits do not include in the case of state pension credit so much of any additional amount which is applicable in the claimant's case under Schedule II to the State Pension Credit Regulations (housing costs) in respect of a period before the decision awarding state pension credit was made.]

Direct payment: more than one loan

2.263 **4.**—(1) This paragraph applies where the borrower is liable to pay mortgage interest in respect of two or more different loans.

[5(2) Subject to the following provisions of this paragraph, the Secretary of State shall pay to the qualifying lender or, if there is more than one qualifying lender, to each qualifying lender—

(a) a sum equal to the mortgage interest determined by reference to paragraph 12 of Schedule 3 to the Income Support Regulations [8or, as the case may be, paragraph 11 of Schedule 2 to the Jobseeker's Allowance Regulations] [26 or paragraph 13 of Schedule 6 to the Employment and Support Allowance Regulations] (standard rate) in respect of each loan made by that lender, plus

(b) any amount payable in accordance with paragraph 7 of Schedule 3 to the Income Support Regulations (transitional protection) attributable to the particular loan; [9. . .]

(c) any additional amount attributable to a particular loan which may, under paragraph 3(5), have been taken into account in calculating the specified part.]

(3) If, by virtue of deductions made under either paragraph 3(2) or 3(3), the specified part is less than the amount payable by the borrower in respect of mortgage interest, then the sum payable under sub-paragraph (2)(a) shall be minus such proportion of the sum subtracted under those sub-paragraphs as is attributable to the particular loan.

(4) Paragraph 3(4) shall apply to reduce the amount payable to a qualifying lender mentioned in sub-paragraph (2) above as it applies to reduce the amount of any relevant benefits payable to a qualifying lender under paragraph 3.

(5) Where the specified part is the part referred to in paragraph 3(8), the Secretary of State shall pay the specified part directly to the qualifying lenders to whom mortgage interest is payable by the borrower in order of the priority of mortgages or (in Scotland) in accordance with the preference in ranking of heritable securities.

[[28] Application of payment where it exceeds borrower's actual mortgage interest

4A.—(1) Subject to sub-paragraph (2), insofar as the sum paid to a qualifying lender under this Schedule in respect of a particular loan exceeds the borrower's liability in respect of the mortgage interest payable on that loan the excess shall be applied by that lender in the following order of priority— 2.264

(a) first, towards the discharge of any liability for arrears of mortgage interest in respect of that loan;

(b) second, towards the discharge of any liability to repay the principal sum, or any other sum payable by the borrower to that lender, in respect of that loan.

(2) Where the borrower is liable to pay mortgage interest to the same qualifying lender in respect of two or more different loans, insofar as the sum paid to that lender under this Schedule in respect of one of those loans ("loan A") exceeds the borrower's liability in respect of the mortgage interest payable on that loan the excess shall be applied by that lender in the following order of priority—

(a) first, towards the discharge of any liability for arrears of mortgage interest payable in respect of loan A;

(b) second, towards the discharge of any liability to repay the principal sum, or any other sum payable by the borrower to that lender, in respect of loan A or (insofar as that liability is not already discharged by the application of any other sum paid to the qualifying lender under this Schedule) any of the other loans.]

Relevant benefits

5. [[7]. . .] 2.265

Time and manner of payments

6. Payments to qualifying lenders under regulation 34A and this Schedule shall be made in arrears at intervals of 4 weeks. 2.266

Fees payable by qualifying lenders

7. For the purposes of defraying the expenses of the Secretary of State in administering the making of payments under regulation 34A and this Schedule a qualifying lender shall pay to the Secretary of State a fee of[[38] £0.39] in respect of each payment made under regulation 34A and this Schedule. 2.267

Qualifying lenders

8. The following bodies and persons shall be qualifying lenders— 2.268

(a) the [[29] Regulator of Social Housing;]

[[33] (aa) ...]

[[34] (aaa) the Greater London Authority;

(b) Housing for Wales;

(c) [[22] Communities Scotland;]

(d) the Development Board for Rural Wales; and

(e) any body incorporated under the Companies Act 1985 whose main objects include the making of loans secured by a mortgage of or a charge over land or (in Scotland) by a heritable security.

Election not to be regarded as a qualifying lender

9.—(1) A body which, or a person who, would otherwise be a qualifying lender may elect not to be regarded as such for the purposes of these Regulations by giving notice of election under this paragraph to the Secretary of State in accordance with sub-paragraphs (2) and (3). 2.269

(2) Subject to sub-paragraph (3), notice of election shall be given in writing—

(a) in the case of the financial year 1992 to 1993, before 23rd May 1992 and shall take effect on that date; and

(b) in the case of any other financial year, before 1st February in the preceding year and shall take effect on 1st April following the giving of the notice.

(3) A body which, or a person who, becomes a qualifying lender during a financial year and who wishes to elect not to be regarded as such for the purposes of these Regulations shall give notice of election in writing within a period of six weeks from the date on which the person or body becomes a qualifying lender.

(4) Regulation 34A shall not apply to a body which, or a person who, becomes a qualifying lender during a financial year for a period of six weeks from the date on which the person or body became a qualifying lender unless, either before the start of that period or at any time during that period, the person or body notifies the Secretary of State in writing that this sub-paragraph should not apply.

(5) A body which, or a person who, has made an election under this paragraph may revoke that election by giving notice in writing to the Secretary of State before 1st February in any financial year and the revocation shall take effect on the 1st April following the giving of the notice.

(6) Where a notice under this paragraph is sent by post it shall be treated as having been given on the day it was posted.

Provision of information

2.270 **10.**—(1) A qualifying lender shall provide the Secretary of State with information relating to—

(a) the mortgage interest payable by a borrower;
(b) the amount of the loan;
(c) the purpose for which the loan is made;
(d) the amount outstanding on the loan on which the mortgage interest is payable;
(e) any change in the amount of interest payable by the borrower;

at the times specified in sub-paragraphs (2) and (3).

[[17] (2) Subject to sub-paragraph (4), the information referred to in heads (a), (b), (c) and (d) of sub-paragraph (1) shall be provided at the request of the Secretary of State when a claim for—

(a) income support [[26], employment and support allowance] or income-based jobseeker's allowance is made and a sum in respect of mortgage interest is to be brought into account in determining the applicable amount; or

(b) state pension credit is made and a sum in respect of housing costs is applicable in the claimant's case in accordance with regulation 6(6)(c) of the State Pension Credit Regulations.]

(3) [[12]Subject to sub-paragraph (4),] the information referred to in heads (d) and (e) of sub-paragraph (1) shall be provided at the request of the Secretary of State—

(a) when a claim for income support [[26], employment and support allowance] [[17] state pension credit] [[8]or income-based jobseeker's allowance] ceases to be paid to a relevant beneficiary; and

(b) once every 12 months notwithstanding that, in relation to head (d), the information may already have been provided during the period of 12 months preceding the date of the Secretary of State's request.

[[12](4) Where a claimant or his partner is a person to whom either paragraph 1A of Schedule 3 to the Income Support (General) Regulations 1987 (housing costs) [[26], paragraph 3 of schedule 6 to the Employment and Support Allowance Regulation (housing costs)] or paragraph 1A of Schedule 2 to the Jobseeker's Allowance Regulations 1996 (housing costs) refers, the information to which sub-paragraphs (2) and (3)(b) refer shall be provided at the request of the Secretary of State on the anniversary of the date on which the housing costs in respect of mortgage interest were first brought into account in determining the applicable amount of the person concerned.]

Recovery of sums wrongly paid

2.271 **11.**—(1) Where sums have been paid to a qualifying lender under regulation 34A which ought not to have been paid for one or both of the reasons mentioned in sub-paragraph (2) of this paragraph, the qualifying lender shall, at the request of the Secretary of State, repay the sum overpaid.

(2) The reasons referred to in sub-paragraph (1) of this paragraph are—

(a) that—

(i) the rate at which the borrower pays mortgage interest has been reduced [[5] or the rate [18 determined in accordance with] paragraph 12 of Schedule 3 to the Income Support Regulations [8or, as the case may be, paragraph 11 of Schedule 2 to the Jobseeker's Allowance Regulations] [26 or paragraph 13 of Schedule 6 to the Employment and Support Allowance Regulation] (standard rate) has been reduced] or the amount outstanding on the loan has been reduced, and

(ii) as a result of this reduction the applicable amount of the relevant beneficiary has also been reduced, but

(iii) no corresponding reduction was made to the specified part; or

(b) subject to paragraph (3), that the relevant beneficiary has ceased to be entitled to any relevant benefits.

(3) A qualifying lender shall only repay sums which ought not to have been paid for the reason mentioned in sub-paragraph (2)(b) of this paragraph if the Secretary of State has requested that lender to repay the sums within a period of 4 weeks starting with the last day on which the relevant beneficiary was entitled to any relevant benefits.]

AMENDMENTS

1. The Social Security (Claims and Payments) Amendment Regulations 1992 (SI 1992/1026) reg.6 and Sch. (May 25, 1992).

2. The Social Security (Claims and Payments) Amendment (No.3) Regulations 1993 (SI 1993/2113) reg.3 (September 27, 1993).

3. The Social Security (Claims and Payments) Amendment (No.3) Regulations 1994 (SI 1994/2944) reg.2 (April 1, 1995).

4. The Social Security (Claims and Payments) Amendment (No.2) Regulations 1994 (SI 1994/2943) reg.16 (April 13, 1995).

5. The Social Security (Income Support and Claims and Payments) Amendment Regulations 1995 (SI 1995/1613) reg.3 and Sch.2 (October 2, 1995).

6. The Social Security (Claims and Payments) Amendment (No.2) Amendment Regulations 1996 (SI 1996/2988) reg.2 (April 1, 1997).

7. The Social Security (Claims and Payments etc.) Amendment Regulations 1996 (SI 1996/672) reg.2(8) (April 4, 1996).

8. The Social Security (Claims and Payments) (Jobseeker's Allowance Consequential Amendments) Regulations 1996 (SI 1996/1460) reg.2(27) (October 7, 1996).

9. The Social Security and Child Support (Miscellaneous Amendments) Regulations 1997 (SI 1997/827) reg.7(3) (April 7, 1997).

10. The Social Security (Child Maintenance Bonus) Regulations 1996 (SI 1996/3195) reg.16(2) (April 7, 1997).

11. The Social Security (Miscellaneous Amendments) Regulations 1997 (SI 1997/454) reg.8(10) (April 6, 1997).

12. The Social Security (Miscellaneous Amendments) (No.4) Regulations 1997 (SI 1997/2305) reg.5 (October 22, 1997).

13. The Social Security (Claims and Payments) Amendment Regulations 2002 (SI 2002/355) reg.2 (April 1, 2002).

14. The Social Security (Claims and Payments) Amendment Regulations 2000 (SI 2000/1366) reg.2, (June 14, 2000).

15. The Social security (Miscellaneous Amendments) Regulations 2001 (SI 2001/488) reg.11 (April 9, 2001).

16. Social Security (Claims and Payments and Miscellaneous Amendments) (No.2) Regulations 2002 (SI 2002/2441) reg.13 (October 23, 2002).

17. The Social Security (Claims and Payments) Amendment Regulations 2004 (SI 2004/576) (April 12, 2004 or first benefit pay day thereafter).

18. Social Security (Housing Costs Amendments) Regulations 2004 (SI 2004/2825) reg.3(b) (November 28, 2004).

19. Social Security (Claims and Payments) Amendment (No.2) Regulations 2005 (SI 2005/777) reg.4 (April 11, 2005).

20. The Social Security (Claims and Payments) Regulations 2006 (SI 2006/551) (April 1, 2006).

21. The Social Security (Housing Costs Amendments) Regulations 2004 (SI 2004/2825) (November 28, 2005).

22. The Social Security (Miscellaneous Amendments) (No.4) Regulations 2006, (SI 2006/2378) (October 1, 2006).
23. The State Pension Credit (Consequential, Transitional and Miscellaneous Provisions) (No. 2) Regulations 2002 (SI 2002/3197) (April 7, 2003).
24. The Social Security (Miscellaneous Amendments) Regulations 2009 (SI 2009/583) reg.3 (April 1, 2009).
25. The Social Security (Housing Costs and Miscellaneous Amendments) Regulations 2007 (SI 2007/3183) (December 17, 2007).
26. The Employment and Support Allowance (Consequential provisions) (No.2) Regulations 2008 (SI 2008/1554) reg.27 (October 27, 2008).
27. The Social Security (Miscellaneous Amendments) Regulations 2010 (SI 2010/510) reg.3(8) (April 1, 2010).
28. The Social Security (Claims and Payments) Amendment Regulations 2010 (SI 2010/796) reg.2 (April 8, 2010).
29. Housing and Regenerations Act 2008 (Consequential Provisions) (No. 2) (Order 2010) (SI 2010/671) art.4 and Sch.1 (April 1, 2010).
30. Social Security (Miscellaneous Amendments) (No. 5) Regulations 2010 (SI 2010/2429) reg.3 (November 1, 2010).
31. The Social Security (Claims and Payments) Amendment Regulations 2011 (SI 2011/679) reg.2 (April 1, 2011).
32. The Social Security (Miscellaneous Amendments) Regulations 2011 (SI 2011/674) reg.4 (April 1 *or* April 4, 2011).
33. The Localism Act 2011 (Regulation of Social Housing) (Consequential Provisions) Order 2012 (SI 2012/641) reg.2(3) (April 1, 2012).
34. The Localism Act 2011 (Housing and Regeneration Functions in Greater London) (Consequential, Transitional and Saving Provisions) (No. 2) Order 2012 (SI 2012/702) art.3 and Sch.1 para.6 (April 1, 2012).
35. The Social Security (Claims and Payments) Amendment Regulations 2013 (SI 2013/456) reg.2 (April 1, 2013).
36. The Social Security (Fees Payable to Qualifying Lenders) (Amendment) Regulations 2014 (SI 2014/485) reg.2 (April 1, 2014).
37. The Pensions Act 2014 (Consequential, Supplementary and Incidental Amendments) Order 2015 (SI 2015/1985) art.9(19) (April 6, 2016).
38. The Social Security (Fees Payable by Qualifying Lenders) (Amendment) Regulations 2017 (SI 2017/270) reg.2 (April 1, 2017).

DEFINITIONS

"instrument for benefit payment"—see reg.2(1).
"jobseeker's allowance"—*ibid.*
"mortgage interest"—see Administration Act s.15A(4).
"qualifying lender"—see Administration Act s.15A(3).
"relevant beneficiary"—see Administration Act s.15A(1).

GENERAL NOTE

2.272 Paragraph 11 only authorises recovery of overpaid interest in the circumstances specified in sub-paras (2) and (3).

In previous editions of this book it was suggested that it was not clear who decides that the interest has been overpaid, and that it was certainly arguable that this is the type of decision that should be made by an adjudication officer, now decision maker. *CIS 288/1994* and *CSIS 98/1994* hold that any decision regarding the recovery of any overpayment of mortgage interest from a qualifying lender is a matter for the Secretary of State, not the adjudication officer. The mortgage interest payment provisions are outside the scope of s.71 of the Administration Act (*CSIS 98/1994*). But in *CIS 5206/1995* the Commissioner reaches the opposite conclusion. He points out that under s.20 of the Administration Act all questions arising on claims or awards of benefit are to be determined by adjudication officers, unless reserved to the Secretary of State (or other bodies). The question of whether the Secretary of State was *entitled to* recover a payment under para.11 (which required consideration of whether the conditions in para.11(2) were satisifed and also required calculation of the amount of the overpayment) was not reserved by para.11 (or any other provision) to the Secretary of State. It therefore fell to be determined by an adjudication officer. Once it had been determined that an overpayment was recoverable, the Secretary of State then had the discretion as to whether to request the lender to repay the sum to him. The process of adjudication was thus the same as that under s.71 of the Act, even though the circumstances in which recovery could be sought were different. Furthermore, where any question of recovery under para.11 arose, the claimant's award must first be reviewed and revised under s.25 (as had been accepted by the Court of Appeal in *Golding*, see below). If not, the Secretary of State would be bound to pay any overpayment recovered from the lender to the claimant, since the money recovered represented part of the benefit due to the claimant. There is thus a conflict between these decisions but *CIS 5206/1995* is cogently argued and it is suggested that it is to be preferred.

Note also that under para.3(1) the amount that will be paid to the qualifying lender by the Secretary of State under reg.34A (the "specified part") is defined by reference to the amount of mortgage interest met in the income support or JSA assessment. Thus, if the claimant disputes the amount that has been awarded for mortgage interest, or maintains that there are no grounds for reviewing the amount of an existing award, he will have a right of appeal to a tribunal in the normal way.

In *R. v Secretary of State for Social Security Ex p. Golding, The Times*, March 15, 2.273
1996, there had been an overpayment of mortgage interest because the claimant's interest rate had reduced. Recovery of the overpayment was implemented by withholding current payments due to the claimant's building society. Brooke J. accepted the claimant's contention that the effect of sub-para.(2)(iii) was that the Secretary of State could only recover an overpayment where an adjudication officer had decided under sub-para.(2)(ii) that a claimant's applicable amount should be reduced but the amount paid to the lender had not changed. Thus the Secretary of State could not recover the overpayment from the lender under para.11 in respect of the period before the adjudication officer's decision. Paragraph 11 only applied to overpayments made after that decision (i.e. as a result of the decision not being implemented). The result of this decision would have been that in effect recovery of any overpayment would be governed by s.71 of the Administration Act (since it would normally be the period between the reduction in the interest rate and the adjudication officer's review decision that would be in issue, assuming the adjudication officer's decision was implemented promptly).

The Court of Appeal on July 1, 1996 reversed Brooke J.'s decision. It was held that in sub-para.(2)(ii), the applicable amount means the amount as determined by the adjudication officer's assessment current at the date when the question is asked. Thus, once there had been a review with retrospective effect of Mr Golding's entitlement to take account of the reduction in interest rates, there was a reduction for that retrospective period in his applicable amount, so that sub-para.(2)(ii) was met. Sub-paragraph (2)(iii) was also met, because the "specified part" actually paid to the lender in that past period could not be reduced. Therefore the overpayment was repayable by the lender. The Court of Appeal rejected Mr Golding's argument that the condition in sub-para.(1) that the sums "ought not to have been paid" was not met, because the sums were paid under the current adjudication officer's assessment. The provisions were to be interpreted so as to be consistent with the clear statutory intention of dealing with the built-in problem under the direct payment scheme of annual retrospective notification of interest rate changes under para.10. Note the circumstances in which there can be no review on a reduction in interest rates where the claimant's liability remains constant (Adjudication Regulations reg.63(7)).

The Court of Appeal did express concern over the method of recovery adopted by the Secretary of State, who had not asked the lender to repay the overpayment, but had made deductions from the amounts of mortgage interest currently being paid direct to the lender. The concern was that that might put the claimant into arrears. The Secretary of State accepted that he could only use the set-off method if it did not adversely affect the position of the claimant. The Court of Appeal considered that that would only be so if each deduction was accompanied in the lender's accounting system by a corresponding credit to the claimant's interest account. The Department has apparently carried out a review of the arrangements for recovery of overpayments from lenders.

2.274 It should be noted that para.11 only applies where the overpayment has occurred for the reasons specified in sub-para.(2) and not, for example, where it is due to an incorrect amount of capital being taken into account.

Until April 1997, deductions could be made from a claimant's benefit in respect of mortgage interest arrears under para.3(5) (the April 1996 rate was £2.40). This is no longer possible if the lender is covered by the mortgage payments direct scheme. *CIS 15146/1996* holds that it was for the adjudication officer to decide whether such deductions were to be made and that a decision to alter the amount of a deduction had to be made by way of review, as this was not one of the up-rating changes which took effect automatically under s.159 of the Act without the need for a review decision. Furthermore, it was necessary to investigate whether there were in fact mortgage arrears, as the existence of arrears had to be proved in order to justify the deduction (see *R(IS) 14/95* which had adopted the same approach in relation to deductions under para.5 of Sch.9). Adjudication officers and tribunals were not limited to determining whether there was sufficient income support in payment to sustain the direct payment.

SCHEDULE 9B

Deductions from Benefit in Respect of Child Support Maintenance and Payment to Persons with Care

Interpretation

2.275 **1.** In this Schedule—

"the Act" means the Child Support Act 1991,

"beneficiary" means a person who has been awarded a specified benefit and includes each member of a joint-claim couple awarded joint-claim jobseeker's allowance,

[7 "fee" means any collection fee under Part 3 of the Child Support Fees Regulations 2014 which is payable by the non-resident parent,]

"maintenance" [2, except in paragraph 3,] means maintenance which a non-resident parent is liable to pay under the Act at a flat rate of child support maintenance (or would be so liable but for a variation having been agreed to), and that rate applies (or would have applied) because he falls within paragraph 4(1)(b) or (c) or 4(2) of Schedule 1 to the Act, and includes such maintenance payable at a transitional rate in accordance with Regulations made under section 29(3)(a) of the Child Support, Pensions and Social Security Act 2000,

"specified benefit" means either a benefit, pension or allowance mentioned in section 5(2) of the Social Security Administration Act 1992 and which is prescribed for the purpose of paragraph 4(1)(b) or (c) of Schedule 1 to the Act or a war disablement pension or a war widow's pension within the meaning of section 150(2) of the Social Security Contributions and Benefits Act 1992.

Deductions

2.276 **2.**—(1) Subject to paragraphs 5 and 6, the Secretary of State may deduct from a specified benefit awarded to a beneficiary, an amount equal to the amount of maintenance [7 and any fee] which is payable by the beneficiary (or in the case of income support [3, state pension credit [4, income-based jobseekers allowance or income-related employment and support allowance] payable either by the beneficiary or his partner) and pay the amount deducted to or among the person or persons with care in discharge (in whole or in part) of the liability to pay maintenance. [7, and retain any amount deducted in discharge of any liability to pay a fee.]

(2) A deduction [7 for maintenance and fees] may only be made from one of the specified benefits in any one week.

[5 (2A) Where paragraph 5 (flat rate maintenance) of Schedule 7 (deductions from benefit in respect of child support maintenance and payment to persons with care) to the 2013 Regulations applies, the Secretary of State shall not make deductions under paragraphs 5 and 6 of this Schedule, unless the amount of "specified benefit" within the meaning of paragraph 1 of Schedule 7 to the 2013 Regulations is insufficient to meet the deduction under paragraph 5 of that Schedule.]

(3) No deduction may be made unless the amount of the relevant specified benefit is not less than the total of the amounts to be deducted under this Schedule plus 10 pence.

Arrears

3.—(1) Except where income support [3, state pension credit] [4, income-based jobseekers allowance or income-related employment and support allowance] is payable to the beneficiary or his partner, the Secretary of State may deduct the sum of [7 £1.20] per week from a specified benefit which the beneficiary has been awarded and, subject to sub-paragraph (2), pay the amount deducted to or among the person or persons with care in discharge (in whole or in part) of the beneficiary's liability to pay arrears of maintenance [7, and retain any amount deducted in discharge of any liability to pay a fee.]. 2.277

(2) Deductions made under sub-paragraph (1) may be retained by the Secretary of State in the circumstances set out in regulation 8 of the Child Support (Arrears, Interest and Adjustment of Maintenance Assessments) Regulations 1992.

[2 (3) In sub-paragraph (1) "maintenance" means child support maintenance as defined by section 3(6) of the Act—

(a) before the amendment of the definition of such maintenance by section 1(2)(a) of the Child Support, Pensions and Social Security Act 2000;
(b) after the amendment of the definition; or
(c) both before and after the amendment of the definition,

and includes maintenance payable at a transitional rate in accordance with regulations made under section 29(3)(a) of that Act.]

Apportionment

4. Where maintenance is payable to more than one person with care, the amount deducted [7 in respect of maintenance] shall be apportioned between the persons with care in accordance with paragraphs 6, 7 and 8 of Schedule 1 to the Act. 2.278

Flat rate maintenance

5.—(1) This sub-paragraph applies where the beneficiary and his partner are each liable to pay maintenance at a flat rate in accordance with paragraph 4(2) of Schedule 1 to the Act and either of them has been awarded income support [3, state pension credit] [4, income-based jobseekers allowance or income-related employment and support allowance]. 2.279

(2) Where sub-paragraph (1) applies, an amount not exceeding [6 the flat rate of maintenance] [7 and any fee] may be deducted in respect of the sum of both partners' liability to pay maintenance [7 and any fee], in the proportions described in regulation 4(3) of the Child Support (Maintenance Calculations and Special Cases) Regulations 2000 [6 or regulation 44(3) of the Child Support Maitenance Calculation Regulation 2012] and shall be paid in discharge (in whole or in part) of the respective liabilities to pay maintenance [7 or retained in discharge of any liability to pay a fee.].

Flat rate maintenance (polygamous marriage)

6.—(1) This sub-paragraph applies where two or more members of a polygamous marriage are each liable to pay maintenance at a flat rate in accordance with paragraph 4(2) of Schedule 1 to the Act and any member of the polygamous marriage has been awarded income support [3, state pension credit] [4, income-based jobseekers allowance or income-related employment and support allowance]. 2.280

(2) Where sub-paragraph (1) applies, an amount not exceeding [6 the flat rate of maintenance] [7 and any fee] may be deducted in respect of the sum of all the members' liability to pay maintenance [7 , and any fee], in the proportions described in regulation 4(3) of the Child Support (Maintenance Calculations and Special Cases) Regulations 2000 [6 or regulation 44(3) of the Child Support Maintenance Calculation Regulation 2012] and shall be paid in discharge (in whole or in part) of the respective liabilities to pay maintenance [7 or retained in discharge of any liability to pay a fee.].

(3) In this paragraph "polygamous marriage" means any marriage during the subsistence of which a party to it is married to more than one person and the ceremony of marriage took place under the law of a country which permits polygamy.

Notice

2.281 **7.** When the Secretary of State commences making deductions, he shall notify the beneficiary in writing of the amount and frequency of the deduction and the benefit from which the deduction is made and shall give further such notice when there is a change to any of the particulars specified in the notice.

General

2.282 **8.** A deduction made in accordance with this Schedule is a deduction by way of recovery for the purposes of regulation 40(3) of the Income Support (General) Regulations 1987 [[4], regulation 104 of the Employment and Support Allowance Regulation] and regulation 103(3) of the Jobseeker's Allowance Regulations 1996."

AMENDMENTS

1. The Social Security (Claims and Payments) Amendment Regulations 2001 (SI 2001/18) reg.2 (January 31, 2001).
2. Social Security (Claims and Payments) Amendment (No.2) Regulations 2002 (SI 2002/1950) reg.3 (entry into force tied to entry into force of s.43 of the Child Support Act 1991 as substituted by s.21 of the Child Support, Pensions and Social Security Act 2000: March 3, 2003 in relation to certain cases, see SI 2003/192; date to be appointed for remaining cases: see Child Support, Pensions and Social Security Act 2000 s.86(2)).
3. State Pension Credit (Consequential, Transitional and Miscellaneous Provisions) Regulations 2002, SI 2002/3019 reg.14 (April 7, 2003).
4. The Employment and Support Allowance (Consequential provisions) (No.2) Regulations 2008 (SI 2008/1554) reg.28 (October 27, 2008).
5. The Social Security (Miscellaneous Amendments) (No. 2) Regulations 2013 (SI 2013/1508) reg.2(4) (July 29, 2013).
6. The Child Support and Claims and Payments (Miscellaneous amendments and Change to the Minimum Amount of Liability) Regulations 2013 (SI 2013/1654) reg.3 (July 29, 2013).
7. The Child Support Fees Regulations 2014 (SI 2014/612) reg.14 (August 11, 2014).

GENERAL NOTE

2.283 This schedule empowers the Secretary of State to deduct an amount in respect of certain child support maintenance liabilities from certain social security benefits where the person in receipt of the benefit is a non-resident parent. That sum is than paid to the person with the care of the child.

Regulation 3 of the amending regulations (SI 2001/18) contain a transitional provision as follows:

> "No deductions shall be made under paragraph 7A or 7B of Schedule 9 to the Claims and Payments Regulations in respect of maintenance to which Schedule 9B applies."

See annotations to reg.35 for comment on the precedence to be accorded to child support payments and the relationship between Sch.9 and Sch.9B.

[[1] SCHEDULE 9ZC **Regulations 4ZC and 32ZA**

ELECTRONIC COMMUNICATION

PART 1

INTRODUCTION

Interpretation

2.284 **1.** In this Schedule "official computer system" means a computer system maintained by or on behalf of the Secretary of State for the sending, receiving, processing or storing of any claim, certificate, notice, information or evidence.

PART 2

ELECTRONIC COMMUNICATION—GENERAL PROVISIONS

Conditions for the use of electronic communication

[6 "(1) The Secretary of State may use an electronic communication in connection with claims for, and awards of— 2.285

(a) carer's allowance;
(b) attendance allowance;
[7 (ba) bereavement support payment;]
(c) disability living allowance;
(d) graduated retirement benefit;
(e) a jobseeker's allowance;
(f) a retirement pension;
(g) state pension under Part 1 of the Pensions Act 2014;
(h) shared additional pension;
(i) industrial injuries benefit;
(j) an employment and support allowance.

(1A) The Secretary of State may use an electronic communication in connection with awards of—

(a) incapacity benefit;
(b) income support;
(c) state pension credit.]

(2) A person other than the Secretary of State may use an electronic communication in connection with the matters referred to in [6 sub-paragraphs (1) and (1A)] if the conditions specified in sub-paragraphs (3) to (6) are satisfied.

(3) The first condition is that the person is for the time being permitted to use an electronic communication by an authorisation given by means of a direction of the Secretary of State.

(4) The second condition is that the person uses an approved method of—

(a) authenticating the identity of the sender of the communication;
(b) electronic communication;
(c) authenticating any claim, certificate, notice, information or evidence delivered by means of an electronic communication; and
(d) subject to sub-paragraph (7), submitting to the Secretary of State any claim, certificate, notice, information or evidence.

(5) The third condition is that any claim, certificate, notice, information or evidence sent by means of an electronic communication is in a form approved for the purpose of this Schedule.

(6) The fourth condition is that the person maintains such records in written or electronic form as may be specified in a direction given by the Secretary of State.

(7) Where the person uses any method other than the method approved by the Secretary of State, of submitting any claim, certificate, notice, information or evidence, that claim, certificate, notice, information or evidence shall be treated as not having been submitted.

(8) In this paragraph "approved" means approved by means of a direction given by the Secretary of State for the purposes of this Schedule.

Use of intermediaries

3. The Secretary of State may use intermediaries in connection with— 2.286

(a) the delivery of any claim, certificate, notice, information or evidence by means of an electronic communication; and
(b) the authentication or security of anything transmitted by such means,

and may require other persons to use intermediaries in connection with those matters.

PART 3

ELECTRONIC COMMUNICATION—EVIDENTAL PROVISIONS

Effect of delivering information by means of electronic communication

4.—(1) Any claim, certificate, notice, information or evidence which is delivered by means of an electronic communication shall be treated as having been delivered, in the manner or form required by any provision of these Regulations, on the day the conditions imposed— 2.287

(a) by this Schedule; and

(b) by or under an applicable enactment,

are satisfied.

(2) The Secretary of State may, by a direction, determine that any claim, certificate, notice, information or evidence is to be treated as delivered on a different day (whether earlier or later) from the day provided for in sub-paragraph (1).

(3) Information shall not be taken to have been delivered to an official computer system by means of an electronic communication unless it is accepted by the system to which it is delivered.

Proof of identify of sender or recipient of information

2.288 **5.** If it is necessary to prove, for the purpose of any legal proceedings, the identity of—

(a) the sender of any claim, certificate, notice, information or evidence delivered by means of an electronic communication to an official computer system; or

(b) the recipient of any such claim, certificate, notice, information or evidence delivered by means of an electronic communication from an official computer system,

the sender or recipient, as the case may be, shall be presumed to be the person whose name is recorded as such on that official computer system.

Proof of delivery of information

2.289 **6.**—(1) If it is necessary to prove, for the purpose of any legal proceedings, that the use of an electronic communication has resulted in the delivery of any claim, certificate, notice, information or evidence this shall be presumed to have been the case where—

(a) any such claim, certificate, notice, information or evidence has been delivered to the Secretary of State, if the delivery of that claim, certificate, notice, information or evidence has been recorded on an official computer system; or

(b) any such certificate, notice, information or evidence has been delivered by the Secretary of State, if the delivery of that certificate, notice, information or evidence has been recorded on an official computer system.

(2) If it is necessary to prove, for the purpose of any legal proceedings, that the use of an electronic communication has resulted in the delivery of any such claim, certificate, notice, information or evidence, this shall be presumed not to be the case, if that claim, certificate, notice, information or evidence delivered to the Secretary of State has not been recorded on an official computer system.

(3) If it is necessary to prove, for the purpose of any legal proceedings, when any such claim, certificate, notice, information or evidence sent by means of an electronic communication has been received, the time and date of receipt shall be presumed to be that recorded on an official computer system.

Proof of content of information

2.290 **7.** If it is necessary to prove, for the purpose of any legal proceedings, the content of any claim, certificate, notice, information or evidence sent by means of an electronic communication, the content shall be presumed to be that recorded on an official computer system.]

AMENDMENTS

1. The Social Security (Electronic Communications) (Carer's Allowance) Order 2003 (SI 2003/2800) reg.2 (December 1, 2003).
2. The Social Security (Electronic Communications) (Miscellaneous Benefits) Order 2005 (SI 2005/3321) (January 30, 2006).
3. The Social Security (Electronic Communications) Order 2011 (SI 2011/1498) reg.4(4) (June 20, 2011).
4. The Social Security (Electronic Communications) (No.2) Order 2011 (SI 2011/2943) (January 23, 2012).
5. The Pensions Act 2014 (Consequential, Supplementary and Incidental Amendments) Order 2015 (SI 2015/1985) art.9(20) (April 6, 2016).
6. Social Security (Claims and Payments) Amendment Regulations 2016 (SI 2016/544) reg.2 (June 15, 2016).
7. The Pensions Act 2014 (Consequential, Supplementary and Incidental Amendments) Order 2017 (SI 2017/422) art.10 (April 6, 2017).

GENERAL NOTE

For a case exploring the issues when an electronic claim goes wrong, see *CW v SSWP (JSA)* [2016] UKUT 114 discussed in the annotations to reg.4ZC at 2.63 above. 2.291

[[1] SCHEDULE 9C **Regulations 4C and 32A**

ELECTRONIC COMMUNICATION

PART 1

INTRODUCTION

Interpretation

1. In this Schedule "official computer system" means a computer system maintained by or on behalf of the Secretary of State for the– 2.292

(a) sending or receiving of any claim, certificate, notice, information or evidence; or

(b) processing or storing of any claim, certificate, notice, information or evidence.

PART 2

ELECTRONIC COMMUNICATION—GENERAL PROVISIONS

Conditions for the use of electronic communication

2.—(1) The Secretary of State may use an electronic communication in connection with claims for, and awards of, child benefit and elections under regulation 6A of the Social Security (Guardian's Allowances) Regulations 1975 (prescribed manner of making an election). 2.293

(2) A person other than the Secretary of State may use an electronic communication in connection with the matters referred to in sub-paragraph (1) if the conditions specified in sub-paragraphs (3) to (6) are satisfied.

(3) The first condition is that the person is for the time being permitted to use an electronic communication by an authorisation given by means of a direction of the Secretary of State.

(4) The second condition is that the person uses an approved method of–

(a) authenticating the identity of the sender of the communication;

(b) electronic communication;

(c) authenticating any claim, certificate, notice, information or evidence delivered by means of an electronic communication; and

(d) subject to sub-paragraph (7), submitting to the Secretary of State any claim, certificate, notice, information or evidence.

(5) The third condition is that any claim, certificate, notice, information or evidence sent by means of an electronic communication is in a form approved for the purpose of this Schedule.

(6) The fourth condition is that the person maintains such records in written or electronic form as may be specified in a direction given by the Secretary of State.

(7) Where the person uses any method other than the method approved by the Secretary of State, of submitting any claim, certificate, notice, information or evidence, that claim, certificate, notice, information or evidence shall be treated as not having been submitted.

(8) In this paragraph "approved" means approved by means of a direction given by the Secretary of State for the purposes of this Schedule.

Use of intermediaries

3. The Secretary of State may use intermediaries in connection with– 2.294

(a) the delivery of any claim, certificate, notice, information or evidence by means of an electronic communication; and

(b) the authentication or security of anything transmitted by such means, and may require other persons to use intermediaries in connection with those matters.

PART 3

ELECTRONIC COMMUNICATION—EVIDENTIAL PROVISIONS

Effect of delivering information by means of electronic communication

2.295 4. —(1) Any claim, certificate, notice, information or evidence which is delivered by means of an electronic communication shall be treated as having been delivered, in the manner or form required by any provision of these Regulations, on the day the conditions imposed–

(a) by this Schedule; and

(b) by or under an applicable enactment,

are satisfied.

(2) The Secretary of State may, by a direction, determine that any claim, certificate, notice, information or evidence is to be treated as delivered on a different day (whether earlier or later) from the day provided for in sub-paragraph (1).

Proof of identity of sender or recipient of information

2.296 5. If it is necessary to prove, for the purpose of any legal proceedings, the identity of–

(a) the sender of any claim, certificate, notice, information or evidence delivered by means of an electronic communication to an official computer system; or

(b) the recipient of any such claim, certificate, notice, information or evidence delivered by means of an electronic communication from an official computer system, the sender or recipient, as the case may be, shall be presumed to be the person recorded as such on that official computer system.

Proof of delivery of information

2.297 6. —(1) If it is necessary to prove, for the purpose of any legal proceedings, that the use of an electronic communication has resulted in the delivery of any claim, certificate, notice, information or evidence this shall be presumed to have been the case where–

(a) any such claim, certificate, notice, information or evidence has been delivered to the Secretary of State, if the delivery of that claim, certificate, notice, information or evidence has been recorded on an official computer system; or

(b) any such certificate, notice, information or evidence has been delivered by the Secretary of State, if the delivery of that certificate, notice, information or evidence has been recorded on an official computer system.

(2) If it is necessary to prove, for the purpose of any legal proceedings, that the use of an electronic communication has resulted in the delivery of any such claim, certificate, notice, information or evidence, this shall be presumed not to be the case, if that claim, certificate, notice, information or evidence delivered to the Secretary of State has not been recorded on an official computer system.

(3) If it is necessary to prove, for the purpose of any legal proceedings, when any such claim, certificate, notice, information or evidence sent by means of an electronic communication has been received, the time of receipt shall be presumed to be that recorded on an official computer system.

Proof of content of information

2.298 7. If it is necessary to prove, for the purpose of any legal proceedings, the content of any claim, certificate, notice, information or evidence sent by means of an electronic communication, the content shall be presumed to be that recorded on an official computer system.]

AMENDMENT

2.299 1. Inserted by The Social Security (Electronic Communications) (Child Benefit) Order 2002 (SI 2002/1789) (October 28, 2002).

The Universal Credit, Personal Independence Payment, Jobseeker's Allowance and Employment and Support Allowance (Claims and Payments) Regulations 2013

(SI 2013/380)

COMMENCEMENT: APRIL 8, 2013—FOR THE PURPOSE OF PERSONAL INDEPENDENCE PAYMENT

COMMENCEMENT: APRIL 2, 2013—FOR THE PURPOSES OF UNIVERSAL CREDIT, JOBSEEKER'S ALLOWANCE AND EMPLOYMENT AND SUPPORT ALLOWANCE

PART 1

GENERAL

1. Citation and commencement 2.300
2. Interpretation
3. Use of electronic communications
4. Consequential amendments
5. Disapplication of section 1(1A) of the Administration Act

PART 2

CLAIMS

6. *Revoked.*
7. Claims not required for entitlement to an employment and support allowance in certain cases
8. Making a claim for universal credit
9. Claims for universal credit by members of a couple
10. Date of claim for universal credit
11. Making a claim for personal independence payment
12. Date of claim for personal independence payment
13. Making a claim for an employment and support allowance by telephone
14. Date of claim for an employment and support allowance where claim made by telephone
15. Making a claim for an employment and support allowance in writing
16. Date of claim for an employment and support allowance where claim made in writing
17. Claim for an employment and support allowance where no entitlement to statutory sick pay
18. Special provision where it is certified that a woman is expected to be confined or where she has been confined
19. Making a claim for a jobseeker's allowance: attendance at an appropriate office
20. Date of claim where a person claiming a jobseeker's allowance is required to attend at an appropriate office
21. Making a claim for a jobseeker's allowance in writing
22. Date of claim for a jobseeker's allowance where claim made in writing
23. Making a claim for a jobseeker's allowance by telephone

Part 3

Evidence, information and notification of changes of circumstances

Part 4

Payments

PART 5

THIRD PARTIES

PART 6

MOBILITY COMPONENT OF PERSONAL INDEPENDENCE PAYMENT

SCHEDULES

The Secretary of State, in exercise of the powers conferred upon him by the provisions set out in Schedule 1 to these Regulations, makes the following Regulations.

In accordance with section 172(1)(**1**) of the Social Security Administration Act 1992, the Secretary of State has referred the proposals for these Regulations to the Social Security Advisory Committee.

The Secretary of State has consulted with organisations representing qualifying lenders likely to be affected by the fee specified in paragraph 9(2) of Schedule 5 to the Regulations (direct payment to lender of deductions in respect of interest on secured loans)(**2**).

In accordance with section 176(2)(b) of the Social Security Administration Act 1992 and in so far as these Regulations relate to housing benefit, the Secretary of State has obtained the agreement of organisations appearing to him to be representative of the authorities concerned that proposals in respect of these Regulations should not be referred to them.

PART 1

GENERAL

Citation and commencement

2.301 **1.—**(1) These Regulations may be cited as the Universal Credit, Personal Independence Payment, Jobseeker's Allowance and Employment and Support Allowance (Claims and Payments) Regulations 2013.

(2) For the purpose of personal independence payment these Regulations come into force on 8th April 2013.

(3) For the purposes of universal credit, jobseeker's allowance and employment and support allowance these Regulations come into force on 29th April 2013.

GENERAL NOTE

2.302 It is particularly important to note the commencement provisions in relation to the matters covered by these regulations, especially when considering benefits other than universal credit. The provisions affecting a personal independence payment entered into force on April 8, 2013, while those relating to universal credit and new-style employment and support allowance and jobseeker's allowance entered into force on April 29, 2013. Care must be taken to apply the right regulations to old-style and new-style employment and support allowance and jobseeker's allowance.

In particular, the new regulations signal the move to online claiming of benefit as the primary channel of communication between the Department and a claimant.

Interpretation

2.303 This section has no associated Explanatory Memorandum

2. —In these Regulations—

"the 1991 Act" means the Child Support Act 1991;

"the 2012 Act" means the Welfare Reform Act 2012;

"the Administration Act" means the Social Security Administration Act 1992;

"the Contributions and Benefits Act" means the Social Security Contributions and Benefits Act 1992;

"the Jobseeker's Allowance Regulations" means the Jobseeker's Allowance Regulations 2013;

"the Personal Independence Payment Regulations" means the Social Security (Personal Independence Payment) Regulations 2013;

"the Universal Credit Regulations" means the Universal Credit Regulations 2013;

"appropriate office" means—

(a) an office of the Department for Work and Pensions or any other place designated by the Secretary of State in relation to any case or class of case as a place to, or at which, any claim, notice, document, evidence or other information may be sent, delivered or received for the purposes of these Regulations and includes a postal address specified by the Secretary of State for that purpose; or

(b) in the case of a person who is authorised or required by these Regulations to use an electronic communication for any purpose, an address to which such communications may be sent in accordance with Schedule 2;

"assessment period" has the meaning given by regulation 21 of the Universal Credit Regulations;

"attendance allowance" means an allowance payable by virtue of section 64 of the Contributions and Benefits Act;

"benefit", except in regulation 60 and Schedules 5 and 6, means universal credit, personal independence payment, a jobseeker's allowance or an employment and support allowance;

"child" has the meaning given by section 40 of the 2012 Act;

"claimant" in relation to—

(a) universal credit, has the meaning given by section 40 of the 2012 Act;

(b) personal independence payment, means any person who is a claimant for the purposes of regulations made under Part 4 (personal independence payment) of that Act;

(c) a jobseeker's allowance, has the meaning given by section 35(1) of the Jobseekers Act 1995; and

(d) an employment and support allowance, has the meaning given by section 24(1) of the Welfare Reform 2007 Act;

"couple" has the meaning given by section 39 of the 2012 Act;

"disability living allowance" means an allowance payable by virtue of section 71 of the Contributions and Benefits Act;

"earned income" has the meaning given by regulation 52 of the Universal Credit Regulations;

"electronic communication" has the meaning given by section 15(1) of the Electronic Communications Act 2000;

"employment and support allowance" means an allowance under Part 1 of the Welfare Reform Act 2007 as amended by the provisions of Schedule 3, and Part 1 of Schedule 14, to the 2012 Act that remove references to an income-related allowance;

"jobseeker's allowance" means an allowance under the Jobseekers Act 1995 as amended by the provisions of Part 1 of Schedule 14 to the 2012 Act that remove references to an income-based allowance;

"limited capability for work" has the meaning given by section 1(4) of the Welfare Reform Act 2007;

"local authority" has the meaning given by section 191 of the Administration Act;

"maternity allowance" means an allowance payable by virtue of section 35 of the Contributions and Benefits Act;

"official computer system" means a computer system maintained by or on behalf of the Secretary of State to—

(a) send or receive any claim or information; or

(b) process or store any claim or information;

"partner" means one of a couple;

"personal independence payment" means the allowance under Part 4 of the 2012 Act;

"qualifying young person" has the meaning given by regulation 5 of the Universal Credit Regulations;

"regular and substantial caring responsibilities for a severely disabled person" has the meaning given by regulation 30 of the Universal Credit Regulations;

"universal credit" means the benefit under Part 1 of the 2012 Act;
"writing" includes writing produced by means of electronic communications used in accordance with Schedule 2.

Use of electronic communications

2.304 **3.**—Schedule 2 makes provision as to the use of electronic communications

Consequential amendments

2.305 **4.**—Schedule 3 makes amendments to other regulations which are consequential upon these Regulations.

Disapplication of section 1(1A) of the Administration Act

2.306 **5.** Section 1(1A) of the Administration Act (requirements in respect of a national insurance number) is not to apply to a child or a qualifying young person in respect of whom universal credit is claimed.

PART 2

Claims

Claims not required for entitlement to universal credit in certain cases

2.307 **6.** [1 . . .]

Amendment

1. Revoked by the Universal Credit (Digital Service) Amendment Regulations 2014 (SI 2014/2887) reg.3(2)(a) (November 26, 2014). The revocation is subject to a saving provision in reg.5 of SI 2014/2887.

Claims not required for entitlement to an employment and support allowance in certain cases

2.308 [1 **7.**—(1) It is not to be a condition of entitlement to an employment and support allowance that a claim be made for it where—

(a) the claimant has made and is pursuing an appeal against a relevant decision of the Secretary of State, and
(b) the appeal relates to a decision to terminate or not to award an employment and support allowance for which a claim was made.

(2) In this regulation—

"appellate authority" means the First-tier Tribunal, the Upper Tribunal, the Court of Appeal, the Court of Session, or the Supreme Court; and
"relevant decision" means—

(a) a decision that embodies the first determination by the Secretary of State that the claimant does not have limited capability for work; or
(b) a decision that embodies the first determination by the Secretary of State that the claimant does not have limited capability for work since a previous determination by the Secretary of State or appellate authority that the claimant does have limited capability for work.]

AMENDMENT

1. The Employment and Support Allowance (Repeat Assessments and Pending Appeal Awards) (Amendment) Regulations 2015 (SI 2015/437) reg.6 (March 30, 2015).

Making a claim for universal credit

8.—(1) Except as provided in paragraph (2), a claim for universal credit must be made by means of an electronic communication in accordance with the provisions set out in Schedule 2 and completed in accordance with any instructions given by the Secretary of State for that purpose. 2.309

(2) A claim for universal credit may be made by telephone call to the telephone number specified by the Secretary of State if the claim falls within a class of case for which the Secretary of State accepts telephone claims or where, in any other case, the Secretary of State is willing to do so.

(3) A claim for universal credit made by means of an electronic communication in accordance with the provisions set out in Schedule 2 is defective if it is not completed in accordance with any instructions of the Secretary of State.

(4) A claim made by telephone in accordance with paragraph (2) is properly completed if the Secretary of State is provided during that call with all the information required to determine the claim and the claim is defective if not so completed.

(5) If a claim for universal credit is defective the Secretary of State must inform the claimant of the defect and of the relevant provisions of regulation 10 relating to the date of claim.

(6) The Secretary of State must treat the claim as properly made in the first instance if—

(a) in the case of a claim made by telephone, the person corrects the defect; or

(b) in the case of a claim made by means of an electronic communication, a claim completed in accordance with any instructions of the Secretary of State is received at an appropriate office,

within one month, or such longer period as the Secretary of State considers reasonable, from the date on which the claimant is first informed of the defect.

Claims for universal credit by members of a couple

9.—(1) Where a person is a member of a couple and may make a claim as a single person by virtue of regulation 3(3) (couples) of the Universal Credit Regulations, but instead makes a claim for universal credit jointly, that claim is to be treated as a claim made by that person as a single person. 2.310

(2) Where a claim for universal credit is made jointly by a member ("M1") of a polygamous marriage with another member of the polygamous marriage ("M2"), that claim is to be treated as a claim made by M1 as a single person where—

(a) M1 is not a party to an earlier marriage in the polygamous marriage, and

(b) any party to an earlier marriage is living in the same household as M1 and M2.

(3) In paragraph (2) "polygamous marriage" means a marriage during

which a party to it is married to more than one person and which took place under the laws of a country which permits polygamy.

(4) The Secretary of State may treat a claim made by members of a couple as single persons as a claim made jointly by the couple where it is determined by the Secretary of State that they are a couple.

(5) Where the Secretary of State considers that one member of a couple is unable to make a joint claim with the other member of that couple, the other member of the couple may make a claim jointly for both of them.

[2 (6) Where an award of universal credit to joint claimants is terminated because they cease to be a couple an award may be made, without a claim, to either or each one of them—

(a) as a single person; or

(b) if either of them has formed a new couple with a person who is already entitled to universal credit, jointly with that person.]

(7) Where awards of universal credit to two single claimants are terminated because they form a couple who are joint claimants, it is not to be a condition of entitlement to universal credit that the couple make a claim for it and universal credit may be awarded to them jointly.

(8) A couple who are joint claimants are to be treated as making a claim for universal credit where—

[2 (a) one of them ceased to be entitled to an award of universal credit (whether as a single person or as a member of a different couple) on the formation of that couple;] and

(b) the other member of the couple did not have an award of universal credit as a single person before formation of the couple,

[1 and the claim is to be treated as made on the day after the member of the couple mentioned in sub-paragraph (a) ceased to be entitled to universal credit.]

(9) In relation to an award which may be made by virtue of paragraph (6) or (7) without a claim being required, a claimant and every person by whom or on whose behalf, sums by way of universal credit are receivable must supply in such manner and at such times as the Secretary of State may determine such information or evidence as the Secretary of State may require in connection with the formation or dissolution of a couple.

(10) Where an award of universal credit to joint claimants is terminated because one of them has died it is not to be a condition of entitlement to universal credit that the surviving partner makes a claim for it.

AMENDMENTS

1. The Social Security (Miscellaneous Amendments) No.2) Regulations 2013 (SI 2013/1508) reg.6 (July 29, 2013).

2. The Universal Credit (Digital Service) Amendment Regulations 2014 (SI 2014/2887) reg.3 (November 26, 2014). There are savings provisions in reg.5 of SI 2014/2887.

Date of claim for universal credit

2.311 **10.**—(1) Where a claim for universal credit is made, the date on which the claim is made is—

(a) subject to sub-paragraph (b), in the case of a claim made by means of an electronic communication in accordance with regulation 8(1), the date on which the claim is received at an appropriate office;

(b) in the case of a claim made by means of an electronic communication in accordance with regulation 8(1), where the claimant receives assistance at home or at an appropriate office from the Secretary of State, or a person providing services to the Secretary of State, which is provided for the purpose of enabling that person to make a claim, the date of first notification of a need for such assistance;

(c) subject to sub-paragraph (d), in the case of a claim made by telephone in accordance with 8(2), the date on which that claim is properly completed in accordance with regulation 8(4); or

(d) where the Secretary of State is unable to accept a claim made by telephone in accordance with regulation 8(2) on the date of first notification of intention to make the claim, the date of first notification, provided a claim properly completed in accordance with regulation 8(4) is made within one month of that date,

or the first day in respect of which the claim is made if later than the above.

(2) In the case of a claim which is defective by virtue of regulation 8, the date of claim is to be the first date on which the defective claim is received or made but is treated as properly made in the first instance in accordance with regulation 8(6).

Making a claim for personal independence payment

11.—(1) A claim for personal independence payment must be made— 2.312

(a) in writing on a form authorised by the Secretary of State for that purpose and completed in accordance with the instructions on the form;

(b) by telephone call to the telephone number specified by the Secretary of State; or

(c) by receipt by the claimant of a telephone call from the Secretary of State made for the purpose of enabling a claim for personal independence payment to be made,

unless in any case or class of case the Secretary of State decides only to accept a claim made in one of the ways specified in paragraph (a), (b) or (c).

(2) In the case of a claim made in writing the claim must be sent to or received at the appropriate office.

(3) A claim for personal independence payment made in writing is defective if it is not completed in accordance with any instructions of the Secretary of State.

(4) A claim made by telephone in accordance with paragraph (1) is properly completed if the Secretary of State is provided during that call with all the information required to determine the claim and the claim is defective if not so completed.

(5) If a claim for personal independence payment is defective the Secretary of State must inform the claimant of the defect and of the relevant provisions of regulation 12 relating to the date of claim.

(6) The Secretary of State must treat the claim as properly made in the first instance if a claim completed in accordance with any instructions of the Secretary of State is received within one month, or such longer period as the Secretary of State may consider reasonable, from the date on which the claimant is first informed of the defect.

(7) Paragraph (8) applies where—

(a) a person ("P1") makes a claim for personal independence payment on behalf of another person ("P2") whom P1 asserts to be a person unable for the time being to act; and

(b) the Secretary of State makes a decision not to appoint P1 under regulation 57.

(8) The Secretary of State must treat the claim made by P1 as properly made by P2 in the first instance if a further claim made by P2 is received within one month, or such longer period as the Secretary of State may consider reasonable, from the date the Secretary of State notified the decision not to appoint P1 under regulation 57.

GENERAL NOTE

2.313 The intention is that claims will be initiated by telephone in the first instance (and the Department's publicity makes reference to this), but the Explanatory Memorandum indicates that an online service is planned for introduction in 2014. However, this regulation provides also for paper claims until such time as the Secretary of State decides to accept claims made only through a particular medium.

Date of claim for personal independence payment

2.314 **12.**—(1) Subject to paragraph (4), where a claim for personal independence payment is made in accordance with regulation 11 the date on which the claim is made is—

(a) in the case of a claim in writing made by means of an electronic communication in accordance with the provisions set out in Schedule 2, the date on which the claim is received at the appropriate office;

(b) in the case of a claim made by telephone, the date on which a claim made by telephone is properly completed; or

(c) where a person first notifies an intention to make a claim and provided that a claim made in writing produced other than by means of an electronic communication is properly completed and received at the appropriate office designated by the Secretary of State in that claimant's case within one month or such longer period as the Secretary of State considers reasonable of the date of first notification, the date of first notification,

or the first day in respect of which the claim is made if later than the above.

(2) In the case of a claim which is defective by virtue of regulation 11(3) or (4)—

(a) subject to sub-paragraph (b) and paragraph (4), the date of claim is to be the first date on which the defective claim is received or made but is treated as properly made in the first instance in accordance with regulation 11(6);

(b) the date of claim is to be the date of first notification of an intention to make a claim where a claim made by a person to whom paragraph (1)(c) applies is defective but is treated as properly made in the first instance in accordance with regulation 11(6).

(3) In the case of a claim which is treated as properly made by the claimant in accordance with regulation 11(8), the date on which the claim is made is the date on which it was received in the first instance.

(4) Where a further claim made by a person ("P2") in the circumstances set out in regulation 11(8) is defective and that further claim is treated as properly made in the first instance in accordance with regulation 11(6), the date of claim is to be the date on which the claim made by the person ("P1") whom the Secretary of State decided not to appoint under regulation 57 was received in the first instance.

(5) In a case where the Secretary of State decides not to award personal

independence payment following a claim for it being made on behalf of another expressly on the ground of terminal illness (which has the meaning given by section 82(4) of the 2012 Act), the date of claim is to be—

(a) the date that claim was made if a further claim, made in accordance with regulation 11, is received within one month, or such longer period as the Secretary of State may consider reasonable, from the date the Secretary of State notified the decision not to award personal independence payment on the ground of terminal illness; or

(b) the date that claim was made where the further claim is defective but is treated as properly made in the first instance in accordance with regulation 11(6).

Making a claim for an employment and support allowance by telephone

13.—(1) Except where the Secretary of State directs in any case or class of case that a claim must be made in writing, a claim for an employment and support allowance may be made by telephone call to the telephone number specified by the Secretary of State. 2.315

(2) Where the Secretary of State, in any particular case, directs that the person making the claim approves a written statement of the person's circumstances provided for the purpose by the Secretary of State, a telephone claim is not a valid claim unless the person complies with the direction.

(3) A claim made by telephone in accordance with paragraph (1) is properly completed if the Secretary of State is provided during that call with all the information required to determine the claim and the claim is defective if not so completed.

(4) Where a telephone claim is defective, the Secretary of State must advise the person making it of the defect and of the effect on the date of claim of the provisions of regulation 14.

(5) If the person corrects the defect so that the claim then satisfies the requirements of paragraph (3) and does so within one month, or such longer period as the Secretary of State considers reasonable, of the date the Secretary of State first drew attention to the defect, the Secretary of State must treat the claim as if it had been properly made in the first instance.

Date of claim for an employment and support allowance where claim made by telephone

14. In the case of a telephone claim, the date on which the claim is made is to be the first date on which— 2.316

(a) a claim made by telephone is properly completed;

(b) a person first notifies the Secretary of State of an intention to make a claim, provided that a claim made by telephone is properly completed within one month or such longer period as the Secretary of State considers reasonable of first notification; or

(c) a defective claim is received but is treated as properly made in the first instance in accordance with regulation 13(5),

or the first day in respect of which the claim is made if later than the above.

Making a claim for an employment and support allowance in writing

15.—(1) A claim for an employment and support allowance may be made to the Secretary of State in writing on a form authorised by the 2.317

Secretary of State for that purpose and must be completed in accordance with the instructions on the form.

(2) A written claim for an employment and support allowance, which is made on the form approved for the time being, is properly completed if completed in accordance with the instructions on the form and defective if not so completed.

(3) If a written claim is defective when first received, the Secretary of State must advise the person making it of the defect and of the effect on the date of claim of the provisions of regulation 16.

(4) If the person corrects the defect so that the claim then satisfies the requirements of paragraph (2) and does so within one month, or such longer period as the Secretary of State considers reasonable, of the date the Secretary of State first drew attention to the defect, the Secretary of State must treat the claim as if it had been properly made in the first instance.

Date of claim for an employment and support allowance where claim made in writing

2.318 **16.** In the case of a written claim for an employment and support allowance, the date on which the claim is made is to be the first date on which—

(a) a properly completed claim is received in an appropriate office;

(b) a person first notifies an intention to make a claim, provided that a properly completed claim form is received in an appropriate office within one month, or such longer period as the Secretary of State considers reasonable, of first notification; or

(c) a defective claim is received but is treated as properly made in the first instance in accordance with regulation 15(4),

or the first day in respect of which the claim is made if later than the above.

Claims for an employment and support allowance where no entitlement to statutory sick pay

2.319 **17.**—(1) Paragraph (2) applies to a claim for an employment and support allowance for a period of limited capability for work in relation to which the claimant gave the claimant's employer a notice of incapacity under regulation 7 of the Statutory Sick Pay (General) Regulations 1982 and for which the claimant has been informed in writing by the employer that there is no entitlement to statutory sick pay.

(2) A claim to which this paragraph applies is to be treated as made on the date accepted by the claimant's employer as the first day of incapacity, provided that the claimant makes the claim within the period of 3 months beginning with the day on which the claimant is informed in writing by the employer that the claimant was not entitled to statutory sick pay.

Special provisions where it is certified that a woman is expected to be confined or where she has been confined

2.320 **18.** Where, in a certificate issued or having effect as issued under the Social Security (Medical Evidence) Regulations 1976, it has been certified that it is to be expected that a woman will be confined and she makes a claim for maternity allowance in expectation of that confinement, any such claim may, unless the Secretary of State otherwise directs, be treated as a claim for an employment and support allowance, made in respect of any days in the period beginning with either—

(a) the beginning of the sixth week before the expected week of confinement; or

(b) the actual date of confinement,

whichever is the earlier, and ending in either case on the 14th day after the actual date of confinement.

(2) Where, in a certificate issued under the Social Security (Medical Evidence) Regulations 1976 it has been certified that a woman has been confined and she claims maternity allowance within three months of the date of her confinement, her claim may be treated in the alternative or in addition as a claim for an employment and support allowance for the period beginning with the date of her confinement and ending 14 days after that date.

Making a claim for a jobseeker's allowance: attendance at an appropriate office

19. A person wishing to make a claim for a jobseeker's allowance, unless the Secretary of State otherwise directs, is required to attend for the purpose of making a claim for that allowance, in person at an appropriate office or such other place, and at such time, as the Secretary of State may specify in that person's case. 2.321

Date of claim where a person claiming a jobseeker's allowance is required to attend at an appropriate office

20.—(1) Subject to regulation 29(6), where a person is required to attend in accordance with regulation 19, if the person subsequently attends for the purpose of making a claim for a jobseeker's allowance at the place and time specified by the Secretary of State and, if so requested, provides a properly completed claim form at or before the time when the person is required to attend, the claim is to be treated as made on whichever is the later of the date of first notification of intention to make that claim or the first day in respect of which the claim is made. 2.322

(2) Where a person who is required to attend in accordance with regulation 19 without good cause fails to attend at either the place or time specified in that person's case, or does not, if so requested, provide a properly completed claim form at or before the time when the person is required to attend, the claim is to be treated as made on the first day on which the person does attend at the specified place or time or does provide a properly completed claim form, or if later the first day in respect of which the claim is made.

(3) The Secretary of State may direct that the time for providing a properly completed claim form may be extended to a date no later than the date one month after the date of first notification of intention to make that claim.

Making a claim for a jobseeker's allowance in writing

21.—(1) Except where a person is required to attend in accordance with regulation 19, a claim for a jobseeker's allowance may be made in writing on a form authorised by the Secretary of State for that purpose and may be delivered or sent to the Secretary of State at an appropriate office. 2.323

(2) A claim made in accordance with paragraph (1) must be completed in accordance with the instructions on the form.

(3) A written claim for a jobseeker's allowance made under this regulation or regulation 20, which is made on the form approved for the time being, is properly completed if completed in accordance with the instructions on the form and defective if not so completed.

(4) If a written claim made under this regulation is defective when first received, the Secretary of State must advise the person making it of the defect and of the effect on the date of claim of the provisions of regulation 22.

(5) If that person corrects the defect so that the claim then satisfies the requirements of paragraph (3) and does so within one month, or such longer period as the Secretary of State considers reasonable, from the date the Secretary of State first drew attention to the defect, the claim must be treated as having been properly made in the first instance.

Date of claim for a jobseeker's allowance where claim made in writing

2.324 **22.** Subject to regulation 29(6), in the case of a written claim for a jobseeker's allowance made under regulation 21, the date on which the claim is made or treated as made is to be the first date on which—

(a) a properly completed claim is received in an appropriate office;

(b) a person first notifies an intention to make a claim, provided that a properly completed claim form is received in an appropriate office within one month or such longer period as the Secretary of State considers reasonable of first notification; or

(c) a defective claim is received but is treated as properly made in the first instance in accordance with regulation 21(5),

or the first day in respect of which the claim is made if later than the above.

Making a claim for a jobseeker's allowance by telephone

2.325 **23.**—(1) Except where a person is required to attend in accordance with regulation 19, or where the Secretary of State in any case directs that the claim must be made in writing in accordance with regulation 21, a claim for a jobseeker's allowance may be made by telephone call to the telephone number specified by the Secretary of State where such a claim falls within a class of case for which the Secretary of State accepts telephone claims or in any other case where the Secretary of State is willing to do so.

(2) A claim made by telephone in accordance with paragraph (1) is properly completed if the Secretary of State is provided during that call with all the information required to determine the claim and the claim is defective if not so completed.

(3) Where a telephone claim is defective, the Secretary of State must advise the person making it of the defect and of the effect on the date of claim of the provisions of regulation 24.

(4) If the person corrects the defect so that the claim then satisfies the requirements of paragraph (2) and does so within one month, or such longer period as the Secretary of State considers reasonable, of the date the Secretary of State first drew attention to the defect, the Secretary of State must treat the claim as if it had been properly made in the first instance.

Date of claim for a jobseeker's allowance where claim made by telephone

24. Subject to regulation 29(6), in the case of a telephone claim made under regulation 23, the date on which the claim is made or treated as made is to be the first date on which— 2.326

(a) a claim made by telephone is properly completed;

(b) a person first notifies an intention to make a claim, provided that a claim made by telephone is properly completed within one month or such longer period as the Secretary of State considers reasonable of first notification; or

(c) a defective claim is received but is treated as properly made in the first instance in accordance with regulation 23(4),

or the first day in respect of which the claim is made if later than the above.

Interchange with claims for other benefits

25.—(1) The Secretary of State may treat a claim for an employment and support allowance by a woman in addition or in the alternative as a claim for maternity allowance. 2.327

(2) The Secretary of State may treat a claim for a maternity allowance in addition or in the alternative as a claim for an employment and support allowance.

(3) Where it appears that a person who has made a claim for personal independence payment is not entitled to it but may be entitled to disability living allowance or attendance allowance, the Secretary of State may treat any such claim alternatively, or in addition, as a claim for either disability living allowance or attendance allowance as the case may be.

(4) Where it appears that a person who has made a claim for disability living allowance or attendance allowance is not entitled to it but may be entitled to personal independence payment, the Secretary of State may treat any such claim alternatively, or in addition, as a claim for personal independence payment.

(5) In determining whether the Secretary of State should treat a claim as made alternatively or in addition to another claim ("the original claim") under this regulation the Secretary of State must treat the alternative or additional claim, whenever made, as having been made at the same time as the original claim.

Time within which a claim for universal credit is to be made

26.—(1) Subject to the following provisions of this regulation, a claim for universal credit must be made on the first day of the period in respect of which the claim is made. 2.328

(2) Where the claim for universal credit is not made within the time specified in paragraph (1), the Secretary of State is to extend the time for claiming it, subject to a maximum extension of one month, to the date on which the claim is made, if—

(a) any one or more of the circumstances specified in paragraph (3) applies or has applied to the claimant; and

(b) as a result of that circumstance or those circumstances the claimant could not reasonably have been expected to make the claim earlier.

(3) The circumstances referred to in paragraph (2) are—

(a) the claimant was previously in receipt of a jobseeker's allowance or an employment and support allowance and notification of expiry of entitlement to that benefit was not sent to the claimant before the date that the claimant's entitlement expired;

[1 (aa) the claimant was previously in receipt of an existing benefit (as defined in the Universal Credit (Transitional Provisions) Regulations 2014) and notification of expiry of entitlement to that benefit was not sent to the claimant before the date that the claimant's entitlement expired;]

(b) the claimant has a disability;

(c) the claimant has supplied the Secretary of State with medical evidence that satisfies the Secretary of State that the claimant had an illness that prevented the claimant from making a claim;

(d) the claimant was unable to make a claim in writing by means of an electronic communication used in accordance with Schedule 2 because the official computer system was inoperative;

(e) [2 . . .]

(f) where—

(i) the Secretary of State decides not to award universal credit to members of a couple cause one of the couple does not meet the basic condition in section 4(1)(e) of the 2012 Act;

(ii) they cease to be a couple; and

(iii) the person who did meet the basic condition in section 4(1)(e) makes a further claim as a single person;

(g) where—

(i) an award of universal credit to joint claimants has been terminated because one of the couple does not meet the basic condition in section 4(1)(e) of the 2012 Act;

(ii) they cease to be a couple; and

(iii) the person who did meet the basic condition in section 4(1)(e) makes a further claim as a single person.

(4) In the case of a claim for universal credit made by each of joint claimants, the prescribed or claiming is not to be extended under paragraph (2) unless both claimants satisfy that paragraph.

[2 (5) In the case of a claim for universal credit referred to in regulation 21(3C) of the Universal Credit Regulations (assessment period applied from a previous award within the last 6 months) the claim for universal credit must be made before the end of the assessment period in respect of which it is made.]

AMENDMENTS

1. The Universal Credit (Transitional Provisions) Regulations 2014 (SI 2014/1230) reg.15 (June 16, 2014).

2. The Universal Credit (Digital Service) Amendment Regulations 2014 (SI 2014/2887) reg.3 (November 26, 2014). There are savings provisions in reg.5 of SI 2014/2887.

GENERAL NOTE

2.329 *AM v SSWP (UC)* [2017] UKUT 131 (AAC) considers what is meant by the official computer system being "inoperative". The claimant had been confused by a question concerning his expected take-home pay (which was relevant to the gateway conditions for universal credit) which had resulted in his being treated as not entitled to universal credit and advised to claim a jobseeker's allowance. Judge Rowland accepted that the question which only allowed either an affirmative or a negative answer was unsatisfactory. The claimant had lost out on two days' benefit and was seeking to have his claim for universal credit back-dated. Judge Rowland concluded that the unsatisfactory nature of the online question was not such as to render the official computer system as inoperative. Consequently, the claimant could not establish a ground for the back-dating of his award of universal credit.

Time within which a claim for personal independence payment is to be made

27. A claim for personal independence payment must be made on the first day of the period in respect of which the claim is made. 2.330

Time within which a claim for an employment and support allowance is to be made

28. A claim for an employment and support allowance must be made on the first day of the period in respect of which the claim is made or within the period of three months immediately following that day. 2.331

Time within which a claim for a jobseeker's allowance is to be made

29.—(1) Subject to paragraphs (2) and (4), a claim for a jobseeker's allowance must be made on the first day of the period in respect of which the claim is made. 2.332

(2) In a case where the claim is not made within the time specified in paragraph (1), the Secretary of State is to extend the time for claiming a jobseeker's allowance, subject to a maximum extension of three months, to the date on which the claim is made, where—

(a) any one or more of the circumstances specified in paragraph (3) applies or has applied to the claimant; and

(b) as a result of that circumstance or those circumstances the claimant could not reasonably have been expected to make the claim earlier.

(3) The circumstances referred to in paragraph (2) are—

(a) the claimant has difficulty communicating because—

(i) the claimant has learning, language or literacy difficulties; or

(ii) the claimant is deaf or blind,

and it was not reasonably practicable for the claimant to obtain assistance from another person to make the claim;

(b) the claimant was caring for a person who is ill or disabled and it was not reasonably practicable for the claimant to obtain assistance from another person to make the claim;

(c) the claimant was given information by an officer of the Department for Work and Pensions which led the claimant to believe that a claim for a jobseeker's allowance would not succeed;

(d) the claimant was given written advice by a solicitor or other professional adviser, a medical practitioner, a local authority or a person working in a Citizens Advice Bureau or agency, which led the claimant to believe that a claim for a jobseeker's allowance would not succeed;

(e) the claimant was required to deal with a domestic emergency affecting the claimant and it was not reasonably practicable for the claimant to obtain assistance from another person to make the claim; or

(f) the claimant was prevented by adverse weather conditions from attending an appropriate office.

(4) In a case where the claim is not made within the time specified in paragraph (1), the prescribed time for claiming a jobseeker's allowance is to be extended, subject to a maximum extension of one month, to the date on which the claim is made, where—

(a) any one or more of the circumstances specified in paragraph (5) applies or has applied to the claimant; and

(b) as a result of that circumstance or those circumstances the claimant could not reasonably have been expected to make the claim earlier.

(5) The circumstances referred to in paragraph (4) are—

(a) the appropriate office where the claimant would be expected to make a claim was closed and alternative arrangements were not available;

(b) the claimant was unable to attend the appropriate office due to difficulties with the claimant's normal mode of transport and there was no reasonable alternative available;

(c) there were adverse postal conditions;

(d) the claimant was previously in receipt of an employment and support allowance and notification of expiry of entitlement to that benefit was not sent to the claimant before the date that the entitlement expired;

(e) the claimant had ceased to be a member of a couple within the period of one month before the claim was made;

(f) during the period of one month before the claim was made a close relative of the claimant had died and for this purpose "close relative" means partner, parent, son, daughter, brother or sister;

(g) the claimant was unable to make telephone contact with the appropriate office where the claimant would be expected to notify an intention of making a claim because the telephone lines to that office were busy or inoperative;

(h) the claimant was unable to make contact by means of an electronic communication used in accordance with Schedule 2 where the claimant would be expected to notify an intention of making a claim because the official computer system was inoperative.

(6) In a case where the time for claiming a jobseeker's allowance is extended under paragraph (2) or (4), the claim is to be treated as made on the first day of the period in respect of which the claim is, by reason of the operation of those paragraphs, timeously made.

Amendment of claim

2.333 **30.**—(1) A person who has made a claim for benefit may amend it at any time before a determination has been made on the claim by notice in writing received at an appropriate office, by telephone call to a telephone number specified by the Secretary of State or in such other manner as the Secretary of State may decide or accept.

(2) Any claim amended in accordance with paragraph (1) may be treated as if it had been so amended in the first instance.

Withdrawal of claim

31.—(1) A person who has made a claim for benefit may withdraw it at any time before a determination has been made on it by notice in writing received at an appropriate office, by telephone call to a telephone number specified by the Secretary of State or in such other manner as the Secretary of State may decide or accept. 2.334

(2) Any notice of withdrawal given in accordance with paragraph (1) has effect when it is received.

Advance claim for and award of universal credit 2.335

32.—(1) This regulation applies where—

(a) although a person does not satisfy the conditions of entitlement to universal credit on the date on which a claim is made, the Secretary of State is of the opinion that unless there is a change of circumstances that person will satisfy those conditions for a period beginning on a day not more than one month after the date on which the claim is made; and

(b) the case falls within a class for which Secretary of State accepts advance claims or is a case where Secretary of State is otherwise willing to do so.

(2) The Secretary of State is to treat the claim as if made on the first day of that period.

(3) The Secretary of State may award universal credit accordingly, subject to the requirement that the person satisfies the conditions for entitlement on the first day of that period.

Advance claim for and award of personal independence payment

33.—(1) Where, although a person does not satisfy the requirements for entitlement to personal independence payment on the date on which the claim is made, the Secretary of State is of the opinion that unless there is a change of circumstances the person will satisfy those requirements for a period beginning on a day ("the relevant day") not more than 3 months after the date on which the decision on the claim is made, the Secretary of State may award personal independence payment from the relevant day subject to the condition that the person satisfies the requirements for entitlement on the relevant day. 2.336

(2) A person who has an award of personal independence payment may make a further claim for personal independence payment during the period of 6 months immediately before the existing award expires.

(3) Where a person makes a claim in accordance with paragraph (2) the Secretary of State may—

(a) treat the claim as if made on the first day after the expiry of the existing award; and

(b) award personal independence payment accordingly, subject to the condition that the person satisfies the requirements for entitlement on that first day after the expiry of the existing award.

GENERAL NOTE

This regulation permits advance awards of a personal independence payment, and also makes provision for renewal claims to be made in advance of the renewal date and which will take effect from that renewal date. 2.337

Advance claim for an award of an employment and support allowance or a jobseeker's allowance

2.338 **34.** Where, although a person does not satisfy the requirements of entitlement to an employment and support allowance or a jobseeker's allowance on the date on which a claim is made, the Secretary of State is of the opinion that unless there is a change of circumstances that claimant will satisfy those requirements for a period beginning on a day ("the relevant day") not more than three months after the date on which the claim is made, then the Secretary of State may—

(a) treat the claim as if made for a period beginning with the relevant day; and

(b) award an employment and support allowance or a jobseeker's allowance accordingly, subject to the condition that the person satisfies the requirements for entitlement when those benefits become payable under an award.

Attendance in person

2.339 **35.** Except in a case where regulation 9 of the Personal Independence Payment Regulations applies, every person who makes a claim for benefit, other than a jobseeker's allowance, or any person entitled to benefit, other than a jobseeker's allowance, and any other person by whom, or on whose behalf, payments by way of such a benefit are receivable, must attend at such place and on such days and at such times as the Secretary of State may direct, for the purpose of supplying any information or evidence under regulations 37, 38, 39 and 41, if reasonably so required by the Secretary of State.

Duration of awards

2.340 **36.**—(1) A claim for universal credit is to be treated as made for an indefinite period and any award of universal credit on that claim is to be made for an indefinite period.

(2) The provisions of Schedule 4 are to have effect in relation to claims for a jobseeker's allowance made during periods connected with public holidays.

PART 3

EVIDENCE, INFORMATION AND NOTIFICATION OF CHANGES OF CIRCUMSTANCES

Evidence and information in connection with a claim

2.341 **37.**—(1) Subject to regulation 8 of the Personal Independence Payment Regulations, paragraphs (2) and (3) apply to a person who makes a claim for benefit, other than a jobseeker's allowance, or on whose behalf a claim is made.

(2) The Secretary of State may require the person to supply information or evidence in connection with the claim, or any question arising out of it, as the Secretary of State considers appropriate.

(3) The person must supply the Secretary of State with the information or evidence in such manner as the Secretary of State determines within one

month of first being required to do so or such longer period as the Secretary of State considers reasonable.

(4) Where joint claimants have made a claim for universal credit, information relating to that claim may be supplied by the Secretary of State to either or both members of the couple for any purpose connected with the claim.

(5) Where a person is a member of a couple and may make a claim as a single person by virtue of regulation 3(3) (couples) of the Universal Credit Regulations and entitlement to or the amount of any universal credit is or may be affected by the circumstances of their partner, the Secretary of State may require the partner to do any of the following, within one month of being required to do so or such longer period as the Secretary of State may consider reasonable—

(a) to confirm the information given about the partner's circumstances;

(b) to supply information or evidence in connection with the claim, or any question arising out of it, as the Secretary of State may require.

(6) The Secretary of State may require a landlord or a rent officer to supply information or evidence in connection with a claim for universal credit that may include in the calculation of an award an amount in respect of housing costs, and any information or evidence so requested must be supplied within one month of the request or such longer period as the Secretary of State considers reasonable.

(7) Every person providing relevant childcare as defined in regulation 35 of the Universal Credit Regulations, in a case where the calculation of a claimant's award of universal credit may include an amount in respect of childcare costs under regulation 31 of those Regulations, must supply such information or evidence in connection with the claim made by the claimant, or any question arising out of it, as may be required by the Secretary of State, and must do so within one month of being required to do so or such longer period as the Secretary of State may consider reasonable.

(8) In this regulation any reference to a person or joint claimants making a claim for a benefit, other than a jobseeker's allowance, is to be interpreted as including a person or joint claimants in a case where it is not a condition of entitlement to benefit that a claim be made for it.

(9) In this regulation any reference to a claim for a benefit, other than a jobseeker's allowance, is to be interpreted as including a potential award of benefit in a case where it is not a condition of entitlement to benefit that a claim be made for it.

Evidence and information in connection with an award

38.—(1) This regulation, apart from paragraph (7), applies to any person entitled to benefit, other than a jobseeker's allowance, and any other person by whom, or on whose behalf, payments by way of such a benefit are receivable. 2.342

(2) Subject to regulation 8 of the Personal Independence Payment Regulations, a person to whom this regulation applies must supply in such manner as the Secretary of State may determine and within the period applicable under regulation 45(4)(a) of the Universal Credit, Personal Independence Payment, Jobseeker's Allowance and Employment and Support Allowance (Decisions and Appeals) Regulations 2013 such information or evidence as the Secretary of State may require for determining

whether a decision on the award of benefit should be revised under section 9 of the Social Security Act 1998 or superseded under section 10 of that Act.

(3) A person to whom this regulation applies must supply in such manner and at such times as the Secretary of State may determine such information or evidence as the Secretary of State may require in connection with payment of the benefit awarded.

(4) A person to whom this regulation applies must notify the Secretary of State of any change of circumstances which the person might reasonably be expected to know might affect—

(a) the continuance of entitlement to benefit;
(b) the amount of benefit awarded; or
(c) the payment of benefit,

as soon as reasonably practicable after the change occurs.

(5) A notification of any change of circumstances under paragraph (4) must be given—

(a) in writing or by telephone (unless the Secretary of State determines in any case that notice must be given in a particular way or to accept notice given otherwise than in writing or by telephone); or
(b) in writing if in any class of case the Secretary of State requires written notice (unless the Secretary of State determines in any case to accept notice given otherwise than in writing),

and must be sent or delivered to, or received at, the appropriate office.

(6) Where universal credit has been awarded to joint claimants, information relating to that award may be supplied by the Secretary of State to either or both members of the couple for any purpose connected with that award.

(7) Every person providing relevant childcare as defined in regulation 35 of the Universal Credit Regulations, in a case where the claimant's award of universal credit includes an amount in respect of childcare costs under regulation 31 of those Regulations, must supply such information or evidence in connection with the award, or any question arising out of it, as the Secretary of State may require, and must do so within one month of being required to do so or such longer period as the Secretary of State may consider reasonable.

(8) Where the calculation of an award of universal credit includes, by virtue of regulation 29 of the Universal Credit Regulations, an amount in respect of the fact that a claimant has regular and substantial caring responsibilities for a severely disabled person, the Secretary of State may require a person to whom this regulation applies to furnish a declaration signed by such severely disabled person confirming the particulars respecting the severely disabled person which have been given by that person.

Alternative means of notifying changes of circumstances

2.343 **39.** In such cases and subject to such conditions as the Secretary of State may specify, the duty in regulation 38(4) to notify a change of circumstances may be discharged by notifying the Secretary of State as soon as reasonably practicable—

(a) where the change of circumstances is a birth or death, through a local authority, or a county council in England, by personal attendance at an office specified by that authority or county council, provided the Secretary of State has agreed with that authority or county council for it to facilitate such notification; or

(b) where the change of circumstances is a death, by telephone to a telephone number specified for that purpose by the Secretary of State.

Information to be provided to rent officers

40.—(1) The Secretary of State must provide to the rent officer such information as the rent officer may reasonably require to carry out functions under section 122 of the Housing Act 1996. 2.344

(2) The information referred to in paragraph (1) may include information required to make a determination under the Rent Officers Order and may include—

(a) the name and address of a universal credit claimant in respect of whom the Secretary of State has applied for a determination;
(b) the amount of any rent (within the meaning of paragraph 2 of Schedule 1 to the Universal Credit Regulations) (meaning of payments in respect of accommodation);
(c) the amount of any service charge payments (within the meaning of paragraph 2 of Schedule 1 to the Universal Credit Regulations);
(d) the number of bedrooms in the accommodation in respect of which a determination is made;
(e) the name and address of a claimant's landlord.

(3) A landlord must provide to the rent officer such information or evidence as the rent officer may reasonably require to make a determination in accordance with the Rent Officers Order and which the rent officer is not able to obtain from the Secretary of State.

(4) The evidence referred to in paragraph (3) may include evidence as to whether a property is let at an Affordable Rent within the meaning in Schedule 2 to the Rent Officers Order.

(5) In this regulation and regulation 37 "landlord" means any person to whom a claimant or partner is liable to make payments in respect of the occupation of the claimant's accommodation.

(6) In this regulation "the Rent Officers Order" means the Rent Officer (Universal Credit Functions) Order 2013.

Evidence and information required from pension fund holders

41.—(1) Where a claimant or the claimant's partner is aged not less than 60 and is a member of, or a person deriving entitlement to a pension under a personal pension scheme or an occupational pension scheme, such a person must, where the Secretary of State so requires, furnish the following information— 2.345

(a) the name and address of the pension fund holder;
(b) such other information including any reference or policy number as is needed to enable the personal pension scheme or occupational pension scheme to be identified.

(2) Where the pension fund holder receives from the Secretary of State a request for details concerning the personal pension scheme or occupational pension scheme relating to a person to whom paragraph (1) refers, the pension fund holder must provide the Secretary of State with any information to which the following paragraph refers.

(3) The information to which this paragraph refers is—

(a) where the purchase of an annuity under a personal pension scheme or occupational pension scheme has been deferred, the amount of any income which is being withdrawn from the personal pension scheme or occupational pension scheme;

(b) in the case of—

(i) a personal pension scheme or occupational pension scheme where income withdrawal is available, the maximum amount of income which may be withdrawn from the scheme; or

(ii) a personal pension scheme or occupational pension scheme where income withdrawal is not available, the maximum amount of income which might be withdrawn from the fund if the fund were held under a personal pension scheme or occupational pension scheme where income withdrawal was available,

calculated by or on behalf of the pension fund holder by means of tables prepared from time to time by the Government Actuary which are appropriate for this purpose.

(4) In this regulation any reference to a claimant is to be interpreted as including a person in a case where it is not a condition of entitlement to benefit that a claim be made for it.

(5) This regulation does not apply to a person claiming personal independence payment.

(6) In this regulation—

(a) "pension fund holder" means with respect to a personal pension scheme or an occupational pension scheme, the trustees, managers or scheme administrators of the scheme concerned;

(b) "personal pension scheme" means—

(i) a personal pension scheme as defined by section 1 of the Pension Schemes Act 1993(22);

(ii) an annuity contract or trust scheme approved under section 620 or 621 of the Income and Corporation Taxes Act 1988 or a substituted contract within the meaning of section 622(3) of that Act which is treated as having become a registered pension scheme by virtue of paragraph 1(1)(f) of Schedule 36 to the Finance Act 2004;

(iii) a personal pension scheme approved under Chapter 4 of Part 14 of the Income and Corporation Taxes Act 1988 which is treated as having become a registered pension scheme by virtue of paragraph 1(1)(g) of Schedule 36 to the Finance Act 2004;

(c) "occupational pension" means any pension or other periodical payment under an occupational pension scheme but does not include any discretionary payment out of a fund established for relieving hardship in particular cases.

Notification for purposes of sections 111A and 112 of the Administration Act

2.346 **42.** Regulations 43 to 44 below prescribe the person to whom, and manner in which, a change of circumstances must be notified for the purposes of sections 111A(1A) to (1G) and 112(1A) to (1F) of the Administration Act (offences relating to failure to notify a change of circumstances).

Notification of changes of circumstances affecting a jobseeker's allowance or an employment and support allowance for purposes of sections 111A and 112 of the Administration Act

43.—(1) Subject to paragraphs (2) and (3), where the benefit affected by the change of circumstances is a jobseeker's allowance or an employment and support allowance, notice must be given to the Secretary of State at the appropriate office— 2.347

(a) in writing or by telephone (unless the Secretary of State determines in any case that notice must be in writing or may be given otherwise than in writing or by telephone); or

(b) in writing if in any class of case the Secretary of State requires written notice (unless the Secretary of State determines in any case to accept notice given otherwise than in writing).

(2) Where the notice in writing referred to in paragraph (1) is given or sent by an electronic communication that notice must be given or sent in accordance with the provisions set out in Schedule 2 to these Regulations (electronic communications).

(3) In such cases and subject to such conditions as the Secretary of State may specify, the duty in regulation 38(4) of these Regulations or regulation 31(4) of the Jobseeker's Allowance Regulations to notify a change of circumstances may be discharged by notifying the Secretary of State as soon as reasonably practicable—

(a) where the change of circumstances is a birth or death, through a local authority, or a county council in England, by personal attendance at an office specified by that authority or county council, provided the Secretary of State has agreed with that authority or county council for it to facilitate such notification; or

(b) where the change of circumstances is a death, by telephone to a telephone number specified for that purpose by the Secretary of State.

Notification of changes of circumstances affecting personal independence payment or universal credit for purposes of sections 111A and 112 of the Administration Act

44.—(1) Subject to paragraphs (2) and (3), where the benefit affected by the change of circumstances is personal independence payment or universal credit, notice must be given to the Secretary of State ("S") at the appropriate office— 2.348

(a) in writing or by telephone (unless S determines in any case that notice must be in writing or may be given otherwise than in writing or by telephone); or

(b) in writing if in any class of case S requires written notice (unless S determines in any case to accept notice given otherwise than in writing).

(2) Where the notice in writing referred to in paragraph (1) is given or sent by an electronic communication that notice must be given or sent in accordance with the provisions set out in Schedule 2 to these Regulations (electronic communications).

(3) In such cases and subject to such conditions as the Secretary of State may specify, the duty in regulation 38(4) to notify a change of circumstances may be discharged by notifying the Secretary of State as soon as reasonably practicable—

(a) where the change of circumstances is a birth or death, through a local authority, or a county council in England, by personal attendance at an office specified by that authority or county council, provided the Secretary of State has agreed with that authority or county council for it to facilitate such notification; or

(b) where the change of circumstances is a death, by telephone to a telephone number specified for that purpose by the Secretary of State.

PART 4

PAYMENTS

Time of payment: general provision

2.349 **45.** Subject to the other provisions of this Part, benefit is to be paid in accordance with an award as soon as is reasonably practicable after the award has been made.

Direct credit transfer

2.350 **46.**—[1 (1) The Secretary of State may arrange for benefit to be paid by way of direct credit transfer into a bank or other account nominated by the person entitled to benefit, a person acting on their behalf under regulation 57(1) or a person referred to in regulation 57(2).]

(2) A Jobseeker's Allowance or an Employment and Support Allowance are to be paid in accordance with paragraph (1) within seven days of the last day of each successive period of entitlement.

AMENDMENT

1. The Universal Credit and Miscellaneous Amendments (No.2) Regulations 2014 (SI 2014/2888), reg.5(3) (November 26, 2014).

Payment of universal credit

2.351 **47.**—(1) Universal credit is payable monthly in arrears in respect of each assessment period unless in any case or class of case the Secretary of State arranges otherwise.

(2) Where universal credit is to be paid in accordance with regulation 46, it is to be paid within seven days of the last day of the assessment period but if it is not possible to pay universal credit within that period of seven days, it is to be paid as soon as reasonably practicable thereafter.

(3) In respect of an award of universal credit which is the subject of an arrangement for payment under regulation 46, the Secretary of State may make a particular payment by credit transfer otherwise than is provided by paragraph (2), if it appears to the Secretary of State appropriate to do so for the purpose of—

(a) paying any arrears of benefit; or

(b) making a payment in respect of a terminal period of an award or for any similar purpose.

(4) Where the Secretary of State has arranged for universal credit to be

paid in accordance with regulation 46, joint claimants may nominate a bank or other account into which that benefit is to be paid.

(5) Where joint claimants of universal credit have not nominated a bank or other account into which that benefit is to be paid, the Secretary of State may nominate a bank or other account.

(6) The Secretary of State may, in any case where the Secretary of State considers it is in the interests of—

(a) the claimants;

(b) a child or a qualifying young person for whom one or both of the claimants are responsible; or

(c) a severely disabled person, where the calculation of an award of universal credit includes, by virtue of regulation 29 of the Universal Credit Regulations, an amount in respect of the fact that a claimant has regular and substantial caring responsibilities for that severely disabled person,

arrange that universal credit payable in respect of joint claimants be paid wholly to only one member of the couple or be split between the couple in such proportion as the Secretary of State considers appropriate.

(7) Where a superseding decision takes effect in accordance with paragraph 26 of Schedule 1 to the Universal Credit, Personal Independence Payment, Jobseeker's Allowance and Employment and Support Allowance (Decisions and Appeals) Regulations 2013, the amount payable in respect of that last assessment period is to be calculated as follows—

$$N \times \left\{\frac{A \times 12}{365}\right\}$$

where N is the number of days in the period and A is the amount calculated in relation to that period as if it were an assessment period of one month.

Payment of personal independence payment

48.—(1) Subject to the following provisions of this regulation and regulation 50, personal independence payment is to be paid at intervals of four weeks in arrears. 2.352

(2) In the case of any person to whom section 82 of the 2012 Act (terminal illness) applies, the Secretary of State may arrange that personal independence payment is to be paid at intervals of one week in advance.

(3) Where the amount of personal independence payment payable is less than £5.00 a week the Secretary of State may arrange that it is to be paid in arrears at such intervals as may be specified not exceeding 12 months.

Days for payment of personal independence payment

49.—(1) Subject to the following provisions of this regulation, a personal independence payment is payable on the day of the week on which the Secretary of State makes a decision to award that benefit, except that where that decision is made on a Saturday or a Sunday the benefit is to be paid on such day of the week as the Secretary of State may direct in any case. 2.353

(2) The Secretary of State may, in any case or class of case, arrange that personal independence payment or any part of it be paid on any day of the week.

(3) Where personal independence payment is in payment to any person

and the day on which it is payable is changed, it is to be paid at a daily rate of 1/7th of the weekly rate in respect of any of the days for which payment would have been made but for that change.

(4) Where there is a change in the amount of any personal independence payment payable, or where entitlement to personal independence payment ends, and these events do not occur on the day of the week referred to in paragraph (1) or (2), personal independence payment is to be paid at a daily rate of 1/7th of the weekly rate.

Payment of personal independence payment at a daily rate between periods in hospital or other accommodation

2.354 **50.**—(1) Personal independence payment is to be paid in respect of any person, for any day falling within a period to which paragraph (2) applies, at the daily rate (which is to be equal to 1/7th of the weekly rate) and personal independence payment payable in pursuance of this regulation is to be paid weekly or as the Secretary of State may direct in any case.

(2) This paragraph applies to any period which is not a period of residence—

(a) but which commences immediately following such a period; and
(b) on the first day of which it is expected that, before the expiry of the term of 28 days beginning with that day, the person will commence another period of residence.

(3) Where paragraph (2) applies, the period referred to in that paragraph is to end—

(a) at the expiry of the term of 28 days beginning with the first day of the period referred to in that paragraph; or
(b) if earlier, on the day before the day which is the first day of a period of residence.

(4) In this regulation a "period of residence" means a period of residence where—

(a) the person is a resident of a care home, as defined in section 85(3) of the 2012 Act, and no amount of personal independence payment which is attributable to the daily living component is payable in respect of the person by virtue of regulation 28(1) of the Personal Independence Payment Regulations(29); or
(b) the person is undergoing medical or other treatment as an in-patient at a hospital or similar institution and no amount of personal independence payment which is attributable to the daily living component or the mobility component is payable in respect of the person by virtue of regulation 29 of the Personal Independence Payment Regulations,

and such period is to be deemed to begin on the day after the day on which the person enters the care home, hospital or similar institution and to end on the day before the day on which the person leaves the care home, hospital or similar institution.

Payment of an employment and support allowance

2.355 **51.**—(1) Subject to paragraphs (3) to (8), an employment and support allowance paid in accordance with regulation 46 is to be paid fortnightly in arrears on the day of the week determined in accordance with paragraph (2).

(2) The day specified for the purposes of paragraph (1) is the day in column (2) which corresponds to the series of numbers in column (1) which includes the last two digits of the claimant's national insurance number—

(1)	(2)
00 to 19	Monday
20 to 39	Tuesday
40 to 59	Wednesday
60 to 79	Thursday
80 to 99	Friday

(3) The Secretary of State may, in any case or class of case, arrange that the claimant be paid otherwise than fortnightly.

(4) In respect of an award of an employment and support allowance which is the subject of an arrangement for payment under regulation 46, the Secretary of State may make a particular payment by credit transfer otherwise than as provided by paragraph (1), if it appears to the Secretary of State appropriate to do so for the purpose of—

(a) paying any arrears of benefit; or
(b) making a payment in respect of a terminal period of an award or for any similar purpose.

(5) The Secretary of State may, in any case or class of case, arrange that an employment and support allowance be paid on any day of the week and where it is in payment to any person and the day on which it is payable is changed, it is to be paid at a daily rate of 1/7th of the weekly rate in respect of any of the days for which payment would have been made but for that change.

(6) Where the weekly amount of an employment and support allowance is less than £1.00 it may be paid in arrears at intervals of not more than 13 weeks.

(7) Where the weekly amount of an employment and support allowance is less than 10 pence that allowance is not payable.

(8) Where an employment and support allowance is normally payable in arrears and the day on which that benefit is payable by reason of paragraph (2) is affected by office closure, it may for that benefit week be paid wholly in advance or partly in advance and partly in arrears and on such day as the Secretary of State may direct.

(9) Where under paragraph (8) an employment and support allowance is paid either in advance or partly in advance and partly in arrears it is for any other purposes to be treated as if it were paid in arrears.

(10) For the purposes of paragraph (8), "benefit week" means a period of seven days beginning or ending with such day as the Secretary of State may direct.

(11) For the purposes of paragraph (8), "office closure" means a period during which an appropriate office is closed in connection with a public holiday.

(12) For the purposes of paragraph (11), "public holiday" means—

(a) in England and Wales, Christmas Day, Good Friday or a bank holiday under the Banking and Financial Dealings Act 1971(**a**);

(b) in Scotland, a bank holiday under the Banking and Financial Dealings Act 1971 or a local holiday.

Payment of a jobseeker's allowance

2.356 **52.**—(1) Subject to paragraphs (2) to (4), a jobseeker's allowance paid in accordance with regulation 46 is to be paid fortnightly in arrears unless in any case or class of case the Secretary of State arranges otherwise.

(2) In respect of an award of a jobseeker's allowance which is the subject of an arrangement for payment under regulation 46, the Secretary of State may make a particular payment by credit transfer otherwise than as provided by paragraph (1), if it appears to the Secretary of State appropriate to do so for the purpose of—

(a) paying any arrears of benefit; or

(b) making a payment in respect of a terminal period of an award or for any similar purpose.

(3) Where the amount of a jobseeker's allowance is less than £1.00 a week the Secretary of State may direct that it is to be paid at such intervals, not exceeding 13 weeks, as may be specified in the direction.

(4) Where a jobseeker's allowance is normally payable in arrears and the day on which that benefit is normally payable is affected by office closure, it may for that benefit week be paid wholly in advance or partly in advance and partly in arrears and on such day as the Secretary of State may direct.

(5) Where under paragraph (4) a jobseeker's allowance is paid either in advance or partly in advance and partly in arrears it is for any other purposes to be treated as if it were paid in arrears.

(6) For the purposes of paragraph (4), "benefit week" means a period of seven days ending with a day determined in accordance with the definition of that term in regulation 2(2) (general interpretation) of the Jobseeker's Allowance Regulations.

(7) For the purposes of paragraph (4), "office closure" means a period during which an appropriate office is closed in connection with a public holiday.

(8) For the purposes of paragraph (7), "public holiday" means—

(a) in England and Wales, Christmas Day, Good Friday or a bank holiday under the Banking and Financial Dealings Act 1971;

(b) in Scotland, a bank holiday under the Banking and Financial Dealings Act 1971 or a local holiday.

Fractional amounts of benefit

2.357 **53.** Where the amount of any benefit payable would, but for this regulation, include a fraction of a penny, that fraction is to be disregarded if it is less than half a penny and is otherwise to be treated as a penny.

Payment to persons under age 18

2.358 **54.** Where a benefit is paid to a person under the age of 18, a direct credit transfer under regulation 46 into any such person's account, or the receipt by the person of a payment made by some other means, is sufficient discharge for the Secretary of State.

Extinguishment of right to payment if payment is not obtained within the prescribed period

55.—(1) The right to payment of any sum by way of benefit is to be extinguished where payment of that sum is not obtained within the period of 12 months from the date on which the right is treated as having arisen. 2.359

(2) For the purposes of this regulation, the right to payment of any sum by way of benefit is to be treated as having arisen—

(a) where notice is given or sent that the sum contained in the notice is ready for collection, on the date of the notice or, if more than one such notice is given or sent, the date of the first such notice;

(b) in relation to any such sum which the Secretary of State has arranged to be paid by means of direct credit transfer in accordance with regulation 46 into a bank or other account, on the due date for payment of the sum or in the case of universal credit on the date of payment of the sum; or

(c) in relation to any such sum to which neither sub-paragraph (a) or (b) applies, on such date as the Secretary of State determines.

(3) The giving or sending of a notice under paragraph (2)(a) is effective for the purposes of that paragraph, even where the sum contained in that notice is more or less than the sum which the person concerned has the right to receive.

(4) Where a question arises whether the right to payment of any sum by way of benefit has been extinguished by the operation of this regulation and the Secretary of State is satisfied that—

(a) the Secretary of State first received written notice requesting payment of that sum after the expiration of 12 months from the date on which the right is treated as having arisen;

(b) from a day within that period of 12 months and continuing until the day the written notice was given, there was good cause for not giving the notice; and

(c) no payment has been made under the provisions of regulation 46 (direct credit transfer),

the period of 12 months is extended to the date on which the Secretary of State decides that question, and this regulation is to apply accordingly as though the right to payment had arisen on that date.

(5) This regulation applies to a person appointed under regulation 57(1) to act on behalf of a claimant or a person referred to in regulation 57(2) as it applies to a claimant.

Payments on death

56.—(1) On the death of a person who has made a claim for benefit, the Secretary of State may appoint such person as the Secretary of State thinks fit to proceed with the claim and any related issue of revision, supersession or appeal under the Social Security Act 1998. 2.360

(2) Subject to paragraphs (6) and (7), any sum payable by way of benefit which is payable under an award on a claim proceeded with under paragraph (1) may be paid or distributed by the Secretary of State to or amongst persons over the age of 16 claiming as personal representatives, legatees, next of kin or creditors of the deceased and the provisions of regulation 55 (extinguishment of right to payment if payment is not obtained within the prescribed period) are to apply to any such payment or distribution.

(3) Subject to paragraphs (2), (6) and (7), any sum payable by way of benefit to the deceased, payment of which the deceased had not obtained at the date of the deceased's death, may, unless the right to payment was already extinguished at that date, be paid or distributed to or amongst any persons mentioned in paragraph (2), and regulation 55 is to apply to any such payment or distribution, except that, for the purpose of that regulation, the period of 12 months is to be calculated from the date on which the right to payment of any sum is treated as having arisen in relation to any such person and not from the date on which that right is treated as having arisen in relation to the deceased.

(4) A direct credit transfer under regulation 46 into an account in the name of any person mentioned in paragraph (2), or the receipt by such a person of a payment made by some other means, is sufficient discharge for the Secretary of State for any sum so paid.

(5) Where the Secretary of State is satisfied that any sum payable by way of benefit under paragraph (2) or (3), or part of it, is needed for the well-being of any person under the age of 16, the Secretary of State may obtain sufficient discharge for it by paying the sum or part of it to a person over that age who satisfies the Secretary of State that that person will apply the sum so paid for the well-being of the person under the age of 16.

(6) Paragraphs (2) and (3) are not to apply in any case unless written application for the payment of any sum is made to the Secretary of State within 12 months from the date of the deceased's death or within such longer period as the Secretary of State may allow in any case.

(7) The Secretary of State may dispense with strict proof of the title of any person claiming in accordance with the provisions of this regulation.

(8) In paragraph (2) "next of kin" means—

(a) in England and Wales, the persons who would take beneficially on an intestacy;

(b) in Scotland, the persons entitled to the moveable estate of the deceased on intestacy.

PART 5

THIRD PARTIES

Persons unable to act

2.361 57.—(1) Where a person ("P1") is, or may be, entitled to benefit (whether or not a claim for benefit has been made by P1 or on P1's behalf) but P1 is unable for the time being to act, the Secretary of State may, if all the conditions in paragraph (2) and the additional conditions in paragraph (3) are met, appoint a person ("P2") to carry out the functions set out in paragraph (4).

(2) The conditions are that—

(a) no deputy has been appointed by the Court of Protection under Part 1 of the Mental Capacity Act 2005;

(b) no receiver has been appointed under Part 7 of the Mental Health Act 1983 who is treated as a deputy by virtue of the Mental Capacity Act 2005 with power to claim or receive benefit on P1's behalf;

(c) no attorney with a general power, or a power to claim or receive benefit, has been appointed by P1 under the Powers of Attorney Act 1971, the Enduring Powers of Attorney Act 1985(35), the Mental Capacity Act 2005 or otherwise; and

(d) in Scotland, P1's estate is not being administered by a judicial factor or any guardian acting or appointed under the Adults with Incapacity (Scotland) Act 2000 who has power to claim or receive benefit on P1's behalf.

(3) The additional conditions are that—

(a) P2 has made a written application to the Secretary of State to be appointed; and

(b) if P2 is a natural person, P2 is over the age of 18.

(4) The functions are exercising on behalf of P1 any right to which P1 may be entitled and receiving and dealing on behalf of P1 with any sums payable to P1.

(5) Anything required by these Regulations to be done by or in relation to P1 may be done by or in relation to P2 or any person mentioned in paragraph (2).

(6) Where a person has been appointed under regulation 82(3) of the Housing Benefit Regulations 2006 by a relevant authority within the meaning of those Regulations to act on behalf of another in relation to a benefit claim or award, the Secretary of State may, if the person so appointed agrees, treat that person as if the Secretary of State had appointed that person under paragraph (1).

(7) A direct credit transfer under regulation 46 into the account of P2 or any person mentioned in paragraph (2), or the receipt by such a person of a payment made by some other means, is sufficient discharge for the Secretary of State for any sum paid.

(8) An appointment under paragraph (1) or (6) comes to an end if—

(a) the Secretary of State at any time revokes it;

(b) P2 resigns P2's office having given one month's notice in writing to the Secretary of State of an intention to do so; or

(c) the Secretary of State is notified that any condition in paragraph (2) is no longer met.

Payment to another person on the claimant's behalf

58.—(1) The Secretary of State may direct that universal credit be paid wholly or in part to another person on the claimant's behalf if this appears to the Secretary of State necessary to protect the interests of— **2.362**

(a) the claimant;

(b) their partner;

(c) a child or qualifying young person for whom the claimant or their partner or both are responsible; or

(d) a severely disabled person, where the calculation of the award of universal credit includes, by virtue of regulation 29 of the Universal Credit Regulations, an amount in respect of the fact that the claimant has regular and substantial caring responsibilities for that severely disabled person.

(2) The Secretary of State may direct that personal independence payment be paid wholly to another person on the claimant's behalf if this appears to the Secretary of State necessary to protect the interests of the claimant.

Direct payment to lender of deductions in respect of interest on secured loans

2.363 **59.**— Schedule 5 has effect where section 15A(1) of the Administration Act (payment out of benefit of sums in respect of mortgage interest etc.) applies in relation to a case where a claimant is entitled to universal credit.

Deductions which may be made from benefit and paid to third parties

2.364 **60.** —Except as provided for in regulation 59 and Schedule 5, deductions may be made from may be made to third parties on behalf of a claimant in accordance with the provisions of Schedule 6 and Schedule 7.

Part 6

Mobility component of personal independence payment

Cases where mobility component of personal independence payment not payable

2.365 **61.**—(1) Subject to the following provisions of this regulation, personal independence payment by virtue of entitlement to the mobility component is not payable to any person who would otherwise be entitled to it during any period in respect of which that person has received, or is receiving, any payment—

(a) by way of grant under section 5 of, and paragraph 10 of Schedule 1 to, the National Health Service Act 2006, section 5 of, and paragraph 10 of Schedule 1 to, the National Health Service (Wales) Act 2006 or section 46 of the National Health Service (Scotland) Act 1978 towards the costs of running a private car;

(b) of mobility supplement under—

   (i) the Naval, Military and Air Forces etc., (Disablement and Death) Service Pensions Order 2006;

   (ii) the Personal Injuries (Civilians) Scheme 1983; or

   (iii) the Order referred to in paragraph (i) by virtue of the War Pensions (Naval Auxiliary Personnel) Scheme 1964, the Pensions (Polish Forces) Scheme 1964, the War Pensions (Mercantile Marine) Scheme 1964 or an Order of Her Majesty in relation to the Home Guard dated 21st or 22nd December 1964 or in relation to the Ulster Defence Regiment dated 4th January 1971; or

(c) out of public funds which the Secretary of State is satisfied is analogous to a payment under sub-paragraph (a) or (b).

(2) Paragraph (3) applies where a person in respect of whom personal independence payment is claimed for any period has received any such payment as is referred to in paragraph (1) for a period which, in whole or in part, covers the period for which personal independence payment is claimed.

(3) Such payment referred to in paragraph (1) is to be treated as an aggregate of equal weekly amounts in respect of each week in the period for which it is made and, where in respect of any such week a person is treated as having a weekly amount so calculated which is less than the weekly rate

of mobility component of personal independence payment to which, apart from paragraph (1), they would be entitled, any personal independence payment to which that person may be entitled for that week is to be payable at a weekly rate reduced by the weekly amount so calculated.

Payment of personal independence payment on behalf of a claimant (Motability)

62.—(1) This regulation applies where— 2.366

(a) personal independence payment is payable in respect of a claimant by virtue of entitlement to the mobility component at the enhanced rate; and

(b) under arrangements made or negotiated by Motability, an agreement has been entered into by or on behalf of the claimant for the hire or hire-purchase of a vehicle.

(2) Where this regulation applies, the Secretary of State may arrange that any personal independence payment by virtue of entitlement to the mobility component at the enhanced rate be paid in whole or in part on behalf of the claimant in settlement of liability for payments due under the agreement mentioned in paragraph (1).

(3) Subject to regulations 63 and 64, in the case of the hire of a vehicle, an arrangement made by the Secretary of State under paragraph (2) terminates—

(a) where the vehicle is returned to the owner at or before the expiration of the term of hire or any agreed extension of the term of hire, on expiry of the period of the term or extended term;

(b) where the vehicle is retained by or on behalf of the claimant with the owner's consent after the expiration of the term of hire or any agreed extension of the term of hire, on expiry of the period of the term or extended term; or

(c) where the vehicle is retained by or on behalf of the claimant otherwise than with the owner's consent after the expiration of the term of hire or any agreed extension of the term of hire, or its earlier termination, on expiry of whichever is the longer of the following periods—

  (i) the period ending with the return of the vehicle to the owner; or

  (ii) the period of the term of hire or any agreed extension of the term of hire.

(4) Subject to regulations 63 and 64 in the case of a hire-purchase agreement, an arrangement made by the Secretary of State under paragraph (2) terminates—

(a) on the purchase of the vehicle; or

(b) where the vehicle is returned to, or is repossessed by, the owner under the terms of the agreement before the completion of the purchase, at the end of the original period of the agreement.

(5) In this regulation "Motability" means the company, set up under that name as a charity and originally incorporated under the Companies Act 1985 and subsequently incorporated by Royal Charter.

[1 Recovery of expenses

62A.—(1) Paragraph 2 applies where— 2.367

(a) an agreement referred to in regulation 62(1)(b) has been entered into; and

(b) a relevant provider is receiving payments of personal independence payment in settlement of liability for payments due under that agreement.

(2) The Secretary of State may require the relevant provider to make payments to meet the reasonable expenses of the Secretary of State in administering the making of the payments of personal independence payment to the relevant provider.

(3) The method by which the expenses under paragraph (2) are to be met is for the Secretary of State to issue an invoice to the relevant provider setting out the expenses that have been incurred and for the relevant provider to pay the sum stated to the Secretary of State.

(4) The first invoice issued by the Secretary of State may recover expenses incurred between 21st July 2016 and the date of the invoice.

(5) Subsequently the Secretary of State may issue invoices no more frequently than annually and only in respect of expenses incurred since the period covered by the previous invoice.

(6) The expenses that the Secretary of State may take into account for the purposes of paragraph (2) include—

(a) the salaries and other costs relating to the employment of staff wholly engaged in the administering of the payments of personal independence payment and where staff have other responsibilities, an apportioned amount of those costs; and

(b) overheads, including rent and other shared costs, relating to those staff.

(7) In determining what expenses were reasonably incurred in administering the making of payments of personal independence payment to a relevant provider, the Secretary of State must have regard to any agreement between the Secretary of State and the relevant provider concerning the level of service to be provided by the Secretary of State in the making of such payments to that relevant provider.]

AMENDMENT

1. Inserted by the Social Security (Expenses of Paying Sums in Relation to Vehicle Hire) Regulations 2016 (SI 2016/674) reg.5 (July 21, 2016).

Power for the Secretary of State to terminate an arrangement (Motability)

2.368 **63.** The Secretary of State may terminate an arrangement under regulation 62(2) on such date as the Secretary of State decides—

(a) if requested to do so by the owner of the vehicle to which the arrangement relates; or

(b) if it appears to the Secretary of State that the arrangement is causing undue hardship to the claimant and that it should be terminated earlier than provided for by regulation 62(3) or (4).

Restriction on duration of arrangements by the Secretary of State (Motability)

2.369 **64.** The Secretary of State must terminate an arrangement under regulation 62(2) where the Secretary of State is satisfied that—

(a) the vehicle to which the arrangement relates has been returned to the owner; and

(b) the expenses of the owner arising out of the hire or hire-purchase agreement have been recovered following the return of the vehicle.

SCHEDULE 1 — POWERS EXERCISED IN MAKING THESE REGULATIONS

1. The following provisions of the Administration Act— 2.370
- (a) section 1(1), (1C);
- (b) section 5(1)(a), (b), (c), (d), (g), (i), (j), (k), (l), (m), (p), (q), (1A), (2A), (2B), (2C), (3B);
- (c) section 7A(2)(b);
- (d) section 15A(2);
- (e) section 111A(1A)(d), (1B)(d), (1D)(c), (1E)(c);
- (f) section 112(1A)(d), (1B)(d), (1C)(c), (1D)(c);
- (g) section 189(1) and (5) to (6);
- (h) section 191.

2. Paragraph 7A of Schedule 2 to the Abolition of Domestic Rates etc. (Scotland) Act 1987.

3. Paragraph 6 of Schedule 4 to the Local Government Finance Act 1988.

4. Section 24(2)(b), (c) and (d) and section 30 of the Criminal Justice Act 1991.

5. Section 43(2) of the 1991 Act.

6. Paragraphs 1 and 6(2)(b) of Schedule 4 and paragraph 6 of Schedule 8 to, the Local Government Finance Act 1992.

7. Sections 32 and 92 of, and paragraph 3(1)(a), (b), (2)(a), (b) and (c) of Schedule 1 to the 2012 Act.

SCHEDULE 2 — ELECTRONIC COMMUNICATIONS

PART 1

USE OF ELECTRONIC COMMUNICATIONS

Use of electronic communications by the Secretary of State

1. The Secretary of State may use an electronic communication in connection with claims for, and awards of, any benefit. 2.371

Conditions for the use of electronic communications by other persons

2.—(1) A person other than the Secretary of State may use an electronic communication in connection with the matters referred to in paragraph 1 if the conditions specified in sub-paragraphs (2) to (5) are satisfied. 2.372

(2) The first condition is that the person is for the time being permitted to use an electronic communication for the purpose in question by an authorisation given by means of a direction of the Secretary of State.

(3) The second condition is that the person uses an approved method of—
- (a) authenticating the identity of the sender of the communication where required to do so;
- (b) electronic communication;
- (c) authenticating any claim or information delivered by means of an electronic communication; and
- (d) subject to sub-paragraph (6), submitting any claim or information to the Secretary of State.

(4) The third condition is that any claim or information sent by means of an electronic communication is in an approved form.

(5) The fourth condition is that the person maintains such records as may be specified in a direction given by the Secretary of State.

(6) Where the person uses any method other than the method approved by the Secretary of State of submitting any claim or information, it is to be treated as not having been submitted.

(7) In this paragraph "approved" means approved by means of a direction given by the Secretary of State for the purposes of this Schedule.

Use of intermediaries

3. The Secretary of State may use intermediaries in connection with— 2.373
- (a) the delivery of any claim or information by means of an electronic communication; and
- (b) the authentication or security of anything transmitted by such means,

and may require other persons to use intermediaries in connection with those matters.

PART 2

EVIDENTIAL PROVISIONS

Effect of delivering information by electronic communications

2.374 **4.**—(1) Any claim or information which is delivered by means of an electronic communication is to be treated as having been delivered in the manner or form required by any provision of these Regulations on the day on which the conditions imposed—

(a) by this Schedule; and
(b) by or under an applicable enactment (except to the extent that the condition thereby imposed is incompatible with this Schedule),

are satisfied.

(2) The Secretary of State may, by a direction, determine that any claim or information is to be treated as delivered on a different day (whether earlier or later) from the day specified in sub-paragraph (1).

(3) Any claim or information is not to be taken to have been delivered to an official computer system by means of an electronic communication unless it is accepted by the system to which it is delivered.

Proof of delivery

2.375 **5.**—(1) The use of an approved method of electronic communication is to be presumed, unless the contrary is proved, to have resulted in delivery—

(a) in the case of any claim or information falling to be delivered to the Secretary of State, if the delivery of that claim or information is recorded on an official computer system; or
(b) in the case of any information that falls to be delivered by the Secretary of State, if the despatch of that information is recorded on an official computer system.

(2) The use of an approved method of electronic communication is to be presumed, unless the contrary is proved, not to have resulted in delivery—

(a) in the case of any claim or information falling to be delivered to the Secretary of State, if the delivery of that claim or information is not recorded on an official computer system; or
(b) in the case of information that falls to be delivered by the Secretary of State, if the despatch of that information is not recorded on an official computer system.

(3) The time and date of receipt of any claim or information sent by an approved method of electronic communication is to be presumed, unless the contrary is proved, to be that recorded on an official computer system.

Proof of identity

2.376 **6.**—(1) The identity of—

(a) the sender of any claim or information delivered by means of an electronic communication to an official computer system; or
(b) the recipient of any claim or information delivered by means of an electronic communication from an official computer system,

is to be presumed, unless the contrary is proved, to be the person whose name is recorded as such on that official computer system.

(2) Any claim or information delivered by an approved method of electronic communication on behalf of another person ("P") is to be deemed to have been delivered by P unless P proves that it was delivered without P's knowledge or connivance.

Proof of content

2.377 **7.** The content of any claim or information sent by means of an electronic communication is to be presumed, unless the contrary is proved, to be that recorded on an official computer system.

Schedule 3 – Consequential Amendments

Amendments made by this Schedule have been incorporated in the regulations which are amended. 2.378

Schedule 4 – Special Provisions relating to Claims for a Jobseeker's Allowance during periods connected with Public Holidays [Regulation 36(2)]

1. In this Schedule and regulation 36(2)— 2.379

(a) "public holiday" means—

(i) in England and Wales, Christmas Day, Good Friday or a bank holiday under the Banking and Financial Dealings Act 1971,

(ii) in Scotland, a bank holiday under the Banking and Financial Dealings Act 1971 or a local holiday;

(b) "Christmas and New Year holidays" means—

(i) in England and Wales, the period beginning at the start of Christmas Day and terminating at the end of New Year's Day, or if New Year's Day is a Sunday at the end of 2nd January,

(ii) in Scotland, the period beginning at the start of Christmas Day and terminating at the end of 2nd January, or where New Year's Day is a Saturday or a Sunday terminating at the end of 3rd January;

(c) "Easter Holidays" means the period beginning at the start of Good Friday and terminating at the end of Easter Monday;

(d) "office closure" means a period during which an appropriate office is closed in connection with a public holiday.

2. Where a claim for a jobseeker's allowance is made during any period set out in paragraph 3, the Secretary of State may treat that claim as a claim for a period, to be specified in a decision of the Secretary of State, not exceeding— 2.380

(a) 35 days after the date of the claim where the claim is made during the period specified in sub-paragraph (a) of paragraph 3; or

(b) 21 days after the date of claim where the claim is made during the period specified in either sub-paragraph (b) or (c) of paragraph 3.

3. For the purposes of paragraph 2 the periods are— 2.381

(a) in the case of Christmas and New Year holidays, a period beginning with the start of the before the first day of office closure and terminating at the end of the last day of office closure;

(b) in the case of Easter Holidays, a period beginning with the start of the 16th day before the first day of office closure and terminating at the end of the last day of office closure;

(c) in the case of any other public holiday, a period beginning with the start of the 14th day re the first day of office closure and terminating at the end of the last day of office closure.

Schedule 5 – Direct Payment to Lender of Deductions in respect of Interest on Secured Loans [Regulation 59]

Interpretation

1.—(1) In this Schedule— 2.382

"housing costs element" means an amount in respect of housing costs which is included in a claimant's award of universal credit under section 11(1) of the 2012 Act;

"qualifying lender" means (subject to paragraph 10)—

(a) the bodies or persons listed in paragraphs (a) to (g) of section 15A(3) of the Administration Act;

(b) the Regulator of Social Housing;

(c) the Greater London Authority; and

(d) any body incorporated under the Companies Act 1985(**c**), the main objects of which include the making of loans secured by—

(i) a mortgage of or charge over land, or

(ii) in Scotland a heritable security;

"loan interest payments" has the meaning given by paragraph 5 of Schedule 1 to the Universal Credit Regulations;

"relevant claimant" has the meaning given in paragraph 2(1);

"specified benefits", in relation to a relevant claimant, means the benefits specified in paragraph 2(2)—

(a) to which the relevant claimant is entitled; or

(b) where the relevant claimant is a member of a couple, to which the other member of the couple is entitled;

"standard rate" means the standard rate of interest determined under paragraph 12 of Schedule 5 to the Universal Credit Regulations.

(2) References in this Schedule to a relevant claimant who meets the payment condition or the liability condition are to a claimant who meets those conditions in accordance with regulation 25 of the Universal Credit Regulations (the housing costs element).

Relevant claimants and benefits from which payments are to be made

2.383 **2.**—(1) For the purposes of this Schedule, "relevant claimant" means a claimant—

(a) who is entitled to universal credit;

(b) whose maximum amount for the purposes of universal credit includes the housing costs element; and

(c) whose amount of housing costs element is calculated by reference to loan interest payments (whether or not that amount is calculated by reference to any other description of payment).

(2) Direct payments of loan interest may be made under paragraph 3 from any of the following benefits—

(a) universal credit; and

(b) if the maximum amount to which the relevant claimant is entitled for the purposes of universal credit is insufficient for the purposes of this Schedule—

(i) a jobseeker's allowance, or

(ii) an employment and support allowance.

Circumstances in which direct payments of loan interest to be made

2.384 **3.**—(1) If the circumstances set out in sub-paragraph (2) apply to a relevant claimant in respect of a loan, the Secretary of State is to pay part of the specified benefits directly to the qualifying lender to whom the loan interest payments in respect of the loan are payable.

(2) The circumstances are that—

(a) a loan was made in respect of which loan interest payments are payable to a qualifying lender;

(b) the relevant claimant (or either joint claimant) meets the payment condition and liability condition in respect of loan interest payments on the loan;

(c) those payments are taken into account in calculating the amount of housing costs element to be included in the relevant claimant's award of universal credit; and

(d) the amount included in respect of those payments is calculated by reference to the standard rate.

(3) The part of the specified benefits which is to be paid under sub-paragraph (1) is the amount calculated under paragraphs 4 and 5 in respect of the relevant claimant.

Determining the amount to be paid to a qualifying lender

2.385 **4.**—(1) Where the circumstances set out in paragraph 3(2) apply to a relevant claimant in respect of one loan only, the amount that is to be paid under paragraph 3 directly to the qualifying lender is to be calculated as follows.

Step 1

Find the amount in respect of the loan interest payments which is calculated under paragraph 10 of Schedule 5 to the Universal Credit Regulations (amount in respect of interest on loans).

Step 2

Deduct from the amount resulting from step 1 a sum equivalent to so much of any amount payable in the circumstances described in sub-paragraph (2) as represents payments in respect of loan interest.

(2) This sub-paragraph applies where a payment is being made under a policy of insurance taken out by a relevant claimant to insure against the risk of not being able to maintain repayments of loan interest to a qualifying lender.

(3) The amount to be paid directly to the qualifying lender in respect of the relevant claimant is—

(a) the amount resulting from sub-paragraph (1); or

(b) where the aggregate amount of all of the specified benefits is less than the amount resulting from sub-paragraph (1), the aggregate amount of all those benefits less one penny.

Determining the amount to be paid to a qualifying lender: more than one loan

5.—(1) Where the circumstances set out in paragraph 3(2) apply to a relevant claimant in respect of more than one loan, the amount that is to be paid under paragraph 3 directly to each of the qualifying lenders to whom loan interest payments are payable is to be calculated as follows. 2.386

(2) Where loan interest payments on two or more loans are payable to the same qualifying lender, the amount to be paid directly to that lender is found by—

(a) in respect of each of those loans, calculating an amount in accordance with Steps 1 and 2 of paragraph 4(1); and

(b) adding those amounts together.

(3) Where loan interest payments are payable to more than one qualifying lender, the amount to be paid directly to each lender is found by—

(a) where loan interest payments are payable to a qualifying lender in respect of one loan only, calculating an amount in accordance with Steps 1 and 2 of paragraph 4(1) in respect of the loan;

(b) where loan interest payments are payable to a qualifying lender in respect of more than one loan, calculating an amount in accordance with sub-paragraph (2).

(4) The amount to be paid directly to the qualifying lender in respect of the relevant claimant is—

(a) the amount resulting from sub-paragraph (2) or (3) in respect of that lender; or

(b) where the aggregate amount of all of the specified benefits is less than the sum of the amounts resulting from sub-paragraph (2) or (3), the amount determined under sub-paragraph (5).

(5) For the purposes of sub-paragraph (4)(b)—

(a) the overall total of the amounts to be paid directly to the qualifying lenders is the aggregate amount of all of the specified benefits less one penny; and

(b) that amount is to be paid directly to qualifying lenders as follows—

(i) the qualifying lender in whose case the amount resulting from sub-paragraph (2) or (3) is the largest is to be paid first,

(ii) if anything remains, the qualifying lender in whose case the amount resulting from sub-paragraph (2) or (3) is next largest is to be paid next, and so on until nothing remains.

(6) In the application of sub-paragraph (5)(b) in any case where the amount resulting from sub- paragraph (2) or (3) is the same in respect of two or more qualifying lenders, the available amount is to be divided equally between them.

Qualifying lenders to apply direct payments in discharge of borrower's liability

6. Where a direct payment is made under paragraph 3 to a qualifying lender in respect of a relevant claimant, the lender must apply the amount of the payment towards discharging the liability to make loan interest payments in respect of which the direct payment was made. 2.387

Application by qualifying lenders of any amount which exceeds liability

7.—(1) This paragraph applies where, in respect of a relevant claimant— 2.388

(a) any direct payment is made under paragraph 3 to a qualifying lender; and

(b) the amount paid exceeds the amount of the loan interest payments payable.

(2) Unless sub-paragraph (3) applies, the qualifying lender must apply the amount of the excess as follows—

(a) first, towards discharging the amount of any liability of the relevant claimant for arrears of loan interest payments in respect of the loan in question; and

(b) if any amount of the excess is then remaining, towards discharging any liability of the relevant claimant to repay—

(i) the principal sum in respect of the loan, or

(ii) any other sum payable by the relevant claimant to that lender in respect of the loan.

(3) Where loan interest payments on two or more loans are payable to the same qualifying lender, the lender must apply the amount of the excess as follows—

(a) first, towards discharging the amount of any liability of the relevant claimant for arrears of loan interest payments in respect of the loan in respect of which the excess amount was paid; and

(b) if any amount of the excess is then remaining, towards discharging any liability of the relevant claimant to repay—

(i) in respect of the loan referred to in paragraph (a), the principal sum or any other sum payable by the relevant claimant to that lender, or

(ii) in respect of any other loan, any sum payable by the relevant claimant to that lender where the liability to pay that sum has not already discharged under this Schedule.

Time and manner of payments

2.389 **8.** Direct payments under paragraph 3 are to be made in monthly instalments in arrears.

Fees payable by qualifying lenders

2.390 **9.**—(1) A fee is payable by a qualifying lender to the Secretary of State for the purpose of meeting the expenses of the Secretary of State in administering the making of direct payments to qualifying lenders under paragraph 3.

(2) The fee is [[1] £0.39] in respect of each occasion on which a direct payment is made to the qualifying lender.

Election not to be regarded as a qualifying lender

2.391 **10.**—(1) A body or person who would otherwise be within the definition of "qualifying lender" in paragraph 1(1)—

(a) may elect not to be regarded as such by giving notice to the Secretary of State in writing; and

(b) may revoke any such notice by giving a further notice in writing.

(2) In respect of any financial year, a notice under sub-paragraph (1) which is given not later than the 1st February before the start of the financial year takes effect on 1st April following the giving of the notice.

(3) Where a body or person becomes a qualifying lender in the course of a financial year—

(a) any notice of an election by the body or person under sub-paragraph (1)(a) must be given within 6 weeks ("the initial period") of the date of their becoming a qualifying lender; and

(b) no direct payments may be made under paragraph 3 to the body or person before the expiry of the initial period.

(4) But sub-paragraph (3)(b) does not apply in any case where—

(a) the body or person gives the Secretary of State notice in writing that that provision should not apply; and

(b) that notice is given before the start of the initial period or before that period expires.

(5) In relation to a notice under sub-paragraph (1)—

(a) where the notice is given by an electronic communication, it must be given in accordance with the provisions set out in Schedule 2 (electronic communications);

(b) where the notice is sent by post, it is to be treated as having been given on the day the notice was received.

Provision of information

11.—(1) A qualifying lender must, in respect of a relevant claimant, provide the Secretary of State with information as to— **2.392**

(a) the loan interest payments in respect of which the relevant claimant meets the payment condition and the liability condition;
(b) the amount of the loan;
(c) the purpose for which the loan was made;
(d) the amount outstanding on the loan;
(e) the amount of arrears of loan interest payments due in respect of the loan;
(f) any change in the amount of the loan interest payable; and
(g) the redemption of the loan.

(2) The information referred to in sub-paragraph (1)(a) to (e) must be provided at the request of the Secretary of State where—

(a) a claim is made for universal credit; or
(b) the housing costs element is to be included in an award of universal credit otherwise than on the making of a claim,

and loan interest payments payable to the qualifying lender are taken into account in determining the amount of the relevant claimant's housing costs element.

(3) The information referred to in sub-paragraph (1)(f) must be provided at such times, or in the case of the information referred to in sub-paragraph (1)(d) at such other times, as the Secretary of State may determine.

(4) The information referred to in sub-paragraph (1)(g) must be provided to the Secretary of State immediately once the qualifying lender has received notice that the loan is to be redeemed.

Recovery of sums wrongly paid

12.—(1) In the following circumstances, a qualifying lender must at the request of the Secretary of State repay any amount paid to the lender under paragraph 3 which ought not to have been paid. **2.393**

(2)Those circumstances are that, in respect of a relevant claimant—

(a) an amount calculated by reference to loan interest payments payable to the qualifying lender ceases to be included in the relevant claimant's housing costs element;
(b) a specified benefit ceases to be paid to a relevant claimant;
(c) the loan in respect of which loan interest payments are payable has been redeemed; or
(d) both of the conditions set out in sub-paragraphs (3) and (4) are met.

(3) The first condition is that the amount of the relevant claimant's housing costs element is reduced as a result of—

(a) the standard rate having been reduced; or
(b) the amount outstanding on the loan having been reduced.

(4) The second condition is that no corresponding reduction was made to the amount calculated in respect of the qualifying lender under paragraph 4 or 5.

(5) A qualifying lender is not required to make a repayment in the circumstances described in sub-paragraph (2)(a) or (b) unless the Secretary of State's request is made before the end of the period of two months starting with the date on which the thing described in that provision ceased.

AMENDMENT

1. The Social Security (Fees Payable by Qualifying Lenders) (Amendment) Regulations 2017 (SI 2017/270) reg.3 (April 1, 2017).

SCHEDULE 6 – DEDUCTIONS FROM BENEFIT AND DIRECT PAYMENT TO THIRD PARTIES [REGULATION 60]

Interpretation

1. In this Schedule— **2.394**

"assessment period" has the meaning given by regulation 21 (assessment periods) of the Universal Credit Regulations;

"the work allowance" means, in relation to any claimant, the amount applicable to that claimant under regulation 22(2) (deduction of income and work allowance) of the Universal Credit Regulations;

"child element" means, in relation to any claimant, any amount included in the claimant's award of universal credit under regulation 24 (the child element) of the Universal Credit Regulations;

"the Community Charges Regulations" means the Community Charges (Deductions from Income Support) (No. 2) Regulations 1990;

"the Community Charges (Scotland) Regulations" means the Community Charges (Deductions from Income Support) (Scotland) Regulations 1989;

"the Council Tax Regulations" means the Council Tax (Deductions from Income Support) Regulations 1993;

"the Fines Regulations" means the Fines (Deductions from Income Support) Regulations 1992;

"standard allowance" means, in relation to any claimant, any amount included in the claimant's award of universal credit under section 9(1) of the 2012 Act;

"water charges" means—

(a) as respects England and Wales, any water and sewerage charges under Chapter 1 of Part 5 of the Water Industry Act 1991;

(b) as respects Scotland, any such charges established by Scottish Water under a charges scheme made under section 29A of the Water Industry (Scotland) Act 2002;

[4 . . .]

General

2.395 **2.**—(1) The Secretary of State may deduct an amount from a claimant's award of universal credit and pay that amount to a third party in accordance with the following provisions of this Schedule to discharge (in whole or part) a liability of the claimant to that third party. as the Secretary of State may direct.

Limitations applicable to deductions made under this Schedule

2.396 **3.**—(1) The Secretary of State may not deduct an amount from a claimant's award of universal credit under this Schedule and pay that amount to a third party if, in relation to any assessment period, that would—

(a) reduce the amount payable to the claimant to less than one penny; or

(b) result in more than three deductions being made, in relation to that assessment period, under one or more of the provisions mentioned in sub-paragraph (2).

(2) The provisions are—

(a) paragraph 6 (housing costs) of this Schedule;

(b) paragraph 7 (rent and service charges included in rent) of this Schedule;

(c) paragraph 8 (fuel costs) of this Schedule;

(d) paragraph 9 (water charges) of this Schedule;

(e) paragraph 10 (payments in place of payments of child support maintenance) of this Schedule;

(f) paragraph 11 (eligible loans) of this Schedule;

(g) paragraph 12 (integration loans) of this Schedule;

(h) regulation 3 (deductions from income support etc.) of the Community Charges Regulations;

(i) regulation 3 (deductions from income support etc.) of the Community Charges (Scotland) Regulations;

(j) regulation 5 (deduction from debtor's income support etc.) of the Council Tax Regulations; and

(k) regulation 4 (deductions from offender's income support etc.) of the Fines Regulations.

(3) The aggregate amount deducted from a claimant's award of universal credit in relation to any assessment period and paid to a third party under paragraphs 8 (fuel costs) and 9 (water charges) of this Schedule must not, without the claimant's consent, exceed a sum equal to [4 25%] of the aggregate of the standard allowance and any child element

Maximum amount

2.397 **4.**—(1) Except as provided for in sub-paragraph (4), the Secretary of State may not deduct an amount from a claimant's award of universal credit under a provision mentioned in paragraph 5(2) of this Schedule if, in relation to any assessment period, that would result in the Secretary of State deducting an amount in excess of [4 40%] of the standard allowance ("the maximum amount") from the claimant's award under one or more relevant provisions.

(2) The relevant provisions are—

(a) those mentioned in paragraph 5(2) of this Schedule;
(b) section 26 (higher-level sanctions) of the 2012 Act;
(c) section 27 (other sanctions) of the 2012 Act;
(d) section 71ZG (recovery of payments on account) of the Administration Act(**c**);
(e) section 6B of the Social Security Fraud Act 2001 ("the 2001 Act");
(f) section 7 of the 2001 Act; and
(g) section 9 of the 2001 Act (**c**).

(3) For the purposes of determining whether the maximum amount would be exceeded, no account is to be taken of any liability for continuing need mentioned in—
(a) paragraph 8(4)(b) (fuel costs) of this Schedule; or
(b) paragraph 9(6)(b) or (7)(b)(water charges) of this Schedule.

(4) Subject to paragraph 3 of this Schedule, the Secretary of State may deduct an amount from the claimant's award under paragraph 6 (housing costs), [3 . . .] or paragraph 8 (fuel costs) [3, or the minimum amount which may be deducted under paragraph 7 (rent and service charges included in rent)] of this Schedule and pay that amount to a third party where the deduction appears to the Secretary of State to be in the claimant's best interests, even though the deduction would result in the maximum amount being exceeded.

Priority as between certain debts

5.—(1) This paragraph applies to a claimant ("C") where, in relation to any assessment period— 2.398
(a) a deduction could otherwise be made from C's award under more than one of the provisions mentioned in sub-paragraph (2); and
(b) the amount of universal credit payable to C in relation to that assessment period is insufficient to enable the Secretary of State to meet all of the liabilities for which in C's case deductions may be made under those provisions or the deduction, were it to be made, would mean that the maximum amount referred to in paragraph 4(1) would be exceeded.

(2) The provisions are—
(a) paragraph 6 (housing costs of this Schedule);
(b) paragraph 7 (rent and service charges included in rent) [3 where the amount of the deduction equals 10% of the standard allowance];
(c) paragraph 8 (fuel costs) of this Schedule;
(d) regulation 3 (deductions from income support etc.) of the Community Charges Regulations, regulation 3 (deductions from income support etc.) of the Community Charges (Scotland) Regulations or (because no such payments are being made in C's case) regulation 5 (deduction from debtor's income support etc.) of the Council Tax Regulations;
(e) regulation 4 (deductions from offender's income support etc.) of the Fines Regulations where the amount of the deduction equals 5% of the standard allowance;
(f) paragraph 9 (water charges) of this Schedule;
(g) paragraph 10 (payments in place of child support maintenance) of this Schedule;
(h) Schedule 7 (deductions from benefit in respect of child support maintenance and payment to persons with care) to these Regulations;
(i) section 78(2) (recovery of social fund awards) of the Administration Act;
(j) section 71ZH(1)(a) or (b) (recovery of hardship payments etc.) of the [5 Administration Act];
(k) section 115A (penalty as alternative to prosecution) of the Administration Act where an overpayment is recoverable from a person by, or due from a person to, the Secretary of State or an authority under or by virtue of section 71 (overpayments – general), section 75 (overpayments of housing benefit) or section 71ZB (recovery of overpayments of certain benefits) of that Act;
(l) section 71 (overpayments – general), section 71ZC (deduction from benefit) or section 75(4) (overpayments of housing benefit) of the Administration Act or an overpayment of working tax credit or child tax credit, where in each case, the overpayment (or part of it) is the result of fraud;
(m) section 115C(4) (incorrect statements etc.) and section 115D(1) (failure to disclose information) of the Administration Act;
(n) section 71 (overpayments – general), section 71ZC (deduction from benefit) or section 75(4) (overpayments of housing benefit) of the Administration Act or an overpayment of working tax credit or child tax credit, where in each case, the overpayment (or part of it) is not the result of fraud;
(o) paragraph 12 (integration loans) of this Schedule;
(p) paragraph 11 (eligible loans) of this Schedule;

[3 (pa) paragraph 7 (rent and service charges included in rent) where the amount of deduction exceeds the minimum amount that may be deducted under that paragraph;]

(q) regulation 4 (deductions from offender's income support etc.) of the Fines Regulations where the amount of the deduction exceeds the minimum amount that may be deducted in accordance with those Regulations.

(3) Where this paragraph applies to a claimant, the Secretary of State must make a deduction under any of the provisions mentioned sub-paragraph (2) in accordance with sub-paragraphs (4) and (5).

(4) The Secretary of State must give priority to any such deductions in the order in which they are listed in sub-paragraph (2), with housing costs having the priority.

(5) Where two or more provisions mentioned in any single paragraph of sub-paragraph (2) apply to the claimant, unless the Secretary of State directs otherwise, those deductions have equal priority with each other and the amount of such deductions are to be apportioned accordingly.

(6) For the purposes of sub-paragraph (2)(l) and (n), an overpayment is the result of fraud if, in relation to that overpayment or that part of it, the claimant—

(a) has been found guilty of an offence whether under statute or otherwise;

(b) made an admission after caution of deception or fraud for the purpose of obtaining benefit under the Administration Act, or in the case of a tax credit, under the Tax Credits Act 2002; or

(c) agreed to pay a penalty under section 115A of the Administration Act (penalty as an alternative to prosecution) and the agreement has not been withdrawn.

Housing costs

2.399 **6.**—(1) This paragraph applies where the following condition is met.

(2) The condition is that in any assessment period the claimant is in debt for any item of housing costs which is included in the claimant's award of universal credit under Schedule 5 (housing costs element for owner-occupiers) to the Universal Credit Regulations.

(3) Where this paragraph applies, but subject to sub-paragraph (4), the Secretary of State may, in such cases and circumstances as the Secretary of State may determine, in relation to that assessment period deduct an amount from the claimant's award equal to 5% of the standard allowance in respect of any debt mentioned in sub-paragraph (2) and pay that amount or those amounts to the person to whom any such debt is owed.

(4) Before the Secretary of State may commence (or re-commence) making deductions in respect of any such debt, the claimant's earned income (or in the case of joint claimants their combined earned income) in relation to the previous assessment period must not exceed the work allowance.

(5) No amount may be deducted under this paragraph in respect of owner-occupier payments within the meaning of paragraph 4 of Schedule 1 (meaning of payments in respect of accommodation) to the Universal Credit Regulations in any case where those payments—

(a) are required to be paid directly to a qualifying lender under regulation 59 of these Regulations; or

(b) would have been required to be paid to a body which, or a person who, would otherwise have been a qualifying lender but for an election given under paragraph 10 of Schedule 5 to these Regulations.

(6) As between liability for items of housing costs to which this paragraph applies, liabilities in respect of owner-occupier payments (within the meaning of paragraph 4(1) of Schedule 1 (meaning of payments in respect of accommodation) to the Universal Credit Regulations) are to have priority over all other items.

Rent and service charges included in rent

2.400 **7.**—(1) This paragraph applies where all of the following conditions are met.

(2) The first condition is that in any assessment period the claimant—

(a) has an award of universal credit which includes an amount under Schedule 4 (housing costs element for renters) to the Universal Credit Regulations; or

(b) occupies exempt accommodation and has an award of housing benefit under section 130 (housing benefit) of the Contributions and Benefits Act.

(3) The second condition is that the claimant is in debt for any—

(a) rent payments;

(b) service charges which are paid with or as part of the claimant's rent.

(4) The third condition is that the claimant occupies the accommodation to which the debt relates.

(5) Where this paragraph applies, but subject to sub-paragraphs (6) and (7), the Secretary of State may, in such cases and circumstances as the Secretary of State may determine, deduct in relation to that assessment period an amount from the claimant's award [3 which is no less than 10% and no more than 20%] of the standard allowance and pay that amount to the person to whom the debt is owed.

(6) Before the Secretary of State may commence (or re-commence) making deductions in respect of such a debt, the claimant's earned income (or in the case of joint claimants their combined earned income) in relation to the previous assessment period must not exceed the work allowance.

(7) The Secretary of State must stop making such deductions if, in relation to the three assessment periods immediately preceding the date on which the next deduction could otherwise be made, the claimant's earned income (or in the case of joint claimants their combined earned income) equals or exceeds the work allowance.

(8) In this paragraph—

"exempt accommodation" has the meaning given by paragraph 1 of Schedule 1 (interpretation) to the Universal Credit Regulations;

"rent payments" includes any elements included in the claimant's rent which would not fall to be treated as rent under the Housing Benefit Regulations 2006 or as rent payments under the Universal Credit Regulations;

"service charges" includes any items in a charge for services in respect of the accommodation occupied by the claimant which would not fall to be treated as service charges under the Universal Credit Regulations.

Fuel costs

8.—(1) This paragraph applies where the following condition is met. 2.401

(2) The condition is that in any assessment period the claimant is in debt for any [1 fuel item].

(3) Where this paragraph applies, but subject to sub-paragraphs (5) and (6), the Secretary of State may, in such cases and circumstances as the Secretary of State may determine, deduct in relation to that assessment period the following amounts from the claimant's award and pay them to the person to whom the payment is due.

(4) The amount which may be deducted in respect of any fuel item is—

(a) an amount equal to 5% of the standard allowance; and

(b) an additional amount which the Secretary of State estimates is equal to the average monthly cost necessary to meet the claimant's continuing need for [1 the fuel in respect of which the debt arose, plus such monthly amount as is required to meet any payments required to be made under a green deal plan within the meaning of section 1 of the Energy Act 2011 ("the 2011 Act")], except where current consumption is paid for by other means such as a pre-payment meter.

(5) Before the Secretary of State may commence (or re-commence) making deductions in respect of such a debt, the claimant's earned income (or in the case of joint claimants their combined earned income) in relation to the previous assessment period must not exceed the work allowance.

(6) The Secretary of State must stop making such deductions if, in relation to the three assessment periods immediately preceding the date on which the next deduction could otherwise be made, the claimant's earned income (or in the case of joint claimants their combined earned income) equals or exceeds the work allowance.

(7) As between liabilities for items of gas or electricity, the Secretary of State must give priority to whichever liability the Secretary of State considers it would, having regard to the circumstances and to any requests of the claimant, be appropriate to discharge.

[1 (8) In this paragraph, "fuel item" means –

(a) any charge for mains gas, including for the reconnection of mains gas;

(b) any charge for mains electricity and including any charge for the disconnection and reconnection of mains electricity and including any payments required to be made under a green deal plan within the meaning of section 1 of the 2011 Act.]

Water charges

9.—(1) This paragraph applies where the following condition is met. 2.402

(2) The condition is that in any assessment period the claimant is in debt for water charges, including any charges for reconnection ("the original debt").

(3) Where this paragraph applies, but subject to sub-paragraphs (4) and (5), the Secretary of State may, in such cases and circumstances as the Secretary of State may determine, deduct an amount from the claimant's award in accordance with sub-paragraphs (6) to (8) and pay it to

a water undertaker to whom the payment is due or to the person or body authorised to collect water charges for that undertaker.

(4) Before the Secretary of State may commence (or re-commence) making deductions in respect of such a debt, the claimant's earned income (or in the case of joint claimants their combined earned income) in relation to the previous assessment period must not exceed the work allowance.

(5) The Secretary of State must stop making such deductions if, in relation to the three assessment periods immediately preceding the date on which the next deduction could otherwise be made, the claimant's earned income (or in the case of joint claimants their combined earned income) equals or exceeds the work allowance.

(6) Where water charges are determined by means of a water meter, the amount to be deducted under this paragraph in relation to any assessment period is to be—

(a) an amount equal to 5% of the standard allowance towards discharging the original debt; and

(b) an additional amount which the Secretary of State estimates to be the average monthly cost necessary to meet the claimant's continuing need for water consumption.

(7) Where water charges are determined otherwise than by means of a water meter, the amount to be deducted in relation to any assessment period under this paragraph is to be—

(a) the amount referred to in sub-paragraph (6)(a); and

(b) an additional amount equal to the cost necessary to meet the continuing need for water consumption in that assessment period.

(8) Where the claimant is in debt to two water undertakers—

(a) only one amount under sub-paragraph (6)(a) or (7)(a) may be deducted;

(b) a deduction in respect of an original debt for sewerage may only be made after the whole debt in respect of an original debt for water has been paid; and

(c) deductions in respect of continuing charges for both water and for sewerage may be made at the same time.

(9) In this paragraph "water undertaker" means—

(a) in relation to any area in England and Wales, a company holding an appointment as a water undertaker or a sewerage undertaker under the Water Industry Act 1991; or

(b) in relation to any area in Scotland, Scottish Water.

Payments in place of payments of child support maintenance

2.403 **10.**—(1) This paragraph applies where the Secretary of State has determined that section 43 (contribution to maintenance by deduction from benefit) of the 1991 Act and regulation 28 (contribution to maintenance by deduction from benefit) of the Child Support (Maintenance Assessments and Special Cases) Regulations 1992(**c**) apply in relation to the claimant.

(2) Where this paragraph applies, the Secretary of State must, if satisfied that there is sufficient universal credit in payment (but subject to paragraphs 1, 4 and 5 of this Schedule), determine that an amount is to be deducted from the claimant's award for transmission to the person or persons entitled to receive that amount under or by virtue of the 1991 Act.

(3) Not more than one deduction may be made under this paragraph in relation to any assessment period.

(4) The amount of universal credit which may be deducted in relation to any assessment period id to a third party under this paragraph is to be an amount equal to 5% of the standard allowance.

Eligible loans

2.404 **11.**—(1) This paragraph applies where [2 in any assessment period the claimant is in arrears in respect of a loan entered into (whether solely or jointly) with an eligible lender in respect of an eligible loan].

(2) [2 . . .]

(3) [2 . . .]

(4) Where the claimant has an award of universal credit, the Secretary of State may, in such cases and circumstances as the Secretary of State may determine, deduct in relation to the assessment period referred to in sub-paragraph (2) an amount from the claimant's award equal to 5% of the standard allowance and pay that amount to the eligible lender towards discharging the amount owing under the loan agreement.

(5) In a case where the claimant has an award of universal credit but the amount payable to the claimant in relation to that assessment period is insufficient to enable such a deduction to be made, the Secretary of State may instead deduct a weekly amount equal to 5% of the personal allowance for a single claimant aged not less than 25 from any employment and support allowance or jobseeker's allowance awarded to the claimant and pay that amount to the eligible lender.

(6) In a case where the claimant does not have an award of universal credit, but has an award of an employment and support allowance or a jobseeker's allowance, the Secretary of State may deduct a weekly amount equal to 5% of the personal allowance for a single claimant aged not less than 25 from any such award and pay that amount to the eligible lender.

(7) The Secretary of State must not make deductions from a claimant's employment and support allowance or a jobseeker's allowance under this paragraph if that would reduce the amount payable to the claimant to less than 10 pence.

(8) In this paragraph—

"eligible benefit" means—

(a) an employment and support allowance;

(b) a jobseeker's allowance;

(c) universal credit;

"eligible lender" means—

(a) a body registered under section 1 (societies which may be registered) of the Industrial and Provident Societies Act 1965;

(b) a credit union within the meaning of section 1 (registration under the Industrial and Provident Societies Act 1965) of the Credit Unions Act 1979;

(c) a charitable institution within the meaning of section 58(1) (interpretation of Part 2) of the Charities Act 1992;

(d) a body entered on the Scottish Charity Register under section 3 (Scottish Charities Register) of the Charities and Trustee Investment (Scotland) Act 2005;

(e) a community interest company within the meaning of Part 2 of the Companies (Audit, Investigations and Community Enterprise) Act 2004,

which, except for a credit union, is licensed under the Consumer Credit Act 1974 and which the Secretary of State considers is an appropriate body to which payments on behalf of the claimant may be made in respect of loans made by that body;

"eligible loan" means a loan made by a lender who is, at the time the loan agreement is made, an eligible lender, to a claimant except a loan which—

(a) is secured by a charge or pledge;

(b) is for the purpose of business or self-employment; or

(c) was made by means of a credit card;

"loan agreement" means an agreement between the eligible lender and the claimant in respect of an eligible loan;

"5% of the personal allowance" means 5% of the personal allowance applicable in the claimant's case, rounded up (in any case where that calculation produces a result which is not a multiple of five pence) to the next higher multiple of five pence.

Integration loans

12.—(1) This paragraph applies where [2 the claimant has an integration loan which is recoverable by deductions]. 2.405

(2) [2 . . .]

(3) [2 . . .]

(4) Where this paragraph applies, the amount payable by deductions in any assessment period is to be equal to 5% of the standard allowance.

(5) In this paragraph, "integration loan which is recoverable by deductions" means an integration loan which is made under the Integration Loans for Refugees and Others Regulations 2007 and which is recoverable from the claimant by deductions from the claimant's award of universal credit under regulation 9 of those Regulations.

AMENDMENTS

1. The Social Security (Miscellaneous Amendments) Regulations 2013 (SI 2013/443) reg.10 (April 29, 2013).

2. The Universal Credit and Miscellaneous Amendments Regulations 2014 (SI 2014/597) reg.5 (April 28, 2014).

3. The Universal Credit and Miscellaneous Amendments (No.2) Regulations 2014 (SI 2014/2888) reg.6 (November 26, 2014).

4. The Social Security (Miscellaneous Amendments) No 2) Regulations 2013 (SI 2013/1508) reg.6 (July 29, 2013).

5. The Universal Credit and Miscellaneous Amendments Regulations 2015 (SI 2015/1754) reg.9 (November 3, 2015).

SCHEDULE 7 – DEDUCTIONS FROM BENEFIT IN RESPECT OF CHILD SUPPORT MAINTENANCE AND PAYMENT TO PERSONS WITH CARE [REGULATION 60]

Interpretation

2.406 1. In this Schedule—

"beneficiary" means a person who has been awarded a specified benefit;

[1 "fee" means any collection fee under Part 3 of the Child Support Fees Regulations 2014 which is payable by the non-resident parent;]

"maintenance", except in paragraph 3, means child support maintenance which a non-resident parent is liable to pay under the 1991 Act at a flat rate (or would be so liable but for a variation having been agreed to) where that rate applies (or would have applied) because the non-resident parent falls within paragraph 4(1)(b), (c) or (2) of Schedule 1 to the 1991 Act, and includes such maintenance payable at a transitional rate in accordance with regulations made under section 29(3)(a) of the Child Support, Pensions and Social Security Act 2000;

"person with care" has the same meaning as in section 3 (meaning of certain terms used in this Act) of the 1991 Act;

"specified benefit" means—

(a) an employment and support allowance;

(b) a jobseeker's allowance;

(c) universal credit.

Deductions

2.407 **2.**—(1) Subject to the following provisions of this paragraph and to paragraph 5 (flat rate maintenance), the Secretary of State may deduct from any specified benefit awarded to a beneficiary, an amount equal to the amount of maintenance [1 and any fee] which is payable by the beneficiary and pay the amount deducted to or among the person or persons with care in discharge (in whole or in part) of the liability to pay maintenance [1, and retain any amount deducted in discharge of any liability to pay a fee.].

(2) A deduction [1 for maintenance and fees] may only be made from one specified benefit in respect of the same period.

(3) No amount may be deducted under this Schedule from any employment and support allowance or any jobseeker's allowance awarded to the claimant if that would reduce the amount of the benefit payable to the claimant to less than 10 pence.

(4) No amount may be deducted from any universal credit awarded to the claimant under this Schedule if that would reduce the amount payable to the claimant to less than one penny.

Arrears

2.408 **3.**—(1) Except where universal credit is awarded to the beneficiary, the Secretary of State may deduct the sum of [1 £1.20] per week from any employment and support allowance or jobseeker's allowance which the beneficiary has been awarded and, subject to sub-paragraph (2), pay the amount deducted to or among the person or persons with care in discharge (in whole or in part) of the beneficiary's liability to pay arrears of maintenance [1, and retain an amount deducted in discharge of any liability to pay a fee.].

(2) Deductions made under sub-paragraph (1) may be retained by the Secretary of State in the circumstances set out in regulation 8 of the Child Support (Arrears, Interest and Adjustment of Maintenance Assessments) Regulations 1992.

(3) In sub-paragraph (1) "maintenance" means child support maintenance as defined by section 3(6) of the 1991 Act whether before or after the amendment of the definition of such maintenance by section 1(2)(a) of the Child Support, Pensions and Social Security Act 2000, and includes maintenance payable at a transitional rate in accordance with regulations made under section 29(3)(a) of that Act.

Apportionment

2.409 **4.** Where maintenance is payable to more than one person with care, the amount deducted [1 in respect of maintenance] must be apportioned between the persons with care in accordance with paragraphs 6, 7 and 8 of Schedule 1 (maintenance assessments) to the 1991 Act.

Flat rate maintenance

5.—(1) This paragraph applies where the beneficiary and that person's partner are each liable to pay maintenance at a flat rate in accordance with paragraph 4(2) of Schedule 1 to the 1991 Act and either of them has been awarded universal credit (whether as a single claimant or as joint claimants). **2.410**

(2) Where this paragraph applies, an amount not exceeding an amount equal to the flat rate of maintenance [1 and any fee] may be deducted from such an award in respect of the total liability of both partners to pay maintenance [1 and any fee], in the proportions described in regulation 4(3) of the Child Support (Maintenance Calculations and Special Cases) Regulations 2001 or regulation 44(3) of the Child Support Maintenance Calculation Regulations 2012 and must be paid in discharge (in whole or in part) of the respective liabilities to pay maintenance [1 or retained in discharge of any liability to pay a fee.].

Notice

6. Where the Secretary of State commences making deductions under this Schedule, the Secretary of State must notify the beneficiary in writing of the amount and frequency of the deduction and the benefit from which the deduction is made and must give further such notice when there is a change to any of the particulars specified in the notice. **2.411**

AMENDMENT

1. The Child Support Fees Regulations 2014 (SI 2014/612) reg.15 (August 11, 2014).

The Social Security and Child Support (Decisions and Appeals) Regulations 1999

(SI 1999/991)

ARRANGEMENT OF REGULATIONS

PART I

GENERAL

PART II

REVISIONS, SUPERSESSIONS AND OTHER MATTERS (SOCIAL SECURITY AND CHILD SUPPORT)

CHAPTER I

REVISIONS

CHAPTER II

SUPERSESSIONS

CHAPTER III

OTHER MATTERS

PART III

SUSPENSION, TERMINATION AND OTHER MATTERS

CHAPTER I

SUSPENSION AND TERMINATION

CHAPTER II

OTHER MATTERS

PART IV

RIGHTS OF APPEAL AND PROCEDURE FOR BRINGING APPEALS

CHAPTER I

GENERAL

General appeals matters not including child support appeals

General appeals matters including child support appeals

PART V

APPEAL TRIBUNALS FOR SOCIAL SECURITY CONTRACTING OUT OF PENSIONS, VACCINE DAMAGE AND CHILD SUPPORT

PART VI

REVOCATIONS

SCHEDULES

Schedule 3 *Revoked.*
Schedule 3A Date from which superseding decision takes effect where a claimant is in receipt of Income Support or Jobseeker's Allowance.
Schedule 3B Date on which change of circumstances takes effect where claimant entitled to State Pension Credit.
Schedule 3C Date from which change of circumstances takes effect where claimant entitled to Employment and Support Allowance.
Schedule 4 *Omitted.*

Whereas a draft of this Instrument was laid before Parliament in accordance with section 80(1) of the Social Security Act 1998 and approved by resolution of each House of Parliament;

Now, therefore, the Secretary of State for Social Security, in exercise of powers set out in Schedule 1 to this Instrument and of all other powers enabling him in that behalf, with the concurrence of the Lord Chancellor in so far as the Regulations are made under section 6(3) of the Social Security Act 1998, by this Instrument, which contains only regulations made by virtue of, or consequential upon, those provisions of the Social Security Act 1998 and which is made before the end of the period of six months beginning with the coming into force of those provisions, after consultation with the Council on Tribunals in accordance with section 8 of the Tribunals and Inquiries Act 1992, hereby makes the following Regulations:

PART I

GENERAL

Citation, commencement [28 , application and interpretation]

2.413 **1.**—(1) These Regulations may be cited as the Social Security and Child Support (Decisions and Appeals) Regulations 1999.

(2) These Regulations shall come into force—

(a) in so far as they relate to child support and for the purposes of this regulation and regulation 2 on 1st June, 1999;

(b) in so far as they relate to—

  (i) industrial injuries benefit, guardian's allowance and child benefit; and

  (ii) a decision made under the Pension Schemes Act 1993 by virtue of section 170(2) of that Act;

on 5th July, 1999;

(c) in so far as they relate to retirement pension, widow's benefit, incapacity benefit, severe disablement allowance and maternity allowance, on 6th September, 1999;

(d) in so far as they relate to [3 working families' tax credit and disabled person's tax credit], on 5th October, 1999;

(e) in so far as they relate to attendance allowance, disability living allowance, invalid care allowance, jobseeker's allowance, credits of contributions or earnings, home responsibilities protection and vaccine damage payments, on 18th October, 1999; and

(f) for all remaining purposes, on 29th November, 1999.

[28 (2A) In so far as these Regulations relate to—

(a) an employment and support allowance payable under the Welfare Reform Act, they apply only in so far as the Act has effect apart from the amendments made by Schedule 3 and Part 1 of Schedule 14 to the Welfare Reform Act 2012 ("the 2012 Act") (removing references to an income-related allowance);
(b) a jobseeker's allowance payable under the Jobseekers Act 1995, they apply only in so far as the Act has effect apart from the amendments made by Part 1 of Schedule 14 to the 2012 Act (removing references to an income-based allowance).

(2B) These Regulations do not apply to universal credit (within the meaning of Part 1 of the Welfare Reform Act 2012) or personal independence payment (within the meaning of Part 4 of that Act).]

(3) In these Regulations, unless the context otherwise requires—

"the Act" means the Social Security Act 1998;

"the 1997 Act" means the Social Security (Recovery of Benefits) Act 1997;

[6 "the Arrears, Interest and Adjustment of Maintenance Assessments Regulations" means the Child Support (Arrears, Interest and Adjustment of Maintenance Assessments) Regulations 1992;]

[10 "assessed income period" is to be construed in accordance with sections 6 and 9 of the State Pension Credit Act;]

"the Claims and Payments Regulations" means the Social Security (Claims and Payments) Regulations 1987;

"appeal" means an appeal to [22 the First-tier Tribunal];

[32 [33 . . .];

"bereavement benefit" means—

[33 (a) bereavement support payment under section 30 of the Pensions Act 2014; or]

(c) a widowed parent's allowance;

[33 . . .]]

[1 "the Board" means the Commissioners of [32 for Her Majesty's Revenue and Customs];]

"claimant" means—

(a) any person who is a claimant for the purposes of section 191 of the Administration Act [10 section 35(1) of the Jobseekers Act or [18 , section 17(1) of the State Pension Credit Act or section 24(1) of the Welfare Reform Act]] or any other person from whom benefit is alleged to be recoverable; and
(b) any person subject to a decision of [1 an officer of the Board] under the Pension Schemes Act 1993;

[22 . . .]

[21 [27 . . .]]

[32 "contribution-based jobseeker's allowance" means a contribution-based jobseeker's allowance under Part 1 of the Jobseekers Act;]

[18 "contributory employment and support allowance" means a contributory allowance under Part 1 of the Welfare Reform Act;]

[29 "couple" means—

(a) two people who are married to, or civil partners of, each other and are members of the same household; or
(b) two people who are not married to, or civil partners of, each other but are living together as a married couple;]

"the date of notification" means—

(a) the date that notification of a decision of the Secretary of State [3 or an officer of the Board] is treated as having been given or sent in accordance with regulation 2(b); [25 . . .]

(b) in the case of a social fund payment arising in accordance with regulations made under section 138(2) of the Contributions and Benefits Act—

(i) the date seven days after the date on which the Secretary of State makes his decision to make a payment to a person to meet expenses for heating;

(ii) where a person collects the instrument of payment at a post office, the date the instrument is collected;

(iii) where an instrument of payment is sent to a post office for collection but is not collected and a replacement instrument is issued, the date on which the replacement instrument is issued; or

(iv) where a person questions his failure to be awarded a payment for expenses for heating, the date on which the notification of the Secretary of State's decision given in response to that question is issued; [25 ; or

(c) where notification of a decision of the Secretary of State is sent by means of an electronic communication (within the meaning given in section 15(1) of the Electronic Communications Act 2000), the date on which the notification is sent.]

[17 "the Deferral of Retirement Pensions etc. Regulations" means the Social Security (Deferral of Retirement Pensions, Shared Additional Pension and Graduated Retirement Benefit) (Miscellaneous Provisions) Regulations 2005;]

[9 "designated authority" means—

(a) the Secretary of State;

(b) a person providing services to the Secretary of State;

(c) a local authority;

(d) a person providing services to, or authorised to exercise any functions of, any such authority.]

[18 "the Employment and Support Allowance Regulations" means the Employment and Support Allowance Regulations 2008;

[24 "failure determination" means a determination by the Secretary of State under regulation 61(2) of the Employment and Support Allowance Regulations or regulation 8(2) of the Employment and Support Allowance (Work-Related Activity) Regulations 2011 that a claimant has failed to satisfy a requirement of regulation 54 of the Employment and Support Allowance Regulations (requirement to take part in a work-focused interview) or regulation 3 of the Employment and Support Allowance (Work-Related Activity) Regulations 2011 (requirement to undertake work-related activity).]

[4 "family" has the same meaning as in section 137 of the Contributions and Benefits Act;]

[22 . . .]

[17 "the Graduated Retirement Benefit Regulations" means the Social Security (Graduated Retirement Benefit) Regulations 2005;]

[18 "income-related employment and support allowance" means an income-related allowance under Part 1 of the Welfare Reform Act;

"the Income Support Regulations" means the Income Support (General) Regulations 1987;

[30 "Income Support Work-Related Activity Regulations" means the Income Support (Work-Related Activity) and Miscellaneous Amendments Regulations 2014;]

"the Jobseeker's Allowance Regulations" means the Jobseeker's Allowance Regulations 1996;

[6 "a joint-claim couple" has the same meaning as in section 1(4) of the Jobseekers Act 1995;

"a joint-claim jobseeker's allowance" has the same meaning as in section 1(4) of the Jobseekers Act 1995;]

[22 . . .]

[18 "'limited capability for work'" has the same meaning as in section 1(4) of the Welfare Reform Act;

[19 "the Lump Sum Payments Regulations" means the Social Security (Recovery of Benefits) (Lump Sum Payments) Regulations 2008;]

[7 [23 . . .]]

[5 "the Maintenance Calculation Procedure Regulations" means the Child Support (Maintenance Calculation Procedure) Regulations 2000;

"the Maintenance Calculations and Special Cases Regulations" means the Child Support (Maintenance Calculations and Special Cases) Regulations 2000;]

[22 . . .]

[15 . . .]

[8 "official error" means an error made by—

(a) an officer of the Department for Work and Pensions [21 [27 . . .]] or the Board acting as such which no person outside the Department or the [21 , the Commission] Inland Revenue caused or to which no person outside the Department [21 [27 . . .]] or the Inland Revenue materially contributed;

(b) a person employed by a designated authority acting on behalf of the authority, which no person outside that authority caused or to which no person outside that authority materially contributed,

but excludes any error of law which is shown to have been an error by virtue of a subsequent decision of [22 the Upper Tribunal] or the court;]

[22 . . .]

[22 . . .]

[22 . . .]

[22 . . .]

[8 "partner" means—

(a) where a person is a member of [16 a couple] the other member of that couple; or

(b) where a person is polygamously married to two or more members of his household, any such member;]

"party to the proceedings" means the Secretary of State [21 [27 . . .]] [3 or, as the case may be, the Board or an officer of the Board,] and any other person—

(a) who is one of the principal parties for the purposes of sections 13 and 14;

(b) who has a right of appeal to [22 the First-tier Tribunal] under section 11(2) of the 1997 Act, section 20 of the Child Support Act [6 . . .] [13, section 2B(6) of the Administration Act] or section 12(2);

[22. . .]

"referral" means a referral of an application for a departure direction to [22 the First-tier Tribunal] under section 28D(1)(b) of the Child Support Act;

[5 "relevant credit" means a credit of contributions or earnings resulting from a decision in accordance with regulations made under section 22(5) of the Contributions and Benefits Act;]

[26 "relevant other child" is to be interpreted by reference to paragraph 10C(2) of Schedule 1 to the Child Support Act];

[6 except where otherwise provided "relevant person" means—

(a) a person with care;

(b) a non-resident parent;

(c) a parent who is treated as a non-resident parent under regulation 8 of the Maintenance Calculations and Special Cases Regulations;

(d) a child, where the application for a maintenance calculation is made by that child under section 7 of the Child Support Act,

in respect of whom a maintenance calculation has been applied for, [22 . . .], or is or has been in force;]

[31 "shared additional pension" means a shared additional pension under section 55A or 55AA of the Contributions and Benefits Act;]

[10 "state pension credit" means the benefit payable under the State Pension Credit Act;

"State Pension Credit Act" means the State Pension Credit Act 2002;

"State Pension Credit Regulations" means the State Pension Credit Regulations 2002;]

[3 "tax credit" means working families' tax credit or disabled person's tax credit, construing those terms in accordance with section 1(1) of the Tax Credits Act 1999;]

[2 "the Transfer Act" means the Social Security Contributions (Transfer of Functions, etc.) Act 1999.]

[7 "the Variations Regulations" means the Child Support (Variations) Regulations 2000;]

[18 "'the Welfare Reform Act'" means the Welfare Reform Act 2007;]

[32 "widowed parent's allowance" means an allowance under section 39A of the Contributions and Benefits Act;]

[14 "work focused-interview" means an interview in which a person is required to take part in accordance with regulations made under section 2A or 2AA of the Administration Act;]

[1 (3A) In these Regulations as they relate to any decision made under the Pension Schemes Act 1993 by virtue of section 170(2) of that Act, any reference to the Secretary of State is to be construed as if it were a reference to an officer of the Board.]

(4) In these Regulations, unless the context otherwise requires, a reference—

(a) to a numbered section is to the section of the Act bearing that number;

(b) to a numbered Part is to the Part of these Regulations bearing that number;

(c) to a numbered regulation or Schedule is to the regulation in, or Schedule to, these Regulations bearing that number;
(d) in a regulation or Schedule to a numbered paragraph is to the paragraph in that regulation or Schedule bearing that number;
(e) in a paragraph to a lettered or numbered sub-paragraph is to the sub-paragraph in that paragraph bearing that letter or number.

AMENDMENTS

1. Social Security Contributions (Transfer of Functions, etc.) Act 1999 (Commencement No.2 and Consequential and Transitional Provisions) Order 1999 (SI 1999/1662) art.3(2) (July 5, 1999).
2. Social Security and Child Support (Decisions and Appeals) Amendment (No.3) Regulations 1999 (SI 1999/1670) reg.2(2) (July 5, 1999).
3. Tax Credits (Decisions and Appeals) (Amendment) Regulations 1999 (SI 1999/2570) regs 3 and 4 (October 5, 1999). Note that amendments made by these regulations only have effect with respect to tax credit under the Tax Credits Act 1999 (reg.1(2) of the Amendment Regulations).
4. Social Security and Child Support (Miscellaneous Amendments) Regulations 2000 (SI 2000/1596) reg.14 (June 19, 2000).
5. Social Security Amendment (Joint Claims) Regulations 2001 (SI 2001/518) reg.4(a) (March 19, 2001).
6. Child Support (Decisions and Appeals) (Amendment) Regulations 2000 (SI 2000/3185) reg.2 (various dates as provided in reg.1(1)).
7. Social Security (Breach of Community Order) (Consequential Amendments) Regulations 2001 (SI 2001/1711) reg.2(2)(a) (October 15, 2001).
8. Social Security and Child Support (Decisions and Appeals) (Miscellaneous Amendments) Regulations 2002 (SI 2002/1379) reg.2 (May 20, 2002).
9. Social Security (Jobcentre Plus Interviews) Regulations 2002 (SI 2002/1703) Sch.2 para.6(a) (September 30, 2002).
10. State Pension Credit (Consequential, Transitional and Miscellaneous Provisions) Regulations 2002 (SI 2002/3019) reg.16 (April 7, 2003).
11. Child Benefit and Guardian's Allowance (Decisions and Appeals) Regulations 2003 (SI 2003/916) reg.36 (April 7, 2003). Note that this amendment replaces the words "regulation 27" only so far as the definition relates to child benefit and guardian's allowance. See the annotation to this definition.
12. Social Security and Child Support (Miscellaneous Amendments) Regulations 2003 (SI 2003/1050) reg.3(1) (May 5, 2003).
13. Social Security (Jobcentre Plus Interviews for Partners) Regulations 2003 (SI 2003/1886) reg.15(2) (April 12, 2004).
14. Social Security (Working Neighbourhoods) Regulations 2004 (SI 2004/959) reg.24(2) (April 26, 2004).
15. Social Security, Child Support, and Tax Credits (Decisions and Appeals) Amendment Regulations 2004 (SI 2004/3368) reg.2(2) (December 21, 2004).
16. Civil Partnership (Consequential Amendments) Regulations 2005 (SI 2005/2878) reg.8(2) (December 5, 2005).
17. Social Security (Deferral of Retirement Pensions, Shared Additional Pension and Graduated Retirement Benefit) (Miscellaneous Provisions) Regulations 2005 (SI 2005/2677) reg.9(2) (April 6, 2006).
18. Employment and Support Allowance (Consequential Provisions) (No.2) Regulations 2008 (SI 2008/1554) regs 29 and 30 (July 27, 2008).
19. Social Security (Recovery of Benefits) (Lump Sum Payments) Regulations 2008 (SI 2008/1596) Sch.2 para.1(a) (October 1, 2008).
20. Child Support (Consequential Provisions) Regulations 2008 (SI 2008/2543), reg.4(1) and (2) (October 27, 2008).
21. Child Support (Consequential Provisions) (No.2) Regulations 2008 (SI 2008/2656) reg.4 (November 1, 2008).

22. Tribunals, Courts and Enforcement Act 2007 (Transitional and Consequential Provisions) Order 2008 (SI 2008/2683) Sch.1 paras 95 and 96 (November 3, 2008), subject to a saving under art.3 for reasons explained in the note to ss.5–7 of the Social Security Act 1998.

23. Welfare Reform Act 2009, (Section 26) (Consequential Amendments) Regulations 2010 (SI 2010/424) reg.4(1) and (2) (March 22, 2010).

24. Employment and Support Allowance (Work-Related Activity) Regulations 2011 (SI 2011/1349) reg.21 (June 1, 2011).

25. Social Security (Electronic Communications) Order 2011 (SI 2011/1498) art.5 (June 20, 2011).

26. Child Support (Miscellaneous Amendments) Regulations 2011 (SI 2011/1464) reg.2(1) and (2) (July 4, 2011).

27. Public Bodies (Child Maintenance and Enforcement Commission: Abolition and Transfer of Functions) Order 2012 (SI 2012/2007) art.3(2) and Sch. para.113(1) and (2) (August 1, 2012).

28. Universal Credit, Personal Independence Payment, Jobseeker's Allowance and Employment and Support Allowance (Decisions and Appeals) Regulations 2013 (SI 2013/381) reg.55 (April 8, 2013 in relation to personal independence payment and April 29, 2013 for other purposes).

29. Marriage (Same Sex Couples) Act 2013 (Consequential Provisions) Order 2014 (SI 2014/107) art.2 and Sch.1 para.26 (March 13, 2014, in England and Wales) and Marriage and Civil Partnership (Scotland) Act 2014 and Civil Partnership Act 2004 (Consequential Provisions and Modifications) Order 2014 (SI 2014/3229) Sch.6 para.18 (December 16, 2014, in Scotland).

30. Income Support (Work-Related Activity) and Miscellaneous Amendments Regulations 2014 (SI 2014/1097) reg.12(1) and (2) (April 28, 2014).

31. Pensions Act 2014 (Consequential, Supplementary and Incidental Amendments) Order 2015 (SI 2015/1985) art.18(1) and (2) (April 6, 2016).

32. Social Security (Credits, and Crediting and Treatment of Contributions) (Consequential and Miscellaneous Amendments) Regulations 2016 (SI 2016/1145) reg.4(1) and (2) (January 1, 2017).

33. Pensions Act 2014 (Consequential, Supplementary and Incidental Amendments) Order 2017 (SI 2017/422) art.15(1) and (2) (April 6, 2017, subject to a saving).

Definitions

"the Child Support Act"—see s.84 of the Social Security Act 1998.

"the Contributions and Benefits Act"—see s.84 of the Social Security Act 1998.

General Note

Paragraphs (2A) and (2B)

2.414 These Regulations do not apply to those benefits to which the Universal Credit, Personal Independence Payment, Jobseeker's Allowance and Employment and Support Allowance (Decisions and Appeals) Regulations 2013 apply. Note, however, that that means that these Regulations continue to apply to income-related jobseeker's allowance and employment and support allowance. They will also continue to apply to contribution-based jobseeker's allowance and employment and support allowance to the extent that those benefits do not fall within the scope of reg.1(3) of the 2013 Regulations after April 29, 2013.

Paragraph (3)

2.415 The definition of "the Claims and Payments Regulations" is out of sequence due to a drafting error.

The definitions of "the Arrears, Interest and Adjustment of Maintenance Assessments Regulations", "the Maintenance Calculation Procedure Regulations", the Maintenance Calculations and Special Cases Regulations", "relevant other child", "relevant person" and "Variations Regulations" are omitted for purposes of cases where child support maintenance is calculated under the scheme introduced by the Child Maintenance and Other Payments Act 2008 (see the Child Support (Meaning of Child and New Calculation Rules) (Consequential and Miscellaneous Amendment) Regulations 2012 (SI 2012/2785), reg.6.). Amendments have also been made to regs 4, 30 and 33 and a number of regulations not included in this volume have been omitted altogether, solely for those purposes. This seems an unnecessarily complicated method of drafting, leaving in force two versions of these Regulations. Since these child support amendments are not relevant to social security cases, this volume takes no account of them.

"the Board"

Except in regs 3(8H), 11A and 38A, references to the Board are of virtually no practical effect because they are relevant only to decisions in respect of tax credits paid under the Tax Credits Act 1999, which were abolished in 2003. Decisions in respect of child benefit and guardian's allowance are made by HMRC under the Child Benefit and Guardian's Allowance (Decisions and Appeals) Regulations 2003. **2.416**

"official error"

The definition of "official error" is important because it is a ground for revision under reg.3, whereas a mistake of fact or law that is not an "official error" is a ground of supersession under reg.6 and a supersession is usually effective from a later date than a revision. **2.417**

Adjudication officers under the pre-1998 Act system of adjudication were "officers of the Department . . . acting as such" and so an error by an adjudication officer can constitute an "official error" (*R(CS) 3/04*, not following *R(I) 5/02*). However, there is no "official error" where an error is made by an authority in its capacity as an employer rather than in its capacity as an administrator of benefits (*EM v LB Waltham Forest* [2009] UKUT 245 (AAC), *Kingston-Upon-Hull CC v DM (HB)* [2010] UKUT 234 (AAC) (subsequently upheld on appeal without reference to this point)).

Only clear and obvious mistakes amount to errors in this context and a failure to elucidate facts not disclosed by a claimant is unlikely to suffice (*R(SB) 10/91* and *R(SB) 2/93*). However, failing to ask a question on a standard claim form (or otherwise) can amount to an "official error" (*MB v Christchurch BC (HB)* [2014] UKUT 201 (AAC); [2014] AACR 39). There is also no "official error" where a decision is made without investigating a possible discrepancy in the evidence or on incomplete evidence, partly because in such cases a claimant is likely to have contributed to any error (*R(H) 1/04, R(H) 2/04*). In *KW v Lancaster CC (HB)* [2011] UKUT 266 (AAC), there was held to be no official error where the substantial cause of the overpayment of housing benefit was the claimant's ex-partner's late payment of child support maintenance, even if the delays involved might have been contributed to by the Child Support Agency not taking enforcement action.

Since it was decided in *CDLA/1707/2005* that a tribunal is entitled to substitute a revision for a supersession or refusal to supersede (see the annotation to s.12(2) of the Social Security Act 1998, above), there have been a number of new decisions on the meaning of "official error". In *CDLA/393/2006*, the Commissioner regarded the adjudication officer's reliance on the claim form without obtaining further evidence as "a failure in the proper standards of administration" but found that the claimant's mother had contributed to the error by the way in which she had completed the claim form. There was therefore no "official error". He said that "in judging what was a material contribution a common sense approach should be taken, rather than a highly refined analysis of causation" and that the way the claim form had been completed should not be seen as merely the setting for the adjudication officer's error.

This echoes what was said in *R. (Sier) v Cambridge CC Housing Benefit Review Board* [2001] EWCA Civ 1523, the effect of which was summarised in *SN v London Borough of Hounslow (HB)* [2010] UKUT 57 (AAC) (at [19]): **2.418**

"The issue before the Court of Appeal was whether a claimant who had obtained a series of benefit overpayments by not disclosing the facts that he had another property (on which he also claimed benefit), and further had ceased to qualify for income support, could avoid recovery on the ground of 'official error' when the DSS, as it then was, had failed to send the authority the usual notification of his income support being stopped.... the Court of Appeal decision emphasises that the approach to causation in such cases is to be concerned with the practical question of what really caused the overpayments in question to be made. The unanimous (and perhaps not very surprising) conclusion was ... that a claimant who has got benefit by not disclosing relevant facts is not able to turn the case into one of 'overpayment caused by official error' by saying that if only officialdom had been more vigilant he would have been spotted."

In *CH/687/2006*, the claimant was overpaid housing benefit because the amount of her partner's incapacity benefit changed due to the length of time he had been incapable of work. The Deputy Commissioner reviewed the cases and held that there was no official error. Although the local authority had known that the incapacity benefit in payment when the award was made was only short-term incapacity benefit, which would inevitably be replaced by a higher rate if the claimant's partner continued to be incapable of work, the local authority had been entitled to presume that any change in the rate of incapacity benefit would be reported to it. This can therefore be seen as another case where the claimant contributed to the error. In *CPC/206/2005*, the Commissioner stated that the term "official error" is not confined to errors of law but said that it "involves more than merely taking a decision that another decision-maker with the same information would not take". He considered that it would not be helpful further to explain what the term meant. However, he found an official error in the case because "no Secretary of State or decision-maker acting reasonably could have [made the decision under appeal]". That would have been an error of law and it is perhaps difficult to envisage an official error that would not be an error of law in its public law sense (see the annotation to s.11 of the Tribunals Courts and Enforcement Act 2007). An "official error" is not revealed merely because a decision made some time ago in the light of current medical opinion is shown to have been wrong as a result of a change in medical opinion (*R(AF) 5/07*). There will merely have been a mistake of fact justifying supersession.

Generally, notification of a change of circumstances must be made to the office dealing with the relevant benefit and so, if information is not acted on because it has been sent to another office, a claimant will generally have contributed to the error. However, that will not inevitably be the case. In *CH/2567/2007*, the Commissioner had regard to confusing nomenclature (such that even officials got it wrong and the tribunal was confused), the proliferation of correspondence, the repeated notification of the relevant facts to one department that ought to have passed the information to another and the complication of the benefit position (such that the claimant could not reasonably have been expected to realise there had been an overpayment) and he concluded that the claimant had not contributed to the official error involved in one department failing to pass information on to another.

2.419 Generally also, notification of a change of circumstances must be made in writing unless given by telephone (although there are exceptions, see regs 32–32B of the Social Security (Claims and Payments) Regulations 1987). However, even though there had been a duty to make the notification in writing in *West Somerset DC v JA (HB)* [2010] UKUT 190 (AAC), there was "official error" when the claimant gave oral notice of a change of circumstances and the local authority neither acted upon that notification nor informed the claimant that written notice was required. Unusually, none of the notices issued by the local authority that were before the Upper Tribunal had referred to the duty under the legislation relevant to that case to notify a change of circumstances in writing. Had any of them done so, there would presumably have arisen the question whether the requirement to give notice in writing had been waived by the officer receiving the oral notification.

The concluding words of the amended definition are imprecise but it is now fairly clear that they apply where the official was acting in accordance with a general Departmental misunderstanding of the law that has been shown to be wrong by a decision of the Upper Tribunal or court that need not itself have directly involved the particular claimant in respect of whom the error was made. The jurisprudential difficulties arising because the Upper Tribunal and courts only declare the law to be as it has always been and because the misunderstanding may not have been shared by anyone outside the Department are familiar ones. However, in *R(P)2/09*, a Tribunal of Commissioners did not dwell on those theoretical problems and gave the words their practical meaning, deciding that there had been no official error where the Department had been shown by a decision of the European Court of Justice to have been misapplying European Community law. The consequence was that the claimant, who had made an application for revision or supersession shortly after the Court's decision, was entitled to have it treated only as an application for supersession effiective from the date it was made, insofar as she needed to rely on the decision of the Court but could have it treated as an application for revision insofar as she could rely upon domestic legislation. The issue was considered in greater depth in *JK v SSWP (DLA)* [2013] UKUT 218 (AAC), where it was pointed out that "the court" is not defined but the judge nonetheless found the term to include the European Court of Justice and further found the restriction implied by the concluding words of the definition of "official error" not to be contrary to European Union law. A decision is not "shown" to be wrong by a decision of a Commissioner if it was plainly wrong on a clear reading of legislation (*BD v SSWP (DLA)* [2013] UKUT 216 (AAC)). Where a decision is wrong both for a reason subsequently revealed by a court and for some other reason, the concluding words of this definition do not prevent the decision from being revised in a way that corrects both errors (*R(P) 2/09* and *BD v SSWP (DLA)*). An order made by a Court by consent is not a "decision" for these purposes (*R(FC) 3/98*).

The definition of "official error" does not include errors of tribunals and, in any event, there is no power to revise a decision of a tribunal. Nor is there any power under reg.6 to supersede a decision of a tribunal on the ground of error of law. The consequence is that, where the Secretary of State makes the same official error in a number of cases and some claimants appeal unsuccessfully to the First-tier Tribunal but others do not appeal, it is possible to revise the decisions in order to correct the error in those cases where claimants did not appeal but the error cannot be corrected retrospectively by the Secretary of State in the cases where the claimant did appeal. It was held in *ED v SSWP (DLA)* [2013] UKUT 583 (AAC) that there are sound reasons of principle why the Secretary of State's power to overturn a decision of a tribunal are limited and therefore, even where the official error is a breach of European Union law, this inability to correct the error retrospectively is not itself contrary to European Union law. It is always open to the claimant to make a new claim. It may sometimes also be possible for the claimant to appeal to the Upper Tribunal, so as to correct the error from the date that the earlier decision was effective but that would have involved an impermissible extension of time in *ED*.

"party to the proceedings"

In *CA/1014/1999*, it was held that, where the Secretary of State had decided that an overpayment was recoverable from a claimant but had made no decision in respect of the claimant's appointee, the claimant's appointee was not a "party to the proceedings" against whom the tribunal could make a recoverability decision, even though the appointee had brought the proceedings on behalf of the claimant (and had an express right of appeal under reg.25). However, in *CTC/3543/2004*, the same Commissioner held that, where Her Majesty's Revenue and Customs had made a decision to the effect that a tax credit was recoverable from both the husband and the wife, the husband was a "party to the proceedings" before the tribunal even though only his wife had appealed (although acting through her husband). 2.420

Where the Secretary of State has made a decision that an overpayment is recoverable from both a claimant and the claimant's appointee, an appeal brought by the appointee should be treated as an appeal brought on behalf of both the claimant and the appointee unless it is clear that an appeal on behalf of only one of them was intended (*R(A) 2/06*). Even if an appeal by only one of them is intended, *CA/1014/1999* is clearly distinguishable and whichever has not appealed will be a "party to the proceedings", as in *CTC/3543/2004*.

Service of notices or documents

2.421 **2.** Where, by any provision of the Act [3, of the Child Support Act] or of these Regulations—

(a) any notice or other document is required to be given or sent [4. . .] to an officer authorised by the Secretary of State [1 or to an officer of the Board], that notice or document shall be treated as having been so given or sent on the day that it is received [4. . .] by an officer authorised by the Secretary of State [1 or by an officer of the Board], as the case may be, and

(b) any notice (including notification of a decision of the Secretary of State [2 or of an officer of the Board] or other document is required to be given or sent to any person other than [4. . .] [1 [4. . .] an officer] authorised by the Secretary of State [1 or an officer of the Board], as the case may be, that notice or document shall, if sent by post to that person's last known address, be treated as having been given or sent on the day that it was posted.

AMENDMENTS

1. Tax Credits (Decisions and Appeals) (Amendment) Regulations 1999 (SI 1999/2570) reg.5 (October 5, 1999). Note that amendments made by these regulations only have effect with respect to tax credit (reg.1(2) of the Amendment Regulations).

2. Tax Credits (Decisions and Appeals) (Amendment) Regulations 2000 (SI 2000/127) reg.2 (February 14, 2000). This amendment has effect with respect only to tax credit (reg.1(2) of the amending Regulations).

3. Child Support (Decisions and Appeals) (Amendment) Regulations 2000 (SI 2000/3185) reg.3 (various dates as provided by reg.1(1)).

4. Tribunals, Courts and Enforcement Act 2007 (Transitional and Consequential Provisions) Order 2008 (SI 2008/2683) Sch.1 paras 95 and 97 (November 3, 2008), subject to a saving under art.3 for reasons explained in the note to ss.5–7 of the Social Security Act 1998.

DEFINITIONS

"the Act"—see reg.1(3).
"the Board"—*ibid.*
"the Child Support Act"—see s.39(1) of the Social Security Act 1998.

GENERAL NOTE

2.422 This regulation re-enacts reg.1(3) of the Social Security (Adjudication) Regulations 1995.

In *R(IB)4/02*, it was held that, where a document had, under reg.53(4) as then in force, to be sent to a chairman or member of a tribunal, para.(a) did not apply. Paragraph (b) applied instead so that the document was sent when posted and not when it was received. Regulation 53(4) has been revoked but the reasoning still holds good when a document must be sent to anyone not mentioned in para.(a). A document may be sent by fax and is received for the purposes of reg.2(a) when it is successfully transmitted to, and received by, a fax machine, irrespective of when it is actually collected from the fax machine *(R(DLA)3/05)*.

In *CG/2973/2004*, the Commissioner had to consider whether the claimant had made a claim for benefit on a certain date. A claim is generally effective only when received. The position is therefore similar to that under reg.2(a), relating to documents to be sent to the Secretary of State. The Commissioner accepted that the claimant had posted a claim form but found that it was more likely to have been lost in the post before it reached the building where it was to be opened than lost in that building or subsequently. Strictly speaking, it was therefore unnecessary for him to consider whether, the claimant having succeeded in showing that the form had been posted, the burden of proving that the letter was lost after arrival at that building rested on her or whether the burden of proving that it was lost before then rested on the Secretary of State. However, having heard full legal argument, he said that the burden would have lain on the claimant to prove delivery so that, if it had been impossible to say where the letter was more likely to have been lost, the claimant would still have failed. He preferred *CIS/306/2003* to *CSIS/48/1992* and *CIS/759/1992*. An appeal against the Commissioner's decision was dismissed (*Levy v Secretary of State for Work and Pensions* [2006] EWCA Civ 890 (reported as *R(G) 2/06*). This decision was distinguished in *R. (Latimer) v Bury Magistrates' Court* [2008] EWHC 2213 (Admin) on the ground that it was based on the statutory language. In the absence of such language, it was held, the appropriate inference to be drawn where it is common ground that a letter has been posted is that it was received, this being a presumption based on the application of common sense rather than a presumption of law.

The "last known address" to which documents must be sent for para.(b) to apply need not be the person's last known *residence* because the concepts are different. Moreover, the sender must consider the address to be reliable and, if he does not, should take reasonable steps to see whether a more reliable one exists (*CCS/2288/2005*). This approach exists to aid the innocent claimant and not the one who has failed to take reasonable steps to keep the relevant authority aware of his whereabouts. Generally, an authority is entitled to rely on a claimant to inform it of any move.

Part II

Revisions, Supersessions and Other Matters Social Security and Child Support

Chapter I

Revisions

Revision of decisions

3.—(1) Subject to the following provisions of this regulation, any decision of the Secretary of State [3 or the Board or an officer of the Board] under section 8 or 10 ("the original decision") may be revised by him [3 or them] if— 2.423

[10(a) he or they commence action leading to revision within one month of the date of notification of the original decision; or

(b) an application for a revision is received by the Secretary of State or the Board or an officer of the Board at the appropriate office—

(i) subject to regulation 9A(3), within one month of the date of notification of the original decision;

(ii) where a written statement is requested under [35 paragraph (3)(b) of regulation 3ZA or] paragraph(1)(b) of regulation 28 and is provided within the period specified in head (i), within 14 days of the expiry of that period;

(iii) where a written statement is requested under [35 paragraph (3)(b) of regulation 3ZA or] paragraph(1)(b) of regulation 28 and is provided after the period specified in head (i), within 14 days of the date on which the statement is provided; or

(iv) within such longer period as may be allowed under regulation 4.]

(2) Where the Secretary of State [3 or the Board or an officer of the Board] requires further evidence or information from the applicant in order to consider all the issues raised by an application under paragraph (1)(b) ("the original application"), he [3 or they] shall notify the applicant that further evidence or information is required and the decision may be revised—

(a) where the applicant provides further relevant evidence or information within one month of the date of notification or such longer period of time as the Secretary of State [3 or the Board or an officer of the Board] may allow; or

(b) where the applicant does not provide such evidence or information within the time allowed under sub-paragraph (a), on the basis of the original application.

(3) In the case of a payment out of the social fund in respect of maternity or funeral expenses, a decision under section 8 may be revised where the application is made—

(a) within one month of the date of notification of the decision, or if later

(b) within the time prescribed for claiming such a payment under regulation 19 of, and Schedule 4 to, the Claims and Payments Regulations, or

(c) within such longer period of time as may be allowed under regulation 4.

(4) In the case of a decision made under the Pension Schemes Act 1993 by virtue of section 170(2) of that Act, the decision may be revised at any time by [2 an officer of the Board] where it contains an error.

[10 (4A) Where there is an appeal against an original decision (within the meaning of paragraph (1)) within the time prescribed [21 by Tribunal Procedure Rules], but the appeal has not been determined, the original decision may be revised at any time.]

(5) A decision of the Secretary of State [3 *Board or an officer of the Board*] under section 8 or 10—

(a) [18 except where paragraph (5ZA) applies] which arose from an official error; or

(b) [17 except in a case to which sub-paragraph (c) or (d) applies,] where the decision was made in ignorance of, or was based upon a mistake as to, some material fact and as a result of that ignorance of or mistake as to that fact, the decision was more advantageous to the claimant than it would otherwise have been but for that ignorance or mistake,

[3 *(bb) which was made in ignorance of, or was based on a mistake as to some material fact,*]

(c) [1 [17 subject to subparagraph (d),] where the decision is a disability benefit decision, or is an incapacity benefit decision where there has been an incapacity determination [19 or is an employment and support allowance decision where there has been a limited capability for work determination] (whether before or after the decision), which was made in ignorance of, or was based upon a mistake as to, some material fact in relation to a disability determination embodies in or necessary to the disability benefit decision, [19 , the incapacity determination or the limited capability for work determination], and—

(i) as a result of that ignorance or mistake as to that fact the decision was more advantageous to the claimant than it would otherwise have been but for that ignorance or mistake and,

(ii) the Secretary of State is satisfied that at the time the decision was made the claimant or payee knew or could reasonably have been expected to know of the fact in question and that it was relevant to the decision,]

[17 (d) where the decision [19 is an employment and support allowance decision,] is a disability benefit decision, or is an incapacity benefit decision, which was made in ignorance of, or was based upon a mistake as to, some material fact not in relation to the [19 limited capability for work determination,] incapacity or disability determination embodied in or necessary to [19 the employment and support allowance decision,] the incapacity benefit decision or disability benefit decision, and as a result of that ignorance of, or mistake as to that fact, the decision was more advantageous to the claimant than it would otherwise have been but for the ignorance or mistake,]

may be revised at any time by the Secretary of State [3 *by the Board or an officer of the Board at any time not later than the end of the period of six years immediately following the date of the decision or, where ignorance of the material fact referred to in sub-paragraph (b) was caused by the fraudulent or negligent conduct of the claimant, not later than the end of the period of twenty years immediately following the date of the decision.*]

[18 (5ZA) This paragraph applies where—

(a) the decision which would otherwise fall to be revised is a decision to award a benefit specified in paragraph (5ZB), whether or not the award has already been put in payment;

(b) that award was based on the satisfaction by a person of the contribution conditions, in whole or in part, by virtue of credits of earnings for incapacity for work or approved training in the tax years from 1993–94 to 2007–08;

(c) the official error derives from the failure to transpose correctly information relating to those credits from the Department for Work and Pensions' Pension Strategy Computer System to Her Majesty's Revenue and Customs' computer system (NIRS2) or from related clerical procedures; and

(d) that error has resulted in an award to the claimant which is more advantageous to him than if the error had not been made.

(5ZB) The specified benefits are—

(a) bereavement allowance;

[40 (aa) bereavement support payment under section 30 of the Pensions Act 2014;]

(b) contribution-based jobseeker's allowance;

(c) incapacity benefit;

(d) retirement pension;

(e) widowed mother's allowance;

(f) widowed parent's allowance; [19 . . .]

(g) widow's pension. [19 and

(h) contributory employment and support allowance].

(5ZC) In paragraph (5ZA)(b), "tax year" has the meaning ascribed to it by section 122(1) of the Contributions and Benefits Act.]

[10 (5A) Where—

(a) the Secretary of State or the Board or an officer of the Board, as the case may be, makes a decision under section 8 or 10, or that decision is revised under section 9, in respect of a claim or award ("decision A") and the claimant appeals against decision A;

(b) decision A is superseded or the claimant makes a further claim which is decided ("decision B") after the claimant made the appeal but before the appeal results in a decision by [21 the First-tier Tribunal] ("decision C"); and

(c) the Secretary of State or the Board or an officer of the board, as the case may be, would have made decision B differently if he or they had been aware of decision C at the time he or they made decision B,

decision B may be revised at any time.]

[17 (5B) A decision by the Secretary of State under section 8 or 10 awarding incapacity benefit may be revised at any time if—

(a) it incorporates a determination that the condition in regulation 28(2)(b) of the Social Security (Incapacity for Work) (General) Regulations 1995 (conditions for treating a person as incapable of work until the personal capability assessment is carried out) is satisfied;

(b) the condition referred to in sub-paragraph (a) was not satisfied at the time when the further claim was first determined; and

(c) there is a period before the award which falls to be decided.]

[19 (5C) A decision of the Secretary of State under section 10 made in consequence of a failure determination may be revised at any time if it contained an error to which the claimant did not materially contribute;

[23 ....]]

[29 (5D) A decision by the Secretary of State under section 8 or 10 awarding an employment and support allowance may be revised at any time if—

(a) it incorporates a determination that the conditions in regulation 30 of the Employment and Support Allowance Regulations are satisfied;

(b) the condition referred to in sub-paragraph (a) was not satisfied at the time when the claim was made; and

(c) there is a period before the award which falls to be decided.]

[27 (5E) A decision under section 8 or 10 awarding an employment and support allowance may be revised if—

(a) the decision of the Secretary of State awarding an employment and support allowance was made on the basis that the claimant had made and was pursuing an appeal against a decision of the Secretary of State that the claimant did not have limited capability for work ("the original decision"); and

(b) the appeal to the First-tier Tribunal in relation to the original decision is successful.

(5F) A decision under section 8 or 10 awarding an employment and support allowance may be revised if—

(a) the person's current period of limited capability for work is treated as a continuation of another such period under regulation 145(1) [32 . . .] of the Employment and Support Allowance Regulations; and

(b) regulation 7(1)(b) of those Regulations applies.]

[29 (5G) Where—

(a) a person's entitlement to an employment and support allowance is terminated because of a decision which embodies a determination that the person does not have limited capability for work;
(b) the person appeals that decision to the First-tier Tribunal;
(c) before or after that decision is appealed by the person, that person claims and there is a decision to award–
  (i) income support, or
  (ii) jobseeker's allowance; and
(d) the decision referred to in sub-paragraph (a) is successfully appealed,

the decision to award income support or jobseeker's allowance may be revised.

(5H) Where—

(a) a conversion decision within the meaning of regulation 5(2)(b) of the Employment and Support Allowance (Transitional Provisions, Housing Benefit and Council Tax Benefit) (Existing Awards) (No. 2) Regulations 2010 (deciding whether an existing award qualifies for conversion) is made in respect of a person;
(b) the person appeals that decision to the First-tier Tribunal;
(c) before or after that decision is appealed by the person, that person claims and there is a decision to award–
  (i) income support, or
  (ii) jobseeker's allowance; and
(d) the decision referred to in sub-paragraph (a) is successfully appealed,

the decision to award income support or jobseeker's allowance may be revised.]

[31 (5I) Where—

(a) a decision to terminate a person's entitlement to a contributory employment and support allowance is made because of section 1A of the Welfare Reform Act (duration of contributory allowance); and
(b) it is subsequently determined, in relation to the period of entitlement before that decision, that the person had or is treated as having had limited capability for work-related activity,

the decision to terminate that entitlement may be revised.]

[37 (5J) A decision by the Secretary of State under section 8 awarding an employment and support allowance may be revised at any time where—

(a) it is made immediately following the last day of a period for which the claimant was treated as capable of work or as not having limited capability for work under regulation 55ZA of the Jobseeker's Allowance Regulations or regulation 46A of the Jobseeker's Allowance Regulations 2013 (extended period of sickness) and that period lasted 13 weeks; and
(b) it is not a decision which embodies a determination that the claimant is treated as having limited capability for work under regulation 30 of the Employment and Support Allowance Regulations (conditions for treating a claimant as having limited capability for work until a determination about limited capability for work has been made).]

(6) [33 A decision of the Secretary of State under section 8 or 10 that a jobseeker's allowance is reduced in accordance with section 19 or 19A of the Jobseeker's Act or regulation 69B of the Jobseeker's Allowance Regulations may be revised at anytime by the Secretary of State.]

[5 (6A) A relevant decision within the meaning of section 2B(2) [13 or (2A)] of the Administration Act may be revised at any time if it contains an error.]

[34 (6B) A decision of the Secretary of State under section 8 or 10 awarding a jobseeker's allowance may be revised where the Secretary of State makes a decision under regulation 69B (the period of a reduction under section 19B: claimants ceasing to be available for employment etc.) of the Jobseeker's Allowance Regulations ("the JSA Regulations") that the amount of the award is to be reduced in accordance with regulations 69B and 70 of the JSA Regulations.]

[9 (7) Where—

(a) the Secretary of State or an officer of the Board makes a decision under section 8 or 10 awarding benefit to a claimant ("the original award"); and

(b) an award of another relevant benefit or an increase in the rate of another relevant benefit is made to the claimant or a member of his family for a period which includes the date on which the original award took effect,

the Secretary of State or an officer of the Board, as the case may require, may revise the original award.]

[14 (7ZA) Where—

(a) the Secretary of State makes a decision under section 8 or 10 awarding income support [23 income-based jobseeker's allowance,] [19, state pension credit or an income-related employment and support allowance] to a claimant ("the original award");

(b) the claimant has a non-dependant within the meaning of regulation 3 of the Income Support Regulations [23 , regulation 2 of the Jobseeker's Allowance Regulations] [19 or regulation 71 of the Employment and Support Allowance Regulations] or a person residing with him within the meaning of paragraph 1(1)(a)(ii), (b)(ii) or (c)(iii) of Schedule I to the State Pension Credit Regulations ("the non-dependant");

(c) but for the non-dependant—

(i) a severe disability premium would be applicable to the claimant under regulation 17(1)(d) of the Income Support Regulations [23 , regulation 83(e) or 86A(c) of the Jobseeker's Allowance Regulations] [19 or regulation 67 of the Employment and Support Allowance Regulations]; or

(ii) an additional amount would be applicable to the claimant as a severe disabled person under regulation 6(4) of the State Pension Credit Regulations; and

(d) after the original award the non-dependant is awarded benefit which—

(i) is for a period which includes the date on which the original award took effect; and

(ii) is such that a severe disability premium becomes applicable to the claimant under paragraph 13(3)(a) of Schedule 2 to the Income Support Regulations [23, paragraph 15(4)(a) or 20I(3)(a) of Schedule 1 to the Jobseeker's Allowance Regulations] [19 , paragraph 6(4)(a) of Schedule 4 to the Employment and Support Allowance Regulations] or an additional amount for severe disability becomes applicable to him under paragraph 2(2)(a) of Schedule I to the State Pension Credit Regulations,

the Secretary of State may revise the original award.]

[10 (7A) Where a decision as to a claimant's entitlement to a disablement pension under section 103 of the Contributions and Benefits Act is revised by the Secretary of State, or changed on appeal, a decision of the Secretary of State as to the claimant's entitlement to reduced earnings allowance under paragraph 11 or 12 of Schedule 7 to that Act may be revised at any time provided that the revised decision is more advantageous to the claimant than the original decision.]

[14 (7B) A decision under regulation 22A of the Income Support Regulations (reduction in applicable amount where the claimant is appealing against a decision which embodies a determination that he is not incapable of work) may be revised if the appeal is successful [16 or lapses].

(7C) Where a person's entitlement to income support is terminated because of a determination that he is not incapable of work and [16 the decision which embodies that determination is revised or] he subsequently appeals the decision [16 which embodies] that determination and is entitled to income support under regulation 22A of the Income Support Regulations, the decision to terminate entitlement may be revised.]

[23 (7CC) Where—

(a) a person's entitlement to income support is terminated because of a determination that the person is not incapable of work;
(b) the person subsequently claims and is awarded jobseeker's allowance; and
(c) the decision which embodies the determination that the person is not incapable of work is revised or successfully appealed,

the Secretary of State may revise the decisions to terminate income support entitlement and to award jobseeker's allowance.

[36 (7CD) A decision of the Secretary of State under section 10 of the Act made in consequence of a determination under regulation 6(2) of the Income Support Work-Related Activity Regulations that a claimant has failed to satisfy a requirement of regulation 2 of those Regulations (requirement to undertake work-related activity) may be revised at any time if it contained an error to which the claimant did not materially contribute.]

[15 (7D) Where—

(a) a person elects for an increase of—
    (i) a Category A or Category B retirement pension in accordance with paragraph A1 or 3C of Schedule 5 to the Contributions and Benefits Act (pension increase or lump sum where entitlement to retirement pension is deferred);
    (ii) a shared additional pension in accordance with paragraph 1 of Schedule 5A to that Act (pension increase or lump sum where entitlement to shared additional pension is deferred); or, as the case may be,
    (iii) graduated retirement benefit in accordance with paragraph 12 or 17 of Schedule 1 to the Graduated Retirement Benefit Regulations (further provisions replacing section 36(4) of the National Insurance Act 1965: increases of graduated retirement benefit and lump sums);
(b) the Secretary of State decides that the person or his partner is entitled to state pension credit and takes into account the increase of pension or benefit in making or superseding that decision; and

(c) the person's election for an increase is subsequently changed in favour of a lump sum in accordance with regulation 5 of the Deferral of Retirement Pensions etc. Regulations or, as the case may be, paragraph 20D of Schedule 1 to the Graduated Retirement Benefit Regulations,

the Secretary of State may revise the state pension credit decision.

[38 (7DA) The Secretary of State may revise the state pension credit decision where—

(a) a person chooses under—
 (i) section 8(2) of the Pensions Act 2014 (choice of lump sum or survivor's pension under section 9 in certain cases) to be paid a state pension under section 9 of that Act (survivor's pension based on inheritance of deferred old state pension); or
 (ii) Regulations made under section 10 of the Pensions Act 2014 (inheritance of graduated retirement benefit) which make provision corresponding or similar to section 8(2) to be paid a state pension under Regulations made under section 10 which make provision corresponding or similar to section 9 of that Act;

(b) the Secretary of State—
 (i) decides that the person or their partner is entitled to state pension credit; and
 (ii) takes into account the state pension mentioned in sub-paragraph (a) in making or superseding that decision; and

(c) the person's choice for a state pension mentioned in sub-paragraph (a) is subsequently altered in favour of a lump sum in accordance with—
 (i) regulation 6 of the State Pension Regulations 2015 (changing a choice of lump sum or survivor's pension); or
 (ii) Regulations made under section 10 of the Pensions Act 2014 which make provision corresponding or similar to regulation 6 of the State Pension Regulations 2015.

(7DB) The Secretary of State may revise an award of a state pension under Part 1 of the Pensions Act 2014 where—

(a) the person makes a choice under—
 (i) section 8(2) of the Pensions Act 2014; or
 (ii) Regulations under section 10 of that Act which make provision corresponding or similar to section 8(2); and

(b) the person subsequently alters their choice in accordance with—
 (i) regulation 6 of the State Pension Regulations 2015; or
 (ii) Regulations under section 10 of the Pensions Act 2014 which make provision corresponding or similar to regulation 6 of the State Pension Regulations 2015.]

(7E) Where—

(a) a person is awarded a Category A or Category B retirement pension, shared additional pension or, as the case may be, graduated retirement benefit;

(b) an election is made, or treated as made, in respect of the award in accordance with paragraph A1 or 3C of Schedule 5 or paragraph 1 of Schedule 5A to the Contributions and Benefits Act or, as the case may be, in accordance with paragraph 12 or 17 of Schedule 1 to the Graduated Retirement Benefit Regulations; and

(c) the election is subsequently changed in accordance with regulation 5 of the Deferral of Retirement Pensions etc. Regulations or, as the case may be, paragraph 20D of Schedule 1 to the Graduated Retirement Benefit Regulations,

the Secretary of State may revise the award.]

[30 (7EA) The Secretary of State may revise a decision made under regulation 18(1) that a person ceases to be entitled to a benefit specified in paragraph (7EB).

(7EB) Those benefits are—

(a) a Category A or Category B retirement pension; .

(b) a shared additional pension;

(c) graduated retirement benefit;]

[38 (d) a state pension under Part 1 of the Pensions Act 2014.]

[16 (7F) A decision under regulation 17(1)(d) of the Income Support Regulations that a person is no longer entitled to a disability premium because of a determination that he is not incapable of work may be revised where the decision which embodies that determination is revised or his appeal against the decision is successful.]

(8) A decision of the Secretary of State [3 or the Board of an officer of the Board] which is specified in Schedule 2 to the Act or is prescribed in regulation 27 (decisions against which no appeal lies) may be revised at any time.

[7 (8A) [24 . . .]]

[8 (8B) [25 Where—

(a) a restriction is imposed on a person under section 6B, 7, 8 or 9 of the Social Security Fraud Act 2001 (loss of benefit provisions) as result of the person—

(i) being convicted of an offence by a court; or

(ii) agreeing to pay a penalty as an alternative to prosecution under section 115A of the Administration Act or section 109A of the Social Security Administration (Northern Ireland) Act 1992, and

(b) that conviction is quashed or set aside by that or any other court, or the person withdraws his agreement to pay a penalty,

a decision of the Secretary of State made under section 8(1)(a) or made under section 10 in accordance with regulation 6(2)(j) or (k) may be revised at any time.]]

[20 (8C) A decision made under section 8 or 10 ("the original decision") may be revised at any time—

(a) where, on or after the date of the original decision—

(i) a late paid contribution is treated as paid under regulation 5 of the Social Security (Crediting and Treatment of Contributions and National Insurance Numbers) Regulations 2001 (treatment of late paid contributions where no consent, connivance or negligence by the primary contributor) on a date which falls on or before the date on which the original decision was made;

(ii) a direction is given under regulation 6 of those Regulations (treatment of contributions paid late through ignorance or error) that a late contribution shall be treated as paid on a date which falls on or before the date on which the original decision was made; or

(iii) an unpaid contribution is treated as paid under regulation 60 of the Social Security (Contributions) Regulations 2001 (treatment of unpaid contributions where no consent, connivance or negligence by the primary contributor) on a date which falls on or before the date on which the original decision was made; and

(b) where any of paragraphs (i), (ii) or (iii) apply, either an award of benefit would have been made or the amount of benefit awarded would have been different.]

[22 (8D) A decision made under section 8 or 10 may be revised at any time where, by virtue of regulation 6C (treatment of Class 3 contributions paid under section 13A of the Act) of the Social Security (Crediting and Treatment of Contributions, and National Insurance Numbers) Regulations 2001, a contribution is treated as paid on a date which falls on or before the date on which the decision was made.]

[39 (8E) A decision in relation to a claim for a contribution-based jobseeker's allowance or a contributory employment and support allowance may be revised at any time where—

(a) on or after the date of the decision a contribution is treated as paid as set out in regulation 7A of the Social Security (Crediting and Treatment of Contributions, and National Insurance Numbers) Regulations 2001 (treatment of Class 2 contributions paid on or before the due date); and

(b) by virtue of the contribution being so treated, the person satisfies the contribution conditions of entitlement listed in column 2 of the table in paragraph (8G) in relation to a contribution-based jobseeker's allowance or a contributory employment and support allowance.

(8F) A decision to award a benefit listed in column 1 of the table in paragraph (8G) may be revised at any time where, on or after the date of the decision—

(a) any of the circumstances set out in paragraph (8H) occur; and

(b) by virtue of the circumstance occurring, the person ceases to satisfy the contribution conditions of entitlement listed in the corresponding entry in column 2 of that table.

(8G) The table referred to in paragraphs (8E) and (8F) is as follows—

1. Benefit	*2. Contribution conditions of entitlement*
Contribution-based jobseeker's allowance	the conditions set out in section 2(1)(a) and (b) of the Jobseekers Act
Contributory employment and support allowance	the first and second conditions set out in paragraphs 1(1) and 2(1) of Schedule 1 to the Welfare Reform Act
[40 Bereavement support payment under section 30 of the Pensions Act 2014]	[40 the contribution conditions set out in section 31 of the Pensions Act 2014 (bereavement support payment: contributions and amendments)]
Widowed parent's allowance	the contribution conditions set out in paragraph 5(2) and (3) of Schedule 3 to the Contributions and Benefits Act
[40 . . .]	[40 . . .]
Category A or Category B retirement pension under Part II of the Contributions and Benefits Act	the contribution conditions set out in paragraph 5(2) and (3) or, as the case may be, 5A(2) of Schedule 3 to the Contributions and Benefits Act
State pension under Part 1 of the Pensions Act 2014	the conditions of entitlement to a state pension in section 2(1)(b) or, as the case may be, 2(2)(b) or 4(1)(b) and (c) of the Pensions Act 2014

(8H) The circumstances are—

(a) a Class 2 contribution is repaid to a person in consequence of an amendment or correction of the person's relevant profits under section 9ZA or 9ZB of the Taxes Management Act 1970 (amendment or correction of return by taxpayer or officer of the Board); or

(b) a Class 2 contribution is returned to a person under regulation 52 of the Social Security (Contributions) Regulations 2001 (contributions paid in error); or

(c) a Class 1 or Class 2 contribution paid by a person to Her Majesty's Revenue and Customs under section 223 of the Finance Act 2014 (accelerated payment in respect of notice given while tax enquiry is in progress) is repaid to the person.

(8I) A decision to award a benefit specified in paragraph (8K) may be revised at any time where, on or after the date of the decision—

(a) any of the circumstances set out in paragraph (8H) occur; and

(b) by virtue of the circumstances occurring, the decision was more advantageous to the claimant than it would otherwise have been.

(8J) A decision to award a benefit specified in paragraph (8K), or a decision that that benefit is not payable, may be revised at any time where, on or after the date of the decision, a contribution is treated as paid by the relevant day by virtue of regulation 7(1) of the Social Security (Crediting and Treatment of Contributions, and National Insurance Numbers) Regulations 2001 (treatment for the purpose of any contributory benefit of contributions paid under certain provisions relating to the payment and collection of contributions).

(8K) The benefits specified in this paragraph are—

(a) a bereavement benefit;

(b) Category A or Category B retirement pension under Part II of the Contributions and Benefits Act;

(c) a state pension under Part 1 of the Pensions Act 2014.]

[[4] (9) Paragraph (1) shall not apply in respect of—

(a) a relevant change of circumstances which occurred since the decision [[12] had effect] [[14] or, in the case of an advance award under regulation 13, 13A or 13C of the Claims and Payments Regulations, since the decision was made,]or where the Secretary of State has evidence or information which indicates that a relevant change of circumstances will occur; [[19] . . .]

(b) a decision which relates to an attendance allowance or a disability living allowance where the person is terminally ill, within the meaning of section 66(2)(a) of the Contributions and Benefit Act, unless an application for revision which contains an express statement that the person is terminally ill is made either by—

(i) the person himself; or

(ii) any other person purporting to act on his behalf whether or not that other person is acting with his knowledge or authority,

but where such an application is received a decision may be so revised notwithstanding that no claim under section 66(1) or, as the case may be, 72(5) or 73(12) of that Act has been made;] [[19] nor

(c) a decision which relates to an employment and support allowance where the claimant is terminally ill, within the meaning of regulation 2(1) of the Employment and Support Allowance Regulations unless the claimant makes an application which contains an express statement that he is terminally ill and where such an application is made, the decision may be revised.".

(10) The Secretary of State [[3] or the Board] may treat an application for a supersession as an application for a revision.

(11) In this regulation and regulation 7, "appropriate office" means

(a) the office of the [[10] Department for Work and Pensions] the address of which is indicated on the notification of the original decision; or

(b) in the case of a person who has claimed jobseeker's allowance, the office specified by the Secretary of State in accordance with regulation 23 of the Jobseeker's Allowance Regulations [[2]; or

(c) in the case of a contributions decision which falls within Part II of Schedule 3 to the Act, any National Insurance Contributions office of the Board or any office of the [[10] Department for Work and Pensions]; or

(d) in the case of a decision made under the Pension Schemes Act 1993 by virtue of section 170(2) of that Act, any National Insurance Contributions office of the Board;] [[3] or

(e) in the case of a person who has claimed working families' tax credit or disabled person's tax credit, a Tax Credits Office, the address of which is indicated on the notification of the original decision;] [[5] or

[[11](f) in the case of a person who is, or would be, required to take part in a work-focused interview, an office of the Department for Work and Pensions which is designated by the Secretary of State as a Jobcentre Plus Office or an office of a designated authority which displays the **one** logo.]

[[39] (12) In this regulation—

"relevant day" has the meaning given in regulation 7(3)(b) of the Social Security (Crediting and Treatment of Contributions, and National Insurance Numbers) Regulations 2001;

"relevant profits" has the meaning given in section 11(3) of the Contributions and Benefits Act.]

AMENDMENTS

1. Social Security and Child Support (Decisions and Appeals) Amendment (No.2) Regulations 1999 (SI 1999/1623) reg.2 (July 5, 1999).

2. Social Security Contributions (Transfer of Functions, etc.) Act 1999 (Commencement No.2 and Consequential and Transitional Provisions) Order 1999 (SI 1999/1662) art.3(3) (July 5, 1999).

3. Tax Credits (Decisions and Appeals) (Amendment) Regulations 1999 (SI 1999/ 2570) reg.6 (October 5, 1999). Note that amendments made by these regulations only have effect with respect to tax credit (reg.1(2) of the Amendment Regulations). In the case of para.(5) the amendments are substituted in relation to tax credit; for this reason the substituted words in relation to tax credit are shown in italics.

4. Social Security and Child Support (Decisions and Appeals), Vaccine Damage Payments and Jobseeker's Allowance (Amendment) Regulations 1999 (SI 1999/2677) reg.6 (October 18, 1999).

5. Social Security (Work-focused Interviews) Regulations 2000 (SI 2000/897) reg.16(5) and Sch.6 para.3 (April 3, 2000).

6. Social Security (Joint Claims: Consequential Amendments) Regulations 2000 (SI 2000/1982) reg.5(a) (March 19, 2001).

7. Social Security (Breach of Community Order) (Consequential Amendments) Regulations 2001 (SI 2001/1711) reg.2(2)(b) (October 15, 2001).

8. Social Security (Loss of Benefit) (Consequential Amendments) Regulations 2002 (SI 2002/490) reg.8(a) (April 1, 2002).

9. Social Security (Claims and Payments and Miscellaneous Amendments) Regulations 2002 (SI 2002/428) reg.4(2) (April 2, 2002).

10. Social Security and Child Support (Decisions and Appeals) (Miscellaneous Amendments) Regulations 2002 (SI 2002/1379) reg.3(e) (May 20, 2002).

11. Social Security (Jobcentre Plus Interviews) Regulations 2002 (SI 2002/1703) Sch.2 para.6(b) (September 30, 2002).

12. Social Security and Child Support (Miscellaneous Amendments) Regulations 2003 (SI 2003/1050) reg.3(2) (May 5, 2003).

13. Social Security (Jobcentre Plus Interviews for Partners) Regulations 2003 (SI 2003/1886) reg.15(3) (April 12, 2004).

14. Social Security, Child Support and Tax Credits (Miscellaneous Amendments) Regulations 2005 (SI 2005/337) reg.2(2) (March 18, 2005).

15. Social Security (Deferral of Retirement Pensions, Shared Additional Pension and Graduated Retirement Benefit) (Miscellaneous Provisions) Regulations 2005 (SI 2005/2677) reg.9(3) (April 6, 2006).

16. Social Security (Miscellaneous Amendments) (No.2) Regulations 2006 (SI 2006/832) reg.5(2) (April 10, 2006).

17. Social Security (Miscellaneous Amendments) (No.4) Regulations 2007 (SI 2007/2470) reg.3(2)–(5) (September 24, 2007).

18. Social Security (National Insurance Credits) Amendment Regulations 2007 (SI 2007/2582) reg.3 (October 1, 2007).

19. Employment and Support Allowance (Consequential Provisions) (No. 2) Regulations 2008 (SI 2008/1554) regs 29 and 31 (July 27, 2008).

20. Social Security (Miscellaneous Amendments) (No. 5) Regulations 2008 (SI 2008/2667) reg.3(1) and (2) (October 30, 2008).

21. Tribunals, Courts and Enforcement Act 2007 (Transitional and Consequential Provisions) Order 2008 (SI 2008/2683) Sch.1 paras 95 and 98 (November 3, 2008).

22. Social Security (Additional Class 3 National Insurance Contributions) Amendment Regulations 2009 (SI 2009/659), reg.2 (April 6, 2009).

23. Social Security (Miscellaneous Amendments) (No.2) Regulations 2009 (SI 2009/1490) reg.3 (July 13, 2009).

24. Welfare Reform Act 2009 (Section 26) (Consequential Amendments) Regulations 2010 (SI 2010/424) reg.4(1) and (3) (March 22, 2010).

25. Social Security (Loss of Benefit) Amendment Regulations 2010 (SI 2010/1160) reg.3(1) and (2) (April 1, 2010).

26. Jobseeker's Allowance (Sanctions for Failure to Attend) Regulations 2010 (SI 2010/509) reg.3(1) and (2) (April 6, 2010).

27. Social Security (Miscellaneous Amendments) (No.3) Regulations 2010 (SI 2010/840) reg.7(1) and (2) (June 28, 2010).

28. Jobseeker's Allowance (Mandatory Work Activity Scheme) Regulations 2011 (SI 2011/688) reg.18(a) (April 25, 2011).

29. Social Security (Miscellaneous Amendments) (No. 3) Regulations 2011 (SI 2011/2425) reg.12 (October 31, 2011).

30. Social Security (Suspension of Payment of Benefits and Miscellaneous Amendments) Regulations 2012 (SI 2012/824) reg.4(1) and (2) (April 17, 2012).

31. Employment and Support Allowance (Duration of Contributory Allowance) (Consequential Amendments) Regulations 2012 (SI 2012/913) reg.5 (May 1, 2012).

32. Employment and Support Allowance (Amendment of Linking Rules) Regulations 2012 (SI 2012/919) reg.2 (May 1, 2012).

33. Jobseeker's Allowance (Sanctions) (Amendment) Regulations 2012 (SI 2012/2568) reg.6(1) and (2) (October 22, 2012).

34. Social Security (Miscellaneous Amendments) (No.2) Regulations 2012 (SI 2012/2575) reg.4 (November 5, 2012).

35. Social Security, Child Support, Vaccine Damage and Other Payments (Decisions and Appeals) (Amendment) Regulations 2013 (SI 2013/2380) reg.4(1) and (2) (October 28, 2013).

36. Income Support (Work-Related Activity) and Miscellaneous Amendments Regulations 2014 (SI 2014/1097) reg.12(1) and (3) (April 28, 2014).

37. Jobseeker's Allowance (Extended Period of Sickness) Amendment Regulations 2015 (SI 2015/339) reg.7(1) and (2) (March 30, 2015).

38. Pensions Act 2014 (Consequential, Supplementary and Incidental Amendments) Order 2015 (SI 2015/1985) art.18(1), (3) and (4) (April 6, 2016).

39. Social Security (Credits, and Crediting and Treatment of Contributions) (Consequential and Miscellaneous Amendments) Regulations 2016 (SI 2016/1145) reg.4(1) and (3) (January 1, 2017).

40. Pensions Act 2014 (Consequential, Supplementary and Incidental Amendments) Order 2017 (SI 2017/422) art.15(1) and (3) (April 6, 2017, subject to a saving).

DEFINITIONS

"the Administration Act"—see s.84 of the Social Security Act 1998.
"appeal"—see reg.1(3).
"appropriate office"—see para.(11).
"bereavement benefit"—see reg.1(3).
"the Board"—*ibid.*
"claimant"—*ibid.*
"the Claims and Payments Regulations"—*ibid.*
"the Contributions and Benefits Act"—see s.84 of the Social Security Act 1998.
"contribution-based jobseeker's allowance—see reg.1(3).
"contributory employment and support allowance"—*ibid.*
"the date of notification"—*ibid.*
"the Deferral of Retirement Pensions etc. Regulations"—*ibid.*
"designated authority"—*ibid.*
"disability benefit decision"—see reg.7A(1).
"disability determination"—*ibid.*
"employment and support allowance decision"—*ibid.*
"the Employment and Support Allowance Regulations"—see reg.1(3).
"failure determination"—*ibid.*
"family"—*ibid.*
"the Graduated Retirement Benefit Regulations"—*ibid.*
"incapacity benefit decision"—see reg.7A(1).
"incapacity determination"—*ibid.*
"income-related employment and support allowance"—see reg.1(3).
"Income Support Work-Related Activity Regulations"—*ibid.*
"the Jobseekers Act"—see s.84 of the Social Security Act 1998.
"the Jobseeker's Allowance Regulations"—see reg.1(3).
"limited capability for work determination"—see reg.7A(1).
"official error"—See reg.1(3).
"original decision"—see para.(1).
"payee"—see reg.7A(1).
"relevant benefit"—see s.39(1) of the Social Security Act 1998.
"relevant day"—see para.(12).
"relevant profits"—*ibid.*
"tax credit"—see reg.1(3).
"tax year"–see para.(ZC).
"widowed parent's allowance"—see reg.1(3).
"work-focused interview"—*ibid.*

General Note

This regulation provides for the circumstances in which a decision may be revised under s.9 of the Social Security Act 1998, whereas reg.6 provides for the circumstances in which a decision may be superseded under s.10. There are three main distinctions between revision and supersession. First, only decisions of the Secretary of State may be revised, whereas not only decisions of the Secretary of State but also decisions of tribunals may be superseded. Secondly, revisions have effect from the date from which the decision being revised was effective (see s.9(3) of the Social Security Act 1998) unless a mistake was made in respect of that date, in which case the correct date is used (reg.5). Supersessions are usually effective from a later date (s.10(5) or reg.7). Thirdly, there is no right of appeal to a tribunal against a decision to revise or not to revise, whereas there is a right of appeal under s.12 against a decision to supersede or not to supersede. Instead, a decision to revise and, in limited circumstances, a decision not to revise, extends the time for appealing against the decision that has been revised (see s.9(5) of the 1998 Act and the annotation to it. **2.424**

The first and third of these distinctions give rise to considerable problems where there is an appeal to a tribunal and the tribunal considers that a decision expressed as a revision should have been expressed as a supersession or vice versa. These problems were explored by a Tribunal of Commissioners in *R(IB)2/04* and *R(IS)15/04* (see the annotations to s.12 of the 1998 Act and para.(c) in the second column of the first row of the table in Sch.1 to the Tribunal Procedure (First-tier Tribunal) (Social Entitlement Chamber) Rules 2008). It is arguable that many of the problems are caused by the wide scope of reg.3, which appears to be based on the premise that if it is intended that a new decision should take place from the same date as the decision that is being reconsidered, the new decision must be expressed as a revision rather than a supersession. That approach is unnecessary, as appears to be accepted where it is desired that a new decision given on reconsideration of a decision of a tribunal should take effect from the same date as the original decision, because provision can be made by regulations under s.10(6) for a supersession to take effect from the same date as the decision that has been superseded (see reg.7(5)). If the grounds for revision contained in paras (4) and (5)–(8C) were instead grounds for supersession, many of the problems identified by the Tribunal of Commissioners would be removed. That would leave revision available only for cases where a decision is looked at again within a month or so of its being made or pending an appeal. It is only in those circumstances that the first and third of the distinctions drawn above suggest that revision is more appropriate than supersession.

In addition to the circumstances outlined in this regulation, decisions in respect of advance claims may be revised under regs 13(2), 13A(3) and 13C(3) of the Social Security (Claims and Payments) Regulations 1987 (*R(IB)2/04* at paras 106 and 107). A further power to revise is conferred by s.25(4) of the Social Security Act 1998 in respect of decisions made while a test case is pending before the Upper Tribunal or court.

Note that, for the purpose of the migration of claimants from incapacity benefit to employment and support allowance, regs 6 and 16 of, and Sch.3 to, the Employment and Support Allowance (Transitional Provisions, Housing Benefit and Council Tax Benefit) (Existing Awards) (No.2) Regulations 2010 (SI 2010/1907), apply the 1999 Regulations to conversion decisions, treating a conversion decision as though it were a decision as to entitlement to employment and support allowance made on a claim. Regulation 17 of those Regulations, as amended by reg.9 of the Employment and Support Allowance (Transitional Provisions, Housing Benefit and Council Tax Benefit) (Existing Awards) (No.2) (Amendment) Regulations 2010 (SI 2010/2430), provides: **2.425**

> "Where, on or after the effective date of any person's conversion decision, the Secretary of State is notified of any change of circumstances or other relevant event which occurred before that date and would have been relevant to the existing award or awards, the Secretary of State—

(a) must treat any award–

(i) converted by virtue of regulation 14(2) (conversion decision that existing award qualifies for conversion), or

(ii) terminated by virtue of regulation 14(2B)(a) (termination of an existing award of incapacity benefit or severe disablement allowance where entitlement to award of income support continues), regulation 14(3) (termination of award of an employment and support allowance where that entitlement already exists) or regulation 15(2) (termination of existing awards which do not qualify for conversion),

as if that award had not been converted or terminated;

(b) must treat any entitlement to be credited with earnings terminated by virtue of regulation 14(5) or 15(3) as if it had not been terminated;

(c) must treat any entitlement to a disability premium terminated by virtue of regulations 14(2B)(b), 15(2B) or 15(6) as if it had not been terminated;

(d) must take account of the change of circumstances or other relevant event for the purposes of determining whether to revise or supersede a decision ("the earlier decision") relating to the award or awards in respect of which the conversion decision was made;

(e) in an appropriate case, must revise or supersede the earlier decision;

(f) if any earlier decision is revised or superseded, must determine whether to revise the conversion decision made in relation to P; and

(g) in an appropriate case, must revise that conversion decision."

Note that paras (1)(a) and (9)(a) are modified by the 2010 Regulations (see below).

Paragraphs (1)–(3)

2.426 These allow a decision to be put right "on any ground" where the claimant applies for a revision within one month of the original decision being notified (but note the extension of time permitted where there has been a correction or request for reasons (see para.(1)(b)) or under para.(3)(b) in the case of a social fund payment or under reg.4). They also allow revision where the Secretary of State notices the error within that time. Note that the time for appealing against the original decision runs from the date the decision is revised *or is not revised* following an application under these paras (s.9(5) of the Social Security Act 1998 and para.(c) in the second column of the first row of the table in Sch.1 to the Tribunal Procedure (First-tier Tribunal) (Social Entitlement Chamber) Rules 2008), so that a claimant is not prejudiced by seeking a revision before appealing.

A decision may now be revised under para.(4A) at any time while an appeal is pending against it. This makes it possible to avoid a tribunal hearing altogether where the Secretary of State is prepared to concede the case in its entirety.

Note also that para.25A(1)(a) of Sch.2 to the Employment and Support Allowance (Transitional Provisions, Housing Benefit and Council Tax Benefit) (Existing Awards) (No.2) Regulations 2010 (SI 2010/1907), as amended by reg.17(1) and (12) of the Employment and Support Allowance (Transitional Provisions, Housing Benefit and Council Tax Benefit) (Existing Awards) (No.2) (Amendment) Regulations 2010 (SI 2010/2430), specifically provides that, with effect from October 1, 2010, reg.3(1)(a) of the 1999 Regulations is to be read as if, in the case of a revision of a decision to award jobseeker's allowance made following the reinstatement of an existing award in accordance with reg.15(5) of the Employment and Support Allowance (Transitional Provisions, Housing Benefit and Council Tax Benefit) (Existing Awards) (No.2) Regulations 2010, the words "within one month of the date of notification of the original decision" were omitted. Thus an error in a reinstated award of jobseeker's allowance may be corrected at any time.

Paragraph (4A)

This allows the Secretary of State to revise any decision while an appeal is pending in circumstances where it has not been, or could not be, revised under para.(1) or (3). The effect is that the appeal lapses under s.9(6) unless the revised decision is no more advantageous to the appellant than the decision that has been revised (see reg.30). 2.427

Paragraph (5)

Normally, a decision based on a mistake of law or fact made by the Secretary of State can only be superseded under reg.6(2)(b) unless the error is detected in time to allow revision under paras (1)–(3). Supersession will be effective only from the date the application was made (see s.10(5) of the Social Security Act 1998). Paragraph (5) provides for such a decision to be revised rather than superseded where either there has been an official error or else there has been an overpayment (which might be recoverable under s.71 of the Social Security Administration Act 1992) due to a mistake of fact). In effect, the time limit is removed because revisions generally take effect from the same date as the original decision (see s.9(3) of the Social Security Act 1998). 2.428

"Official error" is defined in reg.1. In *R(IS)15/04* (subsequently approved by the Court of Appeal in *Beltekian v Westminster CC* [2004] EWCA Civ 1784 (reported as *R(H)8/05*)), the Tribunal of Commissioners noted that a claimant might wish to assert that there were grounds for revision for "official error", whereas a claimant would not wish to rely on para.(5)(b) or (c). Consequently, a claimant might wish to challenge a refusal to revise under para.(5)(a) but, due to there being no right of appeal against a decision under s.9 not to revise and to the time limits for an appeal against the original decision, might be unable to do so save by way of an application for judicial review. The burden of proving that there was an "official error" lies on the claimant where it is he who is applying for revision, but it is for the Secretary of State to produce evidence of the supersession or revision that is in issue before the tribunal (*CH/3439/2004*).

Note that para.(5)(c) protects claimants of disability benefits or incapacity benefits from the full rigour of para.(b) in most cases and effectively prevents there from being a recoverable overpayment where a claimant could not reasonably have known a fact of which the Secretary of State was ignorant, or as to which he made a mistake, or could not reasonably have known that it was relevant. It does not protect the claimant who reasonably did not know that the Secretary of State was ignorant of, or had made a mistake as to, an obviously relevant fact of which he was aware, but that is presumably because in such cases any overpayment is unlikely to be recoverable anyway due to the lack of any misrepresentation or failure to disclose a material fact. More importantly, para.(5)(d) limits the effect of para.(5)(c) so that, where the ignorance or mistake relates to an issue other than the extent of the claimant's incapacity or disability, the general rule in para.(5)(b) applies.

In *AL v SSWP (IB)* [2013] UKUT 476 (AAC), the Upper Tribunal followed *JL v SSWP (DLA)* [2011] UKUT 293 (AAC); [2012] AACR 14, decided in relation to reg.7(2)(c), and held that a decision could not be revised under reg.3(5)(d) in respect of a period before September 24 2007, when that subparagraph was first inserted.

In *JA v SSWP (DLA)* [2014] UKUT 44 (AAC), the judge said that it was not obvious why revision was considered appropriate in the circumstances covered by para.(5), rather than those being grounds for a supersession effective from the same date as the decision being superseded, and he suggested that para.(5) could give rise to practical anomalies and introduced a wholly unnecessary degree of complication into decision-making. 2.429

Paragraphs (5ZA)–(5ZC)

The amendment to para.(5)(a) and the insertion of paras (5ZA)–(5ZC) make it unnecessary to revise decisions awarding the benefits listed in para.(5ZB) made as a 2.430

result of errors in claimants' favour in transposing information on the Department for Work and Pensions' computer system to Her Majesty's Revenue and Customs computer system. The claimants continue to receive the benefits.

Paragraph (5A)

2.431 This enables the Secretary of State to apply a tribunal's decision to any decision made while the appeal was pending, thus making it unnecessary for the claimant to appeal against the further decisions. The paragraph was required because, since the Social Security Act 1998 came into force, it has not been possible to refer to the tribunal questions arising while an appeal is pending or simply not to determine the questions on the basis that the tribunal could deal with all issues down to the date of decision. Although the Tribunal of Commissioners in *R(IS) 15/04*, considered that para.(5)(a) was the only part of reg.3, other than paras. (1) to (3) upon which a claimant might wish to rely, it was suggested in *CDLA/3323/2003* that para.(5A) is another provision. The Commissioner held that he was not precluded by "decision B" from making a decision on an appeal from "decision C" that covered the same period as "decision B", in case the Secretary of State declined to revise "decision B" and the claimant was left without any remedy because the time for appealing had expired. He held that "decision B" lapsed in the light of his new award.

Paragraph (5B)

2.432 Regulation 28 of the Social Security (Incapacity for Work) (General) Regulations 1995 provided that a person was to be deemed to satisfy the personal capability assessment before the assessment was carried out if a medical certificate was provided and he or she has not failed a personal capability assessment in the last six months (subject to certain exceptions). In *R(IB) 1/01*, it was held that, where those conditions were not satisfied, the claimant was still entitled to benefit in respect of the claim if he or she subsequently passed the personal capability assessment and, in *R(IB) 8/04*, it was held that a new claim was not necessary once the six months had elapsed. Paragraph (5B) enabled the Secretary of State to revise a decision awarding benefit from a date later than the date of claim (presumably because the claimant had failed a personal capability assessment less than six months before the date of claim but six months before the date from which the award was made) if the claimant subsequently satisfied the personal capability assessment. Since incapacity benefit has now been abolished, this paragraph has effectively been replaced by para.(5D) which applies to employment and support allowance.

2.433 *Paragraph (5C)*

This provides a fairly wide power to revise decisions relating to employment and support allowance that have resulted in sanctions.

Paragraph (5D)

2.434 This paragraph replaces with effect from October 31, 2011 an almost identical paragraph revoked from July 13, 2009, the difference being that subpara.(a) refers to "conditions" in the plural. It is in similar terms to para (5B) and presumably has been made for the same reason after the Secretary of State had second thoughts about the revocation. The explanatory note to the amending regulations suggests that this paragraph enables the Secretary of State "to revise a decision at any time where there is a non-medical change of circumstances relating to an ESA decision". Whatever the true effect is, it is not that broad.

Paragraph (5E)

2.435 When a claimant appeals against a decision of the Secretary of State to the effect that he or she does not have limited capability for work, the claimant is often awarded employment and support allowance at the basic rate while the appeal is pending, without a new claim being made (see reg.3(j) of the Social Security

(Claims and Payments) Regulations 1987) and for as long as medical certificates are provided (see reg.30 of the Employment and Support Allowance Regulations 2008 — in Vol.I). If the appeal is unsuccessful, withdrawn, struck out or discontinued, that award is terminated (under reg.147A(5) of the 2008 Regulations). If, however, the appeal is successful, para.(5E) permits the award to be revised, for which purpose any finding of fact embodied in or necessary to the decision of the First-tier Tribunal is to be treated as binding up to the date of any relevant change of circumstances (see reg.147A(6) and (7) of the 2008 Regulations). Revision is necessary because the effect of the First-tier Tribunal's decision will be that the claimant is entitled to include the work-related activity component or support component in addition to the basic rate. Thus, implementation of the decision of the First-tier Tribunal is in practice generally effected through this form of revision rather than more directly.

Notwithstanding, s.9(3) of the Social Security Act 1998, which provides that a revision is effective from the date the original decision "took, or was to take, effect", a revision under para.(5E) will take effect from the end of the assessment phase in a case where reg.7(38) would have had that effect if the original decision had been favourable to the claimant (*NC v SSWP (ESA)* [2015] UKUT 147 (AAC)).

Paragraph (5F)

The validity of this paragraph was questioned in *SSWP v PT (ESA)* [2011] UKUT 317 (AAC); [2012] AACR 17, although the judge also suggested that it might be validly made under s.9(1) of the Social Security Act 1998 and it is not easy to see why that should not be so. The judge also did not find the paragraph easy to interpret and his decision implicitly raises the question whether it is actually necessary or whether it was inserted as a result of the Department misunderstanding the way the provisions mentioned in it work. **2.436**

Paragraphs (5G) and (5H)

These paragraphs are both concerned with the situation that arises where a claimant's appeal against a decision to the effect that there was no entitlement to employment and support allowance is successful but he or she has been awarded income support or jobseeker's allowance while the appeal was pending. They enable the award of income support or jobseeker's allowance to be revised in the light of the successful appeal so as to prevent double entitlement. The benefit already paid under the revised award may be treated as having been paid on account of the award of employment and support allowance (see reg.5 of the Social Security (Payments on account, Overpayments and Recovery) Regulations 1988). **2.437**

Paragraph (5I)

Section 1A of the Welfare Reform Act 2007 (in Vol.I) has the effect that a person who does not have limited capability for work-related activity ceases to be entitled to contributory employment and support allowance after a year. This paragraph deals with the situation where an award is terminated under that provision while an appeal is pending against the decision that the claimant did not have limited capability for work-related activity and the appeal is subsequently allowed, although it also deals with cases where, after the award was terminated, it is revised or superseded in favour of the claimant from a date before the termination. The paragraph allows the award to be reinstated from the date it was terminated, as well as being increased so as to include the support component. **2.438**

Paragraphs (6) to (6B)

These paragraphs are concerned with the revision of decisions to impose sanctions in relation to jobseeker's allowance (para.(6)) or in relation to failures to attend work-focused interviews (para.(6A)) and with the revision of awards following a decision to impose a sanction in relation to jobseeker's allowance (para.(6B)). **2.439**

In *CJSA/2375/2000*, the claimant was twice disqualified for failing to attend training courses. The second disqualification was for four weeks because there had been the previous disqualification. An appeal against the first disqualification was allowed by a tribunal. The Commissioner, hearing an appeal against a decision by a tribunal dismissing an appeal against the second disqualification, said that the Secretary of State should have revised the second disqualification under the former version of para.(6) following the first tribunal's decision, in order to reduce the period to two weeks. This would more clearly have been appropriate under the new version. The odd use of the single word "anytime" in para.(6) is in the Queen's Printer's version of the amending Regulations.

Paragraph (7)

2.440 There are many instances where an award of benefit affects entitlement to another benefit awarded earlier. If the second award is made in respect of a period which includes the date from which a decision in respect of the first benefit took effect, that earlier decision is revised under this paragraph. If entitlement under the second award arises only after that date, the earlier decision is superseded under reg.6(2)(e) instead. Note that the earlier decision must have resulted in an "award" of benefit. It is suggested that that does not include a refusal of benefit, because the same term is used in sub-para.(b) in relation to the second decision and it is fairly clear that only an increase in entitlement under the second decision, and not a decrease in entitlement, gives rise to a revision under this paragraph. Where a decision in respect of one benefit is affected by a decision in respect of another benefit that is *less* favourable to a claimant, neither this paragraph nor reg.6(2)(e) applies and any consequent revision or supersession must be made under some other provision.

Paragraph (7ZA)

2.441 This enables an award of income support, income-based jobseeker's allowance, employment and support allowance or state pension credit to be revised in circumstances where the award was made while a non-dependant was awaiting determination of a claim for benefit and, as a result of a favourable decision on the non-dependant's claim, the first claimant becomes entitled to a severe disability premium.

Paragraph (7A)

2.442 This enables a decision as to entitlement to reduced earnings allowance to be revised in favour of the claimant following a favourable revision of, or a successful appeal against, a decision in respect of disablement benefit.

Paragraphs (7B) and (7C)

2.443 These paragraphs and paras (7CC) and (7F) date from before the introduction of employment and support allowance, when income support could be claimed on the ground of incapacity for work. Decisions about capacity for work were, in practice, always made in the context of entitlement to incapacity benefit or incapacity "credits". A person who had been entitled to income support on the ground of incapacity for work and was then found not to be incapable of work for the purposes of incapacity benefit or credits was likely to have the award of income support terminated but, if he or she appealed against the incapacity determination, a fresh award of income would be made at a reduced rate until the appeal was determined. These paragraphs had the effect that, if the appeal was unsuccessful or lapsed because the incapacity determination was revised, the income support decision could be revised. Paragraph (7CC) applied if jobseeker's allowance was claimed and awarded while the appeal against the incapacity determination was pending. If the appeal was successful, the termination of income support and the award of jobseeker's allowance could both be revised so that the award of income support could be reinstated in place of the award of jobseeker's allowance. Paragraph (7F) applied if the claimant remained entitled to income support on other grounds (e.g. being a single parent) at a lower rate due to the loss of the disability premium while the appeal against the incapacity determination was pending. Again, there could be a revision of the reduced award of income support if the appeal was successful.

Paragraph (7CC)

See the note to paras (7B) and (7C). 2.444

Paragraphs (7D) to (7E)

Where entitlement to certain pensions has been deferred or inherited, the claimant may elect to have either an increase in the pension or a lump sum. These paragraphs enable awards of state pension credit and the relevant pensions to be revised following a change in such an election. 2.445

Paragraphs (7EA) and (7EB)

These paragraphs provide a wide power to revise a decision to terminate an award of a retirement or state pension following the suspension of payments. A refusal to exercise the power is not appealable but presumably the power exists partly in case the Department loses contact with a pensioner, so that arrears can be paid when contact is resumed. 2.446

Paragraph (7F)

See the note to paras (7B) and (7C). 2.447

Paragraph (8)

See the note to reg.6(2)(d). 2.448

Paragraphs (8A) and (8B)

Paragraph (8A) is concerned with the now repealed provisions enabling benefit to be reduced if the claimant had breached a community order imposed by a court. Paragraph (8B) is concerned with the loss of benefit following a conviction or an agreement to pay a penalty in respect of an offence relating to the obtaining of benefit. Both paragraphs enable a decision to be revised if the determination or conviction is set aside or quashed or the agreement to pay a penalty is withdrawn. 2.449

Paragraphs (8C) to (8K)

These paragraphs enable a decision in respect of entitlement to a contributory benefit to be revised if, on or after the date on which the decision was made, it is decided either that a contribution should be treated as having been paid before that date or that a contribution that had been paid should be repaid, with the result that the entitlement decision is shown to have been wrong from the outset. Note, however, that reg.4 of the Social Security (Crediting and Treatment of Contributions and National Insurance Numbers) Regulations 2001 has the effect that in some circumstances late paid contributions are treated as having been paid only when they are actually paid, so that if they affect the amount of an award of a bereavement benefit, retirement pension or state pension the award will fall to be superseded under reg.6(2)(sa) rather than being revised, and that it has the effect that in some other circumstances late paid contributions are treated as not having been paid at all. 2.450

Paragraph (9)

On an appeal against a decision as revised, it is not possible for the appeal tribunal to have regard to any change of circumstances arising between the date of the original decision and the date of revision (*R(CS) 1/03*). 2.451

Note that, for the purpose of the migration of claimants onto employment and support allowance, para.25A(1) of Sch.2 to the Employment and Support Allowance (Transitional Provisions, Housing Benefit and Council Tax Benefit) (Existing Awards) (No.2) Regulations 2010 (SI 2010/1907) ("the 2010 Regulations"), as amended by reg.17(1) and (12) of the Employment and Support Allowance (Transitional

Provisions, Housing Benefit and Council Tax Benefit) (Existing Awards) (No.2) (Amendment) Regulations 2010 (SI 2010/2430), specifically provides that, with effect from October 1, 2010, reg.3 of the 1999 Regulations "is to be read as if—

(a) . . .;

(b) in the case of a conversion decision where there has been a change of circumstances to which regulation 12(4) of the 2010 Regulations (calculation of transitional addition) applies, paragraph (9)(a) were omitted; and

(c) in paragraph (9)(a), for "in the case of an advance award under regulation 13, 13A or 13C of the Claims and Payments Regulations" there were substituted, "in the cases of an advance award under regulation 13, 13A or 13C of the Claims and Payments Regulations or a conversion decision within the meaning of regulation 5(2)(a) of the 2010 Regulations".

Paragraph (10)

2.452 An application for supersession may be treated as an application for revision. Regulation 6(5) provides that an application for revision may be treated as an application for supersession.

For the powers of the First-tier Tribunal to treat a revision as a refusal to supersede and vice versa, see the note to s.12 of the Social Security Act 1998.

2.453 **[1 Consideration of revision before appeal**

3ZA. (1) This regulation applies in a case where—

(a) the Secretary of State gives a person written notice of a decision under section 8 or 10 of the Act (whether as originally made or as revised under section 9 of that Act); and

(b) that notice includes a statement to the effect that there is a right of appeal in relation to the decision only if the Secretary of State has considered an application for a revision of the decision.

(2) In a case to which this regulation applies, a person has a right of appeal under section 12(2) of the Act in relation to the decision only if the Secretary of State has considered on an application whether to revise the decision under section 9 of the Act.

(3) The notice referred to in paragraph (1) must inform the person—

(a) of the time limit specified in regulation 3(1) or (3) for making an application for a revision; and

(b) that, where the notice does not include a statement of the reasons for the decision ("written reasons"), he may, within one month of the date of notification of the decision, request that the Secretary of State provide him with written reasons.

(4) Where written reasons are requested under paragraph (3)(b), the Secretary of State must provide them within 14 days of receipt of the request or as soon as practicable afterwards.

(5) Where, as the result of paragraph (2), there is no right of appeal against a decision, the Secretary of State may treat any purported appeal as an application for a revision under section 9 of the Act.]

AMENDMENT

1. Social Security, Child Support, Vaccine Damage and Other Payments (Decisions and Appeals) (Amendment) Regulations 2013 (SI 2013/2380) reg.4(1) and (3) (October 28, 2013).

DEFINITIONS

"the Act"—see reg.1(3).
"appeal" —*ibid.*

GENERAL NOTE

This regulation is made under s.12(3A) and (3B) of the Social Security Act 1998 and it enables the Secretary of State to require a person to apply for a revision before exercising their right of appeal. This is known as "mandatory reconsideration" and harks back to s.33 of the Social Security Administration Act 1992 which had the effect that an appeal relating to attendance allowance or disability living allowance could be brought only following a decision made under s.30 on review. Those provisions were repealed in 1999, when the 1998 Act came into force, and were not re-enacted presumably because requiring a review in all cases created delay that was not justified by improved decision-making and a reduction in the number of appeals. This time, the idea is that the review should be more intensive, with claimants being telephoned to discuss the case, so that evidence is elicited and the decision fully explained and there is an increased likelihood of the right decision being made by the Secretary of State and of claimants only appealing when they have realistic prospects of success. This reduces the need to revise decisions under reg.3(4A) after appeals have been lodged and so it is no longer necessary for appeals to be lodged with the Secretary of State. Instead, they are now lodged with the First-tier Tribunal under r.22 of the Tribunal Procedure (First-tier Tribunal) (Social Entitlement Chamber) Rules 2008. However, note that the regulation applies only where the decision being challenged was made on or after October 28, 2013. 2.454

Note, also, that this regulation applies only where the right of appeal arises under s.12 of the 1998 Act (see para.(2)). Equivalent provision (e.g. reg.9ZB below) is made in respect of some other rights of appeal to the Social Entitlement Chamber of the First-tier Tribunal but by no means all. 2.455

Mandatory reconsideration is not uncontroversial. It can cause delay and there is clearly a risk that some claimants with meritorious cases may be dissuaded from appealing by assurances given over the telephone by the Department for Work and Pensions that the challenged decision is right and cannot be revised. A fall in the number of appeals is not an advantage to the extent that it results in wrong decisions being maintained. There also appears at first sight to be no right of appeal against a decision not to extend the time for applying for a revision under reg.3(1) or (3) or not to accept that an adequate application for revision has been made where, for instance, the Department wrongly tells a claimant that an application for revision must be in writing or that the usual one month time limit for applications under reg.3(1) or (3) cannot be extended. A person may therefore be deprived of his or her right of appeal through a mistake by the Department against which there is no redress short of an application for judicial review. The Social Security Advisory Committee has considered the impact of "mandatory reconsideration" in a study published in July 2016 (Occasional Paper No.18), which may be found at *https://www.gov.uk/government/publications/government-response-ssac-report-on-decision-making-and-mandatory-reconsideration* (accessed April 2017), together with the Government's responses to its recommendations.

Moreover, the legislation is not drafted as clearly as might have been desirable.

Paragraph (1) does not require the Secretary of State to issue a notice complying with subpara.(b) in all cases where the original decision has not already been the subject of reconsideration, although it seems currently to be his policy to do so. Its terms enable the Secretary of State to decide that certain classes of decision, or even individual decisions, should be appealable without the claimant first being obliged to seek reconsideration. Whether he issues a notice complying with subpara.(b) is a matter within his discretion. The regulation does not even expressly forbid the Secretary of State from issuing a notice complying with subpara.(b) when a decision in respect of which such a notice has already been issued has been revised. However, para.03012 in vol.1 of the *Decision Maker's Guide* makes it clear that the policy intention is that: "Once a decision has been subjected to mandatory reconsideration, further dispute rights are not dependent upon a further mandatory reconsideration". The notice issued with the revised decision in those circumstances should be the "notice of the result of mandatory reconsideration", which should be issued in duplicate so that, if the claimant wishes to appeal, they can send one copy to the First-tier Tribunal as required by r.22(4)(a)(i) of the Tribunal Procedure (First-tier Tribunal) (Social Entitlement Chamber) Rules 2008. However, there is scope for confusion if, as sometimes happens, the Secretary of State does not issue a notice in the standard form so that a clerk to the First-tier Tribunal receiving it does not know that there has in fact been consideration of the question whether the challenged decision should be revised and that there is therefore a right of appeal against the decision. A clerk has the power to refuse to admit an appeal if it is not accompanied by a notice of the result of mandatory reconsideration and may well do so if the notice of the decision does not bear the words "mandatory reconsideration" even though a notice without those words may in fact be a "notice of the result of mandatory reconsideration" for the purpose of the Rules. However, a clerk's refusal to admit an appeal should contain a notice that the claimant may ask that the issue be considered afresh by a judge under r.4(3) of the 2008 Rules.

2.456 Where a notice complying with para.(1)(b) is issued, it is para.(2) that operates to restrict the right of appeal. It is to be noted that it does not say under which paragraph of reg.3 any application for revision should be made, although para.(3)(a) clearly anticipates applications being made under reg.3(1) or (3). There are time limits for making applications under those provisions and, although time may be extended by the Secretary of State under reg.4, there is no right of appeal against a refusal to extend time and it is doubtful that the Secretary of State can be said to have "considered . . . whether to revise the decision" if he has refused to extend the time for applying for the revision. However, an application under reg.3(5)(a), for instance, does not need to be made within any specific time. If a claimant is refused an extension of time for making an application under reg.3(1) but makes an unsuccessful application under reg.3(5)(a), it may be arguable that the terms of para.(2) of this regulation are satisfied and they may appeal against the original decision.

If written reasons are provided following a request under para.(3)(b), the usual one-month time limit for applying for a revision under reg.3(1) is automatically extended (see reg.3(1)(b)(ii) and (iii)). However, there is no equivalent extension of time in relation to applications under reg.3(3) (relating to social fund payments for maternity or funeral expenses), despite what para.(3) of this regulation might suggest. Therefore, if a claimant has delayed applying for a revision of a decision in respect of a payment for maternity of funeral expenses and in consequence the usual one-month time limit has passed, they must rely on the Secretary of State exercising his discretionary power to extend time under reg.4.

Paragraph (5) enables the Secretary of State to treat a purported appeal as an application for revision. This would appear to apply whether the appeal is lodged with the Secretary of State in error or whether it is lodged with the First-tier Tribunal and then copied to the Secretary of State, although in the latter case the date of the application for revision is likely to be taken to be the date the appeal was received by the Secretary of State rather than when it was received by the First-tier Tribunal. Note that para.(5) applies only where there is no right of appeal. It will therefore not apply where the original decision was made before October 28, 2013 or was for any other reason not accompanied by a notice of the type mentioned in para.(1). In such a case, the Secretary of State will still be entitled to consider revising the decision under reg.3(4A) but the appeal will have been valid so that the Secretary of State will be obliged to send a response to the appeal to the First-tier Tribunal if the original decision is not revised in the claimant's favour.

3A. *Omitted.* 2.457

3B. *Omitted.* 2.458

Late application for a revision

4.—(1) The time limit for making an application for a revision specified in regulation 3(1) or (3) [2 or 3A(1)(a)] may be extended where the conditions specified in the following provisions of this regulation are satisfied. 2.459

(2) An application for an extension of time shall be made by [2 the relevant person,] the claimant or a person acting on his behalf.

(3) An application shall—

(a) contain particulars of the grounds on which the extension of time is sought and shall contain sufficient details of the decision which it is sought to have revised to enable that decision to be identified; and

(b) be made within 13 months of the date of notification of the decision which it is sought to have revised [3, but if the applicant has requested a statement of the reasons in accordance with [6 regulation 3ZA(3)(b) or] regulation 28(1)(b) the 13 month period shall be extended by—

(i) if the statement is provided within one month of the notification, an additional 14 days; or

(ii) if it is provided after the elapse of a period after the one month ends, the length of that period and an additional 14 days.]

(4) An application for an extension of time shall not be granted unless the applicant satisfies the Secretary of State [5 , the Commission] [1 or the Board or an officer of the Board] that—

(a) it is reasonable to grant the application;

(b) the application for revision has merit [6 , except in a case to which regulation 3ZA or 3B applies.]; and

(c) special circumstances are relevant to the application and as a result of those special circumstances it was not practicable for the application to be made within the time limit specified in regulation 3 [2 or 3A].

(5) In determining whether it is reasonable to grant an application, the Secretary of State [5 , the Commission] [1 or the Board or an officer of the Board] shall have regard to the principle that the greater the amount of time that has elapsed between the expiration of the time specified in regulation 3(1) and (3) [2 and regulation 3A(1)(a)] for applying for a revision and the making of the application for an extension of time, the more compelling should be the special circumstances on which the application is based.

(6) In determining whether it is reasonable to grant the application for an extension of time [6 , except in a case to which regulation 3ZA or 3B applies,], no account shall be taken of the following—

(a) that the applicant or any person acting for him was unaware of or misunderstood the law applicable to his case (including ignorance or misunderstanding of the time limits imposed by these Regulations); or

(b) that [4 the Upper Tribunal] or a court has taken a different view of the law from that previously understood and applied.

(7) An application under this regulation for an extension of time which has been refused may not be renewed.

AMENDMENTS

1. Tax Credits (Decisions and Appeals) (Amendment) Regulations 1999 (SI 1999/2570) reg.7 (October 5, 1999). Note that amendments made by these regulations only have effect with respect to tax credit (reg.1(2) of the Amendment Regulations).

2. Child Support (Decisions and Appeals) (Amendment) Regulations 2000 (SI 2000/3185) reg.6 (various dates as provided by reg.1(1)).

3. Social Security, Child Support and Tax Credits (Miscellaneous Amendments) Regulations 2005 (SI 2005/337) reg.2(3) (March 18, 2005).

4. Tribunals, Courts and Enforcement Act 2007 (Transitional and Consequential Provisions) Order 2008 (SI 2008/2683) Sch.1 paras 95 and 100 (November 3, 2008).

5. Child Support (Miscellaneous Amendments) Regulations 2009 (SI 2009/396) reg.4(1) and (3) (April 6, 2009).

6. Social Security, Child Support, Vaccine Damage and Other Payments (Decisions and Appeals) (Amendment) Regulations 2013 (SI 2013/2380) reg.4(1) and (5) (October 28, 2013).

DEFINITIONS

"the Board"—see reg.1(3).
"claimant"—*ibid.*
"the date of notification"—see reg.1(3).
"relevant person"—*ibid.*

GENERAL NOTE

2.460 Amendments made by reg.6 of the Child Support (Meaning of Child and New Calculation Rules) (Consequential and Miscellaneous Amendment) Regulations 2012 (SI 2012/2785) and effective only for the purpose of certain child support cases are not included in this volume.

Paragraph (1)

2.461 It was held in *R(TC)1/05* that a tribunal did not have jurisdiction to consider whether the Inland Revenue ought, under reg.4, to have extended the time for applying for revision. In that case, the relevant decision was made on April 22, 2002, the claimant sought reconsideration on November 11, 2002 and the Inland Revenue refused to extend the time for applying for revision and therefore refused to revise the decision on November 25, 2002. The claimant appealed. There is no right of appeal against a revision or refusal to revise and so the appeal had to be treated as an appeal against the decision of April 22, 2002. The time for appealing against a decision is not extended under reg.31 when the application for revision is made late and time is not extended under reg.4. In those circumstances (and subject to the possibility that the decision of April 22, 2002 had not been sent to the claimant), the appeal should have been treated as having been late and therefore invalid, unless the tribunal extended the time for appealing. On the facts of *R(TC)1/05*, it made no difference whether the time for applying for revision was extended under reg.4 or whether the time for appealing was extended under reg.31, but the Commissioner pointed out that the test for extending the time for applying for revision is now different from that for extending the time for appealing. He also pointed out that the 13-month absolute time limit for appeals now to be found in r.23(5) of the Tribunal Procedure (First-tier Tribunal) (Social Entitlement Chamber) Rules 2008 means that in some cases an appeal could be valid only if the time for applying for revision had been extended. It seems regrettable that a tribunal should not have the power to determine whether the Secretary of State ought to have extended time under reg.4, especially as the exercise the Secretary of State is required to perform is not all that simple and a considerable amount of money may turn on it. This is particularly so now that an application for revision may be required before a claimant can exercise their right of appeal (see, e.g. 3ZA). On the other hand, the most stringent provisions of paras (4) and (6) are relaxed in such cases.

Paragraphs (4)–(6)

Where an application for revision is required before a person may exercise a right of appeal, the merits test in para.(4)(b) is disapplied and so is para.(6). 2.462

Departmental guidance in DMG Memo 20/13 emphasises that, notwithstanding para.(4)(c), "Applicants are *not* expected to show unexpected or exceptional circumstances" and that an extension of time should be allowed "where the person is able to explain why their application for a revision is late and is reasonable". This approach appears justified in the light of *R(S) 3/79* and *R(I) 1/90*, in which it was held that reasonable ignorance of the law or a reasonable mistake as to the law could make it not "practicable" to take action. (In *R(S) 3/79*, reference was made to *Dedman v British Building and Engineering Appliances Ltd* [1974] I.C.R. 53 and *Wall's Meat Co Ltd v Khan* [1979] I.C.R. 52 but it was suggested that, in the social security context, one should focus only on the reasonableness of any ignorance or mistake on the part of the claimant in the light of any advice they received or should have sought, and not on the reasonableness of an advisor's ignorance or mistake.)

Nonetheless, one unsatisfactory feature of these paragraphs is that, even where the admission of a late application or revision is a prerequisite of an appeal, they prevent the Secretary of State from admitting a late application simply because it has obvious merit and a lot is at stake. Paragraph (4)(c) always requires that there has to have been a good reason for the delay and minor inexcusable delay may therefore result in a disproportionate loss.

Moreover, it is not obvious that the draftsman of para.(6) had *R(S) 3/79* and *R(I) 1/90* in mind. Paragraph (6)(a) provides that ignorance of, or a mistake as to, the law is not relevant to whether it is "reasonable to grant the application" (the para.(4)(a) issue) which is of doubtful effect if such ignorance or mistake is relevant to whether there are "special circumstances" (the para.(4)(c) issue). 2.463

As regards para.6(a), if a claimant is ignorant of a time limit due to the Secretary of State failing to provide the information required by reg.3ZA(3)(a), time will presumably be extended without difficulty. However, a provision requiring that misunderstandings of the law must be ignored seems to owe more to administrative convenience than individual justice.

Paragraph (6)(b) raises all sorts of questions. Understood by whom? Presumably not the appellant because the view must also be different from that previously "applied". Although, is it the understanding of the Department for Work and Pensions as a whole that matters or of a particular local office? Whatever the answers to these questions, it is not easy to see what sub-para.(b) adds to sub-para.(a) in practical terms.

The draftsman of the Public Bodies (Child Maintenance and Enforcement Commission: Abolition and Transfer of Functions) Order 2012 (SI 2012/2007) appears to have overlooked the need to remove the references in these paragraphs to the Commission (i.e. the Child Maintenance and Enforcement Commission) when it was abolished with effect from August 1, 2012, although those Regulations did remove the definition in reg.1(3).

Paragraph (7)

This prevents repeat out-of-time applications under reg.3(1) or (3) but it does not prevent the claimant from applying for revision under another provision, such as reg.3(5)(a) in respect of which there is no time limit or from applying for a supersession, although a supersession would almost always be effective from a later date. 2.464

Date from which a decision revised under section 9 takes effect

5.—[2 (1)] Where, on a revision under section 9, the Secretary of State [1 2.465

or the Board or an officer of the Board] decides that the date from which the decision under section 8 or 10 ("the original decision") took effect was erroneous, the decision under section 9 shall take effect on the date from which the original decision would have taken effect had the error not been made.

[2 (2) Where—

(a) a person attains pensionable age, claims a retirement pension after the prescribed time for claiming and the Secretary of State decides ("the original decision") that he is not entitled because—

(i) in the case of a Category A retirement pension, the person has not satisfied the contribution conditions; or

(ii) in the case of a Category B retirement pension, the person's spouse [3 or civil partner] has not satisfied the contribution conditions;

(b) in accordance with regulation 50A of the Social Security (Contributions) Regulations 2001(Class 3 contributions: tax years 1996–97 to 2001–02) the Board subsequently accepts Class 3 contributions paid after the due date by the claimant or, as the case may be, the spouse [3 or civil partner];

(c) in accordance with regulation 6A of the Social Security (Crediting and Treatment of Contributions, and National Insurance Numbers) Regulations 2001 the contributions are treated as paid on a date earlier than the date on which they were paid; and

(d) the Secretary of State revises the original decision in accordance with regulation 11A(4)(a),

the revised decision shall take effect from—

(i) 1st October 1998; or

(ii) the date on which the claimant attained pensionable age in the case of a Category A pension, or, in the case of a Category B pension, the date on which the claimant's spouse [3 or civil partner] attained pensionable age,

whichever is later."

AMENDMENTS

1. Tax Credits (Decisions and Appeals) (Amendment) Regulations 1999 (SI 1999/2570) reg.8 (October 5, 1999). Note that amendments made by these regulations only have effect with respect to tax credit (reg.1(2) of the Amendment Regulations).

2. Social Security (Retirement Pensions) Amendment Regulations 2004 (SI 2004/2283) reg.3 (September 27, 2004).

3. Civil Partnership (Consequential Amendments) Regulations 2005 (SI 2005/2878) reg.8(3) (December 5, 2005).

DEFINITION

"the Board"—see reg.1(3).

GENERAL NOTE

2.466 These paragraphs provide the exceptions to the general rule in s.9(3) of the Social Security Act 1998 that a revision takes effect from the same date as the original decision that has been revised.

Paragraph(1) deals with the obvious case where the effective date of the original decision was wrong.

Paragraph(2) is linked to reg.6(31) and (32) of the Social Security (Claims and Payments) Regulations 1987 and deals with a problem caused by the failure from

1996 to 2003 to inform contributors of deficiencies in their contribution records so that they could pay voluntary Class 3 contributions to make up the deficit. By regulation 50A of the Social Security (Contributions) Regulations 2001, claimants are being allowed to pay their contributions very late. Regulation 6(31) of the 1987 Regulations enables a late claim based on those contributions to be made and this amendment allows an earlier decision disallowing a claim to be revised with effect from October 1, 1998 or the date the claimant or, where appropriate, the claimant's spouse or civil partner reached pensionable age. Without these amendments, the new claim or the revision might be effective from a much later date and that might be unfair because, having discovered about the deficiency, the claimant might have delayed claiming on what was then a correct understanding that there was nothing that could be done about it.

5A. *Omitted.* 2.467

Chapter II

Supersessions

Supersession of decisions

6.—(1) Subject to the following provisions of this regulation, for the purposes of section 10, the cases and circumstances in which a decision may be superseded under that section are set out in paragraphs (2) to (4). 2.468

(2) A decision under section 10 may be made on the Secretary of State's [2 or the Board's] own initiative or on an application made for the purpose on the basis that the decision to be superseded—

(a) is one in respect of which—

(i) there has been a relevant change of circumstances since the decision [11 had effect [15 or, in the case of an advance award under regulation 13, 13A or 13C of the Claims and Payments Regulations [17 or regulation 146 of the Employment and Support Allowance Regulations], since the decision was made]; or

(ii) it is anticipated that a relevant change of circumstances will occur;

(b) is a decision of the Secretary of State [2 or the Board or an officer of the Board] other than a decision to which sub-paragraph (d) refers and—

(i) the decision was erroneous in point of law, or it was made in ignorance of, or was based upon a mistake as to, some material fact; and

(ii) an application for a supersession was received by the Secretary of State [2 or the Board], or the decision by the Secretary of State [2 or the Board] to act on his [2 or their] own initiative was taken, more than one month after the date of notification of the decision which is to be superseded or after the expiry of such longer period of time as may have been allowed under regulation 4;

[11 (c) is a decision of [19 [25 an appeal tribunal, the First-tier Tribunal, the Upper Tribunal or of a Commissioner]]—

(i) that was made in ignorance of, or was based upon a mistake as to, some material fact; or

(ii) that was made in accordance with section 26(4)(b), in a case where section 26(5) applies;]

(d) is a decision which is specified in Schedule 2 to the Act or is prescribed in regulation 27 (decisions against which no appeal lies); [11 . . .]

[5 (e) is a decision where—

(i) the claimant has been awarded entitlement to a relevant benefit; and

(ii) [9 subsequent to the first day of the period to which that entitlement relates], the claimant or a member of his family becomes entitled to [9 . . .] another relevant benefit or an increase in the rate of another relevant benefit;]

[15 (ee) is an original award within the meaning of regulation 3(7ZA) and sub-paragraphs (a) to (c) and (d)(ii) of regulation 3(7ZA) apply but not sub-paragraph (d)(i);]

[3 (f) [26 is a decision that a jobseeker's allowance is payable at the full rate to which the claimant would be entitled in the absence of any reduction where the award is reduced under section 19 of the Jobseekers Act;]]

[24 (fa) [26 is a decision that a jobseeker's allowance is payable at the full rate to which the claimant would be entitled in the absence of any reduction where the award is reduced under section 19A of the Jobseekers Act;]]

[1 (g) is an incapacity benefit decision where there has been an incapacity determination (whether before or after the decision) and where, since the decision was made, the Secretary of State has received medical evidence following an examination in accordance with regulation 8 of the Social Security (Incapacity for Work) (General) Regulations 1995 from a [18 health care professional] referred to in paragraph (1) of that regulation;] [4 [11 . . .]

(h) is one in respect of a person who—

(i) is subsequently the subject of a separate decision or determination as to whether or not he took part in a work-focused interview;

(ii) had been held not to have taken part in a work-focused interview but who had, subsequent to the decision to be superseded, attained the age of 60 or ceased to reside in an area in which there is a requirement to take part in a work-focused interview [13 or, in the case of a partner who was required to take part in a work-focused interview [14 in accordance with regulations made under section 2AA of the Administration Act, ceased to be a partner for the purposes of those regulations or is no longer a partner to whom the requirement to take part in a work-focused interview under those regulations applies];]

[7 (i) [20 . . .]]

[8 (j) is a decision of the Secretary of State that a sanctionable benefit is payable to a claimant where that benefit ceases to be payable or falls to be reduced under section [21 6B,] 7 or 9 of the Social Security Fraud Act 2001 and for this purpose "sanctionable benefit" has the [21 meaning given in section 6A] of that Act;

(k) is a decision of the Secretary of State that a joint-claim jobseeker's allowance is payable where that allowance ceases to be payable or falls to be reduced under section 8 of the Social Security Fraud Act 2001;]

[10 (l) is a relevant decision for the purposes of section 6 of the State Pension Credit Act and—

(i) on making that decision, the Secretary of State specified a period as the assessed income period; and

(ii) that period has ended or is about to end;]

[12 (m) is a relevant decision for the purposes of section 6 of the State Pension Credit Act in a case where—

(i) the information and evidence required under regulation 32(6)(a) of the Claims and Payments Regulations has not been provided in accordance with the time limits set out in regulation 32(6)(c) of those Regulations;

(ii) the Secretary of State was prevented from specifying a new assessed income period under regulation 10(1) of the State Pension Credit Regulations; and

(iii) the information and evidence required under regulation 32(6)(a) of the Claims and Payments Regulations has since been provided;]

[15 (n) is a decision by [19 [25 an appeal tribunal or] the First-tier Tribunal] confirming a decision by the Secretary of State terminating a claimant's entitlement to income support because he no longer falls within the category of person specified in paragraph 7 of Schedule 1B to the Income Support Regulations (persons incapable of work) and a further [19[25 decision of an appeal tribunal or the First-tier Tribunal]] subsequently determines that he is incapable of work;]

[16 (o) is a decision that a person is entitled to state pension credit and—

(i) the person or his partner makes, or is treated as having made, an election for a lump sum in accordance with—

(aa) paragraph A1 or 3C of Schedule 5 to the Contributions and Benefits Act;

(bb) paragraph 1 of Schedule 5A to that Act; or, as the case may be,

(cc) paragraph 12 or 17 of Schedule 1 to the Graduated Retirement Benefit Regulations;

or

(ii) such a lump sum is repaid in consequence of an application to change an election for a lump sum in accordance with regulation 5 of the Deferral of Retirement Pensions etc. Regulations or, as the case may be, paragraph 20D of Schedule 1 to the Graduated Retirement Benefit Regulations;]

[28 (oa) is a decision that a person is entitled to state pension credit and—

(i) the person—

(aa) chooses under section 8(2) of the Pensions Act 2014, or under Regulations under section 10 of that Act which make provision corresponding or similar to section 8(2), to be paid a lump sum; or

(bb) is entitled to a lump sum under section 8(4) of the Pensions Act 2014, or under Regulations under section 10 of that Act which make provision corresponding or similar to section 8(4), because the person has failed to choose within the period mentioned in section 8(3); or

(ii) such a lump sum is repaid in consequence of an application—

(aa) to alter the choice mentioned in paragraph (i)(aa) in accordance with regulation 6 of the State Pension Regulations 2015 or Regulations made under section 10 of the Pensions Act 2014 which make provision corresponding or similar to regulation 6 of the State Pension Regulations 2015; or

(bb) to make a late choice in accordance with regulation 4(4) of the State Pension Regulations 2015 (when a choice of lump sum or survivor's pension may be made) or Regulations made under section 10 of the Pensions Act 2014 which make provision corresponding or similar to regulation 4(4) of the State Pension Regulations 2015;]

[[17] (p) is a decision awarding employment and support allowance where there has been a failure determination;

(q) is a decision made in consequence of a failure determination where the reduction ceases to have effect under of regulation 64 of the Employment and Support Allowance Regulations;

(r) [[23] is an employment and support allowance decision where, since the decision was made, the Secretary of State has—

(i) received medical evidence from a health care professional approved by the Secretary of State, or

(ii) made a determination that the claimant is to be treated as having limited capability for work in accordance with regulation 20, 25, 26 or 33(2) of the Employment and Support Allowance Regulations;]]

[[18] (s) is a decision where on or after the date on which the decision was made, a late or unpaid contribution is treated as paid under—

(i) regulation 5 of the Social Security (Crediting and Treatment of Contributions and National Insurance Numbers) Regulations 2001 (treatment of late paid contributions where no consent, connivance or negligence by the primary contributor) on a date which falls on or before the date on which the original decision was made;

(ii) regulation 6 of those Regulations (treatment of contributions paid late through ignorance or error) on a date which falls on or before the date on which the original decision was made; or

(iii) regulation 60 of the Social Security (Contributions) Regulations 2001 (treatment of unpaid contributions where no consent, connivance or negligence by the primary contributor) on a date which falls on or before the date on which the original decision was made;]

[[29] (sa) is a decision where on or after the date on which the decision was made, a late contribution is treated as paid by virtue of regulation 4 of the Social Security (Crediting and Treatment of Contributions, and National Insurance Numbers) Regulations 2001 for the purposes of entitlement to—

(i) a bereavement benefit;

(ii) a Category A or Category B retirement pension under Part II of the Contributions and Benefits Act; or

(iii) a state pension under Part 1 of the Pensions Act 2014;]

[[27] (t) is a decision awarding income support where there has been a determination by the Secretary of State under regulation 6(2) of the Income Support Work-Related Activity Regulations that a person has failed to undertake work-related activity;

(u) is a decision made in consequence of a determination by the Secretary of State that a person has failed to undertake work-related activity where a reduction under regulation 8(1) of the Income Support Work-Related Activity Regulations ceases to have effect by virtue of regulation 9 of those Regulations.]

(3) A decision which may be revised under regulation 3 may not be superseded under this regulation except where—

(a) circumstances arise in which the Secretary of State [2 or the Board or an officer of the Board] may revise that decision under regulation 3; and

(b) further circumstances arise in relation to that decision which are not specified in regulation 3 but are specified in paragraph (2) or (4).

(4) Where the Secretary of State requires [2 or the Board require] further evidence or information from the applicant in order to consider all the issues raised by an application under paragraph (2) ("the original application"), he [2 or they] shall notify the applicant that further evidence or information is required and the decision may be superseded—

(a) where the applicant provides further relevant evidence or information within one month of the date of notification or such longer period of time as the Secretary of State [2 or the Board] may allow; or

(b) where the applicant does not provide such evidence or information within the time allowed under sub-paragraph (a), on the basis of the original application.

(5) The Secretary of State [2 or the Board] may treat an application for a revision or a notification of a change of circumstances as an application for a supersession.

(6) The following events are not relevant changes of circumstances for the purposes of paragraph (2)—

(a) the repayment of a loan to which regulation 66A of the Income Support Regulations or regulation 136 of the Jobseeker's Allowance Regulations applies; [17 , regulation 137 of the Employment and Support Allowance Regulations]

(b) [15 . . .]

[3 (c) the fact that a person has become terminally ill, within the meaning of section 66(2)(a) of the Contributions and Benefits Act, unless an application for supersession which contains an express statement that the person is terminally ill is made either by—

(i) the person himself; or

(ii) any other person purporting to act on his behalf whether or not that other person is acting with his knowledge or authority;

and where such an application is received a decision may be so superseded notwithstanding that no claim under section 66(1) or, as the case may be, 72(5) or 73(12) of that Act has been made.]

(7) In paragraph (6)(b), "nursing home" and "residential care home" have the same meanings as they have in regulation 19 of the Income Support Regulations.

[10 (8) In relation to the assessed income period, the only change of circumstances relevant for the purposes of paragraph (2)(a) is that the assessed income period ends in accordance with section 9(4) of the State Credit Pension Act or the regulations made under section 9(5) of that Act.]

AMENDMENTS

1. Social Security and Child Support (Decisions and Appeals) Amendment (No.2) Regulations 1999 (SI 1999/1623) reg.2 (July 5, 1999).
2. Tax Credits (Decisions and Appeals) (Amendment) Regulations 1999 (SI 1999/2570) reg.9 (October 5, 1999). Note that amendments made by these regulations only have effect with respect to tax credit (reg.1(2) of the Amendment Regulations).
3. Social Security and Child Support (Decisions and Appeals), Vaccine Damage Payments and Jobseeker's Allowance (Amendment) Regulations 1999 (SI 1999/2677) reg.7 (October 18, 1999).
4. Social Security (Work-focused Interviews) Regulations 2000 (SI 2000/897) reg.16(5) and Sch.6 para.4 (April 3, 2000).
5. Social Security and Child Support (Miscellaneous Amendments) Regulations 2000 (SI 2000/1596) reg.16 (June 19, 2000).
6. Social Security (Joint Claims: Consequential Amendments) Regulations 2000 (SI 2000/1982) reg.5(b) (March 19, 2001).
7. Social Security (Breach of Community Order) (Consequential Amendments) Regulations 2001 (SI 2001/1711) reg.2(2)(c) (October 15, 2001).
8. Social Security (Loss of Benefit) (Consequential Amendments) Regulations 2002 (SI 2002/490) reg.8(b) (April 1, 2002).
9. Social Security (Claims and Payments and Miscellaneous Amendments) Regulations 2002 (SI 2002/428) reg.4(3) (April 2, 2002).
10. State Pension Credit (Consequential, Transitional and Miscellaneous Provisions) Regulations 2002 (SI 2002/3019) reg.17 (April 7, 2003).
11. Social Security and Child Support (Miscellaneous Amendments) Regulations 2003 (SI 2003/1050) reg.3(3) (May 5, 2003).
12. State Pension Credit (Transitional and Miscellaneous Provisions) Amendment Regulations 2003 (SI 2003/2274) reg.5(2) (October 6, 2003).
13. Social Security (Jobcentre Plus Interviews for Partners) Regulations 2003 (SI 2003/1886) reg.15(4) (April 12, 2004).
14. Social Security (Working Neighbourhoods) Regulations 2004 (SI 2004/959) reg.24(3) (April 26, 2004).
15. Social Security, Child Support and Tax Credits (Miscellaneous Amendments) Regulations 2005 (SI 2005/337) reg.2(4) (March 18, 2005).
16. Social Security (Deferral of Retirement Pensions, Shared Additional Pension and Graduated Retirement Benefit) (Miscellaneous Provisions) Regulations 2005 (SI 2005/2677) reg.9(4) (April 6, 2006).
17. Employment and Support Allowance (Consequential Provisions) (No.2) Regulations 2008 (SI 2008/1554) regs 29 and 32 (July 27, 2008).
18. Social Security (Miscellaneous Amendments) (No.5) Regulations 2008 (SI 2008/2667) reg.3(1) and (3) (October 30, 2008).
19. Tribunals, Courts and Enforcement Act 2007 (Transitional and Consequential Provisions) Order 2008 (SI 2008/2683) Sch.1 paras 95 and 101 (November 3, 2008).
20. Welfare Reform Act 2009 (Section 26) (Consequential Amendments) Regulations 2010 (SI 2010/424) reg.4(1) and (4) (March 22, 2010).
21. Social Security (Loss of Benefit) Amendment Regulations 2010 (SI 2010/1160) reg.3(1) and (3) (April 1, 2010).
22. Jobseeker's Allowance (Sanctions for Failure to Attend) Regulations 2010 (SI 2010/509) reg.3(1) and (3) (April 6, 2010).
23. Social Security (Miscellaneous Amendments) (No.3) Regulations 2010 (SI 2010/840) reg.7(1) and (3) (June 28, 2010).
24. Jobseeker's Allowance (Mandatory Work Activity Scheme) Regulations 2011 (SI 2011/688) reg.18(b) (April 25, 2011).

25. Social Security and Child Support (Supersession of Appeal Decisions) Regulations 2012 (SI 2012/1267) reg.4(1) and (2) (November 3, 2008, the retrospective effect being permitted by s.103(2)(b) of the Welfare Reform Act 2012).

26. Jobseeker's Allowance (Sanctions) (Amendment) Regulations 2012 (SI 2012/2568) reg.6(1) and (3) (October 22, 2012).

27. Income Support (Work-Related Activity) and Miscellaneous Amendments Regulations 2014 (SI 2014/1097) reg.12(1) and (4) (April 28, 2014).

28. Pensions Act 2014 (Consequential, Supplementary and Incidental Amendments) Order 2015 (SI 2015/1985) art.18(1) and (5) (April 6, 2016).

29. Social Security (Credits, and Crediting and Treatment of Contributions) (Consequential and Miscellaneous Amendments) Regulations 2016 (SI 2016/1145) reg.4(1) and (4) (January 1, 2017).

DEFINITIONS

"the Act"—see reg.1(3).
"appeal tribunal"–see s.17(7) of the Social Security Act 1998.
"assessed income period"—*ibid.*
"bereavement benefit"—*ibid.*
"the Board"—*ibid.*
"claimant"—*ibid.*
"Commissioner"–see s.17(7) of the Social Security Act 1998.
"the Contributions and Benefits Act"—see s.84 of the Social Security Act 1998.
"the date of notification"—see reg.1(3).
"the Deferral of Retirement Pensions etc. Regulations"—*ibid.*
"employment and support allowance decision"—see reg.7A(1).
"the Employment and Support Allowance Regulations"—see reg.1(3).
"failure determination"—*ibid.*
"family"—*ibid.*
"the Graduated Retirement Benefit Regulations"—*ibid.*
"health care professional"—see s.39(2) of the Social Security Act 1998.
"incapacity benefit decision"—see reg.7A(1).
"incapacity determination"—*ibid.*
"the Income Support Regulations"—see reg.1(3).
"Income Support Work-Related Activity Regulations"—*ibid.*
"the Jobseekers Act"—see s.84 of the Social Security Act 1998.
"the Jobseeker's Allowance Regulations"—see reg.1(3).
"a joint-claim jobseeker's allowance"—*ibid.*
"nursing home"—see para.(7).
"payee"—see reg.7A(1).
"relevant benefit"—see s.39(1) of the Social Security Act 1998.
"residential care home"—see para.(7).
"State Pension Credit Act"—see reg.1(3).
"work-focused interview"—*ibid.*

GENERAL NOTE

Paragraph (1)

This regulation is made under s.10(3) of the Social Security Act 1998. 2.469

In *Wood v Secretary of State for Work and Pensions* [2003] EWCA Civ 53 (reported as *R(DLA) 1/03*), the Court of Appeal overruled *R(DLA) 6/02* and held that a decision may be superseded only if one of the conditions in paras (2)–(4) is satisfied. If a claimant has applied for supersession and the conditions are not met, the Secretary of State must refuse to supersede. That is the natural meaning of the provisions but the Tribunal of Commissioners deciding *R(DLA) 6/02* had thought it necessary to give a strained construction to reg.6 because they understood s.12(9) of the 1998 Act precluded an appeal against a refusal to supersede, which would have been unfair. The majority of the Court of Appeal acknowledged that it was difficult to give both reg.6 and s.12(9) a literal construction but they preferred to give an extended construction to s.12(9), holding that there is an appeal against a refusal to supersede, and to take a more literal approach to reg.6, which certainly makes it easier to apply reg.6.

Where a decision is superseded and then the superseding decision is itself superseded, the body making that third decision must be satisfied that there are grounds for superseding the first decision as well as the second decision if the outcome is to be different from that of the first decision (*R(DLA) 1/06*).

2.470 It was held by a Tribunal of Commissioners in *R(IB)2/04*, adopting at para.10(4) a suggestion made by Rix L.J. in *Wood*, that the ground of supersession which is found to exist must form the basis of the supersession in the sense that the original decision can only be altered in a way which follows from that ground. This overrules *R(A) 1/90*, although no reference was made to that decision by the Tribunal of Commissioners.

However, there is still a question whether the use of the word "may" in paras (1) and (2) means that the Secretary of State need not supersede even if he finds that one of the conditions in paras (2)–(4) is satisfied. In *Wood*, Rix L.J. regarded a superseded decision as an altered decision, which might imply that supersession of an award necessarily implied a change in the claimant's entitlement so that there was no scope for supersession without there being a different outcome. Such an approach would be rather different from that taken in the context of reviews under earlier legislation (see the note to para.(2)(a)(i) below). But, now that it has been established that there is a right of appeal against a refusal to supersede, there is no practical difference between a refusal to supersede and a decision to supersede "at the same rate", at least at the time the decision is given. There may be a difference later to the extent that, if there is a later supersession, the nature of an earlier decision may determine which decision must be superseded but, even then, it is difficult to see how the outcome in terms of entitlement to benefit could be affected. It may well be that there are two or more perfectly acceptable legal analyses, each producing the same practical result and any one of which can properly be applied without the decision-maker erring in law.

There may be no practical difference between a refusal to supersede and a supersession "at the same rate" but, in *CIS/6249/1999*, the Commissioner decided that the Secretary of State had a limited discretion to refuse to supersede even where grounds of supersession existed and any supersession would result in a change in entitlement. Although a power may appear discretionary, there is often a duty to exercise it in a particular way in order that the purpose for which the power is given is not frustrated (*Julius v Lord Bishop of Oxford* (1880) L.R. 5 App. Cas. 214) and therefore the Secretary of State is for practical purposes normally bound to supersede a decision if the conditions for supersession are met and would result in a change of entitlement. However, in *CIS/6249/1999*, there was a competing duty not to abuse power by reviewing an award of income support in respect of a period in the past in circumstances where the claimant would have been unfairly prejudiced. The facts of the case illustrate the operation of the principle. The claimant was an asylum seeker entitled to "urgent cases" payments of income support to which he was not entitled if he had any capital in the form of liquid assets. In October 1995, he had been paid almost £900, representing about 11 weeks' arrears of income support, which he paid into a bank. As long as it remained in his bank, that sum should have disentitled him from income support. In October 1996, he told a visiting officer that he still had £787 but benefit continued in payment until 1998, when a decision was made disentitling him from February 25, 1998. In principle, the claimant had not been entitled to income support from October 1995, but there was no question of the overpayment being recoverable as the Benefits Agency had known he had the money in October 1995. On the other hand, deciding that the claimant had not been entitled to income support throughout the period from October 1995 to February 1998 would have prevented the claimant from being paid any benefit in the future because the claimant would have been unable to show he was entitled to benefit immediately before February 5, 1996 and would have been deprived of the transitional protection given to asylum seekers in receipt of benefit at that date. Had benefit been stopped in October 1995, when it should have been, the claimant would undoubtedly have qualified for benefit again before February 5, 1996. The Commissioner considered that reviewing entitlement before February 25, 1998 would have been so unfair as to be an abuse of power. The same approach would presumably be appropriate in respect of supersession.

CIS/6249/1999 was distinguished (and to some extent its correctness was doubted) in *R1/07 (IB)*, where it was held that it was not an abuse of power for a decision to be superseded retrospectively in a case where the claimant had sought advice from the Department for Social Development about working while claiming incapacity benefit but had not been advised that he was required to give notice of any work in writing. The claimant had acted honestly at all times but, as the Commissioner observed, there was no question of the recovery of any overpaid benefit and she considered that any unfairness to the claimant did not outweigh the public interest in ensuring that a correct decision as to entitlement was made. It is not clear from the decision whether the claimant had in fact lost anything to which he would have been entitled had he not received the wrong advice except, presumably, credited contributions during the material period in the past. If a loss of entitlement in the past meant a loss of current entitlement because different contribution years had to be taken into account, that was not recorded. However, the Commissioner did point out that the claimant might have a remedy in the courts if he had suffered any loss. 2.471

Although it appears necessary first to determine whether one of the cases in para. (2) applies and then determine what the outcome should be, the two stages need not be kept rigidly apart. In *CDLA/5469/1999*, the Deputy Commissioner pointed out that the fact that a tribunal must, as a first step *in their deliberations*, ask themselves whether there are grounds for supersession does not translate into a rule of practice that the question whether grounds for supersession exist must be treated as a preliminary issue *in the hearing*. In most cases involving ignorance or mistake as to a material fact, he suggests, the tribunal should, after the hearing, first ask itself simply what the facts are that are material to the issue to be decided. Only then should it ask whether the original decision was made in ignorance of any of those facts. If the answer is yes, it can then give its own decision on the basis of the facts found. In *CSDLA/765/2004*, the Commissioner took the opposite approach and suggested that a hearing should initially be restricted to taking evidence relevant to a ground of supersession, but that was not followed in *CSDLA/637/2006*, where the Commissioner said:

> "It is sensible rather that a tribunal hears all the evidence, including what is potentially relevant to current entitlement, but without yet making a final determination with respect to that, in order to compare present circumstances with those which surrounded the original award."

Then, it is generally necessary to consider whether there are grounds for supersession, before making a final decision on entitlement, particularly where the question of entitlement involves an element of judgment. Thus, in *CS v SSWP (DLA)* [2011] UKUT 509 (AAC), the First-tier Tribunal erred in considering whether the claimant was "virtually unable to walk" at the material time without identifying a relevant change of circumstances since the decision being superseded, because that "failed ... to give proper protection to the judgment of the original decision maker".

Nonetheless, it may sometimes be a legitimate inference from a finding that the claimant does not satisfy the conditions of entitlement to benefit that an earlier award was based on a mistake of law or fact or that that there has been a change of circumstances so that the earlier award may be superseded (*CDLA/1820/1998*), although that applies only where no reasonable person could find the conditions 2.472

of entitlement currently to be satisfied. It is then appropriate to presume that the ground of supersession is the one least unfavourable to the claimant (*Cooke v Secretary of State for Social Security* [2001] EWCA Civ 734 (reported as *R(DLA) 6/01*)). In *CSDLA/637/2006*, however, the Commissioner pointed out that drawing such an inference did not imply that an original award made by a tribunal, as opposed to the Secretary of State, could be superseded, because an error of law is not a ground for superseding a tribunal's decision. She rejected the Secretary of State's contention that it should be presumed that the earlier tribunal had not erred in law and she consequently upheld a decision to the effect that grounds for supersession had not been made out.

The Secretary of State may supersede a decision either on an application or on his own initiative. Where he considers a claimant's application for supersession but reduces entitlement rather than increasing it, he must be treated as having superseded the original decision on his own initiative, rather than on the claimant's application (*R(IB)2/04*, at para.95). That is necessary to avoid the claimant being unfairly prejudiced in respect of the date from which the decision is effective under s.10(5) of the 1998 Act. For the same reason, where a claimant appeals against a decision made on his or her application for supersession and a tribunal makes a decision that is less favourable to the claimant than the decision that is being superseded, the decision will be effective from the date on which it would have been effective if the Secretary of State had acted on his own initiative (*R(IB)2/04*, at para.97). It has been held that if the Secretary of State considers a case on his own motion but decides not to change the award, he is bound nonetheless to issue a decision refusing to revise or supersede the decision, or revising or superseding it "at the same rate" (*CTC/2979/2001*). However, that was doubted in *CDLA/705/2002* and, in *CI/1547/2001*, it was said that the Secretary of State was nearly always bound to issue a decision on a claimant's application but need not do so when considering a case on his own motion. If a decision is given simply in terms of a new award without supersession being mentioned but in circumstances where the new award could be made only on supersession, the defect can be cured by a tribunal giving the decision in the correct form (*R(IB)2/04*, at para.76). However, if the tribunal never discover that the decision should have been a supersession, because they are unaware that there was an award current when the decision was made, the tribunal's decision may well be set aside because it is impossible to infer that circumstances justifying a different outcome on supersession were made out (*CDLA/9/2001*).

Section 10(3) permits regulations to be made prescribing the procedure by which a supersession may be made, but no regulation has been made prescribing the form of an application and the question whether a letter amounts to an application for supersession does not fall within the exclusive jurisdiction of the Secretary of State. A letter providing information about a change of circumstances will often imply a request for supersession (see para.(5)) but not all letters to the Department carry a clear implication to that effect and it may sometimes be difficult to determine whether, in reconsidering a decision, the Secretary of State is acting on his own initiative or in response to an application. This would not matter were it not for the impact the distinction may have on the date from which the application is effective (see s.10(5) of the Social Security Act 1998). It is doubtful whether giving information to a medical advisor during a medical examination amounts to an application for supersession, even though a notification of a change of circumstances may be treated as an application for supersession under para.(5), but the Secretary of State can made a supsersession decision of his own motion when the information is passed to him (*CI/954/2006*).

2.473 A final assessment of disablement made under the legislation replaced by the 1998 Act implies that there was no disablement after the end of the award, and so has ongoing effect and requires supersession as well as a new claim for benefit (*R(I) 5/02*), whereas an assessment under the 1998 Act carries no such implication and, after it expires, requires just a new claim.

Save in the many instances where reg.7 or Schs 3A–3C provide otherwise, a supersession is effective from the date on which it was made, if the supersession was made on the Secretary of State's own initiative, or on the date of application when the suppression was made on the application of a claimant or other interested person (s.10(5) of the 1998 Act). In *CI/1547/2001*, it was suggested that all appeals against assessment decisions should also be treated as appeals against the consequent entitlement decisions because the provisions for supersession and revision, are too limited, having regard to the dates from which they are effective, to deal satisfactorily with the consequences of a successful appeal on assessment alone. In *CI/954/2006*, the Commissioner made the same point in respect of an application to supersede an assessment of disablement. He also held that, where a person who had been awarded disablement benefit suffered another industrial accident, a claim for disablement benefit in respect of the second accident might have to be treated in the alternative as an application for supersession of the first award and he pointed out that there is an anomolous difference in the extent to which a claim and an application for supersession can be backdated.

Note that payment of benefit may be suspended under reg.16 while consideration is being given to susperseding an award. In a case where payment of attendance allowance was terminated on supersession, because a local authority was paying care home fees, but the claimant was in dispute with a financial adviser and it was possible that money to pay the fees retrospectively would be forthcoming, payment ought merely to have been suspended (*CA/3800/2006; SSWP v DA* [2009] UKUT 214 (ACC)). It made a difference because, if payments were superseded, it was not possible to reinstate them from the date they were terminated by way of a further supersession. Indeed, a three-judge panel in *SSWP v JL (DLA)* [2011] UKUT 293 (AAC); [2012] AACR 14 has held that suspension of payment under reg.16 rather than supersession under reg.6 should normally be the default position where a claimant of attendance allowance or disability allowance first goes into long-term care. 2.474

Even if an award of benefit is a possession within art.1 of Protocol 1 to the European Convention on Human Rights, its removal under the provisions for supersession is not in breach of the Convention (*CDLA/3908/2001*). 2.475

For the purpose of the migration of claimants from incapacity benefit to employment and support allowance, regs 6 and 16 of, and Sch.3 to, the Employment and Support Allowance (Transitional Provisions, Housing Benefit and Council Tax Benefit) (Existing Awards) (No.2) Regulations 2010 (SI 2010/1907), apply the 1999 Regulations to conversion decisions, treating a conversion decision as though it were a decision as to entitlement to employment and support allowance made on a claim. For the terms of reg.17 to the 2010 Regulations, see the annotation to reg.3 above. Note that para.(2)(a)(i) is modified by the 2010 Regulatons (see below).

Paragraph (2)

There is some degree of overlap between the sub-paras (e.g. (a)(i) and (e)) but this is not of particular significance. In *DS v SSWP (PIP)* [2016] UKUT 538 (AAC); [2017] AACR 19, decided under the equivalent provisions in the Universal Credit, Personal Independence Payment, Jobseeker's Allowance and Employment and Support Allowance (Decisions and Appeals) Regulations 2013, the judge referred to the different dates from which a supersession might be effective under the equivalent of reg.7 or Schs 3A–3C (which provide numerous exceptions to the general rule under s.10(5) that a supersession is effective from the date it is made or the application for it was made) and said: 2.476

> "15. . . . In my view, all grounds of supersession can apply in so far as the conditions they contain are made out, without any artificial rules to try to make them mutually exclusive. So far as decisions that are advantageous to the claimant go, there is then no difficulty in applying a general principle that the claimant should be able to take the benefit of whatever ground gives the most advantage. So far as decisions that are not advantageous to the claimant are concerned, which will in the great majority of cases be supersessions carried out at the Secretary of State's

own initiative, I do not see why the same principle cannot apply. The Secretary of State is entitled to rely on whatever of the grounds of supersession that are made out that result in what he says is the correct position being applied for the longest period."

However, he also held that, if the Secretary of State chose to rely on a simpler and more administratively-convenient ground and was content for the superseding decision to take effect from the date on which it was made rather than from an earlier date that would be more favourable to him, he was entitled to do so, subject to the power of the First-tier Tribunal in the event of an appeal to consider another ground of supersession if its potential application was clearly apparent from the evidence before it.

Paragraph (2)(a)(i)

2.477 In *R(I) 56/54*, the Commissioner said: "A relevant change of circumstances postulates that the decision has ceased to be correct". This means that only an award may be superseded on the ground of change of circumstances. A decision that a claimant is not entitled to benefit at all may not be superseded on that ground. Instead, the claimant must make a new claim. *R(I)56/54* also suggests that a change of circumstances is relevant only if it would result in a different "outcome decision". The same approach was taken in *Wood v Secretary of State for Work and Pensions* [2003] EWCA Civ 53 (reported as *R(DLA) 1/03*) but the Court did not refer to *Saker v Secretary of State for Social Services, The Times*, January 16, 1988 (reported as an appendix to *R(I) 2/88*) in which Nicholls L.J. considered what might amount to a "material" fact for the purposes of a provision similar to para.(2)(b)(i) and said that a fact was material "if it was one which, had it been known to the medical board, would have called for serious consideration by the board and might well have affected its decision". On the other hand, in *CIB/2338/2000*, the Commissioner said that the "subtleties based on the *Saker* decision, under which a change maybe relevant without justifying a different outcome, have no place in the scheme of adjudication under the 1998 Act" and, in *CIS/3655/2007*, he effectively held that *Saker* no longer applied because the effect of *Wood* is that reg.6 prescribes "outcome criteria" rather than "threshold criteria". In practical terms there is probably nothing to choose between the *Wood* approach and the *Saker* approach because a refusal to supersede has the same effect as a supersession "at the same rate". In other words, properly applied, either approach produces the same outcome, a point acknowledged in *CIS/3655/2007*.

A new medical opinion is not itself a change of circumstances but a new medical report may reveal not only a new opinion but also new clinical findings which would show a change of circumstances (*R(IS) 2/97* and *Cooke v Secretary of State for Social Security* [2001] EWCA Civ 734 (reported as *R(DLA) 6/01*)). A lessening of care needs is itself a change of circumstances (*R1/05(DLA)*).

A change of circumstances includes a change in the law due to the coming into force of a statutory provision (*Chief Adjudication Officer v McKiernon* (reported as R(I) 2/94)). Any supersession for such a change of circumstances is effective from the date of the legislative change (reg.7(30) and (30A)). By contrast, a binding decision of the Upper Tribunal or a court states the law as it has always been and so is not ordinarily considered to change the law (*In Re Spectrum Plus Ltd* [2005] UKHL 41; [2005] 2 AC 680). This does not create any difficulty where such a decision shows that an earlier decision of the Secretary of State was wrong in law, because the Secretary of State's decision may be superseded under reg.6(2)(b). However, reg.6(2)(b) permits supersession only of decisions of the Secretary of State and it was suggested by the majority in *SSWP v TJ (JSA)* [2015] UKUT 56 (AAC) that, for the purposes of social security adjudication, the making of the binding decision may need to be treated as a change of circumstances affecting the understanding of the law so that a decision of the First-tier Tribunal given before the binding decision was given can be superseded under reg.6(2)(a)(i). Otherwise, where an award of benefit has been made for an indefinite period by the First-tier Tribunal rather than the Secretary of State, it would not be possible to supersede the decision even prospectively so as to give effect to the binding decision from the date it was handed down. (This issue did not actually arise in that case and it was not considered by the Court of Appeal in the subsequent appeal, *Secretary of State for Work and Pensions v Reilly* [2016] EWCA Civ 413; [2017] Q.B. 257; [2017] AACR 14.)

Although reg.6(2)(a)(i) enables the Secretary of State to supersede a decision on the ground that there has been a change of circumstances "since the decision had effect", a Tribunal of Commissioners has suggested that it would be improper for the Secretary of State to supersede on that ground where the decision being superseded was that of a tribunal and, because the change of circumstances occurred before the decision under appeal and the tribunal was well aware of it, the tribunal could have taken it into account notwithstanding s.12(8)(b) of the Social Security Act 1998 but did not do so (*R(IS) 2/08*). "The Secretary of State should abide by a tribunal's decision in such circumstances." If he considers that the change of circumstances has not properly been taken into account, his remedy is to appeal.

See reg.7(2) for the date from which the supersession is effective. 2.478

For the purpose of the migration of claimants from incapacity benefit to employment and support allowance, para.25A(2) of Sch.2 to the Employment and Support Allowance (Transitional Provisions, Housing Benefit and Council Tax Benefit) (Existing Awards) (No.2) Regulations 2010 (SI 2010/1907) ("the 2010 Regulations"), as amended by reg.17(1) and (12) of the Employment and Support Allowance (Transitional Provisions, Housing Benefit and Council Tax Benefit) (Existing Awards) (No.2) (Amendment) Regulations 2010 (SI 2010/2430), provides that, with effect from October 1, 2010, reg.6(2)(a)(i) of the 1999 Regulations is to be read as if for "in the case of an advance award under regulation 13, 13A or 13C of the Claims and Payments Regulations or regulation 146 of the Employment and Support Allowance Regulations" there were substituted "in the cases of an advance award under regulation 13, 13A or 13C of the Claims and Payments Regulations or regulation 146 of the Employment and Support Allowance Regulations or a conversion decision within the meaning of regulation 5(2)(a) of the 2010 Regulations".

Paragraph (2)(a)(ii)

Section 8(2) of the Social Security Act 1998 provides that, when the Secretary of State makes a decision on a claim, he is precluded from taking account of circumstances not obtaining at the date of his decision. There is no equivalent provision in s.10 in respect of supersessions and this head expressly permits the Secretary of State to anticipate a change of circumstances. This is obviously a useful provision allowing the Secretary of State to act immediately to make the appropriate adjustment when a claimant informs him that his circumstances are about to change. However, it raises some interesting questions. For instance, what ground of supersession would there be if the anticipated change of circumstances did not take place? Perhaps supersession or revision on the ground of mistake of fact would be appropriate? More problematic is that a tribunal is precluded by s.12(8)(b) from having regard to any change of circumstances not obtaining at the date of the Secretary of State's decision and would therefore apparently be bound to ignore the change of circumstances that the Secretary of State had anticipated, even if the tribunal found that the change of circumstances had occurred. It must presumably be inferred that the passage of time is a change of circumstances for the purpose of reg.6(2)(a) even though it is not for the purpose of s.12(8)(b) (*R(DLA) 4/05*). Also, the amendment to this head made in respect of advance awards does not apply to an award made on supersession under this very head so that it might be difficult to supersede a decision in the light of an unanticipated change of circumstances occurring between the date of supersession and the date from which the supersession was effective. 2.479

consider the evidence lying behind the decision being superseded. However, where a claimant submits that his or her condition is unchanged since an earlier assessment, the findings made on the earlier assessment may well be relevant as evidence of the claimant's present condition, particularly if the condition is variable and any examination is likely to be only a snapshot (*CIB/2338/2000*). Commissioners were therefore highly critical of a rumoured proposal to destroy all records of personal capability assessments so that they were not available to decision-makers or tribunals concerned with subsequent supersessions (*CIB/1972/2000, CIB/3667/2000, CIB/378/2001, CIB/3179/2000*). In *CIB/3985/2001*, it was held that, where a claimant had stated that his condition had not changed since he had previously satisfied a personal capability assessment, the Secretary of State ought to make the report on that assessment available because the claimant had identified that as relevant evidence and was unable to produce it himself. Where the Secretary of State had not produced that evidence, the tribunal had to proceed on the basis that they had before them an implied request for an adjournment. That meant they had to consider whether the evidence was potentially relevant, in the light of the other evidence before them and, in the circumstances of the case under consideration, the tribunal erred in law in failing to adjourn and direct the Secretary of State to produce the evidence. There was nothing to suggest that the earlier assessments had ceased to be relevant because, for instance, there had been a supervening operation or injury. In those circumstances, it was not sufficient for the tribunal to rely on the new assessment when the claimant's argument was that earlier assessments would show it to be incomplete and insufficient. The need to provide a tribunal with proper information about the adjudication history behind a decision, explaining the basis of previous awards and the grounds upon which the last award has been superseded, has again been emphasised by a Tribunal of Commissioners in Northern Ireland in *R1/04(IB)*.

2.486 Another Tribunal of Commissioners in Northern Ireland, having analysed several of the cases mentioned above, held that the Department for Social Development should list details of all previous assessment determinations within the current claim, which the Department had said "should be straightforward in most cases . . . from computer records" but that the assessment reports themselves need only be provided "in a limited class of case, where there is an assertion that there has been no change in the claimant's condition, and where the evidence associated with the previous adjudication history is relevant to that submission or, for example, where the claimant's medical condition, and the evidence associated with the previous adjudication history assists in the assessment of the claimant's overall capacity" (*JC v DSD (IB)* [2011] NICom 177; [2014] AACR 30). See also *FN v SSWP (ESA)* [2015] UKUT 670 (AAC); [2016] AACR 24, mentioned in the annotation to reg.6(2)(r) below.

Another consequence of it being unnecessary to find a change of circumstances since, or error in, an earlier decision is that a decision-maker is entitled to make a different judgement on the same facts so that, even if a tribunal accept that a claimant's condition has not changed since an earlier favourable assessment and they cannot identify an error of fact or law in that earlier decision, they may decide that the claimant is not entitled to benefit. Nonetheless, the burden of proving grounds for supersession always lies on the person seeking supersession so that, where a claimant had been entitled to incapacity benefit, it was for the Secretary of State to justify terminating the award by superseding it under reg.6(2)(g). However, it was pointed out in *CIB/1509/2004* that the burden of proof must be considered in two stages. For reg.6(2)(g) to apply at all, the Secretary of State must have received the necessary medical evidence following an appropriate medical examination. On an appeal to a tribunal, it was plainly for the Secretary of State to produce that evidence but he invariably did so and therefore that was not usually a live issue. The second stage was considering whether the claimant still satisfied the conditions for entitlement to benefit and so continued to be entitled to benefit notwithstanding that the requirements of reg.6(2)(g) are met. The Commissioner referred to *Kerr v Department for Social Development* [2004] UKHL 23; [2004] 1 W.L.R. 1372 (also reported as an appendix to *R1/04(SF)* (see the annotation to s.3(1) of the Tribunals, Courts and Enforcement

Act 2007, where Baroness Hale talked of "a co-operative process of investigation" (at [62]) and said that "it will rarely be necessary to resort to concepts taken from adversarial litigation such as the burden of proof" (at [63]). A tribunal must have regard to all the evidence produced in the investigation and decide the case on the balance of probabilities. The Commissioner followed *CIS/427/1991* in holding that the burden of proof is relevant only: (a) if there is no relevant evidence on an issue (despite an adequate investigation) or (b) if the evidence on the issue is so evenly balanced that it is impossible to determine where the balance of probabilities lies. When superseding a decision on his own initiative, the burden of proof lies on the Secretary of State at both stages so that, in the few cases when it is relevant at the second stage, the case should be decided in favour of the claimant. Normally there is sufficient evidence to enable a tribunal to form a clear view one way or the other. That evidence includes the earlier decision and so, where it is decided to supersede it to the disadvantage of the claimant, it may be necessary for a tribunal's reasons to refer to the earlier decision (*R(M) 1/96*). Decisions that appear inconsistent and are not adequately explained tend to bring the adjudication system into disrepute *(R(A) 2/83)*.

In *CIB/313/2002* and *R(IB)2/04,* at para.125, Commissioners suggested that reg.6(2)(g) was applicable only where the award to be superseded was based on a personal capability assessment (see the definition of "incapacity determination" in reg.7A) and that where, for instance, an award was based on deemed incapacity under reg.28 of the Social Security (Incapacity for Work) (General) Regulations 1995, the proper basis for supersession was reg.6(2)(a)(i). However, in neither case was the point determined because the result would have been the same whichever provision was applied. In *CSIB/501/2003* (subsequently approved by the Court of Appeal in *Hooper v Secretary of State for Work and Pensions* [2007] EWCA Civ 495 (reported as *R(IB) 4/07*)), it was held that a decision to award invalidity benefit could not be "an incapacity benefit decision" and therefore could not be superseded under reg.6(2)(g). Presumably it could have been superseded under reg.6(2)(a)(i) but the Deputy Commissioner left such issues to be considered by the Secretary of State.

Paragraph (2)(r)

See the note to para.(2)(g), which makes equivalent provision in respect of incapacity benefit decisions. 2.487

In *MC v SSWP (ESA)* [2014] UKUT 125 (AAC); [2014] AACR 35, it was recorded that it was always the Secretary of State's practice to issue a decision following a work capability assessment and inform the claimant that they might appeal if dissatisfied with it. It could be argued that reg.6(2) prescribes circumstances in which a decision *may* be superseded and that, where a claimant has not applied for a supersession and the Secretary of State does not consider that an award need be altered in the light of a medical report, there is no requirement for the Secretary of State to issue any formal decision, far less a decision to supersede, although the claimant should no doubt be informed that, in the light of the result of their recent medical examination, the award will continue as before. Nonetheless, the judge said that the practice seemed desirable and was permissible and, indeed, that it was arguably required. He suggested that, where a decision made under s.10 of the Social Security Act 1998 on the Secretary of State's own initiative makes no difference to the existing award, it might be better to describe it as a decision not to supersede or as a decision to supersede but to replace the original decision with a decision to the same effect, rather than as a refusal to supersede. (There seems no reason why a decision made on the Secretary of State's own initiative not to supersede should not be treated as an appealable decision in the same way as a refusal to supersede following an application made by a claimant (see the note to s.12(9) of the 1998 Act).)

Where a decision is made during the "assessment period" (in broad terms, the first thirteen weeks of a period of entitlement to employment and support allowance), a decision that is adverse to the claimant and results in the termination of an award takes effect immediately but a decision in favour of the claimant takes effect only from the end of the assessment period (see reg.7(38) and (40)), which is the earliest date from which an award may be increased to include the work-related activity component or the support component (see ss.2(2)(a) and (3)(a) and 4(4)(a) and (5)(a) of the Welfare Reform Act 2007 — in Vol.I). In *NC v SSWP (ESA)* [2015] UKUT 147 (AAC), the Secretary of State failed to take account of the temporary effects of an operation undergone by the claimant the day before his decision terminating the claimant's award. The claimant said that those effects had passed after two weeks, which was before the end of the assessment period. The Secretary of State could have terminated the award under para.(2)(a)(ii) from the date that he expected the effects would have passed, rather than terminating it under para.(2)(r), but neither the First-tier Tribunal nor the Upper Tribunal could give a decision to that effect because they were precluded by s.12(8)(b) of the Social Security Act 1998 from taking into account a change of circumstances after the date of the Secretary of State's decision.

In *ST v SSWP (ESA)* [2012] UKUT 469 (AAC), it was held that a report of a previous medical examination that a claimant "passed" is often relevant and that, if he has it in his possession, the Secretary of State should send a copy if he considers it *is* relevant and should at least inform the First-tier Tribunal that he has the report in any other case because it *may* be relevant. In *FN v SSWP (ESA)* [2015] UKUT 670 (AAC); [2016] AACR 24, a three-judge panel has broadly agreed with what was said in that case and also with *JC v DSD (IB)* [2011] NICom 177 (mentioned in the annotation to reg.6(2)(g)) but has stressed that the previous adjudication history and associated evidence is not always relevant and that, even if the Secretary of State has not produced all the information and evidence that he should have produced with his response to an appeal, it does not necessarily follow that the First-tier Tribunal will err in proceeding in the absence of the evidence. It said –

> "79. . . . We can envisage a situation where a First-tier Tribunal considers that it has sufficient relevant evidence before it to determine the issues arising in the appeal without the requirement to call for evidence which is missing because the Secretary of State has failed in his duty to provide it.
>
> 80. . . . Our view is that the first choice for the tribunal should not be to adjourn but to get on with the task of determining the issues arising in the appeal when satisfied that it has the necessary relevant evidence before it. It might be the case that having weighed and assessed the appellant's oral evidence, the tribunal might be satisfied that the evidence is credible, should be accepted and the appeal be allowed. . . ."

It is suggested that the question for the First-tier Tribunal is not just whether it has sufficient evidence to enable it to determine the issues before it but whether it has sufficient evidence to do so *fairly* in a case where the evidence before it suggests a decision adverse to the claimant. This may involve an assessment of the probable helpfulness to the claimant of evidence that the Secretary of State could produce but has not produced. So, in *AM v SSWP (ESA)* [2013] UKUT 458 (AAC) (again broadly approved by the three-judge panel), which was a "conversion" case so that the tests applied in the earlier assessments were different from those to be applied in the current assessment, it was held that the First-tier Tribunal was entitled to conclude that it had enough evidence upon which to determine the appeal without obtaining the reports from previous assessments.

2.488 *Paragraphs (2)(s)*

It is not easy to see when supersession under this subparagraph would be appropriate rather than revision under reg.3(8C), unless the decision being superseded were that of a tribunal. Any supersession is effective from the date on which the late or unpaid contribution is treated as paid (see reg.7(8A)), which, if this subparagraph is to apply at all, must be "on a date which falls on or before the date on which the original decision was made". One wonders whether there has been an error and this subparagraph was intended to apply where the contribution is treated as paid on a date *after* the original decision was made.

Paragraph (2)(sa) 2.489

This paragraph applies where a late paid contribution is treated as paid when it is actually paid, rather than when it should have been paid, and so the supersession is effective accordingly under reg.7(43). See reg.3(8C) to (8K) for circumstances in which the late payment of contributions (or the repayment of contributions) may justify revision.

Paragraph (5)

An application for revision may be treated as an application for supersession. 2.490
Regulation 3(10) provides that an application for supersession may be treated as an application for revision. For the power of an appeal tribunal to treat a supersession as a refusal to revise and vice versa, see the note to s.12 of the Social Security Act 1998.

6A. *Omitted.* 2.491

6B. *Omitted.* 2.492

Date from which a decision superseded under section 10 takes effect

7.—[4 (1) This regulation— 2.493

[12 (a) is, except for [14 paragraphs (2)(b) [27 , (bb)] [26 or (be)], (29) and (30)], subject to Schedules3A [26 , 3B and 3C]; and]

(b) contains exceptions to the provisions of section 10(5) as to the date from which a decision under section 10 which supersedes an earlier decision is to take effect.]

(2) Where a decision under section 10 is made on the ground that there has been, or it is anticipated that there will be, a relevant change of circumstances since the decision [14 had effect] [19 or, in the case of an advance award, since the decision was made], the decision under section 10 shall take effect—

[4 (a) from the date the change occurred or, where the change does not have effect until a later date, from the first date on which such effect occurs where—

(i) the decision is advantageous to the claimant; and

(ii) the change was notified to an appropriate office within one month of the change occurring or within such longer period as may be allowed under regulation 8 for the claimant's failure to notify the change on an earlier date;]

(b) where the decision is advantageous to the claimant and the change was notified to an appropriate office more than one month after the change occurred or after the expiry of any such longer period as may have been allowed under regulation 8—

(i) in the case of a claimant who is in receipt of income support [12, jobseeker's allowance [26, state pension credit or an employment and support allowance] and benefit is paid in arrears, from the beginning of the benefit week in which the notification was made;

(ii) in the case of a claimant who is in receipt of income support [12, jobseeker's allowance [26 , state pension credit or an employment and support allowance]] and benefit is paid in advance and the date of notification is the first day of a benefit week from that date and otherwise, from the beginning of the benefit week following the week in which the notification was made; or

(iii) in any other case, the date of notification of the relevant change of circumstances; or

[27 (bb) where the decision is advantageous to the claimant and is made on the Secretary of State's own initiative—

(i) except where paragraph (ii) applies, from the beginning of the benefit week in which the Secretary of State commenced action with a view to supersession; or

(ii) in the case of a claimant who is in receipt of income support, jobseeker's allowance or state pension credit where benefit is paid in advance and the Secretary of State commenced action with a view to supersession on a day which was not the first day of the benefit week, from the beginning of the benefit week following the week in which the Secretary of State commenced such action;

(bc) where—

(i) the claimant is a disabled person or a disabled person's partner;

(ii) the decision is advantageous to the claimant; and

(iii) the decision is made in connection with the cessation of payment of a carer's allowance relating to that disabled person,

the day after the last day for which carer's allowance was paid to a person other than the claimant or the claimant's partner;]

[[24] (bd) [[25] . . .]]

[[26] (be) in the case of a claimant who is in receipt of an employment and support allowance and the claimant makes an application which contains an express statement that he is terminally ill within the meaning of regulation 2(1) of the Employment and Support Allowance Regulations, from the date the claimant became terminally ill;]

(c) where the decision is not advantageous to the claimant—

(i) [[4] . . .]

[[1](ii) in the case of a disability benefit decision, or an incapacity benefit decision where there has been an incapacity determination [[29] or an employment and support allowance decision where there has been a limited capability for work determination] (whether before or after the decision), where the Secretary of State is satisfied that in relation to a disability determination embodied in or necessary to the disability benefit decision, or the incapacity determination [[29] or an employment and support allowance decision where there has been a limited capability for work determination], the claimant or payee failed to notify an appropriate office of a change of circumstances which regulations under the Administration Act required him to notify, and the claimant or payee, as the case may be, knew or could reasonably have been expected to know that the change of circumstances should have been notified,

(aa) from the date on which the claimant or payee, as the case may be, ought to have notified the change of circumstances, or

(bb) if more than one change has taken place between the date from which the decision to be superseded took effect and the date of the superseding decision, from the date on which the first change ought to have been notified, or

(iii) [[22] . . .]

[[22](iv) in the case of a disability benefit decision, where the change of circumstances is not in relation to the disability determination embodied in or necessary to the disability benefit decision, from the date of the change; or

(v) in any other case, except in the case of a decision which supersedes a disability benefit decision, from the date of the change.]

[25 (2A) [27 . . .]]

[26 (3) For the purposes of paragraphs (2) and (8) "benefit week" has the same meaning, as the case may be, as in—

(a) regulation 2(1) of the Income Support Regulations;
(b) regulation 1(3) of the Jobseeker's Allowance Regulations;
(c) regulation 1(2) of the State Pension Credit Regulations; or
(d) regulation 2(1) of the Employment and Support Allowance Regulations.]

(4) In paragraph (2) a decision which is to the advantage of the claimant includes a decision specified in regulation 30(2)(a) to (f).

[7 (5) Where the Secretary of State supersedes a decision made by [28[39 an appeal tribunal, the First-tier Tribunal, the Upper Tribunal or a Commissioner]] on the grounds specified in regulation 6(2)(c) [14 (i)] (ignorance of, or mistake as to, a material fact), the decision under section 10 shall take effect, in a case where, as a result of that ignorance of or mistake as to material fact, the decision to be superseded was more advantageous to the claimant than it would otherwise have been and which either—

(a) does not relate to a disability benefit decision or an incapacity benefit decision where there has been an incapacity determination; or
(b) relates to a disability decision or an incapacity benefit decision where there has been an incapacity determination, and the Secretary of State is satisfied that at the time the decision was made the claimant or payee knew or could reasonably have been expected to know of the fact in question and that it was relevant to the decision.

from the date on which the decision of [28[39 an appeal tribunal, the First-tier Tribunal, the Upper Tribunal or a Commissioner]] took, or was to take, effect.]

(6) Any decision made under section 10 in consequence of a decision which is a relevant determination for the purposes of section 27 shall take effect as from the date of the relevant determination.

[19 (6A) Where—

(a) there is a decision which is a relevant determination for the purposes of section 27 and the Secretary of State makes a benefit decision of the kind specified in section 27(1)(b);
(b) there is an appeal against the determination;
(c) after the benefit decision payment is suspended in accordance with regulation 16(1) and (3)(b)(ii); and
(d) on appeal a court, within the meaning of section 27, reverses the determination in whole or in part,

a consequential decision by the Secretary of State under section 10 which supersedes his earlier decision under sub-paragraph (a) shall take effect from the date on which the earlier decision took effect.]

[22 (7) A decision which is superseded in accordance with regulation 6(2)(e) or (ee) shall be superseded—

(a) subject to sub-paragraph (b), from the date on which entitlement arises to the other relevant benefit referred to in regulation 6(2)(e)(ii) or (ee) or to an increase in the rate of that other relevant benefit; or
(b) where the claimant or his partner—
    (i) is not a severely disabled person for the purposes of section 135(5) of the Contributions and Benefits Act (the applicable amount) or section 2(7) of the State Pension Credit Act

(guarantee credit) [26 or paragraph 6 of Schedule 4 to the Employment and Support Allowance Regulations;]

(ii) by virtue of his having—

(aa) a non-dependant as defined by regulation 3 of the Income Support Regulations [38 , regulation 2 of the Jobseeker's Allowance Regulations] [26 or regulation 71 of the Employment and Support Allowance Regulations]; or

(bb) a person residing with him for the purposes of paragraph 1 of Schedule 1 to the State Pension Credit Regulations whose presence may not be ignored in accordance with paragraph 2 of that Schedule,

at the date the superseded decision would, but for this sub-paragraph, have had effect,

from the date on which the claimant or his partner ceased to have a non-dependant or person residing with him or from the date on which the presence of that person was first ignored.]

[21 (7A) Where a decision is superseded in accordance with regulation 6(2)(o) [44 or (oa)], the superseding decision shall take effect from the day on which a lump sum, or a payment on account of a lump sum, is paid or repaid if that day is the first day of the benefit week but, if it is not, from the next following such day.]

[3 (8) [40 A decision to which regulation 6(2)(f) applies shall take effect from the beginning of the period specified in regulation 69(6) of the Jobseeker's Allowance Regulations.]]

[35 (8ZA) [40 A decision to which regulation 6(2)(fa) applies shall take effect from the beginning of the period specified in regulation 69A(3) of the Jobseeker's Allowance Regulations.]]

[36 (8ZB) [40 . . .]]

[27 (8A) Where a decision is superseded in accordance with regulation 6(2)(s), the superseding decision shall take effect from the date on which the late or unpaid contribution is treated as paid]

[4 (9) [37 Except where paragraph (9A) applies,] a decision relating to attendance allowance or disability living allowance which is advantageous to the claimant and which is made under section 10 on the basis of a relevant change of circumstances shall take effect from—

[14 (a) where the decision is made on the Secretary of State's own initiative—

(i) the date on which the Secretary of State commenced action with a view to supersession; or

(ii) subject to paragraph (30), in a case where the relevant circumstances are that there has been a change in the legislation in relation to attendance allowance or disability living allowance, the date on which that change in the legislation had effect;]

(b) where—

(i) the change is relevant to the question of entitlement to a particular rate of benefit; and

(ii) the claimant notifies the change before a date one month after he satisfied the conditions of entitlement to that rate or within such longer period as may be allowed under regulation 8,

the [27 date on which] he satisfied those conditions;

(c) where—

(i) the change is relevant to the question of whether benefit is payable; and

(ii) the claimant notifies the change before a date one month after the change or within such longer period as may be allowed under regulation 8,

the [27 date on which] the change occurred; or

(d) in any other case, the date of the application for the superseding decision.]

[37 (9A) Where—

(a) on or after 8th March 2001, the claimant had an award of attendance allowance, carer's allowance, or the care component of disability living allowance;

(b) the Secretary of State made a superseding decision in accordance with regulation 6(2)(a) to end that award on the ground that there had been, or it was anticipated that there would be, a relevant change of circumstances as a result of the claimant moving, or planning to move, from Great Britain to an EEA state or Switzerland; and

(c) the Secretary of State supersedes that decision in accordance with regulation 6(2)(b)(i) on the ground that it was erroneous in point of law, the superseding decision referred to in sub-paragraph (c) shall take effect from 18th October 2007.]

(10) A decision as to an award of incapacity benefit, which is made under section 10 because section 30B(4) of the Contributions and Benefits Act applies to the claimant, shall take effect as from the date on which he became entitled to the highest rate of the care component of disability living allowance.

(11) A decision as to an award of incapacity benefit or severe disablement allowance, which is made under section 10 because the claimant is to be treated as incapable of work under regulation 10 of the Social Security (Incapacity for Work) (General) Regulations 1995 (certain persons with a severe condition to be treated as incapable of work), shall take effect as from the date he is to be treated as incapable of work.

(12) Where this paragraph applies, a decision under section 10 may be made so as to take effect as from such date not more than eight weeks before—

(a) the application for supersession; or

(b) where no application is made, the date on which the decision under section 10 is made,

as is reasonable in the particular circumstances of the case.

(13) Paragraph (12) applies where—

(a) the effect of a decision under section 10 is that there is to be included in a claimant's applicable amount an amount in respect of a loan which qualifies under—

(i) paragraph 15 or 16 of Schedule 3 to the Income Support Regulations; or

(ii) paragraph 14 or 15 of Schedule 2 to the Jobseeker's Allowance Regulations; [12 or

(iii) paragraph 11 or 12 of Schedule II to the State Pension Credit Regulations; [26 or]]

[26 (iv) paragraph 16 or 17 of Schedule 6 to the Employment and Support Allowance Regulations; and]

(b) that decision could not have been made earlier because information necessary to make that decision, requested otherwise than in accordance with paragraph 10(3)(b) of Schedule 9A to the Claims and

Payments Regulations (annual requests for information), had not been supplied to the Secretary of State by the lender.

(14) Subject to paragraph (23), where a claimant is in receipt of income support and his applicable amount includes an amount determined in accordance with Schedule 3 to the Income Support Regulations (housing costs), and there is a reduction in the amount of eligible capital owing in connection with a loan which qualifies under paragraph 15 or 16 of that Schedule, a decision made under section 10 shall take effect—

(a) on the first anniversary of the date on which the claimant's housing costs were first met under that Schedule; or

(b) where the reduction in eligible capital occurred after the first anniversary of the date referred to in sub-paragraph (a), on the next anniversary of that date following the date of the reduction.

(15) Where a claimant is in receipt of income support and payments made to that claimant which fall within paragraph 29 or 30(1)(a) to (c) of Schedule 9 to the Income Support Regulations have been disregarded in relation to any decision under section 8 or 10 and there is a change in the amount of interest payable—

(a) on a loan qualifying under paragraph 15 or 16 of Schedule 3 to those Regulations to which those payments relate; or

(b) on a loan not so qualifying which is secured on the dwelling occupied as the home to which those payments relate,

a decision under section 10 which is made as a result of that change in the amount of interest payable shall take effect on whichever of the dates referred to in paragraph (16) is appropriate in the claimant's case.

(16) The date on which a decision under section 10 takes effect for the purposes of paragraph (15) is—

(a) the date on which the claimant's housing costs are first met under paragraph 6(1)(a), 8(1)(a) or 9(2)(a) of Schedule 3 to the Income Support Regulations; or

(b) where the change in the amount of interest payable occurred after the date referred to in sub-paragraph (a), on the date of the next alteration in the standard rate following the date of that change.

(17) In paragraph (16), "standard rate" has the same meaning as it has in paragraph 1(2) of Schedule 3 to the Income Support Regulations.

[[12] (17A) For the purposes of state pension credit—

(a) paragraph (14) shall apply as if the reference to—

(i) "income support and his applicable amount" was a reference to "state pension credit and his appropriate minimum guarantee";

(ii) "Schedule 3 to the Income Support Regulations" was a reference to "Schedule II to the State Pension Credit Regulations"; and

(iii) "paragraph 15 or 16" was a reference to "paragraph 11 or 12";

(b) paragraphs (15) to (17) shall not apply.]

[[16] (17B) Paragraph 17C applies where—

(a) a claimant is awarded state pension credit;

(b) the claimant or his partner is aged 65 or over;

(c) his appropriate minimum guarantee (as defined by the State Pension Credit Act) includes housing costs determined in accordance with Schedule II to the State Pension Credit Regulations; and

(d) after the date from which sub-paragraph (c) applies—

(i) a non-dependant (as defined in that Schedule) begins to reside with the claimant; or

(ii) a non-dependant's income increases and this affects the applicable amount of the claimant's housing costs.

(17C) In the circumstances specified in paragraph (17B) a decision made under section 10 shall take effect—

(a) where there is more than one change of the kind specified in paragraph (17B)(d) in respect of the same non-dependant within the same 26 week period, 26 weeks after the date on which the first such change occurred; and

(b) in any other circumstances, 26 weeks after the date on which a change specified in paragraph (17B)(d) occurred.]

[[26] (17D) Except in a case where paragraph (23) applies, where a claimant is in receipt of an employment and support allowance and his applicable amount includes an amount determined in accordance with Schedule 6 to the Employment and Support Allowance Regulations (housing costs), and there is a reduction in the amount of eligible capital owing in connection with a loan which qualifies under paragraph 16 or 17 of that Schedule, a decision made under section 10 shall take effect—

(a) on the first anniversary of the date on which the claimant's housing costs were first met under that Schedule; or

(b) where the reduction in eligible capital occurred after the first anniversary of the date referred to in sub-paragraph (a), on the next anniversary of that date following the date of the reduction.

(17E) Where a claimant is in receipt of an employment and support allowance and payments made to that claimant which fall within paragraph 31 or 32(1)(a) to (c) of Schedule 8 to the Employment and Support Allowance Regulations have been disregarded in relation to any decision under section 8 or 10 and there is a change in the amount of interest payable—

(a) on a loan qualifying under paragraph 16 or 17 of Schedule 6 to those Regulations to which those payments relate; or

(b) on a loan not so qualifying which is secured on the dwelling occupied as the home to which those payments relate,

a decision under section 10 which is made as a result of that change in the amount of interest payable shall take effect on whichever of the dates referred to in paragraph (17F) is appropriate in the claimant's case.

(17F) The date on which a decision under section 10 takes effect for the purposes of paragraph (17E) is—

(a) the date on which the claimant's housing costs are first met under paragraph 8(1)(a), 9(1)(a) or 10(2)(a) of Schedule 6 to the Employment and Support Allowance Regulations; or

(b) where the change in the amount of interest payable occurred after the date referred to in sub-paragraph (a), on the date of the next alteration in the standard rate following the date of that change.

(17G) In paragraph (17F) "standard rate" has the same meaning as it has in paragraph 13(2) of Schedule 6 to the Employment and Support Allowance Regulations.

(17H) Where the decision is superseded in accordance with regulation 6(2)(a)(i) and the relevant circumstances are that the claimant has a non-dependant who has become entitled to main phase employment and support allowance, the superseding decision shall take effect from the date the main phase employment and support allowance is first paid to the non-dependant.]

(18) Subject to paragraph (24) and, except in a case to which paragraph (23) applies, where a claimant is in receipt of a jobseeker's allowance and his applicable amount includes an amount determined in accordance with Schedule 2 to the Jobseeker's Allowance Regulations (housing costs), and there is a reduction in the amount of eligible capital owing in connection with a loan which qualifies under paragraph 14 or 15 of that Schedule, a decision under section 10 made as a result of that reduction shall take effect—

(a) on the first anniversary of the date on which the claimant's housing costs were first met under that Schedule; or

(b) where the reduction in eligible capital occurred after the first anniversary of the date referred to in sub-paragraph (a), on the next anniversary of that date following the date of the reduction.

(19) Where a claimant is in receipt of a jobseeker's allowance and payments made to that claimant which fall within paragraph 30 or 31(1)(a) to (c) of Schedule 7 to the Jobseeker's Allowance Regulations have been disregarded in relation to any decision under section 8 or 10 and there is a change in the amount of interest payable—

(a) on a loan qualifying under paragraph 14 or 15 of Schedule 2 to those Regulations to which those payments relate; or

(b) on a loan not so qualifying which is secured on the dwelling occupied as the home to which those payments relate,

any decision under section 10 which is made as a result of that change in the amount of interest payable shall take effect on whichever of the dates referred to in paragraph (20) is appropriate in the claimant's case.

(20) The date on which a decision under section 10 takes effect for the purposes of paragraph (19) is—

(a) the date on which the claimant's housing costs are first met under paragraph 6(1)(a), 7(1)(a) or 8(2)(a) of Schedule 2 to the Jobseeker's Allowance Regulations; or

(b) where the changes in the amount of interest payable occurred after the date referred to in sub-paragraph (a), on the date of the next alteration in the standard rate following the date of that change.

(21) In paragraph (20), "standard rate" has the same meaning as it has in paragraph 1(2) of Schedule 2 to the Jobseeker's Allowance Regulations.

(22) Where—

(a) a claimant was paid benefit in respect of October 6, 1996 in accordance with an award of income support;

(b) that claimant's applicable amount includes an amount determined in accordance with Schedule 3 to the Income Support Regulations (housing costs);

(c) that claimant is treated as having been awarded a jobseeker's allowance by virtue of regulation 7 of the Jobseeker's Allowance (Transitional Provisions) Regulations 1996 (jobseeker's allowance to replace income support and unemployment benefit); and

(d) a decision is made under section 10 in consequence of a reduction in the amount of eligible capital owing in connection with a loan which qualifies under paragraph 15 or 16 of Schedule 3 to the Income Support Regulations,

the decision under section 10 referred to in sub-paragraph (d) shall take effect on the next anniversary of the date on which housing costs were first met which occurs after the reduction.

[13 (23) Where, in any case to which paragraph (14), (17A) [16 . . .] [26, 17D] or (18) applies, a claimant has been continuously in receipt of, or treated as having been continuously in receipt of income support, a jobseeker's allowance [26 , an employment and support allowance] or state pension credit, or one of those benefits followed by the other, and he or his partner continues to receive any of those benefits, the anniversary to which those paragraphs refer shall be—

(a) in the case of income support [26 , jobseeker's allowance or employment and support allowance], the anniversary of the earliest date on which benefit in respect of those mortgage interest costs became payable;

(b) in the case of state pension credit, the relevant anniversary date determined in accordance with paragraph 7 of Schedule II to the State Pension Credit Regulations.]

(24) Where—

(a) it has been determined that the amount of a jobseeker's allowance payable to a young person is to be reduced under regulation 63 of the Jobseeker's Allowance Regulations because paragraph (1)(b)(iii), (c), (d), (e) or (f) of that regulation (reduced payments under section 17 of the Jobseekers Act) applied in his case; and

(b) the decision made in consequence of sub-paragraph (a) falls to be superseded by a decision under section 10 because the Secretary of State has subsequently issued a certificate under section 17(4) of the Jobseekers Act with respect to the failure in question,

the decision under section 10 shall take effect as from the same date as the decision made in consequence of sub-paragraph (a) has effect.

[5 [17 (25) In a case where a decision ("the first decision") has been made that a person failed without good cause to take part in a work-focused interview, the decision under section 10 shall take effect as from—

(a) the first day of the benefit week to commence for that person following the date of the first decision; or

(b) in a case where a partner has failed without good cause to take part in a work-focused interview [18 in accordance with regulations made under section 2AA of the Administration Act]—

(i) the first day of the benefit week to commence for the claimant [18 (meaning the person who has been awarded benefit within section 2AA(2) of the Administration Act at a higher rate referable to that partner)] following the date of the first decision; or

(ii) if that date arises five days or less after the day on which the first decision was made, as from the first day of the second benefit week to commence for the claimant following the date of the first decision.]

(26) In paragraph (25), "benefit week" means any period of 7 days corresponding to the week in respect of which the relevant social security benefit is due to be paid.]

[9 (27) [31 . . .]]

[10 (28) A decision to which regulation 6(2)(j) or (k) applies shall take effect from the first day of the disqualification period prescribed for the purposes of section [32 6B or] 7 of the Social Security Fraud Act 2001.]

[12 (29) [15 Subject to paragraphs (29A) and (29B), a] decision to which regulation 6(2)(l) (state pension credit) refers shall take effect from the day following the day on which the assessed income period ends if that day is the first day of the claimant's benefit week, but if it is not, from the next following such day.]

[15 (29A) A decision to which regulation 6(2)(l) applies, where—

(a) the decision is advantageous to the claimant; and

(b) the information and evidence required under regulation 32(1) of the Claims and Payments Regulations has not been provided within the period allowed under that regulation,

shall take effect from the day the information and evidence required under that regulation is provided if that day is the first day of the claimant's benefit week, but, if it is not, from the next following such day.

(29B) A decision to which regulation 6(2)(l) applies, where—

(a) the decision is disadvantageous to the claimant; and

(b) the information and evidence required under regulation 32(1) of the Claims and Payments Regulations has not been provided within the period allowed under that regulation,

shall take effect from the day after the period allowed under that regulation expired.

(29C) Except where there is a change of circumstances during the period in which the Secretary of State was prevented from specifying a new assessed income period under regulation 10(1) of the State Pension Credit Regulations, a decision to which regulation 6(2)(m) applies shall take effect from the day on which the information and evidence required under regulation 32(6)(a) of the Claims and Payments Regulations was provided.]

[14 (30) Where a decision is superseded in accordance with regulation 6(2)(a)(i) and the relevant circumstances are that there has been a change in the legislation in relation to a relevant benefit, the decision under section 10 shall take effect from the date on which that change in the legislation had effect.

[30 (30A) Where a decision is superseded in accordance with regulation 6(2)(a)(ii) and the relevant change of circumstances is the coming into force of a change in the legislation in relation to a relevant benefit, the decision under section 10 shall take effect from the date on which that change in the legislation takes effect.]

(31) Where a decision is superseded in accordance with regulation 6(2)(a)(ii) and the relevant circumstances are that—

(a) a personal capability assessment has been carried out in the case of a person to whom section 171C(4) of the Contributions and Benefits Act applies; and

(b) the own occupation test remains applicable to him under section 171B(3) of that Act,

the decision under section 10 shall take effect on the day [27 . . .] on which the own occupation test is no longer applicable to that person.

(32) For the purposes of paragraph (31)—

(a) "personal capability assessment" has the same meaning as in regulation 24 of the Social Security (Incapacity for Work) (General) Regulations 1995;

(b) "own occupation test" has the same meaning as in section 171B(2) of the Contributions and Benefits Act.

(33) A decision to which regulation 6(2)(c)(ii) applies shall take effect from the date on which [39 the decision of the appeal tribunal, the First-tier Tribunal, the Upper Tribunal or the Commissioner] would have taken effect had it been decided in accordance with the determination of the [28 Upper Tribunal] [39 or the Commissioner] or the court in the appeal referred to in section 26(1)(b).]

[19 (34) A decision which supersedes a decision specified in regulation 6(2)(n) shall take effect from the effective date of the Secretary of State's decision to terminate income support which was confirmed by the decision specified in regulation 6(2)(n).]

[26 (35) [41 . . .]

(36) [41 A decision made in accordance with regulation 6(2)(p) shall take effect —

(a) on the first day of the benefit week in which the failure determination was made where, on the date of that determination, the claimant has not been paid an employment and support allowance since the failure to which that determination relates; or

(b) in any other case, on the first day of the benefit week after the end of the benefit week in respect of which the claimant was last paid an employment and support allowance]

(37) A decision made in accordance with regulation 6(2)(q) shall take effect from the first day of the benefit week in which the reduction mentioned in that sub-paragraph ceased to have effect.

(38) [34 A decision made in accordance with regulation 6(2)(r) that embodies a determination that the claimant has—

(a) limited capability for work; or

(b) limited capability for work-related activity; or

(c) limited capability for work and limited capability for work-related activity

which is the first such determination shall take effect from [43 the day after the last day of the relevant period as defined in regulation 4(4) of the Employment and Support Allowance Regulations].]

(39) A decision made in accordance with regulation 6(2)(r), following an application by the claimant, that embodies a determination that the claimant has limited capability for work-related activity shall take effect from the date of the application.]

[34 (40) A decision made in accordance with regulation 6(2)(r) that embodies a determination that the claimant has—

(a) limited capability for work; or

(b) limited capability for work-related activity; or

(c) limited capability for work and limited capability for work-related activity

where regulation 5 of the Employment and Support Allowance Regulations (assessment phase – previous claimants) applies shall take effect from the beginning of the 14th week of the person's continuous period of limited capability for work.]

[42 (41) A decision made in accordance with regulation 6(2)(t) shall take effect from the first day of the next benefit week following the day on which the determination mentioned in that sub-paragraph was made.

(42) A decision made in accordance with regulation 6(2)(u) shall take effect from the first day of the benefit week in which the reduction mentioned in that sub-paragraph ceased to have effect.]

[45 (43) Where the decision is superseded in accordance with regulation 6(2)(sa), the superseding decision shall take effect from the date on which the contributions are treated as paid in accordance with regulation 4(7) of the Social Security (Crediting and Treatment of Contributions, and National Insurance Numbers) Regulations 2001 for the purposes of entitlement to—

(i) a bereavement benefit;
(ii) a Category A or Category B retirement pension under Part II of the Contributions and Benefits Act; or
(iii) a state pension under Part 1 of the Pensions Act 2014.]

AMENDMENTS

1. Social Security and Child Support (Decisions and Appeals) Amendment (No.2) Regulations 1999 (SI 1999/1623) reg.4 (July 5, 1999).

2. Tax Credits (Decisions and Appeals) (Amendment) Regulations 1999 (SI 1999/2570) reg.10 (October 5, 1999). Note that amendments made by these regulations only have effect with respect to tax credit (reg.1(2) of the Amendment Regulations).

3. Social Security and Child Support (Decisions and Appeals), Vaccine Damage Payments and Jobseeker's Allowance (Amendment) Regulations 1999 (SI 1999/2677) reg.8 (October 18, 1999).

4. Social Security Act 1998 (Commencement No.12 and Consequential and Transitional Provisions) Order 1999 (SI 1999/3178) art.3(19) and Sch.19 para.1 (November 29, 1999).

5. Social Security and Child Support (Decisions and Appeals) Amendment Regulations 2000 (SI 2000/119) reg.2 (February 17, 2000).

6. Social Security (Work-focused Interviews) Regulations 2000 (SI 2000/897) reg.16(5) and Sch.6 para.5 (April 3, 2000).

7. Social Security and Child Support (Miscellaneous Amendments) Regulations 2000 (SI 2000/1596) reg.17 (June 19, 2000).

8. Social Security (Joint Claims: Consequential Amendments) Regulations2000 (SI 2000/1982) reg.5(c) (March 19, 2001).

9. Social Security (Breach of Community Order) (Consequential Amendments) Regulations 2001 (SI 2001/1711) reg.2(2)(d) (October 15, 2001).

10. Social Security (Loss of Benefit) (Consequential Amendments) Regulations 2002 (SI 2002/490) reg.8(c) (April 1, 2002).

11. Social Security (Claims and Payments and Miscellaneous Amendments) Regulations 2002 (SI 2002/428) reg.4(4) (April 2, 2002).

12. State Pension Credit (Consequential, Transitional and Miscellaneous Provisions) Regulations 2002 (SI 2002/3019) reg.18 (April 7, 2003).

13. State Pension Credit (Consequential, Transitional and Miscellaneous Provisions) (No.2) Regulations 2002 (SI 2002/3197) reg.6 (April 7, 2003).

14. Social Security and Child Support (Miscellaneous Amendments) Regulations 2003 (SI 2003/1050) reg.3(5) (May 5, 2003).

15. State Pension Credit (Transitional and Miscellaneous Provisions) Amendment Regulations 2003 (SI 2003/2274) reg.5(3) (October 6, 2003).

16. State Pension Credit (Miscellaneous Amendments) Regulations 2004 (SI 2004/647) reg.2 (April 5, 2004).

17. Social Security (Jobcentre Plus Interviews for Partners) Regulations 2003 (SI 2003/1886) reg.15(5) (April 12, 2004).

18. Social Security (Working Neighbourhoods) Regulations 2004 (SI 2004/959) reg.24(4) (April 26, 2004).

19. Social Security, Child Support and Tax Credits (Miscellaneous Amendments) Regulations 2005 (SI 2005/337) reg.2(5) (March 18, 2005).

20. Social Security (Housing Benefit, Council Tax Benefit, State Pension Credit and Miscellaneous Amendments) Regulations 2004 (SI 2004/2327) reg.4 (April 4, 2005).

21. Social Security (Deferral of Retirement Pensions, Shared Additional Pension and Graduated Retirement Benefit) (Miscellaneous Provisions) Regulations 2005 (SI 2005/2677) reg.9(5) (April 6, 2006).

22. Social Security (Miscellaneous Amendments) (No.2) Regulations 2006 (SI 2006/832) reg.5(3) (April 10, 2006).

23. Social Security (Miscellaneous Amendments) (No.3) Regulations 2006 (SI 2006/2377) reg.3(2) (October 2, 2006).
24. Social Security (Miscellaneous Amendments) (No.4) Regulations 2007 (SI 2007/2470) reg.3(6) and (7) (September 24, 2007).
25. Social Security (Miscellaneous Amendments) (No.2) Regulations 2008 (SI 2008/1042) reg.2 (May 19, 2008).
26. Employment and Support Allowance (Consequential Provisions) (No.2) Regulations 2008 (SI 2008/1554) regs 29 and 33 (July 27, 2008).
27. Social Security (Miscellaneous Amendments) (No.5) Regulations 2008 (SI 2008/2667) reg.3(1) and (4) (October 30, 2008).
28. Tribunals, Courts and Enforcement Act 2007 (Transitional and Consequential Provisions) Order 2008 (SI 2008/2683) Sch.1 paras 95 and 104 (November 3, 2008).
29. Social Security (Miscellaneous Amendments) (No.2) Regulations 2009 (SI 2009/1490) reg.3 (July 13, 2009).
30. Social Security (Miscellaneous Amendments) Regulations 2010 (SI 2010/510) reg.4(1) and (2) (March 4, 2010).
31. Welfare Reform Act 2009 (Section 26) (Consequential Amendments) Regulations 2010 (SI 2010/424) reg.4(1) and (5) (March 22, 2010).
32. Social Security (Loss of Benefit) Amendment Regulations 2010 (SI 2010/1160) reg.3(1) and (4) (April 1, 2010).
33. Jobseeker's Allowance (Sanctions for Failure to Attend) Regulations 2010 (SI 2010/509) reg.3(1) and (4) (April 6, 2010).
34. Social Security (Miscellaneous Amendments) (No.3) Regulations 2010 (SI 2010/840) reg.7(1) and (4) (June 28, 2010).
35. Jobseeker's Allowance (Mandatory Work Activity Scheme) Regulations 2011 (SI 2011/688) reg.18(c) (April 25, 2011).
36. Jobseeker's Allowance (Employment, Skills and Enterprise Scheme) Regulations 2011 (SI 2011/917) reg.17 (May 20, 2011).
37. Social Security (Disability Living Allowance, Attendance Allowance and Carer's Allowance) (Miscellaneous Amendments) Regulations 2011 (SI 2011/2426) reg.2 (October 31, 2011).
38. Social Security (Miscellaneous Amendments) Regulations 2012 (SI 2012/757) reg.17 (April 1, 2012).
39. Social Security and Child Support (Supersession of Appeal Decisions) Regulations 2012 (SI 2012/1267) reg.4(1) and (5) (November 3, 2008, the retrospective effect being permitted by s.103(2)(b) of the Welfare Reform Act 2012).
40. Jobseeker's Allowance (Sanctions) (Amendment) Regulations 2012 (SI 2012/2568) reg.6(1) and (4) (October 22, 2012).
41. Employment and Support Allowance (Sanctions) (Amendment) Regulations 2012 (SI 2012/2756) reg.8 (December 3, 2012).
42. Income Support (Work-Related Activity) and Miscellaneous Amendments Regulations 2014 (SI 2014/1097) reg.12(1) and (5) (April 28, 2014).
43. Jobseeker's Allowance (Extended Period of Sickness) Amendment Regulations 2015 (SI 2015/339) reg.7(1) and (3) (March 30, 2015).
44. Pensions Act 2014 (Consequential, Supplementary and Incidental Amendments) Order 2015 (SI 2015/1985) art.18(1) and (6) (April 6, 2016).
45. Social Security (Credits, and Crediting and Treatment of Contributions) (Consequential and Miscellaneous Amendments) Regulations 2016 (SI 2016/1145) reg.4(1) and (5) (January 1, 2017).

DEFINITIONS

"appeal tribunal"–see s.17(7) of the Social Security Act 1998.
"appropriate office"—see reg.3(11).
"assessed income period"—see reg.1(3).
"bereavement benefit"—*ibid.*

"benefit week"—see para.(3).
"the Board"—see reg.1(3).
"claimant"—*ibid.*
"the Claims and Payments Regulations"—*ibid.*
"Commissioner"–see s.17(7) of the Social Security Act 1998.
"the Contributions and Benefits Act"—see s.84 of the Social Security Act 1998.
"disability benefit decision"—see reg.7A(1).
"disability determination"—*ibid.*
"the Employment and Support Allowance Regulations"—see reg.1(3).
"failure determination"—*ibid.*
"incapacity benefit decision"—See reg.7A(1).
"incapacity determination"—*ibid.*
"the Income Support Regulations"—see reg.1(3).
"the Jobseekers Act"—see s.84 of the Social Security Act 1998.
"the Jobseeker's Allowance Regulations"—see reg.1(3).
"a joint-claim jobseeker's allowance"—*ibid.*
"limited capability for work"—*ibid.*
"payee"—see reg.7A(1).
"standard rate"—see paras(17) and (21).
"state pension credit"—see reg.1(3).
"State Pension Credit Regulations"—*ibid.*
"work-focused interview"—*ibid.*

General Note

2.494 This regulation is not quite as complicated as it looks at first sight. As is explained in para.(1), the regulation provides exceptions to the general rule that a supersession decision takes effect from the date it is made or, where applicable, the date the application for supersession was made (s.10(5) of the Social Security Act 1998). The structure of the regulations is as follows:

Paragraph (1):	Introductory.
Paragraphs (2)–(4):	Supersession for change of circumstances.
Paragraph (5):	Supersession of a tribunal or Commissioner's decision for error of fact.
Paragraphs (6) and 6(A):	Supersession following a test case.
Paragraph (7):	Supersession following an award of another relevant benefit.
Paragraph (7A):	Supersession following a change in election whether to receive an increase in pension or a lump sum following a deferral of pension.
Paragraph (8):	Supersession of an award of jobseeker's allowance following a finding of voluntary unemployment.
Paragraph (8ZA):	Supersession of an award of jobseeker's allowance following the imposition of sanctions for failure to take part in employment schemes.
Paragraph (8A):	Supersession where a late or unpaid contribution has been treated as paid.
Paragraphs (9) and (9A):	Supersession advantageous to claimant of an award of attendance allowance or disability living allowance.
Paragraph (10):	Supersession of an award of short-term incapacity benefit to increase the rate following an award of the highest rate of the care component of disability living allowance.
Paragraph (11):	Supersession of an award of incapacity benefit following a determination that the claimant is to be treated as incapable of work because he or she is suffering from a severe condition.
Paragraphs (12)	Supersession in an income support or jobseeker's allowance

and (13):	case where information about housing costs was not supplied to the Secretary of State by a lender.
Paragraph (14):	Supersession in an income support case where there has been a reduction in the amount of eligible capital owing in respect of a loan.
Paragraphs (15)–(17):	Supersession in an income support case where the claimant has been receiving payments under an insurance policy in respect of housing costs and there has been a change in the amount of interest payable.
Paragraph (17A):	Supersession in a state pension credit case where there has been a reduction in the amount of eligible capital owing in respect of a loan.
Paragraphs (17B) and (17C):	Supersession in a state pension credit case where a non-dependant commences residing with the claimant or has an increase in income.
Paragraph (17D):	Supersession in an employment and support allowance case where there has been a reduction in the amount of capital owing on a loan.
Paragraphs (17E) to (17G):	Supersession in an employment and support allowance case where the claiamant has been receiving payments under an insurance policy in respect of housing costs and there has been a change in the amount of interest payable.
Paragraph (17H):	Supersession in an employment and support allowance case where a non-dependant becomes entitled to main phase employment and support allowance.
Paragraph (18):	Supersession in a jobseeker's allowance case where there has been a reduction in the amount of eligible capital owing in respect of a loan.
Paragraphs (19)–(21):	Supersession in a jobseeker's allowance case where the claimant has been receiving payments under an insurance costs in respect of housing costs and there has been a change in the amount of interest payable.
Paragraph (22):	Supersession in case where a claimant was transferred from income support to jobseeker's allowance on October 6, 1996 and there has been a reduction in the amount of eligible capital owing in respect of a loan.
Paragraph (23):	Supplementary to paras (14)–(18) in a case where a person has been in receipt of more than one of income support, jobseeker's allowance and state pension credit.
Paragraph (24):	Supersession in a case where the claimant is a young person and was receiving a reduced amount of jobseeker's allowance on account of failing to complete a course and the Secretary of State has issued a certificate stating that the claimant had good cause for failing to complete the course.
Paragraphs (25) and (26):	Supersession following a determination that the claimant has failed without good cause to take part in a work-focused interview.
Paragraph (27):	Supersession in order to reduce benefit because an offender has breached a community order.
Paragraph (28):	Supersession in order to remove benefit because a person has been convicted of benefit offences.
Paragraphs (29)–(29B):	Supersession in a state pension credit case on the ending of an assessed income period.
Paragraph (29C):	Supersession where late provision of information or evidence has delayed the specification of a new assessed income period.
Paragraphs (30) and (30A):	Supersession following a change in relevant legislation.

Paragraphs (31) and (32):	Supersession following a personal capability assessment carried out before the all work test becomes applicable.
Paragraph (33):	Supersession of a decision determined by a tribunal or Commissioner under s.26 of the Social Security Act 1998 while a test case was pending.
Paragraph (34):	Supersession of a decision of a tribunal in relation to income support where another tribunal has subsequently decided that the claimant is incapable of work.
Paragraphs (35) to (37):	Supersession in an employment and support allowance case where there has been a failure determination.
Paragraphs (38) to (40):	Supersession in an employment and support allowance case following receipt of a new medical opinion.
Paragraphs (41) and (42):	Supersession following a determination that a claimant of income support has failed to undertake work-related activity or to end a reduction made in consequence of such a determination.
Paragraph (43):	Supersession following the late payment of contributions for a bereavement benefit, a retirement pension or a state pension.

Note that Schs 3A, 3B and 3C make further provision in respect of income-related benefits and sometimes, but not always, take precedence over the provisions of this regulation (see para.(1)).

Paragraph (1)

2.495 Section 10(5) of the Social Security Act 1998 provides that a supersession decision takes effect from the date it is made or, where applicable, the date the application for supersession was made. Schedule 3A provides further refinement for income support and jobseeker's allowance cases as do Sch.3B for state pension credit cases and Sch.3C for employment and support allowance cases. Subparagraph (a) has the effect that those Schedules take precedence over most, but not all, of the other paragraphs of this regulation. The exceptions are paras (2)(b) or (bb) (changes of circumstances advantageous to a claimant), (29) (certain decisions relating to state pension credit) or (30) (change of legislation). Where a case is not covered by this regulation or by those schedules, s.10(5) applies.

Paragraph (2)

2.496 A supersession on the ground of change of circumstances advantageous to the claimant is effective from the date of the change if the change is notified within a month (or such longer period as is allowed under reg.8) but is otherwise effective only from the date of notification. In *PH v SSWP (DLA)* [2013] UKUT 268 (AAC), it was held that a firmer prognosis amounted to a change of circumstances that could justify a supersession extending an award of disability living allowance but the judge said that it was difficult to see how reg.7(2)(a)(ii) could apply in such a context so that, in order to be effective, any application for supersession would have to be made before the award expired. In practice, a renewal claim would generally be made instead and the issue arose in that case only because the claimant had not made a renewal claim but had successfully appealed against a supersession decision terminating her award prematurely. A claimant who does notify a change of circumstances within one month is entitled to rely on reg.7(2)(a) even if he or she then fails to answer a further question from the Secretary of State within a month (*YZ v SSWP (ESA)* [2016] UKUT 430 (AAC)).

Where the change is not advantageous to the claimant, the supersession is generally effective from the date of change or, in the case of incapacity and disability cases, from the date when the change should have been reported. Presumably, para.(2) does not apply to those attendance allowance and disability living allowance cases where para.(9) applies or, indeed, to any cases where any of paras (10)–(34) applies and the latter provision is in mandatory terms. However, it was suggested in *SK v*

SSWP (JSA) [2013] UKUT 138 (AAC) that there may be a mere discretion where para.(12) is concerned, because that provision is expressed in discretionary terms.

It was pointed out in that case that notifying a change of circumstances or providing information about such a change is not necessarily the same as applying for a supersession, so that any supersession in the light of the information might be on the Secretary of State's initiative and therefore within the scope of subpara.(bb), rather than subpara.(b). It was also held that, where a change of circumstances in fact takes place *after* the date on which the Secretary of State "commenced action with a view to supersession" by asking for information, the change is effective from the date of the change of circumstances.

The inclusion of a reference to a disabled person's partner in head (i) of the new version of reg.7(2)(bc) reverses the effect of *SSWP v JJ* [2009] UKUT 2 (AAC). **2.497**

See reg.7A for definitions material to para.(2)(c). Regulation 7(2)(c) is concerned to ensure that an appropriate effective date is fixed where the effect of a supersession due to a change of circumstances is that benefit has been overpaid and the overpayment is likely to be recoverable under s.71 of the Social Security Administration Act 1992. (Regulation 3(5)(b) and (c) makes similar provision by way of revision where the original decision was made in ignorance of, or on a mistake as to, a material fact). Section 71(5A) of the 1992 Act provides that an overpayment can generally be recovered only if a decision has properly been given in terms of revision or supersession, a point reiterated in *CIS/4434/2004*. If the decision is in terms of supersession, there will only be an overpayment if the date from which the supersession is effective is before the date on which payment ceased. It is therefore not surprising that the question whether a claimant has "failed to notify" a change of circumstances for the purposes of reg.7(2)(c)(ii) was found in *CDLA/1823/2004* to be similar to the familiar question whether a person has "failed to disclose" a change of circumstances for the purposes of s.71. The Commissioner noted that the phrase "regulations under the Administration Act" refers to reg.32 of the Social Security (Claims and Payments) Regulations 1987, which was considered in some detail in the context of s.71 by the Court of Appeal in *B v Secretary of State for Work and Pensions* [2005] EWCA Civ 929; [2005] 1 W.L.R. 3796 (also reported as *R(IS) 9/06*). He suggested that there will be a failure to notify a change of circumstances if there is a breach of clear and unambiguous instructions, as was the position in *R(IS) 9/06* but that otherwise the issue is likely to be whether the Secretary of State could reasonably have expected the claimant to notify him of the material fact. Determining the question whether reg.7(2)(c)(ii) applies may, therefore, require some evidence as to the instructions given to the claimant. See also *R(A) 2/06*. The practice of dealing with the recovery of overpayments separately from decisions as to entitlement may lead to the same complex issues of fact being considered twice.

The application of head (ii) is particularly important in relation to attendance allowance, disability living allowance, severe disablement allowance and industrial injuries disablement benefit because heads (ii), (iv) and (v) have the combined effect that supersessions are not retrospective where the change of circumstances relates to a "disability determination" as defined in reg.7A, except where the claimant both was required to notify the change of circumstances and knew or could reasonably have been expected to know that the change of circumstances should be notified. This means that, except where the claimant has clearly been at fault, there is no overpayment and so any question of the recoverability of an overpayment simply does not arise.

The revocation of reg.7(2)(c)(iii) and its replacement with heads (iv) and (v), which contain no exceptions in respect of incapacity determinations, deals with the anomalies revealed in such incapacity benefit cases as *R(IB) 1/05* and *CIB/763/2004*, where there had been changes of circumstances but no failure by the claimant to disclose them (so that head (ii) did not apply) but the Commissioner found that head (iii) did not apply either. Now, any supersession will be effective from the date of the change of circumstances by virtue of head (v). That, of course, will be at least as early as the date applicable under head (ii) and it might seem odd at first sight that a supersession may be effective from an earlier date when there has been no failure **2.498** to disclose a change of circumstances than where there has been. However, this only acts to the disadvantage of a claimant where a payment of benefit has not already been made. If it has already been made, it will not be recoverable due to the lack of a failure to disclose the change of circumstances. If the payment has not already been made, there are obvious reasons why the supersession should take effect from the date of the change so that only the benefit to which the claimant is properly entitled is paid.

It was held in *SSWP v JL (DLA)* [2011] UKUT 293 (AAC); [2012] AACR 14 that the deletion of reg.7(2)(c)(iii) and the insertion of heads (iv) and (v) were not retrospective and enable a supersession to take effect only from April 10, 2006 or a later date although the amendments can apply where the relevant change of circumstances occurred on an earlier date. The question whether a supersession can take effect from an earlier date must therefore be determined under the legislation in force at that date.

There may also still be some difficulties in incapacity cases due to the practice of determining that a person is incapable of work in the contest of "credits" and then relying on that determination when determining entitlement to income support (see reg.10). In *CIB/1599/2005*, the claimant was in receipt of income support on the basis of a decision, made for the purposes of incapacity credits, that he was incapable of work. He failed to inform the social security office that he had taken some casual employment. The Commissioner held that reg.7(2)(c)(ii) did not apply because the claimant was not required by "regulations under the Administration Act" to notify his change of circumstances. Regulation 32 of the Social Security (Claims and Payments) Regulations 1987 applies only to benefit cases and not to "credits" cases. That meant that the "credits" decision could not be superseded with effect from a date before it was made. Given the terms of reg.10, that in turn presumably also limited the scope for superseding the award of income support retrospectively, although the Commissioner expressed no view on that issue.

Paragraph (5)

2.499 This provides consistency between, on the one hand, revision and supersession of decisions of the Secretary of State on the ground of error of fact (under regs 3(5) and 6(2)(b)) and, on the other hand, supersession of decisions of tribunals on the ground of error of fact (under reg.6(2)(c)). However, in *JA v SSWP (DLA)* [2014] UKUT 44 (AAC), the judge drew attention to the anomalies that can arise because a decision of the Secretary of State may be altered on revision in the same circumstances as a decision of a tribunal may be altered on supersession and asked whether the distinction was necessary. A decision of a tribunal cannot be revised under s.9 of the Social Security Act 1998 but he said that it was not obvious why the grounds of revision in reg.3(5) were not grounds of supersession to which this paragraph might apply.

Paragraph (6)

2.500 Where a decision of the Secretary of State is superseded under reg.6(2)(b)(i) because it has been shown to have been erroneous in point of law by a decision of the Upper Tribunal or a court involving a different claimant, the supersession will be effective from the date of the decision of the Upper Tribunal or court. However, showing that a decision was based on a mistake of law rather than a different understanding of the facts may not be easy (*MP v SSWP* [2010] UKUT 130 (AAC)).

There is a question as to whether para.(6) is compatible with European Union law in a case where an error is revealed by a decision of the Court of Justice of the European Union, because a ruling of that Court is not a determination within the scope of s.27(1) of the Social Security Act 1998, whereas a ruling of a superior British court is. That question was considered but not answered in *JK v SSWP (DLA)* [2013] UKUT 218 (AAC).

Paragraphs (8) and (8ZA)

2.501 These paragraphs are concerned with the commencement date of a period of reduction in the amount of jobseeker's allowance, imposed where a claimant is considered to be voluntarily unemployed or as a sanction.

Paragraph (9)

Supersessions of decisions concerning attendance allowance and disability living allowance on the ground of changes of circumstances which are disadvantageous to claimants are dealt with under para.(2)(c). This paragraph deals with supersessions on the grounds of changes of circumstances that are advantageous to the claimant. A claimant is given a month in which to notify the relevant office of the change of circumstances, but *SSWP v DA* [2009] UKUT 214 (AAC) confirms that the month runs from the end of the qualifying period for a higher rate of benefit following a change of circumstances, rather than the date of the change of circumstances itself. It is difficult to envisage a situation in which para.(9)(c) can operate because if the claimant was not entitled to any benefit before the change occurred, a claim would have been appropriate rather than a supersession (*R(I) 56/54*). Perhaps its use is envisaged in cases where a claimant becomes terminally ill during the qualifying period, although it is arguable that, even then, a new claim would be appropriate. Paragraph (9)(b) is in terms similar to para.(2)(b) with variations that seem designed merely to take account of the qualifying periods for attendance allowance and disability living allowance and to require the supersession to be effective from the first pay day after the claimant qualifies for the new rate. 2.502

Paragraph (9A)

March 8, 2001 was the date the European Court of Justice decided *Jauch v Pensionsversicherungsanstalt der Arbeiter* (C-215/99) and October 18, 2007 was the date the Court gave a ruling in *Commission of the European Communities v European Parliament and Council of the European Union* (C-299/05) [2007] E.C.R. I–8695, applying principles established in *Jauch*, that had the effect that it was, and had previously been, unlawful for the Secretary of State to terminate an award of attendance allowance, carer's allowance or the care component of disability living allowance on the ground that a person was moving from Great Britain to elsewhere in the European Economic Area or to Switzerland. This paragraph enables a person whose award of one of these benefits was terminated on that ground after the decision in *Jauch* to be re-awarded benefit from the date of the Court's later judgment. It is arguable that "a superseding decision" in subpara.(b) includes a superseding decision made by the Secretary of State that was upheld on an appeal to an appeal tribunal. 2.503

Paragraphs (12)–(23)

The original provisions are all concerned with changes in housing costs and contain provisions similar to those previously found in regs 63 and 63A of the Social Security (Adjudication) Regulations 1995. This is not true of all the inserted paragraphs. 2.504

Paragraph (13) is not predicated on delay by a lender, but simply on the late supply of information for any reason. However, the relationship between para.(12) and para.(2) is such that there appears to be a mere discretion to apply para.(12) rather than para.(2) and, in any event, in a jobseeker's allowance case, para.(12) does not prevail over para.7 of Sch.3A, due to the effect of para.(1)(a) (*SK v SSWP (JSA)* [2013] UKUT 138 (AAC)).

Paragraphs (31) and (32)

With the abolition of incapacity benefit, these paragraphs have become redundant. 2.505

Paragraphs (38)–(40)

Where a decision is made during the "assessment phase" of employment and support allowance (broadly during the first thirteen weeks of a period of entitlement, but less in some circumstances), a decision that is *adverse* to the claimant and results in the termination of an award takes effect immediately under s.10(5) of the Social Security Act 1998. However, paras (38) and (40) have the effect that a 2.506

decision *in favour* of the claimant takes effect only from the end of the "assessment phase", because that is the earliest date from which an award may be increased so as to include the work-related activity component or the support component (see ss.2(2)(a) and (3)(a) and 4(4)(a) and (5)(a) of the Welfare Reform Act 2007 — in Vol.I). Paragraph (38) applies in the ordinary case and para.(40) applies where a person ceases to be entitled to employment and support allowance after less than thirteen weeks but becomes entitled again within twelve weeks.

The purpose of para.(39) is less clear since it appears merely to duplicate the effect of s.10(5) of the 1998 Act. Perhaps it is thought necessary, for the avoidance of doubt, because grounds given by a claimant for an application for supersession are unlikely to invoke reg.6(2)(r) rather than, say, reg.6(2)(a)(i) or (b) and so the obtaining of the medical evidence justifying supersession under reg.6(2)(r) may have been entirely on the Secretary of State's initiative and, indeed, unrelated to the application made by the claimant.

[1 [4 Definitions for the purposes of Chapters I and II]

2.507 **7A.**—(1) For the purposes of regulations 3(5)(c), 6(2)(g) [56(2)(r)] [2, 7(2)(c) and (5)]—

"disability benefit decision" means a decision to award a relevant benefit embodied in or necessary to which is a disability determination,

"disability determination" means—

(a) in the case of a decision as to an award of an attendance allowance or a disability living allowance, whether the person satisfies any of the conditions in section 64, 72(1) or 73(1) to (3), as the case may be, of the Contributions and Benefits Act,

(b) in the case of a decision as to an award of severe disablement allowance, whether the person is disabled for the purpose of section 68 of the Contributions and Benefits Act, or

(c) in the case of a decision as to an award of industrial injuries benefit, whether the existence or extent of any disablement is sufficient for the purposes of section 103 or 108 of the Contributions and Benefits Act or for the benefit to be paid at the rate which was in payment immediately prior to that decision;

[4 "employment and support allowance decision" means a decision to award a relevant benefit or relevant credit embodied in or necessary to which is a determination that a person has or is to be treated as having limited capability for work under Part 1 of the Welfare Reform Act;]

"incapacity benefit decision" means a decision to award a relevant benefit [2 or relevant credit] embodied in or necessary to which is a determination that a person is or is to be treated as incapable of work under Part XIIA of the Contributions and Benefits Act [3 or an award of long term incapacity benefit under regulation 17(1) (transitional awards of long-term incapacity benefit) of the Social Security (Incapacity Benefit) (Transitional) Regulations 1995],

"incapacity determination" means a determination whether a person is incapable of work by applying the [2 personal capability assessment] in regulation 24 of the Social Security (Incapacity for Work) (General) Regulations 1995 or whether a person is to be treated as incapable of work in accordance with regulation 10 (certain persons with a severe condition to be treated as incapable of work) or 27 (exceptional circumstances) of those Regulations, and

[4 "limited capability for work determination" means a determination whether a person has limited capability for work by applying the test of limited capability for work or whether a person is to be treated as having limited capability for work in accordance with regulation 20 of the Employment and Support Allowance Regulations;]

"payee" means a person to whom a benefit referred to in paragraph (a), (b) or (c) of the definition of "disability determination", or a benefit referred to in the definition of "incapacity benefit decision" [4 or "employment and support allowance decision"] is payable.

(2) Where a person's receipt of or entitlement to a benefit ("the first benefit") is a condition of his being entitled to any other benefit, allowance or advantage ("a second benefit") and a decision is revised under regulation 3(5)(c) or a superseding decision is made under regulation 6(2) to which regulation 7(2)(c)(ii) applies, the effect of which is that the first benefit ceases to be payable, or becomes payable at a lower rate than was in payment immediately prior to that revision or supersession, a consequent decision as to his entitlement to the second benefit shall take effect from the date of the change in his entitlement to the first benefit.]

AMENDMENTS

1. Social Security and Child Support (Decisions and Appeals) Amendment (No.2) Regulations 1999 (SI 1999/1623) reg.5 (July 5, 1999).
2. Social Security and Child Support (Miscellaneous Amendments) Regulations 2000 (SI 2000/1596) reg.18 (June 19, 2000).
3. Social Security (Miscellaneous Amendments) (No.4) Regulations 2007 (SI 2007/2470) reg.3(8) (September 24, 2007).
4. Employment and Support Allowance (Consequential Provisions) (No. 2) Regulations 2008 (SI 2008/1554) regs 29 and 34 (July 27, 2008).
5. Social Security (Miscellaneous Amendments) (No.3) Regulations 2010 (SI 2010/840) reg.7(1) and (5) (June 28, 2010).

DEFINITIONS

"the Contributions and Benefits Act"—see s.84 of the Social Security Act 1998.
"the Employment and Support Allowance Regulations"—see reg.1(3).
"limited capability for work"—*ibid.*
"relevant benefit"—see s.39(1) of the Social Security Act 1998.
"relevant credit"—see reg.1(3).
"the Welfare Reform Act"—*ibid.*

GENERAL NOTE

"disability determination"

In *CA/2650/2006*, the Commissioner held that the reference to s.64 of the Contributions and Benefits Act (which has a different structure from that in ss. 72 and 73) in head (a) of the definition of "disability determination" refers only to "determinations whether the conditions set out in section 64(2) and (3) were satisfied (and possibly extending to age and non-entitlement to DLA)" and so does not extend to determinations as to residence or presence. **2.508**

7B. *Omitted.* **2.509**

7C. *Omitted.* **2.510**

Effective date for late notifications of change of circumstances

2.511 **8.**—(1) For the purposes of regulation 7(2) [2 and (9)], a longer period of time may be allowed for the notification of a change of circumstances in so far as it affects the effective date of the change where the conditions specified in the following provisions of this regulation are satisfied.

(2) An application for the purposes of regulation 7(2) [2 or (9)] shall be made by the claimant or a person acting on his behalf.

(3) The application referred to in paragraph (2) shall—

(a) contain particulars of the relevant change of circumstances and the reasons for the failure to notify the change of circumstances on an earlier date; and

[4 (b) be made—

(i) within 13 months of the date the change occurred; or

(ii) in the case of an application for the purposes of regulation 7(9)(b), within 13 months of the date on which the claimant satisfied the conditions of entitlement to the particular rate of benefit.]

(4) An application under this regulation shall not be granted unless the Secretary of State is satisfied [1 or the Board are satisfied] that—

(a) it is reasonable to grant the application;

(b) the change of circumstances notified by the applicant is relevant to the decision which is to be superseded; and

(c) special circumstances are relevant to the application and as a result of those special circumstances it was not practicable for the applicant to notify the change of circumstances within one month of the change occurring.

(5) In determining whether it is reasonable to grant the application, the Secretary of State [1 or the Board] shall have regard to the principle that the greater the amount of time that has elapsed between the date one month after the change of circumstances occurred and the date the application for the purposes of regulation 7(2) [2 or (9)] is made, the more compelling should be the special circumstances on which the application is based.

(6) In determining whether it is reasonable to grant an application, no account shall be taken of the following—

(a) that the applicant or any person acting for him was unaware of, or misunderstood, the law applicable to his case (including ignorance or misunderstanding of the time limits imposed by these Regulations); or

(b) that a [3 the Upper Tribunal] or a court has taken a different view of the law from that previously understood and applied.

(7) An application under this regulation which has been refused may not be renewed.

AMENDMENTS

1. Tax Credits (Decisions and Appeals) (Amendment) Regulations 1999 (SI 1999/2570) reg.11 (October 5, 1999). Note that amendments made by these regulations only have effect with respect to tax credit (reg.1(2) of the Amendment Regulations).

2. Social Security and Child Support (Decisions and Appeals) Amendment Regulations 2000 (SI 2000/119) reg.3 (February 17, 2000).

3. Tribunals, Courts and Enforcement Act 2007 (Transitional and Consequential Provisions) Order 2008 (SI 2008/2683) Sch.1 paras 95 and 106 (November 3, 2008).

4. Social Security (Miscellaneous Amendments) Regulations 2010 (SI 2010/510) reg.4(1) and (3) (March 4, 2010).

DEFINITIONS

"the Board"—see reg.1(3).
"claimant"—*ibid.*

GENERAL NOTE

Paragraph (6)(b)
See the note to reg.4(6)(b) which is in similar terms. 2.512

CHAPTER III

OTHER MATTERS

Certificates of recoverable benefits

9. A certificate of recoverable benefits may be reviewed under section 10 of the 1997 Act where the Secretary of State is satisfied that— 2.513
(a) a mistake (whether in computation of the amount specified or otherwise) occurred in the preparation of the certificate;
(b) the benefit recovered from a person who makes a compensation payment (as defined in section 1 of the 1997 Act) is in excess of the amount due to the Secretary of State;
(c) incorrect or insufficient information was supplied to the Secretary of State by the person who applied for the certificate and in consequence the amount of benefit specified in the certificate was less than it would have been had the information supplied been correct or sufficient; or
(d) a ground for appeal is satisfied under section 11 of the 1997 Act.

DEFINITIONS

"the 1997 Act"—see reg.1(3).
"appeal"—*ibid.*

GENERAL NOTE

These grounds of review are very wide. In *CCR/3391/2005*, the Commissioner suggested that the Secretary of State should always consider reviewing a decision against which an appeal has been brought, so that unnecessary cases did not reach tribunals. Regulation 9(d) may have been drafted with such an approach in mind. A submission to a tribunal would then, in effect, be an explanation for the Secretary of State not reviewing the decision in the light of the grounds of appeal. Where the appellant was the compensator, grounds of appeal were often accompanied by a considerable amount of new evidence obtained in the course of defending the compensation proceedings. Considering a review was, in such circumstances, the first opportunity the Secretary of State has to take such evidence into account. Regulation 9ZB is intended to ensure that a review now takes place *before* any appeal is brought, although it is still possible to review a decision again in the light of any further evidence provided with a notice of appeal. 2.514

[1 Review of certificates

2.515 **9ZA.**—(1) A certificate may be reviewed under section 10 of the 1997 Act where the Secretary of State is satisfied that—

(a) a mistake (whether in the computation of the amount specified or otherwise) occurred in the preparation of the certificate;

(b) the lump sum payment recovered from a compensator who makes a compensation payment (as defined in section 1A(5) of the 1997 Act) is in excess of the amount due to the Secretary of State;

(c) incorrect or insufficient information was supplied to the Secretary of State by the compensator who applied for the certificate and in consequence the amount of lump sum payment specified in the certificate was less than it would have been had the information supplied been correct or sufficient;

(d) a ground for appeal is satisfied under section 11 of the 1997 Act or an appeal has been made under that section; or

(e) a certificate has been issued and, for any reason, a recoverable lump sum payment was not included in that certificate.

(2) In this regulation and regulations 1(3) in paragraph (b) of the definition of "party to the proceedings", [3 29 [4 . . .]], where applicable—

(a) any reference to the 1997 Act is to be construed so as to include a reference to that Act as applied by regulation 2 of the Lump Sum Payments Regulations and, where applicable, as modified by Schedule 1 to those Regulations;

(b) [2 "certificate" means a certificate of recoverable lump sum payments, including where any of the amounts is nil;]

(c) "lump sum payment" is a payment to which section 1A(2) of the 1997 Act applies;

(d) "P" is to be construed in accordance with regulations 4(1)(a)(i) and 5 of the Lump Sum Payments Regulations.]

AMENDMENTS

1. Social Security (Recovery of Benefits) (Lump Sum Payments) Regulations 2008 (SI 2008/1596) Sch.2 para.1(b) (October 1, 2008).

2. Social Security (Miscellaneous Amendments) (No.3) Regulations 2008 (SI 2008/2365) reg.6(1) and (4) (October 1, 2008).

3. Tribunals, Courts and Enforcement Act 2007 (Transitional and Consequential Provisions) Order 2008 (SI 2008/2683) Sch.1 paras 95 and 107 (November 3, 2008).

4. Social Security, Child Support, Vaccine Damage and Other Payments (Decisions and Appeals) (Amendment) Regulations 2013 (SI 2013/2380) reg.4(1) and (10)(a) (October 28, 2013, subject to a saving).

DEFINITIONS

"the 1997 Act"—see reg.1(3) and para.(2)(a).
"certificate"—see para.(2)(b).
"lump sum payment"—see para.(2)(c).
"P"—see para.(2)(d).

[1 Consideration of review before appeal

2.516 **9ZB.** (1) This regulation applies in a case where—

(a) the Secretary of State has issued a certificate of recoverable benefits or certificate of recoverable lump sum payments; and

(b) that certificate is accompanied by a notice to the effect that there is a right of appeal in relation to the certificate only if the Secretary of State has considered an application for review of the certificate.

(2) In a case to which this regulation applies, a person has a right of appeal under section 11 of the 1997 Act against the certificate only if the Secretary of State has considered an application for review of the certificate under section 10 of that Act.]

AMENDMENT

1. Social Security, Child Support, Vaccine Damage and Other Payments (Decisions and Appeals) (Amendment) Regulations 2013 (SI 2013/2380) reg.4(1) and (6) (October 28, 2013).

DEFINITIONS

"the 1997 Act"—see reg.1(3).
"appeal"—*ibid.*

GENERAL NOTE

This regulation is made under s.11(2A) and (2B) of the Social Security (Recovery of Benefits) Act 1997 and makes, for appeals under that Act, provision equivalent to reg.3ZA(1) and (2). For the power to treat a purported appeal as an application for review where there is no right of appeal as a result of this provision, see reg.29(6). 2.517

[1 Correction of accidental errors

9A.—(1) Accidental errors in a decision of the Secretary of State or an officer of the Board under a relevant enactment within the meaning of section 28(3), or in any record of such a decision, may be corrected by the Secretary of State or an officer of the Board, as the case may be, at any time. 2.518

(2) A correction made to, or to the record of, a decision shall be deemed to be part of the decision, or of that record, and the Secretary of State or an officer of the Board shall give a written notice of the correction as soon as practicable to the claimant.

(3) In calculating the time within which an application can be made under regulation 3(1)(b) for a decision to be revised [2. . .] there shall be disregarded any day falling before the day on which notice was given of the decision or to the record thereof under paragraph (2).]

AMENDMENTS

1. Social Security and Child Support (Decisions and Appeals) (Miscellaneous Amendments) Regulations 2002 (SI 2002/1379) reg.4 (May 20, 2002).

2. Tribunals, Courts and Enforcement Act 2007 (Transitional and Consequential Provisions) Order 2008 (SI 2008/2683) Sch.1 paras 95 and 108 (November 3, 2008).

DEFINITIONS

"appeal"—see reg.1(3).
"the Board"—*ibid.*
"claimant"—*ibid.*

[1 Effect of determination as to capacity or capability for work

2.519 **10.**—(1) This regulation applies to a determination whether a person—

(a) is capable or incapable of work;

(b) is to be treated as capable or incapable of work;

(c) has or does not have limited capability for work; or

(d) is to be treated as having or not having limited capability for work.

(2) A determination (including a determination made following a change of circumstances) as set out in paragraph (1) which is embodied in or necessary to a decision under Chapter II of Part I of the Act or on which such a decision is based shall be conclusive for the purposes of any further decision.]

AMENDMENT

1. Employment and Support Allowance (Consequential Provisions) (No.2) Regulations 2008 (SI 2008/1554) regs 29 and 36 (July 27, 2008).

DEFINITIONS

"the Act"—see reg.1(3).
"limited capability for work"—*ibid.*

GENERAL NOTE

2.520 Note that a decision that a person was *not*, or was not to be treated as, incapable of work was not of continuing effect. Consequently, it operated to allow supersession of any award of benefit current at the time it was made but it did not operate so as to prevent a person from making a new claim or a further application for supersession, although might not be entitled to benefit while a new assessment was arranged (*R(IB)1/01* and *R(IB)2/01*).

Secretary of State to determine certain matters

2.521 **11.** Where, in relation to a determination for any purpose to which Part XIIA of the Contributions and Benefits Act [1 or Part 1 of the Welfare Reform Act] applies, an issue arises as to—

(a) whether a person is, or is to be treated as, capable or incapable of work in respect of any period; or

[1 (aa) whether a person is, or is to be treated as, having or not having limited capability for work; or]

(b) whether a person is terminally ill,

that issue shall be determined by the Secretary of State, notwithstanding that other matters fall to be determined by another authority.

AMENDMENT

1. Employment and Support Allowance (Consequential Provisions) (No.2) Regulations 2008 (SI 2008/1554) regs 29 and 37 (July 27, 2008).

DEFINITIONS

"the Contributions and Benefits Act"—see s.84 of the Social Security Act 1998.
"limited capability for work"—see reg.1(3).

[1 Issues for decision by officers of Inland Revenue

2.522 **11A.**—(1) Where, on consideration of any claim or other matter, it appears to the Secretary of State that an issue arises which, by virtue of section 8 of the Transfer Act, falls to be decided by an officer of the Board, he shall refer that issue to the Board.

(2) Where—

(a) the Secretary of State has decided any claim or other matter on an assumption of facts—

(i) as to which there appeared to him to be no dispute, but

(ii) concerning which, had an issue arisen, that issue would have fallen, by virtue of section 8 of the Transfer Act, to be decided by an officer of the Board; and

(b) an application for revision or an application for supersession [2 or an appeal] is made in relation to the decision of that claim or other matter; and

(c) it appears to the Secretary of State on [2 receipt of the application or appeal] that such an issue arises,

he shall refer that issue to the Board.

(3) Pending the final decision of any issue which has been referred to the Board in accordance with paragraph (1) or (2) above, the Secretary of State may—

(a) determine any other issue arising on consideration of the claim or other matter or, as the case may be, of the application,

(b) seek a preliminary opinion of the Board on the issue referred and decide the claim or other matter or, as the case may be, the application in accordance with that opinion on that issue; or

(c) defer making any decision on the claim or other matter or, as the case may be, the application.

(4) On receipt by the Secretary of State of the final decision of an issue which has been referred to the Board in accordance with paragraph (1) or (2) above, the Secretary of State that—

(a) in a case to which paragraph (3)(b) above applies—

(i) consider whether the decision ought to be revised under section 9 or superseded under section 10, and

(ii) if so, revise it, or, as the case may be, make a further decision which supersedes it; or

(b) in a case to which paragraph (3)(a) or (c) above applies, decide the claim or other matter or, as the case may be, the application,

in accordance with the final decision of the issue so referred.

(5) In paragraphs (3) and (4) above "final decision" means the decision of an officer of the Board under section 8 of the Transfer Act or the determination of any appeal in relation to that decision.]

AMENDMENTS

1. Social Security and Child Support (Decisions and Appeals) Amendment (No.3) Regulations 1999 (SI 1999/1623) reg.2(3) (July 5, 1999).

2. Social Security and Child Support (Decisions and Appeals) (Miscellaneous Amendments) Regulations 2002 (SI 2002/1379) reg.5 (May 20, 2002).

DEFINITIONS

"appeal"—see reg.1(3).

"the Board"—*ibid.*

"claim"—by virtue of s.39(2) of the Social Security Act 1998, see s.191 of the Social Security Administration Act 1992.

"final decision"—see para.(5).

"the Transfer Act"—see reg.1(3).

GENERAL NOTE

2.523 The Inland Revenue has been merged into Her Majesty's Revenue and Customs (HMRC). Some decisions fall to be made by HMRC by virtue of s.170 of the Pensions Schemes Act 1993 (rather than by virtue of s.8 of the Social Security Contributions (Transfer of Functions, etc.) Act 1999) but the Secretary of State may refer to HMRC issues for determination under the 1993 Act notwithstanding that this regulation does not apply (*R(P) 1/04*).

Decision of the Secretary of State relating to industrial injuries benefit

2.524 **12.**—(1) This regulation applies where, for the purpose of a decision of the Secretary of State relating to a claim for industrial injuries benefit under Part V of the Contributions and Benefits Act an issue to be decided is—

(a) the extent of a personal injury for the purposes of section 94 of that Act;
(b) whether the claimant has a disease prescribed for the purposes of section 108 of that Act or the extent of any disablement resulting from such a disease; or
(c) whether the claimant has a disablement for the purposes of section 103 of that Act or the extent of any such disablement.

(2) In connection with making a decision to which this regulation applies, the Secretary of State may refer an issue, together with any relevant evidence or information available to him, including any evidence or information provided by or on behalf of the claimant, to a [1 health care professional approved by the Secretary of State] who has experience in such of the issues specified in paragraph (1) as are relevant to the decision, for such report as appears to the Secretary of State to be necessary for the purpose of providing him with information for use in making the decision.

(3) In making a decision to which this regulation applies, the Secretary of State shall have regard to (among other factors)—

(a) all relevant medical reports provided to him in connection with that decision; and
(b) the experience, in such of the issues specified in paragraph (1) as are relevant to the decision, of any [1 health care professional] who has provided a report, including a [1 health care professional approved by the Secretary of State] who has provided a report following an examination required by the Secretary of State under section 19.

AMENDMENT

1. Social Security (Miscellaneous Amendments) (No.2) Regulations 2007 (SI 2007/1626) reg.4(2) (July 3, 2007).

DEFINITIONS

"claimant"—see reg.1(3).
"health care professional"—see s.39(2) of the Social Security Act 1998.
"industrial injuries benefit"—by virtue of s.39(2) of the Social Security Act 1998, see s.191 of the Social Security Administration Act 1992.
"medical practitioner"—*ibid.*

General Note

Adjudicating medical authorities have been abolished and so all decisions which an adjudication officer would, or might, have referred to such authorities under the Social Security Administration Act 1992 are now decided by the Secretary of State on the basis of medical advice which, since 2007, may be given by a health care professional other than a doctor. Approved health care professionals receive special training to make an assessment of the disabling effects of an impairment and relate this to the relevant legislation in order to provide advice or reports for those making decisions on behalf of the Secretary of State. Even where a health care professional has not examined a claimant, his or her opinion may be taken into account as evidence, provided the tribunal can identify the factual basis on which the opinion was given. On appeal, para.(3)(b) makes it necessary for a tribunal to know the health care professional's professional qualification and area of expertise (see also *CDLA/2466/2007*). 2.525

See s.30 of the Social Security Act 1998 for the effect of an earlier declaration that the claimant has suffered personal injury by accident.

[1 Recrudescence of a prescribed disease

12A.—(1) This regulation applies to a decision made under sections 108 to 110 of the Contributions and Benefits Act where a disease is subsequently treated as a recrudescence under regulation 7 of the Social Security (Industrial Injuries) (Prescribed Diseases) Regulations 1985. 2.526

(2) Where this regulation applies Chapter II of Part I of the Act shall apply as if section 8(2) did not apply.]

Amendment

1. Social Security and Child Support (Miscellaneous Amendments) Regulations 2000 (SI 2000/1596) reg.19 (June 19, 2000).

Definition

"the Contributions and Benefits Act"—see s.84 of the Social Security Act 1998.

Income support and social fund determinations on incomplete evidence

13.—(1) Where, for the purpose of a decision under section 8 or 10— 2.527

[1 (a) a determination falls to be made by the Secretary of State as to what housing costs are to be included in—

(i) a claimant's applicable amount by virtue of regulation 17(1)(e) or 18(1)(f) of, and Schedule 3 to, the Income Support Regulations; [2 . . .]

(ii) a claimant's appropriate minimum guarantee by virtue of regulation 6(6)(c) and Schedule II to the State Pension Credit Regulations; [2 or]]

[2 (iii) a claimant's applicable amount under regulation 67(1)(c) or 68(1)(d) of the Employment and Support Allowance Regulations; and]

(b) it appears to the Secretary of State that he is not in possession of all of the evidence or information which is relevant for the purposes of such a determination,

he shall make the determination on the assumption that the housing costs to be included in the claimant's [1 applicable amount or, as the case may be, appropriate minimum guarantee are those] that can be immediately determined.

AMENDMENT

1. Pensions Act 2014 (Consequential, Supplementary and Incidental Amendments) Order 2015 (SI 2015/1985) art.18(1) and (7) (April 6, 2016).

Effect of alteration in the component rates of income support and jobseeker's allowance

2.530 **14.**—(1) Section 159 of the Administration Act (effect of alteration in the component rates of income support) shall not apply to any award of income support in force in favour of a person where there is applicable to that person—

(a) any amount determined in accordance with regulation 17(2) to (7) of the Income Support Regulations; or

(b) any protected sum determined in accordance with Schedule 3A or 3B of those Regulations; or

(c) any transitional addition, personal expenses addition or special transitional addition applicable under Part II of the Income Support (Transitional) Regulations 1987 (transitional protection).

(2) Where section 159 of the Administration Act does not apply to an award of income support by virtue of paragraph (1), a decision under section 10 may be made in respect of that award for the sole purpose of giving effect to any change made by an order under section 150 of the Administration Act.

(3) Section 159A of the Administration Act (effect of alterations in the component rates of jobseeker's allowance) shall not apply to any award of a jobseeker's allowance in force in favour of a person where there is applicable to that person any amount determined in accordance with regulations 87 of the Jobseeker's Allowance Regulations.

(4) Where section 159A of the Administration Act does not apply to an award of a jobseeker's allowance by virtue of paragraph (3), a decision under section 10 may be made in respect of that award for the sole purpose of giving effect to any change made by an order under section 150 of the Administration Act.

[[1] (5) Section 159B of the Administration Act (effect of alterations affecting state pension credit) shall not apply to any award of state pension credit in favour of a person where in relation to that person the appropriate minimum guarantee includes an amount determined under paragraph 6 of Part III of Schedule I to the State Pension Credit Regulations.

(6) Where section 159B of the Administration Act does not apply to an award of state pension credit by virtue of paragraph (5), a decision under section 10 may be made in respect of that award for the sole purpose of giving effect to any change made to an award under section 150 of the Administration Act.]

AMENDMENT

1. State Pension Credit (Consequential Transitional and Miscellaneous Provisions) Regulations 2002 (SI 2002/3019) reg.20 (April 7, 2003).

DEFINITIONS

"the Administration Act"—see s.84 of the Social Security Act 1998.
"the Income Support Regulations"—see reg.1(3).

"the Jobseeker's Allowance Regulations"—*ibid.*
"state pension credit"—*ibid.*
"State Pension Credit Regulations"—*ibid.*

[1 Termination of award of income support [2 , jobseeker's allowance or employment and support allowance]

14A.—(1) This regulation applies in a case where an award of income support [2 , a jobseeker's allowance or an employment and support allowance] ("the existing benefit") exists in favour of a person and, if that award did not exist and a claim was made by that person or his partner for [2 an employment and support allowance,] a jobseeker's allowance or, as the case may be, income support ("the alternative benefit"), an award of the alternative benefit would be made on that claim. 2.531

(2) In a case to which this regulation applies, if a claim for the alternative benefit is made the Secretary of State may bring to an end the award of the existing benefit if he is satisfied that an alternative benefit will be made on that claim.

(3) Where, under paragraph (2), the Secretary of State brings an award of the existing benefit to an end he shall do so with effect from the day immediately preceding the first day on which an award of the alternative benefit takes effect.

(4) Where an award of a jobseeker's allowance is made in accordance with the provisions of this regulation, paragraph 4 of Schedule 1 to the Jobseeker's Act (waiting days) shall not apply.]

[2 (5) Where an award of an employment and support allowance is made in accordance with the provisions of this regulation, paragraph 2 of Schedule 2 to the Welfare Reform Act (waiting days) shall not apply.]

AMENDMENTS

1. Social Security and Child Support (Decisions and Appeals) (Miscellaneous Amendments) Regulations 2002 (SI 2002/1379) reg.6 (May 20, 2002).
2. Employment and Support Allowance (Consequential Provisions) (No.2) Regulations 2008 (SI 2008/1554) regs 29 and 39 (July 27, 2008).

DEFINITIONS

"the alternative benefit"—see para.(1).
"the Jobseekers Act"—see s.84 of the Social Security Act 1998.
"the Welfare Reform Act"—see reg.1(3).

Jobseeker's allowance determinations on incomplete evidence

15. Where, for the purpose of a decision under section 8 or 10— 2.532

(a) a determination falls to be made by the Secretary of State as to whether—
  (i) in relation to any person, the applicable amount falls to be reduced or disregarded to any extent by virtue of section 15 of the Jobseekers Act (persons affected by trade disputes); or
  (ii) for the purposes of regulation 54(2) to (4) of the Jobseeker's Allowance Regulations (relevant education), a person is by virtue of that regulation, to be treated as receiving relevant education; and

(b) it appears to the Secretary of State that he is not in possession of all of the evidence or information which is relevant for the purposes of such a determination.

he shall make the determination on the assumption that the relevant evidence or information which is not in his possession is adverse to the claimant.

DEFINITIONS

"claimant"—see reg.1(3).
"the Jobseekers Act"—see s.84 of the Social Security Act 1998.
"the Jobseeker's Allowance Regulations"—see reg.1(3).

2.533 **15A.–15D.** *Omitted.*

PART III

SUSPENSION, TERMINATION AND OTHER MATTERS

CHAPTER I

SUSPENSION AND TERMINATION

Suspension in prescribed cases

2.534 **16.**—(1) Subject to paragraph (2), the Secretary of State [1 or the Board] may suspend payment of a relevant benefit, in whole or in part, in the circumstances prescribed in paragraph (3).

(2) The Secretary of State shall suspend payment of a jobseeker's allowance in the circumstances prescribed in paragraph (3)(a)(i) or (ii) where the issue or one of the issues is whether a person, who has claimed a jobseeker's allowance, is or was available for employment or whether he is or was actively seeking employment.

(3) The prescribed circumstances are that—

(a) it appears to the Secretary of State [1 or the Board] that—

(i) an issue arises whether the conditions for entitlement to a relevant benefit are or were fulfilled;

(ii) an issue arises whether a decision as to an award of a relevant benefit should be revised under section 9 or superseded under section 10;

(iii) an issue arises whether any amount paid or payable to a person by way of, or in connection with a claim for, a relevant benefit is recoverable under section 71(overpayments), 71A (recovery of jobseeker's allowance: severe hardship cases) or 74 (income support and other payments) of the Administration Act or regulations made under any of those sections; or

(iv) the last address notified to him [1 or them] of a person who is in receipt of a relevant benefit is not the address at which that person is residing; or

(b) an appeal is pending against—

(i) a decision of an [3 the First-tier Tribunal, the Upper Tribunal] or a court;

(ii) a decision given in a different case by [3 the Upper Tribunal] or a court, and it appears to the Secretary of State [1 or the Board] that, if the appeal were to be determined in a particular way, an issue would arise as to whether the award of a relevant benefit (whether the same benefit or not) in the case itself ought to be revised or superseded.

[2(4) For the purposes of section 21(3)(c) an appeal is pending where a decision of [3 the First-tier Tribunal, the Upper Tribunal] or a court has been made and the Secretary of State—

(a) is awaiting receipt of that decision or (in the case of [3 a decision of the First-tier Tribunal]) is considering whether to apply for a statement of the reasons for it, or has applied for such a statement and is awaiting receipt thereof; or

(b) has received that decision or (in the case [3 a decision of the First-tier Tribunal]) the statement of the reasons for it, and is considering whether to apply for [3 permission] to appeal, or where [3 permission] to appeal has been granted, is considering whether to appeal;

and the Secretary of State shall give written notice of his proposal to make a request for a statement of the reasons for a tribunal decision, to apply for leave to appeal, or to appeal, as soon as reasonably practicable.]

AMENDMENTS

1. Tax Credits (Decisions and Appeals) (Amendment) Regulations 1999 (SI 1999/2570) reg.12 (October 5, 1999). Note that amendments made by these regulations only have effect with respect to tax credit under the Tax Credit Act 1999 (reg.1(2) of the Amendment Regulations).

2. Social Security and Child Support (Miscellaneous Amendments) Regulations 2000 (SI 2000/1596) reg.20 (June 19, 2000).

3. Tribunals, Courts and Enforcement Act 2007 (Transitional and Consequential Provisions) Order 2008 (SI 2008/2683) Sch.1 paras 95 and 109 (November 3, 2008).

DEFINITIONS

"the Administration Act"—see s.84 of the Social Security Act 1998.

"the Board"—see reg.1(3).

"relevant benefit"—see s.39(1) of the Social Security Act 1998.

GENERAL NOTE

This regulation provides for the suspension of payments while a question about entitlement is being decided. Entitlement may be terminated under the usual powers of revision or supersession (see regs 3 and 6) or if information is not provided (see reg.18). Regulation 20 provides for the reinstatement of payments where entitlement is not terminated from the beginning of the period of suspension or some earlier date. 2.535

There is no appeal against a decision to suspend payments under this regulation (see Sch.2 para.24). The claimant is expected to wait until the decision is made as to entitlement. In principle, a suspension is subject to judicial review but, in *R. (Sanneh) v Secretary of State for Work and Pensions* [2012] EWHC 1840 (Admin), an application for judicial review of a decision to suspend benefit while the Secretary of State was pursuing an application for permission to appeal to the Upper Tribunal did not "get off the ground" where "the claimant and her child lived sustainably (though not lavishly)", although it was accepted that in principle a suspension decision could be challenged on "well-recognised grounds such as irrationality".

A further application by the same claimant failed when it was conceded that she would never in practice leave the United Kingdom as a result of economic pressure, because she would be eligible to receive support from a local authority under s.17 of the Children Act 1989 which would inevitably prevent her and her daughter facing destitution and homelessness and ensure that neither European Union law nor the European Convention on Human Rights would be breached (*R. (Sanneh) v Secretary of State for Work and Pensions* [2013] EWHC 793 (Admin)).

In *CA/3800/2006*, a claimant entitled to attendance allowance had been paying her own nursing home fees. However, she got into financial difficulties because her money had been badly invested by a financial adviser and the local authority started paying the fees. The claimant was in dispute with her financial adviser and eventually recovered a substantial sum that required her to reimburse the local authority for the fees it had paid. It was held that it had been inappropriate to supersede the award of attendance allowance so as to terminate payment when the local authority started paying the fees because it was impossible to reinstate the payments with effect from the date they had been terminated on a supersession following the reimbursement of the local authority. Instead, because the claimant had been in dispute with her financial adviser, the Secretary of State should merely have suspended payment on the ground that an issue within the scope of reg.16(3)(a)(ii) had arisen. The Commissioner revised the first supersession on the ground of "official error" so that payments could be reinstated from the date they had been stopped. This decision has been followed in *SSWP v DA* [2009] UKUT 214 (AAC) and has been approved by a three-judge panel in *SSWP v JL (DLA)* [2011] UKUT 293 (AAC); [2012] AACR 14. Indeed it was held in the latter case that suspension of payment under reg.16 rather than supersession under reg.6 should normally be the default action where a claimant of attendance allowance or disability allowance goes into long-term care.

Paragraph (1) confers a discretion on the Secretary of State and, where the Secretary of State receives information to the effect that the claimant is being overpaid benefit, the overpayment does not cease to be due to any misrepresentation or failure to disclose by the claimant (so as not to be recoverable under s.71 of the Social Security Administration Act 1992) merely because the Secretary of State does not suspend payments before the claimant is interviewed (*JA v SSWP (DLA)* [2014] UKUT 44 (AAC)).

Provision of information or evidence

2.536 **17.**—(1) This regulation applies where the Secretary of State requires information or evidence for a determination whether a decision awarding a relevant benefit should be—

(a) revised under section 9; or
(b) superseded under section 10.

(2) For the purposes of paragraph (1), the following persons must satisfy the requirements of paragraph (4)—

(a) a person in respect of whom payment of a benefit has been suspended in the circumstances prescribed in regulation 16(3)(a);
(b) a person who has made an application for a decision of the Secretary of State to be revised or superseded;
[3 (c) a person from whom the Secretary of State requires information or evidence under regulation 32(1) of the Claims and Payments Regulations;
(ca) a person from whom the Secretary of State requires documents, certificates or other evidence under regulation 24(5) or (5A) of the Jobseeker's Allowance Regulations;]
(d) a person who qualifies for income support by virtue of paragraph 7 of Schedule 1B to the Income Support Regulations;

(e) a person whose entitlement to benefit is conditional upon his being, or being treated as, incapable of work;

[1 (f) a person whose entitlement to an employment and support allowance is conditional on his having, or being treated as having, limited capability for work.]

(3) The Secretary of State shall notify any person to whom paragraph (2) refers of the requirements of this regulation.

(4) A person to whom paragraph (2) refers must either—

(a) supply the information or evidence within—

[3 (i) a period of 14 days beginning with the date on which the notification under paragraph (3) was sent to him or such longer period as the Secretary of State allows in that notification; or]

(ii) such longer period as he satisfies the Secretary of State is necessary in order to enable him to comply with the requirement; or

(b) satisfy the Secretary of State within the [3 period applicable under"] sub-paragraph (a)(i) that either—

(i) the information or evidence required of him does not exist; or

(ii) that it is not possible for him to obtain it.

[3 (4A) In relation to a person to whom paragraph (2)(ca) refers, paragraph (4)(a)(i) has effect as if for "14 days" there were substituted "7 days".]

(5) The Secretary of State may suspend the payment of a relevant benefit, in whole or in part, to any person to whom paragraph (2)(b) to [2 (f)] applies who fails to satisfy the requirements of paragraph (4).

(6) In this regulation, "evidence" includes evidence which a person is required to provide in accordance with regulation 2 of the Social Security (Medical Evidence) Regulations 1976.

AMENDMENTS

1. Employment and Support Allowance (Consequential Provisions) (No.2) Regulations 2008 (SI 2008/1554) regs 29 and 40 (July 27, 2008).

2. Social Security (Miscellaneous Amendments) (No.3) Regulations 2010 (SI 2010/840) reg.7(1) and (6) (June 28, 2010).

3. Social Security (Suspension of Payment of Benefits and Miscellaneous Amendments) Regulations 2012 (SI 2012/824) reg.4(1) and (3) (April 17, 2012).

DEFINITIONS

"the Claims and Payments Regulations"—see reg.1(3).
"evidence"—see para.(6).
"the Income Support Regulations"—see reg.1(3).
"limited capability for work"—*ibid.*
"relevant benefit"—see s.39(1) of the Social Security Act 1998.

GENERAL NOTE

A different version of this regulation (reproduced in editions of this work up to 2005) was enacted by reg.13 of the Tax Credits (Decisions and Appeals) (Amendment) Regulations 1999 (SI 1999/2570) with effect from October 5, 1999 in respect of working families' tax credit and disabled person's tax credit, payable under the Tax Credits Act 1999 until 2003. 2.537

Termination in cases of failure to furnish information or evidence

18.—(1) Subject to paragraphs (2), (3) and (4), the Secretary of State shall decide that where a person— 2.538

(a) whose benefit has been suspended in accordance with regulation 16 and who subsequently fails to comply with an information requirement made in pursuance of regulation 17; or
(b) whose benefit has been suspended in accordance with regulation 17(5),

that person shall cease to be entitled to that benefit from the date on which payment was suspended except where entitlement to benefit ceases on an earlier date other than under this regulation.

(2) Paragraph (1)(a) shall not apply where not more than one month has elapsed since the information requirement was made in pursuance of regulation 17.

(3) Paragraph (1)(b) shall not apply where not more than one month has elapsed since the first payment was suspended in accordance with regulation 17.

(4) Paragraph (1) shall not apply where benefit has been suspended in part under regulation 16 or, as the case may be, regulation 17.

GENERAL NOTE

2.539 A different version of this regulation (reproduced in editions of this work up to 2005) was enacted by reg.13 of the Tax Credits (Decisions and Appeals) (Amendment) Regulations 1999 (SI 1999/2570) with effect from October 5, 1999 in respect of working families' tax credit and disabled person's tax credit, payable under the Tax Credits Act 1999 until 2003.

A decision that entitlement has ceased under reg.18(1) will usually be a supersession decision against which an appeal lies (*R(H) 4/08*). A refusal to allow a home visit is not, in itself, a refusal to provide information and there can usually be no termination if the claimant has not been given a deadline under reg.17(3) and (4) by which the information must be provided. Moreover, notwithstanding the exception at the end of para.(1), any termination under reg.18 is effective only from the date of the suspension unless there are alternative grounds for revision or supersession from an earlier date (*CH/2995/2006*). This approach was followed in *GZ v SSWP* [2009] UKUT 93 (AAC), where the Secretary of State discovered in March 2008 that the claimant's partner had been in receipt of working tax credit since February 15, 2008. On April 3, 2008, payment of income-based jobseeker's allowance to the claimant was suspended and he was asked to provide information about his partner's work and receipt of tax credit. He failed to do so and the Secretary of State purported to terminate entitlement from February 15, 2008 under reg.18 solely due to the failure to provide the information requested. The judge, referring to *CH/2995/2006*, pointed out that the question whether the claimant was entitled to benefit before April 3, 2008 depended largely on whether the claimant's partner was actually working, which had not been addressed by the Secretary of State. He therefore substituted a decision to the effect that the termination under reg.18 was effective only from April 3, leaving the Secretary of State to make a further decision in respect of the earlier period if he wished to do so.

In *R(H)1/09*, a claimant of council tax benefit had an annual turnover below £15,000 and so was not required to produce a profit and loss account for tax purposes and had not done so. The local authority had no reason not to believe that he had no such account. It failed to inform the claimant of the council tax benefit provision equivalent to reg.17(4)(b) and did not ask for any alternative evidence when informed by the claimant that he did not have any accounts and that his expenses were simply the same as the previous year. The Deputy Commissioner held that there were no grounds for terminating the award of benefit under the equivalent of reg.18. If the local authority or tribunal had considered that the amount claimed for expenses was unrealistic, they could have asked for further evidence or simply recalculated the claimant's entitlement to council tax benefit on the basis that he had no, or a smaller amount of, expenses.

Note that reg.3(7EA) provides a wide power to revise a decision under this regulation to terminate an award of a retirement or state pension following the suspension of payments.

Suspension and termination for failure to submit to medical examination

19.—(1) Except where regulation 8 of the Social Security (Incapacity for Work) (General) Regulations 1995 [3 . . .] (where a question arises as to whether a person is capable of work) [3 or regulation 23 of the Employment and Support Allowance Regulations (where a question arises whether a person has limited capability for work) applies], the Secretary of State [1or the Board] may require a person to submit to a medical examination by a [2 health care professional approved by the Secretary of State] where that person is in receipt of a relevant benefit, and either— 2.540

(a) the Secretary of State considers [1or the Board consider] it necessary to satisfy himself [1or themselves] as to the correctness of the award of the benefit, or of the rate at which it was awarded; or

(b) that person applies for a revision or supersession of the award and the Secretary of State considers [1 or the Board consider] that the examination is necessary for the purpose of making his [1 or their] decision.

(2) The Secretary of State [1 or the Board] may suspend payment of a relevant benefit in whole or in part, to a person who fails, without good cause, on two consecutive occasions to submit to a medical examination in accordance with requirements under paragraph (1) except where entitlement to benefit is suspended on an earlier date other than under this regulation.

(3) Subject to paragraph (4), the Secretary of State [1 or the Board] may determine that the entitlement to a relevant benefit of a person, in respect of whom payment of such a benefit has been suspended under paragraph (2), shall cease from a date not earlier than the date on which payment was suspended except where entitlement to benefit ceases on an earlier date other than under this regulation.

(4) Paragraph (3) shall not apply where not more than one month has elapsed since the first payment was suspended under paragraph (2).

AMENDMENTS

1. Tax Credits (Decisions and Appeals) (Amendment) Regulations 1999 (SI 1999/2570) reg.14 (October 5, 1999). Note that amendments made by these regulations have effect only with respect to tax credit under the Tax Credit Act 1999 (reg.1(2) of the Amendment Regulations).

2. Social Security (Miscellaneous Amendments) (No.2) Regulations 2007 (SI 2007/1626) reg.4(3) (July 3, 2007).

3. Employment and Support Allowance (Consequential Provisions) (No.2) Regulations 2008 (SI 2008/1554) regs 29 and 41 (July 27, 2008).

DEFINITIONS

"the Board"—see reg.1(3).
"the Employment and Support Allowance Regulations"—*ibid.*
"health care professional"—see s.39 of the Social Security Act 1998.

"limited capability for work"—see reg.1(3).
"medical examination"—by virtue of s.39(2) of the Social Security Act 1998, see s.191 of the Social Security Administration Act 1992.
"medical practitioner"—*ibid.*
"relevant benefit"—see s.39(1) of the Social Security Act 1998.

GENERAL NOTE

2.541 Whereas s.19 of the Social Security Act 1998 provides for the obtaining of a report for the purpose of determining a claim, this regulation provides for the obtaining of a report for the purpose of deciding whether an award should be revised or superseded. In *CDLA/2335/2001*, the claimant's award of disability living allowance was terminated because he had failed to attend two consecutive appointments for medical examinations. The claimant's appeal to a tribunal was dismissed and he appealed to a Commissioner. The Commissioner criticised the submission provided to the tribunal on behalf of the decision-maker, which had failed to include any reference to the statutory provision under which the award had been terminated. The Secretary of State conceded that the relevant provision was reg.19 and that the conditions for terminating an award of benefit under para.(3) were not met because, contrary to para.(2), benefit had been suspended before there had been any suggestion that the claimant should attend an appointment for an examination and, contrary to para.(4), more than a month had elapsed since the suspension. The Secretary of State's representative explained that the automated system used to generate decisions was unable to generate a decision in conformity with reg.19 and the decision-maker had used the "least inappropriate" code available. The claimant had said that, following the termination of the award of benefit, he had offered to attend a medical examination but that offer had been rebuffed. The Commissioner observed that a termination under reg.19(3) is effective only until the claimant makes a new claim and that, if the claimant had made such an offer, he should have been told he could make a new claim and that a medical examination would then be arranged.

A decision that entitlement has ceased under reg.19(3) will usually be a supersession decision against which an appeal lies (*R(H) 4/08* and see also para.22 of *CH/2995/2006*). A decision under reg.19(3) cannot be justified merely because there has been a purported suspension under reg.19(2). The conditions for such a suspension must actually have been satisfied (*CDLA/5167/2001*). This will usually involve consideration of whether the claimant had "good cause" for failing to "submit to a medical examination". Presumably those phrases have the same meaning in this regulation as they do in similar provisions, including s.19 of the Social Security Act 1998. See the annotation to that section, above.

Making of payments which have been suspended

2.542 **20.**—(1) Subject to paragraphs (2) and (3), payment of a benefit suspended in accordance with regulation 16 [1 or 17] shall be made where—

(a) in a case to which regulation 16(2) or (3)(a)(i) to (iii) applies, the Secretary of State is satisfied [2 or the Board are satisfied] that the benefit suspended is properly payable and no outstanding issues remain to be resolved;
(b) in a case to which regulation 16(3)(a)(iv) applies, the Secretary of State is satisfied [2 or the Board are satisfied] that the has [2 or they have] been notified of the address at which the person is residing;
(c) [3 . . .];
(d) [1 in a case to which regulation 17(5) applies, the Secretary of State is satisfied that the benefit is properly payable and the requirements of regulation 17(4) have been satisfied.]

[2 (d) *in a case to which regulation 18(1) applies, the Board are satisfied that the benefit suspended is properly payable and the requirements of regulation 17(2), (4), (5) or (7) have been satisfied.*]

[3 (2) Where regulation 16(3)(b)(i) applies, payment of a benefit suspended shall be made if the Secretary of State—

(a) does not, in the case of a decision of [4 the First-tier Tribunal], apply for a statement of the reasons for that decision within the period [4 specified under Tribunal Procedure Rules];

(b) does not, in the case of a decision of [4 the First-tier Tribunal, the Upper Tribunal] or a court, make an application for [4 permission] to appeal and (where [4 the Upper Tribunal] to appeal is granted) make the appeal within the time prescribed for the making of such applications and appeals;

(c) withdraws an application for [4 permission] to appeal or the appeal; or

(d) is refused [4 permission]to appeal, in circumstances where it is not open to him to renew the application for leave or to make a further application for leave to appeal.

(3) Where regulation 16(3)(b)(ii) applies, payment of a benefit suspended shall be made if the Secretary of State, in relation to the decision of [4 the Upper Tribunal] or the court in a different case—

(a) does not make an application for [4 permission] to appeal and (where [4 permission] to appeal is granted) make the appeal within the time prescribed for the making of such applications and appeals;

(b) withdraws an application for [4 permission] to appeal or the appeal; or

(c) is refused [4 permission] to appeal, in circumstances where it is not open to him to renew the application for [4 permission] or to make a further application for [4 permission] to appeal.]

(4) Payment of benefit which has been suspended in accordance with regulation 19 for failure to submit to a medical examination shall be made where the Secretary of State is satisfied [2 or the Board are satisfied] that it is no longer necessary for the person referred to in that regulation to submit to a medical examination.

AMENDMENTS

1. Social Security and Child Support (Decisions and Appeals) Amendment (No.2) Regulations 1999 (SI 1999/1623) reg.6 (July 5, 1999).

2. Tax Credits (Decisions and Appeals) (Amendment) Regulations 1999 (SI 1999/2570) reg.15 (October 5, 1999). Note that amendments made by these Regulations have effect only with respect to tax credit under the Tax Credit Act 1999 (reg.1(2) of the Amendment Regulations). There are thus two forms of para.(1)(d) as the second form is only substituted for the purposes of tax credit.

3. Social Security and Child Support (Miscellaneous Amendments) Regulations 2000 (SI 2000/1596) reg.21 (June 19, 2000).

4. Tribunals, Courts and Enforcement Act 2007 (Transitional and Consequential Provisions) Order 2008 (SI 2008/2683) Sch.1 paras 95 and 110 (November 3, 2008).

DEFINITIONS

"the Board"—see reg.1(3).

"medical examination"—by virtue of s.39(2) of the Social Security Act 1998, see s.191 of the Social Security Administration Act 1992.

Chapter II

Other Matters

Decisions involving issues that arise on appeal in other cases

2.543 **21.**—(1) For the purposes of section 25(3)(b) (prescribed cases and circumstances in which a decision may be made on a prescribed basis) a case which satisfies the condition in paragraph (2) is a prescribed case.

(2) The condition is that the claimant would be entitled to the benefit to which the decision which falls to be made relates, even if the appeal in the other case referred to in section 25(1)(b) were decided in a way which is the most unfavourable to him.

(3) For the purposes of section 25(3)(b), the prescribed basis on which the Secretary of State [1 or the Board] may make the decision is as if—

(a) the appeal in the other case which is referred to in section 25(1)(b) had already been determined; and

(b) that appeal had been decided in a way which is the most unfavourable to the claimant.

(4) The circumstance prescribed under section 25(5)(c), where an appeal is pending against a decision for the purposes of that section, even though an appeal against the decision has not been brought (or, as the case may be, an application for [2 permission] to appeal against the decision has not been made) but the time for doing so has not yet expired, is where the Secretary of State [1 or the Board—

(a) certifies in writing that he is [1, or certify in writing that they are,] considering appealing against that decision; and

(b) considers [1, or consider,] that, if such an appeal were to be dete rmined in a particular way—

(i) there would be no entitlement to benefit in a case to which section 25(1)(a) refers; or

(ii) the appeal would affect the decision in that case in some other way.

Amendments

1. Tax Credits (Decisions and Appeals) (Amendment) Regulations 1999 (SI 1999/2570) reg.16 (October 5, 1999). Note that amendments made by these regulations only have effect with respect to tax credit under the Tax Credit Act 1999 (reg.1(2) of the Amendment Regulations).

2. Tribunals, Courts and Enforcement Act 2007 (Transitional and Consequential Provisions) Order 2008 (SI 2008/2683) Sch.1 paras 95 and 111 (November 3, 2008).

Definitions

"the Board"—see reg.1(3).
"claimant"—*ibid.*

Appeals involving issues that arise in other cases

2.544 **22.** The circumstance prescribed under section 26(6)(c), where an appeal is pending against a decision in the case described in section 26(1)(b) even though an appeal against the decision has not been brought (or, as the case may be, an application for [2 permission] to appeal against the decision has not been made) but the time for doing so has not yet expired, is where the Secretary of State [1 or the Board—

(a) certifies in writing that he is [1, or certify in writing that they are,] considering appealing against that decision; and

(b) considers [1, or consider,] that, if such an appeal were already determined, it would affect the determination of the appeal described in section 26(1)(a).

AMENDMENTS

1. Tax Credits (Decisions and Appeals) (Amendment) Regulations 1999 (SI 1999/2570) reg.17 (October 5, 1999). Note that amendments made by these regulations only have effect with respect to tax credit under the Tax Credit Act 1999 (reg.1(2) of the Amendment Regulations).

2. Tribunals, Courts and Enforcement Act 2007 (Transitional and Consequential Provisions) Order 2008 (SI 2008/2683) Sch.1 paras 95 and 112 (November 3, 2008).

DEFINITION

"the Board"—see reg.1(3).

23. *Omitted.* 2.545

24. *Omitted.* 2.546

PART IV

RIGHTS OF APPEAL AND PROCEDURE FOR BRINGING APPEALS

CHAPTER I

GENERAL

General appeals matters not including child support appeals

Other persons with a right of appeal

25. For the purposes of [3 section 12(2)] [5 but subject to regulation 3ZA,], the following other persons have a right to appeal to [4 the First-tier Tribunal]— 2.547

[2 (ai) any person who has been appointed by the Secretary of State or the Board under regulation 30(1) of the Claims and Payments Regulations (payments on death) to proceed with the claim of a person who has made a claim for benefit and subsequently died;

(aii) any person who is appointed by the Secretary of State to claim benefit on behalf of a deceased person and who claims the benefit under regulation 30(5) and (6) of the Claims and Payments Regulations;

(aiii) any person who is appointed by the Secretary of State to make a claim for reduced earnings allowance or disablement benefit in the name of a person who has died and who claims under regulation 30(6A) and (6B) of the Claims and Payments Regulations;]

(a) any person appointed by the Secretary of State [1 or the Board] under regulation 33(1) of the Claims and Payments Regulations (persons unable to act) to act on behalf of another;
(b) any person claiming attendance allowance or disability living allowance on behalf of another under section 66(2)(b) of the Contributions and Benefits Act or, as the case may be, section 76(3) of that Act (claims on behalf of terminally ill persons);
(c) in relation to a pension scheme, any person who, for the purposes of Part X of the Pension Schemes Act 1993, is an employer, member, trustee or manager by virtue of section 146(8) of that Act.

AMENDMENTS

1. Tax Credits (Decisions and Appeals) (Amendment) Regulations 1999 (SI 1999/2570) reg.18 (October 5, 1999). Note that amendments made by these regulations only have effect with respect to tax credit under the Tax Credit Act 1999 (reg.1(2) of the Amendment Regulations).
2. Social Security and Child Support (Decisions and Appeals) (Miscellaneous Amendments) Regulations 2002 (SI 2002/1379) reg.7 (May 20, 2002).
3. Social Security, Child Support and Tax Credits (Decisions and Appeals) Regulations 2004 (SI 2004/3368) reg.2(3) (December 21, 2004).
4. Tribunals, Courts and Enforcement Act 2007 (Transitional and Consequential Provisions) Order 2008 (SI 2008/2683) Sch.1 paras 95 and 115 (November 3, 2008).
5. (Social Security, Child Support, Vaccine Damage and Other Payments (Decisions and Appeals) (Amendment) Regulations 2013 (SI 2013/2380) reg.4(1) and (7) (October 28, 2013).

DEFINITIONS

"appeal"—see reg.1(3).
"the Board"—see reg.1(3).
"the Claims and Payments Regulations"—*ibid.*
"the Contributions and Benefits Act"—see s.84 of the Social Security Act 1998.

GENERAL NOTE

2.548 In *CA/1014/1999*, an appointee appealed on behalf of a claimant against a decision that an overpayment was recoverable from the claimant. It was held that the tribunal were not entitled to consider whether it was recoverable from the appointee, who was not a "party to the proceedings" as that term is defined in reg.1. However, where an appeal is brought against a decision that an overpayment is recoverable from both the claimant and the appointee, the appeal will generally be regarded as having been brought on behalf of both of them and, even if it is not, both will be parties to the proceedings (*R(A) 2/06*).

Decisions against which an appeal lies

2.549 **26.** [6 Subject to regulation 3ZA,] an appeal shall lie to [4 the First-tier Tribunal] against a decision made by the Secretary of State [1 or an officer of the Board]—
(a) as to whether a person is entitled to a relevant benefit for which no claim is required by virtue of regulation 3 of the Claims and Payments Regulations; or
(b) as to whether a payment be made out of the social fund to a person to meet expenses for heating by virtue of regulations made under section 138(2) of the Contributions and Benefits Act (payments out of the social fund); [2 or

(c) under Schedule 6 to the Contributions and Benefits Act (assessment of extent of disablement) in relation to sections 103 (disablement benefit) and 108 (prescribed diseases) of that Act for the purposes of industrial injuries benefit under Part V of that Act;] [3 or

(d) under section 59 of, and Schedule 7 to, the Welfare Reform and Pensions Act 1999 (couples to make joint-claim for jobseeker's allowance) where one member of the couple is working and the Secretary of State has decided that both members of the couple are not engaged in remunerative work] [5 ; or

(e) under, or by virtue of regulations made under, section 23A (contributions credits for relevant parents or carers) of the Contributions and Benefits Act.]

AMENDMENTS

1. Tax Credits (Decisions and Appeals) (Amendment) Regulations 1999 (SI 1999/2570) reg.19 (October 5, 1999). Note that amendments made by these regulations only have effect with respect to tax credit under the Tax Credit Act 1999 (reg.1(2) of the Amendment Regulations).

2. Social Security and Child Support (Miscellaneous Amendments) Regulations 2000 (SI 2000/1596) reg.22 (June 19, 2000).

3. Social Security Amendment (Joint Claims) Regulations 2001 (SI 2001/518) reg.4(b) (March 19, 2001).

4. Tribunals, Courts and Enforcement Act 2007 (Transitional and Consequential Provisions) Order 2008 (SI 2008/2683) Sch.1 paras 95 and 116 (November 3, 2008).

5. Pensions Act 2007 (Supplementary Provision) Order 2009 (SI 2009/2715) art.2 (April 6, 2010).

6. (Social Security, Child Support, Vaccine Damage and Other Payments (Decisions and Appeals) (Amendment) Regulations 2013 (SI 2013/2380) reg.4(1) and (8) (October 28, 2013).

DEFINITIONS

"appeal"—see reg.1(3).
"the Board"—see reg.1(3).
"the Claims and Payments Regulations"—*ibid.*
"the Contributions and Benefits Act"—see s.84 of the Social Security Act 1998.
"relevant benefit"—see s.89(1) of the Social Security Act 1998.

GENERAL NOTE

Paragraph (c) enables there to be an appeal against an assessment of disablement **2.550** independently of any appeal against a decision awarding, or refusing to award, benefit. This creates difficulties. In *CI/1547/2001*, it was suggested that all appeals against assessment decisions should also be treated as appeals against the consequent entitlement decisions because the provisions for supersession and revision are too limited, having regard to the dates from which they are effective, to deal satisfactorily with the consequences of a successful appeal on assessment alone. For the same reason, an application to supersede an assessment of disablement should generally be treated as also an application to supersede the underlying award (*CI/954/2006*).

A final assessment of disablement made under the legislation replaced by the Social Security Act 1998 Act implies that there was no disablement after the end of the award, and so has ongoing effect and requires supersession of the assessment as well as a new claim for benefit (*R(I) 5/02*). However, an assessment under the 1998 Act carries no such implication and, after it expires, requires just a new claim (*DT v SSWP (II)* [2015] UKUT 509 (AAC)).

Decisions against which no appeal lies

2.551 **27.**—(1) No appeal lies to [1 the First-tier Tribunal] against a decision set out in Schedule 2.

(2) In paragraph (1) and Schedule 2, "decision" includes determinations embodied in or necessary to a decision.

(3) [1 . . .].

AMENDMENT

1. Tribunals, Courts and Enforcement Act 2007 (Transitional and Consequential Provisions) Order 2008 (SI 2008/2683) Sch.1 paras 95 and 117 (November 3, 2008).

DEFINITIONS

"appeal"—see reg.1(3).
"decision"—see para.(2).

GENERAL NOTE

2.552 See note to Sch.2.

Notice of decision against which appeal lies

2.553 **28.**—(1) A person with a right of appeal under the Act or these Regulations against any decision of the Secretary of State [1 or the Board or an officer of the Board] shall—

(a) be given written notice of the decision against which the appeal lies;
(b) be informed that, in a case where that written notice does not include a statement of the reasons for that decision, he may, within one month of the date of notification of that decision, request that the Secretary of State [1 or the Board or an officer of the Board] provide him with a written statement of the reasons for that decision; and
(c) be given written notice of his right of appeal against that decision.

(2) Where a written statement of the reasons for the decision is not included in the written notice of the decision and is requested under paragraph (1)(b), the Secretary of State [1 or the Board or an officer of the Board] shall provide that statement within 14 days of receipt of the request [2 or as soon as practicable afterwards].

AMENDMENTS

1. Tax Credits (Decisions and Appeals) (Amendment) Regulations 1999 (SI 1999/2570) reg.20 (October 5, 1999). Note that amendments made by these regulations only have effect with respect to tax credit under the Tax Credit Act 1999 (reg.1(2) of the Amendment Regulations).

2. Social Security, Child Support and Tax Credits (Miscellaneous Amendments) Regulations 2005 (SI 2005/337) reg.2(6) (March 18, 2005).

DEFINITIONS

"the Act"—see reg.1(3).
"appeal"—*ibid.*
"the Board"—*ibid.*
"the date of notification"—*ibid.*

GENERAL NOTE

Paragraph (1)

There may be circumstances in which a failure to comply with the duties imposed by this regulation may invalidate the decision altogether (see *C3/07-08(IS)*, in which the Deputy Commissioner considered that computer-generated letters could not be reconciled with the statutory provisions for decision-making). The same approach has been taken by the High Court in relation to immigration decisions. Thus, in *R.(E (Russia)) v Secretary of State for the Home Department* [2012] EWCA Civ 357; [2012] 1 W.L.R. 3198, it was held that an immigration decision was invalid when it was accompanied by advice that wrongly stated that the right of appeal against it could be exercised only from outside the United Kingdom. However, in *R(P) 1/04*, it was held that a failure to issue notice of a decision simply had the effect that the time for appealing against the decision did not start to run. The same is true where a decision is issued but it incorrectly tells the claimant that benefit has been awarded for life when it has been awarded only for a limited period. The decision is valid but time for appealing runs from when the claimant is informed of the true nature of the decision (*CDLA/3440/2003*). It is suggested that, where a decision is issued, a failure to provide the information required by sub-para.(c) also has the effect that the decision is valid but that the time for appealing against it does not start to run. If that is so, the time for appealing would run from when the claimant does become aware of his rights. In *C10/07-08(IS)*, a Deputy Commissioner in Northern Ireland has considered, in the context of the Northern Ireland equivalent to s.71(5A) of the Social Security Administration Act 1992 (which provides that a decision cannot usually be made as to whether the overpayment of benefit is recoverable (a "recoverability decision") until the award has been superseded or revised (an "entitlement decision") and an award of the correct amount of entitlement (if any) has been substituted), the effect of a failure to give notice of the entitlement decision before the recoverability decision is made. He held that a failure to give notice of the entitlement decision did not invalidate it or the recoverability decision but that, on an appeal against the recoverability decision, steps should be taken to ensure that there had been no prejudice to the claimant through the failure to give notice of the entitlement decision by, for instance, adjourning so that the claimant could also appeal against the entitlement decision. However, he contemplated that, if prejudice could not otherwise be avoided, it might be necessary to allow the claimant's appeal against the recoverability decision. 2.554

In child support cases, there is always likely to be prejudice because the interests of a third party entitled to rely on the decision have to be taken into account. In those circumstances, time has been held to run from the date of a decision even though the parties have been misled into thinking they had no right of appeal (*CCS/5515/2002*).

It is arguable that a statement of reasons only counts as such for the purposes of sub-para.(b) if it is adequate but the adequacy of a statement of reasons is very much a matter of judgment and depends on the issues arising in the particular case. A request made under para.(1)(b) extends the time for appealing but, presumably, only if it is properly made and the notice really does not include an adequate statement of reasons. Accordingly, the cautious claimant will treat any purported statement of reasons as being adequate for the purpose and will ensure that the appeal is lodged within the usual one month time limit, even if a fuller explanation is expected in the Secretary of State's submission to the tribunal.

A failure to refer to the fact that a decision is a supersession can, like most other defects, be cured by a tribunal giving a decision in the proper form (*R(IB)2/04*). On the other hand, if a tribunal does not realise that a decision under appeal was, or should have been, a supersession rather than a decision on a new claim, the tribunal's decision is liable to be set aside if it is impossible to infer that any ground for altering the decision on supersession was made out (*CDLA/9/2001*).

Further particulars required relating to certificate of recoverable benefits [1 or, as the case may be, recoverable lump sum payments] appeals

2.555 **29.**—(1) [2 . . .]

(2) [2 . . .]

(3) [3 . . .]

(4) [3 . . .]

(5) [3 . . .]

(6) [3 The Secretary of State may treat any—

(a) purported appeal (where, as the result of regulation 9ZB(2) (consideration of review before appeal), there is no right of appeal);

(b) appeal relating to the certificate of recoverable benefits; or

(c) appeal relating to the certificate of recoverable lump sum payments,

as an application for review under section 10 of the 1997 Act.]

AMENDMENTS

1. Social Security (Recovery of Benefits) (Lump Sum Payments) Regulations 2008 (SI 2008/1596) Sch.2 para.1(c), (i) (October 1, 2008).

2. Tribunals, Courts and Enforcement Act 2007 (Transitional and Consequential Provisions) Order 2008 (SI 2008/2683) Sch.1 paras 95 and 118 (November 3, 2008).

3. Social Security, Child Support, Vaccine Damage and Other Payments (Decisions and Appeals) (Amendment) Regulations 2013 (SI 2013/2380) reg.4(1), (9) and (10)(b) (October 28, 2013, save where notice of the certificate of recoverable benefits or recoverable lump sum payments was posted to the appellant's last known address before that date—see reg.8(1) and (3)).

DEFINITIONS

"the 1997 Act"—see reg.1(3).
"appeal"—*ibid.*

GENERAL NOTE

2.556 Paragraphs (3) to (5) made provision for the Secretary of State to obtain particulars omitted from a notice of appeal and they remain in force in respect of appeals relating to certificates issued before October 28, 2013, which must be lodged with the Secretary of State rather than the First-tier Tribunal. When that saving ceases to apply, the heading of the regulation will have become anachronistic.

General appeals matters including child support appeals

Appeal against a decision which has been [2 replaced or] revised

2.557 **30.**—(1) An appeal against a decision of the Secretary of State [5 [6 . . .]] [1 or the Board or an officer of the Board] shall not lapse where the decision [2 is treated as replaced by a decision under section 11 of the Child Support Act by section 28F(5) of that Act, or is revised under section 16 of that Act] or section 9 before the appeal is determined and the decision as [2 replaced or] revised is not more advantageous to the appellant than the decision before it was [2 replaced or] revised.

(2) Decisions which are more advantageous for the purposes of this regulation include decisions where—

(a) any relevant benefit paid to the appellant is greater or is awarded for a longer period in consequence of the decision made under section 9;
(b) it would have resulted in the amount of relevant benefit in payment being greater but for the operation of any provision of the Administration Act or the Contributions and Benefits Act restricting or suspending the payment of, or disqualifying a claimant from receiving, some or all of the benefit;
(c) as a result of the decision, a denial or disqualification for the receiving of any relevant benefit, is lifted, wholly or in part;
(d) it reverses a decision to pay benefit to a third party;
[3(dd) it reverses a decision under section 29(2) that an accident is not an industrial accident;]
(e) in consequence of the revised decision, benefit paid is not recoverable under section 71, 71A or 74 of the Administration Act or regulations made under any of those sections, or the amount so recoverable is reduced; or
(f) a financial gain accrued or will accrue to the appellant in consequence of the decision.

(3) Where a decision as [2 replaced under section 28F(5) of the Child Support Act, or as revised under section 16 of that Act] or under section 9 is not more advantageous to the appellant than the decision before it was [2 replaced or] revised, the appeal shall be treated as though it had been brought against the decision as [2 replaced or] revised.

(4) The appellant shall have a period of one month from the date of notification of the decision as [2 replaced or] revised to make further representations as to the appeal.

(5) After the expiration of the period specified in paragraph (4), or within that period if the appellant consents in writing, the appeal to the [4 First-tier Tribunal] shall proceed except where, in the light of the further representations from the appellant, the Secretary of State [5 [6 . . .]] [1 or the Board or an officer of the Board] further revises his [1, or revise their,] decision and that decision is more advantageous to the appellant than the decision before it was [2 replaced or] revised.

AMENDMENTS

1. Tax Credits (Decisions and Appeals) (Amendment) Regulations 1999 (SI 1999/2570) reg.21 (October 5, 1999). Note that amendments made by these regulations only have effect with respect to tax credit under the Tax Credit Act 1999 (reg.1(2) of the Amendment Regulations).

2. Child Support (Decisions and Appeals) (Amendment) Regulations 2000 (SI 2000/3185) reg.11 (various dates as provided by reg.1(1)).

3. Social Security, Child Support and Tax Credits (Miscellaneous Amendments) Regulations 2005 (SI 2005/337) reg.2(7) (March 18, 2005).

4. Tribunals, Courts and Enforcement Act 2007 (Transitional and Consequential Provisions) Order 2008 (SI 2008/2683) Sch.1 paras 95 and 119 (November 3, 2008).

5. Child Support (Miscellaneous Amendments) Regulations 2009 (SI 2009/396) reg.4(1) and (14) (April 6, 2009).

6. Public Bodies (Child Maintenance and Enforcement Commission: Abolition and Transfer of Functions) Order 2012 (SI 2012/2007) art.3(2) and Sch. para.113(1) and (12) (August 1, 2012).

DEFINITIONS

"the Administration Act"—see s.84 of the Social Security Act 1998.
"appeal"—see reg.1(3).
"the Board"—*ibid.*
"the Child Support Act"—see s.84 of the Social Security Act 1998.
"the Contributions and Benefits Act"—*ibid.*
"the date of notification"—see reg.1(3).
"relevant benefit"—see s.39(1) of the Social Security Act 1998.

GENERAL NOTE

2.558 Paragraph (1) provides an exception to the general rule that an appeal lapses when the decision under appeal is revised (see s.9(6) of the Social Security Act 1998). It makes it unnecessary for the claimant to submit a fresh appeal where the decision under appeal is replaced by a decision that is no more favourable to the claimant. Paragraph (2), however, makes it clear that a fresh appeal will be required where the new decision is only partially favourable to a claimant as well as when it is wholly favourable. However, an appeal does not lapse merely because, on reconsideration, the Secretary of State considers that the claimant scores more points on a work capability assessment but still not enough for entitlement to employment and support allowance (*AJ v SSWP (ESA)* [2014] UKUT 208 (AAC)). In *R(IS) 2/08*, a decision was made in 2003 to the effect that the claimant was not entitled to income support from May 17, 2002. When the claimant appealed, the decision was revised and income support was paid in respect of the period from May 17, 2002 to July 31, 2002. It was held that reg.30(2)(a) did not require the appeal to be treated as having lapsed in respect of the period from August 1, 2002. The Tribunal of Commissioners said—

> ". . . where a period before the date of the original decision is in issue and a revision affects only part of that period, it seems to us that there are many circumstances in which it can be appropriate to regard the decision as being more advantageous to the appellant only in respect of that part of the period and not the remainder of the period. This is particularly so where the Secretary of State knows very well that the revision does not deal with the main issue raise by the appeal and that it would be a waste of time to treat the appeal as having lapsed and to require the appellant to start all over again."

Subparagraph (dd) has effect only in relation to industrial accident declarations made under the now-repealed s.29(2) otherwise than in the course of a claim for benefit. It is probably meant to apply not only to cases where the reversed decision was to the effect that an accident was not an industrial accident but also to cases where it was to the effect that an alleged industrial accident was not an accident at all or did not even take place.

Amendments made to this regulation by reg.6 of the Child Support (Meaning of Child and New Calculation Rules) (Consequential and Miscellaneous Amendment) Regulations 2012 (SI 2012/2785) and effective only for the purpose of certain child support cases are not included in this volume.

2.559 **30A.** *Omitted.*

2.560 **31.** [1 . . .]

AMENDMENT

1. Tribunals, Courts and Enforcement Act 2007 (Transitional and Consequential Provisions) Order 2008 (SI 2008/2683) Sch.1 paras 95 and 121 (November 3, 2008).

2.561 **32.** [1 . . .]

AMENDMENT

1. Social Security, Child Support, Vaccine Damage and Other Payments (Decisions and Appeals) (Amendment) Regulations 2013 (SI 2013/2380) reg.4(1) and (10)(c) (October 28, 2013, subject to a saving—see the note to reg.34).

33. [1 . . .]

AMENDMENT

1. Social Security, Child Support, Vaccine Damage and Other Payments (Decisions and Appeals) (Amendment) Regulations 2013 (SI 2013/2380) reg.4(1) and (10)(d) (October 28, 2013, subject to a saving—see the note to reg.34).

34. [1 . . .]

AMENDMENT

1. Social Security, Child Support, Vaccine Damage and Other Payments (Decisions and Appeals) (Amendment) Regulations 2013 (SI 2013/2380) reg.4(1) and (10)(e) (October 28, 2013, subject to savings—see below).

GENERAL NOTE

The revocation of regs 32–34 does not apply to appeals where notice of the Secretary of State's decision was posted to the appellant's last known address before October 28, 2013 (see reg.8(1) and (3) of the 2013 Amendment Regulations), because such appeals must be lodged with the Secretary of State, rather than the First-tier Tribunal, under r.23 of the Tribunal Procedure (First-tier Tribunal) (Social Entitlement Chamber) Rules 2008. Regulation 32 permitted the Secretary of State to extend the time for appealing and was arguably unnecessary in the light of r.23(4) of the 2008 Rules. Regulation 33 made provision as to the address to which appeals were to be sent and the obtaining by the Secretary of State of particulars omitted from a notice of appeal. Regulation 34 provided for the appointment of a person to act in place of a party to proceedings who had died. **2.562**

Regulation 34 also remains in force for the limited purpose explained in the note to ss.5–7 of the Social Security Act 1998.

The revocation of reg.34 in other cases arguably leaves a lacuna not yet filled by the 2008 Rules. Although there seems to be no reason why there should not be an appointment under reg.30(1) of the Social Security (Claims and Payments) Regulations 1987 after an appeal relating to a claim for benefit has been lodged, in other cases where an appointment could previously have been made under reg.34 it is likely that an appeal will have to be abated until someone has been appointed to administer the deceased's estate.

PART V

APPEAL TRIBUNALS FOR SOCIAL SECURITY CONTRACTING OUT OF PENSIONS, VACCINE DAMAGE AND CHILD SUPPORT

35.–38. [1 . . .] **2.563**

AMENDMENT

1. Tribunals, Courts and Enforcement Act 2007 (Transitional and Consequential Provisions) Order 2008 (SI 2008/2683) Sch.1 paras 95 and 124 (November 3, 2008), subject to a saving under art.1(3).

GENERAL NOTE

2.564 Except for parts of reg.36, these regulations remain in force in Scotland for the limited purpose explained in the note to ss.5–7 of the Social Security Act 1998.

[1Appeals raising issues for decision by officers of Inland Revenue

2.565 **38A.**—(1) Where, [2 a person has appealed to [3 the First-tier Tribunal and it appears to the First-tier Tribunal,] that an issue arises which, by virtue of section 8 of the Transfer Act, falls to be decided by an officer of the Board, that tribunal [2 [3 . . .] shall—

(a) refer the appeal to the Secretary of State pending the decision of that issue by an officer of the Board; and

(b) require the Secretary of State to refer that issue to the Board;

and the Secretary of State shall refer that issue accordingly.

(2) Pending the final decision of any issue which has been referred to the Board in accordance with paragraph (1) above, the Secretary of State may revise the decision under appeal, or make a further decision superseding that decision, in accordance with his determination of any issue other than one which has been so referred.

(3) On receipt by the Secretary of State of the final decision of an issue which has been referred in accordance with paragraph (1) above, he shall consider whether the decision under appeal ought to be revised under section 9 or superseded under section 10, and—

(a) if so, revise it or, as the case may be, make a further decision which supersedes it; or

(b) if not, forward the appeal to the [3 First-tier Tribunal] which shall determine the appeal in accordance with the final decision of the issue so referred.

(4) In paragraphs (2) and (3) above, "final decision" has the same meaning as in regulation 11A(3) and (4).]

AMENDMENTS

1. Social Security and Child Support (Decisions and Appeals) Amendment (No.3) Regulations 1999 (SI 1999/1670) reg.2(4) (July 5, 1999).

2. Social Security and Child Support (Decisions and Appeals) (Miscellaneous Amendments) Regulations 2002 (SI 2002/1379) reg.12 (May 20, 2002).

3. Tribunals, Courts and Enforcement Act 2007 (Transitional and Consequential Provisions) Order 2008 (SI 2008/2683) Sch.1 paras 95 and 125 (November 3, 2008).

DEFINITIONS

"appeal"—see reg.1(3).
"the Board"—*ibid.*
"final decision"—by virtue of para.(4), see reg.11A(5).
"the Transfer Act"—see reg.1(3).

GENERAL NOTE

2.566 The Inland Revenue has been merged into Her Majesty's Revenue and Customs (HMRC). The process envisaged by this regulation has not always worked well, as HMRC has not always made the type of decision required by the First-tier Tribunal or, indeed, any decision at all. The consequence of criticism is that HMRC has now agreed that the First-tier Tribunal (or the Upper Tribunal) may refer cases straight to them and they will then endeavour to deal with them within three months (*SSWP v TB (RP)* [2010] UKUT 88 (AAC); [2010] AACR 38).

Some decisions fall to be made by HMRC by virtue of s.170 of the Pensions Schemes Act 1993 (rather than by virtue of s.8 of the Social Security Contributions (Transfer of Functions, etc.) Act 1999) but the Tribunal may refer to HMRC issues for determination under the 1993 Act notwithstanding that this regulation does not apply (*R(P) 1/04*). It might be necessary to adjourn the hearing before the Tribunal while the question was being decided and procedures akin to those laid down in paras (2) and (3) could be followed.

39. – 47. [1 . . .] 2.567

AMENDMENT

1. Tribunals, Courts and Enforcement Act 2007 (Transitional and Consequential Provisions) Order 2008 (SI 2008/2683) Sch.1 paras 95 and 126 (November 3, 2008), subject to a saving under art.1(3).

GENERAL NOTE

Except for regs 41, 44 and 45, these regulations remain in force in Scotland for the limited purpose explained in the note to ss.5–7 of the Social Security Act 1998. 2.568

48. [1 . . .] 2.569

AMENDMENT

1. Social Security, Child Support and Tax Credits (Decisions and Appeals) Regulations 2004 (SI 2004/3368) reg.2(8) (December 21, 2004).

49. – 58. [1 . . .] 2.570

AMENDMENT

1. Tribunals, Courts and Enforcement Act 2007 (Transitional and Consequential Provisions) Order 2008 (SI 2008/2683) Sch.1 paras 95 and 126 (November 3, 2008), subject to a saving under art.1(3).

GENERAL NOTE

Except for regs 50 and 52, these regulations remain in force in Scotland for the limited purpose explained in the note to ss.5–7 of the Social Security Act 1998. 2.571

[1 Appeal to [2 the Upper Tribunal] by a partner

58A. A partner within the meaning of section 2AA(7) of the Administration Act (full entitlement to certain benefits conditional on work-focused interview for partner) may appeal to [2 the Upper Tribunal] under section 14 from a decision of [2 the First-tier Tribunal] in respect of a decision specified in section 2B(2A) and (6) of the Administration Act.] 2.572

AMENDMENTS

1. Social Security, Child Support and Tax Credits (Miscellaneous Amendments) Regulations 2005 (SI 2005/337) reg.2(19) (March 19, 2005).
2. Tribunals, Courts and Enforcement Act 2007 (Transitional and Consequential Provisions) Order 2008 (SI 2008/2683) Sch.1 paras 95 and 127 (November 3, 2008).

DEFINITION

"the Administration Act"—see reg.1(3).

GENERAL NOTE

2.573 This regulation, made under s.14(3)(b) of the Social Security Act 1998, was necessary because a partner does not fall within the term "claimant" in s.14(3)(b). It has presumably been retained lest there be a case where a partner did not have a right of appeal under s.11 of the Tribunals, Courts and Enforcement Act 2007 as a "party".

PART VI

REVOCATIONS

2.574 **59.**—*Omitted.*

SCHEDULE 1

2.575 PROVISIONS CONFERRING POWERS EXERCISED IN MAKING THESE REGULATIONS

Column (1) Provision		*Column (2) Relevant Amendments*
Vaccine Damage Payments Act 1979	Section 4(2) and (3)	The Act, Section 46
Child Support Act 1991	Section 7A(1)	The Act, Section 47
	Section 16(6)	The Act, Section 40
	Section 20(5) and (6)	The Act, Section 42
	Section 28ZA(2)(b) and (4)(c)	The Act, Section 43
	Section 28ZB(6)(c)	The Act, Section 43
	Section 28ZC(7)	The Act, Section 44
	Section 28ZD(1) and (2)	The Act, Section 44
	Section 46B	The Act, Schedule 7, paragraph 44
	Section 51(2)	The Act, Schedule 7, paragraph 46
	Schedule 4A, paragraph 8	The Act, Schedule 7, paragraph 53
Social Security Administration Act 1992	Section 5(1)(hh)	The Act, Section 74
	Section 159	The Act, Schedule 7, paragraph 95
	Section 159A	The Act, Schedule 7, paragraph 96
Pension Schemes Act 1993	Section 170(3)	The Act, Schedule 7, paragraph 131
Social Security (Recovery of Benefits) Act 1997	Section 10	The Act, Schedule 7, paragraph 149
	Section 11(5)	
Social Security Act 1998	Section 6(3)	

Section 7(6)
Section 9(1), (4) and (6)
Section 10(3) and (6)
Section 11(1)
Section 12(2) and (3), (6) and (7)
Section 14(10)(a) and (11)
Section 16(1) and Schedule 5
Section 17
Section 18(1)
Section 20
Section 21(1) to (3)
Section 22
Section 23
Section 24
Section 25(3)(b) and (5)(c)
Section 26(6)(c)
Section 28(1)
Section 31(2)
Section 79(1) and (3) to (7)
Section 84
Schedule 1, paragraphs 7, 11 and 12
Schedule 2, paragraph 9
Schedule 3, paragraphs 1, 4 and 9

SCHEDULE 2 — Regulation 27

Decisions Against Which No Appeal Lies

Child benefit

1. A decision of the Secretary of State as to whether an educational establishment be recognised for the purposes of Part IX of the Contributions and Benefits Act. **2.576**

2. A decision of the Secretary of State to recognise education provided otherwise than at a recognised educational establishment.

3. A decision of the Secretary of State made in accordance with the discretion conferred upon him by the following provisions of the Child Benefit (Residence and Persons Abroad) Regulations 1976—

(a) regulation 2(2)(c)(iii) (decision relating to a child's temporary absence abroad);
(b) regulation 7(3) (certain days of absence abroad disregarded).

4. A decision of the Secretary of State made in accordance with the discretion conferred upon him by regulation 2(1) or (3) of the Child Benefit (General) Regulations 1976 (provisions relating to contributions and expenses in respect of a child).

Claims and payments

[5 **5.** A decision, being a decision of the Secretary of State unless specified below as a decision of the Board, under the following provisions of the Claims and Payments Regulations— **2.577**

[8 (a) regulation 4(3) or (3B) (which partner should make a claim for income support or jobseeker's allowance);]
[9 (aa) regulation 4I (which partner should make a claim for an employment and support allowance);]
(b) [8 . . .];
[8 (bb) regulation 4D(7) (which partner should make a claim for state pension credit);]
(c) [8 . . .];
(d) [8 . . .];
(e) [8 . . .];
(f) regulation 7 (decision by the Secretary of State or the Board as to evidence and information required);
(g) regulation 9 and Schedule 1 (decision by the Secretary of State or the board as to interchange of claims with claims for other benefits);

(h) regulation 11 (treating claim for maternity allowance as claim for incapacity benefit [9 or employment and support allowance]);
(i) regulation 15(7) (approving form of particulars required for determination of retirement pension questions in advance of claim);
(j) regulations 20 to 24 (decisions by the Secretary of State or the Board as to the time and manner of payments);
(k) regulation 25(1) (intervals of payment of attendance allowance and disability living allowance where claimant is expected to return to hospital);
(l) regulation 26 (manner and time of payment of income support);
(m) regulation 26A (time and intervals of payment of jobseeker's allowance);
[7 (mm) regulation 26B (payment of state pension credit);]
[9 (mn) regulation 26C (manner and time of payment of employment and support allowance);]
(n) regulation 27(1) and (1A) (decision by the Board as to manner and time of payment of tax credits);
(o) regulation 30 (decision by the Secretary of State or the Board as to claims or payments after death of claimant);
(p) regulation 30A (payment of arrears of joint-claim jobseeker's allowance where nominated person can no longer be traced);
(q) regulation 31 (time and manner of payment of industrial injuries gratuities);
(r) regulation 32 (decision by the Secretary of State or the Board where person unable to act);
(s) regulation 33 (appointments by the Secretary of State or the Board where person unable to act);
(t) regulation 34 (decision by the Secretary of State or the Board as to paying another person on a beneficiaries behalf);
(u) regulation 34A(1) (payment, out of benefit, of mortgage interest to qualifying lender);
(v) regulation 35(2) (payment to third person of maternity expenses or expenses for heating in cold weather);
(w) regulation 36 (decision by the Secretary of State or the Board to pay partner as alternative payee);
(x) regulation 38 (decision by the Secretary of State or the Board as to the extinguishment of right to payment of sums by way of benefit where payment not obtained within the prescribed period, except a decision under paragraph (2A) (payment requrested after expiration of prescribed period));
(y) regulations 42 to 46 (mobility component of disability living allowance and disability living allowance for children;
(z) regulation 47(2) and (3) (return of instruments of payment etc. to the Secretary of State or the Board).]

[13 *Schemes that were Contracted-out Pension Schemes*]

2.578 **6.** A decision of the Secretary of State under section 109 of the Pension Schemes Act 1993 or any Order made under it (annual increase of guaranteed minimum pensions).

Decisions depending on other cases

2.579 **7.** A decision of the Secretary of State under section 25 or 26 (decisions and appeals depending on other cases).

Deductions

2.580 **8.** A decision which falls to be made by the Secretary of State under the Fines (Deductions from Income Support) Regulations 1992, other than [1 a decision whether benefit is sufficient for a deduction to be made].

9.—(1) Except in relation to a decision to which sub-paragraph (2) applies, any decision of the Secretary of State under the Community Charges (Deductions from Income Support) (No.2) Regulations 1990, the Community Charges (Deductions from Income Support) (Scotland) Regulations 1989 or the Council Tax (Deductions from Income Support) Regulations 1993.

(2) This sub-paragraph applies to a decision—
(a) whether there is an outstanding sum due of the amount sought to be deducted;
(b) whether benefit is sufficient for a deduction to be made; and
(c) on the priority to be given to any deduction.

European Community regulations

10. An authorization given by the Secretary of State in accordance with article 22(1) or (1) of Council Regulation (EEC) No.1408/71 on the application of social security schemes to employed persons, to self-employed persons and to members of their families moving within the Community. 2.581

Expenses

11. A decision of the Secretary of State whether to pay expenses to any person under section 180 of the Administration Act. 2.582

Guardian's allowance

12. A decision of the Secretary of State relating to the giving of a notice under regulation 5(8) of the Social Security (Guardian's Allowance) Regulations 1975 (children whose surviving parents are in prison or legal custody). 2.583

Income support

13. A decision of the Secretary of State [3 . . .] made in accordance with paragraph (1) or (2) of regulation 13 (income support and social fund determinations on incomplete evidence). 2.584

[6 State pension credit

13A. A decision of the Secretary of State made in accordance with paragraph (1) or (3) of regulation 13 in relation to state pension credit (determination on incomplete evidence).] 2.585

Industrial injuries benefit

14. A decision of the Secretary of State relating to the question whether— 2.586

(a) disablement pension be increased under section 104 of the Contributions and Benefits Act (constant attendance); or

(b) disablement pension be further increased under section 105 of the Contributions and Benefits Act (exceptionally severe disablement);

and if an increase is to be granted or renewed, the period for which and the amount at which it is payable.

15. A decision of the Secretary of State under regulation 2(2) of the Social Security (Industrial Injuries and Diseases) Miscellaneous Provisions Regulations 1986 as to the length of any period of interruption of education which is to be disregarded.

16. A decision of the Secretary of State to approve or not to approve a person undertaking work for the purposes of regulation 17 of the Social Security (General Benefit) Regulations 1982.

17. A decision of the Secretary of State as to how the limitations under Part VI of Schedule 7 to the Contributions and Benefits Act on the benefit payable in respect of any death are to be applied in the circumstances of any case.

Invalid vehicle scheme

18. A decision of the Secretary of State relating to the issue of certificates under regulation 13 of, and Schedule 2 to, the Social Security (Disability Living Allowance) Regulations 1991. 2.587

Jobseeker's allowance

19.—(1) A decision of the Secretary of State under Chapter IV of Part II of the Jobseeker's Allowance Regulations as to the day and the time a claimant is to attend at a job centre. 2.588

(2) A decision of the Secretary of State as to the day of the week on which a claimant is required to provide a signed declaration under regulation 24(10) of the Jobseeker's Allowance Regulations.

(3) A decision of the Secretary of State [3 . . .] made in accordance with regulation 15 (Jobseeker's allowance determinations on incomplete evidence).

[10 . . .] 2.589

Payments on account, overpayments and recovery

2.590 **20.** A decision of the Secretary of State under the Social Security (Payments on account, Overpayments and Recovery) Regulations 1988, except a decision of the Secretary of State under the following provisions of those Regulations—

(a) [12 . . .]
(b) [12 . . .]
(c) regulation 5 as to the offsetting of a prior payment against a subsequent award;
(d) regulation 11(1) as to whether a payment in excess of entitlement has been credited to a bank or other account;
(e) regulation 13 as to the sums to be deducted in calculating recoverable amounts;
(f) regulation 14(1) as to the treatment of capital to be reduced;
(g) regulation 19 determining a claimant's protected earnings; and
(h) regulation 24 whether a determination as to a claimant's protected earnings is revised or superseded.

[12 **20A.** A decision of the Secretary of State under the Social Security (Payments on Account of Benefit) Regulations 2013 except a decision under regulation 10 of those Regulations.]

Persons abroad

2.591 **21.** A decision of the Secretary of State made under—

(a) regulation 2(1)(a) of the Social Security Benefit (Persons Abroad) Regulations 1975 whether to certify that it is consistent with the proper administration of the Contributions and Benefits Act that a disqualification under section 113(1)(a) of that Act should not apply;
(b) regulation 9(4) or (5) of those Regulations whether to allow a person to avoid disqualification for receiving benefit during a period of temporary absence from Great Britain longer than that specified in the regulation.

Reciprocal Agreements

2.592 **22.** A decision of the Secretary of State made in accordance with an Order made under section 179 of the Administration Act (reciprocal agreements with countries outside the United Kingdom).

Social fund awards

2.593 **23.** A decision of the Secretary of State under section 78 of the Administration Act relating to the recovery of social fund awards.

Suspension

2.594 **24.** A decision of the Secretary of State relating to the suspension of a relevant benefit or to the payment of such a benefit which has been suspended under Part III.

Up-rating

2.595 **25.** A decision of the Secretary of State relating to the up-rating of benefits under Part X of the Administration Act.

[2 **26.** Any decision treated as a decision of the Secretary of State whether or not to waive or defer a work-focused interview.]

Loss of Benefit

2.596 [4 **27.** [11 (1) In the circumstances referred to in sub-paragraph (2), a decision of the Secretary of State that a sanctionable benefit as defined in section 6A(1) of the Social Security Fraud Act 2001 is not payable (or is to be reduced) pursuant to section 6B, 7, 8 or 9 of that Act as a result of—

(a) a conviction for one or more benefit offences in one set of proceedings;
(b) an agreement to pay a penalty under section 115A of the Administration Act (penalty as alternative to prosecution) or section 109A of the Social Security Administration (Northern Ireland) Act 1992 (the corresponding provision for Northern Ireland) in relation to a benefit offence;
(c) a caution in respect of one or more benefit offences; or
(d) a conviction for one or more benefit offences in each of two sets of proceedings, the

later offence or offences being committed within the period of 5 years after the date of any of the convictions for a benefit offence in the earlier proceedings.

(2) The circumstances are that the only ground of appeal is that any of the convictions was erroneous, or that the offender (as defined in section 6B(1) of the Social Security Fraud Act 2001) did not commit the benefit offence in respect of which there has been an agreement to pay a penalty or a caution has been accepted.]]

AMENDMENTS

1. Social Security Act 1998 (Commencement No.12 and Consequential and Transitional Provisions) Order 1999 (SI 1999/3178) art.3(19) and Sch.19 para.2 (November 29, 1999).

2. Social Security (Work-focused Interviews) Regulations 2000 (SI 2000/897), reg.16(5) and Sch.6 para.7 (April 3, 2000).

3. Social Security and Child Support (Miscellaneous Amendments) Regulations 2000 (SI 2000/1596) reg.34 (June 19, 2000).

4. Social Security (Loss of Benefit) Regulations 2001 (SI 2001/4022) reg.21 (April 1, 2002).

5. Social Security and Child Support (Decisions and Appeals) (Miscellaneous Amendments) Regulations 2002 (SI 2002/1379) reg.21 (May 20, 2002).

6. State Pension Credit (Consequential, Transitional and Miscellaneous Provisions) Regulations 2002 (SI 2002/3019) reg.21 (April 7, 2003).

7. State Pension Credit (Decisions and Appeals—Amendments) Regulations 2003 (SI 2003/1581) reg.2 (June 18, 2003).

8. Social Security, Child Support and Tax Credits (Decisions and Appeals) Regulations 2004 (SI 2004/3368) reg.2(9) (December 21, 2004).

9. Employment and Support Allowance (Consequential Provisions) (No.2) Regulations 2008 (SI 2008/1554) regs 29 and 42 (July 27, 2008).

10. Welfare Reform Act 2009 (Section 26) (Consequential Amendments) Regulations 2010 (SI 2010/424) reg.4(1) and (6) (March 22, 2010).

11. Social Security (Loss of Benefit) Amendment Regulations 2010 (SI 2010/1160) reg.3(1) and (5) (April 1, 2010).

12. Social Security (Payment on Account of Benefit) Regulations 2013 (SI 2013/383) reg.21 (April 1, 2013, subject to a saving in respect of interim payments paid under the 1988 Regulations).

13. Pensions Act 2014 (Abolition of Contracting-out for Salary Related Pension Schemes) (Consequential Amendments and Savings) Order 2016 (SI 2016/200) art.15 (April 6, 2016).

DEFINITIONS

"the Administration Act"—see s.84 of the Social Security Act 1998.
"the Claims and Payments Regulations"—see reg.1(3).
"the Contributions and Benefits Act"—see s.84 of the Social Security Act 1998.
"decision"—see reg.27(2).
"the Jobseeker's Allowance Regulations"—see reg.1(3).
"relevant benefit"—see s.39(1) of the Social Security Act 1998.
"state pension credit"—see reg.1(3).
"work-focused interview"—*ibid.*

GENERAL NOTE

Before December 21, 2004, para.5(a)–(e) had the effect that decisions under regs **2.597**
4, 4A, 4D and 6 of the Social Security (Claims and Payments) Regulations 1987 as to whether a claim had been properly made were unappealable and that was also the effect of the original form of para.5 that was replaced from May 20, 2002. Now the only decisions under those regulations that are not appealable are decisions as to which of two partners should make claims where the partners do not agree.

If reg.27 is made under s.12(2) of the Social Security Act 1998, it is arguable that much of Sch.2 to the Regulations is ultra vires, having regard to s.12(3). It is not easy to see why, for instance, a decision of the Secretary of State that an educational establishment be recognised for the purposes of child benefit or to recognise education provided otherwise than at such a recognised establishment (paras 1 and 2 of Sch.2) is not a decision "that relates to the conditions of entitlement" to child benefit, as indeed it may be in child support cases as opposed to child benefit cases (*CF v CMEC (CSM)* [2010] UKUT 39 (AAC)). The fact that a large element of discretion is involved is not material. There is no reason in principle why such a discretion should not be exercised by a tribunal. There may be sound reasons for restricting the rights of appeal in cases where there is a large element of pure discretion (see *TD v SSWP (CSM)* [2013] UKUT 282 (AAC); [2014] AACR 7, holding that judicial review provided an adequate remedy in such cases) and, of course, there was no right of appeal under the old legislation, but it is arguable that neither of those considerations carries much weight against the clear language of s.12(3). On the other hand, it is arguable that reg.27 is made under para.9 of Sch.2 to the Act, which is in much broader terms than s.12. Both regulation-making powers are to be found in Sch.1 to the Regulations. What the point is in having s.12(2) qualified by s.12(3) when there is the broader unqualified power in the same Act is unclear but an argument that a broad power should be regarded as qualified by the scope of the narrower power found little sympathy in *R. v Secretary of State for Social Security, Ex p. Moore, The Times*, March 9, 1993 (but see now *R. (BAPIO Action Ltd) v Secretary of State for the Home Department* [2008] UKHL 27; [2008] 1 A.C. 1003).

The question of the validity of this Schedule has been considered in four Commissioners' decisions without any very clear resolution of these issues. In the first two cases, the Schedule was held to be valid as far as it affected the individual cases, but different grounds were given. In *CJSA/69/2001*, the Commissioner considered that this Schedule was made under s.12(2) of the 1998 Act but held that para.5 was intra vires insofar as it then prohibited any appeal against a decision by the Secretary of State under reg.4 of the Social Security (Claims and Payments) Regulations 1987 that a claim was to be treated as not made until the claimant provided his P45. He pointed out that s.12(3) applies only in respect of a benefit for which a claim has been validly made. However, he declined to determine whether or not the claim *had* been validly made, accepting the submission of the Secretary of State that a right of appeal could arise only after the Secretary of State had decided that a claim had been validly made and that it was beyond the power of a tribunal to consider whether the condition of reg.4(1B)(b) of the 1987 Regulations (or reg.4(1B)(d) which might have been more relevant) was met. It is suggested that an alternative construction of s.12(3) would be that it is necessary for there to be a right of appeal against any decision as to whether or not a claim was valid. *CF/3565/2001*, decided a few days later by a different Commissioner who was apparently unaware of the approach taken in *CJSA/69/2001*, concerned a decision of the Secretary of State not to recognise education provided otherwise than at a recognised educational establishment, which the Commissioner held to fall within para.2 of this Schedule. The Commissioner held that this Schedule was validly made under s.12(1)(a) of, and para.9 of Sch.2 to, the 1998 Act. In fact, as was noted in *CJSA/69/2001*, s.12(1) is not listed in Sch.1 to the Regulations as being a power under which the Regulations were made, doubtless because it does not independently confer any power to make regulations. Curiously, the Commissioner in *CJSA/69/2001* stated that Sch.3 was also not listed in Sch.1 to the Regulations when it is, although it is not clear why the Commissioner mentioned it at all as it is irrelevant. Even more curiously, he did not mention para.9 of Sch.2, which *does* confer the relevant power to make regulations relied upon in *CF/3565/2001* and is also listed in Sch.1 to the Regulations. Equally, the Commissioner deciding *CF/3565/2001* did not consider the argument that the Schedule might have been made under s.12(2) of the 1998 Act. He did however reject a broader argument that the Schedule was ultra vires because it was inconsistent with the European Convention on Human Rights. He held, applying *R. (Alconbury Developments Ltd) v Secretary of State for the Environment,*

Transport and the Regions [2001] UKHL 23; [2001] [2003] 2 A.C. 295, that judicial review was an adequate remedy in the case before him, although he left open the question whether the Schedule would be ultra vires for the purposes of other cases.

In *R(IS) 6/04*, the Commissioner again had a challenge to para.5 in its first form and the question was whether an appeal lay against the Secretary of State's decision that the claimant had not complied with the prescribed requirements for making a valid claim. The Commissioner considered it unnecessary to say how the regulation-making power in para.9 of Sch.2 to the Act should be construed or whether para.5 of Sch.2 to the Regulations had been made under that power because he agreed with the construction of s.12 applied in *CJSA/69/2001* so that, even applying the approach more favourable to the claimant, he considered that para.5 was validly made when the Regulations first came into force. However, he held the absence of a right of appeal to be incompatible with art.6 of the European Convention on Human Rights and so disapplied the paragraph insofar as it was necessary to do so to ensure that a claimant was entitled to appeal against a decision as to whether or when a claim had been validly made in accordance with the prescribed requirements. This restored the position to what it had been before the Social Security Act 1998 had come into force (*R(U) 9/60*). The Secretary of State withdrew an appeal to the Court of Appeal and subsequently amended para.5(a) in order to provide a right of appeal against a decision that a claim had not been validly made. It does not necessarily follow, however, that he accepted that the Commissioner's decision as to the application of art.6 of the Convention was correct. Indeed, in *R(H)3/05*, leading counsel for one of the claimants acknowledged that the reasoning in *R(IS)6/04* had been overtaken by that in *Runa Begum v Tower Hamlets London (First Secretary of State intervening)* [2003] UKHL 5; [2003] 2 A.C. 430 in which it was held by the House of Lords that there was no breach of art.6 of the Convention where an appeal from a local authority's decision in respect of their duties to homeless people lay only on a point of law. One possible inference to be drawn from the House of Lords' decision is that judicial review of the unappealable decisions listed in Sch.2 of these Regulations, or the similar provisions relating to housing benefit and council tax benefit in issue in *R(H)3/05*, is an adequate remedy under the Convention. However, counsel submitted that the House of Lords' conclusion in *Runa Begum*, that there was no unfairness in not having an appeal on a point of fact, was reached against the background of a system of internal review by a different officer of appropriate seniority, whereas, in housing benefit and council tax cases, such system of internal review as there had formerly been had been replaced by an appeal to a tribunal, which is the procedure available in other social security cases. In the absence of as sophisticated a system of review as there was in *Runa Begum*, he argued, there had to be a right of appeal on questions of fact. It was unnecessary for the Tribunal of Commissioners to express a view on that argument and they did not do so. Now that judicial review has adapted so as to be able to include a review of the merits of a decision as well as its legality, where that is required (see *Secretary of State for the Home Department v MB* [2006] EWCA Civ 1140; [2007] Q.B. 415), arguments that it does not provide an adequate remedy for the purposes of the Convention are more difficult to run and they may have become even more so now that is has become possible for judicial review cases to be transferred to the Upper Tribunal (see the note to s.15 of the Tribunals, Courts and Enforcement Act 2007). See, on the other hand, *ZM and AB v HMRC (TC)* [2013] UKUT 547 (AAC); [2014] AACR 17 in which the Upper Tribunal drew a distinction between issues of fact, in respect of which it was held that an appeal did lie under a similar provision in the Tax Credits Act 2002 because judicial review would not in practice be an adequate remedy, and issues of discretion, in which it was held that judicial review was as effective a remedy and an appeal did not lie. In *CI v HMRC (TC)* [2014] UKUT 158 (AAC), the Upper Tribunal declined to draw such a distinction on the ground that it was "over-technical" but, on this approach, much of Sch.2 to the 1999 Regulations would be inconsistent with art.6 of the European Convention on Human Rights and it is suggested that the more subtle approach in *ZM and AB*, 2.598

which is consistent with *SSWP v AK (CA)* [2014] UKUT 415 (AAC), is to be preferred.

The fourth case in which an ultra vires challenge to Sch.2 was raised is *Campbell v Secretary of State for Work and Pensions* [2005] EWCA Civ 989, where the Court of Appeal agreed with a Tribunal of Commissioners that a decision under the Convention on Social Security between Great Britain and Jamaica was a decision on payability rather than entitlement, because the convention was given force by the Social Security (Jamaica) Order 1997 which was made under s.179 of the Social Security Administration Act 1992. Section 12(3) of the Social Security Act 1998 therefore did not come into play and the decision was unappealable by virtue of para.22 of Sch.2 to the Regulations, read with para.9 of Sch.2 to the Act.

In this Schedule, "decision" includes determinations embodied in or necessary to a decision (see reg.27(2)).

2.599 **Schedule 3.** *Revoked.*

[1SCHEDULE 3A **Regulation 7(1)(a)**

DATE FROM WHICH SUPERSEDING DECISION TAKES EFFECT WHERE A CLAIMANT IS IN RECEIPT OF INCOME SUPPORT OR JOBSEEKER'S ALLOWANCE.

Income Support

2.600 **1.** Subject to paragraphs 2 to 6, where the amount of income support payable under an award is changed by a superseding decision made on the ground of a change of circumstances, that superseding decision shall take effect—

(a) where income support is paid in arrears, from the first day of the benefit week in which the relevant change of circumstances occurs or is expected to occur; or

(b) where income support is paid in advance, from the date of the relevant change of circumstances, or the day on which the relevant change of circumstances is expected to occur, if either of those days is the first day of the benefit week and otherwise from the next following such day, and

for the purposes of this paragraph any period of residence in temporary accommodation under arrangements for training made under section 2 of the Employment and Training Act 1973 or section 2 of the Enterprise and New Towns (Scotland) Act 1990 for a period which is expected to last for seven days or less shall not be regarded as a change of circumstances.

2. In the cases set out in paragraph 3, the superseding decision shall take effect from the day on which the relevant change of circumstances occurs or is expected to occur.

3. The cases referred to in paragraph 2 are where—

(a) income support is paid in arrears and entitlement ends, or is expected to end, for a reason other than that the claimant no longer satisfies the provisions of section 124(1)(b) of the Contributions and Benefits Act;

[2(aa) income support is being paid from 8th April 2002 to persons who, immediately before that day, had a preserved right for the purposes of the Income Support Regulations;]

(b) a child or young person referred to in regulation 16(6) of the Income Support Regulations (child in care of local authority or detained in custody) lives, or is expected to live, with the claimant for part only of the benefit week;

(c) [5 . . .]

(d) a person referred to in paragraph 1, 2, 3 or 18 of Schedule 7 to the Income Support Regulations—

 (i) ceases, or is expected to cease, to be a patient; or

 (ii) a member of his family ceases, or is expected to cease, to be a patient, in either case for a period of less than a week;

(e) a person referred to in paragraph 8 of Schedule 7 to the Income Support Regulations—

 (i) ceases to be a prisoner; or

 (ii) becomes a prisoner;

(f) a person to whom section 126 of the Contributions and Benefits Act (trade disputes) applies—

(i) becomes incapable of work by reason of disease or bodily or mental disablement; or
(ii) enters the maternity period (as defined in section 126(2) of that Act) or the day is known on which that person is expected to enter the maternity period;

(g) during the currency of the claim, a claimant makes a claim for a relevant social security benefit—
(i) the result of which is that his benefit week changes; or
(ii) under regulation 13 of the Claims and Payment Regulations and an award of that benefit on the relevant day for the purposes of that regulation means that his benefit week is expected to change;

[7 (h) regulation 9 of the Social Security (Disability Living Allowance) Regulations 1991 (persons in certain accommodation other than hospitals) applies, or ceases to apply, to the claimant for a period of less than one week [8 ; or]

(i) regulations under section 86(1) (hospital in-patients) of the Welfare Reform Act 2012 apply, or cease to apply, to the claimant for a period of less than one week.]

4. A superseding decision made in consequence of a payment of income being treated as paid on a particular day under regulation 31(1)(b) [4 (2) or (3)] or 39C(3) of the Income Support Regulations (date on which income is treated as paid) shall take effect from the day on which that payment is treated as paid.

5. Where—
(a) it is decided upon supersession on the ground of a relevant change of circumstances [5 or change specified in paragraph 12 and 13] that the amount of income support is, or is to be, reduced; and
(b) the Secretary of State certifies that it is impracticable for a superseding decision to take effect from the day prescribed in the preceding paragraphs of this Schedule (other than where paragraph 3(g) or 4 applies),

that superseding decision shall take effect—
(i) where the relevant change has occurred, from the first day of the benefit week following that in which that superseding decision is made; or
(ii) where the relevant change is expected to occur, from the first day of the benefit week following that in which that change of circumstances is expected to occur.

6. Where—
(a) a superseding decision ("the former supersession") was made on the ground of a relevant change of circumstances in the cases set out in paragraphs 3(b) to (g); and
(b) that superseding decision is itself superseded by a subsequent decision because the circumstances which gave rise to the former supersession cease to apply ("the second change"),

that subsequent decision shall take effect from the date of the second change.

Jobseeker's Allowance

7. Subject to paragraphs 8 to 11, where a decision in respect of a claim for jobseeker's allowance is superseded on the ground that there has been or there is expected to be, a relevant change of circumstances, the supersession shall take effect from the first day of the benefit week (as defined in regulation 1(3) of the Jobseeker's Allowance Regulations) in which that relevant change of circumstances occurs or is expected to occur. **2.601**

8. Where the relevant change of circumstances giving rise to the supersession is that—
(a) entitlement to jobseeker's allowance ends, or is expected to end, for a reason other than that the claimant no longer satisfies the provisions of section 3(1)(a) [2 or 3A(1)(a)] of the Jobseekers Act; or

[3 (aa) jobseeker's allowance is being paid from 8th April 2002 to persons who, immediately before that day, had a preserved right for the purposes of the Jobseeker's Allowance Regulations;]

(b) a child or young person who is normally in the care of a local authority or who is detained in custody lives, or is expected to live, with the claimant for a part only of the benefit week; or
(c) [5 . . .]
(d) the partner of the claimant or a member of his family ceases, or is expected to cease, to be a hospital in-patient for a period of less than a week; [2 or,
(e) a joint-claim couple ceases to be [6 couple]],

the supersession shall take effect from the date that the relevant change of circumstances occurs or is expected to occur.

9. Where the relevant change of circumstances giving rise to a supersession is any of those specified in paragraph 8, and, in consequences of those circumstances ceasing to apply, a further superseding decision is made, that further superseding decision shall take effect from the date that those circumstances ceased to apply.

10. Where, under the provisions of regulation 96 or 102C(3) of the Jobseeker's Allowance Regulations, income is treated as paid on a certain date and that payment gives rise, or is expected to give rise, to a relevant change of circumstance resulting in a supersession, that supersession shall take effect from that date.

11. Where a relevant change of circumstances [5 or change specified in paragraphs 12 and 13] occurs which results, or is expected to result, in a reduced award of jobseeker's allowance then, if the Secretary of State is of the opinion that it is impracticable for a supersession to take effect in accordance with [5 paragraph 12 or] the preceding paragraphs of this Schedule, the supersession shall take effect from the first day of the benefit week following that in which the relevant change of circumstances occurs.]

[5*Changes other than changes of circumstances*

2.602 **12.** Where an amount of income support or jobseeker's allowance payable under an award is changed by a superseding decision specified in paragraph 13 the superseding decision shall take effect—

(a) in the case of a change in respect of income support, from the day specified in paragraph 1(a) or (b) for a change of circumstances; and

(b) in the case of a change in respect of jobseeker's allowance, from the day specified in paragraph 7 for a change of circumstances.

13. The following are superseding decisions for the purposes of paragraph 12—

(a) a decision which supersedes a decision specified in regulation 6(2)(b) to (ee); and

(b) a superseding decision which would, but for paragraph 12, take effect from a date specified in regulation 7(5) to (7), (12) to (16), (18) to (20), (22), (24) and (33).]

AMENDMENTS

1. Social Security and Child Support (Miscellaneous Amendments) Regulations 2000 (SI 2000/1596) reg.35 (June 19, 2000).

2. Social Security Amendment (Joint Claim) Regulations 2001 (SI 2001/518) reg.4(c) (March 19, 2001).

3. Social Security Amendment (Residential Care and Nursing Homes) Regulations 2002 (SI 2002/398) reg.3 (April 8, 2002).

4. Social Security (Working Tax Credit and Child Tax Credit) (Consequential Amendments) (No.3) Regulations 2003 (SI 2003/1731) reg.5 (August 8, 2003).

5. Social Security, Child Support and Tax Credits (Miscellaneous Amendments) Regulations 2005 (SI 2005/337) reg.2(21) (March 19, 2005).

6. Civil Partnership (Consequential Amendments) Regulations 2005 (SI 2005/2878) reg.8(4) (December 5, 2005).

7. Social Security (Miscellaneous Amendments) (No. 3) Regulations 2006 (SI 2006/2377) reg.3(3) (October 2, 2006).

8. Personal Independence Payment (Supplementary Provisions and Consequential Amendments) Regulations 2013 (SI 2013/388) reg.8 and Sch. para.21 (April 8, 2013).

DEFINITIONS

"the Claims and Payments Regulations"—see reg.1(3).
"the Contributions and Benefits Act"—see s.84 of the Social Security Act 1998.
"the Income Support Regulations"—see reg.1(3).
"the Jobseekers Act"—see s.84 of the Social Security Act 1998.
"the Jobseeker's Allowance Regulations"—see reg.1(3).
"a joint-claim couple"—*ibid.*
"superseding decision"—see para.13.

GENERAL NOTE

2.603 Paragraphs 12 and 13 have the effect that any change to an existing award of income support or jobseeker's allowance takes place from the start of a benefit week. However, this does not apply where a change of circumstances is favourable to a claimant or is due to a change of legislation, because in such cases reg.7(2)(b) or (bb) or (30) takes precedence over this Schedule (see reg.7(1)(a)). This Schedule takes precedence over all other paragraphs of reg.7.

[1 SCHEDULE 3B

Date on Which Change of Circumstances Takes Effect Where Claimant Entitled to State Pension Credit

1. Where the amount of state pension credit payable under an award is changed by a superseding decision made on the ground that there has been a relevant change of circumstances, that superseding decision shall take effect from the following days— **2.604**

(a) for the purpose only of determining the day on which an assessed income period begins under section 9 of the State Pension Credit Act, from the day following the day on which the last previous assessed income period ended; and

(b) [6 except as provided in the following paragraphs–

(i) where state pension credit is paid in advance, from the day that change occurs or is expected to occur if either of those days is the first day of a benefit week but if it is not from the next following such day;

(ii) where state pension credit is paid in arrears, from the first day of the benefit week in which that change occurs or is expected to occur.]

[7 **2.** Subject to paragraph 3, where the relevant change is that—

(a) the claimant's income or the income of the claimant's partner (other than deemed income from capital) has changed;

(b) the claimant or the claimant's partner becomes entitled to—

(i) disability living allowance (middle or higher rate care component); or

(ii) attendance allowance; [8 . . .]

[8 (iii) personal independence payment (standard or enhanced rate daily living component under section 78 of the Welfare Reform Act 2012); or]

[9 (iv) armed forces independence payment under the Armed Forces and Resrve Forces (Compensation Scheme) Order 2011; or]

(c) the claimant or the claimant's partner again receives [8 any of the allowances or payments] mentioned in sub-paragraph (b) above immediately after the end of the period specified in paragraph 2A,

the superseding decision shall take effect on the first day of the benefit week in which that change occurs or if that is not practicable in the circumstances of the case, on the first day of the next following benefit week.

2A. A period specified for the purposes of paragraph 2 is a period when the claimant or the claimant's partner is maintained free of charge while undergoing medical or other treatment as an in-patient in—

(a) a hospital or similar institution under—

(i) the National Health Service 2006;

(ii) the National Health Service (Wales) Act 2006; or

(iii) the National Health Service (Scotland) Act 1978; or

(b) a hospital or similar institution maintained or administered by the Defence Council.]

3. Paragraph 2 shall not apply where the only relevant change is that working tax credit under the Tax Credits Act 2002 becomes payable or becomes payable at a higher rate.

4. A superseding decision shall take effect from the day the change of circumstances occurs or is expected to occur if—

(a) the person ceases to be or becomes a prisoner, and for this purpose "prisoner" has the same meaning as in regulation 1(2) of the State Pension Credit Regulations; or

(b) whilst entitled to state pension credit a claimant is awarded another social security benefit and in consequence of that award his benefit week changes or is expected to change.

[2 **5.** In a case where the relevant circumstance is that the claimant ceased to be a patient, if he becomes a patient again in the same benefit week, the superseding decision in respect of ceasing to be a patient shall take effect from the first day of the week in which the change occured.]

6. In paragraph 5, "patient" means a person (other than a prisoner) who is regarded as receiving free in-patient treatment within the meaning of the [4 Social Security (Hospital In-Patients) Regulations 2005.]

[3 **7.** [5 Subject to [6 paragraph 8A], where] an amount of state pension credit payable under an award is changed by a superseding decision specified in paragraph 8 the superseding decision shall take effect from the day specified in paragraph 1(b).

8. The following are superseding decisions for the purposes of paragraph 7—

(a) a decision which supersedes a decision specified in regulation 6(2)(b) to (ee) and (m); and

(b) a superseding decision which would, but for paragraphs 2 and 7, take effect from a date specified in regulation 7(5) to (7), (12) to (16) and (29C).]

[6 **8A.** Where the relevant change of circumstances is the death of the claimant, the superseding decision shall take effect on the first day of the benefit week next following the date of death.]

[5 **9.** [6 . . .]

10. [6 . . .]

11. In this Schedule, "benefit week" means—

(a) where state pension credit is paid in advance, the period of 7 days beginning on the day on which, in the claimant's case, that benefit is payable;

(b) where state pension credit is paid in arrears, the period of 7 days ending on the day on which, in the claimant's case, that benefit is payable.]

Amendments

1. State Pension Credit (Consequential, Transitional and Miscellaneous Provisions) Regulations 2002 (SI 2002/3019) reg.22 (April 7, 2003).
2. State Pension Credit (Transitional and Miscellaneous Provisions) Amendment Regulations 2003 (SI 2003/2274) reg.5(4) (October 6, 2003).
3. Social Security (Miscellaneous Amendments) (No.2) Regulations 2006 (SI 2006/832) reg.5(4) (April 10, 2006).
4. Social Security (Miscellaneous Amendments) (No.4) Regulations 2007 (SI 2007/2470) reg.3(9) (September 24, 2007).
5. Social Security (Miscellaneous Amendments) Regulations 2010 (SI 2010/510) reg.4(1) and (4) (March 4, 2010).
6. Social Security (Miscellaneous Amendments) Regulations 2011 (SI 2011/674) reg.8 (April 11, 2011).
7. Social Security (Miscellaneous Amendments) Regulations 2013 (SI 2013/443) reg.5(a) and (c) (April 2, 2013).
8. Social Security (Miscellaneous Amendments) Regulations 2013 (SI 2013/443) reg.5(b) (April 8, 2013).
9. Armed Forces and Reserve Forces Compensation Scheme (Consequential Provisions: Subordinate Legislation) Order 2013 (SI 2013/591) art.7 and Sch. para.15 (April 8, 2013).

Definitions

"assessed income period"—see reg.1(3).
"benefit week"–see para.(11).
"patient"—see para.6.
"state pension credit"—see reg.1(3).
"State Pension Credit Act"—*ibid.*
"State Pension Credit Regulations"—*ibid.*

General Note

2.605 This Schedule takes precedence over reg.7, except where reg.7(2)(b) or (bb), (29) or (30) applies (see reg.7(1)(a)). The misspelling of what should read as "occurred" in para.5 occurs in the Queen's Printer's copy of the statutory instrument.

[1 SCHEDULE 3C

Date From Which Change of Circumstances Takes Effect Where Claimant Entitled to Employment and Support Allowance

1. Subject to paragraphs 2 to 7, where the amount of an employment and support allowance payable under an award is changed by a superseding decision made on the ground of a change of circumstances, that superseding decision shall take effect from the first day of the benefit week in which the relevant change of circumstances occurs or is expected to occur. **2.606**

2. In the cases set out in paragraph 3, the superseding decision shall take effect from the day on which the relevant change of circumstances occurs or is expected to occur.

3. The cases referred to in paragraph 2 are where—

(a) entitlement ends, or is expected to end, for a reason other than that the claimant no longer satisfies the provisions of paragraph 6(1)(a) of Schedule 1 to the Welfare Reform Act;

(b) a child or young person referred to in regulation 156(6)(d) or (h) of the Employment and Support Allowance Regulations (child in care of local authority or detained in custody) lives, or is expected to live, with the claimant for part only of the benefit week;

(c) a person referred to in paragraph 12 of Schedule 5 to the Employment and Support Allowance Regulations—

(i) ceases, or is expected to cease, to be a patient; or

(ii) a member of the person's family ceases, or is expected to cease, to be a patient, in either case for a period of less than a week;

(d) a person referred to in paragraph 3 of Schedule 5 to the Employment and Support Allowance Regulations—

(i) ceases to be a prisoner; or

(ii) becomes a prisoner;

(e) during the currency of the claim a claimant makes a claim for a relevant social security benefit—

(i) the result of which is that his benefit week changes; or

(ii) in accordance with regulation 13 of the Claims and Payments Regulations and an award of that benefit on the relevant day for the purposes of that regulation means that his benefit week is expected to change.

[2 (f) regulation 9 of the Social Security (Disability Living Allowance) Regulations 1991 (persons in care homes) applies, or ceases to apply, to the claimant for a period of less than one week; or

(g) regulations under section 85(1) of the Welfare Reform Act 2012 (care home residents) apply, or cease to apply, to the claimant for a period of less than one week.]

4. A superseding decision made in consequence of a payment of income being treated as paid on a particular day under regulation 93 of the Employment and Support Allowance Regulations (date on which income is treated as paid) shall take effect from the day on which that payment is treated as paid.

5. Where—

(a) it is decided upon supersession on the ground of a relevant change of circumstances or change specified in paragraphs 9 and 10 that the amount of an employment and support allowance is, or is to be, reduced; and

(b) the Secretary of State certifies that it is impracticable for a superseding decision to take effect from the day prescribed in paragraph 9 or the preceding paragraphs of this Schedule (other than where paragraph 3(e) or 4 applies),

that superseding decision shall take effect—

(i) where the relevant change has occurred, from the first day of the benefit week following that in which that superseding decision is made; or

(ii) where the relevant change is expected to occur, from the first day of the benefit week following that in which that change of circumstances is expected to occur.

6. Where—

(a) a superseding decision ("the former supersession") was made on the ground of a relevant change of circumstances in the cases set out in paragraph 3(b) to (e); and

(b) that superseding decision is itself superseded by a subsequent decision because the circumstances which gave rise to the former supersession cease to apply ("the second change"), that subsequent decision shall take effect from the date of the second change.

7. In the case of an employment and support allowance decision where there has been a limited capability for work determination, where—

(a) the Secretary of State is satisfied that, in relation to a limited capability for work determination, the claimant or payee failed to notify an appropriate office of a change of circumstances which regulations under the Administration Act required him to notify; and

(b) the claimant or payee, as the case may be, could reasonably have been expected to know that the change of circumstances should have been notified,

the superseding decision shall take effect—

(i) from the date on which the claimant or payee, as the case may be, ought to have notified the change of circumstances; or

(ii) if more than one change has taken place between the date from which the decision to be superseded took effect and the date of the superseding decision, from the date on which the first change ought to have been notified.

Changes other than changes of circumstances

8. Where—

(a) the Secretary of State supersedes a decision made by an appeal tribunal or a Commissioner on the grounds specified in regulation 6(2)(c)(i) (ignorance of, or mistake as to, a material fact);

(b) the decision to be superseded was more advantageous to the claimant because of the ignorance or mistake than it would otherwise have been; and

(c) the material fact—

(i) does not relate to the limited capability for work determination embodied in or necessary to the decision; or

(ii) relates to a limited capability for work determination embodied in or necessary to the decision and the Secretary of State is satisfied that at the time the decision was made the claimant or payee, as the case may be, knew or could reasonably have been expected to know of it and that it was relevant,

the superseding decision shall take effect from the first day of the benefit week in which the decision of the appeal tribunal or the Commissioner took effect or was to take effect.

9. Where an amount of an employment and support allowance payable under an award is changed by a superseding decision specified in paragraph 10 the superseding decision shall take effect from the day specified in paragraph 1 for a change of circumstances.

10. The following are superseding decisions for the purposes of paragraph 9—

(a) a decision which supersedes a decision specified in regulation 6(2)(b) and (d) to (ee); and

(b) a superseding decision which would, but for paragraph 9, take effect from a date specified in regulation 7(6), (7), (12), (13), (17D) to (17F), and (33).]

AMENDMENTS

1. Employment and Support Allowance (Consequential Provisions) (No.2) Regulations 2008 (SI 2008/1554) regs 29 and 43 (July 27, 2008).

2. Social Security (Miscellaneous Amendments) (No.3) Regulations 2013 (SI 2013/2536) reg.8 (October 29, 2013).

2.607 Schedules 3D and **4.** *Omitted.*

The Universal Credit, Personal Independence Payment, Jobseeker's Allowance and Employment and Support Allowance (Decisions and Appeals) Regulations 2013

(SI 2013/381)

Made *25th February 2013*

Coming into force in accordance with Regulation 1

CONTENTS

PART 1

GENERAL

PART 2

REVISION

CHAPTER 1

REVISION ON ANY GROUND

CHAPTER 2

REVISION ON SPECIFIC GROUNDS

CHAPTER 3

PROCEDURE AND EFFECTIVE DATE

PART 3

SUPERSESSIONS

CHAPTER 1

GROUNDS FOR SUPERSESSION

CHAPTER 2

SUPERSEDING DECISIONS: LIMITATIONS AND PROCEDURE

CHAPTER 3

EFFECTIVE DATES FOR SUPERSESSIONS

PART 4

OTHER MATTERS REALTING TO DECISION-MAKING

PART 5

SUSPENSION

PART 6

TERMINATION

PART 7

APPEALS

SCHEDULES

The Secretary of State makes the following Regulations in exercise of the powers conferred by sections:
– 5(1A), 159D(1) and (6), 189(1), (4) to (6) and section 191 of the Social Security Administration Act 1992;
– 9(1), (4) and (6), 10(3) and (6), 10A, 11(1), 12(2), (3), (3A), (3B), (6) and (7)(b), 16(1), 17, 18(1), 21(1) to (3), 22 and 23, 25(3)(b) and (5)(c), 26(6)(c), 28(1), 31(2), 79(1) and (4) to (7) and 84 of, and paragraph 9 of Schedule 2, paragraphs 1, 4 and 9 of Schedule 3 and Schedule 5 to, the Social Security Act 1998.
A draft of this instrument was laid before and approved by a resolution of each House of Parliament in accordance with section 80(1) of the Social Security Act 1998.
The Social Security Advisory Committee has agreed that the proposals in respect of these Regulations should not be referred to it.

PART 1

GENERAL

Citation, commencement and application

2.609 **1.**—(1) These Regulations may be cited as the Universal Credit, Personal Independence Payment, Jobseeker's Allowance and Employment and Support Allowance (Decisions and Appeals) Regulations 2013.

(2) They come into force—

(a) in so far as they relate to personal independence payment and for the purposes of this regulation, on 8th April 2013;

(b) for all remaining purposes, on 29th April 2013.

(3) These Regulations apply in relation to—

(a) an employment and support allowance payable under Part 1 of the 2007 Act as amended by Schedule 3 and Part 1 of Schedule 14 to the 2012 Act (to remove references to an income-related allowance);

(b) a jobseeker's allowance payable under the Jobseekers Act as amended by Part 1 of Schedule 14 to the 2012 Act (to remove references to an income-based allowance);

(c) personal independence payment; and

(d) universal credit.

DEFINITIONS

"the 2007 Act"–see reg.2.
"the 2012 Act"–see reg.2.
"the Jobseekers Act"–see reg.2.
"personal independence payment"–see reg.2.
"universal credit"–see reg.2.

GENERAL NOTE

2.610 These Regulations are similar to the Social Security and Child Benefit (Decisions and Appeals) Regulations 1999 but it has been decided to have these separate Regulations for the "working age" benefits introduced by the Welfare Reform Act 2012, including the "new style" contributory employment and support allowance and jobseeker's allowance, rather than further complicate those Regulations and the opportunity has been taken to simplify the drafting and divide up some of the longer provisions.

Interpretation

2.611 **2.** In these Regulations—

"the 1998 Act" means the Social Security Act 1998;

"the 2007 Act" means the Welfare Reform Act 2007;

"the 2012 Act" means the Welfare Reform Act 2012;

"the Administration Act" means the Social Security Administration Act 1992;

"appeal", except where the context otherwise requires, means an appeal to the First-tier Tribunal established under the Tribunals, Courts and Enforcement Act 2007;

"appropriate office" means—

(a) in the case of a contributions decision which falls within Part 2 (contributions decisions) of Schedule 3 (decisions against which an appeal lies) to the 1998 Act, any National Insurance Contributions office of HMRC or any office of the Department for Work and Pensions; or
(b) in any other case, the office of the Department for Work and Pensions, or other place, the address of which is specified on the notification of the original decision referred to in regulation 5(1) (revision on any grounds);

"assessment period" is to be construed in accordance with regulation 21 (assessment periods) of the Universal Credit Regulations;

"benefit" means a benefit or an allowance in relation to which these Regulations apply;

"benefit week" has the same meaning as in—
(a) regulation 2 (interpretation) of the Employment and Support Allowance Regulations 2013 in the case of an employment and support allowance;
(b) regulation 2 (general interpretation) of the Jobseeker's Allowance Regulations 2013, in the case of a jobseeker's allowance;

"child" means a person under the age of 16;

"claimant" means—
(a) any person who has claimed—
  (i) an employment and support allowance;
  (ii) a jobseeker's allowance;
  (iii) personal independence payment;
(b) in the case of universal credit, any person who is a claimant for the purposes of section 40 (interpretation) of the 2012 Act; and
(c) any other person from whom an amount of benefit is alleged to be recoverable;

"the Claims and Payments Regulations 2013" means the Universal Credit, Personal Independence Payment, Jobseeker's Allowance and Employment and Support Allowance (Claims and Payments) Regulations 2013;

"the Contributions and Benefits Act" means the Social Security Contributions and Benefits Act 1992;

"the date of notification", in relation to a decision of the Secretary of State, means the date on which the notification of the decision is treated as having been given or sent in accordance with—
(a) regulation 3 (service of documents); or
(b) where the notification is given or sent using an electronic communication, Schedule 2 (electronic communications) to the Claims and Payments Regulations 2013;

"designated authority" means—
(a) the Secretary of State; or
(b) a person providing services to the Secretary of State;

"electronic communication" has the same meaning as in section 15(1) of the Electronic Communications Act 2000;

"employment and support allowance" means an employment and support allowance in relation to which these Regulations apply;

"the Fraud Act" means the Social Security Fraud Act 2001;

"fraud penalty", in relation to any claimant of an employment and support allowance, a jobseeker's allowance or universal credit, means

PART 2

REVISION

CHAPTER 1

REVISION ON ANY GROUNDS

Revision on any grounds

2.616 5.—(1) Any decision of the Secretary of State under section 8 or 10 of the 1998 Act ("the original decision") may be revised by the Secretary of State if—

(a) the Secretary of State commences action leading to the revision within one month of the date of notification of the original decision; or

(b) an application for a revision is received by the Secretary of State at an appropriate office within—

(i) one month of the date of notification of the original decision (but subject to regulation 38(4)(correction of accidental errors));

(ii) 14 days of the expiry of that period if a written statement of the reasons for the decision is requested under regulation 7 (consideration of revision before appeal) or regulation 51 (notice of a decision against which an appeal lies) and that statement is provided within the period specified in paragraph (i);

(iii) 14 days of the date on which that statement was provided if the statement was requested within the period specified in paragraph (i) but was provided after the expiry of that period; or

(iv) such longer period as may be allowed under regulation 6 (late application for a revision).

(2) Paragraph (1) does not apply—

(a) in respect of a relevant change of circumstances which occurred since the decision had effect or, in the case of an advance award under regulation 32, 33 or 34 of the Claims and Payments Regulations 2013, since the decision was made;

(b) where the Secretary of State has evidence or information which indicates that a relevant change of circumstances will occur;

(c) in respect of a decision which relates to an employment and support allowance or personal independence payment where the claimant is terminally ill, unless the application for a revision contains an express statement that the claimant is terminally ill.

DEFINITIONS

"the 1998 Act"–see reg.2.
"appeal"–see reg.2.
"appropriate office"–see reg.2.
"claimant"–see reg.2.

"the Claims and Payments Regulations 2013"–see reg.2.
"the date of notification"–see reg.2.
"employment and support allowance"–by virtue of reg.2, see reg.1(3)(a).
"personal independence payment"–see reg.2.
"terminally ill"–see reg.2.

GENERAL NOTE

This regulation is equivalent to reg.3(1) and (9) of the Social Security and Child Support (Decisions and Appeals) Regulations 1999. See the notes to those provisions. The broad power of revision is conferred by s.9 of the Social Security Act 1998 and this regulation is made in exercise of the regulation-making powers conferred by that section. The power of revise on an application made under para. (1)(b) is likely to become more significant in the light of reg.7, which will require claimants to apply for a revision before exercising their right to appeal. 2.617

Late application for a revision

6.—(1) The Secretary of State may extend the time limit specified in regulation 5(1) (revision on any grounds) for making an application for a revision if all of the following conditions are met. 2.618

(2) The first condition is that the person wishing to apply for the revision has applied to the Secretary of State at an appropriate office for an extension of time.

(3) The second condition is that the application—

(a) explains why the extension is sought;
(b) contains sufficient details of the decision to which the application relates to enable it to be identified; and
(c) is made within 13 months of the latest date by which the application for revision should have been received by the Secretary of State in accordance with regulation 5(1)(b)(i) to (iii).

(4) The third condition is that the Secretary of State is satisfied that it is reasonable to grant the extension.

(5) The fourth condition is that the Secretary of State is satisfied that due to special circumstances it was not practicable for the application for revision to be made within the time limit specified in regulation 5(1)(b)(i) to (iii) (revision on any grounds).

(6) In determining whether it is reasonable to grant an extension of time, the Secretary of State must have regard to the principle that the greater the amount of time that has elapsed between the end of the time limit specified in regulation 5(1)(b)(i) to (iii) (revision on any grounds) and the date of the application, the more compelling should be the special circumstances on which the application is based.

(7) An application under this regulation which has been refused may not be renewed.

DEFINITION

"appropriate office"–see reg.2.

GENERAL NOTE

This regulation is equivalent to reg.4 of the Social Security and Child Support (Decisions and Appeals) Regulations 1999, save that it does not reproduce reg.4(6) 2.619

which is an unsatisfactory provision restricting the power to extend time. See the note to reg.4(1) of the 1999 Regulations.

Consideration of revision before appeal

2.620 **7.**—(1) This regulation applies in a case where—

(a) the Secretary of State gives a person written notice of a decision under section 8 or 10 of the 1998 Act (whether as originally made or as revised under section 9 of that Act); and

(b) that notice includes a statement to the effect that there is a right of appeal in relation to the decision only if the Secretary of State has considered an application for a revision of the decision.

(2) In a case to which this regulation applies, a person has a right of appeal under section 12(2) of the 1998 Act in relation to the decision only if the Secretary of State has considered on an application whether to revise the decision under section 9 of that Act.

(3) The notice referred to in paragraph (1) must inform the person—

(a) of the time limit under regulation 5(1) (revision on any grounds) for making an application for a revision; and

(b) that, where the notice does not include a statement of the reasons for the decision ("written reasons"), the person may, within one month of the date of notification of the decision, request that the Secretary of State provide written reasons.

(4) Where written reasons are requested under paragraph (3)(b), the Secretary of State must provide that statement within 14 days of receipt of the request or as soon as practicable afterwards.

(5) Where, as the result of paragraph (2), there is no right of appeal against a decision, the Secretary of State may treat any purported appeal as an application for a revision under section 9 of the 1998 Act.

DEFINITIONS

"the 1998 Act"–see reg.2.
"appeal"–see reg.2.
"the date of notification"–see reg.2.

GENERAL NOTE

2.621 This regulation is equivalent to reg.3ZA of the Social Security and Child Support (Decisions and Appeals) Regulations 1999, although this provision came into effect six months earlier. See the note to that provision.

CHAPTER 2

REVISION ON SPECIFIC GROUNDS

Introduction

2.622 **8.** A decision of the Secretary of State under section 8 or 10 of the 1998 Act may be revised at any time by the Secretary of State in any of the cases and circumstances set out in this Chapter.

DEFINITION

"the 1998 Act"–see reg.2.

GENERAL NOTE

This Chapter reproduces the relevant provisions of reg.3(4A) to (8K) of the Social Security and Child Support (Decisions and Appeals) Regulations 1999 in a more digestible form. See the beginning of the note to reg.3 of the 1999 Regulations for the differences between revision and supersession, dealt with under regs 22 of 37 of these Regulations. Regulation 32 has the effect that revision takes precedence over supersession where both might otherwise be possible. **2.623**

Official error, mistake etc.

9. A decision may be revised where the decision— **2.624**
(a) arose from official error; or
(b) was made in ignorance of, or was based on a mistake as to, some material fact and as a result is more advantageous to a claimant than it would otherwise have been.

DEFINITIONS

"claimant"–see reg.2.
"official error"–see reg.2.

GENERAL NOTE

This regulation is equivalent to reg.3(5)(a) and (b) of the Social Security and Child Support (Decisions and Appeals) Regulations 1999. See the note to that reg.3(5), and also to reg.1(3) of the 1999 Regulations for the scope of "official error". However, note that the complications of reg.3(5)(c) and (d) have not been reproduced in these Regulations with the result that questions as to whether a claimant could reasonably have been expected to be aware of a material fact or that it was relevant to a decision will arise only in respect of recoverability decisions in respect of personal independence payment under s.71 of the Social Security Administration Act 1992 and will not determine whether a decision as to entitlement to personal independence payment or an employment and support allowance should be revised retrospectively rather than superseded only prospectively. **2.625**

Decisions against which no appeal lies

10. A decision may be revised where the decision is one which is— **2.626**
(a) specified in Schedule 2 (decisions against which no appeal lies) to the 1998 Act; or
(b) prescribed by regulation 50(2) (decisions which may or may not be appealed).

DEFINITIONS

"the 1998 Act"–see reg.2.
"appeal" see reg.2.

GENERAL NOTE

This regulation is equivalent to reg.3(8) of the Social Security and Child Support (Decisions and Appeals) Regulations 1999. **2.627**

Decisions where there is an appeal

2.628 **11.**—(1) A decision may be revised where there is an appeal against the decision within the time prescribed by the Tribunal Procedure Rules but the appeal has not been decided.

(2) Where—

(a) the Secretary of State makes a decision under section 8 or 10 of the 1998 Act or such a decision is revised under section 9(1) of the 1998 Act ("decision A");

(b) the claimant appeals against decision A;

(c) after the appeal has been made, but before it results in a decision by the First-tier Tribunal, the Secretary of State makes another decision ("decision B") which—

(i) supersedes decision A; or

(ii) decides a further claim by the claimant;

(d) after the making of decision B, the First-tier Tribunal makes a decision on the appeal ("decision C"); and

(e) the Secretary of State would have made decision B differently if, at the time, the Secretary of State had been aware of decision C,

the Secretary of State may revise decision B.

DEFINITIONS

"the 1998 Act"–see reg.2.
"appeal"–see reg.2.
"claimant"–see reg.2.
"the Tribunal Procedure Rules"–see reg.2.

GENERAL NOTE

2.629 This regulation is equivalent to reg.3(4A) and (5A) of the Social Security and Child Support (Decisions and Appeals) Regulations 1999. See the note to those provisions. Regulation 7 may result in fewer revisions under reg.11(1) than there might otherwise have been. However, there will still be cases where new evidence is provided during the course of appeal proceedings or where the act of responding to an appeal alerts a decision-maker to an error in the original decision that was missed on revision and so para.(1) is likely to remain useful.

Award of another benefit

2.630 **12.** Where—

(a) the Secretary of State makes a decision to award a benefit to a claimant ("the original award"); and

(b) an award of another relevant benefit or of an increase in the rate of another relevant benefit is made to the claimant or, in the case of universal credit, to a member of their family, for a period which includes the date on which the original award took effect,

the Secretary of State may revise the original award.

DEFINITIONS

"benefit"–see reg.2.
"claimant"–see reg.2.
"family"–see reg.2.
"relevant benefit"–see reg.2.
"universal credit"–see reg.2.

General Note

This regulation is equivalent to reg.3(7) of the Social Security and Child Support (Decisions and Appeals) Regulations 1999. See the note to that provision. 2.631

Advance awards etc.

13. A decision pursuant to regulation 32, 33 or 34 of the Claims and Payments Regulations 2013 to make an advance award of benefit may be revised if the conditions for entitlement are found not to have been satisfied at the start of the period for which the claim is treated as having been made. 2.632

Definitions

"benefit"–see reg.2.
"the Claims and Payments Regulations 2013"–see reg.2.

General Note

Under previous legislation, the power to revise advance awards was to be found in the provisions of the Social Security (Claims and Payments) Regulations 1987 making provision for advance claims and awards (see in particular regs 13(2) and 13A(3)) rather than in reg.3 of the Social Security and Child Support (Decisions and Appeals) Regulations 1999. See the notes to those regulations. It seems that this rule is intended to apply only to advance awards made on initial claims, because specific provision for awards made on renewal claims for personal independence payment is made in reg.18(1). 2.633

Sanctions cases etc.

14.—(1) The following decisions may be revised— 2.634

(a) a decision that the amount of an employment and support allowance is to be reduced by virtue of section 11J(1) (sanctions) of the 2007 Act;
(b) a decision that the amount of a jobseeker's allowance is to be reduced by virtue of section 6J (higher-level sanctions) or 6K(1) (other sanctions) of the Jobseekers Act;
(c) a decision that the amount of universal credit is to be reduced by virtue of section 26(1) (higher-level sanctions) or 27(1) (other sanctions) of the 2012 Act.

(2) A decision under section 6B, 7 or 9 ("the loss of benefit provisions") of the Fraud Act that benefit ceases to be payable or falls to be reduced as a result of the person—

(a) being convicted of an offence; or
(b) agreeing to pay a penalty as an alternative to prosecution,

may be revised where that conviction is quashed or set aside by a court or where the person withdraws the agreement to pay the penalty.

Definitions

"the 2007 Act"–see reg.2.
"the 2012 Act"–see reg.2.
"benefit"–see reg.2.
"employment and support allowance"–by virtue of reg.2, see reg.1(3)(a).
"the Fraud Act"–see reg.2.
"the Jobseekers Act"–see reg.2.

"jobseeker's allowance"–by virtue of reg.2, see reg.1(3)(b).
"universal credit"–see reg.2.

GENERAL NOTE

2.635 This regulation is equivalent to reg.3(6) and (8B) of the Social Security and Child Support (Decisions and Appeals) Regulations 1999.

The formatting error in the Queen's Printer's version has been corrected here.

Other decisions relating to an employment and support allowance

2.636 **15.**—(1) A decision awarding an employment and support allowance may be revised in any of the following circumstances.

(2) The first circumstance is where—

(a) the decision was made on the basis that the claimant had made and was pursuing an appeal against a decision of the Secretary of State that the claimant did not have limited capability for work ("the original decision"); and

(b) the appeal in relation to the original decision is successful.

(3) The second circumstance is where—

(a) the decision incorporates a determination that the conditions in regulation 26(2) (conditions for treating claimant as having limited capability for work until a determination about limited capability for work has been made) of the Employment and Support Allowance Regulations 2013 are satisfied;

(b) those conditions were not satisfied when the claim was made; and

(c) a decision falls to be made concerning entitlement to that award in respect of a period before the date on which the award took effect.

(4) The third circumstance is where the claimant's current period of limited capability for work is treated as a continuation of another such period under regulation 86 (linking period) of the Employment and Support Allowance Regulations 2013.

[1 (4A) The fourth circumstance is where the decision—

(a) immediately follows the last day of a period for which the claimant was treated as capable of work or as not having limited capability for work under regulation 55ZA of the Jobseeker's Allowance Regulations or regulation 46A of the Jobseeker's Allowance Regulations 2013 (extended period of sickness) and that period lasted 13 weeks; and

(b) is not a decision which embodies a determination that the person is treated as having limited capability for work under regulation 26 of the Employment and Support Allowance Regulations 2013 (conditions for treating a claimant as having limited capability for work until a determination about limited capability for work has been made).]

(5) A decision terminating a person's entitlement to an employment and support allowance may be revised where—

(a) that entitlement was terminated because of section 1A (duration of contributory allowance) of the 2007 Act; and

(b) it is subsequently determined, in relation to the period of entitlement before that decision, that the person had or is treated as having had limited capability for work-related activity.

AMENDMENT

1. Jobseeker's Allowance (Extended Period of Sickness) Amendment Regulations 2015 (SI 2015/339) reg.8(1) and (2) (March 30, 2015).

DEFINITIONS

"the 2007 Act"–see reg.2.
"appeal"–see reg.2.
"claimant"–see reg.2.
"employment and support allowance"–by virtue of reg.2, see reg.1(3)(a).
"limited capability for work"–see reg.2.

GENERAL NOTE

This regulation is equivalent to reg.3(5D), (5E), (5F), (5I) and (5J) of the Social Security and Child Support (Decisions and Appeals) Regulations 1999. **2.637**

Other decisions relating to a jobseeker's allowance

16.—(1) A decision awarding a jobseeker's allowance may be revised in any of the following circumstances. **2.638**

(2) The first circumstance is where—

(a) the Secretary of State makes a conversion decision (within the meaning of regulation 5(2)(b) of the Employment and Support Allowance (Transitional Provisions, Housing Benefit and Council Tax Benefit) (Existing Awards) (No. 2) Regulations 2010 (deciding whether an existing award qualifies for conversion)) in respect of a person;
(b) the person appeals against that decision;
(c) before or after the appeal is made, there is a decision to award a jobseeker's allowance as the result of a claim being made by that person; and
(d) the appeal in relation to the conversion decision referred to in sub-paragraph (a) is successful.

(3) The second circumstance is where—

(a) a person's entitlement to an employment and support allowance is terminated because of a decision which embodies a determination that the person does not have limited capability for work;
(b) the person appeals against that decision;
(c) before or after the appeal is made, there is a decision to award a jobseeker's allowance as the result of a claim being made by that person; and
(d) the appeal in relation to the termination decision referred to in sub-paragraph (a) is successful.

DEFINITIONS

"appeal"–see reg.2.
"employment and support allowance"–by virtue of reg.2, see reg.1(3)(a).
"jobseeker's allowance"–by virtue of reg.2, see reg.1(3)(b).
"limited capability for work"–see reg.2.

GENERAL NOTE

This regulation is equivalent to reg.3(5G) and (5H) of the Social Security and Child Support (Decisions and Appeals) Regulations 1999. **2.639**

Contributions cases

2.640 **17.**—(1) A decision ("the original decision") may be revised where—

(a) on or after the date of the original decision—

(i) a late paid contribution is treated under regulation 5 (treatment of late paid contributions where no consent, connivance or negligence by the primary contributor) of the Social Security (Crediting and Treatment of Contributions and National Insurance Numbers) Regulations 2001 ("the Crediting Regulations") as paid on a date which falls on or before the date on which the original decision was made;

(ii) a direction is given under regulation 6 (treatment of contributions paid late through ignorance or error) of those Regulations that a late paid contribution is to be treated as paid on a date which falls on or before the date on which the original decision was made; or

(iii) an unpaid contribution is treated under regulation 60 (treatment of unpaid contributions where no consent, connivance or negligence by the primary contributor) of the Social Security (Contributions) Regulations 2001 as paid on a date which falls on or before the date on which the original decision was made; and

(b) either an award of benefit would have been made or the amount of benefit awarded would have been different.

(2) A decision may be revised where, by virtue of regulation 6C (treatment of Class 3 contributions paid under section 13A of the Act) of the Crediting Regulations, a contribution is treated as paid on a date which falls on or before the date on which the decision was made.

[1 (3) A decision in relation to a claim for a jobseeker's allowance or an employment and support allowance may be revised at any time where—

(a) on or after the date of the decision a contribution is treated as paid as set out in regulation 7A of the Social Security (Crediting and Treatment of Contributions, and National Insurance Numbers) Regulations 2001 (treatment of Class 2 contributions paid on or before the due date); and

(b) by virtue of the contribution being so treated, the person satisfies the contribution conditions of entitlement specified in paragraph (6) in relation to that benefit.

(4) A decision to award a jobseeker's allowance or an employment and support allowance may be revised at any time where on or after the date of the decision—

(a) any of the circumstances in paragraph (5) occur; and

(b) by virtue of the circumstance occurring, the person ceases to satisfy the contribution conditions of entitlement specified in paragraph (6) in relation to that benefit.

(5) The circumstances are—

(a) a Class 2 contribution is repaid to a person in consequence of an amendment or correction of the person's relevant profits under section 9ZA or 9ZB of the Taxes Management Act 1970 (amendment or correction of return by taxpayer or officer of the Board);

(b) a Class 2 contribution is returned to a person under regulation 52 of the Social Security (Contributions) Regulations 2001 (contributions paid in error); or

(c) a Class 1 or a Class 2 contribution paid by a person to Her Majesty's Revenue and Customs under section 223 of the Finance Act 2014 (accelerated payment in respect of notice given while tax enquiry is in progress) is repaid to the person.

(6) The contribution conditions of entitlement are—

(a) in relation to a jobseeker's allowance, the conditions set out in section 2(1)(a) and (b) of the Jobseekers Act (the contribution-based conditions); or

(b) in relation to an employment and support allowance, the first and second conditions set out in paragraphs 1(1) and 2(1) of Schedule 1 to the 2007 Act (conditions relating to national insurance).

(7) In this regulation "relevant profits" has the meaning given in section 11(3) of the Contributions and Benefits Act.]

AMENDMENT

1. Social Security (Credits, and Crediting and Treatment of Contributions) (Consequential and Miscellaneous Amendments) Regulations 2016 (SI 2016/1145) reg.4(1) and (5) (January 1, 2017).

DEFINITIONS

"benefit"—see reg.2.
"the Contributions and Benefits Act"—*ibid.*
"the Crediting Regulations"—see para.(1)(a)(i).
"employment and support allowance"—see reg.2.
"the Jobseekers Act"—*ibid.*
"jobseeker's allowance"—*ibid.*
"relevant profits"—see para.(7).

GENERAL NOTE

This regulation is equivalent to reg.3(8C) to 8(H) of the Social Security and Child Support (Decisions and Appeals) Regulations 1999. **2.641**

Other decisions relating to personal independence payment

18.—(1) Where the Secretary of State makes a decision awarding personal independence payment which takes effect immediately after the expiry of an existing award under regulation 33(3) (advance claim for and award of personal independence payment) of the Claims and Payments Regulations 2013, that decision may be revised if the requirements for entitlement are found not to have been met on the date on which the decision takes effect. **2.642**

(2) A decision that personal independence payment is not payable to a person for any period may be revised where—

(a) the Secretary of State determines that the person meets the condition in section 85(2) of the 2012 Act (care home residents where the costs of qualifying services are borne out of local or public funds) on incomplete evidence in accordance with regulation 39(5); and

(b) after that determination is made, any of the costs of the qualifying services are recovered from the person for whom they are provided.

(3) A decision of the Secretary of State made in consequence of a negative determination may be revised at any time if it contains an error to which the claimant did not materially contribute.

DEFINITIONS

"the 2012 Act"–see reg.2.
"claimant"–see reg.2.
"the Claims and Payments Regulations 2013"–see reg.2.
"personal independence payment"–see reg.2.

GENERAL NOTE

Paragraph (1)

2.643 This is equivalent to provision made in respect of disability living allowance in reg.13C(3) of the Social Security (Claims and Payments) Regulations 1987 and permits an award on a continuation claim made in advance of the renewal date to be revised if the conditions of entitlement are not in fact satisfied on the renewal date.

Paragraph (2)

2.644 This is a helpful new provision, enabling the Secretary of State to revise a decision that a personal independence payment is not payable because the costs of accommodation are borne out of public or local funds if part of the costs are subsequently recovered from the claimant. The benefit can then be paid, as it would have been if the claimant had been contributing to the costs from the outset.

Paragraph (3)

2.645 The term "negative determination" is not defined but a footnote to this provision in the Queen's Printer's version of these Regulations refers to s.80(6) of the Welfare Reform Act 2012, where the term is defined solely for the purpose of s.80(5)(a) as—

"a determination that a person does not meet the requirements of—
(a) section 78(1)(a) and (b) or (2)(a) and (b) (daily living component);
(b) section 79(1)(a) to (c) or (2)(a) to (c) (mobility component)."

This does not make it clear whether or not, in these Regulations, the term refers only to such a determination that has been treated as having been made by virtue of regulations made under s.80(5)(a) for breach of a requirement to provide information or evidence or participate in a consultation without a good reason. In fact, regs 8(3) and 9(2) of the Social Security (Personal Independence Payment) Regulations 2013 (see Vol.I) require a "negative determination" to be made where there has been a breach of such requirements without good reason, rather than treating one as having been made. Again, those Regulations do not define the term, but it seems probable that it was intended that at least determinations made under those provisions should fall within the scope of "negative determination" in this regulation and reg.26. The view expressed in *KB v SSWP (PIP)* [2016] UKUT 537 (AAC) is that "negative determination" in these Regulations refers *only* to determinations under regs 8 and 9 of those Regulations.

Other decisions relating to universal credit

2.646 **19.**—(1) Where the Secretary of State has reduced the amount of an award of universal credit as a consequence of regulation 81 (reduction of universal credit) of the Universal Credit Regulations, that decision may be revised.

(2) A decision in relation to universal credit which adopts a determi-

nation made under the Rent Officers Order 2013 may be revised at any time in consequence of a rent officer's redetermination made under that Order which resulted in an increase in the amount which represents rent for the purposes of calculating the housing costs element in universal credit.

DEFINITION

"the Rent Officers Order 2013"–see reg.2.
"the Universal Credit Regulations"–see reg.2.
"universal credit"–see reg.2.

CHAPTER 3

PROCEDURE AND EFFECTIVE DATE

Procedure for making an application for a revision

20.—(1) The Secretary of State may treat an application for a supersession under section 10 of the 1998 Act as an application for a revision under section 9 of that Act. 2.647

(2) The following paragraph applies where the Secretary of State, in order to consider all the issues raised by the application, requires further evidence or information from a person who has applied for a revision ("the applicant").

(3) The Secretary of State must notify the applicant that—

(a) the further evidence or information specified in the notification is required;
(b) if the applicant provides the relevant evidence or information within one month of the date of notification or such longer period as the Secretary of State may allow, the decision may be revised taking such evidence or information into account; and
(c) if the applicant does not provide such evidence or information within that period, the decision may be revised using such evidence or information as was submitted with the application for revision.

DEFINITION

"the 1998 Act"–see reg.2.
"the date of notification"–see reg.2.

GENERAL NOTE

Paragraph (1) is equivalent to reg.3(10) of the Social Security and Child Support (Decisions and Appeals) Regulations 1999. See reg.32(1) below. 2.648

Effective date of a revision

21. Where, on a revision under section 9 of the 1998 Act, the Secretary of State decides that the date from which the decision under section 8 or 10 of that Act ("the original decision") took effect was wrong, the revision takes effect from the date from which the original decision would have taken effect had the error not been made. 2.649

DEFINITION

"the 1998 Act"–see reg.2.

GENERAL NOTE

2.650 This regulation is equivalent to reg.5 of the Social Security and Child Support (Decisions and Appeals) Regulations 1999. The general rule in s.9(3) of the Social Security Act 1998 is that a revision takes effect from the same date as the decision being revised. This regulation provides an exception in a case where the decision is being revised, at least in part, precisely because the date from which it was effective was wrong.

PART 3

SUPERSESSIONS

CHAPTER 1

GROUNDS FOR SUPERSESSION

Introduction

2.651 **22.** Subject to regulation 32 (decisions which may not be superseded), the Secretary of State may make a decision under section 10 ("a superseding decision") of the 1998 Act in any of the cases and circumstances set out in this Chapter.

DEFINITION

"the 1998 Act"–see reg.2.

GENERAL NOTE

2.652 This regulation is equivalent to reg.6(1) of the Social Security and Child Support (Decisions and Appeals) Regulations 1999 and the rest of this Chapter reproduces the relevant provisions of reg.6(2) in a more digestible form. See the beginning of the note to reg.3 of the 1999 Regulations for the differences between revision and supersession. Regulation 32 has the effect that revision takes precedence over supersession where both might otherwise be possible. See the note to reg.6(1) of the 1999 Regulations for general observations about supersessions.

Regulation 11 of the Social Security (Personal Independence Payment) Regulations 2013 (see Vol.I) has the effect that the Secretary of State may at any time determine afresh whether a person in receipt of personal independence payment remains unable to carry out daily living activities and mobility activities. In *KB v SSWP (PIP)* [2016] UKUT 537 (AAC), the judge expressed the view, in obiter dicta but nonetheless persuasively, that such a determination did not determine entitlement; any change of entitlement would be determined in a consequential revision or supersession depending on the facts of the case. Moreover, such a determination did not in itself constitute a change of circumstances for the purpose of reg.23 of these Regulations and neither was it a "negative determination" for the purposes of reg.26(2).

Changes of circumstances

23.—(1) The Secretary of State may supersede a decision in respect of which— **2.653**

(a) there has been a relevant change of circumstances since the decision to be superseded had effect or, in the case of an advance award under regulation 32, 33 or 34 of the Claims and Payments Regulations 2013, since it was made; or

(b) it is expected that a relevant change of circumstances will occur.

(2) The fact that a person has become terminally ill is not a relevant change of circumstances for the purposes of paragraph (1) unless an application for supersession is made which contains an express statement that the person is terminally ill.

DEFINITIONS

"the Claims and Payments Regulations 2013"–see reg.2.
"terminally ill"–see reg.2.

GENERAL NOTE

This is equivalent to reg.6(2)(a) and (6)(c) of the Social Security and Child Support (Decisions and Appeals) Regulations 1999. See the note to reg.6(2)(a) of the 1999 Regulations. The date from which the supersession decision is effective is determined by Sch.1 or, if none of the provisions in the Schedule applies, by s.10(5) of the Social Security Act 1998. A determination under reg.11 of the Social Security (Personal Independence Payment) Regulations 2013 (see Vol.I) does not in itself constitute a change of circumstances for the purpose this regulation (*KB v SSWP (PIP)* [2016] UKUT 537 (AAC)). **2.654**

Error of law, ignorance, mistake etc.

24. A decision of the Secretary of State, other than one to which regulation 25 (decisions against which no appeal lies) refers, may be superseded where— **2.655**

(a) the decision was wrong in law, or was made in ignorance of, or was based on a mistake as to, some material fact; and

(b) an application for a supersession was received, or a decision was taken by the Secretary of State to act on the Secretary of State's own initiative, more than one month after the date of notification of the decision to be superseded or after the expiry of such longer period as may have been allowed under regulation 6 (late application for a revision).

DEFINITIONS

"appeal"–see reg.2.
"the date of notification"–see reg.2.

GENERAL NOTE

This is equivalent to reg.6(2)(b) of the Social Security and Child Support (Decisions and Appeals) Regulations 1999. See the note to that provision. The date from which the supersession decision is effective is determined by reg.35(3) in the case of jobseeker's allowance or employment and support allowance, by reg.35(4) in the case of universal credit and by s.10(5) of the Social Security Act 1998 in the case of personal independence payment. **2.656**

Decisions against which no appeal lies

2.657 **25.** A decision specified in Schedule 2 (decisions against which no appeal lies) to the 1998 Act or prescribed in regulation 50(2) (decisions which may or may not be appealed) may be superseded.

DEFINITIONS

"the 1998 Act"–see reg.2.
"appeal"–see reg.2.

GENERAL NOTE

2.658 This is equivalent to reg.6(2)(d) of the Social Security and Child Support (Decisions and Appeals) Regulations 1999. Like that provision, it is difficult to understand at first sight how it can be effective given that it overlaps with reg.10 and reg.32 prevents a decision from being superseded if it can be revised. See the note to reg.6(2)(d) for a possible explanation. The date from which a supersession under this regulation is effective is determined either under s.10(5) of the Social Security Act 1998 or under reg.35 in the same way as for decisions under reg.24.

Medical evidence and limited capability for work etc.

2.659 **26.**—(1) An employment and support allowance decision, a personal independence payment decision or universal credit decision may be superseded where, since the decision was made, the Secretary of State has—

(a) received medical evidence from a healthcare professional or other person approved by the Secretary of State; or

[1 (b) made a determination that the claimant is to be treated as having—

(i) limited capability for work in accordance with regulation 16, 21, 22 or 29 of the Employment and Support Allowance Regulations 2013; or

(ii) limited capability for work or for work and work-related activity in accordance with Part 5 (capability for work or work-related activity) of the Universal Credit Regulations.]

(2) The decision awarding personal independence payment may be superseded where there has been a negative determination.

(3) In this regulation—

"an employment and support allowance decision", "personal independence payment decision" and "universal credit decision" each has the meaning given in Schedule 1 (effective dates for superseding decisions made on the ground of a change of circumstances);

"healthcare professional" means—

(a) a registered medical practitioner;

(b) a registered nurse; or

(c) an occupational therapist or physiotherapist registered with a regulatory body established by an Order in Council under section 60 (regulation of health professions, social workers, other care workers etc.) of the Health Act 1999.

AMENDMENT

1. Universal Credit and Miscellaneous Amendments Regulations 2014 (SI 2014/597) reg.6 (April 28, 2014).

DEFINITIONS

"claimant"—see reg.2

"employment and support allowance decision"—by virtue of para.(3), see Sch.1 para.11

"healthcare professional"—see para.(3)

"limited capability for work"—see reg.2

"personal independence payment"—see reg.2

"personal independence payment decision"—by virtue of para.(3), see Sch.1 para.19.

"the Universal Credit Regulations"—see reg.2

"universal credit decision"—by virtue of para.(3), see Sch.1 para.30

GENERAL NOTE

Paragraph (1) is equivalent to reg.6(2)(r) of the Social Security and Child Support (Decisions and Appeals) Regulations 1999. See the note to that provision. The date from which the supersession decision is effective is determined by reg.35(6)–(9). **2.660**

The term "negative determination", used in para.(2) is not defined but, in *KB v SSWP (PIP)* [2016] UKUT 537 (AAC), it was suggested that only a determination under regs 8 or 9 of the Social Security (Personal Independence Payment) Regulations 2013 (see Vol.I), in consequence of a failure to provide information or participate in a consultation, was a "negative determination" and that an adverse determination under reg.11 of those Regulations was not. See the note to reg.18.

In *SF v SSWP (PIP)* [2016] UKUT 481 (AAC), the Upper Tribunal accepted a submission on behalf of the Secretary of State to the effect that supersession under reg.26 was appropriate only as a last resort where there was no other ground of supersession such as change of circumstances under reg.23. However, that view was not accepted in *DS v SSWP (PIP)* [2016] UKUT 538 (AAC); [2017] AACR 19, in which the judge referred to the different dates from which a supersession on the ground of change of circumstances might be effective under Sch.1 (depending on, for instance, whether the supersession was advantageous or not to the claimant and whether and when the claimant might reasonably have been expected to notify the change of circumstances) and said:

> "15. . . . In my view, all grounds of supersession can apply in so far as the conditions they contain are made out, without any artificial rules to try to make them mutually exclusive. So far as decisions that are advantageous to the claimant go, there is then no difficulty in applying a general principle that the claimant should be able to take the benefit of whatever ground gives the most advantage. So far as decisions that are not advantageous to the claimant are concerned, which will in the great majority of cases be supersessions carried out at the Secretary of State's own initiative, I do not see why the same principle cannot apply. The Secretary of State is entitled to rely on whatever of the grounds of supersession that are made out that result in what he says is the correct position being applied for the longest period. But if the Secretary of State chooses to rely on the simpler ground of supersession in regulation 26(1)(a), without going to all the bother of investigating and thinking about what the claimant should or should not have realised needed to be notified in the past, and is content for the superseding decision to take effect from the date on which it is made, I do not see why on appeal a tribunal should be obliged to consider all the elements of regulation 23(1) on relevant change of circumstances first. . . . A tribunal would always retain the discretion under section 12(8)(a) of the Social Security Act 1998 to consider regulation 23(1) in a case in which the Secretary of State has relied only on regulation 26(1)(a) if the potential application of regulation 23(1) is clearly apparent from the evidence before it (which may be different from or more extensive than that before the Secretary of State)."

On the other hand, both judges were agreed that reasons for a decision under reg.26 might need to explain why the decision was different from a previous decision (see *R(M) 1/96* and *R. (Viggers) v Pensions Appeal Tribunal* [2009] EWCA Civ 1321; [2010] AACR 19).

Sanctions cases

2.661 **27.**—(1) A decision as to the amount of an award of benefit may be superseded where the amount of that award is to be reduced by virtue of—

(a) section 11J(1) (sanctions) of the 2007 Act;
(b) section 6J(1) (higher-level sanctions) or 6K(1) (other sanctions) of the Jobseekers Act; or
(c) section 26(1) (higher-level sanctions) or 27(1) (other sanctions) of the 2012 Act.

(2) A decision reducing an award of benefit by virtue of any of those provisions may be superseded where the reduction falls to be suspended or terminated.

DEFINITIONS

"the 2007 Act"—see reg.2.
"the 2012 Act"—see reg.2.
"benefit"—see reg.2.
"the Jobseekers Act"—see reg.2.

GENERAL NOTE

2.662 This regulation is equivalent to reg.6(2)(f), (fa), (p) and (q) of the Social Security and Child Support (Decisions and Appeals) Regulations 1999. The date from which the supersession decision is effective is determined by reg.35(10) or (11).

Loss of benefit cases

2.663 **28.** A decision that a benefit is payable to a claimant may be superseded where that benefit ceases to be payable or falls to be reduced by virtue of section 6B, 7 or 9 of the Fraud Act (loss of benefit provisions).

DEFINITIONS

"benefit"—see reg.2.
"claimant"—see reg.2.
"the Fraud Act"—see reg.2.

GENERAL NOTE

2.664 This regulation is equivalent to reg.6(2)(i) of the Social Security and Child Support (Decisions and Appeals) Regulations 1999. The date from which the supersession decision is effective is determined by reg.35(12).

Contributions cases

2.665 **29.** The Secretary of State may supersede a decision ("the original decision") where, on or after the date on which the decision is made, a late or an unpaid contribution is treated as paid under—

(a) regulation 5 of the Social Security (Crediting and Treatment of Contributions and National Insurance Numbers) Regulations 2001 (treatment of late paid contributions where no consent, connivance or negligence by the primary contributor) on a date which falls on or before the date on which the original decision was made;

(b) regulation 6 of those Regulations (treatment of contributions paid late through ignorance or error) on a date which falls on or before the date on which the original decision was made; or
(c) regulation 60 of the Social Security (Contributions) Regulations 2001 (treatment of unpaid contributions where no consent, connivance or negligence by the primary contributor) on a date which falls on or before the date on which the original decision was made.

GENERAL NOTE

This regulation is equivalent to reg.6(2)(s) of the Social Security and Child Support (Decisions and Appeals) Regulations 1999. The date from which the supersession decision is effective is determined by reg.35(13). **2.666**

Housing costs: universal credit

30.—(1) A decision in relation to universal credit which adopts a determination made under the Rent Officers Order 2013 may be superseded where, in consequence of a rent officer's redetermination made in under that Order, the amount which represents rent for the purposes of calculating the housing costs element in universal credit is reduced. **2.667**

DEFINITIONS

"the Rent Officers Order 2013"—see reg.2.
"universal credit"—see reg.2.

GENERAL NOTE

This regulation is equivalent to reg.7(2)(c) of the Housing Benefit and Council Tax Benefit (Decisions and Appeals) Regulations 2001 (SI 2001/1002). The date from which the supersession decision is effective is determined by reg.35(14). **2.668**

Tribunal decisions

31. The Secretary of State may supersede a decision of the First-tier Tribunal or Upper Tribunal which— **2.669**
(a) was made in ignorance of, or was based upon a mistake as to, some material fact; or
(b) in a case where section 26(5) (appeals involving issues that arise in other cases) of the 1998 Act applies, was made in accordance with section 26(4)(b) of that Act.

DEFINITIONS

"the 1998 Act"—see reg.2.
"appeal"—see reg.2.

GENERAL NOTE

This regulation is equivalent to reg.6(2)(c) of the Social Security and Child Support (Decisions and Appeals) Regulations 1999. See the note to that provision. **2.670**

(5) A superseding decision made in consequence of a decision which is a relevant determination for the purposes of section 27 of the 1998 Act (restrictions on entitlement to benefit in certain cases of error) takes effect from the date of the relevant determination.

(6) In the case of an employment and support allowance, a superseding decision made in accordance with regulation 26(1) (medical evidence and limited capability for work etc.), following an application by the claimant, that embodies a determination that the claimant has limited capability for work-related activity, takes effect from the date of the application.

(7) In the case of an employment and support allowance, a superseding decision made on the Secretary of State's own initiative in accordance with regulation 26(1) that embodies a determination that the claimant has—

(a) limited capability for work; or
(b) limited capability for work-related activity; or
(c) limited capability for work and limited capability for work-related activity,

takes effect from [1 the day after the last day of the relevant period as defined in regulation 5(4) of the Employment and Support Allowance Regulations 2013] where the determination is the first such determination.

(8) In the case of an employment and support allowance where regulation 6 of the Employment and Support Allowance Regulations 2013 (assessment phase – previous claimants) applies, a superseding decision made in accordance with regulation 26(1) of these Regulations that embodies a determination that the claimant has—

(a) limited capability for work; or
(b) limited capability for work-related activity; or
(c) limited capability for work and limited capability for work-related activity,

takes effect from the beginning of the 14th week of the claimant's continuous period of limited capability for work.

(9) In the case of universal credit, a superseding decision made in accordance with regulation 26(1) that embodies a determination that the claimant has limited capability for work or limited capability for work and work-related activity takes effect—

(a) in a case to which regulation 28(1) (period for which the LCW or LCWRA element is not to be included) of the Universal Credit Regulations applies, from the beginning of the assessment period specified in that paragraph; or
(b) in any other case, from the beginning of the assessment period in which the decision (if made on the Secretary of State's own initiative) or the application for a supersession was made.

(10) A superseding decision to which regulation 27(1) (sanctions cases: reduction in an award) applies takes effect from the beginning of the period specified in—

(a) regulation 54 of the Employment and Support Allowance Regulations 2013, where the decision relates to the start of a reduction in the amount of an employment and support allowance;
(b) regulation 56 of the Employment and Support Allowance Regulations 2013, where the decision relates to ending the suspension of a such a reduction where a fraud penalty ceases to apply;
(c) regulation 22 of the Jobseeker's Allowance Regulations 2013, where

the decision relates to the start of a reduction in the amount of a jobseeker's allowance;

(d) regulation 24 of the Jobseeker's Allowance Regulations 2013, where the decision relates to ending the suspension of such a reduction where a fraud penalty ceases to apply;

(e) regulation 106 of the Universal Credit Regulations, where the decision relates to the start of a reduction in the amount of universal credit;

(f) regulation 108 of the Universal Credit Regulations, where the decision relates to ending the suspension of such a reduction where a fraud penalty ceases to apply.

(11) A superseding decision to which regulation 27(2) (sanctions cases: suspension and termination of a reduction) applies takes effect from the beginning of the period specified in—

(a) regulation 56 of the Employment and Support Allowance Regulations 2013, where the decision relates to the start of a suspension where a fraud penalty applies;

(b) regulation 57 of the Employment and Support Allowance Regulations 2013, where the decision relates to the termination of a reduction in the amount of an employment and support allowance;

(c) regulation 24 of the Jobseeker's Allowance Regulations 2013, where the decision relates to the start of a suspension where a fraud penalty applies;

(d) regulation 25 of the Jobseeker's Allowance Regulations 2013, where the decision relates to the termination of a reduction in the amount of a jobseeker's allowance;

(e) regulation 108 of the Universal Credit Regulations, where the decision relates to the start of a suspension where a fraud penalty applies;

(f) regulation 109 of the Universal Credit Regulations, where the decision relates to the termination of a reduction in the amount of an award of universal credit.

(12) A superseding decision to which regulation 28 (loss of benefit provisions) applies takes effect from the date prescribed for the purposes of section 6B or 7 of the Fraud Act.

(13) Where a decision is superseded in accordance with regulation 29 (contributions cases), the superseding decision takes effect from the date referred to in regulation 29(a), (b) or (c) on which the late or unpaid contribution is treated as paid.

(14) A superseding decision made in consequence of a redetermination in accordance with regulation 30 (housing costs: universal credit) takes effect on the first day of the first assessment period following the day on which that redetermination is received by Secretary of State.

AMENDMENT

1. Jobseeker's Allowance (Extended Period of Sickness) Amendment Regulations 2015 (SI 2015/339) reg.8(1) and (3) (March 30, 2015).

DEFINITIONS

"the 1998 Act"—see reg.2.
"appeal"—see reg.2.
"assessment period"—see reg.2.

"benefit"—see reg.2.
"benefit week"—see reg.2.
"claimant"—see reg.2.
"employment and support allowance"—by virtue of reg.2, see reg.1(3)(a).
"the Fraud Act"—see reg.2.
"jobseeker's allowance"—by virtue of reg.2, see reg.1(3)(b).
"limited capability for work"—see reg.2.
"the Universal Credit Regulations"—see reg.2.
"universal credit"—see reg.2.

General Note

2.678 This regulation is somewhat simpler than reg.7 of the Social Security and Child Support (Decisions and Appeals) Regulations 1999, but this is partly because the provisions equivalent to some of the complicated provisions in reg.7(2) of the 1999 Regulations relating to changes of circumstances are to be found in Sch.1 to these Regulations. The structure is as follows—

Paragraph (1)	Supersession for change of circumstances.
Paragraphs (2)–(4)	Supersession under reg.24 for ignorance or mistake of fact or under reg.25 of an unappealable decision.
Paragraph (5)	Supersession following a test case.
Paragraphs (6)–(8)	Supersession under reg.26 of employment and support allowance decisions related to a limited capability for work or limited capability for work-related activities.
Paragraph (9)	Supersession under reg.26 of universal credit decisions related to a limited capability for work or limited capability for work-related activities.
Paragraphs. (10) and (11)	Supersession under reg.27 relating to reductions imposed as sanctions.
Paragraph (12)	Supersession under reg.28 in order to remove benefit because a person has been convicted of benefit offences.
Paragraph (13)	Supersession under reg.29 following the late payment of contributions.
Paragraph (14)	Supersession under reg.30 of universal credit decisions following a re-determination of housing costs.

Note that the reference only to reg.24 in para.(2)(a) means that paras (3) and (4) do not apply where the supersession is of a tribunal decision and therefore made under reg.31.

Effective dates for superseding decisions where changes notified late

2.679 **36.**—(1) For the purposes of regulation 35(1) (effective dates: Secretary of State decisions) and paragraphs 6, 14 and 21 of Schedule 1 (effective dates for superseding decisions made on the ground of a change of circumstances), the Secretary of State may extend the time allowed for a person ("the applicant") to give notice of a change of circumstances in so far as it affects the effective date of the change if all of the following conditions are met.

(2) The first condition is that an application is made to the Secretary of State at an appropriate office for an extension of time.

(3) The second condition is that the application—

(a) contains particulars of the change of circumstances and the reasons for the failure to give notice of the change of circumstances on an earlier date; and

(b) is made—
  (i) within 13 months of the date on which the change occurred; or
  (ii) in the case of personal independence payment where a notification is given under paragraph 15 of Part 2 of Schedule 1 (effective dates for superseding decisions made on the ground of a change of circumstances), within 13 months of the date on which the claimant first satisfied the conditions of entitlement to the particular rate of personal independence payment.

(4) The third condition is that the Secretary of State is satisfied that it is reasonable to grant the extension.

(5) The fourth condition is that the change of circumstances notified by the applicant is relevant to the decision which is to be superseded.

(6) The fifth condition is that the Secretary of State is satisfied that, due to special circumstances, it was not practicable for the applicant to give notice of the change of circumstances within the relevant notification period.

(7) In determining whether it is reasonable to grant an extension of time—
(a) the Secretary of State must have regard to the principle that the greater the amount of time that has elapsed between the end of the relevant notification period and the date of the application, the more compelling should be the special circumstances on which the application is based;
(b) no account must be taken of the fact that the applicant or any person acting for them was unaware of, or misunderstood, the law applicable to the case (including ignorance or misunderstanding of the time limits imposed by these Regulations); and
(c) no account must be taken of the fact that the Upper Tribunal or a court has taken a different view of the law from that previously understood and applied.

(8) An application under this regulation which has been refused may not be renewed.

(9) In this regulation, "the relevant notification period" means—
(a) in the case of universal credit, the assessment period in which the change of circumstances occurs; or
(b) in any other case, a period of one month, beginning with the date on which the change of circumstances occurred.

DEFINITIONS

"appropriate office"–see reg.2.
"assessment period"–see reg.2.
"claimant"–see reg.2.
"personal independence payment"–see reg.2.
"universal credit"–see reg.2.

GENERAL NOTE

This regulation is equivalent to reg.8 of the Social Security and Child Support (Decisions and Appeals) Regulations 1999. **2.680**

Effective dates: tribunal cases

37.—(1) This paragraph applies where— **2.681**

(a) the Secretary of State supersedes a decision of the First-tier Tribunal or the Upper Tribunal on the ground that it is made in ignorance of, or based on a mistake as to, a material fact in accordance with regulation 31(a) (tribunal decisions), and

(b) as a result of that ignorance or mistake, the decision to be superseded was more advantageous to the claimant than it would otherwise have been.

(2) In a case where paragraph (1) applies where the decision relates to—

(a) a jobseeker's allowance;

(b) personal independence payment,

the superseding decision takes effect from the date on which the decision of the First-tier Tribunal or the Upper Tribunal took, or was to take, effect.

(3) In a case where paragraph (1) applies and the decision relates to an employment and support allowance or universal credit where—

(a) the material fact does not relate to a limited capability for work determination embodied in or necessary to the decision; or

(b) the material fact does relate to such a determination and the Secretary of State is satisfied that at the time the decision was made the claimant knew or could reasonably be expected to know of it and that it was relevant,

the superseding decision takes effect from the first day of the benefit week or (as the case may be) the assessment period in which in the Tribunal's decision took or was to take effect.

(4) Where the Secretary of State supersedes a decision of the First-tier Tribunal or the Upper Tribunal in accordance with regulation 31(b) (tribunal decisions), the decision takes effect—

(a) if the decision relates to personal independence payment, from the date on which the decision of the First-tier Tribunal or the Upper Tribunal would have taken effect had it been decided in accordance with the determination of the Upper Tribunal or the court in the appeal referred to in section 26(1)(b) of the 1998 Act;

(b) if the decision relates to a jobseeker's allowance or an employment and support allowance, from the first day of the benefit week in which the Tribunal's decision would have taken effect had it been so decided;

(c) if the decision relates to universal credit, from the first day of the assessment period in which the Tribunal's decision would have taken effect had it been so decided.

(5) Paragraph (6) applies where—

(a) the Upper Tribunal, or the court as defined in section 27(7) (restrictions on entitlement to benefit in certain cases of error) of the 1998 Act, determines an appeal as mentioned in subsection (1)(a) of that section ("the relevant determination");

(b) the Secretary of State makes a decision of the kind specified in subsection (1)(b) of that section;

(c) there is an appeal against the relevant determination;

(d) after the Secretary of State's decision, payment is suspended in accordance with regulation 44 (suspension in prescribed cases); and

(e) on appeal a court, within the meaning of section 27, reverses the relevant determination in whole or part.

(6) A consequential decision by the Secretary of State under section 10 of the 1998 Act which supersedes an earlier decision of the Secretary of

State under paragraph (5)(b) takes effect from the date on which the earlier decision took effect.

DEFINITIONS

"the 1998 Act"–see reg.2.
"appeal"–see reg.2.
"assessment period"–see reg.2.
"benefit"–see reg.2.
"benefit week"–see reg.2.
"claimant"–see reg.2.
"employment and support allowance"–by virtue of reg.2, see reg.1(3)(a).
"jobseeker's allowance"–by virtue of reg.2, see reg.1(3)(b).
"limited capability for work determination"–see reg.2.
"personal independence payment"–see reg.2.
"universal credit"–see reg.2.

PART 4

OTHER MATTERS RELATING TO DECISION- MAKING

Correction of accidental errors

38.—(1) An accidental error in a decision of the Secretary of State, or in any record of such a decision, may be corrected by the Secretary of State at any time. **2.682**

(2) Such a correction is to be treated as part of that decision or of that record.

(3) The Secretary of State must give written notice of the correction as soon as practicable to the person to whom the decision was given.

(4) In calculating the time within which an application may be made under regulation 5 (revision on any grounds) for a decision to be revised, no account is to be taken of any day falling before the day on which notice of the correction was given.

GENERAL NOTE

This regulation is equivalent to reg.9A of the Social Security and Child Support (Decisions and Appeals) Regulations 1999. **2.683**

Determinations on incomplete evidence

39.—(1) The following provisions of this regulation apply for the purposes of a decision under section 8 or 10 of the 1998 Act. **2.684**

(2) Where—

(a) a determination falls to be made by the Secretary of State concerning the matter mentioned in paragraph (3); and

(b) it appears to the Secretary of State that the Secretary of State is not in possession of all of the evidence or information which is relevant for the purposes of the determination,

the Secretary of State must make the determination on the assumption that the relevant evidence or information which is not in the Secretary of State's possession is adverse to the claimant.

(3) The matter is whether, for the purposes of regulation 45 (relevant education) of the Jobseeker's Allowance Regulations 2013 a person is by virtue of that regulation to be treated as receiving relevant education.

(4) Where—

(a) a determination falls to be made by the Secretary of State as to what costs are to be included in claimant's award of universal credit under section 11 (housing costs) of the 2012 Act; and

(b) it appears to the Secretary of State that the Secretary of State is not in possession of all of the evidence or information which is relevant for the purposes of the determination,

the Secretary of State may make the determination on the assumption that the costs to be included in the claimant's award under that section are those that the Secretary of State is able to determine using such evidence or information as is in the Secretary of State's possession.

(5) Where, in the case of personal independence payment—

(a) a determination falls to be made by the Secretary of State as to whether a person meets the condition in section 85(2) (care home residents where the costs of qualifying services are borne out of local or public funds) of the 2012 Act; and

(b) it appears to the Secretary of State that, having made reasonable enquiries, the Secretary of State is not in possession of all of the evidence or information which is or could be relevant for the purposes of the determination,

the Secretary of State may make the determination using such information or evidence as is in the Secretary of State's possession.

DEFINITIONS

"the 1998 Act"–see reg.2.
"the 2012 Act"–see reg.2.
"claimant"–see reg.2.
"personal independence payment"–see reg.2.
"universal credit"–see reg.2.

GENERAL NOTE

2.685 This regulation is equivalent to reg.13 of the Social Security and Child Support (Decisions and Appeals) Regulations 1999.

Determinations as to limited capability for work

2.686 **40.**—(1) Where, in relation to an award of an employment and support allowance, the Secretary of State makes a determination (including a determination made following a change of circumstances) whether a person—

(a) has or does not have limited capability for work; or

(b) is to be treated as having or not having limited capability for work,

which is embodied in or necessary to a decision under Chapter 2 of Part 1 of the 1998 Act (decisions and appeals) or on which such a decision is based, that determination is to be conclusive for the purposes of any further decision relating to such an allowance.

(2) Paragraph (1) applies to determinations made in relation to universal credit as it applies in the case of an employment and support allowance.

(3) Where, in relation to any purpose for which Part 1 (employment and support allowance) of the 2007 Act or Part 1 (universal credit) of the 2012 Act applies, a determination falls to be made as to whether a person—

(a) is, or is to be treated as, having or not having limited capability for work; or

(b) is terminally ill,

that issue is to be determined by the Secretary of State, notwithstanding the fact that any other matter falls to be determined by another authority.

DEFINITIONS

"the 1998 Act"–see reg.2.
"the 2007 Act"–see reg.2.
"the 2012 Act"–see reg.2.
"appeal"–see reg.2.
"employment and support allowance"–by virtue of reg.2, see reg.1(3)(a).
"limited capability for work"–see reg.2.
"terminally ill"–see reg.2.
"universal credit"–see reg.2.

GENERAL NOTE

This regulation is equivalent to regs 10 and 11 of the Social Security and Child Support (Decisions and Appeals) Regulations 1999. **2.687**

Effect of alterations affecting universal credit

41.—(1) Subject to paragraph (3), an alteration in the amount of a person's employed earnings (within the meaning of regulation 55(1) of the Universal Credit Regulations) made in accordance with Chapter 2 of Part 6 (earned income) of the Universal Credit Regulations in consequence of information provided to the Secretary of State by HMRC is prescribed for the purposes of section 159D(1)(b)(vi) (effect of alterations affecting universal credit) of the Administration Act. **2.688**

(2) For the purposes of this regulation, "alteration" means an increase or decrease in such earnings.

(3) Where the person disputes the figure used in accordance with regulation 55 (employed earnings) of the Universal Credit Regulations to calculate employed earnings in relation to any assessment period, the Secretary of State must—

(a) inform the person that they may request that the Secretary of State gives a decision in relation to the amount of universal credit payable in relation to that assessment period; and

(b) where such a decision is requested, give it within 14 days of receiving the request or as soon as practicable afterwards.

(4) Paragraph (3) does not affect the validity of anything done under section 159D(2) or (3) of the Administration Act in relation to the person's award.

(5) A decision made in accordance with paragraph (3) takes effect on the date on which the alteration under section 159(D)(2) or (3) came into force in relation to the person.

DEFINITIONS

"the Administration Act"–see reg.2.
"assessment period"–see reg.2.
"HMRC"–see reg.2.
"the Universal Credit Regulations"–see reg.2.
"universal credit"–see reg.2.

GENERAL NOTE

Where the Secretary of State makes a decision under reg.41(3), reg.61(5) of the Universal Credit Regulations 2013 (see Vol.V) applies so as to enable him either **2.689** to treat a payment of employed earnings received in one assessment period as paid in a later period or to disregard information received about a payment of employed earnings.

Issues for HMRC

2.690 **42.**—(1) Where, on consideration of any claim or other matter, it appears to the Secretary of State that an issue arises which, by virtue of section 8 of the Transfer Act, falls to be decided by an officer of HMRC, the Secretary of State must refer that issue to HMRC.

(2) Where—

(a) the Secretary of State has decided any claim or other matter on an assumption of facts—

(i) which appeared to the Secretary of State not to be in dispute, but

(ii) concerning which, had an issue arisen, that issue would have fallen, by virtue of section 8 of the Transfer Act, to be decided by HMRC;

(b) an application for a revision or supersession is made, or an appeal is brought, in relation to that claim or other matter; and

(c) it appears to the Secretary of State on receipt of that application or appeal that such an issue arises,

the Secretary of State must refer that issue to HMRC.

(3) Pending the final decision of any issue which has been referred to HMRC in accordance with paragraph (1) or (2), the Secretary of State may—

(a) determine any other issue arising on consideration of the claim, application or other matter,

(b) seek a preliminary opinion from HMRC on the issue referred and decide the claim, application or other matter in accordance with that opinion; or

(c) defer making any decision on the claim, application or other matter.

(4) On receipt by the Secretary of State of the final decision of an issue which has been referred to HMRC under paragraph (1) or (2), the Secretary of State must—

(a) In a case where the Secretary of State made a decision under paragraph (3)(b), decide whether to revise the decision under section 9 of the 1998 Act or to supersede it under section 10 of that Act;

(b) in a case to which paragraph (3)(a) or (c) applies, decide the claim, application or other matter in accordance with the final decision of the issue so referred.

(5) In this regulation—

(a) "final decision" means the decision of HMRC under section 8 (decisions by officers of Board) of the Transfer Act or the determination of any appeal in relation to that decision; and

(b) "the Transfer Act" means the Social Security Contributions (Transfer of Functions, etc.) Act 1999.

DEFINITIONS

"the 1998 Act"–see reg.2.
"appeal"–see reg.2.
"HMRC"–see reg.2.

General Note

This regulation is equivalent to reg.11A of the Social Security and Child Support (Decisions and Appeals) Regulations 1999. **2.691**

Appeals raising issues for HMRC

43.—(1) This regulation applies where— **2.692**

(a) a person has appealed to the First-tier Tribunal and it appears to the First-tier Tribunal that an issue arises which, by virtue of section 8 of the Transfer Act, falls to be decided by HMRC; and

(b) the tribunal has required the Secretary of State to refer that issue to HMRC.

(2) Pending the final decision of any issue which has been referred to HMRC in accordance with paragraph (1), the Secretary of State may revise the decision under appeal under section 9 of the 1998 Act, or make a further decision under section 10 of that Act superseding that decision, in accordance with the Secretary of State's determination of any issue other than one which has been so referred.

(3) On receipt by the Secretary of State of the final decision of an issue which has been referred to HMRC in accordance with paragraph (1), the Secretary of State must consider whether the decision under appeal ought to be revised or superseded under the 1998 Act, and—

(a) if so, revise it or make a further decision which supersedes it; or

(b) if not, invite the First-tier Tribunal to determine to appeal.

(4) In this regulation, "final decision" and "Transfer Act" have the same meaning as in regulation 42 (issues for HMRC).

Definitions

"the 1998 Act"–see reg.2.
"appeal"–see reg.2.
"HMRC"–see reg.2.

General Note

This regulation is equivalent to reg.38A of the Social Security and Child Support (Decisions and Appeals) Regulations 1999. **2.693**

Part 5

Suspension

Suspension in prescribed cases

44.—(1) The Secretary of State may suspend, in whole or part, payment of any benefit to a person ("P") in the circumstances described in paragraph (2). **2.694**

(2) The circumstances are where—

(a) it appears to the Secretary of State that—

(i) an issue arises whether the conditions for entitlement to the benefit are or were fulfilled;

(ii) an issue arises whether a decision relating to an award of the benefit should be revised under section 9 or superseded under section 10 of the 1998 Act,

(iii) an issue arises whether any amount of benefit paid to P is recoverable under or by virtue of section 71ZB, 71ZG or 71ZH of the Administration Act,
(iv) the last address notified to the Secretary of State of P is not the address at which P resides,

(b) an appeal is pending in P's case against a decision of the First-tier Tribunal, the Upper Tribunal or a court; or
(c) an appeal is pending against a decision given by the Upper Tribunal or a court in a different case and it appears to the Secretary of State that, if the appeal were to be decided in a particular way, an issue would arise as to whether the award of any benefit to P (whether the same benefit or not) ought to be revised or superseded.

(3) For the purposes of section 21(2)(c) (suspension in prescribed circumstances) of the 1998 Act, where an appeal against the decision has not been brought or an application for permission to appeal against the decision has not been made but the time for doing so has not yet expired, an appeal is pending in the circumstances described in paragraph (4).

(4) The circumstances are where a decision of the First-tier Tribunal, the Upper Tribunal or a court has been made and the Secretary of State—

(a) is awaiting receipt of that decision; or
(b) in the case of a decision of the First-tier Tribunal, is considering whether to apply for a statement of reasons for the decision or has applied for such a statement and is awaiting receipt; or
(c) has received that decision or, if it is a decision of the First-tier Tribunal has received the statement of reasons for it, and is considering whether to apply for permission to appeal, or where permission to appeal has been granted, is considering whether to appeal.

(5) Where payment of any benefit is suspended as the result of paragraph (2)(b) or (c), the Secretary of State must, as soon as reasonably practicable, give written notice to P of any proposal to—

(a) request a statement of the reasons for a tribunal decision;
(b) apply for permission to appeal; or
(c) make an appeal.

DEFINITIONS

"the 1998 Act"—see reg.2.
"benefit"—see reg.2.

GENERAL NOTE

2.695 This regulation is equivalent to reg.16 of the Social Security and Child Support (Decisions and Appeals) Regulations 1999.

Provision of information or evidence

2.696 **45.**—(1) This regulation applies where the Secretary of State requires information or evidence from a person mentioned in paragraph (2) ("P") in order to determine whether a decision awarding a benefit should be revised under section 9 of the 1998 Act or superseded under section 10 of that Act.

(2) The persons are—

(a) a person in respect of whom payment of any benefit has been suspended in the circumstances set out in regulation 44(2)(a) (suspension in prescribed cases);

(b) a person who has made an application for a decision of the Secretary of State to be revised or superseded;
(c) a person from whom the Secretary of State requires information or evidence under regulation 38(2) (evidence and information in connection with an award) of the Claims and Payments Regulations 2013;
(d) a person from whom the Secretary of State requires documents, certificates or other evidence under regulation 31(3) (evidence and information) of the Jobseeker's Allowance Regulations 2013;
(e) a person whose entitlement to an employment and support allowance or universal credit is conditional on their having, or being treated as having, limited capability for work.

(3) The Secretary of State must notify P of the requirements of this regulation.

(4) P must either—
(a) supply the information or evidence within—
(i) a period of 14 days beginning with the date on which the notification under paragraph (3) was given or sent to P or such longer period as the Secretary of State allows in that notification, or
(ii) such longer period as P satisfies the Secretary of State is necessary in order to comply with the requirements, or
(b) satisfy the Secretary of State within the period applicable under sub-paragraph (a)(i) that either—
(i) the information or evidence does not exist, or
(ii) it is not possible for P to obtain it.

(5) In relation to a person to whom paragraph (2)(d) refers, paragraph (4)(a)(i) has effect as if for "14 days" there were substituted "7 days".

(6) The Secretary of State may suspend the payment of a benefit, in whole or part, to any person to whom paragraph (2)(b), (c), (d) or (e) applies who fails to satisfy the requirements of paragraph (4).

(7) In this regulation, "evidence" includes evidence which a person is required to provide in accordance with regulation 2 (evidence of incapacity for work, limited capability for work and confinement) of the Social Security (Medical Evidence) Regulations 1976(3).

DEFINITIONS

"the 1998 Act"–see reg.2.
"the Administration Act"–see reg.2.
"benefit"–see reg.2.
"the Claims and Payments Regulations 2013"–see reg.2.
"employment and support allowance"–by virtue of reg.2, see reg.1(3)(a).
"limited capability for work"–see reg.2.
"universal credit"–see reg.2.

GENERAL NOTE

This regulation is equivalent to reg.17 of the Social Security and Child Support (Decisions and Appeals) Regulations 1999. 2.697

Making of payments which have been suspended

46. The Secretary of State must pay a benefit which has been suspended where— 2.698

(a) in a case where regulation 44(2)(a) (suspension in prescribed cases) applies, the Secretary of State is satisfied that the benefit is properly payable and that there are no outstanding issues to be resolved;
(b) in a case to which regulation 45(6) (provision of information or evidence) applies, the Secretary of State is satisfied that the benefit is properly payable and that the requirements of regulation 45(4) have been satisfied;
(c) in a case to which regulation 44(2)(b) (suspension in prescribed cases) applies, the Secretary of State—
    (i) does not, in the case of a decision of the First-tier Tribunal, apply for a statement of the reasons for that decision within the period specified under the Tribunal Procedure Rules;
    (ii) does not, in the case of a decision of the First-tier Tribunal, the Upper Tribunal or a court, make an application for permission to appeal or (where permission to appeal is granted) make the appeal within the time prescribed for the making of such application or appeal;
    (iii) withdraws an application for permission to appeal or withdraws the appeal; or
    (iv) is refused permission to appeal, in circumstances where it is not open to the Secretary of State to renew the application for permission or to make a further application for permission to appeal;
(d) in a case to which regulation 44(2)(c) (suspension in prescribed cases) applies, the Secretary of State, in relation to the decision of the Upper Tribunal or a court in a different case—
    (i) does not make an application for permission to appeal or (where permission to appeal is granted) make the appeal within the time prescribed for the making of such application or appeal;
    (ii) withdraws an application for permission to appeal or withdraws the appeal;
    (iii) is refused permission to appeal, in circumstances where it is not open to the Secretary of State to renew the application for permission or to make a further application for permission to appeal.

DEFINITIONS

"benefit"—see reg.2.
"the Tribunal Procedure Rules"—see reg.2.

GENERAL NOTE

2.699 This regulation is equivalent to reg.20 of the Social Security and Child Support (Decisions and Appeals) Regulations 1999.

PART 6

TERMINATION

Termination for failure to furnish information or evidence

47.—(1) This regulation applies where payment of a benefit to a person ("P") has been suspended in full under— 2.700

(a) regulation 44 (suspension in prescribed cases) and P subsequently fails to comply with a requirement for information or evidence under regulation 45 (provision of information or evidence) and more than one month has elapsed since the requirement was made; or

(b) regulation 45(6) and more than one month has elapsed since the first payment was suspended.

(2) In a case to which this regulation applies, except where entitlement ceases on an earlier date other than under this regulation, the Secretary of State must decide that P ceases to be entitled to that benefit with effect from the date on which the payment of the benefit was suspended.

DEFINITION

"benefit"—see reg.2.

GENERAL NOTE

This regulation is broadly equivalent to reg.18 of the Social Security and Child Support (Decisions and Appeals) Regulations 1999 but is considerably clearer. A termination is a form of supersession (*R(H) 4/08*) and there is therefore a right of appeal to the First-tier Tribunal under s.12 of the Social Security Act 1998. See the note to reg.18 of the 1999 Regulations for further commentary. 2.701

Termination in the case of entitlement to alternative benefits

48.—(1) This paragraph applies where an award of a jobseeker's allowance ("the existing benefit") exists in favour of a person and, if that award did not exist and a claim was made by that person for an employment and support allowance ("the alternative benefit"), an award of the alternative benefit would be made on that claim. 2.702

(2) This paragraph applies where an award of an employment and support allowance ("the existing benefit") exists in favour of a person and, if that award did not exist and a claim was made by that person for a jobseeker's allowance ("the alternative benefit"), an award of the alternative benefit would be made on that claim.

(3) In a case where paragraph (1) or (2) applies, if a claim for the alternative benefit is made, the Secretary of State may bring to an end the award of the existing benefit if satisfied that an award of the alternative benefit will be made.

(4) Where the Secretary of State brings an award of the existing benefit to an end under paragraph (3), the Secretary of State must end the award on the day immediately preceding the first day on which an award of the alternative benefit takes effect.

(5) Where an award of a jobseeker's allowance is made in accordance with this regulation, paragraph 4 of Schedule 1 to the Jobseekers Act (waiting days) does not apply.

(6) Where an award of an employment and support allowance is made in accordance with this regulation, paragraph 2 (waiting days) of Schedule 2 (supplementary provisions) to the 2007 Act does not apply.

DEFINITIONS

"the 2007 Act"–see reg.2.
"benefit"–see reg.2.
"employment and support allowance"–by virtue of reg.2, see reg.1(3)(a).
"the Jobseekers Act"–see reg.2.
"jobseeker's allowance"–by virtue of reg.2, see reg.1(3)(b).

GENERAL NOTE

2.703 This regulation applies where it is decided that a person entitled to jobseeker's allowance should be entitled to employment and support allowance or vice versa and ensures that there is no gap in entitlement.

PART 7

APPEALS

Other persons with a right of appeal

2.704 **49.** In addition to the claimant, but subject to regulation 7 (consideration of revision before appeal), the following persons have the right of appeal under section 12(2) of the 1998 Act—

(a) any person appointed by the Secretary of State under regulation 56 (payments on death) of the Claims and Payments Regulations 2013 to proceed with the claim of a person who claimed benefit and subsequently died;
(b) any person appointed by the Secretary of State under regulation 57 (persons unable to act) of those Regulations to act on behalf of another;
(c) any person claiming personal independence payment on behalf of another under section 82(5) of the 2012 Act (terminal illness); and
(d) in the case of a decision under section 71ZB, 71ZG or 71ZH of the Administration Act to recover any amount paid by way of benefit, any person from whom such an amount is recoverable, but only if their rights, duties or obligations are affected by that decision.

DEFINITIONS

"the 1998 Act"–see reg.2.
"the 2012 Act"–see reg.2.
"appeal"–see reg.2.
"benefit"–see reg.2.
"claimant"–see reg.2.
"the Claims and Payments Regulations 2013"–see reg.2.
"personal independence payment"–see reg.2.

GENERAL NOTE

2.705 This regulation is equivalent to reg.25 of the Social Security and Child Support (Decisions and Appeals) Regulations 1999.

Decisions which may or may not be appealed

50.—(1) An appeal lies against a decision set out in Schedule 2 (decisions against which an appeal lies). **2.706**

(2) No appeal lies against a decision set out in Schedule 3 (decisions against which no appeal lies).

(3) In paragraph (2) and Schedule 3, "decision" includes a determination embodied in or necessary to a decision.

DEFINITION

"appeal"–see reg.2.

GENERAL NOTE

This regulation is equivalent to regs 26 and 27 of the Social Security and Child Support (Decisions and Appeals) Regulations 1999. **2.707**

Notice of a decision against which an appeal lies

51.—(1) This regulation applies in the case of a person ("P") who has a right of appeal under the 1998 Act or these Regulations. **2.708**

(2) The Secretary of State must—

(a) give P written notice of the decision and of the right to appeal against that decision; and

(b) inform P that, where that notice does not include a statement of the reasons for the decision, P may, within one month of the date of notification of that decision, request that the Secretary of State provide a written statement of the reasons for that decision.

(3) If the Secretary of State is requested under paragraph (2)(b) to provide a written statement of reasons, the Secretary of State must provide such a statement within 14 days of the request or as soon as practicable afterwards.

DEFINITIONS

"the 1998 Act"–see reg.2.
"appeal"–see reg.2.
"the date of notification"–see reg.2.

GENERAL NOTE

This regulation is equivalent to reg.28 of the Social Security and Child Support (Decisions and Appeals) Regulations 1999. **2.709**

Appeals against decisions which have been revised

52.—(1) An appeal against a decision of the Secretary of State does not lapse where— **2.710**

(a) the decision is revised under section 9 of the 1998 Act before the appeal is decided; and

(b) the decision of the Secretary of State as revised is not more advantageous to the appellant than the decision before it was revised.

(2) In a case to which paragraph (1) applies, the appeal must be treated as though it had been brought against the decision as revised.

(3) The Secretary of State must inform the appellant that they may,

within one month of the date of notification of the decision as revised, make further representations as to the appeal.

(4) After the end of that period, or within that period if the appellant consents in writing, the appeal to the First-tier Tribunal must proceed, except where—

(a) the Secretary of State further revises the decision in light of further representations from the appellant; and

(b) that decision is more advantageous to the appellant than the decision before it was revised.

(5) Decisions which are more advantageous for the purpose of this regulation include those where—

(a) the amount of any benefit payable to the appellant is greater, or any benefit is awarded for a longer period, as a result of the decision;

(b) the decision would have resulted in the amount of benefit in payment being greater but for the operation of any provision of the Administration Act or the Contributions and Benefits Act restricting or suspending the payment of, or disqualifying a claimant from receiving, some or all of the benefit;

(c) as a result of the decision, a denial or disqualification for the receipt of any benefit is lifted, wholly or in part;

(d) the decision reverses a decision to pay benefit to a third party instead of to the appellant;

(e) in consequence of the decision, benefit paid is not recoverable under section 71ZB, 71ZG or 71ZH of the Administration Act or regulations made under any of those sections, or the amount so recoverable is reduced; or

(f) a financial gain accrued or will accrue to the appellant in consequence of the decision.

DEFINITIONS

"the 1998 Act"–see reg.2.
"the Administration Act"–see reg.2.
"appeal"–see reg.2.
"benefit"–see reg.2.
"the Contributions and Benefits Act"–see reg.2.
"the date of notification"–see reg.2.
"writing"–see reg.2.

GENERAL NOTE

2.711 This regulation is equivalent to reg.30 of the Social Security and Child Support (Decisions and Appeals) Regulations 1999.

Decisions involving issues that arise on appeal in other cases

2.712 **53.**—(1) For the purposes of section 25(3)(b) of the 1998 Act (prescribed cases and circumstances in which a decision may be made on a prescribed basis)—

(a) a prescribed case is a case in which the claimant would be entitled to the benefit to which the decision relates, even if the other appeal referred to in section 25(1)(b) of the 1998 Act were decided in a way which is the most unfavourable to the claimant; and

(b) the prescribed basis on which the Secretary of State may make the decision is as if—
  (i) the other appeal referred to in section 25(1)(b) of the 1998 Act had already been decided; and
  (ii) that appeal had been decided in a way which is the most unfavourable to the claimant.

(2) For the purposes of section 25(5)(c) of the 1998 Act (appeal treated as pending against a decision in a different case, even though an appeal against the decision has not been brought or an application for permission to appeal against the decision has not been made but the time for doing so has not yet expired), the prescribed circumstances are that the Secretary of State—

(a) certifies in writing that the Secretary of State is considering appealing against that decision; and
(b) considers that, if such an appeal were to be decided in a particular way—
  (i) there would be no entitlement to benefit in that case; or
  (ii) the appeal would affect the decision in that case in some other way.

DEFINITIONS

"the 1998 Act"–see reg.2.
"benefit"–see reg.2.
"claimant"–see reg.2.
"writing"–see reg.2.

GENERAL NOTE

This regulation is equivalent to reg.21 of the Social Security and Child Support (Decisions and Appeals) Regulations 1999. **2.713**

Appeals involving issues that arise in other cases

54. For the purposes of section 26(6)(c) of the 1998 Act (appeal is treated as pending against a decision in a different case, even though an appeal against the decision has not been brought or an application for permission to appeal has not been made but the time for doing so has not yet expired) the prescribed circumstances are that the Secretary of State— **2.714**

(a) certifies in writing that the Secretary of State is considering appealing against that decision; and
(b) considers that, if such an appeal were already decided, it would affect the determination of the appeal referred to in section 26(1)(a) of the 1998 Act.

DEFINITIONS

"the 1998 Act"–see reg.2.
"writing"–see reg.2.

GENERAL NOTE

This regulation is equivalent to reg.22 of the Social Security and Child Support (Decisions and Appeals) Regulations 1999. **2.715**

55. *Omitted.* **2.716**

Regulation 35

SCHEDULE 1

EFFECTIVE DATES FOR SUPERSEDING DECISIONS MADE ON THE GROUND OF A CHANGE OF CIRCUMSTANCES

PART 1

EMPLOYMENT AND SUPPORT ALLOWANCE AND JOBSEEKER'S ALLOWANCE

2.717 **1.** Subject to the following provisions of this Part and to Part 4, in the case of an employment and support allowance or a jobseeker's allowance, a superseding decision made on the ground of a change of circumstances takes effect from the first day of the benefit week in which the relevant change of circumstances occurs or is expected to occur.

2. Paragraph 1 does not apply where—

(a) the superseding decision is not advantageous to the claimant; and

(b) there has been an employment and support allowance decision where the Secretary of State is satisfied that, in relation to a limited capability for work determination, the claimant—

(i) failed to notify an appropriate office of a change of circumstances which the claimant was required by regulations under the Administration Act to notify; and

(ii) could not reasonably have been expected to know that the change of circumstances should have been notified.

3. Where a relevant change of circumstances results, or is expected to result, in a reduced award and the Secretary of State is of the opinion that it is impracticable for a superseding decision to take effect from the day set out in paragraph 1, that superseding decision takes effect—

(a) where the relevant change has occurred, from the first day of the benefit week following that in which that superseding decision is made; or

(b) where the relevant change is expected to occur, from the first day of the benefit week following that in which that change of circumstances is expected to occur.

4. Where entitlement ends, or is expected to end, as the result of a change of circumstances, the superseding decision takes effect from the day on which the relevant change of circumstances occurs or is expected to occur.

5. In the case of an employment and support allowance where a person who is subject to—

(a) section 45A or 47 of the Mental Health Act 1983 (power of higher courts to direct hospital admission; removal to hospital of persons serving sentences of imprisonment etc.);

(b) section 59A (hospital direction) of the Criminal Procedure (Scotland) Act 1995; or

(c) section 136 (transfer of prisoners for treatment for mental disorder) of the Mental Health (Care and Treatment) (Scotland) Act 2003,

ceases, or is expected to cease, to be detained in a hospital (as defined in the Act, or the Act of the Scottish Parliament, to which the person is subject) for a period of less than a week, a superseding decision related to that person's departure from, or return to, hospital takes effect from the day on which that change of circumstances occurs or is expected to occur.

6. Where the superseding decision is advantageous to the claimant and the change of circumstances was notified to an appropriate office more than one month after the change occurred or after the expiry of such longer period as may be allowed under regulation 36 (effective dates for superseding decisions where changes notified late), the superseding decision takes effect from the beginning of the benefit week in which the notification was given.

7. In the case of an employment and support allowance decision where the Secretary of State is satisfied that, in relation a limited capability for work determination, the claimant—

(a) failed to notify an appropriate office of a change of circumstances which the claimant was required by regulations under the Administration Act to notify; and

(b) could reasonably have been expected to know that the change of circumstances should have been notified,

the superseding decision takes effect in accordance with paragraph 8.

8. The superseding decision takes effect—

(a) from the date on which the claimant ought to have notified the change of circumstances; or

(b) if more than one change has taken place between the date from which the decision to be superseded took effect and the date of the superseding decision, from the date on which the first change ought to have been notified.

9. In the case of a claimant who makes an application for a supersession which contains an express statement that they are terminally ill, the superseding decision takes effect from the date on which the claimant became terminally ill.

10. Where the superseding decision is advantageous to the claimant and is made on the Secretary of State's own initiative, the decision takes effect from the beginning of the benefit week in which the Secretary of State commenced action with a view to supersession.

11. In this Part—

"employment and support allowance decision" means a decision to award an employment and support allowance embodied in or necessary to which is a determination that the claimant has, or is to be treated as having, limited capability for work;

"week" means a period of 7 days, beginning with midnight between Saturday and Sunday.

PART 2

PERSONAL INDEPENDENCE PAYMENT

12. Subject to the following provisions of this Part and to Part 4, in the case of personal independence payment, a superseding decision made on the ground of a change of circumstances takes effect on the date on which the relevant change of circumstances occurs or is expected to occur. **2.718**

13. Paragraph 12 does not apply where—

(a) the superseding decision is not advantageous to the claimant; and

(b) there has been a personal independence payment decision where the Secretary of State is satisfied that, in relation to such a decision, the claimant—

(i) failed to notify an appropriate office of a change of circumstances which the claimant was required by regulations under the Administration Act to notify; and

(ii) could not reasonably have been expected to know that the change of circumstances should have been notified.

14. Except in a case where paragraph 15 or 31 applies, where the superseding decision is advantageous to the claimant and the change of circumstances was notified to an appropriate office more than one month after the change occurred or after the expiry of such longer period as may be allowed under regulation 36 (effective dates for superseding decisions where changes notified late), the superseding decision takes effect from the date of notification of the change.

15. Where—

(a) the change is relevant to entitlement to a particular rate of personal independence payment; and

(b) the claimant notifies an appropriate office of the change no later than one month after the date on which they first satisfied the conditions of entitlement to that rate or within such longer period as may be allowed by regulation 36 (effective dates for superseding decisions where changes notified late),

the superseding decision takes effect from the date on which the claimant first satisfied those conditions.

16. Where the Secretary of State is satisfied that, in relation to a personal independence payment decision, the claimant—

(a) failed to notify an appropriate office of a change of circumstances which the claimant was required by regulations under the Administration Act to notify; and

(b) could reasonably have been expected to know that the change of circumstances should have been notified,

the superseding decision takes effect in accordance with paragraph 17.

17. The superseding decision takes effect—

(a) from the date on which the claimant ought to have notified the change of circumstances; or

(b) if more than one change has taken place between the date from which the decision to be superseded took effect and the date of the superseding decision, from the date on which the first change ought to have been notified.

18. Where the superseding decision is advantageous to the claimant and is made on the Secretary of State's own initiative, the decision takes effect from the date on which the Secretary of State commenced action with a view to supersession.

19. In paragraphs 13 and 16, "personal independence payment decision" means a decision to award personal independence payment, embodied in or necessary to which is a determination whether the claimant satisfies any of the requirements in section 78(1) and (2) (daily living component) or section 79(1) and (2) (mobility component) of the 2012 Act.

PART 3

UNIVERSAL CREDIT

2.719 **20.** Subject to the following paragraphs and to Part 4, in the case of universal credit, a superseding decision made on the ground of a change of circumstances takes effect from the first day of the assessment period in which that change occurred or is expected to occur.

21. Except in a case to which paragraph 22 or 31 applies, where the superseding decision is advantageous to the claimant and the change of circumstances was notified to an appropriate office after the end of the assessment period in which the change occurred or after the expiry of such longer period as may be allowed under regulation 36 (effective dates for superseding decisions where changes notified late), the superseding decision takes effect from the first day of the assessment period in which the notification was given.

22. In the case of a person to whom regulation 61 (information for calculating earned income) of the Universal Credit Regulations applies, where—

(a) the relevant change of circumstances is that the person's employed earnings are reduced; and

(b) the person provides such information for the purposes of calculating those earnings at such times as the Secretary of State may require,

the superseding decision takes effect from the first day of the assessment period in which that change occurred.

23. In the case of a universal credit decision where the Secretary of State is satisfied that, in relation to a limited capability for work determination, the claimant—

(a) failed to notify an appropriate office of a change of circumstances which the claimant was required by regulations under the Administration Act to notify; and

(b) could reasonably have been expected to know that the change of circumstances should have been notified,

the superseding decision takes effect in accordance with paragraph 24.

24. The superseding decision takes effect—

(a) from the first day of the assessment period in which the claimant ought to have notified the change of circumstances; or

(b) if more than one change has taken place between the date from which the decision to be superseded took effect and the date of the superseding decision, from the first day of the assessment period in which the first change ought to have been notified.

25. Where—

(a) the superseding decision is not advantageous to the claimant; and

(b) there has been a universal credit decision where the Secretary of State is satisfied that, in relation to a limited capability for work determination, the claimant—

(i) failed to notify an appropriate office of a change of circumstances which the claimant was required by regulations under the Administration Act to notify; and

(ii) could not reasonably have been expected to know that the change of circumstances should have been notified,

the superseding decision takes effect on the first day of the assessment period in which the Secretary of State makes that decision.

26. Where, in any assessment period, a claimant—

(a) reaches the qualifying age for state pension credit under the State Pension Credit Act 2002; and

(b) has made an advance claim for an award of state pension credit,

a superseding decision made in consequence of the person reaching that age takes effect on the date on which that change of circumstances occurs or is expected to occur.

27. A superseding decision of the Secretary of State to make or to cease making a hardship payment takes effect in accordance with regulation 117 (period of hardship payments) of the Universal Credit Regulations.

28. In the case of a claimant who makes an application for a supersession which contains an express statement that they are terminally ill, the superseding decision takes effect from the first day of the assessment period in which the claimant became terminally ill.

29. Where the superseding decision is advantageous to a claimant and is made on the Secretary of State's own initiative, it takes effect from the first day of the assessment period in which the Secretary of State commenced action with a view to supersession.

30. In this Part, "a universal credit decision" means a decision to award universal credit embodied in or necessary to which is a determination that the claimant has or is to be treated as having limited capability for work.

PART 4

COMMON PROVISIONS

31.—(1) This paragraph applies in relation to an award of personal independence payment or universal credit where the change of circumstances is that the claimant or, in the case of universal credit, a member of their family, becomes entitled to another relevant benefit, ceases so to be entitled or the rate of another such benefit alters. **2.720**

(2) Where this paragraph applies, the superseding decision takes effect from—

(a) where the superseding decision concerns universal credit, the first day of the assessment period in which—

(i) the entitlement to the other benefit arises;

(ii) the entitlement to the other benefit ends; or

(iii) entitlement to a different rate of the other benefit arises;

(b) where the superseding decision concerns personal independence payment, the date on which—

(i) the entitlement to the other benefit arises;

(ii) the entitlement to the other benefit ends; or

(iii) entitlement to a different rate of the other benefit arises.

(3) For the purpose of sub-paragraph (1), where the superseding decision relates to personal independence payment, "relevant benefit" includes any payment made under any of the provisions mentioned in regulation 61(1) (cases where mobility component of personal independence payment not payable) of the Claims and Payments Regulations 2013.

32. Where the change of circumstances is that there has been a change in the legislation in relation to any benefit, the superseding decision takes effect from the date on which that change in the legislation had effect.

33. Where the change of circumstances is the expected coming into force of a change in the legislation in relation to any benefit, the superseding decision takes effect from the date on which that change in the legislation takes effect

DEFINITIONS

"the 2012 Act"–see reg.2.
"the Administration Act"–see reg.2.
"appropriate office"–see reg.2.
"assessment period"–see reg.2.
"benefit"–see reg.2.
"benefit week"–see reg.2.
"claimant"–see reg.2.
"the Claims and Payments Regulations 2013"–see reg.2.
"the date of notification"–see reg.2.
"employment and support allowance"–by virtue of reg.2, see reg.1(3)(a).
"family"–see reg.2.
"jobseeker's allowance"–by virtue of reg.2, see reg.1(3)(b).
"limited capability for work"–see reg.2.
"limited capability for work determination"–see reg.2.
"personal independence payment"–see reg.2.
"relevant benefit"–see reg.2.
"terminally ill"–see reg.2.
"the Universal Credit Regulations"–see reg.2.
"universal credit"–see reg.2.

GENERAL NOTE

This regulation is equivalent to Sch.3A and Sch.3B to the Social Security and Child Support (Decisions and Appeals) Regulations 1999 and makes equivalent provision for universal credit. It also makes provision equivalent to some paragraphs of reg.7 of the 1999 Regulations. **2.721**

Regulation 50(1)

SCHEDULE 2

DECISIONS AGAINST WHICH AN APPEAL LIES

2.722 **1.** A decision as to whether a person is entitled to a benefit for which no claim is required by virtue of regulation 6, 7 or 9(6) and (7) of the Claims and Payments Regulations 2013.

DEFINITIONS

"appeal"–see reg.2.
"benefit"–see reg.2.
"the Claims and Payments Regulations 2013"–see reg.2.

GENERAL NOTE

2.723 This Schedule, read with reg.50(1), is equivalent to reg.26(a) of the Social Security and Child Support (Decisions and Appeals) Regulations 1999.

Regulation 50(2)

SCHEDULE 3

DECISIONS AGAINST WHICH NO APPEAL LIES

Claims and Payments

2.724 **1.** A decision under any of the following provisions of the Claims and Payments Regulations 2013—

(a) regulation 18 (special provisions where it is certified that a woman is expected to be confined or where she has been confined);
(b) regulation 25 (interchange with claims for other benefits);
(c) regulation 37 (evidence and information in connection with a claim);
(d) regulation 46 (direct credit transfer);
(e) regulation 47 (payment of universal credit);
(f) regulation 48 (payment of personal independence payment);
(g) regulation 49 (days for payment of personal independence payment);
(h) regulation 50(1) (payment of personal independence payment at a daily rate between periods in hospital or other accommodation);
(i) regulation 51 (payment of an employment and support allowance);
(j) regulation 52 (payment of a jobseeker's allowance);
(k) regulation 55, except a decision under paragraph (4) (extinguishment of right to payment if payment is not obtained within the prescribed period);
(l) regulation 56 (payments on death);
(m) regulation 57 (persons unable to act);
(n) regulation 58 (payment to another person on the claimant's behalf);
(o) regulation 59 (direct payment to lender of deductions in respect of interest on secured loans);
(p) Part 6 (mobility component of personal independence payment).

Other Jobseeker's Allowance Decisions

2.725 **2.** A decision made in accordance with regulation 39(2) (jobseeker's allowance determinations on incomplete evidence) of these Regulations.

Other Decisions relating to Universal Credit

2.726 **3.** A decision in default of a nomination under regulation 21(4) (assessment periods) of the Universal Credit Regulations.

4. A decision in default of an election under regulation 29 (award to include the carer element) of the Universal Credit Regulations.

5. A decision as to the amount of universal credit to which a person is entitled, where it appears to the Secretary of State that the amount is determined by reference to the claimant's entitlement to an increased amount of universal credit in the circumstances referred to in section 160C(2) (implementation of increases in universal credit due to attainment of a particular age) of the Administration Act.

6. So much of a decision as adopts a decision of a rent officer under an order made by virtue of section 122 of the Housing Act 1996 (decisions of rent officers for the purposes of universal credit).

Suspension

7. A decision of the Secretary of State relating to suspending payment of benefit, or to the payment of a benefit which has been suspended, under Part 5 (suspension) of these Regulations. **2.727**

Decisions Depending on Other Cases

8. A decision of the Secretary of State in accordance with section 25 or 26 of the 1998 Act (decisions and appeals depending on other cases). **2.728**

Expenses

9. A decision of the Secretary of State whether to pay travelling expenses under section 180 of the Administration Act. **2.729**

Deductions

10. A decision of the Secretary of State under the Fines (Deductions from Income Support) Regulations 1992, other than a decision whether benefit is sufficient for a deduction to be made. **2.730**

11. Any decision of the Secretary of State under the Community Charges (Deductions from Income Support) (No. 2) Regulations 1990, the Community Charges (Deductions from Income Support) (Scotland) Regulations 1989 or the Council Tax (Deductions from Income Support) Regulations 1993, except a decision—

(a) whether there is an outstanding sum due of the amount sought to be deducted;
(b) whether benefit is sufficient for the deduction to be made; or
(c) on the priority of the deductions.

Loss of Benefit

12.—(1) In the circumstances referred to in sub-paragraph (2), a decision of the Secretary of State that a sanctionable benefit as defined in section 6A(1) of the Fraud Act is not payable (or is to be reduced) pursuant to section 6B, 7 or 9 of that Act as a result of— **2.731**

(a) a conviction for one or more benefit offences in one set of proceedings;
(b) an agreement to pay a penalty as an alternative to prosecution;
(c) a caution in respect of one or more benefit offences; or
(d) a conviction for one or more benefit offences in each of two sets of proceedings, the later offence or offences being committed within the period of 5 years after the date of any of the convictions for a benefit offence in the earlier proceedings.

(2) The circumstances are that the only ground of appeal is that any of the convictions was erroneous, or that the offender (as defined in section 6B(1) of the Fraud Act) did not commit the benefit offence in respect of which there has been an agreement to pay a penalty or a caution has been accepted.

Payments on Account, Overpayments and Recovery

13. In the case of personal independence payment, a decision of the Secretary of State under the Social Security (Payments on account, Overpayments and Recovery) Regulations **2.732**

1988, except a decision of the Secretary of State under the following provisions of those Regulations—

(a) regulation 5, as to the offsetting of a prior payment against a subsequent award;
(b) regulation 11(1), as to whether a payment in excess of entitlement has been credited to a bank or other account;
(c) regulation 13, as to the sums to be deducted in calculating recoverable amounts.

14. A decision of the Secretary of State under the Social Security (Payments on Account of Benefit) Regulations 2013, except a decision under regulation 10 (bringing payments on account of benefit into account) of those Regulations.

15. A decision of the Secretary of State under the Social Security (Overpayments and Recovery) Regulations 2013, except a decision of the Secretary of State under the following provisions of those Regulations—

(a) regulation 4(3), as to the person from whom an overpayment of a housing payment is recoverable;
(b) regulation 7, as to the treatment of capital to be reduced;
(c) regulation 8, as to the sums to be deducted in calculating recoverable amounts;
(d) regulation 9 (sums to be deducted: change of dwelling).

Reciprocal Agreements

2.733 **16.** A decision of the Secretary of State made in accordance with an Order made under section 179 (reciprocal agreements with countries outside the United Kingdom) of the Administration Act.

European Community Regulations

2.734 **17.** An authorisation given by the Secretary of State in accordance with Article 22(1) or 55(1) of Council Regulation (EEC) No 1408/71 on the application of social security schemes to employed persons, to self-employed persons and to members of their families moving within the European Union.

Up-rating

2.735 **18.** A decision of the Secretary of State relating to the up-rating of benefits under Part 10 (review and alteration of benefits) of the Administration Act.

Definitions

"the 1998 Act"–see reg.2.
"the Administration Act"–see reg.2.
"appeal"–see reg.2.
"assessment period"–see reg.2.
"benefit"–see reg.2.
"claimant"–see reg.2.
"the Claims and Payments Regulations 2013"–see reg.2.
"employment and support allowance"–by virtue of reg.2, see reg.1(3)(a).
"the Fraud Act"–see reg.2.
"jobseeker's allowance"–by virtue of reg.2, see reg.1(3)(b).
"personal independence payment"–see reg.2.
"the Universal Credit Regulations"–see reg.2.
"universal credit"–see reg.2.

General Note

2.736 This Schedule is equivalent to Sch.2 to the Social Security and Child Support (Decisions and Appeals) Regulations 1999. See the note to that Schedule.

The Social Security (General Benefit) Regulations 1982

(SI 1982/1408) (AS AMENDED)

ARRANGEMENT OF REGULATIONS

PART I

General

Regs 5-47 and schedules omitted.

The Secretary of State for Social Services, in exercise of the powers conferred upon him by sections 50(4), 56(7), 57(5), 58(3), 60(4) and (7), 61(1), 62(2), 67(1), 68(2), 70(2), 72(1) and (8), 74(1), 81(6), 82(5) and (6), 83(1), 85(1), 86(2) and (5), 90(2), 91(1), 119(3) and (4) and 159(3) of, and paragraphs 2, 3 and 6 of Schedule 8, paragraphs 1 and 8 of Schedule 9 and Schedule 14 of the Social Security Act 1975 and of all other powers enabling him in that behalf, hereby makes the following regulations, which only consolidate the regulation hereby revoked, and which accordingly, by virtue of paragraph 20 of Schedule 3 to the Social Security Act 1980, are not subject to the requirements of section 10 of that Act for prior reference to the Social Security Advisory Committee and, by virtue of section 141(2) and paragraph 12 of Schedule 16 of the Social Security Act 1975, do not require prior reference to the Industrial Injuries Advisory Council:—

PART I

GENERAL

Citation, commencement and application

1.—(1) These regulations may be cited as the Social Security (General Benefit) Regulations 1982 and shall come into operation on 4th November, 1982. 2.738

(2) In these regulations, unless the context otherwise requires—

"the Act" means the Social Security Act 1975;

[7 . . .]

"the Child Benefit Act" means the Child Benefit Act 1975;

"child benefit" means benefit under Part I of the Child Benefit Act;

[1 "determining authority" means, as the case may require, the Secretary of State, [5 the First-tier Tribunal or the Upper Tribunal]

"entitled to child benefit" includes treated as so entitled;

"industrial injuries benefit" means [2. . .] disablement benefit and industrial death benefit payable under section 50 of the Act;

"parent" has the meaning assigned to it by section 24(3) of the Child Benefit Act;

[4 "shared additional pension" means a shared additional pension under section 55A [6 or 55AA] of the Social Security Contributions and Benefits Act 1992;]

"standard rate of increase" means the amount specified in Part IV or Part V of Schedule 4 to the Act as the amount of an increase of the benefit in question for an adult dependant;

"the Workmen's Compensation Act" means the Workmen's Compensation Acts 1925 to 1945, or the enactments repealed by the Workmen's Compensation Act 1925 or the enactments repealed by the Workmen's Compensation Act 1906;

and other expressions have the same meanings as in the Act.

(3) Unless the context otherwise requires, any reference in these regulation—

(a) to a numbered section is to the section of the Act bearing that number;

(b) to a numbered regulation is a reference to the regulation bearing that number in these regulations and any reference in a regulation to a numbered paragraph is a reference to the paragraph of that regulation bearing that number.

AMENDMENTS

1. The Social Security Act 1998 (Commencement No.8, and Savings and Consequential and Transitional Provisions) Order 1999 (SI 1999/1958) Sch.5 (July 4, 1999).

2. The Social Security (Abolition of Injury Benefit) (Consequential) Regulations 1983 (SI 1983/186) reg.13 (April 6, 1983).

3. The Social Security (Benefits for Widows and Widowers) (Consequential Amendments) Regulations 2000 (SI 2000/1483) reg.8 (April 9, 2001).

4. The Social Security (Shared Additional Pension) (Miscellaneous Amendments) Regulations 2005 (SI 2005/1551) (July 6, 2005).

5. The Tribunals, Courts and Enforcement Act 2007 (Transitional and Consequential Provisions) Order 2008 (SI 2008/2683) reg.24 (November 3, 2008).

6. The Pensions Act 2014 (Consequential, Supplementary and Incidental Amendments) Order 2015 (SI 2015/1985) art.7 (April 6, 2016).

7. The Pensions Act 2014 (Consequential, Supplementary and Incidental Amendments) Order 2017 (SI 2017/422) art.8 (April 6, 2017).

Exceptions from disqualification for imprisonment etc.

2.739 **2.**—(1) The following provisions of this regulation shall have effect to except benefit from the operation of [section 113(1)(b) of the Social Security Contributions and Benefits Act 1992] which provides that (except where regulations otherwise provide) a person shall be disqualified for receiving any benefit and an increase of benefit shall not be payable in respect of any person as the beneficiary's [8 spouse or civil partner], for any period during which that person is undergoing imprisonment or detention in legal custody (hereinafter in this regulation referred to as "the said provisions").

(2) The said provisions shall not operate to disqualify a person for receiving [1incapacity benefit], [2attendance allowance, disability living allowance], widow's benefit, [11 widowed parent's allowance] child's special allowance, maternity allowance, [7 a shared additional pension] retirement pension of any category, age addition, [3severe disablement allowance], [4. . .disablement benefit], [5. . .reduced earnings allowance,

retirement allowance] or industrial death benefit or to make an increase of benefit not payable in respect of a person as the beneficiary's [8 spouse or civil partner], for any period during which that person is undergoing imprisonment or detention in legal custody in connection with a charge brought or intended to be brought against him in criminal proceedings, or pursuant to any sentence or order for detention made by a court in such proceedings, unless, in relation to him, a penalty is imposed at the conclusion of those proceedings or, in the case of default of payment of a sum adjudged to be paid on conviction, a penalty is imposed in respect of such default.

(3) The said provisions shall not operate to disqualify a person for receiving any benefit (not being a guardian's allowance or death grant), or to make an increase of benefit not payable in respect of a person as the beneficiary's [8 spouse or civil partner], for any period during which that person [10 P is detained in a hospital or similar institution in Great Britain as a person suffering from mental disorder unless P satisfied the following conditions.]

[10 (4) The first condition is that—

(a) P is being detained under section 45A or 47 of the Mental Health Act 1983 (power of higher courts to direct hospital admission; removal to hospital of persons serving sentences of imprisonment etc.); and

(b) in any case where there is in relation to P a release date within the meaning of section 50(3) of that Act, P is being detained on or before the day which the Secretary of State certifies to be that release date.

(4A) The second condition is that P is being detained under—

(a) section 59A of the Criminal Procedure (Scotland) Act 1995 (hospital direction); or

(b) section 136 of the Mental Health (Care and Treatment) (Scotland) Act 2003 (transfer of prisoners for treatment of mental disorder).]

is undergoing detention in legal custody after the conclusion of criminal proceedings if it is a period during which [10 ("P")] unless—

(5) The said provisions shall not operate to disqualify a person for receiving a guardian's allowance or death grant.

[5(6) Subject to paragraph (7), the said provisions shall not operate to disqualify a person for receiving disablement benefit, other than any increase of that benefit, for any period during which he is undergoing imprisonment or detention in legal custody.]

(7) The amount payable by virtue of the last preceding paragraph by way of any disablement pension or pensions in respect of any period, other than a period in respect of which that person is excepted from disqualification by virtue of the provisions of paragraph (3) of this regulation, during which that person is and has continuously been undergoing imprisonment or detention in legal custody, shall not exceed the total amount payable by way of such pension or all such pensions for a period of one year.

(8) For the purposes of this regulation—

(a) "court" means any court in the United Kingdom, the Channel Islands or the Isle of Man or in any place to which the Colonial Prisoners Removal Act 1884 applies or any naval court-martial, army court-martial or air force court-martial within the meaning of the Courts-Martial (Appeals) Act 1968, or the Courts-Martial Appeal Court;

(b) "hospital or similar institution" means any place (not being a prison, a detention centre, a Borstal institution, a young offenders institution or a remand centre, and not being at or in any such place) in which persons suffering from mental disorder are or may be received for care or treatment;

(c) "penalty" means a sentence of imprisonment, Borstal training or detention under section 53 of the Children and Young Persons Act 1933 or under section 57(3) of the Children and Young Persons (Scotland) Act 1937 or under section 208(3) and 416(4) of the Criminal Proceedings (Scotland) Act 1975 or an order for detention in a detention centre;

(d) in relation to a person who is liable to be detained in Great Britain as a result of any order made under the Colonial Prisoners Removal Act 1884, references to a prison shall be construed as including references to a prison within the meaning of that Act;

(e) [9. . .]

(f) [9. . .]

(g) criminal proceedings against any person shall be deemed to be concluded upon his being found insane in those proceedings so that he cannot be tried or his trial cannot proceed.

(9) Where a person outside Great Britain is undergoing imprisonment or detention in legal custody and, in similar circumstances in Great Britain, he would have been excepted, by the operation of any of the preceding paragraphs of this regulation, from disqualification under the said provisions (referred to in paragraph (1)) for receiving the benefit claimed, he shall not be disqualified for receiving that benefit by reason only of his said imprisonment or detention.

(10) Paragraph (9) applies to increases of benefit not payable under the said provisions as it applied to disqualification for receiving benefit.

Amendments

1. The Social Security (Incapacity Benefit) (Consequential and Transitional Amendments and Savings) Regulations 1995 (SI 1995/829) reg.16 (April 13, 1995).

2. The Disability Living Allowance and Disability Working Allowance (Consequential Provisions) Regulations 1991 (SI 1991/2742) reg.11 (April 6, 1992).

3. The Social Security (Severe Disablement Allowance) Regulations 1984 (SI 1984/1303) reg.11 (November 29, 1984).

4. The Social Security (Abolition of Injury benefit) (Consequential) Regulations 1983 (SI 1983/186) reg.13 (April 6, 1983).

5. The Social Security (Industrial Injuries and Diseases) (Miscellaneous Amendments) Regulations 1996 (SI 1996/425) reg.4 (March 24, 1996).

6. The Social Security (Benefits for Widows and Widowers) (Consequential Amendments) Regulations 2000 (SI 2000/1483) reg.6 (April 9, 2001).

7. The Social Security (Shared Additional Pension) (Miscellaneous Amendments) Regulations 2005 (SI 2005/1551) (July 6, 2005).

8. The Social Security (Civil Partnership) (Consequential Amendments) Regulations 2005 (SI 2005/2878) (December 5, 2005).

9. The Social Security (Hospital In-Patients) Regulations 2005 (SI 2005/3360) reg.3 (April 10, 2006).

10. The Social Security (Persons Serving a Sentence of Imprisonment Detained in Hospital) Regulations 2010 (SI 2010/442) reg.2(2) (March 25, 2010).

11. The Pensions Act 2014 (Consequential, Supplementary and Incidental Amendments) Order 2017 (SI 2017/422) art.8 (April 6, 2017).

DEFINITIONS

"the Act"—reg.1.
"benefit"—C & BA 1992 s.122.
"court"—para.(8)(a).
"Great Britain"—by art.1 of the Union with Scotland Act 1706, this means England, Scotland and Wales.
"hospital or similar institution"—para.(8)(b).
"penalty"—para.(8)(c).
"the said provisions"—para.(1).

GENERAL NOTE

Persons who can bring themselves within the terms of this regulation can escape the disqualification from benefit provided for in s.113(1)(b) of the Contributions and Benefits Act. Different rules apply to different benefits. **2.740**

Under para.(2) the disqualification applies in cases of imprisonment in connection with criminal proceedings where such penalty is imposed at the conclusion of proceedings. Imprisonment outside the exercise of criminal jurisdiction does not disqualify from benefit: *R(S)8/79*. It is now established that "penalty" in this paragraph includes the imposition of a suspended sentence and that a suspended sentence amounts to a sentence of imprisonment: *R(S)1/71*.

Paragraph (3) deals with the transfer of offenders from prison to hospital as mental patients under the mental health legislation. The disqualification in such circumstances exists only for the length of the original sentence: *R(P)2/57* reversing *R(S)9/56*. Provision is made for the Secretary of State to issue a certificate which is conclusive as to the earliest date on which the original sentence would come to an end had the person not been transferred to hospital.

A Commissioner has ruled in *CSS/239/2007* that, without a certificate of the type referred to in reg.2(4) of the General Benefit Regulations, an appellant could not obtain the advantage of the regulation. Paragraphs 8–10 of the decision address questions arising in relation to devolved government in Scotland.

A challenge relating to the exclusion from benefits of prisoners transferred to mental hospital under these regulations as being in breach of art.14 of the European Convention when read with art.1 of Protocol No.1 has failed with one exception: see *R. (on the application of EM) v Secretary of State for Work and Pensions* [2009] EWHC 454 (Admin). The excepted class is a small group (there were 45 such persons in detention when the case was decided) of what are described as "technical lifers", namely those, although sentenced to life imprisonment, are treated by the Secretary of State after transfer to hospital as though they had been made the subject of a hospital order under s.37 of the Mental Health Act 1983 and to a restriction order under s.41 of that Act.

Suspension of payment of benefit during imprisonment etc.

3.—(1) Subject to the following provisions of this regulation, the payment to any person of any benefit— **2.741**

(a) which is excepted from the operation of [section 113(1)(b) of the Social Security Contributions and Benefits Act 1992] by virtue of the provisions of regulation 2(2), (5) and (6) or by any of those paragraphs as applied by regulation 2(9); or

(b) which is payable otherwise than in respect of a period during which he is undergoing imprisonment or detention in legal custody;

shall be suspended while that person is undergoing imprisonment or detention in legal custody.

(2) Paragraph (1) shall not operate to require the payment of any benefit to be suspended while the beneficiary is liable to be detained in a hospital or

similar institution as defined in regulation 2(8)(b) during a period for which in his case, benefit to which regulation 2(3) applies is or would be excepted from the operation of the said [section 113(1)] by virtue of the provision of regulation 2(3).

(3) A guardian's allowance or death grant, or any benefit to which paragraph (1)(b) applies may nevertheless be paid while the beneficiary is undergoing imprisonment or detention in legal custody to any person appointed for the purpose by the Secretary of State to receive and deal with any sums payable on behalf of the beneficiary on account of that benefit, and the receipt of any person so appointed shall be a good discharge to the Secretary of State and the National Insurance Fund for any sum so paid.

(4) Where, by virtue of this regulation, payment of benefit under [Part V of the Social Security Contribution and Benefits Act 1992] is suspended for any period, the period of suspension shall not be taken into account in calculating any period under the provisions of regulation 22 of the Social Security (Claims and Payments) Regulations 1979 (extinguishment of right to sums payable by way of benefit which are not obtained within the prescribed time).

Interim payments by way of benefit under the Act

2.742 **4.**—(1) Where, under arrangements made by the Secretary of State with the consent of the Treasury, payment by way of benefit has been made pending determination of a claim for it without due proof of the fulfilment of the relevant conditions or otherwise than in accordance with the provisions of the Act and orders and regulations made under it, the payment so made shall, for the purposes of those provisions, but subject to the following provisions of this regulation, be deemed to be a payment of benefit duly made.

(2) When a claim for benefit in connection with which a payment has been made under arrangements such as are referred to in paragraph (1) above is determined by a determining authority—

(a) if that authority decides that nothing was properly payable by way of the benefit in respect of which the payment was made or that the amount properly payable by way of that benefit was less than the amount of the payment, it may, if appropriate, direct that the whole or part of the overpayment be treated as paid on account of benefit (whether benefit under the Act or the Supplementary Benefits Act 1976) which is properly payable, but subject as aforesaid shall require repayment of the overpayment; and

(b) if that authority decides that the amount properly payable by way of the benefit in respect of which the payment was made equals or exceeds the amount of that payment, it shall treat that payment as paid on account of the benefit properly payable.

(3) Unless before a payment made under arrangements such as are mentioned in paragraph (1) above has been made to a person that person had been informed of the effect of sub-paragraph (a) of paragraph (2) above as it relates to repayment of an overpayment, repayment of an overpayment shall not be required except where the determining authority is satisfied that[1] he, or any person acting for him, has, whether fraudulently or otherwise, misrepresented or failed to disclose any material fact and that the

interim payment has been made in consequence of the misrepresentation or failure.]

(4) An overpayment required to be repaid under the provisions of this regulation shall, without prejudice to any other method of recovery, be recoverable by deduction from any benefit then or thereafter payable to the person by whom it is to be repaid or any persons entitled to receive his benefit on his death.

AMENDMENT

1. The Social Security (Payments on account, Overpayment and Recovery) Regulations 1987 (SI 1987/491) reg.19 (April 6, 1987).

GENERAL NOTE

This regulation has not been repealed by the Overpayments Regulations because its provisions will still be needed for cases where the relevant determination was made before April 6, 1987. As time passes the provision will fall into disuse, and will in due course be revoked. **2.743**

The Social Security (Information-sharing in relation to Welfare Services etc.) Regulations 2012

(SI 2012/1483) (AS AMENDED)

ARRANGEMENT OF REGULATIONS

PART 1

GENERAL

PART 2

INFORMATION-SHARING IN RELATION TO PROVISION OF OVERNIGHT CARE ETC. UNDER SECTION 130 OF THE 2012 ACT

PART 3

INFORMATION-SHARING IN RELATION TO WELFARE SERVICES ETC. UNDER SECTIONS 131 TO 133 OF THE 2012 ACT

PART 4

INFORMATION-SHARING IN RELATION TO COUNCIL TAX UNDER SECTIONS 131 TO 133 OF THE 2012 ACT

PART 5

INFORMATION-SHARING IN RELATION TO SOCIAL SECURITY BENEFITS UNDER SECTION 131(2) OF THE 2012 ACT

The Secretary of State for Work and Pensions makes the following Regulations in exercise of the powers conferred by sections 130(2) and (7), 131(1), (3) and (11), 132(8) and 133(1) and (2) of the Welfare Reform Act 2012.

In respect of provisions in these Regulations relating to housing benefit, the Secretary of State has consulted with organisations appearing to him to be representative of the authorities concerned.

GENERAL NOTE

2.745 These regulations contain detailed provisions for the sharing of information between agencies connected with welfare services, council tax and social security benefits. They prescribe the extent of information sharing under SS.130–133 of the Welfare Reform Act 2012.

PART 1

GENERAL

Citation and commencement

2.746 **1.** These Regulations may be cited as the Social Security (Information-sharing in relation to Welfare Services etc.) Regulations 2012 and come into force on 2nd July 2012.

Interpretation

2. In these Regulations— **2.747**

"the 2012 Act" means the Welfare Reform Act 2012;

"the benefit cap" means the benefit cap (if any) which is provided for in regulations under section 96 of the 2012 Act;

"the Contributions and Benefits Act" means the Social Security Contributions and Benefits Act 1992;

[1 "council tax reduction scheme"—

(a) in England and Wales, has the meaning given in section 13A(9) of the Local Government Finance Act 1992 and (in England) includes a default scheme within the meaning of paragraph 4 of Schedule 1A to that Act [2 and (in Wales) includes a default scheme within the meaning of paragraph 6(1)(e) of Schedule 1B to that Act]; and

(b) in Scotland, means a means-tested reduction to an individual's council tax liability in accordance with the Council Tax Reduction (Scotland) Regulations 2012 or the Council Tax Reduction (State Pension Credit) (Scotland) Regulations 2012;]

"disabled person's badge" means a badge issued under section 21 of the Chronically Sick and Disabled Persons Act 1970 (badges for display on motor vehicles used by disabled persons);

[2 "the healthy start scheme" means the scheme established by the Healthy Start Scheme and Welfare Food (Amendment) Regulations 2005;]

"housing benefit" means housing benefit under section 130 of the Contributions and Benefits Act;

"housing benefit claimant" means a person who has made a claim for or is in receipt of housing benefit;

"the Housing Benefit Regulations" means the Housing Benefit Regulations 2006;

"the Housing Benefit (State Pension Credit) Regulations" means the Housing Benefit (Persons who have attained the qualifying age for state pension credit) Regulations 2006;

"housing support services" means—

in England, non-statutory assistance;

in Wales, services provided under the supporting people programme in Wales;

in Scotland, services of a type falling within the Schedule to the Housing (Scotland) Act 2001 (Housing Support Services) Regulations 2002);

"landlord" includes a person to whom rent allowance is payable under the Housing Benefit Regulations or regulation 76 of the Housing Benefit (State Pension Credit) Regulations (circumstances in which payment is to be made to a landlord), as the case may require;

[2 "local welfare provision" means occasional financial or other assistance given by a local authority, the Scottish Ministers or the Welsh Ministers, or a person authorised to exercise any function of theirs or providing a service to them, to or in respect of individuals for the purpose of—

(a) meeting, or helping to meet, an immediate short term need—

(i) arising out of an exceptional event or exceptional circumstances; and

(ii) that requires to be met in order to avoid a risk to the well-being of an individual; or

(b) enabling individuals to establish or maintain a settled home, where those individuals have been or, without the assistance, might otherwise be—

(i) in prison, hospital, a residential care establishment or other institution; or

(ii) homeless or otherwise living an unsettled way of life;]

"non-statutory assistance" means assistance provided by a local authority in England, in the form of the funding, planning, monitoring or delivery of housing-related support services for the purpose of enabling people aged 16 or over to overcome barriers to participation in society by assisting such people to live more independently within their home or community, but does not include the grant of a tenancy or the provision of accommodation;

[2 offence relating to a council tax reduction" means—

(a) any criminal offence in connection with the making of an application for a reduction under a council tax reduction scheme;

(b) any criminal offence in connection with the award of a reduction under a council tax reduction scheme;

(c) any criminal offence committed for the purpose of facilitating the commission (whether or not by the same person) of an offence of a kind referred to in paragraph (a) or (b); or

(d) any attempt or conspiracy to commit an offence of a kind referred to in paragraph (a) or (b);]

"regulations relating to under-occupation" means regulations (if any) that have been made under section 130A of the Contributions and Benefits Act which restrict, by reference to the number of bedrooms in relation to the number of people occupying the dwelling as their home, the amount of housing benefit available to housing benefit claimants whose landlord is a social landlord or local authority;

"rent" is to be construed in accordance with regulation 2(1) of the Housing Benefit Regulations or regulation 2(1) of the Housing Benefit (State Pension Credit) Regulations, as the case may require;

"residential care" means—

(a) in England and Wales, the provision of accommodation together with nursing and personal care in a care home as defined in section 3 of the Care Standards Act 2000;

(b) in Scotland, the provision of accommodation together with nursing, personal care or personal support by a care home service as defined in paragraph 2 of Schedule 12 to the Public Services Reform (Scotland) Act 2010;

[3 "social landlord" means—

(a) in a case to which the Housing Benefit Regulations apply, a landlord falling within regulation 13C(5)(a)(i), (ii) or (iii) of those Regulations;

(b) in a case to which the Housing benefit (State Pension Credit) Regulations apply, a landlord falling within regulation 13C(5)(a)(i), (ii) or (iii) of those Regulations;

(c) in a case to which the Universal Credit Regulations 2013 apply, a provider of social housing within the definition given in paragraph 2 of Schedule 4 (housing costs element for renters) to those Regulations;]

"the supporting people programme in Wales" means the programme of assistance provided by local authorities in Wales, in the form of the funding, planning, monitoring or delivery of housing-related support services for the purpose of enabling people aged 16 or over to overcome barriers to participation in society by assisting such people to live more independently within their home or community, other than through the grant of a tenancy or the provision of accommodation;

[2 troubled families programme" means any programme of assistance provided by a local authority] in England, for the purpose of engaging with households who face multiple disadvantages (such as crime, worklessness, truancy and anti-social behaviour), in the form of the funding, planning, monitoring or delivery of support services which assist members of such households to obtain employment, education or training, improve school attendance, or address crime and anti-social behaviour.

[2 "universal credit" means universal credit under Part 1 of the 2012 Act.]

[3 "universal credit claimant" means a person who has made a claim for or has an award of universal credit;

"universal support initiative" means any initiative under which advice, assistance or support is provided by the Secretary of State or any qualifying person listed in regulation 10(1)(e) to a universal credit claimant for the purposes of assisting them with—

(a) managing their claim for or award of universal credit, including accessing and using online services, or

(b) managing their financial affairs.]

AMENDMENTS

1. The Social Security (Information-sharing in relation to Welfare Services etc.) (Amendment) Regulations 2013 (SI 2013/41) reg.2(2) (February 11, 2013).

2. The Social Security (Information-sharing in relation to Welfare services etc.) Amendment and Prescribed Bodies Regulations 2013 (SI 2013/454) reg.3 (April 1, 2013).

3. The Social Security (Information-sharing in relation to Welfare Services etc.) (Amendment) Regulations 2015 (SI 2015/46) reg.2(2) (February 13, 2015).

PART 2

INFORMATION-SHARING IN RELATION TO PROVISION OF OVERNIGHT CARE ETC. UNDER SECTION 130 OF THE 2012 ACT

Prescribed information

3.—(1) The information prescribed under section 130(2)(c) of the 2012 Act (information held by a local authority) is— 2.748

(a) whether a resident is meeting in full the cost of the provision to them of residential care and if so the date this commenced and the period over which the cost is intended to be met;

(b) whether the local authority is funding or has funded in full or in part the cost of the provision to a resident of residential care and if so—

(i) the date from which the funding commenced and the period covered or intended to be covered by it;

(ii) the date when the funding stopped or is intended to stop;
(iii) the enactment under which the funding is being or was provided;
(iv) whether there exists any agreement enabling the local authority to recover the cost of the funding on the sale of the resident's home and if so, whether that recovery has commenced or when it is intended to commence; and
(v) whether the local authority has entered into a deferred payment agreement with the resident and if so the date this commenced and the period the agreement is intended to cover.

(2) In this regulation—
(a) "deferred payment agreement" has the meaning given in section 55(3) of the Health and Social Care Act 2001 or (in Scotland) section 6(2) of the Community Care and Health (Scotland) Act 2002;
(b) "resident" means a recipient of residential care.

Prescribed benefits

2.749 **4.** The benefits prescribed under section 130(7)(d) of the 2012 Act are—
(a) attendance allowance under section 64 of the Contributions and Benefits Act;
(b) disability living allowance under section 71 of the Contributions and Benefits Act
(c) income-based jobseeker's allowance within the meaning given in section 1(4) of the Jobseekers Act 1995;
(d) income-related employment and support allowance payable in accordance with section 1(2)(b) of the Welfare Reform Act 2007;
(e) income support under section 124 of the Contributions and Benefits Act; [1 . . .]
(f) state pension credit under section 1 of the State Pension Credit Act 2002 [1 ; and
(g) personal independence payment under Part 4 of the 2012 Act.]

AMENDMENT

1. The Personal Independence Payments (Supplementary Provisions and Consequential Amendments) Regulations 2013 (SI 2013/388) reg.8 and Sch. para.48 (April 8, 2013).

PART 3

INFORMATION-SHARING IN RELATION TO WELFARE SERVICES [1 . . .] UNDER SECTIONS 131 TO 133 OF THE 2012 ACT

Supply of relevant information by the Secretary of State

2.750 **5.**—(1) The purposes prescribed under section 131(1) of the 2012 Act [1 in relation to welfare services] (purposes for which the Secretary of State or a person providing services to the Secretary of State may supply relevant information to a qualifying person) are—

[2 (a) determining a person's eligibility or continued eligibility for—

(i) a disabled person's badge;
(ii) assistance under the healthy start scheme; or
(iii) local welfare provision;]

(b) determining whether to make to any person any grant or payment listed in paragraph (2) and if so the amount of any such grant or payment;

(c) determining whether a person applying for or receiving a welfare service listed in paragraph (3) is liable to contribute towards the cost of that service and if so the amount of that contribution; [2 . . .]

[2 "(d) where the qualifying person is a local authority in England—
(i) identifying households eligible for support under a troubled families programme;
(ii) providing appropriate types of advice, support and assistance to members of such households under such programmes; and
(iii) monitoring and evaluating such programmes;]

[2 "(e) discharging any functions under Part 7 of the Housing Act 1996 or (in Scotland) Part 2 of the Housing (Scotland) Act 1987; and

(f) identifying, and providing appropriate types of advice, support and assistance to, persons in receipt of a relevant social security benefit who are or may be affected by—
(i) the benefit cap;
(ii) regulations relating to under-occupation.]

[3 (g) where the qualifying person is a social landlord and the relevant information is limited to information referred to in paragraph (3A), determining whether a universal credit claimant, whose award includes or is likely to include a housing costs element in respect of accommodation provided by that social landlord, needs advice, assistance or support in relation to managing their financial affairs;

(h) where the qualifying person is listed in regulation 10(1)(e) and the Secretary of State or any qualifying person listed in regulation 10(1)(e) determines that a universal credit claimant needs advice, assistance or support under a universal support initiative—
(i) providing such advice, assistance or support to that person; and
(ii) monitoring and evaluating the provision of such advice, assistance or support.]

(2) The grants and payments referred to in paragraph (1)(b) are—
(a) a disability adaptation grant;
(b) a disabled facilities grant;
(c) a discretionary housing payment.

(3) The welfare services referred to in paragraph (1)(c) are—
(a) housing support services;
(b) the provision of domiciliary care;
(c) the provision of residential care.

[3 (3A) The information referred to in paragraph (1)(g) is information confirming—
(a) the identity of the universal credit claimant;
(b) that the universal credit claimant has a tenancy with the social landlord;
(c) the date on which the universal credit claimant made a claim for or was awarded universal credit; or
(d) in a case where universal credit has been awarded to the universal credit claimant—

(i) the date on which the next payment of universal credit is due to be paid;
(ii) whether the next payment is the first payment under the award; or
(iii) the amount of housing costs element in the next payment under the award.]

(4) In this regulation—
(a) "disability adaptation grant" means a grant paid under Part 2 of the Housing (Scotland) Act 2006 to assist with the adaptation of a house for a disabled person to make it suitable for the accommodation, welfare or employment of that person;
(b) "disabled facilities grant" means a grant paid under Chapter 1 of Part 1 of the Housing Grants, Construction and Regeneration Act 1996;
(c) "discretionary housing payment" means a payment made pursuant to regulation 2(1) of the Discretionary Financial Assistance Regulations 2001;
(d) "domiciliary care" means care or assistance of any description provided to an adult person by reason of their age, health or any disability, whether provided continuously or not and whether or not provided at a place where they live, but excludes care or assistance provided to a person in residential care.
[3 (e) "housing costs element" means an amount in respect of housing costs which is included in an award of universal credit under section 11 of the 2012 Act.]

AMENDMENTS

1. The Social Security (Information-sharing in relation to Welfare Services etc.) (Amendment) Regulations 2013 (SI 2013/41) reg.2 (February 11, 2013).
2. The Social Security (Information-sharing in relation to Welfare services etc.) Amendment and Prescribed Bodies Regulations 2013 (SI 2013/454) reg.3 (April 1, 2013).
3. The Social Security (Information-sharing in relation to Welfare Services etc.) (Amendment) Regulations 2015 (SI 2015/46) reg.2(3) (February 13, 2015).

Holding purposes

2.751 **6.—**(1) The purposes prescribed under section 131(3) of the 2012 Act as purposes for which relevant information must be held by a qualifying person in order for them to use or supply it as set out in that subsection, are any of the following—
[1 (a) determining a person's eligibility or continued eligibility for—
(i) a disabled person's badge;
(ii) assistance under the healthy start scheme;
(iii) housing support services; or
(iv) local welfare provision;]
(b) determining whether to make to any person any grant or payment listed in regulation 5(2) and if so the amount of any such grant or payment;
(c) determining whether a person applying for or receiving a welfare service listed in regulation 5(3) is liable to contribute towards the cost of that service and if so the amount of that contribution;

[1 (d) where the qualifying person is a local authority in England, a person providing services to a local authority in England relating to a troubled families programme, or a person who falls within regulation 10(1)(b)—

(i) identifying households eligible for support under a troubled families programme;

(ii) providing appropriate types of advice, support and assistance to members of such households under such programmes; and

(iii) monitoring and evaluating such programmes;]

(e) discharging any functions under Part 7 of the Housing Act 1996(a) or (in Scotland) Part 2 of the Housing (Scotland) Act 1987(b);

(f) determining whether a person is in receipt of housing benefit;

(g) determining the size of a dwelling occupied by a [1 person in receipt of a relevant social security benefit] and the number of persons occupying that dwelling as their home;

(h) identifying [1 persons in receipt of a relevant social security benefit] who are or may be affected by regulations relating to under-occupation, and providing appropriate types of advice, support and assistance to such persons;

(i) identifying [1 persons in receipt of a relevant social security benefit] who are or may be affected by the benefit cap, and providing appropriate types of advice, support and assistance to such persons;

(j) determining the amount of housing benefit payable to a housing benefit claimant by reference to the local housing allowance;

(k) [2 . . .]

(l) determining whether a [1 person in receipt of a relevant social security benefit] is likely to have difficulty in managing their financial affairs;

(m) determining the probability that a housing benefit claimant will pay their rent;

(n) determining whether the landlord of a housing benefit claimant—

(i) was to provide qualifying welfare services to that housing benefit claimant but has not done so, or

(ii) is to provide qualifying welfare services to that housing benefit claimant but is unlikely to do so;

(o) determining whether—

(i) the landlord of a housing benefit claimant is a social landlord,

(ii) a housing benefit claimant occupies as their home a dwelling which is exempt accommodation,

(iii) the tenancy of a housing benefit claimant is an excluded tenancy,

(iv) a housing benefit claimant occupies as their home a houseboat, caravan or mobile home, or

(v) a housing benefit claimant resides in a hostel.

[1 "(p) identifying the amount of housing costs included in an award of universal credit by reference to the local housing allowance.]

[3 (q) where the qualifying person is listed in regulation 10(1)(e)—

(i) providing advice, assistance or support to a universal credit claimant under a universal support initiative; and

(ii) monitoring and evaluating the provision of such advice, assistance or support.]

(2) In this regulation—

(a) "excluded tenancy" means a tenancy of a type falling within any of paragraphs 4 to 11 of Schedule 2 to the Housing Benefit Regulations or paragraphs 4 to 11 of Schedule 2 to the Housing Benefit (State Pension Credit) Regulations, as the case may require;

(b) "exempt accommodation" has the meaning given in paragraph 4(10) of Schedule 3 to the Housing Benefit and Council Tax Benefit (Consequential Provisions) Regulations 2006 (transitional and savings provision);

(c) "hostel" has the meaning given in regulation 2(1) of the Housing Benefit Regulations or regulation 2(1) of the Housing Benefit (State Pension Credit) Regulations, as the case may require;

(d) "local housing allowance" means an allowance determined in accordance with paragraph 2 of Schedule 3B to the Rent Officers Order;

(e) "Rent Officers Order" means the Rent Officers (Housing Benefit Functions) Order 1997 or (in Scotland) the Rent Officers (Housing Benefit Functions) (Scotland) Order 1997;

AMENDMENTS

1. The Social Security (Information-sharing in relation to Welfare services etc.) Amendment and Prescribed Bodies Regulations 2013 (SI 2013/454) reg.3 (April 1, 2013).

2. The Council Tax Benefit Abolition (Consequential Provision) Regulations 2013 (SI 2013/458) reg.3 (April 1, 2013).

3. The Social Security (Information-sharing in relation to Welfare Services etc.) (Amendment) Regulations 2015 (SI 2015/46) reg.2(4) (February 13, 2015).

Using purposes connected with welfare services and housing benefit

2.752 **7.—**(1) This regulation applies to relevant information held by a qualifying person for any purpose listed in regulation 6 except the [1 purposes listed in regulation 6(1)(a)(ii), (iv) or (d)].

(2) The purposes set out in paragraph (3) are prescribed—

(a) under section 131(3)(a) of the 2012 Act as purposes for which the information may be used by that qualifying person; and

(b) subject to regulation 11, under section 131(3)(b) of the 2012 Act as purposes for use in relation to which the information may be supplied by that qualifying person to another qualifying person.

(3) The purposes are any purposes connected with—

[1 "(a) the purposes referred to in regulation 6(1)(a)(i) or (iii), (b), (c), (e), (h) or (i);]

(b) applying any of the following regulations—

(i) regulation 13C(5) of the Housing Benefit Regulations (cases where a maximum rent (LHA) is not to be determined);

(ii) regulation 96(3) or (3A) of the Housing Benefit Regulations(d) (circumstances in which payment may be made to a landlord);

(iii) regulation 13C(5) of the Housing Benefit (State Pension Credit) Regulations (cases where a maximum rent (LHA) is not to be determined);

(iv) regulation 77(3) or (3A) of the Housing Benefit (State Pension Credit) Regulations(e) (circumstances in which payment may be made to a landlord);

(c) determining whether the qualifying person who uses the information or to whom it is supplied holds other relevant information about a [1 person in receipt of a relevant social security benefit] for any purpose prescribed in regulation 6.

AMENDMENT

1. The Social Security (Information-sharing in relation to Welfare services etc.) Amendment and Prescribed Bodies Regulations 2013 (SI 2013/454) reg.3 (April 1, 2013).

Using purposes connected with [1 a troubled families programme]

8.—(1) This regulation applies to relevant information held by a qualifying person which is a local authority in England [1 or a person who falls within regulation 10(1)(b)] for the purpose listed in regulation [1 6(1)(d)] or the purpose listed in regulation [1 6(1)(i)]. 2.753

(2) The purposes set out in paragraph (3) are prescribed—

(a) under section 131(3)(a) of the 2012 Act as purposes for which the information may be used by that qualifying person; and

(b) under section 131(3)(b) of the 2012 Act as purposes for use in relation to which the information may be supplied by that qualifying person to another qualifying person.

(3) The purposes are any purposes connected with [1 troubled families programme].

(4) This regulation permits relevant information to be supplied to another qualifying person only where that other qualifying person is also a local authority in England [1 or a person who falls within regulation 10(1)(b)].

[1 (5) The references in regulations 8(1) and (4) to a local authority in England include references to a person providing services to a local authority in England relating to a troubled families programme.]

AMENDMENT

1. The Social Security (Information-sharing in relation to Welfare services etc.) Amendment and Prescribed Bodies Regulations 2013 (SI 2013/454) reg.3 (April 1, 2013).

Using purposes connected with under-occupation and benefit cap

9.—(1) This regulation applies to relevant information held by a qualifying person for any purpose listed in regulation [1 6(1)(f)] to (i). 2.754

(2) The purposes set out in paragraph (3) are prescribed—

(a) under section 131(3)(a) of the 2012 Act as purposes for which the information may be used by that qualifying person; and

(b) under section 131(3)(b) of the 2012 Act as purposes for use in relation to which the information may be supplied by that qualifying person to another qualifying person.

(3) The purposes are any purposes connected with—

(a) identifying [1 persons in receipt of a relevant social security benefit] who are or may be affected by regulations relating to under-occupation, and providing appropriate types of advice, support and assistance to such persons;

(b) identifying housing benefit claimants who are or may be affected by the benefit cap, and

providing appropriate types of advice, support and assistance to such persons.

AMENDMENT

1. The Social Security (Information-sharing in relation to Welfare services etc.) Amendment and Prescribed Bodies Regulations 2013 (SI 2013/454) reg.3 (April 1, 2013).

[1 Using purposes connected with the healthy start scheme

2.755 **9A.**—(1) This regulation applies to relevant information held by the Secretary of State for Health or by a person providing services to the Secretary of State for Health, as a qualifying person for the purpose listed in regulation 6(1)(a)(ii).

(2) The purposes set out in paragraph (3) are prescribed—

(a) under section 131(3)(a) of the 2012 Act as purposes for which the information may be used by that qualifying person; and

(b) under section 131(3)(b) of the 2012 Act as purposes for use in relation to which the information may be supplied by that qualifying person to another qualifying person.

(3) The purposes are any purposes connected with the healthy start scheme.]

(4) This regulation permits relevant information to be supplied to another qualifying person only where that other qualifying person is the Secretary of State for Health or a person providing services to the Secretary of State for Health relating to the healthy start scheme.]

AMENDMENT

1. Inserted by The Social Security (Information-sharing in relation to Welfare services etc.) Amendment and Prescribed Bodies Regulations 2013 (SI 2013/454) reg.3 (April 1, 2013).

[1 Using purposes connected with local welfare provision

2.756 **9B.**—(1) This regulation applies to relevant information held by a qualifying person listed in regulation 10(1)(d) or section 131(11)(a) to (c) of the 2012 Act for the purpose listed in regulation 6(1)(a)(iv).

(2) The purposes set out in paragraph (3) are prescribed—

(a) under section 131(3)(a) of the 2012 Act as purposes for which the information may be used by a qualifying person; and

(b) subject to regulation 11, under section 131(3)(b) of the 2012 Act as purposes for use in relation to which the information may be supplied by that qualifying person to another qualifying person.

(3) The purposes are any purposes connected with local welfare provision.

(4) This regulation permits relevant information to be supplied to another qualifying person only where that other qualifying person is listed in regulation 10(1)(d) or section 131(11)(a) to (c) of the 2012 Act.]

AMENDMENT

1. Inserted by The Social Security (Information-sharing in relation to Welfare services etc.) Amendment and Prescribed Bodies Regulations 2013 (SI 2013/454) reg.3 (April 1, 2013).

[1 Using purposes connected with a universal support initiative

9C.—(1) This regulation applies to relevant information held by a qualifying person listed in regulation 10(1)(e) for the purposes listed in regulation 6(1)(q). 2.757

(2) The purposes set out in paragraph (3) are prescribed—

(a) under section 131(3)(a) of the 2012 Act as purposes for which the information maybe used by that qualifying person; and

(b) under section 131(3)(b) of the 2012 Act as purposes for use in relation to which the information may be supplied by that qualifying person to another qualifying person.

(3) The purposes are any purposes connected with—

(a) providing advice, assistance or support to a universal credit claimant under a universal support initiative; and

(b) monitoring and evaluating the provision of such advice, assistance or support.

(4) This regulation permits relevant information to be supplied to another qualifying person only where that other qualifying person is listed in regulation 10(1)(e).]

AMENDMENT

1. The Social Security (Information-sharing in relation to Welfare Services etc.) (Amendment) Regulations 2015 (SI 2015/46) reg.2(5) (February 13, 2015).

Qualifying persons

[1 **10.**—(1) The following persons are prescribed as qualifying persons under section 131(11)(g) of the 2012 Act— 2.758

(a) for the purposes of regulations [2 5(1)(g)] 6(1)(f) to (i) and 9, a social landlord;

(b) for the purposes of regulations 6(1)(d) and 8, a person who carries out activities in connection with a troubled families programme;

(c) for the purposes of regulations 5(1)(a)(ii), 6(1)(a)(ii) and 9A—

(i) the Secretary of State for Health;

(ii) a person providing services to the Secretary of State for Health relating to the healthy start scheme;

(d) for the purposes of regulations 5(1)(a)(iii), 6(1)(a)(iv) and 9B—

(i) the Scottish Ministers;

(ii) a person authorised to exercise any function of the Scottish Ministers relating to local welfare provision;

(iii) a person providing to the Scottish Ministers services relating to local welfare provision;

(iv) the Welsh Ministers;

(v) a person authorised to exercise any function of the Welsh Ministers relating to local welfare provision;

(vi) a person providing to the Welsh Ministers services relating to local welfare provision.

[2 (e) for the purposes of regulations 5(1)(h), 6(1)(q), 9C, 16(d) and 17(3)(c)—
(i) a person listed in section 131(11)(a), (b) or (c) of the 2012 Act,
(ii) a member of the National Association of Citizens Advice Bureaux or the Scottish Association of Citizens Advice Bureaux,
(iii) a credit union within section 1 of the Credit Unions Act 1979,
(iv) a social landlord,
(v) a charity entered in the register of charities maintained under Part 4 of the Charities Act 2011 or a body entered on the register of charities maintained under the Charities and Trustee Investment (Scotland) Act 2005.]

(2) The provisions of section 132 of the 2012 Act (offence of unlawful disclosure) apply to—
(a) the qualifying persons listed in paragraph (1) other than the Secretary of State for Health, the Scottish Ministers and the Welsh Ministers; and
(b) any person ("A") associated with a qualifying person listed in paragraph (1)(a), (c)(i), (d)(i) or (iv) by reason of A's office or employment or otherwise.]

AMENDMENT

1. Substituted by The Social Security (Information-sharing in relation to Welfare services etc.) Amendment and Prescribed Bodies Regulations 2013 (SI 2013/454) reg.3 (April 1, 2013).
2. The Social Security (Information-sharing in relation to Welfare Services etc.) (Amendment) Regulations 2015 (SI 2015/46) reg.2(6) (February 13, 2015).

Excepted matters

2.759 **11.**—(1) Regulation 7(2)(b) does not permit relevant information held by a Welsh body or a Scottish body for a purpose listed in regulation [1 6(1)(a)(i) or (iii)], (b), (c) or (e) to be supplied by that body to another qualifying person for use in relation to the same or any other such purpose.

[1 "(1A) Regulation 9B(2)(b) does not permit relevant information held by a Welsh body or a Scottish body to be supplied by that body to another qualifying person for use in relation to any purpose connected with local welfare provision.]

(2) This regulation does not apply if the information was supplied by, or is derived from information supplied to another person by, the Secretary of State or a person providing services to the Secretary of State or a person engaged in the administration of housing benefit.

AMENDMENT

1. The Social Security (Information-sharing in relation to Welfare services etc.) Amendment and Prescribed Bodies Regulations 2013 (SI 2013/454) reg.3 (April 1, 2013).

[1 PART 4

INFORMATION-SHARING IN RELATION TO COUNCIL TAX UNDER SECTIONS 131 TO 133 OF THE 2012 ACT

Supply of relevant information by the Secretary of State

12.—The purposes prescribed under section 131(1) of the 2012 Act in relation to council tax (purposes for which the Secretary of State or a person providing services to the Secretary of State may supply relevant information to a qualifying person) are— 2.760

(a) making a council tax reduction scheme;
(b) determining a person's entitlement or continued entitlement to a reduction under a council tax reduction scheme.]
[2 "(c) preventing, detecting, securing evidence of, or prosecuting the commission of, an offence relating to a council tax reduction.]

AMENDMENTS

1. Inserted by the Social Security (Information-sharing in relation to Welfare Services etc.) (Amendment) Regulations 2013 (SI 2013/41) reg.2(5) (February 11, 2013).
2. The Social Security (Information-sharing in relation to Welfare services etc.) Amendment and Prescribed Bodies Regulations 2013 (SI 2013/454) reg.3 (April 1, 2013).

[1 Holding purposes

13.—The purposes prescribed under section 131(3) of the 2012 Act in relation to council tax as purposes for which relevant information must be held by a qualifying person in order for them to use or supply it as set out in that subsection, are— 2.761

(a) making a council tax reduction scheme;
(b) determining a person's entitlement or continued entitlement to a reduction under a council tax reduction scheme.]
[2 "(c) preventing, detecting, securing evidence of, or prosecuting the commission of, an offence relating to a council tax reduction.]

AMENDMENTS

1. Inserted by the Social Security (Information-sharing in relation to Welfare Services etc.) (Amendment) Regulations 2013 (SI 2013/41) reg.2(5) (February 11, 2013).
2. The Social Security (Information-sharing in relation to Welfare services etc.) Amendment and Prescribed Bodies Regulations 2013 (SI 2013/454) reg.3 (April 1, 2013).

[1 Using purposes

[2 **14.**—(1) This regulation applies to relevant information held by a qualifying person for any purpose listed in regulation 13. 2.762

(2) The purposes set out in paragraph (3) are prescribed—
(a) under section 131(3)(a) of the 2012 Act as purposes for which the information may be used by that qualifying person; and
(b) subject to regulation 15, under section 131(3)(b) of the 2012 Act as purposes for use in relation to which the information may be supplied by that qualifying person to another qualifying person.

(3) The purposes are any purposes connected with—
(a) making a council tax reduction scheme;
(b) determining a person's entitlement or continued entitlement to a reduction under a council tax reduction scheme;
(c) preventing, detecting, securing evidence of, or prosecuting the commission of, an offence relating to a council tax reduction;
(d) any proceedings in connection with a reduction under a council tax reduction scheme before—
(i) the Valuation Tribunal for England, established under Part 1 of Schedule 11 to the Local Government Finance Act 1988(**5**);
(ii) the Valuation Tribunal for Wales, established under Part 2 of Schedule 11 to the Local Government Finance Act 1988; or
(iii) a valuation appeal committee established under section 29 of the Local Government etc. (Scotland) Act 1994(**6**);
(e) the purposes referred to in regulation 6(1)(a)(i) or (iii), (b) or (c).]]

AMENDMENTS

1. Inserted by the Social Security (Information-sharing in relation to Welfare Services etc.) (Amendment) Regulations 2013 (SI 2013/41) reg.2(5) (February 11, 2013).
2. The Social Security (Information-sharing in relation to Welfare services etc.) Amendment and Prescribed Bodies Regulations 2013 (SI 2013/454) reg.3 (April 1, 2013).

[1 Excepted matters

2.763 **15.**—(1) Subject to paragraph (2), regulation 14 does not permit relevant information held by a Welsh body or a Scottish body to be supplied by that body to another qualifying person for use in relation to that purpose.

(2) Paragraph (1) does not apply if the information was supplied by, or is derived from, information supplied to another person by the Secretary of State (or a person providing services to the Secretary of State) or a person engaged in the administration of housing benefit.]

AMENDMENT

1. Inserted by the Social Security (Information-sharing in relation to Welfare Services etc.) (Amendment) Regulations 2013 (SI 2013/41) reg.2(5) (February 11, 2013).

[1 PART 5

INFORMATION-SHARING IN RELATION TO SOCIAL SECURITY BENEFITS UNDER SECTION 131(2) OF THE 2012 ACT

Holding purposes

2.764 **16.** The purposes prescribed under section 131(2) of the 2012 Act (supply of information to the Secretary of State or service provider for purposes relating to relevant social security benefit) as purposes for which relevant information must be held by a qualifying person in order for them to supply it as set out in that subsection, are any of the following—
(a) determining whether a person occupies as their home a dwelling which falls within paragraph 4(1)(b) of Schedule 3 to the Housing

Benefit and Council Tax Benefit (Consequential Provisions) Regulations 2006(7);

(b) determining whether a person has, or is likely to have, difficulty in managing their financial affairs;

(c) where the qualifying person is a local authority in England—

(i) identifying households eligible for support under a troubled families programme;

(ii) providing appropriate types of advice, support and assistance to members of such households under such programmes; and

(iii) monitoring and evaluating such programmes.]

[2 (d) where the qualifying person is listed in regulation 10(1)(e)—

(i) providing advice, assistance or support to a universal credit claimant under a universal support initiative; and

(ii) monitoring and evaluating the provision of such advice, assistance or support.]

AMENDMENTS

1. Inserted by The Social Security (Information-sharing in relation to Welfare services etc.) Amendment and Prescribed Bodies Regulations 2013 (SI 2013/454) reg.3 (April 1, 2013).

2. The Social Security (Information-sharing in relation to Welfare Services etc.) (Amendment) Regulations 2015 (SI 2015/46) reg.2(7) (February 13, 2015).

[1 Prescribed purposes relating to a relevant social security benefit

17.—(1) This regulation applies to relevant information held by a qualifying person for any purpose listed in regulation 16. 2.765

(2) The purposes set out in paragraph (3) are prescribed under section 131(2) of the 2012 Act as purposes for which the information may be supplied to the Secretary of State or a person providing services to the Secretary of State.

(3) Those purposes are—

(a) in relation to the purposes prescribed in regulation 16(a) and (b), any purpose connected with the administration of universal credit;

(b) in relation to any purpose prescribed in regulation 16(c)—

(i) any purpose connected with providing appropriate types of advice, support and assistance to a person in connection with their receipt of a relevant social security benefit; and

(ii) any purpose connected with monitoring and evaluating the effect of participation in a troubled families programme on receipt of a relevant social security benefit.]

[2 (c) in relation to either of the purposes prescribed in regulation 16(d)—

(i) providing advice, assistance or support to a universal credit claimant under a universal support initiative; and

(ii) monitoring and evaluating the provision of such advice, assistance or support.]

AMENDMENTS

1. Inserted by The Social Security (Information-sharing in relation to Welfare services etc.) Amendment and Prescribed Bodies Regulations 2013 (SI 2013/454) reg.3 (April 1, 2013).

2. The Social Security (Information-sharing in relation to Welfare Services etc.) (Amendment) Regulations 2015 (SI 2015/46) reg.2(8) (February 13, 2015).

The Social Security (Information-sharing in relation to Welfare Services etc.) Amendment and Prescribed Bodies Regulations 2013

(SI 2013/454)

COMMENCEMENT: APRIL 1, 2013

ARRANGEMENT OF REGULATIONS

The Secretary of State for Work and Pensions makes the following Regulations in exercise of the powers conferred by sections 131(1), (2), (3), (11) and (12), 132(8) and 133(1) and (2) of the Welfare Reform Act 2012(**1**).

Citation, commencement and interpretation

2.767 **1.**—(1) These Regulations may be cited as the Social Security (Information-sharing in relation to Welfare Services etc.) Amendment and Prescribed Bodies Regulations 2013.

(2) They come into force on 1st April 2013.

(3) In these Regulations "the 2012 Act" means the Welfare Reform Act 2012.

Prescription of Scottish bodies and Welsh bodies

2.768 **2.**—(1) The following are prescribed as Scottish bodies for the purpose of paragraph (d) of the definition of that term in section 131(12) of the 2012 Act—

(a) the Scottish Ministers;
(b) a person authorised to exercise any function of the Scottish Ministers relating to welfare services;
(c) a person providing to the Scottish Ministers services relating to welfare services.

(2) The following are prescribed as Welsh bodies for the purpose of paragraph (d) of the definition of that term in section 131(12) of the 2012 Act—

(a) the Welsh Ministers;
(b) a person authorised to exercise any function of the Welsh Ministers relating to welfare services;
(c) a person providing to the Welsh Ministers services relating to welfare services.

The Social Security (Jobcentre Plus Interviews) Regulations 2002

(SI 2002/1703) (AS AMENDED)

ARRANGEMENT OF REGULATIONS

The Secretary of State for Work and Pensions, in exercise of the powers conferred upon him by sections 2A(1), (3) to (6) and (8), 2B(6) and (7), 5(1)(a) and (b), 6(1)(a) and (b), 7A, 189(1), (4) and (5) and 191 of the Social Security Administration Act 1992 and section 68 of, and paragraphs 3(1), 4(4), 6(8), 20(3) and 23(1) of Schedule 7 to, the Child Support, Pensions and Social Security Act 2000, and of all other powers enabling him in that behalf, after consultation with the Council on Tribunals in accordance with section 8(1) of the Tribunals and Inquiries Act 1992 and in respect of provisions in these Regulations relating to housing benefit and council tax benefit with organisations appearing to him to be representative of the authorities concerned, and after agreement by the Social Security Advisory Committee that proposals in respect of these Regulations should not be referred to it, hereby makes the following Regulations:

Citation and commencement

1. These Regulations may be cited as the Social Security (Jobcentre Plus Interviews) Regulations 2002 and shall come into force on 30th September 2002. 2.770

Interpretation and application

2.771 **2.**—(1) In these Regulations, unless the context otherwise requires—

"the 1998 Act" means the Social Security Act 1998;

"benefit week" means any period of seven days corresponding to the week in respect of which the relevant specified benefit is due to be paid;

[3 . . .]

[8 . . .]

"interview" means a work-focused interview with a person who has claimed a specified benefit and which is conducted for any or all of the following purposes—

(a) assessing that person's prospects for existing or future employment (whether paid or voluntary);

(b) assisting or encouraging that person to enhance his prospects of such employment;

(c) identifying activities which that person may undertake to strengthen his existing or future prospects of employment;

(d) identifying current or future employment or training opportunities suitable to that person's needs; and

(e) identifying educational opportunities connected with the existing or future employment prospects or needs of that person;

[3 "lone parent" has the meaning it bears in regulation 2(1) of the Income Support (General) Regulations 1987;]

"officer" means a person who is an officer of, or who is providing services to or exercising functions of, the Secretary of State;

[6 "pensionable age", in the case of a man born before 6th April 1955, means the age when a woman born on the same day as the man would attain pensionable age;]

[3 "relevant benefit" means income support other than income support where one of the following paragraphs of Schedule 1B to the Income Support (General) Regulations 1987 applies—

(a) paragraph 7 (persons incapable of work), or

(b) paragraph 24 or 25 (persons appealing against a decision which embodies a determination that they are not incapable of work);]

[8 "relevant interview" means an interview under these Regulations in relation to the claimant's current award of a specified benefit;]

[3 "specified benefit" means income support, incapacity benefit and severe disablement allowance;]

[3 "specified person" means—

(a) a lone parent, or

(b) a person who claims—

(i) incapacity benefit,

(ii) income support where paragraph 7 (persons incapable of work) of Schedule 1B to the Income Support (General) Regulations 1987 applies,

(iii) income support where paragraph 24 or 25 (persons appealing against a decision which embodies a determination that they are not incapable of work) of Schedule 1B to the Income Support (General) Regulations 1987 applies, or

(iv) severe disablement allowance.]

(2) For the purposes of these Regulations—

(a) a person shall be deemed to be in remunerative work where he is in remunerative work within the meaning prescribed in [4 regulation 6 of the Housing Benefit Regulations 2006]; but
(b) a person shall be deemed not to be in remunerative work where—
  (i) he is not in remunerative work in accordance with subparagraph (a) above; or
  (ii) he is in remunerative work in accordance with sub-paragraph (a) above and is not entitled to income support but would not be prevented from being entitled to income support solely by being in such work; and
(c) a person shall be deemed to be engaged in part-time work where he is engaged in work for which payment is made but he is not engaged or deemed to be engaged in remunerative work.

[8 (2A) For the purposes of section 2A(2A)(b) of the Social Security Administration Act 1992 and these Regulations, a lone parent is to be treated as responsible for, and a member of the same household as, a child under the age of one only where the lone parent would be treated as being responsible for, and a member of the same household as, such a child under regulations 15 and 16 of the Income Support (General) Regulations 1987, if references in those Regulations to income support were to a specified benefit.]

(3) Except in a case where regulation 16(2) applies [5. . .] regulations 3 to 15 apply in respect of a person who makes a claim for a specified benefit on or after 30th September 2002 at an office of the Department for Work and Pensions which is designated by the Secretary of State as a Jobcentre Plus Office or at an office of a relevant authority (being a person within section 72(2) of the Welfare Reform and Pensions Act 1999) which displays the **one** logo.

(4) Where a claim for benefit is made by a person ("the appointee") on behalf of another, references in these Regulations to a person claiming benefit shall be treated as a reference to the person on whose behalf the claim is made and not to the appointee.

(5) In these Regulations, unless the context otherwise requires, a reference—
(a) to a numbered regulation is to a regulation in these Regulations bearing that number;
(b) in a regulation to a numbered paragraph or sub-paragraph is to the paragraph or sub-paragraph in that regulation bearing that number;
(c) to a numbered Schedule is to the Schedule to these Regulations bearing that number.

AMENDMENTS

1. The Social Security Amendment (Carer's Allowance) Regulations 2002 (SI 2002/2497) Sch.2 (October 28, 2002).
2. Social Security (Working Neighbourhoods) Regulations 2004 (SI 2004/959) reg.26(2) (April 26, 2004).
3. The Social Security (Work-focused Interviews) Amendment Regulations 2005 (SI 2005/2727) (October 31, 2005).
4. The Housing Benefit and Council Tax Benefit (Consequential Provisions) Regulations 2006 (SI 2006/217) Sch.2 para.21 (March 6, 2006).
5. The Social Security (Working Neighbourhoods) Miscellaneous Amendment Regulations 2006 (SI 2006/909) (April 24, 2006).
6. The Social Security (Work-focused Interviews etc.) (Equalisation of

State Pension Age) Amendment Regulations 2010 (SI 2010/563) reg.6(2) (April 6, 2010).

7. Local Education Authorities and Children's Services Authorities (Integration of Functions) (Local and Subordinate Legislation) Order 2010 (SI 2010/1172) Sch.3 para.45 (May 5, 2010).

8. The Social Security (Miscellaneous Amendments) (No.3) Regulations 2011 (SI 2011/2425) reg.14 (October 31, 2011).

Requirement for person claiming a specified benefit to take part in an interview

2.772 **3.**—(1) Subject to regulations 6 to 9, a person who—

[1 (a) either—

(i) makes a claim for a relevant benefit, or

(ii) is entitled to a specified benefit other than a relevant benefit;]

[1 (b) on the day on which he [claims a specified benefit], has attained the age of 16 but has not attained [2 pensionable age]; [4 . . .]

(c) is not in remunerative work, [4 ; and

(d) is not a lone parent who—

(i) makes a claim for or is entitled to income support; and

(ii) falls within paragraph 1 (lone parents) of Schedule 1B (prescribed categories of person) to the Income Support (General) Regulations 1987]

is required to take part in an interview.

(2) An officer shall, except where paragraph (3) applies, conduct the interview.

(3) An officer may, if he considers it appropriate in all the circumstances, arrange for a person who has not attained the age of 18 to attend an interview with [3 such person as the Secretary of State may specify.]

AMENDMENTS

1. The Social Security (Work-focused Interviews) Amendment Regulations 2005 (SI 2005/2727) (October 31, 2005).

2. The Social Security (Work-focused Interviews etc.) (Equalisation of State Pension Age) Amendment Regulations 2010 (SI 2010/563) reg.6(3) (April 6, 2010).

3. The Social Security (Miscellaneous Amendments) (No. 3) Regulations 2011 (SI 2011/2425) reg.14 (October 31, 2011).

4. The Social Security (Work-focused Interviews for Lone Parents and Partners) (Amendment) Regulations 2011 (SI 2011/2428) reg.3 (October 31, 2011).

2.773 [1 Continuing entitlement to full amount of specified benefit dependent on an interview

4.—(1) This paragraph applies to a person who—

(a) is not a lone parent who is entitled to income support who falls within paragraph 1 (lone parents) of Schedule 1B (prescribed categories of person) to the Income Support (General) Regulations 1987;

(b) has not attained pensionable age; and

(c) is entitled to a specified benefit.

(2) Subject to regulations 6 to 9, a person to whom paragraph (1) applies is required to take part in an interview as a condition of continuing to be entitled to the full amount of benefit which is payable apart from

these Regulations where paragraph (3) and either paragraph (4) or (5) apply.

(3) This paragraph applies to a person who has taken part in a relevant interview or who would have taken part in such an interview but for—

(a) the requirement being waived in accordance with regulation 6; or

(b) the requirement being deferred in accordance with regulation 7.

(4) This paragraph applies to a person when any of the following circumstances arise—

(a) the person's entitlement to carer's allowance ceases whilst entitlement to a specified benefit continues;

(b) the person becomes engaged or ceases to be engaged in part-time work;

(c) the person has been undergoing education or training arranged by the officer and that education or training comes to an end; or

(d) the person attains the age of 18 and has not previously taken part in a relevant interview.

(5) This paragraph applies where a person has not been required to take part in a relevant interview for at least 36 months.]

AMENDMENT

This regulation inserted by The Social Security (Work-focused Interviews for Lone Parents and Partners) (Amendment) Regulations 2011 (SI 2011/2428) reg.3 (October 31, 2011).

[1 Continuing entitlement to full amount of income support dependent on an interview: lone parents who fall within paragraph 1 of Schedule 1B to the Income Support (General) Regulations 1987

4ZA.—(1) Subject to regulations 4A and 6 to 9, this regulation applies to a lone parent who— 2.774

(a) is entitled to income support;

(b) falls within paragraph 1 (lone parents) of Schedule 1B (prescribed categories of person) to the Income Support (General) Regulations 1987; and

(c) has not attained pensionable age.

(2) A lone parent to whom this regulation applies is required to take part in an interview if the lone parent has not taken part in or been required to take part in a relevant interview.

(3) This paragraph applies to a lone parent to whom this regulation applies who is aged 18 or over and has—

(a) taken part,

(b) failed to take part, or

(c) been treated as taking part,

in a relevant interview.

(4) A lone parent to whom paragraph (3) applies is required to take part in an interview every six months after the date on which the lone parent—

(a) last took part,

(b) last failed to take part, or

(c) was last treated as having taken part,

in a relevant interview.

(5) An officer shall, except where paragraph (6) applies, conduct the interview.

(6) An officer may, if he considers it appropriate in all the circumstances, arrange for a person who has not attained the age of 18 to attend an interview with such person as the Secretary of State may specify.]

AMENDMENT

This regulation inserted by The Social Security (Work-focused Interviews for Lone Parents and Partners) (Amendment) Regulations 2011 (SI 2011/2428) reg.3 (October 31, 2011).

[1 Requirement for certain lone parents to take part in an interview

2.775 **4A.**—(1) This regulation applies to a lone parent who—

(a) [3 is aged 18 or over and] is entitled to income support and is a person to whom paragraph 1 (lone parents) of Schedule 1B to the Income Support (General) Regulations 1987 applies; [5 and]

(b) does not fall within any other paragraph of that Schedule;

(c) [5 . . .]

[5 (2) Subject to regulations 7 to 9, a lone parent to whom this regulation applies is required to take part in one or more interviews as a condition of continuing to be entitled to the full amount of benefit which is payable to him part from these Regulations.]

(3) A lone parent who—

(a) is required to take part in an interview under this regulation, or

(b) has had a requirement to take part in an interview under this regulation waived or deferred,

is not required to take part in an interview under [4 regulation 4ZA] unless this regulation ceases to apply to him.]

AMENDMENTS

1. The Social Security (Lone Parents and Miscellaneous Amendments) Regulations 2008 (SI 2008/3051) reg.8 (November 24, 2008).

2. Social Security (Lone Parents and Miscellaneous Amendments) Regulations 2008 (SI 2008/3051) reg.10 (October 25, 2010).

3. The Social Security (Miscellaneous Amendments) (No. 3) Regulations 2011 (SI 2011/2425) reg.14 (October 31, 2011).

4. The Social Security (Work-focused Interviews for Lone Parents and Partners) (Amendment) Regulations 2011 (SI 2011/2428) reg.3 (October 31, 2011).

5. Income Support (Work-Related Activity) and Miscellaneous Amendments Regulations 2014 (SI 2014/1097), reg.14(2) (April 28, 2014).

GENERAL NOTE

2.776 Note that Pt 1 of the Schedule to the Social Security (Lone Parents and Miscellaneous Amendments) Regulations 2008 (SI 2008/3051) contains special commencement provision for certain existing claimants.

[1 Time when interview is to take place

2.777 **5.—**(1) Where the claimant is not a lone parent entitled to income support who falls within paragraph 1 (lone parents) of Schedule 1B (prescribed categories of person) to the Income Support (General) Regulations 1987, an officer shall arrange for an interview to take place as soon as reasonably practicable after—

(a) the expiry of eight weeks after the date the claim for a specified benefit, other than a relevant benefit, is made;

(b) the claim for a relevant benefit is made;
(c) the requirement under regulation 4(2) arises;
(d) in a case where regulation 7(1) applies, the time when that requirement is to apply by virtue of regulation 7(2); or
(e) the requirement to take part in a relevant interview arises, in a case where the requirement to take part in an interview arises because the youngest child a lone parent is responsible for, and a member of the same household as, has attained the age of one.

(2) Where the claimant is a lone parent entitled to income support who falls within paragraph 1 of Schedule 1B to the Income Support (General) Regulations 1987, an officer shall arrange for an interview to take place [2 . . .]—

(a) [2 as soon as reasonably practicable after] the requirement to take part in a relevant interview arises, in a case where the requirement to take part in an interview arises because the youngest child a lone parent is responsible for, and a member of the same household, has attained the age of one;
[2 (aa) in a case where regulation 4A(2) applies, on such a date as may be determined by the officer; or]
(b) in any other case [2 as soon as reasonably practicable after]
(i) [2 . . .]
(ii) where regulation 4ZA(2) (first interview) applies [2 . . .], the expiry of 6 months beginning on the date on which the requirement to attend an interview arises;
(iii) where [2 . . .] regulation 4ZA(3) [2 . . .] (subsequent interviews) applies, the requirement to attend an interview arises; or
(iv) in a case where regulation 7(1) applies, the time when that requirement is to apply by virtue of regulation 7(2).]

AMENDMENTS

1. This regulation inserted by The Social Security (Work-focused Interviews for Lone Parents and Partners) (Amendment) Regulations 2011 (SI 2011/2428) reg.3 (October 31, 2011).

2. Income Support (Work-Related Activity) and Miscellaneous Amendments Regulations 2014 (SI 2014/1097), reg.14(3) (April 28, 2014).

Waiver of requirement to take part in an interview

6.—(1) [1 Except in a case where a requirement is imposed by virtue of regulation 4A(2), a] requirement imposed by these Regulations to take part in an interview shall not apply where an officer determines that an interview would not— 2.778

(a) be of assistance to the person concerned; or
(b) be appropriate in the circumstances.

(2) A person in relation to whom a requirement to take part in an interview has been waived under paragraph (1) shall be treated for the purposes of—

(a) regulation 3,4 [1 or 4ZA]; and
(b) any claim for, or entitlement to, a specified benefit,

as having complied with that requirement.

AMENDMENT

1. Income Support (Work-Related Activity) and Miscellaneous Amendments Regulations 2014 (SI 2014/1097) (April 28, 2014).

Deferment of requirement to take part in an interview

2.779 **7.**—(1) [1 Subject to regulation 8(4)] an officer may determine, in the case of any particular person, that the requirement to take part in an interview shall be deferred at the time the claim is made or the requirement to take part in an interview arises or applies because an interview would not at that time—

(a) be of assistance to that person; or
(b) be appropriate in the circumstances.

(2) Where the officer determines in accordance with paragraph (1) that the requirement to take part in an interview shall be deferred, he shall also determine when that determination is made, the time when the requirement to take part in an interview is to apply in the person's case.

(3) Where a requirement to take part in an interview has been deferred in accordance with paragraph (1), then until—

(a) a determination is made under regulation 6(1);
(b) the person takes part in an interview; or
(c) a relevant decision has been made in relation to that person in accordance with regulation 11(4),

that person shall be treated for the purposes of any claim for, or entitlement to, a specified benefit as having complied with that requirement.

AMENDMENT

1. The Social Security (Work-focused Interviews for Lone Parents and Partners) (Amendment) Regulations 2011 (SI 2011/2428) reg.3 (October 31, 2011).

Exemptions

2.780 **8.**—(1) Subject to paragraph (2), persons who, on the day on which the claim for a specified benefit is made or the requirement to take part in an interview under regulation [5 4 or 4A or 7(2)] arises or applies—

(a) are engaged in remunerative work; or
(b) are claiming, or are entitled to, a jobseeker's allowance, shall be exempt from the requirement to take part in an interview.

(2) Paragraph (1)(b) shall not apply where—

(a) a joint-claim couple (as defined for the purposes of section 1(4) of the Jobseekers Act 1995) have claimed a jobseeker's allowance; and
(b) a member of that couple is a person to whom regulation 3D(1)(c) of the Jobseeker's Allowance Regulations 1996 (further circumstances in which a joint-claim couple may be entitled to a jointclaim jobseeker's allowance) applies.

[1 (3) A person who, on the day on which the claim for a specified benefit is made or the requirement to take part in an interview under regulation 4 or 7(2) arises or applies is—

(a) required to take part in an interview; or
(b) not required to take part in an interview by virtue of—
    (i) a waiver of a requirement; or
    (ii) a deferment of an interview,

under the [4 Social Security (Incapacity Benefit Work-focused Interviews)

Regulations 2008.] [6 . . .] shall be exempt from the requirement to take part in an interview.]

[6 (4) The requirement to take part in an interview under regulations 3, 4, 4ZA [7 , 4A] or 7(2) does not apply to a lone parent who is responsible for, and a member of the same household as, a child under the age of one.]

AMENDMENTS

1. The Social Security (Incapacity Benefit Work-focused Interviews) Regulations 2003 (SI 2003/2439) (October 27, 2003).

2. The Social Security (Work-focused Interviews) Amendment Regulations 2005 (SI 2005/2727) (October 31, 2005).

3. The Social Security (Work-focused Interviews for Lone Parents) Amendment Regulations 2007 (SI 2007/1034) (April 30, 2007).

4. The Social Security (Incapacity Benefit Work-focused Interviews) Regulations 2008 (SI 2008/2928) reg.12 (December 15, 2008).

5. The Social Security (Lone Parents and Miscellaneous Amendments) Regulations 2008 (SI 2008/3051) reg.8 (November 24, 2008).

6. The Social Security (Work-focused Interviews for Lone Parents and Partners) (Amendment) Regulations 2011 (SI 2011/2428) reg.3 (October 31, 2011).

7. Income Support (Work-Related Activity) and Miscellaneous Amendments Regulations 2014 (SI 2014/1097), reg.14(5) (April 29, 2014).

Claims for two or more specified benefits

9. A person who would otherwise be required under these Regulations to take part in interviews relating to more than one specified benefit— 2.781

(a) is only required to take part in one interview; and

(b) that interview counts for the purposes of all those benefits.

The interview

10.—(1) The officer shall inform a person who is required to take part in an interview of the place and time of the interview. 2.782

(2) The officer may determine that an interview is to take place in the person's home where it would, in his opinion, be unreasonable to expect that person to attend elsewhere because that person's personal circumstances are such that attending elsewhere would cause him undue inconvenience or endanger his health.

Taking part in an interview

11.—(1) The officer shall determine whether a person has taken part in an interview. 2.783

[1 (2) A person who has not taken part in an interview under these Regulations before 31st October 2005 shall be regarded as having taken part in his first interview under these Regulations if—

(a) he attends for the interview at the place and time notified to him by the officer;

(b) where he is a specified person, he participates in discussions with the officer in relation to the specified person's employability, including any action the specified person and the officer agree is reasonable and they are willing to take in order to help the specified person enhance his employment prospects;

(c) he provides answers (where asked) to questions and appropriate information about—

(i) the level to which he has pursued any educational qualifications;
(ii) his employment history;
(iii) any vocational training he has undertaken;
(iv) any skills he has acquired which fit him for employment;
(v) any paid or unpaid employment he is engaged in;
(vi) any medical condition which, in his opinion, puts him at a disadvantage in obtaining employment;
(vii) any caring or childcare responsibilities he has;
(viii) his aspirations for future employment;
(ix) any vocational training or skills which he wishes to undertake or acquire; and
(x) his work related abilities; and

(d) where he is a specified person, he assists the officer in the completion of an action plan which records the matters discussed in relation to sub-paragraph (b) above.

(2A) A person who has taken part in an interview under these Regulations before 31st October 2005 shall be regarded as having taken part in his first interview under these Regulations after 30th October 2005 if—

(a) he attends for the interview at the place and time notified to him by the officer;
(b) where he is a specified person, he participates in discussions with the officer in relation to the specified person's employability, including any action the specified person and the officer agree is reasonable and they are willing to take in order to help the specified person enhance his employment prospects;
(c) he participates in discussions with the officer—
(i) in relation to the person's employability or any progress he might have made towards obtaining employment; and
(ii) in order to consider any of the programmes and support available to help the person obtain employment;
(d) he provides answers (where asked) to questions and appropriate information about—
(i) the content of any report made following his personal capability assessment, insofar as that report relates to the person's capabilities and employability;
and
(ii) his opinion as to the extent to which his medical condition restricts his ability to obtain employment; and
(e) where he is a specified person, he assists the officer in the completion of an action plan which records the matters discussed in relation to sub-paragraph (b) above.

(2B) A person shall be regarded as having taken part in any subsequent interview under these Regulations if—

(a) he attends for the interview at the place and time notified to him by the officer;
(b) he participates in discussions with the officer—
(i) in relation to the person's employability or any progress he might have made towards obtaining employment; and
(ii) in order to consider any of the programmes and support available to help the person obtain employment;
(c) where he is a specified person, he participates in discussions with the officer—

(i) about any action the specified person or the officer might have taken as a result of the matters discussed in relation to paragraphs (2)(b) or (2A)(b) above; and

(ii) about how, if at all, the action plan referred to in paragraphs (2)(d) or (2A)(e) above should be amended;

(d) he provides answers (where asked) to questions and appropriate information about—

(i) the content of any report made following his personal capability assessment, insofar as that report relates to the person's capabilities and employability;

and

(ii) his opinion as to the extent to which his medical condition restricts his ability to obtain employment; and

(e) where he is a specified person, he assists the officer in the completion of any amendment of the action plan referred to in paragraphs (2)(d) or (2A)(e) above in light of the matters discussed in relation to sub-paragraphs (b) and (c) above and the information provided in relation to sub-paragraph (d) above.]

(3) A person who has not attained the age of 18 shall also be regarded as having taken part in an interview if he attends an interview with [2 a person specified by the Secretary of State under regulation 3(3)] at the place and time notified to him by an officer.

(4) Where an officer determines that a person has failed to take part in an interview and good cause has not been shown for that failure within five working days of the [3 date on which the person was notified of his failure to take part in an interview], a relevant decision shall be made for the purposes of section 2B of the Social Security Administration Act 1992.

[3 (5) Where a notice under paragraph (4) is sent by post it is take to have been received on the second working day after it is sent.]

AMENDMENTS

1. The Social Security (Work-focused Interviews) Amendment Regulations 2005 (SI 2005/2727) (October 31, 2005).

2. The Social Security (Miscellaneous Amendments) (No.3) Regulations 2011 (SI 2011/2425) reg.14 (October 31, 2011).

3. Income Support (Work-Related Activity) and Miscellaneous Amendments Regulations 2014 (SI 2014/1097), reg.14(6) (April 29, 2014).

Failure to take part in an interview

12.—(1) A person in respect of whom a relevant decision has been made in accordance with regulation 11(4) shall, subject to paragraph (12), suffer the consequences set out below. 2.784

(2) Those consequences are—

(a) where the interview arose in connection with a claim for a [2 relevant benefit], that the person to whom the claim relates is to be regarded as not having made a claim for a [2 relevant benefit];

(b) where an interview which arose in connection with a claim for a [2 relevant benefit] was deferred and benefit became payable by virtue of regulation 7(3), that the person's entitlement to that benefit shall terminate from the first day of the next benefit week following the date on which the relevant decision was made;

(c) where the claimant has an award of benefit and the requirement for the interview arose under regulation [5 4, 4ZA or 4A], [2 or by virtue of the claimant falling within regulation 3(1)(a)(ii),] the claimant's benefit shall be reduced as from the first day of the next benefit week following the day the relevant decision was made, by a sum equal (but subject to paragraphs (3) and (4)) to 20 per cent. of the amount applicable [4 . . .] in respect of a single claimant for income support aged not less than 25.

(3) Benefit reduced in accordance with paragraph (2)(c) shall not be reduced below ten pence per week.

(4) Where two or more specified benefits are in payment to a claimant, a deduction made in accordance with this regulation shall be applied, except in a case to which paragraph (5) applies, to the specified benefits in the following order of priority—

(a) income support;
(b) incapacity benefit;
(c) [2. . .];
(d) [2. . .];
(e) severe disablement allowance.

(5) Where the amount of the reduction is greater than some (but not all) of the specified benefits listed in paragraph (4), the reduction shall be made against the first benefit in that list which is the same as, or greater than, the amount of the reduction.

(6) For the purpose of determining whether a specified benefit is the same as, or greater than, the amount of the reduction for the purposes of paragraph (5), ten pence shall be added to the amount of the reduction.

(7) In a case where the whole of the reduction cannot be applied against any one specified benefit because no one benefit is the same as, or greater than, the amount of the reduction, the reduction shall be applied against the first benefit in payment in the list of priorities at paragraph (4) and so on against each benefit in turn until the whole of the reduction is exhausted or, if this is not possible, the whole of the specified benefits are exhausted, subject in each case to ten pence remaining in payment.

(8) [4 . . .]

(9) Where a claimant whose benefit has been reduced in accordance with this regulation [6 satisfies a compliance condition], the reduction shall cease to have effect on the first day of the benefit week in which the [6 compliance condition was satisfied].

[6 (9A) In paragraph (9) "compliance condition" means a requirement to—

(a) take part in an interview; or
(b) undertake work-related activity.]

(10) For the avoidance of doubt, a person who is regarded as not having made a claim for any benefit because he failed to take part in an interview shall be required to make a new claim in order to establish entitlement to any specified benefit.

(11) For the purposes of determining the amount of any benefit payable, a claimant shall be treated as receiving the amount of any specified benefit which would have been payable but for a reduction made in accordance with this regulation.

(12) The consequences set out in this regulation shall not apply in the

case of a person who brings new facts to the notice of the Secretary of State within one month of the date on which the decision was notified and—

(a) those facts could not reasonably have been brought to the Secretary of State's notice within five working days of the [6 date on which the person was notified of his failure to take part in an interview]; and

(b) those facts show that he had good cause for his failure to take part in the interview.

(13) In paragraphs (2) and (12), the "decision" means the decision that the person failed without good cause to take part in an interview.

AMENDMENTS

1. The Social Security Amendment (Carer's Allowance) Regulations 2002 (SI 2002/2497) Sch.2 (October 28, 2002).

2. The Social Security (Work-focused Interviews) Amendment Regulations 2005 (SI 2005/2727) (October 31, 2005).

3. The Social Security (Lone Parents and Miscellaneous Amendments) Regulations 2008 (SI 2008/3051) reg.8 (November 24, 2008).

4. The Social Security (Miscellaneous Amendments) (No. 3) Regulations 2011 (SI 2011/2425) reg.14 (October 31, 2011).

5. The Social Security (Work-focused Interviews for Lone Parents and Partners) (Amendment) Regulations 2011 (SI 2011/2428) reg.3 (October 31, 2011).

6. Income Support (Work-Related Activity) and Miscellaneous Amendments Regulations 2014 (SI 2014/1097), reg.14(7) (April 28, 2014).

[1 Circumstances where the amount of benefit payable to a claimant is not to be reduced in accordance with regulation 12(2)(c)

12A.—(1) The amount of benefit payable to a claimant is not to be reduced in accordance with regulation 12(2)(c) if that amount— 2.785

(a) is at the time the relevant decision falls to be made in respect of the current failure, being paid at a reduced rate in accordance with regulation 12(2)(c), regulations 7(3) and 8 of the Social Security (Work-focused Interviews for Lone Parents) and Miscellaneous Amendments Regulations 2000 or regulation 8(1) and (2) of the Income Support (Work-Related Activity) and Miscellaneous Amendments Regulations 2014; and

(b) was last reduced not more than two weeks before the date of the current failure.

(2) In paragraph (1) "current failure" means a failure which may, in the case of a claimant who has an award of benefit, lead to a reduction in benefit under regulation 12(2)(c) in relation to which the Secretary of State has not yet determined whether the amount of benefit payable to the claimant is to be reduced in accordance with that regulation.]

AMENDMENT

1. Inserted by the Income Support (Work-Related Activity) and Miscellaneous Amendments Regulations 2014 (SI 2014/1097), reg.14(8) (April 28, 2014).

Circumstances where regulation 12 does not apply

13. The consequences of a failure to take part in an interview set out in regulation 12 shall not apply where— 2.786

(a) he is no longer required to take part in an interview as a condition for continuing to be entitled to the full amount of benefit which is payable apart from these Regulations; or

(b) the person attains [[1] pensionable age].

AMENDMENT

1. The Social Security (Work-focused Interviews etc.) (Equalisation of State Pension Age) Amendment Regulations 2010 (SI 2010/563) reg.6(5) (April 6, 2010).

Good cause

2.787 **14.** Matters to be taken into account in determining whether a person has shown good cause for his failure to take part in an interview include—

(a) that the person misunderstood the requirement to take part in the interview due to any learning, language or literacy difficulties of the person or any misleading information given to the person by the officer;

(b) that the person was attending a medical or dental appointment, or accompanying a person for whom the claimant has caring responsibilities to such an appointment, and that it would have been unreasonable, in the circumstances, to rearrange the appointment;

(c) that the person had difficulties with his normal mode of transport and that no reasonable alternative was available;

(d) that the established customs and practices of the religion to which the person belongs prevented him attending on that day or at that time;

(e) that the person was attending an interview with an employer with a view to obtaining employment;

(f) that the person was actually pursuing employment opportunities as a self-employed earner;

(g) that the person or a dependant of his or a person for whom he provides care suffered an accident, sudden illness or relapse of [[1] a physical or mental health condition];

(h) that he was attending the funeral of a close friend or relative on the day fixed for the interview;

(i) that a disability from which the person suffers made it impracticable for him to attend at the time fixed for the interview.

AMENDMENT

1. The Social Security (Work-focused Interviews) Amendment Regulations 2005 (SI 2005/2727) (October 31, 2005).

Appeals

2.788 **15.**—(1) This regulation applies to any relevant decision made under regulation 11(4) or any decision under section 10 of the 1998 Act superseding such a decision.

(2) This regulation applies whether the decision is as originally made or as revised under section 9 of the 1998 Act.

(3) In the case of a decision to which this regulation applies, the person

in respect of whom the decision was made shall have a right of appeal under section 12 of the 1998 Act to [1 the First-tier Tribunal]

AMENDMENT

1. The Tribunals, Courts and Enforcement Act 2007 (Transitional and Consequential Provisions) Order 2008 (SI 2008/2683) reg.178 (November 3, 2008).

Revocations and transitional provision

16.—(1) Subject to paragraph (2), the Social Security (Work-focused Interviews) Regulations 2000 ("the 2000 Regulations") and the Social Security (Jobcentre Plus Interviews) Regulations 2001 ("the 2001 Regulations") are hereby revoked to the extent specified in Schedule 1. **2.789**

(2) Notwithstanding paragraph (1), both the 2000 Regulations (except for regulations 4, 5 and 12(2)(a) and (b)) and the 2001 Regulations (except for regulations 3 and 11(2)(a) and (b)) [2 . . .] shall continue to apply as if these Regulations had not come into force for the period specified in paragraph (3) in the case of a person who, on the day before the day on which these Regulations come into force, [3—

(a) is a relevant person for the purposes of those Regulations,

(b) is entitled to income support, and

(c) does not fall within paragraph 7, 24 or 25 of Schedule 1B to the Income Support (General) Regulations 1987(**9**) (prescribed categories of person).]

(3) The period specified for the purposes of paragraph (2) shall be the period beginning on the day on which these Regulations come to force and ending on the day on which the person—

(a) ceases to be a relevant person for the purposes of the 2000 Regulations or, as the case may be, the 2001 Regulations;

(b) is not entitled to any specified benefit for the purposes of those Regulations; or

(c) attains [4 pensionable age],

whichever shall first occur.

AMENDMENTS

1. Social Security (Working Neighbourhoods) Regulations 2004 (SI 2004/959) reg.26(4) (April 26, 2004).

2. The Social Security (Working Neighbourhoods) Miscellaneous Amendment Regulations 2006 (SI 2006/909) (April 24, 2006).

3. The Social Security (Lone Parents and Miscellaneous Amendments) Regulations 2008 (SI 2008/3051) reg.9 (October 26, 2009).

4. The Social Security (Work-focused Interviews etc.) (Equalisation of State Pension Age) Amendment Regulations 2010 (SI 2010/563) reg.6(6) (April 6, 2010).

GENERAL NOTE

Regulation 3(3)–(5) of the Social Security (Incapacity Benefit Work-focused Interviews) (Amendment) Regulations 2009 (SI 2009/1541) further provides: **2.790**

"(3) Regulation 12 (failure to take part in an interview) of the 2000 Regulations and regulation 11 (failure to take part in an interview) of the 2001 Regulations (as saved by regulation 16(2) of the 2002 Regulations) continue to have effect as if the amendment set out in paragraph (2) above had not been made in respect of a person who immediately before 26th October 2009 is—

(a) entitled to a specified benefit as defined in the principal Regulations, and

(b) subject to the consequences specified in regulation 12 of the 2000 Regulations or regulation 11 of the 2001 Regulations.

(4) Any other provisions of the 2000 Regulations and the 2001 Regulations (as saved by regulation 16(2) of the 2002 Regulations, but disregarding the amendment in paragraph (2) above) continue to have effect insofar as it is necessary to give full effect to paragraph (3) above.

(5) For the purposes of regulation 9(8), (9) and (11) (consequences of failure to take part in a work-focused interview) of the principal Regulations, a person referred to in paragraph (3)(a) above is deemed to be subject to the consequences under regulation 9(1) of the principal Regulations; and as from the date on which these Regulations come into force, regulation 12 of the 2000 Regulations and regulation 11 of the 2001 Regulations cease to apply to that person."

Amendments to regulations

2.791 *Omitted.*

2.792 *Schedules 1 and 2 omitted.*

The Social Security (Jobcentre Plus Interviews for Partners) Regulations 2003

(SI 2003/1886)

ARRANGEMENT OF REGULATIONS

GENERAL NOTE

2.794 These controversial regulations extend the scheme of work-focused interviews to the partners of claimants, and cover five benefits: income support, income-based jobseeker's allowance, incapacity benefit, severe disablement allowance and carer's allowance. The pattern follows that to be found in the earlier regulations relating to work-focused interviews in other contexts. But those regulations apply only where the claim was made after the commencement date of the regulations where both the partners are between the ages of 18 and 60; these regulations apply whenever benefit is in payment and whenever the claim is through a Jobcentre Plus office. A further distinction is that the interview under these regulations is a once and for all interview without there being provisions for follow-up interviews. Failure to participate results in a deduction equal to 20 per cent of the single adult applicable amount for income support. Both partners have an independent right of appeal, so that both can, in principle, appeal against the same decision.

Whereas a draft of this instrument was laid before Parliament in accordance with s.190(1) of the Social Security Administration Act 1992 and approved by resolution of each House of Parliament;

Now, therefore, the Secretary of State for Work and Pensions, in exercise of the powers conferred upon him by ss.2AA(1) and (4)–(7), 2B(6), 189(1) and (4)–(6) and 191 of the Social Security Administration Act 1992 and of all other powers enabling him in that behalf, after consultation with the Council on Tribunals in accordance with s.8(1) of the Tribunals and Inquiries Act 1992, by this instrument, which contains only regulations made by virtue of, or consequential upon, section 2AA of the Social Security Administration Act 1992 and which is made before the end of the period of 6 months beginning with the coming into force of that provision, hereby makes the following Regulations:

Citation and commencement

1. These Regulations may be cited as the Social Security (Jobcentre Plus Interviews for Partners) Regulations 2003 and shall come into force on 12th April 2004. **2.795**

Interpretation [4 . . .]

2.—(1) In these Regulations— **2.796**

"the 1998 Act" means the Social Security Act 1998;

"benefit week" means any period of seven days corresponding to the week in respect of which the relevant specified benefit is due to be paid;

"claimant" means a claimant of a specified benefit who has a partner to whom these Regulations apply;

[2 "couple" means—

(a) a man and woman who are married to each other and are members of the same household;

(b) a man and woman who are not married to each other but are living together as husband and wife;

(c) two people of the same sex who are civil partners of each other and are members of the same household; or

(d) two people of the same sex who are not civil partners of each other but are living together as if they were civil partners,

and for the purposes of paragraph (d), two people of the same sex are to be regarded as living together as if they were civil partners if, but only if, they would be regarded as living together as husband and wife were they instead two people of the opposite sex;]

"interview" means a work-focused interview with a partner which is conducted for any or all of the following purposes—

(a) assessing the partner's prospects for existing or future employment (whether paid or voluntary);

(b) assisting or encouraging the partner to enhance his prospects of such employment;
(c) identifying activities which the partner may undertake to strengthen his existing or future prospects of employment;
(d) identifying current or future employment or training opportunities suitable to the partner's needs; and
(e) identifying educational opportunities connected with the existing or future employment prospects or needs of the partner;

"officer" means a person who is an officer of, or who is providing services to or exercising functions of, the Secretary of State;

"partner" means a person who is a member of the same couple as the claimant, or, in a case where the claimant has more than one partner, a person who is a partner of the claimant by reason of a polygamous marriage, but only where—

(a) [4 . . .]
(b) both the partner and the claimant have attained the age of 18 but have not attained [5 pensionable age];

[5 "pensionable age", in the case of a man born before 6th April 1955, means the age when a woman born on the same day as the man would attain pensionable age;]

"polygamous marriage" means any marriage during the subsistence of which a party to it is married to more than one person and the ceremony of marriage took place under the law of a country which permits polygamy;

"specified benefit" means a benefit to which section 2AA applies.

[6 (2) For the purposes of these Regulations a person is to be treated as responsible for, and a member of the same household as, a child only where the person would be treated as being responsible for, and a member of the same household as, such a child under regulations 15 and 16 of the Income Support (General) Regulations 1987, if references in those Regulations to income support were to a specified benefit.]

AMENDMENTS

1. Social Security (Working Neighbourhoods) Regulations 2004 (SI 2004/959) reg.27(2) (April 26, 2004).
2. The Civil Partnership (Pensions, Social Security and Child Support) (Consequential etc. Provisions) Order 2005 (SI 2005/2877) (December 5, 2005).
3. The Social Security (Working Neighbourhoods) Miscellaneous Amendment Regulations 2006 (SI 2006/909) (April 24, 2006).
4. The Social Security (Jobcentre Plus Interviews for Partners) Amendment Regulations 2008 (SI 2008/759) (April 28, 2008).
5. The Social Security (Work-focused Interviews etc.) (Equalisation of State Pension Age) Amendment Regulations 2010 (SI 2010/563) reg.7 (April 6, 2010).
6. The Social Security (Work-focused Interviews for Lone Parents and Partners) (Amendment) Regulations 2011 (SI 2011/2428) reg.4 (October 31, 2011).

[1 Partner of a person claiming a specified benefit to take part in an interview

2.797 **3.**—(1) Subject to regulations 5 to 8, a partner to whom this regulation applies is required to take part in an interview as a condition of the claimant continuing to be paid the full amount of a specified benefit which is payable apart from these Regulations.

(2) This regulation applies to a partner of a person claiming a specified benefit where—

(a) the claimant has been continuously entitled to a specified benefit for at least 26 weeks;

(b) the claimant has been awarded the benefit at a higher rate referable to the partner;

(c) the benefit is administered from a designated Jobcentre Plus Office(**4**); and

(d) the partner has not taken part or been required to take part in an interview under these Regulations.

(3) Where a requirement to take part in an interview arises under this regulation in relation to a particular specified benefit, the requirement also applies in relation to any other specified benefit in payment to the claimant at a higher rate referable to his partner on the date set for the interview and notified to the partner in accordance with regulation 9(1).]

AMENDMENT

1. The Social Security (Jobcentre Plus Interviews for Partners) Amendment Regulations 2008 (SI 2008/759) (April 28, 2008).

[[1] Partner of a person claiming jobseeker's allowance to take part in an interview where child or qualifying young person in household

3A.—(1) Subject to regulations 5 to 8, a partner to whom this regulation applies is required to take part in an interview as a condition of the claimant continuing to be paid the full amount of a jobseeker's allowance which is payable apart from these Regulations. **2.798**

(2) This regulation applies to a partner of a person claiming a jobseeker's allowance where—

(a) the claimant or the partner is responsible for a child or qualifying young person who is a member of that person's household;

(b) the claimant has been continuously entitled to a jobseeker's allowance for at least 26 weeks;

(c) the claimant has been awarded that benefit at a higher rate referable to the partner;

(d) the benefit is administered at a designated Jobcentre Plus Office; and

(e) the partner has taken part or failed to take part in an interview under these Regulations.

(3) The requirement to take part in an interview under this regulation arises every six months, on a date to be determined in accordance with paragraphs (4) and (5).

(4) Where the interview referred to in paragraph (2)(e) was on a date before 28th October 2007—

(a) the requirement arises for the first time on 28th April 2008; and

(b) it then arises again every six months after the date on which the partner last took part or failed to take part in an interview.

(5) Where the interview referred to in paragraph (2)(e) was on a date on or after 28th October 2007, the requirement arises every six months after the date on which the partner last took part or failed to take part in an interview.

(6) For the purposes of paragraph (2)(a), "child" and "qualifying young person" are to be construed in accordance with section 142 of the Social Security Contributions and Benefits Act 1992(**5**).

(7) References in paragraphs (2)(e), (4) and (5) to a partner having taken part in an interview are to be construed as including cases where the partner is treated as having taken part in an interview under regulation 5 or 6.]

AMENDMENT

1. The Social Security (Jobcentre Plus Interviews for Partners) Amendment Regulations 2008 (SI 2008/759) (April 28, 2008).

Time when interview is to take place

2.799 **4.** An officer shall arrange for an interview to take place as soon as reasonably practicable after—

(a) the requirement under regulation [[1] 3 or 3A] arises; or
(b) in a case where regulation 6(1) applies, the time when that requirement is to apply by virtue of regulation 6(2).

AMENDMENT

1. The Social Security (Jobcentre Plus Interviews for Partners) Amendment Regulations 2008 (SI 2008/759) (April 28, 2008).

Waiver of requirement to take part in an interview

2.800 **5.**—(1) A requirement imposed by these Regulations to take part in an interview shall not apply where an officer determines that an interview would not—

(a) be of assistance to the partner concerned; or
(b) be appropriate in the circumstances.

(2) A partner in relation to whom a requirement to take part in an interview has been waived under paragraph (1) shall be treated [[1] . . .] as having complied with that requirement.

AMENDMENT

1. The Social Security (Jobcentre Plus Interviews for Partners) Amendment Regulations 2008 (SI 2008/759) (April 28, 2008).

Deferment of requirement to take part in an interview

2.801 **6.**—(1) An officer may determine, in the case of any particular partner, that the requirement to take part in an interview shall be deferred at the time that the requirement to take part in it arises or applies because an interview would not at that time—

(a) be of assistance to the partner concerned; or
(b) be appropriate in the circumstances.

(2) Where the officer determines in accordance with paragraph (1) that the requirement to take part in an interview shall be deferred, he shall also, when that determination is made, determine the time when the requirement to take part in an interview is to apply in the partner's case.

(3) Where a requirement to take part in an interview has been deferred in accordance with paragraph (1), then until—

(a) a determination is made under regulation 5(1);
(b) the partner takes part in an interview; or
(c) a relevant decision has been made in accordance with regulation 10(3),

the partner shall be treated for the purposes of regulation 3 as having complied with that requirement.

Exemption

[1 **7.** A partner who, on the day on which the requirement to take part in an interview arises or applies under regulation 3, 3A or 6(2) is— 2.802

(a) in receipt of a specified benefit as a claimant in his own right, or

(b) a member of a couple, one of whom is responsible for, and a member of the same household as, a child under the age of one,

is exempt from the requirement to take part in an interview.]

AMENDMENT

1. This version of reg.7 introduced by The Social Security (Work-focused Interviews for Lone Parents and Partners) (Amendment) Regulations 2011 (SI 2011/2428) reg.4 (October 31, 2011).

Claims for two or more specified benefits

8. A partner who would otherwise be required under these Regulations to take part in interviews relating to more than one specified benefit— 2.803

(a) is only required to take part in one interview during any period where the claimant is in receipt of two or more specified benefits concurrently; and

(b) that interview counts for the purposes of each of those benefits.

The interview

9.—(1) An officer shall inform a partner who is required to take part in an interview of the date, place and time of the interview. 2.804

(2) The officer may determine that an interview is to take place in the partner's home where it would, in his opinion, be unreasonable to expect the partner to attend elsewhere because the partner's personal circumstances are such that attending elsewhere would cause him undue inconvenience or endanger his health.

(3) An officer shall conduct the interview.

Taking part in an interview

10.—(1) The officer shall determine whether a partner has taken part in an interview. 2.805

(2) A partner shall be regarded as having taken part in an interview if and only if—

(a) he attends for the interview at the place and time notified to him by the officer; and

(b) he provides answers (where asked) to questions and appropriate information about—

(i) the level to which he has pursued any educational qualifications;

(ii) his employment history;

(iii) any vocational training he has undertaken;

(iv) any skills he has acquired which fit him for employment;

(v) any paid or unpaid employment he is engaged in;

(vi) any medical condition which, in his opinion, puts him at a disadvantage in obtaining employment; and

(vii) any caring or childcare responsibilities he has.

(3) Where an officer determines that a partner has failed to take part in an interview and good cause has not been shown either by the partner or

by the claimant for that failure within five working days of the day on which the interview was to take place, a relevant decision shall be made for the purposes of section 2B of the Social Security Administration Act 1992 and the partner and the claimant shall be notified accordingly.

Failure to take part in an interview

2.806 **11.**—(1) Where a relevant decision has been made in accordance with regulation 10(3), subject to paragraph (11), the specified benefit payable to the claimant in respect of which the requirement for the partner to take part in an interview under regulation [1 3 or 3A] arose shall be reduced, either as from the first day of the next benefit week following the day on which the relevant decision was made, or, if that date arises five days or less after the day on which the relevant decision was made, as from the first day of the second benefit week following the date of the relevant decision.

(2) The deduction made to benefit in accordance with paragraph (1) shall be by a sum equal (but subject to paragraphs (3) and (4)) to 20 per cent. of the amount applicable [3 . . .] in respect of a single claimant for income support aged not less than 25.

(3) Benefit reduced in accordance with paragraph (1) shall not be reduced below ten pence per week.

(4) Where two or more specified benefits are in payment to a claimant, in relation to each of which a requirement for the partner to take part in an interview had arisen under [1 these Regulations], a deduction made in accordance with this regulation shall be applied, except in a case to which paragraph (5) applies, to those benefits in the following order of priority—

(a) an income-based jobseeker's allowance;

[2 (aa) an income-related employment and support allowance under Part 1 of the Welfare Reform Act 2007 (employment and support allowance);]

(b) income support;

(c) incapacity benefit;

(d) severe disablement allowance;

(e) carer's allowance.

(5) Where the amount of the reduction is greater than some (but not all) of those benefits, the reduction shall be made against the first benefit in the list in paragraph (4) which is the same as, or greater than, the amount of the reduction.

(6) For the purpose of determining whether a benefit is the same as, or greater than, the amount of the reduction for the purposes of paragraph (5), ten pence shall be added to the amount of the reduction.

(7) In a case where the whole of the reduction cannot be applied against any one benefit because no one benefit is the same as, or greater than, the amount of the reduction, the reduction shall be applied against the first benefit in the list of priorities at paragraph (4) and so on against each benefit in turn until the whole of the reduction is exhausted or, if this is not possible, the whole of those benefits are exhausted, subject in each case to ten pence remaining in payment.

(8) [3 . . .]

(9) Where the partner of a claimant whose benefit has been reduced in accordance with this regulation subsequently takes part in an interview, the reduction shall cease to have effect on the first day of the benefit week in which the requirement to take part in an interview was met.

(10) For the purposes of determining the amount of any benefit payable, a claimant shall be treated as receiving the amount of any specified benefit which would have been payable but for a reduction made in accordance with this regulation.

(11) Benefit shall not be reduced in accordance with this regulation where the partner or the claimant brings new facts to the notice of the Secretary of State within one month of the date on which the decision that the partner failed without good cause to take part in an interview was notified and—

- (a) those facts could not reasonably have been brought to the Secretary of State's notice within five working days of the day on which the interview was to take place; and
- (b) those facts show that he had good cause for his failure to take part in the interview.

AMENDMENTS

1. The Social Security (Jobcentre Plus Interviews for Partners) Amendment Regulations 2008 (SI 2008/759) (April 28, 2008).

2. The Employment and Support Allowance (Consequential Provisions) (No.2) Regulations 2008 (SI 2008/1554) reg.71 (October 27, 2008).

3. The Social Security (Miscellaneous Amendments) (No.3) Regulations 2011 (SI 2011/2425) reg.16 (October 31, 2011).

Circumstances where regulation 11 does not apply

12. The reduction of benefit to be made under regulation 11 shall not apply as from the date when a partner who failed to take part in an interview ceases to be a partner for the purposes of these Regulations or is no longer a partner to whom [1 regulation 3 or 3A applies] 2.807

AMENDMENT

1. The Social Security (Jobcentre Plus Interviews for Partners) Amendment Regulations 2008 (SI 2008/759) (April 28, 2008).

Good cause

13. Matters to be taken into account in determining whether the partner or the claimant has shown good cause for the partner's failure to take part in an interview include— 2.808

- (a) that the partner misunderstood the requirement to take part in an interview due to any learning, language or literacy difficulties of the partner or any misleading information given to the partner by the officer;
- (b) that the partner was attending a medical or dental appointment, or accompanying a person for whom the partner had caring responsibilities to such an appointment, and that it would have been unreasonable, in the circumstances, to rearrange the appointment;
- (c) that the partner had difficulties with his normal mode of transport and that no reasonable alternative was available;
- (d) that the established customs and practices of the religion to which the partner belongs prevented him attending on that day or at that time;

(e) that the partner was attending an interview with an employer with a view to obtaining employment;
(f) that the partner was actually pursuing employment opportunities as a self-employed earner;
(g) that the partner, claimant or a dependant or a person for whom the partner provides care suffered an accident, sudden illness or relapse of a chronic condition;
(h) that he was attending the funeral of a close friend or relative on the day fixed for the interview;
(i) that a disability from which the partner suffers made it impracticable for him to attend at the time fixed for the interview.

Appeals

2.809 **14.**—(1) This regulation applies to any relevant decision made under regulation 10(3) or any decision under section 10 of the 1998 Act superseding such a decision.

(2) This regulation applies whether the decision is as originally made or as revised under section 9 of the 1998 Act.

(3) In the case of a decision to which this regulation applies, the partner in respect of whom the decision was made and the claimant shall each have a right of appeal under section 12 of the 1998 Act to [1 the First-tier Tribunal]

AMENDMENT

1. The Tribunals, Courts and Enforcement Act 2007 (Transitional and Consequential Provisions) Order 2008 (SI 2008/2683) Sch.1 para.237 (November 3, 2008).

2.810 **15.** *Omitted.*

The Social Security (Loss of Benefit) Regulations 2001

(SI 2001/4022)

2.811 *Made* — *18th December 2001*
Coming into force — *1st April 2002*

Whereas a draft of this instrument was laid before Parliament in accordance with section 11(3) of the Social Security Fraud Act 2001, section 80(1) of the Social Security Act 1998 and section 5A(3) of the Pensions Appeal Tribunals Act 1943 and approved by resolution of each House of Parliament.

Now, therefore, the Secretary of State, in exercise of the powers conferred by sections 7(3) to (6), 8(3) and (4), 9(2) to (5), 10(1) and (2) and 11(1) of the Social Security Fraud Act 2001, section 189(4) of the Social Security Administration Act 1992, sections 79(4) and 84 of, and paragraph 9 of Schedule 2 to, the Social Security Act 1998 and section 5A(2) of the Pensions Appeal Tribunals Act 1943, and of all other powers enabling him in that behalf, by this Instrument, which is made before the end of the period of 6 months beginning with the coming into force of sections 7 to 13 of the Social Security Fraud Act 2001 and which contains only regulations made by virtue of, or consequential upon, those sections, hereby makes the following Regulations:

PART I

GENERAL

Citation, commencement and interpretation

1.—(1) These Regulations may be cited as the Social Security (Loss of Benefit) Regulations 2001 and shall come into force on 1st April 2002. **2.812**

(2) In these Regulations, unless the context otherwise requires—

[3 "the 2007 Act" means the Welfare Reform Act 2007;

"the 2012 Act" means the Welfare Reform Act 2012;]

"the Act" means the Social Security Fraud Act 2001;

[3 "the Administration Act" means the Social Security Administration Act 1992;]

[5 "armed forces independence payment" means armed forces independence payment under the Armed Forces and Reserve Forces Compensation Scheme Order 2011;]

"the Benefits Act" means the Social Security Contributions and Benefits Act 1992;

[3 "the ESA Regulations" means the Employment and Support Allowance Regulations 2008;]

"the Council Tax Benefit Regulations" means the Council Tax Benefit Regulations 2006;

[1 "the Council Tax Benefit (State Pension Credit) Regulations" means the Council Tax Benefit (Persons who have attained pensionable age for state pension credit) Regulations 2006;

"the Housing Benefit Regulations" means the Housing Benefit Regulations 2006;

"the Housing Benefit (State Pension Credit) Regulations" means the Housing Benefit (Persons who have attained pensionable age for state pension credit) Regulations 2006;]

"the Income Support Regulations" means the Income Support (General) Regulations 1987;

"the Jobseekers Act" means the Jobseekers Act 1995;

"the Jobseeker's Allowance Regulations" means the Jobseeker's Allowance Regulations 1996;

[6 "the UC Regulations" means the Universal Credit Regulations 2013;

"assessment period" has the same meaning as in the UC Regulations;]

"claimant" in a regulation means the person claiming the sanctionable benefit referred to in that regulation;

[2 "the determination day" means (subject to paragraph (2A)) the day on which the Secretary of State determines that a restriction under—

(a) section 6B or 7 of the Act would be applicable to the offender were the offender in receipt of a sanctionable benefit;

(b) section 8 of the Act would be applicable to the offender were the offender a member of a joint-claim couple which is in receipt of a joint-claim jobseeker's allowance; or

(c) section 9 of the Act would be applicable to the offender's family member were that member in receipt of income support, jobseeker's allowance, state pension credit, employment and support allowance, housing benefit or council tax benefit;]

"disqualification period" means the period in respect of which the restrictions on payment of a relevant benefit apply in respect of an offender in accordance with section [2 6B(11) or] 7(6) of the Act and shall be interpreted in accordance with [2 regulations 1A and 2]; and

[6 "income-based jobseeker's allowance" means an income-based allowance under the Jobseekers Act as it has effect apart from the amendments made by Part 1 of Schedule 14 to the 2012 Act (to remove references to an income-based allowance);

"income-related employment and support allowance" means an income-related allowance under the Part 1 of the 2007 Act as it has effect apart from the amendments made by Schedule 3 and Part 1 of Schedule 14 to the 2012 Act (to remove references to an income-related allowance);

"joint claimant" means each of joint claimants as defined in section 40 of the 2012 Act;]

"offender" means the person who is subject to the restriction in the payment of his benefit in accordance with section [2 6B or] 7 of the Act.

[2 "pay day" in relation to a sanctionable benefit means the day on which that benefit is due to be paid;

[4 "personal independence payment" means the allowance under Part 4 of the 2012 Act;]

"relevant authority" in relation to housing benefit or council tax benefit means the relevant authority administering the benefit of the offender or the offender's family member.]

[6 "universal credit" means the benefit payable under Part 1 of the 2012 Act.]

[2 (2A) Where, for the purposes of section 6B of the Act, the disqualifying event is an agreement to pay a penalty as referred to in section 6B(1)(b) of the Act, the determination day is the 28th day after the day referred to in the definition of that term in paragraph (2).]

(3) Expressions used in these Regulations which are defined either for the purposes of the Jobseekers Act or for the purposes of the Jobseeker's Allowance Regulations shall, except where the context otherwise requires, have the same meaning as for the purposes of that Act or, as the case may be, those Regulations.

(4) In these Regulations, unless the context otherwise requires, a reference—

(a) to a numbered regulation is to the regulation in these Regulations bearing that number;

(b) in a regulation to a numbered paragraph is to the paragraph in that regulation bearing that number.

AMENDMENTS

1. Housing Benefit and Council Tax Benefit (Consequential Provisions) Regulations 2006 (SI 2006/217) Sch.2 para.20(2) (March 6, 2006).

2. Social Security (Loss of Benefit) Amendment Regulations 2010 (SI 2010/1160) reg.2(1) and (2) (April 1, 2010).

3. Social Security (Loss of Benefit) Amendment Regulations 2013 (SI 2013/385) regs 2 and 3(a), (b) and (c) (April 1, 2013).
4. Social Security (Loss of Benefit) Amendment Regulations 2013 (SI 2013/385) regs 2 and 3(f) (April 8, 2013).
5. Armed Forces and Reserve Forces Compensation Scheme (Consequential Provisions: Subordinate Legislation) Order 2013 (SI 2013/591) art.7 and Sch. para.22(1) and (2) (April 8, 2013).
6. Social Security (Loss of Benefit) (Amendment) Regulations 2013 (SI 2013/385) regs 2 and 3(d), (e) and (g) (April 29, 2013).

[1 Disqualification period: section 6B(11) of the Act

1A.—(1) The first day of the disqualification period for the purposes of section 6B(11) of the Act ("DQ-day") shall be as follows. **2.813**

(2) This paragraph applies where on the determination day—

(a) the offender is in receipt of a sanctionable benefit [2 other than a benefit to which paragraph (5A) applies] [3 or universal credit];
(b) the offender is a member of a joint-claim couple which is in receipt of a joint-claim jobseeker's allowance; or
(c) the offender's family member is in receipt of income support, jobseeker's allowance, state pension credit, employment and support allowance, housing benefit or council tax benefit.

(3) Where paragraph (2) applies and paragraph (4) does not apply (but subject to paragraph (7))—

(a) in relation to a sanctionable benefit which is paid in arrears, DQ-day is the day following the first pay day after the end of the period of 28 days beginning with the determination day; and
(b) in relation to a sanctionable benefit which is paid in advance, DQ-day is the first pay day after the end of the period of 28 days beginning with the determination day.

(4) This paragraph applies where on the determination day the offender or (as the case may be) the offender's family member is in receipt of—

(a) either housing benefit or council tax benefit or both of those benefits; and
(b) no other sanctionable benefit.

(5) Where paragraph (4) applies—

(a) in relation to housing benefit or council tax benefit which is paid in arrears, DQ-day is the day following the first pay day after the end of the period of 28 days beginning with the first day after the determination day on which the Secretary of State is notified by the relevant authority that the offender or the offender's family member is in receipt of either housing benefit or council tax benefit (or both of those benefits) or has been awarded either or both of those benefits; and
(b) in relation to housing benefit or council tax benefit which is paid in advance, DQ-day is the first pay day after the end of the period of 28 days beginning with the first day after the determination day on which the Secretary of State is so notified by the relevant authority.

[2 (5A) This paragraph applies where on the determination day the offender or, as the case may be, the offender's family member is in receipt of a sanctionable benefit which is neither payable wholly in advance nor wholly in arrears and no other sanctionable benefit.]

(6) Where [2 paragraph (5A) applies or where there is no sanctionable benefit payable on the determination day], DQ-day is the first day after the end of the period of 28 days beginning with the determination day.

[3 (6A) Paragraph (6B) applies where, on the determination day, the offender or, as the case may be, the offender's family member is in receipt of universal credit.

(6B) Where this paragraph applies, DQ-day is—

(a) if the first day after the end of the period of 28 days beginning with the determination day is the first day of an assessment period, that day;

(b) if the first day after the end of the period of 28 days beginning with the determination day is not the first day of an assessment period, the first day of the next assessment period after that day.]

(7) Where on the determination day—

(a) paragraph (2) [3 or (6A)] applies in the case of an offender or (as the case may be) the offender's family member, but

(b) that person ceases to be in receipt of a benefit referred to in [3 those paragraphs] before the first day of the disqualification period that would apply by virtue of paragraph (3) [3 or (6B)],

DQ-day is the first day after the end of the period of 28 days beginning with the determination day.]

AMENDMENTS

1. Social Security (Loss of Benefit) Amendment Regulations 2010 (SI 2010/1160) reg.2(1) and (3) (April 1, 2010).

2. Social Security (Loss of Benefit) (Amendment) Regulations 2013 (SI 2013/385) regs 2 and 4(1), (2), (4) and (5) (April 1, 2013).

3. Social Security (Loss of Benefit) (Amendment) Regulations 2013 (SI 2013/385) regs 2 and 4(3), (6) and (7) (April 29, 2013).

[1 Disqualification period: section 7(6) of the Act

2.814 **2.**—(1) The first day of the disqualification period for the purposes of section 7(6) of the Act ("DQ-day") shall be as follows.

(2) This paragraph applies where on the determination day—

(a) the offender is in receipt of a sanctionable benefit [2 other than a benefit to which paragraph (5A) applies] [3 or universal credit];

(b) the offender is a member of a joint-claim couple which is in receipt of a joint-claim jobseeker's allowance; or

(c) the offender's family member is in receipt of income support, jobseeker's allowance, state pension credit, employment and support allowance, housing benefit or council tax benefit.

(3) Where paragraph (2) applies and paragraph (4) does not apply—

(a) in relation to a sanctionable benefit which is paid in arrears, DQ-day is the day following the first pay day after the end of the period of 28 days beginning with the determination day; and

(b) in relation to a sanctionable benefit which is paid in advance, DQ-day is the first pay day after the end of the period of 28 days beginning with the determination day.

(4) This paragraph applies where on the determination day the offender or (as the case may be) the offender's family member is in receipt of—

(a) either housing benefit or council tax benefit or of both of those benefits; and

(b) no other sanctionable benefit.

(5) Where paragraph (4) applies—

(a) in relation to housing benefit or council tax benefit which is paid in arrears, DQ-day is the day following the first pay day after the end of the period of 28 days beginning with the first day after the determination day on which the Secretary of State is notified by the relevant authority that the offender or the offender's family member is in receipt of either housing benefit or council tax benefit (or both of those benefits) or has been awarded either or both of those benefits; and

(b) in relation to housing benefit or council tax benefit which is paid in advance, DQ-day is the first pay day after the end of the period of 28 days beginning with the first day after the determination day on which the Secretary of State is so notified by the relevant authority.

[2 (5A) This paragraph applies where on the determination day the offender or, as the case may be, the offender's family member is in receipt of a sanctionable benefit which is neither payable wholly in advance nor wholly in arrears and no other sanctionable benefit.]

(6) Where [2 paragraph (5A) applies or where there is no sanctionable benefit payable on the determination day], DQ-day is the first day after the end of the period of 28 days beginning with the determination day on which the Secretary of State decides to award—

(a) a sanctionable benefit to the offender;

(b) a joint-claim jobseeker's allowance to a joint-claim couple of which the offender is a member; or

(c) [3 universal credit,] income support, jobseeker's allowance, state pension credit or employment and support allowance to the offender's family member.

[3 (6A) Paragraph (6B) applies where on the determination day, the offender or, as the case may be, the offender's family member is in receipt of universal credit.

(6B) Where this paragraph applies, DQ-day is—

(a) if the first day after the end of the period of 28 days beginning with the determination day is the first day of an assessment period, that day;

(b) if the first day after the end of the period of 28 days beginning with the determination day is not the first day of an assessment period, the first day of the next assessment period after that day.]

(7) For the purposes of the preceding provisions of this regulation [2 but except where paragraph (8) applies], DQ-day is to be no later than 5 years and 28 days after the date of the conviction of the offender for the benefit offence in the later proceedings referred to in section 7(1) of the Act; and section 7(9) of the Act (date of conviction and references to conviction) shall apply for the purposes of this paragraph as it applies for the purposes of section 7 of the Act.]

[2 (8) Where the date of the conviction of the offender for the benefit offence in the later proceedings is on or after 1st April 2013 and on the determination day—

(a) paragraph (2) or (6A) applies in the case of an offender or, as the case may be, an offender's family member; but

(b) that person ceases to be in receipt of a benefit referred to in those paragraphs before the first day of the disqualification period that would apply by virtue of paragraph (3) or (6B),

This regulation applied to income-related employment and support allowance from October 27, 2008 until April 1, 2013 and continues to do so by virtue of reg.7(6) of the Social Security (Loss of Benefit) (Amendment) Regulations 2013 (SI 2013/385) in relation to a person whose payment of income-related employment and support allowance was being reduced in accordance with this regulation on April 1, 2013 or where the offence in respect of which income-related employment and support allowance falls to be reduced was committed before that date. In other cases, reg.3ZA now makes provision in respect of income-related employment and support allowance.

[1 Reduction of income-related employment and support allowance

2.818 **3ZA.**—(1) Subject to paragraphs (4) and (5), any payment of an income-related employment and support allowance which falls to be made to an offender in respect of any week in the disqualification period or to an offender's family member in respect of any week in the relevant period is to be reduced in accordance with paragraph (2).

(2) The amount of the reduction is to be—

(a) where the offender or, as the case may be, the offender's family member, is pregnant or seriously ill, a sum equivalent to 20 per cent.;

(b) where the offender or, as the case may be, the offender's family member is subject to no work-related requirements for the purpose of section 11D of the 2007 Act(1), a sum equivalent to 40 per cent.;

(c) in any other case, a sum equivalent to 100 per cent.,

of the applicable amount for a single claimant specified in paragraph 1(1) of Schedule 4 to the ESA Regulations on the day specified in paragraph (3).

(3) The specified day is—

(a) where a payment to the offender falls to be reduced, on the first day of the disqualification period; or

(b) where a payment to the offender's family member falls to be reduced, on the first day of the relevant period.

(4) Payment must not be reduced under paragraph (2) to below 10 pence per week.

(5) A reduction under paragraph (2) must, if it is not a multiple of 5 pence, be rounded to the nearest such multiple or, if it is a multiple of 2.5 pence but not of 5 pence, to the next lower multiple of 5 pence.

(6) Where the rate of an income-related employment and support allowance payable to an offender or an offender's family member changes, the rules set out above for a reduction in the allowance payable are to be applied to the new rate and any adjustment to the reduction shall take effect from the first day of the first benefit week to start after the date of change.

(7) In paragraph (6), "benefit week" has the same meaning as in regulation 2(1) of the ESA Regulations.]

AMENDMENT

1. Social Security (Loss of Benefit) (Amendment) Regulations 2013 (SI 2013/385) regs 2 and 8 (April 1, 2013).

GENERAL NOTE

2.819 Before April 1, 2013, reg.3 provided for the reduction of income-related employment and support allowance. See the note to that regulation.

[1 Reduction of universal credit

3ZB.–(1) Any payment of universal credit which falls to be made to an offender or an offender's family member ("O") in respect of an assessment period wholly or partly within a disqualification period is to be reduced in accordance with paragraph (2) or (5). **2.820**

(2) Except where paragraph (5) applies and subject to paragraphs (6) and (7), the amount of the reduction is to be calculated by multiplying the daily reduction rate by the number of days in the assessment period or, if lower, the number of days in the assessment period to which the reduction is to relate.

(3) The daily reduction rate for the purposes of paragraph (2) is, unless paragraph (4) applies, an amount equal to the amount of the standard allowance applicable to the award multiplied by 12 and divided by 365.

(4) The daily reduction rate for the purposes of paragraph (2) is 40 per cent. of the rate calculated in accordance with paragraph (3) if, at the end of the assessment period—

(a) O, or where O is a joint claimant, the other joint claimant ("J"), falls within section 19 of the 2012 Act (claimant subject no work-related requirements) by virtue of—
   (i) subsection (2)(c) of that section (responsible carer for a child under the age of 1), or
   (ii) regulation 89(1)(c), (d) or (f) of the UC Regulations (adopter, claimants within 11 weeks before, or 15 weeks after, confinement or responsible foster parent of a child under the age of 1); or

(b) O or, as the case may be, O or J, falls within section 20 of the 2012 Act (claimant subject to work-focused interview only).

(5) Where the disqualification period ends during an assessment period, the amount of the reduction for that assessment period is to be calculated by multiplying the daily reduction rate under paragraph (3) or, as the case may be, paragraph (4) by the number of days in that assessment period which are within the disqualification period.

(6) The amount of the daily reduction rate in paragraphs (3) and (4) is to be rounded down to the nearest 10 pence.

(7) The amount of the reduction under paragraph (2) in respect of any assessment period must not exceed the amount of the standard allowance which is applicable to O in respect of that period.

(8) Where the rate of universal credit payable to O or as the case may be, to O and J, changes, the rules set out above for a reduction in the universal credit payable are to be applied to the new rate and any adjustment to the reduction is to take effect from the first day of the first assessment period to start after the date of the change.

(9) In the case of joint claimants—

(a) each joint claimant is considered individually for the purpose of determining the rate applicable under paragraph (3) or (4); and

(b) half of any applicable rate is applied to each joint claimant accordingly.

(10) In this regulation, "standard allowance" means the allowance of that name, the amount of which is set out in regulation 36 of the UC Regulations.]

AMENDMENT

1. Social Security (Loss of Benefit) (Amendment) Regulations 2013 (SI 2013/385) regs 2 and 9 (April 29, 2013).

[1 Reduction in state pension credit

2.821 **3A.**—(1) Subject to the following provisions of this regulation, state pension credit shall be payable in the case of an offender for any week comprised in the disqualification period or in the case of an offender's family member for any week comprised in the relevant period, as if the rate of benefit were reduced—

(a) where the offender or the offender's family member is pregnant or seriously ill, by 20 per cent. of the relevant sum; or

(b) where sub-paragraph (a) does not apply, by 40 per cent. of the relevant sum.

(2) In paragraph (1), the "relevant sum" is the amount applicable—

(a) except where sub-paragraph (b) applies, in respect of a single claimant aged not less than 25 under paragraph 1(1) of Schedule 2 to the Income Support Regulations; or

(b) if the claimant's family member is the offender and the offender has not attained the age of 25, the amount applicable in respect of a person of the offender's age under paragraph 1(1) of Part I of that Schedule,

on the first day of the disqualification period or, as the case may be, on the first day of the relevant period.

(3) Payment of state pension credit shall not be reduced under this regulation to less than 10 pence per week.

(4) A reduction under paragraph (1) shall, if it is not a multiple of 5 pence, be rounded to the nearest such multiple or, if it is a multiple of 2.5 pence but not of 5 pence, to the next lower multiple of 5 pence.

(5) Where the rate of state pension credit payable to an offender or an offender's family member changes, the rules set out above for a reduction in the credit payable shall be applied to the new rate and any adjustment to the reduction shall take effect from the first day of the first benefit week to start after the date of change.

(6) In paragraph (5), "benefit week" has the same meaning as in regulation 1(2) of the State Pension Credit Regulations 2002.

(7) A person of a prescribed description for the purposes of the definition of "family" in section 137(1) of the Benefits Act as it applies for the purpose of this regulation is—

(a) a person who is an additional spouse for the purposes of section 12(1) of the State Pension Credit Act 2002 (additional spouse in the case of polygamous marriages);

(b) a person [2 who is a qualifying young person for the purposes of section 142(2)] of the Benefits Act.]

AMENDMENTS

1. State Pension Credit Regulations 2002 (SI 2002/1792) reg.25(3) (October 6, 2003).

2. Social Security (Loss of Benefit) (Amendment) Regulations 2013 (SI 2013/385) regs 2 and 10 (April 1, 2013).

Reduction of joint-claim jobseeker's allowance

4. In respect of any part of the disqualification period when section 8(2) of the Act does not apply, the reduced rate of joint-claim jobseeker's allowance payable to the member of that couple who is not the offender shall be— 2.822

(a) in any case in which the member of the couple who is not the offender satisfies the conditions set out in section 2 of the Jobseekers Act (contribution-based conditions), a rate equal to the amount calculated in accordance with section 4(1) of that Act;

(b) in any case where the couple are a couple in hardship for the purposes of regulation 11, a rate equal to the amount calculated in accordance with regulation 16;

(c) in any other case, a rate calculated in accordance with section 4(3A) of the Jobseekers Act save that the applicable amount shall be the amount determined by reference to paragraph 1(1) of Schedule 1 to the Jobseeker's Allowance Regulations as if the member of the couple who is not the offender were a single claimant.

PART III

HARDSHIP

Meaning of "person in hardship"

5.—(1) In this Part of these Regulations, a "person in hardship" means, for the purposes of regulation 6, a person, other than a person to whom paragraph (3) or (4) applies, where— 2.823

(a) she is a single woman who is pregnant and in respect of whom the Secretary of State is satisfied that, unless a jobseeker's allowance is paid, she will suffer hardship;

(b) he is a single person who is responsible for a young person and the Secretary of State is satisfied that, unless a jobseeker's allowance is paid, the young person will suffer hardship;

(c) he is a member of [2 a couple] where—

[2 (i) at least one member of the couple is a woman who is pregnant; and]

(ii) the Secretary of State is satisfied that, unless a jobseeker's allowance is paid, the woman will suffer hardship;

(d) he is a member of a polygamous marriage and—

(i) one member of the marriage is pregnant; and

(ii) the Secretary of State is satisfied that, unless a jobseeker's allowance is paid, that woman will suffer hardship;

(e) he is a member of [2 a couple] or of a polygamous marriage where—

(i) one or both members of the couple, or one or more members of the polygamous marriage, are responsible for a child or young person; and

(ii) the Secretary of State is satisfied that, unless a jobseeker's allowance is paid, the child or young person will suffer hardship;

(f) he has an award of a jobseeker's allowance which includes or would, if a claim for a jobseeker's allowance from him were to succeed, have included in his applicable amount a disability premium and the Secretary of State is satisfied that, unless a jobseeker's allowance is paid, the person who would satisfy the conditions of entitlement to that premium would suffer hardship;

(g) he suffers, or his partner suffers, from a chronic medical condition which results in functional capacity being limited or restricted by physical impairment and the Secretary of State is satisfied that—
   (i) the suffering has already lasted, or is likely to last, for not less than 26 weeks; and
   (ii) unless a jobseeker's allowance is paid to that person, the probability is that the health of the person suffering would, within 2 weeks of the Secretary of State making his decision, decline further than that of a normally healthy adult and that person would suffer hardship;

(h) he does, or his partner does, or in the case of a person who is married to more than one person under a law which permits polygamy, at least one of those persons does, devote a considerable portion of each week to caring for another person who—
   (i) is in receipt of an attendance allowance [6 , the care component of disability living allowance at one of the two higher rates prescribed under section 72(4) of the Benefits Act [7 , armed forces independence payment] or the daily living component of personal independence payment at the standard or enhanced rate in accordance with section 78 of the 2012 Act];
   (ii) has claimed either attendance allowance [6 , disability living allowance [7 , armed forces independence payment] or personal independence payment], but only for so long as the claim has not been determined, or for 26 weeks from the date of claiming, whichever is the earlier; [6 . . .]
   (iii) has claimed either attendance allowance or disability living allowance and has an award of either attendance allowance or the care component of disability living allowance at one of the two higher rates prescribed under section 72(4) of the Benefits Act for a period commencing after the date on which that claim was made; [6 [7 . . .]
   (iv) has claimed personal independence payment and has an award of the daily living component of personal independence payment at the standard or enhanced rate in accordance with section 78 of the 2012 Act for a period commencing after the date on which that claim was made;] [7 or
   (v) has claimed armed forces independence payment and has an award for a period commencing after the date on which that claim was made,]

   and the Secretary of State is satisfied, after taking account of the factors set out in paragraph (5), in so far as they are appropriate to the particular circumstances of the case, that the person providing the care will not be able to continue doing so unless a jobseeker's allowance is paid to the offender;

(i) he is a person or is the partner of a person to whom section 16 of the Jobseekers Act applies by virtue of a direction issued by the

Secretary of State, except where the person to whom the direction applies does not satisfy the requirements of section 1(2)(a) to (c) of that Act;

(j) he is a person—

(i) to whom section 3(1)(f)(iii) of the Jobseekers Act (persons under the age of 18) applies, or is the partner of such a person; and

(ii) in respect of whom the Secretary of State is satisfied that the person will, unless a jobseeker's allowance is paid, suffer hardship; or

(k) he is a person—

(i) who, pursuant to the Children Act 1989, was being looked after by a local authority;

(ii) with whom the local authority had a duty, pursuant to that Act, to take reasonable steps to keep in touch; or

(iii) who, pursuant to that Act, qualified for advice and assistance from a local authority,

but in respect of whom head (i), (ii) or (iii) above, as the case may be, had not applied for a period of 3 years or less as at the date on which he complies with the requirements of regulation 9; and

(iv) who, as at the date on which he complies with the requirements of regulation 9, is under the age of 21.

(2) Except in a case to which paragraph (3) or (4) applies, a person shall, for the purposes of regulation 7, be deemed to be a person in hardship where, after taking account of the factors set out in paragraph (5) in so far as they are appropriate to the particular circumstances of the case, the Secretary of State is satisfied that he or his partner will suffer hardship unless a jobseeker's allowance is paid to him.

(3) In paragraphs (1) and (2), a person shall not be deemed to be a person in hardship—

(a) where he is entitled, or his partner is entitled, to income support or where he or his partner fall within a category of persons prescribed for the purpose of section 124(1)(e) of the Benefits Act; [4 or]

(b) during any period in respect of which it has been determined that a jobseeker's allowance is not payable to him pursuant to section [3 8] [5 of the Jobseekers Act (attendance, information and evidence) or that it be reduced pursuant to section 19 or 19A or 19B of that Act (circumstances in which a jobseeker's allowance is reduced)];

(c) [4 . . .]

(4) Paragraph (1)(h) shall not apply in a case where the person being cared for resides in a [1 care home, an Abbeyfield Home or an independent hospital].

(5) Factors which, for the purposes of paragraphs (1) and (2), the Secretary of State is to take into account in determining whether the person is a person in hardship are

(a) the presence in that person's family of a person who satisfies the requirements for a disability premium specified in paragraphs 13 and 14 of Schedule 1 to the Jobseeker's Allowance Regulations or for a disabled child premium specified in paragraph 16 of that Schedule to those Regulations;

(b) the resources which, without a jobseeker's allowance, are likely to

than 25 or a member of a couple or polygamous marriage where one member is aged not less than 18 but less than 25 and the other member or, in the case of a polygamous marriage each other member, is a person under 18 who is not eligible for an income-based jobseeker's allowance under section 3(1)(f)(iii) of the Jobseekers Act or is not subject to a direction under section 16 of that Act, the amount specified in paragraph 1(1)(d) of Schedule 1 to the Jobseeker's Allowance Regulations;

(b) where the claimant is a single claimant aged not less than 25 or a member of a couple or a polygamous marriage (other than a member of a couple or polygamous marriage to whom sub-paragraph (a) applies) at least one of whom is aged not less than 18, the amount specified in paragraph 1(1)(e) of Schedule 1 to the Jobseeker's Allowance Regulations.

(2) A reduction under paragraph (1) shall, if it is not a multiple of 5p, be rounded to the nearest such multiple or, if it is a multiple of 2.5p but not of 5p, to the next lower multiple of 5p.

PART IV

HARDSHIP FOR JOINT-CLAIM COUPLES

Application of Part and meaning of "couple in hardship"

2.829 **11.**—(1) This Part of these Regulations applies in respect of any part of the disqualification period when section 8(2) of the Act would otherwise apply.

(2) In this Part of these Regulations, a "couple in hardship" means, for the purposes of [3 regulation 12], a joint-claim couple, other than a couple to whom paragraph (4) or (5) applies, who are claiming a jointclaim jobseeker's allowance jointly where at least one member of that couple is an offender and where—

(a) [1 care home, an Abbeyfield Home or an independent hospital] and the Secretary of State is satisfied that, unless a joint-claim jobseeker's allowance is paid, she will suffer hardship;

(b) one or both members of the couple are members of a polygamous marriage, one member of the marriage is pregnant and the Secretary of State is satisfied that, unless a joint-claim jobseeker's allowance is paid, she will suffer hardship;

(c) the award of a joint-claim jobseeker's allowance includes, or would, if a claim for a jobseeker's allowance from the couple were to succeed, have included in their applicable amount a disability premium and the Secretary of State is satisfied that, unless a joint-claim jobseeker's allowance is paid, the member of the couple who would have caused the disability premium to be applicable to the couple would suffer hardship;

(d) either member of the couple suffers from a chronic medical condition which results in functional capacity being limited or restricted by physical impairment and the Secretary of State is satisfied that—

(i) the suffering has already lasted or is likely to last, for not less than 26 weeks; and

(ii) unless a joint-claim jobseeker's allowance is paid, the probability is that the health of the person suffering would, within two weeks of the Secretary of State making his decision, decline further than that of a normally healthy adult and the member of the couple who suffers from that condition would suffer hardship;

(e) either member of the couple, or where a member of that couple is married to more than one person under a law which permits polygamy, one member of that marriage, devotes a considerable portion of each week to caring for another person who—

(i) is in receipt of an attendance allowance [4 , the care component of disability living allowance at one of the two higher rates prescribed under section 72(4) of the Benefits Act [5 , armed forces independence payment] or the daily living component of personal independence payment at the standard or enhanced rate in accordance with section 78 of the 2012 Act];

(ii) has claimed either attendance allowance [4 , disability living allowance [5 , armed forces independence payment] or personal independence payment], but only for so long as the claim has not been determined, or for 26 weeks from the date of claiming, whichever is the earlier; [4 . . .]

(iii) has claimed either attendance allowance or disability living allowance and has an award of either attendance allowance or the care component of disability living allowance at one of the two higher rates prescribed under section 72(4) of the Benefits Act for a period commencing after the date on which that claim was made; [4 [5 . . .]

(iv) has claimed personal independence payment and has an award of the daily living component of personal independence payment at the standard or enhanced rate in accordance with section 78 of the 2012 Act for a period commencing after the date on which that claim was made;] [5 or

(v) has claimed armed forces independence payment and has an award for a period commencing after the date on which that claim was made,]

and the Secretary of State is satisfied, after taking account of the factors set out in paragraph (6) in so far as they are appropriate to the particular circumstances of the case, that the person providing the care will not be able to continue doing so unless a joint-claim jobseeker's allowance is paid; or

(f) section 16 of the Jobseekers Act applies to either member of the couple by virtue of a direction issued by the Secretary of State, except where the member of the joint-claim couple to whom the direction applies does not satisfy the requirements of section 1(2)(a) to (c) of that Act;

(g) section 3A(1)(e)(ii) of the Jobseekers Act (member of joint-claim couple under the age of 18) applies to either member of the couple and the Secretary of State is satisfied that unless a jointclaim jobseeker's allowance is paid, the couple will suffer hardship; or

(h) one or both members of the couple is a person—

(i) who, pursuant to the Children Act 1989, was being looked after by a local authority;

(ii) with whom the local authority had a duty, pursuant to that Act, to take reasonable steps to keep in touch; or

(iii) who, pursuant to that Act, qualified for advice or assistance from a local authority,

but in respect of whom head (i), (ii) or (iii) above, as the case may be, had not applied for a period of 3 years or less as at the date on which the requirements of regulation 15 are complied with; and

(iv) who, as at the date on which the requirements of regulation 15 are complied with, is under the age of 21.

(3) Except in a case to which paragraph (4) or (5) applies, a joint-claim couple shall, for the purposes of [3 regulation 13], be deemed to be a couple in hardship where the Secretary of State is satisfied, after taking account of the factors set out in paragraph (6) in so far as they are appropriate to the particular circumstances of the case, that the couple will suffer hardship unless a joint-claim jobseeker's allowance is paid.

(4) In paragraphs (2) and (3), a joint-claim couple shall not be deemed to be a "couple in hardship"—

(a) where one member of the couple is entitled to income support or falls within a category of persons prescribed for the purposes of section 124(1)(e) of the Benefits Act; or

(b) during a period in respect of which it has been determined that both members of the couple are subject [3 or are treated as subject] to sanctions for the purposes of section [3 8 or] 20A of the Jobseekers Act ([3 attendance, information and evidence;] denial or reduction of joint-claim jobseeker's allowance).

(5) Paragraph (2)(e) shall not apply in a case where the person being cared for resides in a [2 care home, an Abbeyfield Home or an independent hospital].

(6) Factors which, for the purposes of paragraphs (2) and (3), the Secretary of State is to take into account in determining whether a joint-claim couple will suffer hardship are—

(a) the presence in the joint-claim couple of a person who satisfies the requirements for a disability premium specified in paragraphs 20H and 20I of Schedule 1 to the Jobseeker's Allowance Regulations;

(b) the resources which, without a joint-claim jobseeker's allowance, are likely to be available to the joint-claim couple, the amount by which these resources fall short of the amount applicable in their case in accordance with regulation 16 (applicable amount of joint-claim couple in hardship cases), the amount of any resources which may be available to the joint-claim couple from any person in the couple's household who is not a member of the family and the length of time for which those factors are likely to persist;

(c) whether there is a substantial risk that essential items, including food, clothing, heating and accommodation, will cease to be available to the joint-claim couple, or will be available at considerably reduced levels, the hardship that will result and the length of time those factors are likely to persist.

(7) In determining the resources available to the offender's family under paragraph (6)(b), any training premium or top-up payment paid pursuant to the Employment and Training Act 1973 shall be disregarded.

AMENDMENTS

1. Social Security (Care Homes and Independent Hospitals) Regulations 2005 (SI 2005/2687) reg.15(3) (October 24, 2005).

2. Civil Partnership (Pensions, Social Security and Child Support) (Consequential etc. Provisions) Order 2005 (SI 2005/2877) Sch.3 para.34(3) (December 5, 2005).

3. Social Security (Loss of Benefit) Amendment Regulations 2010 (SI 2010/1160) reg.2(1) and (8) (April 1, 2010).

4. Social Security (Loss of Benefit) (Amendment) Regulations 2013 (SI 2013/385) regs 2 and 12 (April 8, 2013).

5. Armed Forces and Reserve Forces Compensation Scheme (Consequential Provisions: Subordinate Legislation) Order 2013 (SI 2013/591) art.7 and Sch. para.22(1) and (4) (April 8, 2013).

Circumstances in which a joint-claim jobseeker's allowance is payable where a joint-claim couple is a couple in hardship

12.—(1) This regulation applies where a joint-claim couple is a couple in hardship within the meaning of regulation 11(2) and is subject to the provisions of regulations 14 and 15. 2.830

(2) A joint-claim jobseeker's allowance shall be payable to a couple in hardship even though section 8(2) of the Act prevents payment of a joint-claim jobseeker's allowance to the couple or section 8(3) of the Act reduces the amount of a joint-claim jobseeker's allowance payable to the couple but the allowance shall be payable under this paragraph only if and for so long as—

(a) the joint-claim couple satisfy the other conditions of entitlement to a joint-claim jobseeker's allowance; or

(b) one member satisfies those conditions and the other member comes within any paragraph in Schedule A1 to the Jobseeker's Allowance Regulations (categories of members not required to satisfy conditions in section 1(2B)(b) of the Jobseekers Act).

Further circumstances in which a joint-claim jobseeker's allowance is payable to a couple in hardship

13.—(1) This regulation applies to a couple in hardship falling within regulation 11(3) and is subject to the provisions of regulations 14 and 15. 2.831

(2) A joint-claim jobseeker's allowance shall be payable to a couple in hardship even though section 8(2) of the Act prevents payment of a joint-claim jobseeker's allowance to the couple or section 8(3) of the Act reduces the amount of a joint-claim jobseeker's allowance payable to the couple but the allowance—

(a) shall not be payable under this paragraph in respect of the first 14 days of the prescribed period; and

(b) shall be payable thereafter only where the conditions of entitlement to a joint-claim jobseeker's allowance are satisfied or where one member satisfies those conditions and the other member comes within any paragraph in Schedule A1 to the Jobseeker's Allowance Regulations (categories of members not required to satisfy conditions in section 1(2B)(b) of the Jobseekers Act).

Conditions for payment of a joint-claim jobseeker's allowance

2.832 **14.**—(1) A joint-claim jobseeker's allowance shall not be payable in accordance with regulation 12 or 13 except where either member of the couple has—

(a) furnished on a form approved for the purpose by the Secretary of State or in such other form as he may in any particular case approve, a statement of the circumstances he relies upon to establish entitlement under regulation 11(2) or, as the case may be, 11(3); and

(b) signed the statement.

(2) The completed and signed form shall be delivered by a member of the couple to such office as the Secretary of State may specify.

Provision of information

2.833 **15.** For the purposes of section 8(4)(b) of the Act, a member of the couple shall provide to the Secretary of State information as to the circumstances of the alleged hardship of the couple.

Applicable amount of joint-claim couple in hardship cases

2.834 **16.**—(1) The weekly applicable amount of a couple to whom a joint-claim jobseeker's allowance is payable in accordance with this Part shall be reduced by a sum equivalent to 40 per cent. or, in a case where a member of the joint-claim couple is either pregnant or seriously ill or where a member of the joint-claim couple is a member of a polygamous marriage and one of those members is either pregnant or seriously ill, 20 per cent of the following amount—

(a) where one member of the joint-claim couple or of the polygamous marriage is aged not less than 18 but less than 25 and the other member or, in the case of a polygamous marriage, each other member, is a person under 18 to whom section 3A(1 (e)(ii) of the Jobseekers Act applies or is not subject to a direction under section 16 of that Act, the amount specified in paragraph 1(1)(d) of Schedule 1 to the Jobseeker's Allowance Regulations;

(b) where one member of the joint-claim couple or at least one member of the polygamous marriage (other than a member of a couple or polygamous marriage to whom sub-paragraph (a) applies) is aged not less than 18, the amount specified in paragraph 1(1)(e) of Schedule 1 to the Jobseeker's Allowance Regulations.

(2) A reduction under paragraph (1) shall, if it is not a multiple of 5p, be rounded to the nearest such multiple or, if it is a multiple of 2.5p but not of 5p, to the next lower multiple of 5p.

[1 PART 4A

HARDSHIP: INCOME-RELATED EMPLOYMENT AND SUPPORT ALLOWANCE

Payment of income-related employment and support allowance to specified persons

16A—(1) Subject to regulation 16B, an income-related employment and support allowance is payable in accordance with the following provisions of this Part to an offender or an offender's family member ("O") where— 2.835

(a) O meets the conditions for entitlement to that allowance;
(b) the amount of the allowance otherwise payable to O is subject to a reduction under regulation 3ZA above or regulation 63 of the ESA Regulations; and
(c) the Secretary of State is satisfied that O, their partner or a child or qualifying young person for whom they are responsible, will be in hardship unless such a payment is made.

(2) The Secretary of State must take the following matters into account in determining whether a person is in hardship for the purpose of paragraph (1)(c)—

(a) whether O's partner or a person in O's family satisfies the requirements for a disability premium specified in paragraphs 6 and 7 of Schedule 4 to the ESA Regulations, or for an element of child tax credit in respect of a child or young person who is disabled or severely disabled within the meaning of regulation 8 of the Child Tax Credit Regulations 2002;
(b) the household's available resources without a payment under paragraph (1), including resources from persons who are not members of the household;
(c) the difference between the available resources and the amount of a payment under paragraph (1) that O would receive;
(d) whether there is a substantial risk that the household will not have access to essential items (including food, clothing, heating and accommodation), or will have access to such essential items at considerably reduced levels, without a payment under paragraph (1); and
(e) the length of time that the factors set out in sub-paragraphs (b) to (d) are likely to continue.

(3) In paragraphs (1) and (2), "partner", "child" and "qualifying young person" have the same meaning as they have in the ESA Regulations.]

AMENDMENT

1. Social Security (Loss of Benefit) (Amendment) Regulations 2013 (SI 2013/385) regs 2 and 13 (April 1, 2013).

[1 Requirements for payments under regulation 16A(1)

16B The Secretary of State must not make a payment under regulation 16A(1) unless O — 2.836

(a) completes and submits an application in a form approved for the purpose by the Secretary of State, or in such other form as the Secretary of State accepts as sufficient, in such manner as the Secretary of State determines; and

(b) provides such information or evidence relating to the matters specified in regulation 16A(2)(b) to (d) as the Secretary of State may require, in such manner as the Secretary of State determines.]

AMENDMENT

1. Social Security (Loss of Benefit) (Amendment) Regulations 2013 (SI 2013/385) regs 2 and 13 (April 1, 2013).

[1 Amount of payment under regulation 16A(1)

2.837 **16C.**—(1) The amount of a payment under regulation 16A(1) is 60 per cent. of the prescribed amount for a single claimant as set out in paragraph (1)(a) of Part 1 of Schedule 4 to the ESA Regulations.

(2) A payment calculated in accordance with paragraph (1) is to be, if it is not a multiple of 5 pence, rounded to the nearest such multiple or, if it is a multiple of 2.5 pence but not of 5 pence, to the next lower multiple of 5 pence.]

AMENDMENT

1. Social Security (Loss of Benefit) (Amendment) Regulations 2013 (SI 2013/385) regs 2 and 13 (April 1, 2013).

[1 PART 4B

HARDSHIP: UNIVERSAL CREDIT

2.838 Payment of universal credit to specified persons

16D.–(1) Subject to regulation 16E, universal credit is payable in accordance with the following provisions of this Part to an offender or an offender's family member ("O") or where O is a joint claimant, to O and the other joint claimant ("J"), where the Secretary of State is satisfied that they are in hardship.

(2) For the purposes of paragraph (1), O or, as the case may be, O and J must be considered as being in hardship only where—

(a) they meet the conditions for entitlement to universal credit;
(b) they cannot meet their immediate and most basic and essential needs, specified in paragraph (3), or the immediate and most basic and essential needs of a child or qualifying young person for whom O is, or O and J are, responsible only because the amount of their award has been reduced under—
  (i) section 26 or 27 of the 2012 Act by the daily reduction rate determined in accordance with regulation 111 of the UC Regulations; or
  (ii) regulation 3ZB above by the daily reduction rate determined in accordance with paragraph (3) or (4) of that regulation;
(c) they have made every effort to access alternative sources of support to meet, or partially meet, such needs; and
(d) they have made every effort to cease to incur any expenditure which does not relate to such needs.

(3) The needs referred to in paragraph (2) are—

(a) accommodation;
(b) heating;

(c) food;
(d) hygiene.

(4) In paragraph (2)(b), "child" and "qualifying young person" have the same meaning as in Part 1 of the 2012 Act and whether or not O is, or O and J are, responsible for a child or qualifying young person is to be determined in accordance with regulation 4 of the UC Regulations.]

AMENDMENT

1. Social Security (Loss of Benefit) (Amendment) Regulations 2013 (SI 2013/385) regs 2 and 14 (April 29, 2013).

[1 Requirements for payments under regulation 16D(1)

16E. The Secretary of State must not make a payment under regulation 16D(1) unless— 2.839

(a) O completes and submits or, as the case may be, O and J complete and submit, an application in a form approved for the purpose by the Secretary of State, or in such other form as the Secretary of State accepts as sufficient, in such manner as the Secretary of State determines;
(b) O furnishes or, as the case may be, O and J furnish, such information or evidence relating to the matters specified in regulation 16D(2)(b) to (d) as the Secretary of State may require, in such manner as the Secretary of State determines; and
(c) O accepts or, as the case may be O and J accept, that any such payments that are paid are recoverable and may be recovered in accordance with section 71ZH of the Administration Act, except in such cases as the Secretary of State determines otherwise.]

AMENDMENT

1. Social Security (Loss of Benefit) (Amendment) Regulations 2013 (SI 2013/385) regs 2 and 14 (April 29, 2013).

[1 Period in respect of which payments under regulation 16D(1) are to be made

16F. A payment under regulation 16D(1) is to be made in respect of— 2.840

(a) a period which—
  (i) begins with the date on which the application under regulation 16E(a) is submitted or, if later, the date on which all of the conditions in regulation 16D(2) are met; and
  (ii) ends with the day before the date on which O's, or as the case may be, O and J's next full payment of universal credit for an assessment period is due to be made (or would be made but for a reduction under regulation 3ZB); or
(b) where the period calculated in accordance with paragraph (a) is 7 days or less, that period plus a further period ending with the day referred to in paragraph (a)(ii) or, if sooner, the last day in respect of which O's, or as the case may be, O and J's award is reduced in accordance with regulation 3ZB.

AMENDMENT

1. Social Security (Loss of Benefit) (Amendment) Regulations 2013 (SI 2013/385) regs 2 and 14 (April 29, 2013).]

[1 The amount of payments under regulation 16D(1)

2.841 **16G.** The amount of a payment under regulation 16D(1) for each day in respect of which such a payment is to be is made is to be determined in accordance with the formula—

$$60\% \text{ of } \left(\frac{A \times 12}{365}\right)$$

where A is equal to the amount of the reduction in the amount of O's award or, as the case may be, the amount of O and J's award, calculated under regulation 3ZB for the assessment period preceding the assessment period in which an application is submitted under regulation 16E(a).]

AMENDMENT

1. Social Security (Loss of Benefit) (Amendment) Regulations 2013 (SI 2013/385) regs 2 and 14 (April 29, 2013).

[1 Recoverability of payments made under regulation 16D(1)

2.842 **16H.** Payments made under regulation 16D(1) are recoverable by virtue of section 71ZH of the Administration Act as if they were hardship payments under regulation 116 of the UC Regulations and for this purpose, regulation 119 of those Regulations applies to payments under regulation 16D(1) as it applies to such hardship payments.]

AMENDMENT

1. Social Security (Loss of Benefit) (Amendment) Regulations 2013 (SI 2013/385) regs 2 and 14 (April 29, 2013).

PART V

HOUSING BENEFIT AND COUNCIL TAX BENEFIT

2.843 **17.** *Omitted.*

2.844 **18.** *Omitted.*

PART VI

DEDUCTIONS FROM BENEFITS AND DISQUALIFYING BENEFITS

Social security benefits not to be sanctionable benefits

2.845 **19.** The following social security benefits are to be treated as a disqualifying benefit but not a sanctionable benefit—

(a) constant attendance allowance payable under [1 article 8 of the Naval, Military and Air Forces Etc. (Disablement and Death) Service Pensions Order 2006] ("the Order") or article 14 or 43 of the Personal Injuries (Civilians) Scheme 1983 ("the Scheme");

(b) exceptionally severe disablement allowance payable under [1 article 9 of the Order] or article 15 or 44 of the Scheme;
(c) mobility supplement payable under [1 article 26A] of the Order or article 25A or 48A of the Scheme;
(d) constant attendance allowance and exceptionally severe disablement allowance, payable under sections 104 and 105 respectively of the Benefits Act where a disablement pension is payable under section 103 of that Act; and
(e) [2 bereavement support payment payable under section 30 of the Pensions Act 2014.]

AMENDMENTS

1. Social Security (Loss of Benefit) (Amendment) Regulations 2013 (SI 2013/385) regs 2 and 15 (April 1, 2013).
2. Pensions Act 2014 (Consequential, Supplementary and Incidental Amendments) Order 2017 (SI 2017/422) art.20 (April 6, 2017, subject to a saving).

[1 Benefits to be treated as neither sanctionable nor disqualifying

19A. Each of the following benefits is to be treated as neither a sanctionable benefit nor a disqualifying benefit— **2.846**
(a) statutory adoption pay;
(b) statutory paternity pay;
(c) health in pregnancy grant.]

AMENDMENT

1. Social Security (Loss of Benefit) Amendment Regulations 2010 (SI 2010/1160) reg.2(1) and (11) (April 1, 2010).

Deductions from benefits

20. Any restriction in section [1 6B,] 7, 8 or 9 of the Act shall not apply in relation to payments of benefit to the extent of any deduction from the payments which falls to be made under regulations made under section 5(1)(p) of the Social Security Administration Act 1992 for, or in place of, child support maintenance and for this purpose, "child support maintenance" means such maintenance which is payable under the Child Support Act 1991. **2.847**

AMENDMENT

1. Social Security (Loss of Benefit) Amendment Regulations 2010 (SI 2010/1160) reg.2(1) and (12) (April 1, 2010).

PART VII

OTHER AMENDMENTS

21. *Omitted.* **2.848**
22. *Omitted.* **2.849**

The Social Security (Medical Evidence) Regulations 1976

(SI 1976/615) (AS AMENDED)

ARRANGEMENT OF REGULATIONS

SCHEDULES

The Secretary of State for Social Services, in exercise of powers conferred upon him by section 115(1) of, and Schedule 13 to, the Social Security Act 1975 and of all other powers enabling him in that behalf, after reference to the National Insurance Advisory Committee hereby makes the following regulations:

Citation, commencement, and interpretation

2.851 **1.** (1) These regulations may be cited as the Social Security (Medical Evidence) Regulations 1976, and shall come into operation on 4th October 1976.

(2) In these regulations, unless the context otherwise requires—

"the Act" means the Social Security Act 1975;

[[2] "the Contributions and Benefits Act" means the Social Security Contributions and Benefits Act 1992;]

[[4] "the Employment and Support Allowance Regulations" means the Employment and Support Allowance Regulations 2008;]

[[5] "limited capability for work" has the meaning—

(a) for the purposes of employment and support allowance, given in section 1(4) of the Welfare Reform Act 2007; and

(b) for the purposes of universal credit, given in section 37 of the Welfare Reform Act 2012;"

"limited capability for work assessment" means the assessment of whether a person has limited capability for work—

(a) for the purposes of old style ESA, under Part 5 of the Employment and Support Allowance Regulations;

(b) for the purposes of new style ESA, under Part 4 of the Employment and Support Allowance Regulations 2013;

(c) for the purposes of universal credit, under Part 5 of the Universal Credit Regulations 2013;]

[3 "personal capability assessment" means the assessment provided for in section 171C of the Contributions and Benefits Act;]

[1 "registered midwife" means a midwife who is registered as a midwife with the United Kingdom Central Council for Nursing, Midwifery and Health Visiting under the Nurses, Midwives and Health Visitors Act 1979;]

"doctor" means a registered medical practitioner;

"signature" means, in relation to any statement or certificate given in accordance with these regulations, the name by which the person giving that statement or certificate, as the case may be, is usually known (any name other than the surname being either in full or otherwise indicated) written by that person in his own handwriting; and "signed" shall be construed accordingly.

(3) Any reference in these regulations to any provisions made by or contained in any enactment or instrument shall, except in so far as the context otherwise requires, be construed as a reference to that provision as amended or extended by any enactment or instrument and as including a reference to any provision which it re-enacts or replaces, or which may re-enact or replace it, with or without modification.

(4) The rules for the construction of Acts of Parliament contained in the Interpretation Act 1889 shall apply in relation to this instrument and in relation to the revocation effected by it as if this instrument, the regulations revoked by it and regulations revoked by the regulations so revoked were Acts of Parliament, and as if each revocation were a repeal.

[5 (5) For the purposes of the definition of "limited capability for work assessment" in paragraph (2)—

(a) "old style ESA" means an allowance under Part 1 of the Welfare Reform Act 2007 as that Part has effect apart from the amendments made by Schedule 3, and Part 1 of Schedule 14, to the Welfare Reform Act 2012 that remove references to an income-related allowance; and

(b "new style ESA" means an allowance under Part 1 of the Welfare Reform Act 2007 as amended by the provisions of Schedule 3, and Part 1 of Schedule 14, to the Welfare Reform Act 2012 that remove references to an income-related allowance.]

AMENDMENTS

1. The Social Security (Medical Evidence) Amendment Regulations 1987 (SI 1987/409) reg.2 (April 6, 1987).

2. The Social Security (Medical Evidence) Amendment Regulations 1994 (SI 1994/2975) reg.2 (April 13, 1995).

3. The Social Security (Incapacity for Work) Miscellaneous Amendments Regulations 1999 (SI 1999/3109) reg.5(a) (April 3, 2000).

4. The Employment and Support Allowance (Consequential provisions) (No.2) Regulations 2008 (SI 2008/1554) reg.68 (October 27, 2008).

5. The Universal Credit (Consequential Supplementary, Incidental and Miscellaneous Provisions) Regulations 2013 (SI 2013/630) reg.24 (April 29, 2013).

Evidence of incapacity for work [8 , limited capability for work] and confinement

[9 **2.**—(1) Subject to regulation 5 and paragraph (1A) below, where a person claims to be entitled to any benefit, allowance or advantage (other than industrial injuries benefit or statutory sick pay) and entitlement to that benefit, allowance or advantage depends on that person being incapable of work or 2.852

having limited capability for work, then in respect of each day until that person has been assessed for the purposes of the personal capability assessment or the limited capability for work assessment they shall provide evidence of such incapacity or limited capability by means of a statement given by a doctor in accordance with the rules set out in Part 1 of Schedule 1 to these Regulations.

(1A) Where it would be unreasonable to require a person to provide a statement in accordance with paragraph (1) above that person shall provide such other evidence as may be sufficient to show that they are incapable of work or have limited capability for work so that they should refrain (or should have refrained) from work by reason of some specific disease or bodily or mental disability.]

(2) Every person to whom paragraph (1) applies [[2] who has not been assessed for the purposes of the [[6] personal capability assessment]] [[8] or the limited capability for work assessment] shall, before he returns to work, furnish evidence of the date on which he became fit for work either in accordance with rule 10 of Part 1 of Schedule 1 to these regulations, or by such other means as may be sufficient in the circumstances of the case.

[[7] (3) Every woman who claims maternity benefit shall furnish evidence—

(a) where the claims is made in respect of expectation of confinement, that she is pregnant and as to the stage which she has reached in her pregnancy; or

(b) where the claim is made by virtue of the fact of confinement, that she has been confined;

and shall furnish such evidence by means of a maternity certificate given by a doctor or by as registered midwife [not earlier than the beginning of the 20th week before the week in which she is expected to be confined] in accordance with the rules set out in Part I of Schedule 2 to these regulations in the appropriate form set out in Part II of that Schedule or by such other means as may be sufficient in the circumstances of any particular case.]

AMENDMENTS

1. The Social Security (Medical Evidence, Claims and Payments) Amendments Regulations 1982 (SI 1982/699) reg.2 (June 14, 1982).

2. The Social Security (Medical Evidence) Amendment Regulations 1994 (SI 1994/2975) reg.2 (April 13, 1995).

3. The Social Security (Medical Evidence) Amendment Regulations 1992 (SI 1992/2471) reg.3 (March 9, 1992).

4. The Social Security (Incapacity for Work) Miscellaneous Amendments Regulations 1995 (SI 1995/987) reg.4 (April 13, 1995.)

5. The Social Security (Incapacity) Miscellaneous Amendments Regulations 2000 (SI 2000/590) reg.6 (April 3, 2000).

6. The Social Security (Incapacity for Work) Miscellaneous Amendments Regulations 1999 (SI 1999/3109) reg.5(b) (April 3, 2000).

7. The Social Security (Medical Evidence) and Statutory Maternity Pay (Medical Evidence) (Amendment) Regulations 2001 (SI 2001/2931) reg.2 (September 28, 2001).

8. The Employment and Support Allowance (Consequential provisions) (No.2) Regulations 2008 (SI 2008/1554) reg.68 (October 27, 2008).

9. The Social Security (Medical Evidence) and Statutory Sick Pay (Medical Evidence) (Amendment) Regulations 2010 (SI 2010/137) reg.2(2) (April 6, 2010).

GENERAL NOTE

2.853 In *R(15) 8/93,* the Commissioner ruled that the reference in the regulation to "such other means as may be sufficient in the particular circumstances of any particular case" meant that evidence of incapacity need not be in the form of a medical certificate. This means that medical certificates other than in the form set out in the Schedule may be acceptable as well as evidence from the claimant himself or herself (para.14). Whether such evidence is sufficient is a matter for determination by the decision-maker or tribunal. Failure to consider this issue will be an error of law.

In *CIB/17533/1996* the Commissioner addressed an issue which was being argued by a number of representatives, namely that there was no jurisdiction to make an all work test determination where the adjudication officer had requested the claimant to obtain the special Form Med. 4 and this form was not available to the adjudication officer when the decision was made. Form Med. 4 is the special form which specifically directs doctors to consider capacity for *all* work in certifying incapacity for work. The Commissioner concludes that "the somewhat legalistic proposition that a decision by an adjudication officer made without a form MED4 is a nullity or is erroneous in law cannot in my view be sustained" (para.8 of Common Appendix).

Regulation 3 revoked by The Social Security (Claims and Payments) Regulations 1979 (SI1979/628) reg.32 (July 9, 1979). **2.854**

Regulation 4 revoked by The Social Security (Medical Evidence, Claims and Payments) Amendments Regulations 1982 (SI1982/699) reg.2 (June 14, 1982). **2.855**

[1 Self-certificate for first 7 days of a spell of incapacity for work [4 or limited capability for work]

5.—[2 (1) [3 The evidence of incapacity [4 or limited capability for work] required for the purposes of determining entitlement to a benefit, allowance or advantage referred to in regulation 2(1)]— **2.856**

(a) for a spell of incapacity which lasts for less than 8 days,
(b) in respect of any of the first 7 days of a longer spell of incapacity;
may consist of a self certificate instead of a certificate in the form of a statement in writing given by a doctor in accordance with regulation 2(1).]
[4 (c) for a period of limited capability for work which lasts less than 8 days; or
(d) in respect of any of the first 7 days of a longer period of limited capability for work.]

(2) For the purpose of this regulation:—

[4 "self-certificate means either—
(i) a declaration made by the claimant in writing, on a form approved for the purpose by the Secretary of State; or
(ii) where the claim has made a claim for employment and support allowance in accordance with regulation 4G of the Social Security (Claims and Payments) Regulations 1987, an oral declaration by the claimant,
that the claimant has been unfit for work from a date or for a period specified in the declaration and may include a statement that the claimant expects to continue to be unfit for work on days subsequent to the date on which it is made;]

[3 "spell of incapacity" has the meaning given to it by section 171B(3) of the Contributions and benefits Act.]]

AMENDMENTS

1. The Social Security (Medical Evidence, Claims and Payments) Amendments Regulations 1982 (SI 1982/699) reg.2 (June 14, 1982).

2. The Social Security (Medical Evidence, Claims and Payments) Amendment Regulations 1989 (SI 1989/1686) reg.2 (October 9, 1989).
3. The Social Security (Medical Evidence) Amendment Regulations 1994 (SI 1994/2975) reg.2 (April 13, 1995).
4. The Employment and Support Allowance (Consequential Provisions) (No. 2) Regulations 2008 (SI 2008/1554) reg.68 (October 27, 2008).

[[1] SCHEDULE 1 **Regulation 2(1)(a)**

PART 1

RULES

2.857 1. In these rules, unless the context otherwise requires—
"assessment" means either a consultation between a patient and a doctor which takes place in person or by telephone or a consideration by a doctor of a written report by another doctor or other health care professional;
"condition" means a specific disease or bodily or mental disability;
"doctor" means a registered medical practitioner, not being the patient;
"other health care professional" means a person (other than a registered medical practitioner and not being the patient) who is a registered nurse, a registered midwife, an occupational therapist or physiotherapist registered with a regulatory body established by an Order in Council under section 60 of the Health Act 1999(6), or a member of any profession regulated by a body mentioned in section 25(3) of the National Health Service Reform and Health Care Professions Act 2002;
"patient" means the person in respect of whom a statement is given in accordance with these rules.

2. Where a doctor issues a statement to a patient in accordance with an obligation arising under a contract, agreement or arrangement under Part 4 of the National Health Service Act 2006 or Part 4 of the National Health Service (Wales) Act 2006 or Part 1 of the National Health Service (Scotland) Act 1978 the doctor's statement shall be in a form set out at Part 2 of this Schedule and shall be signed by that doctor.

3. Where a doctor issues a statement in any case other than in accordance with rule 2, the doctor's statement shall be in the form set out in Part 2 of this Schedule or in a form to like effect and shall be signed by the doctor attending the patient.

4. A doctor's statement must be based on an assessment made by that doctor.

5. A doctor's statement shall be completed in ink or other indelible substance and shall contain the following particulars—
(a) the patient's name;
(b) the date of the assessment (whether by consultation or consideration of a report as the case may be) on which the doctor's statement is based;
(c) the condition in respect of which the doctor advises the patient they are not fit for work;
(d) a statement, where the doctor considers it appropriate, that the patient may be fit for work;
(e) a statement that the doctor will or, as the case may be will not, need to assess the patient's fitness for work again;
(f) the date on which the doctor's statement is given;
(g) the address of the doctor,

and shall bear, opposite the words "Doctor's signature", the signature in ink of the doctor making the statement.

6. Subject to rule 8, the condition in respect of which the doctor is advising the patient is not fit for work or, as the case may be, which has caused the patient's absence from work shall be specified as precisely as the doctor's knowledge of the patient's condition at the time of the assessment permits.

7. Where a doctor considers that a patient may be fit for work the doctor shall state the reasons for that advice and where this is considered appropriate, the arrangements which the patient might make, with their employer's agreement, to return to work.

8. The condition may be specified less precisely where, in the doctor's opinion, disclosure of the precise condition would be prejudicial to the patient's well-being, or to the patient's position with their employer.

9. A doctor's statement may be given on a date after the date of the assessment on which it is based, however no further statement shall be furnished in respect of that assessment other than a doctor's statement by way of replacement of an original which has been lost, in which case it shall be clearly marked "duplicate".

10. Where, in the doctor's opinion, the patient will become fit for work on a day not later than 14 days after the date of the assessment on which the doctor's statement is based, the doctor's statement shall specify that day.

11. Subject to rules 12 and 13, the doctor's statement shall specify the minimum period for which, in the doctor's opinion, the patient will not be fit for work or, as the case may be, for which they may be fit for work.

12. The period specified shall begin on the date of the assessment on which the doctor's statement is based and shall not exceed 3 months unless the patient has, on the advice of a doctor, refrained from work for at least 6 months immediately preceding that date.

13. Where—

(a) the patient has been advised by a doctor that they are not fit for work and, in consequence, has refrained from work for at least 6 months immediately preceding the date of the assessment on which the doctor's statement is based; and

(b) in the doctor's opinion, the patient will not be fit for work for the foreseeable future,

instead of specifying a period, the doctor may, having regard to the circumstances of the particular case, enter, after the words "case for", the words "an indefinite period".

Part 2

Form of Doctor's Statement 2.858

STATEMENT OF FITNESS FOR WORK
FOR SOCIAL SECURITY OR STATUTORY SICK PAY

Patient's name: Mr, Mrs, Miss, Ms

I assessed your case on: / /

and, because of the following condition(s):

I advise you that:

☐ you are not fit for work.

☐ you may be fit for work taking account of the following advice:

If available, and with your employer's agreement, you may benefit from:

☐ a phased return to work ☐ amended duties

☐ altered hours ☐ workplace adaptations

Comments, including functional effects of your condition(s):

This will be the case for [ ]

or from [/ /] to [/ /]

I will/will not need to assess your fitness for work again at the end of this period.
(Please delete as applicable)

Doctor's signature [ ]

Date of statement [/ /]

Doctor's address [ ]

AMENDMENT

1. The Social Security (Medical Evidence) and Statutory Sick Pay (Medical Evidence) (Amendment) Regulations 2010 (SI 2010/137) reg.2(3) (April 6, 2010).

2.859 SCHEDULES 1A AND 1B *repealed by* The Social Security (Medical Evidence) and Statutory Sick Pay (Medical Evidence) (Amendment) Regulations 2010 (SI 2010/137) reg.2(4) (April 6, 2010).

[1]SCHEDULE 2 **Regulation 2(3)**

PART I

RULES

2.860 **1.** In these rules any reference to a woman is a reference to the woman in respect of whom a maternity certificate is given in accordance with these rules.

2. A maternity certificate shall be given by a doctor or registered midwife attending the woman and shall not be given by the woman herself.

3. The maternity certificate shall be on a form provided by the Secretary of State for the purpose and the wording shall be that set out in the appropriate part of the form specified in Part II of this Schedule.

4. Every maternity certificate shall be completed in ink or other indelible substance and shall contain the following particulars—

(a) the woman's name;
(b) the week in which the woman is expected to be confined or, if the maternity certificate is given after confinement, the date of that confinement and the date the confinement was expected to take place [2 . . .];
(c) the date of the examination on which the maternity certificate is based;
(d) the date on which the maternity certificate is signed; and
(e) the address of the doctor or where the maternity certificate is signed by a registered midwife the personal identification number given to her by the United Kingdom Central Council for Nursing, Midwifery and Health Visiting ("UKCC") on her registration in Part 10 of the register maintained under section 10 of the Nurses, Midwives and Health Visitors Act 1979 and the expiry date of that registration,

and shall bear opposite the word "Signature", the signature of the person giving the maternity certificate written after there has been entered on the maternity certificate the woman's name and the expected date or, as the case may be, the date of the confinement.

5. After a maternity certificate has been given, no further maternity certificate based on the same examination shall be furnished other than a maternity certificate by way of replacement of an original which has been lost or mislaid, in which case it shall be clearly marked "duplicate".

[2]PART II

FORM OF CERTIFICATE

MATERNITY CERTIFICATE **2.861**

Please fill in this form in ink

Name of patient

Fill in this part if you are giving the certificate before the confinement
Do not fill this in more [3 than 20 weeks] before the week the baby is expected.

I certify that I examined you on the date given below. In my opinion you can expect to have your baby in the week that includes . . . ./. . . . ./. . . . .

Week means a period of 7 days starting on a Sunday and ending on a Saturday.

Fill in this part if you are giving the certificate after the confinement.
I certify that I attended you in connection with the birth which took place on . . . ./. . . . ./. . . . . when you were delivered of a child [ ] children. In my opinion your baby was expected in the week that includes . . . ./. . . . ./. . . . .

Date of examination . . . ./. . . . ./. . . . . .

Date of signing . . . ./. . . . ./. . . . .

Signature

Registered midwives

Please give your UKCC Personal Identification Number and the expiry date of your registration with the UKCC.

Doctors
Please stamp your name and address here [4 (unless the form has been stamped, in Wales, by a Local health Board in whose medical performers list you are included or, in Scotland,] by the Health Board in whose primary medical services performers list you are included)] in whose medical list you are included.

AMENDMENTS

1. The Social Security (Medical Evidence) Amendment Regulations 1987 (SI 1987/409) reg.4 (April 6, 1987).

2. The Social Security (Miscellaneous Provisions) Amendment Regulations 1991 (SI 1991/2284) reg.21 (November 1, 1991).

3. General Medical Services and Personal Medical Services Transition and Consequential Provisions Order 2004 (SI 2004/865) Sch.1 (April 1, 2004).

4. The National Treatment Agency (Abolition) and the Health and Social Care Act 2012 (Consequential, Transitional and Saving Provisions) Order 2013 (SI 2013/235) art.11 and Sch.2 Pt.1 para.6(3) (April 1, 2013).

The Social Security (Notification of Change of Circumstances) Regulations 2001

(SI 2001/3252)

Made	*26th September 2001*
Laid before Parliament	*2nd October 2001*
Coming into force	*18th October 2001*

ARRANGEMENT OF REGULATIONS

GENERAL NOTE

2.863 Section 16 of the Social Security Fraud Act 2001 (c.11), which came fully into force on October 18, 2001, amends the Administration Act 1992 to create new offences relating to failure to notify a change of circumstances, which affects entitlement to benefit. The requirements of the offences under the amended provisions of the Administration Act (which are not reproduced in Vol.III) are, broadly, fourfold (1) there has been a change of circumstances affecting entitlement to benefit, (2) the change is not excluded by regulations from changes which are required to be notified, (3) the person knows that the change affects entitlement to benefit, and (4) the person dishonestly fails to give a prompt notification in the prescribed manner to the prescribed person. These regulations set out the matter prescribed by the statute for the purposes of the criminal offences. The explanatory note to the regulations indicates that they are intended to mirror the existing requirements prescribed for the purposes of claims and payments under ss.5 and 6 of the Administration Act. The regulations are reproduced here so that those dealing with questions arising in the appeal tribunals and elsewhere in relation to claims for benefit are aware of the existence of these requirements under the criminal law. They may be referred to in overpayment cases.

The Secretary of State for Work and Pensions, in exercise of the powers conferred on him by ss.111A(1A), (1B), (1D) and (1E), 112(1A) to (1D), 189(1), (3) and (4) and 191 of the Social Security Administration Act 1992 and of all other powers enabling him in that behalf, and after consultation in respect of provisions of these Regulations relating to housing benefit and council tax benefit with organisations appearing to him to be representative of the authorities concerned, by this

Instrument, which is made before the end of the period of six months from the coming into force of s.16 of the Social Security Fraud Act 2001, hereby makes the following Regulations:

Citation and commencement

1. These Regulations may be cited as the Social Security (Notification of Change of Circumstances) Regulations 2001 and shall come into force on 18th October 2001. **2.864**

Notification for purposes of sections 111A and 112 of the Social Security Administration Act 1992

2. Regulations 3 to 5 below prescribe the person to whom, and manner in which, a change of circumstances must be notified for the purposes of sections 111A(1A) to (1G) and 112(1A) to (1F) of the Social Security Administration Act 1992 (offences relating to failure to notify a change of circumstances). **2.865**

Change affecting jobseeker's allowance

3.—(1) [2 Subject to [3 paragraphs (1ZA) and(1A),] where the benefit affected by the change of circumstances is a jobseeker's allowance, notice must be given [1 . . .] to the Secretary of State [1 . . .] at the office that the claimant is required to attend in accordance with a notification given to him under regulation 23 of the Jobseeker's Allowance Regulations 1996— **2.866**

[1 (a) in writing or by telephone (unless the Secretary of State determines in any particular case that notice must be in writing or may be given otherwise than in writing or by telephone); or

(b) in writing if in any class of case he requires written notice (unless he determines in any particular case to accept notice given otherwise than in writing).]

[3 (1ZA) Where the notice in writing referred to in paragraph (1) is given or sent by an electronic communication that notice must be given or sent in accordance with the provisions set out in Schedule 9ZC to the Social Security (Claims and Payments) Regulations 1987 (electronic communication).]

[2 "(1A) In such cases and subject to such conditions as the Secretary of State may specify, notice may be given to the Secretary of State—

(a) where the change of circumstances is a birth or death, through a relevant authority, or a county council in England, by personal attendance at an office specified by that authority or county council, provided the Secretary of State has agreed with that authority or county council for it to facilitate such notification;

(b) where the change of circumstances is a death, by telephone to a telephone number specified for that purpose by the Secretary of State.]

(2) In [2 paragraph (1)] "Secretary of State" includes a person designated as an employment officer by an order made by the Secretary of State under section 8(3) of the Jobseekers Act 1995.

[2 (3) In paragraph (1A) "relevant authority" has the same meaning as in regulation 4(2).]

AMENDMENTS

1. The Social Security (Miscellaneous Amendments) (No.2) Regulations 2006 (SI 2006/832) reg.2 (April 10, 2006).
2. The Social Security (Notification of Changes of Circumstances) Regulations 2010 (SI 2010/444) reg.4(2) (April 5, 2010).
3. The Social Security (Electronic Communications) Order 2011 (SI 2011/1498) reg.6 (June 20, 2011).

Change affecting housing benefit or council tax benefit

2.867 **4.**—[3 (1) Subject to paragraphs (1A) to [4 (1D)], where the benefit affected by the change of circumstances is housing benefit or council tax benefit, notice must be given to the relevant authority at the designated office—

(a) in writing; or
(b) by telephone—
 (i) where the relevant authority has published a telephone number for that purpose or for the purposes of making a claim unless the authority determines that in any particular case or class of case notification may not be given by telephone; or
 (ii) in any case or class of case where the relevant authority determines that notice may be given by telephone; or
(c) by any other means which the relevant authority agrees to accept in any particular case.]

[2 (1A) In such cases and subject to such conditions as the Secretary of State may specify, notice may be given to the Secretary of State—

(a) where the change of circumstances is a birth or death, through a relevant authority, or a county council in England, by person attendance at an office specified by that authority or county council, provided the Secretary of State has agreed with that authority or county council for it to facilitate such notification; or
(b) where the change of circumstances is a death, by telephone to a telephone number specified for that purpose by the Secretary of State.

(1B) Paragraph (1A) only applies if the authority administering the claimant's housing benefit or council tax benefit agrees with the Secretary of State that notifications may be made in accordance with that paragraph.]

[3 (1C) Notice may be given to the appropriate DWP office by telephone where all the following conditions are met—

(a) the claimant or the claimant's partner is in receipt of income support or a jobseeker's allowance;
(b) the change of circumstances is that the claimant or the claimant's partner starts employment;
(c) as a result of the change, either entitlement to housing benefit or council tax benefit will end, or the amount of benefit will be reduced; and
(d) a telephone number has been provided for this purpose.]

(1D) Where—

(a) the change of circumstances required to be notified is a death; and
(b) the authority administering the claimant's housing benefit or council tax benefit agrees with the Secretary of State that notifications may be made in accordance with paragraph (1A).

Notice in writing may be given or sent to the Secretary of State by an electronic communication in accordance with the provisions set out in Schedule 9ZC to the Social Security (Claims and Payments) Regulation 1987 (electronic communication).

(1E) The provisions set out in that Schedule shall apply to such notice as they apply for the purposes of regulation 32ZA of the Social Security (Claims and Payments) Regulations 1987 (information given electronically).

(2) In this regulation [3 "appropriate DWP office",] [2 "claimant",] "designated office" and "relevant authority" have the same meaning as in the [1 Housing Benefit Regulations 2006, Housing Benefit (Persons who have attained the qualifying age for state pension credit) Regulations 2006, Council Tax Benefit Regulations 2006, and Council Tax Benefit (Persons who have attained the qualifying age for state pension credit) Regulations 2006.]

AMENDMENTS

1. The Housing Benefit and Council Tax Benefit (Consequential Provisions) Regulations 2006 (SI 2006/217) Sch.2 para.9 (March 6, 2006).
2. The Social Security (Notification of Changes of Circumstances) Regulations 2010 (SI 2010/444) reg.4(3) (April 5, 2010).
3. The Housing Benefit and Council Tax Benefit (Miscellaneous Amendments) Regulations 2010 (SI 2010/2449) reg.7 (October 11, 2010).
4. The Social Security (Electronic Communications) (No.2) Order 2011 (SI 2011/2943) reg.3 (January 23, 2012).

Change affecting other benefit payment or advantage

5.—(1) [2 Subject to [5 paragraphs (1ZZA) and (1ZA)] where the benefit or other payment or advantage affected by the change of circumstances is not a jobseeker's allowance, housing benefit or council tax benefit, notice must be given [3 . . .] to the Secretary of State [3 at the appropriate office— 2.868

(a) in writing or by telephone (unless the Secretary of State determines in any particular case that notice must be in writing or may be given otherwise than in writing or by telephone); or
(b) in writing if in any class of case he requires written notice (unless he determine in any particular case to accept notice given otherwise than in writing)]

[4 (1ZZA) In such cases and subject to such conditions as the Secretary of State may specify, notice may be given to the Secretary of State—

(a) where the change of circumstances is a birth or death, through a relevant authority, or a county council in England, by personal attendance at an office specified by that authority or county council, provided the Secretary of State has agreed with that authority or county council for it to facilitate such notification; or
(b) where the change of circumstances is a death, by telephone to a telephone number specified for that purpose by the Secretary of State.]

[2 (1ZA) Where this paragraph applies, where the notice in writing referred to in paragraph (1) is given or sent by an electronic communication that notice must be given or sent in accordance with the provisions set out in Schedule 9ZC to the Social Security (Claims and Payments) Regulations

1987 (electronic communication). (1ZB) Paragraph (1ZA) applies in relation to carer's allowance.]

[5 (1ZB) Paragraph (1ZA) applies in relation to—

(a) attendance allowance;
(b) carer's allowance;
(c) disability living allowance
(d) an employment and support allowance;
[6 (da) incapacity benefit;]
(e) income support]
[6 (f) retirement pension;
[7 (fa) a state pension under Part 1 of the Pensions Act 2014,]
(g) state pension credit.]

[1 (1A) The reference in paragraph (1) to notice "in writing" includes where that notice relates to child benefit, notice given or sent in accordance with Schedule 9C to the Social Security (Claims and Payments) Regulations 1987 (electronic communication).]

[4 (2) In this regulation—

"the appropriate office" has the same meaning as in the Social Security (Claims and Payments) Regulations 1987;

"relevant authority" has the same meaning as in regulation 4(2).]

AMENDMENTS

1. The Social Security (Electronic Communications) (Child Benefit) Order 2002 (SI 2002/1789) art.8 (October 28, 2002). These regulations are revoked with effect from December 1, 2003 by the Social Security (Electronic Communications) (Carer's Allowance) Order 2003 (SI 2003/2800) reg.4.

2. The Social Security (Electronic Communications) (Carer's Allowance) Order 2003 (SI 2003/2800) reg.3 (December 1, 2003).

3. The Social Security (Notification of Change of Circumstances) Regulations 2003 (SI 2003/3209) reg.3 (January 6, 2004).

4. The Social Security (Notification of Changes of Circumstances) Regulations 2010 (SI 2010/444) reg.4(4) (April 5, 2010).

5. The Social Security (Electronic Communications) Order 2011 (SI 2011/1498) reg.6 (June 20, 2011).

6. The Social Security (Electronic Communications) (No.2) Order 2011 (SI 2011/2943) reg.3 (January 23, 2012).

7. The Pensions Act 2014 (Consequential, Supplementary and Incidental Amendments) Order 2015 (SI 2015/1985) art.23 (April 6, 2016).

The Social Security (Overpayments and Recovery) Regulations 2013

(SI 2013/384)

GENERAL NOTE

2.869 These are the "2013 rules" which apply to:

- recovery of overpayments of universal credit, new-style contribution-based JSA and new-style contribution-based ESA claimed on or after April 29, 2013; and
- recovery of court costs incurred in recovering overpayments, certain advances of universal credit, hardship payments, financial penalties for benefit offences, and civil penalties.

The rules relating to the recovery of overpayments of other benefits are to be found in the Payments on Account etc Regulations at paras 2.915–2.955 below.

PART 1

GENERAL

PART 2

RECOVERABILITY

PART 3

PREVENTION OF DUPLICATION OF PAYMENTS

PART 4

CALCULATION OF RECOVERABLE AMOUNT OF AN OVERPAYMENT

PART 5

THE PROCESS OF RECOVERY

PART 6

RECOVERY BY DEDUCTION FROM EARNINGS

2.871 The Secretary of State for Work and Pensions makes the following Regulations in exercise of the powers conferred by sections 71(4), (6)(a) and (b), (8) and (9A) to (9C), 71ZA, 71ZB(2)(b) to (5), 71ZC(1) to (3), 71ZD, 71ZF 71ZG(5), 71ZH(5), 74(2), 75(4), (5)(a) and (8) to (10), 78(2) and (3C) to (3E), 115B(4A), 115C(5), 115D(5), 189(1), (4) to (6) and 191 of the Social Security Administration Act 1992(**1**) ("the Act") and paragraphs 1(1) and 6(b) of Schedule 6 to the Welfare Reform Act 2012.

In accordance with section 173(1)(b) of the Act, the Secretary of State has obtained the agreement of the Social Security Advisory Committee that proposals in respect of these Regulations should not be referred to it.

In relation to provisions in these Regulations relating to housing benefit, in accordance with section 176(1) of the Act, consultation has taken place with organisations appearing to the Secretary of State to be representative of the authorities concerned.

PART 1

GENERAL

IN FORCE FROM APRIL 8, 2013

Citation and commencement

2.872 **1.**—(1) These Regulations may be cited as the Social Security (Overpayments and Recovery) Regulations 2013.

(2) The following provisions of these Regulations come into force on 8th April 2013—

(a) this Part;
(b) Part 6 and Schedules 1 and 2;
(c) regulation 31 except paragraphs (2)(b), (d), (e) and (g), (4)(b) and (7)(b);
(d) regulation 33(1), (2)(a) and (c) and (3); and
(e) regulation 34(1), (2)(a) and (c) and (3).

(3) All other provisions of these Regulations come into force on 29th April 2013.

Interpretation

2. In these Regulations— 2.873

"the Act" means the Social Security Administration Act 1992;
"the 1995 Act" means the Jobseekers Act 1995;
"the 2007 Act" means the Welfare Reform Act 2007;
"the 2012 Act" means the Welfare Reform Act 2012;
"the UC Regulations" means the Universal Credit Regulations 2013;
"the UC etc. Claims and Payments Regulations" means the Universal Credit, Personal Independence Payment, Jobseeker's Allowance and Employment and Support Allowance (Claims and Payments) Regulations 2013;
"assessment period" has the same meaning as in the UC Regulations;
"claimant" means the person who has claimed the benefit concerned;
"couple" has the same meaning as in Part 1 of the 2012 Act;
"employment and support allowance" means an allowance under Part 1 of the 2007 Act as amended by the provisions of Schedule 3, and Part 1 of Schedule 14, to the 2012 Act that remove references to an income-related allowance;
"housing costs" means any amount included in an award of universal credit in respect of rent payments as defined in paragraph 2 of Schedule 1 to the UC Regulations;
"jobseeker's allowance" means an allowance under the 1995 Act as amended by the provisions of Part 1 of Schedule 14 to the 2012 Act that remove references to an income-based allowance;
"liable person" means the person from whom a recoverable amount is recoverable;
"overpayment" means an amount of—

(a) universal credit, jobseeker's allowance or employment and support allowance which may be recovered by the Secretary of State by virtue of section 71ZB(1) of the Act;
(b) working tax credit or child tax credit which may be recovered under section 29 of the Tax Credits Act 2002 as modified by paragraph 10 of the Schedule to the Universal Credit (Transitional Provisions) Regulations 2013;

"overpayment period" means the period over which an overpayment accrues;
"partner" means, where the person being referred to is a member of a couple, the other member of the couple;
"recoverable amount" is to be construed in accordance with regulation 3;
"universal credit" means universal credit under Part 1 of the 2012 Act.

PART 2

RECOVERABILITY

IN FORCE FROM APRIL 29, 2013

Recoverable amounts

2.874 **3.** (1) In these Regulations, "recoverable amount" means—

(a) subject to regulations 7 to 9, the amount of any overpayment; and
(b) any other amount recoverable under any provision of the Act specified in paragraph (2).

(2) Those provisions are—

(a) section 71ZE(3) (costs of court action etc.);
(b) section 71ZG (recovery of payments on account);
(c) section 71ZH (recovery of hardship payments);
(d) section 115B(4)(recovery of penalties imposed as an alternative to prosecution);
(e) section 115C(4) (recovery of civil penalties for incorrect statements); and
(f) section 115D(4) (recovery of civil penalties for failure to disclose information).

Persons from whom an overpayment may be recovered

2.875 **4.** (1) The following paragraphs apply for determining the person from whom an overpayment is recoverable in the circumstances specified in those paragraphs.

(2) Where the payee is a person appointed under regulation 57 of the UC etc. Claims and Payments Regulations or a person to whom the Secretary of State has directed that payment be made in accordance with regulation 58 of those Regulations, then the overpayment is recoverable from the claimant in addition to the payee.

(3) Where the payee is a person to whom universal credit, jobseeker's allowance or employment and support allowance has been paid pursuant to Schedule 6 to the UC etc. Claims and Payments Regulations (payments to third parties), then, to the extent that the amount paid does not exceed the amount payable to the payee under that Schedule, the overpayment is recoverable from the claimant instead of the payee.

(4) Paragraphs (5) to (7) apply only in relation to overpayments of housing costs.

(5) Where the Secretary of State is satisfied that an overpayment occurred in consequence of any change of dwelling occupied by the claimant as their home, then if the claimant and the payee are not the same person, the overpayment is recoverable from the claimant in addition to the payee.

(6) Where the Secretary of State is satisfied that an overpayment occurred in consequence of a misrepresentation, or a failure to disclose a material fact (in either case, whether fraudulent or otherwise), by any person ("M"), then, if M and the payee are not the same person, the overpayment is recoverable from M instead of the payee.

(7) Where the Secretary of State is satisfied that an overpayment occurred for a reason other than that mentioned in paragraph (5) or (6), then, except

where paragraph (2) or (8) applies in relation to the overpayment, if the claimant and the payee are not the same person, the overpayment is recoverable from the claimant instead of the payee.

(8) This paragraph applies where the overpayment occurred due to the amount of the payment exceeding the amount of housing costs for which the claimant is liable.

(9) In this regulation, "payee" means the person to whom the overpayment has been paid.

Circumstances in which a determination need not be reversed, varied, revised or superseded prior to recovery

5. Section 71ZB(3) of the Act (recoverability of an overpayment dependent on reversal, variation, revision or supersession) does not apply where the circumstances of the overpayment do not provide a basis for the decision pursuant to which the payment was made to be revised under section 9 of the Social Security Act 1998 or superseded under section 10 of that Act. **2.876**

PART 3

PREVENTION OF DUPLICATION OF PAYMENTS

IN FORCE FROM APRIL 29, 2013

Duplication and prescribed income

6. (1) The income prescribed for the purpose of section 71ZB(5) of the Act (duplication of payments: universal credit) is any income which falls to be taken into account in accordance with Chapters 2 and 3 of Part 6 of the UC Regulations. **2.877**

(2) The date prescribed for the payment of income for the purpose of that subsection is—

(a) where the payment of income is made in respect of a specific day or period, that day or the first day of that period;

(b) where the payment of income is not so made, the day or first day of the period to which it is fairly attributable.

PART 4

CALCULATION OF RECOVERABLE AMOUNT OF AN OVERPAYMENT

Diminution of capital

7. (1) Paragraph (2) applies where— **2.878**

(a) there is an overpayment of universal credit which occurred as a consequence of an error relating to the amount of a person's capital; and

(b) the overpayment period is 3 months or more.

(2) Where this paragraph applies, the Secretary of State must, for the purpose only of calculating the recoverable amount of that overpayment—

(a) at the end of the first 3 months of the overpayment period, treat the amount of that capital as having been reduced by the amount of universal credit overpaid during those 3 months;

(b) at the end of each subsequent period of 3 months, if any, of the overpayment period, treat the amount of that capital as having been further reduced by the amount of universal credit overpaid during the immediately preceding 3 months.

(3) Capital is not to be treated as reduced over any period other than 3 months in any circumstances other than those for which paragraph (2) provides.

Sums to be deducted

2.879 **8.** (1) In calculating the recoverable amount of an overpayment of jobseeker's allowance or employment and support allowance, the Secretary of State must deduct the amounts specified in paragraphs (2) and (3).

(2) Any amount which has been offset under regulation 16.

(3) Any additional amount of universal credit which was not payable to the claimant or their partner under the original or any other determination but which should have been determined to be payable in respect of all or part of the overpayment period to the claimant, or to the claimant and their partner jointly—

(a) on the basis of the claim for universal credit as presented to the Secretary of State;

(b) on the basis of that claim as it would have appeared if any change of circumstances, except a change of the dwelling which the claimant occupies as their home, had been notified at the time that change occurred;

(c) where the overpayment arose by virtue of a misrepresentation or a failure to disclose a material fact, on the basis that that misrepresentation or failure had been remedied prior to the award being made; or

(d) where the overpayment arose by virtue of an error made by, or on behalf of, the Secretary of State, on the basis that that error had not been made.

Sums to be deducted: change of dwelling

2.880 **9.** (1) This regulation applies where an overpayment of housing costs has occurred in the following circumstances—

(a) the claimant has moved from the dwelling previously occupied as their home ("dwelling A") to another dwelling which they occupy as their home ("dwelling B");

(b) they have been awarded housing costs in respect of dwelling A to which they are not entitled because they are no longer occupying or treated as occupying dwelling A as their home; and

(c) housing costs are payable to the same person in respect of the claimant's occupation of dwelling B as it was paid to in respect of dwelling A.

(2) In calculating the recoverable amount of the overpayment, the Secretary of State may, at his or her discretion, deduct an amount equal to the claimant's entitlement to housing costs for the assessment period in respect of dwelling B for the number of assessment periods equal to the number of assessment periods during which the claimant was overpaid housing costs in respect of dwelling A.

(3) Where a sum has been deducted under paragraph (2), an equivalent sum is to be treated as having been paid in respect of the claimant's entitlement to housing costs in respect of dwelling B for the number of assessment

periods equal to the number of assessment periods during which the claimant was overpaid housing costs in respect of dwelling A.

PART 5

THE PROCESS OF RECOVERY

IN FORCE FROM APRIL 29, 2013

Recovery by deduction from benefits

10. (1) Subject to regulations 11 to 14, the Secretary of State may recover a recoverable amount from a liable person by deduction from the benefits specified in paragraph (2) which are payable to them. **2.881**

(2) Those benefits are—

(a) benefits under Parts 2 to 5 of the Social Security Contributions and Benefits Act 1992;

(b) universal credit;

(c) jobseeker's allowance;

(d) employment and support allowance;

(e) state pension credit payable under the State Pension Credit Act 2002; [1 . . .]

(f) personal independence payment payable under Part 4 of the 2012 Act. [1 ; and]

[1 (g) a state pension under Part 1 of the Pensions Act 2014.]

AMENDMENT

1. The Pensions Act 2014 (Consequential, Supplementary and Incidental Amendments) Order 2015 (SI 2015/1985) art.42 (April 6, 2016).

Recovery by deduction from universal credit

11. (1) The following paragraphs apply where the recoverable amount falls to be recovered by deduction from universal credit payable to the liable person. **2.882**

(2) Subject to paragraphs (5) to (9), regulation 10 is to apply to the amount of universal credit to which the liable person is presently entitled to the extent that there may be recovered in any one assessment period—

(a) in a case to which paragraph (3) applies, an amount equivalent to not more than [1 40 per cent.] of the appropriate universal credit standard allowance;

(b) in a case to which paragraph (4) applies but paragraph (3) does not apply, an amount equivalent to not more than [1 25 per cent.] of that allowance; and

(c) in any other case, an amount equivalent to not more than [1 15 per cent.] of that allowance.

(3) This paragraph applies where deductions from universal credit are made to recover from the liable person—

(a) the whole or part of an overpayment in respect of which the liable person has—

(i) been found guilty of an offence whether under statute or otherwise;

(ii) made an admission after caution of deception or fraud for the purpose of obtaining benefit under the Act or a tax credit under the Tax Credits Act 2002; or

(iii) agreed to pay a penalty under section 115A of the Act (penalty as an alternative to prosecution) and the agreement has not been withdrawn; or

(b) a payment which is recoverable by virtue of section 71ZH of the Act (hardship payments).

(4) This paragraph applies where amounts are deducted from earned income in an award of universal credit by virtue of regulation 22(1)(b) of the UC Regulations (adjustment to take account of income and amount of earnings disregarded).

(5) Paragraph (2) is subject to paragraphs 4 and 5 of Schedule 6 to the UC etc. Claims and Payments Regulations (payments to third parties).

[1 (6) For the purpose of paragraph (2), where the relevant percentage of the appropriate universal credit standard allowance results in a fraction of a penny, that fraction is to be disregarded if it is less than half a penny and otherwise it is to be treated as a penny.]

(7) No deduction made under paragraph (2) is to be applied so as to reduce the universal credit in respect of an assessment period to less than 1 penny.

(8) The limitations in paragraph (2) do not apply where the deduction falls to be made from any payment of arrears of universal credit other than any arrears caused by the operation of regulation 46 of the Universal Credit, Personal Independence Payment, Jobseeker's Allowance and Employment and Support Allowance (Decisions and Appeals) Regulations 2013 (making of payments which have been suspended).

(9) The limitations in paragraph (2) do not apply where—

(a) the recoverable amount is an overpayment of housing costs; and

(b) the person from whom that amount falls to be recovered is not the claimant.

(10) In this regulation and in regulation 14, "admission after caution" means—

(a) in England and Wales, an admission after a caution has been administered in accordance with a Code issued under the Police and Criminal Evidence Act 1984;

(b) in Scotland, admission after a caution has been administered, such admission being duly witnessed by two persons.

(11) In paragraph (2), "the appropriate universal credit standard allowance" means the appropriate universal credit standard allowance included in the award of universal credit made to the liable person, or to the liable person and their partner as joint claimants, by virtue of regulation 36 of the UC Regulations.

AMENDMENT

1. The Social Security (Miscellaneous Amendments) (No. 2) Regulations 2013 (SI 2013/1508) reg.5 (July 29, 2013).

Recovery by deduction from jobseeker's allowance

2.883 **12.** (1) The following paragraphs apply where the recoverable amount falls to be recovered by deduction from jobseeker's allowance payable to the liable person.

(2) Subject to paragraphs (3) and (4), regulation 10 is to apply to the amount of a jobseeker's allowance to which the liable person is presently entitled to the extent that there may be recovered in respect of any benefit week an amount equivalent to 40 per cent. of the age-related amount applicable to the liable person as specified in regulation 49 of the Jobseeker's Allowance Regulations 2013.

(3) Paragraph (2) is subject to paragraphs 4 and 5 of Schedule 6 to the UC etc. Claims and Payments Regulations (payments to third parties).

(4) Where the amount deductible under paragraph (2) is not a multiple of five pence, it is to be rounded up to the next higher such multiple.

(5) In paragraph (2), "benefit week" has the same meaning as in regulation 2(1) of the Jobseeker's Allowance Regulations 2013.

Recovery by deduction from employment and support allowance

13. (1) The following paragraphs apply where the recoverable amount falls to be recovered by deduction from employment and support allowance payable to the liable person. 2.884

(2) Subject to paragraphs (3) and (4), regulation 10 is to apply to the amount of an employment and support allowance to which the liable person is presently entitled to the extent that there may be recovered in respect of any one benefit week an amount equivalent to 40 per cent. of the age-related amount applicable to the liable person as specified in regulation 62(1)(b) of the Employment and Support Allowance Regulations 2013.

(3) Paragraph (2) is subject to paragraphs 4 and 5 of Schedule 6 to the UC etc. Claims and Payments Regulations (payments to third parties).

(4) Where the amount deductible under paragraph (2) is not a multiple of five pence, it is to be rounded up to the next higher such multiple.

(5) In paragraph (2), "benefit week" has the same meaning as in regulation 2 of the Employment and Support Allowance Regulations 2013.

Recovery by deduction from state pension credit

14. (1) The following paragraphs apply where the recoverable amount falls to be recovered by deduction from state pension credit payable to the liable person. 2.885

(2) Subject to paragraphs (4) and (5), regulation 10 is to apply to the amount of state pension credit to which the liable person is presently entitled to the extent that there may be recovered in any one benefit week—

(a) in a case to which paragraph (3) applies, an amount equivalent to not more than 5 times 5 per cent. of the standard allowance for a single person aged 25 or over under regulation 36 of the UC Regulations; and

(b) in any other case, an amount equivalent to not more than 3 times 5 per cent. of that allowance.

(3) This paragraph applies where deductions from state pension credit are made to recover from the liable person—

(a) the whole or part of an overpayment in respect of which the liable person has—

(i) been found guilty of an offence whether under statute or otherwise;

(ii) made an admission after caution of deception or fraud for the purpose of obtaining universal credit, jobseeker's allowance or employment and support allowance; or

(iii) agreed to pay a penalty under section 115A of the Act (penalty as an alternative to prosecution) and the agreement has not been withdrawn; or

(b) a payment which is recoverable by virtue of section 71ZH of the Act (hardship payments).

(4) Where the amount deductible under paragraph (2) is not a multiple of five pence, it is to be rounded up to the next higher such multiple.

(5) No deduction made under paragraph (2) is to be applied so as to reduce the state pension credit in respect of a benefit week to less than 10 pence.

(6) In this regulation, "benefit week" has the same meaning as in regulation 2(1) of the State Pension Credit Regulations 2002.

Restrictions on recovery of rent and consequent notifications

2.886 **15.** (1) Paragraph (2) applies where, pursuant to section 71ZC(2)(b) of the Act, an amount of housing costs has been, or falls to be, recovered by deduction from benefit paid to a person ("the landlord") to discharge (in whole or in part) an obligation owed to the landlord by the person on whose behalf the recoverable amount was paid ("the tenant").

(2) Where, in respect of the overpayment of that amount, the landlord has—

(a) been found guilty of an offence whether under statute or otherwise; or

(b) agreed to pay a penalty under section 115A of the Act (penalty as an alternative to prosecution) and the agreement has not been withdrawn,

that obligation is to be taken to be discharged by the amount of the deduction.

(3) In any case to which paragraph (2) applies or will apply when recovery is made, the Secretary of State must notify both the landlord and the tenant—

(a) that the overpayment that it has recovered or that the Secretary of State has determined to recover ("that sum") is, or will be, one to which paragraph (2) applies; and

(b) that the landlord has no right in relation to that sum against the tenant, and that the tenant's obligation to the landlord is to be taken to be discharged by the amount so recovered.

Offsetting

2.887 **16.** (1) Paragraph (2) applies where a person has been paid a sum of benefit under a decision ("the original decision") which is subsequently—

(a) revised or further revised;

(b) superseded or further superseded; or

(c) set aside on an appeal.

(2) Any universal credit, jobseeker's allowance or employment and support allowance paid in respect of a period covered by the subsequent decision is to be offset against arrears of entitlement to benefit under that decision and, except to the extent that the universal credit, jobseeker's allowance or employment and support allowance exceeds the arrears, is to be treated as properly paid on account of them.

(3) Where an amount has been deducted under regulation 8 or 9 (sums to be deducted in calculating recoverable overpayments), an equivalent sum is to be offset against any arrears of entitlement under the subsequent decision except to the extent that the sum exceeds the arrears and is to be treated as properly paid on account of them.

(4) No amount may be offset under paragraph (2) which is an overpayment.

(5) In this regulation, "subsequent decision" means the decision referred to in paragraph (1)(a), (b) or (c) which was taken in relation to the original decision.

PART 6

RECOVERY BY DEDUCTION FROM EARNINGS

IN FORCE FROM APRIL 8, 2013

Interpretation of Part 6

17.—(1) In this Part— 2.888

"appropriate authority", in relation to any recoverable amount, means—

(a) the Secretary of State; or

(b) an authority administering housing benefit if the recoverable amount is recoverable by that authority under section 115B(4)(a), 115C or 115D of the Act,

and where a notice has been issued, "the appropriate authority" means the appropriate authority which issued the notice;

"notice" means a notice issued by an appropriate authority requiring an employer to make deductions from earnings to be paid by the employer to a liable person employed by them and to pay corresponding amounts to that appropriate authority in respect of the recovery of a recoverable amount from the liable person;

"pay-day" in relation to a liable person means an occasion on which earnings are paid to them or the day on which such earnings would normally fall to be paid;

"protected earnings proportion", in relation to a deduction by an employer from a liable person's net earnings, is 60 per cent. of the liable person's net earnings during the period to which the deduction relates, as calculated by the liable person's employer on the relevant pay-day.

(2) In this Part, subject to paragraph (3), "earnings" means any sums payable to a person—

(a) by way of wages or salary (including any fees, bonus, commission, overtime pay or other emoluments payable in addition to wages or salary payable under a contract of service);

(b) by way of pension which is paid with wages or salary (including an annuity in respect of past service, whether or not rendered to the person paying the annuity, and including periodical payments by way of compensation for the loss, abolition or relinquishment, or diminution in the emoluments, of any office or employment); or

(c) by way of statutory sick pay.

(3) "Earnings" does not include—

(a) sums payable by any public department of the Government of Northern Ireland or of a territory outside the United Kingdom;

(b) pay or allowances payable to the liable person as a member of Her Majesty's forces other than pay or allowances payable by their employer to them as a special member of a reserve force (within the meaning of the Reserve Forces Act 1996);

(c) other pensions, allowances or benefit payable under any enactment relating to social security;
(d) pension or allowances payable in respect of disablement or disability;
(e) guaranteed minimum pension within the meaning of the Pension Schemes Act 1993;
(f) working tax credit payable under section 10 of the Tax Credits Act 2002;
(g) sums paid to reimburse expenses wholly and necessarily incurred in the course of the employment.

(4) "Net earnings" means the residue of earnings after deduction of—
(a) income tax;
(b) primary Class I contributions under Part 1 of the Social Security Contributions and Benefits Act 1992;
(c) amounts deductible by way of contributions to a superannuation scheme which provides for the payment of annuities or lump sums—
(i) to the employee on retirement at a specified age or on becoming incapacitated at some earlier age; or
(ii) on the employee's death or otherwise, to their personal representative, widow, surviving civil partner, relatives or dependants.

(5) Where these Regulations refer to a notice or notification being given or sent, if sent by post to the last known address of the recipient, it is to be treated as having been given or sent on the day on which it is posted.

Exemption from this Part

2.889 **18.** This Part does not impose any obligation on an employer who is carrying on a business which is—
(a) a new business; or
(b) an existing micro-business during the exemption period,
and Schedule 1 has effect for the purpose of this regulation.

Notices

2.890 **19.**—(1) A notice must be given or sent to—
(a) the liable person; and
(b) any employer of the liable person who is to make deductions from the liable person's earnings in accordance with the notice.

(2) A notice must specify—
(a) the full name and address of the liable person;
(b) the name of the employer at whom the notice is directed;
(c) where known, the liable person's place of work, the nature of their work and any staff number, pay roll number or similar identifying number;
(d) the liable person's national insurance number;
[[1] (e) the deduction or rate of deduction to be made in accordance with regulation 20.]
(f) the protected earnings proportion;
(g) the address to which amounts deducted from earnings are to be sent if paid by cheque; and
(h) details of the account into which such amounts are to be transferred if paid by direct credit transfer.

(3) The notice has effect from the next pay-day which falls a minimum of 22 days after the day on which it is given or sent.

(4) References in paragraphs (1) to (3) to a notice include references to a notice as varied in accordance with regulation 25(1).

AMENDMENT

1. The Social Security (Overpayments and Recovery) Amendment Regulations 2015 (SI 2015/499) reg.4 (April 6, 2015).

Amount to be deducted by employer

20.—(1) This regulation applies where an employer has received from an appropriate authority a notice in respect of a liable person in their employment. 2.891

(2) Subject to the following provisions of this regulation, the employer must, each pay-day, make a deduction in accordance with paragraph (3) [[1] or (38)] from the net earnings which it would otherwise pay to the liable person on that pay-day.

(3) [[1] Except where paragraph (3B) applies, the amount to be deducted is—]

(a) where the liable person's earnings are payable weekly, the percentage of their earnings specified in column 2 of Table A in Schedule 2 opposite the band in column 1 of that Table within which their net earnings payable on their pay-day fall;

(b) where the liable person's earnings are payable monthly, the percentage of their earnings specified in column 2 of Table B in that Schedule opposite the band in column 1 of that Table within which their net earnings payable on their pay-day fall; or

(c) a lower amount calculated in the manner specified by the appropriate authority in the notice.

[[1] (3A) Paragraph (3B) applies where deductions from earnings are made to recover from the liable person the whole or part of an overpayment in respect of which the liable person has been found guilty of an offence whether under statute or otherwise.

(3B) Where this paragraph applies, the amount to be deducted by the employer is—

(a) where the liable person's earnings are payable weekly, the percentage of their earnings specified in column 2 of Table C in Schedule 2 opposite the band in column 1 of that Table within which their net earnings payable on their pay-day fall;

(b) where the liable person's earnings are payable monthly, the percentage of their earnings specified in column 2 of Table D in Schedule 2 opposite the band in column 1 of that Table within which their net earnings payable on their pay-day fall; or

(c) a lower amount calculated in the manner specified by the appropriate authority in the notice.]

(4) Where any amount calculated under paragraph (3) [[1] or (3B)] includes a fraction of a penny, it is to be rounded to the nearest whole penny with a result of exactly half a penny being rounded down to the nearest whole penny below.

[[1] (5) The employer must continue to make deductions in accordance with paragraph (3) or (3B) unless and until—

(a) they are notified by the appropriate authority that the notice—

(i) has been varied in accordance with regulation 2

(ii) has been discharged under regulation 26; or
(iii) has lapsed under regulation 27; or

(b) the employer considers that, as a result of deductions under this regulation, the balance of the recoverable amount which falls to be recovered from the liable person is nil.]

(6) Where, on any pay-day ("the relevant pay-day"), the employer fails to deduct an amount under paragraph (3) [1 or (3B)] or deducts an amount less than the amount specified in that paragraph, the employer must, on the next available pay-day or pay-days, first deduct the amount required to be deducted under paragraph (3) [1 or (3B)] for that pay-day and then the difference between the amount, if any, which was deducted on the relevant pay-day and the amount which should have been deducted on that pay-day.

(7) Where a deduction made in accordance with paragraph (3) [1, or (3B)] or (6) would reduce the amount paid to the liable person below the protected earnings proportion, the employer must deduct only such amount as will result in the employer paying the liable person an amount equal to the protected earnings proportion.

(8) Where, on any pay-day ("the relevant pay-day"), the employer deducts more than the amount required to be deducted under paragraph (3), the employer must, on the next available pay-day or pay-days, deduct only the amount required to be deducted under paragraph (3) [1 or (3B)] less the difference between the amount which was deducted on the relevant pay-day and the amount which should have been deducted on that pay-day.

(9) Where, on any pay-day, an employer makes a deduction from the earnings of a liable person in accordance with the notice, they may also deduct an additional amount not exceeding £1 in respect of their administrative costs and such deduction for administrative costs may reduce the amount which the employer pays to the liable person on that pay-day below the protected earnings proportion.

AMENDMENT

1. The Social Security (Overpayments and Recovery) Amendment Regulations 2015 (SI 2015/499) reg.5 (April 6, 2015).

Employer to notify liable person of deduction

2.892 **21.**—[1 (1) An employer making a deduction from earnings for the purposes of these Regulations must notify the liable person in writing of the amount of the deduction including any amount deducted for administrative costs under regulation 20(9).]

(2) Such notification must be given or sent not later than the pay-day on which the deduction is made or, where that is impracticable, not later than the following pay-day.

[1 (3) An employer must, within 28 days of receiving a written request from the liable person, provide the liable person with an explanation in writing of how the first amount referred to in paragraph (1) was calculated.]

AMENDMENT

1. The Social Security (Overpayments and Recovery) Amendment Regulations 2015 (SI 2015/499) reg.6 (April 6, 2015).

Payment by employer to the appropriate authority

22.—(1) Amounts deducted by an employer pursuant to regulation 20 (other than any administrative costs deducted under paragraph (9) of that regulation) must be paid by the employer to the appropriate authority by the 19th day of the month following the month in which the deduction is made. **2.893**

(2) Such payment may be made—

(a) by cheque;

(b) by direct credit transfer; or

(c) by such other method as the appropriate authority may permit.

(3) The employer must keep a record of every amount paid to an appropriate authority pursuant to paragraph (1) and of the employee in respect of whom each such amount was paid.

Information to be provided by the liable person

23.—[1 (1) An employer making a deduction from earnings for the purposes of these Regulations must notify the liable person in writing of the amount of the deduction including any amount deducted for administrative costs under regulation 20(9).] **2.894**

(2) A notification under paragraph (1)(b) must include the following details—

(a) the name and address of their employer or employers if more than one;

(b) the amount of their earnings or expected earnings; and

(c) their place of work, nature of their work and any staff number, pay roll number or similar identifying number.

Duty of employers and others to notify appropriate authority

24.—(1) In this regulation, "P" means the liable person. **2.895**

(2) Where a notice is given or sent to a person who is believed to be an employer of P but P is not in that person's employment, that person must notify the appropriate authority of that fact in writing, at the address specified in the notice, within 10 days after the day on which the notice is given or sent.

(3) In paragraphs (4) and (5), "E" means an employer of P.

(4) Where a notice is given or sent to E but E believes that there is no obligation on them under this Part by virtue of regulation 18 and Schedule 1, E must notify the appropriate authority of that fact in writing, at the address specified in the notice, within 10 days after the day on which the notice is given or sent.

(5) Where E is required to make deductions under a notice and P ceases to be in their employment, E must notify the appropriate authority of that fact in writing, at the address specified in the notice, within 10 days after the day on which P ceased to be in their employment.

Power to vary notices

25.—(1) The appropriate authority may vary a notice so as to— **2.896**

(a) decrease any amount to be deducted under regulation 20; or

(b) with the agreement of the liable person, increase any such amount but only to the extent that such deductions will result in the employer paying the liable person an amount more than, or equal to, the protected earnings proportion.

(2) Where a notice has been varied and a copy of the notice as varied has been given or sent in accordance with regulation 19(1) and (4), any employer who is liable to make deductions under the notice must comply with the notice as varied from the day it takes effect by virtue of regulation 19(3).

Discharge of notices

2.897 **26.**—(1) The appropriate authority must discharge a notice where the recoverable amount is no longer outstanding.

(2) The appropriate authority may discharge a notice where—

(a) it appears to them to be defective;

(b) it appears to them that it is ineffective or that some other method of recovering the recoverable amount would be more effective; or

(c) the liable person agrees with the appropriate authority to pay the recoverable amount by another method.

(3) A notice may be considered to be defective for the purpose of paragraph (2)(a) where it does not comply with the requirements of regulation 19(2) and such failure to comply has made it impracticable for an employer to comply with their obligations under these Regulations.

(4) Notification of the discharge of the notice under paragraph (1) or (2) must be given or sent to the liable person and the employer from whom deductions from the liable person's earnings were being made.

(5) Where a notice is discharged by virtue of paragraph (2)(b) or (c), regulation 22 nevertheless applies in respect of any deductions made in respect of the employment but not yet paid to the appropriate authority.

Lapse of notices

2.898 **27.**—(1) Where a liable person in respect of whom deductions are being made in accordance with a notice ceases to be in the employment of an employer, subject to paragraph (2), the notice is to lapse immediately after the pay-day coinciding with, or, if none, the pay-day following, the termination of the employment.

(2) Where a notice lapses by virtue of paragraph (1), regulation 22 nevertheless applies in respect of any deductions made or to be made in respect of the employment but not yet paid to the appropriate authority.

Crown employment

2.899 **28.** Where a liable person is in the employment of the Crown and a notice is to be sent in respect of that person, then for the purposes of these Regulations—

(a) the chief officer for the time being of the Department, office or other body in which the liable person is employed is to be treated as having the liable person in their employment (any transfer of the liable person from one Department, office or body to another being treated as a change of employment); and

(b) any earnings paid by the Crown or a minister of the Crown, or out of the public revenue of the United Kingdom, is to be treated as paid by that chief officer.

Priority as between notices and orders requiring deduction from earnings

2.900 **29.**—(1) In this regulation—

"child support order" means a deduction from earnings order under Part

3 of the Child Support (Collection and Enforcement) Regulations 1992(26);

"other deduction order" means an order, other than a child support order, under any other enactment relating to England and Wales which requires deduction from a person's earnings.

(2) Paragraphs (3) to (10) have effect subject to paragraph (11).

(3) Paragraph (4) applies where an employer would otherwise be obliged, on any pay-day, to make deductions from the earnings which it would otherwise pay to the liable person on that pay-day under two or more notices.

[1 (4) Where this paragraph applies, the employer must make deductions under any later notice as if the earnings to which it relates were the residue of the liable person's earnings after the making of any deduction to comply with any earlier notice.]

(5) Paragraph (6) applies where an employer would otherwise be obliged, on any pay-day, to make deductions from the earnings which it would otherwise pay to the liable person on that pay-day, under one or more notices and one or more child support orders.

(6) Where this paragraph applies, the employer must first make deductions under the child support order or orders and then make deductions under the notice or notices.

(7) In England and Wales, paragraph (8) applies where an employer would otherwise be obliged, on any pay-day, to make deductions from the earnings which it would otherwise pay to the liable person on that pay-day, under one or more notices and one or more other deduction orders.

(8) Where this paragraph applies, the employer must—

(a) in a case where there is at least one other deduction order in effect on the first pay-day in respect of which deductions would otherwise be made under the notice, first make deductions under the other deduction order or orders and then under any notice or notices;

(b) in any other case, make deductions under the other deduction order and the notices according to the respective dates on which they were made, disregarding any later notice or order until deductions have been made under the earlier one.

(9) In Scotland, paragraph (10) applies where an employer would otherwise be obliged, on any pay-day, to make deductions from the earnings which it would otherwise pay to the liable person on that pay-day, under one or more notices and one or more diligences against earnings.

(10) Where this paragraph applies, the employer must—

(a) in a case where there is a diligence against earnings in effect on the first pay-day in respect of which deductions would otherwise be made under the notice, first make deductions under any diligence against earnings and then under any notice;

(b) in any other case, make deductions under any notice and then under any diligence against earnings.

(11) An employer may only make deductions under paragraph (4), (6), (8) or (10) up to the extent that such deductions will result in the employer paying the liable person an amount equal to or greater than the protected earnings proportion.

AMENDMENT

1. The Social Security (Overpayments and Recovery) Amendment Regulations 2015 (SI 2015/499) reg.7 (April 6, 2015).

Offences

2.901 **30.** A person who fails to comply with any of the following provisions of this Part is guilty of an offence punishable on summary conviction by a fine not exceeding level 3 on the standard scale—
(a) regulation 20(2);
(b) regulation 22(1);
(c) regulation 22(3);
(d) regulation 23.

Regulation 18

SCHEDULE 1

EXEMPTION FOR EXISTING MICRO-BUSINESSES AND NEW BUSINESSES

Micro-businesses

2.902 1. A micro-business is a business that has fewer than 10 employees (see paragraphs 6 to 8).

Existing micro-businesses

2.903 2. An existing micro-business is a business that was a micro-business immediately before 8th April 2013.

New businesses

2.904 3.—(1) A new business is a business which a person, or a number of persons, ("P") begins to carry on during the period beginning on 8th April 2013 and ending on 31st March 2014.

(2) But a business is not a new business if—
(a) P has, at any time during the period of 6 months ending immediately before the date on which P begins to carry on the business, carried on another business consisting of the activities of which the business consists (or most of them); or
(b) P carries on the business as a result of a transfer (within the meaning of sub-paragraph (3)).

(3) P carries on a business as a result of a transfer if P begins to carry on the business on another person ceasing to carry on the activities of which it consists (or most of them) in consequence of arrangements involving P and the other person.

(4) For this purpose, P is to be taken to begin to carry on a business on another person ceasing to carry on such activities if—
(a) P begins to carry on the business otherwise than in partnership on such activities ceasing to be carried on by persons in partnership; or
(b) P is a number of persons in partnership who begin to carry on the business on such activities ceasing to be carried on—
(i) by a person, or a number of persons, otherwise than in partnership;
(ii) by persons in partnership who do not consist only of all the persons who constitute P; or

(iii) partly as mentioned in paragraph (i) and partly as mentioned in paragraph (ii).

(5) P is not to be regarded as beginning to carry on a business for the purposes of sub-paragraph (1) if—

(a) before P begins to carry on the business, P is a party to arrangements under which P may (at any time during the period beginning on 8th April 2013 and ending on 31st March 2014) carry on, as part of the business, activities carried on by any other person; and

(b) the business would have been prevented by sub-paragraph (2)(b) from being a new business if—

(i) P had begun to carry on the activities when beginning to carry on the business; and

(ii) the other person had at that time ceased to carry them on.

(6) "Arrangements" includes an agreement, understanding, scheme, transaction or series of transactions (whether or not legally enforceable).

The exemption period: existing micro-businesses

4.—(1) This paragraph defines the exemption period in relation to an existing micro-business. **2.905**

(2) The exemption period starts on 8th April 2013 and ends on the day after a grace period in relation to the business ends, if the grace period is one in which the business grows (see paragraphs 5 and 6).

(3) The following are grace periods in relation to a business for the purposes of this paragraph—

(a) the 6-month period that starts with the first day after 8th April 2013 on which the business has 10 or more employees;

(b) the 6-month period that starts after the end of a grace period (the "earlier grace period") that is not one in which the business grows, in accordance with sub-paragraph (4) or (5).

(4) If the business has 10 or more employees on the day after the end of the earlier grace period, the next grace period starts on that day.

(5) If the business has fewer than 10 employees on that day, the next grace period starts on the next day on which the business has 10 or more employees.

Grace periods in which business grows

5.—(1) For the purposes of this Schedule, a grace period is one in which a business grows if A is greater than B, where— **2.906**

(a) A is the number of days in the grace period when the business has 10 or more employees; and

(b) B is the number of days in the grace period when the business has fewer than 10 employees.

Number of employees of a business

6. For the purposes of this Schedule, the number of employees of a business is calculated as follows— **2.907**

TH/37.5

where TH is the total number of hours per week for which all the employees of the business are contracted to work.

Employees of a business

2.908 7. For the purposes of this Schedule, the employees of a business are the persons who are employed for the purposes of the business in connection with any of the activities of which the business consists.

Employees

2.909 8.—(1) In this Schedule, "employee" means an individual who has entered into, or works under, a contract of employment.

(2) In sub-paragraph (1) "contract of employment" means a contract of service, whether express or implied, and (if it is express) whether oral or in writing.

Franchises

2.910 9. For the purposes of this Schedule, a business that is carried on pursuant to a franchise agreement is treated as part of the business of the franchisor (and not as a separate business carried on by the franchisee).

Regulation 20(2) [1 and (3B)]

SCHEDULE 2

AMOUNTS TO BE DEDUCTED BY EMPLOYERS

TABLE A: [1 CASES WHERE REGULATION 20(3) APPLIES]

2.911 **WHERE EARNINGS ARE PAID WEEKLY**

AMOUNT OF NET EARNINGS	DEDUCTION (PER CENT. OF NET EARNINGS)
[1 £100 or less]	Nil
Exceeding £100 but not exceeding £160	3
Exceeding £160 but not exceeding £220	5
Exceeding £220 but not exceeding £270	7
Exceeding £270 but not exceeding £375	11
Exceeding £375 but not exceeding £520	15
Exceeding £520	20

TABLE B: [1 CASES WHERE REGULATION 20(3B) APPLIES]

WHERE EARNINGS ARE PAID MONTHLY 2.912

AMOUNT OF NET EARNINGS	DEDUCTION (PER CENT. OF NET EARNINGS)
[1 £430 or less]	Nil
Exceeding £430 but not exceeding £690	3
Exceeding £690 but not exceeding £950	5
Exceeding £950 but not exceeding £1,160	7
Exceeding £1,160 but not exceeding £1,615	11
Exceeding £1,615 but not exceeding £2,240	15
Exceeding £2,240	20

[1 TABLE C: CASES WHERE REGULATION 20(3B) APPLIES

WHERE EARNINGS ARE PAID WEEKLY 2.913

AMOUNT OF NET EARNINGS	DEDUCTION (PER CENT. OF NET EARNINGS)
£100 or less	5
Exceeding £100 but not exceeding £160	6
Exceeding £160 but not exceeding £220	10
Exceeding £220 but not exceeding £270	14
Exceeding £270 but not exceeding £375	22
Exceeding £375 but not exceeding £520	30
Exceeding £520	40

TABLE D: CASES WHERE REGULATION 20(3B) APPLIES

WHERE EARNINGS ARE PAID WEEKLY 2.914

AMOUNT OF NET EARNINGS	DEDUCTION (PER CENT. OF NET EARNINGS)
£430 or less	5
Exceeding £430 but not exceeding £690	6
Exceeding £690 but not exceeding £950	10
Exceeding £950 but not exceeding £1,160	14

AMOUNT OF NET EARNINGS	DEDUCTION (PER CENT. OF NET EARNINGS)
Exceeding £1,160 but not exceeding £1,615	22
Exceeding £1,615 but not exceeding £2,240	30
Exceeding £2,240	40]

AMENDMENT

1. The Social Security (Overpayments and Recovery) Amendment Regulations 2015 (SI 2015/499) reg.8 (April 6, 2015).

The Social Security (Payments on Account, Overpayments and Recovery) Regulations 1988

(SI 1988/664) (AS AMENDED)

GENERAL NOTE

2.915 These regulations relate to "old style" recovery of overpayments. Recovery of overpayments of universal credit, contribution-based JSA, and contribution-based ESA claimed on or after April 29, 2013 (together with certain court costs) are recoverable under the Social Security (Overpayments and Recovery) Regulations 2013 (SI 2013/384) set out at 2.869–2.914 above. Care should be taken to apply the relevant set of regulations to any overpayment in issue.

ARRANGEMENT OF REGULATIONS

PART I

GENERAL

PART II

INTERIM PAYMENTS

PART III

OFFSETTING

Part IV

Prevention of Duplication of Payments

Part V

Direct Credit Transfer Overpayments

Part VI

Revision of Determination and Calculation of Amount Recoverable

Part VII

The Process of Recovery

Part VIII

Recovery by Deductions from Earnings Following Trade Dispute

Whereas a draft of the following Regulations was laid before Parliament in accordance with the provisions of section 83(3)(b) of the Social Security Act 1986 and approved by resolution of each House of Parliament.

Now, therefore, the Secretary of State for Social services, in exercise of the powers conferred upon him by sections 23(8), 27, 51(1)(t) and (u), 53, 83(1), 84(1) and 89 of that Act and all other powers enabling him in that behalf, by this instrument, which contains only regulations made under the sections of the Social Security Act 1986 specified above and provisions consequential on those sections and which is made before the end of a period of 12 months from the commencement of those sections, makes the following Regulations:

PART I

GENERAL

Citation, commencement and interpretation

2.917 **1.**—(1) These regulations may be cited as the Social Security (Payments on account, Overpayments and Recovery) Regulations 1988 and shall come into force on 6th April 1988.

(2) In these Regulations, unless the context otherwise requires—

[13 "the 2012 Act" means the Welfare Reform Act 2012;]

"the Act" means the Social Security Act 1986;

[10 "the Administration Act" means the Social Security Administration Act 1992;]

[5 "adjudicating authority" means, as the case may require, the Secretary of State, [12 the First-tier Tribunal or the Upper Tribunal;]]

"benefit" means [9 a jobseeker's allowance, state pension credit [13 personal independence payment,] [11 , an employment and support allowance] and] any benefit under the Social Security Act 1975 [SSCBA, Parts II to V], [15 , a state pension under Part 1 of the Pensions Act 2014] child benefit, family credit, income support and [1any social fund payment under sections 32(2)(a) and 32(2A) of the Act [SSCBA, section 138(1)(a) and (2)] [3and any incapacity benefit under sections 30A(1) and (5) of the Contributions and Benefits Act]];

[16 . . .]

"bereavement payment" means the sum specified in Part II of Schedule

4 to the Contributions and Benefits Act and referred to in section 36 of that Act;]

[6"the Board" means the Commissioners of Inland Revenue]

"child benefit" means benefit under Part I of the Child Benefit Act 1975 [SSCBA, Part IX];

"the Claims and Payments Regulations" means the Social Security (Claims and Payments) Regulations 1987;

[3"the Contributions and Benefits Act" means the Social Security Contributions and Benefits Act 1992;]

[2"disability living allowance" means a disability living allowance under section 37ZA of the Social Security Act 1975 [SSCBA, s.71];

[7 "disabled person's tax credit" means a disabled person's tax credit under section 129 of the Contributions and Benefits Act and, in relation to things done, or falling to be done, prior to 5th October 1999, shall include a reference to disability working allowance;] [7. . .]

[14 "employment and support allowance" means, for the purposes of Parts 3 to 6, employment and support allowance under Part 1 of the 2007 Act as that Part has effect apart from the amendments made by Schedule 3, and Part 1 of Schedule 14, to the 2012 Act that remove references to an income-related allowance;]

[11 "the Employment and Support Allowance Regulations" means the Employment and Support Allowance Regulations 2008;]

"guardian's allowance" means an allowance under section 38 of the Social Security Act 1975 [SSCBA, s.77];

"income support" means income support under Part II of the Act [SSCBA, Part VII] and includes personal expenses addition, special transitional addition and transitional addition as defined in the Income Support (Transitional) Regulations 1987;

"Income Support Regulations" means the Income Support (General) Regulations 1987;

[14 "jobseeker's allowance" means, for the purposes of Parts 3 to 6, jobseeker's allowance under the 1995 Act as that Act has effect apart from the amendments made by Part 1 of Schedule 14 to the 2012 Act that remove references to an income-based allowance;]

[4 "Jobseeker's Allowance Regulations" means the Jobseeker's Allowance Regulations 1996;]

[14 "personal independence payment" means the allowance under Part 4 of the 2012 Act;]

[13 "personal independence payment" means the allowance under Part 4 of the 2012 Act;]

"severe disablement allowance" means an allowance under section 36 of the Social Security Act 1975 [SSCBA, s.68].

[9 "state pension credit" means the benefit payable under the State Pension Credit Act 2002;

"the State Pension Credit Regulations" means the State Pension Credit Regulations 2002]

[7 "start notification" means a notification of entitlement to tax credit furnished to an employer by the Board, referred to in section 6(2)(a) of the Tax Credits Act 1999;

"tax credit" means working families' tax credit or disabled person's tax credit;

[14 "universal credit" means universal credit under Part 1 of the 2012 Act;]

[11 "the Welfare Reform Act means the Welfare Reform Act 2007;]
"working families' tax credit" means working families' tax credit under section 128 of the Contributions and Benefits Act and, in relation to things done, or falling to be done, prior to 5th October 1999 shall include a reference to family credit.]

(3) Unless the context otherwise requires, any reference in these regulations to a numbered Part or regulation is a reference to the Part or regulation bearing that number in these Regulations and any reference in a regulation to a numbered paragraph is a reference to the paragraph of that regulation bearing that number.

AMENDMENTS

1. The Social Security (Payments on account, Overpayments and Recovery) Amendments Regulations 1989 (SI 1989/136) reg.3 (February 27, 1989).
2. The Disability Living Allowance and Disability Working Allowance (Consequential Provisions) Regulations 1991 (SI 1991/2742) reg.15 (April 6, 1992).
3. The Social Security (Incapacity Benefit) (Consequential and Transitional Amendments and Savings) Regulations 1995 (SI 1995/829) reg.21(2) (April 13, 1995).
4. The Social Security and Child Support (Jobseeker's Allowance) (Consequential Amendments) Regulations 1996 (SI 1996/1345) reg.23(2) (October 7, 1996).
5. The Social Security Act 1998 (Commencement No.12 and Consequential and Transitional Provisions) Order 1999 (SI 1999/3178) Sch.9 para.1 (November 29, 1999).
6. For tax credits purposes only these words substituted by The Tax Credits (Payments on Account, Overpayments and Recovery) (Amendment) Regulations 1999 (SI 1999/2571) reg.3 (October 5, 1999).
7. The Tax Credits (Payments on Account, Overpayments and Recovery) (Amendment) Regulations 1999 (SI 1999/2571) reg.3 (October 5, 1999).
8. The Social Security (Benefits for Widows and Widowers) (Consequential Amendments) Regulations 2000 (SI 2000/1483) reg.10 (April 9, 2001).
9. State Pension Credit (Consequential, Transitional and Miscellaneous Provisions) Regulations 2002 (SI 2002/3019) reg.24 (October 6, 2003).
10. The Social Security, Child Support and Tax Credits (Miscellaneous Amendments) Regulations 2005 (SI 2005/337) reg.10 (March 18, 2005).
11. The Employment and Support Allowance (Consequential Provisions) (No. 2) Regulations 2008 (SI 2008/1554) reg.52 (October 27, 2008).
12. The Tribunals, Courts and Enforcement Act 2007 (Transitional and Consequential Provisions) Order 2008 (SI 2008/2683) Sch.1 para.44 (November 3, 2008).
13. The Social Security (Overpayments and Recovery) Regulations 2013 (SI 2013/384) reg.31(2) (April 8, 2013).
14. The Social Security (Overpayment and Recovery Regulations 2013 (SI 2013/384) reg.31(1)(d)–(g) (April 29, 2013).
15. The Pensions Act 2014 (Consequential, Supplementary and Incidental Amendments) Order 2015 (SI 2015/1985) art.11(2) (April 6, 2016).
16. The Pensions Act 2014 (Consequential, Supplementary and Incidental Amendments) Order 2017 (SI 2017/422) art.13 (April 6, 2017).

PART II

INTERIM PAYMENTS

2.918 Regs 2–4 revoked.

General note

Regulation 19 of the Social Security (Payments on Account of Benefit) Regulations 2013 (SI 2013/383) revokes Pt II of these Regulations with effect from April 1, 2013, subject to savings in respect of applications for interim payments made before April 1, 2013 and interim payments made pursuant to applications made before April 1, 2013. 2.919

Part III

Offsetting

Offsetting prior payment against subsequent award

5.—(1) Subject to [2 paragraphs (1A) [7, (2A) and (6)] and] regulation 6 (exception from offset of recoverable overpayment), any sum paid in respect of a period covered by a subsequent determination in any of the cases set out in paragraph (2) shall be offset against arrears of entitlement under the subsequent determination and, except to the extent that the sum exceeds the arrears, shall be treated as properly paid on account of them. 2.920

[2(1A) In paragraph (1) the reference to "any sum paid" shall, in relation to tax credit, include a reference to any amount or calculation of tax credit payable in respect of a period to the date of subsequent determination, which is included in a start notification given by the Board to an employer, and for the payment of which the employer remains responsible.]

(2) Paragraph (1) applies in the following cases—

[6 *Case 1: Payment pursuant to a decision which is revised or superseded, or overturned on appeal*

Where a person has been paid a sum by way of benefit [or by way of a shared additional pension under section 55A [11 or 55AA] of the Social Security Contributions and Benefits Act 1992] pursuant to a decision which is subsequently revised under section 9 of the Social Security Act 1998, superseded under Section 10 of that Act or overturned on appeal.]

Case 2: Award or payment of benefit in lieu

Where a person has been paid a sum by way benefit under the original award and it is subsequently determined, . . ., that another benefit [10 or, as the case may be, universal credit] should be awarded or is payable in lieu of the first.

Case 3: Child benefit and severe disablement allowance

Where either—

(a) a person has been awarded and paid child benefit for a period in respect of which severe disablement allowance [9 , employment and support allowance for those persons with limited capability for work in relation to your in accordance with paragraph 4 of Schedule 1 to the Welfare Reform Act 2007] [4 or incapacity benefit for persons incapacitated in youth in accordance with section 30(A)(1)(b) and (2A) of the Contributions and Benefits Act] is subsequently determined to be payable to the child concerned, or

(b) severe disablement allowance [4 or incapacity benefit for persons incapacitated in youth in accordance with section 30(A)(1)(b) and (2A) of the Contributions and Benefits Act] is awarded and paid for a period in respect of which child benefit is subsequently awarded to someone else, the child concerned in the subsequent determination being the beneficiary of the original award.

Case 4: Increase of benefit for dependant

Where a person has been paid a sum by way of an increase in respect of a dependent person under the original award and it is subsequently determined that that other person is entitled to benefit for that period, or that a third person is entitled to the increase for that period in priority to the beneficiary of the original award.

Case 5: Increase of benefit for partner

Where a person has been paid a sum by way of an increase in respect of a partner (as defined in regulation 2 of the Income Support Regulations) and it is subsequently determined that that other person is entitled to benefit for that period.

[2 (2A) In paragraph (2), Case 2 shall not apply where either—

(a) the sum paid under the original award, or

(b) the subsequent decision on the revision, supersession or appeal,

referred to in the Case (but not both) is or relates to tax credit.]

(3) Where an amount has been deducted under regulation 13(b) (sums to be deducted in calculating recoverable amounts) an equivalent sum shall be offset against any arrears of entitlement of that person under a subsequent award of [5 income support, state pension credit and] [1, or income-based jobseeker's allowance] [8 or an income related employment and support allowance] for the period to which the deducted amount relates.

(4) Where child benefit which has been paid under an award in favour of a person (the original beneficiary) is subsequently awarded to someone else for any week, the benefit shall nevertheless be treated as properly paid if it was received by someone other than the original beneficiary, who—

(a) either had the child living with him or was contributing towards the cost of providing for the child at a weekly rate which was not less than the weekly rate under the original award, and

(b) could have been entitled to child benefit in respect of that child for that week had a claim been made in time.

(5) Any amount which is treated, under paragraph (4), as properly paid shall be deducted from the amount payable to the beneficiary under the subsequent award.

[7 (6) Subject to regulation 6, any sums under—

(a) Schedule 5 or 5A to the Contributions and Benefits Act (pension increases or lump sum where entitlement to retirement pension or shared additional pension is deferred);

(b) Schedule 1 to the Social Security (Graduated Retirement Benefit) Regulations 2005 (increases or lump sum where entitlement to greaduate retirement benefit is deferred);

[11 (c) sections 8 or 9 of the Pensions Act 2014; or

(d) Regulations under section 10 of that Act which make provision corresponding or similar to sections 8 or 9 of that Act,]

Paid pursuant to a decision which is subsequently revised under section 9 of the Social Security Act 1998, superseded under section 10 of that Act or overturned on appeal, shall be offset against any sums due under the subsequent determination and, except to the extent that the sum exceeds the amount now due, shall be treated as properly paid on account of it.]

AMENDMENTS

1. The Social Security and Child Support (Jobseeker's Allowance) (Consequential Amendments) Regulations 1996 (SI 1996/1345) reg.23(5) and (6) (October 7, 1996).
2. The Tax Credits (Payments on Account, Overpayments and Recovery) (Amendment) Regulations 1999 (SI 1999/2571) reg.7 (October 5, 1999).
3. The Social Security Act 1998 (Commencement No.11 and Transitional Provisions) Order 1999 (SI 1999/2860) Sch.4 (October 18, 1999).
4. The Social Security (Incapacity Benefits) Miscellaneous Amendments Regulations 2000 (SI 2000/3120) reg.5 (April 6, 2001).
5. State Pension Credit (Consequential, Transitional and Miscellaneous Provisions) Regulations 2002 (SI 2002/3019) reg.24 (October 6, 2003).
6. The Social Security (Shared Additional Pension) (Miscellaneous Amendments) Regulations 2005 (SI 2005/1551) (July 6, 2005).
7. The Social Security (Deferral of Retirement Pensions etc.) Regulations 2006 (SI 2006/516) (April 6, 2006).
8. The Employment and Support Allowance (Consequential Provisions) (No. 2) Regulations 2008 (SI 2008/1554) reg.52 (October 27, 2008).
9. Social Security (Miscellaneous Amendments) (No. 3) Regulations 2010 (SI 2010/840) reg.3 (June 28, 2010).
10. The Social Security (Overpayments and Recovery) Regulations 2013 (SI 2013/384) reg.31(3) (April 29, 2013).
11. The Pensions Act 2014 (Consequential, Supplementary and Incidental Amendments) Order 2015 (SI 2015/1985) art.11(3) (April 6, 2016).

GENERAL NOTE

This regulation contains important powers to deal with cases where a subsequent award of one benefit replaces an earlier award of a different benefit. It enables the benefit originally awarded to be treated as paid on account of the benefit subsequently awarded. The circumstances in which the power is available are spelled out in the five cases listed in the regulation. Tribunals may need to refer to this power when the result of their decision is to substitute one benefit for another which has already been awarded. 2.921

In *Brown v Secretary of State for Work and Pensions* [2006] EWCA Civ 89, reported as *R(DLA) 2/07*, the Court of appeal, interpreting reg.5(1) ruled that where payments of disability living allowance had been suspended because there has been an overpayment, and a new decision made, payments subsequently awarded could not be offset against the irrecoverable overpayment, since the amount of payments would vary depending on how long it took for the new decision to be reached.

Exception from offset of recoverable overpayment

6. No amount may be offset under regulation 5(1) which has been determined to be a recoverable overpayment for the purposes of section 53(1) of the Act [SSAA, section 71(1)]. 2.922

PART IV

PREVENTION OF DUPLICATION OF PAYMENTS

Duplication and prescribed income

7.—[1 (1) For the purposes of section 74(1) of the Social Security Administration Act 1992 ([4 income support, state pension credit and] [6, income-based jobseeker's allowance, income-related employment and 2.923

support allowance] and other payments), a person's prescribed income is—

(a) income required to be taken into account in accordance with Part V of the Income Support Regulations [3or, as the case may be, Part VIII of the Jobseeker's Allowance Regulations] [4 or Part III of the State Pension Credit Regulations] [5 or Part 10 of the Employment and Support Allowance Regulations], except for the income specified in sub-paragraph (b); and]

[2(b) income which, if it were actually paid, would be required to be taken into account in accordance with Chapter VIIA of Part V of the Income Support Regulations [3or, as the case may be, Chapter VIII of Part VIII of the Jobseeker's Allowance Regulations] (child support maintenance); [5 or Chapter 9 of Part 10 to the Employment and Support Allowance Regulations (child support)] but only in so far as it relates to the period beginning with the effective date of the maintenance assessment under which it is payable, as determined in accordance with regulation 30 of the Child Support (Maintenance Assessment Procedure) Regulations 1992, and ending with the first day which is a day specified by the Secretary of State under regulation 4(1) of the Child Support (Collection and Enforcement) Regulations 1992 as being a day on which payment of child support maintenance under that maintenance assessment is due.]

(2) The prescribed date in relation to any payment of income prescribed by [1paragraph (1)(a)] is—

(a) where it is made in respect of a specific day or period, that day or the first day of the period;

(b) where it is not so made, the day or the first day of the period to which it is fairly attributable.

[2(3) Subject to paragraph (4), the prescribed date in relation to any payment of income prescribed by paragraph (1)(b) is the last day of the maintenance period, determined in accordance with regulation 33 of the Child Support (Maintenance Assessment Procedure) Regulations 1992, to which it relates.

(4) Where the period referred to in paragraph (1)(b) does not consist of a number of complete maintenance periods the prescribed date in relation to income prescribed by that sub-paragraph which relates to any part of that period which is not a complete maintenance period is the last day of that period.]

AMENDMENTS

1. The Social Security (Payments on account, Overpayments and Recovery) Amendment Regulations 1993 (SI 1993/650) reg.2, as amended by The Social Security (Miscellaneous Provisions) Amendment Regulations 1993 (SI 1993/846) reg.4 (April 5, 1993).

2. The Social Security (Payments on account, Overpayments and Recovery) Amendment Regulations 1993 (SI 1993/650) reg.2, as amended by The Social Security (Miscellaneous Provisions) Amendment Regulations 1993 (SI 1993/846) reg.4 (April 5, 1993).

3. The Social Security and Child Support (Jobseeker's Allowance) (Consequential Amendments) Regulations 1996 (SI 1996/1345) reg.23(3) (October 7, 1996).

4. State Pension Credit (Consequential, Transitional and Miscellaneous Provisions) Regulations 2002 (SI 2002/3019) reg.24 (October 6, 2003).

5. The Employment and Support Allowance (Consequential Provisions) (No. 2) Regulations 2008 (SI 2008/1554) reg.52 (October 27, 2008).
6. The Employment and Support Allowance (Miscellaneous Amendments) Regulations 2008 (SI 2008/2428) reg.22 (October 27, 2008).

GENERAL NOTE

See the notes to s.74(1) of the Administration Act. 2.924

Under s.54 of the Child Support Act 1991 "maintenance assessment" means an assessment of maintenance made under that Act, including, except where regulations prescribe otherwise, an interim assessment. Under reg.30 of the Child Support (Maintenance Assessment Procedure) Regulations 1992, the effective date of a new assessment is usually, when the application was made by the person with care of the child, the date on which a maintenance enquiry form was sent to the absent parent or, where the application was made by the absent parent, the date on which an effective maintenance form was received by the Secretary of State. Arrears will inevitably accrue while the assessment is being made. In the meantime income support or income-based JSA can be paid in full to the parent with care. When the arrears are paid, the amount of "overpaid" income support or JSA is recoverable under s.74(1) of the Administration Act.

See the notes to reg.60C of the Income Support (General) Regulations for the interaction with payments of other arrears of child support maintenance, which are excluded from the operation of s.74(1). Note also s.74A of the Administration Act and regs 55A and 60E of the Income Support Regulations and regs 119 and 127 of the Jobseeker's Allowance Regulations.

Duplication and prescribed payments

8.—(1) For the purposes of section [8 74(2) of the Administration Act] (recovery of amount of benefit awarded because prescribed payment not made on prescribed date), the payment of any of the following is a prescribed payment— 2.925

[12 (za) a state pension under Part 1 of the Pensions Act 2014,]

(a) any benefit under the Social Security Act 1975 [SSCBA, Parts II to V] other than any grant or gratuity or a widow's payment;

[11 (aa) any personal independence payment;]

(b) any child benefit;

(c) any family credit;

(d) any war disablement pension or war widow's pension which is not in the form of a gratuity and any payment which the Secretary of State accepts as analogous to any such pension;

(e) any allowance paid under the Job Release Act 1977;

(f) any allowance payable by or on behalf of [2Scottish Enterprise Highlands and Islands Enterprise or] [1the Secretary of State] to or in respect of a person for his maintenance for any period during which he is following a course of training or instruction provided or approved by [2Scottish Enterprise Highlands and Islands Enterprise or] [1the Secretary of State]

(g) any payment of benefit under the legislation of any member State other than the United Kingdom concerning the branches of social security mentioned in Article 4(1) of Regulation (EEC) No.1408/71 on the application of social security schemes to employed persons, to self-employed persons and to members of their families moving within the Community, whether or not the benefit has been acquired by virtue of the provisions of that Regulation;

[3. . .]
[13 (i) any widowed parent's allowance under section 39A of the Contributions and Benefits Act;]
[8 (j) any contribution-based jobseeker's allowance within the meaning of section 1(4) of the Jobseekers Act.]
[9 (k) payments under the Financial Assistance Scheme Regulations 2005.]
[10 (l) a contributory employment and support allowance.]

(2) The prescribed date, in relation to any payment prescribed by paragraph (1) is the date by which receipt of or entitlement to that benefit would have to be notified to the Secretary of State if it were to be taken into account in determining, whether [5by way of revision or supersession], the amount of or entitlement to [7 income support, [11 universal credit,] a state pension credit] [4, or income-based jobseeker's allowance][10 or income-related employment and support allowance].

AMENDMENTS

1. Employment Act 1989 Sch.5 paras 1 and 4 (November 16, 1989).
2. The Enterprise (Scotland) Consequential Amendments Order 1991 (SI 1991/387) art.14 (April 1, 1991).
3. The Tax Credits (Payments on Account, Overpayments and Recovery) (Amendment) Regulations 1999 (SI 1999/2571) reg.8 (October 5, 1999).
4. The Social Security and Child Support (Jobseeker's Allowance) (Consequential Amendments) Regulations 1996 (SI 1996/1345) reg.23(5) and (6) (October 7, 1996).
5. The Social Security Act 1998 (Commencement No.11 and Transitional Provisions) Order 1999 (SI 1999/2680) Sch.4 (October 18, 1999).
6. The Social Security (Benefits for Widows and Widowers) (Consequential Amendments) Regulations 2000 (SI 2000/1483) reg.10 (April 9, 2001).
7. State Pension Credit (Consequential, Transitional and Miscellaneous Provisions) Regulations 2002 (SI 2002/3019) reg.24 (October 6, 2003).
8. The Social Security, Child Support and Tax Credits (Miscellaneous Amendments) Regulations 2005 (SI 2005/337) reg.10 (March 18, 2005).
9. The Social Security (Payments on account, Overpayments and Recovery) Amendment Regulations 2005 (SI 2005/3476) (January 19, 2006).
10. The Employment and Support Allowance (Consequential Provisions) (No. 2) Regulations 2008 (SI 2008/1554) reg.52 (October 27, 2008).
11. The Social Security (Overpayments and Recovery) Regulations 2013 (SI 2013/384 reg.31(4) (April 29, 2013).
12. The Pensions Act 2014 (Consequential, Supplementary and Incidental Amendments) Order 2015 (SI 2015/1985) art.11(4) (April 6, 2016).
13. The Pensions Act 2014 (Consequential, Supplementary and Incidental Amendments) Order 2017 (SI 2017/422) art.13 (April 6, 2017).

GENERAL NOTE

2.926 See the notes to s.74(2) of the Administration Act.

R(IS) 14/94 concerned an overpayment of income support which arose from the award of invalid care allowance. The claimant was an elderly widow, whose daughter was her appointee. Income support was paid to the widow. The daughter was in receipt of invalid care allowance in respect of her mother. Recovery was sought under s.27 of the Social Security Act 1986 (now s.74 of the Administration Act) from the widow.

The claimant argued that the words in reg.8(2) "taken into account" meant that only the claimant's resources and requirements were to be considered. The Commissioner rejects such a narrow reading of the words and says that "the words 'into account' should be given a wide interpretation and in the context include 'take notice of'."

Duplication and maintenance payments

9. For the purposes of section 27(3) of the Act [SSAA, section 74(3)] (recovery of amount of benefit awarded because maintenance payments not made), the following benefits are prescribed— 2.927

(a) child benefit;
(b) increase for dependants of any benefit under the Social Security Act 1975 [SSCBA, Parts II to V];
(c) child's special allowance under section 31 of the Social Security Act 1975 [SSCBA, section 56]; and
(d) guardian's allowance.

GENERAL NOTE

See the notes to s.74(3) of the Administration Act. 2.928

Conversion of payments made in a foreign currency

10. Where a payment of income prescribed by regulation 7(1), or a payment prescribed by regulation 8(1), is made in a currency other than sterling, its value in sterling, for the purposes of section 27 of the Act [SSAA, section 74] and this Part, shall be determined, after conversion by the Bank of England, or by [1any institution which is authorised under the Banking Act 1987], as the net sterling sum into which it is converted, after any banking charge or commission on the transaction has been deducted. 2.929

AMENDMENT

1. The Social Security (Payments on Account, Overpayments and Recovery) (Amendment) Regulations 1988 (SI 1988/688) reg.2(2) (April 11, 1988).

PART V

DIRECT CREDIT TRANSFER OVERPAYMENTS

Recovery of overpayments by automated or other direct credit transfer

11.— [4 (A1) This regulation applies only in respect of payments of benefit to which section 71 of the Administration Act applies.] 2.930

(1) [1 Subject to paragraph (4)] where it is determined by the adjudicating authority that a payment in excess of entitlement has been credited to a bank or other account under an arrangement for automated or other direct credit transfer made in accordance with regulation 21 of the Claims and Payments Regulations and that the conditions prescribed by paragraph (2) are satisfied, the excess, or the specified part of it to which the Secretary of State's certificate relates, shall be recoverable under this regulation.

(2) The prescribed conditions for recoverability under paragraph (1) are as follows—

(a) the Secretary of State has certified that the payment in excess of entitlement, or a specified part of it, is materially due to the arrangements for payments to be made by automated or other direct credit transfer; and

[2 (b) notice of the effect to which this regulation would have, in the event

of an overpayment, was given to the beneficiary or to a person acting form his—
(i) in writing, where the claim was made in writing; or
(ii) either orally or in writing, where the claim was made by telephone

[3 before the arrangement came into effect.]

(3) Where the arrangement was agreed to before April 6, 1987 the condition prescribed by paragraph (2)(b) need not be satisfied in any case where the application for benefit to be paid by automated or other direct credit transfer contained a statement, or was accompanied by a written statement made by the applicant, which complied with the provisions of regulation 16A(3)(b) and (8) of the Social Security (Claims and Payments) Regulations 1979 or, as the case may be, regulation 7(2)(b) and (6) of the Child Benefit (Claims and Payments) Regulations 1984.

[1 Where the payment mention in paragraph (1) is a payment of tax credit, paragraphs (1) and (2) shall apply with the modifications that—
(a) in paragraph (1) for the words "Secretary of State" there is substituted the words "Board's", and
(b) in paragraph (2) for the words "Secretary of State" there is substituted the word "Board".]

AMENDMENTS

1. The Tax Credits (Payments on Account, Overpayments and Recovery) (Amendment) Regulations 1999 (SI 1999/2571) reg.9 (October 5, 1999).

2. The Social Security (Claims and Payments and Payments on account, Overpayments and Recovery) Amendment Regulations 2005 (SI 2005/34) reg.3 (May 2, 2005).

3. The Social Security (Miscellaneous Amendments) Regulations 2012 (SI 2012/757) reg.16 (April 1, 2012).

4. The Social Security (Overpayments and Recovery) Regulations 2013 (SI 2013/384 reg.31(5) (April 29, 2013).

PART VI

CALCULATION OF AMOUNT RECOVERABLE

Circumstances in which determination need not be revised

2.931 **12.** [2 Section 71(5) or (5A) of the Administration Act] (recoverability dependent on reversal, variation, revision [1 or supersession] of determination) shall not apply where the fact and circumstances of the misrepresentation or non-disclosure do not provide a basis for [1 the decision pursuant to which the payment was made to be revised under section 9 of the Social Security Act 1998 or superseded under section 10 of that Act.]

AMENDMENTS

1. The Social Security Act 1998 (Commencement No.9, and Savings and Consequential and Transitional Provisions) Order 1999 (SI 1999/2422) Sch.8 (September 6, 1999).

2. The Social Security, Child Support and Tax Credits (Miscellaneous Amendments) Regulations 2005 (SI 2005/337) reg.10 (March 18, 2005).

General Note

See the notes to s.71(5A) of the Administration Act. 2.932

Sums to be deducted in calculating recoverable amounts

13.—[6 (1) Subject to paragraphs (1C) and (2), in calculating an amount recoverable under section 71(1) of the Administration Act or under regulation 11 ("the overpayment"), the adjudicating authority must deduct— 2.933

(a) any amount which has been offset under Part 3;

(b) any additional amount of a benefit specified in paragraph (1A) which was not payable under the original, or any other, determination but which should have been determined to be payable in respect of all or part of the overpayment period to the claimant or their partner—

(i) on the basis of the claim as presented to the adjudicating authority; or

(ii) on the basis that any misrepresentation or failure to disclose a material fact had been remedied prior to the award being made.

(1A) The specified benefits are—

(a) universal credit;

(b) income support;

(c) state pension credit;

(d) income-based jobseeker's allowance; and

(e) income-related employment and support allowance.

(1B) In paragraph (1), "overpayment period" means the period over which the overpayment accrued.

(1C) No other deduction is to be made in respect of any other entitlement to benefit which may be, or might have been, determined to exist.]

[2 (2) Paragraph (1) shall apply to tax credit only where both—

(a) The overpayment of benefit referred to in paragraph (1), and

(b) The amount referred to in sub-paragraph (a) of that paragraph,

Are tax credit, and with the modification that sub-paragraph (b) of that paragraph is omitted.]

Amendments

1. The Social Security and Child Support (Jobseeker's Allowance) (Consequential Amendments) Regulations 1996 (SI 1996/1345) reg.23(5) and (6) (October 7, 1996).

2. The Tax Credits (Payments on Account, Overpayments and Recovery) (Amendment) Regulations 1999 (SI 1999/2571) reg.11 (October 5, 1999).

3. State Pension Credit (Consequential, Transitional and Miscellaneous Provisions) Regulations 2002 (SI 2002/3019) reg.24 (October 6, 2003).

4. The Employment and Support Allowance (Consequential Provisions) (No. 2) Regulations 2008 (SI 2008/1554) reg.52 (October 27, 2008).

5. The Social Security (Recovery) (Amendment) Regulations 2012 (SI 2012/645) reg.2(1) (April 1, 2012).

6. The Social Security (Overpayments and Recovery) Regulations 2013 (SI 2013/384) reg.31(6) (April 8, 2013).

General Note

See the notes to s.71(1) and (2) of the Administration Act, 1992 for important case law affecting this provision. 2.934

In *CP/5257/1999* the Commissioner interpreted the poorly drafted reg.13 by holding that:

(a) the regulation is not limited to overpayments of income support or income-based jobseeker's allowance, but covers overpaid benefit other than these two benefits; and

(b) the regulation only applies where the benefit sought to be offset is income support or income-based jobseeker's allowance.

In *CIS/1777/2000* a different Commissioner said:

> "[Regulation 13] was amended to include a reference to income-based jobseeker's allowance when that benefit was introduced in 1996. I do not read the provision as authorising the deduction from an overpayment of jobseeker's allowance that would have been paid if a claim for that benefit has been made rather than a claim for income support. Head (i) refers to the claim as presented—the claim as presented was for income support. Head (ii) refers to the claim as it would have appeared if the facts had been correctly represented—if the facts had been correctly known, the claim would have appeared as a claim for income support to which the claimant was not entitled. The claimant might have been advised by the Department of Social Security to make a claim for an income based jobseeker's allowance, but that would have been a different claim—there is no power for the Secretary of State to treat a claim for income support as a claim for income based jobseeker's allowance in the alternative under Schedule 1 to the Social Security (Claims and Payments) Regulations 1987." (See [9]).

The interpretation of the regulation was revisited in *CIS/2291/2001* following the 1999 amendments. The Commissioner concludes:

> "17. Although the wording is particularly obscure for such an important and potentially severe rule, the effect is clear. Anyone who is working or capable of work so as to exclude them from income support must claim jobseeker's allowance. If they do not, and they continue to receive income support, they risk losing both the income support actually received and the jobseeker's allowance they might have received.
>
> 18. Regulation 13 does not contain any discretion. That rests with the Secretary of State in deciding whether and how to collect any overpayment. No doubt the Secretary of State will take into account whether the public purse has in reality lost the sum claimed as overpaid or some other amount."

2.935 In *CDLA/3768/2002*, the Commissioner said:

> "15. . . . the decision maker acting for the Secretary of State [in presenting the case to the tribunal] should first consider whether any amount has been offset under Part III (regulations 5 and 6 of the Social Security (Payments on Account, Overpayments and Recoveries) Regulations 1988. This may call for further enquiry, bearing in mind always that it is for the Secretary of State to meet any problems arising from conflicts of evidence or absence of proof of any relevant issue . . .
>
> 16. The other issues that regulation 13(1) requires the decision maker and tribunal to identify and deduct is:
>
> > 'any additional amount of income support or income-based jobseeker's allowance which was not payable under the original or any other determination, but which should have been determined to be payable on the basis of the claim as presented to the adjudicating authority or on the basis of the claim as it would have appeared had the misrepresentation or nondisclosure been remedied before the determination'.
>
> I have removed the punctuation for the reasons given in *CIS/2291/2001*. Regulation 13(1) then emphasises that no other deduction shall be made for any other actual or hypothetical entitlement."

In the particular circumstances of the case in *CIS/0546/2008*, a Deputy Commissioner decided that the appellant was entitled to the application of the set off provisions in reg.13 in the context of a claim for income support. Benefit had been stopped when it was established that the appellant and her partner were living together as husband and wife. It appeared that the appellant had not been given the opportunity to elect to make a claim for income support for herself, her partner and the children. In this case, there was a claim for income support affecting the appellant. There was an issue which "should have been determined". This meant that the appellant was entitled to have reg.13 applied to offset all or part of the overpayment which was recoverable from her.

The Administrative Court in *Larusai v Secretary of State for Work and Pensions*, [2003] EWHC 371 (Admin) was called upon to consider the relationship of benefits administered by the Department and tax credits administered by the Board of Inland Revenue in relation to the offsetting of benefits where there are recoverable overpayments of benefits administered by the Department. The claimant had been overpaid income support which was recoverable, but argued that a notional entitlement to working families tax credit should be set off against the overpayment notwithstanding the absence of such a provision in reg.13. The claimant argued that the Secretary of State in exercising his discretion as to the amount of the recoverable overpayment had acted unlawfully in failing to deduct a notional amount of working families tax credit from the overpayment. The decision was never likely to require the Secretary of State to exercise his discretion in the way for which the claimant argued, but the decision is interesting for the way in which the Administrative Court responded to the claimant's arguments: **2.936**

(1) The claimant argued that the Secretary of State's approach in treating tax credits as different from benefits administered by the Department and so precluding any discretionary offset of working families tax credit was irrational. The Court did not accept this, seeing nothing irrational in attempts to change the perception of claimants about the difference between benefits which required a person to be out of work and those which were payable to people in work.

(2) The claimant argued that the policy of the Secretary of State had departed from its own guidelines in pursuing a policy of exercising its discretion only in "exceptional circumstances". The Court concluded that this was a matter of phraseology and did not render the policy unlawful.

(3) The claimant argued that the decision to recover the whole of the overpaid income support without deduction of a notional entitlement to working families tax credit constituted a penal sanction (it appears that the claimant would have been entitled to something in the order of £2,000 by way of working families tax credit). Since the policy in reg.13 was to secure full recovery subject to the specified offsets and since the notional amount of working families tax credit did not constitute a debt by the Department to the claimant, it could not be said that there was anything which could be characterised as a penal sanction; there was no basis for the claimant's argument.

(4) The Court said that an argument based on the Government securing a windfall equal to the notional amount of the working families tax credit was misconceived. It "misrepresents the structural position, as well as the law, to describe this as 'a windfall to the State.'" (See [30].)

(5) The claimant raised the question of hardship resulting from the requirement to repay overpaid benefit. The Court simply notes that the Secretary of State has been provided with full details of the claimant's circumstances, that there is inevitably an element of hardship when overpaid benefit is recovered, but that it "is not for this court, unless it is satisfied that there has been an unlawful exercise of discretion, to form a view about the financial margins with which this case, or any case, might give rise to." (See [32].)

See also *Department for Work and Pensions v Richards*, [2005] EWCA Crim 491.

Public Records Act 1958

2.937 *R(IS) 1/05* gives guidance on the significance of the Public Records Act 1958 to the retention of documents by the Department, and the onus of proof where a claimant asserts that there has been an underpayment of benefit in the past which reduces the amount of a recoverable overpayment. The overpayment at issue in this case had arisen as a result of admitted false statements made by the claimant which resulted in the award of income support. The point of contention was whether the claimant could offset the substantial overpayment by underpayments of benefit in circumstances where many of the relevant documents had long since been destroyed by the Department under its document retention policy.

The requirements of the Public Records Act 1958 were seen as something of a red herring, and the Commissioner has little time for them, noting, "It is difficult to believe that these elaborate procedures [in the 1958 Act] were ever intended to apply to social security claim forms". In fairness, the claimant's representative had abandoned this point in arguing the case before the Commissioner.

The onus of proof in cases such as this was a rather more substantial point, particularly in the light of the House of Lords in *Kerr v Department for Social Development* [2004] UKHL 23. The Commissioner sees no real difference in the views expressed by Lady Hale in *Kerr* and the long-established wisdom that "if a particular matter relates to the qualifying conditions of entitlement it is a claimant who must bear the consequences of ignorance; however, if what is in issue constitute an exception to such conditions, then the Department bears the burden of establishing that factor which operates to disentitled the claimant". (See [43]). The issue which arises under reg.13 is distinct from the recovery of the overpayment; it is not necessarily related to the period which is covered by the s.71 revision or supersession nor to the same benefit the subject of recovery. The Commissioner concludes:

> "If, as is trite law, one who submits an initial claim for benefit has the burden of showing that its qualifying conditions are met, it can hardly be the case that one who must pay benefit back because it has been demonstrated that she should never have had it, has an easier task in establishing a similar entitlement to offset against the proven debt. In my judgement, nothing in principle or on account of the statutory language or from the structure of the overpayment scheme or to further its consistency can justify such a departure from what is usual and right." (para.47)

Quarterly diminution of capital

2.938 **14.**—(1) For the purposes of section 53(1) of the Act [SSAA, section 71(1)], where income support, [4 or state pension credit] [2, or income-based jobseeker's allowance] [5 , or income-related employment and support allowance] [1, working families' tax credit or disabled person's tax credit] has been overpaid in consequence of a misrepresentation as to the capital a claimant possesses or a failure to disclose its existence, the adjudicating authority shall treat that capital as having been reduced at the end of each quarter from the start of the overpayment period by the amount overpaid by way of income support, [4 or state pension credit] [2, or income based jobseeker's allowance] [5 , or income-related employment and support allowance] [1 working families' tax credit or disabled person's tax credit] within that quarter.

(2) Capital shall not be treated as reduced over any period other than a quarter or in any circumstances other than those for which paragraph (1) provides.

(3) In this regulation—

"a quarter" means a period of 13 weeks starting with the first day on which the overpayment period began and ending on the 90th consecutive day thereafter;

"overpayment period" is a period during which income support [3 or an income based jobseeker's allowance,] [5 , or income-related employment and support allowance] [1 working families' tax credit or disabled person's tax credit] is overpaid in consequence of a misrepresentation as to capital or a failure to disclose its existence.

AMENDMENTS

1. The Tax Credits (Payments on Account, Overpayments and Recovery) (Amendment) Regulations 1999 (SI 1999/2571) reg.12 (October 5, 1999).

2. The Tax Credits (Payments on Account, Overpayments and Recovery) (Amendment) Regulations 1999 (SI 1996/2571) reg.23(5) and (6) (October 7, 1996).

3. The Social Security (Jobseeker's Allowance and Payments on account) (Miscellaneous Amendments) Regulations 1996 (SI 1996/2519) reg.3(2) (October 7, 1996).

4. State Pension Credit (Consequential, Transitional and Miscellaneous Provisions) Regulations 2002 (SI 2002/3019) reg.24 (October 6, 2003).

5. The Employment and Support Allowance (Consequential Provisions) (No. 2) Regulations 2008 (SI 2008/1554) reg.52 (October 27, 2008).

GENERAL NOTE

See the notes to s.71(1) and (2) of the Administration Act. 2.939

On the proper interpretation of the rule in reg.14, see *CIS/2570/2007* and *CIS/2365/2007*. See also for a discussion of the proper approach to the application of the diminishing capital rule on successive claims to benefit, *MP v SSWP* [2009] UKUT 193 (AAC).

In *R(IS) 10/08*, the Commissioner effectively holds that capital held by a child should be subject to the diminishing capital rules if an overpayment arises as a result of capital held by a child of the family unit seeking entitlement to income support.

PART VII

THE PROCESS OF RECOVERY

Recovery by deduction from benefits

15.—(1) Subject to regulation 16, where any amount is recoverable under sections 27 or 53(1) of the Act [SSAA, sections 74 or 71(1)], or under these Regulations, that amount shall be recoverable by the Secretary of State from any of the benefits prescribed by the next paragraph, to which the person from whom [1the amount is determined] to be recoverable is entitled. 2.940

(2) The following benefits are prescribed for the purposes of this regulation—

(a) subject to paragraphs (1) and (2) of regulation 16, any benefit under the Social Security Act 1975 [SSCBA, Parts II to V];

[10(aa) a state pension under Part 1 of the Pensions Act 2014,]

(b) subject to paragraphs (1) and (2) of regulation 16, any child benefit;

(c) [5. . .]

(d) subject to regulation 16, any income support [7 an employment and support allowance] [6 or state pension credit], [4or a jobseeker's allowance].

[2(e) [5. . .];
[3(f) any incapacity benefit.]
[8 (g) personal independence payment;]
[9 (h) universal credit.]

AMENDMENTS

1. The Social Security (Payments on account, Overpayments and Recovery) Amendments Regulations 1988 (SI 1988/688) reg.2(3) (April 11, 1988).
2. The Disability Living Allowance and Disability Working Allowance (Consequential Provisions) Regulations 1991 (SI 1991/2742) reg.15 (April 6, 1992).
3. The Social Security (Incapacity Benefit) (Consequential and Transitional Amendments and Savings) Regulations 1991 (SI 1995/829) reg.21(3) (April 13, 1995).
4. The Social Security (Jobseeker's Allowance and Payments on account) (Miscellaneous Amendments) Regulations 1996 (SI 1996/2519) reg.3(3) (October 7, 1996).
5. The Social Security (Jobseeker's Allowance and Payments on account) (Miscellaneous Amendments) Regulations 1996 (SI 1996/2519) reg.13 (October 5, 1999).
6. State Pension Credit (Consequential, Transitional and Miscellaneous Provisions) Regulations 2002 (SI 2002/3019) reg.24 (October 6, 2003).
7. The Employment and Support Allowance (Consequential Provisions) (No. 2) Regulations 2008 (SI 2008/1554) reg.52 (October 27, 2008).
8. The Social Security (Overpayments and Recovery) Regulations 2013 (SI 2013/384) reg.31(7) (April 8, 2013).
9. The Social Security (Overpayment and Recovery Regulations 2013 (SI 2013/384) reg.31(7)(b) (April 29, 2013).
10. The Pensions Act 2014 (Consequential, Supplementary and Incidental Amendments) Order 2015 (SI 2015/1985) art.11(5) (April 6, 2016).

Limitations on deductions from prescribed benefits

2.941 **16.**—(1) Deductions may not be made from entitlement to the benefits prescribed by paragraph (2) except as a means of recovering an overpayment of the benefit from which the deduction is to be made.

(2) The benefits [1prescribed] for the purposes of paragraph (1) are guardian's allowance, [2. . .] and child benefit.

[15 (2A) Paragraphs (3) to (7) do not apply where paragraph (7A) applies.]

(3) Regulation 15 shall apply without limitation to any payment of arrearsof benefit other than any arrears caused by the operation of [12 regulation 20 of the Social Security and Child Support (Decisions and Appeals) Regulations 1999 (making of payments which have been suspended)]

(4) Regulation 15 shall apply to the amount of [5benefit] to which a person is presently entitled only to the extent that there may [17 . . .] be recovered in respect of any one benefit week—

(a) in a case to which paragraph (5) applies, not more than the amount there specified; and
(b) in any other case, 3 times 5 per cent of the personal allowance for a single claimant aged not less than 25, that 5 per cent being, where it is not a multiple of 5 pence, rounded to the next higher such multiple.

[6(4A) Paragraph (4) shall apply to the following benefits—

(a) income support;
(b) an income-based jobseeker's allowance;
(c) where, if there was no entitlement to a contribution-based jobseeker's allowance, there would be entitlement to an income-based jobseeker's allowance at the same rate, a contribution-based jobseeker's allowance.]

[11 (d) state pension credit.]
[13 (e) an income-related employment and support allowance;
(f) where, if there was no entitlement to a contributory employment and support allowance, there would be entitlement to an income-related employment and support allowance at the same rate, a contributory employment and support allowance.]

[9 (5) Where a person responsible for the misrepresentation or failure to disclose a material fact has, by reason thereof—
(a) been found guilty of an offence whether under statute or otherwise; or
(b) made an admission after caution of deception or fraud for the purpose of obtaining benefit; or
(c) agreed to pay a penalty under section 115A of the Social Security Administration Act 1992 and the agreement has not been withdrawn,

the amount mentioned in paragraph (4)(a) [17 shall, subject to paragraph (5ZA), be 8 times] 5 per cent. of the personal allowance for a single claimant aged not less than 25, that 5 per cent. being, [14 where it is not a multiple of 5 pence, rounded to the next higher such multiple]]

[17 (5ZA) In a case to which paragraph (5) applies, where deductions fall to be made under Schedule 9 to the Claims and Payments Regulations (payments to third parties), the total of the amount deductible under paragraph (5) and the amount deductible under that Schedule shall not exceed 8 times 5 per cent. of the personal allowance mentioned in paragraph (5).

(5ZB) Paragraph (4)(b) is subject to paragraphs 8 and 9 of Schedule 9 to the Claims and Payments Regulations.]

[6(5A) Regulation 15 shall apply to an amount of a contribution-based jobseeker's allowance, other than a contribution-based jobseeker's allowance to which paragraph (4) applies in accordance with paragraph (4A)(c), to which a person is presently entitled only to the extent that there may, subject to paragraphs 8 and 9 of Schedule 9 to the Claims and Payments Regulations be recovered in respect of any one benefit week a sum equal to one third of the age-related amount applicable to the claimant under section 4(1)(a) of the Jobseekers Act 1995.

(5B) For the purposes of paragraph (5A) where the sum that would otherwise fall to be deducted includes a fraction of a penny, the sum to be deducted shall be rounded down to the nearest whole penny.]

(6) [5 Where—
(a) in the calculation of the income of a person to whom income support is payable, the amount of earnings or other income falling to be taken into account is reduced by paragraphs 4 to 9 of Schedule 8 to the Income Support Regulations (sums to be disregarded in the calculation of earnings) or paragraphs 15 and 16 of Schedule 9 to those Regulations (sums to be disregarded in the calculation of income other than earnings); or
(b) in the calculation of the income of a person to whom income-based jobseeker's allowance is payable, the amount of earnings or other income falling to be taken into account is reduced by paragraphs 5 to 12 of Schedule 6 to the Jobseeker's Allowance Regulations (sums to be disregarded in the calculation of earnings) or paragraphs 15 and 17 of Schedule 7 to those Regulations (sums to be disregarded in the calculation of income other than earnings),

[11 or

(c) in the calculation of the income of a person to whom state pension credit is payable, the amount of earnings or other income falling to be taken into account is reduced in accordance with paragraph 1 of Schedule 4 (sums to be disregarded in the calculation of income other than capital), or Schedule 6 (sums disregarded from claimant's earnings) to the State Pension Credit Regulations,] [13 or

(d) in the calculation of the income of a person to whom income-related employment and support allowance is payable, the amount of earnings or other income falling to be taken into account is reduced by paragraph 7 of Schedule 7 to the Employment and Support Allowance Regulations (sums to be disregarded in the calculation of earnings) or paragraphs 16 and 17 of Schedule 8 to those Regulations (sums to be disregarded in the calculation of income other than earnings),]

the weekly amount] applicable under paragraph (4) may be increased by not more than half the amount of the reduction, [16 ...].

(7) Regulation 15 shall not be applied to a specified benefit so as to reduce the benefit in any one benefit week to less than 10 pence.

[15 (7A) This paragraph applies where the benefit from which the deduction is to be made under regulation 15 is universal credit.

(7B) Where paragraph (7A) applies, regulation 11 of the Social Security (Overpayments and Recovery) Regulations 2013 applies in relation to those deductions as it applies to deductions from universal credit for the recovery of recoverable amounts under those Regulations.]

(8) In this regulation—

[9 'admission after caution' means—

(i) in England and Wales, an admission after a caution has been administered in accordance with a Code issued under the Police and Criminal Evidence Act 1984;

in Scotland, an admission after a caution has been administered, such admission being duly witnessed by two persons;]

"benefit week" means the week corresponding to the week in respect of which the benefit is paid;

[11 "personal allowance for a single claimant aged not less than 25" means—

(a) in the case of a person who is entitled to [13 an employment and support allowance,] income support or state pension credit, the amount for the time being specified in paragraph 1(1)(e) of column (2) of Schedule 2 to the Income Support Regulations; or

(b) in the case of a person who is entitled to income-based jobseeker's allowance, the amount for the time being specified in paragraph 1(1)(e) of column (2) of Schedule 1 to the Jobseeker's Allowance Regulations;]

"specified benefit" means—

(a) a jobseeker's allowance;

(b) income support when paid alone or together with any incapacity benefit, retirement pension or severe disablement allowance in a combined payment in respect of any period;

(c) if incapacity benefit, retirement pension or severe disablement allowance is paid concurrently with income support in respect of any period but not in a combined payment, income support and such of those benefits as are paid concurrently;

(d) state pension credit when paid alone or together with any retirement pension, incapacity benefit or severe disablement allowance in a combined payment in respect of any period;

(e) if retirement pension, incapacity benefit or severe disablement allowance is paid concurrently with state pension credit in respect of any period but not in a combined payment, state pension credit and such of those benefits as are paid concurrently, but does not include any sum payable by way of child maintenance bonus in accordance with section 10 of the Child Support Act 1995 and the Social Security (Child Maintenance Bonus) Regulations 1996.] [[13] and

(f) an employment and support allowance,]

but does not include any sum payable by way of child maintenance bonus in accordance with section 10 of the Child Support Act 1995 and the Social Security (Child Maintenance Bonus) Regulations 1996.]

AMENDMENTS

1. The Social Security (Payments on account, Overpayments and Recovery) Amendments Regulations 1988 (SI 1988/688) reg.2(4) (April 11, 1988).

2. The Disability Living Allowance and Disability Working Allowance (Consequential Provisions) Regulations 1991 (SI 1991/2742) reg.15 (April 6, 1992).

3. The Social Security (Incapacity Benefit) (Consequential and Transitional Amendments and Savings) Regulations 1995 (SI 1995/829) reg.21(4) (April 13, 1995).

4. The Social Security (Claims and Payments, etc.) Amendment Regulations 1996 (SI 1996/672) reg.4 (April 4, 1996).

5. The Social Security and Child Support (Jobseeker's Allowance) (Consequential Amendments) Regulations 1996 (SI 1996/1345) reg.23(4) (October 7, 1996).

6. The Social Security (Jobseeker's Allowance and Payments on account) (Miscellaneous Amendments) Regulations 1996 (SI 1996/2519) reg.3(4) (October 7, 1996).

7. The Social Security (Child Maintenance Bonus) Regulations 1996 (SI 1996/3195) reg.16(3) (April 7, 1997).

8. The Social Security (Miscellaneous Amendments) Regulations 1997 (SI 1997/454) reg.8(10) (April 6, 1997).

9. The Social Security (Payments on Account, Overpayment and Recovery) Amendment Regulations 2000 (SI 2000/2336) reg.2 (October 2, 2000).

10. The Social Security (Claims and Payments and Miscellaneous Amendments) (No.2) Regulations 2002 (SI 2002/2441) reg.134 (October 23, 2002).

11. State Pension Credit (Consequential, Transitional and Miscellaneous Provisions) Regulations 2002 (SI 2002/3019) reg.24 (October 6, 2003).

12. The Social Security, Child Support and Tax Credits (Miscellaneous Amendments) Regulations 2005 (SI 2005/337) reg.10 (March 18, 2005).

13. The Employment and Support Allowance (Consequential Provisions) (No.2) Regulations 2008 (SI 2008/1554) reg.52 (October 27, 2008).

14. The Social Security (Recovery) (Amendment) Regulations 2012 (SI 2012/645) reg.3(1) (April 1, 2012).

15. The Social Security (Overpayments and Recovery) Regulations 2013 (SI 2013/384) reg.31(8) (April 8, 2013).

16. The Universal Credit, Personal Independence Payment, Jobseeker's Allowance and Employment and Support Allowance (Claims and Payments) Regulations 2013 (SI 2013/380) Sch.3 para.2 (April 29, 2013).

17. The Social Security (Overpayments and Recovery) Amendments Regulations 2015 (SI 2015/499) reg.2 (April 6, 2015).

Recovery from couples

2.942 **17.** In the case of an overpayment of income support [3 or state pension credit] [2, or income-based jobseeker's allowance] [5 or income-related employment and support allowance] [1, family credit or disability working allowance] to one of [4 a couple], the amount recoverable by deduction, in accordance with regulation 15, may be recovered by deduction from income support [3 or state pension credit] [2, or income-based jobseeker's allowance] [5 or income-related employment and support allowance] [1, family credit or disability working allowance] payable to either of them, provided that the two of them are [4 a couple] at the date of the deduction.

AMENDMENTS

1. The Disability Living Allowance and Disability Working Allowance (Consequential Provisions) Regulations 1991 (SI 1991/2742) reg.15 (April 6, 1992).
2. The Social Security and Child Support (Jobseeker's Allowance) (Consequential Amendments) Regulations 1996 (SI 1996/1345) reg.23(5) and (6) (October 7, 1996).
3. State Pension Credit (Consequential, Transitional and Miscellaneous Provisions) Regulations 2002 (SI 2002/3019) reg.24 (October 6, 2003).
4. The Civil Partnership (Pensions, Social Security and Child Support) (Consequential etc. Provisions) Order 2005 (SI 2005/2877) (December 5, 2005).
5. The Employment and Support Allowance (Consequential Provisions) (No. 2) Regulations 2008 (SI 2008/1554) reg.52 (October 27, 2008).

PART VIII

RECOVERY BY DEDUCTIONS FROM EARNINGS FOLLOWING TRADE DISPUTE

Recovery by deductions from earnings

2.943 **18.**—(1) Any sum paid to a person on an award of income support made to him by virtue of section 23(8) of the Act [SSCBA, section 127] (effect of return to work after a trade dispute) shall be recoverable from him in accordance with this Part of these Regulations.

(2) In this Part, unless the context otherwise requires—

"available earnings" means the earnings, including any remuneration paid by or on behalf of an employer to an employee who is for the time being unable to work owing to sickness, which remain payable to a claimant on any pay-day after deduction by his employer of all amounts lawfully deductible by the employer otherwise than by virtue of a deduction notice;

"claimant" means a person to whom an award is made by virtue of section 23(8) of the Act [SSCBA, section 127];

"deduction notice" means a notice under regulation 20 or 25;

"employment" means employment (including employment which has been suspended but not terminated) in remunerative work, and related expressions shall be construed accordingly;

"pay-day" means an occasion on which earnings are paid to a claimant;

"protected earnings" means protected earnings as determined by an adjudicating authority, in accordance with regulation 19(2), under regulation 19(1)(a) or 24;

"recoverable amount" means the amount (determined in accordance with regulation 20(3) or (5) or regulation 25(2)(a)) by reference to which deductions are to be made by an employer from a claimant's earnings by virtue of a deduction notice;

"repaid by the claimant" means paid by the claimant directly to the Secretary of State by way of repayment of income support otherwise recoverable under this Part of these Regulations.

(3) Any notice or other document required or authorised to be given or sent to any person under the provisions of this Part shall be deemed to have been given or sent if it was sent by post to that person in accordance with paragraph (6) of regulation 27 where that regulation applies and, in any other case, at his ordinary or last known address or in the case of an employer at the last place of business where the claimant to which it relates is employed, and if so sent to have been given or sent on the day on which it was posted.

Award and protected earnings

19.—(1) Where an adjudicating authority determines that a person claiming income support is entitled by virtue of section 23(8) of the Act [SSCBA, section 127] (effect of return to work after a trade dispute) and makes an award to him accordingly he shall determine the claimant's protected earnings (that is to say the amount below which his actual earnings must not be reduced by any deduction made under this Part). 2.944

(2) The adjudicating authority shall include in his decision—

(a) the amount of income support awarded together with a statement that the claimant is a person entitled by virtue of section 23(8) of the Act [SSCBA, section 127] and that accordingly any sum paid to him on that award will be recoverable from him as provided in this Part;

(b) the amount of the claimant's protected earnings, and

(c) a statement of the claimant's duty under regulation 28 (duty to give notice of cessation or resumption of employment).

[1(3) The protected earnings of the claimant shall be the sum determined by—

(a) taking the sum specified in paragraph (4),

(b) adding the sum specified in paragraph (5), and

(c) subtracting from the result any child benefit which falls to be taken into account in calculating his income for the purposes of Part V of the Income Support Regulations.]

(4) The sum referred to in paragraph (3)(a) shall be the aggregate of the amounts calculated under regulation 17(a) to (d), 18(a) to (e), 20 or 21, as the case may be, of the Income Support Regulations.

(5) The sum referred to in paragraph (3)(b) shall be £27 except where the sum referred to in paragraph (3)(a) includes an amount calculated under regulation 20 in which case the sum shall be £8.00.

AMENDMENT

1. The Social Security (Payments on account, Overpayments and Recovery) Amendments Regulations 1988 (SI 1988/688) reg.2(5) (April 11, 1988).

Service and contents of deduction notices

20.—(1) Where the amount of income support has not already been repaid by the claimant, the Secretary of State shall serve a deduction notice on the employer of the claimant. 2.945

(2) A deduction notice shall contain the following particulars—
(a) particulars enabling the employer to identify the claimant;
(b) the recoverable amount;
(c) the claimant's protected earnings as specified in the notification of award.

(3) Subject to paragraph (5) the recoverable amount shall be—
(a) the amount specified in the decision as having been awarded to the claimant by way of income support; reduced by
(b) the amount (if any) which has been repaid by the claimant before the date of the deduction notice.

(4) If a further award relating to the claimant is made the Secretary of State shall cancel the deduction notice (giving written notice of the cancellation to the employer and the claimant) and serve on the employer a further deduction notice.

(5) The recoverable amount to be specified in the further deduction notice shall be the sum of—
(a) the amount determined by applying paragraph (3) to the further award; and
(b) the recoverable amount specified in the cancelled deduction notice less any part of that amount which before the date of the further notice has already been deducted by virtue of the cancelled notice or repaid by the claimant.

Period for which deduction notice has effect

2.946 **21.**—(1) A deduction notice shall come into force when it is served on the employer of the claimant to whom it relates and shall cease to have effect as soon as any of the following conditions is fulfilled—
(a) the notice is cancelled by virtue of regulation 20(4) or paragraph (2) of this regulation;
(b) the claimant ceases to be in the employment of the person on whom the notice was served;
(c) the aggregate of—
(i) any part of the recoverable amount repaid by the claimant on or after the date of the deduction notice, and
(ii) the total amount deducted by virtue of the notice,
reaches the recoverable amount;
(d) there has elapsed a period of 26 weeks beginning with the date of the notice.

(2) The Secretary of State may at any time give a direction in writing cancelling a deduction notice and—
(a) he shall cause a copy of the direction to be served on the employer concerned and on the claimant;
(b) the direction shall take effect when a copy of it is served on the employer concerned.

Effect of deduction notice

2.947 **22.**—(1) Where a deduction notice is in force the following provisions of this regulation shall apply as regards any relevant pay-day.

(2) Where a claimant's earnings include any bonus, commission or other similar payment which is paid other than on a day on which the remainder of his earnings is paid, then in order to calculate his available earnings for

the purposes of this regulation any such bonus, commission or other similar payment shall be treated as being paid to him on the next day of payment of the remainder of his earnings instead of on the day of actual payment.

(3) If on a relevant pay-day a claimant's available earnings—

(a) do not exceed his protected earnings by at least £1, no deduction shall be made;

(b) do exceed his protected earnings by at least £1, his employer shall deduct from the claimant's available earnings one half of the excess over his protected earnings,

so however that where earnings are paid other than weekly the amount of the protected earnings and the figure of £1 shall be adjusted accordingly, in particular—

(c) where earnings are paid monthly, they shall for this purpose be treated as paid every five weeks (and the protected earnings and the figure of £1 accordingly multiplied by five);

(d) where earnings are paid daily, the protected earnings and the figure of £1 shall be divided by five,

and if, in any case to which sub-paragraph (c) or (d) does not apply, there is doubt as to the adjustment to be made this shall be determined by the Secretary of State on the application of the employer or the claimant.

(4) Where on a relevant pay-day earnings are payable to the claimant in respect of more than one pay-day the amount of the protected earnings and the figure of £1 referred to in the preceding paragraph, adjusted where appropriate in accordance with the provisions of that paragraph, shall be multiplied by the number of pay-days to which the earnings relate.

(5) Notwithstanding anything in paragraph (3)—

(a) the employer shall not make a deduction on a relevant pay-day if the claimant satisfies him that up to that day he has not obtained payment of the income support to which the deduction notice relates;

(b) the employer shall not on any relevant pay-day deduct from the claimant's earnings by virtue of the deduction notice an amount greater than the excess of the recoverable amount over the aggregate of all such amounts as, in relation to that notice, are mentioned in regulation 21(1)(c)(i) and (ii); and

(c) where the amount of any deduction which by this regulation the employer is required to make would otherwise include a fraction of 1p, that amount shall be reduced by that fraction.

(6) For the purpose of this regulation "relevant pay-day" means any pay-day beginning with—

(a) the first pay-day falling after the expiration of the period of one month from the date on which the deduction notice comes into force; or

(b) if the employer so chooses, any earlier pay-day after the notice has come into force.

Increase of amount of award on appeal or [1 otherwise]

23. If the amount of the award is increased, whether on appeal or [1 other- 2.948
wise], this Part shall have effect as if on the date on which the amount of the award was increased—

(a) the amount of the increase was the recoverable amount; and

(b) the claimant's protected earnings [1, where a notice of variation of protected earnings is given under regulation 24, were the earnings stated in the notice]

AMENDMENT

1. The Social Security Act 1998 (Commencement No.12, and Consequential and Transitional Provisions) Order 1999 (SI 1999/3178) Sch.9 (November 29, 1999).

[1 Notice of variation] of protected earnings

2.949 [1 . . .] **24.**—(1) [1 . . .]

[1 (2) The Secretary of State shall give a claimant's employer written notice varying the deduction notice where a decision as to a claimant's protected earnings is revised or superseded.]

(3) Variation of a deduction notice under paragraph (2) shall take effect either from the end of the period of 10 working days beginning with the day on which notice of the variation is given to the employer or, if the employer so chooses, at any earlier time after notice is given.

AMENDMENT

1. The Social Security Act 1998 (Commencement No.12 and Consequential and Transitional Provisions) Order 1999 (SI 1999/3178) Sch.9 (November 29, 1999).

Power to serve further deduction notice on resumption of employment

2.950 **25.**—(1) Where a deduction notice has ceased to have effect by reason of the claimant ceasing to be in the employment of the person on whom the notice was served, the Secretary of State may, if he thinks fit, serve a further deduction notice on any person by whom the claimant is for the time being employed.

(2) Notwithstanding anything in the foregoing provisions of these Regulations, in any such deduction notice—

(a) the recoverable amount shall be equal to the recoverable amount as specified in the previous deduction notice less the aggregate of—
  (i) the total of any amounts required to be deducted by virtue of that notice, and
  (ii) any additional part of that recoverable amount repaid by the claimant on or after the date of that notice,

or, where this regulation applies in respect of more than one such previous notice, the aggregate of the amounts as so calculated in respect of each such notice;

(b) the amount specified as the claimant's protected earnings shall be the same as that so specified in the last deduction notice relating to him which was previously in force or as subsequently [1 varied].

AMENDMENT

1. The Social Security Act 1998 (Commencement No.12 and Consequential and Transitional Provisions) Order 1999 (SI 1999/3178) Sch.9 (November 29, 1999).

Right of Secretary of State to recover direct from claimant

2.951 **26.** Where [1, at any time, it is not practicable for the Secretary of State] by means of a deduction notice, to effect recovery of the recoverable amount or of so much of that amount as remains to be recovered from the claimant, the amount which remains to be recovered shall, by virtue of this regulation, be recoverable from the claimant by the Secretary of State.

AMENDMENT

1. The Social Security Act 1998 (Commencement No.12 and Consequential and Transitional Provisions) Order 1999 (SI 1999/3178) Sch.9 (November 29, 1999).

Duties and liabilities of employers

27.—(1) An employer shall keep a record of the available earnings of each claimant who is an employee in respect of whom a deduction notice is in force and of the payments which he makes in pursuance of the notice. 2.952

(2) A record of every deduction made by an employer under a deduction notice on any pay-day shall be given or sent by him to the Secretary of State, together with payment of the amount deduced, by not later than the 19th day of the following month.

(3) Where by reason only of the circumstances mentioned in regulation 22(5)(a) the employer makes no deduction from a claimant's weekly earnings on any pay-day he shall within 10 working days after that pay-day give notice of that fact to the Secretary of State.

(4) Where a deduction notice is cancelled by virtue of regulation 20(4) or 21(2) or ceases to have effect by virtue of regulation 21(1) the employer shall within 10 working days after the date on which the notice is cancelled or, as the case may be, ceases to have effect—

(a) return the notice to the Secretary of State and, where regulation 21(1) applies, give notice of the reason for its return;

(b) give notice, in relation to each relevant pay-day (as defined in regulation 22(6)), of the available earnings of the claimant and of any deduction made from those earnings.

(5) If on any pay-day to which regulation 22(3)(b) applies the employer makes no deduction from a claimant's available earnings, or makes a smaller deduction than he was thereby required to make, and in consequence any amount is not deducted while the deduction notice, or any further notice which under regulation 20(4) cancels that notice, has effect—

(a) the amount which is not deducted shall, without prejudice to any other method of recovery from the claimant or otherwise, be recoverable from the employer by the Secretary of State; and

(b) any amount so recovered shall, for the purposes of these Regulations, be deemed to have been repaid by the claimant.

(6) All records and notices to which this regulation applies shall given or sent to the Secretary of State, on a form approved by him, at such office of the [1Department of Social Security] as he may direct.

AMENDMENT

1. The Transfer of Functions (Health and Social Security) Order 1988 (SI 1988/1843) art.3(4) (November 28, 1988).

Claimants to give notice of cessation or resumption of employment

28.—(1) Where a claimant ceases to be in the employment of a person on whom a deduction notice relating to him has been duly served knowing that the full amount of the recoverable amount has not been deducted from his earnings or otherwise recovered by the Secretary of State, he shall give notice within 10 working days to the Secretary of State of his address and of the date of such cessation of employment. 2.953

(2) Where on or after such cessation the claimant resumes employment (whether with the same or some other employer) he shall within 10 working days give notice to the Secretary of State of the name of the employer and of the address of his place of employment.

Failure to notify

2.954 **29.** If a person fails to comply with any requirement under regulation 27 or 28 to give notice of any matter to the Secretary of State he shall be guilty of an offence and liable on summary conviction to a fine not exceeding—

(a) for any one offence, level 3 on the standard scale; or

(b) for an offence of continuing any such contravention, £40 for each day on which it is so continued.

[1 PART 8A

RECOVERY BY DEDUCTION FROM EARNINGS: OTHER CASES

Recovery by deduction from earnings: other cases

2.955 **29A.**—(1) Any amount which is recoverable by virtue of section 71(1) or (4), 71ZA or 78(1) of the Administration Act may be recovered by the Secretary of State by deduction from the earnings of the person from whom it is recoverable.

(2) Part 6 of the Social Security (Overpayments and Recovery) Regulations 2013 applies in relation to recovery by deduction from the earnings of a person specified in paragraph (1) by the Secretary of State as it applies to recovery by deduction from the earnings of persons of recoverable amounts under that Part of those Regulations by an appropriate authority.]

AMENDMENT

1. Inserted by The Social Security (Overpayments and Recovery) Regulations 2013 (SI 2013/384) reg.31(9) (April 8, 2013).

The Social Security (Payments on Account of Benefit) Regulations 2013

(SI 2013/383)

COMMENCEMENT: APRIL 1, 2013

PART 1

GENERAL

PART 2

PAYMENTS ON ACCOUNT OF BENEFIT

PART 3

BUDGETING ADVANCES

PART 4

CONSEQUENTIAL AMENDMENTS, REVOCATIONS AND SAVINGS

The Secretary of State for Work and Pensions makes the following Regulations in exercise of the powers conferred by sections 5(1)(r), 189(1), (4) to (6) and 191 of the Social Security Administration Act 1992 and section 84 of, and paragraph 9 of Schedule 2 to, the Social Security Act 1998.

In accordance with section 80(1)(b) of the Social Security Act 1998, a draft of this instrument was laid before Parliament and approved by a resolution of each House of Parliament.

This instrument contains only regulations made by virtue of, or consequential upon, sections 101(1) and 104(1) of the Welfare Reform Act 2012 and is made before the end of the period of 6 months beginning with the coming into force of those sections.

PART 1

GENERAL

Citation and commencement

2.957 **1.**—(1) These Regulations may be cited as the Social Security (Payments on Account of Benefit) Regulations 2013.

(2) They come into force—

(a) for the purposes of this Part and Part 2 (except the provisions specified in paragraph (3)) and Part 4, on 1st April 2013;

(b) for all other purposes, on 29th April 2013.

(3) The specified provisions are—

(a) in regulation 2(1)

(i) the definitions of "the UC etc. Claims and Payments Regulations", "the Universal Credit Regulations" and "universal credit";

(ii) paragraph (a) of the definition of "couple";

(b) regulation 2(2) and (3)(a);

(c) regulation 3(1)(a) and (2)(a)(i) and (b)(i);

(d) regulation 5(3)(a);

(e) regulation 7(2); and

(f) regulation 8(2).

Interpretation

2.958 **2.**—(1) In these Regulations—

"the 1995 Act" means the Jobseekers Act 1995;

"the 2007 Act" means the Welfare Reform Act 2007;

"the 2012 Act" means the Welfare Reform Act 2012;

"the Contributions and Benefits Act" means the Social Security Contributions and Benefits Act 1992;

"the 1988 Regulations" means the Social Security (Payments on account, Overpayments and Recovery) Regulations 1988;

"the Claims and Payments Regulations" means the Social Security (Claims and Payments) Regulations 1987;

[Definitions not yet in force omitted]

"partner" means, where the person being referred to is a member of a couple, the other member of the couple;

[Definition not yet in force omitted].

(2) *Omitted.*

(3) In these Regulations, "writing" includes writing produced by means of electronic communications and, where such communications are used by the Secretary of State—

(a) *Omitted.*

(b) Schedule 9ZC to the Claims and Payments Regulations,

has effect in connection with notices required to be given or sent under regulations 8 and 17 as it has effect in connection with claims for, and awards of, any benefit to which those Regulations apply.

PART 2

PAYMENTS ON ACCOUNT OF BENEFIT

Definition of "benefit"

3. (1) In this Part, "benefit" means any of the following— 2.959

(a) universal credit;
(b) employment and support allowance;
(c) income support;
(d) jobseeker's allowance;
(e) state pension credit;
(f) benefit under Parts 2 to 5 of the Contributions and Benefits Act except attendance allowance [1 , disability living allowance and guardian's allowance].

[2 (g) a state pension under Part 1 of the Pensions Act 2014.]

(2) For the purpose of paragraph (1)—

(a) "employment and support allowance" means an allowance under—
  (i) Part 1 of the 2007 Act as amended by Schedule 3, and Part 1 of Schedule 14, to the 2012 Act (to remove references to an income-related allowance); and
  (ii) Part 1 of the 2007 Act as it has effect apart from the amendments made by Schedule 3, and Part 1 of Schedule 14, to the 2012 Act;
(b) "jobseeker's allowance" means an allowance under—
  (i) the 1995 Act as amended by Part 1 of Schedule 14 to the 2012 Act (to remove references to an income-based allowance); and
  (ii) the 1995 Act as it has effect apart from the amendments made by Part 1 of Schedule 14 to the 2012 Act.

AMENDMENTS

1. The Social Security (Miscellaneous Amendments) (No. 2) Regulations 2013 (SI 2013/1508) reg.7(2) (July 29, 2013).
2. The Pensions Act 2014 (Consequential, Supplementary and Incidental Amendments) Order 2015 (SI 2015/1985) art.41 (April 6, 2016).

Payments on account of benefit

4.—(1) The Secretary of State may, subject to paragraph (2), make a payment on account of benefit to a person ("A") in accordance with this Part. 2.960

(2) Paragraph (1) does not apply pending the determination of an appeal relating to the benefit on account of which the payment would otherwise have been made.

Payment on account of benefit where there is no award of benefit

5.—(1) The Secretary of State may make a payment on account of benefit to A if— 2.961

(a) either of paragraphs (2) or (3) applies;
(b) it appears to the Secretary of State likely that the conditions of

entitlement for benefit are satisfied [1 (or will be satisfied during the period in respect of which the payment is to be made)]; and

(c) the Secretary of State is satisfied that A is in financial need.

(2) This paragraph applies where A has made a claim for benefit but the claim has not yet been determined.

(3) This paragraph applies where A is not required to make a claim for benefit by virtue of—

(a) *Omitted.*

(b) regulation 3 of the Claims and Payments Regulations (claims not required for entitlement to benefit in certain cases) (16),

but an award of benefit has not yet been made.

AMENDMENT

1. The Universal Credit and Miscellaneous Amendments (No. 2) Regulations 2014 (SI 2014/2888), reg.5(1)(a) (November 26, 2014).

Payment on account of benefit where there is an award of benefit

2.962 6.—(1) The Secretary of State may make a payment on account of benefit to A if—

(a) an award of benefit has been made to A;

(b) any of paragraphs (2) to (5) applies; and

(c) the Secretary of State is satisfied that A is in financial need.

(2) This paragraph applies where—

(a) A currently satisfies the conditions of entitlement to that benefit; and

(b) the date on which the first payment of that benefit to A is due to be made in accordance with the award has not yet been reached.

(3) This paragraph applies where—

(a) the first payment of that benefit has been made to A in accordance with the award;

(b) the period in respect of which that payment was made is shorter than the period in respect of which subsequent payments of that benefit are to be made in accordance with that award should entitlement continue; and

(c) the date on which a subsequent payment of that benefit is due to be made to A has not yet been reached.

(4) This paragraph applies where there has been a change of circumstances which would increase the amount of benefit payable under the award and—

(a) the award has not yet been revised or superseded to reflect that change; or

(b) the award has been revised or superseded to reflect that change but the date on which the payment of benefit is due to be made in accordance with the revised or superseded award has not yet been reached.

(5) This paragraph applies where—

(a) A is entitled to a payment of that benefit pursuant to the award; and

(b) it is impracticable to make some or all of that payment on the day on which it is due.

Definition of financial need

2.963 7.—(1) A is in financial need for the purposes of regulation 5(1)(c) or 6(1)(c) where the circumstances in regulation 5(2) or (3) or, as the case may be, 6(2), (3), (4) or (5) result in a serious risk of damage to the health or safety of A or any member of their family.

(2) *Omitted.*

(3) Where the payment on account of benefit is to be on account of a benefit specified in regulation 3(1)(b) to [1 (g)], for the purpose of paragraph (1), "family" has the meaning given in section 137(1) of the Contributions and Benefits Act.

AMENDMENT

1. The Pensions Act 2014 (Consequential, Supplementary and Incidental Amendments) Order 2015 (SI 2015/1985) art.41 (April 6, 2016).

Requirement for notice

8.—(1) The Secretary of State must, on or before making a payment on account of benefit to A, give or send notice in writing to A of their liability— **2.964**

(a) to have the amount of the payment on account of benefit deducted from subsequent payments of benefit; and

(b) to repay the amount of any payment on account of benefit to the extent that it is not deducted from subsequent payments of benefit.

(2) *Omitted.*

[1 "Payment by direct credit transfer

9. A payment on account of benefit may be paid by way of direct credit transfer into a bank account or other account nominated by A or a person acting on A's behalf.] **2.965**

AMENDMENT

1. The Universal Credit and Miscellaneous Amendments (No. 2) Regulations 2014 (SI 2014/2888), reg.5(1)(b) (November 26, 2014).

Bringing payments on account of benefit into account

10. Where it is practicable to do so, a payment on account of benefit— **2.966**

(a) which was made in anticipation of an award of benefit, is to be offset by the Secretary of State against the sum payable to A under the award of benefit on account of which it was made;

(b) whether or not made in anticipation of an award, which is not offset under paragraph (a), is to be deducted by the Secretary of State from—

(i) the sum payable to A under the award of benefit on account of which it was made; or

(ii) any sum payable under any subsequent award of that benefit to A.

PART 3

BUDGETING ADVANCES

Payment of budgeting advances

11.—(1) The Secretary of State may make a payment on account of universal credit to a person ("B") in accordance with this Part. **2.967**

(2) A payment under this Part is to be known as a budgeting advance.

(a) the penalty applies where it appears to the Secretary of State or authority that there are grounds for instituting proceedings against the person for an offence relating to an act or omission on the part of the person in relation to any benefit;
(b) if an overpayment attributable to the act or omission had been made, the overpayment would have been recoverable under section 71, 71ZB, 71A, 75 or 76 of the 1992 Act;
(c) the penalty is £350;
(d) a person who agrees to pay the penalty may withdraw the agreement within 14 days (including the date of the agreement) by notifying the Secretary of State or authority in the manner specified by the Secretary of State or authority; if the person withdraws the agreement, so much of the penalty as has already been recovered shall be repaid and he will no longer be immune from proceedings for an offence;
(e) if it is decided on review or appeal (or in accordance with regulations) that any overpayment attributable to the act or omission would not have been recoverable or due, so much of the penalty as has already been recovered shall be repaid;
(f) the payment of a penalty does not give the person immunity from prosecution in relation to any overpayment or any other offence not relating to an overpayment.]

(2) The notice [1 in either case] shall set out–
(a) the manner specified by the Secretary of State or authority by which the person may agree to pay a penalty;
(b) the manner specified by the Secretary of State or authority by which the person may notify the withdrawal of his agreement to pay a penalty.

AMENDMENT

1. The Social Security (Miscellaneous Amendments) Regulations 2014 (SI 2014/591) reg.5 (April 28, 2014).

GENERAL NOTE

2.980 Regulation 4(5) of The Social Security (Miscellaneous Amendments) Regulations 2014 provides that the amendments made by these regulations shall apply "only where the offence in respect of which the notice is given is committed wholly on or after 8th May 2012."

The Social Security (Persons Required to Provide Information) Regulations 2013

(SI 2013/1510)

IN FORCE OCTOBER 1, 2013

ARRANGEMENT OF REGULATIONS

The Secretary of State for Work and Pensions makes the following Regulations in exercise of the powers conferred by sections 109B(2)(ia), 189(1) and (5) and 191 of the Social Security Administration Act 1992.

In accordance with section 176(1) of that Act, the Secretary of State has consulted with organisations appearing to him to be representative of the authorities concerned.

This instrument has not been referred to the Social Security Advisory Committee because it contains only regulations made by virtue of section 110 of the Welfare Reform Act 2012 and is made before the end of the period of 6 months beginning with the coming into force of that section.

Citation and commencement

1. (1) These Regulations may be cited as the Social Security (Persons Required to Provide Information) Regulations 2013. 2.982

(2) They come into force on 1st October 2013.

Persons required to provide information

2. (1) The following are prescribed as descriptions of persons for the purpose of section 109B(2)(ia) of the Social Security Administration Act 1992 (power of authorised officers to require information)— 2.983

(a) a person who provides relevant childcare;

(b) a person to whom a person in receipt of universal credit ("C") is liable to make rent payments in respect of accommodation which C occupies, or purports to occupy, as their home where C's award of universal credit includes an amount in respect of such payments;

(c) a rent officer to the extent that the information required relates to the rent officer's functions under section 122 of the Housing Act 1996;

(d) a local authority which administers a council tax reduction scheme to the extent that the information required relates to such a scheme.

(2) In this regulation—

(a) "UC Regulations" means the Universal Credit Regulations 2013(**5**);

(b) "council tax reduction scheme"—

(i) in England and Wales, has the meaning given in section 13A(9) of the Local Government Finance Act 1992 and includes a default scheme within the meaning of paragraph 4 of Schedule

1A (or in Wales paragraph 6(1)(e) of Schedule 1B) to that Act; and
(ii) in Scotland, means a means-tested reduction to an individual's council tax liability in accordance with the Council Tax Reduction (Scotland) Regulations 2012 or the Council Tax Reduction (State Pension Credit) (Scotland) Regulations 2012;
(c) "relevant childcare" has the meaning given in regulation 35 of the UC Regulations;
(d) "rent payments" has the meaning given in paragraph 2 of Schedule 1 to the UC Regulations;
(e) "universal credit" means universal credit under Part 1 of the Welfare Reform Act 2012.

The Social Security Act 1998 (Prescribed Benefits) Regulations 2006

(SI 2006/2529)

Made	*14th September 2006*
Laid before Parliament	*21st September 2006*
Coming into force	*16th October 2006*

2.984 The Secretary of State for Work and Pensions makes the following Regulations in exercise of the powers conferred by sections 8(3)(h), 79(1) and 84 of the Social Security Act 1998.

In accordance with section 173(1)(b) of the Social Security Administration Act 1992, the Secretary of State has obtained the agreement of the Social Security Advisory Committee that proposals in respect of these Regulations need not be referred to it.

Citation and commencement

2.985 **1.**—(1) These Regulations may be cited as the Social Security Act 1998 (Prescribed Benefits) Regulations 2006 and shall come into force on 16th October 2006.

Prescribed benefits

2.986 **2.** The benefits prescribed for the purposes of section 8(3)(h) of the Social Security Act 1998 (decisions by Secretary of State) are—
(a) the following benefits under the Social Security Act 1975—
(i) sickness benefit under section 14;
(ii) unemployment benefit under section 14;
(iii) invalidity pension under section 15;
(iv) invalidity allowance under section 16;
(v) attendance allowance under section 35; and
(vi) mobility allowance under section 37A;
(b) supplementary benefit under the Supplementary Benefit Act 1976.

GENERAL NOTE

2.987 Except for attendance allowance, the benefits listed are benefits that had been abolished before the Social Security Act 1998 Act came into force and are therefore not within the scope of s.8(3)(a) to (g) of that Act. Attendance allowance has presumably been included from an abundance of caution because it is now payable only to people over the age of 65, whereas until 1992 it was payable to younger people.

The need for this provision was revealed by *CDLA/2999/2004*, in which it was held that, because the transitional provision made when the 1998 Act came into force relies on the concept of a "relevant benefit" as defined by s.8(3), there was no power to make a supersession decision under s.10 of the 1998 Act in respect of mobility allowance, with the consequence that an overpayment of mobility allowance could not be recovered under s.71 of the Social Security Administration Act 1992. It is not entirely clear why the scope of s.8(3) of the 1998 Act has not been made precisely the same as the scope of s.71 of the 1992 Act (see para.4(1) of Sch.10 to the 1992 Act) but perhaps it was thought unlikely that any wider prescription would be required in practice. It is doubtful that the omission of the second "s" from the short title of the Supplementary Benefits Act 1976 is significant.

The Employment Protection (Recoupment of [Benefits]) Regulations 1996

(SI 1996/2349)

Made	*10th September 1996*
Laid before Parliament	*11th September 1996*
Coming into force	*7th October 1996*

The Secretary of State in exercise of the powers conferred on him by section 16 and section 41(4) of the Industrial Tribunals Act 1996, section 58(1) of the Social Security Administration Act 1992, and of all other powers enabling him in that behalf, and after reference to the Social Security Advisory Committee in so far as is required by section 172 of the Social Security Administration Act 1992, and after consultation with the Council on Tribunals, in so far as is required by section 8 of the Tribunals and Inquiries Act 1992, hereby makes the following Regulations:— 2.988

PART I

INTRODUCTORY

Citation and Commencement

1. These Regulations may be cited as the Employment Protection (Recoupment of [1 Benefits] Regulations 1996 and shall come into force on 7th October 1996. 2.989

AMENDMENT

1. Universal Credit (Consequential, Supplementary, Incidental and Miscellaneous Provisions) Regulations 2013 (SI 2013/630) reg.50(1) and (3) (April 29, 2013).

GENERAL NOTE

These Regulations began life as the Employment Protection (Recoupment of Jobseeker's Allowance and Income Support) Regulations 1996 and were renamed 2.990

when they were extended to universal credit, although they had already been extended to income-related (but not contributory) employment and support allowance without a change of name.

Interpretation

2.991 **2.**—(1) In these Regulations, unless the context otherwise requires, the following expressions have the meanings hereby assigned to them respectively, that is to say—

"the 1992 Act" means the Trade Union and Labour Relations (Consolidation) Act 1992;

"the 1996 Act" means the Employment Rights Act 1996;

"prescribed element" has the meaning assigned to it in Regulation 3 below and the Schedule to these Regulations;

"protected period" has the same meaning as in section 189(5) of the 1992 Act;

"protective award" has the same meaning as in section 189(3) of the 1992 Act;

"recoupable benefit" means any jobseeker's allowance [2 , income-related employment and support allowance] [3 , universal credit] or income support as the case may be, which is recoupable under these Regulations;

"recoupment notice" means a notice under these Regulations;

"Secretary of the Tribunals" means the Secretary of the Central Office of the [1 Employment] Tribunals (England and Wales) or, as the case may require, the Secretary of the Central Office of the [1 Employment] Tribunals (Scotland) for the time being;

[3 "universal credit" means universal credit under Part 1 of the Welfare Reform Act 2012]

(2) In the Schedule to these Regulations references to sections are references to sections of the 1996 Act unless otherwise indicated and references in column 3 of the table to the conclusion of the tribunal proceedings are references to the conclusion of the proceedings mentioned in the corresponding entry in column 2.

(3) For the purposes of these Regulations (and in particular for the purposes of any calculations to be made by an [1 employment tribunal] as respects the prescribed element) the conclusion of the tribunal proceedings shall be taken to occur—

(a) where the [1 employment tribunal] at the hearing announces the effect of its decision to the parties, on the date on which that announcement is made;

(b) in any other case, on the date on which the decision of the tribunal is sent to the parties.

(4) References to parties in relevant [1 employment tribunal] proceedings shall be taken to include references to persons appearing on behalf of parties in a representative capacity.

(5) References in these Regulations to anything done, or to be done, in, or in consequence of, any tribunal proceedings include references to anything done, or to be done, in, or in consequence of any such proceedings as are in the nature of a review, or re-hearing or a further hearing consequent on an appeal.

AMENDMENTS

1. Employment Rights (Dispute Resolution) Act 1998, s.1(2)(a) (August 1, 1998).
2. Social Security (Miscellaneous Amendments) (No.5) Regulations 2010 (SI 2010/2429) reg.5 (November 1, 2010).
3. Universal Credit (Consequential, Supplementary, Incidental and Miscellaneous Provisions) Regulations 2013 (SI 2013/630) reg.50(1) and (4) (April 29, 2013).

PART II

INDUSTRIAL TRIBUNAL PROCEEDINGS

Application to payments and proceedings

3.—(1) Subject to paragraph (2) below these Regulations apply— 2.992
(a) to the payments described in column 1 of the table contained in the Schedule to these Regulations, being, in each case, payments which are the subject of [1 employment tribunal] proceedings of the kind described in the corresponding entry in column 2 and the prescribed element in relation to each such payment is so much of the relevant monetary award as is attributable to the matter described in the corresponding entry in column 3; and
(b) to payments of remuneration in pursuance of a protective award.

(2) The payments to which these Regulations apply by virtue of paragraph (1)(a) above include payments in proceedings under section 192 of the 1992 Act and, accordingly, where an order is made on an employee's complaint under that section, the relevant protective award shall, as respects that employee and to the appropriate extent, be taken to be subsumed in the order made under section 192 so that the provisions of these Regulations relating to monetary awards shall apply to payments under that order to the exclusion of the provisions relating to protective awards, but without prejudice to anything done under the latter in connection with the relevant protective award before the making of the order under section 192.

AMENDMENT

1. Employment Rights (Dispute Resolution) Act 1998 s.1(2)(a) (August 1, 1998).

Duties of the [1 employment tribunals] and of the Secretary of the Tribunals in respect of monetary awards

4.—(1) Where these Regulations apply, no regard shall be had, in assessing the amount of a monetary award, to the amount of any jobseeker's allowance [2 , income-related employment and support allowance] [3 , universal credit] or any income support which may have been paid to or claimed by the employee for a period which coincides with any part of a period to which the prescribed element is attributable. 2.993

(2) Where the [1 employment tribunal] in arriving at a monetary award makes a reduction on account of the employee's contributory fault or on account of any limit imposed by or under the 1992 Act or 1996 Act, a proportionate reduction shall be made in arriving at the amount of the prescribed element.

(3) Subject to the following provisions of this Regulation it shall be the duty of the [1 employment tribunal] to set out in any decision which includes a monetary award the following particulars—

(a) the monetary award;
(b) the amount of the prescribed element, if any;
(c) the dates of the period to which the prescribed element is attributable;
(d) the amount, if any, by which the monetary award exceeds the prescribed element.

(4) Where the [1 employment tribunal] at the hearing announces to the parties the effect of a decision which includes a monetary award it shall inform those parties at the same time of the amount of any prescribed element included in the monetary award and shall explain the effect of Regulations 7 and 8 below in relation to the prescribed element.

(5) Where the [1 employment tribunal] has made such an announcement as is described in paragraph (4) above the Secretary of the Tribunals shall forthwith notify the Secretary of State that the tribunal has decided to make a monetary award including a prescribed element and shall notify him of the particulars set out in paragraph (3) above.

(6) As soon as reasonably practicable after the Secretary of the Tribunals has sent a copy of a decision containing the particulars set out in paragraph (3) above to the parties he shall send a copy of that decision to the Secretary of State.

(7) In addition to containing the particulars required under paragraph (3) above, any such decision as is mentioned in that paragraph shall contain a statement explaining the effect of Regulations 7 and 8 below in relation to the prescribed element.

(8) The requirements of paragraphs (3) to (7) above do not apply where the tribunal is satisfied that in respect of each day falling within the period to which the prescribed element relates the employee has neither received nor claimed jobseeker's allowance [2 , income-related employment and support allowance] [3 , universal credit] or income support.

AMENDMENTS

1. Employment Rights (Dispute Resolution) Act 1998 s.1(2)(a) (August 1, 1998).

2. Social Security (Miscellaneous Amendments) (No.5) Regulations 2010 (SI 2010/2429) reg.5 (November 1, 2010).

3. Universal Credit (Consequential, Supplementary, Incidental and Miscellaneous Provisions) Regulations 2013 (SI 2013/630) reg.50(1) and (5) (April 29, 2013).

Duties of the [1 employment tribunals] and of the Secretary of the Tribunals in respect of protective awards

2.994 **5.** (1) Where, on a complaint under section 189 of the 1992 Act, an [1 employment tribunal]—

(a) at the hearing announces to the parties the effect of a decision to make a protective award; or
(b) (where it has made no such announcement) sends a decision to make such an award to the parties; the Secretary of the Tribunals shall forthwith notify the Secretary of State of the following particulars relating to the award—
   (i) where the [1 employment tribunal] has made such an announcement as is described in paragraph (1)(a) above, the date of the

hearing or where it has made no such announcement, the date on which the decision was sent to the parties;
(ii) the location of the tribunal;
(iii) the name and address of the employer;
(iv) the description of the employees to whom the award relates; and
(v) the dates of the protected period.

(2)(a) Where an [1 employment tribunal] makes such an announcement as is described in paragraph (1)(a) above in the presence of the employer or his representative it shall advise him of his duties under Regulation 6 below and shall explain the effect of Regulations 7 and 8 below in relation to remuneration under the protective award.

(b) Without prejudice to (a) above any decision of an [1 employment tribunal] to make a protective award under section 189 of the 1992 Act shall contain a statement advising the employer of his duties under Regulation 6 below and an explanation of the effect of Regulations 7 and 8 below in relation to remuneration under the protective award.

AMENDMENT

1. Employment Rights (Dispute Resolution) Act 1998 s.1(2)(a) (August 1, 1998).

Duties of the employer to give information about protective awards

6.—(1) Where an [1 employment tribunal] makes a protective award under section 189 of the 1992 Act against an employer, the employer shall give to the Secretary of State the following information in writing— 2.995
(a) the name, address and national insurance number of every employee to whom the award relates; and
(b) the date of termination (or proposed termination) of the employment of each such employee.

(2) Subject to paragraph (3) below the employer shall comply with paragraph (1) above within the period of ten days commencing on the day on which the [1 employment tribunal] at the hearing announces to the parties the effect of a decision to make a protective award or (in the case where no such announcement is made) on the day on which the relevant decision is sent to the parties.

(3) Where, in any case, it is not reasonably practicable for the employer to comply with paragraph (1) above within the period applicable under paragraph (2) above he shall comply as soon as reasonably practicable after the expiration of that period.

AMENDMENT

1. Employment Rights (Dispute Resolution) Act 1998 s.1(2)(a) (August 1, 1998).

PART III

RECOUPMENT OF BENEFIT

Postponement of Awards

7.—(1) This Regulation shall have effect for the purpose of postponing relevant awards in order to enable the Secretary of State to initiate recoupment under Regulation 8 below. 2.996

(2) Accordingly—

(a) so much of the monetary award as consists of the prescribed element;

(b) payment of any remuneration to which an employee would otherwise be entitled under a protective award, shall be treated as stayed (in Scotland, sisted) as respects the relevant employee until—

(i) the Secretary of State has served a recoupment notice on the employer; or

(ii) the Secretary of State has notified the employer in writing that he does not intend to serve a recoupment notice.

(3) The stay or sist under paragraph (2) above is without prejudice to the right of an employee under section 192 of the 1992 Act to present a complaint to an [1 employment tribunal] of his employer's failure to pay remuneration under a protective award and Regulation 3(2) above has effect as respects any such complaint and as respects any order made under section 192(3) of that Act.

AMENDMENT

1. Employment Rights (Dispute Resolution) Act 1998 s.1(2)(a) (August 1, 1998).

Recoupment of Benefit

2.997 **8.**—(1) Recoupment shall be initiated by the Secretary of State serving on the employer a recoupment notice claiming by way of total or partial recoupment of jobseeker's allowance [1 , income-related employment and support allowance] [2 , universal credit] or income support the appropriate amount, computed, as the case may require, under paragraph (2) or (3) below.

(2) In the case of monetary awards the appropriate amount shall be whichever is the less of the following two sums—

(a) the amount of the prescribed element (less any tax or social security contributions which fall to be deducted therefrom by the employer); or

(b) [2 (i)] the amount paid by way of or paid as on account of jobseeker's allowance [1 , income-related employment and support allowance] or income support to the employee for any period which coincides with any part of the period to which the prescribed element is attributable. [2 ; or

(ii) in the case of an employee entitled to an award of universal credit for any period ("the UC period") which coincides with any part of the period to which the prescribed element is attributable, any amount paid by way of or on account of universal credit for the UC period that would not have been paid if the person's earned income for that period was the same as immediately before the period to which the prescribed element is attributable].

(3) In the case of remuneration under a protective award the appropriate amount shall be whichever is the less of the following two sums—

(a) the amount (less any tax or social security contributions which fall to be deducted therefrom by the employer) accrued due to the employee in respect of so much of the protected period as falls before the date on which the Secretary of State receives from the employer the information required under Regulation 6 above; or

(b) [2 (i)] the amount paid by way of or paid as on account of jobseeker's allowance [1 , income-related employment and support allowance] or income support to the employee for any period which coincides with any part of the protected period falling before the date described in (a) above [2; or

(ii) in the case of an employee entitled to an award of universal credit for any period ("the UC period") which coincides with any part of the protected period falling before the date described in (a) above, any amount paid by way of or on account of universal credit for the UC period that would not have been paid if the person's earned income for that period was the same as immediately before the protected period].

(4) A recoupment notice shall be served on the employer by post or otherwise and copies shall likewise be sent to the employee and, if requested, to the Secretary of the Tribunals.

(5) The Secretary of State shall serve a recoupment notice on the employer, or notify the employer that he does not intend to serve such a notice, within the period applicable, as the case may require, under paragraph (6) or (7) below, or as soon as practicable thereafter.

(6) In the case of a monetary award the period shall be—

(a) in any case in which the tribunal at the hearing announces to the parties the effect of its decision as described in Regulation 4(4) above, the period ending 21 days after the conclusion of the hearing or the period ending 9 days after the decision has been sent to the parties, whichever is the later; or

(b) in any other case, the period ending 21 days after the decision has been sent to the parties.

(7) In the case of a protective award the period shall be the period ending 21 days after the Secretary of State has received from the employer the information required under Regulation 6 above.

(8) A recoupment notice served on an employer shall operate as an instruction to the employer to pay, by way of deduction out of the sum due under the award, the recoupable amount to the Secretary of State and it shall be the duty of the employer to comply with the notice. The employer's duty under this paragraph shall not affect his obligation to pay any balance that may be due to the employee under the relevant award.

(9) The duty imposed on the employer by service of the recoupment notice shall not be discharged by payment of the recoupable amount to the employee during the postponement period or thereafter if a recoupment notice is served on the employer during the said period.

(10) Payment by the employer to the Secretary of State under this Regulation shall be a complete discharge in favour of the employer as against the employee in respect of any sum so paid but without prejudice to any rights of the employee under Regulation 10 below.

(11) The recoupable amount shall be recoverable by the Secretary of State from the employer as a debt.

[2 (12) For the purposes of paragraphs (2)(b)(ii) and (3)(b)(ii), "earned income" has the meaning given in regulation 52 of the Universal Credit Regulations 2013.]

AMENDMENTS

1. Social Security (Miscellaneous Amendments) (No.5) Regulations 2010 (SI 2010/2429) reg.5 (November 1, 2010).

2. Universal Credit (Consequential, Supplementary, Incidental and Miscellaneous Provisions) Regulations 2013 (SI 2013/630) reg.50(1) and (6) (April 29, 2013).

GENERAL NOTE

2.998 When assessing compensation, an employment tribunal must make a gross award, ignoring any jobseeker's allowance, income-related employment and support allowance, universal credit or income support paid to the employee during the relevant period, (reg.4(1)) and must give the Secretary of State details of the award (regs 4 and 5). The award is then postponed under reg.7 to allow the Secretary of State to recoup under reg.8 from the employer the amount of the relevant benefits paid to the employee during the relevant period. Note that contributory employment and support allowance cannot be recouped. The relevant period is the period in respect of which compensation for loss of pay or arrears of pay is awarded but ends at the date of the employment tribunal's decision if the award covers a period in the future (reg.3 and Sch. and see *Homan v A1 Bacon Co Ltd* [1996] I.C.R. 721). The Secretary of State serves a recoupment notice on the employer who must pay the recoupable amount to the Secretary of State, by way of deduction out of the sum due under the award, and then pay the balance of the award to the employee (reg.8(8)). An employee may give notice to the Secretary of State that he does not accept the amount specified in the recoupment notice (reg.10(1)) and may appeal to the First-tier Tribunal against any decision of the Secretary of State in response to such a notice (reg.10(2B)).

Order made in secondary proceedings

2.999 **9.**—(1) In the application of any of the above provisions in the case of—

(a) proceedings for an award under section 192 of the 1992 Act; or
(b) proceedings in the nature of a review, a re-hearing or a further hearing consequent on an appeal,

it shall be the duty of the [1 employment tribunal] or, as the case may require, the Secretary of State, to take the appropriate account of anything done under or in consequence of these Regulations in relation to any award made in the original proceedings.

(2) For the purposes of this Regulation the original proceedings are—

(a) where paragraph (1)(a) above applies the proceedings under section 189 of the 1992 Act; or
(b) where paragraph (1)(b) above applies the proceedings in respect of which the re-hearing, the review or the further hearing consequent on an appeal takes place.

AMENDMENT

1. Employment Rights (Dispute Resolution) Act 1998 s.1(2)(a) (August 1, 1998).

PART IV

DETERMINATION [2 . . .] OF BENEFIT RECOUPED

Provisions relating to determination of amount paid by way of or paid as on account of benefit

2.1000 **10.**—(1) Without prejudice to the right of the Secretary of State to recover from an employer the recoupable benefit, an employee on whom a copy of a recoupment notice has been served in accordance with Regulation 8 above may, within 21 days of the date on which such notice was served on him or within such further time as the Secretary of State may for special reasons allow, give notice in writing to the Secretary of State that he does not accept that the amount specified in the recoupment notice in respect of jobseeker's allowance [4 , income-related employment and support allowance] [5 , universal credit] or income support is correct.

[2 (2) Where an employee has given notice in writing to the Secretary of State under paragraph (1) above that he does not accept that an amount specified in the recoupment notice is correct, the Secretary of State shall make a decision as to the amount of jobseeker's allowance [4 , income-related employment and support allowance] [5 , universal credit] or, as the case may be, income support paid in respect of the period to which the prescribed element is attributable or, as appropriate, in respect of so much of the protected period as falls before the date on which the employer complies with Regulation 6 above.

(2A) The Secretary of State may revise either upon application made for the purpose or on his own initiative a decision under paragraph (2) above.

(2B) The employee shall have a right of appeal to [3 the First-tier Tribunal] against a decision of the Secretary of State whether as originally made under paragraph (2) or as revised under paragraph (2A) above.

(2C) The Social Security and Child Support (Decisions and Appeals) Regulations 1999 shall apply for the purposes of paragraphs (2A) and (2B) above as though a decision of the Secretary of State under paragraph (2A) above were made under section 9 of the 1998 Act and any appeal from such a decision were made under section 12 of that Act.

(2D) In this Regulation "the 1998 Act" means the Social Security Act 1998.

(3) Where the Secretary of State recovers too much money from an employer under these Regulations the Secretary of State shall pay to the employee an amount equal to the excess.]

(4) In any case where, after the Secretary of State has recovered from an employer any amount by way of recoupment of benefit, the decision given by the [1 employment tribunal] in consequence of which such recoupment took place is set aside or varied on appeal or on a re-hearing by the industrial tribunal, the Secretary of State shall make such repayment to the employer or payment to the employee of the whole or part of the amount recovered as he is satisfied should properly be made having regard to the decision given on appeal or re-hearing.

Amendments

1. Employment Rights (Dispute Resolution) Act 1998 s.1(2)(a) (August 1, 1998).

2. The Social Security Act 1998 (Commencement No.12 and Consequential and Transitional Provisions) Order 1999 (SI 1999/3178) (November 29, 1999).

3. Tribunals, Courts and Enforcement Act 2007 (Transitional and Consequential Provisions Order 2008 (SI 2008/2683) Sch.1 para.73 (November 3, 2008).

4. Social Security (Miscellaneous Amendments) (No.5) Regulations 2010 (SI 2010/2429) reg.5 (November 1, 2010).

5. Universal Credit (Consequential, Supplementary, Incidental and Miscellaneous Provisions) Regulations 2013 (SI 2013/630) reg.50(1) and (7) (April 29, 2013).

General Note

The jurisdiction of the Secretary of State and the tribunal is confined to the question of the amount of jobseeker's allowance, income-related employment and support allowance , universal credit or income support paid in respect of the relevant period. In *R(JSA) 3/03*, it was held that no reduction could be made to the recoupable amount to take account of the loss of tax credits caused by the loss of employment. Presumably the loss of such benefits can be claimed from the employer as a head of compensation (see *Neal v Bingle* [1998] Q.B. 466). 2.1001

Revocation and Transition Provision

2.1002 **11.** *Omitted.*

SCHEDULE **Regulation 3**

2.1003 TABLE RELATING TO MONETARY AWARDS

Column 1	**Column 2**	**Column 3**
Payment	**Proceedings**	**Matter to which prescribed element is attributable**
1. Guarantee payments under section 28.	1. Complaint under section 34.	1. Any amount found to be due to the employee and ordered to be paid under section 34(3) for a period before the conclusion of the tribunal proceedings.
2. Payments under any collective agreement having regard to which the appropriate Minister has made an exemption order under section 35.	2. Complaint under section 35(4).	2. Any amount found to be due to the employee and ordered to be paid under section 34(3), as applied by section 35(4), for a period before the conclusion of the tribunal proceedings.
3. Payments of remuneration in respect of a period of suspension on medical grounds under section 64 and section 108(2).	3. Complaint under section 70.	3. Any amount found to be due to the employee and ordered to be paid under section 70(3) for a period before the conclusion of the tribunal proceedings.
4. Payments of remuneration in respect of a period of suspension on maternity grounds under section 68.	4. Complaint under section 70.	4. Any amount found to be due to the employee and ordered to be paid under section 70(3) for a period before the conclusion of the tribunal proceedings.
5. Payments under an order for reinstatement under section 114(1).	5. Complaint of unfair dismissal under section 111(1).	5. Any amount ordered to be paid under section 114(2)(a) in respect of arrears of pay for a period before the conclusion of the tribunal proceedings.
6. Payments under an order for re-engagement under section 117(8).	6. Complaint of unfair dismissal under section 111(1).	6. Any amount ordered to be paid under section 115(2)(d) in respect of arrears of pay for a period before the conclusion of the tribunal proceedings.
7. Payments under an award of compensation for unfair dismissal in cases falling under section 112(4) (cases where no order for reinstatement or re-engagement has been made).	7. Complaint of unfair dismissal under section 111(1).	7. Any amount ordered to be paid and calculated under section 123 in respect of compensation for loss of wages for a period before the conclusion of the tribunal proceedings.
8. Payments under an award of compensation for unfair dismissal under	8. Proceedings in respect of non-compliance with order.	8. Any amount ordered to be paid and calculated under section 123 in

Column 1	Column 2	Column 3
Payment	**Proceedings**	**Matter to which prescribed element is attributable**
section 117(3) where reinstatement order not complied with.		respect of compensation for loss of wages for a period before the conclusion of the tribunal proceedings.
9. Payments under an award of compensation for unfair dismissal under section 117(3) where re-engagement order not complied with.	9. Proceedings in respect of non-compliance with order.	9. Any amount ordered to be paid and calculated under section 123 in respect of compensation for loss of wages for a period before the conclusion of the tribunal proceedings.
10. Payments under an interim order for reinstatement under section 163(4) of the 1992 Act.	10. Proceedings on an application for an order for interim relief under section 161(1) of the 1992 Act.	10. Any amount found to be due to the complainant and ordered to be paid in respect of arrears of pay for the period between the date of termination of employment and the conclusion of the tribunal proceedings.
11. Payments under an interim order for re-engagement under section 163(5)(a) of the 1992 Act.	11. Proceedings on an application for an order for interim relief under section 161(1) of the 1992 Act.	11. Any amount found to be due to the complainant and ordered to be paid in respect of arrears of pay for the period between the date of termination of employment and the conclusion of the tribunal proceedings.
12. Payments under an order for the continuation of a contract of employment under section 163(5)(b) of the 1992 Act where employee reasonably refuses re-engagement.	12. Proceedings on an application for an order for interim relief under section 161(1) of the 1992 Act.	12. Any amount found to be due to the complainant and ordered to be paid in respect of arrears of pay for the period between the date of termination of employment and the conclusion of the tribunal proceedings.
13. Payments under an order for the continuation of a contract of employment under section 163(6) of the 1992 Act where employer fails to attend or is unwilling to reinstate or re-engage.	13. Proceedings on an application for an order for interim relief under section 161(1) of the 1992 Act.	13. Any amount found to be due to the complainant and ordered to be paid in respect of arrears of pay for the period between the date of termination of employment and the conclusion of the tribunal proceedings.
14. Payments under an order for the continuation of a contract of employment under sections 166(1) and (2) of the 1992 Act where reinstatement or re-engagement order not complied with.	14. Proceedings in respect of non-compliance with order.	14. Any amount ordered to be paid to the employee by way of compensation under section 166(1)(b) of the 1992 Act for loss of wages for the period between the date of termination of employment and the conclusion of the tribunal proceedings.
15. Payments under an order for compensation under sections 166(3)–(5) of the 1992 Act where	15. Proceedings in respect of non-compliance with order.	15. Any amount ordered to be paid to the employee by way of compensation under section 166(3)–(4) of the 1992

Column 1	Column 2	Column 3
Payment	**Proceedings**	**Matter to which prescribed element is attributable**
order for the continuation of contract of employment not complied with.		Act for loss of wages for the period between the date of termination of employment and the conclusion of the tribunal proceedings.
16. Payments under an order under section 192(3) of the 1992 Act on employer's default in respect of remuneration due to employee under protective award. proceedings.	16. Complaint under section 192(1) of the 1992 Act.	16. Any amount ordered to be paid to the employee in respect of so much of the relevant protected period as falls before the date of the conclusion of the tribunal

The Social Security (Recovery of Benefits) Regulations 1997

(SI 1997/2205)

ARRANGEMENT OF REGULATIONS

The Secretary of State for Social Security, in exercise of the powers conferred by section 189(4), (5) and (6) of the Social Security Administration Act 1992 and sections 4(9), 14(2), (3) and (4), 16(1) and (2), 18, 19, 21(3), 23(1), (2), (5) and (7), 29 and 32 of, and paragraphs 4 and 8 of Schedule 1 to, the Social Security (Recovery of Benefits) Act 1997, and of all other powers enabling her in that behalf, hereby makes the following Regulations:

Citation, commencement and interpretation

2.1005 **1.**—(1) These Regulations may be cited as the Social Security (Recovery of Benefits) Regulations 1997 and shall come into force on 6th October 1997.

(2) In these Regulations—

"the 1992 Act" means the Social Security Administration Act 1992;

"the 1997 Act" means the Social Security (Recovery of Benefits) Act 1997;

"commencement day" means the day these Regulations come into force;

"compensator" means a person making a compensation payment;

"Compensation Recovery Unit" means the Compensation Recovery Unit of the Department of Social Security at [1 Durham House, Washington, Tyne and Wear, NE38 7SP].

(3) A reference in these Regulations to a numbered section or Schedule is a reference, unless the context otherwise requires, to that section of or Schedule to the 1997 Act.

AMENDMENT

1. Social Security (Recovery of Benefits) (Miscellaneous Amendments) Regulations 2000 (SI 2000/3030) reg.2 (December 4, 2000).

DEFINITION

"compensation payment"—see s.1(4) of the Social Security (Recovery of Benefits) Act 1997.

GENERAL NOTE

Although the Compensation Recovery Unit remains in Washington, its postal address is now: Compensation Recovery Unit, Post Handling Site B, Wolverhampton, WV99 2FR. Its website is: *www.gov.uk/government/collections/cru.* 2.1006

Exempted trusts and payments

2.—(1) The following trusts are prescribed for the purposes of paragraph 4 of Schedule 1— 2.1007

(a) the Macfarlane Trust established on 10th March 1988 partly out of funds provided by the Secretary of State to the Haemophilia Society for the relief of poverty or distress among those suffering from haemophilia;

(b) the Macfarlane (Special Payments) Trust established on 29th January 1990 partly out of funds provided by the Secretary of State, for the benefit of certain persons suffering from haemophilia;

(c) the Macfarlane (Special Payments) (No.2) Trust established on 3rd May 1991 partly out of funds provided by the Secretary of State, for the benefit of certain persons suffering from haemophilia and other beneficiaries;

(d) the Eileen Trust established on 29th March 1993 out of funds provided by the Secretary of State for the benefit of persons eligible for payment in accordance with its provisions;

[1(e) a trust established out of funds provided by the Secretary of State in respect of persons who suffered, or who are suffering, from variant Creutzfelt-Jakob disease for the benefit of persons eligible for interim payments in accordance with its provisions;

(f) a trust established out of funds provided by the Secretary of State in respect of persons who suffered, or who are suffering, from variant Creutzfelt-Jakob disease for the benefit of persons eligible for payments, other than interim payments, in accordance with its provisions;]

[4 (g) the UK Asbestos Trust established on 10th October 2006, for the benefit of certain persons suffering from asbestos-related diseases;

(h) the EL Scheme Trust established on 23rd November 2006, for the benefit of certain persons suffering from asbestos-related diseases.]

(2) The following payments are prescribed for the purposes of paragraph 8 of Schedule 1—

(a) any payment to the extent that it is made—
  (i) in consequence of an action under the Fatal Accidents Act 1976; or
  (ii) in circumstances where, had an action been brought, it would have been brought under that Act;

(b) any payment to the extent that it is made in respect of a liability arising by virtue of section 1 of the Damages (Scotland) Act 1976;

(c) any payment made under the Vaccine Damage Payments Act 1979 to or in respect of the injured person;

(d) any award of compensation made to or in respect of the injured person under the Criminal Injuries Compensation Act 1995 or by the Criminal Injuries Compensation Board under the Criminal Injuries Compensation Scheme 1990 or any earlier scheme;

(e) any compensation payment made by British Coal in accordance with the NCB Pneumoconiosis Compensation Scheme set out in the Schedule to an agreement made on the 13th September 1974 between the National Coal Board, the National Union of Mine Workers, the National Association of Colliery Overmen Deputies and Shot-firers and the British Association of Colliery Management;

(f) any payment made to the injured person in respect of sensorineural hearing loss where the loss is less than than 50 dB in one or both ears;

(g) any contractual amount paid to an employee by an employer of his in respect of a period of incapacity for work;

(h) any payment made under the National Health Service (Injury Benefits) Regulations 1995 or the National Health Service (Scotland) (Injury Benefits) Regulations 1974;

(i) any payment made by or on behalf of the Secretary of State for the benefit of persons eligible for payment in accordance with the provisions of a scheme established by him on 24th April 1992 or, in Scotland, on 10th April 1992;

[2 (j) any payment made from the Skipton Fund, the ex-gratia payment scheme administered by the Skipton Fund Limited, incorporated on 25th March 2004, for the benefit of certain persons suffering from hepatitis C and other persons eligible for payments in accordance with the scheme's provisions;]

[3 (k) any payment made from the London Bombings Relief Charitable Fund, the company limited by guarantee (number 5505072) and registered charity of that name established on 11th July for the purpose of (amongst other things) relieving sickness, disability or financial need of victims (including families or dependants of victims) of the terrorist attacks carried out in London on 7th July 2005;]

[5 (l) any payment made by MFET Limited, a company limited by guarantee (number 7121661) of that name, established for the purpose in particular of making payments in accordance with arrangements made with the Secretary of State to persons who have acquired HIV as a result of treatment by the NHS with blood or blood products;]

[6 (m) any payment made from the Caxton Foundation, the charitable trust of that name established on 28th March 2011 out of funds provided by the Secretary of State for the benefit of certain persons suffering from hepatitis C and other persons eligible for payment in accordance with its provisions;]

[7 (n) any payment made from the Scottish Infected Blood Support Scheme administered by the Common Services Agency (constituted by section 10 of the National Health Service (Scotland) Act 1978).]

AMENDMENTS

1. Social Security Amendment (Capital Disregards and Recovery of Benefits) Regulations 2001 (SI 2001/1118) reg.4 (April 12, 2001).
2. Social Security (Miscellaneous Amendments) (No.2) Regulations 2004 (SI 2004/1141) reg.7 (May 12, 2004).
3. Income-related Benefits (Amendment) (No.2) Regulations 2005 (SI 2005/3391) reg.6 (December 12, 2005).
4. Social Security (Recovery of Benefits) Amendment) Regulations 2007 (SI 2007/357) reg.2 (March 12, 2007).
5. Social Security (Miscellaneous Amendments) (No.2) Regulations 2010 (SI 2010/641) reg.5 (March 11, 2010).
6. Social Security (Miscellaneous Amendments) (No.3) Regulations 2011 (SI 2011/2425) reg.11 (October 31, 2011).
7. Social Security (Scottish Infected Blood Support Scheme) Regulations 2017 (SI 2017/329) reg.2 (April 3, 2017).

DEFINITIONS

"compensation payment"—see s.1(4) of the Social Security (Recovery of Benefits) Act 1997.

"payment"—see s.29 of the Social Security (Recovery of Benefits) Act 1997.

Information to be provided by the compensator

3.—The following information is prescribed for the purposes of section 23(1): **2.1008**

(a) the full name and address of the injured person;
(b) where known, the date of birth or national insurance number of that person, or both if both are known;
(c) where the liability arises, or is alleged to arise, in respect of an accident or injury, the date of the accident or injury;
(d) the nature of the accident, injury or disease; and
(e) where known, and where the relevant period may include a period prior to 6th April 1994, whether, at the time of the accident or injury or diagnosis of the disease, the person was employed under a contract of service, and, if he was, the name and address of his employer at that time and the person's payroll number.

DEFINITION

"injured person"—see s.1(4) of the Social Security (Recovery of Benefits) Act 1997.

Information to be provided by the injured person

4. The following information is prescribed for the purposes of section 23(2): **2.1009**

(a) whether the accident, injury or disease resulted from any action taken by another person, or from any failure of another person to act, and, if so, the full name and address of that other person;
(b) whether the injured person has claimed or may claim a compensation payment, and, if so, the full name and address of the person against whom the claim was or may be made;
(c) the amount of any compensation payment and the date on which it was made;
(d) the listed benefits claimed, and for each benefit the date from which it was first claimed and the amount received in the period beginning with that date and ending with the date the information is sent;
(e) in the case of a person who has received statutory sick pay during the relevant period and prior to 6th April 1994, the name and address of any employer who made those payments to him during the relevant period and the dates the employment with that employer began and ended; and
(f) any changes in the medical diagnosis relating to the condition arising from the accident, injury or disease.

DEFINITIONS

"compensation payment"—see s.1(4) of the Social Security (Recovery of Benefits) Act 1997.
"injured person"—*ibid.*
"listed benefit"—see s.29 of the Social Security (Recovery of Benefits) Act 1997.

Information to be provided by the employer

2.1010 **5.** The following information is prescribed for the purposes of section 23(5):
(a) the amount of any statutory sick pay the employer has paid to the injured person since the first day of the relevant period and before 6th April 1994;
(b) the date the liability to pay such statutory sick pay first arose and the rate at which it was payable;
(c) the date on which such liability terminated; and
(d) the causes of incapacity for work during any period of entitlement to statutory sick pay during the relevant period and prior to 6th April 1994.

DEFINITION

"injured person"—see s.1(4) of the Social Security (Recovery of Benefits) Act 1997.

Provision of information

2.1011 **6.** A person required to give information to the Secretary of State under regulations 3 to 5 shall do so by sending it to the Compensation Recovery Unit not later than 14 days after—
(a) where he is a person to whom regulation 3 applies, the date on which he receives a claim for compensation from the injured person in respect of the accident, injury or disease;
(b) where he is a person to whom regulation 4 or 5 applies, the date on which the Secretary of State requests the information from him.

DEFINITION

"Compensation Recovery Unit"—see reg.1(2).

Application for a certificate of recoverable benefits

7.—(1) The following particulars are prescribed for the purposes of section 21(3)(a) (particulars to be included in an application for a certificate of recoverable benefits): **2.1012**

(a) the full name and address of the injured person;
(b) the date of birth and, where known, the national insurance number of that person;
(c) where the liability arises or is alleged to arise in respect of an accident or injury, the date of the accident or injury;
(d) the nature of the accident, injury or disease;
(e) where the person liable, or alleged to be liable, in respect of the accident, injury or disease, is the employer of the injured person, or has been such an employer, the information prescribed by regulation 5.

(2) An application for a certificate of recoverable benefits is to be treated for the purposes of the 1997 Act as received by the Secretary of State on the day on which it is received by the Compensation Recovery Unit, or if the application is received after normal business hours, or on a day which is not a normal business day at that office, on the next such day.

DEFINITIONS

"the 1997 Act"—see reg.1(2).
"Compensation Recovery Unit"—*ibid.*
"injured person"—see s.1(4) of the Social Security (Recovery of Benefits) Act 1997.
"recoverable benefit"—*ibid.*

Payments into court

8.—(1) Subject to the provisions of this regulation, where a party to an action makes a payment into court which, had it been paid directly to another party to the action ("the relevant party"), would have constituted a compensation payment— **2.1013**

(a) the making of that payment shall be treated for the purposes of the 1997 Act as the making of a compensation payment;
(b) a current certificate of recoverable benefits shall be lodged with the payment; and
(c) where the payment is calculated under section 8, the compensator must give the relevant party the information specified in section 9(1), instead of the person to whom the payment is made.

(2) The liability under section 6(1) to pay an amount equal to the total amount of the recoverable benefits shall not arise until the person making the payment into court has been notified that the whole or any part of the payment into court has been paid out of court to or for the relevant party.

(3) Where a payment into court in satisfaction of his claim is accepted by the relevant party in the initial period, then as respects the compensator in question, the relevant period shall be taken to have ended, if it has not done

so already, on the day on which the payment into court (or if there were two or more such payments, the last of them) was made.

(4) Where, after the expiry of the initial period, the payment into court is accepted in satisfaction of the relevant party's claim by consent between the parties, the relevant period shall end, if it has not done so already, on the date on which application to the court for the payment is made.

(5) Where, after the expiry of the initial period, payment out of court is made wholly or partly to or for the relevant party in accordance with an order of the court and in satisfaction of his claim, the relevant period shall end, if it has not done so already, on the date of that order.

(6) In paragraphs (3), (4) and (5), "the initial period" means the period of 21 days after the receipt by the relevant party to the action of notice of the payment into court having been made.

(7) Where a payment into court is paid out wholly to or for the party who made the payment (otherwise than to or for the relevant party to the action) the making of the payment into court shall cease to be regarded as the making of a compensation payment.

(8) A current certificate of recoverable benefits in paragraph (1) means one that is in force as described in section 4(4).

GENERAL NOTE

2.1014 See the note to s.16(1) and (2) of the Social Security (Recovery of Benefits) Act 1997, under which this regulation is made.

Reduction of compensation: complex cases

2.1015 **9.**—(1) This regulation applies where—

(a) a compensation payment in the form of a lump sum (an "earlier payment") has been made to or in respect of the injured person; and
(b) subsequently another such payment (a "later payment") is made to or in respect of the same injured person in consequence of the same accident, injury or disease.

(2) In determining the liability under section 6(1) arising in connection with the making of the later payment, the amount referred to in that sub-section shall be reduced by any amount paid in satisfaction of that liability as it arose in connection with the earlier payment.

(3) Where—

(a) a payment made in satisfaction of the liability under section 6(1) arising in connection with an earlier payment is not reflected in the certificate of recoverable benefits in force at the time of a later payment, and
(b) in consequence, the aggregate of payments made in satisfaction of the liability exceeds what it would have been had that payment been so reflected,

the Secretary of State shall pay the compensator who made the later payment an amount equal to the excess.

(4) Where—

(a) a compensator receives a payment under paragraph (3), and
(b) the amount of the compensation payment made by him was calculated under section 8,

then the compensation payment shall be recalculated under section 8, and the compensator shall pay the amount of the increase (if any) to the person to whom the compensation payment was made.

(5) Where both the earlier payment and the later payment are made by the same compensator, he may—

(a) aggregate the gross amounts of the payments made by him;

(b) calculate what would have been the reduction made under section 8(3) if that aggregate amount had been paid at the date of the last payment on the basis that—

(i) so much of the aggregate amount as is attributable to a head of compensation listed in column (1) of Schedule 2 shall be taken to be the part of the gross amount which attributable to that head, and

(ii) the amount of any recoverable benefits shown against any head in column (2) of that Schedule shall be taken to be the amount determined in accordance with the most recent certificate of recoverable benefits;

(c) deduct from that reduction calculated under sub-paragraph (b) the amount of the reduction under section 8(3) from any earlier payment; and

(d) deduct from the latest gross payment the net reduction calculated under sub-paragraph (c) (and accordingly the latest payment may be nil).

(6) Where the Secretary of State is making a refund under paragraph (3), he shall send to the compensator (with the refund) and to the person to whom the compensation payment was made a statement showing—

(a) the total amount that has already been paid by that compensator to the Secretary of State;

(b) the amount that ought to have been paid by that compensator; and

(c) the amount to be repaid to that compensator by the Secretary of State.

(7) Where the reduction of a compensation payment is recalculated by virtue of paragraph (4) or (5) the compensator shall give notice of the calculation to the injured person.

General Note

This regulation is made under ss.18(1)–(3) and 19 of the Social Security (Recovery of Benefits) Act 1997 and is concerned with cases where more than one lump-sum compensation payment is made to a victim in respect of a single accident, injury or disease. (Structured settlements involving periodical payments are dealt with in reg.10). Regulation 9 covers cases where the same compensator makes more than one lump-sum payment and also cases where different compensators make payments because they all contributed to the accident, injury or disease. However, it makes no attempt at apportionment of liability for recoverable benefits between different compensators. It is concerned only to ensure that there is not double recovery and it does not even attempt that in a case where benefit has been paid as a result of two different injuries each attributable to a different accident. See *R(CR)2/04* and the note to s.1 of the Act for the way that liability is attributed in such a case. Where two compensators are liable in respect of the same accident, injury or disease, the one making the first compensation payment is likely to have the greater liability to the Secretary of State and must seek a contribution from the other so that they each bear a fair share of the liability for benefits. **2.1016**

Paragraph (2) simply provides that when a second compensation payment is made, the Secretary of State should not recover benefits that were recovered when the earlier payment was made. Paragraph (3) provides for a refund to the compensator if benefits are erroneously recovered for a second time. Paragraph (4) provides that, where the compensator has reduced under s.8 of the Act the amount of compensation paid to the victim (in effect recovering from the victim the benefits that the victim had received and the compensator had to pay to the Secretary of State), he must recalculate the s.8 reduction in the light of a refund under para.(3) and pay the appropriate amount, if any, to the victim. Where the same compensator made both the compensation payments, he may aggregate them for the purpose of recalculating the appropriate s.8 reduction under para.(4) (para.(5)). Paragraphs (6) and (7) require the victim to be told by the Secretary of State about any refund under para.(3) and by the compensator about any recalculation under paras (4) and (5).

Structured settlements

2.1017 **10.**—(1) This regulation applies where—

(a) in final settlement of an injured person's claim, an agreement is entered into—
   (i) for the making of periodical payments (whether of an income or capital nature); or
   (ii) for the making of such payments and lump sum payments; and

(b) apart from the provisions of this regulation, those payments would fall to be treated for the purposes of the 1997 Act as compensation payments.

(2) Where this regulation applies, the provisions of the 1997 Act and these Regulations shall be modified in the following way—

(a) the compensator in question shall be taken to have made on that day a single compensation payment;
(b) the relevant period in the case of the compensator in question shall be taken to end (if it has not done so already) on the day of settlement;
(c) payments under the agreement referred to in paragraph (1)(a) shall be taken not to be compensation payments;
(d) paragraphs (5) and (7) of regulation 11 shall not apply.

(3) Where any further payment falls to be made to or in respect of the injured person otherwise than under the agreement in question, paragraph (2) shall be disregarded for the purpose of determining the end of the relevant period in relation to that further payment.

(4) In any case where—

(a) the person making the periodical payments ("the secondary party") does so in pursuance of arrangements entered into with another ("primary party") (as in a case where the primary party purchases an annuity for the injured person from the secondary party), and
(b) apart from those arrangements, the primary party would have been regarded as the compensator,

then for the purposes of the 1997 Act, the primary party shall be regarded as the compensator and the secondary party shall not be so regarded.

(5) In this regulation "the day of settlement" means—

(a) if the agreement referred to in paragraph (1)(a) is approved by a court, the day on which that approval is given; and
(b) in any other case, the day on which the agreement is entered into.

GENERAL NOTE

This regulation is made under s.8(4)–(6) of the Social Security (Recovery of Benefits) Act 1997. 2.1018

Where a final settlement is reached in the form of an agreement that involves the making of periodical payments (whether of a capital or income nature and whether or not they are combined with sum lump sums), the compensator is treated as having made a compensation payment on the day the agreement is reached. That is when the "relevant period" under s.3 of the Act is taken to have ended and when the compensator becomes liable to make a payment to the Secretary of State under s.6. Further payments under the agreement (by whomever they are made (see para.(4)) do not count as compensation payments (para.(2)(c)) but any payments outside it will (para.(3)) and reg.9 will apply to them.

Adjustments

11.—(1) Where the conditions specified in subsection (1) and paragraphs (a) and (b) of subsection (2) of section 14 are satisfied, the Secretary of State shall pay the difference between the amount that has been paid and the amount that ought to have been paid to the compensator. 2.1019

(2) Where the conditions specified in subsection (1) and paragraphs (a) and (b) of subsection (3) of section 14 are satisfied, the compensator shall pay the difference between the total amounts paid and the amount that ought to have been paid to the Secretary of State.

(3) Where the Secretary of State is making a refund under paragraph (1), or demanding payment of a further amount under paragraph (2), he shall send to the compensator (with the refund or demand) and to the person to whom the compensation payment was made a statement showing—

(a) the total amount that has already been paid to the Secretary of State;
(b) the amount that ought to have been paid; and
(c) the difference, and whether a repayment by the Secretary of State or a further payment to him is required.

(4) This paragraph applies where—

(a) the amount of the compensation payment made by the compensator was calculated under section 8; and
(b) the Secretary of State has made a payment under paragraph (1).

(5) Where paragraph (4) applies, the amount of the compensation payment shall be recalculated under section 8 to take account of the fresh certificate of recoverable benefits and the compensator shall pay the amount of the increase (if any) to the person to whom the compensation payment was made.

(6) This paragraph applies where—

(a) the amount of the compensation payment made by the compensator was calculated under section 8;
(b) the compensator has made a payment under paragraph (2); and
(c) the fresh certificate of recoverable benefits issued after the review or appeal was required as a result of the injured person or other person to whom the compensation payment was made supplying to the compensator information knowing it to be incorrect or insufficient with the intent of enhancing the compensation payment calculated under section 8, and the compensator supplying that information to the Secretary of State without knowing it to be incorrect or insufficient.

(7) Where paragraph (6) applies, the compensator may recalculate the compensation payment under section 8 to take account of the fresh certificate of recoverable benefits and may require the repayment to him by the person to whom he made the compensation payment of the difference (if any) between the payment made and the payment as so recalculated.

General Note

2.1020 This is a key provision. Paragraphs (1)–(3) simply provide for the appropriate refund or demand for further payment to be made by the Secretary of State following a review or appeal. Of more practical importance are paras (4) and (5) requiring that, where there is a refund, the compensator must recalculate any reduction in a compensation payment made under s.8 of the Social Security (Recovery of Benefits) Act 1997 and pay the amount of any increase in the compensation payment to the claimant. That means that a compensator does not have any practical interest in challenging a certificate for recoverable benefits insofar as he has reduced the claimant's compensation to take account of the benefits (*R(CR) 2/03*). Unfortunately, it appears that these paragraphs are sometimes overlooked even by experienced insurance companies with the result that they retain money due to claimants. Paragraphs (6) and (7) make similar provision for cases where there is a demand for a further payment, only in those circumstances they have the effect that the claimant may have to make a further payment to the compensator. They operate only if the claimant knowingly supplied incorrect, or insufficient, information to the compensator and the compensator innocently passed it on to the Secretary of State.

Transitional provisions

2.1021 **12.**—(1) In relation to a compensation payment to which by virtue of section 2 the 1997 Act applies and subject to paragraph (2), a certificate of total benefit issued under Part IV of the 1992 Act shall be treated on or after the commencement date as a certificate of recoverable benefits issued under the 1997 Act and the amount of total benefit treated as that of recoverable benefits.

(2) Paragraph (1) shall not apply to a certificate of total benefit which specifies an amount in respect of disability living allowance without specifying whether that amount was, or is likely to be, paid wholly by way of the care component or the mobility component or (if not wholly one of them) specifying the relevant amount for each component.

[1(3) Any appeal under section 98 of the 1992 Act made on or after 6th October 1997 which has not been determined before 29th November 1999 shall be referred to an appeal tribunal constituted in accordance with paragraph (31) below.

(3A) Any appeal duly made before 6th October 1997 which has not been referred to a medical appeal tribunal or a social security appeal tribunal shall be referred to and determined by an appeal tribunal constituted in accordance with paragraph (3I) below.

(3B) Any appeal duly made before 6th October 1997 and referred to a medical appeal tribunal shall be determined by an appeal tribunal constituted in accordance with paragraph (3I) below which shall determine all issues.

(3C) Any appeal duly made before 6th October 1997 and referred to a social security appeal tribunal shall be determined by an appeal tribunal which shall consist of a legally qualified panel member and in making its determination, the appeal tribunal shall be bound by any decision of a medical appeal tribunal to which a question under section 98(5) of the 1992 Act was referred.

(3D) An appeal tribunal constituted in accordance with paragraph (3I) below shall completely rehear any appeal made under section 98 of the 1992 Act which stands adjourned immediately before 29th November 1999.

(3E) Where a Commissioner holds that the decision of a medical appeal tribunal or a social security appeal tribunal on an appeal made before 6th October 1997 was erroneous in law and refers the case to an appeal tribunal, that appeal tribunal shall be constituted in accordance with paragraph (3I) below and shall determine all issues in accordance with the Commissioner's direction.

(3F) Regulation 11 of the Social Security (Recoupment) Regulations 1990 ("the 1990 Regulations") and regulation 12 of those Regulations shall have effect in relation to any appeal under section 98 of the 1992 Act made on or after 6th October 1997 with the modification that for the word "chairman" in each place in which it occurs there were substituted the words "legally qualified panel member".

(3G) Regulation 13 of the 1990 Regulations shall have effect in relation to any appeal under section 98 of the 1992 Act made on or after 6th October 1997.

(3H) Any other transitional question arising from an appeal made under section 98 of the 1992 Act in consequence of the coming into force of the Social Security and Child Support (Decisions and Appeals) Regulations 1999 ("the 1999 Regulations") shall be determined by a legally qualified panel member who may for this purpose give such directions consistent with these regulations as are necessary.

(3I) For the purposes of paragraphs (3) to (3B) and (3E) above an appeal tribunal shall be constituted under Chapter I of Part I of the Social Security Act 1998 as though the appeal were made under section 11(1)(b) of the 1997 Act.

(3J) In this regulation, "legally qualified panel member" has the meaning it bears in regulation 1(3) of the 1999 Regulations.]

(4) Paragraph (5) applies where—

(a) an amount has been paid to the Secretary of State under section 82(1)(b) of the 1992 Act,
(b) liability arises on or after the commencement day to make a payment under section 6(1), and
(c) the compensation payments which give rise to the liability to make both payments are to or in respect of the same injured person in consequence of the same accident, injury or disease.

(5) Where this paragraph applies, the liability under section 6 shall be reduced by the payment (or aggregate of the payments, if more than one) described in paragraph (4)(a).

(6) Where—

(a) a payment into court has been made on a date prior to the commencement day but the initial period, as defined in section 93(6) of the 1992 Act, in relation to that payment, expires on or after the commencement day; and
(b) the payment into court is accepted by the other party to the action in the initial period,

that payment into court shall be treated as a compensation payment to which the 1992 Act, and not the 1997 Act, applies.

(7) Where a payment into court has been made prior to the commencement day, remains in court on that day and paragraph (6) does not apply, that payment into court shall be treated as a payment to which the 1997 Act applies, but paragraph (1) (b) and (c) of regulation 8 shall not apply.

AMENDMENT

1. Social Security Act 1998 (Commencement No.12 and Consequential and Transitional Provisions) Order 1999 (SI 1999/3178) art.3(17) and Sch.17 (November 29, 1999).

GENERAL NOTE

2.1022 This regulation has been amended in such a way that it now makes transitional provision not only for the coming into force of the Social Security (Recovery of Benefits) Act 1997 but also for the coming into force of the Social Security Act 1998.

The Social Security (Recovery of Benefits) (Lump Sum Payments) Regulations 2008

(SI 2008/1596)

Made	*18th June 2008*
Laid before Parliament	*25th June 2008*
Coming into force	*1st October 2008*

2.1023 The Secretary of State for Work and Pensions makes the following Regulations in exercise of the powers conferred by section 189(4) and (6) of the Social Security Administration Act 1992, sections 1A, 14(2), (3) and (4), 18, 19, 21(3), 23(1), (2) and (7) and 29 of, and paragraphs 4 and 8 of Schedule 1 to, the Social Security (Recovery of Benefits) Act 1997, section 79(6) of the Social Security Act 1998 and section 53 of the Child Maintenance and Other Payments Act 2008, which contains only regulations made by virtue of, or consequential on sections 54 and 57(2) of the Child Maintenance and Other Payments Act 2008 and which are made before the end of a period of 6 months beginning with the coming into force of those sections:

PART 1

GENERAL

Citation, commencement and interpretation

2.1024 **1.**—(1) These Regulations may be cited as the Social Security (Recovery of Benefits) (Lump Sum Payments) Regulations 2008 and shall come into force on 1st October 2008.

(2) In these Regulations—

"the Act" means the Social Security (Recovery of Benefits) Act 1997;

[1 "the 2014 Act" means the Mesothelioma Act 2014;]

"compensator" means a person making a compensation payment [1 and includes the scheme administrator who makes a payment in accordance with the Diffuse Mesothelioma Payment Scheme;];

"Compensation Recovery Unit" means the Compensation Recovery Unit of the Department for Work and Pensions at Durham House, Washington, Tyne and Wear, NE38 7SF;

[1 "Diffuse Mesothelioma Payment Scheme" means the scheme established by the Diffuse Mesothelioma Payment Scheme Regulations 2014;]

[1 "lump sum payment" means a payment to which any of paragraphs (a) to (d) of section 1A(2) of the Act applies,] except in relation to regulation 18(1)(b);

"recoverable benefits" has the same meaning as in section 1(4)(c) of the Act;

[1 "recoverable lump sum payment"—

(a) in relation to a compensation payment which is a payment under the Diffuse Mesothelioma Payment Scheme, means any specified lump sum payment which is recoverable by virtue of regulation 4A;

(b) in relation to any other description of compensation payment, means any lump sum payment which is recoverable by virtue of regulation 4;

"specified lump sum payment" means a lump sum payment within paragraph (a), (b) or (c) of section 1A(2) of the Act.]

AMENDMENT

1. Social Security (Recovery of Benefits) (Lump Sum Payments) (Amendment) Regulations 2014 (SI 2014/1456) reg.2 and Sch. paras 1 and 2 (July 1, 2014).

GENERAL NOTE

Although the Compensation Recovery Unit remains in Washington, its postal address is now: Compensation Recovery Unit, Post Handling Site B, Wolverhampton, WV99 2FR. Its website is: *www.gov.uk/government/collections/cru.* 2.1025

Application of the Act

2.—(1) The provisions of the Act specified in paragraph (2) apply for the purposes of these Regulations with the modifications, where appropriate, prescribed in Schedule 1. 2.1026

(2) The specified provisions are—

(a) section 1(3) (cases in which this Act applies);
(b) sections 10 to 14 (reviews and appeals);
(c) sections 15 and 17 (courts);
(d) sections 18 and 19 (reduction of compensation: complex cases);
(e) sections 20 to 23 (miscellaneous);
(f) sections 26 and 27 (provisions relating to Northern Ireland);
(g) sections 28 to 31 (general);
(h) section 33 (consequential amendments and repeals);
(i) section 34(1) and (3) (short title and extent);
(j) Schedule 1 (compensation payments—exempted payments and power to disregard small payments).

3. *Omitted.* 2.1027

[1 Recovery of lump sum payments from compensation payment made otherwise than under Diffuse Mesothelioma Payment Scheme]

2.1028 **4.**—(1) The Secretary of State may recover the amount of [1 a lump sum payment] where—

(a) a compensation payment in consequence of a disease is made to or in respect of—

(i) a person ("P"); or

(ii) a dependant of P,

to whom, or in respect of whom, a lump sum payment has been, or is likely to be, made; and

[1 (ab) the compensation payment is not a payment under the Diffuse Mesothelioma Payment Scheme; and]

(b) the compensation payment is made in consequence of the same disease as the lump sum payment.

[1 (1A) The Secretary of State may also recover the amount of lump sum payments to which section 1A(2)(d) of the Act applies where—

(a) any such payment has been, or is likely to be, made to one or more dependants of P;

(b) by virtue of a notice given under section 3(3) of the 2014 Act, any other dependant of P has ceased to be eligible for a lump sum payment to which section 1A(2)(d) of the Act applies; and

(c) a compensation payment in consequence of P's diffuse mesothelioma is made to that other dependant.]

(2) In paragraph (1), references to a payment made in consequence of a disease—

(a) are references to a payment made by or on behalf of a person who is, or is alleged to be, liable to any extent in respect of the disease; but

(b) do not include references to a payment mentioned in Part 1 of Schedule 1 to the Act.

AMENDMENT

1. Social Security (Recovery of Benefits) (Lump Sum Payments) (Amendment) Regulations 2014 (SI 2014/1456) reg.2 and Sch. paras 1 and 3 (July 1, 2014).

[1 Recovery of specified lump sum payments from compensation payment under Diffuse Mesothelioma Payment Scheme

2.1029 **4A.** The Secretary of State may recover the amount of a specified lump sum payment where—

(a) a compensation payment in consequence of diffuse mesothelioma is made to or in respect of P, or to a dependant of P, and a lump sum payment has been, or is likely to be, made to P or in respect of P;

(b) that compensation payment is a payment under the Diffuse Mesothelioma Payment Scheme; and

(c) the disease in consequence of which the specified lump sum payment was made is also diffuse mesothelioma.]

AMENDMENT

1. Social Security (Recovery of Benefits) (Lump Sum Payments) (Amendment) Regulations 2014 (SI 2014/1456) reg.2 and Sch. paras 1 and 4 (July 1, 2014).

Application of these Regulations to a dependant of P

5.—(1) Subject to paragraph (2), in these Regulations and any provision of the Act as modified any reference to P is to be construed as if it included a reference to a dependant of P where that dependant is the person to whom, or in respect of whom, a lump sum payment is made. 2.1030

(2) Paragraph (1) does not apply in relation to regulations 4, 10(7) and 12(7) and sections 15 and 23(2) of, and paragraphs 3(a) and 5(1) of Part 1 of Schedule 1 to, the Act.

Compensation payments to which these Regulations apply

6. [1 —(1) Except as stated in paragraph (2),] these Regulations apply in relation to compensation payments made on or after the day on which section 54 of the Child Maintenance and Other Payments Act 2008 comes into force. 2.1031

[1 (2) In any case where—

(a) the lump sum payment falls within section 1A(2)(d) of the Act; or

(b) paragraphs (a) to (c) of regulation 4A apply;

these Regulations apply only in relation to compensation payments which are made on or after 31st March 2014.]

AMENDMENT

1. Social Security (Recovery of Benefits) (Lump Sum Payments) (Amendment) Regulations 2014 (SI 2014/1456) reg.2, Sch. paras 1 and 5 (July 1, 2014).

Exempted trusts and payments

7.—(1) The following trusts are prescribed for the purposes of paragraph 4 of Schedule 1 to the Act— 2.1032

(a) the Macfarlane Trust established on 10th March 1988 partly out of funds provided by the Secretary of State to the Haemophilia Society for the relief of poverty or distress among those suffering from haemophilia;

(b) the Macfarlane (Special Payments) Trust established on 29th January 1990 partly out of funds provided by the Secretary of State, for the benefit of certain persons suffering from haemophilia;

(c) the Macfarlane (Special Payments) (No. 2) Trust established on 3rd May 1991 partly out of funds provided by the Secretary of State, for the benefit of certain persons suffering from haemophilia and other beneficiaries;

(d) the Eileen Trust established on 29th March 1993 out of funds provided by the Secretary of State, for the benefit of persons eligible for payment in accordance with its provisions;

(e) a trust established out of funds provided by the Secretary of State in respect of persons who suffered, or who are suffering, from variant Creutzfeldt-Jakob disease for the benefit of persons eligible for interim payments in accordance with its provisions;

(f) a trust established out of funds provided by the Secretary of State in respect of persons who suffered, or who are suffering, from variant Creutzfeldt-Jakob disease for the benefit of persons eligible for payments, other than interim payments, in accordance with its provisions;

[1 (g) the UK Asbestos Trust established on 10th October 2006 for the benefit of certain persons suffering from asbestos-related diseases [4 provided that any payment made in respect of diffuse mesothelioma out of this Trust is not made to or in respect of a person who has received a payment under the Diffuse Mesothelioma Payment Scheme];

(h) the EL Scheme Trust established on 23rd November 2006 for the benefit of certain persons suffering from asbestos-related diseases.]

(2) The following payments are prescribed for the purposes of paragraph 8 of Schedule 1 to the Act—

(a) any payment made under the Vaccine Damage Payments Act 1979 to or in respect of P;

(b) any award of compensation made to or in respect of P under the Criminal Injuries Compensation Act 1995 or by the Criminal Injuries Compensation Board under the Criminal Injuries Compensation Scheme 1990 or any earlier scheme or under the Criminal Injuries Compensation (Northern Ireland) Order 2002;

(c) any payment made to P in respect of sensorineural hearing loss where the loss is less than 50 decibels in one or both ears;

(d) any contractual amount paid to P by an employer of P in respect of a period of incapacity for work;

(e) any payment made under the National Health Service (Injury Benefits) Regulations 1995, the National Health Service (Scotland) (Injury Benefits) Regulations 1998 or the Health and Personal Social Services (Injury Benefits) Regulations (Northern Ireland) 2001;

(f) any payment made by or on behalf of the Secretary of State for the benefit of persons eligible for payment in accordance with the provisions of a scheme established by the Secretary of State on 24th April 1992 or, in Scotland, on 10th April 1992;

(g) any payment made from the Skipton Fund, the ex-gratia payment scheme administered by the Skipton Fund Limited, incorporated on 25th March 2004, for the benefit of certain persons suffering from hepatitis C and other persons eligible for payment in accordance with the scheme's provisions;

(h) any payment made from the London Bombings Relief Charitable Fund, the company limited by guarantee (number 5505072) and registered charity of that name established on 11th July 2005 for the purpose of (amongst other things) relieving sickness, disability or financial need of victims (including families or dependants of victims) of the terrorist attacks carried out in London on 7th July 2005;

[2 (i) any payment made by MFET Limited, a company limited by guarantee (number 7121661) of that name, established for the purpose in particular of making payments in accordance with arrangements made with the Secretary of State to persons who have acquired HIV as a result of treatment by the NHS with blood or blood products;]

[3 (j) any payment made from the Caxton Foundation, the charitable trust of that name established on 28th March 2011 out of funds provided by the Secretary of State for the benefit of certain persons suffering from hepatitis C and other persons eligible for payment in accordance with its provisions;]

[5 (k) any payment made from the Scottish Infected Blood Support Scheme administered by the Common Services Agency (constituted by section 10 of the National Health Service (Scotland) Act 1978).]

AMENDMENTS

1. Social Security (Recovery of Benefits) (Lump Sum Payments) (Amendment) Regulations 2009 (SI 2009/1494) reg.2 (July 13, 2009).
2. Social Security (Miscellaneous Amendments) (No.2) Regulations 2010 (SI 2010/641) reg.13 (March 11, 2010).
3. Social Security (Miscellaneous Amendments) (No.3) Regulations 2011 (SI 2011/2425) reg.24 (October 31, 2011).
4. Social Security (Recovery of Benefits) (Lump Sum Payments) (Amendment) Regulations 2014 (SI 2014/1456) reg.2 and Sch. paras 1 and 6 (July 1, 2014).
5. Social Security (Scottish Infected Blood Support Scheme) Regulations 2017 (SI 2017/329) reg.9 (April 3, 2017).

PART 2

CERTIFICATES

Applications for certificates

8.—(1) Before making a compensation payment the compensator must apply to the Secretary of State for a certificate. 2.1033

(2) Where the compensator applies for a certificate, the Secretary of State must—
- (a) send to the compensator a written acknowledgment of receipt of the application; and
- (b) issue the certificate before the end of the period of 4 weeks.

(3) An application for a certificate is to be treated for the purposes of the Act as received by the Secretary of State on the day on which it is received by the Compensation Recovery Unit, or if the application is received after normal business hours, or on a day which is not a normal business day at that office, on the next such day.

Information contained in certificates

9.—(1) Subject to paragraph (2), a certificate must specify— 2.1034
- (a) the amounts;
- (b) which of the type of payments referred to in section 1A(2) of the Act applies; and
- (c) the dates,

of any lump sum payments which have been, or are likely to have been paid.

(2) Where the type of payment is an extra-statutory payment the certificate may specify that type of payment as if it were a payment to which section 1A(2)(a) applies.

[2 (2A) Where a certificate has been applied for by the scheme administrator, the certificate may contain information which would assist the scheme administrator in making a determination in accordance with the Diffuse Mesothelioma Payment Scheme.]

(3) The Secretary of State may estimate, in such manner as the Secretary of State thinks fit the amount of the lump sum payments specified in the certificate.

(4) Where the Secretary of State issues a certificate, the information contained in that certificate must be provided to—

(a) the person who appears to the Secretary of State to be P; or

(b) any person who the Secretary of State thinks will receive a compensation payment in respect of P.

(5) A person to whom a certificate is issued or who is provided with information under [1 paragraph (4)] is entitled to particulars of the manner in which any amount, type of payment or date specified in the certificate has been determined, if that person applies to the Secretary of State for those particulars.

AMENDMENTS

1. The Social Security (Miscellaneous Amendments) (No. 3) Regulations 2008 (SI 2008/2365) reg.6(1) and (2) (October 1, 2008).

2. Social Security (Recovery of Benefits) (Lump Sum Payments) (Amendment) Regulations 2014 (SI 2014/1456) reg.2 and Sch. paras 1 and 7 (July 1, 2014).

PART 3

LIABILITY OF PERSON PAYING COMPENSATION

Liability to pay Secretary of State amount of lump sum payments

2.1035 **10.**—(1) A person who makes a compensation payment in any case is liable to pay the Secretary of State an amount equal to the total amount of—

(a) in a case to which paragraph (2) applies, the recoverable lump sum payments; or

(b) in a case to which paragraph (3) applies, the compensation payment.

(2) Paragraph (1)(a) applies to a case where—

(a) the compensation payment is equal to, or more than, any recoverable lump sum payments; or

(b) a dependant is a beneficiary of part of a compensation payment made in respect of P, that part of the compensation payment is equal to, or more than, any recoverable lump sum payments which have been made to that dependant.

(3) Paragraph 1(b) applies to a case where—

(a) the compensation payment; or

(b) a dependant is a beneficiary of part of a compensation payment made in respect of P, and recoverable lump sum payments have been made to that dependant, the share of the compensation payment,

[1 is less than the recoverable lump sum payments]

(4) The liability referred to in paragraph (1) arises—

(a) immediately before the compensation payment or, if there is more than one, the first of them is made;

(b) prior to any liability to pay the Secretary of State an amount equal to the total amount of the recoverable benefits payable under section 6 of the Act.

[1 (4A) In any case where recoverable lump sum payments include one or more lump sum payments to which section 1A(2)(d) of the Act applies, the liability referred to in paragraph (1) in respect of those lump sum payments arises prior to any such liability in respect of any other recoverable lump sum payment.]

(5) No amount becomes payable under this regulation before the end of the period of 14 days following the day on which the liability arises.

(6) Subject to paragraph (4), an amount becomes payable under this regulation at the end of the period of 14 days beginning with the day on which a certificate is first issued showing that the amount of recoverable lump sum payment to which it relates has been or is likely to have been paid.

(7) [1 Subject to paragraph (8),] in the case of a lump sum payment which has been made to a dependant of P, this regulation applies only to the extent to which the compensator is making any payment—

(a) (i) under the Fatal Accidents Act 1976;

(ii) to the extent that it is made in respect of a liability arising by virtue of section 1 of the Damages (Scotland) Act 1976; or

(iii) under the Fatal Accidents (Northern Ireland) Order 1977, to that dependant; or

(b) in respect of P, and that dependant is an intended beneficiary of part or all of that payment.

[1 (8) In the case of a lump sum payment to which section 1A(2)(d) of the Act applies which has been made to one or more dependants of P, this regulation also applies to the extent that the compensator is making any of the payments listed in—

(a) paragraph (7)(a), where such a payment is made to another dependant of P who has ceased to be eligible for a lump sum payment to which section 1A(2)(d) of the Act applies by virtue of having given notice under section 3(3) of the 2014 Act;

(b) paragraph (7)(b), where such a dependant is an intended beneficiary of that payment.]

AMENDMENT

1. Social Security (Recovery of Benefits) (Lump Sum Payments) (Amendment) Regulations 2014 (SI 2014/1456) reg.2 and Sch. paras 1 and 8 (July 1, 2014).

Recovery of payment due under regulation 10

11.—(1) This regulation applies where a compensator has made a compensation payment but— 2.1036

(a) has not applied for a certificate; or

(b) has not made a payment to the Secretary of State under regulation 10 before the end of the period allowed under that regulation.

(2) The Secretary of State may—

(a) issue the compensator who made the compensation payment with a certificate, if none has been issued; or

(b) issue that compensator with a copy of the certificate or (if more than one has been issued) the most recent one,

and (in either case) issue that compensator with a demand that payment of any amount due under regulation 10 be made immediately.

(3) The Secretary of State may, in accordance with paragraphs (4) and (5), recover the amount for which a demand for payment is made under paragraph (2) from the compensator who made the compensation payment.

(4) If the compensator who made the compensation payment resides or carries on business in England and Wales and a county court so orders, any amount recoverable under paragraph (3) is recoverable by execution issued from the county court or otherwise as if it were payable under an order of that court.

(5) If the compensator who made the payment resides or carries on business in Scotland, any amount recoverable under paragraph (3) may be enforced in like manner as an extract registered decree arbitral bearing a warrant for execution issued by the sheriff court of any sheriffdom in Scotland.

(6) A document bearing a certificate which—

(a) is signed by a person authorised to do so by the Secretary of State; and

(b) states that the document, apart from the certificate, is a record of the amount recoverable under paragraph (3),

is conclusive evidence that that amount is so recoverable.

(7) A certificate under paragraph (6) purporting to be signed by a person authorised to do so by the Secretary of State is to be treated as so signed unless the contrary is proved.

Part 4

Reduction Of Compensation Payment

Reduction of compensation payment

2.1037 **12.**—(1) [1 Except where regulation 12A applies,] this regulation applies in a case where, in relation to any compensation payment in consequence of a disease made to, or in respect of P, a lump sum payment has been, or is likely to be made to, or in respect of P.

(2) In such a case, any claim of a person to receive the compensation payment is to be treated for all purposes as discharged if—

(a) that person is paid the amount (if any) of the compensation payment calculated in accordance with this regulation; and

(b) if the amount of the compensation payment so calculated is nil, that person is given a statement saying so by the compensator who (apart from this regulation) would have paid the gross amount of the compensation payment.

(3) For an award of compensation for which paragraph (1) is satisfied, so much of the gross amount of the compensation payment as is equal to the amount of the lump sum payment is to be reduced (to nil, if necessary) by deducting the amount of the recoverable lump sum payment.

(4) Paragraph (3) is to have effect as if a requirement to reduce a payment by deducting an amount which exceeds that payment were a requirement to reduce that payment to nil.

(5) The amount of the compensation payment calculated in accordance with this regulation is—

(a) the gross amount of the compensation payment;

less

(b) the reductions made under paragraph (3),

(and, accordingly, the amount may be nil).

(6) The reduction specified in paragraph (3) is to be attributed to the heads of compensation in the following order—

(a) damages for non-pecuniary loss;

(b) damages for pecuniary loss,

and, the reduction is to be made before any reduction in respect of recoverable benefits under section 8 of the Act.

(7) [1 Subject to paragraph (8),] where the lump sum payment has been made to a dependant of P, the reduction specified in paragraph (3) may be attributed—

(a) to any damages awarded to that dependant—

(i) under the Fatal Accidents Act 1976;

(ii) to the extent that they are made in respect of a liability arising by virtue of section 1 of the Damages (Scotland) Act 1976; or

(iii) under the Fatal Accidents (Northern Ireland) Order 1977,

other than those paid for funeral expenses;

(b) to any part of a compensation payment paid in respect of P, where that dependant is an intended beneficiary of part or all of that compensation.

[1 (8) In the case of a lump sum payment to which section 1A(2)(d) of the Act applies which has been made to one or more dependants of P, this regulation also applies to the extent that the compensator is making any of the payments listed in—

(a) paragraph (7)(a), where such a payment is made to another dependant of P who has ceased to be eligible for a lump sum payment to which section 1A(2)(d) of the Act applies by virtue of having given notice under section 3(3) of the 2014 Act;

(b) paragraph (7)(b), where such a dependant is an intended beneficiary of that payment.]

AMENDMENT

1. Social Security (Recovery of Benefits) (Lump Sum Payments) (Amendment) Regulations 2014 (SI 2014/1456) reg.2 and Sch. paras 1 and 9 (July 1, 2014).

[1 Reduction of compensation payment under Diffuse Mesothelioma Payment Scheme

12A.—(1) This regulation applies in a case where the compensation payment is a payment under the Diffuse Mesothelioma Payment Scheme. 2.1038

(2) The gross amount of the compensation payment—

(a) is to be reduced by the amount of the recoverable lump sum payments; and

(b) accordingly, is to be reduced to nil in any case where the amount of the recoverable lump sum payments is equal to or greater than the gross amount of the compensation payment.

(3) The reduction in paragraph (2) is to be made before any reduction in respect of recoverable benefits under section 8A of the Act.

(4) Any claim by a person to receive the compensation payment is to be treated for all purposes as discharged if—

(a) the person is paid the gross amount of the compensation payment less the amount of the recoverable lump sum payments; or

(b) the amount of the recoverable lump sum payments is equal to or greater than the gross amount of the compensation payment and the person is given a statement by the scheme administrator saying that the compensation payment has been reduced to nil.

(5) In the application of paragraph (4) to any case where the compensation payment is to be made to two or more dependants of P, the deduction of the amount of the recoverable lump sum payments is to be made before calculating the amount to be paid to each dependant in accordance

with regulation 16(2)(iii) of the Diffuse Mesothelioma Payment Scheme Regulations 2014.]

AMENDMENT

1. Social Security (Recovery of Benefits) (Lump Sum Payments) (Amendment) Regulations 2014 (SI 2014/1456) reg.2 and Sch. paras 1 and 10 (July 1, 2014).

[1 Regulations 12 and 12A]: supplementary

2.1039 **13.**—(1) A compensator who makes a compensation payment calculated in accordance with regulation 12 [1 or 12A] must inform the person to whom the payment is made—

(a) that the payment has been so calculated; and

(b) of the date for payment by reference to which the calculation has been made.

(2) If the amount of a compensation payment calculated in accordance with regulation 12 [1 or 12A] is nil, a compensator giving a statement saying so is to be treated for the purposes of these Regulations as making a payment within regulation 4(1)(a) [1 or 4A(a) (as the case may be)] on the day on which the statement is given.

(3) Where a compensator—

(a) makes a compensation payment calculated in accordance with regulation 12 [1 or 12A]; and

(b) if the amount of the compensation payment so calculated is nil, gives a statement saying so,

the compensator is to be treated, for the purpose of determining any rights and liabilities in respect of contribution or indemnity, as having paid the gross amount of the compensation payment.

(4) For the purposes of these Regulations—

(a) the gross amount of the compensation payment is the amount of the compensation payment apart from regulation 12 [1 or 12A]; and

(b) the amount of any recoverable lump sum payment is the amount determined in accordance with the certificate.

AMENDMENT

1. Social Security (Recovery of Benefits) (Lump Sum Payments) (Amendment) Regulations 2014 (SI 2014/1456) reg.2 and Sch. paras 1 and 11 (July 1, 2014).

Reduction of compensation: complex cases

2.1040 **14.**—(1) This regulation applies where—

(a) a compensation payment in the form of a lump sum (an "earlier payment") has been made to or in respect of P; and

(b) subsequently another such payment (a "later payment") is made to or in respect of the same P in consequence of the same disease.

(2) In determining the liability under regulation 10(1) arising in connection with the making of the later payment, the amount referred to in that regulation is to be reduced by any amount paid in satisfaction of that liability as it arose in connection with the earlier payment.

(3) Where—

(a) a payment made in satisfaction of the liability under regulation 10(1) arising in connection with an earlier payment is not reflected in the certificate in force at the time of a later payment; and

(b) in consequence, the aggregate of payments made in satisfaction of the liability exceeds what it would have been had that payment been so reflected,

the Secretary of State is to pay the compensator who made the later payment an amount equal to the excess.

(4) Where—

(a) a compensator receives a payment under paragraph (3); and

(b) the amount of the compensation payment made by that compensator was calculated under regulation 12 [[1] or 12A],

then the compensation payment is to be recalculated under regulation 12 [[1] or 12A], and the compensator must pay the amount of the increase (if any) to the person to whom the compensation payment was made.

(5) Where both the earlier payment and the later payment are made by the same compensator, that compensator may—

(a) aggregate the gross amounts of the payments made;

(b) calculate what would have been the reduction made under regulation 12(3) if that aggregate amount had been paid at the date of the last payment on the basis that—

(i) the aggregate amount is to be taken to be the gross amount; and

(ii) the amount of any recoverable lump sum payment is to be taken to be the amount determined in accordance with the most recent certificate;

(c) deduct from that reduction calculated under sub-paragraph (b) the amount of the reduction under regulation 12(3) from any earlier payment; and

(d) deduct from the latest gross payment the net reduction calculated under sub-paragraph (c) (and accordingly the latest payment may be nil).

(6) Where a refund is made under paragraph (3), the Secretary of State is to send the compensator (with the refund) and the person to whom the compensation payment was made a statement showing—

(a) the total amount that has already been paid by that compensator to the Secretary of State;

(b) the amount that ought to have been paid by that compensator; and

(c) the amount to be repaid to that compensator by the Secretary of State.

(7) Where the reduction of a compensation payment is recalculated by virtue of paragraph (4) or (5) the compensator must give notice of the calculation to P.

AMENDMENT

1. Social Security (Recovery of Benefits) (Lump Sum Payments) (Amendment) Regulations 2014 (SI 2014/1456) reg.2 and Sch. paras 1 and 12 (July 1, 2014).

PART 5

MISCELLANEOUS

Information to be provided by the compensator

2.1041 **15.** The following information is prescribed for the purposes of sections 21(3)(a) and 23(1) of the Act—

(a) the full name and address of P;

(b) where known, the date of birth or national insurance number of P, or both if both are known; and

(c) the nature of the disease.

Information to be provided by P [1 and the scheme administrator]

2.1042 **16.** [1 —(1)] The following information is prescribed for the purposes of [1 section 23(2)(a) of the Act]—

(a) whether P has claimed or may claim a compensation payment, and if so, the full name and address of the person against whom the claim was or may be made;

(b) the amount of any compensation payment and the date on which it was made;

(c) the amount of the lump sum payment claimed, the type of that payment and the date on which it was paid.

[1 (2) For the purposes of section 23(2)(b) of the Act, the prescribed information is the amount of the lump sum payment falling within section 1A(2)(d) and the date on which it was paid.]

AMENDMENT

1. Social Security (Recovery of Benefits) (Lump Sum Payments) (Amendment) Regulations 2014 (SI 2014/1456) reg.2 and Sch. paras 1 and 13 (July 1, 2014).

Provision of information

2.1043 **17.** A person required to give information to the Secretary of State under regulation 15 or 16 is to do so by sending it to the Compensation Recovery Unit not later than 14 days after—

(a) where the person is one to whom regulation 15 applies, the date on which the compensator receives a claim for compensation from P in respect of the disease;

(b) where the person is one to whom regulation 16 applies, the date on which the Secretary of State requests the information from P [1 or the scheme administrator, as the case may be].

AMENDMENT

1. Social Security (Recovery of Benefits) (Lump Sum Payments) (Amendment) Regulations 2014 (SI 2014/1456) reg.2 and Sch. paras 1 and 14 (July 1, 2014).

Periodical payments

2.1044 **18.**—(1) This regulation applies where in final settlement of P's claim, an agreement is entered into—

(a) for the making of periodical payments (whether of an income or capital nature); or

(b) for the making of such payments and lump sum payments,

and, those payments would fall to be treated for the purposes of the Act as compensation payments.

(2) Where this regulation applies—

(a) the compensator in question is to be taken to have made a single compensation payment on the day of settlement;

(b) the total of the payments due to be made under the agreement referred to in paragraph (1) are to be taken to be a compensation payment for the purposes of the Act; and

(c) that single compensation payment is a payment from which lump sum payments may be recovered under these Regulations.

(3) In any case where—

(a) the person making the periodical payments ("the secondary party") does so in pursuance of arrangements entered into with another ("the primary party") (as in a case where the primary party purchases an annuity for P from the secondary party); and

(b) apart from those arrangements, the primary party would have been regarded as the compensator,

then for the purposes of the Act, the primary party is to be regarded as the compensator and the secondary party is not to be so regarded.

(4) In this regulation—

"the day of settlement" means—

(a) if the agreement referred to in paragraph (1) is approved by a court, the day on which that approval is given; and

(b) in any other case, the day on which the agreement is entered into;

"a single compensation payment" means the total amount of the payments due to be made under the agreement referred to in paragraph (1).

Adjustments

19.—(1) Where the conditions specified in subsection (1) and paragraphs (a) and (b) of subsection (2) of section 14 of the Act are satisfied, the Secretary of State is to pay the difference between the amount that has been paid and the amount that ought to have been paid to the compensator. **2.1045**

(2) Where the conditions specified in subsection (1) and paragraphs (a) and (b) of subsection (3) of section 14 of the Act are satisfied, the compensator is to pay the difference between the amount that has been paid and the amount that ought to have been paid to the Secretary of State.

(3) Where the Secretary of State is making a refund under paragraph (1), or demanding a payment of a further amount under paragraph (2), the Secretary of State is to send to the compensator (with the refund or demand) and to the person to whom the compensation payment was made a statement showing—

(a) the total amount that has already been paid to the Secretary of State;

(b) the amount that ought to have been paid; and

(c) the difference, and whether a repayment by the Secretary of State or a further payment by the compensator to the Secretary of State is required.

(4) This paragraph applies where—

(a) the amount of the compensation payment by the compensator was calculated under regulation 12; and

(b) the Secretary of State has made a payment under paragraph (1).

(5) Where paragraph (4) applies, the amount of the compensation payment is to be recalculated under regulation 12 to take account of the fresh certificate and the compensator must pay the amount of the increase (if any) to the person to whom the compensation payment was made.

[[1] (5A) This paragraph applies where—

(a) the amount of the payment made by the compensator was calculated under regulation 12A; and

(b) the Secretary of State has made a payment under paragraph (1).

(5B) Where paragraph (5A) applies, the amount of the compensation payment is to be recalculated under regulation 12A to take account of the fresh certificate and the compensator must pay the amount of the increase (if any) to the applicant as defined by regulation 3 of the Diffuse Mesothelioma Payment Scheme Regulations 2014.]

(6) This paragraph applies where—

(a) the amount of the compensation payment made by the compensator was calculated under regulation 12;

(b) the compensator has made a payment under paragraph (2); and

(c) the fresh certificate issued after the review or appeal was required as a result of P or such other person to whom the compensation payment was made supplying to the compensator information, knowing it to be incorrect or insufficient, with the intent of enhancing the compensation payment calculated under regulation 12, and the compensator supplying that information to the Secretary of State without knowing it to be incorrect or insufficient.

(7) Where paragraph (6) applies, the compensator may recalculate the compensation payment under regulation 12 to take account of the fresh certificate and may require the repayment of the difference (if any) between the payment made and the payment as so recalculated by the person to whom the compensator made the compensation payment.

[[1] (8) This paragraph applies where—

(a) the amount of the payment made by the compensator was calculated under regulation 12A; and

(b) the fresh certificate issued after the review or appeal was required as a result of any applicant for payment under the Diffuse Mesothelioma Payment Scheme supplying to the compensator information knowing it to be incorrect or insufficient, and the compensator supplying that information to the Secretary of State without knowing it to be incorrect or insufficient.

(9) Where paragraph (8) applies, the compensator may recalculate the compensation payment under regulation 12A to take account of the fresh certificate and may require the repayment by the applicant responsible for supplying the incorrect or insufficient information of the difference (if any) between the payment made and the payment so recalculated.]

AMENDMENT

1. Social Security (Recovery of Benefits) (Lump Sum Payments) (Amendment) Regulations 2014 (SI 2014/1456) reg.2 and Sch. paras 1 and 15 (July 1, 2014).

SCHEDULE 1

MODIFICATION OF CERTAIN PROVISIONS OF THE ACT

1. This Schedule applies to any case to which regulation 4 [3 or 4A] applies. **2.1046**

2. Where this Schedule applies, section 1 (cases in which this Act applies) is to apply as if in subsection (3), for "Subsection (1)(a)" there were substituted "Section 1A(1)(a)".

3. Where this Schedule applies, section 10 (review of certificates of recoverable benefits) is to apply as if in—

(a) the heading and in subsection (1), there were omitted "of recoverable benefits" in each place it occurs;
(b) subsection (3), for "benefits" there were substituted "lump sum payments, except where that certificate has been reviewed under regulation 9ZA(1)(e) of the Social Security and Child Support (Decisions and Appeals) Regulations 1999 (review of certificates),".

4. Where this Schedule applies, section 11 (appeals against certificates of recoverable benefits) is to apply as if in—

(a) the heading and in subsections (1) and (2)(a), there were omitted "of recoverable benefits" in each place it occurs;
(b) subsection (1)(a), there were omitted ", rate or period";
(c) subsection (1)(b)—
 (i) for "listed benefits" there were substituted "[3 recoverable lump sum payments]";
 (ii) there were omitted "accident, injury or";
(d) subsection (1)(c)—
 (i) for "listed benefits" there were substituted [3 recoverable lump sum payments];
 (ii) for "the injured person during the relevant period" there were substituted "P";
(e) subsection (1)(d), for "1(1)(a)" there were substituted "1A(1)(a)";
(f) subsection (2)(aa) for "section 7(2)(a)" there were substituted "regulation 11(2)(a) of the Lump Sum Payments Regulations";
(g) subsection (2)(b), for "section 8 [3 or 8A]) the injured person" there were substituted "regulation 12 [3 or 12A] of the Lump Sum Payments Regulations) P";
(h) subsection (3), for "section 6" there were substituted "regulation 10 of the Lump Sum Payments Regulations".

5. Where this Schedule applies, section 12 (reference of questions to [2 First-tier Tribunal]) is to apply as if in—

(a) [2 . . .]
(b) subsection (3), there were omitted "accident, injury or";
(c) subsection (4)(a), for "amounts, rates and periods" there were substituted "amount, type and date of payments";
(d) subsections (4)(a) and (c), there were omitted "of recoverable benefits" in each place it occurs.

6. [1 Where this Schedule applies, section 13 (appeal to [2 Upper Tribunal]) is to apply [3 as if in subsection (2)—

(a) in paragraph (b), there were omitted "of recoverable benefits";
(b) in paragraph (bb), for "section 7(2)(a)" there were substituted "regulation 11(2)(a) of the Lump Sum Payments Regulations";
(c) in paragraph (c), for "section 8 or 8A) the injured person" there were substituted "regulation 12 or 12A of the Lump Sum Payments Regulations) P".]]

7. Where this Schedule applies, section 14 (reviews and appeals: supplementary) is to apply as if in—

(a) subsection (1), there were omitted "of recoverable benefits";
(b) subsections (2) and (3), for "section 6" there were substituted "regulation 10 of the Lump Sum Payments Regulations" in each place it occurs;
(c) subsection (4), for "section 8 [3 or 8A]" there were substituted "regulation 12 [3 or 12A] of the Lump Sum Payments Regulations".

8. Where this Schedule applies, for section 15 (court orders) is to apply as if there were substituted—

"15.—(1) This section applies where a court makes an order for a compensation payment to be made in a case where a compensation payment is to be made to a dependant of P—

(a) under the Fatal Accidents Act 1976 (c. 30);
(b) to the extent that it is made in respect of a liability arising by virtue of section 1 of the Damages (Scotland) Act 1976 (c. 13);

(c) under the Fatal Accidents (Northern Ireland) Order 1977 (S.I. 1977/1251 (N.I. 18)); or
(d) in respect of P, where that dependant is an intended beneficiary of part or all of that compensation,

and a lump sum payment has been made to that dependant, unless the order is made with the consent of that dependant and the person by whom the payment is to be made.

(2) The court must specify in the order the amount of the payment made—

(a) under the Fatal Accidents Act 1976;
(b) to the extent that it is made in respect of a liability arising by virtue of section 1 of the Damages (Scotland) Act 1976;
(c) under the Fatal Accidents (Northern Ireland) Order 1977; or
(d) in respect of P, where a dependant of P is an intended beneficiary of part or all of that compensation,

which is attributable to each or any dependant of P who has received a lump sum payment.".

9. Where this Schedule applies, section 17 (benefits irrelevant to assessment of damages) is to apply as if—

(a) in the heading for "benefits" there were substituted "lump sum payments";
(b) there were omitted "accident, injury or";
(c) for "listed benefits" there were substituted "lump sum payments".

10. Where this Schedule applies, section 18 (lump sum and periodical payments) is to apply as if—

(a) in subsection (1)—
 (i) for "the injured person" there were substituted "P";
 (ii) there were omitted "accident, injury or";
(b) in subsection (2), for "section 8" there were substituted "regulation 12 of the Lump Sum Payments Regulations";
(c) for subsection (3) there were substituted—
 "(3) For the purposes of subsection (2), the regulations may provide for—
 (a) the gross amounts of the compensation payments to be aggregated and for the aggregate amount to be the gross amount of the compensation payment for the purposes of regulation 12 of the Lump Sum Payments Regulations; and
 (b) for the amount of any lump sum payment to be taken to be the amount determined in accordance with the most recent certificate.";
(d) in subsection (4), for "the injured person's" there were substituted "P's";
(e) in subsection (5), there were omitted paragraph (a).

11. Where this Schedule applies, section 19 (payments by more than one person) is to apply as if in—

(a) subsection (1)—
 (i) for "injured person" there were substituted "P";
 (ii) there were omitted "accident, injury or";
(b) subsection (2)—
 (i) for "section 6" there were substituted "regulation 10 of the Lump Sum Payments Regulations";
 (ii) for "benefits" there were substituted "lump sum payments";
(c) subsection (3)—
 (i) in paragraph (a), for "benefits" there were substituted "lump sum payments";
 (ii) in paragraph (b), for "section 8 [3 or 8A]" there were substituted "regulation 12 [3 or 12A] of the Lump Sum Payments Regulations".

12. Where this Schedule applies, section 20 (amounts overpaid under section 6) is to apply as if in—

(a) the heading and in subsection (1), for "section 6" there were substituted "regulation 10 of Lump Sum Payments Regulations" in each place it occurs;
(b) subsection (4)(a), for "section 8 [3 or 8A]" there were substituted "regulation 12 [3 or 12A] of the Lump Sum Payments Regulations".

13. Where this Schedule applies, section 21 (compensation payments to be disregarded) is to apply as if in—

(a) subsections (1) and (5)(a), for "sections 6 and 8 [3 or 8A]" there were substituted "regulations 10 and 12 [3 or 12A] of the Lump Sum Payments Regulations" in each place it occurs;
(b) subsection (2)(a), there were omitted "of recoverable benefits";
(c) subsection (3)(a)—
 (i) for "the injured person" there were substituted "P";
 (ii) there were omitted "accident, injury or";

(d) subsection (4), for "section 4" there were substituted "regulation 8 of the Lump Sum Payments Regulations";
(e) subsection (5)(b), for "section 6" there were substituted "regulation 10 of the Lump Sum Payments Regulations".

14. Where this Schedule applies, section 22(1) (liability of insurers) is to apply as if—
(a) in paragraph (a), there were omitted "accident, injury or";
(b) for "section 6" there were substituted "regulation 10 of the Lump Sum Payments Regulations".

15. Where this Schedule applies, section 23 (provision of information) is to apply as if—
(a) in subsection (1), for—
(i) "any accident, injury or" there were substituted "a";
(ii) "any person ("the injured person")" there were substituted "P";
(iii) "the injured person" there were substituted "P";
(b) in subsection (1)(a), there were omitted "accident, injury or";
[3 (ba) after subsection (1)(b) there were inserted—
", and
(c) where the compensation which is sought is a payment under the Diffuse Mesothelioma Payment Scheme, subsection (6A) applies.";
(c) for subsection (2), there were substituted—
"(2) Where P or a dependant of P, receives or claims a lump sum payment which is or is likely to be paid in respect of the disease suffered by P [3 —
(a) the prescribed information about the disease must be given to the Secretary of State by P or a dependant of P, as the case may be;
(b) the prescribed information about any lump sum payment which falls within section 1A(2)(d) must be given to the Secretary of State by the scheme administrator.]
(d) in subsection (3), for "listed benefit" there were substituted "lump sum payment";
(e) in subsection (4)—
(i) for "any accident, injury or" there were substituted "a";
(ii) there were omitted ", or any damage to property,";
(f) there were omitted subsections (5), (6) and (8).

16. Where this Schedule applies, section 26 (residence of the injured person—Northern Ireland) is to apply as if—
(a) in subsections (1)(a) and (b)(i), (2)(a), (b) and (c) and (3)(d)(ii), there were omitted "of recoverable benefits" in each place it occurs;
(b) in subsections (1)(c)(ii) and (2)(c)(i), for "section 6" there were substituted "regulation 10 of the Lump Sum Payments Regulations";
(c) in subsections (1) and (2), for "injured person's address" there were substituted "address of P";
(d) for subsection (3)(a), there were substituted—
"(a) "the address of P" is the address first notified in writing to the person making the payment by or on behalf of P as the residence of P (or if P had died, by or on behalf of the person entitled to receive the compensation payment as the last residence of P),";
(e) in subsection (3)(d)(i) and the heading to this section, for "the injured person" there were substituted "P" in each place it occurs.

17. Where this Schedule applies, section 27 (jurisdiction of courts—Northern Ireland) is to apply as if in—
(a) subsections (1) and (2), for "section 7" there were substituted "regulation 11 of the Lump Sum Payments Regulations" in each place it occurs;
(b) subsection (3)(a)(i), for—
(i) "the injured person" the first time it occurs, there were substituted "P";
(ii) "the injured person or, if he" there were substituted "P or, if P".

18. Where this Schedule applies, section 29 (general interpretation) is to apply as if—
(a) there were omitted the following definitions—
(i) "benefit";
(ii) "compensation scheme for motor accidents";
(iii) "listed benefit";
(b) in the appropriate place, there were inserted the following definitions—
(i) "certificate" means a certificate which includes amounts in respect of recoverable benefits and of recoverable lump sum payments, including where any of those amounts are nil;
(ii) "P" is to be construed in accordance with regulation 5 of the Lump Sum Payments Regulations;

(iii) "recoverable lump sum payments" means any lump sum payments which are recoverable by virtue of regulation 4 [3 or 4A] of the Lump Sum Payments Regulations;

(iv) "the Lump Sum Payments Regulations" means the Social Security (Recovery of Benefits) (Lump Sum Payments) Regulations 2008.

19. Where this Schedule applies, Part 1 of Schedule 1 (compensation payments—exempted payments) is to apply as if—

(a) in paragraph 2 and 3(a), for "the injured person" there were substituted "P" in each place it occurs;

(b) in paragraph 3(a) and (b) there were omitted "accident, injury or" in each place it occurs;

(c) for paragraph 5(1) there were substituted—

"(1) Any payment made to P or a dependant of P by an insurer under the terms of any contract of insurance entered into between P and the insurer before the date on which P or a dependant of P first claims a lump sum payment in consequence of the disease in question suffered by P.";

(d) in paragraph 6 for "an accident, injury or" there were substituted "a".

20. Where this Schedule applies, paragraph 9 of Part 2 of Schedule 1 (compensation payments—power to disregard small payments) is to apply as if in—

(a) sub-paragraph (1), for "sections 6 and 8" there were substituted "regulations 10 and 12 of the Lump Sum Payments Regulations";

(b) sub-paragraph (3)(a)—

(i) for "injured person" there were substituted "P";

(ii) there were omitted "accident, injury or".

AMENDMENTS

1. Social Security (Miscellaneous Amendments) (No.3) Regulations 2008 (SI 2008/2365) reg.6 (October 1, 2008).

2. Tribunals, Courts and Enforcement Act 2007 (Transitional and Consequential Provisions Order 2008 (SI 2008/2683) Sch.1 para.344 (November 3, 2008).

3. Social Security (Recovery of Benefits) (Lump Sum Payments) (Amendment) Regulations 2014 (SI 2014/1456) reg.2 and Sch. paras 1 and 16 (July 1, 2014).

GENERAL NOTE

2.1047 This Schedule applies, with modifications, a number of the provisions relating to adjudication in the 1997 Act to the recovery of lump sum payments under these Regulations. In particular, ss.9 to 14 of the 1997 Act, relating to reviews and appeals, are applied as modified. In *Aviva Insurance Ltd v SSWP* [2015] UKUT 613 (AAC); [2016] AACR 29, it was accepted that, having regard to *R(CR) 1/02*, a compensator was in principle entitled to argue on an appeal to the First-tier Tribunal that the payment made to the claimant under the Pneumoconiosis etc. (Workers' Compensation) Act 1979 that the Secretary of State now sought to recover ought not to have been made because the Secretary of State had misconstrued the 1979 Act when awarding the payment. However, the argument advanced by the compensator was rejected on its merits.

SCHEDULE 2

2.1048 *Omitted.*

The Social Security (Work-focused Interviews for Lone Parents) and Miscellaneous Amendments Regulations 2000

(SI 2000/1926)

ARRANGEMENT OF REGULATIONS

The Secretary of State for Social Security, in exercise of the powers conferred upon him by sections 123(1)(d) and (e) and 137(1) of the Social Security Contributions and Benefits Act 1992 and sectons 2A(1), (3)(b) to (f), (4), (5)(a) and (b), (6), (7) and (8), 2B(2), (6) and (7), 2C, 189(4) to (7A) and 191 of the Social Security Administration Act 1992 and of all other powers enabling him in that behalf, after consultation with the Council on Tribunals in accordance with section 8(1) of the Tribunals and Inquiries Act 1992 and in respect of provisions in these Regulations relating to housing benefit and council tax benefit with organisations appearing to him to be representative of the authorities concerned and after agreement by the Social Security Advisory Committee that proposals in respect of these Regulations should not be referred to it, hereby makes the following Regulations:

Citation, commencement and interpretation

1.—(1) These Regulations may be cited as the Social Security (Work-focused Interviews for Lone Parents) and Miscellaneous Amendments Regulations 2000. 2.1050

(2) This Regulation and paragraphs 2 to 5 of Schedule 2 and regulation 10 in so far as it relates to those paragraphs shall come into force on 14th August 2000.

(3) Regulations 2 to 9, paragraph 1 of Schedule 2 and regulation 10 in so far as it relates to that paragraph shall—

(a) come into force on 30th October 2000 in respect of lone parents who on that date—

(i) live in an area identified in Schedule 1: and
(ii) are not entitled to income support;

(b) subject to sub-paragraph (a), come into force on 30th April 2001 in respect of lone parents who on that date—
(i) are not entitled to income support; or
(ii) are entitled to income support and are not—
(aa) responsible for; and
(bb) living in the same household as,
a child under the age of 13;

(c) subject to the preceding sub-paragraphs, come into force on 1st April 2002 in respect of lone parents who on that date are entitled to income support and are not—
(i) responsible for; and
(ii) living in the same household as,
a child under the age of 9;

(d) subject to the preceding sub-paragraphs, where a lone parent—
(i) is responsible for and living in the same household as a child whose 13th birthday occurs in the period beginning on 1st May 2001 and ending on 31st March 2002; and
(ii) is not on the date of the 13th birthday responsible for and living in the same household as a younger child,
come into force in respect of that lone parent on the date of that child's 13th birthday;

(e) subject to the preceding sub-paragraphs, where a loneparent—
(i) is responsible for and living in the same household as a child whose 9th birthday occurs in the period beginning on 2nd April 2002 and ending on 6th April 2003; and
(ii) is not on the date of the 9th birthday responsible for and living in the same household as a younger child,
come into force in respect of that lone parent on the date of that child's 9th birthday; and

[[1] (f) subject to the preceding sub-paragraphs, come into force on 7th April 2003 in respect of lone parents who on that date are entitled to income support and are not responsible for and living in the same household as a child under the age of 5 years and 3 months;

[[3] (g) subject to the preceding sub-paragraphs, come into force on 5th April 2004 in respect of a lone parent who on that date is entitled to income support and is responsible for an living in the same household as a child.]
come into force in respect of that lone parent on the date that child reaches the age of 5 years and 3 months.]

(4) In these Regulations, unless the context otherwise requires—
"the 1998 Act" means the Social Security Act 1998;
"benefit week" means any period of seven days corresponding to the week in respect of which income support is due to be paid;
"lone parent" has the meaning it bears in regulation 2(1) of the Income Support (General) Regulations 1987;
"interview" means a work-focused interview with a lone parent conducted for any or all of the following purposes—
(a) assessing that person's prospects for existing or future employment (whether paid or voluntary);

(b) assisting or encouraging that person to enhance his prospects of such employment;
(c) identifying activities which that person may undertake to strengthen his existing or future prospects of employment;
(d) identifying current or future employment or training opportunities suitable to that person's needs; and
(e) identifying educational opportunities connected with the existing or future employment prospects or needs of that person; and

"officer" means an officer of, or providing services to, the Secretary of State.

[4 "pensionable age", in the case of a man born before 6th April 1955, means the age when a woman born on the same day as the man would attain pensionable age.]

[5 "relevant interview" means an interview under these Regulations in relation to the lone parent's current award of income support.]

(5) In these Regulations, unless the context otherwise requires, a reference—
(a) to a numbered regulation is to a regulation in these Regulations bearing that number;
(b) in a regulation to a numbered paragraph or sub-paragraph is to the paragraph or sub-paragraph in that regulation bearing that number;
(c) to a numbered Schedule is to the Schedule to these Regulations bearing that number.

[5 (6) For the purposes of section 2A(2A)(b) of the Social Security Administration Act 1992 and these Regulations, a lone parent is to be treated as responsible for, and a member of the same household as, a child under the age of one where the lone parent is treated as being responsible for and a member of the same household as such a child under regulations 15 and 16 of the Income Support (General) Regulations 1987.]

AMENDMENTS

1. The Social Security (Work-focused Interviews for Lone Parents) Amendment Regulations 2002 (SI 2002/670) reg.2 (April 8, 2002).
2. The Social Security (Work-focused Interviews for Lone Parents) Amendment Regulations 2003 (SI 2003/400) reg.2 (April 7, 2003).
3. The Social Security (Miscellaneous Amendments) Regulations 2004 (SI 2004/565) reg.7 (April 5, 2004).
4. The Social Security (Work-focused Interviews etc.) (Equalisation of State Pension Age) Amendment Regulations 2010 (SI 2010/563) reg.4(2) (April 6, 2010).
5. The Social Security (Work-focused Interviews for Lone Parents and Partners) (Amendment) Regulations 2011 (SI 2011/2428) reg.2 (October 31, 2011).

[1 Requirement for certain lone parents entitled to income support to take part in an interview

2.—(1) Subject to this regulation and regulations 2ZA and 4 to 6, a lone parent who falls within paragraph 1 (lone parents) of Schedule 1B (prescribed categories of person) to the Income Support (General) Regulations 1987(7) and paragraph (2) or (3) is required to take part in an interview. 2.1051

(2) A lone parent falls within this paragraph if the lone parent is entitled to income support and has not taken part or been required to take part in a relevant interview.

(3) A lone parent falls within this paragraph if the lone parent has—

(a) taken part;

(b) failed to take part; or

(c) been treated as having taken part,

in a relevant interview.

(4) Where a lone parent falls within paragraph (3) the requirement to take part in an interview arises every six months after the date on which the lone parent—

(a) last took part;

(b) last failed to take part; or

(c) was last treated as having taken part,

in a relevant interview.

(5) Where a determination has been made in relation to a lone parent under regulation 6(1) (waiver) the lone parent is to be treated for the purposes of paragraph (2) of this regulation as if he has not taken part or been required to take part in a relevant interview.]

AMENDMENT

1. This version of the regulation introduced by the Social Security (Work-focused Interviews for Lone Parents and Partners) (Amendment) Regulations 2011 (SI 2011/2428) reg.2 (October 31, 2011).

[1 Requirement for certain lone parents to take part in an interview

2.1052 **2ZA.**—(1) This regulation applies to a lone parent if—

(a) he is entitled to income support and is a person to whom paragraph 1 (lone parents) of schedule 1B to the Income Support (General) Regulations 1987 applies; [5 and]

(b) no other paragraph of that Schedule applies to him; [5 . . .]

(c) [5 . . .]

[5 (2) Subject to regulations 4 and 5, a lone parent to whom this regulation applies is required to take part in one or more interviews as a condition of continuing to be entitled to the full amount of benefit which is payable to him part from these Regulations.]

AMENDMENTS

1. Inserted by The Social Security (Lone Parents and Miscellaneous Amendments) Regulations 2008 (SI 2008/3051) reg.5 (November 23, 2008).

2. Social Security (Lone Parents and Miscellaneous Amendments) Regulations 2008 (SI 2008/3051) reg.7 (October 25, 2010).

3. The Social Security (Work-focused Interviews for Lone Parents and Partners) (Amendment) Regulations 2011 (SI 2011/2428) reg.2 (October 31, 2011).

4. The Social Security (Lone Parents and Miscellaneous Amendments) Regulations 2012 (SI 2012/874) (May 21, 2012).

5. Income Support (Work-Related Activity) and Miscellaneous Amendments Regulations 2014 (SI 2014/1097), reg.13(2) (April 28, 2014).

GENERAL NOTE

2.1053 Note that the Schedule to The Social Security (Lone Parents and Miscellaneous Amendments) Regulations 2012 (SI 2012/874) contains special commencement provisions for certain classes of claimant.

2.1054 **2A** [1 ...]

AMENDMENT

1. Omitted under The Social Security (Work-focused Interviews for Lone Parents and Partners) (Amendment) Regulations 2011 (SI 2011/2428) reg.2 (October 31, 2011).

[1 General requirement for lone parents entitled to income support to take part in an interview

2ZB.—(1) Subject to regulations 4 to 6, this regulation applies to a lone parent who does not fall within paragraph 1 (lone parents) of Schedule 1B (prescribed categories of person) to the Income Support (General) Regulations 1987 and is entitled to income support. 2.1055

(2) A lone parent to whom this regulation applies is required to take part in an interview—

(a) where paragraph (3) applies to them; or

(b) where paragraph (4) and either paragraph (5) or (6) applies to them.

(3) This paragraph applies to a lone parent who has not taken part or been required to take part in a relevant interview.

(4) This paragraph applies to a lone parent who has taken part in a relevant interview or who would have taken part in such an interview but for—

(a) the requirement being deferred in accordance with regulation 5, or

(b) the requirement being waived in accordance with regulation 6.

(5) This paragraph applies to a lone parent when any of the following circumstances arise—

(a) the lone parent's entitlement to carer's allowance ceases whilst entitlement to income support continues;

(b) the lone parent becomes engaged or ceases to be engaged in part-time work;

(c) the lone parent has been undergoing education or training arranged by an officer and that education or training comes to an end; or

(d) the lone parent attains the age of 18 and has not previously taken part in a relevant interview.

(6) This paragraph applies where a lone parent has not been required to take part in a relevant interview for at least 36 months.]

AMENDMENT

1. Inserted by The Social Security (Work-focused Interviews for Lone Parents and Partners) (Amendment) Regulations 2011 (SI 2011/2428) reg.2 (October 31, 2011).

2B [1 . . .] 2.1056

AMENDMENT

1. Omitted under The Social Security (Miscellaneous Amendments) Regulations 2011 (SI 2011/674) reg.9 (April 1 *or* April 4, 2011).

[1 The interview

2C. —[2 (1) An interview under these Regulations shall take place— 2.1057

(a) where regulation 2ZA applies, on such date as may be determined by an officer;

(b) in any other case, as soon as is reasonably practicable after the date on which the requirement to take part in the interview arises.]

(2) An officer shall inform the lone parent of the place and time of the interview.

(3) An officer may determine that an interview is to take place in the lone parent's home where it would, in the opinion of the officer, be unreasonable to expect that lone parent to attend elsewhere because that lone parent's personal circumstances are such that attending elsewhere would—

(a) cause him undue inconvenience, or
(b) endanger his health.

AMENDMENTS

1. Inserted by The Social Security (Work-focused Interviews for Lone Parents) Amendment Regulations 2007 (SI 2007/1034) (April 30, 2007).

2. Income Support (Work-Related Activity) and Miscellaneous Amendments Regulations 2014 (SI 2014/1097), reg.13(3) (April 28, 2014).

Taking part in an interview

2.1058 **3.**—(1) An officer shall determine whether a lone parent has taken part in an interview.

[[1] (2) Subject to regulations 5(2) and 6(2), a lone parent who has not taken part in an interview under these Regulations before 31st October 2005 shall be regarded as having taken part in his first interview under these Regulations if—

(a) he attends for the interview at the place and time notified to him by the officer;
(b) he participates in discussions with the officer in relation to the lone parent's employability, including any action the lone parent and the officer agree is reasonable and they are willing to take in order to help the lone parent enhance his employment prospects;
(c) he provides answers (where asked) to questions and appropriate information about—
  (i) the level to which he has pursued any educational qualifications;
  (ii) his employment history;
  (iii) any vocational training he has undertaken;
  (iv) any skills he has acquired which fit him for employment;
  (v) any paid or unpaid employment he is engaged in;
  (vi) any medical condition which, in his opinion, puts him at a disadvantage in obtaining employment;
  (vii) any caring or childcare responsibilities he has;
  (viii) his aspirations for future employment;
  (ix) any vocational training or skills which he wishes to undertake or acquire; and
  (x) his work related abilities; and
(d) he assists the officer in the completion of an action plan which records the matters discussed in relation to sub-paragraph (b) above.

(2A) Subject to regulations 5(2) and 6(2), a lone parent who has taken part in an interview under these Regulations before 31st October 2005 shall be regarded as having taken part in his first interview under these Regulations after 30th October 2005 if—

(a) he attends for the interview at the place and time notified to him by the officer;

(b) he participates in discussions with the officer in relation to the lone parent's employability, including any action the lone parent and the officer agree is reasonable and they are willing to take in order to help the lone parent enhance his employment prospects;

(c) he participates in discussions with the officer—

(i) in relation to the lone parent's employability or any progress he might have made towards obtaining employment; and

(ii) in order to consider any of the programmes and support available to help the lone parent obtain employment;

(d) he provides answers (where asked) to questions and appropriate information about—

(i) the content of any report made following his personal capability assessment, insofar as that report relates to the lone parent's capabilities and employability; and

(ii) his opinion as to the extent to which his medical condition restricts his ability to obtain employment; and

(e) he assists the officer in the completion of an action plan which records the matters discussed in relation to sub-paragraph (b) above.

(2B) Subject to regulations 5(2) and 6(2), a lone parent shall be regarded as having taken part in any subsequent interview under these Regulations if—

(a) he attends for the interview at the place and time notified to him by the officer;

(b) he participates in discussions with the officer—

(i) in relation to the lone parent's employability or any progress he might have made towards obtaining employment;

(ii) about any action the lone parent or the officer might have taken as a result of the matters discussed in relation to paragraph (2)(b) or (2A)(b) above;

(iii) about how, if at all, the action plan referred to in paragraphs (2)(d) or (2A)(e) above should be amended; and

(iv) in order to consider any of the programmes and support available to help the lone parent obtain employment;

(c) he provides answers (where asked) to questions and appropriate information about—

(i) the content of any report made following his personal capability assessment, insofar as that report relates to the lone parent's capabilities and employability; and

(ii) his opinion as to the extent to which his medical condition restricts his ability to obtain employment; and

(d) he assists the officer in the completion of any amendment of the action plan referred to in paragraphs (2)(d) or (2A)(e) above in light of the matters discussed in relation to sub-paragraph (b) above and the information provided in relation to sub-paragraph (c) above.]

AMENDMENT

1. The Social Security (Work-focused Interviews) Amendment Regulations 2005 (SI 2005/2727) (October 31, 2005).

[1 Circumstances where requirement to take part in an interview does not apply

2.1059 **4.**—(1) [8 Regulation 2 [9, 2ZA] and 2ZB] shall not apply where the lone parent—

(a) has attained [6 pensionable age];

(b) has not attained the age of 18; or

(c) is—

(i) required to take part in an interview, or

(ii) not required to take part in an interview by virtue of—

(aa) a waiver of a requirement, or

(bb) a deferment of an interview, under the Social Security (Work-focused Interviews) Regulations 2000, the Social Security (Jobcentre Plus Interviews) Regulations 2001, the Social Security (Jobcentre Plus Interviews) Regulations 2002, [3 or the Social Security (Incapacity Benefit Work-focused Interviews) Regulations 2003.]

[8 (1A) [9 Regulation 2 and 2ZA] shall not apply to a lone parent who is treated as responsible for, and a member of the same household as, a child who is under the age of one.]

(2) [2. . .]

[3 (3) [9. . .]

AMENDMENTS

1. The Social Security (Work-focused Interviews) Amendment Regulations 2005 (SI 2005/2727) (October 31, 2005).

2. The Social Security (Working Neighbourhoods) Miscellaneous Amendment Regulations 2006 (SI 2006/909) (April 24, 2006).

3. The Social Security (Work-focused Interviews for Lone Parents) Amendment Regulations 2007 (SI 2007/1034) (April 30, 2007).

4. The Social Security (Incapacity Benefit Work-focused Interviews) Regulations 2008 (SI 2008/2928) reg.12 (December 15, 2008).

5. The Social Security (Lone Parents and Miscellaneous Amendments) Regulations 2008 (SI 2008/3051) reg.5 (November 23, 2008).

6. The Social Security (Work-focused Interviews etc.) (Equalisation of State Pension Age) Amendment Regulations 2010 (SI 2010/563) reg.4(3) (April 6, 2010).

7. The Social Security (Miscellaneous Amendments) Regulations 2011 (SI 2011/674) reg.9 (April 1 *or* April 4, 2011).

8. The Social Security (Work-focused Interviews for Lone Parents and Partners) (Amendment) Regulations 2011 (SI 2011/2428) reg.2 (October 31, 2011).

9. Income Support (Work-Related Activity) and Miscellaneous Amendments Regulations 2014 (SI 2014/1097), reg.13(4) (April 28, 2014).

Deferment of requirement to take part in an interview

2.1060 **5.**—(1) A requirement by virtue of these Regulations to take part in an interview shall not apply to a person until a date determined by an officer where he determines that an interview would not [1 until] that time be—

(a) of assistance to that person; or

(b) appropriate in the circumstances.

(2) Except for the purpose of [2 regulations [4 2, 2ZA and 2A]], where an officer has made a decision under paragraph (1), the person to whom that decision relates shall be treated for the purposes of any claim

for, or entitlement to, income suppport as having complied with the requirement to take part in an interview until an officer decides whether that person took part in the interview which had been deferred under paragraph (1).

AMENDMENTS

1. The Social Security (Claims and Information and Work-focused Interviews for Lone Parents) Amendment Regulations 2001 (SI 2001/1189) reg.3 (April 23, 2001).
2. The Social Security (Work-focused Interviews) Amendment Regulations 2005 (SI 2005/2727) (October 31, 2005).
3. The Social Security (Lone Parents and Miscellaneous Amendments) Regulations 2008 (SI 2008/3051) reg.5 (November 23, 2008).
4. The Social Security (Miscellaneous Amendments) Regulations 2011 (SI 2011/674) reg.9 (April 1 *or* April 4, 2011).

Waiver

6.—(1) A requirement imposed by [3 regulations 2(1) and 2ZB(2)] to take part in an interview shall not apply if an officer determines that an interview would not be— **2.1061**

(a) of assistance to the lone parent; or
(b) appropriate in the circumstances.

(2) A person in relation to whom a requirement to take part in an interview has been waived under paragraph (1) shall be treated for the purposes of—

(a) [2 2 [3. . .] and 2A]; and
(b) any claim for, or entitlement to, income support,

as having complied with that requirement.

AMENDMENTS

1. The Social Security (Work-focused Interviews) Amendment Regulations 2005 (SI 2005/2727) (October 31, 2005).
2. The Social Security (Miscellaneous Amendments) Regulations 2011 (SI 2011/674) reg.9 (April 1 *or* April 4, 2011).
3. Income Support (Work-Related Activity) and Miscellaneous Amendments Regulations 2014 (SI 2014/1097), reg.13(5) (April 28, 2014).

Consequence of failure to take part in an interview

7.—(1) Subject to paragraphs [6 (2), (5) and (5A) and regulations 5 and 6, [5 the consequence specified in paragraph (3) ensues] if a person does not— **2.1062**

(a) take part in any interview when required to do so; and
(b) show good cause for not taking part in an interview before the end of five working days following the [6 date on which the person was notified of his failure to take part in the interview]

[6 (1A) Where a notice under paragraph (1)(b) is sent by post it is taken to have been received on the second working day after it was sent.]

(2) In a case where within one month of the date on which the decision was notified to a lone parent that he failed without good cause to take part in an interview—

(a) he brings new facts to the notice of an officer which could not reasonably have been brought to an officer's notice within five working days of the [6 date on which the person was notified of his failure to take part in the interview]; and

(b) those facts show that he had good cause for his failure to take part in the interview

paragraph (1)(b) shall apply with the modification that for the words "five working days following" there were substituted the words "one month of".

[5 (3) the income support of a lone parent to whom paragraph (1) applies shall be reduced in accordance with regulation 8.]

(4) Where an interview which arose in connection with a claim was deferred and benefit became payable in accordance with regulation 5(2), the person's entitlement to income support shall terminate as from the first day of the next benefit week following the date the decision was made that the person failed without good cause to take part in an interview.

(5) For the purposes of this regulation and regulation 8(1), matters to be taken into account in determining whether a person has shown good cause for his failure to take part in an interview include—

(a) that the lone parent misunderstood the requirement to take part in the interview due to any learning, language or literacy difficulties of the lone parent or any misleading information given to him by an officer;

(b) that the lone parent was attending a medical or dental appointment, or accompanying someone for whom he has caring responsibilities to such an appointment, and that it would be unreasonable, in the circumstances, to have rearranged that appointment;

(c) that the lone parent had difficulties with his normal mode of transport and that no reasonable alternative was available;

(d) that the established customs and practices of the religion to which that lone parent belongs prevented him attending at the time and place for the interview notified to him by an officer;

(e) that the lone parent was attending an interview with an employer with a view to obtaining employment;

(f) that the lone parent was pursuing employment opportunities as a self-employed earner;

(g) that a dependant of the lone parent or someone for whom the lone parent provides care suffered an accident, sudden illness or relapse of [1 a physical or mental health condition];

(h) that the lone parent was attending a funeral of a close friend or relative on the day fixed for the interview; and

(i) that a disability from which the lone parent suffers made it impracticable for him to attend at the time fixed for the interview.

[6 (5A) The amount of income support payable to a person is not to be reduced in accordance with paragraph (3) if that amount—

(a) is, at the time a decision falls to be made in respect of the current failure, being paid at a reduced rate in accordance with paragraph (3) and regulation 8, regulation 12(2)(c) of the Social Security (Jobcentre Plus Interviews) Regulations 2002 or regulation 8(1) and (2) of the Income Support (Work-Related Activity) and Miscellaneous Amendments Regulations 2014; and

(b) was last reduced not more than two weeks before the date of the current failure.

(5B) In paragraph (5A), "current failure" means a failure which may, in the case of a claimant who has an award of income support, lead to a reduction in income support under paragraph (3) and regulation 8 in relation to which the Secretary of State has not yet determined whether the amount of income support payable to the person is to be reduced in accordance with that paragraph and regulation.]

(6) For the avoidance of doubt, a person who is regarded as not having made a claim for income support because he failed to take part in an interview shall be required to make a new claim for income support in order to establish entitlement to that benefit.

AMENDMENTS

1. The Social Security (Work-focused Interviews) Amendment Regulations 2005 (SI 2005/2727) (October 31, 2005).

2. The Social Security (Work-focused Interviews for Lone Parents) Amendment Regulations 2007 (SI 2007/1034) (April 30, 2007).

3. The Social Security (Lone Parents and Miscellaneous Amendments) Regulations 2008 (SI 2008/3051) reg.5 (November 23, 2008).

4. The Social Security (Miscellaneous Amendments) Regulations 2011 (SI 2011/674) reg.9 (April 1 *or* April 4, 2011).

5. The Social Security (Work-focused Interviews for Lone Parents and Partners) (Amendment) Regulations 2011 (SI 2011/2428) reg.2 (October 31, 2011).

6. Income Support (Work-Related Activity) and Miscellaneous Amendments Regulations 2014 (SI 2014/1097), reg.13(6) (April 29, 2014).

Reduction of income support

8.—(1) Subject to paragraphs (2) and (3), any payment of income support which falls to be made to a person after the date on which an officer decided under these Regulations that that person had not— 2.1063

(a) taken part; and

(b) shown good cause for not taking part,

in an interview shall be reduced as from the first day of the next benefit week following the date the decision was made, by a sum equal to 20 per cent of the income applicable (specified in Part I of Schedule 2 to the Income Support (General) Regulations 1987) [2 . . .] in respect of a single claimant for income support aged not less than 25.

(2) Payment shall not be reduced under paragraph (1) below 10 pence per week.

(3) A reduction under this regulation shall cease to have effect as regards a person from whichever is the earlier of—

(a) the date on which that person attains [1 pensionable age];

(b) the date on which that person ceased to be a lone parent; [3 . . .]

(c) the first day of the benefit week in which that person [4 satisfies a compliance condition] [3 "and;

(d) the first day of the benefit week in which regulation 4(1A) first applies to that person.]

[4 (4) In paragraph (3)(c), "compliance condition" means a requirement to—

(a) take part in an interview; or

(b) undertake work-related activity.]

AMENDMENTS

1. The Social Security (Work-focused Interviews etc.) (Equalisation of State Pension Age) Amendment Regulations 2010 (SI 2010/563) reg.4(4) (April 6, 2010).

2. The Social Security (Miscellaneous Amendments) (No.3) Regulations 2011 (SI 2011/2425) reg.13 (October 31, 2011).

3. The Social Security (Work-focused Interviews for Lone Parents and Partners) (Amendment) Regulations 2011 (SI 2011/2428) reg.2 (October 31, 2011).

4. Income Support (Work-Related Activity) and Miscellaneous Amendments Regulations 2014 (SI 2014/1097), reg.13(7) (April 29, 2014).

Appeals

2.1064 **9.**—(1) This regulation applies to any relevant decision made under these Regulations or any decision under section 10 of the 1998 Act (decisions superseding earlier decisions) superseding such a decision.

(2) This regulation applies—

(a) whether the decision is as originally made or as revised under section 9 of the 1998 Act (revision of decisions); and

(b) as if any decision made, superseded or revised otherwise than by the Secretary of State was a decision made, superseded or revised by him.

(3) In the case of a decision to which this regulation applies, the person in respect of whom the decision was made shall have a right of appeal under section 12 of the 1998 Act [[1] (appeal to First-tier Tribunal) to the First-tier Tribunal]

AMENDMENT

1. The Tribunals, Courts and Enforcement Act 2007 (Transitional and Consequential Provisions) Order 2008 (SI 2008/2683) reg.140 (November 3, 2008).

SCHEDULE 1 **Regulation 1(3)(a)**

2.1065 AREAS WHERE THESE REGULATIONS COME INTO FORCE ON 30TH OCTOBER 2000 IN RESPECT OF LONE PARENTS WHO ARE NOT ENTITLED TO INCOME SUPPORT

For the purposes of regulation 1(3)(a), the areas are—

(a) the areas of Shropshire County Council and Telford Wrekin District Council; and

(b) the following postcode districts—

DH2 1AA to DH2 1BO
DH2 1XA to DH2 1XQ
DH3 1 and DH3 2
NE8 and NE9
NE10 0
NE10 8 and NE10 9
NE11
NE16 3 to NE16 5
NE16 6NX to NE16 6PE
NE16 8
NE17 7AA to NE17 7HE
NE17 7HG to NE17 7LM
NE17 7TA to NE17 7ZZ
NE21 1
NE21 4 to NE21 6
NE31 1 to NE31 5
NE32 2 to NE32 4
NE33
NE34 0
NE34 6 to NE34 9
NE35 1 and NE35 9
NE36 0 and NE36 1
NE39

NE40 3 to NE40 4
NE42 5 to NE42 6
NE43 7
SR6 7.

(c) The area of Five Council excluding the following postcode districts—
DD 6 8 and DD 6 9
KY 14 6
KY 16 0
KY 16 9.

AMENDMENT

1. The Social Security (Work-focused Interviews for Lone Parents) Amendment Regulations 2002 (SI 2002/670) reg.2 (April 8, 2002).

Schedule 2 omitted. **2.1066**

[1 SCHEDULE 3] **Regulation 2B(1)**

[2 . . .] **2.1067**

AMENDMENTS

1. Inserted by The Social Security (Work-focused Interviews for Lone Parents) Amendment Regulations 2007 (SI 2007/1034) (April 30, 2007).
2. The Social Security (Miscellaneous Amendments) Regulations 2011 (SI 2011/674) reg.9 (April 1 *or* April 4, 2011).

SECTION B

HMRC-ADMINISTERED BENEFITS

Note

The administration and initial adjudication of claims for child benefit and guardian's allowance are the responsibility of Her Majesty's Revenue and Customs but are governed by the Social Security Administration Act 1992 and the Social Security Act 1998. Separate regulations have been made under those Acts for these benefits and they are reproduced in this section. They are naturally similar to, although they do not exactly replicate, the regulations made by the Secretary of State for Work and Pensions that are in Section A above. Where no specific annotation is provided to regulations reproduced in this section, readers are advised to check the annotation of the corresponding provision in Section A.

For equivalent legislation in respect of other HMRC-administered benefits, see Vol.IV.

The Child Benefit and Guardian's Allowance (Administration) Regulations 2003

(SI 2003/492)

Made — *5th March 2003*
Laid before Parliament — *5th March 2003*
Coming into force — *7th April 2003*

ARRANGEMENT OF REGULATIONS

PART I

GENERAL

PART II

CLAIMS AND AWARDS

PART III

PAYMENTS

SCHEDULE 1

POWERS EXERCISED IN MAKING THESE REGULATIONS

SCHEDULE 2

ELECTRONIC COMMUNICATIONS

PART I GENERAL

PART II GENERAL

PART III EVIDENTIAL PROVISIONS

SCHEDULE 3

REVOCATIONS

The Commissioners of Inland Revenue, in exercise of the powers conferred upon them by the provisions set out in Schedule 1, hereby make the following Regulations:

PART I

GENERAL

Citation, commencement and effect

1.—(1) These Regulations may be cited as the Child Benefit and Guardian's Allowance (Administration) Regulations 2003 and shall come into force on 7th April 2003 immediately after the commencement of section 50 of the Tax Credits Act 2002 for the purposes of entitlement to payment of child benefit and guardian's allowance. **2.1069**

(2) These Regulations have effect only in relation to—

(a) child benefit and guardian's allowance under the Contributions and Benefits Act; and

(b) child benefit and guardian's allowance under the Contributions and Benefits (NI) Act.

Interpretation

2.1070 **2.** In these Regulations—

"the adjudicating authority" means—

(a) the Board;

(b) an appeal tribunal constituted under Chapter 1 of Part 1 of the Social Security Act 1998 or [2 . . .]

(c) a Commissioner [2 . . .] to whom an appeal lies under Article 15 of that Order;

[2 (d) the First-tier Tribunal or the Upper Tribunal]

"the Administration Act" means the Social Security Administration Act 1992;

"the Administration (NI) Act" means the Social Security Administration (Northern Ireland) Act 1992;

[3 "appropriate office" means—

(a) Waterview Park, Washington, Tyne and Wear; or

(b) any other office specified in writing by the Board.]

"the approved form" has the meaning given by regulation 5(1)(a);

"the Board" means the [1 Commissioners for Her Majesty's Revenue and Customs];

"the Contributions and Benefits Act" means the Social Security Contributions and Benefits Act 1992;

"the Contributions and Benefits (NI) Act" means the Social Security Contributions and Benefits (Northern Ireland) Act 1992;

"interim payment" has the meaning given by regulation 22(1);

"married couple" means a man and a woman who are married to each other and are neither—

(a) separated under a court order, nor

(b) separated in circumstances in which the separation is likely to be permanent;

"partner" means a member of a married or an unmarried couple;

"relevant authority" means—

(a) in relation to child benefit or guardian's allowance under the Contributions and Benefits Act, the Secretary of State or a person providing services to the Secretary of State;

(b) in relation to child benefit or guardian's allowance under the Contributions and Benefits (NI) Act, the Department for Social Development in Northern Ireland or a person providing services to that Department;

"unmarried couple" means a man and a woman who are not a married couple but are living together as husband and wife;

"writing" includes writing produced by electronic communications used in accordance with Schedule 2.

AMENDMENTS

1. The Child Benefit and Guardian's Allowance (Miscellaneous Amendments) Regulations 2006 (SI 2006/203) (April 10, 2006).

2. The Tribunals, Courts and Enforcement Act 2007 (Transitional and Consequential Provisions) Order 2008 (SI 2008/2683) reg.211 (November 3, 2008).

3. The Child Benefit and Guardian's Allowance (Miscellaneous Amendments) Regulations 2009 (SI 2009/3268) reg.3(2) (January 1, 2010).

Use of electronic communications

3. Schedule 2 (the use of electronic communications) has effect. 2.1071

Notification for purposes of sections 111A and 112 of the Administration Act and sections 105A and 106 of the Administration (NI) Act

4.—(1) This regulation prescribes the person to whom, and manner in which, a change of circumstances must be notified for the purposes of sections 111A(1A) to (1G) and 112(1A) to (1F) of the Administration Act and sections 105A(1A) to (1G) and 106(1A) to (1F) of the Administration (NI) Act (offences relating to failure to notify a change of circumstances). 2.1072

(2) Notice of the change of circumstances must be given to the Board, or, where relevant, a relevant authority, in writing (except where they determine or it determines, in any particular case, that they or it will accept a notice other than in writing) by delivering or sending it to an appropriate office.

PART II

CLAIMS AND AWARDS

Making a claim

5.—[1 (1) A claim, or an extension of a claim, for child benefit or guardian's allowance must be made— 2.1073

(a) to the Board, in writing and completed on a form approved or authorised by the Board for the purpose of the claim; or

(b) in such other manner as the Board may decide having regard to all the circumstances.]

(2) The person making the claim must deliver or send it to an appropriate office.

(3) Subject to regulation 10, the claim is made on the date on which it is received by the appropriate office.

AMENDMENT

1. The Child Benefit and Guardian's Allowance (Miscellaneous Amendments) Regulations 2009 (SI 2009/3268) reg.3(3) (January 1, 2010).

Time within which claims to be made

[1 **6.**—(1) The time within which a claim for child benefit or guardian's allowance is to be made is 3 months beginning with any day on which, apart from satisfying the conditions for making the claim, the person making the claim is entitled to the benefit or allowance. 2.1074

(2) Paragraph (1) shall not apply where—

(a) a person has been awarded child benefit or guardian's allowance while he was present and residing in great Britain, or Northern Ireland;

(b) at a time when payment of the award has not been suspended or terminated (under regulations 18 to 20 of the Child Benefit and

Guardian's Allowance (Decisions and Appeals) Regulations 2003 or otherwise), he take up residence in Northern Ireland, or Great Britain as the case may be ("the new country of residence"); and

(c) a new claim for that benefit or allowance is made in the new country of residence, for a period commencing on the later of—

(i) the date of the change of residence referred to in sub-paragraph (b), or

(ii) the date on which, apart from satisfying the conditions for making the claim, the person became entitled to the benefit or allowance under the legislation of the new country of residence.]

[[2] (d) a person who has claimed asylum and, on or after 6th April 2004, makes a claim for that benefit or allowance and satisfies the following conditions—

(i) the person is notified that he has been recorded as a refugee by the Secretary of State; and

(ii) he claims that benefit or allowance within 3 months of receiving that notification.

(3) In a case falling within paragraph (2)(d) the person making the claim shall be treated as having made it on the date when he submitted his claim for asylum.]

AMENDMENTS

1. The Child Benefit and Guardian's Allowance) (Administration) (Amendment No.3) Regulations 2003 (SI 2003/2107) reg.6 (September 3, 2003).

2. The Child Benefit and Guardian's Allowance (Miscellaneous Amendments) Regulations 2004 (SI 2004/761) reg.2 (April 6, 2004).

GENERAL NOTE

2.1075 *HMRC v AA* [2012] UKUT 121 (AAC) concerned a claimant who was the beneficiary of the decisions of the Administrative Court of April 8, 2008 and April 9, 2009 that the extension of the period before which those subject to immigration control could apply for indefinite leave to remain from four years to five years could not be applied to certain categories of migrants.

The claimant had claimed child benefit on September 3, 2008. He subsequently asked for the award to be backdated to August 28, 2007 on the grounds that following the judicial reviews, he was retrospectively deemed to have indefinite leave to remain from August 28, 2007.

The First-tier tribunal had applied the provisions in reg.6(2)(d) relating to those who had claimed asylum and been recorded as refugees by analogy to the circumstances presented by the claimant. HMRC appealed to the Upper Tribunal, where the Judge decided that the provisions relating to refugees could not be interpreted to include those in the claimant's circumstances. The limitation in the regulations that the award of child benefit could be backdated for a maximum period of three months applied to the claimant.

Evidence and information

2.1076 **7.**—(1) A person making a claim for child benefit or guardian's allowance must furnish such certificates, documents, information and evidence in connection with the claim, or any question arising out of it, as may be required by the Board.

(2) A person required under paragraph (1) to furnish certificates, documents, information and evidence must do so—

(a) within one month of being required by the Board to do so; or
(b) within such longer period as the Board may consider reasonable.

[1 (3) If a person is required, by virtue of paragraph (1) to furnish a certificate of a [2 the birth or adoption of a child or qualifying young person], the certificate so produced must be either an original certificate or a copy authenticated in such manners as would render it admissible in proceedings in any court in the jurisdiction in which the copy was made.]

AMENDMENTS

1. Child Benefit and Guardian's Allowance (Administration) (Amendment) Regulations 2004 (SI 2004/1240) (May 1, 2004).

2. The Child Benefit and Guardian's Allowance (Miscellaneous Amendments) Regulations 2006 (SI 2006/203) (April 10, 2006).

GENERAL NOTE

This provision would appear to reflect the rather more legalistic approach the Board of Inland Revenue adopt to some issues, since the Department for Work and Pensions never seem to have felt the need for such a provision. 2.1077

Amending claims

8.—(1) A person who has made a claim for child benefit or guardian's allowance may amend it by giving to the Board or a relevant authority notice in writing in accordance with paragraph (2). 2.1078

(2) A notice under paragraph (1) must be delivered or sent to an appropriate office at any time before a determination has been made on the claim.

(3) The Board may treat a claim amended in accordance with this regulation as if it had been so amended when first made.

Withdrawing claims

9.—(1) A person who has made a claim for child benefit or guardian's allowance may withdraw it by giving notice in writing to the Board or a relevant authority. 2.1079

(2) A notice of withdrawal given in accordance with paragraph (1) has effect when it is received by an appropriate office.

Defective applications

10.—(1) If an appropriate office receives a defective application, the Board or the relevant authority may refer it back to the person making it or supply him with the approved form for completion. 2.1080

(2) Where—

(a) in accordance with paragraph (1), a defective application has been referred back, or an approved form supplied, to a person; and
(b) a claim is received by an appropriate office—
    (i) within the period of one month beginning with the date on which the defective application was referred back or the approved form was supplied; or
    (ii) within such longer period as the Board may consider reasonable,

the claim shall be treated as having been made on the date on which the appropriate office received the defective application.

(3) "Defective application" means an intended claim which—

(a) is made on an approved form which has not been completed in accordance with the instructions on it; or
(b) is in writing but is not made on the approved form.

Claims for child benefit treated as claims for guardian's allowance and vice versa

2.1081 **11.**—(1) Where it appears to the Board that a person who has made a claim for child benefit in respect of a child [1 or qualifying young person] may be entitled to guardian's allowance in respect of the same child [1 or qualifying young person], the Board may treat, either in the alternative or in addition, the claim as being a claim for guardian's allowance by that person.

(2) Where it appears to the Board that a person who has made a claim for guardian's allowance in respect of a child [1 or qualifying young person] may be entitled to child benefit in respect of the same child [1 or qualifying young person], the Board may treat, either in the alternative or in addition, the claim as being a claim for child benefit by that person.

AMENDMENT

1. The Child Benefit and Guardian's Allowance (Miscellaneous Amendments) Regulations 2006 (SI 2006/203) (April 10, 2006).

Advance claims and awards

2.1082 **12.**—(1) This regulation applies where a person who has made a claim for child benefit or guardian's allowance does not satisfy the requirements for entitlement on the date on which the claim is made.

(2) If the Board are of the opinion that, unless there is a change of circumstances, the person will satisfy those requirements for a period beginning with a date ("the relevant date") not more than 3 months after the date on which the claim is made, they—
(a) may treat the claim as if made for a period beginning with the relevant date; and
(b) may award the benefit or allowance accordingly, subject to the condition that the person satisfies the requirements for entitlement when the benefit or allowance becomes payable under the award.

(3) If the requirements for entitlement are found not to have been satisfied on the relevant date, a decision under paragraph (2)(b) to award benefit may be revised under—
(a) in relation to child benefit and guardian's allowance under the Contributions and Benefits Act, section 9 of the Social Security Act 1998;
(b) in relation to child benefit and guardian's allowance under the Contributions and Benefits (NI) Act, Article 10 the Social Security (Northern Ireland) Order 1998.

Date of entitlement under an award for the purposes of payability

2.1083 **13.**—(1) This regulation applies where child benefit or guardian's allowance is awarded for a period of a week or weeks and the earliest date on which entitlement would commence is not a Monday.

(2) For the purposes of determining the day from which the benefit or allowance is to become payable, entitlement shall be treated as beginning on the Monday next following the earliest date referred to in paragraph (1).

Effective date of change of rate

14. Where a change in the rate of child benefit or guardian's allowance would take effect, but for this regulation, on a day which would not be the appropriate pay day for the benefit or allowance, the change shall take effect from the appropriate pay day next following. 2.1084

Duration of claims and awards

15.—(1) Subject to paragraphs (2) and (3), a claim for child benefit or guardian's allowance shall be treated as made for an indefinite period and any award shall be made for an indefinite period. 2.1085

(2) If it would be inappropriate to treat a claim as made and to make an award for an indefinite period (for example, where a relevant change of circumstances is reasonably to be expected in the near future), the claim shall be treated as made for a definite period which is appropriate in the circumstances and any award shall be made for that period.

(3) In any case where benefit or allowance is awarded in respect of days subsequent to the date on which the claim was made, the award shall be subject to the condition that the person by whom the claim was made satisfies the requirements for entitlement.

PART III

PAYMENTS

[1 Payment by direct credit transfer

16.—(1) Child benefit or guardian's allowance shall be paid in accordance with paragraphs (2) to (6) unless paid in accordance with regulation 17. 2.1086

(2) Payment of child benefit or guardian's allowance [3 . . .] shall be made by direct credit transfer into a bank or other account that [2 the person entitled to the benefit or allowance has] notified to the Board(a) for the purpose of payment of—

(a) a benefit described in section 5(2) of the Social Security Administration Act 1992;

(b) a benefit described in section 5(2) of the Social Security Administration (Northern Ireland Act) 1992; or

(c) a tax credit described in section 1 of the Tax Credits Act 2002, to which that person is entitled.

(3) If a person entitled to child benefit is also entitled to guardian's allowance, the allowance shall be paid into the same bank or other account as that into which the child benefit is paid under this regulation.

(4) The bank account or other account into which the Board may make payment of the allowance or benefit must be—

(a) in the name of—

(i) the person entitled to the benefit or allowance ("the person"),

(ii) the person's partner, or

(iii) a person acting on behalf of the person; or

(b) in the joint names of the person and—

(i) the person's partner, or
(ii) a person acting on the person's behalf.

(5) Subject to paragraph (6), the benefit or allowance shall be paid within seven days of the last day of each successive period of entitlement.

(6) The Board may make a particular payment by direct credit transfer otherwise than is provided by paragraph (5) if it appears to them appropriate to do so for the purpose of—

(a) paying any arrears of benefit or allowance, or
(b) making a payment in respect of a terminal period of an award for any similar purpose.]

AMENDMENTS

1. Child Benefit and Guardian's Allowance (Administration) (Amendment) Regulations 2010 (SI 2010/2459) reg.2 (November 1, 2010).

2. Child Benefit and Guardian's Allowance (Administration) (Amendment) Regulations 2016 (SI 2016/681) reg.2 (July 21, 2016).

[1 Payment by other means

2.1087 **17.—**(1) Child benefit or guardian's allowance may be paid by a means other than by direct credit transfer where it appears to the Board to be appropriate to do so in the circumstances of a particular case.

(2) If a person entitled to child benefit is also entitled to guardian's allowance, the allowance shall be paid in the same manner as that in which the child benefit is paid under this regulation.

(3) An instrument of payment issued by the Board pursuant to this regulation shall—

(a) remain the property of the Board, and
(b) be returned immediately to the Board (or such person as the Board may direct) if the person who has the instrument—
  (i) is required to do so by the Board; or
  (ii) ceases to be entitled to any part of the benefit or allowance to which the instrument relates.]

AMENDMENT

1. Child Benefit and Guardian's Allowance (Administration) (Amendment) Regulations 2010 (SI 2010/2459) reg.2 (November 1, 2010).

Time of payment

2.1088 **18.**—(1) Subject to paragraphs (2) to (4), child benefit and guardian's allowance shall be paid in accordance with an award as soon as reasonably practicable after the award has been made.

(2) Child benefit shall be paid—

(a) if a person entitled to it makes an election under regulation 19 or 20, weekly beginning with the first convenient date after the election has been made;
(b) in any other case, in the last week of each successive period of four weeks of the period of entitlement.

(3) Where benefit is paid at four-weekly intervals in accordance with paragraph (2)(b), the Board must arrange for it to be paid weekly if they are satisfied that payment at intervals of four weeks is causing hardship.

(4) If a person who has made a claim for child benefit is also entitled to

guardian's allowance, the allowance shall be paid at the same intervals as the child benefit.

(5) The Board must take steps to notify persons to whom child benefit or guardian's allowance is payable of the arrangements they have made for payment in so far as those arrangements affect those persons.

Persons who may elect to have child benefit paid weekly

19.—(1) A person may make an election under this regulation to have child benefit paid weekly if— 2.1089

(a) he is a lone parent; [2 . . .]

(b) he or his partner is receiving—

(i) income support; or

(ii) an income-based allowance payable under Part 1 of the Jobseekers Act 1995 or Part 2 of the Jobseekers (Northern Ireland) Order 1995.

[2 (iii) an income-related employment and support allowance within the meaning in Part 1 of the Welfare Reform Act 2007 or Part 1 of the Welfare Reform Act (Northern Ireland) 2007; or

(iv) a state pension credit within the meaning in the State Pension Credit Act 2002 or the State Pension Credit Act (Northern Ireland) 2002.]

[3 (v) universal credit under Part 1 of the Welfare Reform Act 2012.]

(2) "Lone parent" means a person who has no partner and is entitled to child benefit in respect of a child [1 or qualifying young person] for whom he is responsible.

(3) A person making an election under this regulation—

(a) must furnish, in such manner and at such times as the Board may determine, such certificates, documents, other information or facts as the Board may require which may affect his right to receive payment of the benefit weekly; and

(b) as soon as reasonably practicable after any change of circumstances which he might reasonably be expected to know might affect that right, must notify the Board in writing of that change in accordance with paragraph (4).

(4) A notification under paragraph (3)(b) must be delivered or sent to an appropriate office as regards the Board.

AMENDMENTS

1. The Child Benefit and Guardian's Allowance (Miscellaneous Amendments) Regulations 2006 (SI 2006/203) (April 10, 2006).

2. The Child Benefit and Guardian's Allowance (Miscellaneous Amendments) Regulations 2009 (SI 2009/3268) reg.3(4) (January 1, 2010).

3. The Universal Credit (Consequential Supplementary, Incidental and Miscellaneous Provisions) Regulations 2013 (SI 2013/630) reg.81 (April 29, 2013).

Elections for weekly payment by persons to whom child benefit was payable for a period beginning before and ending after 15th March 1982

20.—(1) This regulation applies to a person to whom child benefit is payable for an uninterrupted period beginning before and ending after 15th March 1982. 2.1090

(2) A person to whom this regulation applies may make an election to have the benefit paid weekly after 15th March 1982 if—

(a) he makes it before the end of the period of 26 weeks beginning with the day on which benefit was payable for the first four weeks in respect of which arrangements for four-weekly payment were made;

(b) in the case of benefit under the Contributions and Benefits Act, he was absent from Great Britain on 15th March 1982 for any of the reasons specified in paragraph (3) and he makes the election before the end of the period of 26 weeks beginning with the first week in respect of which benefit became payable to him in Great Britain on his return; or

(c) in the case of benefit under the Contributions and Benefits (NI) Act, he was absent from Northern Ireland on 15th March 1982 for any of the reasons specified in paragraph (3) and he makes the election before the end of the period of 26 weeks beginning with the first week in respect of which benefit became payable to him in Northern Ireland on his return.

(3) The reasons specified in this paragraph are that the person—

(a) was a serving member of the forces;

(b) was the spouse of such a serving member; or

(c) was living with such a serving member as husband or wife.

(4) "Serving member of the forces" means a person, other than one mentioned in Part 2 of Schedule 6 to the Social Security (Contributions) Regulations 2001, who, being over the age of 16 years, is a member of any establishment or organisation specified in Part 1 of that Schedule (being a member who gives full pay service) but does not include any such person while absent on desertion.

Manner of making elections under regulations 19 and 20

2.1091 **21.**—(1) This regulation applies to elections under regulations 19 and 20.

(2) An election—

(a) must be made by notice in writing to the Board; and

(b) must be delivered or sent to an appropriate office as regards the Board.

(3) An election is made on the date on which it is received by the appropriate office.

(4) Where a person has made an election, child benefit is payable weekly so long as—

(a) he remains continually entitled to it; and

(b) in the case of an election under regulation 19, the conditions specified in paragraph (1)(a) or (b) of that regulation continue to be satisfied.

(5) A person who has made an election may cancel it at any time by giving to the Board a notice in writing which must be sent or delivered to an appropriate office as regards the Board.

(6) The Board must give effect to a notice given in accordance with paragraph (5) as soon as reasonably practicable after receiving it.

Interim payments

2.1092 **22.**—[1 (1) If the condition in any sub-paragraph of paragraph (1A) is satisfied, the Board may make a payment on account ("an interim payment") of any child benefit or guardian's allowance to which it appears to them that a person—

(a) is or may be entitled, were a claim made,

(b) where sub-paragraph (a) of paragraph (1A) applies, would or might be entitled, were a claim made,

(c) where sub-paragraph (b) of that paragraph applies, would or might be entitled, were the national insurance number condition satisfied.

(1A) The conditions are that—

(a) a claim for benefit or allowance has not been made in accordance with these Regulations and it is impracticable for such a claim to be made immediately;

(b) a claim has been made in accordance with these Regulations, the conditions of entitlement are satisfied other than the national insurance number condition, and it is impracticable for that condition to be satisfied immediately;

(c) a claim for the benefit or allowance has been so made but it is impracticable for it, or an application or appeal relating to it, to be determined immediately;

(d) an award of the benefit or allowance has been made but it is impracticable for the person entitled to it to be paid immediately other than by means of an interim payment.]

(2) Paragraph (1) does not apply pending the determination of an appeal [[1] . . .]

(3) On or before the making of an interim payment, the Board must give the person to whom payment is to be made notice in writing of his liability under regulations 41 and 42 to have it brought into account and to repay any overpayment.

[[1] (4) In this regulation "the national insurance number condition" means the condition imposed—

(a) in Great Britain by section 13(1A) and (1B), of the Administration Act (requirement for claim to be accompanied by details of national insurance number);

(b) in Northern Ireland, by section 11(1A) and (1B) of the Administration (NI) Act.]

AMENDMENT

1. The Child Benefit and Guardian's Allowance (Miscellaneous Amendments) Regulations 2005 (SI 2005/343) reg.8 (March 18, 2005).

Information to be given and changes to be notified

23.—(1) This regulation applies to any person entitled to child benefit or guardian's allowance and any person by whom, or on whose behalf, payments of such benefit or allowance are receivable. 2.1093

(2) A person to whom this regulation applies must furnish in such manner and at such times as the Board may determine such information or evidence as the Board may require for determining whether a decision on an award—

(a) in relation to benefit or allowance under the Contributions and Benefits Act, should be revised under section 9 or superseded under section 10 of the Social Security Act 1998;

(b) in relation to benefit or allowance under the Contributions and

Benefits (NI) Act, should be revised under Article 10 or superseded under Article 11 of the Social Security (Northern Ireland) Order 1998.

(3) A person to whom this regulation applies must furnish in such manner and at such times as the Board may determine such information and evidence as the Board may require in connection with the payment of the benefit or allowance.

(4) A person to whom this regulation applies must notify the Board or a relevant authority of any change of circumstances which he might reasonably be expected to know might affect—

(a) the continuance of entitlement to the benefit or allowance; or
(b) the payment of it,

as soon as reasonably practicable after the change occurs.

(5) A notification under paragraph (4)—

(a) must be given by notice in writing or orally; and
(b) must be sent, delivered or given to the appropriate office.

Fractional amounts of benefit or allowance

2.1094 **24.** Where the amount of any child benefit or guardian's allowance payable includes a fraction of a penny, that fraction—

(a) if it is less than a half, shall be disregarded;
(b) if it is a half or more, shall be treated as a whole penny.

Payments to persons under the age of 18 years

2.1095 **25.** Where a sum of child benefit or guardian's allowance is paid to a person under the age of 18 years (whether on his own behalf or on behalf of another), either of the following is a sufficient discharge to the Board for the sum paid—

(a) a direct credit transfer under [1 regulation 16] into the person's account;
(b) the receipt by the person of a payment made by some other means.

AMENDMENT

1. Child Benefit and Guardian's Allowance (Administration) (Amendment) Regulations 2010 (SI 2010/2459) reg.2 (November 1, 2010).

Extinguishment of right to payment if payment is not obtained within the prescribed period

2.1096 **26.**—[1 (1) A person's right to payment of any sum of child benefit or guardian's allowance shall be extinguished if payment of that sum has not been obtained within 12 months of the issue by the Board of a cheque or other instrument of payment to that person.]

(2)–(5) [1 . . .]

(6) This regulation has effect in relation to a person authorised or appointed to act on behalf of a person entitled to child benefit or guardian's allowance in the same manner as it has effect in relation to such a person.

AMENDMENT

1. The Child Benefit and Guardian's Allowance (Miscellaneous Amendments) Regulations 2009 (SI 2009/3268) reg.3(5) (January 1, 2010).

PART IV

THIRD PARTIES

Persons who may act on behalf of those unable to act

27.—(1) Anything required by these regulations to be done by or to any person who is for the time being unable to act may be done by or to— 2.1097

(a) in England and Wales, a receiver appointed by the Court of Protection with power to claim, or, as the case may be, receive, the benefit or allowance on behalf of the person;

(b) in Scotland, [1 guardian acting or appointed under the Adults with Incapacity (Scotland) Act 2000] who is administering the estate of the person;

(c) in Northern Ireland, a controller appointed by the High Court, with power to claim, or, as the case may be, receive, the benefit or allowance on behalf of the person; or

(d) a person appointed under regulation 28(2) to act on behalf of the person.

(2) Where a sum of child benefit or guardian's allowance is paid to a receiver or other person mentioned in paragraph (1)(a), (b), (c) or (d), either of the following is a sufficient discharge to the Board for the sum paid—

(a) a direct credit transfer under [2 regulation 16] into the person's account;

(b) the receipt by the person of a payment made by some other means.

AMENDMENTS

1. The Child Benefit and Guardian's Allowance (Miscellaneous Amendments) Regulations 2005 (SI 2005/343) reg.10 (March 18, 2005).

2. Child Benefit and Guardian's Allowance (Administration) (Amendment) Regulations 2010 (SI 2010/2459) reg.2 (November 1, 2010).

Appointment of persons to act on behalf of those unable to act

28.—(1) This regulation applies where— 2.1098

(a) a person is for the time being unable to act;

(b) the person is, or is alleged to be, entitled to child benefit or guardian's allowance (whether or not a claim for the benefit or allowance has been made by him or on his behalf); and

(c) no receiver or other person mentioned in regulation 27(1)(a), (b) or (c) has been appointed in relation to the person.

(2) The Board may appoint a person who—

(a) has applied in writing to them to act on behalf of the person who is unable to act, and

(b) if a natural person, is over the age of 18 years,

to exercise, on behalf of the person who is unable to act, any right relating to child benefit or guardian's allowance to which that person may be entitled and to receive and deal on his behalf with any sums payable to him in respect of the benefit or allowance.

(3) Where an appointment has been made under paragraph (2)—

(a) the Board may at any time revoke it; and

(b) the person appointed may resign from the appointment after having given one month's notice in writing to the Board of his intention to do so.

(4) An appointment made under paragraph (2) shall terminate when the Board are notified that a receiver or other person mentioned in regulation 27(1)(a), (b) or (c) has been appointed.

Persons who may proceed with a claim made by a person who has died

2.1099 **29.**—(1) The Board may appoint such person as they think fit to proceed with a claim for child benefit or guardian's allowance [1, and to deal with any issue related to the revision of, supersession of, or appeal in connection with a decision on, that claim] which has been made by a person who has died.

(2) Subject to regulation 32(2), the Board may pay or distribute any sum payable under an award on a claim proceeded with under paragraph (1) to or among—

(a) persons over the age of 16 years claiming as personal representatives, legatees, next of kin or creditors of the person who has died; and
(b) if the person who has died was illegitimate, any other persons over that age.

(3) "Next of kin" means—

(a) in England and Wales, and in Northern Ireland, the persons who would take beneficially on an intestacy;
(b) in Scotland, the persons entitled to the moveable estate of the deceased on intestacy.

(4) Where a sum is paid under paragraph (2) to a person, either of the following is a sufficient discharge to the Board for the sum paid—

(a) a direct credit transfer under [2 regulation 16] into the person's account;
(b) the receipt by the person of a payment made by some other means.

(5) If the Board consider that a sum or part of a sum which may be paid or distributed under paragraph (2) is needed for the benefit of a person under the age of 16 years, they may obtain a good discharge for that sum by paying it to a person over that age whom they are satisfied will apply the sum for the benefit of the person under that age.

(6) Regulation 26 (extinguishment of right) applies to a payment or distribution made under paragraph (2).

AMENDMENTS

1. The Child Benefit and Guardian's Allowance (Miscellaneous Amendments) Regulations 2009 (SI 2009/3268) reg.3(5) (January 1, 2010).
2. Child Benefit and Guardian's Allowance (Administration) (Amendment) Regulations 2010 (SI 2010/2459) reg.2 (November 1, 2010).

Persons who may receive payments which a person who has died had not obtained

2.1100 **30.**—(1) This regulation applies where a person who has died had not obtained at the date of his death a sum of child benefit or guardian's allowance which was payable to him.

(2) Subject to regulation 32(2), the Board may, unless the right to

payment had already been extinguished at the date of death, pay or distribute the sum to or amongst the persons mentioned in regulation 29(2) (a) and (b).

(3) Regulation 26 (extinguishment of right) applies to a payment or distribution made under paragraph (2), except that, for the purposes of paragraph (1) of that regulation, the period of 12 months shall be calculated from the date on which the right to payment is treated as having arisen to the person to whom the payment or distribution is made (and not from the date on which that right is treated as having arisen in relation to the person who has died).

Person who may make a claim on behalf of a person who has died

31.—(1) If the conditions specified in paragraph (2) are satisfied, a claim may be made in the name of a person who has died for any child benefit or guardian's allowance to which he would have been entitled if he had claimed it in accordance with these Regulations. 2.1101

(2) Subject to paragraph (3), the following conditions are specified in this paragraph—

- (a) within 6 months of the date of death an application must have been made in writing to the Board for a person, whom the Board think fit to be appointed to make the claim, to be so appointed;
- (b) a person must have been appointed by the Board to make the claim; and
- (c) the person so appointed must have made the claim not more than 6 months after the appointment.

(3) Subject to paragraphs (4) and (5), if the Board certify that to do so would be consistent with the proper administration of the Contributions and Benefits Act, the period of 6 months mentioned in paragraph (2)(a) or (c) shall be extended by such period (not exceeding 6 months) as may be specified in the certificate.

(4) If a certificate given under paragraph (3) specifies a period by which the period of 6 months mentioned in paragraph (2)(a) shall be extended, the period of 6 months mentioned in paragraph (2)(c) shall be shortened by a period corresponding to the period so specified.

(5) No certificate shall be given under paragraph (3) which would enable a claim to be made more than 12 months after the date of death. For the purposes of this paragraph, any period between the date on which the application for a person to be appointed to make the claim is made and the date on which that appointment is made shall be disregarded.

(6) A claim made in accordance with this regulation shall be treated for the purposes of these Regulations as if it had been made on the date of his death by the person who has died.

Regulations 29, 30 and 31: supplementary

32.—(1) The Board may dispense with strict proof of the title of a person claiming in accordance with regulation 29, 30 or 31. 2.1102

(2) Neither paragraph (2) of regulation 29 nor paragraph (2) of regulation 30 applies unless written application for payment of the sum under that paragraph is made to the Board within 12 months from the date of death or such longer period as the Board may allow.

Payment to one person on behalf of another

2.1103 **33.**—(1) Subject to paragraph (2), the Board may direct that child benefit or guardian's allowance shall be paid, wholly or in part, to another natural person on behalf of the person entitled to it.

(2) The Board may not make a direction under paragraph (1) unless they are satisfied that it is necessary for protecting the interests of—

(a) the person entitled to the benefit or allowance; or

(b) any child [1 or qualifying young person] in respect of whom the benefit or allowance is payable.

AMENDMENT

1. The Child Benefit and Guardian's Allowance (Miscellaneous Amendments) Regulations 2006 (SI 2006/203) (April 10, 2006).

Payment to partner as alternative payee

2.1104 **34.**—(1) Subject to paragraph (2), where a member of a married couple or an unmarried couple is entitled to child benefit or guardian's allowance, the Board may make arrangements whereby that benefit or allowance, as well as being payable to the person entitled to it, may, in the alternative, be paid to that person's partner on behalf of that person.

(2) Paragraph (1) does not apply to guardian's allowance where a wife has elected that the allowance is not to be paid to her husband in accordance with regulation 10 of the Guardian's Allowance (General) Regulations 2003 (prescribed manner of making an election under section 77(9) of the Contributions and Benefits Act and section 77(9) of the Contributions and Benefits (NI) Act).

PART V

OVERPAYMENTS AND RECOVERY

Recovery of overpayments by direct credit transfer

2.1105 **35.**—(1) If the adjudicating authority determines that—

(a) a payment of child benefit or guardian's allowance in excess of entitlement has been credited to a bank account or other account under an arrangement for direct credit transfer made in accordance with [1 regulation 16]; and

(b) the conditions specified in paragraph (2) are satisfied,
the excess, or the specified part of it to which the certificate referred to in sub-paragraph (a) of that paragraph relates, shall be recoverable.

(2) The following conditions are specified in this paragraph—

(a) the Board must have certified that the payment in excess of entitlement, or a specified part of it, is materially due to the arrangement for payments to be made by direct credit transfer; and

(b) subject to paragraph (3), notice of the effect which this regulation would have, in the event of an overpayment, must have been given in writing to the person entitled to the benefit or allowance, or to a person acting in his behalf, [1 before the Board made the arrangement for the payment of child benefit or guardian's allowance into that account].

(3) In the case of an arrangement relating to child benefit which was agreed to before 6th April 1987, the condition specified in paragraph (2)(b) need not be satisfied in any case where the application for the benefit to be paid by direct credit transfer contained a statement, or was accompanied by a written statement made by the applicant, which complied with the provisions specified in paragraph (4).

(4) The provisions specified in this paragraph are—

(a) in relation to child benefit under the Contributions and Benefits Act, regulation 7(2)(b) and (6) of the Child Benefit (Claims and Payments) Regulations 1984;

(b) in relation to child benefit under the Contributions and Benefits (NI) Act, regulation 7(2)(b) and (6) of the Child Benefit (Claims and Payments) Regulations (Northern Ireland) 1985.

AMENDMENT

1. Child Benefit and Guardian's Allowance (Administration) (Amendment) Regulations 2010 (SI 2010/2459) reg.2 (November 1, 2010).

Circumstances in which determination need not be reversed, varied, revised or superseded

36.—(1) This regulation applies where, whether fraudulently or otherwise, a person has misrepresented, or failed to disclose, material facts which do not provide a basis for the determination in pursuance of which an amount of child benefit or guardian's allowance was paid— 2.1106

(a) in relation to benefit or allowance under the Contributions and Benefits Act, to be revised under section 9 or superseded under section 10 of the Social Security Act 1998;

(b) in relation to benefit or allowance under the Contributions and Benefits (NI) Act, to be revised under Article 10 or superseded under Article 11 of the Social Security (Northern Ireland) Order 1998.

(2) Where this regulation applies—

(a) in relation to an amount mentioned in paragraph (1) relating to child benefit or guardian's allowance under the Contributions and Benefits Act, neither subsection (5) nor (5A) of section 71 of the Administration Act (recoverability dependent on reversal, variation, revision or supersession of determination) applies;

(b) in relation to an amount mentioned in paragraph (1) relating to child benefit or guardian's allowance under the Contributions and Benefits (NI) Act, neither subsection (5) nor (5A) of section 69 of the Administration (NI) Act (recoverability dependent on reversal, variation, revision or supersession of determination) applies.

Calculating recoverable amounts

37. Where there has been an overpayment of child benefit or guardian's allowance, in calculating the amounts recoverable under section 71(1) of the Administration Act, section 69(1) of the Administration (NI) Act or regulation 35, the adjudicating authority must deduct any amount which is offset under regulation 38. 2.1107

Offsetting prior payments of child benefit and guardian's allowance against arrears payable by virtue of a subsequent determination

2.1108 **38.**—(1) Subject to regulation 40, in either of the cases specified in paragraphs (2) and (3)—

(a) a sum of child benefit paid for a period covered by a subsequent determination shall be offset against any arrears of entitlement to the benefit payable for that period by virtue of the subsequent determination;

(b) a sum of guardian's allowance paid for a period covered by a subsequent determination shall be offset against any arrears of entitlement to the allowance payable for that period by virtue of the subsequent determination, and, except to the extent that it exceeds them, the sum so paid shall be treated as properly paid on account of the arrears.

(2) The case specified in this paragraph is where a person has been paid a sum pursuant to a determination which subsequently—

(a) is revised under section 9 or superseded under section 10 of the Social Security Act 1998;

(b) is revised under Article 10 or superseded under Article 11 of the Social Security (Northern Ireland) Order 1998; or

(c) is overturned on appeal.

(3) The case specified in this paragraph is where a person has been paid a sum for a period by way of an increase in respect of a dependent person and it is subsequently determined that—

(a) the dependent person is entitled to the benefit or allowance for that period; or

(b) a third person is entitled to the increase for that period in priority to the person who has been paid.

(4) Where child benefit which has been paid under an award in favour of a person ("the first claimant") is subsequently awarded to another ("the second claimant") for any week, the benefit shall nevertheless be treated as properly paid if it was received by someone (other than the first claimant) who—

(a) had [1 the child or qualifying young person] living with him or was contributing towards the cost of providing for [1 the child or qualifying young person] at a weekly rate which was not less than the weekly rate under the original award; and

(b) could have been entitled to child benefit in respect of [1 that child or qualifying young person] for that week had a claim been made in time.

(5) Any amount which is treated under paragraph (4) as properly paid shall be deducted from the amount payable to the second claimant under the subsequent award.

AMENDMENT

1. The Child Benefit and Guardian's Allowance (Miscellaneous Amendments) Regulations 2006 (SI 2006/203) (April 10, 2006).

Offsetting prior payments of income support or jobseeker's allowance against arrears of child benefit or guardian's allowance payable by virtue of a subsequent determination

2.1109 **39.**—(1) This regulation applies where—

(a) a person has been paid a sum by way of income support or jobseeker's allowance; and

(b) it is subsequently determined that—
   (i) child benefit or guardian's allowance should be awarded or is payable in lieu of the income support or jobseeker's allowance; and
   (ii) the income support or jobseeker's allowance was not payable.

(2) Subject to regulation 40, any sum of income support or jobseeker's allowance in respect of the period covered by the subsequent determination—
(a) shall be offset against any arrears of entitlement to the child benefit or guardian's allowance payable for that period by virtue of that determination; and
(b) except to the extent that it exceeds them, the sum so paid shall be treated as properly paid on account of the arrears.

Exception from offset of recoverable overpayment

40. No amount may be offset under regulation 38(1) or 39(2) which has been determined to be a recoverable overpayment for the purposes of section 71(1) of the Administration Act or section 69(1) of the Administration (NI) Act. 2.1110

Bringing interim payments into account

41.—(1) Subject to paragraph (2), if it is practicable to do so— 2.1111
(a) any interim payment made in anticipation of an award of child benefit or guardian's allowance shall be ofset by the adjudicating authority in reduction of the benefit or allowance to be awarded;
(b) any interim payment (whether or not made in anticipation of an award) which is not offset under sub-paragraph (a) shall be deducted by the Board from—
   (i) the sum payable under the award of benefit or allowance on account of which the interim payment was made; or
   (ii) any sum payable under any subsequent award of the benefit or allowance to the same person.

(2) Paragraph (1) does not apply unless the Board have given the notice required by regulation 22(3).

Recovery of overpaid interim payments

42.—(1) Subject to paragraph (2), if the adjudicating authority, in the circumstances specified in either of paragraphs (3) and (4), has determined that an interim payment has been overpaid, it shall determine the amount of the overpayment. 2.1112

(2) Paragraph (1) does not apply unless the Board have given the notice required by regulation 22(3).

(3) The circumstances specified in this paragraph are where an interim payment has been made under regulation 22(1)(a) and (b) and—
(a) the recipient has failed to make a claim in accordance with these Regulations as soon as practicable;
(b) the recipient has made a defective application and the Board have not treated the claim as duly made under regulation 10;
(c) it has been determined that—

(i) there is no entitlement on the claim;
(ii) the entitlement is less than the amount of the interim payment; or
(iii) the benefit or allowance on the claim is not payable; or
(d) the claim has been withdrawn.

(4) The circumstances specified in this paragraph are where an interim payment has been made under regulation 22(1)(c) which exceeds the entitlement under the award of benefit on account of which the interim payment was made.

(5) The amount of any overpayment determined under paragraph (1) shall be recoverable by the Board in the same manner as it would be if it were recoverable under—

(a) in relation to child benefit or guardian's allowance under the Contributions and Benefits Act, section 71(1) of the Administration Act;
(b) in relation to child benefit or guardian's allowance under the Contributions and Benefits (NI) Act, section 69(1) of the Administration (NI) Act.

[1 Recovery of overpayments from awards of child benefit and guardian's allowance

2.1113 **42A.**—(1) Where any amount of child benefit or guardian's allowance is recoverable from a person under—

(a) section 71(1) of the Administration Act,
(b) section 69(1) of the Administration (NI) Act, or
(c) regulation 35(1) or 42(5),

That amount may be recovered by the adjudicating authority from any child benefit or guardian's allowance payable to that person.

(2) For the purposes of paragraph (1), child benefit or guardian's allowance payable includes any payment of arrears of child benefit or guardian's allowance other than a payment of arrears required to be made by regulation 21(1) of the Child Benefit and Guardian's Allowance (Decisions and Appeals) Regulations 2003.]

AMENDMENT

1. Inserted by The Child Benefit and Guardian's Allowance (Administration) (Amendment) Regulations 2012 (SI 2012/1074) reg.3 (May 8, 2012).

PART VI

REVOCATIONS AND TRANSITIONAL PROVISIONS

Revocations

2.1114 **43.** The subordinate legislation specified in column (1) of Parts 1 and 2 of Schedule 3, in so far as it relates to child benefit or guardian's allowance, is revoked to the extent mentioned in column (3) of that Schedule.

Transitional provisions

44.—(1) Anything done or commenced under any provision of the instruments revoked by regulation 43, so far as relating to child benefit or guardian's allowance, is to be treated as having been done or as being continued under the corresponding provision of these Regulations. **2.1115**

(2) The revocation by regulation 43 of an instrument which itself revoked an earlier instrument subject to savings does not prevent the continued operation of those savings, in so far as they are capable of continuing to have effect.

(3) "Instrument" includes a Statutory Rule of Northern Ireland.

SCHEDULE 1

Preamble

POWERS EXERCISED IN MAKING THESE REGULATIONS

1. The following provisions of the Administration Act— **2.1116**

(a) section 5(1)(a), (b), (c), (d), (g), (h), (hh), (i), (j), (k), (l), (m), (p), (q) and (r) and (2) (a) and (g);
(b) section 7(1), (2) and (3)(a);
(c) section 71(4), (5), (5A), (6), (7) and (11)(a) and (f);
(d) section 111A(1A), (1B), (1D) and (1E);
(e) section 112(1A) to (1D);
(f) section 189(1), (4), (5) and (6);
(g) section 191.

2. The following provisions of the Administration (NI) Act—

(a) section 5(1)(a), (b), (c), (d), (g), (h), (hh), (i), (j), (k), (l), (m), (n), (q), (r), (s) and (t) and (2)(a) and (g);
(b) section 69(4), (5), (5A), (6), (7) and (11)(a) and (f);
(c) section 105A(1A), (1B), (1D) and (1E);
(d) section 106(1A) to (1D);
(e) section 165(1), (4), (5), (6) and (11A);
(f) section 167(1).

3. Sections 9(1) and 84 of the Social Security Act 1998.

4. Articles 2(2) and 10(1) of the Social Security (Northern Ireland) Order 1998.

5. Sections 132 and 133(1) and (2) of the Finance Act 1999.

6. Sections 50(1) and (2)(b) and (d) and 54(2) of the Tax Credits Act 2002.

Regulation 3 SCHEDULE 2

ELECTRONIC COMMUNICATIONS

PART I

GENERAL

Introduction

1. This Schedule supersedes the Social Security (Electronic Communications) (Child Benefit) Order 2002 which was made under section 8 of the Electronic Communications Act 2000. **2.1117**

Interpretation

2.—(1) In this Schedule— **2.1118**

"electronic communications" includes any communications by means of a telecommunication system (within the meaning of the Telecommunications Act 1984);

"official computer system" means a computer system maintained by or on behalf of the Board—

(a) to send or receive information; or
(b) to process or store information.

(2) References in this Schedule to the delivery of information and to information shall be construed in accordance with section 132(8) of the Finance Act 1999.

Scope of this Schedule

2.1119 **3.** This Schedule applies to the delivery of information to or by the Board, the delivery of which is authorised or required by these Regulations.

PART II

GENERAL

Use of electronic communications by the Board

2.1120 **4.** The Board may only use electronic communications in connection with the matters referred to in paragraph 3 if—

(a) the recipient has indicated that he consents to the Board using electronic communications in connection with those matters; and
(b) the Board have not been informed that that consent has been withdrawn.

Restrictions on the use of electronic communications by persons other than the Board

2.1121 **5.**—(1) A person other than the Board may only use electronic communications in connection with the matters referred to in paragraph 3 if the conditions specified in subparagraphs (2) to (5) are satisfied.

(2) The first condition is that the person is for the time being permitted to use electronic communications for the purpose in question by an authorisation given by means of a specific or general direction of the Board.

(3) The second condition is that the person uses—

(a) an approved method for authenticating the identity of the sender of the communication;
(b) an approved method of electronic communications; and
(c) an approved method for authenticating any information delivered by means of electronic communications.

(4) The third condition is that any information sent by means of electronic communications is in an approved form (including the manner in which the information is presented).

(5) The fourth condition is that the person maintains such records in written or electronic form as may be specified in a specific or general direction given by the Board.

(6) "Approved" means approved for the purposes of this Schedule, and for the time being, by means of a specific or general direction given by the Board.

Use of intermediaries

2.1122 **6.** The Board may use intermediaries in connection with—

(a) the delivery of information by means of electronic communications in connection with the matters referred to in paragraph 3; and
(b) the authentication or security of anything transmitted by any such means, and may require other persons to use intermediaries in connection with those matters.

PART III

EVIDENTIAL PROVISIONS

Effect of delivering information by means of electronic communications

2.1123 **7.**—(1) Information which is delivered by means of electronic communications shall be treated as having been delivered in the manner or form required by any provision of these Regulations if, but only if, all the conditions imposed by—

(a) this Schedule,
(b) any other applicable enactment (except to the extent that the condition thereby imposed is incompatible with this Schedule); and
(c) any specific or general direction given by the Board,

are satisfied.

(2) Information delivered by means of electronic communications shall be treated as having been delivered on the day on which the last of the conditions imposed as mentioned in subparagraph (1) is satisfied.

This is subject to the following qualifications.

(3) The Board may by a general or specific direction provide for information to be treated

as delivered upon a different date (whether earlier or later) than that given by sub-paragraph (2).

(4) Information shall not be taken to have been delivered to an official computer system by means of electronic communications unless it is accepted by the system to which it is delivered.

Proof of content

8.—(1) A document certified by an officer of the Board to be a printed-out version of any information delivered by means of electronic communications under this Schedule on any occasion shall be evidence, unless the contrary is proved, that that information— **2.1124**

(a) was delivered by means of electronic communications on that occasion; and

(b) constitutes the entirety of what was delivered on that occasion.

(2) A document purporting to be a certificate given in accordance with sub-paragraph (1) shall be presumed to be such a certificate unless the contrary is proved.

Proof of identity of sender or recipient

9. The identity of— **2.1125**

(a) the sender of any information delivered to an official computer system by means of electronic communications under this Schedule, or

(b) the recipient of any information delivered by means of electronic communications from an official computer system,

shall be presumed, unless the contrary is proved, to be the person recorded as such on an official computer system.

Information delivered electronically on another's behalf

10. Any information delivered by an approved method of electronic communications on behalf of any person shall be deemed to have been delivered by him unless he proves that it was delivered without his knowledge or connivance. **2.1126**

Proof of delivery of information

11.—(1) The use of an authorised method of electronic communications shall be presumed, unless the contrary is proved, to have resulted in the delivery of information— **2.1127**

(a) in the case of information falling to be delivered to the Board, if the delivery of the information has been recorded on an official computer system;

(b) in the case of information falling to be delivered by the Board, if the despatch of the information has been recorded on an official computer system.

(2) The use of an authorised method of electronic communications shall be presumed, unless the contrary is proved, not to have resulted in the delivery of information—

(a) in the case of information falling to be delivered to the Board, if the delivery of the information has not been recorded on an official computer system;

(b) in the case of information falling to be delivered by the Board, if the despatch of the information has not been recorded on an official computer system.

(3) The time of receipt of any information sent by an authorised means of electronic communications shall be presumed, unless the contrary is proved, to be that recorded on an official computer system.

Use of unauthorised means of electronic communications

12.—(1) Sub-paragraph (2) applies to information which is required to be delivered to the Board in connection with the matters mentioned in paragraph 3. **2.1128**

(2) The use of a means of electronic communications, for the purpose of delivering any information to which this paragraph applies, shall be conclusively presumed not to have resulted in the delivery of that information, unless—

(a) that means of electronic communications is for the time being approved for delivery of information of that kind; and

(b) the sender is approved for the use of that means of electronic communications in relation to information of that kind.

Regulation 43 SCHEDULE 3

REVOCATIONS

PART I

REVOCATIONS APPLICABLE TO GREAT BRITAIN

2.1129 *Omitted*

PART II

REVOCATIONS APPLICABLE TO NORTHERN IRELAND

2.1130 *Omitted*

The Child Benefit and Guardian's Allowance (Administrative Arrangements) Regulations 2003

(SI 2003/494)

Made	*5th March 2003*
Laid before Parliament	*5th March 2003*
Coming into force	*7th April 2003*

ARRANGEMENT OF REGULATIONS

The Commissioners of Inland Revenue, in exercise of the powers conferred upon them by sections 58 and 65(1), (2), (7) and (9) of the Tax Credits Act 2002, hereby make the following Regulations:

Citation and commencement

2.1132 **1.** These Regulations may be cited as the Child Benefit and Guardian's Allowance (Administrative Arrangements) Regulations 2003 and shall come into force on 7th April 2003 immediately after the Child Benefit and Guardian's Allowance (Administration) Regulations 2003.

Interpretation

2.1133 **2.** In these Regulations—

"the Board" means the [1 Commissioners for the Majesty's Revenue and Customs];

"defective application" has the meaning given by regulation 10(3) of the principal Regulations;

"the principal Regulations" means the Child Benefit and Guardian's Allowance (Administration) Regulations 2003;

"relevant authority" means—

(a) the Secretary of State;

(b) the Department for Social Development in Northern Ireland; or

(c) a person providing services to the Secretary of State or that Department.

AMENDMENT

1. The Child Benefit and Guardian's Allowance (Miscellaneous Amendments) Regulations 2006 (SI 2006/203) (April 10, 2006).

Provision of information or evidence to relevant authorities

3.—(1) Information or evidence relating to child benefit or guardian's allowance which is held— 2.1134

(a) by the Board; or

(b) by a person providing services to the Board, in connection with the provision of those services,

may be provided to a relevant authority for the purposes of, or for any purposes connected with, the exercise of that relevant authority's functions under the principal Regulations.

(2) Information or evidence relating to child benefit and guardian's allowance may be provided to a relevant authority by persons other than the Board (whether or not persons by whom claims or notifications relating to child benefit or guardian's allowance are or have been made or given).

Giving of information or advice by relevant authorities

4. A relevant authority to which a claim or notification is or has been made or given by a person in accordance with the principal Regulations may give information or advice relating to child benefit and guardian's allowance to that person. 2.1135

Recording, verification and holding, and forwarding, of claims etc. received by relevant authorities

5.—(1) A relevant authority may record and hold— 2.1136

(a) claims and notifications received by virtue of the any of the principal Regulations; and

(b) information or evidence received by virtue of regulation 3(2).

(2) Subject to paragraphs (3) and (4), a relevant authority or a person providing services to the Board must forward to the Board such a claim or notification, or such information or evidence, as soon as reasonably practicable after being satisfied that it is complete.

(3) Before forwarding a claim or notification in accordance with paragraph (2), a relevant authority must verify whether the details of the claim or notification are consistent with any details held by it which have been provided in connection with a relevant claim for benefit that relates to—

(a) the person by whom the claim for child benefit or guardian's allowance is or has been made; or

(b) [1 the child or qualifying young person in respect to whom] the child benefit or guardian's allowance is payable.

(4) Before forwarding a claim in accordance with paragraph (2), a relevant authority must verify that—

(a) any national insurance number provided in respect of the person by whom the claim is made exists and has been allocated to that person;
(b) the matters verified in accordance with sub-paragraph (a) accord with—
(i) its own records; or
(ii) in the case of a person providing services to the Secretary of State or the Department for Social Development in Northern Ireland, records held by the Secretary of State or that Department.

(5) Before forwarding a claim in accordance with paragraph (2), a relevant authority may verify the existence of any original document provided by the person making the claim which is required to be returned to him.

(6) If a relevant authority cannot locate any national insurance number in respect of a person by whom such a claim is made, it must forward to the Board or a person providing services to the Board the claim.

(7) "National insurance number" means the national insurance number allocated within the meaning of—
(a) regulation 9 of the Social Security (Crediting and Treatment of Contributions, and National Insurance Numbers) Regulations 2001; or
(b) regulation 9 of the Social Security (Crediting and Treatment of Contributions, and National Insurance Numbers) Regulations (Northern Ireland) 2001.

(8) "Claim for benefit" means a claim for—
(a) a benefit in relation to which—
(i) the Secretary of State has functions under the Social Security Contributions and Benefits Act 1992; or
(ii) the Department for Social Development in Northern Ireland has functions under the Social Security Contributions and Benefits (Northern Ireland) Act 1992; or
(b) a jobseeker's allowance under—
(i) the Jobseekers Act 1995; or
(ii) the Jobseekers (Northern Ireland) Order 1995.
[2 (c) universal credit under Part 1 of the Welfare Reform Act 2012.]

AMENDMENTS

1. The Child Benefit and Guardian's Allowance (Miscellaneous Amendments) Regulations 2006 (SI 2006/203) (April 10, 2006).

2. The Universal Credit (Consequential Supplementary, Incidental and Miscellaneous Provisions) Regulations 2013 (SI 2013/630) reg.82 (April 29, 2013).

The Child Benefit and Guardian's Allowance (Decisions and Appeals) Regulations 2003

(SI 2003/916)

Made	*27th March 2003*
Coming into force	*7th April 2003*

ARRANGEMENT OF REGULATIONS

PART 1

GENERAL

PART 2

REVISION OF DECISIONS

PART 3

SUPERSEDING DECISIONS

PART 4

SUSPENSION AND TERMINATION

2.1138 Whereas a draft of this instrument was laid before Parliament in accordance with section 80(1) of the Social Security Act 1998 and Article 75(1A) of the Social Security (Northern Ireland) Order 1998 and approved by resolution of each House of Parliament;

Now, therefore, the Commissioners of Inland Revenue, in exercise of the powers conferred upon them by the provisions set out in Schedule 1 and, in accordance with section 8 of the Tribunals and Inquiries Act 1992, after consultation with the Council on Tribunals, hereby make the following Regulations:

PART 1

GENERAL

Citation, commencement and effect

1.—(1) These Regulations may be cited as the Child Benefit and Guardian's Allowance (Decisions and Appeals) Regulations 2003 and shall come into force on 7th April 2003 immediately after the commencement of section 50 of the Tax Credits Act 2002 for the purposes of entitlement to payment of child benefit and guardian's allowance. **2.1139**

(2) These Regulations have effect only in relation to—

(a) child benefit and guardian's allowance under the Contributions and Benefits Act; and

(b) child benefit and guardian's allowance under the Contributions and Benefits (NI) Act.

Interpretation

2.—(1) In these Regulations— **2.1140**

"the 1998 Act" means the Social Security Act 1998;

"the Administration Act" means the Social Security Administration Act 1992;

"the Administration (NI) Act" means the Social Security Administration (Northern Ireland) Act 1992;

"the Administration Regulations" means the Child Benefit and Guardian's Allowance (Administration) Regulations 2003;

"appeal tribunal" means—

[[1] . . .] in relation to child benefit or guardian's allowance under the Contributions and Benefits (NI) Act, an appeal tribunal constituted under Chapter 1 of Part 2 of the 1998 Order;

[[2] "the appropriate office" [[3] (except in regulation 31)] means—

(a) Waterview Park, Washington, Tyne and Wear; or

(b) any other office specified in writing by the Board.]

"the Board" means the Commissioners of Inland Revenue;

"claimant" means a person who has claimed child benefit or guardian's allowance and includes, in relation to an award or decision, a beneficiary under the award or a person affected by the decision;

"clerk to the appeal tribunal" means—

[[1] . . .] in relation to child benefit or guardian's allowance under the Contributions and Benefits (NI) Act, a clerk assigned to the appeal tribunal in accordance with regulation 37 of the Decisions and Appeals Regulations (NI);

"Commissioner" means—

[[1] . . .] in relation to child benefit or guardian's allowance under the Contributions and Benefits (NI) Act, the Chief Social Security Commissioner or any other Social Security Commissioner appointed under the 1998 Order and includes a tribunal of two or more Commissioners constituted under Article 16(7);

"the Contributions and Benefits Act" means the Social Security Contributions and Benefits Act 1992;

"the Contributions and Benefits (NI) Act" means the Social Security Contributions and Benefits (Northern Ireland) Act 1992;

"the Decisions and Appeals Regulations" means the Social Security and Child Support (Decisions and Appeals) Regulations 1999;

"the Decisions and Appeals Regulations (NI)" means the Social Security and Child Support (Decisions and Appeals) Regulations (Northern Ireland) 1999;

"family" has—

(a) in relation to child benefit and guardian's allowance under the Contributions and Benefits Act, the meaning given by section 137 of that Act;

(b) in relation to child benefit and guardian's allowance under the Contributions and Benefits (NI) Act, the meaning given by section 133 of that Act;

"legally qualified panel member" means—

[1 . . .] in relation to child benefit or guardian's allowance under the Contributions and Benefits (NI) Act, a panel member who satisfies the requirements of paragraph 1 of Schedule 2 to the Decisions and Appeals Regulations (NI);

"the Northern Ireland Department" means the Department for Social Development in Northern Ireland;

"the 1998 Order" means the Social Security (Northern Ireland) Order 1998;

"panel" means the panel constituted under [1 . . .] or Article 7;

"panel member" means a person appointed to the panel;

"party to the proceedings" means the Board and any other person who—

(a) is one of the principal parties for the purposes of sections 13 and 14 or Articles 14 and 15; or

(b) has a right of appeal to an appeal tribunal under section 12(2) or Article 13(2);

"relevant benefit" means child tax credit under the Tax Credits Act 2002 and—

(a) in relation to child benefit or guardian's allowance under the Contributions and Benefits Act, any of the benefits mentioned in section 8(3);

(b) in relation to child benefit or guardian's allowance under the Contributions and Benefits (NI) Act, any of the benefits mentioned in Article 9(3);

"superseding decision" has the meaning given by regulation 13(1);

"writing" includes writing produced by electronic communications used in accordance with regulation 4.

(2) In these Regulations—

(a) a reference to a numbered section without more is a reference to the section of the 1998 Act bearing that number;

(b) a reference to a numbered Article without more is a reference to the Article of the 1998 Order bearing that number.

AMENDMENTS

1. Tribunals, Courts and Enforcement Act 2007 (Transitional and Consequential Provisions) Order 2008 (SI 2008/2683) Sch.1 paras 212 and 213 (November 3, 2008).
2. Child Benefit and Guardian's Allowance (Miscellaneous Amendments) Regulations 2009 (SI 2009/3268) reg.4 (January 1, 2010).
3. Tax Credits, Child Benefit and Guardian's Allowance Reviews and Appeals Order 2014 (SI 2014/886) art.5(1) and (2) (April 6, 2014).

GENERAL NOTE

"the Board" 2.1141

The definition of "the Board" must be read in the light of the Commissioners for Revenue and Customs Act 2005. Section 5(2)(a) vests all the functions of the former Commissioners of Inland Revenue in the Commissioners for Her Majesty's Revenue and Customs and s.4(1) provides that the Commissioners and the officers of Revenue and Customs may together be referred to as Her Majesty's Revenue and Customs.

Service of notices or documents

3.—(1) Where, under any provision of these Regulations— 2.1142

(a) a notice or other document is required to be given or sent to the clerk to the appeal tribunal or the Board, the notice or document is to be treated as having been so given or sent on the day that it is received by the clerk or the Board;

(b) a notice (including notification of a decision of the Board) or other document is required to be given or sent to any person other than clerk to the appeal tribunal or the Board, the notice or document is, if sent by post to that person's last known address, to be treated as having been given or sent on the day that it was posted.

(2) In these Regulations, "the date of notification", in relation to a decision of the Board, means the date on which notification of the decision is treated under paragraph (1)(b) as having been given or sent.

DEFINITIONS

"the Board"—see reg.2(1).
"clerk to the appeal tribunal"—*ibid*.

GENERAL NOTE

Paragraph (1)

See the note to reg.2 of the Social Security and Child Support (Decisions and Appeals) Regulations 1999 to which this is equivalent. 2.1143

Paragraph (2)

This has the effect that whenever the phrase "the date of notification" is used in subsequent provisions in these Regulations, it refers to the date on which notification of a decision of the Board is treated under para.(1)(b) as having been given or sent. 2.1144

Use of electronic communications

4.—(1) Schedule 2 to the Administration Regulations (the use of electronic communications) applies to the delivery of information to or by the Board which is authorised or required by these Regulations 2.1145 in the same manner as it applies to the delivery of information to or by the Board which is authorised or required by the Administration Regulations.

(2) References in paragraph (1) to the delivery of information shall be construed in accordance with section 132(8) of the Finance Act 1999.

DEFINITIONS

"the Administration Regulations"—see reg.2(1).
"the Board"—*ibid.*

PART 2

REVISION OF DECISIONS

Revision of decisions within a prescribed period or on an application

2.1146 **5.**—(1) Subject to paragraph (3), if the conditions specified in paragraph (2) are satisfied—

(a) a decision under section 8 or 10 may be revised by the Board under section 9; and
(b) a decision under Article 9 or 11 may be revised by them under Article 10.

(2) The conditions specified in this paragraph are that—

(a) the Board commence action leading to the revision within one month of the date of notification of the decision; or
(b) subject to regulation 6, an application for the revision was received by the Board at the appropriate office—
   (i) within one month of the date of notification of the decision;
   (ii) if a written statement of the reasons for the decision requested under regulation 26(1)(b) was provided within the period specified in paragraph (i), within 14 days of the expiry of that period; or
   (iii) if such a statement was provided after the period specified in paragraph (i), within 14 days of the date on which the statement was provided.

(3) Paragraph (1) does not apply in respect of a relevant change of circumstances which occurred since the decision [1 had effect (or, in the case of an advance award under regulation 12 of the Child Benefit and Guardian's Allowance (Administration) Regulations 2003 (advance claims and awards), was made)] or where the Board have evidence or information which indicates that a relevant change of circumstances will occur.

AMENDMENT

1. Child Benefit and Guardian's Allowance (Miscellaneous Amendments) Regulations 2005 (SI 2005/343) reg.3 (March 18, 2005).

DEFINITIONS

"the appropriate office"—see reg.2(1).
"the Board"—*ibid.*
"the date of notification"—see reg.3(2).

General Note

This regulation provides for revision of a decision where the Board or the claimant takes action within one month of the date of notification of the decision. It is equivalent to reg.3(1) and (9)(a) of the Social Security and Child Support (Decisions and Appeals) Regulations 1999. The time for making an application may be extended if a request for reasons has been made promptly (para.(2)(b)(ii) and (iii)) or where the conditions of reg.6 are met. The time for appealing against a decision is extended if an application is made for revision, so that the claimant is not prejudiced by first having sought a revision (see reg.28(2)). **2.1147**

Late applications for revision of decisions

6.—(1) The Board may extend the time limits specified in regulation 5(2)(b)(i) to (iii) if the first and second conditions are satisfied. **2.1148**

(2) The first condition is that an application for an extension of time must be made to the Board by the claimant or a person acting on his behalf.

(3) The second condition is that the application for the extension of time must—

(a) contain particulars of the grounds on which the extension is sought;
(b) contain sufficient details of the decision which it is sought to have revised so as to enable it to be identified; and
(c) be made within 13 months of the latest date by which the application for revision should have been received by the Board in accordance with regulation 5(2)(b).

(4) An application for an extension of time must not be granted unless the Board are satisfied that—

(a) it is reasonable to grant it;
(b) the application for revision has merit; and
(c) special circumstances are relevant to the application for an extension of time as a result of which it was not practicable for the application for revision to be made within the time limits specified in regulation 5(2)(b)(i) to (iii).

(5) In determining whether it is reasonable to grant an application for an extension of time, the Board must have regard to the principle that the greater the amount of time that has elapsed between the expiration of the time limits specified in regulation 5(2)(b)(i) to (iii) and the making of the application, the more compelling the special circumstances mentioned in paragraph (4)(c) should be.

(6) In determining whether it is reasonable to grant an application for an extension of time, the Board must take no account of the following—

(a) that the applicant or any person acting for him was unaware of, or misunderstood, the law applicable to his case (including being unaware of, or misunderstanding, the time limits imposed by these Regulations); or
(b) that a Commissioner [[1] , the Upper Tribunal] or a court has taken a different view of the law from that previously understood and applied.

(7) An application for an extension of time which has been refused may not be renewed.

AMENDMENT

1. Tribunals, Courts and Enforcement Act 2007 (Transitional and Consequential Provisions) Order 2008 (SI 2008/2683) Sch.1 paras 212 and 214 (November 3, 2008).

DEFINITIONS

"the Board"—see reg.2(1).
"claimant"—*ibid.*
"Commissioner"—*ibid.*

GENERAL NOTE

2.1149 This is equivalent to reg.4 of the Social Security and Child Support (Decisions and Appeals) Regulations 1999.

Procedure for revision of decisions on an application

2.1150 **7.**—(1) The Board may treat—

(a) an application for a decision under section 10 as an application for a revision under section 9;
(b) an application for a decision under Article 11 as an application for a revision under Article 10.

(2) Paragraph (3) applies where, in order to consider all the issues raised by an application for such a revision, the Board require further evidence or information from the applicant.

(3) Where this paragraph applies, the Board must notify the applicant that further evidence or information is required and—

(a) if the applicant provides relevant further evidence or information within one month of the date of notification or such longer period of time as the Board may allow, the decision may be revised;
(b) if the applicant does not provide such evidence or information within that time, the decision may be revised on the basis of the application.

DEFINITIONS

"the Board"—see reg.2(1).
"the date of notification"—see reg.3(2).

GENERAL NOTE

Paragraph (1)

2.1151 This is equivalent to reg.3(10) of the Social Security and Child Support (Decisions and Appeals) Regulations 1999 and provides for an application for a superseding decision to be treated as an an application for revision. Regulation 14(1) makes provision for an application for a revision to be treated as an application for superseding decision.

Paragraphs (2) and (3)

2.1152 These are equivalent to reg.3(2) of the Social Security and Child Support (Decisions and Appeals) Regulations 1999.

Revision of decisions against which there has been an appeal

8.—(1) In the circumstances prescribed by paragraph (2), any of the following decisions may be revised by the Board at any time— 2.1153

(a) a decision under section 8 or 10;
(b) a decision under Article 9 or 11.

(2) The circumstances prescribed by this paragraph are circumstances where there is an appeal to an appeal tribunal [1 or the First-tier Tribunal] against the decision within the time prescribed by regulation 28, or in a case to which [1 regulations 29 and 29A apply within the time prescribed by those regulations] but the appeal has not been determined.

(3) If—

(a) the Board make one of the following decisions ("the original decision")—
 (i) a decision under section 8 or 10 or one under section 9(1) revising such a decision; or
 (ii) a decision under Article 9 or 11 or one under Article 10(1) revising such a decision;
(b) the claimant appeals to an appeal tribunal against the original decision;
(c) after the appeal has been made, but before it results in a decision by the appeal tribunal, the Board make a second decision which—
 (i) supersedes the original decision in accordance with section 10 or Article 11; or
 (ii) decides a further claim for child benefit or guardian's allowance by the claimant; and
(d) the Board would have made their second decision differently if, at the time they made it, they had been aware of the decision subsequently made by the appeal tribunal,

the second decision may be revised by the Board at any time.

AMENDMENT

1. Tribunals, Courts and Enforcement Act 2007 (Transitional and Consequential Provisions) Order 2008 (SI 2008/2683) Sch.1 paras 212 and 215 (November 3, 2008).

DEFINITIONS

"appeal tribunal"—see reg.2(1).
"the Board"—*ibid.*
"claimant"—*ibid.*

GENERAL NOTE

This is equivalent to reg.3(5A) of the Social Security and Child Support (Decisions and Appeals) Regulations 1999 and enables a decision made while an appeal to a tribunal is pending to be revised in the light of the tribunal's decision. 2.1154

Revision of decisions against which no appeal lies

9.—(1) In the case prescribed by paragraph (2), any of the following decisions may be revised by the Board at any time— 2.1155

(a) a decision under section 8 or 10;
(b) a decision under Article 9 or 11.

(2) The case prescribed by this paragraph is the case of decisions which—

(a) are specified in—

(i) Schedule 2 to the 1998 Act; or

(ii) Schedule 2 to the 1998 Order; or

(b) are prescribed by regulation 25 (decisions against which no appeal lies).

DEFINITION

"the Board"—see reg.2(1).

GENERAL NOTE

2.1156 This is equivalent to reg.3(8) of the Social Security and Child Support (Decisions and Appeals) Regulations 1999.

Revision of decisions arising from official error etc.

2.1157 **10.**—(1) In the circumstances prescribed by paragraph (2), any of the following decisions may be revised by the Board at any time—

(a) a decision under section 8 or 10;

(b) a decision under Article 9 or 11.

(2) The circumstances prescribed by this paragraph are circumstances where the decision—

(a) arose from an official error; or

(b) was made in ignorance of, or was based upon a mistake as to, some material fact and, as a result of that ignorance of, or mistake as to, that fact, is more advantageous to the claimant than it would otherwise have been.

(3) "Official error" means an error made by—

(a) an officer of the Board acting as such, which no person outside the Inland Revenue caused or to which no such person materially contributed; or

(b) a person employed by a person providing services to the Board and acting as such which no other person who was not so employed caused or to which no such other person materially contributed,

but does not include an error of law which is shown to have been an error by virtue of a subsequent decision of a Commissioner [1 , the Upper Tribunal] or the court.

AMENDMENT

1. Tribunals, Courts and Enforcement Act 2007 (Transitional and Consequential Provisions) Order 2008 (SI 2008/2683) Sch.1 paras 212 and 216 (November 3, 2008).

DEFINITIONS

"the Board"—see reg.2(1).

"claimant"—*ibid.*

"Commissioner"—*ibid.*

"Inland Revenue", by virtue of s.39(2) of the Social Security Act 1998, see s.191 of the Social Security Administration Act 1992.

"official error"—see para.(3).

GENERAL NOTE

This is equivalent to reg.3(5) of the Social Security and Child Support (Decisions and Appeals) Regulations 1999. For the interpretation of the definition of "official error", see the note to reg.1(3) of the 1999 Regulations. 2.1158

Revision of decisions following the award of another relevant benefit

11.—(1) In the circumstances prescribed by paragraph (2), any of the following decisions may be revised by the Board at any time— 2.1159

(a) a decision under section 8 or 10;

(b) a decision under Article 9 or 11.

(2) The circumstances prescribed by this paragraph are circumstances where—

(a) the decision awards child benefit or guardian's allowance to a person; and

(b) an award of another relevant benefit, or of an increase in the rate of another relevant benefit, is made to that person or a member of his family for a period which includes the date on which the decision took effect.

DEFINITIONS

"the Board"—see reg.2(1).
"family"—*ibid.*
"relevant benefit"—*ibid.*

GENERAL NOTE

This is equivalent to reg.3(7) of the Social Security and Child Support (Decisions and Appeals) Regulations 1999. A decision may be revised where a later decision in respect of a relevant benefit affects entitlement under the earlier decision from the date it took effect. If the later decision affects entitlement under the earlier decision from a later date, the earlier decision is superseded under reg.13(2)(e) instead of being revised. 2.1160

Date as from which revised decisions take effect

12. If the Board decide that— 2.1161

(a) on a revision under section 9, the date as from which the decision under section 8 or 10 took effect was erroneous; or

(b) on a revision under Article 10, the date as from which the decision under Article 9 or 11 took effect was erroneous,

the revision shall take effect as from the date from which the decision would have taken effect had the error not been made.

DEFINITION

"the Board"—see reg.2(1).

GENERAL NOTE

This is equivalent to reg.5 of the Social Security and Child Support (Decisions and Appeals) Regulations 1999 and provides the exception to the general rule imposed by s.9(3) of the Social Security Act 1998 that a revision is effective from the same date as the decision being revised. The exception is where a ground for the revision is that the effective date of the original decision was wrong. 2.1162

PART 3

SUPERSEDING DECISIONS

Cases and circumstances in which superseding decisions may be made

2.1163 **13.**—(1) Subject to regulation 15, the Board may make a decision under section 10 or Article 11 ("a superseding decision"), either on their own initiative or on an application received by them at an appropriate office, in any of the cases and circumstances prescribed by paragraph (2).

(2) The cases and circumstances prescribed by this paragraph are cases and circumstances where the decision to be superseded is—

(a) a decision in respect of which—
 (i) there has been a relevant change of circumstances since it [1 had effect (or, in the case of an advance award under regulation 12 of the Child Benefit and Guardian's Allowance (Administration) Regulations 2003 (advance claims and awards), was made)]; or
 (ii) it is anticipated that there will be such a change;
(b) a decision (other than one to which sub-paragraph (d) refers)—
 (i) which was erroneous in point of law, or was made in ignorance of, or was based upon a mistake as to, some material fact; and
 (ii) in relation to which an application for a superseding decision was received by the Board, or a decision by the Board to act on their own initiative was taken, more than one month after the date of notification of the decision to be superseded or after the expiry of such longer period of time as may have been allowed under regulation 6;
(c) a decision of an appeal tribunal [2 the First-tier Tribunal, the Upper Tribunal] or a Commissioner which—
 (i) was made in ignorance of, or was based upon a mistake as to, some material fact;
 (ii) in a case to which subsection (5) of section 26 applies, was dealt with in accordance with subsection (4)(b) of that section; or
 (iii) in a case to which paragraph (5) of Article 26 applies, was dealt with in accordance with paragraph (4)(b) of that Article;
(d) a decision—
 (i) specified in Schedule 2 to the 1998 Act;
 (ii) specified in Schedule 2 to the 1998 Order; or
 (iii) prescribed by regulation 25 (decisions against which no appeal lies); or
(e) a decision where—
 (i) the claimant has been awarded entitlement to child benefit or guardian's allowance; and
 (ii) subsequent to the first day of the period to which that entitlement relates, the claimant or a member of his family becomes entitled to, or to an increase in the rate of, another relevant benefit.

AMENDMENTS

1. Child Benefit and Guardian's Allowance (Miscellaneous Amendments) Regulations 2005 (SI 2005/343) reg.4 (March 18, 2005).

2. Tribunals, Courts and Enforcement Act 2007 (Transitional and Consequential Provisions) Order 2008 (SI 2008/2683) Sch.1 paras 212 and 217 (November 3, 2008).

DEFINITIONS

"appeal tribunal"—see reg.2(1).
"appropriate office"—*ibid.*
"the Board"—*ibid.*
"claimant"—*ibid.*
"Commissioner"—*ibid.*
"the date of notification"—see reg.3(2).
"family"—see reg.2(1).
"relevant benefit"—*ibid.*
"superseding decision"—see para.(1).

GENERAL NOTE

Paragraph (1)

This is equivalent to reg.6(1) of the Social Security and Child Support (Decisions and Appeals) Regulations 1999. See the note to that provision. One difference is the use of the phrase "superseding decision" instead of "supersession" but this seems to be only a matter of style. 2.1164

Paragraph (2)

This is equivalent to reg.6(2)(a)–(e) of the 1999 Regulations, the other subparagraphs of reg.6(2) of the 1999 regulations not being relevant to child benefit or guardian's allowance. 2.1165

The context, as well as a comparison with the 1999 Regulations, makes it clear that the "decision" in subpara.(b) refers only to decisions of the Board. Decisions of tribunals and Commissioners fall to be superseded on the ground of ignorance of, or mistake as to, a material fact only under subpara.(c). Subpara.(b)(ii) prevents any overlap with reg.5. In subpara.(d) "decision" also refers only to decisions of the Board, because the relevant decisions do not fall within the jurisdiction of tribunals or Commissioners but, in subparas (a) and (e), "decision" includes decisions of tribunals and Commissioners.

Subparagraph (e) provides for supersession only where the later decision affects entitlement under the earlier decision from a date later than the date from which the earlier decision was effective. If the later decision has effect from the date from which the earlier decision was effective, revision under reg.11 is appropriate if the earlier decision was a decision of the Board. If the earlier decision was a decision of a tribunal or Commissioner, it is not clear that there will always be grounds for supersession, save under subpara.(a)(i), which is unlikely to produce the appropriate degree of backdating.

A superseding decision is effective from the date it is made (s.10(5) of the Social Security Act 1998), save where reg.16 provides otherwise.

See further the note to reg.6 of the 1999 Regulations.

Procedure for making superseding decisions on an application

14.—(1) The Board may treat— 2.1166

(a) an application for a revision under section 9 as an application for a decision under section 10;

(b) an application for a revision under Article 10 as an application for a decision under Article 11.

(2) Paragraph (3) applies where, in order to consider all the issues raised

by an application for a superseding decision, the Board require further evidence or information from the applicant.

(3) Where this paragraph applies, the Board must notify the applicant that further evidence or information is required and—

(a) if the applicant provides further relevant evidence or information within one month of the date of notification or such longer period of time as the Board may allow, the decision to be superseded may be superseded;

(b) if the applicant does not provide such evidence or information within that period, the decision to be superseded may be superseded on the basis of the application.

DEFINITIONS

"the Board"—see reg.2(1).
"the date of notification"—see reg.3(2).
"superseding decision"—by virtue of reg.2(1), see reg.13(1).

GENERAL NOTE

Paragraph (1)

2.1167 This is equivalent to reg.6(5) of the Social Security and Child Support (Decisions and Appeals) Regulations 1999. It permits an application for revision to be treated as an application for supersession. Regulation 7(1) permits an application for supersession to be treated as an application for revision. See the note to s.12 of the Social Security Act 1998 for a discussion of the question whether, on appeal, a tribunal may treat a superseding decision as a refusal to revise or a revision as a refusal to supersede.

Paragraphs (2) and (3)

2.1168 These are equivalent to reg.6(4) of the 1999 Regulations.

Interaction of revisions and superseding decisions

2.1169 **15.**—(1) This regulation applies to any decision in relation to which circumstances arise in which the decision may be revised under section 9 or Article 10.

(2) A decision to which this regulation applies may not be superseded by a superseding decision unless—

(a) circumstances arise in which the Board may revise the decision in accordance with Part 2;
and

(b) further circumstances arise in relation to the decision which—
  (i) are not specified in any of the regulations in Part 2; but
  (ii) are prescribed by regulation 13(2) or are ones where a superseding decision may be made in accordance with regulation 14(3).

DEFINITIONS

"the Board"—see reg.2(1).
"superseding decision"—by virtue of reg.2(1), see reg.13(1).

GENERAL NOTE

2.1170 This is equivalent to reg.6(3) of the Social Security and Child Support (Decisions and Appeals) Regulations 1999.

Date as from which superseding decisions take effect

16.—(1) This regulation prescribes cases or circumstances in which a superseding decision shall take effect as from a prescribed date other than the date on which it was made or, where applicable, the date on which the application for it was made. 2.1171

(2) If a superseding decision is made on the basis that—

(a) there has been a relevant change of circumstances since the decision to be superseded had effect [1 (or, in the case of an advance award, was made)]; or

(b) it is anticipated there will be such a change,

it shall take effect as from the earliest date prescribed by paragraphs (3) to (8).

(3) In any case where the superseding decision is advantageous to the claimant and notification of the change was given in accordance with any enactment or subordinate legislation under which that notification was required, the date prescribed by this paragraph is—

(a) if the notification was given within one month of the change occurring or such longer period as may be allowed under regulation 17, the date the change occurred or, if later, the first date on which the change has effect; or

(b) if the notification was given after the period mentioned in subparagraph (a), the date of notification of the change.

(4) In any case where the superseding decision is advantageous to the claimant and is made on the Board's own initiative, the date prescribed by this paragraph is the date on which the Board commenced action with a view to the supersession.

(5) In any case where the superseding decision is not advantageous to the claimant, the date prescribed by this paragraph is the date of the change.

(6) Decisions which are advantageous to claimants include those mentioned in regulation 27(5).

(7) If—

(a) the Board supersede a decision made by an appeal tribunal [2 the First-tier Tribunal, the Upper Tribunal] or a Commissioner in accordance with paragraph (i) of regulation 13(2)(c); and

(b) as a result of the ignorance or mistake referred to in that paragraph, the decision to be superseded was more advantageous to the claimant than it would otherwise have been,

the superseding decision shall take effect as from the date on which the decision of the appeal tribunal or the Commissioner took, or was to take, effect.

(8) If the Board supersede a decision made by an appeal tribunal [2 the First-tier Tribunal, the Upper Tribunal] or a Commissioner in accordance with paragraph (ii) or (iii) of regulation 13(2)(c), the superseding decision shall take effect as from the date on which it would have taken effect had it been decided in accordance with the determination of [2 the Upper Tribunal,] the Commissioner or the court in the appeal referred to in section 26(1)(b) or Article 26(1)(b).

(9) If a superseding decision is made in consequence of a decision which is a relevant determination for the purposes of section 27 or Article 27, it shall take effect as from the date of the relevant determination.

[1 (9A) Where—

(a) a Commissioner [2, the Upper Tribunal] or the court determines an appeal as mentioned in section 27(1)(a) or Article 27(1)(a) ("the relevant determination") and the Board make a decision of the kind specified in section 27(1)(b) or Article 27(1)(b);
(b) there is an appeal against the relevant determination;
(c) after the Board's decision, payment is suspended in accordance with regulation 18(1) and (3)(b); and
(d) on appeal the court reverses the relevant determination in whole or in part,

a consequential decision by the Board under section 10 or Article 11 which supersedes the earlier decision referred to in sub-paragraph (a) above shall take effect from the date on which that earlier decision took effect.

In this paragraph "the court" has the meaning given in section 27 or Article 27 (as the case requires).]

(10) If the Board supersede a decision in accordance with subparagraph (e) of regulation 13(2), the superseding decision shall take effect as from the date on which entitlement arises—

(a) to the other relevant benefit referred to in paragraph (ii) of that sub-paragraph; or
(b) to an increase in the rate of that benefit.

AMENDMENTS

1. Child Benefit and Guardian's Allowance (Miscellaneous Amendments) Regulations 2005 (SI 2005/343) reg.5 (March 18, 2005).

2. Tribunals, Courts and Enforcement Act 2007 (Transitional and Consequential Provisions) Order 2008 (SI 2008/2683) Sch.1 paras 212 and 218 (November 3, 2008).

DEFINITIONS

"appeal tribunal"—see reg.2(1).
"the Board"—*ibid.*
"claimant"—*ibid.*
"Commissioner"—*ibid.*
"prescribed"—see s.84 of the Social Security Act 1998.
"relevant benefit"—see reg.2(1).
"superseding decision"—by virtue of reg.2(1), see reg.13(1).

GENERAL NOTE

2.1172 This is equivalent to reg.7(1)–(7) and (33) of the Social Security and Child Support (Decisions and Appeals) Regulations 1999. See the notes to reg.7 of the 1999 Regulations. (The other provisions of reg.7 of the 1999 Regulations have no relevance to child benefit or guardian's allowance.)

Effective date for late notifications of change of circumstances

2.1173 **17.**—(1) For the purposes of paragraph (3) of regulation 16, the Board may allow a longer period of time than the period of one month mentioned in sub-paragraph (a) of that paragraph for the notification of a change of circumstances if the first and second conditions are satisfied.

(2) The first condition is that an application for the purposes of regulation 16(3) must be made by the claimant or a person acting on his behalf.

(3) The second condition is that the application for the purposes of regulation 16(3) must—

(a) contain particulars of the relevant change of circumstances and the reasons for the failure to notify the change on an earlier date; and

(b) be made within 13 months of the date on which the change occurred.

(4) An application under this regulation must not be granted unless the Board are satisfied that—

(a) it is reasonable to grant it;

(b) the change of circumstances notified by the applicant is relevant to the decision which is to be superseded; and

(c) special circumstances are relevant to the application as a result of which it was not practicable for the applicant to notify the change of circumstances within one month of the change occurring.

(5) In determining whether it is reasonable to grant an application for the purposes of regulation 16(3), the Board must have regard to the principle that the greater the amount of time that has elapsed between the date one month after the change of circumstances occurred and the date the application is made, the more compelling the special circumstances mentioned in paragraph (4)(c) should be.

(6) In determining whether it is reasonable to grant an application for the purposes of regulation 16(3), the Board must take no account of the following—

(a) that the applicant or any person acting for him was unaware of, or misunderstood, the law applicable to his case (including being unaware of, or misunderstanding, the time limits imposed by these Regulations); or

(b) that a Commissioner [[1], the Upper Tribunal] or a court has taken a different view of the law from that previously understood and applied.

(7) An application for the purposes of regulation 16(3) which has been refused may not be renewed.

Amendment

1. Tribunals, Courts and Enforcement Act 2007 (Transitional and Consequential Provisions) Order 2008 (SI 2008/2683) Sch.1 paras 212 and 219 (November 3, 2008).

Definitions

"the Board"—see reg.2(1).
"claimant"—*ibid.*
"Commissioner"—*ibid.*

General Note

This is equivalent to reg.8 of the Social Security and Child Support (Decisions and Appeals) Regulations 1999. **2.1174**

PART 4

SUSPENSION AND TERMINATION

Suspension in prescribed cases

2.1175 **18.**—(1) The Board may suspend payment of child benefit or guardian's allowance, in whole or in part, in the circumstances prescribed by paragraph (2) or (3).

(2) The circumstances prescribed by this paragraph are circumstances where it appears to the Board that—

(a) an issue arises as to whether the conditions for entitlement to the benefit or allowance are or were fulfilled;

(b) an issue arises as to whether a decision relating to an award of the benefit or allowance should be—

(i) revised under section 9 or Article 10; or

(ii) superseded under section 10 or Article 11;

(c) an issue arises as to whether any amount paid or payable to a person by way of, or in connection with a claim for, the benefit or allowance is recoverable under—

(i) section 71 of the Administration Act;

(ii) section 69 of the Administration (NI) Act; or

(iii) regulations made under either of those sections;

(d) the last address notified to them of a person who is in receipt of the benefit or allowance is not the address at which that person is residing; or

(e) the details of a bank account or other account which has been notified to them and to which payment of the benefit or allowance by way of a credit is to be made to a person are incorrect.

(3) The circumstances prescribed by this paragraph are where—

(a) an appeal is pending against a decision of an appeal tribunal, [1 the First-tier Tribunal, the Upper Tribunal,] a Commissioner or a court; or

(b) an appeal is pending against a decision given in a different case by a Commissioner [1 , the Upper Tribunal] or a court (whether or not relating to child benefit or guardian's allowance) and it appears to the Board that, if the appeal were to be determined in a particular way, an issue would arise as to whether the award of child benefit or guardian's allowance should be revised or superseded.

(4) For the purposes of section 21(3)(c) and Article 21(3)(c), the prescribed circumstances are circumstances where an appeal tribunal, [1 the First-tier Tribunal, the Upper Tribunal,] a Commissioner or a court has made a decision and the Board—

(a) are awaiting receipt of the decision or, in the case of an appeal tribunal [1 or First-tier Tribunal] decision, are considering whether to apply for a statement of the reasons for it;

(b) in the case of an appeal tribunal decision, [1 or First-tier Tribunal] have applied for, and are awaiting receipt of, such a statement; or

(c) have received the decision, or, in the case of an appeal tribunal [1 or First-tier Tribunal] decision, such a statement, and are considering—

(i) whether to apply for leave [1 or permission] to appeal; or
(ii) where leave [1 or permission] to appeal has been granted, whether to appeal.

(5) In the circumstances prescribed by paragraph (4), the Board must give written notice, as soon as reasonably practicable, to the person in respect of whom payment has been or is to be suspended of their proposal—

(a) to make a request for a statement of the reasons for an appeal tribunal [1 or First-tier Tribunal] decision;
(b) to apply for leave [1 or permission] to appeal; or
(c) to appeal.

AMENDMENT

1. Tribunals, Courts and Enforcement Act 2007 (Transitional and Consequential Provisions) Order 2008 (SI 2008/2683) Sch.1 paras 212 and 220 (November 3, 2008).

DEFINITIONS

"the Administration Act"—see reg.2(1).
"the Administration (NI) Act"—*ibid.*
"appeal tribunal"—*ibid.*
"the Board"—*ibid.*
"Commissioner"—*ibid.*
"prescribed"—see s.84 of the Social Security Act 1998.

Provision of information or evidence

19.—(1) This regulation applies where the Board require information or evidence for a determination whether a decision awarding child benefit or guardian's allowance should be— 2.1176

(a) revised under section 9 or Article 10; or
(b) superseded under section 10 or Article 11.

(2) A person to whom this paragraph applies must—

(a) supply the information or evidence within—
 (i) the period of one month beginning with the date on which the notification under paragraph (4) was sent to him; or
 (ii) such longer period as he satisfies the Board is necessary in order to enable him to comply with the requirement; or
(b) satisfy the Board within the period of time specified in subparagraph (a)(i) that—
 (i) the information or evidence required of him does not exist; or
 (ii) it is not possible for him to obtain it.

(3) A person to whom paragraph (2) applies is any of the following—

(a) a person in respect of whom payment of the benefit or allowance has been suspended in the circumstances prescribed by regulation 18(2);
(b) a person who has made an application for the decision to be revised or superseded;
(c) a person who fails to comply with the provisions of regulation 23 of the Administration Regulations in so far as they relate to information, facts or evidence required by the Board.

(4) The Board must notify a person to whom paragraph (2) applies of the requirements of that paragraph.

(5) The Board may suspend the payment of benefit or allowance, in whole or in part, to a person falling within paragraph (3)(b) or (c) who fails to satisfy the requirements of paragraph (2).

DEFINITIONS

"the Administration Regulations"—see reg.2(1).
"the Board"—*ibid.*

Termination in cases of failure to furnish information or evidence

2.1177 **20.**—(1) Subject to paragraph (3), this regulation applies where—

(a) a person whose benefit or allowance has been suspended under regulation 18 subsequently fails to comply with a requirement for information or evidence under regulation 19 and more than one month has elapsed since the requirement was made; or
(b) a person's benefit or allowance has been suspended under regulation 19(5) and more than one month has elapsed since the first payment was so suspended.

(2) The Board must decide that the person ceases to be entitled to the benefit or allowance from the date on which payment was suspended except where entitlement to the benefit or allowance ceases on an earlier date.

(3) This regulation does not apply where benefit or allowance has been suspended in part under regulation 18 or 19.

DEFINITION

"the Board"—see reg.2(1).

Making of payments which have been suspended

2.1178 **21.**—(1) Payment of benefit or allowance suspended in accordance with regulation 18 or 19 must be made in any of the circumstances prescribed by paragraphs (2) to (5).

(2) The circumstances prescribed by this paragraph are circumstances where—

(a) in a case to which regulation 18(2)(a), (b) or (c) applies, the Board are satisfied that—
  (i) the benefit or allowance suspended is properly payable; and
  (ii) no outstanding issues remain to be resolved;
(b) in a case to which regulation 18(2)(d) applies, the Board are satisfied that they have been notified of the address at which the person is residing;
(c) in a case to which regulation 18(2)(e) applies, the Board are satisfied that they have been notified of the correct details of the bank account or other account to which payment of the benefit or allowance by way of a credit is to be made to the person.

(3) The circumstances prescribed by this paragraph are circumstances where, in a case to which regulation 18(3)(a) applies, the Board—

(a) in the case of a decision of an appeal tribunal, [1 or the First-tier Tribunal] do not apply for a statement of the reasons for that decision within the period of one month specified in—
  (i) in relation to child benefit and guardian's allowance under the Contributions and Benefits Act, regulation 53(4) of the Decisions and Appeals Regulations;
  (ii) in relation to child benefit and guardian's allowance under the

Contributions and Benefits (NI) Act, regulation 53(4) of the Decisions and Appeals Regulations (NI);

(b) in the case of a decision of an appeal tribunal, [1 First-tier Tribunal, the Upper Tribunal] a Commissioner or a court—

(i) do not make an application for leave [1 or permission] to appeal within the time prescribed for the making of such an application; or

(ii) where leave [1 or permission] to appeal is granted, do not make the appeal within the time prescribed for the making of it;

(c) withdraw an application for leave [1 or permission] to appeal or the appeal; or

(d) are refused leave [1 or permission] to appeal in circumstances where it is not open to them to renew the application, or to make a further application, for such leave [1 or permission].

(4) The circumstances prescribed by this paragraph are circumstances where, in a case to which regulation 18(3)(b) applies, the Board, in relation to the decision of the Commissioner [1 , the Upper Tribunal] or the court in the different case—

(a) do not make an application for leave [1 or permission] to appeal within the time prescribed for the making of such an application;

(b) where leave [1 or permission] to appeal is granted, do not make the appeal within the time prescribed for the making of it;

(c) withdraw an application for leave [1 or permission] to appeal or the appeal; or

(d) are refused leave [1 or permission] to appeal in circumstances where it is not open to them to renew the application, or to make a further application, for such leave [1 or permission].

(5) The circumstances prescribed by this paragraph are circumstances where, in a case to which paragraph (5) of regulation 19 applies, the Board are satisfied that—

(a) the benefit or allowance suspended is properly payable; and

(b) the requirements of paragraph (2) of that regulation have been satisfied.

AMENDMENT

1. Tribunals, Courts and Enforcement Act 2007 (Transitional and Consequential Provisions) Order 2008 (SI 2008/2683) Sch.1 paras 212 and 221 (November 3, 2008).

DEFINITIONS

"appeal tribunal"—see reg.2(1).
"the Board"—*ibid.*
"Commissioner"—*ibid.*
"the Contributions and Benefits Act"—*ibid.*
"the Contributions and Benefits (NI) Act"—*ibid.*
"the Decisions and Appeals Regulations"—*ibid.*
"the Decisions and Appeals (NI) Regulations"—*ibid.*

Part 5

Other Matters

Decisions involving issues that arise on appeal in other cases

2.1179 **22.**—(1) A case which satisfies the condition specified in paragraph (2) is a prescribed case for the purposes of section 25(3)(b) and Article 25(3)(b) (prescribed cases and circumstances in which a decision may be made on a prescribed basis).

(2) The condition specified in this paragraph is that the claimant would be entitled to the benefit or allowance to which the decision which falls to be made relates, even if the appeal in the other case referred to in section 25(1)(b) or Article 25(1)(b) were decided in a way which is the most unfavourable to him.

(3) For the purposes of subsection (3)(b) of section 25 and paragraph (3)(b) of Article 25, the prescribed basis on which the Board may make the decision is as if—

- (a) the appeal in the other case which is referred to in subsection (1)(b) of that section, or paragraph (1)(b) of that Article, had already been determined; and
- (b) that appeal had been decided in a way which is the most unfavourable to the claimant.

(4) For the purposes of subsection (5)(c) of section 25 and paragraph (5)(c) of Article 25 (prescribed circumstances in which, for the purposes of the section or the Article, an appeal is pending against a decision), the prescribed circumstances are circumstances where the Board—

- (a) certify in writing that they are considering appealing against that decision; and
- (b) consider that, if such an appeal were to be determined in a particular way—
  - (i) there would be no entitlement to the benefit or allowance in a case to which subsection (1)(a) of that section, or paragraph (1)(a) of that Article, refers; or
  - (ii) the appeal would affect the decision in that case in some other way.

Definitions

"the Board"—see reg.2(1).
"claimant"—*ibid.*
"prescribed"—see s.84 of the Social Security Act 1998.

Appeals involving issues that arise on appeal in other cases

2.1180 **23.** For the purposes of subsection (6)(c) of section 26 and paragraph (6)(c) of Article 26 (prescribed circumstances in which an appeal against a decision which has not been brought, or an application for leave [1 or permission] to appeal has not been made, but the time for so doing has not yet expired, is pending for the purposes of the section or the Article), the prescribed circumstances are circumstances where the Board—

- (a) certify in writing that they are considering appealing against that decision; and
- (b) consider that, if such an appeal were already determined, it would

affect the determination of the appeal described in subsection (1)(a) of that section or paragraph (1)(a) of that Article.

AMENDMENT

1. Tribunals, Courts and Enforcement Act 2007 (Transitional and Consequential Provisions) Order 2008 (SI 2008/2683) Sch.1 paras 212 and 222 (November 3, 2008).

DEFINITION

"the Board"—see reg.2(1).

PART 6

RIGHTS OF APPEAL AND PROCEDURE FOR BRINGING APPEALS

Other persons with a right of appeal

24. For the purposes of section 12(2) and Article 13(2), the following persons are prescribed— 2.1181

(a) any person appointed by the Board under regulation 28(1) of the Administration Regulations to act on behalf of another who is unable to act;

(b) any person appointed by the Board under regulation 29(1) of those regulations to proceed with the claim of a person who has made a claim for benefit or allowance and subsequently died;

(c) any person who, having been appointed by the Board under paragraph (2) of regulation 31 of those regulations to claim on behalf of a deceased person, makes a claim in accordance with that regulation.

DEFINITIONS

"the Administration Regulations"—see reg.2(1).
"prescribed"—see s.84 of the Social Security Act 1998.

GENERAL NOTE

See the note to reg.25 of the Social Security and Child Support (Decisions and Appeals) Regulations 1999. 2.1182

Decisions against which no appeal lies

25.—(1) Subject to paragraph (2), for the purposes of section 12(2) and Article 13(2), the decisions set out in Schedule 2 are prescribed as decisions against which no appeal lies to an appeal tribunal [1 or to the First-tier Tribunal]. 2.1183

(2) Paragraph (1) shall not have the effect of prescribing any decision that relates to the conditions of entitlement to child benefit or guardian's allowance for which a claim has been validly made or for which no claim is required.

(3) In this regulation and Schedule 2, "decision" includes any determination embodied in or necessary to a decision.

Amendment

1. Tribunals, Courts and Enforcement Act 2007 (Transitional and Consequential Provisions) Order 2008 (SI 2008/2683) Sch.1 paras 212 and 223 (November 3, 2008).

Definitions

"appeal tribunal"—see reg.2(1).
"prescribed"—see s.84 of the Social Security Act 1998.

General Note

2.1184 Paragraph (2) reiterates what is said in s.12(3) of the Social Security Act 1998. As para.9 of Sch.2 to the Act is not listed among the powers exercised in making these Regulations (see Sch.1), Sch.2 to these Regulations must be made under s.12. For the implication of that, see the note to Sch.2 to the Social Security and Child Support (Decisions and Appeals) Regulations 1999.

Notice of decision against which appeal lies

2.1185 **26.**—(1) A person with a right of appeal under the 1998 Act, the 1998 Order or these Regulations against a decision of the Board must—

(a) be given written notice of the decision against which the appeal lies;
(b) be informed that, in a case where that written notice does not include a statement of the reasons for that decision, he may, within one month of the date of notification of that decision, request that the Board provide him with a written statement of the reasons for that decision; and
(c) be given written notice of his right of appeal against that decision.

(2) If the Board are requested under paragraph (1)(b) to provide a written statement of the reasons for the decision, they [1 shall provide the statement within 14 days of receipt of the request or as soon as practicable afterwards].

Amendment

1. Child Benefit and Guardian's Allowance (Miscellaneous Amendments) Regulations 2005 (SI 2005/343) reg.6 (March 18, 2005).

Definitions

"the 1998 Act"—see reg.2(1).
"the Board"—*ibid.*
"the 1998 Order"—*ibid.*

General Note

2.1186 See the note to reg.28 of the Social Security and Child Support (Decisions and Appeals) Regulations 1999.

Appeals against decisions which have been revised

2.1187 **27.**—(1) This regulation applies where—

(a) a decision—
  (i) under section 8 or 10 is revised under section 9; or
  (ii) under Article 9 or 11 is revised under Article 10, before an appeal against that decision is determined; and
(b) the decision as revised is not more advantageous to the appellant than the decision before it was revised.

(2) The appeal shall not lapse and is to be treated as though it had been brought against the decision as revised.

(3) The appellant shall have a period of one month from the date of notification of the decision as revised to make further representations as to the appeal.

(4) After the expiration of the period specified in paragraph (3), or within that period if the appellant consents in writing, the appeal shall proceed unless, in the light of the further representations from the appellant, the Board further revise their decision and that decision is more advantageous to the appellant than the decision before it was revised.

(5) Decisions which are more advantageous to the appellant include those in consequence of which—

- (a) child benefit or guardian's allowance paid to him is greater or is awarded for a longer period;
- (b) the amount of benefit or allowance in payment would have been greater but for the operation of—
  - (i) any provision of the Administration Act or the Administration (NI) Act; or
  - (ii) any provision of the Contributions and Benefits Act, or any provision of the Contributions and Benefits (NI) Act, restricting or suspending the payment of, or disqualifying a claimant from receiving, some or all of the benefit or allowance;
- (c) a denial or disqualification for the receiving of benefit or allowance is lifted wholly or in part;
- (d) a decision to pay benefit or allowance to a third party is reversed;
- (e) benefit or allowance paid is not recoverable under—
  - (i) section 71 of the Administration Act or section 69 of the Administration (NI) Act; or
  - (ii) regulations made under either of those sections;
- (f) the amount of benefit or allowance paid which is recoverable as mentioned in sub-paragraph (e) is reduced; or
- (g) a financial gain accrues or will accrue to the appellant in consequence of the decision.

DEFINITIONS

"the Administration Act"—see reg.2(1).
"the Administration (NI) Act"—*ibid.*
"the Board"—*ibid.*
"claimant"—*ibid.*
"the Contributions and Benefits Act"—*ibid.*
"the Contributions and Benefits (NI) Act"—*ibid.*
"the date of notification"—see reg.3(2).
"writing"—see reg.2(1).

GENERAL NOTE

Like reg.30 of the Social Security and Child Support (Decisions and Appeals) Regulations 1999, this provides an exception to the general rule that an appeal lapses when the decision under appeal is revised (see s.9(6) of the Social Security Act 1998 and the note to s.9(5)). **2.1188**

28. *Omitted.* **2.1189**

29. *Omitted.* **2.1190**

[1 Late appeals to the First-tier Tribunal

29A. In respect of an appeal to the First-tier Tribunal, the Board may treat a late appeal as made in time in accordance with Tribunal Procedure **2.1191**

Rules if the Board is satisfied that it is in the interests of justice, but no appeal shall in any event be brought more than one year after the expiration of the last day for appealing under [2 those rules].

AMENDMENTS

1. Tribunals, Courts and Enforcement Act 2007 (Transitional and Consequential Provisions) Order 2008 (SI 2008/2683) Sch.1 paras 212 and 226 (November 3, 2008).
2. Tax Credits, Child Benefit and Guardian's Allowance Reviews and Appeals Order 2014 (SI 2014/886) art.5(1) and (4) (April 6, 2014).

GENERAL NOTE

2.1192 This regulation merely serves to narrow the Board's power not to object under r.22(8)(a) of the Tribunal Procedure (First-tier Tribunal (Social Entitlement Chamber) Rules 2008 to a late appeal being admitted by the First-tier Tribunal. The point of it doing so is unclear. The equivalent provision in reg.32 of the Social Security and Child Support (Decisions and Appeals) Regulations 1999 has been revoked. The absolute time limit duplicates r.22(8)(b).

Interests of justice

2.1193 **30.**—(1) For the purposes of paragraph (5)(b) of regulation 29 [1 and regulation 29A], it is not in the interests of justice to grant an application [1 or, as the case may be, treat the appeal as made in time][. . .] unless the panel member is satisfied, or the Board are satisfied, that—

(a) the special circumstances specified in paragraph (2) are relevant [1 . . .]; or
(b) some other special circumstances exist which are wholly exceptional and relevant [1 . . .],

and, as a result of those special circumstances, it was not practicable for the appeal to be brought within the time limit [2 . . .].

(2) The special circumstances specified in this paragraph are that—

(a) the applicant or a partner or dependant of the applicant has died or suffered serious illness;
(b) the applicant is not resident in the United Kingdom; or
(c) normal postal services were disrupted.

(3) "Partner" means—

(a) where a person is a member of a married couple or an unmarried couple, the other member of that couple; or
(b) where a person is polygamously married to two or more members of his household, any such member.

(4) In determining whether it is in the interests of justice to grant an application under regulation 29 [1 or, as the case may be, treat the appeal as made in time under regulation 29A], the panel member or the Board must have regard to the principle that the greater the amount of time that has elapsed between the expiration of the time within which the appeal is to be brought [2 . . .]and the making of the application [1 or, as the case may be, submission of a notice of appeal] the more compelling the special circumstances mentioned in paragraph (1) should be.

(5) In determining whether it is in the interests of justice to grant an application under regulation 29 [1 or, as the case may be, treat the appeal as made in time under regulation 29A], the panel member or the Board must take no account of the following—

(a) that the applicant or any person acting for him was unaware of or misunderstood the law applicable to his case (including ignorance or misunderstanding of the time limits imposed by these Regulations); or

(b) that a Commissioner [1 , the Upper Tribunal] or a court has taken a different view of the law from that previously understood and applied.

AMENDMENTS

1. Tribunals, Courts and Enforcement Act 2007 (Transitional and Consequential Provisions) Order 2008 (SI 2008/2683) Sch.1 paras 212 and 227 (November 3, 2008).

2. Tax Credits, Child Benefit and Guardian's Allowance Reviews and Appeals Order 2014 (SI 2014/886) art.5(1), (5) and (6) (April 6, 2014).

DEFINITIONS

"the Board"—see reg.2(1).
"Commissioner"—*ibid.*
"partner"— see para.(3).

GENERAL NOTE

This is an extraordinarily narrow approach to the interests of justice and appears pointless now that appeals are lodged with the First-tier Tribunal because the First-tier Tribunal has a simple discretionary power, to be exercised judicially of course, to extend time under r.5(3)(a) of the Tribunal Procedure (First-tier Tribunal) (Social Entitlement Chamber) Rules 2008. The equivalent provision in reg.32 of the Social Security and Child Support (Decisions and Appeals) Regulations 1999, upon which this regulation was clearly based, has been revoked. **2.1194**

Paragraph (5)

If the claimant is ignorant of the time limit for appealing because the Board has failed to provide the information required by reg.26(1)(c), it is arguable that the notice of decision is defective and time for appealing has not started to run. Otherwise subpara.(a) has the effect that the claimant cannot rely on the Board's failure to provide advice it was legally required to provide, which would be unfair if the First-tier Tribunal's powers were also limited by this regulation. It is not clear whether, for the purposes of subpara.(b), the comparison is with the previous understanding of the whole of HMRC, or a particular office or those giving guidance to decision-makers. Whatever the answer, it is not easy to see what, in practice, subpara.(b) really adds to subpara.(a). **2.1195**

31. *Omitted.* **2.1196**
32. *Omitted.* **2.1197**

Death of a party to an appeal

33.—(1) In any proceedings, on the death of a party to those proceedings (other than a member of the Board), the Board may appoint such person as they think fit to proceed with the appeal in the place of such deceased party. **2.1198**

(2) A grant of probate, confirmation or letters of administration to the estate of the deceased party, whenever taken out, shall have no effect on an appointment made under paragraph (1).

(3) If a person appointed under paragraph (1) has, prior to the date of such appointment, taken any action in relation to the appeal on behalf of the deceased party, the effective date of appointment by the Board shall be the day immediately prior to the first day on which such action was taken.

DEFINITION

"the Board"—see reg.2(1).

GENERAL NOTE

2.1199 This was equivalent to reg.34 of the Social Security and Child Support (Decisions and Appeals) Regulations 1999 which has been revoked.

PART VII

REVOCATIONS, TRANSITIONAL PROVISIONS AND CONSEQUENTIAL AMENDMENTS

Revocations

2.1200 **34.** The following provisions are hereby revoked—

(a) in so far as they relate to child benefit or guardian's allowance under the Contributions and Benefits Act, Parts 2, 3 and 4 of, and Schedule 2 to, the Decisions and Appeals Regulations;

(b) in so far as they relate to child benefit or guardian's allowance under the Contributions and Benefits (NI) Act, Parts 2, 3 and 4 of, and Schedule 1 to, the Decisions and Appeals Regulations (NI).

DEFINITIONS

"the Contributions and Benefits Act"—see reg.2(1).
"the Contributions and Benefits (NI) Act"—*ibid.*
"the Decisions and Appeals Regulations"—*ibid.*
"the decision and Appeals (NI) Regulations"—*ibid.*

Transitional provisions

2.1201 **35.** Anything done or commenced under any provision revoked by regulation 34, so far as relating to child benefit or guardian's allowance, is to be treated as having been done or as being continued under the corresponding provision of these Regulations.

2.1202 **36.** *Omitted.*

2.1203 **37.** *Omitted.*

SCHEDULE 1 **Preamble**

POWERS EXERCISED IN MAKING THESE REGULATIONS

2.1204 **1.** Section 5(1)(hh) of the Administration Act.

2. Section 5(1)(hh) of the Administration (NI) Act.

3. The following provisions of the 1998 Act—

(a) section 9(1), (4) and (6);
(b) section 10(3) and (6);
(c) section 12(2), (3), (6) and (7);
(d) section 16(1) and paragraphs 1 to 4 and 6 of Schedule 5;
(e) section 21;
(f) section 22;
(g) section 23;
(h) section 25(3)(b) and (5)(c);
(i) section 26(6)(c);
(j) section 79(1), (2A) and (4) to (7);
(k) section 84.

4. The following provisions of the 1998 Order—
(a) Article 2(2);
(b) Article 10(1), (4) and (6);
(c) Article 11(3) and (6);
(d) Article 13(2), (3), (6) and (7);
(e) Article 16(1) and paragraphs 1 to 4 and 6 of Schedule 4;
(f) Article 21;
(g) Article 22;
(h) Article 23;
(i) Article 25(3)(b) and (5)(c);
(j) Article 26(6)(c);
(k) Article 74(1) and (3) to (6).

5. Sections 132 and 133(1) and (2) of the Finance Act 1999.

6. The following provisions of the Tax Credits Act 2002—
(a) section 50(1) and (2)(e) and (f);
(b) section 54(2);
(c) paragraphs 15 and 19 of Schedule 4.

DEFINITIONS

"the 1998 Act"—see reg.2(1).
"the Administration Act"—*ibid.*
"the Administration (NI) Act"—*ibid.*
"the 1998 Order"—*ibid.*

SCHEDULE 2 — **Regulation 25**

DECISIONS AGAINST WHICH NO APPEAL LIES

PART I

DECISIONS MADE UNDER PRIMARY LEGISLATION

1. A decision of the Board whether to recognise, for the purposes of Part 9 of the Contributions and Benefits Act or Part 10 of the Contributions and Benefits (NI) Act— **2.1205**
(a) an educational establishment; or
(b) education provided otherwise than at a recognised educational establishment.

2. A decision of the Board whether to pay expenses to any person under—
(a) sections 180 and 180A of the Administration Act; or
(b) section 156 of the Administration (NI) Act.

3. A decision of the Treasury relating to the up-rating of child benefit or guardian's allowance under—
(a) Part 10 of the Administration Act; or
(b) Part 9 of the Administration (NI) Act.

4. A decision of the Board under—
(a) section 25 or 26; or
(b) Article 25 or 26.

PART II

DECISIONS MADE UNDER SECONDARY LEGISLATION

5. A decision of the Board relating to— **2.1206**
(a) the suspension of child benefit or allowance under Part 4; or
(b) the payment of such a benefit or allowance which has been so suspended.

6. A decision of the Board under any of the following provisions of the Administration Regulations—
(a) [1 . . .]
(b) regulation 7 (decision as to evidence and information required);
(c) [1 . . .]
(d) regulation 11 (decision as to claims for child benefit treated as claims for guardian's allowance and vice versa);
(e) regulation 18 (decision as to the time of payments);

(f) regulation 19 (decision as to elections to have child benefit paid weekly);
(g) regulation 23 (decision as to information to be given);
(h) regulation 26 (decision as to extinguishment of right to payment if payment is not obtained within the prescribed period) other than a decision under paragraph (5) (decision as to payment request after expiration of prescribed period);
(i) regulation 28 (decision as to appointments where person unable to act);
(j) regulations 29 to 32 (decisions as to claims or payments after death of claimant);
(k) regulation 33 (decision as to paying a person on behalf of another);
(l) regulation 34 (decision as to paying partner as alternative payee);
(m) Part 5 other than a decision under—
  (i) regulation 35(1) (decision as to whether a payment in excess of entitlement has been credited to a bank or other account);
  (ii) regulation 37 (decision as to the sums to be deducted in calculating recoverable amounts);
  (iii) regulation 38 (decision as to the offsetting of a prior payment of child benefit or guardian's allowance against arrears of child benefit or guardian's allowance payable by virtue of a subsequent determination);
  (iv) regulation 39 (decision as to the offsetting of a prior payment of income support or jobseeker's allowance against arrears of child benefit or guardian's allowance payable by virtue of a subsequent determination);
  (v) regulation 41(1) (decision as to bringing interim payments into account);
  (vi) regulation 42(1) (decision as to the overpayment of an interim payment).

7. A decision of the Board made in accordance with the discretion conferred upon them by the following regulations of the Child Benefit (General) Regulations 2003—
(a) regulation 4(1) or (4) (provisions relating to contributions and expenses in respect of a child);
(b) regulation 24(1)(c) or 28(1)(c) (decisions relating to a child's temporary absence abroad).

8. A decision of the Board relating to the giving of a notice under regulation 8(2) of the Guardian's Allowance (General) Regulations 2003 (children whose surviving parents are in prison or legal custody).

9. A decision of the Board made in accordance with an Order made under—
(a) section 179 of the Administration Act (reciprocal agreements with countries outside the United Kingdom); or
(b) section 155 of the Administration (NI) Act (reciprocal agreements with countries outside the United Kingdom).

PART III

OTHER DECISIONS

2.1207 **10.** An authorization given by the Board in accordance with Article 22(1) or 55(1) of Council Regulation (EEC) No.1408/71 on the application of social security schemes to employed persons, to self-employed persons and to members of their families moving within the Community.

AMENDMENT

1. Child Benefit and Guardian's Allowance (Decisions and Appeals) (Amendment) Regulations 2004 (SI 2004/3377) reg.2(3) (December 21, 2004).

DEFINITIONS

"the Administration Act"—see reg.2(1).
"the Administration (NI) Act"—*ibid.*
"the Administration Regulations"—*ibid.*
"the Board"—*ibid.*
"the Contributions and Benefits Act"—*ibid.*
"the Contributions and Benefits (NI) Act"—*ibid.*

GENERAL NOTE

2.1208 See the notes to reg.25 of these Regulations and Sch.2 to the Social Security and Child Support (Decisions and Appeals) Regulations 1999.

PART III

EUROPEAN UNION LAW

The Treaty of Lisbon (Changes in Terminology) Order 2011

(SI 2011/1043)

The Secretary of State is a Minister designated for the purposes of section 2(2) of the European Communities Act 1972 in relation to changes in terminology or numbering arising out of the Treaty of Lisbon Amending the Treaty on European Union and the Treaty Establishing the European Community signed at Lisbon on 13 December 2007. 3.1

The Secretary of State makes the following Order in exercise of the powers conferred by:

(a) section 3(4) and (5) of the European Union (Amendment) Act 2008(**c**) (to the extent that the Order applies to provisions contained in (i) an Act of Parliament passed before 19 June 2008, or (ii) an instrument made before 19 June 2008 under an Act of Parliament), and

(b) section 2(2) of the European Communities Act 1972 (to the extent that the Order applies to provisions contained in (i) an Act of Parliament passed on or after 19 June 2008, (ii) an instrument made on or after 19 June 2008 under an Act of Parliament, (iii) an Act of the Scottish Parliament, or (iv) an instrument made under an Act of the Scottish Parliament):

PART 1

CITATION AND COMMENCEMENT

Citation

1. This Order may be cited as the Treaty of Lisbon (Changes in Terminology) Order 2011. 3.2

Commencement

2. This Order comes into force on 22nd April 2011. 3.3

PART 2

AMENDMENTS TO ACTS OF PARLIAMENT, ACTS OF THE SCOTTISH PARLIAMENT AND CERTAIN STATUTORY INSTRUMENTS

Application

3.—(1) The amendments made by this Part apply to provisions contained in— 3.4

(a) an Act of Parliament,

(b) an Act of the Scottish Parliament, or

(c) an instrument made under an Act of Parliament or an Act of the Scottish Parliament (or both).

(2) The amendments made by this Part do not apply to—

(a) an instrument falling within article 8(1),

(b) an Order in Council mentioned in section 24(5)(c), (e) or (g) of the Interpretation Act 1978 (Northern Ireland legislation),
(c) the European Communities Act 1972,
(d) the Interpretation Act 1978,
(e) the European Union (Amendment) Act 2008,
(f) the title of an Act or statutory instrument,
(g) a reference to the title of an Act or statutory instrument,
(h) a reference to the title of an item of European Community legislation, or
(i) a reference to a term defined in an item of European Community legislation.

(3) The amendments made by this Part do not apply to a reference that relates only to things done before 1 December 2009 (the date on which the Treaty of Lisbon entered into force) and do not affect any other reference in its application to things done before that date.

European Community – European Union

3.5 **4.**—(1) For references to the European Communities or to the European Community or the European Coal and Steel Community (including references to "the Communities", "the Community", "the EC" or "the EEC") substitute references to the European Union.

(2) Paragraph (1) does not apply to—
(a) the use of "Community", "EC" or "EEC" as an adjective (but see article 6);
(b) a reference that forms part of a reference to a treaty (but see article 5).

Article 310 of the Treaty of Amsterdam

3.6 **5.** For references to "Article 310 of the Treaty of Amsterdam amending the Treaty on European Union, the Treaties establishing the European Communities and certain related Acts" substitute "Article 217 of the Treaty on the Functioning of the European Union".

"Community"

3.7 **6.**—(1) In the following terms (which were defined by the European Communities Act 1972 as it had effect before the passing of the European Union (Amendment) Act 2008) for the word "Community" substitute "EU"—
(a) Community treaties,
(b) Community customs duty,
(c) Community institution,
(d) Community instrument,
(e) Community obligation, and
(f) enforceable Community right.

(2) In the following terms, and in those terms preceded by the word "European", for "Community", or as the case may be "European Community", substitute "EU"—
(a) Community law,
(b) Community legislation, and
(c) Community provision.

(3) Where the term mentioned in paragraph (1) or (2) is preceded by the word "a", for "a" substitute "an".

(4) Paragraphs (1) to (3) do not apply where the term mentioned in paragraph (1) or (2) forms part of a reference to a treaty.

(5) Paragraph (2) does not apply to the term "specified Community provision" where used in an enactment containing a definition of that term.

Miscellaneous

7. Schedule 1, which contains miscellaneous amendments, has effect. 3.8

PART 3

AMENDMENTS TO CERTAIN LEGISLATION RELATING TO WALES

Application

8.—(1) The amendments made by this Part apply to provisions contained in an instrument made under an Act of Parliament by the Assembly constituted by the Government of Wales Act 1998 or by the Welsh Ministers (whether alone or with any other person), other than an instrument that is made in the English language only. 3.9

(2) The amendments made by this Part do not apply to—

(a) the title of a statutory instrument,

(b) a reference to the title of an Act or statutory instrument,

(c) a reference to the title of an item of European Community legislation, or

(d) a reference to a term defined in an item of European Community legislation.

(3) The amendments made by this Part do not apply to a reference that relates only to things done before 1 December 2009 (the date on which the Treaty of Lisbon entered into force) and do not affect any other reference in its application to things done before that date.

European Community – European Union

9.—(1) For references to the European Communities or to the European Community (including references to "the Communities", "the Community", "the EC" or "the EEC") substitute references to the European Union. 3.10

(2) For references to Cymunedau Ewropeaidd (European Communities) or to Cymuned Ewropeaidd (European Community) (including references expressed by the word "Cymuned" (Community) or "Cymunedau" (Communities), and any abbreviated, grammatically mutated or other forms of any of those references) substitute references to Undeb Ewropeaidd (European Union) and make any consequential grammatical amendments that are necessary.

(3) Paragraph (1) does not apply to—

(a) the use of "Community", "EC" or "EEC" as an adjective (but see article 10);

(b) a reference that forms part of a reference to a treaty.

(4) Paragraph (2) does not apply to—

(a) the use of "Cymuned" or "Cymunedol" (Community), or any abbreviated form of Cymunedau Ewropeaidd (European Communities) or Cymuned Economaidd Ewropeaidd (European Economic Community) (or any grammatically mutated forms of any of those terms), as an adjective (but see article 10);

(b) a reference that forms part of a reference to a treaty.

Terms defined by the European Communities Act 1972

3.11 **10.**—(1) In the following terms (which were defined by the European Communities Act 1972 as it had effect before the passing of the European Union (Amendment) Act 2008) for the word "Community" substitute "EU"—

(a) Community treaties,
(b) Community customs duty,
(c) Community institution,
(d) Community instrument,
(e) Community obligation, and
(f) enforceable Community right.

(2) In the following terms (which correspond to the relevant English language terms which were defined by the European Communities Act 1972 as it had effect before the passing of the European Union (Amendment) Act 2008) (including any grammatically mutated or other forms of the following terms) for the words "Cymuned" and "Cymunedol" (Community) (including any grammatically mutated or other form of those words) substitute "UE" (EU) and make any consequential grammatical amendments that are necessary—

(a) cytuniadau'r Gymuned or cytuniadau Cymunedol (Community treaties),
(b) tollau'r Gymuned or tollau Cymunedol (Community customs duty),
(c) sefydliad Cymuned or sefydliad Cymunedol (Community institution),
(d) offeryn Cymuned, offeryn y Gymuned or offeryn Cymunedol (Community instrument),
(e) rhwymedigaeth Gymuned or rhwymedigaeth Gymunedol (Community obligation), and
(f) hawl Gymuned orfodadwy or hawl Gymunedol orfodadwy (enforceable Community right).

(3) In the following terms, and in those terms preceded by the word "European", for "the Community", or as the case may be "European Community", substitute "EU"-

(a) Community law;
(b) Community legislation;
(c) Community provision.

(4) For "cyfraith y Gymuned" or "cyfraith Gymunedol" (Community law), and for those terms followed by the word "Ewropeaidd" (including any grammatically mutated or other forms of those terms) substitute "cyfraith yr UE" (EU law) and make any consequential grammatical amendments that are necessary.

(5) For "deddfwriaeth y Gymuned" or "deddfwriaeth Gymunedol" (Community legislation) and for those terms followed by the word "Ewropeaidd" (including any grammatically mutated or other forms of those terms) substitute "deddfwriaeth yr UE" (EU legislation) and make any consequential grammatical amendments that are necessary.

(6) For "darpariaeth Gymuned", "darpariaeth y Gymuned" or "darpariaeth Gymunedol" (Community provision) and for those terms followed by the word "Ewropeaidd" (including any grammatically mutated or other forms of those terms) substitute "darpariaeth UE" (EU provision) and make any consequential grammatical amendments that are necessary.

(7) Where the term mentioned in paragraph (1) or (3) is preceded by the word "a", for "a" substitute "an".

(8) Paragraphs (1) to (7) do not apply where the term mentioned in paragraph (1), (2), (3), (4), (5) or (6) forms part of a reference to a treaty.

(9) Paragraph (3) does not apply to the term "specified Community provision" where used in an enactment containing a definition of that term.

(10) Paragraph (6) does not apply to the term "darpariaeth Gymunedol benodedig" (or any grammatically mutated or other form of that term) where used in an enactment containing a definition of that term.

Miscellaneous

11. Schedule 2, which contains miscellaneous amendments, has effect. **3.12**

Schedules omitted. **3.13**

European Communities Act 1972

(1972 c.68) (As amended)

Arrangement of sections reproduced

Preamble

An Act to make provision in connection with the enlargement of the European Communities to include the United Kingdom, together with (for certain purposes) the Channel Islands, the Isle of Man and Gibraltar.

[October 17, 1972]

Short title and interpretation.

1.(1) This Act may be cited as the European Communities Act 1972. **3.15**

(2) In this Act [1 . . .]—

[2 "the EU" means the European Union, being the Union established by the Treaty on European Union signed at Maastricht on 7th February 1992 (as amended by any later Treaty),]

"the Communities" means the European Economic Community, the European Coal and Steel Community and the European Atomic Energy Community;

"the Treaties" or [3 "the EU Treaties"] means, subject to subsection (3) below, the pre-accession treaties, that is to say, those described in Part I of Schedule 1 to this Act, taken with—

(a) the treaty relating to the accession of the United Kingdom to the European Economic Community and to the European Atomic Energy Community, signed at Brussels on the 22nd January 1972; and

(b) the decision, of the same date, of the Council of the European

Communities relating to the accession of the United Kingdom to the European Coal and Steel Community; [4 and

(c) the treaty relating to the accession of the Hellenic Republic to the European Economic Community and to the European Atomic Energy Community, signed at Athens on 28th May 1979; and

(d) the decision, of 24th May 1979, of the Council relating to the accession of the Hellenic Republic to the European Coal and Steel Community;] [5 and]

[6 (e) the decisions of the Council of 7th May 1985, 24th June 1988, 31st October 1994, 29th September 2000 and 7th June 2007 on the Communities' system of own resources;]

[7 (g) the treaty relating to the accession of the Kingdom of Spain and the Portuguese Republic to the European Economic Community and to the European Atomic Energy Community, signed at Lisbon and Madrid on 12th June 1985; and

(h) the decision, of 11th June 1985, of the Council relating to the accession of the Kingdom of Spain and the Portuguese Republic to the European Coal and Steel Community;] [8and]

[8 (j) the following provisions of the Single European Act signed at Luxembourg and The Hague on 17th and 28th February 1986, namely Title II (amendment of the treaties establishing the Communities) and, so far as they relate to any of the Communities or any Community institution, the preamble and Titles I (common provisions) and IV (general and final provisions);] [9 and]

[9 (k) Titles II, III and IV of the Treaty on European Union signed at Maastricht on 7th February 1992, together with the other provisions of the Treaty so far as they relate to those Titles, and the Protocols adopted at Maastricht on that date and annexed to the Treaty establishing the European Community with the exception of the Protocol on Social Policy on page 117 of Cm 1934;] [10 and]

[10 (l) the decision, of 1st February 1993, of the Council amending the Act concerning the election of the representatives of the European Parliament by direct universal suffrage annexed to Council Decision 76/787/ECSC, EEC, Euratom of 20th September 1976; [11 and]

[11 (m) the Agreement on the European Economic Area signed at Oporto on 2nd May 1992 together with the Protocol adjusting that Agreement signed at Brussels on 17th March 1993; [12 and]

[12 (n) the treaty concerning the accession of the Kingdom of Norway, the Republic of Austria, the Republic of Finland and the Kingdom of Sweden to the European Union, signed at Corfu on 24th June 1994;] [13 and]

[13 (o) the following provisions of the Treaty signed at Amsterdam on 2nd October 1997 amending the Treaty on European Union, the Treaties establishing the European Communities and certain related Acts—

(i) Articles 2 to 9,

(ii) Article 12, and

(iii) the other provisions of the Treaty so far as they relate to those Articles,

and the Protocols adopted on that occasion other than the Protocol on Article J.7 of the Treaty on European Union;] [14 and]

[14 (p) the following provisions of the Treaty signed at Nice on 26th February

2001 amending the Treaty on European Union, the Treaties establishing the European Communities and certain related Acts—
(i) Articles 2 to 10, and
(ii) the other provisions of the Treaty so far as they relate to those Articles,
and the Protocol adopted on that occasion; [[15] . . .]
[[16] (q) the treaty concerning the accession of the Czech Republic, the Republic of Estonia, the Republic of Cyprus, the Republic of Latvia, the Republic of Lithuania, the Republic of Hungary, the Republic of Malta, the Republic of Poland, the Republic of Slovenia and the Slovak Republic to the European Union, signed at Athens on 16th April 2003;] [[17] and]
[[15] (r) the treaty concerning the accession of the Republic of Bulgaria and Romania to the European Union, signed at Luxembourg on 25th April 2005;]
[[17] (s) the Treaty of Lisbon Amending the Treaty on European Union and the Treaty Establishing the European Community signed at Lisbon on 13th December 2007 (together with its Annex and protocol), excluding any provision that relates to, or in so far as it relates to or could be applied in relation to, the Common Foreign and Security Policy;] and [[3] any other treaty entered into by the EU (except in so far as it relates to, or could be applied in relation to, the Common Foreign and Security Policy)], with or without any of the member States, or entered into, as a treaty ancillary to any of the Treaties, by the United Kingdom; and any expression defined in Schedule 1 to this Act has the meaning there given to it.
[[18] (t) the Protocol amending the Protocol (No. 36) on transitional provisions annexed to the Treaty on European Union, to the Treaty on the Functioning of the European Union and to the Treaty establishing the European Atomic Energy Community, signed at Brussels on 23 June 2010; [[19] and—]
[[19] (u) the treaty concerning the accession of the Republic of Croatia to the European Union, signed at Brussels on 9 December 2011; and
(v) the Protocol on the concerns of the Irish people on the Treaty of Lisbon, adopted at Brussels on 16 May 2012;]

(3) If Her Majesty by Order in Council declares that a treaty specified in the Order is to be regarded as one of [[3] the EU Treaties] as herein defined, the Order shall be conclusive that it is to be so regarded; but a treaty entered into by the United Kingdom after the 22nd January 1972, other than a pre-accession treaty to which the United Kingdom accedes on terms settled on or before that date, shall not be so regarded unless it is so specified, nor be so specified unless a draft of the Order in Council has been approved by resolution of each House of Parliament.

(4) For purposes of subsections (2) and (3) above, "treaty" includes any international agreement, and any protocol or annex to a treaty or international agreement.

AMENDMENTS

1. Words repealed by Interpretation Act 1978 (c.30) s.25, Sch.3.
2. European Union (Amendment) Act 2008 (c.7) s.3(1) (December 1, 2009).
3. European Union (Amendment) Act 2008 (c.7) Sch.1(1) para.1 (December 1, 2009).

4. European Communities (Greek Accession) Act 1979 (c.57) s.1. (December 20, 1979).
5. European Communities (Finance) Act 2001 (c.22) s.1 (December 4, 2001).
6. European Communities (Finance) Act 2008 (c.1) s.1 (February 19, 2008).
7. European Communities (Spanish and Portuguese Accession) Act 1985 (c.75) s.1 (December 19, 1985).
8. European Communities (Amendment) Act 1986 (c.58) s.1 (November 7, 1986).
9. European Communities (Amendment) Act 1993 (c.32) s.1(1) (July 23, 1993).
10. European Parliamentary Elections Act 1993 (c.41) s.3(2) (November 5, 1993).
11. European Economic Area Act 1993 (c.51) s.1 (November 5, 1993).
12. European Union (Accessions) Act 1994 (c.38) s.1 (November 3, 1994).
13. European Communities (Amendment) Act 1998 (c.21) s.1 (June 11, 1998).
14. European Communities (Amendment) Act 2002 (c.3) s.1 (February 26, 2002).
15. European Union (Accessions) Act 2006 (c.2) s.1 (February 16, 2006).
16. European Union (Accessions) Act 2003 (c.35) s.1 (November 13, 2003).
17. European Union (Amendment) Act 2008 (c.7) s.2 (December 1, 2009).
18. European Union Act 2011 s.15(2) (July 19, 2011).
19. European Union (Croatian Accession and Irish Protocol) Act 2013 s.3 (January 31, 2013).

GENERAL NOTE

3.16 *United Kingdom withdrawal from the European Union*

On June 23, 2016, the people of the United Kingdom voted to leave the European Union. In announcing his intention to resign once his successor has been appointed, the Prime Minister indicated that he would leave it to his successor to put a resolution to Parliament which would authorize the giving of formal notice to the Secretary General of the Council of the United Kingdom's intention to withdraw from the Union in accordance with art.50 TEU. That article provides for a two-year period (which may be extended by unanimous decision of the Council) during which the terms of withdrawal from the Union are negotiated. In the interim period, the provisions of European Union law continue to apply. Unless a withdrawal agreement is concluded earlier, the Treaties only cease to apply at the end of the two-year period (or any extension of it).

In *R (on the application of Miller and Dos Santos) v Secretary of State for Exiting the European Union* [2016] EWHC 2768 (Admin), a high-powered Administrative Court decided that Parliament must be involved in the decision to trigger the process of leaving the European Union for which Article 50 of the Treaty on European Union provides. On January 24, 2017, the Supreme Court upheld that judgment: [2017] UKSC 5. On March 16, 2017 the very short European Union (Notification of Withdrawal) Act 2017 received the Royal Assent; and on March 29, 2017, a letter giving notice of the United Kingdom's withdrawal from the European Union was hand delivered to the President of the European Council. For the full text of the letter, see *https://www.gov.uk/government/publications/prime-ministers-letter-to-donald-tusk-triggering-article-50*

The ramifications of withdrawal cannot be under-estimated. Simply repealing the European Communities Act 1972 would not, of itself, put the United Kingdom in the position it was in prior to its accession in 1973, or, indeed, any later date. On the effective date of withdrawal, European Union Regulations would cease to apply. Those provisions of Regulations which the United Kingdom wishes to retain would need to be enacted in national law. The same is not true of the provisions of Directives. Directives require implementation, and national law implementing the requirements of Directives would remain as national law unless and until repealed by the United Kingdom government, though without any obligation to interpret national law in a manner to secure compatibility with the requirements of the relevant Directive.

Some detail on how this will be achieved (through the "Great Repeal Bill") can be found in the White Paper, *Legislating for the United Kingdom's Withdrawal from the European Union*, Cm 9446 (March 2017).

It is also highly likely that the withdrawal negotiations will need to address the rights of those with acquired rights (United Kingdom nationals abroad as well as nationals of other Member States in the United Kingdom) under European Union law. This might well be particularly complex in the field of social security.

The Member States

The Member States of the European Union (with the date of their entry) are as follows: 3.17

Austria (January 1, 1995)
Belgium (January 1, 1958)
Bulgaria (January 1, 2007)
Croatia (July 1, 2013)
Cyprus (May 1, 2004)
Czech Republic (May 1, 2004)
Denmark (January 1, 1973)
Estonia (May 1, 2004)
Finland (January 1, 1995)
France (January 1, 1958)
Germany (January 1, 1958)
Greece (January 1, 1981)
Poland (May 1, 2004)
Hungary (May 1, 2004)
Ireland (January 1, 1973)
Italy (January 1, 1958)
Latvia (May 1, 2004)
Lithuania (May 1, 2004)
Luxembourg (January 1, 1958)
Malta (May 1, 2004)
Netherlands (January 1, 1958)
Portugal (January 1, 1986)
Romania (January 1, 2007)
Slovakia (May 1, 2004)
Slovenia (May 1, 2004)
Spain (January 1, 1986)
Sweden (January 1, 1995)
United Kingdom (January 1, 1973)

Croatia

Croatia became the 28th Member State on July 1, 2013. Section 4 of the European Union (Croatian Accession and Irish Protocol) Act 2013 contains powers to make regulations concerning free movement for Croatian nationals as workers. Section 2 of Annex V to the Treaty concerning the accession of the Republic of Croatia, [2012] OJ L112/6, contains transitional provisions relating to the free movement of persons. In essence, there will be a two-year period within which national restrictions on workers will be applied followed by a further three-year period during which they may be applied. Austria, Malta, the Netherlands and the United Kingdom have notified the Commission that they will maintain restrictions on the free movement of workers for the period July 1, 2015 to June 30, 2018. From July 1, 2018 to June 30, 2020, Member States will only be able to apply restrictions in the case of "serious disturbances of their labour market or a threat of such disturbances." However, Croatian nationals who work lawfully for 12 months in a Member State (other than Croatia) will be assimilated with those with full rights under the Treaty on European Union and European secondary legislation. 3.18

There are three additional countries which, with the Member States, form the countries of the European Economic Area (EEA):

Iceland	(January 1, 1994)
Liechtenstein	(January 1, 1994)
Norway	(January 1, 1994)

The status of the Isle of Man

The Isle of Man is a Crown Dependency. As such the Isle of Man is self-governing. The Isle of Man is not part of the United Kingdom but is a territory for whose international relations the United Kingdom is responsible in international law. The United Kingdom is responsible for the defence of the Isle of Man and for providing 3.19

consular services. The Island makes an annual contribution to the United Kingdom in recognition of defence and other common services provided on its behalf.

The Isle of Man is not part of the European Union but it has a special, limited, relationship with the European Union set out in Protocol 3 to the United Kingdom's Treaty of Accession. In essence, the Isle of Man is part of the customs union allowing free movement of goods between the Isle of Man and the Member States of the European Union, but, apart from art.4 of the Protocol, other provisions of European Union law do not apply to the Isle of Man.

Article 4 of Protocol 3 provides:

"The authorities of [the Isle of Man] shall apply the same treatment to all natural and legal persons of the Community."

The Social Security (Isle of Man) Order 1977 (SI 1977/2150) (as amended) and The Social Security Reciprocal Agreement (Isle of Man) Order 2016 (SI 2016/157) make provision for modification and adaptation of the social security legislation to co-ordinate social security provision between the Isle of Man and the United Kingdom.

The status of the Channel Islands (Bailiwicks of Jersey and Guernsey)

3.20 The Channel Islands consist of the bailiwicks of Jersey and Guernsey and are Crown Dependencies. As such they are self-governing with their own legal system. Jersey comprises the island of Jersey and uninhabited islets such as the Minquiers and Écréhous. Guernsey comprises the islands of Guernsey, Sark, Alderney, Brecqhou, Herm, Jethou and Lihou.

The Channel Islands are not part of the United Kingdom but are territory for whose international relations the United Kingdom is responsible in international law.

Like the Isle of Man, the Channel Islands are not part of the European Union but they have a special, limited, relationship with the European Union set out in Protocol 3 to the United Kingdom's Treaty of Accession. In essence, the Channel Islands are part of the customs union allowing free movement of goods between the Channel Islands and the Member States of the European Union, but, apart from art.4 of the Protocol, other provisions of European Union law do not apply to the Channel Islands.

The Social Security (Jersey and Guernsey) Order 1994 (SI 1994/2802) (as amended) makes provision for modification and adaptation of the social security legislation to co-ordinate social security provision between the Jersey and Guernsey, and the United Kingdom.

The status of Gibraltar

3.21 Gibraltar was ceded in perpetuity by Spain to Great Britain under the Treaty of Utrecht 1713. It is a British Crown Colony. It is not part of the United Kingdom. This separate status is recognised under national law, international law and European Union law.

In *Spain v United Kingdom* (C-145/04) [2006] E.C.R. I-7917, the Court of Justice described the status of Gibraltar as follows:

"19. In Community law, Gibraltar is a European territory for whose external relations a Member State is responsible within the meaning of Article 299(4) EC and to which the provisions of the EC Treaty apply. The Act concerning the conditions of accession of the Kingdom of Denmark, Ireland and the United Kingdom of Great Britain and Northern Ireland and the adjustments to the Treaties (OJ 1972 L 73, p. 14) provides, however, that certain parts of the Treaty are not to apply to Gibraltar."

In particular, European Union law on citizenship of the Union and the free movement of persons do apply to Gibraltar.

The Family Allowances, National Insurance and Industrial Injuries (Gibraltar) Order 1974 (SI 1974/555) makes provision for modification and adaptation of the social security legislation to co-ordinate social security provision between Gibraltar and the United Kingdom. See also *R(IS) 8/06*.

The evolution of the treaties

3.22 The following table shows the evolution of the treaties:

Date	Title	Entry into force
1951	Treaty of Paris (signed 18 April 1951) ECSC Treaty	July 23, 1952 Expired July 23, 2002
1957	Treaty of Rome (signed 25 March 1957 EEC Treaty	January 1, 1958
1957	Euratom Treaty (signed 25 March 1957)	January 1, 1958
1965	Merger Treaty (signed 8 April 1965) ECSC and EEC to share Commission and Council	July 1, 1967
1986	Single European Act (signed 17 February 1986)	July 1, 1987
1992	Treaty of Maastricht (signed 7 February 1992) Known as the Treaty on European Union	November 1, 1993
1997	Treaty of Amsterdam (signed 2 October 1997)	May 1, 1999
2001	Treaty of Nice (signed 26 February 2001)	February 1, 2003
2004	Treaty establishing a Constitution for Europe (signed 29 October 2004)	*Abandoned*
2007	Treaty of Lisbon (signed 13 December 2007)	December 1, 2009

The Treaty of Lisbon came into force on December 1, 2009. This amends both the Treaty on European Union and the EC Treaty. The EC Treaty is renamed the Treaty on the Functioning of the European Union. The two key treaties are now known as the *Treaty on European Union* (TEU) and the *Treaty on the Functioning of the European Union* (TFEU). The result of this change in nomenclature is that the term "Community law" has now effectively been replaced by the term "European Union law" to describe the law flowing from the treaties and the case-law of the Court of Justice.

The Treaty of Lisbon (Changes in Terminology) Order 2011 (SI 2011/1043), (which entered into force on April 22, 2011) makes textual changes to much UK legislation to take account of the entry into force of the Treaty of Lisbon. There is no change to the law, simply to the terms used in the legislation to ensure a greater degree of congruence with the terminology used as a result of changes made by the Treaty of Lisbon. The main changes are that references to "EC" generally become references to "EU", and references to the "Community" generally become references to the "Union".

The beneficiaries of European Union law

European Union law generally applies to nationals of the Member States and of the additional countries of the EEA. European Union law rules on social security are generally co-ordinating rules permitting different social security systems to operate together in order to enhance the free movement of workers. These rules are extended to their nationals of the EEA countries by the EEA Treaty. For this reason the term "EEA country" or countries is frequently used to describe those countries whose nationals are beneficiaries of the European Union rules on social security. 3.23

In addition, nationals of Switzerland are covered by the rules in reg.1408/71 with effect from June 1, 2002. From June 1, 2003, third country nationals who have been lawfully resident in two Member States are covered by the co-ordinating regulation under reg.859/2003/EC, which is reproduced later in this volume.

Regulation 1408/71 is replaced with effect from May 1, 2010 by reg.883/2004, but the earlier regulation will remain important both for EEA and Swiss nationals until such time as they are brought within the new regime.

General implementation of Treaties

2.—(1) All such rights, powers, liabilities, obligations and restrictions from time to time created or arising by or under the Treaties, and all such remedies and procedures from time to time provided for by or under the Treaties, as in accordance with the Treaties are without further enactment to be given legal effect or used in the United Kingdom shall be recognised 3.24

and available in law, and be enforced, allowed and followed accordingly; and the expression [3 "enforceable EU right"] and similar expressions shall be read as referring to one to which this subsection applies.

(2) Subject to Schedule 2 to this Act, at any time after its passing Her Majesty may by Order in Council, and any designated Minister or department may by [2 by order, rules, regulations or scheme], make provision—

(a) for the purpose of implementing any Community obligation of the United Kingdom, or enabling any such obligation to be implemented, or of enabling any rights enjoyed or to be enjoyed by the United Kingdom under or by virtue of the Treaties to be exercised; or

(b) for the purpose of dealing with matters arising out of or related to any such obligation or rights or the coming into force, or the operation from time to time, of subsection (1) above;

and in the exercise of any statutory power or duty, including any power to give directions or to leg is late by means of orders, rules, regulations or other subordinate instrument, the person entrusted with the power or duty may have regard to the [3 objects of the EU] and to any such obligation or rights as afore said.

In this subsection "designated Minister or department" means such Minister of the Crown or government department as may from time to time be designated by Order in Council in relation to any matter or for any purpose, but subject to such restrictions or conditions (if any) as may be specified by the Order in Council.

(3) There shall be charged on and issued out of the Consolidated Fund or, if so determined by the Treasury, the National Loans Fund the amounts required to meet any [3 EU obligation] to make payments to any of the Communities or member States, or any [3 EU obligation] in respect of contributions to the capital or reserves of the European Investment Bank or in respect of loans to the Bank, or to redeem any notes or obligations issued or created in respect of any such Community obligation; and, except as otherwise provided by or under any enactment—

(a) any other expenses incurred under or by virtue of the Treaties or this Act by any Minister of the Crown or government department may be paid out of moneys provided by Parliament; and

(b) any sums received under or by virtue of the Treaties or this Act by any Minister of the Crown or government department, save for such sums as may be required for disbursements permitted by any other enactment, shall be paid into the Consolidated Fund or, if so determined by the Treasury, the National Loans Fund.

(4) The provision that may be made under subsection (2) above includes, subject to Schedule 2 to this Act, any such provision (of any such extent) as might be made by Act of Parliament, and any enactment passed or to be passed, other than one contained in this Part of this Act, shall be construed and have effect subject to the foregoing provisions of this section; but, except as may be provided by any Act passed after this Act, Schedule 2 shall have effect in connection with the powers conferred by this and the following sections of this Act to make Orders in Council [2 or orders, rules, regulations or schemes].

(5) [1 . . .] and the references in that subsection to a Minister of the

Crown or government department and to a statutory power or duty shall include a Minister or department of the Government of Northern Ireland and a power or duty arising under or by virtue of an Act of the Parliament of Northern Ireland.

(6) A law passed by the legislature of any of the Channel Islands or of the Isle of Man, or a colonial law (within the meaning of the Colonial Laws Validity Act 1865) passed or made for Gibraltar, if expressed to be passed or made in the implementation of the Treaties and of the obligations of the United Kingdom there under, shall not be void or inoperative by reason of any inconsistency with or repugnancy to an Act of Parliament, passed or to be passed, that extends to the Island or Gibraltar or any provision having the force and effect of an Act there (but not including this section), nor by reason of its having some operation outside the Island or Gibraltar; and any such Act or provision that extends to the Island or Gibraltar shall be construed and have effect subject to the provisions of any such law.

AMENDMENTS

1. Northern Ireland Constitution Act 1973 s.41.
2. Legislative and Regulatory Reform Act 2006 c.51 Pt.3 s.27(1) (January 8, 2007).
3. European Union (Amendment) Act 2008 (c.7) Sch.1(1) para.1 (December 1, 2009).

MODIFICATION

The operation of this section is modified in relation to Scotland by the Scotland Act 1998 s.15 and Sch.8 and the Scotland Act 1998 (Transfer of Functions to the Scottish Ministers etc.) Order 1999, (SI 1999/1750), and in relation to Northern Ireland by the Northern Ireland Act 1998 and the Northern Ireland Assembly Act 1973.

GENERAL NOTE

The binding nature of European Union law

European Union law is binding on United Kingdom courts and tribunals by virtue of this section. Any rule of law qualifying as "an enforceable EU right" is to be given legal effect in the law of the United Kingdom. Whenever there is a conflict between United Kingdom law and European Union law, the rule of European Union law is to prevail: see s.2(4). **3.25**

European Union legislation

European Union law takes a variety of forms but the forms most likely to be met in tribunals and before the Commissioners are *regulations* and *directives*. **3.26**

Article 288 TFEU, formerly art.249 EC, provides that regulations are to have the force of law in all the Member States without further implementation, whereas directives are addressed to Member States and require conversion (if necessary) into national law.

Regulations retain their character as European Union law and are binding in all Member States in exactly the same way as that Member State's primary legislation.

Individuals may rely on the provisions of regulations by citing them just as if they were statutory provisions emanating from the United Kingdom Parliament. Indeed, they may be regarded as superior to national legislation since no national legislature can alter the form of a Union regulation. **3.27**

Directives are a form of legislation which is intended to enable European Union law to be enacted in each Member State in the manner which best fits the legal traditions of that Member State. So the obligation is to achieve the result required by the directive, but the choice of form and method is for each Member State to select.

There is a requirement that each Member State to whom a directive is addressed must notify the Commission of the national law which implements the requirements of the directive.

Every piece of European Union secondary legislation must find its authority in a provision of the treaties. This is known as the legal basis or legal base for the measure. Legal base is important because the provision of the Treaty under which it is made will set out the decision-making procedure to be followed. This has generated disputes between the institutions, where an institution takes the view that the secondary legislation should have been made under a Treaty provision which requires its greater involvement in that procedure than under the provision under which the Council has adopted it. The two most important doctrines developed in the case law of the Court of Justice of the European Union (hereafter "Court of Justice") are: (a) the supremacy of European Union law, and (b) the direct effect of European Union law.

Supremacy

3.28 The supremacy of European Union law requires that any conflict between a rule of European Union law and a rule of national law must be decided in favour of the rule of European Union law. See *R. v Secretary of State for Transport Ex p Factortame* (C-213/89) [1990] E.C.R. I-2433; [1990] 3 C.M.L.R. 1. Note the requirements of the doctrine as re-affirmed in this case, which involved a procedural rule in English law which operated as a barrier to a remedy under European Union law; significantly, it involved the non-application of a United Kingdom statute.

Direct effect

3.29 A helpful distinction drawn by some commentators is between direct applicability and direct effect.

Direct applicability refers to the *status* of the source of a rule of European Union law, and refers to those sources which are automatically law in the national legal orders of all the Member States. Treaty articles have this character, as do regulations. It is not open to a Member State to interfere with the direct application of a regulation in the national legal order. This preserves the Union nature of the source of obligation throughout all the Member States. If you know that an article of a particular regulation gives you a right in your own national legal order, you can be sure that the same right is provided in all the national legal orders under the same article of the same regulation. The only difference is that it will be in another official language of the European Union.

The attribute of direct applicability is a feature of the supremacy of European Union law.

3.30 Note that in some areas the Member States have transferred sole competence to legislate to the Union; one purpose for such transfers of sovereignty is to ensure the uniform application of law throughout the Union. This is sometimes called the doctrine of *pre-emption*. The effect is that once an area is occupied by European Union law, Member States cannot legislate in that area.

Direct effect refers to the *content* of a rule, and describes its capacity to give rise to rights for individuals which they can plead before national courts, and which national courts must recognise.

Just as it is the case that not every provision of national law gives rise to rights for individuals, so too it is the case that not every provision of European Union law gives rise to direct effect. It is necessary to consider the scope and wording of any provision in order to deter mine whether it is capable of giving rise to direct effect.

Where the status of the provision of European Union law in issue is one which has the attribute of direct applicability, it is simply a matter of interpretation to determine whether direct effect arises. So, in the case of Treaty articles and regulations, the requirements for direct effect are that the rule in question: **3.31**

- is sufficiently clear and precise; and
- is unconditional.

The direct effect of directives has given rise to particular problems, since art.288 TFEU, formerly art.249 EC, provides that directives are:

- addressed to the Member States; and
- are binding as to the result to be achieved; but
- leave the choice of form and methods to the national authorities of the Member States.

All Directives give Member States a time limit within which to implement the requirements of the directive. They are obliged to inform the Commission of the action taken to implement the directive. Failure to implement a directive by the deadline is likely to result in action being taken by the Commission to bring the Member State before the Court of Justice under art.258 TFEU, formerly art.226 EC, for failing to fulfil its obligations under the Treaty.

Proper and complete implementation of a directive results in individuals acquiring rights under the implementing national law.

It is now accepted that, where the deadline for implementation has passed without the Directive's being implemented or without its being implemented properly, a Directive can give rise to direct effect where it contains an obligation as to the result to be achieved which meets the requirements for direct effect set out above, *provided that* the party against whom the right is asserted is the state or "an emanation of the State". This is called a vertical relationship, and so vertical direct effect of directives is said to be permitted. Note particularly the definition of what constitutes an emanation of the state in *Foster v British Gas* (C-188/89) [1990] E.C.R. I-3313; [1990] 2 C.M.L.R. 833.

However, the Court of Justice has ruled that the direct effect of directives does not arise where the right is being asserted against another private party. This is called a horizontal relationship, and so horizontal direct effect of directives is said not to be possible. There are a number of reasons for this:

1. To do so would impose an insuperable burden on private parties. Whereas it is justifiable to refuse to permit the State and its emanations from being able to plead the State's wrong doing to avoid its liabilities, it would be wrong to impose a similar burden on a private party.

2. Directives are addressed to Member States. To allow the horizontal direct effect of directives would be to remove the distinction between regulations and directives. It would also provide an incentive for Member States not to implement directives, since they would take effect in any event after the expiry of the time for implementation.

The doctrine of indirect effect

To mitigate the harshness of a rule relating to the direct effect of directives as between private parties, the Court of Justice has imposed obligations on national authorities and national courts to interpret national law compatibly with the requirements of directives so far as it is possible to do so. This obligation flows from the duty of solidarity to be found in art.4(3) TEU, formerly art.10 EC. **3.32**

State liability for breaches of European Union law

3.33 The Court of Justice has developed rules which ensure the effective enjoyment of European Union rights for individuals. The Court has even fashioned the requirement for a remedy where a Member State has failed either wholly or in part to implement a directive, and the relationship between the parties is a horizontal one.

However, the remedy is available wherever there has been a breach of European Union law of sufficient seriousness to engage the remedy.

Under the *Francovich* line of cases, courts in the Member States are obliged to compensate individuals who have suffered loss as a result of infringements of European Union law by Member States. Three conditions for liability are required:

- the rule of European Union law grants rights to individuals and the content of those rights is clearly identifiable;
- the breach by the Member State is sufficiently serious to trigger liability for loss; and
- there is a direct causal link between the breach of the rule by the Member State and the loss suffered by the individuals concerned.

This important remedy has been refined in subsequent case law. This is helpfully summarised in the decision of the House of Lords of October 28, 1999 in *R. v Secretary of State for Transport Ex p. Factortame Ltd (No.5)*, HL, [2000] 1 A.C. 524; [1999] 3 W.L.R. 1062; [1999] 4 All E.R. 906; [1999] 3 C.M.L.R. 597.

For guidance on the application of limitation periods to *Francovich* actions, see *Spencer v SSWP,* and *Moore v Secretary of State for Transport,* [2008] EWCA Civ 750.

However, neither the First-tier Tribunal nor the Upper Tribunal is the forum to argue for damages under the *Francovich* line of authority. Claims for damages for breach of European Union law are claims in tort and must be brought in the county courts or the High Court. Neither tribunal has any jurisdiction in respect of such claims: *Secretary of State for Employment v Mann and others* [1997] I.C.R. 209 (CA).

The European Union law doctrine of the effective enjoyment of European Union law rights

3.34 The case law has established that national law must afford the same remedies in relation to the enforcement of European Union law as are available for the enforcement of national law. This has come to be known as the doctrine of the effective enjoyment of European Union law rights and operates on the basis of two principles: see, for example, *Peterbroeck* v *Belgium* (C-312/93) [1995] E.C.R. I-4599, at [12]).

The principle of *equivalence* requires that the conditions laid down by national law for the pursuit of European Union rights are not discriminatory by comparison with those relating to domestic claims. The principle of *effectiveness* requires that any restrictions imposed must not be such as to render the reliance on European Union rights virtually impossible or excessively difficult. The doctrine applies regardless of the source of the European Union right on which the individual is relying: it may be a Treaty provision, regulation or directive, or indeed any other instrument having legal effect. The case law of the Court of Justice on the application of this doctrine to national time limits has proved difficult.

The issue first arose in the context of Ireland's failure fully to implement Dir.79/7. In *McDermott v Minister for Social Welfare* (286/85) [1987] E.C.R. 1453; [1987] 2 C.M.L.R. 607, the Court of Justice ruled that art.4(1) of Dir.79/7 could be relied on by individuals as from December 23, 1984. In *Emmott* v *Minister for Social Welfare and Attorney General* (208/90) [1991] E.C.R. I-4269, the Court of Justice ruled as incompatible with European Union law a limitation period operative under national law which had the effect of completely defeating the claimant's reliance on European Union law entitlements. The case arose in the context of failures by the Irish Government to implement the requirements of Directive 79/7 on equal treatment of men and women in matters pertaining to social security. Mrs

Emmott sought payment of her disability benefit at the same rate paid to married men. Ultimately she began judicial review proceedings but the national authorities pleaded that her application was time-barred since the time limit was three months from the date when the grounds of the application first arose. This completely defeated her claim.

The Court of Justice ruled that where directives had not been properly implemented by a Member State, that State could not rely on national rules on time limits to defeat entirely a claim arising from the Member State failure. **3.35**

The scope of that decision has been clarified in later case law. In *Steenhorst Neerings* (C-338/91) [1993] E.C.R. I-5475, the Court of Justice ruled that national provisions which simply limit the period prior to the date of claim for which benefit entitlement may be claimed were not inconsistent with European Union law.

In *Steenhorst Neerings*, the Court of Justice said:

> "21. It should be noted first that, unlike the rule of domestic law fixing time-limits for bringing actions, the rule described in the question referred for a preliminary ruling in this case does not affect the right of individuals to rely on Directive 79/7 in proceedings before the national courts against a defaulting Member State. It merely limits the retroactive effect of claims made for the purpose of obtaining the relevant benefits.
>
> 22. The time-bar resulting from the expiry of the time-limit for bringing proceedings serves to ensure that the legality of administrative decisions cannot be challenged indefinitely. The judgment in Emmott indicates that that requirement cannot prevail over the need to protect the rights conferred on individuals by the direct effect of provisions in a directive so long as the defaulting Member State responsible for those decisions has not properly transposed the provisions into national law.
>
> 23. On the other hand, the aim of the rule restricting the retroactive effect of claims for benefits for incapacity for work is quite different from that of a rule imposing mandatory time-limits for bringing proceedings. As the Government of the Netherlands and the defendant in the main proceedings explained in their written observations, the first type of rule, of which examples can be found in other social security laws in the Netherlands, serves to ensure sound administration, most importantly so that it may be ascertained whether the claimant satisfied the conditions for eligibility and so that the degree of incapacity, which may well vary over time, may be fixed. It also reflects the need to preserve financial balance in a scheme in which claims submitted by insured persons in the course of a year must in principle be covered by the contributions collected during that same year.
>
> 24. The reply to the first question must therefore be that Community law does not preclude the application of a national rule of law whereby benefits for incapacity for work are payable not earlier than one year before the date of claim, in the case where an individual seeks to rely on rights conferred directly by Article 4(1) of Directive 79/7 with effect from 23 December 1984 and where on the date the claim for benefit was made the Member State concerned had not yet properly transposed that provision into national law."

The ruling in *Steenhorst Neerings* was followed in *Johnson v Chief Adjudication Officer* (C-410/92) [1994] E.C.R. I-5483, where the Court said: **3.36**

> "26. However, it is clear from the judgment in *Steenhorst-Neerings* that the solution adopted in *Emmott* was justified by the particular circumstances of that case, in which a time-bar had the result of depriving the applicant of any opportunity whatever to rely on her right to equal treatment under the directive.
>
> 27. The Court pointed out in *Steenhorst-Neerings* (paragraph 20) that in *Emmott* the applicant in the main proceedings had relied on the judgment of the Court in Case 286/85 *McDermott v Minister for Social Welfare* [1987] E.C.R. 1453 in order

to claim entitlement by virtue of Article 4(1) of Directive 79/7, with effect from 23 December 1984, to invalidity benefits under the same conditions as those applicable to men in the same situation. The administrative authorities had then declined o adjudicate on her claim since Directive 79/7 was the subject of proceedings pending before a national court. Finally, even though Directive 79/7 had still not been correctly transposed into national law, it was claimed that the proceedings she had brought to obtain a ruling that her claim should have been accepted were out of time.

28. In contrast, the rule at issue in *Steenhorst-Neerings* did not affect the right of individuals to rely on Directive 79/7 in proceedings before the national courts against a defaulting Member State but merely limited to one year the retroactive effect of claims for benefits for incapacity for work.

29. The Court concluded (paragraph 24) that Community law did not preclude the application of a national rule of law whereby benefits for incapacity for work were payable not earlier than one year before the date of claim, in the case where an individual sought to rely on rights conferred directly by Article 4(1) of Directive 79/7 with effect from 23 December 1984 and where on the date the claim for benefit was made the Member State concerned had not yet properly transposed that provision into national law.

30. In the light of the foregoing, the national rule which adversely affects Mrs Johnson's action before the Court of Appeal is similar to that at issue in *Steenhorst-Neerings*. Neither rule constitutes a bar to proceedings; they merely limit the period prior to the bringing of the claim in respect of which arrears of benefit are payable."

Walker-Fox v SSWP [2005] EWCA Civ 1441, reported as *R(IS) 3/06* is the appeal against the decision in *CIS/0488/2004*. The judgment contains a detailed discussion of the authorities; in particular, the Court of Appeal was keen to limit the situations in which the *Emmott* case would apply to circumstances close to the situation which arose in that case. In allowing the Secretary of State's appeal the Court of Appeal considered that the Deputy Commissioner had erred in confusing "the *making* of a claim with the *outcome* of a claim. The real question is whether it was virtually impossible or excessively difficult to *make* the claim" (at [46] of the judgment). The Court of Appeal concluded that it was not.

A Commissioner has for the first time had to consider whether European Union law principles on effective enjoyment of European Union rights requires the grant of interim relief in a case where payments of disability living allowance were stopped when the claimant moved to Spain and where a Commissioner had referred questions to the Court of Justice under art.234 EC. In *R(DLA) 4/99* and *R(DLA) 5/99* the Commissioner does not directly answer the question since he proceeds on the assumption that there might be such a power but does not consider that the claimant's case met the necessary threshold of being "strongly arguable" as distinct from being merely "arguable". Despite this conclusion the decision raises many of the difficult issues which would arise if the Commissioners (and now, the Upper Tribunal) were to have such a power. It could well follow that First-tier Tribunals enjoyed a similar power. A particular difficulty is that Tribunals and the Upper Tribunal are concerned with entitlement, whereas the mechanics of payment are matters for the Secretary of State alone. Such a distinction of role (which has, of course, for many purposes been removed by the Social Security Act 1998 without removing all the possible problems) might not be able to survive an onslaught relying on European authority on remedies before national judicial bodies.

The appellant in the case sought a judicial review of the Commissioner's decision in *R. v Social Security Commissioner Ex p. Snares*, reported as *R(DLA) 4/99*. The Divisional Court concluded that the Commissioner could not be faulted in the way he had exercised any discretion he had in the case. The case does not advance matters beyond what the Commissioner said. The trend of the case law of the Court of Justice is, however, that European Union law requires national judicial authorities to have the power to give legal effect to rights arising under EU law. An example of where this might be problematic is the absence of any express power to award interest on late benefit or costs: see *R(FC)2/90*.

Decisions on, and proof of, Treaties and Community instruments, etc.

3.—(1) For the purposes of all legal proceedings any question as to the meaning or effect of any of the Treaties, or as to the validity, meaning or effect of any [[2] EU instrument], shall be treated as a question of law (and, if not referred to the European Court, be for determination as such in accordance with the principles laid down by and any relevant [[1] decision of the European Court [[2] . . .])]. **3.37**

(2) Judicial notice shall be taken of the Treaties, of the Official Journal of the Communities and of any decision of, or expression of opinion by the European Court [[2] . . .] on any such question as aforesaid; and the Official Journal shall be admissible as evidence of any instrument or other act thereby communicated of [[2] the EU].

(3) Evidence of any instrument issued by a [[2] EU institution], including any judgment or order of the European Court [[2] . . .], or of any document in the custody of a [[2] EU institution], or any entry in or extract from such a document, may be given in any legal proceedings by production of a copy certified as a true copy by an official of that institution; and any document purporting to be such a copy shall be received in evidence without proof of the official position or hand writing of the person signing the certificate.

(4) Evidence of any [[2] EU instrument] may also be given in any legal proceedings—

(a) by production of a copy purporting to be printed by the Queen's Printer;

(b) where the instrument is in the custody of a government department (including a department of the Government of Northern Ireland), by production of a copy certified on behalf of the department to be a true copy by an officer of the department generally or specially authorised so to do; and any document purporting to be such a copy as is mentioned in paragraph (b) above of an instrument in the custody of a department shall be received in evidence without proof of the official position or hand writing of the person signing the certificate, or of his authority to do so, or of the document being in the custody of the department.

(5) *Omitted.*

AMENDMENTS

1. European Communities (Amendment) Act 1986 (c.58) s.2 (November 7, 1986).
2. European Union (Amendment) Act 2008 (c.7) Sch.1 para.1 (December 1, 2009).

GENERAL NOTE

Questions as to the meaning and effect of the treaties and of any European Union secondary legislation are questions of law. Where such questions are decided by **3.38** national courts or tribunals, they are to be decided in accordance with principles laid down in any decision of the Court of Justice or General Court, formerly the Court of First Instance. In deciding such questions, judicial notice is to be taken of the treaties and secondary legislation as well as of decisions of the Union courts.

Extracts from the Treaty on European Union

Title I

Common Provisions

Article 1
(ex Article 1 TEU)

3.39 By this Treaty, the HIGH CONTRACTING PARTIES establish among themselves a EUROPEAN UNION, hereinafter called "the Union" on which the Member States confer competences to attain objectives they have in common.

This Treaty marks a new stage in the process of creating an ever closer union among the peoples of Europe, in which decisions are taken as openly as possible and as closely as possible to the citizen.

The Union shall be founded on the present Treaty and on the Treaty on the Functioning of the European Union (hereinafter referred to as "the Treaties"). Those two Treaties shall have the same legal value. The Union shall replace and succeed the European Community.

Article 2

3.40 The Union is founded on the values of respect for human dignity, freedom, democracy, equality, the rule of law and respect for human rights, including the rights of persons belonging to minorities. These values are common to the Member States in a society in which pluralism, non-discrimination, tolerance, justice, solidarity and equality between women and men prevail.

Article 3
(ex Article 2 TEU)

3.41 1. The Union's aim is to promote peace, its values and the well-being of its peoples.

2. The Union shall offer its citizens an area of freedom, security and justice without internal frontiers, in which the free movement of persons is ensured in conjunction with appropriate measures with respect to external border controls, asylum, immigration and the prevention and combating of crime.

3. The Union shall establish an internal market. It shall work for the sustainable development of Europe based on balanced economic growth and price stability, a highly competitive social market economy, aiming at full employment and social progress, and a high level of protection and improvement of the quality of the environment. It shall promote scientific and technological advance.

It shall combat social exclusion and discrimination, and shall promote social justice and protection, equality between women and men, solidarity between generations and protection of the rights of the child.

It shall promote economic, social and territorial cohesion, and solidarity among Member States.

It shall respect its rich cultural and linguistic diversity, and shall ensure that Europe's cultural heritage is safeguarded and enhanced.

4. The Union shall establish an economic and monetary union whose currency is the euro.

5. In its relations with the wider world, the Union shall uphold and promote its values and interests and contribute to the protection of its citizens. It shall contribute to peace, security, the sustainable development of the Earth, solidarity and mutual respect among peoples, free and fair trade, eradication of poverty and the protection of human rights, in particular the rights of the child, as well as to the strict observance and the development of international law, including respect for the principles of the United Nations Charter.

6. The Union shall pursue its objectives by appropriate means commensurate with the competences which are conferred upon it in the Treaties.

General Note

The Court has frequently found its inspiration for an interpretation of a particular provision of the Treaty or of secondary legislation by reference to the objectives of the Union as set out in what is now arts 3-6: for example, *Levin v Staatssecretaris van Justitie* (53/81) [1982] E.C.R. 1035 (See [15] of the judgment), though the terms of the predecessors of these articles have been found not to be sufficiently precise to give rise to direct effect: *Giménez Zaera v Instituto Nacional de la Seguridad Social* (126/86) [1987] E.C.R. 3697 (See [11] of judgment in relation to art.2 EC). 3.42

Article 4

1. In accordance with Article 5, competences not conferred upon the Union in the Treaties remain with the Member States. 3.43

2. The Union shall respect the equality of Member States before the Treaties as well as their national identities, inherent in their fundamental structures, political and constitutional, inclusive of regional and local self-government. It shall respect their essential State functions, including ensuring the territorial integrity of the State, maintaining law and order and safeguarding national security. In particular, national security remains the sole responsibility of each Member State.

3. Pursuant to the principle of sincere cooperation, the Union and the Member States shall, in full mutual respect, assist each other in carrying out tasks which flow from the Treaties.

The Member States shall take any appropriate measure, general or particular, to ensure fulfilment of the obligations arising out of the Treaties or resulting from the acts of the institutions of the Union.

The Member States shall facilitate the achievement of the Union's tasks and refrain from any measure which could jeopardise the attainment of the Union's objectives.

Article 5
(ex Article 5 TEC)

3.44 1. The limits of Union competences are governed by the principle of conferral. The use of Union competences is governed by the principles of subsidiarity and proportionality.

2. Under the principle of conferral, the Union shall act only within the limits of the competences conferred upon it by the Member States in the Treaties to attain the objectives set out therein.

Competences not conferred upon the Union in the Treaties remain with the Member States.

3. Under the principle of subsidiarity, in areas which do not fall within its exclusive competence, the Union shall act only if and in so far as the objectives of the proposed action cannot be sufficiently achieved by the Member States, either at central level or at regional and local level, but can rather, by reason of the scale or effects of the proposed action, be better achieved at Union level.

The institutions of the Union shall apply the principle of subsidiarity as laid down in the Protocol on the application of the principles of subsidiarity and proportionality. National Parliaments ensure compliance with the principle of subsidiarity in accordance with the procedure set out in that Protocol.

4. Under the principle of proportionality, the content and form of Union action shall not exceed what is necessary to achieve the objectives of the Treaties.

The institutions of the Union shall apply the principle of proportionality as laid down in the Protocol on the application of the principles of subsidiarity and proportionality.

Article 6
(ex Article 6 TEU)

3.45 1. The Union recognises the rights, freedoms and principles set out in the Charter of Fundamental Rights of the European Union of 7 December 2000, as adapted at Strasbourg, on 12 December 2007, which shall have the same legal value as the Treaties.

The provisions of the Charter shall not extend in any way the competences of the Union as defined in the Treaties.

The rights, freedoms and principles in the Charter shall be interpreted in accordance with the general provisions in Title VII of the Charter governing its interpretation and application and with due regard to the explanations referred to in the Charter, that set out the sources of those provisions.

2. The Union shall accede to the European Convention for the Protection of Human Rights and Fundamental Freedoms. Such accession shall not affect the Union's competences as defined in the Treaties.

3. Fundamental rights, as guaranteed by the European Convention for the Protection of Human Rights and Fundamental Freedoms and as they

result from the constitutional traditions common to the Member States, shall constitute general principles of the Union's law.

GENERAL NOTE

The text of the Charter of Fundamental Rights of the European Union can be found on the europa website *http://europa.eu/index_en.htm* [Accessed June 7, 2010], and is reproduced below at paras 3.122–3.180. **3.46**

Protocol No.30 contains provisions on the application of the Charter of Fundamental Rights of the European Union to Poland and the United Kingdom. Its operative provisions are:

Article 1

1. The Charter does not extend the ability of the Court of Justice of the European Union, or any court or tribunal of Poland or of the United Kingdom, to find that the laws, regulations or administrative provisions, practices or action of Poland or of the United Kingdom are inconsistent with the fundamental rights, freedoms and principles that it reaffirms.
2. In particular, and for the avoidance of doubt, nothing in Title IV of the Charter creates justiciable rights applicable to Poland or the United Kingdom except in so far as Poland or the United Kingdom has provided for such rights in its national law.

Article 2

To the extent that a provision of the Charter refers to national laws and practices, it shall only apply to Poland or the United Kingdom to the extent that the rights or principles that it contains are recognised in the law or practices of Poland or of the United Kingdom.

Protocol No. 8 provides a little more detail on the accession of the European Union to the European Convention on Human Rights.

The status of Protocol No. 30

On a reference from the Court of Appeal in *NS v SSHD* (C-411/10), the Advocate General, in her Opinion, has addressed some remarks on the effect of Protocol No 30. Since they are the first judicial remarks from the Luxembourg Court on this question, they merit reproduction here (footnotes omitted): **3.47**

"165. By its seventh question, the referring court asks the Court to clarify the content and scope of Protocol (No 30) on the application of the Charter of Fundamental Rights of the European Union to Poland and to the United Kingdom, annexed to the Treaty on European Union and the Treaty on the Functioning of the European Union. It essentially asks whether, having regard to that Protocol, the provisions of the Charter of Fundamental Rights which are relevant to the present case can take full effect in the legal order of the United Kingdom.

166. With this question, the referring court thus wishes to ascertain whether, and if so to what extent, Protocol No 30 can be regarded as an 'opt-out' from the Charter of Fundamental Rights for the United Kingdom and the Republic of Poland.

167. In my view, the question whether Protocol No 30 is to be regarded as a general opt-out from the Charter of Fundamental Rights for the United Kingdom and the Republic of Poland can be easily answered in the negative. This conclusion is suggested by an analysis of the wording of Protocol No 30, having particular regard to its recitals.

168. Under Article 1(1) of Protocol No 30, the Charter does not extend the ability of the Court of Justice of the European Union, or any court or tribunal of Poland or of the United Kingdom, to find that the laws, regulations or administrative provisions, practices or action of Poland or of the United Kingdom are inconsistent with the fundamental rights, freedoms and principles that it reaffirms.

169. According to its wording, Article 1(1) of Protocol No 30 therefore makes clear that the Charter of Fundamental Rights does not have the effect of either shifting powers at the expense of the United Kingdom or Poland or of extending the field of application of EU law beyond the powers of the European Union as established in the Treaties. Article 1(1) of Protocol No 30 thus merely reaffirms the normative content of Article 51 of the Charter of Fundamental Rights, which seeks to prevent precisely such an extension of EU powers or of the field of application of EU law. Article 1(1) of the Protocol does not therefore, in principle, call into question the validity of the Charter of Fundamental Rights for the United Kingdom and for Poland.

170. This view is confirmed in the recitals in the preamble to the Protocol, which confirms, in several places, the fundamental validity of the Charter of Fundamental Rights in the Polish and the English legal orders. For example, the third recital states that under Article 6 TEU the Charter is to be *applied* and *interpreted* by the courts of Poland and of the United Kingdom strictly in accordance with the explanations referred to in that article. Reference is made in the eighth and ninth recitals to the wish of Poland and the United Kingdom to clarify *certain aspects of the application of the Charter* and the *application of the Charter in relation to the laws and administrative action of Poland and of the United Kingdom*.

171. Whilst Article 1(1) of Protocol No 30 does not call into question the validity of the Charter of Fundamental Rights, but should merely be regarded as an express confirmation of the normative content of Article 51 of the Charter of Fundamental Rights, Article 1(2) of Protocol No 30 appears to seek to clarify the validity of individual provisions of the Charter in the legal orders of the United Kingdom and Poland. Under Article 1(2) of Protocol No 30, nothing in Title IV of the Charter creates justiciable rights applicable to Poland or the United Kingdom except in so far as such rights are provided for in their respective national laws.

172. Article 1(2) of Protocol No 30 relates to the social fundamental rights and principles grouped together under Title IV of the Charter of Fundamental Rights (Article 27 to 38). That title, entitled 'Solidarity', is regarded as one of the most controversial areas in the evolution of the Charter. There was dispute not only over the fundamental question whether social rights and principles should be incorporated into the Charter, but also how many social rights should be included, how they should be organised in detail, what binding force they should have, and whether they should be classified as fundamental rights or as principles.

173. With the statement that Title IV of the Charter of Fundamental Rights does not create justiciable rights applicable to Poland or the United Kingdom, Article 1(2) of Protocol No 30 first reaffirms the principle, set out in Article 51(1) of the Charter, that the Charter does not create justiciable rights as between private individuals. However, Article 1(2) of Protocol No 30 also appears to rule out new EU rights and entitlements being derived from Articles 27 to 38 of the Charter of Fundamental Rights, on which those entitled could rely against the United Kingdom or against Poland.

174. Because the contested fundamental rights in the present case are not among the social fundamental rights and principles set out in Title IV of the Charter of Fundamental Rights, however, there is no need to examine in any greater detail here the question of the precise validity and scope of Article 1(2) of Protocol No 30. It is sufficient to refer to the 10th recital in the preamble to

Protocol No 30, according to which references in that protocol to the operation of specific provisions of the Charter are strictly without prejudice to the operation of other provisions of the Charter.

175. Article 2 of Protocol No 30 provides, lastly, that where a provision of the Charter refers to national laws and practices, it only applies to Poland or the United Kingdom to the extent that the rights or principles that it contains are recognised in the law or practices of Poland or of the United Kingdom.

176. In the light of the abovementioned recitals, it is not possible to infer from Article 2 of Protocol No 30 a general opt-out from the Charter of Fundamental Rights for the United Kingdom and the Republic of Poland. Moreover, Article 2 of Protocol No 30 applies solely to provisions of the Charter of Fundamental Rights which make reference to national laws and practices. That is not the case with the provisions of the Charter which are relevant in the present case.

177. In the light of the foregoing, the seventh question must be answered to the effect that the interpretation of Protocol No 30 has not produced any findings which could call into question the validity for the United Kingdom of the provisions of the Charter of Fundamental Rights which are relevant in the present case."

The Grand Chamber of the Court of Justice has essentially taken the same view in its judgment of December 21, 2011:

"116. By its seventh question in Case C-411/10, the Court of Appeal (England & Wales) (Civil Division) asks, in essence, whether, in so far as the preceding questions arise in respect of the obligations of the United Kingdom, the answers to the second to sixth questions should be qualified in any respect so as to take account of Protocol (No 30).

117. As noted by the EHRC, that question arises because of the position taken by the Secretary of State before the High Court of Justice (England & Wales) (Administrative Court) that the provisions of the Charter do not apply in the United Kingdom.

118. Even if the Secretary of State no longer maintained that position before the Court of Appeal (England & Wales) (Civil Division), it must be noted that Protocol (No 30) provides, in Article 1(1), that the Charter is not to extend the ability of the Court of Justice or any court or tribunal of Poland or of the United Kingdom, to find that the laws, regulations administrative provisions, practices or action of Poland or of the United Kingdom are inconsistent with the fundamental rights, freedoms and principles that it affirms.

119. According to the wording of that provision, as noted by the Advocate General in points 169 and 170 of her Opinion in Case C-411/10, Protocol (No 30) does not call into question the applicability of the Charter in the United Kingdom or in Poland, a position which is confirmed by the recitals in the preamble to that protocol. Thus, according to the third recital in the preamble to Protocol (No 30), Article 6 TEU requires the Charter to be applied and interpreted by the courts of Poland and of the United Kingdom strictly in accordance with the explanations referred to in that article. In addition, according to the sixth recital in the preamble to that protocol, the Charter reaffirms the rights, freedoms and principles recognised in the Union and makes those rights more visible, but does not create new rights or principles.

120. In those circumstances, Article 1(1) of Protocol (No 30) explains Article 51 of the Charter with regard to the scope thereof and does not intend to exempt the Republic of Poland or the United Kingdom from the obligation to comply with the provisions of the Charter or to prevent a court of one of those Member States from ensuring compliance with those provisions.

121. Since the rights referred to in the cases in the main proceedings do not form part of Title IV of the Charter, there is no need to rule on the interpretation of Article 1(2) of Protocol (No 30).

122. The answer to the seventh question in Case C-411/10 is therefore that, in so far as the preceding questions arise in respect of the obligations of the United Kingdom, the answers to the second to sixth questions referred in Case C-411/10 do not require to be qualified in any respect so as to take account of Protocol (No 30)."

Article 19

3.48 1. The Court of Justice of the European Union shall include the Court of Justice, the General Court and specialised courts. It shall ensure that in the interpretation and application of the Treaties the law is observed.

Member States shall provide remedies sufficient to ensure effective legal protection in the fields covered by Union law.

2. The Court of Justice shall consist of one judge from each Member State. It shall be assisted by Advocates-General.

The General Court shall include at least one judge per Member State.

The Judges and the Advocates-General of the Court of Justice and the Judges of the General Court shall be chosen from persons whose independence is beyond doubt and who satisfy the conditions set out in

Articles 253 and 254 of the Treaty on the Functioning of the European Union. They shall be appointed by common accord of the governments of the Member States for six years. Retiring Judges and Advocates-General may be reappointed.

3. The Court of Justice of the European Union shall, in accordance with the Treaties:

(a) rule on actions brought by a Member State, an institution or a natural or legal person;
(b) give preliminary rulings, at the request of courts or tribunals of the Member States, on the
interpretation of Union law or the validity of acts adopted by the institutions;
(c) rule in other cases provided for in the Treaties.

Article 50

3.49 1. Any Member State may decide to withdraw from the Union in accordance with its own constitutional requirements.

2. A Member State which decides to withdraw shall notify the European Council of its intention. In the light of the guidelines provided by the European Council, the Union shall negotiate and conclude an agreement with that State, setting out the arrangements for its withdrawal, taking account of the framework for its future relationship with the Union. That agreement shall be negotiated in accordance with Article 218(3) of the Treaty on the Functioning of the European Union. It shall be concluded on behalf of the Union by the Council, acting by a qualified majority, after obtaining the consent of the European Parliament.

3. The Treaties shall cease to apply to the State in question from the date of entry into force of the withdrawal agreement or, failing that, two

years after the notification referred to in paragraph 2, unless the European Council, in agreement with the Member State concerned, unanimously decides to extend this period.

4. For the purposes of paragraphs 2 and 3, the member of the European Council or of the Council representing the withdrawing Member State shall not participate in the discussions of the European Council or Council or in decisions concerning it.

A qualified majority shall be defined in accordance with Article 238(3)(b) of the Treaty on the Functioning of the European Union.

5. If a State which has withdrawn from the Union asks to rejoin, its request shall be subject to the procedure referred to in Article 49.

GENERAL NOTE

ON JUNE 23, 2016, the people of the United Kingdom voted to leave the European Union. Article 50 TEU sets out the process by which a Member State withdraws from the Union. See also the note at 3.16 above. 3.50

Extracts from the Treaty on the Functioning of the European Union

GENERAL NOTE

In order to assist users of this book in matching the provisions of the Treaty on the Functioning of the European Union with key provisions formerly in the EC Treaty, the following table of equivalences is offered. 3.51

Table of Equivalences

TREATY ON THE FUNCTIONING OF THE EUROPEAN UNION

3.52

Old numbering of the EC Treaty	**New numbering of the Treaty on the Functioning of the European Union**
Article 2	*Repealed, but replaced in substance by Article 3 TEU*
Article 3(1)	*Repealed*
Article 3(2)	*Repealed, but replaced in substance by Articles 3-6 TEU*
Article 5	*Replaced in substance by Article 5 TEU*
Article 10	*Repealed, but replaced in substance by Article 4(3) TEU*
Article 12	Article 18 *(now in Part Two on Citizenship of the Union)*
Article 13	Article 19 *(now in Part Two on Citizenship of the Union)*
Article 14	Article 26 *(now in Part Three on Community Policies)*
Article 17	Article 20
Article 18	Article 21
Article 19	Article 22
Article 20	Article 23
Article 21	Article 24
Article 22	Article 25
Article 39	Article 45
Article 40	Article 46
Article 41	Article 47
Article 42	Article 48
Article 43	Article 49
Article 220	*Repealed but replaced in substance by Article 19 TEU*
Article 226	Article 258
Article 227	Article 259
Article 228	Article 260
Article 230	Article 263
Article 231	Article 264
Article 234	Article 267
Article 308	Article 352

Part Two

Non-Discrimination and Citizenship of the Union

Article 18
(ex Article 12 TEC)

3.53 Within the scope of application of the Treaties, and without prejudice to any special provisions contained therein, any discrimination on grounds of nationality shall be prohibited.

The European Parliament and the Council, acting in accordance with the ordinary legislative procedure, may adopt rules designed to prohibit such discrimination.

General Note

3.54 This is the general prohibition of discrimination on grounds of nationality, which applies wherever the provisions of the treaty apply. In *Martínez Sala v Freistaat Bayern* (C-85/96) [1998] E.C.R. I-2691, it was held that a person lawfully resident in Germany could rely on the principle of discrimination to gain access to social security benefits in Germany notwithstanding that she was not a worker under European Union law. A crucial aspect of the case which is not fully explained is what constitutes lawful residence in a Member State. See also the case law discussed in the annotations to art.21 TFEU below.

Article 19
(ex Article 13 TEC)

3.55 1. Without prejudice to the other provisions of the Treaties and within the limits of the powers conferred by them upon the Union, the Council, acting unanimously in accordance with a special legislative procedure and after obtaining the consent of the European Parliament, may take appropriate action to combat discrimination based on sex, racial or ethnic origin, religion or belief, disability, age or sexual orientation.

2. By way of derogation from paragraph 1, the European Parliament and the Council, acting in accordance with the ordinary legislative procedure, may adopt the basic principles of Union incentive measures, excluding any harmonisation of the laws and regulations of the Member States, to support action taken by the Member States in order to contribute to the achievement of the objectives referred to in paragraph 1.

Article 20
(ex Article 17 TEC)

3.56 1. Citizenship of the Union is hereby established. Every person holding the nationality of a Member State shall be a citizen of the Union. Citizenship of the Union shall be additional to and not replace national citizenship.

2. Citizens of the Union shall enjoy the rights and be subject to the duties provided for in the Treaties. They shall have, *inter alia*:

(a) the right to move and reside freely within the territory of the Member States;

(b) the right to vote and to stand as candidates in elections to the European Parliament and in municipal elections in their Member State of residence, under the same conditions as nationals of that State;
(c) the right to enjoy, in the territory of a third country in which the Member State of which they are nationals is not represented, the protection of the diplomatic and consular authorities of any Member State on the same conditions as the nationals of that State;
(d) the right to petition the European Parliament, to apply to the European Ombudsman, and to address the institutions and advisory bodies of the Union in any of the Treaty languages and to obtain a reply in the same language.

These rights shall be exercised in accordance with the conditions and limits defined by the Treaties and by the measures adopted thereunder.

General Note

The allocation of nationality to individuals is a matter for each Member State to determine, subject to very limited intervention by European Union law. These qualifications mean that it will not be open to a Member State to deny that an individual has the nationality of a Member State even though certain rules of its own civil justice system operate in a way which does not recognise the nationality. An example is the *Micheletti* (C-369/90) [1992] E.C.R. I-4239. Micheletti held both Argentinean and Italian nationality. Prior to moving to Spain, he had been resident in Argentina for some time. Under certain Spanish rules, this meant that he was treated as an Argentinean national and his Italian nationality was not recognised. He was refused a residence permit on this basis. The Court of Justice ruled that a Member State could not use its internal law on nationality to deny recognition to a dual national of the nationality of another Member State. Nor is it necessary to have a passport as evidence of the holding of the nationality of a Member State if the nationality can be established by other means: see *Giagounidis* (C-376/89) [1991] E.C.R. I-1069. **3.57**

The laws of the Member States govern changes of nationality just as they govern the attribution of nationality.

Ruiz Zambrano (C–34/09) Judgment of March 8, 2011 is authority for the proposition that rights of residence may flow from art.20 TFEU independently of rights arising under the Citizenship Directive. The Grand Chamber ruled in a case concerning the status of the Colombian father of two children born in, and consequently holding the nationality of, Belgium as follows:

"40. Article 20 TFEU confers the status of citizen of the Union on every person holding the nationality of a Member State (see, inter alia, *D'Hoop* (C–224/98) [2002] E.C.R. I–6191, para.27, and *Garcia Avello* (C–148/02) [2003] E.C.R. I–11613, para.21). Since Mr Ruiz Zambrano's second and third children possess Belgian nationality, the conditions for the acquisition of which it is for the Member State in question to lay down (see, to that effect, inter alia, *Rottmann* (C–135/08) [2010] E.C.R. I–0000, para.39), they undeniably enjoy that status (see, to that effect, *Garcia Avello*, para.21, and *Zhu and Chen*, para.20).
41. As the Court has stated several times, citizenship of the Union is intended to be the fundamental status of nationals of the Member States (see, inter alia, *Grzelczyk* (C–184/99) [2001] E.C.R. I–6193, para.31; *Baumbast and R* (C–413/99) [2002] E.C.R. I–7091, para.82; *Garcia Avello*, para.22; *Zhu and Chen*, para.25; and *Rottmann*, para.43).
42. In those circumstances, Article 20 TFEU precludes national measures which have the effect of depriving citizens of the Union of the genuine enjoyment of the substance of the rights conferred by virtue of their status as citizens of the Union (see, to that effect, *Rottmann*, para.42).
43. A refusal to grant a right of residence to a third country national with depend-

ent minor children in the Member State where those children are nationals and reside, and also a refusal to grant such a person a work permit, has such an effect.
44. It must be assumed that such a refusal would lead to a situation where those children, citizens of the Union, would have to leave the territory of the Union in order to accompany their parents. Similarly, if a work permit were not granted to such a person, he would risk not having sufficient resources to provide for himself and his family, which would also result in the children, citizens of the Union, having to leave the territory of the Union. In those circumstances, those citizens of the Union would, as a result, be unable to exercise the substance of the rights conferred on them by virtue of their status as citizens of the Union.
45. Accordingly, the answer to the questions referred is that art.20 TFEU is to be interpreted as meaning that it precludes a Member State from refusing a third country national upon whom his minor children, who are European Union citizens, are dependent, a right of residence in the Member State of residence and nationality of those children, and from refusing to grant a work permit to that third country national, in so far as such decisions deprive those children of the genuine enjoyment of the substance of the rights attaching to the status of European Union citizen."

3.58 *Dereci* (C-256/11) Judgment of November 15, 2011, ruled that European Union law and, in particular, its provisions on citizenship of the Union, must be interpreted as meaning that it does not preclude a Member State from refusing to allow a third country national to reside on its territory, where that third country national wishes to reside with a member of their family who is a citizen of the Union residing in the Member State of which they have nationality, who has never exercised their right to freedom of movement, provided that such refusal does not lead, for the Union citizen concerned, to the denial of the genuine enjoyment of the substance of the rights conferred by virtue of their status as a citizen of the Union, which is a matter for the referring court to verify.

The combined effects of the judgments in the *Zambrano* and *Dereci* cases led to arguments that there was a right to reside where a refusal to recognise such a right might have the result that children who are citizens of the Union might have to leave their country of residence regardless of the nationality of their parents. It is now abundantly clear that these judgments do not go that far.

O and S v Maahanmuuttovirasto; and *Maahanmuuttovirasto v L* (C-356/11 and C-357/11) consider the Court's judgment in *Ruiz-Zambrano* in the context of applications for rights of residence under Council Directive 2003/86/EC of September 22, 2003 on the right to family reunification, [2003] OJ L251/12.

3.59 The facts in (C-356/11) arose in the context of an application for a residence permit for Mr O which had been sponsored by Ms S. Ms S, a national of Ghana, had permanent residence in Finland by reason of her marriage to a Finnish national. The couple had a child who acquired Finnish nationality and has always lived in Finland. The couple divorced; the father remained in Finland, but Ms S has sole custody of the child. Ms S had studied, taken maternity leave, qualified for a trade and been gainfully employed in Finland. She subsequently married Mr O, a national of Côte d'Ivoire, with whom she subsequently had a child in Finland, who holds Ghanaian nationality. Ms S and Mr O live together in Finland. Mr O was refused a residence permit and that decision was challenged in the Finnish courts.

The facts in (C-357/11) are similar in many respects but also differ in some material elements. Ms L, a national of Algeria, had permanent residence in Finland by reason of her marriage to a Finnish national, with whom she had a child who acquired Finnish nationality and has always lived in Finland. The couple divorced; the father remained in Finland, but Ms L has sole custody of the child. Ms L subsequently married Mr M, a national of Algeria. A child of this relationship was born in Finland, but by that time Mr M was in Algeria. Ms L, as sponsor, sought a residence permit for Mr M, but this was refused.

The Court of Justice confirms following its decision in the *Dereci* case (C-256/11), Judgment of November 15, 2011, the Citizenship Directive did not apply to these situations since the Finnish children of the marriages had never exercised any rights of free movement under Union law (at [42]). The Court then considers the position under the *Ruiz-Zambrano* doctrine. The Court confirms that the doctrine can apply to the situation of third country nationals who are seeking residence permits on the basis of family reunification:

> "47. The criterion of the denial of the genuine enjoyment of the substance of the rights conferred by the status of citizen of the Union referred, in the *Ruiz Zambrano* and *Dereci and Others* cases, to situations characterised by the circumstance that the Union citizen had, in fact, to leave not only the territory of the Member State of which he was a national but also that of the European Union as a whole.
> 48. That criterion is therefore specific in character inasmuch as it relates to situations in which a right of residence, exceptionally, may not be refused to a third country national who is a family member of a national of a Member State, as the effectiveness of the Union citizenship enjoyed by that national would otherwise be undermined (*Dereci and Others*, paragraph 67).
> 49. In the present case, it is for the referring court to establish whether the refusal of the applications for residence permits submitted on the basis of family reunification in circumstances such as those at issue in the main proceedings entails, for the Union citizens concerned, a denial of the genuine enjoyment of the substance of the rights conferred by their status.
> 50. When making that assessment, it must be taken into account that the mothers of the Union citizens hold permanent residence permits in the Member State in question, so that, in law, there is no obligation either for them or for the Union citizens dependent on them to leave the territory of that Member State or of the European Union as a whole.
> 51. For the purpose of examining whether the Union citizens concerned would be unable, in fact, to exercise the substance of the rights conferred by their status, the question of the custody of the sponsors' children and the fact that the children are part of reconstituted families are also relevant. First, since Ms S and Ms L have sole custody of the Union citizens concerned who are minors, a decision by them to leave the territory of the Member State of which those children are nationals, in order to preserve the family unit, would have the effect of depriving those Union citizens of all contact with their biological fathers, should such contact have been maintained up to the present. Secondly, any decision to stay in the territory of that Member State in order to preserve the relationship, if any, of the Union citizens who are minors with their biological fathers would have the effect of harming the relationship of the other children, who are third country nationals, with their biological fathers.
> 52. However, the mere fact that it might appear desirable, for economic reasons or in order to preserve the family unit in the territory of the Union, for members of a family consisting of third country nationals and a Union citizen who is a minor to be able to reside with that citizen in the territory of the Union in the Member State of which he is a national is not sufficient in itself to support the view that the Union citizen would be forced to leave the territory of the Union if such a right of residence were not granted (see, to that effect, *Dereci and Others*, paragraph 68).
> 53. In connection with the assessment, mentioned in paragraph 49 above, which it is for the referring court to carry out, that court must examine all the circumstances of the case in order to determine whether, in fact, the decisions refusing residence permits at issue in the main proceedings are liable to undermine the effectiveness of the Union citizenship enjoyed by the Union citizens concerned.
> 54. Whether the person for whom a right of residence is sought on the basis of family reunification lives together with the sponsor and the other family members is not decisive in that assessment, since it cannot be ruled out that some family members who are the subject of an application for family reunification may arrive in the Member State concerned separately from the rest of the family.
> 55. It should also be noted that, contrary to the submissions of the German and Italian Governments, while the principles stated in the *Ruiz Zambrano* judgment

apply only in exceptional circumstances, it does not follow from the Court's case-law that their application is confined to situations in which there is a blood relationship between the third country national for whom a right of residence is sought and the Union citizen who is a minor from whom that right of residence might be derived.
56. On the other hand, both the permanent right of residence of the mothers of the Union citizens concerned who are minors and the fact that the third country nationals for whom a right of residence is sought are not persons on whom those citizens are legally, financially or emotionally dependent must be taken into consideration when examining the question whether, as a result of the refusal of a right of residence, those citizens would be unable to exercise the substance of the rights conferred by their status. As the Advocate General observes in point 44 of his Opinion, it is the relationship of dependency between the Union citizen who is a minor and the third country national who is refused a right of residence that is liable to jeopardise the effectiveness of Union citizenship, since it is that dependency that would lead to the Union citizen being obliged, in fact, to leave not only the territory of the Member State of which he is a national but also that of the European Union as a whole, as a consequence of such a refusal (see *Ruiz Zambrano*, paragraphs 43 and 45, and *Dereci and Others*, paragraphs 65 to 67).
57. Subject to the verification which it is for the referring court to carry out, the information available to the Court appears to suggest that there might be no such dependency in the cases in the main proceedings.
58. In the light of the foregoing, it must be stated that Article 20 TFEU must be interpreted as not precluding a Member State from refusing to grant a third country national a residence permit on the basis of family reunification where that national seeks to reside with his spouse, who is also a third country national and resides lawfully in that Member State and is the mother of a child from a previous marriage who is a Union citizen, and with the child of their own marriage, who is also a third country national, provided that such a refusal does not entail, for the Union citizen concerned, the denial of the genuine enjoyment of the substance of the rights conferred by the status of citizen of the Union, that being for the referring court to ascertain.
59. Should that court find that, in the circumstances of the cases before it, such a denial does not follow from the refusals of residence permits at issue in the main proceedings, that would be without prejudice to the question whether, on the basis of other criteria, inter alia by virtue of the right to the protection of family life, Mr O and Mr M could not be refused a right of residence. That question must be addressed in the framework of the provisions on the protection of fundamental rights which are applicable in each case (see *Dereci* at [69])."

In [61]–[74], the Court of Justice examines the application of the Family Reunification Directive to the circumstances of these cases, but then goes on to remind the referring court that assessments it makes in applying Union law must respect the fundamental rights set out in the Charter of Fundamental Rights, most notably art.7 on respect for family life, and art.24 on the rights of the child.

3.60 These principles were applied in *SSWP v RR (IS)* [2013] UKUT 21 (AAC), reported as [2013] AACR 20, in ruling that a German national with a daughter who was a citizen of the Union could claim no right to reside on the basis of the *Zambrano* principles. That decision also noted the judgment of the Court of Appeal in *Harrison (Jamaica) v Secretary of State for the Home Department* [2012] EWCA Civ 1736 to the same effect.

The Court of Appeal has overruled the decision in *SSWP v JS (IS)* [2013] UKUT 490 (AAC) in a combined decision in *Sanneh v SSWP, Scott v London Borough of Croydon, Birmingham CC v Merali, R (on the application of HC) v SSWP* [2015] EWCA Civ 49. In a complex decision which concerns the situation both before and after the amendments made by a whole series of amendment regulations (SI 2012/2587; SI 2012/2588; and SI 2012/2612) the effect of which was, from November 8, 2012, to disqualify from a range of income-related benefits those with a right to reside arising under art.20 following the *Zambrano* case ("the 2012 amendments"). This group is described as *Zambrano* carers. They are, by definition, not citizens of the Union, but are third country nationals.

In a significant development of the case-law, the Court of Appeal ruled that *Zambrano* carers have a right to reside from the date on which the carer ceased to be liable to be removed from the United Kingdom (that is, on the birth of a child who is a citizen of the Union for whom care is provided, or upon becoming the primary carer of a citizen of the Union, in both cases where the citizen of the Union might have to leave the European Union if the carer might be obliged to leave) and not just from the later date on when measures are taken, or are imminent, to seek the removal of the carer from the United Kingdom.

In relation to the circumstances of the *Sanneh* case (the appeal against the decision in *SSWP v JS*), since Sanneh was a *Zambrano* carer in June 2011 when she claimed income support, she was entitled to that benefit since her circumstances predated the 2012 amendments.

The Court of Appeal decides that the rights of *Zambrano* carers are not the same as the rights of citizens of the Union, although the requirement that the EU national's citizenship is effective under EU law requires Member States to provide basic support. Such support was wholly a matter for national law, and assistance provided under s.17 of the Children Act 1989 might well suffice.

The Court of Appeal concluded that the exclusion of *Zambrano* carers by the 2012 amendments was not directly discriminatory. It was accepted that the amendments were indirectly discriminatory, but the Court ruled that the difference in treatment was justifiable both under EU law and under the European Convention on Human Rights. Finally, the Court concluded that in making the amending regulations, the Secretary of State had not failed to comply with the general public sector equality duty under s.149 of the Equality Act 2010.

The second and third questions referred by the Court of Appeal in *Secretary of State for the Home Department v NA* (C-115/15) [2015] OJ C171/20 are:

> "2. Does an EU citizen have an EU law right to reside in a host member state under Articles 20 and 21 of the TFEU in circumstances where the only state within the EU in which the citizen is entitled to reside is his state of nationality, but there is a finding of fact by a competent tribunal that the removal of the citizen from the host member state to his state of nationality would breach his rights under Article 8 of the ECHR or Article 7 of the Charter of Fundamental Rights of the EU?
>
> 3. If the EU citizen in (2) (above) is a child, does the parent having sole care of that child have a derived right of residence in the host member state if the child would have to accompany the parent on removal of the parent from the host member state?"

The Court of Justice issued its decision in *Secretary of State for the Home Department v NA* (C-115/15) on June 30, 2016. The Court ruled that the answer to the second and third questions raised by the Court of Appeal is:

> "81. In the light of the foregoing, the answer to the second and third questions is as follows:
>
> — Article 20 TFEU must be interpreted as meaning that it does not confer a right of residence in the host Member State either on a minor Union citizen, who has resided since birth in that Member State but is not a national of that State, or on a parent who is a third-country national and who has sole custody of that minor, where they qualify for a right of residence in that Member State under a provision of secondary EU law.
> — Article 21 TFEU must be interpreted as meaning that it confers on a minor Union citizen a right of residence in the host Member State, provided that that citizen satisfies the conditions set out in Article 7(1) of Directive 2004/38, which it is for the referring court to determine. If so,

> that same provision allows the parent who is the primary carer of that Union citizen to reside with that citizen in the host Member State."

H C Chavez-Vilchez and others (C-133/15), Judgment of May 10, 2017 concerned the rights of a child who is a citizen of the Union who has one parent who is a citizen of the Union and one parent who is a third-country national. All the circumstances of the child's situation must be considered and such assessment must have regard to the best interests of the child. Such an assessment can take account of the willingness of the parent who is a citizen of the Union to assume sole responsibility for the day-to-day care of the child. It is permissible to require the third-country national parent to provide evidence of the effects of a refusal to grant that parent a right of residence. But this does not absolve the Member State from itself making a full assessment of the situation in the light of all the specific circumstances.

Article 21
(ex Article 18 TEC)

3.61 1. Every citizen of the Union shall have the right to move and reside freely within the territory of the Member States, subject to the limitations and conditions laid down in the Treaties and by the measures adopted to give them effect.

2. If action by the Union should prove necessary to attain this objective and the Treaties have not provided the necessary powers, the European Parliament and the Council, acting in accordance with the ordinary legislative procedure, may adopt provisions with a view to facilitating the exercise of the rights referred to in paragraph 1.

3. For the same purposes as those referred to in paragraph 1 and if the Treaties have not provided the necessary powers, the Council, acting in accordance with a special legislative procedure, may adopt measures concerning social security or social protection. The Council shall act unanimously after consulting the European Parliament.

General Note

Infringement proceedings against the United Kingdom

3.62 The Commission has indicated that it has initiated proceedings before the Court of Justice arguing that the "right to reside" test as an additional condition to habitual residence constitutes unlawful discrimination under the European Union rules on the co-ordination of social security systems: see Press Release IP/13/475 of May 30, 2013. The right to reside test is closely linked to the free movement of persons. The case was lodged with the Court on June 27, 2014 and is *Commission v United Kingdom* (C-308/14).

In Case C-308/14, on October 6, 2015, Advocate General Cruz Villalón expressed the opinion that the challenged United Kingdom legislation did not breach European Union law. He said,

> "99. In conclusion, I consider that it does not constitute discrimination prohibited by Article 4 of Regulation 883/2004 if national legislation provides that, when examining claims for social benefits such as child benefit or child tax credit, the Member State's authorities may carry out the checks necessary to ensure that nationals of other Member States claiming those benefits are lawfully resident in its territory. However, for that purpose, the authorities responsible for carrying out those checks will, in any case, from a procedural point of view, have to observe the principles described above, in particular, the principle of proportionality, as well as the provisions of the second paragraph of Article 14(2), Article 15(1), and Article 30 and 31 of Directive 2004/38."

The Court, in its judgment of June 14, 2016, dismissed the Commission's action. The Commission's complaint related only to child benefit and child tax credit under the provisions of Regulation 883/2004. The Court accepted that these benefits were social security benefits within the scope of Regulation 883/2004 but essentially rejected the Commission's complaint that the right to reside test added a condition supplementary to that of habitual residence which was to be found in the Regulation. It was merely the United Kingdom's expression of it. It was accepted that the condition does give rise to unequal treatment because United Kingdom nationals can comply more readily than nationals of other Member States. However, the Court found that the difference in treatment could be justified by the legitimate objective of protecting the finances of the host Member State provided that it does not go beyond what is necessary to attain that objective: paras 78-84.

Preliminary note on the scope of these annotations

This commentary seeks to set out the content of European Union law as set out in art.21, in the context of secondary legislation and elaborated in decisions of the Court of Justice in Luxembourg, and the key authorities in the national legal order. It covers some of the case law in the national legal order on the "right to reside". But it does not purport to cover all the decisions of the Commissioners, and now, the Upper Tribunal on the "right to reside". For a useful overview of the European authorities and the United Kingdom legislation, see *SSWP v IA* [2009] UKUT 35 (AAC). Much more detail on the now numerous individual decisions in the national legal order on the right to reside can be found in the commentary to reg.21AA of the Income Support (General) Regulations 1987 in Vol.II of this work. **3.63**

Relevant secondary legislation

The most important secondary legislation is now the Citizenship Directive (Directive 2004/38, which is reproduced later in this volume at paras 3.202–3.294). This is both an immigration code for citizens of the Union, and a statement of the rights which migrants enjoy at various stages of their social or economic integration into the life of the host Member State. **3.64**

The line of cases discussed below has implications for the United Kingdom which has made entitlement to means-tested benefits conditional upon the claimant having: (a) a right to reside, and (b) being habitually resident, in the United Kingdom, the Channel islands, the Isle of Man or the Republic of Ireland (see, for example, reg.21AA Income Support General Regulations 1987). The "right to reside" is not defined in primary national legislation, but it is clear both from secondary legislation and from decisions of courts and tribunals that such a right may flow from European Union law.

Considerable substance is given to the citizenship approach to the right to move and reside in a Member State other than that of a person's own nationality in the Citizenship Directive. Though the drafting of that Directive may be criticized, (and there is evidence that it has been implemented in an incomplete manner in *all* Member States), it constitutes both an immigration code for nationals of the Member States, and gives citizens substantive rights according to the length of their residence. It marks a significant de-coupling of entitlements from economic activity, rather attaching them to the status of citizen of the Union than to migrant workers and other economically active persons. Decisions of the Luxembourg Court on the interpretation of the Directive are dealt with in the commentary to the relevant provision of the Directive.

In addition, certain provisions of Reg.1612/68 and its successor, Reg.492/2011 (reproduced later in this volume at paras 3.173–3.191) will assist those who are, or have been, workers. Some of the principles originally limited to workers may now also be available for those who are, or have been, self-employed, since the rights of those who are or have been economically active are increasingly being read as identical. **3.65**

Finally, in some cases the co-ordinating rules now to be found in reg.883/2004 (reproduced later in this volume at paras 3.269–3.446) may assist citizens of the Union who are not United Kingdom nationals in securing access to benefits here.

The underlying philosophy of the Luxembourg Court

3.66 The Luxembourg Court has repeated the following statement about the impact of citizenship of the Union sufficiently frequently that it can be regarded as an underlying principle in dealing with questions arising as a result of the holding of the status:

> "[Citizenship of the Union is] destined to be the fundamental status of nationals of the Member States, enabling those who find themselves in the same situation to receive the same treatment in law irrespective of their nationality, subject to such exceptions as are expressly provided for."

This quote is from *Gottwald* (C-103/08) Judgment of October 1, 2009 [2009] E.C.R. I-9117, at [23]. See also, among many examples, *Bidar* (C-209/03) [2005] E.C.R. I-2119, at [31]; *Schempp* (C-403/03) [2005] E.C.R. 6421, at [15]; *Orfanopoulos and Oliveri* (C-482/01 and C-493/01) [2004] E.C.R. I-5257, at [65]; *Garcia Avello* (C-148/02) [2003] E.C.R. 11613, at [22]; and *Grzelcyk* (C-184/99) [2001] E.C.R. I-6193, at [31].

See now also the important *Ruiz Zambrano* (C–34/09) Judgment of March 8, 2011, reported in the commentary to art.20 TFEU.

Rights flowing directly from art.21 TFEU

3.67 At first sight, art.21 TFEU (and its predecessor, art.18 EC) would appear to give no new rights; it simply refers to rights set out elsewhere in the Treaty. But the Luxembourg Court in *Baumbast and R* (C-413/99) [2002] E.C.R. I-7091 ruled that rights of residence may flow directly from what was then art.18 EC where there was a lacuna in the scheme of the treaties. The issue arose when the United Kingdom authorities refused to renew the residence permit of Baumbast, a German national resident here with his Colombian wife and the children of the family. Baumbast had been a worker in the United Kingdom but was at the material time working outside the European Union for a company established in Germany. The family was of independent means and had private health insurance in Germany, but no comprehensive sickness insurance in the United Kingdom (as required by the operative directive at the time, which was the predecessor to the Citizenship Directive). The Court ruled:

> "83. Moreover, the Treaty on European Union does not require that citizens of the Union pursue a professional or trade activity, whether as an employed or self-employed person, in order to enjoy the rights provided in Part Two of the EC Treaty, on citizenship of the Union. Furthermore, there is nothing in the text of that Treaty to permit the conclusion that citizens of the Union who have established themselves in another Member State in order to carry on an activity as an employed person there are deprived, where that activity comes to an end, of the rights which are conferred on them by the EC Treaty by virtue of that citizenship.
>
> 84. As regards, in particular, the right to reside within the territory of the Member States under Article 18(1) EC, that right is conferred directly on every citizen of the Union by a clear and precise provision of the EC Treaty. Purely as a national of a Member State, and consequently a citizen of the Union, Mr Baumbast therefore has the right to rely on Article 18(1) EC."

The Court noted the limitations to which art.18 EC referred, and noted the requirements which applied in relation to self-sufficiency and sickness insurance in the relevant Directive at the time, but ruled that such limitations had to be applied proportionately. It followed:

> "92. In respect of the application of the principle of proportionality to the facts of the Baumbast case, it must be recalled, first, that it has not been denied that Mr Baumbast has sufficient resources within the meaning of Directive 90/364; second, that he worked and therefore lawfully resided in the host Member State for several years, initially as an employed person and subsequently as a self-employed person; third, that during that period his family also resided in the host Member State and

remained there even after his activities as an employed and self-employed person in that State came to an end; fourth, that neither Mr Baumbast nor the members of his family have become burdens on the public finances of the host Member State and, fifth, that both Mr Baumbast and his family have comprehensive sickness insurance in another Member State of the Union.

93. Under those circumstances, to refuse to allow Mr Baumbast to exercise the right of residence which is conferred on him by Article 18(1) EC by virtue of the application of the provisions of Directive 90/364 on the ground that his sickness insurance does not cover the emergency treatment given in the host Member State would amount to a disproportionate interference with the exercise of that right."

This decision was re-inforced by the Court's judgment in *Zhu and Chen* (C-200/02) [2004] E.C.R. I-9925, which recognised the right under art.18 EC of a newborn baby with the nationality of the Republic of Ireland to reside in the United Kingdom. The consequence was that the parents of the child (who were Chinese nationals) also had a parasitic right to reside in order to make the baby's right of residence practical and effective.

The issue of proportionality has come to play an important part in the determination of cases both before the Luxembourg Court and before national tribunals and courts.

The limitations of the *Zhu and Chen* case are illustrated in *Alokpa, Moudoulou and Moudoulou v Ministre du Travail, de l'Emploi et de l'Immigration* (C-86/12) Judgment of October 10, 2013. Alokpa was a national of Togo living in Luxembourg, where her twin sons were born. The father was a French national and acknowledged his paternity on their birth. The twins were granted French nationality. The mother and the twins continued to live in Luxembourg with their mother. They had never moved to any other Member State. The Court of Justice observed that there were two grounds of distinction with the circumstances in the *Zhu and Chen* case. There, the child had been born in Ireland and so acquired Irish nationality. The family then moved back to the United Kingdom where they were self-sufficient. The Chinese parents acquired a derivative right through the child under art.21 TFEU and art.7(1)(b) of the Citizenship Directive. That was apparently not the case here, and so art.21 TFEU did not require the Luxembourg authorities to grant the mother a right to reside. Nor did art.20 TFEU assist the mother, since the consequence of Luxembourg refusing her a right to reside would not mean that the twins (who were citizens of the Union) would be required to leave the territory of the European Union altogether. The mother would have a derivate right to reside in France as sole carer of the twins since their birth.

Some basic propositions from the Luxembourg case-law

There is now a line of cases which suggests that entitlement to social benefits in a Member State may flow from the holding of citizenship of the Union coupled with lawful residence in a Member State. 3.68

In *Martínez Sala* (C-85/96) [1998] E.C.R. I-2691, Maria Martínez Sala, a Spanish national lawfully resident in Germany, found herself in need of financial support from the state. The Court of Justice ruled that the prohibition of discrimination on grounds of nationality applied in this case and that she was entitled to obtain social assistance on the same basis as German nationals. But a key point in the case was that the referring court had stated that the claimant's residence in Germany was lawful.

Grzelczyk (C-184/99) [2001] E.C.R. I-6193, concerned a French student undertaking higher education in Belgium. For the first three years of the course, he managed to maintain himself, but ran into financial difficulties in his fourth year of study and sought help from the State. The referring court did not regard Grzelczyk as a worker and so he could derive no help from the provisions applicable to workers. He appeared to be a student; the Directive on the free movement of students expressly provides that students are not entitled to maintenance grants from the

State as a matter of EU law entitlement, though this was without prejudice to their entitlement to social security on the same basis as nationals of the State of residence. Nevertheless the Court of Justice ruled that Grzelczyk was lawfully resident in Belgium as a student by reason of being a citizen of the Union and was entitled to receive the same support that would be afforded to a Belgian student in the same circumstances by reason of the operation of art.12 EC. The declaration made on entry to the Member State of residence was of an expectation, based on reasonable conclusions at the time, of an ability to be self-sufficient for the duration of the course.

3.69 *Trojani* (C-456/02) [2004] E.C.R. I-7573, takes this further. Trojani was a single man of French nationality. He clearly fell on hard times. He was living in a Salvation Army hostel in Belgium under an arrangement where he undertook various jobs for the hostel as part of a personal rehabilitation scheme, in exchange for which he received board and lodging and a small monetary allowance each week. He claimed the minimex (the minimum subsistence allowance in Belgium). His claim was refused on the grounds that he was not a Belgian national. Trojani brought proceedings before the Labour Court in Brussels to challenge this refusal. That Court referred questions to the Court of Justice. The Luxembourg Court advised that Trojani did not appear to be a worker by reason of the nature of his activities in the hostel where he lived. The second argument essentially concerned the possible entitlement of Trojani to the minimex as a person exercising his right to reside in Belgium as a citizen of the European Union. The Advocate General concluded that it was open to Belgium to deny Trojani a right of residence because he did not have the means to support himself. The Court was a little more circumspect. Referring to the ruling in the *Baumbast* case, the Court indicates that it would not be disproportionate to deny Trojani a right of residence on the basis that he did not have the means to be self sufficient. In other words, he had no *European Union* right to reside. But the Court went on to note that he may have a right to reside under *national law*, since he had been issued with a residence permit under national law by the municipal authorities in Brussels. The Court made three points (at [41]–[46] of its judgment):

(1) Social assistance falls within the scope of the EC Treaty.
(2) A citizen of the Union who is not economically active may rely on the prohibition of discrimination on grounds of nationality where he has been "lawfully resident" in the host Member State "for a certain time or possesses a residence permit" (para.43).
(3) Restricting entitlement to social assistance to the nationals of the host Member State constitutes discrimination on grounds of nationality contrary to art.12 EC.

It would follow that, if the national court concluded that Trojani was "lawfully resident" in Belgium under *national law*, then the prohibition of discrimination in EU law would be engaged, and the restriction of entitlement to the minimex to Belgian nationals in the circumstances of this case would breach the equality provisions of the EC Treaty.

In *Minister voor Immigratie, Integatie en Asiel v O and S* (456/12 and 457/12), Judgment of March 12, 2014, the Court ruled that art.21(1) TFEU must be interpreted as meaning that where a Union citizen has created or strengthened a family life with a third country national during genuine residence, pursuant to and in conformity with the conditions set out in art.7(1) and (2) and art.16(1) and (2) of the Citizenship Directive in a Member State other than that of which they are a national, the provisions of that directive apply by analogy where that Union citizen returns, with the family member in question, to their Member State of origin. It followed that the conditions for granting a derived right of residence to a third country national who is a family member of that Union citizen, in the latter's Member State of origin, should not, in principle, be more strict than those provided for by the Citizenship Directive for the grant of a derived right of residence to a third country national who is a family member of a Union citizen who has exercised their right of freedom of movement by becoming established in a Member State other than the Member State of which they are a national.

Residence requirements as conditions of entitlement

Residence requirements as conditions of entitlement to social assistance are not prohibited, but they must be proportionate in their application to any particular claimant. 3.70

Collins (C-138/02) [2004] E.C.R. I-2703, concerned a man who came to the United Kingdom to look for work. He held the nationality of the United States and Ireland. Though he had worked in the United Kingdom many years before, the time gap meant that he could not be considered to be a worker at the time of his claim. He was subject to the requirement, under national law, that he show habitual residence in the United Kingdom before he could become entitled to income-based jobseeker's allowance. The Court of Justice recognised that it was legitimate to impose a requirement that the person seeking the benefit had established a genuine link with the employment market of the State in which he was seeking an unemployment benefit. Furthermore, a residence-based test was not, of itself, inappropriate provided that its scope and application were clear and proportionate to establish the necessary link. See the commentary on art.7 of reg.492/2011, formerly reg.1612/68 below for a discussion of the decision of the Commissioner following the ruling of the Court of Justice, and the appeal against that decision in *Collins v SSWP*, reported as *R(JSA) 3/06*.

The dramatic impact of the citizenship provisions is also illustrated by the judgment of the Court of Justice in *Bidar* (C-209/03) [2005] E.C.R. I-2119. This case concerned a claim for a student loan by a French national who had come to the United Kingdom some years earlier and had completed his secondary education here. The Court of Justice recalled what it described as "settled case-law" (at [32]) that a citizen of the European Union lawfully resident in the territory of the host Member State can rely on art.12 EC (now art.18 TFEU) in all situations which fall within the material scope of the EC Treaty. Prior to this case, the award of financial support to students for their living expenses, whether in the form of grants or loans, had been considered to be outside the material scope of the EC Treaty. But the Court says that developments in EU law, especially the introduction of citizenship of the Union called for a change in that position. Such matters are now to be treated as within the scope of the EC Treaty for all the reasons set out in the judgment. The Court of Justice went on to rule that the application of the prohibition of discrimination meant that a person lawfully resident in the host Member State who has received a substantial part of his secondary education in that Member State and so has established a genuine link with the society of that State must be treated in the same manner as a national of that state. See also *Jacqueline Förster v Hoofdirectie van de Informatie Beheer Groep* (C-158/07) [2008] E.C.R. I-8507, which upholds the limitation in the Citizenship Directive disentitling citizens of the Union in a Member State other than that of their nationality to financial support for their studies until they have acquired permanent residence.

There must be a clear justification for any residence clause. *Turpeinen* (C-520/04) [2006] E.C.R. I-10685, ruled that art.18 EC outlaws national legislation under which the income tax charged on a retirement pension paid by an institution of the Member State concerned to a person in another Member State exceeds the tax charged on a pension payable to a resident of the Member State concerned, where that pension constitutes all or nearly all of the person's income. Similarly, *Nerkowska* (C-499/06) [2008] E.C.R. I-3993, decides that art.18 EC must be interpreted as precluding legislation of a Member State under which it refuses, generally and in all circumstances, to pay to its nationals a benefit granted to civilian victims of war or repression solely because they are not resident in the territory of that Member State throughout the period of payment of the benefit, but in the territory of another Member State. 3.71

But in *De Cuyper* (C-406/04) [2006] E.C.R. I-6947, the Court of Justice ruled that freedom of movement and residence, conferred on citizens of the Union under art.18 EC, does not preclude a residence clause, which is imposed on an unemployed person over 50 years of age who is exempt from the requirement to establish that he was available for work, as a condition for the retention of his entitlement to unemployment benefit. De Cuyper, a Belgian national, was born in 1942. He was no longer required to "submit to the local control procedures" in connection with his entitlement to unemployment benefit because he was over 50 years of age. Following a routine check, it was established that he spent considerable periods each year living in France. He was subsequently refused unemployment benefit. The Court of Justice concluded that the benefit in question was an unemployment benefit (as distinct from a pre-retirement benefit) and that, although the restriction on his right of movement if he was to remain entitled to unemployment benefit was a restriction on his right to free movement, the requirement for residence was objectively justifiable having regard to the need to monitor the employment and family situation of unemployed persons. There was no less restrictive measure capable of meeting the monitoring requirement.

In *D'Hoop* (C-224/98) [2002] E.C.R. I-6191, the court ruled that limiting access to a benefit for unemployed graduates to those who had undertaken their secondary education in Belgium had the potential to discriminate unlawfully against those who had exercised their rights of free movement. D'Hoop had undertaken her secondary education in France. She was penalised retrospectively for the past exercise of her rights of free movement under art.18 EC. Unless objective justification could be shown for the particular residence rule, it would breach art.18 EC when read with art.12 EC.

National authorities

3.72 Courts and tribunals in England and Wales have taken a narrow view of the right to reside flowing from art.18 EC, and the Citizenship Directive.

So in *Ali v Secretary of State for the Home Department* [2006] EWCA Civ 484, the Court of Appeal ruled that the right to reside under art.18 EC was not an unfettered right, that a parent could not claim a derivative right to reside by reason of a five-year-old child of that person being in primary education in the United Kingdom, and that a spouse (a Dutch national residing in the United Kingdom) who has not worked in the United Kingdom was not a worker under EU law.

CIS/3573/2005, decided by a Tribunal of Commissioners, concerned a Swedish national born in Somalia who had come to live in the United Kingdom. She had not worked in the United Kingdom, and claimed income support. The Tribunal of Commissioners said:

> "31. Both the Treaty of Rome, as amended, and EEC Directive 90/364 make it entirely clear that national governments are entitled to restrict the right to residence of European Union nationals and to restrict any social assistance to them, even if they are, in fact, resident under a lawful right of entrance and no steps have been taken for their removal. Mr Knafler submitted that the reality of the situation is that no steps will ever be taken to remove the claimant as, even if she were removed, she would have an immediate right of re-entry. However, in our view having a right of re-entry is somewhat different to fulfilling conditions for social assistance."

3.73 A series of cases decided by a Tribunal of Commissioners (*CIS/3573/2005*; *CPC/2920/2005*; *CIS/2559/2005*; *CIS/2680/2005*; *and CH/2484/2005*) has determined that non-economically active nationals of the Member States (and of the EEA countries) do not acquire a right to reside under EU law and any discrimination which arises as a consequence of such nationals being required to establish a right to reside is objectively justified and proportionate.

A memorandum (Memo DMG Vol.2 01/06) from the Department for Work and Pensions indicates that the changes consequent upon the entry into force of Directive 2004/38/EC (the "Citizenship Directive") do not alter the position. That proposition is looking increasingly questionable in the light of recent rulings of the Luxembourg Court, since it is based on the (unspoken) premise that the Citizenship Directive is purely a consolidating measure, when it is at least arguable that it develops the rights attached to Citizenship of the Union; it certainly introduces a new EU right of permanent residence.

The decisions of the Tribunal of Commissioners have been largely upheld by the Court of Appeal in *Abdirahman v SSWP, Abdirahman v Leicester CC and SSWP*, and *Ullusow v SSWP* [2007] EWCA Civ 657, reported as *R(IS) 8/07*. On the European points raised in argument, the Court of Appeal concluded that the rights claimed by the claimants were not within the scope of application of the EC Treaty, and so the prohibition of discrimination in art.12 EC did not apply. They further held that the claimants had no "right to reside" under national law, and so side-stepped the possible consequences of the decision of the Court of Justice in *Trojani*, which had ruled that equal treatment was required where a person had a right to reside in the country under national law (in that case, Trojani held a national residence permit—sof course, there is no direct equivalent under United Kingdom law). Of particular significance is that the Court of Appeal considered that the relevant Directive was Directive 90/364/EEC, which has been repealed by the Citizenship Directive. The Court of Appeal also ruled that the requirement that a claimant has the "right to reside" as a precondition to entitlement to benefit was not incompatible with European Union Law.

In *Zalewska v Department of Social Development*, Judgment of Northern Ireland 3.74
Court of Appeal of May 9, 2007, the Northern Ireland Court of Appeal has dismissed an appeal from the decision of the Commissioner in C 6/05-06, in essence, to similar effect, though this case concerned the rights of nationals from some of the new Member States which joined in May 2004. The Court concluded that the Acts of Accession by which the new Member States joined the European Union permitted Member States to derogate from the EU provisions in art.39 EC. During the transitional period, the rights of nationals of the designated new Member States arose solely under national law. The steps taken by the United Kingdom were reasonable and proportionate under the permitted derogations and so did not go beyond what was permitted. The House of Lords has upheld this decision in *Zalewska v Department for Social Development* [2008] UKHL 67, reported as *R1/09 (IS)*. In a 3-2 decision, the House of Lords decided that the United Kingdom regulations establishing the regime for A8 nationals (requiring them to register their work and to have an uninterrupted period of 12 months in employment before becoming assimilated with workers under art.39 EC) were not inconsistent with obligations arising under the EC Treaty. The difference of opinion related to the issue of proportionality. Baroness Hale and Lord Neuberger considered that the scheme adopted was disproportionate in that the complete disenfranchisement from the protection of social security went beyond the scope of the permissible derogation in the Treaty of Accession.

For an example of a case where the Secretary of State conceded that it would be disproportionate to refuse a person a right to reside, see *JK v SSWP (PC)* [2017] UKUT 179 (AAC).

RM v SSWP [2010] UKUT 238 (AAC) considers the claim of a Polish national to a right of residence flowing from art.21 (formerly art.18 EC). The claimant is a young woman who had spent the best part of 10 years in the United Kingdom, initially as a child when her father came to the United Kingdom, but latterly in her own right. She had undertaken some short-term work, but had then become pregnant and had to cease work. Her claim was that she had a right of residence under the *Baumbast* principles since there was a lacuna in the scheme in the Treaty and it would be unfair or disproportionate to refuse to recognise her right of residence in the United Kingdom. The judge reminds us that there is a difference between a lacuna in the scheme of the Treaty (and its implementing legislation), and a deliberate omission. In this case it could not be said that there was an accidental omission—and this was all the clearer since the claimant was an A8 national. But the judge does refer to the unsatisfactory position under which a claimant who is a national of the one of the Member States cannot establish their immigration status in the United Kingdom. He says that there "is a clear need for the benefit authorities to be able to refer arguable cases to the immigration authorities for a decision that will be effective from the date from which benefit was claimed . . ." (para.15).

The claimant took the case on appeal to the Court of Appeal, which upheld the decision of the Upper Tribunal: [2012] EWCA Civ 1952. The appeal then proceeded to the Supreme Court where it was joined with the appeal of *Samin* [2012] EWCA Civ 1468. In *Mirga v SSWP; Samin v Westminster CC* [2016] UKSC 1; [2016] AACR 26, the Supreme Court, after considering the latest authorities from the Court of Justice, concluded that Mirga did not have a right to reside since she could not establish that she was a worker (she had not worked as an accession State worker for more than a year). Unsurprisingly, in the light of the authorities, the Supreme Court saw nothing wrong with the requirements of the national provisions in relation to the claimant's rights under the Treaties; nor was it disproportionate to refuse her social assistance in the circumstances she presented. The category of circumstances where proportionality would come into play was exceptional.

In *SSWP v PS-B (IS)* [2016] UKUT 511 (AAC), Judge Jacobs considers the *Mirga* judgment, emphasising the exceptional nature of circumstances which would justify a conclusion that it would be disproportionate not to regard a person as not having a right to reside in the United Kingdom for the purpose of claiming income-related benefits. See also *SSWP v AC (UC)* [2017] UKUT 130 (AAC).

In *CIS/3875/2005* the Commissioner found that a French national could not claim a right to reside under EU law based on his being a recipient of services. It may be significant that the Commissioner did not consider the controversial *Carpenter* case *Carpenter v Secretary of State for the Home Department* (C-60/00) [2002] E.C.R. I-6279). See also *CIS/3182/2005* which concerned a Dutch national who had also worked for about six weeks before giving up work because she was pregnant. The Commissioner concluded that she had no right to reside under the United Kingdom regulations.

3.75 In *SS v Slough BC (HB)* [2011] UKUT 128 (AAC), the Upper Tribunal judge has reconsidered the opinions he had expressed in *CH/3314/2005* on the application of the requirement that work be genuine and effective to the exclusion of work that is purely marginal and ancillary. The decision contains a detailed review of the authorities, noting that ultimately the test has to be applied by national courts. The Upper Tribunal judge notes that "what is regarded as marginal where a right of residence is in issue may not necessarily be the same as what is marginal in equal treatment and employment rights cases." (At [20]). The judge goes on to say:

> "26. I therefore prefer the approach . . . of simply considering what is proportionate. It is fair and gives effect to one of the overarching principles of Community law. Moreover, proportionality is an approach that enables all possibly relevant matters to be taken into consideration. . .".

CH/1400/2006 concerned a woman who was a Slovenian national. She had entered the United Kingdom with her three children in September 2003. She began a postgraduate course in contemporary cinema culture in September 2004. In July 2005 she applied for housing benefit, and had appealed against its refusal. The tribunal had held that she had a right to reside under EU law as a person receiving services, namely the education on the course on which she was enrolled at the time of her claim. The Commissioner allowed the local authority's appeal on the grounds that the claimant was a person from abroad. In coming to that conclusion, he relied on *Humbel* (C-263/86) [1988] E.C.R. 5365, and *Wirth* (C-109/92) [1993] E.C.R. I-6447 in concluding that the provision of education was not the provision of services. It is certainly possible to read paras 18 and 19 of the Luxembourg Court's ruling in *Wirth* as *not applying* to the provision of a course in a University where a student is paying (as in this case) full cost fees because she has the status of an overseas student (some of the circumstances appear to have related to a period prior to accession to the Union by Slovenia). The Commissioner went on to consider whether the claimant had a right to reside as a student under the terms of the Students Directive (Directive 93/96/EEC) but concluded that this Directive required a student to have "sufficient resources to avoid becoming a burden on the social assistance system of the host Member State". However, in coming to that conclusion the Commissioner does not refer to Case *Grzelczyk (*C-184/99) where the Court accepted that, in the case of students, what was required was an assurance of sufficient resources, which may be frustrated by the passage of time, and which does not preclude access to national assistance. The Commissioner also rejected a final argument based on reg.1408/71. It seems that no argument was presented based upon *Trojani* (C-456/02) on the grounds that the claimant was lawfully resident in the United Kingdom, and on these grounds alone was entitled to equal treatment. The Court of Appeal has upheld the Commissioner's decision in *CIS/2358/2006* in *Kaczmarek v SSWP* [2008] EWCA Civ 1310; *R(IS) 5/09;* this was a case concerning a Polish student who had worked in the United Kingdom but had ceased work following the birth of a daughter. Two key issues arose for the Court of Appeal. Having regard to art.12, does the reference to lawful residence "for a certain time" in the *Trojani* case give rise to an eligibility based on residence of unspecified but significant duration and of a type which evidences a degree of social integration in the host Member State? Maurice Kay L.J., giving the judgment of the Court, ruled that it did not, stating that "eligibility is primarily and more appropriately a matter for normative regulation . . . ." (at [16]). It is suggested that this may not be the view taken by the Luxembourg Court were the matter to be raised before them. Although there is much debate about the significance of the Luxembourg Court's decision in the *Trojani* case, it can certainly be read as indicating that lawful residence for a certain, and unspecified, time which evidences a degree of social integration does give rise to the right to be treated equally with nationals. It is also true that the old system of residence permits (abandoned in Directive 2004/38/EC) did not require lawful presence for a significant period in order to obtain it. It was obtainable through employment which might then come to an end through no fault of the permit holder after very short duration without prejudice to the rights of the permit holder under the residence permit. The permit was always regarded as merely being evidence of rights arising under the EC Treaty and not as conferring those rights.

The second question was whether, under art.18 EC, it was disproportionate to deny a right of residence to a person in the position of the appellant. Having regard to what might be regarded as corresponding provisions in Directive 2004/38/ EC, Maurice Kay L.J. concluded that he was not dealing with a lacuna in the scheme in the EC Treaty. It was accordingly not disproportionate to deny the appellant a right to reside.

In *CIS/408/2006*, the Commissioner said that, in his view, Directive 2004/38/ **3.76**
EC "sets a standard by reference to which proportionality must be judged for the purpose of art.18(1) in a case arising before the directive came into force." (See [33]) This case is an important authority on when a burden on the public purse will be regarded as reasonable, though the decision may turn on its rather special facts (which involved the rights of a Cameroon national married to a French national). The Commissioner summarises the position as follows:

> "54. In my judgment, having regard to all these considerations, the claimant's wife's right of free movement for the purpose of working, guaranteed to her by Article 39 of the Treaty, would be infringed if she and the claimant were not recognised as having the right to reside in the United Kingdom in the circumstances of this case. There was a lacuna in the directives in force at the time of the claimant's claim for income support and there is now a lacuna in Directive 2004/38/ EC but I am satisfied that the claimant and his wife retained rights of residence by virtue of Article 18(1) of the Treaty. Where a worker exercising

rights under Article 39 of the Treaty in the United Kingdom is obliged to cease work and cannot be available for alternative work due to a need to care for his or her spouse who is a not a citizen of the Union but who is temporarily seriously disabled, they both retain rights of residence in the United Kingdom in the circumstances that arise in this case. Among those circumstances are the facts that—

(a) the disabled person had been exercising his Community law right to work in the United Kingdom and had become temporarily incapable of work;
(b) the disability had first manifested itself some considerable time after the disabled person had arrived in the United Kingdom, after he had married and after he had started work;
(c) the disabled person had qualified for free National Health Service treatment by virtue of his period of residence in the United Kingdom, which was at least in part by virtue of his right of residence under Community law, and was continuing to undergo such treatment while being cared for by his wife; the recognition of the claimant's right of residence under Community law when he married had led to him losing the opportunity of establishing a right of residence in his own right as a refugee.

Whether any of those circumstances is determinative can be decided when the need arises. (If point (a) is not determinative, it may follow that a person retains a right of residence while temporarily unable to be available for work due to the need to care for a dependant child, although, I would suggest, only where the child's need for care is temporary and is wholly due to the seriousness of the disability rather than the child's age.)"

In *CIS/4010/2006*, which concerned a French woman who had lived in the United Kingdom for just over a year and had become pregnant, the Commissioner noted:

"9. The claimant argues that it is enough that she had been living in the United Kingdom for just over a year. She refers to *CIS/3182/2005* and relies on Articles 12 and 18 of the EC Treaty. I do not agree that a year's residence is long enough. When considering Article 18, regard must be had to the standard set by Directive 2004/38/EC under which a right of permanent residence giving access to social assistance to people who are not economically active is not generally acquired until after five years' residence, although there are specified exceptions, and, in the light of *Abdirahman v. SSWP* [2007] EWCA Civ 657, it is clear that Article 12 cannot be relied upon independently."

However, the Commissioner makes no reference to art.24(2) of Directive 2004/38 which provides that "the host Member State shall not be obliged to confer entitlement to social assistance during the first three months of residence"; it remains to be seen what this provision means in the light of the other provisions of the Directive. That same provision also makes reference to entitlement to grant maintenance aid for studies only after a period of residence of five years. See *CIS/419/2007* which considered the position of a Polish student whose studies were in suspense, and who was found not to have a right of residence. For an example of a judgment exploring some of the issues raised in the line of cases referred to in these annotations, including issues of student status and entitlement to reside as the parent of a child born in the United Kingdom, see the decision of the Court of Appeal in *Jeleniewicz v SSWP* [2008] EWCA Civ 1163, reported as *R(IS) 3/09*, upholding the Commissioner's decision in *CIS/1545/2007*. The Court of Appeal concluded that the Commissioner was right to rule that a claimant, a Polish national, could not rely on a claimed right to reside by a young child (without any independent means of support) whose father (with whom the claimant was no longer living) was said to have a right to reside in the

United Kingdom as a student. The case before the Commissioner was characterised by a lack of clear evidence on a number of key issues. The Court of Appeal noted that the claimed right to reside was "doubly indirect in law".

In *CIS/185/2008,* the Commissioner relied on art.18 EC in finding that the claimant— a Portuguese national—had a right to reside. The claimant had come to the United Kingdom in January 1998; she appears to have worked almost continuously until the summer of 2002. She then took maternity leave until April 2003, when she chose not to return to work. She claimed she received income support until April 26, 2004. She then returned to work until March 2007, when she decided to give up work to spend more time with her children. Her claim for income support was refused on the grounds that she had no "right to reside". She held a residence permit valid from May 13, 2000 until May 13, 2005. Taking account of the effect of the residence permit, the Commissioner concluded that the claimant had become permanently resident under the national legislation implementing Directive 2004/38/EC. He went on to consider whether a right of permanent residence could have been acquired by reason of the claimant's having worked continuously for five years before her maternity leave had ended. The Commissioner accepted that a right of permanent residence under the Directive could *not* have been acquired prior to its entry into force (an issue covered by the reference to the Luxembourg Court made by the Court of Appeal in *SSWP v Lassal,* [2009] EWCA Civ 157), but, referring to his decisions in *CIS/2358/2006* and *CIS/408/2006,* concludes that the claimant had, in any event, acquired a right of residence under art.18 EC during the earlier period. He goes on to observe: 3.77

> "It does appear inconsistent with the concept of citizenship of the Union to deny a right of residence in a Member State to a person who has lived in that State for nine years and been a worker for eight of those years, including a continuous period of over five years. On the other hand, applying the approach I have taken in *CIS/2358/2006* and *CIS/408/2006*, the question would arise whether it could be said that there was a lacuna in the Directive, in which case a national court or tribunal could apply Article 18(1) of the EC Treaty, or whether the Directive had deliberately been given the effect it had despite it appearing to be inconsistent with the EC Treaty, in which case a national court or tribunal would be obliged to refer the case to the European Court of Justice. In view of the conclusions I have already reached in favour of the claimant, it is unnecessary for me to consider that question further". (See [22].)

In *W (China) and X (China) v Secretary of State for the Home Department* [2006] EWCA Civ 1494, rather surprisingly, distinguished the decision of the Court of Justice in the *Chen* case *Zhu and Chen* (C-200/02) [2004] E.C.R. I-9925) in which it had held that third country nationals who were the parents of a Union citizen—in this case a baby born in Northern Ireland who thereby became entitled to Irish citizenship—had a right to reside in a Member State since otherwise the entitled of the child to reside would be rendered nugatory. The Court of Appeal indicated disagreement with the decision in the *Chen* case on the grounds that certain matters were not argued. In approaching the case in the way it did, the Court of Appeal focused exclusively on the technical requirements of Directive 90/364, giving it a priority which the Court of Justice had not, and arguably failed to give sufficient weight to the growing case law on rights flowing from Union citizenship provided in the Treaty.

European Convention on Social and Medical Assistance ETS 14 of December 11, 1953

As a postscript to the commentary on the right to reside and art.21 TFEU, it should be noted that the Court of Appeal has also ruled that escape from the exclusion of persons from abroad (with its requirements for a right to reside and habitual residence) cannot arise under the European Convention on Social and Medical Assistance (ECSMA). In *Yesoloz v London Borough of Camden and SSWP,* [2009] EWCA Civ 415, Pill L.J., delivering the judgment of the Court, said: 3.78

"31. Whether the appellant has a right to reside in the United Kingdom depends on the construction of the appropriate statute or statutory instrument, in this case regulation 10 of the 2006 [Housing Benefit] Regulations. The appellant must establish that she has a right to reside. Otherwise she is a "person from abroad" and not entitled to housing benefit. Regulation 10(3B) specifies many categories of persons who are not "persons from abroad". It was, and was intended to be, a comprehensive list. The need, in this context, for a clear and specific classification is obvious.

32. The categories do not include nationals of states party to ECSMA. In those circumstances, such persons cannot be said to have a right to reside either because of their position in the schedule to the 2000 Regulations [SI 2000/636], or because the introduction of the concept of right to reside was primarily aimed at nationals of A8 states, or because there is no powerful reason in public policy for depriving them of the right to reside, or by reason of any combination of those factors. The inclusion of paragraph 4 in part 1 to the schedule to the 2000 Regulations, whatever its purpose, does not, in my view, carry for paragraph 4 persons the implication of entitlement to a right to reside."

PART THREE

UNION POLICIES AND INTERNAL ACTIONS

TITLE I

THE INTERNAL MARKET

Article 26
(ex Article 14 TEC)

3.79 1. The Union shall adopt measures with the aim of establishing or ensuring the functioning of the internal market, in accordance with the relevant provisions of the Treaties.

2. The internal market shall comprise an area without internal frontiers in which the free movement of goods, persons, services and capital is ensured in accordance with the provisions of the Treaties.

3. The Council, on a proposal from the Commission, shall determine the guidelines and conditions necessary to ensure balanced progress in all the sectors concerned.

TITLE IV

FREE MOVEMENT OF PERSONS, SERVICES AND CAPITAL

CHAPTER 1

WORKERS

Article 45
(ex Article 39 TEC)

3.80 1. Freedom of movement for workers shall be secured within the Union.

2. Such freedom of movement shall entail the abolition of any discrimination based on nationality between workers of the Member States as regards employment, remuneration and other conditions of work and employment.

3. It shall entail the right, subject to limitations justified on grounds of public policy, public security or public health:

(a) to accept offers of employment actually made;
(b) to move freely within the territory of Member States for this purpose;
(c) to stay in a Member State for the purpose of employment in accordance with the provisions governing the employment of nationals of that State laid down by law, regulation or administrative action;
(d) to remain in the territory of a Member State after having been employed in that State, subject to conditions which shall be embodied in regulations to be drawn up by the Commission.

4. The provisions of this Article shall not apply to employment in the public service.

General Note

Preliminary remarks

The activities of the Union include an internal market characterised by the abolition, as between Member States, of obstacles to the free movement of goods, persons, services and capital: art.26 TFEU. 3.81

Free movement of persons is generally regarded as encompassing workers, establishment, and services under arts 45-62 TFEU. Note that art.21 TFEU recognises the rights of free movement under these provisions as incidents of citizenship of the Union.

Beneficiaries of the provisions on free movement are nationals of the Member States.

So-called reverse discrimination is permitted under which a Member State treats its own nationals less favourably than the European standard where there is no factor linking the situation to one contemplated by the Treaty. But the rights deriving from European Union law can be pleaded against the State of which the person is a national if there is some connecting factor to the situations contemplated by European Union law: *Volker Steen* (C-332/90) and (C-132/93) [1992] E.C.R. I-341 and [1994] E.C.R. I-2715.

In many cases, reference will also need to be made to provisions of the Citizenship Directive, which is reproduced below at paras 3.140–3.205.

Directive 2014/54/EU of April 16, 2014 on measures facilitating the exercise of rights conferred in the context of freedom of movement for workers, [2014] OJ L128/1, has a deadline for implementation of May 21, 2016. It contains provisions on defence of rights, the promotion of equal treatment, a requirement for dialogue, and access to information.

Defining who are workers

The concept of "worker" in art.45 TFEU is wider than those actually in employment. All those who are beneficiaries of the rights set out in art.45 are accordingly to be regarded as workers. In *SSWP v RR (IS)* [2013] UKUT 21 (AAC), reported as [2013] AACR 20, a three-judge panel said: 3.82

> "35. Article [45 TFEU] contemplates a number of situations encompassing the whole of a person's working life, and beyond. It expressly provides for Union citizens (a) a right of free movement between the Member States for the purpose of accepting an offer of employment actually made, (b) a right to stay in a Member State for those who are actually in work, and (c) a right to remain when a period of actual work ends either on retirement or through accident or ill health. Both

the case-law of the Court of Justice and European secondary legislation elaborate the conditions for the exercise of the rights enshrined in Article 39 EC, but the secondary legislation cannot limit the rights set out in the Treaty itself."

On its terms, art.45 encompasses three distinct rights attaching to persons within the article's concept of workers:

(a) the right to move to and stay in another Member State for the purpose of accepting an offer of employment actually made: art.45(3)(a) and (b);
(b) the right to stay in another Member State as a person actually in work: art.45(3)(c); and
(c) the right to remain in another Member State when employment ends in accordance with conditions set out in secondary legislation: art.45(3)(d).

In *SSWP v RR (IS)* the three-judge panel found that a person who had entered the United Kingdom holding the offer of a job, but whose ability to take up that offer was frustrated for a period of five months initially by problems in finding accommodation suitable for working from home and later by serious ill health remained within the terms of what is now art.45(3)(a) and (b). It was significant that the First-tier tribunal had found that the job offer remained open at all material times. The circumstances of the claimant in this case should be distinguished from those of a person who comes to the United Kingdom to seek work. Such persons are work seekers, whose position is considered below.

In *SSWP v RO (JSA)* [2015] UKUT 533 (AAC), Judge West emphasised that *SSWP v RR (IS)* did not decide that jobseekers are workers within art.45; the effect of the decision did not go beyond establishing that persons falling squarely within the wording of art.45(a) and (b) constituted workers within the definition in art.45; that is, those holding an offer of employment who move for the purposes of accepting such an offer.

3.83 Where a person is in work, European Union law determines who constitutes a worker in this sense under art.45: *Hoekstra* (75/63)[1964] E.C.R. 177. There is both a formal test and a sufficiency test. It is logical to apply the formal test first. *Lawrie-Blum* (66/85) [1986] E.C.R. 2121 determines that persons are workers if: (1) they are obliged to provide services for another, (2) in return for reward (monetary of otherwise: *Steymann* (196/87) [1988] E.C.R. 6159), and (3) are subject to the direction and control of that other person.

Levin (53/81) [1982] E.C.R. 1035 established that, in order to be workers, persons must be in work which is effective and genuine and not on such a small scale as to be regarded as purely marginal and ancillary.

Those in low-paid, part-time work are workers, provided that their work is effective and genuine: *Kempff* (C-139/85) [1986] E.C.R. 1741 and *Raulin* (C-357/89) [1992] E.C.R. I-1027. For a consideration of this line of cases by a national court, see *Mohamed Barry v London Borough of Southwark* [2008] EWCA Civ 1440. But work whose objective is not primarily economic, as for example in an artificially constructed work situation designed to encourage those recovering from drug dependence to establish a regular pattern of activity, will not render those engaged in it workers: *Bettray* (344/87) [1989] E.C.R. 1621.

3.84 *Genc v Land Berlin* (C–14/09) [2010] E.C.R. I–931 is a case on the interpretation of the concept of a worker under art.6 of the Decision of the Association Council on the development of the EEC-Turkey Association. It is generally assumed that the term has the same meaning as in art.45 TFEU. Genc worked for 5.5 hours per week at an hourly rate of €7.87. The judgment accordingly has the potential to be of assistance in determining when a part-time worker is a worker under European Union law. The Luxembourg Court advised:

"26. Although the fact that a person works for only a very limited number of hours in the context of an employment relationship may be an indication that the activities performed are marginal and ancillary (Case C-357/89 *Raulin* [1992]

ECR I-1027, paragraph 14), the fact remains that, independently of the limited amount of the remuneration for and the number of hours of the activity in question, the possibility cannot be ruled out that, following an overall assessment of the employment relationship in question, that activity may be considered by the national authorities to be real and genuine, thereby allowing its holder to be granted the status of 'worker' within the meaning of Article 39 EC.

27. The overall assessment of Ms Genc's employment relationship makes it necessary to take into account factors relating not only to the number of working hours and the level of remuneration but also to the right to 28 days of paid leave, to the continued payment of wages in the event of sickness, and to a contract of employment which is subject to the relevant collective agreement, in conjunction with the fact that her contractual relationship with the same undertaking has lasted for almost four years.

28. Those factors are capable of constituting an indication that the professional activity in question is real and genuine."

This judgment is the subject of detailed consideration in *SS v Slough BC* [2011] UKUT 128 (AAC).

JA v SSWP (ESA) [2012] UKUT 122 (AAC), reported as [2013] AACR 15, considered whether an arrangement under which a person was paid cash in hand without deducting PAYE tax or national insurance contributions for work done would, of itself, prevent the person from being classified as a worker under the terms of art.45. The judge concludes that it would not even if such a contract was illegal (See [8]–[14] of the decision explore the issue of illegal employment contracts). In ruling that employment under an illegal contract does not, of itself preclude worker status under art.45, the judge had this to say:

"19. The Court has qualified its definition of worker. The services have to be economic, genuine and effective, not marginal and ancillary. Again, the focus is on the factual position, on the nature of the services, not on the legal relationship within which they are performed. In other words, the Court has defined worker as an economic status, not a legal one. It has legal consequences, but it is not necessarily legal in nature. That is consistent with giving a broad scope to a fundamental freedom of the Union. Most work takes place within a legal relationship of an employment contract. But it need not do so. To limit it to a particular category of contractual relationship would limit its scope. And that would be incompatible with the fundamental nature of the freedom of movement.

20. There is also this to consider. Worker is an EU concept. That means that it has an autonomous meaning in EU law; it does not depend on the law of the member State in which the activity is undertaken. This is essential if freedom of movement for workers is to be effective as an EU right. The judge in this case applied particular domestic rules of public policy on the enforceability of contracts. There may well be the same or similar rules in other member States. But there may also be differences of substance or detail; it would be surprising if there were not. To allow States to apply their own rules is contrary to the EU nature of the concept: *Hoekstra v Bestuur der Bedrijfsvereniging voor Dertailhandel en Ambachten* [1964] ECR 177."

A person who has been the victim of trafficking is not prevented from arguing that he or she is a worker on ordinary principles: *EG v SSWP (JSA)* [2016] UKUT 445 (AAC).

A person does not cease to be a worker for the purposes of art.45 simply by ceasing to be employed. So a German worker whose employment ended not long after it had started when she suffered a back injury did not, by that reason alone, cease to be a worker: *CIS/3890/2005*. A period of maternity leave does not interrupt self-employment: *CIS/1042/2008*, nor prevent a person from continuing to be treated as a worker: *CIS/0185/2008*. **3.85**

The same is true of a period of sick leave where the person's contract of employment nevertheless subsists: *BS v SSWP* [2009] UKUT 16 (AAC).

In *VW v SSWP (SPC)* [2014] UKUT 573 (AAC) Judge Ward ruled that a person who had undertaken work for three periods of two or four weeks many years before the date of the claim under appeal, and who received board and lodging, reimbursement and certain other expenses in exchange for his work, was not a worker within art.45 TFEU (see paras 21–50).

In *Ioannidis* (C-258/04) [2005] E.C.R. I-8275, the Luxembourg Court avoided ruling on the interpretation of arts 12, 17 and 18 EC, but did rule that it is contrary to art.39 EC and to art.7(2) of reg.1612/68 for a Member State to refuse to grant a tideover allowance to a national of another Member State seeking their first employment, who is not the dependent child of a migrant worker residing in the Member State granting the allowance, solely on the ground that the claimant completed their secondary education in another Member State. See also *D'Hoop* (C-224/98) [2002] E.C.R. I-6191.

The DWP guidance on whether an EEA national is a worker or self-employed person is set out in Memo DMG 21/14 of September 2014.

Work seekers

3.86 Work seekers enjoy a limited right of entry and residence as a matter of European Union Law: *Royer* (48/75) [1976] E.C.R. 497 and *Tsiotras* (C-171/91) [1993] E.C.R. I-2925. Even after an initial period seeking work, a Member State may not be able to deport a person who has not found work if they can show a genuine chance of finding work in the immediate future: *Antonissen* (C-292/89) [1991] E.C.R. I-745.

SSWP v MB and linked cases (JSA) [2016] UKUT 372 (AAC); [2017] AACR 6 establishes that the provisions in national legislation requiring certain jobseekers to show compelling evidence of a genuine prospect of gaining employment (the so-called "genuine prospect of work" test) cannot go beyond what is required by applying the tests laid down in the *Antonissen* case without risking being in breach of the requirements of European Union law. This is an important decision which calls into question the compatibility of some of the Departmental guidance on the operation of the genuine prospect of work test.

In *OS v SSWP (JSA)* [2017] UKUT 107 (AAC) Judge Ward concludes that post-decision job outcomes can provide evidence of a claimant's prospects of work, but also notes that post-decision failure to secure employment may also be taken into account. Section 12(8)(b) of the Social Security Act 1998 does not preclude inferences being drawn from events which occurred after the date of the decision under appeal in this context (para.6).

But work seekers may not, as a result of the application of European Union law, enjoy other social rights accorded to those who have found work: *Lebon* (316/85) [1987] E.C.R. 2811. Note that the citizenship line of cases discussed in the annotations to art.21 may require some reconsideration of the law as stated in *Lebon*. Those now in the position of Lebon who are lawfully resident in the host Member State and have the necessary link with the host Member State are entitled to be treated equally with nationals of that State even though they are not workers in the strict sense. Such persons will, however, after three months of residence, need to show that they have a right to reside under art.7 of Dir.2004/38/EC (the Citizenship Directive, which is reproduced below).

Exceptions and limitations

3.87 The rights are subject to exceptions and limitations.

Limitations may be imposed on grounds of public policy, public health and public security; the application of these limitations is spelled out in the Citizenship Directive. The public policy ground requires the presence of a genuine, present and sufficiently serious threat to the requirements of public policy affecting one of the fundamental interests of society: *Bouchereau* (30/77) [1977] E.C.R. 1999. The genuineness of the limitation is tested by looking at the regulation of the objectionable conduct within the Member State: *Adoui and Cornuaille* (115 & 116/81) [1982] E.C.R. 1665.

Article 45(4) TFEU excludes employment in the public service. A functional test has been adopted for identifying such employment: it must involve the exercise of powers conferred by public law, and responsibility for safeguarding the interests of either central and local government: *Commission v Belgium* (149/79) [1980] E.C.R. 3881 and [1982] E.C.R. 1845.

Artide 45(3)(d): the right to remain

Article 45(3)(d) gives former workers the right to remain after a period of work "subject to conditions which shall be embodied in regulations to be drawn up by the Commission." It is odd that this wording was not tidied up in amendments made by the Treaty of Lisbon. The right to remain was formerly governed by Commission Regulation 1251/70/EEC of June 29, 1970, [1970] OJ L142/24, but that regulation has been repealed by Commission Regulation 635/2006/EC of April 25, 2006 [2006] OJ L112/9, which entered into force on April 27, 2006. Regulation 635/2006 states that the right to remain is now governed by art.17 of Dir.2004/38 (the Citizenship Directive) and suggests that those exercising the right to remain have enhanced rights under the provisions of the Citizenship Directive on permanent residence. But analysis of the position under Commission Regulation 1251/70 and the Citizenship Directive reveals that the right to remain under the former regulation, once acquired, was retained without the possibility of its loss. The regulation made no provision for the loss of the right to remain. In contrast, art.17 of the Citizenship Directive does contain provisions governing the loss of the status of permanent residence. See also the commentary on art.17 of the Citizenship Directive at paras 3.265–3.267, below. **3.88**

Enlargement, free movement and access to social security benefits

Ten new states joined the European Union on May 1, 2004, two further states on January 1, 2007, and Croatia on January 1, 2013. There are detailed Treaties of Accession with these new Member States. In relation to the law of the internal market relating to workers, there are transitional periods over which the full application of the Treaty rules will be phased in. The Europe Agreements, which paved the way for membership, did not give a right of access to the labour markets of the Member States for nationals of the applicant countries. The result is that virtually all nationals from the new Member States who were, prior to May 1, 2004 or January 1, 2007, workers in the territories of the 15 existing Member States were there as a result of the application national immigration rules or of the provisions of bilateral agreements between the countries in question. Those lawfully resident in one of the Member States acquired rights under the Europe Agreements, and from the date of entry of the Member State into the European Union will acquire rights under the EC Treaty, now the TFEU. **3.89**

In the past, it has been common to have transitional periods for the implementation of certain provisions of the Treaty. These have been followed by, or coupled with, a period during which safeguard measures may be taken if there is serious or persistent disruption of the labour market as a result of the exercise of the free movement rights. In the case of the accession of Spain and Portugal, a transitional period of seven to 10 years for the free movement of workers was agreed, though the full operation of the Treaty provisions was achieved after six years.

The 2004 and 2007 enlargements were accompanied by a very high level of concern about the potential of labour migration to disturb the labour markets of some Member States. Such concerns have flowed from geographic proximity, (leading to a prediction that labour migration will be concentrated in the so-called "frontline" Member States) considerable variations in earnings levels, differential levels of unemployment, and a concern that there will be a greater propensity for labour migration than with earlier enlargements. It is important to realise that the transitional period covers only the right of movement for the purposes of employment. There has been an immediate right to move for the purposes of study or residence, or establishment. The arrangements for the 2004 and 2007 enlargements allow national rules to govern free movement of workers for a significant period. The transitional arrangements for the A8 countries came to an end on April 30, 2011. For Romania and Bulgaria, transitional arrangements continued until the end of 2013. For Croatia, the transitional arrangements will not come to an end until June, 30 2020.

The specific arrangements in relation to the United Kingdom are set out in Vol.II.

Article 48
(ex Article 42 TEC)

3.90 The European Parliament and the Council shall, acting in accordance with the ordinary legislative procedure, adopt such measures in the field of social security as are necessary to provide freedom of movement for workers; to this end, they shall make arrangements to secure for employed and selfemployed migrant workers and their dependants:

(a) aggregation, for the purpose of acquiring and retaining the right to benefit and of calculating the amount of benefit, of all periods taken into account under the laws of the several countries;
(b) payment of benefits to persons resident in the territories of Member States.

Where a member of the Council declares that a draft legislative act referred to in the first subparagraph would affect important aspects of its social security system, including its scope, cost or financial structure, or would affect the financial balance of that system, it may request that the matter be referred to the European Council. In that case, the ordinary legislative procedure shall be suspended. After discussion, the European Council shall, within four months of this suspension, either:

(a) refer the draft back to the Council, which shall terminate the suspension of the ordinary legislative procedure; or
(b) take no action or request the Commission to submit a new proposal; in that case, the act originally proposed shall be deemed not to have been adopted.

General Note

3.91 This article provides for the co-ordination of social security rules in the Member States in order to minimise a potential barrier to the free movement of workers. Co-ordination requires co-operation between the Member States to provide interchange between different national social security systems. The Luxembourg Court has frequently drawn attention to the distinction between harmonisation and co-ordination and noted that the substantive and procedural difference between the social security systems of the Member States remain unaffected by what is now art.48 and its secondary legislation: *Pinna* (41/84) [1986] E.C.R. 1, 24–5. But it has also been established that those exercising the right of freedom of movement should not lose advantages in the field of social security; this has come to be known as the *Petroni* principle: *Petroni* (24/75) [1975] E.C.R. 1149, at [13].

Three general principles emerge from the complex rules of co-ordination which can be found in Reg. 883/2004 and the case law:

Article 48

1. A national of a Member State is not to be disqualified from entitlement to benefits on the grounds of nationality or on a change of country or residence within the European Union.
2. A national of a Member State may become entitled to a benefit by having contributions or qualifying periods of employment or residence in one Member State aggregated with those arising in another Member State.
3. A national of a Member State should not be better off in relation to entitlement to benefits by reason of his or her exercise of rights to move freely between Member States.

There have been three regulations seeking to co-ordinate the social security systems of the Member States:

(1) Regulation 3 of September 25, 1958 ([1958] OJ L30/561), in force from January 1, 1959 to March 31, 1973.

(2) Regulation 1408/71 (consolidated version at [1997] OJ L28/4), in force from April 1, 1973 to April 30, 2010.

(3) Regulation 883/2004 ([2004] OJ L200/1) in force from May 1, 2010.

Regulation 883/2004 is reproduced at paras 3.295–3.500 below.

CHAPTER 2

RIGHT OF ESTABLISHMENT

Article 49
(ex Article 43 TEC)

Within the framework of the provisions set out below, restrictions on the freedom of establishment of nationals of a Member State in the territory of another Member State shall be prohibited. Such prohibition shall also apply to restrictions on the setting-up of agencies, branches or subsidiaries by nationals of any Member State established in the territory of any Member State. 3.92

Freedom of establishment shall include the right to take up and pursue activities as self-employed persons and to set up and manage undertakings, in particular companies or firms within the meaning of the second paragraph of Article 54, under the conditions laid down for its own nationals by the law of the country where such establishment is effected, subject to the provisions of the Chapter relating to capital.

GENERAL NOTE

The rights of persons who are self-employed are governed by this article. Just as European Union law defines which persons are workers, so too European Union law defines which persons constitute self-employed persons. In *Jany* (C-268/99) [2001] E.C.R. I-8615, the Luxembourg Court defined the following three characteristics as those of self-employment: 3.93

(1) There is no relationship of subordination concerning the choice of activity, working conditions and conditions of remuneration.

(2) The activity is engaged under the person's own responsibility.

(3) The remuneration is paid in full to the person so engaged directly.

Like employment, limitations may be applied by Member States on the grounds of public policy, public security or public health.

Activities which involve "the exercise of official authority" are excluded from the freedom under art.51(1) TFEU.

SSWP v HH (SPC) [2015] UKUT 583 (AAC) is an example of when self-employment will be regarded as not genuine and effective economic activity, but rather purely marginal and ancillary activity which does not qualify the claimant to be regarded as a self-employed person under art.49.

In *DV v SSWP* [2017] UKUT 155 (AAC), Judge Markus QC concluded that a First-tier Tribunal had addressed all the right questions in determining that a Romanian national, who claimed to be self-employed selling *The Big Issue*, did not qualify as a self-employed person under art.49. This was essentially because the economic activity did not constitute effective and genuine work to the exclusion of work that was marginal or ancillary.

Chapter 3

Services

Article 56
(ex Article 49 TEC)

3.94 Within the framework of the provisions set out below, restrictions on freedom to provide services within the Union shall be prohibited in respect of nationals of Member States who are established in a Member State other than that of the person for whom the services are intended.

The European Parliament and the Council, acting in accordance with the ordinary legislative procedure, may extend the provisions of the Chapter to nationals of a third country who provide services and who are established within the Union.

General note

3.95 Art.56 provides for the free movement of services. It is supplemented, in particular, by the provisions of Directive 2006/123/EC of the European Parliament and Council of December 12, 2006 on services in the internal market, [2006] OJ L376/36 ("the Services Directive"), whose date for implementation was December 28, 2009.

NB v HMRC (TC) [2016] NICom 47 is an instructive decision of a Tribunal of Commissioners in Northern Ireland in relation to the right to the child care element of tax credits where the child care provider was situated outside the United Kingdom—in this case in the Republic of Ireland. In particular, the United Kingdom government could not set discriminatory limits on the grant of financial assistance for child care services by reason of the fact that the service provider was established in another Member State.

Section 5

The Court of Justice of the European Union

Article 258
(ex Article 226 TEC)

If the Commission considers that a Member State has failed to fulfil an obligation under the Treaties, it shall deliver a reasoned opinion on the matter after giving the State concerned the opportunity to submit its observations. 3.96

If the State concerned does not comply with the opinion within the period laid down by the Commission, the latter may bring the matter before the Court of Justice of the European Union.

Article 259
(ex Article 227 TEC)

A Member State which considers that another Member State has failed to fulfil an obligation under the Treaties may bring the matter before the Court of Justice of the European Union. 3.97

Before a Member State brings an action against another Member State for an alleged infringement of an obligation under the Treaties, it shall bring the matter before the Commission.

The Commission shall deliver a reasoned opinion after each of the States concerned has been given the opportunity to submit its own case and its observations on the other party's case both orally and in writing.

If the Commission has not delivered an opinion within three months of the date on which the matter was brought before it, the absence of such opinion shall not prevent the matter from being brought before the Court.

Article 260
(ex Article 228 TEC)

1. If the Court of Justice of the European Union finds that a Member State has failed to fulfil an obligation under the Treaties, the State shall be required to take the necessary measures to comply with the judgment of the Court. 3.98

2. If the Commission considers that the Member State concerned has not taken the necessary measures to comply with the judgment of the Court, it may bring the case before the Court after giving that State the opportunity to submit its observations. It shall specify the amount of the lump sum or penalty payment to be paid by the Member State concerned which it considers appropriate in the circumstances.

If the Court finds that the Member State concerned has not complied with its judgment it may impose a lump sum or penalty payment on it.

This procedure shall be without prejudice to Article 259.

3. When the Commission brings a case before the Court pursuant to Article 258 on the grounds that the Member State concerned has failed to fulfil its obligation to notify measures transposing a directive adopted

under a legislative procedure, it may, when it deems appropriate, specify the amount of the lump sum or penalty payment to be paid by the Member State concerned which it considers appropriate in the circumstances.

If the Court finds that there is an infringement it may impose a lump sum or penalty payment on the Member State concerned not exceeding the amount specified by the Commission. The payment obligation shall take effect on the date set by the Court in its judgment.

Article 261
(ex Article 229 TEC)

3.99 Regulations adopted jointly by the European Parliament and the Council, and by the Council, pursuant to the provisions of the Treaties, may give the Court of Justice of the European Union unlimited jurisdiction with regard to the penalties provided for in such regulations.

Article 263
(ex Article 230 TEC)

3.100 The Court of Justice of the European Union shall review the legality of legislative acts, of acts of the Council, of the Commission and of the European Central Bank, other than recommendations and opinions, and of acts of the European Parliament and of the European Council intended to produce legal effects *vis-à-vis* third parties. It shall also review the legality of acts of bodies, offices or agencies of the Union intended to produce legal effects *vis-à-vis* third parties.

It shall for this purpose have jurisdiction in actions brought by a Member State, the European Parliament, the Council or the Commission on grounds of lack of competence, infringement of an essential procedural requirement, infringement of the Treaties or of any rule of law relating to their application, or misuse of powers.

The Court shall have jurisdiction under the same conditions in actions brought by the Court of Auditors, by the European Central Bank and by the Committee of the Regions for the purpose of protecting their prerogatives.

Any natural or legal person may, under the conditions laid down in the first and second paragraphs, institute proceedings against an act addressed to that person or which is of direct and individual concern to them, and against a regulatory act which is of direct concern to them and does not entail implementing measures.

Acts setting up bodies, offices and agencies of the Union may lay down specific conditions and arrangements concerning actions brought by natural or legal persons against acts of these bodies, offices or agencies intended to produce legal effects in relation to them.

The proceedings provided for in this Article shall be instituted within two months of the publication of the measure, or of its notification to the plaintiff, or, in the absence thereof, of the day on which it came to the knowledge of the latter, as the case may be.

Article 264
(ex Article 231 TEC)

If the action is well founded, the Court of Justice of the European Union shall declare the act concerned to be void. **3.101**

However, the Court shall, if it considers this necessary, state which of the effects of the act which it has declared void shall be considered as definitive.

Article 267
(ex Article 234 TEC)

The Court of Justice of the European Union shall have jurisdiction to give preliminary rulings concerning: **3.102**

(a) the interpretation of the Treaties;

(b) the validity and interpretation of acts of the institutions, bodies, offices or agencies of the Union;

Where such a question is raised before any court or tribunal of a Member State, that court or tribunal may, if it considers that a decision on the question is necessary to enable it to give judgment, request the Court to give a ruling thereon.

Where any such question is raised in a case pending before a court or tribunal of a Member State against whose decisions there is no judicial remedy under national law, that court or tribunal shall bring the matter before the Court.

If such a question is raised in a case pending before a court or tribunal of a Member State with regard to a person in custody, the Court of Justice of the European Union shall act with the minimum of delay.

General Note

Any national court or tribunal can refer questions on the interpretation of the Treaties, and on the validity and interpretation of Union legislation to the Court of Justice under this article. The objective of the procedure is a partnership between national courts and tribunals and the Luxembourg Court to ensure the uniform application in all Member States of European Union law. **3.103**

Courts other than final appeal courts have a *discretion* to make a reference, whereas final appeal courts have a *duty* to refer questions for consideration by the Luxembourg Court where answers to those questions are necessary to enable the national court to deter mine the question before it.

The effect of a court or tribunal seeking a ruling is that the national proceedings stand adjourned pending the receipt of the ruling of the Luxembourg Court. The case is then relisted for determination before the national court or tribunal in the light of the ruling of the Luxembourg Court on the point of European Union law. The Luxembourg Court is careful not to determine the point arising under national law.

It is an error of law for a tribunal to fail to address a point of European Union law raised in the course of an appeal: *R(SB)6/91*, at para.5, and *R(S)2/93*.

Care should be taken whenever a tribunal is called upon to decide an issue involving a national of an EEA country. If a case involves a national of an EEA country, inquiry should be made to determine whether the provisions of European Union law apply to that person and assist in qualifying them for benefit. Failure to do so is an error of law: *CIS/771/1997*.

The Luxembourg Court of Justice has stressed in *Rheinmühlen* (166/73) [1974]

E.C.R. 33, 38, that the objective of the preliminary ruling procedure is a partnership between national courts and tribunals and the Luxembourg Court with a view to ensuring the uniform application of European Union law in all the Member States.

3.104 Under the procedure, the Luxembourg Court advises on the meaning of European Union law put to it by a national court or tribunal. The discretion as to whether a reference is made is a wide one, and may be exercised by the court or tribunal of its own notion or on application for the court or tribunal to consider doing so by the parties. The leading case of the Luxembourg Court on the exercise of the discretion to refer is *Irish Creamery Milk Suppliers Association v Ireland* (36 and 71/80) [1981] E.C.R. 735. The principles laid down in this case have been approved in *Campus Oil v Minister for Industry and Energy* (72/83) [1984] E.C.R. 2727; and *Pretore di Salo v Persons Unknown* (14/86) [1987] E.C.R. 2545. The following points emerge from this line of cases:

1. It is for the national court or tribunal to decide at what stage of proceedings it is appropriate for a preliminary ruling to be requested.
2. In order to assist the Luxembourg Court of Justice, it is essential for the national court or tribunal to define the legal context in which the reference is made.
3. This suggests that in some cases it might well be appropriate for the facts in the case to be established and for questions of purely national law to be settled at the time of the reference.
4. Attempts to fetter or limit the discretion of the national court or tribunal are inconsistent with European Union law.
5. The discretion to refer is that of the national court or tribunal and not that of the parties.

Practice in English courts and tribunals has been influenced by the guide lines expressed by Lord Denning in *Bulmer v Bollinger (No.2)* [1974] Ch 401, but these are not binding on any court or tribunal and aspects of them are inconsistent with statements of the Luxembourg Court. Distilling a considerable body of case law and adding points specific to the social security jurisdictions, the following factors are relevant in the determination by a First-tier Tribunal or the Upper Tribunal of the exercise of the discretion to refer questions to the Luxembourg Court, namely whether:

1. a serious point of Union law arises in the case which has been fully argued by the parties;
2. the relevant facts have been found or are substantially agreed;
3. the point of law will be substantially determinative of the case;
4. there is any European Union authority precisely or closely in point;
5. there is any national authority addressing the point of European Union law; and
6. it seems certain that at some stage in the life of the case, it will have to be referred to the Luxembourg Court.

The expense and delay caused by an inappropriate reference will be issues every adjudicating body will consider. The factors set out above are consistent with European Union law on the exercise of the discretion to refer. The absence of full argument on the European Union law point—from both the claimant and the Secretary of State—(and full argument is likely to be rare in First-tier Tribunals) suggests that caution should be the order of the day before the First-tier Tribunals. On the other hand, tribunals should not be inhibited from making a reference if the relevant facts have been found, if the point has been fully argued, if the tribunal concludes that the appeal turns on the proper interpretation of a point of European Union law, if there is no relevant authority which suggests that the question of interpretation is free from doubt, and if it seems certain that at some stage a reference will need to be made to resolve the question. It is probably fair to say that such circumstances will not be commonplace in the First-tier Tribunals.

The Luxembourg Court has itself issued guidance for national courts and tribunals on the making of references and this is reproduced at the end of the annotations to this article. **3.105**

Although there are prescribed forms of order for references from the High Court the Luxembourg Court does not make any formal requirements as to form: see CPR r.68. The adjudicating body is responsible for drafting the questions it wishes to refer. The question should be couched in terms which pose a general question of law rather than the specific issues raised in the case. The questions should be self-contained and self-explanatory, since they will be notified to the Commission, Council and the Member States under art.20 of the Statute of the Court. Those so notified may choose within two months of the notification to submit written observations on the questions raised. Though the only requirement is the formulation of questions for the Luxembourg Court, it will be helpful to the court to provide the following further information:

1. the facts of the case;
2. the relevant provisions of United Kingdom law;
3. the relevant provisions of European Union law;
4. a summary of the contentions of the parties on the question or questions referred; and
5. if necessary, the reasons why the answers to the questions referred are considered necessary to decide the case.

A ruling given by the Luxembourg Court is binding on the national court or tribunal as to the interpretation of the EU law in question. It will also bind future courts or tribunals determining similar questions: see s.3(1), European Communities Act 1972.

In *CIS/501/1993* the Commissioner had to consider whether he had jurisdiction to consider the validity of a reference to the Luxembourg Court made by a tribunal. The Commissioner, of course, only has jurisdiction when there is a "final" decision of a tribunal. The question was whether a reference could be regarded as a final decision.

The Commissioner relied on RSC Ord.114 r.6 and *R. v International Stock Exchange of the United Kingdom and the Republic of Ireland Ltd Ex p. Else (1982) Ltd* [1993] Q.B. 534 in holding that an order referring questions to the Luxembourg Court is to be treated as a final decision against which appeal will lie. He then set aside the decision to refer since the answer to the question posed was clearly not "necessary" to enable the tribunal to resolve the issue before it. The Commissioner also makes reference to the guidelines set down by the Court of Appeal in *Bulmer*. Those guidelines are, as noted above, not wholly consistent with statements made by the Luxembourg Court and care should be taken in relying exclusively upon them without referring to the relevant decisions of the Luxembourg Court of Justice and subsequent decisions of the United Kingdom courts: see generally A. Arnull, "References to the European Court" (1990) 15 E.L.Rev. 375.

The Luxembourg Court's updated Information Note [2009] OJ C297/1 of December 5, 2009 reads as follows:

Information Note

on references from national courts for a preliminary ruling

I. General

3.106 1. The preliminary ruling system is a fundamental mechanism of European Union law aimed at enabling national courts to ensure uniform interpretation and application of that law in all the Member States.

2. The Court of Justice of the European Union has jurisdiction to give preliminary rulings on the interpretation of European Union law and on the validity of acts of the institutions, bodies, offices or agencies of the Union. That general jurisdiction is conferred on it by Article 19(3)(b) of the Treaty on European Union (OJEU 2008 C 115, p.13) ('the TEU') and Article 267 of the Treaty on the Functioning of the European Union (OJEU 2008 C 115, p. 47) ('the TFEU').

3. Article 256(3) TFEU provides that the General Court is to have jurisdiction to hear and determine questions referred for a preliminary ruling under Article 267, in specific areas laid down by the Statute. Since no provisions have been introduced into the Statute in that regard, the Court of Justice alone has jurisdiction to give preliminary rulings.

4. While Article 267 TFEU confers on the Court of Justice a general jurisdiction, a number of provisions exist which lay down exceptions to or restrictions on that jurisdiction. This is true in particular of Articles 275 and 276 TFEU and Article 10 of Protocol (No 36) on Transitional Provisions of the Treaty of Lisbon (OJEU 2008 C 115, p.322).

5. The preliminary ruling procedure being based on cooperation between the Court of Justice and national courts, it may be helpful, in order to ensure that that cooperation is effective, to provide the national courts with the following information.

6. This practical information, which is in no way binding, is intended to provide guidance to national courts as to whether it is appropriate to make a reference for a preliminary ruling and, should they proceed, to help them formulate and submit questions to the Court.

The role of the Court of Justice in the preliminary ruling procedure

3.107 7. Under the preliminary ruling procedure, the Court's role is to give an interpretation of European Union law or to rule on its validity, not to apply that law to the factual situation underlying the main proceedings, which is the task of the national court. It is not for the Court either to decide issues of fact raised in the main proceedings or to resolve differences of opinion on the interpretation or application of rules of national law.

8. In ruling on the interpretation or validity of European Union law, the Court makes every effort to give a reply which will be of assistance in resolving the dispute, but it is for the referring court to draw the appropriate conclusions from that reply, if necessary by disapplying the rule of national law in question.

The decision to submit a question to the Court

The originator of the question

3.108 9. Under Article 267 TFEU, any court or tribunal of a Member State, in so far as it is called upon to give a ruling in proceedings intended to arrive at a decision of a judicial nature, may as a rule refer a question to the Court of Justice for a preliminary ruling ([1]). Status as a court or tribunal is interpreted by the Court of Justice as a self-standing concept of European Union law.

[1] Article 10(1) to (3) of Protocol No 36 provides that the powers of the Court of Justice in relation to acts adopted before the entry into force of the Treaty of Lisbon (OJ 2007 C 306, p. 1) under Title VI of the TEU, in the field of police cooperation and judicial cooperation in criminal matters, and which have not since been amended, are, however, to remain the same for a maximum period of five years from the date of entry into force of the Treaty of Lisbon (1 December 2009). During that period, such acts may, therefore, form the subject-matter of a reference for a preliminary ruling only where the order for reference is made by a court of a Member State which has accepted the jurisdiction of the Court of Justice, it being a matter for each State to determine whether the right to refer a question to the Court is to be available to all of its national courts or is to be reserved to the courts of last instance.

10. It is for the national court alone to decide whether to refer a question to the Court of Justice for a preliminary ruling, whether or not the parties to the main proceedings have requested it to do so.

References on interpretation

11. Any court or tribunal **may** refer a question to the Court of Justice on the interpretation of a rule of European Union law if it considers it necessary to do so in order to resolve a dispute brought before it. **3.109**

12. However, courts or tribunals against whose decisions there is no judicial remedy under national law **must, as a rule**, refer such a question to the Court, unless the Court has already ruled on the point (and there is no new context that raises any serious doubt as to whether that case-law may be applied), or unless the correct interpretation of the rule of law in question is obvious.

13. Thus, a court or tribunal against whose decisions there is a judicial remedy may, in particular when it considers that sufficient guidance is given by the case-law of the Court of Justice, itself decide on the correct interpretation of European Union law and its application to the factual situation before it. However, a reference for a preliminary ruling may prove particularly useful, at an appropriate stage of the proceedings, when there is a new question of interpretation of general interest for the uniform application of European Union law in all the Member States, or where the existing case-law does not appear to be applicable to a new set of facts.

14. It is for the national court to explain why the interpretation sought is necessary to enable it to give judgment.

References on determination of validity

15. Although national courts may reject pleas raised before them challenging the validity of acts of an institution, body, office or agency of the Union, the Court of Justice has exclusive jurisdiction to declare such an act invalid. **3.110**

16. All national courts **must** therefore refer a question to the Court when they have doubts about the validity of such an act, stating the reasons for which they consider that that act may be invalid.

17. However, if a national court has serious doubts about the validity of an act of an institution, body, office or agency of the Union on which a national measure is based, it may exceptionally suspend application of that measure temporarily or grant other interim relief with respect to it. It must then refer the question of validity to the Court of Justice, stating the reasons for which it considers the act to be invalid.

The stage at which to submit a question for a preliminary ruling

3.111 18. A national court or tribunal may refer a question to the Court for a preliminary ruling as soon as it finds that a ruling on the point or points of interpretation or validity is necessary to enable it to give judgment; it is the national court which is in the best position to decide at what stage of the proceedings such a question should be referred.

19. It is, however, desirable that a decision to seek a preliminary ruling should be taken when the national proceedings have reached a stage at which the national court is able to define the factual and legal context of the question, so that the Court of Justice has available to it all the information necessary to check, where appropriate, that European Union law applies to the main proceedings. It may also be in the interests of justice to refer a question for a preliminary ruling only after both sides have been heard.

The form of the reference for a preliminary ruling

3.112 20. The decision by which a national court or tribunal refers a question to the Court of Justice for a preliminary ruling may be in any form allowed by national law as regards procedural steps. It must however be borne in mind that it is that document which serves as the basis of the proceedings before the Court and that it must therefore contain such information as will enable the latter to give a reply which is of assistance to the national court. Moreover, it is only the actual reference for a preliminary ruling which is notified to the interested persons entitled to submit observations to the Court, in particular the Member States and the institutions, and which is translated.

21. Owing to the need to translate the reference, it should be drafted simply, clearly and precisely, avoiding superfluous detail.

22. A maximum of about 10 pages is often sufficient to set out in a proper manner the context of a reference for a preliminary ruling. The order for reference must be succinct but sufficiently complete and must contain all the relevant information to give the Court and the interested persons entitled to submit observations a clear understanding of the factual and legal context of the main proceedings. In particular, the order for reference must:

— include a brief account of the subject-matter of the dispute and the relevant findings of fact, or, at least, set out the factual situation on which the question referred is based;
— set out the tenor of any applicable national provisions and identify, where necessary, the relevant national case-law, giving in each case precise references (for example, a page of an official journal or specific law report, with any internet reference);
— identify the European Union law provisions relevant to the case as accurately as possible;
— explain the reasons which prompted the national court to raise the

question of the interpretation or validity of the European Union law provisions, and the relationship between those provisions and the national provisions applicable to the main proceedings;

— include, if need be, a summary of the main relevant arguments of the parties to the main proceedings.

In order to make it easier to read and refer to the document, it is helpful if the different points or paragraphs of the order for reference are numbered.

23. Finally, the referring court may, if it considers itself able, briefly state its view on the answer to be given to the questions referred for a preliminary ruling.

24. The question or questions themselves should appear in a separate and clearly identified section of the order for reference, generally at the beginning or the end. It must be possible to understand them without referring to the statement of the grounds for the reference, which will however provide the necessary background for a proper assessment.

The effects of the reference for a preliminary ruling on the national proceedings

25. A reference for a preliminary ruling calls for the national proceedings to be stayed until the Court of Justice has given its ruling. **3.113**

26. However, the national court may still order protective measures, particularly in connection with a reference on determination of validity (see point 17 above).

Costs and legal aid

27. Preliminary ruling proceedings before the Court of Justice are free of charge and the Court does not rule on the costs of the parties to the main proceedings; it is for the national court to rule on those costs. **3.114**

28. If a party has insufficient means and where it is possible under national rules, the national court may grant that party legal aid to cover the costs, including those of lawyers' fees, which it incurs before the Court. The Court itself may also grant legal aid where the party in question is not already in receipt of legal aid under national rules or to the extent to which that aid does not cover, or covers only partly, costs incurred before the Court.

Communication between the national court and the Court of Justice

29. The order for reference and the relevant documents (including, where applicable, the case file or a copy of the case file) are to be sent by the national court directly to the Court of Justice, by registered post (addressed to the Registry of the Court of Justice, L-2925 Luxembourg, telephone +352 4303-1). **3.115**

30. The Court Registry will stay in contact with the national court until a ruling is given, and will send it copies of the procedural documents.

31. The Court of Justice will send its ruling to the national court. It would welcome information from the national court on the action taken upon its ruling in the national proceedings and, where appropriate, a copy of the national court's final decision.

II. The Urgent preliminary ruling procedure (PPU)

32. This part of the note provides practical information on the urgent preliminary ruling procedure applicable to references relating to the area of freedom, security and justice. The procedure is governed by Article **3.116**

23a of Protocol (No 3) on the Statute of the Court of Justice of the European Union (OJEU 2008 C 115, p. 210) and Article 104b of the Rules of Procedure of the Court of Justice. National courts may request that this procedure be applied or request the application of the accelerated procedure under the conditions laid down in Article 23a of the Protocol and Article 104a of the Rules of Procedure.

Conditions for the application of the urgent preliminary ruling procedure

3.117 33. The urgent preliminary ruling procedure is applicable only in the areas covered by Title V of Part Three of the TFEU, which relates to the area of freedom, security and justice.

34. The Court of Justice decides whether this procedure is to be applied. Such a decision is generally taken only on a reasoned request from the referring court. Exceptionally, the Court may decide of its own motion to deal with a reference under the urgent preliminary ruling procedure, where that appears to be required.

35. The urgent preliminary ruling procedure simplifies the various stages of the proceedings before the Court, but its application entails significant constraints for the Court and for the parties and other interested persons participating in the procedure, particularly the Member States.

36. It should therefore be requested only where it is absolutely necessary for the Court to give its ruling on the reference as quickly as possible. Although it is not possible to provide an exhaustive list of such situations, particularly because of the varied and evolving nature of the rules of European Union law governing the area of freedom, security and justice, a national court or tribunal might, for example, consider submitting a request for the urgent preliminary ruling procedure to be applied in the following situations: in the case, referred to in the fourth paragraph of Article 267 TFEU, of a person in custody or deprived of his liberty, where the answer to the question raised is decisive as to the assessment of that person's legal situation or, in proceedings concerning parental authority or custody of children, where the identity of the court having jurisdiction under European Union law depends on the answer to the question referred for a preliminary ruling.

The request for application of the urgent preliminary ruling procedure

3.118 37. To enable the Court to decide quickly whether the urgent preliminary ruling procedure should be applied, the request must set out the matters of fact and law which establish the urgency and, in particular, the risks involved in following the normal preliminary ruling procedure.

38. In so far as it is able to do so, the referring court should briefly state its view on the answer to be given to the question(s) referred. Such a statement makes it easier for the parties and other interested persons participating in the procedure to define their positions and facilitates the Court's decision, thereby contributing to the rapidity of the procedure.

39. The request for the urgent preliminary ruling procedure must be submitted in a form that enables the Court Registry to establish immediately that the file must be dealt with in a particular way. Accordingly, the request should be submitted in a document separate from the order for reference itself, or in a covering letter expressly setting out the request.

40. As regards the order for reference itself, it is particularly important that it should be succinct where the matter is urgent, as this will help to ensure the rapidity of the procedure.

Communication between the Court of Justice, the national court and the parties

41. As regards communication with the national court or tribunal and the parties before it, national courts or tribunals which submit a request for an urgent preliminary ruling procedure are requested to state the e-mail address or any fax number which may be used by the Court of Justice, together with the e-mail addresses or any fax numbers of the representatives of the parties to the proceedings. **3.119**

42. A copy of the signed order for reference together with a request for the urgent preliminary ruling procedure can initially be sent to the Court by e-mail (ECJ-Registry@curia.europa.eu) or by fax (+352 43 37 66). Processing of the reference and of the request can then begin upon receipt of the e-mailed or faxed copy. The originals of those documents must, however, be sent to the Court Registry as soon as possible. **3.120**

Article 352
(ex Article 308 TEC)

1. If action by the Union should prove necessary, within the framework of the policies defined in the Treaties, to attain one of the objectives set out in the Treaties, and the Treaties have not provided the necessary powers, the Council, acting unanimously on a proposal from the Commission and after obtaining the consent of the European Parliament, shall adopt the appropriate measures. Where the measures in question are adopted by the Council in accordance with a special legislative procedure, it shall also act unanimously on a proposal from the Commission and after obtaining the consent of the European Parliament. **3.121**

2. Using the procedure for monitoring the subsidiarity principle referred to in Article 5(3) of the Treaty on European Union, the Commission shall draw national Parliaments' attention to proposals based on this Article.

3. Measures based on this Article shall not entail harmonisation of Member States' laws or regulations in cases where the Treaties exclude such harmonisation.

4. This Article cannot serve as a basis for attaining objectives pertaining to the common foreign and security policy and any acts adopted pursuant to this Article shall respect the limits set out in Article 40, second paragraph, of the Treaty on European Union.

Charter of Fundamental Rights of the European Union

[2007] OJ C303/1 of December 14, 2007

General Note

The entry into force of the Treaty of Lisbon has significantly changed the status of the Charter of Fundamental Rights of the European Union. It is no longer a document to which the Luxembourg Court makes occasional reference as inspira- **3.122** tion for determining the content of the fundamental rights protection inherent in European Union law, but it is now a document to which is given "the same legal value as the Treaties" under art.6 TEU.

In the case of the United Kingdom, this is subject to the provisions in Protocol No.30 quoted in the annotations to art.6 TEU. Few commentators have been bold enough to suggest that the Luxembourg Court will regard the provisions of the Protocol as a complete opt out of the application of the rules in the Charter to the United Kingdom. In any event there are important rules on the field and scope of application of the Charter in its arts 51 and 52.

On the significance of Protocol No. 30, see the comments of both the Advocate General and the Court of Justice in its judgment in *NS v SSHD* (C–411/10) judgment of December 21, 2011.

The European Parliament, the Council and the Commission solemnly proclaim the following text as the Charter of Fundamental Rights of the European Union.

Charter of Fundamental Rights of the European Union

Preamble

3.123 The peoples of Europe, in creating an ever closer union among them, are resolved to share a peaceful future based on common values.

Conscious of its spiritual and moral heritage, the Union is founded on the indivisible, universal values of human dignity, freedom, equality and solidarity; it is based on the principles of democracy and the rule of law. It places the individual at the heart of its activities, by establishing the citizenship of the Union and by creating an area of freedom, security and justice.

The Union contributes to the preservation and to the development of these common values while respecting the diversity of the cultures and traditions of the peoples of Europe as well as the national identities of the Member States and the organisation of their public authorities at national, regional and local levels; it seeks to promote balanced and sustainable development and ensures free movement of persons, services, goods and capital, and the freedom of establishment.

To this end, it is necessary to strengthen the protection of fundamental rights in the light of changes in society, social progress and scientific and technological developments by making those rights more visible in a Charter.

This Charter reaffirms, with due regard for the powers and tasks of the Union and for the principle of subsidiarity, the rights as they result, in particular, from the constitutional traditions and international obligations common to the Member States, the European Convention for the Protection of Human Rights and Fundamental Freedoms, the Social Charters adopted by the Union and by the Council of Europe and the case-law of the Court of Justice of the European Union and of the European Court of Human Rights. In this context the Charter will be interpreted by the courts of the Union and the Member States with due regard to the explanations prepared under the authority of the Praesidium of the Convention which drafted the Charter and updated under the responsibility of the Praesidium of the European Convention.

Enjoyment of these rights entails responsibilities and duties with regard to other persons, to the human community and to future generations.

The Union therefore recognises the rights, freedoms and principles set out hereafter.

Title I

Dignity

Article 1

Human dignity

Human dignity is inviolable. It must be respected and protected. 3.124

Article 2

Right to life

1. Everyone has the right to life. 3.125
2. No one shall be condemned to the death penalty, or executed.

Article 3

Right to the integrity of the person

1. Everyone has the right to respect for his or her physical and mental integrity. 3.126

2. In the fields of medicine and biology, the following must be respected in particular

(a) the free and informed consent of the person concerned, according to the procedures laid down by law;
(b) the prohibition of eugenic practices, in particular those aiming at the selection of persons;
(c) the prohibition on making the human body and its parts as such a source of financial gain;
(d) the prohibition of the reproductive cloning of human beings.

Article 4

Prohibition of torture and inhuman or degrading treatment or punishment

No one shall be subjected to torture or to inhuman or degrading treatment or punishment. 3.127

Article 5

Prohibition of slavery and forced labour

1. No one shall be held in slavery or servitude. 3.128
2. No one shall be required to perform forced or compulsory labour.
3. Trafficking in human beings is prohibited.

TITLE II

FREEDOMS

Article 6

Right to liberty and security

3.129 Everyone has the right to liberty and security of person.

Article 7

Respect for private and family life

3.130 Everyone has the right to respect for his or her private and family life, home and communications.

Article 8

Protection of personal data

3.131 1. Everyone has the right to the protection of personal data concerning him or her.

2. Such data must be processed fairly for specified purposes and on the basis of the consent of the person concerned or some other legitimate basis laid down by law. Everyone has the right of access to data which has been collected concerning him or her, and the right to have it rectified.

3. Compliance with these rules shall be subject to control by an independent authority.

Article 9

Right to marry and right to found a family

3.132 The right to marry and the right to found a family shall be guaranteed in accordance with the national laws governing the exercise of these rights.

Article 10

Freedom of thought, conscience and religion

3.133 1. Everyone has the right to freedom of thought, conscience and religion. This right includes freedom to change religion or belief and freedom, either alone or in community with others and in public or in private, to manifest religion or belief, in worship, teaching, practice and observance.

2. The right to conscientious objection is recognised, in accordance with the national laws governing the exercise of this right.

Article 11

Freedom of expression and information

3.134 1. Everyone has the right to freedom of expression. This right shall include freedom to hold opinions and to receive and impart information

Article 11

and ideas without interference by public authority and regardless of frontiers.

2. The freedom and pluralism of the media shall be respected.

Article 12

Freedom of assembly and of association

1. Everyone has the right to freedom of peaceful assembly and to freedom of association at all levels, in particular in political, trade union and civic matters, which implies the right of everyone to form and to join trade unions for the protection of his or her interests. **3.135**

2. Political parties at Union level contribute to expressing the political will of the citizens of the Union.

Article 13

Freedom of the arts and sciences

The arts and scientific research shall be free of constraint. Academic freedom shall be respected. **3.136**

Article 14

Right to education

1. Everyone has the right to education and to have access to vocational and continuing training. **3.137**

2. This right includes the possibility to receive free compulsory education.

3. The freedom to found educational establishments with due respect for democratic principles and the right of parents to ensure the education and teaching of their children in conformity with their religious, philosophical and pedagogical convictions shall be respected, in accordance with the national laws governing the exercise of such freedom and right.

Article 15

Freedom to choose an occupation and right to engage in work

1. Everyone has the right to engage in work and to pursue a freely chosen or accepted occupation. **3.138**

2. Every citizen of the Union has the freedom to seek employment, to work, to exercise the right of establishment and to provide services in any Member State.

3. Nationals of third countries who are authorised to work in the territories of the Member States are entitled to working conditions equivalent to those of citizens of the Union.

Article 16

Freedom to conduct a business

3.139 The freedom to conduct a business in accordance with Union law and national laws and practices is recognised.

Article 17

Right to property

3.140 1. Everyone has the right to own, use, dispose of and bequeath his or her lawfully acquired possessions. No one may be deprived of his or her possessions, except in the public interest and in the cases and under the conditions provided for by law, subject to fair compensation being paid in good time for their loss. The use of property may be regulated by law in so far as is necessary for the general interest.

2. Intellectual property shall be protected.

Article 18

Right to asylum

3.141 The right to asylum shall be guaranteed with due respect for the rules of the Geneva Convention of 28 July 1951 and the Protocol of 31 January 1967 relating to the status of refugees and in accordance with the Treaty on European Union and the Treaty on the Functioning of the European Union (hereinafter referred to as 'the Treaties').

Article 19

Protection in the event of removal, expulsion or extradition

3.142 1. Collective expulsions are prohibited.

2. No one may be removed, expelled or extradited to a State where there is a serious risk that he or she would be subjected to the death penalty, torture or other inhuman or degrading treatment or punishment.

TITLE III

EQUALITY

Article 20

Equality before the law

3.143 Everyone is equal before the law.

Article 21

Article 21

Non-discrimination

1. Any discrimination based on any ground such as sex, race, colour, ethnic or social origin, genetic features, language, religion or belief, political or any other opinion, membership of a national minority, property, birth, disability, age or sexual orientation shall be prohibited. **3.144**

2. Within the scope of application of the Treaties and without prejudice to any of their specific provisions, any discrimination on grounds of nationality shall be prohibited.

Article 22

Cultural, religious and linguistic diversity

The Union shall respect cultural, religious and linguistic diversity. **3.145**

Article 23

Equality between women and men

Equality between women and men must be ensured in all areas, including employment, work and pay. **3.146**

The principle of equality shall not prevent the maintenance or adoption of measures providing for specific advantages in favour of the under-represented sex.

Article 24

The rights of the child

1. Children shall have the right to such protection and care as is necessary for their well-being. They may express their views freely. Such views shall be taken into consideration on matters which concern them in accordance with their age and maturity. **3.147**

2. In all actions relating to children, whether taken by public authorities or private institutions, the child's best interests must be a primary consideration.

3. Every child shall have the right to maintain on a regular basis a personal relationship and direct contact with both his or her parents, unless that is contrary to his or her interests.

Article 25

The rights of the elderly

The Union recognises and respects the rights of the elderly to lead a life of dignity and independence and to participate in social and cultural life. **3.148**

Article 26

Integration of persons with disabilities

3.149 The Union recognises and respects the right of persons with disabilities to benefit from measures designed to ensure their independence, social and occupational integration and participation in the life of the community.

TITLE IV

SOLIDARITY

Article 27

Workers' right to information and consultation within the undertaking

3.150 Workers or their representatives must, at the appropriate levels, be guaranteed information and consultation in good time in the cases and under the conditions provided for by Union law and national laws and practices.

Article 28

Right of collective bargaining and action

3.151 Workers and employers, or their respective organisations, have, in accordance with Union law and national laws and practices, the right to negotiate and conclude collective agreements at the appropriate levels and, in cases of conflicts of interest, to take collective action to defend their interests, including strike action.

Article 29

Right of access to placement services

3.152 Everyone has the right of access to a free placement service.

Article 30

Protection in the event of unjustified dismissal

3.153 Every worker has the right to protection against unjustified dismissal, in accordance with Union law and national laws and practices.

Article 31

Fair and just working conditions

1. Every worker has the right to working conditions which respect his or her health, safety and dignity. 3.154

2. Every worker has the right to limitation of maximum working hours, to daily and weekly rest periods and to an annual period of paid leave.

Article 32

Prohibition of child labour and protection of young people at work

The employment of children is prohibited. The minimum age of admission to employment may not be lower than the minimum school-leaving age, without prejudice to such rules as may be more favourable to young people and except for limited derogations. 3.155

Young people admitted to work must have working conditions appropriate to their age and be protected against economic exploitation and any work likely to harm their safety, health or physical, mental, moral or social development or to interfere with their education.

Article 33

Family and professional life

1. The family shall enjoy legal, economic and social protection. 3.156

2. To reconcile family and professional life, everyone shall have the right to protection from dismissal for a reason connected with maternity and the right to paid maternity leave and to parental leave following the birth or adoption of a child.

Article 34

Social security and social assistance

1. The Union recognises and respects the entitlement to social security benefits and social services providing protection in cases such as maternity, illness, industrial accidents, dependency or old age, and in the case of loss of employment, in accordance with the rules laid down by Union law and national laws and practices. 3.157

2. Everyone residing and moving legally within the European Union is entitled to social security benefits and social advantages in accordance with Union law and national laws and practices.

3. In order to combat social exclusion and poverty, the Union recognises and respects the right to social and housing assistance so as to ensure a decent existence for all those who lack sufficient resources, in accordance with the rules laid down by Union law and national laws and practices.

GENERAL NOTE

3.158 This provision, which deals explicitly with social security and social assistance is certain to be cited in national tribunals as providing support for claimed entitlements. Rather like the introduction of citizenship of the Union, it will remain to be seen what the Luxembourg Court makes of the provisions of this article, and whether it will fill what might be regarded simply as a restatement of rights contained elsewhere as importing something more than those other provisions contain.

Article 35

Health care

3.159 Everyone has the right of access to preventive health care and the right to benefit from medical treatment under the conditions established by national laws and practices. A high level of human health protection shall be ensured in the definition and implementation of all the Union's policies and activities.

Article 36

Access to services of general economic interest

3.160 The Union recognises and respects access to services of general economic interest as provided for in national laws and practices, in accordance with the Treaties, in order to promote the social and territorial cohesion of the Union.

Article 37

Environmental protection

3.161 A high level of environmental protection and the improvement of the quality of the environment must be integrated into the policies of the Union and ensured in accordance with the principle of sustainable development.

Article 38

Consumer protection

3.162 Union policies shall ensure a high level of consumer protection.

TITLE V

CITIZENS' RIGHTS

Article 39

Right to vote and to stand as a candidate at elections to the European Parliament

1. Every citizen of the Union has the right to vote and to stand as a candidate at elections to the European Parliament in the Member State in which he or she resides, under the same conditions as nationals of that State. **3.163**

2. Members of the European Parliament shall be elected by direct universal suffrage in a free and secret ballot.

Article 40

Right to vote and to stand as a candidate at municipal elections

Every citizen of the Union has the right to vote and to stand as a candidate at municipal elections in the Member State in which he or she resides under the same conditions as nationals of that State. **3.164**

Article 41

Right to good administration

1. Every person has the right to have his or her affairs handled impartially, fairly and within a reasonable time by the institutions, bodies, offices and agencies of the Union. **3.165**

2. This right includes:

(a) the right of every person to be heard, before any individual measure which would affect him or her adversely is taken;

(b) the right of every person to have access to his or her file, while respecting the legitimate interests of confidentiality and of professional and business secrecy;

(c) the obligation of the administration to give reasons for its decisions.

3. Every person has the right to have the Union make good any damage caused by its institutions or by its servants in the performance of their duties, in accordance with the general principles common to the laws of the Member States.

4. Every person may write to the institutions of the Union in one of the languages of the Treaties and must have an answer in the same language.

Article 42

Right of access to documents

3.166 Any citizen of the Union, and any natural or legal person residing or having its registered office in a Member State, has a right of access to documents of the institutions, bodies, offices and agencies of the Union, whatever their medium.

Article 43

European Ombudsman

3.167 Any citizen of the Union and any natural or legal person residing or having its registered office in a Member State has the right to refer to the European Ombudsman cases of maladministration in the activities of the institutions, bodies, offices or agencies of the Union, with the exception of the Court of Justice of the European Union acting in its judicial role.

Article 44

Right to petition

3.168 Any citizen of the Union and any natural or legal person residing or having its registered office in a Member State has the right to petition the European Parliament.

Article 45

Freedom of movement and of residence

3.169 1. Every citizen of the Union has the right to move and reside freely within the territory of the Member States.

2. Freedom of movement and residence may be granted, in accordance with the Treaties, to nationals of third countries legally resident in the territory of a Member State.

Article 46

Diplomatic and consular protection

3.170 Every citizen of the Union shall, in the territory of a third country in which the Member State of which he or she is a national is not represented, be entitled to protection by the diplomatic or consular authorities of any Member State, on the same conditions as the nationals of that Member State.

TITLE VI

JUSTICE

Article 47

Right to an effective remedy and to a fair trial

Everyone whose rights and freedoms guaranteed by the law of the Union are violated has the right to an effective remedy before a tribunal in compliance with the conditions laid down in this Article. **3.171**

Everyone is entitled to a fair and public hearing within a reasonable time by an independent and impartial tribunal previously established by law. Everyone shall have the possibility of being advised, defended and represented.

Legal aid shall be made available to those who lack sufficient resources in so far as such aid is necessary to ensure effective access to justice.

GENERAL NOTE

For a case on the interpretation of art.47, see *DEB Deutsche Energiehandels- und Beratungsgesellschaft mbH v Bundesrepublik Deutschland* (C–279/09) Judgment of December 22, 2010. **3.172**

Article 48

Presumption of innocence and right of defence

1. Everyone who has been charged shall be presumed innocent until proved guilty according to law. **3.173**

2. Respect for the rights of the defence of anyone who has been charged shall be guaranteed.

Article 49

Principles of legality and proportionality of criminal offences and penalties

1. No one shall be held guilty of any criminal offence on account of any act or omission which did not constitute a criminal offence under national law or international law at the time when it was committed. Nor shall a heavier penalty be imposed than the one that was applicable at the time the criminal offence was committed. If, subsequent to the commission of a criminal offence, the law provides for a lighter penalty, that penalty shall be applicable. **3.174**

2. This Article shall not prejudice the trial and punishment of any person

for any act or omission which, at the time when it was committed, was criminal according to the general principles recognised by the community of nations.

3. The severity of penalties must not be disproportionate to the criminal offence.

Article 50

Right not to be tried or punished twice in criminal proceedings for the same criminal offence

3.175 No one shall be liable to be tried or punished again in criminal proceedings for an offence for which he or she has already been finally acquitted or convicted within the Union in accordance with the law.

TITLE VII

GENERAL PROVISIONS GOVERNING THE INTERPRETATION AND APPLICATION OF THE CHARTER

Article 51

Field of application

3.176 1. The provisions of this Charter are addressed to the institutions, bodies, offices and agencies of the Union with due regard for the principle of subsidiarity and to the Member States only when they are implementing Union law. They shall therefore respect the rights, observe the principles and promote the application thereof in accordance with their respective powers and respecting the limits of the powers of the Union as conferred on it in the Treaties.

2. The Charter does not extend the field of application of Union law beyond the powers of the Union or establish any new power or task for the Union, or modify powers and tasks as defined in the Treaties.

GENERAL NOTE

3.177 *Iida* (C-40/11) Judgment of November 12, 2012, provides some guidance on the interpretation of art.51. The case concerned a Japanese man who was the father and the spouse of German nationals. The family was living in Germany, but the relationship between the spouses broke down, and the mother and daughter moved to Austria in connection with the mother's work. The father maintained regular contact with his daughter. He sought a residence permit as a family member of a Union citizen since it gave him greater immigration security than his current status. He also elected not to apply for a long-term residence permit under the provisions of Directive 2003/109/EC [2003] OJ L16/44. The Court of Justice ruled that his circumstances did not bring him within the definitions in art.2 of the Citizenship Directive (see update below on this issue). Among the father's subsidiary arguments was reliance on art.7 (Respect for private and family life) and art.24 (Rights of the child) in the Charter. But the Court ruled that Charter did not apply. The father was not within the personal scope of the Citizenship Directive, and, because he had elected not to apply for a long-term residence permit under Directive 2003/109, "his situation shows no connection with European Union law." (para.80). It could not therefore be said that the actions of the German authorities were actions when they were implementing Union law, and consequently those actions could not be examined by reference to rights set out in the Charter (para.81). The Advocate General had taken a different view on this point. *Åklageren v Fransson* (C-617/10), Judgment of February 26, 2013, suggests that broad view should be taken of when matters fall within the scope of European Union law.

Article 52

Scope and interpretation of rights and principles

1. Any limitation on the exercise of the rights and freedoms recognised by this Charter must be provided for by law and respect the essence of those rights and freedoms. Subject to the principle of proportionality, limitations may be made only if they are necessary and genuinely meet objectives of general interest recognised by the Union or the need to protect the rights and freedoms of others. 3.178

2. Rights recognised by this Charter for which provision is made in the Treaties shall be exercised under the conditions and within the limits defined by those Treaties.

3. In so far as this Charter contains rights which correspond to rights guaranteed by the Convention for the Protection of Human Rights and Fundamental Freedoms, the meaning and scope of those rights shall be the same as those laid down by the said Convention. This provision shall not prevent Union law providing more extensive protection.

4. In so far as this Charter recognises fundamental rights as they result from the constitutional traditions common to the Member States, those rights shall be interpreted in harmony with those traditions.

5. The provisions of this Charter which contain principles may be implemented by legislative and executive acts taken by institutions, bodies, offices and agencies of the Union, and by acts of Member States when they are implementing Union law, in the exercise of their respective powers. They shall be judicially cognisable only in the interpretation of such acts and in the ruling on their legality.

6. Full account shall be taken of national laws and practices as specified in this Charter.

7. The explanations drawn up as a way of providing guidance in the interpretation of this Charter shall be given due regard by the courts of the Union and of the Member States.

Article 53

Level of protection

Nothing in this Charter shall be interpreted as restricting or adversely affecting human rights and fundamental freedoms as recognised, in their respective fields of application, by Union law and international law and by international 3.179

agreements to which the Union or all the Member States are party, including the European Convention for the Protection of Human Rights and Fundamental Freedoms, and by the Member States' constitutions.

Article 54

Prohibition of abuse of rights

3.180 Nothing in this Charter shall be interpreted as implying any right to engage in any activity or to perform any act aimed at the destruction of any of the rights and freedoms recognised in this Charter or at their limitation to a greater extent than is provided for herein.

Regulation (EU) No 492/2011 of the European Parliament and of the Council of 5 April 2011 on freedom of movement for workers within the Union (codification) (Text with EEA relevance)

[2011] OJ L141/1

Entry into Force: June 16, 2011

General note

3.181 Regulation 492/2011 merely consolidates and codifies the rules in repealed Reg.1612/68/EEC as amended so that there is an up to date statement of the rights which flow from being a worker under art.45 TFEU. It follows that the case law under Reg.1612/68 can be transposed directly to the corresponding provisions of the new regulation. Annex II of the new regulation contains a correlation table with the provisions of the former regulation.

Directive 2014/54/EU of April 16, 2014 on measures facilitating the exercise of rights conferred in the context of freedom of movement for workers, [2014] OJ L128/1, has a deadline for implementation of May 21, 2016. It contains provisions on defence of rights, the promotion of equal treatment, a requirement for dialogue, and access to information. This Directive is mainly concerned with rights flowing from art.45 TFEU and arts 1-10 of Regulation 492/2011.

The European Parliament and The Council of The European Union

3.182 Having regard to the Treaty on the Functioning of the European Union, and in particular Article 46 thereof,

Having regard to the proposal from the European Commission,

After transmission of the draft legislative act to the national parliaments,

Having regard to the opinion of the European Economic and Social Committee (1),

Acting in accordance with the ordinary legislative procedure (2),

Whereas:

(1) Regulation (EEC) No 1612/68 of the Council of 15 October 1968 on freedom of movement for workers within the Community (3) has been substantially amended several times (4). In the interests of clarity and rationality the said Regulation should be codified.

(2) Freedom of movement for workers should be secured within the Union. The attainment of this objective entails the abolition of any discrimination based on

nationality between workers of the Member States as regards employment, remuneration and other conditions of work and employment, as well as the right of such workers to move freely within the Union in order to pursue activities as employed persons subject to any limitations justified on grounds of public policy, public security or public health.

(3) Provisions should be laid down to enable the objectives laid down in Articles 45 and 46 of the Treaty on the Functioning of the European Union in the field of freedom of movement to be achieved.

(4) Freedom of movement constitutes a fundamental right of workers and their families. Mobility of labour within the Union must be one of the means by which workers are guaranteed the possibility of improving their living and working conditions and promoting their social advancement, while helping to satisfy the requirements of the economies of the Member States. The right of all workers in the Member States to pursue the activity of their choice within the Union should be affirmed.

(5) Such right should be enjoyed without discrimination by permanent, seasonal and frontier workers and by those who pursue their activities for the purpose of providing services.

(6) The right of freedom of movement, in order that it may be exercised, by objective standards, in freedom and dignity, requires that equality of treatment be ensured in fact and in law in respect of all matters relating to the actual pursuit of activities as employed persons and to eligibility for housing, and also that obstacles to the mobility of workers be eliminated, in particular as regards the conditions for the integration of the worker's family into the host country.

(7) The principle of non-discrimination between workers in the Union means that all nationals of Member States have the same priority as regards employment as is enjoyed by national workers.

(8) The machinery for vacancy clearance, in particular by means of direct cooperation between the central employment services and also between the regional services, as well as by coordination of the exchange of information, ensures in a general way a clearer picture of the labour market. Workers wishing to move should also be regularly informed of living and working conditions.

(9) Close links exist between freedom of movement for workers, employment and vocational training, particularly where the latter aims at putting workers in a position to take up concrete offers of employment from other regions of the Union. Such links make it necessary that the problems arising in this connection should no longer be studied in isolation but viewed as interdependent, account also being taken of the problems of employment at the regional level. It is therefore necessary to direct the efforts of Member States toward coordinating their employment policies,

Have Adopted This Regulation.

Chapter I

Employment, equal treatment and workers' families

Section 2

Employment and equality of treatment

Article 7

1. A worker who is a national of a Member State may not, in the territory of another Member State, be treated differently from national workers by reason of 3.183

his nationality in respect of any conditions of employment and work, in particular as regards remuneration, dismissal, and, should he become unemployed, reinstatement or re-employment.

2. He shall enjoy the same social and tax advantages as national workers.

3. He shall also, by virtue of the same right and under the same conditions as national workers, have access to training in vocational schools and retraining centres.

4. Any clause of a collective or individual agreement or of any other collective regulation concerning eligibility for employment, remuneration and other conditions of work or dismissal shall be null and void in so far as it lays down or authorises discriminatory conditions in respect of workers who are nationals of the other Member States.

DERIVATION

3.184 Article 7 of Regulation 1612/68/EEC.

GENERAL NOTE

Eligibility under art.7

3.185 This provision protects workers and the Regulation has no application to self-employed persons. However, the Luxembourg Court is increasingly viewing the rights enjoyed by those who are economically active as not being dependent upon the nature of their economic activity, but on their status as citizens of the Union. Were the point to arise, the Luxembourg Court would probably determine that the prohibition of discrimination required Member States to accord to self-employed persons similar benefits to those which arise under this provision for employed persons.

Paragraph 2

3.186 If a national of a Member State is a worker within the meaning of this Regulation, then art.7(2) may often be a better passport to entitlement to a social security benefit than the co-ordinating rules in Reg.883/2004, or reliance on citizenship of the Union. There is no limitation in relation to the material scope of this Regulation; this provision covers social assistance as well as social security falling within Regulation 883/2004. The worker is entitled to be treated in exactly the same way as someone in a similar position who is a national of the Member State. See, for examples, *R(IS) 4/98* and *R(IS) 12/98*, which concerned, respectively, entitlement to a funeral payment, and entitlement to income support.

Defining workers for the purpose of Title II of former Regulation 1612/68 was at the heart of the appeal in *CJSA/4065/1999*, in which the Commissioner referred questions to the Luxembourg Court. The ruling of the Luxembourg Court can be found in *Collins v SSWP* (C-138/02) [2004] E.C.R. I–2703, annexed to *R.(JSA)* 3/06. Collins held both Irish and American nationality. He had been a student in the United Kingdom for a semester in 1978, and in 1980 and 1981 had spent about ten months working in part-time casual work in the United Kingdom. He subsequently worked in the United States and in South Africa. In 1998 he returned to the United Kingdom to look for work, and shortly afterwards claimed an income-based jobseeker's allowance. This was refused because he was not regarded as being habitually resident in the United Kingdom.

The Advocate General and the Court used different reasoning in reaching essentially the same conclusion. The Advocate General began his Opinion by recalling the rights of citizens of the Union under art.39 EC (now art.45 TFEU), but also noted that a person must have the status of actually being a "worker" (as distinct from a "work seeker") before he or she could rely on art.7(2) of Regulation 1612/68. The Advocate General went on to note that the habitual residence test is, in principle, indirectly discriminatory since it is easier for United Kingdom nationals to fulfil the requirement than nationals of other Member States. However, the Advocate General considered that a condition as to residence which makes it possible to ascertain the degree of connection with the host Member State and the links which the claimant has with the domestic employment market may be justified in order to avoid the movement of persons for the purpose of taking advantage of non-contributory benefits and to prevent abuses. The Advocate General accordingly proposed that the answer to the questions posed by the Commissioner should that Community law as it then stood does not require that an income-based social security benefit be provided to a citizen of the Union who seeks work in a Member State with whose employment market he lacks any connection or link.

The Luxembourg Court concludes that a person in Collins' situation is not a "worker" for the purposes of Title II of Regulation 1612/68, although it is for the national adjudicating authorities to determine whether the term "worker", as used in the national legislation, is to be understood in the same sense. The link with the earlier employment is too remote to permit his classification as a worker in 1998.

Furthermore, Collins did not have a right to reside in the United Kingdom solely on the basis of Council Directive 68/360 (a predecessor to some of the rules now to be found in the Citizenship Directive). Finally, the Court concluded:

> ". . . the right to equal treatment laid down in Art.48(2) (now 39(2)) of the Treaty, read in conjunction with Arts 6 (now 12) and 8 (now 17) of the Treaty, does not preclude legislation which makes entitlement to a jobseeker's allowance conditional on a residence requirement, in so far as that requirement may be justified on the basis of objective considerations that are independent of nationality of the persons concerned and proportionate to the legitimate aim of the national provisions". (At [73]).

CJSA/4065/1999, March 4, 2005, is the Commissioner's decision following the reference in *Collins*. On the status of Collins as a worker for the purposes of Regulation 1612/68 in the JSA Regulations, the Commissioner had this to say:

> "In my judgment, the reference in regulation 85(4) of the JSA Regulations to a 'workers for the purposes of [Regulation 1612/68]' must have been intended to have a narrower effect than a reference to a person within the scope of application of the Regulation as a whole. By 'worker' is meant a person who falls within the Community concept of worker in relation to the parts of Regulation 1612/68 that expressly confer entitlements on people in their capacity as workers, rather than in their capacity as nationals of a Member State. That restricts the meaning on the reference in the JSA Regulations to persons who are workers for the purposes of Title II of Part I of Regulation 1612/68. The meaning does not extend to persons who are entitled to assistance under Title I of Part I (in particular Article 5) or who fall only within the broader sense of 'worker' mentioned in paragraph 32 of the ECJ's judgment." (See para.16.)

The Commissioner then turned to the Luxembourg Court's conclusions on European Union law requirements in relation to justification for the requirement to establish habitual residence, and found that the test of justification and proportionality is met by the habitual residence test as a condition of entitlement to a means-tested jobseeker's allowance. However, he added a proviso: for the application of the requirement for any day to be proportionate in any particular case, the answer to the question, "Has the point been reached that the relevant national authority has become satisfied of the genuineness of the claimant's search for work?" must be in the negative. The Commissioner's decision was largely upheld by the Court of Appeal in *Collins v SSWP* [2006] EWCA Civ 376, annexed to *R.(JSA) 3/06*. However, the Court of Appeal concluded that the Commissioner erred in concluding that in order to render the habitual residence test compatible with Community law it was necessary to introduce the proviso set out above. The result is that the habitual residence test alone is, in the view of the Court of Appeal, sufficient to secure compatibility with European Union law on access to a jobseekers allowance. 3.187

The *Hartmann* case in the Court of Justice (*Hartmann v Freistaat Bayern* (C-212/05) [2007] E.C.R. I–6303) also concerned the definition of "worker" for the purposes of art.7(2). Mr and Mrs Hartmann are a married couple with three children. Before the couple married in 1990, Mr Hartmann lived and worked in Germany. Following the marriage he moved to Austria, but continued to work in Germany. Claims for a German child-raising allowance were refused on the grounds that the applicant, Mrs Hartmann, was not resident in Germany. Regulation 1408/71 was not applicable because Mr Hartmann was a civil servant, and at the material time, civil servants were not included within the personal scope of that regulation; they now are. Mr Hartmann became a frontier worker, living in Austria but working in Germany.

The question was whether a person who had moved his residence, not in connection with his employment, but for other reasons, could be considered to be a worker for the purposes of Regulation 1612/68. The Advocate General came to a different conclusion from that reached by the court, but his discussion of the issues provides helpful background to the judgment of the court. The Luxembourg Court concluded that Mr Hartmann was a worker within the meaning of that term in art.7(2) of Regulation 1612/68; his motivation for moving his country of residence, unconnected as it was with his employment, did not justify refusing him the status of migrant worker. The Court then moves on to consider whether the ability of Mrs Hartmann to claim a German child-raising allowance constitutes a social advantage for Mr Hartmann; in other words, does the indirect nature of the benefit of equal treatment extend to the spouse of a worker? The benefit claimed has as one of its conditions of entitlement that the person claiming it devotes herself to the raising of children and has no full-time employment. The Luxembourg Court considers that the benefit is a social advantage for the worker since the income contributes to the overall family expenses, which would otherwise fall exclusive on the parent who was working. A residence requirement is capable of discriminating against workers who do not reside in Germany, and would require objective justification and proportionality to be established. The Court reported that the German authorities exercised some discretion in relation to the residence requirement in the case of frontier workers. For the Court this meant that residence was not the only connecting link with Germany; and it followed that the allowance could not be refused on Mrs Hartmann's application.

3.188 The *Geven* case, (*Geven (*C-213/05) [2007] E.C.R. I–6347) decided on the same day, also concerned an application for a German child-raising allowance in rather difference circumstances. Ms Geven is a Dutch national. When her son was born she was living in the Netherlands with her husband. After the statutory maternity protection period and during her son's first year, she worked in Germany for between three and 14 hours a week. Her claim for a child-raising allowance in Germany was refused on the grounds that she was neither resident in Germany nor in more than minor employment. The Court confirmed that the allowance is a social advantage within the scope of Reg.1612/68. But, contrary to its conclusion in the *Hartmann* case, the Court concluded that the requirement for a substantial link with the German labour market established by the nature of the employment is capable of constituting a legitimate justification for a refusal to grant the social advantage at issue. In cases where a person is not currently working but has worked in the past in a period which is sufficiently closely connected in time to the claim for benefit, it will be important to recall that a person does not automatically lose worker status simply by reason of the employment ending. It is the circumstances in which the work ends which must be considered.

In *Ninni-Orasche* (C-413/01) [2003] E.C.R. I–13187, the Luxembourg Court was considering a reference from Verwaltungsgerichthof in Austria concerning an Italian national, Franca Ninni-Orasche, who had been married to an Austrian national since January 1993, and had been resident in Austria since November 1993. Ninni-Orasche had been employed as a waitress between July 6 and September 25, 1995;

she also had some duties as a cashier and in relation to stock control. She was also undertaking part-time study and subsequently passed examinations qualifying her for admission to an Austrian university. She was refused financial support for her studies. The question was whether she was a worker for the purposes of art.39 EC (now art.45 TFEU), and more particularly Regulation 1612/68, since she would then appear potentially to be entitled to financial support for her studies under art.7(2) of the Regulation (provided other conditions were satisfied). The Court concluded that the short-term work Ninni-Orasche had undertaken qualified her as a worker under art.39 EC "provided that the activity performed as an employed person is not purely marginal or ancillary" (at [32]). This is an issue to be determined by the national courts. Furthermore, a person would not be treated as voluntarily unemployed merely because the initial contract of employment was for a fixed term which has expired. See also observations in *R(IS) 12/98*.

MR v HMRC (TC) [2011] UKUT 40 (AAC) concerned a claim for the 50 Plus element of working tax credit by a Polish migrant who had been in receipt of unemployment benefit in Poland prior to his arrival in the United Kingdom to work. He claimed working tax credit with the 50 Plus element, but was refused because the conditions of entitlement required the claimant to have been in receipt of one of a number of specified UK benefits. The claimant argued that his Polish benefit equated to one of these benefits and that he was entitled to the supplement under art.7(2) of Regulation 1612/68.

The judge concludes that the requirement to be in receipt of a specified UK benefit was indirectly discriminatory on grounds of nationality, that the justification put forward by HMRC (tackling low employment in the over-50 age group, increasing the output of the UK economy, and reducing the United Kingdom's social security bill) was not proportionate, and that, accordingly, the requirement to be in receipt of a UK qualifying benefit should be disapplied in the claimant's case. The judge accepted the legitimacy of the aims, but found that the response had to justify the discriminatory effect of the provisions. The arguments put forward did not do that. The ongoing practical importance of the decision is limited since the 50 Plus element of working tax credit is to be abolished from April 2012. However, the decision is a good illustration of the application of an entitlement flowing from art.7(2) of Reg.1612/68. **3.189**

Commission v The Netherlands (C-542/09) Judgment of June 14, 2012, concerned the permissibility of a Dutch condition of entitlement for an award of funding higher education outside the Netherlands that the person be eligible for funding for higher education in the Netherlands *and* has resided in the Netherlands for three out of the six years preceding enrolment at the higher education establishment abroad. The Commission brought infringement proceedings, arguing that the conditions of entitlement amounted to indirect discrimination against migrant workers, and was incompatible with the obligations in art.7 of Reg.1612/68 (now Reg.492/2011). The Court agreed that it was indirect discrimination which was not permitted unless it could be objectively justified. The Court rejected the argument that the conditions of entitlement were needed in order to avoid an unreasonable financial burden falling on the state. Ultimately it was the prioritisation of the length of residence to the exclusion of other considerations that resulted in the Court declaring that the Netherlands had failed to fulfil its obligations under the Treaty.

The significance of this case is that it shows that arguments based on indirect discrimination flowing from conditions of entitlement have to be assessed individually in each case. The detailed reasoning of the Court draws together a wide range of authorities in the field, as does the typically robust Opinion of Advocate General Sharpston. See also *Prete* (C-367/11) Judgment of October 25, 2012, which comes to a similar conclusion on the same reasoning in the context of rights flowing from what is now art.45 TFEU in relation to a requirement for eligibility for a tideover allowance (a special benefit for young persons seeking their first job) that they had completed at least six years of studies in Belgium.

Paragraph (3)

3.190 This provision is concerned with the worker's access to vocational training. It is art.10 which deals with the education of the children of workers.

Article 9

3.191 1. A worker who is a national of a Member State and who is employed in the territory of another Member State shall enjoy all the rights and benefits accorded to national workers in matters of housing, including ownership of the housing he needs.

2. A worker referred to in paragraph 1 may, with the same right as nationals, put his name down on the housing lists in the region in which he is employed, where such lists exist, and shall enjoy the resultant benefits and priorities.

If his family has remained in the country whence he came, they shall be considered for this purpose as residing in the said region, where national workers benefit from a similar presumption.

DERIVATION

3.192 Article 9 of Regulation 1612/68/EEC.

GENERAL NOTE

3.193 The predecessor to art.9 has not been, but might be, raised in cases concerning entitlement to housing benefit. Article 9 certainly makes clear that provision of housing and benefits related to housing must be provided to workers from other Member States on the same basis as provision for workers who are UK nationals.

SECTION 3

Workers' families

Article 10

3.194 The children of a national of a Member State who is or has been employed in the territory of another Member State shall be admitted to that State's general educational, apprenticeship and vocational training courses under the same conditions as the nationals of that State, if such children are residing in its territory.

Member States shall encourage all efforts to enable such children to attend these courses under the best possible conditions.

DERIVATION

3.195 Article 12 of Regulation 1612/68/EEC.

GENERAL NOTE

3.196 For an elaboration of the rights contained in the predecessor to this article, see *Echternach and Moritz* (389 and 390/87) [1989] E.C.R. 723. In *Baumbast and R* (C–413/99) [2002] E.C.R. I–7091, the Luxembourg Court recognised the right of a parent, who was a third country national and the primary carer of children, to reside in the United Kingdom in order for the children to be able to exercise their right to education.

The rights of children under art.10 give rise to an independent right to reside in the host Member State which is not dependent upon the children, or their primary carer, being economically self-sufficient and holding comprehensive sickness insurance: *Ibrahim* (C–310/08) [2010] E.C.R. I–1065; and *Teixeira* (C–480/08) Judgment of February 23, 2010, [2010] E.C.R. I–1107. Nor is it necessary for the child to have started in education while the parent was actually in work; it is enough that the parent has been a worker. The primary carer has a right of residence in order to make the rights of the children to education practical and effective, but the right to reside of the carer will cease when the child completes his or her education.

In *Alarape and Tijani* (C-529/11) Judgment of May 8, 2013, the Court of Justice has ruled that periods of residence by family members on the sole basis of art.12 of Reg.1612/68 (now art.10 of Reg.492/11) in circumstances where no rights to reside arise under the Citizenship Directive do not constitute periods to be taken into account in computing the period required in order to acquire permanent resident status under art.16 of the Citizenship Directive. However, the same case also confirms that the parent of a child who has attained the age of majority and remains in education may continue to have a derived right of residence "if the child remains in need of the presence and care of that parent in order to be able to continue and to complete his or her education" (at [31]). The answer to that question is to be determined by the national authorities taking account of all the circumstances.

Following the rulings in the *Ibrahim* and *Teixeira* cases, the Department issued Memo DMG 30/10 offering guidance on the application of the rulings but this has been amended by Memo DMG 21/12. This stresses the impact the rulings will have on a range of means-tested benefits, not just housing benefit. The following points are made:

- The beneficiaries of the rulings must be children citizens of the Union or an EEA national, and the parent must be or have been a worker (not a work seeker).
- General education runs from the start of primary education, and excludes play school and pre-school schemes. But it may include education after the age of 18.
- The child may retain an entitlement to reside in connection with education even where the parent leaves to United Kingdom.
- Absence which is other than temporary will break the child's right to reside.

The issue in *SSWP v IM (IS)* [2011] UKUT 231 (AAC) concerned the stage at which general educational courses begin for the purposes of art.12 of Reg.1612/68. The judge decided that, in the circumstances of the appeal before him, the right under art.12 arises when a child enters compulsory education at around the age of five (see [17]). However, note that the judge specifically states that his conclusion relates only to England and that there may be differences in Wales or Scotland and only to the position in late 2006 and early 2007. The law has been changed from 2008 (see [3]).

In *Shabani v Secretary of State for the Home Department* [2013] UKUT 315 (IAC) the Secretary of State for the Home Department conceded that the primary carer of a child of a Union citizen who has been employed in the host Member State is entitled to a derivative right of residence once that child has entered into reception class education. The Secretary of State also indicated that the definition of "education" was to be reviewed.

MDB, MADB (a minor), and GRDB (a minor) v SSHD [2012] EWCA Civ 1015 **3.197**
is a judgment of the Court of Appeal which holds that a person who, in a period of residence of several years, had worked for only 80 hours in a 10-week period earning around £1,000 did not constitute a worker either for the purposes of art.12 of Regulation 1612/68 (the predecessor of this provision). As a consequence the entitlement of the children to remain in the United Kingdom under art.12 failed. In the proceedings, it had been conceded that the test for being a "worker" was the same under Regulation 1612/68 and under the Citizenship Directive. The Court expressed some reservations about that concession, but did not pursue the point.

In *SSWP v LC (IS)* [2011] UKUT 108 (AAC), reported as [2013] AACR 6, the Upper Tribunal judge made a reference to the Court of Justice in Luxembourg in the following terms:

"The following questions are referred to the European Court of Justice for a preliminary ruling:
"In circumstances where a claimant:

(a) is a citizen of Poland;
(b) came to the United Kingdom before her country acceded to the EU;
(c) established herself in self- employment within the meaning of Article 49 TFEU (ex at. 43 TEC);
(d) remained here, and continued in self- employment, following accession;
(e) is no longer in self- employment; and
(f) is the primary carer of a child who came to the United Kingdom and entered general education after accession and after she ceased to be established in self- employment,

does the claimant have a right to reside in the United Kingdom on the basis that (individually or cumulatively):

(a) Regulation 1612/68 applies, together with the reasoning of the European Court of Justice in *Baumbast and R v Secretary of State for the Home Department* (C–413/99) [2002] E.C.R. I–7091, *London Borough of Harrow v Ibrahim* (C–310/08) and *Teixeira v London Borough of Lambeth* (C–480/08);
(b) there is a general principle of EU law that equates the position of workers and the self- employed;
(c) it would impede or deter the freedom of establishment if the claimant did not have a right to reside?"

A reference in almost identical terms was made in a case involving a Czech national by the same judge in *SSWP v MP (IS)* [2011] UKUT 109 (AAC), reported as [2013] AACR 6.

3.198 The responses of the Court of Justice to these references is not altogether satisfactory, in part because the United Kingdom government made concessions in the cases which deprived the Court of the opportunity to respond fully to some of the questions. In particular, the Secretary of State accepted that both Czop and Punakova had a right to reside for the purposes of their claims to income support. In Ms Czop's case that arose because she had attained permanent residence in the United Kingdom (she was either self-employed or self-sufficient under the terms of the Directive for the required period). In Ms Punakova's case that arose because she had a right of residence as the primary carer of a child in education because her partner had worked in the United Kingdom and their child had "installed himself" in the United Kingdom while the father was a worker. The Secretary of State further conceded that there was no requirement for a congruent period during which the parent was in work and the child was in education.

SSWP v Czop, SSWP v Punakova (C-147/11) and (C-148/11) Judgment of September 6, 2012, reported as [2013] AACR 6, are the responses to questions referred in *SSWP v LC (IS)* [2011] UKUT 108 (AAC) and *SSWP v MP (IS)* [2011] UKUT 109 (AAC). The response to the questions raised shows a stark contrast between employment and self-employment when the rights flowing from what is now art.10 are considered. The Court of Justice advised that art.12 of Regulation 1612/68 (and it would follow also art.10 of Reg.492/2011) concerns only employed persons, and cannot be interpreted as applying also to self-employed persons. In the case of *Punakova,* it was established that she was the primary carer of a child whose father had been employed in the United Kingdom, and so had a right of residence. That, however, was not the case in *Czop*. It was not necessary to explore further the position of self-employed persons compared with employed persons, since the United Kingdom government produced information at the hearing showing the Lucja Czop had a right of permanent residence under art.16(1) of the Citizenship Directive at the material time.

SSWP v Margita Punakova [2012] UKUT 352 (AAC) and *SSWP v Lucja Czop*

[2012] UKUT 351 (AAC) are the final decisions dismissing the appeals of the Secretary of State. The judge also makes some brief observations on the questions he had raised which had not needed to be answered by the Court of Justice in the context of the information and arguments put by the United Kingdom government before the Court of Justice.

In *Hrabkova v Secretary of State for Work and Pensions* [2017] EWCA Civ 794, the Court of Appeal ruled that *Czop (C-147/11)* had definitively determined that art.12 of Regulation 1612/68 (and by implication art.10 of Regulation 492/2011) could not apply to Ms Czop because she was a self-employed person, and not a worker (that is, an employee). Furthermore, arguments based on treating employed persons and self-employed persons as having the same rights because there would otherwise be discrimination were ill-founded.

RM v SSWP (IS) [2014] UKUT 401 (AAC) decides that the logic of the structure of the reasoning of the Court of Justice in responding to references in the *Czop* and *Punakova* cases means that the children of self-employed persons are not entitled to a right of residence as primary carers under art.12 of Regulation 1612/68; and it would follow the successor provision in art.10.

SSWP v RR (IS) [2013] UKUT 21 (AAC), reported as [2013] AACR 20, a decision of a three-judge panel, clarifies two matters relating to the application of the rights contained in what is now art.10. The panel concluded that the rights could be relied on where the child in question is a British national, and considers that the proposition to the contrary in para.17 of *SSWP v SW (IS)* [2011] UKUT 508 is not good law. The second issue related to the circumstances in which the rights in art.10 would be lost where the worker leaves the United Kingdom. The panel ruled:

> "79. In our view, rights relating to the process of integration of a Union citizen who has exercised rights of free movement do not last forever. This much is clear in relation, for example, to the acquisition of the right of permanent residence under Articles 16 and 17 of the Citizenship Directive. Under Article 16(4) the right of permanent residence can be lost 'through absence from the host Member State for a continuous period of two years.'
>
> 80. We have concluded that whether an absence from the host Member results in the loss of the ability to claim the integration rights in [art.10] will be a matter to be determined in the light of all the circumstances of each case. Where a person has established an habitual residence in another Member State for a substantial period, we consider that the right to rely on a period of employment in an earlier period of residence in order to trigger the rights in [art.10] will be lost. Where the absence can properly be characterised as temporary having regard to all the circumstances, the right will not be lost. We observe that the test will always arise by considering what has happened in the past rather than what might happen in the future.
>
> 81. The most relevant factors will be (a) the reasons why the person ceased to be resident in the host Member State in which the rights are being asserted; (b) the activities which the person undertook in the country to which he or she went, including economic activity in that country; (c) the roots which the person put down in the new country of residence; (d) the contact and its quality which the person retained with the host Member State; and (e) the length of absence from the host Member State. The longer the absence, the more difficult it will be to rely on the earlier period in work."

In *IP v SSWP (IS)* [2015] UKUT 691, Judge Jacobs, relying on *ONAFTS V Radia Hadj Ahmed* (C-45/12), Judgment of June 13, 2013, concluded that a child's parent can only benefit from what is now art.10 if that child is the child of someone who is or has been a worker. It will not assist a claimant that her current partner who is not the father of the child is or has been a worker. In *IP v SSWP* neither parent of the child had ever been a worker.

Article 10 is drafted in terms very similar to art.12 of former Regulation 1612/68, which was the subject of Judge Wright's decision in *HMRC v IT (CTC)* [2016] UKUT 252 (AAC). The claimant was a national of Romania and so was an "A2 national" whose rights under European Union law were limited under the accession arrangements for Romania. The claimant had never worked in authorised work, (because he had not registered the work under the applicable workers' registration arrangements for Romanian—and Bulgarian—nationals) although he had undertaken some work. Judge Wright considered whether the use of the term "worker" in art.12 of Regulation 1612/68 (and it would follow in art.10 of Regulation 492/2011) covered the claimant, since the derogation in the accession arrangements only referred to arts 1–6 of Regulation 1612/68. Judge Wright concludes that it did not since the claimant had never been admitted to the United Kingdom's employment market. Judge Wright explains at paras 31–55 how and why his conclusions are not inconsistent with the outcome in *SSWP v JS* [2010] UKUT 347 (AAC).

The fourth question referred by the Court of Appeal in *Secretary of State for the Home Department v NA* (C-115/15) [2015] OJ C171/20 is:--

> "4. Does a child have a right to reside in the host Member State pursuant to Article 12 of Regulation (EEC) No 1612/68/EEC_(now Article 10 of Regulation 492/2011/EU) if the child's Union citizen parent, who has been employed in the host Member State, has ceased to reside in the host Member State before the child enters education in that state?"

The Court of Justice issued its decision in *Secretary of State for the Home Department v NA* (C-115/15) on June 30, 2016. The Court ruled that the answer to the fourth question raised by the Court of Appeal is as follows:

> "68. In the light of the foregoing, the answer to the fourth question is that Article 12 of Regulation 1612/68 must be interpreted as meaning that a child and a parent who is a third-country national and who has sole custody of that child qualify for a right of residence in the host Member State, under that provision, in a situation, such as that in the main proceedings, where the other parent is a Union citizen and worked in that Member State, but has ceased to reside there before the child began to attend school in that Member State."

CHAPTER IV

Final Provisions

Article 36

3.199 1. This Regulation shall not affect the provisions of the Treaty establishing the European Atomic Energy Community which deal with eligibility for skilled employment in the field of nuclear energy, nor any measures taken in pursuance of that Treaty.

Nevertheless, this Regulation shall apply to the category of workers referred to in the first subparagraph and to members of their families in so far as their legal position is not governed by the above-mentioned Treaty or measures.

2. This Regulation shall not affect measures taken in accordance with Article 48 of the Treaty on the Functioning of the European Union.

3. This Regulation shall not affect the obligations of Member States arising out of special relations or future agreements with certain non-European countries or territories, based on institutional ties existing on 8 November 1968, or agreements in existence on 8 November 1968 with certain non-European countries or territories, based on institutional ties between them.

Workers from such countries or territories who, in accordance with this provision, are pursuing activities as employed persons in the territory of one of those Member States may not invoke the benefit of the provisions of this Regulation in the territory of the other Member States.

DERIVATION

Article 42 of Regulation 1612/68/EEC. 3.200

GENERAL NOTE

Following the amendment of the EC Treaty art.51 of the EEC Treaty became art.42 EC, and is now art.48 TFEU which refers to the adoption of measures in the field of social security. In *C50/90- 00* (DLA) a Commissioner in Northern Ireland concluded that the effect of art.42(2) can be to preclude the application of art.7(2) where the matter is governed by Regulation 1408/71 (a regulation made under art.51 (now 42 EC) of the EEC Treaty). The case concerned a claimant for a disability living allowance on the basis of European Union law; the claimant was at all relevant times resident in Ireland. She later claimed a disability living allowance in Northern Ireland where she worked, arguing that art.7(2) meant that the residence and presence conditions could not be applied to her. The Commissioner upheld the decision of the tribunal that she could not maintain the art.7(2) right since disability living allowance was a benefit falling within art.10a of Regulation 1408/71, which alone applied to her situation. She said: 3.201

> "28. It does not appeal to me that Article 42(2) can be given anything other than its plain meaning, i.e. that Regulation (EEC)1612/68 is not to affect measures taken under Article 51. The provisions of that regulation cannot have any effect on such measures".

In *CIS/825/2001* a Commissioner in England, while not dissenting from the decision of the Commissioner in Northern Ireland, disagreed with the reasoning, since it was too wide. The Commissioner in England said:

> "43. I conclude from both the specific comments of the Court in *EC Commission v French Republic* and from the absence of the point being taken by or to the Court in other cases that the 'plain meaning' attached to Article 42(2) in C 50/99- 00 (DLA) is too wide. The right granted by Article 7(2) of Regulation 1612/68 is a fundamental aspect of the freedom of movement of workers—and, perhaps it should now be said, of European citizens. It is one of the essential aspects of the freedom granted by Article 39 (formerly Article 48) of the Treaty, securing the freedom of movement of workers. Regulation 1408/71 is about coordinating social security systems under Article 42 (formerly 51) of the Treaty by adopting 'such measures as are necessary to provide freedom of movement of workers'. Those Articles pursue parallel aims, and I do not readily read a final provision in Regulation 1612/68 as undercutting those parallel aims so as to reduce a worker's rights under Article 7 of that Regulation unless there is clear reason to do so. The reason to do so, as the European Court reflects, is that there is some provision of Regulation 1408/71 in application which provides a benefit to a worker in a different way to Regulation 1612/68 but, by reason of the purposes of those Regulations, to the same end. In other words, it is an example of what used to be given the Latin tag *specialia generalibus derogant*—a specific rule derogates from a general rule. But, in this context, both rules are concerned with granting rights and not restricting them".

In *SSWP v Bobezes* [2005] EWCA Civ 111, (the appeal against the Commissioner's decision in *CIS/825/2001*) reported as *R(IS) 6/05*, the Court of Appeal alluded to the question of whether art.42 precluded the application of art.7 of Regulation 1612/68 to the claimant's case. Lord Slynn said:

> "15. Despite all these arguments based on the European Court's authorities the real point for the purpose of this case is that, when considering whether there is discrimination against Mr Bobezes in the application of . . . the United Kingdom Regulation, there is no difference between Article 3 [of Regulation 1408/71] and Article 7 [of Regulation 1612/68]. . . . Both unequivocally

prohibit the different treatment of migrant workers and national workers in the grant and payment of the allowance. … Despite the Secretary of State's argument [that it was essential for the court to decide under which of the two regulations the matter had to be resolved] I do not consider that it would be appropriate in the circumstances for the court to review all the authorities and to express an opinion on what is at best a theoretical question with no consequences for the parties to this appeal."

Directive 2004/38/EC of the European Parliament and of the Council of 29 April 2004 on the right of citizens of the Union and their family members to move and reside freely within the territory of the Member States amending Regulation (EEC) No 1612/68 and repealing Directives 64/221/EEC, 68/360/EEC, 72/194/EEC, 73/148/EEC, 75/34/EEC, 75/35/EEC, 90/364/EEC, 90/365/EEC and 93/96/EEC

[2004] OJ L229/35 CORRIGENDUM [2005] OJ L197/34

Date for implementation: April 30, 2006

General Note

3.202 The Immigration (European Economic Area) Regulations 2006 (SI 2006/1003), as amended, implemented into United Kingdom law the requirements of the Directive. The Immigration (European Economic Area) Regulations 2016 (SI 2016/1052) consolidate and amend the Immigration (European Economic Area) Regulations 2006 (SI 2006/1003), as amended, and came fully into force on February 1, 2017. These regulations are reproduced in *Volume II: Income Support, Jobseeker's Allowance, State Pension Credit and the Social Fund.*

The following two documents may assist in the proper interpretation of the requirements of the Directive, since they set out the Commission's view on such matters:

Report from the Commission to the European Parliament and the Council on the application of Directive 2004/38/EC on the right of citizens of the Union and their family members to move and reside freely within the territory of the Member States, COM(2008) 840/3.

Communication from the Commission to the European Parliament and the Council on guidance for better transposition and application of Directive 2004/38/EC on the right of citizens of the Union and their family members to move and reside freely within the territory of the Member States, COM(2009) 313/4.

Relationship between Regulation (EC) No 883/2004 and Directive No 2004/38/EC is a useful note published by the European Commission's Employment, Social Affairs and Inclusion Directorate in January 2011. It is one of a series of explanatory notes on the key concepts of modernised coordination, which can be found at *http://ec.europa.eu/social/main.jsp?catId=866&langId=en&furtherPubs=yes* [Accessed May 24, 2012].

The European Parliament and the Council of the European Union

3.203 *Having regard* to the Treaty establishing the European Community, and in particular Articles 12, 18, 40, 44 and 52 thereof,

Having regard to the proposal from the Commission,

Having regard to the opinion of the European Economic and Social Committee,

Having regard to the opinion of the Committee of the Regions, *Acting in accordance* with the procedure laid down in Article 251 of the Treaty,

Whereas:

(1) Citizenship of the Union confers on every citizen of the Union a primary and individual right to move and reside freely within the territory of the Member States, subject to the limitations and conditions laid down in the Treaty and to the measures adopted to give it effect.

(2) The free movement of persons constitutes one of the fundamental freedoms of the internal market, which comprises an area without internal frontiers, in which freedom is ensured in accordance with the provisions of the Treaty.

(3) Union citizenship should be the fundamental status of nationals of the Member States when they exercise their right of free movement and residence. It is therefore necessary to codify and review the existing Community instruments dealing separately with workers, self employed persons, as well as students and other inactive persons in order to simplify and strengthen the right of free movement and residence of all Union citizens.

(4) With a view to remedying this sector-by-sector, piecemeal approach to the right of free movement and residence and facilitating the exercise of this right, there needs to be a single legislative act to amend Council Regulation (EEC) No 1612/68 of 15 October 1968 on freedom of movement for workers within the Community, and to repeal the following acts: Council Directive 68/360/EEC of 15 October 1968 on the abolition of restrictions on movement and residence within the Community for workers of Member States and their families, Council Directive 73/148/EEC of 21 May 1973 on the abolition of restrictions on movement and residence within the Community for nationals of Member States with regard to establishment and the provision of services, Council Directive 90/364/ EEC of 28 June 1990 on the right of residence, Council Directive 90/365/EEC of 28 June 1990 on the right of residence for employees and self-employed persons who have ceased their occupational activity and Council Directive 93/96/EEC of 29 October 1993 on the right of residence for students.

(5) The right of all Union citizens to move and reside freely within the territory of the Member States should, if it is to be exercised under objective conditions of freedom and dignity, be also granted to their family members, irrespective of nationality. For the purposes of this Directive, the definition of "family member" should also include the registered partner if the legislation of the host Member State treats registered partnership as equivalent to marriage.

(6) In order to maintain the unity of the family in a broader sense and without prejudice to the prohibition of discrimination on grounds of nationality, the situation of those persons who are not included in the definition of family members under this Directive, and who therefore do not enjoy an automatic right of entry and residence in the host Member State, should be examined by the host Member State on the basis of its own national legislation, in order to decide whether entry and residence could be granted to such persons, taking into consideration their relationship with the Union citizen or any other circumstances, such as their financial or physical dependence on the Union citizen.

(7) The formalities connected with the free movement of Union citizens within the territory of Member States should be clearly defined, without prejudice to the provisions applicable to national border controls.

(8) With a view to facilitating the free movement of family members who are not nationals of a Member State, those who have already obtained a residence card should be exempted from the requirement to obtain an entry visa within the meaning of Council Regulation (EC) No 539/2001 of 15 March 2001 listing the third countries whose nationals must be in possession of visas when crossing the external borders and those whose nationals are exempt from that requirement (1) or, where appropriate, of the applicable national legislation.

(9) Union citizens should have the right of residence in the host Member State for a period not exceeding three months without being subject to any conditions or any formalities other than the requirement to hold a valid identity card or passport, without prejudice to a more favourable treatment applicable to job-seekers as recognised by the case-law of the Court of Justice.

(10) Persons exercising their right of residence should not, however, become an unreasonable burden on the social assistance system of the host Member State during an initial period of residence. Therefore, the right of residence for Union citizens and their family members for periods in excess of three months should be subject to conditions.

(11) The fundamental and personal right of residence in another Member State is conferred directly on Union citizens by the Treaty and is not dependent upon their having fulfilled administrative procedures.

(12) For periods of residence of longer than three months, Member States should have the possibility to require Union citizens to register with the competent authorities in the place of residence, attested by a registration certificate issued to that effect.

(13) The residence card requirement should be restricted to family members of Union citizens who are not nationals of a Member State for periods of residence of longer than three months.

(14) The supporting documents required by the competent authorities for the issuing of a registration certificate or of a residence card should be comprehensively specified in order to avoid divergent administrative practices or interpretations constituting an undue obstacle to the exercise of the right of residence by Union citizens and their family members.

(15) Family members should be legally safeguarded in the event of the death of the Union citizen, divorce, annulment of marriage or termination of a registered partnership. With due regard for family life and human dignity, and in certain conditions to guard against abuse, measures should therefore be taken to ensure that in such circumstances family members already residing within the territory of the host Member State retain their right of residence exclusively on a personal basis.

(16) As long as the beneficiaries of the right of residence do not become an unreasonable burden on the social assistance system of the host Member State they should not be expelled. Therefore, an expulsion measure should not be the automatic consequence of recourse to the social assistance system. The host Member State should examine whether it is a case of temporary difficulties and take into account the duration of residence, the personal circumstances and the amount of aid granted in order to consider whether the beneficiary has become an unreasonable burden on its social assistance system and to proceed to his expulsion. In no case should an expulsion measure be adopted against workers, self-employed persons or job-seekers as defined by the Court of Justice save on grounds of public policy or public security.

(17) Enjoyment of permanent residence by Union citizens who have

chosen to settle long term in the host Member State would strengthen the feeling of Union citizenship and is a key element in promoting social cohesion, which is one of the fundamental objectives of the Union. A right of permanent residence should therefore be laid down for all Union citizens and their family members who have resided in the host Member State in compliance with the conditions laid down in this Directive during a continuous period of five years without becoming subject to an expulsion measure.

(18) In order to be a genuine vehicle for integration into the society of the host Member State in which the Union citizen resides, the right of permanent residence, once obtained, should not be subject to any conditions.

(19) Certain advantages specific to Union citizens who are workers or self-employed persons and to their family members, which may allow these persons to acquire a right of permanent residence before they have resided five years in the host Member State, should be maintained, as these constitute acquired rights, conferred by Commission Regulation (EEC) No 1251/70 of 29 June 1970 on the right of workers to remain in the territory of a Member State after having been employed in that State (1) and Council Directive 75/34/EEC of 17 December 1974 concerning the right of nationals of a Member State to remain in the territory of another Member State after having pursued therein an activity in a self-employed capacity.

(20) In accordance with the prohibition of discrimination on grounds of nationality, all Union citizens and their family members residing in a Member State on the basis of this Directive should enjoy, in that Member State, equal treatment with nationals in areas covered by the Treaty, subject to such specific provisions as are expressly provided for in the Treaty and secondary law.

(21) However, it should be left to the host Member State to decide whether it will grant social assistance during the first three months of residence, or for a longer period in the case of job-seekers, to Union citizens other than those who are workers or self-employed persons or who retain that status or their family members, or maintenance assistance for studies, including vocational training, prior to acquisition of the right of permanent residence, to these same persons.

(22) The Treaty allows restrictions to be placed on the right of free movement and residence on grounds of public policy, public security or public health. In order to ensure a tighter definition of the circumstances and procedural safeguards subject to which Union citizens and their family members may be denied leave to enter or may be expelled, this Directive should replace Council Directive 64/221/EEC of 25 February 1964 on the coordination of special measures concerning the movement and residence of foreign nationals, which are justified on grounds of public policy, public security or public health.

(23) Expulsion of Union citizens and their family members on grounds of public policy or public security is a measure that can seriously harm persons who, having availed themselves of the rights and freedoms conferred on them by the Treaty, have become genuinely integrated into the host Member State. The scope for such measures should therefore be limited in accordance with the principle of proportionality to take account of the degree of integration of the persons concerned, the length of their residence in the host Member State, their age, state of health, family and economic situation and the links with their country of origin.

(24) Accordingly, the greater the degree of integration of Union citizens and their family members in the host Member State, the greater the degree of protection against expulsion should be. Only in exceptional circumstances, where there are imperative grounds of public security, should an expulsion measure be taken against Union citizens who have resided for many years in the territory of the host Member State, in particular when they were born and have resided there throughout their life. In addition, such exceptional circumstances should also apply to an expulsion measure taken against minors, in order to protect their links with their family, in accordance with the United Nations Convention on the Rights of the Child, of 20 November 1989.

(25) Procedural safeguards should also be specified in detail in order to ensure a high level of protection of the rights of Union citizens and their family members in the event of their being denied leave to enter or reside in another Member State, as well as to uphold the principle that any action taken by the authorities must be properly justified.

(26) In all events, judicial redress procedures should be available to Union citizens and their family members who have been refused leave to enter or reside in another Member State.

(27) In line with the case-law of the Court of Justice prohibiting Member States from issuing orders excluding for life persons covered by this Directive from their territory, the right of Union citizens and their family members who have been excluded from the territory of a Member State to submit a fresh application after a reasonable period, and in any event after a three year period from enforcement of the final exclusion order, should be confirmed.

(28) To guard against abuse of rights or fraud, notably marriages of convenience or any other form of relationships contracted for the sole purpose of enjoying the right of free movement and residence, Member States should have the possibility to adopt the necessary measures.

(29) This Directive should not affect more favourable national provisions.

(30) With a view to examining how further to facilitate the exercise of the right of free movement and residence, a report should be prepared by the Commission in order to evaluate the opportunity to present any necessary proposals to this effect, notably on the extension of the period of residence with no conditions.

(31) This Directive respects the fundamental rights and freedoms and observes the principles recognised in particular by the Charter of Fundamental Rights of the European Union. In accordance with the prohibition of discrimination contained in the Charter, Member States should implement this Directive without discrimination between the beneficiaries of this Directive on grounds such as sex, race, colour, ethnic or social origin, genetic characteristics, language, religion or beliefs, political or other opinion, membership of an ethnic minority, property, birth, disability, age or sexual orientation.

Have Adopted this Directive

Chapter I

General Provisions

Article 1

Subject

This Directive lays down: 3.204

(a) the conditions governing the exercise of the right of free movement and residence within the territory of the Member States by Union citizens and their family members;

(b) the right of permanent residence in the territory of the Member States for Union citizens and their family members;

(c) the limits placed on the rights set out in (a) and (b) on grounds of public policy, public security or public health.

General Note

Directive 2004/38 is frequently referred to as "the Citizenship Directive". It is more than a consolidation of existing law, and is more than merely an immigration code, since it spells out rights which migrants enjoy in the host Member State. 3.205

The United Kingdom government had initially taken the view that the Directive was a self-contained code, and that, since its entry into force, it constituted the sole basis for the conditions governing the exercise of the right of residence in the Member States. That position was firmly rejected in *Teixeira* (C-480/08) Judgment of February 23, 2010. The Luxembourg Court, sitting as a Grand Chamber, said that one of the aims of the Directive is "to simplify and strengthen the right of free movement and residence of all Union citizens" (at [60]). The Advocate General was even more trenchant in her rejection of the United Kingdom's position:

> "Moreover the directive undeniably applies to all Union citizens and their family members. Nevertheless, it does not contain comprehensive and definitive rules to govern every conceivable right of residence of those Union citizens and their family members." (para.48 of the Opinion)

In its judgment in *Ibrahim* (C-310/08) issued on the same day, the Grand Chamber makes the same point, noting that the Citizenship Directive was "designed to be consistent" with the judgment in the *Baumbast* case: (at [44]–[47]).

Article 2

Definitions

For the purposes of this Directive: 3.206

1. "Union citizen" means any person having the nationality of a Member State;

2. "family member" means:

(a) the spouse;

(b) the partner with whom the Union citizen has contracted a registered partnership, on the basis of the legislation of a Member State, if the legislation of the host Member State treats registered partnerships as equivalent to marriage and in accordance with the conditions laid down in the relevant legislation of the host Member State;

(c) the direct descendants who are under the age of 21 or are dependants and those of the spouse or partner as defined in point (b);

(d) the dependent direct relatives in the ascending line and those of the spouse or partner as defined in point (b);

3. "host Member State" means the Member State to which a Union citizen moves in order to exercise his/her right of free movement and residence.

General Note

3.207 The Directive extends the scope of the family in terms of rights flowing from the Directive. Under the previous regime, the family of a worker included the spouse, children under the age of 21, and children over the age of 21 together with relatives in the ascending line of the worker and spouse who are actually dependent on the worker. Family members need not be citizens of the Union, though many will be. This list is extended by art.2(2) of the Citizenship Directive to include those in civil partnerships. This extends the notion of spouse to include the recognition of unmarried partner status where this exists in the legislation of the Member States. The language is clearly broad enough to encompass same-sex relationships, but there is a requirement that the host Member State treats such partnerships as equivalent to marriage in the same circumstances. There is also the limitation that the registered partnership on which the mover is depending arises under the law of one of the Member States.

Eind (C-291/05) [2007] E.C.R. I-10719, was decided under provisions of Regulation 1612/68 which have been repealed and re-enacted in slightly different form in the Citizenship Directive. Article 10 of Reg.1612/68 provided (so far as relevant):

> "1. The following shall, irrespective of their nationality, have the right to install themselves with a worker who is a national of one Member State and who is employed in the territory of another Member State:
> (a) his spouse and their descendants who are under the age of 21 or are dependants; . . ."

The case concerned the position of third country nationals who are relatives of a citizen of the Union. Mr Eind, a Dutch national, moved to the United Kingdom in February 2000 where he found work. In December 2000 he was joined by his 11-year-old daughter, Rachel, who came direct to the United Kingdom from Suriname. The United Kingdom authorities accepted that Rachel was entitled to reside in the United Kingdom as the daughter of a worker. In October 2001, Mr Eind and his daughter went to The Netherlands. Mr Eind did not work there because of ill health. Rachel was refused a residence permit on the grounds that her father was not a worker for EU law purposes. When that decision was challenged, questions were referred to the Luxembourg Court. Relying in part on *Mattern and Cikotic* (C-10/05) [2006] E.C.R. I-3145, the court ruled that:

> ". . . the right of a third-country national who is a member of the family of a Community worker to install himself with that worker may be relied on only in the Member State where that worker resides." (See [24]).

3.208 So it followed that the Dutch authorities were not bound by the grant of a right to reside by another Member State even where that decision is made under art.10 of Reg.1612/68. However, that was not the end of the story. Any refusal to grant the family the possibility of returning to the Member State of origin would be an obstacle to free movement. Rachel Eind was entitled to reside in The Netherlands with her father by reason of art.10 of Reg.1612/68. Both the judgment of the Court and the Opinion of the Advocate General are silent on the Citizenship Directive, since they were concerned with events occurring before the entry into force of the Citizenship Directive. But it is worth noting one difference between the wording of Reg.1612/68 and the Citizenship Directive. In the *Eind* case the Court, following the *Mattern and Cikotic* case, interpreted arts 10 and 11 of Regulation 1612/68 as meaning that the rights could only be relied on *in the State in which the person was a worker*. Though the line of reasoning covers a range of provisions of the Citizenship Directive, it is arguable that this limitation no longer applies.

PM v SSHD [2011] UKUT 89 (IAC) rules that there is no difference in entitlements of a spouse who is not a national of one of the EEA countries and of a spouse who is such a national. The decision was made in the context of a married couple (a Turkish woman married to an Italian national) who were no longer living in the same household, but where social contact was retained and where the father visited his son twice a week and provided financial support for him.

Iida (C-40/11) Judgment of November 8, 2012, concerned a Japanese man who was separated, but not divorced, from his German wife. The family included a daughter who held German, Japanese and American nationalities. Following the separation, the mother and the daughter moved to Austria as a consequence of the mother's work. The father provided maintenance and kept up regular contact with his daughter. The father, who was lawfully resident in Germany and entitled to long-term residence there (but had chosen not to apply for such a permit), sought a residence card as a family member of a Union citizen since this would give him greater security than the discretionary extensions to his residence in Germany which applied to his current immigration status. The Court ruled that, in these circumstances, he did not fall within the terms of art.3, which presupposes that the direct relative in the ascending line is dependent upon the child and not the reverse. Nor could he benefit as the spouse of a Union citizen, since he had not accompanied or joined her in a Member State other than that of which the spouse is a national. The rights in art.3 applied could only be relied on in the Member State in which the Union citizen resides.

Nor did arts 20 or 21 TFEU assist the father. In the circumstances of this case, the Court considered that the refusal to grant the father a right of residence derived from the Union citizenship of the mother, and that the daughter would not be liable to deny them the genuine enjoyment of the substance of rights flowing from citizenship of the Union. Nor did the Charter of Fundamental Rights assist, since the father had chosen not to apply for a long-term residence permit under Directive 2003/109, and so his situation had no connection with European Union law.

In *Reyes v Migrationsverket* (C-423/12), Judgment of January 16, 2014, the Court of Justice has ruled that art.2(2)(c) must be interpreted as meaning that a Member State cannot require a direct descendant who is 21 years old or older to show that they have tried unsuccessfully to secure employment or subsistence in the Member State or country of origin in order to qualify as a dependant. Nor is the dependant precluded from seeking to obtain employment in the Member State to which they move as a dependant.

Dependency

Although it concerns the interpretation of an earlier Directive, some guidance on the approach to determining dependence can be found in *Yunying Jia v Migrationsverket* (C-1/05) [2007] E.C.R. I-1,where the Luxembourg Court ruled: **3.209**

> "Article 1(1)(d) of Council Directive 73/148/EEC of 21 May 1973 on the abolition of restrictions on movement and residence within the Community for nationals of Member States with regard to establishment and the provision of services is to be interpreted to the effect that 'dependent on them' means that members of the family of a Community national established in another Member State within the

meaning of Article 43 EC need the material support of that Community national or his or her spouse in order to meet their essential needs in the State of origin of those family members or the State from which they have come at the time when they apply to join that Community national. Article 6(b) of that directive must be interpreted as meaning that proof of the need for material support may be adduced by any appropriate means, while a mere undertaking from the Community national or his or her spouse to support the family members concerned need not be regarded as establishing the existence of the family members' situation of real dependence."

In *CIS/2100/2007* the Commissioner analysed and discussed the European authorities on the notion of dependence under earlier secondary legislation of the European Union. He concludes that the case-law is authority for the following propositions: (a) a person is only a dependant if he or she actually receives support from another; (b) there need be no right to that support and it is irrelevant that there are alternative sources of support available; and (c) the support must be material, although not necessarily financial, and must provide for, contribute towards, the basic necessities of life.

Pedro v SSWP [2009] EWCA Civ 1358; [2010] AACR 18, is an important decision of the Court of Appeal on the interpretation of the Citizenship Directive. It makes a number of comments on its interpretation in the United Kingdom in the light of recent authorities of the Luxembourg Court. Its particular concern, however, was with the proper interpretation of art.2(2)(d) and the requirements for dependency set out in that provision. Goldring L.J., delivering the judgment of the court said:

"67. Article 2(2) does not specify when the dependency has to have arisen. Neither does it require that the relative must be dependent in the country of origin. Article 3(2)(a), on the other hand, requires actual dependency at a particular time and place. That difference, as I have said, is reflected by Article 8(5)(d) as compared with 8(5)(e). It cannot be an accident of drafting. It contemplates, as it seems to me, that where in an Article 2(2)(d) case reliance is placed on dependency, it can be proved by a document from the host state without input from the state of origin. Taking Article 2(2)(d) together with Article 8(5)(d), suggests that dependency in the state of origin need not be proved for family members. It is sufficient if, as is alleged here, the dependency arises in the host state. Such an interpretation reflects the policy of the Directive to strengthen and simplify the realisation of realistic free movement rights of Union citizens compatibly with their family rights. On the one hand, close family members of Union citizens can move freely with Union citizens who might otherwise be inhibited from exercising their rights of free movement. On the other, Member States are merely obliged . . . to give open-minded consideration to those extended family members who have demonstrable need. Such an interpretation, as well as being in accordance with the language of the Citizens' Directive, is consistent with the approach of the European Court of Justice in *Metock* [84–9]."

Article 3

Beneficiaries

3.210 1. This Directive shall apply to all Union citizens who move to or reside in a Member State other than that of which they are a national, and to their family members as defined in point 2 of Article 2 who accompany or join them.

2. Without prejudice to any right to free movement and residence the persons concerned may have in their own right, the host Member State shall, in accordance with its national legislation, facilitate entry and residence for the following persons:

(a) any other family members, irrespective of their nationality, not falling under the definition in point 2 of Article 2 who, in the country from which they have come, are dependants or members of the household of the Union citizen having the primary right of residence, or where serious health grounds strictly require the personal care of the family member by the Union citizen;

(b) the partner with whom the Union citizen has a durable relationship, duly attested.

The host Member State shall undertake an extensive examination of the personal circumstances and shall justify any denial of entry or residence to these people.

GENERAL NOTE

The obligation under art.3 is to "facilitate" entry and residence for persons not listed in art.2, including "the partner with whom the Union citizen has a durable relationship, duly attested." This would include opposite sex couples where there is no registered partnership arrangement for such relationships (as in the United Kingdom). Some substance is given to the concept of facilitation by the last sentence of art.3, which requires the host Member State to undertake an extensive examination of the personal circumstances of the persons concerned, and to justify any refusal of entry or residence. **3.211**

KG and AK v Secretary of State for the Home Department [2008] EWCA Civ 13 concerned the interpretation of art.3. KG is a national of Sri Lanka. In November 2000 he arrived "clandestinely" in the United Kingdom and claimed asylum, but that claim was refused. He nevertheless remained in the United Kingdom without leave to remain. He had a brother who had been granted refugee status in Germany and had acquired German nationality in 2001. In January 2006 the brother came to the United Kingdom and applied for a residence permit. KG then immediately applied to stay in the United Kingdom as the brother of a Union citizen. Since KG was not an art.2 family member, (that is, spouse, partner under a registered partnership, son or daughter under the age of 21 or dependent on the citizen of the Union, or a dependent relative in the ascending line of the citizen or spouse/partner) his entitlement to reside in the United Kingdom turned on the art.3 provisions relating to "other family members". Here the obligation (so far as relevant to the circumstances of this case) of the Member State is "in accordance with its national legislation, [to] facilitate entry and residence" of other family members who "are dependants or members of the household of the Union citizen... ." Before denying entry or residence, the Member State is required to "undertake an extensive examination of the personal circumstances." The national implementing legislation, The Immigration (European Economic Area) Regulations 2006, required other family members to arrive in the United Kingdom from *another Member State*. KG had arrived in the United Kingdom from Sri Lanka. Accordingly, it was argued that the national legislation did not correctly transpose the requirements of the Directive. KG argued that the expression in the Directive "who, in the country from which they have come, are dependants or members of the household of the Union citizen" had to be read as referring to any country and not just to a Member State. KG argued that he had been a member of the household of a Union citizen in Sri Lanka between 1968 and 1992. It is inherent in the Court of Appeal's judgment that the Citizenship Directive is essentially a consolidation of the earlier law. Buxton L.J., giving the lead judgment, says:

> ". . . the assumptions and procedures of Directive 2004/38 do not mark a fundamental change from the previous state of the law. In particular . . . Directive 2004/38 proceeds not by replacing but by amending the workers' Regulation 1612/68." (At [17].)

It was argued that the Directive placed considerable emphasis on family reunion and that its terms should be interpreted and transposed with due respect for this principle. But the court said:

> "Put shortly, Community law recognises rights of movement on the part of relations not in order to support family values as such, but in order to make real the right of movement of the Union citizen: who may be deterred from exercising that right if he cannot take his relevant family with him. That is the constant theme of the cases that we were shown in support of the attempt to assert the doctrine of family reunion." (See [33].)

3.212 The court concluded:

> "The tight relationship between the exercise of rights by the Union citizen and the requirement that the [other family members] accompanying or joining him should have been his dependants or members of his household in the country from which they have come very strongly suggests that that relationship should have existed in the country from which the *Union citizen* has come, and thus have existed immediately before the Union citizen was accompanied or joined by the [other family member]. It seems wholly unlikely that when article 10(2) of Regulation 1612/68 and article 3(2)(a) of Directive 2004/38 introduce the requirement of dependence on and membership of the household of the Union citizen in the country from which the [other family member] has come, they can have had in mind anything other than dependence on the Union citizen in the country movement from which by the Union citizen is the whole basis of his rights and, thus of the rights of the [other family member]." (At [65].)

That judgment now needs to be read in the light of the Luxembourg Court's judgment in *Metock* (C-127/08) [2008] E.C.R. I-6241. This is a very significant case on the interpretation of art.3 on a reference from the Irish courts. It concerns national implementation of art.3 which has some similarities with implementation in the United Kingdom, and has important implications for the interpretation of the United Kingdom's national regulations implementing the Directive. This makes it worth setting out the circumstances of some of the individuals whose cases were the subject of this reference.

Metock is a national of Cameroon who arrived in Ireland in June 2006 and whose application for asylum failed.

Ikeng, born a national of Cameroon acquired United Kingdom nationality and resided and worked in Ireland since late in 2006. Metock and Ikeng met in Cameroon in 1994 and had been in a stable relationship. There are two children. They were married in Ireland in October 2006. An application for a residence card for Metock was refused on the grounds that he did not satisfy the requirement of the Irish regulations that he had resided lawfully in another Member State prior to the application.

Mr Ikogho was also a failed asylum seeker; he was subject to a deportation order at the material time. Mrs Ikogho, a United Kingdom national, had lived and worked in Ireland since 1996. Mr and Mrs Ikogho met in Ireland in 2004 and were married in June 2006. An application for a residence card was refused on the grounds that Mr Ikogho was staying illegally in Ireland at the time of his marriage.

Chinedu, a national of Nigeria is also a failed asylum seeker. Babucke is a woman of German nationality lawfully resident in Ireland. Chinedu and Babucke married in July 2006. An application for a residence card was refused on the grounds that Chinedu did not meet the condition in the national regulations of lawful residence in another Member State prior to the application.

3.213 The applicants all argued that the Irish regulations implementing the Directive were incompatible with it. Their argument was that a national of a non-member country who becomes a family member of a Union citizen while that citizen is resident in a Member State other than that of which he is a national accompanies that citizen within the meaning of arts 3(1) and 7(2) of the Directive. The Irish Government argued that the Directive does not preclude the imposition of a condition of prior lawful residence in another Member State in the national implementing legislation. The Luxembourg Court observed that nothing in the Directive makes the application of its provisions conditional on persons having previously resided in a Member State. The court concluded:

> "... Directive 2004/38 confers on all nationals of non-member countries who are family members of a Union citizen within the meaning of part 2 of Article 2 of that directive, and accompany or join the Union citizen in a Member State other than that of which he is a national, rights of entry into and residence in the host Member State, regardless of whether the national of a non-member country has already been lawfully resident in another Member State." (At [70].)

The court went on to consider cases where rights arose from marriage and concluded:

> "... Article 3(1) of Directive 2004/38 must be interpreted as meaning that a national of a non-member country who is the spouse of a Union citizen residing in a Member State whose nationality he does not possess and who accompanies or joins that Union citizen benefits from the provisions of that directive, irrespective of when and where their marriage took place and of how the national of a non-member country entered the host Member State." (At [99].)

For some observations by the Court of Appeal on the propositions in *KG* in the light of the Luxembourg's judgments in *Metock,* see *Bigia v Entry Clearance Officer* [2009] EWCA Civ 79.

Some of the difficulties identified in this line of case-law are explored in a decision of the Immigration and Asylum Chamber of the Upper Tribunal in *SSHD v MR, FI and MR* [2010] UKUT 449 (IAC), where the Chamber has referred questions to the Court of Justice in Luxembourg on the proper interpretation of art.3(2) and the evidence required for the issue of a residence card under art.10 of the Directive. 3.214

Rahman, Islam and Rahman (C-83/11) is a reference from the Immigration and Asylum Chamber of the Upper Tribunal. The Advocate General gave his Opinion on March 27, 2012. He proposed that art.3(2) requires Member States to adopt the necessary measures to facilitate entry into, and residence in, their territory for beneficiaries of art.3. This meant that the persons concerned must have the possibility to obtain a right of entry and residence following an extensive examination of their application in the light of all the circumstances of their cases. They were entitled to a reasoned decision in the event of refusal of their application, but the provision does not require Member States to recognise an automatic right of entry and residence. The provision is capable of giving rise to direct effect in order to "disapply the particular provisions which would restrict its scope." (At [109]). The Advocate General concluded:

> "(2) The primary law of the European Union, in particular its provisions on Union citizenship and the protection of private and family life, and Article 3(2) of Directive 2004/38 preclude a Member State from refusing a national of a non-member country who comes with the scope of that provision residence in its territory, where that national wishes to reside with a member of his family who is a Union citizen, since such refusal has the effect of unjustifiably impeding the exercise of the right of the Union citizen concerned to move and reside freely within the territory of the Member States or causes a disproportionate impairment of his rights to respect for private and family life, which must be ascertained by the referring court." (At [109].)

For the ruling of the Court, see below.

Dereci (C–256/11) Judgment of November 15, 2011, is a judgment of the Grand Chamber on a reference from the Austrian courts. The cases concerns a number of third country nationals (Turkish, Nigerian and Sri Lankan) who had married Austrian nationals. The Austrian nationals had never exercised any free movement rights under European Union law. The third country nationals all claimed to have 3.215

a right to reside in Austria as family members of a citizen of the Union. The Grand Chamber considered that the claims made by the third country nationals were without merit. The provisions of Directive 2004/38 simply did not apply. There was no right to reside where the citizen of the Union had never exercised any rights under European Union law. Nor was this a situation where refusal to recognise the right to reside would result in a denial of the enjoyments of citizenship rights. The third country nationals are not citizens of the Union, and the denial of a right to reside for them does not have the inevitable consequence that the family members of the third country national could not exercise their rights as citizens of the Union anywhere in the Union (paras 63–9). But a national court must always consider whether the refusal of a right of residence for the third country national "undermines the right to respect for private and family life provided for in Article 7 of the Charter [of Fundamental Rights of the European Union.] On the other hand, if it takes the view that that situation is not covered by European Union law, it must undertake that examination in the light of Article 8(1) of the ECHR." (At [72].)

Memo DMG 7/12, commenting on the effect of the *Zambrano* and *Dereci* decisions states that:

> "*Zambrano* can never apply in the case of a dependent UK national child whose parent is an EU national because the primary carer will always be able to reside within the Union in their state of nationality and the child will also be able to reside in that state."

That is too sweeping a statement since it ignores the requirement spelled out in *Dereci* that the right to respect for family life either under art.7 of the Charter of Fundamental Rights or art.8 ECHR will always need to be considered. That consideration is relevant whether the individual is a citizen of the Union or a third-country national.

The Administrative Court has, in *R (on the application of Lounes) v Secretary of State for the Home Department* [2016] EWHC 436 (Admin) referred the following question to the Court of Justice:

> "Where a Spanish national and Union citizen:
>
> (i) moves to the United Kingdom, in exercise of her right to free movement under Directive 2004/38/EC; and
> (ii) resides in the United Kingdom in the exercise of her right under Article 7 or Article 16 of Directive 2004/38/EC; and
> (iii) subsequently acquires British citizenship, which she holds in addition to her Spanish nationality, as a dual national; and
> (iv) several years after acquiring British citizenship, marries a third country national with whom she resides in the United Kingdom;
>
> are she and her spouse both beneficiaries of Directive 2004/38/EC, within the meaning of Article 3(1), whilst she is residing in the United Kingdom, and holding both Spanish nationality and British citizenship?"

Advocate General Bot gave his Opinion on May 30, 2017. He proposed answering the questions raised by the Administrative Court as follows:

(1) A person who has exercised rights under the Citizenship Directive, has acquired permanent residence under the Directive, and has then obtained the nationality of the host Member State, ceases to be a beneficiary of the provisions in the Citizenship Directive. This is because they have become a national of the host Member State.

(2) However, this does not mean that European Union law ceases to have any relevance. The United Kingdom had argued that the matter became solely governed by national law. That was not correct. National law had to be applied in the context of European Union law. Article 21(1) TFEU required

that such a person must be afforded rights no less favourable than those in the Citizenship Directive. This included the conditions for granting a derived right of residence to a third-country national spouse.

Article 3(2)

Secretary of State for the Home Department v Rahman, Islam and Rahman (C-83/11) Judgment of September 5, 2012 (Grand Chamber), establishes a number of propositions in relation to the interpretation of art.3(2): **3.216**

(a) Member States are not required to grant every application for entry and residence submitted by family members of a Union citizen falling within art.3(2), but their legislation must contain criteria which enable applicants to obtain a decision which is founded on full consideration of their personal circumstances. Any rejection must be reasoned.

(b) Member States have a wide discretion in determining the relevant criteria. However, those criteria must be compatible with the concept of facilitating entry, and must be consistent with the notion of dependency, and not be such as to render that provision ineffective.

(c) Decisions must be subject to judicial review of their merits.

(d) The situation of dependence required must exist in the country from which the family member concerned comes at the very least at the time when that person applies to join the Union citizen.

(e) Member States are free to impose particular requirements relating to the nature and duration of dependence provided that they do not exceed what is reasonably required and do not deprive the concept of all effectiveness.

The Court of Appeal has applied the decision in the *Rahman, Islam and Rahman* case in *Oboh v SSHD* [2013] EWCA Civ 1525 in deciding that dependency had to be established in the country from which the person comes. The Court rejected an argument that the provision also covers the situation of a person whose dependency arose only in the country to which that person moved.

For some observations on the application of the principle established in *Surinder Singh (C-370/90)* [1992] ECR I-4265 to the rights set out in art.3(2), see *JS v DSD (JSA)* [2015] NI Com 53.

Article 3(2)(b): "durable relationship"

Article 3(2)(b) requires Member States to facilitate the entry and residence of the partner of a Union citizen, with whom that citizen has a "durable relationship". The provision has been implemented in the United Kingdom through reg.8(5) of the Immigration (European Economic Area) Regulation 2006, which provides: **3.217**

> "A person satisfies the condition in this paragraph if the person is a partner of an EEA national (other than a civil partner) and can prove to the decision-maker that he is in a durable relationship with the EEA national."

In *CIS/0612/2008* the Commissioner ruled that the concept of a "durable relationship" must be given an EU law meaning. He went on to say that the concepts in art.3(2)(b) are expressed "in ordinary words that do not require definition and can be left to the relevant fact-finding body" (para.30). However, he considered that there was an element of ambiguity in the notion of durability in that it "may mean that it has lasted or that it is capable of lasting" (para.36), although plainly it was the relationship with the partner rather than the partnership itself that had to display this quality. The relationship may have existed prior to the persons becoming partners. Subject to these considerations the question of the durability of the relationship was one of fact.

CHAPTER II

RIGHT OF EXIT AND ENTRY

Article 4

Right of exit

3.218 1. Without prejudice to the provisions on travel documents applicable to national border controls, all Union citizens with a valid identity card or passport and their family members who are not nationals of a Member State and who hold a valid passport shall have the right to leave the territory of a Member State to travel to another Member State.

2. No exit visa or equivalent formality may be imposed on the persons to whom paragraph 1 applies.

3. Member States shall, acting in accordance with their laws, issue to their own nationals, and renew, an identity card or passport stating their nationality.

4. The passport shall be valid at least for all Member States and for countries through which the holder must pass when travelling between Member States. Where the law of a Member State does not provide for identity cards to be issued, the period of validity of any passport on being issued or renewed shall be not less than five years.

Article 5

Right of entry

3.219 1. Without prejudice to the provisions on travel documents applicable to national border controls, Member States shall grant Union citizens leave to enter their territory with a valid identity card or passport and shall grant family members who are not nationals of a Member State leave to enter their territory with a valid passport. No entry visa or equivalent formality may be imposed on Union citizens.

2. Family members who are not nationals of a Member State shall only be required to have an entry visa in accordance with Regulation (EC) No.539/2001 or, where appropriate, with national law. For the purposes of this Directive, possession of the valid residence card referred to in Article 10 shall exempt such family members from the visa requirement. Member States shall grant such persons every facility to obtain the necessary visas. Such visas shall be issued free of charge as soon as possible and on the basis of an accelerated procedure.

3. The host Member State shall not place an entry or exit stamp in the passport of family members who are not nationals of a Member State provided that they present the residence card provided for in Article 10.

4. Where a Union citizen, or a family member who is not a national of a Member State, does not have the necessary travel documents or, if required, the necessary visas, the Member State concerned shall, before turning them back, give such persons every reasonable opportunity to obtain the neces-

sary documents or have them brought to them within a reasonable period of time or to corroborate or prove by other means that they are covered by the right of free movement and residence.

5. The Member State may require the person concerned to report his/her presence within its territory within a reasonable and non- discriminatory period of time. Failure to comply with this requirement may make the person concerned liable to proportionate and non-discriminatory sanctions.

General Note

Regulation 539/2001/EC does not apply to the United Kingdom. 3.220

Chapter III

Right of Residence

Article 6

Right of residence for up to three months

1. Union citizens shall have the right of residence on the territory of another Member State for a period of up to three months without any conditions or any formalities other than the requirement to hold a valid identity card or passport. 3.221

2. The provisions of paragraph 1 shall also apply to family members in possession of a valid passport who are not nationals of a Member State, accompanying or joining the Union citizen.

Article 7

Right of residence for more than three months

1. All Union citizens shall have the right of residence on the territory of another Member State for a period of longer than three months if they: 3.222

(a) are workers or self-employed persons in the host Member State; or

(b) have sufficient resources for themselves and their family members not to become a burden on the social assistance system of the host Member State during their period of residence and have comprehensive sickness insurance cover in the host Member State; or

(c) — are enrolled at a private or public establishment, accredited or financed by the host Member State on the basis of its legislation or administrative practice, for the principal purpose of following a course of study, including vocational training; and

— have comprehensive sickness insurance cover in the host Member State and assure the relevant national authority, by means of a declaration or by such equivalent means as they may choose, that they have sufficient resources for themselves and their family members not to become a burden on the social assistance system of the host Member State during their period of residence; or

(d) are family members accompanying or joining a Union citizen who satisfies the conditions referred to in points (a), (b) or (c).

2. The right of residence provided for in paragraph 1 shall extend to family members who are not nationals of a Member State, accompanying or joining the Union citizen in the host Member State, provided that such Union citizen satisfies the conditions referred to in paragraph 1(a), (b) or (c).

3. For the purposes of paragraph 1(a), a Union citizen who is no longer a worker or self-employed person shall retain the status of worker or self-employed person in the following circumstances:

(a) he/she is temporarily unable to work as the result of an illness or accident;

(b) he/she is in duly recorded involuntary unemployment after having been employed for more than one year and has registered as a job-seeker with the relevant employment office;

(c) he/she is in duly recorded involuntary unemployment after completing a fixed-term employment contract of less than a year or after having become involuntarily unemployed during the first twelve months and has registered as a jobseeker with the relevant employment office. In this case, the status of worker shall be retained for no less than six months;

(d) he/she embarks on vocational training. Unless he/she is involuntarily unemployed, the retention of the status of worker shall require the training to be related to the previous employment.

4. By way of derogation from paragraphs 1(d) and 2 above, only the spouse, the registered partner provided for in Article 2(2)(b) and dependent children shall have the right of residence as family members of a Union citizen meeting the conditions under 1(c) above. Article 3(2) shall apply to his/her dependent direct relatives in the ascending lines and those of his/her spouse or registered partner.

General Note

Infringement proceedings against the United Kingdom

3.223 For details of the infringement proceedings which the Commission has brought before the Court of Justice in relation to the right to reside test, see the annotations to art.21 TFEU at paras 3.62–3.78 above.

Introduction

3.224 Where an issue arises as to whether a person has a continuing right to reside beyond three months under European Union law, the proper interpretation of this Article of the Directive will be central to the consideration of that issue. Despite the constitutional overtones of rights attaching to citizenship of the Union, it remains the case that there is a difference in European Union law entitlements between those who are, or have been, economically active and those who are economically inactive. That raises questions as to when a person who has, in the past, been economically active loses the status of being an economically active person. In a nutshell, those who have been workers or self-employed persons who fall on hard times are better placed to claim support from the host Member State than those who have never been economically active. The other big questions arising under art.7 relate to the requirement not to be an unreasonable burden on the social assistance system of the host Member State, and the requirement to hold comprehensive sickness insurance cover in the host Member State.

It seems that arguments based on the level of integration a citizen has achieved are unlikely to be of assistance. In *Wadi Samin v City of Westminster* [2012] EWCA Civ 1468, a case on appeal from a county court in a housing assistance case, Hughes L.J., delivering the judgment of the court, said:

> "33. . . . Mr Carter's further submission, that when answering the question [whether the interruption of work is temporary or permanent] one should have regard to the degree of integration which the worker has achieved, should be rejected. Of course it is true that the underlying principle of the European and English legislation alike is to accord rights of increasing strength as the integration of the EU citizen progresses. That is the principle which underlies the sliding scale of rights set out in the Directive . . . .. So, where the question arises whether the generally stated power of expulsion on public policy grounds is exercisable or not, it is plainly right to take into account the level of integration and this is expressly stipulated by Article 28 of the Directive. But this general principle is already given effect by the specific provisions of Article 7. There is no occasion to add it as a further step required of those whose job it is to determine whether an absence from work is temporary or not, and to do so would both complicate their task and render outcomes potentially inconsistent. The Article 7(3)(a) question will after all normally arise only in the case of a limited class of integration, namely those who have been in the destination State for something more than three months but less than five years."

That proposition is, however, framed rather more in the context of the rules relating to expulsion, and not expressly in the context of a framework in the Citizenship Directive in which there is no obligation to grant social assistance in the first three months of residence, and a requirement of complete equality of treatment once permanent residence is achieved. In this context, a debate remains about the proper treatment of those with residence of more than three months but less than five years. Otherwise, the Citizenship Directive would provide that a Member State need not grant social assistance until permanent residence is achieved. In this context, the degree of social integration achieved might well have some relevance. It can be argued that art.7 is really about measuring the degree of social integration which gives rise both to a right to reside, and potentially to social assistance if that should be needed.

There can be more than one basis on which a person has a right to reside

Note that a person may have a right to reside on more than one basis. When an issue arises about a right to reside, then that may flow from a provision at first sight unconnected with the benefit claimed. An example would be a person who could claim to retain the status of a self-employed person who is claiming jobseeker's allowance. The right to reside flowing from the retention of the status of a self-employed person is sufficient to meet the requirement to have a right to reside for the purposes of claiming jobseeker's allowance. The judge in *SSWP v JB (JSA)* [2011] UKUT 96 (AAC) said: 3.225

> "7. There is in principle no reason why a person may not have a right to reside on a number of bases. A person who is a worker may also have a permanent right to reside. Each member of a couple who are both working has a right to reside both as a worker and as a family member of the other. And so on. For immigration purposes, this may be of no significance. However, it is potentially of significance for the purposes of benefit entitlement.
> 8. There is, therefore, no reason why a claimant who remains in self-employment may not rely on that status for the purposes of a claim for a jobseeker's allowance while seeking employment as a worker."

Determinations by the Secretary of State do not automatically port across to local authorities considering entitlement to housing benefit. The local authority must consider these matters for itself: *EP v SSWP (JSA)* [2016] UKUT 445 (AAC). This takes on added significance now that those in receipt of income-related JSA as jobseekers (as distinct from jobseekers with retained worker status) are no longer eligible to receive housing benefit.

Article 7(1)(a): workers and self-employed persons

3.226 A person who has attained the status of a worker under art.45 TFEU or of a self-employed person under art.49 TFEU has a right of residence. On the loss of that status other than by voluntary action, the worker can rely on art.7 of Reg.492/2011 in order to receive the same assistance as would be offered to a national of the host Member State in the same circumstances. Such rights would also seem to flow for the self-employed person through the application of the principle of equal treatment to be found in art.18 TFEU, though this proposition has yet to be clearly established. Joined Cases *SSWP v Czop, SSWP v Punakova* (C-147/11 and C-148/11) Judgment of September 6, 2012, established that the rights in Regulation 1612/68 (and it would therefore follow in Regulation 492/2011) are only for workers and not self-employed persons.

In *SSWP v SY (IS)* [2012] UKUT 233 (AAC) the judge ruled that being a fosterer only in receipt of allowances intended to cover the time and cost of caring for the child did not constitute self-employment within art.49 TFEU such that the person could claim a right to reside. Nor did the activity fall within the ambit of the provisions of the art.56 TFEU on services, since that provision contemplates a situation of the person providing the service and the recipient of those services being in different Member States.

A similar approach was taken to the claim that a person in receipt of a carer's allowance. Such a person is not a worker or self-employed person: *JR v SSWP (IS); JR v Leeds CC (HB)* [2014] UKUT 154 (AAC).

However, the term "workers" must be interpreted as including all those within the express terms of art.45 TFEU, and so will include those who enter a Member State holding an offer of employment: *SSWP v RR (IS)* [2013] UKUT 21, reported as [2013] AACR 20, at [53].

Retaining the status of worker or self-employed person: some general points

3.227 Article 7(3) lays down the circumstances in which a person who has been a worker or self-employed person retains that status. Some of the bases for retention of the status are clear and obvious; others are not. In considering whether a person has ceased to be a worker, it will be important to consider the contractual position. So, there would appear to be no difficulty in concluding that a person on maternity or paternity leave remained a worker, since the contract of employment subsists in such cases: *CIS/4237/2007*. Equally it would seem that a person who is self-employed and who takes a period of maternity leave from that self-employment remains a self-employed person: *CIS/1042/2008*.

JS v SSWP [2010] UKUT 240 (AAC) discusses the circumstances in which a person remains a self- employed person notwithstanding that there is no current work being undertaken in that capacity. The judge points out that, although art.7 includes provisions on the retention of worker status (that is, status as an employee) under the Treaty, art.7 is largely silent on the retention of self-employed status. Whether self-employed status has been abandoned or lost, or retained, will depend on the particular circumstances of each case, and the significance of any change in the self-employed person's personal circumstances: see para.8 of the decision.

R (on the application of Marian Tilianu) v Social Fund Inspector and SSWP [2010] EWCA Civ 1397 established that the provisions of art.7(3)(b) and (c) apply only to workers and not to self-employed persons.

3.228 *SSWP v AL (JSA)* [2010] UKUT 451 (AAC) followed *JS v SSWP* and the Upper Tribunal judge pointed out that such cases were to be distinguished from the situation in *Tilianu*, which had not considered retention of self-employed status but only looked at whether someone formerly self-employed could retain worker status.

RJ v SSWP (JSA) [2011] UKUT 477 (AAC), reported as [2012] AACR 28, is a decision from Scotland applying the *Tilianu* judgment in the context of a claim by a Polish national for a jobseeker's allowance. The judge confirms that a self-employed person who is not actually working as such but is engaged in other activities of self-employment does not cease to be a self-employed person. The case was remitted to a First-tier Tribunal for them to make findings of fact on the nature and extent of the activities being undertaken. However, once it is established that the self-employment has come to an end in all respects, the person will not fall within the provisions of art.7(3). The judge follows *Tilianu* and explains why the Upper Tribunal sitting in Scotland should respect decisions of the Court of Appeal for England and Wales (at [13]). Finally, the judge rejected an argument that the right to reside test constituted a restriction on freedom of establishment prohibited under art.49 TFEU. There was no reason to make a reference in this case (at [16]).

Retaining the status of worker or self-employed person: illness or accident: art.7(3)(a)

The definition of when a person is "temporarily unable to work as a result of illness" under art.7(3)(a) has been considered in the context of the meaning of "permanent incapacity to work" in art.17 in a number of cases in the Court of Appeal. See the cases referred to in the annotations to art.17 below. 3.229

Article 7(3)(a) does not provide that a parent who is temporarily unable to work because their child is ill or has suffered an accident retains their status as a worker: *CIS/3182/2005* and *CIS/599/2007*.

Shabani v Secretary of State for the Home Department [2013] UKUT 315 (IAC) confirms that a woman who has left the labour market in order to look after her children does not retain her status as a worker: *SSWP v Dias* [2009] EWCA Civ 807 applied.

Since pregnancy is not an illness, the position of those who stop work for reasons connected with pregnancy remains unclear. *JS Prix v SSWP* [2011] EWCA Civ 806, (reported as [2012] AACR 7) is the judgment of the Court of Appeal dismissing the appeal by the claimant against the decision in *SSWP v JS (IS)* [2010] UKUT 131 (AAC). The claimant, a French national, came to the United Kingdom in July 2006 and worked. She then enrolled on a teacher training course, but withdrew from her studies in February 2008 when she became pregnant. She undertook some agency work, but stopped working when she was six months' pregnant. Her search for less demanding work proved unsuccessful and she then claimed income support which was refused on the grounds that she did not have a right to reside. The Court of Appeal ruled that a person who ceases work for reasons other than those set out in art.7(3) ceases to be a worker. Pregnancy is not an illness. Nor did the Court consider that there was an oversight, since art.16(3) makes special provision in relation to absences resulting from pregnancy. Arguments based on alleged discrimination in the right to reside test were dismissed in the light of the Court of Appeal judgment in *Abdirahman* and of the Supreme Court in *Patmalniece*. The Supreme Court gave the claimant permission to appeal, and has referred the following questions to the Court of Justice:

1. Is the right of residence conferred upon a "worker" in art.7 of the Citizenship Directive to be interpreted as applying only to those: (i) in an existing employment relationship, (ii) (at least in some circumstances) seeking work, or (iii) covered by the extensions in art.7(3), or is the Article to be interpreted as not precluding the recognition of further persons who remain "workers" for this purpose?
2. (i) If the latter, does it extend to a woman who reasonably gives up work, or seeking work, because of the physical constraints of the late stages of pregnancy (and the aftermath of childbirth)?
   (ii) If so, is she entitled to the benefit of the national law's definition of when it is reasonable for her to do so?

The court's judgment in *Jessy Saint Prix v Secretary of State for Work and Pensions* (C-507/12) was delivered on June 19, 2014. The court ruled that the concept of "worker" was not limited to the situations listed in art.7 of the Citizenship Directive, but had to be considered in the wider context of the scope of art.45 TFEU. The court ruled:

> "Article 45 TFEU must be interpreted as meaning that a woman who gives up work, or seeking work, because of the physical constraints of the late stages of pregnancy and the aftermath of childbirth retains the status of 'worker', within the meaning of that article, provided she returns to work or finds another job within a reasonable period after the birth of her child."

The judgment will present some problems in the context of claims for benefit, since the return to work will be at some time in the future. On the facts of the case before the court, the claimant had, in fact, returned to work some three months after the birth of her child. The judgment also covers the situation of a person who gives up seeking work by reason of her pregnancy but with an intention to find a job after the birth of her child.

The DWP guidance in response to the judgment in *Jessy Saint-Prix v SSWP* (C-507/120 is set out in Memo DMG 25/14 of October 2014. Paragraph 9 provides:

> "Where a claimant indicates that they have an intention to return to their previous job or that they will find another job, the [decision maker] can award IS for a fixed period until the end of the 15 week period after the expected date of confinement. If the claimant subsequently does not return to work, a recovery of the IS paid will not be required."

The judgment of the Court of Justice of June 19, 2014 in *Jessy Saint-Prix v SSWP (C-507/12)* [2015] 1 CMLR 5 left open a number of questions about how the new approach to entitlement to benefit during a maternity period would operate. The most significant of those questions have been answered in *SSWP v SFF; ADR v SSWP; and CS v London Borough of Barnet and SSWP* [2015] UKUT 502 (AAC); [2016] AACR 16. Judge Ward comes to the following conclusions on what he labels "the Saint-Prix right":

(a) The right is to be assessed prospectively, since, for the right to be effective, a woman will need a decision at the time of her claim, and not once she has subsequently returned to work or to seeking work (paras 20-24).

(b) The right is available to those who are workers by virtue of actually having been in employment and to those who are no longer working by who retain the right to be treated as a worker. Judge Ward leaves open the question of whether a person who is a worker within art.45 TFEU solely by reason of being a work seeker enjoys the right (para.25).

(c) The start of the right is determined on the facts of each case, but in practice this will generally be the start of the eleven weeks prior to the expected date of confinement (para.26).

(d) The duration of the right will also be determined by the facts of each case which must be viewed in the context of the 52 week period of ordinary maternity leave and additional maternity leave combined (paras 27-37).

(e) Obviously an actual return to work in some form will suffice, but it will also suffice if the woman returns to seeking work where the conditions of art.7(3) (b) or (c) of the Citizenship Directive are complied with (paras 38-43).

The period during which a woman enjoys the right contributes to the period of time necessary to acquire a permanent right of residence under art.16 of the Citizenship Directive (para.44).

See also Memo DMG 5/16 of March 2016.

The question of whether the ruling of the Court of Justice in the *Saint-Prix* case could be applied by analogy to those who have been self-employed rather than workers was considered in *HMRC v HD* and *HMRC v GP* [2017] UKUT 11 (AAC), but was not finally determined in those cases. In one of them, further facts found by Judge Ward enabled him to conclude that the appellant remained a self-employed person with right to reside, and did not need to rely on the *Saint-Prix* principles. In the other case, Judge Ward is considering the submissions of the parties on whether to stay the proceedings pending the outcome of a reference to the Court of Justice by the Court of Appeal in the Republic of Ireland in *Gusa v Minister for Social Protection and others* [2016] IECA 237 which raise the issue: see paras 34 and 35.

Retaining the status of worker: involuntary unemployment: art.7(3)(b) and (c)

Article 7(3)(b) and (c) concern the circumstances in which persons who have been workers retain that status following involuntary unemployment. According to national authorities, the provisions have no application to those who have been self-employed: *SSWP v RK*, [2009] UKUT 209 (AAC) and *R (on the application of Marian Tilianu) v Social Fund Inspector and SSWP*, [2010] EWCA Civ 1397, but note the cases mentioned above in relation to art.7(1)(a) which discuss when a person in self-employment ceases to have such a status. **3.230**

Some of the difficulties in relation to art.7(3)(b) and (c) have arisen because there is no specific procedure under United Kingdom social security law for a person to record their involuntary unemployment other than by claiming a jobseeker's allowance. Many of the difficulties have arisen in connection with claims for income support.

There are different requirements for those who have completed employment "for more than one year" (art.7(3)(b)) and those whose employment has been for less than a year (art.7(3)(c)).

It remains to be established whether two periods of employment can be aggregated to meet the more than one year requirement in art.7(3)(b). In *SSWP v MK (IS)* [2013] UKUT 163 the Secretary of State conceded for the purposes of that case only that two periods of employment separated by a period of about a month could be aggregated, but reserved the right to argue the point in another case. **3.231**

In addition to the qualifying period of employment, there are three requirements in art.7(3)(b) and (c):

(a) there must be involuntary unemployment;

(b) that involuntary unemployment must be duly recorded; and

(c) the claimant must have registered as a jobseeker with the relevant employment office.

SSWP v MM (IS) [2015] UKUT 128 (AAC) concerned a Polish national who had a significant employment record, followed by a period in receipt of JSA, followed by a period in receipt of maternity allowance. When the maternity allowance ended, the claimant made a claim for income support as a lone parent. The Secretary of State refused the claim on the grounds that the claimant did not have a right to reside. Judge White concluded that she had retained her status as a worker on the completion of her periods of employment and that this did not end when she was in receipt of a maternity allowance, since this was a benefit connected with work. The key issue was whether she retained worker status under art.7(3)(b) when she claimed income support, some eleven months after initially retaining the status when her employment ended. Judge White noted that art.7(3)(b) is silent on the duration for which the status is retained, but that art.7(3)(c) (which concerns those with work of less than a year's duration when they retain the status) indicates that the status is to be retained for "no less than six months". He therefore concluded that retention for a period of eleven months was not inappropriate for retention of the status in the absence of some intervening event which indicated that the claimant had removed herself from the labour market. There was nothing to indicate this in the circumstances of this case: receipt of maternity allowance did not, of itself, constitute such an event. In this case, there was evidence that the claimant remained registered with employment agencies indicating an intention to return to work when her circumstances permitted.

Involuntary unemployment: In *IA v SSWP* [2009] UKUT 35 (AAC) the judge observed:

3.232 The six months' limit in art.7(3)(c) and the prohibition on expulsion in art.14(4)(b) reflect the [Luxembourg] Court's answer in *Antonissen*, but the Directive does not translate the Court's reasoning in that case into a right to reside for those [who] are not in the labour market. (See [23].)

The concept of involuntary unemployment under art.7 has been explained in *SSWP v MK (IS)* [2013] UKUT 163:

"42. The starting point is *R(IS) 12/98*, an authority of long standing. The case concerned a French national who had worked as an *au pair* who claimed income support following the end of the *au pair* arrangement. If she could show that she was a worker who had retained her worker status, she would be entitled to income support under regulation 21(3)(a) of the Income Support (General) Regulations 1987 as then in force as a person who was a worker for the purposes of Regulation 1612/68/EEC. As such, she would be treated as being habitually resident in the United Kingdom.
43. In considering whether a person was in involuntary unemployment for the purposes of retaining worker status under Regulation 1612/68, Commissioner Mesher said:

> . . . it does not matter in itself whether the previous employment was left voluntarily or involuntarily. The question is whether the circumstances of the leaving, and in particular the person's intentions and actions at the time, indicate that the person was still in the labour market or not. (para.21)

44. In the joined cases of *CH/3314/2005* and *CIS/3315/2005*, the Commissioner was considering the position of a person who gave up work because of the pressures of childcare responsibilities. After citing the passage quoted above from R(IS) 12/98, the Commissioner said:

> Thus, it seems to me, the term "voluntarily unemployed" must be regarded as focussing on the question whether the claimant is still in the labour market rather than on the circumstances in which he or she has ceased to be employed, although the latter may be material as evidence as to whether or not the claimant is genuinely still in the labour market. (para.11)

45. The Secretary of State cited a number of paragraphs of the judgment of the Court of Justice of the European Communities in Case C-413/01 *Ninni-Orasche* [2003] ECR I-13217 on the distinction between being voluntarily unemployed and being involuntarily unemployed. Mr Cross says the effect of this decision on the earlier authorities is that it is not the correct approach to involuntary unemployment to focus only on whether a person remains in the labour market *after* they have left their employment. The reasons why the employment has ended are also relevant and should be considered.
46. In my view, in determining whether persons are in involuntary unemployment for the purposes of Article 7 of the Citizenship Directive, the proper question is whether they remain engaged in the labour market. In determining the answer to that question, the reasons why the previous employment ended, the intentions of the person concerned, and their actions and the circumstances obtaining after they have left employment are all relevant matters.
47. I do not read paragraph 11 of *CIS/3315/2005* as saying that the reasons why a person stopped work are not relevant in determining whether a person remains

engaged in the labour market. Those reasons are a relevant consideration, not the determining factor. They provide the context for a person's activities after they have left their employment."

Duly recorded: the involuntary unemployment must be duly recorded. This will usually be accomplished through a claim for a jobseeker's allowance, but it would seem that (in the absence of specific provisions in connection with a claim for income support) it may be established by other means in claims for income support. 3.233

Registered as a jobseeker with the relevant employment office: ZW v SSWP [2009] UKUT 25 (AAC) concerned, in part, whether participation in a work-focused interview in connection with an income support claim was or involved registration sufficient to satisfy art.7(3)(b) and (c) (implemented in national law as reg.6(2)(b) of the Immigration (European Economic Area) Regulations 2006). The judge concluded that the concept of registration in this Article should be interpreted as being evidence of remaining in contact with the labour market. However, the concept in the Article is not an autonomous one: "What is required is that the Union citizen register in accordance with the particular arrangements in the host State." (See [24].) 3.234

It followed that a work-focused interview did not: "provide an opportunity for claimants to register for work . . . the interview is not itself registration not does it involve registration. It is at best a preliminary stage." (See [27].)

A three-judge panel in *SSWP v FE* [2009] UKUT 287 (AAC) considered the requirements which must be met under art.7(3)(c) by a person in order to retain her worker status, and so secure an entitlement to income support. This was appealed unsuccessfully by the Secretary of State as *SSWP v Elmi* [2011] EWCA Civ 1403 (reported as [2012] AACR 22). There were important factual concessions made in the case, most notably that the claimant had established that she was seeking work by ticking a box on the habitual residence questionnaire. The core issue was, therefore, what procedures the claimant needed to complete to establish that she met the requirement to "register as a job-seeker with the relevant employment office." In upholding the First-tier Tribunal, the majority concluded as follows:

"29. We conclude that the Secretary of State has not shown that the UK has defined specific mechanisms as being the only ways in which an individual can, for the purposes of Article 7(3)(c) "register as a job-seeker with the relevant employment office". That being so, the tribunal was entitled to hold that the Secretary of State's factual concessions meant that the claimant succeeded in her appeal. In summary:

a. What the Directive contemplates is that a claimant has done what is needed in order to have his or her name recorded as looking for work by the relevant employment office
b. Whether or not this has been done is a question of fact
c. There is no rule of law that such registration can be effected only by way of registering for jobseeker's allowance or national insurance credits, less still only by successfully claiming one or other of those benefits
d. Nor was there at the material time an administrative practice to that effect (even assuming—without deciding—that to be a lawful way of implementing the Directive)
e. Successfully claiming jobseeker's allowance or national insurance credits will no doubt provide sufficient evidence to satisfy Article 7(3)(c); but
f. Those who are able to show not merely that they were seeking work, but that they had done what is needed in order to have their name recorded as looking for work by the relevant employment office will meet the registration requirement of Article 7(3)(c).
g. It being conceded that the claimant had stated on the Habitual Residence Test documents that she was seeking work and that the extent of the work being sought was sufficient, it follows that she met the relevant test."

In *SSWP v Elmi* [2011] EWCA Civ 1403 the Court of Appeal dismissed the 3.235

Secretary of State's appeal against the decision of the Upper Tribunal. The Court of Appeal ruled that the Secretary of State could not rely on art.7(3)(c) of the Citizenship Directive to fill in a gap in national law where no provision had been made in relation to a claim for income support for a person to register as a jobseeker. Consequently the claimant was not excluded from entitlement to income support. In the course of his judgment, Maurice Kay L.J. cast some doubt on the correctness of *ZW v SSWP* [2009] UKUT 25 (AAC) in ruling that participation in a work-focused interview does not amount to registration pursuant to art.7(3)(c). However, the judgment indicates that there is nothing to preclude the Parliament from legislating for the position for which the Secretary of State was contending, and that such legislation, if drafted in reasonable terms, would be compatible with the Citizenship Directive (para.22 of the judgment of Maurice Kay L.J.). See now also Memo DMG 34/11 for the Department's guidance on dealing with the issues raised in this judgment.

SSWP v MK (IS) [2013] UKUT 163 (followed in *VP v SSWP (JSA)* [2014] UKUT 32 (AAC); [2014] AACR 25) considered the timeliness within which the requirements of art.7(3)(b) must be met if worker status is to be retained:

> "69. I have concluded that where there is delay of more than a very few days between the end of employment and the completion of the formalities required to take the benefit of Article 7(3)(b) of the Citizenship Directive, the proper approach is to ask whether, having regard to all the circumstances of the case, there has been undue delay in meeting the requirements of the Citizenship Directive. I believe that an approach which focuses on undue delay is likely to be more easily and more consistently applied by decision makers and tribunals than a requirement for prompt completion of the requirements.
> 70. What then is involved in a test of undue delay? There must be a full enquiry into the reasons for, and circumstances of, any delay in completing the requirements specified in Article 7(3)(b) of the Citizenship Directive. In practice, that will be delay in making a claim for a jobseeker's allowance, since that is the normal means by which the requirements are met.
> 71. Undertaking this enquiry will require decision makers and tribunals to make full and careful findings of fact about what a claimant did between the ending of employment and the completion of the requirements of Article 7(3)(b) of the Citizenship Directive. In the light of those findings, decision makers and tribunals are required to exercise a judgment as to whether there are reasonable grounds for the delay such that it is not right to regard it as an undue delay.
> 72. It follows that the longer the delay, the more compelling must be the reasons for it. I do not specify any outer limit beyond which a delay will necessarily be regarded as an undue delay."

In *FT v (1) LB of Islington and (2) SSWP (HB)* [2015] UKUT 121 (AAC), Judge Ward ruled that there had not been undue delay in registering as a jobseeker between June 10 and 24 August 2012 because the jobseeker showed that she had previously obtained employment quickly; she had savings to tide her over; and she had provided evidence of her steps to find work during the period of the delay. In *SSWP v MM (IS)* [2015] UKUT 128 (AAC) Judge White found that there was not undue delay for a period of five weeks before registering as a jobseeker, since the claimant remained registered with an agency (which had been providing her with work) and claimed as soon as it became apparent that there was no further work.

Retaining the status of worker: vocational training: art.7(3)(d)

3.236 This provision seeks to encapsulate decisions of the Court of Justice which have recognised that a person can retain their status as a worker where they cease work but embark on vocational training. A distinction is made between those who are in involuntary unemployment and those who are not. Those in involuntary unemployment do not need to show any relationship to their previous work, whereas those not in involuntary unemployment must show a relationship to their previous work. The rationale would seem to be that those in involuntary unemployment will retain their worker status while retraining in a different type of work.

The leading European case is *Ninni-Orasche* (C-431-01) [2003] E.C.R. I-13217.

Persons who are self-sufficient: art.7(1)(b)

This provision enables those who are not economically active, but who are financially independent to have a right to reside under the Directive, provided that they are not a burden on the social assistance system of the host Member State and have comprehensive sickness insurance cover there. The difficulties arise where people have exercised the right of free movement, have not yet attained permanent residence under art.16 of the Directive, and find themselves in need of support from the host Member State. There are two central issues: (a) the limits of self-sufficiency; and (b) the requirements concerning health insurance. 3.237

In *Pensionversicherungsanstalt v Brey* (C-140/12), Judgment of September 19, 2013, the Court of Justice addresses the relationship between Reg.883/2004 and the Citizenship Directive and the entitlement of those who are not economically active to be self-sufficient in order to have a right to reside for more than three months.

The court ruled that the definition of social assistance was not the same in both instruments. It had been argued that any benefit falling within Reg.883/2004 (even special non-contributory benefits) could not constitute social assistance for the purposes of the Citizenship Directive. The court rejects this proposition. The concept of social assistance for the purposes of the Citizenship Directive is defined by reference to the purpose of the benefit (see [60]–[62] of the judgment). However, the court immediately goes on to say:

> "63. Consequently, the fact that a national of another Member State who is not economically active may be eligible, in light of his low pension, to receive [social assistance] could be an indication that that national does not have sufficient resources to avoid becoming an unreasonable burden on the social assistance system of the host Member State for the purposes of Article 7(1)(b) of Directive 2004/38 . . . .
> 64. However, the competent national authorities cannot draw such conclusions without first carrying out an overall assessment of the specific burden which granting that benefit would place on the national social assistance system as a whole, by reference to the personal circumstances characterizing the individual situation of the person concerned."

This means that it is not compatible with EU law to have a blanket rule. The court ruled that there must always be an assessment of the burden an individual claim would place on the social security system which takes account of such factors as the length of residence, the amount and regularity of any income, the amount of benefit and the period for which it is available, and the overall personal circumstances of the claimant. This was a case in which the claimant was seeking a top-up benefit because of his low pension income. The court said: 3.238

> "78. . . . . In addition, in order to ascertain more precisely the extent of the burden which [the] grant [of social assistance] would place on the national social assistance system, it may be relevant . . . to determine the proportion of the beneficiaries of that benefit who are Union citizens in receipt of a retirement pension in another Member State."

The requirement for the measure to be proportionate would not be satisfied unless such an individualised assessment was undertaken.

The application of the *Brey* judgment has been subject to detailed consideration in *VP v SSWP (JSA)* [2014] UKUT 32 (AAC); [2014] AACR 25, at [71]–[97]. The case concerned a national of Lithuania who had done a certain amount of work, mostly of a seasonal nature, and had got by for five years without reliance on social security benefits. The decision establishes that self-sufficiency has to be looked at from the beginning of the five-year period relied on for attaining permanent residence where that is what is sought. While there is little limitation over the source of the resources a person relies upon, the legislation presupposes a degree of stability. The judge follows immigration cases in deciding that it is not possible to rely on wages to assert self-sufficiency against the Member State in which those wages are earned. The appellant could not establish that he had sufficient resources to bring himself within art.7(1)(b).

The judge, at [106]–[107], considered that the *Brey* judgment did not mean that a claimant can merely say that the burden they pose by claiming is not unreasonable, since it erodes to nothing the protection provided for Member States by the self-sufficiency provisions in art.7(1)(b). Properly understood, the *Brey* judgment addresses the position of someone who has established an art.7 right to reside but where something then occurs which necessitates a claim for benefit.

The judgment of September 15, 2015 in the *Alimanovic case* (C-67/14) requires some reconsideration of the scope of the Court's judgment in the *Brey case* (C-140/12), and certainly places much less emphasis on rights flowing from citizenship of the Union than the Court had done on the *Dano case* (C-333/13) where the Court had repeated its mantra that citizenship of the Union is a "fundamental status" leading to a requirement for equal treatment.

The *Alimanovic case* concerned entitlements flowing solely from holding the status of being a work seeker. Under German legislation, the claimants were refused a subsistence benefit (which the Court characterized as "social assistance") following their loss of retained worker status under art.7(3)(c) of the Citizenship Directive. The claimants' status was solely that of work seekers. The Court re-affirms its decision in the *Dano case* that Union citizens can only claim social assistance on the basis of art.24(2) of the Citizenship Directive when their residence meets the conditions set out in the Directive. Recalling its decision in *Vatsouras and Koupatantze* (C-22/08 and C-23/08), the Court notes the entitlement to social assistance during the six month period during which worker status is retained under art.7(3)(c) and the possibility that a right to residence as work seekers might arise on the ending of the period of retained worker status. However, the derogation in art.24(2) permits Member States to refuse social assistance where claimants' right of residence falls within art.14(4)(b). Those in this situation would, following the *Brey case*, seem to be entitled to an individual assessment of their circumstances, but the Court says:

> "59. . . ., although the Court has held that Directive 2004/38 requires a Member State to take account of the individual situation of the person concerned before it adopts an expulsion measure or finds that the residence of that person is placing an unreasonable burden on its social assistance system (judgment in *Brey* . . .), no such individual assessment is necessary in circumstances such as those at issue in the main proceedings.
>
> 60. Directive 2004/38, establishing a gradual system as regards the retention of the status of 'worker' which seeks to safeguard the right of residence and access to social assistance, itself takes into consideration various factors characterising the individual situation of each applicant for social assistance, and, in particular, the duration of the exercise of any economic activity."

It followed that the German legislation was not in breach of the requirements of the Citizenship Directive.

The effect of the judgment in the *Alimanovic case* on the judgment in the *Brey case* is far from clear. The two judgments can only stand side by side if the obligation arising under art.7(1)(b) for an individual assessment of whether a claimant is an unreasonable burden on the social assistance of the host Member State can somehow be decoupled from the consideration of entitlement to social assistance for those falling within art.14(4)(b). That seems an exceedingly subtle distinction.

The second interim decision in *AMS v SSWP (PC)* [2017] UKUT 48 (AAC) considers the extent to which the decision in *Brey* case has survived the decisions in *Dano* and *Alimanovic* cases. It contains an extensive review of the authorities. Judge Ward considers that the decisions after the *Brey* case have excluded it from "applying outside its proper home of Article 7(1)(b), but have not overruled it." (para.45). Judge Ward regards the following factors as relevant where a *Brey* review is still required:

- the personal circumstances characterising the individual situation of the person concerned;
- some assessment of the amounts prescribed as meeting a person's requirements by the benefits legislation;
- factors bearing on the burden on the Member State's social assistance system having regard to the duration of residence, the amount of the benefit, and the period for which it is available;
- any income of the person and its source.

However, what is required is a "collective assessment" (para. 51).

Self-sufficiency: Article 8(4) of the Directive contains guidance on what constitute sufficient resources. This must be assessed in the light of the personal situation of each person. Any amount set cannot be higher than the threshold below which nationals of the host Member State become eligible for means-tested benefits, or, if there is no such figure, the minimum social security pension paid in that state. If the resources are provided by a third party, they must be accepted: *Commission v Belgium* (C-408/03) [2006] E.C.R. I- 2647, at [40] and following. National authorities are permitted to make checks, but cannot limit the nature of, or evidence establishing the existence of, the resources available to periodic payments; the available resources can be in the form of capital: *Commission v Italy* (C-424/98) [2000] E.C.R. I- 4001, at [37]. 3.239

For a decision exploring the requirement of sufficiency of resources under art.7(1) (b) in the context of a claim for housing benefit and council tax benefit, see *SG v Tameside MBC* [2010] UKUT 243 (AAC). This judgment also records a concession by the Secretary of State (who had been joined in the appeal to the Upper Tribunal) that the appellant had adequate health insurance under arrangements applicable because she held an exported invalidity benefit from Sweden which entitled her to medical treatment within the NHS (at [20]–[28] of the Decision).

A burden on the social assistance system: the Preamble (recital 16) gives some guidance on determining when a person has become an unreasonable burden on the social assistance system of the host Member State. Such determination has to be made in the context in which the Directive only exempts the host Member State from any consideration of entitlement to social assistance in the first three months of a migrant's residence: see Recital 10 in the Preamble. It is only receipt of social assistance than can be considered relevant in determining whether a person has become an unreasonable burden on the social assistance system. Three factors are to be taken into account. First, it is relevant to consider how long the person is likely to need assistance set in the context of the length of time the person has resided in the host Member State. Secondly, all the circumstances of the person and their family must be taken into account, including the degree of integration into the host Member State. Finally, consideration can be given as to the total amount of assistance granted, the person's history of needing social assistance, and the extent to which the person has in the past contributed to the economy of the host state through the payment of taxes and social security contributions. Article 14(3) of the Directive provides that a person cannot be expelled as an automatic consequence of making a claim for social assistance. 3.240

3.241 *Comprehensive sickness insurance cover:* What constitutes comprehensive sickness insurance cover has proved to be controversial with the Commission changing its view. It had originally indicated that what was required was health insurance whether through the public or private sector, which does not create a burden on the public finances of the host Member State. It has subsequently taken the view that provision through the National Health Service in the United Kingdom suffices: see comments at [103]–[104] of *VP v SSWP (JSA)* [2014] UKUT 32 (AAC); [2014] AACR 25. The judge in *VP* analysed the authorities, most notably *FK (Kenya) v Secretary of State for the Home Department* [2010] EWCA Civ 1302, and concluded that NHS cover does not constitute comprehensive sickness insurance cover for the purposes of art.7(1)(b).

In *SSWP v LL (PC)* [2014] UKUT 136 (AAC) the judge follows *VP v SSWP,* though expresses some reservations about whether the European legislation intended to set so high a hurdle for those exercising rights of free movement where there is a residence-based health system.

The meaning of comprehensive sickness insurance cover has been considered by the Court of Appeal in *Ahmad v Secretary of State for the Home Department* [2014] EWCA Civ 988. The Court upholds the decision of the Upper Tribunal (IAT), and approves the reasoning of the judge in *VP v SSWP,* concluding:

> "70. . . . If an EEA national enters the UK and is not involved in an economically active activity, for example because she is a student, her residence and that of her family members will not be lawful unless she has CSIC [comprehensive sickness insurance cover] while she is a student in the five years following her arrival.
> 71. So Mrs Ahmad had to have CSIC while she was a student. This condition must be strictly complied with. The fact that she would be entitled to treatment under the NHS, and was thus at all times in substantially the same position as she would have been had she had CSIC, is nothing to the point. Her failure to take out CSIC put the host state at risk of having to pay for healthcare at a time when the Ahmads had not then achieved the status of permanent resident and she was not economically active."

3.242 In some situations it has been argued that the European Health Insurance Card (EHIC) issued under the provisions of Reg.883/2004 meets these requirements, although the EHIC is intended to passport the migrant to health care which is immediately required on a temporary presence in another Member State.

In *SSWP v GS (PC)* [2016] UKUT 394 (AAC); [2017] AACR 7; Judge Ward explores, among other things, whether the European Health Insurance Card (EHIC) for which provision is made in art.22 of Regulation 1408/71 and art.19 of Regulation 883/2004 can constitute comprehensive sickness insurance cover. Judge Ward notes that the EHIC is designed to provide health cover for urgently required treatment during a "stay" in a Member State. However, the term "stay" is defined in the co-ordinating regulations as temporary residence. It can only assist a person whose residence is temporary. In unusual situations, a stay can be for a lengthy period. In *Case C-255/13 I v Health Service Executive,* ECLI: EU: C:2014:1291, the stay lasted for eleven years. In the case before Judge Ward, the claimant could not establish that he was temporarily resident in the United Kingdom, and his holding of an EHIC did not assist him. Furthermore, the provision only assisted a person in the United Kingdom whose "competent state" under the co-ordinating regulations was *not* the United Kingdom.

For some, their rights under Chapter 1 of Title III of Reg.883/2004 may result in their having comprehensive sickness insurance cover in the host Member State. This is certainly the case for pensioners.

Students: art.7(1)(c)

3.243 The position of students is clear from the wording of the provision. The requirements in relation to comprehensive sickness insurance cover are the same as for those who are self-sufficient, though the EHIC may well constitute sufficient health care protection in these cases.

The position in relation to the sufficiency of resources is more generous than in the case of those who are self-sufficient, since the student only has to show a realistic expectation of sufficiency of resources during their studies. That expectation may be frustrated by events during the course of their studies: see *Grzelczyk* (C-184/99) [2001] E.C.R. I- 6193.

Those who have a right to reside without the need to show that they are self-sufficient

It is only students and economically inactive persons whose residence is subject to the requirement to have sufficient resources to avoid becoming an unreasonable burden on the social assistance system of the host Member State. The Luxembourg Court confirmed in *Ibrahim* (C-310/08) [2010] E.C.R. I-1065, and *Teixeira* (C-480/08) [2010] E.C.R. I-1107 that those who could show a right of residence flowing from other provisions of European Union law as primary carers of children in education were not subject to the requirement to show that their residence did not involve an unreasonable burden on the social assistance system of the host Member State. That requirement only applied where European Union law expressly provided for it. 3.244

Article 8

Administrative formalities for Union citizens

1. Without prejudice to Article 5(5), for periods of residence longer than three months, the host Member State may require Union citizens to register with the relevant authorities. 3.245

2. The deadline for registration may not be less than three months from the date of arrival. A registration certificate shall be issued immediately, stating the name and address of the person registering and the date of the registration. Failure to comply with the registration requirement may render the person concerned liable to proportionate and non-discriminatory sanctions.

3. For the registration certificate to be issued, Member States may only require that

— Union citizens to whom point (a) of Article 7(1) applies present a valid identity card or passport, a confirmation of engagement from the employer or a certificate of employment, or proof that they are self-employed persons,

— Union citizens to whom point (b) of Article 7(1) applies present a valid identity card or passport and provide proof that they satisfy the conditions laid down therein,

— Union citizens to whom point (c) of Article 7(1) applies present a valid identity card or passport, provide proof of enrolment at an accredited establishment and of comprehensive sickness insurance cover and the declaration or equivalent means referred to in point (c) of Article 7(1).

Member States may not require this declaration to refer to any specific amount of resources.

4. Member States may not lay down a fixed amount which they regard as "sufficient resources", but they must take into account the personal

situation of the person concerned. In all cases this amount shall not be higher than the threshold below which nationals of the host Member State become eligible for social assistance, or, where this criterion is not applicable, higher than the minimum social security pension paid by the host Member State.

5. For the registration certificate to be issued to family members of Union citizens, who are themselves Union citizens, Member States may require the following documents to be presented:

(a) a valid identity card or passport;

(b) a document attesting to the existence of a family relationship or of a registered partnership;

(c) where appropriate, the registration certificate of the Union citizen whom they are accompanying or joining;

(d) in cases falling under points (c) and (d) of Article 2(2), documentary evidence that the conditions laid down therein are met;

(e) in cases falling under Article 3(2)(a), a document issued by the relevant authority in the country of origin or country from which they are arriving certifying that they are dependants or members of the household of the Union citizen, or proof of the existence of serious health grounds which strictly require the personal care of the family member by the Union citizen;

(f) in cases falling under Article 3(2)(b), proof of the existence of a durable relationship with the Union citizen.

GENERAL NOTE

3.246 In *SSWP v EM* [2009] UKUT 44 (AAC), the judge considers the effect of the *permissive, not required,* registration scheme which a Member State may establish under art.8. The judge observes:

> "13. The most important distinction between Article 8 of Directive 2004/38/EC and Directive 68/360/EEC, which was among the Directives that it replaced, is that, under the new Directive, there is no requirement to have a registration scheme and there is no requirement placed on a Member State to issue registration certificates if there is no scheme. Nor is anything said in Directive 2004/38/ EC as to the effect of a registration certificate or as to the period for which it is valid. However, it may be inferred from paragraph (2) of Article 8 that the certificate operates, firstly, as evidence that the holder has complied with a requirement to register imposed by a Member State in conformity with paragraph (1) and is therefore not liable to the sanctions permitted under paragraph (2) and, secondly, as evidence that, at the date of issue, the applicant was a citizen of the European Union with a right of residence under Article 7(1). On that basis, there is no reason to limit the period of a registration certificate's validity. The passing of time cannot logically affect its value as evidence of the position at the date of issue. Thus, there is nothing to suggest that a registration certificate has the same effect as a residence permit which, it could be inferred from the earlier Directives, had continuing effect until it expired or was withdrawn because otherwise it would not perform the designated function of proving a right of residence."

The judge rejected arguments that the registration certificate had the same effect as the former residence permit. That must be right. The former residence permit was a document required to be provided under EU law as evidence of a person's entitlement in a Member State other than that of his or her nationality under the EC Treaty. The case law clearly established that it was merely evidence of Treaty rights and did not grant them. By contrast the scheme of registration under art.8 is a discretionary national scheme which a Member State may choose to set up as a matter of its own internal administration. It follows that the effect of the registration certificate will be determined under national law, although that national law must be applied consistently with EU law entitlements.

Article 9

Administrative formalities for family members who are not nationals of a Member State

1. Member States shall issue a residence card to family members of a Union citizen who are not nationals of a Member State, where the planned period of residence is for more than three months. 3.247

2. The deadline for submitting the residence card application may not be less than three months from the date of arrival.

3. Failure to comply with the requirement to apply for a residence card may make the person concerned liable to proportionate and non-discriminatory sanctions.

Article 10

Issue of residence cards

1. The right of residence of family members of a Union citizen who are not nationals of a Member State shall be evidenced by the issuing of a document called "Residence card of a family member of a Union citizen" no later than six months from the date on which they submit the application. A certificate of application for the residence card shall be issued immediately. 3.248

2. For the residence card to be issued, Member States shall require presentation of the following documents:

(a) a valid passport;

(b) a document attesting to the existence of a family relationship or of a registered partnership;

(c) the registration certificate or, in the absence of a registration system, any other proof of residence in the host Member State of the Union citizen whom they are accompanying or joining;

(d) in cases falling under points (c) and (d) of Article 2(2), documentary evidence that the conditions laid down therein are met;

(e) in cases falling under Article 3(2)(a), a document issued by the relevant authority in the country of origin or country from which they are arriving certifying that they are dependants or members of the household of the Union citizen, or proof of the existence of serious health grounds which strictly require the personal care of the family member by the Union citizen;

(f) in cases falling under Article 3(2)(b), proof of the existence of a durable relationship with the Union citizen.

Article 11

Validity of the residence card

3.249 1. The residence card provided for by Article 10(1) shall be valid for five years from the date of issue or for the envisaged period of residence of the Union citizen, if this period is less than five years.

2. The validity of the residence card shall not be affected by temporary absences not exceeding six months a year, or by absences of a longer duration for compulsory military service or by one absence of a maximum of 12 consecutive months for important reasons such as pregnancy and childbirth, serious illness, study or vocational training, or a posting in another Member State or a third country.

Article 12

Retention of the right of residence by family members in the event of death or departure of the Union citizen

3.250 1. Without prejudice to the second subparagraph, the Union citizen's death or departure from the host Member State shall not affect the right of residence of his/her family members who are nationals of a Member State.

Before acquiring the right of permanent residence, the persons concerned must meet the conditions laid down in points (a), (b), (c) or (d) of Article 7(1).

2. Without prejudice to the second subparagraph, the Union citizen's death shall not entail loss of the right of residence of his/her family members who are not nationals of a Member State and who have been residing in the host Member State as family members for at least one year before the Union citizen's death.

Before acquiring the right of permanent residence, the right of residence of the persons concerned shall remain subject to the requirement that they are able to show that they are workers or self-employed persons or that they have sufficient resources for themselves and their family members not to become a burden on the social assistance system of the host Member State during their period of residence and have comprehensive sickness insurance cover in the host Member State, or that they are members of the family, already constituted in the host Member State, of a person satisfying these requirements. "Sufficient resources" shall be as defined in Article 8(4).

Such family members shall retain their right of residence exclusively on a personal basis.

3. The Union citizen's departure from the host Member State or his/her death shall not entail loss of the right of residence of his/her children or of the parent who has actual custody of the children, irrespective of nationality, if the children reside in the host Member State and are enrolled at an educational establishment, for the purpose of studying there, until the completion of their studies.

Article 13

Retention of the right of residence by family members in the event of divorce, annulment of marriage or termination of registered partnership

1. Without prejudice to the second subparagraph, divorce, annulment of the Union citizen's marriage or termination of his/her registered partnership, as referred to in point 2(b) of Article 2 shall not affect the right of residence of his/her family members who are nationals of a Member State. 3.251

Before acquiring the right of permanent residence, the persons concerned must meet the conditions laid down in points (a), (b), (c) or (d) of Article 7(1).

2. Without prejudice to the second subparagraph, divorce, annulment of marriage or termination of the registered partnership referred to in point 2(b) of Article 2 shall not entail loss of the right of residence of a Union citizen's family members who are not nationals of a Member State where:

(a) prior to initiation of the divorce or annulment proceedings or termination of the registered partnership referred to in point 2(b) of Article 2, the marriage or registered partnership has lasted at least three years, including one year in the host Member State; or

(b) by agreement between the spouses or the partners referred to in point 2(b) of Article 2 or by court order, the spouse or partner who is not a national of a Member State has custody of the Union citizen's children; or

(c) this is warranted by particularly difficult circumstances, such as having been a victim of domestic violence while the marriage or registered partnership was subsisting; or

(d) by agreement between the spouses or partners referred to in point 2(b) of Article 2 or by court order, the spouse or partner who is not a national of a Member State has the right of access to a minor child, provided that the court has ruled that such access must be in the host Member State, and for as long as is required.

Before acquiring the right of permanent residence, the right of residence of the persons concerned shall remain subject to the requirement that they are able to show that they are workers or self-employed persons or that they have sufficient resources for themselves and their family members not to become a burden on the social assistance system of the host Member State during their period of residence and have comprehensive sickness insurance cover in the host Member State, or that they are members of the family, already constituted in the host Member State, of a person satisfying these requirements. "Sufficient resources" shall be as defined in Article 8(4).

Such family members shall retain their right of residence exclusively on personal basis.

General Note

In *ONAFTS v Radia Hadj Ahmed* (C-45/12) Judgment of June 13, 2013, the Court of Justice ruled that arts 13(2) and 14 of the Citizenship Directive, read in conjunction with art.18 TFEU, must be interpreted as not precluding the legisla- 3.252

tion of a Member State which subjects the grant of guaranteed family benefits to a third country national who falls within the following characterisation:

- that third-country national obtained, less than five years earlier, a permit to reside in a Member State in order to join, not in the context of marriage or registered partnership, a national of another Member State, by whom she has a child who has the nationality of the latter Member State;
- only that national of another Member State has the status of worker;
- in the meantime the cohabitation of the third-country national and the national of another Member State has come to an end; and
- both children are members of their mother's household

to a requirement of five years residence even though its own nationals are not subject to a similar requirement.

The first of four questions referred to the Court of Justice by the Court of Appeal in *Secretary of State for the Home Department v NA* (C-115/15) [2015] OJ C171/20 is:

> "Must a third country national ex-spouse of a Union citizen be able to show that their former spouse was exercising Treaty rights in the host Member state at the time of their divorce in order to retain a right of residence under Article 13(2) of Directive 2004/38/EC?"

The Court of Justice issued its decision in *Secretary of State for the Home Department v NA* (C-115/15) on June 30, 2016. The Court ruled that the answer to the first question raised by the Court of Appeal is as follows:

> "51. In the light of the foregoing, the answer to the first question is that Article 13(2)(c) of Directive 2004/38 must be interpreted as meaning that a third-country national, who is divorced from a Union citizen at whose hands she has been the victim of domestic violence during the marriage, cannot rely on the retention of her right of residence in the host Member State, on the basis of that provision, where the commencement of divorce proceedings post-dates the departure of the Union citizen spouse from that Member State."

Article 14

Retention of the right of residence

3.253 1. Union citizens and their family members shall have the right of residence provided for in Article 6, as long as they do not become an unreasonable burden on the social assistance system of the host Member State.

2. Union citizens and their family members shall have the right of residence provided for in Articles 7, 12 and 13 as long as they meet the conditions set out therein. In specific cases where there is a reasonable doubt as to whether a Union citizen or his/her family members satisfies the conditions set out in Articles 7, 12 and 13, Member States may verify if these conditions are fulfilled. This verification shall not be carried out systematically.

3. An expulsion measure shall not be the automatic consequence of a Union citizen's or his or her family member's recourse to the social assistance system of the host Member State.

4. By way of derogation from paragraphs 1 and 2 and without prejudice to the provisions of Chapter VI, an expulsion measure may in no case be adopted against Union citizens or their family members if:

(a) the Union citizens are workers or self-employed persons, or

(b) the Union citizens entered the territory of the host Member State in order to seek employment. In this case, the Union citizens and their family members may not be expelled for as long as the Union citizens can provide evidence that they are continuing to seek employment and that they have a genuine chance of being engaged.

GENERAL NOTE

Article 14(4)(b) codifies the position established under *Antonissen* (C-292/89) [1991] E.C.R. I-745 to the effect that work seekers have a right under art.39 EC to be in a Member State while looking for work provided that they have a genuine prospect of securing employment. This is also reflected in the Immigration (European Economic Area) Regulations 2006 which implement the Directive: see reg.6(1)(a) referring to jobseekers. This analysis of the legal position was accepted by the Commissioner in *R(IS) 8/08*. 3.254

SSWP v MB and linked cases (JSA) [2016] UKUT 372 (AAC); [2017] AACR 6; establishes that the provisions in national legislation requiring certain jobseekers to show compelling evidence of a genuine prospect of gaining employment (the so-called "genuine prospect of work" test) cannot go beyond what is required by applying the tests laid down in the *Antonissen* case without risking being in breach of the requirements of European Union law. This is an important decision which calls into question the compatibility of some of the Departmental guidance on the operation of the genuine prospect of work test.

In *OS v SSWP (JSA)* [2017] UKUT 107 (AAC) Judge Ward concludes that post-decision job outcomes can provide evidence of a claimant's prospects of work, but also notes that post-decision failure to secure employment may also be taken into account. Section 12(8)(b) of the Social Security Act 1998 does not preclude inferences being drawn from events which occurred after the date of the decision under appeal in this context (para.6).

Note *ONAFTS v Radia Hadj Ahmed* (C-35/12) Judgment of June 13, 2013 referred to in the annotations to art.13.

Article 15

Procedural safeguards

1. The procedures provided for by Articles 30 and 31 shall apply by analogy to all decisions restricting free movement of Union citizens and their family members on grounds other than public policy, public security or public health. 3.255

2. Expiry of the identity card or passport on the basis of which the person concerned entered the host Member State and was issued with a registration certificate or residence card shall not constitute a ground for expulsion from the host Member State.

3. The host Member State may not impose a ban on entry in the context of an expulsion decision to which paragraph 1 applies.

Chapter IV

Right of Permanent Residence

Section I

Eligibility

Article 16

General rule for Union citizens and their family members

3.256 1. Union citizens who have resided legally for a continuous period of five years in the host Member State shall have the right of permanent residence there. This right shall not be subject to the conditions provided for in Chapter III.

2. Paragraph 1 shall apply also to family members who are not nationals of a Member State and have legally resided with the Union citizen in the host Member State for a continuous period of five years.

3. Continuity of residence shall not be affected by temporary absences not exceeding a total of six months a year, or by absences of a longer duration for compulsory military service, or by one absence of a maximum of 12 consecutive months for important reasons such as pregnancy and childbirth, serious illness, study or vocational training, or a posting in another Member State or a third country.

4. Once acquired, the right of permanent residence shall be lost only through absence from the host Member State for a period exceeding two consecutive years.

General note

3.257 The right of permanent residence is an innovation in the Directive. The status is a particularly valuable one, since it removes all restrictions on the beneficiary's residence, and guarantees them equality of treatment in every respect with nationals of the host Member State. It is, however, not entirely permanent, since it can be lost following absence from the host Member State for a period exceeding two consecutive years.

DWP guidance on the right of permanent residence is contained in Memo DMG 16/15.

Who can rely on the Directive?

3.258 The provision refers to "Union citizens". However, in *McCarthy* (C–434/09) Judgment of May 5, 2011, the Court ruled, in a reference from the Supreme Court, that a woman holding both UK and Irish nationality, who had lived all her life in the United Kingdom, and had never exercised her rights to move as a Union citizen, could not rely on the Citizenship Directive. This meant that she could not claim the more favourable treatment EU law made for the admission of her Jamaican husband to the United Kingdom than was available under national immigration law. Nor could she rely on art.21 TFEU since there was no denial of the right of free movement; the non-application of EU law would not have the effect of impeding in any way her own exercise of her rights of free movement.

At first glance this judgment does not appear to be consistent with the earlier judgment of the Grand Chamber in *Ruiz Zambrano* (C–34/09) Judgment of March 8, 2011. In this case a Colombian couple had come from Colombia to Belgium in 1999 where they had sought unsuccessfully to obtain refuges status. Nevertheless they had remained in Belgium, where the man had worked. Two children were born in Belgium and acquired Belgian nationality by reason of their birth there. The father became unemployed and claimed unemployment benefits. These were refused, essentially on the grounds that he had no right to reside in Belgium. The Employment Tribunal in Brussels referred questions to the Luxembourg Court. Here the children who were Union citizens had lived nowhere other than Belgium. Nevertheless, the Grand Chamber ruled that they could rely on EU Law. The Court ruled that the Citizenship Directive did not apply:

> "39. It should be observed at the outset that, under Article 3(1) of Directive 2004/38, entitled '[b]eneficiaries', that directive applies to 'all Union citizens who move to or reside in a Member State other than that of which they are a national, and to their family members . . .'. Therefore, that directive does not apply to a situation such as that at issue in the main proceedings."

That was not, however, the end of the matter, since the children were Union citizens and would be deprived of the benefits of that citizenship if they were not entitled to remain in Belgium. That required their father to be entitled to reside and to work in Belgium. There would otherwise be a breach of art.20 TFEU.

The Court in *McCarthy* distinguished its judgment in *Ruiz Zambrano*. Denial of EU law rights for the Ruiz Zambrano children would have resulted in their exclusion from Belgium, and negate the benefits of Union citizenship. That was not the effect of the inapplicability of EU law to Mrs McCarthy's situation. In *Ruiz Zambrano* the national measure had the effect of depriving the Union citizens of the genuine enjoyment of the substance of the rights conferred by virtue of that status, and of impeding the exercise of free movement rights. There were no such consequences for Mrs McCarthy.

What do the words "resided legally" mean?

In *McCarthy* (C–434/09) Judgment of May 5, 2011, the Supreme Court had asked a question about the meaning of the words "resided legally" for the purposes of art.16 of the Citizenship Directive, but the Court ruled that it did not need to answer that question in view of the answer it had given to the first question the Supreme Court had referred to the Luxembourg Court. 3.259

In *Dias* (C–325/09) Advocate General's Opinion of February 17, 2011, the Advocate General says:

> "74. ... the wording of Article 16(1) of Directive 2004/38 is open. It precludes neither an interpretation accordingly to which only periods of residence on the basis of European Union law are taken into account, nor one going beyond that to include periods of residence which occurred on the basis of provisions of national law."

Despite that statement, the reasoning of the Advocate General in a long and intricate Opinion appears to veer in favour of entitlement to permanent residence being dependent upon residence in accordance with the provisions of the Directive. Note too that recital 17 to the Directive refers to residence "in compliance with the conditions laid down in the Directive." This issue is not addressed directly in the judgment of July 21, 2011.

The Court of Justice has disagreed with the Opinion of Advocate General Bot in *Ziolkowski and Szeja* (C-424/10 and C-425/10) Judgment of December 21, 2011, in ruling that art.16 of the Citizenship Directive: 3.260

> "must be interpreted as meaning that a Union citizen who has been resident on the sole basis of the national law of that Member State cannot be regarded as

having acquired the right of permanent residence under that provision if, during that period of residence, he did not satisfy the conditions laid down in Article 7(1) of the directive."

But periods of residence prior to a Member State's accession may be taken into account "provided those periods were completed in compliance with the conditions laid down in Article 7(1) of the directive."

In *Alarape and Tijani* (C-529/11) Judgment of May 8, 2013, the Court of Justice has ruled that periods of residence by family members on the sole basis of art.12 of Regulation 1612/68 (now art.10 of Reg.492/11) in circumstances where no rights to reside arise under the Citizenship Directive do not constitute periods to be taken into account in computing the period required in order to acquire permanent resident status under art.16 of the Citizenship Directive.

Computing residence for a continuous period of five years

3.261 It is now firmly established that periods of residence prior to April 30, 2006 (when the Directive entered into force) may be taken into account in determining a person's entitlement to permanent residence status: *Lassal* (C–162/09) Judgment of October 7, 2010. However, since permanent residence is an innovation of the Directive, the new status cannot come into effect from to April 30, 2006.

The *Lassal* case concerned the treatment of gaps in pattern of residence prior to April 30, 2006. On this point, the court ruled that:

> ". . . absences from the host Member State of less than two consecutive years which occurred before 30 April 2006 but following a continuous period of five years' legal residence completed before that date do not affect the acquisition of the right of permanent residence pursuant to Article 16(1)." (See [59].)

Dias (C–325/09) judgment of July 21, 2011, (reported as [2012] AACR 36) concerned a further set of questions relating to acquisition of permanent residence. The claimant had the following pattern of presence in the United Kingdom:

January 1988	arrived in the United Kingdom
May 13, 2000	obtained a five-year residence permit under Directive 68/360; and worked until the summer of 2002
Summer 2002	on maternity leave until April 17, 2003
April 18, 2003	not working until April 26, 2004
April 26, 2004	in work
March 23, 2007	not working and claims benefit

3.262 In the light of the *Lassal* judgment, the United Kingdom accepted that Maria Dias had acquired permanent residence. This did not, however, in the view of the Advocate General, render the need to respond to the questions unnecessary.

In its judgment, the court has provided answers to two questions which relate to the interpretation of art.16. First, the court rules that residence permits issued by national authorities in accordance with Directive 68/360 are declaratory and not constitutive. They grant no rights of residence. The court said:

> "The grant of a residence permit to a national of a Member State is to be regarded, not as a measure giving rise to rights, but as a measure by a Member State serving to prove the individual position of a national of another Member State with regard to provisions of European Union law." (At [48].)

In Maria Dias's particular circumstances, the period covered only by the residence permit in which Maria was not working was of less than two years' duration, and occurred after she had been lawfully resident for more than five years, and so did not preclude her acquiring a right of permanent residence on April 30, 2006.

In *HR (Portugal) v SSHD* [2009] EWCA Civ 371 and *Carvalho v SSHD* [2010] EWCA Civ 1406, the Court of Appeal ruled that time spent in prison does not accrue towards the acquisition of permanent resident status. In *Onuekwere v SSHD* (C-378/12) Judgement of January 16, 2014, the Court of Justice ruled that periods of imprisonment in the host Member State of a third country national, who is a family member of a citizen of the Union who has acquired the right of permanent residence during those periods, cannot be taken into consideration in the context of the acquisition by the third country national of the right of permanent residence. Furthermore, continuity of residence is interrupted by periods of imprisonment.

There is national authority that a period in detention under a hospital order is not equated with a period of imprisonment. In *SSHD v Jo* [2012] UKUT 237 (IAC), the Upper Tribunal concluded that a person under a hospital order after having committed a horrific attack on a pensioner was more akin to that of a person unable to work because of illness. The individual was accordingly able to resist a deportation order since the time in hospital under the order counted in his attaining a right of permanent residence, which gave him additional protection against deportation under art.28 of the Citizenship Directive.

In *Secretary of State for the Home Department v Jovita Ojo* [2015] EWCA Civ 1301, the Court of Appeal ruled:

> "20. In my view none of the authorities to which we were referred supports the proposition that the court can treat the period during which Mrs Ojo ceased to be dependent on her mother as analogous to a period of absence from the United Kingdom. The acquisition of a permanent right of residence depends on continuous residence in a qualifying status and the Directive makes no provision for changes in status of the kind which occurred in this case, nor is there any reason why it should say so. There is a distinction to be drawn between residence and status which makes it inapposite to draw an analogy between the two."

The position of nationals of the Member States joining in 2004 and 2007 3.263

GN (EEA Regulations: Five years' residence) Hungary, [2007] UKAIT 73 had suggested that rights of residence held under national law before a person becomes a citizen of the Union are not relevant for the purpose of art.16(1). Without deciding the matter either way, the Commissioner in *R(IS) 3/08* suggests that the reasoning in the immigration case might need to be re-considered in the light of the possibility of enjoying a right of residence directly under what is now art.21 TFEU.

The position of the Commission in COM(2008) 840/3 is certainly that nationals of the new Member States "enjoy unrestricted right of free movement. Transitional arrangements apply only to access to labour markets." (p.2) This Report further states:

> "Belgium and the UK incorrectly take no account of periods of residence acquired by EU citizens before their countries acceded to the EU". (p.7)

Article 17

Exemptions for persons no longer working in the host Member State and their family members

1. By way of derogation from Article 16, the right of permanent residence in the host Member State shall be enjoyed before completion of a continuous period of five years of residence by: 3.264

(a) workers or self-employed persons who, at the time they stop working, have reached the age laid down by the law of that Member State for entitlement to an old age pension or workers who cease paid employment to take early retirement, provided that they have been working in that Member State for at least the preceding twelve months and have resided there continuously for more than three years. If the law of the host Member State does not grant the right to an old age pension to certain categories of self-employed persons, the age condition shall be deemed to have been met once the person concerned has reached the age of 60;

(b) workers or self-employed persons who have resided continuously in the host Member State for more than two years and stop working there as a result of permanent incapacity to work. If such incapacity is the result of an accident at work or an occupational disease entitling the person concerned to a benefit payable in full or in part by an institution in the host Member State, no condition shall be imposed as to length of residence;

(c) workers or self-employed persons who, after three years of continuous employment and residence in the host Member State, work in an employed or self-employed capacity in another Member State, while retaining their place of residence in the host Member State, to which they return, as a rule, each day or at least once a week. For the purposes of entitlement to the rights referred to in points (a) and (b), periods of employment spent in the Member State in which the person concerned is working shall be regarded as having been spent in the host Member State. Periods of involuntary unemployment duly recorded by the relevant employment office, periods not worked for reasons not of the person's own making and absences from work or cessation of work due to illness or accident shall be regarded as periods of employment.

2. The conditions as to length of residence and employment laid down in point (a) of paragraph 1 and the condition as to length of residence laid down in point (b) of paragraph 1 shall not apply if the worker's or the self-employed person's spouse or partner as referred to in point 2(b) of Article 2 is a national of the host Member State or has lost the nationality of that Member State by marriage to that worker or self-employed person.

3. Irrespective of nationality, the family members of a worker or a self-employed person who are residing with him in the territory of the host Member State shall have the right of permanent residence in that Member State, if the worker or self-employed person has acquired himself the right of permanent residence in that Member State on the basis of paragraph 1.

4. If, however, the worker or self-employed person dies while still working but before acquiring permanent residence status in the host Member State on the basis of paragraph 1, his family members who are residing with him in the host Member State shall acquire the right of permanent residence there, on condition that:

(a) the worker or self-employed person had, at the time of death, resided continuously on the territory of that Member State for two years; or

(b) the death resulted from an accident at work or an occupational disease; or

(c) the surviving spouse lost the nationality of that Member State following marriage to the worker or self-employed person.

GENERAL NOTE

These provisions enable former workers and self-employed persons to acquire permanent residence status in a period shorter than five years, where they are sufficiently integrated into the host Member State (according to the conditions set out in the provision) when they cease employment or self-employment for a variety of reasons. 3.265

Article 45(3)(d) TFEU provides a right to remain in the territory of a Member State after having been employed there "subject to the conditions which shall be embodied in regulations to be drawn up by the Commission." The main beneficiaries are workers who (after a requisite period of work in the host Member State) have come to the end of their working life on reaching state pensionable age or on taking early retirement caused by ill health, accident at work or occupational disease.

Regulation 1251/70/EEC of June 29 1970, [1970] OJ L142/24, originally set out those conditions. That regulation has been repealed by Commission Regulation 635/2006/EC of April 25, 2006, [2006] OJ L112/9 (which entered into force on April 27, 2006). The preamble notes that art.17 of the Citizenship Directive includes the main elements of Reg.1251/70 and "amends them by granting beneficiaries of the right to remain a more privileged status, namely the right of permanent residence."

There may, however, be some issues flowing from the acquisition of a right to remain under the provisions of the repealed regulation and the application of the provisions of art.16 of the Citizenship Directive relating to loss of permanent residence. 3.266

Article 2 of Reg.1251/70 gives a right to remain permanently to those falling within the situations contemplated by the provisions of the article. Article 5 requires the right to remain to be exercised within two years from the time of becoming entitled to the right, but once acquired, Reg.1251/70 makes no provision for the loss of the right. There was no corresponding provision to art.16(4) of the Citizenship Directive under the arrangements put in place by Reg.1251/70, though art.6 of that Regulation did provide for a system of automatic residence permits for those coming within the provisions of the Regulation. It would seem to follow that a person who acquired and exercised a right to remain under Reg.1251/70 many years ago would have retained that right, which was arguably converted into a right of permanent residence under art.16 of the Citizenship Directive on its entry into force, and then could be lost where the conditions set out in art.16(4) apply (absence from the host State for a period exceeding two consecutive years).

In *TG v SSWP (PC)* [2015] UKUT 50 (AAC), Judge Ward has ruled that the right of permanent residence contained in art.17, unlike the corresponding right of permanent residence under art.16, is satisfied by actual residence rather than residence strictly in accordance with the provisions of the Citizenship Directive. This is essentially because it corresponds to a right which had originally been contained in Commission Regulation 1251/70, which contained no limitation on the concept of residence comparable to that found in the Citizenship Directive. The Citizenship Directive was designed to preserve existing rights and so could not limit the nature of the residence upon which the right in art.17 depended. In contrast, the right of permanent residence in art.16 was a new right introduced by the Citizenship Directive, and so could contain more restrictive conditions on the nature of the residence. Judge Ward's detailed reasoning can be found at paras 14–68 of the decision.

This decision is currently under appeal to the Court of Appeal under the name of *Gubeladze v Secretary of State for Work and Pensions.*

See also Memo ADM 4/16 of February 2016.

Permanent incapacity to work

3.267 *Aurelio de Brito v SSHD* [2012] EWCA Civ 709 is an interesting authority in an appeal from the Immigration and Asylum Chamber of the Upper Tribunal, which considers the concept of permanent incapacity for work under art.17. The claimant, a Portuguese national, had come to the United Kingdom in January 2004 and had worked between March 2004 and February 2005. He stopped work because of illness. His employment ended in July 2005, although he continued to receive sickness certification from his doctor. Incapacity benefit was awarded from April 2006, and the claimant has not returned to work. He sought acknowledgement of his right to remain as a former worker who had suffered permanent incapacity for work. The claimant argued that for the period between July 2005 and April 2006 he continued to be treated as a worker under art.7(3)(a) of the Citizenship Directive since his incapacity should properly be regarded as temporary at that time. This would have enabled him to aggregate periods of actual employment and deemed employment in order to meet the requirement that he was a "worker" who had resided for more than two years which would then passport him to permanent residence under the shorter qualifying period in art.17. The Court of Appeal rules that the test of whether the incapacity for work was permanent was an objective one (See [33]). The Upper Tribunal had not erred in concluding that the claimant was permanently incapable of work from July 2005 because it was clear from that date that the claimant was unable to engage with the labour market and has not since worked. It would be for the claimant to show that his medical condition at any given time was temporary; if he or she could not show that the incapacity should be regarded as permanent.

Wadi Samin v City of Westminster [2012] EWCA Civ 1468 is a judgment of the Court of Appeal which applies the conclusions reached in the *Aurelio de Brito* case. It contains a useful summary of the earlier authorities, and concludes:

> "31. This court is bound by *de Brito* and *Konodyba*. We have considered the European cases in some depth because they were not referred to in either decision. If, having done so, there remained a doubt about the proper approach to the meaning of Article 7(3)(a) [of the Citizenship Directive] we ought to refer it to the CJEU. It is important that the application of domestic provisions based on Article 7(3)(a) should be applied consistently across the Union. There is, however, no room for any sensible doubt. The Article, and Regulation 6(2)(a) of the domestic Regulations, contain a specific test, namely whether the interruption is a temporary one or is not. Temporary is to be contrasted with permanent. The question is one of fact in every case; plainly the circumstances which will fall to be examined will vary infinitely. It will generally be helpful to ask whether there is or is not a realistic prospect of a return to work. It will generally not be helpful to ask if the interruption is indefinite; an indefinite absence from work may well not be temporary, but it might be, for example if an injured man is awaiting surgery which can be expected to restore him to fitness to work, but the date when it will be available is uncertain. This approach to the legislation, explained in *de Brito* and *Konodyba*, is entirely consistent with the objectives of the Directive as explained in its recitals and in the European cases."

Article 18

Acquisition of the right of permanent residence by certain family members who are not nationals of a Member State

3.268 Without prejudice to Article 17, the family members of a Union citizen to whom Articles 12(2) and 13(2) apply, who satisfy the conditions laid down therein, shall acquire the right of permanent residence after residing legally for a period of five consecutive years in the host Member State.

Article 19

Section II

Administrative formalities

Article 19

Document certifying permanent residence for Union citizens

1. Upon application Member States shall issue Union citizens entitled to permanent residence, after having verified duration of residence, with a document certifying permanent residence. The document certifying permanent residence shall be issued as soon as possible. 3.269

Article 20

Permanent residence card for family members who are not nationals of a Member State

1. Member States shall issue family members who are not nationals of a Member State entitled to permanent residence with a permanent residence card within six months of the submission of the application. The permanent residence card shall be renewable automatically every 10 years. 3.270

2. The application for a permanent residence card shall be submitted before the residence card expires. Failure to comply with the requirement to apply for a permanent residence card may render the person concerned liable to proportionate and non-discriminatory sanctions.

3. Interruption in residence not exceeding two consecutive years shall not affect the validity of the permanent residence card.

Article 21

Continuity of residence

For the purposes of this Directive, continuity of residence may be attested by any means of proof in use in the host Member State. Continuity of residence is broken by any expulsion decision duly enforced against the person concerned. 3.271

CHAPTER V

PROVISIONS COMMON TO THE RIGHT OF RESIDENCE AND THE RIGHT OF PERMANENT RESIDENCE

Article 22

Territorial scope

The right of residence and the right of permanent residence shall cover the whole territory of the host Member State. Member States may impose territorial restrictions on the right of residence and the right of permanent residence only where the same restrictions apply to their own nationals. 3.272

Article 23

Related rights

3.273 Irrespective of nationality, the family members of a Union citizen who have the right of residence or the right of permanent residence in a Member State shall be entitled to take up employment or self-employment there.

Article 24

Equal treatment

3.274 1. Subject to such specific provisions as are expressly provided for in the Treaty and secondary law, all Union citizens residing on the basis of this Directive in the territory of the host Member State shall enjoy equal treatment with the nationals of that Member State within the scope of the Treaty. The benefit of this right shall be extended to family members who are not nationals of a Member State and who have the right of residence or permanent residence.

2. By way of derogation from paragraph 1, the host Member State shall not be obliged to confer entitlement to social assistance during the first three months of residence or, where appropriate, the longer period provided for in Article 14(4)(b), nor shall it be obliged, prior to acquisition of the right of permanent residence, to grant maintenance aid for studies, including vocational training, consisting in student grants or student loans to persons other than workers, self-employed persons, persons who retain such status and members of their families.

GENERAL NOTE

3.275 In *Vatsouras and Koupatantze* (C-22/08 and C-23/08) [2009] E.C.R. I-4585 the Luxembourg Court dismissed a challenge to the validity of art.24(2).

This Article reflects the European Union law obligation to treat people equally. The key proposition is that those enjoying the right of permanent residence (and their families regardless of their nationality) are entitled to be treated equally in every respect with nationals of the host Member State.

The difficult area is the obligation of equal treatment when a national of another Member State (and note that the Directive has been extended to nationals of the three EEA countries) has been resident for more than three months but less than five years. This is because there is no obligation (but equally no prohibition) to confer entitlement to social assistance in the first three months (or longer where a process of seeking work under art.14(4)(b) is continuing) when there is an unconditional right to reside. Nor is there any entitlement to support for living expenses of students prior to attainment of permanent residence under the Directive. However, this does not mean that, during this period, claims to equal treatment are bound to fail. Any differential treatment during this period must be objectively and reasonably justified and also proportionate in the particular circumstances of the case.

The provision is also without prejudice to the provisions of art.7(2) of Reg.1612/68 (now Regulation 492/2011) which entitle those within the definition of "worker" under Title II of that Regulation to the same social and tax advantages as nationals of the host Member State.

Dano v Jobcenter Leipzig (C-333/13), Judgment of November 11, 2014, confirms that there is no obligation under art.24 (or art.4 of Regulation 883/2004) to pay means-tested benefits (social assistance) to an EU migrant of more than three months standing who has not been a worker, and is not seeking work. The Court notes that art.7(1)(b) requires those who are economically inactive "to meet the condition that they have sufficient resources of their own" in order to have a right of residence (para.75).

In *Vestische Arbeit Jobcenter Kreis Recklinghausen v García-Nieto* (C-299/14), Judgment of February 25, 2016, the Court of Justice has ruled that art.24 does not preclude exclusion from benefits which constitute social assistance, notwithstanding that the benefits are also special non-contributory benefits within art.70 of Regulation 883/2004, of those who fall within art.6(1) of the Directive, that is, those in the first three months of their residence in the host Member State.

Note also the judgment of the Grand Chamber of the Court of Justice in the *Alimanovic case* (C-67/14) discussed above in the annotations to art.7 of the Citizenship Directive.

In *Alhashem v SSWP* [2016] EWCA Civ 395; [2017] AACR 12, the Court of Appeal decided that an income-based employment and support allowance constituted social assistance and not social security under the Citizenship Directive.

Article 25

General provisions concerning residence documents

1. Possession of a registration certificate as referred to in Article 8, of a document certifying permanent residence, of a certificate attesting submission of an application for a family member residence card, of a residence card or of a permanent residence card, may under no circumstances be made a precondition for the exercise of a right or the completion of an administrative formality, as entitlement to rights may be attested by any other means of proof. **3.276**

2. All documents mentioned in paragraph 1 shall be issued free of charge or for a charge not exceeding that imposed on nationals for the issuing of similar documents.

Article 26

Checks

Member States may carry out checks on compliance with any requirement deriving from their national legislation for non nationals always to carry their registration certificate or residence card, provided that the same requirement applies to their own nationals as regards their identity card. In the event of failure to comply with this requirement, Member States may impose the same sanctions as those imposed on their own nationals for failure to carry their identity card. **3.277**

CHAPTER VI

RESTRICTIONS ON THE RIGHT OF ENTRY AND THE RIGHT OF RESIDENCE ON GROUNDS OF PUBLIC POLICY, PUBLIC SECURITY OR PUBLIC HEALTH

Article 27

General principles

1. Subject to the provisions of this Chapter, Member States may restrict the freedom of movement and residence of Union citizens and their family **3.278**

members, irrespective of nationality, on grounds of public policy, public security or public health. These grounds shall not be invoked to serve economic ends.

2. Measures taken on grounds of public policy or public security shall comply with the principle of proportionality and shall be based exclusively on the personal conduct of the individual concerned. Previous criminal convictions shall not in themselves constitute grounds for taking such measures. The personal conduct of the individual concerned must represent a genuine, present and sufficiently serious threat affecting one of the fundamental interests of society. Justifications that are isolated from the particulars of the case or that rely on considerations of general prevention shall not be accepted.

3. In order to ascertain whether the person concerned represents a danger for public policy or public security, when issuing the registration certificate or, in the absence of a registration system, not later than three months from the date of arrival of the person concerned on its territory or from the date of reporting his/her presence within the territory, as provided for in Article 5(5), or when issuing the residence card, the host Member State may, should it consider this essential, request the Member State of origin and, if need be, other Member States to provide information concerning any previous police record the person concerned may have. Such enquiries shall not be made as a matter of routine. The Member State consulted shall give its reply within two months.

4. The Member State which issued the passport or identity card shall allow the holder of the document who has been expelled on grounds of public policy, public security, or public health from another Member State to re-enter its territory without any formality even if the document is no longer valid or the nationality of the holder is in dispute.

Article 28

Protection against expulsion

3.279 1. Before taking an expulsion decision on grounds of public policy or public security, the host Member State shall take account of considerations such as how long the individual concerned has resided on its territory, his/her age, state of health, family and economic situation, social and cultural integration into the host Member State and the extent of his/her links with the country of origin.

2. The host Member State may not take an expulsion decision against Union citizens or their family members, irrespective of nationality, who have the right of permanent residence on its territory, except on serious grounds of public policy or public security.

3. An expulsion decision may not be taken against Union citizens, except if the decision is based on imperative grounds of public security, as defined by Member States, if they:

(a) have resided in the host Member State for the previous 10 years; or

(b) are a minor, except if the expulsion is necessary for the best interests of the child, as provided for in the United Nations Convention on the Rights of the Child of 20 November 1989.

General note

3.280 *P.I.* (C-349/09) judgment of May 22, 2012, concerned the deportation of a serious sex offender. In his Opinion, the Advocate General had drawn a surprising conclusion that a person could not accrue rights under the Directive where his presence involved engagement in serious criminal conduct. The Court does not follow that line of reasoning, but rather builds on earlier case-law in ruling that serious and continuing sexual offences against children (which are referred to in art.83 TFEU in the chapter of the treaty of judicial cooperation in criminal matters—namely, sexual exploitation of children) are capable of coming within the notion of "imperative grounds of public security" and so might justify expulsion of a 10-year resident "as long as the manner in which the offences were committed discloses particularly serious characteristics, which is a matter for the referring court to determine on the basis of an individual examination of the specific case before it."

The Court is clearly taking a broad view of the concept of public security in order to enable Member States to deport those who, despite being long residents in the Member State concerned, have been convicted of a range of particularly serious offences, some of which do not at first sight appear to affect public security. But the Court has rejected any notion that there are hidden conditions attaching to the accrual of permanent residence or 10-year residence for the purposes of the conditions relating to deportation.

Article 29

Public health

1. The only diseases justifying measures restricting freedom of movement shall be the diseases with epidemic potential as defined by the relevant instruments of the World Health Organisation and other infectious diseases or contagious parasitic diseases if they are the subject of protection provisions applying to nationals of the host Member State. **3.281**

2. Diseases occurring after a three-month period from the date of arrival shall not constitute grounds for expulsion from the territory.

3. Where there are serious indications that it is necessary, Member States may, within three months of the date of arrival, require persons entitled to the right of residence to undergo, free of charge, a medical examination to certify that they are not suffering from any of the conditions referred to in paragraph 1. Such medical examinations may not be required as a matter of routine.

Article 30

Notification of decisions

1. The persons concerned shall be notified in writing of any decision taken under Article 27(1), in such a way that they are able to comprehend its content and the implications for them. **3.282**

2. The persons concerned shall be informed, precisely and in full, of the public policy, public security or public health grounds on which the decision taken in their case is based, unless this is contrary to the interests of State security.

3. The notification shall specify the court or administrative authority with which the person concerned may lodge an appeal, the time limit for the appeal and, where applicable, the time allowed for the person to leave the territory of the Member State. Save in duly substantiated cases of urgency,

the time allowed to leave the territory shall be not less than one month from the date of notification.

Article 31

Procedural safeguards

3.283 1. The persons concerned shall have access to judicial and, where appropriate, administrative redress procedures in the host Member State to appeal against or seek review of any decision taken against them on the grounds of public policy, public security or public health.

2. Where the application for appeal against or judicial review of the expulsion decision is accompanied by an application for an interim order to suspend enforcement of that decision, actual removal from the territory may not take place until such time as the decision on the interim order has been taken, except:

— where the expulsion decision is based on a previous judicial decision; or

— where the persons concerned have had previous access to judicial review;

or

— where the expulsion decision is based on imperative grounds of public security under Article 28(3).

3. The redress procedures shall allow for an examination of the legality of the decision, as well as of the facts and circumstances on which the proposed measure is based. They shall ensure that the decision is not disproportionate, particularly in view of the requirements laid down in Article 28.

4. Member States may exclude the individual concerned from their territory pending the redress procedure, but they may not prevent the individual from submitting his/her defence in person, except when his/her appearance may cause serious troubles to public policy or public security or when the appeal or judicial review concerns a denial of entry to the territory.

Article 32

Duration of exclusion orders

3.284 1. Persons excluded on grounds of public policy or public security may submit an application for lifting of the exclusion order after a reasonable period, depending on the circumstances, and in any event after three years from enforcement of the final exclusion order which has been validly adopted in accordance with Community law, by putting forward arguments to establish that there has been a material change in the circumstances which justified the decision ordering their exclusion. The Member State concerned shall reach a decision on this application within six months of its submission.

2. The persons referred to in paragraph 1 shall have no right of entry to the territory of the Member State concerned while their application is being considered.

Article 33

Expulsion as a penalty or legal consequence

1. Expulsion orders may not be issued by the host Member State as a 3.285
penalty or legal consequence of a custodial penalty, unless they conform to the requirements of Articles 27, 28 and 29.

2. If an expulsion order, as provided for in paragraph 1, is enforced more than two years after it was issued, the Member State shall check that the individual concerned is currently and genuinely a threat to public policy or public security and shall assess whether there has been any material change in the circumstances since the expulsion order was issued.

Chapter VII

Final Provisions

Article 34

Publicity

Member States shall disseminate information concerning the rights and 3.286
obligations of Union citizens and their family members on the subjects covered by this Directive, particularly by means of awareness-raising campaigns conducted through national and local media and other means of communication.

Article 35

Abuse of rights

Member States may adopt the necessary measures to refuse, terminate 3.287
or withdraw any right conferred by this Directive in the case of abuse of rights or fraud, such as marriages of convenience. Any such measure shall be proportionate and subject to the procedural safeguards provided for in Articles 30 and 31.

Article 36

Sanctions

Member States shall lay down provisions on the sanctions applicable to 3.288
breaches of national rules adopted for the implementation of this Directive and shall take the measures required for their application. The sanctions laid down shall be effective and proportionate. Member States shall notify the Commission of these provisions not later than 30 April 2006 and as promptly as possible in the case of any subsequent changes.

Article 37

More favourable national provisions

3.289 The provisions of this Directive shall not affect any laws, regulations or administrative provisions laid down by a Member State which would be more favourable to the persons covered by this Directive.

Article 38

Repeals

3.290 1. Articles 10 and 11 of Regulation (EEC) No 1612/68 shall be repealed with effect from 30 April 2006.

2. Directives 64/221/EEC, 68/360/EEC, 72/194/EEC, 73/148/EEC, 75/34/EEC, 75/35/EEC, 90/364/EEC, 90/365/EEC and 93/96/EEC shall be repealed with effect from 30 April 2006.

3. References made to the repealed provisions and Directives shall be construed as being made to this Directive.

Article 39

Report

3.291 No later than 30 April 2008 the Commission shall submit a report on the application of this Directive to the European Parliament and the Council, together with any necessary proposals, notably on the opportunity to extend the period of time during which Union citizens and their family members may reside in the territory of the host Member State without any conditions. The Member States shall provide the Commission with the information needed to produce the report.

Article 40

Transposition

3.292 1. Member States shall bring into force the laws, regulations and administrative provisions necessary to comply with this Directive by 30 April 2006. When Member States adopt those measures, they shall contain a reference to this Directive or shall be accompanied by such a reference on the occasion of their official publication. The methods of making such reference shall be laid down by the Member States.

2. Member States shall communicate to the Commission the text of the provisions of national law which they adopt in the field covered by this Directive together with a table showing how the provisions of this Directive correspond to the national provisions adopted.

Article 41

Entry into force

This Directive shall enter into force on the day of its publication in the *Official Journal of the European Union*. **3.293**

Article 42

Addressees

This Directive is addressed to the Member States. **3.294**

Done at Strasbourg, 29 April 2004.

Regulation (EC) No 883/2004 of the European Parliament and of the Council of 29 April 2004 on the coordination of social security systems

CORRECTED VERSION AS SET OUT IN [2004] OJ L200/1 (7 JUNE 2004)
(*AS AMENDED*)

GENERAL NOTE

An unofficial consolidated text of Regulation 883/2004 as amended by Regulation 988/2009 has been produced by the European Commission, and may be found at: *http://eur-lex.europa.eu/legal-content/EN/TXT/PDF/?uri=CELEX:02004R0883-20130108* [Accessed July 20, 2016]. **3.295**

Applies from May 1, 2010

ARRANGEMENT OF REGULATION

Preamble

TITLE I

GENERAL PROVISIONS

TITLE II

DETERMINATION OF THE LEGISLATION APPLICABLE

TITLE III

SPECIAL PROVISIONS CONCERNING THE VARIOUS CATEGORIES OF BENEFITS

CHAPTER 1

SICKNESS, MATERNITY AND EQUIVALENT PATERNITY BENEFITS

Section 1

Insured persons and members of their families, except pensioners and members of their families

Section 2

Pensioners and members of their families

Section 3

Common provisions

31. General provision
32. Prioritising of the right to benefits in kind—Special rule for the right of members of the family to benefits in the Member State of residence
33. Substantial benefits in kind
34. Over-lapping of long-term care benefits
35. Reimbursements between institutions

CHAPTER 2

BENEFITS IN RESPECT OF ACCIDENTS AT WORK AND OCCUPATIONAL DISEASES

36. Right to benefits in kind and in cash
37. Costs of transport
38. Benefits for an occupational disease where the person suffering from such a disease has been exposed to the same risk in several Member States
39. Aggravation of an occupational disease
40. Rules for taking into account the special features of certain legislation
41. Reimbursements between institutions

CHAPTER 3

DEATH GRANTS

42. Right to grants where death occurs in, or where the person entitled resides in, a Member State other than the competent Member State
43. Provisions of benefits in the event of the death of a pensioner

CHAPTER 4

INVALIDITY BENEFITS

44. Persons subject only to type A legislation
45. Special provisions on aggregation of periods
46. Persons subject either only to type B legislation or to type A and B legislation
47. Aggravation of invalidity
48. Conversion of invalidity benefits into old-age benefits
49. Special provisions for civil servants

CHAPTER 5

OLD-AGE AND SURVIVORS' PENSIONS

50. General provisions
51. Special provisions on aggregation of periods
52. Award of benefits
53. Rules to prevent overlapping
54. Overlapping of benefits of the same kind
55. Overlapping of benefits of a different kind
56. Additional provisions for the calculation of benefits

CHAPTER 6

UNEMPLOYMENT BENEFITS

CHAPTER 7

PRE-RETIREMENT BENEFITS

CHAPTER 8

FAMILY BENEFITS

CHAPTER 9

SPECIAL NON-CONTRIBUTORY BENEFITS

TITLE IV

ADMINISTRATIVE COMMISSION AND ADVISORY COMMITTEE

General Note

3.297 This Regulation is the successor to Regulation 3 ([1958] OJ L30/561), which was in force from January 1, 1959 until March 31, 1973, when it was succeeded by Regulation 1408/71 with effect from April 1, 1973. Regulation 3 was amended 14 times during its lifetime, and Regulation 1408/71 some 37 times. This Regulation needed to be amended even prior to its entry into force.

Like its predecessors, Regulation 883/2004 is coupled with an implementing regulation, Regulation 987/2009 (reproduced below at paras 3.501–3.630, setting out the administrative detail of its implementation. Regulation 883/2004 can be referred to as "the basic regulation", and Regulation 987/2009 as "the implementing regulation".

Regulation 883/2004 builds on the achievements of its predecessors. In the annotations which follow, the earlier case-law is reported where it appears relevant to the proper interpretation and application of the Regulation 883/2004.

There is no official table of derivation matching provisions of Regulation 883/2004 to Regulation 1408/71, but the annotations provide an indication of the corresponding provisions of the earlier regulation as a guide.

Regulation 1408/71 does not, however, cease to have effect altogether on May 1, 2010. It will continue in effect pending:

(a) the application of Regulation 883/2004 to the EEA countries (Iceland, Liechtenstein and Norway) (see below); and

(b) the extension of Regulation 883/2004 to Switzerland under a new agreement with that country (see below).

The United Kingdom and Denmark have contracted out of the extension of Regulation 883/2004 to third country nationals. In relation to these two countries Regulation 859/2003 (reproduced below) will continue to apply, but for all other Member States the position of third country nationals will be governed by Regulation (EU) No. 1231/2010 of November 24, 2010, [2010] OJ L344/1, which entered into force on January 1, 2011.

3.298 For overviews of the regulation and its provisions, see: R. White, "The new European social security regulations in context" (2010) 17 JSSL 144–63, and special double issue of *European Journal of Social Security*, Vol.11, Nos 1–2 (June 2009).

There is a helpful guide by the European Commission to the Regulation designed for the lay person *The EU provisions on social security. Your rights when moving within the European Union. Update 2010,* which can be found on the Union's website. In addition, the European Commission is continuing to produce a series of explanatory notes on aspects of the application of the new regulations, which are also available on the website from the page *http://ec.europa.eu/social/main.jsp?catId=26&langId=en* [Accessed August 3, 2010].

Relationship between Regulation (EC) No 883/2004 and Directive No 2004/38/EC is a useful note published by the European Commission's Employment, Social Affairs and Inclusion Directorate in January 2011. It is one of a series of explanatory notes on the key concepts of modernised coordination, which can be found at *http://ec.europa.eu/social/main.jsp?catId=866&langId=en&furtherPubs=yes* [Accessed May 24, 2012].

3.299 The predecessor Regulation had been extended to the EEA countries (Iceland, Liechtenstein and Norway) under the EEA Agreement, and to Switzerland by a separate agreement. Regulation 883/2004 has been extended to the EEA countries by Decision of the EEA Joint Committee [2011] OJ L262/33, and enters into force on June 1, 2012. The United Kingdom's challenge to the legal base of the Decision extending the operation of Reg.883/2004 to the three EEA countries and to Switzerland has been rejected by the Court of Justice: *United Kingdom v Council* (C-431/11), Judgment of September 26, 2013; and *United Kingdom v Council* (C-656/11), Judgment of February 27, 2014.

THE EUROPEAN PARLIAMENT AND THE COUNCIL OF THE EUROPEAN UNION,

Having regard to the Treaty establishing the European Community, and in particular Articles 42 and 308 thereof, Having regard to the proposal from the Commission presented after consultation with the social partners and the Administrative Commission on Social Security for Migrant Workers[1], **3.300**

Having regard to the Opinion of the European Economic and Social Committee,[2] Acting in accordance with the procedure laid down in Article 251 of the Treaty,[3]

Whereas:

(1) The rules for coordination of national social security systems fall within the framework of free movement of persons and should contribute towards improving their standard of living and conditions of employment.

(2) The Treaty does not provide powers other than those of Article 308 to take appropriate measures within the field of social security for persons other than employed persons.

(3) Council Regulation (EEC) No 1408/71 of 14 June 1971 on the application of social security schemes to employed persons, to self-employed persons and to members of their families moving within the Community[4] has been amended and updated on numerous occasions in order to take into account not only developments at Community level, including judgments of the Court of Justice, but also changes in legislation at national level. Such factors have played their part in making the Community coordination rules complex and lengthy. Replacing, while modernising and simplifying, these rules is therefore essential to achieve the aim of the free movement of persons.

(4) It is necessary to respect the special characteristics of national social security legislation and to draw up only a system of coordination.

(5) It is necessary, within the framework of such coordination, to guarantee within the Community equality of treatment under the different national legislation for the persons concerned.

(6) The close link between social security legislation and those contractual provisions which complement or replace such legislation and which have been the subject of a decision by the public authorities rendering them compulsory or extending their scope may call for similar protection with regard to the application of those provisions to that afforded by this Regulation. As a first step, the experience

1 OJ C 38, 12.2.1999, p.10.

2 OJ C 75, 15.3.2000, p.29.

3 Opinion of the European Parliament of September 3, 2003 (not yet published in the Official Journal). Council Common Position of January 26, 2004 (OJ C 79 E, 30.3.2004, p. 15) and Position of the European Parliament of April 20, 2004 (not yet published in the Official Journal). Decision of the Council of April 26, 2004.

4 OJ L 149, 5.7.1971, p.2. Regulation as last amended by Regulation (EC) No 1386/2001 of the European Parliament and of the Council (OJ L 187, 10.7.2001, p.1).

of Member States who have notified such schemes might be evaluated.

(7) Due to the major differences existing between national legislation in terms of the persons covered, it is preferable to lay down the principle that this Regulation is to apply to nationals of a Member State, stateless persons and refugees resident in the territory of a Member State who are or have been subject to the social security legislation of one or more Member States, as well as to the members of their families and to their survivors.

(8) The general principle of equal treatment is of particular importance for workers who do not reside in the Member State of their employment, including frontier workers.

(9) The Court of Justice has on several occasions given an opinion on the possibility of equal treatment of benefits, income and facts; this principle should be adopted explicitly and developed, while observing the substance and spirit of legal rulings.

(10) However, the principle of treating certain facts or events occurring in the territory of another Member State as if they had taken place in the territory of the Member State whose legislation is applicable should not interfere with the principle of aggregating periods of insurance, employment, self-employment or residence completed under the legislation of another Member State with those completed under the legislation of the competent Member State. Periods completed under the legislation of another Member State should therefore be taken into account solely by applying the principle of aggregation of periods.

(11) The assimilation of facts or events occurring in a Member State can in no way render another Member State competent or its legislation applicable.

(12) In the light of proportionality, care should be taken to ensure that the principle of assimilation of facts or events does not lead to objectively unjustified results or to the overlapping of benefits of the same kind for the same period.

(13) The coordination rules must guarantee that persons moving within the Community and their dependants and survivors retain the rights and the advantages acquired and in the course of being acquired.

(14) These objectives must be attained in particular by aggregating all the periods taken into account under the various national legislation for the purpose of acquiring and retaining the right to benefits and of calculating the amount of benefits, and by providing benefits for the various categories of persons covered by this Regulation.

(15) It is necessary to subject persons moving within the Community to the social security scheme of only one single Member State in order to avoid overlapping of the applicable provisions of national legislation and the complications which could result therefrom.

(16) Within the Community there is in principle no justification for making social security rights dependent on the place of residence of the person concerned; nevertheless, in specific cases, in particular as regards special benefits linked to the economic and social context of the person involved, the place of residence could be taken into account.

(17) With a view to guaranteeing the equality of treatment of all persons occupied in the territory of a Member State as effectively as possible, it is appropriate to determine as the legislation applicable, as a general rule, that of the Member State in which the person concerned pursues his activity as an employed or self-employed person.

[1 (17a) Once the legislation of a Member State becomes applicable to a person under Title II of this Regulation, the conditions for affiliation and entitlement to benefits should be defined by the legislation of the competent Member State while respecting Community law.]

(18) In specific situations which justify other criteria of applicability, it is necessary to derogate from that general rule.

[1 (18a) The principle of single applicable legislation is of great importance and should be enhanced. This should not mean, however, that the grant of a benefit alone, in accordance with this Regulation and comprising the payment of insurance contributions or insurance coverage for the beneficiary, renders the legislation of the Member State, whose institution has granted that benefit, the applicable legislation for that person.]

[2 (18b) In Annex III to Council Regulation (EEC) No 3922/91 of 16 December 1991 on the harmonization of technical requirements and administrative procedures in the field of civil aviation [[1991] OJ L373/4], the concept of "home base" for flight crew and cabin crew members is defined as the location nominated by the operator to the crew member from where the crew member normally starts and ends a duty period, or a series of duty periods, and where, under normal conditions, the operator is not responsible for the accommodation of the crew member concerned. In order to facilitate the application of Title II of this Regulation for flight crew and cabin crew members, it is justified to use the concept of "home base" as the criterion for determining the applicable legislation for flight crew and cabin crew members. However, the applicable legislation for flight crew and cabin crew members should remain stable and the home base principle should not result in frequent changes of applicable legislation due to the industry's work patterns or seasonal demands.]

(19) In some cases, maternity and equivalent paternity benefits may be enjoyed by the mother or the father and since, for the latter, these benefits are different from parental benefits and can be assimilated to maternity benefits strictu sensu in that they are provided during the first months of a new-born child's life, it is appropriate that maternity and equivalent paternity benefits be regulated jointly.

(20) In the field of sickness, maternity and equivalent paternity benefits, insured persons, as well as the members of their families, living or staying in a Member State other than the competent Member State, should be afforded protection.

(21) Provisions on sickness, maternity and equivalent paternity benefits were drawn up in the light of Court of Justice case-law. Provisions on prior authorisation have been improved, taking into account the relevant decisions of the Court of Justice.

(22) The specific position of pension claimants and pensioners and the members of their families makes it necessary to have provisions governing sickness insurance adapted to this situation.

(23) In view of the differences between the various national systems, it is appropriate that Member States make provision, where possible, for medical treatment for family members of frontier workers in the Member State where the latter pursue their activity.

(24) It is necessary to establish specific provisions regulating the non-overlapping of sickness benefits in kind and sickness benefits in cash which are of the same nature as those which were the subject of the judgments of the Court of Justice in Case C-215/99 *Jauch* and C-160/96 *Molenaar*, provided that those benefits cover the same risk.

(25) In respect of benefits for accidents at work and occupational diseases, rules should be laid down, for the purpose of affording protection, covering the situation of persons residing or staying in a Member State other than the competent Member State.

(26) For invalidity benefits, a system of coordination should be drawn up which respects the specific characteristics of national legislation, in particular as regards recognition of invalidity and aggravation thereof.

(27) It is necessary to devise a system for the award of old-age benefits and survivors' benefits where the person concerned has been subject to the legislation of one or more Member States.

(28) There is a need to determine the amount of a pension calculated in accordance with the method used for aggregation and pro-rata calculation and guaranteed by Community law where the application of national legislation, including rules concerning reduction, suspension or withdrawal, is less favourable than the aforementioned method.

(29) To protect migrant workers and their survivors against excessively stringent application of the national rules concerning reduction, suspension or withdrawal, it is necessary to include provisions strictly governing the application of such rules.

(30) As has constantly been reaffirmed by the Court of Justice, the Council is not deemed competent to enact rules imposing a restriction on the overlapping of two or more pensions acquired in different Member States by a reduction of the amount of a pension acquired solely under national legislation.

(31) According to the Court of Justice, it is for the national legislature to enact such rules, bearing in mind that it is for the Community legislature to fix the limits within which the national provisions concerning reduction, suspension or withdrawal are to be applied.

(32) In order to foster mobility of workers, it is particularly appropriate to facilitate the search for employment in the various Member States; it is therefore necessary to ensure closer and more effective coordination between the unemployment insurance schemes and the employment services of all the Member States.

(33) It is necessary to include statutory pre-retirement schemes within the scope of this Regulation, thus guaranteeing both equal treatment and the possibility of exporting pre-retirement benefits as well as the award of family and health-care benefits to the person concerned, in accordance with the provisions of this Regulation; however, the rule on the aggregation of periods should not be included, as only a very limited number of Member States have statutory pre-retirement schemes.

(34) Since family benefits have a very broad scope, affording protection in situations which could be described as classic as well as in others which are specific in nature, with the latter type of benefit having been the subject of the judgments of the Court of Justice in Joined Cases C-245/94 and C-312/94 *Hoever* and *Zachow* and in Case C-275/96 *Kuusijärvi*, it is necessary to regulate all such benefits.

(35) In order to avoid unwarranted overlapping of benefits, there is a need to lay down rules of priority in the case of overlapping of rights to family benefits under the legislation of the competent Member State and under the legislation of the Member State of residence of the members of the family.

(36) Advances of maintenance allowances are recoverable advances intended to compensate for a parent's failure to fulfil his legal obligation of maintenance to his own child, which is an obligation derived from family law. Therefore, these advances should not be considered as a direct benefit from collective support in favour of families. Given these particularities, the coordinating rules should not be applied to such maintenance allowances.

(37) As the Court of Justice has repeatedly stated, provisions which derogate from the principle of the exportability of social security benefits must be interpreted strictly. This means that they can apply only to benefits which satisfy the specified conditions. It follows that Chapter 9 of Title III of this Regulation can apply only to benefits which are both special and non-contributory and listed in Annex X to this Regulation.

(38) It is necessary to establish an Administrative Commission consisting of a government representative from each Member State, charged in particular with dealing with all administrative questions or questions of interpretation arising from the provisions of this Regulation, and with promoting further cooperation between the Member States.

(39) The development and use of data-processing services for the exchange of information has been found to require the creation of a Technical Commission, under the aegis of the Administrative Commission, with specific responsibilities in the field of data-processing.

(40) The use of data-processing services for exchanging data between institutions requires provisions guaranteeing that the documents exchanged or issued by electronic means are accepted as equivalent to paper documents. Such exchanges are to be carried out in accordance with the Community provisions on the protection of natural persons with regard to the processing and free movement of personal data.

(41) It is necessary to lay down special provisions which correspond to the special characteristics of national legislation in order to facilitate the application of the rules of coordination.

(42) In line with the principle of proportionality, in accordance with the premise for the extension of this Regulation to all European Union citizens and in order to find a solution that takes account of any constraints which may be connected with the special characteristics of systems based on residence, a special derogation by means

of an Annex XI – "DENMARK" entry, limited to social pension entitlement exclusively in respect of the new category of non-active persons, to whom this Regulation has been extended, was deemed appropriate due to the specific features of the Danish system and in the light of the fact that those pensions are exportable after a ten-year period of residence under the Danish legislation in force (Pension Act).

(43) In line with the principle of equality of treatment, a special derogation by means of an Annex XI – "FINLAND" entry, limited to residence-based national pensions, is deemed appropriate due to the specific characteristics of Finnish social security legislation, the objective of which is to ensure that the amount of the national pension cannot be less than the amount of the national pension calculated as if all insurance periods completed in any Member State were completed in Finland.

(44) It is necessary to introduce a new Regulation to repeal Regulation (EEC) No 1408/71. However, it is necessary that Regulation (EEC) No 1408/71 remain in force and continue to have legal effect for the purposes of certain Community acts and agreements to which the Community is a party, in order to secure legal certainty.

(45) Since the objective of the proposed action, namely the coordination measures to guarantee that the right to free movement of persons can be exercised effectively, cannot be sufficiently achieved by the Member States and can therefore, by reason of the scale and effects of that action, be better achieved at Community level, the Community may adopt measures in accordance with the principle of subsidiarity as set out in Article 5 of the Treaty. In accordance with the principle of proportionality as set out in that article, this Regulation does not go beyond what is necessary, in order to achieve that objective.

AMENDMENTS

1. Regulation 988/2009 art.1 (May 1, 2010).
2. Regulation 465/2012 [2012] OJ L149/4 art.1 (June 28, 2012).

GENERAL NOTE

3.301 The Preamble to regulations can be an important aid to its interpretation. A number of important points from the Preamble can be identified. The regulation is concerned only with the co-ordination of different social security systems. This regulation is a natural successor to Regulation 1408/71 and retains the principles established in that regulation, but updates them in the light of the case-law of the Luxembourg Court, and provides for the co-ordination of certain additional benefits. At a number of points, the Preamble stresses the application of the principle of proportionality in this field; those called upon to apply and interpret the regulation should take care to recall this.

Regulation 883/2004 is based upon six key principles:

(1) In respect of any claim to benefit, the beneficiary is subject to the social security system of one country alone. This will generally, but by no means always, be the Member State where the person is working at the material time.

(2) All those covered by the co-ordinating rules are subject to the same rights and obligations as nationals of the competent Member State. This is the principle of equal treatment.

(3) Periods of insurance, employment, self-employment and residence accrued in different Member States may be added together where this is necessary to meet the conditions of entitlement to a benefit. This is known as the principle of aggregation.

(4) Subject to considerable limitations which should be strictly construed, benefits to which title has been acquired in one Member State may be taken to another Member State. This is the principle of the exportability of benefits.

(5) The legal effects of entitlement in one Member State, and the facts upon which that entitlement is based must be recognised in other Member States. This is the principle of the assimilation of legal effects and facts (now spelled out in art.5.)

(6) Member States undertake to co-operate in the administration of the co-ordinating rules in the regulation. This can be regarded as the duty of co-operation.

Any decisions made under the regulation should have due regard to the principle of proportionality.

Co-ordination not harmonisation

The regulation, like its predecessors, is concerned with the co-ordination of social security schemes and not with the harmonization of the social security laws of the Member States. The Luxembourg Court has consistently stressed this distinction in its judgments on provisions of Regulation 1408/71. So, for example, in *Hervein and Lorthiois* (C-393 and C-394/99) [2002] E.C.R. I-2829, the Court said: 3.302

"... the system put in place by Regulation No 1408/71 is merely a system of coordination. . . .
. . . it . . . does not follow from [arts 39 and 43 of the Treaty] that, in the absence of harmonisation of the social security legislation, neutrality as regard the complexity, for the persons concerned, of the administration of their social security cover will be guaranteed in all circumstances" (paras 52 and 58).

In *Jörn Petersen* (C-228/07) [2008] E.C.R.1–6989 the Luxembourg Court said:

"... Regulation 1408/71 does not set up a common scheme of social security, but allows different social security schemes to exist and its sole objective is to ensure the coordination of those schemes (Case 21/87 *Borowitz* [1988] ECR 3715, paragraph 23, and Case C-331/06 *Chuck* [2008] ECR I-0000, paragraph 27)". (See [41].)

The purpose of the regulation is to build bridges in order to connect different social security schemes so that those moving within the Union are not disadvantaged as a result of exercising their rights of free movement. However, notwithstanding this important distinction between co-ordination and harmonisation, there are certainly adaptive pressures on Member States as a result of the requirements of co-ordination of benefit schemes which tend to pull Member State policy closer together. So there are limits to the freedom of action of the Member States in relation to their national social security rules. In *Kalsbeek* (100/63) [1964] E.C.R. 565, the Luxembourg Court said:

"Article 51 [now art.48 TFEU] . . . cannot allow [national] regulations to fall short of the objectives which it sets, which are intended to favour freedom of movement for worker and which would be incompatible with any reduction in their rights". (At 574.)

That requirement needs to be read in the context of a statement in a later judgment in *Salgado Alonso* (C-306/03) [2005] E.C.R. I-705: 3.303

"It should be recalled that the Court has consistently held that Member States remain competent to define the conditions for granting a social security benefit, even if they make them more strict, provided that the conditions adopted do not give rise to overt or disguised discrimination between Community workers . . ." (At [27].)

The requirement that workers should not lose advantages in the field of social security has come to be known as "the Petroni principle"; in *Petroni* (24/75) [1975] E.C.R. 1149, the Luxembourg Court said:

"The aim of Articles 48 to 51 [now art.45 to 48 TFEU] would not be attained if, as a consequence of the exercise of their right to freedom of movement, workers were to lose advantages in the field of social security guaranteed them in any event by the laws of a single Member State". (At [13].)

Have Adopted this Regulation:

TITLE I

GENERAL PROVISIONS

Article 1

Definitions

3.304 For the purposes of this Regulation:

(a) "activity as an employed person" means any activity or equivalent situation treated as such for the purposes of the social security legislation of the Member State in which such activity or equivalent situation exists;
(b) "activity as a self-employed person" means any activity or equivalent situation treated as such for the purposes of the social security legislation of the Member State in which such activity or equivalent situation exists;
(c) "insured person", in relation to the social security branches covered by Title III, Chapters 1 and 3, means any person satisfying the conditions required under the legislation of the Member State competent under Title II to have the right to benefits, taking into account the provisions of this Regulation;
(d) "civil servant" means a person considered to be such or treated as such by the Member State to which the administration employing him is subject;
(e) "special scheme for civil servants" means any social security scheme which is different from the general social security scheme applicable to employed persons in the Member State concerned and to which all, or certain categories of, civil servants are directly subject;
(f) "frontier worker" means any person pursuing an activity as an employed or self-employed person in a Member State and who resides in another Member State to which he returns as a rule daily or at least once a week;
(g) "refugee" shall have the meaning assigned to it in Article 1 of the Convention relating to the Status of Refugees, signed in Geneva on 28 July 1951;

(h) "stateless person" shall have the meaning assigned to it in Article 1 of the Convention relating to the Status of Stateless Persons, signed in New York on 28 September 1954;

(i) "member of the family" means

(1) (i) any person defined or recognised as a member of the family or designated as a member of the household by the legislation under which benefits are provided;

(ii) with regard to benefits in kind pursuant to Title III, Chapter 1 on sickness, maternity and equivalent paternity benefits, any person defined or recognised as a member of the family or designated as a member of the household by the legislation of the Member State in which he resides;

(2) If the legislation of a Member State which is applicable under subparagraph (1) does not make a distinction between the members of the family and other persons to whom it is applicable, the spouse, minor children, and dependent children who have reached the age of majority shall be considered members of the family;

(3) If, under the legislation which is applicable under subparagraphs (1) and (2), a person is considered a member of the family or member of the household only if he lives in the same household as the insured person or pensioner, this condition shall be considered satisfied if the person in question is mainly dependent on the insured person or pensioner;

(j) "residence" means the place where a person habitually resides;

(k) "stay" means temporary residence;

(l) "legislation" means, in respect of each Member State, laws, regulations and other statutory provisions and all other implementing measures relating to the social security branches covered by Article 3(1);

This term excludes contractual provisions other than those which serve to implement an insurance obligation arising from the laws and regulations referred to in the preceding subparagraph or which have been the subject of a decision by the public authorities which makes them obligatory or extends their scope, provided that the Member State concerned makes a declaration to that effect, notified to the President of the European Parliament and the President of the Council of the European Union. Such declaration shall be published in the Official Journal of the European Union;

(m) "competent authority" means, in respect of each Member State, the Minister, Ministers or other equivalent authority responsible for social security schemes throughout or in any part of the Member State in question;

(n) "Administrative Commission" means the commission referred to in Article 71;

(o) "Implementing Regulation" means the Regulation referred to in Article 89;

(p) "institution" means, in respect of each Member State, the body or authority responsible for applying all or part of the legislation;

(q) "competent institution" means:

(i) the institution with which the person concerned is insured at the time of the application for benefit; or

(ii) the institution from which the person concerned is or would be entitled to benefits if he or a member or members of his family resided in the Member State in which the institution is situated; or

(iii) the institution designated by the competent authority of the Member State concerned; or

(iv) in the case of a scheme relating to an employer's obligations in respect of the benefits set out in Article 3(1), either the employer or the insurer involved or, in default thereof, the body or authority designated by the competent authority of the Member State concerned;

(r) "institution of the place of residence" and "institution of the place of stay" mean respectively the institution which is competent to provide benefits in the place where the person concerned resides and the institution which is competent to provide benefits in the place where the person concerned is staying, in accordance with the legislation administered by that institution or, where no such institution exists, the institution designated by the competent authority of the Member State concerned;

(s) "competent Member State" means the Member State in which the competent institution is situated;

(t) "period of insurance" means periods of contribution, employment or self-employment as defined or recognised as periods of insurance by the legislation under which they were completed or considered as completed, and all periods treated as such, where they are regarded by the said legislation as equivalent to periods of insurance;

(u) "period of employment" or "period of self-employment" mean periods so defined or recognised by the legislation under which they were completed, and all periods treated as such, where they are regarded by the said legislation as equivalent to periods of employment or to periods of self-employment;

(v) "period of residence" means periods so defined or recognised by the legislation under which they were completed or considered as completed;

[[1] (va) "Benefits in kind" means:

(i) for the purposes of Title III, Chapter 1 (sickness, maternity and equivalent paternity benefits), benefits in kind provided for under the legislation of a Member State which are intended to supply, make available, pay directly or reimburse the cost of medical care and products and services ancillary to that care. This includes long-term care benefits in kind.;

(ii) for the purposes of Title III, Chapter 2 (accidents at work and occupational diseases), all benefits in kind relating to accidents at work and occupational diseases as defined in point (i) above and provided for under the Member States' accidents at work and occupational diseases schemes.]

(w) "pension" covers not only pensions but also lump-sum benefits which can be substituted for them and payments in the form of reimbursement of contributions and, subject to the provisions of Title III, revaluation increases or supplementary allowances;

(x) "pre-retirement benefit" means: all cash benefits, other than an unemployment benefit or an early old-age benefit, provided from a specified age to workers who have reduced, ceased or suspended their remunerative activities until the age at which they qualify for an old-age pension or an early retirement pension, the receipt of which is not conditional upon the person concerned being available to the employment services of the competent State; "early old-age benefit" means a benefit provided before the normal pension entitlement age is reached and which either continues to be provided once the said age is reached or is replaced by another old-age benefit;

(y) "death grant" means any one-off payment in the event of death excluding the lump-sum benefits referred to in subparagraph (w);

(z) "family benefit" means all benefits in kind or in cash intended to meet family expenses, excluding advances of maintenance payments and special childbirth and adoption allowances mentioned in Annex I.

Corresponding Provision of Regulation 1408/71

Article 1.

Amendment

1. Regulation 988/2009 art.1 (May 1, 2010).

General Note

Article 1 contains crucial definitions in the application of the co-ordinating rules it contains. These are autonomous concepts under EU law and are to be applied from a Union perspective. 3.305

The concept of residence

Two particularly important definitions are those of "residence" and "stay". 3.306

Residence is defined as habitual residence which is similar to but not necessarily identical to the concept adopted in United Kingdom regulations as a condition of entitlement to benefit. Residence is contrasted with stay which is temporary residence in a Member State; residence here probably means presence since holidays abroad constitute a stay in another Member State.

For a discussion of the concept of "habitual residence" under European Union law, see *Marinos v Marinos* [2007] EWHC 2047 (Fam); [2007] 2 F.L.R. 1018.

There is guidance in the implementing regulation on the issue of residence. Residence under the regulations refers to "habitual residence", which is an EU concept. Residence plays an important part at a number of points in the operation of the co-ordinating regulation. Among them, of course, is the limitation of the payment of special non-contributory benefits in the Member State of residence. However, such is the nature of "habitual residence" that there is a risk that a person would be found not to have a residence in any Member State. For this reason, art.11 of the implementing regulation provides:

"Elements for determining residence

1. Where there is a difference of views between the institutions of two or more Member States about the determination of the residence of a person to whom the basic Regulation applies, these institutions shall establish by common agree-

ment the centre of interests of the person concerned, based on an overall assessment of all available information relating to relevant facts, which may include, as appropriate:

(a) the duration and continuity of presence on the territory of the Member States concerned;

(b) the person's situation, including:

(i) the nature and the specific characteristics of any activity pursued, in particular the place where such activity is habitually pursued, the stability of the activity, and the duration of any work contract;

(ii) his family status and family ties;

(iii) the exercise of any non-remunerated activity;

(iv) in the case of students, the source of their income;

(v) his housing situation, in particular how permanent it is;

(vi) the Member State in which the person is deemed to reside for taxation purposes.

2. Where the consideration of the various criteria based on relevant facts as set out in paragraph 1 does not lead to agreement between the institutions concerned, the person's intention, as it appears from such facts and circumstances, especially the reasons that led the person to move, shall be considered to be decisive for establishing that person's actual place of residence."

This provision should ensure that a situation does not arise in which a person is not found to be resident in any Member State. However, it remains for national law to determine whether a person meet the conditions for affiliation to its social security system, for example, through thresholds for making contributions: see definition of "insured person" at art.1(c) above.

Article 1(i): definition of "member of the family"

3.307 *PB v SSWP (DLA)* [2016] UKUT 280 (AAC) concerned the past presence test in relation to a claim for a disability living allowance. The factual position was that the claimant was a Czech national who had come to the United Kingdom with his mother in order to live with his sister. The First-tier Tribunal had disallowed the appeal on the grounds that the claimant's sister was not a "member of the family" as defined in art.1(i). However, the claimant's position was governed by national law (regs.2 and 2A of the DLA Regs) and not Regulation 883/2004. Under the national regulations, a genuine and sufficient link with the United Kingdom could be established through the claimant's connection with the sister who had lived and worked in the United Kingdom for some time, and was providing regular care for the claimant.

Article 1(z): definition of "family benefit"

3.308 In *Caisse nationale des prestations familiales v Hiddal and Bernand* (C-216/12 and C-217/12), Judgment of September 19, 2013, the Court has ruled that a parental leave allowance constitutes a family benefit under Regulation 1408/71. Since the definition of "family benefit" is, if anything, wider under Reg.883/2004, such an allowance almost certainly constitutes a family benefit under Reg.883/2004. There is certainly nothing in the Court's reasoning to suggest otherwise.

In *Caisse nationale des prestations familiales v Lachleb* (C-177/12), Judgment of October 24, 2012, the Court ruled that a "child bonus" (which appears to be a form of tax credit) constituted a family benefit under Reg.1408/71. It would also almost certainly constitute a family benefit under Reg.883/2004.

Article 2

Persons covered

1. This Regulation shall apply to nationals of a Member State, stateless persons and refugees residing in a Member State who are or have been subject to the legislation of one or more Member States, as well as to the members of their families and to their survivors. 3.309

2. It shall also apply to the survivors of persons who have been subject to the legislation of one or more Member States, irrespective of the nationality of such persons, where their survivors are nationals of a Member State or stateless persons or refugees residing in one of the Member States.

CORRESPONDING PROVISION OF REGULATION 1408/71

Article 2.

GENERAL NOTE

Regulation 883/2004 contains a much simplified definition of those within its personal scope. However, the simplicity of art.2 is somewhat compromised by additional conditions which apply in relation to particular benefits of the regulation. The following terms are also used in the regulation: "activity as an employed person"; "activity as a self-employed person"; "insured person"; "civil servant"; "frontier worker"; "refugee"; "stateless person"; and "member of the family". Furthermore arts 23–27 refer in a heading to "pensioners", and the text of the articles refers to persons "who receive a pension or pensions under the legislation" of the Member States. So it will often be necessary to show that the additional requirements are met before the benefit of certain provisions of the regulation accrue. 3.310

In order to be a beneficiary of the rules in the regulation, a person must be a citizen of the Union, that is a national of one of the Member States.

Borger (C–516/09) Judgment of March 10, 2011 concerns the interpretation of the term "employed person" under art.1(a) of Regulation 1408/71. As noted above the status of employed person remains relevant under the new regulation.

Ms Borger, an Austrian national living in Austria, gave birth to a son in January 2006. She took unpaid leave from her employer which ultimately lasted until July 2008. In March 2007 she moved to Switzerland where her husband had been working since 2006. Her Austrian childcare allowance was ended on the grounds that Ms Borger was not working, and that the responsibility for paying family benefits rested with the Swiss authorities since the father was working there and all members of the family were living there. Ms Borger argued that the Austrian authorities should pay the benefit until July 2008 since she was in "a *de facto* employment relationship." She further adds that she remained affiliated with the Austrian retirement insurance scheme. The national court's question essentially asked whether Ms Borger remained an employed person during the extension period of her unpaid leave of absence from January to July 2008. The Court points out that in determining whether a person came within the personal scope of Regulation 1408/71, the existence of an employment relationship is irrelevant; the determining factor is whether the person is insured for one or more of the risks covered by the regulation. The Court advised the national court that Ms Borger would remain an employed person during the six-month period in question if she is covered even if only in respect of a single risk, on a compulsory or optional basis under the Austrian social security scheme. 3.311

See also the judgment of the Grand Chamber in *Dodl and Oberhollenzer* (C–543/03) [2005] E.C.R. I-5065, at [30]–[31].

In *ONAFTS v Radia Hadj Ahmed* (C-45/12) Judgment of June 13, 2013, the Court of Justice ruled that Regulation 1408/71:

"must be interpreted as meaning that a third-country national or her daughter, who is also a third-country national, while their situation is the following:

- that third-country national obtained, less than five years earlier, a permit to reside in a Member State in order to join, not in the context of marriage or registered partnership, a national of another Member State, by whom she has a child who has the nationality of the latter Member State;
- only that national of another Member State has the status of worker;
- in the meantime the cohabitation of the third-country national and the national of another Member State has come to an end; and
- both children are members of their mother's household,

do not come within the scope *ratione personae* of that regulation, unless that third-country national or her daughter can be regarded, within the meaning of the national legislation and for its application, as 'members of the family' of the national of another Member State or, where that is not the case, unless they can be regarded as being 'mainly dependent' on him."

The judgment applies equally to similar situations arising under Regulation 883/2004.

Article 3

Matters covered

3.312 1. This Regulation shall apply to all legislation concerning the following branches of social security:

(a) sickness benefits;
(b) maternity and equivalent paternity benefits;
(c) invalidity benefits;
(d) old-age benefits;
(e) survivors' benefits;
(f) benefits in respect of accidents at work and occupational diseases;
(g) death grants;
(h) unemployment benefits;
(i) pre-retirement benefits;
(j) family benefits.

2. Unless otherwise provided for in Annex XI, this Regulation shall apply to general and special social security schemes, whether contributory or non-contributory, and to schemes relating to the obligations of an employer or shipowner.

3. This Regulation shall also apply to the special non-contributory cash benefits covered by Article 70.

4. The provisions of Title III of this Regulation shall not, however, affect the legislative provisions of any Member State concerning a ship-owner's obligations.

[[1] 5. This Regulation shall not apply to:

(a) social and medical assistance or
(b) benefits in relation to which a Member State assumes the liability for damages to persons and provides for compensation, such as those

for victims of war and military action or their consequences; victims of crime, assassination or terrorist acts; victims of damage occasioned by agents of the Member State in the course of their duties; or victims who have suffered a disadvantage for political or religious reasons or for reasons of descent.]

CORRESPONDING PROVISION OF REGULATION 1408/71

Article 4.

AMENDMENT

1. Regulation 988/2009 art.1 (May 1, 2010).

GENERAL NOTE

The two new branches of social security added by Reg.883/2004 are paternity benefits which may be regarded as equivalent to maternity benefits, and pre-retirement benefits. 3.313

The regulation applies to all legislation governing benefits protecting against the ten named risks. The eight earlier social risks are those identified in ILO Convention 102. It does not matter whether the specified benefits are provided under contributory or non-contributory schemes. Special non-contributory benefits are also covered where they provide supplementary, substitute or ancillary cover against the social risk set out in the article, or are specific protection for disabled people. The provision contains an exhaustive list of the branches of social security governed by the regulation. It applies to all legislation concerning the specified branch of social security; legislation is defined in very broad terms in art.1(l). The Luxembourg Court has described the corresponding definition in Reg.1408/71 as "remarkable for its breadth": *Bozzone* (87/76) [1977] E.C.R. 687.

Whether a particular benefit falls within the scope of these 10 branches of social security as well as whether any of the exceptions applies is determined in accordance with European Union law, and not simply the classification of a benefit under the national scheme. The Luxembourg Court has consistently said that whether a benefit is within the material scope of Regulation 1408/71 "rests entirely on the factors relating to each benefit, in particular its purpose and the conditions for its grant": *Gillard* (9/78) [1978] E.C.R. 1661, at [12]. The fact that the benefit has a dual purpose does not exclude it from the material scope of the regulation. So it will be substance and not form which determines whether a benefit falls within the material scope of the regulation.

Commission v Slovak Republic (C-433/13) concerned a complaint by the Commission that the Slovak Republic had breached the requirements of arts 7 and 21 of Regulation 883/2004 in refusing the export of care allowance and allied benefits. However, the Court concluded that, because the Member State retained a discretion over the award of the benefit even where the conditions of entitlement were met, the benefit did "not constitute social security benefits within the meaning of Regulation No 883/2004." (para.83).

In *Molenaar* (C-160/96) [1998] E.C.R. I-843, the Luxembourg Court ruled that care insurance was a benefit intended to supplement sickness insurance and so constituted a sickness benefit for the purpose of Reg.1408/71. This was taken further in *Gaumain-Cerri* and *Barth* (C-502/01 and C-31/02) [2004] E.C.R. I-6483, where the Court ruled that the payment of old-age insurance in respect of carers of a person in receipt of care insurance also constituted a sickness benefit. 3.314

Jörn Petersen (C-228/07) [2008] E.C.R. I-6989, illustrates the need for careful consideration of the classification of benefits. Petersen is a German national who was working in Austria. He claimed an incapacity pension, which was refused. While an appeal against this decision was pending, the Austrian authorities granted Petersen an advance of pension payments under provisions of Austrian law headed "advance pension payments." Petersen was considering returning to Germany and asked for the advance unemployment benefit to be continued after his change of residence. That application was refused. The first question before the Court was whether the benefit was an unemployment benefit or an invalidity benefit. Though the benefit had certain characteristics of both, the Court concluded that the benefit was an unemployment benefit within art.4(1)(g) of Reg.1408/71.

The second question concerned the exportability of the benefit, since Austrian law provided that the benefit was payable subject to a condition of residence in the national territory. The Court noted that the provisions of arts 69 and 71 of reg.1408/71 were not applicable to the present case. However, in exercising their discretion to regulate the scheme, the Austrian authorities were required to exercise their choices having appropriate and proportionate regard to arts 39–42 EC (now arts 45–48 TFEU). The Court concluded that the Austrian Government had not put forward any objective justification for the condition that recipients of the benefit to which Petersen was entitled must be residence on the national territory.

3.315 Note that the United Kingdom, after much argument, eventually conceded that winter fuel payments were an old-age benefit within the material scope of Regulation 1408/71. For background and discussion of the implications, see *Secretary of State for Work and Pensions v Walker-Fox* [2005] EWCA Civ 1441, reported as *R(IS) 3/06*, and *R(IS) 8/06*. *DM v SSWP (IS)* [2014] UKUT 259 (AAC) decides that the principles set out in *Walker-Fox* apply equally to late claims for winter fuel payments following the Secretary of State's acceptance that the *Lucy Stewart* case (C-503/09) [2011] E.C.R. I-6497, [2012] AACR 8, required a consideration in relation to a claim from an EEA national not resident in the United Kingdom of whether the claimant had a genuine and sufficient connection with the United Kingdom.

It is possible that issues will arise as to whether child trust contributions under the Child Trust Funds Act 2004 constitute family benefits within Regulation 1408/71,or Regulation 883/2004 since s.2 of the Act excludes payment of the contribution where child benefit is in payment under the coordination rules, but the child is not resident in the United Kingdom.

The distinction between social security and social assistance

3.316 Social assistance is excluded from the scope of the regulation together with medical assistance, and schemes for war victims. The distinction between social insurance and social assistance used to be more clear cut than it is today. Social insurance as originally conceived related to insurance-based schemes in respect of certain risks against which workers or their employers would insure; it also included provision for what might be regarded as the certainties of life: birth, old age and death. By contrast social assistance is support provided by the State at its discretion on the basis of need. There is also a third group of benefits which are provided on the basis of need, but are a matter of legal entitlement and not discretion. Considerable debate still surrounds the true nature of certain income-based benefits which are means tested but are paid as a matter of legal right to those who meet closely specified conditions of entitlement and at a rate also set out in regulations.

European Union secondary legislation refers to social assistance but does not define it. Nor has the Luxembourg Court provided a definitive definition of social assistance and its relationship with social security. The most comprehensive summary of a line of case-law can be found in the Opinion of Advocate General Kokott in *Skalka* (C-160/02) [2004] E.C.R. I-1771.

The Luxembourg Court has said in a number of cases that a benefit is a social security benefit:

> "in so far as it is granted, without any individual and discretionary assessment of personal needs, to recipients on the basis of a legally defined position and relates to one of the risks expressly listed in Article 4(1) of Regulation No. 1408/71" (*Jauch* (C-215/99) [2001] E.C.R. I-1901, at [25].)

3.317 But the distinction between social security and social assistance is not always easy to draw. *Hughes* (C-78/91) [1992] E.C.R. I-4839 concerned a claim to family credit. The United Kingdom argued that it was social assistance. The Luxembourg Court reiterated its earlier case-law and in doing so addressed a specific objection of the United Kingdom government to the effect that the claimant was not in a legally defined position because the benefit was subject to a means test. The court said that the need to satisfy an individual assessment of needs did not preclude the benefit from being social security, since the criteria applied were objective, legally defined criteria which, if met, conferred an entitlement to the benefit (at [17]). The court went on to find that there was a sufficient link with the family for the benefit to constitute a family benefit falling within art.4(1)(h) of Regulation 1408/71. Advocate General Kokott in *Skalka* questions whether the analysis in *Hughes* should be generalised:

> "53. ... The definition of a social security benefit, as it is construed in that judgment, might, conversely, support the argument that a benefit constitutes social assistance only if it is granted on the basis of an assessment of the needs of the person concerned, which falls within the discretion of the competent authority, rather than on the basis of objective, legally defined criteria.
>
> 54. However, in many national legal orders, social assistance is granted on the basis of objective, legally defined criteria for assessing personal need simply so as to observe the principle of equal treatment. Furthermore, guaranteeing the minimum level of subsistence is no longer considered to be a charitable measure on the part of the State. On the contrary, in many modern welfare States, individuals have such a right as an expression of their human dignity.
>
> 55. It follows that a benefit can display social assistance features, which are the criteria necessary for its classification as a special benefit, even when it is granted according to personal need which can be determined on the basis of objective, legally defined criteria."

In *Perry v Chief Adjudication Officer* [1999] 2 C.M.L.R. 439, reported as *R(IS)4/99*, the Court of Appeal held that income support was not a special non contributory benefit within the meaning of Regulation 1408/71, but this decision must now be read in the light of *Swaddling v Adjudication Officer* (C-90/97) [1999] E.C.R. I-1075, reported as *R(IS)6/99*, in which the Luxembourg Court ruled that income support is a special non-contributory benefit within the meaning of reg.1408/71.

In *CIB/4243/1999*, the Commissioner held that short-term incapacity benefit whether paid at the lower or the higher rate is a sickness benefit for the purposes of Regulation 1408/71, while long-term incapacity benefit was an invalidity benefit for the purposes of the regulation (at para.17).

Certain United Kingdom benefits take the form of a contribution-based benefit **3.318**
and an income-related benefit within the same overall benefit: jobseeker's allowance, and employment and support allowance. The contribution-based component will fall within the scope of the regulation as, respectively, an unemployment benefit, and a sickness or invalidity benefit. The willingness of the Luxembourg Court to unravel national benefit structures became abundantly clear in *Commission v European Parliament and Council* (C-299/05) [2007] E.C.R. I-8695, in which the Court split the care component and the mobility component of disability living allowance. Though not definitively established, it was accepted that the mobility component was a special non-contributory benefit, but the Court ruled that the care component is a form of sickness benefit, whose exportability could not be excluded.

The conclusion that the mobility component is a special non-contributory benefit has been confirmed in *Bartlett, Ramos and Taylor v SSWP* (C-537/09) [2011] E.C.R. I-03417 [2012] AACR 34, although the conclusion in the *Bartlett* case might usefully be compared with the Luxembourg Court's judgment in *Commission v*

Germany (C-206/10) Judgment of May 5, 2011, where the court ruled that a similar sort of benefit in Germany was a sickness benefit, entitlement to which could not be conditioned on residence or habitual residence in Germany.

For the outcome of the *Bartlett, Ramos and Taylor* judgment on its return to the Upper Tribunal, see the commentary to art.70 below.

Short-term incapacity benefit in youth under s.30A of the Contribution and Benefits Act

3.319 *Lucy Stewart* (C–503/09) [2011] E.C.R. I-06497, [2012] AACR 8, concerns the impact of certain provisions of Regulation 1408/71 on entitlement to short-term incapacity benefit in youth, which was introduced in April 2001 as a non-contributory benefit subject to residence and presence conditions.

Lucy Stewart has Down's Syndrome. She is a British national who was born in November 1989 and has always lived with her parents who are both now retired. Lucy has been in receipt of disability living allowance since its inception in April 1992. The family moved to Spain in August 2000. With effect from Lucy's sixteenth birthday, her mother made a claim for short-term incapacity benefit in youth. The conditions of entitlement for the benefit include a requirement set out in the Social Security (Incapacity Benefit) Regulations 1994 that the claimant be "ordinarily resident in Great Britain"; "present in Great Britain"; and "present in Great Britain for a period of, or for periods amounting in aggregate to, not less than 26 weeks in the 52 weeks" prior to the date of claim. Lucy Stewart met none of these residence and presence conditions on her date of claim. When the appeal against the refusal to award the benefit reached the Upper Tribunal, it referred three questions to the Court of Justice enquiring: (1) whether the benefit should be classified as a sickness benefit or an incapacity benefit; (2) if it was a sickness benefit, what impact, if any, Lucy's relationship to her parents had on her entitlement; and (3) if it was an invalidity benefit, whether it was open to the United Kingdom to set conditions on the acquisition of entitlement which are based on residence or past residence in the United Kingdom.

On examination of the conditions of entitlement to the benefit, the Court of Justice concluded that short-term incapacity benefit in youth is an invalidity benefit, where, as in this case, on the date on which the claim is made, the claimant has a permanent or long-term disability (at [54]).

3.320 The Court of Justice rules that all three conditions of entitlement are incompatible with European Union law.

First, the condition of ordinary residence is contrary to art.10(1) of Regulation 1408/71 (at [59]–[70]).

Secondly, the condition of past presence, and thirdly, the condition of presence in Great Britain, are contrary to art.21(1) TFEU. The condition of past presence could not be justified. The Court notes that it is "too exclusive in nature" and "unduly favours an element which is not necessarily representative of the real and effective degree of connection between the claimant . . . and the Mamber State" (at [95]). As such it constituted an "unjustified restriction on the freedoms guaranteed" by art.21(1) TFEU (at [104]). For similar reasons the requirement of presence in Great Britain was also unjustified (at [105]–[109]).

For the Department's guidance following this judgment, see Memo DMG 19/12.

The Court of Appeal has, in *SSWP v Garland* [2014] EWCA Civ 1550 allowed the appeal against the decision in *SSWP v JG (RP)* [2013] UKUT 300 (AAC) ruling that the claimant did not have residence in Gibraltar which qualified for consideration as residence in the United Kingdom and so could not show residence in the United Kingdom for the required period to be entitled to a Category D retirement pension.

Article 4

Equality of treatment

Unless otherwise provided for by this Regulation, persons to whom this Regulation applies shall enjoy the same benefits and be subject to the same obligations under the legislation of any Member State as the nationals thereof. 3.321

Corresponding Provision of Regulation 1408/71

Article 3.

General Note

The obligation in this article is central to the system of co-ordination established by the regulation. It reflects the general constitutional obligation in art.18 TFEU that "any discrimination on grounds of nationality shall be prohibited." 3.322

In *Chateignier* (C-346/05) [2006] E.C.R. I-10951, the Luxembourg Court ruled:

> "Article 39(2) EC and Article 3(1) of Council Regulation (EEC) No 1408/71 of 14 June 1971 . . . are to be interpreted as precluding national legislation under which the competent institution of the Member State of residence denies unemployment benefits to a national of another Member State on the ground that, on the date when the benefit claim was submitted, the person concerned had not completed a specified period of employment in that Member State of residence, whereas there is no such requirement for nationals of that Member State."

The issue of discrimination prohibited by art.3 of Reg.1408/71 was discussed in *SSWP* v *Bobezes*, [2005] EWCA Civ 111, reported as *R(IS) 6/05*. The claimant was a Portuguese national who had been a worker in the United Kingdom who had become permanently incapable of work. He was in receipt of income support including an allowance for a child. When the child when to visit her grandmother in Portugal from August to November 1998, the decision maker concluded that there was no entitlement to the child allowance on the grounds of absence from Great Britain for more than four weeks. The claimant argued that he had been the victim of discrimination prohibited by EU law in that, had the child gone to stay with a grandparent in Great Britain, there would have been a continuing entitlement to the allowance. There was discussion in the Court of Appeal as to whether art.7(2) of Reg.1612/68 applied or art.3 of Reg.1408/71. The Court of Appeal declines to resolve the question of the relationship of these two provisions and proceeds on the basis that the claimant could rely on art.3 of Reg.1408/71. The key question then addressed concerned proof of discrimination. The Secretary of State argued that the claimant must produce statistical evidence to show the claimed discrimination, while the claimant argued that he had to do no more than show that the requirements of the United Kingdom legislation were intrinsically more likely to affect essentially migrant workers. The Court of Appeal concludes that adjudicating authorities should take a:

> "broad approach and to find that indirect discrimination is liable to affect a significant number of migrant workers on the ground of nationality without statistical proof being available". (At [24].)

Lord Slynn said that the proper approach was to compare the children of migrant workers with British children whose families are normally resident here. 3.323

In a decision under art.3 of Reg.1408/71 (the corresponding provision of that Regulation prohibiting discrimination), the judge ruled that there was no discrimination prohibited by art.3: *SF v SSWP and HMRC (HRP)* [2013] UKUT 175 (AAC). In this case a woman had worked in the United Kingdom before moving to Belgium where she received child benefit, but did not work. On claiming a retirement pension the Department refused to credit her with contributions under home responsibilities protection in relation to the relevant years spent in Belgium. The judge ruled that there was no discrimination on grounds of nationality. She was refused home responsibilities protection because she was living in another country and not in receipt of UK child benefit. However, the judge went on to decide that the denial constituted a restriction on free movement which was not objectively justified.

Is the United Kingdom "right to reside" requirement compatible with the prohibition of discrimination under art.4?

3.324 *CPC/1072/2006* was an attempt to use art.3 of Regulation 1408/71 as a means of challenging the requirement of a right to reside as a condition of entitlement to state pension credit. The Commissioner ruled that the Secretary of State's concession that state pension credit fell within the material scope of the regulation was plainly right. This meant that art.3 bit, even though the benefit was listed in Annex IIa as a special non-contributory benefit. The appellant argued that the requirement of a right to reside as a condition of entitlement constituted prohibited discrimination under art.3 which could not be justified.

The appeal wound its way all the way to the Supreme Court, where the appellant's appeal was dismissed: see *Patmalniece v SSWP* [2011] UKSC 11; [2011] AACR 36.

Lord Hope, giving the lead judgment, identified the following issues as raised by the appeal:

(1) whether the conditions of entitlement to State Pension Credit give rise to direct discrimination contrary to art.3 of Regulation 1408/71 (the predecessor to art.4);

(2) if the conditions of entitlement give rise only to indirect discrimination, whether that discrimination can be objectively justified; and

(3) if the indirect discrimination would otherwise be objectively justified, whether that conclusion is undermined by the favourable treatment accorded to Irish nationals.

3.325 After careful analysis of the Luxembourg authorities, notably *Bressol* (C–73/08) Judgment of April 13, 2010, [2010] 3 C.M.L.R. 20, Lord Hope concludes that the requirements must be regarded as indirectly discriminatory. Accordingly, to be lawful, the requirements needed to be justified on the basis of objective considerations independent of the nationality of the persons concerned and to be proportionate to the legitimate aims of the national provisions. The Secretary of State argued that the requirements were designed to concentrate the payment of benefits to those with a close connection with the United Kingdom which could be achieved by an appropriate degree of economic or social integration. That proposition was readily accepted. Rather more troubling was whether this requirement operated independently of the nationality of the persons concerned. The Court (Lord Walker dissenting) accepts that the justification is not defeated by its linkage to nationality; the test is one of economic and social integration which applies also to UK nationals.

That left the third question for consideration: whether the above conclusion was tainted by the preferential treatment of Irish nationals. The Court concludes that the privileged position of Irish nationals is within the special terms of the Protocol first attached to the Treaty of Amsterdam, but now forming Protocol No.20 to the Treaty on European Union, and does not taint the conclusions on the justification of the indirect discrimination contained in the conditions of entitlement for State Pension Credit.

The *Patmalniece* reasoning has been applied and followed by the Upper Tribunal in relation to JSA with the result that the right to reside test has been found to be justifiable in relation to that benefit: *RJ v SSWP (JSA)* [2011] UKUT 477 (AAC), reported as [2012] AACR 28.

It remains just about arguable that the specific conditions of entitlement for other specific benefits might raise a situation in which the indirect discrimination resulting from the application of the right to reside test could not be justified. This is because the specific test in relation to State pension credit (a special non-contributory benefit) which was in issue in *Patmalniece* involved a slight variant on the usual habitual residence/right to reside test of eligibility for the benefit. **3.326**

The Northern Ireland Court of Appeal has over-ruled the decision in *AS v HMRC (CB)* [2013] NI Com 15 (CI/10/11 (CB)) and ruled that the right to reside requirement in relation to entitlement to child benefit is not directly discriminatory under art.3 of Regulation 1408/71 (and, it would follow, art.4 of Regulation 883/2004).

Commission proceedings against the United Kingdom on the "right to reside" test

After a long delay following the issue of a letter before action (Press Release IP/11/1118), the European Commission has announced that it is taking infringement proceedings against the United Kingdom under art.258 TFEU in relation to the right to reside test as it applies to child benefit, child tax credit, income-based jobseeker's allowance, state pension credit, and income-related employment and support allowance. The Commission argues that the habitual residence test is sufficient to establish a genuine connection with the host State without the additional requirement to show a right to reside. From its press release (IP/13/475), the Commission appears to be relying on the principles in both Reg.883/2004 and in the Citizenship Directive. The press release says: **3.327**

"Whereas EU law on the free movement of Union citizens (Directive 2004/38/EC) does allow Member States to restrict access to social assistance, EU rules on social security do not allow for restrictions on social security benefit in the case of EU nationals that are workers, direct family members of workers or habitually resident in the Member State in question."

The Government has indicated that it will defend these proceedings vigorously: see *http://www.bbc.co.uk/news/uk-22712569*. The case number is (C-308/14).

In Case C-308/14, on October 6, 2015, Advocate General Cruz Villalón expressed the opinion that the challenged United Kingdom legislation did not breach European Union law. He said,

> "99. In conclusion, I consider that it does not constitute discrimination prohibited by Article 4 of Regulation 883/2004 if national legislation provides that, when examining claims for social benefits such as child benefit or child tax credit, the Member State's authorities may carry out the checks necessary to ensure that nationals of other Member States claiming those benefits are lawfully resident in its territory. However, for that purpose, the authorities responsible for carrying out those checks will, in any case, from a procedural point of view, have to observe the principles described above, in particular, the principle of proportionality, as well as the provisions of the second paragraph of Article 14(2), Article 15(1), and Article 30 and 31 of Directive 2004/38."

The Court, in its judgment of June 14, 2016, dismissed the Commission's action. The Commission's complaint related only to child benefit and child tax credit under the provisions of Regulation 883/2004. The Court accepted that these benefits were social security benefits within the scope of Regulation 883/2004 but essentially rejected the Commission's complaint that the right to reside test added a condition supplementary to that of habitual residence which was to be found in the Regulation. It was merely the United Kingdom's expression of it. It was accepted that the condition does give rise to unequal treatment because United Kingdom nationals can comply more readily than nationals of other Member States. However, the Court found that the difference in treatment could be justified by the legitimate objective of protecting the finances of the host Member State provided that it does not go beyond what is necessary to attain that objective: paras 78-84.

Asylum seekers

3.328 Article 2 of the regulation brings refugees, as defined in reg.1, within its personal scope. This article provides that those within the personal scope of the regulation are entitled to the same rights as nationals of the Member State in which they are resident. But note that "resident" is defined in art.1 as involving "habitual residence".

In *CF/3662/1999* a person seeking asylum sought to rely on the corresponding provision in reg.1408/71 to obtain a right of entry and residence in the United Kingdom. The Commissioner dismissed the appeal on the authority of *Krasniqi v Chief Adjudication Officer*, (reported as *R(IS) 15/99)*, to the effect that a claimant who has no connection with any Member State of the European Union other than the United Kingdom cannot rely on Regulation 1408/71. That decision is found to be entirely consistent with authority from the Luxembourg Court in *Khalil v Bundesanstalt für Arbeit* (C-95/99–C-98/99) [2001] E.C.R. I-7413.

Article 5

Equal treatment of benefits, income, facts or events

3.329 Unless otherwise provided for by this Regulation and in the light of the special implementing provisions laid down, the following shall apply:

(a) where, under the legislation of the competent Member State, the receipt of social security benefits and other income has certain legal effects, the relevant provisions of that legislation shall also apply to the receipt of equivalent benefits acquired under the legislation of another Member State or to income acquired in another Member State;

(b) where, under the legislation of the competent Member State, legal effects are attributed to the occurrence of certain facts or events, that Member State shall take account of like facts or events occurring in any Member State as though they had taken place in its own territory.

General Note

3.330 This is a new provision of general application in Reg.883/2004. There were similar provisions applying to particular benefits in Reg.1408/71, but the earlier provisions have been elevated in Reg.883/2004 to principles of general application sitting alongside such requirements as equality of treatment and aggregation of periods in arts 4 and 6 respectively.

Under the first paragraph of art.5, where a person's social security entitlements have legal effects in one Member State, those legal effects must be recognised in other Member States. So, if a person is in receipt of an old-age pension in one Member State, another Member State considering a question concerning that person's social security entitlements must recognise that person as a pensioner.

Under the second paragraph of art.5, where the legal effects in one Member State are attributable to the occurrence of certain facts or events determined by the competent institution of that state, those facts and events are to be recognised in other Member States. Under this principle, it is not open to Member State B to question, for example, whether a person determined to have suffered an industrial accident in Member State A actually suffered such an accident. In other words, there must be mutual recognition of factual matters relating to the award of a benefit by a competent Member State.

This provision may, however, not be entirely straight forward in its application, as might be illustrated by reference to *NB v SSWP* [2009] UKUT 273 (AAC). In this case a recipient of incapacity benefit had moved from the United Kingdom to the Republic of Ireland, where she was examined on behalf of the Department by a doctor in Dublin. She complained that the medical examination was inadequate, and the judge remitted the appeal for a fresh decision, having heard that doctors in Dublin appointed to conduct medical examinations on behalf of the Department received no training from the Department, and that the doctor might not have appreciated the significance of variability in the appellant's condition. Since, in this case, the question was not about the recognition of a medical report conducted in another Member State for the purpose of a benefit there, but a medical examination conducted on behalf of the competent authorities in the Member State awarding the benefit, the article would not appear to have any relevance. If, however, the appellant had been found to be incapable of work in Ireland for the purposes of the application of the Irish test of incapacity for work in connection with entitlement to an incapacity pension, then it could well be that her incapacity would have to be accepted by the United Kingdom (or at the very least taken into account) if a question subsequently arose in the United Kingdom about whether or not she was incapable of work. It is suggested that the provision is much more likely to be relevant in relation to long-term benefits—such as, for example, benefits flowing from an industrial injury.

Article 6

Aggregation of periods

Unless otherwise provided for by this Regulation, the competent institution of a Member State whose legislation makes: 3.331

— the acquisition, retention, duration or recovery of the right to benefits,

— the coverage by legislation,

or

— the access to or the exemption from compulsory, optional continued or voluntary insurance,

conditional upon the completion of periods of insurance, employment, self-employment or residence shall, to the extent necessary, take into account periods of insurance, employment, self-employment or residence completed under the legislation of any other Member State as though they were periods completed under the legislation which it applies.

Relevant Provision of the Implementing Regulation

Article 12.

RELEVANT DECISION OF THE ADMINISTRATIVE COMMISSION

Decision No.H6 of December 16, 2010 concerning the application of certain principles regarding the aggregation of periods under Article 6 of Regulation (EC) No 883/2004 on the coordination of social security systems [2011] OJ C45/4.

GENERAL NOTE

3.332 The principle of aggregation of periods of insurance, employment or residence has always been a central feature of the co-ordinating regulations, but the principle is elevated to a general principle, to which there may be exceptions, for the first time in this regulation.

Article 7

Waiving of residence rules

3.333 Unless otherwise provided for by this Regulation, cash benefits payable under the legislation of one or more Member States or under this Regulation shall not be subject to any reduction, amendment, suspension, withdrawal or confiscation on account of the fact that the beneficiary or the members of his family reside in a Member State other than that in which the institution responsible for providing benefits is situated.

CORRESPONDING PROVISION OF REGULATION 1408/71

Article 10.

GENERAL NOTE

3.334 This article should be read in conjunction with art.70 on special non-contributory benefits. It deals with the exportability of cash benefits, and is drawn in wider terms than its predecessor. Regulation 1408/71 applied a general exportability rule only to "invalidity, old-age or survivors' cash benefits, pension for accidents at work or occupational diseases and death grants". Special provisions related to the export, in particular, of sickness and unemployment benefits. The new article simply refers to cash benefits. Unless there are other provisions preventing their export, or making them subject to additional conditions, the general position is that such benefits are exportable.

It will be recalled that in *Stewart (Lucy)* (C–503/09) [2011] E.C.R. I-06497, [2012] AACR 8, the Court of Justice ruled that short-term incapacity benefit in youth is an incapacity benefit as distinct from a sickness benefit. The Court defined sickness benefits as those which "cover the risk connected to a morbid condition involving temporary suspension of the concerned person's activities." (At [37].) By contrast an invalidity benefit "is intended, as a general rule, to cover the risk of disability of a prescribed degree, where it is probable that such disability will be permanent or long-term." (At [38].) The Advocate General in that case had suggested that, even under Regulation 1408/71, it would matter little whether the benefit was characterised as an invalidity benefit or a sickness benefit for the purposes of considering whether it could be exported.

A decision of a three-judge panel in *SSWP v LT (DLA)* [2012] UKUT 282 (AAC) concerned the export rules in Regulation 1408/71 relating to the care component of DLA. Much of the decision concerns specific provisions of Regulation 1408/71. The Upper Tribunal, however, refused to make a reference to the Court of Justice, as requested by the Secretary of State questioning the correctness of the judgment of the Court of Appeal in *HMRC v Ruas* [2010] EWCA Civ 291, which had held that the term "employed person" had a single meaning throughout the

Regulation, and was satisfied if the claimant was insured for any risk falling with Regulation 1408/71. They did so on the basis that they were bound by the judgment of the Court of Appeal and found its reasoning compelling. Furthermore, the Supreme Court had refused the Secretary of State permission to appeal in the case.

The appeal against *SSWP v LT (DLA)* [2012] UKUT 282 (AAC) has been dismissed by the Court of Appeal (*SSWP v Linda Tolley (deceased)* [2013] EWCA Civ 1471). 3.335

The *Tolley case* rumbles on. The Supreme Court in *SSWP v Tolley (deceased, acting by her personal representative)* [2015] UKSC 55 has referred the following questions to the Court of Justice:

"1. Is the care component of the United Kingdom's Disability Living Allowance properly classified as an invalidity rather than a cash sickness benefit for the purpose of Regulation No 1408/71?

2.(i) Does a person who ceases to be entitled to UK Disability Living Allowance as a matter of UK domestic law, because she has moved to live in another member state, and who has ceased all occupational activity before such move, but remains insured against old age under the UK social security system, cease to be subject to the legislation of the UK for the purpose of article 13(2)(f) of Regulation No 1408/71?

(ii) Does such a person in any event remain subject to the legislation of the UK in the light of Point 19(c) of the United Kingdom's annex VI to the Regulation?

(iii) If she has ceased to be subject to the legislation of the UK within the meaning of article 13(2)(f), is the UK obliged or merely permitted by virtue of Point 20 of annex VI to apply the provisions of Chapter 1 of Title III to the Regulation to her?

3. (i) Does the broad definition of an employed person in *Dodl* apply for the purposes of articles 19 to 22 of the Regulation, where the person has ceased all occupational activity before moving to another member state, notwithstanding the distinction drawn in Chapter 1 of Title III between, on the one hand, employed and self-employed persons and, on the other hand, unemployed persons?

(ii) If it does apply, is such a person entitled to export the benefit by virtue zof either article 9 or article 22? Does article 22(1)(b) operate to prevent a claimant's entitlement to the care component of DLA being defeated by a residence requirement imposed by national legislation on a transfer of residence to another member state?"

The Court issued its judgment in *SSWP v Tolley (C-430/15)* on February 1, 2017. The Court confirmed that the care component of a disability living allowance is a sickness benefit and went on to rule:

"2. Article 13(2)(f) of Regulation No 1408/71 . . . must be interpreted as meaning that the fact that a person has acquired rights to an old-age pension by virtue of contributions paid during a given period to the social security scheme of a Member State does not preclude the legislation of that Member State from subsequently ceasing to be applicable to that person. It is for the national court to determine, in the light of the circumstances of the case before it and of the provisions of the applicable national law when that legislation ceased to be applicable to that person.

3. Article 22(1)(b) of Regulation No 1408/71 . . . must be interpreted as preventing legislation of the competent State from making entitlement to an allowance such as that in issue in the main proceedings subject to a condition as to residence and presence on the territory of that Member State.

Article 22(1)(b) and Article 22(2) of Regulation No 1408/71 . . . must be interpreted as meaning that a person in a situation such as that at issue in the main proceedings retains the right to receive the benefits referred to in Article 22(1)(b) after transferring his residence to a Member state other than the competent State, provided that he has obtained authorisation for that purpose."

Regulation 883/2004 states a more generous rule permitting the export of benefits than its predecessor (where the general rule in art.10 applied only to invalidity, old-age or survivor's cash benefits, pensions for accidents at work or occupational diseases and death grants), but still provides certain limitations on the export of certain benefits under the specific rules on particular benefits. Some of those rules are, however, more generous than the rules in Reg.1408/71. For example, art.22 of Reg.1408/71 required authorisation (which could only be refused in limited circumstances) where a beneficiary of sickness benefits wished to move to another Member State. By contrast, art.21 of Reg.883/2004 gives an unconditional right to payment of cash benefits without any provisions on authorisation by the competent state.

Article 8

Relations between this Regulation and other coordination instruments

3.336 1. This Regulation shall replace any social security convention applicable between Member States falling under its scope. Certain provisions of social security conventions entered into by the Member States before the date of application of this Regulation shall, however, continue to apply provided that they are more favourable to the beneficiaries or if they arise from specific historical circumstances and their effect is limited in time. For these provisions to remain applicable, they shall be included in Annex II. If, on objective grounds, it is not possible to extend some of these provisions to all persons to whom the Regulation applies this shall be specified.

2. Two or more Member States may, as the need arises, conclude conventions with each other based on the principles of this Regulation and in keeping with the spirit thereof.

Corresponding Provision of Regulation 1408/71

Article 6.

General Note

3.337 This article gives priority to the provisions of the regulation over social security conventions concluded between the Member States. The predecessor to this provision has given rise to some complex and difficult case law. The essential question was whether advantages arising under the existing conventions were lost when the regulation came into force, and whether this was compatible with the EC Treaty provisions.

In its first decision on this issue in *Walder* (82/72) [1973] E.C.R. 599, the Luxembourg Court ruled that the provisions of art.6 of Reg.1408/71 were mandatory and did not allow for exceptions which were not expressly set out in the Regulation.

Rönfeldt (227/89) [1991] E.C.R. I-323 concerned a German national who had from 1941 to 1957, and so prior to the entry into force of Reg.1408/71 (or its predecessor), worked in Germany before moving to Denmark and working there until 1971 when he returned to Germany. Retirement pension ages were 65 in

Germany and 67 in Denmark; in Germany an early retirement pension could be claimed at 63 provided that a person had completed 35 years of insurance. Rönfeldt claimed an early retirement pension but was refused since the German authorities took the view that contributions paid in Denmark could not be taken into account in Germany until the claimant reached the Danish retirement age of 67. The Court noted that art.45 of Reg.1408/71 required competent institutions to take insurance periods completed in other Member States into account in determining whether a person has acquired, retained or recovered a right to benefit, but art.46 did not require contributions paid elsewhere to be taken into account in calculating the amount of a benefit. This was in contrast to the requirements of a convention between Germany and Denmark. The Court then ruled that it was incompatible with the provisions of the EC Treaty on free movement of workers to deprive a person of advantages which they had acquired under a convention.

The judgment presented very significant problems of administration for the Member States since it would mean that in very many cases multiple computations would be needed because of the number of bilateral and multilateral treaties in existence. The Court clarified its judgment in the *Rönfeldt* case in *Thévenon and Speyer* (475/93) [1995] E.C.R. I-3813. The Court explained that the rule in the *Rönfeldt* case only applied where a right to freedom of movement had been exercised prior to the entry into force; it did not apply where the right of free movement was first exercised after Reg.1408/71 had replaced the provisions of the bilateral convention. The *Rönfeldt* exception applied only to those who had already accrued certain rights under the bilateral convention. It did not preserve the more beneficial rule in the convention for those first exercising their right of free movement under the regime set in place by Reg.1408/71. The consequence is that it is not a requirement for institutions in the Member States to investigate in every claim whether a person might have a more advantageous position under a bilateral or multilateral convention. 3.338

In *Gómez Rodríguez* (C-113/96) [1998] E.C.R. I-2482, the Luxembourg Court ruled that a comparison of rights had to be made only once: at the first determination of benefit entitlement within the terms of Reg.1408/71.

In *Thelen* (C-75/99) [2000] E.C.R. I-9399 and (C-277/99) [2000] E.C.R. I-1261, the Luxembourg Court ruled that the only purpose of the *Rönfeldt* exception was to preserve entitlement to an established social right which was not part of Community law at the time when the national of a Member State relying on it had such an entitlement. The *Rönfeldt* exception was based on a person's legitimate expectation that accrued rights would not be lost.

Article 9

[1 Declarations by the Member States on the scope of this Regulation 3.339

1. The Member States shall notify the European Commission in writing of the declarations made in accordance with point (l) of Article 1, the legislation and schemes referred to in Article 3, the conventions entered into as referred to in Article 8(2), the minimum benefits referred to in Article 58, and the lack of an insurance system as referred to in Article 65a(1), as well as substantive amendments. Such notifications shall indicate the date from which this Regulation will apply to the schemes specified by the Member States therein.

2. These notifications shall be submitted to the European Commission every year and shall be given the necessary publicity.]

Corresponding Provision of Regulation 1408/71

Article 5.

Amendment

1. This version of art.9 is substituted by Regulation 465/2012 [2012] OJ L149/4 art.1(3) (June 28, 2012).

General Note

3.340 In the past the declarations attached to the regulation were often not up to date, but the new system of annual notification to the Commission should improve matters considerably provided that the information is published promptly in the *Official Journal*.

Article 10

Prevention of overlapping of benefits

3.341 Unless otherwise specified, this Regulation shall neither confer nor maintain the right to several benefits of the same kind for one and the same period of compulsory insurance.

Corresponding Provision of Regulation 1408/71

Article 12(1).

Relevant Provision of the Implementing Regulation

Article 10.

General Note

3.342 The rules in the co-ordinating regulations have always had a high degree of complexity, but the basic principles are readily comprehensible. First, that a claimant cannot use the co-ordination rules to acquire title to the same benefit in more than one Member State; and, secondly, that national law may apply its own rules on the overlapping of benefits notwithstanding that title to one of the benefits in issue was acquired under the European Union rules.

This article states the basic principle that the application of the rules in the regulation cannot operate to give rise to a double claim. A claimant cannot use the regulation as the basis for claiming benefits of the same kind in more than one Member State.

But the regulation does not preclude national social security systems from applying overlapping rules even where title to a benefit arises through the operation of the European Union rules. An example would be the application of national law which precluded the overlapping of a sickness benefit with an unemployment benefit. In some Member States entitlement to both benefits may be held at the same time, in other Member States the benefits cannot overlap.

The overlapping rules do not apply to long-term benefits paid on a pro rata basis: art.54(1) of Regulation 883/2004.

Other provisions of the regulation dealing with the overlapping of benefits are:

art.34: Over-lapping of long-term care benefits
arts 53–55: provisions relating to old-age and survivors' benefits
art.68: provisions relating to the overlapping of family benefits

Title II

Determination of the Legislation Applicable

Article 11

General rules

1. Persons to whom this Regulation applies shall be subject to the legislation of a single Member State only. Such legislation shall be determined in accordance with this Title. 3.343

2. For the purposes of this Title, persons receiving cash benefits because or as a consequence of their activity as an employed or self-employed person shall be considered to be pursuing the said activity. This shall not apply to invalidity, old-age or survivors' pensions or to pensions in respect of accidents at work or occupational diseases or to sickness benefits in cash covering treatment for an unlimited period.

3. Subject to Articles 12 to 16:

(a) a person pursuing an activity as an employed or self-employed person in a Member State shall be subject to the legislation of that Member State;

(b) a civil servant shall be subject to the legislation of the Member State to which the administration employing him is subject;

(c) a person receiving unemployment benefits in accordance with Article 65 under the legislation of the Member State of residence shall be subject to the legislation of that Member State;

(d) a person called up or recalled for service in the armed forces or for civilian service in a Member State shall be subject to the legislation of that Member State;

(e) any other person to whom subparagraphs (a) to (d) do not apply shall be subject to the legislation of the Member State of residence, without prejudice to other provisions of this Regulation guaranteeing him benefits under the legislation of one or more other Member States.

4. For the purposes of this Title, an activity as an employed or self-employed person normally pursued on board a vessel at sea flying the flag of a Member State shall be deemed to be an activity pursued in the said Member State. However, a person employed on board a vessel flying the flag of a Member State and remunerated for such activity by an undertaking or a person whose registered office or place of business is in another Member State shall be subject to the legislation of the latter Member State if he resides in that State. The undertaking or person paying the remuneration shall be considered as the employer for the purposes of the said legislation.

[1 5. An activity as a flight crew or cabin crew member performing air passenger or freight services shall be deemed to be an activity pursued in the Member State where the home base, as defined in Annex III to Regulation (EEC) No 3922/91, is located.]

Corresponding Provision of Regulation 1408/71

Article 13.

RELEVANT PROVISIONS OF THE IMPLEMENTING REGULATION

Articles 6 and 15.

AMENDMENT

1. Regulation 465/2012 [2012] OJ L149/4 art.1(4) (June 28, 2012).

GENERAL NOTE

3.344 Title II of the regulation provides a complete system of the conflict of laws for answering questions concerning both jurisdiction and the choice of law to apply to any situation involving an international element between Member States. The basic proposition is that persons to whom the regulation applies are at any given time subject to the legislation of a single Member State only, which will normally apply its own social security laws to the matter subject to the co-ordinating rules in the regulation. The starting point to which there are exceptions is that priority is given to the place of employment or self-employment.

Note that the terms "activity as an employed person" and "activity as a self-employed person" are defined in art.1(a) and (b).

Title II of Reg.883/2004 is rather shorter than its predecessor because the exceptions for those in employment, or self-employment, in two or more Member States at the same time have been brought together. Under art.13, the displacement of the place of work with the place of residence as determining the competent State will only arise where a substantial part of the activity takes place in the Member State of residence. Under art.14(8) of the implementing regulation, in order to be substantial, more than one quarter of the time on the activities will have to take place in the Member State of residence. The Commission has issued a new guide to the legislation applicable in November 2012, entitled *Practical Guide: The Legislation that Applies to Workers in the European Union (EU), the European Economic Area (EEA) and in Switzerland.* It can be found on the European Commission's web pages on EU social security co-ordination: *http://ec.europa.eu/social/main.jsp?catId=849&langId=en* [Accessed June 2013].

3.345 *SSWP v PS* [2009] UKUT 226 (AAC); [2010] AACR 14, is a decision concerning art.13 of Reg.1408/71, but the points it makes are equally pertinent to the effect of the rules for determining the legislation applicable under the new regulation. The claimant had been self-employed in Spain for a number of years, and had paid social security contributions under the Spanish legislation. She became unable to continue her work. As commonly happens in such cases, she returned to the United Kingdom (of which she appears to be a national). She claimed incapacity benefit. Enquiries were made of the Spanish authorities, which do not appear to have been entirely satisfactory, but the outcome was that she was not entitled to sickness benefit in Spain.

The claimant then made an argument that she had last been insured in the United Kingdom because she had a prospective entitlement to national insurance credits. The argument was based on the definitions of "competent institution" and "competent State" found in art.1 of Regulation 1408/71. The judge concludes that art.13 (and, by implication the rules in Title II of Regulation 1408/71) alone determine the applicable law in respect of any single claim for a benefit within the scope of the regulation (see paras 27–32). In this case, the Secretary of State had argued that a national insurance credit could never of itself be insurance for the purposes of Reg.1408/71. The judge said that he preferred to leave the issue for determination in a case where the point was in issue.

The primacy of the place of work

3.346 Person pursuing activities as employed or self-employed persons who live in one Member State but work in another Member State country are subject, for any given claim, to the legislation of the Member State in which they work. This rule applies even if the registered office or centre of administration of an employer is in a different Member State. The Luxembourg Court has even applied the provisions of Title II of Reg.1408/71 by analogy where a situation arises which is not covered directly by its provisions. So in *Aldewereld* (60/93) [1994] E.C.R. I-2991, a question arose as to whether a Dutch national recruited by a company established in Germany and sent to work in Thailand was covered by the legislation of The Netherlands or Germany. The Court concluded that there was a sufficient link with European Union law for that law to apply, and that there was a real and substantial link with Germany in relation to the employment. Aldewereld should accordingly be treated as a person employed in Germany, and the provisions of German social security law would apply to his liability to pay social security contributions.

Even though the terms "activity as an employed person" and "activity as a self-employed person" are defined in art.1(a) and (b), those definitions refer to such activities being treated as either employment or self-employment under the social security legislation of the Member State in which the activity takes place. It follows that the dividing line between employment and self-employment may differ in each Member States. However, in relation to the *location* of the activity, that is a matter to be determined by European Union law. The Court has indicated that the first question to ask is where the occupational activity in question takes place, before then considering whether that activity is employment or self-employment. Consequently, certain national rules making irrebuttable presumptions about the location of occupational activities will be contrary to European Union law: see *Partena ASBL* (C-137/11) Judgment of September 27, 2012, [50]–[59] of the judgment.

It is now clearly established that a person employed to work on an oil rig on the continental shelf of a Member State operated by a company established in that state falls within the provisions of art.13(2)(a) of Reg.1408/71 (the corresponding provision to art.11(3)(a)): *Salemink* (C–347/10) Judgment of the Grand Chamber of January 17, 2012. It follows that the Member State in question cannot subject such persons to the additional requirement that they are resident in that Member State.

Determining the location of self employment may be more complex than determining the location of employment. Given the varied nature of self employment, careful enquiry may be needed in order to determine whether there is a separation of the place of residence and the place of the self employment, especially where the activity is conducted from home. For example, a person who moves to Spain to live there, but who continues his self-employment as a business adviser advising only clients in the United Kingdom may well continue to be self-employed in the United Kingdom. **3.347**

SSWP v AH (CA) [2016] UKUT 148 (AAC) concerned a claim by a daughter who was living in and self-employed in Portugal for carer's allowance in respect of her grandmother who was in receipt of attendance allowance in Portugal. She sought to argue that carer's allowance is so closely connected to attendance allowance that the United Kingdom should be the competent state for its award. However, Judge Turnbull concluded that art.11 is concerned with determining jurisdiction by reference to the claimant of a benefit. Plainly art.11(3)(a) applied to the claimant by reason of her self-employment in Portugal. This meant that Portugal was the competent state for the purposes of the claimant's claim for a sickness benefit within the scheme of classification of benefits in Regulation 883/2004.

Bosmann (C-352/06) [2008] E.C.R. I-3827, concerned the interpretation of art.13(2)(a) of Reg.1408/71 which provides that the competent state is the state in which a person is employed even if they reside in another Member State. The main principle of art.13 is to ensure that there is only one competent state. But does that mean that there can be no entitlement to a benefit under the law of the Member State of residence?

That was the question which arose in this case. Brigitte Bosmann, a Belgian national, worked in The Netherlands, but lived in Germany. When she undertook this employment, the German authorities terminated the award of child benefits for her two children. There was no comparable entitlement under Dutch law since the legislation of that country does not provide for the payment of child benefits for children over 18. At first sight, it would seem that Bosmann was caught by art.13(2)(a) in that, when she became employed in Germany, that country was alone the competent State for the purpose of benefits falling within the scope of Reg.1408/71. But the Luxembourg Court ruled that "the application of provisions from another system of legislation is not thereby always precluded" (at [20]). While European Union law does not *require* the German authorities to pay child benefit in respect of the two children, it does not *exclude* that possibility. How sweeping an exception to the single state rule is introduced by this case remains contentious. One view is that the possibility of dual state competence is limited to family benefit cases where there remain wide variations in both the conditions of entitlement and the level of benefits. The second is that the case establishes that a state other than the competent state *may* elect to pay benefits where a person meets the conditions of entitlement in that state through some linking factor, such as residence, on the basis of national law alone. It is worth observing that the Opinion of Advocate General Mazák came to the opposite view, namely that Bosmann was not entitled to the application of German law so as to receive child benefit.

In Joined Cases *Hudziński and Wawrzyniak* (C-611/10 and C-612/10) Judgment of June 12, 2012 (which involved the interpretation of provisions of Regulation 1408/71), the Court of Justice followed and extended its judgment in *Bosmann*. Two Polish workers worked in Germany respectively as a seasonal worker and as a posted worker. They retained affiliation with the Polish social security system, but both made requests to be subject to unlimited tax liability in Germany on their earnings there, and as a consequence to be entitled to the (higher) family benefits available in Germany. The Court ruled that Reg.1408/71 did not preclude the award of benefits in these circumstances by a state other than the competent state under the Regulation. The required connection with German law was precise and the benefits claimed were financed out of taxation. Such an approach facilitates the free movement of workers. On a subsidiary point, the Court ruled that it would be contrary to European Union law to have an overlapping rule which excluded any entitlement to the German benefit rather than simply reducing it by the amount of the corresponding benefit in Poland.

In *IG v SSWP (AA)* [2016] UKUT 176 (AAC), [2016] AACR 41, considered in detail the application of the principles established in the *Hudziński* case in the context of s.65(7) of Social Security Contributions and Benefits Act 1992, which provides:

> "A person to whom either Regulation (EC) No 1408/71 or Regulation (EC) No 883/2004 applies shall not be entitled to an attendance allowance for a period unless during that period the United Kingdom is competent for payment of sickness benefits in cash to the person for the purposes of Chapter 1 of Title III of the Regulation in question."

Judge Jacobs concludes that s.65(7) is not in breach of the requirements of Regulation 883/2004, and is not covered by the prohibitions suggested in the *Hudziński* case, and related cases.

In *LD v SSWP (DLA)* [2017] UKUT 65 (AAC), Judge Jacobs rules that the care component of a disability living allowance is a sickness benefit and not a "pension" for the purposes of Regulation 883/2004. Consequently, when the claimant became entitled to a pension from the Netherlands that Member State became the competent state for the purpose of the award of sickness benefits, and the United Kingdom was not required to pay such benefits under its domestic legislation.

Giving practical effect to the single state rule

3.348 The Court has interpreted the rules on the applicable legislation in order to ensure that practical effect is given to the scheme in the regulation. The facts of *De Paep* (196/90) [1991] E.C.R. I-4815, were rather unusual. Mrs De Paep owned a vessel on which her husband and son were employed. Following damage to the vessel, it was declared unseaworthy. Despite this it was sailed across the Channel from Belgium to the United Kingdom. During this passage, the vessel was shipwrecked, and the husband and son were lost at sea. Under Belgian law on employment contracts for seamen, contracts of employment automatically terminate when a vessel is declared unseaworthy. The effect in law was that the husband and son were technically not employed on the vessel when it sank. Nor were they flying on a vessel carrying the flag of Belgium (the vessel was registered in the United Kingdom). The Court ruled that neither condition precluded the legislation of Belgium from applying to the claim made by Madeleine De Paep for an annuity by way of compensation for loss sustained as a result of accidents at work following the death of her son. The Court said:

> "... according to the case-law of the Court the provisions of Title II of Regulation No. 1408/71 . . . constitute a complete and uniform system of conflict rules . . . and that those provisions are intended not only to prevent the simultaneous application of a number of national legislative systems and the complications which might ensue, but also to ensure that the persons covered by Regulation No 1408/71 are not left without social security cover because there is no legislation applicable to them. In particular, the conditions concerning the right of a person to become affiliated to a social security scheme may not have the effect of excluding from the scope of the legislation at issue persons to whom it applies pursuant to Regulation No 1408/71 . . ." (para.18).

Bakker (C-106/11) Judgment of June 7, 2012, concerns the interpretation of art.13(2)(c) of Reg.1408/71, but is of relevance in interpreting the first sentence of art.11(4). The Court advised that the jurisdictional rule in art.13(2)(c) must be interpreted as precluding legislation which excludes from affiliation to the national social security system a person who: (a) holds the nationality of that state, (b) does not reside there, but (c) works on board a dredger flying the flag of that Member State and operating outside the territory of the European Union.

Subject to the legislation of the Member State of residence

Article 11(3)(e) states the rule formerly in art.13(2)(f) rather differently. The application of the legislation of the Member State of residence is stated as a general proposition. Article 13(2)(f) was set in the context of a person having given up employment permanently and moving to another Member State. The former provision resolved an uncertainty that had arisen from the decision of the Luxembourg Court in *Ten Holder* (302/84) [1986] E.C.R. 1821, which had suggested that the legislation of the place where a person last worked was applicable to them forever thereafter until such time as the person undertook further employment or self-employment. The Court, however, mitigated its decision in two subsequent cases: *Noij* (C-140/88) [1991] E.C.R. I-387, and *Daalmeijer* (C-245/88) [1991] E.C.R. I-555, ruling that a person who had ceased all work and moved country became subject to the legislation of the state of residence. **3.349**

Article 11(3)(e) is qualified not just by the other articles in Title II of the Regulation, but also by the articles in Title III which makes special provisions concerning the various categories of benefit: *SL v SSWP (DLA)* [2014] UKUT 108 (AAC), with which Judge Jacobs agreed in *SSWP v AK (AA)* [2015] UKUT 110 (AAC), [2015] AACR 27, at para.22–3. See also *AM v SSWP (CA)* [2017] UKUT 26 (AAC).

The application of the principle in former art.13(2)(f) appeared to have become more sweeping than might first have been expected. One of the questions which arose in *Kuusijärvi* (C-275/96) [1998] E.C.R. I-3419, was whether the exception applied where a person had permanently ceased all occupational activity, or whether it also applied where a person had ceased occupational activity in circumstances where it might reasonably be expected that he or she would resume occupational activities at some time in the future. In its judgment the Luxembourg

Court ruled that art.13(2)(f) also applied in the latter situation. This would appear to permit Member States to draft their social security legislation in such a way that they can impose a residence requirement for continued entitlement to benefit acquired in that State.

Previously there were some convoluted provisions in Annex VI of Reg.1408/71 on the application of art.13(2)(f) of that regulation when the United Kingdom was concerned. Those provisions have not been re-enacted in the new regulation. But where a person subject to the legislation of the United Kingdom transfers their residence in the future, similar issues are likely to arise. For a discussion of the meaning the provisions in Annex VI of Reg.1408/71, see *SSWP v LT (DLA)* [2012] UKUT 282 (AAC). The appeal against *SSWP v LT (DLA)* has been dismissed by the Court of Appeal (*SSWP v Linda Tolley (deceased)* [2013] EWCA Civ 1471).The Supreme Court has referred a number of questions to the Court of Justice in the *Tolley case.* These are set out at 3.335 above.

Merely being registered as resident will not be enough to ground jurisdiction. In *Ministertvo práce a sociálních věcí v B* (C-394/13), Judgment of September 11, 2014, the Court of Justice ruled:

> "...Regulation No 883/2004, in particular Article 11 thereof, must be interpreted as precluding a Member State from being regarded as the competent State for the purpose of granting a family benefit to a person on the sole ground that the person concerned is registered as being permanently resident in its territory, where neither that person nor the members of his family work or habitually reside in that Member State."

Liability to pay national insurance contributions

3.350 *CF/1727/2006* contains guidance on the procedure for obtaining a formal decision of the National Insurance Contributions Office as to a person's liability to pay national insurance contributions. That is important for the regulation, since it will also determine which law is applicable to a claim for family benefits.

Disputes about the applicable legislation

3.351 Article 6 of the Implementing Regulation contains rules dealing with situations in which there is a difference of views about the determination of the applicable legislation between competent institutions in the Member States.

Article 12

Special rules

3.352 [1 1. A person who pursues an activity as an employed person in a Member State on behalf of an employer which normally carries out its activities there and who is posted by that employer to another Member State to perform work on that employer's behalf shall continue to be subject to the legislation of the first Member State, provided that the anticipated duration of such work does not exceed 24 months and that he/she is not sent to replace another posted person.]

2. A person who normally pursues an activity as a self-employed person in a Member State who goes to pursue a similar activity in another Member State shall continue to be subject to the legislation of the first Member State, provided that the anticipated duration of such activity does not exceed twenty-four months.

Corresponding Provision of Regulation 1408/71

Article 14(1).

Relevant Provisions of the Implementing Regulation

Articles 14 and 15.

Amendment

1. Regulation 465/2012 [2012] OJ L149/4 art.1(5) (June 28, 2012).

General Note

This provision concerns the rules on the posting of workers. It is an important provision, which has been extended to the movement of self-employed persons in situations analogous to posting by an employer. **3.353**

On the posting of workers, see also:

(a) Decision No.181 of the Administrative Commission of December 13, 2000, [2000] OJ L329/73, which relates only to the system under Reg.1408/71. This Decision is to be substituted by new Decision L2 of the Administrative Commission.

(b) *Practical Guide. The Legislation that applies to workers in the European Union (EU) in the European Economic Area and in Switzerland,* November 2012 *http://ec.europa.eu/social/keyDocuments.jsp?advSearchKey=posting&mode=advancedSubmit&langId=en&search.x=8&search.y=16&search=Search* [Accessed May 1, 2015].

(c) Decision No.A2 of June 12, 2009 of the Administrative Commission concerning the interpretation of art.12 of Regulation (EC) No.883/2004 on the legislation applicable to posted workers and self-employed workers temporarily working outside the competent state.

(d) Decision No.A3 of December 17, 2009 of the Administrative Commission, concerning the aggregation of uninterrupted periods completed under the Regulation No.1408/71 and 883/2004.

There are four conditions which must be satisfied for the posting rules to apply: (1) affected workers must be sent to work abroad by an undertaking to which they are normally attached; (2) the workers must be performing work abroad for the undertaking that sent them abroad; (3) the anticipated duration of the posting must not initially exceed 24 months; and (4) the posting must not be for the purpose of replacing another posted worker.

It is important that there is, throughout the posting, a direct relationship between the undertaking and the posted worker. Such a direct relationship will be present when the following features will be present: (a) a contractual relationship continues to exist between employer and employee; (b) the power to terminate that contract remains with the posting undertaking; (c) the nature of the work undertaken by the posted worker must be determinable by the posting undertaking; and (d) the obligation with regard to the remuneration of the worker rests with the undertaking which concluded the contract, irrespective of who actually makes the payment of that remuneration. **3.354**

Some of the guidance flows from the decision of the Luxembourg Court in *Fitzwilliam Executive Search Ltd* (C-202/97) [2002] E.C.R. I-883. This case concerned the activities of Fitzwilliam in placing workers both in Ireland in the Netherlands in the agricultural and horticultural sectors. The company recruited workers in order for them to be posted. Its turnover in the Netherlands came to exceed that in Ireland. The Dutch authorities took the view that workers engaged by Fitzwilliam in order to be posted to the Netherlands were subject to Dutch law and required to pay Dutch social security contributions. The question which arose in the reference made by the Dutch courts was whether workers recruited for the purpose posting to another Member State were within the posting rules in art.14 of Regulation 1408/71. The Court decided that, for art.14 to apply, the undertaking in question must normally carry on its activities in the sending state, which meant that it habitually carries on significant activities in that state. Performance of management activities which are purely internal in that state cannot justify the use of the posting provisions.

The following are considered in Decision No.181 and the Guide to be helpful indicators of the significance of the activities carried out in the sending state: (a) the place where the undertaking has its registered office and administration; (b) the number and nature of its staff there; (c) the place of recruitment of the posted worker; (d) the place where the majority of contracts are concluded; (e) the law applicable to the contracts signed by the undertaking with its clients and with its workers; and (f) turnover in the sending state and in the Member State(s) to which the workers are sent. The Guide indicates that habitual performance of the activities will be met if the activity has been carried out for four months or more; in the case of lesser periods a case-by-case consideration having regard to all the circumstances is required.

3.355 A person's status as a posted worker was attested by the issue in the sending state of Form E101 which certifies that the holder is subject to the legislation of the issuing state and so is exempt from the application of the legislation of the receiving state. *Barry Banks* (C-178/97) [2000] E.C.R. I-2005 concerned a refusal by the Belgian authorities to accept the validity of a Form E101 issued by the United Kingdom authorities (for which provision was made in arts 11 and 11a of Reg.574/72). Banks was an opera singer who undertook short term contracts singing in Brussels. The Belgian authorities took the view that Banks and his colleagues were employed in Belgium, but they held Forms E101 certifying that they were self-employed persons in the United Kingdom. The Court of Justice ruled that, as long as it had not been withdrawn or declared invalid, the Form E101 certificate is binding on the competent institution of the place where the worker or self-employed person goes. That institution may refer the matter back to the certifying institution for investigation if it suspects fraud, but otherwise must accept the exemption from its own legislation.

These decisions have been affirmed in *Herbosch Kiere NV* (C-2/05) [2006] E.C.R. I-1079.

Note that longer periods of exemption could be secured by an agreement between two Member States under art.17 of Reg.1408/71 (now art.16 of Reg.883/2004).

The Commission has set up a Committee of Experts on Posting of Workers ([2009] OJ L8/26, January 13, 2009) to examine the practical difficulties in the operation of the posting rules in Directive 96/71/EC concerning the posting of workers in the framework of the provision of services. The subject matter is related to the issue of posting under Reg.1408/71 and now Reg.883/2004.

Article 13

Pursuit of activities in two or more Member States

3.356 [1 1. A person who normally pursues an activity as an employed person in two or more Member States shall be subject:

(a) to the legislation of the Member State of residence if he/she pursues a substantial part of his/her activity in that Member State; or
(b) if he/she does not pursue a substantial part of his/her activity in the Member State of residence:

(i) to the legislation of the Member State in which the registered office or place of business of the undertaking or employer is situated if he/she is employed by one undertaking or employer; or

(ii) to the legislation of the Member State in which the registered office or place of business of the undertakings or employers is situated if he/she is employed by two or more undertakings or employers which have their registered office or place of business in only one Member State; or

(iii) to the legislation of the Member State in which the registered office or place of business of the undertaking or employer is situated other than the Member State of residence if he/she is employed by two or more undertakings or employers, which have their registered office or place of business in two Member States, one of which is the Member State of residence; or

(iv) to the legislation of the Member State of residence if he/she is employed by two or more undertakings or employers, at least two of which have their registered office or place of business in different Member States other than the Member State of residence.]

2. A person who normally pursues an activity as a self-employed person in two or more Member States shall be subject to:

(a) the legislation of the Member State of residence if he pursues a substantial part of his activity in that Member State; or

(b) the legislation of the Member State in which the centre of interest of his activities is situated, if he does not reside in one of the Member States in which he pursues a substantial part of his activity.

3. A person who normally pursues an activity as an employed person and an activity as a self-employed person in different Member States shall be subject to the legislation of the Member State in which he pursues an activity as an employed person or, if he pursues such an activity in two or more Member States, to the legislation determined in accordance with paragraph 1.

4. A person who is employed as a civil servant by one Member State and who pursues an activity as an employed person and/or as a self-employed person in one or more other Member States shall be subject to the legislation of the Member State to which the administration employing him is subject.

5. Persons referred to in paragraphs 1 to 4 shall be treated, for the purposes of the legislation determined in accordance with these provisions, as though they were pursuing all their activities as employed or self-employed persons and were receiving all their income in the Member State concerned.

Corresponding Provisions of Regulation 1408/71

Articles 14(2), 14a and 14c.

Relevant Provisions of the Implementing Regulation

Articles 14 and 16.

Amendment

1. Regulation 465/2012 [2012] OJ L149/4 art.1(6) (June 28, 2012).

General Note

3.357 This provision clarifies the former rules relating to those who work simultaneously in two or more Member States, whether as employed or self-employed persons, or a combination of the two. Priority is now given to the Member State of residence if the person pursues a substantial part of his activities there. In order to be substantial, more than one quarter of the time on the activities will have to take place in the Member State of residence under art.14(8) of the implementing regulation.

Article 14

Voluntary insurance or optional continued insurance

3.358 1. Articles 11 to 13 shall not apply to voluntary insurance or to optional continued insurance unless, in respect of one of the branches referred to in Article 3(1), only a voluntary scheme of insurance exists in a Member State.

2. Where, by virtue of the legislation of a Member State, the person concerned is subject to compulsory insurance in that Member State, he may not be subject to a voluntary insurance scheme or an optional continued insurance scheme in another Member State. In all other cases in which, for a given branch, there is a choice between several voluntary insurance schemes or optional continued insurance schemes, the person concerned shall join only the scheme of his choice.

3. However, in respect of invalidity, old age and survivors' benefits, the person concerned may join the voluntary or optional continued insurance scheme of a Member State, even if he is compulsorily subject to the legislation of another Member State, provided that he has been subject, at some stage in his career, to the legislation of the first Member State because or as a consequence of an activity as an employed or self-employed person and if such overlapping is explicitly or implicitly allowed under the legislation of the first Member State.

[1 4. Where the legislation of a Member State makes admission to voluntary insurance or optional continued insurance conditional upon residence in that Member State or upon previous activity as an employed or self-employed person, art.5(b) shall apply only to persons who have been subject, at some earlier stage, to the legislation of that Member State on the basis of an activity as an employed or self-employed person.]

Corresponding Provision of Regulation 1408/71

Article 15.

Amendment

1. Regulation 988/2009 art.1 (May 1, 2010).

Article 15

[1 Contract staff] of the European Communities

3.359 [1 Contract staff] of the European Communities may opt to be subject to the legislation of the Member State in which they are employed, to the legislation of the Member State to which they were last subject or to the legislation of the Member State whose nationals they are, in respect of provisions other than those relating to family allowances, provided under the scheme applicable to such staff. This right of option, which may be exercised once only, shall take effect from the date of entry into employment.

AMENDMENT

1. Regulation 988/2009 art.1 (May 1, 2010).

RELEVANT PROVISION OF THE IMPLEMENTING REGULATION

Article 17.

Article 16

Exceptions to Articles 11 to 15

1. Two or more Member States, the competent authorities of these Member States or the bodies designated by these authorities may by common agreement provide for exceptions to Articles 11 to 15 in the interest of certain persons or categories of persons. 3.360

2. A person who receives a pension or pensions under the legislation of one or more Member States and who resides in another Member State may at his request be exempted from application of the legislation of the latter State provided that he is not subject to that legislation on account of pursuing an activity as an employed or self-employed person.

CORRESPONDING PROVISION OF REGULATION 1408/71

Article 17.

RELEVANT PROVISION OF THE IMPLEMENTING REGULATION

Article 18.

GENERAL NOTE

This provision was used in *Brusse* (101/83) [1984] E.C.R. 2223 to "rescue" a claimant from a long gap in his contribution record in the United Kingdom. The terms of the agreement covered a period before the United Kingdom was a Member State of the European Community but was expressly made under art.17 of Regulation 1408/71 in relation to the period from January 1, 1973 (when the United Kingdom acceded). The Luxembourg Court ruled that agreements under art.17 could be retrospective; the test was whether the agreement was in the interests of the worker concerned. 3.361

This approach was confirmed in *van Gestel* (C-454/93) [1995] E.C.R. I-1707. The scope of agreements under the provision is accordingly very wide, provided that the parties are satisfied that the terms of the agreement are in the interests of certain persons or categories of persons.

Title III

Special Provisions Concerning the Various Categories of Benefits

Chapter 1

Sickness, maternity and equivalent paternity benefits

General Note

3.362 The provisions on sickness benefits include the provision of benefits in kind (treatment in all its forms) and benefits in cash. Regulation 883/2004 recasts the provisions to make a greater separation in the provisions concerned with benefits in kind and benefits in cash. The law on benefits in kind is now very complex, and the rules in reg.883/2004 may not be entirely consistent with the interpretation of obligations flowing from provisions of the Treaty on the Functioning of the European Union. Benefits in kind are the responsibility of the Department of Health and are outside the scope of this work. The annotations to the provisions of this chapter of the regulation are accordingly concerned solely with benefits in cash.

In this area the concepts of residence and stay have particular importance, although that mostly arises in relation to benefits in kind: for example, where a person falls ill in a Member State where they are staying and needs medical treatment.

The provisions of this chapter make a distinction between those who are pensioners and others. But the regulation only defines the term "pension" non-exhaustively (in art.1(w)) not the term "pensioner". Though there is likely to be little difficulty in regarding those in receipt of an old-age pension within the material scope of the regulation, there is likely to be some difficulty in determining when receipt of other benefits qualifies the beneficiary as a "pensioner". For example, is someone in receipt of a long-term invalidity pension where the Member State operates a Type A invalidity pension (that is, one paid on fixed scales which are not tied to periods of insurance, though there may be a requirement for a minimum period of insurance), a pensioner?

The Department has issued two memos concerning the award of sickness benefits: Memo DMG 26/15 *Deciding the competent State to pay cash sickness benefits,* and Memo DMG 27/15 *Action to take once competency has been decided.* Both memos are dated November 2015.

Relevant Provisions of the Implementing Regulation

See generally, Ch.1 of Title III, though much of these provisions is about benefits in kind.

SECTION 1

INSURED PERSONS AND MEMBERS OF THEIR FAMILIES, EXCEPT PENSIONERS AND MEMBERS OF THEIR FAMILIES

Article 17

Residence in a Member State other than the competent Member State

An insured person or members of his family who reside in a Member State other than the competent Member State shall receive in the Member State of residence benefits in kind provided, on behalf of the competent institution, by the institution of the place of residence, in accordance with the provisions of the legislation it applies, as though they were insured under the said legislation. 3.363

CORRESPONDING PROVISION OF REGULATION 1408/71

Article 19.

GENERAL NOTE

Article 17 would appear to be contemplating a situation in which a person is resident other than in the competent state at the material time. It addresses the situation in which a person is, for example, working in one Member State (the competent state), but living in another Member State. This would seem to have been confirmed in *Keller* (C–145/03) [2005] E.C.R. I–2529, where in a situation where the claimant for benefits in kind was resident in the competent state declined to answer a question about the corresponding provision of Reg.1408/71, on the basis that art.22 of Reg.1408/71 (now art.19 of Reg.883/2004) applied to her situation. 3.364

See also commentary on *Lucy Stewart* (C–503/09) in the annotations to art.3.

Article 18

Stay in the competent Member State when residence is in another Member State—Special rules for the members of the families of frontier workers

1. Unless otherwise provided for by paragraph 2, the insured person and the members of his family referred to in Article 17 shall also be entitled to benefits in kind while staying in the competent Member State. The benefits in kind shall be provided by the competent institution and at its own expense, in accordance with the provisions of the legislation it applies, as though the persons concerned resided in that Member State. 3.365

[1 2. The members of the family of a frontier worker shall be entitled to benefits in kind during their stay in the competent Member State.

Where the competent Member State is listed in Annex III however, the members of the family of a frontier worker who reside in the same

Member State as the frontier worker shall be entitled to benefits in kind in the competent Member State only under the conditions laid down in Article 19(1).]

CORRESPONDING PROVISION OF REGULATION 1408/71

Article 20.

AMENDMENT

1. Regulation 988/2009 art.1 (May 1, 2010).

Article 19

Stay outside the competent Member State

3.366 1. Unless otherwise provided for by paragraph 2, an insured person and the members of his family staying in a Member State other than the competent Member State shall be entitled to the benefits in kind which become necessary on medical grounds during their stay, taking into account the nature of the benefits and the expected length of the stay. These benefits shall be provided on behalf of the competent institution by the institution of the place of stay, in accordance with the provisions of the legislation it applies, as though the persons concerned were insured under the said legislation.

2. The Administrative Commission shall establish a list of benefits in kind which, in order to be provided during a stay in another Member State, require for practical reasons a prior agreement between the person concerned and the institution providing the care.

CORRESPONDING PROVISION OF REGULATION 1408/71

Article 22.

RELEVANT DECISIONS OF THE ADMINISTRATIVE COMMISSION

Decision No.S3 of June 12, 2009 defining the benefits covered by Articles 19(1) and 27(1) of Regulation 883/2004 of the European Parliament and of the Council and Article 25(A)(3) of Regulation (EC) No 987/2009 of the European Parliament and of the Council [2010] OJ C106/40.

GENERAL NOTE

3.367 In *I v Health Service Executive* (C-255/13) Judgment of June 5, 2014, the Court ruled as follows:

> "Article 1(j) and (k) of Regulation (EC) No 883/2004 . . . must be interpreted as meaning that, for the purpose of Article 19(1) or Article 20(1) and (2) of that regulation, where a European Union national who was resident in one Member State suffers a sudden serious illness while on holiday in a second Member State and is compelled to remain in the latter State for 11 years as a result of that illness and the fact that specialist medical care is available close to the place where he lives, such a person must be regarded as 'staying' in the second Member State if the habitual centre of his interests is in the first Member State. It is for the national court to determine the habitual centre of such a person's interests by carrying out an assessment of all the relevant facts and taking into account that person's

intention, as may be discerned from those facts, the mere fact that that person has remained in the second Member State for a long time not being sufficient in itself alone for him to be regarded as residing in that Member State." (para.59).

Article 20

Travel with the purpose of receiving benefits in kind—Authorisation to receive appropriate treatment outside the Member State of residence

1. Unless otherwise provided for by this Regulation, an insured person travelling to another Member State with the purpose of receiving benefits in kind during the stay shall seek authorisation from the competent institution. **3.368**

2. An insured person who is authorised by the competent institution to go to another Member State with the purpose of receiving the treatment appropriate to his condition shall receive the benefits in kind provided, on behalf of the competent institution, by the institution of the place of stay, in accordance with the provisions of the legislation it applies, as though he were insured under the said legislation. The authorisation shall be accorded where the treatment in question is among the benefits provided for by the legislation in the Member State where the person concerned resides and where he cannot be given such treatment within a time-limit which is medically justifiable, taking into account his current state of health and the probable course of his illness.

3. Paragraphs 1 and 2 shall apply mutatis mutandis to the members of the family of an insured person.

4. If the members of the family of an insured person reside in a Member State other than the Member State in which the insured person resides, and this Member State has opted for reimbursement on the basis of fixed amounts, the cost of the benefits in kind referred to in paragraph 2 shall be borne by the institution of the place of residence of the members of the family. In this case, for the purposes of paragraph 1, the institution of the place of residence of the members of the family shall be considered to be the competent institution.

Corresponding Provision of Regulation 1408/71

Article 22.

Article 21

Cash benefits

1. An insured person and members of his family residing or staying in a Member State other than the competent Member State shall be entitled to cash benefits provided by the competent institution in accordance with the legislation it applies. By agreement between the competent institution and the institution of the place of residence or stay, such benefits may, however, be provided by the institution of the place of residence or stay at the expense of the competent institution in accordance with the legislation of the competent Member State. **3.369**

2. The competent institution of a Member State whose legislation stipulates that the calculation of cash benefits shall be based on average income or on an average contribution basis shall determine such average income or average contribution basis exclusively by reference to the incomes confirmed as having been paid, or contribution bases applied, during the periods completed under the said legislation.

3. The competent institution of a Member State whose legislation provides that the calculation of cash benefits shall be based on standard income shall take into account exclusively the standard income or, where appropriate, the average of standard incomes for the periods completed under the said legislation.

4. Paragraphs 2 and 3 shall apply mutatis mutandis to cases where the legislation applied by the competent institution lays down a specific reference period which corresponds in the case in question either wholly or partly to the periods which the person concerned has completed under the legislation of one or more other Member States.

Corresponding Provision of Regulation 1408/71

Article 19.

Relevant Provisions of the Implementing Regulation

Articles 27–29.

General Note

3.370 Where the person claiming a sickness benefit has been employed or self-employed and falls ill in a Member State while not working, then the competent state will be the Member State in which that person was last insured as an employed or self-employed person.

The determination of the applicable legislation in relation to entitlement to sickness benefits was considered by the Luxembourg Court in *Coppola v Insurance Officer* (150/82) [1983] E.C.R. 43. The Court ruled:

> "11. By virtue of [art.13(2)(a) of reg.1408/71], and in the absence of contrary provisions referring to the particular type of benefit in question, only the legislation of the State in whose territory the worker is employed is therefore applicable. Although that provision does not expressly mention the case of a worker who is not employed when he seeks sickness benefit, it is appropriate to interpret it as meaning that, where necessary, it refers to the legislation of the State in whose territory the worker was last employed.
>
> 12. It follows from the fact that, by virtue of Article 13(2)(a), the legislation of only one Member State is applicable, that the institution or institutions of a single Member State, namely the State in whose territory the worker is or was last employed, must be considered competent for the purpose of the application of Article 18(1) . . ."

Article 22

Pension claimants

3.371 1. An insured person who, on making a claim for a pension, or during the investigation thereof, ceases to be entitled to benefits in kind under the legislation of the Member State last competent, shall remain entitled to benefits in kind under the legislation of the Member State in which he resides, provided that the pension claimant satisfies the insurance conditions of the legislation of the Member State referred to in paragraph 2. The right to benefits in kind in the Member State of residence shall also apply to the members of the family of the pension claimant.

2. The benefits in kind shall be chargeable to the institution of the Member State which, in the event of a pension being awarded, would become competent under Articles 23 to 25.

CORRESPONDING PROVISION OF REGULATION 1408/71

Article 26.

SECTION 2

PENSIONERS AND MEMBERS OF THEIR FAMILIES

Article 23

Right to benefits in kind under the legislation of the Member State of residence

A person who receives a pension or pensions under the legislation of two or more Member States, of which one is the Member State of residence, and who is entitled to benefits in kind under the legislation of that Member State, shall, with the members of his family, receive such benefits in kind from and at the expense of the institution of the place of residence, as though he were a pensioner whose pension was payable solely under the legislation of that Member State. 3.372

CORRESPONDING PROVISION OF REGULATION 1408/71

Article 27.

GENERAL NOTE

Regulation 883/2004 (like its predecessor Reg.1408/71) does not define the term pensioner, but does in art.1(w) define "pension". While plainly a person in receipt of an old-age pension is a pensioner for the purposes of the regulation, what about those in receipt of other benefits on a long-term basis? The issue was addressed in *JS v SSWP (DLA)* [2012] AACR 7 in relation to Reg.1408/71 and it was suggested that pensions would include payments of incapacity benefit, employment and support allowance, and disability living allowance. In *KS v SSWP (DLA)* [2014] UKUT 19 (AAC) *JS* was followed in deciding that a person in receipt of a severe disablement allowance would also be a pensioner. The position is likely to be similar under the provisions of Reg.883/2004. 3.373

The position of pensioners is rather different from those who are still economically active. In essence, they carry the protection of the state taking their pension with them when they move to another country. This has given rise to a number of appeals in the United Kingdom where a pensioner resident in the United Kingdom claims a disability living allowance here.

This is illustrated in slightly different circumstances in *SL v SSWP (DLA)* [2014]

UKUT 108 (AAC). The appellant was an Irish national who had spent time working in both the United Kingdom and Ireland. He was in receipt of state retirement pensions from both the United Kingdom and Ireland. He had moved to Ireland and was at the material time living there. He had been in receipt of a disability living allowance in the United Kingdom which had been stopped when he moved to Ireland. He sought to resurrect his entitlement following the determination by the Court of Justice that the care component of a disability living allowance is a cash sickness benefit. His entitlement was considered under both Regulation 1408/71 and Regulation 883/2004. Since the appellant was a pensioner and was resident in Ireland, Ireland was the competent state in relation to the payment of cash sickness benefits through a combination of arts 21, 23, and 29. This meant that he was not entitled to reinstatement of his disability living allowance award. Note the provisions of art.6 of Regulation 987/2009 for resolving a difference of views about the determination of the applicable legislation or about which institution should provide benefits. These operate in a way which protects the claimant from delays inherent in resolving the difference of views by requiring the provisional application of the legislation of one of the Member States concerned.

Article 24

No right to benefits in kind under the legislation of the Member State of residence

3.374 1. A person who receives a pension or pensions under the legislation of one or more Member States and who is not entitled to benefits in kind under the legislation of the Member State of residence shall nevertheless receive such benefits for himself and the members of his family, insofar as he would be entitled thereto under the legislation of the Member State or of at least one of the Member States competent in respect of his pensions, if he resided in that Member State. The benefits in kind shall be provided at the expense of the institution referred to in paragraph 2 by the institution of the place of residence, as though the person concerned were entitled to a pension and benefits in kind under the legislation of that Member State.

2. In the cases covered by paragraph 1, the cost of benefits in kind shall be borne by the institution as determined in accordance with the following rules:

(a) where the pensioner is entitled to benefits in kind under the legislation of a single Member State, the cost shall be borne by the competent institution of that Member State;

(b) where the pensioner is entitled to benefits in kind under the legislation of two or more Member States, the cost thereof shall be borne by the competent institution of the Member State to whose legislation the person has been subject for the longest period of time; should the application of this rule result in several institutions being responsible for the cost of benefits, the cost shall be borne by the institution applying the legislation to which the pensioner was last subject.

Corresponding Provision of Regulation 1408/71

Article 28.

General note

3.375 See also commentary on *Lucy Stewart* (C–503/09) in the annotations to art.3.

Helder and Farrington v College voor zorgverzekeringen (C-321/12) Judgment of October 10, 2013, concerns the interpretation of art.28(2)(b) of Regulation 1408/71 which corresponds to the provisions of art.24(2)(b) of Regulation 883/2004. The

Court ruled that art.28(2)(b) should be interpreted as meaning that the "legislation" to which the pensioner has been subject for the longest period of time, for the purposes of that provision, refers to the legislation concerning pensions.

Article 25

Pensions under the legislation of one or more Member States other than the Member State of residence, where there is a right to benefits in kind in the latter Member State

Where the person receiving a pension or pensions under the legislation of one or more Member States resides in a Member State under whose legislation the right to receive benefits in kind is not subject to conditions of insurance, or of activity as an employed or self-employed person, and no pension is received from that Member State, the cost of benefits in kind provided to him and to members of his family shall be borne by the institution of one of the Member States competent in respect of his pensions determined in accordance with Article 24(2), to the extent that the pensioner and the members of his family would be entitled to such benefits if they resided in that Member State. **3.376**

Corresponding Provision of Regulation 1408/71

Article 28a.

Article 26

Residence of members of the family in a Member State other than the one in which the pensioner resides

Members of the family of a person receiving a pension or pensions under the legislation of one or more Member States who reside in a Member State other than the one in which the pensioner resides shall be entitled to receive benefits in kind from the institution of the place of their residence in accordance with the provisions of the legislation it applies, insofar as the pensioner is entitled to benefits in kind under the legislation of a Member State. The costs shall be borne by the competent institution responsible for the costs of the benefits in kind provided to the pensioner in his Member State of residence. **3.377**

Corresponding Provision of Regulation 1408/71

Article 29.

Article 27

Stay of the pensioner or the members of his family in a Member State other than the Member State in which they reside—Stay in the competent Member State—Authorisation for appropriate treatment outside the Member State of residence

1. Article 19 shall apply mutatis mutandis to a person receiving a **3.378**

pension or pensions under the legislation of one or more Member States and entitled to benefits in kind under the legislation of one of the Member States which provide his pension(s) or to the members of his family who are staying in a Member State other than the one in which they reside.

2. Article 18(1) shall apply mutatis mutandis to the persons described in paragraph 1 when they stay in the Member State in which is situated the competent institution responsible for the cost of the benefits in kind provided to the pensioner in his Member State of residence and the said Member State has opted for this and is listed in Annex IV.

3. Article 20 shall apply mutatis mutandis to a pensioner and/or the members of his family who are staying in a Member State other than the one in which they reside with the purpose of receiving there the treatment appropriate to their condition.

4. Unless otherwise provided for by paragraph 5, the cost of the benefits in kind referred to in paragraphs 1 to 3 shall be borne by the competent institution responsible for the cost of benefits in kind provided to the pensioner in his Member State of residence.

5. The cost of the benefits in kind referred to in paragraph 3 shall be borne by the institution of the place of residence of the pensioner or of the members of his family, if these persons reside in a Member State which has opted for reimbursement on the basis of fixed amounts. In these cases, for the purposes of paragraph 3, the institution of the place of residence of the pensioner or of the members of his family shall be considered to be the competent institution.

CORRESPONDING PROVISION OF REGULATION 1408/71

Article 31.

RELEVANT DECISIONS OF THE ADMINISTRATIVE COMMISSION

Decision No.S3 of June 12, 2009 defining the benefits covered by Articles 19(1) and 27(1) of Regulation 883/2004 of the European Parliament and of the Council and Article 25(A)(3) of Regulation (EC) No 987/2009 of the European Parliament and of the Council [2010] OJ C106/40.

Article 28

Special rules for retired frontier workers

3.379 [[1] A frontier worker who has retired because of old-age or invalidity is entitled in the event of sickness to continue to receive benefits in kind in the Member State where he/she last pursued his/her activity as an employed or self-employed person, in so far as this is a continuation of treatment which began in that Member State. "Continuation of treatment" means the continued investigation, diagnosis and treatment of an illness for its entire duration.

The first subparagraph shall apply *mutatis mutandis* to the members of the family of the former frontier worker unless the Member State where the frontier worker last pursued his/her activity is listed in Annex III.]

2. A pensioner who, in the five years preceding the effective date of an old-age or invalidity pension has been pursuing an activity as an employed or self-employed person for at least two years as a frontier worker shall be entitled to benefits in kind in the Member State in which he pursued such an activity as a frontier worker, if this Member State and the Member State

in which the competent institution responsible for the costs of the benefits in kind provided to the pensioner in his Member State of residence is situated have opted for this and are both listed in Annex V.

3. Paragraph 2 shall apply mutatis mutandis to the members of the family of a former frontier worker or his survivors if, during the periods referred to in paragraph 2, they were entitled to benefits in kind under Article 18(2), even if the frontier worker died before his pension commenced, provided he had been pursuing an activity as an employed or self-employed person as a frontier worker for at least two years in the five years preceding his death.

4. Paragraphs 2 and 3 shall be applicable until the person concerned becomes subject to the legislation of a Member State on the basis of an activity as an employed or self-employed person.

5. The cost of the benefits in kind referred to in paragraphs 1 to 3 shall be borne by the competent institution responsible for the cost of benefits in kind provided to the pensioner or to his survivors in their respective Member States of residence.

Relevant Provision of the Implementing Regulation

Article 29.

Amendment

1. Regulation 988/2009 art.1 (May 1, 2010).

Article 29

Cash benefits for pensioners

1. Cash benefits shall be paid to a person receiving a pension or pensions under the legislation of one or more Member States by the competent institution of the Member State in which is situated the competent institution responsible for the cost of benefits in kind provided to the pensioner in his Member State of residence. Article 21 shall apply mutatis mutandis. **3.380**

2. Paragraph 1 shall also apply to the members of a pensioner's family.

Corresponding Provision of Regulation 1408/71

Article 28.

General note

See annotation to art.23. **3.381**

Article 30

Contributions by pensioners

1. The institution of a Member State which is responsible under the legislation it applies for making deductions in respect of contributions for sickness, maternity and equivalent paternity benefits, may request and recover such deductions, calculated in accordance with the legislation it applies, only to the extent that the cost of the benefits under Articles 23 to 26 is to be borne by an institution of the said Member State. **3.382**

2. Where, in the cases referred to in Article 25, the acquisition of sickness, maternity and equivalent paternity benefits is subject to the payment of contributions or similar payments under the legislation of a Member State in which the pensioner concerned resides, these contributions shall not be payable by virtue of such residence.

CORRESPONDING PROVISION OF REGULATION 1408/71

Article 33.

RELEVANT PROVISION OF THE IMPLEMENTING REGULATION

Article 30.

GENERAL NOTE

3.383 In *Nikula* (C-50/05) [2006] E.C.R. I-7029, the Luxembourg Court ruled that art.33(1) of Reg.1408/71 does not preclude the inclusion, in the basis of calculation in determining sickness insurance contributions in the Member State of residence, of pensions paid by the institutions of another Member State, provided that the sickness insurance contributions do not exceed the amount of pension paid in then Member State of residence. But art.39 EC (now art.45 TFEU) does preclude the amount of pensions received from institutions of another Member State being taken into account if contributions have already been paid in the other state out of the income from work received in that state. It is for the person concerned to prove that the earlier contributions were in fact paid.

SECTION 3

COMMON PROVISIONS

Article 31

General provision

3.384 Articles 23 to 30 shall not apply to a pensioner or the members of his family who are entitled to benefits under the legislation of a Member State on the basis of an activity as an employed or self-employed person. In such a case, the person concerned shall be subject, for the purposes of this Chapter, to Articles 17 to 21.

CORRESPONDING PROVISION OF REGULATION 1408/71

Article 34.

Article 32

Prioritising of the right to benefits in kind—Special rule for the right of members of the family to benefits in the Member State of residence

3.385 1. An independent right to benefits in kind based on the legislation of a Member State or on this Chapter shall take priority over a derivative right to benefits for members of a family. A derivative right to benefits in kind shall, however, take priority over independent rights, where the independent right in the Member State of residence exists directly and solely on the basis of the residence of the person concerned in that Member State.

2. Where the members of the family of an insured person reside in a Member State under whose legislation the right to benefits in kind is not subject to conditions of insurance or activity as an employed or self-employed person, benefits in kind shall be provided at the expense of the competent institution in the Member State in which they reside, if the spouse or the person caring for the children of the insured person pursues an activity as an employed or self-employed person in the said Member State or receives a pension from that Member State on the basis of an activity as an employed or self-employed person.

Article 33

Substantial benefits in kind

1. An insured person or a member of his family who has had a right to a prosthesis, a major appliance or other substantial benefits in kind recognised by the institution of a Member State, before he became insured under the legislation applied by the institution of another Member State, shall receive such benefits at the expense of the first institution, even if they are awarded after the said person has already become insured under the legislation applied by the second institution. **3.386**

2. The Administrative Commission shall draw up the list of benefits covered by paragraph 1.

Corresponding Provision of Regulation 1408/71

Article 24.

Article 34

Overlapping of long-term care benefits

1. If a recipient of long-term care benefits in cash, which have to be treated as sickness benefits and are therefore provided by the Member State competent for cash benefits under Articles 21 or 29, is, at the same time and under this Chapter, entitled to claim benefits in kind intended for the same purpose from the institution of the place of residence or stay in another Member State, and an institution in the first Member State is also required to reimburse the cost of these benefits in kind under Article 35, the general provision on prevention of overlapping of benefits laid down in Article 10 shall be applicable, with the following restriction only: if the person concerned claims and receives the benefit in kind, the amount of the benefit in cash shall be reduced by the amount of the benefit in kind which is or could be claimed from the institution of the first Member State required to reimburse the cost. **3.387**

2. The Administrative Commission shall draw up the list of the cash benefits and benefits in kind covered by paragraph 1.

3. Two or more Member States, or their competent authorities, may agree on other or supplementary measures which shall not be less advantageous for the persons concerned than the principles laid down in paragraph 1.

RELEVANT PROVISION OF THE IMPLEMENTING REGULATION

Article 31.

GENERAL NOTE

3.388 The rationale for this provision can be found in Recital (24) of the Preamble.

The approach adopted by the Court of Justice in looking to substance rather than form has meant that the category of benefits which are classified as sickness benefits has extended beyond those benefits which are intended to cover the loss of income consequent upon a period of illness. Sickness benefits now include benefits intended to improve the state of health and life of persons reliant on care. This can give rise to difficulties in relation to overlapping of benefits, as was illustrated in the *da Silva Martins* (C–388/09) Judgment of June 30, 2011, [2011] ECR 5737 which involved the interplay between benefits in Germany and in Portugal.

Article 35

Reimbursements between institutions

3.389 1. The benefits in kind provided by the institution of a Member State on behalf of the institution of another Member State under this Chapter shall give rise to full reimbursement.

2. The reimbursements referred to in paragraph 1 shall be determined and effected in accordance with the arrangements set out in the Implementing Regulation, either on production of proof of actual expenditure, or on the basis of fixed amounts for Member States the legal or administrative structures of which are such that the use of reimbursement on the basis of actual expenditure is not appropriate.

3. Two or more Member States, and their competent authorities, may provide for other methods of reimbursement or waive all reimbursement between the institutions coming under their jurisdiction.

CORRESPONDING PROVISION OF REGULATION 1408/71

Article 36.

RELEVANT PROVISIONS OF THE IMPLEMENTING REGULATION

Chapter 1 of Title IV.

Chapter 2

Benefits in Respect of Accidents at Work and Occupational Diseases

General Note

This chapter contains provisions covering accidents at work and occupational diseases. Though these provisions (and their predecessors) are detailed and substantial, they appear to give rise to fewer difficulties than certain other types of benefit. This may, in part, be because Member States do not make entitlement to benefits for accidents at work and occupational diseases conditional upon the completion of particular periods of insurance. So, the provisions of this chapter do not need to deal with rules of aggregation. **3.390**

Under Title II the competent state is normally the state in which the claimant is working. Chapter 2 makes modifications to that rule. Article 36, reflecting the approach adopted in relation to sickness benefits, provides that persons habitually resident in a country other than that in which they work are to receive benefits in the State in which they reside. The distinction familiar from the sickness benefit rules between benefits in kind and cash benefits is repeated.

Benefits in kind are provided on behalf of the competent state in accordance with the legislation of the country of residence as if the beneficiary were insured there. They are re-imbursed by the competent state. Cash benefits are, however, provided by the competent institution in accordance with the legislation of the competent state.

It is in the nature of some occupational diseases that they develop as a result of prolonged exposure to a particular environment. Article 38 deals with situations where the claimant has been exposed to the same risk in Member States. In such cases, the starting point is that benefits are to be awarded exclusively under the legislation of the last of those Member States whose conditions of entitlement are satisfied. So, if a claimant does not meet the conditions of entitlement in the last Member State, that country is required to forward to application to the next Member State in line to see whether the conditions of entitlement are met there. **3.391**

Where there is a subsequent aggravation of the injury or disease, little difficulty arises if the person has not been engaged in an occupation likely to cause aggravation of the disease in another country. The first country continues to have jurisdiction over the matter: art.39(a). But where there has been some engagement in an occupation likely to cause an aggravation in another country, the first country continues to be liable for the benefits under its own legislation for the disease ignoring the aggravation, while the second country is required to pay a supplement which is the difference between the amount it would have awarded if the disease had first occurred under its own legislation and the amount of benefit to which there is entitlement under its own legislation having regard to the aggravation: art.39(b).

The two awards from different countries do not overlap: art.39(c).

Article 36

Right to benefits in kind and in cash

[1 1. Without prejudice to any more favourable provisions in paragraphs 2 and 2a of this Article, Articles 17, 18(1),19(1) and 20(1) shall also apply to benefits relating to accidents at work or occupational diseases]. **3.392**

2. A person who has sustained an accident at work or has contracted

an occupational disease and who resides or stays in a Member State other than the competent Member State shall be entitled to the special benefits in kind of the scheme covering accidents at work and occupational diseases provided, on behalf of the competent institution, by the institution of the place of residence or stay in accordance with the legislation which it applies, as though he were insured under the said legislation.

[2 2a. The competent institution may not refuse to grant the authorisation provided for in Article 20(1) to a person who has sustained an accident at work or who has contracted an occupational disease and who is entitled to benefits chargeable to that institution, where the treatment appropriate to his/her condition cannot be given in the Member State in which he/she resides within a time-limit which is medically justifiable, taking into account his/her current state of health and the probable course of the illness.]

3. Article 21 shall also apply to benefits falling within this Chapter.

CORRESPONDING PROVISION OF REGULATION 1408/71

Article 52.

RELEVANT PROVISIONS OF THE IMPLEMENTING REGULATION

Articles 33–35.

AMENDMENTS

1. Regulation 998/2009 art.1 (May 1, 2010).
2. Regulation 465/2012 [2012] OJ L149/4 art.1(7) (June 28, 2012).

Article 37

Costs of transport

3.393 1. The competent institution of a Member State whose legislation provides for meeting the costs of transporting a person who has sustained an accident at work or is suffering from an occupational disease, either to his place of residence or to a hospital, shall meet such costs to the corresponding place in another Member State where the person resides, provided that that institution gives prior authorisation for such transport, duly taking into account the reasons justifying it. Such authorisation shall not be required in the case of a frontier worker.

2. The competent institution of a Member State whose legislation provides for meeting the costs of transporting the body of a person killed in an accident at work to the place of burial shall, in accordance with the legislation it applies, meet such costs to the corresponding place in another Member State where the person was residing at the time of the accident.

CORRESPONDING PROVISION OF REGULATION 1408/71

Article 59.

Article 38

Benefits for an occupational disease where the person suffering from such a disease has been exposed to the same risk in several Member States

When a person who has contracted an occupational disease has, under the legislation of two or more Member States, pursued an activity which by its nature is likely to cause the said disease, the benefits that he or his survivors may claim shall be provided exclusively under the legislation of the last of those States whose conditions are satisfied. **3.394**

Corresponding Provision of Regulation 1408/71

Article 57.

Relevant Provisions of the Implementing Regulation

Articles 36 and 37.

General note

SSWP v OF (by MF) (II) [2011] UKUT 448 (AAC) is a decision concerning art.57(1) of Reg.1408/71, which is drafted in identical terms to art.38. The claimant had worked in Ireland and the United Kingdom. He had contracted lung cancer. The Secretary of State took the view that the competent state was Ireland because that was where he had last worked. The Judge established in evidence that the claimant could not succeed in any claim in Ireland, since lung cancer was not a prescribed disease under the Irish industrial injuries scheme. Furthermore the First-tier Tribunal had erred in law in determining that the claim should be dealt with under United Kingdom law on the grounds that the level of exposure to asbestos had been far more significant while the claimant was working in the United Kingdom rather than in Ireland. Article 57(1)—and it would follow also art.38—do not require any examination of the relative likelihood of exposure to asbestos, but simply of whether the claimant pursued in more than one Member State an activity which by its nature is likely to cause the industrial disease. Since the claimant could not satisfy the conditions of entitlement in Ireland, the legislation of the last of the Member States whose conditions are satisfied is the United Kingdom, which was accordingly the competent State to determine this claim. **3.395**

Article 39

Aggravation of an occupational disease

In the event of aggravation of an occupational disease for which a person suffering from such a disease has received or is receiving benefits under the legislation of a Member State, the following rules shall apply: **3.396**

(a) if the person concerned, while in receipt of benefits, has not pursued, under the legislation of another Member State, an activity as an employed or self-employed person likely to cause or aggravate the disease in question, the competent institution of the first Member State shall bear the cost of the benefits under the provisions of the legislation which it applies, taking into account the aggravation;

(b) if the person concerned, while in receipt of benefits, has pursued such an activity under the legislation of another Member State, the competent institution of the first Member State shall bear the cost of the benefits under the legislation it applies without taking the aggravation into account. The competent institution of the second Member State shall grant a supplement to the person concerned, the amount of which shall be equal to the difference between the amount of benefits due after the aggravation and the amount which would have been due prior to the aggravation under the legislation it applies, if the disease in question had occurred under the legislation of that Member State;

(c) the rules concerning reduction, suspension or withdrawal laid down by the legislation of a Member State shall not be invoked against persons receiving benefits provided by institutions of two Member States in accordance with subparagraph (b).

CORRESPONDING PROVISION OF REGULATION 1408/71

Article 60.

RELEVANT PROVISION OF THE IMPLEMENTING REGULATION

Article 38.

Article 40

Rules for taking into account the special features of certain legislation

3.397 1. If there is no insurance against accidents at work or occupational diseases in the Member State in which the person concerned resides or stays, or if such insurance exists but there is no institution responsible for providing benefits in kind, those benefits shall be provided by the institution of the place of residence or stay responsible for providing benefits in kind in the event of sickness.

2. If there is no insurance against accidents at work or occupational diseases in the competent Member State, the provisions of this Chapter concerning benefits in kind shall nevertheless be applied to a person who is entitled to those benefits in the event of sickness, maternity or equivalent paternity under the legislation of that Member State if that person sustains an accident at work or suffers from an occupational disease during a residence or stay in another Member State. Costs shall be borne by the institution which is competent for the benefits in kind under the legislation of the competent Member State.

3. Article 5 shall apply to the competent institution in a Member State as regards the equivalence of accidents at work and occupational diseases which either have occurred or have been confirmed subsequently under the legislation of another Member State when assessing the degree of incapacity, the right to benefits or the amount thereof, on condition that:

(a) no compensation is due in respect of an accident at work or an occupational disease which had occurred or had been confirmed previously under the legislation it applies; and

(b) no compensation is due in respect of an accident at work or an occupational disease which had occurred or had been confirmed subsequently, under the legislation of the other Member State under which the accident at work or the occupational disease had occurred or been confirmed.

Article 40

CORRESPONDING PROVISION OF REGULATION 1408/71

Article 61.

Article 41

Reimbursements between institutions

1. Article 35 shall also apply to benefits falling within this Chapter, and reimbursement shall be made on the basis of actual costs. 3.398

2. Two or more Member States, or their competent authorities, may provide for other methods of reimbursement or waive all reimbursement between the institutions under their jurisdiction.

CORRESPONDING PROVISION OF REGULATION 1408/71

Article 63.

RELEVANT PROVISIONS OF THE IMPLEMENTING REGULATION

Chapter 1 of Title IV.

CHAPTER 3

DEATH GRANTS

Article 42

Right to grants where death occurs in, or where the person entitled resides in, a Member State other than the competent Member State

1. When an insured person or a member of his family dies in a Member State other than the competent Member State, the death shall be deemed to have occurred in the competent Member State. 3.399

2. The competent institution shall be obliged to provide death grants payable under the legislation it applies, even if the person entitled resides in a Member State other than the competent Member State.

3. Paragraphs 1 and 2 shall also apply when the death is the result of an accident at work or an occupational disease.

CORRESPONDING PROVISION OF REGULATION 1408/71

Article 65.

RELEVANT PROVISION OF THE IMPLEMENTING REGULATION

Article 42.

Article 43

Provision of benefits in the event of the death of a pensioner

3.400 1. In the event of the death of a pensioner who was entitled to a pension under the legislation of one Member State, or to pensions under the legislations of two or more Member States, when that pensioner was residing in a Member State other than that of the institution responsible for the cost of benefits in kind provided under Articles 24 and 25, the death grants payable under the legislation administered by that institution shall be provided at its own expense as though the pensioner had been residing at the time of his death in the Member State in which that institution is situated.

2. Paragraph 1 shall apply mutatis mutandis to the members of the family of a pensioner.

Corresponding Provision of Regulation 1408/71

Article 66.

Relevant Provision of the Implementing Regulation

Article 42.

Chapter 4

Invalidity Benefits

General Note

3.401 Whereas the regulation adopts an approach to short-term benefits which results generally in one Member State being responsible for the payment of such benefits, such an approach is applied less easily to long-term benefits, since, under such a system, a Member State may become liable to pay a long-term benefit for a substantial period without having received contributions to support that benefit.

The general approach to long-term benefits is that each Member State pays its proportionate share of the pension. The position becomes more complicated in the case of invalidity pensions, since the Member States take two fundamentally different approaches to invalidity benefits.

Some Member States operate invalidity benefits in much the same way as they operate old age benefits. These are known as Type B schemes.

3.402 Other Member States have schemes under which invalidity benefit is paid on fixed scales (which may be related to the level of previous earnings) which are not tied to periods of insurance, though there may be a requirement for a minimum period of insurance. These schemes are known as Type A schemes.

The United Kingdom scheme is a Type A scheme. Co-ordination of Type A and Type B schemes presents particular difficulties. The effect of the provisions of the Regulation can be summarised as follows:

Article 44

1. Claimant insured in a single country.	Entitled to invalidity benefits calculated in accordance with the legislation of that country.
2. Claimant insured in more than one country where the amount of invalidity benefit is determined by reference to the length of insurance.	Entitled to invalidity benefits from each country in accordance with the periods of insurance. The calculation is as for old-age pensions.
3. Claimant insured in more than one country where the amount of the invalidity benefit is independent of the length of insurance periods.	Entitled to invalidity benefits from the country in which the claimant became an invalid (even if this is lower than the benefits paid in any of the other countries where the claimant has been insured).
4. Claimant first insured in a country where the amount of the invalidity benefit depends on the length of insurance periods and then in a country where the amount of invalidity benefit is independent of the length of insurance periods.	Entitled to invalidity benefit from the first country in accordance with the periods of insurance, and an invalidity benefit from the second country which may be reduced to take account of the benefit received from the first country.
5. Claimant first insured in a country where the amount of the pension is independent of the length of in insurance periods and then in a country where the amount of invalidity. Benefit depends on the length of insurance periods.	Entitled to invalidity benefit from the first country and an invalidity benefit from the second country accordance with the periods of insurance.

Article 44

Persons subject only to type A legislation

1. For the purposes of this Chapter, "type A legislation" means any legislation under which the amount of invalidity benefits is independent of the duration of the periods of insurance or residence and which is expressly included by the competent Member State in Annex VI, and "type B legislation" means any other legislation. 3.403

2. A person who has been successively or alternately subject to the legislation of two or more Member States and who has completed periods of insurance or residence exclusively under type A legislations shall be entitled to benefits only from the institution of the Member State whose legislation was applicable at the time when the incapacity for work followed by invalidity occurred, taking into account, where appropriate, Article 45, and shall receive such benefits in accordance with that legislation.

3. A person who is not entitled to benefits under paragraph 2 shall receive the benefits to which he is still entitled under the legislation of another Member State, taking into account, where appropriate, Article 45.

4. If the legislation referred to in paragraph 2 or 3 contains rules for the reduction, suspension or withdrawal of invalidity benefits in the case of overlapping with other income or with benefits of a different kind within the meaning of Article 53(2), Articles 53(3) and 55(3) shall apply mutatis mutandis.

CORRESPONDING PROVISION OF REGULATION 1408/71

Article 37.

RELEVANT PROVISIONS OF THE IMPLEMENTING REGULATION

Articles 45–47.

Article 45

Special provisions on aggregation of periods

3.404 The competent institution of a Member State whose legislation makes the acquisition, retention or recovery of the right to benefits conditional upon the completion of periods of insurance or residence shall, where necessary, apply Article 51(1) mutatis mutandis.

CORRESPONDING PROVISION OF REGULATION 1408/71

Article 38.

Article 46

Persons subject either only to type B legislation or to type A and B legislation

3.405 1. A person who has been successively or alternately subject to the legislation of two or more Member States, of which at least one is not a type A legislation, shall be entitled to benefits under Chapter 5, which shall apply mutatis mutandis taking into account paragraph 3.

2. However, if the person concerned has been previously subject to a type B legislation and suffers incapacity for work leading to invalidity while subject to a type A legislation, he shall receive benefits in accordance with Article 44, provided that:

— he satisfies the conditions of that legislation exclusively or of others of the same type, taking into account, where appropriate, Article 45, but without having recourse to periods of insurance or residence completed under a type B legislation, and

— he does not assert any claims to old-age benefits, taking into account Article 50(1).

3. A decision taken by an institution of a Member State concerning the degree of invalidity of a claimant shall be binding on the institution of any other Member State concerned, provided that the concordance between the legislation of these Member States on conditions relating to the degree of invalidity is acknowledged in Annex VII.

CORRESPONDING PROVISION OF REGULATION 1408/71

Article 40.

Article 46

RELEVANT PROVISION OF THE IMPLEMENTING REGULATION

Article 49.

GENERAL NOTE

In *Leyman v INAMI* (C-3/08) [2009] E.C.R. I-9085, the Luxembourg Court ruled: 3.406

> "Article 39 EC must be interpreted as precluding application by the competent authorities of a Member State of national legislation which, in accordance with Article 40(3)(b) of Regulation (EEC) No 1408/71 . . . , makes acquisition of the right to invalidity benefits subject to the condition that a period of primary incapacity of one year has elapsed, where such application has the result that a migrant worker has paid into the social security scheme of that Member State contributions on which there is no return and is therefore at a disadvantage by comparison with a non-migrant worker."

Article 47

Aggravation of invalidity

1. In the case of aggravation of an invalidity for which a person is receiving benefits under the legislation of one or more Member States, the following provisions shall apply, taking the aggravation into account: 3.407

(a) the benefits shall be provided in accordance with Chapter 5, applied mutatis mutandis;

(b) however, where the person concerned has been subject to two or more type A legislations and since receiving benefit has not been subject to the legislation of another Member State, the benefit shall be provided in accordance with Article 44(2).

2. If the total amount of the benefit or benefits payable under paragraph 1 is lower than the amount of the benefit which the person concerned was receiving at the expense of the institution previously competent for payment, that institution shall pay him a supplement equal to the difference between the two amounts.

3. If the person concerned is not entitled to benefits at the expense of an institution of another Member State, the competent institution of the Member State previously competent shall provide the benefits in accordance with the legislation it applies, taking into account the aggravation and, where appropriate, Article 45.

CORRESPONDING PROVISION OF REGULATION 1408/71

Article 41.

Article 48

Conversion of invalidity benefits into old-age benefits

1. Invalidity benefits shall be converted into old-age benefits, where appropriate, under the conditions laid down by the legislation or 3.408

legislations under which they are provided and in accordance with Chapter 5.

2. Where a person receiving invalidity benefits can establish a claim to old-age benefits under the legislation of one or more other Member States, in accordance with Article 50, any institution which is responsible for providing invalidity benefits under the legislation of a Member State shall continue to provide such a person with the invalidity benefits to which he is entitled under the legislation it applies until paragraph 1 becomes applicable in respect of that institution, or otherwise for as long as the person concerned satisfies the conditions for such benefits.

3. Where invalidity benefits provided under the legislation of a Member State, in accordance with Article 44, are converted into old-age benefits and where the person concerned does not yet satisfy the conditions laid down by the legislation of one or more of the other Member States for receiving those benefits, the person concerned shall receive, from that or those Member States, invalidity benefits from the date of the conversion.

Those invalidity benefits shall be provided in accordance with Chapter 5 as if that Chapter had been applicable at the time when the incapacity for work leading to invalidity occurred, until the person concerned satisfies the qualifying conditions for old-age benefit laid down by the national legislations concerned or, where such conversion is not provided for, for as long as he is entitled to invalidity benefits under the latter legislation or legislations.

4. The invalidity benefits provided under Article 44 shall be recalculated in accordance with Chapter 5 as soon as the beneficiary satisfies the qualifying conditions for invalidity benefits laid down by a type B legislation, or as soon as he receives old-age benefits under the legislation of another Member State.

Corresponding Provisions of Regulation 1408/71

Articles 43 and 51.

Article 49

Special provisions for civil servants

3.409 Articles 6, 44, 46, 47 and 48 and Article 60(2) and (3) shall apply mutatis mutandis to persons covered by a special scheme for civil servants.

Corresponding Provision of Regulation 1408/71

Article 43a.

Chapter 5

Old-Age and Survivors' Pensions

Article 50

General provisions

1. All the competent institutions shall determine entitlement to benefit, under all the legislations of the Member States to which the person concerned has been subject, when a request for award has been submitted, unless the person concerned expressly requests deferment of the award of old-age benefits under the legislation of one or more Member States. 3.410

2. If at a given moment the person concerned does not satisfy, or no longer satisfies, the conditions laid down by all the legislations of the Member States to which he has been subject, the institutions applying legislation the conditions of which have been satisfied shall not take into account, when performing the calculation in accordance with Article 52(1) (a) or (b), the periods completed under the legislations the conditions of which have not been satisfied, or are no longer satisfied, where this gives rise to a lower amount of benefit.

3. Paragraph 2 shall apply mutatis mutandis when the person concerned has expressly requested deferment of the award of old-age benefits.

4. A new calculation shall be performed automatically as and when the conditions to be fulfilled under the other legislations are satisfied or when a person requests the award of an old-age benefit deferred in accordance with paragraph 1, unless the periods completed under the other legislations have already been taken into account by virtue of paragraph 2 or 3.

Corresponding Provision of Regulation 1408/71

Article 44.

Relevant Provision of the Implementing Regulation

Article 51.

Relevant Decision of the Administrative Commission

Decision No P1 of June 12, 2009 on the interpretation of arts 50(4), 58 and 87(5) of Regulation (EC) No.883/2004 for the award of Invalidity, Old-Age and Survivor's benefits.

Article 51

Special provisions on aggregation of periods

1. Where the legislation of a Member State makes the granting of certain benefits conditional upon the periods of insurance having been completed 3.411

only in a specific activity as an employed or self-employed person or in an occupation which is subject to a special scheme for employed or self-employed persons, the competent institution of that Member State shall take into account periods completed under the legislation of other Member States only if completed under a corresponding scheme or, failing that, in the same occupation, or where appropriate, in the same activity as an employed or self-employed person.

If, account having been taken of the periods thus completed, the person concerned does not satisfy the conditions for receipt of the benefits of a special scheme, these periods shall be taken into account for the purposes of providing the benefits of the general scheme or, failing that, of the scheme applicable to manual or clerical workers, as the case may be, provided that the person concerned had been affiliated to one or other of those schemes.

2. The periods of insurance completed under a special scheme of a Member State shall be taken into account for the purposes of providing the benefits of the general scheme or, failing that, of the scheme applicable to manual or clerical workers, as the case may be, of another Member State, provided that the person concerned had been affiliated to one or other of those schemes, even if those periods have already been taken into account in the latter Member State under a special scheme.

[[1] 3. Where the legislation or specific scheme of a Member State makes the acquisition, retention or recovery of the right to benefits conditional upon the person concerned being insured at the time of the materialisation of the risk, this condition shall be regarded as having been satisfied if that person has been previously insured under the legislation or specific scheme of that Member State and is, at the time of the materialisation of the risk, insured under the legislation of another Member State for the same risk or, failing that, if a benefit is due under the legislation of another Member State for the same risk. The latter condition shall, however, be deemed to be fulfilled in the cases referred to in Article 57.]

AMENDMENT

1. Regulation 988/2009 art.1 (May 1, 2010).

CORRESPONDING PROVISIONS OF REGULATION 1408/71

Articles 45 and 53.

Tomaszewska (C–440/09) Judgment of March 3, 2011 concerned the interpretation of art.45 of Regulation 1408/71 which largely corresponds to art.51(1). Ms Tomaszewska had completed periods of contribution for a retirement pension in Poland and the Czech Republic, but her application for an early retirement pension was rejected on the grounds that she had not met the necessary conditions of entitlement. The dispute concerned the operation of a requirement that "non-contribution periods" must not exceed one-third of the total contributions periods. In the instant case contribution periods in another Member State were not taken into consideration for the purpose of determining the maximum limit for non-contribution periods in relation to contribution periods. There was a difference of treatment depending upon where the contribution periods arose, which put the claimant in a less favourable position than if she had completed all the periods within Poland. The court ruled that the contribution periods completed by the claimant in any other Member State must be treated for all purposes in the same way as contribution periods completed in Poland.

Article 52

Award of benefits

1. The competent institution shall calculate the amount of the benefit that would be due: 3.412

(a) under the legislation it applies, only where the conditions for entitlement to benefits have been satisfied exclusively under national law (independent benefit);

(b) by calculating a theoretical amount and subsequently an actual amount (pro-rata benefit), as follows:

(i) the theoretical amount of the benefit is equal to the benefit which the person concerned could claim if all the periods of insurance and/or of residence which have been completed under the legislations of the other Member States had been completed under the legislation it applies on the date of the award of the benefit. If, under this legislation, the amount does not depend on the duration of the periods completed, that amount shall be regarded as being the theoretical amount;

(ii) the competent institution shall then establish the actual amount of the pro-rata benefit by applying to the theoretical amount the ratio between the duration of the periods completed before materialisation of the risk under the legislation it applies and the total duration of the periods completed before materialisation of the risk under the legislations of all the Member States concerned.

2. Where appropriate, the competent institution shall apply, to the amount calculated in accordance with subparagraphs 1(a) and (b), all the rules relating to reduction, suspension or withdrawal, under the legislation it applies, within the limits provided for by Articles 53 to 55.

3. The person concerned shall be entitled to receive from the competent institution of each Member State the higher of the amounts calculated in accordance with subparagraphs 1(a) and (b).

[1 4. Where the calculation pursuant to paragraph 1(a) in one Member State invariably results in the independent benefit being equal to or higher than the pro rata benefit, calculated in accordance with paragraph 1(b), the competent institution shall waive the pro rata calculation, provided that:

(i) such a situation is set out in Part 1 of Annex VIII;

(ii) no legislation containing rules against overlapping, as referred to in Articles 54 and 55, is applicable unless the conditions laid down in Article 55(2) are fulfilled; and

(iii) Article 57 is not applicable in relation to periods completed under the legislation of another Member State in the specific circumstances of the case.]

[1 Notwithstanding the provisions of paragraphs 1, 2and 3, the pro rata calculation shall not apply to schemes providing benefits in respect of which periods of time are of no relevance to the calculation, subject to such schemes being listed in part 2 of Annex VIII. In such cases, the person concerned shall be entitled to the benefit calculated in accordance with the legislation of the Member State concerned.]

CORRESPONDING PROVISION OF REGULATION 1408/71

Article 46.

RELEVANT PROVISIONS OF THE IMPLEMENTING REGULATION

Articles 43 and 50.

AMENDMENT

1. Regulation 988/2009 art.1 (May 1, 2010).

GENERAL NOTE

3.413 This article is at the heart of the treatment of entitlement to old age pensions where a person has contribution records in more than one Member State. Article 51 contains the basic aggregation rule requiring the competent institution of a Member State to take account of periods of insurance, employment or self-employment completed in another Member State as if they had been completed there.

In *Murru* (2/72) [1972] E.C.R. 333, the Luxembourg Court ruled that a period of unemployment could be assimilated to a period of employment under EU rules if the legislation of the country under which the period of unemployment had been completed so provided. Periods are aggregated under EU rules even where they would not be aggregated under the legislation of the state of the competent institution: *Fabrizii* (113–114/92 and 156/92) [1993] E.C.R. I-6707.

Article 52 sets out the basis for determining the award of benefits. Each Member State to whose legislation the claimant has been subject must undertake the following computation. Periods of less than one year are generally ignored: art.57.

3.414 First it calculates the pension entitlement to which claimant would be entitled if that country applies only its own legislation.

Next, the first step in the second calculation is taken: regard is had to the total period to be taken into account under the legislation of all the relevant countries. Each country then determines the amount of pension to which that would give entitlement: this is known as the "theoretical amount". The second step in the second calculation is to calculate what proportion of the theoretical amount the ratio of years completed in the country doing the calculation to the total years bears. This is called the "actual amount". So in the case of a claim who had spent ten years out of 40 years taken into account under the legislation of the country in question, the actual amount would be one quarter of the theoretical amount. But the actual amount is not what the claimant necessarily receives since this must first be compared with the amount calculated solely under the legislation of the country of claim. The higher of these two amounts is awarded.

Each country to whose legislation the claimant has been subject makes this calculation and awards a pension on the basis of the calculation. So pensioners will receive a pension made up of contributions from each of the Member States to whose legislation they have been subject.

3.415 See art.58 for a provision guaranteeing a minimum pension. The purpose is to ensure a basic standard of living where a person has a series of relatively short periods of employment of self employment in several Member States.

The specific rules on the overlapping of benefits in arts 53–55 display characteristics of technicality and complexity, and are not always easy to understand. But note that they do not apply to benefits calculated in accordance with this article. This means that the individual pro rata pensions calculated in accordance with the formula in this article are protected against the rules on the overlapping of benefits.

Article 53

Rules to prevent overlapping

1. Any overlapping of invalidity, old-age and survivors' benefits calculated or provided on the basis of periods of insurance and/or residence completed by the same person shall be considered to be overlapping of benefits of the same kind. 3.416

2. Overlapping of benefits which cannot be considered to be of the same kind within the meaning of paragraph 1 shall be considered to be overlapping of benefits of a different kind.

3. The following provisions shall be applicable for the purposes of rules to prevent overlapping laid down by the legislation of a Member State in the case of overlapping of a benefit in respect of invalidity, old age or survivors with a benefit of the same kind or a benefit of a different kind or with other income:

(a) the competent institution shall take into account the benefits or incomes acquired in another Member State only where the legislation it applies provides for benefits or income acquired abroad to be taken into account;

(b) the competent institution shall take into account the amount of benefits to be paid by another Member State before deduction of tax, social security contributions and other individual levies or deductions, unless the legislation it applies provides for the application of rules to prevent overlapping after such deductions, under the conditions and the procedures laid down in the Implementing Regulation;

(c) the competent institution shall not take into account the amount of benefits acquired under the legislation of another Member State on the basis of voluntary insurance or continued optional insurance;

(d) if a single Member State applies rules to prevent overlapping because the person concerned receives benefits of the same or of a different kind under the legislation of other Member States or income acquired in other Member States, the benefit due may be reduced solely by the amount of such benefits or such income.

CORRESPONDING PROVISION OF REGULATION 1408/71

Article 46a.

GENERAL NOTE

This provision introduces the abstract notion of benefits of the same kind and benefits of a different kind. In *Schmidt* (C-98/94) [1995] E.C.R. I-2559, the Luxembourg Court said: 3.417

> "The Court has consistently held that social security benefits must be regarded, irrespective of the characteristics peculiar to different national legal systems, as being of the same kind when their purpose and object as well as the basis on which they are calculated and the conditions for granting them are identical (see the judgment in Case 197/85 *ONPTS v Stefanutti* [1987] ECR 3855, paragraph 12). On the other hand, characteristics which are purely formal must not be

considered relevant criteria for the classification of benefits (judgment in *Van Gestel* [Case 37/86 [1987] E.C.R. 3589] paragraph 10". (At [24].)

This case is also testimony to the difficulty of applying this test, since the Advocate General and the Court disagreed on whether a pensions awarded to a divorced person on the contributions of her former spouse and a pension awarded to a person on her own contributions were benefits of the same kind under European Union law. The Advocate General concluded that they were, but the Court disagreed and ruled that they were not.

Article 54

Overlapping of benefits of the same kind

3.418 1. Where benefits of the same kind due under the legislation of two or more Member States overlap, the rules to prevent overlapping laid down by the legislation of a Member State shall not be applicable to a pro-rata benefit.

2. The rules to prevent overlapping shall apply to an independent benefit only if the benefit concerned is:

(a) a benefit the amount of which does not depend on the duration of periods of insurance or residence,
or

(b) a benefit the amount of which is determined on the basis of a credited period deemed to have been completed between the date on which the risk materialised and a later date, overlapping with:

(i) a benefit of the same type, except where an agreement has been concluded between two or more Member States to avoid the same credited period being taken into account more than once,
or

(ii) a benefit referred to in subparagraph (a).

The benefits and agreements referred to in subparagraphs (a) and (b) are listed in Annex IX.

Corresponding Provision of Regulation 1408/71

Article 46b.

General Note

3.419 The term "independent benefit" is defined in art.52(1)(a).

Article 55

Overlapping of benefits of a different kind

3.420 1. If the receipt of benefits of a different kind or other income requires the application of the rules to prevent overlapping provided for by the legislation of the Member States concerned regarding:

(a) two or more independent benefits, the competent institutions shall

divide the amounts of the benefit or benefits or other income, as they have been taken into account, by the number of benefits subject to the said rules;
however, the application of this subparagraph cannot deprive the person concerned of his status as a pensioner for the purposes of the other Chapters of this Title under the conditions and the procedures laid down in the Implementing Regulation;

(b) one or more pro-rata benefits, the competent institutions shall take into account the benefit or benefits or other income and all the elements stipulated for applying the rules to prevent overlapping as a function of the ratio between the periods of insurance and/or residence established for the calculation referred to in Article 52(1)(b)(ii);

(c) one or more independent benefits and one or more pro-rata benefits, the competent institutions shall apply mutatis mutandis subparagraph (a) as regards independent benefits and subparagraph (b) as regards pro-rata benefits.

2. The competent institution shall not apply the division stipulated in respect of independent benefits, if the legislation it applies provides for account to be taken of benefits of a different kind and/or other income and all other elements for calculating part of their amount determined as a function of the ratio between periods of insurance and/or residence referred to in Article 52(1)(b)(ii).

3. Paragraphs 1 and 2 shall apply mutatis mutandis where the legislation of one or more Member States provides that a right to a benefit cannot be acquired in the case where the person concerned is in receipt of a benefit of a different kind, payable under the legislation of another Member State, or of other income.

CORRESPONDING PROVISION OF REGULATION 1408/71

Article 46c.

Article 56

Additional provisions for the calculation of benefits

1. For the calculation of the theoretical and pro-rata amounts referred to in Article 52(1)(b), the following rules shall apply: **3.421**

(a) where the total length of the periods of insurance and/or residence completed before the risk materialised under the legislations of all the Member States concerned is longer than the maximum period required by the legislation of one of these Member States for receipt of full benefit, the competent institution of that Member State shall take into account this maximum period instead of the total length of the periods completed; this method of calculation shall not result in the imposition on that institution of the cost of a benefit greater than the full benefit provided for by the legislation it applies. This provision shall not apply to benefits the amount of which does not depend on the length of insurance;

(b) the procedure for taking into account overlapping periods is laid down in the Implementing Regulation;

(c) if the legislation of a Member State provides that the benefits are to be calculated on the basis of incomes, contributions, bases of contributions, increases, earnings, other amounts or a combination of more than one of them (average, proportional, fixed or credited), the competent institution shall:

(i) determine the basis for calculation of the benefits in accordance only with periods of insurance completed under the legislation it applies;

(ii) use, in order to determine the amount to be calculated in accordance with the periods of insurance and/or residence completed under the legislation of the other Member States, the same elements determined or recorded for the periods of insurance completed under the legislation it applies;

[1 where necessary] in accordance with the procedures laid down in Annex XI for the Member State concerned.

[1 (d) In the event that point (c) is not applicable because the legislation of a Member State provides for the benefit to be calculated on the basis of elements other than periods of insurance or residence which are not linked to time, the competent institution shall take into account, in respect of each period of insurance or residence completed under the legislation of any other Member State, the amount of the capital accrued, the capital which is considered as having been accrued or any other element for the calculation under the legislation it administers divided by the corresponding units of periods in the pension scheme concerned.]

2. The provisions of the legislation of a Member State concerning the revalorisation of the elements taken into account for the calculation of benefits shall apply, as appropriate, to the elements to be taken into account by the competent institution of that Member State, in accordance with paragraph 1, in respect of the periods of insurance or residence completed under the legislation of other Member States.

AMENDMENT

1. Regulation 988/2009 art.1 (May 1, 2010).

CORRESPONDING PROVISION OF REGULATION 1408/71

Article 47.

Article 57

Periods of insurance or residence of less than one year

3.422 1. Notwithstanding Article 52(1)(b), the institution of a Member State shall not be required to provide benefits in respect of periods completed under the legislation it applies which are taken into account when the risk materialises, if:

— the duration of the said periods is less than one year,
and

— taking only these periods into account no right to benefit is acquired under that legislation.

Article 57

For the purposes of this Article, "periods" shall mean all periods of insurance, employment, self-employment or residence which either qualify for, or directly increase, the benefit concerned.

2. The competent institution of each of the Member States concerned shall take into account the periods referred to in paragraph 1, for the purposes of Article 52(1)(b)(i).

3. If the effect of applying paragraph 1 would be to relieve all the institutions of the Member States concerned of their obligations, benefits shall be provided exclusively under the legislation of the last of those Member States whose conditions are satisfied, as if all the periods of insurance and residence completed and taken into account in accordance with Articles 6 and 51(1) and (2) had been completed under the legislation of that Member State.

[1 4. This Article shall not apply to schemes listed in Part 2 of Annex VIII.]

CORRESPONDING PROVISION OF REGULATION 1408/71

Article 48.

For a case about a claim for long-term incapacity benefit which turned on art.48 of Reg.1408/71 (which is in the same terms as art.57), see *ML v SSWP (IB)* [2011] UKUT 390 (AAC), reported as [2012] AACR 27.

AMENDMENT

1. Regulation 988/2009 art.1 (May 1, 2010).

Article 58

Award of a supplement

1. A recipient of benefits to whom this Chapter applies may not, in the Member State of residence and under whose legislation a benefit is payable to him, be provided with a benefit which is less than the minimum benefit fixed by that legislation for a period of insurance or residence equal to all the periods taken into account for the payment in accordance with this Chapter. **3.423**

2. The competent institution of that Member State shall pay him throughout the period of his residence in its territory a supplement equal to the difference between the total of the benefits due under this Chapter and the amount of the minimum benefit.

CORRESPONDING PROVISION OF REGULATION 1408/71

Article 50.

RELEVANT PROVISION OF THE IMPLEMENTING REGULATION

Article 51.

RELEVANT DECISION OF THE ADMINISTRATIVE COMMISSION

Decision No.P1 of June 12, 2009 on the interpretation of arts 50(4), 58 and 87(5) of Regulation (EC) No.883/2004 for the award of Invalidity, Old-Age and Survivor's benefits.

Article 59

Recalculation and revaluation of benefits

3.424 1. If the method for determining benefits or the rules for calculating benefits are altered under the legislation of a Member State, or if the personal situation of the person concerned undergoes a relevant change which, under that legislation, would lead to an adjustment of the amount of the benefit, a recalculation shall be carried out in accordance with Article 52.

2. On the other hand, if, by reason of an increase in the cost of living or changes in the level of income or other grounds for adjustment, the benefits of the Member State concerned are altered by a percentage or fixed amount, such percentage or fixed amount shall be applied directly to the benefits determined in accordance with Article 52, without the need for a recalculation.

Corresponding Provision of Regulation 1408/71

Article 51.

Article 60

Special provisions for civil servants

3.425 1. Articles 6, 50, 51(3) and 52 to 59 shall apply mutatis mutandis to persons covered by a special scheme for civil servants.

2. However, if the legislation of a competent Member State makes the acquisition, liquidation, retention or recovery of the right to benefits under a special scheme for civil servants subject to the condition that all periods of insurance be completed under one or more special schemes for civil servants in that Member State, or be regarded by the legislation of that Member State as equivalent to such periods, the competent institution of that State shall take into account only the periods which can be recognised under the legislation it applies.

If, account having been taken of the periods thus completed, the person concerned does not satisfy the conditions for the receipt of these benefits, these periods shall be taken into account for the award of benefits under the general scheme or, failing that, the scheme applicable to manual or clerical workers, as the case may be.

3. Where, under the legislation of a Member State, benefits under a special scheme for civil servants are calculated on the basis of the last salary or salaries received during a reference period, the competent institution of that State shall take into account, for the purposes of the calculation, only those salaries, duly re-valued, which were received during the period or periods for which the person concerned was subject to that legislation.

Corresponding Provision of Regulation 1408/71

Article 51a.

CHAPTER 6

UNEMPLOYMENT BENEFITS

GENERAL NOTE

The provisions of Reg.1408/71 dealing specifically with unemployment benefit demonstrated an overly cautious view by the Member States of the motives of unemployed persons moving between the Member States. The provisions of reg.883/2004 are only marginally more generous. 3.426

Provision is made in art.61 for periods of employment or insurance to be aggregated in order to determine entitlement to unemployment benefits. But there is a sting in the tail of the provision. Aggregation is only possible under the legislation of the country in which the person claiming "lastly" completed periods of insurance or employment. The result is, for example, that a British national living and working in Germany who becomes unemployed cannot return to the United Kingdom and claim jobseeker's allowance on the basis of contributions to the German scheme, because he or she will not have lastly completed a period of insurance in the United Kingdom unless he or she comes within the scope of art.65: see below. This territorial limitation on aggregation seems unnecessarily restrictive, and has been the subject of criticism: See, for example, N. Wikeley, "Migrant Workers and Unemployment Benefit in the European Community" [1988] J.S.W.L. 300.

The severity of the same rule in Reg.1408/71 is illustrated in *Gray v Adjudication Officer* (C-62/91) [1992] E.C.R. I-2737. Gray, a British national, had lived and worked in Spain running a restaurant from 1971 to 1990. He returned to the United Kingdom after selling the business without having registered as unemployed in Spain. He claimed unemployment benefit in the United Kingdom, and appealed the refusal to award him the benefit to the Bognor Regis social security appeal tribunal. It was argued by the adjudication officer that there was no entitlement in the United Kingdom because the claimant was last insured in Spain. Furthermore since he had not registered as unemployed in Spain, no question could arise as to any entitlement under art.69 of Reg.1408/71. The tribunal also concluded that the claimant had been habitually resident in Spain and so could not take the benefit of the rules in art.71 of Reg.1408/71. The lay members of the tribunal (the lawyer chairman of the tribunal considered that the provisions were consistent with the Treaty rules) clearly saw an injustice and felt that certain provisions of arts 67 and 69 of Reg.1408/71 militated against the Treaty rules on free movement of persons. They clearly insisted (as they were entitled to) that a reference be made concerning the validity of the provisions in question. The Luxembourg Court, however, concluded that there was no factor of such a kind as to affect the validity of the provisions in issue. Both conferred on workers rights which they would not otherwise enjoy.

Article 61

Special rules on aggregation of periods of insurance, employment or self-employment

1. The competent institution of a Member State whose legislation makes the acquisition, retention, recovery or duration of the right to benefits conditional upon the completion of either periods of insurance, employment 3.427

or self-employment shall, to the extent necessary, take into account periods of insurance, employment or self-employment completed under the legislation of any other Member State as though they were completed under the legislation it applies.

However, when the applicable legislation makes the right to benefits conditional on the completion of periods of insurance, the periods of employment or self-employment completed under the legislation of another Member State shall not be taken into account unless such periods would have been considered to be periods of insurance had they been completed in accordance with the applicable legislation.

2. Except in the cases referred to in Article 65(5)(a), the application of paragraph 1 of this Article shall be conditional on the person concerned having the most recently completed, in accordance with the legislation under which the benefits are claimed:

— periods of insurance, if that legislation requires periods of insurance,
— periods of employment, if that legislation requires periods of employment,
or
— periods of self-employment, if that legislation requires periods of self-employment.

CORRESPONDING PROVISION OF REGULATION 1408/71

Article 67.

RELEVANT PROVISION OF THE IMPLEMENTING REGULATION

Article 54.

GENERAL NOTE

3.428 *ONEM v M, and M v ONEM* (C-284/15), Judgment of April 7, 2016 concerned the interpretation of Art.67 of Regulation 1408/71 whose provisions are almost identical with those of Art.61. The Court concluded that Art.67 of Regulation 1408/71 did not preclude a Member State from refusing to aggregate periods of employment necessary to qualify for unemployment benefit to supplement income from part-time employment where the part-time employment was not preceded by any period of insurance or of employment in that Member State.

Article 62

Calculation of benefits

3.429 1. The competent institution of a Member State whose legislation provides for the calculation of benefits on the basis of the amount of the previous salary or professional income shall take into account exclusively the salary or professional income received by the person concerned in respect of his last activity as an employed or self-employed person under the said legislation.

2. Paragraph 1 shall also apply where the legislation administered by the competent institution provides for a specific reference period for the determination of the salary which serves as a basis for the calculation of benefits and where, for all or part of that period, the person concerned was subject to the legislation of another Member State.

Article 62

3. By way of derogation from paragraphs (1) and (2), as far as the [[1] unemployed persons] covered by Article 65(5)(a) are concerned, the institution of the place of residence shall take into account the salary or professional income received by the person concerned in the Member State to whose legislation he was subject during his last activity as an employed or self-employed person, in accordance with the Implementing Regulation.

AMENDMENT

1. Regulation 988/2009 art.1 (May 1, 2010).

CORRESPONDING PROVISION OF REGULATION 1408/71

Article 68.

RELEVANT PROVISION OF THE IMPLEMENTING REGULATION

Article 54.

GENERAL NOTE

This article, like its predecessor, provides that where unemployment benefit is linked to a previous wage or salary, the salary or wages to be taken into account are those in respect of the last employment in that state: *Fellinger* (67/79) [1980] E.C.R. 535. However, where the amount of benefit varies with the number of members of the family, members of the family residing in another Member State are to be treated as residing in the competent state. **3.430**

Article 63

[[1] Special provisions for the waiving of residence rules

For the purpose of this Chapter, Article 7 shall apply only in the cases provided for by Articles 64, 65 and 65a and within the limits prescribed therein.] **3.431**

AMENDMENT

1. Regulation 465/2012 [2012] OJ L149/4 art.1(8) (June 28, 2012).

Article 64

Unemployed persons going to another Member State

1. A wholly unemployed person who satisfies the conditions of the legislation of the competent Member State for entitlement to benefits, and who goes to another Member State in order to seek work there, shall retain his entitlement to unemployment benefits in cash under the following conditions and within the following limits: **3.432**

(a) before his departure, the unemployed person must have been registered as a person seeking work and have remained available to the employment services of the competent Member State for at least four weeks after becoming unemployed. However, the competent services or institutions may authorise his departure before such time has expired;

(b) the unemployed person must register as a person seeking work with the employment services of the Member State to which he has gone, be subject to the control procedure organised there and adhere to the conditions laid down under the legislation of that Member State. This condition shall be considered satisfied for the period before registration if the person concerned registers within seven days of the date on which he ceased to be available to the employment services of the Member State which he left. In exceptional cases, the competent services or institutions may extend this period;

(c) entitlement to benefits shall be retained for a period of three months from the date when the unemployed person ceased to be available to the employment services of the Member State which he left, provided that the total duration for which the benefits are provided does not exceed the total duration of the period of his entitlement to benefits under the legislation of that Member State; the competent services or institutions may extend the period of three months up to a maximum of six months;

(d) the benefits shall be provided by the competent institution in accordance with the legislation it applies and at its own expense.

2. If the person concerned returns to the competent Member State on or before the expiry of the period during which he is entitled to benefits under paragraph 1(c), he shall continue to be entitled to benefits under the legislation of that Member State. He shall lose all entitlement to benefits under the legislation of the competent Member State if he does not return there on or before the expiry of the said period, unless the provisions of that legislation are more favourable. In exceptional cases the competent services or institutions may allow the person concerned to return at a later date without loss of his entitlement.

3. Unless the legislation of the competent Member State is more favourable, between two periods of employment the maximum total period for which entitlement to benefits shall be retained under paragraph 1 shall be three months; the competent services or institutions may extend that period up to a maximum of six months.

4. The arrangements for exchanges of information, cooperation and mutual assistance between the institutions and services of the competent Member State and the Member State to which the person goes in order to seek work shall be laid down in the Implementing Regulation.

CORRESPONDING PROVISION OF REGULATION 1408/71

Article 69.

RELEVANT PROVISION OF THE IMPLEMENTING REGULATION

Article 55.

GENERAL NOTE

3.433 This article provides a limited right to export unemployment benefit for up to six months where the person goes to another Member State for the purpose of seeking work. Strict conditions surround the right to export the benefit, and failure to return to the competent state within the six-month period normally results in the loss of all entitlement to benefits under the legislation of the competent state. The right to export unemployment benefit could previously only be exercised once in any period of unemployment, but the new provision enables the move to be exercised more than once within the total period. The normal maximum period is three months, but this may be extended by the competent institution to a maximum period of six months

In *Testa, Maggio and Vitale* (41, 121 and 796/79) [1980] E.C.R. 1979, the validity of art.69(2) of Reg.1408/71 was questioned in circumstances where each of three Italian nationals lost the residual entitlement to unemployment benefit in Germany when they did not return within three months to Germany from an authorised stay in Italy in order to look for work there. In two of the cases, the later return was explained by an intervening illness. The Luxembourg Court readily concluded that there was nothing to impugn the validity of the provisions of art.69(2) which provided that all entitlement to unemployment benefit would cease if the beneficiary did not return to the competent state before the expiry of the authorised period of absence. There was, according to the court, a clear advantage to the person in that they were, during their period of absence abroad, exempt from the controls applicable in the competent state (even though they would be subject to the controls in the country to which they went). The only glimmer of hope related to the court's advice on how the discretion to extend the period in exceptional cases should be applied: see also *Coccioli* (139/78) [1979] E.C.R. 991. First, retrospective applications for extensions of the period were admissible. Secondly, the competent institution in exercising its discretion must take account of the principle of proportionality in European Union law. In each case, the institution must consider the extent to which the three-month period has been exceeded, the reasons for the delay in returning, and the seriousness of the legal consequences arising from the delay. This would, presumably, include consideration of the residual amount of benefit which might be forfeit if all entitlement were to cease.

In *Rydergård* (C-215/00) [2002] E.C.R. I–1817, the Luxembourg Court ruled that the period of four weeks referred to in art.69(1)(a) of Reg.1408/71 (now art.64(10(a) need not be completed without a break. Short breaks—for example, where the claimant moved to a child caring benefit because her child was ill for just a few days—would not cause the four week qualifying period to start to run all over again.

Relevant Recommendations of the Administrative Commission

Recommendation No U2 of June 12, 2009 of the Administrative Commission concerning the application of art.64(1)(a) of Regulation (EC) No.883/2004 to unemployed persons accompanying their spouses or partners pursuing a professional or trade activity in a Member State other than the competent state.

Article 65

Unemployed persons who resided in a Member State other than the competent State

1. A person who is partially or intermittently unemployed and who, during his last activity as an employed or self-employed person, resided in a Member State other than the competent Member State shall make himself available to his employer or to the employment services in the competent Member State. He shall receive benefits in accordance with the legislation of the competent Member State as if he were residing in that Member State. These benefits shall be provided by the institution of the competent Member State. 3.434

2. A wholly unemployed person who, during his last activity as an employed or self-employed person, resided in a Member State other than the competent Member State and who continues to reside in that Member State or returns to that Member State shall make himself available to the employment services in the Member State of residence. Without prejudice to Article 64, a wholly unemployed person may, as a supplementary step, make himself available to the employment services of the Member State in which he pursued his last activity as an employed or self-employed person.

An unemployed person, other than a frontier worker, who does not return to his Member State of residence, shall make himself available to the employment services in the Member State to whose legislation he was last subject.

3. The unemployed person referred to in the first sentence of paragraph 2 shall register as a person seeking work with the competent employment services of the Member State in which he resides, shall be subject to the control procedure organised there and shall adhere to the conditions laid down under the legislation of that Member State. If he chooses also to register as a person seeking work in the Member State in which he pursued his last activity as an employed or self-employed person, he shall comply with the obligations applicable in that State.

4. The implementation of the second sentence of paragraph 2 and of the second sentence of paragraph 3, as well as the arrangements for exchanges of information, cooperation and mutual assistance between the institutions and services of the Member State of residence and the Member State in which he pursued his last occupation, shall be laid down in the Implementing Regulation.

5. (a) The unemployed person referred to in the first and second sentences of paragraph 2 shall receive benefits in accordance with the legislation of the Member State of residence as if he had been subject to that legislation during his last activity as an employed or self-employed person. Those benefits shall be provided by the institution of the place of residence.

(b) However, a worker other than a frontier worker who has been provided benefits at the expense of the competent institution of the Member State to whose legislation he was last subject shall firstly receive, on his return to the Member State of residence, benefits in accordance with Article 64, receipt of the benefits in accordance with (a) being suspended for the period during which he receives benefits under the legislation to which he was last subject.

6. The benefits provided by the institution of the place of residence under paragraph 5 shall continue to be at its own expense. However, subject to paragraph 7, the competent institution of the Member State to whose legislation he was last subject shall reimburse to the institution of the place of residence the full amount of the benefits provided by the latter institution during the first three months. The amount of the reimbursement during this period may not be higher than the amount payable, in the case of unemployment, under the legislation of the competent Member State. In the case referred to in paragraph 5(b), the period during which benefits are provided under Article 64 shall be deducted

from the period referred to in the second sentence of this paragraph. The arrangements for reimbursement shall be laid down in the Implementing Regulation.

7. However, the period of reimbursement referred to in paragraph 6 shall be extended to five months when the person concerned has, during the preceding 24 months, completed periods of employment or self-employment of at least 12 months in the Member State to whose legislation he was last subject, where such periods would qualify for the purposes of establishing entitlement to unemployment benefits.

8. For the purposes of paragraphs 6 and 7, two or more Member States, or their competent authorities, may provide for other methods of reimbursement or waive all reimbursement between the institutions falling under their jurisdiction.

CORRESPONDING PROVISION OF REGULATION 1408/71

Article 71.

RELEVANT PROVISION OF THE IMPLEMENTING REGULATION

Article 56, and Ch.2 of Title IV.

RELEVANT DECISIONS AND RECOMMENDATIONS OF THE ADMINISTRATIVE COMMISSION

Decision No U2 of June 12, 2009 of the Administrative Commission concerning the scope of art.65(2) of Regulation (EC) No.883/2004 on the right to unemployment benefits of wholly unemployed persons other than frontier workers who were resident in the territory of a Member State other than the competent Member State during their last period of employment or self-employment.

Decision No U3 of June 12, 2009 of the Administrative Commission concerning the scope of the concept of "partial unemployment" applicable to the unemployed persons referred to in art.65(1) of Regulation (EC) No 883/2004.

Recommendation No U1 of June 12, 2009 of the Administrative Commission concerning the legislation applicable to unemployed persons engaging in part-time professional or trade activity in a Member State other than the State of residence.

GENERAL NOTE

Some of the rigours of the limited aggregation and exportability rules is moder- **3.435**
ated by the provisions of art.65, which concern situations in which the claimant was residing, during their last period of work, in a country other than the competent State.

Since the provisions are exceptions to the rules elsewhere in this chapter of the regulation, the Luxembourg Court has said, in relation to the predecessor rules, that they must be strictly interpreted: *di Paolo* (76/76) [1977] E.C.R. 315, at [12] and [13].

In *Jeltes, Peeters and Arnold* (C-443/11) Judgment of April 11, 2013, the Court of Justice ruled that the provisions of art.65 are not to be interpreted in the light of the judgment in *Miethe* (1/85) [1986] E.C.R. 1837. In the *Miethe* case, the Court of Justice had ruled that the relevant provision of Reg.1408/71 should be interpreted as permitting atypical frontier workers to claim unemployment benefit in the Member State where they worked rather than in the Member State where they resided. What made them atypical was that, although they lived in one Member State and worked in another, their links with the Member State in which they worked were such that their best chance of securing employment was in that Member State rather than the Member State of residence.

[1 *Article 65a*

Special provisions for wholly unemployed self- employed frontier workers where no unemployment benefits system covering self-employed persons exists in the Member State of residence

3.436 1. By way of derogation from Article 65, a wholly unemployed person who, as a frontier worker, has most recently completed periods of insurance as a self-employed person or periods of self-employment recognised for the purposes of granting unemployment benefits in a Member State other than his/her Member State of residence and whose Member State of residence has submitted notification that there is no possibility for any category of self-employed persons to be covered by an unemployment benefits system of that Member State, shall register with and make himself/herself available to the employment services in the Member State in which he/she pursued his/her last activity as a self-employed person and, when he/she applies for benefits, shall continuously adhere to the conditions laid down under the legislation of the latter Member State. The wholly unemployed person may, as a supplementary step, make himself/herself available to the employment services of the Member State of residence.

2. Benefits shall be provided to the wholly unemployed person referred to in paragraph 1 by the Member State to whose legislation he/she was last subject in accordance with the legislation which that Member State applies.

3. If the wholly unemployed person referred to in paragraph 1 does not wish to become or remain available to the employment services of the Member State of last activity after having been registered there, and wishes to seek work in the Member State of residence, Article 64 shall apply mutatis mutandis, except Article 64(1)(a). The competent institution may extend the period referred to in the first sentence of Article 64(1)(c) up to the end of the period of entitlement to benefits.]

AMENDMENT

1. Inserted by Regulation 465/2012 [2012] OJ L149/4 art.1(9) (June 28, 2012).

CHAPTER 7

PRE-RETIREMENT BENEFITS

Article 66

Benefits

3.437 When the applicable legislation makes the right to pre-retirement benefits conditional on the completion of periods of insurance, of employment or of self-employment, Article 6 shall not apply.

GENERAL NOTE

3.438 The provisions of the regulation on pre-retirement benefits are exceedingly brief, consisting of this single article which excludes the provisions in art.6 on aggregation of periods of insurance from applicability in this field. This means that acquiring title to a pre-retirement benefit must be achieved solely under the provisions of the national social security system which has the benefit. Paragraph (33) of the Preamble indicates that the aggregation principle does not apply because only a few Member States have statutory pre-retirement benefits. That is not a convincing reason for excluding for pre-retirement benefits the possibility of aggregation. Pre-retirement benefits are defined at length in art.1(x):

> " 'pre-retirement benefit' means: all cash benefits, other than an unemployment benefit or an early old-age benefit, provided from a specified age to workers who have reduced, ceased or suspended their remunerative activities until the age at which they qualify for an old-age pension or an early retirement pension, the receipt of which is not conditional upon the person concerned being available to the employment services of the competent State; 'early old-age benefit' means a benefit provided before the normal pension entitlement age is reached and which either continues to be provided once the said age is reached or is replaced by another old-age benefit".

The definition distinguishes a pre-retirement benefit from either an early old-age benefit or unemployment benefit. It will be interesting to see whether the case law on substance over form raises questions of the classification of benefits for those not expected to be employed further before reaching a Member state's statutory retirement age, as, for example in *De Cuyper* (C-406/04) [2006] E.C.R. I-6947. The most significant advantage for those in receipt of a pre-retirement benefit is the ability to export the benefit if they move to another Member State.

Chapter 8

Family Benefits

General Note

The provisions of Regulation 883/2004 on family benefits are significantly different from those in Regulation 1408/71. Following the entry into force of Regulation 883/2004 on May 1, 2010, this was initially overlooked in submissions to tribunals, as Judge Jacobs noted in *BM v HMRC* [2015] UKUT 526 (AAC). 3.439

What constitutes a family benefit is defined in broad terms in art.1(z). There are many kinds of family benefit in the Member States; and the basis on which they are awarded varies considerably. In the United Kingdom, the following are family benefits: child benefit, child tax credit, guardian's allowance, and increases in other benefits for an adult or a child. On child tax credit, see *AW v HMRC (TC)* [2011] UKUT 322 (AAC); [2012] AACR 18.

The provisions of Regulation 883/2004 on family benefits represent a simplification of the earlier rules, but entitlement to family benefits under the Regulation remains a complex area for co-ordination. The reasons are that entitlement may flow from the activity of either parent, and it is not uncommon for the insured person to be living in a different Member State from family members. The regulation is concerned with co-ordination and not harmonisation but, in the case of family benefits, it has been decided to allow families to receive up to the higher rate of family benefit having regard to entitlement arising in two Member States.

Suppose that Member State A pays £15.00 per week per child in child benefit, while Member State B pays £20.00 per week per child. One parent works in Member State A and one parent in Member State B. If the parent in Member State B claims, the outcome is simple. The higher amount is payable. If the parent in Member State A claims, then provision is made for a supplementary payment to top up the child benefit to the higher rate.

Art.67 states the general rules. Art.68 contains provisions in the event of overlapping. These are not always easy to understand and apply.

Art.60 of Regulation 987/2009 sets out the way the competent institutions should deal with claims for family benefits.

Article 67

Members of the family residing in another Member State

3.440 A person shall be entitled to family benefits in accordance with the legislation of the competent Member State, including for his family members residing in another Member State, as if they were residing in the former Member State. However, a pensioner shall be entitled to family benefits in accordance with the legislation of the Member State competent for his pension.

Corresponding Provision of Regulation 1408/71

Article 73.

Relevant Provision of the Implementing Regulation

Article 60.

General Note

3.441 Article 67 states two general rules:

(a) A person is entitled to family benefits for their family members (including those residing in another Member State) in accordance with the legislation of the competent Member State.

(b) There is a different rule for pensioners, where the Member State competent in relation to the pension is the competent Member State.

Family members of the person claiming who are residing in another Member State are treated as though they were residing in the competent Member State. The term "member of the family" is defined in art.1(i) and should be noted carefully, since it dovetails with provisions of national law.

Nephews and nieces are not family members of a person in the United Kingdom for the purposes of art.67: *KT v HMRC (CB)* [2013] UKUT 151 (AAC).

Divorce does not end membership of a family. In *Slanina* (C-363/08) judgment of November 26, 2009, the Luxembourg Court was considering a case in which a divorced mother and her child moved from Austria to Greece following the breakdown of the marriage, where entitlement to a family benefit for the child under Austrian social security legislation had been terminated. The Court ruled that, notwithstanding the divorce, provided that the child remained a "member of the family" within art.1(f)(i) of Regulation 1408/71, entitlement to the family benefit payable to the mother under the Austrian system continued.

It appeared that the mother had undertaken work in Greece. Under Greek social security law, employment gives rise to entitlement to family benefits. If the mother became entitled to family benefit in Greece because of her employment, that would, the Court ruled, have the effect of suspending any entitlement to family benefits under Austrian social security law up to the value of the allowances paid in Greece. It follows that if the Austrian benefit was higher, the Austrian authorities would be required to pay a supplement to bring the level of the Greek benefit up to the level of the Austrian benefit under what is now art.68 of Regulation 883/2004.

Würker v Familienkasse Nürnberg (C-32/13) judgment of February 27, 2014, ruled that a benefit in Germany in the form of a pension for bringing up children which is granted, in the event of death, to the former spouse of the deceased for the purposes of bringing up the children of that former spouse is covered by the concept of a "pension" for the purposes of art.67

Article 68

Priority rules in the event of overlapping

1. Where, during the same period and for the same family members, benefits are provided for under the legislation of more than one Member State the following priority rules shall apply: **3.442**

(a) in the case of benefits payable by more than one Member State on different bases, the order of priority shall be as follows: firstly, rights available on the basis of an activity as an employed or self-employed person, secondly, rights available on the basis of receipt of a pension and finally, rights obtained on the basis of residence;

(b) in the case of benefits payable by more than one Member State on the same basis, the order of priority shall be established by referring to the following subsidiary criteria:

   (i) in the case of rights available on the basis of an activity as an employed or self-employed person: the place of residence of the children, provided that there is such activity, and additionally, where appropriate, the highest amount of the benefits provided for by the conflicting legislations. In the latter case, the cost of benefits shall be shared in accordance with criteria laid down in the Implementing Regulation;

   (ii) in the case of rights available on the basis of receipt of pensions: the place of residence of the children, provided that a pension is payable under its legislation, and additionally, where appropriate, the longest period of insurance or residence under the conflicting legislations;

   (iii) in the case of rights available on the basis of residence: the place of residence of the children.

2. In the case of overlapping entitlements, family benefits shall be provided in accordance with the legislation designated as having priority in accordance with paragraph 1. Entitlements to family benefits by virtue of other conflicting legislation or legislations shall be suspended up to the amount provided for by the first legislation and a differential supplement shall be provided, if necessary, for the sum which exceeds this amount. However, such a differential supplement does not need to be provided for children residing in another Member State when entitlement to the benefit in question is based on residence only.

3. If, under Article 67, an application for family benefits is submitted to the competent institution of a Member State whose legislation is applicable, but not by priority right in accordance with paragraphs 1 and 2 of this Article:

(a) that institution shall forward the application without delay to the competent institution of the Member State whose legislation is applicable by priority, inform the person concerned and, without prejudice to the provisions of the Implementing Regulation concerning the provisional award of benefits, provide, if necessary, the differential supplement mentioned in paragraph 2;

(b) the competent institution of the Member State whose legislation is applicable by priority shall deal with this application as though it were submitted directly to itself, and the date on which such an application was submitted to the first institution shall be considered as the date of its claim to the institution with priority.

Corresponding Provisions of Regulation 1408/71

Articles 72a, 75 and 76.

Relevant Provisions of the Implementing Regulation

Articles 58 and 60.

Relevant Decisions of the Administrative Commission

Decision No F1 of June 12, 2009 concerning the interpretation of art.68 of Regulation (EC) No.883/2004 relating to priority rules in the event of overlapping of family benefits.

Decision No.F2 of June 23, 2015 on the exchange of data between institutions for the purposes of granting family benefits. [2016] OJ C52/11.

General Note

3.443 The interpretation of art.68 is particularly difficult. This is partly because it uses terms which frequently appear in national social security legislation, but such terms do not necessarily mean the same thing as in national law. Often they plainly do not.

The first question is when art.68 applies. The heading is "Priority rules *in the event* of overlapping" (emphasis added). This suggests that art.68 is only of relevance where there is actual overlapping, that is, where there are competing claims or overlapping awards. Support for this can be found in the *Trapkowski* case (C-378/14) judgment of October 22, 2015. The father, a Polish national, resided in Germany. He was divorced from his wife who lived in Poland with their son. She worked in Poland, but did not receive or apply for family benefits in Poland or in Germany. The father claimed a family benefit for his son in Germany. The Court of Justice ruled:

> "As regards the applicability of the priority rules laid down in Article 68(1) of Regulation No 883/2004 it should be recalled that, according to the settled case-law of the Court, for a finding that such overlapping is present in a given case, it is not enough for such benefits to be due in the relevant child's Member State of residence and to be, in parallel, merely capable of being due in another Member State, where one of the parents of that child works (judgment in *Schwemmer*, C-16/09, EU:C:2010:605, paragraph 52 and the case-law cited)."

The Court found that Art.68 did not apply. This approach was followed in *JL v HMRC (CB)* [2017] UKUT 193 (AAC). The claimant was a Polish national who had come to the United Kingdom in 2012 and had worked here ever since. He was divorced but had a son who was living with his mother in Poland. The father was sending money to Poland to support his son, as well as providing some support in kind. It was accepted that when both the cash payments and the additional support were aggregated, the claimant was providing support at least at the relevant weekly amount of child benefit for the son. HMRC argued that the priority claimant was the mother and so the father was not entitled to child benefit in the United Kingdom. Judge White disagreed, concluding that art.68 did not apply and that the father was entitled to child benefit for his son.

Where art.68 does apply, it sets out an order of priority in dealing with claims. The article refers to "the legislation designated as having priority" under art.68(1), but it may be easier to think in terms of a primary competent Member State and a secondary competent Member State.

Where there is overlapping of benefits, family benefits are paid under art.68(2) in accordance with the legislation of the primary competent Member State.

Entitlement under the legislation of the secondary competent Member State is suspended up to the amount of benefit paid under the legislation of the primary competent Member State. However, if the amount of benefit under the legislation of the secondary competent Member State is higher than that under the legislation of the primary competent Member State, then the secondary competent Member State pays a supplement equal to the difference. There is one exception set out in the last sentence of art.68(2).

The order of priority (or the scheme for determining the primary and secondary competent Member State) is set out in art.68(1).

Where the basis for paying a family benefit is *different*, then the primary competent Member State will be determined in the following order of priority: **3.444**

(1) The Member State where the claimant's rights flow from his or her status as an employed or self-employed person;

(2) The Member State where the claimant's rights flow from his or her status as a pensioner;

(3) The Member State where the claimant's rights flow from his or her residence in the Member State.

Where the basis for paying a family benefit is *the same*, art.68(1)(b) sets out some subsidiary rules, and the place of residence of the children becomes relevant.

The order of priority turns on whether the basis on which the two Member States concerned pay the benefit is the same or different. What is meant here by the "basis" on which the benefit is payable? Furthermore, what does "rights" refer to in the phrases "rights available on the basis of" in art.68(1)? It is suggested that "basis" refers to the national conditions of entitlement for the benefit, and "rights" refers to the way in which a Member State is the competent State having regard to art.11 of Regulation 883/2004 and other provisions of the regulation (for example, the special position of pensioners).

Careful reading of art.68(1) suggests that the term "basis", on which a family benefit is payable, must refer to the conditions of entitlement under the relevant national provisions for the family benefit in question. For example, child benefit in the United Kingdom is based on residence: s.146 of the Social Security Contributions and Benefits Act 1992. The starting point is to examine the national law on entitlement to determine the basis on which it is paid, and then to compare that basis with the basis for the award in the other Member State in order to decide whether the two schemes have the same basis. Quite what constitutes the same basis is far from clear.

Taking this example further, it has already been noted that the underlying basis of United Kingdom child benefit is residence. There is however the further condition that the claimant is responsible for a child or qualifying young person. In Poland, child benefit is based on residence, but is also subject to a means test. Does that mean that, when comparing the basis for an award in the United Kingdom and Poland, the basis is the same or different because of the different qualifying conditions? In other words, do you look at the overall conditions of entitlement or just the principle connecting factor to the Member State? The answer will make a considerable difference to which Member State is the primary competent Member State. It is certainly arguable in this example that the basis of entitlement is *not* the same, and this would seem to be the better view. If that is correct, then priority is given to the Member State where rights flow from activity as an employed or self-employed person. The rights of a Polish national working in the United Kingdom flow from that economic activity (this is the basis on which the United Kingdom is the competent State under art.11 in this example), and this would suggest that the primary competent Member State is the United Kingdom under art.68(1)(a). Looking at the same set of circumstances from Poland, then the rights of the other parent (who is an employee in Poland) do not flow from the economic activity but from residence in Poland. Poland is the secondary competent Member State.

If the basis is regarded as the same in this example (because both countries use residence as the starting point), then priority would be given under art.68(1)(b)(i) to the place of residence of the children.

Information about the basis of any family benefit in another Member State should be provided to tribunals by HMRC, and will be a question of fact. HMRC should have this information where it is relevant because of their communications with the social security institutions of the other Member State concerned.

This rather convoluted set of rules is designed to provide that where the application of the priority rules means that, where the family benefits are not the most favourable available among the rules of the relevant Member States, a differential supplement must be paid by the institutions of the Member State with the higher family benefits in order to top up the benefits paid by the Member State accorded priority under the priority rules.

Article 68(3)

3.445 At first sight art.68(3) seems to be a provision of general application, but it should be noted that art.68 only applies where there is actual overlapping, that is, where there are competing claims or awards. Naturally, where a claim for a family benefit indicates a possible link with another Member State (usually because the children are in a different Member State with one of their parents), then enquiries will need to be made between social security institutions to check that the children exist and that there is no competing claim for the family benefit. This is done using Forms F001 and F002. If there has been no claim for benefit in the other Member State, then art.68 does not apply.

Decision No.F1 of the Administrative Commission provides additional guidance on when rights will flow from an activity as an employed or self-employed person. It extends the meaning of "activity as an employed or self-employed person" to include temporary suspension of the activity:

(a) during sickness, maternity, accident at work, occupational disease or unemployment, if wages or benefits, excluding pensions, are payable in respect of the contingencies listed above;

(b) during paid leave, strike or lock-out; and

(c) unpaid leave for child-raising if the leave is deemed equivalent to such an activity as an employed or self-employed person in accordance with the relevant legislation.

See also art.60 of Regulation 987/2009 and the commentary on it. That article sets out the administrative process for dealing with claims, and for dealing with any differences of view which arise on the determination of the primary and secondary competent Member States.

[1 *Article 68a*

Provision of benefits

3.446 In the event that family benefits are not used by the person to whom they should be provided for the maintenance of the members of the family, the competent institution shall discharge its legal obligations by providing those benefits to the natural or legal person in fact maintaining the members of the family, at the request and through the agency of the institution in their Member State of residence or of the designated institution or body appointed for that purpose by the competent authority of their Member State of residence.]

Article 68a

Amendment

1. Inserted by Regulation 988/2009 art.1 (May 1, 2010).

General note

Article 68a was inserted by amendment to address the rare situation in which family benefits are not being applied for the benefit of the family member in respect of whom they are paid, and enables them to be re-routed to the person in fact maintaining the family members for whom the benefit is paid. 3.447

Article 69

Additional provisions

1. If, under the legislation designated by virtue of Articles 67 and 68, no right is acquired to the payment of additional or special family benefits for orphans, such benefits shall be paid by default, and in addition to the other family benefits acquired in accordance with the abovementioned legislation, under the legislation of the Member State to which the deceased worker was subject for the longest period of time, insofar as the right was acquired under that legislation. If no right was acquired under that legislation, the conditions for the acquisition of such right under the legislations of the other Member States shall be examined and benefits provided in decreasing order of the length of periods of insurance or residence completed under the legislation of those Member States. 3.448

2. Benefits paid in the form of pensions or supplements to pensions shall be provided and calculated in accordance with Chapter 5.

Relevant Provision of the Implementing Regulation

Article 61.

Chapter 9

Special Non-Contributory Cash Benefits

Article 70

General provision

1. This Article shall apply to special non-contributory cash benefits which are provided under legislation which, because of its personal scope, objectives and/or conditions for entitlement, has characteristics both of the social security legislation referred to in Article 3(1) and of social assistance. 3.449

2. For the purposes of this Chapter, "special non-contributory cash benefits" means those which:

(a) are intended to provide either:

(i) supplementary, substitute or ancillary cover against the risks covered by the branches of social security referred to in Article 3(1), and which guarantee the persons concerned a minimum subsistence income having regard to the economic and social situation in the Member State concerned;

or

(ii) solely specific protection for the disabled, closely linked to the said person's social environment in the Member State concerned,

and

(b) where the financing exclusively derives from compulsory taxation intended to cover general public expenditure and the conditions for providing and for calculating the benefits are not dependent on any contribution in respect of the beneficiary. However, benefits provided to supplement a contributory benefit shall not be considered to be contributory benefits for this reason alone,

and

(c) are listed in Annex X.

3. Article 7 and the other Chapters of this Title shall not apply to the benefits referred to in paragraph 2 of this Article.

4. The benefits referred to in paragraph 2 shall be provided exclusively in the Member State in which the persons concerned reside, in accordance with its legislation. Such benefits shall be provided by and at the expense of the institution of the place of residence.

CORRESPONDING PROVISION OF REGULATION 1408/71

Article 10a.

GENERAL NOTE

Introduction

3.450 The concept of special non-contributory benefits was introduced into Reg.1408/71 by Reg.1247/92/EEC, [1992] OJ L/136/1 with effect from June 1, 1992.

Such benefits are benefits which provide "supplementary, substitute or ancillary cover" in respect of the risks set out in what was then art.4 of Reg.1408/71, or "solely as specific protection for the disabled".

By an amendment in 2005 additional qualifying words were added which refer to minimum subsistence income benefits and qualify the benefits for disabled people by referring to their being "closely linked to the said person's social environment in the Member State concerned."

The significance of the designation of a benefit as a special non-contributory benefit is *not* that it is taken outside the scope of reg.1408/71, and now Reg.883/2004, completely, but that it is payable only on the territory of the competent state. The United Kingdom's list of benefits included in Annex IIa of Reg.1408/71 was always among the longer lists of such benefits.

Listing in the Annex is not conclusive—benefits must be special non-contributory benefits in substance

3.451 The nature of disability living allowance was considered in *Snares v The Adjudication Officer* (C-20/96) [1997] E.C.R. I-6057, reported as *R(DLA) 5/99*, and of attendance allowance in *Partridge v The Adjudication Officer* (C-297/96) [1998] E.C.R. I-3467, reported as *R(A) 1/99*. The Luxembourg Court took the view that the listing of the benefit in Annex IIa must be accepted as establishing the nature of the benefit; the absence of a revised declaration under art.5 of Reg.1408/71 did not prejudice this position. The result was the same in *Partridge*.

It was accepted in the Court of Appeal in *Perry v Chief Adjudication Officer*, reported as *R(IS) 4/99* that income support is a special non-contributory benefit.

This was confirmed in a ruling from the Luxembourg Court in *Swaddling v Adjudication Officer* (C-90/97) [2009] E.C.R. I-1097, reported as *R(IS) 6/99*, but that ruling also indicated the effect of the benefit remaining one within the scope of Reg.1408/71 for other purposes.

Though it is a precondition for claiming that a benefit is a special non-contributory benefit that it is listed in Annex IIa (now Annex X), that is not conclusive as to its status. It remains open to the Luxembourg Court to determine that the benefit is a supplement to one of the benefits within the material scope of the regulation: *Jauch* (C-215/99) [2001] E.C.R. I-1901, and Case C-43/99 *Leclere (*C-43/99) [2001] E.C.R. I-4265. This case rather took the Member States by surprise, since they had assumed that inclusion in Annex IIa was conclusive. But the Luxembourg Court ruled that it must examine in cases where the issue arose whether a benefit genuinely qualified as a special non-contributory benefit; specification in Annex IIa was not conclusive. The fallout from the decision in *Jauch and Leclere* is that claims that benefits are special non-contributory benefits can now be subject to more detailed enquiry if that matter comes before the Luxembourg Court 3.452

In *Skalka* (C-160/02) [2004] E.C.R. I-1771 the Luxembourg Court had to consider the status of a supplementary pension in Austria, which was listed in Annex IIa. In essence this is a topping up pension to bring a pensioner's income up to a certain level. It was, however, only payable to people habitually resident in Austria. Skalka was an Austrian national who had retired early and moved to Spain. The Luxembourg Court accepted that it was a special non-contributory benefit. There was clear evidence that the benefit was non-contributory. At [22] the court said:

> "22. A special benefit within the meaning of Article 4(2a) of Regulation No 1408/71 is defined by its purpose. It must either replace or supplement a social security benefit and be by its nature social assistance justified on economic and social grounds and fixed by legislation setting objective criteria (see to that effect Case C-20/96 *Snares* [1997] ECR I-6057, paragraphs 33, 42 and 43, Case C-297/96 *Partridge* [1998] ECR I-3467, paragraph 34, and Case C-43/99 *Leclère and Deaconescu* [2001] ECR I-4265, paragraph 32).
>
> 26. As all the interveners have stated, the Austrian compensatory supplement tops up a retirement pension or an invalidity pension. It is by nature social assistance in so far as it is intended to ensure a minimum means of subsistence for its recipient where the pension is insufficient. Its grant is dependent on objective criteria defined by law. Consequently, it must be classified as a 'special benefit' within the meaning of Regulation No 1408/71."

In *Silvia Hosse* (C-286/03) [2006] E.C.R. I-1771, the Grand Chamber of the Luxembourg Court was faced with a reference concerning a German care allowance. It was regional benefit, but that did not prove to be material to the Court's ruling. The Court noted that the Union institutions were entitled to legislate for certain exceptions to the principle of exportability of social security benefits, but recapitulated its earlier case law on the classification of benefits. The Court then explained why the German benefit was not a special non-contributory benefit:

> "36. The scheme of Regulation No 1408/71 shows that the concept of 'social security benefit' within the meaning of Article 4(1) and the concept of 'special non-contributory benefit' within the meaning of Article 4(2a) and (2b) of the regulation are mutually exclusive. A benefit which satisfies the conditions of a 'social security benefit' within the meaning of Article 4(1) of Regulation No 1408/71 therefore cannot be analysed as a 'special non-contributory benefit".
>
> 37. A benefit may be regarded as a social security benefit in so far as it is granted to the recipients, without any individual and discretionary assessment of personal needs, on the basis of a legally defined position and relates to one

of the risks expressly listed in Article 4(1) of Regulation No 1408/71 (see, inter alia, Case 249/83 *Hoeckx* [1985] ECR 973, paragraphs 12 to 14; Case C-78/91 *Hughes* [1992] ECR I-4839, paragraph 15; Case C-160/96 *Molenaar* [1998] ECR I-843, paragraph 20; and *Jauch*, paragraph 25).

38. It follows that benefits which are granted objectively on the basis of a legally defined position and are intended to improve the state of health and life of persons reliant on care have the essential purpose of supplementing sickness insurance benefits, and must be regarded as 'sickness benefits' within the meaning of Article 4(1)(a) of Regulation No 1408/71 (*Molenaar*, paragraphs 24 and 25, and *Jauch* paragraph 28).

39. A care allowance such as that granted under the SPGG is intended to compensate, in the form of a flat-rate contribution, for the additional expenditure resulting from the recipients' condition of reliance on care, in particular the cost of the assistance it is necessary to provide them with.

40. The amount of such a care allowance depends of the degree of reliance on care. It corresponds to the time spent on care, expressed in terms of hours per month. Assessment of reliance on care is regulated in detail in a measure laying down a classification according to degrees of reliance. The other income of the person reliant on care has no effect on the amount of the care allowance.

41. The allowance is paid to persons who do not receive any pension under the Federal provisions. Those persons are essentially members of the families of socially insured persons, recipients of social assistance, disabled workers, and persons receiving pensions from the provinces and municipalities.

42. Consequently, while a care allowance such as that at issue in the main proceedings may have a different system from that applicable to the German benefits of insurance against reliance on care at issue in *Molenaar* and the Austrian federal care allowance at issue in *Jauch*, it none the less remains of the same kind as those benefits.

43. Moreover, as the Court observed in *Jauch*, the conditions for the grant of care allowance and the way in which it is financed cannot have the intention or the effect of changing the character of care allowance as analysed in the *Molenaar* and *Jauch* judgments. The fact that the grant of the benefit is not necessarily linked to payment of a sickness insurance benefit or a pension awarded on a basis other than sickness insurance cannot therefore change that analysis.

44. In those circumstances, even if they have their own particular characteristics, such benefits must be regarded as sickness benefits within the meaning of Article 4(1)(a) of Regulation No 1408/71.

45. In the light of the above factors, one of the conditions necessary for Article 4(2b) of Regulation No 1408/71 to apply, namely the classification of the benefit in question as a 'special benefit', is not satisfied. There is thus no longer any need to consider whether the other conditions laid down in that article are satisfied."

3.453 *Kersbergen-Lap and Dams-Schipper* (C-154/05) [2006] E.C.R. I-6249, raised the question of whether an incapacity benefit for disabled young people who had never worked constituted a special non-contributory benefit. Two recipients of the benefit had moved to France and Germany respectively, and the payment of the benefit had been stopped. It was again easy to conclude that the benefit was non-contributory, and as in the earlier cases the focus was on whether the benefit was special. The Third Chamber concluded:

"30. A special benefit within the meaning of Article 4(2a) of Regulation No 1408/71 is defined by its purpose. It must either replace or supplement a social security benefit and be by its nature social assistance justified on economic and social grounds and fixed by legislation setting objective criteria (see Case C-160/02 *Skalka* [2004] ECR I-5613, paragraph 25, and case-law cited).

31. As was pointed out by the Netherlands Government, the Wajong benefit is

a replacement allowance intended for those who do not satisfy the conditions of insurance for obtaining invalidity benefit under Article 4(1)(b) of Regulation No 1408/71. By guaranteeing a minimum income to a socially disadvantaged group (disabled young people), the Wajong benefit is by its nature social assistance justified on economic and social grounds. Moreover, it is granted according to objective criteria defined by law.

32. With regard to the fact that the benefit at issue in the main proceedings is granted without any means test or needs assessment being carried out, as was pointed out by the Commission, the majority of disabled young people would not have sufficient means of subsistence if they did not receive that benefit.

33. Further, that benefit is closely linked to the socio-economic situation in the Netherlands since it is based on the minimum wage and the standard of living in that Member State. The Court has in the past accepted that the grant of benefits closely linked with the social environment may be made subject to a condition of residence in the State of the competent institution (see, to that effect, Case 313/86 *Lenoir* [1988] ECR 5391, paragraph 16; Case C-20/96 *Snares* [1997] ECR I-6057, paragraph 42; and Case C-43/99 *Leclerc and Deaconescu* [2001] ECR I-4265, paragraph 32).

34. It follows that a benefit under the Wajong must be classified as a special benefit within the meaning of Regulation No 1408/71."

José Perez Naranjo (C-265/05) [2007] E.C.R. I-347, 2007, concerned a supplementary old-age allowance payable in France. Perez Naranjo was a Spanish national who had worked in France but then return to Spain. Since November 1991 he has been in receipt of a French old-age pension. His claim for the supplementary allowance was refused. In this case the Grand Chamber quickly concluded that the benefit was a special benefit; it was similar to both social security and social assistance, and so had a mixed character which meant it had to be regarded as a special benefit (at [35]). The question of whether it was contributory was rather more complex and required an examination of the financing of the benefit. It is acknowledged that this is an enquiry which might better be resolved following consideration in the national courts (at [36]). In connection with this enquiry the Court observes that it is necessary to consider whether there is an identifiable link between the supplementary allowance and the general social contribution on earned income and substitute income. In a steer to the national court, the Grand Chamber says:

". . . even if the part of the general social contribution based on earned income and substitute income must be regarded as a contribution rather than financing from public resources, the link between that contribution and the supplementary allowance is not sufficiently identifiable for that allowance to be classified as a contributory benefit." (At [52].)

In *Hendrix* (C-287/05) [2007] E.C.R. I-6909, the Grand Chamber ruled:

"1. A benefit such as that provided under the Law on provision of incapacity benefit to disabled young people (Wet arbeidsongeschiktheidsvoorziening jonggehandicapten) of 24 April 1997 must be regarded as a special non-contributory benefit within the meaning of Article 4(2a) of Council Regulation (EEC) No 1408/71 of 14 June 1971 on the application of social security schemes to employed persons, to self-employed persons and to members of their families moving within the Community, as amended and updated by Council Regulation (EC) No 118/97 of 2 December 1996, as amended by Council Regulation (EC) No 1223/98 of 4 June 1998, with the result that only the coordinating provision in Article 10a of that regulation must be applied to persons who are in the situation of the applicant in the main proceedings and that payment of that benefit may validly be reserved to persons who reside on the territory of the Member State which provides the benefit. The fact that the person concerned previously received a benefit for disabled young people which was exportable is of no relevance to the application of those provisions.

2. Article 39 EC and Article 7 of Regulation (EEC) No 1612/68 of the Council

of 15 October 1968 on freedom of movement for workers within the Community must be interpreted as not precluding national legislation which applies Article 4(2a) and Article 10a of Regulation No 1408/71, as amended and updated by Regulation No 118/97, as amended by Regulation No 1223/98, and provides that a special non-contributory benefit listed in Annex IIa to Regulation No 1408/71 may be granted only to persons who are resident in the national territory. However, implementation of that legislation must not entail an infringement of the rights of a person in a situation such as that of the applicant in the main proceedings which goes beyond what is required to achieve the legitimate objective pursued by the national legislation. It is for the national court, which must, so far as possible, interpret the national legislation in conformity with Community law, to take account, in particular, of the fact that the worker in question has maintained all of his economic and social links to the Member State of origin."

Disability living allowance

3.454 The issue of what are genuinely special non-contributory benefits was raised in an action for annulment brought by the Commission against the European Parliament and Council, arguing that the legislators had acted beyond their powers in agreeing to the inclusion of certain benefits by three Member States in Annex IIa. The United Kingdom benefits in issue were attendance allowance, carer's allowance, and disability living allowance. In *Commission v European Parliament and Council* (C-299/05) [2007] E.C.R. I-8695, the Court has ruled that attendance allowance, carer's allowance, and the care component of a disability living allowance constitute sickness benefits and not special non-contributory benefits. The problem of the care component being part of a single benefit, namely, disability living allowance, is acknowledged, with the possibility of severing the two components of the allowance. To give the United Kingdom an opportunity to reconstitute the two components of the disability living allowance as separate benefits, the Court attached a temporal limitation to its judgment in the following terms:

"74. It is necessary, however, for the Court to state that the straightforward annulment of the inclusion of the DLA in the list in Annex IIa as amended would lead to the United Kingdom being forced to grant the 'mobility' element of that benefit to an unspecified number of recipients throughout the European Union, although the fact that that part of the DLA is in the nature of a non-contributory benefit cannot be disputed and it could lawfully be included in that list as a non-exportable benefit.

75. That fact warrants the Court exercising the power expressly conferred on it by the second paragraph of Article 231 EC in the event of annulment of a regulation, provisionally to maintain the effects of inclusion of the DLA as regards solely the 'mobility' part so that, within a reasonable period, appropriate measures can be taken to include it in Annex IIa as amended."

The decision makes it clear that attendance allowance, carer's allowance and the care component of a disability living allowance (together referred to below as "the relevant benefits") are exportable from May 5, 2005 (the date Reg.1408/71 was amended) where entitlement has been established and the only issue is termination of payment by reason of time spent outside Great Britain. Furthermore, no change to the structure of disability living allowance has yet been put in place, which leaves claimants and tribunals in some uncertainty as to how to proceed. There remains some uncertainty as to how far back the United Kingdom Government may need to go in order to divide disability living allowance into a component which is exportable and one which is (arguably) not: see *JS v SSWP* [2009] UKUT 81 (AAC).

The following would seem to be the most likely scenarios and their outcomes on the basis of the judgment in *Commission v European Parliament and Council*:

(1) Appeals against refusals to pay the relevant benefits which relate to periods on or after May 5, 2005 should be allowed. Claims in relation to earlier periods (and indeed some new claims which seek to go back only to May 5, 2005) will almost certainly run into difficulties in relation to time limits.

(2) Appeals concerning disability living allowance which concern both components should be allowed in relation to the care component in relation to periods to which they apply on or after May 5, 2005.

(3) Appeals concerning only the mobility component or periods before May 5, 2005 are likely to be more complex. The mobility component issue is complicated because its status as a special non-contributory benefit was conceded rather than established before the Luxembourg Court. This leaves open a possible challenge to its status. Cases involving time limits raise the application of the anti-test case rule in s.27 of the Social Security Act 1998. That provision does not apply because the change in the law has not arisen in the context of an appeal, but in the context of an action under art.230 EC taken by one Community institution against two other Community institutions seeking the annulment of parts of Community legislation. It is a direct action before the Luxembourg Court rather than a reference in appeal proceedings before the national courts.

GS v SSWP (DLA) [2015] UKUT 687 (AAC) decides that the "age 65 cut off" in the DLA scheme does not breach EU law.

For guidance from the Department on the export of attendance allowance, the care component of disability living allowance, and carer's allowance, see Memo DMG 28/10 of April 2010 available on the Department's website. 3.455

A reference has been made by the Upper Tribunal on the application of the principles in this case to the mobility component of disability living allowance in *RB v Secretary of State for Work and Pensions,* [2009] UKUT 286 (AAC). In *Bartlett, Ramos and Taylor v Secretary of State for Work and Pensions* (C-537/09) [2011] E.C.R. I-03417, [2012] AACR 34, the Luxembourg Court has ruled that the mobility component of disability living allowance is a special non-contributory benefit. For the decisions of the Upper Tribunal on the return of the case from the Court of Justice, see *NG v SSWP (DLA)* [2012] UKUT 26 (AAC) (reported as [2012] AACR 35); *RB v SSWP (DLA)* [2012] UKUT 28 (AAC); and *JT v SSWP (DLA)* [2012] UKUT 27 (AAC) (reported as [2012] AACR 39).

Note too that reg.6(35) and (36) of the Claims and Payments Regulations makes amendments to allow certain claims where a supersession to remove entitlement to the care component by the Secretary of State was incompatible with the judgment of the Court of Justice in *Commission v European Parliament and Council* (C-299/05) [2007] E.C.R. I-8730.

The benefits listed in Annex X

The United Kingdom list the following benefits in Annex X: 3.456

(a) State Pension Credit (State Pension Credit Act 2002 and State Pension Credit Act (Northern Ireland) 2002).

It was held in *EC v SSWP,* [2010] AACR 39, that state pension credit is a special non-contributory benefit which is not exportable.

(b) Income-based allowances for jobseekers (Jobseekers Act 1995 and Jobseekers (Northern Ireland) Order 1995).

(c) Income Support (Social Security Contributions and Benefits Act 1992 and Social Security Contributions and Benefits (Northern Ireland) Act 1992).

(d) Disability Living Allowance mobility component (Social Security Contributions and Benefits Act 1992 and Social Security Contributions and Benefits (Northern Ireland) Act 1992).

Other United Kingdom authorities

In *SC v SSWP* [2010] UKUT 108 (AAC), the judge found that Italian civil invalidity benefit is a "special non-contributory benefit", and so receipt of this benefit could not count towards the 364 days of entitlement to an equivalent of short-term incapacity benefit in order to qualify for long-term incapacity benefit. 3.457

Title IV

Administrative Commission and Advisory Committee

Article 71

Composition and working methods of the Administrative Commission

3.458 1. The Administrative Commission for the Coordination of Social Security Systems (hereinafter called "the Administrative Commission") attached to [1 the European Commission] shall be made up of a government representative from each of the Member States, assisted, where necessary, by expert advisers. A representative of [1 the European Commission] shall attend the meetings of the Administrative Commission in an advisory capacity.

[2 2. The Administrative Commission shall act by a qualified majority as defined by the Treaties, except when adopting its rules which shall be drawn up by mutual agreement among its members.

Decisions on questions of interpretation referred to in Article 72(a) shall be given the necessary publicity.]

3. Secretarial services for the Administrative Commission shall be provided by [1 the European Commission].

Corresponding Provision of Regulation 1408/71

Article 80.

Amendments

1. Regulation 465/2012 [2012] OJ L149/4 art.1(1) (June 28, 2012).
2. Regulation 465/2012 [2012] OJ L149/4 art.1(10) (June 28, 2012).

Article 72

Tasks of the Administrative Commission

3.459 The Administrative Commission shall:

(a) deal with all administrative questions and questions of interpretation arising from the provisions of this Regulation or those of the Implementing Regulation, or from any agreement concluded or arrangement made thereunder, without prejudice to the right of the authorities, institutions and persons concerned to have recourse to the procedures and tribunals provided for by the legislation of the Member States, by this Regulation or by the Treaty;

(b) facilitate the uniform application of Community law, especially by promoting exchange of experience and best administrative practices;

(c) foster and develop cooperation between Member States and their institutions in social security matters in order, inter alia, to take into account particular questions regarding certain categories of persons; facilitate realisation of actions of cross-border cooperation activities in the area of the coordination of social security systems;

(d) encourage as far as possible the use of new technologies in order to facilitate the free movement of persons, in particular by modernising procedures for exchanging information and adapting the information flow between institutions for the purposes of exchange by electronic means, taking account of the development of data processing in each Member State; the Administrative Commission shall adopt the common structural rules for data processing services, in particular on security and the use of standards, and shall lay down provisions for the operation of the common part of those services;

(e) undertake any other function falling within its competence under this Regulation and the Implementing Regulation or any agreement or arrangement concluded thereunder;

(f) make any relevant proposals to [1 the European Commission] concerning the coordination of social security schemes, with a view to improving and modernising the Community "acquis" by drafting subsequent Regulations or by means of other instruments provided for by the Treaty;

(g) establish the factors to be taken into account for drawing up accounts relating to the costs to be borne by the institutions of the Member States under this Regulation and to adopt the annual accounts between those institutions, based on the report of the Audit Board referred to in Article 74.

CORRESPONDING PROVISION OF REGULATION 1408/71

Article 81.

AMENDMENT

1. Regulation 465/2012 [2012] OJ L149/4 art.1 (June 28, 2012).

GENERAL NOTE

The Administrative Commission from time to time makes decisions on the interpretation and application of provisions of the basic regulation and the implementing regulation. These are for guidance, but often provide very helpful guidance; they also often address concerns which have been expressed by Member States in the meetings of the Administrative Commission. Decisions of the Administrative Commission are available on the European Commission website, accessible from *http://ec.europa.eu/social/main.jsp?catId=868* [Accessed April 14, 2017]. The most significant are published in the C series of the *Official Journal*. **3.460**

Decision No H1 of the Administrative Commission of June 12, 2009 concerning the framework for the transition from Regulations (EEC) No.1408/71 and No.574/72 to regulations (EC) No.883/2004 and No [. . .] and the application of Decisions and Recommendations of the Administrative Commission for the coordination of social security systems, provides detailed information on the applicability of Decisions made in relation to Reg.1408/71 which (a) will have no successor under the new regulations; (b) have substituted Decisions and Regulations covering corresponding provisions of the new regulations; and (c) are still to be adapted for the new regulations.

Article 73

Technical Commission for Data Processing

3.461 1. A Technical Commission for Data Processing (hereinafter called the "Technical Commission") shall be attached to the Administrative Commission. The Technical Commission shall propose to the Administrative Commission common architecture rules for the operation of data-processing services, in particular on security and the use of standards; it shall deliver reports and a reasoned opinion before decisions are taken by the Administrative Commission pursuant to Article 72(d). The composition and working methods of the Technical Commission shall be determined by the Administrative Commission.

2. To this end, the Technical Commission shall:

(a) gather together the relevant technical documents and undertake the studies and other work required to accomplish its tasks;

(b) submit to the Administrative Commission the reports and reasoned opinions referred to in paragraph 1;

(c) carry out all other tasks and studies on matters referred to it by the Administrative Commission;

(d) ensure the management of Community pilot projects using data-processing services and, for the Community part, operational systems using data-processing services.

Article 74

Audit Board

3.462 1. An Audit Board shall be attached to the Administrative Commission. The composition and working methods of the Audit Board shall be determined by the Administrative Commission.

The Audit Board shall:

(a) verify the method of determining and calculating the annual average costs presented by Member States;

(b) collect the necessary data and carry out the calculations required for establishing the annual statement of claims of each Member State;

(c) give the Administrative Commission periodic accounts of the results of the implementation of this Regulation and of the Implementing Regulation, in particular as regards the financial aspect;

(d) provide the data and reports necessary for decisions to be taken by the Administrative Commission under Article 72(g);

(e) make any relevant suggestions it may have to the Administrative Commission, including those concerning this Regulation, in connection with subparagraphs (a), (b) and (c);

(f) carry out all work, studies or assignments on matters referred to it by the Administrative Commission.

Article 75

Advisory Committee for the Coordination of Social Security Systems

1. An Advisory Committee for the Coordination of Social Security Systems (hereinafter referred to as "Advisory Committee") is hereby established, comprising, from each Member State: 3.463

(a) one government representative;
(b) one representative from the trade unions;
(c) one representative from the employers' organisations.

For each of the categories referred to above, an alternate member shall be appointed for each Member State.

The members and alternate members of the Advisory Committee shall be appointed by the Council. The Advisory Committee shall be chaired by a representative of [[1] the European Commission]. The Advisory Committee shall draw up its rules of procedure.

2. The Advisory Committee shall be empowered, at the request of [[1] the European Commission], the Administrative Commission or on its own initiative:

(a) to examine general questions or questions of principle and problems arising from the implementation of the Community provisions on the coordination of social security systems, especially regarding certain categories of persons;
(b) to formulate opinions on such matters for the Administrative Commission and proposals for any revisions of the said provisions.

Corresponding Provision of Regulation 1408/71

Article 82.

Amendment

1. Regulation 465/2012 [2012] OJ L149/4 art.1 (June 28, 2012).

Title V

Miscellaneous Provisions

Article 76

Cooperation

1. The competent authorities of the Member States shall communicate to each other all information regarding: 3.464

(a) measures taken to implement this Regulation;
(b) changes in their legislation which may affect the implementation of this Regulation.

2. For the purposes of this Regulation, the authorities and institutions of the Member States shall lend one another their good offices and act as though implementing their own legislation. The administrative assistance given by the said authorities and institutions shall, as a rule, be free of

charge. However, the Administrative Commission shall establish the nature of reimbursable expenses and the limits above which their reimbursement is due.

3. The authorities and institutions of the Member States may, for the purposes of this Regulation, communicate directly with one another and with the persons involved or their representatives.

4. The institutions and persons covered by this Regulation shall have a duty of mutual information and cooperation to ensure the correct implementation of this Regulation.

The institutions, in accordance with the principle of good administration, shall respond to all queries within a reasonable period of time and shall in this connection provide the persons concerned with any information required for exercising the rights conferred on them by this Regulation.

The persons concerned must inform the institutions of the competent Member State and of the Member State of residence as soon as possible of any change in their personal or family situation which affects their right to benefits under this Regulation.

5. Failure to respect the obligation of information referred to in the third subparagraph of paragraph 4 may result in the application of proportionate measures in accordance with national law. Nevertheless, these measures shall be equivalent to those applicable to similar situations under domestic law and shall not make it impossible or excessively difficult in practice for claimants to exercise the rights conferred on them by this Regulation.

6. In the event of difficulties in the interpretation or application of this Regulation which could jeopardise the rights of a person covered by it, the institution of the competent Member State or of the Member State of residence of the person concerned shall contact the institution(s) of the Member State(s) concerned. If a solution cannot be found within a reasonable period, the authorities concerned may call on the Administrative Commission to intervene.

7. The authorities, institutions and tribunals of one Member State may not reject applications or other documents submitted to them on the grounds that they are written in an official language of another Member State, recognised as an official language of the Community institutions in accordance with Article 290 of the Treaty.

CORRESPONDING PROVISION OF REGULATION 1408/71

Article 84.

RELEVANT DECISIONS OF THE ADMINISTRATIVE COMMISSION

Decision No A1 of June 12, 2009 of the Administrative Commission concerning the establishment of a dialogue and conciliation procedure concerning the validity of documents, the determination of the applicable legislation and the provision of benefits under Regulation (EC) No.883/2004.

GENERAL NOTE

3.465 Article 4(3) TEU (re-enacting a provision formerly found in art.10 EC) contains an over-arching obligation to co-operate in carrying out the tasks which flow from the Treaties. This provision is specific expression of that duty in the context of the co-ordination of the social security systems of the Member States within the framework of this regulation.

Article 77

Protection of personal data

1. Where, under this Regulation or under the Implementing Regulation, the authorities or institutions of a Member State communicate personal data to the authorities or institutions of another Member State, such communication shall be subject to the data protection legislation of the Member State transmitting them. Any communication from the authority or institution of the receiving Member State as well as the storage, alteration and destruction of the data provided by that Member State shall be subject to the data protection legislation of the receiving Member State. 3.466

2. Data required for the application of this Regulation and the Implementing Regulation shall be transmitted by one Member State to another Member State in accordance with Community provisions on the protection of natural persons with regard to the processing and free movement of personal data.

Article 78

Data processing

1. Member States shall progressively use new technologies for the exchange, access and processing of the data required to apply this Regulation and the Implementing Regulation. [1 the European Commission] shall lend its support to activities of common interest as soon as the Member States have established such data-processing services. 3.467

2. Each Member State shall be responsible for managing its own part of the data-processing services in accordance with the Community provisions on the protection of natural persons with regard to the processing and the free movement of personal data.

3. An electronic document sent or issued by an institution in conformity with this Regulation and the Implementing Regulation may not be rejected by any authority or institution of another Member State on the grounds that it was received by electronic means, once the receiving institution has declared that it can receive electronic documents. Reproduction and recording of such documents shall be presumed to be a correct and accurate reproduction of the original document or representation of the information it relates to, unless there is proof to the contrary.

4. An electronic document shall be considered valid if the computer system on which the document is recorded contains the safeguards necessary in order to prevent any alteration, disclosure or unauthorised access to the recording. It shall at any time be possible to reproduce the recorded information in an immediately readable form. When an electronic document is transferred from one social security institution to another, appropriate security measures shall be taken in accordance with the Community provisions on the protection of natural persons with regard to the processing and the free movement of personal data.

AMENDMENT

1. Regulation 465/2012 [2012] OJ L149/4 art.1 (June 28, 2012).

Article 79

Funding of activities in the social security field

3.468 In connection with this Regulation and the Implementing Regulation, [1 the European Commission] may fund in full or in part:

(a) activities aimed at improving exchanges of information between the social security authorities and institutions of the Member States, particularly the electronic exchange of data;

(b) any other activity aimed at providing information to the persons covered by this Regulation and their representatives about the rights and obligations deriving from this Regulation, using the most appropriate means.

AMENDMENT

1. Regulation 465/2012 [2012] OJ L149/4 art.1 (June 28, 2012).

Article 80

Exemptions

3.469 1. Any exemption from or reduction of taxes, stamp duty, notarial or registration fees provided for under the legislation of one Member State in respect of certificates or documents required to be produced in application of the legislation of that Member State shall be extended to similar certificates or documents required to be produced in application of the legislation of another Member State or of this Regulation.

2. All statements, documents and certificates of any kind whatsoever required to be produced in application of this Regulation shall be exempt from authentication by diplomatic or consular authorities.

Article 81

Claims, declarations or appeals

3.470 Any claim, declaration or appeal which should have been submitted, in application of the legislation of one Member State, within a specified period to an authority, institution or tribunal of that Member State shall be admissible if it is submitted within the same period to a corresponding authority, institution or tribunal of another Member State. In such a case the authority, institution or tribunal receiving the claim, declaration or appeal shall forward it without delay to the competent authority, institution or tribunal of the former Member State either directly or through the competent authorities of the Member States concerned. The date on which such claims, declarations or appeals were submitted to the authority, institution or tribunal of the second Member State shall be considered as the date of their submission to the competent authority, institution or tribunal.

CORRESPONDING PROVISION OF REGULATION 1408/71

Article 86.

GENERAL NOTE

A claim made to a competent institution in a Member State other than the competent State is to be forwarded to the competent Member State without delay and is to be treated by that Member State as a claim made in time if it was received within the relevant time limit in the first Member State. 3.471

In *SSWP v AK (AA)* [2015] UKUT 110 (AAC), Judge Jacobs explained the operation of art.81 as follows:

> "29. Applying [Article 81] requires this approach. In order for Article 81 to apply, two conditions must be satisfied. First, the Secretary of State or the tribunal must decide that the United Kingdom is not the competent State for the benefit claimed. Second, there must be no evidence that is sufficient to show a difference of view between competing member States. If, and only if, both of those conditions are satisfied, the Secretary of State must submit the claim to the other potentially competent State under the Article."

Article 82

Medical examinations

Medical examinations provided for by the legislation of one Member State may be carried out at the request of the competent institution, in another Member State, by the institution of the place of residence or stay of the claimant or the person entitled to benefits, under the conditions laid down in the Implementing Regulation or agreed between the competent authorities of the Member States concerned. 3.472

CORRESPONDING PROVISION OF REGULATION 1408/71

Article 87.

Article 83

Implementation of legislation

Special provisions for implementing the legislation of certain Member States are referred to in Annex XI. 3.473

Article 84

Collection of contributions and recovery of benefits

1. Collection of contributions due to an institution of one Member State and recovery of benefits provided by the institution of one Member State 3.474

but not due may be effected in another Member State in accordance with the procedures and with the guarantees and privileges applicable to the collection of contributions due to the corresponding institution of the latter Member State and the recovery of benefits provided by it but not due.

2. Enforceable decisions of the judicial and administrative authorities relating to the collection of contributions, interest and any other charges or to the recovery of benefits provided but not due under the legislation of one Member State shall be recognised and enforced at the request of the competent institution in another Member State within the limits and in accordance with the procedures laid down by the legislation and any other procedures applicable to similar decisions of the latter Member State. Such decisions shall be declared enforceable in that Member State insofar as the legislation and any other procedures of that Member State so require.

3. Claims of an institution of one Member State shall in enforcement, bankruptcy or settlement proceedings in another Member State enjoy the same privileges as the legislation of the latter Member State accords to claims of the same kind.

4. The procedure for implementing this Article, including costs reimbursement, shall be governed by the Implementing Regulation or, where necessary and as a complementary measure, by means of agreements between Member States.

CORRESPONDING PROVISION OF REGULATION 1408/71

Article 92.

RELEVANT PROVISIONS OF THE IMPLEMENTING REGULATION

Chapter 3 of Title IV.

Article 85

Rights of institutions

3.475 1. If a person receives benefits under the legislation of one Member State in respect of an injury resulting from events occurring in another Member State, any rights of the institution responsible for providing benefits against a third party liable to provide compensation for the injury shall be governed by the following rules:

(a) where the institution responsible for providing benefits is, under the legislation it applies, subrogated to the rights which the beneficiary has against the third party, such subrogation shall be recognised by each Member State;

(b) where the institution responsible for providing benefits has a direct right against the third party, each Member State shall recognise such rights.

2. If a person receives benefits under the legislation of one Member State in respect of an injury resulting from events occurring in another Member State, the provisions of the said legislation which determine the cases in which the civil liability of employers or of their employees is to be excluded shall apply with regard to the said person or to the competent institution.

Paragraph 1 shall also apply to any rights of the institution responsible for providing benefits against employers or their employees in cases where their liability is not excluded.

Article 85

3. Where, in accordance with Article 35(3) and/or Article 41(2), two or more Member States or their competent authorities have concluded an agreement to waive reimbursement between institutions under their jurisdiction, or, where reimbursement does not depend on the amount of benefits actually provided, any rights arising against a liable third party shall be governed by the following rules:

(a) where the institution of the Member State of residence or stay accords benefits to a person in respect of an injury sustained in its territory, that institution, in accordance with the provisions of the legislation it applies, shall exercise the right to subrogation or direct action against the third party liable to provide compensation for the injury;

(b) for the application of (a):

 (i) the person receiving benefits shall be deemed to be insured with the institution of the place of residence or stay, and

 (ii) that institution shall be deemed to be the institution responsible for providing benefits;

(c) Paragraphs 1 and 2 shall remain applicable in respect of any benefits not covered by the waiver agreement or a reimbursement which does not depend on the amount of benefits actually provided.

CORRESPONDING PROVISION OF REGULATION 1408/71

Article 93.

Article 86

Bilateral agreements

As far as relations between, on the one hand, Luxembourg and, on the other hand, France, Germany and Belgium are concerned, the application and the duration of the period referred to in Article 65(7) shall be subject to the conclusion of bilateral agreements. 3.476

TITLE VI

TRANSITIONAL AND FINAL PROVISIONS

Article 87

Transitional provisions

1. No rights shall be acquired under this Regulation for the period before its date of application. 3.477

2. Any period of insurance and, where appropriate, any period of employment, self-employment or residence completed under the legislation of a Member State prior to the date of application of this Regulation in the Member State concerned shall be taken into consideration for the determination of rights acquired under this Regulation.

3. Subject to paragraph 1, a right shall be acquired under this Regulation

even if it relates to a contingency arising before its date of application in the Member State concerned.

4. Any benefit which has not been awarded or which has been suspended by reason of the nationality or place of residence of the person concerned shall, at the request of that person, be provided or resumed with effect from the date of application of this Regulation in the Member State concerned, provided that the rights for which benefits were previously provided have not given rise to a lump-sum payment.

5. The rights of a person to whom a pension was provided prior to the date of application of this Regulation in a Member State may, at the request of the person concerned, be reviewed, taking into account this Regulation.

6. If a request referred to in paragraph 4 or 5 is submitted within two years from the date of application of this Regulation in a Member State, the rights acquired under this Regulation shall have effect from that date, and the legislation of any Member State concerning the forfeiture or limitation of rights may not be invoked against the persons concerned.

7. If a request referred to in paragraph 4 or 5 is submitted after the expiry of the two-year period following the date of application of this Regulation in the Member State concerned, rights not forfeited or not time-barred shall have effect from the date on which the request was submitted, subject to any more favourable provisions under the legislation of any Member State.

[1 8. If, as a result of this Regulation, a person is subject to the legislation of a Member State other than that determined in accordance with Title II of Regulation(EEC) No 1408/71, that legislation shall continue to apply while the relevant situation remains unchanged and in any case for no longer than 10 years from the date of application of this Regulation unless the person concerned requests that he/she be subject to the legislation applicable under this Regulation. The request shall be submitted within 3 months after the date of application of this Regulation to the competent institution of the Member State whose legislation is applicable under this Regulation if the person concerned is to be subject to the legislation of that Member State as of the date of application of this Regulation. If the request is made after the time limit indicated, the change of applicable legislation shall take place on the first day of the following month.]

9. Article 55 of this Regulation shall apply only to pensions not subject to Article 46c of Regulation (EEC) No 1408/71 on the date of application of this Regulation.

10. The provisions of the second sentences of Article 65(2) and (3) shall be applicable to Luxembourg at the latest two years after the date of application of this Regulation.

[1 10a. The entries in Annex III corresponding to Estonia, Spain, Italy, Lithuania, Hungary and the Netherlands shall cease to have effect 4 years after the date of application of this Regulation.

10b. The list contained in Annex III shall be reviewed no later than 31 October 2014 on the basis of a report by the Administrative Commission. That report shall include an impact assessment of the significance, frequency, scale and costs, both in absolute and in relative terms, of the application of the provisions of Annex III. That report shall also include the possible effects of repealing those provisions for those Member States which continue to be listed in that Annex after the date referred to in paragraph 10a. In the light of that report, the Commission shall decide whether to submit a proposal concerning a review of the list, with the aim in principle of repealing the list unless the report of the Administrative Commission provides compelling reasons not to do so.]

11. Member States shall ensure that appropriate information is provided regarding the changes in rights and obligations introduced by this Regulation and the Implementing Regulation.

AMENDMENT

1. Regulation 988/2009 art.1 (May 1, 2010).

RELEVANT DECISIONS OF THE ADMINISTRATIVE COMMISSION

Decision No H1 of the Administrative Commission of June 12, 2009 concerning the framework for the transition from Reg.(EEC) No.1408/71 and No.574/72 to Regs (EC) No.883/2004 and No [. . .] and the application of Decisions and Recommendations of the Administrative Commission for the co-ordination of social security systems.

Decision No.P1 of June 12, 2009 on the interpretation of arts 50(4), 58 and 87(5) of Regulation (EC) No.883/2004 for the award of Invalidity, Old-Age and Survivor's benefits.

GENERAL NOTE

Note the remarks of the Court of Justice in *Jeltes, Peeters and Arnold* (C-443/11) Judgment of April 11, 2013, on the operation of art.87 in the context of claims for unemployment benefit by atypical frontier workers: see [47]–[62] of the judgment). **3.478**

In *SSWP v PW (CA)* [2013] UKUT 296 (AAC), the judge ruled that the transitional provision in art.87(8):

> "applies to preserve entitlement that has already been established. If so, it allows that entitlement to continue for no longer than 10 years. It does not, on my understanding, allow a claimant to rely on it in order to establish entitlement from a date after Regulation 883/2004 came into force. That is the only interpretation that is consistent with the nature of a transitional provision. If it allowed a claimant to make a claim and rely on Regulation 1408/71 for ten years, it would effectively postpone the replacement of that Regulation by Regulation 883/2004 and have the effect that two Regulations were fully in force simultaneously. Neither of those results is impossible, but they are so unlikely and unusual that a clear and express provision would be needed to produce that outcome. There is no such provision." (At [5].)

KG v SSWP (DLA) [2015] UKUT 146 (AAC) concerned a claimant who had moved to Spain in January 2012, and wished to export the mobility component of her disability living allowance in reliance on the transitional protection contained in art.95b(8) of Regulation 1408/71. Judge Jacobs ruled that she could not rely on the transitional protection in Regulation 1408/71, since she had never relied on that Regulation because she had throughout the period when that Regulation was in force been in the United Kingdom. The transitional protection in art.87(8) of Regulation 883/2004 only operates to preserve entitlement that has already been established. The claimant could only rely on the provisions of Regulation 883/2004 and they did not entitle her to export the mobility component, which the Court of Justice of the European Union had ruled in *Bartlett, Ramos and Taylor v SSWP* (C-537/09) [2011] E.C.R. I-03417, [2012] AACR 34, was a special non-contributory benefit which was not exportable.

[1 Article 87a

Transitional provision for application of Regulation (EU) No 465/2012

3.479 1. If as a result of the entry into force of Regulation (EU) No 465/2012, a person is subject, in accordance with Title II of this Regulation, to the legislation of a different Member State than that to which he/she was subject before that entry into force, the legislation of the Member State applicable before that date shall continue to apply to him/her for a transitional period lasting for as long as the relevant situation remains unchanged and, in any case, for no longer than 10 years from the date of entry into force of Regulation (EU) No 465/2012. Such a person may request that the transitional period no longer applies to him/her. Such request shall be submitted to the institution designated by the competent authority of the Member State of residence. Requests submitted by 29 September 2012 shall be deemed to take effect on 28 June 2012. Requests submitted after 29 September 2012 shall take effect on the first day of the month following that of their submission.

2. No later than 29 June 2014, the Administrative Commission shall evaluate the implementation of the provisions laid down in Article 65a of this Regulation and present a report on their application. On the basis of this report, the European Commission may, as appropriate, submit proposals to amend those provisions.]

AMENDMENT

1. Inserted by Regulation 465/2012 [2012] OJ L149/4 art.1(11) (June 28, 2012).

Article 88

Updating of the Annexes

3.480 The Annexes of this Regulation shall be revised periodically.

GENERAL NOTE

3.481 It is the intention that it should be much more straightforward in the future to amend the annexes to the regulation than has been the case in the past, when information in the annexes has lagged behind the realities of the social security systems of the Member States.

Article 89

Implementing Regulation

3.482 A further Regulation shall lay down the procedure for implementing this Regulation.

Article 90

Article 90

Repeal

1. Council Regulation (EEC) No 1408/71 shall be repealed from the date of application of this Regulation. 3.483

However, Regulation (EEC) No 1408/71 shall remain in force and shall continue to have legal effect for the purposes of:

(a) Council Regulation (EC) No 859/2003 of 14 May 2003 extending the provisions of Regulation (EEC) No 1408/71 and Regulation (EEC) No 574/72 to nationals of third countries who are not already covered by those provisions solely on the ground of their nationality,[5] for as long as that Regulation has not been repealed or modified;

(b) Council Regulation (EEC) No 1661/85 of 13 June 1985 laying down the technical adaptations to the Community rules on social security for migrant workers with regard to Greenland,[6] for as long as that Regulation has not been repealed or modified;

(c) the Agreement on the European Economic Area[7] and the Agreement between the European Community and its Member States, of the one part, and the Swiss Confederation, of the other part, on the free movement of persons[8] and other agreements which contain a reference to Regulation (EEC) No 1408/71, for as long as those agreements have not been modified in the light of this Regulation.

2. References to Regulation (EEC) No 1408/71 in Council Directive 98/49/EC of 29 June 1998 on safeguarding the supplementary pension rights of employed and self-employed persons moving within the Community[9] are to be read as referring to this Regulation.

Article 91

Entry into force

This Regulation shall enter into force on the twentieth day after its publication in the Official Journal of the European Union. 3.484

It shall apply from the date of entry into force of the Implementing Regulation.

This Regulation shall be binding in its entirety and directly applicable in all Member States.

---

5 OJ L 124, 20.5.2003, p.1.

6 OJ L 160, 20.6.1985, p.7.

7 OJ L 1, 3.1.1994, p.1.

8 OJ L 114, 30.4.2002, p. 6. Agreement as last amended by Decision No 2/2003 of the EU-Swiss Committee (OJ L 187, 26.7.2003, p.55).

9 OJ L 209, 25.7.1998, p.46.

General Note

3.485 Although the regulation entered into force in May 2004, it did not apply until the implementing regulation had been finalised and published in the *Official Journal.* The regulation applies from May 1, 2010.

Paragraphs 24–30 of *Reichel-Albert* (C-522/10) Judgment of July 19, 2012, provide a useful reminder of the temporal effect of European Union law and the transition from Reg.1408/71 and Reg.883/2004 following the entry into force of Reg.883/2004 on May 1, 2010.

Done at Strasbourg, 29 April 2004.

Annex I

Advances of Maintenance Payments and Special Childbirth and Adoption Allowances

(Article 1(z))

I. Advances of maintenance payments

3.486 [1 . . .] BELGIUM

Advances of maintenance allowances under the law of 21 February 2003 creating a maintenance payments agency within the federal public service, Finance Department

[1 BULGARIA

Maintenance payments made by the State under Article 92 of the Family Code.]

[1 . . .] DENMARK

Advance payment of child support laid down in the Act on Child Benefits
Advance payment of child support consolidated by Law No 765 of 11 September 2002

[1 . . .] GERMANY

Advances of maintenance payments under the German law on advances of maintenance payments (Unterhaltsvorschussgesetz) of 23 July 1979.

[1 ESTONIA

Maintenance allowances under the Maintenance Allowance Act of 21 February 2007.

SPAIN

Advances of maintenance payments under the Royal Decree 1618/2007 of 7 December 2007.]

[1 . . .] FRANCE

Family support allowance paid to a child one of whose parents or both of whose parents are in default or are unable to meet their maintenance obligations or the payment of a maintenance allowance laid down by a court decision

[2CROATIA

Temporary advances paid by Centres for Social Welfare on the basis of the obligation to provide temporary maintenance pursuant to the Family Act (OG 116/03, as amended).]

[1 LITHUANIA

Payments from the Children's Maintenance Fund under the Law on the Children's Maintenance Fund.

LUXEMBOURG

Advances and recover of maintenance payments within the meaning of the Act of 26 July 1980.]

[1 . . .] AUSTRIA

Advances of maintenance payments under the Federal Law on the grant of advances of child maintenance (Unterhaltsvorschussgesetz 1985 – UVG)

[1 POLAND

Benefits from the Alimony Fund under the Act of Assistance to the Persons Entitled to Alimony.]

[1 . . .] PORTUGAL

Advances of maintenance payments (Act No 75/98, 19 November, on the guarantee of maintenance for minors).

[1 SLOVENIA

Maintenance replacement in accordance with the Act of Public Guarantee and Maintenance Fund of the Republic of Slovenia of 25 July 2006.

SLOVAKIA

Substitute alimony benefit (substitute maintenance payment) pursuant to the Act No 452/2004 Coll. On substitute alimony benefit as amended by later regulations.]

[1 . . .] FINLAND

Maintenance allowance under the Security of Child Maintenance Act (671/1998)

[1 . . .] SWEDEN

Maintenance allowance under the Maintenance Support Act (1996:1030)

II Special childbirth and adoption allowances

[1 . . .] BELGIUM

Childbirth allowance and adoption grant.

[1 BULGARIA

Maternity lump sum allowance (Law on Family Allowances for Children).

CZECH REPUBLIC

Childbirth allowance.

ESTONIA

(a) Childbirth allowance;
(b) Adoption allowance.]

[1 . . .] SPAIN

[1 Single payment birth and adoption grants.

[1 . . .] FRANCE

Birth or adoption grants as part of the "early childhood benefit" [1 , except when they are paid to a person who remains subject to French legislation pursuant to Article 12 or Article 16.]

[2 CROATIA

One-off cash benefit for a newborn child under the Maternity and Parental Benefits Act (OG 85/08, as amended) One-off cash benefit for an adopted child under the Maternity and Parental Benefits Act (OG 85/08, as amended) One-off cash benefits for a newborn child or an adopted child provided by regulations on local and regional self-government pursuant to Article 59 of the Maternity and Parental Benefits Act (OG 85/08, as amended).]

[1 LATVIA

(a) Childbirth grant;
(b) Adoption allowance.

LITHUANIA

Child lump sum grant.]

[1 . . .] LUXEMBOURG

Antenatal allowances
Childbirth allowances

HUNGARY

Maternity grant.

POLAND

Single payment birth grant (Act on Family Benefits).

ROMANIA

(a) Childbirth allowance;
(b) Layette for newborn children.

SLOVENIA

Childbirth grant.

SLOVAKIA

(a) Childbirth allowance;
(b) Supplement to childbirth allowance.]

[1 . . .] FINLAND

Maternity package, maternity lump-sum grant and assistance in the form of a lump sum intended to offset the cost of international adoption pursuant to the Maternity Grant Act

AMENDMENTS

1. Regulation 988/2009 art.1 (May 1, 2010).
2. Regulation 517/2013 art.1(b) (July 1, 2013).

[1 ANNEX II

PROVISIONS OF CONVENTIONS WHICH REMAIN IN FORCE AND WHICH, WHERE APPLICABLE, ARE RESTRICTED TO THE PERSONS COVERED THEREBY

(Article 8(1))

General comments

It is to be noted that the provisions of bilateral conventions which do not fall within the scope of this Regulation and which remain in force between Member States are not listed in this Annex. This includes obligations between Member States arising from conventions providing, for example, for provisions regarding aggregation of insurance periods fulfilled in a third country. 3.487

Provisions of social security conventions remaining applicable:

BELGIUM-GERMANY

Articles 3 and 4 of the Final Protocol of 7 December 1957 to the General Convention of that date, as set out in the Complementary Protocol of 10 November 1960 (reckoning of insurance periods completed in some border regions before, during and after the Second World War).

BELGIUM-LUXEMBOURG

Convention of 24 March 1994 on social security for frontier workers (relating to the complementary flat rate reimbursement).

BULGARIA-GERMANY

Article 28(1)(b) of the Convention on social security of 17 December 1997 (maintenance of conventions concluded between Bulgaria and the former German Democratic Republic for persons who already received a pension before 1996).

[2 BULGARIA-CROATIA
Article 35(3) of the Convention on Social Security of 14 July 2003 (recognition of periods of insurance completed until 31 December 1957 at the expense of the contracting state in which the insured person resided on 31 December 1957).]

BULGARIA-AUSTRIA

Article 38(3) of the Convention on social security of 14 April 2005 (reckoning of periods of insurance completed before27 November 1961); the application of that provision remains restricted to the persons covered by that Convention.

BULGARIA-SLOVENIA

Article 32(2) of the Convention on Social Security of 18 December 1957 (reckoning of periods of insurance completed until 31 December 1957).

CZECH REPUBLIC-GERMANY

Article 39(1)(b) and (c) of the Convention on Social Security of 27 July 2001 (maintenance of the convention concluded between the former Czechoslovak Republic and the former German Democratic Republic for persons who already received a pension before 1996; reckoning of periods of insurance completed in one of the contracting States for persons who already received a pension for these periods on 1 September 2002 from the other contracting State, while residing in its territory).

CZECH REPUBLIC-CYPRUS

Article 32(4) of the Convention on Social Security of 19 January 1999 (determining competence for the calculation of periods of employment completed under the relevant Convention of 1976); the application of that provision remains restricted to the persons covered by it.

CZECH REPUBLIC-LUXEMBOURG

Article 52(8) of the Convention on Social Security of 17 November 2000 (reckoning of pension insurance periods for political refugees).

CZECH REPUBLIC-AUSTRIA

Article 32(3) of the Convention on social security of 20 July 1999 (reckoning of periods of insurance completed before 27 November 1961); the application of that provision remains restricted to the persons covered by it.

CZECH REPUBLIC-SLOVAKIA

Articles 12, 20 and 33 of the Convention on Social Security of 29 October 1992 (Article 12 determines competence for a grant of survivor's benefits; Article 20 determines competence for calculation of insurance periods completed until the day of dissolution of the Czech and Slovak Federal Republic; Article 33 determines competence for payment of pensions awarded before the day of the dissolution of the Czech and Slovak Federal Republic).

DENMARK-FINLAND

Article 7 of the Nordic Convention on social security of 18 August 2003 (concerning coverage of extra travel expenses in case of sickness during stay in another Nordic country increasing the cost of return travel to the country of residence).

DENMARK-SWEDEN

Article 7 of the Nordic Convention on social security of 18 August 2003 (concerning coverage of extra travel expenses in case of sickness during stay in another Nordic country increasing the cost of return travel to the country of residence).

GERMANY-SPAIN

Article 45(2) of the Social Security Convention of 4 December 1973 (representation by diplomatic and consular authorities).

GERMANY-FRANCE

(a) Complementary Agreement No 4 of 10 July 1950 to the General Convention of the same date, as set out in Supplementary Agreement No 2 of 18 June 1955 (reckoning of periods of insurance completed between 1 July 1940and 30 June 1950);
(b) Title I of that Supplementary Agreement No 2 (reckoning of periods of insurance completed before 8 May 1945);
(c) points 6, 7 and 8 of the General Protocol of 10 July 1950 to the General Convention of the same date (administrative arrangements);
(d) Titles II, III and IV of the Agreement of 20 December 1963 (social security in the Saar).

[[2] GERMANY-CROATIA

Article 41 of the Convention on Social Security of 24 November 1997 (settlement of rights acquired before 1 January 1956 under the social security scheme of the other contracting state) application of that provision remains restricted to the persons covered by it.]

GERMANY-LUXEMBOURG

Articles 4, 5, 6 and 7 of the Convention of 11 July 1959 (reckoning of insurance periods completed between September 1940 and June 1946).

GERMANY-HUNGARY

Article 40(1)(b) of the Convention on social security of 2 May 1998 (maintenance of the convention concluded between the former German Democratic Republic and Hungary for persons who already received a pension before 1996).

GERMANY-NETHERLANDS

Articles 2 and 3 of Complementary Agreement No 4 of 21 December 1956 to the Convention of 29 March 1951 (settlement of rights acquired under the German social insurance scheme by Dutch workers between 13 May 1940 and 1 September 1945).

GERMANY-AUSTRIA

(a) Article 1(5) and Article 8 of the Convention on Unemployment Insurance of 19 July 1978 and Article 10 of the Final Protocol to this Convention (granting of unemployment allowances to frontier workers by the previous State of employment) shall continue to apply to persons who have exercised an activity as a frontier worker on or before 1 January 2005 and become unemployed before 1 January 2011;
(b) Article 14(2)(g), (h), (i) and (j) of the Convention on social security of 4 October 1995 (determination of competencies between both countries with regard to former insurance cases and acquired insurance periods); the application of that provision remains restricted to the persons covered by it.

GERMANY-POLAND

(a) Convention of 9 October 1975 on old-age and work injury provisions, under the conditions and the scope defined by Article 27(2) to (4) of the Convention on social security of 8 December 1990 (maintenance of legal status, on the basis of the Convention of 1975, of the persons who had established their residence in the territory of Germany or Poland before 1 January 1991 and who continue to reside there);
(b) Articles 27(5) and 28(2) of the Convention on social security of 8 December 1990 (maintenance of entitlement to a pension paid on the basis of the Convention of 1957 concluded between the former German Democratic Republic and Poland; reckoning of periods of insurance completed by Polish employees under the Convention of 1988 concluded between the former German Democratic Republic and Poland).

GERMANY-ROMANIA

Article 28(1)(b) of the Convention on social security of 8 April 2005 (maintenance of the Convention concluded between the former German Democratic Republic and Romania for persons who already received a pension before1996).

GERMANY-SLOVENIA

Article 42 of the Convention on social security of 24 September 1997 (settlement of rights acquired before 1 January1956 under the social security scheme of the other contracting state); the application of that provision remains restricted to the persons covered by it.

GERMANY-SLOVAKIA

Article 29(1), second and third subparagraphs of the Agreement of 12 September 2002 (maintenance of the Convention concluded between the former Czechoslovak Republic and the former German Democratic Republic for persons who already received a pension before 1996; reckoning of periods of insurance completed in one of the contracting States for persons who already received a pension for these periods on 1 December 2003 from the other contracting State, while residing in its territory).

GERMANY-UNITED KINGDOM

(a) Article 7(5) and (6) of the Convention on social security of 20 April 1960 (legislation applicable to civilians serving in the military forces);
(b) Article 5(5) and (6) of the Convention on unemployment insurance of 20 April 1960 (legislation applicable to civilians serving in the military forces).

IRELAND-UNITED KINGDOM

Article 19(2) of the Agreement of 14 December, 2004 on social security (concerning the transfer and reckoning of certain disability credits).

SPAIN-PORTUGAL

Article 22 of the General Convention of 11 June 1969 (export of unemployment benefits). This entry will remain valid for 2 years from the date of application of this Regulation.

[2 CROATIA-ITALY

(a) The Agreement between Yugoslavia and Italy on Regulation of Mutual Obligations in Social Insurance with Reference to Paragraph 7 of Annex XIV to the Peace Treaty, concluded by exchange of notes on 5 February 1959 (reckoning of periods of insurance completed before 18 December 1954); the application remains restricted to the persons covered by that Agreement;
(b) Article 44(3) of the Convention on Social Security between the Republic of Croatia and the Italian Republic of 27 June 1997, concerning ex Zone B of the Free Territory of Trieste (reckoning of periods of insurance completed before 5 October 1956); the application of that provision remains restricted to persons covered by that Convention.

CROATIA-HUNGARY

Article 43(6) of the Convention on Social Security of 8 February 2005 (recognition of periods of insurance completed until 29 May 1956 at the expense of the contracting state in which the insured person resided on 29 May 1956).

CROATIA-AUSTRIA

Article 35 of the Convention on Social Security of 16 January 1997 (reckoning of periods of insurance completed before 1 January 1956); the application of that provision remains restricted to the persons covered by it.

CROATIA-SLOVENIA

(a) Article 35(3) of the Agreement on Social Security of 28 April 1997 (recognition of periods with bonus under the legislation of the former common State);
(b) Articles 36 and 37 of the Agreement on Social Security of 28 April 1997 (benefits acquired before 8 October 1991 remain the obligation of the contracting state that granted them; pensions granted between 8 October 1991 and 1 February 1998, the date of entry into force of the said Agreement, in respect of the periods of insurance completed in the other contracting state until 31 January 1998, are subject to recalculation).]

ITALY-SLOVENIA

(a) Agreement on regulation of mutual obligations in social insurance with reference to paragraph 7 of Annex XIV to the Peace Treaty, concluded by exchange of notes on 5 February 1959 (reckoning of periods of insurance completed before 18 December 1954); the application of that provision remains restricted to the persons covered by that Agreement;
(b) Article 45(3) of the Convention on social security of 7 July 1997 concerning ex-Zone B of the Free Territory of Trieste (reckoning of periods of insurance completed before 5 October 1956); the application of that provision remains restricted to the persons covered by that Convention.

LUXEMBOURG-PORTUGAL

Agreement of 10 March 1997 (on the recognition of decisions by institutions in one contracting party concerning the state of invalidity of applicants for pensions from institutions in the other contracting party).

LUXEMBOURG-SLOVAKIA

Article 50(5) of the Convention on Social Security of 23 May 2002 (reckoning of pension insurance periods for political refugees).

HUNGARY-AUSTRIA

Article 36(3) of the Convention on social security of 31 March 1999 (reckoning of periods of insurance completed before 27 November 1961); the application of that provision remains restricted to the persons covered by it.

HUNGARY-SLOVENIA

Article 31 of the Convention on social security of 7 October 1957 (reckoning of periods of insurance completed before29 May 1956); the application of that provision remains restricted to the persons covered by it.

HUNGARY-SLOVAKIA

Article 34(1) of the Convention on social security of 30 January 1959 (Article 34(1) of that Convention provides that the insurance periods awarded before the day of signing that Convention are the insurance periods of the contracting State on which territory the entitled person had a residence); the application of that provision remains restricted to the persons covered by it.

AUSTRIA-POLAND

Article 33(3) of the Convention on social security of 7 September 1998 (reckoning of periods of insurance completed before 27 November 1961); the application of that provision remains restricted to the persons covered by it.

AUSTRIA-ROMANIA

Article 37(3) of the Agreement on social security of 28 October 2005 (reckoning of periods of insurance completed before 27 November 1961); the application of that provision remains restricted to the persons covered by it.

AUSTRIA-SLOVENIA

Article 37 of the Convention on social security of 10 March 1997 (reckoning of periods of insurance completed before1 January 1956); the application of that provision remains restricted to the persons covered by it.

AUSTRIA-SLOVAKIA

Article 34(3) of the Convention of 21 December 2001 on Social Security (reckoning of periods of insurance completed before 27 November 1961); the application of that provision remains restricted to the persons covered by it.

FINLAND-SWEDEN

Article 7 of the Nordic Convention on social security of 18 August 2003 (concerning coverage of extra travel expenses in case of sickness during stay in another Nordic country increasing the cost of return travel to the country of residence).]

AMENDMENTS

1. Inserted by Regulation 988/2009 art.1 (May 1, 2010).
2. Regulation 517/2013 art.1(b) (July 1, 2013).

[1 Annex III

RESTRICTION OF RIGHTS TO BENEFITS IN KIND FOR MEMBERS OF THE FAMILY OF A FRONTIER WORKER

(referred to in Article 18(2))

3.488 DENMARK

ESTONIA (this entry will be valid during the period referred to in Article 87(10a))

IRELAND

SPAIN (this entry will be valid during the period referred to in Article 87(10a))

[2 CROATIA]

ITALY (this entry will be valid during the period referred to in Article 87(10a))

LITHUANIA (this entry will be valid during the period referred to in Article 87(10a))

HUNGARY (this entry will be valid during the period referred to in Article 87(10a))

NETHERLANDS (this entry will be valid during the period referred to in Article 87(10a))

FINLAND

SWEDEN

UNITED KINGDOM.]

AMENDMENTS

1. Regulation 988/2009 art.1 (May 1, 2010).
2. Regulation 517/2013 art.1(b) (July 1, 2013).

ANNEX IV

MORE RIGHTS FOR PENSIONERS RETURNING TO THE COMPETENT MEMBER STATE

(Article 27(2))

3.489 BELGIUM

[1 BULGARIA

CZECH REPUBLIC]

Annex IV

GERMANY

GREECE

SPAIN

FRANCE

[1 CYPRUS]

[1 . . .]

LUXEMBOURG

[1 POLAND

SLOVENIA]

AUSTRIA

SWEDEN

AMENDMENT

1. Regulation 988/2009 art.1 (May 1, 2010).

ANNEX V

MORE RIGHTS FOR FORMER FRONTIER WORKERS WHO RETURN TO THEIR PREVIOUS MEMBER STATE OF ACTIVITY AS AN EMPLOYED OR SELF-EMPLOYED PERSON (APPLICABLE ONLY IF THE MEMBER STATE IN WHICH THE COMPETENT INSTITUTION RESPONSIBLE FOR THE COSTS OF THE BENEFITS IN KIND PROVIDED TO THE PENSIONER IN HIS MEMBER STATE OF RESIDENCE IS SITUATED ALSO APPEARS ON THE LIST)

(Article 28(2))

BELGIUM **3.490**

GERMANY

SPAIN

FRANCE

LUXEMBOURG

AUSTRIA

PORTUGAL

ANNEX VI

IDENTIFICATION OF TYPE A LEGISLATION WHICH SHOULD BE SUBJECT TO SPECIAL COORDINATION

(Article 44(1))

3.491 [1 CZECH REPUBLIC

Full disability pension for persons whose total disability arose before reaching 18 years of age and who were not insured for the required period (Section 42 of the Pension Insurance Act No 155/1995 Coll.).

ESTONIA

(a) Invalidity pensions granted before 1 April 2000 under the State Allowances Act and which are retained under the State Pension Insurance Act.
(b) National pensions granted on the basis of invalidity according to the State Pension Insurance Act.
(c) Invalidity pensions granted according to the Defence Forces Service Act, Police Service Act, Prosecutor's Office Act, Status of Judges Act, Members of the Riigikogu Salaries, Pensions and Other Social Guarantees Act and President of the Republic Official Benefits Act.]

[1 . . .] GREECE

Legislation relating to the agricultural insurance scheme (OGA), under Law No 4169/1961

[3 CROATIA

(a) Invalidity pension due to occupational injury or disease according to Article 52(5) of the Pension Insurance Act (OG 102/98, as amended).
(b) Physical damage allowance according to Article 56 of the Pension Insurance Act (OG 102/98, as amended).]

[1 LATVIA

Invalidity pensions (third group) under Article 16(1)(2) of the Law on State Pensions of 1 January 1996.]

[2 HUNGARY

As from 1 January 2012 pursuant to Act CXCI of 2011 on the benefits of persons with changed working capacity and amendments of certain other acts:

(a) the rehabilitation benefit;
(b) the invalidity benefit.

SLOVAKIA

Invalidity pension for a person who became invalid as a dependent child or during full-time doctoral studies while under the age of 26 years and who is always deemed to have fulfilled the required period of insurance (Article 70(2), Article 72(3) and Article 73(3) and (4) of Act No 461/2003 on social insurance as amended).]

[1 . . .] IRELAND

[1 Part 2, Chapter 17 of the Social Welfare Consolidation Act 2005.]

[1 FINLAND

National Pensions to persons who are born disabled or become disabled at an early age (the National Pension Act,568/2007);

Invalidity pensions determined according to transitional rules and awarded prior to 1 January 1994 (Act on Enforcement of the National Pensions Act, 569/2007).]

[1 . . .] SWEDEN

Income-related sickness benefit and activity compensation [2 (Chapter 34 of the Social Insurance Code (2010:110)).]

[2 UNITED KINGDOM

Employment and Support Allowance

(a) Great Britain
Part 1 of the Welfare Reform Act 2007.

(b) Northern Ireland
Part 1 of the Welfare Reform Act (Northern Ireland) 2007.]

AMENDMENTS

1. Regulation 988/2009 art.1 (May 1, 2010).
2. Regulation 1224/2012 art.1 (January 8, 2013).
3. Regulation 517/2013 art.1(b) (July 1, 2013).

Annex VII

CONCORDANCE BETWEEN THE LEGISLATIONS OF MEMBER STATES ON CONDITIONS RELATING TO THE DEGREE OF INVALIDITY

(Article 46(3) of the Regulation)

Belgium

3.492

Member State	Schemes administered by institutions of Member States which have taken a decision recognising the degree of invalidity	Schemes administered by Belgian institutions on which the decision is binding in cases of concordance				
		General scheme	Miners' scheme		Mariners' scheme	Ossom
			General invalidity	Occupational invalidity		
FRANCE	1. General scheme:					
	– Group III (constant attendance)	Concordance	Concordance	Concordance	Concordance	No concordance
	– Group II	Concordance	Concordance	Concordance	Concordance	No concordance
	– Group I	Concordance	Concordance	Concordance	Concordance	No concordance
	2. Agricultural scheme					
	– Total, general invalidity	Concordance	Concordance	Concordance	Concordance	No concordance
	– Two-thirds general invalidity	Concordance	Concordance	Concordance	Concordance	No concordance
	– Constant attendance	Concordance	Concordance	Concordance	Concordance	No concordance
	3. Miners' scheme:					
	– Partial, general invalidity	Concordance	Concordance	Concordance	Concordance	No concordance
	– Constant attendance	Concordance	Concordance	Concordance	Concordance	No concordance
	– Occupational invalidity	No concordance	No concordance	Concordance	No concordance	No concordance
	4. Mariners' scheme:					
	– General invalidity	Concordance	Concordance	Concordance	Concordance	No concordance
	– Constant attendance	Concordance	Concordance	Concordance	Concordance	No concordance
	– Occupational invalidity	No concordance	No concordance	No concordance	No concordance	No concordance
ITALY	1. General scheme:					
	– Invalidity — manual workers	No concordance	Concordance	Concordance	Concordance	No concordance
	– Invalidity — clerical staff	No concordance	Concordance	Concordance	Concordance	No concordance
	2. Mariners' scheme:					
	– Unfitness for seafaring	No concordance	No concordance	No concordance	No concordance	No concordance

Member State	Schemes administered by institutions of Member States which have taken a decision recognising the degree of invalidity	Schemes administered by French institutions on which the decision is binding in cases of concordances											
		General scheme			Agricultural scheme			Miners' scheme			Mariners' scheme		
		Group I	Group II	Group III Constant attendance	2/3 Invalidity	Total invalidity	Constant attendance	2/3 General invalidity	Constant attendance	Occupational invalidity	2/3 General invalidity	Total occupational invalidity	Constant attendance
BELGIUM	1. General scheme	Concordance	No concordance	No concordance	Concordance	No concordance	No concordance	Concordance	No concordance	No concordance	No concordance	No concordance	No concordance
	2. Miners' scheme												
	– partial general invalidity	Concordance	No concordance	No concordance	Concordance	No concordance	No concordance	Concordance	No concordance	No concordance	No concordance	No concordance	No concordance
	– occupational invalidity	No concordance	No concordance	No concordance	No concordance	No concordance	No concordance	No concordance	No concordance	Concordance (2)			
	3. Mariners' scheme	Concordance (1)	No concordance	No concordance	Concordance (1)	No concordance	No concordance	Concordance (1)	No concordance	No concordance	No concordance	No concordance	No concordance
ITALY	1. General scheme												
	– invalidity — manual workers	Concordance	No concordance	No concordance	Concordance	No concordance	No concordance	Concordance	No concordance	No concordance	No concordance	No concordance	No concordance
	– invalidity — clerical staff	Concordance	No concordance	No concordance	Concordance	No concordance	No concordance	Concordance	No concordance	No concordance	No concordance	No concordance	No concordance
	2. Mariners' scheme												
	– unfitness for seafaring	No concordance	No concordance	No concordance	No concordance	No concordance	No concordance	No concordance	No concordance	No concordance	No concordance	No concordance	No concordance

(1) In so far as the invalidity recognised by the Belgian institutions is general invalidity.
(2) Only if the Belgian institution has recognised that the worker is unfit for work underground or at ground level.

AMENDMENT

1. Regulation 998/2009 art.1(May 1, 2010).

ITALY

3.493

Member State	Schemes administered by institutions of Member States which have taken a decision recognising the degree of invalidity	Schemes administered by Italian institutions on which the decision is binding in cases of concordance		
		General scheme		Mariners unfit for navigation
		Manual workers	Clerical staff	
BELGIUM	1. General scheme	No concordance	No concordance	No concordance
	2. Miners' scheme			
	– partial general invalidity	Concordance	Concordance	No concordance
	– occupational invalidity	No concordance	No concordance	No concordance
	3. Mariners' scheme	No concordance	No concordance	No concordance
FRANCE	1. General scheme			
	– Group III (constant attendance)	Concordance	Concordance	No concordance
	– Group II	Concordance	Concordance	No concordance
	– Group I	Concordance	Concordance	No concordance
	2. Agricultural scheme			
	– total general invalidity	Concordance	Concordance	No concordance
	– partial general invalidity	Concordance	Concordance	No concordance
	– constant attendance	Concordance	Concordance	No concordance
	3. Miners' scheme			
	– partial general invalidity	Concordance	Concordance	No concordance
	– constant attendance	Concordance	Concordance	No concordance
	– occupational invalidity	No concordance	No concordance	No concordance
	4. Mariners' scheme			
	– partial general invalidity	No concordance	No concordance	No concordance
	– constant attendance	No concordance	No concordance	No concordance
	– occupational invalidity			

[1 Annex VIII

Cases in Which the Pro Rata Calculation shall be Waived or shall Not Apply

(Article 52(4) and 52(5))

Part 1: Cases in which the pro rata calculation shall be waived pursuant to Article 52(4) 3.494

DENMARK

All applications for pensions referred to in the law on social pensions, except for pensions mentioned in Annex IX.

IRELAND

All applications for state pension (transition), state pension (contributory), widow's (contributory) pension and widower's (contributory) pension.

CYPRUS

All applications for old age, invalidity, widow's and widower's pensions.

LATVIA

(a) All applications for invalidity pensions (Law on State Pensions of 1 January 1996);
(b) All applications for survivor's pensions (Law on State pensions of 1 January 1996; Law on State funded pensions of 1 July 2001).

LITHUANIA

All applications for State social insurance survivor's pensions calculated on the basis of the basic amount of survivor's pension (Law on State Social Insurance Pensions).

NETHERLANDS

All applications for old-age pensions under the law on general old-age insurance (AOW).

AUSTRIA

(a) All applications for benefits under the Federal Act of 9 September 1955 on General Social Insurance – ASVG, the Federal Act of 11 October 1978 on social insurance for self-employed persons engaged in trade and commerce—GSVG, the Federal Act of 11 October 1978 on social insurance for self-employed farmers—BSVG and the Federal Act of 30 November 1978 on social insurance for the self-employed in the liberal professions (FSVG);
(b) All applications for invalidity pensions based on a pension account pursuant to the General Pensions Act (APG) of18 November 2004;
[3 (c) All applications for survivors' pensions based on a pension account

pursuant to the General Pensions Act (APG) of 18 November 2004, with the exception if cases under Part 2.]

(d) All applications for invalidity and survivors' pensions of the Austrian Provincial Chambers of Physicians (Landesärztekammer) based on basic provision (basic and any supplementary benefit, or basic pension);

(e) All applications for permanent occupational invalidity support and survivors' support from the pension fund of the Austrian Chamber of Veterinary Surgeons;

(f) All applications for benefits from occupational invalidity, widows and orphans pensions according to the statutes of the welfare institutions of the Austrian bar associations, Part A.

[3 All applications for benefits under the Notary Insurance Act of 3 February 1972 – NVG 1972.]

POLAND

All applications for disability pensions, old-age pensions under the defined benefits scheme and survivors' pensions.

[2 PORTUGAL

All applications for invalidity, old-age and survivors' pension claims, except for the cases where the totalised periods of insurance completed under the legislation of more than one Member State are equal to or longer than 21 calendar years but the national periods of insurance are equal or inferior to 20 years, and the calculation is made under Articles 32 and 33 of Decree-Law No 187/2007 of 10 May 2007.]

SLOVAKIA

(a) All applications for survivors' pension (widow's pension, widower's and orphan's pension) calculated according to the legislation in force before 1 January 2004, the amount of which is derived from a pension formerly paid to the deceased;

(b) All applications for pensions calculated pursuant to Act No 461/2003 Coll. on social security as amended.

[3 SWEDEN

(a) Applications for a guarantee pension in the form of an old-age pension (Chapter 66 and 67 of the Social Insurance Code (2010:110));

(b) Applications for a guarantee pension in the form of a survivor's pension (Chapter 81 of the Social Insurance Code (2010: 110)).]

UNITED KINGDOM

All applications for retirement pension, widows' and bereavement benefits, with the exception of those for which during a tax year beginning on or after 6 April 1975:

(i) the party concerned had completed periods of insurance, employment or residence under the legislation of the United Kingdom and another Member State; and one (or more) of the tax years was not considered a qualifying year within the meaning of the legislation of the United Kingdom;

(ii) the periods of insurance completed under the legislation in force in the United Kingdom for the periods prior to 5 July 1948 would be taken into account for the purposes of Article 52(1) (b) of the Regulation by application of the periods of insurance, employment or residence under the legislation of another Member State.

All applications for additional pension pursuant to the Social Security Contributions and Benefits Act 1992, section 44,and the Social Security Contributions and Benefits (Northern Ireland) Act 1992, section 44.

Part 2: Cases in which Article 52(5) applies

BULGARIA

Old age pensions from the Supplementary Compulsory Pension Insurance, under Part II, Title II, of the Social Insurance Code. 3.495

[5 CZECH REPUBLIC

Pensions paid from the Second Pillar scheme establishedby Act No 426/2011 Coll., on pension savings.]

[3 DENMARK

(a) Personal pensions;
(b) Benefits in the event of death (accrued based on contributions to Arbejdsmarkedets Tillægspension related to the time before 1 January 2002);
(c) Benefits in the event of death (accrued based on contributions to Arbejdsmarkedets Tillægspension related to the time after 1 January 2002) referred to in the Consolidated Act on Labour Market Supplementary Pensions (Arbejdsmarkedets Tillægspension) 942:2009).]

ESTONIA

Mandatory funded old-age pension scheme.

FRANCE

Basic or supplementary schemes in which old-age benefits are calculated on the basis of retirement points.

[4 CROATIA

Pensions from the compulsory insurance scheme based on the individual capitalised savings according to the Compulsory and Voluntary Pension Funds Act (OG 49/99, as amended) and the Act on Pension Insurance Companies and Payment of Pensions Based on Individual Capitalised Savings (OG 106/99, as amended), except in the cases provided by Articles 47 and 48 of the Compulsory and Voluntary Pensions Funds Act (invalidity pension based on general incapacity to work and survivor's pension).]

LATVIA

Old-age pensions (Law on State pensions of 1 January 1996; Law on State funded pensions of 1 July 2001).

HUNGARY

Pension benefits based on membership of private pension funds.

AUSTRIA

[5 (a) Old-age pensions and survivor's pensions derived thereof based on a pension account pursuant to the General Pensions Act (APG) of 18 November 2004;]

(b) Compulsory allowances under Article 41 of the Federal Law of 28 December 2001, BGBl I Nr. 154 on the general salary fund of Austrian pharmacists (Pharmazeutische Gehaltskasse für Österreich);

(c) Retirement and early retirement pensions of the Austrian Provincial Chambers of Physicians based on basic provision (basic and any supplementary benefit, or basic pension), and all pension benefits of the Austrian Provincial Chambers of Physicians based on additional provision (additional or individual pension);

(d) Old-age support from the pension fund of the Austrian Chamber of Veterinary Surgeons;

(e) Benefits according to the statutes of the welfare institutions of the Austrian bar associations, Parts A and B, with the exception of applications for benefits from disability, widows' and orphans' pensions according to the statutes of the welfare institutions of the Austrian bar associations, Part A;

(f) Benefits by the welfare institutions of the Federal Chamber of Architects and Consulting Engineers under the Austrian Civil Engineers' Chamber Act (Ziviltechnikerkammergesetz) 1993 and the statutes of the welfare institutions, with the exception of benefits on grounds of occupational invalidity and survivors' benefits deriving from the last-named benefits;

(g) Benefits according to the statute of the welfare institution of the Federal Chamber of Professional Accountants and Tax Advisors under the Austrian Professional Accountants and Tax Advisors' Act (Wirtschaftstreuhand-berufsgesetz).

POLAND

Old-age pensions under the defined contribution scheme.

[2 PORTUGAL

Supplementary pensions granted pursuant to Decree-Law No 26/2008 of 22 February 2008 (public capitalisation scheme).]

SLOVENIA

Pension from compulsory supplementary pension insurance.

SLOVAKIA

Mandatory old-age pension saving.

[3 SWEDEN

Income pensions and premium pensions (Chapters 62 and 64 of the Social Insurance Code (2010:110)).]

UNITED KINGDOM

Graduated retirement benefits paid pursuant to the National Insurance Act 1965, sections 36 and 37, and the National Insurance Act (Northern Ireland) 1966, sections 35 and 36.]

AMENDMENTS

1. Regulation 988/2009 art.1 (May 1, 2010).
2. Regulation 1244/2010 [2010] OJ L338/35 art.1 (January 11, 2011).
3. Regulation 1224/2012 art.1 (January 8, 2013).
4. Regulation 517/2013 art.1(b) (July 1, 2013).
5. Regulation 1372/2013 art.1(1) (January 1, 2014).

ANNEX IX

BENEFITS AND AGREEMENTS WHICH ALLOW THE APPLICATION OF ARTICLE 54

I. Benefits referred to in Article 54(2)(a) of the Regulation, the amount of which is independent of the length of periods of insurance or residence completed

[1 . . .] BELGIUM

Benefits relating to the general invalidity scheme, the special invalidity 3.496
scheme for miners and the special scheme for merchant navy mariners Benefits on insurance for self-employed persons against incapacity to work Benefits relating to invalidity in the overseas social insurance scheme and the invalidity scheme for former employees of the Belgian Congo and Ruanda-Urundi

[1 . . .] DENMARK

The full Danish national old-age pension acquired after 10 years' residence by persons who will have been awarded a pension by 1 October 1989.

[1 . . .] IRELAND

Type A Invalidity Pension

[1 . . .] GREECE

Benefits under Law No 4169/1961 relating to the agricultural insurance scheme (OGA)

[1 . . .] SPAIN

Survivors' pensions granted under the general and special schemes, with the exception of the Special Scheme for Civil Servants

[1 . . .] FRANCE

Invalidity pension under the general social security system or under the agricultural workers scheme.

Widower's or widow's invalidity pension under the general social security system or under the agricultural workers scheme where it is calculated on the basis of the deceased spouse's invalidity pension settled in accordance with Article 52(1)(a).

[1 LATVIA

Invalidity pensions (third group) under Article 16(1)(2) of the Law on State Pensions of 1 January 1996.]

[2 NETHERLANDS

Disability Insurance Act of 18 February 1966, as amended (WAO).

Self-employed Persons Disablement Benefits Act of 24 April 1997, as amended (WAZ).

General Surviving Relatives Act of 21 December 1995 (ANW).

The Work and Income according to Labour Capacity Act of 10 November 2005 (WIA).]

[1 . . .] FINLAND

[1 National pensions to persons who are born disabled or become disabled at an early age (the National Pensions Act, 568/2007);

National pensions and spouse's pensions determined according to the transitional rules and awarded prior to the 1 of January 1994 (Act on Enforcement of the National Pensions Act, 569/2007);

The additional amount of child's pension when calculating independent benefit according to the National Pension Act (the National Pension Act, 568/2007).]

[1 . . .] SWEDEN

[1 Swedish income-related sickness compensation and activity compensation [3 (Chapter 34 of the Social Insurance Code (2010:110)).]

Swedish guarantee pension and guaranteed compensation which replaced the full Swedish state pensions provided under the legislation on the state pension which applied before 1 January 1993, and the full state pension awarded under the transitional rules of the legislation applying from that date.]

II. Benefits referred to in Article 54(2)(b) of the Regulation, the amount of which is determined by reference to a credited period deemed to have been completed between the date on which the risk materialised and a later date

[1 . . .] GERMANY

3.497 Invalidity and survivors' pensions, for which account is taken of a supplementary period.

Old-age pensions, for which account is taken of a supplementary period already acquired.

[1 . . .] SPAIN

The pensions for retirement or retirement for permanent disability (invalidity) under the Special Scheme for Civil Servants due under Title I of the consolidated text of the Law on State Pensioners if at the time of materialisation of the risk the beneficiary was an active civil servant or treated as such; death and survivors' (widows'/widowers', orphans' and parents') pensions due under Title I of the consolidated text of the Law on State Pensioners if at the time of death the civil servant was active or treated as such.

[1 . . .] ITALY

Italian pensions for total incapacity for work (inabilità).

[1 LATVIA

Survivors' pension calculated on the basis of assumed insurance periods (Article 23(8) of the Law on State Pensions of 1 January 1996).

LITHUANIA

(a) State social insurance work incapacity pensions, paid under the Law on State Social Insurance Pensions;
(b) State social insurance survivors' and orphans' pensions, calculated on the basis of the work incapacity pension of the deceased under the Law on State Social Insurance Pensions.]

[1 . . .] LUXEMBOURG

Invalidity and survivors' pensions.

[1 SLOVAKIA

(a) Slovak invalidity pension and survivors' pension derived therefrom;
(b) [3]

[1 . . .] FINLAND

Employment pensions for which account is taken of future periods according to the national legislation

[3 SWEDEN

Sickness compensation and activity compensation in the form of guarantee compensation (Chapter 35 of the Social Insurance Code (2010: 110))

Widow's pension calculated on the basis of credited insurance periods (Chapter 84 of the Social Insurance Code (2010: 110)).]

III. Agreements referred to in Article 54(2)(b)(i) of the Regulation intended to prevent the same credited period being taken into account two or more times:

The Social Security Agreement of 28 April 1997 between the Republic of Finland and the Federal Republic of Germany **3.498**

The Social Security Agreement of 10 November 2000 between the Republic of Finland and the Grand Duchy of Luxembourg

[1 Nordic Convention on social security of 18 August 2003.]

AMENDMENTS

1. Regulation 988/2009 art.1 (May 1, 2010).
2. Regulation 1244/2010 [2010] OJ L338/35 art.1 (January 11, 2011).
3. Regulation 1224/2012 art.1 (January 8, 2013).

[1 ANNEX X

SPECIAL NON-CONTRIBUTORY CASH BENEFITS

(Article 70(2)(c))

BELGIUM

3.499 (a) Income replacement allowance (Law of 27 February 1987);
(b) Guaranteed income for elderly persons (Law of 22 March 2001).

BULGARIA

Social Pension for old age (Article 89 of the Social Insurance Code).

CZECH REPUBLIC

Social allowance (State Social Support Act No 117/1995 Sb.).

DENMARK

Accommodation expenses for pensioners (Law on individual accommodation assistance, consolidated by Law No 204of 29 March 1995).

GERMANY

(a) Basic subsistence income for the elderly and for persons with reduced earning capacity under Chapter 4 of Book XII of the Social Code;
(b) Benefits to cover subsistence costs under the basic provision for jobseekers unless, with respect to these benefits, the eligibility requirements for a temporary supplement following receipt of unemployment benefit (Article 24(1)of Book II of the Social Code) are fulfilled.

ESTONIA

(a) Disabled adult allowance (Social Benefits for Disabled Persons Act of 27 January 1999);
(b) State unemployment allowance (Labour Market Services and Support Act of 29 September 2005).

IRELAND

(a) Jobseekers' allowance (Social Welfare Consolidation Act 2005, Part 3, Chapter 2);
(b) State pension (non-contributory) (Social Welfare Consolidation Act 2005, Part 3, Chapter 4);

(c) Widow's (non-contributory) pension and widower's (non-contributory) pension (Social Welfare Consolidation Act2005, Part 3, Chapter 6);
(d) Disability allowance (Social Welfare Consolidation Act 2005, Part 3, Chapter 10);
(e) Mobility allowance (Health Act 1970, Section 61);
(f) Blind pension (Social Welfare Consolidation Act 2005, Part 3, Chapter 5).

GREECE

Special benefits for the elderly (Law 1296/82).

SPAIN

(a) Minimum income guarantee (Law No 13/82 of 7 April 1982);
(b) Cash benefits to assist the elderly and invalids unable to work (Royal Decree No 2620/81 of 24 July 1981);
(c) (i) Non-contributory invalidity and retirement pensions as provided for in Article 38(1) of the Consolidated Text of the General Law on Social Security, approved by Royal Legislative Decree No 1/1994 of 20 June 1994; and
(ii) the benefits which supplement the above pensions, as provided for in the legislation of the Comunidades Autonómas, where such supplements guarantee a minimum subsistence income having regard to the economic and social situation in the Comunidades Autonómas concerned;
(d) Allowances to promote mobility and to compensate for transport costs (Law No 13/1982 of 7 April 1982).

FRANCE

(a) Supplementary allowances of:
(i) the Special Invalidity Fund; and
(ii) the Old Age Solidarity Fund in respect of acquired rights (Law of 30 June 1956, codified in Book VIII of the Social Security Code);
(b) Disabled adults' allowance (Law of 30 June 1975, codified in Book VIII of the Social Security Code);
(c) Special allowance (Law of 10 July 1952, codified in Book VIII of the Social Security Code) in respect of acquired rights;
(d) Old-age solidarity allowance (ordinance of 24 June 2004, codified in Book VIII of the Social Security Code) as of1 January 2006.

ITALY

(a) Social pensions for persons without means (Law No 153 of 30 April 1969);
(b) Pensions and allowances for the civilian disabled or invalids (Laws No 118 of 30 March 1971, No 18 of 11 February 1980 and No 508 of 23 November 1988);
(c) Pensions and allowances for the deaf and dumb (Laws No 381 of 26 May 1970 and No 508 of 23 November1988);
(d) Pensions and allowances for the civilian blind (Laws No 382 of 27 May 1970 and No 508 of 23 November 1988);

(e) Benefits supplementing the minimum pensions (Laws No 218 of 4 April 1952, No 638 of 11 November 1983and No 407 of 29 December 1990);
(f) Benefits supplementing disability allowances (Law No 222 of 12 June 1984);
(g) Social allowance (Law No 335 of 8 August 1995);
(h) Social increase (Article 1(1) and (12) of Law No 544 of 29 December 1988 and successive amendments).

CYPRUS

(a) Social Pension (Social Pension Law of 1995 (Law 25(I)/95), as amended);
(b) Severe motor disability allowance (Council of Ministers' Decisions Nos 38210 of 16 October 1992, 41370 of1 August 1994, 46183 of 11 June 1997 and 53675 of 16 May 2001);
(c) Special grant to blind persons (Special Grants Law of 1996 (Law 77(I)/96), as amended).

LATVIA

(a) State Social Security Benefit (Law on State Social Benefits of 1 January 2003);
(b) Allowance for the compensation of transportation expenses for disabled persons with restricted mobility (Law on State Social Benefits of 1 January 2003).

LITHUANIA

(a) Social assistance pension (Law of 2005 on State Social Assistance Benefits, Article 5);
(b) Relief compensation (Law of 2005 on State Social Assistance Benefits, Article 15);
(c) transport compensation for the disabled who have mobility problems (Law of 2000 on Transport Compensation, Article 7).

LUXEMBOURG

Income for the seriously disabled (Article 1(2), Law of 12 September 2003), with the exception of persons recognized as being disabled workers and employed on the mainstream labour market or in a sheltered environment.

HUNGARY

(a) Invalidity annuity (Decree No 83/1987 (XII 27) of the Council of Ministers on Invalidity Annuity);
(b) Non-contributory old age allowance (Act III of 1993 on Social Administration and Social Benefits);
(c) Transport allowance (Government Decree No 164/1995 (XII 27) on Transport Allowances for Persons with Severe Physical Handicap).

MALTA

(a) Supplementary allowance (Section 73 of the Social Security Act (Cap. 318) 1987);
(b) Age pension (Social Security Act (Cap. 318) 1987).

NETHERLANDS

[2 (a) Work and Employment Support for Disabled Young Persons Act of 24 April 1997 (Wet Wajong).

(b) Supplementary Benefits Act of 6 November 1986 (TW).

AUSTRIA

Compensatory supplement (Federal Act of 9 September 1955 on General Social Insurance — ASVG, Federal Act of11 October 1978 on Social insurance for persons engaged in trade and commerce — GSVG and Federal Act of 11 October 1978 on Social insurance for farmers BSVG).

POLAND

Social pension (Act of 27 June 2003 on social pensions).

PORTUGAL

(a) Non-contributory State old-age and invalidity pension (Decree-Law No 464/80 of 13 October 1980);

(b) Non-contributory widowhood pension (Regulatory Decree No 52/81 of 11 November 1981);

(c) Solidarity supplement for the elderly (Decree – Law No 232/2005 of 29 December 2005, amended by Decree –Law No 236/2006 of 11 December 2006).

SLOVENIA

(a) State pension (Pension and Disability Insurance Act of 23 December 1999);

(b) Income support for pensioners (Pension and Disability Insurance Act of 23 December 1999);

(c) Maintenance allowance (Pension and Disability Insurance Act of 23 December 1999).

SLOVAKIA

(a) Adjustment awarded before 1 January 2004 to pensions constituting the sole source of income;

(b) Social pension which has been awarded before 1 January 2004.

FINLAND

(a) Housing allowance for pensioners (Act concerning the Housing Allowance for pensioners, 571/2007);

(b) Labour market support (Act on Unemployment Benefits 1290/2002);

(c) Special assistance for immigrants (Act on Special Assistance for Immigrants, 1192/2002).

SWEDEN

(a) Housing supplements for persons receiving a pension (Law 2001:761);

(b) Financial support for the elderly (Law 2001:853).

UNITED KINGDOM

(a) State Pension Credit (State Pension Credit Act 2002 and State Pension Credit Act (Northern Ireland) 2002);
(b) Income-based allowances for jobseekers (Jobseekers Act 1995 and Jobseekers (Northern Ireland) Order 1995);
(c) [2 . . .]
(d) Disability Living Allowance mobility component (Social Security Contributions and Benefits Act 1992 and Social Security Contributions and Benefits (Northern Ireland) Act 1992).
[2 (e) Employment and Support Allowance Income-related (Welfare Reform Act 2007 and Welfare Reform Act (Northern Ireland) 2007).]

AMENDMENTS

1. Regulation 988/2009 art.1 (May 1, 2010).
2. Regulation 465/2012 [2012] OJ L149/4 art.1(12) (June 28, 2012).

[1 ANNEX XI

SPECIAL PROVISIONS FOR THE APPLICATION OF THE LEGISLATION OF THE MEMBER STATES

(Article 51(3), 56(1) and 83)

BULGARIA

3.500 Article 33(1) of the Bulgarian Health Insurance Act shall apply to all persons for whom Bulgaria is the competent Member State under Chapter 1 of Title III of this Regulation.;

CZECH REPUBLIC

For the purposes of defining members of the family according to Article 1(i), "spouse" also includes registered partners as defined in the Czech act no. 115/2006 Coll., on registered partnership.;

DENMARK

1. (a) For the purpose of calculating the pension under the "lov om social pension" (Social Pension Act), periods of activity as an employed or self-employed person completed under Danish legislation by a frontier worker or a worker who has gone to Denmark to do work of a seasonal nature are regarded as periods of residence completed in Denmark by the surviving spouse in so far as, during those periods, the surviving spouse was linked to the abovementioned worker by marriage without separation from bed and board or de facto separation on grounds of incompatibility, and provided that, during those periods, the spouse resided in the territory of another Member State.

For the purposes of this point, "work of a seasonal nature" means work which, being dependent on the succession of the seasons, automatically recurs each year.

(b) For the purpose of calculating the pension under the "lov om social pension" (Social Pension Act), periods of activity as an employed or self-employed person completed under Danish legislation before 1 January 1984by a person to whom point 1(a) does not apply shall be regarded as periods of residence completed in Denmark by the surviving spouse, in so far as, during those periods, the surviving spouse was linked to the person by marriage without separation from bed and board or de facto separation on grounds of incompatibility, and provided that, during those periods, the spouse resided in the territory of another Member State.

(c) Periods to be taken into account under points (a) and (b) shall not be taken into consideration if they coincide with the periods taken into account for the calculation of the pension due to the person concerned under the legislation on compulsory insurance of another Member State or with the periods during which the person concerned received a pension under such legislation. These periods shall, however, be taken into consideration if the annual amount of the said pension is less than half the basic amount of the social pension.

2. (a) Notwithstanding the provisions of Article 6 of this Regulation, persons who have not been gainfully employed in one or more Member States are entitled to a Danish social pension only if they have been, or have previously been, permanent residents of Denmark for at least 3 years, subject to the age limits prescribed by Danish legislation. Subject to Article 4 of this Regulation, Article 7 does not apply to a Danish social pension to which entitlement has been acquired by such persons.

(b) The abovementioned provisions do not apply to Danish social pension entitlement for the members of the family of persons who are or have been gainfully employed in Denmark, or for students or the members of their families.

3. The temporary benefit for unemployed persons who have been admitted to the ledighedsydelse (flexible job' scheme)(Law No 455 of 10 June 1997) is covered by Title III, Chapter 6 of this Regulation. As regards unemployed persons going to another Member State, Articles 64 and 65 will be applicable when this Member State has similar employment schemes for the same category of persons.

4. Where the beneficiary of a Danish social pension is also entitled to a survivor's pension from another Member State, these pensions for the implementation of Danish legislation shall be regarded as benefits of the same kind within the meaning of Article 53(1) of this Regulation, subject to the condition, however, that the person whose periods of insurance or of residence serve as the basis for the calculation of the survivor's pension had also acquired a right to a Danish social pension.

GERMANY

1. Notwithstanding Article 5(a) of this Regulation and Article 5(4) point 1 of the Sozialgesetzbuch VI (Volume VI of the Social Code), a person who receives a full old-age pension under the legislation of another

Member State may request to be compulsorily insured under the German pension insurance scheme.

[2 2. Notwithstanding Article 5(a) of this Regulation and Article 7 of the Sozialgesetzbuch VI (Volume VI of the Social Code), a person who is compulsorily insured in another Member State or receives an old-age pension under the legislation of another Member State may join the voluntary insurance scheme in Germany.]

3. For the purpose of granting cash benefits under §47(1) of SGB V, §47(1) of SGB VII and §200(2) of the Reichsversicherungsordnung to insured persons who live in another Member State, German insurance schemes calculate net pay, which is used to assess benefits, as if the insured person lived in Germany, unless the insured person requests an assessment on the basis of the net pay which he actually receives.

4. Nationals of other Member States whose place of residence or usual abode is outside Germany and who fulfil the general conditions of the German pension insurance scheme may pay voluntary contributions only if they had been voluntarily or compulsorily insured in the German pension insurance scheme at some time previously; this also applies to stateless persons and refugees whose place of residence or usual abode is in another Member State.

5. The pauschale Anrechnungszeit (fixed credit period) pursuant to Article 253 of the Sozialgesetzbuch VI (Volume VI of the Social Code) shall be determined exclusively with reference to German periods.

6. In cases where the German pension legislation, in force on 31 December 1991, is applicable for the recalculation of a pension, only the German legislation applies for the purposes of crediting German Ersatzzeiten (substitute periods).

7. The German legislation on accidents at work and occupational diseases to be compensated for under the law governing foreign pensions and on benefits for insurance periods which can be credited under the law governing foreign pensions in the territories named in paragraph 1(2)(3) of the Act on affairs of displaced persons and refugees(Bundesvertriebenenge setz) continues to apply within the scope of application of this Regulation, notwithstanding the provisions of paragraph 2 of the Act on foreign pensions (Fremdrentengesetz).

8. For the calculation of the theoretical amount referred to in Article 52(1)(b)(i) of this Regulation, in pension schemes for liberal professions, the competent institution shall take as a basis, in respect of each of the years of insurance completed under the legislation of any other Member State, the average annual pension entitlement acquired during the period of membership of the competent institution through the payment of contributions.

ESTONIA

For the purpose of calculating parental benefits, periods of employment in Member States other than Estonia shall be considered to be based on the same average amount of Social Tax as paid during the periods of employment in Estonia with which they are aggregated. If during the reference year the person has been employed only in other Member States, the calculation of the benefit shall be considered to be based on the average Social Tax paid in Estonia between the reference year and the maternity leave.

IRELAND

1. Notwithstanding Articles 21(2) and 62 of this Regulation, for the purposes of calculating the prescribed reckonable weekly earnings of an insured person for the grant of sickness or unemployment benefit under Irish legislation, an amount equal to the average weekly wage of employed persons in the relevant prescribed year shall be credited to that insured person in respect of each week of activity as an employed person under the legislation of another Member State during that prescribed year.

2. Where Article 46 of this Regulation applies, if the person concerned suffers incapacity for work leading to invalidity while subject to the legislation of another Member State, Ireland shall, for the purposes of Section 118(1)(a) of the Social Welfare Consolidation Act 2005, take account of any periods during which, in respect of the invalidity that followed that incapacity for work, he/she would have been regarded as being incapable of work under Irish legislation.

GREECE

1. Law No 1469/84 concerning voluntary affiliation to the pension insurance scheme for Greek nationals and foreign nationals of Greek origin is applicable to nationals of other Member States, stateless persons and refugees, where the persons concerned, regardless of their place of residence or stay, have at some time in the past been compulsorily or voluntarily affiliated to the Greek pension insurance scheme.

2. Notwithstanding Article 5(a) of this Regulation and Article 34 of Law 1140/1981, a person who receives a pension in respect of accidents at work or occupational diseases under the legislation of another Member State may request to be compulsorily insured under the legislation applied by OGA, to the extent that he/she pursues an activity falling within the scope of that legislation.

SPAIN

1. For the purposes of implementing Article 52(1)(b)(i) of this Regulation, the years which the worker lacks to reach the pensionable or compulsory retirement age as stipulated under Article 31(4) of the consolidated version of the Ley de Clases Pasivas del Estado (Law on State Pensioners) shall be taken into account as actual years of service to the State only if at the time of the event in respect of which invalidity or death pensions are due, the beneficiary was covered by Spain's special scheme for civil servants or was performing an activity assimilated under the scheme, or if, at the time of the event in respect of which the pensions are due, the beneficiary was performing an activity that would have required the person concerned to be included under the State's special scheme for civil servants, the armed forces or the judiciary, had the activity been performed in Spain.

2. (a) Under Article 56(1)(c) of this Regulation, the calculation of the theoretical Spanish benefit shall be carried out on the basis of the actual contributions of the person during the years immediately preceding payment of the last contribution to Spanish social security. Where, in the calculation of the basic amount for the pension, periods of insurance and/or residence under the legislation of other Member States have to be taken into account, the contribution basis in Spain

which is closest in time to the reference periods shall be used for the aforementioned periods, taking into account the development of the retail price index.

(b) The amount of the pension obtained shall be increased by the amount of the increases and revaluations calculated for each subsequent year for pensions of the same nature.

3. Periods completed in other Member States which must be calculated in the special scheme for civil servants, the armed forces and the judicial administration, will be treated in the same way, for the purposes of Article 56 of this Regulation, as the periods closest in time covered as a civil servant in Spain.

4. The additional amounts based on age referred to in the Second Transitional Provision of the General Law on Social Security shall be applicable to all beneficiaries of the Regulation who have contributions to their name under the Spanish legislation prior to 1 January 1967; it shall not be possible, by application of Article 5 of this Regulation, to treat periods of insurance credited in another Member State prior to the aforementioned date as being the same as contributions paid in Spain, solely for the present purposes. The date corresponding to 1 January 1967 shall be1 August 1970 for the Special Scheme for Seafarers and 1 April 1969 for the Special Social Security Scheme for Coal Mining.

FRANCE

1. [2 . . .]

2. For persons receiving benefits in kind in France pursuant to Articles 17, 24 or 26 of this Regulation who are resident in the French departments of Haut-Rhin, Bas-Rhin or Moselle, benefits in kind provided on behalf of the institution of another Member State which is responsible for bearing their cost include benefits provided by both the general sickness insurance scheme and the obligatory supplementary local sickness insurance scheme of Alsace-Moselle.

3. French legislation applicable to a person engaged, or formerly engaged, in an activity as an employed or self-employed person for the application of Chapter 5 of Title III of this Regulation includes both the basic old-age insurance scheme(s) and the supplementary retirement scheme(s) to which the person concerned was subject.

CYPRUS

For the purpose of applying the provisions of Articles 6, 51 and 61 of this Regulation, for any period commencing on or after 6 October 1980, a week of insurance under the legislation of the Republic of Cyprus is determined by dividing the total insurable earnings for the relevant period by the weekly amount of the basic insurable earnings applicable in the relevant contribution year, provided that the number of weeks so determined shall not exceed the number of calendar weeks in the relevant period.

MALTA

Special provisions for civil servants

(a) Solely for the purposes of the application of Articles 49 and 60 of this Regulation, persons employed under the Malta Armed Forces Act

(Chapter 220 of the Laws of Malta), the Police Act (Chapter 164 of the Laws of Malta) and the Prisons Act (Chapter 260 of the Laws of Malta) shall be treated as civil servants.

(b) Pensions payable under the above Acts and under the Pensions Ordinance (Chapter 93 of the Laws of Malta) shall, solely for the purposes of Article 1(e) of the Regulation, be considered as "special schemes for civil servants".

NETHERLANDS

1. Health care insurance

(a) As regards entitlement to benefits in kind under Dutch legislation, persons entitled to benefits in kind for the purpose of the implementation of Chapters 1 and 2 of Title III of this Regulation shall mean:

(i) persons who, under Article 2 of the Zorgverzekeringswet (Health Care Insurance Act), are obliged to takeout insurance under a health care insurer; and

(ii) in so far as they are not already included under point (i), members of the family of active military personnel who are living in another Member State and persons who are resident in another Member State and who, under this Regulation are entitled to health care in their state of residence, the costs being borne by the Netherlands.

(b) The persons referred to in point 1(a)(i) must, in accordance with the provisions of the Zorgverzekeringswet (Health Care Insurance Act) take out insurance with a health care insurer, and the persons referred to in point 1(a)(ii) must register with the College voor zorgverzekeringen (Health Care Insurance Board).

(c) The provisions of the Zorgverzekeringswet (Health Care Insurance Act) and the Algemene Wet Bijzondere Ziektekosten (General Act on Exceptional Medical Expenses) concerning liability for the payment of contributions shall apply to the persons referred to in point (a) and the members of their families. In respect of members of the family, the contributions shall be levied on the person from whom the right to health care is derived with the exception of the members of the family of military personnel living in another Member State, who shall be levied directly.

(d) The provisions of the Zorgverzekeringswet (Health Care Insurance Act) concerning late insurance shall apply *mutatis mutandis* in the event of late registration with the College voor zorgverzekeringen (Health Care Insurance Board) in respect of the persons referred to in point 1(a)(ii).

(e) Persons entitled to benefits in kind by virtue of the legislation of a Member State other than the Netherlands who reside in the Netherlands or stay temporarily in the Netherlands shall be entitled to benefits in kind in accordance with the policy offered to insured persons in the Netherlands by the institution of the place of residence or the place of stay, taking into account Article 11(1), (2) and (3) and Article 19(1) of the Zorgverzekeringswet (Health Care Insurance Act), as well as to benefits in kind provided for by the Algemene Wet Bijzondere Ziektekosten (General Act on Exceptional Medical Expenses).

(f) For the purposes of Articles 23 to 30 of this Regulation, the following benefits (in addition to pensions covered by Title III, Chapters 4 and 5 of this Regulation) shall be treated as pensions due under Dutch legislation:

— pensions awarded under the Law of 6 January 1966 on pensions for civil servants and their survivors(Algemene burgerlijke pensioenwet) (Netherlands Civil Service Pensions Act),

— pensions awarded under the Law of 6 October 1966 on pensions for military personnel and their survivors (Algemene militaire pensioenwet) (Military Pensions Act),

— benefits for incapacity for work awarded under the Law of 7 June 1972 on benefits for incapacity for work for military personnel (Wetarbeidsongeschiktheidsvoorziening militairen) (Military Personnel Incapacity for Work Act),

— pensions awarded under the Law of 15 February 1967 on pensions for employees of the NV Nederlandse Spoorwegen (Dutch Railway Company) and their survivors (Spoorwegpensioenwet) (Railway Pensions Act),

— pensions awarded under the Reglement Dienstvoorwaarden Nederlandse Spoorwegen (Regulation governing conditions of employment of the Netherlands Railway Company),

— benefits awarded to retired persons before reaching the pensionable age of 65 years under a pension designed to provide income for former employed persons in their old age, or benefits provided in the event of premature exit from the labour market under a scheme set up by the state or by an industrial agreement for persons aged 55 or over,

— benefits awarded to military personnel and civil servants under a scheme applicable in the event of redundancy, superannuation and early retirement.

[[3] (fa) Any person as referred to in Article 69(1) of the Zorgverzekeringswet (Health Care Insurance Act) who, on the last day of the month preceding that in which he or she reaches the age of 65, is receiving a pension or benefit which, on the basis of paragraph 1(f) of this Section is treated as a pension payable under Dutch legislation, shall be regarded as a pension claimant as referred to in Article 22 of this Regulation until he or she reaches the pension age as referred to in Article 7a of the Algemene Ouderdomswet (General Old Age Pensions Act).]

(g) [[2] . . .]

[[2] (h) For the purposes of Article 18(1) of this Regulation, the persons referred to in point 1(a)(ii) of this Annex who stay temporarily in the Netherlands shall be entitled to benefits in kind in accordance with the policy offered to insured persons in the Netherlands by the institution of the place of stay, taking into account Article 11(1), (2) and (3) and Article 19(1) of the Zorgverzekeringswet (Health Care Insurance Act), as well as to benefits in kind provided for by the Algemene Wet Bijzondere Ziektekosten (General Act on Exceptional Medical Expenses).]

2. Application of the Algemene Ouderdomswet (AOW) (Dutch legislation on general old-age insurance)

(a) The reduction referred to in Article 13(1) of the Algemene

Ouderdomswet (AOW) ([2 General Old Age Pensions Act]) shall not be applied for calendar years before 1 January 1957 during which a recipient not satisfying the conditions for having such years treated as periods of insurance:

— resided in the Netherlands between the ages of 15 and 65, or
— while residing in another Member State, worked in the Netherlands for an employer established in the Netherlands, or
— worked in another Member State during periods regarded as periods of insurance under the Dutch social security system.

By way of derogation from Article 7 of the AOW, anyone who resided or worked in the Netherlands in accordance with the above conditions only prior to 1 January 1957 shall also be regarded as being entitled to a pension.

(b) The reduction referred to in Article 13(1) of the AOW shall not apply to calendar years prior to 2 August 1989during which, between the ages of 15 and 65, a person who is or was married was not insured under the above legislation, while being resident in the territory of a Member State other than the Netherlands, if these calendar years coincide with periods of insurance completed by the person's spouse under [2 the sbove legislation] or with calendar years to be taken into account under point 2(a), provided that the couple's marriage subsisted during that time.

By way of derogation from Article 7 of the AOW, such a person shall be regarded as entitled to a pension.

(c) The reduction referred to in Article 13(2) of the AOW shall not apply to calendar years before 1 January 1957during which a pensioner's spouse who fails to satisfy the conditions for having such years treated as periods of insurance:

— resided in the Netherlands between the ages of 15 and 65, or
— while residing in another Member State, worked in the Netherlands for an employer established in the Netherlands, or
— worked in another Member State during periods regarded as periods of insurance under the Netherlands social security system.

(d) The reduction referred to in Article 13(2) of the AOW shall not apply to calendar years prior to 2 August 1989 during which, between the ages of 15 and 65, a pensioner's spouse resident in a Member State other than the Netherlands was not insured under the above legislation, if those calendar years coincide with periods of insurance completed by the pensioner under that legislation or with calendar years to be taken into account under point 2(a), provided that the couple's marriage subsisted during that time.

(e) Points 2(a), 2(b), 2(c) and 2(d) shall not apply to periods which coincide with:

— periods which may be taken into account for calculating pension rights under the old-age insurance legislation of a Member State other than the Netherlands, or
— periods for which the person concerned has drawn an old-age pension under such legislation.

Periods of voluntary insurance under the system of another Member State shall not be taken into account for the purposes of this provision.

(f) Points 2(a), 2(b), 2(c) and 2(d) shall apply only if the person concerned has resided in one or more Member States for 6 years after the age of 59 and only for such time as that person is resident in one of those Member States.

(g) By way of derogation from Chapter IV of the AOW, anyone resident in a Member State other than the Netherlands whose spouse is covered by compulsory insurance under that legislation shall be authorised to takeout voluntary insurance under that legislation for periods during which the spouse is compulsorily insured.

This authorisation shall not cease where the spouse's compulsory insurance is terminated as a result of his death and where the survivor receives only a pension under the Algemene nabestaandenwet ([2 General Surviving Relatives Act]).

In any event, the authorisation in respect of voluntary insurance ceases on the date on which the person reaches the age of 65.

The contribution to be paid for voluntary insurance shall be set in accordance with the provisions relating to the determination of the contribution for voluntary insurance under the AOW. However, if the voluntary insurance follows on from a period of insurance as referred to in point 2(b), the contribution shall be set in accordance with the provisions relating to the determination of the contribution for compulsory insurance under the AOW, with the income to be taken into account being deemed to have been received in the Netherlands.

(h) The authorisation referred to in point 2(g) shall not be granted to anyone insured under another Member State's legislation on pensions or survivors' benefits.

(i) Anyone wishing to take out voluntary insurance under point 2(g) shall be required to apply for it to the Social Insurance Bank (Sociale Verzekeringsbank) not later than 1 year after the date on which the conditions for participation are fulfilled.

3. Application of the Algemene nabestaandenwet (ANW) ([2 General Surviving Relatives Act])

(a) Where the surviving spouse is entitled to a survivor's pension under the Algemene Nabestaandenwet (ANW)(General Surviving Relatives Act) pursuant to Article 51(3) of this Regulation, that pension shall be calculated in accordance with Article 52(1)(b) of this Regulation.

For the application of these provisions, periods of insurance prior to 1 October 1959 shall also be regarded as periods of insurance completed under Dutch legislation if during those periods the insured person, after the age of 15:

— resided in the Netherlands, or
— while resident in another Member State, worked in the Netherlands for an employer established in the Netherlands, or
— worked in another Member State during periods regarded as periods of insurance under the Dutch social security system.

(b) Account shall not be taken of the periods to be taken into consideration under point 3(a) which coincide with periods of compulsory insurance completed under the legislation of another Member State in respect of survivor's pensions.

(c) For the purposes of Article 52(1)(b) of this Regulation, only periods of insurance completed under Dutch legislation after the age of 15 shall be taken into account as periods of insurance.

(d) By way of derogation from Article 63a(1) of the ANW, a person resident in a Member State other than the Netherlands whose spouse is compulsorily insured under the ANW shall be authorised to take out voluntary insurance under [2 the above legislation], provided that such insurance has already begun by the date of application of this Regulation, but only for periods during which the spouse is compulsorily insured.

This authorisation shall cease as from the date of termination of the spouse's compulsory insurance under than, unless the spouse's compulsory insurance is terminated as a result of his death and where the survivor only receives a pension under the ANW.

In any event, the authorisation in respect of voluntary insurance ceases on the date on which the person reaches the age of 65.

The contribution to be paid for voluntary insurance shall be set in accordance with the provisions relating to the determination of contributions for voluntary insurance under the ANW. However, if the voluntary insurance follows on from a period of insurance as referred to in point 2(b), the contribution shall be set in accordance with the provisions relating to the determination of contributions for compulsory insurance under the ANW, with the income to be taken into account being deemed to have been received in the Netherlands.

4. Application of Dutch legislation relating to incapacity for work

(a) Where, pursuant to Article 51(3) of this Regulation, the person concerned is entitled to a Netherlands invalidity benefit, the amount referred to in Article 52(1)(b) of this Regulation for calculating that benefit shall be determined:

(i) where, prior to the occurrence of incapacity for work, the person last exercised an activity as an employed person within the meaning of Article 1(a) of this Regulation:

— in accordance with the provisions laid down in the Wet op arbeidsongeschiktheidsverzekering(WAO) ([2 Disability Insurance Act]) if the incapacity for work occurred before 1 January 2004, or

— in accordance with the provisions laid down in the Wet Werk en inkomen naar arbeidsvermogen (WIA) ([2 Self-employed Persons Development Benefits Act]) if the incapacity for work occurred on or after 1 January 2004;

(ii) where, prior to the occurrence of the incapacity for work, the person concerned last exercised an activity as a self-employed person within the meaning of Article 1 (b) of this Regulation, in accordance with the provisions laid down in the Wet arbeidsongeschiktheidsverzekering zelfstandigen (WAZ) (Self-employed Persons Act on Incapacity for Work) if the incapacity for work occurred before 1 August 2004.

(b) In calculating benefits under either the WAO, WIA or the WAZ, the Netherlands institutions shall take account of:

— periods of paid employment, and periods treated as such, completed in the Netherlands before 1 July1967,

— periods of insurance completed under the WAO,

— periods of insurance completed by the person concerned, after the age of 15, under the Algemene Arbeidsongeschiktheidswet (AAW) (General Act on Incapacity for Work), in so far as these do not coincide with the periods of insurance completed under the WAO,
— periods of insurance completed under the WAZ,
— periods of insurance completed under the WIA.

AUSTRIA

1. For the purpose of acquiring periods in the pension insurance, attendance at a school or comparable educational establishment in another Member State shall be regarded as equivalent to attendance at a school or educational establishment pursuant to Articles 227(1)(1) and 228(1)(3) of the Allgemeines Sozialversicherungsgesetz (ASVG) (General Social Security Act), Article 116(7) of the Gewerbliches Sozialversicherungsgesetz (GSVG) (Federal Act on Social Insurance for Persons engaged in Trade and Commerce) and Article 107(7) of the Bauern-Sozialversicherungsgesetz(BSVG) (Social Security Act for Farmers), when the person concerned was subject at some time to Austrian legislation on the grounds that he pursued an activity as an employed or self-employed person, and the special contributions provided for under Article 227(3) of the ASVG, Article 116(9) of the GSVG and Article 107(9) of the BSGV for the purchase of such periods of education, are paid.

2. For the calculation of the pro rata benefit referred to in Article 52(1)(b) of this Regulation, special increments for contributions for supplementary insurance and the miners' supplementary benefit under Austrian legislation shall be disregarded. In these cases the pro rata benefit calculated without those contributions shall, if appropriate, be increased by unreduced special increments for contributions for supplementary insurance and the miners' supplementary benefit.

3. Where pursuant to Article 6 of this Regulation substitute periods under an Austrian pension insurance scheme have been completed, but these cannot form a basis for calculation pursuant to Articles 238 and 239 of the Allgemeines Sozialversicherungsgesetz (ASVG) (General Social Security Act), Articles 122 and 123 of the Gewerbliches Sozialversicherungsgesetz (GSVG) (Federal Act on Social Insurance for Persons engaged in Trade and Commerce) and Articles 113 and 114 of the Bauern-Sozialversicherungsgesetz (BSVG) (Social Security Act for Farmers), the calculation basis for periods of childcare pursuant to Article 239 of the ASVG, Article 123 of the GSVG and Article 114of the BSVG shall be used.

FINLAND

1. For the purposes of determining entitlement and of calculating the amount of the Finnish national pension under Articles 52 to 54 of this Regulation, pensions acquired under the legislation of another Member State are treated in the same way as pensions acquired under Finnish legislation.

2. When applying Article 52(1)(b)(i) of this Regulation for the purpose of calculating earnings for the credited period under Finnish legislation on earnings-related pensions, where an individual has pension insurance

periods based on activity as an employed or self-employed person in another Member State for part of the reference period under Finnish legislation, the earnings for the credited period shall be equivalent to the sum of earnings obtained during the part of the reference period in Finland, divided by the number of months for which there were insurance periods in Finland during the reference period.

SWEDEN

1. When parental leave allowance is paid under Article 67 of this Regulation to a member of the family who is not employed, the parental leave allowance is paid at a level corresponding to the basic or lowest level.

2. For the purpose of calculating parental leave allowance in accordance with Chapter 4, paragraph 6 of the Lag(1962:381) om allmän försäkring (the National Insurance Act) for persons eligible for a work-based parental leave allowance, the following shall apply:

For a parent for whom sickness benefit generating income is calculated on the basis of income from gainful employment in Sweden, the requirement to have been insured for sickness benefit above the minimum level for at least240 consecutive days preceding the child's birth shall be satisfied if, during the period mentioned, the parent had income from gainful employment in another Member State corresponding to insurance above the minimum level.

3. The provisions of this Regulation on the aggregation of insurance periods and periods of residence shall not apply to the transitional provisions in the Swedish legislation on entitlement to guarantee pension for persons born in or before 1937 who have been resident in Sweden for a specified period before applying for a pension (Act 2000:798).

4. For the purpose of calculating income for notional income-related sickness compensation and income-related activity compensation in accordance with Chapter 8 of the Lag (1962:381) om allmän försäkring (the National Insurance Act), the following shall apply:

(a) where the insured person, during the reference period, has also been subject to the legislation of one or more other Member States on account of activity as an employed or self-employed person, income in the Member State(s) concerned shall be deemed to be equivalent to the insured person's average gross income in Sweden during the part of the reference period in Sweden, calculated by dividing the earnings in Sweden by the number of years over which those earnings accrued;

(b) where the benefits are calculated pursuant to Article 46 of this Regulation and persons are not insured in Sweden, the reference period shall be determined in accordance with Chapter 8, paragraphs 2 and 8 of the abovementioned Act as if the person concerned were insured in Sweden. If the person concerned has no pension-generating income during this period under the Act on income-based old-age pension (1998:674), the reference period shall be permitted to run from the earlier point in time when the insured person had income from gainful activity in Sweden.

5. (a) For the purpose of calculating notional pension assets for income-based survivor's pension (Act 2000:461), if the requirement in Swedish legislation for pension entitlement in respect of at least

three out of the 5 calendar years immediately preceding the insured person's death (reference period) is not met, account shall also be taken of insurance periods completed in other Member States as if they had been completed in Sweden. Insurance periods in other Member States shall be regarded as based on the average Swedish pension base. If the person concerned has only 1 year in Sweden with a pension base, each insurance period in another Member State shall be regarded as constituting the same amount.

(b) For the purpose of calculating notional pension credits for widows' pensions relating to deaths on or after1 January 2003, if the requirement in Swedish legislation for pension credits in respect of at least two out of the 4 years immediately preceding the insured person's death (reference period) is not met and insurance periods were completed in another Member State during the reference period, those years shall be regarded as being based on the same pension credits as the Swedish year.

UNITED KINGDOM

1. Where, in accordance with United Kingdom legislation, a person may be entitled to a retirement pension if:

(a) the contributions of a former spouse are taken into account as if they were that person's own contributions; or

(b) the relevant contribution conditions are satisfied by that person's spouse or former spouse,

then provided, in each case, that the spouse or former spouse is or had been exercising an activity as an employed or self-employed person, and had been subject to the legislation of two or more Member States, the provisions of Chapter 5 of Title III of this Regulation shall apply in order to determine entitlement under United Kingdom legislation. In this case, references in the said Chapter 5 to "periods of insurance" shall be construed as references to periods of insurance completed by:

(i) a spouse or former spouse where a claim is made by:
- — a married woman, or
- — a person whose marriage has terminated otherwise than by the death of the spouse; or

(ii) a former spouse, where a claim is made by:
- — a widower who immediately before pensionable age is not entitled to widowed parent's allowance, or
- — a widow who immediately before pensionable age is not entitled to widowed mother's allowance, widowed parent's allowance or widow's pension, or who is only entitled to an age-related widow's pension calculated pursuant to Article 52(1)(b) of this Regulation, and for this purpose "age-related widow's pension" means a widow's pension payable at a reduced rate in accordance with section 39(4) of the Social Security Contributions and Benefits Act 1992.

2. For the purposes of applying Article 6 of this Regulation to the provisions governing entitlement to attendance allowance, carer's allowance and disability living allowance, a period of employment, self-employment or residence completed in the territory of a Member State other than the United Kingdom shall be taken into account in so far as is necessary to satisfy conditions as to required periods of presence in the

United Kingdom, prior to the day on which entitlement to the benefit in question first arises.

3. For the purposes of Article 7 of this Regulation, in the case of invalidity, old-age or survivors' cash benefits, pensions for accidents at work or occupational diseases and death grants, any beneficiary under United Kingdom legislation who is staying in the territory of another Member State shall, during that stay, be considered as if he resided in the territory of that other Member State.

4. Where Article 46 of this Regulation applies, if the person concerned suffers incapacity for work leading to invalidity while subject to the legislation of another Member State, the United Kingdom shall, for the purposes of Section 30A (5) of the Social Security Contributions and Benefits Act 1992, take account of any periods during which the person concerned has received, in respect of that incapacity for work:

(i) cash sickness benefits or wages or salary in lieu thereof; or

(ii) benefits within the meaning of Chapters 4 and 5 of Title III of this Regulation granted in respect of the invalidity which followed that incapacity for work, under the legislation of the other Member State, as though they were periods of short-term incapacity benefit paid in accordance with Sections 30A (1)-(4) of the Social Security Contributions and Benefits Act 1992.

In applying this provision, account shall only be taken of periods during which the person would have been incapable of work within the meaning of United Kingdom legislation.

5. (1) For the purpose of calculating an earnings factor in order to determine entitlement to benefits under United Kingdom legislation, for each week of activity as an employed person under the legislation of another Member State, and which commenced during the relevant income tax year within the meaning of United Kingdom legislation, the person concerned shall be deemed to have paid contributions as an employed earner, or have earnings on which contributions have been paid, on the basis of earnings equivalent to two-thirds of that year's upper earnings limit.

(2) For the purposes of Article 52(1)(b)(ii) of this Regulation, where:

(a) in any income tax year starting on or after 6 April 1975, a person carrying out activity as an employed person has completed periods of insurance, employment or residence exclusively in a Member State other than the United Kingdom, and the application of point 5(1) above results in that year being counted as a qualifying year within the meaning of United Kingdom legislation for the purposes of Article 52(1)(b)(i)of this Regulation, he shall be deemed to have been insured for 52 weeks in that year in that other Member State;

(b) any income tax year starting on or after 6 April 1975 does not count as a qualifying year within the meaning of United Kingdom legislation for the purposes of Article 52(1)(b)(i) of this Regulation, any periods of insurance, employment or residence completed in that year shall be disregarded.

(3) For the purpose of converting an earnings factor into periods of insurance, the earnings factor achieved in the relevant income tax year within the meaning of United Kingdom legislation shall be divided by that year's lower earnings limit. The result shall be

expressed as a whole number, any remaining fraction being ignored. The figure so calculated shall be treated as representing the number of weeks of insurance completed under United Kingdom legislation during that year, provided that such figure shall not exceed the number of weeks during which in that year the person was subject to that legislation.

AMENDMENTS

1. Regulation 988/2009 art.1 (May 1, 2010).
2. Regulation 465/2012 [2012] OJ L149/4 art.1(12) (June 28, 2012).
3. Regulation 1872/2013 art.1(2) (January 1, 2014).

Regulation (EC) No 987/2009 of the European Parliament and of the Council

of 16 September 2009

laying down the procedure for implementing Regulation (EC) No 883/2004 on the coordination of social security systems

[2009] OJ L284/1

Applies from May 1, 2010

ARRANGEMENT OF REGULATION

3.501 *Preamble*

TITLE I

GENERAL PROVISIONS

CHAPTER I

Definitions

CHAPTER II

Provisions concerning cooperation and exchange of data

CHAPTER III

Other general provisions for the application of the basic Regulation

TITLE II

DETERMINATION OF THE LEGISLATION APPLICABLE

Title III

Special Provisions Concerning the Various Categories of Benefits

Chapter I

Sickness, maternity and equivalent paternity benefits

Chapter II

Benefits in respect of accidents at work and occupational diseases

Chapter III

Death grants

Chapter IV

Invalidity benefits and old-age and survivors' pensions

Chapter V

Unemployment benefits

Chapter VI

Family benefits

TITLE IV

FINANCIAL PROVISIONS

CHAPTER I

Reimbursement of the cost of benefits in application of Article 35 and Article 41 of the basic Regulation

Section 1

Reimbursement on the basis of actual expenditure

Section 2

Reimbursement on the basis of fixed amounts

Section 3

Common Provisions

CHAPTER II

Reimbursement of unemployment benefits pursuant to Article 65 of the basic Regulation

CHAPTER III

Recovery of benefits provided but not due, recovery of provisional payments and contributions, offsetting and assistance with recovery

Section 1

Principles

Section 2

Offsetting

Section 3

Recovery

TITLE V

MISCELLANEOUS, TRANSITIONAL AND FINAL PROVISION

The European Parliament and the Council of the European Union,

3.502 Having regard to the Treaty establishing the European Community, and in particular Articles 42 and 308 thereof,

Having regard to Regulation (EC) No 883/2004 of the European Parliament and of the Council of 29 April 2004 on the coordination of social security systems,[10] and in particular Article 89 thereof,

Having regard to the proposal from the Commission,

Having regard to the Opinion of the European Economic and Social Committee,[11]

Acting in accordance with the procedure laid down in Article 251 of the Treaty,[12]

Whereas:

(1) Regulation (EC) No 883/2004 modernises the rules on the coordination of Member States' social security systems, specifying the measures and procedures for implementing them and simplifying them for all the players involved. Implementing rules should be laid down.

(2) Closer and more effective cooperation between social security institutions is a key factor in allowing the persons covered by Regulation (EC) No 883/2004 to access their rights as quickly as possible and under optimum conditions.

(3) Electronic communication is a suitable means of rapid and reliable data exchange between Member States' institutions. Processing data electronically should help speed up the procedures for everyone involved. The persons concerned should also benefit from all the guarantees provided for in the Community provisions on the protection of natural persons with regard to the processing and free movement of personal data.

(4) Availability of the details (including electronic details) of those national bodies likely to be involved in implementing Regulation (EC) No 883/2004, in a form which allows them to be updated in real time, should facilitate exchanges between Member States' institutions. This

10 OJ L 166, 30.4.2004, p.1.
11 OJ C 324, 30.12.2006, p.59.
12 Opinion of the European Parliament of July 9, 2008 (not yet published in the Official Journal), Council Common Position of 17 December2008 (OJ C 38 E, 17.2.2009, p.26) and Position of the European Parliament of April 22, 2009. Council Decision of July 27, 2009.

approach, which focuses on the relevance of purely factual information and its immediate accessibility to citizens, is a valuable simplification which should be introduced by this Regulation.

(5) Achieving the smoothest possible operation and the efficient management of the complex procedures implementing the rules on the coordination of social security systems requires a system for the immediate updating of Annex 4. The preparation and application of provisions to that effect calls for close cooperation between the Member States and the Commission, and their implementation should be carried out rapidly, in view of the consequences of delays for citizens and administrative authorities alike. The Commission should therefore be empowered to establish and manage a database and ensure that it is operational at least from the date of entry into force of this Regulation. The Commission should, in particular, take the necessary steps to integrate into that database the information listed in Annex 4.

(6) Strengthening certain procedures should ensure greater legal certainty and transparency for the users of Regulation (EC) No 883/2004. For example, setting common deadlines for fulfilling certain obligations or completing certain administrative tasks should assist in clarifying and structuring relations between insured persons and institutions.

(7) The persons covered by this Regulation should receive from the competent institution a timely response to their requests. The response should be provided at the latest within the time-limits prescribed by the social security legislation of the Member State in question, where such time-limits exist. It would be desirable for Member States whose social security legislation does not make provision for such time-limits to consider adopting them and making them available to the persons concerned as necessary.

(8) The Member States, their competent authorities and the social security institutions should have the option of agreeing among themselves on simplified procedures and administrative arrangements which they consider to be more effective and better suited to the circumstances of their respective social security systems. However, such arrangements should not affect the rights of the persons covered by Regulation (EC) No 883/2004.

(9) The inherent complexity of the field of social security requires all institutions of the Member States to make a particular effort to support insured persons in order to avoid penalising those who have not submitted their claim or certain information to the institution responsible for processing this application in accordance with the rules and procedures set out in Regulation (EC) No 883/2004 and in this Regulation.

(10) To determine the competent institution, namely the one whose legislation applies or which is liable for the payment of certain benefits, the circumstances of the insured person and those of the family members must be examined by the institutions of more than one Member State. To ensure that the person concerned is protected for the duration of the necessary communication between institutions, provision should be made for provisional membership of a social security system.

(11) Member States should cooperate in determining the place of residence of persons to whom this Regulation and Regulation (EC) No 883/2004 apply and, in the event of a dispute, should take into consideration all relevant criteria to resolve the matter. These may include criteria referred to in the appropriate Article of this Regulation.

(12) Many measures and procedures provided for in this Regulation are intended to ensure greater transparency concerning the criteria which the institutions of the Member States must apply under Regulation (EC) No 883/2004. Such measures and procedures are the result of the case-law of the Court of Justice of the European Communities, the decisions of the Administrative Commission and the experience of more than 30 years of application of the coordination of social security systems in the context of the fundamental freedoms enshrined in the Treaty.

(13) This Regulation provides for measures and procedures to promote the mobility of employees and unemployed persons. Frontier workers who have become wholly unemployed may make themselves available to the employment services in both their country of residence and the Member State where they were last employed. However, they should be entitled to benefits only from their Member State of residence.

(14) Certain specific rules and procedures are required in order to define the legislation applicable for taking account of periods during which an insured person has devoted time to bringing up children in the various Member States.

(15) Certain procedures should also reflect the need for a balanced sharing of costs between Member States. In particular in the area of sickness, such procedures should take account of the position of Member States which bear the costs of allowing insured persons access to their healthcare system and the position of Member States whose institutions bear the cost of benefits in kind received by their insured persons in a Member State other than that in which they are resident.

(16) In the specific context of Regulation (EC) No 883/2004, it is necessary to clarify the conditions for meeting the costs of sickness benefits in kind as part of scheduled treatments, namely treatments for which an insured person goes to a Member State other than that in which he is insured or resident. The obligations of the insured person with regard to the application for prior authorisation should be specified, as should the institution's obligations towards the patient with regard to the conditions of authorisation. The consequences for the chargeability of the costs of care received in another Member State on the basis of an authorisation should also be clarified.

(17) This Regulation, and especially the provisions concerning the stay outside the competent Member State and concerning scheduled treatment, should not prevent the application of more favourable national provisions, in particular with regard to the reimbursement of costs incurred in another Member State.

(18) More binding procedures to reduce the time needed for payment of these claims between Member States' institutions are essential in order to maintain confidence in the exchanges and meet the need for sound management of Member States' social security systems. Procedures for the processing of claims relating to sickness and unemployment benefits should therefore be strengthened.

(19) Procedures between institutions for mutual assistance in recovery of social security claims should be strengthened in order to ensure more effective recovery and smooth functioning of the coordination rules. Effective recovery is also a means of preventing and tackling abuses and fraud and a way of ensuring the sustainability of social security schemes. This involves the adoption of new procedures, taking as a basis a number of existing

provisions in Council Directive 2008/55/EC of 26 May 2008 on mutual assistance for the recovery of claims relating to certain levies, duties, taxes and other measures.[13] Such new recovery procedures should be reviewed in the light of the experience after five years of implementation and adjusted if necessary, in particular to ensure they are fully operable.

(20) For the purposes of provisions on mutual assistance regarding the recovery of benefits provided but not due, the recovery of provisional payments and contributions and the offsetting and assistance with recovery, the jurisdiction of the requested Member State is limited to actions regarding enforcement measures. Any other action falls under the jurisdiction of the applicant Member State.

(21) The enforcement measures taken in the requested Member State do not imply the recognition by that Member State of the substance or basis of the claim.

(22) Informing the persons concerned of their rights and obligations is a crucial component of a relationship of trust with the competent authorities and the Member States' institutions. Information should include guidance on administrative procedures. The persons concerned may include, depending on the situation, the insured persons, their family members and/or their survivors or other persons.

(23) Since the objective of this Regulation, namely the adoption of coordination measures in order to guarantee the effective exercise of the free movement of persons, cannot be sufficiently achieved by the Member States and can therefore, by reason of its scale and effects, be better achieved at Community level, the Community may adopt measures, in accordance with the principle of subsidiarity as set out in Article 5 of the Treaty. In accordance with the principle of proportionality, as set out in that Article, this Regulation does not go beyond what is necessary to achieve that objective.

(24) This Regulation should replace Council Regulation (EEC) No 574/72 of 21 March 1972 fixing the procedure for implementing Regulation (EEC) No 1408/71 on the application of social security schemes to employed persons and their families moving within the Community,[14]

HAVE ADOPTED THIS REGULATION:

13 OJ L 150, 10.6.2008, p.28.
14 OJ L 74, 27.3.1972, p.1.

Title I

General Provisions

Chapter I

Definitions

Article 1

Definitions

3.503 1. For the purposes of this Regulation:

(a) "basic Regulation" means Regulation (EC) No 883/2004;

(b) "implementing Regulation" means this Regulation; and

(c) the definitions set out in the basic Regulation shall apply.

2. In addition to the definitions referred to in paragraph 1,

(a) "access point" means an entity providing:

  (i) an electronic contact point;

  (ii) automatic routing based on the address; and

  (iii) intelligent routing based on software that enables automatic checking and routing (for example, an artificial intelligence application) and/or human intervention;

(b) "liaison body" means any body designated by the competent authority of a Member State for one or more of the branches of social security referred to in Article 3 of the basic Regulation to respond to requests for information and assistance for the purposes of the application of the basic Regulation and the implementing Regulation and which has to fulfil the tasks assigned to it under Title IV of the implementing Regulation;

(c) "document" means a set of data, irrespective of the medium used, structured in such a way that it can be exchanged electronically and which must be communicated in order to enable the operation of the basic Regulation and the implementing Regulation;

(d) "Structured Electronic Document" means any structured document in a format designed for the electronic exchange of information between Member States;

(e) "transmission by electronic means" means the transmission of data using electronic equipment for the processing (including digital compression) of data and employing wires, radio transmission, optical technologies or any other electromagnetic means;

(f) "Audit Board" means the body referred to in Article 74 of the basic Regulation.

Article 2

CHAPTER II

Provisions concerning cooperation and exchanges of data

Article 2

Scope and rules for exchanges between institutions

1. For the purposes of the implementing Regulation, exchanges between Member States' authorities and institutions and persons covered by the basic Regulation shall be based on the principles of public service, efficiency, active assistance, rapid delivery and accessibility, including e-accessibility, in particular for the disabled and the elderly. **3.504**

2. The institutions shall without delay provide or exchange all data necessary for establishing and determining the rights and obligations of persons to whom the basic Regulation applies. Such data shall be transferred between Member States directly by the institutions themselves or indirectly via the liaison bodies.

3. Where a person has mistakenly submitted information, documents or claims to an institution in the territory of a Member State other than that in which the institution designated in accordance with the implementing Regulation is situated, the information, documents or claims shall be resubmitted without delay by the former institution to the institution designated in accordance with the implementing Regulation, indicating the date on which they were initially submitted. That date shall be binding on the latter institution. Member State institutions shall not, however, be held liable, or be deemed to have taken a decision by virtue of their failure to act as a result of the late transmission of information, documents or claims by other Member States' institutions.

4. Where data are transferred indirectly via the liaison body of the Member State of destination, time limits for responding to claims shall start from the date when that liaison body received the claim, as if it had been received by the institution in that Member State.

Article 3

Scope and rules for exchanges between the persons concerned and institutions

1. Member States shall ensure that the necessary information is made available to the persons concerned in order to inform them of the changes introduced by the basic Regulation and by the implementing Regulation to enable them to assert their rights. They shall also provide for user friendly services. **3.505**

2. Persons to whom the basic Regulation applies shall be required to forward to the relevant institution the information, documents or supporting evidence necessary to establish their situation or that of their families, to establish or maintain their rights and obligations and to determine the applicable legislation and their obligations under it.

3. When collecting, transmitting or processing personal data pursuant to their legislation for the purposes of implementing the basic Regulation, Member States shall ensure that the persons concerned are able to exercise fully their rights regarding personal data protection, in accordance with Community provisions on the protection of individuals with regard to the processing of personal data and the free movement of such data.

4. To the extent necessary for the application of the basic Regulation and the implementing Regulation, the relevant institutions shall forward the information and issue the documents to the persons concerned without delay and in all cases within any time limits specified under the legislation of the Member State in question.

The relevant institution shall notify the claimant residing or staying in another Member State of its decision directly or through the liaison body of the Member State of residence or stay. When refusing the benefits it shall also indicate the reasons for refusal, the remedies and periods allowed for appeals. A copy of this decision shall be sent to other involved institutions.

GENERAL NOTE

3.506 In *SSWP v HR (AA)* [2014] UKUT 571 (AAC), [2015] AACR 26, Judge Jacobs has drawn attention to the objectives contained in this article in dealing with a case concerning a difference of view between Member State institutions about which State was the competent State for the purposes of a claim for a sickness benefit. See also annotation to art.6 of Regulation 987/2009.

Article 4

Format and method of exchanging data

3.507 1. The Administrative Commission shall lay down the structure, content, format and detailed arrangements for exchange of documents and structured electronic documents.

2. The transmission of data between the institutions or the liaison bodies shall be carried out by electronic means either directly or indirectly through the access points under a common secure framework that can guarantee the confidentiality and protection of exchanges of data.

3. In their communications with the persons concerned, the relevant institutions shall use the arrangements appropriate to each case, and favour the use of electronic means as far as possible. The Administrative Commission shall lay down the practical arrangements for sending information, documents or decisions by electronic means to the person concerned.

Article 5

Legal value of documents and supporting evidencc issued in another Member State

3.508 1. Documents issued by the institution of a Member State and showing the position of a person for the purposes of the application of the basic Regulation and of the implementing Regulation, and supporting evidence on the basis of which the documents have been issued, shall be accepted by the institutions of the other Member States for as long as they have not been withdrawn or declared to be invalid by the Member State in which they were issued.

2. Where there is doubt about the validity of a document or the accuracy of the facts on which the particulars contained therein are based, the institution of the Member State that receives the document shall ask the issuing institution for the necessary clarification and, where appropriate, the withdrawal of that document. The issuing institution shall reconsider the grounds for issuing the document and, if necessary, withdraw it.

3. Pursuant to paragraph 2, where there is doubt about the information provided by the persons concerned, the validity of a document or supporting evidence or the accuracy of the facts on which the particulars contained therein are based, the institution of the place of stay or residence shall, insofar as this is possible, at the request of the competent institution, proceed to the necessary verification of this information or document.

4. Where no agreement is reached between the institutions concerned, the matter may be brought before the Administrative Commission by the competent authorities no earlier than one month following the date on which the institution that received the document submitted its request. The Administrative Commission shall endeavour to reconcile the points of view within six months of the date on which the matter was brought before it.

Article 6

Provisional application of legislation and provisional granting of benefits

1. Unless otherwise provided for in the implementing Regulation, where there is a difference of views between the institutions or authorities of two or more Member States concerning the determination of the applicable legislation, the person concerned shall be made provisionally subject to the legislation of one of those Member States, the order of priority being determined as follows: **3.509**

(a) the legislation of the Member State where the person actually pursues his employment or self-employment, if the employment or self-employment is pursued in only one Member State;

[1 (b) the legislation of the Member State of residence if the person concerned pursues employment or self-employment in two or more Member States and performs part of his/her activity or activities in the Member State of residence, or if the person concerned is neither employed nor self-employed;

(c) in all other cases, the legislation of the Member State, the application of which was first requested if the person pursues an activity, or activities, in two or more Member States.]

2. Where there is a difference of views between the institutions or authorities of two or more Member States about which institution should provide the benefits in cash or in kind, the person concerned who could claim benefits if there was no dispute shall be entitled, on a provisional basis, to the benefits provided for by the legislation applied by the institution of his place

of residence or, if that person does not reside on the territory of one of the Member States concerned, to the benefits provided for by the legislation applied by the institution to which the request was first submitted.

3. Where no agreement is reached between the institutions or authorities concerned, the matter may be brought before the Administrative Commission by the competent authorities no earlier than one month after the date on which the difference of views, as referred to in paragraph 1 or 2 arose. The Administrative Commission shall seek to reconcile the points of view within six months of the date on which the matter was brought before it.

4. Where it is established either that the applicable legislation is not that of the Member State of provisional membership, or the institution which granted the benefits on a provisional basis was not the competent institution, the institution identified as being competent shall be deemed retroactively to have been so, as if that difference of views had not existed, at the latest from either the date of provisional membership or of the first provisional granting of the benefits concerned.

5. If necessary, the institution identified as being competent and the institution which provisionally paid the cash benefits or provisionally received contributions shall settle the financial situation of the person concerned as regards contributions and cash benefits paid provisionally, where appropriate, in accordance with Title IV, Chapter III, of the implementing Regulation.

Benefits in kind granted provisionally by an institution in accordance with paragraph 2 shall be reimbursed by the competent institution in accordance with Title IV of the implementing Regulation.

AMENDMENT

1. Regulation 465/2012 [2012] OJ L149/4 art.2(1) (June 28, 2012).

GENERAL NOTE

3.510 The procedure for which this article makes provision seems to be underused. There are occasions in which there is a dispute over entitlement to sickness benefits; see for example *SL v SSWP (DLA)* [2014] UKUT 108 (AAC). The article covers differences of views about the applicable legislation, as well as about which institution or authorities should provide the benefits for which a claim has been made.

Article 6 effectively insulates the claimant from the resolution of a difference of view by requiring the claimant to be made provisionally subject to the legislation of one of the Member States concerned pending the resolution between the relevant bodies of the difference of view. Article 6(3) even includes an internal resolution procedure involving the Administrative Commission.

The provisions of this article may need to be read with art.81 of Regulation 883/2004 which provide for the forwarding of claims by the competent institutions of one Member State to those of another Member State.

The procedures in this article should be distinguished from the particular procedures in art.11 for determining the residence of a person where there is a difference of views on that aspect of any determination under Regulation 883/2004.

In *SSWP v HR (AA)* [2014] UKUT 571 (AAC), [2015] AACR 26, Judge Jacobs has given detailed guidance on the operation of this article in a case in which there was a difference of view between the United Kingdom and Swedish authorities on which was the competent institution for the award of sickness benefits. The Secretary of State accepted that in a claim for an attendance allowance by a Swedish national resident in the United Kingdom, the legislation of the State of residence should be provisionally applied under the terms of the article. The decision under appeal had been a refusal of the claim on the grounds that the United Kingdom was not the competent State. A difference of view does not require formal decisions from different authorities (see paras 16–19).

Judge Jacobs goes on to provide guidance in three typical situations which can arise. The first situation arises where the United Kingdom concludes that it is the competent State under Regulation 883/2004. Here the only remaining issues will be the application of national law to the claim which has been made (para.26).

The second situation arises where the Secretary of State decides that the United Kingdom is not the competent State and another Member State has expressed a different view. Here there is a difference of view and art.6 must be applied. If the claimant meets the conditions of entitlement under national law to the United Kingdom benefit, the United Kingdom is required to apply its legislation on a provisional basis to award the benefit. No appeal should arise since the claimant will be receiving the benefit (para.27).

The third situation arises where the Secretary of State decides that the United Kingdom is not the competent State, and there is no indication of a difference of view with any other Member State. Here the Secretary of State will be likely to refuse the claim, but is also under a duty under art.81 of Regulation 883/2004 to forward the claim without delay to the State which it considers to be the competent State. This could generate a difference of view which would trigger the operation of the procedures in art.6. Judge Jacobs concludes that any difficulties about the date of claim and the date from which payment could be made will be governed by European Union law which will override any limitations contained in national law (paras 28–31).

SSWP v AK (AA) [2015] UKUT 110 (AAC), [2015] AACR 27, deals with the situation where there was no disagreement on the issue of which Member State was the competent State for the purposes of Regulation 883/2004. Judge Jacobs says:

> "28. On the basis that the United Kingdom was not the competent State for the claimant's attendance allowance, the Secretary of State was entitled, indeed obliged, to refuse the claim. But that was not all. Article 81 of Regulation 883/2004 provides for what should happen when the Secretary of State considers that another State is the competent State: . . .
>
> 29. Applying [Article 81] requires this approach. In order for Article 81 to apply, two conditions must be satisfied. First, the Secretary of State or the tribunal must decide that the United Kingdom is not the competent State for the benefit claimed. Second, there must be no evidence that is sufficient to show a difference of view between competing member States. If, and only if, both of those conditions are satisfied, the Secretary of State must submit the claim to the other potentially competent State under the Article.
>
> 30. If the other State subsequently decides that it is not the competent State, there will be a difference of view. The case must then be dealt with in accordance with *Secretary of State for Work and Pensions v HR*. . . . ."

What constitutes a difference of view remains contentious, and was considered in *SSWP v FF* [2015] UKUT 288 (AAC), where Judge Jacobs said:

> "11. As a result of decisions I have given in *HR* and other cases, the correct approach to cases like this one has become clear. It depends on whether there has been a difference of view. Article 6(2) says nothing about the form in which that difference must be expressed or the nature of the evidence required to show it. In particular, it does not say that it must be formally expressed in a decision. The only issue for the domestic authorities in this country – the decision-maker, the First-tier Tribunal and the Upper Tribunal – is whether the evidence is sufficient to satisfy them that the two competing States hold different views on the issue. The United Kingdom takes the view that France is the competent State. The claimant says that he approached the French authorities and was told that they would not pay benefit for caring for someone in the United Kingdom. I have no reason to doubt what he says. Given their attitude, it is understandable

why he did not press the matter by making a formal claim for the equivalent of a carer's allowance in France. A formal decision is not required, as I have said. The failure of the Secretary of State's officials to elicit any response from their French counterparts is some indication of the difficulty that the claimant would face if required to produce some more formal evidence. His difficulty in that regard would be compounded by the fact that he now lives here. His evidence is sufficient to satisfy me that there is a difference of view in this case.

12. The Secretary of State's representative has argued that the application of Regulation 883/2004 is clear: France is the competent State, not the United Kingdom. That may be right, but it is not how Article 6(2) operates. That provision is triggered by a difference of view. It takes the decision out of the hands of the States to ensure a single, binding decision. It prevents claimants being left in the position of each State refusing to accept responsibility. That is its purpose and it applies regardless of how clear any particular State considers the answer to be.

13. As there is a difference of view, Article 6(2) applies. The tribunal went wrong in law by not applying that provision. I set its decision aside and re-make it to provide for the Secretary of State to investigate and decide the claim under domestic legislation and, if necessary, to make a provisional award pending resolution by the Administrative Commission."

Article 7

Provisional calculation of benefits and contributions

3.511 1. Unless otherwise provided for in the implementing Regulation, where a person is eligible for a benefit, or is liable to pay a contribution in accordance with the basic Regulation, and the competent institution does not have all the information concerning the situation in another Member State which is necessary to calculate definitively the amount of that benefit or contribution, that institution shall, on request of the person concerned, award this benefit or calculate this contribution on a provisional basis, if such a calculation is possible on the basis of the information at the disposal of that institution.

2. The benefit or the contribution concerned shall be recalculated once all the necessary supporting evidence or documents are provided to the institution concerned.

CHAPTER III

Other general provisions for the application of the basic Regulation

Article 8

Administrative arrangements between two or more Member States

3.512 1. The provisions of the implementing Regulation shall replace those laid down in the arrangements for the application of the conventions referred to in Article 8(1) of the basic Regulation, except the provisions concerning the arrangements concerning the conventions referred to in Annex II to the basic Regulation, provided that the provisions of those arrangements are included in Annex 1 to the implementing Regulation.

2. Member States may conclude between themselves, if necessary,

arrangements pertaining to the application of the conventions referred to in Article 8(2) of the basic Regulation provided that these arrangements do not adversely affect the rights and obligations of the persons concerned and are included in Annex 1 to the implementing Regulation.

Article 9

Other procedures between authorities and institutions

1. Two or more Member States, or their competent authorities, may agree procedures other than those provided for by the implementing Regulation, provided that such procedures do not adversely affect the rights or obligations of the persons concerned. 3.513

2. Any agreements concluded to this end shall be notified to the Administrative Commission and listed in Annex 1 to the implementing Regulation.

3. Provisions contained in implementing agreements concluded between two or more Member States with the same purpose as, or which are similar to, those referred to in paragraph 2, which are in force on the day preceding the entry into force of the implementing Regulation and are included in Annex 5 to Regulation (EEC) No 574/72, shall continue to apply, for the purposes of relations between those Member States, provided they are also included in Annex 1 to the implementing Regulation.

Article 10

Prevention of overlapping of benefits

Notwithstanding other provisions in the basic Regulation, when benefits due under the legislation of two or more Member States are mutually reduced, suspended or withdrawn, any amounts that would not be paid in the event of strict application of the rules concerning reduction, suspension or withdrawal laid down by the legislation of the Member States concerned shall be divided by the number of benefits subjected to reduction, suspension or withdrawal. 3.514

Article 11

Elements for determining residence

1. Where there is a difference of views between the institutions of two or more Member States about the determination of the residence of a person to whom the basic Regulation applies, these institutions shall establish by common agreement the centre of interests of the person concerned, based on an overall assessment of all available information relating to relevant facts, which may include, as appropriate: 3.515

(a) the duration and continuity of presence on the territory of the Member States concerned;

(b) the person's situation, including:

(i) the nature and the specific characteristics of any activity pursued, in particular the place where such activity is habitually pursued, the stability of the activity, and the duration of any work contract;
(ii) his family status and family ties;
(iii) the exercise of any non-remunerated activity;
(iv) in the case of students, the source of their income;
(v) his housing situation, in particular how permanent it is;
(vi) the Member State in which the person is deemed to reside for taxation purposes.

2. Where the consideration of the various criteria based on relevant facts as set out in paragraph 1 does not lead to agreement between the institutions concerned, the person's intention, as it appears from such facts and circumstances, especially the reasons that led the person to move, shall be considered to be decisive for establishing that person's actual place of residence.

Article 12

Aggregation of periods

3.516 1. For the purposes of applying Article 6 of the basic Regulation, the competent institution shall contact the institutions of the Member States to whose legislation the person concerned has also been subject in order to determine all the periods completed under their legislation.

2. The respective periods of insurance, employment, self-employment or residence completed under the legislation of a Member State shall be added to those completed under the legislation of any other Member State, insofar as necessary for the purposes of applying Article 6 of the basic Regulation, provided that these periods do not overlap.

3. Where a period of insurance or residence which is completed in accordance with compulsory insurance under the legislation of a Member State coincides with a period of insurance completed on the basis of voluntary insurance or continued optional insurance under the legislation of another Member State, only the period completed on the basis of compulsory insurance shall be taken into account.

4. Where a period of insurance or residence other than an equivalent period completed under the legislation of a Member State coincides with an equivalent period on the basis of the legislation of another Member State, only the period other than an equivalent period shall be taken into account.

5. Any period regarded as equivalent under the legislation of two or more Member States shall be taken into account only by the institution of the Member State to whose legislation the person concerned was last compulsorily subject before that period. In the event that the person concerned was not compulsorily subject to the legislation of a Member State before that period, the latter shall be taken into account by the institution of the Member State to whose legislation the person concerned was compulsorily subject for the first time after that period.

6. In the event that the time in which certain periods of insurance or residence were completed under the legislation of a Member State cannot be determined precisely, it shall be presumed that these periods do not overlap

with periods of insurance or residence completed under the legislation of another Member State, and account shall be taken thereof, where advantageous to the person concerned, insofar as they can reasonably be taken into consideration.

Article 13

Rules for conversion of periods

1. Where periods completed under the legislation of a Member State are expressed in units different from those provided for by the legislation of another Member State, the conversion needed for the purpose of aggregation under Article 6 of the basic Regulation shall be carried out under the following rules: 3.517

(a) the period to be used as the basis for the conversion shall be that communicated by the institution of the Member State under whose legislation the period was completed;

(b) in the case of schemes where the periods are expressed in days the conversion from days to other units, and vice versa, as well as between different schemes based on days shall be calculated according to the following table:

Scheme based on	*1 day corresponds to*	*1 week corresponds to*	*1 month corresponds to*	*1 quarter corresponds to*	*Maximum of days in one calendar year*
5 days	9 hours	5 days	22 days	66 days	264 days
6 days	8 hours	6 days	26 days	78 days	312 days
7 days	6 hours	7 days	30 days	90 days	360 days

(c) in the case of schemes where the periods are expressed in units other than days,

(i) three months or 13 weeks shall be equivalent to one quarter, and vice versa;

(ii) one year shall be equivalent to four quarters, 12 months or 52 weeks, and vice versa;

(iii) for the conversion of weeks into months, and vice versa, weeks and months shall be converted into days in accordance with the conversion rules for the schemes based on six days in the table in point (b);

(d) in the case of periods expressed in fractions, those figures shall be converted into the next smaller integer unit applying the rules laid down in points (b) and (c). Fractions of years shall be converted into months unless the scheme involved is based on quarters;

(e) if the conversion under this paragraph results in a fraction of a unit, the next higher integer unit shall be taken as the result of the conversion under this paragraph.

2. The application of paragraph 1 shall not have the effect of producing, for the total sum of the periods completed during one calendar year, a total exceeding the number of days indicated in the last column in the table in paragraph 1(b), 52 weeks,12 months or four quarters.

If the periods to be converted correspond to the maximum annual amount of periods under the legislation of the Member State in which they have been completed, the application of paragraph 1shall not result within one calendar year in periods that are shorter than the possible maximum annual amount of periods provided under the legislation concerned.

3. The conversion shall be carried out either in one single operation covering all those periods which were communicated as an aggregate, or for each year, if the periods were communicated on a year-by-year basis.

4. Where an institution communicates periods expressed in days, it shall at the same time indicate whether the scheme it administers is based on five days, six days or seven days.

TITLE II

DETERMINATION OF THE LEGISLATION APPLICABLE

Article 14

Details relating to Articles 12 and 13 of the basic Regulation

3.518 1. For the purposes of the application of Article 12(1) of the basic Regulation, a "person who pursues an activity as an employed person in a Member State on behalf of an employer which normally carries out its activities there and who is posted by that employer to another Member State" shall include a person who is recruited with a view to being posted to another Member State, provided that, immediately before the start of his employment, the person concerned is already subject to the legislation of the Member State in which his employer is established.

2. For the purposes of the application of Article 12(1) of the basic Regulation, the words "which normally carries out its activities there" shall refer to an employer that ordinarily performs substantial activities, other than purely internal management activities, in the territory of the Member State in which it is established, taking account of all criteria characterising the activities carried out by the undertaking in question. The relevant criteria must be suited to the specific characteristics of each employer and the real nature of the activities carried out.

3. For the purposes of the application of Article 12(2) of the basic Regulation, the words "who normally pursues an activity as a self-employed person" shall refer to a person who habitually carries out substantial activities in the territory of the Member State in which he is established. In particular, that person must have already pursued his activity for some time before the date when he wishes to take advantage of the provisions of that Article and, during any period of temporary activity in another Member State, must continue to fulfil, in the Member State where he is established, the requirements for the pursuit of his activity in order to be able to pursue it on his return.

4. For the purposes of the application of Article 12(2) of the basic Regulation, the criterion for determining whether the activity that a self-employed person goes to pursue in another Member State is "similar" to the

self-employed activity normally pursued shall be that of the actual nature of the activity, rather than of the designation of employed or self-employed activity that may be given to this activity by the other Member State.

[[1] 5. For the purposes of the application of Article 13(1) of the basic Regulation, a person who "normally pursues an activity as an employed person in two or more Member States" shall refer to a person who simultaneously, or in alternation, for the same undertaking or employer or for various undertakings or employers, exercises one or more separate activities in two or more Member States.

5a. For the purposes of the application of Title II of the basic Regulation, "registered office or place of business" shall refer to the registered office or place of business where the essential decisions of the undertaking are adopted and where the functions of its central administration are carried out.

For the purposes of Article 13(1) of the basic Regulation, an employed flight crew or cabin crew member normally pursuing air passenger or freight services in two or more Member States shall be subject to the legislation of the Member State where the home base, as defined in Annex III to Council Regulation (EEC) No 3922/91 of 16 December 1991 on the harmonization of technical requirements and administrative procedures in the field of civil aviation [[1991] OJ L373/4], is located.

5b. Marginal activities shall be disregarded for the purposes of determining the applicable legislation under Article 13 of the basic Regulation. Article 16 of the implementing Regulation shall apply to all cases under this Article.]

6. For the purposes of the application of Article 13(2) of the basic Regulation, a person who "normally pursues an activity as a self-employed person in two or more Member States" shall refer, in particular, to a person who simultaneously or in alternation pursues one or more separate self-employed activities, irrespective of the nature of those activities, in two or more Member States.

7. For the purpose of distinguishing the activities under paragraphs 5 and 6 from the situations described in Article 12(1)and (2) of the basic Regulation, the duration of the activity in one or more other Member States (whether it is permanent or of an ad hoc or temporary nature) shall be decisive. For these purposes, an overall assessment shall be made of all the relevant facts including, in particular, in the case of an employed person, the place of work as defined in the employment contract.

8. For the purposes of the application of Article 13(1) and (2)of the basic Regulation, a "substantial part of employed or self-employed activity" pursued in a Member State shall mean a quantitatively substantial part of all the activities of the employed or self-employed person pursued there, without this necessarily being the major part of those activities.

To determine whether a substantial part of the activities is pursued in a Member State, the following indicative criteria shall be taken into account:

(a) in the case of an employed activity, the working time and/or the remuneration; and
(b) in the case of a self-employed activity, the turnover, working time, number of services rendered and/or income.

In the framework of an overall assessment, a share of less than 25 % in respect of the criteria mentioned above shall be an indicator that a substantial part of the activities is not being pursued in the relevant Member State.

9. For the purposes of the application of Article 13(2)(b) of the basic Regulation, the "centre of interest" of the activities of a self-employed person shall be determined by taking account of all the aspects of that person's occupational activities, notably the place where the person's fixed and permanent place of business is located, the habitual nature or the duration of the activities pursued, the number of services rendered, and the intention of the person concerned as revealed by all the circumstances.

10. For the determination of the applicable legislation under paragraphs 8 and 9, the institutions concerned shall take into account the situation projected for the following 12 calendar months.

11. If a person pursues his activity as an employed person in two or more Member States on behalf of an employer established outside the territory of the Union, and if this person resides in a Member State without pursuing substantial activity there, he shall be subject to the legislation of the Member State of residence.

AMENDMENT

1. Regulation 465/2012 [2012] OJ L149/4 art.2(2) (June 28, 2012).

Article 15

Procedures for the application of Article 11(3)(b) and (d), Article 11(4) and Article 12 of the basic Regulation (on the provision of information to the institutions concerned)

3.519 1. Unless otherwise provided for by Article 16 of the implementing Regulation, where a person pursues his activity in a Member State other than the Member State competent under Title II of the basic Regulation, the employer or, in the case of a person who does not pursue an activity as an employed person, the person concerned shall inform the competent institution of the Member State whose legislation is applicable thereof, whenever possible in advance. [That institution shall issue the attestation referred to in Article 19(2) of the implementing Regulation to the person concerned and shall without delay make information concerning the legislation applicable to that person, pursuant to Article 11(3)(b) or Article 12 of the basic Regulation, available to the institution designated by the competent authority of the Member State in which the activity is pursued.]

2. Paragraph 1 shall apply *mutatis mutandis* to persons covered by Article 11(3)(d) of the basic Regulation.

3. An employer within the meaning of Article 11(4) of the basic Regulation who has an employee on board a vessel flying the flag of another Member State shall inform the competent institution of the Member State whose legislation is applicable thereof whenever possible in advance. That institution shall, without delay, make information concerning the legislation applicable to the person concerned, pursuant to Article 11(4) of the basic Regulation, available to the institution designated by the competent authority of the Member State whose flag, the vessel on which the employee is to perform the activity, is flying.

AMENDMENT

1. Regulation 465/2012 [2012] OJ L149/4 art.2(3) (June 28, 2012).

Article 16

Article 16

Procedure for the application of Article 13 of the basic Regulation

1. A person who pursues activities in two or more Member States shall inform the institution designated by the competent authority of the Member State of residence thereof. 3.520

2. The designated institution of the place of residence shall without delay determine the legislation applicable to the person concerned, having regard to Article 13 of the basic Regulation and Article 14 of the implementing Regulation. That initial determination shall be provisional. The institution shall inform the designated institutions of each Member State in which an activity is pursued of its provisional determination.

3. The provisional determination of the applicable legislation, as provided for in paragraph 2, shall become definitive within two months of the institutions designated by the competent authorities of the Member States concerned being informed of it, in accordance with paragraph 2, unless the legislation has already been definitively determined on the basis of paragraph 4, or at least one of the institutions concerned informs the institution designated by the competent authority of the Member State of residence by the end of this two-month period that it cannot yet accept the determination or that it takes a different view on this.

4. Where uncertainty about the determination of the applicable legislation requires contacts between the institutions or authorities of two or more Member States, at the request of one or more of the institutions designated by the competent authorities of the Member States concerned or of the competent authorities themselves, the legislation applicable to the person concerned shall be determined by common agreement, having regard to Article 13 of the basic Regulation and the relevant provisions of Article 14 of the implementing Regulation.

Where there is a difference of views between the institutions or competent authorities concerned, those bodies shall seek agreement in accordance with the conditions set out above and Article 6 of the implementing Regulation shall apply.

5. The competent institution of the Member State whose legislation is determined to be applicable either provisionally or definitively shall without delay inform the person concerned.

6. If the person concerned fails to provide the information referred to in paragraph 1, this Article shall be applied at the initiative of the institution designated by the competent authority of the Member State of residence as soon as it is appraised of that person's situation, possibly via another institution concerned.

Article 17

Procedure for the application of Article 15 of the basic Regulation

Contract staff of the European Communities shall exercise the right of option provided for in Article 15 of the basic Regulation when the employment contract is concluded. The authority empowered to conclude the contract shall inform the designated institution of the Member State for 3.521

whose legislation the contract staff member of the European Communities has opted.

Article 18

Procedure for the application of Article 16 of the basic Regulation

3.522 A request by the employer or the person concerned for exceptions to Articles 11 to 15 of the basic Regulation shall be submitted, whenever possible in advance, to the competent authority or the body designated by the authority of the Member State, whose legislation the employee or person concerned requests be applied.

Article 19

Provision of information to persons concerned and employers

3.523 1. The competent institution of the Member State whose legislation becomes applicable pursuant to Title II of the basic Regulation shall inform the person concerned and, where appropriate, his employer(s) of the obligations laid down in that legislation. It shall provide them with the necessary assistance to complete the formalities required by that legislation.

2. At the request of the person concerned or of the employer, the competent institution of the Member State whose legislation is applicable pursuant to Title II of the basic Regulation shall provide an attestation that such legislation is applicable and shall indicate, where appropriate, until what date and under what conditions.

Article 20

Cooperation between institutions

3.524 1. The relevant institutions shall communicate to the competent institution of the Member State whose legislation is applicable to a person pursuant to Title II of the basic Regulation the necessary information required to establish the date on which that legislation becomes applicable and the contributions which that person and his employer(s) are liable to pay under that legislation.

2. The competent institution of the Member State whose legislation becomes applicable to a person pursuant to Title II of the basic Regulation shall make the information indicating the date on which the application of that legislation takes effect available to the institution designated by the competent authority of the Member State to whose legislation that person was last subject.

Article 21

Article 21

Obligations of the employer

1. An employer who has his registered office or place of business outside the competent Member State shall fulfil all the obligations laid down by the legislation applicable to his employees, notably the obligation to pay the contributions provided for by that legislation, as if he had his registered office or place of business in the competent Member State. 3.525

2. An employer who does not have a place of business in the Member State whose legislation is applicable and the employee may agree that the latter may fulfil the employer's obligations on its behalf as regards the payment of contributions without prejudice to the employer's underlying obligations. The employer shall send notice of such an arrangement to the competent institution of that Member State.

Title III

Special Provisions Concerning the Various Categories of Benefits

Chapter I

Sickness, maternity and equivalent paternity benefits

Article 22

General implementing provisions

1. The competent authorities or institutions shall ensure that any necessary information is made available to insured persons regarding the procedures and conditions for the granting of benefits in kind where such benefits are received in the territory of a Member State other than that of the competent institution. 3.526

2. Notwithstanding Article 5(a) of the basic Regulation, a Member State may become responsible for the cost of benefits in accordance with Article 22 of the basic Regulation only if, either the insured person has made a claim for a pension under the legislation of that Member State, or in accordance with Articles 23 to 30 of the basic Regulation, he receives a pension under the legislation of that Member State.

Article 23

Regime applicable in the event of the existence of more than one regime in the Member State of residence or stay

If the legislation of the Member State of residence or stay comprises more than one scheme of sickness, maternity and paternity insurance for 3.527

more than one category of insured persons, the provisions applicable under Articles 17, 19(1), 20, 22, 24 and 26 of the basic Regulation shall be those of the legislation on the general scheme for employed persons.

Article 24

Residence in a Member State other than the competent Member State

3.528 1. For the purposes of the application of Article 17 of the basic Regulation, the insured person and/or members of his family shall be obliged to register with the institution of the place of residence. Their right to benefits in kind in the Member State of residence shall be certified by a document issued by the competent institution upon request of the insured person or upon request of the institution of the place of residence.

2. The document referred to in paragraph 1 shall remain valid until the competent institution informs the institution of the place of residence of its cancellation.

The institution of the place of residence shall inform the competent institution of any registration under paragraph 1 and of any change or cancellation of that registration.

3. This Article shall apply *mutatis mutandis* to the persons referred to in Articles 22, 24, 25 and 26 of the basic Regulation.

Article 25

Stay in a Member State other than the competent Member State

A. Procedure and scope of right

3.529 1. For the purposes of the application of Article 19 of the basic Regulation, the insured person shall present to the health care provider in the Member State of stay a document issued by the competent institution indicating his entitlement to benefits in kind. If the insured person does not have such a document, the institution of the place of stay, upon request or if otherwise necessary, shall contact the competent institution in order to obtain one.

2. That document shall indicate that the insured person is entitled to benefits in kind under the conditions laid down in Article 19 of the basic Regulation on the same terms as those applicable to persons insured under the legislation of the Member State of stay.

3. The benefits in kind referred to in Article 19(1) of the basic Regulation shall refer to the benefits in kind which are provided in the Member State of stay, in accordance with its legislation, and which become necessary on medical grounds with a view to preventing an insured person from being forced to return, before the end of the planned duration of stay, to the competent Member State to obtain the necessary treatment.

B. Procedure and arrangements for meeting the costs and providing reimbursement of benefits in kind

3.530 4. If the insured person has actually borne the costs of all or part of the benefits in kind provided within the framework of Article 19 of the basic

Regulation and if the legislation applied by the institution of the place of stay enables reimbursement of those costs to an insured person, he may send an application for reimbursement to the institution of the place of stay. In that case, that institution shall reimburse directly to that person the amount of the costs corresponding to those benefits within the limits of and under the conditions of the reimbursement rates laid down in its legislation.

5. If the reimbursement of such costs has not been requested directly from the institution of the place of stay, the costs incurred shall be reimbursed to the person concerned by the competent institution in accordance with the reimbursement rates administered by the institution of the place of stay or the amounts which would have been subject to reimbursement to the institution of the place of stay, if Article 62 of the implementing Regulation had applied in the case concerned.

The institution of the place of stay shall provide the competent institution, upon request, with all necessary information about these rates or amounts.

6. By way of derogation from paragraph 5, the competent institution may undertake the reimbursement of the costs incurred within the limits of and under the conditions of the reimbursement rates laid down in its legislation, provided that the insured person has agreed to this provision being applied to him/her.

7. If the legislation of the Member State of stay does not provide for reimbursement pursuant to paragraphs 4 and 5 in the case concerned, the competent institution may reimburse the costs within the limits of and under the conditions of the reimbursement rates laid down in its legislation, without the agreement of the insured person.

8. The reimbursement to the insured person shall not, in any event, exceed the amount of costs actually incurred by him/her.

9. In the case of substantial expenditure, the competent institution may pay the insured person an appropriate advance as soon as that person submits the application for reimbursement to it.

C. Family Members

10. Paragraphs 1 to 9 shall apply *mutatis mutandis* to the members of the 3.531
family of the insured person.

Article 26

Scheduled treatment

A. Authorisation procedure

1. For the purposes of the application of Article 20(1) of the basic 3.532
Regulation, the insured person shall present a document issued by the competent institution to the institution of the place of stay. For the purposes of this Article, the competent institution shall mean the institution which bears the cost of the scheduled treatment; in the cases referred to in Article 20(4) and 27(5) of the basic Regulation, in which the benefits in kind provided in the Member State of residence are reimbursed on the basis

of fixed amounts, the competent institution shall mean the institution of the place of residence.

2. If an insured person does not reside in the competent Member State, he shall request authorisation from the institution of the place of residence, which shall forward it to the competent institution without delay.

In that event, the institution of the place of residence shall certify in a statement whether the conditions set out in the second sentence of Article 20(2) of the basic Regulation are met in the Member State of residence.

The competent institution may refuse to grant the requested authorisation only if, in accordance with the assessment of the institution of the place of residence, the conditions set out in the second sentence of Article 20(2) of the basic Regulation are not met in the Member State of residence of the insured person, or if the same treatment can be provided in the competent Member State itself, within a time-limit which is medically justifiable, taking into account the current state of health and the probable course of illness of the person concerned.

The competent institution shall inform the institution of the place of residence of its decision.

In the absence of a reply within the deadlines set by its national legislation, the authorisation shall be considered to have been granted by the competent institution.

3. If an insured person who does not reside in the competent Member State is in need of urgent vitally necessary treatment, and the authorisation cannot be refused in accordance with the second sentence of Article 20(2) of the basic Regulation, the authorisation shall be granted by the institution of the place of residence on behalf of the competent institution, which shall be immediately informed by the institution of the place of residence.

The competent institution shall accept the findings and the treatment options of the doctors approved by the institution of the place of residence that issues the authorisation, concerning the need for urgent vitally necessary treatment.

4. At any time during the procedure granting the authorisation, the competent institution shall retain the right to have the insured person examined by a doctor of its own choice in the Member State of stay or residence.

5. The institution of the place of stay shall, without prejudice to any decision regarding authorisation, inform the competent institution if it appears medically appropriate to supplement the treatment covered by the existing authorisation.

B. Meeting the cost of benefits in kind incurred by the insured person

3.533 6. Without prejudice to paragraph 7, Article 25(4) and (5) of the implementing Regulation shall apply *mutatis mutandis*.

7. If the insured person has actually borne all or part of the costs for the authorised medical treatment him or herself and the costs which the competent institution is obliged to reimburse to the institution of the place of stay or to the insured person according to paragraph 6 (actual cost) are lower than the costs which it would have had to assume for the same treatment in the competent Member State (notional cost), the competent institution shall reimburse, upon request, the cost of treatment incurred by the insured person up to the amount by which the notional cost exceeds the actual cost. The reimbursed sum may not, however, exceed the costs actu-

ally incurred by the insured person and may take account of the amount which the insured person would have had to pay if the treatment had been delivered in the competent Member State.

C. Meeting the costs of travel and stay as part of scheduled treatment

8. Where the national legislation of the competent institution provides for the reimbursement of the costs of travel and stay which are inseparable from the treatment of the insured person, such costs for the person concerned and, if necessary, for a person who must accompany him/her, shall be assumed by this institution when an authorisation is granted in the case of treatment in another Member State. 3.534

D. Family members

9. Paragraphs 1 to 8 shall apply *mutatis mutandis* to the members of the family of the insured persons. 3.535

Article 27

Cash benefits relating to incapacity for work in the event of stay or residence in a Member State other than the competent Member State

A. Procedure to be followed by the insured person

1. If the legislation of the competent Member State requires that the insured person presents a certificate in order to be entitled to cash benefits relating to incapacity for work pursuant to Article 21(1) of the basic Regulation, the insured person shall ask the doctor of the Member State of residence who established his state of health to certify his incapacity for work and its probable duration. 3.536

2. The insured person shall send the certificate to the competent institution within the time limit laid down by the legislation of the competent Member State.

3. Where the doctors providing treatment in the Member State of residence do not issue certificates of incapacity for work, and where such certificates are required under the legislation of the competent Member State, the person concerned shall apply directly to the institution of the place of residence. That institution shall immediately arrange for a medical assessment of the person's incapacity for work and for the certificate referred to in paragraph 1 to be drawn up. The certificate shall be forwarded to the competent institution forthwith.

4. The forwarding of the document referred to in paragraphs 1,2 and 3 shall not exempt the insured person from fulfilling the obligations provided for by the applicable legislation, in particular with regard to his employer. Where appropriate, the employer and/or the competent institution may call upon the employee to participate in activities designed to promote and assist his return to employment.

B. Procedure to be followed by the institution of the Member State of residence

5. At the request of the competent institution, the institution of the place of residence shall carry out any necessary administrative checks or medical 3.537

examinations of the person concerned in accordance with the legislation applied by this latter institution.

The report of the examining doctor concerning, in particular, the probable duration of the incapacity for work, shall be forwarded without delay by the institution of the place of residence to the competent institution.

C. Procedure to be followed by the competent institution

3.538 6. The competent institution shall reserve the right to have the insured person examined by a doctor of its choice.

7. Without prejudice to the second sentence of Article 21(1) of the basic Regulation, the competent institution shall pay the cash benefits directly to the person concerned and shall, where necessary, inform the institution of the place of residence thereof.

8. For the purposes of the application of Article 21(1) of the basic Regulation, the particulars of the certificate of incapacity for work of an insured person drawn up in another Member State on the basis of the medical findings of the examining doctor or institution shall have the same legal value as a certificate drawn up in the competent Member State.

9. If the competent institution refuses the cash benefits, it shall notify its decision to the insured person and at the same time to the institution of the place of residence.

D. Procedure in the event of a stay in a Member State other than the competent Member State

3.539 10. Paragraphs 1 to 9 shall apply *mutatis mutandis* when the insured person stays in a Member State other than the competent Member State.

Article 28

Long-term care benefits in cash in the event of stay or residence in a Member State other than the competent Member State

A. Procedure to be followed by the insured person

3.540 1. In order to be entitled to long-term care benefits in cash pursuant to Article 21(1) of the basic Regulation, the insured person shall apply to the competent institution. The competent institution shall, where necessary, inform the institution of the place of residence thereof.

B. Procedure to be followed by the institution of the place of residence

3.541 2. At the request of the competent institution, the institution of the place of residence shall examine the condition of the insured person with respect to his need for long-term care. The competent institution shall give the institution of the place of residence all the information necessary for such an examination.

C. Procedure to be followed by the competent institution

3.542 3. In order to determine the degree of need for long-term care, the competent institution shall have the right to have the insured person examined by a doctor or any other expert of its choice.

Article 28

4. Article 27(7) of the implementing Regulation shall apply *mutatis mutandis*.

D. Procedure in the event of a stay in a Member State other than the competent Member State

5. Paragraphs 1 to 4 shall apply *mutatis mutandis* when the insured person stays in a Member State other than the competent Member State. 3.543

E. Family members

6. Paragraphs 1 to 5 shall apply *mutatis mutandis* to the members of the family of the insured person. 3.544

Article 29

Application of Article 28 of the basic Regulation

If the Member State where the former frontier worker last pursued his activity is no longer the competent Member State, and the former frontier worker or a member of his family travels therewith the purpose of receiving benefits in kind pursuant to Article 28 of the basic Regulation, he shall submit to the institution of the place of stay a document issued by the competent institution. 3.545

Article 30

Contributions by pensioners

If a person receives a pension from more than one Member State, the amount of contributions deducted from all the pensions paid shall under no circumstances be greater than the amount deducted in respect of a person who receives the same amount of pension from the competent Member State. 3.546

Article 31

Application of Article 34 of the basic Regulation

A. Procedure to be followed by the competent institution

1. The competent institution shall inform the person concerned of the provision contained in Article 34 of the basic Regulation regarding the prevention of overlapping of benefits. The application of such rules shall ensure that the person not residing in the competent Member State is entitled to benefits of at least the same total amount or value as those to which he would be entitled if he resided in that Member State. 3.547

2. The competent institution shall also inform the institution of the place of residence or stay about the payment of long-term care cash benefits where the legislation applied by the latter institution provides for the long-term care benefits in kind included in the list referred to in Article 34(2) of the basic Regulation.

B. Procedure to be followed by the institution of the place of residence or stay

3.548 3. Having received the information provided for in paragraph 2, the institution of the place of residence or stay shall without delay inform the competent institution of any long-term care benefit in kind intended for the same purpose granted under its legislation to the person concerned and of the rate of reimbursement applicable thereto.

4. The Administrative Commission shall lay down implementing measures for this Article where necessary.

Article 32

Special implementing measures

3.549 1. When a person or a group of persons are exempted upon request from compulsory sickness insurance and such persons are thus not covered by a sickness insurance scheme to which the basic Regulation applies, the institution of another Member State shall not, solely because of this exemption, become responsible for bearing the costs of benefits in kind or in cash provided to such persons or to a member of their family under Title III, Chapter I, of the basic Regulation.

2. For the Member States referred to in Annex 2, the provisions of Title III, Chapter I, of the basic Regulation relating to benefits in kind shall apply to persons entitled to benefits in kind solely on the basis of a special scheme for civil servants only to the extent specified therein.

The institution of another Member State shall not, on those grounds alone, become responsible for bearing the costs of benefits in kind or in cash provided to those persons or to members of their family.

3. When the persons referred to in paragraphs 1 and 2 and the members of their families reside in a Member State where the right to receive benefits in kind is not subject to conditions of insurance, or of activity as an employed or self-employed person, they shall be liable to pay the full costs of benefits in kind provided in their country of residence.

CHAPTER II

BENEFITS IN RESPECT OF ACCIDENTS AT WORK AND OCCUPATIONAL DISEASES

Article 33

Right to benefits in kind and in cash in the event of residence or stay in a Member State other than the competent Member State

3.550 1. For the purposes of the application of Article 36 of the basic Regulation, the procedures laid down in Articles 24 to 27 of the implementing Regulation shall apply *mutatis mutandis*.

2. When providing special benefits in kind in connection with accidents at work and occupational diseases under the national legislation of the Member State of stay or residence, the institution of that Member State shall without delay inform the competent institution.

Article 34

Procedure in the event of an accident at work or occupational disease which occurs in a Member State other than the competent Member State

1. If an accident at work occurs or an occupational disease is diagnosed for the first time in a Member State other than the competent Member State, the declaration or notification of the accident at work or the occupational disease, where the declaration or notification exists under national legislation, shall be carried out in accordance with the legislation of the competent Member State, without prejudice, where appropriate, to any other applicable legal provisions in force in the Member State in which the accident at work occurred or in which the first medical diagnosis of the occupational disease was made, which remain applicable in such cases. The declaration or notification shall be addressed to the competent institution. 3.551

2. The institution of the Member State in the territory of which the accident at work occurred or in which the occupational disease was first diagnosed, shall notify the competent institution of medical certificates drawn up in the territory of that Member State.

3. Where, as a result of an accident while travelling to or from work which occurs in the territory of a Member State other than the competent Member State, an inquiry is necessary in the territory of the first Member State in order to determine any entitlement to relevant benefits, a person may be appointed for that purpose by the competent institution, which shall inform the authorities of that Member State. The institutions shall cooperate with each other in order to assess all relevant information and to consult the reports and any other documents relating to the accident.

4. Following treatment, a detailed report accompanied by medical certificates relating to the permanent consequences of the accident or disease, in particular the injured person's present state and the recovery or stabilisation of injuries, shall be sent upon request of the competent institution. The relevant fees shall be paid by the institution of the place of residence or of stay, where appropriate, at the rate applied by that institution to the charge of the competent institution.

5. At the request of the institution of the place of residence or stay, where appropriate, the competent institution shall notify it of the decision setting the date for the recovery or stabilisation of injuries and, where appropriate, the decision concerning the granting of a pension.

Article 35

Disputes concerning the occupational nature of the accident or disease

1. Where the competent institution disputes the application of the legislation relating to accidents at work or occupational diseases under Article 36(2) of the basic Regulation, it shall without delay inform the institution of the place of residence or stay which provided the benefits in kind, which will then be considered as sickness insurance benefits. 3.552

2. When a final decision has been taken on that subject, the competent

institution shall without delay inform the institution of the place of residence or stay which provided the benefits in kind.

Where an accident at work or occupational disease is not established, benefits in kind shall continue to be provided as sickness benefits if the person concerned is entitled to them.

Where an accident at work or occupational disease is established, sickness benefits in kind provided to the person concerned shall be considered as accident at work or occupational disease benefits from the date on which the accident at work occurred or the occupational disease was first medically diagnosed.

3. The second subparagraph of Article 6(5) of the implementing Regulation shall apply *mutatis mutandis*.

Article 36

Procedure in the event of exposure to the risk of an occupational disease in more than one Member State

3.553 1. In the case referred to in Article 38 of the basic Regulation, the declaration or notification of the occupational disease shall be sent to the competent institution for occupational diseases of the last Member State under the legislation of which the person concerned pursued an activity likely to cause that disease.

When the institution to which the declaration or notification was sent establishes that an activity likely to cause the occupational disease in question was last pursued under the legislation of another Member State, it shall send the declaration or notification and all accompanying certificates to the equivalent institution in that Member State.

2. Where the institution of the last Member State under the legislation of which the person concerned pursued an activity likely to cause the occupational disease in question establishes that the person concerned or his survivors do not meet the requirements of that legislation, inter alia, because the person concerned had never pursued in that Member State an activity which caused the occupational disease or because that Member State does not recognise the occupational nature of the disease, that institution shall forward without delay the declaration or notification and all accompanying certificates, including the findings and reports of medical examinations performed by the first institution to the institution of the previous Member State under the legislation of which the person concerned pursued an activity likely to cause the occupational disease in question.

3. Where appropriate, the institutions shall reiterate the procedure set out in paragraph 2 going back as far as the equivalent institution in the Member State under whose legislation the person concerned first pursued an activity likely to cause the occupational disease in question.

Article 37

Exchange of information between institutions and advance payments in the event of an appeal against rejection

3.554 1. In the event of an appeal against a decision to refuse benefits taken by the institution of one of the Member States under the legislation of which the person concerned pursued an activity likely to cause the occupational disease in question, that institution shall inform the institution to which the declaration or notification was sent, in accordance with the procedure provided for in Article 36(2) of the implementing Regulation, and shall subsequently inform it when a final decision is reached.

2. Where a person is entitled to benefits under the legislation applied by the institution to which the declaration or notification was sent, that institution shall make the advance payments, the amount of which shall be determined, where appropriate, after consulting the institution which made the decision against which the appeal was lodged, and in such a way that overpayments are avoided. The latter institution shall reimburse the advance payments made if, as a result of the appeal, it is obliged to provide those benefits. That amount will then be deducted from the benefits due to the person concerned, in accordance with the procedure provided for in Articles 72 and 73 of the implementing Regulation.

3. The second subparagraph of Article 6(5) of the implementing Regulation shall apply *mutatis mutandis*.

Article 38

Aggravation of an occupational disease

In the cases covered by Article 39 of the basic Regulation, the claimant must provide the institution in the Member State from which he is claiming entitlement to benefits with details concerning benefits previously granted for the occupational disease in question. That institution may contact any other previously competent institution in order to obtain the information it considers necessary. **3.555**

Article 39

Assessment of the degree of incapacity in the event of occupational accidents or diseases which occurred previously or subsequently

Where a previous or subsequent incapacity for work was caused by an accident which occurred when the person concerned was subject to the legislation of a Member State which makes no distinction according to the origin of the incapacity to work, the competent institution or the body designated by the competent authority of the Member State in question shall: **3.556**

(a) upon request by the competent institution of another Member State, provide information concerning the degree of the previous or subsequent incapacity for work, and where possible, information making it possible to determine whether the incapacity is the result of an accident at work within the meaning of the legislation applied by the institution in the other Member State;

(b) take into account the degree of incapacity caused by these previous or subsequent cases when determining the right to benefits and the amount, in accordance with the applicable legislation.

Article 40

Submission and investigation of claims for pensions or supplementary allowances

3.557 In order to receive a pension or supplementary allowance under the legislation of a Member State, the person concerned or his survivors residing in the territory of another Member State shall submit, where appropriate, a claim either to the competent institution or to the institution of the place of residence, which shall send it to the competent institution.

The claim shall contain the information required under the legislation applied by the competent institution.

Article 41

Special implementing measures

3.558 1. In relation to the Member States referred to in Annex 2, the provisions of Title III, Chapter 2 of the basic Regulation relating to benefits in kind shall apply to persons entitled to benefits in kind solely on the basis of a special scheme for civil servants, and only to the extent specified therein.

2. Article 32(2) second subparagraph and Article 32(3) of the implementing Regulation shall apply *mutatis mutandis*.

CHAPTER III

DEATH GRANTS

Article 42

Claim for death grants

3.559 For the purposes of applying Articles 42 and 43 of the basic Regulation, the claim for death grants shall be sent either to the competent institution or to the institution of the claimant's place of residence, which shall send it to the competent institution.

The claim shall contain the information required under the legislation applied by the competent institution.

CHAPTER IV

INVALIDITY BENEFITS AND OLD-AGE AND SURVIVORS' PENSIONS

Article 43

Additional provisions for the calculation of benefit

1. For the purposes of calculating the theoretical amount and the actual amount of the benefit in accordance with Article 52(1)(b) of the basic Regulation, the rules provided for in Article 12(3), (4), (5) and (6) of the implementing Regulation shall apply. **3.560**

2. Where periods of voluntary or optional continued insurance have not been taken into account under Article 12(3) of the implementing Regulation, the institution of the Member State under whose legislation those periods were completed shall calculate the amount corresponding to those periods under the legislation it applies. The actual amount of the benefit, calculated in accordance with Article 52(1)(b) of the basic Regulation, shall be increased by the amount corresponding to periods of voluntary or optional continued insurance.

3. The institution of each Member State shall calculate, under the legislation it applies, the amount due corresponding to periods of voluntary or optional continued insurance which, under Article 53(3)(c) of the basic Regulation, shall not be subject to another Member State's rules relating to withdrawal, reduction or suspension.

Where the legislation applied by the competent institution does not allow it to determine this amount directly, on the grounds that that legislation allocates different values to insurance periods, a notional amount may be established. The Administrative Commission shall lay down the detailed arrangements for the determination of that notional amount.

Article 44

Taking into account of child raising-periods

1. For the purposes of this Article, 'child-raising period' refers to any period which is credited under the pension legislation of a Member State or which provides a supplement to a pension explicitly for the reason that a person has raised a child, irrespective of the method used to calculate those periods and whether they accrue during the time of child-raising or are acknowledged retroactively. **3.561**

2. Where, under the legislation of the Member State which is competent under Title II of the basic Regulation, no child-raising period is taken into account, the institution of the Member State whose legislation, according to Title II of the basic Regulation, was applicable to the person concerned on the grounds that he or she was pursuing an activity as an employed or self-employed person at the date when, under that legislation, the child-raising

period started to be taken into account for the child concerned, shall remain responsible for taking into account that period as a child-raising period under its own legislation, as if such child-raising took place in its own territory.

3. Paragraph 2 shall not apply if the person concerned is, or becomes, subject to the legislation of another Member State due to the pursuit of an employed or self-employed activity.

GENERAL NOTE

3.562 The factual situation which arose in *Reichel-Albert* (C-522/10) Judgment of July 19, 2012, preceded the entry into force of Reg.883/2004 which could not therefore apply, but Reg.1408/71 contained no specific rules on child-raising periods. The Court therefore had to fall back on general principles, but was clearly aware of the specific rules to be found in art.44.

Doris Reichel-Albert, a German national, had worked in Germany for a number of years, followed by a period of unemployment. She and her family moved to Belgium from 1980 to 1986 as a result of her husband's work. Two children were born in Belgium, and the mother undertook no work or self-employment in Belgium. She had only ever paid contributions in Germany. The family appears subsequently to have returned to Germany. The German authorities rejected her claims to have child-raising periods in Belgium taken into account and credited for the purposes of later entitlement to an old-age pension. The Court concluded that German law applied to the claimant and that Belgium had not become the competent state in relation to her claim for the periods concerned. The permissibility of the German rules fell to be assessed in the light of art.21 TFEU. The Court concluded:

> "42. National legislation which places some of its nationals at a disadvantage simply because they have exercised their freedom to move and to reside in another Member State thereby gives rise to inequality of treatment, contrary to the principles which underpin the status of citizenship of the Union, that is, the guarantee of the same treatment in law in the exercise of the citizen's freedom to move . . . ".

Any provision on its face incompatible with these requirements needed to be objectively justified and proportionate in its effect. The German authorities had not even argued this, and the German provisions were found to be incompatible with the rights flowing from art.21 TFEU.

Article 45

Claim for benefits

A. Submission of the claim for benefits under type A legislation under Article 44(2) of the basic Regulation

3.563 1. In order to receive benefits under type A legislation under Article 44(2) of the basic Regulation, the claimant shall submit a claim to the institution of the Member State, whose legislation was applicable at the time when the incapacity for work occurred followed by invalidity or the aggravation of such invalidity, or to the institution of the place of residence, which shall forward the claim to the first institution.

2. If sickness benefits in cash have been awarded, the expiry date of the period for awarding these benefits shall, where appropriate, be considered as the date of submission of the pension claim.

Article 45

3. In the case referred to in Article 47(1) of the basic Regulation, the institution with which the person concerned was last insured shall inform the institution which initially paid the benefits of the amount and the date of commencement of the benefits under the applicable legislation. From that date benefits due before aggravation of the invalidity shall be withdrawn or reduced to the supplement referred to in Article 47(2) of the basic Regulation.

B. Submission of other claims for benefits

4. In situations other than those referred to in paragraph 1, the claimant shall submit a claim to the institution of his place of residence or to the institution of the last Member State whose legislation was applicable. If the person concerned was not, at anytime, subject to the legislation applied by the institution of the place of residence, that institution shall forward the claim to the institution of the last Member State whose legislation was applicable. 3.564

5. The date of submission of the claim shall apply in all the institutions concerned.6.

By way of derogation from paragraph 5, if the claimant does not, despite having been asked to do so, notify the fact that he has been employed or has resided in other Member States, the date on which the claimant completes his initial claim or submits a new claim for his missing periods of employment or/and residence in a Member State shall be considered as the date of submission of the claim to the institution applying the legislation in question, subject to more favourable provisions of that legislation.

Article 46

Certificates and information to be submitted with the claim by the claimant

1. The claim shall be submitted by the claimant in accordance with the provisions of the legislation applied by the institution referred to in Article 45(1) or (4) of the implementing Regulation and be accompanied by the supporting documents required by that legislation. In particular, the claimant shall supply all available relevant information and supporting documents relating to periods of insurance (institutions, identification numbers), employment (employers) or self-employment (nature and place of activity) and residence (addresses) which may have been completed under other legislation, as well as the length of those periods. 3.565

2. Where, in accordance with Article 50(1) of the basic Regulation, the claimant requests deferment of the award of old-age benefits under the legislation of one or more Member States, he shall state that in his claim and specify under which legislation the deferment is requested. In order to enable the claimant to exercise that right, the institutions concerned shall, upon the request of the claimant, notify him of all the information available to them so that he can assess the consequences of concurrent or successive awards of benefits which he might claim.

3. Should the claimant withdraw a claim for benefits provided for under the legislation of a particular Member State, that withdrawal shall not be

considered as a concurrent withdrawal of claims for benefits under the legislation of other Member States.

Article 47

Investigation of claims by the institutions concerned

A. Contact institution

3.566 1. The institution to which the claim for benefits is submitted or forwarded in accordance with Article 45(1) or (4) of the implementing Regulation shall be referred to hereinafter as the "contact institution". The institution of the place of residence shall not be referred to as the contact institution if the person concerned has not, at any time, been subject to the legislation which that institution applies.

In addition to investigating the claim for benefits under the legislation which it applies, this institution shall, in its capacity as contact institution, promote the exchange of data, the communication of decisions and the operations necessary for the investigation of the claim by the institutions concerned, and supply the claimant, upon request, with any information relevant to the Community aspects of the investigation and keep him/her informed of its progress.

B. Investigation of claims for benefits under type A legislation under Article 44 of the basic Regulation

3.567 2. In the case referred to in Article 44(3) of the basic Regulation, the contact institution shall send all the documents relating to the person concerned to the institution with which he was previously insured, which shall in turn examine the case.

3. Articles 48 to 52 of the implementing Regulation shall not be applicable to the investigation of claims referred to in Article 44 of the basic Regulation.

C. Investigation of other claims for benefits

3.568 4. In situations other than those referred to in paragraph 2, the contact institution shall, without delay, send claims for benefits and all the documents which it has available and, where appropriate, the relevant documents supplied by the claimant to all the institutions in question so that they can all start the investigation of the claim concurrently. The contact institution shall notify the other institutions of periods of insurance or residence subject to its legislation. It shall also indicate which documents shall be submitted at a later date and supplement the claim as soon as possible.

5. Each of the institutions in question shall notify the contact institution and the other institutions in question, as soon as possible, of the periods of insurance or residence subject to their legislation.

6. Each of the institutions in question shall calculate the amount of benefits in accordance with Article 52 of the basic Regulation and shall notify the contact institution and the other institutions concerned of its decision, of the amount of benefits due and of any information required for the purposes of Articles 53 to 55 of the basic Regulation.

Article 47

7. Should an institution establish, on the basis of the information referred to in paragraphs 4 and 5 of this Article, that Article 46(2) or Article 57(2) or (3) of the basic Regulation is applicable, it shall inform the contact institution and the other institutions concerned.

Article 48

Notification of decisions to the claimant

1. Each institution shall notify the claimant of the decision it has taken in accordance with the applicable legislation. Each decision shall specify the remedies and periods allowed for appeals. Once the contact institution has been notified of all decisions taken by each institution, it shall send the claimant and the other institutions concerned a summary of those decisions. A model summary shall be drawn up by the Administrative Commission. The summary shall be sent to the claimant in the language of the institution or, at the request of the claimant, in any language of his choice recognised as an official language of the Community institutions in accordance with Article 290 of the Treaty. 3.569

2. Where it appears to the claimant following receipt of the summary that his rights may have been adversely affected by the interaction of decisions taken by two or more institutions, the claimant shall have the right to a review of the decisions by the institutions concerned within the time limits laid down in the respective national legislation. The time limits shall commence on the date of receipt of the summary. The claimant shall be notified of the result of the review in writing.

Article 49

Determination of the degree of invalidity

1. Where Article 46(3) of the basic Regulation is applicable, the only institution authorised to take a decision concerning the claimant's degree of invalidity shall be the contact institution, if the legislation applied by that institution is included in Annex VII to the basic Regulation, or failing that, the institution whose legislation is included in that Annex and to whose legislation the claimant was last subject. It shall take that decision as soon as it can determine whether the conditions for eligibility laid down in the applicable legislation are met, taking into account, where appropriate, Articles 6 and 51 of the basic Regulation. It shall without delay notify the other institutions concerned of that decision. 3.570

Where the eligibility criteria, other than those relating to the degree of invalidity, laid down in the applicable legislation are not met, taking into account Articles 6 and 51 of the basic Regulation, the contact institution shall without delay inform the competent institution of the last Member State to whose legislation the claimant was subject. The latter institution shall be authorised to take the decision concerning the degree of invalidity of the claimant if the conditions for eligibility laid down in the applicable legislation are met. It shall without delay notify the other institutions concerned of that decision.

When determining eligibility, the matter may, if necessary have to be referred back, under the same conditions, to the competent institution in respect of invalidity of the Member State to whose legislation the claimant was first subject.

2. Where Article 46(3) of the basic Regulation is not applicable, each institution shall, in accordance with its legislation, have the possibility of having the claimant examined by a medical doctor or other expert of its choice to determine the degree of invalidity. However, the institution of a Member State shall take into consideration documents, medical reports and administrative information collected by the institution of any other Member State as if they had been drawn up in its own Member State.

Article 50

Provisional instalments and advance payment of benefit

3.571 1. Notwithstanding Article 7 of the implementing Regulation, any institution which establishes, while investigating a claim for benefits, that the claimant is entitled to an independent benefit under the applicable legislation, in accordance with Article 52(1)(a) of the basic Regulation, shall pay that benefit without delay. That payment shall be considered provisional if the amount might be affected by the result of the claim investigation procedure.

2. Whenever it is evident from the information available that the claimant is entitled to a payment from an institution under Article 52(1)(b) of the basic Regulation, that institution shall make an advance payment, the amount of which shall be as close as possible to the amount which will probably be paid under Article 52(1)(b) of the basic Regulation.

3. Each institution which is obliged to pay the provisional benefits or advance payment under paragraphs 1 or 2 shall inform the claimant without delay, specifically drawing his attention to the provisional nature of the measure and any rights of appeal in accordance with its legislation.

Article 51

New calculation of benefits

3.572 1. Where there is a new calculation of benefits in accordance with Articles 48(3) and (4), 50(4) and 59(1) of the basic Regulation, Article 50 of the implementing Regulation shall be applicable *mutatis mutandis*.

2. Where there is a new calculation, withdrawal or suspension of the benefit, the institution which took the decision shall inform the person concerned without delay and shall inform each of the institutions in respect of which the person concerned has an entitlement.

Article 52

Measures intended to accelerate the pension calculation process

1. In order to facilitate and accelerate the investigation of claims and the payment of benefits, the institutions to whose legislation a person has been subject shall: 3.573

(a) exchange with or make available to institutions of other Member States the elements for identifying persons who change from one applicable national legislation to another, and together ensure that those identification elements are retained and correspond, or, failing that, provide those persons with the means to access their identification elements directly;

(b) sufficiently in advance of the minimum age for commencing pension rights or before an age to be determined by national legislation, exchange with or make available to the person concerned and to institutions of other Member States information (periods completed or other important elements) on the pension entitlements of persons who have changed from one applicable legislation to another or, failing that, inform those persons of, or provide them with, the means of familiarising themselves with their prospective benefit entitlement.

2. For the purposes of applying paragraph 1, the Administrative Commission shall determine the elements of information to be exchanged or made available and shall establish the appropriate procedures and mechanisms, taking account of the characteristics, administrative and technical organisation, and the technological means at the disposal of national pension schemes. The Administrative Commission shall ensure the implementation of those pension schemes by organising a follow-up to the measures taken and their application.

3. For the purposes of applying paragraph 1, the institution in the first Member State where a person is allocated a Personal Identification Number (PIN) for the purposes of social security administration should be provided with the information referred to in this Article.

Article 53

Coordination measures in Member States

1. Without prejudice to Article 51 of the basic Regulation, where national legislation includes rules for determining the institution responsible or the scheme applicable or for designating periods of insurance to a specific scheme, those rules shall be applied, taking into account only periods of insurance completed under the legislation of the Member State concerned. 3.574

2. Where national legislation includes rules for the coordination of special schemes for civil servants and the general scheme for employed persons, those rules shall not be affected by the provisions of the basic Regulation and of the implementing Regulation.

Chapter V

Unemployment Benefits

Article 54

Aggregation of periods and calculation of benefits

3.575 1. Article 12(1) of the implementing Regulation shall apply *mutatis mutandis* to Article 61 of the basic Regulation. Without prejudice to the underlying obligations of the institutions involved, the person concerned may submit to the competent institution a document issued by the institution of the Member State to whose legislation he was subject in respect of his last activity as an employed or self-employed person specifying the periods completed under that legislation.

[1 2. For the purposes of applying Article 62(3) of the basic Regulation, the competent institution of the Member State to whose legislation the person concerned was subject in respect of his/her last activity as an employed or self- employed person shall, without delay, at the request of the institution of the place of residence, provide it with all the information necessary to calculate unemployment benefits which can be obtained in the Member State where it is situated, in particular the salary or professional income received.]

3. For the purposes of applying Article 62 of the basic Regulation and notwithstanding Article 63 thereof, the competent institution of a Member State whose legislation provides that the calculation of benefits varies with the number of members of the family shall also take into account the members of the family of the person concerned residing in another Member State as if they resided in the competent Member State. This provision shall not apply where, in the Member State of residence of members of the family, another person is entitled to unemployment benefits calculated on the basis of the number of members of the family.

Amendment

1. Regulation 465/2012 [2012] OJ L149/4 art.2(4) (June 28, 2012).

Article 55

Conditions and restrictions on the retention of the entitlement to benefits for unemployed persons going to another Member State

3.576 [1 1. In order to be covered by Article 64 or Article 65a of the basic Regulation, the unemployed person going to another Member State shall inform the competent institution prior to his/her departure and request a document certifying that he/she retains his/her entitlement to benefits under the conditions laid down in Article 64(1)(b) of the basic Regulation.]

That institution shall inform the person concerned of his obligations and shall provide the abovementioned document which shall include the following information:

(a) the date on which the unemployed person ceased to be available to the employment services of the competent State;

(b) the period granted in accordance with Article 64(1)(b) of the basic Regulation in order to register as a person seeking work in the Member State to which the unemployed person has gone;

(c) the maximum period during which the entitlement to benefits may be retained in accordance with Article 64(1)(c) of the basic Regulation;

(d) circumstances likely to affect the entitlement to benefits.

2. The unemployed person shall register as a person seeking work with the employment services of the Member State to which he goes in accordance with Article 64(1)(b) of the basic Regulation and shall provide the document referred to in paragraph 1 to the institution of that Member State. If he has informed the competent institution in accordance with paragraph 1 but fails to provide this document, the institution in the Member State to which the unemployed person has gone shall contact the competent institution in order to obtain the necessary information.

3. The employment services in the Member State to which the unemployed person has gone to seek employment shall inform the unemployed person of his obligations.

4. The institution in the Member State to which the unemployed person has gone shall immediately send a document to the competent institution containing the date on which the unemployed person registered with the employment services and his new address.

If, in the period during which the unemployed person retains entitlement to benefits, any circumstance likely to affect the entitlement to benefits arises, the institution in the Member State to which the unemployed person has gone shall send immediately to the competent institution and to the person concerned a document containing the relevant information.

At the request of the competent institution, the institution in the Member State to which the unemployed person has gone shall provide relevant information on a monthly basis concerning the follow-up of the unemployed person's situation, in particular whether the latter is still registered with the employment services and is complying with organised checking procedures.

5. The institution in the Member State to which the unemployed person has gone shall carry out or arrange for checks to be carried out, as if the person concerned were an unemployed person obtaining benefits under its own legislation. Where necessary, it shall immediately inform the competent institution if any circumstances referred to in paragraph 1(d) arise.

6. The competent authorities or competent institutions of two or more Member States may agree amongst themselves specific procedures and time-limits concerning the follow-up of the unemployed person's situation as well as other measures to facilitate the job-seeking activities of unemployed persons who go to one of those Member States under Article 64 of the basic Regulation.

[[1] 7. Paragraphs 2 to 6 shall apply *mutatis mutandis* to the situation covered by Article 65a(3) of the basic Regulation.]

Amendment

1. Regulation 465/2012 [2012] OJ L149/4 art.2(5) (June 28, 2012).

Article 56

Unemployed persons who resided in a Member State other than the competent Member State

3.577 [1 1. Where the unemployed person decides, in accordance with Article 65(2) or Article 65a(1) of the basic Regulation, to make himself/herself also available to the employment services in the Member State not providing the benefits, by registering there as a person seeking work, he/she shall inform the institution and the employment services of the Member State providing the benefits.

At the request of the employment services of the Member State not providing the benefits, the employment services in the Member State that is providing the benefits shall send the relevant information concerning the unemployed person's registration and his/her search for employment.

2. Where the legislation applicable in the Member States concerned requires the fulfilment of certain obligations and/or job-seeking activities by the unemployed person, the obligations and/or job-seeking activities by the unemployed person in the Member State providing the benefits shall have priority.

The non-fulfilment by the unemployed person of all the obligations and/or job-seeking activities in the Member State which does not provide the benefits shall not affect the benefits awarded in the other Member State.]

3. For the purposes of applying Article 65(5)(b) of the basic Regulation, the institution of the Member State to whose legislation the worker was last subject shall inform the institution of the place of residence, when requested to do so by the latter, whether the worker is entitled to benefits under Article 64 of the basic Regulation.

Amendment

1. Regulation 465/2012 [2012] OJ L149/4 art.2(6) (June 28, 2012).

Article 57

Provisions for the application of Articles 61, 62, 64 and 65 of the basic Regulation regarding persons covered by a special scheme for civil servants

3.578 1. Articles 54 and 55 of the implementing Regulation shall apply *mutatis mutandis* to persons covered by a special unemployment scheme for civil servants.

2. Article 56 of the implementing Regulation shall not apply to persons covered by a special unemployment scheme for civil servants. An unemployed person who is covered by a special unemployment scheme for civil servants, who is partially or wholly unemployed, and who, during his last employment, was residing in the territory of a Member State other than the competent State, shall receive the benefits under the special unemployment

scheme for civil servants in accordance with the provisions of the legislation of the competent Member State as if he were residing in the territory of that Member State. Those benefits shall be provided by the competent institution, at its expense.

Chapter VI

Family Benefits

Article 58

Priority rules in the event of overlapping

For the purposes of applying Article 68(1)(b)(i) and (ii) of the basic Regulation, where the order of priority cannot be established on the basis of the children's place of residence, each Member State concerned shall calculate the amount of benefits including the children not resident within its own territory. In the event of applying Article 68(1)(b)(i), the competent institution of the Member State whose legislation provides for the highest level of benefits shall pay the full amount of such benefits and be reimbursed half this sum by the competent institution of the other Member State up to the limit of the amount provided for in the legislation of the latter Member State. 3.579

Article 59

Rules applicable where the applicable legislation and/or the competence to grant family benefits changes

1. Where the applicable legislation and/or the competence to grant family benefits change between Member States during a calendar month, irrespective of the payment dates of family benefits under the legislation of those Member States, the institution which has paid the family benefits by virtue of the legislation under which the benefits have been granted at the beginning of that month shall continue to do so until the end of the month in progress. 3.580

2. It shall inform the institution of the other Member State or Member States concerned of the date on which it ceases to pay the family benefits in question. Payment of benefits from the other Member State or Member States concerned shall take effect from that date.

Article 60

Procedure for applying Articles 67 and 68 of the basic Regulation

3.581 1. The application for family benefits shall be addressed to the competent institution. For the purposes of applying Articles 67and 68 of the basic Regulation, the situation of the whole family shall be taken into account as if all the persons involved were subject to the legislation of the Member State concerned and residing there, in particular as regards a person's entitlement to claim such benefits. Where a person entitled to claim the benefits does not exercise his right, an application for family benefits submitted by the other parent, a person treated as a parent, or a person or institution acting as guardian of the child or children, shall be taken into account by the competent institution of the Member State whose legislation is applicable.

2. The institution to which an application is made in accordance with paragraph 1 shall examine the application on the basis of the detailed information supplied by the applicant, taking into account the overall factual and legal situation of the applicant's family.

If that institution concludes that its legislation is applicable by priority right in accordance with Article 68(1) and (2) of the basic Regulation, it shall provide the family benefits according to the legislation it applies.

If it appears to that institution that there may be an entitlement to a differential supplement by virtue of the legislation of another Member State in accordance with Article 68(2) of the basic Regulation, that institution shall forward the application, without delay, to the competent institution of the other Member State and inform the person concerned; moreover, it shall inform the institution of the other Member State of its decision on the application and the amount of family benefits paid.

3. Where the institution to which the application is made concludes that its legislation is applicable, but not by priority right in accordance with Article 68(1) and (2) of the basic Regulation, it shall take a provisional decision, without delay, on the priority rules to be applied and shall forward the application, in accordance with Article 68(3) of the basic Regulation, to the institution of the other Member State, and shall also inform the applicant thereof. That institution shall take a position on the provisional decision within two months.

If the institution to which the application was forwarded does not take a position within two months of the receipt of the application, the provisional decision referred to above shall apply and the institution shall pay the benefits provided for under its legislation and inform the institution to which the application was made of the amount of benefits paid.

4. Where there is a difference of views between the institutions concerned about which legislation is applicable by priority right, Article 6(2) to (5) of the implementing Regulation shall apply. For this purpose the institution of the place of residence referred to in Article 6(2) of the implementing Regulation shall be the institution of the child's or children's place of residence.

5. If the institution which has supplied benefits on a provisional basis has paid more than the amount for which it is ultimately responsible, it may claim reimbursement of the excess from the institution with primary

responsibility in accordance with the procedure laid down in Article 73 of the implementing Regulation.

General Note

This article sets out the administrative process for handling claims under art.67 and art.68. It will be important to determine whether the claim falls within art.67 or art.68. Article 67 applies where there is no overlapping of benefits and art.68 applies in the event of competing claims or awards (see annotations to those articles). **3.582**

Paragraph 1 provides that the situation of the whole family is to be considered as if all the persons involved were subject to the legislation of the Member State concerned. This would seem to include both parents and all the children of the family.

Quite what the phrase "person entitled to claim the benefit does not exercise his right" means is on the face of it unclear. However, some assistance in the interpretation of art.60 can be found in the *Trapkowski* case.

The *Trapkowski* case (C-378/14) judgment of October 22, 2015, concerned the interpretation of art.60 of Regulation 987/2009 which sets out the procedure for applying arts.67 and 68 of Regulation 883/2004. The father was resident in Germany and was divorced from the mother who lived in Poland with their son. In August 2012 the father claimed family benefits for the son; he had been at various times in work and in receipt of unemployment benefits. At the date of claim, he was in receipt of unemployment benefit. Meanwhile, the mother was at the material time in paid employment in Poland, but had not claimed family benefits there (or in Germany).

The German authorities refused the father's claim because it was principally the mother who was entitled to family benefit under German law. That decision was appealed and the Bundesfinanzhof referred questions to the Court of Justice. In response to the first question referred by the national court, the Court of Justice ruled:

> "38. It is apparent from a combined reading of Article 67 of Regulation No 883/2004 and Article 60(1) of Regulation No 987/2009, first, that a person may claim family benefits for members of his family who reside in a Member State other than that responsible for paying those benefits and, second, that the possibility to apply for family benefits is granted not only to persons who reside in the Member State required to pay the family benefits, but also to all the 'persons concerned', who may claim those benefits, including the parents of the child for whom the benefits are claimed.
> 39. Accordingly, given that the parents of the child for whom family benefits are claimed fall within the definition of 'persons concerned' within the meaning of Article 60(1) of Regulation No 987/2009, authorised to claim payment of those benefits, it is conceivable that a parent who resides in a Member State other than that required to pay those benefits is the person entitled to receive those benefits, if all the other conditions laid down by national law are also met.
> 40. It is for the competent national authority to determine the persons who, in accordance with national law, have a right to family benefits."

In response to the second question referred, the Court said:

> "42. By its second question, the referring court asks essentially whether Article 60(1), third sentence, of Regulation No 987/2009 must be interpreted as meaning that the parent of the child for whom family benefits are paid, who resides in the Member State required to pay those benefits, must be granted entitlement to those benefits because the other parent, who resides in another Member State, has not made an application for family benefits.
> 43. To answer that question, it should be recalled, as a preliminary point, that Regulations No 987/2009 and No 883/2004 do not determine the persons entitled to family benefits, even though they lay down the rules which enable the persons entitled to claim those benefits to be determined.

44. The persons entitled to family benefits are, as is clear from Article 67 of Regulation No 883/200, to be determined in accordance with national law.
45. Furthermore, it must be observed that Article 60(1), third sentence, of Regulation No 987/2009 provides that where a person entitled to claim the benefits does not exercise his right, the competent institutions of the Member States must take into account such applications made by the persons or institutions mentioned in that provision which include the 'other parent'.
46. First, it appears both from the wording and the general scheme of Article 60(1) of Regulation No 987/2009 that a distinction must be made between making a claim for family benefits and the right to receive such benefits.
47. Second, it is also clear from the wording of that article that it is sufficient if one of the persons able to claim the benefit of those family benefits makes an application for such benefits, so that the competent institution of the Member State must take that application into consideration.
48. However, EU law does not preclude such an institution, by applying national law, from finding that the person entitled to receive child benefits is a person other than the person who made the application for those benefits.
49. Therefore, where all the conditions for the grant of child benefits have been met and those benefits are actually granted, the issue as to which parent is regarded under national law as the person entitled to receive such benefits is irrelevant (see, to that effect, judgment in *Hoever* and *Zachow*, C-245/94 and C-312/94, . . ., paragraph 37)."

Article 61

Procedure for applying Article 69 of the basic Regulation

3.583 For the purposes of applying Article 69 of the basic Regulation, the Administrative Commission shall draw up a list of the additional or special family benefits for orphans covered by that Article. If there is no provision for the institution competent to grant, by priority right, such additional or special family benefits for orphans under the legislation it applies, it shall without delay forward any application for family benefits, together with all relevant documents and information, to the institution of the Member State to whose legislation the person concerned has been subject, for the longest period of time and which provides such additional or special family benefits for orphans. In some cases, this may mean referring back, under the same conditions, to the institution of the Member State under whose legislation the person concerned has completed the shortest of his or her insurance or residence periods.

Title IV

Financial Provisions

Chapter I

Reimbursement of the cost of benefits in application of Article 35 and Article 41 of the basic Regulation

Section 1

Reimbursement on the Basis of Actual Expenditure

Article 62

Principles

1. For the purposes of applying Article 35 and Article 41 of the basic Regulation, the actual amount of the expenses for benefits in kind, as shown in the accounts of the institution that provided them, shall be reimbursed to that institution by the competent institution, except where Article 63 of the implementing Regulation is applicable. 3.584

2. If any or part of the actual amount of the expenses for benefits referred to in paragraph 1 is not shown in the accounts of the institution that provided them, the amount to be refunded shall be determined on the basis of a lump-sum payment calculated from all the appropriate references obtained from the data available. The Administrative Commission shall assess the basest be used for calculation of the lump-sum payment and shall decide the amount thereof.

3. Higher rates than those applicable to the benefits in kind provided to insured persons subject to the legislation applied by the institution providing the benefits referred to in paragraph 1 may not be taken into account in the reimbursement.

Section 2

Reimbursement on the Basis of Fixed Amounts

Article 63

Identification of the Member States concerned

1. The Member States referred to in Article 35(2) of the basic Regulation, whose legal or administrative structures are such that the use of reimbursement on the basis of actual expenditure is not appropriate, are listed in Annex 3 to the implementing Regulation. 3.585

2. In the case of the Member States listed in Annex 3 to the implementing Regulation, the amount of benefits in kind supplied to:

(a) family members who do not reside in the same Member State as the insured person, as provided for in Article 17 of the basic Regulation; and to

(b) pensioners and members of their family, as provided for in Article 24(1) and Articles 25 and 26 of the basic Regulation;

shall be reimbursed by the competent institutions to the institutions providing those benefits, on the basis of a fixed amount established for each calendar year. This fixed amount shall be as close as possible to actual expenditure.

Article 64

Calculation method of the monthly fixed amounts and the total fixed amount

3.586 1. For each creditor Member State, the monthly fixed amount per person (Fi) for a calendar year shall be determined by dividing the annual average cost per person (Yi), broken down by age group (i), by 12 and by applying a reduction (X) to the result in accordance with the following formula:

Fi = Yi*1/12*(1-X)

Where:

— the index (i = 1, 2 and 3) represents the three age groups used for calculating the fixed amounts:

i = 1: persons aged under 20,

i = 2: persons aged from 20 to 64,

i = 3: persons aged 65 and over,

— Yi represents the annual average cost per person in age group i, as defined in paragraph 2,

— the coefficient X (0,20 or 0,15) represents the reduction as defined in paragraph 3,

2. The annual average cost per person (Yi) in age group i shall be obtained by dividing the annual expenditure on all benefits in kind provided by the institutions of the creditor Member State to all persons in the age group concerned subject to its legislation and residing within its territory by the average number of persons concerned in that age group in the calendar year in question. The calculation shall be based on the expenditure under the schemes referred to in Article 23 of the implementing Regulation.

3. The reduction to be applied to the monthly fixed amount shall, in principle, be equal to 20 % (X = 0,20). It shall be equal to 15 % (X = 0,15) for pensioners and members of their family where the competent Member State is not listed in Annex IV to the basic Regulation.

4. For each debtor Member State, the total fixed amount for a calendar year shall be the sum of the products obtained by multiplying, in each age group i, the determined monthly fixed amounts per person by the number of months completed by the persons concerned in the creditor Member State in that age group.

The number of months completed by the persons concerned in the creditor Member State shall be the sum of the calendar months in a calendar year during which the persons concerned were, because of their residence in the territory of the creditor Member State, eligible to receive benefits in kind in that territory at the expense of the debtor Member State. Those months shall be determined from an inventory kept for that purpose by the institution of the place of residence, based on documentary evidence of the entitlement of the beneficiaries supplied by the competent institution.

5. No later than 1 May 2015, the Administrative Commission shall present a specific report on the application of this Article and in particular on the reductions referred to in paragraph 3. On the basis of that report, the Administrative Commission may present a proposal containing any amendments which may prove necessary in order to ensure that the calculation of fixed amounts comes as close as possible to the actual expenditure incurred and the reductions referred to in paragraph 3 do not result in unbalanced payments or double payments for the Member States.

6. The Administrative Commission shall establish the methods for determining the elements for calculating the fixed amounts referred to in paragraphs 1 to 5.

7. Notwithstanding paragraphs 1 to 4, Member States may continue to apply Articles 94 and 95 of Regulation (EEC) No 574/72 for the calculation of the fixed amount until 1 May 2015, provided that the reduction set out in paragraph 3 is applied.

Article 65

Notification of annual average costs

1. The annual average cost per person in each age group for a specific year shall be notified to the Audit Board at the latest by the end of the second year following the year in question. If the notification is not made by this deadline, the annual average cost per person which the Administrative Commission has last determined for a previous year will be taken. 3.587

2. The annual average costs determined in accordance with paragraph 1 shall be published each year in the *Official Journal of the European Union.*

SECTION 3

COMMON PROVISIONS

Article 66

Procedure for reimbursement between institutions

1. The reimbursements between the Member States concerned shall be made as promptly as possible. Every institution concerned shall be obliged to reimburse claims before the deadlines mentioned in this Section, as soon as it is in a position to do so. A dispute concerning a particular claim shall not hinder the reimbursement of another claim or other claims. 3.588

There is no requirement to consider requests introduced after the time-limit referred to in the first paragraph.

Articles 66(1) and 67(5) to (7) of the implementing Regulation shall apply *mutatis mutandis*.

From the end of the 18-month period referred to in Article 67(5)of the implementing Regulation, interest may be charged by the creditor institution on outstanding claims. The interest shall be calculated in accordance with Article 68(2) of the implementing Regulation.

The maximum amount of the reimbursement referred to in the third sentence of Article 65(6) of the basic Regulation is in each individual case the amount of the benefit to which a person concerned would be entitled according to the legislation of the Member State to which he was last subject if registered with the employment services of that Member State. However, in relations between the Member States listed in Annex 5 to the implementing Regulation, the competent institutions of one of those Member States to whose legislation the person concerned was last subject shall determine the maximum amount in each individual case on the basis of the average amount of unemployment benefits provided under the legislation of that Member State in the preceding calendar year.

CHAPTER III

RECOVERY OF BENEFITS PROVIDED BUT NOT DUE, RECOVERY OF PROVISIONAL PAYMENTS AND CONTRIBUTIONS, OFFSETTING AND ASSISTANCE WITH RECOVERY

SECTION 1

PRINCIPLES

Article 71

Common provisions

3.593 For the purposes of applying Article 84 of the basic Regulation and within the framework defined therein, the recovery of claims shall, wherever possible, be by way of offsetting either between the institutions of Member States concerned, or vis-à-vis the natural or legal person concerned in accordance with Articles 72 to 74 of the implementing Regulation. If it is not possible to recover all or any of the claim via this offsetting procedure, the remainder of the amount due shall be recovered in accordance with Articles 75 to 85 of the implementing Regulation.

SECTION 2

OFFSETTING

Article 72

Benefits received unduly

1. If the institution of a Member State has paid undue benefits to a person, that institution may, within the terms and limits laid down in the legislation it applies, request the institution of any other Member State responsible for paying benefits to the person concerned to deduct the undue amount from arrears or on-going payments owed to the person concerned regardless of the social security branch under which the benefit is paid. The institution of the latter Member State shall deduct the amount concerned subject to the conditions and limits applying to this kind of offsetting procedure in accordance with the legislation it applies in the same way as if it had made the overpayments itself, and shall transfer the amount deducted to the institution that has paid undue benefits. **3.594**

2. By way of derogation from paragraph 1, if, when awarding or reviewing benefits in respect of invalidity benefits, old-age and survivors' pensions pursuant to Chapter 4 and 5 of Title III of the basic Regulation, the institution of a Member State has paid to a person benefits of undue sum, that institution may request the institution of any other Member State responsible for the payment of corresponding benefits to the person concerned to deduct the amount overpaid from the arrears payable to the person concerned. After the latter institution has informed the institution that has paid an undue sum of these arrears, the institution which has paid the undue sum shall within two months communicate the amount of the undue sum. If the institution which is due to pay arrears receives that communication within the deadline it shall transfer the amount deducted to the institution which has paid undue sums. If the deadline expires, that institution shall without delay pay out the arrears to the person concerned.

3. If a person has received social welfare assistance in one Member State during a period in which he was entitled to benefits under the legislation of another Member State, the body which provided the assistance may, if it is legally entitled to reclaim the benefits due to the person concerned, request the institution of any other Member State responsible for paying benefits in favour of the person concerned to deduct the amount of assistance paid from the amounts which that Member State pays to the person concerned.

This provision shall apply *mutatis mutandis* to any family member of a person concerned who has received assistance in the territory of a Member State during a period in which the insured person was entitled to benefits under the legislation of another Member State in respect of that family member.

The institution of a Member State which has paid an undue amount of assistance shall send a statement of the amount due to the institution of the other Member State, which shall then deduct the amount, subject to the conditions and limits laid down for this kind of offsetting procedure in accordance with the legislation it applies, and transfer the amount without delay to the institution that has paid the undue amount.

Article 73

Provisionally paid benefits in cash or contributions

3.595 1. For the purposes of applying Article 6 of the implementing Regulation, at the latest three months after the applicable legislation has been determined or the institution responsible for paying the benefits has been identified, the institution which provisionally paid the cash benefits shall draw up a statement of the amount provisionally paid and shall send it to the institution identified as being competent.

The institution identified as being competent for paying the benefits shall deduct the amount due in respect of the provisional payment from the arrears of the corresponding benefits it owes to the person concerned and shall without delay transfer the amount deducted to the institution which provisionally paid the cash benefits.

If the amount of provisionally paid benefits exceeds the amount of arrears, or if arrears do not exist, the institution identified as being competent shall deduct this amount from ongoing payments subject to the conditions and limits applying to this kind of offsetting procedure under the legislation it applies, and without delay transfer the amount deducted to the institution which provisionally paid the cash benefits.

2. The institution which has provisionally received contributions from a legal and/or natural person shall not reimburse the amounts in question to the person who paid them until it has ascertained from the institution identified as being competent the sums due to it under Article 6(4) of the implementing Regulation.

Upon request of the institution identified as being competent, which shall be made at the latest three months after the applicable legislation has been determined, the institution that has provisionally received contributions shall transfer them to the institution identified as being competent for that period for the purpose of settling the situation concerning the contributions owed by the legal and/or natural person to it. The contributions transferred shall be retroactively deemed as having been paid to the institution identified as being competent.

If the amount of provisionally paid contributions exceeds the amount the legal and/or natural person owes to the institution identified as being competent, the institution which provisionally received contributions shall reimburse the amount in excess to the legal and/or natural person concerned.

Article 74

Costs related to offsetting

3.596 No costs are payable where the debt is recovered via the offsetting procedure provided for in Articles 72 and 73 of the implementing Regulation.

Article 75

SECTION 3

RECOVERY

Article 75

Definitions and common provisions

1. For the purposes of this Section: 3.597
- "claim" means all claims relating to contributions or to benefits paid or provided unduly, including interest, fines, administrative penalties and all other charges and costs connected with the claim in accordance with the legislation of the Member State making the claim;
- "applicant party" means, in respect of each Member State, any institution which makes a request for information, notification or recovery concerning a claim as defined above,
- "requested party" means, in respect of each Member State, any institution to which a request for information, notification or recovery can be made.

2. Requests and any related communications between the Member States shall, in general, be addressed via designated institutions.

3. Practical implementation measures, including, among others, those related to Article 4 of the implementing Regulation and to setting a minimum threshold for the amounts for which a request for recovery can be made, shall be taken by the Administrative Commission.

Article 76

Requests for information

1. At the request of the applicant party, the requested party shall provide any information which would be useful to the applicant party in the recovery of its claim. 3.598

In order to obtain that information, the requested party shall make use of the powers provided for under the laws, regulations or administrative provisions applying to the recovery of similar claims arising in its own Member State.

2. The request for information shall indicate the name, last known address, and any other relevant information relating to the identification of the legal or natural person concerned to whom the information to be provided relates and the nature and amount of the claim in respect of which the request is made.

3. The requested party shall not be obliged to supply information:

(a) which it would not be able to obtain for the purpose of recovering similar claims arising in its own Member State;

(b) which would disclose any commercial, industrial or professional secrets; or

(c) the disclosure of which would be liable to prejudice the security of or be contrary to the public policy of the Member State.

4. The requested party shall inform the applicant party of the grounds for refusing a request for information.

Article 77

Notification

3.599 1. The requested party shall, at the request of the applicant party, and in accordance with the rules in force for the notification of similar instruments or decisions in its own Member State, notify the addressee of all instruments and decisions, including those of a judicial nature, which come from the Member State of the applicant party and which relate to a claim and/or to its recovery.

2. The request for notification shall indicate the name, address and any other relevant information relating to the identification of the addressee concerned to which the applicant party normally has access, the nature and the subject of the instrument or decision to be notified and, if necessary the name, address and any other relevant information relating to the identification of the debtor and the claim to which the instrument or decision relates, and any other useful information.

3. The requested party shall without delay inform the applicant party of the action taken on its request for notification and, particularly, of the date on which the decision or instrument was forwarded to the addressee.

Article 78

Request for recovery

3.600 1. The request for recovery of a claim, addressed by the applicant party to the requested party, shall be accompanied by an official or certified copy of the instrument permitting its enforcement, issued in the Member State of the applicant party and, if appropriate, by the original or a certified copy of other documents necessary for recovery.

2. The applicant party may only make a request for recovery if:

(a) the claim and/or the instrument permitting its enforcement are not contested in its own Member State, except in cases where the second subparagraph of Article 81(2) of the implementing Regulation is applied;

(b) it has, in its own Member State, applied appropriate recovery procedures available to it on the basis of the instrument referred to in paragraph 1, and the measures taken will not result in the payment in full of the claim;

(c) the period of limitation according to its own legislation has not expired.

3. The request for recovery shall indicate:

(a) the name, address and any other relevant information relating to the identification of the natural or legal person concerned and/or to the third party holding his or her assets;

Article 78

(b) the name, address and any other relevant information relating to the identification of the applicant party;
(c) a reference to the instrument permitting its enforcement, issued in the Member State of the applicant party;
(d) the nature and amount of the claim, including the principal, the interest, fines, administrative penalties and all other charges and costs due indicated in the currencies of the Member States of the applicant and requested parties;
(e) the date of notification of the instrument to the addressee by the applicant party and/or by the requested party;
(f) the date from which and the period during which enforcement is possible under the laws in force in the Member State of the applicant party;
(g) any other relevant information.

4. The request for recovery shall also contain a declaration by the applicant party confirming that the conditions laid down in paragraph 2 have been fulfilled.

5. The applicant party shall forward to the requesting party any relevant information relating to the matter which gave rise to the request for recovery, as soon as this comes to its knowledge.

Article 79

Instrument permitting enforcement of the recovery

1. In accordance with Article 84(2) of the basic Regulation, the instrument permitting enforcement of the claim shall be directly recognised and treated automatically as an instrument permitting the enforcement of a claim of the Member State of the requested party. **3.601**

2. Notwithstanding paragraph 1, the instrument permitting enforcement of the claim may, where appropriate and in accordance with the provisions in force in the Member State of the requested party, be accepted as, recognised as, supplemented with, or replaced by an instrument authorising enforcement in the territory of that Member State.

Within three months of the date of receipt of the request for recovery, Member States shall endeavour to complete the acceptance, recognition, supplementing or replacement, except in cases where the third subparagraph of this paragraph applies. Member States may not refuse to complete these actions where the instrument permitting enforcement is properly drawn up. The requested party shall inform the applicant party of the grounds for exceeding the three-month period.

If any of these actions should give rise to a dispute in connection with the claim and/or the instrument permitting enforcement issued by the applicant party, Article 81 of the implementing Regulation shall apply.

Article 80

Payment arrangements and deadlines

1. Claims shall be recovered in the currency of the Member State of the requested party. The entire amount of the claim that is recovered by the **3.602**

requested party shall be remitted by the requested party to the applicant party.

2. The requested party may, where the laws, regulations or administrative provisions in force in its own Member State so permit, and after consulting the applicant party, allow the debtor time to pay or authorise payment by instalment. Any interest charged by the requested party in respect of such extra time to pay shall also be remitted to the applicant party.

From the date on which the instrument permitting enforcement of the recovery of the claim has been directly recognised in accordance with Article 79(1) of the implementing Regulation, or accepted, recognised, supplemented or replaced in accordance with Article 79(2) of the implementing Regulation, interest shall be charged for late payment under the laws, regulations and administrative provisions in force in the Member State of the requested party and shall also be remitted to the applicant party.

Article 81

Contestation concerning the claim or the instrument permitting enforcement of its recovery and contestation concerning enforcement measures

3.603 1. If, in the course of the recovery procedure, the claim and/or the instrument permitting its enforcement issued in the Member State of the applicant party are contested by an interested party, the action shall be brought by this party before the appropriate authorities of the Member State of the applicant party, in accordance with the laws in force in that Member State. The applicant party shall without delay notify the requested party of this action. The interested party may also inform the requested party of the action.

2. As soon as the requested party has received the notification or information referred to in paragraph 1 either from the applicant party or from the interested party, it shall suspend the enforcement procedure pending the decision of the appropriate authority in the matter, unless the applicant party requests otherwise in accordance with the second subparagraph of this paragraph. Should the requested party deem it necessary, and without prejudice to Article 84 of the implementing Regulation, it may take precautionary measures to guarantee recovery insofar as the laws or regulations in force in its own Member State allow such action for similar claims.

Notwithstanding the first subparagraph, the applicant party may, in accordance with the laws, regulations and administrative practices in force in its own Member State, request the requested party to recover a contested claim, in so far as the relevant laws, regulations and administrative practices in force in the requested party's Member State allow such action. If the result of the contestation is subsequently favourable to the debtor, the applicant party shall be liable for the reimbursement of any sums recovered, together with any compensation due, in accordance with the legislation in force in the requested party's Member State.

3. Where the contestation concerns enforcement measures taken in the Member State of the requested party, the action shall be brought before the appropriate authority of that Member State in accordance with its laws and regulations.

Article 81

4. Where the appropriate authority before which the action is brought in accordance with paragraph 1 is a judicial or administrative tribunal, the decision of that tribunal, insofar as it is favourable to the applicant party and permits recovery of the claim in the Member State of the applicant party, shall constitute the "instrument permitting enforcement" within the meaning of Articles 78 and 79 of the implementing Regulation and the recovery of the claim shall proceed on the basis of that decision.

Article 82

Limits applying to assistance

1. The requested party shall not be obliged: 3.604

(a) to grant the assistance provided for in Articles 78 to 81 of the implementing Regulation if recovery of the claim would, because of the situation of the debtor, create serious economic or social difficulties in the Member State of the requested party, insofar as the laws, regulations or administrative practices in force in the Member State of the requested party allow such action for similar national claims;

(b) to grant the assistance provided for in Articles 76 to 81 of the implementing Regulation, if the initial request under Articles 76 to 78 of the implementing Regulation applies to claims more than five years old, dating from the moment the instrument permitting the recovery was established in accordance with the laws, regulations or administrative practices in force in the Member State of the applicant party at the date of the request. However, if the claim or instrument is contested, the time limit begins from the moment that the Member State of the applicant party establishes that the claim or the enforcement order permitting recovery may no longer be contested.

2. The requested party shall inform the applicant party of the grounds for refusing a request for assistance.

Article 83

Periods of limitation

1. Questions concerning periods of limitation shall be governed as follows: 3.605

(a) by the laws in force in the Member State of the applicant party, insofar as they concern the claim and/or the instrument permitting its enforcement; and

(b) by the laws in force in the Member State of the requested party, insofar as they concern enforcement measures in the requested Member State.

Periods of limitation according to the laws in force in the Member State of the requested party shall start from the date of direct recognition or from the date of acceptance, recognition, supplementing or replacement in accordance with Article 79 of the implementing Regulation.

2. Steps taken in the recovery of claims by the requested party in

1405

pursuance of a request for assistance, which, if they had been carried out by the applicant party, would have had the effect of suspending or interrupting the period of limitation according to the laws in force in the Member State of the applicant party, shall be deemed to have been taken in the latter State, in so far as that effect is concerned.

Article 84

Precautionary measures

3.606 Upon reasoned request by the applicant party, the requested party shall take precautionary measures to ensure recovery of a claim in so far as the laws and regulations in force in the Member State of the requested party so permit.

For the purposes of implementing the first paragraph, the provisions and procedures laid down in Articles 78, 79, 81 and 82 of the implementing Regulation shall apply *mutatis mutandis*.

Article 85

Costs related to recovery

3.607 1. The requested party shall recover from the natural or legal person concerned and retain any costs linked to recovery which it incurs, in accordance with the laws and regulations of the Member State of the requested party that apply to similar claims.

2. Mutual assistance afforded under this Section shall, as a rule, be free of charge. However, where recovery poses a specific problem or concerns a very large amount in costs, the applicant and the requested parties may agree on reimbursement arrangements specific to the cases in question.

3. The Member State of the applicant party shall remain liable to the Member State of the requested party for any costs and any losses incurred as a result of actions held to be unfounded, as far as either the substance of the claim or the validity of the instrument issued by the applicant party is concerned.

Article 86

Review clause

3.608 1. No later than the fourth full calendar year after the entry into force of the implementing Regulation, the Administrative Commission shall present a comparative report on the time limits set out in Article 67(2), (5) and (6) of the implementing Regulation.

On the basis of this report, the European Commission may, as appropriate, submit proposals to review these time limits with the aim of reducing them in a significant way.

Article 86

2. No later than the date referred to in paragraph 1, the Administrative Commission shall also assess the rules for conversion of periods set out in Article 13 with a view to simplifying those rules, if possible.

3. No later than 1 May 2015, the Administrative Commission shall present a report specifically assessing the application of Chapters I and III of Title IV of the implementing Regulation, in particular with regard to the procedures and time limits referred to in Article 67(2), (5) and (6) of the implementing Regulation and to the recovery procedures referred to in Articles 75 to 85 of the implementing Regulation.

In the light of this report, the European Commission may, if necessary, submit appropriate proposals to make these procedures more efficient and balanced.

TITLE V

MISCELLANEOUS, TRANSITIONAL AND FINAL PROVISIONS

Article 87

Medical examination and administrative checks

1. Without prejudice to other provisions, where a recipient or a claimant of benefits, or a member of his family, is staying or residing within the territory of a Member State other than that in which the debtor institution is located, the medical examination shall be carried out, at the request of that institution, by the institution of the beneficiary's place of stay or residence in accordance with the procedures laid down by the legislation applied by that institution. **3.609**

The debtor institution shall inform the institution of the place of stay or residence of any special requirements, if necessary, to be followed and points to be covered by the medical examination.

2. The institution of the place of stay or residence shall forward a report to the debtor institution that requested the medical examination. This institution shall be bound by the findings of the institution of the place of stay or residence.

The debtor institution shall reserve the right to have the beneficiary examined by a doctor of its choice. However, the beneficiary may be asked to return to the Member State of the debtor institution only if he or she is able to make the journey without prejudice to his health and the cost of travel and accommodation is paid for by the debtor institution.

3. Where a recipient or a claimant of benefits, or a member of his family, is staying or residing in the territory of a Member State other than that in which the debtor institution is located, the administrative check shall, at the request of the debtor institution, be performed by the institution of the beneficiary's place of stay or residence.

Paragraph 2 shall also apply in this case.

4. Paragraphs 2 and 3 shall also apply in determining or checking the state of dependence of a recipient or a claimant of the long-term care benefits mentioned in Article 34 of the basic Regulation.

5. The competent authorities or competent institutions of two or more Member States may agree specific provisions and procedures to improve fully or partly the labour-market readiness of claimants and recipients and their participation in any schemes or programmes available in the Member State of stay or residence for that purpose.

6. As an exception to the principle of free-of-charge mutual administrative cooperation in Article 76(2) of the basic Regulation, the effective amount of the expenses of the checks referred to in paragraphs 1 to 5 shall be refunded to the institution which was requested to carry them out by the debtor institution which requested them.

Article 88

Notifications

3.610 1. The Member States shall notify the European Commission of the details of the bodies defined in Article 1(m), (q) and (r) of the basic Regulation and Article 1(2)(a) and (b) of the implementing Regulation, and of the institutions designated in accordance with the implementing Regulation.

2. The bodies specified in paragraph 1 shall be provided with an electronic identity in the form of an identification code and electronic address.

3. The Administrative Commission shall establish the structure, content and detailed arrangements, including the common format and model, for notification of the details specified in paragraph 1.

4. Annex 4 to the implementing Regulation gives details of the public database containing the information specified in paragraph 1. The database shall be established and managed by the European Commission. The Member States shall, however, be responsible for the input of their own national contact information into this database. Moreover, the Member States shall ensure the accuracy of the input of the national contact information required under paragraph 1.

5. The Member States shall be responsible for keeping the information specified in paragraph 1 up to date.

Article 89

Information

3.611 1. The Administrative Commission shall prepare the information needed to ensure that the parties concerned are aware of their rights and the administrative formalities required in order to assert them. This information shall, where possible, be disseminated electronically via publication online on sites accessible to the public. The Administrative Commission shall ensure that the information is regularly updated and monitor the quality of services provided to customers.

2. The Advisory Committee referred to in Article 75 of the basic

Article 89

Regulation may issue opinions and recommendations on improving the information and its dissemination.

3. The competent authorities shall ensure that their institutions are aware of and apply all the Community provisions, legislative or otherwise, including the decisions of the Administrative Commission, in the areas covered by and within the terms of the basic Regulation and the implementing Regulation.

Article 90

Currency conversion

For the purposes of applying the basic Regulation and the implementing Regulation, the exchange rate between two currencies shall be the reference rate published by the European Central Bank. The date to be taken into account for determining the exchange rate shall be fixed by the Administrative Commission. **3.612**

Article 91

Statistics

The competent authorities shall compile statistics on the application of the basic Regulation and the implementing Regulation and forward them to the secretariat of the Administrative Commission. Those data shall be collected and organised according to the plan and method defined by the Administrative Commission. The European Commission shall be responsible for disseminating the information. **3.613**

Article 92

Amendment of the Annexes

Annexes 1, 2, 3, 4 and 5 to the implementing Regulation and Annexes VI, VII, VIII and IX to the basic Regulation may be amended by Commission Regulation at the request of the Administrative Commission. **3.614**

Article 93

Transitional provisions

Article 87 of the basic Regulation shall apply to the situations covered by the implementing Regulation. **3.615**

Article 94

Transitional provisions relating to pensions

3.616 1. Where the contingency arises before the date of entry into force of the implementing Regulation in the territory of the Member State concerned and the claim for pension has not been awarded before that date, such claim shall give rise to a double award, in as much as benefits must be granted, pursuant to such contingency, for a period prior to that date:

(a) for the period prior to the date of entry into force of the implementing Regulation in the territory of the Member State concerned, in accordance with Regulation (EEC) No 1408/71, or with agreements in force between the Member States concerned;

(b) for the period commencing on the date of entry into force of the implementing Regulation in the territory of the Member State concerned, in accordance with the basic Regulation.

However, if the amount calculated pursuant to the provisions referred to under point (a) is greater than that calculated pursuant to the provisions referred to under point (b), the person concerned shall continue to be entitled to the amount calculated pursuant to the provisions referred to under point (a).

2. A claim for invalidity, old age or survivors' benefits submitted to an institution of a Member State from the date of entry into force of the implementing Regulation in the territory of the Member State concerned shall automatically necessitate the reassessment of the benefits which have been awarded for the same contingency prior to that date by the institution or institutions of one or more Member States, in accordance with the basic Regulation; such reassessment may not give rise to any reduction in the amount of the benefit awarded.

Article 95

Transitional period for electronic data exchanges

3.617 1. Each Member State may benefit from a transitional period for exchanging data by electronic means as provided for by Article 4(2) of the implementing Regulation.

These transitional periods shall not exceed 24 months from the date of entry into force of the implementing Regulation.

However, if the delivery of the necessary Community infrastructure (Electronic Exchange of Social Security information — EESSI) is significantly delayed with regard to the entry into force of the implementing Regulation, the Administrative Commission may agree on any appropriate extension of these periods.

2. The practical arrangements for any necessary transitional periods referred to in paragraph 1 shall be laid down by the Administrative Commission with a view to ensuring the necessary data exchange for the application of the basic Regulation and the implementing Regulation.

Article 96

Repeal

1. Regulation (EEC) No 574/72 is repealed with effect from 1 May 2010. **3.618**

However, Regulation (EEC) No 574/72 shall remain in force and continue to have legal effect for the purposes of:

(a) Council Regulation (EC) No 859/2003 of 14 May 2003extending the provisions of Regulation (EEC) No 1408/71and Regulation (EEC) No 574/72 to nationals of third countries who are not already covered by those provisions solely on the grounds of their nationality,[15] until such time as that Regulation is repealed or amended;

(b) Council Regulation (EEC) No 1661/85 of 13 June 1985 laying down the technical adaptations to the Community rule son social security for migrant workers with regard to Greenland,[16] until such time as that Regulation is repealed or amended;

(c) the Agreement on the European Economic Area,[17] the Agreement between the European Community and its Member States, of the one part, and the Swiss Confederation, of the other, on the free movement of persons[18] and other agreements containing a reference to Regulation (EEC) No 574/72, until such time as those agreements are amended on the basis of the implementing Regulation.

2. In Council Directive 98/49/EC of 29 June 1998 on safeguarding the supplementary pension rights of employed and self-employed persons moving within the Community,[19] and more generally in all other Community acts, the references to Regulation (EEC) No 574/72 shall be understood as referring to the implementing Regulation.

Article 97

Publication and entry into force

This Regulation shall be published in the *Official Journal of the European Union*. It shall enter into force on 1 May 2010. **3.619**

This Regulation shall be binding in its entirety and directly applicable in all Member States.

Done at Strasbourg, 16 September 2009.

---

15 OJ L 124, 20.5.2003, p.1.
16 OJ L 160, 20.6.1985, p.7.
17 OJ L 1, 3.1.1994, p.1.
18 OJ L 114, 30.4.2002, p.6.
19 OJ L 209, 25.7.1998, p.46.

Annex 1

Implementing Provisions for Bilateral Agreements Remaining in Force and New Bilateral Implementing Agreements

(referred to in Article 8(1) and Article 9(2) of the implementing Regulation)

BELGIUM — DENMARK

3.620 The Exchange of Letters of 8 May 2006 and 21 June 2006 on the Agreement of reimbursement with the actual amount of the benefit provided to members of the family of an employed or self-employed person insured in Belgium, where the family member resides in Denmark and to pensioners and/or members of their family insured in Belgium but residing in Denmark.

BELGIUM—GERMANY

The Agreement of 29 January 1969 on the collection and recovery of social security contributions.

BELGIUM—IRELAND

The Exchange of Letters of 19 May and 28 July 1981 concerning Articles 36(3) and 70(3) of Regulation (EEC) No 1408/71 (reciprocal waiving of reimbursement of the costs of benefits in kind and of unemployment benefits under Chapters 1 and 6 of Title III of Regulation (EEC) No 1408/71) and Article 105(2) of Regulation (EEC) No 574/72 (reciprocal waiving of reimbursement of the costs of administrative checks and medical examinations).

BELGIUM—SPAIN

The Agreement of 25 May 1999 on the reimbursement of benefits in kind according to the provisions of Regulations (EEC) No 1408/71 and No 574/72.

BELGIUM—FRANCE

(a) The Agreement of 4 July 1984 relating to medical examinations of frontier workers resident in one country and working in another
(b) The Agreement of 14 May 1976 on the waiving of reimbursement of the costs of administrative checks and medical examinations, adopted pursuant to Article 105(2) of Regulation (EEC) No 574/72
(c) The Agreement of 3 October 1977 implementing Article 92 of Regulation (EEC) No 1408/71 (recovery of social security contributions)
(d) The Agreement of 29 June 1979 concerning the reciprocal waiving of reimbursement provided for in Article 70(3) of Regulation (EEC) No 1408/71 (costs of unemployment benefit)
(e) The Administrative Arrangement of 6 March 1979 on the procedures

for the implementation of the Additional Convention of 12 October 1978 on social security between Belgium and France in respect of its provisions relating to self-employed persons

(f) The Exchange of Letters of 21 November 1994 and 8 February 1995 concerning the procedures for the settlement of reciprocal claims pursuant to Articles 93, 94, 95 and 96 of Regulation (EEC) No 574/72

BELGIUM—ITALY

(a) The Agreement of 12 January 1974 implementing Article 105(2) of Regulation (EEC) No 574/72
(b) The Agreement of 31 October 1979 implementing Article 18(9) of Regulation (EEC) No 574/72
(c) The Exchange of Letters of 10 December 1991 and 10 February 1992 concerning the reimbursement of reciprocal claims under Article 93 of Regulation (EEC) No 574/72
(d) The Agreement of 21.11.2003 on the terms for settling reciprocal claims under Articles 94 and 95 of Council Regulation (EEC) No 574/72

BELGIUM—LUXEMBOURG

(a) The Agreement of 28 January 1961 on the recovery of social security contributions
(b) The Agreement of 16 April 1976 on the waiving of reimbursement of the costs of administrative checks and medical examinations, as provided for in Article 105(2) of Regulation (EEC) No 574/72

BELGIUM—NETHERLANDS

(a) [1...]
(b) The Agreement of 13 March 2006 on health care insurance
(c) The Agreement of 12 August 1982 on sickness, maternity and invalidity insurance

BELGIUM—UNITED KINGDOM

(a) The Exchange of Letters of 4 May and 14 June 1976 regarding Article 105(2) of Regulation (EEC) No 574/72 (waiving of reimbursement of the costs of administrative checks and medical examinations)
(b) The Exchange of Letters of 18 January and 14 March 1977 regarding Article 36(3) of Regulation (EEC) No 1408/71 (arrangement for reimbursement or waiving of reimbursement of the costs of benefits in kind provided under the terms of Chapter 1 of Title III of Regulation (EEC) No 1408/71) as amended by the Exchange of Letters of 4 May and 23 July 1982 (agreement for reimbursement of costs incurred under Article 22(1)(a) of Regulation (EEC) No 1408/71)

BULGARIA—CZECH REPUBLIC

Article 29(1) and (3) of the Agreement of 25 November 1998 and Article 5(4) of the Administrative Arrangement of 30 November 1999 on the waiving of reimbursement of the costs of administrative checks and medical examinations.

BULGARIA—GERMANY

Articles 8 to 9 of the Administrative Agreement on implementing the Convention on social security of 17 December 1997 in the pension field.

CZECH REPUBLIC—SLOVAKIA

Articles 15 and 16 of the Administrative Arrangement of 8 January 1993 concerning the specification of a seat of the employer and the place of residence for the purposes of application of Article 20 of the Convention of 29 October 1992 on social security.

DENMARK—IRELAND

The Exchange of Letters of 22 December 1980 and 11 February 1981 on the reciprocal waiving of reimbursement of the costs of benefits in kind granted under insurance for sickness, maternity, accidents at work and occupational diseases, and of unemployment benefits and of the costs of administrative checks and medical examinations (Articles 36(3), 63(3) of Regulation (EEC) No 1408/71 and Article 105(2) of Regulation (EEC) No 574/72).

DENMARK—GREECE

Agreement of 8 May 1986 on the partial reciprocal waiving of reimbursement in respect of benefits in kind for sickness, maternity, accidents at work and occupational diseases and waiving of reimbursement in respect of administrative checks and medical examinations.

DENMARK—SPAIN

Agreement of 11 December 2006 of advance payment, time-limits and reimbursement with the actual amount of the benefit provided to members of the family of an employed or self-employed person insured in Spain, where the family member resides in Denmark and to pensioners and/or members of their family insured in Spain but residing in Denmark.

DENMARK — FRANCE

[3 . . .]

DENMARK — ITALY

[4 . . .]

DENMARK — LUXEMBOURG

[1 . . .]

DENMARK — NETHERLANDS

[3 . . .]

DENMARK — PORTUGAL

The Agreement of 17 April 1998 on the partial waiving of reimbursement of costs of benefits in kind under insurance for sickness, maternity, accidents at work and occupational diseases and administrative checks and medical examinations.

DENMARK — FINLAND

Article 15 of the Nordic Convention on Social Security of 18 August 2003: Agreement on the reciprocal waiver of refund pursuant to Articles 36, 63 and 70 of Regulation (EEC) No 1408/71 (cost of benefits in kind in respect of sickness and maternity, accidents at work and occupational diseases, and unemployment benefits) and Article 105 of Regulation (EEC) No 574/72 (costs of administrative checks and medical examinations).

DENMARK — SWEDEN

Article 15 of the Nordic Convention on Social Security of 18 August 2003: Agreement on the reciprocal waiver of refund pursuant to Articles 36, 63 and 70 of Regulation (EEC) No 1408/71 (cost of benefits in kind in respect of sickness and maternity, accidents at work and occupational diseases, and unemployment benefits) and Article 105 of Regulation (EEC) No 574/72 (costs of administrative checks and medical examinations).

DENMARK — UNITED KINGDOM

The Exchange of Letters of 30 March and 19 April 1977 as modified by an Exchange of Letters of 8 November 1989 and of10 January 1990 on agreement of waiving of reimbursement of the costs of benefits in kind and administrative checks and medical examinations.

GERMANY — FRANCE

The Agreement of 26 May 1981 implementing Article 92 of Regulation (EEC) No 1408/71 (collection and recovery of social security contributions).

GERMANY — ITALY

The Agreement of 3 April 2000 on the collection and recovery of social security contributions.

GERMANY — LUXEMBOURG

(a) The Agreement of 14 October 1975 on the waiving of reimbursement of the costs of administrative checks and medical examinations, adopted pursuant to Article 105(2) of Regulation (EEC) No 574/72
(b) The Agreement of 14 October 1975 on the collection and recovery of social security contributions
(c) The Agreement of 25 January 1990 relating to the application of Articles 20 and 22(1)(b) and (c) of Regulation (EEC) No 1408/71

GERMANY — NETHERLANDS

[1 . . .]

GERMANY — AUSTRIA

Section II, Number 1, and section III of the Agreement of 2 August 1979 on the implementation of the Convention on unemployment insurance of 19 July 1978 shall continue to apply to persons who have exercised an activity as a frontier worker on or before 1 January 2005 who become unemployed before 1 January 2011.

GERMANY — POLAND

The Agreement of 11 January 1977 on the implementation of the Convention of 9 October 1975 on old-age pensions and benefits for accidents at work.

ESTONIA — UNITED KINGDOM

The Arrangement finalised on 29 March 2006 between the Competent Authorities of the Republic of Estonia and of the United Kingdom under Articles 36(3) and 63(3) of Regulation (EEC) No 1408/71 establishing other methods of reimbursement of the costs of benefits in kind provided under this Regulation by both countries with effect from 1 May 2004.

IRELAND — FRANCE

The Exchange of Letters of 30 July 1980 and 26 September 1980 concerning Articles 36(3) and 63(3) of Regulation (EEC) No 1408/71 (reciprocal waiving of reimbursement of the costs of benefits in kind) and Article 105(2) of Regulation (EEC) No 574/72 (reciprocal waiving of reimbursement of the costs of administrative checks and medical examinations).

IRELAND — LUXEMBOURG

The Exchange of Letters of 26 September 1975 and 5 August 1976 concerning Articles 36(3) and 63(3) of Regulation (EEC) No 1408/71 and Article 105(2) of Regulation (EEC) No 574/72 (waiving of reimbursement of the costs of benefits in kind provided pursuant to Chapter 1 or 4 of Title III of Regulation (EEC) No 1408/71, and of the costs of administrative checks and medical examinations referred to in Article 105 of Regulation (EEC) No 574/72).

IRELAND — NETHERLANDS

The Exchange of Letters of 22 April and 27 July 1987 concerning Article 70(3) of Regulation (EEC) No 1408/71 (waiving of costs of reimbursement in respect of benefits awarded in application of Article 69 of Regulation (EEC) No 1408/71) and Article 105(2) of Regulation (EEC) No 574/72 (waiving of the reimbursement of the costs of administrative checks and medical examinations referred to in Article 105 of Regulation (EEC) No 574/72).

IRELAND — SWEDEN

The Agreement of 8 November 2000 on the waiving of reimbursement of the costs of benefits in kind of sickness, maternity, accidents at work and occupational diseases, and the costs of administrative and medical controls

IRELAND — UNITED KINGDOM

The Exchange of Letters of 9 July 1975 regarding Articles 36(3) and 63(3) of Regulation (EEC) No 1408/71 (arrangement for reimbursement or waiving of reimbursement of the costs of benefits in kind provided under the terms of Chapter 1 or 4 of Title III of Regulation (EEC) No 1408/71) and Article 105(2) of Regulation (EEC) No 574/72 (waiving of reimbursement of the costs of administrative checks and medical examinations).

GREECE — NETHERLANDS

[3 . . .]

SPAIN — FRANCE

The Agreement of 17 May 2005 establishing the specific arrangements for the management and settlement of reciprocal claims in respect of health care benefits pursuant to Regulations (EEC) No 1408/71 and (EEC) No 574/72

SPAIN — ITALY

The Agreement on a new procedure for the improvement and simplification of reimbursements of costs for health care of21 November 1997 concerning Article 36(3) of Regulation (EEC) No 1408/71 (reimbursement of sickness and maternity benefits in kind) and Articles 93, 94, 95, 100 and 102(5) of Regulation (EEC) No 574/72 (procedures for the refund and sickness and maternity insurance benefits and late claims).

SPAIN — NETHERLANDS

[3 . . .]

SPAIN — PORTUGAL

(a) [3 . . .]
(b) The Agreement of 2 October 2002 laying down detailed arrangements for the management and settlement of reciprocal claims for health care with a view to facilitating and accelerating the settlement of these claims

SPAIN — SWEDEN

The Agreement of 1 December 2004 on the reimbursement of the costs of benefits in kind provided under Regulations (EEC) No 1408/71 and (EEC) No 574/72

SPAIN — UNITED KINGDOM

The Agreement of 18 June 1999 on the reimbursement of costs for benefits in kind granted pursuant to the provisions of Regulations (EEC) No 1408/71 and (EEC) No 574/72.

FRANCE — ITALY

(a) The Exchange of Letters of 14 May and 2 August 1991 concerning the terms for settling reciprocal claims under Article 93 of Regulation (EEC) No 574/72
(b) The supplementary Exchange of Letters of 22 March and 15 April 1994 concerning the procedures for the settlement of reciprocal debts under the terms of Articles 93, 94, 95 and 96 of Regulation (EEC) No 574/72
(c) The Exchange of Letters of 2 April 1997 and 20 October 1998 modifying the Exchange of Letters mentioned under points (a) and (b) concerning the procedures for the settlement of reciprocal debts under the terms of Articles 93, 94, 95 and 96 of Regulation (EEC) No 574/72
(d) The Agreement of 28 June 2000 waiving reimbursement of the costs referred to in Article 105(1) of Regulation (EEC) No 574/72 for administrative checks and medical examinations requested under Article 51 of the abovementioned Regulation

FRANCE — LUXEMBOURG

(a) [2 . . .]
(b) [2 . . .]
[3 (a) The Agreement of 2 July 1976 on the waiving of reimbursement of the costs of administrative checks and medical examinations provided for in Article 105(2) of Council Regulation (EEC) No 574/72 of 21 March 1972
[4 (b) The Exchange of Letters of 17 July and 20 September 1995 concerning the terms for settling reciprocal claims under Articles 93, 95 and 96 of Regulation (EECV) 574/72 and the Exchange of Letters dated 10 July and 30 August 2013.]]

FRANCE — NETHERLANDS

[3 The Agreement of 28 April 1997 on the waiving of reimbursement of the costs of administrative checks and medical examinations pursuant to Article 105 of Regulation (EEC) No 574/72.]
(b) [3 . . .]
(c) [3 . . .]

FRANCE — PORTUGAL

The Agreement of 28 April 1999 laying down special detailed rules governing the administration and settlement of reciprocal claims for medical treatment pursuant to Regulations (EEC) No 1408/71 and EEC No 574/72.

FRANCE — UNITED KINGDOM

(a) The Exchange of Letters of 25 March and 28 April 1997 regarding Article 105(2) of Regulation (EEC) No 574/72 (waiving of reimbursement of the costs of administrative checks and medical examinations)
(b) The Agreement of 8 December 1998 on the specific methods of determining the amounts to be reimbursed for benefits in kind pursuant to Regulations (EEC) No 1408/71 and (EEC) No 574/72

ITALY — LUXEMBOURG

Article 4(5) and (6) of the Administrative Arrangement of 19 January 1955 on the implementing provisions of the General Convention on Social Security (sickness insurance for agricultural workers).

ITALY — NETHERLANDS

[3 . . .]

ITALY — UNITED KINGDOM

The Arrangement signed on 15 December 2005 between the Competent Authorities of the Italian Republic and of the United Kingdom under Articles 36(3) and 63(3) of Regulation (EEC) No 1408/71 establishing other methods of reimbursement of the costs of benefits in kind provided under this Regulation by both countries with effect from 1 January 2005.

LUXEMBOURG — NETHERLANDS

The Agreement of 1 November 1976 on the waiving of reimbursement of the costs of administrative checks and medical examinations adopted pursuant to Article 105(2) of Regulation (EEC) No 574/72.

LUXEMBOURG — SWEDEN

The Arrangement of 27 November 1996 on the reimbursement of expenditure in the field of social security

LUXEMBOURG — UNITED KINGDOM

The Exchange of Letters of 18 December 1975 and 20 January 1976 regarding Article 105(2) of Regulation (EEC) No 574/72 (waiving of reimbursement of the costs entailed in administrative checks and medical examinations referred to in Article 105 of Regulation (EEC) No 574/72).

HUNGARY — UNITED KINGDOM

The Arrangement finalised on 1 November 2005 between the Competent Authorities of the Republic of Hungary and of the United Kingdom under Articles 35(3) and 41(2) of Regulation (EEC) No 883/2004 establishing other methods of reimbursement of the costs of benefits in kind provided under that Regulation by both countries with effect from 1 May 2004.

MALTA — UNITED KINGDOM

The Arrangement finalised on 17 January 2007 between the Competent Authorities of Malta and of the United Kingdom under Articles 35(3) and 41(2) of Regulation (EEC) No 883/2004 establishing other methods of reimbursement of the costs of benefits in kind provided under that Regulation by both countries with effect from 1 May 2004.

NETHERLANDS — PORTUGAL

[1 . . .]

NETHERLANDS — UNITED KINGDOM

[3 The second sentence of Article 3 of the Administrative Arrangement of 12 June 1956 on the implementation of the Convention of 11 August 1954.]

(b) [3 . . .]

PORTUGAL — UNITED KINGDOM

The Arrangement of 8 June 2004 establishing other methods of reimbursement of the costs of benefits in kind provided by both countries with effect from 1 January 2003.

FINLAND — SWEDEN

Article 15 of the Nordic Convention on Social Security of 18 August 2003: Agreement on the reciprocal waiver of refund pursuant to Articles 36, 63 and 70 of Regulation (EEC) No 1408/71 (cost of benefits in kind in respect of sickness and maternity, accidents at work and occupational diseases, and unemployment benefits) and Article 105 of Regulation (EEC) No 574/72 (costs of administrative checks and medical examinations).

FINLAND — UNITED KINGDOM

The Exchange of Letters 1 and 20 June 1995 concerning Articles 36(3) and 63(3) of Regulation (EEC) No 1408/71 (reimbursement or waiving of reimbursement of the cost of benefits in kind) and Article 105(2) of Regulation (EEC) 574/72 (waiving of reimbursement of the cost of administrative checks and medical examinations).

SWEDEN — UNITED KINGDOM

The Arrangement of 15 April 1997 concerning Article 36(3) and Article 63(3) of Regulation (EEC) No 1408/71 (reimbursement or waiving of reimbursement of the cost of benefits in kind) and Article 105(2) of Regulation (EEC) No 574/72 (waiving of refunds of the costs of administrative checks and medical examinations).

AMENDMENTS

1. Regulation 1244/2010 [2010] OJ L338/35 art.2(1) (January 11, 2011).
2. Regulation 1224/2012 art.2 (January 8, 2013).
3. Regulation 1372/2013 art.2 (January 1, 2014).
4. Regulation1368/2014 art.1 (January 1, 2015).

Annex 2

Special Schemes for Civil Servants

(referred to in [1 Articles 32(2) and 41(1)] of the implementing Regulation)

A. Special schemes for civil servants which are not covered by Title III, Chapter 1 of Regulation (EC) No 883/2004 concerning benefits in kind

Germany

Special sickness scheme for civil servants. 3.621

B. Special schemes for civil servants which are not covered by Title III, Chapter 1 of Regulation (EC) No 883/2004, with the exception of Article 19, paragraph 1 of Article 27 and Article 35, concerning benefits in kind

Spain

Special scheme of social security for civil servants. 3.622
Special scheme of social security for the armed forces.
Special scheme of social security for the court officials and administrative staff

C. Special schemes for civil servants which are not covered by Title III, Chapter 2 of Regulation (EC) No 883/2004 concerning benefits in kind.

Germany

Special accident scheme for civil servants 3.623

Amendment

1. Regulation 1244/2010 [2010] OJ L338/35 art.2(2) (January 11, 2011).

Annex 3

Member States Claiming the Reimbursement of the Cost of Benefits in Kind on the Basis of Fixed Amounts

(referred to in Article 63(1) of the implementing Regulation)

IRELAND 3.624

SPAIN

[1CYPRUS]

[1 . . .]

[1 . . .]

THE NETHERLANDS

PORTUGAL

FINLAND

SWEDEN

UNITED KINGDOM

AMENDMENT

1. Regulation 1224/2012 art.2 (January 8, 2013).

ANNEX 4

DETAILS OF THE DATABASE REFERRED TO IN ARTICLE 88(4) OF THE IMPLEMENTING REGULATION

1. Content of the database

3.625 An electronic directory (URL) of the bodies concerned shall indicate:

(a) the names of the bodies in the official language(s) of the Member State as well as in English

(b) the identification code and the EESSI electronic addressing

(c) their function in respect of the definitions in Article 1(m), (q) and (r) of the basic Regulation and Article 1(a) and (b) of the implementing Regulation

(d) their competence as regards the different risks, types of benefits, schemes and geographical coverage

(e) which part of the basic Regulation the bodies are applying

(f) the following contact details: postal address, telephone, telefax, e-mail address and the relevant URL address

(g) any other information necessary for the application of the basic Regulation or the implementing Regulation.

2. Administration of the database

3.626 (a) The electronic directory is hosted in EESSI at the level of the European Commission.

(b) Member States are responsible for collecting and checking the necessary information of bodies and for the timely submission to the European Commission of any entry or change of the entries falling under their responsibility.

3. Access

3.627 Information used for operational and administrative purposes is not accessible to the public.

4. Security

3.628 All modifications to the database (insert, update, delete) shall be logged. Prior to accessing the Directory for the purposes of modifying entries, users shall be identified and authenticated. Prior to any attempt of a modification of an entry, the user's authorisation to perform this action will be checked. Any unauthorised action shall be rejected and logged.

5. Language Regime

The general language regime of the database is English. The name of bodies and their contact details should also be inserted in the official language(s) of the Member State. **3.629**

Annex 5

Member States Determining, on a Reciprocal Basis, the Maximum Amount of Reimbursement Referred to in the Third Sentence of Article 65(6) of the Basic Regulation, on the Basis of the Average Amount of Unemployment Benefits Provided Under their Legislations in the Preceding Calendar Year

(referred to in Article 70 of the implementing Regulation)

BELGIUM **3.630**

CZECH REPUBLIC

[1 DENMARK]

GERMANY

[2 NETHERLANDS]

AUSTRIA

SLOVAKIA

FINLAND

Amendments

1. Regulation 1224/2012 art.2 (January 8, 2013).
2. Regulation 1372/2013 art.2(2) (January 1, 2014).

Council Regulation (EC) No 859/2003 of 14 May 2003 Extending the Provisions of Regulation (EEC) No 1408/71 and Regulation (EEC) No 574/72 to Nationals of Third Countries Who are not Already Covered by Those Provisions Solely on the Ground of Their Nationality

[2003] OJ L124/1

General Note

As the Preamble makes clear, there had, for some years, been concern that nationals of countries other than EEA countries and Switzerland ("participating countries") were at a disadvantage in that there was no provision for co-ordination of the social security rules of two or more participating countries for the benefit of third country nationals who had lawfully lived and worked in the European Union. **3.631**

This regulation seeks to ameliorate their circumstances by extending, with effect from June 1, 2003, the provisions of Reg.1408/71 to such third country nationals where they have had contact with two or more participating countries. Note that the regulation extends the provisions of Reg.1408/71 to such situations.

Regulation 1231/2010 of November 24, 2010, [2010] OJ L344/1, extends the provisions of Reg.883/2004 to nationals of third countries, but the United Kingdom is not participating in this new regime. For the United Kingdom, Reg.859/2003 will continue to govern such matters through the extension of the provisions of Reg.1408/71. Happily, it seems that Reg.859/2003 has not generated litigation before the Court of Justice, but the United Kingdom decision does mean that Regulation 1408/71 lives on beyond May 1, 2010 in relation to third country nationals.

For comment on the external dimension of social security-co-ordination, see *Communication from the Commission to the European Parliament, the Council, the European Economic and Social Committee and the Committee of the Regions. The External Dimension of EU Social Security Coordination*, COM(2012) 153 final, March 30, 2012.

The Council of the European Union

3.632 Having regard to the Treaty establishing the European Community and in particular Article 63, point 4 thereof,

Having regard to the proposal from the Commission,[1]

Having regard to the opinion of the European Parliament,[2]

Whereas:

1. As its special meeting in Tampere on 15 and 16 October 1999, the European Council proclaimed that the European Union should ensure fair treatment of third-country nationals who reside legally in the territory of its Member States, grant them rights and obligations comparable to those of EU citizens, enhance non-discrimination in economic, social and cultural life and approximate their legal status to that of Member States' nationals.

2. In its resolution of 27 October 1999,[3] the European Parliament called for prompt action on promises of fair treatment for third-country nationals legally resident in the Member States and on the definition of their legal status, including uniform rights as close as possible to those enjoyed by the citizens of the European Union.

3. The European Economic and Social Committee has also appealed for equal treatment of Community nationals and third-country nationals in the social field, notably in its opinion of 26 September 1991 on the status of migrant workers from third countries.[4]

4. Article 6(2) of the Treaty on European Union provides that the Union shall respect fundamental rights, as guaranteed by the European Convention on the Protection of Human Rights and Fundamental Freedoms signed in Rome on 4 November 1950 and as they result from the constitutional traditions common to the Member States, as general principles of Community law.

5. This Regulation respects the fundamental rights and observes the principles recognised in particular by the Charter of Fundamental Rights of the European Union, in particular the spirit of its Article 34(2).

6. The promotion of a high level of social protection and the raising of the standard of living and quality of life in the Member States are objectives of the Community.

7. As regards the conditions of social protection of third-country nationals, and in particular the social security scheme applicable to them, the Employment and Social Policy Council argued in its conclusions of 3

December 2001 that the coordination applicable to third-country nationals should grant them a set of uniform rights as near as possible to those enjoyed by EU citizens.

8. Currently, Council Regulation (EEC) No 1408/71 of 14 June 1971 on the application of social security schemes to employed persons and their families moving within the Community,[5] which is the basis for the coordination of the social security schemes of the different Member States, and Council Regulation (EEC) No 574/72 of 21 March 1972, laying down the procedure for implementing Regulation (EEC) No 1408/71,[6] apply only to certain third-country nationals. The number and diversity of legal instruments used in an effort to resolve problems in connection with the coordination of the Member States' social security schemes encountered by nationals of third countries who are in the same situation as Community nationals give rise to legal and administrative complexities. They create major difficulties for the individuals concerned, their employers, and the competent national social security bodies.

9. Hence, it is necessary to provide for the application of the coordination rules of Regulation (EEC) No 1408/71 and Regulation (EEC) No 574/72 to third-country nationals legally resident in the Community who are not currently covered by the provisions of these Regulations on grounds of their nationality and who satisfy the other conditions provided for in this Regulation; such an extension is in particular important with a view to the forthcoming enlargement of the European Union.

10. The application of Regulation (EEC) No 1408/71 and Regulation (EEC) No 574/72 to these persons does not give them any entitlement to enter, to stay or to reside in a Member State or to have access to its labour market.

11. The provisions of Regulation (EEC) No 1408/71 and Regulation (EEC) No 574/72 are, by virtue of this Regulation, applicable only in so far as the person concerned is already legally resident in the territory of a Member State. Being legally resident is therefore a prerequisite for the application of these provisions.

12. The provisions of Regulation (EEC) No 1408/71 and Regulation (EEC) No 574/72 are not applicable in a situation which is confined in all respects within a single Member State. This concerns, inter alia, the situation of a third country national who has links only with a third country and a single Member State.

13. The continued right to unemployment benefit, as laid down in Article 69 of Regulation (EEC) No 1408/71, is subject to the condition of registering as a job-seeker with the employment services of each Member State entered. Those provisions may therefore apply to a third-country national only provided he/she has the right, where appropriate pursuant to his/her residence permit, to register as a job-seeker with the employment services of the Member State entered and the right to work there legally.

14. Transitional provisions should be adopted to protect the persons covered by this Regulation and to ensure that they do not lose rights as a result of its entry into force.

15. To achieve these objectives it is necessary and appropriate to extend the scope of the rules coordinating the national social security schemes by adopting a Community legal instrument which is binding and directly applicable in every Member State which takes part in the adoption of this Regulation.

16. This Regulation is without prejudice to rights and obligations arising from international agreements with third countries to which the Community is a party and which afford advantages in terms of social security.

17. Since the objectives of the proposed action cannot be sufficiently achieved by the Member States and can therefore, by reason of the scale or effects of the proposed action, be better achieved at Community level, the Community may take measures in accordance with the principle of subsidiarity enshrined in Article 5 of the Treaty. In compliance with the principle of proportionality as set out in that Article, this Regulation does not go beyond what is necessary to achieve these objectives.

18. In accordance with Article 3 of the Protocol on the position of the United Kingdom and Ireland annexed to the Treaty on the European Union and to the Treaty establishing the European Community, Ireland and the United Kingdom gave notice, by letters of 19 and 23 April 2002, of their wish to take part in the adoption and application of this Regulation.

19. In accordance with Articles 1 and 2 of the Protocol on the position of Denmark annexed to the Treaty on the European Union and to the Treaty establishing the European Community, Denmark is not taking part in the adoption of this Regulation and is not therefore bound by or subject to it,

FOOTNOTES

1. OJ C 126 E, 28.5.2002, p.388.
2. Opinion of 21 November 2002.
3. OJ C 154, 5.6.2000, p.63.
4. OJ C 339, 231.12.1991, p.82.
5. OJ L 149, 5.7.1971, p.2; Regulation last amended by Regulation (EC) No 1386/2001 of the European parliament and of the Council (OJ L187, 10.7.2001, p.1).
6. OJ L 74, 27.3.1972, p.1; Regulation last amended by Commission Regulation (EC) No 410/2002 (OJ L 62, 5.3.2002, p.17).

Has Adopted this Regulation

Article 1

3.633 Subject to the provisions of the Annex to this Regulation, the provisions of Regulation (EEC) No 1408/71 and Regulation (EEC) No 574/72 shall apply to nationals of third countries who are not already covered by those provisions solely on the ground of their nationality, as well as to members of their families and to their survivors, provided they are legally resident in the territory of a Member State and are in a situation which is not confined in all respects within a single Member State.

GENERAL NOTE

3.634 This short article enfranchises third country nationals into the scheme for the co-ordination of social security found in the two principal regulations where they are not already within that scheme. Some third country nationals are already covered by the rules in Reg.1408/71, namely, stateless persons, refugees and members of families and survivors of Community nationals in the circumstances set out in Reg.1408/71.

The condition for third country nationals is that they are "lawfully resident" in the territory of a Member State. This phrase is not defined, but will have to be applied by national authorities in accordance with their immigration laws. The most likely way forward will be that Member States will regard as lawfully resident all those whose immigration status is compliant with national requirements. But see for discussion of the phrase in a different context, *Szoma v Secretary of State for Work and Pensions* [2005] UKHL 64, reported as *R(IS) 2/01*, in which the House of Lords ruled that, under UK social security regulations and in the context of asylum seekers, persons subject to immigration control are lawfully present in the United Kingdom.

Note too that the extension of Reg.1408/71 to third country nationals only relates to the co-ordination of schemes within the participating countries, and so has no application where the third country national has only had contact with the social security system of one Member State. So, for example, the regulation does not apply where an Australian national is living and working in the UK, and has had no contact with the social security system of any other Member State.

Article 2

1. This Regulation shall not create any rights in respect of the period before 1 June 2003. **3.635**

2. Any period of insurance and, where appropriate, any period of employment, self-employment or residence completed under the legislation of a Member State before 1 June 2003 shall be taken into account for the determination of rights acquired in accordance with the provisions of this Regulation.

3. Subject to the provisions of paragraph 1, a right shall be acquired under this Regulation even if it relates to a contingency arising prior to 1 June 2003.

4. Any benefit that has not been awarded or that has been suspended on account of the nationality or the residence of the person concerned shall, at the latter's request, be awarded or resumed from 1 June 2003, provided that the rights for which benefits were previously awarded did not give rise to a lump-sum payment.

5. The rights of persons who prior to 1 June 2003, obtained the award of a pension may be reviewed at their request, account being taken of the provisions of this Regulation.

6. If the request referred to in paragraph 4 or paragraph 5 is lodged within two years from 1 June 2003, rights deriving from this Regulation shall be acquired from that date and the provisions of the legislation of any Member State on the forfeiture or lapse of rights may not be applied to the persons concerned.

7. If the request referred to in paragraph 4 or paragraph 5 is lodged after expiry of the deadline referred to in paragraph 6, rights not forfeited or lapsed shall be acquired from the date of such request, subject to any more favourable provisions of the legislation of any Member State.

General Note

This article deals with the temporal effect of the extension of the system of co-ordination to third country nationals. Rights may not be acquired prior to June 1, 2003, but periods of insurance or residence before that date may be taken into account in determining entitlement to a right accruing after June 1, 2003. So, periods of contribution prior to June 1, 2003 may be taken into account in determining whether there is entitlement to a benefit payable with effect from June 1, 2003 or later. **3.636**

Article 3

3.637 This Regulation shall enter into force on the first day of the month following its publication in the Official Journal of the European Union.

This Regulation shall be binding in its entirety and directly applicable in the Member States in accordance with the Treaty establishing the European Community.

Done at Brussels, 14 May 2003.

ANNEX

SPECIAL PROVISIONS REFERRED TO IN ARTICLE 1

I. GERMANY

3.638 In the case of family benefits, this Regulation shall apply only to third-country nationals who are in possession of a residence permit meeting the definition in German law of the "Aufenthaltserlaubnis" or "Aufenthaltsberechtigung".

II. AUSTRIA

3.639 In the case of family benefits, this Regulation shall apply only to third-country nationals who fulfil the conditions laid down by Austrian legislation for permanent entitlement to family allowances.

Council Directive 79/7/EEC of December 19 1978 on the Progressive Implementation of the Principle of Equal Treatment for Men and Women in Matters of Social Security

[1979] OJ L6/24

THE COUNCIL OF THE EUROPEAN COMMUNITIES,

3.640 *Having regard* to the Treaty establishing the European Economic Community, and in particular Article 235 thereof,

Having regard to the proposal from the Commission,[1]

Having regard to the opinion of the European Parliament,[2]

Having regard to the opinion of the Economic and Social Committee,[3] whereas Article 1 (2) of Council Directive 76/207 of February 9 1976 on the implementation of the principle of equal treatment for men and women as regards access to employment, vocational training and promotion, and working conditions[4] provides that, with a view to ensuring the progressive implementation of the principle of equal treatment in matters of social security, the Council, acting on a proposal from the Commission, will adopt provisions defining its substance its scope and the arrangements for its application;

whereas the Treaty does not confer the specific powers required for this purpose;

whereas the principle of equal treatment in matters of social security should be implemented in the first place in the statutory schemes which provide protection against the risks of sickness, invalidity, old age, accidents at work, occupational diseases and unemployment, and in social assistance in so far as it is intended to supplement or replace the abovementioned schemes;

whereas the implementation of the principle of equal treatment in matters of social security does not prejudice the provisions relating to the protection of women on the ground of maternity;

whereas, in this respect, Member States may adopt specific provisions for women to remove existing instances of unequal treatment,

HAS ADOPTED THIS DIRECTIVE:

FOOTNOTES

1. [1977] O.J. C34/3.
2. [1977] O.J. C299/13.
3. [1977] O.J. C180/36.
4. [1976] O.J. L39/40.

GENERAL NOTE

The Union institutions recognised that moves to secure the principle of equal treatment for men and women would be incomplete without the inclusion of provisions dealing with social security. Directive 79/7 was made under art.235 EC, and was part of the programme of legislation flowing from the commitment to equal pay for equal work to be found in art.141 (ex art.119) EC, rather than part of the programme for securing the free movement of workers. **3.641**

Unfortunately a number of concepts in the directive have been interpreted slightly differently from what might be regarded as corresponding provisions of Reg.1408/71 now Reg.883/2004. Furthermore, the coverage of Dir.79/7 is not the same as that of Reg.1408/71 in terms of the benefits covered.

The Directive was required to be implemented in all the Member States from and including December 23, 1984.

Article 1

The purpose of this Directive is the progressive implementation, in the field of social security and other elements of social protection provided for in Article 3, of the principle of equal treatment for men and women in **3.642** matters of social security, hereinafter referred to as "the principle of equal treatment".

Article 2

3.643 This Directive shall apply to the working population—including self-employed persons, workers and self-employed persons whose activity is interrupted by illness, accident or involuntary unemployment and persons seeking employment—and to retired or invalided workers and selfemployed persons.

GENERAL NOTE

3.644 Those within the personal scope of this Directive are not the same as those who are within the personal scope of Regulation 883/2004. The Directive applies to the "working population". There is a link with employment (which includes selfemployment) related social security benefits in the Directive which makes it more limited than the concept of insured persons under Regulation 883/2004.

The Court of Justice has given a very wide meaning to the term "working population", holding that it covers any worker, including those who are seeking work: *Van Damme* (C-280/94) [1996] E.C.R. I-179. It extends to include someone who gives up work to care for a sick relative: *Drake v Chief Adjudication Officer* (150/85) [1986] E.C.R. 1995. But it does not include those who have never worked in a paid capacity: *Achterberg te Riele* (48/88, 106/88 and 107/88) [1989] E.C.R. 1963. Nor does it cover someone who gives up work to look after healthy children, since this is not one of the risks covered in art.3: *Johnson v Chief Adjudication Officer (Johnson I)* (C-31/90) [1991] E.C.R. 3723, reported as *R(S) 1/95*.

In *CG/5425/1995* the Commissioner held that the Directive did not apply to a woman who had last worked in 1949, and who claimed invalid care allowance to look after her mother in 1989. It is clear that there must be a causal link between giving up work and the incidence of one of the risks covered by art.3.

Article 3

3.645 1. This Directive shall apply to:

(a) statutory schemes which provide protection against the following risks:
- — sickness,
- — invalidity,
- — old age,
- — accidents at work and occupational diseases,
- — unemployment;

(b) social assistance, in so far as it is intended to supplement or replace the schemes referred to in (a).

2. This Directive shall not apply to the provisions concerning survivors' benefits nor to those concerning family benefits, except in the case of family benefits granted by way of increases of benefits due in respect of the risks referred to in paragraph 1(a).

3. With a view to ensuring implementation of the principle of equal treatment in occupational schemes, the Council, acting on a proposal from the Commission, will adopt provisions defining its substance, its scope and the arrangements for its application.

GENERAL NOTE

In *Drake v Chief Adjudication Officer* (150/85) [1986] E.C.R. 1995, the Court of Justice said that: 3.646

> "Article 3(1) must be interpreted as including any benefit which in a broad sense forms part of one of the statutory schemes referred to or a social assistance provision intended to supplement or replace such a scheme." (At [21]).

In *R. v Secretary of State for Social Security Ex p. Smithson* (C-243/90) [1992] E.C.R. I-467, the Court explained:

> "In order to fall within the scope of the Directive, the benefit must be directly and effectively linked to the protection against one of the risks specified in Article 3(1)." (At [14].)

In *Brachner* (C-123/10) Judgment of October 20, 2011, the Court of Justice ruled that an annual pension adjustment scheme operating in Austria fell within the material scope of the Directive, and was subject to the prohibition of discrimination between men and women in art.4(1) of the Directive.

R(A)2/94 holds that attendance allowance is an "invalidity benefit" within the meaning of art.10 of Reg.1408/71. It follows that it also falls within the scope of this directive, as will disability living allowance. The position is not changed by the categorisation of those benefits as special non-contributory benefits which are not exportable under Reg.1408/71. 3.647

The Court of Justice has ruled that income support constitutes social assistance: *Jackson and Cresswell v Chief Adjudication Officer* (C-63/91 and C-64/91) [1992] E.C.R. I-4737 (printed as appendix to *R(IS)10/91*). But discriminatory treatment may fall foul of Council Directive 76/207 on the implementation of the principle of equal treatment for men and women as regards access to employment, vocational training and promotion and working conditions, [1976] OJ L39/40. A similar view has been taken in relation to family credit (which subsequently became working families tax credit until that later benefit was abolished), see *Meyers v Adjudication Officer* (C-116/94) [1995] E.C.R. I-2131, reported as *R(FC)2/98*.

The classification of family credit (later working families' tax credit) proved to later be somewhat problematic. It was classified as a family benefit for the purposes of reg.1408/71: *Hughes v Chief Adjudication Officer* (C-78/91) [1992] E.C.R. I-4839. However, it could arguably be regarded as having provided protection against the risk of unemployment through its role in topping up low pay.

In *R. v Secretary of State for Health Ex p. Richardson* (C-137/94) [1995] E.C.R. I-3407, the Court ruled that free prescription charges fell within the material scope of the directive; it did not matter that these were regarded as a health benefit in the United Kingdom. In *R. v Secretary of State for Social Security Ex p. Taylor* (C-382/98) Judgment of December 16, 1999 [1999] E.C.R. I-8955, the Court ruled that winter fuel payments under the social fund were also within the material scope of the Directive. 3.648

In *Hockenjos v Secretary of State for Social Security*, Court of Appeal, May 2, 2001 [2001] EWCA Civ. 624, the Court of Appeal ruled that there is one statutory scheme for a jobseeker's allowance and that the benefit is one which provides protection against the risk of unemployment. Accordingly the benefit falls within the scope of art.3 of the Directive.

In *CPC/4177/2005*, the Commissioner decided that state pension credit is a benefit falling within the scope of Directive 79/7.

See also *R(P) 1/95* and *R(P) 1/96.*

Article 4

3.649 **1.** The principle of equal treatment means that there shall be no discrimination whatsoever on ground of sex either directly, or indirectly by reference in particular to marital or family status, in particular as concerns:

— the scope of the schemes and the conditions of access thereto,
— the obligation to contribute and the calculation of contributions,
— the calculation of benefits including increases due in respect of a spouse and for dependants and the conditions governing the duration and retention of entitlement to benefits.

2. The principle of equal treatment shall be without prejudice to the provisions relating to the protection of women on the grounds of maternity.

GENERAL NOTE

3.650 The Court of Justice has ruled that art.4 outlaws both direct and indirect forms of discrimination: *Teuling* (30/85) [1987] E.C.R. 2497, and *Molenbroek* (C-226/91) [1992] E.C.R. I-5943.

The test to be applied was laid down in *Commission v Belgium* (C-229/89) [1991] E.C.R. I-2205:

> "Article 4(1) of Directive 79/7 precludes less favourable treatment from being accorded to a social group when it is shown to be made up of a much greater number of persons of one or other sex, unless the provision in question is 'based on objectively justified factors unrelated to any discrimination on grounds of sex'." (At [13].)

In *Brachner* (C-123/10) Judgment of October 20, 2011, the Court of Justice ruled that art.4(1) would preclude a national scheme for the up-rating of pensions where statistical data showed that the method of calculating the increase leads to the exclusion from an exceptional pension increase of a significantly higher percentage of female pensioners than male pensioners. If a national court came to such a conclusion, art.4(1) would not permit that differentiation to be justified on the basis that women who have worked become entitled to a pension at an earlier age than men, or that they are likely to receive their pension over a longer period. In similar vein, a scheme which requires a proportionally greater contribution from part-time worker (the vast proportion of whom are women) than from full-time workers in order to qualify for a contributory retirement pension will be contrary to art.4: *Moreno* (C-385/11) Judgment of November 22, 2012.

3.651 Note that in *Blaik v Chief Adjudication Officer*, reported as *R(SB)6/91*, the Court of Appeal decided that a difference of treatment accorded to a man and a woman on the ground of differing marital or family status (in the context of supplementary benefit) was not indirect discrimination within art.4 and so did not breach Dir.79/7.

In *CIB/230/2000*, the Commissioner had to consider whether the provisions of regs 4 and 5 of the Overlapping Benefits Regulations resulted in discrimination prohibited by the Directive. The claimant had been in receipt of widow's pension since July 1995; she subsequently became entitled to incapacity benefit, but the adjudication officer decided that the benefit was not payable to her because it overlapped with widow's pension on the application of Regs 4 and 5 of the Overlapping Benefits Regulations. The claimant argued that there was discrimination contrary to Dir.79/7/EEC relying on *A M van Gemert-Derks v Bestuur van de Nieuwe Industriële Bedrijfsvereniging* (C-337/91) [1993] E.C.R. I-5435, which decided that, although survivors' benefits are outside the scope of the Directive, art.4 precludes a national rule which withdraws from widows who are unfit for work the benefits applicable to that risk on their being granted a widow's pension, if that withdrawal is not the result of a voluntary renunciation by the beneficiary and is not applicable to widowers who are entitled to benefits for incapacity to work.

The Secretary of State argued before the Commissioner that: (1) there was a difference between a withdrawal of benefit and an adjustment of the amount payable, and (2) it was essential that the withdrawl should involve a drop in income. The Commissioner rejected both those arguments. The Commissioner says that "what matters is the practical effect that the claimant was to receive nothing by way of incapacity benefit" (at [12]). On the second issue, the Commissioner notes,

> "The principle was stated clearly and unequivocally in [*van Gemert-Derks*] that there is discrimination whenever women are deprived of a right to claim a benefit which men continue to receive in the same situation." (At [13].)

Addressing the issue in the case, the Commissioner says,

> ". . . if I had to, I would conclude that in the present case regulation 4(5) of the Overlapping Benefits Regulations, as applied to incapacity benefit and women in receipt or claiming widow's pension discriminated against women for the purposes of Directive 79/7. However, since below I have concluded that there is nevertheless objective justification for that discrimination, so that Article 4(1) of the Directive is not breached, I do not have to reach a final decision on this point." (At [20].)

Addressing the issue of objective justification, the Commissioner concluded that reg.4(5) of the Overlapping Benefits Regulations served the aim of co-ordinating the social security system, which is unrelated to any discrimination based on sex. So the Commissioner concludes that, if there was prima facie discrimination on grounds of sex contrary to Dir.79/7 in the application of Reg.4(5) to the claimant, the discrimination was objectively justified (at [33]).

In *Secretary of State for Social Security v Walter* [2001] EWCA Civ 1913; [2002] 3.652
1 C.M.L.R. 27 (reported as *R(JSA)3/02*) the Court of Appeal held that there was no breach of Dir.79/7 in the context of a claim by a student, whose studies were in suspense, and who had claimed a jobseeker's allowance. She challenged the regulations as directly discriminatory against pregnant women.

A Tribunal of Commissioners in *R(JSA)4/03* has held that the rule in Reg.51(2)(c) of the Jobseeker's Allowance Regulations 1996 affects disproportionately more women than men and cannot be objectively justified. It is accordingly incompatible with art.4 of Dir.79/7 and has no effect. Regulation 51(2)(c) provides that the number of hours persons or their partners are engaged in remunerative work is to be determined by disregarding those periods in which they are not required to work where they work at a school or other educational establishment or some other place of employment and the cycle of work consists of one year but with school holidays or similar vacations during which they do not work.

In *CJSA/4890/1998* the Commissioner ruled that Reg.77(1), (2) and (3)(b) of the JSA Regulations on child additions and family premium discriminates unlawfully on grounds of sex. Statistical information had been presented to the Commissioner which showed that 92 per cent of men who shared the care of their children for at least 104 nights a year could not get child additions in income-based JSA because they did not receive child benefit as compared with 8 per cent of women sharing care who could not get the addition for that reason.

In *Hockenjos v Secretary of State for Social Security*, Judgment of December 21, 3.653
2004 [2004] EWCA Civ 1749, the Court of Appeal has allowed the claimant's appeal against the decision of the Commissioner in *CJSA/4890/2003* and dismissed the Department's cross appeal. It will be recalled that *Hockenjos v Secretary of State for Social Security* [2001] EWCA Civ 624 (and referred to in the annotations to art.3) was the decision of the Court of Appeal determining that jobseeker's allowance was a benefit falling within the material scope of the Directive. This decision

of the Court of Appeal deals with the substance of the claimant's claim to entitlement to additional amounts in respect of his children (the child premium) and to the family premium. Though he had shared care of the children, child benefit was paid to the children's mother which precluded payment of the additions to the claimant.

All three judges in the Court of Appeal reach the same conclusion by somewhat different lines of reasoning on the detail of the case. The Department conceded that the conditions of entitlement for child additions to a jobseeker's allowance, which linked these to entitlement to child benefit, were indirectly discriminatory, but argued that the discrimination could be objectively justified. The claimant was a man with shared care of his children following his separation from his wife. The Department argued that the link with entitlement to child benefit ensured consistency of decision-making. Scott Baker L.J., delivering the first judgment said:

> "45. According, in my judgment the position is this. The law is set out in the European Court's judgment in *Seymour-Smith*. The Secretary of State must first show that the discriminatory rule reflects a legitimate aim of social policy. Next he must show that the aim is unrelated to any discrimination based on sex and finally that he could reasonably consider that the means chosen are suitable for attaining that aim. Built into this final question is the balance between holding fast to the Community's fundamental principles on the one hand and the Member State's freedom to achieve its own social policy on the other."

Scott Baker L.J. concludes that Regs 77(1), (2), (3) and (5) are discriminatory contrary to art.4 of the Directive and have not been justified by the Secretary of State.

The question of the remedy to be applied once this conclusion was reached clearly troubled the Court of Appeal, and there was an ultimately fruitless excursion into the possible impact of the Apportionment Act 1870. The conclusion reached is that the proper remedy is for the whole allowance to be paid to the claimant in respect of each child, since both children met the test of being members of the claimant's household for whom he was responsible. This is because there is no provision in the jobseeker's allowance scheme permitting the splitting of the additions for children.

3.654 The alleged unlawful discrimination in *CIB/3933/2001* arose in the context of claims to for an increase of incapacity benefit for children. The parents were separated, but the children lived with their father for part of the week. He was refused an increase in his incapacity benefit for the children because he was not in receipt of child benefit for the children. He argued that the requirement that a person be in receipt of child benefit in order to be entitled to the increased constituted unlawful discrimination between men and women. The Commissioner accepted that men were more likely to be adversely affected by this requirement but that it was objectively justified on the grounds that, in most cases where parents are separated, it is mothers who undertake the greater proportion of the practical responsibility for caring for children of the family.

The alleged unlawful discrimination in *R(IB)5/04* arose in the context of the age requirements in relation to entitlement to an incapacity benefit. The claimant, a woman, became incapable of work when she was 64. If she had been a man, she would have paid contribution and would have been eligible to claim incapacity benefit at that age. The Commissioner felt bound by the decision in *Graham* to rule that the alleged discrimination was not unlawful under the provisions of the Directive. However, he stayed the case on the basis that proceeding might be brought to enable the claimant to pay contributions, but in the absence of such proceedings the appeal is to be treated as dismissed. The appeal was definitively dismissed on March 26, 2004 since the claimant had indicated that no such proceedings were to be brought.

Issues arising under the Gender Recognition Act 2004

In *MB v SSWP (RP)* [2013] UKUT 290 (AAC) the judge rules that the requirement in s.4 of the Gender Recognition Act 2004 not to be married in order to get a full gender recognition certificate does not breach the requirement of equal treatment in art.4 of the Directive.The Court of Appeal has, in *MB v SSWP* [2014] EWCA Civ 1112 dismissed the appeal against the decision in *MB v SSWP (RP)* [2013] UKUT 290 (AAC). The Supreme Court gave permission to appeal, and has referred the following question to the Court of Justice of the European Union [2016] UKSC 53: **3.655**

> "18. The question referred is whether Council Directive 79/7 EEC precludes the imposition in national law of a requirement that, in addition to satisfying the physical, social and psychological criteria for recognising a change of gender, a person who has changed gender must also be unmarried in order to qualify for a state retirement pension."

In *Richards v Secretary of State for Work and Pensions* (C-423/04), reported as *R(P) 1/07*, the Court of Justice has ruled that art.4(1) of the Directive precludes legislation which denies a person, who has undergone male-to-female gender reassignment, entitlement to a retirement pension on the ground that she has not reached the age of 65, when she would have been entitled to such a pension at the age of 60 had she been held to be a woman as a matter of national law. This is the response to the Commissioner's reference in *CP/0428/2004*. Following the receipt of the opinion of the Luxembourg court, the Commissioner issued a short decision under file as *CP/0428/2004* in terms consented to by the parties, awarding the appellant retirement pension from her 60th birthday and stating simply that this was in the light of the judgment of the Luxembourg Court and for the reasons given by that court on what was seen to be a determinative issue in respect of the claim under appeal. See now Departmental Guidance in Memo DMG 06/07.

On the application of the principle established in the *Richards* case to a case in which the claimant had not by the date of the decision under appeal undergone gender reassignment surgery, see *CP/3485/2003*.

CIB/2248/2006 concerned a claim to incapacity benefit by a female to male transsexual. The claimant, who was born on August 18,1942, and his gender at birth was registered as female. He began to live as a man from the age of 19, and underwent gender re-assignment surgery early in 2003. His assigned gender from that date was male, but his registered gender remained as female. The claimant reached the age of 60 in August 2002 (when his registered gender remained female). He had not option but to claim a retirement pension on the cessation of his entitlement to incapacity benefit on attaining the age of 60. On November 30, 2005 the claimant obtained a gender recognition certificate as a man. He was then 63. His entitlement to retirement pension ceased. He reclaimed incapacity benefit on December 2, 2005, but his claim was refused. The Commissioner first considered any issue arising under the European Convention on Human Rights, but could not conclude that it was possible to interpret s.30A of the Contributions and Benefits Act in such a way as to avoid the discrimination on grounds of sex which arose when art.8 was read together with art.14 of the European Convention. **3.656**

The Commissioner then turned to the application of Directive 79/7/EEC to the circumstances presented by the appellant. The Commissioner concludes that there is a breach of the equal treatment requirement in art.4:

> "37. Persons who are incapable of work and whose legal gender changes from female to male between the ages of 60 and 65 are entitled to incapacity benefit until the age of 60, then to a retirement pension until the change in their legal gender. Thereafter, depending on the time that has elapsed, they may be entitled to neither. That makes them unique in that the link between the loss of incapacity benefit and entitlement to a retirement pension is broken. And it is broken

solely because of the change in legal gender between those ages. The claimant has not been treated equally with persons in the other categories because his legal gender changed as a result of having acquired an assigned gender. Unlike the persons in every other category, he is deprived of the opportunity of ensuring a continuity between entitlement to incapacity benefit and a retirement pension. . . .

38. That effect is a direct result of the change in the claimant's legal gender and prohibited by the wording of Article 4(1). Alternatively, it is attributable to the acquisition of the claimant's acquisition of an assigned gender and is prohibited on the authority of *Richards.*"

But once again the Commissioner finds, for the same reasons as in relation to the European Convention, that interpretation is of no assistance. But a remedy can be provided by disapplying the national law to the extent necessary to remove the prohibited discriminatory treatment:

"43. The 2004 Act fails to comply with Article 4, because it deprives the claimant of the link between entitlement to incapacity benefit and a retirement pension. I can remove that discrimination by disapplying the legislation to the extent necessary in order to allow that link to be maintained in the circumstances of his case. For practical purposes, that result can be achieved by deciding the claim for incapacity benefit as if it was made the day that his entitlement previously ceased. The claimant must, of course, be incapable of work, but for other purposes the gap in entitlement is to be disregarded."

3.657 The key points decided by the Tribunal of Commissioners in *R(P)2/09, CSP/503/2007* and *R(P)1/09* (which issued separate decisions in each of the cases before them) were as follows. The Gender Recognition Act 2004 had not removed the possibility of a direct effect claim based on art.4 of the Directive on the grounds that equal treatment was absent when the position of a transsexual of the acquired gender was compared with that of a non-transsexual member of the acquired gender. Such claims could apply to periods both prior and subsequent to the entry into force of the Gender Recognition Act 2004. In *CSP/503/2007* and *CP/1425/2007* the applicants were entitled from the date of their applications to be given the automatic increase in the weekly rate under s.55 of the Contributions and Benefits Act appropriate to a woman whose pension had started later than its earliest possible date, for a deferment period measured from when the appellants could first have insisted on their pension under the Directive as a woman down to its actual start at the age of 65. In this regard, the Tribunal of Commissioners concluded that the special provisions in Sch.5 of the Gender Recognition Act 2004 are over-ridden as they fall short of the achievement of equal treatment of two comparable groups.

However, whether a person's change of gender is to be recognised for the purposes of the right to equal treatment under the Directive is to be determined by applying the substantive provisions of the Gender Recognition Act 2004 even as regards periods prior to the entry into force of the recognition machinery in the national legal order. *CP/3485/2003* is followed and approved. The Tribunal of Commissioners indicates its view (not strictly necessary for the cases before them) that this means that there is no right to a pension as a single woman while still married as a man to another.

Timbrell v SSWP, [2010] EWCA Civ 701, [2011] AACR 13, dealt with a claim for a retirement pension made by a male-to-female transsexual who claimed a retirement pension from the age of 60 in 2002 before the passing of the Gender Recognition Act 2004. At the time the appellant was married. She subsequently underwent gender re-assignment surgery, but remained married and continued to live with her spouse as a married couple. The Court of Appeal ruled that the appellant's case could not be considered "through spectacles that are coloured by the subsequent enactment of the GRA and the terms of its provisions": at [38].

The proper approach was to consider the application of Dir.79/7 in the light of the ruling in the *Richards* case. Aikens L.J. giving the judgment of the Court of Appeal says:

> "... the critical question is whether Directive 79/7, in particular Article 4, applies to a situation where, as was the case prior to the GRA, English law and legislation had no means at all of giving legal recognition toa change of gender of a person who had successfully undergone gender re-assignment for the purposes of obtaining a retirement pension. Was the UK bound to ensure that, with regard to those who acquired a different gender, there would be no discrimination whatsoever, either direct or indirect, on the ground of sex, with regard either to the scope of the Category A pension scheme or the conditions of access to that scheme?" (At [41].)

The answer to that question is clear; art.4(1) of the Directive precludes legislation which denies a person legal recognition of their acquired gender. There could not be a legal vacuum, nor was the matter one in which the appellant could simply seek damages for failure to implement the Directive fully in the sphere of pension entitlement. The precise form of the remedy would be a declaration to be agreed subsequently. But the outcome is clear, the appellant is entitled to claim a pension from the age of 60 notwithstanding her failure to comply with all the requirements subsequently set out in the Gender Recognition Act 2004.

For a case considering the position following the *Timbrell* judgment (and where the Gender Recognition Act 2004 did not apply), see *SP v SSWP (RP)* [2013] UKUT 156 (AAC). Unless there is an earlier claim which has been made but upon which no decision has been given (as in the *Timbrell* case), the only remedy is arrears on the basis of a deferred pension going back to April 27, 2006 (the date of the judgment of the Court of Justice in *Richards*).

Article 5

Member States shall take the measures necessary to ensure that any laws, regulations and administrative provisions contrary to the principle of equal treatment are abolished. **3.658**

Article 6

Member States shall introduce into their national legal systems such measures as art necessary to enable all persons who consider themselves wronged by failure to apply the principle of equal treatment to pursue their claims by judicial process, possibly after recourse to other competent authorities. **3.659**

General Note

In *R. v Secretary of State for Social Security Ex p. Sutton* (C-66/95) [1997] E.C.R. I-2163, the Court of Justice ruled that art.6 required a judicial process which would ensure that those who had been wronged by discrimination prohibited by the directive could get the benefit to which they were entitled, but went on to rule that "the payment of interest on arrears of benefits cannot be regarded as an essential component of the right as so defined." (At [25].) Contrast certain decisions under the European Convention on Human Rights which seem to assume that just **3.660** satisfaction under the Convention will require the payment of interest: see annotations to art.41 ECHR.

Article 7

3.661 **1.** This Directive shall be without prejudice to the right of Member States to exclude from its scope:

(a) the determination of pensionable age for the purposes of granting old-age and retirement pensions and the possible consequences thereof for other benefits;

(b) advantages in respect of old-age pension schemes granted to persons who have brought up children; the acquisition of benefit entitlements following periods of interruption of employment due to the bringing up of children;

(c) the granting of old-age or invalidity benefit entitlements by virtue of the derived entitlements of a wife;

(d) the granting of increases of long-term invalidity, old-age, accidents at work and occupational disease benefits for a dependent wife;

(e) the consequences of the exercise, before the adoption of this Directive, of a right of option not to acquire rights or incur obligations under a statutory scheme.

2. Member States shall periodically examine matters excluded under paragraph 1 in order to ascertain, in the light of social developments in the matter concerned, whether there is justification for maintaining the exclusions concerned.

General Note

3.662 Cases involving the Directive frequently raise issues of the scope of the derogations to be found in this article. The Court of Justice always takes the view that exceptions should be strictly construed, whereas freedoms are to be liberally construed.

Artide 7(1)(a)

3.663 In *R. v Secretary of State for Social Security Ex p. Equal Opportunities Commission* (C-9/91) [1992] E.C.R. I-4297, the Court of Justice ruled that art.7(1)(a) permitted a Member State which retained differential pensionable ages for men and women and in which pensions were funded from contributions to retain a system under which men continued to be contribute for five years longer than women in order to be entitled to the same basic pension and by requiring men who work until the age of 65 to pay contributions whereas a woman who chooses to work beyond the age of 60 is not required to continue to pay contributions. The difference in treatment must, however, be necessarily linked to the difference in the statutory pensionable age.

In *Thomas v Secretary of State for Social Security* (C-328/91) [1993] E.C.R. I-1247, reported as *R(G) 2/94*, the Court of Justice was called upon to rule on the nature of non-contributory invalidity benefits having regard to whether the different entitlement of men and women were such as to have "possible consequences . . ." for the purposes of prescribing different pensionable ages within the meaning of art.7(1)(a). The Court ruled that the situations envisaged by the words "possible consequences thereof for other benefits" were limited to the forms of discrimination which are necessarily and objectively linked to the difference in retirement age.

In *Secretary of State for Social Security v Graham* (C-92/94) [1995] E.C.R. I-2521, reported as *R(S)2/95*, concerned entitlement to invalidity benefit and the differential requirements applied to men and women. Rose Graham was 58 when she ceased work after several years in self-employment. As a person within five years of pensionable age who was not entitled to the invalidity allowance component of invalidity benefit; when she reached the age of 60 her entitlement to an invalidity pension was limited to the amount of her retirement pension (a condition which does not apply to a man until the age of 65), and her retirement was taxable whereas invalidity pension was tax-free. The claimant argued that the differential treatment was neither necessarily nor objectively linked to the difference in retirement age. The court's somewhat unsatisfactory reasoning holds that the differential treatment is within the exception having regard to the coherence of the social security system. It is estimated that there were almost 40,000 look-alike cases affected by the decision. Where there are appeals on the grounds of links between invalidity benefit or unemployment benefit (by analogy), they seem certain to fail.

By contrast in *R. v Secretary of State for Health Ex p. Richardson* (C-137/94) 3.664
[1995] E.C.R. I-3407, it was held that the discriminatory treatment of men and women in relation to the restriction of entitlement to free prescriptions to those over retirement age unlawfully discriminated against men, since there was no necessary or objective link to pensionable age in the case of this social benefit. See also *R. v Secretary of State for Social Security Ex p. Taylor* (C-382/98) Judgment of December 16, 1999, [1999] E.C.R. I-8955, in which the Court ruled that the different conditions of entitlement for man and women to winter fuel payments under the social fund could not be justified under the derogations in this article.

In *Haackert v Pensionsversicherungsanstalt der Angestellten* (C-303/02) Judgment of March 4, 2004, the Court of Justice ruled that the exception in art.7(1)(a) applied to early old-age pension schemes with different entitlement ages for men and women because of the close link with the age at which old-age pensions, which were not awarded early, would arise. In the circumstances of the case before the court, the early old-age pension operated as a substitute for the old-age pension.

In *CIB/13368/1996* the Commissioner ruled that the claimant (and all women whose entitlement to incapacity benefit derives from industrial injury or prescribed disease) are entitled to continue to receive the benefit after the age of 60 and before reaching the age of 65 since there is a breach of the principle of equal treatment in the United Kingdom regulations which does not fall within the exemption in art.7(1)(a) but this decision was set aside, by consent, in the Court of Appeal on June 20, 2000 in *Chief Adjudication Officer v Rowlands*, because it was accepted that, in the light of the decision of the Court of Justice in *Hepple v Adjudication Officer* (C-196/98) Judgment of May 23, 2000, [2000] E.C.R. I-3701, the Commissioner's decision could not be upheld. In *Hepple*, the Court of Justice ruled that, in relation to reduced earnings allowance, the age conditions were held to fall within the exception in art.7(1)(a) in order to preserve coherence between the rules on reduced earnings allowance and the rules on old age pensions. The Court said that discrimination of the kind at issue in the main proceedings is objectively and necessarily linked to the difference between the retirement age for men and that for women, to that it is covered by the derogation for which art.7(1)(a) of the Directive provides (para.34 of the judgment). A key issue in the case had been the permissibility of introducing age conditions which differ according to sex *after* the date for implementation of the Directive.

Artide 7(1)(c)

In *R(P) 1/96* the Commissioner held that the question of whether United 3.665
Kingdom contribution requirements breached the prohibition of discrimination in Dir.79/7 is a question of law and so was not be determined by the Secretary of State. The claimant, who had been married more than once, was arguing that the failure to take into account her first husband's contributions in determining her entitlement to a retirement pension constituted indirect discrimination against women. The Commissioner considered that such discrimination as there might bewas permitted by art.7(1)(c).

PART IV

HUMAN RIGHTS LAW

Human Rights Act 1998

(1998 c.42)

Arrangement of Sections

GENERAL NOTE

4.2 This Act has been described as "the first historic step . . . towards a constitutional Bill of Rights" (A. Lester, and D. Pannick (eds), *Human Rights Law and Practice* (Butterworths: London, 1999), para.1.44. It followed a Labour consultation paper of December 1996 entitled *Bringing Rights Home*, a manifesto commitment by the Labour Party in 1997, and an October 1997 White Paper entitled *Rights Brought Home: The Human Rights Bill*, Cmnd.3782.

The Act entered into force on October 2, 2000: The Human Rights Act 1998 (Commencement No.2) Order 2000 (SI 2000/1851). The commencement of each section is noted in the annotation to each section.

The UK has been a party to the European Convention on Human Rights since September 23, 1953 and has recognised the right of individual petition under the Convention continuously since January 14, 1966. Until this Act come into force, rights accruing for individuals under the Convention could not be invoked directly to determine whether they have been victims of a violation of the rights protected by the Convention. Individuals within the jurisdiction could only use the "ordinary" law of the land to secure their rights. If they believed that these have been denied them by the state or a part of the state, and they have sought redress under the national legal order (exhausted domestic remedies in the language of the Convention), they have been able to make an application to the Commission of Human Rights (prior to November 1, 1998) and direct to the Court of Human Rights (from November 1, 1998) claiming to be victims of a violation of one of the rights protected. If the application is admitted, then the Court of Human Rights may adjudicate on the issue. The Convention organs, which are part of the Council of Europe, are located in Strasbourg; they should not be confused with the institutions of the European Union. The Court of Justice of the European Union is located in Luxembourg.

Introduction

The Convention Rights

1.—(1) In this Act "the Convention rights" means the rights and fundamental freedoms set out in— 4.3

(a) Articles 2 to 12 and 14 of the Convention,
(b) Articles 1 to 3 of the First Protocol, and
[2 (c) Article 1 of the Thirteenth Protocol,]

as read with Articles 16 to 18 of the Convention.

(2) Those Articles are to have effect for the purposes of this Act subject to any designated derogation or reservation (as to which see sections 14 and 15).

(3) The Articles are set out in Schedule 1.

(4) The [1 Secretary of State] may by order make such amendments to this Act as he considers appropriate to reflect the effect, in relation to the United Kingdom, of a protocol.

(5) In subsection (4) "protocol" means a protocol to the Convention—

(a) which the United Kingdom has ratified; or
(b) which the United Kingdom has signed with a view to ratification.

(6) No amendment may be made by an order under subsection (4) so as to come into force before the protocol concerned is in force in relation to the United Kingdom.

COMMENCEMENT

October 2, 2000: the Human Rights Act 1998 (Commencement No.2) Order 2000 (SI 2000/1851).

AMENDMENTS

1. The Secretary of State for Constitutional Affairs Order 2003 (SI 2003/1887) (August 19, 2003).
2. Human Rights Act 1998 (Amendment) Order 2004 (SI 2004/1574) (June 22, 2004).

GENERAL NOTE

The Preamble to the Act describes its objective as to give "further effect" to the rights and freedoms guaranteed by the European Convention on Human Rights. The further effect given to the rights encompassed by the Act is their effect within the national legal order, so that they can be invoked directly in proceedings before United Kingdom courts and tribunals. This is the scheme of incorporation adopted for the United Kingdom. The late former President of the Court has expressed the advantages of incorporation as follows, 4.4

> "It has in fact two advantages: it provides the national court with the possibility of taking account of the Convention and the Strasbourg case-law to resolve the dispute before it, and at the same time it gives the European organs an opportunity to discover the views of the national courts regarding the interpretation of the Convention and its application to a specific set of circumstances. The dialogue

which thus develops between those who are called upon to apply the Convention on the domestic level and those who must do so on the European level is crucial for an effective protection of the rights guaranteed under the Convention." (Rolv Ryssdal, Speech at the ceremony for the 40th anniversary of the European Convention on Human Rights at Trieste, 18 December 1990, Council of Europe document Court (90) 318, 2.)

Convention rights are defined in subs.(1) as arts 2–12 and 14 of the Convention itself, together with certain articles of the First and Sixth Protocols as read with arts 16–18 of the Convention. These articles are set out in Sch.1. Their effect is subject to the terms of any derogation under art.15 of the Convention or any reservation filed by the UK Government. Derogations are governed in more detail by s.14, and reservations by s.15; any current derogations and reservations are set out in Sch.3. The Secretary of State is given power to amend the Act to give effect to rights contained in protocols to the Convention which have not yet been ratified by the UK. For example, the UK Government has indicated that consideration is being given to ratification of certain provisions of the Seventh Protocol, but not of the Fourth Protocol.

Convention rights as defined in s.1 do not include art.1 which provides that parties to the Convention "shall secure to everyone within their jurisdiction the rights and freedoms" set out in arts 2–18 of the Convention. Nor do they include art.13 which gives a right to an effective remedy in the following terms:

"Everyone whose rights and freedoms as set forth in this Convention are violated shall have an effective remedy before a national authority notwithstanding that the violation has been committed by persons acting in an official capacity."

The incorporation of art.1 among Convention rights named by the Act is probably not necessary since the purpose of the Act is to give effect to Convention rights within the national legal order. However, it should be noted that the rights given by the Convention are not linked in any way to the nationality of an individual; they are guaranteed to all within the UK's jurisdiction. This differs from many rights given by EU law where the beneficiaries are nationals of the Member States of the European Union.

4.5 The failure to include art.13 among the Convention rights may be more problematic, though the Lord Chancellor stoutly argued that its inclusion was not necessary because the Act gives effect "to Article 13 by establishing a scheme under which Convention rights can be raised before out domestic courts": HL Vol.583 col.475 (November 18, 1997). In the Commons, the Home Secretary made a similar point. There is apparently some concern that inclusion of the article might lead all manner of courts and tribunals to "invent" new remedies for violation of Convention rights. The Act is cautious on the issue of remedies where a violation is found: see commentary to s.8. However, both the Lord Chancellor and the Home Secretary conceded that in considering any question of remedies, courts or tribunals may have regard to the terms of art.13 under s.2 of the Act. However, situations may arise where the scheme of the Act arguably does not offer an effective remedy for the violation, though it should be noted that the nature and scope of the effectiveness of the remedy required under art.13 has hardly been touched on in the Strasbourg case law.

An example might help to illustrate the possible lacuna. Suppose a claimant before an appeal tribunal succeeds in persuading the tribunal that there has been an excessive delay in giving judgment on an appeal; This would constitute a violation of art.6(1) ECHR. In this type of case, the Court of Human Rights has often awarded some compensation for the delay, but an appeal tribunal has no power to award compensation, or interest on late benefit. This would leave the individual without a remedy unless the mere statement that there was a violation was considered sufficient in the circumstances of the case. Any claim for compensation would have to be the subject of separate (and wholly novel) proceedings in a different forum. It is at least arguable that making a person in this position go to two judicial bodies for a remedy for the same violation is a failure to provide an effective remedy.

Interpretation of Convention rights

2.—(1) A court or tribunal determining a question which has arisen in connection with a Convention right must take into account any— **4.6**

(a) judgment, decision, declaration or advisory opinion of the European Court of Human Rights,

(b) opinion of the Commission given in a report adopted under Article 31 of the Convention,

(c) decision of the Commission in connection with Article 26 or 27(2) of the Convention, or

(d) decision of the Committee of Ministers taken under Article 46 of the Convention,

whenever made or given, so far as, in the opinion of the court or tribunal, it is relevant to the proceedings in which that question has arisen.

(2) Evidence of any judgment, decision, declaration or opinion of which account may have to be taken under this section is to be given in proceedings before any court or tribunal in such manner as may be provided by rules.

(3) In this section "rules" means rules of court or, in the case of proceedings before a tribunal, rules made for the purposes of this section—

(a) by [[1] . . .] [[2] the Lord Chancellor or] the Secretary of State, in relation to any proceedings outside Scotland;

(b) by the Secretary of State, in relation to proceedings in Scotland; or

(c) by a Northern Ireland department, in relation to proceedings before a tribunal in Northern Ireland—

  (i) which deals with transferred matters; and

  (ii) for which no rules made under paragraph (a) are in force.

Commencement

October 2, 2000: The Human Rights Act 1998 (Commencement No.2) Order 2000 (SI 2000/1851).

Amendments

1. The Secretary of State for Constitutional Affairs Order 2003 (SI 2003/1887) (August 19, 2003).

2. The Transfer of Functions (Lord Chancellor and Secretary of State) Order 2005 (SI 2005/3429) (January 12, 2006).

General Note

Introduction

This section requires courts and tribunals to have regard to the Strasbourg case law, past, present and future, in deciding any question relating to a Convention right. Note that the Strasbourg case law is not binding. There are two reasons for this. First, it will not always be easy to transplant directly the point being made by the Strasbourg organ where the case involves the complexities of other legal systems. Secondly, the Convention sets a minimum standard; one possibly dramatic effect of incorporation is that the United Kingdom authorities will set a higher standard than the common European standard which is set by the Strasbourg organs. **4.7**

The section refers to dispositions of three Strasbourg organs: the Commission, the Court and the Committee of Ministers. In order to understand the reasons for this, both the old and the new Strasbourg systems must be understood.

The "old" system of protection

4.8 The Convention, in its original form, created two organs "to ensure the observance of the engagements undertaken by the High Contracting Parties": the European Commission of Human Rights and the European Court of Human Rights. The main function of these two organs, sometimes collectively referred to as the Strasbourg organs, (together with the Committee of Ministers discussed later) was to deal with applications made by states and by individuals alleging violations of the Convention. Under old art.24, any state party to the Convention could refer to the Commission any alleged breach of the provisions of the Convention by another State party. Under old art.25, the Commission could receive applications from any person, non-governmental organization, or group of individuals claiming to be the victim of a violation by one of the Member States of the rights set forth in the Convention and any relevant Protocols. The procedure differed depending on whether the application is made under art.24 or 25; what follows describes the process in relation to individual applications under art.25.

Once an application was registered, the Commission first considered, and issued a *decision* on, whether the application met the admissibility requirements. If it did not, that was an end of the matter. If the application was declared admissible, the Commission went on to conduct an investigation into the merits of the complaint and to consider whether there had been a violation of the Convention. The result was a *report* from the Commission expressing an *opinion* (which is not legally binding) as to whether or not there has been a violation. The report was communicated on a confidential basis to the applicant and to the state concerned and was delivered to the Committee of Ministers, the political organ of the Council of Europe. Throughout this time, attempts would have been made to secure a friendly settlement "on the basis of respect for human rights".

Final decisions on cases on which the Commission had reported and which had not resulted in a friendly settlement were made by the Committee of Ministers, or the Court of Human Rights. Recognition of the jurisdiction of the Court was technically voluntary under old art.46 of the Convention. Within three months of the transmission of the Commission report to the Committee of Ministers, the application could be referred to the Court for determination by the Commission, the defendant state, or the state whose national was alleged to be the victim. The applicant had no standing to refer the application to the Court, unless the defendant state was a party to Protocol 9. Where this was so, the applicant could refer the matter to the Court, but (unless it was also referred to the Court by the Commission or a state) it first had to be submitted to a panel of three judges, who could decide unanimously that the application should not be considered by the Court because it did not raise a serious question affecting the interpretation or application of the Convention.

4.9 If the case was referred to the Court and heard by it, there was a full judicial procedure, and even where Protocol 9 had not been ratified, some accommodations were made which allowed limited participation by the applicant. The Courts at in plenary session or in Chambers of nine. Decisions were made by a majority of the judges present and voting, with the President enjoying a casting vote if this was necessary. Separate opinions could be attached to the judgment of the majority.

Those cases which were not referred to the Court within three months of transmission of the Commission's report to the Committee of Ministers were automatically referred to the Committee of Ministers for final decision. The practice of the Committee of Ministers in recent years was simply to endorse the Commission report without any further investigation of the merits of the case.

The use of a political organ was a compromise to ensure that all applications resulted in a final determination. In the early years, there were states which had not recognised the competence of the Court, and there have always been cases which no one has referred to the Court.

The "new" system of protection

Protocol 11 has amended the Convention to make provision for a new wholly judicial system of determination of applications. The Commission and the Court have been replaced from November 1, 1998 by a new permanent Court, which handles both the admissibility and merits phases of application. The Court is also charged with seeking to secure friendly settlement of matters before it. **4.10**

Individual applications are made to the Court under art.34 and individuals have full standing before the Court. Complaints are initially considered by a three-judge committee which will consider whether the application meets the Convention's admissibility criteria, but it can only rule an application to be inadmissible if it is unanimous. These criteria have not changed and flow from the terms of arts 34 and 35 and involve the consideration of nine questions:

1. Can the applicant claim to be a victim?
2. Is the defendant State a party to the Convention?
3. Have domestic remedies been exhausted?
4. Is the application filed within the six-month time-limit?
5. Is the application signed?
6. Has the application been brought before?
7. Is the application compatible with the Convention?
8. Is the application manifestly ill-founded?
9. Is there an abuse of the right of petition?

Those cases which are not ruled inadmissible by the three judge committee are put before a seven judge chamber of the Court, which will include the judge sitting in respect of the defendant state. The chamber will consider the written arguments of the parties, investigate the material facts if these are in contention, and hear oral argument. This stage of the proceedings concludes with a decision whether the complaint is admissible and whether a friendly settlement is possible. There follows a consideration of the merits. In many cases, the admissibility and merits phases are now joined.

Certain cases of special difficulty may be relinquished by a chamber to a Grand Chamber of 17 judges: art.30. It is also possible for any party to a judgment of a chamber to request referral of the judgment to a Grand Chamber. In such cases, a panel of five judges of the Grand Chamber decides whether or not to accept the request. Many such requests are denied. In 2008, 295 such requests were made, of which 10 were accepted.

Protocol 14 enters into force

Protocol No.14 to the European Convention has, after many years of delay, been ratified by the Russian Federation, and the text of the Convention as amended by Protocol No.14 took effect from June 1, 2010. The text of the Convention as amended can be found on the Court's website. **4.11**

There are no changes to the Convention rights listed in the Schedule to the Human Rights Act 1998, but there are significant changes to the admissibility rules, to the way in which the Strasbourg Court works, and to the potential sanctions for failure by a respondent State to comply with a judgment of the Strasbourg Court.

Single judge formations of the Court will in future be able to declare an application inadmissible in clear cut cases where the application is wholly without merit: see changes to arts 26 and 27.

A new admissibility criterion is added to art.35, under which the Court shall declare an application inadmissible if it considers that: **4.12**

> "the applicant has not suffered a significant disadvantage, unless respect for human rights as defined in the Convention and the Protocols thereto requires an examination of the application on the merits and provided that no case may be rejected on this ground which has not been duly considered by a domestic tribunal."

There is no definition of "significant disadvantage", but there are three safeguards against this criterion being used inappropriately: (1) respect for human rights might nevertheless justify consideration of the application; (2) the application of Convention rights to the claim must have been considered before the national courts or tribunals; and (3) for two years from June 1, 2010 only Chambers and the Grand Chamber will be able to apply the criterion.

Three judge formations (committees) which currently have jurisdiction only in relation to questions of admissibility will be able to make judgments on the merits in clear-cut cases where the case-law on the interpretation of the Convention is well settled: amended art.28.

4.13 In relation to the execution of judgments, the Committee of Ministers may request an interpretation of a final judgment for the purpose of facilitating the supervision of its execution: amended art.46(3). Where the Committee of Ministers considers that a state is refusing to abide by a final judgment of the Court, it may refer to the Court the question whether that state has failed to fulfil its obligation under art.46(1). If the Court finds a violation of that obligation, it shall refer it back to the Committee of Ministers for consideration of the measures to be taken: amended art.46(4) and (5).

For more detail see the Report of the Joint Committee on Human Rights on *Protocol No.14 to the European Convention on Human Rights,* HLP 8 HC106 of December 8, 2004.

Which authorities are the most important?

4.14 Though the section requires courts and tribunals to have regard to authorities from all three Strasbourg organs, but there can be little doubt that the most important are the judgments of the Court of Human Rights.

Too great a reliance should not be placed on decisions on admissibility of any antiquity, since these have not always been fully reasoned and where the decision is to declare an application inadmissible are, by definition, not based on any comprehensive consideration of the merits. Furthermore the volume of such decisions has been such that the quality of the reasoning in admissibility decisions can be opaque. How much can be learned from a decision which outlines some facts as asserted in the application and then decides that the application is "manifestly ill-founded"? In many cases no observations had been sought from the respondent government.

Authorities on the interpretation of the concept of a "victim" of a violation of the Convention may be particularly persuasive, because of the drafting of s.7(7): see commentary to that section. The same view is taken of the concept of "just satisfaction" in s.8(3): see commentary to that section.

The relationship between Strasbourg judgments and national judgments

4.15 *Kay v Lambeth LBC, Leeds CC v Price* [2006] UKHL 10, [2006] 2 A.C. 465 provides guidance for courts and tribunals when faced with a judgment of the Court of Human Rights which conflicts with an earlier binding authority of a national court. Both Justice and Liberty were permitted to intervene in the case. The Court rejected the argument that a lower court could depart from what would otherwise be a binding precedent of a higher court where there was a later judgment of the Court of Human Rights which was clearly inconsistent with the judgment of the higher court. The effect of the House of Lords ruling is that the development of case law will be influenced by the judgments of the Court of Human Rights, but that legal certainty can only be maintained if conflicts between decisions of the Court of Human Rights and those of national courts are determined within the hierarchy of courts in the national legal order.

There are aftershocks of this decision in the social security context in the context of whether non-contributory benefits are "possessions" within art.1 of Protocol 1. So, for example, both *Couronne* and *CIS/1757/2006* (para.40) decide that they were bound to follow *Reynolds* and *Campbell R (H)1/05* in the Court of Appeal to the effect that non-contributory benefits are not possessions, notwithstanding the decision of the Grand Chamber to the contrary in *Stec*. It is understood that CPAG are concerned about this approach and have raised the matter with the Department for Work and Pensions. There is certain to be further case law on this point in the social security context. In such litigation it would be argued that the special circumstances of the post-Court of Appeal litigation in *Reynolds* would provide grounds for *not* following the general rule laid down in *Kay*.

In *R. (on the application of RJM) v Secretary of State for Work and Pensions,* [2008] UKHL 63, the House of Lords addressed the questions touched on in *Kay*. Lord Neuberger said:

> "64. Where the Court of Appeal considers that an earlier decision of this House, which would otherwise be binding on it, may be, or even is clearly, inconsistent with a subsequent decision of the ECtHR, then (absent wholly exceptional circumstances) the court should faithfully follow the decision of the House, and leave it to your Lordships to decide whether to modify or reverse its earlier decision. To hold otherwise would be to go against what Lord Bingham decided. As a matter of principle, it should be for this House, not for the Court of Appeal, to determine whether one of its earlier decisions has been overtaken by a decision of the ECtHR. As a matter of practice, as the recent decision of this House in *Animal Defenders* [2008] 2 WLR 781 shows, decisions of the ECtHR are not always followed as literally as some might expect. As to what would constitute exceptional circumstances, I cannot do better than to refer back to the exceptional features which Lord Bingham identified as justifying the Court of Appeal's approach in *East Berkshire* [2004] QB 558: see *Kay* [2006] 2 AC 465, para 45."

But the position in relation to the Court of Appeal's respect for its own previous decisions is different:

> "65. When it comes to its own previous decisions, I consider that different considerations apply. It is clear from what was said in *Young* [1944] KB 718 that the Court of Appeal is freer to depart from its earlier decisions than from those of this House: a decision of this House could not, I think, be held by the Court of Appeal to have been arrived at per incuriam. Further, more recent jurisprudence suggests that the concept of per incuriam in this context has been interpreted rather generously—see the discussion in the judgment of Lloyd L.J. in *Desnousse v Newham London Borough Council* [2006] EWCA Civ 547, [2006] QB 831, paras 71 to 75.
>
> 66. The principle promulgated in *Young* [1944] KB 718 was, of course, laid down at a time when there were no international courts whose decisions had the domestic force which decisions of the ECtHR now have, following the passing of the 1998 Act, and in particular section 2(1)(a). In my judgment, the law in areas such as that of precedent should be free to develop, albeit in a principled and cautious fashion, to take into account such changes. Accordingly, I would hold that, where it concludes that one of its previous decisions is inconsistent with a subsequent decision of the ECtHR, the Court of Appeal should be free (but not obliged) to depart from that decision."

Legislation

Interpretation of legislation

3.—(1) So far as it is possible to do so, primary legislation and subordinate legislation must be read and given effect in a way which is compatible with the Convention rights. 4.16

(2) This section—

(a) applies to primary legislation and subordinate legislation whenever enacted;

(b) does not affect the validity, continuing operation or enforcement of any incompatible primary legislation; and

(c) does not affect the validity, continuing operation or enforcement of any incompatible subordinate legislation if (disregarding any possibility of revocation) primary legislation prevents removal of the incompatibility.

COMMENCEMENT

October 2, 2000: The Human Rights Act 1998 (Commencement No.2) Order 2000 (SI 2000/1851).

GENERAL NOTE

4.17 There is a powerful new principle of statutory interpretation here: so far as it is *possible* to do so, primary and secondary legislation whenever enacted *must* be read in a way which is compatible with Convention rights whenever a question of Convention rights is in issue. The requirement applies to all users of the legislation; it does not apply solely to courts and tribunals, nor does it require that a public authority (see s.6) is a party to the issue raised.

The principle is clearly mandatory and strongly so. A judge writing in a journal has said that the section creates a rebuttable presumption in favour of an interpretation consistent with Convention rights: Lord Steyn, "Incorporation and Devolution—A Few Reflections on the Changing Scene" [1998] E.H.R.L.R. 153, 155.

However, where primary legislation cannot be read compatibly with Convention rights, then a court or tribunal does not have the power to strike down or ignore the incompatible primary legislation. Certain courts may, however, declare the legislation incompatible with Convention rights. This preserves the sovereignty of Parliament and is one of the clever features of the Act that have enabled it to fit into the constitutional traditions of the UK.

4.18 Where secondary legislation cannot be read compatibly with Convention rights, two possibilities will arise. First, if the incompatibility of the secondary legislation is required by the primary legislation under which it is made, then the status of the secondary legislation is the same as that of incompatible primary legislation. Its validity, continuing operation and enforcement are unaffected. But if the incompatibility is not required by the primary legislation, then it cannot be said to be within the powers of the primary legislation under which it is enacted, and any court or tribunal (and seemingly anyone called on to interpret that legislation) can disregard it: its validity, continuing operation and enforcement will be affected.

To some extent, this obligation to force an interpretation from a statutory provision is not entirely new, since European Union law requires legislation implementing the requirements of EU law to be read, so far as it is possible to do so, in a manner which achieves the objectives of the treaties: see the view taken in the House of Lords in *Webb v EMO Air Cargo (UK) Ltd* [1992] 2 All E.R. 929.

The application of the rule of interpretation in s.3 has now been the subject of comment in the highest courts of the United Kingdom.

4.19 The distinction between interpretation and legislation had been made by Lord Woolf C.J., in the Court of Appeal in *Poplar Housing and Regeneration Community Association Ltd v Donoghue* [2002] Q.B. 48,

> "It is difficult to overestimate the importance of section 3. It applies to legislation passed both before and after the Human Rights Act 1998 came into force. Subject to the section not requiring the court to go beyond what is possible, it is mandatory in its terms. . . . Now, when section 3 applies, the courts have to adjust

their traditional role in relation to interpretation so as to give effect to the direction contained in section 3. It is as though legislation which predates the Human Rights Act 1998 and conflicts with the Convention has to be treated as being subsequently amended to incorporate the language of section 3. . . . Section 3 does not entitle the court to *legislate* (its task is still one of *interpretation*, but interpretation in accordance with the direction contained in section 3. . . .

The most difficult task which courts face is distinguishing between legislation and interpretation. Here practical experience of seeking to apply section 3 will provide the best guide. However, if it is necessary in order to obtain compliance to radically alter the effect of the legislation this will be an indication that more than interpretation is involved."

In *R. v A (Complainant's Sexual History) (No. 2)* [2002] A.C. 45, the House of Lords has commented on the effect of the obligation in s.3 in the context of the interpretation of s.41 of the Youth Justice and Criminal Evidence Act 1999 in relation to the evidence which may be adduced in rape trials. Lord Steyn said,

". . . the interpretative obligation under section 3 is a strong one. It applies even if there is no ambiguity in the language in the sense of the language being capable of two different meanings. It is an emphatic adjuration by the legislature . . . Section 3 places a duty on the court to strive to find a possible interpretation compatible with Convention rights. Under ordinary methods of interpretation a court may depart from the language of the statute to avoid absurd consequences: section 3 goes much further. . . . Section 3 . . . requires a court to find an interpretation compatible with Convention rights if it is possible to do so. . . . In accordance with the will of Parliament as reflected in section 3 it will sometimes be necessary to adopt an interpretation which linguistically may appear strained. The techniques to be used will not only involve the reading down of express language in a statute but also the implication of provisions. A declaration of incompatibility is a measure of last resort. It must be avoided unless it is plainly impossible to do so."

Lord Hope of Craighead said,

"The rule of construction which section 3 lays down is quite unlike any previous rule of statutory interpretation. There is no need to identify an ambiguity or absurdity. Compatibility with Convention rights is the sole guiding principle. That is the paramount object which the rule seeks to achieve. But the rule is only a rule of interpretation. It does not entitle the judges to act as legislators."

The court also endorsed the distinction between interpretation and legislation identifed by Lord Woolf C.J. in the *Poplar Housing* case. 4.20

This point was also reiterated by the House of Lords in *Re S (FC); Re S and Re W* [2002] 2 All E.R. 192, where Lord Nicholls said,

"In applying section 3 courts must be ever mindful of this outer limit. The Human Rights Act reserves the amendment of primary legislation to Parliament. By this means the Act seeks to preserve parliamentary sovereignty. The Act maintains the constitutional boundary. Interpretation of statutes is a matter for the courts; the enactment of statutes, and the amendment of statutes, are matters for Parliament. . . . The area of real difficulty lies in identifying the limits of interpretation in a particular case. . . . For present purposes it is sufficient to say that a meaning which departs substantially from a fundamental feature of an Act of Parliament is likely to have crossed the boundary between interpretation and amendment. This is especially so where the departure has important practical repercussions which the court is not equipped to evaluate. In such a case the overall contextual setting may leave no scope for rendering the statutory provision Convention compliant by legitimate use of the process of interpretation."

In *Ghaidan v Godin-Mendoza*, [2004] UKHL 30, the House of Lords ruled that the policy reasons for giving a statutory tenancy to the survivor of a cohabiting heterosexual couple applied equally to the survivor of a cohabiting homosexual couple. In so holding, they interpreted paras.2 and 3 of Sch.1 to the Rent Act 1977 to secure compatibility with Convention rights. This avoided less favourable treatment of homosexual couples in the enjoyment of their Convention rights under art.8 ECHR which could not be objectively justified.

4.21 The case is important for its re-affirmation of the approach which should be adopted in reading and giving effect to primary and subordinate legislation in a way which is compatible with Convention rights. Significantly, the judges in the House of Lords did not attempt to write words into or delete words from the statutory provisions in issue, preferring simply to indicate what the substantive effect of those provisions should be (see opinion of Lord Nicholls at [35]). The task of interpretation under s.3 required courts, if necessary, to depart from the unambiguous meaning of a legislative provision in order to ensure respect for Convention rights. Lord Steyn said that declarations of incompatibility under s.4 were remedies of last resort, and that s.3 represents the principal remedial measure. Lord Steyn also indicated that there had been a tendency to concentrate too much on linguistic features of particular legislative provisions; what was required was a broad purposive approach concentrating on the Convention right in issue. Lord Rodger said,

> "123. Attaching decisive importance to the precise adjustments required to the language of any particular provision would reduce the exercise envisaged by s.3(1) to a game where the outcome would depend in part on the particular turn of phrase chosen by the draftsman and in part on the skill of the court in devising brief formulae to make the provision compatible with Convention rights. The statute book is the work of many different hands in different parliaments over hundreds of years and, even today, two different draftsmen might choose different language to express the same proposition. In enacting s.3(1), it cannot have been the intention of parliament to place those asserting their rights at the mercy of the linguistic choices of the individual who happened to draft the provision in question. What matters is not so much the particular phraseology chosen by the draftsman as the substance of the measure which Parliament has enacted in those words. Equally, it cannot have been the intention of Parliament to place a premium on the skill of those called on to think up a neat way round the draftsman's language. Parliament was not out to devise an entertaining parlour game for lawyers, but, so far as possible, to make legislation operate compatibly with Convention rights. This means concentrating on matters of substance, rather than on matters of mere language.
>
> 124. Sometimes it may be possible to isolate a particular phrase which causes the difficulty and to read in words that modify it so as to remove the incompatibility. Or else the court may read in words that qualify the provision as a whole. At other times the appropriate solution may be to read down the provision so that it falls to be given effect in a way that is compatible with the Convention rights in question. In other cases the easiest solution may be to put the offending part of the provision into different words which convey the meaning that will be compatible with those rights. The preferred technique will depend on the particular provision and also, in reality, on the person doing the interpreting. This does not matter since they are simply different means of achieving the same substantive result. However, precisely because s.3(1) is to be operated by many others besides the courts, and because it is concerned with interpreting and not with amending the offending provision, it respectfully seems to me that it would be going too far to insist that those using the section to interpret legislation should match the standards to be expected of a parliamentary draftsman amending the provision: *cf. R. v Lambert* [2002] 2 A.C. 545 at 585, para.80, *per* Lord Hope of Craighead. It is enough that the interpretation placed on the

provision should be clear, however it may be expressed and whatever the precise means adopted to achieve it."

The proper approach to the application of s.3 would appear in the light of all the authorities to involve a number of steps. First, it is necessary to identify the legislative provision which it is argued breaches Convention rights: see *R. v A (No.2)* [2002] A.C. 45. Then consideration should be given to whether that provision involves a breach of Convention rights: see *Poplar Housing and Regeneration Community Association Ltd v Donoghue* [2002] Q.B. 48. If there is, then a s.3 interpretation is needed and the focus here should be on compatibility with the Convention right. This can be achieved by reading in Convention rights, that is, by implying words in the legislative provision to secure compatibility with Convention rights; or by reading down, that is, by applying a narrower interpretation in order to secure compatibility. But it is not necessary to specify the precise rewording of the provision: see *Ghaidan v Godin-Mendoza* above.

The limits of interpretation are reached where the required construction conflicts with the express words of a legislative provision: see *R. (Anderson) v Secretary of State for the Home Department* [2003] 1 A.C. 837. The same conclusion will be reached if there is a conflict with the legislative provision by necessary implication. Finally, the limits of construction are reached when the construction placed on the provision alters the statutory scheme in a fundamental way.

In *R(G) 2/04*, the Commissioner, following the decision of the Court of Appeal in *R. (Hooper) v Secretary of State for Work and Pensions* [2003] 1 W.L.R 2623 in this respect—which was not in issue in the appeal to the House of Lords—decided that the words of the statute admitted of only one interpretation. The effect of this was to preclude a man from claiming widow's benefit in respect of a spouse who died before April 9, 2001. See annotations to art.14 ECHR for more detail on this line of cases.

Declaration of incompatibility

4.—(1) Subsection (2) applies in any proceedings in which a court determines whether a provision of primary legislation is compatible with a Convention right. 4.22

(2) If the court is satisfied that the provision is incompatible with a Convention right, it may make a declaration of that incompatibility.

(3) Subsection (4) applies in any proceedings in which a court determines whether a provision of subordinate legislation, made in the exercise of a power conferred by primary legislation, is compatible with a Convention right.

(4) If the court is satisfied—

(a) that the provision is incompatible with a Convention right, and

(b) that (disregarding any possibility of revocation) the primary legislation concerned prevents removal of the incompatibility,

it may make a declaration of that incompatibility.

(5) In this section "court" means—

[2 the Supreme Court;]

(b) the Judicial Committee of the Privy Council;

[3 Court Martial Appeal Court;]

(d) in Scotland, the High Court of Justiciary sitting otherwise than as a trial court or the Court of Session;

(e) in England and Wales or Northern Ireland, the High Court or the Court of Appeal.

[1 (f) the Court of Protection, in any matter being dealt with by the President of the Family Division, the [4 Chancellor of the High Court] or a puisne judge of the High Court.]

(6) A declaration under this section ("a declaration of incompatibility")—

(a) does not affect the validity, continuing operation or enforcement of the provision in respect of which it is given; and
(b) is not binding on the parties to the proceedings in which it is made.

COMMENCEMENT

October 2, 2000: The Human Rights Act 1998 (Commencement No.2) Order 2000 (SI 2000/1851).

AMENDMENTS

1. Mental Capacity Act 2005 Sch.6 para.43 (October 1, 2007).
2. Constitutional Reform Act 2005 Sch.9(1) para.66(2) (October 1, 2009).
3. Armed Forces Act 2006 Sch.16 para.156 (October 31, 2009).
4. Crime and Courts Act 2013 Sch.14(3) para.5(5) (October 1, 2013).

GENERAL NOTE

4.23 This section gives certain courts power to make declarations of incompatibility where primary or secondary legislation cannot be read compatibly with Convention rights. It is a discretionary power available to the higher courts only. It arises in any proceedings; there is again no requirement that one of the parties is a public authority. Neither First-tier tribunals nor the Upper Tribunal have the power to make declarations of incompatibility.

It is perhaps unfortunate that the only routes to declarations of incompatibility in the social security jurisdiction are appeal from the Upper Tribunal to the Court of Appeal, or taking judicial review proceedings in the High Court against a decision of a First-tier tribunal or the Upper Tribunal, assuming in the latter case that judicial review lies against the Upper Tribunal.

A judge of the Upper Tribunal has now given guidance on how either a First-tier Tribunal or the Upper Tribunal should proceed when faced with a case where the only possible remedy for a claimant would be a declaration of compatibility. *SH v SSWP (JSA)* [2011] UKUT 428 (AAC) concerned an appeal by a claimant who had been refused a jobseeker's allowance on the grounds that he did not meet the contribution conditions. He argued that there was discrimination contrary to art.14 ECHR as between those who were employed and paid Class 1 contributions and those who had formerly been self-employed whose Class 2 and 4 contributions did not count towards building an entitlement to a contribution-based jobseeker's allowance. The judge took the view that he was faced with a case where, were he to accept the contentions of the appellant, the only possible remedy available would be a declaration of incompatibility under s.4, which it was not within the competence of the Upper Tribunal to make. That was the position here, since the contribution conditions are set out in primary legislation in terms which are "far too clear to permit any other interpretation." (At [16].) In these circumstances, after reviewing the authorities, the judge provided guidance on how the Upper Tribunal (or indeed a First-tier Tribunal in the same situation) should proceed in the following terms:

"21. The extent to which it is appropriate for the Upper Tribunal, in a case where the only possible remedy would be a declaration of incompatibility, to enter into the merits of the claimant's contentions that legislation infringes the Convention must in my judgment depend on the circumstances of the particular case. In the present case full consideration of the justification argument is likely to require evidence from the Secretary of State. I see no point in my making directions for the filing of such evidence, with a view to my expressing an opinion on whether the alleged discrimination is justified, when (a) the Claimant may not be prepared to incur the risk of liability for costs which would be involved in appealing to the Court of Appeal, and (b) the Court of Appeal might hold that the claim fails in any event for want of a sufficient 'personal characteristic'. It does not seem to me that there is any point in my purporting to decide points which are arguable, when I would have no jurisdiction to grant any remedy. I therefore dismiss the appeal without further ado.

22. Nor would I presently be inclined to give permission to appeal to the Court of Appeal, were the Claimant to make an application for permission. It seems to me that it should be left for the Court of Appeal to decide whether it is appropriate for it to entertain the case, and what directions for the filing of evidence by the Secretary of State should be made. However, if the Claimant wishes to apply for permission, he should make the application, and I will formally consider and decide it."

Judge Wikeley has followed *SH v SSWP (JSA)* [2011] UKUT 428 (AAC) in *AB v SSWP (JSA)* [2013] UKUT 288 (AAC). He found that tribunal did not err in law when it found that the claimant could not succeed before it in an argument that the abatement rule under which occupational pension payments were taken into account in determining entitlement to contribution-based jobseeker's allowance constituted indirect discrimination which could not be justified. 4.24

The effect of a declaration of incompatibility is not to declare the legislation invalid, inoperative or unenforceable, and so does not give rise to any claim for damages for breach of the Human Rights Act: *Re K: A Child*, Court of Appeal, November 15, 2000 [2001] 2 All E.R. 719. The impeached provision will continue in full force and effect pending any amendment. The effect of a declaration of incompatibility is to put the Government on notice of the incompatibility. The Government may then choose to take the remedial action provided for in s.10 of and Sch.2 to the Act.

On July 10, 2003, the House of Lords ruled on the appeal in *Wilson v Secretary of State for Trade and Industry* [2003] UKHL 40. They reversed the decision of the Court of Appeal to make a declaration of incompatibility in respect of s.127 of the Consumer Credit Act 1974.

Wilson had borrowed £5,000 from First County Trust on the security of her BMW 318 convertible. The loan agreement added a £250 document fee to the £5,000 loan, thus mis-stating the amount of the loan as £5,250. In 1999 Wilson issued a claim in the county court, inter alia, for a declaration that the loan agreement was unenforceable because it did not contain all the prescribed terms. The county court ruled in the lender's favour, but this was reversed in the Court of Appeal, but adjourned to enable Convention rights arguments to be considered. The Secretary of State argued that the Court had no power to make a declaration of incompatibility because the agreement pre-dated October 2, 2000, the date the Human Rights Act 1998 entered into force. However, the Court said that the act which violated Convention rights was not the agreement but any order of the Court making the loan agreement unenforceable. They went on to make a declaration of incompatibility. 4.25

The House of Lords has ruled that the Human Rights Act 1998 is not to be applied retrospectively, and so there was no jurisdiction in the Court of Appeal to make the declaration of incompatibility. A statute concerned with Convention rights could not render acts unlawful which were lawful when they were undertaken, since this would impose retrospective liability.

Their Lordships did go on to consider whether the provisions of s.127 were compatible with Convention rights. The section imposed a mandatory sanction designed to ensure that lenders directed their minds to compliance with their obligations. It was a measure for the protection of the consumer, the weaker party in such transactions. This appeared to be in the view of the court not a violation of Convention rights in relation to the loans covered by the section (up to £25,000). In these circumstances there was no lack of proportionality in the sanction for failure to comply with the requirements of the legislation.

In *R(IS)12/04* the Commissioner concludes that a tribunal's lack of power to make a declaration of incompatibility is not a good reason for not dealing fully with human rights issues raised before tribunals. The Commissioner notes that in some circumstances, tribunals do have the power to declare subordinate legislation to have been invalidly made. The tribunal's reasons were found to be inadequate 4.26

because they had dismissed detailed human rights arguments on the basis that they could not make a declaration of inadmissibility under s.4.

In its admissibility decision of June 18, 2002 in *Hobbs v United Kingdom (App.63684/00)*, the Court of Human Rights ruled that a declaration of incompatibility is not an effective remedy within the meaning of art.35 of the Convention for the purpose of the rule requiring an applicant to exhaust domestic remedies. The Court rejected the Government's invitation to reconsider this position in its admissibility decision of March 16, 2004 in *Walker v United Kingdom (App.37212/02)*. The Court was strongly influenced by the fact that a declaration of incompatibility was not binding on the parties.

This view has been confirmed by the Grand Chamber of the Strasbourg Court in *Burden v United Kingdom* (App. 13378/05), judgment of April 28, 2008, at [40]–[44].

Right of Crown to intervene

4.27 **5.**—(1) Where a court is considering whether to make a declaration of incompatibility, the Crown is entitled to notice in accordance with rules of court.

(2) In any case to which subsection (1) applies—

(a) a Minister of the Crown (or a person nominated by him),
(b) a member of the Scottish Executive,
(c) a Northern Ireland Minister,
(d) a Northern Ireland department,

is entitled, on giving notice in accordance with rules of court, to be joined as a party to the proceedings.

(3) Notice under subsection (2) may be given at any time during the proceedings.

(4) A person who has been made a party to criminal proceedings (other than in Scotland) as the result of a notice under subsection (2) may, with leave, appeal to the [1 Supreme Court] against any declaration of incompatibility made in the proceedings.

(5) In subsection (4)—

"criminal proceedings" includes all proceedings before the [2 Courts-Martial Appeal Court]; and

"leave" means leave granted by the court making the declaration of incompatibility or by the [1 Supreme Court].

COMMENCEMENT

October 2, 2000: The Human Rights Act 1998 (Commencement No.2) Order 2000 (SI 2000/1851).

AMENDMENTS

1. Constitutional Reform Act 2005 Sch.9(1) para.66(3) (October 1, 2009).
2. Armed Forces Act 2006 Sch.16 para.156 (October 31, 2009).

Public authorities

Acts of public authorities

4.28 **6.**—(1) It is unlawful for a public authority to act in a way which is incompatible with a Convention right.

(2) Subsection (1) does not apply to an act if—

(a) as the result of one or more provisions of primary legislation, the authority could not have acted differently; or

(b) in the case of one or more provisions of, or made under, primary legislation which cannot be read or given effect in a way which is compatible with the Convention rights, the authority was acting so as to give effect to or enforce those provisions.

(3) In this section "public authority" includes—

(a) a court or tribunal, and

(b) any person certain of whose functions are functions of a public nature,

but does not include either House of Parliament or a person exercising functions in connection with proceedings in Parliament.

(4) [[1] . . .].

(5) In relation to a particular act, a person is not a public authority by virtue only of subsection (3)(b) if the nature of the act is private.

(6) "An act" includes a failure to act but does not include a failure to—

(a) introduce in, or lay before, Parliament a proposal for legislation; or

(b) make any primary legislation or remedial order.

COMMENCEMENT

October 2, 2000: The Human Rights Act 1998 (Commencement No.2) Order 2000 (SI 2000/1851).

AMENDMENT

1. Constitutional Reform Act 2005, Sch.18(5) para.1 (October 1, 2009).

GENERAL NOTE

The obligation in s.6(1) is at the heart of the scheme of incorporation in the Act. 4.29
It could be said that all the other provisions flow from the requirement that public authorities of any kind act compatibly with Convention rights. Note that there is a "defence" in s.6(2) where there was a statutory requirement to act in a particular manner. Here there will, of course, be an incompatibility between the statutory provision and Convention rights.

The key concept in the section is that of a public authority. This includes courts and tribunals, but not either House of Parliament, and is extended to "any person certain of whose functions are functions of a public nature" The difficult two words become very difficult 12 words. Only "certain" of the authority's functions need be of a public nature, and there is no liability in respect of the exercise of their functions of a private nature.

The question of what constitutes a public authority is reminiscent of the definitional problem of determining what are "emanations of the State" for the purposes of the horizontal application of EC Directives. The test is certainly not the same, but the same difficulties will arise in determining those institutions at the margins of State power which constitute public authorities. The definition will require judicial interpretation, but it is clearly a functional test.

There is, however, no doubt that the Department and all its constituent parts 4.30
constitute public authorities, as, of course, do the tribunals and other judicial bodies. All must act compatibly with Convention rights. This means that they must take up obvious Convention points even if they are not raised by the parties, since otherwise they would be acting unlawfully by acting in a manner which is not compatible with Convention rights.

In *Poplar Housing and Regeneration Community Association Ltd v Donoghue* [2002] Q.B. 48, the Court of Appeal provided some useful guidance on the definition of the notion of a public authority as defined in the section. The definition is to be given a generous interpretation. Hybrid bodies which exercised both public and private functions were public authorities only in relation to acts of a public nature and not acts of a private nature. But the fact that a public regulatory body supervised a body did not necessarily indicate that any act subject to supervision was an act of a public nature.

On the concept of "public authority" for the purposes of this Act, see also *Parochial Church Council of the Parish of Aston Cantlow and Wilmcote with Billesley, Warwickshire v Wallbank* [2004] 1 A.C. 546; [2003] UKHL 37; [2003] 3 W.L.R. 283; and *Hampshire CC v Beer t/a Hammer Trout Farm* [2003] EWCA Civ 1056; [2004] 1 W.L.R. 233.

4.31 In the *Aston Cantlow* case, Lord Nicholls said,

> "12. What, then, is the touchstone to be used in deciding whether a function is public for this purpose? Clearly there is no single test of universal application. There cannot be, given the diverse nature of governmental functions and the variety of means by which these functions are discharged today. Factors to be taken into account include the extent to which in carrying out the relevant function the body is publicly funded, or is exercising statutory powers, or is taking the place of central government or local authorities, or is providing a public service."

For a detailed consideration of the concept of "public authority" and the way in which the courts are approaching the determination of this issue, see generally *The Meaning of Public Authority under the Human Rights Act.* Seventh Report of the Joint Committee on Human Rights of Session 2003–04 HL Paper 39 HC 382, which can be found at *http://www.publications.parliament.uk/pa/jt2003/04/jtselect/jtrights/39/39.pdf.*

The Joint Committee expresses some concern about the way the courts are interpreting the concept, but commends the approach adopted by the House of Lords in the *Aston Cantlow* case.

The duty of courts to act compatibly and precedent

4.32 In *Leeds CC v Price* [2006] UKHL 10, the House of Lords ruled that in almost all cases where there is a conflict between authorities of the Court of Human Rights in Strasbourg and of a superior court in the United Kingdom, an inferior court or tribunal in the United Kingdom should follow the decision of the national court. That is a controversial proposition, but the rule may well not apply if the point at issue is not in dispute between the parties. So, for example, in *Esfandiari* [2006] EWCA Civ 282, reported as *R(IS) 11/06*, neither party contested the proposition that all benefits count as possessions following the decision of the Court of Human Rights in *Stec*, even though an earlier Court of Appeal decision has ruled that means-tested benefits cannot be treated as "possessions" for the purpose of art.1 of Protocol 1. This may simply be an illustration of the Court of Appeal not regarding the House of Lords ruling as applying to them, or, perhaps rather more likely, that there was recent and specific Strasbourg authority on the point. There is certainly authority that in such circumstances, any court or tribunal should not lightly depart from germane Strasbourg case law: see *Attorney General's reference No 4 of 2002* [2004] UKHL 43, at [33]; and *Anderson* [2002] UKHL 46, at [17]–[18].

See further annotations to s.2, para.4.09.

Section 6(2)

4.33 The proper interpretation of subs.(2) is discussed in the judgment of the House of Lords in *Hooper* [2005] UKHL 29: see [2]–[6], [41]–[52], [62]–[83], [91]–[96], and [101]–[126].

In July 2008, the House of Lords again considered this aspect of the Act in *Doherty v Birmingham CC* [2008] UKHL 57 in a case which concerned the obtaining of a possession order against a traveller under a procedure which it was argued would breach art.8 of the Convention (on which see *Connors v United Kingdom,* (App.66746/01) May 24 2004, (2005) 40 EHRR 9; and *McCann v United Kingdom,* (App.19009/04) May 13, 2008). In the course of their deliberations, the House gives detailed consideration to the circumstances in which a breach of the Act will be avoided because of the operation of s.6(2)(b). The position adopted in earlier cases was re-affirmed. The House confirmed that three distinct situations can arise under the provision. The first is where a decision to exercise or not to exercise a power that is given in primary legislation would inevitably give rise to a violation of Convention rights. The second is at the opposite end of the spectrum where no statutory provision concerns the exercise of discretion by a public body which acts in violation of Convention rights; such action will be unlawful under s.6(1) because s.6(2)(b) cannot apply. The third situation is said to lie in the middle:

> "This is where the act or omission takes place within the context of a scheme which primary legislation has laid down that gives general powers, such as powers of management, to a public authority. . . . The answer to the question whether or not s.6(2)(b) applies will depend on the extent to which the act or omission can be said to give effect to any of the provisions of the scheme that is to be found in the statutes." (At [39], per Lord Hope of Craighead.)

The House has indicated that there are two possible gateways by which a violation of Convention rights might be addressed in such situations. The first gateway provides two possibilities. The first is that the use of the interpretative obligation in s.3 results in an interpretation which avoids the violation which is alleged. The second is that the interpretative obligation does not help, but that a court of sufficient seniority can give a declaration of incompatibility under s.4 which results in a remedial order under s.10. The second gateway involves an argument that the public authority whose decision is challenged has made an improper use of its powers; this route offers a procedural protection in that the court will consider whether the public authority acted unreasonably in the *Wednesbury* sense in taking the action that it did (See [52]–[55]).

Proceedings

7.—(1) A person who claims that a public authority has acted (or proposes to act) in a way which is made unlawful by section 6(1) may— **4.34**

(a) bring proceedings against the authority under this Act in the appropriate court or tribunal, or

(b) rely on the Convention right or rights concerned in any legal proceedings,

but only if he is (or would be) a victim of the unlawful act.

(2) In subsection (1)(a) "appropriate court or tribunal" means such court or tribunal as may be determined in accordance with rules; and proceedings against an authority include a counterclaim or similar proceeding.

(3) If the proceedings are brought on an application for judicial review, the applicant is to be taken to have a sufficient interest in relation to the unlawful act only if he is, or would be, a victim of that act.

(4) If the proceedings are made by way of a petition for judicial review in Scotland, the applicant shall be taken to have title and interest to sue in relation to the unlawful act only if he is, or would be, a victim of that act.

(5) Proceedings under subsection (1)(a) must be brought before the end of—

(a) the period of one year beginning with the date on which the act complained of took place; or

(b) such longer period as the court or tribunal considers equitable having regard to all the circumstances,

but that is subject to any rule imposing a stricter time limit in relation to the procedure in question.

(6) In subsection (1)(b) "legal proceedings" includes—

(a) proceedings brought by or at the instigation of a public authority; and

(b) an appeal against the decision of a court or tribunal.

(7) For the purposes of this section, a person is a victim of an unlawful act only if he would be a victim for the purposes of Article 34 of the Convention if proceedings were brought in the European Court of Human Rights in respect of that act.

(8) Nothing in this Act creates a criminal offence.

(9) In this section "rules" means—

(a) in relation to proceedings before a court or tribunal outside Scotland, rules made by [1 . . .] [2 the Lord Chancellor or] the Secretary of State for the purposes of this section or rules of court,

(b) in relation to proceedings before a court or tribunal in Scotland, rules made by the Secretary of State for those purposes,

(c) in relation to proceedings before a tribunal in Northern Ireland—

(i) which deals with transferred matters; and

(ii) for which no rules made under paragraph (a) are in force, rules made by a Northern Ireland department for those purposes,

and includes provision made by order under section 1 of the Courts and Legal Services Act 1990.

(10) In making rules, regard must be had to section 9.

(11) The Minister who has power to make rules in relation to a particular tribunal may, to the extent he considers it necessary to ensure that the tribunal can provide an appropriate remedy in relation to an act (or proposed act) of a public authority which is (or would be) unlawful as a result of section 6(1), by order add to—

(a) the relief or remedies which the tribunal may grant; or

(b) the grounds on which it may grant any of them.

(12) An order made under subsection (11) may contain such incidental, supplemental, consequential or transitional provision as the Minister making it considers appropriate.

(13) "The Minister" includes the Northern Ireland department concerned.

COMMENCEMENT

October 2, 2000: The Human Rights Act 1998 (Commencement No.2) Order 2000 (SI 2000/1851).

AMENDMENTS

1. The Secretary of State for Constitutional Affairs Order 2003 (SI 2003/1887) (August 19, 2003).

2. The Transfer of Functions (Lord Chancellor and Secretary of State) Order 2005 (SI 2005/3429) (January 12, 2006).

GENERAL NOTE

Introduction

4.35 This section is full of difficulty. A person who believes that a public authority has acted unlawfully by not acting in a manner compatible with Convention rights may bring proceedings under s.7. Such a person must under subs.(7) show that they would be a victim for the purposes of art.34 of the Convention if proceedings were brought before the Court of Human Rights in respect of the allegedly unlawful act.

The section refers to at least three different types of proceedings: (1) the so-called new "constitutional tort" under subs.(1)(a); (2) judicial review under subs.(3); and (3) "any legal proceedings" in subs.(1)(b).

Changes to the Civil Procedures Rules to accommodate these proceedings left a number of questions unanswered.

Standing to raise the complaint: the victim requirement

Under subs.(7) which applies to the whole section, only a person who can show that they would fall within the victim requirement under art.34 of the Convention has standing to complain of the unlawful act by the public authority. The concept of "victim" is a particular concept under Convention case law, and for this reason the interpretative requirement to have regard to Convention case law must be particularly strong since otherwise the specific reference to art.34 in subs.(7) would be otiose. Article 34 has replaced art.25 in the original version of the Convention prior to its amendment by Protocol 11. **4.36**

Fortunately, the Strasbourg authorities—and here admissibility decisions of the Commission under the "old" system of protection (see commentary to s.2) will be particularly useful—have been generous in the matter of standing to make an application under the Convention.

The term "person" under the Convention (*personne physique* in the French text) clearly refers only to natural persons, but the Commission has accepted applications from corporate and unincorporated bodies whose rights under the Convention have been violated. So complaints have been accepted from companies, partnerships, trades unions, churches, political parties, and numerous other types of institution. It would seem that only public bodies themselves are excluded from the possibility of making an individual petition. Furthermore, there are no restrictions on grounds of nationality, residence or any other status.

Standing has been extended to representative complaints, for example, by parents on behalf of children where that is appropriate, though there is no age limit for making an application: App.10929/84 *Nielsen v Denmark* (1986) 46 D.R. 55 and App.22920/93 *MB v United Kingdom* (1994) 77-A D.R. 42. Equally, there is no bar to application by persons under a disability: App.1572/62 *X v Austria* (1962) 5 Yearbook 238. **4.37**

Associations have no standing to bring actions in a representative capacity: App.10581/83 *Norris and National Gay Federation v Ireland* (1984) 44 D.R. 132, though if they provide evidence that they are acting on behalf of specified individuals, the application may be accepted: App.10983/84 *Confédération des Syndicats me´dicaúx franc¸ais et Fédération nationale des Infirmiers v France* (1986) 47 D.R. 225.

In some cases potential victims may make an application, such as in cases where covert surveillance might take place without any notification of the possibility to the individual: *Klass v Germany*, judgment of September 6, 1978, Series A No.28; (1979–80) 2 E.H.R.R. 214.

The Commission and the Court will not, however, countenance an application in the abstract as a means of testing the compatibility of provisions of a national legal order: App.9297/81 *X Association v Sweden* (1982) 28 D.R. 204. Drawing the distinction between potential victims and claims in the abstract is not always easy: see App.10039/82 *Leigh v United Kingdom* (1984) 38 D.R. 74. **4.38**

In *Director General of Fair Trading v Proprietary Association of Great Britain*, Court of Appeal, July 26, 2001 [2001] EWCA Civ 1217 (sometimes referred to as *Re medicaments (No.4))*, the Court of Appeal made some passing, and inconclusive comments on the nature of the "victim requirement" under s.7. The Court expressly avoided dealing with the possible distinction between interest groups which are really associations of interested individuals which might be regarded as a group of individuals each of whom may be regarded as a victim and broader representative groups (examples given are Amnesty International or the Joint Council for the Welfare of Immigrants) which have special expertise but who cannot be classified as a collection of victims. The Court simply stated that each case must be decided in its own context.

Note the discussion of the victim requirement (particularly victim status and retrospectivity) in the judgment of the House of Lords in *Hooper* [2005] UKHL 29: see [53]–[59].

Subsection (1)(a): the new constitutional tort

4.39 A person who can show that they meet the victim test may bring proceedings against the authority "in the appropriate court or tribunal". This is to be determined in accordance with rules to be made, outside Scotland, by the Lord Chancellor or the Secretary of State. The Civil Procedure Rules simply map this action onto the existing division of responsibilities between the county courts and the High Court.

The time limits for such an action are, however, specified in subs.(5). The action is to be brought within one year of the date on which the act complained of took place or such longer period as the court or tribunal considers equitable having regard to all the circumstances. There is a proviso that both the one year time limit and any extension of it is to be without prejudice to any rule imposing a stricter time limit "in relation to the procedure in question." An example would be judicial review where the normal time limit is three months unless this is extended by the court. However, where an action is brought under a procedure with a longer limitation period, it would seem that the longer limitation period will apply; such proceedings would not, however, arise under subs.(1)(a) but presumably under subs.(1)(b).

Under s.9(1), where the unlawful act of which the applicant complains is a judicial act, it is stated that proceedings under s.7(1)(a) may be brought only by exercising a right of appeal, seeking judicial review against those bodies susceptible to judicial review, or "in such other forum as may be prescribed by rules."

Judicial review: subss.(3) and (4)

4.40 Where the proceedings are by way of judicial review on the grounds that a public authority has acted unlawfully, the normal sufficient interest test of standing (which would permit action by a representative body or a pressure group) is replaced by a test that the applicant must satisfy the victim test in subs.(7).

Raising Convention rights in any legal proceedings: subs.(1)(b)

4.41 Convention rights may be raised in any legal proceedings, provided that the person can show that they would be a victim under art.34 of the Convention. So a person bringing proceedings on a well-established cause of action can raise his or her Convention rights at any time. Indeed, the court or tribunal is under a duty by virtue of s.6(1) to take obvious Convention points since they are under a duty to act in a manner compatible with the Convention.

Apart from judicial review claims (which may be important if a person is seeking the possibility of a money remedy), Convention rights are most likely to be raised in the course of appeals to the First-tier Tribunal and the Upper Tribunal. The commentary to the Convention rights set out in Sch.1 gives some indication of the sorts of issues which might be raised under them.

In *CSIB/973/1999* a Scottish Commissioner warns of the need for responsible resort to the taking of human rights points. He complains of a point which was "in the nature of a wrap up omnibus ground of appeal placed before the Commissioners no doubt in the hope that there was something in the point." The Commissioner regrets the absence of rules setting out the manner in which human rights points are to be taken before the Commissioners. He goes on to indicate the content of those rules; this might assist those contemplating raising human rights points before both tribunals and Commissioners. The provision of the Convention which it is argued has been breached should be identified, together with the remedy sought in respect of the breach. The legal principles and authorities relied on and any error of law by the tribunal which it is asserted were made consequent on the breach should also be identified. Such points should be taken on proper notice so that both parties can research them and focus on them in their arguments to the adjudicating body. That is, no doubt, good advice, but the duty in s.6(1) on public authorities to act compatibly with Convention rights means that adjudicating bodies must themselves consider obvious points arising under the Convention even if they are not raised by the parties.

In *R(IS)12/04* the Commissioner reminds tribunals of the need to address fully arguments based on Convention rights in the following terms, 4.42

"13. Finally, it is necessary to consider the adequacy of the tribunal's reasons. I agree with the Secretary of State that a tribunal's lack of any power to make a declaration of incompatibility is not a good reason for not dealing fully with Human Rights issues, particularly since a tribunal may have power in some cases to declare subordinate legislation to have been invalidly made-see *Chief Adjudication Officer v Foster* [1993] 1 All E.R. 705. The claimant in this appeal clearly went to considerable trouble to set out his arguments under the Human Rights Act clearly and comprehensively in response to the chairman's direction, and I consider that he was entitled to a much fuller explanation of the tribunal's reasons for rejecting his arguments than the very short passage at the end of the statement of reasons set out above. The reasons for the tribunal's rejection of the claimant's discrimination arguments are not apparent from the statement, and I therefore consider that, in all the circumstances, the tribunal's reasons were inadequate."

The Court of Appeal in *R. (on the application of Hooper, Withey, Naylor and Martin v Secretary of State for Work and Pensions* [2003] EWCA Civ 813 addresses at [29]–[46] the question of when a person becomes a victim within the meaning of s.7, and did not find the application of Strasbourg case law to be satisfactory. The Strasbourg authorities appeared to provide that only when a man has made a claim to a benefit is he in a position to complain that he is not being treated in the same way as a woman, and so, only then, would become a victim for the purposes of art.34 of the Convention. The Court of Appeal describes as "unattractive" an argument raised by the United Kingdom Government before the Court of Human Rights in *White v United Kingdom* (App.53134/99), admissibility decision of June 7, 2001, that the claimant was not a victim because he had not claimed on the official form, notwithstanding that this was designed specifically for widows. Differing from the views expressed by Moses J. in the court below, the Court of Appeal concludes that it is not necessary for the claim to be made in writing in order to constitute the applicant as a victim for the purpose of asserting his Convention rights. The Court of Appeal says, ". . . we can see no reason in principle why an oral claim, made and rejected, should not suffice to constitute a claim." Note, however, that the oral claim is not a perfected claim for the purposes of the Claims and Payments Regulations, simply for the purposes of giving a person standing to claim Convention rights as a victim of a violation of those rights. This aspect of the Court of Appeal's decision was accepted by the House of Lords, [2005] UKHL 29.

Judicial remedies

8.—(1) In relation to any act (or proposed act) of a public authority which the court finds is (or would be) unlawful, it may grant such relief or remedy, or make such order, within its powers as it considers just and appropriate. 4.43

(2) But damages may be awarded only by a court which has power to award damages, or to order the payment of compensation, in civil proceedings.

(3) No award of damages is to be made unless, taking account of all the circumstances of the case, including—

(a) any other relief or remedy granted, or order made, in relation to the act in question (by that or any other court), and

(b) the consequences of any decision (of that or any other court) in respect of that act,

the court is satisfied that the award is necessary to afford just satisfaction to the person in whose favour it is made.

(4) In determining—

(a) whether to award damages, or

(b) the amount of an award,

the court must take into account the principles applied by the European Court of Human Rights in relation to the award of compensation under Article 41 of the Convention.

(5) A public authority against which damages are awarded is to be treated—

(a) in Scotland, for the purposes of section 3 of the Law Reform (Miscellaneous Provisions) (Scotland) Act 1940 as if the award were made in an action of damages in which the authority has been found liable in respect of loss or damage to the person to whom the award is made;

(b) for the purposes of the Civil Liability (Contribution) Act 1978 as liable in respect of damage suffered by the person to whom the award is made.

(6) In this section—

"court" includes a tribunal;

"damages" means damages for an unlawful act of a public authority; and

"unlawful" means unlawful under section 6(1).

COMMENCEMENT

October 2, 2000: The Human Rights Act 1998 (Commencement No.2) Order 2000 (SI 2000/1851).

GENERAL NOTE

4.44 Section 8(1) grants a broad competence, but the nature of the remedies available will vary according to the forum. The relief, remedy or order open to the court or tribunal must be one already within its powers. So the Act gives no new competence to decision-making bodies to provide a remedy for a violation of a Convention right. The decision not to extend the powers of all courts and tribunals to include new remedies for violations of Convention rights was apparently motivated by a concern that there would be an explosion of damages awards in this area across a wide range of decision-making bodies. This was the same concern which led to the exclusion of art.13 of the Convention from the incorporated rights. There is, accordingly, a wide but not unlimited range of remedies available for breaches of Convention rights.

The drafting of s.8 reveals a concern that damages for violations of Convention rights should be contained. Section 8(2) provides that damages for an unlawful act of a public authority under the Act may be awarded only by a court (or tribunal) which has power to award damages, or to order the payment of compensation, in civil proceedings. Furthermore, damages, though not the remedy of last resort, are circumscribed since they are not to be made unless the court is satisfied that the award is necessary to afford just satisfaction to the person in whose favour the award is made, having regard to all the circumstances of the case, and in particular any other remedy or relief granted and the consequences of any decision in respect of the breach of Convention rights: subs.(3). As noted above, decisions about the award of damages and the amount of damages are to be informed by reference to the case law of the Court of Human Right in awarding just satisfaction.

A number of observations need to be made about the structure of s.8. It assumes that the range of remedies currently available to United Kingdom courts will be adequate to remedy breaches of Convention rights. It seeks to discourage an explosion of damages awards. The Lord Chancellor indicated that the intent was to match the awards victims would get if they received just satisfaction under art.41: HL Vol.582 col.1232, November 3, 1997. It establishes a system in which the luck of the forum will determine whether duplication of litigation will be needed to secure a money remedy. A good example would be an appeal heard by an appeal tribunal, which has no power to award damages, and it has been established that it has no power award interest on the late payment of benefit; This undoubtedly follows from the reasoning of the Social Security Commissioner in *R(FC)2/90*; see also the decision of the Court of Justice in *R. v Secretary of State for Social Security; Ex p. Sutton* [1997] E.C.R. I-2163; [1997] 2 C.M.L.R. 382. Nor it seems would any other court. Yet the Court of Human Rights has awarded interest on the late payment of benefit: *Schuler-Zgraggen v Switzerland*, judgment of June 24, 1993, Series A, No.263; (1993) 16 E.H.R.R. 405. In the early days of Community law, an action for a declaration was one means of securing a judicial statement of an entitlement under Community law. This would seem to be the only route open within the national legal order to a victim who had only received social security benefit to which he or she was entitled some years late and who wished to raise the claim for interest on the late payment. Otherwise, such a person would have to raise the complaint that no interest was available before the Court in Strasbourg.

Perhaps the most pertinent point to make is that the deference to the provisions of the Convention on just satisfaction in the national legislation is misplaced. The provisions in art.41 of the Convention on affording just satisfaction are a safety net where the national legal order does not offer full compensation for the breach of the Convention. **4.45**

The starting point is that the national legal order should determine what remedies are appropriate for breaches of the Convention. Such an obligation flows from art.13 of the Convention. Indeed, it could be argued that the effect of s.8 replicates the failures of earlier years to recognise what was demanded by the Convention. It assumes that the current panoply of remedies available in the national legal order meets the requirements of the Convention. It also reveals a deep anxiety about damages as a remedy for breach of a Convention right.

The potential gap in remedies available can, however, be cured under the rule-making power in s.7(11) and (12) which enables additional powers to be given to tribunals to add to the remedies open to them, and to define the grounds on which any additional remedies may be granted.

Where the act complained of is a judicial act, damages as a remedy is limited to compensation for unlawful detention awarded in accordance with art.5(5): s.9(3). **4.46**

In *CSIS/460/2002,* the Commissioner makes some comments on the nature of remedies for a violation of Convention rights in the context of an argument that one remedy could be to order a permanent stay of the proceedings. The Commissioner concludes,

> "A tribunal has no power to impose a permanent stay of an appeal. There is no express statutory provision nor can one be implied by virtue of necessity. Mr Orr drew an analogy with an appeal abating. However that derives from a principle of common law and is not a stay by a court or tribunal. Where an appellant dies before the determination of the appeal, the appeal is not terminated by that fact. However, unless and until there is an appointment of someone to proceed with the appeal or there is a personal representative, then no-one is legally competent to take the appeal forward. In such circumstances, the appeal is considered as automatically 'abated', by which is meant suspended. It can nevertheless be revived by the appropriate procedure. Any statement by a tribunal or a Commissioner that an appeal has been abated is thus for clarification only. Abatement is therefore very different from the power to grant a permanent stay. Such a concept could in any event give no advantage to the respondent as it would leave outstanding the adverse decision. The Secretary of State is not legally obliged to contine the customary suspension of recovery procedures and would have no reason to do so if the appeal is permanently stayed." (para.49)

See also discussion of remedies in *Dyer v Watson* [2002] 4 All E.R. 1, especially the analysis by Lord Millett at [128]–[133].

Judicial acts

4.47 **9.**—(1) Proceedings under section 7(1)(a) in respect of a judicial act may be brought only

(a) by exercising a right of appeal;

(b) on an application (in Scotland a petition) for judicial review; or

(c) in such other forum as may be prescribed by rules.

(2) That does not affect any rule of law which prevents a court from being the subject of judicial review.

(3) In proceedings under this Act in respect of a judicial act done in good faith, damages may not be awarded otherwise than to compensate a person to the extent required by Article 5(5) of the Convention.

(4) An award of damages permitted by subsection (3) is to be made against the Crown; but no award may be made unless the appropriate person, if not a party to the proceedings, is joined.

(5) In this section—

"appropriate person" means the Minister responsible for the court concerned, or a person or government department nominated by him;

"court" includes a tribunal;

"judge" includes a member of a tribunal, a justice of the peace [[1] (or, in Northern Ireland, a lay magistrate)] and a clerk or other officer entitled to exercise the jurisdiction of a court;

"judicial act" means a judicial act of a court and includes an act done on the instructions, or on behalf, of a judge; and

"rules" has the same meaning as in section 7(9).

Commencement

October 2, 2000: The Human Rights Act 1998 (Commencement No.2) Order 2000 (SI 2000/1851).

Amendment

1. The Justice (Northern Ireland) Act 2002 (Commencement No.8) Order 2005 SR 2005/109 art.2 Sch. (April 1, 2005).

Remedial action

Power to take remedial action

4.48 **10.**—(1) This section applies if—

(a) a provision of legislation has been declared under section 4 to be incompatible with a Convention right and, if an appeal lies—

(i) all persons who may appeal have stated in writing that they do not intend to do so;

(ii) the time for bringing an appeal has expired and no appeal has been brought within that time; or

(iii) an appeal brought within that time has been determined or abandoned; or

(b) it appears to a Minister of the Crown or Her Majesty in Council that, having regard to a finding of the European Court of Human Rights made after the coming into force of this section in proceedings against the United Kingdom, a provision of legislation is incompatible with an obligation of the United Kingdom arising from the Convention.

(2) If a Minister of the Crown considers that there are compelling reasons for proceeding under this section, he may by order make such amendments to the legislation as he considers necessary to remove the incompatibility.

(3) If, in the case of subordinate legislation, a Minister of the Crown considers—

(a) that it is necessary to amend the primary legislation under which the subordinate legislation in question was made, in order to enable the incompatibility to be removed, and

(b) that there are compelling reasons for proceeding under this section,

he may by order make such amendments to the primary legislation as he considers necessary.

(4) This section also applies where the provision in question is in subordinate legislation and has been quashed, or declared invalid, by reason of incompatibility with a Convention right and the Minister proposes to proceed under paragraph 2(b) of Schedule 2.

(5) If the legislation is an Order in Council, the power conferred by subsection (2) or (3) is exercisable by Her Majesty in Council.

(6) In this section "legislation" does not include a Measure of the Church Assembly or of the General Synod of the Church of England.

(7) Schedule 2 makes further provision about remedial orders.

COMMENCEMENT

October 2, 2000: The Human Rights Act 1998 (Commencement No.2) Order 2000 (SI 2000/1851).

GENERAL NOTE

This section and Sch.2 make provision for a fast-track Parliamentary procedure to respond to a declaration of incompatibility by a court. **4.49**

Other rights and proceedings

Safeguard for existing human rights

11.—A person's reliance on a Convention right does not restrict— **4.50**

(a) any other right or freedom conferred on him by or under any law having effect in any part of the United Kingdom; or

(b) his right to make any claim or bring any proceedings which he could make or bring apart from sections 7 to 9.

COMMENCEMENT

October 2, 2000: The Human Rights Act 1998 (Commencement No.2) Order 2000 (SI 2000/1851).

GENERAL NOTE

4.51 The rights given to persons under s.7 to complain of unlawful acts by public authorities in acting in a manner incompatible with the Convention does not limit in any way existing rights under UK law. The new rights are additional to existing rights and not in substitution for them.

Freedom of expression

4.52 **12.**—(1) This section applies if a court is considering whether to grant any relief which, if granted, might affect the exercise of the Convention right to freedom of expression.

(2) If the person against whom the application for relief is made ("the respondent") is neither present nor represented, no such relief is to be granted unless the court is satisfied—

(a) that the applicant has taken all practicable steps to notify the respondent; or

(b) that there are compelling reasons why the respondent should not be notified.

(3) No such relief is to be granted so as to restrain publication before trial unless the court is satisfied that the applicant is likely to establish that publication should not be allowed.

(4) The court must have particular regard to the importance of the Convention right to freedom of expression and, where the proceedings relate to material which the respondent claims, or which appears to the court, to be journalistic, literary or artistic material (or to conduct connected with such material), to—

(a) the extent to which—

(i) the material has, or is about to, become available to the public; or

(ii) it is, or would be, in the public interest for the material to be published;

(b) any relevant privacy code.

(5) In this section—

"court" includes a tribunal; and

"relief" includes any remedy or order (other than in criminal proceedings).

COMMENCEMENT

October 2, 2000: The Human Rights Act 1998 (Commencement No.2) Order 2000 (SI 2000/1851).

GENERAL NOTE

4.53 This section is a response to concerns expressed by media interests that the Act would limit freedom of expression by giving priority to the development of privacy under art.8 of the Convention. The section is not needed, since the Strasbourg case law makes it clear that a balance has to be struck between the privacy of the individual and the freedom of the press.

Freedom of thought, conscience and religion

4.54 **13.**—(1) If a court's determination of any question arising under this Act might affect the exercise by a religious organisation (itself or its members collectively) of the Convention right to freedom of thought, conscience and religion, it must have particular regard to the importance of that right.

(2) In this section "court" includes a tribunal.

COMMENCEMENT

October 2, 2000: The Human Rights Act 1998 (Commencement No.2) Order 2000 (SI 2000/1851).

GENERAL NOTE

This section was included in response to concerns expressed on behalf of religious groups that priority would be given to other provisions of the Convention than the provision on freedom of religion in art.9 and that churches would find themselves being required in the name of human rights to do things contrary to their tenets. Like s.12, this section is not needed, since the Strasbourg case law makes it clear that a balance has to be struck between the pluralism of a modern democratic societies and respect for religious and personal beliefs. 4.55

Derogations and reservations

Derogations

14.—(1) In this Act "designated derogation" means— 4.56

[. . .[1]] any derogation by the United Kingdom from an Article of the Convention, or of any protocol to the Convention, which is designated for the purposes of this Act in an order made by the Secretary of State.

(2) [. . .[1]].

(3) If a designated derogation is amended or replaced it ceases to be a designated derogation.

(4) But subsection (3) does not prevent the [[2] Secretary of State] from exercising his power under subsection (1)[. . .[1]] to make a fresh designation order in respect of the Article concerned.

(5) The [[2] Secretary of State] must by order make such amendments to Schedule 3 as he considers appropriate to reflect—

(a) any designation order; or

(b) the effect of subsection (3).

(6) A designation order may be made in anticipation of the making by the United Kingdom of a proposed derogation.

COMMENCEMENT

October 2, 2000: The Human Rights Act 1998 (Commencement No.2) Order 2000 (SI 2000/1851).

AMENDMENTS

1. The Human Rights Act (Amendment) Order 2001 (SI 2001/1216) art.2 (April 1, 2001).

2. The Secretary of State for Constitutional Affairs Order 2003 (SI 2003/1887) (August 19, 2003).

Reservations

15.—(1) In this Act "designated reservation" means— 4.57

(a) the United Kingdom's reservation to Article 2 of the First Protocol to the Convention; and

(b) any other reservation by the United Kingdom to an Article of the Convention, or of any protocol to the Convention, which is designated for the purposes of this Act in an order made by the Secretary of State.

(2) The text of the reservation referred to in subsection (1)(a) is set out in Part II of Schedule 3.

(3) If a designated reservation is withdrawn wholly or in part it ceases to be a designated reservation.

(4) But subsection (3) does not prevent the [[1] Secretary of State] from exercising his power under subsection (1)(b) to make a fresh designation order in respect of the Article concerned.

(5) The [[1] Secretary of State] must by order make such amendments to this Act as he considers appropriate to reflect—

(a) any designation order; or

(b) the effect of subsection (3).

Commencement

October 2, 2000: The Human Rights Act 1998 (Commencement No.2) Order 2000 (SI 2000/1851).

Amendment

1. The Secretary of State for Constitutional Affairs Order 2003 (SI 2003/1887) (August 19, 2003).

Period for which designated derogations have effect

4.58 **16.**—(1) If it has not already been withdrawn by the United Kingdom, a designated derogation ceases to have effect for the purposes of this Act—

[. . .[1]] at the end of the period of five years beginning with the date on which the order designating it was made.

(2) At any time before the period—

(a) fixed by subsection (1) [. . .[1]], or

(b) extended by an order under this subsection,

comes to an end, the [[2] Secretary of State] may by order extend it by a further period of five years.

(3) An order under section 14(1)[. . .[1]] ceases to have effect at the end of the period for consideration, unless a resolution has been passed by each House approving the order.

(4) Subsection (3) does not affect—

(a) anything done in reliance on the order; or

(b) the power to make a fresh order under section 14(1)[. . .[1]].

(5) In subsection (3) "period for consideration" means the period of forty days beginning with the day on which the order was made.

(6) In calculating the period for consideration, no account is to be taken of any time during which—

(a) Parliament is dissolved or prorogued; or

(b) both Houses are adjourned for more than four days.

(7) If a designated derogation is withdrawn by the United Kingdom, the [[2] Secretary of State] must by order make such amendments to this Act as he considers are required to reflect that withdrawal.

Commencement

October 2, 2000: The Human Rights Act 1998 (Commencement No.2) Order 2000 (SI 2000/1851).

AMENDMENTS

1. The Human Rights Act (Amendment) Order 2001 (SI 2001/1216) art.3 (April 1, 2001).
2. The Secretary of State for Constitutional Affairs Order 2003 (SI 2003/1887) (August 19, 2003).

Periodic review of designated reservations

17.—(1) The appropriate Minister must review the designated reservation referred to in section 15(1)(a)— **4.59**

(a) before the end of the period of five years beginning with the date on which section 1(2) came into force; and

(b) if that designation is still in force, before the end of the period of five years beginning with the date on which the last report relating to it was laid under subsection (3).

(2) The appropriate Minister must review each of the other designated reservations (if any)—

(a) before the end of the period of five years beginning with the date on which the order designating the reservation first came into force; and

(b) if the designation is still in force, before the end of the period of five years beginning with the date on which the last report relating to it was laid under subsection (3).

(3) The Minister conducting a review under this section must prepare a report on the result of the review and lay a copy of it before each House of Parliament.

COMMENCEMENT

October 2, 2000: The Human Rights Act 1998 (Commencement No.2) Order 2000 (SI 2000/1851).

Judges of the European Court of Human Rights

Section 18 omitted. **4.60**

Parliamentary procedure

Statements of compatibility

19.—(1) A Minister of the Crown in charge of a Bill in either House of Parliament must, before Second Reading of the Bill— **4.61**

(a) make a statement to the effect that in his view the provisions of the Bill are compatible with the Convention rights ("a statement of compatibility"); or

(b) make a statement to the effect that although he is unable to make a statement of compatibility the government nevertheless wishes the House to proceed with the Bill.

(2) The statement must be in writing and be published in such manner as the Minister making it considers appropriate.

COMMENCEMENT

Section 19 entered into force on November 24, 1998: (SI 1998/2882).

General Note

4.62 Part of the scheme of the Act is to require improved pre-legislative scrutiny of legislation to ensure its compliance with Convention rights. The use of the section to date has been disappointing, since no reasoning is publicly available to elaborate a simple Ministerial statement that the provisions of a Bill are compatible with Convention rights.

Reviews carried out by the Parliamentary Joint Committee on Human Rights are rather more rigorous.

Supplemental

4.63 *Section 20 omitted.*

Interpretation, etc.

4.64 **21.**—(1) In this Act—

"amend" includes repeal and apply (with or without modifications);

"the appropriate Minister" means the Minister of the Crown having charge of the appropriate authorised government department (within the meaning of the Crown Proceedings Act 1947);

"the Commission" means the European Commission of Human Rights;

"the Convention" means the Convention for the Protection of Human Rights and Fundamental Freedoms, agreed by the Council of Europe at Rome on 4th November 1950 as it has effect for the time being in relation to the United Kingdom;

"declaration of incompatibility" means a declaration under section 4;

"Minister of the Crown" has the same meaning as in the Ministers of the Crown Act 1975;

"Northern Ireland Minister" includes the First Minister and the deputy First Minister in Northern Ireland;

"primary legislation" means any—

(a) public general Act;
(b) local and personal Act;
(c) private Act;
(d) Measure of the Church Assembly;
(e) Measure of the General Synod of the Church of England;
(f) Order in Council—
  (i) made in exercise of Her Majesty's Royal Prerogative;
  (ii) made under section 38(1)(a) of the Northern Ireland Constitution Act 1973 or the corresponding provision of the Northern Ireland Act 1998; or
  (iii) amending an Act of a kind mentioned in paragraph (a), (b) or (c);

and includes an order or other instrument made under primary legislation (otherwise than by the National Assembly for Wales, a member of the Scottish Executive, a Northern Ireland Minister or a Northern Ireland department) to the extent to which it operates to bring one or more provisions of that legislation into force or amends any primary legislation;

"the First Protocol" means the protocol to the Convention agreed at Paris on March 20 1952;

[[1]. . .]

"the Eleventh Protocol" means the protocol to the Convention (restructuring the control machinery established by the Convention) agreed at Strasbourg on May 11 1994;

[1 "the Thirteenth Protocol" means the protocol to the Convention (concerning the abolition of the death penalty in all circumstances agreed at Vilnius on 3rd May 2002;]

"subordinate legislation" means any—

(a) Order in Council other than one—

(i) made in exercise of Her Majesty's Royal Prerogative;

(ii) made under section 38(1)(a) of the Northern Ireland Constitution Act 1973 or the corresponding provision of the Northern Ireland Act 1998; or

(iii) amending an Act of a kind mentioned in the definition of primary legislation;

(b) Act of the Scottish Parliament;

[2 (ba) Measure of the National Assembly for Wales;

(bb) Act of the National Assembly for Wales;]

(c) Act of the Parliament of Northern Ireland;

(d) Measure of the Assembly established under section 1 of the Northern Ireland Assembly Act 1973;

(e) Act of the Northern Ireland Assembly;

(f) order, rules, regulations, scheme, warrant, byelaw or other instrument made under primary legislation (except to the extent to which it operates to bring one or more provisions of that legislation into force or amends any primary legislation);

(g) order, rules, regulations, scheme, warrant, byelaw or other instrument made under legislation mentioned in paragraph (b), (c), (d) or (e) or made under an Order in Council applying only to Northern Ireland;

(h) order, rules, regulations, scheme, warrant, byelaw or other instrument made by a member of the Scottish Executive, [2 Welsh Ministers, the First Minister for Wales, the Counsel General to the Welsh Assembly Government,] a Northern Ireland Minister or a Northern Ireland department in exercise of prerogative or other executive functions of Her Majesty which are exercisable by such a person on behalf of Her Majesty;

"transferred matters" has the same meaning as in the Northern Ireland Act 1998; and

"tribunal" means any tribunal in which legal proceedings may be brought.

(2) The references in paragraphs (b) and (c) of section 2(1) to Articles are to Articles of the Convention as they had effect immediately before the coming into force of the Eleventh Protocol.

(3) The reference in paragraph (d) of section 2(1) to Article 46 includes a reference to Articles 32 and 54 of the Convention as they had effect immediately before the coming into force of the Eleventh Protocol.

(4) The references in section 2(1) to a report or decision of the Commission or a decision of the Committee of Ministers include references to a report or decision made as provided by paragraphs 3, 4 and 6 of Article 5 of the Eleventh Protocol (transitional provisions).

(5) [3 . . .]

COMMENCEMENT

Section 21(5) entered into force on November 9, 1998. The remainder of the section entered into force on October 2, 2000: The Human Rights Act 1998 (Commencement No.2) Order 2000 (SI 2000/1851).

AMENDMENTS

1. Human Rights Act 1998 (Amendment) Order 2004 (SI 2004/1574) art.2(2) (June 22, 2004).

2. Government of Wales Act 2006 Sch.10 para.56(4) (May 3, 2007 immediately after the ordinary election as specified in 2006 c.32 s.161(1); May 25, 2007 immediately after the end of the initial period for purposes of functions of the Welsh Ministers, the First Minister, the Counsel General and the Assembly Commission and in relation to the Auditor General and the Comptroller and Auditor General as specified in 2006 c.32 s.161(4)-(5)).

3. Armed Forces Act 2006 Sch.17 para.1 (October 31, 2009).

Short title, commencement, application and extent

4.65 **22.**—(1) This Act may be cited as the Human Rights Act 1998.

(2) Sections 18, 20 and 21(5) and this section come into force on the passing of this Act.

(3) The other provisions of this Act come into force on such day as the Secretary of State may by order appoint; and different days may be appointed for different purposes.

(4) Paragraph (b) of subsection (1) of section 7 applies to proceedings brought by or at the instigation of a public authority whenever the act in question took place; but otherwise that subsection does not apply to an act taking place before the coming into force of that section.

(5) This Act binds the Crown.

(6) This Act extends to Northern Ireland.

(7) Section 21(5), so far as it relates to any provision contained in the Army Act 1955, the Air Force Act 1955 or the Naval Discipline Act 1957, extends to any place to which that provision extends.

GENERAL NOTE

4.66 This section entered into force on November 9, 1998.

Subsection (4), which entered into force on November 9, 1998, provides that the lawfulness of an act of a public authority may be called into question in proceedings under s.7(1)(b) (any legal proceedings in which Convention rights are raised) whenever that act took place if those proceedings are begun by a public authority. In other words, it has a retrospective effect in this regard, but if the proceedings are brought other than by a public authority, no complaint can be made about an act of a public authority prior to the entry into force of s.7(1)(b).

The issue of the possible retrospective application of the Human Rights Act 1998 in the context of tribunal decisions would appear to have been laid to rest; the position is neatly summarised in *R(IS)3/02*, where the Commissioner concludes:

> "The effect and interaction of sections 3, 6, 7 and 22 of the Human Rights Act in relation to appeals from inferior tribunal decisions given before 2 October 2000 was much debated before me but the argument that Mr Cox [of Counsel] sought to advance in this appeal, that the 1998 Act had a retrospective effect extending even to turning past lawful decisions of courts and tribunals into unlawful ones in United Kingdom law from 2 October 2000 and to obliging appellate courts to reverse the effect retrospectively from that date onwards, has now conclusively been shown to be untenable: see *R v Lambert* [2001] 3 W.L.R. 206, affirming

what was said by Sir Andrew Morritt V-C in *Wilson v First County Trust Ltd (No.2)* [2001] 3 W.L.R. 42, 51; and cf also the recent decision of the Tribunal of Scots Commissioners in case *CSDLA 1019/99*." (At para.15.)

A tribunal sitting on or after October 2, 2000 on an appeal against a decision made before October 2, 2000 cannot consider Convention points, since s.12(8)(b) of the SSA 1998 confines the tribunal to the state of United Kingdom law at the time the decision was given, and cannot be interpreted in any other way. It might be observed, however, that there may be circumstances in which the Convention provides assistance in the interpretation of existing UK law without there being a situation in which a claimant can be said to be relying on Convention rights as provided by s.7 of the HRA 1998 *(CDLA/1338/2001)*. **4.67**

See also *R(IS) 6/04, CSIS/460/2002,* and *CCS/1306/2001.* The latter summarises at para.22 the case law on the extent to which Convention rights can be relied upon prior to October 2, 2000.

Schedules

Schedule 1

The Articles

Part I

The Convention

Rights and Freedoms

Article 2—Right to life

1. Everyone's right to life shall be protected by law. No one shall be deprived of his life intentionally save in the execution of a sentence of a court following his conviction of a crime for which this penalty is provided by law. **4.68**

2. Deprivation of life shall not be regarded as inflicted in contravention of this Article when it results from the use of force which is no more than absolutely necessary:

(a) in defence of any person from unlawful violence;
(b) in order to effect a lawful arrest or to prevent the escape of a person lawfully detained;
(c) in action lawfully taken for the purpose of quelling a riot or insurrection.

General Note

This article is unlikely to have much relevance in the social security jurisdiction. It is not a vehicle for arguing for a particular allocation of resources by the state. So arguments that without the payment of benefit, a person's life will be at risk and so the state cannot be said to be protecting by law everyone's right to life are destined to fail. This would appear to follow from those cases where the relatives of murder victims have sought to argue that the police failed to protect the victim: App.9837/82 *M v United Kingdom and Ireland* (1986) 47 D.R. 27. **4.69**

Article 3—Prohibition of torture

No one shall be subjected to torture or to inhuman or degrading treatment or punishment. **4.70**

General Note

This article is concerned with conduct which attains at least a minimum level of severity. It is not concerned with anything which a person might find degrading. See *Ireland v United Kingdom*, judgment of January 18, 1978, Series A No.25; (1979–80) 2 E.H.R.R. 25, [162] of the judgment, and *Tyrer v United Kingdom*, judgment of April 25, 1978, Series A No.26; (1979–80) 2 E.H.R.R.1, at [30] of the judgment. The effect of setting a high threshold is that trivial complaints, and even activity **4.71** which is considered undesirable or illegal, will not fall within the scope of the article unless they cause sufficiently serious suffering or humiliation to the victim. The assessment of seriousness is relative. In its judgment in *Ireland v United Kingdom*, the Court suggested that the following factors are relevant in determining the existence of inhuman treatment: the duration of the treatment, its physical and mental effects, and the sex, age, and state of health of the victim. But it should also be remembered that the Convention is a "living instrument" whose standards are not set in stone; it receives a living interpretation and must be considered in the light of present day circumstances.

It follows that arguments, for example, that a medical examination in connection with a benefit claim was felt to be degrading or inhuman by the claimant will fall well below the threshold required to engage this article even where the doctor behaves improperly.

In *R. (on the application of Joanne Reynolds) v Secretary of State for Work and Pensions*, judgment of March 7, 2002, [2002] EWHC 426, it was argued that a failure to pay the claimant more than £41.35 per week by way of social security constituted degrading treatment. Wilson J. gives this argument short shrift, pointing out that "Article 3 proscribes ill-treatment of a depth which the level of payment to Ms Reynolds wholly fails to reach."

4.72 In *Secretary of State for the Home Department v Limbuela, Tesema and Adam* [2004] EWCA Civ 540, the Court of Appeal ruled that the refusal to provide State support for three asylum seekers, who had not applied for asylum within three days of their arrival in the United Kingdom under s.55 of the Nationality, Immigration and Asylum Act 2002, engaged their Convention rights under art.3. Carnwath L.J. said that the case raised the question of the level of abject destitution to which such individuals must sink before their suffering reaches the minimum threshold for art.3 to bite. Shelter was regarded as a basic amenity and the threat of not having access to shelter in the future could come within the ambit of inhuman and degrading treatment under art.3. Laws L.J. dissented. Carnwath L.J. said,

> "118. ... I acknowledge with gratitude the illumination provided by Laws L.J.'s powerful discussion of the scope of Art.3, and its application in the present context. As he says, the legal reality is a spectrum. At one end is state-authorised violence. At the other are to be found executive decisions in exercise of lawful policy objectives, which have consequences for individuals so severe that 'the court is bound to limit the State's right to implement the policy on Art.3 grounds'. I agree also with much of his analysis of the consequences of that distinction, and of the correct approach to the task of drawing the line in an individual case.
>
> 119. Laws L.J. accepts that Art.3 may be engaged by a particular 'vulnerability' in the individual, or external circumstances which make it impossible for him to find food and other basic amenities. Where, with respect, I part company from him is in his view that, on the evidence available to us, the judges were not entitled to find that such circumstances existed in the present cases. I would add that I find it difficult not to regard shelter of some form from the elements at night (even if it is limited as it was in *T's* case) as a 'basic amenity', at least in winter and bad weather... ."

The appeal of the Secretary of State against the decision of the Court of Appeal has been dismissed by a unanimous House of Lords, [2005] UKHL 66.

The judgment is important because it sets out circumstances within the context of state support for individuals which fall within the ambit of inhuman and degrading treatment in art.3.

Article 4—Prohibition of slavery and forced labour

4.73 **1.** No one shall be held in slavery or servitude.

2. No one shall be required to perform forced or compulsory labour.

3. For the purpose of this Article the term "forced or compulsory labour" shall not include:
(a) any work required to be done in the ordinary course of detention imposed according to the provisions of Article 5 of this Convention or during conditional release from such detention;
(b) any service of a military character or, in case of conscientious objectors in countries where they are recognised, service exacted instead of compulsory military service;
(c) any service exacted in case of an emergency or calamity threatening the life or well-being of the community;
(d) any work or service which forms part of normal civic obligations.

GENERAL NOTE

Being required to be available for work as a condition of entitlement to benefit will not constitute forced or compulsory labour. 4.74

The applicant, in *Stummer v Austria* (App 37452/06), Judgment of the Grand Chamber of July 7, 2011, sought to argue that a requirement to work in prison without affiliation to the old-age pension system could no longer be regarded as "work required to be done in the ordinary course of detention." The Grand Chamber disagreed noting a lack of European consensus on this issue. Such practice as there was did not warrant the interpretation for which the applicant argued.

In joined decisions *CSJSA/495/2007* and *CJSA/505/2007*, the Commissioner dismissed as unarguable a complaint by an appellant that the requirements of the New Deal programme with its obligation to participate in an intensive activity period employment programme constituted a modern form of slavery.

The fourth issue determined by the Supreme Court in *R (on the application of Reilly) v SSWP* [2013] UKSC 68 was whether the conditionality requirements for entitlement to jobseeker's allowance involving participation in work or work-related activity constituted force labour under art.4. The Supreme Court after consideration of the key Strasbourg authorities concluded that they did not.

Article 5—Right to liberty and security

1. Everyone has the right to liberty and security of person. No one shall be deprived of his liberty save in the following cases and in accordance with a procedure prescribed by law: 4.75
(a) the lawful detention of a person after conviction by a competent court;
(b) the lawful arrest or detention of a person for non-compliance with the lawful order of a court or in order to secure the fulfilment of any obligation prescribed by law;
(c) the lawful arrest or detention of a person effected for the purpose of bringing him before the competent legal authority on reasonable suspicion of having committed an offence or when it is reasonably considered necessary to prevent his committing an offence or fleeing after having done so;
(d) the detention of a minor by lawful order for the purpose of educational supervision or his lawful detention for the purpose of bringing him before the competent legal authority;
(e) the lawful detention of persons for the prevention of the spreading of infectious diseases, of persons of unsound mind, alcoholics or drug addicts or vagrants;
(f) the lawful arrest or detention of a person to prevent his effecting an unauthorised entry into the country or of a person against whom action is being taken with a view to deportation or extradition.

2. Everyone who is arrested shall be informed promptly, in a language which he understands, of the reasons for his arrest and of any charge against him.

3. Everyone arrested or detained in accordance with the provisions of paragraph 1 (c) of this Article shall be brought promptly before a judge or other officer authorised by law to exercise judicial power and shall be entitled to trial within a reasonable time or to release pending trial. Release may be conditioned by guarantees to appear for trial.

4. Everyone who is deprived of his liberty by arrest or detention shall be entitled to take proceedings by which the lawfulness of his detention shall be decided speedily by a court and his release ordered if the detention is not lawful.

5. Everyone who has been the victimof arrest or detention in contravention of the provisions of this Article shall have an enforceable right to compensation.

GENERAL NOTE

4.76 There are two parts to the protections afforded by art.5. First, it prohibits detention save in the exhaustive list of circumstances listed in para.(1). Secondly, it offers a set of procedural guarantees for those detained. Though the article refers to liberty and security of the person, the Strasbourg organs have not treated liberty and security as different concepts; there is no authority for arguing that security of the person refers to physical integrity independent of liberty. The article has little application in the field of social security.

Article 6—Right to a fair trial

4.77 **1.** In the determination of his civil rights and obligations or of any criminal charge against him, everyone is entitled to a fair and public hearing within a reasonable time by an independent and impartial tribunal established by law. Judgment shall be pronounced publicly but the press and public may be excluded from all or part of the trial in the interest of morals, public order or national security in a democratic society, where the interests of juveniles or the protection of the private life of the parties so require, or to the extent strictly necessary in the opinion of the court in special circumstances where publicity would prejudice the interests of justice.

2. Everyone charged with a criminal offence shall be presumed innocent until proved guilty according to law.

3. Everyone charged with a criminal offence has the following minimum rights:

(a) to be informed promptly, in a language which he understands and in detail, of the nature and cause of the accusation against him;

(b) to have adequate time and facilities for the preparation of his defence;

(c) to defend himself in person or through legal assistance of his own choosing or, if he has not sufficient means to pay for legal assistance, to be given it free when the interests of justice so require;

(d) to examine or have examined witnesses against him and to obtain the attendance and examination of witnesses on his behalf under the same conditions as witnesses against him;

(e) to have the free assistance of an interpreter if he cannot understand or speak the language used in court.

GENERAL NOTE

The structure of these annotations

4.78 Introductory remarks: (para.4.79)

Does the adjudication of social security disputes involve the determination of civil rights and obligations?: (para.4.80)

The application of art.6 to appeal proceedings: (para.4.81)

The right of access to a court: (para.4.82)

An overview of the requirements of fair trial under art.6: (para.4.83)

Equality of arms: (para.4.84)

A judicial process: (para.4.85)

Appearance in person: (para.4.86)

Effective participation: (para.4.87)

A reasoned decision: (para.4.88)

An independent and impartial tribunal established by law: (para.4.89)

A public hearing: (para.4.90)

A public judgment: (para.4.91)

Judgment in a reasonable time: (para.4.92)

Criminal charges: (para.4.93)

Introductory remarks

Article 6 is central to the scheme of protection in the Convention, and has generated the largest number of applications and judgments. Article 6 is an omnibus provision which contains a blueprint for what constitutes a fair trial. Although it has generated an extensive case law, there are few areas where the adjudication of social security disputes presents concerns about compatibility with the requirements of art.6. This is because the rules of procedure applicable to both First-tier Tribunals and the Upper Tribunal contain provisions which effectively guarantee the rights enshrined in art.6. There is also a long tradition of respect for a broadly construed notion of natural justice in the tribunals. Nevertheless, there are issues to be considered, and there is no cause for complacency in ensuring that those before the tribunals get a fair trial within the ambit of art.6. **4.79**

There have been statements by Commissioners and judges of the Upper Tribunal recognising the significance of art.6. In *CJSA/5100/2001,* a case not long after the entry into force of the Human Rights Act 1998, one Commissioner noted:

> "5. I choose to explain my decision in term's of the claimant's Convention right to a fair hearing under article 6(1) of the European Convention on Human Rights and Fundamental Freedoms. In particular, I rely on the equality of arms principle that has developed in the jurisprudence of the Strasbourg authorities as part of that right. It requires that the procedure followed by the tribunal must strike a fair balance between the parties so that none is at a disadvantage as against the others. . .
>
> 6. I could, no doubt, have reached the same conclusion under domestic principles of natural justice. However, the Human Rights Act 1998 provides a convenient opportunity for Commissioners to rebase their decisions on procedural fairness in fresh terms. In my view, this would be desirable. I am sure that tribunals are familiar with the principles of natural justice. However, increasingly the cases that come to me suggest that they are not applying them. If there is a common theme in those cases, it is that the tribunal has not provided a procedural balance between the parties. The introduction of the language of balance would provide a touchstone for tribunals."

See also comments in *CIB/2751/2002,* and *DG v SSWP (ESA)* [2010] UKUT 409 (AAC).

In *R. (on the application of Thompson) v The Law Society* [2002] EWCA Civ 167. Clarke L.J., delivering the judgment of the Court of Appeal with which his colleagues agreed, summarised the proper approach to issues of fair trial as follows:

> "The key point as a matter of principle is that the question whether the procedure satisfies article 6(1), where there is a determination of civil rights and obligations, must be answered by reference to the whole process. The question in each case is whether the process involves a court or courts having 'full jurisdiction to deal with the case as the nature of the decision requires'. There may be cases in which a public and oral hearing is required at first instances and other cases where it is not, just as there may be cases in which the potential availability of judicial review will not be sufficient to avoid a breach of article 6(1)".

What follows presents some observations on the structure and content of art.6, and how its provisions apply in the First-tier Tribunal and the Upper Tribunal.

Does the adjudication of social security disputes involve the determination of civil rights and obligations?

Article 6 is concerned with the determination of civil rights and obligations, and of criminal charges (see further below on criminal charges). Initially there was some uncertainty as to whether art.6 covered proceedings of an administrative nature, **4.80** since it had been argued that the concept of civil rights and obligations concerned only disputes having a private law character. It is, however, now firmly established that art.6 does cover social security adjudication, whether or not the benefit is contributory or non-contributory: *Feldbrugge v The Netherlands,* Series A No.99; (1986) 8 E.H.R.R. 425; *Deumeland v Germany,* Series A No.120; (1986) 8 E.H.R.R. 448; and *Salesi v Italy,* Series A No.257-E; (1998) 26 E.H.R.R. 187. The Strasbourg Court recapitulated its case-law in *Schuler-Zgraggen v Switzerland,* Series A No.263; (1993) 16 E.H.R.R. 405, where it said:

> "... the development in the law that was initiated by [the] judgments [in *Feldbrugge* and *Deumeland*] and the principle of equality of treatment warrant taking the view that today the general rule is that Article 6(1) does apply in the field of social insurance, including even welfare assistance." (at [46].)

See also *Schouten and Meldrum v The Netherlands,* Series A No.304; (1994) 19 E.H.R.R. 432.

In *Stevens and Knight v United Kingdom* (App.28918/85), decision of September 9, 1998, the Commission, in an admissibility decision, simply ignored arguments that the determination of claims to sickness benefit, statutory sick pay and invalidity benefit did not constitute the determination of civil rights and obligations.

Numerous national authorities have adopted the approach taken by the Strasbourg Court: see, for example, *CDLA/5413/1999.* In *Wood v Secretary of State for Work and Pensions* [2003] EWCA Civ 53 (see [24]) (reported as *R(DLA) 1/03*) the Secretary of State made a concession (quite unnecessary in the light of the Strasbourg authorities) which would appear to mean that all social security appeals involve the determination of civil rights and obligations and so attract the protection of art.6. See also *R(IS) 6/04,* but note para.68 of *R(H) 3/05.*

In a housing case, *Begum v Tower Hamlets LBC* [2003] UKHL 5, the House of Lords also took a broad view of what constitutes the determination of civil rights and obligations (without making any definitive ruling on what does and does not fall within this formulation in art.6) and went on to make a number of pertinent comments on what constitutes independence and impartiality for the purposes of the article. A decision by a rehousing manager employed by a local authority reviewing a decision to offer a particular property to the applicant was held not to constitute an "independent and impartial tribunal" for the purposes of art.6, but a determination on review by the county court "on any point of law arising from the decision" even one which did not permit the making of fresh findings of fact did meet the requirements of art.6.

The application of art.6 to appeal proceedings

4.81 The initial decision made by a decision maker does not attract the protection of art.6, since there must be a dispute—*contestation* in French—before art.6 bites. Thus, the first instance adjudication of social security disputes arises in proceedings before the First-tier Tribunal. But does art.6 also apply to appeals from decisions of the First-tier Tribunal?

Article 6 does not require Contracting States to have a system of appeals from decisions at first instance in civil cases: *De Cubber v Belgium,* Series A No.86; (1985) 7 E.H.R.R. 236, at [32], but if the state does provide a system of appeals, it too must comply with the guarantees to be found in art.6(1): *Fejde v Sweden,* Series A No.212-C; (1994) 17 E.H.R.R. 14, at [32]. It follows that a defect at first instance might be corrected at the appellate stage of the proceedings. Where there is an appeal, the requirement to exhaust domestic remedies before a complaint can be made under the Convention means that it must be used, and it will then be the totality of the domestic proceedings which is considered by the Strasbourg Court. It will always be necessary to look at the character of the appellate proceedings to determine the extent to which they are able to remedy any deficiency at first instance.

A fair appeal is unlikely to be able to correct a defect arising from a structural problem in the first instance court or tribunal which results in its not being an independent and impartial tribunal: *De Cubber v Belgium*, Series A No.86; (1985) 7 E.H.R.R. 236, at [33]. There is a suggestion that the quashing by an appeal court on the specific ground that the first instance court or tribunal was not independent and impartial might have cured the defect, but this could amount to recognition that there was no right to a court in the particular instance. This is a right which the Strasbourg Court has read into art.6 (see below).

There has been an ongoing debate in English law concerning the adequacy of judicial review as a remedy for what might be regarded as an earlier breach of Convention rights. In *CTC/0031/2006* the Commissioner considered this question in the context of an appeal concerning the backdating of a claim to Child Tax Credit. The Commissioner dismissed the appeal on the grounds that the acceptance of a "manner" of claiming is an administrative act involving the exercise of discretion. Accordingly, judicial review was an adequate remedy and there was no basis for the argument that art.6 required the recognition of a right to appeal to a tribunal on this question.

The right of access to a court

The Strasbourg Court has recognised that art.6 must contain a right of access to a court for the determination of a particular issue. So the prohibition (at the time) in English Prison Rules on bringing a defamation action against a prison officer, who was alleged to have accused the prisoner wrongly of having assaulted him, violated this right: *Golder v United Kingdom*, Series A No.18; (1979–80) 1 E.H.R.R. 524. A similar conclusion was reached in a case originating from Ireland where there was no procedure by which a father could challenge a decision of the authorities placing his daughter for adoption: *Keegan v Ireland*, Series A No.290; (1994) 18 E.H.R.R. 342. The right might even include a right to some sort of representation in order to make the right effective. In *Airey v Ireland*, Series A No.32; (1979–80) 2 E.H.R.R. 305, the applicant had been unable to find a lawyer to act for her because of her financial position and the absence of legal aid. She needed a separation order to protect her from her husband who was prone to violence towards her. The procedure was complex and not such as could be managed effectively by a litigant in person. The Court concluded that, in such circumstances, art.6 requires the provision of legal assistance where "such assistance proves indispensable for an effective access to court." (at [26]) The case is sometimes wrongly read too sweepingly as imposing an obligation on state to have a legal aid scheme, at least for complex litigation. The judgment is rather more limited; it will be necessary to look at the nature of the right being protected by the litigation, what is at stake for the applicant, and the complexity of the procedure before the particular decision-making body in making a judgment as to whether art.6 requires a state to provide legal assistance. 4.82

In *CJSA/5101/2001* the claimant sought to rely on the *Airey* case to ground an entitlement to legal representation. The Commissioner stated:

> "The claimant has no right to legal representation under British law in a social security case, and the European Convention on Human Rights does not give him that right. I have no power under British law to grant him legal representation and the European Convention on Human Rights, again does not give me that power." (at para.9.)

Though undoubtedly correct in the circumstances of the case before him, it is not entirely inconceivable that a set of circumstances might arise in which the *Airey* test would require the provision legal assistance and possibly legal representation in order to satisfy the requirements of art.6.

Following the passing of the Legal Aid, Sentencing and Punishment of Offenders Act 2012, the availability of legally aided advice, assistance and representation for social security adjudication is severely limited, although there was a late concession by the Government which has resulted in legal advice and assistance being available following a refusal of permission to appeal to the Upper Tribunal by the First-tier Tribunal, which encompasses advice and assistance on appeals (as they must be) on a point of law to the Upper Tribunal, and thereafter to the Court of Appeal and Supreme Court. The only possibility for legal aid for representation (as distinct from advice and assistance) would appear to be those situations in which the requirements of the Legal Aid, Sentencing and Punishment of Offenders Act 2012, s.10 are met. Section 10 provides:

"**10. Exceptional cases**

(1) Civil legal services other than services described in Part 1 of Schedule 1 are to be available to an individual under this Part if subsection (2) or (4) is satisfied.

(2) This subsection is satisfied where the Director—

(a) has made an exceptional case determination in relation to the individual and the services, and

(b) has determined that the individual qualifies for the services in accordance with this Part,

(and has not withdrawn either determination).

(3) For the purposes of subsection (2), an exceptional case determination is a determination—

(a) that it is necessary to make the services available to the individual under this Part because failure to do so would be a breach of—

(i) the individual's Convention rights (within the meaning of the Human Rights Act 1998), or

(ii) any rights of the individual to the provision of legal services that are enforceable EU rights, or

(b) that it is appropriate to do so, in the particular circumstances of the case, having regard to any risk that failure to do so would be such a breach.

(4) This subsection is satisfied where—

(a) the services consist of advocacy in proceedings at an inquest under the Coroners Act 1988 into the death of a member of the individual's family,

(b) the Director has made a wider public interest determination in relation to the individual and the inquest, and

(c) the Director has determined that the individual qualifies for the services in accordance with this Part,

(and neither determination has been withdrawn).

(5) For the purposes of subsection (4), a wider public interest determination is a determination that, in the particular circumstances of the case, the provision of advocacy under this Part for the individual for the purposes of the inquest is likely to produce significant benefits for a class of person, other than the individual and the members of the individual's family.

(6) For the purposes of this section an individual is a member of another individual's family if—

(a) they are relatives (whether of the full blood or half blood or by marriage or civil partnership),

(b) they are cohabitants (as defined in Part 4 of the Family Law Act 1996), or

(c) one has parental responsibility for the other."

See also the Civil Legal Aid (Preliminary Proceedings) Regulations 2013 (SI 2013/265), and the *Lord Chancellor's Exceptional Funding Guidance (Non-Inquests) https://www.gov.uk/government/uploads/system/uploads/attachment_data/file/332858/legal-aid-chancellors-guide-exceptional-funding-non-inquests.pdf*

The Upper Tribunal has on occasion been critical of the refusal of legal aid: see, for example, *JC v SSWP (ESA)* [2014] UKUT 352 (AAC) at para.63.

There are separate provisions relating to judicial review proceedings under which advice, assistance and representation may be available.

Civil legal aid in Scotland is the province of the Scottish Civil Legal Aid Board *http://www.slab.org.uk* and the availability of both advice and assistance, and representation, appears to be significantly more generous than the provision in England and Wales.

Part of the decision of the Tribunal of Commissioners in *CIB/3645/2002* concerned an argument that the absence of a right of appeal in the social security legislation contravened the claimant's rights under art.6. The Tribunal of Commissioners ruled that the decision that the claimant was, or was not, permanently incapacitated for work at the time of leaving Great Britain for Jamaica concerned the payability of benefit while the claimant was in Jamaica rather his entitlement to the benefit. The decision was accordingly not within the scope of the Social Security Act 1998, s.12(3). Furthermore art.6 was not relevant because art.6 had "no part to play in the ambit of substantive rights, as opposed to procedural rights." (at para.43.), since art.13(2) of the Social Security (Jamaica) Order 1997 (SI 1997/871) provided a subjective test, under which the Secretary of State determined whether benefit was to continue to be payable abroad where he considered the claimant likely to be permanently incapacitated for work on leaving Great Britain. The Tribunal of Commissioners indicates that it has not come to this decision lightly and adds a rider in para.54 of its decision:

> "Finally, we should make clear that our decision is limited to the issues before us. On the basis of the decision of Mr Commissioner Howell Q.C. in *CIB/3654/2002* [this appears to be an erroneous reference, which should be to *CIS/540/2002*, now reported as *R(IS) 6/04*], it may be arguable that that the Human Rights Act and Art.6 of the European Convention may require rights of appeal to be granted against decisions under reciprocal agreement provisions in respect of which rights of appeal had existed previously. There may also be other cases in which it may be arguable that para.22 of Sch.2 of the Decisions and Appeals Regulations does not restrict certain rights of appeal without deciding whether the provision is ultra vires (as found in *CIB/3586/2000* (starred decision 15/00)). We express no view on the correctness of those decisions."

The appeal against this decision was dismissed by the Court of Appeal: *Campbell v SSWP* [2005] EWCA Civ. 989.

An overview of the requirements of fair trial under art.6

The Strasbourg organs have indicated that art.6(1) demands not only an overall requirement of a fair hearing but also the presence of specific features in order for there to be a fair trial. The overall requirement has been summarised as follows: **4.83**

> "The effect of Article 6(1) is, inter alia, to place the 'tribunal' under a duty to conduct a proper examination of the submissions, arguments and evidence adduced by the parties, without prejudice to its assessment of whether they are relevant to its decision." (*Kraska v Switzerland*, Series A No.254-B; (1994) 18 E.H.R.R. 188, at [30]).

It is important that the general requirements for a fair trial are appreciated, since they continue to be developed in specific circumstances by the Strasbourg Court. Certain of the requirements are of a general nature, whereas others are more specifically stated in art.6. This over-riding requirement of fairness reflects five inherent requirements for a fair trial and four explicit requirements set out in art.6.

The inherent requirements are: (a) *égalité des armes*, or "equality of arms"; (b) a judicial process; (c) a right to appearance in person; (d) a right to effective participation; and (e) a right to a reasoned decision.

The explicit rights are to: (a) an independent and impartial tribunal established by law; (b) a public hearing; (c) a public judgment; and (d) judgment in a reasonable time.

Each of these nine ingredients of the fair trial will now be considered.

Equality of arms

4.84 Equality of arms is an inelegant translation of *égalité des armes*. An idiomatic translation is more helpful, namely procedural equality. In national law, this has long been an inherent aspect of natural justice. Procedural equality requires that each party has a broadly equal opportunity to present a case in circumstances which do not place one of the parties as a substantial disadvantage as regards the opposing party (see *Dombo Beheer BV v The Netherlands*, Series A No.274-A; (1994) 18 E.H.R.R. 213, at [33]).

In an expansive reading of the Strasbourg case law, the Commissioner in *CDLA/2748/2002* draws on specific case-law relating to criminal proceedings in art.6(3)(e) on the provision of interpretation and translation to suggest that art.6 requires that effective and efficient interpretation and translation is a feature of tribunal adjudication where the claimant needs this. He says that "a failure of interpretation must therefore affect the fairness of the tribunal hearing." (para.11).

A judicial process

4.85 A judicial process requires each side to have the opportunity to have knowledge of and comment on the observations filed or evidence adduced by the opposing party: *Ruiz-Mateos v Spain*, Series A No.262; (1993) 16 E.H.R.R. 505, at [63]. Non-disclosure of material by one side to the other is likely to give rise to violations of this feature of a fair trial, as might issues of the circumstances in which evidence was acquired. In *Feldbrugge v The Netherlands*, Series A No.99; (1986) 8 E.H.R.R. 425, the applicant complained that she had not had a proper opportunity to present her case. The Court found that the proceedings before the President of the Appeals Board "were not attended to a sufficient degree, by one of the principal guarantees of a judicial procedure" (at [44]) in that, although the applicant had been afforded the opportunity to comment on her condition during the medical examinations, she was neither able to present oral argument nor to file written pleadings before the President of the Appeals Board; nor was she able to consult the two reports of the consultants and to formulate objections to them.

Appearance in person

4.86 Can a trial be fair if there is no right of appearance in person? The Strasbourg Court has considered in some detail the importance of a right to appearance in person in *Elo v Finland* (App.30742), judgment of September 26, 2006. The case concerned accident compensation and it was held that written submissions were sufficient to meet the requirements of a fair trial. The Court considers that the "question is whether hearing oral evidence from the applicant and the doctors treating him could have produced anything relevant and decisive which was not already encompassed in the written evidence and submissions." In the circumstances of this case, the Court concluded that oral evidence would have added little to the written submissions. The Strasbourg Court has adopted a distinctly pragmatic approach to this aspect of art.6, as it has to some other rights forming part of the article.

Effective participation

4.87 Mere presence at a trial may not be sufficient. There must also be an ability to participate in the proceedings in an effective manner. The principal authority relates to the treatment of juveniles in the criminal process: *T v United Kingdom* (App.24724/94) and *V v United Kingdom* (App.24888/94), (2000) 30 E.H.R.R. 121; and *SC v United Kingdom* (App.60958/00), (2005) 40 E.H.R.R. 226.

In *Schuler-Zgraggen v Switzerland*, Series A No.263; (1993) 16 E.H.R.R. 405, (which was principally concerned with the right to a public hearing) the applicant had not availed herself of the opportunity to request a hearing, but nevertheless complained that the proceedings were unfair because the Federal Insurance Court had not ordered a hearing of its own motion. The Court accepted the arguments of the Government that purely written proceedings did not in the circumstances of this case prejudice the interests of the litigant. It was accepted that a written procedure would offer advantages of efficiency and speed which might be jeopardised if oral hearings became the rule. The Court ruled:

> "The Court reiterates that the public character of court hearings constitutes a fundamental principle enshrined in Article 6(1). Admittedly, neither the letter nor the spirit of this provision prevents a person from waiving of his own free will, either expressly or tacitly, the entitlement to have his case heard in public, but any such waiver must be made in an unequivocal manner and must not run counter to any important public interest." (at [58].)

The possibility of holding "paper hearings" before the First-tier Tribunal is unlikely to generate any possibility of a lack of fairness (either in relation to appearance in person or effective participation) under art.6 for a number of reasons. Firstly, an appellant always has the opportunity to request an oral hearing. Furthermore, in all cases, r.27 (decision with or without a hearing) of the First-tier Tribunal's rules of procedure requires the tribunal, regardless of the wishes of the parties, always to consider whether it is able to decide the appeal without an oral hearing. The decisions of the Upper Tribunal on the proper application of r.27 discussed in the annotations to that rule (paras 5.288–5.297 below) show that art.6 considerations are at the heart of the requirement to show that the rule has been considered in cases where the tribunal proceeds in the absence of the parties.

A reasoned decision

The requirement for a reasoned decision is regarded as implicit in the notion of a fair trial. The level of reasoning need not be detailed. If a court or tribunal gives reasons, then the requirement for a reasoned decision is prima facie met, but a decision which on its face shows that it was made on a basis not open to the judge cannot be said to be a reasoned decision (see *De Moor v Belgium*, Series A No.292-A; (1994) 18 E.H.R.R. 372). For a case in which a violation of art.6 was found because of the inadequacy of the reasons for rejecting certain medical evidence in a social security context, see *H.A.L. v Finland* (App.38267/97), judgment of January 27, 2004. **4.88**

The use of short-form decisions in tribunals is unlikely to fall foul of this provision, since a party is entitled to a full statement of reasons on application within one month of the day on which the decision notice was notified to the parties. Decisions of the Upper Tribunal are given in full, except a decision made with the consent of the parties to set aside a tribunal decision and remit the case for a rehearing by the tribunal, or otherwise to dispose of the appeal.

An independent and impartial tribunal established by law

The requirement that there is an independent and impartial tribunal established by law includes a subjective and an objective element. The subjective test involves an enquiry into whether the particular judge in the case was actually biased, or lacking in independence or impartiality. Propriety will be presumed in the absence of specific evidence of bias. The objective test involves determination of whether the court or tribunal offers guarantees sufficient to exclude any legitimate doubt about its impartiality or independence. This can include both specific difficulties caused by certain persons being involved in particular decisions, as well as what might be called structural problems with the forum for the resolution of the dispute. A good example of structural problems can be found in the English courts-martial cases, which have determined that the role (at the time) of the convening officer in the management of the prosecution case conflicted with his role as convenor of the court-martial, in particular his appointment of its members (who were subordinate **4.89** in rank to himself and fell within his chain of command) (see *Findlay v United Kingdom* (App.22107/93), (1997) 24 E.H.R.R. 221; and *Coyne v United Kingdom* (App.25942/94), *The Times*, October 24, 1997, ECHR.

Tsfayo v United Kingdom (App. 60860/00), (2009) 48 E.H.R.R. 457, is now of historical interest, but a violation of art.6 was found on the grounds that the Housing Benefit Review Board was not an independent and impartial tribunal. However, the comments in the case on the relationship between appeals and other remedies are of considerable significance, and it was suggested that, for this reason, the United Kingdom would seek to have the case referred to the Grand Chamber. That does not appear to have happened. Note in relation to the *Tsfayo* case, the admissibility decision of the Strasbourg Court in *BH v United Kingdom* (App.59580/00), decision of September 25, 2007.

The issue of an independent and impartial tribunal raises the question of bias by one or more members of the court or tribunal. This has provided to be a contentious issue in relation, in particular, to the medical members of certain social security tribunals. This issue is considered in detail in the annotations to the Tribunals, Courts and Enforcement Act 2007 s.3 see below at 5.25–5.26) and that material is not repeated here.

A public hearing

4.90 Publicity is seen as one of the guarantees of the fairness of a trial, but the requirement for hearings to be in public is surrounded by a substantial list of circumstances in which the presumption of public hearings is displaced. It is now also clear that interlocutory matters do not have to be in public. So the Commission has rejected a complaint that interlocutory proceedings before a High Court Master in Chambers without elaborating its reasons violated art.6: *X v United Kingdom* (App.3860/68), (1970) 30 CD 70. A similar view would almost certainly be taken of proceedings for permission to appeal. As already noted, a written procedure may suffice provided that there are proper opportunities for requesting or ordering an oral hearing.

In *DF v SSWP* [2015] UKUT 143 (AAC), Judge Gamble held that pre-publication of the hearing lists for scheduled appeal hearings did not breach the requirements for a public hearing in art.6. Judge Gamble said:

> "25. . . . . The minimum requirement of a public hearing, in my view, is that it takes place within reasonable office hours and at a publicly recognised court or tribunal hearing centre. That is so even if no pre-publicity of listed cases is available unless that can be shown in any case to be a stratagem to deprive a claimant of a public hearing. . . . ."

A public judgment

4.91 Article 6(1), on its face, requires that judgment is pronounced publicly, and this requirement is not expressed to be subject to the list of limitations which apply to a public trial. The leading case is *Pretto v Italy*, Series A No.71; (1984) 6 E.H.R.R. 182, and adopts a pragmatic view to the right. The Court seems to have been very accommodating to a wide range of practice in this regard among the Contracting States, indicating that the form of publicity to be given to a judgment is to be assessed in the light of special features of particular proceedings. It certainly appears to be the case that nothing more than the formal disposition need be announced publicly, and it seems that the public availability of the outcome is as important as the matter being read out in open court. So in the *Pretto* case, the availability of the disposition in the court registry was considered to meet the requirements for public pronouncement of the judgment.

Judgment in a reasonable time

4.92 Article 6(1) provides that litigants are entitled to judgment in a reasonable time. Complaints of violations of this requirement have been the single most numerous sort of alleged violation of the Convention. Such cases have rarely involved the United Kingdom (but see *Robins v United Kingdom*, (1998) 26 E.H.R.R. 527).

For a pithy statement of how the courts and tribunals of England and Wales deal with the requirement that judgment be given within a reasonable time, see *Bond v Dunster Properties Ltd* [2011] EWCA Civ 455, at [1]–[6].

Though the case law is voluminous, the principles can be stated quite simply. The first task is to determine the period or periods in issue, before moving on to consider the reasonableness of the length of the proceedings. The period in issue will include any appellate proceedings. In forming judgments on the reasonableness of the length of the proceedings, the following factors are relevant: the complexity of the case, the behaviour of the applicant, the conduct of the judicial authorities, and what is at stake for the applicant. However, backlogs of judicial business are not a defence to unreasonable delays. In *Deumeland v Germany,* Series A No.120; (1986) 8 E.H.R.R. 448, the period in issue was ten years, seven months and three weeks from the application to the Berlin Social Security Court to the rejection of the application to the Bundesverfassungericht. The claim to benefit involved a straightforward factual issue involving no great legal complexity, but the behaviour of Klaus Deumeland had protracted the proceedings. Detailed examination of the progress of the case through the various courts showed that the case had lain dormant before the Berlin Social Security Court for significant periods, and the period taken to resolve the second set of proceedings before the appellate body was excessive. There was a violation of the right to judgment within a reasonable time, but it is significant that the Court also finds that the mere declaration of a violation was in the circumstances of the case considered to be adequate just satisfaction under what is now art.41 of the Convention. A delay of a little over six years in the *Salesi v Italy,* Series A No.257-E; (1998) 26 E.H.R.R. 187, was also found to constitute a violation of art.6(1).The reasonableness of the time taken to give judgment must be determined in each case in the light of its own particular circumstances. On the remedies for a breach of the right, see the judgment of the Grand Chamber in *Scordino v Italy (No.1)* (App.36813/97), (2007) 45 E.H.R.R. 207.

The issue of judgment within a reasonable time in the social security context was raised in *R(IS) 1/04,* where the claimant argued that the (it should be said not wholly unusual) lengthy period before an overpayment decision was taken meant that there was a breach of art.6. An overpayment decision was made on October 14, 2000 in respect of an overpayment which had arisen in 1994 and 1995. The Commissioner concludes that for the purposes of the measurement of time in the context of a complaint that judgment has not been given within a reasonable time, time started running on October 14, 2000, since it was at that point that a dispute arose; a different Commissioner in *R(IS) 2/04* takes the same view at para.20. That was enough to dispose of the point since a tribunal determined the appeal in May 2001 which was manifestly within a reasonable time. The claimant had also sought to suggest that overpayment decisions were in the nature of criminal charges. The Commissioner, after careful consideration of the authorities, concludes that overpayment decisions involve the determination of civil rights and obligations and not the determination of a criminal charge (see [12]–[17]).

See also *CIS/4220/2002,* which draws on the decision of the Court in *Dyer v Watson* [2002] 4 All E.R. 1.

In *AS v SSWP (CA)* [2015] UKUT 592 (AAC); [2016] AACR 22, Judge Wright considered how a First-tier Tribunal should deal with an established claim that there has not been judgment in a reasonable time contrary to art.6 ECHR. The issue of delay arose in the following circumstances. The Secretary of State made an entitlement decision on September 4, 2004 in respect of non-entitlement to carer's allowance arising from April 16, 2001. But it was not until January 5, 2007 that an overpayment decision was made. There was then a further five-year delay before a letter which was dated April 11, 2007 was accepted as an appeal against the overpayment decision. The tribunal's decision was made in May 2014. In considering at paras 49-56 how the tribunal should have responded to this issue, Judge Wright assumes that the delays would amount to a failure to give judgment in a reasonable time in breach of Article 6 of the European Convention. He concludes that it will usually be the case that a tribunal must proceed to determine the appeal notwithstanding the delay, and cannot simply not proceed on the grounds that there has been an unreasonable delay. The person affected must seek a remedy elsewhere in the form of compensation, and the tribunal has no power to award compensation: see *Cocchiarella v Italy (App.64886/01)* Judgment of Grand Chamber of March 29, 2006.

In *Bullerwell v United Kingdom* (App.48013/99), (2003) 36 E.H.R.R. CD 76, the Strasbourg Court ruled as inadmissible a complaint that judgment was not given in a reasonable time in an industrial injuries benefit case which involved four hearings by a medical appeal tribunal, three appeals to the Commissioner, and an application for judicial review which resulted in an unsuccessful appeal to the Court of Appeal. The outcome is unsurprising even though the first appeal was lodged in July 1991 and the trail of litigation ended in July 1998 when the House of Lords refused a petition for leave to appeal the refusal of leave to apply for judicial review. The Court applies its tried and tested methodology of considering the complexity of the case, the parties' conduct and that of the competent authorities, and the importance of what was at stake for the applicant in the litigation. There is nothing significant in the decision but it is an excellent example of the approach of the Court to admissibility of complaints and contains a detailed and fair analysis of the course of these lengthy proceedings.

In its admissibility decision of April 8, 2003 in *Wingrave v United Kingdom* (App.40029/02), the Strasbourg Court had declared inadmissible part of the claim (relating (1) to a breach of contract claim, (2) to the requirement to make a new claim at age 65 for disability living allowance, and (3) concerning the quality of her representation) but adjourned the issue concerning the length of the proceedings. The appeal had been twice remitted for rehearing by the Commissioners and had taken nearly five years to conclude. By a decision of May 18, 2004, the Court declared this aspect of the complaint admissible, but a friendly settlement was subsequently reached under which the applicant's executors received from the respondent State an ex gratia payment of £4,500: decision of November 29, 2005.

In *CDLA/1761/2002* the claimant raised an art.6 issue in relation to the delay (of about six months) in producing the written statement of reasons for the tribunal's decision. The Commissioner did not need to address the argument in full, but rightly notes that art.6 is concerned with the overall length of the proceedings and not with delays in relation to specific parts of the process.

Criminal charges

4.93 A question arises as to whether proceedings for penalty additions to overpayments, and of possible penalty proceedings under the tax credits legislation, as well as determinations of the Upper Tribunal under the Forfeiture Act of 1982, constitute the determination of criminal charges under art.6 and so attract the additional protections for such matters in the article.

The concept of a criminal charge is an autonomous one under the Convention, and so it is not the classification of the matter under national law which is determinative of the issue. National classification is not, however, wholly irrelevant since the Strasbourg organs have always regarded as a criminal charge something so considered by national law.

In other cases the following factors have been taken into account in making the determination: the nature of the "offence", the severity of the sanction imposed having regard in particular to any loss of liberty since this is a principal characteristic of criminal liability: see *Engel v The Netherlands*, Series A No.22; (1979–80) 1 E.H.R.R. 647. Having regard to this case and to the judgment of the Court in *Ravnsborg v Sweden* Series A No.283-B; (1994) 18 E.H.R.R. 38, it is argued that such proceedings would not constitute the determination of a criminal charge. The essence of the penalty provision is civil rather than criminal in nature.

However, in *King v United Kingdom* (App 13881/02), judgment of November 16, 2004, which concerned a penalty determination in relation to tax liabilities, the Strasbourg Court found a violation of art.6(1) on grounds of delay and characterised the penalty proceedings as criminal charges. The question of their classification is, however, not argued in the judgment. The United Kingdom government seems to have accepted that the proceedings did involve a criminal charge. The classification would not matter where the sole issue is delay, but could, in other circumstances, be a matter of importance since criminal charges attract additional protections under art.6. An example would be an entitlement to free legal assistance under art.6(3)(c) where the interests of justice demand this.

Article 7—No punishment without law

1. No one shall be held guilty of any criminal offence on account of any act or omission which did not constitute a criminal offence under national or international law at the time when it was committed. Nor shall a heavier penalty be imposed than the one that was applicable at the time the criminal offence was committed. **4.94**

2. This Article shall not prejudice the trial and punishment of any person for any act or omission which, at the time when it was committed, was criminal according to the general principles of law recognised by civilised nations.

Article 8—Right to respect for private and family life

1. Everyone has the right to respect for his private and family life, his home and his correspondence. **4.95**

2. There shall be no interference by a public authority with the exercise of this right except such as is in accordance with the law and is necessary in a democratic society in the interests of national security, public safety or the economic well-being of the country, for the prevention of disorder or crime, for the protection of health or morals, or for the protection of the rights and freedoms of others.

GENERAL NOTE

Introduction

Article 8 is one of the most open-ended provisions of the Convention and is not yet fully developed in its scope. The concept of private life is very wide and not easily contained within a single comprehensive definition. The protection of private life (as distinct from family life) under art.8 can now be organised under a number of headings: **4.96**

- freedom from interference with physical and psychological integrity, which includes interference with the person, searches of property, surveillance and interception of communications, and the dissemination of images;
- the collection, storage and use of personal information;
- freedom to develop one's identity, which includes discovering information about childhood and parenthood, aspects of the use of names, transsexuality, and cultural identity;
- a right to personal autonomy, which includes sexual preference, and the establishment of a settled circle of friends, and respect for decisions in relation to health and medical treatment;
- the protection of one's living environment;
- protection of the home; and
- protection of correspondence.

Like the series of articles which follows, the rights given in para.(1) are limited by the exceptions listed in para.(2). If there is an interference with one of the rights protected in the first paragraph, then it will be necessary to see whether this is justified under the limitations in the second paragraph. Here the Strasbourg organs have consistently required the interference to be: (1) for one of the specified reasons; (2) in accordance with law; (3) necessary in a democratic society; and (4) proportionate in the sense that there is no other way of protecting the recognised interest which constitutes a lesser interference with the right.

Benefit, family life and private life

4.97 Article 8 of the Convention guarantees respect private life, home and correspondence, for family life, subject to the limitation contained in the article. Family life encompasses ties between near relatives, which certainly extends to children, parents and grandparents, though it is unclear how far it includes relationships between siblings, aunts and uncles. In general the Strasbourg organs have preferred relationships in the vertical line to those in the horizontal line.

In the *CG v Austria* (1737/90) case, the applicant had complained that the refusal to award him the emergency assistance requested violated respect for his family life (presumably on the grounds that refusal of the assistance threatened the break up of, or hardship to, his family); the admissibility decision is not specific on the basis for declaring this part of his complaint admissible (see (1994) 18 E.H.R.R. CD51). Neither the Commission nor the Court found it necessary to consider this aspect of the complaint since they concluded that there was a violation of art.14 read in conjunction with art.1 of Protocol 1. Nevertheless, it remains open for the limits of the protection under art.8 to be explored in the context of entitlements to social security. But it would be fair to say that there are few indications that the Strasbourg organs regard the Convention right here as including an obligation on the State to make payments to families for their support.

In *CJSA/935/1999* the Commissioner made some *obiter* comments on the rights of transsexuals to respect for their identity. The issue had arisen in the context of a claim that the use of the national insurance number in a jobseeker's agreement enabled the claimant's gender at birth to be identified. The decision contains a useful overview of some leading decisions in this area both under European Union law and under the European Convention on Human Rights.

4.98 For the latest summary of the position of transsexuals in the light of recent decisions of the Strasbourg Court, see the opinions of the House of Lords in *Bellinger v Bellinger* [2003] UKHL 21 (April 10, 2003).

But note the decision of the Court of Human Rights in *Grant v United Kingdom (App. 32570/03)*, Judgment of May 23, 2006, which concerned a male-to-female transsexual who had been refused a pension on reaching the age of 60. Initial failures to secure the pension before reaching the age of 65 were re-opened following the grant of a gender recognition certificate under the Gender Recognition Act 2004. Grant succeeded in securing a judgment that the United Kingdom was in breach of art.8 E.C.H.R. from July 2002 when the Court of Human Rights handed down its decision in *Goodwin v United Kingdom* (2002) 35 E.H.R.R. 447.

It is clear from the decision of the Court of Appeal and House of Lords in *R. (on the application of Hooper, Withey, Naylor and Martin) v Secretary of State for Work and Pensions,* [2003] EWCA Civ 813, and [2005] UKHL 29, that benefits for widows and widowers fall within the ambit of art.8. However, income support and income-based jobseeker's allowance schemes do not, according to the Court of Appeal, *per se* engage art.8: see *Carson and Reynolds v Secretary of State for Work and Pensions,* [2003] EWCA Civ 797.

4.99 In *R. (Smith) v Secretary of State for Defence and Secretary of State for Work and Pensions* [2004] EWHC 1797 (Admin), Wilson J. held that respect for private life under art.8 encompasses respect for a person's need for financial support "when under as well as over the age of 60". The case concerned an argument by an ex-wife that she was entitled to payment of that part of a pension which was subject to a pension sharing order below the age of 60 since the pension was so payable to her former husband. The judge held that the provisions governing the payment to the ex-wife of the pension at the age of 60 did not breach her rights under art.8:

> "One cannot say that the impugned provision challenges the principle that the claimant needs financial support before as well as after the age of 60. In making the provision the state has decreed only that provision carved out of pension rights should not result in payment earlier than what is presently regarded, in the context of state provision, as normal pensionable age. In other words pension credits are conferred so as to address later, rather than earlier, need; and, because of the delay in payment suffered by some pension credit members, the real amount of their pension is correspondingly increased. The impugned provision does not derogate from the duty of the divorce court under [the matrimonial legislation] to have regard to a spouse's likely needs prior to the age of 60 in deciding what, of any, order to make for her or his benefit by way of financial provision or property adjustment in addition to the pension sharing order." (At [21(b)].)

In *C1/05-06 (WB)*, *C2/05-06 (WB)*, and *C3/05-06 (WB)*, a Commissioner in Northern Ireland concluded that an absolute three months time limit for claiming widow's benefit does not violate art.8. She said,

> "17. . . . . I am doubtful that the three month time limit for claiming a benefit can in any way be linked to or have a "meaningful connection" with an Article 8 right in the absence of any Article 14 discrimination. However, even if a link exists, it is too tenuous to be within the ambit of the right. The right is not to the benefit but to the respect set out in Article 8. The time limit in no way violates that respect."

In *CP/1183/2007* the Commissioner dismisses in short form the possibility of arguing that differential state retirement ages for men and women can constitute a violation of art.8 when read in conjunction with art.14.

CM v SSWP (DLA) [2013] UKUT 27, reported as [2013] AACR 21, concerned a human rights challenge to the hospital rules under which DLA ceased to be payable for a child under 16 once that child had been in hospital for 84 days. The Judge found that art.8 did not apply. Family life continued during the long period in hospital of a very sick three-year-old child, albeit with additional difficulties. The withdrawal of DLA after 84 days in hospital did not preclude that. Respect for family life could not be said to be violated by failing to continue to pay DLA beyond the 84-day limit in this case. But if the Judge was wrong on that, he concluded that the hospital rule could be justified on grounds of the economic well-being of the country largely for the same reasons he had reached in relation to the human rights point taken under art.14 and art.1 of Prot.1, which is discussed in the annotations to art.14. Although the Upper Tribunal decision was upheld in the Court of Appeal at [2014] EWCA Civ 286, the further appeal to the Supreme Court as *Cameron Mathieson, a deceased child (by his father Craig Mathieson) v SSWP* [2015] UKSC 47, [2015] AACR 44, succeeded on the basis that the rule was manifestly without reasonable foundation.

Surveillance in social security cases

In *R(DLA) 4/02* the claimant argued that covert filming of the claimant in public places by the Department violated her Convention rights under art.8. The 4.100
Commissioner did not agree having regard to the balance which had to be struck between the interests of the individual and those of the community as a whole. In claiming benefit, the claimant had necessarily accepted a degree of interference with her private life. The covert filming had been limited to activities in public and was brief. The information gathered was used only for the purposes of considering the claimant's continuing entitlement to the benefit she had claimed.

In *CIS/1481/2006* which is excoriating about the behaviour of officers of the Department in the matter before him, and critical of the tribunal's approach to the case, a Commissioner has provided very useful guidance on issues concerning the use of surveillance techniques to support decision-making in the Department.

In particular, there is the most helpful guidance about the application of the Regulation of Investigatory Powers Act 2000 (RIPA) to surveillance by the Department. Such action is, of course, frequently attacked as a violation of art.8 ECHR. The Commissioner summarises a detailed section of his decision as follows:

> "50. More generally, where there is a challenge under Article 8 of the European Convention against evidence produced by the Secretary of State, or the conduct or results of surveillance are otherwise challenged before an appeal tribunal, RIPA now provides effective answers. If the Secretary of State provides the tribunal and the claimant with a copy of the application and authorisation for the surveillance, and it is clear that the authorisation covers the surveillance, then the tribunal will usually need to take matters no further. The tribunal may properly take the view that the Secretary of State can rely fully on the evidence obtained from the surveillance without further investigation by itself. If the claimant has continuing or other concerns, then he or she may take them to the investigatory powers tribunal. With that in mind, I suggest that the Secretary of State should, in cases such as this, produce the proper documentation about surveillance to an appellant and the tribunal together with the evidence from the surveillance on which the Secretary of State seeks to rely."

CIS/1481/2006 has been followed in *DG v SSWP (DLA)* [2011] UKUT 14 (AAC), at paras 43–47.

For observations by the Court of Appeal on the issue of surveillance, see *Jones v University of Warwick* [2003] 1 W.L.R. 954.

Article 9—Freedom of thought, conscience and religion

4.101 **1.** Everyone has the right to freedom of thought, conscience and religion; this right includes freedom to change his religion or belief and freedom, either alone or in community with others and in public or private, to manifest his religion or belief, in worship, teaching, practice and observance.

2. Freedom to manifest one's religion or beliefs shall be subject only to such limitations as are prescribed by law and are necessary in a democratic society in the interests of public safety, for the protection of public order, health or morals, or for the protection of the rights and freedoms of others.

GENERAL NOTE

4.102 Reliance on this article to avoid the normal requirements, for example, to pay national insurance contributions are most unlikely to succeed. The Commission has held that a Dutch system of old-age pension insurance, alleged to interfere with the religious duty of caring for old people, did not violate the article: App.1497/62, *Reformed Church of X v The Netherlands* (1962) 5 Y.B. 286; and App.2065/63, *X v The Netherlands* (1965) 8 Y.B. 266.

Article 10—Freedom of expression

4.103 **1.** Everyone has the right to freedom of expression. This right shall include freedom to hold opinions and to receive and impart information and ideas without interference by public authority and regardless of frontiers. This Article shall not prevent States from requiring the licensing of broadcasting, television or cinema enterprises.

2. The exercise of these freedoms, since it carries with it duties and responsibilities, may be subject to such formalities, conditions, restrictions or penalties as are prescribed by law and are necessary in a democratic society, in the interests of national security, territorial integrity or public safety, for the prevention of disorder or crime, for the protection of health or morals, for the protection of the reputation or rights of others, for preventing the disclosure of information received in confidence, or for maintaining the authority and impartiality of the judiciary.

Article 11—Freedom of assembly and association

4.104 **1.** Everyone has the right to freedom of peaceful assembly and to freedom of association with others, including the right to form and to join trade unions for the protection of his interests.

2. No restrictions shall be placed on the exercise of these rights other than such as are prescribed by law and are necessary in a democratic society in the interests of national security or public safety, for the prevention of disorder or crime, for the protection of health or morals or for the protection of the rights and freedoms of others. This Article shall not prevent the imposition of lawful restrictions on the exercise of these rights by members of the armed forces, of the police or of the administration of the State.

Article 12—Right to marry

Men and women of marriageable age have the right to marry and to found a family, according to the national laws governing the exercise of this right. 4.105

Article 14—Prohibition of discrimination

The enjoyment of the rights and freedoms set forth in this Convention shall be secured without discrimination on any ground such as sex, race, colour, language, religion, political or other opinion, national or social origin, association with a national minority, property, birth or other status. 4.106

GENERAL NOTE

The structure of these annotations 4.107

The general structure of art.14 (para.4.108)
The Strasbourg approach to art.14 in the social security context (paras 4.109–4.112)
Some judgments of the Strasbourg Court in social security cases (paras 4.113–4.115)
Positive obligations and art.14 (para.4.116)
National authorities on art.14 read with art.1 of Protocol 1 (paras 4.117–4.122)
Article 14 in conjunction with art.8 (paras 4.123–4.124)

The general structure of art.14

Article 14 prohibits discrimination on the grounds of sex, race, colour, language, religion, political or other opinion, national or social origin, association with a national minority, property, birth or other status. Discrimination can be either direct or indirect: *DH v Czech Republic* (App. 57325/00), November 13, 2007 [Grand Chamber]. In *Esfandiari* [2006] EWCA Civ 282, the Court of Appeal was of the view that an indirect discrimination claim under art.14 should be treated with some care because the case law is limited in this area. The key test will be whether the effects on the disadvantaged group are disproportionately prejudicial. However, this case was decided before the judgment of the Grand Chamber in the *DH* case, which establishes without doubt that art.14 does cover indirect discrimination. 4.108

The protection of art.14 is only applicable in relation to the enjoyment of the rights and freedoms set forth in the Convention. It is the linking of art.14 with another article of the Convention which gives it substance. In order to have effect, it does not have to be shown that there is a violation of the substantive article, merely that the alleged discrimination operates in a field which is covered by the protections afforded by those provisions. Indeed the practice of the Strasbourg Court has been to decline to consider art.14 in conjunction with another article if they find a violation of that article on its face, unless the essence of the complaint is discrimination. The article has proved to be a fruitful source of complaints in social security cases. However, the position of the Strasbourg Court is now well established in relation to complaints of violations of the prohibition of discrimination in the social security context. Since most challenges relate to economic and social policy choices, it has proved relatively easy for states to show that those choices are reasonably and objectively justified.

The Strasbourg approach to art.14 in the social security context

The Strasbourg approach to the determination of complaints raising art.14 issues is threefold: 4.109

(1) Does the complaint of discrimination falls within the sphere or ambit of a protected right?

(2) Can the applicants can properly compare themselves with a class of persons who are treated more favourably?

(3) Can the difference in treatment be reasonably and objectively justified and is it proportionate to its aim?

Nearly all social security cases fall within the scope of art.1 of Protocol 1 (the right to property) following the admissibility decision in the *Stec* case: see below.

In relation to the second issue, the court has, over time, has referred to the comparators as being, or not being, in "similar situations" (*Marckx v Belgium* (App. 6833/74), June 13, 1979, Series A, No. 31, (1979–80) 2 E.H.R.R. 330, [32]) or in "relevantly similar situations" (*Burden v United Kingdom,* (App. 13378/05), April 29, 2008 [Grand Chamber], [60]), or in "analogous situations" (*Stubbings v United Kingdom* (Apps 22083/93 and 22095/93), October 22, 1996, (1997) 23 E.H.R.R. 213, [71]). The phrase "relevantly similar situations" appears to be the currently favoured formulation. The third question is whether the difference in treatment can be justified. The court has made it clear that art.14 is concerned with arbitrary discrimination and so a difference of treatment will only be in breach art.14 if it has no objective or reasonable justification.

Article 14 enumerates certain grounds upon which the prohibition of discrimination is based (such as sex, race, language, and religion) but also leaves the list open by referring to "other status". Where the differential treatment is:

- between men and women (*Van Raalte v Netherlands* (App. 20060/92), February 21, 1997, (1997) 24 E.H.R.R. 503, [39]);
- on grounds of nationality (*Gaygusuz v Austria* (App. 17371/90), September 16, 1996, (1997) 23 E.H.R.R. 364, [42]);
- on grounds of race (*Timishev v Russia,*(Apps. 55762/00 and 55974/00), December 13, 2005, (2007) 44 E.H.R.R. 37, [58]);
- on grounds of religion (*Hoffmann v Austria* (App. 12875/87), June 23, 1993, Series A, No. 255–C, (1994) 17 E.H.R.R. 293, [36]);
- on grounds of legitimacy (*Inze v Austria,* (App. 8695/79), October 28, 1987, Series A, No. 126, (1988) 10 E.H.R.R. 394, [41]); and
- on grounds of sexual orientation (*E.B. v France,* (App. 43546/02), January 22, 2008 [Grand Chamber], [93]);

very weighty reasons are required to justify the differential treatment.

Where the basis for the difference of treatment is grounds of sex or race, the contracting parties enjoy no margin of appreciation and will find it exceedingly difficult to establish objective and reasonable justification.

It follows that the nature of the justification presented will vary with the nature of the differential treatment in issue. While it will be reasonably easy for a contracting party to show that a difference of treatment pursues a legitimate aim, the case law suggests that meeting the test of objective and reasonable justification will vary according to the circumstances of each case. The test is tied in with the margin of appreciation.

4.110 The Strasbourg Court's approach to social security cases is typified by the decision of the Grand Chamber in *Stummer v Austria* (App.37452/02), Judgment of July 7, 2011. The case concerned a complaint by a prisoner that he was the victim of discrimination since as a working prisoner he was not affiliated to the old-age pension system and so was deprived of a pension.

The court first considered whether the complaint was one within the scope of the rights protected by the Convention. This was easy to answer, since the Grand Chamber in its admissibility decision in *Stec v United Kingdom* (Apps No 65731/01 and 65900/01) Decision of September 5, 2005, (2005) 41 E.H.R.R. SE295, held that art.1 of Protocol 1 applied to welfare benefits in general for which a contracting party had provided, whether conditional or not on the payment of contributions. The court had said that art.1 of Protocol 1 does not include a right to receive a social security payment, although where a state creates entitlement to a benefit, it must do so in a manner which is compatible with art.14. The full effect of the *Stec* admissibility decision has been accepted by the House of Lords in *R. (on the application of RJM) v Secretary of State for Work and Pensions* [2008] UKHL 63, where Lord Neuberger says:

> "31. . . . I recognise that the admissibility decision in Stec represents a departure from the principle normally applied to claims which rely on A1P1. However, Stec . . . was a carefully considered decision, in which the relevant authorities and principles were fully canvassed, and where the Grand Chamber of the ECtHR came to a clear conclusion, which was expressly intended to be generally applied by national courts. Accordingly, it seems to me that it would require the most exceptional circumstances before any national court should refuse to apply the decision."

The Strasbourg Court defines discrimination as treating people in a relevantly similar situation differently without an objective and reasonable justification. In order to establish objective and reasonable justification, the state imposing the measure is required to show that the differential treatment pursues a legitimate aim and that there is a reasonable relationship of proportionality between the means employed and the aim sought to be realised (*Stummer,* at [87]). So, when considering art.14, it is best to start by considering differential treatment and only to use the term "discrimination" when that differential treatment cannot be objectively and reasonably justified or shown to be proportionate.

It is very significant that the court has held that, where general measures of economic or social strategy are in issue (and where the differential treatment is not related to the specially protected groups), a wide margin of appreciation (or discretion) is allowed to the state. In such cases, the court will not find a violation unless the measure in issue can be regarded as "manifestly without reasonable foundation." (*Stummer,* at [89].) **4.111**

In the *Stummer* case the grounds of different treatment related to a matter of "other status"; the comparison was between working prisoners and employees not in prison. These groups were regarded as appropriate comparators, which meant that the different treatment required justification. The court considered that the Austrian government had shown a legitimate aim in its different treatment in the following terms "preserving the economic efficiency and overall consistency of the old-age pension system by excluding from benefits person who have not made meaningful contributions" (*Stummer,* at [98]). The court gave lengthy consideration to the question of whether the difference in treatment was proportionate and concluded that it was. It could not be said that the Austrian approach was manifestly without reasonable foundation, and so there was no violation of art.14 read with art.1 of Protocol 1.

Some national case law (referred to in detail in earlier editions of this work) suggested that art.14 was only concerned with differential treatment where the basis of comparison was a "personal characteristic". This led to discussion of what amounted to a personal characteristic. That concern is now largely resolved as not being quite so central to the protection provided by art.14 and must in any event be interpreted broadly.

The opinions of the House of Lords in *Carson and Reynolds* [2005] UKHL 37, [13] and [53]–[54], confirmed the importance of identifying a personal characteristic but also indicated that this is to be interpreted broadly so that it does not simply encompass something a person is born with. So in *Francis v Secretary of State for Work and Pensions* [2005] EWCA Civ 1303, reported as *R(IS) 6/06* the Court of Appeal affirmed the need to identify a personal characteristic but indicated that this need not be immutable and can be the result of the exercise of choice. **4.112**

AL (Serbia) v Secretary of State for the Home Department; R. (on the application of Rudi) v Secretary of State for the Home Department, [2008] UKHL 42, contains a very helpful discussion by Baroness Hale of aspects of art.14 at [20]–[35]. This stresses that Strasbourg case law does not place great emphasis on the identification of an exact comparator, rather asking whether differences in otherwise similar situations justify a different treatment. It is also hinted that too much attention has been focused on the notion of "personal characteristic" which is not central to the Strasbourg case law, although clearly differences based on such matters as sex, race or ethnic origin will require very weighty reasons if they are not to be condemned as violations of art.14. See also the discussion in *R. (on the application of RJM) v Secretary of State for Work and Pensions,* [2008] UKHL 63.

The approach advocated in the *AL (Serbia)* case was followed in *TW v SSWP (PIP)* [2017] UKUT 25 (AAC), which is a decision of a three-judge panel considering whether the transitional regulations relating to conversion from disability living allowance to personal independence payment are discriminatory and invalid. Rather than determine whether those moving from disability living allowance to personal independence payment and those who were making a wholly new claim to a personal independence payment were in an analogous position, the Upper Tribunal focused on whether the claimed difference in treatment could be justified since "arguments on justification may well demonstrate that a claimed comparator is not in a truly analogous position, and therefore that the difference in treatment is not actually due to a personal or other identifiable characteristic of the claimant at all . . ." (para 45). The Upper Tribunal concluded that the transitional regulations were neither discriminatory nor ultra vires.

Some judgments of the Strasbourg Court in social security cases involving the United Kingdom

4.113 The long-awaited judgment of the Court of Human Rights in *Runkee and White v United Kingdom* (Apps 42949/98 and 53134/99) was handed down on May 10, 2007. This finally resolved the position in relation to the litigation concerning widowers' entitlements under the legislation in force prior to April 9, 2001. The court ruled that there was no violation of art.14 taken in conjunction with art.1 of Protocol 1 in connection with non-entitlement to a widow's pension but that there was a violation of art.14 taken in conjunction with art.1 of Protocol 1 concerning non-entitlement to a widow's payment.

See *Hobbs, Richard, Walsh and Geen v United Kingdom* (Apps 63684/00, 63475/00, 63484/00 and 63468/00), November 14, 2006, for the corresponding decision to that in *Runkee and White* in relation to widow's bereavement allowance in which a violation of art.14 taken with art.1 of Protocol 1 was found.

Following the judgment of the House of Lords in *R. v Secretary of State for Work and Pensions, ex parte Carson, R. v Secretary of State for Work and Pensions, ex parte Reynolds* [2005] UKHL 37, ruling that there was no breach of art.14 in relation to the rules on the uprating of pensions to certain pensioners living overseas, application was made to the Strasbourg Court. The Chamber judgment of November 4, 2008 was referred to the Grand Chamber, which delivered judgment in *Carson v United Kingdom,* (App.42184/05) on March 16, 2010. The Grand Chamber ruled by 11 votes to six that the United Kingdom was not in violation of art.14 when read in conjunction with art.1 of Protocol 1. The Strasbourg Court noted that, in order for an issue to arise under art.14, there had to be a difference in the treatment of persons in relevantly similar situations. The judgment of the court did not consider that it sufficed for the applicants to have paid National Insurance contributions in the United Kingdom to place them in a relevantly similar position to all other pensioners, regardless of their country of residence. The applicants were accordingly not in a relevantly similar situation with the group with whom they sought to compare themselves.

4.114 Nor did the judgment of the court consider that the applicants were in a relevantly similar position to pensioners living in countries with which the United Kingdom had concluded a bilateral agreement providing for up-rating. Those living in reciprocal agreement countries were treated differently from those living elsewhere because an agreement had been entered into; and an agreement had been entered into because the United Kingdom considered it to be in its interests. In that connection, states clearly had a right under international law to conclude bilateral social security treaties and indeed this was the preferred method used by the

Member States of the Council of Europe to secure reciprocity of welfare benefits. If entering into bilateral arrangements in the social security sphere obliged a state to confer the same advantages on all those living in all other countries, the right of states to enter into reciprocal agreements and their interest in so doing would effectively be undermined.

The substantive issue in *Stec v United Kingdom* (Apps 65731/01 and 65900/01) April 12, 2006 [Grand Chamber], (2006) 43 E.H.R.R. 47, related to the impact of differential state pensionable ages on entitlement to a reduced earnings allowance. The court found no violation accepting that the process of equalising pensionable age for men and women was legitimate and it was not prepared to criticise the government for not beginning the process sooner.

In *Pearson v United Kingdom* (App.8374/03), August 22, 2006, the Strasbourg Court ruled that the differential age for entitlement to a state retirement pension of 65 for a man and 60 for a woman was objectively justifiable. The court refers to its decision in the *Stec* case (citing [61]–[65]) in finding that the differential state pensionable ages are within the state's margin of appreciation and that it cannot be criticised for not having moved earlier towards equalisation of the pension age for men and women (which will be reached in 2020).

In *Susan Richardson v United Kingdom* (App.26252/08), Decision of April 10, 4.115
2012, the applicant complained that the deferral of payment of a state retirement pension for those born after April 1950 until the age of 65 (for those born before April 1950 the pension was payable from the age of 60) amounted to a violation of art.14 read with art.1 of Protocol 1. The Strasbourg Court declared the application manifestly ill-founded on the grounds that changes as to pensionable age fall within the margin of appreciation of a state and could not be questioned provided that it is shown that the changes are in the general interest, are reasonable, and do not amount to a total loss of pension entitlement (see [24]).

On the same day, the judgment in *Walker v United Kingdom,* (App.37212/02) was delivered. This concerned the requirement for a man to pay national insurance contributions beyond the age of 60 when the liability of a woman ceases. For exactly the same reasons as given in *Pearson,* the Strasbourg Court finds that there is no violation of art.14 read in conjunction with art.1 of Protocol 1.

The same conclusion was also reached in *Barrow v United Kingdom* (App.42735/02), August 22, 2006, in a complaint concerning a woman who suffered a reduction in benefit at the age of 60 where her long-term incapacity benefit was replaced with the state retirement pension. She complained that such a reduction would not arise for a man, for whom the transition would not arise until he reached state pensionable age of 65.

In *B v United Kingdom* (App.36571/06), Judgment of February 14, 2012, (reported as [2012] AACR 39) the Court of Human Rights considered that differential treatment of: (a) persons who did not have the capacity to understand the obligation to report, and (b) persons who did have this capacity, could be justified as pursuing the legitimate aim of "ensuring the smooth operation of the welfare system and the facilitation of the recovery of overpaid benefits" (see [59]) which was reasonably and objectively justifiable. Nor did the contested provision breach the requirement of proportionality: public authorities should not be prevented from correcting mistakes—even their own—in the award of benefits and to hold otherwise would result in the unjust enrichment of the benefit recipient. There were safeguards in the United Kingdom system and no interest was charged on overpaid benefit which was recovered.

Positive obligations and art.14

The issue of positive obligations under art.14 requires that the matter first 4.116
be within the ambit of the article. However, once that is established, there is an obligation to take steps to prevent any discrimination prohibited by the article. This has come to be known as the *Thlimmenos* principle from the case of

Thlimmenos v Greece, (App.34369/97), April 6, 2000, (2001) 31 E.H.R.R. 411: the right not to be discriminated against in the enjoyment of rights falling within the scope of the Convention will be violated where contracting parties fail to treat persons in different situations differently without any objective and reasonable justification for doing so. However, in this context, the contracting parties enjoy a considerable margin of appreciation in assessing whether and to what extent differences in otherwise similar situations justify a difference in treatment: see *Sommerfield v Germany* (App.31871/96) July 8, 2003, Grand Chamber, 2004 38 E.H.R.R. 756.

Burnip v Birmingham CC and SSWP; Trengrove v Walsall MC and SSWP; and *Gorry v Wiltshire Council and SSWP; EHRC intervening* [2012] EWCA Civ 629, reported as [2013] AACR 7, is an important authority on the concept of positive obligations under art.14 in the context of social security entitlements. Maurice Kay L.J. said:

> "17. On behalf of the Secretary of State, Mr Tim Eicke QC submits that the *Thlimmenos* principle is not as wide as is suggested. He submits that there is no example of the courts applying *Thlimmenos* so as to require a state to take positive steps to allocate a greater share of public resources to a particular person or group. The limited instances in which the principle has been invoked concern exclusionary rules (as in *Thlimmenos* itself and *AM (Somalia))*.
> 18. Whilst it is true that there has been a conspicuous lack of cases post-*Thlimmenos* in which a positive obligation to allocate resources has been established, I am not persuaded that it is because of a legal no-go area. I accept that it is incumbent upon a court to approach such an issue with caution and to consider with care any explanation which is proffered by the public authority for the discrimination. However, this arises more at the stage of justification than at the earlier stage of considering whether discrimination has been established. I can see no warrant for imposing a *prior* limitation on the *Thlimmenos* principle. To do so would be to depart from the emphasis in Article 14 cases which, as Baroness Hale demonstrated in *AL (Serbia)* (at paragraph 25), is 'to concentrate on the reasons for the difference in treatment and whether they amount to an objective and reasonable justification'. I would apply the same approach to a *Thlimmenos* failure to treat differently persons whose situations are significantly different."

National authorities on art.14 read with art.1 of Protocol 1

4.117 The saga of the Government's response to the discrimination between men and women which occurred in relation to benefits for widows and widowers was considered by the House of Lords in *R v Secretary of State for Work and Pensions, ex p. Hooper* [2005] UKHL 29 and is discussed in some detail in earlier editions of this work. The matter is now largely of historical interest. For two decisions of Commissioners in this area, see *R(G) 2/04* and *R(G) 1/06*.

In *Esfandiari v Secretary of State for Work and Pensions* [2006] EWCA Civ 282, reported as *R(IS) 11/06*, the Court of Appeal considered whether the funeral payments provisions which restrict the payment of funeral expenses where the funeral is held in the United Kingdom (or in certain cases another country within the European Economic Area) are compatible with the European Convention. The Court was unanimous in concluding that this was not a case of discrimination at all but even if those migrants who wished to bury relatives in their country of origin were a group, then any differential treatment could easily be justified as matters where the state enjoyed a wide margin of appreciation is setting its policy. The Court of Appeal regards the different outcome in European Union law as arising because of the special rights which migrant workers are accorded under what is now the EU Treaty.

In *Couronne v Secretary of State for Work and Pensions, Bontemps v Secretary of State for Work and Pensions* [2006] EWHC 1514 (Admin), it was argued that the refusal to award jobseekers allowance to British Citizens arriving from Mauritius (whose parents had been displaced from the Chagos Islands) constituted discrimination in breach of art.14 when read with art.8 and/or art.1 of Protocol 1. It was argued, inter alia, that the comparator group (British Citizens of Irish ethnic origin) are exempt from the habitual residence test, whereas the claimants were not. The habitual residence test was regarded as a legitimate one aimed at protecting the social security system from claims by those with no genuine connection with the United Kingdom. The decision of the Administrative Court was upheld by the Court of Appeal at [2007] EWCA Civ 1086.

SSWP v Sister IS and Sister KM, [2009] UKUT 200 (AAC) concerned claims by nuns for state pension credit, which were refused on the grounds that they were members of a religious order who are fully maintained by that order. It was argued that the exclusionary provision breached art.14 read with art.1 of Protocol 1. The three-judge panel dismissed this argument relying on Sedley L.J.'s reasoning in *Langley v Bradford MBC,* reported as *R(H) 6/05* that a housing benefit claimant was not a victim under the Human Rights Act 1998, because the discriminatory effect of a provision could be removed without conferring any advantage on her. The three-judge panel said that it was "possible to remove any element of religious discrimination (if there is one) by removing the reference to religion." (At [33].) It followed that the claimants could not establish that they were victims within s.7(1)(b) of the Human Rights Act 1998. 4.118

In *R. (on the application of RJM) v Secretary of State for Work and Pensions* [2008] UKHL 63, the House of Lords ruled that a question of entitlement to a disability premium as part of income support falls within the ambit of art.1 of Protocol 1 such that art.14 is engaged. The House went on to conclude that homelessness was a status within art.14 but that the differential treatment could be justified.

In *HMRC v DH* [2009] UKUT 24 (AAC), the judge decided that the payment of child tax credit to the principal carer does not breach art.14 when read with art.1 of Protocol No.1, since any discrimination against the secondary carer is objectively justified. The appeal against this decision has been dismissed in *Humphreys v HMRC* [2010] EWCA Civ 56. The appeal by the claimant to the Supreme Court has been dismissed in a unanimous decision, [2012] UKSC 18, which agrees that there is discrimination but concludes that it is objectively justified. The reasons for so concluding can be found at [22]–[33].

In *NT v SSWP* [2009] UKUT 37 (AAC), the judge ruled that the age cut-off of 65 for entitlement to the mobility component of a disability living allowance was a matter within the margin of appreciation of the United Kingdom. Consideration of the justification for the choice to legislate an age cut-off date simply required the Secretary of State to provide a rational explanation for the policy of the law in this case. The Secretary of State had, in the consideration of the judge, met that obligation. 4.119

In *CM v SSWP* [2009] UKUT 43 (AAC), the judge ruled that denial of income support to a pregnant student nurse intercalating a period of study was objectively and reasonably justified.

A challenge relating to the exclusion from benefits of prisoners transferred to mental hospital under these regulations as being in breach of art.14 of the European Convention when read with art.1 of Protocol No. 1 has failed with one exception: see *R. (on the application of EM) v Secretary of State for Work and Pensions* [2009] EWHC 454 (Admin). The excepted class is a small group (there were 45 such persons in detention when the case was decided) of what are described as "technical lifers", namely those, although sentenced to life imprisonment, are treated by the Secretary of State after transfer to hospital as though they had been made the subject of a hospital order under s.37 of the Mental Health Act 1983 and to a restriction order under s.41 of that Act.

The Court of Appeal dismissed the appeal against the decision in *SSWP v FS (IS)* [2010] UKUT 198 (AAC) in *Faith Stewart v SSWP* [2011] EWCA Civ 907 (reported as [2012] AACR 9). The Secretary of State conceded that the rules on the eligibility of prisoners to funeral payments under the social fund constituted indirect 4.120

discrimination against prisoners but argued successfully (on different grounds than those taken before the Upper Tribunal) that such discrimination was justified. This was based upon the objectives of the scheme to provide a quick and simple test of eligibility enabling payments to be made without delay, coupled with the complexity of any means-tested approach applicable to prisoners which would be likely to impact upon other groups and to be subject to complaints from those other groups that they were the victims of unlawful discrimination.

The appeals against the decisions of the Upper Tribunal in *Burnip* ([2011] UKUT 23), *Trengrove* ([2011] UKUT 172), and *Gorry* ([2011] UKUT 198) were consolidated before the Court of Appeal, which gave judgment in these cases on May 15, 2012: *Burnip v Birmingham CC and SSWP; Trengrove v Walsall MC and SSWP*; and *Gorry v Wiltshire Council and SSWP; EHRC intervening* [2012] EWCA Civ 629, reported as [2013] AACR 7. *Burnip* and *Trengrove* concerned disabled individuals who required 24-hour care and therefore needed an additional bedroom for their carer, while *Gorry* concerned two disabled daughters who each required their own bedroom because of their disabilities, when girls of the same age without their disabilities would normally be able to share a bedroom. The appeals concerned the absence in the housing benefit rules of provisions allowing more than one bedroom where the beneficiary had a disability which either precluded their sharing a bedroom with a sibling or required a carer to live in. The challenge sought to establish that there was a positive obligation to treat those in different circumstances differently. In allowing all three appeals in a unanimous decision, the Court of Appeal considers that there is a prima facie case of discrimination in the failure to treat the situations of disabled and non-disabled people differently and that the Secretary of State could not justify that difference in treatment. The circumstances of two of the appellants had, by the time of the judgment, been resolved by amendments to the housing benefit regulations but that of the third (Gorry) had not, and this required further amendments to the regulations required (see SI 2013/2828).

In *VL v SSWP (IS)* [2011] UKUT 227, the Upper Tribunal judge ruled that the removal of income support from lone parents whose children had reached the age of 12 did not constitute discrimination on grounds of sex, since the Secretary of State had provided a rational explanation for the policy of the law and the methods of achieving the objectives of the policy are proportionate.

4.121 In *AY v SSWP (RP)* [2011] UKUT 324 (AAC), the judge found that there was a breach of art.14 when read with art.1 of Protocol 1 in the following rather unusual circumstances:

> "42. The argument advanced on Mrs Yates's behalf relies on a comparison with a man in Mrs Yates's circumstance who had married a woman whose circumstances were identical to those of the late Mr Yates. The tribunal correctly found that such a man would be entitled to Category B pension while the hypothetical woman was alive, but following her death would have been entitled to Category B pension under section 51 [of the Contributions and Benefits Act] at an up-rated rate."

The judge came to the conclusion that there was discrimination which could not be justified. He concluded:

> "68. I reach this conclusion without enthusiasm. The Human Rights Court has held that the freezing of the pensions of emigrants is compatible with the Convention. Regulation 5 of the Persons Abroad Regulations bore harshly on Mr and Mrs Yates because of the length of Mr Yates's retirement abroad, during decades of high inflation, but it represented the consistent policy of successive governments and it seems somewhat anomalous that I am required to disapply regulation 5(3)(aa) judicially because of the Secretary of State's failure to make equivalent provision for a small number of non-resident made Category B pensioners. That, however, seems to me to be the effect of the law that I am required to apply."

CM v SSWP (DLA) [2013] UKUT 27, reported as [2013] AACR 21, concerned a human rights challenge to the hospital rules under which DLA ceased to be payable for a child under 16 once that child had been in hospital for 84 days. The challenge arose in the context of the care provided by parents of a very sick three-year-old who was in hospital for more than 84 days and in respect of whom payment of DLA was withdrawn. The judge readily found that the issue came within the ambit art.1 of Protocol 1. He also concluded that there was an issue of status involved: that of being disabled so as to require hospital treatment for more than 84 days. There was differential treatment of those requiring hospital admission for more than 84 days and those nor requiring hospital admission extending beyond 84 days. However, the judge ruled that the differential treatment could be justified on economic grounds, accepting that bright-line rules were permitted. Since this was not discrimination on one of the protected grounds (such as sex or race), the test was whether the distinction which had been drawn was manifestly without reasonable foundation. The judge considered that it could not be considered so. Nor could any argument based on positive obligations following the *Thlimmenos* principle succeed.

The appeal against this decision was dismissed by the Court of Appeal as *AM (by his father CM) v Secretary of State for Work and Pensions* [2014] EWCA Civ 286, reported as [2014] AACR 18. However, the further appeal to the Supreme Court as *Cameron Mathieson, a deceased child (by his father Craig Mathieson) v SSWP* [2015] UKSC 47, [2015] AACR 44, resulted in the Supreme Court unanimously allowing the appeal. The Supreme Court acknowledged that in the area of welfare benefits a court will not interfere with policy choices unless the resulting rule was manifestly without reasonable foundation. Bright-line rules will not be invalidated merely because there are some hard cases which fall on the wrong side of it. In this case the claimant's circumstances were not a hard case but were typical of difficulties the whole class would face. Provision by the State for children in hospital did not overlap with the needs for which disability living allowance provided, and so the rule was manifestly without reasonable foundation. The Supreme Court considered the conclusion in harmony with the provisions of the UN Convention on the Rights of the Child and the UN Convention on the Rights of Persons with Disabilities. The Supreme Court did not, however, disapply the provisions for the suspension of disability living allowance, leaving it to the Secretary of State to determine what measures now needed to be taken to remedy the violation of human rights which arose as a result of the 84 day rule.

The Court of Appeal in *Obrey, Snodgrass and Shadforth v SSWP* [2013] EWCA Civ 1584 has dismissed the appeal against the decision in *SSWP and Warwick DC v OB, JS and JS (CTB)* [2012] UKUT 489 (AAC) which held that the provisions of the housing benefit legislation which causes entitlement to cease after persons have been in hospital for 52 weeks, though indirectly discriminatory in respect of those with a mental illness, was capable of objective justification since the "bright line" provision was a policy matter not "manifestly without reasonable foundation." **4.122**

R (MA) v SSWP and Birmingham CC [2014] EWCA Civ 13 concerned the "bedroom tax" and dismissed the appeal of the claimants in respect of their challenge that there was unfair treatment of disabled claimants. The differential treatment was justified and the scheme was not unlawful. *R (on the application of Rutherford and others) v Secretary of State for Work and Pensions* [2016] EWCA Civ 29 rules that the different treatment for children, with regard to the bedroom tax rules, constitutes discriminatory treatment which is manifestly without reasonable foundation contrary to art.14. The judgment is under appeal to the Supreme Court, where it is to be listed to be heard alongside *R (on the application of MA and others) v Secretary of State for Work and Pensions.*

A similar challenge to the "benefit cap" provisions failed in the Court of Appeal in *R (SG) v SSWP* [2014] EWCA Civ 156. Although the benefit cap had a disproportionate impact on women, its imposition was not manifestly without foundation; the government objective of changing what was described as a welfare dependency culture was a legitimate aim of the measure. The Supreme Court has, by a majority of 3 to 2, upheld the judgment of the Court of Appeal in *R (SG) v Secretary of State* [2015] UKSC 16, in ruling that the benefit cap was not unlawful, though concerns were expressed by three judges that the benefit cap was not compatible with duties of the United Kingdom under the United Nations Convention on the Rights of the Child. That Convention was, however, not incorporated into United Kingdom law and so could not be relied on in making a case that there was unlawful discrimination on grounds of sex under art.14 of the ECHR.

In *JH v HMRC (CHB)* [2015] UKUT 479 (AAC); [2016] AACR 15, Judge Levenson disapplies the provisions of reg.3(3) of the Child Benefit (General) Regulations 2006 as being in breach of art.14 when read with art.1 of Protocol 1 in refusing child benefit in respect of an 18-year old on the autistic spectrum ("the young person") who was being educated at home under arrangements funder by the local authority. The preclusion of benefit in such cases where the home schooling had not started before the young person was 16 years of age amounted to a difference of treatment which required justification if it was not to be unlawful discrimination. No justification was found for the difference in treatment in relation to the age when home schooling started, and this was accepted by HMRC.

Article 14 in conjunction with art.8

4.123 A number of art.14 claims have also made use of art.8 on family and private life but since the admissibility decision in *Stec,* it has been more usual simply to rely on art.14 read with art.1 of Protocol 1.

However, complaints under art.14 in conjunction with art.8 have been raised in relation to widow's benefits: see *Willis v United Kingdom* (App.36042/97), June 11, 2002, [2002] 35 E.H.R.R. 21; *Runkee and White v United Kingdom* (Apps 42949/98 and 53134/99), Judgments of May 10, 2007); *Thomas v United Kingdom* (App.63701/00), July 17, 2008; and to state pensions: *Carson v United Kingdom* (App.42184/05), November 4, 2008. In all these cases, the Strasbourg Court examined the case using the link to property rights rather than the link to private and family life in art.8.

In national proceedings, there have been cases arguing that the housing benefit scheme and child support falls within the sphere of application of art.8. However, the complex discussions in both the Court of Appeal and the House of Lords which arose in *Secretary of State for Work and Pensions v M; Langley v Bradford Metropolitan DC and Secretary of State for Work and Pensions* [2004] EWCA Civ 1343; and *Secretary of State for Work and Pensions v M* [2006] UKHL 11 would not now be necessary in relation to the housing benefit scheme and probably also the child support system, since art.1 of Protocol 1 would be regarded as engaged following the *Stec* decision.

4.124 In *Francis v Secretary of State for Work and Pensions* [2005] EWCA Civ 1303 (the appeal against *CIS/1965/2003*, reported as *R(IS) 6/06)*, the Court of Appeal found that the refusal to award a maternity grant constituted discrimination contrary to art.14 of the Convention. The Secretary of State had conceded that the circumstances presented by Ms Francis engaged art.8 of the Convention. Ms Francis argued that her situation as a person with a residence order in respect of a child born to her sister was analogous to that of an adopter under the Adoption Act 1976. There was no objective justification for the difference in treatment.

In *R(P) 2/06* a Tribunal of Commissioners concluded that the United Kingdom rules preventing the payment of widows' benefits to widows of polygamous marriages in the circumstances of the cases before them did not fall foul of the prohibition of discrimination in art.14 when read with art.8. The Tribunal of Commissioners was unanimous as to the outcome, although one Commissioner's line of reasoning differs from that of his two colleagues.

Article 8 was raised (as well as art.1 of Protocol 1) in *R (SG) v SSWP* [2014]

EWCA Civ 156, the challenge to the "benefit cap" measures. The Court of Appeal accepted that art.8 was engaged but determined the point on the same grounds as the claims which linked art.1 of Protocol 1 to the art. 14 prohibition.

Article 16—Restrictions on political activity of aliens

Nothing in Articles 10, 11 and 14 shall be regarded as preventing the High Contracting Parties from imposing restrictions on the political activity of aliens. **4.125**

Article 17—Prohibition of abuse of rights

Nothing in this Convention may be interpreted as implying for any State, group or person any right to engage in any activity or perform any act aimed at the destruction of any of the rights and freedoms set forth herein or at their limitation to a greater extent than is provided for in the Convention. **4.126**

Article 18—Limitation on use of restrictions on rights

The restrictions permitted under this Convention to the said rights and freedoms shall not be applied for any purpose other than those for which they have been prescribed. **4.127**

PART II

THE FIRST PROTOCOL

Article 1—Protection of property

Every natural or legal person is entitled to the peaceful enjoyment of his possessions. No one shall be deprived of his possessions except in the public interest and subject to the conditions provided for by law and by the general principles of international law. The preceding provisions shall not, however, in any way impair the right of a State to enforce such laws as it deems necessary to control the use of property in accordance with the general interest or to secure the payment of taxes or other contributions or penalties. **4.128**

GENERAL NOTE

Introduction

The protection of property rights as human rights presents particular problems, and it is therefore not surprising that agreement could not be reached on their inclusion in the Convention as originally drafted. A right to property is included in art.1 of Protocol 1, but its content is broadly framed and the permissible restrictions are broad in scope. **4.129**

Though drafted rather differently, the structure of the provision is similar to that found in arts 8–11. There is a general right to peaceful enjoyment of possessions. Interferences can, however, be justified on the conditions set out in the article which include references both to the "public interest" and the "general interest"; this is the test of proportionality that pervades the Convention's consideration of interferences and requires the balancing of the interests of the individual against the collective interest.

The Court has repeatedly said that the article comprises three distinct rules: *Sporrong and Lönnroth v Sweden*, (Apps 7151-2/75), September 23, 1982, Series A, No. 52, (1983) 5 E.H.R.R. 35, at [61]. See, more recently, *Jahn v Germany* (Apps 46720/99, 72203/01, and 72552/01), June 30, 2005 [Grand Chamber], (2006) 42 E.H.R.R. 49, ECHR 2005-VI, at [78]; and *Hutten-Czapska v Poland* (App.35014/97), June 19, 2006 [Grand Chamber], (2007) 45 E.H.R.R. 52, ECHR 2006-VIII, at [157]. First, everyone is entitled to peaceful enjoyment of their possessions. Secondly, deprivation of possessions is subject to certain conditions. Finally, contracting parties are entitled to control the use of property where it is in the general interest. But these are not distinct rules, since the second and third rules relate to interferences with the peaceful enjoyment of possessions which may be justified in the general interest.

Once it has been established that the applicant has an interest which can be classified as a possession, the general approach of the Strasbourg Court is to consider **4.130** first whether there has been a deprivation of possessions, followed by consideration of whether there has been a control of the use of possessions, since these are matters specifically dealt with by the article. Only if there has been neither deprivation of possessions nor a control of their use does the Court consider, as a separate issue, whether there has been some other interference with the peaceful enjoyment of possessions. Such interferences will, however, only be unlawful if they are not in the general interest. In its more recent case law, the Court has brought together the tests it applies in relation to deprivations, the control of the use of property, and to other interferences with property, so that the questions the Court will ask in each of these circumstances raise essentially the same issues.

Possessions have been defined in broad terms by both the Commission and the Court. In this context, it is worth noting that the French text of the Convention uses the term "*biens*" which connotes a very broad range of property rights. The term has an autonomous meaning; it extends beyond physical goods, and covers a wide range of rights and interests which may be classified as assets.

Social security payments and pensions

4.131 Entitlements arising under pension and social security schemes have proved difficult to classify; the position was for some time unclear. A distinction had been drawn in the case law between benefits which were paid on the basis of contributions, and those which were paid without reference to contributions. But the case law did not always seem to maintain this distinction. However, the admissibility decision of the Grand Chamber in the *Stec* case (*Stec v United Kingdom* (Apps 65731/01 and 65900/01), Decision of July 6, 2005 [Grand Chamber], (2005) 41 E.H.R.R. SE18) has clarified matters.

An example of the ambiguity caused by the earlier case law can be found in the *Gaygusuz* case (*Gaygusuz v Austria* (App. 17371/90), September 16, 1996, (1997) 23 E.H.R.R. 364). Gaygusuz was a Turkish national who had worked in Austria, where he had paid contributions under the Austrian social security scheme. He had experienced periods of unemployment and periods when he was unfit for work. He applied for an advance on his retirement pension as a form of emergency assistance, but was refused because he was not an Austrian national. He complained that there had been a violation of art.14 when read in conjunction with art.1 of Protocol 1. The first question was whether the substance of the claim was a matter within the scope of the article, since otherwise art.14 could not be brought into play. Both the Commission and the Court concluded that the article was applicable but for different reasons. The Commission concluded that the article was brought into play because the obligation to pay "taxes or other contributions" falls within its field of application. The Court, however, concluded that the link with the obligation to pay taxes or other contributions was not required. That was sufficient to engage the anti-discrimination provision in art.14 and to find a violation since the discrimination between nationals and non-nationals was blatant. The Court took the same approach in the *Koua Poirrez* case (*Koua Poirrez v France* (App.40892/98), September 30, 2003, (2005) 40 E.H.R.R. 12, at [37]).

In the *Stec* case, the Grand Chamber accepted that the *Gaygusuz* case was ambiguous on the significance of contributions in bringing a claim within the scope of art.1 of Protocol 1 for the purpose of claiming discriminatory treatment which breached art.14 of the Convention. The Grand Chamber lays down a new approach which is to be applied in future cases, relying on an interpretation which renders the rights in the Convention practical and effective rather than theoretical and illusory. The Grand Chamber also referred to the Court's case law under art.6 which had brought disputes concerned all forms of social security within the scope of that article. The Court concluded that, whenever persons can assert a right to a welfare benefit under national law, art.1 of Protocol 1 applies. The Court goes on to note that the bringing of social security fairly and squarely within the scope of art.1 of Protocol 1 does not create any right to acquire property. However, if a Contracting

Party does create rights to social security benefits, the benefit schemes must be operated in a manner which is compatible with the prohibition of discrimination set out in art.14.

Attempts have been made to argue that the suspension of retirement pension for those serving terms of imprisonment breached the property rights in art.1 of Protocol 1, but the applications were declared inadmissible (Apps 27004/95, *Josef Szrabjer v United Kingdom*, and 27011/95, *Walter Clarke v United Kingdom*, Decisions of October 23, 1997) and invalidity benefit (App.27537/95, *George Carlin v United Kingdom*, Decision of December 3, 1997). The public interest was served by avoiding a situation in which prisoners enjoyed the advantage of accumulating a lump sum by receiving a State benefit without any outgoing living expenses. Arguments based on discrimination between prisoners and non-prisoners were dismissed as a comparison of two different factual situations. Other comparisons were also found to be without merit. See also discussion of benefits for widowers in the commentary on art.14 above. For a Grand Chamber judgment which considered the entitlement of those working in prison to affiliation to the old-age pension system, see *Stummer v Austria* (App.37452/02), Judgment of July 7, 2011. **4.132**

In *CP/4762/2001* the Commissioner found that the provisions under which a person became entitled to a retirement pension normally with effect from the Monday following their 65th birthday gives rise to no Convention issue either under art.1 of Protocol 1, nor under that provision when read in conjunctions with art.14

In *CP/0281/2002*, the Commissioner ruled that there was no breach of art.1 of Protocol 1 as a consequence of the requirement under the Pension Schemes Act 1993 that any additional pension is reduced by the amount of any guaranteed minimum pension payable to a person.

In *R. (Smith) v Secretary of State for Defence and Secretary of State for Work and Pensions* [2004] EWHC 1797 (Admin), Wilson J. held that a non-contributory pension under the Armed Forces Pension Scheme was a possession within the ambit of art.1 of Protocol 1. This extended to the spouse of the pension holder following the making of a pension-sharing order. However, art.1 of Protocol 1 does not guarantee a right to a pension of a particular amount, nor payment from a particular time. **4.133**

In *R(P) 1/06*, the Commissioner ruled that the three months' time limit on the backdating of a claim for retirement pension did not constitute a deprivation of property contrary to art.1 of Protocol 1. Nor was there any question of a claim based on discrimination by reading art.14 together with art.1 of Protocol 1.

In *R1/07 (IB)* a Commissioner in Northern Ireland said:

> "15. I consider there is no merit in the submission based on art.1 of Protocol 1. There is no inbuilt Convention right to any State benefit. A State is not obliged to provide benefit. The right to benefit only arises when the conditions therefore (which are provided under domestic legislation) are satisfied. In this case they were not so satisfied. The claimant was not entitled to the benefit because he worked and his work did not fall within the categories of exempt work. The basic rule in relation to IB is that those who work are not entitled to it. The benefit is, after all, an incapacity for work benefit. There are exceptions to this basic rule but they relate only to certain categories of work. The relevant category here includes that the work be work of which the required notice is given. Working on the assumption that the domestic law requirement of written notice within 42 days is valid, there is no entitlement to IB if work is done which does not come within an exempt category. art.1 of Protocol 1 is not therefore invoked, there being no property to enjoy. The claimant is not being asked to repay benefit incorrectly paid. His benefit entitlement is merely being determined according to the applicable statutory conditions of entitlement."

See also annotations to art.14.

Article 2—Right to education

4.134 No person shall be denied the right to education. In the exercise of any functions which it assumes in relation to education and to teaching, the State shall respect the right of parents to ensure such education and teaching in conformity with their own religious and philosophical convictions.

GENERAL NOTE

4.135 The full scope of this right is yet to be determined. The existing case law is mainly concerned with primary education, but the Commission has not ruled out the application of the provision to higher education (see, for example, *Sulak v Turkey* (1996) 84 D.R. 101). The confused state of the exclusion of students in full-time higher education from entitlement to most social security benefits might well leave the United Kingdom exposed to challenge under this provision. On the assumption that the provision applies to higher education, it could be argued that students are currently required to abandon their courses completely in order to become eligible for certain social security benefits with the result that they lose entitlement to the balance of finance to support their studies if they wish to return to their courses later on. This could be argued to operate to deny them the right to an education.

In *Douglas v North Tyneside MBC and Secretary of State for Education and Skills* [2003] EWCA Civ 1847, the Court of Appeal ruled that tertiary education falls within the ambit of art.2 of Protocol 1. The Court of Appeal held that, although there was no European or domestic authority establishing clearly that tertiary education falls within the ambit of art.2 of Protocol 1, the Convention was a living instrument and the number of adults in higher education had grown. There was no principle that the article applied only to earlier stages of education, and so tertiary education falls within the ambit of the article. The case turned on the application of art.14 when read in conjunction with art.2 of Protocol 1, and is discussed in the update to the annotations on art.14 above.

Article 3—Right to free elections

4.136 The High Contracting Parties undertake to hold free elections at reasonable intervals by secret ballot, under conditions which will ensure the free expression of the opinion of the people in the choice of the legislature.

PART III

ARTICLE 1 OF THE THIRTEENTH PROTOCOL

Omitted (concerns the abolition of the death penalty).

4.137 *Schedule 2 omitted.*

SCHEDULE 3

DEROGATION AND RESERVATION

4.138 [. . .]

PART II

RESERVATION

4.139 At the time of signing the present (First) Protocol, I declare that, in view of certain provisions of the Education Acts in the United Kingdom, the principle affirmed in the second sentence of Article 2 is accepted by the United Kingdom only so far as it is compatible with the provision of efficient instruction and training, and the avoidance of unreasonable public expenditure.

Dated March 20, 1952. Made by the United Kingdom Permanent Representative to the Council of Europe.

GENERAL NOTE

The derogations of 1988 and 1989 in respect of art.5(3) of the Convention were withdrawn by the Government on February 26, 2001. The amendments to the Act were made by The Human Rights Act (Amendment) Order 2001 (SI 2001/1216) which entered into force on April 1, 2001. **4.140**

The derogation contained in the Human Rights Act (Designated Derogation) Order 2001 (SI 2001/3644) in force from November 13, 2001 contained derogations from the provisions of art.5(1) to permit the detention of foreign nationals in the United Kingdom under the Anti-terrorism, Crime and Security Act 2001. That derogation has been withdrawn and effect is given to its withdrawal by the repeal of P I of Sch.3 to the Human Rights Act 1998 by the Human Rights Act 1998 (Amendment) Order 2005 (SI 2005/1071) with effect from April 8, 2005.

Schedule 4 omitted. **4.141**

PART V

TRIBUNALS

Tribunals, Courts and Enforcement Act 2007

(2007 c.15)

CONTENTS

PART 1

TRIBUNAL JUDICIARY: AND INQUIRIES

CHAPTER 1

TRIBUNAL JUDICIARY: INDEPENDENCE AND SENIOR PRESIDENT

CHAPTER 2

FIRST-TIER TRIBUNAL AND UPPER TRIBUNAL

Establishment

Members and composition of tribunals

Review of decisions and appeals

"Judicial review"

An Act to make provision about tribunals and inquiries; to establish an Administrative Justice and Tribunals Council; to amend the law relating to judicial appointments and appointments to the Law Commission; to amend the law relating to the enforcement of judgments and debts; to make further provision about the management and relief of debt; to make provision protecting cultural objects from seizure or forfeiture in certain circumstances; to amend the law relating to the taking of possession of land affected by compulsory purchase; to alter the powers of the High Court in judicial review applications; and for connected purposes.
[19th July 2007]

PART 1

TRIBUNALS AND INQUIRIES

CHAPTER 1

TRIBUNAL JUDICIARY: INDEPENDENCE AND SENIOR PRESIDENT

1. *Omitted.* 5.2

Senior President of Tribunals

2.—(1) Her Majesty may, on the recommendation of the Lord Chancellor, appoint a person to the office of Senior President of Tribunals. 5.3

(2) Schedule 1 makes further provision about the Senior President of Tribunals and about recommendations for appointment under subsection (1).

(3) A holder of the office of Senior President of Tribunals must, in carrying out the functions of that office, have regard to—
(a) the need for tribunals to be accessible,
(b) the need for proceedings before tribunals—
(i) to be fair, and
(ii) to be handled quickly and efficiently,
(c) the need for members of tribunals to be experts in the subject-matter of, or the law to be applied in, cases in which they decide matters, and
(d) the need to develop innovative methods of resolving disputes that are of a type that may be brought before tribunals.

(4) In subsection (3) "tribunals" means—
(a) the First-tier Tribunal,
(b) the Upper Tribunal,

(c) employment tribunals, [1 and]
(d) the Employment Appeal Tribunal, [1 . . .]
(e) [1 . . .]

AMENDMENT

1. Transfer of Functions of the Asylum and Immigration Tribunal Order 2010 (SI2010/21) Sch.1 paras 36 and 37 (February 15, 2010).

GENERAL NOTE

5.4 Sir Ernest Ryder is the third Senior President of Tribunals. Like his predecessors, he is a Lord Justice of Appeal (i.e. a judge of the Court of Appeal) in England and Wales but, as Senior President of Tribunals, he exercises functions throughout the United Kingdom.

Part 4 of Sch.1, which is not reproduced in this work, confers on the Senior President of Tribunals functions in relation to judges and members of relevant tribunals (those listed in subs.(4) and also those tribunals listed in Pts 1–4 of Sch.6 that have not yet been abolished) that are equivalent to the functions the Lord Chief Justice of England and Wales has in relation to judges in the courts under the Constitutional Reform Act 2005. In addition, this Act and other provisions, such as s.15A of the Social Security Act 1998, confer on him a wide number of functions, which (apart from the power to make orders under s.7(9)) he may delegate to other members of the judiciary or to staff (see s.8). By virtue of s.3(4), he presides over both the First-tier Tribunal and the Upper Tribunal.

CHAPTER 2

FIRST-TIER TRIBUNAL AND UPPER TRIBUNAL

Establishment

The First-tier Tribunal and the Upper Tribunal

5.5 **3.**—(1) There is to be a tribunal, known as the First-tier Tribunal, for the purpose of exercising the functions conferred on it under or by virtue of this Act or any other Act.

(2) There is to be a tribunal, known as the Upper Tribunal, for the purpose of exercising the functions conferred on it under or by virtue of this Act or any other Act.

(3) Each of the First-tier Tribunal, and the Upper Tribunal, is to consist of its judges and other members.

(4) The Senior President of Tribunals is to preside over both of the First-tier Tribunal and the Upper Tribunal.

(5) The Upper Tribunal is to be a superior court of record.

GENERAL NOTE

5.6 This section came into force on November 3, 2008 when the functions of the appeal tribunals constituted under the Social Security Act 1998 and the Social Security Commissioners appointed under that Act were, subject to one exception (see the note to ss.5–7 of the Social Security Act 1998), transferred to the two new tribunals established under this section. The functions of some other tribunals, outside the scope of this work, were transferred to these new tribunals at the same time (see the Transfer of Tribunal Functions Order 2008) and the functions of many others have been transferred since.

Subsection (1)

As explained in the annotation to s.7, the First-tier Tribunal is divided into seven chambers and most social security cases in the First-tier Tribunal are allocated to the Social Entitlement Chamber. The main tribunal administration for such cases is based at five regional centres in England and Wales and one in Scotland, but hearings take place at a large number of venues around Great Britain. More details about the First-tier Tribunal may be found at *https://www.gov.uk/social-security-child-support-tribunal.* 5.7

The First-tier Tribunal has only the functions conferred upon it by statute. The function of hearing appeals in social security cases is conferred by numerous provisions. The principal one is s.12 of the Social Security Act 1998 and the note to that provision above lists the others. The First-tier Tribunal can consider allegations of unlawful behaviour by Government Departments and agencies to the extent that it might be relevant to an appeal, e.g. amounting to an abuse of process preventing a fair hearing, but it has no jurisdiction to deal with other allegations of unlawful behaviour—see *Foulser v HMRC* [2013] UKUT 38 (TCC) in which it was specifically pointed out that the First-tier Tribunal had only the powers conferred upon it by legislation and such further powers as it was necessary to imply so that it could carry out its functions fairly.

In *R. (C) v First-tier Tribunal* [2016] EWHC 707 (Admin), it was held that, even though it had no express statutory power to do so, the First-tier Tribunal had an implied power to appoint a litigation friend in circumstances where a party lacked capacity to conduct proceedings and such an appointment was required by the common law concept of procedural fairness.

Similarly, the First-tier Tribunal can give effect to a legitimate expectation arising out of Department for Work and Pensions guidance as to the way in which legislation is to be applied in practice (*SB v Oxford CC (HB)* [2014] UKUT 166 (AAC)) but it cannot give effect to any expectation arising out of advice given by a Government Department that is inconsistent with the legislation (*HMRC v Noor* [2013] UKUT 71 (TCC)).

The point that an expectation based on a representation or "promise" made by an official cannot be *legitimate* if giving effect to the representation would prevent the lawful operation of a statutory scheme has been reiterated in *PS v SSWP (CSM)* [2016] UKUT 437 (AAC). The judge added:

> "58. There is, moreover, in my judgment nothing surprising about this conclusion. It has its correlate in the numerous authorities holding similarly that estoppel cannot prevent a statutory duty from being carried out: see *R(CS) 2/97*, *R(P) 1/80*, *R(SB) 1/83*, *R(SB) 4/91* and *R(JSA) 4/04*. Both estoppel and legitimate expectation are based fundamentally on fairness (in the latter as a counter to abuse of power), whether that is procedural fairness or substantive fairness. But neither legal test can, in my judgment, enable fairness to require the Secretary of State to act contrary to duties entrusted to him under an Act of Parliament."

The relevance of Departmental guidance has more recently been considered by the Court of Appeal in *R. (Ingenious Media Holdings plc) v Revenue and Customs Commissioners* [2015] EWCA Civ 173; [2015] 1 W.L.R. 3183, (subsequently reversed on appeal in *R. (Ingenious Media Holdings plc) v Revenue and Customs Commissioners* [2016] UKSC 54; [2016] 1 W.L.R. 4164, but without reference to this point). Sir Robin Jacob, with whom Tomlinson and Moore-Bick L.J.J. agreed, said of HMRC's *Information Disclosure Guide*:

> "31. This was issued by HMRC mainly but not exclusively for the guidance of its officials. Substantial parts are nonetheless available to the public. However it is elementary that guides of this sort can have no binding effect on the proper construction of a statute. The law is made by Parliament, not pamphlets. Of course a guide by civil servants writing their interpretation of what the law means and how it would apply to particular cases, can in everyday practice be useful. But it

is not definitive. It is like a commentary on a statute by an academic: it may be considered by a court as a view of what the statute may mean.

32. Such a Guide may even be useful as an aid in considering whether or not a government action was reasonable, should such a question arise. It may also be relevant in considering what might, in circumstances where the question arises, amount to a legitimate expectation as to how a government department may act. But such an expectation has its limits: one cannot really have a legitimate expectation of the meaning of a statute from a pamphlet."

Nor, strictly speaking, can there be a legitimate expectation based on a policy of which the citizen is unaware. However, good administration requires that citizens be treated in accordance with a policy adopted by a Government department unless there are good reasons for not doing so and, in the absence of any reasons for departing from a policy, the courts will require conformity to it where it is favourable to the claimant. Accordingly, a respondent to an appeal to the First-tier Tribunal fails in his or her duty to draw relevant matters to the attention of the tribunal if no mention is made of the favourable policy in the response to the appeal (*Mandalia v Secretary of State for the Home Department* [2015] UKSC 59; [2015] 1 W.L.R. 4546).

Proceedings before the First-tier Tribunal in social security cases are intended to be fairly informal. Legal representation is very rare and legal aid is not available, even for advice about applying to the First-tier Tribunal for permission to appeal to the Upper Tribunal on a point of law. On the other hand, many claimants have non-lawyer representatives.

The general approach to be taken by tribunals considering appeals in the social security context has been the subject of a considerable amount of case law.

The inquisitorial role of the tribunal and the burden of proof

5.8 It has long been recognised that proceedings before tribunals are inquisitorial rather than adversarial and this has been confirmed by the House of Lords in *Kerr v Department for Social Development* [2004] UKHL 23; [2004] 1 W.L.R. 1372 (also reported as an appendix to *R1/04(SF)*), where some of the consequences of this approach were considered. Baroness Hale of Richmond said:

"61. Ever since the decision of the Divisional Court in *R. v Medical Appeal Tribunal (North Midland Region), Ex p. Hubble* [1958] 2 Q.B. 228, it has been accepted that the process of benefits adjudication is inquisitorial rather than adversarial. Diplock J. as he then was said this of an industrial injury benefit claim at p.240:

'A claim by an insured person to benefit under the Act is not truly analogous to a *lis inter partes*. A claim to benefit is a claim to receive money out of the insurance funds . . . Any such claim requires investigation to determine whether any, and if so, what amount of benefit is payable out of the fund. In such an investigation, the minister or insurance officer is not a party adverse to the claimant. If analogy be sought in the other branches of the law, it is to be found in an inquest rather than an action.'

62. What emerges from all this is a co-operative process of investigation in which both the claimant and the department play their part. The department is the one which knows what questions it needs to ask and what information it needs to have in order to determine whether the conditions of entitlement have been met. The claimant is the one who generally speaking can and must supply that information. But where the information is available to the department rather than the claimant, then the department must take the necessary steps to enable it to be traced.

63. If that sensible approach is taken, it will rarely be necessary to resort to concepts taken from adversarial litigation such as the burden of proof. The first question will be whether each partner in the process has played their part. If there is still ignorance about a relevant matter then generally speaking it should be determined

against the one who has not done all that they reasonably could to discover it. As Mr Commissioner Henty put it in *CIS/5321/1998*: 'a claimant must to the best of his or her ability give such information to the AO as he reasonably can, in default of which a contrary inference can always be drawn.' The same should apply to information which the department can reasonably be expected to discover for itself."

In that particular case the claimant had been unable to tell the department whether either his brother or sister, with whom he had lost contact, was in receipt of relevant benefits. The department could have discovered that information had they had the brother's and sister's dates of birth, which the claimant could have given them but for which the department never asked. It was held that the department could not rely on their failure to ask questions which would have led to the right answer to defeat the claim.

Where all relevant questions have been asked and there are still things unknown, it was held in *Kerr* that it has to be decided who should bear the consequences of the collective ignorance. If the ignorance concerns a matter relevant to conditions of entitlement, the claimant has to bear the consequences but if the ignorance concerns an exception to those conditions, the department must bear the consequences. In *Kerr*, the claimant was prima facie entitled to a funeral payment but would not be entitled if his brother or sister was not receiving benefit or had capital. The ignorance as to whether they were receiving benefit or had capital was therefore ignorance concerning an exception to entitlement and the department had to bear the burden and pay the claim. Lord Hope of Craighead set out, at [16], the following basic principles to be applied where the information available to a decision-maker falls short of what is needed for a clear decision one way or the other.

"(1) Facts which may reasonably be supposed to be within the claimant's own knowledge are for the claimant to supply at each stage in the inquiry.
(2) But the claimant must be given a reasonable opportunity to supply them. Knowledge as to the information that is needed to deal with his claim lies with the department, not with him.
(3) So it is for the department to ask the relevant questions. The claimant is not to be faulted if the relevant questions to show whether or not the claim is excluded by the Regulations were not asked.
(4) The general rule is that it is for the party who alleges an affirmative to make good his allegation. It is also a general rule that he who desires to take advantage of an exception must bring himself within the provisions of the exception. As Lord Wilberforce observed, exceptions are to be set up by those who rely on them: *Nimmo v Alexander Cowan & Sons Ltd* [1968] A.C. 107, 130."

It is suggested that the tribunal in *Kerr* would not necessarily have been obliged to determine the case in the claimant's favour when the case first came before them. The inquisitorial role of tribunals obliges them to ask questions that the Secretary of State should have asked but has not (*R(IS) 11/99*). It would have been open to the tribunal to ask the claimant whether he knew the dates of birth of his brother and sister and, if the answer was in the affirmative, to give the department the opportunity of investigating the matter further. However, the question whether to adjourn in those circumstances is a matter within the discretion of the tribunal and the department cannot expect always to be given a chance to do something it could perfectly well have done earlier. By the time *Kerr* reached the courts, it was doubtless felt to be a bit late for the department to be making further enquiries. 5.9

Kerr was decided in the context of a claim. It is suggested, however, that it is reasonably clear that, on an appeal against a supersession decision made on the Secretary of State's own initiative, it is the Secretary of State who must bear the burden of ignorance as to whether there are grounds for supersession because it is he who must assert that there are grounds for supersession.

In the light of *Kerr*, it was held in *CIS/213/2004* that, where a question of French law arose when considering a claimant's possible interest in a property in France, it was reasonable to require the Secretary of State to obtain the necessary evidence of French law. (Questions of foreign law are treated as question of fact as to which expert witnesses may give evidence.) The Commissioner's approach was approved on appeal (*Martin v Secretary of State for Work and Pensions* [2009] EWCA Civ 1289; [2010] AACR 9), it also being held that there were no matters of French law on which additional expert evidence was required in that case.

5.10 In *SSWP v OF (II)* [2011] UKUT 448 (AAC), industrial injuries benefit was payable under United Kingdom law only if the claimant was not entitled to benefit under Irish law. The Upper Tribunal, substituting a decision of the First-tier Tribunal, held that it was not necessary to wait for a formal decision by the Irish benefit authorities on a claim, even though one could have been expected under the implementing legislation (then Council Regulation (EEC) 574/72). It received evidence of Irish law in the form of a leaflet issued by the Irish Department of Social Protection and a statement made by the Irish benefit authorities to the Secretary of State.

In *PM v SSWP (IS)* [2014] UKUT 474 (AAC), the claimant was a 19-year old foreign national who had been in care following estrangement from her father and who, the First-tier Tribunal had been told, was too distressed to attend the hearing. Her entitlement to income support depended on whether her father was a "worker" under European Union law at the material time and the Upper Tribunal held that her circumstances required the First-tier Tribunal to obtain the relevant information through the Secretary of State, who could have obtained the information himself with a bit more effort.

The effect of the tribunal having an inquisitorial role was considered by a Tribunal of Commissioners in *R(IS) 17/04*. In 2002, the Secretary of State had superseded awards of benefit from 1988, amounting to some £30,000. The claimant appealed and the Secretary of State made a written submission and produced a considerable amount of evidence. A tribunal chairman directed that a presenting officer attend the hearing to put the Secretary of State's case. In the event, two investigating officers attended as witnesses but there was no presenting officer and a short adjournment established that none would attend. On the basis that the burden of proof lay on the Secretary of State and that the written material was not sufficient in the light of the specific direction that there be a presenting officer, the tribunal allowed the claimant's appeal without putting to her the Secretary of State's case. The Tribunal of Commissioners held the tribunal to have erred. The written material had been sufficient to raise a case for the claimant to answer and the inquisitorial role of the tribunal required the tribunal "to ascertain and determine the true amount of social security benefit to which the claimant was properly entitled", which, once the tribunal had decided not to adjourn, entailed putting the case raised by the Secretary of State's written material to the claimant and enabling her representative to question the witnesses. The Tribunal of Commissioners rejected a submission that a tribunal could not act fairly if it "descended into the arena" and they referred to another decision of a Tribunal of Commissioners, *R(S) 4/82*, where it was said that it was legitimate for a tribunal to put questions, even probing questions, to a claimant to deal with the obvious points that arose on an appeal. However, questions from a tribunal have to be put carefully and phrased neutrally and a tribunal Judge must avoid the risk described in *Southwark LBC v Kofi-Adu* [2006] EWCA Civ 281 that his descent into the arena "may so hamper his ability properly to evaluate and weigh the evidence before him as to impair his judgment, and may *for that reason* render the trial unfair" (emphasis of the Court of Appeal). In *CS v SSWP (DLA)* [2011] UKUT 509 (AAC), it was held still to be inappropriate for the Secretary of State to include in a response to an appeal a request that the First-tier Tribunal ask the claimant particular questions with a view to removing entitlement from an earlier date than he had done. Rather than asking the First-tier Tribunal to take on a role adverse to the claimant, he should have sent a presenting officer to explore the issues at the hearing, having given the claimant notice of them in the response.

Plainly it is better that the Secretary of State be represented in highly contentious or complex cases and the Tribunal of Commissioners in *R(IS) 17/04* recorded both the Secretary of State's declared policy "to appear by way of a presenting officer at every tribunal hearing where the tribunal had made a direction requiring a presenting officer to attend" and the Secretary of State's acceptance of a recommendation of the National Audit Office that he should himself identify complex cases where spending money on presenting officers might achieve greater financial savings.

The Tribunal of Commissioners cited with approval *CI/1021/2001*, where it was held that a tribunal is not entitled to rely upon a "failure to discharge the burden of proof as a substitute for a proper enquiry where there is evidence that there is something into which there needs to be an enquiry". A similar approach led a Tribunal of Commissioners in Northern Ireland to hold a tribunal to have erred when, at a "paper hearing", it had incomplete evidence that raised important issues it could not answer and it failed to adjourn in order to give the claimant the opportunity of attending (*R1/02(IB)*). However, it does not follow from *R(IS) 17/04* that decision-making bodies need make no effort to present evidence to a tribunal. In *CTC/2090/2004*, the Board of Inland Revenue failed to provide any evidence to a tribunal on the question whether the claimant or his ex-wife had the main responsibility for their daughter. That was important because it determined which of the parents was entitled to child tax credit. Both of the parents had claimed child tax credit and it had been awarded to the claimant's ex-wife. The Board did not ask for an adjournment and did not even send an officer to the hearing. The tribunal heard evidence from the claimant as to which parent had the main responsibility for the child and allowed his appeal. The Board appealed on the ground that its position was neutral and that as child tax credit could not be awarded to both parents, the tribunal's inquisitorial jurisdiction required it to summons the claimant's ex-wife to provide evidence against the claimant in her interest. The Commissioner gave that argument short shrift. Being neutral did not justify inactivity on the Board's part. In the light of *Kerr*, it had been the Board's duty to investigate the cases of both parents properly and avoid inconsistent decisions, which clearly meant enquiring themselves into the question of which parent had the main responsibility. However, the tribunal's decision would not be binding on the claimant's ex-wife and the tribunal had been entitled to assume that the Board was content for the claimant's appeal to be determined without information being obtained from his ex-wife. In other words, the tribunal's inquisitorial duty in respect of the father's claim had been satisfied by obtaining relevant evidence from him. **5.11**

What, however, is made plain in *R(IS) 17/04* is that the inquisitorial role of the tribunal is not brought into play only for the purpose of assisting a claimant. A tribunal is part of the machinery for determining the true entitlement of a claimant. It follows that a tribunal is at liberty to follow its own view of a case even if that does not coincide with the view of either the claimant or the Secretary of State (*R. v Deputy Industrial Injuries Commissioner, Ex p. Moore* [1965] 1 Q.B. 456 (C.A.) (also reported as an appendix to *R(I) 4/65*)). Where medical issues arise in a case, a tribunal will often have a medically qualified practitioner among its members. It is entitled to rely on its own medical expertise and will not routinely obtain medical evidence from a claimant's doctor, even if a claimant asks it to do so, although it has power to obtain a medical report in some cases (see r.25(3) of and Sch.2 to the Tribunal Procedure (First-tier Tribunal) (Social Entitlement Chamber) Procedure Rules 2008).

In *SB v HMRC (CHB)* [2013] UKUT 24 (AAC), the First-tier Tribunal was criticised for not acting inquisitorially when it concentrated entirely on the arguments advanced by HMRC based on the documentary evidence and failed to ask the claimant any questions about the more basic point in issue, which was whether she was responsible for her child at the material time. The judge pointed out that there were really only three possibilities: (1) the claimant was responsible for her child; (2) the child was hers but someone else was responsible for her; and (3) the child was not hers at all. Since there was no evidence supporting (2) and (3) and such evidence as there was made them inherently unlikely anyway, the tribunal needed "to step back, take a reality check, and explore whether there was indeed any further evidence supporting (1)". Apart from the evidence the claimant could have given about her care of the child, she had referred in her grounds of appeal to a related tax credit claim and, had the tribunal investigated, it would have discovered that the claim had been allowed by HMRC and that the evidence the claimant was said not to have been provided to HMRC in her child benefit claim had been provided to HMRC in the tax credit claim. This was a fact that the officer dealing with the child benefit claim could have discovered by using internal information systems.

However, there are limits to the inquisitorial rule of the First-tier Tribunal. In *JB v SSWP* [2009] UKUT 61 (AAC), the chairman of the appeal tribunal had personally telephoned a doctor's surgery to check the authenticity of documents that had been produced by a claimant. It was held that the chairman had "stopped being a judge and become both an investigator and a witness" and that, as the claimant had already been given an opportunity to prove the authenticity of the documents, the tribunal should either have proceeded on the basis that she had failed to prove their authenticity or have set in motion enquiries by a third person, possibly the tribunal's clerk. On the other hand, it was held in *HI v SSWP (ESA)* [2014] UKUT 238 (AAC) that the First-tier Tribunal had not erred in law in using Google Maps to check the claimant's evidence as to the distance from her home to a supermarket, because a tribunal is entitled to make use of information that it has obtained for itself. However, it did err in law by not putting its finding to the claimant at the hearing because the claimant would have been able to point out that the First-tier Tribunal's estimate of the distance was grossly wrong, either because it had measured the distance between the wrong points or else had misread the scale.

Evidence

5.12 *Kerr* is not authority for the proposition that social security authorities are under any obligation to obtain information available to other Government departments or authorities (*Amos v Secretary of State for the Home Department* [2011] EWCA Civ 552; [2011] 1 W.L.R. 2952), at any rate where the claimant can as reasonably be expected to obtain the information. However, it may be arguable that the emphasis in *Kerr* on the duty of the department to cooperate in the investigation of cases has some implications for the standard of evidence that should be expected from the department so far as its own records are concerned. In *R(IS) 11/92*, the Commissioner held that no adverse inference was to be drawn against the department where it had destroyed documents in a general "weeding" programme rather with any specific intention of destroying evidence. However, the three-judge panel in *SSWP v TJ (JSA)* [2015] UKUT 56 (AAC) (in a part of its decision that was not the subject of the appeal to the Court of Appeal in *Secretary of State for Work and Pensions v Reilly* [2016] EWCA Civ 413; [2017] Q.B. 257; [2017] AACR 14) accepted that an intention to destroy evidence is not essential for the drawing of an adverse inference against a spoliator and moreover that the destruction itself need not be deliberate, although it held that it was relevant in the case before it that, although the claimant could no longer remember what documents he had been given, he would at one time have known. A tribunal should probably be slow to disbelieve a claimant who does assert that a document was not received if the department's inability to produce contrary evidence is due to the reckless weeding of documents that should have been seen to be relevant to foreseeable proceedings. Even more is that true when documents have been destroyed while a case has been pending. In *Post Office Counters Ltd v Mahida* [2003] EWCA Civ 1583, the Court of Appeal held a judge to have erred in allowing the Post Office to rely on secondary evidence when the defendant's ability to challenge it had been undermined by the Post Office's own loss or destruction of original documents before proceedings were brought but when proceedings might have been contemplated. In the First-tier Tribunal, there is no rule that a fact can be proved only by the best evidence that might be obtained (*SA v LB Ealing (HB)* [2012] UKUT 437 (AAC)). Moreover, although certified evidence of a decision of the Secretary of State is conclusive as to the existence of the decision (Social Security Act 1998, s.39ZA), secondary evidence of the terms of a decision is acceptable where there were plainly grounds for a decision that produced the outcome that had been achieved, particularly as the law generally presumes, in the absence of evidence to the contrary, that that which ought to have been done has in fact been done (*CIB/3838/2003*). There is no general duty on the Secretary of State to provide evidence in the form of certified statements, a computer screen print being sufficient to prove that a document has been issued albeit not conclusive (*JM v SSWP (ESA)* [2013] UKUT 234 (AAC); [2014] AACR 5). Similarly, it may be inferred from a record that a document has been "issued" that it was actually posted (*Secretary of State for Work and Pensions v Roach* [2006] EWCA Civ 1746 (reported as *R(CS) 4/07*)). In *CIB/62/2008*, the Commissioner refused leave to appeal because the claimant had delayed making an application for over six months, with the result that the tribunal's file, which would probably have contained evidence that would either have corroborated the claimant's claim that he had asked for an oral hearing and not been granted one or would have contradicted it, had been destroyed. As the claimant was largely to blame for the lack of evidence, the Commissioner held that he would be unable to overcome the presumption that procedures had been properly followed.

In *R(IB) 7/05*, the Commissioner held that it was not necessary for the Secretary of State to follow the certification procedure under s.7 of the the Electronic Communications Act 2000 when there was a challenge to the authenticity of an electronic signature. This approach has also been taken in relation to evidence gathered through surveillance. The conduct of surveillance is governed by the Regulation of Investigatory Powers Act 2000. Evidence gained by illegal surveillance is not inadmissible, although the circumstances in which evidence is obtained illegally may make it of little weight (*CIS/1481/2006*, in which the Commissioner criticised the Department for Work and Pensions for refusing to provide the evidence gathered in the surveillance upon which the reports of the surveillance were based and *BS v SSWP (DLA)* [2016] UKUT 73 (AAC); [2016] AACR 32, where in fact the only flaw was the failure of the Secretary of State to produce the certificate and the First-tier Tribunal was held to have been entitled to accept the presenting officer's evidence that authorisation had been obtained). It is also not necessarily a breach of the rules of natural justice to admit a witness statement from an investigator where the investigator is not present at the hearing and so cannot be questioned, although, if contested, such evidence is clearly likely to be given less weight than evidence that has been tested through cross-examination (*CSIS/21/2008*, permission to appeal against which was refused in *Williamson v SSWP* [2010] CSIH 4) and, particularly where a great deal of money is at stake, the tribunal may require the witnesses to attend, as was done in *R(IS) 17/04*).

A statutory declaration is generally to be given more weight than a simple written statement but, in *SA v SSWP (BB)* [2013] UKUT 436 (AAC); [2014] AACR 20, it was held that the First-tier Tribunal had gone too far in stating that such a declaration should be accepted unless there was "the strongest possible evidence" to the contrary.

If a tribunal directs any body (including an agency of the Department for Work and Pensions) to disclose information in its possession, that body may not rely on the Data Protection Act 1998 to justify ignoring the direction, because s.35(1) provides that "[p]ersonal data are exempt from the non-disclosure provisions where the disclosure is required by or under any enactment, by any rule of law or by the order of a court". If the body considers that the material should not be disclosed, its remedy lies in an application to the tribunal for a variation of the direction (*Regina (Davies) v The Commissioners Office and the Child Support Agency* [2008] EWHC 334 (Admin)). 5.13

In *CCS/3749/2003*, it was held that a tribunal should refuse to consider any information about proceedings relating to children of a court sitting in private (because use of the information by a party is potentially a contempt of court) but was entitled to hear evidence about ancillary relief proceedings that had taken in place in private.

The distinction arises because it is not a contempt of court to disclose to a tribunal information about proceedings before a court sitting in private unless the case comes within one of the categories specified in s.12(1)(a)–(d) of the Administration of Justice Act 1960, or the court has expressly prohibited publication of the information under s.12(1)(e) of that Act (*AF Noonan Ltd v Bournemouth and Boscombe AFC* [2007] EWCA Civ 848; [2007] 1 W.L.R. 2614). However, evidence disclosed to a court sitting in private may be regarded as confidential and should not usually be disclosed without the permission of the court (*CCS/3749/2003*), although permission is not difficult to obtain if the relevant document really is relevant to an issue before a tribunal (*CCS/1495/2005*). Rule 12.73(1)(c) of the Family Procedure Rules 2010, read with para.2.1 of Practice Direction 12G, makes it unnecessary (subject to a court's direction) for the court's permission to be obtained if a party wishes to disclose information about proceedings relating to children held in private to a tribunal hearing a child support appeal. No similar provision has been made in respect of social security cases, where the issue is less likely to arise, but, in *CCR/3425/2003*, the Commissioner held that a tribunal did not err in considering medical reports that a compensator seeking to avoid liability under the Social Security (Recovery of Benefits) Act 1997 had obtained in civil proceedings brought by the claimant and had disclosed to the Secretary of State.

On the other hand, in *JC v SSWP (PIP)* [2016] UKUT 533 (AAC) where a representative had obtained 350 pages of medical records and had sent them to the First-tier Tribunal without reading them and therefore without noticing that they included the minutes of a highly sensitive child protection conference, marked "strictly confidential" and with a warning that they should "not be copied or shown, or their contents discussed, with any person without the permission of the child protection co-ordination unit or the court", the Upper Tribunal directed that the representative inform the child protection co-ordination unit of the unauthorised disclosure of child protection information and that the confidential minutes be removed from its file. It said that, in principle, the First-tier Tribunal should have made directions along the same lines. Presumably, if a tribunal discovers that documents are confidential after they have been copied to the parties, it should normally direct the parties to make arrangements for the copies' destruction.

Adverse inferences

5.14 Where a person fails to produce evidence that he or she could reasonably be expected to produce, it may be justifiable to make findings of fact against that person. The inference is drawn where the likely explanation for the evidence not being produced is that it would be unfavourable to the claimant. Often it can be inferred that it would be sufficient to disentitle the claimant altogether, but that will not always be so. Thus, a claimant's refusal to produce bank statements, or other evidence of the amount of capital or income he or she possessed, may make it appropriate to infer that he or she had capital or income sufficient to disqualify him or her from an income-related benefit at the material date (*R(SB) 34/83*, *R(H) 3/05*). Although in proceedings where the burden of proof is important the drawing of an adverse inference may not be permissible unless there is some other evidence of the material fact, that is not so in proceedings where there is a substantial inquisitorial element such as family proceedings (*Prest v Petrodel Resources Limited* [2013] UKSC 34; [2013] 2 A.C. 415 at [45]) or social security cases (*SSWP v HS (JSA)* [2016] UKUT 272 (AAC)). However, as made clear in those cases, this is not a licence to engage in pure speculation; regard must be had to the inherent probabilities and to any explanation, even if not a complete justification, offered for the failure to provide the relevant evidence. Thus, save in obvious cases, it may be necessary for reasons to be given for drawing an adverse inference. Indeed, a failure to produce evidence may not be sufficient to justify drawing an adverse inference unless the party concerned has failed to comply with a formal direction or summons issued by the tribunal, perhaps with an express warning that an adverse inference might be drawn in the event of a failure to comply (*R(CS) 6/05*). It is clear from the cases cited that drawing an adverse inference is not a penalty. Drawing an adverse inference is therefore unlikely to be appropriate merely because evidence has been provided late, unless the circumstances justify ignoring the evidence altogether (*CIB/4253/2004*).

Opinion evidence

Tribunals are not bound by the common law rules of evidence such as, for instance, the rule that evidence of opinion, as opposed to evidence of fact, is usually inadmissible unless given by an expert and so, in *CDLA/2014/2004*, a tribunal erred in refusing to allow a disability consultant to give evidence of his opinion. However, it does not follow that those rules of evidence have no relevance at all. Tribunals have no power to override any privilege of a witness not to give evidence, such as the privilege attaching to solicitor-client communications and the privilege against self-incrimination (*LM v LB Lewisham* [2009] UKUT 2019 (AAC); [2010] AACR 12). Furthermore, the common law rules of evidence may be relevant in the evaluation of evidence because the considerations which have led to the evidence being inadmissible often mean that it has little weight. Thus, in *CDLA/2014/2004*, there might have been good reasons for treating the disability consultant's evidence with caution, but it was wrong to refuse to consider it at all. Similarly, in *Hampshire CC v JP* [2009] UKUT 239 (AAC); [2010] AACR 15, the Upper Tribunal held that the weight to be given to an expert's opinion on a matter beyond his or her professional expertise "is likely to be limited and reliance on such an opinion is likely to require some explanation by a tribunal", although the opinion would not be inadmissible in proceedings before a tribunal. 5.15

In *R.(RS) v First-tier Tribunal (CIC)* [2012] UKUT 205 (AAC), a three-judge panel held that, in relying on opinion evidence of a police officer as to what had happened during the course of a crime "the tribunal appears to have misconceived – and perhaps abrogated – its duty". It was for the First-tier Tribunal to form a view as to what had happened, rather than relying on the police officer to do so. However, it is suggested that it might have been different had the tribunal properly considered and then adopted the police officer's reasoning. An appeal against the Upper Tribunal's decision was allowed in *R.(RS) v First-tier Tribunal* [2013] EWCA Civ 1040; [2013] AACR 34 but the point that the Upper Tribunal had made about relying on the police officer's opinion on a matter strictly beyond his expertise was not challenged and was accepted as a reason why the case still had to be remitted to the First-tier Tribunal.

Disability consultants are now relied upon not just by claimants but also by the Secretary of State. An "approved disability analyst" may be a doctor but alternatively may be another health care professional who has received special training to make an assessment of the disabling effects of an impairment and relate this to the relevant legislation in order to provide advice or reports for those making decisions on behalf of the Secretary of State (see ss.19 and 39). Even where such analysts have not examined a claimant, their opinions may be taken into account as evidence, provided the tribunal can identify the factual basis on which any opinion was given. It will usually also be necessary for the tribunal to know the professional qualification and areas of expertise of the analyst so that the weight to be attached to any particular aspect of the report may be assessed (*CDLA/2466/2007*).

In *R(DLA) 3/99*, the Commissioner held that it was wrong for a tribunal to accept evidence of an examining medical practitioner on the basis that it must normally prevail over other evidence, even though in practice, once a proper weighing exercise had been carried out without giving an examining medical practitioner's evidence any special weight, the examining medical practitioner's evidence might be accepted in the majority of cases. Equally, a tribunal is not entitled to arrive at a view of the credibility of the claimant and then, as a separate exercise, consider whether that finding might be shifted by the expert evidence available; "The evidence has to be looked at as a whole" (*AJ (Cameroon) v Secretary of State for the*

Home Department [2007] EWCA Civ 373). Even where an expert's evidence is found convincing, a tribunal is entitled to accept evidence from a blameless and honest witness that conflicts with it and conclude that, although it cannot identify an error in the expert's evidence, some such error must exist (*Armstrong v First York Ltd* [2005] EWCA Civ 277; [2005] 1 W.L.R. 2751). In *CIB/3074/2003*, the Commissioner suggested that a distinction could be drawn in some cases between the weight to be given to clinical findings of an examining medical officer and the weight to be given to his or her assessment as to the claimant's capabilities in the light of those findings.

> "13. In *CIB/15663/1996*, deputy Commissioner Fellner (as she then was) stated that a tribunal was entitled to give full weight to an examining medical officer's findings. A tribunal should of course give full weight to all the evidence, but may often be justified in regarding clinical findings of an examining medical officer as reliable, although even clinical findings should not be regarded as conclusive and may in some cases be displaced by other evidence. However, the impact of any given degree of loss of function will vary from claimant to claimant. In some cases (such as incontinence) a clinical examination will often give very little indication of the extent of impairment of the activities which need to be considered in carrying out the personal capability assessment, although in such cases the examining medical practitioner will often be able to make an informed assessment of the degree of impairment on the basis of the claimant's medical history and other evidence of functional ability. The examining medical officer's choice of a descriptor will therefore generally require the exercise of judgment to a greater or lesser degree, and a tribunal may therefore not necessarily give the same weight to an examining medical officer's choice of descriptors as it does to clinical findings on examination."

Child witnesses

5.16 In *R(DLA) 3/06*, the foster parent and appointee of the 12-year old claimant, who was alleged to have learning difficulties and behavioural problems, did not arrange for her to attend the hearing to give oral evidence, despite a summons. The Tribunal of Commissioners said:

> "[W]e consider the approach of the tribunal to the child claimant—in summonsing the child to give evidence, and then in drawing an adverse inference from the fact that she did not attend (despite the view of the local authority, her carer and a clinical psychologist that her attendance might have an adverse effect upon her)—was inappropriate and unlawful as breaching the claimant's right to a fair hearing."

The Tribunal of Commissioners gave general guidance as to the circumstances in which a child's evidence should be heard (see the note to r.27 of the Tribunal Procedure (First-tier Tribunal) (Social Entitlement Chamber) Rules 2008).

Use of the tribunal's own expertise or observations

5.17 Even in the courts, a judge is entitled to take a point not advanced by the parties but the Court of Appeal has emphasised that fairness requires that the parties be given an opportunity to comment on the point (*Murphy v Wyatt* [2011] EWCA Civ 408; [2011] 1 W.L.R. 2129). To what extent a party to proceedings may be taken to have waived the right to that opportunity by not attending or being represented at a hearing was not an issue considered by the Court and may depend on the circumstances of the case and the nature of the new issue. However, if the tribunal includes a doctor among its members and the doctor puts a different interpretation on the same clinical findings from that advanced in a report before the tribunal, it may be impossible for the parties or their representatives effectively to comment without seeking medical advice and, therefore, an adjournment may be necessary even if the parties are present

(*Evans v Secretary of State for Social Security* (reported as *R(I) 5/94*), *Butterfield v Secretary of State for Defence* [2002] EWHC 2247 (Admin)). In most other cases, it will be reasonable to expect the parties or their representatives to comment at the hearing on a point raised by the tribunal, without any adjournment. This approach also applies where a tribunal makes new findings as a consequence of a medical examination (*MB v DSD (II)* [2010] NICom 133; [2011] AACR 41) or where informal observation of a claimant during a hearing raises an issue in the minds of the tribunal. Where a tribunal observes a claimant acting in a way that seems inconsistent with a claimed level of disability, it has been said that "there is usually no excuse not to put observations to a party, as it can rarely be the case that the perceived inconsistency between a claimant's evidence and what is being observed does not strike any or all of the tribunal members at the time" (*CSDLA/288/2005*). However, in *R(DLA) 8/06*, the Commissioner held that there was not always a duty to put observations to a party where, for instance, the observation merely confirmed a view the tribunal would have formed anyway. In such circumstances, it can be argued that the observation does not really raise a new issue. The Commissioner also held that it was not necessary to explain the legal significance of an observation before obtaining a comment. In any event, it does not follow that a tribunal necessarily errs in law in not putting observations to a claimant even where it would be good practice to do so. As has been pointed out in *CSDLA/463/2007*, if, on appeal, a claimant does not indicate that the opportunity to comment would have led to a comment that might have made a difference to the outcome of the case (whether a suggestion that the observation was inaccurate or a suggestion that the observation was not as significant as the tribunal thought), it is difficult to see that the claimant will have suffered any unfairness. Procedural irregularities do not amount to errors of law unless they result in unfairness or injustice (*R(DLA)3/08*).

Nonetheless, in *ML v SSWP (ESA)* [2012] UKUT 19 (AAC), the First-tier Tribunal was held to have erred in law in going on a site visit, with the claimant and her representative, on the grounds that the Secretary of State, who was not present, had not been asked for his consent, that the purpose of expedition was to test the accuracy of the claimant's evidence rather than better to understand it and that the judge had not continued the record of proceedings after the visit and recorded the claimant's representative's comments made during it. See also *JB v SSWP (ESA)* [2009] UKUT 61 (AAC) and *HI v SSWP (ESA)* [2014] UKUT 238 (AAC), mentioned above.

Relying on decisions of other bodies

The First-tier Tribunal may rely upon, but is not bound by, findings of fact made, or inferentially made by, other bodies including other social security decision-makers (*GB v LB Hillingdon (HB)* [2010] UKUT 11 (AAC)), tax inspectors (*R(FC) 1/91*), the former asylum and immigration tribunal (*R (Nahar) v Social Security Commissioners* [2001] EWHC 1049 (Admin), affirmed on a different point [2002] EWCA Civ 859) and courts (*RC v SSWP* [2009] UKUT 62 (AAC) and *DF v Disclosure and Barring Service* [2015] UKUT 199 (AAC)). In *RC v SSWP*, the Upper Tribunal said— **5.18**

> "Tribunals must make the best findings they can on the information and evidence available to them. The information may include findings made by previous tribunals and family courts. The significance of those findings will depend on their reliability and relevance. In assessing their reliability, tribunals must consider: (i) the evidence on which they were based; (ii) the nature of the fact-finding process (for example, whether the parent was subject to cross-examination); and (iii) the evidence now available. If there is no evidence to the contrary, tribunals may be entitled to conclude that the findings previously made are sufficient and reliable in the child support context. Whether or not this is so will depend on their relevance in the particular case. In assessing the relevance of previous findings, tribunals

must consider: (iv) the facts that are relevant to the issue before the tribunal; (v) the precision with which they have to be found in order to apply the legislation; (vi) whether the previous findings relate, or can be related by other evidence, to the time now in issue; and (vii) the extent to which the issues in the previous proceedings affected the evidence that was obtained or the facts that were found."

A conviction is not conclusive evidence of the facts that must necessarily have been found by the criminal court, but it was held in *AM v SSWP (DLA)* [2013] UKUT 94 (AAC) that, in the absence of convincing new evidence, public policy precludes the convicted person from challenging the findings of primary fact lying behind the conviction and the conviction is relevant even if obtained after the decision of the Secretary of State being challenged. However, in *KL v SSWP (DLA)* [2015] UKUT 222 (AAC), it was accepted by the same judge that public policy does not always preclude the convicted person from challenging the findings behind the conviction. It all depends on the circumstances, such as whether the claimant was represented in the criminal proceedings and whether there is new evidence, even if the claimant pleaded guilty. See to the same effect *DF v Disclosure and Barring Service* [2015] UKUT 199 (AAC). However, in *Newcastle CC v LW (HB)* [2013] UKUT 123 (AAC), it was held to be contrary to public policy to allow a person to resile from a plea of guilty in criminal proceedings so as to argue that she had pleaded guilty to a charge of failing to disclose a material fact only to avoid more serious charges relating to mortgage fraud and fraud in relation to "the right to buy". Persons other than a convicted defendant are, of course, never bound by findings made in criminal proceedings.

Subsection (2)

5.19 The Upper Tribunal's principal function is hearing appeals on points of law brought under s.11 from decisions of the First-tier Tribunal. In the social security field, it also deals with references of questions arising under s.4 of the Forfeiture Act 1982 and it has a "'judicial review'" jurisdiction (see ss.15–21 of this Act). It is divided into four Chambers (see s.7).

When deciding cases, "an important function of the Upper Tribunal is to develop structured guidance on the use of expressions which are central to the scheme, and so to reduce the risk of inconsistent results by different panels at the First-tier level": (*R. (Jones) v First-tier Tribunal* [2013] UKSC 19; [2013] 2 A.C. 48; [2013] AACR 25).

Appeals from the Social Entitlement Chamber of the First-tier Tribunal (which includes most social security cases) are allocated to the Administrative Appeals Chamber, which has its main offices in London and Edinburgh, where the social security cases are administered, and other offices in Cardiff and Belfast. Many of its cases are dealt with on paper but hearings take place at its offices and also in Manchester, Leeds and, less often, in other venues.

Legal aid is no longer available for oral advocacy in social security cases before the Upper Tribunal in England and Wales except where there would otherwise be a breach of art.6 of the European Convention on Human Rights or European Union law, but it remains available for advice and written advocacy. Where it appears to the Upper Tribunal to be essential that a claimant be legally represented, it is often able to put the claimant in touch with a pro bono representative. In Scotland, legal aid does remain available, subject to tests of means and merits. In practice, most claimants are unrepresented or have non-lawyer representatives both in England and Wales and in Scotland.

Further information about the Administrative Appeals Chamber and a link to its decided cases (and those of the former Social Security and Child Support Commissioners) are available at *https://www.gov.uk/administrative-appeals-tribunal.*

Precedent

5.20 An important function of the Upper Tribunal is the giving of guidance to the First-tier Tribunal and first-instance decision-makers. It was well established that decisions on matters of legal principle of Social Security Commissioners and Child Support Commissioners in Great Britain were binding on appeal tribunals and the Secretary of State (*R(I) 12/75*). The giving of opinions on matters of law was the reason that Commissioners, and their forerunner, the Umpire appointed under the National Insurance Act 1911, were established and the binding effect of their decisions has been implicitly recognised in statutory provisions (see now ss.25–27 of the Social Security Act 1998). In *Dorset Healthcare NHS Foundation Trust v MH* [2009] UKUT 4 (AAC), a three-judge panel of the Administrative Appeals Chamber of the Upper Tribunal held that the principles laid down in *R(I) 12/75* should be applied to decisions of the Upper Tribunal. Thus, both decisions of the Upper Tribunal and decisions of Commissioners in Great Britain are binding on the First-tier Tribunal and on the Secretary of State, where the decisions are on matters of legal principle.

Where there are conflicting decisions of the Upper Tribunal or Commissioners, a decision of a three-judge panel of the Upper Tribunal or of a Tribunal of Commissioners in Great Britain (which consisted of three Commissioners) must be followed by the First-tier Tribunal or the Secretary of State in preference to a decision of a single judge or Commissioner (*Dorset Healthcare NHS Foundation Trust v MH* [2009] UKUT 4 (AAC)). Generally, a decision of the Upper Tribunal in a social security, child support, war pension or armed forces compensation case that has been reported in the Administrative Appeals Chamber Reports published by The Stationery Office or a reported decision of a Commissioner should be followed by the First-tier Tribunal or the Secretary of State in preference to an unreported decision, because decisions are reported only if they command the general assent of the majority of the permanent judges of the Administrative Appeals Chamber of the Upper Tribunal or, in the past, the majority of Commissioners (*R(I) 12/75*). However, where a reported decision has been carefully considered in a later, unreported, decision and not followed, that presumption does not apply (*R1/00(FC)*), particularly if the later decision is too recent to have been considered for reporting (*CIB/1205/2005*). Different considerations may apply when considering the relative weight to be given to reported and unreported decisions of the Upper Tribunal in other chambers because the judges themselves have no role in the reporting of the decisions.

Decisions of Commissioners in Northern Ireland are not strictly binding on the First-tier Tribunal or the Secretary of State in Great Britain but are highly persuasive (*R(SB) 1/90*) and should usually be followed as a matter of comity unless they conflict with a decision of the Upper Tribunal or a Commissioner in Great Britain. Indeed, a decision of a single judge of the Upper Tribunal should be followed in preference even to a decision of a Tribunal of Commissioners in Northern Ireland (*CC v SSWP (ESA)* [2015] UKUT 62 (AAC). Equally, of course, appeal tribunals and the Department for Social Development in Northern Ireland are not strictly bound by decisions of the Upper Tribunal or Commissioners in Great Britain but will generally follow them (*R1/05(IB)*).

Decisions of superior courts on points of legal principle must be followed by the First-tier Tribunal and the Secretary of State (*R(I) 12/75*), although this may technically be a matter of comity where the decision was made in a different jurisdiction within the United Kingdom (*Clarke v Frank Staddon Ltd* [2004] EWCA Civ 422).

Strictly speaking, it is only that part of a decision of the Upper Tribunal, a Commissioner or a court that is both on a point of legal principle and vital to the decision that must be followed. Other comments are to be regarded as merely persuasive, although the weight to be attached to them depends, as a matter of common sense, on the extent to which the judge or Commissioner intended reliance to be placed on them and on the extent to which they were the subject of argument before the judge or Commissioner. Indeed, even where a point of legal principle was essential to a decision of the Upper Tribunal or Commissioner, it is not strictly binding if the point was conceded and so the Upper Tribunal or Commissioner was not required to decide it but could merely assume its correctness (*Secretary of* 5.21

State for Work and Pensions v Deane [2010] EWCA Civ 699; [2011] 1 W.L.R. 743; [2010] AACR 42).

In one case, *CDLA/2288/2007*, it was held that, where a Commissioner has made a decision on a question of fact in the light of detailed medical evidence, that decision is binding on tribunals, unless it can be distinguished or has been overtaken by later medical research which at least casts significant doubt on its accuracy. However, it has been made plain in *MN (Somalia) v Secretary of State for the Home Department* [2014] UKSC 40; [2014] 1 W.L.R. 2064 that, while the Upper Tribunal is entitled to give persuasive guidance on matters of fact, its decisions on factual issues cannot be binding. The further guidance on severe mental impairment given in *NMcM v SSWP (DLA)* [2014] UKUT 312 (AAC) must be read in that light.

Precedent in the Upper Tribunal

5.22 The Upper Tribunal itself generally follows its own decisions on matters of legal principle "in the interests of comity and to secure certainty and avoid confusion". However, it recognises that "a slavish adherence to this could lead to the perpetuation of error", in a jurisdiction where most decisions are given without the assistance of legal submissions by professional representatives acting for the parties, and so a single judge will not follow a decision of another single judge if satisfied that it was wrong (*Dorset Healthcare NHS Foundation Trust v MH* [2009] UKUT 4 (AAC)). Similarly, a three-judge panel will generally follow a decision of another three-judge panel or a decision of a Tribunal of Commissioners but will not do so if satisfied that it was wrong (*R(U) 4/88*). However, a single judge of the Administrative Appeals Chamber will always follow a decision of a three-judge panel (*Dorset Healthcare*). This has the effect that a serious difference of opinion can be resolved by a single judge referring a case to the Chamber President with a view to a three-judge panel being appointed to decide it. The precise status of a two-judge panel remains uncertain. In the Court of Appeal, a two-judge court is treated in the same way as a three-judge court (*Cave v Robinson Jarvis & Rolf* [2001] EWCA Civ 245; [2002] 1 W.L.R. 581), but different considerations may apply in the Upper Tribunal.

The Upper Tribunal takes the same approach to decisions of other tribunals and courts of equivalent seniority as it takes to its own decisions (*R(IS) 3/08*, where a Commissioner considered a decision of the asylum and immigration tribunal presided over by a senior immigration judge to be of equal status). Decisions of the Employment Appeal Tribunal and the Crown Court and some decisions of county courts and sheriff courts are likely to fall into this category. However, in *TG v SSWP (SPC)* [2015] UKUT 50 (AAC), it was noted that, while the criteria for directing that a case be heard by a three-judge panel are the same in the Immigration and Asylum Chamber of the Upper Tribunal as they are in the Administrative Appeals Chamber, it is not considered that a single judge of the Immigration and Asylum Chamber is bound to follow a decision of a three-judge panel, except in a "starred" or "country guidance" case. Nonetheless, the judge considered that a single judge of the Administrative Appeals Chamber should follow any decision of a three-judge panel in the Asylum and Immigration Chamber "unless there are compelling reasons not to".

In *EC v SSWP (ESA)* [2015] UKUT 618 (AAC), a single judge of the Upper Tribunal concluded that there were compelling reasons for disagreeing with a Tribunal of Social Security Commissioners in Northern Ireland on the ground that he had been provided by the Secretary of State with far more extra-statutory material that it was legitimate to take into account in construing the relevant legislation than the Northern Ireland Department for Social Development had provided to the Tribunal of Commissioners. He considered that he should treat a Tribunal of Commissioners in the same way as he would a three-judge panel of the Upper Tribunal, but it seems doubtful that a single judge would generally feel entitled to disagree with a three-judge panel on such grounds. It is arguable that better reasons why the single judge, being satisfied that the decision of the Tribunal of Commissioners was wrong, was justified in not following it would have been that Northern Ireland decisions are not strictly binding, that it was impossible to convene a judicial panel at that level capable of resolving the different views in a way that was equally authoritative in both jurisdictions and that the difference of legal view was going to be of limited effect because the relevant legislation had already been amended.

The Upper Tribunal is clearly bound by decisions of the High Court or the Outer House of the Court of Session when those courts are exercising their supervisory jurisdiction over the Upper Tribunal (see the note to s.13(8), below). However, where the Upper Tribunal is effectively exercising a jurisdiction formerly exercised by the High Court, it is not bound to follow a decision of a High Court judge exercising that jurisdiction before its transfer to the Upper Tribunal (*Chief Supplementary Benefit Officer v Leary* [1985] 1 W.L.R. 84 (also reported as an appendix to *R(SB) 6/85*); *R(AF) 1/07*). This is true even if the High Court was exercising its supervisory jurisdiction over an inferior tribunal, rather than merely an appellate jurisdiction (*Secretary of State for Justice v RB* [2010] UKUT 454 (AAC); [2012] AACR 31). Moreover, in *Gilchrist v Revenue and Customs Commissioners* [2014] UKUT 162 (TCC); [2015] Ch. 183, it was held that the Upper Tribunal, as a "superior court of record", was not bound by High Court decisions in tax cases, notwithstanding that many High Court decisions were given on appeal from decisions of the special commissioners for income tax whose functions have been transferred to the Upper Tribunal. It was pointed out that many High Court judges now sit regularly in the Tax and Chancery Chamber of the Upper Tribunal and it was said that: "Although of course conceptually possible, it would be surprising if a decision of a High Court judge sitting in the High Court would be binding on a High Court judge sitting in the Upper Tribunal but not if sitting in the High Court". Nonetheless, the status of decisions of the High Court given otherwise than in the exercise of its supervisory jurisdiction over the Upper Tribunal or in jurisdictions subsequently transferred to the Upper Tribunal has not formally been determined. Nor has the status in Scotland of decisions of the Outer House of the Court of Session, which in many, but not all, respects is equivalent to the High Court in England and Wales.

However, while it appears from *R(SB) 52/83* that a three-judge panel may be prepared not to follow a decision of a divisional court (i.e. a court of two or more judges of the High Court sitting together), a single judge of the Upper Tribunal will always follow a decision of a divisional court as a matter of judicial comity (*Salisbury Independent Living v Wirral MBC (HB)* [2011] UKUT 44 (AAC); [2012] AACR 37), treating it effectively as though it were a decision of a three-judge panel of the Upper Tribunal.

Judges of the Upper Tribunal in England and Wales applying the law of England 5.23
and Wales are bound by decisions of the Court of Appeal and will always, as a matter of comity and practicality, follow decisions of the Inner House of the Court of Session or the Court of Appeal in Northern Ireland that are not in conflict with decisions of the Court of Appeal, although they are not strictly bound by them (*Secretary of State for Work and Pensions v Deane* [2010] EWCA Civ 699). Similarly, Judges of the Upper Tribunal in Scotland applying the law of Scotland are bound by decisions of the Inner House of the Court of Session and, subject to that, will ordinarily follow decisions of the Court of Appeal in England and Wales or the Court of Appeal in Northern Ireland. In *RJ v SSWP (JSA)* [2011] UKUT 477 (AAC); [2012] AACR 28, a judge sitting in Scotland considered that he would be entitled to decline to follow a decision of the Court of Appeal if he was satisfied that it was clearly wrong, but the point did not arise because he did not consider the relevant decision to be wrong at all. Should there ever be a conflict between decisions of the Court of Appeal and the Court of Session, judges in England and Wales would follow the Court of Appeal and judges in Scotland would follow the Inner House of the Court of Session and the Secretary of State's decision-makers would also have to make different decisions depending on which side of the border the cases arose. Presumably steps would be taken, by way of an appeal to the Supreme Court or by legislation, to remove the conflict as rapidly as possible.

Commissioners in Northern Ireland are in a similar position, not being strictly bound by either decisions of the Court of Appeal in England and Wales or decisions of the Court of Session (*R 1/05(IB)*).

All Upper Tribunal judges and Commissioners are bound by decisions of the Supreme Court and by decisions of its predecessor, the House of Lords although, in *Willers v Joyce (No.2)* [2016] UKSC 44; [2016] 3 W.L.R. 534, it was recorded that the "traditional view in Scotland has been that, subject to some possible exceptions, judgments of the House of Lords in English appeals are at most highly persuasive rather than strictly binding".

The justices of the Supreme Court and their predecessors, the Law Lords, have generally made up the membership of the judicial committee of the Privy Council, which is the final court of appeal for United Kingdom overseas territories and crown dependencies and a number of smaller members, or former members, of the Commonwealth but, even so, its decisions on appeal from overseas courts are not binding in the United Kingdom. Therefore, until recently, a decision of the Court of Appeal had to be followed by the Upper Tribunal in England and Wales even if it had been criticised by the Privy Council (*Re Spectrum Plus Ltd* [2004] EWCA Civ 670; [2004] Ch. 337).

However, in *Willers v Joyce (No.2)*, the Supreme Court has declared that, when deciding that previous authority binding in England and Wales is wrong on a matter of English law, the Privy Council may now direct that courts in England and Wales should treat its decision as representing the law of England and Wales and so, presumably, of Northern Ireland where the common law applies in the same way as it does in England and Wales.

5.24 As with decisions of the Upper Tribunal, strictly speaking, only the reasoning vital to the decision of a court is binding and other comments are not but, where those other comments are made after full argument and expressly for the purpose of giving guidance, they should be followed by the Upper Tribunal except in quite exceptional circumstances (*R(IB)4/04*). Indeed, a decision of the Court of Appeal deciding a point of principle for the purpose of clarifying the law must be followed, even if that part of the decision is obiter and even if it appears to be inconsistent with previous decisions of the Court of Appeal or the House of Lords (*Sayce v TNT (UK) Ltd* [2011] EWCA Civ 1583; [2012] 1 W.L.R. 1261). Moreover, a considered view on a question of jurisdiction upon which the Court of Appeal had requested argument must be regarded as an essential element of the reasoning of the case and is therefore binding and it is not appropriate for judges in lower courts to say obiter that they consider such a view expressed by the Court of Appeal is wrong (*R. (Nirula) v First-tier Tribunal (Asylum and Immigration Chamber)* [2012] EWCA Civ 1436; [2013] 1 W.L.R. 1090). A decision of the Court of Appeal refusing permission to appeal to that Court is not a full decision for these purposes and, while reasons given by the Court of Appeal for refusing permission are not to be disregarded lightly, their value as precedent must be assessed taking account of all relevant factors, in particular whether the Court heard substantial argument and whether the reasons were given fully (*CCS/2567/1998*, applying *Clark v University of Humberside and Lincolnshire* [2000] 1 W.L.R. 1988, and see also *R(IS) 15/96*).

Decisions of the European Court of Human Rights must be taken into account (Human Rights Act 1998, s.2) but do not take precedence over a binding decision of a domestic court unless the decision of the domestic court predates, and cannot survive, the coming into force of the Human Rights Act 1998 (*Kay v Lambeth LBC* [2006] UKHL 10; [2006] 2 A.C. 465 as explained in *R (RJM) v Secretary of State for Work and Pensions* [2008] UKHL 63; [2009] 1 A.C. 311). The effect of the extensive case law on the duty to "take account" of decisions of the European Court of Human Rights on the interpretation of the ambit of a provision of the Convention itself, as opposed to decisions on how a provision in the Convention is to apply to particular factual circumstances, has been neatly summarised in *R. (Hicks) v Commissioner of Police of the Metropolis* [2014] EWCA Civ 3; [2014] 1 W.L.R. 2152 at [80].

Decisions of the Court of Justice of the European Union (formerly the European Court of Justice) determine European Union law, which takes precedence over domestic law (European Communities Act 1972 s.2(4)) and so such decisions are always binding. Where domestic legislation is inconsistent with European Union legislation or European Union directives having direct effect, tribunals must disapply the domestic legislation (*R. (Manson) v Ministry of Defence* [2005] EWCA Civ 1678; [2006] I.C.R. 355, *R(JSA) 4/03*). However, they remain bound by decisions of the superior courts. Indeed, a decision of the Court of Appeal remains binding even if there is a pending appeal against it in which the Supreme Court has referred questions to the Court of Justice of the European Union (*Miskovic v Secretary of State for Work and Pensions* [2011] EWCA Civ 16; [2012] AACR 11). In *R. (Probyn) v First Secretary of State* [2005] EWHC 398 (Admin), Burton J. considered himself obliged to follow a decision of the Court of Appeal dismissing a renewed application for permission to apply for judicial review even though it was arguably inconsistent with subsequent decisions of the European Court of Justice. He accordingly dismissed the application for permission to apply for judicial review that was before him on the basis that a renewed application could be made to the Court of Appeal which was the appropriate court for deciding whether its earlier decision should be followed. The same approach could not be taken if the Upper Tribunal found itself in a similar position on an application for permission to appeal, because there is no right to appeal against a refusal of permission to appeal (see s.13(8)(c)). In this situation, the need to get the case before the Court of Appeal might suggest that permission to appeal to the Upper Tribunal should be granted with the appeal then possibly being dismissed fairly summarily. Permission to appeal to the Court of Appeal could then be granted against the substantive decision.

Subsection (3)

The judges of the First-tier Tribunal include all the legally qualified chairmen of the tribunals whose functions have been transferred to the First-tier Tribunal and the members of the First-tier Tribunal include all the other members of those tribunals. The judges of the Upper Tribunal include the former Social Security Commissioners and Child Support Commissioners and the deputy Commissioners and the former presidents of abolished tribunals. Members of the Upper Tribunal sit with judges hearing appeals from the Disclosure and Barring Service and traffic commissioners and some appeals from the Information Commissioner, which are beyond the scope of this work. There is also a broad power to nominate judges from the courts to sit in the First-tier Tribunal and Upper Tribunal and to assign judges and members of the employment tribunal to chambers of the First-tier Tribunal. For the composition of a tribunal for the purpose of deciding individual cases, see the First-tier Tribunal and Upper Tribunal (Composition of Tribunal) Order 2008. 5.25

Apart from judges, the members of the First-tier Tribunal hearing social security appeals are either doctors, other people with experience of disability or looking after disabled people or accountants. There is no requirement that a medically-qualified member of the First-tier Tribunal should be a specialist in the field of medicine in any particular case before the Tribunal (*ED v SSWP* [2009] UKUT 206 (AAC)). Even in an unusual case, any qualified doctor will usually be able to decide as between competing views (*CSI/146/2003*).

Quite a number of medically qualified tribunal members also work as health care professionals providing reports for use by the Secretary of State when determining claims. In *Gillies v Secretary of State for Work and Pensions* [2006] UKHL 2; [2006] 1 W.L.R. 781 (also reported as *R(DLA) 5/06*), the House of Lords considered whether it was proper for a person who acted as an examining medical practitioner in some cases to sit as a member of a tribunal when reports of other examining medical practitioners were being challenged by claimants. Lord Hope of Craighead pointed out that the "fair-minded and informed observer" by whose standards fairness is to be judged must be taken to be neither complacent nor unduly sensitive or suspicious and to be able distinguish between what is relevant and what is irrelevant and decide what weight should be given to facts that are relevant. He then said:

> "18. ... A fair-minded observer who had considered the facts properly would appreciate that professional detachment and the ability to exercise her own independent judgment on medical issues lay at the heart of [the examining medical practitioner's] relationship with the [Benefits] Agency. He would also appreciate that she was just as capable of exercising those qualities when sitting as a medical member of a disability appeal tribunal. So there is no basis for a finding that there was a reasonable apprehension of bias on the ground that Dr Armstrong had a predisposition to favour the interests of the Benefits Agency... .
> "20. ... The fair-minded observer would understand that there was a crucial difference between approaching the issues which the tribunal had to decide with a predisposition in favour of the views of the EMP, and drawing upon her medical knowledge and experience when testing those views against the other evidence. He would appreciate, looking at the matter objectively, that he knowledge and experience could cut both ways as she would be just as well placed to spot the weaknesses in these reports as to spot their strengths. He would have no reason to think, in the absence of other facts indicating the contrary, that she would not apply her medical knowledge and experience in just the same impartial way when she was sitting as a tribunal member as she would when she was acting as an EMP.
> 21. ... The observer would appreciate that Dr Armstrong's experience of working as an EMP would be likely to be of benefit to her, and through her to the other tribunal members, when she was evaluating the EMP report. The exercise of her independent judgment, after all, was the function that she was expected to perform as the tribunal's medical member. Her experience in the preparation of these reports was an asset which was available, through her, for the other tribunal members to draw upon when they were considering the whole of the evidence... .
> 23. The fact is that the bringing of experience to bear when examining evidence and reaching a decision upon it has nothing to do with bias. The purpose of disqualification on the ground of apparent bias is to preserve the administration of justice from anything that might detract from the basic rules of fairness. One guiding principle is to be found in the concept of independence... . There is no suggestion that that principle was breached in this case. The other principle is to be found in the concept of impartiality—that justice must not only be done but be seen to be done. This too has at its heart the need to maintain public confidence in the integrity of the administration of justice. Impartiality consists in the absence of a predisposition to favour the interests of either side in the dispute. Therein lies the integrity of the adjudication system. But its integrity is not compromised by the use of specialist knowledge or experience when the judge or tribunal member is examining the evidence."

5.26 Lord Rodger of Earlsferry pointed out that the approach adopted on behalf of the claimant in that case might lead to an argument that a member of a tribunal who was disabled should be disqualified on the ground that they would be likely to be partial to the disabled person claiming benefit. He also said that "the position might have been different if there had been any reason to suppose that the [examining medical practitioners] were a close-knit group sharing an esprit de corps". Baroness Hale made a similar point and emphasised that the Tribunal of Commissioners *(CSDLA/1019/1999)* had rejected the suggestion that an examining medical practitioner was a "Benefits Agency doctor" rather than an independent expert adviser. Doctors frequently have to review each others' decisions. She further observed that the Benefits Agency had no particular interest in the outcome of any individual case and was not realistically in a position to influence the doctor's decision one way or the other. Accordingly, the House of Lords held that there was no apparent bias.

There is, nonetheless, a difficulty that must arise if some health care professionals sit also as members of tribunals. Inevitably, there will be cases where the report of such a health care professional has to be considered by a panel of the First-tier Tribunal of which the judge or disability qualified member knows the health care professional because he or she has been the medically qualified member of a tribunal on which they have sat on a previous occasion. In *Secretary of State for Work and Pensions v Cunningham*, 2004 S.L.T. 1007 (also reported as *R(DLA) 7/04*) the issue was whether there was apparent bias when a tribunal had to consider a report by an examining medical practitioner who had sat 22 times as a member of a tribunal with the chairman and 14 times with the member of the tribunal with a disability qualification. The Court of Session held that there was an apprehension of bias applying *Lawal v Northern Spirit Ltd* [2003] UKHL 35; [2003] I.C.R. 856, in which the House of Lords held there to have been apparent bias where one party to proceedings before the Employment Appeal Tribunal was represented by a barrister who had previously sat as a part-time judge of that tribunal with the lay members before whom he was appearing. *Cunningham* was cited in argument in *Gillies* but is not mentioned in the speeches of the House of Lords. It is suggested that a case like *Cunningham* turns not on whether health care professionals are "a close-knit group sharing an esprit de corps" but on whether the tribunal is. As a tribunal must work together in a way that health care professionals do not, *Cunningham* can be distinguished from *Gillies* and it is suggested that it is unaffected by the later case. In *Cunningham*, the Court of Session declined to give guidance as to how often a member of a tribunal had to have sat with an examining medical practitioner before there was apparent bias. In *CSDLA/364/2005*, decided before the House of Lords' decision in *Gillies*, it was held that a chairman was disqualified from hearing an appeal if he had sat with the examining medical practitioner only once. However, that decision was not followed in *R(DLA) 3/07* and was subsequently reversed by the Court of Session, without reasons, when the claimant withdrew her opposition to the Secretary of State's appeal. In *R(DLA) 3/07*, the Commissioner referred to *Locabail (UK) Ltd v Bayfield Properties Ltd* [1999] EWCA Civ 3004; [2000] Q.B. 451 in which it was suggested that each case had to be determined on its facts, that any doubts had to be resolved in favour of recusal and that "[t]he greater the passage of time between the event relied on as showing a danger of bias and the case in which the objection is raised, the weaker (other things being equal) the objection will be" but held that there was a reasonable apprehension of bias where the chairman of the tribunal had sat on a tribunal with the health care professionals whose report was being considered on three occasions, the last being three and a half months before the relevant hearing. The practical answer to the problem revealed in these cases is for those responsible for tribunals to ensure that medically qualified tribunal members who are also health care professionals do not sit in the areas where they usually act as health care professionals, so that they only rarely sit with judges and other members who might subsequently have to consider their reports.

Subsection (5)

The precise significance of the Upper Tribunal being a "superior court of record" 5.27
remains uncertain. In *R.(Cart) v Upper Tribunal (Public Law Project intervening)* [2011] UKSC 28; [2012] 1 A.C. 663; [2011] AACR 38, Lady Hale said at [43] that being a superior court of record empowered it to set precedent. However, the precedential status of decisions of the former Social Security Commissioners, who were not a superior court of record, had long been recognised as a practical consequence of their appellate status and had been implicitly recognised in statute (see s.27 of the Social Security Act 1998 as originally enacted). In *Advocate General for Scotland v Eba* [2011] UKSC 29; [2012] 1 A.C. 710; [2011] AACR 39, it was pointed out at [16] that "superior court of record" was a term that "is unknown to the law of Scotland and has never been applied to any of the Scottish courts", although it has been applied to other tribunals exercising a jurisdiction throughout Great Britain. The Supreme Court held that, when used in respect of courts in parts of the United

Kingdom other than Scotland, the term is used "to indicate a court that keeps a permanent record of its acts and proceedings and has power to punish for contempt". However, it has been felt necessary to give the Upper Tribunal a separate statutory power to punish for contempt in England and Wales and Northern Ireland as well as in Scotland (see s.25). In the end, the use of the term may merely be a declaration of status: it appears to be used where the judges of a tribunal or court include judges of at least the status of High Court judges. (Contrary to what the Supreme Court understood (see *Eba* at [15]), the Transport Tribunal was merely a court of record, like a county court, and not a superior court of record (see Transport Act 1985 Sch.4 para.1).) In any event, it was held in *Cart* and *Eba* that the fact that the Upper Tribunal is a superior court of record does not make it immune from judicial review by, respectively, the High Court or the Court of Session (see the note to s.13(8) below). On the other hand, it has been held that one effect of this subsection is to make it quite clear that the Upper Tribunal must be regarded as a "court" for the purposes of s.42 of the Senior Courts Act 1981 so that, even if a civil proceedings order does not bar a person from bringing proceedings in the First-tier Tribunal without the permission of the High Court, it certainly prevents the person from doing so in the Upper Tribunal (*AO v Shepway DC (HB)* [2013] UKUT 9 (AAC)).

In *CL (Vietnam) v Secretary of State for the Home Department* [2008] EWCA Civ 1551; [2009] 1 W.L.R. 1873, Sedley L.J. raised the question whether an undertaking given by the Secretary of State to the Asylum and Immigration Tribunal, which was not a superior court of record, was enforceable and had any legal force. Presumably that issue does not arise in relation to the Upper Tribunal in the light of s.3(5), but it might in relation to the First-tier Tribunal.

Members and composition of tribunals

5.28 **4. to 6A.** *Omitted.*

Chambers: jurisdiction and Presidents

5.29 **7.**—(1) The Lord Chancellor may, with the concurrence of the Senior President of Tribunals, by order make provision for the organisation of each of the First-tier Tribunal and the Upper Tribunal into a number of chambers.

(2) There is—

(a) for each chamber of the First-tier Tribunal, and

(b) for each chamber of the Upper Tribunal,

to be a person, or two persons, to preside over that chamber.

(3) A person may not at any particular time preside over more than one chamber of the First-tier Tribunal and may not at any particular time preside over more than one chamber of the Upper Tribunal (but may at the same time preside over one chamber of the First-tier Tribunal and over one chamber of the Upper Tribunal).

(4) A person appointed under this section to preside over a chamber is to be known as a Chamber President.

(5) Where two persons are appointed under this section to preside over the same chamber, any reference in an enactment to the Chamber President of the chamber is a reference to a person appointed under this section to preside over the chamber.

(6) The Senior President of Tribunals may (consistently with subsections (2) and (3)) appoint a person who is the Chamber President of a chamber to preside instead, or to preside also, over another chamber.

(7) The [1 Senior President of Tribunals] may (consistently with subsec-

tions (2) and (3)) appoint a person who is not a Chamber President to preside over a chamber.

(8) Schedule 4 (eligibility for appointment under subsection (7), appointment of Deputy Chamber Presidents and Acting Chamber Presidents, assignment of judges and other members of the First-tier Tribunal and Upper Tribunal, and further provision about Chamber Presidents and chambers) has effect.

(9) Each of the Lord Chancellor and the Senior President of Tribunals may, with the concurrence of the other, by order—

(a) make provision for the allocation of the First-tier Tribunal's functions between its chambers;
(b) make provision for the allocation of the Upper Tribunal's functions between its chambers;
(c) amend or revoke any order made under this subsection.

AMENDMENT

1. Crime and Courts Act 2013 s.20 and Sch.13 paras 42 and 43 (October 1, 2013).

GENERAL NOTE

The First-tier Tribunal is organised into seven chambers by art.2 of the First-tier Tribunal and Upper Tribunal (Chambers) Order 2010 (SI 2010/2655). By art.6, there are assigned to the Social Entitlement Chamber of the First-tier Tribunal— **5.30**

"all functions relating to appeals—

(a) in cases regarding support for asylum seekers, failed asylum seekers, persons designated under section 130 of the Criminal Justice and Immigration Act 2008 or the dependants of any such persons;
(b) in criminal injuries compensation cases;
(c) regarding entitlement to, payments of, or recovery or recoupment of payments of, social security benefits, child support, vaccine damage payment, health in pregnancy grant and tax credits, with the exception of—
    (i) appeals under section 11 of the Social Security Contributions (Transfer of Functions, etc.) Act 1999 (appeals against decisions of Her Majesty's Revenue and Customs);
    (ii) appeals in respect of employer penalties or employer information penalties (as defined in section 63(11) and (12) of the Tax Credits Act 2002;
    (iii) appeals under regulation 28(3) of the Child Trust Funds Regulations 2004;
(d) regarding saving gateway accounts with the exception of appeals against requirements to account for an amount under regulations made under section 14 of the Saving Gateway Accounts Act 2009;
(e) regarding child trust funds with the exception of appeals against requirements to account for an amount under regulations made under section 22(4) Child Trust Funds Act 2004 in relation to section 13 of that Act;
(ea) appealable decisions within the meaning of section 56(3) of the Childcare Payments Act 2014;
(f) regarding payments in consequence of diffuse mesothelioma;
(g) regarding a certificate or waiver decision in relation to NHS charges;
(h) regarding entitlement to be credited with earnings or contributions;
(i) against a decision as to whether an accident was an industrial accident."

The excepted cases mentioned in paras (c), (d) and (e) are assigned to the Tax Chamber under art.7. Note, however, that decisions made by HMRC under arrangements made under s.17 of the 1999 Act do not fall within exception (i) in para.(c) since appeals against such decisions are not brought under s.11 of that Act (*SF v SSWP (HRP)* [2013] UKUT 175 (AAC)).

Asylum support cases, falling within the scope of para.(a), were previously determined by adjudicators and criminal injuries compensation cases, falling within the scope of para.(b), were previously determined by the Criminal Injuries Compensation Appeals Panel, both of which were entirely separate from the appeal tribunals that determined social security and child support cases. Although the Social Entitlement Chamber is a single entity in legal terms, its administration still continues to reflect the old divisions, with asylum support appeals and criminal injuries compensation cases (which are outside the scope of this work) being administered separately in central offices while social security and child support cases are administered regionally.

5.31 The Presidents of the Social Entitlement Chamber and the Tax Chamber are, respectively, Judge John Aitken and Judge Colin Bishopp (who is shortly to retire and will be replaced by Upper Tribunal Judge Sinfield from October 11, 2017).

The Upper Tribunal is organised into four chambers by art.9. By art.10, there are assigned to the Administrative Appeals Chamber of the Upper Tribunal, inter alia, all appeals against decisions of the Social Entitlement Chamber of the First-tier Tribunal, all references under s.9(5)(b) or under r.7(3) of the Tribunal Procedure (First-tier Tribunal) (Social Entitlement Chamber) Rules 2008 by that Chamber, all determinations and decisions under the Forfeiture Act 1982 and most judicial review cases. Appeals and references from the Tax Chamber of the First-tier Tribunal and some judicial review cases are allocated to the Tax and Chancery Chamber of the Upper Tribunal under art.13. Complex cases transferred from the Tax Chamber of the First-tier Tribunal to the Upper Tribunal are also allocated to the Tax and Chancery Chamber under art.13.

The Presidents of the Administrative Appeals Chamber and the Tax and Chancery Chamber are, respectively, Mr Justice Charles and Mrs Justice Rose.

Article 14 enables the Senior President of Tribunals to resolve any question of doubt as to the chamber to which a case should be allocated and art.15 gives a president of a chamber to which a case is allocated a broad power to transfer a case to another chamber of the same tribunal, with the agreement of that chamber's president.

Senior President of Tribunals: power to delegate

5.32 **8.**—(1) The Senior President of Tribunals may delegate any function he has in his capacity as Senior President of Tribunals—

(a) to any judge, or other member, of the Upper Tribunal or First-tier Tribunal;

(b) to staff appointed under section 40(1).

[[1] (1A) A function under paragraph 1(1) or 2(1) of Schedule 2 may be delegated under subsection (1) only to a Chamber President of a chamber of the Upper Tribunal.]

(2) Subsection (1) does not apply to functions of the Senior President of Tribunals [[1] under any of the following—

section 7(7);
section 7(9);
paragraph 2(1) of Schedule 3;
paragraph 7(1) of Schedule 3;
paragraph 2 of Schedule 4;
paragraph 5(1) and (3) of Schedule 4;
paragraph 5(5) to (8) of Schedule 4;
paragraph 5A(2)(a) of Schedule 4;
paragraph 5A(3)(a) of Schedule 4.]

(3) A delegation under subsection (1) is not revoked by the delegator's becoming incapacitated.

(4) Any delegation under subsection (1) that is in force immediately before a person ceases to be Senior President of Tribunals continues in force until varied or revoked by a subsequent holder of the office of Senior President of Tribunals.

(5) The delegation under this section of a function shall not prevent the exercise of the function by the Senior President of Tribunals.

AMENDMENT

1. Crime and Courts Act 2013 s.20 and Sch.13 paras 42 and 44 (October 1, 2013).

GENERAL NOTE

Any function delegated to a Chamber President may be further delegated to another judge or a member of staff, under Sch.4 para.4. 5.33

Although that provision has not been amended, it is implicit that it cannot allow a Chamber President further to delegate a function mentioned in subs.(1A) that has been delegated to him or her.

Review of decisions and appeals

Review of decision of First-tier Tribunal

9.—(1) The First-tier Tribunal may review a decision made by it on a matter in a case, other than a decision that is an excluded decision for the purposes of section 11(1) (but see subsection (9)). 5.34

(2) The First-tier Tribunal's power under subsection (1) in relation to a decision is exercisable—

(a) of its own initiative, or

(b) on application by a person who for the purposes of section 11(2) has a right of appeal in respect of the decision.

(3) Tribunal Procedure Rules may—

(a) provide that the First-tier Tribunal may not under subsection (1) review (whether of its own initiative or on application under subsection (2)(b)) a decision of a description specified for the purposes of this paragraph in Tribunal Procedure Rules;

(b) provide that the First-tier Tribunal's power under subsection (1) to review a decision of a description specified for the purposes of this paragraph in Tribunal Procedure Rules is exercisable only of the tribunal's own initiative;

(c) provide that an application under subsection (2)(b) that is of a description specified for the purposes of this paragraph in Tribunal Procedure Rules may be made only on grounds specified for the purposes of this paragraph in Tribunal Procedure Rules;

(d) provide, in relation to a decision of a description specified for the purposes of this paragraph in Tribunal Procedure Rules, that the First-tier Tribunal's power under subsection (1) to review the decision of its own initiative is exercisable only on grounds specified for the purposes of this paragraph in Tribunal Procedure Rules.

(4) Where the First-tier Tribunal has under subsection (1) reviewed a decision, the First-tier Tribunal may in the light of the review do any of the following—

(a) correct accidental errors in the decision or in a record of the decision;
(b) amend reasons given for the decision;
(c) set the decision aside.

(5) Where under subsection (4)(c) the First-tier Tribunal sets a decision aside, the First-tier Tribunal must either—

(a) re-decide the matter concerned, or
(b) refer that matter to the Upper Tribunal.

(6) Where a matter is referred to the Upper Tribunal under subsection (5)(b), the Upper Tribunal must re-decide the matter.

(7) Where the Upper Tribunal is under subsection (6) re-deciding a matter, it may make any decision which the First-tier Tribunal could make if the First-tier Tribunal were re-deciding the matter.

(8) Where a tribunal is acting under subsection (5)(a) or (6), it may make such findings of fact as it considers appropriate.

(9) This section has effect as if a decision under subsection (4)(c) to set aside an earlier decision were not an excluded decision for the purposes of section 11(1), but the First-tier Tribunal's only power in the light of a review under subsection (1) of a decision under subsection (4)(c) is the power under subsection (4)(a).

(10) A decision of the First-tier Tribunal may not be reviewed under subsection (1) more than once, and once the First-tier Tribunal has decided that an earlier decision should not be reviewed under subsection (1) it may not then decide to review that earlier decision under that subsection.

(11) Where under this section a decision is set aside and the matter concerned is then re-decided, the decision set aside and the decision made in re-deciding the matter are for the purposes of subsection (10) to be taken to be different decisions.

General Note

5.35 This convoluted section replaces s.13(2) of the Social Security Act 1998. Note that s.13(3) of the 1998 Act remains in place.

Subsections (1)–(3)

5.36 At first sight, this section provides a very broad power to review a decision. However, r.40(2) of the Tribunal Procedure (First-tier Tribunal) (Social Entitlement Chamber) Rules 2008 provides that a decision may be reviewed only where there has been an application for permission to appeal and only if there was an error of law in the decision, so that the circumstances in which there may be a review are similar to those that formerly existed is under s.13(2) of the 1998 Act. (As decisions in respect of criminal injuries compensation and asylum support are excluded decisions, there is no power of review in such cases.) For what amounts to an error of law, see the note to s.11 and, for the general effect of r.40 and its validity, see the note to that rule.

Because exercising a power of review requires a finding that there has been an error of law, it is difficult to envisage it being appropriate to review a decision and then take no action, rather than refusing to review it (*VH v Suffolk CC (SEN)* [2010] UKUT 203 (AAC)), unless perhaps the case had ceased to have any practical purpose but there was nevertheless some advantage in simply declaring there to have been an error.

A decision should be reviewed only where it is clearly wrong in law, because otherwise the First-tier Tribunal would be usurping the Upper Tribunal's function of determining appeals on contentious points of law. Nonetheless, there are degrees of clarity and the likelihood of the party in whose favour the original decision was made objecting to the review may be an important consideration when deciding whether a review is appropriate (*R.(RB) v First-tier Tribunal (Review)* [2010] UKUT 160 (AAC); [2010] AACR 41). Claimants are probably more likely in practice to object than the Secretary of State. On the other hand, if a decision is reviewed without first giving a party an opportunity to object, r.40(4) of the 2008 Rules enables the review decision to be set aside if an objection is subsequently received from that party.

There is no general rule that it is inappropriate for a judge to consider whether to review his own decision (*AA v Cheshire and Wirral Partnership NHS Foundation Trust* [2009] UKUT 195 (AAC); [2011] AACR 37). However, in the Social Entitlement Chamber to which social security cases are allocated, para.11 of the Senior President of Tribunals' practice statement on the composition of tribunals (see the note to art.2 of the First-tier Tribunal and Upper Tribunal (Composition of Tribunal) Order 2008, below) requires applications for permission to appeal and reviews to be dealt with by salaried judges, who consequently decide whether to review their own decisions and also those of fee-paid judges sitting in their districts. Apparent attempts by one fee-paid judge to prevent his decisions from being reviewed by purporting to consider whether to review his decisions when they were made were held to be ineffective in *LM v SSWP* [2009] UKUT 185 (AAC) because the effect of r.40(2)(a) of the 2008 Rules is that a power to consider a review under s.9 arises only when an application for permission to appeal is made. **5.37**

There is no appeal against a decision to review, or not to review, an earlier decision (see s.11(5)(d)(i)).

Subsection (4)

Note that, upon a review, the tribunal is not limited to setting aside its decision but may instead correct its decision or amend its reasons. **5.38**

The power to correct decisions overlaps with the power under r.36 of the Tribunal Procedure (First-tier Tribunal) (Social Entitlement Chamber) Rules 2008. and, in view of subs.(10), it may be important to identify which of the two powers is being exercised.

The power to amend reasons may be useful where the tribunal has simply failed to explain part of its reasoning but there are limits to the extent to which additional reasons may be given. Although the three-judge panel deciding *JS v SSWP (DLA)* [2013] UKUT 100 (AAC) declined to define "amend", it did state that the power "must not be used to correct defective reasoning or to provide a commentary on the grounds of appeal" and that the amended reasons "must be the reasons that led the tribunal to decide as it did, flawed though they may be, not a later attempt to rationalise the decision". In *SSWP v CM (ESA)* [2012] UKUT 436 (AAC), the Upper Tribunal was sceptical as to whether additional reasons provided on review represented the original reasoning, on the ground that if the First-tier Tribunal had really addressed the more difficult issue in the case dealt with in the additional reasons it was unlikely that it would have mentioned in the original reasons only the easier issue. In both that decision and in *JS v SSWP (DLA)*, the Upper Tribunal said that the power to amend reasons may be exercised only by the presiding judge (or—it was said in the latter case—exceptionally, another member) of the panel that heard the case. However, as noted above, para.11 of the Senior President of Tribunals' practice statement on the composition of tribunals requires reviews to be dealt with by salaried judges. It is difficult for a salaried judge to review a decision where the appropriateness of a review depends on whether or not the reasons of a decision made by a fee-paid judge can be amended satisfactorily. Because the power to amend the reasons for a decision arises only where there has been a review, it is necessary, due to the effect of r.40(1)(b) of the Tribunal Procedure (First-tier Tribunal) (Social Entitlement Chamber) Rules 2008, for the salaried judge to identify an error of law before the case is referred to the fee-paid judge for the reasons to be amended. It might be better if a salaried judge could refer the whole application for permission to appeal and the question of review to the fee-paid judge in such a case. As it is, it may be necessary for the salaried judge at least to leave the fee-paid judge a choice of either amending the reasons or setting the original decision aside. An alternative approach, suggested in *JS v SSWP (DLA)*, would be for the salaried judge to seek representations from the parties before referring the case to fee-paid judge in which case, as the three-judge panel pointed out, the party not making the application for permission to appeal will be able to consider whether to concede that the decision is erroneous in point of law so that it must be set aside under s.13(3) of the Social Security Act 1998. However, note that r.40(4) of the Tribunal Procedure (First-tier Tribunal) (Social Entitlement Chamber) Rules 2008 enables the First-tier Tribunal to make what is in effect a provisional decision without first obtaining representations on the basis that it may reconsider the decision in the light of representations made afterwards. This may often be a more proportionate approach.

5.39 The problems caused by the Practice Statement on the composition of the First-tier Tribunal had been illustrated in *AS v SSWP (ESA)* [2011] UKUT 159 (AAC). The substantive decision had been made by a panel of which the presiding judge was fee-paid. The statement of reasons failed to deal with a certain issue and, upon an application for permission to appeal being received, the salaried judge referred the case to the fee-paid judge who purported to rectify the omission by correcting the statement under r.36 of the Tribunal Procedure (First-tier Tribunal) (Social Entitlement Chamber) Rules 2008. In the light of the correction, the salaried judge refused to review the decision and refused permission to appeal. The Upper Tribunal held that the correction went further than allowed by r.36 (see the annotation to that rule) and that there were no grounds for review because the salaried judge had not been satisfied that there was an error of law. One difficulty, not expressly mentioned by the Upper Tribunal, was that the corrections made by the fee-paid judge could not have been made by the salaried judge under s.9(4)(a) or (b) because the reasons for them were not within his knowledge. He could only have set the decision aside altogether. As it was, the Upper Tribunal declined to take any action on the appeal on the basis that it could have regard to the additional reasons provided by the fee-paid judge, even though she had been wrong to provide them by way of a correction. With those reasons, the decision of the First-tier Tribunal was sound in fact and law.The three-judge panel deciding *JS v SSWP (DLA)* approved that approach. There is no appeal against a decision to take no action or not to take any particular action or to set aside a decision under this subsection (see s.11(5)(d)(ii) and (iii)). However, there appears to be a right of appeal against a decision to correct an error or amend reasons.

A discrete part of a decision may be set aside, but it is the decision and not the reasoning that is set aside and it may introduce unforeseen complications if a decision is not set aside in its entirety (*Essex County Council v TB (SEN)* [2014] UKUT 559 (AAC).

Subsections (5)(b), (6) and (7)

5.40 A case may be referred to the Upper Tribunal under s.9(5)(b) only if the First-tier Tribunal's decision has been set aside under s.9(4)(c), which, in the light of r.40(2) of the Tribunal Procedure (First-tier Tribunal) (Social Entitlement Chamber) Rules 2008, requires the First-tier Tribunal to be satisfied that there was an error of law in its decision. Therefore, in *LM v HMRC (CHB)* [2016] UKUT 389 (AAC) where the First-tier Tribunal, considering an application for permission to appeal to the Upper Tribunal, said nothing about the merits of the grounds of appeal or about setting aside its decision but merely said that "[t]he matter shall be referred to the Upper Tribunal in accordance with section 9(5)(b) of the Act", the Upper Tribunal treated the First-tier Tribunal as having given permission to appeal, rather than as having referred the case. Reference was made to *JS v SSWP (DLA)* [2013] UKUT 100 (AAC); [2013] AACR 30 which "provides a helpful explanation of the steps needed to be taken in order for a District Tribunal Judge to properly review a First-tier Tribunal's decision, steps which are needed in order to properly 'refer' an appeal to the Upper Tribunal under section 9(5)(b) of the Tribunals, Courts and Enforcement Act 2007".

It may be appropriate to set aside a decision and then refer the case to the Upper Tribunal if it is clear that the decision is wrong on one ground but the case raises another point that merits the attention of the Upper Tribunal and will arise whatever findings are made when re-deciding the case. This is perhaps most likely to arise where a judge has reviewed a decision, set it aside and referred it for re-determination without obtaining representations from the parties and then representations are made under r.40(4) of the Tribunal Procedure (First-tier Tribunal) (Social Entitlement Chamber) Rules 2008. The judge may be disinclined to set aside the whole review but may be persuaded that the case should be considered by the Upper Tribunal as would have been the case had permission to appeal, rather than a review, been granted in the first place.

However, references under s.9(5)(b) have generally been discouraged by the Upper Tribunal, because they prevent the Upper Tribunal from remitting the case should any issues of fact need determining, or re-determining, in the light of its decision on the law. A grant of permission to appeal gives the Upper Tribunal more flexibility.

There is no appeal against a decision to refer, or not to refer, a matter to the Upper Tribunal (see s.11(5)(d)(iv)).

Subsection (8)

This tends to suggest that there need not be a complete rehearing if the reason 5.41
for a decision being set aside does not vitiate findings made as part of the original decision. If this is so, it may be appropriate in some cases (subject to the views of the parties) for a judge setting aside a decision on the papers to give a new decision straightaway on the basis that it is clear what decision the tribunal should have given on its findings of fact. However, this may be impossible where s.13(3) of the 1998 Act requires the case to be referred to a differently constituted First-tier Tribunal.

Subsection (9)

Presumably this subsection was included in case the power under para.15(1) of 5.42
Sch.5 was not fully exercised. It enables a correction of a decision under subs.(4)(c) to set aside a decision.

Subsections (10) and (11)

If a decision is corrected under subs.(4)(a) or amended reasons are given under 5.43
subs.(4)(b), there can be no further review of that decision, although there seems no reason why there should not be a correction under the separate power in r.36 of the Tribunal Procedure (First-tier Tribunal) (Social Entitlement Chamber) Rules 2008. The lack of any further power of review makes it particularly important for the parties to have the opportunity to make representations. On the other hand, obtaining representations before reviewing a decision would be time-consuming and cause delay in those cases where the parties were content with the review. Rule 40(4) therefore provides that, if a party has not had an opportunity to make representations before action is taken on a review, it may do so afterwards and ask that the action be set aside. It also provides that parties must be given notice of the right to make such representations where action is taken without the views of the parties being obtained first. In *AM v SSWP* [2009] UKUT 224 (AAC), that was not done.

There can also be no review once there has been a refusal to review. Rule 39(2) has the effect that a tribunal refusing to review a decision will automatically consider whether to grant permission to appeal. The restriction imposed by subs.(10) is unfortunate if two parties apply for a review and the less meritorious application is rejected before the second application is received.

However, where a decision is set aside under subs.(4)(c), a decision substituted for it under subs.(5)(a) is treated as a different decision and may itself be reviewed. It is also the substituted decision against which any appeal must be brought because the decision that has been set aside is an "excluded decision" under s.11(5)(e).

Review of decision of Upper Tribunal

5.44 **10.**—(1) The Upper Tribunal may review a decision made by it on a matter in a case, other than a decision that is an excluded decision for the purposes of section 13(1) (but see subsection (7)).

(2) The Upper Tribunal's power under subsection (1) in relation to a decision is exercisable—

(a) of its own initiative, or

(b) on application by a person who for the purposes of section 13(2) has a right of appeal in respect of the decision.

(3) Tribunal Procedure Rules may—

(a) provide that the Upper Tribunal may not under subsection (1) review (whether of its own initiative or on application under subsection (2)(b)) a decision of a description specified for the purposes of this paragraph in Tribunal Procedure Rules;

(b) provide that the Upper Tribunal's power under subsection (1) to review a decision of a description specified for the purposes of this paragraph in Tribunal Procedure Rules is exercisable only of the tribunal's own initiative;

(c) provide that an application under subsection (2)(b) that is of a description specified for the purposes of this paragraph in Tribunal Procedure Rules may be made only on grounds specified for the purposes of this paragraph in Tribunal Procedure Rules;

(d) provide, in relation to a decision of a description specified for the purposes of this paragraph in Tribunal Procedure Rules, that the Upper Tribunal's power under subsection (1) to review the decision of its own initiative is exercisable only on grounds specified for the purposes of this paragraph in Tribunal Procedure Rules.

(4) Where the Upper Tribunal has under subsection (1) reviewed a decision, the Upper Tribunal may in the light of the review do any of the following—

(a) correct accidental errors in the decision or in a record of the decision;

(b) amend reasons given for the decision;

(c) set the decision aside.

(5) Where under subsection (4)(c) the Upper Tribunal sets a decision aside, the Upper Tribunal must re-decide the matter concerned.

(6) Where the Upper Tribunal is acting under subsection (5), it may make such findings of fact as it considers appropriate.

(7) This section has effect as if a decision under subsection (4)(c) to set aside an earlier decision were not an excluded decision for the purposes of section 13(1), but the Upper Tribunal's only power in the light of a review under subsection (1) of a decision under subsection (4)(c) is the power under subsection (4)(a).

(8) A decision of the Upper Tribunal may not be reviewed under subsection (1) more than once, and once the Upper Tribunal has decided that an earlier decision should not be reviewed under subsection (1) it may not then decide to review that earlier decision under that subsection.

(9) Where under this section a decision is set aside and the matter concerned is then re-decided, the decision set aside and the decision made in re-deciding the matter are for the purposes of subsection (8) to be taken to be different decisions.

GENERAL NOTE

This section is in terms that are very similar to s.9, save that there is no equivalent of s.9(5)(b), (6) and (7). However, the power of review is even more severely curtailed by Tribunal Procedure Rules, being limited to cases where the Upper Tribunal has overlooked a piece of legislation or a binding authority or there has been a binding decision of a superior court since the Upper Tribunal's decision was given (see rr.45(1) and 46 of the Tribunal Procedure (Upper Tribunal) Rules 2008). 5.45

Right to appeal to Upper Tribunal

11.—(1) For the purposes of subsection (2), the reference to a right of appeal is to a right to appeal to the Upper Tribunal on any point of law arising from a decision made by the First-tier Tribunal other than an excluded decision. 5.46

(2) Any party to a case has a right of appeal, subject to subsection (8).

(3) That right may be exercised only with permission (or, in Northern Ireland, leave).

(4) Permission (or leave) may be given by—

(a) the First-tier Tribunal, or

(b) the Upper Tribunal, on an application by the party.

(5) For the purposes of subsection (1), an "excluded decision" is—

(a) any decision of the First-tier Tribunal on an appeal made in exercise of a right conferred by the Criminal Injuries Compensation Scheme in compliance with section 5(1)(a) of the Criminal Injuries Compensation Act 1995 (appeals against decisions on reviews),

[[1] (aa) any decision of the First-tier Tribunal on an appeal made in exercise of a right conferred by the Victims of Overseas Terrorism Compensation Scheme in compliance with section 52(3) of the Crime and Security Act 2010,]

(b) any decision of the First-tier Tribunal on an appeal under section 28(4) or (6) of the Data Protection Act 1998 (appeals against national security certificate),

(c) any decision of the First-tier Tribunal on an appeal under section 60(1) or (4) of the Freedom of Information Act 2000 (appeals against national security certificate),

(d) a decision of the First-tier Tribunal under section 9—

(i) to review, or not to review, an earlier decision of the tribunal,

(ii) to take no action, or not to take any particular action, in the light of a review of an earlier decision of the tribunal,

(iii) to set aside an earlier decision of the tribunal, or

(iv) to refer, or not to refer, a matter to the Upper Tribunal,

(e) a decision of the First-tier Tribunal that is set aside under section 9 (including a decision set aside after proceedings on an appeal under this section have been begun), or

(f) any decision of the First-tier Tribunal that is of a description specified in an order made by the Lord Chancellor.

(6) A description may be specified under subsection (5)(f) only if—

(a) in the case of a decision of that description, there is a right to appeal to a court, the Upper Tribunal or any other tribunal from the decision and that right is, or includes, something other than a right (however expressed) to appeal on any point of law arising from the decision, or

(b) decisions of that description are made in carrying out a function transferred under section 30 and prior to the transfer of the function under section 30(1) there was no right to appeal from decisions of that description.

(7) Where—

(a) an order under subsection (5)(f) specifies a description of decisions, and

(b) decisions of that description are made in carrying out a function transferred under section 30,

the order must be framed so as to come into force no later than the time when the transfer under section 30 of the function takes effect (but power to revoke the order continues to be exercisable after that time, and power to amend the order continues to be exercisable after that time for the purpose of narrowing the description for the time being specified).

(8) The Lord Chancellor may by order make provision for a person to be treated as being, or to be treated as not being, a party to a case for the purposes of subsection (2).

Amendment

1. Crime and Security Act 2010 s.48(4) and Sch.2 para.5 (April 8, 2010).

General Note

Subsection (1)

5.47 In *LS v LB Lambeth (HB)* [2010] UKUT 461 (AAC); [2011] AACR 27, a three-judge panel has decided that there is a right of appeal under s.11 against any decision of the First-tier Tribunal that is not an "excluded decision" (for the meaning of which, see subs.(5)). It was pointed out that, by making an order under subs.(5)(f) and (6)(b), the Lord Chancellor could have preserved the effect of *Morina v SSWP* [2007] EWCA Civ 749; [2007] 1 W.L.R. 3033 (also reported as *R(IS)* 6/07) (in which it was decided that certain interlocutory decisions in social security cases were not "decisions" for the purpose of the right of appeal under s.14 of the Social Security Act 1998) but had not done so.

Nonetheless, interlocutory appeals in respect of decisions made under Tribunal Procedure Rules have not been encouraged. The duty under r.33(2)(c) of the Tribunal Procedure (First-tier Tribunal) (Social Entitlement Chamber) Rules to inform a person of the right of appeal applies only to a decision which finally disposes of all issues in the proceedings and the three-judge panel itself said that:

> "it will be open to both the First-tier Tribunal and the Upper Tribunal to refuse permission to bring an interlocutory appeal on the ground that it is premature. The circumstances of the individual case must be considered. It is one thing to grant permission for an interlocutory appeal in a case where the final hearing may last for a fortnight. It is another to do so where the final hearing is likely to last about an hour, as is often the case in social security appeals. Moreover, as was suggested in *Dorset Healthcare NHS Foundation Trust v MH* [2009] UKUT 4 (AAC) at [19], where case-management decisions are being challenged, the First-tier Tribunal can treat an application for permission to appeal as an application for a new direction if it is satisfied that the challenged direction is not appropriate."

It must follow that, at least in most social security cases, parties will not be prejudiced by waiting until there has been a final decision in the case and relying on an error in an interlocutory decision as grounds of appeal against the final decision, instead of appealing against the interlocutory decision itself.

"POINT OF LAW"

An appeal against any other decision lies only on a "point of law". Even though it has been recognised that the Upper Tribunal may have more flexibility in determining what is or is not a point of law than the courts do (*R. (Jones) v First-tier Tribunal* [2013] UKSC 19; [2013] 2 A.C. 48; [2013] AACR 25), judges of the Upper Tribunal may be expected to resist any attempt by an appellant to present an appeal on facts as raising questions of law, even if they have grave doubts about the decision under appeal. No appeal on a question of law should be allowed to be turned into a rehearing of parts of the evidence (*Yeboah v Crofton* [2002] EWCA Civ 794; [2002] I.R.L.R. 634). However, once a judge is satisfied that a decision is erroneous in point of law, he or she is entitled to determine any outstanding questions of fact (see s.12(2)(b)(ii) and (4)). **5.48**

The meaning of "point of law" was considered by the Court of Appeal in *Nipa Begum v Tower Hamlets LBC* [2000] 1 W.L.R. 306 in a case where a homeless person appealed to the county court under s.204 of the Housing Act 1996 against a decision of a housing authority. An appeal lay "on any point of law arising from" such a decision and the Court of Appeal held that the county court had powers akin to those available on an application for judicial review in the High Court and so could quash a decision on the ground of procedural error, lack of vires, irrationality or inadequacy of reasons as well as for straightforward errors of legal interpretation.

In *R(A) 1/72* and *R(IS) 11/99*, Social Security Commissioners had made similar lists of errors that would amount to errors of law, rather than of fact. More recently, in *R(I) 2/06* and *R(DLA) 3/08*, Tribunals of Commissioners have referred to the judgment of the Court of Appeal in *R (Iran) v Secretary of State for the Home Department* [2005] EWCA Civ 982, offering a "brief summary of the points of law that will most often be encountered in practice". These were—

> "(i) Making perverse or irrational findings on a matter or matters that were material to the outcome ('material matters');
> (ii) Failing to give reasons or any adequate reasons for findings on material matters;
> (iii) Failing to take into account and/or resolve conflicts of fact or opinion on material matters;
> (iv) Giving weight to immaterial matters;
> (v) Making a material misdirection of law on any material matter;
> (vi) Committing or permitting a procedural or other irregularity capable of making a material difference to the outcome or the fairness of proceedings;
> (vii) Making a mistake as to a material fact which could be established by objective and uncontentious evidence, where the appellant and/or his advisers were not responsible for the mistake, and where unfairness resulted from the fact that a mistake was made."
>
> "Each of these grounds for detecting any error of law contains the word 'material' (or 'immaterial'). Errors of law of which it can be said that they would have made no difference to the outcome do not matter."

The seven points identified by the Court of Appeal and the issue of "materiality" are considered in more detail below.

The meaning of "a point of law" is the same in Scotland as in England and Wales, but there are many different ways of expressing it. In *HMRC v Murray Group Holdings Ltd* [2015] CSIH 77, the Inner House of the Court of Session said—

> "[42] Although the concept of appeal on a point of law might seem simple, it has given rise to considerable controversy; indeed in the well-known case of *Edwards* v *Bairstow*, [1956] AC 14, an appeal was taken to the House of Lords to adjudicate upon differences of approach that had developed between the Scottish and English courts. We are of opinion that an appeal on a point of law covers four

different categories of case. The first of these categories is appeals on the general law: the content of its rules. In tax appeals these are largely statutory, but the interpretation of a particular statutory provision may be a matter of general law, and tax law also includes a number of general non-statutory rules, such as the redirection principle and the *Ramsay* principle, both of which are relevant to this case. The second category comprises appeals on the application of the law to the facts as found by the First-tier Tribunal. This is in our opinion a clear example of an appeal on a point of law: it is the application of the general rules to particular factual situations that defines the frontiers of a legal rule and thus its practical scope. Furthermore, it is the application of the general rules to particular facts that brings about the development of those rules to meet new situations. For these reasons we consider that an appeal on the application of the general law to a particular factual situation must be regarded as being on a point of law. This is illustrated by the facts of *Edwards* v *Bairstow*. There the House of Lords, reversing the decisions of the General Commissioners and lower courts, held that a transaction involving the acquisition of spinning plant, dividing it into lots and selling those lots at a profit was an adventure in the nature of trade. In holding otherwise, the Commissioners and the lower courts had misdirected themselves as to the meaning and proper application of the expression "adventure . . . in the nature of trade" found in the relevant taxing statute, the Income Tax Act 1918: see Lord Radcliffe at [1956] AC 36–37.

[43] The third category of appeal on a point of law is where the Tribunal has made a finding "for which there is no evidence or which is inconsistent with the evidence and contradictory of it": *IRC* v *Fraser*, 1942 SC 493, at 497–498, per LP Normand. This runs into a fourth category, comprising cases where the First-tier Tribunal has made a fundamental error in its approach to the case: for example, by asking the wrong question, or by taking account of manifestly irrelevant considerations, or by arriving at a decision that no reasonable tax tribunal could properly reach. In such cases we conceive that the Court of Session and the Upper Tribunal have power to interfere with the decision of the First-tier Tribunal as disclosing an error on a point of law: *Edwards* v *Bairstow*, per Lord Radcliffe at [1956] AC 36."

The Court also observed that decisions of the First-tier Tribunal relating to tax frequently involve elements of evaluation and judgment and that: "In general, a court, or the Upper Tribunal, should be slow to interfere with the decision of the First-tier Tribunal in cases of this nature." Nonetheless: "It is a matter of degree: the higher the factual component in the evaluative exercise, the slower the court should be to interfere, but correspondingly if the factual component is relatively low and the legal component is high the court may properly interfere."

Although the Court did not draw any distinction between the position of a court and the position of the Upper Tribunal, it is clear that, since one of the reasons why appellate bodies do not interfere is the specialist nature of the First-tier Tribunal, there may be some cases where the Upper Tribunal can properly interfere but an appellate court would not, because the Upper Tribunal may be able to claim as much relevant expertise as the First-tier Tribunal (see below and the annotation to s.13(1) and (2)). This point did not arise for consideration in that case because the Upper Tribunal dismissed the appeal from the First-tier Tribunal and the Court of Session decided that they were both wrong in law.

Challenging findings of fact

5.49 The Court of Appeal's points (i), (iii), (iv) and (vii) and the third and fourth of the Court of Session's points show the limited grounds on which findings of fact may be challenged.

The Court of Appeal emphasised what a demanding concept "perversity" was and so did the Tribunal of Commissioners in *R(I) 2/06*, citing *Murrell v Secretary of State for Social Services* (reported as an appendix to *R(I) 3/84*) in which it was said that an assessment of disablement is perverse only if it is "so wildly wrong that it can be set aside".

In *Yeboah v Crofton* [2002] EWCA Civ 794; [2002] I.R.L.R. 634, Mummery LJ said that an appeal based on perversity "ought only to succeed where an overwhelming case is made out that the Employment Tribunal reached a decision which no reasonable tribunal, on a proper appreciation of the evidence and the law, would have reached". However, it is clear from the judgment of Irwin J in *British Broadcasting Corporation v Information Commissioner* [2009] EWHC 2348 (Admin) and from the decision of the Court of Appeal in *Department for Work and Pensions v Information Commissioner* [2016] EWCA Civ 758; [2017] 1 W.L.R. 1 that these are merely expressions of the deference that should be paid to the conclusions of a specialist or expert tribunal. In the latter case, Lloyd-Jones LJ said:

> "34. .... Given such expertise in a Tribunal, it is entirely understandable that a reviewing court or Tribunal will be slow to interfere with its findings and evaluation of facts in areas where that expertise has a bearing. This may be regarded not so much as requiring that a different, enhanced standard must be met as an acknowledgement of the reality that an expert Tribunal can normally be expected to apply its expertise in the course of its analysis of facts. It has been described in various ways in the cases. I agree with Irwin J. that the formulation employed by Mummery LJ in *Yeboah* requiring an overwhelming case, may perhaps be the high water mark of this consideration, although the formulation employed by Sir John Donaldson MR in *Murrell* (so wildly wrong as to merit being set aside) would be a close rival."

The other members of the Court agreed with that analysis, although they reached a different conclusion as to the result of the appeal in that particular case. As to the relative expertise of the Upper Tribunal and the First-tier Tribunal, see the observations in *R. (Jones) v First-tier Tribunal* [2013] UKSC 19; [2013] 2 A.C. 48; [2013] AACR 25 and *R. (Hutton) v First-tier Tribunal* [2016] EWCA Civ 1305 to which reference is made in the annotation to s.13(1) and (2) below.

A finding of fact is also perverse if it "was wholly unsupported by any evidence" (*Iran*) or it is based on a misunderstanding that "is plain and incontrovertible and where there is no room for difference about it" (*Braintree DC v Thompson* [2005] EWCA Civ 178, a housing benefit case in which the Court of Appeal said that a Deputy Commissioner had not been entitled to substitute his view of the facts for the view of the tribunal). It is particularly difficult to show that a decision is perverse where it required an element of judgment (such as, for instance, whether the claimant was virtually unable to walk). In *Moyna v Secretary of State for Work and Pensions* [2003] UKHL 44, [2003] 1 W.L.R. 1929 (also reported as *R(DLA) 7/03*), Lord Hoffmann, with whom the other members of the House of Lords agreed, said:

> "In any case in which a tribunal has to apply a standard with a greater or lesser degree of imprecision and to take a number of factors into account, there are bound to be cases in which it will be impossible for a reviewing court to say that the tribunal must have erred in deciding the case either way: see *George Mitchell (Chesterhall) Ltd v Finney Lock Seeds Ltd* [1983] 2 A.C. 803, 815–816."

If perversity is not shown, it is usually necessary to show some flaw in the reasoning instead, either because a finding is irrational (i.e. there is something illogical in the reasoning leading to it) or because the tribunal has failed to take into account a relevant matter or has given weight to an irrelevant matter. In order to show that any of these errors has been made, it is necessary to analyse the tribunal's statement of reasons. On the other hand, merely pointing to a different analysis of the evidence from that adopted by the tribunal is not sufficient to show an error of law (*Secretary of State for Work and Pensions v Roach* [2007] EWCA Civ 1746 (reported as *R(CS) 4/07*)).

One recent decision in which the First-tier Tribunal's reasoning was held to be flawed is *JH v HMRC (TC)* [2015] UKUT 397 (AAC), where the judge said –

"6. The assessment of the credibility or plausibility of a witness's evidence is primarily a question of fact for the tribunal. In *HK v Secretary of State for the Home Department* [2006] EWCA Civ 1037 Neuberger LJ said, at [30], that rejection of an account on grounds of implausibility must be done "on reasonably drawn inferences and not simply on conjecture or speculation". In addition, a tribunal may properly draw on its common sense and ability, as practical and informed people, to identify what is or is not plausible.

7. In *Gheisari v Secretary of State for the Home Department* [2004] EWCA Civ 1854 (with which Neuberger LJ agreed) the Court of Appeal emphasised that an account that is unlikely may nonetheless be true, just as a likely account may turn out to be untrue. Faced with an account which a tribunal considers to be improbable, its task is to appraise the evidence and the individual who gave the evidence, and decide whether it is true – *Gheisari* at [12], [13] and [16]. It may not be necessary for a tribunal to carry out a strict two stage test (improbability followed by truth), but:

> 'What would be wrong would be to say . . .. that because evidence is inherently unlikely it inevitably follows that it is wrong. An unlikely description may, upon a consideration of the circumstances as a whole, including the judge's assessments of the witness and any explanations he gives, be a true one.'
>
> (Pill LJ in *Gheisari* at [21])

8. The above discussions were made in the context of asylum appeals, where inherent improbability may be particularly unhelpful because '[m]uch of the evidence is referable to societies with customs and circumstances which are very different from those of which the members of the fact-finding tribunal have any (even second-hand) experience.' (*HK* at [29]). It follows that inherent improbability may be more helpful in cases where the evidence is closer to the experiences of the tribunal, but it will nonetheless only be a component of the overall task which is to decide whether a witness's account did occur not whether it was likely to have occurred. The general approach set out in *HK* and *Gheisari* is apt in cases such as the present. I note that it was followed by the Court of Session Outer House in an appeal concerning a decision relating to the educational needs of a learning disabled child: *G v Argyll and Bute Council* [2008] CSOH 61 at [157].

9. It also follows from this approach that it will generally be inappropriate for a tribunal to appraise evidence by reference to what a reasonable person would have done. The question for the tribunal is what the individual in question is likely to have done, not what some other (hypothetical or actual) person would have done. As both Sedley LJ and Pill LJ said in *Gheisari*, the fact-finder should appraise the person giving the evidence (paragraphs [13] and [21] respectively).

10. Judged by reference to this guidance, the tribunal's decision in the present appeal was made in error of law. The tribunal did not accept the appellant's evidence because it considered that it was improbable. It did so on the basis of what the tribunal would have expected a person in her position to have done, and in one instance the tribunal expressly applied the test of a "reasonable" person in the appellant's position. The tribunal did not, whether as part of a single fact-finding process or by considering the evidence in stages, consider whether the appellant's account was true rather than improbable. Had it done so, the tribunal would have had to consider matters such as the appellant's particular circumstances and her explanation for her actions or those of Mr W, and would have had to assess what it was likely that she or he would have done. Unfortunately, because of the underlying error in the tribunal's approach, in a number of respects it did not ask the appellant to provide an explanation for her actions and choices."

5.50 Although tribunals may be found to have erred in the way they have dealt with the evidence before them, Commissioners have pointed out that tribunals cannot be criticised for not taking account of evidence that was not before them at all. In *CDLA/7980/1995*, the Commissioner said that—

> "Finality is another important principle. Parties cannot demand a rehearing simply because, at the original hearing, they failed to adduce the right evidence, failed to ask the right questions or failed to advance the right arguments."

However, the Court of Appeal's point (vii) in the *Iran* case is a limited exception to this approach, derived from *E v Secretary of State for the Home Department* [2004] EWCA Civ 49; [2004] Q.B. 1044 in which the Court of Appeal considered how the general principles for the admission of fresh evidence on appeals, laid down in *Ladd v Marshall* [1954] 1 W.L.R. 1489, should be applied in administrative law cases. The requirements are quite strict: that the evidence that the First-tier Tribunal made a mistake of fact should be "objective and uncontentious", that the mistake should not have been the fault of the relevant party or that party's representative and that the mistake should have caused unfairness. Whether the mistake was the fault of a party or a representative often depends on whether they failed to use "reasonable diligence" in providing evidence to the First-tier Tribunal. Whether the mistake caused unfairness may require consideration of its importance of the mistake to the decision and whether the claimant has an alternative remedy. The context has to be taken into account when considering both these issues.

In *DG v SSWP (II)* [2013] UKUT 474 (AAC), it was held that there is no failure of reasonable diligence in obtaining evidence where the evidence was not obtained because the person relying on it had no reason to suppose that the point to which it was directed would be relevant. In that case, the First-tier Tribunal had not believed the claimant when she said that she had broken her wrist and consequently thought she was exaggerating her symptoms. Her appeal to the Upper Tribunal was allowed in the light of x-ray evidence showing clearly that she had broken her wrist.

The Court of Appeal has also warned against undue consideration of a claimant's fault in a social security context. In *Hussain v Secretary of State for Work and Pensions* [2016] EWCA Civ 1428, Bean LJ, with whom Tomlinson and Floyd LJJ agreed, said:

> "27. There are cases in which an over strict application of the first principle against a party who appeared without representation, as Mr Hussain did in the First-tier Tribunal, can be contrary to the overriding objective of dealing with cases justly. I prefer, therefore, rather than asking whether a consultant's report could have been obtained with reasonable diligence before the hearing in the FTT, to concentrate on the question of whether it would have been potentially decisive in Mr Hussain's favour or at least have had an important influence on the result of the appeal. . . ."

In that case, the claimant was unsuccessful because the report did not address issues relevant to the case and so did not "call into question" the decision that the First-tier Tribunal had upheld.

Where neither the conditions for the Court of Appeal's point (vii) nor the conditions for the traditional grounds identified in points (i), (iii) and (iv) are met, the only remedy for a mistake of fact made by the First-tier Tribunal is an application for supersession under reg.6(2)(c) of the Social Security and Child Support (Decisions and Appeals) Regulations 1999, reg.13(2)(c) of the Child Benefit and Guardian's Allowance (Decisions and Appeals) Regulations 2003 or reg.31(a) of the Universal Credit, Personal Independence Payment, Jobseeker's Allowance and Employment and Support Allowance (Decisions and Appeals) Regulations 2013. The value of that remedy may be limited by the date from which any such supersession can be effective.

Challenging misdirections of law

5.51 It is much more obvious that a misdirection of law (e.g. the tribunal misunderstanding or overlooking a regulation or making a mistake about the law of property), the Court of Appeal's point (v) in the *Iran* case, is an error of law. It is also a misdirection of law for the First-tier Tribunal to act in excess of its jurisdiction (*Secretary of State for the Home Department v VM (Jamaica)* [2017] EWCA Civ 255) or to rely upon a regulation that is ultra vires (*Foster v Chief Adjudication Officer* [1993] A.C. 754 (also reported as *R(IS) 22/93*)), including on procedural grounds (*Howker v Secretary of State for Work and Pensions* [2002] EWCA Civ 1623 (reported as *R(IB) 3/03*), or is inconsistent with European Community law (see s.2(4) of the European Communities Act 1972). However, unless the claimant can rely on the direct effect of a European Union directive, the Upper Tribunal may be unable to provide a remedy if disapplying an ultra vires regulation is not itself enough and it would be necessary to read in an alternative provision (see the observations of Baroness Hale of Richmond JSC in *Humphries v Revenue and Customs Commissioners* [2012] UKSC 18; [2012] 1 W.L.R. 1545; [2012] AACR 46, at [34]).

In *VL v SSWP (IS)* [2011] UKUT 227 (AAC); [2012] AACR 10, it was held that the Upper Tribunal has the power to find subordinate legislation to be invalid not only if it is made beyond the powers conferred by the enabling legislation but also if it conflicts with statutory rights already conferred by other primary legislation. However, it was pointed out that there is only a conflict in cases where there is no other reasonable way to exercise such statutory rights. On one analysis, this is all a question of construction of the enabling power, which can be said to be qualified by the other primary legislation.

It was also reaffirmed in *VL v SSWP (IS)* that the Upper Tribunal may admit arguments under the European Convention on Human Rights notwithstanding that they have not been raised before the First-tier Tribunal. The judge gave short shrift to arguments based on s.12(8)(a) of the Social Security Act 1998 and the practice of the Court of Appeal on appeals from specialist tribunals, pointing out as regards the latter that the Upper Tribunal is itself a specialist tribunal in respect of social security law and probably more so than the First-tier Tribunal which deals mainly with issues of fact and evidence and rarely has the benefit of submissions by legally qualified representatives. The judge also referred to *Miskovic v Secretary of State for Work and Pensions* [2011] EWCA Civ 16; [2012] AACR 11, mentioned in the annotation to s.13(3)–(5) of this Act, for the more flexible approach the Court of Appeal has itself taken recently.

5.52 In an appeal brought on human rights grounds, it has been held that the question for an appellate court is not whether a lower court of tribunal has directed itself correctly but whether there has been a breach of the European Convention on Human Rights (*Belfast CC v Miss Behavin' Ltd* [2007] UKHL 19; [2007] 1 W.L.R. 1420). This has to be read in the light of *In re B (a child) (Care Proceedings: Threshold Criteria)* [2013] UKSC 33; [2013] 1 W.L.R. 1911, where Lord Neuberger of Abbotsbury PSC said that "the court system as a whole must fairly determine for itself whether the requirement of proportionality is met, but that does not mean that each court up the appeal chain does so". However, in practice it may be necessary for the Upper Tribunal to consider human rights points for itself simply because any argument before the First-tier Tribunal is likely to have been fairly limited and so it will be fairly easy to show that it has not had adequate regard to all material considerations.

The Upper Tribunal declined to find there to have been an error of law where, on an appeal by the Secretary of State, both parties agreed that there had been a technical error by the First-tier Tribunal in the light of *R(PC) 1/07* but the judge considered that a carefully negotiated settlement reached before *R(PC) 1/07* was decided should not be set at naught, that there was arguably not a "clear error of law" and that the calculation in issue was in any event based on broad brush figures (*SSWP v DL (SPC)* [2013] UKUT 29 (AAC); [2013] AACR 22). The judge considered the alternative approach of finding there to be an error of law but declining to set aside the First-tier Tribunal's decision (see s.12(2)(a)), which would presumably have had the same practical effect, but rejected it.

Inadequate reasons

The standard of reasoning required from tribunals by the Court of Appeal's point (ii) and the requirement to resolve conflicts (see point (iii)) is considered in detail in the note to r.34 of the Tribunal Procedure (First-tier Tribunal) (Social Entitlement Chamber) Rules 2008. The reasons should be sufficient to avoid "substantial doubt as to whether the [tribunal] erred in law" on any of the other grounds identified in the *Iran* case, but they "need refer only to the main issues in the dispute, not to every consideration" (*South Bucks DC v Porter (No.2)* [2004] UKHL 33; [2004] 1 W.L.R. 1953 at [36]. In the *Iran* case itself, the Court of Appeal referred to *Eagil Trust Co Ltd v Pigott-Brown* [1985] 3 All E.R. 119, 122, where Griffiths L.J. said that, "if it be that the judge has not dealt with a particular argument but it can be seen that there are grounds on which he would have been entitled to reject it, this court should assume that he acted on those grounds unless the appellant can point to convincing reasons leading to a contrary conclusion." 5.53

Procedural and other irregularities

Whether a breach of procedural rules renders a decision invalid or erroneous in point of law is to be determined by considering whether the legislature intended that to be the effect of such a breach (*R(DLA) 3/08*, and *JM v SSWP (ESA)* [2013] UKUT 234; [2014] AACR 5, both citing *R. v Soneji* [2005] UKHL 49; [2006] 1 A.C. 340). Therefore, not every procedural error entitles a party to have a decision set aside on appeal. It largely depends on whether there was any unfairness as a result of the breach. This is point (vi) in the *Iran* case. 5.54

The old distinction between "mandatory" and "directory" requirements is no longer regarded as helpful. Instead, it is necessary to consider the language of the legislation and the legislator's intention against the factual situation and seek to do what is just in all the circumstances. This involves considering whether the procedural requirement is satisfied by "substantial" compliance with it and, if so, whether there has in fact been such substantial compliance or whether non-compliance had been waived. If there has not been sufficient compliance and non-compliance has not been waived, consideration should also be given to the intended consequence of non-compliance because it does not necessarily follow from an applicant's failure to comply with a procedural requirement that the application is a nullity (*R. v Secretary of State for the Home Department, Ex p. Jeyeanthan* [2000] 1 W.L.R. 354).

Consideration must be given to whether the breach of procedural rules might have made any difference to the decision of the tribunal or whether a party to the proceedings has lost anything (such as the opportunity of advancing a particular argument on appeal) as a result of the breach, so that a rehearing is the only way of remedying the breach. For this reason, a breach of a requirement to keep a record of proceedings will render a decision of a tribunal erroneous in point of law if the lack of a record of proceedings makes it difficult to determine whether or not the tribunal has provided an adequate statement of reasons (*R(DLA) 3/08*). On the other hand, a failure to provide any summary of reasons in a decision notice will not render the decision erroneous in point of law because the remedy is to apply for a full statement of reasons (*CIB/4497/1998*). The most commonly relied upon breach is a breach of the statutory duty to give reasons for a decision (see the note to r.34 of the Tribunal Procedure (First-tier Tribunal) (Social Entitlement Chamber) Rules 2008), although this is considered in the *Iran* case to be an entirely separate type of error of law, perhaps because there would be a common law duty to give reasons even if the legislation imposed no duty.

When considering breaches of procedural rules, fairness is judged by reference to the three "rules of natural justice", which are that every party should have a proper opportunity to present his or her case, that there should be no bias and 5.55

that a decision should be based on the evidence. Even where there is no breach of a statutory provision, breach of the rules of natural justice will amount to at least an irregularity. The scope of the rules is fairly broad but it has nonetheless been suggested that judges ought to express their decisions in terms of the parties' right to a fair hearing under art.6(1) of the European Convention on Human Rights rather than in terms of the rules of natural justice which are apt to be misunderstood (*CJSA/5100/2001* and the linked cases *CIB/2751/2002 and CS/3202/2002*) even if the practical differences are not great. In *CSDLA/773/2004*, the judge disagreed and said that the issue was whether there had been a breach of the rules of natural justice and that any assertion that a convention right had been breached had to be raised as a separate issue. It is suggested that that goes too far in the opposite direction and that, while a tribunal is entitled to focus on the common law questions, those questions must now be considered in the light of art.6 of the Convention. Indeed, the Court of Appeal has doubted that the standard of fairness set by the common law is any weaker than that set by art.6 (*R. (Maftah) v Secretary of State for Foreign and Commonwealth Affairs* [2011] EWCA Civ 350; [2012] Q.B. 477).

In *R. v Secretary of State for the Home Department, Ex p. Al-Mehdawi* [1990] 1 A.C. 876 it was said to be incorrect to state simply that a party to a dispute who has not been heard through no fault of his own has been denied justice. In that case, notice of the hearing had been given to the party's solicitors but they had wrongly addressed their letter telling the party of the hearing. Although the House of Lords accepted that a decision of a tribunal may be erroneous in point of law where the tribunal has been entirely blameless but there had been some fault on the part of the other party, they held that there was no error of law in that case because the solicitors had had notice. Service on a solicitor was also treated as service on a claimant in *Tkachuk v Secretary of State for Work and Pensions* [2007] EWCA Civ 515 (reported as *R(IS) 3/07*). However, in social security cases, notices of hearings and decisions are usually sent both to the claimant and any representative. In *CCS/6302/1999*, a decision was set aside because a party had not received notice of the appeal due to the Child Support Agency failing to tell the clerk to the tribunal of his change of address. In *CIB/5227/1999*, the claimant simply did not receive the letter from the clerk inviting him to seek an oral hearing and there was no fault on the part of either the tribunal or the Benefits Agency. The Commissioner distinguished *Al-Mehdawi* and did not base his decision to allow the appeal on there having been any fault of anyone (although presumably the failure of the letter to arrive was attributable to someone). He just said that there had been a fundamental unfairness about the proceedings before the tribunal. That was not so in *CIB/4533/1999*, where the claimant's representative had not been sent notice of the hearing but notice was sent to the claimant, who made a mistake about the date and appeared three days late. It was held that the claimant had not been denied a hearing, notwithstanding the lack of notice to his representative, and his appeal to the Commissioner was dismissed.

The rule that a party must have a proper opportunity to present their case is interpreted in a practical sense. Thus, a party was denied that right where he was misled by an official leaflet into thinking that a request for a postponement would be granted without it being necessary to give reasons for the request (*GC v SSWP (ESA)* [2014] UKUT 224 (AAC)) and also where the First-tier Tribunal proceeded to hear a case even though the claimant's representative had been unable to obtain instructions because the claimant was in prison (*JM v SSD (WP)* [2014] UKUT 358 (AAC); [2015] AACR 7). However, it is not necessarily a breach of the rules of natural justice for a tribunal to cite authoritative decisions that were not mentioned during the course of the proceedings before the tribunal. The question is whether the proceedings were unfair and that depends on whether it might reasonably be considered that the case has been decided on a basis that could not have been anticipated by the parties so that they did not have a proper opportunity of addressing the tribunal on the relevant issues (*Sheridan v Stanley Cole (Wainfleet) Ltd* [2003] EWCA Civ 1046; [2003] 4 All E.R. 1181). A judge is not entitled to decide an appeal on a basis contrary to that on which it has been argued without giving the parties an opportunity to comment (*Sayce v TNT (UK) Ltd* [2011] EWCA Civ 1583; [2012] 1 W.L.R. 1261).

The rule against bias was considered in detail in *Locabail (UK) Ltd v Bayfield Properties Ltd* [1999] EWCA Civ 3004; [2000] Q.B. 451. It has the effect that, where a member of a tribunal has any direct personal interest, apart from the most trivial, in the outcome of proceedings, they are automatically disqualified from hearing the case, irrespective of their knowledge of the interest. In cases where there is no direct personal interest, the question is whether the circumstances would lead a fair-minded and informed observer to conclude that there was a real possibility that the tribunal was biased, in the sense that the tribunal member might unfairly regard with favour or disfavour a party in the proceedings (*Porter v Magill* [2001] UKHL 67; [2002] 2 A.C. 357) and, on appeal, it will be relevant whether the tribunal member knew of the connection with the party because, if he or she did not, no favour or disfavour would have been shown. It was stressed in *CS/1753/2000* that the issue was whether there was a likelihood of bias, not whether there was actual bias. Appearances are therefore important and a decision may be set aside if a tribunal member gives the appearance of having fallen asleep (*Stansbury v Datapulse* [2003] EWCA Civ 1951; [2004] I.C.R. 523) but, in *Locobail* itself, it was stressed that "[t]he mere fact that a judge, earlier in the same case or in a previous case, had commented adversely on a party or witness, or found the evidence of a party or witness to be unreliable, would not without more found a sustainable objection". Judicial continuity may be positively desirable where the same factual issues arise in two separate cases and is permissible provided the tribunal approaches the second case with an open mind. Thus, it is not unlawful for the question whether an overpayment has arisen and is recoverable to be determined by a tribunal with the same constitution as one that has previously decided that the claimant was not entitled to benefit during the period in issue (*R(IS) 1/09*), applying *AMEC Capital Projects Ltd v Whitefriars City Estates Ltd* [2004] EWCA 1418; [2005] 1 All E.R. 723). On the other hand, in *CCS/1876/2006*, the Commissioner made the point that the mere fact that a tribunal chairman is not bound to recuse himself when he has previously decided a case against a party before him does not mean that he is not entitled to arrange for the appeal to be heard by another chairman if he considers it desirable do so in order to strengthen the party's confidence in the fairness of the procedures and if undue expense will not be involved. See also *KU v Bradford MBC* [2009] UKUT 15 (AAC), where the authorities are considered in some detail. 5.56

In *Lawal v Northern Spirit Ltd* [2003] UKHL 35; [2003] I.C.R. 856, the House of Lords held there to have been apparent bias where a party was represented by a barrister who had previously sat as a part-time judge with lay members of the Employment Appeal Tribunal before whom he was appearing. *Lawal* was followed in *Secretary of State for Work and Pensions v Cunningham* [2004] S.L.T. 1007 (also reported as *R(DLA) 7/04*), where a tribunal had relied on a medical report by an examining medical practitioner with whom two members of the tribunal had sat previously and the Court of Session held there had been apparent bias. On the other hand, in *Gillies v Secretary of State for Work and Pensions* [2006] UKHL 2; [2006] 1 W.L.R. 781, it was held by the House of Lords that there was no appearance of bias merely because a member of a tribunal also acted as an examining medical practitioner for the Secretary of State. (For further discussion of *Cunningham* and *Gillies*, see the note to s.3(3).) A long-standing personal friendship with a witness will also give rise to an appearance of bias and a judge was wrong to take into account the inconvenience to the parties in having to adjourn when he refused to recuse himself. "There was either a real possibility of bias, in which case the judge was disqualified by the principle of judicial impartiality, or there was not, in which case there was no valid objection to trial by him." (*AWG Group Ltd v Morrison* [2006] EWCA Civ 6; [2006] 1 W.L.R. 1163 at [20]). Friendship with an advocate will not give rise to an appearance of bias unless the advocate is "a domestic partner of the judge or any other person of either sex in a close personal relationship with the judge" or "a companion or employee of the judge and who lives in the judge's household" (*Guide to Judicial Conduct*, para.7.2.8, which also says that a judge should not try a case in which his or her spouse, children, children-in-law or other close relative living in the judge's household is an advocate). The *Statement of Principles of Judicial Ethics for the Scottish Judiciary* similarly states that "[a] judge should not normally sit on a case in which a member of the judge's family appears as advocate" (para.5.6) but does not attempt a definition of "family". In *SW v SSWP (IB)* [2010] UKUT 73 (AAC), an argument that there was an appearance of bias was rejected in so far as it was based on the judge knowing the claimant's representative and having previously employed her but was accepted in so far as it was based on the judge having previously been a partner in a solicitors' firm that was still acting for the claimant in respect of a claim for criminal injuries compensation arising out of the same disabilities that gave rise to the claim for incapacity benefit that was before the judge. Nor was there apparent bias where a witness had been the judge's research supervisor at university 30 years earlier (*Resolution Chemicals Ltd v H Lundbeck A/S* [2013] EWCA Civ 1515; [2014] 1 W.L.R. 1943). A judge is not normally assumed to endorse all the views expressed in publications of an organisation of which she or he is a member and so is not to be regarded as tainted by the views of other members of the organisation, provided the organisation's published aims and objectives are in themselves unobjectionable (*Helow v Advocate General for Scotland* [2008] UKHL 62; [2008] 1 W.L.R. 2416).

A party can waive the right to object to the lack of independence of a member of a tribunal but any such waiver must be voluntary, informed and unequivocal (*Millar v Dickson* [2001] UKPC D4; [2002] 1 W.L.R. 1615). However, in *CSDLA/ 444/2002*, it was pointed out, referring to *CS/343/1994* and *CDLA/2050/2002*, that, if objection to the constitution of a tribunal is not taken *before* a hearing, a party does run a substantial risk of being taken to have waived the right to object. It was held that the claimant in *CSDLA/444/2002* had not waived the right to object to the members of the tribunal. Although her lay representative had been aware of a relevant decision of a Tribunal of Commissioners on the point, she could not have been expected fully to understand the legal issues involved. The Court of Session did not consider the question of waiver when dismissing the appeal against the Commissioner's decision (*Cunningham* (see above)) but the Commissioner's approach was entirely consistent with that more recently taken by the Court of Appeal when a party delayed asking the judge who had committed him to prison for contempt of court to recuse himself from trying the main actions (*JSC BTA Bank v Ablyazov (No.9)* [2012] EWCA Civ 1551; [2013] 1 W.L.R. 1845).

5.57 It is normally a breach of the rules of natural justice for a member of a tribunal to absent themselves while a witness is giving oral evidence and later to return to participate in the decision. However, there is no breach where a party agreed to that procedure and the agreement is voluntary, informed and unequivocal. Moreover, in the absence of any evidence to the contrary, a tribunal is entitled to rely on the agreement of a properly qualified advocate without checking that their client also agreed. See *R. (Hill) v Institute of Chartered Accountants in England and Wales* [2013] EWCA Civ 555; [2014] 1 W.L.R. 86. The Court considered that there had been no breach of the rules of natural justice, rather than that there had been a breach but that it had been waived because there had been agreement in advance. Its decision rested partly on Mr Hill himself not having had second thoughts during a six-week adjournment following the irregularity but that appears to have been regarded as confirming that he had indeed given voluntary and informed consent to the procedure in advance, having been present and having raised no objection at the time. The advocate in that case was a solicitor and it is arguable that a different approach should be taken where there is a lay representative, by analogy with *CSDLA/444/2002*.

A tribunal may legitimately give assistance to the parties by telling them what it thinks of the evidence it has heard so far, but it may not form, or give the impression of having formed, a firm view in favour of one side's credibility when the other side has not yet called its evidence on the relevant point. To do so suggests bias. However, again, where there is such a manifestation of bias, attention should be drawn to it straightaway, because the Upper Tribunal or a court may not look favourably on an allegation of bias if the dissatisfied party has taken his or her chance on the outcome of the case and found it unwelcome (*Amjad v Steadman-Byrne* [2007] EWCA Civ 625; [2007] 1 W.L.R. 2484). Where a member of a tribunal makes it clear through comments or body language that he or she is unimpressed by evidence that is being given, that may be a rational reaction to the evidence even though it may be discourteous or even intemperate. In those circumstances, it does not show that the tribunal member had a closed mind or was biased, with the result that the tribunal's decision is not vitiated (*Ross v Micro Focus Ltd* UKEAT/304/09).

In *MB v Barnet, Enfield and Haringey Mental Health NHS Trust* [2011] UKUT 328 (AAC), a hearing was held to be unfair where, without giving the applicant's counsel an opportunity to comment, the presiding judge effectively told the applicant that his case was hopeless and that he should withdraw it in order to preserve a right to make another application. It was held that, although the judge was trying to be helpful, "he went far too far" and it was suggested that he "could have put the matter more tentatively and helpfully". The Upper Tribunal referred to *R. (S) v Mental Health Review Tribunal* [2002] EWHC 2522 (Admin), where Stanley Burnton J. held that there was an absence of impartiality where a member of a tribunal "expresses himself in such a way as to give rise to a reasonable apprehension that he has a preconceived concluded opinion". However, it seems unlikely that the appeal to the Upper Tribunal in *MB* would have been allowed had the Upper Tribunal not considered that the judge might, on the facts of the case, have been wrong in his assessment of the advantage to the applicant in withdrawing. The case was distinguished in *GB v SW London & St George's Mental Health NHS Trust* [2013] UKUT 58 (AAC).

Claims that there has been a breach of the rules of natural justice need to be particularised – i.e., the details of what is alleged need to be spelled out clearly – and, if they are, the Upper Tribunal will admit evidence to prove them (*R(M) 1/89*). The need to obtain proper evidence as to what occurred at the hearing from those who were present has been reiterated in *Singh v Secretary of State for the Home Department* [2016] EWCA Civ 492. In particular, the Upper Tribunal will usually obtain statements from members of the First-tier Tribunal, unless the appellant's case is clearly contradicted by, or is adequately supported by, other evidence such as a full record of proceedings (which the Upper Tribunal will be slow to go behind if it contradicts the appellant's case (*CS/343/1994*)) and, even if the allegation appears to be supported by other evidence, the members will be given an opportunity to comment if allegations of personal misconduct are made (*CDLA/5574/2002*).

The materiality of errors

In the *Iran* case, the Court of Appeal stressed the point that only "material" errors of law are important. An error is not material only if the tribunal "would have been *bound* to have reached the same conclusion, notwithstanding the error of law", given findings it made that are not tainted by the error (*Detamu v Secretary of State for the Home Department* [2006] EWCA Civ 604). Errors that would make no difference may be ignored and Commissioners and the Upper Tribunal have often simply dismissed an appeal despite identifying an error of law because the identified error would have made no difference. On the other hand, Commissioners and the Upper Tribunal have frequently set aside decisions on the ground of error of law only to substitute a decision to the same effect as the tribunal's. This is not necessarily inconsistent. It has to be borne in mind that, in social security cases, the Secretary of State has wide, but not unlimited, powers to supersede a decision of a tribunal or a Commissioner on the ground of mistake of fact or change of circumstances and the way in which a decision is expressed may well affect those powers. It may therefore be important for the Upper Tribunal to correct an error made by a tribunal even though the correction has no immediate effect on the amount of benefit payable to the claimant. **5.58**

Subsection (2)

5.59 A "party" is presumably a person who was, or should have been, a party to the proceedings before the First-tier Tribunal. Note that s.13 of the Social Security (Recovery of Benefits) Act 1997 and s.14 of the Social Security Act 1998 make additional (and largely unnecessary) provision as to who may appeal to the Upper Tribunal under this section. Subsection (8) permits further provision to be made as to who may or may not exercise the right of appeal.

A potential witness who is not a "party" cannot challenge by way of an appeal a refusal by the First-tier Tribunal to set aside a summons it has issued. However, the refusal could be challenged in judicial review proceedings and, in England and Wales, the proceedings could be brought in the Upper Tribunal because they would fall within the scope of the practice direction made by the Lord Chief Justice under s.18(6) of this Act (*CB v Suffolk CC (Enforcement Reference)* [2010] UKUT 413 (AAC); [2011] AACR 22). Similarly, it has been held that a person seeking to be added to proceedings is not a "party" until added so that any challenge to a refusal to add him or her must be made by way of an application for judicial review (*Salisbury Independent Living v Wirral BC (HB)* [2011] UKUT 44 (AAC); [2012] AACR 37). On the other hand, a person may be added as a party to proceedings in the First-tier Tribunal after a final decision has been made so as to be enable him or her to appeal (*Razzaq v Charity Commission for England and Wales* [2016] UKUT B46 (TCC)), at least in circumstances where the person could not reasonably have been expected to apply to be added as a party before the decision was made, and in *In re W(A Child) (Care Proceedings: Non-Party Appeal)* [2016] EWCA Civ 1140; [2017] 1 W.L.R., it has been held that witnesses in the High Court who were not formally parties in that Court but had gained the practical status of interveners, were to be regarded as parties entitled to appeal to the Court of Appeal so as to challenge findings made against them. The latter case can perhaps be analysed as a case where, had the case been in a tribunal, the witnesses ought to have been made parties or, alternatively can perhaps be distinguished on the ground that judicial review was not available as a remedy because it does not lie against the High Court.

The scope of the right of appeal is largely defined by subs.(1). Note, however, that this right of appeal exists alongside a right of appeal on questions of fact in penalty appeals under paras 2(2) and 4(1) of Sch.2 to the Tax Credits Act 2002 and s.21(10) of the Child Trust Funds Act 2004.

5.60 An appeal will not usually be considered if it has ceased to have any practical importance in the particular case concerned unless there is a good reason for doing so in the public interest because, for instance, there are likely to be a large number of similar cases and the point in issue is a discrete point of statutory construction (*R. v Secretary of State for the Home Department, ex parte Salem* [1999] 1 A.C. 450, *KF v Birmingham & Solihull Mental Health NHS Foundation Trust* [2010] UKUT 185 (AAC); [2011] AACR 3). However, a single ground of appeal that has ceased to be of practical importance in an individual case may be considered where it is related to other grounds of appeal (*Hampshire CC v JP* [2009] UKUT 239 (AAC); [2010] AACR 15).

In *Office of Communications v Floe Telecom Limited* [2009] EWCA Civ 47, tribunals were discouraged from giving unnecessary guidance in a case where an appeal was brought against such guidance and the Court of Appeal felt obliged to determine the appeal. It said, at [21]:

> "Specialist tribunals seem to be more prone than ordinary courts to yield to the temptation of generous general advice and guidance. The wish to be helpful to users is understandable. It may even be commendable. But bodies established to adjudicate on disputes are not in the business of giving advisory opinions to litigants or potential litigants. They should take care not to be, or to feel, pressured by the parties or by interveners or by critics to do things which they are not intended, qualified or equipped to do. In general, more harm than good is likely to be done by deciding more than is necessary for the adjudication of the actual dispute".

In *Fish Legal v Information Commissioner* [2015] UKUT 52 (AAC); [2015] AACR 33, a three-judge panel declined to lay down broad principles that might assist the Information Commissioner and the First-tier Tribunal in other cases. It explained that, while it had tried to be helpful, the nature of the issue before it did not allow it to lay down general principles in the way that had been suggested, it had to act in the context of the case and not write a treatise and it was inappropriate to give the guidance "because guidance must be based either on a wide range of experience, such as the judges of this Chamber have in social security matters, or on detailed evidence covering the scope of the guidance, such as the Immigration and Asylum Chamber receives in its Country Guidance cases". In relation to the matter on which guidance was sought, it had neither the accumulated experience nor the evidence.

However, a lot depends on the context and, in particular, the attitude of the party, usually a public body, at whom the guidance is principally aimed. Guidance that is not strictly necessary to a decision is likely to be mere obiter dicta and is not strictly binding. Indeed, it is often proffered as a suggestion rather than a requirement, where it is a matter of good practice rather than a matter of determination of the law, because it is not open to a judge sitting in a court or tribunal to lay down a mandatory procedure to be complied with in all cases within the course of giving a judgment or decision in an individual case, as that would be to make a practice direction without compliance with the requirements of s.23 (*Bovale Ltd v Secretary of State for Communities and Local Government* [2009] EWCA Civ 171; [2009] 1 W.L.R. 2274). Provided care is taken and a tribunal is appropriately "qualified or equipped", the giving of guidance may be valuable to all concerned. The problem in the *Ofcom* case seems to have been that the guidance was on matters that had been the subject of detailed argument and could not be ignored and yet was unwelcome to the public authority that was expected to apply it. Worse, much of it was wrong.

In *SSWP v LC* [2009] UKUT 153 (AAC), concessions made before the First-tier Tribunal on behalf of the Secretary of State did not prevent the Secretary of State from appealing successfully against the First-tier Tribunal's decision even though the First-tier Tribunal's decision was clearly based on the concessions.

Subsections (3) and (4)

Permission must first be sought from the First-tier Tribunal (r.21(2) of the Tribunal Procedure (Upper Tribunal) Rules 2008), which gives the First-tier Tribunal the opportunity to consider reviewing its decision under s.9 and so remove the necessity for an appeal. Therefore, although the Upper Tribunal may waive the requirement first to apply to the First-tier Tribunal, it will seldom do so unless already seised of the applicant's case and, in particular, will not do so to enable the applicant to defeat an absolute time bar (*MA v SSD* [2009] UKUT 57 (AAC), disagreeing with *HM v SSWP* [2009] UKUT 40 (AAC) on the issue whether there was a power to waive the requirement). **5.61**

Permission to appeal may be granted on grounds other than those raised by the parties (*Krasniqi v Secretary of State for the Home Department* [2006] EWCA Civ 391). Similarly, unless permission has been expressly refused in respect of some grounds or has otherwise been explicitly granted on limited grounds, a grant of permission is not to be taken as being limited and it is unnecessary for any party to make an application for permission in order to advance new grounds, the Upper Tribunal having adequate case-management powers to avoid unfairness to other parties (*DL-H v Devon Partnership NHS Trust* [2010] UKUT 102 (AAC)). Nonetheless, a judge considering an application for permission to appeal is not bound to trawl through the papers looking for grounds of appeal that have not been advanced by the applicant (*R. (Anayet Begum) v Social Security Commissioner* [2002] EWHC 401 (Admin)). The same approach has been taken in the Court of Session in *Mooney v SSWP*, 2004 S.L.T. 1141 (also reported *sub. nom. Mooney v Social Security Commissioner* as *R(DLA)5/04*). In that case, it was unsuccessfully argued that a Commissioner should have granted leave to appeal on the ground that a tribunal had failed to ask a claimant certain questions. Lord Brodie regarded it as significant that the claimant had failed to aver that the questions would have elicited any favourable evidence and also that the claimant had been represented and his representative had failed to adduce the evidence).

There is no appeal against a refusal of permission to appeal. Where the First-tier Tribunal refuses permission, the remedy is to apply to the Upper Tribunal. It is not open to the First-tier Tribunal to reconsider its refusal of permission (*R(U) 10/55*) unless there are grounds for the refusal to be set aside under r.37 of the Tribunal Procedure (First-tier Tribunal) (Social Entitlement Chamber) Rules 2008. Where the Upper Tribunal refuses permission, there is no right of appeal because such a decision is an excluded decision under s.13(8)(c), although judicial review may lie on limited grounds (see the note to s.3(5)). Consequently, there is no power of review under s.9 but it appears from *RC v SSWP* [2009] UKUT 62 (AAC); [2011] AACR 38, [26] that the Upper Tribunal may nonetheless reconsider a refusal of permission to appeal on general principles. In any event, if the conditions of r.43 of the Tribunal Procedure (Upper Tribunal) Rules 2008 are satisfied, a refusal of permission by the Upper Tribunal may be set aside and reconsidered.

Subsections (5)–(7)

5.62 Subject to the point made in the note to subs.(2), there is a right of appeal to the Upper Tribunal against all decisions of the Social Entitlement Chamber of the First-tier Tribunal except decisions concerned with criminal injuries compensation (excluded under subs.(5)(a)), certain review decisions (excluded under subs.(5)(d)), decisions set aside on review (excluded under subs.(5)(e)) and decisions concerned with asylum support (excluded by art.2 (a) of the Appeals (Excluded Decisions) Order 2009 (SI 2009/275, as amended), made under subs.(5)(f)).

In principle, judicial review will lie where there is no right of appeal and, in the case of decisions excluded under subs.(5)(a) and (d) in England and Wales, applications may be made to the Upper Tribunal (see the note to s.18(6)). However, where decisions are excluded under subs.(5)(d), there will usually be another decision that can be challenged (albeit sometimes made later) or another remedy and so permission to apply for judicial review may be refused if, for instance, an applicant is challenging a review decision and it is considered that he or she should wait for the case to be re-decided (*R.(RB) v First-tier Tribunal (Review)* [2010] UKUT 160 (AAC); [2010] AACR 41).

Note that decisions under section 9(4)(a) and (b) to correct accidental errors or amend reasons are *not* excluded by subs.(5)(d)(ii) and (iii) and so are appealable.

Subsection (5)(e) seems unnecessary.

Subsection (8)

5.63 No relevant order has been made but note that s.13 of the Social Security (Recovery of Benefits) Act 1997, s.14 of the Social Security Act 1998 and legislation concerning housing benefit, council tax benefit and child support maintenance (outside the scope of this work) make further provision as to who may appeal to the Upper Tribunal under this section.

Proceedings on appeal to Upper Tribunal

5.64 **12.**—(1) Subsection (2) applies if the Upper Tribunal, in deciding an appeal under section 11, finds that the making of the decision concerned involved the making of an error on a point of law.

(2) The Upper Tribunal—

(a) may (but need not) set aside the decision of the First-tier Tribunal, and

(b) if it does, must either—
(i) remit the case to the First-tier Tribunal with directions for its reconsideration, or
(ii) re-make the decision.

(3) In acting under subsection (2)(b)(i), the Upper Tribunal may also—
(a) direct that the members of the First-tier Tribunal who are chosen to reconsider the case are not to be the same as those who made the decision that has been set aside;
(b) give procedural directions in connection with the reconsideration of the case by the First-tier Tribunal.

(4) In acting under subsection (2)(b)(ii), the Upper Tribunal—
(a) may make any decision which the First-tier Tribunal could make if the First-tier Tribunal were re-making the decision, and
(b) may make such findings of fact as it considers appropriate.

General Note

Subsection (2)(a) expressly permits the Upper Tribunal to refuse to set aside a decision of the First-tier Tribunal even if it is erroneous in point of law. Certainly courts will generally dismiss an appeal on a point of law where satisfied that the result of decision under appeal was correct even if the decision was otherwise flawed. However, it can be important to substitute a decision based on correct reasoning if there is any possibility of there being a subsequent application for supersession and judges of the Upper Tribunal therefore often set aside a decision only to substitute a decision to the same effect makes explicit that an appeal need not be allowed if an error of law would not have made any difference to the outcome. On the other hand, if there is no point in a case being re-decided even where the decision is flawed and not necessarily correct, the Upper Tribunal will not set it aside but will, in effect, merely declare it to be erroneous in point of law (see *BB v South London and Maudsley NHS Trust* [2009] UKUT 157 (AAC), *Hampshire CC v JP* [2009] UKUT 239 (AAC); [2010] AACR 15 and *KF v Birmingham & Solihull Mental Health NHS Foundation Trust* [2010] UKUT 185 (AAC); [2011] AACR 3, all decisions of three-judge panels). This situation is less likely to occur in the social security context. 5.65

In *ZB v SSWP (CSM)* [2013] UKUT 367 (AAC), it was said that, although a person who had been barred from taking part in proceedings in the First-tier Tribunal was entitled to appeal to the Upper Tribunal against the decision in those proceedings, the fact that they had been so barred might have a bearing on how the Upper Tribunal would exercise its power under s.12(2)(a) to refuse to set aside a decision of the First-tier Tribunal notwithstanding that it has found that the making of the decision involved an error of law. In that case, the Upper Tribunal found that the appellant had not suffered any significant injustice as a result of the First-tier Tribunal's failure to provide a fuller statement of reasons and it declined to set aside the decision. It has been held that, if a case where a party had previously been barred by the First-tier Tribunal is remitted, the party is no longer barred because the proceedings are different (*SL v SSWP (CSM)* [2014] UKUT 128 (AAC)).

Subsection (2)(b) gives the Upper Tribunal a wide discretion as to whether it remits a case to the First-tier Tribunal or re-makes the decision itself. The express power to re-make a decision puts the Upper Tribunal in the same position as its principal predecessor, the Social Security Commissioners, to whom at one time appeals had lain on points of fact as well as law. It is in contrast to the position of the Employment Appeal Tribunal which, it has been held in *Jafri v Lincoln College* [2014] EWCA Civ 449; [2014] I.C.R. 920, is bound to remit a matter when allowing an appeal if the matter is in dispute and more than one outcome is possible, however well placed it might otherwise be to take a decision itself. Relevant considerations are likely to be whether there will be a non-legal member of the First-tier Tribunal with relevant expertise and whether a further, or any, hearing is necessary. Thus, where it is unlikely that a claimant will be present or represented at a hearing before the First-tier Tribunal if the case is remitted to it and both parties have made full submissions in writing, the Upper Tribunal is likely to take the view that it should re-make the decision itself (*VB v SSWP* [2008] UKUT 15 (AAC)). The Upper Tribunal's power to re-make the decision itself makes it appropriate to receive evidence and it is likely to wish to have any relevant evidence before it decides whether or not to allow the appeal. "Forcing a party to produce additional evidence only if and when it is required could lead to inefficiency and delay" (*VH v Suffolk CC (SEN)* [2010] UKUT 203 (AAC)).

It has been held by a three-judge panel of the Immigration and Asylum Chamber of the Upper Tribunal in *VOM v SSHD* [2016] UKUT 410 (IAC) that a right of appeal to the Court of Appeal under s.13 against a decision to set aside a decision of the First-tier Tribunal under s.12(2)(a) does not arise until the Upper Tribunal has disposed of the case under s.12(2)(b). Thus, the Upper Tribunal refused to entertain an application for permission to appeal where, having set aside a decision, it had adjourned proceedings with a view to re-making the decision on a future date. The Court of Appeal did not go that far in *Secretary of State for Work and Pensions v Slavin* [2011] EWCA Civ 1515; [2012] AACR 30 when, in similar circumstances, Richards LJ said at [37] that "it would have been much better for the judge to determine the outstanding issue so that an appeal to this court, if an appeal had still been necessary, could have been considered by reference to a full set of relevant facts". Indeed, it is hard to see that an appellate court is necessarily less able to properly determine an appeal in those circumstances than it would be if the case had been remitted to the First-tier Tribunal (where it is clear that there is a right of appeal before the decision has been re-made by the First-tier Tribunal—see *AA(Iraq) v Secretary of State for the Home Department* [2017] EWCA Civ 944 in which *VOM* was distinguished) or if there had been a formal direction that the question whether there had been an error of law in the First-tier Tribunal's decision had been taken as a preliminary issue; it is suggested that it rather depends on the circumstances of the particular case and that the approach to be taken to the question whether an application for permission to appeal should be considered before the proceedings have been concluded should be regarded as a matter of practice rather than jurisdiction. In any event, some of the matters relied upon in *VOM* apply only in the Immigration and Asylum Chamber of the Upper Tribunal and not also in the Administrative Appeals Chamber.

5.66 In *AW v SSWP (IB)* [2013] UKUT 20 (AAC) the Upper Tribunal left open the question whether, having allowed an appeal against a decision of the First-tier Tribunal not to admit, or to strike out, an appeal made to that Tribunal, it was entitled not only to decide that the appeal to the First-tier Tribunal should be admitted or not struck out but also to determine that appeal. The judge considered that, even if he had the power to do so, he should determine the appeal made to the First-tier Tribunal only if all parties consented to him doing so. One party declined to give consent. Subsection (3)(a) requires a positive direction to be made if is intended that a case that is remitted to the First-tier Tribunal is to be heard by a differently constituted tribunal. Subsection.(3)(b) makes it plain that other procedural directions may be given as well as directions under subs.(2)(b)(i) on the law and under subs.(3)(a) as to the constitution of the tribunal.

The Upper Tribunal should identify outstanding issues of fact or law before referring a case to another tribunal, because otherwise a tribunal is likely to find its role unclear (*Secretary of State for Work and Pensions v Menary-Smith* [2006] EWCA Civ 1751). To like effect, a Tribunal of Commissioners said in *R(IB) 2/07* that it was wrong to suggest that a Commissioner allowing an appeal necessarily had to refer a case to another tribunal, just because no witness had attended to give evidence before the Commissioner and there was a dispute between the parties as to the decision that should be substituted for one that had been set aside. Neither party in that case had suggested there was any material evidence not recorded in the papers or that anything turned on a dispute about that evidence. If the evidence was not in issue, the dispute between the parties was likely to be one of law that a Commissioner should resolve. Similarly, where a tribunal's findings of primary fact are adequate and the reasoning supporting those findings is also adequate, it is wrong to suggest that the Upper Tribunal should refer the case to another tribunal to identify grounds for supersession. The Upper Tribunal can perform that exercise itself under subs.(2)(b)(ii) without making new findings of primary fact (*CDLA/4217/2001*). It was, however, emphasised in *JA (Ghana) v Secretary of State for the Home Department* [2015] EWCA Civ 1031 that remittal will be appropriate if there are issues of credibility or reliability that a party has not had a satisfactory opportunity to address at an oral hearing (e.g., because although there was a hearing before the First-tier Tribunal the relevant findings cannot be relied upon in the light of the First-tier Tribunal's error of law) and it is not convenient for the Upper Tribunal to hold a hearing for the purpose of resolving the issues. Moreover, it was held in that case that, where the Upper Tribunal has made a finding of fact on any issue before remitting a case, the First-tier Tribunal is bound by that finding even if there is no specific direction to that effect. This is consistent with the approach taken in *Kuteh v Secretary of State for Education* [2014] EWCA Civ 1586, where it was held that the Upper Tribunal was bound by a finding made by the Administrative Court when quashing a decision before remitting a case. However, where a case is remitted by the Upper Tribunal to a panel of the First-tier Tribunal that is constituted differently from the panel whose decision has been set aside, the new panel is not entitled to adopt a finding made by the previous panel *only* because the Upper Tribunal has held that particular finding not to be vitiated by any error of law or has not commented on it, although it may adopt the finding for other reasons and must adopt it if directed to do so by the Upper Tribunal (*KK v SSWP (DLA)* [2015] UKUT 417 (AAC)).

See also *Sarkar v Secretary of State for the Home Department* [2014] EWCA Civ 195) in which it was made very plain that, where the error of law does not vitiate a finding of the First-tier Tribunal on a particular issue, the Upper Tribunal may, if it re-makes the decision itself, adopt the finding without considering further evidence or, if it remits the case, issue directions under s.12(2)(b)(i) limiting the scope of the First-tier Tribunal's reconsideration so that it must decide the case on the basis of that finding. In such a case, the Upper Tribunal may even decide to direct that the decision be re-made by the same members who previously decided the case, requiring them to address an issue they had previous failed to consider or to give the reasons they had previously failed to give (*Shah v NHS England* [2013] UKUT 538 (AAC)). However, this will seldom be appropriate or necessary in the social security context, where hearings are generally short and oral evidence from witnesses other than the parties is rare and where it will often be administratively simpler to arrange an entirely new panel rather than reconstitute an earlier one. On the other hand, in the absence of any such practical advantage, it would still be wrong to remit a case to the same panel if that would give rise to "reasonably perceived unfairness to the affected parties" or "damage to the public confidence in the decision making process" (*HCA International Ltd v Competition and Markets Authority* [2015] EWCA Civ 492; [2015] 1 W.L.R. 4341).

Where a case has been remitted to the First-tier Tribunal, the First-tier Tribunal is **5.67**
not entitled to decide that the Upper Tribunal had no jurisdiction to give the decision and on that ground refuse to rehear the case. In *Nesbitt's Application* [2013] NIQB 111; [2014] AACR 31, the High Court in Northern Ireland quashed a decision of the President of appeal tribunals who refused to rehear a case that had been remitted by the Chief Social Security Commissioner with a direction that it be reheard. The President had taken the view that the Chief Commissioner had had no jurisdiction to hear the case because the claimant had validly withdrawn his appeal, even though the Chief Commissioner had expressly determined, following an extensive analysis, that the case had not been withdrawn. Treacy J. held that: "Even if the Commissioner had no jurisdiction, it still would not have been open to the [President] to simply reject it and in effect overturn the Commissioner's decision himself. . . . In the

absence of adjudication by a court of appropriate jurisdiction on the Commissioner's jurisdiction to hear the appeal his decision remains extant and binding on the [President] regardless of the President's view as to its legality." See also *Rochdale MBC v KW (No.2)* [2015] EWCA Civ 1054; [2016] 1 W.L.R. 198, where it was held that a judge of the Court of Protection had been bound by a consent order of the Court of Appeal and it was futile and inappropriate for him to seek to undermine it by complaining that it was ultra vires or wrong for any other reason.

If a case is referred to a differently constituted tribunal, it is usual for the decision that has been set aside to be included in the papers. That is not inappropriate. Even if their findings of fact cannot be relied upon, issues identified by the first tribunal may well be of assistance to the new tribunal, although it must be careful not to be influenced by the discredited findings (*Swash v Secretary of State for the Home Department* [2006] EWCA Civ 1093; [2007] 1 W.L.R. 1264). There may, however, be special circumstances in which the Upper Tribunal setting the first decision aside considers that the interests of justice require the case to be heard by a tribunal that has not seen that decision and he or she will be able to issue appropriate directions to ensure that that happens (*ibid.*).

If a decision of a tribunal has been superseded while an appeal against it has been pending, it is necessary to consider the effect of the supersession on the appeal or vice versa. If the supersession was under reg.6(2)(c) of the Social Security and Child Support (Decisions and Appeals) Regulations 1999 (ignorance of, or mistake as to, fact), there may be circumstances in which the appeal to the Upper Tribunal should be treated as having lapsed, particularly if the supersession has given the claimant all that he or she seeks on the appeal. Where an appeal, or part of an appeal, has lapsed, it must be struck out under r.8(2) of the Tribunal Procedure (Upper Tribunal) Rules 2008 (*LS v HMRC (TC)* [2017] UKUT 275 (AAC)). If the appeal is not treated as having lapsed and is allowed, the supersession decision is generally allowed to stand, and the decision to be made by the Upper Tribunal or another tribunal following the setting aside of the first tribunal's decision is made in respect of a period ending immediately before the supersession took effect. This approach was held in *R(DLA)2/04* to be justifiable where the parties are content with the outcome of the supersession or where it is plain that supersession would have been appropriate whatever the outcome of the appeal because there had been an obvious change of circumstances or, perhaps, new medical evidence justifying supersession under reg.6(2)(g) of the Social Security and Child Support (Decisions and Appeals) Regulations 1999 in an incapacity benefit case. In *R(DLA)2/04* itself, the claimant had both appealed against and applied for supersession of a decision of a tribunal. The appeal was successful and a Commissioner had referred the case to another tribunal. The application for supersession had failed and the claimant's appeal came before the same tribunal as the remitted appeal. The new tribunal made an award on the remitted appeal and did not limit it on account of the failed supersession application. No award was made on the supersession appeal. On further appeals, the Commissioner held that that was the correct approach where, as in that case, the application for supersession had been under reg.6(2)(c) (error of fact). He advanced three rules:

> "1. An application for supersession that results in a refusal to supersede the original decision does not terminate the period under consideration on an appeal against the original decision.
> 2. Live proceedings arising out of an application for supersession based on ignorance of, or a mistake as to, a material fact lapse when the decision to be superseded is set aside on appeal (provided that there is no further appeal in respect of the original decision).
> 3. Live proceedings arising out of an application for supersession based on a change of circumstances do not lapse when the decision to be superseded is set aside on appeal (but the application may have to be treated as an application for supersession of a different decision or, perhaps, as a new claim, depending on the circumstances)."

The second and third rules arise because a tribunal a hearing an appeal against the original decision must correct any error of fact in the original decision but, by virtue of s.12(8)(b) of the Social Security Act 1998, must not take account of any subsequent change of circumstances. In *CDLA/3948/2002*, a different Commissioner also held that a supersession of a tribunal's decision became ineffective when the Commissioner set the tribunal's decision aside. Latham L.J. considered that approach to be correct and refused leave to appeal (*Farrington v Secretary of State for Work and Pensions* [2004] EWCA Civ 435). 5.68

Where the Upper Tribunal sets aside a decision of a tribunal awarding benefit for a fixed period, the period in issue before the Commissioner or a tribunal to whom the case is remitted is not necessarily limited by the fact that there has been a decision on a renewal claim, although the award on the renewal claim must be treated as having lapsed if an award on the original claim is made in respect of the same period and any benefit paid as a result of the renewal claim must be treated as having been paid on account of the decision eventually made on the earlier claim *(CDLA/3323/2003)*.

The Upper Tribunal has no power to make a declaration of incompatibility under s.4 of the Human Rights Act 1998. In *SH v SSWP (JSA)* [2011] UKUT 428 (AAC), the Judge considered that, there being no other grounds on which the claimant could possibly succeed but it being arguable that the primary legislation in issue was incompatible with the Convention, he should dismiss the appeal before him summarily and grant permission to appeal to the Court of Appeal which can make a declaration of incompatibility. However, he said that the extent to which the Upper Tribunal should enter into the merits of a claimant's contentions in such a case would depend on the particular circumstances of the case. In the case before him, dealing with the arguments would have required the filing of detailed evidence which would ultimately have been unnecessary if the claimant was not minded to take the case to the Court of Appeal due to the risk of an adverse costs order should he lose In *R. (Kaiyam) v Secretary of State for Justice* [2013] EWCA Civ 1587; [2014] 1 W.L.R. 1208, the Court of Appeal took a similar approach where it was bound by House of Lords authority not to follow subsequent decisions of the European Court of Human Rights. However, in *AB v SSWP (JSA)* [2013] UKUT 288 (AAC) which was another case where the Upper Tribunal considered it unnecessary to consider arguments under the Human Rights Act 1998 because it had no power to make a declaration of incompatibility, the judge declined to grant permission to appeal because, although the case undoubtedly raised a point of principle, he considered that it was best left to the Court of Appeal to decide whether it raised an *important* point of principle or there was some other compelling reason to hear the appeal (see the annotation to s.13(6) and (7)).

A third approach was taken in *PL v SSWP (JSA)* [2016] UKUT 177 (AAC), where the judge decided to consider, and give reasons for rejecting, an argument that primary legislation was incompatible with the Convention and then refused permission to appeal. She took that approach partly because doing so might assist the Court of Appeal if the claimant were to seek permission to appeal but mainly because her view was that the human rights challenge to the legislation was fundamentally flawed and she considered that it might be helpful to the claimant if she were to explain why she had reached that view.

There can be difficulties even where subordinate legislation is in issue. In *Humphries v Revenue and Customs Commissioners* [2012] UKSC 18; [2012] 1 W.L.R. 1545; [2012] AACR 46, Baroness Hale of Richmond JSC observed (at [34]) that it was not obvious how a remedy could be provided on a statutory appeal if it was held that part of a regulation should be disapplied because it was inconsistent with the European Convention on Human Rights but it was then necessary to read in an alternative provision in order to overcome the effect of primary legislation. However, in *SSWP v Carmichael (HB)* [2017] UKUT 174 (AAC), the Upper Tribunal held that, in the light of *Mathieson v Secretary of State for Work and Pensions* [2015] UKSC 47; [2015] 1 W.L.R. 3250; [2015] AACR 44, where secondary legislation could not be read compatibly with the

Convention but was not mandated by primary legislation, a tribunal could simply direct that benefit be awarded on a basis that it was satisfied was compatible with the Convention. The Secretary of State has been given permission to appeal.

Right to appeal to Court of Appeal etc.

5.69 **13.**—(1) For the purposes of subsection (2), the reference to a right of appeal is to a right to appeal to the relevant appellate court on any point of law arising from a decision made by the Upper Tribunal other than an excluded decision.

(2) Any party to a case has a right of appeal, subject to subsection (14).

(3) That right may be exercised only with permission (or, in Northern Ireland, leave).

(4) Permission (or leave) may be given by—

(a) the Upper Tribunal, or

(b) the relevant appellate court,

on an application by the party.

(5) An application may be made under subsection (4) to the relevant appellate court only if permission (or leave) has been refused by the Upper Tribunal.

(6) The Lord Chancellor may, as respects an application under subsection (4) that falls within subsection (7) and for which the relevant appellate court is the Court of Appeal in England and Wales or the Court of Appeal in Northern Ireland, by order make provision for permission (or leave) not to be granted on the application unless the Upper Tribunal or (as the case may be) the relevant appellate court considers—

(a) that the proposed appeal would raise some important point of principle or practice, or

(b) that there is some other compelling reason for the relevant appellate court to hear the appeal.

[[1] (6A) Rules of court may make provision for permission not to be granted on an application under subsection (4) to the Court of Session that falls within subsection (7) unless the court considers—

(a) that the proposed appeal would raise some important point of principle[[2] or practice], or

(b) that there is some other compelling reason for the court to hear the appeal.]

(7) An application falls within this subsection if the application is for permission (or leave) to appeal from any decision of the Upper Tribunal on an appeal under section 11.

(8) For the purposes of subsection (1), an "excluded decision" is—

(a) any decision of the Upper Tribunal on an appeal under section 28(4) or (6) of the Data Protection Act 1998 (appeals against national security certificate),

(b) any decision of the Upper Tribunal on an appeal under section 60(1) or (4) of the Freedom of Information Act 2000 (appeals against national security certificate),

(c) any decision of the Upper Tribunal on an application under section 11(4)(b) (application for permission or leave to appeal),

(d) a decision of the Upper Tribunal under section 10—

(i) to review, or not to review, an earlier decision of the tribunal,

(ii) to take no action, or not to take any particular action, in the light of a review of an earlier decision of the tribunal, or

(iii) to set aside an earlier decision of the tribunal,

(e) a decision of the Upper Tribunal that is set aside under section 10 (including a decision set aside after proceedings on an appeal under this section have been begun), or

(f) any decision of the Upper Tribunal that is of a description specified in an order made by the Lord Chancellor.

(9) A description may be specified under subsection (8)(f) only if—

(a) in the case of a decision of that description, there is a right to appeal to a court from the decision and that right is, or includes, something other than a right (however expressed) to appeal on any point of law arising from the decision, or

(b) decisions of that description are made in carrying out a function transferred under section 30 and prior to the transfer of the function under section 30(1) there was no right to appeal from decisions of that description.

(10) Where—

(a) an order under subsection (8)(f) specifies a description of decisions, and

(b) decisions of that description are made in carrying out a function transferred under section 30,

the order must be framed so as to come into force no later than the time when the transfer under section 30 of the function takes effect (but power to revoke the order continues to be exercisable after that time, and power to amend the order continues to be exercisable after that time for the purpose of narrowing the description for the time being specified).

(11) Before the Upper Tribunal decides an application made to it under subsection (4), the Upper Tribunal must specify the court that is to be the relevant appellate court as respects the proposed appeal.

(12) The court to be specified under subsection (11) in relation to a proposed appeal is whichever of the following courts appears to the Upper Tribunal to be the most appropriate—

(a) the Court of Appeal in England and Wales;

(b) the Court of Session;

(c) the Court of Appeal in Northern Ireland.

(13) In this section except subsection (11), "the relevant appellate court", as respects an appeal, means the court specified as respects that appeal by the Upper Tribunal under subsection (11).

(14) The Lord Chancellor may by order make provision for a person to be treated as being, or to be treated as not being, a party to a case for the purposes of subsection (2).

(15) Rules of court may make provision as to the time within which an application under subsection (4) to the relevant appellate court must be made.

Amendments

1. Crime and Courts Act 2013 s.23 (July 15, 2013).
2. Criminal Justice and Courts Act 2015 s.83(2) (April 13, 2015).

General Note

Subsections (1) and (2)

There is no right of appeal against an "excluded decision", for the meaning of which see subs.(8). There is also no right of appeal against a refusal of permission to appeal to the Upper Tribunal even where such a refusal of permission is not an **5.70** excluded decision (*Sarfraz v Disclosure and Barring Service* [2015] EWCA Civ 544; [2015] 1 W.L.R. 4441; [2015] AACR 35), although such a refusal of permission may be challenged by way of an application for judicial review without the special procedural restrictions imposed on a challenge to a refusal of permission to appeal from the First-tier Tribunal (see the note to subss.(8) to (10)). There would also be no right of appeal against a ruling of the Upper Tribunal on an issue that did not actually arise in the case in question and was merely intended to give guidance in other cases, because there is no formal jurisdiction to give such a ruling and no party has a sufficient interest in it (*Re X (Court of Protection Practice)* [2015] EWCA Civ 599; [2016] 1 W.L.R. 227).

For the "relevant appellate court", see subss.(11)–(13).

An appeal lies only on a point of law (for the meaning of which, see the note to s.11(1)) and, where the appeal is against a decision on an appeal under s.11, only if it would raise some important point of principle or practice or there is some other compelling reason for the relevant appellate court to hear the appeal (see the note to subss.(6) and (6A)). Courts are generally reluctant to consider appeals that have ceased to have any practical importance in the particular case concerned, although they may do so if there is a good reason in the public interest (*R. v Secretary of State for the Home Department, ex parte Salem* [1999] 1 A.C. 450).

A "party" is presumably a person who was, or should have been, a party to the proceedings before the Upper Tribunal. See the annotation to s.11(2). Note that s.15 of the Social Security Act 1998 makes additional (and largely unnecessary) provision as to who may appeal to the Upper Tribunal under this section. Subsection (14) permits further provision to be made as to who may or may not exercise the right of appeal.

5.71 Where the claimant is the appellant in a social security case, the respondent will be either the Secretary of State for Work and Pensions or Her Majesty's Revenue and Customs (*not* the Upper Tribunal). Service should be effected on the Solicitor to the Department for Work and Pensions, Caxton House, Tothill Street, London SW1H 9NA or on the Solicitor to Her Majesty's Revenue and Customs, South West Wing, Bush House, Strand, London WC2B 4RD, as appropriate.

On an appeal under this section, the Court of Appeal has all the powers of the Upper Tribunal (see the Senior Courts Act s.15(3) and also CPR r.52.20) and also the powers conferred by s.14. The court exercises a degree of self-restraint when considering whether a specialist tribunal has got the law wrong (*AH (Sudan) v Secretary of State for the Home Department* [2007] UKHL 49; [2008] 1 A.C. 678, [30]) but less so where the Upper Tribunal has found the First-tier Tribunal to have erred in law on conventional procedural grounds (*AP (Trinidad and Tobago) v Secretary of State for the Home Department* [2011] EWCA Civ 551), although a decision of the Upper Tribunal that a determination by the First-tier Tribunal is inadequately reasoned would be treated with respect by the Court of Appeal (*PK (Congo) v Secretary of State for the Home Department* [2013] EWCA Civ 1500), presumably because the Upper Tribunal considers the adequacy of reasons given by the First-tier Tribunal on a daily basis and effectively sets the standard of reasoning required.

Because appeals from the First-tier Tribunal to the Upper Tribunal and from the Upper Tribunal to an appellate court are both confined to points of law, the issue in an appellate court is often whether the Upper Tribunal was right to find, or not to find, that the First-tier Tribunal erred in law so that the focus, where only conventional public law issues are raised, is simply on whether the First-tier Tribunal erred in law. However, in *R. (Jones) v First-tier Tribunal* [2013] UKSC 19; [2013] 2 A.C. 48; [2013] AACR 25, Lord Hope said—

> "A pragmatic approach should be taken to the dividing line between law and fact, so that the expertise of tribunals at the first-tier and that of the Upper Tribunal can be used to best effect. An appeal court should not venture too readily into this area by classifying issues as issues of law which are really best left for determination by specialist appellate tribunals."

Jones was a case where the Upper Tribunal had rejected a challenge to the decision of the First-tier Tribunal (and in fact did not give any general guidance to promote consistency in decision-making) and the Court of Appeal had overturned its decision but, in a case where the Upper Tribunal has found the First-tier Tribunal to have erred in law and has, under s.12(2)(b)(ii) substituted its own decision for that of the First-tier Tribunal, the implication of it being difficult to decide whether issues are questions of fact or questions of law is that the focus of an appellate court should be on whether the Upper Tribunal's approach was wrong, rather than on whether the First-tier Tribunal's approach was wrong (*per* Lord Carnwath in *Revenue and Customs Commissioners v Pendragon Plc* [2015] UKSC 37; [2015] 1 W.L.R. 2838). Although the Upper Tribunal only had jurisdiction to intervene if the First-tier Tribunal had erred in law, that was not the *main* issue in the case, which had turned on the understanding of a tax law principle and the evaluation of facts in that context rather than on any significant issue of primary fact.

In *R.(MM) v Secretary of State for Work and Pensions* [2013] EWCA Civ 1565; [2016] AACR 11, the Court of Appeal accepted that the Upper Tribunal (Administrative Appeals Chamber) did not have a special expertise in discrimination issues as far as interpretation of the legislation was concerned but its judges were "specialists who are daily dealing with the practices in the social welfare field and are far better equipped than this court to analyse and assess the evidence relating to the particular difficulties which [mental health patients] may face in handling procedures" so that the court would be even more cautious than usual about overturning a finding which was one of mixed law and fact. Similarly, in *Obrey v Secretary of State for Work and Pensions* [2013] EWCA Civ 1584, it was said that "the question whether the indirectly discriminatory effect of a particular rule in the benefits system because it does not distinguish between mental patients and other patients in hospital is, or is not, 'manifestly without reasonable foundation' is very far from being an issue of 'constitutional significance'. On the contrary, it is precisely the kind of issue that is best left for evaluation and judgment by a specialist appellate tribunal with a particular expertise in the field of social security law." In that case, Sullivan L.J. referred to the judgment of Lord Hope in *R.(Jones) v First-tier Tribunal*

However, when the Supreme Court refused permission to appeal, it did so "[w]hile not endorsing the breadth of the Court of Appeal's observations on deference to an expert tribunal on questions of proportionality". Moreover, in *Mathieson v Secretary of State for Work and Pensions* [2015] UKSC 47; [2015] 1 W.L.R. 3250; [2015] AACR 19, the Supreme Court differed from the Upper Tribunal on the question whether social security legislation resulting in unequal treatment was justified because it considered there had been an error of law in the Upper Tribunal's analysis and it had fuller evidence before it.

In *R.(Hutton) v First-tier Tribunal* [2016] EWCA Civ 1305, Gross LJ, with whom Rafferty and Floyd LJJ agreed, considered the comments of Baroness Hale of Richmond and Lord Hope of Craighead in *AH (Sudan)* and of Lord Hope and Lord Carnwath in *R.(Jones) v First-tier Tribunal* and continued—

"57. Pulling the threads together:

(i) First, this Court should exercise restraint and proceed with caution before interfering with decisions of specialist tribunals. Not only do such tribunals have the expertise which the "ordinary" courts may not have but when a specialised statutory scheme has been entrusted by Parliament to tribunals, the Court should not venture too readily into their field.

(ii) Secondly, if a tribunal decision is clearly based on an error of law, then it must be corrected. This Court should not, however, subject such decisions to inappropriate textual analysis so as to discern an error of law when, on a fair reading of the decision as a whole, none existed. It is probable, as Baroness Hale said, that in understanding and applying the law within their area of expertise, specialist tribunals will have got it right.

Moreover, the mere fact that an appellate tribunal or a court would have reached a different conclusion, does not constitute a ground for review or for allowing an appeal.

(iii) Thirdly, it is of the first importance to identify the tribunal of fact, to keep in mind that it and only it will have heard the evidence and to respect its decisions. When determining whether a question was one of "fact" or "law", this Court should have regard to context, as I would respectfully express it ("pragmatism", "expediency" or "policy", *per Jones*), so as to ensure both that decisions of tribunals of fact are given proper weight and to provide scope for specialist appellate tribunals to shape the development of law and practice in their field.

(iv) Fourthly, it is important to note that these authorities not only address the relationship between the courts and specialist appellate tribunals *but also* between specialist first-tier tribunals and appellate tribunals."

In *Secretary of State for Work and Pensions v Robertson* [2015] CSIH 82, the Court of Session held the appeal by the Secretary of State to be incompetent because the Secretary of State had been successful before the Upper Tribunal. Despite his success, the Secretary of State had wished to appeal because, in the course of its decision, the Upper Tribunal had held that a regulation was invalid and the Secretary of State considered that, unless the Court of Session held it to be wrong, he would be bound to follow that finding to the disadvantage of other claimants. The Court of Session held that, because it had not been necessary for the Upper Tribunal to consider whether the regulation was invalid and its finding on that point formed no part of its reason for dismissing the claimant's appeal, the point of law did not arise from the Upper Tribunal's decision. The implication is presumably that the Secretary of State had been wrong to consider that he would be obliged to follow the finding in other cases because it was only *obiter dicta*, although the Court of Session refrained from saying so on the ground that "how the appellant chooses to act is a matter for him".

Normally English and Welsh law is regarded as foreign law in Scotland (and *vice versa*) and so is treated as a matter of fact that has to be proved by evidence. However, where the First-tier Tribunal and Upper Tribunal exercise jurisdiction throughout Great Britain, they are taken to have judicial knowledge of both English and Welsh law and Scots law, wherever they are sitting, so that proof of the law of either part of Great Britain is unnecessary. It follows that, where the Court of Session hears an appeal from the Upper Tribunal in a tax case or social security case, it also is to be taken to have judicial knowledge of English and Welsh law (*HMRC v Murray Group Holdings Ltd* [2015] CSIH 77 at [50]).

It has been held by a three-judge panel of the Immigration and Asylum Chamber of the Upper Tribunal in *VOM v SSHD* [2016] UKUT 410 (IAC) that a right of appeal against a decision of the Upper Tribunal to set aside a decision of the First-tier Tribunal under s.12(2)(a) does not arise until the Upper Tribunal has disposed of the case under s.12(2)(b). However, see the observations on that decision in the annotation to s.12 above.

Subsections (3)–(5)

5.72 Permission to appeal must first be sought from the Upper Tribunal, which gives the Upper Tribunal the opportunity to consider reviewing its decision under s.10 and so remove the necessity for an appeal. If permission is refused by the Upper Tribunal, permission may be sought from the relevant appellate court. It is important for respondents to bear this in mind if they seek not just to resist the appellant's grounds of appeal or to support the Upper Tribunal's decision on a ground that the Upper Tribunal did not consider (which requires the filing of a respondent's notice) but also to argue that the decision should be upheld on a ground that the Upper Tribunal rejected. In those circumstances, there must be a cross-appeal and that requires permission. Moreover, subs.(5) requires the respondent to seek permission to cross-appeal from the Upper Tribunal in the first instance, even though the case is already pending in the Court of Appeal.

Where a case does not raise an important point of principle or practice, a party is unlikely to be granted permission to appeal on grounds not advanced before the Upper Tribunal if the Upper Tribunal gave a clear opportunity to argue the point by indicating its provisional views (*Secretary of State for Work and Pensions v DH (a child)* [2004] EWCA Civ 16 (reported as *R(DLA) 1/04*)). The Court said that it was "of the utmost value, on an appeal from a specialist tribunal, to have the considered views of the points at issue of that specialist tribunal before testing them on appeal". They were not impressed by the argument that the Commissioner's decision would remain an unfortunate precedent, saying that if the issue was that important it was because there were many similar cases and therefore the Secretary of State would be able to find another case in which to advance his arguments before a Commissioner and, if necessary, the Court.

The Court might have taken a different view had the appellant before them been an unrepresented claimant before the Commissioner. In *Miskovic v Secretary of State for Work and Pensions* [2011] EWCA Civ 16; [2012] AACR 11, the Court of Appeal rejected an argument, advanced by the Secretary of State, that it was precluded from considering points not argued before the Upper Tribunal and accepted that it could do so, provided it would not be unfair to the other party. This is also the approach of the Court of Session (*HMRC v Murray Group Holdings Ltd* [2015] CSIH 77 at [39]). The Court of Appeal also said that it might be reluctant to consider a new point unless all the facts potentially relevant to the correct determination of the point had been found. However, in a jurisdiction where an appeal lies only on a point of law, which includes a failure to find material facts, and where the Court can remit the matter to a tribunal to make further findings, it is not easy to see why there should be such reluctance as long as the absence of findings does not make the determination of the point of law too speculative. In any event, if a ground is raised that was not advanced on the appeal before the Upper Tribunal, the Upper Tribunal should consider obtaining the other party's view on it before granting permission (*RH v South London and Maudsley NHS Foundation Trust* [2010] EWCA Civ 1273; [2011] AACR 14). A case cannot be said to raise an important point of principle unless the point has not already been established and a party applying for permission to appeal should clearly identify the points of law that are said to raise general points of principle (*Secretary of State for Work and Pensions v Cattrell* [2011] EWCA Civ 572; [2011] AACR 35).

For the procedure for applying to the Upper Tribunal for permission to appeal, 5.73
see rr. 44 and 45 of the Tribunal Procedure (Upper Tribunal) Rules 2008. Note that r.44(6)(b) provides that, where the Upper Tribunal refuses to extend the time for applying for permission to appeal, it must refuse permission to appeal, thus satisfying the condition of subs.(5) and reversing the effect of *White v Chief Adjudication Officer* [1986] 2 All E.R. 905 (also reported as an appendix to *R(S) 8/85*). In *White*, it had been held that a Commissioner's refusal to extend time for applying for leave to appeal to the Court of Appeal did not amount to a refusal of leave and was challengeable only by way of a application for judicial review. Now, if permission is refused by the Upper Tribunal on the ground of delay, it is possible for the applicant simply to make an application to the relevant appellant court for permission to appeal, although that court will of course have regard to the delay in applying to the Upper Tribunal.

For the procedure for applying to the Court of Appeal in England and Wales for permission to appeal, see CPR Pt 52. Note that a grant of permission may be set aside by the Court of Appeal under CPR r.52.18, but only "where there is a compelling reason for doing so".

The Upper Tribunal has no express power to grant permission to appeal only on conditions as to costs and it is perhaps doubtful whether it can properly do so. If it does not have the power, it could refuse permission indicating that it is leaving the question of permission to the appellate court so that the imposition of conditions may be considered. If it does impose conditions, any challenge to the conditions by the would-be appellant must be by way of a renewed application to the appellate court for permission to appeal (*R. (Medical Justice) v Secretary of State for the Home Department* [2011] EWCA Civ 269; [2011] 1 W.L.R. 2852). Making a renewed application to the appellate court is also what a would-be appellant must do if he or she fails to comply with any conditions imposed by the Upper Tribunal but still wishes to appeal (*Masri v Consolidated Contractors International Co SAL* [2011] EWCA Civ 898; [2012] 1 W.L.R. 223).

Subsections (6), (6A) and (7)

5.74 The Appeals from the Upper Tribunal to the Court of Appeal Order 2008 (SI 2008/2834) provides that permission to appeal from a decision of the Upper Tribunal to the Court of Appeal may not be given unless one of the conditions set out in subs.(6)(a) and (b) applies. Although the Order does not say so, it can apply only to appeals against decisions of the Upper Tribunal given on appeals under s.11, because subs.(7) limits the order-making power in subs.(6) to such cases (*Clarise Properties Ltd v Rees* [2015] EWCA Civ 1118). Its effect is duplicated in CPR r.52.7, which makes it clear that the requirement that a second appeal would raise an important point of principle or practice is additional to the test for first appeals which is that the appeal would "have a real prospect of success". If only one of a number of grounds of appeal raises an important point of principle or practice, the Upper Tribunal should carefully consider whether the grant of permission should be limited to that ground (*RH v South London and Maudsley NHS Foundation Trust* [2010] EWCA Civ 1273; [2011] AACR 14).

In *PR (Sri Lanka) v Secretary of State for the Home Department* [2011] EWCA Civ 988; [2012] 1 W.L.R. 73, the Court said that, in this context, a point of principle or practice:

> "should be not merely important, but one which calls for attention by the higher courts, specifically the Court of Appeal, rather than being left to be determined within the specialised tribunal system".

It was also held that "compelling" in "some other compelling reason" means legally compelling and indicates that the case must have very high prospects of success. The seriousness of the consequences for the individual or the political importance of the case may be additional grounds but are not by themselves capable of amounting to compelling reasons. Permission was refused in all three cases before the Court. On the other hand, it was held in *JD (Congo) v Secretary of State for the Home Department (Public Law Project intervening)* [2012] EWCA Civ 327; [2012] 1 W.L.R. 3273 that the fact that the Upper Tribunal's decision will have very adverse consequences for the person seeking permission to appeal may, in combination with a strong argument that there has been an error of law, amount to "some other compelling reason" for granting permission to appeal. The point was made that the test is intended to be higher than the ordinary test—a real prospect of success—which is why the argument that there has been an error of law must be "strong".

Subsection (6) does not apply to appeals to the Court of Session in Scotland. The Rules of the Court of Session were nonetheless amended in 2008 to have precisely the same effect but that amendment was held to be invalid (*KP v Secretary of State for the Home Department* [2012] CSIH 38). Consequently, subs.(6A) was inserted with effect from July 15, 2013 and r.41.57 of the Rules of the Court of Session was promptly made under it, coming into force on August 19, 2013. This purportedly brought the position in Scotland into line with that in England and Wales and Northern Ireland but it was then realised that the words "in practice", which appear in subs.(6)(a), did not appear in subs.(6A)(a) and, accordingly, the rule was amended to omit those words with effect from November 11, 2013. Those words were inserted into subs.(6A)(a) with effect from April 13, 2015, but r.41.57 has not been re-amended in accordance with that amendment.

Subsections (8)–(10)

Note that subs.(8)(d)(ii) and (iii) does not exclude the right of appeal in respect of decisions made under s.10(4)(a) or (b) to correct accidental errors in earlier decisions or amend reasons. Subsection (8)(e) seems unnecessary. Insofar as it relates to the Upper Tribunal, the Appeals (Excluded Decisions) Order 2009 (SI 2009/275, as amended by SI 2010/41) made under subs.(8)(f) is concerned only with decisions made by the Tax and Chancery Chamber and the Immigration and Asylum Chamber. 5.75

In practice, the most important exclusion is the denial of a right of appeal against refusals of permission to appeal to the Upper Tribunal from the First-tier Tribunal (subs.(8)(c)). There is also no right of appeal against a refusal of permission to appeal to the Upper Tribunal from other bodies (*Sarfraz v Disclosure and Barring Service* [2015] EWCA Civ 544; [2015] 1 W.L.R. 4441; [2015] AACR 35) but that is on general policy grounds and not because such a refusal of permission is an excluded decision. Although an excluded decision may be challenged by way of an application to the High Court or Court of Session for judicial review, the cases in which a refusal of permission to appeal may be challenged are limited to those which raise some important point of principle or practice or where there is some other some other compelling reason for the High Court or Court of Session to hear the case (see *R. (Cart) v Upper Tribunal (Public Law Project intervening)* [2011] UKSC 28; [2012] 1 A.C. 663; [2011] AACR 38 in relation to England and Wales and *Advocate General for Scotland v Eba* [2011] UKSC 29; [2012] 1 A.C. 710; [2011] AACR 39 in relation to Scotland). In England and Wales, this approach has been incorporated into the Civil Procedure Rules as a condition for the grant of permission to apply for judicial review of a decision of the Upper Tribunal refusing permission to appeal against a decision of the First-tier Tribunal (CPR r.54.7A(7)(b)). The time limit for making such an application for permission is only "16 days after the date on which notice of the Upper Tribunal's decision was sent to the applicant" (*ibid.*, para.(3)). There is no right to renew before the Administrative Court such an application for judicial review where it has been refused on paper without an oral hearing (*ibid.*, para.(8)). On the other hand, if permission is granted, the court will make a final order quashing the refusal of permission without a further hearing, unless a party other than the applicant requests a hearing within 14 days after service of the order granting permission (*ibid.*, para.(9)). If there is such a request, so that the application is challenged, the substantive application is determined applying the well-established grounds for judicial review, without considering again whether the test for the granting of permission is satisfied (*R. (HS) v Upper Tribunal (Immigration and Asylum Chamber)* [2012] EWHC 3126 (Admin)).

It is not always necessary for an applicant to persuade the High Court that the decision of the First-tier Tribunal was wrong in law. However, where the application for judicial review involves a contention that the Upper Tribunal either misunderstood or failed to give effect to the relevant law and the High Court is satisfied, after making full allowance for the expertise of both tribunals, that a ground of appeal to the Upper Tribunal was clearly right, it should say so in order to explain its reasons for finding the Upper Tribunal to have misunderstood or misapplied the law and it does not usurp the Upper Tribunal's function in doing so (*R. (G) v Upper Tribunal* [2016] EWHC 239 (Admin); [2016] 1 W.L.R. 3417).

The approach taken in *Cart* and *Eba* would probably apply also to challenges to decisions excluded under subs.(8)(d), (e) and possibly (f) but it appears to have been conceded by counsel for the Government that no such limitation would apply to challenges to decisions excluded under subs.(8)(a) or (b) (see *Eba*, at [20]).

The test for applying for permission to apply for judicial review being the same as the test for permission to appeal, the approach taken in *PR (Sri Lanka) v Secretary of State for the Home Department* (see the annotation to subss.(6), (6A and (7) above) has been applied in judicial review cases, both in England and Wales (*R. (Khan) v Upper Tribunal (Immigration and Asylum Chamber)* [2011] EWHC 2763 (Admin)) and in Scotland (*Oke, Petitioner* [2012] CSOH 50). However, in *R. (Kuteh) v Upper Tribunal (Administrative Appeals Chamber)* [2012] EWHC 2196 (Admin), the judge 5.76

found there to have been a serious procedural error by the First-tier Tribunal in not having regard to a particular piece of evidence and that the Upper Tribunal, when refusing permission to appeal, had either failed to appreciate that the First-tier Tribunal had not considered the evidence or did not appreciate that its failure to consider the evidence vitiated its decision. The approach of the Upper Tribunal was itself therefore vitiated by a serious procedural irregularity or a failure to apply the rules of natural justice or fairness and, in the unusual circumstances of the case, there was a "compelling reason" to allow the judicial review challenge. Moreover, that finding not only obliged the Upper Tribunal to grant permission to appeal but also obliged it to allow the appeal. This was because it was bound by law to proceed on the footing that the First-tier Tribunal had perpetrated a serious procedural irregularity which was not merely academic or hypothetical, even though the appellant might have been fortunate in the result he had obtained from the High Court (*Kuteh v Secretary of State for Education* [2014] EWCA Civ 1586).

The 16-day time limit in England and Wales expires before the time for applying for a setting aside under r.43 of the Tribunal Procedure (Upper Tribunal) Rules 2008, although promptly pursing an unsuccessful application for setting aside might be considered a ground for extending the time for applying for permission to apply for judicial review in an individual case.

There is a question as to whether there is any right of appeal against such a refusal to set aside a refusal of permission to appeal. In *Samuda v Secretary of State for Work and Pensions* [2014] EWCA Civ 1, a two-judge Court of Appeal sat to consider an application for permission to appeal, presumably with a view to answering that question. Unfortunately, it seems to have understood that, in considering whether to set aside the refusal of permission, the Upper Tribunal was considering whether to review it under s.10. The Court therefore dismissed the application on the ground that there was no power to review an "excluded decision" (see s.10(1)) and that, in any event, any purported refusal to review would itself be an "excluded decision" under s.13(8)(d). However, r.43 is made under a rule-making power that is not related to s.10 and it is suggested that the real question is simply whether s.13(8)(c) is to be construed as extending to any refusal to set aside a refusal of permission to appeal under r.43 (or a refusal to make a correction to a refusal of permission to appeal under r.42) in order to give full effect to the legislature's intention. That remains to be determined on another occasion. However, a narrow view of the exclusion of a right of appeal has been taken in the context of analogous legislation relating to appeals from a county court, under which there was no right of appeal to the Court of Appeal from a decision of a circuit judge refusing permission to appeal to himself from a decision of a district judge. It has been held that that does not preclude an appeal against a decision to strike out an application for permission to appeal to a circuit judge and that, in the circumstances of the case, an order drawn as a dismissal of an application for permission to appeal was in fact a striking out of the application so that an appeal lay to the Court of Appeal (*Patel v Mussa* [2015] EWCA Civ 434; [2015] 1 W.L.R. 4788).

Subsections (11)–(13)

5.77 The Upper Tribunal must specify the relevant appellate court even if it refuses permission to appeal, so that the applicant knows to which court to renew the application. In a social security case, the relevant appellate court will generally be where the claimant lives but there is a considerable element of discretion where there are more than two parties or where the claimant has moved. Relevant considerations are likely to be the convenience of the parties and whether the case raises a point of law where the law may not be the same in all parts of the United Kingdom.

Subsection (14)

5.78 No relevant order has been made but note that s.13 of the Social Security (Recovery of Benefits) Act 1997, s.14 of the Social Security Act 1998 and legislation concerning housing benefit, council tax benefit and child support maintenance (outside the scope of this work) make further provision as to who may appeal to an appellate court under this section.

Subsection (15)

In England and Wales, see C.P.R r.52.2 and PD 52D para.3.3, under which the time limit for filing an appellant's notice is now "within 28 days of the date on which notice of the Upper Tribunal's decision on permission to appeal to the Court of Appeal is sent to the appellant". Before October 1, 2012, the time limit for appeals from the Administrative Appeals Chamber was 42 days, which had always been the time limit for appeals from Social Security Commissioners. It was then surprisingly reduced to 21 days until October 1, 2014, when it was increased to the current 28 days to bring it into line with the time limit for appeals from other chambers. 5.79

Note, however, that from October 3, 2016, the time limit is only 7 days where the application for permission to appeal follows a refusal by the Upper Tribunal to give permission to appeal against a refusal of permission to bring judicial review proceedings and, if permission to appeal was refused by the Upper Tribunal at a hearing (which is rare in the Administrative Appeals Chamber), it runs from the date of the hearing (CPR r.52.9(3)).

Generally, a successful appellant in the Court of Appeal is entitled to recover their costs of the proceedings in the Court of Appeal, even where an appeal is disposed of by consent (*AL (Albania) v Secretary of State for the Home Department* [2012] EWCA Civ 710; [2012] 1 W.L.R. 2898).

Formerly, Chapter 41 of the Rules of the Court of Session made similar provision in Scotland to that made at the time in England and Wales. The time limit remains 42 days in Scotland but Chapter 41 was rewritten with effect from September 27, 2011 without due regard to the practice of the Upper Tribunal of giving its decisions in writing which has the effect that applications for permission are inevitably made on paper some time after the substantive decision is given. Whereas r.41.26(2) provides that an appeal must be lodged within 42 days of a decision granting permission to appeal being intimated to the appellant, r.41.2(4) provides that an application for permission to appeal must be made within 42 days of the date on which the decision appealed against was intimated to the appellant. This means that the time for applying to the court expires before the time for applying to the Upper Tribunal. It is to be hoped there will soon be a further amendment to restore the previous position.

Proceedings on appeal to Court of Appeal etc.

14.—(1) Subsection (2) applies if the relevant appellate court, in deciding an appeal under section 13, finds that the making of the decision concerned involved the making of an error on a point of law. 5.80

(2) The relevant appellate court—

(a) may (but need not) set aside the decision of the Upper Tribunal, and

(b) if it does, must either—

(i) remit the case to the Upper Tribunal or, where the decision of the Upper Tribunal was on an appeal or reference from another tribunal or some other person, to the Upper Tribunal or that other tribunal or person, with directions for its reconsideration, or

(ii) re-make the decision.

(3) In acting under subsection (2)(b)(i), the relevant appellate court may also—

(a) direct that the persons who are chosen to reconsider the case are not to be the same as those who—

(i) where the case is remitted to the Upper Tribunal, made the decision of the Upper Tribunal that has been set aside, or

(ii) where the case is remitted to another tribunal or person, made the decision in respect of which the appeal or reference to the Upper Tribunal was made;

(b) give procedural directions in connection with the reconsideration of the case by the Upper Tribunal or other tribunal or person.

(4) In acting under subsection (2)(b)(ii), the relevant appellate court—

(a) may make any decision which the Upper Tribunal could make if the Upper Tribunal were re-making the decision or (as the case may be) which the other tribunal or person could make if that other tribunal or person were re-making the decision, and

(b) may make such findings of fact as it considers appropriate.

(5) Where—

(a) under subsection (2)(b)(i) the relevant appellate court remits a case to the Upper Tribunal, and

(b) the decision set aside under subsection (2)(a) was made by the Upper Tribunal on an appeal or reference from another tribunal or some other person,

the Upper Tribunal may (instead of reconsidering the case itself) remit the case to that other tribunal or person, with the directions given by the relevant appellate court for its reconsideration.

(6) In acting under subsection (5), the Upper Tribunal may also—

(a) direct that the persons who are chosen to reconsider the case are not to be the same as those who made the decision in respect of which the appeal or reference to the Upper Tribunal was made;

(b) give procedural directions in connection with the reconsideration of the case by the other tribunal or person.

(7) In this section "the relevant appellate court", as respects an appeal under section 13, means the court specified as respects that appeal by the Upper Tribunal under section 13(11).

GENERAL NOTE

5.81 The Court of Appeal is a creature of statute and has only the powers conferred upon it by legislation. On an appeal from the Upper Tribunal, it has all the powers of the Upper Tribunal (Senior Courts Act s.15(3) and also CPR r.52.20) and also the powers conferred by this section. However, it does not have a power to make a declaration unless the Upper Tribunal had such a power, which it would in judicial review proceedings but not when hearing an appeal from the First-tier Tribunal. However, it has a power to grant a declaration of incompatibility under s.4 of the Human Rights Act 1998 if it determines that a provision of primary legislation is incompatible with a Convention right. In *Humphries v Revenue and Customs Commissioners* [2012] UKSC 18; [2012] 1 W.L.R. 1545; [2012] AACR 46, Baroness Hale of Richmond JSC observed (at [34]) that it was not obvious how a remedy could be provided on a statutory appeal if it was held that a provision in subordinate legislation should be disapplied because it was inconsistent with the European Convention on Human Rights but it was then necessary to read in an alternative provision in order to overcome the effect of primary legislation that was not in itself incompatible with a Convention right. This highlights a difficulty with the reasoning in *Francis v Secretary of State for Work and Pensions* [2005] EWCA Civ 1303 (also reported as *R(IS) 6/06*), in which the Court of Appeal declined to read additional words into a regulation and instead asserted a power to make a declaration (*not* a declaration of incompatibility), perhaps forgetting that the proceedings before it had not been brought by way of an application for judicial review. In that case, the Court of Appeal might perhaps have chosen to disapply the word "only" in the regulation in order to achieve the desired effect. However, no such "blue pencil" approach was possible in *Burnip v Birmingham CC* [2012] EWCA Civ 629, reported as [2013] AACR 7, decided the day before *Humphries*, in which the Court followed *Francis* in granting a declaration. Perhaps the Court of Appeal could constitute itself as the High Court for the purposes of making a declaration. In any event, the Court of Appeal will soon be able to consider this issue further, because the Secretary of State has been given permission to appeal from the decision of the Upper Tribunal in *SSWP v Carmichael (HB)* [2017] UKUT 174 (AAC), where it held that, in the light of *Mathieson v Secretary of State for Work and Pensions* [2015] UKSC 47; [2015] 1 W.L.R. 3250; [2015] AACR 44, a tribunal could direct that benefit be awarded on a basis that it was satisfied was compatible with the Convention where secondary legislation could not be read compatibly with the Convention but was not mandated by primary legislation. Different considerations may apply in the Court of Session.

It was made plain in *McAllister v Secretary of State for Work and Pensions,* 2003 S.L.T. 1195 that, before allowing an appeal against a decision of a person or body exercising statutory powers, the Court of Session in Scotland requires to be satisfied that there are proper grounds for doing so. Therefore, a written argument must be submitted, on the basis of which the Court will decide whether the case should be listed for hearing. In England and Wales, the Court of Appeal readily allows appeals by consent, without considering their merits but usually only if satisfied that the parties' consent to allow the appeal is based on apparently competent legal advice and if the parties have advanced plausible reasons to show that the decision of the lower court was wrong. It would not generally do so if, for instance, it was aware that the decision of the lower court had been reported and was causing difficulties. See *Rochdale MBC v KW (No.2)* [2015] EWCA Civ 1054; [2016] 1 W.L.R. 198, where it was held that a judge of the Court of Protection had been bound by a consent order of the Court of Appeal and it was futile and inappropriate for him to seek to undermine it by complaining that it was ultra vires or wrong for any other reason. There have been a number of instances where decisions of Commissioners or the Upper Tribunal have been set aside by the Court of Appeal without the Court considering the merits of the appeal. Although such a decision given by the Court of Appeal is not binding on anyone other than for the purposes of that particular case (*R(FC) 1/97*), it can create difficulties because the decision that has been set aside plainly cannot be regarded as binding either, although the reasoning may still be regarded as persuasive. The law is thus left uncertain.

[1 Appeal to Supreme Court: grant of certificate by Upper Tribunal

14A.—(1) If the Upper Tribunal is satisfied that— 5.82

(a) the conditions in subsection (4) or (5) are fulfilled in relation to the Upper Tribunal's decision in any proceedings, and

(b) as regards that decision, a sufficient case for an appeal to the Supreme Court has been made out to justify an application under section 14B,

the Upper Tribunal may grant a certificate to that effect.

(2) The Upper Tribunal may grant a certificate under this section only on an application made by a party to the proceedings.

(3) The Upper Tribunal may grant a certificate under this section only if the relevant appellate court as regards the proceedings is—

(a) the Court of Appeal in England and Wales, or

(b) the Court of Appeal in Northern Ireland.

(4) The conditions in this subsection are that a point of law of general public importance is involved in the decision of the Upper Tribunal and that point of law is—

(a) a point of law that—

(i) relates wholly or mainly to the construction of an enactment or statutory instrument, and
(ii) has been fully argued in the proceedings and fully considered in the judgment of the Upper Tribunal in the proceedings, or

(b) a point of law—
(i) in respect of which the Upper Tribunal is bound by a decision of the relevant appellate court or the Supreme Court in previous proceedings, and
(ii) that was fully considered in the judgments given by the relevant appellate court or, as the case may be, the Supreme Court in those previous proceedings.

(5) The conditions in this subsection are that a point of law of general public importance is involved in the decision of the Upper Tribunal and that—

(a) the proceedings entail a decision relating to a matter of national importance or consideration of such a matter,
(b) the result of the proceedings is so significant (whether considered on its own or together with other proceedings or likely proceedings) that, in the opinion of the Upper Tribunal, a hearing by the Supreme Court is justified, or
(c) the Upper Tribunal is satisfied that the benefits of earlier consideration by the Supreme Court outweigh the benefits of consideration by the Court of Appeal.

(6) Before the Upper Tribunal decides an application made to it under this section, the Upper Tribunal must specify the court that would be the relevant appellate court if the application were an application for permission (or leave) under section 13.

(7) In this section except subsection (6) and in sections 14B and 14C, "the relevant appellate court", as respects an application, means the court specified as respects that application by the Upper Tribunal under subsection (6).

(8) No appeal lies against the grant or refusal of a certificate under subsection (1).]

AMENDMENT

1. Criminal Justice and Courts Act 2015 s.64 (August 8, 2016).

GENERAL NOTE

5.83 Sections 14A to 14C provide for "leapfrog" appeals straight to the Supreme Court from the Upper Tribunal, thus putting the Upper Tribunal in the same position as the High Court (see ss.12 to 16 of the Administration of Justice Act 1969). Note that, by virtue of s.14A(3), the new sections do not apply if the relevant appellate court would be the Court of Session in Scotland. Section 14C excludes the operation of s.14A in certain types of case.

The circumstances in which the Upper Tribunal might issue a certificate under s.14A will be very rare, particularly where only the conditions of s.14A(4)(a) are satisfied. Note that even where a certificate is issued, the Upper Tribunal may not itself give permission to appeal to the Supreme Court. If the Supreme Court refuses permission, the would-be appellant may appeal to the Court of Appeal. Section 14C(3) provides that a certificate may not be issued under s.14A unless the Upper Tribunal would have given permission to appeal to the Court of Appeal but it does not expressly provide that a certificate is to be taken as the grant of such permission in the event of the Supreme Court refusing permission to appeal to that court.

[1 Appeal to Supreme Court: permission to appeal

14B.—(1) If the Upper Tribunal grants a certificate under section 14A in relation to any proceedings, a party to those proceedings may apply to the Supreme Court for permission to appeal directly to the Supreme Court. 5.84

(2) An application under subsection (1) must be made—

(a) within one month from the date on which that certificate is granted, or

(b) within such time as the Supreme Court may allow in a particular case.

(3) If on such an application it appears to the Supreme Court to be expedient to do so, the Supreme Court may grant permission for such an appeal.

(4) If permission is granted under this section—

(a) no appeal from the decision to which the certificate relates lies to the relevant appellate court, but

(b) an appeal lies from that decision to the Supreme Court.

(5) An application under subsection (1) is to be determined without a hearing.

(6) Subject to subsection (4), no appeal lies to the relevant appellate court from a decision of the Upper Tribunal in respect of which a certificate is granted under section 14A until—

(a) the time within which an application can be made under subsection (1) has expired, and

(b) where such an application is made, that application has been determined in accordance with this section.]

AMENDMENT

1. Criminal Justice and Courts Act 2015 s.64 (August 8, 2016).

[1 Appeal to Supreme Court: exclusions

14C.—(1) No certificate may be granted under section 14A in respect of a decision of the Upper Tribunal in any proceedings where, by virtue of any enactment (other than sections 14A and 14B), no appeal would lie from that decision of the Upper Tribunal to the relevant appellate court, with or without the permission (or leave) of the Upper Tribunal or the relevant appellate court. 5.85

(2) No certificate may be granted under section 14A in respect of a decision of the Upper Tribunal in any proceedings where, by virtue of any enactment, no appeal would lie from a decision of the relevant appellate court on that decision of the Upper Tribunal to the Supreme Court, with or without the permission (or leave) of the relevant appellate court or the Supreme Court.

(3) Where no appeal would lie to the relevant appellate court from the decision of the Upper Tribunal except with the permission (or leave) of the Upper Tribunal or the relevant appellate court, no certificate may be granted under section 14A in respect of a decision of the Upper Tribunal unless it appears to the Upper Tribunal that it would be a proper case for giving permission (or leave) to appeal to the relevant appellate court.

(4) No certificate may be granted under section 14A in respect of a decision or order of the Upper Tribunal made by it in the exercise of its jurisdiction to punish for contempt.]

AMENDMENT

1. Criminal Justice and Courts Act 2015 s.64 (August 8, 2016).

"Judicial review"

Upper Tribunal's "judicial review" jurisdiction

5.86 **15.**—(1) The Upper Tribunal has power, in cases arising under the law of England and Wales or under the law of Northern Ireland, to grant the following kinds of relief—

(a) a mandatory order;
(b) a prohibiting order;
(c) a quashing order;
(d) a declaration;
(e) an injunction.

(2) The power under subsection (1) may be exercised by the Upper Tribunal if—

(a) certain conditions are met (see section 18), or
(b) the tribunal is authorised to proceed even though not all of those conditions are met (see section 19(3) and (4)).

(3) Relief under subsection (1) granted by the Upper Tribunal—

(a) has the same effect as the corresponding relief granted by the High Court on an application for judicial review, and
(b) is enforceable as if it were relief granted by the High Court on an application for judicial review.

(4) In deciding whether to grant relief under subsection (1)(a), (b) or (c), the Upper Tribunal must apply the principles that the High Court would apply in deciding whether to grant that relief on an application for judicial review.

(5) In deciding whether to grant relief under subsection (1)(d) or (e), the Upper Tribunal must—

(a) in cases arising under the law of England and Wales apply the principles that the High Court would apply in deciding whether to grant that relief under section 31(2) of the Supreme Court Act 1981 on an application for judicial review, and
(b) in cases arising under the law of Northern Ireland apply the principles that the High Court would apply in deciding whether to grant that relief on an application for judicial review.

[[1] (5A) In cases arising under the law of England and Wales, subsections (2A) and (2B) of section 31 of the Senior Courts Act 1981 apply to the Upper Tribunal when deciding whether to grant relief under subsection (1) as they apply to the High Court when deciding whether to grant relief on an application for judicial review.

(5B) If the tribunal grants relief in reliance on section 31(2B) of the Senior Courts Act 1981 as applied by subsection (5A), the tribunal must certify that the condition in section 31(2B) as so applied is satisfied.]

(6) For the purposes of the application of subsection (3)(a) in relation to cases arising under the law of Northern Ireland—

(a) a mandatory order under subsection (1)(a) shall be taken to correspond to an order of mandamus,

(b) a prohibiting order under subsection (1)(b) shall be taken to correspond to an order of prohibition, and
(c) a quashing order under subsection (1)(c) shall be taken to correspond to an order of certiorari.

AMENDMENT

1. Criminal Justice and Courts Act 2015 s.84(4) (August 8, 2016).

GENERAL NOTE

Subsections (1) to (5)

Sections 15 to 21 introduce the novel concept of a tribunal exercising "judicial review" powers. The provisions are set out in this work because "judicial review" proceedings in relation to the First-tier Tribunal (and perhaps some other "judicial review" proceedings in the social security sphere) are likely to find their way to the Upper Tribunal. **5.87**

Section 18(6) enables the Lord Chief Justice of England and Wales or the Lord Chief Justice of Northern Ireland to issue a Practice Direction having the effect that cases falling within a specified class will be within the jurisdiction of the Upper Tribunal subject to the other conditions mentioned in s.18 being met. Such cases must be started by making an application for "judicial review" directly to the Upper Tribunal under s.16. If an application is made to the court in such a case, the court will be bound to transfer the case to the Upper Tribunal under s.31A of the Supreme Court Act 1981 or s.25A of the Judicature (Northern Ireland) Act 1978, as the case may be, both those provisions having been inserted into the relevant Acts by s.19 of this Act. Those provisions also permit any case that does not fall within a class specified in a Practice Direction but where other conditions are satisfied to be transferred to the Upper Tribunal on a case-by-case basis. Relevant considerations will include the expertise of the Upper Tribunal in those areas in which it exercises an appellate jurisdiction (including social security law), which might point towards a transfer, and the role and standing of the High Court, which might suggest refusing a transfer in a particularly novel, complex or important case. It is always possible for the High Court to transfer a case with a recommendation that it be heard in the Upper Tribunal by a High Court judge, so as to achieve "the best of both worlds", but, even when a High Court judge is sitting, the Upper Tribunal has no power to make a declaration of incompatibility under s.4 of the Human Rights Act 1998. Another consideration that may be particularly relevant where there is an unrepresented litigant, is the less formal procedure in the Upper Tribunal which permits, for instance, a decision to be made without a hearing. If a case that is not within a specified class is started in the Upper Tribunal in error, the Upper Tribunal must transfer it to the High Court in England and Wales (i.e. the Administrative Court) or the High Court in Northern Ireland, as the case requires, under s.18(3).

By virtue of ss.20 and 21, the position in Scotland is similar, the main difference being that cases cannot be started in the Upper Tribunal.

The main difference between "judicial review" proceedings seeking a "quashing order" or its equivalent in respect of a tribunal decision and an appeal is that the tribunal that made the decision will itself be the respondent in "judicial review" proceedings, although it will seldom take an active part and will usually leave any application to be contested by the "interested party" (who would be the respondent in an appeal). However, another major difference is that, in judicial review proceedings, the Upper Tribunal has a far more limited power to give a final decision rather than remitting the case to the lower tribunal (compare ss.12 and 17). An application for a "mandatory order" or its equivalent might be sought if it was claimed that a tribunal had failed or refused to make a decision and a "prohibiting order" or its equivalent might be sought if it was desired to prevent a tribunal from making a decision.

Subsections (5A) and (5B)

5.88 These subsections do not apply in relation to any case where the application for relief was received by the Upper Tribunal before August 8, 2016 (Criminal Justice and Courts Act 2015 (Commencement No. 4 and Transitional Provisions) Order 2016 (SI 2016/717) art.6).

Nor do they apply to cases where the law of Northern Ireland applies. Perhaps unnecessarily, s.16(3C) to (3F) makes equivalent provision in relation to applications for permission to bring judicial review proceedings in cases under the law of England and Wales.

Subsections (2A) and (2B) were inserted into s.31 of the Senior Courts Act 1981 with effect from April 13, 2015 by s.84(1) of the same Act as inserted subss.(5A) and (5B) into this section and they provide:

"(2A) The High Court—

(a) must refuse to grant relief on an application for judicial review, and

(b) may not make an award under subsection (4) on such an application,

if it appears to the court to be highly likely that the outcome for the applicant would not have been substantially different if the conduct complained of had not occurred.

(2B) The court may disregard the requirements in subsection (2A)(a) and (b) if it considers that it is appropriate to do so for reasons of exceptional public interest."

The reference to "subsection (4)" in s.31(2A)(b) is to the High Court's power to award "damages, restitution or the recovery of a sum due". See s.16(6) of the 2007 Act for the Upper Tribunal's equivalent power and s.16(6A) for provision equivalent to s.31(2A)(b) of the 1981 Act.

Before all these amendments, the High Court and Upper Tribunal generally exercised its discretion to withhold judicial review if satisfied that an error of law had not made a difference to the outcome. However, apart from the fact that s.16(3C)(b) makes it mandatory for the Upper Tribunal to consider the issue where the respondent asks it to do so on an application for permission, the new statutory test is expressed in terms of it being "highly likely" that the outcome would have been "substantially" different. If this is to be a more rigorous test than they previously applied, it will also be more difficult in many cases. As Blake J said in *R. (Logan) v London Borough of Havering* [2015] EWHC 3193 (Admin) at [59]:

> "In the absence of clear pointers at the time that the flaw was a technical one that made no difference, the court will inevitably be drawn into some degree of speculation or second guessing the decision of the public authority that has the institutional competence to make it."

There is also the question of the extent to which, if the respondent tells the Upper Tribunal that it would have made the same decision irrespective of the claimed error, the Upper Tribunal is entitled to go behind that submission. However, this question will hardly ever arise in practice in the Administrative Appeals Chamber because the respondent in most cases before that Chamber of the Upper Tribunal is the First-tier Tribunal, which seldom takes any part in the proceedings. This, of course, makes s.16(3C)(b) of limited effect too, although if any interested party argues that the claimed error of law would not have made any difference to the outcome the Upper Tribunal would anyway be bound to address the contention in pursuance of its duty to give reasons for its decision.

Application for relief under section 15(1)

5.89 **16.**—(1) This section applies in relation to an application to the Upper Tribunal for relief under section 15(1).

(2) The application may be made only if permission (or, in a case arising under the law of Northern Ireland, leave) to make it has been obtained from the tribunal.

(3) The tribunal may not grant permission (or leave) to make the application unless it considers that the applicant has a sufficient interest in the matter to which the application relates.

(3A) *Not yet in force.*

(3B) *Not yet in force.*

[1 (3C) In cases arising under the law of England and Wales, when considering whether to grant permission to make the application, the tribunal—

(a) may of its own initiative consider whether the outcome for the applicant would have been substantially different if the conduct complained of had not occurred, and

(b) must consider that question if the respondent asks it to do so.

(3D) In subsection (3C) "the conduct complained of" means the conduct (or alleged conduct) of the respondent that the applicant claims justifies the tribunal in granting relief.

(3E) If, on considering the question mentioned in subsection (3C)(a) and (b), it appears to the tribunal to be highly likely that the outcome for the applicant would not have been substantially different, the tribunal must refuse to grant permission.

(3F) The tribunal may disregard the requirement in subsection (3E) if it considers that it is appropriate to do so for reasons of exceptional public interest.

(3G) If the tribunal grants permission in reliance on subsection (3F), the tribunal must certify that the condition in subsection (3F) is satisfied.]

(4) Subsection (5) applies where the tribunal considers—

(a) that there has been undue delay in making the application, and

(b) that granting the relief sought on the application would be likely to cause substantial hardship to, or substantially prejudice the rights of, any person or would be detrimental to good administration.

(5) The tribunal may—

(a) refuse to grant permission (or leave) for the making of the application;

(b) refuse to grant any relief sought on the application.

(6) The tribunal may award to the applicant damages, restitution or the recovery of a sum due if—

(a) the application includes a claim for such an award arising from any matter to which the application relates, and

(b) the tribunal is satisfied that such an award would have been made by the High Court if the claim had been made in an action begun in the High Court by the applicant at the time of making the application.

[1 (6A) In cases arising under the law of England and Wales, subsections (2A) and (2B) of section 31 of the Senior Courts Act 1981 apply to the Upper Tribunal as regards the making of an award under subsection (6) as they apply to the High Court as regards the making of an award under section 31(4) of the Senior Courts Act 1981.

(6B) If the tribunal makes an award in reliance on section 31(2B) of the Senior Courts Act 1981 as applied by subsection (6A), the tribunal must certify that the condition in section 31(2B) as so applied is satisfied.]

(7) An award under subsection (6) may be enforced as if it were an award of the High Court.

(8) Where—

(a) the tribunal refuses to grant permission (or leave) to apply for relief under section 15(1),

(b) the applicant appeals against that refusal, and
(c) the Court of Appeal grants the permission (or leave),

the Court of Appeal may go on to decide the application for relief under section 15(1).

(9) Subsections (4) and (5) do not prevent Tribunal Procedure Rules from limiting the time within which applications may be made.

AMENDMENT

1. Criminal Justice and Courts Act 2015 s.84(5) and (6) (August 8, 2016).

GENERAL NOTE

5.90 See the annotation to s.15.

For the procedure for applying to the Upper Tribunal for judicial review, see rr.27–33A of the Tribunal Procedure (Upper Tribunal) Rules 2008. Those rules also apply to cases transferred to the Upper Tribunal under s.31A of the Supreme Court Act 1981 s.25A of the Judicature (Northern Ireland) Act 1978 or s.20 of this Act.

Quashing orders under section 15(1): supplementary provision

5.91 **17.**—(1) If the Upper Tribunal makes a quashing order under section 15(1)(c) in respect of a decision, it may in addition—

(a) remit the matter concerned to the court, tribunal or authority that made the decision, with a direction to reconsider the matter and reach a decision in accordance with the findings of the Upper Tribunal, or
(b) substitute its own decision for the decision in question.

(2) The power conferred by subsection (1)(b) is exercisable only if—

(a) the decision in question was made by a court or tribunal,
(b) the decision is quashed on the ground that there has been an error of law, and
(c) without the error, there would have been only one decision that the court or tribunal could have reached.

(3) Unless the Upper Tribunal otherwise directs, a decision substituted by it under subsection (1)(b) has effect as if it were a decision of the relevant court or tribunal.

GENERAL NOTE

5.92 Note that the Upper Tribunal has a far more limited power under s.17(1)(b) to substitute a decision for a decision quashed in judicial review proceedings than it does under s.12(2)(b)(ii) to re-make a decision set aside on an appeal. Compare s.12(4) with s.17(2)(c).

Limits of jurisdiction under section 15(1)

5.93 **18.**—(1) This section applies where an application made to the Upper Tribunal seeks (whether or not alone)—

(a) relief under section 15(1), or
(b) permission (or, in a case arising under the law of Northern Ireland, leave) to apply for relief under section 15(1).

(2) If Conditions 1 to 4 are met, the tribunal has the function of deciding the application.

(3) If the tribunal does not have the function of deciding the application, it must by order transfer the application to the High Court.

(4) Condition 1 is that the application does not seek anything other than—

(a) relief under section 15(1);

(b) permission (or, in a case arising under the law of Northern Ireland, leave) to apply for relief under section 15(1);

(c) an award under section 16(6);

(d) interest;

(e) costs.

(5) Condition 2 is that the application does not call into question anything done by the Crown Court.

(6) Condition 3 is that the application falls within a class specified for the purposes of this subsection in a direction given in accordance with Part 1 of Schedule 2 to the Constitutional Reform Act 2005.

(7) The power to give directions under subsection (6) includes—

(a) power to vary or revoke directions made in exercise of the power, and

(b) power to make different provision for different purposes.

(8) Condition 4 is that the judge presiding at the hearing of the application is either—

(a) a judge of the High Court or the Court of Appeal in England and Wales or Northern Ireland, or a judge of the Court of Session, or

(b) such other persons as may be agreed from time to time between the Lord Chief Justice, the Lord President, or the Lord Chief Justice of Northern Ireland, as the case may be, and the Senior President of Tribunals.

(9) Where the application is transferred to the High Court under subsection (3)—

(a) the application is to be treated for all purposes as if it—

(i) had been made to the High Court, and

(ii) sought things corresponding to those sought from the tribunal, and

(b) any steps taken, permission (or leave) given or orders made by the tribunal in relation to the application are to be treated as taken, given or made by the High Court.

(10) Rules of court may make provision for the purpose of supplementing subsection (9).

(11) The provision that may be made by Tribunal Procedure Rules about amendment of an application for relief under section 15(1) includes, in particular, provision about amendments that would cause the application to become transferrable under subsection (3).

(12) For the purposes of subsection (9)(a)(ii), in relation to an application transferred to the High Court in Northern Ireland—

(a) an order of mandamus shall be taken to correspond to a mandatory order under section 15(1)(a),

(b) an order of prohibition shall be taken to correspond to a prohibiting order under section 15(1)(b), and

(c) an order of certiorari shall be taken to correspond to a quashing order under section 15(1)(c).

GENERAL NOTE

Subsection (6)

The Lord Chief Justice of England and Wales has issued *Practice Direction (Upper Tribunal: Judicial Review Jurisdiction)* [2009] 1 W.L.R. 327 specifying the following classes of case: **5.94** "(a) Any decision of the First-tier Tribunal on an appeal made in the exercise of a right conferred by the Criminal Injuries Compensation Scheme in compliance with section 5(1) of the Criminal Injuries Compensation Act 1995 (appeals against decisions on review) and

(b) Any decision of the First-tier Tribunal (other than its Immigration and Asylum Chamber) made under Tribunal Procedure Rules or section 9 of the 2007 Act where there is no right of appeal to the Upper Tribunal and that decision is not an excluded decision within paragraph (b), (c), or (f) of section 11(5) of the 2007 Act."

The Practice Direction does not apply where the applicant seeks a declaration of incompatibility under s.4 of the Human Rights Act 1998.

The words in parenthesis in para.(b) were added by another Practice Direction, dated August 21, 2013, which deals comprehensively with judicial review in the Immigration and Asylum Chamber of the Upper Tribunal.

The effect of *LS v LB Lambeth (HB)* [2010] UKUT 461 (AAC); [2011] AACR 27, in which it was held that an appeal lies against all decisions of the First-tier Tribunal that are not "excluded decisions", appears at first sight to be to limit the scope of para.(b) of the Practice Direction to challenges to decisions excluded from the right of appeal by virtue of s.11(5)(d) and, if it has any practical effect, by s.11(5)(e). However, note that the equivalent provision in Scotland has been interpreted so as to include challenges to procedural omissions as well as to procedural decisions (see the note to s.20(3)).

In practice, the overwhelming majority of judicial review cases brought in the Administrative Appeals Chamber of the Upper Tribunal have been criminal injuries compensation cases within the scope of para.(a) of the Practice Direction. However, applications for judicial review of decisions of the Social Entitlement Chamber of the First-tier Tribunal that fall within the scope of para.(b) are also heard in the Administrative Appeals Chamber of the Upper Tribunal (see art.10(b) of the First-tier Tribunal and Upper Tribunal (Chambers) Order 2010).

Subsection (11)

5.95 See r.33A of the Tribunal Procedure (Upper Tribunal) Rules 2008.

Transfer of judicial review applications from High Court

5.96 **19.**—(1) *Omitted.*

(2) *Omitted.*

(3) Where an application is transferred to the Upper Tribunal under 31A of the Supreme Court Act 1981 or section 25A of the Judicature (Northern Ireland) Act 1978 (transfer from the High Court of judicial review applications)—

(a) the application is to be treated for all purposes as if it—

(i) had been made to the tribunal, and

(ii) sought things corresponding to those sought from the High Court,

(b) the tribunal has the function of deciding the application, even if it does not fall within a class specified under section 18(6), and

(c) any steps taken, permission given, leave given or orders made by the High Court in relation to the application are to be treated as taken, given or made by the tribunal.

(4) Where—

(a) an application for permission is transferred to the Upper Tribunal under section 31A of the Supreme Court Act 1981 (c. 54) and the tribunal grants permission, or

(b) an application for leave is transferred to the Upper Tribunal under section 25A of the Judicature (Northern Ireland) Act 1978 (c. 23) and the tribunal grants leave, the tribunal has the function of deciding any subsequent application brought under the permission or leave, even if the subsequent application does not fall within a class specified under section 18(6).

(5) Tribunal Procedure Rules may make further provision for the purposes of supplementing subsections (3) and (4).

(6) For the purposes of subsection (3)(a)(ii), in relation to an application transferred to the Upper Tribunal under section 25A of the Judicature (Northern Ireland) Act 1978—

(a) a mandatory order under section 15(1)(a) shall be taken to correspond to an order of mandamus,

(b) a prohibiting order under section 15(1)(b) shall be taken to correspond to an order of prohibition, and

(c) a quashing order under section 15(1)(c) shall be taken to correspond to an order of certiorari.

GENERAL NOTE

Subsections (1) and (2) inserted the sections mentioned in subs.(3) into the 1981 and 1978 Acts respectively. Those provisions effectively require the High Court to transfer cases falling within Conditions 1, 2 and 3 of s.18 to the Upper Tribunal and, as amended, permit the transfer of other cases provided they fall within Conditions 1 and 2 of those conditions. See the note to s.15. For Tribunal Procedure Rules made under subs.(5), see rr.27(1) and (2) and 33A(3) of the Tribunal Procedure (Upper Tribunal) Rules 2008. **5.97**

Transfer of judicial review applications from the Court of Session

20.—(1) Where an application is made to the supervisory jurisdiction of the Court of Session, the Court— **5.98**

(a) must, if Conditions 1 [2 and 2 are met, and]

[1 (aa) [2 . . .]]

(b) may, if Conditions 1 [2 and 3] are met, but Condition 2 is not, by order transfer the application to the Upper Tribunal.

(2) Condition 1 is that the application does not seek anything other than an exercise of the supervisory jurisdiction of the Court of Session.

(3) Condition 2 is that the application falls within a class specified for the purposes of this subsection by act of sederunt made with the consent of the Lord Chancellor.

(4) Condition 3 is that the subject matter of the application is not a devolved Scottish matter.

(5) [2 . . .]

[1 (5A) [2 . . .]]

(6) There may not be specified under subsection (3) any class of application which includes an application the subject matter of which is a devolved Scottish matter.

(7) For the purposes of this section, the subject matter of an application is a devolved Scottish matter if it—

(a) concerns the exercise of functions in or as regards Scotland, and

(b) does not relate to a reserved matter within the meaning of the Scotland Act 1998.

(8) In subsection (2), the reference to the exercise of the supervisory jurisdiction of the Court of Session includes a reference to the making of any order in connection with or in consequence of the exercise of that jurisdiction.

AMENDMENTS

1. Borders, Citizenship and Immigration Act 2009 s.53 (August 8, 2011).
2. Crime and Courts Act 2013 s.22(2) (November 1, 2013).

GENERAL NOTE

Subsection (1)

5.99 For the procedure for transfer, see R.C. r.58.7A in relation to mandatory transfers under s.20(1)(a) and r.58(11) in relation to discretionary transfers under s.20(1)(b).

Subsection (3)

5.100 Cases within a class specified under this subsection must be transferred to the Upper Tribunal under s.20(1)(a) if the other condition is satisfied. The Act of Sederunt (Transfer of Judicial Review Applications from the Court of Session) 2008 (SSI 2008/357) specifies "an application which challenges a procedural decision or a procedural ruling of the First-tier Tribunal, established under section 3(1) of the Tribunals, Courts and Enforcement Act 2007". The effect of *LS v LB Lambeth (HB)* [2010] UKUT 461 (AAC); [2011] AACR 27, in which it was held that an appeal lies against all decisions of the First-tier Tribunal that are not "excluded decisions", appears at first sight to be to limit the scope of the act of sederunt to challenges to decisions excluded from the right of appeal by virtue of s.11(5)(d) and, if it has any practical effect, by s.11(5)(e). However, in *Currie, Petitioner* [2009] CSOH 145; [2010] AACR 8, Lord Hodge interpreted the act of sederunt as extending to procedural omissions or oversights giving rise to unfairness. On the other hand, he said that an application that challenged not only such procedural decisions but also errors of law that were not of a procedural nature did not fall within the terms of the act of sederunt.

Note that criminal injuries compensation cases, which are specified in the practice direction made in England and Wales under s.18(6), are not specified in the act of sederunt in Scotland. Not only are such cases therefore not subject to a mandatory transfer from the Court of Session, they cannot even be transferred on a discretionary basis because criminal injuries compensation is a "devolved Scottish matter" so that "Condition (3)" identified in s.20(4) is not satisfied (*Currie, Petitioner*, above). However, as "Condition 3" need not be met as a condition for a mandatory transfer, there is nothing specific in this Act that would prevent an act of sederunt being made to enable criminal injuries compensation cases to be transferred on a mandatory basis if the other conditions were satisfied.

Note also that even cases within a specified class must be started in the Court of Session because, in relation to Scotland, s.20 does not admit to the possibility of cases being started in the Upper Tribunal as is done in ss.15 and 16 (see, in particular, s.16(1)). In *EF v SSWP* [2009] UKUT 92 (AAC) (reported as *R (IB) 3/09*), an application for judicial review made to the Upper Tribunal in Scotland was therefore held to be incompetent.

The Court of Session and the Upper Tribunal may have overlapping jurisdiction in criminal injuries compensation cases having both an English dimension and a Scottish one and a decision has to be made as to where it is more appropriate for a case to be heard, having regard to the facts of the case and its procedural history. In *MB v First-tier Tribunal (CIC)* [2012] UKUT 286 (AAC); [2013] AACR 10 and *NF v First-tier Tribunal (CIC)* [2012] UKUT 287 (AAC); [2013] AACR 11, a three-judge panel considered two cases in both of which the claimant lived in Scotland but the decision being challenged had been made on the papers in England. In the first case, the crime causing injury had been committed in England and, in the second case it had been committed in Scotland. It was held that the Upper Tribunal had jurisdiction in the first case and proceedings were stayed in the second case while the applicant made an application to the Court of Session.

[1 Procedural steps where application transferred

20A.—(1) This section applies where the Court of Session transfers an application under section 20(1). 5.101

(2) It is for the Upper Tribunal to determine—

(a) whether the application has been made timeously, and

(b) whether to grant permission for the application to proceed under section 27B of the Court of Session Act 1988 ("the 1988 Act") (requirement for permission).

(3) Accordingly—

(a) the Upper Tribunal has the same powers in relation to the application as the Court of Session would have had in relation to it under sections 27A to 27C of the 1988 Act,

(b) sections 27C and 27D of that Act apply in relation to a decision of the Upper Tribunal under section 27B(1) of that Act as they apply in relation to such a decision of the Court of Session.

(4) The references in section 27C(3) and (4) of the 1988 Act (oral hearings where permission refused) to a different Lord Ordinary from the one who granted or refused permission are to be read as references to different members of the Tribunal from those of whom it was composed when it refused or granted permission.]

AMENDMENT

1. Courts Reform (Scotland) Act 2014 (Consequential Provisions and Modifications) Order 2015 (SI 2015/700) art.7 (September 22, 2015).

GENERAL NOTE

This section was inserted in consequence of the coming into force of s.89 of the Courts Reform (Scotland) Act 2014 (an Act of the Scottish Parliament), which inserted ss.27A to 27D into the Court of Session Act 1988 and so introduced a requirement that applicants for judicial review in Scotland obtain permission, as in England and Wales. The procedure under ss.27A to 27D, as applied to the Upper Tribunal by this section, is similar to the procedure in the Upper Tribunal in England and Wales, but is not identical. Those sections provide – 5.102

> **"Time limits**
>
> **27A.**—(1) An application to the supervisory jurisdiction of the Court must be made before the end of—
>
> (a) the period of 3 months beginning with the date on which the grounds giving rise to the application first arise, or
>
> (b) such longer period as the Court considers equitable having regard to all the circumstances.
>
> (2) Subsection (1) does not apply to an application to the supervisory jurisdiction of the Court which, by virtue of any enactment, is to be made before the end of a period ending before the period of 3 months mentioned in that subsection (however that first-ending period may be expressed).
>
> **Requirement for permission**
>
> **27B.**—(1) No proceedings may be taken in respect of an application to the supervisory jurisdiction of the Court unless the Court has granted permission for the application to proceed.

(2) Subject to subsection (3), the Court may grant permission under subsection (1) for an application to proceed only if it is satisfied that—

(a) the applicant can demonstrate a sufficient interest in the subject matter of the application, and

(b) the application has a real prospect of success.

(3) Where the application relates to a decision of the Upper Tribunal for Scotland in an appeal from the First-tier Tribunal for Scotland under section 46 of the Tribunals (Scotland) Act 2014, the Court may grant permission under subsection (1) for the application to proceed only if it is satisfied that—

(a) the applicant can demonstrate a sufficient interest in the subject matter of the application,

(b) the application has a real prospect of success, and

(c) either—

(i) the application would raise an important point of principle or practice, or

(ii) there is some other compelling reason for allowing the application to proceed.

(4) The Court may grant permission under subsection (1) for an application to proceed—

(a) subject to such conditions as the Court thinks fit,

(b) only on such of the grounds specified in the application as the Court thinks fit.

(5) The Court may decide whether or not to grant permission without an oral hearing having been held.

Oral hearings where permission refused, etc.

27C.—(1) Subsection (2) applies where, in relation to an application to the supervisory jurisdiction of the Court—

(a) the Court—

(i) refuses permission under subsection 27B(1) for the application to proceed, or

(ii) grants permission for the application to proceed subject to conditions or only on particular grounds, and

(b) the Court decides to refuse permission, or grant permission as mentioned in paragraph (a)(ii), without an oral hearing having been held.

(2) The person making the application may, within the period of 7 days beginning with the day on which that decision is made, request a review of the decision at an oral hearing.

(3) A request under subsection (2) must be considered by a different Lord Ordinary from the one who refused permission or granted permission as mentioned in subsection (1)(a)(ii).

(4) Where a request under subsection (2) is granted, the oral hearing must be conducted before a different Lord Ordinary from the one who refused or so granted permission.

(5) At a review following a request under subsection (2), the Court must consider whether to grant permission for the application to proceed; and subsections (2), (3) and (4) of section 27B apply for that purpose.

(6) Section 28 does not apply—

(a) where subsection (2) applies, or

(b) in relation to the refusal of a request made under subsection (2).

Appeals following oral hearings

27D.—(1) Subsection (2) applies where, after an oral hearing to determine whether or not to grant permission for an application to the supervisory jurisdiction of the Court to proceed, the Court—

(a) refuses permission for the application to proceed, or

(b) grants permission for the application to proceed subject to conditions or only on particular grounds.

(2) The person making the application may, within the period of 7 days beginning with the day on which the Court makes its decision, appeal under this section to the Inner House (but may not appeal under any other provision of this Act).

(3) In an appeal under subsection (2), the Inner House must consider whether to grant permission for the application to proceed; and subsections (2), (3) and (4) of section 27B apply for that purpose.

(4) In subsection (1), the reference to an oral hearing is to an oral hearing whether following a request under section 27C(2) or otherwise.".

There has not been any amendment to the Tribunal Procedure (Upper Tribunal) Rules 2008 to reflect this procedure.

Upper Tribunal's "judicial review" jurisdiction: Scotland

21.—(1) The Upper Tribunal has the function of deciding applications transferred to it from the Court of Session under section 20(1). 5.103

(2) The powers of review of the Upper Tribunal in relation to such applications are the same as the powers of review of the Court of Session in an application to the supervisory jurisdiction of that Court.

(3) In deciding an application by virtue of subsection (1), the Upper Tribunal must apply principles that the Court of Session would apply in deciding an application to the supervisory jurisdiction of that Court.

(4) An order of the Upper Tribunal by virtue of subsection (1)—

(a) has the same effect as the corresponding order granted by the Court of Session on an application to the supervisory jurisdiction of that Court, and

(b) is enforceable as if it were an order so granted by that Court.

(5) Where an application is transferred to the Upper Tribunal by virtue of section 20(1), any steps taken or orders made by the Court of Session in relation to the application (other than the order to transfer the application under section 20(1)) are to be treated as taken or made by the tribunal.

(6) Tribunal Procedure Rules may make further provision for the purposes of supplementing subsection (5).

GENERAL NOTE

For the procedure in the Upper Tribunal, see rr.27, 30(2)–(5) and 31–33 of the Tribunal Procedure (Upper Tribunal) Rules 2008. 5.104

Miscellaneous

Tribunal Procedure Rules

22.—(1) There are to be rules, to be called "Tribunal Procedure Rules", governing— 5.105

(a) the practice and procedure to be followed in the First-tier Tribunal, and

(b) the practice and procedure to be followed in the Upper Tribunal.

(2) Tribunal Procedure Rules are to be made by the Tribunal Procedure Committee.

(3) In Schedule 5—

(a) Part 1 makes further provision about the content of Tribunal Procedure Rules,

(b) Part 2 makes provision about the membership of the Tribunal Procedure Committee,
(c) Part 3 makes provision about the making of Tribunal Procedure Rules by the Committee, and
(d) Part 4 confers power to amend legislation in connection with Tribunal Procedure Rules.

(4) Power to make Tribunal Procedure Rules is to be exercised with a view to securing—
(a) that, in proceedings before the First-tier Tribunal and Upper Tribunal, justice is done,
(b) that the tribunal system is accessible and fair,
(c) that proceedings before the First-tier Tribunal or Upper Tribunal are handled quickly and efficiently,
(d) that the rules are both simple and simply expressed, and
(e) that the rules where appropriate confer on members of the First-tier Tribunal, or Upper Tribunal, responsibility for ensuring that proceedings before the tribunal are handled quickly and efficiently.

(5) In subsection (4)(b) "the tribunal system" means the system for deciding matters within the jurisdiction of the First-tier Tribunal or the Upper Tribunal.

General Note

5.106 This section, and Sch.5, came into force on May 19, 2008. The Tribunal Procedure Committee is similar to the committees that make rules for the courts, being composed mainly of judges and members of tribunals and representatives who appear before tribunals. The Committee is able to keep the Tribunal Procedure Rules under constant review. In the past, some tribunals found it very difficult to get changes made to their rules. Paragraphs 28 and 29 of Sch.5 enable the Lord Chancellor to disallow Rules or require Rules to be made.

There are a number of specific rule-making powers in this Act, not confined to Pt 1 of Sch.5, and in other Acts but they are not to be taken to limit the generality of s.22(1) (see para.1 of Sch.5). The power to make Tribunal Procedure Rules is therefore very wide.

The approach that has been taken is to produce a set of rules for each chamber of the First-tier Tribunal and for the Lands Chamber of the Upper Tribunal and a single set of rules for the other three chambers of the Upper Tribunal. The Tribunal Procedure (First-tier Tribunal) (Social Entitlement Chamber) Rules 2008 and the Tribunal Procedure (Upper Tribunal) Rules 2008 are set out in this volume.

Practice directions

5.107 **23.**—(1) The Senior President of Tribunals may give directions—
(a) as to the practice and procedure of the First-tier Tribunal;
(b) as to the practice and procedure of the Upper Tribunal.

(2) A Chamber President may give directions as to the practice and procedure of the chamber over which he presides.

(3) A power under this section to give directions includes—
(a) power to vary or revoke directions made in exercise of the power, and
(b) power to make different provision for different purposes (including different provision for different areas).

(4) Directions under subsection (1) may not be given without the approval of the Lord Chancellor.

(5) Directions under subsection (2) may not be given without the approval of—

(a) the Senior President of Tribunals, and

(b) the Lord Chancellor.

(6) Subsections (4) and (5)(b) do not apply to directions to the extent that they consist of guidance about any of the following—

(a) the application or interpretation of the law;

(b) the making of decisions by members of the First-tier Tribunal or Upper Tribunal.

(7) Subsections (4) and (5)(b) do not apply to directions to the extent that they consist of criteria for determining which members of the First-tier Tribunal or Upper Tribunal may be chosen to decide particular categories of matter; but the directions may, to that extent, be given only after consulting the Lord Chancellor.

GENERAL NOTE

Practice Directions are a common feature in courts and have also been used in some tribunals. They may be directed at the parties appearing before the tribunals or to the judges and members of tribunals and the staff of tribunals. This section provides for Practice Directions to be issued by the Senior President of Tribunals (who may delegate that function under s.8) or by a Chamber President. The latter may issue a Practice Direction only with the approval of the Senior President of Tribunals. 5.108

Practice Directions may be used to supplement Tribunal Procedure Rules and a failure by a party to comply with a Practice Direction attracts the same consequences as a failure to comply with a direction given by a tribunal in a particular case (see r.7(2) of the Tribunal Procedure (First-tier Tribunal) (Social Entitlement Chamber) Rules 2008 and r.7(2) of the Tribunal Procedure (Upper Tribunal) Rules 2008).

Subsections (4) and (5)(b) provide that a Practice Direction may be issued only with the approval of the Lord Chancellor, but those subsections do not apply to the extent that a Practice Direction consists of guidance about the application or interpretation of the law or the making of decisions by judges and other members of tribunals. Practice Directions as to the criteria for deciding which judges and other members may be chosen to decide particular types of case do not require the approval of the Lord Chancellor but do require that he be consulted.

Practice Direction (First-tier and Upper Tribunals: Welsh Language) [2009] 1 W.L.R. 331, *Practice Direction (First-tier and Upper Tribunals: Witnesses)* [2009] 1 W.L.R. 332 and *Practice Direction (Upper Tribunal: Transcripts)* [2009] 1 W.L.R. 328 are set out in this volume. All practice directions are also published at: *http://www.judiciary.gov.uk/publications-and-reports/practice-directions/tribunals/tribunals-pd.*

It is not open to a judge sitting in a court or tribunal to lay down a mandatory procedure to be complied with in all cases within the course of giving a judgment or decision in an individual case (*Bovale Ltd v Secretary of State for Communities and Local Government* [2009] EWCA Civ 171; [2009] 1 W.L.R. 2274). That would be to make a practice direction without compliance with the requirements of this section. However, judges do have wide powers under Tribunal Procedure Rules to depart from standard procedures in individual cases or groups of cases.

Mediation

24.—(1) A person exercising power to make Tribunal Procedure Rules or give practice directions must, when making provision in relation to mediation, have regard to the following principles— 5.109

(a) mediation of matters in dispute between parties to proceedings is to take place only by agreement between those parties;

(b) where parties to proceedings fail to mediate, or where mediation between parties to proceedings fails to resolve disputed matters, the failure is not to affect the outcome of the proceedings.

(2) Practice directions may provide for members to act as mediators in relation to disputed matters in a case that is the subject of proceedings.

(3) The provision that may be made by virtue of subsection (2) includes provision for a member to act as a mediator in relation to disputed matters in a case even though the member has been chosen to decide matters in the case.

(4) Once a member has begun to act as a mediator in relation to a disputed matter in a case that is the subject of proceedings, the member may decide matters in the case only with the consent of the parties.

(5) Staff appointed under section 40(1) may, subject to their terms of appointment, act as mediators in relation to disputed matters in a case that is the subject of proceedings.

(6) In this section—

"member" means a judge or other member of the First-tier Tribunal or a judge or other member of the Upper Tribunal;

"practice direction" means a direction under section 23(1) or (2);

"proceedings" means proceedings before the First-tier Tribunal or proceedings before the Upper Tribunal.

Supplementary powers of Upper Tribunal

5.110 **25.**—(1) In relation to the matters mentioned in subsection (2), the Upper Tribunal—

(a) has, in England and Wales or in Northern Ireland, the same powers, rights, privileges and authority as the High Court, and
(b) has, in Scotland, the same powers, rights, privileges and authority as the Court of Session.

(2) The matters are—

(a) the attendance and examination of witnesses,
(b) the production and inspection of documents, and
(c) all other matters incidental to the Upper Tribunal's functions.

(3) Subsection (1) shall not be taken—

(a) to limit any power to make Tribunal Procedure Rules;
(b) to be limited by anything in Tribunal Procedure Rules other than an express limitation.

(4) A power, right, privilege or authority conferred in a territory by subsection (1) is available for purposes of proceedings in the Upper Tribunal that take place outside that territory (as well as for purposes of proceedings in the tribunal that take place within that territory).

General Note

5.111 The powers of the High Court and the Court of Session include the power to punish a person for contempt of court. Failure to comply with a direction, order, summons or citation issued by a tribunal is a contempt of court but is unlikely to be punishable unless accompanied by a warning (which is a specific requirement in respect of orders, summonses and citations issued under r.16 of either set of Rules). That a tribunal is a "court" for these purposes is clear from *Pickering v Liverpool Daily Post and Echo Newspapers Limited* [1991] 2 A.C. 370. In *MD v SSWP (Enforcement Reference)* [2010] UKUT 202 (AAC); [2011] AACR 5, it was suggested by a three-judge panel that a warning should spell out the penalties that may be imposed for failure to comply. The maximum punishment that may be imposed is a sentence of two years' imprisonment or an unlimited fine (see ss.14 and 15 of the Contempt of Court Act 1981). When a sentence of imprisonment is imposed, consideration should always be given to suspending it and reference to that consideration should be included in the reasons for the decision to impose the sentence (*Slade v Slade* [2009] EWCA Civ 748; [2010] 1 W.L.R. 1262). At least in England and Wales, there is also power to sequestrate assets. In view of the seriousness of committal proceedings, it was emphasised in *MD v SSWP (Enforcement Reference)* that it is particularly important that procedural rules are complied with in such proceedings. However, because a failure to comply with procedural requirements does not itself invalidate proceedings, an irregularity might be waived where it could not have caused the alleged contemnor any prejudice or injustice.

The three-judge panel also referred to *M v P (Contempt of Court: Committal Order)* [1993] Fam.167, in which it was held that "(a) the contemnor, (b) the alleged 'victim' of the contempt and (c) other users of the court for whom the maintenance of the authority of the court is of supreme importance" all had interests that justice required the court to take into account in contempt cases. It therefore doubted the statement of another three-judge panel in *MR v CMEC* [2010] UKUT 38 (AAC) to the effect that it was not appropriate for parties other than the alleged contemnor to make submissions in contempt proceedings. Indeed, at least in England and Wales, a party may have made an application for the committal. Thus, for instance, in *KJM Superbikes Ltd v Hinton* [2008] EWCA Civ 1280; [2009] 1 W.L.R. 2406, the Court of Appeal considered the circumstances in which a court should entertain an application by a party for the committal of a witness for contempt of court in giving false evidence.

Not only must contempt be proved beyond reasonable doubt but so must any contested facts relevant to a more severe sentence, such as prejudice to other parties or the degree to which there has been subsequent compliance. However, it is for the contemnor to prove, on a balance of probabilities, that a contempt has been purged (see *JSC BTA Bank v Solodchenko (No.2)* [2010] EWHC 2843 (Ch); [2011] 1 W.L.R. 906 in which a number of sentencing principles were considered).

This section gives the Upper Tribunal power to punish for contempt of court 5.112
in relation to its own proceedings. Where a person has failed to comply with a requirement to attend at any place for the purpose of giving evidence to the First-tier Tribunal or otherwise to make themselves available to give evidence to the First-tier Tribunal or to swear an oath for in connection with giving evidence in First-tier Tribunal proceedings, that tribunal may refer the case to the Upper Tribunal which may exercise its powers under this section as though the First-tier Tribunal had been the Upper Tribunal (see r.7(3) of the Tribunal Procedure (First-tier Tribunal) (Social Entitlement Chamber) Rules 2008 and r.7(3) and (4) of the Tribunal Procedure (Upper Tribunal) Rules 2008). See the notes to those rules. Only the Chamber President (or a person to whom the power is delegated by him) has the power to make a reference from the Social Entitlement Chamber of the First-tier Tribunal to the Upper Tribunal in a social security case (see para.10 of the practice statement set out below in the note to art.2 of the First-tier Tribunal and Upper Tribunal (Composition of Tribunal) Order 2008).

Where a power is conferred specifically on the "High Court" by statute, this section cannot be read as having the effect that the Upper Tribunal may also exercise the power. The Upper Tribunal therefore has no power to award *pro bono* costs by virtue of s.194 of the Legal Services Act 2007 (*Raftopoulou v HMRC* [2015] UKUT 630 (TCC)). Nor does this section empower the Upper Tribunal to allow a vexatious litigant subject to a civil proceedings order or an all proceedings order under s.42 of the Senior Courts Act 1981 to bring proceedings before the Upper Tribunal (*IB v Information Commissioner* [2011] UKUT 370 (AAC); [2012] AACR 26). Neither does it allow the Upper Tribunal informally to change a decision given orally before it is issued in writing: an oral decision stands unless amended or set aside through a formal decision on review under s.10 or under r.42 or r.43 of the Tribunal Procedure (Upper Tribunal) Rules 2008 (*Patel v Secretary of State for the Home Department* [2015] EWCA Civ 1175, *Jan v SSHD* [2016] UKUT 336 (IAC)). However, it has been held to empower the Upper Tribunal to appoint a litigation friend to act on behalf of a child in judicial review proceedings in the Immigration and Asylum Chamber (*R. (AM) v Solihull MBC*, reported in *Legal Action*, September 2011, p.5), although in *R. (C.) v First-tier Tribunal* [2016] EWHC 707 (Admin), it was held that even the First-tier Tribunal was entitled to appoint a litigation friend in circumstances where that was required by the common law concept of procedural fairness and so presumably the Upper Tribunal could also do so without needing to rely on s.25. That issue does not generally arise in social security cases due to the power of the Secretary of State to appoint a person to act on behalf of a child claimant (see reg.43 of the Social Security (Claims and Payments) Regulations 1987).

For the meaning of "the production . . . of documents" in subs.(2)(b), see the annotation to r.7(3) of the Tribunal Procedure (First-tier Tribunal) (Social Entitlement Chamber) Rules 2008.

First-tier Tribunal and Upper Tribunal: sitting places

5.113 **26.**—Each of the First-tier Tribunal and the Upper Tribunal may decide a case—

(a) in England and Wales,
(b) in Scotland, or
(c) in Northern Ireland,

even though the case arises under the law of a territory other than the one in which the case is decided.

Enforcement

5.114 **27.**—(1) A sum payable in pursuance of a decision of the First-tier Tribunal or Upper Tribunal made in England and Wales—

(a) shall be recoverable as if it were payable under an order of a county court in England and Wales;
(b) shall be recoverable as if it were payable under an order of the High Court in England and Wales.

(2) An order for the payment of a sum payable in pursuance of a decision of the First-tier Tribunal or Upper Tribunal made in Scotland (or a copy of such an order certified in accordance with Tribunal Procedure Rules) may be enforced as if it were an extract registered decree arbitral bearing a warrant for execution issued by the sheriff court of any sheriffdom in Scotland.

(3) A sum payable in pursuance of a decision of the First-tier Tribunal or Upper Tribunal made in Northern Ireland—

(a) shall be recoverable as if it were payable under an order of a county court in Northern Ireland;
(b) shall be recoverable as if it were payable under an order of the High Court in Northern Ireland.

(4) This section does not apply to a sum payable in pursuance of—

(a) an award under section 16(6), or
(b) an order by virtue of section 21(1).

(5) The Lord Chancellor may by order make provision for subsection (1) or (3) to apply in relation to a sum of a description specified in the order with the omission of one (but not both) of paragraphs (a) and (b).

(6) Tribunal Procedure Rules—

(a) may make provision as to where, for purposes of this section, a decision is to be taken to be made;
(b) may provide for all or any of subsections (1) to (3) to apply only, or

not to apply except, in relation to sums of a description specified in Tribunal Procedure Rules.

Assessors

28.—(1) If it appears to the First-tier Tribunal or the Upper Tribunal that a matter before it requires special expertise not otherwise available to it, it may direct that in dealing with that matter it shall have the assistance of a person or persons appearing to it to have relevant knowledge or experience. 5.115

(2) The remuneration of a person who gives assistance to either tribunal as mentioned in subsection (1) shall be determined and paid by the Lord Chancellor.

(3) The Lord Chancellor may—

(a) establish panels of persons from which either tribunal may (but need not) select persons to give it assistance as mentioned in subsection (1);

(b) under paragraph (a) establish different panels for different purposes;

(c) after carrying out such consultation as he considers appropriate, appoint persons to a panel established under paragraph (a);

(d) remove a person from such a panel.

Costs or expenses

29.—(1) The costs of and incidental to— 5.116

(a) all proceedings in the First-tier Tribunal, and

(b) all proceedings in the Upper Tribunal,

shall be in the discretion of the Tribunal in which the proceedings take place.

(2) The relevant Tribunal shall have full power to determine by whom and to what extent the costs are to be paid.

(3) Subsections (1) and (2) have effect subject to Tribunal Procedure Rules.

(4) In any proceedings mentioned in subsection (1), the relevant Tribunal may—

(a) disallow, or

(b) (as the case may be) order the legal or other representative concerned to meet,

the whole of any wasted costs or such part of them as may be determined in accordance with Tribunal Procedure Rules.

(5) In subsection (4) "wasted costs" means any costs incurred by a party—

(a) as a result of any improper, unreasonable or negligent act or omission on the part of any legal or other representative or any employee of such a representative, or

(b) which, in the light of any such act or omission occurring after they were incurred, the relevant Tribunal considers it is unreasonable to expect that party to pay.

(6) In this section "legal or other representative", in relation to a party to proceedings, means any person exercising a right of audience or right to conduct the proceedings on his behalf.

(7) In the application of this section in relation to Scotland, any reference in this section to costs is to be read as a reference to expenses.

General Note

Subsections (1)–(3)

5.117 Rule 10 of the Tribunal Procedure (First-tier Tribunal) (Social Entitlement Chamber) Rules 2008 provides that the tribunal "shall not make any order in respect of costs (or, in Scotland, expenses)". By virtue of rr.10(1)(b) and (2) of the Tribunal Procedure (Upper Tribunal) Rules 2008, the same approach applies in the Upper Tribunal to appeals from the Social Entitlement Chamber of the First-tier Tribunal and to cases under the Forfeiture Act 1982.

Some courts in England and Wales have a power under s.194 of the Legal Services Act 2007 to order a sum of money to be paid to a prescribed charity (usually an organisation providing *pro bono* representation) where a party being represented *pro bono* has not actually incurred costs or expenses due to the conduct of another party but an order would have been made if the first party had been paying for representation. However, that provision does not apply to tribunals and this section does not empower the First-tier Tribunal or Upper Tribunal to make such an order (*Raftopoulou v HMRC* [2015] UKUT 630 (TCC)).

Subsections (4)–(6)

5.118 These subsections provide for a "wasted costs" order to be made against a representative (rather than a party) whose "improper, unreasonable or negligent act or omission" makes it unreasonable for a party to pay costs he or she has incurred. It is not entirely clear whether such orders may be made by the Social Entitlement Chamber or by the Upper Tribunal on appeal from that chamber or in Forfeiture Act cases. The doubt arises because Tribunal Procedure Rules made under subs.(3) may qualify only subss.(1) and (2). If subs.(4) confers a free-standing power to award costs, that power remains available notwithstanding the Tribunal Procedure Rules. However, the better approach may be that subs.(4) merely defines the circumstances in which the broad power in subs.(2) to determine "by whom" costs are to be paid is to be exercised against representatives. Even if the power is available, it is suggested that it will rarely be appropriate to use it. So far as the representative's own client is concerned, the question of who bears any costs may be thought to be a matter between the representative and the client and, so far as any other party is concerned, it needs to be borne in mind that equally improper, unreasonable or negligent acts by an unrepresented party do not result in any award of costs. Making a wasted costs order where there is no other power to award costs would arguably be merely for punitive or deterrent purposes. Where many claimants rely on the free services of representatives, too liberal a use of wasted costs order might unduly affect that availability of representation.

Chapters 3 to 5

5.119 **30.–45.**—*Omitted.*

Chapter 6

Supplementary

5.120 **46.–48.**—*Omitted.*

Orders and regulations under Part 1: supplemental and procedural provisions

5.121 **49.**—(1) Power—

(a) of the Lord Chancellor to make an order, or regulations, under this Part,

(b) of the Senior President of Tribunals to make an order under section 7(9), or

(c) of the Scottish Ministers, or the Welsh Ministers, to make an order under paragraph 25(2) of Schedule 7,

is exercisable by statutory instrument.

(2) The Statutory Instruments Act 1946 shall apply in relation to the power to make orders conferred on the Senior President of Tribunals by section 7(9) as if the Senior President of Tribunals were a Minister of the Crown.

(3) Any power mentioned in subsection (1) includes power to make different provision for different purposes.

(4) Without prejudice to the generality of subsection (3), power to make an order under section 30 or 31 includes power to make different provision in relation to England, Scotland, Wales and Northern Ireland respectively.

(5) No order mentioned in subsection (6) is to be made unless a draft of the statutory instrument containing it (whether alone or with other provision) has been laid before, and approved by a resolution of, each House of Parliament.

(6) Those orders are—

(a) an order under section 11(8), 13(6) or (14), 30, 31(1), 32, 33, 34, 35, 36, 37 or 42(3);

(b) an order under paragraph 15 of Schedule 4;

(c) an order under section 42(1)(a) to (d) that provides for fees to be payable in respect of things for which fees have never been payable;

(d) an order under section 31(2), (7) or (9), or paragraph 30(1) of Schedule 5, that contains provision taking the form of an amendment or repeal of an enactment comprised in an Act.

(7) A statutory instrument that—

(a) contains—

(i) an order mentioned in subsection (8), or

(ii) regulations under Part 3 of Schedule 9, and

(b) is not subject to any requirement that a draft of the instrument be laid before, and approved by a resolution of, each House of Parliament,

is subject to annulment in pursuance of a resolution of either House of Parliament.

(8) Those orders are—

(a) an order made by the Lord Chancellor under this Part;

(b) an order made by the Senior President of Tribunals under section 7(9).

(9) A statutory instrument that contains an order made by the Scottish Ministers under paragraph 25(2) of Schedule 7 is subject to annulment in pursuance of a resolution of the Scottish Parliament.

(10) A statutory instrument that contains an order made by the Welsh Ministers under paragraph 25(2) of Schedule 7 is subject to annulment in pursuance of a resolution of the National Assembly for Wales.

PARTS 2 TO 7

50.–143.—*Omitted.* 5.122

PART 8

GENERAL

5.123 **144.**—*Omitted.*

Power to make supplementary or other provision

5.124 **145.**—(1) The Lord Chancellor (or, in relation to Chapter 3 of Part 5 only, the Secretary of State) may by order make any supplementary, incidental, consequential, transitory, transitional or saving provision which he considers necessary or expedient for the purposes of, in consequence of, or for giving full effect to, any provision of this Act.

(2) An order under this section may in particular—

(a) provide for any provision of this Act which comes into force before another to have effect, until that other provision has come into force, with modifications specified in the order;

(b) amend, repeal or revoke any enactment other than one contained in an Act or instrument passed or made after the Session in which this Act is passed.

(3) The amendments that may be made by an order under this section are in addition to those made by or under any other provision of this Act.

(4) An order under this section may make different provision for different purposes.

(5) The power to make an order under this section is exercisable by statutory instrument.

(6) A statutory instrument containing an order under this section, unless it is an order to which subsection (7) applies, is subject to annulment in pursuance of a resolution of either House of Parliament.

(7) No order amending or repealing an enactment contained in an Act may be made under this section unless a draft of the order has been laid before and approved by a resolution of each House of Parliament.

5.125 **146.**—*Omitted.*

Extent

5.126 **147.**—(1) Parts 1, 2 and 6 and this Part extend to England and Wales, Scotland and Northern Ireland.

(2) The other provisions of this Act extend only to England and Wales.

(3) Subsections (1) and (2) are subject to subsections (4) and (5).

(4) Unless provided otherwise, amendments, repeals and revocations in this Act extend to any part of the United Kingdom to which the provisions amended, repealed or revoked extend.

(5) The following extend also to the Isle of Man—

(a) section 143(1) and (2),

(b) the repeal by this Act of any provision specified in Part 6 of Schedule 23 that extends to the Isle of Man,

(c) sections 145 and 148(5) to (7) so far as relating to—

(i) section 143(1) and (2), and

(ii) the provisions of this Act by which the repeals mentioned in paragraph (b) are effected, and

(d) this section and section 149.

Commencement

148.—(1) Section 60 comes into force at the end of the period of two months beginning with the day on which this Act is passed. 5.127

(2) The provisions of Chapter 3 of Part 5 come into force in accordance with provision made by the Lord Chancellor or the Secretary of State by order.

(3) The provisions of Part 6 come into force, except as provided by subsection (4), in accordance with provision made by the Secretary of State by order.

(4) The provisions of Part 6 come into force, in so far as they extend to Scotland, in accordance with provision made by the Scottish Ministers by order.

(5) The remaining provisions of this Act, except sections 53, 55, 56, 57, 145, 147, 149, this section and Schedule 11, come into force in accordance with provision made by the Lord Chancellor by order.

(6) An order under this section may make different provision for different purposes.

(7) The power to make an order under this section is exercisable by statutory instrument.

Short title

149.—This Act may be cited as the Tribunals, Courts and Enforcement Act 2007. 5.128

Schedules 1 to 3 *Omitted.* 5.129

SCHEDULE 4

CHAMBERS AND CHAMBER PRESIDENTS: FURTHER PROVISION

PART 1

CHAMBER PRESIDENTS: APPOINTMENT, DELEGATION, DEPUTIES AND FURTHER PROVISION

1. to 3. *Omitted.* 5.130

Delegation of functions by Chamber Presidents

4. (1) The Chamber President of a chamber of the First-tier Tribunal or Upper Tribunal may delegate any function he has in his capacity as the Chamber President of the chamber— 5.131

(a) to any judge, or other member, of either of those tribunals;

(b) to staff appointed under section 40(1).

(2) A delegation under sub-paragraph (1) is not revoked by the delegator's becoming incapacitated.

(3) Any delegation made by a person under sub-paragraph (1) that is in force immediately before the person ceases to be the Chamber President of a chamber continues in force until subsequently varied or revoked by another holder of the office of Chamber President of that chamber.

(4) The delegation under sub-paragraph (1) of a function shall not prevent the exercise of the function by the Chamber President of the chamber concerned.

(5) In this paragraph "delegate" includes further delegate.

5.132 **5. to 8**. *Omitted.*

PART 2

JUDGES AND OTHER MEMBERS OF CHAMBERS: ASSIGNMENT AND JURISDICTION

5.133 **9. to 14.** *Omitted.*

Composition of tribunals

5.134 **15.** (1) The Lord Chancellor must by order make provision, in relation to every matter that may fall to be decided by the First-tier Tribunal or the Upper Tribunal, for determining the number of members of the tribunal who are to decide the matter.

(2) Where an order under sub-paragraph (1) provides for a matter to be decided by a single member of a tribunal, the order—

- (a) must make provision for determining whether the matter is to be decided by one of the judges, or by one of the other members, of the tribunal, and
- (b) may make provision for determining, if the matter is to be decided by one of the other members of the tribunal, what qualifications (if any) that other member must have.

(3) Where an order under sub-paragraph (1) provides for a matter to be decided by two or more members of a tribunal, the order—

- (a) must make provision for determining how many (if any) of those members are to be judges of the tribunal and how many (if any) are to be other members of the tribunal, and
- (b) may make provision for determining—
  - (i) if the matter is to be decided by persons who include one or more of the other members of the tribunal, or
  - (ii) if the matter is to be decided by two or more of the other members of the tribunal,

  what qualifications (if any) that other member or any of those other members must have.

(4) A duty under sub-paragraph (1), (2) or (3) to provide for the determination of anything may be discharged by providing for the thing to be

determined by the Senior President of Tribunals, or a Chamber President, in accordance with any provision made under that sub-paragraph.

(5) Power under paragraph (b) of sub-paragraph (2) or (3) to provide for the determination of anything may be exercised by giving, to the Senior President of Tribunals or a Chamber President, power to determine that thing in accordance with any provision made under that paragraph.

(6) Where under sub-paragraphs (1) to (4) a matter is to be decided by two or more members of a tribunal, the matter may, if the parties to the case agree, be decided in the absence of one or more (but not all) of the members chosen to decide the matter.

(7) Where the member, or any of the members, of a tribunal chosen to decide a matter does not have any qualification that he is required to have under sub-paragraphs (2)(b), or (3)(b), and (5), the matter may despite that, if the parties to the case agree, be decided by the chosen member or members.

(8) Before making an order under this paragraph, the Lord Chancellor must consult the Senior President of Tribunals.

(9) In this paragraph "qualification" includes experience.

General Note

Paragraph 15

See the First-tier Tribunal and Upper Tribunal (Composition of Tribunal) Order 2008, below. The Order makes much use of the power in para.15(4) for an order to leave matters of composition to be determined by the Senior President of Tribunals who who has issued practice statements. The relevant practice statements are set out in the notes to the Order. Note that subpara. (6) provides for a case to be determined in the absence of some (but not all!) members of the tribunal, provided the parties agree. Subparagraph (7) also enables a tribunal to proceed if any of the members of the tribunal does not have the requisite qualifications, provided the parties agree. It is normally a breach of the rules of natural justice for a member of a tribunal to absent themselves for part of a hearing so as not to be present while a witness is giving oral evidence and later to return to participate in the decision. However, even then there was no breach where a party agreed, through his solicitor, to that procedure and the agreement was voluntary, informed and unequivocal (*R. (Hill) v Institute of Chartered Accountants in England and Wales* [2013] EWCA Civ 555; [2014] 1 W.L.R. 86). Thus, if one of the members does not have the relevant qualification, there is a choice between the proceedings being adjourned, the case proceeding without that member and the case proceeding with that member. In this context "member" clearly include a judge, so it would be possible for a hearing to take place without a judge by virtue of either of those paragraphs. However, not only must the parties agree that it is appropriate to proceed but so must the tribunal itself. There are likely to be cases where the lack of the relevant expertise obliges the tribunal to adjourn the proceedings in the interests of justice. Where no-one realises that a member lacks the relevant qualifications, including the member himself or herself, and the tribunal therefore hears the case, the decision of the tribunal is not invalid unless the member deliberately closed his or her eyes to the problem or the lack of relevant qualification has rendered the proceedings unfair (*Coppard v Customs and Excise Commissioners* [2003] EWCA Civ 511; [2003] Q.B. 1428). **5.135**

SCHEDULE 5

PROCEDURE IN FIRST-TIER TRIBUNAL AND UPPER TRIBUNAL

PART 1

TRIBUNAL PROCEDURE RULES

Introductory

5.136 **1.** (1) This Part of this Schedule makes further provision about the content of Tribunal Procedure Rules.

(2) The generality of section 22(1) is not to be taken to be prejudiced by—

(a) the following paragraphs of this Part of this Schedule, or

(b) any other provision (including future provision) authorising or requiring the making of provision by Tribunal Procedure Rules.

(3) In the following paragraphs of this Part of this Schedule "Rules" means Tribunal Procedure Rules.

Concurrent functions

5.137 **2.** Rules may make provision as to who is to decide, or as to how to decide, which of the First-tier Tribunal and Upper Tribunal is to exercise, in relation to any particular matter, a function that is exercisable by the two tribunals on the basis that the question as to which of them is to exercise the function is to be determined by, or under, Rules.

Delegation of functions to staff

5.138 **3.** (1) Rules may provide for functions—

(a) of the First-tier Tribunal, or

(b) of the Upper Tribunal,

to be exercised by staff appointed under section 40(1).

(2) In making provision of the kind mentioned in sub-paragraph (1) in relation to a function, Rules may (in particular)—

(a) provide for the function to be exercisable by a member of staff only if the member of staff is, or is of a description, specified in exercise of a discretion conferred by Rules;

(b) provide for the function to be exercisable by a member of staff only if the member of staff is approved, or is of a description approved, for the purpose by a person specified in Rules.

Time limits

4. Rules may make provision for time limits as respects initiating, or taking any step in, proceedings before the First-tier Tribunal or the Upper Tribunal. 5.139

Repeat applications

5. Rules may make provision restricting the making of fresh applications where a previous application in relation to the same matter has been made. 5.140

Tribunal acting of its own initiative

6. Rules may make provision about the circumstances in which the First-tier Tribunal, or the Upper Tribunal, may exercise its powers of its own initiative. 5.141

Hearings

7. Rules may— 5.142
(a) make provision for dealing with matters without a hearing;
(b) make provision as respects allowing or requiring a hearing to be in private or as respects allowing or requiring a hearing to be in public.

Proceedings without notice

8. Rules may make provision for proceedings to take place, in circumstances described in Rules, at the request of one party even though the other, or another, party has had no notice. 5.143

Representation

9. Rules may make provision conferring additional rights of audience before the First-tier Tribunal or the Upper Tribunal. 5.144

Evidence, witnesses and attendance

10. (1) Rules may make provision about evidence (including evidence on oath and administration of oaths). 5.145

(2) Rules may modify any rules of evidence provided for elsewhere, so far as they would apply to proceedings before the First-tier Tribunal or Upper Tribunal.

(3) Rules may make provision, where the First-tier Tribunal has required a person—
(a) to attend at any place for the purpose of giving evidence,

(b) otherwise to make himself available to give evidence,
(c) to swear an oath in connection with the giving of evidence,
(d) to give evidence as a witness,
(e) to produce a document, or
(f) to facilitate the inspection of a document or any other thing (including any premises),

for the Upper Tribunal to deal with non-compliance with the requirement as though the requirement had been imposed by the Upper Tribunal.

(4) Rules may make provision for the payment of expenses and allowances to persons giving evidence, producing documents, attending proceedings or required to attend proceedings.

Use of information

5.146 **11.** (1) Rules may make provision for the disclosure or non-disclosure of information received during the course of proceedings before the First-tier Tribunal or Upper Tribunal.

(2) Rules may make provision for imposing reporting restrictions in circumstances described in Rules.

Costs and expenses

5.147 **12.** (1) Rules may make provision for regulating matters relating to costs, or (in Scotland) expenses, of proceedings before the First-tier Tribunal or Upper Tribunal.

(2) The provision mentioned in sub-paragraph (1) includes (in particular)—

(a) provision prescribing scales of costs or expenses;
(b) provision for enabling costs to undergo detailed assessment in England and Wales by a county court or the High Court;
(c) provision for taxation in Scotland of accounts of expenses by an Auditor of Court;
(d) provision for enabling costs to be taxed in Northern Ireland in a county court or the High Court;
(e) provision for costs or expenses—
  (i) not to be allowed in respect of items of a description specified in Rules;
  (ii) not to be allowed in proceedings of a description so specified;
(f) provision for other exceptions to either or both of subsections (1) and (2) of section 29.

Set-off and interest

5.148 **13.** (1) Rules may make provision for a party to proceedings to deduct, from amounts payable by him, amounts payable to him.

(2) Rules may make provision for interest on sums awarded (including provision conferring a discretion or provision in accordance with which interest is to be calculated).

Arbitration

14. Rules may provide for Part 1 of the Arbitration Act 1996 (which extends to England and Wales, and Northern Ireland, but not Scotland) not to apply, or not to apply except so far as is specified in Rules, where the First-tier Tribunal, or Upper Tribunal, acts as arbitrator. **5.149**

Correction of errors and setting-aside of decisions on procedural grounds

15. (1) Rules may make provision for the correction of accidental errors in a decision or record of a decision. **5.150**

(2) Rules may make provision for the setting aside of a decision in proceedings before the First-tier Tribunal or Upper Tribunal—

(a) where a document relating to the proceedings was not sent to, or was not received at an appropriate time by, a party to the proceedings or a party's representative,

(b) where a document relating to the proceedings was not sent to the First-tier Tribunal or Upper Tribunal at an appropriate time,

(c) where a party to the proceedings, or a party's representative, was not present at a hearing related to the proceedings, or

(d) where there has been any other procedural irregularity in the proceedings.

(3) Sub-paragraphs (1) and (2) shall not be taken to prejudice, or to be prejudiced by, any power to correct errors or set aside decisions that is exercisable apart from rules made by virtue of those sub-paragraphs.

Ancillary powers

16. Rules may confer on the First-tier Tribunal, or the Upper Tribunal, such ancillary powers as are necessary for the proper discharge of its functions. **5.151**

Rules may refer to practice directions

17. Rules may, instead of providing for any matter, refer to provision made or to be made about that matter by directions under section 23. **5.152**

Presumptions

18. Rules may make provision in the form of presumptions (including, in particular, presumptions as to service or notification). **5.153**

Differential provision

5.154 **19.** Rules may make different provision for different purposes or different areas.

PART 2

5.155 **20.** to **26.**—*Omitted.*

PART 3

MAKING OF TRIBUNAL PROCEDURE RULES BY TRIBUNAL PROCEDURE COMMITTEE

Meaning of "Rules" and "the Committee"

5.156 **27.** In the following provisions of this Part of this Schedule—
"the Committee" means the Tribunal Procedure Committee;
"Rules" means Tribunal Procedure Rules.

Process for making Rules

5.157 **28.** (1) Before the Committee makes Rules, the Committee must—
(a) consult such persons (including such of the Chamber Presidents) as it considers appropriate,
(b) consult the Lord President of the Court of Session if the Rules contain provision relating to proceedings in Scotland, and
(c) meet (unless it is inexpedient to do so).

(2) Rules made by the Committee must be—
(a) signed by a majority of the members of the Committee, and
(b) submitted to the Lord Chancellor.

(3) The Lord Chancellor may allow or disallow Rules so made.

(4) If the Lord Chancellor disallows Rules so made, he must give the Committee written reasons for doing so.

(5) Rules so made and allowed—
(a) come into force on such day as the Lord Chancellor directs, and
(b) are to be contained in a statutory instrument to which the Statutory Instruments Act 1946 applies as if the instrument contained rules made by a Minister of the Crown.

(6) A statutory instrument containing Rules made by the Committee is subject to annulment in pursuance of a resolution of either House of Parliament.

(7) In the case of a member of the Committee appointed under paragraph 24, the terms of his appointment may (in particular) provide that, for the purposes of sub-paragraph (2)(a), he is to count as a member of the Committee only in relation to matters specified in those terms.

Power of Lord Chancellor to require Rules to be made

29. (1) This paragraph applies if the Lord Chancellor gives the Committee written notice that he thinks it is expedient for Rules to include provision that would achieve a purpose specified in the notice. 5.158

(2) The Committee must make such Rules, in accordance with paragraph 28, as it considers necessary to achieve the specified purpose.

(3) Those Rules must be made—

(a) within such period as may be specified by the Lord Chancellor in the notice, or

(b) if no period is so specified, within a reasonable period after the Lord Chancellor gives the notice to the Committee.

PART 4

POWER TO AMEND LEGISLATION IN CONNECTION WITH TRIBUNAL PROCEDURE RULES

Lord Chancellor's power

30. (1) The Lord Chancellor may by order amend, repeal or revoke any enactment to the extent he considers necessary or desirable— 5.159

(a) in order to facilitate the making of Tribunal Procedure Rules, or

(b) in consequence of—

(i) section 22,

(ii) Part 1 or 3 of this Schedule, or

(iii) Tribunal Procedure Rules.

(2) In this paragraph "enactment" means any enactment whenever passed or made, including an enactment comprised in subordinate legislation (within the meaning of the Interpretation Act 1978).

GENERAL NOTE

Paragraph 1

The scope of the power to make Tribunal Procedure Rules in s.22(1) is very broad and is not to be treated as limited by any other rule-making power in this Act, including this Schedule, or indeed in any other Act. 5.160

Paragraph 3

There is no need to make rules for the delegation of purely administrative functions and therefore this paragraph is concerned only with the delegation of judicial functions. 5.161

Paragraph 4

In *JI v HMRC (TC)* [2013] UKUT 199, it was held that, in the light of *Mucelli v Government of Albania* [2009] UKHL 2; [2009] 1 W.L.R. 287, this paragraph did not by itself permit the making of rules that extended time limits laid down in primary legislation. However, in *VK v HMRC (TC)* [2016] UKUT 331 (AAC); [2017] AACR 3, a three-judge panel distinguished *Mucelli* and overruled *JI* and 5.162

held that the time limit for appeals against tax credit decisions made before April 6, 2014, which was then found in s.39 of the Tax Credits Act 2002, could be extended by Tribunal Procedure Rules made under this paragraph.

Paragraph 10

5.163 See s.25 for the powers of the Upper Tribunal to which reference is made in sub-para.(3).

Paragraph 15

5.164 There is potentially some overlap between Tribunal Procedure Rules made under this paragraph and the power to correct or set aside a decision on a review under s.9 or s.10. However, the circumstances in which a decision may be reviewed are likely to be limited and it is likely to be fairly clear which power should be used.

Note that para.15(2) is broader than s.28(1) of the Social Security Act 1998, which it replaces, as it covers any procedural irregularity (which, at one time, some regulations purporting to be made under s.28 of the 1998 Act did).

Paragraphs 27–29

5.165 The Lord Chancellor may disallow Rules or require particular provision to be made in Rules.

5.166 **Schedules 6–23**: *Omitted.*

The Transfer of Tribunal Functions Order 2008

(SI 2008/2833)

Made	*29th October 2008*
Coming into force	*3rd November 2008*

5.167 The Lord Chancellor makes the following Order in exercise of the powers conferred by sections 30(1) and (4), 31(1), (2) and (9), 32(3) and (5), 33(2) and (3), 34(2) and (3), 37(1), 38 and 145 of, and paragraph 30 of Schedule 5 to, the Tribunals, Courts and Enforcement Act 2007. The Scottish Ministers have consented to the making of this order in so far as their consent is required by section 30(7) of that Act.

A draft of this Order was laid before Parliament and approved by a resolution of each House of Parliament in accordance with section 49(5) of that Act.

Citation, commencement, interpretation and extent

5.168 **1.**—(1) This Order may be cited as the Transfer of Tribunal Functions Order 2008 and comes into force on 3rd November 2008.

(2) A reference in this Order to a Schedule by a number alone is a reference to the Schedule so numbered in this Order.

(3) Subject as follows, this Order extends to England and Wales, Scotland and Northern Ireland.

(4) Except as provided by paragraph (5) or (6), an amendment, repeal or revocation of any enactment by any provision of Schedule 3

extends to the part or parts of the United Kingdom to which the enactment extends.

(5) For the purposes of article 3(3)(a) and (b) the following amendments, repeals and revocations made by the provisions of that Schedule do not extend to Scotland—

(a) paragraphs 145 to 147;
(b) paragraph 150;
(c) paragraph 151(d);
(d) paragraph 152;
(e) paragraph 154;
(f) paragraphs 167 to 173; and
(g) paragraph 228(h), (l), (n) and (r).

(6) The amendments and repeals made by paragraphs 198 to 201 of Schedule 3 do not extend to Scotland.

GENERAL NOTE

The reason for paras (5) and (6) is explained in the note to ss.5–7 of the Social Security Act 1998. 5.169

2. *Omitted.* 5.170

Transfer of functions of certain tribunals

3.—(1) Subject to paragraph (3), the functions of the tribunals listed in Table 1 of Schedule 1 are transferred to the First-tier Tribunal. 5.171

(2) Subject to paragraph (3), the functions of the tribunals listed in Table 2 of Schedule 1 are transferred to the Upper Tribunal.

(3) The following functions are not transferred—

(a) the determination by an appeal tribunal constituted under Chapter 1 of Part 1 of the Social Security Act 1998 of an appeal which is referred to such tribunal by the Scottish Ministers, or the Secretary of State on their behalf, pursuant to section 158 (appeal tribunals) of the Health and Social Care (Community Health and Standards) Act 2003 ("the 2003 Act"); and
(b) the determination by a Social Security Commissioner of an appeal made under section 159 (appeal to social security commissioner) of the 2003 Act against a decision falling within sub-paragraph (a).

GENERAL NOTE

The reason for para.(3) is explained in the note to ss.5–7 of the Social Security Act 1998. 5.172

Abolition of tribunals transferred under section 30(1)

4. The tribunals listed in Table 1 and Table 2 of Schedule 1 are abolished except for— 5.173

(a) appeal tribunals constituted under Chapter 1 of Part 1 of the Social Security Act 1998 in respect of Scotland for the purposes of the function described in article 3(3)(a); and
(b) the Social Security Commissioners in respect of Scotland for the purposes of the function described in article 3(3)(b).

GENERAL NOTE

5.174 The reason for the saving is explained in the note to ss.5–7 of the Social Security Act 1998.

5.175 **5. to 8.** *Omitted.*

Minor, consequential and transitional provisions

5.176 **9.**—(1) Schedule 3 contains minor, consequential and supplemental amendments, and repeals and revocations as a consequence of those amendments.

(2) Schedule 4 contains transitional provisions.

SCHEDULE 1

FUNCTIONS TRANSFERRED TO THE FIRST-TIER TRIBUNAL AND UPPER TRIBUNAL

5.177 **Table 1: Functions transferred to the First-tier Tribunal**

Tribunal	*Enactment*
Adjudicator	Section 5 of the Criminal Injuries Compensation Act 1995
Appeal tribunal	Chapter 1 of Part 1 of the Social Security Act 1998
Asylum Support Adjudicators	Section 102 of the Immigration and Asylum Act 1999
Mental Health Review Tribunal for a region of England	Section 65(1) and (1A)(a) of the Mental Health Act 1983
Pensions Appeal Tribunal in England and Wales	Section 8(2) of the War Pensions (Administrative Provisions) Act 1919 and paragraph 1(1) of the Schedule to the Pensions Appeal Tribunals Act 1943
Special Educational Needs and Disability Tribunal	Section 28H of the Disability Discrimination Act 1995 and section 333 of the Education Act 1996
Tribunal, except in respect of its functions under section 4 of the Safeguarding Vulnerable Groups Act 2004	Section 9 of the Protection of Children Act 1999

5.178 **Table 2: Functions transferred to the Upper Tribunal**

Tribunal	*Enactment*
Child Support Commissioner	Section 22 of the Child Support Act 1991
Social Security Commissioner	Schedule 4 to the Social Security Act 1998
Tribunal, in respect of its functions under section 4 of the Safeguarding Vulnerable Groups Act 2006	Section 9 of the Protection of Children Act 1999

5.179 **Schedules 2 and 3.** *Omitted.*

SCHEDULE 4

TRANSITIONAL PROVISIONS

Transitional provisions

1. Subject to article 3(3)(a) any proceedings before a tribunal listed in Table 1 of Schedule 1 which are pending immediately before 3rd November 2008 shall continue on and after 3rd November 2008 as proceedings before the First-tier Tribunal. **5.180**

2. Subject to article 3(3)(b) any proceedings before a tribunal listed in Table 2 of Schedule 1 which are pending immediately before 3rd November 2008 shall continue on and after 3rd November 2008 as proceedings before the Upper Tribunal.

3.—(1) The following sub-paragraphs apply where proceedings are continued in the First-tier Tribunal or Upper Tribunal by virtue of paragraph 1 or 2.

(2) Where a hearing began before 3rd November 2008 but was not completed by that date, the First-tier Tribunal or the Upper Tribunal, as the case may be, must be comprised for the continuation of that hearing of the person or persons who began it.

(3) The First-tier Tribunal or Upper Tribunal, as the case may be, may give any direction to ensure that proceedings are dealt with fairly and, in particular, may—

(a) apply any provision in procedural rules which applied to the proceedings before 3rd November 2008; or

(b) disapply provisions of Tribunal Procedure Rules.

(4) In sub-paragraph (3) "procedural rules" means provision (whether called rules or not) regulating practice or procedure before a tribunal.

(5) Any direction or order given or made in proceedings which is in force immediately before 3rd November 2008 remains in force on and after that date as if it were a direction or order of the First-tier Tribunal or Upper Tribunal, as the case may be.

(6) A time period which has started to run before 3rd November 2008 and which has not expired shall continue to apply.

(7) An order for costs may only be made if, and to the extent that, an order could have been made before 3rd November 2008.

4. Subject to article 3(3)(a) and (b) where an appeal lies to a Child Support or Social Security Commissioner from any decision made before 3rd November 2008 by a tribunal listed in Table 1 of Schedule 1, section 11 of the 2007 Act (right to appeal to Upper Tribunal) shall apply as if the decision were a decision made on or after 3rd November 2008 by the First-tier Tribunal.

5. Subject to article 3(3)(b) where an appeal lies to a court from any decision made before 3rd November 2008 by a Child Support or Social Security Commissioner, section 13 of the 2007 Act (right to appeal to Court of Appeal etc.) shall apply as if the decision were a decision made on or after 3rd November 2008 by the Upper Tribunal.

6. Subject to article 3(3)(a) and (b) any case to be remitted by a court on or after 3rd November 2008 in relation to a tribunal listed in Schedule 1 shall be remitted to the First-tier Tribunal or Upper Tribunal as the case may be.

7. *Omitted.*

GENERAL NOTE

5.181 Before November 3, 2008, the time for applying for leave to appeal to a Social Security Commissioner against a decision of an appeal tribunal could not be extended by more than 12 months. No such absolute limit applies to extensions of the time for appealing to the Upper Tribunal against a decision of the First-tier Tribunal. However, where the absolute time limit for appealing against a decision of an appeal tribunal under the old legislation had expired before November 3, 2008, it would give an impermissible retrospective effect to the new legislation to rely on para.4 of this Schedule to extend the time for appealing against that decision (*LS v LB Lambeth* (HB) [2010] UKUT 461 (AAC), [2011] AACR 27; *ED v SSWP (DLA)* [2013] UKUT 583 (AAC)).

The First-tier Tribunal and Upper Tribunal (Composition of Tribunal) Order 2008

(SI 2008/2835)

Made	*29th October 2008*
Coming into force	*3rd November 2008*

5.182 The Lord Chancellor makes the following Order in exercise of the powers conferred by section 145(1) of, and paragraph 15 of Schedule 4 to, the Tribunals, Courts and Enforcement Act 2007.

In accordance with paragraph 15(8) of that Act the Lord Chancellor has consulted the Senior President of Tribunals.

In accordance with section 49(5) of that Act a draft of this instrument was laid before Parliament and approved by a resolution of each House of Parliament.

Citation and commencement

5.183 **1.** This Order may be cited as the First-tier Tribunal and Upper Tribunal (Composition of Tribunal) Order 2008 and comes into force on 3rd November 2008.

Number of members of the First-tier Tribunal

5.184 **2.**—(1) The number of members of the tribunal who are to decide any matter that falls to be decided by the First-tier Tribunal must be determined by the Senior President of Tribunals in accordance with paragraph (2).

(2) The Senior President of Tribunals must have regard to—

(a) where the matter which falls to be decided by the tribunal fell to a tribunal in a list in Schedule 6 to the Tribunals, Courts and Enforcement Act 2007 before its functions were transferred by order under section 30(1) of that Act, any provision made by or under any enactment for determining the number of members of that tribunal; and

(b) the need for members of tribunals to have particular expertise, skills or knowledge.

GENERAL NOTE

As is permitted by para.15(4) of Sch.4 to the Tribunals Courts and Enforcement Act 2007, this article leaves it to the Senior President of Tribunals to determine the number of members to determine any particular type of case and the qualifications they must have. He has issued practice statements. That for the "Composition of tribunals in social security and child support cases in the social entitlement chamber on or after Augast 1, 2013" is in the following terms— 5.185

"1. In this Practice Statement;

a. 'the 2008 Order' means the First-tier Tribunal and Upper Tribunal (Composition of Tribunal) Order 2008;
b. 'the Qualifications Order' means the Qualifications for Appointment of Members to the First-tier Tribunal and Upper Tribunal Order 2008;
c. 'the 2008 Rules' means the Tribunal Procedure (First-tier Tribunal) (Social Entitlement Chamber) Rules 2008;
d. 'social security and child support case' has the meaning given in rule 1(3) of the 2008 Rules.

2. In exercise of the powers conferred by the 2008 Order the Senior President of Tribunals makes the following determinations and supplementary provision:—
3. The number of members of the Tribunal must not exceed three.
4. Where the appeal relates to an attendance allowance or a disability living allowance under Part III of the Social Security Contributions and Benefits Act 1992, or a personal independence payment under Part 4 of the Welfare Reform Act 2012, the Tribunal must, subject to paragraphs 8 to 13, consist of a Tribunal Judge, a Tribunal Member who is a registered medical practitioner, and a Tribunal Member who has a disability qualification as set out in article 2(3) of the Qualifications Order.
5. Where—

a. the appeal involves the personal capability assessment, as defined in regulation 2(1) of the Social Security (Incapacity for Work)(General) Regulations 1995;
b. the appeal involves the limited capability for work assessment under Part 5 of the Employment and Support Allowance Regulations 2008, under Part 5 of the Universal Credit Regulations 2013 or under Part 4 of the Employment and Support Allowance Regulations 2013;
c. the appeal involves the limited capability for work-related activity assessment under Part 6 of the Employment and Support Allowance Regulations 2008, under Part 5 of the Universal Credit Regulations 2013 or under Part 5 of the Employment and Support Allowance Regulations 2013;
d. the appeal is made under section 11(1)(b) of the Social Security (Recovery of Benefits) Act 1997;
e. the appeal raises issues relating to severe disablement allowance under section 68 of the Social Security Contributions and Benefits Act 1992 or industrial injuries benefit under Part V of that Act (except for an appeal where the only issue is whether there should be a declaration of an industrial accident under section 29(2) of the Social Security Act 1998);
f. the appeal is made under section 4 of the Vaccine Damage Payments Act 1979;
g. the appeal is against a certificate of NHS charges under section 157(1) of the Health and Social Care (Community Health and Standards) Act 2003;
h. the appeal arises under Part IV of the Child Maintenance and Other Payments Act 2008;

the Tribunal must, subject to paragraphs 7 to 14, consist of a Tribunal Judge and a Tribunal Member who is a registered medical practitioner.

6. In any other case the Tribunal must consist of a Tribunal Judge.
7. The Chamber President may determine that the Tribunal constituted under paragraph 5 or 6 must also include—

a. a Tribunal Member who is an accountant within the meaning of Article 2(i) of the Qualifications Order, where the appeal may require the examination of financial accounts;
b. an additional Member who is a registered medical practitioner, where the complexity of the medical issues in the appeal so demands;
c. such an additional Tribunal Judge or Member as he considers appropriate for the purposes of providing further experience for that additional Judge or Member or for assisting the Chamber President in the monitoring of standards of decision-making.

8. Where the Chamber President considers, in a particular case, that a matter that would otherwise be decided in accordance with paragraphs 4 or 5 only raises questions of law and the expertise of any of the other members is not necessary to decide the matter, the Chamber President may direct that the Tribunal must consist of a Tribunal Judge, or a Tribunal Judge and any Tribunal Member whose experience and qualifications are necessary to decide the matter.
9. The powers of the Chamber President referred to in paragraphs 7, 8, 10 and 12 may be delegated to a Regional Tribunal Judge and those referred to in paragraphs 7, 8 and 12 may be delegated to a District Tribunal Judge.
10. A decision, including a decision to give a direction or make an order, made under, or in accordance with, rules 5 to 9, 11, 14 to 19, 25(3), 30, 32, 36, 37 or 41 of the 2008 Rules may be made by a Tribunal Judge, except that a decision made under, or in accordance, with rule 7(3) or rule 5(3)(b) to treat a case as a lead case (whether in accordance with rule 18 (lead cases) or otherwise) of the 2008 Rules must be made by the Chamber President.
11. The determination of an application for permission to appeal under rule 38 of the 2008 Rules and the exercise of the power of review under section 9 of the Tribunals, Courts and Enforcement Act 2007 must be carried out—
    a. where the Judge who constituted or was a member of the Tribunal that made the decision was a fee-paid Judge, by a a judge who holds or has held salaried judicial office; or
    b. where the Judge who constituted or was a member of the Tribunal that made the decision was a salaried Judge, by that Judge or, if it would be impracticable or cause undue delay, by another salaried Tribunal Judge,

    save that, where the decision is set aside under section 9(4)(c) of the Act, the matter may only be re-decided under section 9(5)(a) by a Tribunal composed in accordance with paragraph 4, 5 or 6 above.
12. Where the Tribunal consists of a Tribunal Judge and one or two Tribunal Members, the Tribunal Judge shall be the presiding member. Where the Tribunal comprises more than one Tribunal Judge, the Chamber President must select the presiding member. The presiding member may regulate the procedure of the Tribunal.
13. Under rule 34(2) of the 2008 Rules it will be for the presiding member to give any written statement of reasons.
14. In rule 25(2) (Medical and physical examination in appeals under section 12 of the Social Security Act 1998) of the 2008 Rules "an appropriate member" of the Tribunal is a Tribunal Member who is a registered medical practitioner."

This practice statement replaces earlier ones issued in 2008 and February 2013. It still largely reproduces the previous practice in appeal tribunals constituted under the Social Security Act 1998 although paras 7(b) and 8 introduce an additional element of flexibility.

One respect in which the Practice Statement is less flexible than the previous legislation is the requirement in para.11(a) that applications for permission to appeal against decisions made by fee-paid judges *must* be dealt with by salaried judges or former salaried judges as must any reviews. The previous legislation was permissive. This creates difficulties where a salaried judge is faced with an application for permission based on what happened at the hearing or where he or she considers reasons to be inadequate but thinks they could properly be supplemented, because he or she is not able simply to refer the application for permission to appeal to be dealt with by the fee-paid judge. *SE v SSWP* [2009] UKUT 163 (AAC) and *AM v SSWP* [2009] UKUT 224 (AAC) show that the salaried judge must first review the decision, identifying the error of law, before referring the case to the fee-paid judge to take whatever action is appropriate.

See art.8 for the power to make majority decisions and see para.15(6) and (7) of Sch.4 to the Tribunals, Courts and Enforcement Act 2007 for the power of the First-tier Tribunal to proceed in the absence of a member or with a member who is not appropriately qualified. **5.186**

An appeal against a decision that a claimant is to be treated as not having limited capability for work because he or she has failed without good cause to attend a medical examination is not an appeal that "involves the limited capability for work assessment" for the purposes of para.5(b) of the Practice Statement and so a registered medical practitioner should not usually be a member of the First-tier Tribunal in such a case (*CH v SSWP (ESA)* [2017] UKUT 6 (AAC)). It appears that the registered medical practitioner had been present during the hearing, having sat in the previous case and this case having erroneously been listed before a two-person panel, but the judge had recorded that the case was dealt with by him alone. Accordingly, the claimant's appeal to the Upper Tribunal was dismissed.

Section 5 of, and Sch 1 to, the Interpretation Act 1978 provide that, "unless the contrary intention appears",—

> "'Registered medical practitioner' means a fully registered person within the meaning of the Medical Act 1983 who holds a licence to practise under that Act."

However, that definition does not apply in relation to the qualification of registered medical practitioners to sit as members of the First-tier Tribunal because a contrary intention does appear from the relevant legislation. Thus, a challenge by a claimant to the suitability of a registered medical practitioner to sit on the panel determining his case, based partly on the fact that the medical practitioner was not licensed to practise, was rejected by the Upper Tribunal in *DS v SSWP (PIP)* [2016] UKUT 538 (AAC); [2017] AACR 19. The claimant had looked the medical practitioner up on the General Medical Council's website and had discovered that he was registered but did not have a licence to practise and had also been given a warning for conduct some years earlier that did not meet the standards required of a doctor. The Upper Tribunal pointed out that art.2(2)(a) of the Qualifications for Appointment of Members to the First-tier Tribunal and Upper Tribunal Order 2008 (2018/2692) includes "a registered medical practitioner" among those eligible for appointment as a member of the First-tier Tribunal but that art.1(2) defines that term as "a fully registered person within the meaning of the Medical Act 1983 whether or not they hold a licence to practise under that Act". It also held that whether the doctor was a suitable person in general to sit on any particular panel was a matter for the Chamber President or his delegates in making a selection in accordance with the Practice Statement and that, once a selection to a panel had been made, "the Upper Tribunal cannot go behind that selection on the basis of a claimant's or even its own views about the member's suitability". It was noted that no question of bias had been raised in the case.

In any event, there is no obligation on the Chamber President to ensure that a medically qualified tribunal member sitting in any particular case is a specialist in the field of medicine relevant to the case (*ED v SSWP* [2009] UKUT 206 (AAC)). Even if a case is unusual any medical practitioner will ordinarily be able to deal adequately with competing views (*CSI/146/2003*). In *BT v SSW (II)* [2015] UKUT 98 (AAC), the statement of reasons had included a claim that the medically qualified panel member had "a particular expertise in this area", which the claimant challenged. The Upper Tribunal considered the claim to be "both ill-advised and unnecessary" but held that the First-tier Tribunal had been properly constituted and that the claim of specialisation did not have any material effect on its decision. The judge said:

> "18. Reading the statement of reasons, I am uncertain why it was felt necessary to make the point. The statement contains few references to use of the medical member's expertise and such as there are (para 20 – that a medical examination would not assist and para 30 – anticipated healing time) are not phrased in terms that suggest that reliance was being placed on something that only a specialist would know and a registered medical practitioner without such specialism would not. One can imagine, for instance, the position of a panel member who could say something like "In my career as a consultant in X I have conducted more than 200 procedures of the type you have undergone, without ever having noted the consequences you claim". It seems to me that it is only in the latter circumstances that it might be appropriate to mention the specific specialism of the panel member (and fairness would require the particular knowledge to have been put to the parties for comment). . . ."

If a specialist's report is necessary, it is open to the Tribunal to ask the parties to obtain a relevant opinion or to obtain one itself where s.20 of the Social Security Act 1998 applies.

It is not inappropriate for a doctor who acts as an examining medical practitioner for an agency of the Department for Work and Pensions also to sit as a tribunal member (*Gillies v Secretary of State for Work and Pensions* [2006] UKHL 2; [2006] 1 W.L.R. 781 (also reported as *R(DLA) 5/06*), but it may be inappropriate for a tribunal judge or a tribunal member with a disability qualification to sit on a tribunal considering a medical report compiled by a doctor with whom they have sat on previous occasions (*Secretary of State for Work and Pensions v Cunningham*, 2004 S.L.T. 1007 (also reported as *R(DLA) 7/04*)). In practice, therefore tribunal members do not sit in areas where they act as health care professionals. See further the notes to ss.3 and 11 of the Tribunals, Courts and Enforcement Act 2007.

5.187 The practice of listing employment and support allowance appeals with disability living allowance appeals brought by the same claimant has been held to be unlawful by a three-judge panel of the Upper Tribunal, although only by a majority (*MB v SSWP (ESA and DLA)* [2013] UKUT 111 (AAC); [2014] AACR 1). The issue arose because, under paras 4 and 5 of the practice statement, a tribunal member with a disability qualification must be a member of a panel hearing a disability living allowance case but is not entitled to be a member of a panel hearing an employment and support allowance case. It was even held unlawful for the cases to be heard consecutively, one immediately after the other, on grounds of principle if the employment and support allowance were held first and on grounds of practicality if the disability living allowance case were heard first. The result seems inconvenient.

Until 1999, there was a provision requiring that, where practical, at least one member of a tribunal should be of the same sex as the claimant. Notwithstanding the repeal of that provision, it was said in *CIB/2620/2000*:

> "exceptional cases where the absence of a tribunal member of the same sex as the claimant may inhibit the presentation or understanding of the claimant's case to such an extent that there will be a breach of the requirements of natural justice and of Article 6 of the European Convention on Human Rights if the tribunal is not reconstituted. It is obviously sensible to have a female member of the tribunal, if possible, in a case such as this one; raising as it does sensitive issues relating to a female medical condition. If a claimant specifically raises as an issue the absence from the tribunal of a member of the same sex, it will also be necessary for the tribunal to consider whether there is a real possibility of an injustice if the tribunal is not reconstituted. The repeal of s.46(1) [of the Social Security Administration Act 1992] means that there is no longer a need for the tribunal to consider in every case whether it is practicable for the tribunal to include a member of the same sex as the claimant, but a tribunal will nevertheless be under a duty to raise the matter of its own motion if there is a genuine reason to believe that in the circumstances of the particular case the absence of such a member may lead to injustice."

However, in the case before him, no point had been taken before the tribunal as to the absence of a woman and, although the case was concerned with a female medical condition, the examining medical officer's report was not disputed and the tribunal was not required to investigate any further the effect on the claimant of that condition. Accordingly, a fair-minded and informed observer would not have concluded that there was a real possibility of the hearing having been unfair due to the lack of a woman member of the tribunal and the Commissioner rejected that particular ground of appeal.

Number of members of the Upper Tribunal

3.—(1) The number of members of the tribunal who are to decide any matter that falls to be decided by the Upper Tribunal is one unless determined otherwise under paragraph (2). 5.188

(2) The tribunal may consist of two or three members if the Senior President of Tribunals so determines.

GENERAL NOTE

As is permitted by para.15(4) of Sch.4 to the Tribunals Courts and Enforcement Act 2007, this article leaves it to the Senior President of Tribunals to determine the number of members to determine any particular type of case and the qualifications they must have. He has issued practice statements. That for the composition of tribunals in relation to matters that fall to be decided by the Administrative Appeals Chamber of the Upper Tribunal on or after March 26, 2014 is in the following terms— 5.189

"1. In this Practice Statement;
   a. "the 2007 Act" means the Tribunals, Courts and Enforcement Act 2007;
   b. "the 2008 Order" means the First-tier Tribunal and Upper Tribunal (Composition of Tribunal) Order 2008;
   c. "the 2008 Rules" means the Tribunal Procedure (Upper Tribunal) Rules 2008;
2. In exercise of the powers conferred by the 2008 Order the Senior President of Tribunals makes the following determinations and supplementary provision:—
3. In accordance with articles 3 and 4 of the 2008 Order, any matter that falls to be decided by the Administrative Appeals Chamber of the Upper Tribunal is to be decided by one judge of the Upper Tribunal (or by a Registrar if the Senior President of Tribunals has approved that they may decide the matter) except that—
   a. where the Senior President of Tribunals or the Chamber President considers that the matter involves a question of law of special difficulty or an important point of principle or practice, or that it is otherwise appropriate, the matter is to be decided by two or three judges of the Upper Tribunal;
   b. to e. *Omitted.*
4. to 7. *Omitted*
8. Where more than one member of the Upper Tribunal is to decide a matter, the 'presiding member' for the purposes of article 7 of the 2008 Order and the paragraphs below is—
   a. the senior judge, as determined by the Senior President of Tribunals or Chamber President, if the tribunal is composed under paragraph 3(a), (b)(ii), (c)(ii),(d) or (e)(ii); or
   b. the judge if the tribunal is composed under paragraph 3(b)(i), (c)(i) or (e)(i).
9. Where, under paragraph 3(a), (b), (c), (d) or (e), two or three members of the Upper Tribunal have been chosen to give a decision that will, or may, dispose of proceedings, any ancillary matter that arises before that decision is given may be decided by—
   a. the presiding member; or
   b. by all the members so chosen; or

c. otherwise than at a hearing, by a judge or Registrar (who the Senior President of Tribunals has approved may decide the matter) nominated by the Chamber President or presiding member.

10. Where the Upper Tribunal has given a decision that disposes of proceedings ('the substantive decision'), any matter decided under, or in accordance with, rule 5(3)(l) or Part 7 of the 2008 Rules or section 10 of the 2007 Act must be decided by the same member or members of the Upper Tribunal as gave the substantive decision.

11. Paragraph 10 does not apply where complying with it would be impractical or would cause undue delay and, in such a case, the matter decided under, or in accordance with, rule 5(3)(l) or Part 7 of the 2008 Rules or section 10 of the 2007 Act must be decided by—
   a. if the substantive decision was given by more than one member of the Upper Tribunal and the presiding member or any other judge from that constitution is available, the members of the Upper Tribunal who gave the substantive decision and are available to decide the matter;
   b. otherwise, another judge of the Upper Tribunal nominated by the Chamber President."

Paragraph 3(a) of the Practice Statement provides for the tribunal to be composed of more than one judge in circumstances where a Tribunal of Commissioners could formerly have been constituted under s.16(7) of the Social Security Act 1998, but there is more flexibility. Two or three judges (as opposed to three or more Commissioners, although the power to appoint more than three Commissioners that existed from 1999 was never exercised) may sit to consider a case raising an important point of principle or practice even if it does not involve a question of law of special difficulty. A three-judge panel may be appointed where there has been disagreement between single judges of the Upper Tribunal. The decision of the three-judge panel will resolve the disagreement because a single judge must always follow a three-judge panel (*Dorset Healthcare NHS Foundation Trust v MH* [2009] UKUT 4 (AAC)). A three-judge panel will generally follow a decision of another three-judge panel or a decision of a Tribunal of Commissioners but will not do so if satisfied that it was wrong (*R(U) 4/88*). The precise status of a decision of a two-judge panel has not yet been determined.

A two- or three-judge panel may make a decision by a majority, with the presiding judge having a casting vote where there is a two-judge panel (see art.8).

Tribunal consisting of single member

5.190 **4.**—(1) Where a matter is to be decided by a single member of a tribunal, it must be decided by a judge of the tribunal unless paragraph (2) applies.

(2) The matter may be decided by one of the other members of the tribunal if the Senior President of Tribunals so determines.

General note

5.191 The power to provide for a case to be decided by a single member who is not a judge has not been exercised in relation to social security cases.

Tribunal consisting of two or more members

5.192 **5.** The following articles apply where a matter is to be decided by two or more members of a tribunal.

6. The number of members who are to be judges of the tribunal and the number of members who are to be other members of the tribunal must be determined by the Senior President of Tribunals.

General note

See the practice statements set out in the notes to arts 2 and 3. 5.193

7. The Senior President of Tribunals must select one of the members (the "presiding member") to chair the tribunal.

General note

The function of the Senior President of Tribunals may be delegated (see s.8 of the Tribunals, Courts and Enforcement Act 2007). The Practice Statement relating to the Administrative Appeals Chamber of the Upper Tribunal (see the annotation to art.3) states in para.8 that, where there is more than one judge on a panel, the senior judge will preside but, in other Chambers, including the Social Entitlement Chamber (see para.12 of the Practice Statement set out in the annotation to art.2), it is simply stated that "the Chamber President must select the presiding member". However, there is no need for a specific selection of the presiding member in respect of each panel. The application of a convention that the senior judge presides is sufficient (*HMRC v SDM European Transport Limited* [2016] UKUT 201 (TCC)). 5.194

8. If the decision of the tribunal is not unanimous, the decision of the majority is the decision of the tribunal; and the presiding member has a casting vote if the votes are equally divided.

General note

Tribunal Procedure Rules do not require that either a decision notice or a statement of reasons should indicate whether a decision was unanimous. Nonetheless, in *SSWP v SS (DLA)* [2010] UKUT 384 (AAC); [2011] AACR 24, it was held that there was a material error of law when a decision notice said that a decision was unanimous but the statement of reasons said it had been reached by a majority, without acknowledging the error. Moreover, the judge said that, although there was generally no duty to include in a statement of reasons the reasons for any dissent, if a decision notice did state that a decision was by a majority, there was a duty to include the reasons of the dissenting member and that the same approach applied if a decision notice stated that a decision was unanimous when in fact it had been reached by a majority. However, in *JD v SSD (WP)* [2014] UKUT 379 (AAC), some doubt was expressed as to whether a failure to give reasons for dissent was an error of law rather than merely being a breach of good practice. 5.195

In *PF (Nigeria) v Secretary of State for the Home Department* [2015] EWCA Civ 251; [2015] 1 W.L.R. 5235, it was held that the presiding judge's power to use a casting vote should not be exercised irrespective of the nature and extent of the disagreement between the members of the panel. It could be exercised where there was disagreement as to the law (where the right of appeal on a point of law provides an adequate safeguard), but it should not be exercised where there was disagreement on fundamental issues of primary fact. Instead, the case should be adjourned to be considered by a differently-constituted panel.

The Tribunal Procedure (First-tier Tribunal) (Social Entitlement Chamber) Rules 2008

(SI 2008/2685)

IN FORCE NOVEMBER 3, 2008

CONTENTS

PART 1

INTRODUCTION

PART 2

GENERAL POWERS AND PROVISIONS

PART 3

PROCEEDINGS BEFORE THE TRIBUNAL

CHAPTER 1

BEFORE THE HEARING

CHAPTER 2

HEARINGS

CHAPTER 3

DECISIONS

PART 4

CORRECTING, SETTING ASIDE, REVIEWING AND APPEALING TRIBUNAL DECISIONS

SCHEDULE 1

TIME LIMITS FOR PROVIDING NOTICES OF APPEAL TO THE DECISION MAKER

SCHEDULE 2

ISSUES IN RELATION TO WHICH THE TRIBUNAL MAY REFER A PERSON FOR MEDICAL EXAMINATION UNDER SECTION 20(2) OF THE SOCIAL SECURITY ACT 1998

After consulting in accordance with paragraph 28(1) of Schedule 5 to, the Tribunals, Courts and Enforcement Act 2007, the Tribunal Procedure Committee has made the following Rules in exercise of the powers conferred by sections 20(2) and (3) of the Social Security Act 1998 and sections 9(3), 22 and 29(3) of, and Schedule 5 to, the Tribunals, Courts and Enforcement Act 2007. The Lord Chancellor has allowed the Rules in accordance with paragraph 28(3) of Schedule 5 to the Tribunals, Courts and Enforcement Act 2007.

PART 1

INTRODUCTION

Citation, commencement, application and interpretation

5.197 **1.**—(1) These Rules may be cited as the Tribunal Procedure (First-tier Tribunal) (Social Entitlement Chamber) Rules 2008 and come into force on 3rd November 2008.

(2) [[3] These Rules apply to proceedings before the Social Entitlement Chamber of the First-tier Tribunal.]

(3) In these Rules—

"the 2007 Act" means the Tribunals, Courts and Enforcement Act 2007;

"appeal" includes an application under section 19(9) of the Tax Credits Act 2002;

"appellant" means a person who makes an appeal to the Tribunal, or a person substituted as an appellant under rule 9(1) (substitution of parties);

"asylum support case" means proceedings concerning the provision of support for an asylum seeker [[1] , a failed asylum seeker or a person designated under s.130 of the Criminal Justice and Immigration Act 2008, or the dependants of any such person]

"criminal injuries compensation case" means proceedings concerning the payment of compensation under a scheme made under the Criminal Injuries Compensation Act 1995 [[5] or section 47 of the Crime and Security Act 2010];

"decision maker" means the maker of a decision against which an appeal has been brought;

"dispose of proceedings" includes, unless indicated otherwise, disposing of a part of the proceedings;

"document" means anything in which information is recorded in any form, and an obligation under these Rules to provide or allow access to a document or a copy of a document for any purpose means, unless the Tribunal directs otherwise, an obligation to provide or allow access to such document or copy in a legible form or in a form which can be readily made into a legible form;

"hearing" means an oral hearing and includes a hearing conducted in whole or in part by video link, telephone or other means of instantaneous two-way electronic communication;

"legal representative" [2 a person who, for the purposes of the Legal Services Act 2007, is an authorised person in relation to an activity which constitutes the exercise of a right of audience or the conduct of litigation within the meaning of that Act], an advocate or solicitor in Scotland or a barrister or solicitor in Northern Ireland;

"party" means—

(a) a person who is an appellant or respondent in proceedings before the Tribunal;

(b) a person who makes a reference to the Tribunal under section 28D of the Child Support Act 1991;

(c) a person who starts proceedings before the Tribunal under paragraph 3 of Schedule 2 to the Tax Credits Act 2002; or

(d) if the proceedings have been concluded, a person who was a party under paragraph (a), (b) or (c) when the Tribunal finally disposed of all issues in the proceedings;

"practice direction" means a direction given under section 23 of the 2007 Act;

"respondent" means—

(a) in an appeal against a decision, the decision maker and any person other than the appellant who had a right of appeal against the decision;

(b) in a reference under section 28D of the Child Support Act 1991—

(i) the absent parent or non-resident parent;

(ii) the person with care; and

(iii) in Scotland, the child if the child made the application for a departure direction or a variation;

(c) in proceedings under paragraph 3 of Schedule 2 to the Tax Credits Act 2002, a person on whom it is proposed that a penalty be imposed; or [6 . . .]

[6 (cc) an affected party within the meaning of section 61(5) of the Childcare Payments Act 2014, other than an appellant; or

(d) a person substituted or added as a respondent under rule 9 (substitution and addition of parties);

[4 . . .]

"social security and child support case" means any case allocated to the Social Entitlement Chamber [4 of the First-tier Tribunal] except an asylum support case or a criminal injuries compensation case;

"Tribunal" means the First-tier Tribunal.

AMENDMENTS

1. Tribunal Procedure (Amendment) Rules 2009 (SI 2009/274) r.2 (April 1, 2009).

2. Tribunal Procedure (Amendment) Rules 2010 (SI 2010/43) r.3 (January 18, 2010).

3. Tribunal Procedure (Amendment No.3) Rules 2010 (SI 2010/2653) r.5(1) and (2) (November 29, 2010).

4. Tribunal Procedure (Amendment) Rules 2011 (SI 2011/651) r.4(1) and (2) (April 1, 2011).

5. Tribunal Procedure (Amendment) Rules 2013 (SI 2013/477) rr.22 and 23 (April 8, 2013).

6. Tribunal Procedure (Amendment) Rules 2015 (SI 2015/1510) rr.11 and 12 (August 21, 2015).

Definitions

"the 2007 Act"—see para.(3).
"appellant"—*ibid.*
"asylum support case"—*ibid.*
"criminal injuries compensation case"—*ibid.*
"party"—*ibid.*
"respondent"—*ibid.*
"Tribunal"—*ibid.*

General Note

5.198 By para.(2), these Rules apply to all cases within the Social Entitlement Chamber of the First-tier Tribunal which are those cases formerly dealt with by the appeal tribunals constituted under the Social Security Act 1998, by asylum support adjudicators (known collectively as the "asylum support tribunal") acting under ss.103 and 103A of the Immigration and Asylum Act 1999 and by the adjudicators of the Criminal Injuries Compensation Appeal Panel dealing with cases under schemes made under the Criminal Injuries Compensation Act 1995.

Although there are allocated to the Social Entitlement Chamber a wide variety of cases outside the scope of this work and some that could not properly be called either social security or child support cases, these Rules treat any case within the jurisdiction of the Chamber that is not an asylum support or criminal injuries compensation case as a "social security and child support case".

Note that a "hearing" means an "oral hearing" so that the term "paper hearing" is no longer appropriate for the consideration of a case on the papers. Perhaps "paper determination" will become the commonly used term.

Overriding objective and parties' obligation to co-operate with the Tribunal

5.199 **2.**—(1) The overriding objective of these Rules is to enable the Tribunal to deal with cases fairly and justly.

(2) Dealing with a case fairly and justly includes—

(a) dealing with the case in ways which are proportionate to the importance of the case, the complexity of the issues, the anticipated costs and the resources of the parties;
(b) avoiding unnecessary formality and seeking flexibility in the proceedings;
(c) ensuring, so far as practicable, that the parties are able to participate fully in the proceedings;
(d) using any special expertise of the Tribunal effectively; and
(e) avoiding delay, so far as compatible with proper consideration of the issues.

(3) The Tribunal must seek to give effect to the overriding objective when it—

(a) exercises any power under these Rules; or
(b) interprets any rule or practice direction.

(4) Parties must—

(a) help the Tribunal to further the overriding objective; and
(b) co-operate with the Tribunal generally.

Definitions

"party"—see r.1(3).
"practice direction"—*ibid.*
"Tribunal"—*ibid.*

General Note

It is nowadays conventional for procedural rules in England and Wales to set out clearly their overriding objective in this manner. The overriding objective of these Rules is rather different from that of the Civil Procedure Rules. There, one object is to ensure, so far as practical, that the parties are on an equal footing. It may be thought that that is not achievable in Citizen v State litigation before tribunals and these Rules do not require it. Instead, they emphasise the need to avoid "unnecessary formality" (see para.(2)(b)) and to promote the "enabling role" of tribunals (see para.(2)(c)) and they do not expressly refer to the resources of the tribunal in the way that the Civil Procedure Rules refer to the resources of the court as a matter to be taken into account when making procedural decisions. Perhaps, the key concept is "proportionality" (see para.(2)(a)) which is likely to be relevant in most cases where procedural decisions are being made. Paragraph (2)(b) is also of wide-ranging relevance. It was referred to by the Upper Tribunal in *Sheikh v Care Quality Commission* [2013] UKUT 137 (AAC), in support of the statement that— 5.200

> "Where a person makes an inappropriate type of application but an alternative type of application would have been appropriate in order to achieve the purpose desired by the applicant, the First-tier Tribunal should always treat the application as having been made in the appropriate form, unless that would cause any unfairness to any other party. Form should not triumph over substance . . ."

In that case, the First-tier Tribunal was held to have erred in law in not treating a late appeal as an application for the reinstatement of an earlier appeal.

By para.(3), the tribunal is required to "seek to give effect to" the overriding objective when exercising any power under the Rules or interpreting the Rules or a Practice Direction. Note that this does not extend to the exercise of powers under the Tribunals, Courts and Enforcement Act 2007 or other legislation but the principles of the overriding objective might anyway be relevant to the exercise of such powers. By para.(4), parties must help the tribunal to further the overriding objective and co-operate with the tribunal generally and a failure to do so may, in an extreme case, lead to proceedings being struck out under r.8(3)(b).

In *MA v SSWP* [2009] UKUT 211 (AAC), it was said that it was unlikely that the broad principles in r.2 would dictate the decision of a tribunal when considering whether to adjourn a hearing but that the introduction of the principles freed tribunals from the binding effect of earlier case law, although old cases might still be relevant if their principles were compatible with the overriding objective. 5.201

Indeed, in *AT v SSWP (ESA)* [2010] UKUT 430 (AAC), it was said that r.2 reinforced a duty to deal with cases fairly and justly that already existed. A failure expressly to refer to r.2 is thus unlikely to be an error of law in itself. Moreover, it was pointed out, while a tribunal must consider those factors in para.(2) that are relevant, the list of relevant factors in the paragraph is not exhaustive and not every listed factor will be relevant in every case. Nonetheless, the Upper Tribunal held the First-tier Tribunal to have erred in failing to consider the duty in r.2(2)(c) to ensure that the parties are able to participate fully in the proceedings when it determined an appeal without adjourning notwithstanding that the claimant had been forced to leave the hearing after 10 minutes through illness *(AM v SSWP (ESA)* [2013] UKUT 563 (AAC)). The Upper Tribunal took the same view in *PM v SSWP (IB)* [2013] UKUT 301 (AAC), where the First-tier Tribunal had decided to proceed in the absence of an agoraphobic claimant who had asked for a domiciliary hearing. In that case, it accepted that the First-tier Tribunal was entitled to have regard to the need to avoid delay but it pointed out that r.2(2)(e) was qualified by the words "so far as compatible with proper consideration of the issues." Rule 2(2)(c) was also considered relevant in *SW v SSWP (DLA)* [2015] UKUT 319 (AAC) and *LO v SSWP (ESA)* [2016] UKUT 10 (AAC); [2016] AACR 31 which were both cases where the First-tier Tribunal had not heard oral evidence from claimants who did not wish to attend a hearing due to health conditions and where it was suggested by the Upper Tribunal that a telephone hearing could have been considered. Similarly, it was invoked in *WA v SSWP (CSM)* [2016] UKUT 86 (AAC), where a party had given fear of her ex-partner as a reason for not attending a child support hearing. Steps that the judge said could be taken included writing to the party to reassure her that intimidation would not be tolerated, holding the hearing by videolink or by telephone, the presence of a security guard in the hearing room, laying out the hearing room in a particular way to create physical separation, the use of screens, staging the parties' entrance and departure from the room, and ensuring that their waiting arrangements minimised the risk of contact.

Rule 2 places obligations on the parties as well as on the First-tier Tribunal itself. Reference was made to it in *JC v SSWP (PIP)* [2016] UKUT 533 (AAC), where it was stated that documents should not be sent to the First-tier Tribunal by a representative if they have not been read, because it is necessary to avoid sending irrelevant or confidential documents. It was also suggested that, where a representative asks a claimant's doctor for a copy of the claimant's medical notes, he or she ought to make a proportionate and focussed request rather than requesting all of the records, because an unfocussed request, and one unlimited in time, increased the risk that irrelevant or confidential documents might be sent to the First-tier Tribunal. In that case, which was concerned with an appeal against a personal independence payment decision made in July 2015, 350 pages of medical records going back to at least 1992 had been obtained and sent to the First-tier Tribunal. While recognising that historic documents may sometimes be relevant, the Upper Tribunal suggested that it might have been appropriate in that case to ask the doctor only for the records from, say, January 1, 2013.

Alternative dispute resolution and arbitration

5.202 **3.**—(1) The Tribunal should seek, where appropriate—

(a) to bring to the attention of the parties the availability of any appropriate alternative procedure for the resolution of the dispute; and

(b) if the parties wish and provided that it is compatible with the overriding objective, to facilitate the use of the procedure.

(2) Part 1 of the Arbitration Act 1996 does not apply to proceedings before the Tribunal.

DEFINITIONS

"party"—see r.1(3).
"Tribunal"—*ibid.*

GENERAL NOTE

5.203 Rule 3(1) applies only if there is an alternative procedure available, which there is not in relation to social security cases. The scope for such schemes is limited by the facts that tribunal proceedings in social security cases are relatively cheap, quick and informal and that the conditions of entitlement often allow for little compromise, which means that alternative methods of dispute resolution normally offer little advantage over tribunal proceedings, particularly as there is now more intensive reconsideration of cases before appeals can be brought (see the note to reg.3ZA of the Social Security and Child Support (Decisions and Appeals) Regulations 1999). However, that is not to say that there are no cases that could be better dealt with outside the tribunal process.

PART 2

GENERAL POWERS AND PROVISIONS

Delegation to staff

4.—(1) Staff appointed under section 40(1) of the 2007 Act (tribunal staff and services) may, with the approval of the Senior President of Tribunals, carry out functions of a judicial nature permitted or required to be done by the Tribunal. 5.204

(2) The approval referred to at paragraph (1) may apply generally to the carrying out of specified functions by members of staff of a specified description in specified circumstances.

(3) Within 14 days after the date on which the Tribunal sends notice of a decision made by a member of staff under paragraph (1) to a party, that party may apply in writing to the Tribunal for that decision to be considered afresh by a judge.

DEFINITIONS

"the 2007 Act"—see r.1(3).
"party"—*ibid.*
"Tribunal"—*ibid.*

GENERAL NOTE

There is no need to make provision for the delegation of functions of a purely administrative nature and so this rule refers only to functions of a judicial nature. The Senior President of Tribunals has issued a number of practice statements (available at: *http://www.judiciary.gov.uk/publications/*) setting out the delegation of functions to staff in relation to the Social Entitlement Chamber of the First-tier Tribunal. The earliest of the current statements that relates to social security and child support cases delegates limited functions to any member of staff, still often referred to as a clerk, on or after October 1, 2014. The first, and previously the only function that had been delegated, is that of waiving under r.7(2)(a) the requirement that notice of withdrawal under r.17(1)(a) be in writing. This power is usually exercised when a party has informed a clerk over the telephone that he or she wishes to withdraw and has then been told to send in written confirmation but has failed to do so. A further set of functions relates to the question whether a notice of appeal satisfies the requirements set out in r.22(3) and is accompanied by the documents required by r.22(4) or whether a response to an appeal has been submitted within the time limit imposed by r.24(1)(b) or (c). Where a person has failed to comply with those provisions, a clerk may exercise the powers in r.7(2) to waive the requirement or require it to be remedied or may exercise the powers in r.8(1) and (3)(a) to strike the appeal or response out and then reinstate it under r.8(5). The clerk also has the power to give incidental directions and may extend the time for applying for reinstatement. Note that, whereas in relation to appeals the clerk is concerned with the adequacy of the content and not with whether they are in time, the reverse is true in relation to responses. It appears that initially some clerks believed that they had the power to refuse to admit late appeals, although that is plainly not so because the time for appealing is laid down in r.22(2). Clerks still do not have the wide powers to strike out and reinstate cases, to correct decisions and to issue directions that they enjoyed under the Social Security and Child Support (Decisions and Appeals) Regulations 1999 before the First-tier Tribunal was established on November 3, 2008. Note that, except in relation to compliance with r.22(3) and (4) or the time limits in r.24(1)(b) and (c), a clerk cannot even issue a warning that failure to comply with 5.205

an instruction will, or may, result in a case being struck out; such a warning must be in a direction (see r.8(1) and (3)(a)).

On April 20, 2016, the Senior President of Tribunals issued a further practice statement, approving that "an appropriately trained member of staff . . . designated a 'Tribunal Caseworker' by the Chamber President" may "make all decisions that a judge . . . may make under the Tribunal Procedure (First-tier Tribunal) (Social Entitlement Chamber) Rules 2008 save those which are substantive final decisions". This was issued for a period of six months but was followed by another, dated October 19, 2016, also for a period of six months and then another, dated May 30, 2017, effective for 12 months from the expiry of the preceding one and stating that "a review will take place on or before 17 April 2018".

Meanwhile, on December 1, 2016 a new practice statement was issued, stating:

"1. The Senior President of Tribunals hereby approves that a legally qualified member of staff appointed under section 40(1) of the Tribunals, Courts and Enforcement Act 2007 and designated as a 'Registrar' by the Chamber President, may carry out the functions of the Tribunal Procedure (First-tier Tribunal) (Social Entitlement Chamber) Rules 2008 set out in paragraph 3 below.

2. A Registrar must have been authorised by the Chamber President to exercise those functions. All functions must be exercised under the supervision of a judge and in accordance with guidance issued by the Chamber President.

3. A Registrar may make all decisions that a judge assigned to the Social Security and Child Support /Criminal Injuries Compensation jurisdiction may make under the Tribunal Procedure (First Tier Tribunal) (Social Entitlement Chamber) Rules 2008 save those which are substantive final decisions.

4. In accordance with rule 4(3) of the Tribunal Procedure (First Tier Tribunal) (Social Entitlement Chamber) Rules 2008, within 14 days after the date that the Tribunal sends notice of a decision made by a Registrar pursuant to an approval under paragraph 1 above that party may apply in writing to the Tribunal for the decision to be considered afresh by a judge."

This practice statement is not limited in time like the practice statements of April 20, 2016, October 19, 2016 and May 30, 2017 but otherwise is in identical terms save for one important difference. Registrars authorised to act under the practice statement of December 1, 2016 must be "legally qualified", whereas Tribunal Caseworkers authorised to act under the other practice statements need only be "appropriately trained".

The scope of the delegations under these practice statements is not entirely clear, because at first sight "substantive final decisions" are not decisions that are made under the Rules.

Case management powers

5.206 **5.**—(1) Subject to the provisions of the 2007 Act and any other enactment, the Tribunal may regulate its own procedure.

(2) The Tribunal may give a direction in relation to the conduct or disposal of proceedings at any time, including a direction amending, suspending or setting aside an earlier direction.

(3) In particular, and without restricting the general powers in paragraphs (1) and (2), the Tribunal may—

(a) extend or shorten the time for complying with any rule, practice direction or direction;

[[1] (aa) [[2] . . .]]

(b) consolidate or hear together two or more sets of proceedings or parts

of proceedings raising common issues, or treat a case as a lead case (whether in accordance with rule 18 (lead cases) or otherwise);
(c) permit or require a party to amend a document;
(d) permit or require a party or another person to provide documents, information, evidence or submissions to the Tribunal or a party;
(e) deal with an issue in the proceedings as a preliminary issue;
(f) hold a hearing to consider any matter, including a case management issue;
(g) decide the form of any hearing;
(h) adjourn or postpone a hearing;
(i) require a party to produce a bundle for a hearing;
(j) stay (or, in Scotland, sist) proceedings;
(k) transfer proceedings to another court or tribunal if that other court or tribunal has jurisdiction in relation to the proceedings and—
  (i) because of a change of circumstances since the proceedings were started, the Tribunal no longer has jurisdiction in relation to the proceedings; or
  (ii) the Tribunal considers that the other court or tribunal is a more appropriate forum for the determination of the case; or
(l) suspend the effect of its own decision pending the determination by the Tribunal or the Upper Tribunal of an application for permission to appeal against, and any appeal or review of, that decision.

AMENDMENTS

1. Tribunal Procedure (Amendment No. 4) Rules 2013 (SI 2013/2067) rr.22 and 23 (November 1, 2013).
2. Tribunal Procedure (Amendment) Rules 2015 (SI 2015/1510) rr.11 and 13 (August 21, 2015).

DEFINITIONS

"the 2007 Act"—see r.1(3).
"dispose of proceedings"—*ibid.*
"document"—*ibid.*
"hearing"—*ibid.*
"party"—*ibid.*
"practice direction"—*ibid.*
"Tribunal"—*ibid.*

GENERAL NOTE

Paragraph (1)

This paragraph, which is in conventional terms, permits the Tribunal to vary the way it handles a case so that the procedure is appropriate to the issues that arise and to the level of representation, if any. See also the note to r.30(5). **5.207**

In *Foulser v HMRC* [2013] UKUT 38 (TCC), Morgan J. considered that the power to regulate its own procedure would, in an exceptional case where an order barring HMRC from taking any further part in the proceedings was justified but the case did not fall within the scope of rules equivalent to rr.7 and 8 of these Rules, enable the First-tier Tribunal to make the desired order.

Paragraph (2)

This is in very broad terms and, although para.(3) and r.15(1) set out examples of directions the tribunal may give, they do not restrict the width of the power in this **5.208** paragraph. The power must, however, be exercised so as to give effect to the overriding objective in r.2 (see r.2(3)). It must also be exercised judicially. A judge is not generally entitled to subvert the decision of a Tribunal to adjourn for a medical report by directing that the case be relisted without the report. On the other hand, if the case is relisted and no point is taken about the absence of the report, the Upper Tribunal may take the view that the final decision is not erroneous in point of law *(CSDLA/866/2002)*. For the consequences of failing to comply with a direction, see r.7.

The procedure for applying for and giving directions is to be found in r.6. Note that, where a direction requires something to be done by a particular day, it must be done by 5pm on that day (r.12(1)) but, if that day is not a working day, the act is done in time if it is done on the next working day (r.12(2)).

In principle, an appeal lies against case management decisions but interlocutory appeals are not encouraged and, particularly in social security cases, permission may be refused on the ground that the appellant should await the final decision, which can then be challenged if the party is dissatisfied with it and a material interlocutory decision was erroneous in point of law (*LS v LB Lambeth (HB)* [2010] UKUT 461 (AAC); [2011] AACR 27). An application for permission to appeal made to the First-tier Tribunal may also be taken to be an application under r.6(5) for another direction amending, suspending or setting aside the challenged direction (*Dorset Healthcare NHS Foundation Trust v MH* [2009] UKUT 4 (AAC)).

Paragraph (3)(a)

5.209 Subparagraph (a) confers a very broad discretion. However, time limits ought to be observed and, in the context of a late application for reconsideration of a refusal of permission to apply for judicial review in an immigration case, the Court of Appeal has said that, under the identical rule in the Tribunal Procedure (Upper Tribunal) Rules 2008, a three stage approach should be adopted by (i) assessing the seriousness and significance of the failure to comply with the time limit, (ii) considering why the default occurred and (iii) evaluating all the circumstances of the case, so as to enable the tribunal to deal justly with the application (*R.(Kigen) v Secretary of State for the Home Department* [2015] EWCA Civ 1286; [2016] 1 W.L.R. 723, following the approach taken in *R.(Hysaj) v Secretary of State for the Home Department* [2014] EWCA Civ 1663; [2015] 1 W.L.R. 2472 in relation to time limits for appealing to the Court of Appeal). It has been held by the Immigration and Asylum Chamber of the Upper Tribunal, when quashing a decision of the First-tier Tribunal to extend time for the Secretary of State to apply for permission to appeal to the Upper Tribunal and its grant of permission, that the same approach should be applied by both the First-tier Tribunal and the Upper Tribunal when considering whether to extend time limits (*R.(Onowu) v First-tier Tribunal* [2016] UKUT 185 (IAC)). However, while accepting that the same three-stage framework should be applied in relation to applications for permission to appeal to the Administrative Appeals Chamber of the Upper Tribunal in social security cases, it has been suggested that the very robust approach taken in immigration and asylum cases to delays attributable to the underfunding and overwork of legal services and public bodies may not be appropriate in social security cases, where proceedings are not so adversarial and legal services may be provided by volunteers (*JP v SSWP* [2017] UKUT 149 (AAC)).

In *R.(CD) v First-tier Tribunal (CIC)* [2010] UKUT 181 (AAC); [2011] AACR 1, the judge declined an invitation to give guidance for future cases where an extension of time for appealing was concerned and, in particular, said that it was not appropriate to have regard to any checklist. In this, he adopted the reasoning of Black J. in *R.(Howes) v Child Support Commissioner* [2007] EWHC 559 (Admin) who said that "the factors that are relevant will be dependent upon the circumstances of the individual case". This approach has also been followed in *Ofsted v AF* [2011] UKUT 72 (AAC); [2011] AACR 32, *Information Commissioner v PS* [2011] UKUT 94 (AAC) and *R.(YT) v First-tier Tribunal (CIC)* [2013] UKUT 201 (AAC). In *Ofsted v AF*, the judge expressly distinguished *Jurkowska v Hlmad Ltd*

[2008] EWCA Civ 231, in which the Court of Appeal had sanctioned the detailed guidance given by the Employment Appeal Tribunal, on the ground that the nature of employment disputes was far more adversarial than disputes between citizens and the State should be. In *R(YT) v First-tier Tribunal (CIC)*, it was held that the fact that delay was due to negligence on the part of solicitors and the claimant might have a cause of action against them was relevant but not determinative. Other relevant factors in that case were the length of the delay, the consequences of the delay, the merits of the case, and the claimant's health and personal circumstances. Both the strength of the case and the reasons for the delay are likely to be relevant factors in most cases (*R. (Birmingham CC) v Birmingham Crown Court* [2009] EWHC 3329 (Admin); [2010] 1 W.L.R. 1287).

Another highly relevant factor in deciding whether to extend time is whether the person concerned acted reasonably. Thus, in *Peters v Sat Katar Limited* [2003] EWCA Civ 943, a person appealing to an employment tribunal who had sent her notice of appeal to the tribunal two weeks before the time limit had acted reasonably in not seeking confirmation from the appeal tribunal that the appeal had been received until nearly four weeks after she had sent it, but only because there was no indication in any of the information and guidance published by the tribunal that told her to contact it if she had not received an acknowledgment within a specified period.

"There is always a balance to be drawn between the length and effects of delay and the merits of the case", see *Pant v Secretary of State for the Home Department* [2003] EWCA Civ 1964, per Carnwath L.J. In that case the Court of Appeal declined to give permission to appeal out of time where the delay, caused principally by the appellant's former solicitors but also by her failure to keep touch with what was going on, had been two and a half years. The Court would have given permission to appeal but for the delay and, before rejecting the application, it assured itself that, although there would be some prejudice to the appellant, she could make another claim which would avoid the worst consequences there would otherwise have been in rejecting her case.

Paragraph (3)(b)

Although any judge may consolidate or hear together two or more cases, only the Chamber President (or a person to whom he has delegated the power) has the power to treat a social security case as a lead case (see para.10 of the practice statement set out above in the note to art.2 of the First-tier Tribunal and Upper Tribunal (Composition of Tribunal) Order 2008). In *John v Information Commissioner* [2014] UKUT 444 (AAC), the Upper Tribunal suggested that, where two parties appealed against the same decision, it would be appropriate to direct that the cases be heard together rather than consolidated. It was noted that consolidation had been described in *Zuckerman on Civil Procedure* (3th edn) at para.13.12 as an "arcane process". It has a technical meaning that is arguably inappropriate in appeals to tribunals. 5.210

Paragraph (3)(c)

Sub-paragraph (c) presumably refers to grounds of appeal and other submissions, rather than to evidence, despite the statutory definition. 5.211

Paragraph (3)(d)

Although there is no equivalent here to r.16(3), the principle that a person should not be compelled to produce evidence that he could not be compelled to produce in a court generally applies to privileged documents so that a party should not be directed to produce documents covered by legal advice privilege or litigation privilege (*LM v LB Lewisham* [2009] UKUT 204 (AAC); [2010] AACR 12). On the other hand, it may be arguable that, apart from matters clearly covered by professional privilege, it is open to a judge to direct the disclosure of documents, information or evidence 5.212

even though privilege or confidentiality could be claimed, placing the burden on the party to claim a right to non-disclosure by making an application under r.6(5) and leaving open the question whether an adverse inference should be drawn.

Resort may be had to the issuing of a formal summons, citation or order under r.16 if a person fails to comply with a direction to produce documents or other evidence under this subparagraph. However, the power to direct a person to provide information or submissions must be exercised proportionately. In *DTM v Ketttering BC (CTB)* [2013] UKUT 625 (AAC), it was held perverse to direct the claimant to inform the tribunal whether he wished his appeal to continue and, if so, whether he wished there to be a hearing, on pain of his case being struck out if he did not reply. The case could have been determined without his response.

Paragraph (3)(f), (g) and (h)

5.213 Sub-paragraphs (f), (g) and (h) must be read with rr.27–30.

In sub-para.(h), the distinction between a postponement and an adjournment is that the former occurs before the beginning of the hearing and the latter occurs once the hearing has begun, although an application for an adjournment may be made right at the beginning of a hearing. In *CDLA/3680/1997*, the Commissioner said that "[w]here an application for a postponement is refused—or no reply is received to such an application—it is incumbent on the claimant to take all possible steps to appear, or to have someone appear on his or her behalf, before the tribunal in order to assist the tribunal in considering whether there should be an adjournment". A representative should be ready to argue the case as well as possible if the application for an adjournment is refused.

This regulation is concerned only with the postponement or adjournment of oral hearings. There is no express power to adjourn the paper consideration of a case but such a power is to be implied (see *CDLA/1552/1998*).

A party seeking a postponement of a hearing is expected to give reasons and in *GC v SSWP (ESA)* [2014] UKUT 224 (AAC) the judge was highly critical of a leaflet produced by Her Majesty's Courts and Tribunals Service that implied that a postponement would be granted on request and failed to tell claimants that they should provide reasons. He set aside a decision made in the claimant's absence after the claimant had informed the First-tier Tribunal that he was unable to attend the hearing but did not explain why, although he did have reasons.

In *CSDLA/90/1998*, the Commissioner was highly critical of a local authority representative who had represented a claimant before a tribunal on an application for an adjournment. The claimant had had a prior engagement and the Commissioner found that the representative had indicated to her that she need not attend the tribunal hearing without asking her why the other engagement should take priority. When the tribunal refused to adjourn the hearing the representative had withdrawn. The Commissioner said that the nature of the other engagement should have been explained to the tribunal, that it was not for a representative to tell a claimant not to attend a hearing (because a tribunal were not bound to grant an adjournment merely because the claimant was not there) and that a representative who wished to withdraw should obtain the leave of the tribunal to do so. The claimant had been entitled to expect her representative to argue her case on the basis of the evidence available to him and doing so would not have prevented him from arguing on appeal that the tribunal had erred in refusing the adjournment.

5.214 The power to postpone or adjourn proceedings must not be used arbitrarily or capriciously and, in particular, must not be used in order to defeat the general purpose of the legislation, but otherwise there is a complete discretion so long as it is exercised judicially (*CIS/2292/2000*, citing *Jacobs v Norsalta Ltd* [1977] I.C.R. 189) and in accordance on the overriding objective in r.2(2). Nonetheless, in *CIS/2292/2000*, a tribunal erred in rejecting an application for an adjournment made by the representative of a claimant who was in prison, in circumstances where the claimant's oral evidence had an important part to play.

The overriding objective in r.2(2) may be particularly important where a power to postpone or adjourn a hearing is being considered. It requires a case to be dealt with "in ways that are proportionate to the importance of the case, the complexity of the issues, the anticipated costs and the resources of the parties" and also to the avoidance of delay but only "so far as compatible with proper consideration of the issues". On the other hand, in *MA v SSWP* [2009] UKUT 211 (AAC), it was said that it was unlikely that the broad principles in r.2 would dictate the decision of a tribunal when considering whether to adjourn a hearing but that the introduction of the principles freed tribunals from the binding effect of earlier case law, although old cases might still be relevant if their principles were compatible with the overriding objective. Although whether there should be an adjournment all depends on the facts of a particular case, the judge considered that a tribunal was likely to focus on the questions: (a) what would be the benefit of an adjournment, (b) why was the party asking for the adjournment not ready to proceed, and (c) what impact would an adjournment have on the other party and the operation of the tribunal system. In the case of a request for an adjournment to obtain further evidence, the first of those questions would involve considering what evidence was already before the tribunal, what evidence was likely to be obtained if the proceedings were adjourned, how long it would take to obtain it and whether the tribunal could use its own expertise to compensate for the lack of additional evidence. The judge considered that it would be exceptional for an adjournment that would otherwise be granted to be refused solely on account of the needs of the tribunal system as a whole. In *LO v SSWP (ESA)* [2016] UKUT 10 (AAC); [2016] AACR 31, there arose the question whether, where a claimant states that he or she does not wish to attend a hearing because of disability, a tribunal ought generally to consider whether a telephone hearing would be appropriate. The judge rejected a submission by the Secretary of State that it was unnecessary to do so merely because the claimant had not asked for such a hearing, since it was not the practice of the First-tier Tribunal's administration to inform parties of the possibility of there being a telephone hearing and so claimants could not be expected to ask for one. However, he held that there had been no error of law in the particular case before him. The First-tier Tribunal had given detailed consideration to the question whether there needed to be an adjournment so that the claimant could give evidence and had taken a proportionate approach. Although an offer of a telephone hearing was one possibility that might have been considered, it had not been necessary to do so in that case in order to deal with the issue of adjournment fairly. The claimant might, after all, have declined such an offer. Nonetheless, the implication of the decision is that there may be at least some cases where a failure explicitly to consider whether to offer a telephone hearing will render a decision wrong in law.

In both *CIB/1009/2004* and *CIB/2058/2004*, Commissioners have emphasised 5.215
that the inquisitorial approach of tribunals is not a complete substitute for representation and have cited *R. v Social Security Commissioner, Ex p. Bibi* (unreported, May 23, 2000) in which Collins J. said that, although there is no absolute right to representation, there is an absolute right to be dealt with fairly and that it was hardly unreasonable for a person to wish to be represented by the particular solicitor with whom she had been dealing. Therefore, a claimant's desire to be represented, or to be represented by a particular person, is a factor that ought to be given proper weight in considering whether or not to grant an adjournment. As to the balancing exercise itself, in *CIB/1009/2004* the Commissioner said—

> "13. A tribunal will always require to be persuaded that an adjournment is necessary—because there is always a potential disadvantage in adjourning a case—but the arguments against an adjournment in tribunal proceedings in a social security case may not be quite the same as those applicable in adversarial proceedings in the courts. In particular, the interests of the parties are not usually as closely balanced. In an ordinary social security case, where the Secretary of State does not provide a representative or have witnesses in attendance, there is very little disadvantage

to the Secretary of State in granting the claimant an adjournment. It is usually the claimant himself who suffers the principal disadvantage of delay. If the claimant judges that disadvantage to be less than the disadvantage of proceeding without representation, a tribunal should not too readily substitute its own judgment on the relative weight of those two factors. The main consideration for the tribunal will therefore be whether the adjournment can be justified in the light of the substantial cost of a further hearing and the delay in the determination of another case whose place the adjourned hearing will take. Thus the interests of taxpayers and claimants in general need to be balanced against the interests of the particular appellant.

14. If the claimant is to blame for need to request an adjournment, his interests are likely to be given correspondingly less weight. A claimant's interests may also be given less weight where his representative's fault has led to the request for an adjournment. By agreeing to act for a claimant, a representative takes some responsibility for the case and tribunals are entitled to exert pressure on representatives to behave properly. However, in an environment where most representatives are not qualified lawyers and where most claimants are not paying for the services of their representatives, some care must be taken not to cause injustice to a claimant by visiting upon him the sins of his representative. The tribunal's response must be proportionate, having regard to the consequences for the claimant of possibly losing his appeal."

In *CSDLA/90/1998*, the Commissioner also held that, when representation is undertaken by a local authority, the claimant is entitled to be fully represented by the authority until disposal of the appeal and the local authority must, if necessary, arrange representation through their legal department in order to avoid a postponement or an adjournment of a hearing. In *CIB/1009/2004*, the Commissioner disagreed with that approach and said that a local authority was entitled to limit the power of representatives to call upon other resources of the authority when a particular representative was unavailable due to illness. However, he went on to say that a representative should make reasonable efforts to secure alternative representation, even if that meant cancelling some other appointments, and that that implied that a request for an adjournment due to the non-availability of a representative should contain a clear indication that consideration had been given to the possibility of someone else representing the claimant. In the absence of such an explanation, the tribunal might be entitled to infer that the reasonable efforts had not been made to find alternative representation. However, a failure by a representing authority to make reasonable efforts to secure alternative representation should not have led to a refusal of an adjournment, when further efforts might not have made any difference, the claimant himself was blameless, a lot of money was at stake and the case was not straightforward so that an experienced representative might have assisted the tribunal to reach a conclusion favourable to the claimant.

In *Evans v Secretary of State for Social Security* (reported as *R(I)5/94*), a medical appeal tribunal disagreed with the opinions of two consultants. The Court of Appeal held that, where a tribunal proposed to put a different interpretation on the same clinical findings from that put by another expert, "fairness points to the need for an adjournment so that, where possible, the tribunal's provisional view can be brought to the attention of the claimant's own advisers". A similar approach has been taken by Park J. when hearing an appeal from a Pensions Appeal Tribunal (*Butterfield v Secretary of State for Defence* [2002] EWHC 2247 (Admin)). He said that, when a medically qualified member of a tribunal is the only person present with specialist medical knowledge and he perceives a possible medical objection to the claimant's case that has not been pointed out before, he must draw it to the claimant's attention and it may be necessary to offer the claimant an adjournment so that he has a realistic opportunity to consider the point "however inconvenient and irksome that may be". This makes clear what was probably meant in *Evans*. There need not always be an adjournment but the tribunal's provisional view should be put to the claimant and the claimant should expressly be *offered* an adjournment. See also *MB v DSD (II)*

[2010] NICom 133; [2011] AACR 41, where an appeal tribunal made new findings as a consequence of a medical examination and it was held that fairness required the claimant to have an opportunity to comment on those findings after the examination.

There is no general rule that an appeal to a tribunal should be postponed while related criminal proceedings are pending (*Mote v Secretary of State for Work and Pensions* [2007] EWCA Civ 1324 (reported as *R(IS) 4/08*)). The wishes of the parties will be relevant but will not be determinative. Often a claimant will not wish an appeal to be heard while criminal proceedings are pending lest anything he says at the tribunal hearing is used against him in the criminal trial. However, another claimant may prefer an appeal to be heard first because a finding that he or she was entitled to benefit is likely to undermine a prosecution for obtaining the same benefit by deception. 5.216

Adjournments are sometimes necessary because a member of the tribunal is obliged to stand down to avoid an appearance of bias (see the annotation to s.11 of the Tribunals, Courts and Enforcement Act 2007). In *CCS/1876/2006*, the Commissioner suggested that there might be occasions when it was prudent for a member of a tribunal to stand down in order to strengthen a party's confidence in the fairness of the procedures, even if there was no strict legal duty to do so, but he did acknowledge that the expense of an adjournment had to be kept in mind.

At a hearing following an adjournment, the tribunal may be constituted by one or more members who sat on the earlier tribunal and one or more who did not, if no evidence was taken before the adjournment. If evidence was taken before the adjournment, the tribunal should generally be either entirely the same or entirely differently constituted and, in the latter case, must have a complete rehearing, although it is entitled to accept the recorded evidence of a witness who gave evidence at the first hearing provided the rules of natural justice are not infringed (*R(U) 3/88*).

In fact current practice requires a judge to indicate whether any evidence has been heard at an adjourned hearing and, if it has, the clerk will always arrange for the tribunal to consist either of entirely the same members or entirely different members. This avoids the risk of subconscious bias being carried over from one hearing to the other or of a member remembering evidence from the first hearing that does not appear in the record of proceedings (see *CDLA/2429/2004*). 5.217

In *SW v SSWP (ESA)* [2010] UKUT 295 (AAC), the Upper Tribunal held that there had been a breach of the rules of natural justice simply because the medical member had discussed the case with a different judge before an earlier hearing. No other reason was given for the Upper Tribunal's conclusion, the decision being made by consent. It is suggested that merely having discussed a case with another member of the judiciary, even by way of preparation for an abortive hearing, should not be sufficient by itself to disqualify a judge or member from sitting to decide the case. It is the risk of a member having heard different evidence, or different submissions made by the *parties*, from what has been heard by another member that needs to be guarded against. All the members of the tribunal should determine the case on the basis of the same evidence and submissions.

A judge should not subvert a decision of a tribunal to adjourn for a medical report by immediately directing that the case be relisted without the report (*CSDLA/866/2002*).

An unfair refusal to adjourn may make the final decision of the tribunal erroneous in point of law so that an appeal may be brought against that final decision (*R. v Medical Appeal Tribunal (Midland Region) Ex p. Carrarini* [1966] 1 W.L.R. 883 (also reported as an appendix to *R(I)13/65*) *LS v LB Lambeth (HB)* [2010] UKUT 461 (AAC); [2011] AACR 27). 5.218

A refusal to adjourn was an issue in *CM/449/1990*, where the claim was made on behalf of a child with severe learning difficulties. His mother had written as soon as she was given notice of the hearing to apply for an adjournment on the ground that her son was away in short-term care. The tribunal refused the adjournment and dismissed the appeal, saying that they were not prepared to grant it "due to the high incidence of requests for adjournments". The Commissioner allowed the claimant's appeal on the ground that no reasonable tribunal could have refused the request for an adjournment and also on the ground that the tribunal had based their decision entirely on a wholly irrelevant consideration. It may be arguable that the Commissioner went too far in holding that the prevalence of requests for adjournments can never be a factor to be taken into account in considering such a request, but even if that is right, such a consideration cannot prevail without any regard at all being had to the particular facts and circumstances of the individual case. More recently, a refusal by the First-tier Tribunal to adjourn on the ground, among others, that "it was not in the habit" of adjourning so that a police officer could produce documents that were in dispute, was set aside on the ground that it was unfair in the circumstances of the case (*R.(YR) v First-tier Tribunal (CIC)* [2010] UKUT 204 (AAC)).

A refusal to adjourn should be recorded in the record of proceedings (*R(DLA) 3/08*) and it is desirable for a brief reason for the refusal to be included either in the record of proceedings or in the statement of reasons for the tribunal's decision (*Carpenter v Secretary of State for Work and Pensions* [2003] EWCA Civ 33 (also reported as *R(IB) 6/03*)), although a failure in either of these respects will not necessarily render a tribunal's decision erroneous in point of law. It will, however, do so if the decision appears aberrant without reasons (*R.(Birmingham CC) v Birmingham Crown Court* [2009] EWHC 3329 (Admin); [2010] 1 W.L.R. 1302).

Paragraph (3)(i)

5.219 The inability of the First-tier Tribunal to award costs in social security cases means that it is important that it considers upon whom the financial burden of preparing a bundle is placed. If it wishes the costs to be shared, it should direct both parties to prepare it. See *Eclipse Film Partners No.35 LLP v Revenue and Customs Commissioners (No.2)* [2016] UKSC 24; [2016] 1 W.L.R. 1939.

Paragraph (3)(k)

5.220 Sub-paragraph (k) applies only where the First-tier Tribunal had jurisdiction at the time the proceedings were begun. Otherwise, the Tribunal is required to strike the proceedings out under r.8(2). Rule 5(3)(k)(i) applies where the First-tier Tribunal loses jurisdiction and r.5(3)(k)(ii) applies only where the First-tier Tribunal and another tribunal have concurrent jurisdiction (which may be the case in some circumstances where a person moves to or from Northern Ireland).

Paragraph (3)(l)

5.221 Sub-paragraph (l) permits the effect of a decision to be suspended pending an appeal to the Upper Tribunal. There is no provision enabling the First-tier Tribunal to suspend a decision pending an appeal to it. In earlier editions of this work, it was stated that, although the First-tier Tribunal has no power to suspend the effect of a decision being challenged on appeal to it, judicial review proceedings could be brought in the Administrative Court or the Court of Session in non-social security cases to achieve a suspension pending an appeal, although it would be rare for relief to be granted. One such case which was transferred to the Upper Tribunal and was ultimately unsuccessful, brought while a special educational needs case was pending before the First-tier Tribunal, was *R.(JW) v The Learning Trust* [2009] UKUT 197 (AAC); [2010] AACR 11. However, in *CC & C Ltd v Revenue and Customs Commissioners* [2014] EWCA Civ 1653; [2015] 1 W.L.R. 4043, it was held that, while a court before whom parallel judicial review proceedings challenging the decision against which an appeal had been brought had the formal power to grant interim relief having the effect of suspending the decision until the First-tier Tribunal heard the appeal, it should exercise the power only if it was arguable that the decision was unlawful on a fundamental basis such as being an abuse of power or improper or taken in bad faith, rather than merely being unreasonable. Whether that distinction is important, or whether that case can be distinguished, in the context of social security and other welfare law appeals remains to be determined.

Giving tribunals power to suspend a decision pending an appeal to an appellate tribunal is consistent with the approach taken in the courts, where an appellate court has been held to have an inherent jurisdiction to suspend a decision while an appeal is pending (*Admiral Taverns (Cygnet) Ltd v Daniel* [2008] EWCA Civ 1501; [2009] 1 W.L.R. 2192). However, it is usually unnecessary for the Tribunal to suspend a decision in a social security case concerned with entitlement, due to the Secretary of State's power to suspend payments under reg.16 of the Social Security and Child Support (Decisions and Appeals) Regulations 1999 (see, in particular, reg.16(3)(b)(i) and (4)). In the past, the Secretary of State has generally not taken action to recover an overpayment while an appeal against a decision that the overpayment is recoverable is pending but he could now take the view that an appeal does not require him to stay his hand unless the Tribunal so directs under this provision, which would not necessarily be appropriate as a matter of course and could in any event presumably be limited to part of its decision. The power to suspend the effect of a decision may also be useful in appeals under the Social Security (Recovery of Benefits) Act 1997, because s.14 of that Act and the regulations made under it completely fail to deal with the consequences of a successful appeal to the Upper Tribunal. There is no automatic right to a suspension in any particular case. In *Carmarthenshire CC v MW (SEN)* [2010] UKUT 348 (AAC); [2011] AACR 17, which was concerned with the Upper Tribunal's power to suspend the effect of a decision of the First-tier Tribunal, it was held that there has to be balancing exercise, taking into account the practical consequences of suspending the decision on one side and the practical consequences of not doing so on the other. The chances of the appeal succeeding would be relevant but it was doubted whether a good prospect of the appeal succeeding could operate as a threshold condition, particularly in a case of urgency where the grounds of appeal might not have been formulated.

The First-tier Tribunal is entitled to suspend the effect of its own decision pending its determination of an application for permission to appeal and then, having considered the merits of the application and refused permission to appeal, may refuse to continue the suspension pending a renewed application to the Upper Tribunal (*Cabinet Office v Information Commissioner* [2016] UKUT 476 (AAC)). In such circumstances, the would-be appellant may make an application to the Upper Tribunal for a further suspension.

Procedure for applying for and giving directions

6.—(1) The Tribunal may give a direction on the application of one or more of the parties or on its own initiative. 5.222

(2) An application for a direction may be made—

(a) by sending or delivering a written application to the Tribunal; or

(b) orally during the course of a hearing.

(3) An application for a direction must include the reason for making that application.

(4) Unless the Tribunal considers that there is good reason not to do so, the Tribunal must send written notice of any direction to every party and to any other person affected by the direction.

(5) If a party or any other person sent notice of the direction under paragraph (4) wishes to challenge a direction which the Tribunal has given, they may do so by applying for another direction which amends, suspends or sets aside the first direction.

DEFINITIONS

"hearing"—see r.1(3).
"party"—*ibid.*
"Tribunal"—*ibid.*

GENERAL NOTE

5.223 There is no requirement that a person be given the opportunity to make representations before a direction is given. Plainly it is to be expected that such an opportunity would be given where a direction is to be given at a hearing but in other cases, where an application is made in writing or the tribunal proposes to issue a direction on its own initiative, it is often simpler and more proportionate to make the direction and then see whether anyone objects. If a direction is given and a party or other person affected objects to it, the remedy is to apply for another direction amending, suspending or setting aside the first direction (see para.(5)).

In *Dorset Healthcare NHS Foundation Trust v MH* [2009] UKUT 4 (AAC), the Upper Tribunal emphasised the desirability of the First-tier Tribunal considering whether to vary a direction, either on its own initiative under r.5(3) or on an application under r.6(5), before contemplating granting permission to appeal, at least in a case where the original direction was made without the benefit of full argument.

There is no general duty to give reasons for decisions that do not "dispose of proceedings" (see r.34) but reasons may nonetheless be required for an interlocutory decision that would appear aberrant without reasons (*R.(Birmingham CC) v Birmingham Crown Court* [2009] EWHC 3329 (Admin); [2010] 1 W.L.R. 1287).

Failure to comply with rules etc.

5.224 **7.**—(1) An irregularity resulting from a failure to comply with any requirement in these Rules, a practice direction or a direction, does not of itself render void the proceedings or any step taken in the proceedings.

(2) If a party has failed to comply with a requirement in these Rules, a practice direction or a direction, the Tribunal may take such action as it considers just, which may include—

(a) waiving the requirement;
(b) requiring the failure to be remedied;
(c) exercising its power under rule 8 (striking out a party's case); or
(d) exercising its power under paragraph (3).

(3) The Tribunal may refer to the Upper Tribunal, and ask the Upper Tribunal to exercise its power under section 25 of the 2007 Act in relation to, any failure by a person to comply with a requirement imposed by the Tribunal—

(a) to attend at any place for the purpose of giving evidence;
(b) otherwise to make themselves available to give evidence;
(c) to swear an oath in connection with the giving of evidence;
(d) to give evidence as a witness;
(e) to produce a document; or
(f) to facilitate the inspection of a document or any other thing (including any premises).

DEFINITIONS

"the 2007 Act"—see r.1(3).
"document"—*ibid.*
"party"—*ibid.*
"practice direction"—*ibid.*
"Tribunal"—*ibid.*

GENERAL NOTE

Paragraph (1) 5.225

This is an important provision which enables a tribunal to overlook an immaterial breach of the requirements of any rule, practice direction or direction. Although para.(2) is concerned with the consequences of a party failing to comply with a requirement, it appears to be implicit in para.(1) that a failure by the tribunal itself to comply with a requirement can be waived, provided of course that that does not result in undue unfairness to a party. Note, however, that it does not deal with a breach of any statutory requirement other than one contained in the Rules.

Paragraph (2) 5.226

This sets out the possible procedural consequences of a party failing to comply with a requirement of the Rules, a practice direction or a direction. However, there can be other consequences. Thus, for instance, a failure to comply with a direction to provide evidence may simply lead to the case being heard without the evidence, which will usually be to the disadvantage of the person who failed to provide the evidence. Whether it is appropriate to draw an adverse inference from a failure to provide evidence will depend on the circumstances (*CCS/3757/2004* and see also the note to s.3(1) of the Tribunals, Courts and Enforcement Act 2007).

The powers to strike out a case or refer it to the Upper Tribunal may be used only if an appropriate warning has been given (see r.8(3)(a) and the note to para.(3) of this rule).

The powers in subparas (a), (b) and (c) may be exercised by a clerk where a notice of appeal does not satisfy the requirements set out in r.22(3) or is not accompanied by the documents required by r.22(4) and the power to waive an irregularity under subpara.(a) may be exercised by a clerk where a party has given notice of withdrawal under r.17(1)(a) orally but not in writing (see the note to r.4).

Paragraph (3) 5.227

This enables a breach of a requirement to give evidence or produce or make available a document to be referred to the Upper Tribunal with a view to the Upper Tribunal punishing the person for contempt of court (with a term of imprisonment of up to two years and an unlimited fine) under s.25 of the Tribunals' Courts and Enforcement Act 2007, as applied by r.7(4) of the Tribunal Procedure (Upper Tribunal) Rules 2008. In *CB v Suffolk CC (Enforcement Reference)* [2010] UKUT 413 (AAC); [2011] AACR 22, the Upper Tribunal fined a witness £500 for ignoring a summons issued by the Health, Education and Social Care Chamber of the First-tier Tribunal and, under s.16(3) of the Contempt of Court Act 1981, specified a term of imprisonment of seven days to be served if the fine was not paid within the time allowed. The Upper Tribunal emphasised that, if a person thought that a summons was inappropriate, the proper course of action was to ask the First-tier Tribunal to set it aside (see r.16(4)(a)) and, if that failed, to apply to the Upper Tribunal for judicial review to quash the summons. Simply ignoring a summons was not a legitimate course of action. In *BO v Care Quality Commission (Enforcement Reference)* [2013] UKUT 53 (AAC), a fine of £100, with an alternative of two days imprisonment, was imposed in another case where a summons had been ignored.

It has been held that a response to an appeal required under r.24(1) to (3), which is primarily a submission, is not a "document" within the scope of r.7(3)(e), although the documents that ought to accompany it by virtue of r.24(4) would be (*AP v HMRC (Enforcement Reference)* [2014] UKUT 182 (AAC); [2014] AACR 37). However, it is arguable that the better view, although one that would produce the same result where a decision-maker failed to provide a response to an appeal, is that a written submission is a "document" but that a person cannot "produce" a document that does not exist. In other words, in this context "produce" means "provide" rather than "create". In social security cases, a reference under para.(3) may only be made by the Chamber President (see the Practice Statement on the composition of the First-tier Tribunal in social security and child support cases set out above in the note to art.2 of the First-tier Tribunal and Upper Tribunal (Composition of Tribunals) Order 2008) or a judge to whom he has delegated that function (see para.4 of Sch.4 to the 2007 Act) and is likely to be made only as a matter of last resort. In *MD v SSWP (Enforcement Reference)* [2010] UKUT 202 (AAC); [2011] AACR 5, a three-judge panel said that, before a reference is made, the First-tier Tribunal should be satisfied that all the procedural requirements have been met and, in particular, that any summons, citation or order under r.16 was sent to the correct address and included an appropriate warning and, in the case of a summons or citation, was accompanied by an offer to pay expenses. It would be inappropriate to rely on r.7(1) if there might be any prejudice or injustice to the contemnor. The three-judge panel also suggested that, before making a reference, the First-tier Tribunal should give an alleged contemnor an opportunity to explain their conduct so that it could consider whether the matter did indeed warrant a reference. The implication may be that, even where the relevant direction is not made under r.16, it should contain a warning as to the possible effect of breaching it if the First-tier Tribunal is contemplating a reference in that event.

Paragraph (3)(c) must be read subject to s.5 of the Oaths Act 1978, which permits a person who objects to being sworn to make a solemn affirmation instead.

Striking out a party's case

5.228 **8.**—(1) The proceedings, or the appropriate part of them, will automatically be struck out if the appellant has failed to comply with a direction that stated that failure by a party to comply with the direction would lead to the striking out of the proceedings or that part of them.

(2) The Tribunal must strike out the whole or a part of the proceedings if the Tribunal—

(a) does not have jurisdiction in relation to the proceedings or that part of them; and

(b) does not exercise its power under rule 5(3)(k)(i) (transfer to another court or tribunal) in relation to the proceedings or that part of them.

(3) The Tribunal may strike out the whole or a part of the proceedings if—

(a) the appellant has failed to comply with a direction which stated that failure by the appellant to comply with the direction could lead to the striking out of the proceedings or part of them;

(b) the appellant has failed to co-operate with the Tribunal to such an extent that the Tribunal cannot deal with the proceedings fairly and justly; or

(c) the Tribunal considers there is no reasonable prospect of the appellant's case, or part of it, succeeding.

(4) The Tribunal may not strike out the whole or a part of the proceedings under paragraph (2) or (3)(b) or (c) without first giving the appellant an opportunity to make representations in relation to the proposed striking out.

(5) If the proceedings, or part of them, have been struck out under paragraph (1) or (3)(a), the appellant may apply for the proceedings, or part of them, to be reinstated.

(6) An application under paragraph (5) must be made in writing and received by the Tribunal within 1 month after the date on which the Tribunal sent notification of the striking out to the appellant.

(7) This rule applies to a respondent as it applies to an appellant except that—

(a) a reference to the striking out of the proceedings is to be read as a reference to the barring of the respondent from taking further part in the proceedings; and

(b) a reference to an application for the reinstatement of proceedings which have been struck out is to be read as a reference to an application for the lifting of the bar on the respondent from taking further part in the proceedings.

(8) If a respondent has been barred from taking further part in proceedings under this rule and that bar has not been lifted, the Tribunal need not consider any response or other submission made by that respondent [1 and may summarily determine any or all issues against that respondent].

AMENDMENT

1. Tribunal Procedure (Amendment No.3) Rules 2010 (SI 2010/2653) r.5(1) and (3) (November 29, 2010).

DEFINITIONS

"appellant"—see r.1(3).
"party"—*ibid.*
"respondent"—*ibid.*
"Tribunal"—*ibid.*

GENERAL NOTE

Note that, although paras (1)–(6) are expressed in terms of striking out proceedings brought by the appellant, by virtue of paras (7) and (8) they also provide for barring a respondent from taking further part in the proceedings. A decision to strike out proceedings is one that "disposes of proceedings" so that the parties are entitled to ask for a statement of reasons if one is not supplied with the decision (see r.34). It is suggested that a respondent who has been barred from taking a further part in proceedings is also entitled to a statement of reasons for the barring. 5.229

The powers to strike an appeal out under paras (1) or (3)(a) and then reinstate it under para.(5) may be exercised by a clerk where a notice of appeal does not satisfy the requirements set out in r.22(3) or is not accompanied by the documents required by r.22(4). A clerk may also bar a respondent from taking part in proceedings if a response is not submitted within the time required by r.24(1)(b) or (c). See the note to r.4..

A decision to strike out an appeal under paras (2) or (3) may be made without an oral hearing (see r.27(3)) and the usual reason for the Secretary of State or HMRC applying for the striking out of a social security appeal will be to avoid the cost of a hearing or of preparing a full response with all the accompanying documents. However, there are many occasions when it is appropriate for there to be an oral hearing of a strike-out application so that oral representations may be made. In the social security context, an oral hearing is likely to defeat the purpose of an application under r.8(3)(c) but that is not so in areas of law where an oral hearing of an appeal can take several days. See the note to para.(3) for the need to ensure that striking a case out without a hearing does not result in unfairness.

Paragraph (1)

This provides for an automatic strike out where a person has failed to comply with a direction that carried a warning that, unless there was compliance, the case "will" be struck out. No further exercise of judicial discretion is required for the strike-out to take effect provided that it is clear that there has not been compliance. It is important to distinguish this paragraph from para.(3)(a), which provides for a case to be struck out for failure to comply with a direction that carried a warning that if there was no compliance the case "may" be struck out. In the 5.230

latter case, there needs to be a judicial decision exercising the power to strike out. Because a strike out under para.(1) is automatic, there can be no effective appeal against it. However, it is possible to apply for reinstatement under paras (5) and (6) and then, if necessary, to appeal against a refusal to reinstate the appeal. An alternative approach would be to appeal against the earlier direction insofar as it stated that failure to comply with it would lead to the appeal being struck out (as was done in *Salisbury Independent Living v Wirral MBC (HB)* [2011] UKUT 44 (AAC); [2012] AACR 37).

In *DTM v Ketttering BC (CTB)* [2013] UKUT 625 (AAC), it was held that, because a judge had issued a direction stating that a failure to comply with it "will lead to the striking out of the appeal without any further procedure under rule 8(1) of the Tribunal Procedure (First-tier Tribunal (Social Entitlement Chamber) Rules 2008" and the result of non-compliance was that the appeal was indeed struck out, the First-tier Tribunal no longer had jurisdiction to hear the appeal in the absence of reinstatement under para.(5). The Upper Tribunal substituted its own decision, first reinstating the appeal against the local authority's decision and then determining it.

The direction in that case had actually been given because the claimant had not returned the enquiry form issued by the First-tier Tribunal, asking him whether he wished to withdraw his appeal and, if not, whether he wished there to be an oral hearing. The direction had required the claimant to state within 14 days of the date of the direction whether he wished his appeal to continue. In fact, the direction was not posted to the claimant for a week and the claimant replied to the direction by returning the enquiry form so that it arrived nearly a week after the deadline. The Upper Tribunal said that it had been irrational to issue the direction at all because the failure to return the enquiry form did not prevent the First-tier Tribunal from determining the appeal and, indeed, the failure to return it would have entitled the First-tier Tribunal to determine the appeal without a hearing if it considered that not to be inappropriate (see r.27(1)). The inquisitorial role of the First-tier Tribunal and the overriding objective both pointed towards determining the appeal one way or another, rather than issuing a direction that included words having the effect that non-compliance would lead automatically to striking it out.

Paragraph (2)

5.231 This replaces reg.46(1)(a) of the Social Security and Child Support (Decisions and Appeals) Regulations 1999. However, it is not limited to cases excluded from the scope of s.12 of the Social Security Act 1998 by virtue of Sch.2 to that Act or Sch.2 to the 1999 Regsulations. Moreover, unlike Reg.46, its terms are mandatory, so that a final decision to the effect that the tribunal lacks jurisdiction must always be in the form of a decision to strike out the appeal. Most importantly, whereas in *Morina v Secretary of State for Work and Pensions* [2007] EWCA Civ 749; [2007] 1 W.L.R. 3033 (also reported as *R(IS) 6/07*) the Court of Appeal held that that there was no right of appeal under s.14 of the Social Security Act 1998 against a decision under reg.46(1)(a), in *LS v LB Lambeth (HB)* [2010] UKUT 461 (AAC); [2011] AACR 27 it has been held that there is a right of appeal against any decision of the First-tier Tribunal (other than an "excluded decision" within the scope of s.11(5) of the Tribunals, Courts and Enforcement Act 2007).

Where an appeal has lapsed because the decision under appeal was made under s.16 of the Tax Credits Act 2002 and has been replaced by a decision under s.18, it must be struck out under this provision (*LS v HMRC (TC)* [2017] UKUT 275 (AAC)). Presumably the same approach must be taken where the decision under appeal was made under s.8 or s.10 of the Social Security Act 1998 and has been revised under s.9 to the advantage of the appellant so that s.9(6) applies.

In *AW v Essex CC (SEN)* [2010] UKUT 74 (AAC); [2010] AACR 35 (subsequently reversed by the Court of Appeal without reference to this point), it was emphasised that there was a distinction between the equivalent of para.(2) in the Tribunal Procedure (First-tier Tribunal) (Social Entitlement Chamber) Rules 2008

(SI 2008/2699) and the equivalent of para.(3)(c). It is appropriate to use the latter provision, which is discretionary, where a case appears hopeless but is nonetheless one that the First-tier Tribunal has jurisdiction to consider.

By virtue of para.(4), a party must be given an opportunity to make representations before his or her case is struck out and there will be some cases where justice requires there to be a hearing, notwithstanding r.27(3).

Paragraph (3)

Striking out under para.(3) is discretionary and must be proportionate (see r.2(2)(a) and (3)) so that, where a case is being struck out under sub-para.(a) or (b), regard must be had to both the culpability of the party whose case is being struck out and the amount at stake on the appeal. This point was made in *Alpha Rocks Solicitors v Alade* [2015] EWCA Civ 685; [2015] 1 W.L.R. 4534 in relation to ordinary civil proceedings. The Court of Appeal also held that a judge considering on the papers whether to strike out a case should avoid conducting a mini-trial and should not determine issues of credibility "where oral evidence at least *might* have put a different complexion on the allegations made" (emphasis of the Court). **5.232**

Rule 27(3) permits the Tribunal to strike out a case without a hearing but, by virtue of para.(4), a party must be given an opportunity to make representations before his or her case is struck out under sub-para.(b) or (c). Where an effective opportunity to make representations would require a hearing, it is likely to be simpler and fairer to determine the appeal in the ordinary way instead of striking it out. Thus sub-paras (b) and (c) should probably be used only in clear and obvious cases.

There is no right to make representations before a case is struck out under subpara.(a); instead there is a right to apply for reinstatement after the event, by virtue of paras (5) and (6). In *LB Camden v FG (SEN)* [2010] UKUT 249 (AAC), it was suggested that case management directions directed to a respondent and containing a warning that a failure to comply with them might result in the First-tier Tribunal's use of its powers to strike out a case under r.8 ought to have referred specifically to the equivalents of paras (3)(a), (7) and (8) of this rule and that an order under the equivalent of r.8(3)(a) addressed to a respondent ought to have referred to the equivalent of para.(7) and also to the equivalent of paras (5) and (6). However, in the particular case, the failure was not important because the respondent did protest and its letter was in fact treated as an application for reinstatement under paras (5) and (6).

Sub-paragraph (c) reintroduces a power to strike a case out where it has no reasonable prospect of success. The "appellant's case" is not the same as the "grounds on which the appellant relies" in r.22(3)(f) or r.23(6)(e) and so the First-tier Tribunal must look beyond the appellant's formal grounds of appeal and consider whether there are any other obvious grounds that might have a reasonable prospect of success (*HJ v Information Commissioner* [2016] UKUT 82 (AAC); [2016] AACR 33). An equivalent power in reg.48 of the 1999 Regs was revoked in 2004.

The main, perhaps only, reason why the Secretary of State or HMRC might make an application under sub-para.(c) in a social security case is that it is thought appropriate that the case be determined without a hearing. Whether or not an opportunity to have an oral hearing is required for compliance with the European Convention on Human Rights in a social security case depends on whether or not any oral evidence might make any difference to the outcome (*Fexler v Sweden* ECHR Application No. 36801/06). The judge must still address the issue in the appeal when considering whether to strike a case out under sub-para.(c), but may do so summarily, having given the appellant an opportunity to make representations. In *HMRC v Fairford Group plc (in liquidation)* [2014] UKUT 329 (TCC), the Upper Tribunal said:

> "The First-tier Tribunal must decide whether there is a realistic, as opposed to a fanciful (in the sense of being entirely without substance) prospect of succeeding on the issue at a full hearing. ... The tribunal must avoid conducting a 'mini-trial'. ... [T]he strike out procedure is to deal with cases that are not fit for a full hearing at all."

The advantages of this procedure may not be insignificant in financial terms, given that not only are the costs of a hearing saved but also a case may be struck out by a judge alone without other members. However, striking out a case under sub-para. (c) will clearly not be appropriate where there is a dispute as regards which either oral evidence or the expertise of specialist members might be required. Thus, it was inappropriate to exercise the power to strike out an appeal on the ground that it had no prospect of success so as to deny an appellant an oral hearing in a case where there were disputed issues of fact (*AW v Information Commissioner* [2013] UKUT 30 (AAC)) or a discretion had to be exercised in respect of which oral representations might have been made (*R.(AM) v First-tier Tribunal (CIC)* [2013] UKUT 333 (AAC)). Striking a case out without an oral hearing was also held to be inappropriate when it amounted to a breach of an unqualified promise in guidance notes that there would be an oral hearing of the appeal (*AM v Information Commissioner* [2014] UKUT 239 (AAC)). Thus, in a social security case, striking a case out without an oral hearing is likely to be most appropriate where there is a clear statutory bar to entitlement, such as a time limit or age limit, which the claimant cannot satisfy.

An application by a respondent for the striking out of an appeal under sub-para. (c) should be copied to the claimant and be accompanied by a full response that complies with r.24 unless that would clearly be disproportionate, so that the First-tier Tribunal has all the material necessary to enable it properly to decide whether the appeal has no reasonable prospect of success, the claimant is able to make effective representations and the appeal is ready for determination if it is not struck out (*JT v HMRC (TC)* [2015] UKUT 81 (AAC)).

Paragraphs (5) and (6)

5.233 These paragraphs apply only to cases struck out under para.(1) or (3)(a). In other cases, the Tribunal must give the party an opportunity to make representations *before* a case is struck out. In *Synergy Child Services Ltd v Ofsted* [2009] UKUT 125 (AAC), the Upper Tribunal allowed an appeal lay against a refusal to reinstate a struck-out appeal under the equivalent provisions in the Tribunal Procedure (First-tier Tribunal) (Health, Education and Social Care Chamber) Rules 2008 (SI 2008/2699) and held that, when considering whether to reinstate an appeal, "a Tribunal should have regard to the broad justice of the case, in the light of all the circumstances obtaining at the time the application for reinstatement is being considered". Nonetheless, it said that "[w]here there has been flagrant disobedience by a party, belated compliance or a change of circumstances making compliance irrelevant will not always require a Tribunal to reinstate an appeal".

The need to enforce orders in the courts has been emphasised in *Thevarajah v Riordan* [2015] UKSC 78; [2016] 1 W.L.R. 76, a decision in respect of relief from sanction (in the form of barring the defendant from defending the claim), where it was held that belated compliance with an "unless" order equivalent to the type of direction mentioned in r.8(1) could not amount to a change of circumstances justifying relief unless accompanied by other facts. Moreover, in general, directions made by the First-tier Tribunal should be enforced as rigorously as orders of courts (*BPP Holdings v Commissioners for Her Majesty's Revenue and Customs* [2016] EWCA Civ 121; [2016] 1 W.L.R. 1915, where the Court of Appeal said that the Upper Tribunal had erred in allowing an appeal from a decision of the Tax Chamber of the First-tier Tribunal to bar HMRC from further participation in the taxpayer's appeal in a case where it had not only failed to comply with the order to file replies to certain requests by providing replies that were manifestly inadequate but had also failed to remedy the breach for several months, subsequently pleading a lack of resources but having failed to seek a variation of the order). The circumstances of litigants in person in social security and child support cases may sometimes justify a different approach, but not necessarily.

Where an application for reinstatement has been refused, the party can make another application. This may be justified where, for instance, the first application was rejected in ignorance of a material fact or compelling evidence or where there has been a material change of circumstances (*R.(BD) v First-tier Tribunal (CIC)* [2013] UKUT 332 (AAC)).

In *LB Camden v FG (SEN)* [2010] UKUT 249 (AAC), the decision refusing to lift a bar on a respondent was communicated by telephone initially and then it appears that a letter was sent, "pp'd" on behalf of the judge. The Upper Tribunal recommended that such a decision should be in the form of an order signed by the judge and that it ought to draw attention to the right to make an application under the equivalent of Pt 4 of these Rules, although such notice does not appear to be mandatory where barring a respondent does not dispose of all issues in the proceedings (see r.33). As noted above, it was also suggested that an order under the equivalent of r.8(3)(a) (or, inferentially, r.8(2)) addressed to a respondent ought to refer to the right to make an application under paras (5) and (6). These comments were endorsed in *JP v SSWP (ESA)* [2016] UKUT 48 (AAC), where it was said also that not only was it desirable that judicial decisions be conveyed to the parties in a form that showed that they had been made by a judge but that it was also desirable that they should state by which judge and when they were made.

Paragraphs (7) and (8)

Now that para.(8) has been amended, it is clear that the effect of barring a respondent is to allow the First-tier Tribunal summarily to determine a case, or part of a case, against a respondent, so that barring a respondent can have the same effect as striking out an appellant. Simply striking out a respondent's case would not always be appropriate because it is not always obvious what decision should be put in the place of the one that has been challenged. Sometimes it might be appropriate simply to decide a case in the appellant's favour to the greatest permissible extent. Sometimes it might be appropriate merely to hold a hearing in the absence of the respondent. **5.234**

In *ZB v SSWP (CSM)* [2013] UKUT 367 (AAC), it was held that a person barred under para.(7) from taking further part in proceedings nonetheless does not lose the right to appeal and is therefore also entitled to a statement of reasons. However, the fact that a person has been barred from taking further part in the proceedings so that the First-tier Tribunal is entitled to determine issues against him or her summarily has a bearing on how much detail is required in the statement of reasons and on how the Upper Tribunal exercises its power under s.12(2)(a) of the Tribunals, Courts and Enforcement Act 2007 not to set aside the First-tier Tribunal's decision even if it is satisfied that it is wrong in law. Presumably, it might therefore also be a reason for refusing permission to appeal in a case notwithstanding that there is an arguable point of law. In *ZB* itself, the First-tier Tribunal had in fact largely explained its decision in the decision notice and, although the Upper Tribunal held that the First-tier Tribunal had erred in law in refusing to provide a fuller statement of reasons, the Upper Tribunal refused to set aside the First-tier Tribunal's decision because it considered it to be unlikely that the First-tier Tribunal had erred in its approach to the case and it was therefore not satisfied that the appellant had suffered any significant injustice.

In *SL v SSWP (CSM)* [2014] UKUT 128 (AAC), it was pointed out that barring a person from taking any *further* part in proceedings and determining a case summarily did not entitle the First-tier Tribunal to ignore evidence already provided. The First-tier Tribunal was still required "to act rationally on material of probative value in making its decision", giving proper consideration to submissions made and taking account of evidence submitted, albeit that it could "deal with the respondent's case rather more briefly than would otherwise be required." Perhaps more controversially, it was also held that, if the Upper Tribunal allowed an appeal and remitted the case to the First-tier Tribunal, a bar imposed before the First-tier Tribunal made its first decision no longer applied because the remitted case amounted to different "proceedings". If the bar was properly imposed, it is not obvious why that should necessarily be the case just because an appeal on a different issue had been successful although it might well be appropriate to reconsider whether the bar should continue if the reason for the bar has been remedied. In *CW v SSWP (CSM)* [2014] UKUT 290 (AAC), it was held that a bar comes to an end when a decision disposing of all issues in the proceedings is issued. This is arguably inconsistent with *ZB* because, if a bar has come to an end, there is no reason why it should affect the Upper Tribunal's approach to the case if the Upper Tribunal is satisfied that there was an error of law.

Referring a case to the Upper Tribunal under r.7(3) provides an alternative to barring if it is necessary for evidence to be provided and the drawing of adverse inferences is not appropriate. In the days before these remedies were available, resort could be had to judicial review if the Secretary of State was in default.

In *R. (Davies) v The Commissioners' Office and the Child Support Agency* [2008] EWHC 334 (Admin), Black J. declared irrational the Secretary of State's refusal to comply with a tribunal's directions to disclose evidence. She said that the only proper course for the Secretary of State, if he objected to directions, was to return to the tribunal and seek a variation. See now r.6(5), although there would now also be the possibility of appealing against the directions. The same point was forcefully made by the Court of Appeal in *BPP Holdings v Commissioners for Her Majesty's Revenue and Customs* (see above) in relation to HMRC's failure to comply with an order of the First-tier Tribunal.

Substitution and addition of parties

5.235 **9.**—(1) The Tribunal may give a direction substituting a party if—

(a) the wrong person has been named as a party; or
(b) the substitution has become necessary because of a change in circumstances since the start of proceedings.

(2) The Tribunal may give a direction adding a person to the proceedings as a respondent.

(3) If the Tribunal gives a direction under paragraph (1) or (2) it may give such consequential directions as it considers appropriate.

DEFINITIONS

"party"—see r.1(3).
"respondent"—*ibid.*
"Tribunal"—*ibid.*

GENERAL NOTE

Paragraph (2)

5.236 A person joined as a respondent becomes a party and acquires all the rights of a party, including the right to require there to be a hearing, the right to obtain a statement of reasons and the right to apply for permission to appeal. A person claiming to be affected by a decision, despite not having automatically been a party to the proceedings, and wishing to appeal may even apply to be added as a respondent after the decision has been made (*Razzaq v Charity Commission for England and Wales* [2016] UKUT B46 (TCC)). However, a person whose application to be added as a respondent is refused is not a party and so has no right of appeal under s.11 of the Tribunals, Courts and Enforcement Act 2007, although a challenge to the refusal may be made by way of an application to the Upper Tribunal for judicial review (*Salisbury Independent Living v Wirral BC (HB)* [2011] UKUT 44 (AAC); [2012] AACR 37).

The possibility of using the power to add parties as a means of avoiding injustice may sometimes impose upon the First-tier Tribunal a duty to invite a person to be added as a party, although a person should not be added without their consent unless the law requires it (*ML v Tonbridge Grammar School* [2012] UKUT 283 (AAC); *Bell v Information Commissioner* [2012] UKUT 433 (AAC)).

However, given the wide scope of the definition of "respondent" in r.1(3), it will seldom be necessary to add a party as a respondent in a social security case because a person with an interest in a decision under appeal will usually have had a right of appeal against it and so will automatically be a respondent. In the past, there were at least two types of cases where non-parties were invited to attend hearings. The injured person would sometimes be invited to attend a hearing of an appeal under the Social Security (Recovery of Benefits) Act 1997 brought by a compensator even though there had been no deduction under s.8 of that Act so that the injured person had no right of appeal and no direct interest in the case. A person in receipt of widow's benefit would sometimes be invited to attend a hearing of an appeal against a refusal to award another woman widow's benefit based on contributions paid by the same man where there was a possibility that there might have been polygamous marriages. In both cases, the reason for inviting the non-party was that success by the appellant might logically lead to an award of benefit to the non-party being revised or superseded. The problem was, that, in the unfortunate absence of any power in the Secretary of State to refer the question of revision or supersession to a tribunal, any decision on the first appeal was not binding in relation to the revision or supersession. It would be unfair for it to be binding without the question properly being referred and the non-party being given a clear indication of the grounds upon which there might be revision or supersession. However, if a person is added as a party and has all the rights of a party and is made properly aware of the issues, there is no reason in principle why the decision to which they are a party should not be binding on them. Therefore, in *CM v HMRC (TC)* [2014] UKUT 272 (AAC), the Upper Tribunal suggested that, where there were competing claims for child tax credit, the second claimant could be added as a party to an appeal by the first claimant, against their will if necessary, on the basis that the decision would then be binding on both claimants. In an ordinary social security case, it might be necessary to consider whether s.17(2) of the Social Security Act 1998 carried an implication that the decision would not be formally binding but even if the decision was not formally binding, it would obviously carry practical weight.

No power to award costs

10. The Tribunal may not make any order in respect of costs (or, in Scotland, expenses). 5.237

DEFINITION

"Tribunal"—see r.1(3).

GENERAL NOTE

See the note to s.29 to the Tribunals, Courts and Enforcement Act 2007. 5.238

Representatives

11.—(1) A party may appoint a representative (whether a legal representative or not) to represent that party in the proceedings. 5.239

(2) Subject to paragraph (3), if a party appoints a representative, that party (or the representative if the representative is a legal representative) must send or deliver to the Tribunal written notice of the representative's name and address.

(3) In a case to which rule 23 (cases in which the notice of appeal is to be sent to the decision maker) applies, if the appellant (or the appellant's representative if the representative is a legal representative) provides written notification of the appellant's representative's name and address to the decision maker before the decision maker provides its response to the Tribunal, the appellant need not take any further steps in order to comply with paragraph (2).

(4) If the Tribunal receives notice that a party has appointed a representative under paragraph (2), it must send a copy of that notice to each other party.

(5) Anything permitted or required to be done by a party under these Rules, a practice direction or a direction may be done by the representative of that party, except signing a witness statement.

(6) A person who receives due notice of the appointment of a representative—

(a) must provide to the representative any document which is required to be provided to the represented party, and need not provide that document to the represented party; and

(b) may assume that the representative is and remains authorised as such until they receive written notification that this is not so from the representative or the represented party.

(7) At a hearing a party may be accompanied by another person whose name and address has not been notified under paragraph (2) or (3) but who, with the permission of the Tribunal, may act as a representative or otherwise assist in presenting the party's case at the hearing.

(8) Paragraphs (2) to (6) do not apply to a person who accompanies a party under paragraph (7).

DEFINITIONS

"appeal"—see r.1(3).
"appellant"—*ibid.*
"decision maker"—*ibid.*
"document"—*ibid.*
"hearing"—*ibid.*
"legal representative"—*ibid.*
"party"—*ibid.*
"practice direction"—*ibid.*
"Tribunal"—*ibid.*

GENERAL NOTE

Paragraph (1)

5.240 A party has a right to be represented by any person (subject to their proper behaviour). Thus, under earlier legislation, a chairman erred in refusing to hear submissions by what he described as a "McKenzie friend" and it was an error of law for him to insist that the claimant specify at the beginning of the hearing whether the person accompanying her was going to act as a representative in the conventional sense (*CS/1753/2000*). In *CDLA/2462/2003*, the Commissioner reiterated the point that representatives may also be witnesses.

"8. Tribunals operate less formally than courts. They do not operate rights of audience. They allow, of course, professional legal representation. But they also allow lay representation and assistance from anyone whom the claimant wishes to assist in presenting a case to a tribunal. Given that breadth of representation, it is inevitable that the roles of representative and witness cannot be separated in the way that they would in a court. The same person may wish to put the claimant's case and give evidence in support of that case. The tribunal must take care to distinguish evidence from representation so that the former's provenance is known and can be the subject of questioning by the tribunal and other parties. But, subject to the practicalities of the way in which the taking of evidence is handled, there is no objection in principle to the same person acting in different capacities as a witness and as a representative. Nor is there any reason in principle why the probative value of evidence should depend upon whether or not it came from a representative.

. . .

13. I emphasise that I am concerned here with a representative who wanted to give evidence from his own knowledge. I am not concerned with the different circumstance of a representative who wants to make a statement of the claimant's evidence to the appeal tribunal. Some tribunals refuse a representative the chance to do this. They insist on hearing the evidence from the claimant, allowing the representative to supplement the tribunal's questions to ensure that all the evidence is elicited from the claimant. That is a matter that is within the chairman's control of the procedure under regulation 49(1) [now r.5(1)]. Nothing I have written above affects the use of that power by [a] chairman to control the way that the claimant's own evidence is presented."

In *PM v SSWP (IS)* [2014] UKUT 474 (AAC), the judge expressed surprise that the First-tier Tribunal had not been prepared to accept evidence from the claimant's representative in a case where the claimant was a 19-year old foreign national who had been in care following estrangement from her father and who, the First-tier Tribunal had been told, was too distressed to attend the hearing. The First-tier Tribunal had said that only statements of fact made by representatives as to matters within their own personal knowledge were evidence. The Upper Tribunal referred to *PL v Walsall MBC* [2009] UKUT 27 (AAC), a case where an assertion of a local authority's submission-writer, supported by computer printouts, was held to be sufficient evidence to prove that certain decisions had been made, because the fact that the evidence was not of matters within the submission-writer's personal knowledge merely made it hearsay which might affect its probative worth but did not make it inadmissible. (That statements of fact in a representative's written submission, including the Secretary of State's response to an appeal, may amount to evidence has been reiterated in *AS v SSWP (CA)* [2015] UKUT 592 (AAC); [2016] AACR 22.) The evidence in *PM* had been as to the claimant's father's last known address and place of work, which the Upper Tribunal commented "was likely to prove an uncontroversial issue capable of objective verification and not one where there was any risk of the evidence being compromised if it was mediated through a representative". Similarly, the First-tier Tribunal is entitled to accept evidence given by a presenting officer from his or her knowledge of the relevant files (*BS v SSWP (DLA)* [2016] UKUT 73 (AAC); [2016] AACR 32).

In *JF v SSWP (DLA)* [2012] UKUT 335 (AAC) a claimant complained that a person accompanying her was told not to speak on her behalf. The Upper Tribunal commented that there was no record of the First-tier Tribunal having received any evidence from the companion and that "if someone who has accompanied a claimant wishes to speak, . . . the First-tier Tribunal should remember that that person may well be able to give material evidence and, unless the claimant objects, it should give him or her an opportunity to do so, even if not immediately, and it should then make a note of the evidence as it would evidence from the claimant". It was similarly accepted in *SK v SSWP (ESA)* [2014] UKUT 141 (AAC) that representatives may be able to give useful evidence.

It does not follow that a claimant is always entitled to an adjournment for the purpose of being represented but, if an adjournment is refused, it has to be recognised that the claimant may be disadvantaged unless, of course, the First-tier Tribunal is minded to allow the claimant's appeal anyway. In particular, where a claimant has mental health problems and asks for a postponement or adjournment for the purposes of obtaining representation, the First-tier Tribunal must consider whether the adjournment may be a reasonable adjustment required under the Equality Act 2010 to enable the claimant to overcome a disadvantage suffered as a result of a disability (*DC v SSWP (ESA)* [2014] UKUT 218 (AAC)).

The possible conflict of interest where a person employed by a local authority represents a claimant in a housing benefit case where the same local authority is a party was considered in *CSHC/729/2003*. The Commissioner commended the practice of the representative concerned in drawing claimants' attention to the potential conflict. The Commissioner reserved the question whether he or a tribunal had any power to prevent a representative chosen by a claimant from acting. It is suggested that, in the absence of misconduct by the representative, there is no such power, although the Tribunal could ensure that the claimant had made an informed choice.

No provision is made in these Rules for parties who lack capacity to conduct their own cases or to appoint a representative. However, reg.25 of the Social Security and Child Support (Decisions and Appeals) Regulations 1999 and reg.49 of the Universal Credit, Personal Independence Payment, Jobseeker's Allowance and Employment and Support Allowance (Decisions and Appeals) Regulations 2013 provide that those appointed by the Secretary of State to act on behalf of claimants or their estates in relation to claims may appeal and so presumably they have all the powers of appellants. It may also be implicit that those who have a legal right to claim or receive benefits as executors, deputies appointed by the Court of Protection or, in Scotland, judicial factors or other guardians also have a right to appeal in relation to those benefits. In *YA v Central and North-West London NHS Trust* [2015] UKUT 37 (AAC); [2015] AACR 31 there was left open the question whether, in the absence of any other adequate provision, the First-tier Tribunal could itself appoint a representative for a person who lacked capacity to conduct his or her case but, in *R. (C) v First-tier Tribunal* [2016] EWHC 707 (Admin), it was held that the First-tier Tribunal has the power to appoint a litigation friend (i.e., a person appointed to act on behalf of a party in tribunal proceedings) in circumstances where that is required by the common law concept of procedural fairness and, of course, a litigation friend is entitled to appoint a representative. It was made clear in *YA* that any representative must act in accordance with the appellant's instructions, insofar as the appellant is capable of giving instructions. In *AMA v Greater Manchester West Mental Health NHS Foundation Trust* [2015] UKUT 36 (AAC); [2015] AACR 30 it was held that appointment as a deputy by the Court of Protection does not necessarily entitle the deputy to act in tribunal proceedings on behalf of the patient; it depends on the terms of the Court's order.

Paragraphs (2)–(6)

5.241 These paragraphs provide for the formal appointment of a representative. Notice must be given to the Tribunal (para.(2)) unless an appellant has already given notice to the decision-maker before the decision-maker has sent the response to the appeal to the Tribunal (para.(3)), in which case the decision-maker must inform the Tribunal of the name and address of the appellant's representative (see r.24(4)(c)). A formally appointed representative may act on behalf of the party in all respects (except to sign a witness statement) and should be sent any documents that would otherwise be sent to the party (paras (5) and (6)(a)). However, it is presumably possible for the Tribunal to exclude a representative from a hearing under r.30(5) without excluding the party.

In *MP v SSWP (DLA)* [2010] UKUT 103 (AAC), the claimant had solicitors acting for her. As required by r.23(2), they had sent the notice of appeal to the Secretary of State who had duly informed the Tribunals Service that they were acting, as anticipated by para.(3). However, the Tribunals Service sent an "enquiry form", asking whether a hearing was wanted, only to the claimant, who completed it wrongly. It was held that there had been no breach of r.11(6)(a) because the "enquiry form" was not a document "which is required to be provided", but the judge questioned whether it was sensible not to send a copy to the solicitors and observed that r.11(6)(b) would have permitted it to be sent only to the solicitors.

Paragraphs (7) and (8)

5.242 These paragraphs enable a party who is present at a hearing to be represented or assisted at the hearing by any person, without there having been any formal notice of appointment. Although the Tribunal's permission is required, it is suggested that, unless r.30(5) applies, it will only exceptionally be appropriate for the Tribunal to refuse permission, particularly as the party need only provide a written notice under para.(2) in order to avoid the need for permission. Without a written notice of appointment, a person who acts as a representative at a hearing has no rights as a representative outside the hearing. Obviously, a written notice may be provided at the hearing so that the person becomes entitled to act as a full representative thereafter.

Calculating time

12.—(1) Except in asylum support cases, an act required by these Rules, a practice direction or a direction to be done on or by a particular day must be done by 5pm on that day. 5.243

(2) If the time specified by these Rules, a practice direction or a direction for doing any act ends on a day other than a working day, the act is done in time if it is done on the next working day.

(3) In this rule "working day" means any day except a Saturday or Sunday, Christmas Day, Good Friday or a bank holiday under section 1 of the Banking and Financial Dealings Act 1971.

DEFINITIONS

"asylum support case"—see r.1(3).
"practice direction"—*ibid.*
"working day"—see para.(3).

GENERAL NOTE

Paragraph (3)

Christmas Day and Good Friday are holidays under the common law in England, Wales and Northern Ireland, rather than being bank holidays, which is why they are specifically mentioned in this paragraph. The following days are bank holidays in England, Wales and Northern Ireland, either because they are mentioned in Sch.1 to the 1971 Act or by virtue of Royal proclamations under s.1(2) and (3) of that Act: New Year's Day, Easter Monday, the first Monday in May, the last Monday in May, the last Monday in August, and December 26. In Northern Ireland, there are additional bank holidays on March 17 (St Patrick's Day), by virtue of Sch.1 to the 1971 Act, and July 12 (the anniversary of the Battle of the Boyne), by virtue of a proclamation by the Secretary of State for Northern Ireland under s.1(5) of that Act. Where a bank holiday would otherwise fall on a Saturday or Sunday, the following Monday (and Tuesday, where December 26 is on a Sunday) is substituted. Additional bank holidays may be announced by Royal proclamation and so may variations. Thus, there was an additional bank holiday on April 29, 2011 on the occasion of Prince William's wedding and, in 2012, the late May bank holiday was put back to 4 June and there was an additional bank holiday on 5 June to celebrate the Queen's Diamond Jubilee. 5.244

Scotland has different bank holidays under the 1971 Act but they are not always observed as public holidays as there is a tradition of observing various local public holidays or institutional holidays instead of, or occasionally as well as, bank holidays. The statutory bank holidays, including those announced by Royal proclamation, are New Year's Day, January 2, Good Friday, the first Monday in May, the last Monday in May, the first Monday in August, November 30 (St Andrew's Day), Christmas Day and December 26. Where a bank holiday would otherwise fall on a Saturday or Sunday the following Monday (or Tuesday, where January 2 or December 26 is on a Sunday), is substituted. These, subject to variations or additions announced by Royal proclamation, are the relevant days for the purposes of this rule although Royal Mail does in fact operate on November 30. November 30 is a comparatively recent addition to the list and, where it is observed as a holiday, it is often in place of one of the other bank holidays. Ironically, the clearing banks in Scotland observe the English bank holidays so that they are open on January 2, the first Monday in August and November 30 but are closed on Easter Monday and the last Monday in August.

The relevant days to be treated as bank holidays will depend on the part of the United Kingdom in which the "act"—which will be the receipt of a document where the Rules provide that a document must be received by the Tribunal or a party within a specified time—must be performed. No specific provision is made in respect of local holidays or other causes of postal delays where a party lives outside the United Kingdom but the general power to extend time under r.5(3)(a) may be invoked.

Sending and delivery of documents

5.245 **13.**—(1) Any document to be provided to the Tribunal under these Rules, a practice direction or a direction must be—

(a) sent by pre-paid post or delivered by hand to the address specified for the proceedings;
(b) sent by fax to the number specified for the proceedings; or
(c) sent or delivered by such other method as the Tribunal may permit or direct.

(2) Subject to paragraph (3), if a party provides a fax number, email address or other details for the electronic transmission of documents to them, that party must accept delivery of documents by that method.

(3) If a party informs the Tribunal and all other parties that a particular form of communication (other than pre-paid post or delivery by hand) should not be used to provide documents to that party, that form of communication must not be so used.

(4) If the Tribunal or a party sends a document to a party or the Tribunal by email or any other electronic means of communication, the recipient may request that the sender provide a hard copy of the document to the recipient. The recipient must make such a request as soon as reasonably practicable after receiving the document electronically.

(5) The Tribunal and each party may assume that the address provided by a party or its representative is and remains the address to which documents should be sent or delivered until receiving written notification to the contrary.

DEFINITIONS

"document"—see r.1(3).
"party"—*ibid.*
"practice direction"—*ibid.*
"Tribunal"—*ibid.*

GENERAL NOTE

5.246 In these Rules, a party is usually required to provide, or send, a document so that it is *received* by a certain date. See r.12 for the calculation of time.

A document may be sent by fax and, in *R(DLA) 3/05*, it was held that a fax is received when it is successfully transmitted to, and received by, a fax machine, irrespective of whether anyone actually collects it from the machine. Furthermore, the faxed request for a statement of reasons in that case was received by the clerk to the appeal tribunal when received at the tribunal venue, even though the clerk did not visit that venue until some days later. The Commissioner said that it would have been different if the venue had been a casual venue, such as local authority premises. Here, it was a dedicated venue and the fax number had been given to representatives precisely to enable them to communicate with the clerk. There was nothing in any document issued with the decision notice to indicate that the request for a statement of reasons had to be addressed to a different place.

Where documents are sent by the Tribunal to a party under these Rules, the important date is usually the date they are *sent*. However, a decision of the Tribunal may be set aside under r.37 if it is accepted that notice of hearing or a direction was not in fact received by a party even though it was properly posted. In *R(SB) 55/83*, it was held that a setting aside under what is now r.37 was the *only* remedy in these circumstances, but Commissioners later declined to follow that decision and held that an appeal will lie if a decision is not set aside (*CCS/6302/1999*, *CIB/303/1999*), while endorsing the view expressed in *R(SB) 19/83* that an application for a setting aside is to be preferred. Rule 41 permits the First-tier Tribunal to treat an application for permission to appeal as an application for a setting aside.

Paragraph (1)

When sending documents to the Tribunal, fax may always be used if available but email may be used only if the Tribunal has specifically said so. **5.247**

However, in a guidance note dated March 17, 2016, the Chamber President of the Social Entitlement Chamber of the First-tier Tribunal has permitted the delivery of documents to the Tribunal by electronic means by any party in a social security or child support case who has indicated his or her consent to receiving communications by electronic means.

Paragraphs (2) and (3)

When sending documents to a party, any available method of communication may be used unless the party has specifically said that fax or email may not be used. Any address or number given may be assumed to be still in use until notice to the contrary is given (see para.(5)). **5.248**

Paragraph (4)

This paragraph enables a party or the Tribunal to require a hard copy of a faxed or emailed document to be provided even though the fax or email delivery may have been sufficient for the purpose of complying with a time limit. It might be used, for instance, where a fax is poorly reproduced or where printing a large email attachment would be unduly onerous. Note that it is not necessary to provide a hard copy of a fax or email unless requested to do so. However, where a time limit runs to the date a document is received, it might be wise to send a hard copy if there is any reason to doubt that the document will be received electronically even if sent. **5.249**

Use of documents and information

14.—(1) The Tribunal may make an order prohibiting the disclosure or publication of— **5.250**

(a) specified documents or information relating to the proceedings; or
(b) any matter likely to lead members of the public to identify any person whom the Tribunal considers should not be identified.

(2) The Tribunal may give a direction prohibiting the disclosure of a document or information to a person if—

(a) the Tribunal is satisfied that such disclosure would be likely to cause that person or some other person serious harm; and
(b) the Tribunal is satisfied, having regard to the interests of justice, that it is proportionate to give such a direction.

(3) If a party ("the first party") considers that the Tribunal should give a direction under paragraph (2) prohibiting the disclosure of a document or information to another party ("the second party"), the first party must—

(a) exclude the relevant document or information from any documents that will be provided to the second party; and

(b) provide to the Tribunal the excluded document or information, and the reason for its exclusion, so that the Tribunal may decide whether the document or information should be disclosed to the second party or should be the subject of a direction under paragraph (2).

(4) The Tribunal must conduct proceedings as appropriate in order to give effect to a direction given under paragraph (2).

(5) If the Tribunal gives a direction under paragraph (2) which prevents disclosure to a party who has appointed a representative, the Tribunal may give a direction that the documents or information be disclosed to that representative if the Tribunal is satisfied that—

(a) disclosure to the representative would be in the interests of the party; and

(b) the representative will act in accordance with paragraph (6).

(6) Documents or information disclosed to a representative in accordance with a direction under paragraph (5) must not be disclosed either directly or indirectly to any other person without the Tribunal's consent.

DEFINITIONS

"document"—see r.1(3).
"party"—*ibid.*
"Tribunal"—*ibid.*

GENERAL NOTE

Paragraph (1)

5.251 An order under this paragraph may be directed to an individual and be concerned only with an individual document (e.g. prohibiting an appellant from disclosing to someone else a document disclosed to the appellant by the respondent) or it may be directed to the public in general and effectively amount to a reporting restriction. Hearings of social security cases are usually attended only by those immediately interested in them but most hearings are, in principle, open to the public, including the press (see r.30). It is difficult to envisage it being appropriate to prohibit the publication of any information at all about a hearing held in public but it might often be appropriate to make an order prohibiting the publishing of information that may lead to a child or vulnerable adult being identified if there would otherwise be any serious risk of such publication. It will generally be necessary properly to balance the right of one person to respect of his or her private life under art.8 of the European Convention on Human Rights and the right of another person to freedom of expression under art.10 (see *Re British Broadcasting Corporation* [2009] UKHL 34; [2010] 1 A.C. 145, where it is noteworthy that, although the House of Lords discharged an anonymity order so as to permit the BBC to broadcast an acquitted defendant's name, it saw no need to mention his name itself). See also *In re M (A Patient) (Court of Protection: Reporting Restrictions)* [2011] EWHC 1197 (Fam); [2012] 1 W.L.R. 287.

The existence of the powers conferred by this paragraph is a factor to be borne in mind when deciding under r.30(3) whether a hearing should be in private or in public, which requires consideration of the terms of art.6(1). Preventing the publication of parties' names may be appropriate even if a hearing is in public or the press are admitted to a private hearing (*L v L (Ancillary Relief Proceedings: Anonymity)* [2015] EWHC 2621 (Fam); [2016] 1 W.L.R. 1259).

A breach of an order made under this paragraph is a contempt of court. However, it can be enforced only through an application for committal made to the High Court or, in Scotland, the Court of Session.

A non-party may apply for a variation of an order under para.(1) without applying to be made a party to the proceedings. This was done in *Re X (Reporting restric-*

tion order: Variation) [2015] UKUT 380 (AAC); [2016] AACR 6, where a local authority that had not been a party to proceedings before the Upper Tribunal was aware of them and of an order that had been made under r.14(1) of the Tribunal Procedure (Upper Tribunal) Rules 2008 and sought permission to disclose information relating to the proceedings to the police. Applying guidance given by the Court of Appeal in relation to care proceedings in *Re C (A Minor) (Care Proceedings: Disclosure)* [1997] Fam 76, the order prohibiting publication of any matter likely to lead members of the public to identify certain adults and children was varied so as to permit disclosure of the decision of the Upper Tribunal and the identities of individuals mentioned in it to the police and other relevant bodies for the limited purposes of investigating criminal offences, bringing prosecutions and protecting any child or vulnerable adult. However, if a non-party wishes to challenge the decision on such an application, he or she may need to apply to be added as a party so as to be able to appeal under s.11 of the Tribunals, Courts and Enforcement Act 2007.

Paragraphs (2)–(6)

These paragraphs replace reg.42 of the Social Security and Child Support (Decisions and Appeals) Regulations 1999, although they are not limited to medical advice or evidence. It is suggested that "serious harm" merely means harm that would be sufficiently serious to justify what would otherwise be a breach of the right to a fair hearing guaranteed by art.6 of the European Convention on Human Rights. In effect, the application of this rule requires a person's art.8 rights to be balanced against his or her art.6 rights. In *RM v St Andrew's Healthcare* [2010] UKUT 119 (AAC), a case concerned with the equivalent provision in the Tribunal Procedure (First-tier Tribunal) (Health, Education and Social Care Chamber) Rules 2008 (SI 2008/2699), very substantial weight was given to the art.6 right to a fair hearing in the light of *Secretary of State for the Home Department v AF (No.3)* [2009] UKHL 28; [2010] 2 A.C. 269, but both those cases were concerned with the deprivation of a person's liberty and it is suggested that, in social security cases where less is at stake, the need to avoid serious harm may more often justify non-disclosure, although it will still be very rare. Although "Courts have shown an aversion to permitting counsel to see or hear evidence which he is not at liberty to disclose to his client" (*Browning v Information Commissioner* [2014] EWCA Civ 1050), they will do so where necessary, particularly where it is necessary to protect children and vulnerable adults. However, the consent of the representative to the procedure is always necessary (*C v C (Court of Protection: Disclosure)* [2014] EWHC 131 (Fam); [2014] 1 W.L.R. 2731). In *RM v St Andrew's Healthcare*, the judge also made the point that any order for non-disclosure ought to identify the information that is not to be disclosed, rather than, or as well as, specific documents. The disadvantage of referring only to specific documents is that the information may, unknown to the tribunal, also be contained in other documents that are not covered by the order. A similar balancing exercise was required under the former legislation even before the Human Rights Act 1998 came into effect (*CDLA/1347/1999*, disagreeing with the absolutist view expressed in *CSDLA/5/1995* that "no adverserial dispute should be decided against a party on the basis of evidence not disclosed to them unless that party has been given sufficient indication of the gist of that evidence to give them a proper opportunity to put forward their case"). Provided the risk of harm to the claimant is properly balanced against his or her right to a fair hearing, there is unlikely to be a breach of the European Convention on Human Rights, particularly if the claimant has a representative to whom disclosure has been made (see *R. (Roberts) v Parole Board* [2005] UKHL 45; [2005] 2 A.C. 738). Note the power in r.30(5)(c) to exclude a person from a hearing, and the power in r.33(2) not to provide a full statement of reasons, in order to give effect to a direction under para.(2). 5.252

In *CDLA/1347/1999*, it was suggested that, if a tribunal was minded to reveal evidence that had been withheld on medical advice, it might be prudent to give the medical advisor the opportunity of justifying the advice before revealing the evidence. The Commissioner also agreed with a suggestion that, if reasons for a decision were being given, withheld evidence should be referred to in a supplementary statement of reasons given to the Secretary of State (and the claimant's representative if the evidence had been revealed to him or her) but not given to the claimant. That would have the effect that, in the event of an appeal, the Upper Tribunal would know how the evidence had been approached.

In most cases concerning attendance allowance or disability living allowance, this rule will not give rise to great problems because evidence that a claimant is seriously ill, which is the sort of evidence that would normally be withheld, is evidence that is likely to assist the claimant rather than the reverse. It is in cases concerning disablement benefit, where causation is often in issue, that the problem arises most acutely. There, if a tribunal are satisifed that evidence should be withheld but would be likely to be contested by a claimant if he or she knew of it, it is suggested that they should take care to ensure that it is properly tested by, for example, obtaining a second opinion. If proceedings cannot properly be adversarial, they must be truly inquisitorial. Indeed, if there were contradictory evidence and the claimant would be likely to contest the withheld evidence, a tribunal might well be particularly slow to conclude that this rule should be applied and might choose either to disclose the evidence or else to disregard it. However, it is clear from *In re A (Forced Marriage: Special Advocates)* [2010] EWHC 2438 (Fam); [2012] Fam 102 that a case may sometimes properly be determined by a judge on the basis of information that has not been disclosed to a party and that the appointment of a special advocate in such a case is necessary only if there is something that a special advocate could do that it would not be appropriate for the judge to do.

In *Dorset Healthcare NHS Foundation Trust v MH* [2009] UKUT 4 (AAC), it was made clear that serious harm was not the only ground upon which disclosure of documents may be withheld. In that case, documents were withheld from a patient on the ground of confidentiality but it was not suggested that the tribunal should see the withheld documents. It is doubtful that a tribunal could properly have regard to evidence that had not been disclosed to a party in any circumstances other than those contemplated in this rule unless, perhaps, a legally qualified representative acting for the party was prepared to consent to it doing so despite not being able to obtain the informed consent of the party.

A challenge to the validity of r.13(2) to (8) of the Tribunal Procedure (First-Tier Tribunal) (Immigration and Asylum Chamber) Rules 2014 (SI 2014/2604), equivalent to r.14(2) to (6) of these Rules, was rejected in *R. (Immigration Law Practitioners Association) v Tribunal Procedure Committee* [2016] EWHC 218 (Admin) broadly on the basis that the provisions were not inherently unfair, even though it was difficult to see how they could properly be used in that context.

Evidence and submissions

5.253 **15.**—(1) Without restriction on the general powers in rule 5(1) and (2) (case management powers), the Tribunal may give directions as to—

(a) issues on which it requires evidence or submissions;

(b) the nature of the evidence or submissions it requires;

(c) whether the parties are permitted or required to provide expert evidence;

(d) any limit on the number of witnesses whose evidence a party may put forward, whether in relation to a particular issue or generally;

(e) the manner in which any evidence or submissions are to be provided, which may include a direction for them to be given—

(i) orally at a hearing; or

(ii) by written submissions or witness statement; and

(f) the time at which any evidence or submissions are to be provided.

(2) The Tribunal may—

(a) admit evidence whether or not—
 (i) the evidence would be admissible in a civil trial in the United Kingdom; or
 (ii) the evidence was available to a previous decision maker; or
(b) exclude evidence that would otherwise be admissible where—
 (i) the evidence was not provided within the time allowed by a direction or a practice direction;
 (ii) the evidence was otherwise provided in a manner that did not comply with a direction or a practice direction; or
 (iii) it would otherwise be unfair to admit the evidence.

(3) The Tribunal may consent to a witness giving, or require any witness to give, evidence on oath, and may administer an oath for that purpose.

DEFINITIONS

"decision maker"—see r.1(3).
"hearing"—*ibid.*
"party"—*ibid.*
"practice direction"—*ibid.*
"Tribunal"—*ibid.*

GENERAL NOTE

Paragraph (1)

Rule 6 makes the necessary procedural provision. 5.254

Paragraph (2)

Paragraph (2)(a) makes explicit powers to admit evidence that were formerly implicit. Note that the Tribunal merely has a power to admit evidence that would be inadmissible in a civil trial and it cannot override any privilege of a witness not to give evidence (see the note to s.(3)(1) of the Tribunal, Courts and Enforcement Act 2007). Beyond that, the main consideration will simply be whether the evidence is relevant. 5.255

Paragraph (2)(b) enables evidence to be excluded. This power, like all other powers under the Rules, must be exercised so as to give effect to the overriding objective in r.2 and it will rarely be proportionate to exclude relevant evidence simply because it is provided late, unless some prejudice would be suffered by another party or the delay makes it more difficult for the tribunal to consider the evidence. See *CIB/4253/2004* and also *Nottinghamshire and City of Nottingham Fire Authority v Gladman Commercial Properties Ltd (Nottingham CC, Part 20 defendant)* [2011] EWHC 1918 (Ch); [2011] 1 W.L.R. 3235, in which Peter Smith J. said that:

> "[a] decision to exclude a late amendment or witness statement where there is no identifiable prejudice that cannot be addressed can lead to unfairness in the trial procedure and it is essential that the courts ensure that the overriding objective is followed and all parties have a full and fair hearing consistent with that approach."

He held that the person seeking to introduce the evidence does not have a heavy onus merely because it is late and that lateness is only one factor and all factors should be considered.

Paragraph (3)

This makes explicit that the Tribunal may consent to evidence being given on oath where it is the witness or a party who wishes that to be done. In practice, it is fairly rare for evidence to be given on oath in social security cases. 5.256

By virtue of s.5 of the Oaths Act 1978, any person who objects to being sworn shall be permitted to make his or her solemn affirmation instead of taking an oath. In England, Wales and Northern Ireland, a Christian or Jew usually swears an oath with the New Testament, or, in the case of a Jew, the Old Testament, in his or her uplifted hand (*ibid.*, s.1(1)) but if the person desires to swear without holding the Bible but "with uplifted hand in the form and manner in which an oath is usually administered in Scotland", he or she must be permitted to do so (s.3). In the case of a person who is neither a Christian not a Jew, the oath shall be administered in any lawful manner (*ibid.*, s.1(3)), but such a person may prefer to affirm.

Summoning or citation of witnesses and orders to answer questions or produce documents

5.257 **16.**—(1) On the application of a party or on its own initiative, the Tribunal may—

(a) by summons (or, in Scotland, citation) require any person to attend as a witness at a hearing at the time and place specified in the summons or citation; or
(b) order any person to answer any questions or produce any documents in that person's possession or control which relate to any issue in the proceedings.

(2) A summons or citation under paragraph (1)(a) must—

(a) give the person required to attend 14 days' notice of the hearing or such shorter period as the Tribunal may direct; and
(b) where the person is not a party, make provision for the person's necessary expenses of attendance to be paid, and state who is to pay them.

(3) No person may be compelled to give any evidence or produce any document that the person could not be compelled to give or produce on a trial of an action in a court of law in the part of the United Kingdom where the proceedings are due to be determined.

(4) A summons, citation or order under this rule must—

(a) state that the person on whom the requirement is imposed may apply to the Tribunal to vary or set aside the summons, citation or order, if they have not had an opportunity to object to it; and
(b) state the consequences of failure to comply with the summons, citation or order.

DEFINITIONS

"document"—see r.1(3).
"hearing"—*ibid.*
"party"—*ibid.*
"Tribunal"—*ibid.*

GENERAL NOTE

5.258 This rule includes a power to order the production of documents without requiring attendance at a hearing. A failure to comply with a summons, citation or order under this rule is a contempt of court that may be referred to the Upper Tribunal under r.7(3). The Upper Tribunal has the power to impose a term of imprisonment not exceeding two years and an unlimited fine. In *MD v SSWP (Enforcement Reference)* [2010] UKUT 202 (AAC); [2011] AACR 5, a three-judge panel said that, before a reference is made, the First-tier Tribunal should be satisfied that all the procedural requirements had been met and, in particular, that any summons, citation or order was sent to the correct address and included an appropriate warning and, in the case of a summons or citation, was accompanied by an offer to pay expenses. It is unlikely to be appropriate to waive any such requirements, unless it was clear that there was no prejudice or injustice to the alleged contemnor in doing so.

The three-judge panel also made it clear that the First-tier Tribunal should consider whether attendance is really required before issuing a summons. In that case a doctor had been directed to provide a copy of his patient's medical notes. When he failed to do so, he was summoned to attend a hearing. The Upper Tribunal commented that it was unclear why he had been summoned under s.16(1)(a) instead of being formally ordered under r.16(1)(b) to produce the records and that "an order to compel a practising doctor to attend a hearing should not be made without a very compelling reason for doing so". Nonetheless, it has been made clear in *CB v Suffolk County Council (Enforcement Reference)* [2010] UKUT 413 (AAC); [2011] AACR 22 that it is wrong to draw the impression from *MD v SSWP (Enforcement Reference)* "that a person on whom a witness summons has been served can simply sit back, await any reference to the Upper Tribunal and only then argue that the witness summons was not appropriately issued". An application may be made to the First-tier Tribunal for a summons to be set aside (see para.(4)(a)) and a refusal to set it aside may be challenged by way of an application to the Upper Tribunal for judicial review. If a summons is not successfully challenged, it must be obeyed. In that case, the Upper Tribunal fined a witness £500 for failing to comply with a summons issued by the Health, Education and Social Care Chamber of the First-tier Tribunal.

More controversially, when commenting on the First-tier Tribunal's failure to comply with the requirement under r.16(2)(b) to "make provision for the person's necessary expenses of attendance to be paid", it was said in *MD v SSWP (Enforcement Reference)* that "[a] witness such as a doctor who is ordered to attend a hearing may clearly incur very considerable expenses". That is plainly a material consideration when deciding whether it is proportionate to issue a summons but, in *CB v Suffolk CC (Enforcement Reference)*, it was held that the scheme of expenses for witnesses operated by the Tribunals Service, which was the same as that for jurors and covered travel expenses and loss of earnings up to a fixed limit, was sufficient for compliance with r.16(2)(b) and that it was not necessary to compensate for all financial loss.

In *LB Camden v FG (SEN)* [2010] UKUT 249 (AAC), it was suggested that a summons should be signed by a judge "rather than being pp'd (as happened here) on his or her behalf", but the summons in that case was nonetheless held valid. The importance of conveying judicial documents to the parties in a form that shows not only that they have been made by a judge but also by which judge and when they were made has been emphasised in *JP v SSWP (ESA)* [2016] UKUT 48 (AAC).

This rule does not permit the First-tier Tribunal to issue a summons to a person outside the UK with a view to it being served outside the UK, but there are cases where it may be appropriate to issue a summons so that it may be served personally on a potential witness if he or she visits the UK (*Clavis Liberty Fund 1 LP v Revenue and Customs Commissioners* [2015] UKUT 72 (TCC); [2015] 1 W.L.R. 2949).

A Practice Direction dated 24 February 2015 in respect of Witness Summonses and Orders to Produce Documents has been issued by the Chamber President of the Tax Chamber of the First-tier Tribunal. Although not of direct application in the Social Entitlement Chamber, it contains useful guidance as to the desirability of making a prior request to a witness to attend before applying for a summons, the need for the First-tier Tribunal to be satisfied as to the relevance of the evidence sought, the information to be included in a summons of order, the desirability of a summoned witness providing a witness statement, the rights of parties to approach a summoned witness and the scope and amount of "necessary expenses for attendance" of a witness. It is published at: *https://www.judiciary.gov.uk/publications/first-tier-tribunal-tax-chamber-practice-direction-witness-summonses-and-orders-to-produce-documents/*.

Withdrawal

5.259 **17.**—(1) Subject to paragraph (2), a party may give notice of the withdrawal of its case, or any part of it—

(a) [1 . . .] by sending or delivering to the Tribunal a written notice of withdrawal; or

(b) orally at a hearing.

(2) In the circumstances described in paragraph (3), a notice of withdrawal will not take effect unless the Tribunal consents to the withdrawal.

(3) The circumstances referred to in paragraph (2) are where a party gives notice of withdrawal—

(a) [1 . . .] in a criminal injuries compensation case; [1 . . .]

(b) [1 in a security and child support case where the tribunal has directed that notice of withdrawal shall take effect only with the Tribunal's consent; or

(c) at a hearing.]

[2 (4) An application for a withdrawn case to be reinstated may be made by—

(a) the party who withdrew the case;

(b) where an appeal in a social security and child support case has been withdrawn, a respondent.

(5) An application under paragraph (4) must be made in writing and be received by the Tribunal within 1 month after the earlier of—

(a) the date on which the applicant was sent notice under paragraph (6) that the withdrawal had taken effect; or

(b) if the applicant was present at the hearing when the case was withdrawn orally under paragraph (1)(b), the date of that hearing.]

(6) The Tribunal must notify each party in writing [1 that a withdrawal has taken effect.] under this rule.

Amendments

1. Tribunal Procedure (Amendment) Rules 2013 (SI 2013/477) rr.22 and 24 (April 8, 2013).

2. Tribunal Procedure (Amendment) Rules 2015 (SI 2015/1510) rr.11 and 14 (August 21, 2015).

Definitions

"criminal injuries compensation case"—see r.1(3).
"hearing"—*ibid.*
"party"—*ibid.*
"respondent"—*ibid.*
"social security and child support case"—*ibid.*
"Tribunal"—*ibid.*

General Note

5.260 Paragraphs (1) and (6) replace reg.40 of the Social Security and Child Support (Decisions and Appeals) Regulations 1999. However, there are differences. First, this applies to the withdrawal of a respondent's case as well as to an appeal or reference. Secondly, paras (2) and (3) have the effect that a case cannot be withdrawn without the consent of the Tribunal where a judge has directed that consent is necessary or at a hearing. Thirdly, para.(4)(a) allows a party who has withdrawn a case to apply for it to be reinstated, avoiding the difficulty that arose in *Rydqvist v Secretary of State for Work and Pensions* [2002] EWCA Civ 947; [2002] 1 W.L.R. 3343. Clearly any possible prejudice to the respondent will be highly relevant when the Tribunal is considering whether to permit the case to be reinstated. The existence of the one-month time limit for an application for reinstatement may suggest that an application should be granted if made within that period unless there is a clear reason for not doing so, such as the previous conduct of the party, obvious lack of merit in the case or prejudice to another party.

The right to withdraw part of a case does not enable a claimant to prevent the First-tier Tribunal from adjudicating on part of a decision of the Secretary of State that is favourable to them (*AE v SSWP (ESA)* [2014] UKUT 5 (AAC); [2014] AACR 23). This was because the claimant's "case" was that the unfavourable part of the Secretary of State's was wrong. In the context of that case, the Upper Tribunal held that the First-tier Tribunal was bound in law to consider the other part of the Secretary of State's decision but that would not usually be so due to the effect of s.12(8)(a) of the Social Security Act 1998. In any event, to the extent that support for part of a decision of the Secretary of State might be part of a claimant's case, withdrawal of that part of the case would be an invitation to adjudicate on the issue rather than the reverse. A challenge to part of a decision of the Secretary of State can clearly be withdrawn under this rule but s.12(8)(a) has the effect that the First-tier Tribunal would usually still have the power to consider that part of the decision if it thought it necessary to do so. Therefore, there may not be much point in formally withdrawing only part of a case in the social security context.

The requirement that a notice of withdrawal must be in writing unless given at a hearing may be waived and, indeed, a clerk may waive the requirement (see the note to r.4).

In *WM v SSWP (DLA)* [2015] UKUT 642 (AAC), the Upper Tribunal made it plain that, since the amendments to r.17(1)(a) and (3) in 2013, a withdrawal of a social security or child support case made otherwise than at a hearing is automatically effective unless the First-tier Tribunal has given a direction under para.(3)(b) and that, where a hearing is adjourned, a notice of withdrawal given during the period of the adjournment is not given "at a hearing" for the purposes of para.(3)(c). The judge also held that "rising to eat lunch . . . does not constitute a formal adjournment of the proceedings" and so does not interrupt the hearing for the purposes of this rule; it is only adjournment from one day to another that interrupts a hearing. In the circumstances of that case, the First-tier Tribunal had no power to decline to accept the withdrawal and so had no jurisdiction to make a decision on the appeal that was less favourable to the claimant than the Secretary of State's decision.

However, paragraph (4)(b) now enables a respondent (who might be the decision-maker but might be a third party where, for instance, there has been a joint claim or the case concerns child support maintenance) to object to the withdrawal of a social security or child support appeal by applying for it to be reinstated. A respondent might wish to do so where he or she might be unfairly prejudiced by having to make a new application for supersession or lodge a new appeal or make a new decision, as the case might be, due to the limits on the backdating of supersession decisions and the time limits for appeals. Making such an application for supersession, lodging an appeal or making a decision would usually have been unnecessary while the other proceedings were effective. Thus, the decision-maker may wish to apply for a withdrawn appeal to be reinstated if it appears (e.g., in the light of evidence that emerged in the appeal proceedings before the appeal was withdrawn or in the light of an observation by the First-tier Tribunal) that the decision that was the subject of the appeal was too generous to the claimant but it cannot be revised or superseded with effect from a sufficiently early date. However, it is suggested that the conduct of all parties may be relevant and that an appeal should not necessarily be reinstated if the decision-maker was clearly at fault in making the original decision and the claimant was blameless: in other words, it is suggested that the First-tier Tribunal should consider whether reinstatement would be fair in all the circumstances of the case. It is also suggested that reinstatement will seldom be desirable where the decision-maker could achieve the same result by revising the original decision against which the claimant would then have a fresh right of appeal.

Lead cases

5.261 **18.**—(1) This rule applies if—

(a) two or more cases have been started before the Tribunal;

(b) in each such case the Tribunal has not made a decision disposing of the proceedings; and

(c) the cases give rise to common or related issues of fact or law.

(2) The Tribunal may give a direction—

(a) specifying one or more cases falling under paragraph (1) as a lead case or lead cases; and

(b) staying (or, in Scotland, sisting) the other cases falling under paragraph (1) ("the related cases").

(3) When the Tribunal makes a decision in respect of the common or related issues—

(a) the Tribunal must send a copy of that decision to each party in each of the related cases; and

(b) subject to paragraph (4), that decision shall be binding on each of those parties.

(4) Within 1 month after the date on which the Tribunal sent a copy of the decision to a party under paragraph (3)(a), that party may apply in writing for a direction that the decision does not apply to, and is not binding on the parties to, a particular related case.

(5) The Tribunal must give directions in respect of cases which are stayed or sisted under paragraph (2)(b), providing for the disposal of or further directions in those cases.

(6) If the lead case or cases lapse or are withdrawn before the Tribunal makes a decision in respect of the common or related issues, the Tribunal must give directions as to—

(a) whether another case or other cases are to be specified as a lead case or lead cases; and

(b) whether any direction affecting the related cases should be set aside or amended.

Definitions

"dispose of proceedings"—see r.1(3).
"party"—*ibid.*
"Tribunal"—*ibid.*

General Note

5.262 The effect of this rule could be achieved through case management directions under r.5 but the rule provides an off-the-peg process for dealing with cases raising common or related issues of fact or law. It need not be used if a different process appears more appropriate. If it is used, one or more lead cases are selected and are then treated as binding on the other cases unless, within one month of being sent a copy of the decision in the lead cases, a party in another case objects. Presumably "decision" in para.(3) must include the reasons for the decision. Paragraph (4) appears to allow an objection either on the ground that the lead case is distinguishable and does not apply for that reason or on the ground that the party simply wishes to challenge the decision in the lead case and have his or her case dealt with separately, possibly with a view to appealing. The likelihood of objections on that latter ground may be a reason for not applying this rule in the first place but it would be unfair if parties who were separately represented could not elect to have their own cases decided individually. Note that only the Chamber President (or a person to whom the power is delegated by him) has the power to treat a social security case as a lead case (see para.10 of the practice statement set out above in the note to art.2 of the First-tier Tribunal and Upper Tribunal (Composition of Tribunal) Order 2008).

Where common issues of law arise in social security cases, s.26 of the Social Security Act 1998 may provide an alternative procedure.

[1 Confidentiality in social security and child support cases

19. — (1) Paragraph (4) applies to— 5.263

(a) proceedings under the Child Support Act 1991 in the circumstances described in paragraph (2), other than an appeal against a reduced benefit decision (as defined in section 46(10)(b) of the Child Support Act 1991, as that section had effect prior to the commencement of section 15(b) of the Child Maintenance and Other Payments Act 2008);

(b) proceedings where the parties to the appeal include former joint claimants who are no longer living together in the circumstances described in paragraph (3).

(2) The circumstances referred to in paragraph (1)(a) are that the absent parent, non-resident parent or person with care would like their address or the address of the child to be kept confidential and has given notice to that effect—

(a) in the notice of appeal or when notifying the Secretary of State or the Tribunal of any subsequent change of address; or

(b) within 14 days after an enquiry is made by the recipient of the notice of appeal or the notification referred to in sub-paragraph (a).

(3) The circumstances referred to in paragraph (1)(b) are that one of the former joint claimants would like their address to be kept confidential and has given notice to that effect—

(a) in the notice of appeal or when notifying the decision maker or the tribunal of any subsequent change of address; or

(b) within 14 days after an enquiry is made by the recipient of the notice of appeal or the notification referred to in sub-paragraph (a).

(4) Where this paragraph applies, the Secretary of State or other decision maker and the Tribunal must take appropriate steps to secure the confidentiality of the address and of any information which could reasonably be expected to enable a person to identify the address, to the extent that the address or that information is not already known to each other party.

(5) In this rule—

"absent parent", "non-resident parent" and "person with care" have the meanings set out in section 3 of the Child Support Act 1991;

"joint claimants" means the persons who made a joint claim for a jobseeker's allowance under the Jobseekers Act 1995, a tax credit under the Tax Credits Act 2002 or in relation to whom an award of universal credit is made under Part 1 of the Welfare Reform Act 2012.]

AMENDMENT

1. Tribunal Procedure (Amendment No.3) Rules 2014 (SI 2014/2128) rr.33 to 35 (October 20, 2014).

DEFINITIONS

"absent parent"—see para.(7).

"appeal"—see r.1(3).
"joint claimants"—see para.(7).
"non-resident parent"—*ibid.*
"parent with care"—*ibid.*
"party"—see r.1(3).
"Tribunal"—*ibid.*

General Note

5.264 This rule applies to child support cases and those social security cases in which it is most likely that former partners will both be parties. It is open to the First-tier Tribunal to exercise its case-management powers under r.5 so as to make provision for confidentiality in other types of case should that be appropriate.

5.265 **20.**—*Omitted.*

Expenses in social security and child support cases

5.266 **21.**—(1) This rule applies only to social security and child support cases.

(2) The Secretary of State may pay such travelling and other allowances (including compensation for loss of remunerative time) as the Secretary of State may determine to any person required to attend a hearing in proceedings under section 20 of the Child Support Act 1991, section 12 of the Social Security Act 1998 or paragraph 6 of Schedule 7 to the Child Support, Pensions and Social Security Act 2000.

Definitions

"hearing"—see r.1(3).
"social security and child support case"—*ibid.*

General Note

5.267 This rule reproduces the effect of para.4(1)(a) of Sch.1 to the Social Security Act 1998. (Paragraph 4(1)(b) is replaced by a new s.20A.) It suffers from the same defect as the old provision, which is that it does not apply to all social security cases in which claimants might be required to attend hearings, although in practice the Tribunals Service seems never to have refused to pay expenses to those not within the scope of the old provision (e.g. an injured person appealing under s.11 of the Social Security (Recovery of Benefits) Act 1997).

The rule is also unsatisfactory because it seems unlikely that para.10(4) of Sch.5 to the Tribunals, Courts and Enforcement Act 2007 envisages Rules that give the Secretary of State the power to determine what expenses are to be paid, although it is perhaps more appropriate that the power to determine the level of payment should lie with the Secretary of State rather than the Tribunal Procedure Committee.

Part 3

Proceedings Before the Tribunal

Chapter 1

Before the Hearing

5.268 Cases in which the notice of appeal is to be sent to the Tribunal

22.—(1) [1 This rule applies to all cases except those to which—

(a) rule 23 (cases in which the notice of appeal is to be sent to the decision maker), or
(b) rule 26 (social security and child support cases started by reference or information in writing),

applies.]

(2) An appellant must start proceedings by sending or delivering a notice of appeal to the Tribunal so that it is received—

(a) in asylum support cases, within 3 days after the date on which the appellant received written notice of the decision being challenged;
(b) in criminal injuries compensation cases, within 90 days after the date of the decision being challenged;

[1 (c) in appeals under the Vaccine Damage Payments Act 1979, at any time;
(d) in other cases—
 (i) if mandatory reconsideration applies, within 1 month after the date on which the appellant was sent notice of the result of mandatory reconsideration;
 (ii) if mandatory reconsideration does not apply, within the time specified in Schedule 1 to these Rules [3 (time limits for providing notices of appeal in social security and child support cases where mandatory reconsideration does not apply)].

(3) The notice of appeal must be in English or Welsh, must be signed by the appellant and must state—

(a) the name and address of the appellant;
(b) the name and address of the appellant's representative (if any);
(c) an address where documents for the appellant may be sent or delivered;
(d) the name and address of any respondent [1 other than the decision maker];
(e) [1 . . .]; and
(f) the grounds on which the appellant relies.

(4) The appellant must provide with the notice of appeal—

(a) [1 a copy of—
 (i) the notice of the result of mandatory reconsideration, in any social security and child support case to which mandatory reconsideration applies;
 (ii) the decision being challenged, in any other case;]
(b) any statement of reasons for that decision that the appellant has [1 . . .; and]
(c) any documents in support of the appellant's case which have not been supplied to the respondent; [1 . . .]
(d) [1 . . .].

(5) In asylum support cases the notice of appeal must also—

(a) state whether the appellant will require an interpreter at any hearing, and if so for which language or dialect; and
(b) state whether the appellant intends to attend or be represented at any hearing.

(6) If the appellant provides the notice of appeal to the Tribunal later than the time required by paragraph (2) or by an extension of time allowed under rule 5(3)(a) [2 . . .] (power to extend time)—

(a) the notice of appeal must include a request for an extension of time and the reason why the notice of appeal was not provided in time; and

(b) [1 subject to paragraph (8)] unless the Tribunal extends time for the notice of appeal under rule 5(3)(a) [2 . . .] (power to extend time) the Tribunal must not admit the notice of appeal.

(7) The Tribunal must send a copy of the notice of appeal and any accompanying documents to each other party—

(a) in asylum support cases, on the day that the Tribunal receives the notice of appeal, or (if that is not reasonably practicable) as soon as reasonably practicable on the following day;

(b) in [1 all other] cases, as soon as reasonably practicable after the Tribunal receives the notice of appeal.

[3 (7A) Her Majesty's Revenue and Customs must, upon receipt of the notice of appeal from the Tribunal under the Childcare Payments Act 2014, inform the Tribunal whether there are any affected parties within the meaning of section 61(5) of that Act other than the appellant and, if so, provide their names and addresses.]

[1 (8) Where an appeal in a social security and child support case is not made within the time specified in paragraph (2)—

(a) it will be treated as having been made in time, unless the Tribunal directs otherwise, if it is made within not more than 12 months of the time specified and neither the decision maker nor any other respondent objects;

(b) the time for bringing the appeal may not be extended under rule 5(3)(a) by more than 12 months.

[3 (9) For the purposes of this rule, mandatory reconsideration applies where—

(a) the notice of the decision being challenged includes a statement to the effect that there is a right of appeal in relation to the decision only if the decision-maker has considered an application for the revision, reversal, review or reconsideration (as the case may be) of the decision being challenged; or

(b) the appeal is brought against a decision made by Her Majesty's Revenue and Customs.]]

AMENDMENTS

1. Tribunal Procedure (Amendment) Rules 2013 (SI 2013/477) rr.22 and 25 (April 8, 2013).

2. Tribunal Procedure (Amendment) Rules 2014 (SI 2014/514) rr.21 and 22 (April 6, 2014).

3. Tribunal Procedure (Amendment) Rules 2015 (SI 2015/1510) rr.11 and 15 (August 21, 2015).

DEFINITIONS

"appellant"–see r.1(3).
"asylum support case"–*ibid.*
"criminal injuries compensation case–*ibid.*
"decision maker"–*ibid.*
"document"–*ibid.*
"hearing"–*ibid.*
"mandatory reconsideration"–see para.(9).
"party"–see r.1(3).
"respondent"–*ibid.*
"social security and child support case"–*ibid.*
"Tribunal"–*ibid.*

GENERAL NOTE

Paragraphs (1) and (2)

5.269 Until April 8, 2013, notice of appeal in social security cases was always sent to the decision-maker under r.23. Now, all decisions except those made by local authorities in respect of housing benefit (or the abolished council tax benefit) inform claimants that an appeal should be sent to the First-tier Tribunal. This has been the case in relation to all decisions made by the Secretary of State since October 28, 2013 and in relation to decisions made by HMRC since April 6, 2014.

5.270 *Paragraphs (3) and (4)*

Her Majesty's Courts and Tribunals Service has produced a standard notice of appeal (SSCS1) and accompanying guidance about appeals (SSCS1A). It is not legally necessary to complete a SSCS1, provided that the relevant information required by para.(3) is given with the notice of appeal. However, completing the form ensures that appellants have provided all the correct information and, indeed, also the information mentioned in para.(5) that is not strictly required in social security and child support cases. An extra copy of a refusal to revise or a revised decision is issued to claimants and others so that they can retain one copy while complying with para.(4)(a)(i). Sending that document is likely to be particularly important because it will enable the First-tier Tribunal to identify the relevant office to which the decision maker's copy of the notice of appeal should be sent under para.(7). Claimants are not expected to identify that office in the notice itself (see para.(3)(d)).

Appeals should be sent to the relevant "HMCTS SSCS Appeals Centre". In England and Wales, the address is: PO Box 1203, Bradford BD1 9WP. In Scotland, it is: PO Box 27080, Glasgow G2 9HQ. Clerks at those centres may enforce the requirements of paras (3) and (4) or may waive them (see the note to r.4). It is intended that a copy of the notice of appeal and any accompanying documents should be sent by the First-tier Tribunal to the decision maker and any other respondent within five days at the most. The decision maker will then be expected to provide a response under r.24.

HMCTS is currently developing software that will enable appeals to be submitted on-line.

A typed name can amount to a signature when it has been adopted by the person concerned through his or her signing another document or taking some other active step in an appeal (*R(DLA) 2/98*). In *CIB/460/2003*, the claimant's mother, who had not been appointed to act on behalf of the claimant, signed the appeal. No-one had objected and the claimant himself had signed a form issued by the clerk, asking him, among other things, whether he wanted to withdraw his appeal. He had said "no". The Commissioner rejected a submission made on behalf of the Secretary of State to the effect that the appeal was not valid.

Under r.11(5), a notice of appeal may be signed by a representative provided that written notice of the appointment of the representative is given to the First-tier Tribunal under r.11(2) or (3). In *CO v LB Havering (HB)* [2015] UKUT 28 (AAC), a notice of appeal was held valid even though it was signed by the claimant's solicitor rather than by the claimant personally and the solicitor had not provided the claimant's written authority to act as her representative so that r.11(5) did not apply. (A copy of the notice countersigned by the claimant was received only after the absolute time limit for appealing had expired.) The judge left open the question whether a notice of appeal signed by a representative who neither had written authority nor was not under a professional obligation to act only on instructions should be treated as having been signed by the appellant. However, even if the signature of such a representative does not amount to the appellant's signature, it is arguable in the light of *R(DLA) 2/98* and *CIB/460/2003* that the requirement that the notice be signed personally can be waived under r.7 if the real appellant has subsequently adopted the appeal.

In *CS v SSWP (DLA)* [2011] UKUT 509 (AAC), it was accepted that the First-tier Tribunal had been right to treat an appeal against an entitlement decision as being also an appeal against a related recoverability decision. It is therefore clear that the details provided for the purpose of complying with para.(6)(d) are not to be regarded as conclusive as to the decision being challenged. See also *SSD v CM (WP)* [2017] UKUT 8 (AAC); [2017] AACR 27.

Paragraph (6)

5.271 Giving the reason for delay assists the decision-maker in deciding whether or not to object to a late appeal being treated as made in time under para.(8)(a). It seems unlikely that a failure to comply with this paragraph would be held to render a late appeal invalid; rather it merely increases the likelihood of the decision-maker objecting to the appeal being admitted.

Paragraph (8)(b) makes it clear that the time for appealing cannot be extended under r.5(3)(a) by more than 12 months.

Paragraph (8)

5.272 Subparagraph (a) reverses the effect of *R(TC) 1/05*, in which it was held that an appeal tribunal did not have jurisdiction to hear a late appeal where express consideration had not been given to extending the time for appealing.

Subparagraph (b) imposes an absolute time limit but it has been held that an absolute time limit must be read as being subject to the First-tier Tribunal's discretion so far as that is necessary to avoid a breach of art.6 of the European Convention on Human Rights. Thus, in a really exceptional case, where the appellant has done everything possible to act within time, an appeal lodged after this absolute time limit could be admitted (*Adesina v Nursing and Midwifery Council* [2013] EWCA Civ 818, applied in *KK v Sheffield CC (CTB)* [2015] UKUT 0367 (AAC)).

Having such an absolute time limit prohibiting the bringing of appeals more than a year late is not in itself incompatible with the European Convention on Human Rights (*Denson v Secretary of State for Work and Pensions* [2004] EWCA Civ 462 (reported as *R(CS) 4/04*). Nonetheless, it can work injustice, particularly in a case where an unrepresented claimant has been challenging the wrong decision and nobody tells him or her until it is too late which decision it is that must be challenged if he or she is to succeed in obtaining the benefit sought.

In *RS v SSD* [2008] UKUT 1 (AAC); R(AF) 1/09, it was held that the fact that a Pensions Appeal Tribunal had erroneously admitted an appeal that ought not to have been admitted because it was too late did not oblige the Tribunal to determine the appeal. Instead, it was obliged to decline jurisdiction which, under these Rules, would have required it to strike the appeal out under r.8(2). That general approach was not adopted by the majority of the three-judge panel in *LS v LB Lambeth (HB)* [2010] UKUT 461 (AAC); [2011] AACR 27, but that decision was decided partly under old procedural rules and the procedural history of the case was unusual. Under these Rules, an extension of time is regarded as a case-management direction under r.5(3)(a), so that, even if the simple approach taken in *RS* is not appropriate, an extension that ought not to have been granted should presumably be set aside under r.6(5).

Paragraph (9)

5.273 From October 28, 2013, the Secretary of State has been empowered to issue a notice within the scope of para.(9) in all cases where he is the decision-maker and did not already have that power, so that the would-be appellant is bound to apply for a revision or equivalent reconsideration before exercising a right of appeal (see regs 3ZA, 3B and 9ZB of the Social Security and Child Support (Decisions and Appeals) Regulations 1999, reg.11A of the Vaccine Damage Payments Regulations 1979, reg.4B of the Mesothelioma Lump Sum Payments (Claims and Reconsiderations) Regulations 2008 and new provisions in child support legislation beyond the scope of this work, as well as reg.7 of the Universal Credit, Personal

Independence Payment, Jobseeker's Allowance and Employment and Support Allowance (Decisions and Appeals) Regulations 2013 which had been in force since earlier in 2013). There is no provision for mandatory reconsideration in relation to the recovery of NHS charges, although appeals in those cases are among those now sent to the First-tier Tribunal. In contrast, s.12(3D) of the Social Security Act 1998 (in relation to child benefit and guardian's allowance), s.38(1A) to (1C) of the Tax Credits Act 2002 and s.56(2) of the Childcare Payments Act 2014 ensure that there is *always* a requirement to seek a revision or review before appealing against a decision made by HMRC (except decisions under the Child Trust Funds Act 2004, to which r.23 applies).

Cases in which the notice of appeal is to be sent to the decision maker

23.—(1) [3 This rule applies to [5 appeals under paragraph 6 of Schedule 7 to the Child Support, Pensions and Social Security Act 2000 (housing benefit and council tax benefit: revisions and appeals) or under section 22 of the Child Trust Funds Act 2004].] 5.274

(2) An appellant must start proceedings by sending or delivering a notice of appeal to the decision maker so that it is received [5 no later than the latest of—

(a) in a housing benefit or council tax benefit case—

(i) one month after the date on which notice of the decision being challenged was sent to the appellant;

(ii) if a written statement of reasons for the decision was requested within that month, 14 days after the later of—

(aa) the end of that month; or

(ab) the date on which the written statement of reasons was provided; or

(iii) if the appellant made an application for revision of the decision under regulation 4(1)(a) of the Housing Benefit and Council Tax Benefit (Decisions and Appeals) Regulations 2001 and that application was unsuccessful, one month after the date on which notice that the decision would not be revised was sent to the appellant;

(b) in an appeal under section 22 of the Child Trust Funds Act 2004, the period of 30 days specified in section 23(1) of that Act].]

(3) If the appellant provides the notice of appeal to the decision maker later than the time required by [5 paragraph (2)(a)] the notice of appeal must include the reason why the notice of appeal was not provided in time.

(4) Subject to paragraph (5), where an appeal is not made within the time specified in [5 paragraph (2)], it will be treated as having been made in time [2 if neither the decision maker nor any other respondent objects].

(5) No appeal may be made more than 12 months after the time specified in [5 paragraph (2)].

(6) The notice of appeal must be in English or Welsh, must be signed by the appellant and must state—

(a) the name and address of the appellant;

(b) the name and address of the appellant's representative (if any);

(c) an address where documents for the appellant may be sent or delivered;

(d) details of the decision being appealed; and

(e) the grounds on which the appellant relies.

(7) The decision maker must refer the case to the Tribunal immediately if—

(a) the appeal has been made after the time specified in [5 paragraph (2)] and the decision maker [2 or any other respondent] objects to it being treated as having been made in time; or

(b) the decision maker considers that the appeal has been made more than 12 months after the time specified in [5 paragraph (2)].

[1 (8) Notwithstanding rule 5(3)(a) [4 [5 . . .]] (case management powers) and rule 7(2) (failure to comply with rules etc.), the Tribunal must not extend the time limit in paragraph (5).]

AMENDMENTS

1. Tribunal Procedure (Amendment No.2) Rules 2009 (SI 2009/1975) rr.2 and 3 (September 1, 2009).

2. Tribunal Procedure (Amendment) Rules 2012 (SI 2012/500) r.4 (April 6, 2012).

3. Tribunal Procedure (Amendment) Rules 2013 (SI 2013/477) rr.22 and 26 (April 8, 2013).

4. Tribunal Procedure (Amendment No. 4) Rules 2013 (SI 2013/2067) rr.22 and 26 (November 1, 2013).

5. Tribunal Procedure (Amendment) Rules 2015 (SI 2015/1510) rr.11 and 16 (August 21, 2015).

DEFINITIONS

"appeal"—see r.1(3).
"appellant"—*ibid.*
"decision maker"—*ibid.*
"social security and child support case"—*ibid.*
"Tribunal"—*ibid.*

GENERAL NOTE

Paragraph (1)

5.275 Until April 8, 2013, this rule applied to all social security and child support cases except those within the scope of r.26. However, for most practical purposes it now applies only to appeals against decisions by local authorities concerning housing benefit (or the abolished council tax benefit). Technically, it also applies to appeals against decisions under the Child Trust Funds Act 2004 (see Vol IV) (which are now probably only a theoretical possibility) and to very late appeals against decisions made by HMRC before April 6, 2014. Rule 18 of the Rules that made the 2015 amendments provides that the amendments to r.23 of, and the substitution of Sch.1 to, the 2008 Rules "have no effect in relation to any appeal against a decision made before 6th April 2014 where the decision maker was Her Majesty's Revenue and Customs". This saving makes explicit what would probably be the position anyway: any such appeal must be referred to the First-tier Tribunal which will refuse to admit it on the ground that it is irremediably out of time (unless to do so would be a breach of the European Convention on Human Rights—see the annotation to r.22(8)).

Note that there appears to be a drafting error in that the words "the latest of" in the opening words of para.(2) should presumably be in the opening words of sub-para.(a) rather than where they are.

Paragraphs (2)–(8)

5.276 See the annotations to r.22(3)–(8) and para.5 of Sch.1, which make similar provision albeit not in the same order.

Responses and replies

24.—[1 (1) When a decision maker receives a copy of a notice of appeal from the Tribunal under rule 22(7), the decision maker must send or deliver a response to the Tribunal— 5.277

(a) in asylum support cases, so that it is received within 3 days after the date on which the Tribunal received the notice of appeal;

(b) in—

(i) criminal injuries compensation cases, or

(ii) appeals under the Child Support Act 1991,

within 42 days after the date on which the decision maker received the copy of the notice of appeal; and

(c) in other cases, within 28 days after the date on which the decision maker received the copy of the notice of appeal.

(1A) Where a decision maker receives a notice of appeal from an appellant under rule 23(2), the decision maker must send or deliver a response to the Tribunal so that it is received as soon as reasonably practicable after the decision maker received the notice of appeal.]

(2) The response must state—

(a) the name and address of the decision maker;

(b) the name and address of the decision maker's representative (if any);

(c) an address where documents for the decision maker may be sent or delivered;

(d) the names and addresses of any other respondents and their representatives (if any);

(e) whether the decision maker opposes the appellant's case and, if so, any grounds for such opposition which are not set out in any documents which are before the Tribunal; and

(f) any further information or documents required by a practice direction or direction.

(3) The response may include a submission as to whether it would be appropriate for the case to be disposed of without a hearing.

(4) The decision maker must provide with the response—

(a) a copy of any written record of the decision under challenge, and any statement of reasons for that decision, if they were not sent with the notice of appeal;

(b) copies of all documents relevant to the case in the decision maker's possession, unless a practice direction or direction states otherwise; and

(c) in cases to which rule 23 (cases in which the notice of appeal is to be sent to the decision maker) applies, a copy of the notice of appeal, any documents provided by the appellant with the notice of appeal and (if they have not otherwise been provided to the Tribunal) the name and address of the appellant's representative (if any).

(5) The decision maker must provide a copy of the response and any accompanying documents to each other party at the same time as it provides the response to the Tribunal.

(6) The appellant and any other respondent may make a written submission and supply further documents in reply to the decision maker's response.

(7) Any submission or further documents under paragraph (6) must

be provided to the Tribunal within 1 month after the date on which the decision maker sent the response to the party providing the reply, and the Tribunal must send a copy to each other party.

AMENDMENT

1. Tribunal Procedure (Amendment) Rules 2013 rr.22 and 27(a), as amended by the Tribunal Procedure (Amendment No.3) Rules 2014 (SI 2014/2128) rr.36–37 (October 1, 2014).

DEFINITIONS

"appeal"—see r.1(3).
"appellant"—*ibid.*
"asylum support case"—*ibid.*
"criminal injuries compensation case"—*ibid.*
"decision maker"—*ibid.*
"document"—*ibid.*
"hearing"—*ibid.*
"party"—*ibid.*
"practice direction"—*ibid.*
"respondent"—*ibid.*
"Tribunal"—*ibid.*

GENERAL NOTE

Paragraphs (1)–(5)

5.278 These paragraphs make express provision for the decision-maker's response to an appeal, as to which the Social Security and Child Support (Decisions and Appeals) Regulations 1999 were curiously silent. Originally, they made no provision for any precise time limit in social security and child support cases. In part this was because some time could be taken investigating points raised in the grounds of appeal and deciding whether to revise the decision being challenged under reg.3(4A) of the 1999 Regulations, which would cause the appeal to lapse under s.9(6) of the Social Security Act 1998. With the introduction of "mandatory reconsideration", requiring consideration to be given to revision *before* an appeal is made, that justification for the lack of a time limit evaporated. The new para.(1) imposes time limits within which responses to appeals must be provided by the Secretary of State or HMRC in social security and child support cases where there has been direct lodgement or mandatory reconsideration. These are six weeks from the date that the Secretary of State received a copy of the notice of appeal from the First-tier Tribunal in child support cases and four weeks in other cases. (There were already time limits in asylum support and criminal injuries compensation cases.) Clerks have been given the power to waive the time limit or to strike out a respondent's case for failing to comply with it (see the annotation to r.4 above).

Paragraph (1A) applies to housing benefit cases and the few remaining other cases where the appeal was sent directly to the decision-maker and mandatory reconsideration did not apply. It does not impose a time limit, maintaining the status quo and giving the decision-maker a substantial opportunity to consider whether to revise the decision being challenged before submitting a response.

A response to an appeal should identify the relevant statutory provisions and explain the decision being challenged so that the claimant understands why the decision has been made. Particularly where there is a very large volume of evidence, a response should also do something to help the First-tier Tribunal get to grips with the evidence, which might involve summarising it (*SSWP v G (VDP)* [2015] UKUT 321 (AAC) at [146]). An inadequate submission may make it more important for a presenting officer to attend a hearing although often a tribunal judge will be able to fill in obvious gaps and ensure that the claimant knows what the issues are and has an adequate opportunity to address them. In *MT v SSWP (IS)* [2010] UKUT 382 (AAC), it was held that there was an error of law where, as the Secretary of State's representative conceded:

> "the appeals process may well have run its entire course without the claimant ever [being] told that there was a regulation that governs the diminishment of capital for overpayment purposes".

A response needs to engage with the grounds of appeal so that, for instance, if a claimant specifically argues that she was incapable of work-related activity at the time of the Secretary of State's decision, r.24(2)(e) requires the Secretary of State to explain why the relevant statutory provision is not satisfied on the facts of the case and that carries with it a need to set out, in those cases where there was an arguable risk to a claimant in being required to engage in some forms of work-related activity, the range or type of work-related activity which the claimant might be expected to undertake in the relevant area and to explain why there would be no substantial risk to the claimant's health if he or she were found not to have limited capability for work-related activity (*MN v SSWP (ESA)* [2013] UKUT 262 (AAC); [2014] AACR 6, as read in the light of *IM v SSWP (ESA)* [2014] UKUT 412 (AAC); [2015] AACR 10 and, in relation to "Jobcentre Plus Offers", *KC v SSWP (ESA)* [2017] UKUT 94 (AAC)). Indeed, even in relation to an appeal against a decision that the claimant did not have limited capability for work, it is helpful if a response includes information about the range of work-related activity available in the relevant area so as to enable the First-tier Tribunal, should it allow the appeal, fairly to go on and consider whether the claimant had limited capability for work-related activity (see *IM*).

A Tribunal of Commissioners in Northern Ireland held in *JC v DSD (IB)* [2011] **5.279**
NICom 177; [2014] AACR 30 that, in an incapacity benefit case, the Department for Social Development should list details of all previous assessment determinations within the current claim, which the Department had said "should be straightforward in most cases . . . from computer records", but that the assessments themselves need only be provided "in a limited class of case, where there is an assertion that there has been no change in the claimant's condition, and where the evidence associated with the previous adjudication history is relevant to that submission or, for example, where the claimant's medical condition, and the evidence associated with the previous adjudication history assists in the assessment of the claimant's overall capacity". No reference was made to that decision in *ST v SSWP (ESA)* [2012] UKUT 469 (AAC), in which it was held that, in employment and support allowance cases, the Secretary of State should send with the response any copy of the report of a previous medical examination that is in his possession in a case where the claimant appeals on the ground that their condition is no better than when the previous examination was "passed", because the previous report will necessarily be relevant in the absence of a material supervening event (such as a change in the law or a surgical operation). Even when it is not clear that such a report is relevant, the response should at least inform the First-tier Tribunal whether there are previous reports in the Secretary of State's possession that *might* be relevant.

In *FN v SSWP (ESA)* [2015] UKUT 670 (AAC); [2016] AACR 24, a three-judge panel broadly agreed with both those decisions but stressed that the previous adjudication history and associated evidence is not always relevant to the case under consideration and that, even if the Secretary of State has not produced all the information and evidence that he should have produced with his response to an appeal, it does not necessarily follow that the First-tier Tribunal will err in proceeding in the absence of the evidence. It said –

> "79. . . . We can envisage a situation where a First-tier Tribunal considers that it has sufficient relevant evidence before it to determine the issues arising in the appeal without the requirement to call for evidence which is missing because the Secretary of State has failed in his duty to provide it.

80. . . . Our view is that the first choice for the tribunal should not be to adjourn but to get on with the task of determining the issues arising in the appeal when satisfied that it has the necessary relevant evidence before it. It might be the case that having weighed and assessed the appellant's oral evidence, the tribunal might be satisfied that the evidence is credible, should be accepted and the appeal be allowed. . . ."

It is suggested that the question for the First-tier Tribunal is not just whether it has sufficient evidence to enable it to determine the issues before it but whether it has sufficient evidence to do so *fairly* in a case where the evidence before it suggests a decision adverse to the claimant. This may involve an assessment of the probable helpfulness to the claimant of evidence that the Secretary of State could produce but has not produced. Even if the First-tier Tribunal reasonably decides to proceed in the absence of previous medical reports that it considers the Secretary of State should have produced, it is arguable that, if it decides the case against the claimant, its decision may be set aside for inadvertent procedural error (either under r.37 or on review or appeal) if it transpires that the reports that should have been produced would substantially have supported the claimant's case.

Because good administration requires that citizens be treated in accordance with a policy adopted by a Government department unless there are good reasons for not doing so, a respondent to an appeal to the First-tier Tribunal fails in his or her duty to draw relevant matters to the attention of the tribunal if no mention is made of a policy favourable to the appellant in the response to the appeal (*Mandalia v Secretary of State for the Home Department* [2015] UKSC 59; [2015] 1 W.L.R. 4546). This is relevant where the decision under appeal involved exercising an element of discretion or at least judgment and there is published guidance as to how the discretion or judgment should be exercised. It is presumably not necessary to refer to the policy document itself if the submission is in accordance with it, but a decision of the First-tier Tribunal may well be set aside if the First-tier Tribunal makes a decision that is adverse to a claimant but is inconsistent with a published policy unless a good reason for departing from the policy has been given (see, for instance, *SB v Oxford CC (HB)* [2014] UKUT 166 (AAC)).

In *TM v HMRC (TC)* [2013] UKUT 444 (AAC), HMRC did not send a copy of its response to the claimant, as required by para.(5), because it was not sure that the claimant was still living at the address it held for him and it was concerned about data protection issues. It sent a copy of the response to the First-tier Tribunal with a covering letter asking for directions. The First-tier Tribunal overlooked that request and heard the appeal without the claimant having seen the response. The Upper Tribunal doubted whether the data protection concern was well-founded, given s.35(1) of the Data Protection Act 1998 which exempts data from non-disclosure if "disclosure is required by or under any enactment, by any rule of law or by order of the court". The Upper Tribunal's decision appears to suggest that HMRC should either have withheld the response from the First-tier Tribunal until it had obtained directions or else it should have sent the response to the claimant notwithstanding its concerns. However, it is not clear why the Upper Tribunal apparently thought it was wrong for the HMRC to enclose a copy of the response with its request for directions, although it may have thought that the request for directions would probably not have been overlooked if the response had not been sent with it.

In *JT v HMTC (TC)* [2015] UKUT 81 (AAC), HMRC applied for the striking out of the claimant's appeal but did not send a copy of the application to the claimant. The First-tier Tribunal overlooked the nature of the application and treated it as a response to the appeal, which it heard and dismissed in the claimant's absence. The Upper Tribunal suggested that an application by a respondent for the striking out of an appeal under r.8(3)(c) should be copied to the claimant and be accompanied by a full response that complies with r.24 unless that would clearly be disproportionate, so as to ensure that the First-tier Tribunal has all the material necessary to enable it properly to decide whether the appeal has no reasonable prospect of success, the claimant is able to make effective representations and the appeal is ready for determination if it is not struck out.

In *John v Information Commissioner* [2014] UKUT 444 (AAC), the Upper Tribunal rejected an argument that a respondent was required to cross-appeal or submit a respondent's notice if disagreeing with a decision being challenged on appeal to the First-tier Tribunal. It was held that new issues could be raised in a response and, referring to *Birkett v Department for the Environment, Food and Rural Affairs* [2011] EWCA Civ 1606, that the Upper Tribunal could exercise its case-management powers to prevent unfairness to an appellant. 5.280

The term "document" used in r.24(4)(b) is defined in r.1(3) so as to include recordings of telephone calls and so HMRC, which records calls to its Helpline and retains them for five years, had failed to comply with the provision when it had failed to provide with its response transcripts of highly relevant telephone conversations (*AG v HMRC (TC)* [2013] UKUT 530 (AAC)).

However, statements of fact in the Secretary of State's response to an appeal may amount to evidence and the absence of supporting documentary evidence is not always fatal. In *AS v SSWP (CA)* [2015] UKUT 592 (AAC); [2016] AACR 22, the claimant said that he had telephoned the Carer's Allowance Unit and informed it of his employment and earnings. It was stated in the Secretary of State's response that no record of such a conversation could be found. The Upper Tribunal considered the significance of such statements in responses, saying—

> "The critical issue is what weight is to be attached to them, and that is for the First-tier Tribunal to assess. The blander or broader the statement, the less weight it might be given. However in this case there was a specific evidential statement made in the appeal response that a full search of the CA Unit's clerical records had been made and in my judgment that evidence was entitled to be given weight. The particular weight to be attached to it was a matter for the fact-finding tribunal to evaluate as part of its fact-finding jurisdiction, and does not here give rise to any error of law."

In particular, it was held that there was no rule of law requiring the Secretary of State to produce evidence as to his system for recording telephone conversations.

Similarly, in *BS v SSWP (DLA)* [2016] UKUT 73 (AAC); [2016] AACR 32, the failure of the Secretary of State to produce a document proving authorisation of surveillance under the Regulation of Investigatory Powers Act 2000 was remedied by the First-tier Tribunal's acceptance of oral evidence from the presenting officer that there had been the requisite authorisation in the particular case.

If an appellant is dissatisfied with the disclosure of documents with a response, he or she may apply for a direction under r.5(3)(d) for the disclosure by the respondent of further documents. When the First-tier Tribunal is considering an application for such a direction, there is no presumption that the respondent's expressed view of what is "relevant" for the purposes of r.24(4)(b) must be accepted unless there are clear grounds to for believing the contrary (*SSD v LA (AFCS)* [2011] UKUT 391 (AAC)).

Paragraphs (6) and (7)

These paragraphs make express provision for other parties to reply to the decision-makers response. Again, the 1999 Regs made no such provision but in practice parties were given the opportunity when asked whether they wanted a hearing. A one-month time limit is now provided, but that may be regarded as a minimum period that must be given to the parties before a case is determined and it will seldom be proportionate to refuse to accept a late submission or evidence unless another party would be unduly affected by the delay, particularly where there is to be an oral hearing at which submissions and new evidence can be expected whether or not written notice has been given. 5.281

Following receipt of an appeal, the First-tier Tribunal sends the appellant and any third party an "enquiry form" asking whether they want an oral hearing and whether they have any further evidence to submit. In *MP v SSWP (DLA)* [2010] UKUT 103 (AAC), a paper hearing took place within a week of the Tribunals Service (and, presumably the claimant's representative) receiving the Secretary of State's response and of the "enquiry form" being sent out. It was held that there had been a breach of the rules of natural justice, as the claimant's solicitors had further evidence to send and the claimant had not had the month allowed by subs.(7) in which to send it. The judge said that the First-tier Tribunal had also clearly been wrong to hold that there were no grounds, in those circumstances, for setting the decision aside under r.37. Current practice is for the "enquiry form" to ask the parties to send any further submission or evidence within 28 days of them receiving the response from the decision maker (which in practice gives them the the statutory month).

Medical and physical examination in appeals under section 12 of the Social Security Act 1998

5.282 **25.**—(1) This rule applies only to appeals under section 12 of the Social Security Act 1998.

(2) At a hearing an appropriate member of the Tribunal may carry out a physical examination of a person if the case relates to—

(a) the extent of that person's disablement and its assessment in accordance with section 68(6) of and Schedule 6 to, or section 103 of, the Social Security Contributions and Benefits Act 1992; or

(b) diseases or injuries prescribed for the purpose of section 108 of that Act.

(3) If an issue which falls within Schedule 2 to these Rules (issues in relation to which the Tribunal may refer a person for medical examination) is raised in an appeal, the Tribunal may exercise its power under section 20 of the Social Security Act 1998 to refer a person to a health care professional approved by the Secretary of State for—

(a) the examination of that person; and

(b) the production of a report on the condition of that person.

(4) Neither paragraph (2) nor paragraph (3) entitles the Tribunal to require a person to undergo a physical test for the purpose of determining whether that person is unable to walk or virtually unable to do so.

DEFINITIONS

"hearing"—see r.1(3).
"Tribunal"—*ibid.*

GENERAL NOTE

Paragraph (2)

5.283 For the meaning of "physical examination", see the note to s.20(3) of the Social Security Act 1998. The "appropriate member" will be a registered medical practitioner (see para.14 of the practice statement reproduced above in the note to art.2 of the First-tier Tribunal and Upper Tribunal (Composition of Tribunal) Order 2008).

These are the *only* circumstances in which a person may be examined on an appeal under s.12 of the 1998 Act (see s.20(3)). However, the limitation does not apply in other cases, such as appeals under the Social Security (Recovery of Benefits) Act 1997.

Where the Tribunal has the power to examine a claimant it need not do so if it considers that an examination is unnecessary. It is not always necessary to carry out a physical examination in order to assess functional loss. It may be better in some cases simply to question the claimant about the practical effects of an injury. However, if not minded to conduct a physical examination, it is good practice for the Tribunal to state as much during the course of the hearing so that the claimant has an opportunity to make representation on the point (*R(I) 10/62*, *CI/3384/2006*). Whether a failure to do so renders a decision liable to be set aside on appeal is likely to depend on the circumstances and, in particular, whether the claimant can show that an examination might have led to a different outcome.

In *MB v DSD (II)* [2010] NICom 133; [2011] AACR 41, it was held that, where a tribunal makes new findings of significance in consequence of a medical examination, fairness may require all parties to the proceedings to have an opportunity to comment on those findings, even if that sometimes involves an adjournment to allow the claimant to seek advice. See also *Evans v Secretary of State for Social Services* (reported as *R(I) 5/94*).

Paragraph (4)

This paragraph applies to examinations within para.(3) as well as those within para.(2). It must be presumed to do so by prescribing a "condition" under s.20(2) of the Social Security Act 1998 and thereby extending the limitation imposed by s.20(3)(b), which is otherwise confined to what may be done "at a hearing". 5.284

Social security and child support cases started by reference or information in writing

26.—(1) This rule applies to proceedings under section 28D of the Child Support Act 1991 and paragraph 3 of Schedule 2 to the Tax Credits Act 2002. 5.285

(2) A person starting proceedings under section 28D of the Child Support Act 1991 must send or deliver a written reference to the Tribunal.

(3) A person starting proceedings under paragraph 3 of Schedule 2 to the Tax Credits Act 2002 must send or deliver an information in writing to the Tribunal.

(4) The reference or the information in writing must include—

(a) an address where documents for the person starting proceedings may be sent or delivered;

(b) the names and addresses of the respondents and their representatives (if any); and

(c) a submission on the issues that arise for determination by the Tribunal.

(5) Unless a practice direction or direction states otherwise, the person starting proceedings must also provide a copy of each document in their possession which is relevant to the proceedings.

(6) Subject to any obligation under rule 19(3) (confidentiality in child support cases), the person starting proceedings must provide a copy of the written reference or the information in writing and any accompanying documents to each respondent at the same time as they provide the written reference or the information in writing to the Tribunal.

(7) Each respondent may send or deliver to the Tribunal a written submission and any further relevant documents within one month of the date on which the person starting proceedings sent a copy of the written reference or the information in writing to that respondent.

DEFINITIONS

"document"—see r.1(3).
"practice direction"—*ibid.*
"respondent"—*ibid.*
"social security and child support case"—*ibid.*
"Tribunal"—*ibid.*

GENERAL NOTE

5.286 This rule makes specific provision for certain child support cases initiated by the Secretary of State and tax credit penalty cases initiated by HMRC. Paragraph (7) provides for responses by respondents. A one-month time limit is provided, but that may be regarded as a minimum period that must be given to the respondents before a case is determined and it will seldom be proportionate to refuse to accept a late submission or evidence unless another party would be unduly affected by the delay, particularly where there is to be an oral hearing at which submissions and new evidence can be expected whether or not written notice has been given.

CHAPTER 2

HEARINGS

Decision with or without a hearing

5.287 **27.**—(1) Subject to the following paragraphs, the Tribunal must hold a hearing before making a decision which disposes of proceedings unless—
(a) each party has consented to, or has not objected to, the matter being decided without a hearing; and
(b) the Tribunal considers that it is able to decide the matter without a hearing.

(2) This rule does not apply to decisions under Part 4.

(3) The Tribunal may in any event dispose of proceedings without a hearing under rule 8 (striking out a party's case).

(4) In a criminal injuries compensation case—
(a) the Tribunal may make a decision which disposes of proceedings without a hearing; and
(b) subject to paragraph (5), if the Tribunal makes a decision which disposes of proceedings without a hearing, any party may make a written application to the Tribunal for the decision to be reconsidered at a hearing.

(5) An application under paragraph (4)(b) may not be made in relation to a decision—
(a) not to extend a time limit;
(b) not to set aside a previous decision;
(c) not to allow an appeal against a decision not to extend a time limit; or
(d) not to allow an appeal against a decision not to reopen a case.

(6) An application under paragraph (4)(b) must be received within 1 month after the date on which the Tribunal sent notice of the decision to the party making the application.

DEFINITIONS

"criminal injuries compensation case"—see r.1(3).
"dispose of proceedings"—*ibid.*
"hearing"—*ibid.*
"party"—*ibid.*
"Tribunal"—*ibid.*

GENERAL NOTE

Paragraphs (1) and (2)

Paragraph (1) applies where the decision to be made will be one "which disposes of proceedings". It is primarily concerned with the final substantive decision on an appeal or reference but, were it not for para.(3), it would also apply to decisions to strike out proceedings. Paragraph (2) makes it clear that it does not apply to decisions relating to reviews and permission to appeal to the Upper Tribunal. It is less clear whether it applies to a decision whether or not to extend the time for appealing to the First-tier Tribunal. On one view, a decision not to extend time disposes of proceedings but the better argument may be that it merely prevents the proceedings from being started. However, even where this rule does not require there to be a hearing, it may be appropriate for the Tribunal to direct one under r.5(3)(f). See the annotations to paras (4)–(6), below, but the overriding objective in r.2 requires that a proportionate approach be taken. 5.288

The paragraph has the effect that, where it applies, there must be a hearing if any party wants one. The Secretary of State or HMRC will say whether or not they want a hearing when submitting a response (see r.24(3)), reference or information. The Tribunal asks the other parties whether or not they want a hearing by sending them a form to return. If there is no reply, the party may be taken to have "not objected to the matter being decided without a hearing." In effect, therefore, these paragraphs replace reg.39 of the Social Security and Child Support (Decisions and Appeals) Regulations 1999. However, note that the legislation no longer refers to an approved form on which a party was required to indicate whether or not he wished to have a hearing, so that the basis for the decision in *R3/04(IB)* has been removed, and that the provision in reg.46(1)(d) for simply striking proceedings out if the approved form was not returned by a party has not been re-enacted. Now, a case cannot be struck out for failure to return a form unless the Tribunal has directed the form be returned and has warned the party that being struck out will, or may, be the consequence of not complying with the direction (see r.8(1) and (3)(a)). In *R3/04(IB)*, the requirement to issue an approved form to a party was held to be the reason why a clerk to a tribunal could not rely on an indication in the appellant's letter of appeal that a hearing was not wanted. There may still be reasons why reliance should not be placed on such an indication, not the least of which is that the appellant is unlikely to have been aware of the precise case against him or her before receiving the response to the appeal.

Where a joint claim is made, both claimants are parties. If only one of them has appealed, the other is a respondent as a person who had a right of appeal (see the definition of "respondent" in r.1(3)). Consequently, there should be a hearing unless both have consented to the case being determined on the papers. This is important where they have separated since making the claim, as in *PD v HMRC (TC)* [2010] UKUT 159 (AAC).

Where a claimant asks for a paper determination and asks for it not to take place until a certain date because further evidence will be provided, the tribunal must either wait until that date or inform the claimant that it will not do so (*CDLA/792/2006*). It will seldom be appropriate not to wait for evidence unless the time requested is unreasonably long or there has been previous delay on the part of the claimant. Rule 24(7) implies that an appellant should have at least a month from being issued with a response to an appeal in which to provide further evidence. 5.289

However, it was said in *EZ v SSWP (ESA)* [2013] UKUT 644 (AAC) that an open-ended statement that evidence would be provided at some time did not require the First-tier Tribunal to wait forever and parties and representatives had as much of a duty to keep the First-tier Tribunal informed as to when they expected to be able to provide evidence as the tribunal's staff did to impose deadlines.

Taking part in a hearing before a tribunal does not breach an extended civil restraint order imposed on a vexatious litigant by a county court and where a claimant asked that his case be decided on the papers because he feared he would be in breach of such an order and his requests for information on the issue had been ignored by both the county court and the Tribunals Service, there had been a breach of the rules of natural justice (*JW v SSWP* [2009] UKUT 198 (AAC)).

There are many cases where a claimant really has no realistic prospects of success unless he or she attends an oral hearing and gives evidence. Even though claimants are advised in general terms that the chances of success may be greater at an oral hearing, it may be thought that the mere fact that they are offered the choice will suggest to many that a paper hearing is a not a foolish option. In *CDLA/1347/1999*, it was said that, if a tribunal considering an appeal on the papers was wholly unable to do justice without there being an oral hearing, it ought to adjourn the proceedings, and direct that there be one but that, otherwise, a tribunal was generally entitled to take the view that a claimant who had rejected the option of an oral hearing having had notice of the issues in the case had had an adequate opportunity to put his case and had lost the chance of strengthening it by giving oral evidence. In *R1/02(IB)*, a Tribunal of Commissioners in Northern Ireland set aside a decision of a tribunal who did not adjourn in the face of incomplete evidence raising questions that they could not answer. In *CIS/4248/2001*, the Commissioner held that an oral hearing should have been directed in a case where an apparently unrepresented claimant had opted for a paper hearing of an appeal against a decision that income support amounting to some £10,000 had been overpaid and was recoverable from her, in circumstances where the claimant had put forward a case that was tenable if she was believed.

> "A very great deal of money was at stake. Oral evidence would have assisted the tribunal's assessment of honesty, which was central to the case. She had not, as far as could be seen, had the benefit of advice from anyone with experience of tribunals. Those are all factors that suggest that justice required an oral hearing in this case."

5.290 At one time, there was a standard "record of proceedings" for "paper hearings" in which a judge ticked boxes to confirm not only that the claimant had made such an election but also that the chairman was satisfied that a hearing was not required. Now that that form is no longer used, it may be necessary for a judge to explain why the case was dealt with on the papers and without an adjournment if asked to provide a statement of reasons for the decision. Rule 27(1)(b) expressly requires the First-tier Tribunal to be satisfied that it is able to decide the matter without a hearing. In *MH v Pembrokeshire CC (HB)* [2010] UKUT 28 (AAC), the First-tier Tribunal declined to accept a claimant's assertion that he suffered from a mental disorder, saying that he had not produced medical evidence and had elected a paper hearing. The decision was set aside by the Upper Tribunal because the First-tier Tribunal had given no indication that it had considered adjourning. The judge drew attention to the overriding objective in r.2. No one had told the claimant that he needed to produce medical evidence or ask for a hearing. However, it is clear from *AT v SSWP (ESA)* [2010] UKUT 430 (AAC), in which *MH* was distinguished, that a failure expressly to refer to the overriding objective is unlikely to be an error of law in itself and, while a tribunal must consider those factors in para.(2) that are relevant, not every factor will be relevant in every case.

In *MM v SSWP (ESA)* [2011] 334 (AAC), it was held that the First-tier Tribunal ought to have explained why it considered that para.(1)(b) was satisfied so that no oral hearing was necessary and that a mere reference to the overriding objective in r.2 would not be sufficient if obvious factors pointed the other way. It does not necessarily follow from these cases that reasons must always be given for not holding an oral hearing, but they may be illustrative of the point made in *R. v Higher Education Funding Council, Ex p. Institute of Dental Surgery* [1994] 1 W.L.R. 242, at 263, that, even if there is no general duty to give reasons for interlocutory decisions, a decision is liable to be set aside on the ground of failure to give reasons if, in the absence of reasons, it appears aberrant.

In *DG v SSWP (ESA)* [2010] UKUT 409 (AAC), a decision made on the papers was set aside where a mentally ill claimant had not sought a hearing after being given advice from the jobcentre that he need not do anything, which was held to have been misleading when the claimant had not been made aware of the consequences of the choice.

On the other hand, in *KP v Hertfordshire CC (SEN)* [2010] UKUT 119 (AAC), the Upper Tribunal was not persuaded that there was any duty to hold a hearing of a directions application when no request for a hearing had been made.

On a paper determination, or indeed any hearing not attended by a claimant, it will always be an error of law for a tribunal to remove an award that has already been made unless the claimant has been given specific notice (in the sense of being focussed on their own particular case) that this is under consideration (*CDLA/1480/2006*).

When a decision is set aside by the Upper Tribunal and referred to another tribunal, it is the invariable practice to hold an oral hearing. However, in *CIB/4193/2003*, the Commissioner noted that that was not the practice where a decision was set aside by a legally qualified panel member under s.13 of the Social Security Act 1998 and he suggested that claimants should be given a fresh opportunity to ask for an oral hearing. He commented that some claimants might reassess their prospects of success "on a paper determination" once they had lost a case and had to apply for leave to appeal. On the facts of the case, he held that there had been a breach of the rules of natural justice because the claimant had been inadvertently misled into not asking for the oral hearing she wanted. 5.291

In *CIB/2751/2002 and CS/3202/2002*, the Commissioner considered the difficulties that arise on a request for a domiciliary hearing, where a refusal to allow such a hearing may require the determination of the very issues that arise on the appeal itself. He said that fairness may require that a claimant who is refused a domiciliary hearing is given a further opportunity to provide evidence, perhaps by being visited by an expert appointed under s.7(4) of the Social Security Act 1998, who could then give evidence to the tribunal under reg.50. It is suggested, however, that the reality may be that a domiciliary hearing would not be refused where the judge believed that the claimant might not be able to attend a hearing at an ordinary venue. Nonetheless, domiciliary hearings are rare. Although it was said in *CI/4093/1999* that "[i]f in fact the claimant cannot reasonably be expected to come to the tribunal, then the tribunal must offer to come to the claimant.", it was pointed out in *KO v SSWP (ESA)* [2013] UKUT 544 (AAC) that that decision was of some antiquity. The judge said—

> "Matters have moved on during that time in respect of the desirability of holding domiciliary hearings. It is rare that they are either appropriate or necessary. Enquiries may need to be made as to how an appellant attends other appointments, such as hospital visits. Few people are totally housebound, and it may be that an appellant can attend if transport is provided. If the issue has not become apparent prior to the date the scheduled hearing those enquiries should be made as early as possible on that day in a telephone call to the appellant's home by the clerk at the venue as the case may be able to proceed as listed or later in the day if a taxi could be arranged, or an adjournment may be necessary so that a taxi could be provided on another occasion. If other methods of transport (such as a private ambulance) are under consideration, or if it is thought that the tribunal venue itself may be unsuitable and another venue, whether a hearing centre or a local community facility may be preferable, or, unusually that the issue of a domiciliary visit does arise, the tribunal will want to adjourn the case for the attention of the local District Tribunal

Judge who will know about local options and facilities, and who may direct medical evidence as to the nature of the difficulties in order to assess suitability."

In *DB v Secretary of State for Work and Pensions (DLA)* [2016] UKUT 205 (AAC), the same judge reiterated the point that a difficulty in getting around does not necessarily justify a domiciliary hearing and made the point that technology including telephony can enable a person to participate in a hearing without actually attending (see the definition of "hearing" in r.1(3), which allows hearings to take place by telephone or Skype, although these methods of conducting a hearing seem to be used in the North-West of England more than anywhere else). She rejected a submission on behalf of the Secretary of State that the First-tier Tribunal was not required to consider obtaining medical records or directing a domiciliary hearing or other steps to facilitate participation unless an application was made, but continued:

"45. That does not mean that a tribunal must initiate such enquiries in every case; it need not treat litigants who are unrepresented as if they invariably needed help and guidance. The tribunal process does not consist of the hearing alone. The administrative arm provides information and options to an appellant at the outset and where there is no contra indication in the case papers the tribunal can rely upon the choices a litigant has made. Many appellants do not want to be present at a hearing; they are used to decisions in respect of benefit matters being made without their oral input and are happy to make their points on paper. That is a legitimate position to adopt; it does not necessarily indicate that the person does not know any better, but the tribunal must be alert to the possibility of a genuine lack of understanding of the possibilities. . . ."

The tribunal has considerable latitude in deciding how a hearing will be conducted but it must be fair. If the rules of natural justice (which effectively guarantee a fair hearing) are broken, the decision of the tribunal is liable to be set aside on appeal on the ground that it is erroneous in point of law. See further the annotation to s.11 of the Tribunals, Courts and Enforcement Act 2007.

Evidence at a hearing

5.292 A tribunal is entitled to take account of all that it sees and hears at a hearing but if it sees something that appears important, fairness generally requires that the party concerned should be given an opportunity of commenting on what the tribunal has seen. In *R(DLA) 8/06*, the Commissioner cautioned tribunals against giving too much weight to observations of a claimant's apparent well-being that might be unrepresentative and so be unreliable as evidence of his health generally. Giving a claimant an opportunity to comment enables the claimant to put the observation into a broader context. However, the Commissioner also pointed out that, where an observation merely confirms a conclusion that the tribunal would have reached anyway, a failure to invite the claimant to comment on it will not render the decision erroneous in point of law although, unless a judge makes clear what significance a recorded observation had in the tribunal's reasoning when he or she is writing the statement of reasons, it is likely to be assumed that it must have had an effect on the decision. The Commissioner also made clear that a judge does not have to ask precise questions amounting to a cross-examination of the claimant but can ask an open question that gives a claimant the opportunity to comment. He said—

". . .the chairman did not point out to the claimant the significance of the observations that the tribunal had made. But the claimant must have realised this. He had presented his claim on the basis of pain and exhaustion and the observations were clearly directly relevant to that."

What is important is whether, taking the hearing as a whole, the claimant has an adequate opportunity to address the issues raised by any significant observations.

In *R(DLA) 3/06*, the Tribunal of Commissioners allowed an appeal against a decision of a tribunal who had drawn an adverse inference against a 12-year old claimant, alleged to have learning difficulties and behavioural problems, because her foster parent and appointee had failed to arrange for her to give evidence to the tribunal despite a summons. The Tribunal of Commissioners gave the following general guidance about child witnesses.

"(i) A tribunal should have proper regard to the wishes of a child of sufficiently mature years and understanding who wishes to give evidence in a DLA claim made on his behalf. However, a tribunal should be very cautious before requiring any child to give evidence, and should only call for a child to give evidence if it is satisfied that a just decision cannot otherwise be made. Before reaching such a conclusion, the tribunal should consider first all the other available evidence, and then ask itself whether any necessary additional evidence can be obtained from another source, for example, a health visitor, social worker, teacher, family member or friend, to avoid the need for the child to be called at all.
(ii) In any event, a tribunal should be very slow to exercise its power to require a child to give evidence if that child's parent or carer takes the view that for the child to give evidence may be detrimental to the child's welfare, particularly if there is evidence from a competent professional that to do so might be harmful. It would be wholly exceptional for it to be appropriate for a tribunal to call a child in such circumstances.
(iii) Even if it is those representing the child, rather than the tribunal, who wish the child to give evidence, as *Brown v Secretary of State for the Home Department* (LTA 97/6885/J) indicates, a tribunal has power to disallow the child from giving evidence if it is against the child's interests to do so. If it is proposed that the child gives evidence, the tribunal must consider whether it is in that child's interests to do so.
(iv) The tribunal should bear in mind that the mere presence of a child at a hearing is unlikely to give a reliable indication of the effect of a child's disability in normal circumstances.
(v) Where a decision is taken to call a child to give evidence, after submissions from interested persons (including the parents or carers of the child) a tribunal should give consideration to precisely how that evidence will be taken, so that the interests and welfare of the child are maintained, giving any directions that are appropriate. In doing so the tribunal will bear in mind that a child may perceive what is said at a tribunal hearing very differently from an adult. It will be necessary for the tribunal to identify any matters that the child ought not to hear (e.g. it will not generally be appropriate for a child to hear criticism of those responsible for his or her care) and questions that the child ought not to be asked (e.g. it will not generally be appropriate to question a child about his or her own care needs).
(vi) In addition, where a child is to be called to give evidence, the tribunal will need to give consideration to practical matters such as the geography of the hearing room, having an appropriate adult in close attendance, whether any of the tribunal (including the chairman) should be selected because of experience in dealing with child witnesses and even (in appropriate cases) taking such steps as taking the child's evidence by video link if available, giving directions where appropriate."

See also the practice direction of the Senior President of Tribunals, below. However, although care must be taken when considering whether to hear evidence from a child, there can be no presumption against a child giving evidence and regard must be had to the fairness of the proceedings as well as the interests of the child (*In re W (Children) (Family Proceedings: Evidence)* [2010] UKSC 12; [2010] 1 W.L.R. 701). Indeed, in *JP v SSWP (DLA)* [2014] UKUT 275 (AAC); [2015] AACR 2, the judge pointed out that *In re W* had been decided after *R(DLA) 3/06* and the making of the Practice Direction and he said that para.5 of the Practice Direction was inconsistent with the decision of the Supreme Court in saying that a tribunal *must* decline to hear evidence from a child if it would prejudice the child's welfare.

The Senior President of Tribunals has announced that he will revise the Practice Direction.

Representatives in social security cases are often in a position to give evidence from their own knowledge and it has on several occasions been said that they should not be stopped from doing so (see the note to r.11(1)).

Record of proceedings

5.293 There is no statutory duty upon the presiding tribunal judge to keep a record of proceedings before the First-tier Tribunal. However, there is a general duty to do so (see *R.(AW) v First-tier Tribunal (CIC)* [2013] UKUT 350 (AAC)) and, in any event, the Senior President of Tribunals has issued a Practice Statement dated October 30, 2008 which more or less replaces reg.55 of the Social Security and Child Support (Decisions and Appeals) Regulations 1999. It is in the following terms—

"1. In this Practice Statement "social security and child support case" has the meaning given in rule 1(3) of the Tribunal Procedure (First-tier Tribunal) (Social Entitlement Chamber) Rules 2008.

2. A record of the proceedings at a hearing must be made by the presiding member, or in the case of a Tribunal composed of only one member, by that member.

3. The record must be sufficient to indicate any evidence taken and submissions made and any procedural applications, and may be in such medium as the member may determine.

4. The Tribunal must preserve—
   a. the record of proceedings;
   b. the decisions notice; and
   c. any written reasons for the Tribunal's decision for the period specified in paragraph 5.

5. The specified period is six months form the date of—
   a. the decision made by the Tribunal;
   b. any written reasons for the Tribunal's decision;
   c. any correction under Rule 36 of the above Rules;
   d. any refusal to set aside a decision under Rule 37; or
   e. any determination of an application for permission to appeal against decision, or until the date on which those documents are sent to the Upper Tribunal in connection with an appeal against the decision or an application for permission to appeal, if that occurs within the six months.

6. Any party to the proceedings may within the time specified in paragraph 5 apply in writing for a copy of the record of proceedings and a copy must be supplied to him."

A recording of a hearing is a document for the purposes of s.32 of the Freedom of Information Act 2000 and any question whether the Practice Statement applies or it should be disclosed to someone not entitled to it under the Practice Statement is a matter for the tribunal and not for the Information Commissioner (*Edem v Information Commissioner* [2015] UKUT 210 (AAC)).

The record of proceedings should be a record of what has happened at a hearing and therefore should include not only a note of evidence and submissions but also a record of any procedural application, such as an application for an adjournment, and the tribunal's decision on the application (*R(DLA)3/08*).

In *CB v SSWP (ESA)* [2014] UKUT 545 (AAC), it was stated that "the duration of a hearing must be recorded to demonstrate that the hearing did not begin before the notified time and was of sufficient length to allow the parties to put forward their cases". However, the failure to record the duration of the hearing in that case was only a material error because it meant that there was no indication of the period for which the First-tier Tribunal had found that the claimant had sat without discomfort and so the relevance of the finding was unclear on the claimant's appeal to the Upper Tribunal.

Where an appeal is based on what happened at a hearing, the Upper Tribunal will be slow to go behind a full record of proceedings (*CS/343/1994*) but will admit evidence if it is necessary to do so where a full and particularised allegation is made that the conduct of the hearing led to a breach of the rules of natural justice (*R(M) 1/89*). The Upper Tribunal may obtain statements from those present at the hearing, including the members of the tribunal, but it will not be necessary to obtain statements from members of the tribunal if the appellant's case is supported by other evidence, such as the record of proceedings and the statement of reasons, unless the case involves an allegation of personal misconduct that it would be unfair to find proved without the person concerned having had the opportunity of commenting (*CDLA/5574/2002*). The need to obtain proper evidence as to what occurred at the hearing has been reiterated in *Singh v Secretary of State for the Home Department* [2016] EWCA Civ 492.

However, it is not just in cases where procedural impropriety is alleged that a **5.294** record of proceedings is an important document. Because a statement of reasons ought to deal with the principal points raised by the parties but a tribunal is not always required to consider points that have not been explicitly raised and because a tribunal may have an investigatory role, the record of proceedings may be an important document in a case where it is suggested that the statement of reasons is inadequate or that the tribunal failed to ask questions about a particular issue. It may, however, be supplemented. In *CH/2484/2006*, the Deputy Commissioner said—

> "I appreciate that a record of proceedings is not a complete *verbatim* note and that it is possible for points to be omitted, but if an appellant to the Commissioner wishes to base a submission on the overlooking of evidence or submissions and the evidence or submission are not recorded in the record, it seems to me to be necessary as a general rule for it to equip itself with evidence (such as a statement by someone who was present) that that piece of evidence or submission was in fact made. It should also raise the matter with the other side in advance, so as to avoid surprise and facilitate agreement on the position if possible."

In that case, the local authority was the appellant. Where a claimant is an appellant and the Secretary of State was not present at the hearing before the tribunal, the Secretary of State will not be in a position to dispute a statement by the claimant as to what occurred at that hearing. As suggested above, it will be open to the Upper Tribunal to seek the views of the tribunal but it will not be obliged to do so.

Paragraph 3 of the Practice Statement shows that the "record of proceedings" is a note of the evidence and submissions received at the hearing. This is often taken to refer to the oral evidence and submissions but it probably extends to at least a record of what written evidence was before the tribunal which may in turn imply a duty on someone to keep a copy of that evidence. In practice, the Tribunals Service usually keeps the whole file for six months from the last action on the file, which complies with the duty imposed however the statement is construed.

Until 1999, a record of proceedings had to be kept for 18 months. The duty to **5.295** keep the other documents was first introduced in 2005 and usually makes it unnecessary for a person seeking permission to appeal to the Upper Tribunal to supply copies with the application. All parties should have had copies of the decision notice and any statement of reasons and would have had six months in which to ask for a copy of the record of proceedings. The effect of the six-month period is that it remains necessary for an applicant to provide the documents required to support a very late application for leave to appeal. In *CIB/62/2008*, a claimant who made an application to a tribunal chairman for leave to appeal more than six months late, with the consequence that the tribunal's file had been destroyed, was refused leave to appeal by both the chairman and a Commissioner. The latter held that the claimant's assertion that he had asked for an oral hearing of his appeal before the tribunal which had been refused would not be enough to overcome the presumption that the tribunal proceedings had been properly conducted, when the claimant's own delay had resulted in the probable destruction of the evidence that would either have supported or contradicted his assertion.

The duty to provide a record of proceedings is a duty to provide one that is intelligible or capable of being made intelligible to those to whom it is issued (*R(DLA)3/08*). Providing an illegible document is therefore not sufficient, although one obvious remedy is to ask the clerk to obtain and provide a legible copy. A failure to comply with this duty will not always render the tribunal's decision erroneous in point of law but it will do so if, in a particular case, the consequence is a real possibility of unfairness or injustice. The extent to which a lack of a record of proceedings results in unfairness or injustice may turn on the extent to which the deficiency can be made good by obtaining evidence as to what happened or was said at a hearing from the parties or the tribunal (*ibid*).

In *MK v SSWP (II)* [2014] UKUT 323 (AAC), it was pointed out that, where proceedings are recorded, the recording is the record of proceedings so that it cannot be argued that the record is inadequate on the basis of any omissions in a judge's note. It was also said that in such circumstances the judge's note is personal and so not disclosable in any circumstances. In *AW*, it had been suggested that the confidentiality of the judge's note could be waived in the interests of efficiency given the cost of obtaining a transcript of a recording or the length of time it takes an appellate judge to listen to a recording.

Paragraph (3)

5.296 Where a strike-out decision is made without a hearing, care has to be taken to ensure that the effect is not that the claimant is improperly deprived of a hearing of their appeal (see the note to r.8). In a criminal injuries compensation case, a party whose case has been struck out without a hearing may apply for the decision to be reconsidered at a hearing under para.(4)(b) (*R.(NT) v First-tier Tribunal (CIC)* [2013] UKUT 357 (AAC)).

Paragraphs (4)–(6)

5.297 Rule 27(4)(b) gives a claimant a right to apply for a hearing in a criminal injuries compensation case where the case has been struck out without a hearing in accordance with para.(3) (*R.(NT) v First-tier Tribunal (CIC)* [2013] UKUT 357 (AAC)).

The word "extend" in r.27(5)(c) does not include "waive" (*JM v Advocate General for Scotland* [2013] CSOH 169).

It is not obligatory to determine a case falling within para.(5) without a hearing and it is well-established that procedural fairness may require a person to be offered an oral hearing where legislation does not provide an absolute right to one. Relevant factors were identified in *R.(Osborne) v Parole Board* [2013] UKSC 61; [2014] 1 A.C. 1115 of which the first, and perhaps the most relevant in the social security context, is "where facts which appear . . . to be important are in dispute, or where a significant explanation or mitigation is advanced which needs to be heard orally in order fairly to determine its credibility". In some cases it may also be necessary to provide reasons for refusing an oral hearing (*R.(VAA) v First-tier Tribunal* [2010] UKUT 36 (AAC)). In *R.(AG) v First-tier Tribunal (CIC)* [2013] UKUT 357 (AAC), the Upper Tribunal held that it was not appropriate for the First-tier Tribunal to challenge the honesty or integrity of a claimant where an oral hearing has been refused and that reasons for refusing a hearing need to refer to the specific facts of the case in issue and not just "a standard (or perhaps pro forma) list of reasons". In *R.(TG) v First-tier Tribunal (CIC)* [2013] UKUT 366 (AAC), the Upper Tribunal said that—

"The particular factors in this case which should have prompted the First-tier Tribunal to offer the applicant the opportunity to have an oral hearing include the complexity of the factual background (including the applicant's complaints about the nature of the investigation, her very lengthy (if not always accurate) analysis of the case, her belief that the investigation was bungled, the police complaint investigation, and the continuing trouble between the two families) and the applicant's obvious difficulties in keeping to the most relevant matters when expressing herself in writing."

Entitlement to attend a hearing

28. Subject to rule 30(5) (exclusion of a person from a hearing), each party to proceedings is entitled to attend a hearing. 5.298

DEFINITIONS

"hearing"—see r.1(3).
"party"—*ibid.*

GENERAL NOTE

This makes it plain that, except where r.30(5) applies, a party may always attend a hearing even when the hearing is in private. By virtue of r.11(5) a properly appointed representative also has a right to attend a hearing, whether or not the party does so. By virtue of r.11(7), a party who attends hearing may be accompanied by a person acting as a representative or assistant. 5.299

Notice of hearings

29.—(1) The Tribunal must give each party entitled to attend a hearing reasonable notice of the time and place of the hearing (including any adjourned or postponed hearing) and any changes to the time and place of the hearing. 5.300

(2) The period of notice under paragraph (1) must be at least 14 days except that—

(a) in an asylum support case the Tribunal must give at least 1 day's and not more than 5 days' notice; and

(b) the Tribunal may give shorter notice—

(i) with the parties' consent; or

(ii) in urgent or exceptional circumstances.

DEFINITIONS

"asylum support case"—see r.1(3).
"hearing"—*ibid.*
"party"—*ibid.*
"Tribunal"—*ibid.*

GENERAL NOTE

Where a joint claim is made, both claimants are parties. If only one of them has appealed, the other is a respondent as a person who had a right of appeal (see the definition of "respondent" in r.1(3)). Consequently, both should be notified of a hearing. A failure to do so is unlikely to be of practical importance if the claimants are still living together but it may be important where they have separated, as in *PD v HMRC (TC)* [2010] UKUT 159 (AAC). 5.301

Public and private hearings

5.302 **30.**—(1) Subject to the following paragraphs, all hearings must be held in public.

(2) A hearing in a criminal injuries compensation case must be held in private unless—

(a) the appellant has consented to the hearing being held in public; and
(b) the Tribunal considers that it is in the interests of justice for the hearing to be held in public.

(3) The Tribunal may give a direction that a hearing, or part of it, is to be held in private.

(4) Where a hearing, or part of it, is to be held in private, the Tribunal may determine who is permitted to attend the hearing or part of it.

(5) The Tribunal may give a direction excluding from any hearing, or part of it—

(a) any person whose conduct the Tribunal considers is disrupting or is likely to disrupt the hearing;
(b) any person whose presence the Tribunal considers is likely to prevent another person from giving evidence or making submissions freely;
(c) any person who the Tribunal considers should be excluded in order to give effect to a direction under rule 14(2) (withholding information likely to cause harm); or
(d) any person where the purpose of the hearing would be defeated by the attendance of that person.

(6) The Tribunal may give a direction excluding a witness from a hearing until that witness gives evidence.

DEFINITIONS

"appellant"—see r.1(3).
"criminal injuries compensation case"—*ibid.*
"hearing"—*ibid.*
"Tribunal"—*ibid.*

GENERAL NOTE

Paragraphs (1) and (2)

5.303 Paragraph (1) expresses the general rule, which is that hearings should usually be in public. Paragraph (2), which applies only to criminal injuries compensation cases, is anomalous but continues the previous practice in such cases.

A hearing is in public, notwithstanding the lack of any publication of a list of cases, if it takes place within reasonable office hours at a publicly recognised court or tribunal hearing centre (*DF v SSWP (ESA)* [215] UKUT 143 (AAC)), provided that there is no barrier (such as a locked door) to prevent access by a member of the public wishing to drop in to see how the hearing is being conducted (*Storer v British Gas Plc* [2000] 1 W.L.R. 1237 (CA)). Thus, a hearing by telephone will only be in public if the judge is in an accessible hearing room and the telephone is on loudspeaker.

The fact that a hearing is in public does not necessarily mean that it can be recorded by members of the public. In an unpublished decision dated August 8, 2011, the First-tier Tribunal sitting in Exeter refused to allow the BBC to bring recording equipment into a hearing. The BBC wished to be able to broadcast part of the proceedings as part of a Radio 4 documentary programme about the personal capability assessment for incapacity benefit. The First-tier Tribunal considered *Attorney General v British Broadcasting Corporation* [1981] AC 303 and concluded that the tribunal was a "court" for the purposes of s.9 of the Contempt of Court Act 1981. Although s.9(1)(a) of that Act permits a person to "use in court, or bring into court for use, any tape recorder or other instrument for recording sound" provided he or she has the permission of the court, s.9(1)(b) makes it always a contempt of court to:

> "publish a recording of legal proceedings made by means of any such instrument, or any recording derived directly or indirectly form it, by playing it in the hearing of the public or any section of the public".

The tribunal or court has no power to give permission for a sound recording of proceedings to be broadcast to the public. The First-tier Tribunal therefore refused permission to bring any equipment capable of recording sound, including mobile telephones, into the hearing because part of the reason for making a recording would be so that parts of it could be broadcast. It was further pointed out that the ban on broadcasting also applied to any CD of the proceedings that might be provided by the tribunal to the claimant as a record of the proceedings (see the note to r.27).

Equally, the fact that a hearing is in private does not mean that it is a contempt of court to disclose or publish information about the proceedings, unless an order restricting disclosure or publication has been made under r.14(1) (see s.12 of the Administration of Justice Act 1960, considered in *R. (BD) v First-tier Tribunal (CIC)* [2013] UKUT 332 (AAC)).

Paragraph (3)

Paragraph (3) enables the Tribunal to direct that a particular case be heard in 5.304
private, either in whole or in part. In practice, this does not arise as a live issue in social security cases very often because it is very rare for members of the general public to attend hearings. The issue perhaps arises primarily where one party is accompanied by a large number of people and there arises the question whether it is appropriate for them all to attend the hearing. Directing that a hearing be in private enables the numbers to be regulated under para.(4).

The Rules give no guidance as to how it is to be decided whether or not a hearing is to be in private. Regulation 49(6) of the Social Security and Child Support (Decisions and Appeals) Regulations 1999 provided that a hearing could be in private only—

> "(a) in the interests of national security, morals, public order or children;
>
> (b) for the protection of the private or family life of one or more parties to the proceedings; or
>
> (c) in special circumstances, because publicity would prejudice the interests of justice."

The language was based on art.6(1) of the European Convention on Human Rights, but art.6 is concerned with the right of *a party* to a public hearing. Consequently, as far as art.6 is concerned, a party may waive that right (*Schuler-Zgraggen v Switzerland*, judgment of June 24, 1993, Series A, No.263; (1993) 16 E.H.R.R. 405, at [58]) and consent to a hearing being in private even if those grounds are not made out. Regulation 49(6) did not permit such a waiver. The reason for that may have been that there are other interests in there being a public hearing, not the least of which is the right of the public to see how justice is administered, which includes the right of the press to comment on the administration of justice. That right, too, may require the approach formerly taken in reg.49(6), although the need to protect the private or family life of people other than the parties (e.g. witnesses and people who might be mentioned in evidence) may need to be taken into account so reg.49(6)(b) may have been too narrowly drawn.

However, where the press are not present and where the parties wish a hearing to 5.305
be in private so that the number of people present may be limited to avoid a timid claimant from being overwhelmed and unable properly to present his or her case, it

may be open to a Tribunal to direct that the hearing be in private even if the conditions of the former reg.49(6) are not met, simply on the ground that the interests of justice require that the claimant should be enabled to put his or her case effectively (see r.2(2)(c)).

In all of this, it should not be forgotten that concerns about publicity can be met by the imposition of appropriate reporting restrictions under r.14(1). Generally, it will be preferable for the Tribunal to impose reporting restrictions rather than holding a hearing in private if the reporting restrictions will achieve all that is necessary. On the other hand, if there is a legitimate press interest in a case but a good reason for excluding the general public, it would be possible to admit the press to a hearing held in private under para.(4) (*Independent News and Media Ltd v A* [2010] EWCA Civ 343; [2010] 1 W.L.R. 2262) while, if necessary, prohibiting the publication of the names of the parties (*L v L (Ancillary Relief Proceedings: Anonymity)* [2015] EWHC 2621 (Fam); [2016] 1 W.L.R. 1259).

Even in the courts, it is recognised that the confidential nature of documents that must be considered at a hearing may sometimes justify holding the hearing in private (see, for instance, *Eurasian Natural Resources Corporation Ltd v Dechert LLP* [2014] EWHC 3389 (Ch); [2015] 1 W.L.R. 4621).

In *CIB/2751/2002 and CS/3202/2002*, the Commissioner considered how domiciliary hearings might be affected by the former reg.49(6). He suggested that it might be possible to hold a public hearing near a claimant's home rather than actually in it. Given that few people other than those invited by the parties ever watch tribunal hearings, the problems raised may be more theoretical than real but the legislation does require them to be addressed. The answer may be that, where a domiciliary hearing in a claimant's home is necessary, it will usually be justifiable to hold the hearing in private in order to protect the claimant's private or family life. Presumably a claimant who has asked for a domiciliary hearing can be taken to have waived his rights to privacy to the extent necessary to allow the hearing to take place with other parties being present.

Paragraph (4)

5.306 If a case is to be heard in private, the tribunal has a broad power to determine who may attend it. However, certain people have a right to attend a hearing even if it is in private. By r.28, a party always has a right to be present (subject to r.30(5)) and, the consequence is that, by virtue of r.11(5), so does a properly appointed representative whether the party attends or not. Where a party does attend, he or she may be accompanied by a person acting either as a representative or merely as an assistant (see r.11(7)). Plainly relevant witnesses must be allowed to attend for the purpose of giving evidence.

Beyond that, it is all a matter of discretion, there being no equivalent to reg.49(9) of the 1999 Regulations. It is likely to be desirable for the clerk or usher to be present and also a judge or Chamber President or the Senior President of Tribunals monitoring the tribunal. It is also likely to be appropriate to allow a claimant to be accompanied by a friend or relative even if he or she is there only for moral support and is not providing any actual assistance. As to others, it is suggested that, where a person has a reason for attending other than mere curiosity, the views of the parties should be ascertained and taken into account. In practice, parties seldom object to a person being present if they are made aware of a good reason for his or her presence. It will therefore generally be appropriate to allow people undergoing training to attend, whether the person is a member of the decision-maker's staff, a new judge or member of the Tribunal or a trainee lawyer shadowing the judge.

A journalist may also have a legitimate reason for being present and consideration may need to be given to the question whether reporting restrictions imposed under r.14(1) will provide adequate protection for the parties and other vulnerable people. See the note to that rule.

Paragraph (5)

This paragraph allows any person who would otherwise be entitled to attend a hearing to be excluded, where that is necessary on one of the specified grounds. Plainly the power to exclude a party or representative should be exercised only where there is absolutely no practical alternative. See *R. (Secretary of State for the Home Department) v Inner West London Assistant Deputy Coroner* [2010] EWHC 3098 (Admin); [2011] 1 W.L.R. 2564 for the importance attached to the rights of parties and representatives to be present at hearings. In relation to sub-para.(b), it would be desirable to consider whether alternative methods of giving evidence (e.g. by videolink or from behind a screen) would achieve the necessary effect and be practical. **5.307**

In *WS v SSWP (IB)* [2012] UKUT 202 (AAC), there was evidence in the documents that the claimant was prone to violence and habitually carried a lock knife. The First-tier Tribunal, having discussed the matter with his representative, declined to allow the claimant into the hearing unless he consented to be searched. He did not consent to be searched and so the hearing took place in his absence. The First-tier Tribunal considered that the claimant was absent through his own choice and that view was not challenged. The Upper Tribunal observed that the situation was not covered by r.30(5)(a) because it could not be said that the claimant was "likely to disrupt the hearing" but suggested that it could have relied on the power in r.5(1) to "regulate its own procedure", provided it did not breach art.6 of the European Convention on Human Rights. There would, it considered, not have been a breach of art.6 in the circumstances that arose.

Paragraph (6)

Whether witnesses should be excluded from a hearing until they give evidence depends very much on the circumstances of the case. There is often a fear that dishonest witnesses will tailor their evidence so that it fits with other evidence in the case if they hear that evidence before giving their own. Evidence can often be stronger if it is consistent without the witnesses having had the opportunity of hearing each other's answers to questions. On the other hand, witnesses can often usefully comment on other evidence and can pick up points not mentioned by other witnesses, which is important in social security cases, where parties are seldom represented by lawyers and there is rarely any proper examination-in-chief or cross-examination. Indeed, a representative may often be a witness (see the note to r.11(1)). The Tribunal is given a broad discretion as to how to approach a case. If it intends to exclude witnesses from a hearing, it is suggested it should take the same approach to the witnesses of all parties lest it give the impression of having formed a view that the witnesses of one party only are suspected of dishonesty. **5.308**

Hearings in a party's absence

31. If a party fails to attend a hearing the Tribunal may proceed with the hearing if the Tribunal— **5.309**

(a) is satisfied that the party has been notified of the hearing or that reasonable steps have been taken to notify the party of the hearing; and
(b) considers that it is in the interests of justice to proceed with the hearing.

DEFINITIONS

"hearing"—see r.1(3).
"party"—*ibid.*
"Tribunal"—*ibid.*

GENERAL NOTE

5.310 In *Cooke v Glenrose Fish Co* [2004] I.C.R. 1188, the Employment Appeal Tribunal suggested that an employment tribunal should always at least consider telephoning an appellant who has failed to appear before proceeding in his absence and should ordinarily do so where there was an indication that the appellant had been intending to appear at the hearing because, for instance, solicitors were on the record. An oversight can then be rectified. However, the Employment Appeal Tribunal also held that employment tribunals were entitled to take a robust approach and generally to proceed to hear cases where there was an unexplained absence, because any injustice could be put right on review. The provision in these Rules equivalent to a review would be r.37, which permits the setting aside of a decision where a party or his representative was not present at a hearing. The Employment Appeal Tribunal remarked that "it would appear to be a necessary concomitant of the more stringent attitude encouraged by [the President] that there be the less stringent attitude on a review if a party who has not attended comes forward with a genuine and full explanation and shows that the original hearing was not one from which he deliberately absented himself".

In *PS v SSWP (ESA)* [2017] UKUT 55 (AAC), it was stressed that it did not follow from *Cooke* that the First-tier Tribunal must, as a matter of law, always consider whether to telephone an appellant in the event of an unexplained absence from a hearing in the Social Entitlement Chamber, both for practical reasons and because the decisions in such cases are very fact-specific. In particular, there is usually far less inconvenience to other people in a social security decision being set aside if it subsequently turns out that there was a good reason for the non-attendance than there is in an employment tribunal case.

Where a claimant sent a message to a representative to say she would not be attending a hearing and wished the tribunal to proceed in her absence and the representative made no application for an adjournment, a Commissioner declined to hold the tribunal to have erred in not adjourning (*CSIB/404/2005*). However, he set the tribunal's decision aside for failure to deal adequately with questions concerning the claimant's mental health, even though it was difficult to see how the tribunal could have allowed the claimant's appeal on the evidence before it. That may suggest that, where the claimant's presence is required to establish the facts and the non-attendance might have been attributable, at least in part, to the claimant's mental health, a tribunal really should consider whether an adjournment would be in the interests of justice, just as they would if the claimant had not asked for a hearing (see the annotation to r.27). Of course, a tribunal is entitled to take into account the fact that the claimant has asked for a hearing and then failed to attend it in considering whether justice requires an adjournment and whether attendance in the future is likely.

In *LO v SSWP (ESA)* [2016] UKUT 10 (AAC); [2016] AACR 31, there arose the question whether, where an unrepresented claimant states that he or she does not wish to attend a hearing because of disability, a tribunal ought generally to consider whether a telephone hearing would be appropriate. The judge rejected a submission by the Secretary of State that it was unnecessary to do so merely because the claimant had not asked for such a hearing, since it was not the practice of the First-tier Tribunal's administration to inform parties of the possibility of there being a telephone hearing and so claimants could not be expected to ask for one. However, he held that there had been no error of law in the particular case before him. The First-tier Tribunal had given detailed consideration to the question whether there needed to be an adjournment so that the claimant could give evidence and had taken a proportionate approach. Although an offer of a telephone hearing was one possibility that might have been considered, it had not been necessary to do so in that case in order to deal with the issue of adjournment fairly. The claimant might, after all, have declined such an offer. Nonetheless, the implication of the decision is that there may be at least some cases where a failure explicitly to consider whether to offer a telephone hearing will render a decision wrong in law. Similarly, in *WA v*

SSWP (CSM) [2016] UKUT 86 (AAC), a tribunal had erred in proceeding in the absence of a party who had given fear of her ex-partner as a reason for not attending a child support hearing, without at least considering writing to her to stress that everyone has the right to attend a hearing without fear of intimidation and that the tribunal would not tolerate any attempt by one party to intimidate the other. The judge stated that "[a]ny such communication should record that it is given on a neutral basis; that is without making a finding as to whether any allegations made are accepted" and he pointed out that in some cases it might be necessary to seek the views of one parent before writing to the other. Other steps that he suggested could be taken in such a case included a hearing by video link or the "presence of a security guard in the hearing room, attendance by telephone link, laying out the hearing room in a particular way to create physical separation or possibly use of screens if available, staging the parties' entrance and departure from the room, and their waiting arrangements, to minimise proximity".

Compliance with the conditions of r.31 does not prevent the setting aside of the tribunal's decision under r.37 on the ground that a party or representative was not present at the hearing, if it is just to do so (*KH v SSWP (CSM)* [2012] UKUT 329 (AAC)). Indeed, the existence of r.37 enables the First-tier Tribunal to take a more robust approach under r.31. It follows that compliance with r.31 also does not prevent a decision being set aside on review or appeal on the ground that there has been a breach of the rules of natural justice if it turns out that the First-tier Tribunal drew the wrong conclusions from the evidence available to it. In *GJ v SSWP (CSM)* [2012] UKUT 447 (AAC) it was observed on the absent party's appeal: "The issue is whether Mr J had a fair hearing. It is not whether the tribunal reasonably believed that he did." In *KH v SSWP (CSM)* the Upper Tribunal also approved the statement in *R(SB) 19/83*—

> "As a practical matter it is the duty of the appeal tribunal when a claimant does not attend and is not represented on the appeal to ask the tribunal clerk if the claimant has been properly notified of the hearing . . .. And the record of proceedings should show that this has been done or (where this is the case) how otherwise the tribunal was satisfied that the absent claimant was notified of the hearing."

The Upper Tribunal also emphasised the importance of the First-tier Tribunal showing, at least if a statement of reasons is requested, that the relevant factors have been considered and weighed up. It suggested that best practice would be for an explanation to be included (contemporaneously) in the record of proceedings. **5.311**

The First-tier Tribunal has been held to have erred in failing to consider the duty in r.2(2)(c) to ensure that the parties are able to participate fully in the proceedings when it decided to proceed in the absence of an agoraphobic claimant who had asked for a domiciliary hearing (*PM v SSWP (IB)* [2013] UKUT 301 (AAC)) and when it determined an appeal without adjourning notwithstanding that the claimant had been forced to leave the hearing after 10 minutes through illness *(AM v SSWP (ESA)* [2013] UKUT 563 (AAC)). In *SW v SSWP (DLA)* [2015] UKUT 319 (AAC), the Upper Tribunal referred not only to r.2(2)(c) but also to the Senior President of Tribunals' *Practice Direction (First-tier and Upper Tribunals: Children, Vulnerable Adults and Sensitive Witnesses)* (see below) and said that the First-tier Tribunal should have had regard to that Practice Direction in a case where the claimant had explained why she found it stressful to be around other people and had asked whether the First-tier Tribunal could telephone her on the day of the hearing if it had any questions. However, failing to refer to the Practice Direction in a case where a party is vulnerable is not necessarily an error of law, not least because the Tribunal Procedure Rules, common law and the European Convention on Human Rights all require the First-tier Tribunal to have regard to substantially the same considerations as the Practice Direction (*JH(S) v SSWP (ESA)* [2015] UKUT 567 (AAC)).

There is a continuing duty to consider whether it is in the interests of justice to proceed with a hearing in a party's absence so that, if in the course of considering a case in the absence of a party issues emerge that cannot really be dealt with fairly in the absence of the party, an initial decision to proceed in the parties absence may have to be reconsidered (*KO v SSWP (ESA)* [2013] UKUT 544 (AAC)).

Indeed, this may be so even after a decision has been reached. In *AK v HMRC (TC)* [2016] UKUT 98 (AAC), the claimant had arrived 35 minutes late for a hearing listed for 1½ hours before the First-tier Tribunal, which by then had already decided to dismiss her appeal against HMRC's decision that, in the absence of almost any other evidence, it was to be inferred from a credit reference agency's reports that she had been living with a man as his wife. There was no indication that the First-tier Tribunal had considered re-opening the case (by setting aside its decision if the decision notice had been signed and, if necessary, considered adjourning the hearing) or that it had ascertained the reason for the claimant's lateness or balanced that against the amount at stake in the appeal, which was over £8,600. Moreover, the claimant's oral evidence was likely to be particularly important because HMRC had not interviewed her before making its decision. The Upper Tribunal held that, in the absence of any adequate reasoning, the First-tier Tribunal's failure to consider, or reconsider, the claimant's case when she arrived appeared aberrant and so rendered its substantive decision wrong in law.

Chapter 3

Decisions

Consent orders

5.312 **32.**—(1) The Tribunal may, at the request of the parties but only if it considers it appropriate, make a consent order disposing of the proceedings and making such other appropriate provision as the parties have agreed.

(2) Notwithstanding any other provision of these Rules, the Tribunal need not hold a hearing before making an order under paragraph (1), or provide reasons for the order.

Definitions

"hearing"—see r.1(3).
"party"—*ibid.*
"Tribunal"—*ibid.*

General Note

5.313 A consent order, which necessarily involves a decision by the First-tier Tribunal that it is "appropriate", is a decision that may be set aside under r.37 or on a review or appeal (*R.(LR) v First-tier Tribunal* [2012] UKUT 213 (AAC)). However, consent orders have little place in social security cases before the First-tier Tribunal because decision-makers generally have the power to revise the decision under appeal, which causes the appeal to lapse (see, for instance, s.9(1) and (6) of the Social Security Act 1998 and reg.3(4A) of the Social Security and Child Support (Decisions and Appeals) Regulations 1999).

Notice of decisions

5.314 **33.**—(1) The Tribunal may give a decision orally at a hearing.

(2) Subject to rule 14(2) (withholding information likely to cause harm), the Tribunal must provide to each party as soon as reasonably practicable after making [1 a decision (other than a decision under Part 4) which finally

disposes of all issues in the proceedings or of a preliminary issue dealt with following a direction under rule 5(3)(e)]—

(a) a decision notice stating the Tribunal's decision;
(b) where appropriate, notification of the right to apply for a written statement of reasons under rule 34(3); and
(c) notification of any right of appeal against the decision and the time within which, and the manner in which, such right of appeal may be exercised.

(3) In asylum support cases the notice and notifications required by paragraph (2) must be provided at the hearing or sent on the day that the decision is made.

AMENDMENT

1. Tribunal Procedure (Amendment) Rules 2013 (SI 2013/477) rr.22 and 28 (April 8, 2013).

DEFINITIONS

"asylum support case"—see r.1(3).
"hearing"—*ibid.*
"party"—*ibid.*
"Tribunal"—*ibid.*

GENERAL NOTE

Paragraph (1)

It is common practice to give a decision orally. It used to be considered that such a decision was not effective until written notice of it was given although, if the First-tier Tribunal did change its mind, it was usually required to invite further submissions (*SK (Sri Lanka) v Secretary of State for the Home Department* [2008] EWCA Civ 495, *R(I) 14/71*, *SSD v PY (WP)* [2012] UKUT 116 (AAC); [2012] AACR 44). However, in *Patel v Secretary of State for the Home Department* [2015] EWCA Civ 1175, the Court of Appeal held that a tribunal had no power to change a decision after it had been given orally. It said that the rule in the courts that a decision could be amended until an order was drawn up did not apply in tribunals where there is simply a decision and no distinction between a judgment and an order, it being relevant that there was an express power to give "a decision" orally. The Court's decision was given in the context of the Upper Tribunal's powers and it appears not to have been referred to the power of the Upper Tribunal to set aside decisions (equivalent to r.37 of these Rules), which might have been relevant in that case, but that does not undermine the main thrust of its reasoning which appears equally applicable to the First-tier Tribunal (although the distinction between a decision notice and reasons is clearer in the First-tier Tribunal than in the Upper Tribunal). This issue may not matter a great deal in social security cases in the First-tier Tribunal because decision notices are usually given to the parties before they leave the hearing venue so that there is not much opportunity for a change of mind. 5.315

Paragraph (2)

It is not entirely clear whether "finally disposes of all issues in the proceedings" means something different from "disposes of proceedings" (see the note to r.27 above). 5.316

Although a decision may be made by a majority where the Tribunal is composed of more than one member (see art.8 of the First-tier Tribunal and Upper Tribunal (Composition of Tribunal) Order 2008), there is no longer an express requirement to state whether or not a decision has been made by a majority. However, if a statement is made as to whether a decision was unanimous, it must be accurate. In *SSWP v SS (DLA)* [2010] UKUT 384 (AAC); [2011] AACR 24, it was held that there was a material error of law when a decision notice said that a decision was unanimous but the statement of reasons said it had been reached by a majority, without acknowledging any error.

Where the Secretary of State's decision is defective in form but the tribunal agrees with its substance, it is not necessary for the tribunal to reformulate the Secretary of State's decision in the tribunal's decision notice unless the decision as expressed by the Secretary of State is wrong in some *material* respect (e.g. it states an incorrect ground of supersession) or there is likely to be some practical benefit to the claimant or to the adjudication process in future in reformulating the decision (*R(IB)2/04*, para.82). On the other hand, attempting to reformulate the decision may serve to focus the tribunal's mind on the correct issues and so it may have a value. Where a statement of reasons is requested under r.34(3), the statement should explain what the decision under appeal should have been even if the decision notice does not.

5.317 Where an appeal is against an "outcome decision" expressed in terms of a claimant's entitlement to benefit, a decision notice "should make it absolutely clear whether the tribunal has made an outcome decision (subject, in some cases, to the precise amount being calculated by the Secretary of State) or has remitted the final decision on entitlement to the Secretary of State" (*R(IS) 2/08*).

There is no requirement that a decision notice include any reasons at all but there is nothing forbidding a chairman from including brief reasons in the decision notice and it is suggested that it may often good practice to do so (although differing views have been expressed by Commissioners on this issue, see *CIB/4497/1998* and *CSDLA/551/1999*). Apart from anything else, an unsuccessful party is more likely to ask for a statement of reasons under r.34 if no reasons at all are given for a decision, especially if it arises at a paper determination. Moreover, there are cases where the issue determined by the tribunal is almost bound to arise again and it is then helpful to all concerned if some indication of the First-tier Tribunal's reasoning is included in a decision notice if it will not otherwise be obvious to a person who did not attend the hearing. Thus, it was observed in *MW v SSWP (II)* [2011] UKUT 465 (AAC) that it was unfortunate that previous appeal tribunals allowing appeals by the claimant and making provisional assessments of disablement had not recorded at least a brief reason for rejecting the Secretary of State's submissions, given that the making of a provisional assessment necessarily meant that at least one further assessment would have to be made by the Secretary of State. However, it was not suggested that there was a positive duty to give reasons in such a case in the absence of a request by either party.

Nonetheless, in cases concerned with medical assessments for employment and support allowance, personal independence payment or universal credit, in respect of which a person's entitlement to benefit depends on the number of points scored in respect of prescribed descriptors, the general practice is for a decision notice to record the descriptors in respect of which it has been found that the claimant scored points. In *CP v SSWP (PIP)* [2016] UKUT 444 (AAC), it was stated that, while it was quite proper for the First-tier Tribunal, having concluded that the claimant scored sufficient points for the maximum amount of benefit, not to consider any further descriptors that might have been put in issue, it would be good practice in such a case for the decision notice to state that, given that the points added by the tribunal result in the maximum possible award, it has not been necessary to consider whether further points are merited, so as to avoid misapprehension particularly if a supersession of the award were to be contemplated.

There being no duty to include any reasons at all in a decision notice, where some reasons are given but are inadequate, the consequence is not to render the tribunal's decision erroneous in point of law. The remedy is to apply for a proper statement of reasons under r.34(3) (*CIB/4497/1998*). Such a statement cures any inadequacy in reasons given in a decision notice (*CSDLA/531/2000, CIS/2345/2001*). However, if the reasons in the full statement are inconsistent with the reasons given in a decision notice, the decision of the tribunal will be set aside as erroneous in point of law (*CCR/3396/2000*, *CIS/2345/2001*). In criminal injuries compensation cases, the First-tier Tribunal has had a practice of giving fairly detailed hand-written summary reasons on the decision notice but recording that they are not the full reasons and informing the claimant of the right to ask for full reasons. The Upper Tribunal was critical of a failure of the First-tier Tribunal to provide a full statement of reasons when asked to provide a legible copy of the summary reasons even though, treating them as full reasons, the Upper Tribunal was still able to reject the claimant's challenge to their adequacy (*R.(MC) v First-tier Tribunal (CIC)* [2014] UKUT 544 (AAC)).

Reasons for decisions

34.—(1) In asylum support cases the Tribunal must send a written statement of reasons for a decision which disposes of proceedings (except a decision under Part 4) to each party— 5.318

(a) if the case is decided at a hearing, within 3 days after the hearing; or

(b) if the case is decided without a hearing, on the day that the decision is made.

(2) In all other cases the Tribunal may give reasons for a decision which disposes of proceedings (except a decision under Part 4)—

(a) orally at a hearing; or

(b) in a written statement of reasons to each party.

(3) Unless the Tribunal has already provided a written statement of reasons under paragraph (2)(b), a party may make a written application to the Tribunal for such statement following a decision [1 which finally disposes of—

(a) all issues in the proceedings; or

(b) a preliminary issue dealt with following a direction under rule 5(3)(e).]

(4) An application under paragraph (3) must be received within 1 month of the date on which the Tribunal sent or otherwise provided to the party a decision notice relating to the decision [1 . . .]

(5) If a party makes an application in accordance with paragraphs (3) and (4) the Tribunal must, subject to rule 14(2) (withholding information likely to cause harm), send a written statement of reasons to each party within 1 month of the date on which it received the application or as soon as reasonably practicable after the end of that period.

AMENDMENT

1. Tribunal Procedure (Amendment) Rules 2013 (SI 2013/477) rr.22 and 29 (April 8, 2013).

DEFINITIONS

"asylum support case"—see r.1(3).
"dispose of proceedings"—*ibid.*
"hearing"—*ibid.*
"party"—*ibid.*
"Tribunal"—*ibid.*

General Note

Paragraphs (2)–(5)

5.319 These paragraphs replace reg.53(4) of the Social Security and Child Support (Decisions and Appeals) Regulations 1999 but add two refinements. The first is to make it clear that reasons may be given orally but that a written statement (which could simply be a transcript) may subsequently be requested. The second is to impose a time limit, albeit not absolute, within which a tribunal must provide a statement of reasons. Whether a tribunal would be found to have erred in law because reasons were not provided "as soon as reasonably practicable" after the standard one month in circumstances where delay would not previously have been sufficient to vitiate the decision remains to be seen. Note also that reg.53(5) has not been re-enacted, so that there is no longer any express duty to record the reasons of the dissenting member of the Tribunal where a decision is made by a majority, or even to record that the decision was reached only by a majority, but see the note to r.33.

A refusal to adjourn is not a "decision" for which a statement of reasons may be required under this rule, although an unexplained refusal to adjourn may make a final decision erroneous in point of law unless an explanation that is not perverse may be inferred from the circumstances (*Carpenter v Secretary of State for Work and Pensions* [2003] EWCA Civ 33 (reported as *R(IB) 6/03*)). Indeed, although a duty to give reasons under this rule applies only to decisions that dispose of proceedings, there is a common-law duty to give reasons for any decision that would appear aberrant without reasons (*R.(Birmingham CC) v Birmingham Crown Court* [2009] EWHC 3329 (Admin); [2010] 1 W.L.R. 1287), referred to in *SA v LB Ealing (HB)* [2012] UKUT 437 (AAC)). However, the effect of not providing reasons for an apparently aberrant interlocutory decision for which reasons are not required by this rule may, in practice, be that the decision will be set aside on the ground of perversity rather than explicitly on the ground that no reasons have been given.

MT v SSWP ((IS) [2010] UKUT 382 (AAC) is perhaps an example of this. The First-tier Tribunal was held to have erred in law in failing to give reasons for proceeding with a hearing in the absence of a presenting officer when a judge had earlier directed the attendance of a presenting officer on the basis that such attendance was "essential", but it may be significant that its failure to explain why the presence was no longer regarded as "essential" was compounded by the inadequacy of the Secretary of State's submission and the First-tier Tribunal's failure to explain to the claimant at the hearing what the case against him really was. In the absence of any such apparent irrationality in an interlocutory decision and therefore of any duty to provide reasons at all, summary reasons will be adequate (*KP v Hertfordshire CC (SEN)* [2010] UKUT 233 (AAC)).

A judge's power to write a statement of reasons survives the termination of his or her appointment as a judge. The statement must at least be adopted by the judge (or possibly another member) of the tribunal who heard the appeal. Therefore a statement written by a regional chairman in the erroneous belief that it could not be written by the chairman who heard the appeal because her appointment had come to an end, was not valid (*CIS/2132/1998*).

In *R. (Sturton) v Social Security Commissioner* [2007] EWHC 2957 (Admin), the decision notice was not sent on the day of the hearing to a party who had not been present at the hearing, even though the notice stated that it had been sent then, so that, when that party subsequently obtained a copy and made an application for a statement of reasons within a month of the copy actually being sent to him, the application was in time.

5.320 It is usually an error of law to fail to issue a statement of reasons when a request is made within the prescribed time and there are occasions when an application for leave to appeal should be treated as such a request *(R(IS) 11/99)*. An application for leave to appeal received within the time allowed for asking for a statement of reasons is treated as a request for such a statement (r.38(7)). In both *R(IS) 11/99* and *R3/02(IB)*, it is stated that there are occasions when an error of law can be demonstrated without there being a statement of reasons and that a Commissioner could determine an appeal in those circumstances, although it is obviously not possible to challenge a tribunal's decision on the grounds of inadequacy of reasoning in circumstances where there is no written statement of reasons. Furthermore, a tribunal's decision will not be erroneous in law for breach of the duty to imposed by this rule if the decision notice issued under r.33(2)(a) in fact contains all that would be required in a full statement of reasons *(R(IS) 11/99)*, or if the two documents read together provide an adequate statement between them (*CIS/2345/2001*). The practice of some chairmen of stating that the summary reasons on a decision notice amount to a full statement of reasons has been frowned upon, on the basis that such summary reasons are more likely to contain errors than fuller statements produced in response to a request. In *CSDLA/551/1999*, the Commissioner went as far as to say that it was of no effect and that a separate statement of reasons was required in all cases, but that is not the conventional view and is inconsistent with what was said in *R(IS) 11/99.*

Long decisions need to be properly organised. In *Jasim v Secretary of State for the Home Department* [2006] EWCA Civ 342, the Court of Appeal commented on the "unmanageable length" of some paragraphs in a decision of the Asylum and Immigration Tribunal, one of which ran for almost three pages of single-spaced type. It was suggested that the use of shorter paragraphs, with sub-paragraphs and cross-headings where appropriate, was a useful aid not just to the reader but also to the writer.

Standard form decisions have been frowned upon in *CI/5199/1998* and *CIB/4497/1998*, not on grounds of principle but because they tend to be used not only when appropriate but also when the circumstances of the case make it inappropriate.

In *Peters v Sat Katar Limited* [2003] EWCA Civ 943, the use of standard recitals as reasons revealed that no regard whatsoever had been had to the particular circumstances of a case where the exercise of a discretion required all the circumstances to be taken into account.

This rule includes no express duty to record the tribunal's findings but it is necessary to record a tribunal's findings on any matters in dispute as part of the explanation for its decision (*R(I) 4/02* and also *R2/01(IB*), a decision of a Tribunal of Commissioners in Northern Ireland). Indeed, it has been said in *Evans v Secretary of State for Social Services* (reported as *R(I)5/94*) that there are occasions when a record of the tribunal's findings provides a complete explanation for the decision.

Reasons for interlocutory decisions

Whether reasons are needed for an interlocutory decision is likely to depend on the context. Although an appeal lies against interlocutory decisions (*LS v LB Lambeth (HB)* [2010] UKUT 461 (AAC); [2011] AACR 27), there is no statutory requirement under r.34 to give reasons for decisions that do not finally dispose of all issues in the proceedings and no general common law requirement to do so either, although a decision may be set aside on the ground of a failure to provide reasons if a discretion has been exercised in a particularly unusual manner (*Jones v Governing Body of Burdett Coutts School* [1999] I.C.R. 38, 47) or the decision appears aberrant (*R. v Higher Education Funding Council, Ex p. Institute of Dental Surgery* [1994] 1 W.L.R. 242 at 263). 5.321

Where reasons for interlocutory decisions are requested, they are sometimes conveyed in a letter signed by the clerk to the tribunal. This is not improper, provided that the reasons are those of the tribunal (*R. v Stoke CC, Ex p. Highgate Projects* (1993) 26 H.L.R. 551) and, indeed, it would not necessarily be improper for a clerk to assist in the drafting of reasons (*Virdi v Law Society (Solicitors Disciplinary Tribunal intervening)* [2010] EWCA Civ 100 ; [2010] 1 W.L.R. 2840).

For the need to give reasons for deciding a case without a hearing, see the annotation to r.27(4)–(6) above.

Inconsistency

5.322 In *Sandhu v Secretary of State for Work and Pensions* [2010] EWCA Civ 962, the Court of Appeal held reasons to be flawed for inconsistency when at one point the First-tier Tribunal said that it accepted that the claimant could not put any weight on his right leg and then at another point it found he could walk with crutches. (Using crutches to mobilise without putting weight on one leg is not walking.)

In *CDLA/1807/2003*, the tribunal chairman produced two statements of reasons for the tribunal's decision, the second because he had forgotten he had already written a statement. The reasons differed. The Commissioner commented that the reasons should be a statement of the *tribunal's* reasons and not the chairman's later rationalisation of the conclusion reached by the tribunal and that at least one of the statements plainly did not accurately reflect the tribunal's reasons. He set aside the tribunal's decision. Inexplicable inconsistency between the decision notice and the statement of reasons led to an appeal being allowed in *CCR/3396/2000*.

Majority decisions

5.323 In *SSWP v SS (DLA)* [2010] UKUT 384 (AAC); [2011] AACR 24, it was held that there is no duty to record whether or not a decision is unanimous but there was nonetheless a material error of law when a decision notice said that a decision was unanimous and the statement of reasons said it had been reached by a majority, without acknowledging any error. Moreover, the judge said that, if a decision notice *did* state that a decision was by a majority, there was a duty to include the reasons of the dissenting member and that the same approach applied if a decision notice stated that a decision was unanimous when in fact it had been reached by a majority. However, in *JD v SSD (WP)* [2014] UKUT 379 (AAC), some doubt was expressed as to whether a failure to give reasons for dissent was an error of law rather than merely being a breach of good practice.

Adequate reasons

5.324 The inadequacy of statements of reasons is probably the most common ground upon which decsions are set aside by the Upper Tribunal. The superficiality of many submissions made by both claimants' representatives and the Secretary of State's representatives on this issue has been the subject of adverse comment by Commissioners (see, for example, *CIB/4497/1998* in which it was said that there is no simple formula for writing reasons for a decision).

In *Re Poyser and Mills' Arbitration* [1964] 2 Q.B. 467, 478, Megaw J. said:

> "Parliament provided that reasons shall be given, and in my view that must be read as meaning that proper, adequate reasons must be given. The reasons that are set out must be reasons that will not only be intelligible, but which deal with the substantial points that have been raised."

In *R(A) 1/72*, the Chief Commissioner, considering an appeal from a delegated medical practioner acting on behalf of the Attendance Allowance Board, said:

> "The obligation to give reasons for the decision in [a case involving a conflict of evidence] imports a requirement to do more than only to state the conclusion, and for the determining authority to state that on the evidence the authority is not satisfied that the statutory conditions are met, does no more than this. It affords no guide to the selective process by which the evidence has been accepted, rejected, weighed or considered, or the reasons for any of these things. It is not, of course, obligatory thus to deal with every piece of evidence or to over elaborate, but in an administrative quasi-judicial decision the minimum requirement must

at least be that the claimant, looking at the decision should be able to discern on the face of it the reasons why the evidence has failed to satisfy the authority. For the purpose of the regulation which requires the reasons for the review decision to be set out, a decision based, and only based, on a conclusion that the total effect of the evidence fails to satisfy, without reasons given for reaching that conclusion, will in many cases be no adequate decision at all."

In *R. (Asha Foundation) v Millennium Commission* [2003] EWCA Civ 66 (*The Times*, January 24, 2003), the Court of Appeal considered the approach Sedley J. had taken in *R. v Higher Education Funding Council, Ex p. Institute of Dental Surgery* [1994] 1 W.L.R. 242 to the question of whether there was a duty to give any reasons at all and held that, where there is a duty to give reasons, the same approach should be taken to the question whether reasons were adequate. Sedley J.'s approach required the balancing of a number of considerations, which might vary from case to case. He said:

> "The giving of reasons may among other things concentrate the decision-maker's mind on the right questions; demonstrate to the recipient that this is so; show that the issues have been conscientiously addressed and how the result has been reached or alternatively alert the recipient to a justiciable flaw in the process.
>
> On the other side of the argument, it may place an undue burden on decision-makers; demand an appearance of unanimity where there is diversity; call for the articulation of sometimes inexpressible value judgments; and offer an invitation to the captious to comb the reasons for previously unsuspected grounds of challenge."

Detailed guidance

It was acknowledged in *Baron v Secretary of State for Social Services* (reported as an appendix to *R(M) 6/86*) that there are limits to the extent to which a tribunal can be expected to give reasons for decisions on matters of judgment, such as the distance a claimant could walk without having to stop or the extent of breathlessness and pain which caused him to stop. See also *DC v SSWP* [2009] UKUT 45 (AAC) where the Upper Tribunal said that precise findings as to the distance a person can walk and the time taken are unrealistic and that the First-tier Tribunal should not attempt to make more precise findings than are really justified by the evidence. Assessments of disablement also give rise to difficult judgments. In *CI/636/1993*, the Commissioner said: 5.325

> "Whether or how far the duty in law to give reasons for their decision extends beyond saying that the particular percentage arrived at is in the medical judgment of the tribunal a fair one on these particular facts must depend on the nature of the individual case and the issues that have been raised in it. It seems to me that the position is correctly summarised by the Commissioner in *R(I) 30/61* at paragraph 8: there may well be cases where a mere statement that the tribunal makes an assessment at a particular percentage is in itself a sufficient record, since it implies that they think that is a fair assessment; but in other cases findings of fact and an explanation of reasons will be needed to show that evidence they have accepted or rejected as justifying the making of a smaller or larger assessment, since otherwise the claimant will be left guessing as to the basis on which the decision has been arrived at. And in a case where specific submissions backed with expert medical evidence have been addressed to them on the basis of assessment to be used, it will normally be an error of law for the tribunal simply to state their conclusion in the form of a percentage without making it clear to what extent and for what reasons they are accepting or rejecting the suggested basis, since they will not have carried out the general duty to give reasons on a material issue raised before them: see *R(I) 18/61*, para.13."

In many cases it will be obvious from a finding as to the claimant's loss of faculty what the resulting disablement must have been but in others it is necessary for a tribunal to make specific findings as to the resulting disabilities (*CI/343/1988*). In *CI/1802/2001*, it was again stressed that a decision assessing the extent of a claimant's disablement is likely to be inadequate if the tribunal have not explained the factual basis of their decision.

> "This can often be simply expressed. In many cases it will be enough to say that the evidence given by the claimant about the effect of a particular accident or disease on his or her daily life has been accepted. In some cases, where the claimant's evidence is for some reason found to be unreliable, it may be that the tribunal will state that it felt able to accept only those disabilities which in its expert opinion were likely to flow from problems disclosed on clinical examination. Other cases may need more detail."

However, where a tribunal assesses disablement for the purpose of determining entitlement to disablement benefit and the claimant is not suffering from an injury specified in Sch.2 to the Social Security (General Benefit) Regulations 1982, it is not necessary for the statement of reasons to refer to the prescribed degrees of disablement set against the injuries in that Schedule even though reg.11(8) of those Regulations suggests that the Schedule may act as a general guide to the assessment of disablement (*R(I) 1/04*). See, also, the decision of the Tribunal of Commissioners in *R(I) 2/06*, where the same approach was taken and *CI/1802/2001* was approved. Those were cases involving relatively low assessments. It may be more important to have regard to the Schedule where higher assessments are concerned, but provided that clear findings of fact are recorded and the First-tier Tribunal addresses any specific arguments raised as to the level of the assessment, the Upper Tribunal is unlikely to interfere with its judgment on the ground that its reasoning is inadequate even if it does not expressly refer to the Schedule (*DS v SSD (WP)* [2016] UKUT 51 (AAC)).

5.326 Resorting to describing a Benefits Agency Medical Service doctor as "independent" as a reason for preferring his evidence to medical evidence obtained on behalf of the claimant was described as "irrational" in *CIB/563/2001*, given that the Benefits Agency Medical Service doctor was trained and paid by one of the parties to the proceedings. In any event, that reason was inadequate because the doctor acting on behalf of the claimant had recorded different clinical findings and there was no suggestion that he did not conduct a full examination or failed to take account of the claimant's history.

A Tribunal of Commissioners in Northern Ireland has held in *R 3/01 (IB)* that there is no universal obligation on a tribunal to explain an assessment of credibility. It will usually be sufficient to say that a witness is not believed or is exaggerating. It is the decision that has to be explained. A tribunal is not obliged to give reasons for its reasons. There may be situations when a further explanation will be required but the only standard is that the reasons should explain the decision. Much the same approach has been taken in Great Britain, the authorities being analysed in *CIS/4022/2007*.

In *R3/01(IB)*, the Tribunal of Commissioners also held that a tribunal must record their findings on every descriptor of the all work test that is in issue and those raised by clear implication but that there is no universal rule that individual reasons must be given for the selection of a particular descriptor. The reasons given must explain why the tribunal reached the decision they did but need not always explain why it did not reach any different conclusion. However, it is suggested that there *is* a need to explain why a *specific* contention advanced by a party has not been accepted, at least where the contention is a major part of that party's case. It was said in *Flannery v Halifax Estate Agencies Ltd* [2001] 1 W.L.R. 377, CA, that, where there is expert evidence and analysis advanced by both parties, a statement of reasons must "enter into the issues" in order to explain why the unsuccessful party's evidence has failed to prevail. This was applied in *BB v South London and Maudsley NHS Trust* [2009] UKUT 159 (AAC) and *Hampshire CC v JP (SEN)* [2009] UKUT 239 (AAC); [2010] AACR 15. However, in *English v Emery Reimbold & Strick Ltd.* [2002] ECWA Civ 605; [2002] 1 W.L.R. 2409, the Court of Appeal sought to discourage the "cottage industry" of applications inspired by *Flannery* and followed *Eagil Trust Co Ltd v Pigott-Brown* [1985] 3 All E.R. 119, 122 in which Griffiths L.J. had stressed that there was no duty on a judge in giving his reasons to deal with every argument presented to him. The Court also said that, while a judge will often need to refer to a piece of evidence or to a submission which he has accepted or rejected, provided the reference is clear, it may be unnecessary to detail, or even summarise, the evidence or submission in question.

> "The essential requirement is that the terms of the judgment should enable the parties and any appellate tribunal readily to analyse the reasoning that was essential to the Judge's decision."

Where a tribunal has rejected a claimant's account as to how he came by an injury, it is not bound to make any finding as to how he did come by it, where that would be no more than speculation (*AJ (Cameroon) v Secretary of State for the Home Department* [2007] EWCA Civ 373). However, there will, of course, be cases where a tribunal's finding that the injury was due to a different cause is the explanation for rejecting the claimant's case. In *CCS/1626/2002*, the Commissioner said that a person could hardly complain about the adequacy of findings of fact or reasoning lying behind an estimate of income when the need to make an estimate was due to that person's failure to provide better evidence. In *R(I) 3/03*, a Tribunal of Commissioners criticised the Secretary of State for supporting, by reference to an occasional infelicitous word in a statement of reasons, an unrealistic argument advanced by a claimant to the effect that a tribunal had overlooked a basic proposition of law. They said that there are some propositions of law, such as the nature of the civil burden and standard of proof, that are of such fundamental importance in the work of tribunals that it is almost inconceivable that tribunals will have overlooked them and that it should therefore be assumed that they have understood them unless there is something to show otherwise in the substance of what a tribunal has decided.

Specific guidance as to the approach to be taken in medical cases before tribunals 5.327
has been given by the Court of Appeal in *Evans v Secretary of State for Social Services* (reported as *R(I) 5/94*) where it was said:

> "1. The decision should record the medical question or questions which the tribunal is required to answer. Provided the questions are set out and the answers are directed to the questions it should then be possible for the parties to know the issues to which the tribunal have addressed themselves.
> 2. In cases where the tribunal have medically examined the claimant they should record their findings. These findings by themselves may be sufficient to demonstrate the reason why they have reached a particular conclusion.
> 3. Where, however, the clinical findings do not point to some obvious diagnosis it may be necessary to give a short explanation as to why they have made one diagnosis rather than another. Such an explanation will be important in cases where the tribunal's diagnosis differs from a reasoned diagnosis of another qualified practitioner who has examined the claimant on an earlier occasion.
> 4. A decision on a question of causation may pose particular difficulties when one is examining the adequacy of the reasons for a decision. In some cases it may be sufficient for the tribunal to record that it was not satisfied that the present condition was caused by the relevant trauma. Where, however, a claimant has previously been in receipt of some benefit or allowance (particularly if paid over a long period of time) and there is no question of malingering or bad faith then . . . the tribunal should go further than merely to state a conclusion. If one accepts that

> the underlying principle is fairness the claimant should be given some explanation, which may be very short, to enable him or his advisors to know where the break in causation has been found. Thus it may well be that the claimant will wish to reapply and for this purpose fairness requires that, if possible, he should be told why his claim has failed."

That was in the context of decisions of a medical appeal tribunal who had jurisdiction in respect of certain issues only, including the "medical questions" in respect of mobility allowance and the "disablement questions" in respect of disablement benefit. The reference to "the medical question or questions" must be read against that background and must therefore be taken to refer to the *legal* issues as much as the medical issues in a case.

In *CDLA/5419/1999*, it is pointed out that the fact that a claimant is unsuccessful does not always imply rejection of the medical evidence advanced by him or her. In that case, the claimant's doctor said that the claimant required attention but he did not specify how much. The tribunal accepted that the claimant required some attention but found that it was not sufficient to qualify for disability living allowance. The Commissioner said that the doctor's evidence had therefore not supported the element of the claimant's case upon which she failed and that, in the circumstances of the case, there had been no duty to refer to the doctor's evidence at all. In *HL v SSWP (DLA)* [2011] UKUT 183 (AAC), the Upper Tribunal said:

> "All too often, judges present the tribunal's reasons as if the tribunal had a choice between accepting the evidence of the GP or of the examining medical practitioner. There may be cases where that is so, but in many cases the reports each have their strengths and each their limitations as an assessment of the claimant's disablement. In those cases, what a proper analysis usually requires is for the tribunal to show a balance between the value that can be distilled from each report and its limitations."

5.328 A similar point has been made by a Tribunal of Commissioners in Northern Ireland (*R2/04(DLA)*) and by the Court of Appeal in Northern Ireland (*Quinn v Department for Social Development* [2004] NICA 22). In the former case, however, the Tribunal of Commissioners added that, "where it is evident that the claimant attaches great significance to a letter or report, it may be prudent for a tribunal to say, briefly, that it has read the document but derived no assistance from it" and it may be helpful to say why if the relevance or value of the evidence is likely to be controversial.

In *R(M) 1/96*, the Commissioner held that the fact of a previous award does not raise any presumption in the claimant's favour or result in the need for consistency having to be treated as a separate issue on a renewal claim. However, he said that the requirement for a tribunal to give reasons for its decision means that it is usually necessary for a tribunal to explain why it is not renewing a previous award, unless that is obvious from their findings. That approach was applied by the Court of Appeal in Northern Ireland in *Quinn*. The Court also accepted that, in the circumstances of that particular case, there had been no need for the tribunal to refer to a medical report obtained for the purpose of determining the previous claim. More generally, the mere fact that another tribunal has given more detailed reasons when considering the same issue does not render the briefer reasons of a second tribunal inadequate, particularly when they are based on a clear finding of credibility (*SSWP v AM (IS)* [2010] UKUT 428 (AAC)). On the other hand, where an award for one period is markedly different from an award made in respect of an immediately subsequent period, it may be necessary to explain the difference even though the assessment in respect of the later period would not be binding on it (*R. (Viggers) v Pensions Appeal Tribunal* [2009] EWCA Civ 1321; [2010] AACR 19, in which Ward L.J. said (at [22]): "It is elementary for the principle of public law that there should be, as far as possible, consistency in administrative decisions.") However, Etherton L.J. said (at [26]) that it "would have been sufficient for the Tribunal to say that, having had regard to an having taken into account the 40% assessment, nonetheless in the light of the all the evidence before it and the members' expertise it concluded that the assessment should be that of 6-14% for the earlier period". Perhaps the reality is that, if a tribunal does in fact have regard to an earlier award and is obliged expressly to mention that fact, its other reasoning will generally show, at least implicitly, that it either thought the award in respect of the later period was too generous or that it considered there had been a change of circumstances. However, it is suggested that the parties should be told which of those two possibilities the tribunal had in mind.

Where the First-tier Tribunal finds that a claimant does not score sufficient points under Sch.2 to the Employment and Support Allowance Regulations 2008 for entitlement to employment and support allowance, it will normally be necessary for it also to refer expressly to reg.29(2)(b) in order to show that that provision has not been overlooked. However, the extent to which reasons need be given for not finding that provision to apply depends very much on the circumstances of the case (*NS v SSWP (ESA)* [2014] UKUT 115 (AAC); [2014] AACR 33). It is likely to be necessary to give specific reasons where the First-tier Tribunal has disagreed fundamentally with the appellant about the effects of their condition (*ibid.*) or where the claimant has scored a substantial number of points under mental health descriptors (*AJ v SSWP (ESA)* [2014] UKUT 208 (AAC)). On the other hand, where a represented claimant advances a case in very general terms and presents no evidence of a substantial risk, specific reasons are less likely to be required (*JK v SSWP (ESA)* [2014] UKUT 140 (AAC); [2014] AACR 34).

In *Baron v Secretary of State for Social Services* (reported as an appendix to *R(M) 6/86*), it was said that:

> "The overriding test must always be: is the tribunal providing both parties with the materials which will enable them to know that the tribunal has made no error of law in reaching its findings of fact?"

The approach taken in social security cases is not very different from that taken in other areas of public law. In the context of planning, Lord Brown of Eaton-under-Heywood summarised the effect of case law in *South Bucks DC v Porter (No.2)* [2004] UKHL 33 [2004] 1 W.L.R. 1953 (at [36]): **5.329**

> "The reasons for a decision must be intelligible and they must be adequate. They must enable the reader to understand why the matter was decided as it was and what conclusions were reached on the 'principal important controversial issues', disclosing how any issue of law or fact was resolved. Reasons can be briefly stated, the degree of particularity required depending entirely on the nature of the issues falling for decision. The reasoning must not give rise to a substantial doubt as to whether the decision-maker erred in law, for example by misunderstanding some relevant policy or some other important matter or by failing to reach a rational decision on relevant grounds. But such adverse inference will not readily be drawn. The reasons need refer only to the main issues in the dispute, not to every material consideration. They should enable disappointed developers to assess their prospects of obtaining some alternative development permission, or, as the case may be, their unsuccessful opponents to understand how the policy or approach underlying the grant of permission may impact upon future such applications. Decision letters [which contain statements of reasons] must be read in a straightforward manner, recognising that they are addressed to parties well aware of the issues involved and the arguments advanced. A reasons challenge will only succeed if the party aggrieved can satisfy the court that he has genuinely been substantially prejudiced by the failure to provide an adequately reasoned decision".

In *R(DLA)3/08*, a Tribunal of Commissioners adopted that passage and said that it applied equally to social security cases.

However, in *SP v SSWP* [2009] UKUT 97 (AAC), a deputy judge of the Upper Tribunal held that, if a statement of reasons was inadequate, it was not necessary for the appellant also to show prejudice. He relied upon *Mirza v City of Glasgow Licensing Board* 1996 SC 450 (2nd Div) when distinguishing *South Bucks* on the ground that the latter was a planning case in which the High Court had power to quash a decision only if the applicant had been "substantially prejudiced" by a failure to comply with a duty to give reasons. However, in *Mirza*, the Court of Session had itself followed an earlier decision, *Wordie Property Co Ltd v Secretary of State for Scotland* 1984 S.L.T. 345, where the Lord President, having considered the test of adequacy of reasons, said that "reasons which fail to pass the tests I have just discussed will demonstrate a failure to comply with statutory requirements which cannot have been other than prejudicial to the appellant". In other words, prejudice is part of the test of adequacy of reasons rather than a test to be applied in addition, although it may be observed that, as the Upper Tribunal has an explicit discretion to refuse to set aside a decision even if it is erroneous in point of law (see s.12(2)(a) of the Tribunals, Courts and Enforcement Act 2007), it could require prejudice to be shown at either stage.

Even when reasons are plainly flawed, a decision will not necessarily be set aside. Referring to a decision of a reviewing officer as to whether a homeless person had a priority need for housing, Lord Neuberger said in *Holmes-Moorhouse v London Borough of Richmond upon Thames* [2009] UKHL 7; [2009] 1 W.L.R. 413—

> ". . . a decision can often survive despite the existence of an error in the reasoning advanced to support it. For example, sometimes the error is irrelevant to the outcome; sometimes it is too trivial (objectively, or in the eyes of the decision-maker) to affect the outcome; sometimes it is obvious from the rest of the reasoning, read as a whole, that the decision would have been the same notwithstanding the error; sometimes, there is more than one reason for the conclusion, and the error only undermines one of the reasons; sometimes, the decision is the only one which could rationally have been reached. In all such cases, the error should not (save, perhaps, in wholly exceptional circumstances) justify the decision being quashed."

The European Court of Human Rights has taken much the same approach as the United Kingdom's courts. In *Hirvisari v Finland* 2001, it was said:

> "Although Article 6(1) obliges courts to give reasons for their decisions, it cannot be understood as requiring a detailed answer to every argument. Thus, in dismissing an appeal, an appellate court may, in principle, simply endorse the reasons for the lower court's decision . . . A lower court or authority in turn must give such reasons as to enable the parties to make effective use of any existing rights of appeal."

Delay

5.330 In *R(IS) 5/04*, it was held that a delay in providing reasons did not necessarily render a decision erroneous in point of law. The Commissioner said that a delay in providing reasons may itself amount to a breach of art.6 of the European Convention on Human Rights (although, if the tribunal's decision was not flawed in any other respect, the remedy for such a breach would presumably be an award of damages by a court) and she also held that a delay may be relevant on an appeal because it may indicate that the reasons are unreliable. However, in the particular case before her, where the statement of reasons had been requested on July 1, 2002 and was not sent to the parties until October 29, 2002, the Commissioner found there to have been no error of law. In *R(DLA)3/08*, the Tribunal of Commissioners observed that *R(IS)5/04* appeared to be consistent with *Bangs v Connex South Eastern Ltd* [2005] EWCA Civ 14, in which it was held that there had been no error of law despite the fact that a decision of an employment tribunal was not promulgated until a year after the hearing ended. Delay may give rise to the state's liability to pay compensation to the victim of the delay but, where an appeal against the tribunal's decision lies only on a point of law, the Court of Appeal held that it was not enough to claim that the decision is "unsafe" because of the delay. However, that was before the time limit in para.(5) was introduced and, in any event, there may be exceptional cases in which unreasonable delay in promulgating a decision can properly be treated as a serious procedural error or material irregularity giving rise to a question of law if there is a real risk that, due to the delayed decision, the party complaining was deprived of the substance of his right to a fair trial under art.6 of the Convention. It is necessary to consider whether the delay has caused the tribunal to reach a wrong finding or to overlook or forget evidence. Effectively, therefore, delay is merely a factor to be borne in mind when assessing the adequacy of a statement of reasons. In *Bond v Dunster Properties Ltd* [2011] EWCA Civ 455, a delay of 22 months was not sufficient to make findings of fact unsafe.

Supplementing reasons

In *Barke v SEETEC Business Technology Centre Ltd* [2005] EWCA Civ 578, the **5.331** Court of Appeal approved the practice in the Employment Appeal Tribunal of sifting appeals and inviting employment tribunals to supplement their reasons when the reasons appear to be inadequate. This is done to save the costs of an appeal and of a rehearing where the reasons can adequately be supplemented, although it was recognised in *Barke* that it will not always be appropriate if, for example "the inadequacy of reasoning is on its face so fundamental that there is a real risk that supplementary reasons will be reconstructions of proper reasons, rather than the unexplained actual reasons for the decision". It was also said that the Employment Appeal Tribunal "should always be alive to the danger that an employment tribunal might tailor its response to a request for explanations or further reasons (usually subconsciously rather than deliberately) so as to put the decision in the best possible light". In *Hatungimana v Secretary of State for the Home Department* [2006] EWCA Civ 231, the Court of Appeal declined to apply *Barke* on an appeal from the Asylum and Immigration Tribunal, stressing that the procedural rules of that tribunal were different from those governing employment tribunals. In *CT v SSD* [2009] UKUT 167 (AAC), the Upper Tribunal said, obiter, that, although it might be appropriate, under r.5(3)(n) of the Tribunal Procedure (Upper Tribunal) Rules 2008, to ask a First-tier Tribunal to supplement its reasons before an application for permission to appeal was determined, it would generally be difficult to ask for supplementary reasons at a later stage in the proceedings before the Upper Tribunal because the passage of time would have made it difficult for the First-tier Tribunal to give further reasons. In *CA/4297/2004*, a Commissioner had already distinguished *Barke* and held that a salaried chairman, considering an application for leave to appeal under reg.58(6)(a), had been wrong to ask the fee-paid chairman of the tribunal to supplement his statement of reasons for the tribunal's decision and that the fee-paid chairman had had no power to do so. There are substantial practical arguments against the course taken by the salaried chairman in the case before the Commissioner because some substantial delay was caused as the claimant had to be given the opportunity to comment on the supplemented statement. The Commissioner pointed out that appeals to Commissioners were usually dealt with speedily without oral hearings and that the cost and length of rehearings before tribunals are relatively modest. That is quite apart from the danger referred to by the Commissioner of a fee-paid chairman being led into introducing reasoning on issues that were not in fact considered by the whole tribunal. However, it is arguable that the Commissioner went too far in suggesting that reasons can never be supplemented when an application is made for leave to appeal. A modest expansion of reasons when leave to appeal is being refused (or granted) may be acceptable in some cases (e.g. *R(M) 2/78*). It will be for the Upper Tribunal to consider whether the reasons are reliable against the background of the case. In *CAF/2150/2007*, the Commissioner suggested that additional reasons should be confined to comments on the grounds of appeal and pointed out that, where the tribunal consisted of more than one person, they had to reflect the views of the tribunal as a whole.

In *AS v SSWP (ESA)* [2011] UKUT 159, the Upper Tribunal relied upon additional reasons, wrongly added by the First-tier Tribunal as a correction under r.36, when declining to set aside the First-tier Tribunal's decision.

PART 4

CORRECTING, SETTING ASIDE, REVIEWING AND APPEALING TRIBUNAL DECISIONS

Interpretation

5.332 **35.** In this Part—

"appeal" means the exercise of a right of appeal—

(a) under paragraph 2(2) or 4(1) of Schedule 2 to the Tax Credits Act 2002;

(b) under section 21(10) of the Child Trust Funds Act 2004; or

(c) on a point of law under section 11 of the 2007 Act; and

"review" means the review of a decision by the Tribunal under section 9 of the 2007 Act.

DEFINITIONS

"the 2007 Act"—see r.1(3).
"Tribunal"—*ibid.*

GENERAL NOTE

5.333 The references to the Tax Credits Act 2002 and the Child Trust Funds Act 2004 are to appeals against decisions in penalty cases, where rights of appeal, which are not confined to points of law, remain in force alongside the right of appeal under s.11 of the Tribunals, Courts and Enforcement Act 2007.

Clerical mistakes and accidental slips or omissions

5.334 **36.** The Tribunal may at any time correct any clerical mistake or other accidental slip or omission in a decision, direction or any document produced by it, by—

(a) sending notification of the amended decision or direction, or a copy of the amended document, to all parties; and

(b) making any necessary amendment to any information published in relation to the decision, direction or document.

DEFINITIONS

"document"—see r.1(3).
"party"—*ibid.*
"Tribunal"—*ibid.*

GENERAL NOTE

Rule 36 allows correction only of accidental errors, "such as a typing mistake or misspelling of a name or an omission about which both sides if asked, would agree" (*CI/3887/1999*). It cannot be used to remove an error of law on an issue central to an appeal. If a judge realises, after a decision has been issued, that there is an obvious and fundamental error of law in the decision, a party may be invited to apply for permission to appeal so that the decision may be reviewed and a rehearing directed (*LB Camden v YV* [2012] UKUT 190 (AAC); [2013] AACR 2). 5.335

In *AS v SSWP (ESA)* [2011] UKUT 159, the Upper Tribunal said:

> "16. Rule 36 is by its contents a species of slip rule and should be interpreted in accordance with the nature of that type of provision. As such, it deals with matters that were in the judge's mind when writing but for some reason did not find their way onto the page. Typical examples are the typing error that produces the wrong date or a momentary lapse of concentration that results in the word 'not' being omitted. The rule does not cover matters that the judge had planned to mention but forgot to include. Obviously, it is difficult for the Upper Tribunal to know what was in the judge's mind, but the extent of the changes are an indication. It is difficult to classify the omission of a total of nine lines of explanation as in the same category of mistake as a typing error or a momentary lapse of concentration. For that reason, I decide that the changes made by the presiding judge were not authorised by rule 36."

Nonetheless, the Upper Tribunal then went on to rely upon those reasons when refusing to set aside the First-tier Tribunal's decision. That approach was approved by a three-judge panel in *JS v SSWP (DLA)* [2013] UKUT 100 (AAC). On the other hand, in *CG v SSWP (DLA)* [2011] UKUT 453 (AAC), the Upper Tribunal judge declined to rely on the nine additional paragraphs added to a 10-paragraph decision in order to refute grounds of appeal, when the reasoning was inadequate even with the additional reasons.

A written decision is only effective when it is sent out (*R(I) 14/74*, *SK (Sri Lanka) v Secretary of State for the Home Department* [2008] EWCA Civ 495, *SSD v PY (WP)* [2012] UKUT 116 (AAC); [2012] AACR 44, *re L (Children) (Preliminary Finding: Power to Reverse)* [2013] UKSC 8; [2013] 1 W.L.R. 634). Until then, it may be altered informally. However, a decision given orally is effective when it is announced and so cannot subsequently be changed informally (*Patel v Secretary of State for the Home Department* [2015] EWCA Civ 1175). 5.336

A refusal to correct an acknowledged error of fact in reasons for a decision on the ground that it is not a mere slip may imply that the decision was based on a significant misapprehension of the facts and must be set aside (*Space Airconditioning plc v Guy* [2012] EWCA Civ 1664; [2013] 1 W.L.R. 1293).

A correction no longer automatically extends time limits. Note that a separate power to correct a decision arises on review (see s.9(4)(a) of the Tribunals, Courts and Enforcement Act 2007).

Setting aside a decision which disposes of proceedings

37.—(1) The Tribunal may set aside a decision which disposes of proceedings, or part of such a decision, and re-make the decision, or the relevant part of it, if— 5.337

(a) the Tribunal considers that it is in the interests of justice to do so; and

(b) one or more of the conditions in paragraph (2) are satisfied.

(2) The conditions are—

(a) a document relating to the proceedings was not sent to, or was not received at an appropriate time by, a party or a party's representative;

(b) a document relating to the proceedings was not sent to the Tribunal at an appropriate time;
(c) a party, or a party's representative, was not present at a hearing related to the proceedings; or
(d) there has been some other procedural irregularity in the proceedings.

(3) A party applying for a decision, or part of a decision, to be set aside under paragraph (1) must make a written application to the Tribunal so that it is received no later than 1 month after the date on which the Tribunal sent notice of the decision to the party.

DEFINITIONS

"dispose of proceedings"—see r.1(3).
"document"—*ibid.*
"hearing"—*ibid.*
"party"—*ibid.*
"Tribunal"—*ibid.*

GENERAL NOTE

5.338 The one-month time limit for making an application may be extended under r.5(3)(a).

Note that a separate power to set aside a decision arises on review (see s.9(4)(c) of the Tribunals, Courts and Enforcement Act 2007).

Until a written decision is issued in writing to the parties, it may be recalled without recourse to a formal setting aside under this rule or s.9 of the 2007 Act. However, a decision given orally is effective when it is announced and so cannot subsequently be changed informally (*Patel v Secretary of State for the Home Department* [2015] EWCA Civ 1175). If a claimant merely arrives late after an appeal has been heard but while the other party is still present, there is no reason why, if the parties agree or do not have a good reason for disagreeing and if there is time, the tribunal not should simply start again (*CJ v SSWP (IS)* [2013] UKUT 131(AAC), *AK v HMRC (TC)* [2016] UKUT 98 (AAC)) but, if the decision has been given orally or if a decision notice has been handed to any party, it will be necessary formally to set the first decision aside before rehearing the case.

5.339 Setting aside under r.37 is appropriate where a claimant has not received notice of a hearing that has been properly sent (*R(SB) 19/83*). In *R(SB) 55/83*, it was held that that was the only remedy available to a claimant in those circumstances and that there was no basis upon which a Commissioner could allow an appeal. That approach has been rejected in *CDLA/5413/1999* where it is held that a decision of a tribunal is erroneous in law where notice of a hearing has not been received by a party even though there may have been no breach of the rules of natural justice by the tribunal. See also *CIB/303/1999* and, more recently, *KH v SSWP (CSM)* [2012] UKUT 329 (AAC) in which the Upper Tribunal referred to the clear, albeit obiter, statement in *R(SB) 22/83* that the jurisdiction to set aside on appeal a tribunal's decision on the ground of a breach of the rules of natural justice was additional to the power conferred on the lower tribunal to set aside its decisions. Although the First-tier Tribunal had refused to set aside the decision made in the appellant's absence because it found as a fact that he had had notice of the hearing, the Upper Tribunal did not regard itself as bound by that finding and allowed the appeal on the ground that the appellant had not received notice of the hearing and his presence might have made a difference to the outcome. Moreover, it is now apparent that even the Court of Appeal does not regard a failure to apply for the setting aside of a decision of a lower court where that would have been appropriate to be an absolute bar to an appeal (*Williams v Hinton* [2011] EWCA Civ 1123). In *CIB/5227/1999*, it was pointed out that it was necessary to explain fully the circumstances of the case when making an application for a decision to be set aside. In that case, as in *CDLA/5413/1999*, the reason that the claimant had not received notice of the hearing was that none had been sent because the claimant had not received the clerk's direction requiring him to state whether he wished there to be an oral hearing.

In *CSB/15394/1996* and *CSB/574/1997*, a tribunal refused to set aside a decision on the ground that the claimant's case for the setting aside amounted to an allegation that there had been a breach of the rules of natural justice which was an error of law so that an appeal to a Commissioner was the appropriate course for the claimant to take. The Commissioner hearing the appeal disagreed with that approach. He pointed out that most grounds for setting aside would also be proper grounds for appeal and that the forerunner of this rule existed to provide an expeditious alternative to an appeal. On the other hand, in *CSDLA/303/1998*, the Commissioner held that a claimant was not entitled to raise by way of appeal an issue of fact determined under the forerunner of this rule. The tribunal considering the application for setting aside had found as a fact that a fax allegedly sent to the Independent Tribunal Service had not in fact been sent. The Commissioner held that that question of fact could not be considered on an appeal because "there could be no question of unfairness arising as the claimant had been provided with the remedy of seeking set aside". It is not recorded whether or not the claimant was offered an oral hearing of the application for setting aside, which would have been unusual. It may still be arguable that a finding made on such an application without an oral hearing is not sufficient to remove the Upper Tribunal's jurisdiction to consider the same issue on an appeal.

In *CG/2973/2004*, the Commissioner held a tribunal decision to be erroneous in point of law because medical evidence sent by the claimant in support of an application for an adjournment had not been received by the tribunal. He also held that the fact that the claimant had unsuccessfully tried to have the decision set aside on the same ground did not prevent her from taking the point on appeal to a Commissioner. He observed that the chairman who had refused to set the decision aside had done so on the basis that her presence could not have made any difference to the outcome of her hearing. The case is therefore distinguishable from *CSDLA/303/1998*. The fact that the applicant's presence would not have made any difference is a matter that can legitimately be taken into account when considering whether "to set the decision aside is in the interests of justice" and it would also be relevant to the question whether there had been a breach of the rules of natural justice, but the Commissioner disagreed with the chairman's view of the possible importance of the claimant's evidence.

An appeal against *CG/2973/2004* was dismissed by the Court of Appeal (*Levy v Secretary of State for Work and Pensions* [2006] EWCA Civ 890 (reported as *R(G) 2/06*)), but the relevance of the claimant's application under the forerunner of r.37 was not the subject of argument in the Court of Appeal. 5.340

Paragraph (1)(a) specifically provides that, even where the conditions of para.2 are satisfied, a decision need be set aside only if it is "in the interests of justice to do so". This is consistent with the European Convention on Human Rights. Under the Convention, a person who did not receive notice of a hearing is not entitled as of right to have the decision set aside, unless he has a real prospect of success on a rehearing (*Akram v Adam* [2004] EWCA Civ 1601; [2005] 1 W.L.R. 2762).

Tribunals are entitled to take a robust approach to the non-appearance of parties and to proceed to hear cases in their absence, but a necessary concomitant of such a robust approach must be a greater preparedness to set aside decisions under r.37(2)(c) (*Cooke v Glenrose Fish Co* [2004] I.C.R. 1188, *GA v LB Southwark (HB)* [2013] UKUT 170 (AAC)).

A similar sentiment was expressed in *MP v SSWP (DLA)* [2010] UKUT 103 (AAC) where a claimant was not given the month prescribed by r.24(7) for submitting a reply to a decision-maker's response so that medical evidence held by her representative was not submitted before the appeal was determined on the papers. The First-tier Tribunal refused to set aside its decision on the ground that no element of r.37(2) was satisfied. The Upper Tribunal held that there was a right of appeal against the refusal to set aside and that the case had fallen within both para.(2)(b) 5.341

and para.(2)(d) but in any event he held there to have been a breach of the rules of natural justice and he set aside the substantive decision as well.

In principle, a decision should not be set aside without giving the other party an opportunity of commenting on the application, either before the decision is set aside or afterwards, on the basis that the setting aside may itself be set aside (*GA v LB Southwark (HB)* [2013] UKUT 170 (AAC)). This is particularly important where a public authority is applying for the decision to be set aside. It is less important where a claimant is the applicant only because many public authorities are prepared to waive their right to have an opportunity to comment on the ground that it is not a good use of resources. In *GA v LB Southwark (HB)*, the local authority telephoned the First-tier Tribunal 10 minutes after the hearing of the claimant's appeal was due to start and asked for a postponement. The appeal was against a decision to the effect that some £22,000 in housing benefit and council tax benefit had been overpaid to her and was recoverable. The judge refused the request for a postponement and allowed the claimant's appeal in a decision that did not disclose any error of law. The local authority promptly asked for the decision to be set aside and, four months later, a judge did set the decision aside without the claimant having been given any notice of the setting aside application. The Upper Tribunal allowed the claimant's appeal against the setting aside decision on the ground that she had not been given an opportunity to make representations. It substituted its own decision refusing to set aside the appeal decision on the ground that it was not in the interests of justice to do so because the local authority had not been frank as to its reason for not attending the original hearing, the claimant had had no notice of the setting aside application for four months and, while the local authority had an arguable case on the facts, it could not be said that it was likely to be successful if the substantive appeal were reheard.

Where there has been a breach of natural justice that does not fall within the scope of r.37 and an application under this rule has been rejected for that reason, the judge should consider reviewing the decision if an application for permission to appeal is submitted (*CDLA/792/2006*).

If a case is reheard by a differently constituted tribunal, it is usual for the decision that has been set aside to be included in the papers. That is not inappropriate. Even if their findings of fact cannot be relied upon, issues identified by the first tribunal may well be of assistance to the new tribunal, although it must be careful not to be influenced by the discredited findings (*Swash v Secretary of State for the Home Department* [2006] EWCA Civ 1093; [2007] 1 W.L.R. 1264). There may, however, be special circumstances in which the judge setting the first decision aside considers that the interests of justice require the case to be heard by a tribunal that has not seen that decision and he or she will be able to issue appropriate directions to ensure that that happens (*ibid*).

Application for permission to appeal

5.342 **38.**—(1) This rule does not apply to asylum support cases or criminal injuries compensation cases.

(2) A person seeking permission to appeal must make a written application to the Tribunal for permission to appeal.

(3) An application under paragraph (2) must be sent or delivered to the Tribunal so that it is received no later than 1 month after the latest of the dates that the Tribunal sends to the person making the application—

[1(za) the relevant decision notice;]

(a) written reasons for the decision; [1, if the decision disposes of—

(i) all issues in the proceedings; or

(ii) subject to paragraph (3A), a preliminary issue dealt with following a direction under rule 5(3)(e);]

(b) notification of amended reasons for, or correction of, the decision following a review; or

(c) notification that an application for the decision to be set aside has been unsuccessful.

[1 (3A) The Tribunal may direct that the 1 month within which a party may send or deliver an application for permission to appeal against a decision that disposes of a preliminary issue shall run from the date of the decision that disposes of all issues in the proceedings.]

(4) The date in paragraph (3)(c) applies only if the application for the decision to be set aside was made within the time stipulated in rule 37 (setting aside a decision which disposes of proceedings) or any extension of that time granted by the Tribunal.

(5) If the person seeking permission to appeal sends or delivers the application to the Tribunal later than the time required by paragraph (3) or by any extension of time under rule 5(3)(a) (power to extend time)—

(a) the application must include a request for an extension of time and the reason why the application was not provided in time; and

(b) unless the Tribunal extends time for the application under rule 5(3)(a) (power to extend time) the Tribunal must not admit the application.

(6) An application under paragraph (2) must—

(a) identify the decision of the Tribunal to which it relates;

(b) identify the alleged error or errors of law in the decision; and

(c) state the result the party making the application is seeking.

(7) If a person makes an application under paragraph (2) [1 in respect of a decision that disposes of proceedings or of a preliminary issue dealt with following a direction under rule 5(3)(e)] when the Tribunal has not given a written statement of reasons for its decision—

(a) if no application for a written statement of reasons has been made to the Tribunal, the application for permission must be treated as such an application;

(b) unless the Tribunal decides to give permission and directs that this sub-paragraph does not apply, the application is not to be treated as an application for permission to appeal; and

(c) if an application for a written statement of reasons has been, or is, refused because of a delay in making the application, the Tribunal must only admit the application for permission if the Tribunal considers that it is in the interests of justice to do so.

AMENDMENT

1. Tribunal Procedure (Amendment) Rules 2013 (SI 2013/477) rr.22 and 30 (April 8, 2013).

DEFINITIONS

"appeal"—see r.35.
"asylum support case"—see r.1(3).
"criminal injuries compensation case"—*ibid.*
"dispose of proceedings"—*ibid.*
"party"—*ibid.*
"Tribunal"—*ibid.*

GENERAL NOTE

Paragraphs (3) and (3A)

5.343 Where there is no duty to provide a statement of reasons because the decision is purely interlocutory and neither disposes of the proceedings nor is a decision on a preliminary issue following a direction explicitly directing that the issue be dealt with as a preliminary point, the time for appealing runs from the date of the decision itself. Where a decision is given on a preliminary issue, the First-tier Tribunal can decide whether the time for appealing should run from the final decision disposing of all other issues in the case or from the date of the decision on the preliminary issue itself. Which of the courses of action is appropriate will depend a great deal on the circumstances of the individual case.

Paragraph (5)

5.344 There is no longer an absolute time limit on applications. Previously an application could not be accepted if it was more than a year late. It is still unlikely that permission would be given where there had been such a delay but it is not inconceivable in, say, a case where an unrepresented claimant has been actively challenging some other decision and has not been told that success in that challenge depended on a successful appeal against the decision of the Tribunal.

Rule 5(3)(a) does not expressly require "special reasons" to be shown for an extension of time, as was the position under reg.58 of the Social Security and Child Support (Decisions and Appeals) Regulations 1999, but it is suggested that this may not make any difference because "[t]he concept of special reasons [was] a broad and flexible one" (*R. (Howes) v Social Security Commissioner* [2007] EWHC 559 (Admin)). The reasons for delay were never the only relevant factor (*R(M) 1/87*, applying the approach of the Court of Appeal in *R. v Secretary of State for the Home Department Ex p. Mehta* [1975] 1 W.L.R. 1087). That the merits of the case are also relevant has been confirmed in *R. (Birmingham CC) v Birmingham Crown Court* [2009] EWHC 3329 (Admin); [2010] 1 W.L.R. 1287.

In *CCS/2064/1999*, it was suggested that relevant factors included the strength of the grounds of appeal, the amount of money involved, whether the decision affected current entitlement, whether there was an adequate alternative remedy, the difficulties that the lapse of time might create for making any further findings of fact and the way in which the parties had conducted the case, including their respective contributions to delay. However, in *R. (Howes) v Social Security Commissioner* [2007] EWHC 559 (Admin), Black J., in rejecting an argument that deciding whether there were special reasons required consideration of the factors listed in CPR r.3.9, also disapproved of judge-made lists of relevant considerations and said that "the factors that are relevant will be dependent upon the circumstances of the individual case". The amount of delay is likely to be relevant in most cases but, in *CSDLA/71/1999*, the Commissioner made it plain that "special reasons" for admitting a late application for leave to appeal would not necessarily be found merely because the application was made only two or three days late, even if the applicant had an arguable case on the merits. In that case, the applicant was not helped by the fact that the original explanation for the delay advanced by his representative turned out not to be true and the Commissioner refused leave to appeal. See further the annotation to r.5(3)(a).

Paragraph (7)

5.345 Although the circumstances in which a person can demonstrate an error of law in the absence of a statement of reasons are limited, they are not negligible (see *R(IS) 11/99*). This paragraph makes provision for cases where there is no statement of reasons, either because no application has previously been made or because a statement of reasons has been refused. If there has not already been an application for a statement of reasons, the application for permission to appeal is treated as such an application either instead of, or if it so directs under sub-para.(b), as well as an application for permission to appeal. Sub-paragraph (b) applies only if the Tribunal decides to give permission to appeal either at the same time as issuing a statement of reasons or despite the refusal of such a statement. Where the Tribunal would refuse permission to appeal or would review its decision, it must give the applicant another opportunity to apply for permission to appeal in the light of its decision whether or not to issue a statement of reasons. However, it is arguable that sub-para.(b) does not prevent the Tribunal from treating the application as an application for a correction or setting aside (see r.41).

Sub-paragraph (c) (unlike sub-paras (a) and (b)) applies whether or not there has been a previous application for a statement of reasons. It has the effect of treating the delay in applying for a statement of reasons (which is the only ground upon which a statement of reasons may be refused) in the same way as delay in applying for permission to appeal. The application for permission will not be admitted unless the Tribunal is persuaded that it is in the interests of justice to admit it despite the delay, just as, under para.(5)(b), a late application for permission will not be admitted unless it is in the interests of justice to extend the time for making the application.

Tribunal's consideration of application for permission to appeal

39.—(1) On receiving an application for permission to appeal the Tribunal must first consider, taking into account the overriding objective in rule 2, whether to review the decision in accordance with rule 40 (review of a decision). 5.346

(2) If the Tribunal decides not to review the decision, or reviews the decision and decides to take no action in relation to the decision, or part of it, the Tribunal must consider whether to give permission to appeal in relation to the decision or that part of it.

(3) The Tribunal must send a record of its decision to the parties as soon as practicable.

(4) If the Tribunal refuses permission to appeal it must send with the record of its decision—

(a) a statement of its reasons for such refusal; and

(b) notification of the right to make an application to the Upper Tribunal for permission to appeal and the time within which, and the method by which, such application must be made.

(5) The Tribunal may give permission to appeal on limited grounds, but must comply with paragraph (4) in relation to any grounds on which it has refused permission.

DEFINITIONS

"appeal"—see r.35.
"party"—see r.1(3).
"review"—see r.35.
"Tribunal"—see r.1(3).

GENERAL NOTE

The Senior President of Tribunals has issued a Practice Statement which has the effect of replacing reg.58(6) of the Social Security and Child Support (Decisions and Appeals) Regulations 1999 so that, as before, applications for permission to appeal are considered by salaried judges where the decision was made by, or by a tribunal presided over by, a fee-paid judge (see para.11 of the *Practice Statement on the composition of the tribunals in social security and child support cases in the Social Entitlement Chamber* set out above in the note to art.2 of the First-tier Tribunal and Upper Tribunal (Composition of Tribunal) Order 2008). 5.347

There is no requirement to obtain observations from parties other than the applicant and it is suggested that it is unnecessary to do so unless the Tribunal is contemplating reviewing the decision that is being challenged and, even then, it will not always be necessary to do so because a dissatisfied party may apply for the new decision to be set aside (see r.40(4)).

Paragraphs (1) and (2)

5.348 Before deciding whether or not to grant permission to appeal, the Tribunal must first decide whether or not to review the decision under s.9 of the Tribunals, Courts and Enforcement Act 2007, as limited by r.40. A decision may be reviewed if it is erroneous in point of law (see r.40(2)(b)). However, it does not follow that the effect of r.39(1) is that a decision must be reviewed if it is erroneous in point of law. A decision should be reviewed only if there is a "clear" error of law and regard should also be had to whether the point is contentious, because the First-tier Tribunal must not usurp the Upper Tribunal's function of determining appeals on contentious points of law and because reviewing decisions where there is a dispute between the parties as to the law may cause delay rather than reducing it, which is the point of the power of review (*R. (RB) v First-tier Tribunal (Review)* [2010] UKUT 160 (AAC); [2010] AACR 41). Therefore, the First-tier Tribunal may decide not to review a decision simply because it considers that it should instead grant permission to appeal.

Paragraph (4)

5.349 Reasons for refusing permission to appeal can usually be very brief and will often simply be that the application does not raise any point of law. Reasons can be valuable in persuading an applicant not to make an application to the Upper Tribunal in a hopeless case or in alerting the applicant of the need to rewrite the grounds. If an application raises allegations about the conduct of the Tribunal, it is likely to be desirable to make it clear whether the Tribunal disputes the accuracy of the allegations.

Paragraph (5)

5.350 Except where some grounds advanced are completely misconceived, it may not be helpful to grant a party without a legal representative permission to appeal on limited grounds, because doing so can make an appeal to the Upper Tribunal more complicated and the Upper Tribunal itself generally makes observations and issues directions before any response to an appeal is required, thus focussing the parties' attention on the more important issues. Where a party is represented by a lawyer used to formal pleading, other considerations may apply.

It was said in the 2011/12 edition of this work that "the Upper Tribunal exercises an investigatory approach to appeals and so is not confined by the grounds of appeal or the grounds of permission". However, in *AW v SSWP (IB)* [2012] UKUT 104 (AAC), it was held that that was unsound and that, while the Upper Tribunal is not confined to the grounds of appeal in an ordinary case, it is restricted by specific limitations in a grant of permission to appeal. Otherwise, there is no point in the limitations. In that case, the First-tier Tribunal had failed to comply with the duty imposed by para.(5) to inform the claimant of her right to apply to the Upper Tribunal for permission to appeal on those grounds on which permission had been refused by the First-tier Tribunal and the claimant had not made such an application. Presumably the Upper Tribunal Judge could have invited her to do so had he thought there was anything in the grounds, which he did not.

Review of a decision

40.—(1) This rule does not apply to asylum support cases or criminal injuries compensation cases. 5.351

(2) The Tribunal may only undertake a review of a decision—

(a) pursuant to rule 39(1) (review on an application for permission to appeal); and

(b) if it is satisfied that there was an error of law in the decision.

(3) The Tribunal must notify the parties in writing of the outcome of any review, and of any right of appeal in relation to the outcome.

(4) If the Tribunal takes any action in relation to a decision following a review without first giving every party an opportunity to make representations, the notice under paragraph (3) must state that any party that did not have an opportunity to make representations may apply for such action to be set aside and for the decision to be reviewed again.

DEFINITIONS

"appeal"—see r.35.
"asylum support case"—see r.1(3).
"criminal injuries compensation case"—*ibid.*
"party"—*ibid.*
"review"—see r.35.
"Tribunal—see r.1(3).

GENERAL NOTE

Paragraph (2)

The power of review arises under s.9(1) of the Tribunals, Courts and Enforcement Act 2007. 5.352

Section 9(2) provides for the power of review to be exercised either on the tribunal's initiative or on an application, but s.9(3)(b) enables rules to provide that it is exercisable only on the Tribunal's own initiative. In *JS v Kingston upon Hull CC (HB)* [2014] UKUT 43 (AAC), it was held that para.(2)(a), providing that a decision may be reviewed only on an application for permission to appeal, was not validly made under s.9(3) of the Tribunals, Courts and Enforcement Act 2007, although it was valid under the more general rule-making powers under this Act. The Upper Tribunal considered that the subparagraph had the effect that the First-tier Tribunal was prevented from reviewing a decision on its own initiative. However, it is arguable that it merely limits the circumstances in which the First-tier Tribunal may review a decision on its own initiative, since an application for permission to appeal does not necessarily imply an application for review (even though it may always be treated as one under r.41). Making a rule imposing such a limitation is not expressly authorised by s.9(3). However, although the First-tier Tribunal is not entitled to consider reviewing its decision before an application for permission to appeal is made (*LM v SSWP* [2009] UKUT 185 (AAC)), it can always invite an application for permission to appeal and so the limitation is of little practical importance. The main effect of para.(2)(a) is simply to prevent sequential applications for review and for permission to appeal. The real problem in *JS* was that the review was to the advantage of the local authority but the claimant did not accept that the original decision was wrong.

Paragraph (2)(b), made under s.9(3)(d), limits the ground of review to an error of law. Since appeals under s.11 lie only on points of law, a review therefore provides a way of avoiding an appeal where the appeal would plainly be allowed. For what amounts to an error law for the purposes of para.(2)(b), see the note to s.11. Note that the production of "objective and uncontentious" evidence showing a mistake of fact that has caused unfairness may be sufficient to show an error of law if a lack of reasonable diligence was not the reason for the evidence not being produced before the decision was made. In *DG v SSWP (II)* [2013] UKUT 474 (AAC) there was held to be an error of law when x-ray evidence showed that the First-tier Tribunal's finding that the claimant had not broken her wrist was wrong. There was no lack of reasonable diligence because the claimant could not have expected that she would be disbelieved on that point. Thus it may occasionally be appropriate to review a decision where that decision has prompted the claimant to produce more evidence.

5.353 See s.9(4), (5) and (8) for the powers of the Tribunal on review. These powers are wider than they were under s.13(2) of the Social Security Act 1998 and the similar provisions relating to housing benefit, council tax benefit and child support, which s.9, as limited by this rule, replaces. Note, however, that s.13(3) of the 1998 Act remains in place.

The power of review under s.9 is to be exercised only if there is a "clear" error of law (*R. (RB) v First-tier Tribunal (Review)* [2010] UKUT 160 (AAC); [2010] AACR 41). Because the power to review a decision arises only when an error of law has been identified, it is wrong to refer to the process of considering whether there is an error of law as a review (*VH v Suffolk CC (SEN)* [2010] UKUT 203 (AAC)).

In *SE v SSWP* [2009] UKUT 163 (AAC) and *AM v SSWP* [2009] UKUT 224 (AAC) the Upper Trinunal has also pointed out that, by virtue of subpara.(b), the First-tier Tribunal is not entitled to amend its reasons under s.9(4)(b) of the Tribunals, Courts and Enforcement Act 2007 before it has identified a point of law and it has stressed the importance of the First-tier Tribunal giving parties an opportunity to make representations either before any review or afterwards by way of an application under r.40(4) for the review decision to be set aside.

Paragraph (3)

5.354 Section 11(5)(d) of the 2007 Act has the effect that there is no right of appeal against a decision whether or not to review a decision, to take no action on a review, to set aside a decision on a review or to refer, or not refer, a matter to the Upper Tribunal on review. However, that is because there is always another decision that may be the subject of an appeal. Where the Tribunal refuses to review a decision or reviews it but takes no action, the Tribunal must consider whether to give permission to appeal against the original decision. Where the tribunal reviews a decision and either takes action itself or refers it to the Upper Tribunal to be redecided, there will be a right to apply for permission to appeal against the new decision.

Where a decision is reviewed without all the parties having had the opportunity to make representations, notice must also be given of the right to apply for the new decision to be set aside (see para.(4)).

There is no express duty to give reasons for a review but it will generally be helpful to give some indication for the benefit of the parties and both the judge and any other members whose decision has been set aside and for those who must re-decide the case if that is not done by the reviewing judge straightaway. However, since a decision should be reviewed only where there is a clear error of law, reasons can usually be short and "[o]ften a single sentence is sufficient, where, for instance, all that needs to be done is to draw attention to an overlooked authority or statutory provision or to agree with a ground of appeal" *(R. (RB) v First-tier Tribunal (Review)* [2010] UKUT 160 (AAC); [2010] AACR 41).

Paragraph (4)

5.355 The clear implication of this paragraph is that the Tribunal may either obtain submissions from the parties other than the applicant before reviewing a case or review the case first and then wait to see whether any of the other parties objects. Plainly the second of those approaches may lead to a quicker decision and less work where there is no objection to the review. In *R. (RB) v First-tier Tribunal (Review)* [2010] UKUT 160 (AAC); [2010] AACR 41, it was pointed out that para.(4) enables the First-tier Tribunal to take a robust approach to the question whether a perceived error of law is clear enough to justify a review. However, it was also said that regard had to be had to the likelihood of the previously successful party objecting to the review. In the social security context, where many claimants are unrepresented and might not object in circumstances where a represented party would, some care needs to be taken before decisions are reviewed adversely to them and it may sometimes be preferable to obtain representations before making a review decision rather than afterwards. The Secretary of State, on the other hand, is not only less likely to object but may also positively welcome not being asked to make representations in cases that seem clear to a tribunal judge. If submissions are obtained and all the parties assert that the decision is erroneous in point of law, the Tribunal will be obliged to set the decision aside in those cases where s.13(3) of the Social Security Act 1998 (or an equivalent provision in legislation beyond the scope of this work) applies.

In *SSWP v CM (ESA)* [2012] UKUT 436 (AAC) it has been suggested that the words "the decision to be reviewed again" should be read as "alternative action to be taken", because s.9(10) of the Tribunals, Courts and Enforcement Act 2007 does not allow a second review of a decision. However, this may not be a necessary construction. It might be argued that, if a review decision is set aside in circumstances where a party had not had an opportunity to make representations then it should be treated as never having taken place so as not to prohibit what would otherwise be a second review.

Power to treat an application as a different type of application

41. The Tribunal may treat an application for a decision to be corrected, set aside or reviewed, or for permission to appeal against a decision, as an application for any other one of those things. **5.356**

DEFINITIONS

"appeal"—see r.35.
"review"—*ibid.*
"Tribunal"—see r.1(3).

[1 SCHEDULE 1 rule 22

Time Limits for providing notices of appeal in social security and child support cases where mandatory reconsideration does not apply

5.357

	Type of proceedings	*Time for providing notice of appeal*
1	Appeal against a certification of NHS charges under section 157(1) of the Health and Social Care (Community Health and Standards) Act 2003	(a) 3 months after the latest of— (i) the date on the certificate; (ii) the date on which the compensation payment was made; (iii) if the certificate has been reviewed, the date the certificate was confirmed or a fresh certificate was issued; or (iv) the date of any agreement to treat an earlier compensation payment as having been made in final discharge of a claim made by or in respect of an injured person and arising out of the injury or death; or (b) if the person to whom the certificate has been issued makes an application under section 157(4) of the Health and Social Care (Community Health and Standards) Act 2003, one month after— (i) the date of the decision on that application; or (ii) if the person appeals against that decision under section 157(6) of that Act, the date on which the appeal is decided or withdrawn.
2	Appeal against a waiver decision under section 157(6) of the Health and Social Care (Community Health and Standards) Act 2003	One month after the date of the decision.
3	Appeal against a certificate of NHS charges under section 7 of the Road Traffic (NHS Charges) Act 1999	3 months after the latest of— (a) the date on which the liability under section 1(2) of the Road Traffic (NHS Charges) Act 1999 was discharged; (b) if the certificate has been reviewed, the date the certificate was confirmed or a fresh certificate was issued; or (c) the date of any agreement to treat an earlier compensation payment as having been made in final discharge of a claim made by or in respect of a traffic casualty and arising out of the injury or death.
4	Appeal against a certificate of recoverable benefits under section 11 of the Social Security (Recovery of Benefits) Act 1997	One month after the latest of— (a) the date on which any payment to the Secretary of State required under section 6 of the Social Security (Recovery of Benefits) Act 1997 was made; (b) if the certificate has been reviewed, the date the certificate was confirmed or a fresh certificate was issued;

Type of proceedings	*Time for providing notice of appeal*
	(c) the date of any agreement to treat an earlier compensation payment as having been made in final discharge of a claim made by or in respect of an injured person and arising out of the accident, injury or disease.
5 Cases other than those listed above	The latest of— (a) one month after the date on which notice of the decision being challenged was sent to the appellant; (b) if a written statement of reasons for the decision was requested within that month, 14 days after the later of— (i) the end of that month; or (ii) the date on which the written statement of reasons was provided; (c) if the appellant made an application for the revision of the decision under— (i) regulation 17(1)(a) of the Child Support (Maintenance Assessment Procedure) Regulations 1992; (ii) regulation 3(1) or (3) or 3A(1)(a) of the Social Security and Child Support (Decisions and Appeals) Regulations 1999; (iii) regulation 14(1)(a) of the Child Support Maintenance Calculation Regulations 2012; or (iv) regulation 5 of the Universal Credit, Personal Independence Payment, Jobseeker's Allowance and Employment and Support Allowance (Decisions and Appeals) Regulations 2013, and the application was unsuccessful, one month after the date on which notice that the decision would not be revised was sent to the appellant.]

AMENDMENT

1. Tribunal Procedure (Amendment) Rules 2015 (SI 2015/1510) rr.11 and 17 and Sch. (August 21, 2015).

DEFINITIONS

"appeal"—see r.1(3).
"appellant"—*ibid.*

GENERAL NOTE

Originally, Sch.1 applied just for the purposes of r.23 but, from April 2013 (i.e. during the transition to direct lodgement), it applied to both r.22 and r.23. Now, the time limits for r.23 have been incorporated into that rule and this Schedule applies only in the few cases where a notice of appeal in a social security or child support appeals must be sent to the First-tier Tribunal under r.22 but there is no requirement to apply for reconsideration before lodging the appeal. **5.358**

The first three paragraphs deal with cases concerned with the recovery of NHS charges, which are beyond the scope of this work but where the legislation makes no provision for mandatory reconsideration. Paragraphs 4 and 5 deal with other social security and child support cases where there is no mandatory reconsideration. This will usually be because the Secretary of State has, either by accident or design, not provided the requisite notice with the decision being challenged (see, in relation to social security cases, regs 3ZA(1) and 9ZB(1) of the Social Security and Child Support (Decisions and Appeals) Regulations 1999).

In addition to the re-ordering of the paragraphs and the deletion of those that are now unnecessary, there have been substantive amendments to what is now head (c) in the second column of para.5. First, a reference to the 2013 Regulations has been added, while the reference to housing benefit and council tax benefit legislation has been moved to r.23(2)(a)(iii). Secondly, each of the references to child support legislation is now to sub-para.(a) of para.(1) of the relevant provision, rather than just to para.(1). This gives statutory effect to *AS v SSWP (CSM)* [2012] UKUT 448 (AAC); [2013] AACR 18 and explicitly brings child support cases into line with social security cases so that the time for appealing is automatically extended where there has been an unsuccessful revision only if the application for revision was made within one month (or any longer period allowed by the Secretary of State) of the decision being challenged. A similar amendment has been made in what is now r.23(2)(a)(iii).

The consequence of this, as pointed out by a Tribunal of Commissioners in *R(IS)15/04* (subsequently approved by the Court of Appeal in *Beltekian v Westminster CC* [2004] EWCA Civ 1784 (reported as *R(H)8/05*), is that there is no way of challenging a refusal to revise in a social security case, if it is too late to appeal against the original decision, other than by way of an application for judicial review. This is most unsatisfactory. The Tribunal pointed out that claimants would not wish to apply for revision under reg.3(5) of the 1999 Regulations except on the ground of "official error" because the other grounds for revision result in decisions less favourable to the claimant than the decision that has been revised. However, claimants might well apply for revision under other paragraphs in reg.3 and so the problem is not confined to "official error" cases.

Where it is still possible to appeal against the original decision following a refusal to revise, the Tribunal held in *R(IB)2/04* (at para.39) that the appeal can succeed only if it can be shown that the decision should have been revised. Otherwise, as was pointed out in *CCS/5515/2002*, late appeals could easily be brought by making entirely unmeritorious applications for revision.

Rule 18 of Tribunal Procedure (Amendment) Rules 2015 provides that the amendments to r.23 and the substitution of this Schedule "have no effect in relation to any appeal against a decision made before 6th April 2014 where the decision maker was Her Majesty's Revenue and Customs". This ensures that any such appeal must be referred to the First-tier Tribunal which will refuse to admit it on the ground that it is irremediably out of time (unless to do so would be a breach of the European Convention on Human Rights—see the annotation to r.22(8)).

Rule 25(3)

Schedule 2

Issues In Relation to Which the Tribunal May Refer a Person for Medical Examination under Section 20(2) of the Social Security Act 1998

5.359 An issue falls within this Schedule if the issue—

(a) is whether the claimant satisfies the conditions for entitlement to—

(i) an attendance allowance specified in section 64 and 65(1) of the Social Security Contributions and Benefits Act 1992;

(ii) severe disablement allowance under section 68 of that Act;

(iii) the care component of a disability living allowance specified in section 72(1) and (2) of that Act;

(iv) the mobility component of a disability living allowance specified in section 73(1), (8) and (9) of that Act; [1 . . .]
(v) a disabled person's tax credit specified in section 129(1)(b) of that Act;
[1 (vi) the daily living component of personal independence payment specified in section 78 of the Welfare Reform Act 2012; or
(vii) the mobility component of personal independence payment specified in section 79 of the Welfare Reform Act 2012.]

(b) relates to the period throughout which the claimant is likely to satisfy the conditions for entitlement to an attendance allowance or a disability living allowance;
(c) is the rate at which an attendance allowance is payable;
(d) is the rate at which the care component or the mobility component of a disability living allowance is payable;
(e) is whether a person is incapable of work for the purposes of the Social Security Contributions and Benefits Act 1992;
(f) relates to the extent of a person's disablement and its assessment in accordance with Schedule 6 to the Social Security Contributions and Benefits Act 1992;
(g) is whether the claimant suffers a loss of physical or mental faculty as a result of the relevant accident for the purposes of section 103 of the Social Security Contributions and Benefits Act 1992;
(h) relates to any payment arising under, or by virtue of a scheme having effect under, section 111 of, and Schedule 8 to, the Social Security Contributions and Benefits Act 1992 (workmen's compensation);
(i) is whether a person has limited capability for work or work-related activity for the purposes of the Welfare Reform Act 2007;
[1 (j) is the rate at which the daily living component or mobility component of personal independence payment is payable.]

AMENDMENT

1. Tribunal Procedure (Amendment) Rules 2013 (SI 2013/477) rr.22 and 32 (April 8, 2013).

DEFINITION

"Tribunal"—see r.1(3).

The Tribunal Procedure (Upper Tribunal) Rules 2008

(SI 2008/2698)

IN FORCE NOVEMBER 3, 2008

CONTENTS

PART 1

INTRODUCTION

PART 2

GENERAL POWERS AND PROVISIONS

PART 3

PROCEDURE FOR CASES IN THE UPPER TRIBUNAL

PART 4

JUDICIAL REVIEW PROCEEDINGS IN THE UPPER TRIBUNAL

PART 5

HEARINGS

PART 6

DECISIONS

PART 7

CORRECTING, SETTING ASIDE, REVIEWING AND APPEALING DECISIONS OF THE UPPER TRIBUNAL

After consulting in accordance with paragraph 28(1) of Schedule 5 to, the Tribunals, Courts and Enforcement Act 2007 the Tribunal Procedure Committee has made the following Rules in exercise of the power conferred by sections 10(3), 16(9), 22 and 29(3) and (4) of, and Schedule 5 to, that Act.

The Lord Chancellor has allowed the Rules in accordance with paragraph 28(3) of Schedule 5 to the Tribunals, Courts and Enforcement Act 2007.

PART 1

INTRODUCTION

Citation, commencement, application and interpretation

5.361 **1.**—(1) These Rules may be cited as the Tribunal Procedure (Upper Tribunal) Rules 2008 and come into force on 3rd November 2008.

(2) These Rules apply to proceedings before the Upper Tribunal [2 except proceedings in the Lords Chamber].

(3) In these Rules—

"the 2007 Act" means the Tribunals, Courts and Enforcement Act 2007;

[1 "appellant" means—

(a) a person who makes an appeal, or applies for permission to appeal, to the Upper Tribunal;
(b) in proceedings transferred or referred to the Upper Tribunal from the First-tier Tribunal, a person who started the proceedings in the First-tier Tribunal; or
(c) a person substituted as an appellant under rule 9(1) (substitution and addition of parties);]

[5 "applicant" means—

(a) a person who applies for permission to bring, or does bring, judicial review proceedings before the Upper Tribunal and, in judicial review proceedings transferred to the Upper Tribunal from a court, includes a person who was a claimant or petitioner in the proceedings immediately before they were transferred; or
(b) a person who refers a financial services case [11 or a wholesale energy case] to the Upper Tribunal;]

[2 "appropriate national authority" means, in relation to an appeal, the Secretary of State, the Scottish Ministers [8, the Department of the Environment in Northern Ireland] or the Welsh Ministers, as the case may be;]

[4 "asylum case" means proceedings before the Upper Tribunal on appeal against a decision in proceedings under section 82, 83 or 83A of the Nationality, Immigration and Asylum Act 2002 in which a person claims that removal from, or a requirement to leave, the United Kingdom would breach the United Kingdom's obligations under the Convention relating to the Status of Refugees done at Geneva on 28 July 1951 and the Protocol to the Convention;]

[8 "authorised person" means—

(a) an examiner appointed by the Secretary of State under section 66A of the Road Traffic Act 1988;
(b) an examiner appointed by the Department of the Environment in Northern Ireland under Article 74 of the Road Traffic (Northern Ireland) Order 1995; or
(c) any person authorised in writing by the Department of the Environment in Northern Ireland for the purposes of the Goods Vehicles (Licensing of Operators) Act (Northern Ireland) 2010;

and includes a person acting under the direction of such an examiner or other authorised person, who has detained the vehicle to which an appeal relates;]]

[1 . . .]

[12 "disability discrimination in schools case" means proceedings concerning discrimination in the education of a child or young person or related matters;]

"dispose of proceedings" includes, unless indicated otherwise, disposing of a part of the proceedings;

"document" means anything in which information is recorded in any form, and an obligation under these Rules or any practice direction or direction to provide or allow access to a document or a copy of a document for any purpose means, unless the Upper Tribunal directs otherwise, an obligation to provide or allow access to such document or copy in a legible form or in a form which can be readily made into a legible form;

[4 "fast-track case" means an asylum case or an immigration case where the person who appealed to the First-tier Tribunal—

(a) was detained under the Immigration Acts at a place specified in [13 rule 2(3) of the Schedule to the Tribunal Procedure (First-tier Tribunal) (Immigration and Asylum Chamber) Rules 2014] when the notice of decision that was the subject of the appeal to the First-tier Tribunal was served on the appellant;

(b) remains so detained; and

(c) the First-tier Tribunal or the Upper Tribunal has not directed that the case cease to be treated as a fast-track case;]

[5 "financial services case" means a reference to the Upper Tribunal in respect of—

(a) [9 a decision of the Financial Conduct Authority;

(aa) a decision of the Prudential Regulation Authority;]

(b) a decision of the Bank of England;

(c) a decision of the Pensions Regulator; [11 . . .]

(d) a decision of a person relating to the assessment of any compensation or consideration under the Banking (Special Provisions) Act 2008 or the Banking Act 2009;] [6 or]

[6 (e) any determination, calculation or dispute which may be referred to the Upper Tribunal under the Financial Services and Markets Act 2000 (Contribution to Costs of Special Resolution Regime) Regulations 2010 (and in these Rules a decision in respect of which a reference has been made to the Upper Tribunal in a financial services case includes any such determination, calculation or, except for the purposes of rule 5(5), dispute relating to the making of payments under the Regulations).]

[7 [10 . . .]]

"hearing" means an oral hearing and includes a hearing conducted in whole or in part by video link, telephone or other means of instantaneous two-way electronic communication;

[4 "immigration case" means proceedings before the Upper Tribunal on appeal against a decision in proceedings under section 40A of the British Nationality Act 1981, section 82 of the Nationality, Immigration and Asylum Act 2002, or regulation 26 of the Immigration (European Economic Area) Regulations 2006 that are not an asylum case;]

[10 "immigration judicial review proceedings" means judicial review proceedings which are designated as an immigration matter—

(a) in a direction made in accordance with Part 1 of Schedule 2 to the

Constitutional Reform Act 2005 specifying a class of case for the purposes of section 18(6) of the 2007 Act; or

(b) in an order of the High Court in England and Wales made under section 31A(3) of the Senior Courts Act 1981, transferring to the Upper Tribunal an application of a kind described in section 31A(1) of that Act;]

"interested party" means—

(a) a person who is directly affected by the outcome sought in judicial review proceedings, and has been named as an interested party under rule 28 or 29 (judicial review), or has been substituted or added as an interested party under rule 9 [5 (addition, substitution and removal of parties)] [5. . .]

(b) in judicial review proceedings transferred to the Upper Tribunal under section 25A(2) or (3) of the Judicature (Northern Ireland) Act 1978 or section 31A(2) or (3) of the Supreme Court Act 1981, a person who was an interested party in the proceedings immediately before they were transferred to the Upper Tribunal; [5 and

(c) in a financial services case [11 or a wholesale energy case], any person other than the applicant who could have referred the case to the Upper Tribunal and who has been added or substituted as an interested party under rule 9 (addition, substitution and removal of parties);";

"judicial review proceedings" means proceedings within the jurisdiction of the Upper Tribunal pursuant to section 15 or 21 of the 2007 Act, whether such proceedings are started in the Upper Tribunal or transferred to the Upper Tribunal;

[1 . . .]

"mental health case" means proceedings before the Upper Tribunal on appeal against a decision in proceedings under the Mental Health Act 1983 or paragraph 5(2) of the Schedule to the Repatriation of Prisoners Act 1984;

[3 "national security certificate appeal" means an appeal under section 28 of the Data Protection Act 1998 or section 60 of the Freedom of Information Act 2000 (including that section as applied and modified by regulation 18 of the Environmental Information Regulations 2004);]

"party" means a person who is an appellant, an applicant, a respondent or an interested party in proceedings before the Upper Tribunal, a person who has referred a question [5 or matter] to the Upper Tribunal or, if the proceedings have been concluded, a person who was an appellant, an applicant, a respondent or an interested party when the [10 Upper] Tribunal finally disposed of all issues in the proceedings;

"permission" includes leave in cases arising under the law of Northern Ireland;

"practice direction" means a direction given under section 23 of the 2007 Act;

[14 "QCS Board" means a Board constituted under Part 2 of the Transport Act 2000;

"quality contracts scheme" has the meaning provided for in section 124(3) (quality contracts scheme) of the Transport Act 2000;

"quality contracts scheme case" means proceedings in the Upper Tribunal under Part 2 of the Transport Act 2000;]

[5 "reference", in a financial services case, includes an appeal;]
[3 "relevant minister" means the Minister or designated person responsible for the signing of the certificate to which a national security certificate appeal relates;]
"respondent" means—
(a) in an appeal, or application for permission to appeal, against a decision of another tribunal, any person other than the appellant who—
(i) was a party before that other tribunal;
(ii) [1. . .] or
(iii) otherwise has a right of appeal against the decision of the other tribunal and has given notice to the Upper Tribunal that they wish to be a party to the appeal;
(b) in an appeal [8 other than a road transport case]], the person who made the decision;
(c) in judicial review proceedings—
(i) in proceedings started in the Upper Tribunal, the person named by the applicant as the respondent;
(ii) in proceedings transferred to the Upper Tribunal under section 25A(2) or (3) of the Judicature (Northern Ireland) Act 1978 or section 31A(2) or (3) of the Supreme Court Act 1981, a person who was a defendant in the proceedings immediately before they were transferred;
(iii) in proceedings transferred to the Upper Tribunal under section 20(1) of the 2007 Act, a person to whom intimation of the petition was made before the proceedings were transferred, or to whom the Upper Tribunal has required intimation to be made;
[1 (ca) in proceedings transferred or referred to the Upper Tribunal from the First-tier Tribunal, a person who was a respondent in the proceedings in the First-tier Tribunal;]
(d) in a reference under the Forfeiture Act 1982, the person whose eligibility for a benefit or advantage is in issue; [5 . . .]
[5(da) [9 in a financial services case—
(i) where the case is a multiple regulator case, both the primary and secondary regulator as defined in Schedule 3 to these rules (but subject to the operation of paragraph 4A(3) of that Schedule);
(ii) where the case is a single regulator case, the maker of the decision in respect of which a reference has been made; or]]
[11 (db) in a wholesale energy case, in relation to Great Britain, the Gas and Electricity Markets Authority or, in relation to Northern Ireland, the Northern Ireland Authority for Utility Regulation; or]
(e) a person substituted or added as a respondent under rule 9 (substitution and addition of parties);
[8 "road transport case" means an appeal against a decision of a traffic commissioner or the Department of the Environment in Northern Ireland;]
[1 . . .]
[12 "special educational needs case" means proceedings concerning the education of a child or young person who has or may have special educational needs, including proceedings relating to—

(a) an EHC needs assessment within the meaning of section 36(2) of the Children and Families Act 2014; [14 . . .]

[14(aa) a detained person's EHC needs assessment within the meaning of section 70(5) of the Children and Families Act 2014; or]

(b) an EHC plan within the meaning of section 37(2) of that Act,

of such a child or young person;]

[2 "tribunal" does not include a traffic commissioner;]

[11 "wholesale energy case" means a reference to the Upper Tribunal in respect of a decision of—

(a) in relation to Great Britain, the Gas and Electricity Markets Authority under the Electricity and Gas (Market Integrity and Transparency) (Enforcement etc.) Regulations 2013; or

(b) in relation to Northern Ireland, the Northern Ireland Authority for Utility Regulation under the Electricity and Gas (Market Integrity and Transparency) (Enforcement etc.) Regulations (Northern Ireland) 2013;]

"working day" means any day except a Saturday or Sunday, Christmas Day, Good Friday or a bank holiday under section 1 of the Banking and Financial Dealings Act 1971.

[12 "young person" means, in relation to a special educational needs case or a disability discrimination in schools case, a person over compulsory school age but under 25.]

AMENDMENTS

1. Tribunal Procedure (Amendment) Rules 2009 (SI 2009/274) r.5 (April 1, 2009).

2. Tribunal Procedure (Amendment No.2) Rules 2009 (SI 2009/1975) rr.7 and 8 (September 1, 2009).

3. Tribunal Procedure (Amendment) Rules 2010 (SI 2010/43) rr.5 and 6 (January 18, 2010).

4. Tribunal Procedure (Amendment No.2) Rules 2010 (SI 2010/44) rr.2 and 3 (February 15, 2010).

5. Tribunal Procedure (Upper Tribunal) (Amendment) Rules 2010 (SI 2010/747) rr.2 and 4 (April 6, 2010).

6. Tribunal Procedure (Amendment) Rules 2011 (SI 2011/651) r.8(1) and (2) (April 1, 2011).

7. Tribunal Procedure (Upper Tribunal) (Amendment) Rules 2011 (SI 2011/2343) rr.2 and 4 (October 17, 2011).

8. Tribunal Procedure (Amendment No.2) Rules 2012 (SI 2012/1363) rr.4 and 5 (July 1, 2012).

9. Tribunal Procedure (Amendment No.2) Rules 2013 (SI 2013/606) r.2(1) and (2) (April 1, 2013).

10. Tribunal Procedure (Amendment No. 4) Rules 2013 (SI 2013/2067) rr.2 and 4 (November 1, 2013).

11. Tribunal Procedure (Amendment) Rules 2014 (SI 2014/514) rr.2 and 4 (April 6, 2014).

12. Tribunal Procedure (Amendment No.3) Rules 2014 (SI 2014/2128) rr.2 and 4(a), (c) and (d) (September 1, 2014).

13. Tribunal Procedure (Amendment No.3) Rules 2014 (SI 2014/2128) rr.2 and 4(b) (October 20, 2014).

14. Tribunal Procedure (Amendment) Rules 2015 (SI 2015/1510) rr.2 and 3 (August 21, 2015).

DEFINITIONS

"the 2007 Act"—see para.(3).
"appellant"—*ibid.*
"applicant"—*ibid.*
"interested party"—*ibid.*
"judicial review proceedings"—*ibid.*
"party"—*ibid.*
"permission"—*ibid.*
"practice direction"—*ibid.*
"respondent"—*ibid.*

GENERAL NOTE

The Upper Tribunal has jurisdiction in some "judicial review proceedings", by virtue of ss.15–21 of the Tribunals, Courts and Enforcement Act 2007. Note that the terms "applicant" and "interested party" are used only in relation to such cases and certain financial service cases outside the scope of this work. A person applying for permission to appeal *to* the Upper Tribunal is included within the term "appellant" and in all cases other than judicial review proceedings, every party other than the appellant or person making a reference is a "respondent". A person applying for a decision to be set aside or for permission to appeal *from* the Upper Tribunal is referred to in the Rules merely as "a party applying for . . . " or "a person seeking . . . ". **5.362**

For the meaning of "bank holiday" in the definition of "working day", see the note to r.12(3) of the Tribunal Procedure (First-tier Tribunal) (Social Entitlement Chamber) Rules 2008, above.

The special rules for cases falling within the definition of "fast-track case" have been quashed on the ground that they were unfair and unjust and therefore unlawful (*R. (Detention Action) v First-tier Tribunal (Immigration and Asylum Chamber)* [2015] EWCA Civ 840; [2015] 1 W.L.R. 5341).

Overriding objective and parties' obligation to co-operate with the Upper Tribunal

2.—(1) The overriding objective of these Rules is to enable the Upper Tribunal to deal with cases fairly and justly. **5.363**

(2) Dealing with a case fairly and justly includes—

(a) dealing with the case in ways which are proportionate to the importance of the case, the complexity of the issues, the anticipated costs and the resources of the parties;
(b) avoiding unnecessary formality and seeking flexibility in the proceedings;
(c) ensuring, so far as practicable, that the parties are able to participate fully in the proceedings;
(d) using any special expertise of the Upper Tribunal effectively; and
(e) avoiding delay, so far as compatible with proper consideration of the issues.

(3) The Upper Tribunal must seek to give effect to the overriding objective when it—

(a) exercises any power under these Rules; or
(b) interprets any rule or practice direction.

(4) Parties must—

(a) help the Upper Tribunal to further the overriding objective; and
(b) co-operate with the Upper Tribunal generally.

DEFINITIONS

"party"—see r.1(3).
"practice direction"—*ibid.*

GENERAL NOTE

5.364 See the note to r.2 of the Tribunal Procedure (First-tier Tribunal) (Social Entitlement Chamber) Rules 2008, above.

Alternative dispute resolution and arbitration

5.365 **3.**—(1) The Upper Tribunal should seek, where appropriate—

(a) to bring to the attention of the parties the availability of any appropriate alternative procedure for the resolution of the dispute; and
(b) if the parties wish and provided that it is compatible with the overriding objective, to facilitate the use of the procedure.

(2) Part 1 of the Arbitration Act 1996 does not apply to proceedings before the Upper Tribunal.

DEFINITION

"party"—see r.1(3).

GENERAL NOTE

5.366 Rule 3(1) applies only if there is an alternative procedure available and none currently is. Such a procedure would be useful only where the Upper Tribunal was concerned with a complicated issue of fact, which is very seldom the position in a social security case.

PART 2

GENERAL POWERS AND PROVISIONS

Delegation to staff

5.367 **4.**—(1) Staff appointed under section 40(1) of the 2007 Act (tribunal staff and services) may, with the approval of the Senior President of Tribunals, carry out functions of a judicial nature permitted or required to be done by the Upper Tribunal.

(2) The approval referred to at paragraph (1) may apply generally to the carrying out of specified functions by members of staff of a specified description in specified circumstances.

(3) Within 14 days after the date on which the Upper Tribunal sends notice of a decision made by a member of staff under paragraph (1) to a party, that party may apply in writing to the Upper Tribunal for that decision to be considered afresh by a judge.

DEFINITIONS

"the 2007 Act"—see r.1(3).
"party"—*ibid.*

GENERAL NOTE

5.368 There is no need to make provision for the delegation of functions of a purely administrative nature and so this rule refers only to functions of a judicial nature. The Senior President of Tribunals has issued a Practice Statement (available at:

http://www.judiciary.gov.uk/publications) recording his approval of the delegation of certain functions to legally qualified members of staff of the Upper Tribunal, known as Registrars. The functions that are delegated are—

(a) exercising any case management powers under r.5 except—
  (i) extending time under r.5(3)(a) in relation to the time limits for appeals referred to in rr.21(3) and (6), 22(5), 23(2) and (5) and 44(3), (4) and (6) or in relation to the time limits for judicial review proceedings referred to in rr.28(2), (3) and (7) and 30(5);
  (ii) suspending a decision under r.5(3)(l) or (m);
  (iii) requiring a tribunal to provide reasons for its decision under r.5(3)(n);
(b) dealing with irregularities under r.7(2) (except taking action under r.7(2)(d) or (4));
(c) striking out under r.8(1) or (3)(a) and reinstating proceedings under r.8(5);
(d) giving directions substituting or adding parties under r.9;
(e) summarily assessing costs under r.10(8)(a);
(f) making orders prohibiting disclosure or publication of documents and information under r.14;
(g) giving directions in relation to evidence and submissions under r.15(1);
(h) summoning (or, in Scotland, citing) witnesses and issuing orders to persons to answer questions and produce documents under r.16; and
(i) giving consent to withdraw a case and reinstating a case under r.17.

Case management powers

5.—(1) Subject to the provisions of the 2007 Act and any other enactment, the Upper Tribunal may regulate its own procedure. **5.369**

(2) The Upper Tribunal may give a direction in relation to the conduct or disposal of proceedings at any time, including a direction amending, suspending or setting aside an earlier direction.

(3) In particular, and without restricting the general powers in paragraphs (1) and (2), the Upper Tribunal may—

(a) extend or shorten the time for complying with any rule, practice direction or direction;
(b) consolidate or hear together two or more sets of proceedings or parts of proceedings raising common issues, or treat a case as a lead case;
(c) permit or require a party to amend a document;
(d) permit or require a party or another person to provide documents, information, evidence or submissions to the Upper Tribunal or a party;
(e) deal with an issue in the proceedings as a preliminary issue;
(f) hold a hearing to consider any matter, including a case management issue;
(g) decide the form of any hearing;
(h) adjourn or postpone a hearing;
(i) require a party to produce a bundle for a hearing;
(j) stay (or, in Scotland, sist) proceedings;
(k) transfer proceedings to another court or tribunal if that other court or tribunal has jurisdiction in relation to the proceedings and—
  (i) because of a change of circumstances since the proceedings were started, the Upper Tribunal no longer has jurisdiction in relation to the proceedings; or
  (ii) the Upper Tribunal considers that the other court or tribunal is a more appropriate forum for the determination of the case;
(l) suspend the effect of its own decision pending an appeal or review of that decision;

(m) in an appeal, or an application for permission to appeal, against the decision of another tribunal, suspend the effect of that decision pending the determination of the application for permission to appeal, and any appeal;

(n) [1 require any person, body or other tribunal whose decision is the subject of proceedings before the Upper Tribunal to provide reasons for the decision, or other information or documents in relation to the decision or any proceedings before that person, body or tribunal.]

[2 (4) The Upper Tribunal may direct that a fast-track case cease to be treated as a fast-track case if—

(a) all the parties consent; [6 or]

(b) the Upper Tribunal is satisfied that [6 . . .] the appeal or application could not be justly determined if it were treated as a fast-track case; [6 . . .]

(c) [6 . . .]]

[3 (5) In a financial services case, the Upper Tribunal may direct that the effect of the decision in respect of which the reference has been made is to be suspended pending the determination of the reference, if it is satisfied that to do so would not prejudice—

(a) the interests of any persons (whether consumers, investors or otherwise) intended to be protected by that notice; [4 . . .]

(b) the smooth operation or integrity of any market intended to be protected by that notice; [4 or]

[4 (c) the stability of the financial system of the United Kingdom.]

(6) Paragraph (5) does not apply in the case of a reference in respect of a decision of the Pensions Regulator.]

[5 (7) In a wholesale energy case, the Upper Tribunal may direct that the effect of the decision in respect of which the reference has been made is to be suspended pending the determination of the reference.]

AMENDMENTS

1. Tribunal Procedure (Amendment No.2) Rules 2009 (SI 2009/1975) rr.7 and 9 (September 1, 2009).

2. Tribunal Procedure (Amendment No.2) Rules 2010 (SI 2010/44) rr.2 and 4 (February 15, 2010).

3. Tribunal Procedure (Upper Tribunal) (Amendment) Rules 2010 (SI 2010/747) rr.2 and 5 (April 6, 2010).

4. Tribunal Procedure (Amendment No.2) Rules 2013 (SI 2013/606) r.2(1) and (3) (April 1, 2013).

5.Tribunal Procedure (Amendment) Rules 2014 (SI 2014/514) rr.2 and 4 (April 6, 2014).

6. Tribunal Procedure (Amendment No.3) Rules 2014 (SI 2014/2128) rr.2 and 5 (October 20, 2014).

DEFINITIONS

"the 2007 Act"—see r.1(3).
"dispose of proceedings"—*ibid.*
"document"—*ibid.*
"fast-track case"—*ibid.*
"financial services case"—*ibid.*
"hearing" *ibid.*
"party"—*ibid.*

"permission"—*ibid.*
"practice direction"—*ibid.*
"wholesale energy case"—*ibid.*

GENERAL NOTE

Paragraph (2)

This is in very broad terms and, although para.(3) and r.15(1) set out examples of directions the Upper Tribunal may give, they do not restrict the width of the power in this paragraph. The power must, however, be exercised so as to give effect to the overriding objective in r.2 (see r.2(3)). The procedure for applying for and giving directions is to be found in r.6. Note that, where a direction requires something to be done by a particular day, it must be done by 5pm on that day (r.12(1)) but, if that day is not a working day, the act is done in time if it is done on the next working day (r.12(2)). 5.370

Paragraph (3)

Sub-paragraph (a) is in very broad terms. See the note to r.5(3)(a) of the Tribunal Procedure (First-tier Tribunal) (Social Entitlement Chamber) Rules 2008, above. 5.371

Sub-paragraph (c) presumably refers to grounds of appeal and other submissions, rather than to evidence.

Sub-paragraphs (f), (g) and (h) must be read with rr.34–37. See also the note to r.5(3)(f), (g) and (h) of the Tribunal Procedure (First-tier Tribunal) (Social Entitlement Chamber) Rules 2008, above.

When making a direction for the preparation of a bundle under sub-para.(i) in a case where there is no power, or only a limited power, to award costs, it is important that the Upper Tribunal considers upon whom the financial burden of preparing a bundle should be placed. If it wishes the cost to be shared, it should direct both parties to prepare it. See *Eclipse Film Partners No.35 LLP v Revenue and Customs Commissioners (No.2)* [2016] UKSC 24; [2016] 1 W.L.R. 1939.

Sub-paragraph (k) applies only where the Upper Tribunal had jurisdiction at the time the proceedings were begun. Otherwise, the Tribunal is required to strike the proceedings out under r.8(2). Rule 5(3)(k)(i) applies where the Upper Tribunal loses jurisdiction and r.5(3)(k)(ii) applies only where the Upper Tribunal and another tribunal have concurrent jurisdiction (which may be the case in some circumstances where a person moves to or from Northern Ireland).

Sub-paragraphs (l) and (m) permit the effect of a decision to be suspended pending an appeal from or to the Upper Tribunal. The power to suspend the effect of its own decision conferred by sub-para.(l) does not extend to suspending its precedential effect on other claims pending an appeal (*SSD v AD and MM (No.2)* [2009] UKUT 69 (AAC)), but in social security cases such an extended power is unnecessary in the light of s.25 (and s.26) of the Social Security Act 1998. The First-tier Tribunal also has power to suspend the effect of its decision pending an appeal to the Upper Tribunal (see r.5(3)(l) of the Tribunal Procedure (First-tier Tribunal) (Social Entitlement Chamber) Rules 2008 and so the power in sub-para.(m) is most likely to be invoked where the First-tier Tribunal has refused to suspend the effect of its own decision. It is usually unnecessary to suspend a decision in a social security case concerned with entitlement, due to the Secretary of State's power to suspend payments under reg.16 of the Social Security and Child Support (Decisions and Appeals) Regulations 1999 or reg.44 of the Universal Credit, Personal independence Payment, Jobseeker's Allowance and Employment and Support Allowance (Decisions and Appeals) Regulations 2013. In the past, the Secretary of State has generally not taken action to recover an overpayment while an appeal against a decision that the overpayment is recoverable is pending but he could now take the view that an appeal does not require him to stay his hand unless the tribunal so directs under this provision, which would not necessarily be appropriate as a matter of course and could in 5.372

any event presumably be limited to part of its decision. The power to suspend the effect of a decision may also be useful in appeals against decisions under the Social Security (Recovery of Benefits) Act 1997, because s.14 of that Act and the regulations made under it completely fail to deal with the consequences of a successful appeal to the Upper Tribunal or an appellate court. In *Carmarthenshire CC v MW (SEN)* [2010] UKUT 348 (AAC); [2011] AACR 17, it was held that r.5(3)(m) required a balancing exercise, taking into account the practical consequences of suspending the decision on one side and the practical consequences of not doing so on the other. The chances of the appeal succeeding would be relevant but it was doubted whether a good prospect of the appeal succeeding could operate as a threshold condition, particularly in a case of urgency where the grounds of appeal might not have been formulated.

In *Cabinet Office v Information Commissioner* [2016] UKUT 476 (AAC), the Upper Tribunal continued a suspension of the effect of the First-tier Tribunal's decision for 23 days after issue of his refusal of permission to appeal from that decision, in case the Cabinet Office wished to apply for permission to bring judicial review proceedings. The period was calculated by adding 7 days to the 16-day time limit for applying for judicial review, so as to give the Cabinet Office time to get any application for a further suspension before a judge in the Administrative Court if it wished to do so. It is not clear whether the judge read "review" in r.5(3)(l) as including judicial review or read "appeal" in both that provision and r.5(3)(m) as including an application for judicial review or whether, acting outside the Rules, he exercised an implied power.

Sub-paragraph (n) enables the Upper Tribunal to direct the First-tier Tribunal to provide reasons for its decision. This power has seldom been exercised in social security cases. Given the speed with which the First-tier Tribunal hears and determines cases, it may often be simpler to allow an appeal and direct a rehearing rather than to obtain reasons for a previous decision.

Procedure for applying for and giving directions

5.373 **6.**—(1) The Upper Tribunal may give a direction on the application of one or more of the parties or on its own initiative.

(2) An application for a direction may be made—

(a) by sending or delivering a written application to the Upper Tribunal; or

(b) orally during the course of a hearing.

(3) An application for a direction must include the reason for making that application.

(4) Unless the Upper Tribunal considers that there is good reason not to do so, the Upper Tribunal must send written notice of any direction to every party and to any other person affected by the direction.

(5) If a party or any other person sent notice of the direction under paragraph (4) wishes to challenge a direction which the Upper Tribunal has given, they may do so by applying for another direction which amends, suspends or sets aside the first direction.

Definitions

"hearing"—see r.1(3).
"party"—*ibid.*

General Note

5.374 See the note to r.6 of the Tribunal Procedure (First-tier Tribunal) (Social Entitlement Chamber) Rules 2008, above.

Failure to comply with rules etc.

7.—(1) An irregularity resulting from a failure to comply with any requirement in these Rules, a practice direction or a direction, does not of itself render void the proceedings or any step taken in the proceedings. 5.375

(2) If a party has failed to comply with a requirement in these Rules, a practice direction or a direction, the Upper Tribunal may take such action as it considers just, which may include—

(a) waiving the requirement;
(b) requiring the failure to be remedied;
(c) exercising its power under rule 8 (striking out a party's case); or
(d) except in [1 a mental health case, an asylum case or an immigration case], restricting a party's participation in the proceedings.

(3) Paragraph (4) applies where the First-tier Tribunal has referred to the Upper Tribunal a failure by a person to comply with a requirement imposed by the First-tier Tribunal—

(a) to attend at any place for the purpose of giving evidence;
(b) otherwise to make themselves available to give evidence;
(c) to swear an oath in connection with the giving of evidence;
(d) to give evidence as a witness;
(e) to produce a document; or
(f) to facilitate the inspection of a document or any other thing (including any premises).

(4) The Upper Tribunal may exercise its power under section 25 of the 2007 Act (supplementary powers of the Upper Tribunal) in relation to such non-compliance as if the requirement had been imposed by the Upper Tribunal.

Amendment

1. Tribunal Procedure (Amendment No.2) Rules 2010 (SI 2010/44) rr.2 and 5 (February 15, 2010).

Definitions

"the 2007 Act"—see r.1(3).
"asylum case"—*ibid.*
"document"—*ibid.*
"immigration case"—*ibid.*
"mental health case"—*ibid.*
"party"—*ibid.*
"practice direction"—*ibid.*

General Note

Paragraphs (1) and (2)(a) enable the Upper Tribunal to overlook a breach of a rule, practice direction or direction. On the other hand, under para.2(c), such a breach can lead to a case being struck out under r.8, provided an appropriate warning has been given. Alternatively, the Upper Tribunal may exercise its powers under s.25 of the Tribunals, Courts and Enforcement Act 2007 to punish the person for contempt of court (with a term of imprisonment of up to two years and an unlimited fine). Paragraph (1) may imply a greater power of waiver than exists in para.(2)(a), because an irregularity may be the fault of a lower tribunal (see the examples in the note to r.21(2)) or of the Upper Tribunal, rather than of a party, and it may be too late to remedy it. 5.376

Paragraphs (3) and (4) are concerned with cases where the First-tier Tribunal refers a case to the Upper Tribunal because there has been non-compliance with a summons, order or direction issued by that tribunal in connection with the attendance or examination of witnesses or the production or inspection of documents. They are made under para.10 of Sch.5 to the 2007 Act. A referral is necessary because the First-tier Tribunal does not have its own power to punish for contempt. The impression given by the three-judge panel decisions in *PA v CMEC* [2010] UKUT 283 (AAC), *MR v CMEC* [2010] UKUT 284 (AAC) and *MR v CMEC* [2010] UKUT 285 (AAC) that, on a reference by the First-tier Tribunal for breach of a direction to produce evidence, it was necessary for the Upper Tribunal to make its own direction to produce evidence before it could punish the defaulter for contempt of court has been corrected in the subsequent three-judge panel decision of *MD v SSWP (Enforcement Reference)* [2010] UKUT 202 (AAC); [2011] AACR 5, where it was explained that the Upper Tribunal made its own direction in *MR v CMEC* [2010] UKUT 285 (AAC) because that course was, as a matter of discretion, the course which the Upper Tribunal considered appropriate in all the circumstances. It was expressly stated that it "was not because the exercise of the Upper Tribunal's powers was in any way conditional upon the making of a further order". In *CB v Suffolk CC (Enforcement Reference)* [2010] UKUT 413 (AAC); [2011] AACR 22, the Upper Tribunal fined a witness £500 for failing to comply with a summons issued by the Health, Education and Social Care Chamber of the First-tier Tribunal. See also *BO v Care Quality Commission (Enforcement Reference)* [2013] UKUT 53 (AAC), where a fine of £100 was imposed for non-compliance with a summons.

Paragraph (3)(c) must be read subject to s.5 of the Oaths Act 1978, which permits a person who objects to being sworn to make a solemn affirmation instead.

Striking out a party's case

5.377 **8.**—[2 (1A) Except for paragraph (2), this rule does not apply to an asylum case or an immigration case.]

[3 (1) The proceedings, or the appropriate part of them, will automatically be struck out—

(a) if the appellant or applicant has failed to comply with a direction that stated that failure by the appellant or applicant to comply with the direction would lead to the striking out of the proceedings or part of them; or

[4(b) in immigration judicial review proceedings, when a fee has not been paid, as required, in respect of an application under rule 30(4) or upon the grant of permission.]

(2) The Upper Tribunal must strike out the whole or a part of the proceedings if the Upper Tribunal—

(a) does not have jurisdiction in relation to the proceedings or that part of them; and

(b) does not exercise its power under rule 5(3)(k)(i) (transfer to another court or tribunal) in relation to the proceedings or that part of them.

(3) The Upper Tribunal may strike out the whole or a part of the proceedings if—

(a) the appellant or applicant has failed to comply with a direction which stated that failure by the appellant or applicant to comply with the direction could lead to the striking out of the proceedings or part of them;

(b) the appellant or applicant has failed to co-operate with the Upper

Tribunal to such an extent that the Upper Tribunal cannot deal with the proceedings fairly and justly; or

(c) in proceedings which are not an appeal from the decision of another tribunal or judicial review proceedings, the Upper Tribunal considers there is no reasonable prospect of the appellant's or the applicant's case, or part of it, succeeding.

(4) The Upper Tribunal may not strike out the whole or a part of the proceedings under paragraph (2) or (3)(b) or (c) without first giving the appellant or applicant an opportunity to make representations in relation to the proposed striking out.

(5) If the proceedings have been struck out under paragraph (1) or (3)(a), the appellant or applicant may apply for the proceedings, or part of them, to be reinstated.

(6) An application under paragraph (5) must be made in writing and received by the Upper Tribunal within 1 month after the date on which the Upper Tribunal sent notification of the striking out to the appellant or applicant.

(7) This rule applies to a respondent [1 or an interested party] as it applies to an appellant or applicant except that—

(a) a reference to the striking out of the proceedings is to be read as a reference to the barring of the respondent [1 or an interested party] from taking further part in the proceedings; and

(b) a reference to an application for the reinstatement of proceedings which have been struck out is to be read as a reference to an application for the lifting of the bar on the respondent [1 or an interested party] from taking further part in the proceedings.

(8) If a respondent [1 or an interested party] has been barred from taking further part in proceedings under this rule and that bar has not been lifted, the Upper Tribunal need not consider any response or other submission made by that respondent [1 or interested party, and may summarily determine any or all issues against that respondent or interested party].

AMENDMENTS

1. Tribunal Procedure (Amendment) Rules 2009 (SI 2009/274) r.6 (April 1, 2009).

2. Tribunal Procedure (Amendment No.2) Rules 2010 (SI 2010/44) rr.2 and 6 (February 15, 2010).

3. Tribunal Procedure (Upper Tribunal) (Amendment) Rules 2011 (SI 2011/2343) rr.2 and 5 (October 17, 2011).

4. Tribunal Procedure (Amendment No. 4) Rules 2013 (SI 2013/2067) rr.2 and 5 (November 1, 2013).

DEFINITIONS

"appellant"—see r.1(3).
"applicant"—*ibid.*
"asylum case" – *ibid.*
"immigration case" – *ibid.*
"immigration judicial review proceedings"—*ibid.*
"interested party"—*ibid.*
"party"—*ibid.*
"respondent"—*ibid.*

General Note

5.378 Note that, although paras (1)–(6) are expressed in terms of striking out proceedings brought by the appellant, by virtue of paras (7) and (8) they also provide for barring a respondent from taking further part in the proceedings.

Paragraph (1)

5.379 Subparagraph (a) provides for an automatic strike out where a person has failed to comply with a direction that carried a warning that, unless there was compliance, the case "will" be struck out. In theory, no further judicial act is required for the strike-out to take effect provided that it is clear that there has not been compliance. It is important to distinguish this paragraph from para.(3)(a), which provides for a case to be struck out for failure to comply with a direction that carried a warning that if there was no compliance the case "may" be struck out. In such a case, there needs to be a judicial decision exercising the power to strike out. It is suggested that, unless there has been a previous history of non-compliance with directions and rules, warnings should be of the "may" variety rather than the "will" variety. Note that proceedings struck out under this paragraph may be reinstated on an application under paras (5) and (6).

Subparagraph (b) applies only to "immigration judicial review proceedings" and therefore is not relevant to social security cases. Fees are not payable in respect of social security cases.

Paragraph (2)

5.380 The terms of this paragraph are mandatory, so that a final decision to the effect that the tribunal lacks jurisdiction must always be in the form of a decision to strike out the appeal. This includes a case where the Upper Tribunal lacks jurisdiction because the appeal brought to it has lapsed (*LS v HMRC (TC)* [2017] UKUT 275 (AAC)). By virtue of para.(4), a party must be given an opportunity to make representations before his or her case is struck out and there will be some cases where justice requires there to be a hearing.

Paragraph (3)

5.381 By virtue of para.(4), a party must be given an opportunity to make representations before his or her case is struck out under sub-para.(b). There is no right to make representations before a case is struck out under sub-para.(a); instead there is a right to apply for reinstatement after the event, by virtue of paras (5) and (6). Striking out is discretionary and must be proportionate (see r.2(2)(a)), having regard to the culpability of the party whose case is being struck out and the amount at stake on the appeal (see *Alpha Rocks Solicitors v Alade* [2015] EWCA Civ 685; [2015] 1 W.L.R. 4534). However, in principle, directions of the Upper Tribunal should be enforced as rigorously as orders of the courts (*BPP Holdings v Commissioners for Her Majesty's Revenue and Customs* [2016] EWCA Civ 121; [2016] 1 W.L.R. 1915).

Sub-paragraph (c) introduces a power to strike a case out where it has no reasonable prospect of success, but it has little application to social security cases because it does not apply to appeals from the First-tier Tribunal or judicial review proceedings (presumably because the permission requirement makes it unnecessary in the case of appellants and applicants and there is little advantage in barring respondents in such cases) and there is no appellant or applicant in a reference under the Forfeiture Act 1982. On the other hand, in the absence of a power to certify an application for permission to appeal as being totally without merit so as prevent it being renewed orally when it has been refused on the papers in those jurisdictions where that may be done (see r.22(3) and (4) and compare r.30(4A)), the Upper Tribunal has exercised its power to strike out a renewed application for permission when satisfied that it had no arguable merit and that the applicant had "had more than her day in court at the FTT" (*Gaskin v Information Commissioner* [2016] UKUT 382 (AAC)).

See further the note to r.8(3) of the Tribunal Procedure (First-tier Tribunal) (Social Entitlement Chamber) Rules 2008.

Paragraphs (5) and (6)

These paragraphs apply only to cases struck out under para.(1) or (3)(a). In other cases, the Tribunal must give the party an opportunity to make representations *before* a case is struck out. In *Synergy Child Services Ltd v Ofsted* [2009] UKUT 125 (AAC), it was held that, when considering whether to reinstate an appeal, "a Tribunal should have regard to the broad justice of the case, in the light of all the circumstances obtaining at the time the application for reinstatement is being considered". Nonetheless, "[w]here there has been flagrant disobedience by a party, belated compliance or a change of circumstances making compliance irrelevant will not always require a Tribunal to reinstate an appeal". This must now be read in the light of *BPP Holdings*, mentioned above. 5.382

Paragraphs (7) and (8)

The amendment to the end of para.(8) provides for the summary determination of issues against the respondent or interested party, which is equivalent of striking out part, or the whole, of an appellant or applicant's case. See further the note to r.8(7) and (8) of the Tribunal Procedure (First-tier Tribunal) (Social Entitlement Chamber) Rules 2008. 5.383

[1 Addition, substitution and removal of parties

9.—(1) The Upper Tribunal may give a direction adding, substituting or removing a party as an appellant, a respondent or an interested party. 5.384

(2) If the Upper Tribunal gives a direction under paragraph (1) it may give such consequential directions as it considers appropriate.

(3) A person who is not a party may apply to the Upper Tribunal to be added or substituted as a party.

(4) If a person who is entitled to be a party to proceedings by virtue of another enactment applies to be added as a party, and any conditions applicable to that entitlement have been satisfied, the Upper Tribunal must give a direction adding that person as a respondent or, if appropriate, as an appellant.]

[2 (5) In an asylum case, the United Kingdom Representative of the United Nations High Commissioner for Refugees ("the United Kingdom Representative") may give notice to the Upper Tribunal that the United Kingdom Representative wishes to participate in the proceedings.

(6) If the United Kingdom Representative gives notice under paragraph (5)—

(i) the United Kingdom Representative is entitled to participate in any hearing; and

(ii) all documents which are required to be sent or delivered to parties must be sent or delivered to the United Kingdom Representative.]

AMENDMENTS

1. Tribunal Procedure (Amendment No.2) Rules 2009 (SI 2009/1975) rr.7 and 10 (September 1, 2009).

2. Tribunal Procedure (Amendment No.2) Rules 2010 (SI 2010/44) rr.2 and 7 (February 15, 2010).

DEFINITIONS

"appellant" – *ibid.*
"asylum case" – *ibid.*
"interested party" – *ibid.*
"party"—*ibid.*
"respondent"—*ibid.*

GENERAL NOTE

5.385 See the note to r.9 of the Tribunal Procedure (First-tier Tribunal) (Social Entitlement Chamber) Rules 2008, above. This rule does not permit the substitution of an applicant in judicial review proceedings.

[1 Orders for costs

5.386 **10.**—(1) The Upper Tribunal may not make an order in respect of costs (or, in Scotland, expenses) in proceedings [2 transferred or referred by, or on appeal from] another tribunal except –

[3 (aa) in a national security certificate appeal, to the extent permitted by paragraph (1A);]

(a) in proceedings [2 transferred by, or on appeal from] from the Tax Chamber of the First-tier Tribunal; or

(b) to the extent and in the circumstances that the other tribunal had the power to make an order in respect of costs (or, in Scotland, expenses).

[3 (1A) In a national security certificate appeal—

(a) the Upper Tribunal may make an order in respect of costs or expenses in the circumstances described at paragraph (3)(c) and (d);

(b) if the appeal is against a certificate, the Upper Tribunal may make an order in respect of costs or expenses against the relevant Minister and in favour of the appellant if the Upper Tribunal allows the appeal and quashes the certificate to any extent or the Minister withdraws the certificate;

(c) if the appeal is against the application of a certificate, the Upper Tribunal may make an order in respect of costs or expenses—

(i) against the appellant and in favour of any other party if the Upper Tribunal dismisses the appeal to any extent; or

(ii) in favour of the appellant and against any other party if the Upper Tribunal allows the appeal to any extent.]

(2) The Upper Tribunal may not make an order in respect of costs or expenses under section 4 of the Forfeiture Act 1982.

(3) In other proceedings, the Upper Tribunal may not make an order in respect of costs or expenses except—

(a) in judicial review proceedings;

(b) [3. . .];

(c) under section 29(4) of the 2007 Act (wasted costs) [5 and costs incurred in applying for such costs]; [4. . .]

(d) if the Upper Tribunal considers that a party or its representative has acted unreasonably in bringing, defending or conducting the proceedings. [4 or

(e) if, in a financial services case [7 or a wholesale energy case], the Upper Tribunal considers that the decision in respect of which the reference was made was unreasonable]

(4) The Upper Tribunal may make an order for costs (or, in Scotland, expenses) on an application or on its own initiative.

(5) A person making an application for an order for costs or expenses must —

(a) send or deliver a written application to the Upper Tribunal and to the person against whom it is proposed that the order be made; and

(b) send or deliver with the application a schedule of the costs or expenses claimed sufficient to allow summary assessment of such costs or expenses by the Upper Tribunal.

(6) An application for an order for costs or expenses may be made at any time during the proceedings but may not be made later than 1 month after the date on which the Upper Tribunal sends—

(a) a decision notice recording the decision which finally disposes of all issues in the proceedings; or

(b) [5 notice under rule 17(5) that a withdrawal which ends the proceedings has taken effect.]

(7) The Upper Tribunal may not make an order for costs or expenses against a person (the "paying person") without first—

(a) giving that person an opportunity to make representations; and

(b) if the paying person is an individual and the order is to be made under paragraph (3)(a), (b) or (d), considering that person's financial means.

(8) The amount of costs or expenses to be paid under an order under this rule may be ascertained by—

(a) summary assessment by the Upper Tribunal;

(b) agreement of a specified sum by the paying person and the person entitled to receive the costs or expenses ("the receiving person"); or

(c) assessment of the whole or a specified part of the costs or expenses [5, including the costs or expenses of the assessment,] incurred by the receiving person, if not agreed.

(9) Following an order for assessment under paragraph (8)(c), the paying person or the receiving person may apply—

(a) in England and Wales, to the High Court or the Costs Office of the Supreme Court (as specified in the order) for a detailed assessment of the costs on the standard basis or, if specified in the order, on the indemnity basis; and the Civil Procedure Rules 1998 shall apply, with necessary modifications, to that application and assessment as if the proceedings in the tribunal had been proceedings in a court to which the Civil Procedure Rules 1998 apply;

(b) in Scotland, to the Auditor of the Court of Session for the taxation of the expenses according to the fees payable in that court; or

(c) in Northern Ireland, to the Taxing Office of the High Court of Northern Ireland for taxation on the standard basis or, if specified in the order, on the indemnity basis.]

[5 (10) Upon making an order for the assessment of costs, the [6 Upper] Tribunal may order an amount to be paid on account before the costs or expenses are assessed.]

AMENDMENTS

1. Tribunal Procedure (Amendment) Rules 2009 (SI 2009/274) r.7 (April 1, 2009).

2. Tribunal Procedure (Amendment No.2) Rules 2009 (SI 2009/1975) rr.7 and 10 (September 1, 2009).

3. Tribunal Procedure (Amendment) Rules 2010 (SI 2010/43) rr.5 and 7 (January 18, 2010).
4. Tribunal Procedure (Upper Tribunal) (Amendment) Rules 2010 (SI 2010/747), rr.2 and 6 (April 6, 2010).
5. Tribunal Procedure (Amendment) Rules 2013 (SI 2013/477) rr.49–53 (April 1, 2013).
6. Tribunal Procedure (Amendment No. 4) Rules 2013 (SI 2013/2067) rr.2 and 6 (November 1, 2013).
7. Tribunal Procedure (Amendment) Rules 2014 (SI 2014/514) rr.2 and 6 (April 6, 2014).

DEFINITIONS

"the 2007 Act"—see r.1(3).
"financial services case"—*ibid.*
"national security certificate appeal"—*ibid.*
"party"—*ibid.*
"relevant Minister"—*ibid.*
"wholesale energy case"—*ibid.*

GENERAL NOTE

5.387 The effect of para.(1)(b) is that there is no power to award costs in social security cases on appeal from the First-tier Tribunal, because the First-tier Tribunal has no power to award costs in such cases (see r.10 of the Tribunal Procedure (First-tier Tribunal) (Social Entitlement Chamber) Rules 2008, above, and also the note to s.29 to the Tribunals, Courts and Enforcement Act 2007). Paragraph (2) has the effect that there is no power to award costs in cases under the Forfeiture Act 1982.

In many appeals from the Health, Education and Social Care Chamber, the General Regulatory Chamber, the Immigration and Asylum Chamber (since October 20, 2014) and the Tax Chamber of the First-tier Tribunal, the Upper Tribunal has a power to award costs if a party of its representative has acted unreasonably in bringing, defending or conducting the proceedings. It is clear that the fact that proceedings are unsuccessful does not mean that it was unreasonable to bring them (*Buckinghamshire CC v ST (SEN)* [2013] UKUT 468 (AAC); *DK v NHS England* [2014] UKUT 171 (AAC)).

Paragraph (3) leaves the general discretion to award costs in judicial review proceedings entirely unfettered. However, in *R.(LR) v First-tier Tribunal (HESC)* (Costs) [2013] UKUT 294 (AAC), a three-judge panel presided over by the Senior President of Tribunals has decided that in cases within the exclusive jurisdiction of the Administrative Appeals Chamber of the Upper Tribunal (as opposed to cases transferred to it by the High Court on a discretionary basis) where the respondent is a tribunal, the Upper Tribunal should not make an order for costs where the First-tier Tribunal would not have been able to do so. Thus the powers of the Upper Tribunal to award costs in judicial review proceedings against a tribunal are, at least for most practical purposes, the same as its powers on an appeal from that tribunal under para.(1)(b). This approach was followed in judicial review proceedings in a criminal injuries compensation case in *R.(H) v First-tier Tribunal (CIC)* [2014] UKUT 338 (AAC). However, the judge seems to have overlooked the fact that there is no power to award costs at all in the Social Entitlement Chamber of the First-tier Tribunal so, although he made no order for costs, he did so after considering whether the interested party had acted reasonably in resisting the applicant's case. In *R(MM and DM) v SSWP (Costs)* [2015] UKUT 566 (AAC); [2016] AACR 12, a three-judge panel has held that, in judicial review cases transferred to the Upper Tribunal from the High Court, costs are to be awarded in accordance with the principles that would be applied in the High Court.

Chapter 23 of the admirable *Administrative Court Judicial Review Guide 2016* published by Her Majesty's Courts and Tribunals Service (available at *https://www.gov.uk/government/uploads/system/uploads/attachment_data/file/540607/administrative-court-judicial-review-guide.pdf* [Accessed May 11, 2017]) contains a summary of the current practice as regards costs in the High Court.

For a case on wasted costs in the Immigration and Asylum Chamber of the Upper Tribunal, see *Okondu v Secretary of State for the Home Department* [2014] UKUT 377 (IAC), in which it was held that it was not necessarily improper, unreasonable or negligent to advance an unarguable case.

Notwithstanding the lack of specific provision in this rule, it has been held that the Upper Tribunal has the same power to make protective costs orders, costs capping orders and orders limiting costs in appeals as the High Court has. See *Drummond v HMRC* [2016] UKUT 221 (TCC), where it was said –

> "In exercising the same powers as the High Court to make a PCO, CCO or ACO, I take it as axiomatic that the UT should look to the same rules and criteria that govern the High Court when it exercises those powers, bearing in mind that the UT is governed by the UT Rules and especially the overriding objective in those rules and not the CPR. Whether to make such an order is a matter for the UT, in its discretion, to decide based on its evaluation of the circumstances of the case."

Where there is no power, or only a limited power, to award costs, it is important that, when directing under r.5(3)(i) that a party should prepare a bundle for a hearing, the Upper Tribunal considers upon whom the financial burden of preparing it should be placed. If it wishes the cost to be shared by two parties, it should direct them both to prepare it. See *Eclipse Film Partners No 35 LLP v Revenue and Customs Commissioners (No 2)* [2016] UKSC 24; [2016] 1 W.L.R. 1939.

The Upper Tribunal has no power akin to that conferred on some courts in England and Wales by s.194 of the Legal Services Act 2007 to order a sum of money to be paid to a prescribed charity (usually an organisation providing *pro bono* representation) where a party being represented *pro bono* has not actually incurred costs or expenses due to the conduct of another party but an order would have been made if the first party had been paying for representation (*Raftopoulou v HMRC* [2015] UKUT 630 (TCC)).

Representatives

11.—(1) [5 Subject to paragraph (5A),] a party may appoint a representative (whether a legal representative or not) to represent that party in the proceedings. [4 save that a party in an asylum or immigration case may not be represented by any person prohibited from representing by section 84 of the Immigration and Asylum Act 1999] 5.388

(2) If a party appoints a representative, that party (or the representative if the representative is a legal representative) must send or deliver to the Upper Tribunal [1 . . .] written notice of the representative's name and address.

[1 (2A) If the Upper Tribunal receives notice that a party has appointed a representative under paragraph (2), it must send a copy of that notice to each other party.]

(3) Anything permitted or required to be done by a party under these Rules, a practice direction or a direction may be done by the representative of that party, except signing a witness statement.

(4) A person who receives due notice of the appointment of a representative—

(a) must provide to the representative any document which is required to be provided to the represented party, and need not provide that document to the represented party; and

(b) may assume that the representative is and remains authorised as such until they receive written notification that this is not so from the representative or the represented party.

(5) [5 Subject to paragraph (5B),] at a hearing a party may be accompanied by another person whose name and address has not been notified under paragraph (2) but who, subject to paragraph (8) and with the permission of the Upper Tribunal, may act as a representative or otherwise assist in presenting the party's case at the hearing.

[5 (5A) In [6 immigration judicial review] proceedings, a party may appoint as a representative only a person authorised under the Legal Services Act 2007 to undertake the conduct of litigation in the High Court.

(5B) At a hearing of [6 immigration judicial review] proceedings, rights of audience before the Upper Tribunal are restricted to persons authorised to exercise those rights in the High Court under the Legal Services Act 2007.]

(6) Paragraphs (2) to (4) do not apply to a person who accompanies a party under paragraph (5).

(7) In a mental health case if the patient has not appointed a representative the Upper Tribunal may appoint a legal representative for the patient where—

(a) the patient has stated that they do not wish to conduct their own case or that they wish to be represented; or

(b) the patient lacks the capacity to appoint a representative but the Upper Tribunal believes that it is in the patient's best interests for the patient to be represented.

(8) In a mental health case a party may not appoint as a representative, or be represented or assisted at a hearing by—

(a) a person liable to be detained or subject to guardianship or after-care under supervision, or who is a community patient, under the Mental Health Act 1983; or

(b) a person receiving treatment for mental disorder at the same hospital [2 or] home as the patient.

[1 (9) In this rule "legal representative" means [3 a person who, for the purposes of the Legal Services Act 2007, is an authorised person in relation to an activity which constitutes the exercise of a right of audience or the conduct of litigaton within the meaning of that Act,] [4 a qualified person as defined in section 84(2) of the Immigration and Asylum Act 1999,], an advocate or solicitor in Scotland or a barrister or solicitor in Northern Ireland.]

[4 (10) In an asylum case or an immigration case, an appellant's representative before the First-tier Tribunal will be treated as that party's representative before the Upper Tribunal, unless the Upper Tribunal receives notice–

(a) of a new representative under paragraph (2) of this rule; or

(b) from the appellant stating that they are n longer represented.]

AMENDMENTS

1. Tribunal Procedure (Amendment) Rules 2009 (SI 2009/274) r.6 (April 1, 2009).

2. Tribunal Procedure (Amendment No.2) Rules 2009 (SI 2009/1975) rr.7 and 12 (September 1, 2009).

3. Tribunal Procedure (Amendment) Rules 2010 (SI 2010/43) rr.5 and 8 (January 18, 2010).
4. Tribunal Procedure (Amendment No.2) Rules 2010 (SI 2010/44) rr.2 and 8 (February 15, 2010).
5. Tribunal Procedure (Upper Tribunal) (Amendment) Rules 2011 (SI 2011/2343) rr.2 and 6 (October 17, 2011).
6. Tribunal Procedure (Amendment No. 4) Rules 2013 (SI 2013/2067) rr.2 and 7 (November 1, 2013).

DEFINITIONS

"asylum case"—see r.1(3).
"document"—*ibid.*
"hearing"—*ibid.*
"immigration case"—*ibid.*
"immigration judicial review proceedings"—*ibid.*
"legal representative"—see para.(9).
"mental health case"—see r.1(3).
"party"—*ibid.*
"permission"—*ibid.*
"practice direction"—*ibid.*

GENERAL NOTE

See the note to r.11(1) of the Tribunal Procedure (First-tier Tribunal) (Social Entitlement) Rules 2008. **5.389**

Paragraphs (2)–(4)

These paragraphs provide for the formal appointment of a representative who may then act on behalf of the party in all respects (except to sign a witness statement) and should be sent any documents that would otherwise be sent to the party. However, it is presumably possible for the Upper Tribunal to exclude a representative from a hearing under r.37(4) without excluding the party. **5.390**

Note that representatives, other than solicitors, barristers and advocates, are expected to provide written authority to act, signed by the party. In *CSDLA/2/2001*, two different representatives, each purporting to act on behalf of the same claimant, lodged separate applications for leave to appeal. The Commissioner said that a representative should obtain a fresh mandate from a claimant before sending what would now be an application for permission to appeal to the Upper Tribunal, rather than relying on a mandate obtained before a hearing before a lower tribunal. That would show that the representative had discussed the case with the claimant and had obtained specific instructions to apply for permission to appeal.

Paragraphs (5) and (6)

These paragraphs enable a party who is present at a hearing of a social security case to be represented or assisted at the hearing by any person, without there having been any formal notice of appointment. Although the Tribunal's permission is required, it is suggested that, unless r.37(4) applies, it will only exceptionally be appropriate for the Upper Tribunal to refuse permission, particularly as the party need only provide a written notice under para.(2) in order to avoid the need for permission. Without a written notice of appointment, a person who acts as a representative at a hearing has no rights as a representative outside the hearing. Obviously, a written notice may be provided at the hearing so that the person becomes entitled to act as a full representative thereafter. **5.391**

Paragraphs (7) and (8)

These paragraphs do not apply to social security cases. **5.392**

Calculating time

5.393 **12.**—(1) An act required by these Rules, a practice direction or a direction to be done on or by a particular day must be done by 5pm on that day.

(2) If the time specified by these Rules, a practice direction or a direction for doing any act ends on a day other than a working day, the act is done in time if it is done on the next working day.

(3) In a special educational needs case or a disability discrimination in schools case, the following days must not be counted when calculating the time by which an act must be done—

(a) 25th December to 1st January inclusive; and

(b) any day in August.

[[2] (3A) In an asylum case or an immigration case, when calculating the time by which an act must be done, in addition to the days specified in the definition of "working days" in rule 1 (interpretation), the following days must also not be counted as working days—

(a) 27th to 31st December inclusive; [[4] . . .]

(b) [[4] . . .]]

(4) Paragraph (3) [[2] or (3A)] does not apply where the Upper Tribunal directs that an act must be done by or on a specified date.

[[1] (5) [[3] . . .]]

Amendments

1. Tribunal Procedure (Amendment) Rules 2009 (SI 2009/274) r.9 (April 1, 2009).

2. Tribunal Procedure (Amendment No.2) Rules 2010 (SI 2010/44) rr.2 and 9 (February 15, 2010).

3. Tribunal Procedure (Amendment No.3) Rules 2014 (SI 2014/2128) rr.2 and 6(b) (September 1, 2014).

4. Tribunal Procedure (Amendment No.3) Rules 2014 (SI 2014/2128) rr.2 and 6(a) (October 20, 2014).

Definitions

"asylum case"—see r.1(3).
"disability discrimination in schools case"—*ibid.*
"immigration case"—*ibid.*
"practice direction"—*ibid.*
"special educational needs case"—*ibid.*
"working day"—*ibid.*

Sending and delivery of documents

5.394 **13.**—(1) Any document to be provided to the Upper Tribunal under these Rules, a practice direction or a direction must be—

(a) sent by pre-paid post or [[1] by document exchange, or delivered by hand] to the address specified for the proceedings;

(b) sent by fax to the number specified for the proceedings; or

(c) sent or delivered by such other method as the Upper Tribunal may permit or direct.

(2) Subject to paragraph (3), if a party provides a fax number, email address or other details for the electronic transmission of documents to them, that party must accept delivery of documents by that method.

(3) If a party informs the Upper Tribunal and all other parties that a

particular form of communication, other than pre-paid post or delivery by hand, should not be used to provide documents to that party, that form of communication must not be so used.

(4) If the Upper Tribunal or a party sends a document to a party or the Upper Tribunal by email or any other electronic means of communication, the recipient may request that the sender provide a hard copy of the document to the recipient. The recipient must make such a request as soon as reasonably practicable after receiving the document electronically.

(5) The Upper Tribunal and each party may assume that the address provided by a party or its representative is and remains the address to which documents should be sent or delivered until receiving written notification to the contrary.

[2 (6) Subject to paragraph (7), if a document submitted to the Upper Tribunal is not written in English, it must be accompanied by an English Translation.

(7) In proceedings that are in Wales or have a connection with Wales, a document or translation may be submitted to the [3 Upper] Tribunal in Welsh.]

AMENDMENTS

1. Tribunal Procedure (Amendment) Rules 2009 (SI 2009/274) r.10 (April 1, 2009).

2. Tribunal Procedure (Amendment No.2) Rules 2010 (SI 2010/44) rr.2 and 10 (February 15, 2010).

3. Tribunal Procedure (Amendment No. 4) Rules 2013 (SI 2013/2067) rr.2 and 8 (November 1, 2013).

DEFINITIONS

"asylum case"—see r.1(3).
"document"—*ibid.*
"immigration case"—*ibid.*
"party"—*ibid.*
"practice direction"—*ibid.*

GENERAL NOTE

See the note to r.13 of the Tribunal Procedure (First-tier Tribunal) (Social Entitlement Chamber) Rules 2008, above. **5.395**

Use of documents and information

14.—(1) The Upper Tribunal may make an order prohibiting the disclosure or publication of— **5.396**

(a) specified documents or information relating to the proceedings; or
(b) any matter likely to lead members of the public to identify any person whom the Upper Tribunal considers should not be identified.

(2) The Upper Tribunal may give a direction prohibiting the disclosure of a document or information to a person if—

(a) the Upper Tribunal is satisfied that such disclosure would be likely to cause that person or some other person serious harm; and
(b) the Upper Tribunal is satisfied, having regard to the interests of justice, that it is proportionate to give such a direction.

(3) If a party ("the first party") considers that the Upper Tribunal should give a direction under paragraph (2) prohibiting the disclosure of a document or information to another party ("the second party"), the first party must—

(a) exclude the relevant document or information from any documents that will be provided to the second party; and

(b) provide to the Upper Tribunal the excluded document or information, and the reason for its exclusion, so that the Upper Tribunal may decide whether the document or information should be disclosed to the second party or should be the subject of a direction under paragraph (2).

(4) [[1] . . .]

(5) If the Upper Tribunal gives a direction under paragraph (2) which prevents disclosure to a party who has appointed a representative, the Upper Tribunal may give a direction that the documents or information be disclosed to that representative if the Upper Tribunal is satisfied that—

(a) disclosure to the representative would be in the interests of the party; and

(b) the representative will act in accordance with paragraph (6).

(6) Documents or information disclosed to a representative in accordance with a direction under paragraph (5) must not be disclosed either directly or indirectly to any other person without the Upper Tribunal's consent.

(7) Unless the Upper Tribunal gives a direction to the contrary, information about mental health cases and the names of any persons concerned in such cases must not be made public.

[[1] (8) The Upper Tribunal may, on its own initiative or on the application of a party, give a direction that certain documents or information must or may be disclosed to the Upper Tribunal on the basis that the Upper Tribunal will not disclose such documents or information to other persons, or specified other persons.

(9) A party making an application for a direction under paragraph (8) may withhold the relevant documents or information from other parties until the Upper Tribunal has granted or refused the application.

(10) In a case involving matters relating to national security, the Upper Tribunal must ensure that information is not disclosed contrary to the interests of national security.

(11) The Upper Tribunal must conduct proceedings and record its decision and reasons appropriately so as not to undermine the effect of an order made under paragraph (1), a direction given under paragraph (2) or (8) or the duty imposed by paragraph (10).]

AMENDMENT

1. Tribunal Procedure (Amendment No.2) Rules 2009 (SI 2009/1975) rr.7 and 13 (September 1, 2009).

DEFINITIONS

"document"—see r.1(3).
"mental health case"—*ibid.*
"party"—*ibid.*

GENERAL NOTE

Paragraph (1)

An order under this paragraph may be directed to an individual and be concerned only with an individual document (e.g. prohibiting an appellant from disclosing to someone else a document disclosed to the appellant by the respondent) or it may be directed to the public in general and effectively amount to a reporting restriction. Hearings of social security cases are usually attended only by those immediately interested with them but most hearings are, in principle, open to the public, including the press (see r.37). It is difficult to envisage it being appropriate to prohibit the publication of any information at all about a hearing held in public (despite para. (7)) but it might often be appropriate to make an order prohibiting the publishing of information that may lead to a child or vulnerable adult being identified if there would otherwise be any serious risk of such publication. It will generally be necessary properly to balance the right of one person to respect of his or her private life under art.8 of the European Convention on Human Rights and the right of another person to freedom of expression under art.10 (see *Re British Broadcasting Corporation* [2009] UKHL 34; [2010] 1 A.C. 145, where it is noteworthy that, although the House of Lords discharged an anonymity order so as to permit the BBC to broadcast an acquitted defendant's name, it saw no need to mention his name itself). The existence of the powers conferred by this paragraph is a factor to be borne in mind when deciding under r.37(2) whether a hearing should be in private or in public, which requires consideration of the terms of art.6(1). See also *In re M (A Patient) (Court of Protection: Reporting Restrictions)* [2011] EWHC 1197 (Fam); [2012] 1 W.L.R. 287. Preventing the publication of parties' names may be appropriate even if a hearing is in public or the press are admitted to a private hearing (*L v L (Ancillary Relief Proceedings: Anonymity)* [2015] EWHC 2621 (Fam); [2016] 1 W.L.R. 1259). 5.397

Note para.(11), which requires the Upper Tribunal to conduct its proceedings and record its decisions and reasons appropriately so as not to undermine the effect of its order.

A breach of an order made under this paragraph is a contempt of court and may be punished by the Upper Tribunal under s.25 of the Tribunals, Courts and Enforcement Act 2007 by a term of imprisonment not exceeding two years and an unlimited fine.

A non-party may apply for a variation of an order under para.(1) without applying to be made a party to the proceedings. This was done in *Re X (Reporting restriction order: Variation)* [2015] UKUT 380 (AAC); [2016] AACR 6, where a local authority that had not been a party to proceedings before the Upper Tribunal was aware of them and of an order that had been made under r.14(1) and sought permission to disclose information relating to the proceedings to the police. Applying guidance given by the Court of Appeal in relation to care proceedings in *Re C (A Minor) (Care Proceedings: Disclosure)* [1997] Fam 76, the order prohibiting publication of any matter likely to lead members of the public to identify certain adults and children was varied so as to permit disclosure of the decision of the Upper Tribunal and the identities of individuals mentioned in it to the police and other relevant bodies for the limited purposes of investigating criminal offences, bringing prosecutions and protecting any child or vulnerable adult. If a non-party wishes to challenge the decision on such an application, it is unclear whether he or she must do so by way of an application for judicial review because only a party may appeal under s.13 of the Tribunals, Courts and Enforcement Act 2007 or whether an appeal is permissible. The circumstances in which there may be judicial review of a decision of the Upper Tribunal are limited (*R. (Cart) v Upper Tribunal (Public Law Project intervening)* [2011] UKSC 28; [2012] 1 A.C. 663; [2011] AACR 38) and, in *In re W (A Child) (Care Proceedings: Non-Party Appeal)* [2016] EWCA Civ 1140; [2017] 1 W.L.R. 2415, it was held that witnesses who were not parties to proceedings in the High Court were to be treated as parties for the purpose of the right of appeal to the

Court of Appeal in circumstances where they had effectively acquired the status of interveners and they would otherwise have had no way of challenging findings made against them that were affecting their professional careers.

The Administrative Appeals Chamber of the Upper Tribunal has a general practice of anonymising decisions in social security and child support cases and in many other types of case, when publishing them (other than to the parties) or when referring to them, but this does not amount to the making of orders under r.14(1). Unless a specific order is made, claimants or others who know about the cases are not subject to any reporting restrictions and, indeed, claimants may ask that their cases are not anonymised (*Adams v SSWP (CSM)* [2017] UKUT 9 (AAC)). However, staff in the Department for Work and Pensions, Her Majesty's Revenue and Customs and Her Majesty's Courts and Tribunals Service are prohibited from publishing information acquired in the course of their employment and which relates to a particular person (Social Security Administration Act 1992 s.123; Finance Act 1989 s.182).

Paragraphs (2)–(6)

5.398 See the note to r.14(2)–(6) of the Tribunal Procedure (First-tier Tribunal) (Social Entitlement Chamber) Rules 2008, above. Note para.(11), which requires the Upper Tribunal to conduct its proceedings and record its decisions and reasons appropriately so as not to undermine the effect of its direction. Particularly relevant will be the power in r.37(4)(c) to exclude a person from a hearing, and the power in r.40(2) not to provide a full decision, in order to give effect to a direction under para.(2).

Paragraph (7)

5.399 This paragraph does not apply to social security cases and, in applying to *all* information, appears anomalous.

Paragraphs (8)–(10)

5.400 Although these paragraphs are broadly expressed, they are unlikely to be relevant in social security cases.

Paragraph (11)

5.401 See, in particular, rr.37(4)(c) and 40(3), empowering the Upper Tribunal to exclude a person from proceedings and to record its decision and reasons so as to comply with this duty. Reporting restrictions under para.(1) may also be necessary in order to back up a direction under para.(2).

Evidence and submissions

5.402 **15.**—(1) Without restriction on the general powers in rule 5(1) and (2) (case management powers), the Upper Tribunal may give directions as to—

(a) issues on which it requires evidence or submissions;
(b) the nature of the evidence or submissions it requires;
(c) whether the parties are permitted or required to provide expert evidence, and if so whether the parties must jointly appoint a single expert to provide such evidence;
(d) any limit on the number of witnesses whose evidence a party may put forward, whether in relation to a particular issue or generally;
(e) the manner in which any evidence or submissions are to be provided, which may include a direction for them to be given—
  (i) orally at a hearing; or
  (ii) by written submissions or witness statement; and
(f) the time at which any evidence or submissions are to be provided.

(2) The Upper Tribunal may—
(a) admit evidence whether or not—
(i) the evidence would be admissible in a civil trial in the United Kingdom; or
(ii) the evidence was available to a previous decision maker; or
(b) exclude evidence that would otherwise be admissible where—
(i) the evidence was not provided within the time allowed by a direction or a practice direction;
(ii) the evidence was otherwise provided in a manner that did not comply with a direction or a practice direction; or
(iii) it would otherwise be unfair to admit the evidence.

[1 (2A) In an asylum case or an immigration case—
(a) if a party wishes the Upper Tribunal to consider evidence that was not before the First-tier Tribunal, that party must send or deliver a notice to the Upper Tribunal and any other party—
(i) indicating the nature of the evidence; and
(ii) explaining why it was not submitted to the First-tier Tribunal; and
(b) when considering whether to admit evidence that was not before the First-tier Tribunal, the Upper Tribunal must have regard to whether there has been unreasonable delay in producing that evidence.]

(3) The Upper Tribunal may consent to a witness giving, or require any witness to give, evidence on oath, and may administer an oath for that purpose.

AMENDMENT

1. Tribunal Procedure (Amendment No.2) Rules 2010 (SI 2010/44) rr.2 and 11 (February 15, 2010).

DEFINITIONS

"asylum case"—see r.1(3).
"hearing"—*ibid.*
"immigration case"—*ibid.*
"party"—*ibid.*
"practice direction"—*ibid.*

GENERAL NOTE

See the note to r.15 of the Tribunal Procedure (First-tier Tribunal) (Social Entitlement Chamber) Rules 2008, above. 5.403

Summoning or citation of witnesses and orders to answer questions or produce documents

16.—(1) On the application of a party or on its own initiative, the Upper Tribunal may— 5.404
(a) by summons (or, in Scotland, citation) require any person to attend as a witness at a hearing at the time and place specified in the summons or citation; or
(b) order any person to answer any questions or produce any documents in that person's possession or control which relate to any issue in the proceedings.

(2) A summons or citation under paragraph (1)(a) must—

(a) give the person required to attend 14 days' notice of the hearing or such shorter period as the Upper Tribunal may direct; and

(b) where the person is not a party, make provision for the person's necessary expenses of attendance to be paid, and state who is to pay them.

(3) No person may be compelled to give any evidence or produce any document that the person could not be compelled to give or produce on a trial of an action in a court of law in the part of the United Kingdom where the proceedings are due to be determined.

[1 (4) A person who receives a summons, citation or order may apply to the Upper Tribunal for it to be varied or set aside if they did not have an opportunity to object to it before it was made or issued.

(5) A person making an application under paragraph (4) must do so as soon as reasonably practicable after receiving notice of the summons, citation or order.

(6) A summons, citation or order under this rule must—

(a) state that the person on whom the requirement is imposed may apply to the Upper Tribunal to vary or set aside the summons, citation or order, if they did not have an opportunity to object to it before it was made or issued; and

(b) state the consequences of failure to comply with the summons, citation or order.]

AMENDMENT

1. Tribunal Procedure (Amendment) Rules 2009 (SI 2009/274) r.11 (April 1, 2009).

DEFINITIONS

"document"—see r.1(3).
"hearing"—*ibid.*
"party"—*ibid.*

GENERAL NOTE

5.405 This rule includes a power to order the production of documents without requiring attendance at a hearing. A failure to comply with a summons, citation or order under this rule is a contempt of court that may be punished by the Upper Tribunal with a term of imprisonment not exceeding two years and an unlimited fine under s.25 of the Tribunals, Courts and Enforcement Act 2007. In *MD v SSWP (Enforcement Reference)* [2010] UKUT 202 (AAC); [2011] AACR 5, a three-judge panel suggested that, when committal for contempt is being considered, a failure to comply with any of the procedural requirements is unlikely to be overlooked, unless it was clear that there was no prejudice or injustice to the alleged contemnor in doing so. It also suggested that a warning such as is required by r.16(6)(b) should be in explicit terms, referring to the possibility of imprisonment or a fine.

More controversially, when commenting on a failure to "make provision for the person's necessary expenses of attendance to be paid" (see r.16(2)(b)), it said that "[a] witness such as a doctor who is ordered to attend a hearing may clearly incur very considerable expenses". That is plainly a material consideration when deciding whether it is proportionate to issue a summons at all but it is not clear that r.16(2)(b) requires the payment of anything other than travel and subsistence expenses. Since then, it has been held by another three-judge panel in *CB v Suffolk CC (Enforcement Reference)* [2010] UKUT 202 (AAC); [2011] AACR 22 that the scheme of expenses for witnesses operated by the Tribunals Service, which was the same as that for jurors and covered travel expenses and loss of earnings up to a fixed limit, was sufficient for compliance with r.16(2)(b) and that it was not necessary to compensate for all financial loss.

Withdrawal

17.—(1) Subject to paragraph (2), a party may give notice of the withdrawal of its case, or any part of it— 5.406

(a) [2 . . .] by sending or delivering to the Upper Tribunal a written notice of withdrawal; or

(b) orally at a hearing.

(2) Notice of withdrawal will not take effect unless the Upper Tribunal consents to the withdrawal except in relation to an application for permission to appeal.

(3) A party which has withdrawn its case may apply to the Upper Tribunal for the case to be reinstated.

(4) An application under paragraph (3) must be made in writing and be received by the Upper Tribunal within 1 month after—

(a) the date on which the Upper Tribunal received the notice under paragraph (1)(a); or

(b) the date of the hearing at which the case was withdrawn orally under paragraph (1)(b).

(5) The Upper Tribunal must notify each party in writing [2 that a withdrawal has taken effect]under this rule.

[1 (6) Paragraph (3) does not apply to a financial services case other than a reference against a penalty.]

AMENDMENTS

1. Tribunal Procedure (Upper Tribunal) (Amendment) Rules 2010 (SI 2010/747) rr.2 and 7 (April 6, 2010).

2. Tribunal Procedure (Amendment) Rules 2013 (SI 2013/477) rr.49 and 54 (April 1, 2013).

DEFINITIONS

"financial service case"—see r.1(3).
"hearing"—*ibid.*
"party"—*ibid.*
"permission"—*ibid.*

GENERAL NOTE

This rule replaces reg.26 of the Social Security Commissioners (Procedure) Regulations 1999 but it applies to the withdrawal of a respondent's case as well as to the case of an appellant or person making a reference. The existence of the one-month time limit for an application for reinstatement, which did not exist in the old provision, may suggest that an application should be granted if made within that period unless there is a clear reason for not doing so, such as the previous conduct of the party, obvious lack of merit in the case or prejudice to another party. 5.407

17A. *Omitted.* 5.408

Notice of funding of legal services

5.409 **18.** If a party is granted funding of legal services at any time, that party must as soon as practicable—

(a) (i) if [1 civil legal services (within the meaning of section 8 of the Legal Aid, Sentencing and Punishment of Offenders Act 2012) are provided under arrangements made for the purposes of Part 1 of that Act or by] the Northern Ireland Legal Services Commission, send a copy of the [1 certificate or] funding notice to the Upper Tribunal; or

(ii) if funding is granted by the Scottish Legal Aid Board, send a copy of the legal aid certificate to the Upper Tribunal; and

(b) notify every other party in writing that funding has been granted.

AMENDMENT

1. Tribunal Procedure (Amendment) Rules 2013 (SI 2013/477) rr.49 and 55 (April 1, 2013).

DEFINITION

"party"—see r.1(3).

GENERAL NOTE

5.410 Public funding is rare in social security cases but it is helpful for a judge to know whether a party is funded if he or she is considering directing the party to produce a submission or a bundle of documents.

It will also be relevant in judicial review proceedings and other proceedings where the Upper Tribunal has the power to award costs.

[1 Confidentiality in social security and child support cases

5.411 **19.**—(1) Paragraph (4) applies to an appeal against a decision of the First-tier Tribunal—

(a) in proceedings under the Child Support Act 1991 in the circumstances described in paragraph (2), other than an appeal against a reduced benefit decision (as defined in section 46(10)(b) of the Child Support Act 1991, as that section had effect prior to the commencement of section 15(b) of the Child Maintenance and Other Payments Act 2008); or

(b) in proceedings where the parties to the appeal include former joint claimants who are no longer living together in the circumstances described in paragraph (3).

(2) The circumstances referred to in paragraph (1)(a) are that—

(a) in the proceedings in the First-tier Tribunal in respect of which the appeal has been brought, there was an obligation to keep a person's address confidential; or

(b) an absent parent, non-resident parent or person with care would like their address or the address of the child to be kept confidential and has given notice to that effect to the Upper Tribunal—

(i) in an application for permission to appeal or notice of appeal;

(ii) within 1 month after an enquiry by the Upper Tribunal; or

(iii) when notifying any subsequent change of address after proceedings have been started.

(3 The circumstances referred to in paragraph (1)(b) are that—
(a) in the proceedings in the First-tier Tribunal in respect of which the appeal has been brought, there was an obligation to keep a person's address confidential; or
(b) one of the former joint claimants would like their address to be kept confidential and has given notice to that effect to the Upper Tribunal—
  (i) in an application for permission to appeal or notice of appeal;
  (ii) within 1 month after an enquiry by the Upper Tribunal; or
  (iii) when notifying any subsequent change of address after proceedings have been started.

(4) Where this paragraph applies, the Secretary of State or other decision maker and the Upper Tribunal must take appropriate steps to secure the confidentiality of the address and of any information which could reasonably be expected to enable a person to identify the address, to the extent that the address or that information is not already known to each other party.

(5) In this rule—
"absent parent", "non-resident parent" and "person with care" have the meanings set out in section 3 of the Child Support Act 1991;
"joint claimants" means the persons who made a joint claim for a jobseeker's allowance under the Jobseekers Act 1995, a tax credit under the Tax Credits Act 2002 or in relation to whom an award of universal credit is made under Part 1 of the Welfare Reform Act 2012.]

AMENDMENT

1. Tribunal Procedure (Amendment No.3) Rules 2014 (SI 2014/2128) rr.2 and 7 (October 20, 2014).

DEFINITIONS

"absent parent"—see para.(5).
"joint claimants"—*ibid.*
"non-resident parent"—*ibid.*
"party"—see r.1(3).
"permission"—*ibid.*
"person with care" —see para.(5).

Power to pay expenses and allowances

20.—(1) In proceedings brought under section 4 of the Safeguarding Vulnerable Groups Act 2006 [1. . .], the Secretary of State may pay such allowances for the purpose of or in connection with the attendance of persons at hearings as the Secretary of State may, with the consent of the Treasury, determine. 5.412

(2) Paragraph (3) applies to proceedings on appeal from a decision of—
(a) the First-tier Tribunal in proceedings under the Child Support Act 1991, section 12 of the Social Security Act 1998 or paragraph 6 of Schedule 7 to the Child Support, Pensions and Social Security Act 2000;
(b) the First-tier Tribunal in a war pensions and armed forces case (as defined in the Tribunal Procedure (First-tier Tribunal) (War Pensions and Armed Forces Compensation Chamber) Rules 2008); or

(c) a Pensions Appeal Tribunal for Scotland or Northern Ireland.

(3) The Lord Chancellor (or, in Scotland, the Secretary of State) may pay to any person who attends any hearing such travelling and other allowances, including compensation for loss of remunerative time, as the Lord Chancellor (or, in Scotland, the Secretary of State) may determine.

AMENDMENT

1. Tribunal Procedure (Amendment) Rules 2009 (SI 2009/274) r.12 (April 1, 2009).

DEFINITIONS

"hearing"—see r.1(3).
"judicial review proceedings"—*ibid.*

GENERAL NOTE

5.413 Paragraph (1) does not apply to social security cases. Paragraphs (2) and (3) reproduce the effect of para.3 of Sch.4 to the Social Security Act 1998. Paragraph (2) suffers from the same defect as the old provision, which is that it does not apply to all social security cases in which claimants might be required to attend hearings, although in practice the Tribunals Service seems never to have refused to pay expenses to those not within the scope of the old provision (e.g. an injured person appealing against a decision under the Social Security (Recovery of Benefits) Act 1997).

The rule is also unsatisfactory because it seems unlikely that para.10(4) of Sch.5 to the Tribunals, Courts and Enforcement Act 2007 envisages Rules that give the Secretary of State the power to determine what expenses are to be paid, although it is perhaps more appropriate that the power should lie with the Secretary of State than with the Tribunal Procedure Committee.

5.414 **20A.** *Omitted.*

PART 3

[PROCEDURE FOR CASES IN]THE UPPER TRIBUNAL

Application to the Upper Tribunal for permission to appeal

5.415 **21.**—(1) [[1] . . .]

(2) A person may apply to the Upper Tribunal for permission to appeal to the Upper Tribunal against a decision of another tribunal only if—

(a) they have made an application for permission to appeal to the tribunal which made the decision challenged; and

(b) that application has been refused or has not been admitted. [[3] or has been granted only on limited grounds]

(3) An application for permission to appeal must be made in writing and received by the Upper Tribunal no later than—

(a) in the case of an application under section 4 of the Safeguarding Vulnerable Groups Act 2006, 3 months after the date on which written notice of the decision being challenged was sent to the appellant; [[2] . . .

(aa) [4. . .], in an asylum case or an immigration case where the appellant is in the United Kingdom at the time that the application is made—
   (i) [4 14] days after the date on which notice of the First-tier Tribunal's refusal of permission was sent to the appellant; or
   (ii) if the case is a fast-track case, four working days after the date on which notice of the First-tier Tribunal's refusal of permission was sent to the appellant;

(ab) [4 . . .] or]

(b) otherwise, a month after the date on which the tribunal that made the decision under challenge sent notice of its refusal of permission to appeal, or refusal to admit the application for permission to appeal, to the appellant.

[2 (3A) [4. . .]]

(4) The application must state—

(a) the name and address of the appellant;
(b) the name and address of the representative (if any) of the appellant;
(c) an address where documents for the appellant may be sent or delivered;
(d) details (including the full reference) of the decision challenged;
(e) the grounds on which the appellant relies; and
(f) whether the appellant wants the application to be dealt with at a hearing.

(5) The appellant must provide with the application a copy of—

(a) any written record of the decision being challenged;
(b) any separate written statement of reasons for that decision; and
(c) if the application is for permission to appeal against a decision of another tribunal, the notice of refusal of permission to appeal, or notice of refusal to admit the application for permission to appeal, from that other tribunal.

(6) If the appellant provides the application to the Upper Tribunal later than the time required by paragraph (3) or by an extension of time allowed under rule 5(3)(a) (power to extend time)—

(a) the application must include a request for an extension of time and the reason why the application was not provided in time; and
(b) unless the Upper Tribunal extends time for the application under rule 5(3)(a) (power to extend time) the Upper Tribunal must not admit the application.

(7) If the appellant makes an application to the Upper Tribunal for permission to appeal against the decision of another tribunal, and that other tribunal refused to admit the appellant's application for permission to appeal because the application for permission or for a written statement of reasons was not made in time—

(a) the application to the Upper Tribunal for permission to appeal must include the reason why the application to the other tribunal for permission to appeal or for a written statement of reasons, as the case may be, was not made in time; and
(b) the Upper Tribunal must only admit the application if the Upper Tribunal considers that it is in the interests of justice for it to do so.

[3 (8) In this rule, a reference to notice of a refusal of permission to appeal is to be taken to include a reference to notice of a grant of permission to appeal on limited grounds.]

AMENDMENTS

1. Tribunal Procedure (Amendment No.2) Rules 2009 (SI 2009/1975) rr.7 and 15 (September 1, 2009).
2. Tribunal Procedure (Amendment No.2) Rules 2010 (SI 2010/44) rr.2 and 13 (February 15, 2010).
3. Tribunal Procedure (Amendment) Rules 2014 (SI 2014/514) rr.2 and 7 (April 6, 2014).
4. Tribunal Procedure (Amendment No.3) Rules 2014 (SI 2014/2128) rr.2 and 8 (October 20, 2014).

DEFINITIONS

"appellant"—see r.1(3).
"asylum case"—see r.1(3).
"document"—*ibid.*
"hearing"—*ibid.*
"immigration case"—*ibid.*
"permission"—*ibid.*

GENERAL NOTE

5.416 This replaces regs 9 and 10 of the Social Security Commissioners (Procedure) Regulations 1999 but without the absolute time limit of 13 months and without any express duty on a public authority to notify a claimant that it has made an application.

Paragraph (2)

5.417 Paragraph (2) has given rise to some difficulties. Generally, it will be enforced because an application to the First-tier Tribunal gives it the opportunity to review its decision but there are circumstances where the existence of an irregularity emerges only after a case has apparently been properly brought before the Upper Tribunal or where the Upper Tribunal wishes to give permission in a case related to another one already before it. In such cases waiving the requirement to apply to the lower tribunal for permission might be sensible but there is disagreement as to whether it is permissible.

In *HM v SSWP* [2009] UKUT 40 (AAC), the claimant applied to what was then an appeal tribunal for leave to appeal but was then wrongly told that leave had been granted when in fact no decision had been made. The Upper Tribunal held it had no jurisdiction to consider the appeal, referring to *CSCS/4/2008*, where a Commissioner had said that a breach of the similar requirement in reg.9(1) of the Social Security Commissioners (Procedure) Regulations 1999 had not been the sort of irregularity that could be waived. However, in *MA v SSD* [2009] UKUT 57 (AAC), another judge disagreed with that approach and held that, as the requirement to obtain permission was imposed by the Rules rather than by primary legislation, it could be waived under r.7(2)(a). He did not in fact waive it in that case, where a chairman of a Pensions Appeal Tribunal had purported to grant leave to appeal but had done so unlawfully because the application had been made more than 13 months late, in breach of the absolute time-limit that then applied. The Upper Tribunal judge took the view that the Secretary of State should not have the advantage of the time bar removed retrospectively. If the irregularity was on the part of the Pensions Appeal Tribunal rather then the appellant, it is arguable that the power of waiver arose by implication under r.7(1) rather than expressly under r.7(2)(a) (see the note to r.7), although it is also arguable both that the material irregularity lay in the applicant making her application late and that r.21(2) imposes on an appellant a duty to obtain a valid decision so that the appellant is in any event in breach if the decision is invalid.

In *ZN v LB Redbridge (HB)* [2013] UKUT 503 (AAC), the Upper Tribunal followed *MA v SSD* [2009] UKUT 57 (AAC) in holding that the requirement to obtain a decision of the First-tier Tribunal on an application for permission to appeal could be waived.

The same view has been taken in the Immigration and Asylum Chamber of the Upper Tribunal when the First-tier Tribunal refused to consider the application made to it (*Ved v SSHD* [2014] UKUT 150 (IAC)).

Paragraphs (3)–(7)

Note that, under para.(3), the application must now be *received* by the Upper Tribunal within the time limit. The power to extend time is no longer limited to cases where there are "special reasons" but that may not make much difference in practice because the same considerations are likely to be relevant (see the note to r.38(5) of the Tribunal Procedure (First-tier Tribunal) (Social Entitlement Chamber) Rules 2008, above). Paragraph (7) makes it clear that, where an application for permission made to the First-tier Tribunal was made late but nonetheless accepted, there is no need for the Upper Tribunal to consider that delay (giving effect to *CIB/4791/2001*). Paragraph (7) also makes specific provision for cases where there is no statement of the First-tier Tribunal's reasons due to delay in applying for one. The word "any" in para.(5)(b) has the effect that there is no longer an irregularity just because no statement of reasons is submitted in such a case. However, it remains difficult to demonstrate an error of law without a statement of reasons and, in particular, the First-tier Tribunal's decision cannot be challenged on the ground of inadequacy of reasons in the absence of such a statement or a duty to provide one (*R(IS) 11/99*). 5.418

Decision in relation to permission to appeal

22.—(1) [4 [5 Except where rule 22A (special procedure for providing notice of a refusal of permission to appeal in an asylum case) applies],] if the Upper Tribunal refuses permission to appeal [3 or refuses to admit a late application for permission], it must send written notice of the refusal and of the reasons for the refusal to the appellant. 5.419

(2) If the Upper Tribunal gives permission to appeal—

(a) the Upper Tribunal must send written notice of the permission, and of the reasons for any limitations or conditions on such permission, to each party;

(b) subject to any direction by the Upper Tribunal, the application for permission to appeal stands as the notice of appeal and the Upper Tribunal must send to each respondent a copy of the application for permission to appeal and any documents provided with it by the appellant; and

(c) the Upper Tribunal may, with the consent of the appellant and each respondent, determine the appeal without obtaining any further response.

[1 (3) Paragraph (4) applies where the Upper Tribunal, without a hearing, determines an application for permission to appeal—

(a) against a decision of—

(i) the Tax Chamber of the First-tier Tribunal;

(ii) the Health, Education and Social Care Chamber of the First-tier Tribunal;

[2 (iia) the General Regulatory Chamber of the First-tier Tribunal;]

[3 (iib) the Property Chamber of the First-tier Tribunal;]

(iii) the Mental Health Review Tribunal for Wales; or

(iv) the Special Educational Needs Tribunal for Wales; or

(b) under section 4 of the Safeguarding Vulnerable Groups Act 2006.]

(4) In the circumstances set out at paragraph (3) the appellant may apply for the decision to be reconsidered at a hearing if the Upper Tribunal—

(a) refuses permission to appeal [3 or refuses to admit a late application for permission]; or

(b) gives permission to appeal on limited grounds or subject to conditions.

(5) An application under paragraph (4) must be made in writing and received by the Upper Tribunal within 14 days after the date on which the Upper Tribunal sent written notice of its decision regarding the application to the appellant.

AMENDMENTS

1. Tribunal Procedure (Amendment) Rules 2009 (SI 2009/274) r.14 (April 1, 2009).

2. Tribunal Procedure (Amendment No.2) Rules 2009 (SI 2009/1975) rr.7 and 16 (September 1, 2009).

3. Tribunal Procedure (Amendment) Rules 2014 (SI 2014/514) rr.2 and 8 (April 6, 2014).

4. Tribunal Procedure (Amendment No.2) Rules 2014 (SI 2014/1505) rr.2 and 3 (June 30, 2014).

5. Tribunal Procedure (Amendment No.3) Rules 2014 (SI 2014/2128) rr.2 and 9 (October 20, 2014).

DEFINITIONS

"appellant"—see r.1(3).
"document"—*ibid.*
"hearing"—*ibid.*
"party"—*ibid.*
"permission"—*ibid.*
"respondent"—*ibid.*

GENERAL NOTE

Paragraph (2)

5.420 Generally, applications for permission to appeal are considered without notice to the respondent and, when permission to appeal is granted by the Upper Tribunal, the application stands as the appeal and is sent to the respondent. In social security cases, the Upper Tribunal will have obtained the First-tier Tribunal's file to assist it determine the application and that will form the basis of the bundle of documents sent to the respondent (and to the appellant). The next stage in the proceedings will simply be for the respondent to submit a response under r.24. This is the effect of para.(2)(b).

However, where the respondent has had notice of the application and made submissions on it, it is possible to seek the consent of both parties to the appeal being determined without any further response. This is the effect of para.(2)(c).

In *Patel v Secretary of State for the Home Department* [2015] EWCA Civ 1175, the Court of Appeal held that a tribunal had no power informally to change a decision after it had been given orally. It said that the rule in the courts that a decision could be amended until an order was drawn up did not apply in tribunals where there is simply a decision and no distinction between a judgment and an order, it being relevant that there was an express power in r.40(1) to give a decision orally. Therefore, when a judge had said that he was granting permission to appeal, he could not later during the hearing consider whether he should refuse to admit the application for permission because it was late. The Court appears not to have been referred to the power of the Upper Tribunal to set aside decisions under r.43, which might have been relevant in that case (see *Jan v SSHD* [2016] UKUT 336 (IAC)), but that does not undermine the main thrust of its decision.

Paragraphs (3)–(5)

These paragraphs do not apply to social security cases on appeal from the Social Entitlement Chamber of the First-tier Tribunal. If the person applying for permission to appeal wants an oral hearing in a social security case, it is necessary to say so in the application for permission (see r.21(4)(f)). 5.421

In the absence of a power to certify an application for permission to appeal as being totally without merit so as prevent it being renewed orally under r.22(3) and (4) when it has been refused on the papers (compare r.30(4A)), the Upper Tribunal has exercised its power to strike out a renewed application when satisfied that it had no arguable merit and that the applicant had "had more than her day in court at the FTT" (*Gaskin v Information Commissioner* [2016] UKUT 382 (AAC)).

22A. *Omitted.* 5.422

Notice of appeal

23.—(1) [1 This rule applies— 5.423

(a) to proceedings on appeal to the Upper Tribunal for which permission to appeal is not required, except proceedings to which rule 26A [3 or 26B] applies;

(b) if another tribunal has given permission for a party to appeal to the Upper Tribunal; or

(c) subject to any other direction by the Upper Tribunal, if the Upper Tribunal has given permission to appeal and has given a direction that the application for permission to appeal does not stand as the notice of appeal.

[2 (1A) In an asylum case or an immigration case in which the First-tier Tribunal has given permission to appeal, subject to any direction of the First-tier Tribunal or the Upper Tribunal, the application for permission to appeal sent or delivered to the First-tier Tribunal stands as the notice of appeal and accordingly paragraphs (2) to (6) of this rule do not apply.]

(2) The appellant must provide a notice of appeal to the Upper Tribunal so that it is received within 1 month after—

(a) the date that the tribunal that gave permission to appeal sent notice of such permission to the appellant; or

[5 (b) if permission to appeal is not required, the date on which notice of decision to which the appeal relates—

(i) was sent to the appellant; or

(ii) in a quality contracts scheme case, if the notice was not sent to the appellant, the date on which the notice was published in a newspaper in accordance with the requirement of section 125 (notice and consultation requirements) of the Transport Act 2000.]]

(3) The notice of appeal must include the information listed in rule 21(4) (a) to (e) (content of the application for permission to appeal) and, where the Upper Tribunal has given permission to appeal, the Upper Tribunal's case reference.

(4) If another tribunal has granted permission to appeal, the appellant must provide with the notice of appeal a copy of—

(a) any written record of the decision being challenged;

(b) any separate written statement of reasons for that decision; and

(c) the notice of permission to appeal.

(5) If the appellant provides the notice of appeal to the Upper Tribunal later than the time required by paragraph (2) or by an extension of time allowed under rule 5(3)(a) (power to extend time)—

(a) the notice of appeal must include a request for an extension of time and the reason why the notice was not provided in time; and

(b) unless the Upper Tribunal extends time for the notice of appeal under rule 5(3)(a) (power to extend time) the Upper Tribunal must not admit the notice of appeal.

[[1] (6) When the Upper Tribunal receives the notice of appeal it must send a copy of the notice and any accompanying documents—

(a) to each respondent; or

(b) [[4] in a road transport case, to—

(i) the decision maker;

(ii) the appropriate national authority; and

(iii) in a case relating to the detention of a vehicle, the authorised person.]]

[[5] (7) Paragraph (6)(a) does not apply in a quality contracts scheme case, in respect of which Schedule A1 makes alternative and further provision.]

Amendments

1. Tribunal Procedure (Amendment No.2) Rules 2009 (SI 2009/1975) rr.7 and 17 (September 1, 2009).

2. Tribunal Procedure (Amendment No.2) Rules 2010 (SI 2010/44) rr.2 and 14 (February 15, 2010).

3. Tribunal Procedure (Upper Tribunal) (Amendment) Rules 2010 (SI 2010/747) rr.2 and 8 (April 6, 2010).

4. Tribunal Procedure (Amendment No.2) Rules 2012 (SI 2012/1363 rr.4 and 7 (July 1, 2012).

5. Tribunal Procedure (Amendment) Rules 2015 (SI 2015/1510) rr.2 and 4 (August 21, 2015).

Definitions

"appellant"—see r.1(3).
"appropriate national authority"—*ibid.*
"asylum case—*ibid.*
"authorised person"—*ibid.*
"document"—*ibid.*
"immigration case"—*ibid.*
"party"—*ibid.*
"permission"—*ibid.*
"quality contracts scheme case"—*ibid.*
"respondent"—*ibid.*
"road transport case"—*ibid.*

General Note

Paragraph (1)

5.424 Because r.22(2)(b) has the effect that an application for permission to appeal in a social security case almost invariably stands as an appeal where the Upper Tribunal has granted permission, this rule generally applies only where the First-tier Tribunal has granted permission to appeal.

Paragraph (5)

See the note to r.38(5) of the Tribunal Procedure (First-tier Tribunal) (Social Entitlement Chamber) Rules 2008, above. 5.425

Paragraph (6)

In practice in social security cases, the Upper Tribunal obtains the First-tier Tribunal's file and constructs its own bundle of documents. 5.426

Response to the notice of appeal

24.—[2 (1) This rule and rule 25 do not apply to [5 a road transport case], in respect of which Schedule 1 makes alternative provision. 5.427

(1A) Subject to any direction given by the Upper Tribunal, a respondent may provide a response to a notice of appeal.]

(2) Any response provided under paragraph [3 (1A)] must be in writing and must be sent or delivered to the Upper Tribunal so that it is received—

[4 (a) if an application for permission to appeal stands as the notice of appeal, no later than one month after the date on which the respondent was sent notice that permission to appeal had been granted;

(aa) in a fast-track case, [6 two days] before the hearing of the appeal; or]

[7 (ab) in a quality contracts scheme case, no later than 1 month after the date on which a copy of the notice of appeal is sent to the respondent;]

(b) in any other case, no later than 1 month after the date on which the Upper Tribunal sent a copy of the notice of appeal to the respondent.

(3) The response must state—

(a) the name and address of the respondent;

(b) the name and address of the representative (if any) of the respondent;

(c) an address where documents for the respondent may be sent or delivered;

(d) whether the respondent opposes the appeal;

(e) the grounds on which the respondent relies, including [2 (in the case of an appeal against another tribunal)] any grounds on which the respondent was unsuccessful in the proceedings which are the subject of the appeal, but intends to rely in the appeal; and

(f) whether the respondent wants the case to be dealt with at a hearing.

(4) If the respondent provides the response to the Upper Tribunal later than the time required by paragraph (2) or by an extension of time allowed under rule 5(3)(a) (power to extend time), the response must include a request for an extension of time and the reason why the [1 response] was not provided in time.

(5) When the Upper Tribunal receives the response it must send a copy of the response and any accompanying documents to the appellant and each other party.

[7 (6) Paragraph (5) does not apply in a quality contracts scheme case, in respect of which Schedule A1 makes alternative and further provision.]

AMENDMENTS

1. Tribunal Procedure (Amendment) Rules 2009 (SI 2009/274) r.15 (April 1, 2009).
2. Tribunal Procedure (Amendment No.2) Rules 2009 (SI 2009/1975) rr.7 and 18 (September 1, 2009).
3. Tribunal Procedure (Amendment) Rules 2010 (SI 2010/43) rr.5 and 9 (January 18, 2010).
4. Tribunal Procedure (Amendment No.2) Rules 2010 (SI 2010/44) rr.2 and 15 (February 15, 2010).
5. Tribunal Procedure (Amendment No.2) Rules 2012 (SI 2012/1363) rr.4 and 8 (July 1, 2012).
6. Tribunal Procedure (Amendment No.3) Rules 2014 (SI 2014/2128) rr.2 and 11 (October 20, 2014).
7. Tribunal Procedure (Amendment) Rules 2015 (SI 2015/1510) rr.2 and 5 (August 21, 2015).

DEFINITIONS

"appellant"—see r.1(3).
"document"—*ibid.*
"hearing"—*ibid.*
"party"—*ibid.*
"permission"—*ibid.*
"quality contracts scheme case"— *ibid.*
"respondent"—*ibid.*
"road transport case"—*ibid.*

GENERAL NOTE

5.428 If there is more than one respondent, this rule has the effect that they must make simultaneous responses unless the Upper Tribunal directs otherwise. In practice, it nearly always directs sequential responses from the respondents with the appellant replying after the last respondent has had an opportunity to respond to the appeal.

Appellant's reply

5.429 **25.**—(1) Subject to any direction given by the Upper Tribunal, the appellant may provide a reply to any response provided under rule 24 (response to the notice of appeal).

(2) [1 Subject to paragraph (2A), any] reply provided under paragraph (1) must be in writing and must be sent or delivered to the Upper Tribunal so that it is received within one month after the date on which the Upper Tribunal sent a copy of the response to the appellant.

[1 (2A) In an asylum case or an immigration case, the time limit in paragraph (2) is—

(a) one month after the date on which the Upper Tribunal sent a copy of the response to the appellant, or five days before the hearing of the appeal, whichever is the earlier; and
(b) in a fast-track case, the day of the hearing.

[2 (2B) In a quality contracts scheme case, the time limit in paragraph (2) is 1 month from the date on which the respondent sent a copy of the response to the appellant.]

(3) When the Upper Tribunal receives the reply it must send a copy of the reply and any accompanying documents to each respondent.

[2 (4) Paragraph (3) does not apply in a quality contracts scheme case, in respect of which Schedule A1 makes alternative and further provision.]

AMENDMENTS

1. Tribunal Procedure (Amendment No.2) Rules 2010 (SI 2010/44) rr.2 and 16 (February 15, 2010).

2. Tribunal Procedure (Amendment) Rules 2015 (SI 2015/1510) rr.2 and 6 (August 21, 2015).

DEFINITIONS

"appellant"—see r.1(3).
"asylum case"—*ibid.*
"document"—*ibid.*
"fast track case"—*ibid.*
"immigration case"—*ibid.*
"quality contracts scheme case"—*ibid.*
"respondent"—*ibid.*

GENERAL NOTE

This rule is expressly made subject to a direction by the Upper Tribunal. Where it appears to a judge granting permission to appeal that there is an obvious error in a decision of the First-tier Tribunal, it is common for the judge to direct simultaneous observations from all parties in order to speed up the process. **5.430**

References under the Forfeiture Act 1982

26.—(1) If a question arises which is required to be determined by the Upper Tribunal under section 4 of the Forfeiture Act 1982, the person to whom the application for the relevant benefit or advantage has been made must refer the question to the Upper Tribunal. **5.431**

(2) The reference must be in writing and must include—

(a) a statement of the question for determination;
(b) a statement of the relevant facts;
(c) the grounds upon which the reference is made; and
(d) an address for sending documents to the person making the reference and each respondent.

(3) When the Upper Tribunal receives the reference it must send a copy of the reference and any accompanying documents to each respondent.

(4) Rules 24 (response to the notice of appeal) and 25 (appellant's reply) apply to a reference made under this rule as if it were a notice of appeal.

DEFINITIONS

"document"—see r.1(3).
"respondent"—*ibid.*

GENERAL NOTE

This rule is made under s.4(2) of the Forfeiture Act 1982. **5.432**

[1 Cases transferred or referred to the Upper Tribunal, applications made directly to the Upper Tribunal and proceedings without notice to a respondent

26A.—(1) [2 Paragraphs (2) and (3) apply to— **5.433**

(a) a case transferred or referred to the Upper Tribunal from the First-tier Tribunal; or
(b) a case, other than an appeal or a case to which rule 26 (references

under the Forfeiture Act 1982) applies, which is started by an application made directly to the Upper Tribunal.]

(2) In a case to which this paragraph applies—

(a) the Upper Tribunal must give directions as to the procedure to be followed in the consideration and disposal of the proceedings; [4 ...]

[4 (aa) in a reference under Schedule 1D of the Charities Act 1993, the Upper Tribunal may give directions providing for an application to join the proceedings as a party and the time within which it may be made; and]

(b) the preceding rules in this Part will only apply to the proceedings to the extent provided for by such directions.

(3) If a case or matter to which this paragraph applies is to be determined without notice to or the involvement of a respondent—

(a) any provision in these Rules requiring a document to be provided by or to a respondent; and

(b) any other provision in these Rules permitting a respondent to participate in the proceedings

does not apply to that case or matter.]

[3 (4) Schedule 2 makes further provision for national security certificate appeals transferred to the Upper Tribunal.]

AMENDMENTS

1. Tribunal Procedure (Amendment) Rules 2009 (SI 2009/274) r.16 (April 1, 2009).

2. Tribunal Procedure (Amendment No.2) Rules 2009 (SI 2009/1975) rr.7 and 19 (September 1, 2009).

3. Tribunal Procedure (Amendment) Rules 2010 (SI 2010/43) rr.5 and 10 (January 18, 2010).

4. Tribunal Procedure (Amendment) Rules 2012 (SI 2012/500) r.5 (April 6, 2012).

DEFINITION

"national security certificate appeal"—see r.1(3).

GENERAL NOTE

5.434 This rule makes provision for cases other than appeals and references within the scope of r.26 by effectively leaving it to the Upper Tribunal to give case management directions on a case-by-case basis. It has no application to social security cases, except where a case is referred to the Upper Tribunal under s.9(5)(b) of the Tribunals, Courts and Enforcement Act 2007 or r.7(3) of the Tribunal Procedure (First-tier Tribunal) (Social Entitlement Chamber) Rules 2008.

5.435 **26B.** *Omitted.*

PART 4

JUDICIAL REVIEW PROCEEDINGS IN THE UPPER TRIBUNAL

Application of this Part to judicial review proceedings transferred to the Upper Tribunal

5.436 **27.**—(1) When a court transfers judicial review proceedings to the Upper Tribunal, the Upper Tribunal—

(a) must notify each party in writing that the proceedings have been transferred to the Upper Tribunal; and

(b) must give directions as to the future conduct of the proceedings.

(2) The directions given under paragraph (1)(b) may modify or disapply for the purposes of the proceedings any of the provisions of the following rules in this Part.

(3) In proceedings transferred from the Court of Session under section 20(1) of the 2007 Act, the directions given under paragraph (1)(b) must—

(a) if the Court of Session did not make a first order specifying the required intimation, service and advertisement of the petition, state the Upper Tribunal's requirements in relation to those matters;

(b) state whether the Upper Tribunal will consider summary dismissal of the proceedings; and

(c) where necessary, modify or disapply provisions relating to permission in the following rules in this Part.

DEFINITIONS

"the 2007 Act"—see r.1(3).
"judicial review proceedings"—*ibid.*
"party"—*ibid.*
"permission"—*ibid.*

GENERAL NOTE

This rule applies to judicial review proceedings transferred from a court, as opposed to proceedings started in the Upper Tribunal. Because cases may be transferred at any stage of the proceedings, the Upper Tribunal is given a broad power to give directions as to how the case will proceed and how much of rr.28–33 need apply to the case. At the time these Rules were made, rr. 28 and 29 could not cannot apply to cases transferred by the Court of Session, because there was no requirement to obtain permission to apply for judicial review in Scotland. Instead, the Upper Tribunal could hold a preliminary hearing to consider whether summary dismissal of the proceedings was appropriate, which would be equivalent to a first hearing in the Court of Session and had much the same effect as considering whether to refuse permission to apply for judicial review. Hence para.(3)(b) and r.30(2) and (3)(b). Now there is a requirement for permission (see s.20A of the Tribunals, Courts and Enforcement Act 2007 and the note to that section) but it appears not to have been thought necessary to amend these Rules. 5.437

Applications for permission to bring judicial review proceedings

28.—(1) A person seeking permission to bring judicial review proceedings before the Upper Tribunal under section 16 of the 2007 Act must make a written application to the Upper Tribunal for such permission. 5.438

(2) Subject to paragraph (3), an application under paragraph (1) must be made promptly and, unless any other enactment specifies a shorter time limit, must be sent or delivered to the Upper Tribunal so that it is received no later than 3 months after the date of the decision [1, action or omission] to which the application relates.

(3) An application for permission to bring judicial review proceedings challenging a decision of the First-tier Tribunal may be made later than the time required by paragraph (2) if it is made within 1 month after the date on which the First-tier Tribunal sent—

(a) written reasons for the decision; or

(b) notification that an application for the decision to be set aside has been unsuccessful, provided that that application was made in time.

(4) The application must state—

(a) the name and address of the applicant, the respondent and any other person whom the applicant considers to be an interested party;

(b) the name and address of the applicant's representative (if any);

(c) an address where documents for the applicant may be sent or delivered;

(d) details of the decision challenged (including the date, the full reference and the identity of the decision maker);

(e) that the application is for permission to bring judicial review proceedings;

(f) the outcome that the applicant is seeking; and

(g) the facts and grounds on which the applicant relies.

(5) If the application relates to proceedings in a court or tribunal, the application must name as an interested party each party to those proceedings who is not the applicant or a respondent.

(6) The applicant must send with the application—

(a) a copy of any written record of the decision in the applicant's possession or control; and

(b) copies of any other documents in the applicant's possession or control on which the applicant intends to rely.

(7) If the applicant provides the application to the Upper Tribunal later than the time required by paragraph (2) or (3) or by an extension of time allowed under rule 5(3)(a) (power to extend time)—

(a) the application must include a request for an extension of time and the reason why the application was not provided in time; and

(b) unless the Upper Tribunal extends time for the application under rule 5(3)(a) (power to extend time) the Upper Tribunal must not admit the application.

(8) [[2] Except where rule 28A(2)(a) (special provisions for [[3] immigration judicial review] proceedings) applies,] when the Upper Tribunal receives the application it must send a copy of the application and any accompanying documents to each person named in the application as a respondent or interested party.

AMENDMENTS

1. Tribunal Procedure (Amendment) Rules 2009 (SI 2009/274) r.17 (April 1, 2009).

2. Tribunal Procedure (Upper Tribunal) (Amendment) Rules 2011 (SI 2011/2343) rr.2 and 7 (October 17, 2011).

3. Tribunal Procedure (Amendment No. 4) Rules 2013 (SI 2013/2067) rr.2 and 10 (November 1, 2013).

DEFINITIONS

"the 2007 Act"—see r.1(3).

"applicant"—*ibid.*

"document"—*ibid.*

"immigration judicial review proceedings"—*ibid.*

"interested party"—*ibid.*

"judicial review proceedings"—*ibid.*

"party"—*ibid.*
"permission"—*ibid.*
"respondent"—*ibid.*

GENERAL NOTE

This rule applies to judicial review proceedings started in the Upper Tribunal (see the notes to ss.15 and 18 of the Tribunals, Courts and Enforcement Act 2007) Rule 9 gives the Upper Tribunal wide power to substitute the correct parties and add additional parties where the applicant fails to identify the correct respondent and interested party. Where, as will currently always be the case, the decision being challenged is a decision of the First-tier Tribunal, the respondent will be the First-tier Tribunal and the parties to the case before the First-tier Tribunal, other than the applicant, will be interested parties. **5.439**

Paragraph (3) provides for the extension of the three-month time limit in para.(2) but does not interfere with the requirement in para.(2) that an application be made "promptly" so that, where statements of reasons were provided over three years after the decision in one case and over 18 months after the decision in another, applications that could have been made without statements of reasons were held to be late even though made within a month of the statement of reasons being provided (*R.(CICA) v First-tier Tribunal* [2015] UKUT 299 (AAC); *R.(CICA) v First-tier Tribunal* [2015] UKUT 371 (AAC)).

28A. *Omitted.*

Acknowledgment of service

29.—(1) A person who is sent [3 or provided with] a copy of an application for permission under rule 28(8) (application for permission to bring judicial review proceedings) [3 or rule 28A(2)(a) (special provisions for [4 immigration judicial review] proceedings)] and wishes to take part in the proceedings must [3 provide] to the Upper Tribunal an acknowledgment of service so that it is received no later than 21 days after the date on which the Upper Tribunal sent [3, or in [4 immigration judicial review] proceedings the applicant provided,] a copy of the application to that person. **5.440**

(2) An acknowledgment of service under paragraph (1) must be in writing and state—

(a) whether the person intends to [1 support or] oppose the application for permission;
(b) their grounds for any [1 support or] opposition under sub-paragraph (a), or any other submission or information which they consider may assist the Upper Tribunal; and
(c) the name and address of any other person not named in the application as a respondent or interested party whom the person providing the acknowledgment considers to be an interested party.

[3 (2A) In [4 immigration judicial review] proceedings, a person who provides an acknowledgement of service under paragraph (1) must also provide a copy to—

(a) the applicant; and
(b) any other person named in the application under rule 28(4)(a) or acknowledgement of service under paragraph (2)(c)

no later than the time specified in paragraph (1).]

(3) A person who is sent [3 or provided with] a copy of an application for permission under rule 28(8) [3 or 28A(2)(a)] but does not provide an acknowledgment of service [3 to the Upper Tribunal] may not take part

in the application for permission [2 unless allowed to do so by the Upper Tribunal], but may take part in the subsequent proceedings if the application is successful.

AMENDMENTS

1. Tribunal Procedure (Amendment) Rules 2009 (SI 2009/274) r.18 (April 1, 2009).
2. Tribunal Procedure (Amendment) Rules 2011 (SI 2011/651) r.8(1) and (3) (April 1, 2011).
3. Tribunal Procedure (Upper Tribunal) (Amendment) Rules 2011 (SI 2011/2343) rr.2 and 9 (October 17, 2011).
4. Tribunal Procedure (Amendment No. 4) Rules 2013 (SI 2013/2067) rr.2 and 12 (November 1, 2013).

DEFINITIONS

"immigration judicial review proceedings"—see r.1(3).
"interested party"—*ibid.*
"judicial review proceedings"—*ibid.*
"party"—*ibid.*
"permission"—*ibid.*
"respondent"—*ibid.*

GENERAL NOTE

5.441 This rule, including the 21-day time limit, is based on the procedure in the Administrative Court in England and Wales under CPR rr.54.8 and 54.9. The respondent, i.e. the First-tier Tribunal whose decision is being challenged, will only rarely take part in proceedings, so that it will fall to the interested parties to decide whether or not to oppose the application, just as it does on an appeal.

Decision on permission or summary dismissal, and reconsideration of permission or summary dismissal at a hearing

5.442 **30.**—(1) The Upper Tribunal must send to the applicant, each respondent and any other person who provided an acknowledgment of service to the Upper Tribunal, and may send to any other person who may have an interest in the proceedings, written notice of—

(a) its decision in relation to the application for permission; and

[3 (b) the reasons for any—

(i) refusal of the application or refusal to admit the late application, or

(ii) limitations or conditions on permission.]

(2) In proceedings transferred from the Court of Session under section 20(1) of the 2007 Act, where the Upper Tribunal has considered whether summarily to dismiss of the proceedings, the Upper Tribunal must send to the applicant and each respondent, and may send to any other person who may have an interest in the proceedings, written notice of—

(a) its decision in relation to the summary dismissal of proceedings; and

(b) the reasons for any decision summarily to dismiss part or all of the proceedings, or any limitations or conditions on the continuation of such proceedings.

(3) Paragraph (4) applies where the Upper Tribunal, without a hearing—

[3 (a) determines an application for permission to bring judicial review proceedings by—

(i) refusing permission or refusing to admit the late application, or

(ii) giving permission on limited grounds or subject to conditions];

(b) in proceedings transferred from the Court of Session, summarily dismisses part or all of the proceedings, or imposes any limitations or conditions on the continuation of such proceedings.

(4) [2 Subject to paragraph (4A), in] the circumstances specified in paragraph (3) the applicant may apply for the decision to be reconsidered at a hearing.

[2 (4A) Where the Upper Tribunal refuses permission to bring immigration judicial review proceedings [3 or refuses to admit a late application for permission to bring such proceedings] and considers the application to be totally without merit, it shall record that fact in its decision notice and, in those circumstances, the applicant may not request the decision to be reconsidered at a hearing.]

(5) An application under paragraph (4) must be made in writing and must be sent or delivered to the Upper Tribunal so that it is received within 14 days [1 , or in [2 immigration judicial review] proceedings 9 days,] after the date on which the Upper Tribunal sent written notice of its decision regarding the application to the applicant.

AMENDMENTS

1. Tribunal Procedure (Upper Tribunal) (Amendment) Rules 2011 (SI 2011/2343) rr.2 and 10 (October 17, 2011).

2. Tribunal Procedure (Amendment No. 4) Rules 2013 (SI 2013/2067) rr.2 and 13 (November 1, 2013).

3. Tribunal Procedure (Amendment) Rules 2014 (SI 2014/514) rr.2 and 11 (April 6, 2014).

DEFINITIONS

"the 2007 Act"—see r.1(3).
"applicant"—*ibid.*
"immigration judicial review proceedings"—*ibid.*
"hearing"—*ibid.*
"judicial review proceedings"—*ibid.*
"permission"—*ibid.*
"respondent"—*ibid.*

GENERAL NOTE

This rule is based on the procedure in the Administrative Court in England and Wales under CPR rr.54.10–54.12. An application for permission to apply for judicial review that is refused, or is only partially successful, on paper may be renewed at an oral hearing under paras (3)(a) and (4). Dismissal of judicial review proceedings at a first hearing under RC r.58.9 was the equivalent in Scotland of a refusal of permission to apply for judicial review in England and Wales or Northern Ireland and so equivalent provision for summary dismissal by the Upper Tribunal is made in paras (3)(b) and (4). However, there is now a requirement for permission in Scotland by virtue of s.20A of the Tribunals, Courts and Enforcement Act 2007. This rule has not been amended, perhaps because it is considered unnecessary to do so in view of the terms of s.20A itself. 5.443

For the purposes of para.(4A), which does not apply to social security cases, a claim for judicial review may be "totally without merit" if it is bound to fail, even if it is not abusive or vexatious (*R. (Grace) v Secretary of State for the Home Department* [2014] EWCA Civ 1091; [2014] 1 W.L.R. 3432).

In *R. (Wasif) v Secretary of State for the Home Department (Practice Note)* [2016]

EWCA Civ 82; [2016] 1 W.L.R. 2793, the Court of Appeal has said that the question is essentially whether there is any prospect of a judge being persuaded to grant permission following an oral hearing, bearing in mind that one purpose of a hearing would be to give the claimant an opportunity to address issues that may not have been anticipated in the original grounds. The Court also said that, while reasons for refusing permission that are given in summary form are acceptable when the applicant has the right to renew the application, where certification is made care is needed to ensure that all the applicant's points are identified and addressed. Reasons for certification should be separate from reasons for refusing permission, since the tests are not the same. Finally, the Court said that certification of a case as totally without merit is not appealable as such; any appeal must be against the refusal of permission.

The right to apply under r.30(4) for reconsideration at a hearing when permission has been refused on the papers makes it inappropriate to seek permission to appeal to the Court of Appeal against a refusal of permission on the papers (*R. (MD Afghanistan) v Secretary of State for the Home Department* [2012] EWCA Civ 194; [2012] 1 W.L.R. 2422). An application for permission to appeal is therefore likely to be treated as an application for reconsideration.

In *R. (Kigen) v Secretary of State for the Home Department* [2015] EWCA Civ 1286, [2016] 1 W.L.R. 723, the Court of Appeal gave guidance as to the approach to be taken to extending time under r.5(3)(a) for making an application for reconsideration. Following the approach taken in *R. (Hysaj) v Secretary of State for the Home Department* [2014] EWCA Civ 1663; [2015] 1 W.L.R. 2472 in relation to time limits for appealing to the Court of Appeal, it said that a three-stage approach should be adopted by (i) assessing the seriousness and significance of the failure to comply with the time limit, (ii) considering why the default occurred and (iii) evaluating all the circumstances of the case, so as to enable the tribunal to deal justly with the application.

Responses

5.444 **31.**—(1) Any person to whom the Upper Tribunal has sent notice of the grant of permission under rule 30(1) (notification of decision on permission), and who wishes to contest the application or support it on additional grounds, must provide detailed grounds for contesting or supporting the application to the Upper Tribunal.

(2) Any detailed grounds must be provided in writing and must be sent or delivered to the Upper Tribunal so that they are received not more than 35 days after the Upper Tribunal sent notice of the grant of permission under rule 30(1).

DEFINITION

"permission"—see r.1(3).

GENERAL NOTE

5.445 This rule, including the 35-day time limit, is based on the procedure in the Administrative Court in England and Wales under CPR r.54.14(a).

Applicant seeking to rely on additional grounds

5.446 **32.** The applicant may not rely on any grounds, other than those grounds on which the applicant obtained permission for the judicial review proceedings, without the consent of the Upper Tribunal.

DEFINITIONS

"applicant"—see r.1(3).
"judicial review proceedings"—*ibid.*
"permission"—*ibid.*

GENERAL NOTE

This rule is based on the procedure in the Administrative Court in England and Wales under CPR r.54.15. 5.447

Right to make representations

33. Each party and, with the permission of the Upper Tribunal, any other person, may— 5.448

(a) submit evidence, except at the hearing of an application for permission;
(b) make representations at any hearing which they are entitled to attend; and
(c) make written representations in relation to a decision to be made without a hearing.

DEFINITIONS

"hearing"—see r.1(3).
"party"—*ibid.*
"permission"—*ibid.*

GENERAL NOTE

This rule is based on the procedure in the Administrative Court in England and Wales under CPR rr.54.14(b) and 54, 17. 5.449

[1 Amendments and additional grounds resulting in transfer of proceedings to the High Court in England and Wales

33A.—(1) This rule applies only to judicial review proceedings arising under the law of England and Wales. 5.450

(2) In relation to such proceedings—

(a) the powers of the Upper Tribunal to permit or require amendments under rule 5(3)(c) extend to amendments which would, once in place, give rise to an obligation or power to transfer the proceedings to the High Court in England and Wales under section 18(3) of the 2007 Act or paragraph (3);
(b) except with the permission of the Upper Tribunal, additional grounds may not be advanced, whether by an applicant or otherwise, if they would give rise to an obligation or power to transfer the proceedings to the High Court in England and Wales under section 18(3) of the 2007 Act or paragraph (3).

(3) Where the High Court in England and Wales has transferred judicial review proceedings to the Upper Tribunal under any power or duty and subsequently the proceedings are amended or any party advances additional grounds—

(a) if the proceedings in their present form could not have been transferred to the Upper Tribunal under the relevant power or duty had they been in that form at the time of the transfer, the Upper Tribunal must transfer the proceedings back to the High Court in England and Wales;

(b) subject to sub-paragraph (a), where the proceedings were transferred to the Upper Tribunal under section 31A(3) of the Senior Courts Act 1981 (power to transfer judicial review proceedings to the Upper Tribunal), the Upper Tribunal may transfer proceedings back to the High Court in England and Wales if it appears just and convenient to do so.]

AMENDMENT

1. Tribunal Procedure (Upper Tribunal) (Amendment) Rules 2011 (SI 2011/2343) rr.2 and 11 (October 17, 2011).

DEFINITIONS

"applicant"—see r.1(3).
"judicial review proceedings—*ibid.*
"party"—*ibid.*

GENERAL NOTE

5.451 The Upper Tribunal has only a limited jurisdiction to hear judicial review proceedings (see ss.15–21 of the Tribunals, Courts and Enforcement Act 2007, set out in the main work). Rule 33A makes provision for cases where amendments to such proceedings might make it appropriate for the Upper Tribunal to transfer the case to the High Court in England and Wales, even where the High Court has originally transferred the case to the Upper Tribunal. No equivalent provision has been made in respect of Scotland or Northern Ireland but, so far, there have not been any judicial review proceedings in the Upper Tribunal in those parts of the United Kingdom. There may be some cases where it is appropriate to split the proceedings and transfer to the High Court only that part not within the jurisdiction of the Upper Tribunal but in other cases it will be preferable to keep the proceedings together and, if the Upper Tribunal does not have jurisdiction in respect of part of them, transfer the whole proceedings to the High Court. Alternatively, para.(2)(b) enables the Upper Tribunal to refuse to permit an amendment that might require proceedings to be transferred to the High Court, which would leave the party seeking the amendment to consider bringing separate proceedings in the High Court.

The background to this rule was explained in detail in *R. (B) v Secretary of State for the Home Department* [2016] UKUT 182 (IAC) by Walker J., who was chairman of the Tribunal Procedure Committee when the rule was introduced. The parties had agreed that judicial review proceedings that had been transferred to the Upper Tribunal should be transferred back to the High Court so that it could consider an application for permission to amend the claim to add a claim for a declaration of incompatibility under s.4 of the Human Rights Act 1998. Walker J. pointed out that that was inappropriate in the light of this rule and that the proper procedure was to make the application for permission to amend to the Upper Tribunal, with the proceedings being transferred to the High Court only if the amendment were allowed. On reflection, the parties agreed that such an application would be premature.

PART 5

HEARINGS

Decision with or without a hearing

34.—(1) Subject to [1 paragraphs (2) and (3)], the Upper Tribunal may make any decision without a hearing. 5.452

(2) The Upper Tribunal must have regard to any view expressed by a party when deciding whether to hold a hearing to consider any matter, and the form of any such hearing.

[1 (3) In immigration judicial review proceedings, the Upper Tribunal must hold a hearing before making a decision which disposes of proceedings.

(4) Paragraph (3) does not affect the power of the Upper Tribunal to—

(a) strike out a party's case, pursuant to rule 8(1)(b) or 8(2);

(b) consent to withdrawal, pursuant to rule 17;

(c) determine an application for permission to bring judicial review proceedings, pursuant to rule 30; or

(d) make a consent order disposing of proceedings, pursuant to rule 39,

without a hearing.]

AMENDMENT

1. Tribunal Procedure (Amendment No. 4) Rules 2013 (SI 2013/2067) rr.2 and 14 (November 1, 2013).

DEFINITIONS

"hearing"—see r.1(3).
"immigration judicial review proceedings"—*ibid.*
"party"—*ibid.*

GENERAL NOTE

The European Convention on Human Rights does not require a second-tier tribunal such as the Upper Tribunal to hold an oral hearing where there has been an opportunity to have an oral hearing before the First-Tier tribunal (*Hoppe v Germany* [2003] F.L.R. 384, *Fexler v Sweden* ECtHR Application No. 36801/06). At common law a case can be determined without an oral hearing unless that would be unfair because, for instance, oral evidence is required (*R.(O'Connell) v Parole Board* [2007] EWHC 2591 (Admin); [2008] 1 W.L.R 979) or the case is complex (*R. (Thompson) v Law Society* [2004] EWCA Civ 167; [2004] 1 W.L.R. 2522). It is suggested that the Upper Tribunal is entitled to refuse a request for an oral hearing where oral evidence would be irrelevant and there is no reason to suppose that oral argument could make any difference to the outcome. 5.453

A judge who is minded to reject a claimant's appeal despite the fact that it has been supported by the Secretary of State is not bound to direct an oral hearing if no request for a hearing has been made despite an opportunity having been given (*Miller v Secretary of State for Work and Pensions*, 2002 G.W.D. 25–861, IH).

This rule replaces reg.23 of the Social Security Commissioners (Procedure) Regulations 1999. Regulation 23(2) specifically sated that, where a request for a hearing was made by a party, "the Commissioner shall grant the request unless he is satisfied that the proceedings can properly be determined without a hearing" but the absence of a similar provision in this rule may well make no difference because a refusal of a request for a hearing must be for a good reason. In practice, requests by unrepresented claimants are often refused because the judge is prepared to decide the case in favour of the claimant or because they are made specifically for the purpose of giving evidence in circumstances where the appeal lies on a point of law in respect of which it is clear the claimant will be unable to provide any assistance. It will normally be appropriate to give a written reason for refusing a request for an oral hearing (see r.40(4)). A direction as to whether there will be a hearing falls within the scope of r.5 (see r.5(3)(f)) and so the provisions of r.6 apply. A person applying for permission to appeal to the Upper Tribunal should indicate whether he or she wants the application to be determined at a hearing (see r.21(4)(f)), which is particularly important in social security cases where there is no right to renew orally an application refused on paper. A respondent should indicate whether or not he or she wishes there to be an oral hearing when submitting a response to an appeal or reference (see r.24(3)(f)) and the appellant is usually asked by the Upper Tribunal to do so when replying, although there is no specific provision to that effect in r.25.

Entitlement to attend a hearing

5.454 **35.**—(1) Subject to rule 37(4) (exclusion of a person from a hearing), each party is entitled to attend a hearing.

[1 (2) In a national security certificate appeal the relevant Minister is entitled to attend any hearing.]

AMENDMENT

1. Tribunal Procedure (Amendment) Rules 2010 (SI 2010/43) rr.5 and 11 (January 18, 2010).

DEFINITIONS

"hearing"—see r.1(3).
"national security certificate appeal"—*ibid.*
"party"—*ibid.*
"relevant Minister"—*ibid.*

GENERAL NOTE

5.455 This rule makes it plain that, except where r.37(4) applies, a party may always attend a hearing even when the hearing is in private. By virtue of r.11(3) a properly appointed representative also has a right to attend a hearing, whether or not the party does so. By virtue of r.11(5), a party who attends a hearing may be accompanied by a person acting as a representative or assistant.

Notice of hearings

5.456 **36.**—(1) The Upper Tribunal must give each party entitled to attend a hearing reasonable notice of the time and place of the hearing (including any adjourned or postponed hearing) and any change to the time and place of the hearing.

(2) The period of notice under paragraph (1) must be at least 14 days except that—

(a) in applications for permission to bring judicial review proceedings, the period of notice must be at least 2 working days; [1 . . .
(aa) in a fast-track case the period of notice must be at least one working day; and]
(b) [1 in any case other than a fast-track case] the Upper Tribunal may give shorter notice—

(i) with the parties' consent; or
(ii) in urgent or exceptional cases.

AMENDMENT

1. Tribunal Procedure (Amendment) (No.2) Rules 2010 (SI 2010/44) rr.2 and 17 (February 15, 2010).

DEFINITIONS

"fast-track case"—see r.1(3).
"hearing"—*ibid.*
"judicial review proceedings"—*ibid.*
"party"—*ibid.*
"permission"—*ibid.*
"working day"—*ibid.*

36A. *Omitted.* 5.457

Public and private hearings

37.—(1) Subject to the following paragraphs, all hearings must be held in public. 5.458

(2) The Upper Tribunal may give a direction that a hearing, or part of it, is to be held in private.

[[3] (2A) In a national security certificate appeal, the Upper Tribunal must have regard to its duty under rule 14(10) (no disclosure of information contrary to the interests of national security) when considering whether to give a direction that a hearing, or part of it, is to be held in private.]

(3) Where a hearing, or part of it, is to be held in private, the Upper Tribunal may determine who is entitled to attend the hearing or part of it.

(4) The Upper Tribunal may give a direction excluding from any hearing, or part of it—

(a) any person whose conduct the Upper Tribunal considers is disrupting or is likely to disrupt the hearing;
(b) any person whose presence the Upper Tribunal considers is likely to prevent another person from giving evidence or making submissions freely;
(c) any person who the Upper Tribunal considers should be excluded in order to give effect to [[2] the requirement at rule 14(11) (prevention of disclosure or publication of documents and information)]; or
(d) any person where the purpose of the hearing would be defeated by the attendance of that person [[1] ; or
(e) a person under [[4] 18, other than a young person who is a party in a special educational needs case or a disability discrimination in schools case].]

(5) The Upper Tribunal may give a direction excluding a witness from a hearing until that witness gives evidence.

AMENDMENTS

1. Tribunal Procedure (Amendment) Rules 2009 (SI 2009/274) r.19 (April 1, 2009).
2. Tribunal Procedure (Amendment No.2) Rules 2009 (SI 2009/1975) regs 7 and 20 (September 1, 2009).

3. Tribunal Procedure (Amendment) Rules 2010 (SI 2010/43) regs 5 and 12 (January 18, 2010).
4. Tribunal Procedure (Amendment No.3) Rules 2014 (SI 2014/2128) rr.2 and 13 (September 1, 2014).

DEFINITIONS

"disability discrimination in schools case"—see r.1(3).
"hearing"—*ibid.*
"national security certificate appeal"—*ibid.*
"special educational needs case" —*ibid.*
"young person" —*ibid.*

GENERAL NOTE

Paragraphs (1) and (2)

5.459 These paragraphs replace reg.24(5) of the Social Security Commissioners (Procedure) Regulations 1999. Paragraph (1) expresses the general rule, which is that hearings should usually be in public. Paragraph (2) enables the Upper Tribunal to direct that a particular case be heard in private, either in whole or in part. Although it does not specifically provide that a hearing may take place in public only for "special reasons", as reg.24(5) did, the same considerations will still apply. See the notes to r.30(1) and (3) of the Tribunal Procedure (First-tier Tribunal) (Social Entitlement Chamber) Rules 2008 for the meaning of "in public" and considerations relevant to a decision to hold a hearing in private. As in the First-tier Tribunal, this does not arise as a live issue very often because it is very rare for members of the general public to attend hearings. Where someone does attend, concerns raised by a party can often be met by the imposition of appropriate reporting restrictions under r.14(1). Hearings of the Upper Tribunal are usually recorded. Such a recording is a document for the purposes of s.32 of the Freedom of Information Act 2000 and so the question whether it should be disclosed to any person is a matter for the Upper Tribunal and not for the Information Commissioner (*Edem v Information Commissioner* [2015] UKUT 210 (AAC)).

Paragraph (3)

5.460 If a case is to be heard in private, the tribunal has a broad power to determine who may attend it. However, certain people have a right to attend a hearing even if it is in private. By r.35, a party always has a right to be present (subject to r.37(4)) and, the consequence is that, by virtue of r.11(3), so does a properly appointed representative whether the party attends or not. Where a party does attend, he or she may be accompanied by a person acting either as a representative or merely as an assistant (see r.11(5)). Plainly relevant witnesses must be allowed to attend for the purpose of giving evidence.

Beyond that, it is all a matter of discretion, as it was under reg.24(6)(g) of the Social Security Commissioners (Procedure) Regulations 1999. See the note to r.30(4) of the Tribunal Procedure (First-tier Tribunal) (Social Entitlement Chamber) Rules 2008, above.

Paragraphs (4) and (5)

5.461 See the notes to r.30(5) and (6) of the Tribunal Procedure (First-tier Tribunal) (Social Entitlement Chamber) Rules 2008, above, but note that a power to exclude children has been added.

Hearings in a party's absence

5.462 **38.** If a party fails to attend a hearing, the Upper Tribunal may proceed with the hearing if the Upper Tribunal—

(a) is satisfied that the party has been notified of the hearing or that reasonable steps have been taken to notify the party of the hearing; and
(b) considers that it is in the interests of justice to proceed with the hearing.

DEFINITIONS

"hearing"—see r.1(3).
"party"—*ibid.*

GENERAL NOTE

See the note to r.31 of the Tribunal Procedure (First-tier Tribunal) (Social Entitlement Chamber) Rules 2008, above. **5.463**

PART 6

DECISIONS

Consent orders

39.—(1) The Upper Tribunal may, at the request of the parties but only if it considers it appropriate, make a consent order disposing of the proceedings and making such other appropriate provision as the parties have agreed. **5.464**

(2) Notwithstanding any other provision of these Rules, the [2 Upper] Tribunal need not hold a hearing before making an order under paragraph (1)[1 . . .].

AMENDMENTS

1. Tribunal Procedure (Amendment) Rules 2009 (SI 2009/274) r.20 (April 1, 2009).
2.Tribunal Procedure (Amendment No. 4) Rules 2013 (SI 2013/2067) rr.2 and 15 (November 1, 2013).

DEFINITIONS

"hearing"—see r.1(3).
"party"—*ibid.*

GENERAL NOTE

This rule may not have a great deal of relevance to social security cases because it is concerned with cases where there needs to be an "order" and where "other appropriate provision" may need to be made and it applies only "at the request of the parties". Where the parties are agreed as to the outcome of a social security case before the Upper Tribunal, it is usually sufficient for the judge to give a decision to that effect under r.40, which may be given without reasons if the parties consent. **5.465**

Indeed, in *TG v SSD* [2009] UKUT 282 (AAC), the Upper Tribunal pointed out that a draft consent order whereby the claimant agreed that an appeal would be dismissed but the Secretary of State agreed to make a more favourable decision was unsound because dismissal of the appeal would leave the lower tribunal's decision in existence. It was necessary for the appeal to be allowed and for the Upper Tribunal to exercise the lower tribunal's power to remit the case to the Secretary of State.

Decisions

5.466 **40.**—(1) The Upper Tribunal may give a decision orally at a hearing.

[6 (1A) Subject to paragraph (1B), in immigration judicial review proceedings, a decision which disposes of proceedings shall be given at a hearing.

(1B) Paragraph (1A) does not affect the power of the Upper Tribunal to—

(a) strike out a party's case, pursuant to rule 8(1)(b) or 8(2);
(b) consent to withdrawal, pursuant to rule 17;
(c) determine an application for permission to bring judicial review proceedings, pursuant to rule 30; or
(d) make a consent order disposing of proceedings, pursuant to rule 39,

without a hearing.]

(2) [1 . . .] [4 Except where [7 rule 22 (decision in relation to permission to appeal) or rule 22A (special procedure for providing notice of a refusal of permission to appeal in an asylum case)] applies,] the Upper Tribunal must provide to each party as soon as reasonably practicable after making [5 a decision (other than a decision under Part 7) which finally disposes of all issues in the proceedings or of a preliminary issue dealt with following a direction under r.5(3)(e)]—

(a) a decision notice stating the [5 Upper] Tribunal's decision; and
(b) notification of any rights of review or appeal against the decision and the time and manner in which such rights of review or appeal may be exercised.

(3) [1 Subject to rule [2 14(11) (prevention of disclosure or publication of documents and information)],] the Upper Tribunal must provide written reasons for its decision with a decision notice provided under paragraph (2)(a) unless—

(a) the decision was made with the consent of the parties; or
(b) the parties have consented to the Upper Tribunal not giving written reasons.

(4) The [2 Upper] Tribunal may provide written reasons for any decision to which paragraph (2) does not apply.

[3 (5) In a national security certificate appeal, when the Upper Tribunal provides a notice or reasons to the parties under this rule, it must also provide the notice or reasons to the relevant Minister and the Information Commissioner, if they are not parties.

Amendments

1. Tribunal Procedure (Amendment) Rules 2009 (SI 2009/274) r.21 (April 1, 2009).
2. Tribunal Procedure (Amendment No.2) Rules 2009 (SI 2009/1975) rr.7 and 21 (September 1, 2009).
3. Tribunal Procedure (Amendment) Rules 2010 (SI 2010/43) rr.5 and 13 (January 18, 2010).
4. Tribunal Procedure (Amendment No.2) Rules 2010 (SI 2010/44) rr.2 and 19 (February 15, 2010).
5. Tribunal Procedure (Amendment) Rules 2013 (SI 2013/477) rr.49 and 56 (April 1, 2013).
6. Tribunal Procedure (Amendment No. 4) Rules 2013 (SI 2013/2067) rr.2 and 16 (November 1, 2013).

7. Tribunal Procedure (Amendment No.3) Rules 2014 (SI 2014/2128) rr.2 and 14 (October 20, 2014).

DEFINITIONS

"asylum case"—see r.1(3).
"hearing"—*ibid.*
"immigration judicial review proceedings"—*ibid.*
"national security certificate appeal"—*ibid.*
"party"—*ibid.*
"relevant minister"—*ibid.*

GENERAL NOTE

See the notes to rr.33 and 34 of the Tribunal Procedure (First-tier Tribunal) (Social Entitlement Chamber) Rules 2008, above. Presumably the clause "finally disposes of all issues in the proceedings" includes a decision to strike proceedings out under r.8 but does not include a refusal of permission to appeal, a refusal of permission to apply for judicial review or summary dismissal of judicial review proceedings, in respect of all of which specific provision is made (see rr.22(1), 30(1)(b) and 30(2)(b)). In any event, it is usually good practice to provide reasons for any decision (where they may not be obvious to the parties adversely affected by the decision) and para.(4) makes specific provision for that to be done. 5.467

A decision given by consent without reasons has effect in the particular proceedings in which it is made but is not binding authority in any other case. Therefore, the Secretary of State was wrong to rely upon directions given in such a case when making a written submission to a Social Security Commissioner (*CSDLA/101/2000*). See also the note to r.39 above.

40A. *Revoked* 5.468

PART 7

CORRECTING, SETTING ASIDE, REVIEWING AND APPEALING DECISIONS OF THE UPPER TRIBUNAL

Interpretation

41. In this Part— 5.469

"appeal" [1 ,except in rule 44(2) (application for permission to appeal),] means the exercise of a right of appeal under section 13 of the 2007 Act; and

"review" means the review of a decision by the Upper Tribunal under section 10 of the 2007 Act.

AMENDMENT

1. Tribunal Procedure (Amendment) Rules 2009 (SI 2009/274) r.22 (April 1, 2009).

DEFINITION

"the 2007 Act"—see r.1(3).

Clerical mistakes and accidental slips or omissions

5.470 **42.** The Upper Tribunal may at any time correct any clerical mistake or other accidental slip or omission in a decision or record of a decision by—

(a) sending notification of the amended decision, or a copy of the amended record, to all parties; and

(b) making any necessary amendment to any information published in relation to the decision or record.

DEFINITION

"party"—see r.1(3).

GENERAL NOTE

5.471 See the note to r.36 of the Tribunal Procedure (First-tier Tribunal) (Social Entitlement Chamber) Rules 2008, above. Note that a separate power to correct a decision arises on review (see s.10(4)(a) of the Tribunals, Courts and Enforcement Act 2007).

Setting aside a decision which disposes of proceedings

5.472 **43.**—(1) The Upper Tribunal may set aside a decision which disposes of proceedings, or part of such a decision, and re-make the decision or the relevant part of it, if—

(a) the Upper Tribunal considers that it is in the interests of justice to do so; and

(b) one or more of the conditions in paragraph (2) are satisfied.

(2) The conditions are—

(a) a document relating to the proceedings was not sent to, or was not received at an appropriate time by, a party or a party's representative;

(b) a document relating to the proceedings was not sent to the Upper Tribunal at an appropriate time;

(c) a party, or a party's representative, was not present at a hearing related to the proceedings; or

(d) there has been some other procedural irregularity in the proceedings.

(3) [1 Except where paragraph (4) applies,] a party applying for a decision, or part of a decision, to be set aside under paragraph (1) must make a written application to the Upper Tribunal so that it is received no later than 1 month after the date on which the [2 Upper] Tribunal sent notice of the decision to the party.

[1 (4) In an asylum case or an immigration case, the written application referred to in paragraph (3) must be sent or delivered so that it is received by the Upper Tribunal—

(a) where the person who appealed to the First-tier Tribunal is in the United Kingdom at the time that the application is made, no later than twelve days after the date on which the Upper Tribunal or, as the case may be in an asylum case, the Secretary of State for the Home Department, sent notice of the decision to the party making the application; or

(b) where the person who appealed to the First-tier Tribunal is outside the United Kingdom at the time that the application is made, no later than thirty eight days after the date on which the Upper Tribunal sent notice of the decision to the party making the application.

(5) Where a notice of decision is sent electronically or delivered personally, the time limits in paragraph (4) are ten working days.]

AMENDMENTS

1. Tribunal Procedure (Amendment No.2) Rules 2010 (SI 2010/44) rr.2 and 21 (February 15, 2010).

2. Tribunal Procedure (Amendment No. 4) Rules 2013 (SI 2013/2067) rr.2 and 17 (November 1, 2013).

DEFINITIONS

"asylum case"—see r.1(3).
"dispose of proceedings"—*ibid.*
"document"—*ibid.*
"hearing"—*ibid.*
"immigration case"—*ibid.*
"party"—*ibid.*

GENERAL NOTE

See the note to r.37 of the Tribunal Procedure (First-tier Tribunal) (Social Entitlement Chamber) Rules 2008, above. The one-month time limit for making an application may be extended under r.5(3)(a). Note that a separate power to set aside a decision arises on review (see s.10(4)(c) of the 2007 Act). 5.473

Since, procedural irregularities in the proceedings before the First-tier Tribunal would be relevant to the decision of the Upper Tribunal whether to give permission to appeal or allow an appeal, r.43 is concerned only with procedural irregularities in the proceedings before the Upper Tribunal and so an application under r.43 is not an opportunity to challenge the Upper Tribunal's decision as to whether there was, or arguably was, an irregularity in the proceedings before the First-tier Tribunal (*SK v SSWP (AA)* [2016] UKUT 529 (AAC); [2017] AACR 25). It may, however, be possible to conceive of a case in which an irregularity in the proceedings before the Upper Tribunal was caused by an irregularity in the proceedings before the First-tier Tribunal (e.g., a document going astray in the proceedings in the First-tier Tribunal that therefore was not before the Upper Tribunal when it should have been). In such a case, the Upper Tribunal's decision might be set aside if the irregularity came to light only after that decision was given.

Application for permission to appeal

44.—(1) [5 Subject to [5 paragraphs (4A) and (4B)],] a person seeking permission to appeal must make a written application to the Upper Tribunal for permission to appeal. 5.474

(2) Paragraph (3) applies to an application under paragraph (1) in respect of a decision—

(a) on an appeal against a decision in a social security and child support case (as defined in the Tribunal Procedure (First-tier Tribunal) (Social Entitlement Chamber) Rules 2008);

(b) on an appeal against a decision in proceedings in the War Pensions and Armed Forces Compensation Chamber of the First-tier Tribunal); [1 . . .]

[1 (ba) on an appeal against a decision of a Pensions Appeal Tribunal for Scotland or Northern Ireland; or]

(c) in proceedings under the Forfeiture Act 1982.

(3) Where this paragraph applies, the application must be sent or delivered to the Upper Tribunal so that it is received within 3 months after the date on which the Upper Tribunal sent to the person making the application—

(a) written notice of the decision;

(b) notification of amended reasons for, or correction of, the decision following a review; or

(c) notification that an application for the decision to be set aside has been unsuccessful.

[2 (3A) An application under paragraph (1) in respect of a decision in an asylum case or an immigration case must be sent or delivered to the Upper Tribunal so that it is received within the appropriate period after the Upper Tribunal or, as the case may be in an asylum case, the Secretary of State for the Home Department, sent any of the documents in paragraph (3) to the party making the application.

(3B) The appropriate period referred to in paragraph (3A) is as follows—

(a) where the person who appealed to the First-tier Tribunal is in the United Kingdom at the time that the application is made—

(i) [4 twelve working days]; or

(ii) if the party making the application is in detention under the Immigration Acts, seven working days; and

(b) where the person who appealed to the First-tier Tribunal is outside the United Kingdom at the time that the application is made, thirty eight days.

(3C) Where a notice of decision is sent electronically or delivered personally, the time limits in paragraph (3B) are—

(a) in sub-paragraph (a)(i), ten working days;

(b) in sub-paragraph (a)(ii), five working days; and

(c) in sub-paragraph (b), ten working days.]

[3 (3D) An application under paragraph (1) in respect of a decision in a financial services case must be sent or delivered to the Upper Tribunal so that it is received within 14 days after the date on which the Upper Tribunal sent to the person making the application—

(a) written notice of the decision;

(b) notification of amended reasons for, or correction of, the decision following a review; or

(c) notification that an application for the decision to be set aside has been unsuccessful.]

(4) Where paragraph (3) [2 [3 , (3A) [6 , (3D) or (4C)]]] does not apply, an application under paragraph (1) must be sent or delivered to the Upper Tribunal so that it is received within 1 month after the latest of the dates on which the Upper Tribunal sent to the person making the application—

(a) written reasons for the decision;

(b) notification of amended reasons for, or correction of, the decision following a review; or

(c) notification that an application for the decision to be set aside has been unsuccessful.

[5 (4A) [6 Where a decision that disposes of immigration judicial review proceedings is given at a hearing, a party may apply at that hearing for permission to appeal, and the Upper Tribunal must consider at the hearing whether to give or refuse permission to appeal.]]

[6 (4B) Where a decision that disposes of immigration judicial review proceedings is given at a hearing and no application for permission to appeal is made at that hearing—

(a) the Upper Tribunal must nonetheless consider at the hearing whether to give or refuse permission to appeal; and

(b) if permission to appeal is given to a party, it shall be deemed for the purposes of section 13(4) of the 2007 Act to be given on application by that party.

(4C) Where a decision that disposes of immigration judicial review proceedings is given pursuant to rule 30 and the Upper Tribunal records under rule 30(4A) that the application is totally without merit, an application under paragraph (1) must be sent or delivered to the Upper Tribunal so that it is received within 7 days after the later of the dates on which the Upper Tribunal sent to the applicant—

(a) written reasons for the decision; or

(b) notification of amended reasons for, or correction of, the decision following a review.]

(5) The date in paragraph (3)(c) or (4)(c) applies only if the application for the decision to be set aside was made within the time stipulated in rule 43 (setting aside a decision which disposes of proceedings) or any extension of that time granted by the Upper Tribunal.

(6) If the person seeking permission to appeal provides the application to the Upper Tribunal later than the time required by paragraph (3) [2, (3A)] [3 , (3D)] or (4), or by any extension of time under rule 5(3)(a) (power to extend time)—

(a) the application must include a request for an extension of time and the reason why the application notice was not provided in time; and

(b) unless the Upper Tribunal extends time for the application under rule 5(3)(a) (power to extend time) the Upper Tribunal must refuse the application.

(7) An application under paragraph (1) [5 or (4A)(a)] must—

(a) identify the decision of the [6 Upper] Tribunal to which it relates;

(b) identify the alleged error or errors of law in the decision; and

(c) state the result the party making the application is seeking.

AMENDMENTS

1. Tribunal Procedure (Amendment) Rules 2009 (SI 2009/274) r.23 (April 1, 2009).

2. Tribunal Procedure (Amendment) (No.2) Rules 2010 (SI 2010/44) rr.2 and 22 (February 15, 2010).

3. Tribunal Procedure (Upper Tribunal) (Amendment) Rules 2010 (SI 2010/747) rr.2 and 10 (April 6, 2010).

4. Tribunal Procedure (Amendment) Rules 2011 (SI 2011/651) r.8(1) and (4) (April 1, 2011).

5. Tribunal Procedure (Upper Tribunal) (Amendment) Rules 2012 (SI 2012/2890) rr.2 and 3 (December 11, 2012).

6. Tribunal Procedure (Amendment No. 4) Rules 2013 (SI 2013/2067) rr.2 and 18 (November 1, 2013).

DEFINITIONS

"appeal"—see r.41.
"asylum case"—see r.1(3).
"dispose of proceedings"—*ibid.*
"financial services case"—*ibid.*
"immigration case"—*ibid.*
"immigration judicial review proceedings"—*ibid.*
"judicial review proceedings"—*ibid.*
"party"—*ibid.*
"permission"—*ibid.*
"working day"—*ibid.*

GENERAL NOTE

5.475 Paragraph (3), which prescribes a three-month time limit, applies to social security cases and is more favourable than paras (3A)–(4), which apply to other types of case. This generous time-limit existed under the earlier legislation because it is commonly only at this stage that parties, including the Secretary of State, HMRC and local authorities, first seek legal advice.

Paragraph (4A) was introduced in response to comments by the Court of Appeal in *R. (NB (Algeria)) v Secretary of State for the Home Department* [2012] EWCA Civ 1050. It does not apply to social security cases in the Administrative Appeals Chamber.

Note that para.(6)(b) uses the word "refuse", from which it follows that a decision by the Upper Tribunal not to extend the time for applying for permission to appeal does not prevent the applicant from applying to the appellate court for permission, although the appellate court will, of course, have regard to the delay in applying to the Upper Tribunal. This is because the condition in s.13(5) of the Tribunals, Courts and Enforcement Act 2007 (that permission have been "refused" by the Upper Tribunal before an application may be made to the appellate court) will have been satisfied. Thus, the effect of *White v Chief Adjudication Officer* [1986] 2 All E.R. 905 (also reported as an appendix to *R(S) 8/85*) has at last been reversed. In *White*, it had been held that a Commissioner's refusal to extend time for applying for leave to appeal to the Court of Appeal did not amount to a refusal of leave to appeal and was challengeable only by way of an application for judicial review.

Upper Tribunal's consideration of application for permission to appeal

5.476 **45.**—(1) On receiving an application for permission to appeal the Upper Tribunal may review the decision in accordance with rule 46 (review of a decision), but may only do so if—

(a) when making the decision the Upper Tribunal overlooked a legislative provision or binding authority which could have had a material effect on the decision; or
(b) since the Upper Tribunal's decision, a court has made a decision which is binding on the Upper Tribunal and which, had it been made before the Upper Tribunal's decision, could have had a material effect on the decision.

(2) If the Upper Tribunal decides not to review the decision, or reviews the decision and decides to take no action in relation to the decision or part of it, the Upper Tribunal must consider whether to give permission to appeal in relation to the decision or that part of it.

(3) The Upper Tribunal must [1 provide] a record of its decision to the parties as soon as practicable.

(4) If the Upper Tribunal refuses permission to appeal it must [1 provide] with the record of its decision—

(a) a statement of its reasons for such refusal; and
(b) notification of the right to make an application to the relevant appellate court for permission to appeal and the time within which, and the method by which, such application must be made.

(5) The Upper Tribunal may give permission to appeal on limited grounds, but must comply with paragraph (4) in relation to any grounds on which it has refused permission.

AMENDMENT

1. Tribunal Procedure (Amendment No. 4) Rules 2013 (SI 2013/2067) rr.2 and 19 (November 1, 2013).

DEFINITIONS

"appeal"—see r.41.
"permission"—see r.1(3).
"party"—*ibid.*
"review"—see r.41.

GENERAL NOTE

Paragraphs (1) and (2)

Before deciding whether or not to grant permission to appeal, the Upper Tribunal must first decide whether or not to review the decision under s.10 of the Tribunals, Courts and Enforcement Act 2007, as limited by para.(1). A decision may be reviewed only if the judge overlooked an important piece of legislation or case law or superior court has since made a decision that suggests that the decision of the Upper Tribunal was wrong. An example of the Upper Tribunal having overlooked a legislative provision may be seen in *Wychavon DC v EM (IB)* [2012] UKUT 12 (AAC); [2012] AACR 41, a housing benefit case concerned with a mentally disabled claimant's liability to pay rent. The judge had overlooked s.7 of the Mental Capacity Act 2005 and a decision of the Court of Appeal dealing with the law in relation to the supply of necessaries, consideration of which led him to review his previous decision in favour of the local authority and to decide the case against it. The word "could" is used in both subparas (a) and (b) of para.(1), which perhaps suggests that the Upper Tribunal might set aside a decision before hearing full argument rather than obtaining representations before deciding whether or not the decision should be reviewed. 5.477

Paragraph (4)

Reasons for refusing permission to appeal can usually be very brief and will often simply be that the application does not raise any point of law or does not raise an important point of principle and practice, as required by the Order made under s.13(6) of the 2007 Act (see the note to that provision), or that a new point of law would not have persuaded the judge to reach a different conclusion. Reasons can be valuable in persuading an applicant not to make an application to the appellate court in a hopeless case. If an application raises allegations about the conduct of the Upper Tribunal, it is likely to assist the court if the Upper Tribunal makes it clear whether it disputes the accuracy of the allegations. 5.478

Review of a decision

46.—(1) [1 The Upper Tribunal may only undertake a review of a decision pursuant to rule 45(1) (review on an application for permission to appeal).] 5.479

(2) The Upper Tribunal must notify the parties in writing of the outcome of any review and of any rights of review or appeal in relation to the outcome.

(3) If the Upper Tribunal decides to take any action in relation to a decision following a review without first giving every party an opportunity to make representations, the notice under paragraph (2) must state that any party that did not have an opportunity to make representations may apply for such action to be set aside and for the decision to be reviewed again.

AMENDMENT

1. Tribunal Procedure (Upper Tribunal) (Amendment) Rules 2011 (SI 2011/2343) rr.2 and 12 (October 17, 2011).

DEFINITIONS

"appeal"—see r.41.
"party"—see r.1(3).
"review"—see r.41.

GENERAL NOTE

Paragraph (1)

5.480 The power of review arises under s.10(1) of the Tribunals, Courts and Enforcement Act 2007. Section 10(2) provides for the power to be exercised either on the tribunal's initiative or on an application but s.10(3)(b) enables rules to provide that it is exercisable only on the Upper Tribunal's own initiative. That is what para. (1) of this rule does. A party may not make a free-standing application for a review (although if he or she does, the Upper Tribunal could presumably treat it as an application permission to appeal, despite the absence of an equivalent to r.41 of the Tribunal Procedure (First-tier Tribunal) (Social Entitlement Chamber) Rules 2008) but the Upper Tribunal may review a decision on its own initiative once there has been an application for permission to appeal. Rule 45(1), made under s.10(3)(d), limits the ground of review to cases where the Upper Tribunal overlooked a legislative provision or binding authority or there has since been a new binding authority. Since appeals under s.13 lie only on points of law, a review therefore provides a way of avoiding an appeal where the appeal would plainly be allowed or where the Upper Tribunal ought to deal with an overlooked issue before the question of permission to appeal is considered. See s.10(4), (5) and (6) for the powers of the Upper Tribunal on review.

Paragraph (2)

5.481 Section 13(8)(d) has the effect that there is no right of appeal against a decision whether or not to review a decision, to take no action on a review, to set aside a decision on a review or to refer, or not refer, a matter to the Upper Tribunal on review. However, that is because there is always another decision that may be the subject of an appeal. Where the Upper Tribunal refuses to review a decision or reviews it but takes no action or merely amends its reasons, the Upper Tribunal must consider whether to give permission to appeal against the original decision. Where the tribunal reviews a decision and re-decides the case, there will be a right to apply for permission to appeal against the new decision.

Where a decision is reviewed without all the parties having had the opportunity to make representations, notice must also be given of the right to apply for the new decision to be set aside (see para.(3)).

Paragraph (3)

5.482 The clear implication of this paragraph is that the Upper Tribunal may either obtain submissions from the parties other than the applicant before reviewing a case or review the case first and then wait to see whether any of the other parties objects. Plainly the second of those approaches may lead to a quicker decision and less work where there is no objection to the review. However, it is suggested that that approach is appropriate only where both the ground of review and the appropriate decision are very clear.

[1 Setting aside] a decision in proceedings under the Forfeiture Act 1982

47.—(1) A person who referred a question to the Upper Tribunal under rule 26 (references under the Forfeiture Act 1982) must refer the Upper Tribunal's previous decision in relation to the question to the Upper Tribunal if they— 5.483

(a) consider that the decision should be [1 set aside and re-made under this rule]; or

(b) have received a written application for the decision to be [1 set aside and re-made under this rule] from the person to whom the decision related.

(2) The Upper Tribunal may [1 set aside the decision, either in whole or in part, and re-make it] if—

(a) [1 ...];

(b) the decision was made in ignorance of, or was based on a mistake as to, some material fact; or

(c) there has been a relevant change in circumstances since the decision was made.

[1 (3) Rule 26(2) to (4), Parts 5 and 6 and this Part apply to a reference under this rule as they apply to a reference under rule 26(1).]

AMENDMENT

1. Tribunal Procedure (Upper Tribunal) (Amendment) Rules 2011 (SI 2011/2343) rr.2 and 13 (October 17, 2011).

GENERAL NOTE

Wide grounds for setting aside a decision are provided for in cases under the Forfeiture Act 1982, where the Upper Tribunal is the primary fact-finding body and there is no other mechanism for dealing with errors of fact that might have been made. This rule largely reproduces the effect of reg.15(2) and (3) of the Social Security Commissioners (Procedure) Regulations 1999. The effect of para.(4) of reg.15 has not been reproduced and it is therefore merely left implicit that the Upper Tribunal may determine the date from which a new decision takes effect. 5.484

[1 Power to treat an application as a different type of application

48. The [2 Upper] Tribunal may treat an application for a decision to be corrected, set aside or reviewed, or for permission to appeal against a decision, as an application for any other one of those things.] 5.485

AMENDMENTS

1. Tribunal Procedure (Amendment No.3) Rules 2010 (SI 2010/2653) r.8 (November 29, 2010).

2. Tribunal Procedure (Amendment No. 4) Rules 2013 (SI 2013/2067) rr.2 and 20 (November 1, 2013).

DEFINITIONS

"appeal"—see r.41.
"review"—*ibid.*

5.486 **Schedules A1 to 3.** *Omitted.*

PRACTICE DIRECTIONS

Practice Direction (First-Tier And Upper Tribunals: Child, Vulnerable Adult And Sensitive Witnesses)

5.487 1. In this Practice Direction:

a. "child" means a person who has not attained the age of 18;
b. "vulnerable adult" has the same meaning as in the Safeguarding Vulnerable Groups Act 2006;
c. "sensitive witness" means an adult witness where the quality of evidence given by the witness is likely to be diminished by reason of fear or distress on the part of the witness in connection with giving evidence in the case.

Circumstances under which a child, vulnerable adult or sensitive witness may give evidence

5.488 2. A child, vulnerable adult or sensitive witness will only be required to attend as a witness and give evidence at a hearing where the Tribunal determines that the evidence is necessary to enable the fair hearing of the case and their welfare would not be prejudiced by doing so.

3. In determining whether it is necessary for a child, vulnerable adult or sensitive witness to give evidence to enable the fair hearing of a case the Tribunal should have regard to all the available evidence and any representations made by the parties.

4. In determining whether the welfare of the child, vulnerable adult or sensitive witness would be prejudiced it may be appropriate for the Tribunal to invite submissions from interested persons, such as a child's parents.

5. The Tribunal may decline to issue a witness summons under the Tribunal Procedure Rules or to permit a child, vulnerable adult or sensitive witness to give evidence where it is satisfied that the evidence is not necessary to enable the fair hearing of the case and must decline to do so where the witness's welfare would be prejudiced by them giving evidence.

Manner in which evidence is given

5.489 6. The Tribunal must consider how to facilitate the giving of any evidence by a child, vulnerable adult or sensitive witness.

7. It may be appropriate for the Tribunal to direct that the evidence should be given by telephone, video link or other means directed by the Tribunal, or to direct that a person be appointed for the purpose of the hearing who has the appropriate skills or experience in facilitating the giving of evidence by a child, vulnerable adult or sensitive witness.

8. This Practice Direction is made by the Senior President of Tribunals with the agreement of the Lord Chancellor. It is made in the exercise

of powers conferred by the Tribunals, Courts and Enforcement Act 2007.

LORD JUSTICE CARNWATH
Senior President of Tribunals
30 October 2008

GENERAL NOTE

On July 29, 2014, the then Senior President of Tribunals announced that, in light of *JP v SSWP (DLA)* [2014] UKUT 275 (AAC); [2015] AACR 2 in which it was said that para.5 of this Practice Direction was inconsistent with *In re W (Children) (Family Proceedings: Evidence)* [2010] UKSC 12; [2010] 1 W.L.R. 701, this Practice Direction would be revised and brought into line with developments in the law. See the note to r.27 of the Tribunal Procedure (First-tier Tribunal) (Social Entitlement Chamber) Rules 2008. **5.490**

For the relevance of this Practice Direction to deciding whether to proceed with a hearing in a party's absence, see the annotation to r.31 of those Rules.

In *JH(S) v SSWP (ESA)* [2015] UKUT 567 (AAC), it was suggested that defining "vulnerable adult" by reference to the definition in the Safeguarding Vulnerable Groups Act 2006 no longer made sense in the light of amendments to that Act.

Practice Directions (First-Tier And Upper Tribunals: Use Of The Welsh Language In Tribunals In Wales)

General

1. The purpose of this Practice Direction is to reflect the principle of the Welsh Language Act 1993 that in the administration of justice in Wales, the English and Welsh languages should be treated on a basis of equality. **5.491**
2. In this Practice Direction "Welsh case" means a case which is before the Tribunal in which all "individual parties" are resident in Wales or which has been classified as a Welsh case by the Tribunal. An "individual party" is a party other than a Government Department or Agency. Where not all of the "individual parties" are resident in Wales the Tribunal will decide whether the case should be classified as a Welsh case or not. This has still not been done.

Use of the Welsh language

3. In a Welsh case the Welsh language may be used by any party or witnesses or in any document placed before the Tribunal or (subject to the listing provisions below) at any hearing. **5.492**

Listing

4. Unless it is not reasonably practicable to do so a party, or their representative, must inform the Tribunal 21 days before any hearing in a Welsh case that the Welsh language will be used by the party, their representative, any witness to be called by that party or in any document to be produced by the party. **5.493**
5. Where the proceedings are on appeal to the Upper Tribunal and the

Welsh language was used in the Tribunal below, the Tribunal Manager must make arrangements for the continued use of the Welsh language in the proceedings before the Upper Tribunal.

6. Where practicable, a hearing in which the Welsh language is to be used must be listed before a Welsh speaking Tribunal and, where translation facilities are needed, at a venue with simultaneous translation facilities.

Interpreters

5.494 7. Whenever an interpreter is needed to translate evidence from English into Welsh or from Welsh into English, the Tribunal Manager in whose tribunal the case is to be heard must ensure that the attendance is secured of an interpreter whose name is included in the list of approved interpreters.

Witnesses

5.495 8. When a witness in a case in which the Welsh language may be used is required to give evidence on oath or affirmation the Tribunal must inform the witness that they may be sworn or affirm in Welsh or English as they wish.

9. This Practice Direction is made by the Senior President of Tribunals with the agreement of the Lord Chancellor. It is made in the exercise of powers conferred by the Tribunals, Courts and Enforcement Act 2007.

LORD JUSTICE CARNWATH
Senior President of Tribunals
30 October 2008

Practice Direction (Upper Tribunal: Transcripts Of Proceedings)

5.496 1. At any hearing where the proceedings are recorded such recordings must be preserved by the Tribunal for six months from the date of the hearing to which the recording relates, and any party to the proceedings may, within that period, apply in writing for a transcript and a transcript must be supplied to that party.

2. If a transcript is supplied to a party under paragraph 1, that party must pay for the production and supply of the transcript unless they have applied in writing for, and the Tribunal has given, a direction that the transcript be produced and supplied at public expense.

3. The Tribunal may direct a transcript be supplied at public expense if satisfied that:

a. a recording of the relevant proceedings is in existence; and
b. the party making the application;
    i. has applied, or intends to apply, for permission to challenge the Upper Tribunal's decision in another court and has reasonable grounds for bringing or intending to challenge that decision; or
    ii. has been granted permission to challenge the Upper Tribunal's decision and has brought, or intends to bring, such proceedings; or
    iii. is a respondent to any such challenge to a decision of the Upper Tribunal in another court; and
c. the transcript is necessary for the purpose of challenging the Upper Tribunal's decision; and

d. the party's financial circumstances are such that that party cannot afford to pay for the transcript from their own income or funds.

4. Any transcript of proceedings directed to be supplied at public expense must be restricted to that part of the proceedings necessary for the purposes of any such challenge.
5. For the purposes of considering an application for a transcript at public expense, the Tribunal may give directions, for example, requiring the party to disclose details of their financial circumstances.
6. This Practice Direction is made by the Senior President of Tribunals with the agreement of the Lord Chancellor. It is made in the exercise of powers conferred by the Tribunals, Courts and Enforcement Act 2007.

LORD JUSTICE CARNWATH
Senior President of Tribunals
30 October 2008

General Note

This Practice Direction has the effect that anyone may ask for a transcript of a recording of proceedings but will have to pay for it, except in the circumstances listed in para.3. It is to be noted that the right to a transcript is not a right to a copy of the recording. In relation to the courts, *Practice Direction (Audio Recordings of Proceddings: Access)* [2014] 1 W.L.R. 632 makes it clear that "there is generally no right, either for a party or non-party, to listen to or receive a copy of . . . a recording [so as] to minimise the risk of misuse of . . . recordings". However, that Practice Direction makes provision for a person who has obtained a copy of the official transcript to apply for permission to listen to or receive a recording, although it also makes clear that permission will be granted "only in exceptional circumstances, for example where there is cogent evidence that the official transcript may have been wrongly transcribed." **5.497**

INDEX

LEGAL TAXONOMY
FROM SWEET & MAXWELL

This index has been prepared using Sweet and Maxwell's Legal Taxonomy. Main index entries conform to keywords provided by the Legal Taxonomy except where references to specific documents or non-standard terms (denoted by quotation marks) have been included. These keywords provide a means of identifying similar concepts in other Sweet & Maxwell publications and online services to which keywords from the Legal Taxonomy have been applied. Readers may find some minor differences between terms used in the text and those which appear in the index. Suggestions to *sweetandmaxwell.taxonomy@thomson.com*.

(All references are to paragraph number)